The Embassador and his Functions

GEORGE R.

GEORGE, by the Grace of God, King of *Great Britain*, *France* and *Ireland*, Defender of the Faith, &c. To all to whom these Presents shall come, Greeting. Whereas Our Trusty and Wellbeloved *Bernard Lintott* of Our City of *London*, Bookseller, has humbly represented unto Us, that he is now printing a compleat Translation of a Book, entitled, *The Embassador and his Functions*. To which is added, *An Historical Discourse*, concerning *the Election of the Emperor and the Electors*, by Monsieur *de Wicquefort*, Counsellor in the Councils of State, and Privy-Counsellor to the Duke of *Brunswick* and *Lunenburg*, *Zell*, &c. translated into *English*, from the *French*, by *John Digby*, in Folio. And whereas the said *Bernard Lintott* has informed Us, that he has been at a great Expence in carrying on the said Work, and that the sole Right and Title of the Copy of the said Work is vested in the said *Bernard Lintott*. He has therefore humbly besought Us to grant him Our Royal Licence and Privilege for the sole printing and publishing thereof for the Term of fourteen Years. WE being graciously pleased to encourage so Useful a Work, are willing to condescend to his Request, and do therefore hereby give and grant unto him the said *Bernard Lintott* Our Royal Licence and Privilege for the sole printing and publishing the said Book, entitled, *The Embassador and his Functions*; To which is added, *An Historical Discourse*, concerning *the Election of the Emperor and the Electors*, by Monsieur *de Wicquefort*, Counsellor in the Councils of State, and Privy-Counsellor to the Duke of *Brunswick* and *Lunenburg*, *Zell*, &c. translated into *English* by *John Digby*, for and during the Term of fourteen Years, to be computed from the Day of the Date hereof, strictly charging and prohibiting all Our Subjects within Our Kingdoms and Dominions to reprint or abridge the same either in the like or any other Volume or Volumes whatsoever, or to import, buy, vend, utter or distribute any Copies of the same or any part thereof reprinted beyond the Seas within the said Term of fourteen Years, without the Consent and Approbation of the said *Bernard Lintott*, his Heirs, Executors and Assigns by Writing under his or their Hands and Seals first had and obtained, as they and every of them offending herein will answer the contrary at their Perils, and such other Penalties as by the Laws and Statutes of this our Realm may be inflicted. Whereof the Master, Wardens and Company of Stationers of Our City of *London*, Commissioners and other Officers of Our Customs, and all other Our Officers and Ministers whom it may concern, are to take Notice that due Obedience be given to Our Pleasure herein signified. Given at Our Court at St. *James*'s the 26th Day of *March*, 1716. in the second Year of our Reign.

By His Majesty's Command,

JAMES STANHOPE.

THE
EMBASSADOR
AND HIS
FUNCTIONS:
Written by

Monsieur de *WICQUEFORT*,

Privy-Counsellor to the Duke of *Brunswick* and *Lunenburg, Zell*, &c.

In Two BOOKS.

I. SHEWING, The Right of Sovereigns to send Embassadors. The several Orders of Publick Ministers Of the Birth, Learning, and Age of Embassadors, and the Trust reposed in them : Their Instructions, Letters of Credence, Powers, Passports, Entries, Audiences, Ceremonies, Visits, Apparel, Expences, Domesticks, Privileges, &c The Competition between *France* and *Spain*, and several other Princes and States about Rank

II. TREATING of the Functions of Embassadors : Their Manner of Negotiating Their Liberty of Speech : Their secret Services, Letters, Dispatches. Of their Mediatory Treaties · Of the Treaty of *Westphalia*, and all other Treaties in the last Century : Of Ratifications : The Lives and Characters of the most Illustrious Embassadors, and of several splendid Embassies ; *viz*
I That of Sir *Francis Walsingham* from Q *Elizabeth* to *France*
II The Duke of *Buckingham* to *Spain* and *France*
III Sir *Robert Shirley*, Embassador from the K of *Persia* to K *James 1st*.
IV. Mr *Lockhart* Minister of *England* at the *Pyrenean* Treaty
V The Lord *Falconbridge* to the *French* King at *Dunkirk*
VI The Duke of *Crequi* to *Cromwell*
VII Sir *John Trevor* to *France*.
VIII The Lord *Hollis* to *France*
IX The Earl of *Essex* to *Denmark*
X Sir *William Temple* to the *Hague* and *Nimeguen*

With many other Embassies from *England*, *France*, *Spain*, which afford Useful Historical Relations no where else to be found
Also, A large Account of the Constitution of the *German* Empire, the Manner of Electing their Emperors, of the Electoral College, of the *Golden Bull*, of the Election of the King of the *Romans*, the Rights and Prerogatives of the several Electors, and the Laws and Usages of the Empire

Translated into *English* by Mr. *DIGBY*.

LONDON

Printed for BERNARD LINTOTT between the *Temple-Gates* in *Fleetstreet* And sold by CHARLES KING in *Westminster-Hall*, EDWARD FLEETWOOD at the Foot of the *Parliament-Stair*, and WILLIAM TAYLOR at the *Ship* in *Pater-Noster-Row*. 1716.
Price 25s. small, and 35s. large Paper

THE
EMBASSADOR
AND HIS
FUNCTIONS.

To which is added,

An Hiſtorical Diſcourſe,

Concerning the

ELECTION of the EMPEROR,

AND THE

ELECTORS.

BY

Monſieur de *WICQUEFORT*,

Counſellor in the Councils of State, and Privy-Counſellor to the Duke of *Brunſwick* and *Lunenburg, Zell,* &c

Tranſlated into Engliſh *by* Mr. DIGBY.

LONDON:
Printed for BERNARD LINTOTT, at the *Croſs-Keys* between the *Temple-Gates*.

TO THE
RIGHT HONOURABLE the
Lord DIGBY.

My Lord,

I *Shall not in this Dedication imitate the Practice of most Authors, and take occasion from the Antiquity of Your Family, and its signal Services to the Kingdom; from the Nobility of Your Birth, nor from Your own personal Qualifications, Virtues, and Merits, to swell my Epistle with Your Praises, for tho' no body would better become all that can be said on those Heads than Your* LORDSHIP; *yet I am sensible Your* LORDSHIP's *Humility is as deep as is requisite to support the noble Superstructure You have rais'd thereon; I shall therefore carefully avoid gratifying my Pen in the Pleasure it would otherwise take to indulge it self in the due Praises of so noble a Subject, and forbear saying any thing of You by way of Encomium, as well for fear of offending where I most would please, as because I know that all I could say would be too little, and I should be liable to be censur'd by all that know You for my Temerity in attempting what deserves a better Hand.*

For these Reasons, My Lord, *I shall content my self with acquainting Your* LORDSHIP *that I put this Translation*

Epistle Dedicatory.

Translation under Your Patronage on many Accounts. First, because my Author was a great Man himself, and so worthy Your Protection, next, because the matter he so ingeniously and skillfully handles is not unworthy Your Perusal; and tho' I am not to learn that he is no Stranger to You in his own Language, yet I thought it might be some Satisfaction to You to read him in Your Mother Tongue. But, My Lord, *the chief Reason is, that I think it a good Opportunity to express to Your* Lordship *and the World, the feeling Sense I have of all Your Favours and Bounties to me, which justly intitle You to all that the Remainder of my Life will enable me to do, in any kind whatever, to testify my Gratitude; and till I can give some better Proof thereof, I hope You will, out of Your wonted Goodness, accept of this small Token of it, since I can with the greatest Truth say, that no body can be with more Sincerity, or a more profound Veneration and Respect, than I am,*

My Lord,

Your Lordship's most obliged,

and most obedient humble

Servant and Kinsman,

John Digby.

THE

Author's EPISTLE

TO HIS

MOST SERENE HIGHNESS

GEORGE WILLIAM,

Duke of *Brunſwick* and *Lunenburg*, &c.

May it pleaſe Your Highneſs,

Y Deſign was to digeſt in this Work, that Confuſion which disfigures the Memoirs that have been publiſh'd on the ſame Subject, and to reduce it into a Treatiſe that had both Order and Method. I can ſay that its Beginnings were ſo fortunate, that I might have promis'd my ſelf a favourable Succeſs. But I had hardly form'd the firſt Project of the Second Part, when I was depriv'd of the Means to finiſh it, and indeed to continue it. Since Your moſt Serene Highneſs has permitted me to retire to Your Court, I have been oblig'd to beſtow my Thoughts on Affairs of another Nature, and to apply my ſelf to the Continuation of a Work of a larger Extent, which was formerly deſir'd of me. I therefore made no Scruple to abandon a Matter that was not yet in a Condition to receive a reaſonable Form, and neverthelefs, that I might do no Injury to the Printer, I would not hinder him from giving it to the Publick, to the End he might find an Advantage by it, which I my ſelf could

The *Author's* EPISTLE.

not. It is not without some Reluctancy that I expose this imperfect Piece to the Sight of Your most Serene Highness, and indeed I could never have resolv'd upon it, if I did not know that there is nothing so well finish'd, but your great Skill would enable You to find Fault with; and if I did not consider that Great Princes have this in common with him who is above 'em, That they receive the Vows and Sacrifices of the Rich and the Poor indifferently, and that the Talent of the one and the Mite of the other are equally acceptable to 'em. Small Oblations have their Agreeableness and Merit, as well as Holocausts and Hecatombs. I lay but a small Grain of Incense on the Altar, but it is with a profound Respect, in Acknowledgment of the infinite Favours I every Day receive of Your Serene Highness, and particularly of the Protection You have been pleas'd to honour me with, and for which I render You my most humble Thanks. And as the Happiness of the little Time I have to live depends upon it, I also protest to You, I shall employ all the Moments of it in whatsoever You shall please to require of him who is, with the most submissive Sentiments,

My Lord,

Your most Serene Highness's

most humble, most obedient,

and most devoted Servant,

Wicquefort,

THE CONTENTS.

BOOK I.

Chap		Page
I	Of the Embassador in General,	1
II	It belongs to Sovereigns only to send Embassadors,	6
III	Whether Usurpers, and Governors in Chief can send Embassadors,	17
IV	The Princes of Germany have a Right to send Embassadors to represent them,	25
V	Of the Ministers of the second Order,	33
VI	To whom Embassadors are sent,	44
VII	Of the Birth and Learning of an Embassador,	47
VIII	What Age is proper for an Embassador,	53
IX	Whether Clergymen are proper for Embassies,	57
X	Of Legates,	67
XI	The Prince may employ Strangers in his Embassies, even in their own Countrey,	75
XII	Of the Fidelity of the Embassador,	86
XIII	The Embassador ought to be agreeable,	94
XIV	Of Instructions,	107
XV	Of Letters of Credence,	109
XVI	Of the Embassadors Powers,	116
XVII	Of Passports and Safe-conducts,	121
XVIII	Of the Reception and Entry of the Embassador,	127
XIX	Of Audiences,	148
XX	Of the Honours and Civilities that Embassadors are oblig'd to pay, and of those that are done to Embassadors,	164
XXI	Of the first Visit,	184
XXII	Of some other Civilities which are done to Embassadors, or that Embassadors use towards one another,	192
XXIII	Of the Apparel and Expences of the Embassador,	202
XXIV	Of the Competition between France and Spain,	208
XXV	Of several other Competitions,	220
XXVI	Of Embassies compos'd of several Embassadors,	236
XXVII	Embassadors are inviolable in their Persons,	246
XXVIII	The House and Domesticks of an Embassador are inviolable,	265
XXIX	Embassadors are not always inviolable,	274
XXX	When the Embassador's Functions cease,	282

BOOK II.

Chap		Page
I	Of the Function of the Embassador in general,	294
II	With whom the Embassador ought to negotiate,	301
III	How the Embassador ought to negotiate,	306
IV	The Embassador ought not to meddle with the domestick Affairs of the State where he negotiates,	315
V	The Embassador ought to execute his Orders, and how,	322
VI	Of Prudence and Cunning,	329
VII	Of the Liberty of Speaking,	339
VIII	Of Moderation,	349
IX	It is lawful for an Embassador to corrupt the Ministers of the Court where he resides,	353
X	Of Letters and Dispatches,	357
XI	Of Mediation, and of Embassadors Mediators,	364
XII	Of Treaties,	371
XIII	Of the Treaties of Munster and Osnaburg,	385
XIV	The most considerable Treaties relating to the Affairs of this Age,	391
XV	Of Ratifications,	405
XVI	Of the Report the Embassador makes of his Negotiations,	413
XVII	Of some illustrious Embassadors of our Time,	416

The Contents to the Election of the Emperor, &c.

Chap		Page
I	That the Empire was hereditary in Charlemagne's Time,	437
II	When the Empire began to be elective,	439
III	Of what Nature was the first Election of the Emperors of Germany,	441
IV	That the Electoral College was not instituted by the Emperor Otho III, nor in his Time,	443
V	Whether the Election of the Emperors, Successors to Henry V, was perform'd by seven Electors, and whether the Electoral College was instituted under the Emperors of the House of Suabia,	446
VI	Whether the Electoral College was instituted to the Number of Seven, before the Publication of the Golden Bull,	449
VII	The Golden Bull,	453
i	Of the Safe-conduct of the Electors, and by whom they ought to be guarded,	ibid
ii	Of the Election of the King of the Romans,	455
iii	Of the Place of the Archbishops of Triers, Cologn and Mayence,	456
iv	Of the Princes Electors in general,	ibid
v	Of the Right of the Count Palatin of the Rhine, and of the Duke of Saxony,	457
vi	Of the Comparison of the Electors with the other Princes,	ibid
vii	Of the Succession of the Princes,	ibid
viii	Of the Exemption of the King of Bohemia, and of the Inhabitants of the said Kingdom,	458
ix	Of Mines of Gold, Silver, and other Mettals,	ibid
x	Concerning the Coyn,	ibid
xi	Of the Exemption of the Princes Electors,	459
xii	Of the Assembly of the Princes,	ibid
xiii	Of the Revocation of Privileges,	ibid
xiv	Of those from whom Fiefs are taken away, as being unworthy thereof,	460
xv	Of Conspiracies,	ibid
xvi	Of the Pfalburgers,	ibid
xvii	Of Defiances,	ibid
xviii	The Form of a Summons, or Letters of Intimation,	461
xix	The Form of the Procuration,	ibid
xx	Of the Union between the Princes Electors, and of the Rights which particularly belong to them,	ibid
xxi	Of the Order to be observ'd by the Archbishops in any Procession,	462
xxii	Of the Order the Secular Princes shall observe, who carry the Regalia,	ibid
xxiii	Of the Functions of the Archbishops in the Presence of the Emperor,	ibid
xxiv	* * *	ibid
xxv	Of the Preservation of the Principalities of the Electors entire,	463
xxvi	Of the Imperial Court, and of the Meeting or Session,	464
xxvii	Of the Functions of the Princes Electors in the solemn Courts of the Emperors, or of the King of the Romans,	ibid
xxviii	Of the Imperial and Electoral Tables,	465
xxix	Of the Right of the Officers, when the Princes do Homage for their Fiefs to the Emperor, or to the King of the Romans,	ibid
xxx	Of the Instruction of the Princes Electors in Languages,	466
VIII	Several Remarks on the Golden Bull,	471
IX	Of the Electoral College, and of the Dignity and Power of the Princes Electors in general,	471
X	Of the Ecclesiastical Electors,	480
XI	Of the Secular Princes Electors in general,	488
XII	Of the Vicars of the Empire, and of the Vicars of the Electors,	499
XIII	Of the King of Bohemia,	502
XIV	Of the Duke of Bavaria, Prince Elector of the holy Empire,	514
XV	Of the Duke of Saxony, Prince Elector of the holy Empire,	524
XVI	Of the Marquiss of Brandenburg, Prince Elector of the holy Empire,	533
XVII	Of the Count Palatin of the Rhine, Prince Elector of the holy Empire,	541
XVIII	Of the Preliminaries of the Election, and of the Capitulation,	548
XIX	Of the Election of the Emperor,	559
XX	Of the Effect of the Election,	565

THE EMBASSADOR AND HIS FUNCTIONS.

BOOK I.

CHAP. I.
Of an Embaffador in general.

THERE is no doubt to be made, but the Knowledge of that part of the publick Right, which treats of *Embaffadors* and *foreign Minifters*, is very neceffary, and yet it muft be acknowledg'd that there is nothing fo univerfally unknown. There is not any Kingdom or State that does not make ufe of 'em, yet neverthelefs there is hardly any body that knows what an *Embaffador* is, that is to fay, what are the Qualities that form him, the Rights and Privileges he enjoys, what Civilities are due to his Character, and what are the proper Functions of his Employment. I have therefore often wonder'd, that there has not yet appear'd any perfect Treatife on that Subject, and that among fo many learned Men, who have made Politicks their chiefeft Study, and even among fo many great Men, who have distinguifh'd themfelves in Embaffies, there is not any one who has thought fit to oblige Pofterity fo far, as to prefent it with a Work by fo much the more ufeful, as an Embaffador is a Minifter which the State cannot be without, and at the fame time the Rights and Privileges of Embaffy are the moft illuftrious Marks of Sovereignty.

The greateft part of thofe who have handled this Matter have done it but flightly, and thofe who have compos'd whole Volumes to give us an Idea of a *confummate Embaffador*, furnifh us with nothing but common Places, infomuch that inftead of forming an accomplifh'd Minifter, they extend themfelves on Qualities that are neither proper nor peculiar to him, but without which it is impoffible to be either a good Citizen or an honeft Man. The very Mafters of the Ceremonies, and Introductors of Embaffadors, have been fo remifs and negligent, that except Mr *John Finet*, Mafter of the Ceremonies in *England*, (who has left Memoirs of what pafs'd at the Court in *London* relating to this Subject, while he difcharged the Function of Introductor there) not one has been willing to do that good Office to his Succeffor. M *Girault*, who is an Affiftant or Lieutenant to the Introductors at the Court of *France*, is beyond all doubt the Man, who, of all the Officers, beft underftands this Employment. He holds it from Father to Son, and not being an half yearly Attendant, as the Introductors are, it is impoffible but he muft be very knowing. He is moreover a very worthy, and very able Man, and yet he has not hitherto been prevail'd upon to beftow a little Application, to draw up Memoirs that might regulate the Ceremonial in all the other Courts of *Europe*. In the second Volume of the *Ceremonial of France* are to be found some Remarks that the Count *de Brulon* and Monf. *de Berlize* have made relating to the time they liv'd in, but then there is but a few of 'em, and even they are imperfect, and have neither Series nor Order.

As for my own part, I do not promise here a Treatise, where there shall be nothing wanting, as well because the Matter it self is endless, as because that this Work coming forth during the tediousness of a very rigid and insupportable Captivity, it is impossible but there must almost every where appear some Tokens of the Uneasiness of my Mind, as well as of the Infirmities which are common to all Men, and which I readily acknowledge to be very great in my self. During the time of my Solitude, I had no other Conversation than that of some few of my Books, (which I obtain'd as it were an Alms from the Fiscal) nor any other Diversion than that of Reading. That of modern History has in all times made part of my Occupation, wherein I took Pleasure to remark some Passages which might be useful, (if not to the Composition of a regular and methodical Treatise) at least to lighten the Task of those who, having better Means and larger Capacities than my self, might thereby be able to apply themselves to it with greater Assiduity and Success. But my Misfortunes having made me lose those Thoughts, and having broken all my Measures, have caus'd a Project which in itself was reasonable enough, to be succeeded by this Collection of Examples, which have been publish'd under the Title of *Memoirs relating to Embassadors and publick Ministers*.

They so amply set forth the Exemptions, Immunities, Privileges and Advantages that the *Law of Nations* bestows upon 'em, that, to give 'em some Form of a Treatise, it was (in my Opinion) sufficient to sort 'em, and redress in this third Edition what may be confus'd and irregular in the two former. I know very well, all that I can say will never be able to make it a Science that has its mathematical Principles, or that is founded on demonstrative Reasons, upon which certain and infallible Rules may be made, but however, I think I can reduce all my Discourse to Maxims, wherein will be found something that comes very near to a moral Infallibility.

Princes have a sort of Commerce among themselves as well as other Men, but not being able to confer one with the other in Person, without some Prejudice to their Dignity or Affairs, they have recourse to the Mediation of certain Ministers to whom they give the Character of Embassador, or some other publick Qualification. On this is founded the Necessity of having Embassadors, for Princes not being able to do their Business themselves with other Sovereigns, they are necessitated to employ Persons who represent 'em, who find themselves thereby rais'd to a high pitch of Dignity, in which they receive Honours they could not pretend to without this eminent Quality. When those Persons have the Character of *Publick Representatives*, they are call'd *Embassadors* in a Signification much more restrain'd than that the *Romans* gave to the word *Legatus*, which does not only extend it self to the Ministers of the second Rank, but even to Persons who not being employ'd from Sovereigns, are not within the Protection of the *Law of Nations*. The *Roman* History, and the Laws of ancient *Rome*, give the Quality of *Legatus* not only to the Lieutenant Generals of their Armies, and to the Lieutenant Colonels of their Regiments or Legions, but also to the Messengers the Senate sent to the Generals, and which the Towns subject to their Empire, and the same Generals, sent to the Senate. As I cannot therefore apply to my *Embassador* all that the *Roman* Laws say of their *Legatus*, I thought it was to no purpose to draw from ancient History Examples that did not square with modern Usage, since excepting the Protection, that the *Law of Nations* bestows on the one as well as the other, there is nothing in Antiquity to swell this Work with, which treats only of what is practis'd at this time.

The Word *Embassador, Ambassadore*, or *Embaxador*, is deriv'd from the *Spanish Embiar*, which signifies to send, so that one may say, *That an Embassador is a publick Minister, dispatch'd by a sovereign Prince to some foreign Potentate or State, there to represent his Person, by virtue of a Power, Letters of Credence, or some Commission that notifies his Character*. I am sensible this Definition has not all the parts of which it ought to be compos'd, but as the School does not extend its Jurisdiction to the Matter I am at present treating of, so I do not think I am oblig'd to subject my self to its Laws and Rules. I shall in the next Chapter speak of those who have a Right to send *Embassadors*, and the Powers, as also the Letters of Credence, shall likewise have theirs. I shall therefore be contented to say here, That no body can doubt that an *Embassador* is a publick Minister, as on the other side no body can be ignorant that every publick Minister is not an *Embassador*, but that it is necessary he have the Character of *Representative*, without which he must take his Place among the Ministers of the second Order. The Pope's *Nuncio* has not the Quality of *Embassador*, and yet for all that he is one under a *Latin* Denomination.

All other Ministers, as *Plenipotentiaries* (if they have with this Quality the representing Character) *Internuncios, Envoys, Residents, Agents, Commissioners*, the *Secretaries* of *Embassies*, and even the *Secretaries* of *Embassadors*, who in the Absence of their Masters, or during the Intervals of Embassies, are charg'd with the Prosecution or Sollicitation of Affairs, are also publick Ministers, and as such they enjoy the Protection of the *Law of Nations* in its full extent. This obliges me to speak of 'em as occasion requires, and to shew, that notwithstanding they are not paid the same Civilities that are inseparable from the Character, yet that is no hindrance to their enjoying all the same Advantages which the *Law of Nations*, and the publick Faith, bestows on all those, to whom one may give the Quality of *Legatus*.

I put also into this Number, those Persons whom Princes employ by a verbal Order, provided that he, with whom they are to negociate, acknowledges 'em in that Quality, and gives them a Credit which he would not give to another without Letters. *Henry* IV being in the beginning of this Age advanc'd as far as the Frontiers of *Flanders*, on occasion of the Siege of *Ostend*, which the Arch-Duke *Albert* was carrying on, and the Queen of *England* being come to *Dover*, there was a mighty Commerce of Letters between these two Princes. The Queen wrote one to the King, the last Lines whereof were so obscure, that the King imagining they contain'd something mysterious, thought he ought to have them explain'd, and to that end employ some Minister, whose Favour with his Majesty, and the Confidence he put in him, was sufficiently known, to prevail with the Queen to unfold her Meaning without Scruple. He therefore order'd the Marquis *de Rosny*, who has since made himself known under the Quality of Duke *de Sully*, to cross the Sea under the pretext of taking a trip to *London*, by way of Diversion, because he was well assur'd that the Queen (who without doubt would be inform'd of his Passage) would not fail to speak to him. Accordingly at his landing he found in the Port of *Dover* several *English* Noblemen, who knowing him saluted him, and acquainted the Queen with his Arrival, who immediately sent for him by the Captain of her Guards. She entertain'd him a long time with the common Interest of both Crowns, and the Designs that might be form'd against *Spain*, and sent him back very well satisfy'd. Now he had no Letters of Credence that could give him either Quality or Character, but did not hinder him from discharging the Function of an Embassador, because the Queen, who knew the Confidence his Master repos'd in him, consider'd him as a publick Minister, and beyond all doubt would not have fail'd to have let him enjoy all the Rights and Privileges of that Character if it had been necessary.

This is what may be done betwixt Princes who are in a perfect Amity and good Understanding, but no risque is to be run of this nature, with those who are not, and who perhaps would not have for the Person, the Consideration they are oblig'd to have for the Character.

In the Year 1646, the Court of *France* seeing that the Abbot of St *Nicholas*, tho' a Person of great Ability, could not overcome the rigorous Disposition of Pope *Innocent* X towards the *Barberins*, whose Restoration the King was contriving, resolv'd to send thither the Duke *de Brezé* with the Character of Embassador Extraordinary, or else Prince *Thomas* of *Savoy*, who had no other Qualification but what his Birth entitled him to. But the Duke being kill'd in a Sea-Fight, and the Siege of *Orbitello* being rais'd with little Reputation to the Arms of *France*, the Prince would not appear at *Rome* after that ill Success. He would not take upon him the Character of Embassador that he might not thereby injure that of Prince, but yet he had nevertheless been one in Fact, because he had his *Letters of Credence* to discharge the Functions thereof, and to enjoy the Protection and all other Advantages of the *Law of Nations*. There have been Princes of the Blood of *France* who have been Embassadors to *Spain* and *England*. *Anthony* King of *Navarre* and the Cardinal *de Bourbon* conducted *Isabella* (who was betrothed to the King of *Spain*) to the very Frontiers. The Prince of *Condé* went even to *Madrid*, and the Prince *Daufin*, Son of the Duke of *Montpensier* was chief of the Embassy which *Henry* III sent into *England* to negociate the Marriage of his Brother the Duke of *Alençon*. I shall not speak of the Dukes of *Mayenne* and *Chevreuse*, Princes of the House of *Lorrain*, nor of the Duke *d'Engoulesme*, because Prince *Thomas* pretended to be something more than they, but I do not believe that a younger Son of the Duke of *Savoy* would put himself in Competition with a Cardinal Lantgrave of *Hesse*, which is a Family as illustrious, and at least as ancient, as that of *Savoy*, and yet he appear'd in the Quality of the Emperor's Embassador at a Court where he held a Rank, that neither the Princes, nor even the Duke of *Savoy* himself, can pretend to. The same may be said of Cardinal *Bichi* Embassador from *France*, or the Bishop of *Osnabourg* Prince of the Empire, who was Embassador at *Munster*, not from a crown'd Head, but from the Electoral College, from whence I conclude, that the Character of Embassador does not at all derogate from the Dignity of Prince.

A domestick Example might have convinc'd Prince *Thomas* of the Truth of this Assertion. In the Year 1607, the Duke of *Savoy*, who was his Father, desir'd and obtain'd of the Emperor the Embassy Extraordinary to *Venice*, where they were endeavouring to adjust the Difference that Republick had with Pope *Paul* V. The Duke said he had sought that Employ for three Reasons. The first, because he fear'd, that if the War kindled in *Italy*, he should be the first that would feel the Inconveniencies thereof, the second, that he might thereby destroy the Opinion was had of him, that being an active Prince, and an Enemy to Idleness, he coveted nothing but War, and the third, because it behov'd him to make the Emperor (who talk'd of marrying his Daughter) sensible that Ambition was not his Vice, and that he could accommodate himself to every thing. This Embassy was not put in execution, whether because the Duke had not wherewith to defray the Expence thereof, or that he was not satisfy'd with the Honours the Senate had resolv'd to shew him at his Reception, or because the Treaty betwixt the Pope and the Republick was like to be concluded, before he could have enter'd upon a Negotiation. However it plainly appears from hence, that the Duke of *Savoy* (whose Heart was at least as good as that of the Prince his younger Son's) did not look upon this Employ to be incompatible with his Dignity. In the Year 1641, the States of the United Provinces sent a solemn Embassy to *England* on account of the Marriage of Prince *William*, Son of Prince *Frederick Henry* of *Orange*. After the Marriage was resolv'd upon, Prince *William* went thither in Person, but to prevent the Difficulties the Embassadors might have made, and particularly Foreigners, to give place to his Quality of Prince, he was himself vested with that of *Embassador*.

It might perhaps not be from the purpose to ask here, whether the *Cardinals Protectors* are also publick Ministers? I dare not declare my self in the affirmative, as well because that not one of those who write of the publick Right puts 'em in the Number of Ministers, as because their Functions are very different. The Protector

Protector is no Embaſſador, becauſe he has not the *repreſenting Character*, and on the other ſide, he cannot be a Miniſter of the ſecond Order, becauſe that Quality is infinitely below the Dignity of Cardinal. The Embaſſador enjoys the Protection of the *Law of Nations*, and all the Privileges that depend on it, whereas the *Cardinal Protector* can only have recourſe to the Authority, or rather the Interceſſion of that Crown whoſe Intereſt he protects, and cannot exempt himſelf from the Pope's Juriſdiction. The Embaſſador has a ſet Allowance, the Protector has only either Penſions or Benefices. It is true, that the Protection of the two firſt Crowns, gives a great Authority to the Cardinals, particularly in the Conclave, where they are Heads of Parties, on which account the beſt Families in *Italy*, and ſometimes even the Cardinal Nephews themſelves, ſeek after it with Warmth and Ambition, tho' they would not at the ſame time be conſider'd as publick Miniſters.

I do not diſtinguiſh between *Embaſſadors Ordinary and Extraordinary*, becauſe there is no eſſential Difference between 'em. They ought all to have the ſame perſonal Qualifications, their Letters of Credence, their Inſtructions, their Powers, &c. the one as well as the other equally enjoy all the Prerogatives of *the Law of Nations*. They are both Repreſentatives in the ſame Degree, and I ſhall ſay nothing of the one, that may not alſo be apply'd to the other.

The *Embaſſador* repreſents the Perſon of the the Prince his Maſter, for which reaſon the Quality of *publick Repreſentative* is given him, in a Signification which is peculiar to that Character. The *Venetians* give this Quality to thoſe of their Magiſtrates, who, like *Proveditores*, have Command in their Armies, or Provinces, and even the *Podeſtats*, or Governors of their Towns, aſſume to themſelves the ſame Quality, and cauſe themſelves to be reſpected as ſuch. In the beginning of this Century, *the Count de Vaudemont*, ſecond Son to the Duke of *Lorraine*, being arriv'd in *Italie*, all the *Podeſtats* made him publick Entries, and ſhew'd him other Civilities, but they every where took the upper Hand of him, notwithſtanding the *Doge* did him a great deal more honour, than he is us'd to ſhew to Embaſſadors. The *Repreſentantes* of the *Spaniards* are quite an other thing, altho' it cannot be deny'd, but that a good Embaſſador is alſo a great Theatrical Perſonage, and that to be ſucceſsful in his Profeſſion, he ought to play the Comedian a little.

It is not but I'd have him be a Man of Probity, and that he ſhould poſſeſs with the true Vertue, the Qualities that are able to form ſo agreeable a Mixture of Morality and Politicks, whithout which, a Miniſter makes a very indifferent Figure among the brighter part of the World. But I am not afraid to ſay, (conſidering the Corruption of the preſent Age) that it is not what is abſolutely neceſſary, and that it ſuffices, that an Embaſſador have a noble Exterior and a fine Appearance, from whence he ſhall draw more notable Advantages than from Vertue her ſelf, although it be impoſſible to conceal long the Qualities Nature has beſtow'd, or to amuſe the World with thoſe one has not. Wit diſcovers it ſelf preſently, but it is not ſo eaſy a matter to penetrate into the true Cauſes of Actions, and to find out whether *Paſſion* or *Vertue* be the Spring that gives 'em Motion, and that for this Reaſon, that the one proceeding from the Corruption of Nature, we take more pains to conceal the one, than to acquire the other. This being a thing ſo common to all Mankind in general, nothing more can be requir'd of an Embaſſador, who nevertheleſs cannot always ſatisfy with outward Appearance, but finds himſelf oblig'd on ſome particular Occaſions, to be effectually what he may pretend to be at another time. If he has not a true Foundation of Honour within himſelf, he muſt at leaſt counterfeit an honeſt Principle in his Exterior, that he may not ſcandalize his Character and his Maſter. The Count *de Cantecroix*, the Emperor's Embaſſador at *Venice*, in the Year 1606, made a Bawdy-houſe of his Houſe, he coyn'd falſe Money, he had attempted to murder his Wife, tho' the Aſſaſſins fail'd in their Undertaking, and he had effectually, kill'd his Steward. This gave ſo great a Scandal to the Senate, that they complain'd of it to the Emperor, and cauſ'd him to be recall'd. All this notwithſtanding, they diſmiſs'd him honourably, and made him the uſual Preſent, but the Count being apprehenſive, that his Wife might accompliſh the Stroke he had miſcarry'd in, ſtole out of *Venice*, and left it in the Night, without taking his leave of any Body.

I ſhall not here take notice of thoſe Qualities that are abſolutely requiſite to an Embaſſador, becauſe I deſign 'em particular Chapters, and yet I ſhall not omit ſaying here, that an *Embaſſador* is a uſeleſs Tool, and even dangerous to his Maſter, if he has not an incorruptible Fidelity towards him, and a Zeal, neither inconſiderate, nor ſelf-intereſted, beſides which, he muſt have Ability enough, not to be ridiculous in his Station. He ought moreover to have a perfect Knowledge of the Affairs he is to negotiate, as well as of the Circumſtances of thoſe Princes who have any relation to the Intereſt of his Maſter. It is beſides impoſſible, that the Prince ſhould be aſſur'd of the Fidelity and Capacity of his Miniſter, if he has not given him ſufficient Proofs thereof on other Occaſions, of which the Maſter uſually takes notice in his Commiſſion, which ſerves to make known the Capacity of the one, and the Confidence of the other.

When I ſay that an Embaſſador tranſacts his Maſter's Buſineſs in a Court, or with ſome foreign Power, I on purpoſe decline the word *Negotiate*. All Miniſters of the ſecond Order are *Negotiators*, whereas all *Embaſſadors* are not, neither are all Negotiators *Embaſſadors*. The *Embaſſador* of Obedience, and he who is ſent to be a Witneſs to an Oath, for the Obſervation and Execution of a Treaty of Peace, or to repreſent his Prince at the Ceremonies of a Chriſtening, a Marriage, a Coronation, or a Funeral, negotiate nothing, however this does not hinder 'em from being *Embaſſadors*, and indeed they generally receive more Honour than they who negotiate.

There are, moreover, *Miniſters* who have neither *Quality* nor *Character*, and yet are entitl'd to the Protection of the *Law of Nations*. The *Marquis Spinola*, *Preſident Richardot*, and the other Miniſters, whom the Arch-Duke *Albert*, ſent to the *Hague*, in the Year 1607, to treat of a Peace, were not *Embaſſadors*, which is

The EMBASSADOR and his FUNCTIONS

is Self-evident, by reason their Credentials did not give 'em that Character. They were not at the same time Ministers of the second Order neither, because they were of too high a Rank for an Employ so much beneath 'em, yet they receiv'd the same Honours which would have been paid to the Character of Embassador, and were respected as if they had been such. The Mareschal d'Estrades, while he was yet but a private Captain, and afterwards Colonel, tho' he had no political Qualification, yet he negotiated Affairs of the highest Importance, and was consider'd as a very able and very necessary Minister.

Dossat had solicited the Affairs of France, a long time before Henry IV's Reconciliation, but he was particularly charg'd therewith, only after the Duke of Luxemburg had finish'd the Business of his Embassy; and notwithstanding he had not the Character of Embassador, it was no hindrance to his executing the Functions thereof, or enjoying all the Rights and Priviledges of the Character. There was nothing but the publick Ceremonies that distinguish'd him from an Embassador, at the Audiences, and at the Pope's Chapels. He says himself, that at the Marriage of Philip III King of Spain, and the Arch-Dutchess of Austria, the Solemnities whereof were celebrated at Ferrara, in the Year 1598, the Emperor's, and Venetian Embassadors were standing near the Pope, the Spanish Embassador had no Rank, while he, Dossat, was among the Bishop's Assistants, and administer'd Incense to the new Queen of Spain.

But it is a thing somewhat extraordinary, to give the Quality of Embassador to one who is not design'd to negotiate, and who cannot, for that reason, enjoy the Protection of the Law of Nations. Peter, Lord of Moldavia, having render'd himself odious to his Subjects, and not being very agreeable to the Court at Constantinople, was driven from his Countrey by the Turks, who pursu'd him so vigorously, that all he could do was to fling himself into a Castle he had acquir'd in Transilvania, where he had secur'd his Wife and his most precious Moveables. Here he was besieg'd by John Zapoli, King of Hungary, who forc'd him to surrender, but upon such Conditions, as oblig'd John to permit him to remain in the said Castle in full Liberty. Stephen, who had succeeded his Brother Peter in Moldavia, fearing to be expell'd himself in his turn, made intercession to Soliman to ease him of that Apprehension, by taking from his Brother the Protection of the King of Hungary. Soliman requir'd it of John, who at first pretended he could not abandon that Lord, after having given him his Word to the contrary, but finding himself press'd hard, he yielded at last to the earnest Solicitations of Soliman, and sent him to Constantinople, not as a Prisoner, but with the Quality and Retinue of an Embassador. Peter was very well receiv'd at the Port, and there justify'd his Actions so well, that Soliman not being able to send him back to Moldavia, with which he had invested Stephen, and yet being desirous to spread a good Opinion of his Justice and Generosity, gave him leave to go and live at Pera, where he allow'd him a perfect Liberty to make and receive all sorts of Visits. Stephen dying some time after, Soliman sent him back to his own Countrey, where he caus'd him to be re-establish'd by one of his Bashas. Peter may be said to have had the Quality of Embassador, and yet he was none, neither could he pretend to the Protection of the Law of Nations. He had no Letters of Credence, nor did Soliman acknowledge him for a publick Minister, and the Retinue that accompany'd him, was in effect but an Honourable Guard, compos'd of Persons who had Orders to deliver him up to the Great Turk.

The Quality of Embassadress is of a much later Date than that of Embassador. The word Legatus is Masculine, and the same Laws that prohibit Women the Exercise of publick Offices, debar 'em also of this Employ, which Men of the greatest Ability have much ado to discharge worthily. Indeed formerly, when all Embassies were extraordinary, and lasted no longer than was necessary for the transacting the Affairs they had to negotiate, Embassadors did not take their Wives along with 'em, so that an Embassadress was altogether an unheard of thing. Margaret of Austria, Aunt to the Emperor Charles V. Louisa, Mother of Francis I. Eleonora, his Queen, Mary, Queen of Hungary, and Margaret, Dutchess of Alençon, Sister to the same King Francis, have all perform'd Negotiations and Treaties, but then they were assisted by able Ministers, and they had a Quality much above that of Embassadress. The Marshaless of Guebriant was the first Lady, and the only one if I mistake not, that has had this Quality annex'd to her own Person, and she may perhaps be the last. When therefore I shall speak of an Embassadress, I wou'd be understood to speak of the Wife of an Embassador, who is the Person that makes her enjoy the Protection of the Law of Nations, which is unacquainted with the Quality of Embassadress. The English Lady, of whom Philip de Commines makes so delightful a History, had neither Character nor Quality: But after what he relates of the Ability of this Creature, it must be own'd, that if she was not an Embassadress, she knew perfectly well how to discharge the Functions thereof. The Earl of Warwick was, of all the English Noblemen, he, who had most contributed to the undoing of Henry VI to the ruin of the House of Lancaster, and to the setting up that of York in the Person of Edward IV. He afterwards incurr'd Edward's Displeasure irreconcilably, so that not thinking himself safe in England, he took Shipping, in order to retire to his Government of Calais, taking with him the Duke of Clarence, his Son-in-law, and Brother to Edward. The Earl making a Stop near the Risbank, Vauclere, his Lieutenant in the Government of Calais, who had been plac'd there by himself, fir'd upon him, and forc'd him to put to Sea in order to land in Normandy. Edward was so well pleas'd with Vauclere's Proceeding, that he made him Governor in Chief, but being inform'd afterwards, that this new Governor kept still a Correspondence with the Earl, he began to distrust him, as well as the Refuge Lewis XI gave to the Exiles. What most disturb'd him, was to see his Brother engag'd in the Party of their common Enemies, against the Interest of their House. To make him sensible of the ill Consequences thereof, he made use of a Lady, who under the pre-

C

tence of going to the Earl, on the part of his private Friends, procur'd her self a Passage to *Calais*, and afterwards met with Protection in *France* She outwitted *Vauclere*, and so artfully represented to the Duke of *Clarence*, that certain Ruin would attend him, if he adher'd to the Earl, whatever the Success of Affairs might be, (because the Earl was going to marry his youngest Daughter to the Prince of *Wales*, *Henry* VI's Son) that he promis'd to declare for the King his Brother so soon as ever he had the least favourable Opportunity, and could do it with Success to their mutual Advantage Accordingly he did so, in the first Engagement, and thereby secur'd the Sceptre to his House, which otherwise was just returning to the House of *Lancaster*, which by that Marriage was going to reascend the Throne The most accomplish'd Embassador could not have done more

I shall only add to this, That the Embassies in Ordinary are not of the Appointment of the *Law of Nations*, it being certain, they were not so much as known two hundred Years ago There are still several Nations that are altogether ignorant of 'em *Europe* only admits 'em, and those Princes who would not receive 'em, would, 'tis true, act against the Custom, but not against the *Law of Nations* There are none to be seen at the Court of *Poland*, the *Polanders* not suffering any to reside with 'em willingly

In the Month of *April* 1666, one of the Deputies of the Nobility said in the Diet at *Warsaw*, that the *French* Embassador had nothing to do there that he ought to be look'd upon as a Spy, or rather as a Traytor that it was known he had manag'd several Intrigues against the Tranquility of the State that the King had no need of a Tutor, nor the Crown of foreign Councils that the Residence of the *Embassador* was to be suspected, because *Embassadors are us'd to retire when they have finish'd their Negotiation* that it was above a Year that this was in *Poland*, and what he did there was not known, nor to what his Presence was requisite that he should therefore depart, or *change his Quality of Embassador into that of Resident* This Gentleman did not explain himself well, but nevertheless he confirms what I advanc'd In the beginning of the Year 1668, the Deputies of the Provinces made pressing Instances ten times, that all the Embassadors might be sent away, and that a Law might be made which should regulate the time they should be allow'd to stay, which the King and the Senate oppos'd, but this Opposition also was one of the chief Causes of the breaking up of the Diet

---

CHAP. II

It belongs to Sovereigns only to send Embassadors.

I Have taken notice in the preceding Chapter, that there is not a more illustrious Mark of Sovereignty than the Right of sending and receiving Embassadors When some Years after the Treaty of *Vervins*, the Arch-Duke *Albert* caus'd the first Overtures of a Peace to be made to the United Provinces, the States (to shew that the first Article of their Treaty was to be the Foundation and Establishment of their Liberty and Sovereignty) gave the Quality of Embassadors, to *Francis d'Arsens* and to *Noel Caron*, who till then had done the Business of the State as Agents and the two Kings, of *France* and *England*, acknowledging in those Ministers the representing Character, own'd at the same time the Sovereignty of the State that sent 'em But while *Spain* disputed it with 'em, after the Truce, and that the States were to treat with her at *Munster*, they found themselves by so much the more perplex'd, because they knew that the *Spaniards* would not suffer, that the Quality of Embassador should be clearly express'd in the Powers of their Ministers At first it was propos'd at the *Hague*, to give to their Ministers that, *of Embassadors appointed to the Crown of* Sweden, *and Plenipotentiaries at* Munster, and to give them the same *Character of Embassador* in the Powers they were to take with 'em, to treat with the Ministers of *France*. That at the opening of their Negotiation with those of *Spain*, they should produce that Power, where the Quality *of Embassadors to the Crown of* Sweden was express'd, but moreover they should have no other Power, of which they should make use, in case the *Spaniards* made any Difficulty to acknowledge 'em as Embassadors, and that then, those of *France* should be also oblig'd to be contented with the Quality of Plenipotentiaries D'*Avaux* and *Servien* were mightily scandaliz'd at this Proceeding, and said, that the *Dutch* were not contented to fill their Powers with a Quality which had not been agreed to, and which the *Spaniards* would not suffer, but would also oblige the Ministers of *France* to divest themselves of a Character, which the King had given 'em and under which they had been acknowledg'd for above two Years They said, that this was by so much the more strange, that even the *Spaniards* did not give it themselves in the Powers they had to treat with the *Dutch*, whereas all those, with whom the Ministers of *France* were oblig'd to negotiate, were *Embassadors*, so that it was absolutely necessary they should also have the same Character They moreover said that this would disable the King their Master from employing, for the future, Embassadors, upon occasion of any Treaty with the King of *Spain*, in any place whatever, because the Interest of *France* being inseparable from those of the United Provinces, he would be always oblig'd to follow their Caprice. That they could not comprehend why the States should resent against *France*, an Injury they receiv'd from *Spain*, *which by rejecting this Power, would call their Sovereignty in question*, whereas *France* acknowledg'd knowledg'd 'em as Sovereigns That the *Dutch* would thereby expose themselves without Necessity to an inevitable Affront, by reason the *Spaniards* being punctually inform'd of all the Resolutions the States-General took, would not fail to contest the Quality of their Ministers, if it were but to set that State and *France* at variance, and so expose both the one and the other to the Discretion of their common Enemies That the *Dutch* acted here contrary to the Rules of Prudence, in wilfully drawing on themselves the Refusal of the *Spaniards*, who, by obliging them *to renounce the most conspicuous Token of Sovereignty*, did them a Prejudice, for which *France* could not cause any Reparation to be made For if the *Hollanders* should oblige the Ministers of *France* to renounce the Quality of Embassadors, this voluntary Renunciation would not hinder the King of *France* from causing his Embassadors to be acknowledg'd in all the Courts of the World, whereas it would be disputed every where, to the United Provinces, when once they should be obliged to blot it out of their Powers So that they ought to risque nothing, but be contented to take the Quality of *Embassadors* in the Powers they should shew to the whole Assembly, except the *Spaniards*, for fear the Refusal of these should draw upon 'em that of others, who till then had own'd 'em for Sovereigns

No stronger Argument can be us'd on this Subject, nor that explains it better, for which reason I shall only alledge one Example to make good my Position The *Grisons* are those People of the *Alps* whom the *Romans* call'd *Rœti* They are distinguish'd into three Confederacies, or Communities, and the most considerable (which is call'd the *Grey League*) gives its Name to the other two, of which the one is call'd *the League of the ten Jurisdictions*, and the other *the League of the House of God* The Inhabitants of the *Valteline*, who are subject to the *Grisons*, revolt'd in the Year 1620, and having call'd to their Assistance the Arch-Duke of *Tirol* and the Duke of *Feria*, Governor of *Milan*, the *Grisons* found themselves so incommoded by the Arms of their Neighbours, that they sent to *Milan* to desire Passports for the Deputies, who were to repair thither to negotiate a Peace This was granted 'em, but when their Embassadors or Deputies came there, the Governor would not admit of those of the League of the ten Jurisdictions He said that that League (which formerly made part of the Demesne of the House of *Austria*) having been conquer'd by the Arch-Duke to whom it had sworn Fidelity, he could no longer consider 'em but as a lopp'd off Member, *which being become subject to the Arch-Duke, had no more the Right of sending Embassadors, nor of treating as a free People* The Duke of *Feria* acknowledg'd the other two Leagues as Sovereigns, as they really were, and are still, as is also the third, having recover'd its ancient Rights, and this is what no body can doubt of The Kings of *France* and *Spain* have had their Embassadors with them, and have made Treaties and Alliances with the *Grisons*, as with a free and sovereign People In the Year 1604, the *Grisons* sent to *Venice* seven Embassadors, who were attended by one hundred and fifty Persons, and the Senate defray'd their Expences throughout the whole State, and caus'd 'em to be receiv'd with more Honour than had ever been shewn to any other Embassador

The Reason that makes this Right inseparable from Sovereignty, is, that the Prince who employs an *Embassador* being oblig'd to protect him, as well as he to whom he is employ'd, it is evident that the Minister can hope for this Protection but from him who has the Right of the Sword, and can resent an outrage which is done him in the Person of his Minister, that is to say, that those Sovereigns only who were unaccountable for their Actions, can employ Embassadors because they are oblig'd to protect 'em

From whence we must conclude, that those who are employ'd by Persons that are not Sovereigns, being neither Embassadors nor publick Ministers, notwithstanding they are allow'd the Benefit of the publick Security, yet they cannot pretend to the Protection of the *Law of Nations* The Princes of the Blood, and the other Catholick Lords, who after the Death of *Henry* III declar'd themselves for the lawful Heir, sent the Duke of *Luxemburg* to *Rome* in the Year 1501, but he was no Embassador, because he had no Letters of Credence from his Sovereign, tho' at the same time he took the Journey with the King's Consent It was not the King that order'd him to negotiate, nor that sign'd his Instructions, but some Lords of the same Quality as the Duke, who pray'd him to take upon him this Commission The Cardinal *Joyeuse*, and the Baron of *Senecy*, who went thither since in the behalf of the League, were not Embassadors nor publick Ministers neither, but only Deputies of a criminal and very dangerous Faction, which had set itself up in the State against the Royal Authority, which alone could name and constitute publick Ministers For although the incomparable *H de Groot* makes this Position That when in a State there are two Factions or Parties, whose Power is almost equal, the Ministers both of the one and the other ought equally to enjoy the Protection of the *Law of Nations*, one would think that should extend no farther than to the Commerce the two Parties may have, each with the other Had it not been for the Bravery and personal Merit of *Henry* IV, the Party of the League was beyond Comparison more considerable than the King's, yet neither the Pope, nor the King of *Spain* who protected the Catholick Zealots, ever consider'd their Deputies as publick Ministers It is true that in the Conference at *Surène*, they treated upon the level with the King's Deputies, but then both the one and the other found their Security in their Passports, and not in the *Law of Nations*, which is otherwise very little respected in Civil Wars

The Party of the Parliament at *London* was already very considerable, when it sent *Walter Strickland* to the *Hague* in the Month of September 1642, but as soon as he had demanded Audience, *Boswell*, who was there on the part of the King of *England*, oppos'd it, and represented that the Parliament being but a Body without a Soul, in the Absence, and without the King's Warranty, had neither the Power to determine any thing within the Countrey, nor the Authority to set on foot Negotiations out of the Kingdom, *without the Permission of its Sovereign* Strickland seeing that the States-General (to whom he had sent his Letters of Credence) return'd him no Message, went one Day into one of their Ante-rooms and demanded Audience They sent him word by two Deputies, that his Letter of Credence not being yet translated out of *English*, the States desir'd him to consider if it might not be proper for him to give in his Proposals in Writing, that they might be translated at the same time But he made answer, That he had Orders to deliver 'em by word of Mouth, and that if they delay'd giving him Audience that Day he would take it as a Refusal, and would consider what was proper for him to do This Resolution oblig'd the States to send him a Deputy of each Province, to whom he laid open his Commission, and left with 'em his Proposals in Writing, however he had no publick Audience, notwithstanding the Deputies of the Province of *Holland* ask'd it with as much warmth as himself The States-General came to some Resolutions upon his Memorial, and assur'd him they would always observe an exact Neutrality between the King and the Parliament An Expression that gives to understand, that the States acknowledg'd that there were two Parties form'd in *England*, and that, for particular Reasons, (which cannot be unknown) they had more Consideration for the one than the other They gave sufficient Testimony thereof the second Voyage the same *Strickland* made to the *Hague*, immediately after the Death of the late King, which had not remov'd the Difficulties of his Admission *Dorislaus*, his Colleague, had been murther'd there, so that *Strickland*, not thinking himself safe, made pressing Instances to be admitted and dispatch'd The Deputies of *Holland* seconded his Instances, and continually represented, that Audience could not be refus'd him without breaking the Neutrality, which the States had promis'd to preserve inviolably But all these good Offices were of no use, for the Deputies of the six other Provinces declar'd, They could come to no Resolution in an Affair of this nature, without the express Order of their Principals, who did not explain themselves upon the Matter Insomuch that *Strickland* (who was in continual Uneasiness on the Account of the Accident which had happen'd to *Dorislaus*) seeing the Obstinacy of the six Provinces, back'd by the Authority of the Prince of *Orange*, was invincible, went back to *England* This Proceeding of theirs was the more surprizing, because the State had an Embassador with the same Parliament, whose Minister they treated so unworthily, and which not wanting the means to resent it, soon reveng'd it self so cruelly, that there was all the Reason in the World to repent of the little Regard had been shewn to a Power, which made a great part of *Europe* tremble

In the Year 1643, *Hugh de Burgo*, who was deputed by the *Irish* Catholicks, being at *Brussells*, sollicited a Passport from the States-General to come to the *Hague*, being refus'd it, his Sollicitor desir'd one from the Council of State, which being ignorant of what had pass'd in the Assembly of the States-General order'd him one The States being very much surpris'd to see the Memorial of a Man, to whom they had refus'd leave to enter into the Countrey, caus'd it to be return'd him with his Letters of Credence which he had deliver'd in with it, and order'd him to depart the Countrey in four Days Those Catholicks had declar'd against the Parliament, but they had given the Direction of their Affairs to the Archbishop of *Fermo*, the Pope's Nuncio, so that although the King approv'd of their Intention, yet he did not dare countenance their Proceedings They were Rebels whom the *Law of Nations* does not protect, and whose Emissaries do not deserve the Denomination of Ministers, neither are they so in effect

In making the Right of Embassy inseparable from Sovereignty, we may form two Theses, the Truth of which we must examine in this Chapter, whether all Sovereigns have it, and on the other side, whether all those who are not Sovereigns have no Pretence to it As for the first part, I think I may say, that except the Electors and the Princes of *Germany*, of whom we shall speak in the fourth Chapter, there is no Sovereign but who has that Right, and enjoys the same The Pope sends his *Legates* every where, and has his Nuncios almost in all the Catholick Courts of *Europe*, in *France*, in *Spain*, in *Portugal*, at *Vienna*, *Venice*, *Turin*, *Naples*, and sometimes Nuncios or Internuncios in *Poland*, at *Brussels*, at *Cologn* and elsewhere They have no Function of Ecclesiastical Jurisdiction in *France*, but almost every where else He also sends Bishops, of those who are call'd *in partibus infidelium*, into the Provinces of Catholick Princes, and Protestants, but they are properly speaking but Vicars, and their Function being merely spiritual, they cannot be consider'd as publick Ministers, nor enjoy the Protection of the *Law of Nations*, tho' they are allow'd the publick Security in those Places where they have Admittance

The Emperor has his Embassadors in Ordinary only at *Rome* and at *Maarid*, he only sends Ministers of the second Order to almost all the other Courts, altho' he sends sometimes Extraordinary Embassadors to *Constantinople*, into *Poland*, to *Venice*, and elsewhere

The King of *France* has his Embassadors in Ordinary at *Constantinople*, at *Rome*, *Madrid*, *London*, *Lisbon*, *Venice*, *Turin*, the *Hague*, and at *Soleurre* At *Vienna* he has only a Minister of the second Order, because the *Spanish* Embassador has there the Precedency He has no Minister in Ordinary at the Courts of *Stockholm*, and of *Copenhagen*, nor in *Poland*, but he sends thither Extraordinaries when Affairs require it, as well as to the confederated *Grisons*, and to the Princes of *Germany* and *Italy*

The Embassies of *Spain* are to *Rome*, to *Paris*, *London*, *Lisbon*, *Vienna*, *Venice*, and to the *Swiss Cantons* As for the *Northern* Kings she does as *France* does, sending Embassadors or Ministers Extraordinary, as Occasion requires Since the Peace of *Munster*, there has been two Embassadors in Ordinary from *Spain* at the *Hague*, but in Consideration that the States grew weary of entertaining one at *Madrid*, and that the most important Affairs are for the most part determin'd at *Brussells* with the Governor of the Low Countreys, the King has thought fit to fill that Post with a Minister of the second

The EMBASSADOR and his FUNCTIONS. 9

cond Order, who, in his Quality of Envoy, discharges the Functions of Embassador with as much Sufficiency and Splendor as his Predecessors had done.

The Crown of *England* has its Embassadors in all the Courts I have nam'd, excepting *Vienna* and *Venice*, whither it sends only Extraordinaries. It has one at the Port for the Security of the Commerce, which its Subjects formerly carryed on under the Banner of *France*. It is but of late Years that it has one in *Holland*. After that in the Year 1585 Queen *Elizabeth* had sent the Earl of *Leicester* to the United Provinces to command their Armies, the States permitted her Minister to assist at the Council of State, by reason that the Queen (who had her Garrisons in the *Briel*, at *Flushing*, and in the Fort of *Rammekens*, for the better Security of being rumour'd of those Sums which she had advanc'd,) thought she ought to have a part in their Councils, being she took so great a one in their Fortune. But the States being unwilling to remain any longer under that Dependence, after they were reimbursed by King *James*, and dismiss'd of their Towns, understanding in the Year 1626 that *Ralph* grew was to succeed *Dudley Carleton* in the Embassy in *Holland*, they gave King *Charles* to understand, that his Embassador should be always received with the Respect which was due to his Character, but they could not suffer him to have a Seat in their Council of State, because the Reasons, for which this Advantage had been granted to the Minister of Queen *Elizabeth*, being ceas'd, they could not admit there for the future any of the King should send. That they had declin'd offering any Affront to *Carleton*, by causing him to quit a Post he was in Possession of, because they knew the King intended to recall him in a little time, but that they could not suffer his Successor to fill the same. The *English* were very much offended hereat, and accus'd the State of Ingratitude, but nevertheless they were forc'd to acquiesce, and all the Resentment they shew'd, was, that from that time they sent no more Embassadors to the *Hague*, but only a Minister of the second Order, 'till Sir *William Temple*, having in the Year 1668 concluded the triple Alliance, the King made him reside at the *Hague* in the Quality of Embassador in Ordinary, and in the Year 1674 he sent him back thither as an Extraordinary.

The Republick of *Venice* has its Embassadors in Ordinary, to the best of my Knowledge, only at *Rome*, *Vienna*, *Paris*, in *Spain*, and at *Constantinople*, observing generally this Order, That as that it quits the Embassy of *France* passes into *Spain*, or else the versa out of *Spain* into *France*, and from thence to *Vienna*, from whence, after his limited time of Service, he is employ'd at *Rome*. She has no Embassador in Ordinary with the Duke of *Savoy*, for many Reasons, which I shall take notice of elsewhere. He that is employ'd near the Imperor is of the Quality of *Grand Sage*, at least it is given him in his Letters of Credence, and the other Embassadors have that of *Sage* of *Terra firma*. The Embassy of *Constantinople*, in which the Embassador is of the Quality of *Baily*, is the last, is well as the most laborious of all. It has this Advantage, that, with the Employment

of Embassador, he performs also the Function of Consul and of Judge, not only between the *Venetians*, but also between all those who traffick there under the Banner of St *Mark*, and he is not oblig'd to give an Account of the Money that he is entrusted with, to be distributed among the Ministers of that Court, who are the most self-interested and most avaricious in the whole World. So that it is reckon'd that the Baily may, during his three Years Service, get clear to himself above one hundred thousand Crowns, all Charges defray'd. This Republick also sends sometimes Embassadors into *England*, and to the *Swiss Cantons*, but it is very rarely, and only upon extraordinary Occasions. She also frequently employs Ministers of the second Order, which she takes from amongst her Citizens and seldom from the Nobles. She ever apply'd her self to the making and maintaining Peace between the other Princes of *Europe*, as well because her Preservation depends in a great measure on the repose of *Christendom*, and principally on that of *Italy*, as because the *Turk*, who is the most powerful and most to be dreaded of all her Enemies, always makes his Advantage of the Divisions of Christian Princes. She would willingly therefore have their Strength so equally balanc'd, that she might have no reason to be uneasy on that account, and that their Wars may not invite the *Turk* to extend his Frontiers on the side of *Europe*, and especially in their Neighbourhood.

Formerly there was a very good Correspondence between the Republick of *Venice* and the States of the United Provinces, by reason of the common Interest both the one and the other has, to oppose that of the two great Powers, which might oppress the other, and by that means establish an universal Monarchy in *Christendom*. The same Interest subsists still, however all that the Republick of *Venice* does is to contribute its good Wishes, and its Offices of Mediation, while the United Provinces, by opposing the Progress of the Arms of *France* in *Flanders*, have not been afraid to draw upon themselves all the Strength of that terrible Power, which very much approv'd of their Sentiments, when the Arms of the House of *Austria* were more formidable, and its Intentions more dangerous than they are at present. It is true, the States had a particular Interest to keep the Arms of *France* at a Distance from their Frontiers, and to prevent the Conquest of *Germany*, since that of the Low Countries would have follow'd as a necessary Consequence. But it is also true, that as well on this Occasion, as on many others, the *Venetians* have made use only of Intrigue and Negotiation, so long as the foreign Forces did not approach *Italy*, and did not pass the *Alps*. This good Correspondence was cultivated for many Years by the Embassadors in Ordinary, who were on the part of the two Republicks, at *Venice* and the *Hague*, till this Commerce was interrupted within near these forty Years. The *Venetians* had promis'd to pay yearly to the *Hollanders* certain Subsidies, but perceiving that this remote Friendship was either of no Use, or at least not very necessary, they grew weary of it, and did not trouble themselves much to make good the Alliance they had with the States

D

States Insomuch that these, finding it was altogether neglected on that side, neglected also to supply the Place of *William de Liri* Lord of *Osterwick*, who, upon the Conclusion of his Embassy at *Venice* in the Year 1638, had succeeded to that of *France*, after the Decease of the Baron of *Languerac*. The *Venetian* Embassador from time to time made pressing Instances that they would send a Successor to the Lord of *Osterwick*, but receiving no other Answer than Reproaches of the little Care was taken at *Venice* to execute Treaties, he caus'd himself to be also recall'd, since which time, there has been no *Venetian* Minister at the *Hague*, nor *Dutch* Embassador at *Venice*. It has been more than once propos'd, and even resolv'd upon in the Assembly of the States-General, to renew this good Understanding, and to send a Minister to *Venice*. But forasmuch as the Interest of those who were to be employ'd was more consider'd than that of the State, this Thought was soon laid aside after their Death, and no farther mention has been made of it these many Years.

The *States of the United Provinces* have Embassadors in Ordinary but in *France* and in *England*, where they have always had 'em, ever since they have been acknowledg'd as Sovereigns, till the last Rupture. Formerly they had also one at *Venice*, as I before took notice, but they did not think it advisable to continue that Custom, because the Honour of the Republick's Alliance being destitute of all other Utility, they did not think themselves oblig'd to purchase it. I here speak of the customary and regulated Embassies. It is not long since they had an Embassador in Ordinary at *Madrid*, and another at *Stockholm*, but it may be said, that those Employs were only bestow'd for personal and particular Considerations. *Cornelius Haga* has likewise had the Quality of Embassador, or Orator at the Court of the Great Turk, but as well he, as the others were succeeded by Ministers of the second Order. The States of *Holland* have a right to present to the States General the Person they would have nam'd to the Embassy of *France*, and the States of *Zealand* have the same Advantage, with reference to him that is design'd for the Embassy of *England*, by reason of the Commerce wherein these two Provinces are principally concern'd. *Holland* again has a right to present one of their Province to all the Embassies Extraordinary that are compos'd of two or three Persons. In the Year 1660, the States-General dispatch'd three solemn Embassies, each of which was compos'd of three Embassadors, to deliver their Compliments at *Paris* and *Madrid* upon the *Pirenean* Peace and the Marriage, and in *London* on account of the Restoration of the King of *Great Britain*, and *Holland* which had nam'd two to each of the first, nam'd one also to the last. They have only Ministers of the second Order in most of the other Courts, because the Funds they settle every Year, for this kind of Expence, being regulated, they are oblig'd to husband it, that they may not will themselves in Charges that are not absolutely necessary.

The *Swiss Cantons* have no Embassadors nor Ministers residing, or Ordinary, at *Rome*, in *France*, *Spain*, or elsewhere. He that sollicits their Pensions, and pays the Soldiers in *France*, is not acknowledg'd as a publick Minister, because he has neither Quality nor Character, nor is it maintain'd by the *Cantons*, but by the Officers of the Troops that are in the King's Service. The Pensions which the King of *Spain* pays to some of the Catholick *Cantons*, on the Score of the Alliance he has with 'em, as Duke or *Milan*, are not so considerable as to require a publick Minister to sollicit the Payment thereof. The Advantages they gain'd in the Battels they gave to *Charles* the last Duke of *Burgundy*, and the Expeditions they made into *Italy*, for and against *France*, in the Reigns of *Charles* VIII, *Lewis* XII, and of *Francis* I, procur'd 'em such a high Reputation of Valour, that Princes thought themselves oblig'd to court and even buy their Friendship and Alliance. They have maintain'd themselves in this Acquisition ever since that Time, and receive Embassadors at home, without sending any abroad, unless it be upon very extraordinary Occasions. We may add, that all the *Canton* have not the same Interests nor the same Alliances, a thing the States of the United Provinces have, which are link'd together by a much stricter, and indeed inseparable Band, whereas the *Cantons* being divided on the point of Religion, which is the most important and most dangerous of all, sometimes take Arms one against the other, which has not yet been seen amongst the United Provinces, as it is very probable it never will. Moreover there are some *Can on*, who, out of their Territories, have Subjects who do not acknowledge the other Allies in any thing whatever, which is not to be observ'd among the United Provinces, who jointly and undividedly possess whatever their common Arms have conquer'd or united to the State. The *Cantons* have no particular Funds, neither for Embassies nor for the other Expences of that Nature, but when the *Cantons* send in Embassy any where, they each of 'em name a certain Number of Deputies, and pay 'em.

What I have now said of the *Cantons*, may be said of the three Leagues of the *Grisons*. They form also a Sovereign State, which makes it self be acknowledg'd as such, and is pretty considerable, as well on the account of the Alliance they have with the *Swiss Cantons* as because being Masters of the principal Pass, that make the Communication of *Germany* and *Italy*, *France*, *Spain*, and the Republick of *Venice* have judg'd, that the Friendship of these People was necessary to 'em, and accordingly have been chary of it on several Occasions. In reference to Embassy, the govern themselves as the *Swiss* do.

The Republicks of *Genoa*, *Lucca*, and *Ragusa* have no Embassadors in Ordinary neither, in the chief Courts of *Europe*, except that of *Genoa*, which has sometimes Ministers of the second Order in *France* and in *Spain*.

Excepting the Duke of *Savoy*, who has his Ordinary Embassadors a *Rome*, at *Paris*, and at *Madrid*, the other Princes of *Italy* employ there only Ministers of the second Order, is also at *Venice*, where the Duke of *Savoy* has not a regular and continual Commerce, but only, by Intervals, as it shall be said elsewhere. The great Duke of *Tuscany*, the Dukes of *Mantua*, *Parma*, and *Modena*, cause their Embassadors

The EMBASSADOR and his FUNCTIONS   11

to be acknowledg'd in the first Courts of *Europe*, but they do not keep there any *Ordinaries*.

The Emperor of the *Turks* and the Czar of *Muscovy* are not only Sovereigns, but are so absolute, and reign after so arbitrary a manner, that there is no Difference between their Subjects and Slaves. They also send their Embassadors, and other Ministers, to other Princes, but they do not let 'em reside there. *Philip de Comines* says, "There is a much greater Advantage in "sending Embassadors than in receiving them, "because being Spies that are receiv'd with Ho"nour, they may with the greatest Security carry "on their Intrigues and Cabals, which are "sometimes very dangerous, so that altho' the "Prince, to whom Embassadors are sent, re"ceives the Honour of 'em, yet he that em"ploys them reaps all the Benefit of 'em. But the *Turks* have quite different Politicks. The Port receives the Ministers of all the other Princes, and values it self for the Honour, flattering it self, that it is a kind of Homage that is done it, while she sends none to the other Courts, where she sends only *Chiaous* which do not reside there. The Christian Princes on their side, have their Ministers at *Constantinople*, but only for the Advantage they find thereby, in reference to the Commerce of their Subjects, excepting the Republick of *Venice* who having its Interest to negotiate, is oblig'd to cultivate the Friendship of that Court. The *Turks* do not suffer an Embassador to depart, till he is reliev'd by his Successor, or promises one shall come very speedily. M. *de Nantua*, Embassador from *France*, having fix'd his Design of leaving *Constantinople*, the Divan gave Orders to the *Caimacan* (who is the first Vizier's Lieutenant) to oppose his embarking, till he had caus'd a Successor to be sent to reside in his stead. The Ships which he had provided for his Transportation, were come within sight of the Town, over against the *Seraglio*, so that nothing hindring his Embarcation, he ran the Risque of it: but he was hardly ready to sail, when the Wind, which blew very hard, so entangl'd the Admiral (in which he was) in the Sails of another Ship, that it was impossible for him to pursue his Course: by this means the *Caimican* had sufficient time to give Orders to the Captains of the *Dardanells* to oppose his Passage. The *French* Ships were seiz'd, and the Embassador was order'd to repair to the Court, which was then at *Adrianople*, to give an account of his clandestine Retreat, and to tell the Reason, why the King his Master, had sent so powerful a Succour to the *Venetians* at *Candia*.

The *Czar* entertains no regular Correspondence with other Princes, nor any Ordinary Ministers in their Courts, but sometimes he sends thither Extraordinarys, with such limited Instructions, that they are not allow'd to depart from them in the least, upon pain of Death. The *Muscovites* have some Commerce with *England*, and with the United Provinces, on the account of Trafficks, wherein the *Czar* himself has a good Share. They have heretofore had great Differences with *Poland* and the *Suede*, concerning *Livonia*, but at present the *Muscovites* and the *Polanders* seem to have some common Interest, because the *Turks* and *Tartars* are Enemies to both, and that *Poland* cannot be lost, but *Muscovy* must also be undone.

Supposing then, that the Right of Embassy is inherent to Sovereignty, I shall have no great trouble to establish the Truth of my other Position, and to prove, that they who are not Sovereigns, have not the Privilege of sending Embassadors. Upon this Foundation, I say, that all other Princes that are Subjects, after what manner soever it be, cannot enjoy a Right, that is inseparable from Sovereignty.

The *Dauphin*, Son to *Charles* VII and some *Princes of the Blood*, sent their Embassadors to the Assembly that was holding at *Arras* in the Year 1435. In the Year 1448, the same King sent a solemn Embassy to *Rome*, to endeavour to suppress a Schism, that divided the Church under *Nicholas* V and *Felix* V. The King of *Sicily*, Prince of the Blood of *France* added his Embassadors also, and the *Dauphin* sent thither on his part, the Archbishop of *Embrun*, the Bishop of *St. Paul*, the Lord of *Malcora*, and the Dean of *Cravelis*. But these are things that are out of date, Kings not commonly granting this Right, neither to their Sons, nor Brothers, because it is one of the Flowers of their Crown, and that in a Monarchical State, none but the Monarch himself is Sovereign, all the rest are Subjects, of what Quality soever they be. There is no true Prince that is not Sovereign, or that it is not come from a Sovereign House, altho' he be not Sovereign himself: but this Quality of Prince, without Sovereignty, does not give him the Right of Embassy. The Princes, Younger Sons of *Savoy* and *Lorrain*, who have settled themselves in *France*, altho' they are Strangers, are Subjects, as well as those other Lords, who take the Quality of Prince, on account of *Dombes*, *Taimont*, *Enrichemont*, of *Tingry*, &c. I say the same thing, concerning the Lords of the House of *Bouillon de la Tour*, who within some Years, are acknowledg'd for Princes in *France*, notwithstanding they are not any longer in possession of the Territory of *Sedan*, of which they pretended to be Sovereigns. The late Mademoiselle *de Bouillon*, who dy'd unmarry'd, was become so strangely vain on the Score of this Principality, that she did not scruple to say, that her Sister, (who was marry'd to the Duke *de la Trimouille*, whose House is one of the most illustrious, and best ally'd in all the Kingdom) had marry'd beneath her self, tho' it was known, that the same Duke *de la Trimouille*, being at *Roan* in the Year 1617, in the Assembly of the *Notables*, oblig'd the Duke of *Bouillon* to quit the Bench of Dukes and Peers, to take place among the Marshals of *France*. The Marshal *de Turenne* had the Quality of Prince, but in the Year 1652, because, having left the Party of the Prince of *Condé*, Cardinal *Mazarine* had occasion for his Head and his Heart during the disturbance of the Kingdom. It is not such Princes as these, that have the Right of Embassy, no more than those titular Princes, the King of *Spain* makes in the *Low Countrey*, and particularly in the Kingdom of *Naples* and *Sicily*, where there are Princes that are hardly Noblemen.

The *Cardinals* pretend to be upon the level with Kings, and to take place of all other Princes. We shall have occasion to speak of 'em hereafter, for which reason I shall only take notice here, that Cardinals have no other Advantage over Princes, than that which *Melchisedec*

sedec had over *Abraham*, and that whatever Prerogatives have been annex'd to their Dignity, they have not the Right of sending Embassadors Cardinal *Francis Barbarin* (who was first Minister under the Pontificate of *Urban* VIII his Unkle) employ'd several Persons near the late Queen of *England*, *Henrietta* of *France*, who under the Quality of Agents, did all that a Minister from the Pope could have done, for the Promotion of the Roman Catholick Religion.

He sent thither, in the Year 1639, Count *Charles Rossetti*, who has since been Nuncio at *Cologn*, and made Cardinal, he was not contented to use his utmost Endeavours to obtain Liberty of Conscience, and the Exercise of their Religion, for the Roman Catholicks, but attempted also to change the predominant Religion in the Person of the King. He, who writ the History of those Times, upon very good Memoirs, says, that the Archbishop of *Canterbury* himself was much inclin'd thereto, and resolv'd to follow *Rossetti* to *Rome*, if Cardinal *Barber n* would have ensur'd him a Pension of eight and forty thousand Livres. The People of *London*, coming to understand *Rossetti*'s Intrigues, attack'd him in his House, from whence he sav'd himself at the Queen-Mother's, *Mary de Medicis*, who was then in *England*. The Parliament caus'd him to be sought for there, and oblig'd him to leave the Kingdom, and retire to *Flanders*. He was no publick Minister, since he had no Character, nor Letters of Credence from the Pope, so that he was at most but the Agent of a Cardinal, who could give him neither the one nor the other, for which Reason he could not enjoy the Protection of the *Law of Nations*, but to the extent of the Queen's Power. But neither the Parliament nor the *Londoners* violated the said Law, in the Person of a Man, who having no Character, nor being acknowledg'd for a publick Minister, disturb'd the Tranquillity of the State, by endeavouring to introduce a new Religion, contrary to the Laws of the Kingdom.

It is certain, that Subjects, are so far from having a Right to send Embassadors to their own Prince, that they cannot, without a Crime, make a Deputation to a foreign Prince, without the special Permission of their Sovereign. They who do it, let the Pretext be what it will, are guilty of Rebellion, and High Treason. The Deputies, whom the Subjects employ to their Sovereign as they address themselves to him, only by the way of Remonstrances and Supplications, cannot assume the Quality of publick Ministers, nor lay any Claim to the Protection of the *Law of Nations*, even not in those Countreys, which being govern'd after the Form of States, seem in some measure to share the Sovereignty with their Prince. Most of the Provinces of the Low Countreys, had such illustrious Privileges, that they were within a very small matter of enjoying an entire Liberty. At the beginning of the Troubles, which engag'd 'em in a Civil-War of fourscore Years, the States sent into *Spain the Marquis of Bergen-op-zoom, and the Baron* de Montigny, to endeavour to make *Philip* II relish the means, which might be of use, to prevent the Disorders, that threaten'd the State with all the Misfortunes which have befallen it since. It must

be own'd, they were very ill treated, and it is not doubted, but the Marquis dy'd there a violent Death, as well as the Baron, who resign'd his Life in the hands of the Hangman. It cannot be deny'd neither, that it was an Instance of barbarous Cruelty, and an Effect of *Ph lip*'s anxious, restless and haughty Temper, who, two Years after, did not scruple to sacrifice his only Son, to his Ambition and Jealousy, but then again, it would be wrong to say, that the *Law of Nations* was violated in the Death of those two *Flemish* Lords, because they were not invested with a *Character*, that could shelter them from the Severity of the *Laws*, and of *Justice*, tho' they who have the Administration of it, do not always strictly keep up to it.

Their Principals could not be consider'd as Sovereigns, by that Prince, who was himself Sovereign of the one, as well as of the other, notwithstanding the Privileges and Immunities, which the Provinces enjoy'd, came very near an entire Liberty. Their Deputies were indeed publick Persons, but they were not publick Ministers, and therefore could not pretend to the Protection of the *Law of Nations*, but only to the Enjoyment of the Effect of their Privileges, which might be said to screen em from the Rigour of an unproportionate Justice, but not from that of Cruelty and Tyranny.

Most of the *Provinces of the Low Countreys*, having in the Year 1581, cast off the Yoke of a Domination, which they said was foreign, offer'd it in part to the Duke of *Alençon*, who dying in the Year 1584, and *William*, Prince of *Orange*, being kill'd the same Year, they sent their Deputies to *France*, and offer'd the Sovereignty of their Countrey to King *Henry* III. He was a timorous Prince, and was so perplex'd with the League, that not daring to suffer the Deputies to come to *Paris*, he caus'd 'em to stay at *Roan*, whither he d spatch'd *Brulard*, his Secretary of State, to 'em, who being inform'd of their Intention, made his Report of it, and acquainted them also with the King's, which was quite contrary to that of the States, who were so inconsiderable at that time, that *Brulard* was not so much as provided with a Letter of Credence to the Deputies.

In the beginning of the Year 1585, the States of *Brabant*, of *Guelders*, *Flanders*, *Holland*, *Zeeland*, *Utrecht*, of *Frise*, and of *Mecklen*, sent thither again fifteen Persons of Quality, who besides their general Commission, had also a particular one from each Province.

Henry III who began to be undeceiv'd in the false Zeal, and evil Intentions of the Leaguers, look'd every where about him for Supporting unit their abominable Under akings. He therefore order'd the Deputies to come to *Paris*, after he had made them stay a Fortnight at *Senlis*. They had Audience of the King, and of the Queen-Mother, and had several Conferences with the Ministers. They were also invited to the publick Diversions, where they had an honourable Seat, and among the rest, to the Ceremonies of the Order of the Garter, which Queen *Elizabeth* sent at that time to the King. It is very probable they would have succeeded, if the King had not been necessitated, to give all his Application to the Affairs of his Kingdom, and to employ his whole Strength against the
House

The EMBASSADOR *and his* FUNCTIONS   13

House of *Guise*. The Deputies were given to understand as much, and were presented with Gold Chains after their Audience of Leave, and their Expences were defray'd during their Stay at *Paris*. It is very certain they were not consider'd as Embassadors, since neither in those Times, nor a great while after, did the States give that Character to their Ministers, so that it may be said with some certainty, that they did not put on their Hats, when they had Audience of a Prince who understood himself, and knew very well how to assert what was his due. They were publick Ministers, because that notwithstanding the States were not then acknowledg'd for Sovereigns, yet nevertheless they were so in effect, since they had no Superior since the Abdication.

The Deputies, whom the *Catalonians* sent to *Paris* in the Year 1640, were neither Embassadors, nor publick Ministers, altho' they assum'd that Quality. *Catalonia* had revolted, not with an intent on to erect it self into a Sovereignty, but with a Design to yield it self to an other Sovereign, so that it could only hope from its Revolt, to change its Master, whereby there is always more lost than got. Hereupon I think I ought to observe, that the Historians, especially those of *Spain*, frequently give the Quality of *Embassador*, as wel to those publick Ministers that are employ'd under all kinds of Characters, as to those Persons whom the Princes, who are presumptive Heirs to the Crown, employ'd near their Father, as may be seen in *Henry* Prince of *Asturias*, and in *Charles* Prince of *Viana*, who were presumptive Heirs of *Castile* and *Navarre*, as also to those Commissioners, whom the Kings send to their Subjects, and to those Deputies that the People employ'd to their Sovereign. I know very well, that the *Catalonians* to justify their last Insurrection, made a long Memorial of several Infractions of their Privileges, wherein, amongst other things, they complain'd, that at *Madrid* Prohibition had been made to give to the *Embassadors* of *Catalonia*, any other Quality than that of Syndicks or Agents, and that the Counsellors of *Barcelona* had not been suffer'd to cover themselves in the King's Presence. But as in *Spain* the Honour of being cover'd before the King is not particularly reserv'd to publick Ministers, so we ought to say, that formerly the Title of *Embassador* was so general, that it extended to all Persons publickly employ'd. But then again, since that Character is no longer given but to Representatives, and not to Ministers of the second Order, Those that are employ'd by *the States of a Province*, whatsoever may be their Liberties or Privileges, if it be not absolutely *Independent* and *Sovereign*, they cannot give themselves that Quality, since they are in effect but Syndicks or Deputies. At the same time I don't disown, that *Catalonia* and the other Provinces dependent on the Crown of *Arragon*, have such large Privileges, and so many, that there is not much wanting to the four Orders of the States, (which they stile the four Arms, which consist of the Prelates, the Barons, (which were formerly call'd, *los Ricos Hombres*) the Knights and the Citizens) to make 'em represent in their Assemblies, a kind of free Republick. We see they have frequently sent Embassadors to their Kings, and that they have likewise receiv'd some from foreign Princes and that it may be plain, that the Word is taken in its proper Signification, they make a Distinction betwixt the *Embassador* of the States of the *Province*, and the Deputies of the Town of *Barcelona*. *John*, King of *Arragon*, dying in the Year 1395, the Succession of the Crown became litigious, between *Matthew* Earl of *Foix*, who had marry'd *Jeanne* of *Arragor*, and *Martin*, Uncle to that Princess. *Matthew* sent to the States of the Kingdom the Bishop of *Oleron*, and a Lawyer nam'd *Promyre*, in the Quality of Embassadors to prosecute the Right of his Wife. The States having declar'd themselves in favour of *Martin*, deputed to him the Year following the Archbishop of *Saragossa*, *Don Peter Fernandez d'Ixa*, Commander of *Montauban*, *Don Lopez Ximenez d'Iurea*, *Don Fernand Lopez de Luna*, *Don Garci Lopez de Sese*, *John Fernandez de Heredia*, *James* of the Hospital, and *Stephen Pettinar*. The two last were Burgesses of *Saragossa*, notwithstanding which they had the Quality of *Embassadors* given 'em, as having been nam'd by the States of the Kingdom, whereas the four Jurats and Burgesses, which the Town added to the others, had only that of *Deputies*. These Embassadors, having acquitted themselves of their Complement in a publick Audience, desir'd a private one of the King, at which the Archbishop told him, *That according to the Privileges and Customs of the Kingdom, his Highness was oblig'd to come and give them his Oath in the City of* Saragossa, *immediately after his Accession to the Crown, and that the States were not oblig'd to respect him as their King, nor to receive his Orders and Commands, till he had given 'em that Pleage*. That they had suffer'd the Queen (who had a Power to act in the absence of her Husband) to take the Quality of Queen, and give that of King to her Husband, in the Letters she had dispatch'd to 'em, but at the same time they would have him to be sensible, that they had done it only to destroy the Pretensions of the Earl of *Foix*. That they beseech'd him therefore to grant 'em other Letters, immediately after his taking the Oath, in which he would please to declare, that it should be no Prejudice to 'em hereafter, either in general or particular. And for as much as the King gave 'em to understand, that the War the Earl of *Foix* made against him hinder'd him from going so soon to *Saragossa*, the four Deputies of the City presented to him their Request in Writing, and made a sort of Protestation in form, to that the King, to satisfie 'em, order'd them his Letters Patents, declaring in express terms, that *this Delay should be no Prejudice to them*. And as their *Embassadors* (since they must be call'd by that Name) have been receiv'd by the Kings their Sovereigns, so foreign Kings have honour'd the States of *Arragon* and *Catalonia* with their Embassadors. In the Year 1410, *Charles* VI King of *France*, sent to *Martin* King of *Arragon*, *Girard* Bishop of *St Flour*, *Henry* of *Marle*, first President of the Parliament of *Paris*, *Robert de Chalais*, Seneschal of *Carcassonne*, and *William* or *Giles Vendelle*, to renew the Alliances between the two Crowns. The Advice the Embassadors receiv'd of the Death of *Martin* having stopp'd 'em on their Journey, the King sent them word to pursue their Journey, *and to repair to the States of* Catalonia, which were assembled at *Barcelona*. They receiv'd Audience, wherein they recommended the Rights and Pretensions of *Lewis*, the Son of *Lewis* King of *Sicily*, and of *Toland* of *Arragon*. Two Years after, the same King *Charles* sent to the States of *Catalonia*, who were met again at *Barcelona*, and to those of *Arragon* which had been call'd together at *Alcanniz*, the same Bishop of *St Flour*, the Count *de Vendome*, *Robert de Chalas*, with three or four other Embassadors, who had their Audience the 29th of *December* 1429. But as I observ'd before, the Word Embassador was of a larger Extent in those times. For whatsoever Title may be giv'n to those whom the Subject employs, or to those who are employ'd to Subjects, they are still but Deputies, with this Difference, that the one may enjoy the Protection of the *Law of Nations*, which the Subjects can lay no Claim to.

During the last Commotions of *Naples*, wherein they took to their Arms under *Gennaro Annese*, the Marquis of *Fontenay Marueil* the *French* Embassador at *Rome*, (who gave Sanctuary to the Rebels, and fomented the Rebellion) writing to the People of that revolted City, gave it the Quality of *Republick*, and us'd the Terms of *most serene Highness*, but Cardinal *Mazarin* disapprov'd it very much, and spoke of it as a thing altogether ridiculous and impertinent. He alledg'd that the Title of Highness was always given to the Person, and not to the State, it being a thing unheard of, that it was given to a Republick, tho' it might very well receive that of *most serene*. He esteem'd the Letter of that pretended Republick to be no less odd and unaccountable, which was sign'd *Your most humble Servant*. The same Cardinal gave express Orders to the Marquis of *Fontenay*, to use all his Industry to hinder the *Neapolitans* from sending to the Court of *France*, Persons with any other Character than that of *Deputies*, that it might not be intangled in Inconveniencies, *if the pretended Embassadors of this abortive Republick* should insist upon being treated as those of *Venice* or the United Provinces. Monsieur de *Fontenay* gave the Quality of *Embassador from* France *to the Republick of* Naples, by virtue of a Commission given under the Seal of his Embassy, to a certain Person nam'd *Lewis del Ferro*, who, by the means of a pack of worthless Wretches, call'd the *Lazars*, (of whom he was chief) had most contributed to the prevailing with *Naples* to have recourse to the Protection of *France*. This Embassador, who represented the King his Master in the first Post of *Christendom*, prostituted his own Character, by communicating it to a sorry Fellow who had been a profess'd Pedant, and by giving the Stile of Excellency to one who was such a mad Man, that there are several confin'd that don't deserve it so much. The Duke of *Guise* was so offended at his Extravagancies, that he put him in a Dungeon, and he has since been known to beg at *Paris*.

In the Year 1645, the States of the United Provinces, deliberating on the Instructions of the Plenipotentiaries they were going to send to *Munster*, were for having the Prince of *Orange*'s Opinion concerning the Civilities they were to shew the Ministers of the *Hanse Towns* they might possibly meet with there. The Prince made answer, They should carry it on the level with them, because those Towns do not send Embassadors, but only Deputies, for this reason, that that Right is inseparably unnext to Sovereignty. In the Year 1626 there arriv'd at *London* two Deputies from *Hamburg*, which is of all the *Hanse Towns* that which has the greatest Commerce with *England*. Their Names were *Lundjman* and *Brande*, their Domesticks, who were ignorant of the Consequences thereof, gave 'em the Title of *Embassadors*, but after the Counsel had perus'd their *Letters of Credence*, they found there nothing like it, but only that the Word *ablegavimus* had afforded room for an Error, into which the Court had like to have fall'n. The Domesticks of this sort of Ministers, who make no Distinction between the Terms *Legatus* and *Ablegatus*, make no Difficulty to give the Quality of Excellency to their Masters, tho' at the same time they are only Envoys or Residents, and so easily draw into the same Error those who cannot have a particular Knowledge of the Quality their *Credentials* give 'em. The *English* however did not suffer themselves to be imposed upon, but gave these Ministers to understand that the Word *ablegavimus* could have no other Signification than that *we have deputed*. And indeed it was upon this ground that they regulated the Civilities they shew'd to these deputed Embassadors, all their Reception consisting in the Honour was done 'em, to send *Finet* to them, who was Deputy-Master of the Ceremonies, who conducted 'em to their Audience, and brought 'em back to their own Houses in the Lord High Chamberlain's Coach. The Court of *France* did not so much to *David Penthorn* and *Dederic Muller*, Senators of *Hamburg*, who arrived at *Paris* in the Year 1654. They had Letters of Credence from the *Hanse Towns*, that is to say, from *Lubeck*, *Bremen*, and *Hamburg*, which are the only ones that appear at this time under that Name. The *French* Privateers had taken several of their Merchant-Men, which were carrying into *Spain* (where the City of *Hamburg* has its chiefest Commerce) several Commodities of *Norway* and *Prussia*, which pass'd in *France* for *contraband* Goods, and the Marshal *de la Meilleraye*, Governor of *Britany*, under the Queen-Mother, protected the Privateers, because he was a Gainer by their Depredations. The Intention of the *Hanse Towns* was to secure to themselves the Freedom of Commerce and Navigation, by a good Treaty, by causing them to be renew'd which they had obtain'd from *Charles* IX and *Henry* IV. The Deputies liv'd sumptuously enough, and pretended to be consider'd as Embassadors, by reason that in the Treaty *Henry* IV had granted 'em, their Agents had the Quality of *Embassadors deputed*, but at the very first Overture they made for it they lost all Hopes of obtaining of it. Monsieur *Servien*, who had had considerable Differences with the Deputies of the *Hanse Towns* at *Munster*, spoke of it with Contempt, and the *Comte de Brienne* gave 'em to understand, that if they insisted on their Pretension, their Negotiation would soon have an end. They had Audience of the King and the Queen, paying the usual Respect, not one of the Ministers gave 'em the Hand at his own House, and

The EMBASSADOR and his FUNCTIONS. 15

and all they could obtain, by the means of a confiderable Gratification, was that the Count *de Brienne* was prevail'd upon to let flip into the Treaty the fame Words of *Embaſſadors deputed*, becauſe their *Letters of Credence* gave 'em the Quality of *Ablegati*. But ſuppoſing their Principals had giv'n 'em that of *Legati* or *Embaſſadors*, the Court of *France* wou'd have taken no notice of it, becauſe it does not belong to the *Hanſe Towns* to take upon 'em to be Sovereigns, and to give their Miniſters a Quality, wh ch the Princes of *Germany* have not yet been able to procure for their own. *M. de Brienne* made no great Difficulty to inſert the Quality of *Embaſſadors*, as well becauſe it is found alſo in the Treaty made with *Henry IV*. as by reaſon that Word ſignifies nothing when it is joyn'd with that of *deputed*, the laſt deſtroying the firſt.

In the Relation a Perſon of Quality and publick Capacity has made of the Particulars of the Marriage of the Lady *Henrietta* of *France* with the King of *England*, we find that in the Church of *Noſtre Dame* there was a Bench plac'd for the Nuncio and for the Embaſſadors of *Spain*, *Venice*, and *Savoy*, and about three Foot behind the ſaid Bench was another for the four *Embaſſadors Reſidents*, that is to ſay, for the Miniſters of the ſecond Order.

And indeed it is matter of Amazement, that at this time any Conſideration ſhould be had for the *Teutonick Hanſe*, which being formerly compos'd of ſeventy Towns, has at preſent no Subſiſtence but in the Imagination. There are but three left, as I juſt now obſerv'd, and again, of theſe three, that of *Bremen* retains only the Name of one, that of *Lubeck* contributes little or nothing, and that of *Hamburg* alone furniſhes all the Expences of theſe Deputations, to the End ſhe may thereby preſerve her Commerce under the ſhelter of that great Name, and the Favour of its firſt Reputation. To ſpeak the truth, the *Teutonick Hanſe* never was a State nor a Republick, but barely a Society, united for the greater ſecurity of their Commerce and Navigation. This being indiſputable, I cannot comprehend how the Courts of Princes and Potentates of *Europe* ſhould admit or conſider the Miniſters of a Body, which no longer ſubſiſts, otherwiſe than as ſingle Deputies, ſince while it yet ſubſiſted, and had a being, it could not be conſider'd but as a Society of Merchants, or at moſt but as the Companies that have form'd themſelves for both the *Indies* in the United Provinces, which do not act, but under the Name of the State that protects 'em. Which is by ſo much the more evident, that even when the *Teutonick Hanſe* was ſtill ſomething, and its Power yet conſiderable, it did not form a particular Republick, nor a Sovereign State in *Chriſtendom*. For being compos'd of Towns, which for the moſt part were *Municipals*, and had not the leaſt Token of Sovereignty, but depended on Princes who govern'd 'em as they did their other Subjects, they could together make but barely a Society of Merchants, and not an Alliance of Sovereign to Sovereign. Nay, even at this time, the City of *Hamburg*, which the King of *Denmark* pretends to make part of his Dutchy of *Holſtern*, acts meerly under the Title of *Hanſe*, only becauſe it cannot effect its being declar'd Free Imperial. The two others, on the contrary, glory in being Imperial, be-

cauſe they do not reap any great Benefit from the *Hanſeatick* Society. To which I ſhall add, that whoever will take the Pains to examine the Treaties which the *Hanſe Towns* have at any time heretofore, and even within ſome Years, made in *France* and *England*, will find, that they are only Renovations and Confirmations of thoſe Privileges, Liberties and Immunities, they had formerly obtain'd for the Benefit and Security of their Navigation and Commerce. In the Year 1589, Queen *Elizabeth* gave leave to certain *Engliſh* Lords to fit out ſeveral Men of War, which on the Coaſt of *Spain* took ſeveral Merchant-Ships belonging to the *Hanſe Towns*, which traded to thoſe Parts. Hereupon they ſent their Deputies to *London*, where they made their Complaints, mix'd with Threats and Marks of great Reſentment. The Queen ſent 'em word, that ſhe had warn'd the Towns to leave off that Commerce, and withal had foretold 'em what had ſince happen'd. That their Ships were lawful Prize. That Privileges are particular Laws, which cannot prejudice the Publick Good, which is the ſupreme Law of all. That *in the Privilege granted by Edward to the* Hanſe Towns, there was a Condition, and an expreſs Proviſion, that they ſhould not carry any Merchandiſe nor Commodities to the Enemies of *England*. That what ſhe had done was not without Precedent. That the Neutrality ſubſiſted no longer, when Kindneſs was ſhewn to one of the Parties to the Prejudice of the other, and that the Threats of a few trading Towns did not at all terrifie a Queen, who did not ſtand in fear of the greateſt Powers of *Europe*. It was hereupon that the Advice of the Prince of *Orange* was grounded, it was likewiſe upon this that the States-General founded the Reſolution they took the 11th of *February* 1656, ordaining that for the future *the Deputies Extraordinary of the Hanſe Towns*, ſhould not be conducted to Audience but by the Agent, in one Coach with two Horſes, that they ſhould be ſeated in a Cloth Chair with a back, and that they ſhould be re-conducted home again in the ſame manner.

What I have now ſaid of the Subject and Sovereign, ought alſo to be allow'd of with reference to *Lord* and *Vaſſal*. But as there is a great deal of Difference betwixt a Vaſſal and a Subject, ſo likewiſe is there a great deal of Difference betwixt the Lord of a Fee and the Sovereign. They, *who are in Poſſeſſion of Fees, with the Offices and uſual Conditions, cannot ſend Embaſſadors to their Lord on the account of the Fee, tho' at the ſame time they were in actual Poſſeſſion of other States in full Sovereignty*. Pope *Urban* VIII. would never ſuffer the Duke of *Parma* (who on other Occaſions ſent his Embaſſadors to *Rome* and other Places) to ſend him one, on account of the Difference that was between 'em about the Dutchy of *Caſtro*, which is a Fee of the Apoſtolick See, notwithſtanding the preſſing Inſtances of the two Crowns, and the major part of the Princes and States of *Italy* to that purpoſe. The Pope ſaid poſitively to *Don John de Chumazzero*, Embaſſador Extraordinary from *Spain*, who preſs'd him very much thereto, that he would not admit of any Miniſter from the Duke, and that if he ſent a private Perſon, it would only ſerve to inform the Judges. *That he ought not to send, but to come* Yet if the Vassal possesses with his Fee, other States and Provinces in Sovereignty, it is certain, that he may send Embassadors to his Lord, and elsewhere The King of *England* was formerly Vassal to the Crown of *France*, on the score of the Dutchy of *Normandy* and *Guyenne*, which he held of it, but that did hinder him from being Sovereign on the account of his own Dominions, and in that Quality he not only sent Embassadors to the King of *France*, but also made War against him I say the same of the last Dukes of *Burgundy*, who, together with those Provinces which they held of the Crown of *France*, were in Possession of others, of which they were absolute Sovereigns. They sent Embassadors to the King, and receiv'd 'em from him In the Year 1464, *Lewis* XI sent to *Philip the Good*, Duke of *Burgundy*, a solemn Embassy, consisting of the *Comte d'Eu*, Prince of the Blood, of the Chancellor of *France*, and of the Arch-bishop of *Narbonne* And *Philip* sent to *Lewis* the Bishop of *Tournay*, and the Lord *de Crequy*

This Correspondence was frequent enough between the King and the Duke, and *Philip*, who pretended to carry it on the level with crown'd Heads, affected the Preservation of this Advantage with reference to *France* He was a great Prince, as well on the account of his personal Qualifications, as by reason of his Power His House was regular, and serv'd by half Yearly Waitings, as that of the Kings, to which it was not inferiour, either in Number of Officers, or in Quantity or Quality of Furniture, Plate or Jewels The account *Olivier de la March* gives of his Houshold at the end of his Memoirs, very well deserves to be look'd into *Guy de Rochfort*, Chancellor of *France*, insisted on the Respect that was due to him, when he receiv'd the Homage of the Arch-Duke *Philip*, but when the Ceremony was over, he made it very well known, that he knew how to distinguish between *Philip*, Earl of *Flanders*, and the Arch-Duke, Sovereign Prince of several free and independent Provinces Those Princes, who by vertue of their first Investiture, possess their Fiefs in full Sovereignty, with all the *Rights* of the *Regalia*, so as to owe only simple Homage, notwithstanding it be accompany'd with some Acknowledgments, yet that does not hinder 'em from being Sovereigns in effect, nor from sending Embassadors every where, even to the Lord of the Fief Whatever therefore the Pope said to *Don John de Chumazzero*, and to *Hugh de Lionne*, relating to the Duke of *Parma*, ought to be apply'd to the Dutchy of *Castro*, and not to the Dutchy of *Parma*, because the last, altho' it be a Fief of the See of *Rome*, owes nothing to the Pope, who could not confiscate it from the Duke, even for Felony, and the See of *Rome* will never be able to reunite it to its other Demesnes, unless it should become Caducous for want of Heirs Thus we shall see hereafter, that the Pope gives Audience to the Embassador of *Parma*, with the same Ceremonies that are us'd to the other Princes of *Italy*

Before the Kings of *Arragon* had annex'd the two *Sicilys* to their Crown, the Kings of *Naples* sent their Embassadors to *Rome* and other Places, notwithstanding that Kingdom be a Fief of the Holy See The Kings that have reign'd there, after the Death of *Alfonso* the Magnanimous, us'd to send their Embassadors to *France*, *Spain*, *Venice*, *Milan*, and even to *Rome*, because, having acquitted themselves of the Duty of Homage, and what depended on it, they did not acknowledge the Pope's Authority in point of Temporals The King of *Spain* does the like to this Day, after the Example of all the other Princes of *Italy*, who notwithstanding they hold their Principalities of the See of *Rome*, or of the Empire, do nevertheless possess 'em in full Sovereignty, and have the Right of Embassy in all the Courts of *Europe* I say the same of the Princes of *Germany*, who tho' they are *Vassals of the Empire*, possess their Principalities in full Sovereignty, and enjoy all the Rights that are annex'd to it The Opposition that is form'd against that of Embassy, which cannot be contested with 'em, no more than all the other Rights, obliges me to give 'em a particular Chapter after the next following

Before I put an end to this, I shall say two or three Words concerning the *Deputies* that compose *the Assembly, which represents the States General of the United Provinces* These Provinces are all Sovereign and Independent, except only with respect to the Conditions that make the Foundation of their Union, and of their State In this Quality of Sovereigns they send to the *Hague* Persons that represent 'em, and deliberate and resolve together, what they judge necessary for the common Interest of the Allies Also it must not be doubted, that as such they ought to be consider'd as publick Ministers, whom the *Law of Nations* protects, and that no Violence can be offer'd 'em, either in their Persons or Attendants, without failing in what is their due, by vertue of the publick Security The Quality of Embassadors is not given 'em, as well because they are not sent out of their own State to a foreign Power, as because they are sent to a perpetual Assembly, as Members of the same Body which is the reason why they are not treated and consider'd as publick Ministers, but as Deputies of Provinces, that constitute among themselves the same State and same Republick However they enjoy an entire Security, and are inviolate in their Persons, even to that degree, that the Justice of the Place cannot extend its Jurisdiction to them But it is not so with respect to those Deputies that assist at the Assembly of the same Province wherefore it might be doubted whether it was properly spoken, when it was said, that the Town of *Groningen*, by confining a Gentleman, (whom the neighbouring Country had deputed to the Assembly of the States of the Province) and in causing him to be prosecuted, did violate the *Law of Nations* The States of that Province are compos'd of two Members, to wit, of the Town and of the circumjacent Countrey, which being inseparable from one another, constitute together the Sovereignty of the Province, so that for what relates to the Province in general they cannot act separately I am willing to suppose besides, that the one cannot alone prosecute the Subjects of the other, but I would
not

The EMBASSADOR *and his* FUNCTIONS. 17

not maintain, that in so doing the *Law of Nations* was violated I am of Opinion it were better to say, that in violating the publick Security, they transgress'd against the Treaties which are the Preservation, and the fundamental Law of the Province

CHAP. III.

Whether Usurpers and Governors in Chief can send Embassadors.

I Shall in this Chapter speak of four sorts of Persons First, Of those who possess Countreys and States with a supreme Power and Authority Secondly, Of those who having been driven from their States, do nevertheless retain the Possession thereof In the third place, Of those that abdicate and renounce their Sovereignty And lastly, Of those who not being Sovereigns, do notwithstanding discharge the Functions thereof, by virtue of a Power committed to 'em

Of the first, Some are Sovereigns by Birth, or become so by Election or Conquest, or else they usurp the Sovereignty Lawful Princes have the Right of Embassy beyond dispute, but the Usurper will find some Difficulty to have his Embassadors admitted, even tho' he were absolute Master of the State he has so usurp'd, it the Prince, to whom he sends his Ministers, has not some Interest that obliges him to seek after, or suffer his Friendship *Lewis* XI, who was the Prince of the World that best understood his Interest, did not scruple to purchase that of *Edward* IV, who had usurp'd the Crown of *England* from *Henry* VI, but he despis'd the earnest Sollicitations of *Richard* III, his Brother, and would not so much as see his Embassadors That Tyrant had caus'd his Nephews to be murther'd, the Eldest whereof was his lawful King to whom he had sworn Allegiance, so that be ng both Parricide and Usurper, and having withal so many Enemies in *England,* that *Lewis* had not the least reason to apprehend his coming to disturb his Quiet in *France,* he would have nothing to do with him, and sent back his Embassadors

There is in the Negociation of President *Jeannin,* a Passage which is admirable on this Subject *Charle* Duke of *Sudermania,* having caus'd himself to be crown'd King of *Sweden* in the beginning of this Century, sent into *France James Van Dyke,* and made offer to *Henry* the Great, to renew the Treaties and Alliances that had been formerly betwixt the two Crowns *Van Dyke* represented, that the Advantages that would accrue to *France* from the Commerce with *Sweden* would be so very considerable, that the King listen'd to the Proposals of this Minister, and had a great mind to come to a Conclusion with him There was nothing hinder'd him from it, but only the Action of *Charles,* who had usurp'd the Crown from *Sigismund* his Nephew, after this had been chosen King of *Poland,* which was by so much the more odious, as the Pretext of Religion was the Cause of the Revolution *France* likewise consider'd, that the King of *Denmark,* who was no Friend to *Charles,* might form a Party against him, with the King of *England* his Brother-in-law But notwithstanding all this, *Monsieur de Villeroy,* writing to *Jeannin* on the 8th of *April* 1608, cuts short and says, *All these Reasons and Considerations, shall not hinder the King from tre+t ng w th* Charles, *if he finds it to be for his Interest, and that of his Kingdom* He adds, that *Sigismund* had no other Sentiments than what the Court of *Vienna* inspir'd him with, and that *England* and *Denmark* having no great Consideration for *France,* the King was not oblig'd to have any for them However, it was thought proper to observe some Measures in the matter, and know for certain whether the King would gain his Ends in effect, wherefore *Van Dyke* was sent back to President *Jeannin,* who negotiated at that time in *Holland,* where he might get Information of the State of the Affairs of *Sweden*

If there ever appear'd in any State, a Chief who was at the same time both Tyrant and Usurper, most certainly *Oliver Cromwel* was such and yet for all that, never was there an Usurper so solemnly acknowledg'd Immediately after the Death of the late King, *Don Alonso d. Cardenas,* Embassador from *Spain,* legitimated this bastard Republick, and *Oliver* had no sooner made himself Sovereign, under the Quality of *Protector,* than all the Kings of the Earth prostrated themselves before this Idol To gratifie him, the lawful King, with his Brothers, were driven out of those Kingdoms and Provinces, that ought to have serv'd him as Places of Refuge or Asylums *Loccard,* who was Embassador from the Usurper, was not only receiv'd in *France* with all the Honours that could have been done to the Minister of the first Monarch of Christendom, but *Cardinal Mazarine* even refus'd to see the King of *Great-Britain,* who had travell'd quite through the Kingdom to come to him at the foot of the *Pirenean* Hills, and would not so much as speak to the Person that came from him, and waited at the Door of this chief Minister, who at the same time had daily Conferences with the Usurper's All that the dispossess'd King could obtain was, that the Cardinal gave him leave that the Duke of *Ormond* should speak to him as he pass'd along, and as it were accidentally, as he went from his own Quarters to the Isle of the Conference

The King of *Spain,* who was Brother-in-law to the deceased King, behav'd himself a little better He suffer'd the Son to be in safety at *Brussels,* where he also met with some Civilities and his chief Minister, *Don Lewis de Haro,* at the *Pirenean* Hills, shew'd him that Respect which the Cardinal had refus'd him

The King of *France* being advanc'd as far as the Frontiers of *Flanders,* the Protector sent *Falcanbridge* his Son-in-law to him, to pay him those Civilities, which Sovereigns are us'd to

F shew

shew one another on the like Occasions and the Duke *de Crequy*, one of the first Lords of *France*, next to the Princes, was sent to *London*, to thank the Usurper for his Civilities and that nothing might be wanting to the Ceremony, the Cardinal would have his Nephew *Mancini* accompany the Duke. The Difference that is seen in the Behaviour of these two Kings of *France* and *Spain*, who were both nearly related to the King of *England*, proceeded only from the Difference of their Interest. The *Spanish* Embassador had us'd his utmost Endeavours with the Usurper, to engage him in the Interest of the King his Master, even to the offering him a hundred thousand Crowns *per* Month, two hundred thousand by way of Advance, and an Army of twenty thousand Men, to assist the *English* to re-conquer *Calice*. *Cromwell* had rejected these Offers, and as he fear'd more the Neighbourhood of *France*, than he hop'd for Advantage from the languishing and remote Strength of *Spain*, he sided with the first, whose Friend he became, by that means obliging the other to be so to the King of *Great Britain*, whose three Kingdoms he had usurp'd.

Those Princes to whom Ministers are sent, do not usually examine into the Title of those that employ 'em, they are contented to weigh their Power and Possession, tho' at the same time, unless Interest sways 'em, they are not over forward to acknowledge an Usurper. When their Interest is concern'd, Princes make no great Difficulty to receive Embassadors and Ministers from whomsoever sends 'em. Cardinal *Dossat* explains himself very well on this Head, in the Letter he writes to Monsieur *de Villeroy* of the 23d of *July* 1601, where he says, That Princes, when they see a considerable Power well establish'd, do not mind whether the Potentate, who sends the Embassador or Agent, be lawful or not, and do not enquire so scrupulously into the Title, as it is usual in the Case of buying and changing, but have a regard to the Power and Possession. That if it were necessary to judge of the Title of each Prince before their Ministers were receiv'd, there would be found a great many whose Embassadors would be sent back, but it is not what is customarily look'd into, not even amongst Enemies, who very often send 'em to each other. He instances in the Example of the *Swiss Cantons*, who having been formerly Subjects to the House of *Austria*, have ever sent and receiv'd Embassadors. I dare not say that *John* IV King of *Portugal* was an Usurper, since *France*, *England*, *Sweden*, and the United Provinces acknowledg'd him for a lawful King, after the unanimous Declaration of the States of the Kingdom, yet nevertheless, whatever Instances the Plenipotentiaries of *France* made at *Munster*, the Mediators would never admit his Ministers, nor negotiate with them, as with the other Embassadors The Pope's Nuncio and the *Venetian* Embassador said, That since the Pope nor the Republick had not as yet acknowledg'd the King, they could not treat with those who took the Quality of his Ministers. In the Month of *March* 1641, two Embassadors from *Portugal* being arriv'd at *London*, and having obtain'd Audience, the King told them, That till then he had not own'd any other King of *Portugal* than the King of *Spain*, but since the Embassadors assur'd him, That the Prince they represented had obtain'd the Crown, with the unanimous Consent of the People, and that he was in peaceable Possession of the Kingdom, he had been willing to admit 'em, that he might not injure their Character. The *Venetian* Embassador, who was at that time in *England*, refus'd to see those Embassadors without Orders from their Republick.

Queen *Christina* of *Sweden*, who had admitted and own'd those Ministers, and had caus'd 'em to assist at her Coronation, bethought her self the Day before she abdicated, to send Word to the Resident of *Portugal*, that she acknowledg'd no other King of *Portugal* than *Philip* IV King of *Spain*. But this was only a capricious Humour, whereas the Court of *Rome* had a particular Reason that hinder'd it from owning him. The Pope who is said to be the common Father of the Catholick Princes, and was as the Judge of the Difference, could not determine it without being duly inform'd of the Cause, and without receiving the Opposition of the King of *Spain*, as he would in some measure have decided it, had he admitted and acknowledg'd the *Portugal* Embassador. The Bishop of *Lamego* went to *Rome* in this Quality, but the Pope, who was oblig'd to have some Consideration for the King of *Spain*, hinder'd him from entring in the Day-time, and from appearing with the Tokens of Embassy. This did not hinder his Friends from seeing him, and considering him as an Embassador. The Affair of his Reception had been warmly debated in a particular Congregation of Cardinals, before he came to Town, and forasmuch as the Court of *Rome* was not willing to lose the Profits she receives from that Kingdom, it was concluded, that the Bishop ought to be admitted to Audience without prejudicing the Rights of others. The *Nuncio* that resided at *Madrid* had Orders to try to make this Resolution relish with the Council there, and prevail with it to acquiesce to the Reasons the Pope had for so doing. But the Nuncio met with so great an Opposition, accompany'd with such strong and express Protestations, that he was forc'd to let the Affair drop, for fear the *Spaniards* should take Resolutions that the Pope would not at all have been pleas'd with. So that all the Pontificate of *Urbin* pass'd without any thing being done for the new King of *Portugal*. Cardinal *Antonio*, *Urbin*'s Nephew, protected the Bishop, and *France* was very officious for his Admission, but it was impossible to prevail with the Pope, who would never give him place amongst the publick Ministers. On the contrary, taking Occasion or Pretext from the Rencounter the Bishop had with the *Spanish* Embassador, he oblig'd him to return back to *Lisbon*. Don *Lewis Peirera de Castro* succeeded him, not as Embassador, but as Deputy of the Clergy of *Portugal*, who press'd the Pope hard to provide for the Bishopricks, which being most of 'em vacant, there were not Priests enow to discharge the Service and administer the Sacraments.

The Rencounter the Bishop of *Lamego* had with the Marquis *de los Veles* Embassador from *Spain*, was so considerable, that I think my self obliged to relate the Particulars thereof, which are

are remarkable enough. The Bishop having begun to visit the Cardinals, in order to dispose 'em to favour the Interest of the King his Master, the Spanish Embassador desir'd Cardinal Barbarin not to suffer the Portuguese to appear in publick with so much Pomp and Attendance, because there might arise from thence such a Scandal as might be capable of disturbing the Pope's Repose. Now the Congregation that had the Affairs of Portugal before it, not judging it proper to hinder the Bishop from going abroad, was contented to regulate his Attendants, the Number of his Footmen, and his manner of going about the Town, by ordering him to draw the Curtains of his Coach whenever he met the Spanish Embassador. It was according to this Regulation that the Bishop went the 20th of August 1624 to visit the Marquis de Fontenay Embassador from France, at the same time that the Spanish Embassador made a Visit to Cardinal Roma, whither they brought him Advice that the Bishop was at Monsieur de Fontenay's. He immediately sent one of his Coaches to fetch him a good Number of Fire-Arms, which he caus'd to be distributed to his People, amongst whom there were several Soldiers cloath'd with his Livery. The Embassador, as he took Coach, having perform'd his Visit, gave Orders to his Retinue to let the Bishop of Lamego pass quietly, without any notice, if the Curtains of his Coach were drawn, but if they were not, and the Bishop did not stop to pay his Respects to him, then to hamstring his Horses. The French Embassador, and the Bishop of Lamego, being inform'd that the Spanish Embassador had sent for Arms, made Provision also thereof, and the Bishop being accompany'd by the Domesticks of Monsieur de Fontenay, and what other French Men, Portuguese, and Catalonians could be got together, took Coach also, in order to return home the nearest way. He had not gone far, before his Attendants meeting with that of the Spanish Embassador, several Discharges were heard, no body being able to tell who had fir'd first. The Embassador's two Horses (which the Coachman had on purpose caus'd to rear, thereby to cover his Master) were kill'd, and sav'd the Embassador, who not without Difficulty retir'd into the Palace of Cardinal Albornos, which was in that Neighbourhood, whilst the Bishop also sav'd himself in a House hard by. Don Diego de Vargas, a Valet de Chambre, and a Sicilian, were kill'd on the side of the Spaniards, and the Bishop lost one of the French Embassador's Coachmen, and two Peruvians. All the Friends of the Marquis de los Velez, and all the Partisans of Spain immediately repair'd to his House. So that the Court apprehending some worse Consequences, posted two Companies of Foot and fifty Horse before his Palace, and Orders were given to the Officers not to suffer any body to go out. They did the same before the Bishop's House, besides which, there were Corps de Garde up and down, and the Patrole went about all the Night. The very next Morning the Marquis de Fontenay spoke to the Pope about what had happen'd, as also to Cardinal Barbarin, and demanded Reparation to be made for the Violence that had been offer'd to the Bishop, who, he said, was Embassador from a crown'd Head. The Spanish Embassador made also his Complaints, but not having receiv'd much Satisfaction, he took the Advice of the Cardinals of his Party, and resolv'd to retire to the Kingdom of Naples, because he said, It would be impossible for him to stay at Rome, and not break through the Bounds of that Respect which he would always preserve for the Pope, and which was inconsistent with the Resentment he should be oblig'd to shew. To hinder his withdrawing, the Affair was put under Examination, but after several goings and comings, (during which the Pope made Enquiry into the Matter) he was told at last that it would take up some time to perfect the Informations, which not being finish'd, the Pope could not condemn the Bishop without hearing him, (notwithstanding *he was his Subject*) *by reason of his Character*, but as for his part he had good reason to complain of both the one and the other. The Embassador had resolv'd to depart without taking leave of the Pope, and alter'd his Mind but only at the Request of his Friends, who prevail'd with him to go to Audience, at which he complain'd of both the Cardinal Nephews, who, as he said, had openly declar'd themselves his Enemies. The Pope answer'd him cooly enough, that the Process not being yet duly prepar'd, he could not tell which of the two was in the wrong or in the right. The Embassador went away the same Day, and the Spanish Cardinals retir'd the next Day to Frascati, the other Prelates and Partizans of the Spanish Faction withdrawing themselves likewise.

France, England, and the United Provinces, who had no very good Understanding with Spain at that time, were not contented to acknowledge the King of Portugal, and to admit his Embassadors, but they also declar'd themselves for his Establishment and Interests. Divers other Princes follow'd their Example, and at this time the King of Spain himself receives Embassadors from Portugal, and sends his own thither. I cannot therefore sufficiently wonder, that after a solemn Treaty, which has been concluded between these two Crowns, there are Persons suffer'd at Brussels (to their Shame be it spoken) who make no Scruple to put the King of Portugal in the Number of Usurpers, and have the Impudence to publish in their impertinent Libels, that the Treaty, which Necessity extorted from the Council of Madrid, would not subsist after the said Necessity was over. The Spaniards protest in all their Manifestos and Declarations, that they never violated Treaties, how disadvantageous soever they may have been. To speak the truth, they have not stipulated any great Advantages, in all the Treaties they have made since that of Chateau Cambresis. That of Vervin oblig'd 'em to restore all that they held in France, and the Pirenean Treaty, as well as that of Aix la Chappelle, have extorted from 'em Conditions hard enough, and nevertheless they pretend to have observ'd 'em very religiously, notwithstanding the Rupture in the Year 1673. I should think that the same Author that strives to canonize the Probity and Sincerity of Ferdinand the Catholick, might very well forbear representing the Spanish Ministers as Persons capable of breaking (after the Treaty of Portugal) that

that, which the same Necessity oblig'd the King of *Spain* to conclude with the United Provinces. It is well known, that the major part of Princes, do not observe those Treaties which they can break with any Advantage; but at the same time, there are none that glory in it, or that take pleasure to make known their evil Disposition, as well as Impotency. I say nothing of Prince *Don Pedro*, who during the Life of his Brother, enjoys both his Wife and Crown, and causes his Embassadors to be receiv'd at every where.

It is sufficient that the Prince who causes his Embassadors to be acknowledg'd be in possession of the Sovereignty; hence we may conclude, that he that has been expell'd by a superior Force, or by the Insurrection of his Subjects has been oblig'd to withdraw, retains Possession, till by a formal Treaty he has renounc'd the Countreys which have been conquer'd or usurp'd from him, or till Success has justify'd the Arms of the Subjects. He retains also the Right of Embassy, because the Sovereignty remains in him. *Christierne*, King of *Denmark*, and *John Zapoli*, King of *Hungary*, kept their Ministers in foreign Courts during the time of their Exile. Altho' the *Spaniards* were in possession of the *Upper Navarre*, that is to say, of that part of the Kingdom which is beyond the *Pirenean* Hills, yet that did not hinder *Pius* IV, from giving Audience to the Embassador of *Anthony*, King of *Navarre*, in the Year 1560, and *Gregory* XIII, in the Year 1573, admitted likewise the Embassador of *Henry*, *Anthony*'s Son. It is true, that *Ferdinand*, King of the *Romans*, would not suffer *Jerome Laski*, Embassador from *John Zapoli*, to come into *Germany*, and that he would not grant him a Passport; but then it was, because that *Laski* was to go thither, in order to procure Succour against *Ferdinand*, who pretended himself to the Crown of *Hungary*, as Husband to the Sister of the last deceased King; which notwithstanding, did not hinder *Laski* from being consider'd at *Constantinople* as Embassador from *John*. If at the time of the *Pirenean* Congress, Cardinal *Mazarin* thought it proper to deal other Usage to the Minister of the King of *Great-Britain*, it was not because *France* was ignorant of what might, and even ought to have been done, but because it had other Interests to look to, and was apprehensive, lest the Protector should strike in with the *Spaniards*. This was so powerful a Consideration at that time, that the same Cardinal had oblig'd the King, and the Princes his Brothers, to depart the Kingdom: and he himself refus'd to see the King, who had cross'd all *France*, and was come to the Frontiers of *Spain*, to speak to the Cardinal. However, the Consideration that *France* and other Places had for the Usurper, did not cause the Quality of publick Minister to be call'd in question, nor the Protection of the *Law of Nations* to be deny'd, to those whom the King of *England* employ'd in those Courts where he had still some Interest. The Duke of *Lorrain* (altho' dispossess'd of his Countrey by a superior Force) had for all that his Minister at *Nimmeguen*, even with the Passport of *France* that had dispossess'd him.

The same *Anthony*, King of *Navarre*, which I just now mention'd, being a very weak Prince, suffer'd himself to be continually flatter'd with the false Hopes the *Spaniards* gave him of the Restitution of his Kingdom of *Navarre*, or at least of an Equivalent. A *Bernese* nam'd *Lejeun*, one of the Duke of *Albuquerque*'s Domesticks, told him from the Duke his Master, that if he could resolve with himself to go to *Spain* in Person, and make a Compliment to King *Philip*, he might be assur'd of receiving Satisfaction concerning *Navarre*. Hereupon *Anthony* sent thither the *Sieur d'Odaux*, of the House of *Levy*, with Letters, in which he desir'd a Passport for the Safety of his Journey. *Philip*, who was advis'd of the Subject of the Embassy, gave Audience to *Odaux* in the Presence of *Sebastian de l'Aubepine*, Bishop of *Limoges*, the *French* Embassador, of whom he enquir'd afterwards, whether the King his Master had any knowledge of that Embassy. The Bishop made answer that he could not tell, and that nothing had been writ to him about it: whereupon *Philip* return'd to *Odaux* his Letters of Credence, and caus'd him to be told, that if *Anthony* had no other Motive for his Journey into *Spain*, than to talk with him on the Affairs of *Navarre*, neither he nor his Wife need give themselves that trouble; that they could not be ignorant what were his Sentiments on that Subject, since he had sufficiently explain'd himself at the Congress of *Cercamp*, where the Treaty of *Chasteau Cambresis* had been regulated.

It is no hard matter to guess at the Reason that made *Philip* give this Repulse to the Minister of a dispossess'd King, since he could not have done otherwise, without acknowledging himself to be an Usurper of the Kingdom of *Navarre*. *Henry* II. by consenting that no mention should be made thereof in the Treaty of *Chasteau Cambresis*, consented to the Usurpation, to the Prejudice of the Honour and Interest of the Crown of *France*, which were even prostituted by those who counsell'd him to treat upon such infamous Conditions.

There is a vast deal of difference betwixt a Sovereign, whom a foreign Force or a civil War drives from his Estate, and a Prince that abdicates voluntarily. *He that abdicates or resigns, does no longer retain his Sovereignty*, by renouncing it, renounces also to all the Rights that are dependent on it, and amongst the rest, to that of sending Embassadors or publick Ministers. Birth stamps such a Character on Princes as is indelible, so that to whatsoever Extremity they are driven, there is a Respect due to 'em; but as for the Rights of Sovereignty, they are inseparable from him that is in possession thereof. There is no holding the one without the other. Whosoever is call'd to Sovereignty, either by Birth or by Election, succeeds also to all the Rights that belong to it. They are not communicable to any body whatever, nor can they be reserv'd by him that abdicates, renounces, or resigns, who after Abdication, Renunciation, or Resignation, has no longer any Affairs of State to negotiate. King *Casimir*, by quitting the Crown and *Poland* it self, might be said to leave the World, where he had made a very indifferent Figure: and if Queen *Christina* makes any still, and if any Regard be had to her Ministers, it is because she has a distinguishing Merit, and a Greatness of of Soul, which she could not deprive her self of, when she resign'd the Crown of Sweden. I would stop here, and be contented to add, that the King and Queen were the last of the Posterity of *Jagellon*, and that if the Queen grew tir'd with wearing a Crown that was beneath her, the King quitted it because he was not worthy of t, and was incapable of Governing after the Death of his Wife, were it not, that within some time, they have in a manner oug up at *Brussels* (where they ought to have had some Veneration for that Princess) the Marquis *Monaldeschi*, and spoke after a strange manner of the Execution she had caus'd him to undergo it *Fontainbleau*. I do not doubt but what the Queen did was what he deserv'd, and I know very well that Sovereigns often pass over Formalities. I know also, that without a weighty Reason of State they neither ought nor can dispense with 'em. And I am not afraid to add, that on this occasion the Queen could not act as Sovereign. I shall moreover say that a lawful Power, how absolute soever it may be, (unless it be Despotick, or, to speak more intelligibly, altogether Tyrannical) never gives it self nor its Jurisdiction this Extent of Power, which indeed is never practis'd in the Territories of another. This matter shall be spoke to hereafter, when we treat of the Jurisdiction Embassadors have over their Domesticks, wherefore I shall only here speak a word or two in reference to *Mary* Queen of *Scots*. *John Lesley*, Bishop of *Rosse*, Embassador from *Mary* at *London*, having been convicted of a Conspiracy against the Life of Queen *Elizabeth*, as I shall more particularly take notice of in the 27th Chapter, the best Lawyers of the Kingdom were consulted, to know whether the Minister of a Queen, who had resign'd the Crown to her Son, ought to enjoy the Privilege of the *Law of Nations*. Their Report sav'd the Bishop's Life, because they represented, that besides the having suffer'd that Queen's Minister at the Court, this Princess's Abdication was not voluntary. On the contrary, it is certain, that she was not only a Prisoner when she was forc'd to resign, but that she made a formal Protestation, in the Presence of *Nicholas Throgmorton* the *English* Embassador, against the Violence that was done to her in this Action. Which is so notorious, that in the Year 1568, that is to say, after her Abdication, the same Bishop of *Rosse*, with the Bishop of *Orkney* and some others, were acknowledg'd in the Quality of her Embassadors.

Viceroys and Chief Governors, who have an absolute Power, employ also publick Ministers, who enjoy the Protection of the *Law of Nations*, and to whom they give the Quality of Embassador. While the *English* were still in possession of the Provinces of *Normandy* and *Guyenne*, notwithstanding they were both held of the Crown of *France*, the Governors that commanded there for the King of *England*, negotiated Affairs with the King of *France*, by the Mediation of their Embassadors, and no Objection was made against treating with these subaltern Ministers, because it was well known that their Principals had a substituting Power.

John Baptista de Gattinara, Nephew of that *Mercurin* who was Minister of *Charles* V, had no other Power but what was given him by the Count de Lanoy, Viceroy of *Naples*, when in the Year 1524 he was at *Rome*, and there concluded a Treaty with the Pope, and with the *Florentines*, (leaving to the Republick of *Venice* the liberty to come into it) for the Preservation of *Francis Sforza*, Duke of *Milan*. This Treaty was concluded on the 1st of *April*, and proclaim'd the 1st of *May*, upon the Ratification of the Viceroy, who did not wait for that of the Emperor. The Duke of *Alva*, Viceroy of *Naples*, and Lieutenant General to the Emperor *Charles* V, and to *Philip* his Son in *Italy*, designing to amuse Pope *Paul* IV with some Proposals of an Accommodation, in order to justifie the Rupture, and the War he had resolv'd to make against the *Caraffas*, sent to *Rome*, *Pirrho Loffredi*, Marquis of *Trevico*, whom the Pope caus'd to be confin'd, as soon as the *Spanish* Army had enter'd the Ecclesiastick Territories. The Duke complain'd of it, and reproach'd the Pope with having violated the *Law of Nations* in confining his Minister. The Court of *Rome* has within these few Years seen the Secretary of *Don Pedro of Arragon*, Viceroy of *Naples*, complement Pope *Clement* IX upon his Exaltation, which was very well taken, and the Pope entertain'd him very handsomly. In the Year 1577, *Don John of Austria*, Governor of the Low Countreys, sent a sole Embassy to the Emperor and Princes of *Germany*, and at the same time he dispatch'd the Viscount of *Gand* in the Quality of Embassador to *England*. In the Year 1588 there was a Deputation made of some Ministers of *Spain* and *England*, to *Flanders*. As soon as they communicated their Powers to each other, it appear'd, that that of the Spaniards was sign'd only by the Duke of *Parma*, who was Governor of the Low Countreys, and not by the King. But that did not hinder the *English* from continuing the Conferences, because they could not be ignorant that the general Power the Duke had, imply'd that of *Subdelegation*. *Albert* of *Austria*, while he was yet but *Cardinal*, and Governor of the Low Countreys, sent his Ministers to all the neighbouring Princes, as well in *Germany* as elsewhere, and particularly in the Year 1598, he sent the *Count de Barlaimont*, with *Westerdorp* and *Nikerchen* to *Lubeck*, as to the chief of the *Hansi Towns*, to endeavour to bring 'em to a Rupture with *England* and the United Provinces. This Embassy, if it may be so call'd, was so well receiv'd, that notice was given thereof to the other Towns, which have always been, and will ever be ready to interrupt and disturb the Commerce and Navigation of the *Hollanders*. The Government of *Milan* is one of the most considerable Employments of *Spain*, because that Dutchy being situate in the midst of the States of the Republick of *Venice*, *Genoa*, the *Swiss Cantons*, the Dukes of *Savoy*, *Mantua*, *Parma* and *Modena*, the Governor is so much respected, that as soon as he comes to his Government, all the neighbouring Princes complement him by their Embassadors, and he returns their Civility by sending his to them.

However we must observe, that altho' this Quality be given to the Ministers of Viceroys and chief Governors, yet they are (to speak properly) but Deputies, to whom Honour is

G done

done for the Prince's sake, which the Governor represents.

Don *Alfonso Caffati*, and his three Sons, had been a long time employ'd by the Governor of *Milan* to the *Swiss Cantons*, who had consider'd 'em as Embassadors, notwithstanding they had no Credentials from the King of *Spain*. In the Year 1646, M. de *Caumartin* the *French* Embassador, perceiving that the third of these Brothers, who was therein the same Quality of Embassador, thwarted his Negotiation undertook to affront him by disputing his Character. He said that *Caffati* having Credentials but only from the Governor of *Milan*, he could at most be consider'd but as his Agent, and not as the King of *Spain*'s Minister, and that in this Quality the *Cantons* could not give him Audience in their General Assembly. *Caffati* reply'd, that his Father, and his two Brothers, who had not had any other Letters, had been treated as Embassadors, and the five little *Cantons* which are in Alliance with the State of *Milan* back'd his Pretensions; but *Caumartin* carry'd it against him in the General Assembly, which would not give him Audience, notwithstanding it had been promis'd him. He had it only of the five little *Cantons* which did not give him the Style of Excellency, but only that of Lordship. The Money and Authority of the King of *France* were the Cause of his receiving this Affront. For as I just now took notice, the Governor of *Milan* has a right to send Ministers, to whom the Quality of Embassador is given. One of the best Historians of our time remarks that when, in the Year 1615, *Don Pedro de Toledo* enter'd upon his Government of *Milan*, the Duke of *Savoy* sent an Embassador to him to compliment him, and forasmuch as Don Pedro did not make a handsome Return, (not sending any body to *Turin* of a great while after) his Incivility was talk'd of, as a certain Proof of the little Friendship he had for the Duke. He sent *Andrew Manriquez* to *Venice*, where the Count de *Bethune*, Embassador Extraordinary from *France*, treated with him. *Richardot*, *Taxis*, and *Verreyken*, had indeed their Commission from the Arch-Duke, but they were Embassadors from the King of *Spain*, whose Procurator the Arch-Duke was. The same ought to be said of the Baron de *Bergeyck*, whom the Marquis de *Castelrodrigue*, Governor of the Low Countreys, sent to *Aix la Chapelle* in the Year 1668. The Deputies whom I just now spoke of, and who met in the Year 1588 on the part of the Duke of *Parma*, with the Ministers of *England*, were not Embassadors, *Chiapin Vitelli*, whom the Duke of *Alva*, Governor of the Low Countreys, sent into *England* in the Year 1569, was not Embassador neither.

It is indubitable, *That those who during Interregnums have the Direction of Affairs with a full Power, may send Embassadors*. After the Death of *Sigismund the August*, King of *Poland*, and even after the Election of the Duke of *Anjou*, the Senate of the Kingdom sent a solemn Embassy to *France*, and they who compos'd it were consider'd there and treated as Embassadors, tho' it may be said, that *Poland* being properly but a Republick, the Senate which represents it has a right in it self to send Embassadors, since it lends its Name and Authority even to those the King employs. So that there is no *Interregnum*, any more than there is at *Venice*, upon the Death of the *Doge*. For altho the publick Deliberations are suspended for some Days, it is only to oblige the Senate to proceed to an Election so much the sooner. *Sede vacante*, the *Conclave* may send Embassadors, and there are Examples of it.

In hereditary Kingdoms there is no *Interregnum*, and nevertheless, when the Succession is contested amongst the Heirs, the Estates of the Kingdom may send Embassadors in their own Name. After the Death of *Henry* King of *Portugal*, the *Regents* of the Kingdom sent the Bishop of *Coimbre*, and *Don Emanuel de Melo*, to *Philip* King of *Spain*. Philip, who pretended there was no *Interregnum*, by reason he maintain'd that his Right was indisputable, put it in Deliberation, whether he should receive 'em as Embassadors, or whether he should treat 'em as his Subjects. However he receiv'd them as Embassador, and gave 'em publick Audience; but he did not deal the same Usage to *Ferdinand de Silva*, Embassador in Ordinary from *Portugal*, neither did he invite him to the Chapel after the Death of *Henry*, notwithstanding he had *Letters of Credence* from the Regents. *Charles*, the eldest Son of *John* King of *France*, who was Regent of the Kingdom during the time his Father was a Prisoner in *England*, sent his Embassadors every where as well because in those Days the Regents govern'd in their own Name, as because being Regent in his own Right, and presumptive Heir to the Crown, he was in a manner the Sovereign thereof, since there was then no other in the Kingdom. The Mother of *France*, who was Regent of *France* during the time of her Son's detention at *Madrid*, had only a delegated Power, yet that did not hinder her from sending, in the Year 1524, the Archbishop d'*Embrun*, since Cardinal, *John de Seltz*, first President of the Parliament of *Paris* and *Philip Chabot* Lord of *Brion*, in the Quality of Embassadors, to treat there of the King's Liberty. The illustrious Posterity of this *John de Seltz* invites me to add, that he was always spoke man, tho' at the same time his two Collegues had also the Reputation of being very able Negotiators. He left behind him six Sons, who, except one who was Abbot of St *Vigour*, were all employ'd in Embassies and Negociations of Importance. *Lazarus de Seltz*, his eldest Son, and one of the Gentlemen of the Bed Chamber to the King, was sent to the *Swiss Cantons*, *John Francis* into *Turkey*, *George*, Bishop of *Lavaur*, to the Emperor, and *John Paul*, Bishop of St *Flour*, and *Odes*, to *Rome* and *Venice*.

This Embassy of the Regent receiv'd its Authority, in part, from that of the Estates of the Kingdom, who had a considerable share in the Affairs during the King's detention. But as for an Embassador, or publick Minister, he cannot *subdelegate*, unless he has a special Power for that Purpose. For this Reason, the Count de *Pegnaranda*, when he substituted and subdelegated the Archbishop of *Mechlin*, *Diego de Saavedra*, and *Anthony le Brun*, for the Negotiation at *Munster*, gave them an Instrument whereon he speaks in these Terms. Don *Gaspar de Bracamonte*, Count de *Pegnaranda*, &c. forasmuch

The EMBASSADOR and his FUNCTIONS. 23

much as it has pleas'd the King of Spain, my Master, to give me by his Letters Patents of the twenty fifth of February 1645, full Power and Authority to treat of Peace or Truce with the High and Potent Lords, the States of the United Provinces, which Letters begin thus *Philip, by the Grace of God, King of Spain, &c. I therefore, by virtue of the Power and Authority which his Majesty has given us, by which I can take to my Assistance one or more Persons any by which I am impower'd to substitute, subrogate, and nominate them, to be these Present, name and constitute Brother Joseph de Bergagne Archbishop of Mecklen, Diego de Saavedra, and Anthony le Brun, and all and every of them, Plenipotentiaries at the General Peace at Munster, to whom I have transmitted, and do transmit the same Authority, and same Power with which his Majesty has invested me, and substitute in to myself, to the end that in the Name, and on the Part of his said Majesty, they may negotiate and conclude all Treaties of Peace or Truce, either all together, or each of them in particular, as well in my Absence, as in my Presence, &c.* But then these Ministers were not the Embassadors or Count de Pignerand's, like those which Viceroys and Governors send in their own Name, they had the Quality of Plenipotentiaries of the King of Spain.

I shall illustrate this Matter by one Example more. Gustavus Adolphus, King of Sweden, being kill'd at the Battel of Lutzen the 16th of November 1632, the Crown of Sweden gave the whole Direction of Affairs, and of the War in Germany, to the Chancellor Axel Oxenstiern, with the Quality of Legate or Embassador Plenipotentiary in the Empire. The whole Party acknowledg'd him in this Quality, and all the Princes, except the Electors gave him the Hand. There were some that did it with Reluctancy, and that could not endure that a Gentleman, who was a Stranger should assume an Authority that exceeded that of Sovereign. And in fact he exercis'd it with so much Imperiousness, that it was one of the chief Causes of the particular Peace, which the Elector of Saxony concluded at Prague in the Year 1635, and of the Engagement the Duke of Weimar made with France. Oxenstiern making use of the Power of Legation, nominated Hugh de Groot to the Embassy of France, to which the deceased King had destin'd him, and provided him with Letters of Credence, and his Instructions. Cardinal de Richelieu who was then first Minister of France, oppos'd the Admission of Monsieur de Groot, because, not having Letters from the Senate of Sweden, the general Power of Plenipotentiary did not extend to far, as the Faculty of giving to another the representing Character. Neither was he admitted, till the evil Constitution of Affairs obliging the Chancellor to return into Sweden, and to take his way through France, he represented to the Cardinal, that the same Power that had made him be consider'd in the Treaties he had made with France, ought also to make him be consider'd in the Commission which he had given to Monsieur a Groot, which could not be rejected without destroying at the same time all that had been concluded with him in Germany. The Cardinal, who designd to make use of Sweden, in the Execution of the great Designs he was laying against the House of Austria, suffer'd himself to be overcome, and caus'd Monsieur de Groot to be accepted. He was Embassador of Sweden and not the Chancellor's, who had given him his Commission by virtue of his Procuration, or his full Power.

The Duke of Orleans, Lieutenant General of the Kingdom during the Minority of the present King might in the King's Absence, who was then in Guyenne, subdelegate a Person to treat of the Peace with whomsoever the Arch-Duke Leopold should nominate on his Part, but so as much as this particularly relates to the Powers, we shall speak of it hereafter more seasonably.

Generals of Armies employ also Ministers, who, as publick Persons, ought likewise to enjoy the Protection of the Law of Nations. Philip o. Savoy, Count of Racconis, commanding the Armies of Emanuel Philibert against the Protestants of the Valleys of Piedmont, in the Year 1561, sent to them a Gentleman nam'd Francis de Gilles, who having negotiated and concluded their Accommodation, upon very reasonable Terms, was kill'd the same Night by two of the Inhabitants of the Valleys, as he was returning to the Duke of Savoy's Camp. The Count was extremely exasperated hereat, and complain'd thereof, *as a Violation of the Law of Nations*. Those of the Valley detested the Action, and, to justify themselves, deliver'd up the Authors of the Murther to the Count, who perceiving thereby the Sincerity of their Intent on, was satisfy'd, and procur'd 'em a Peace on the Conditions Gilles had granted them.

Generals make use also of *Trumpets*, and *Drums*, who, having succeeded to the Function of the *Heralds*, enjoy likewise their Rights and Privileges. This Matter alone is sufficient for a whole Volume, so that as it cannot make a part of that I am now handling, I shall be contented to say, that the *Law of Nations* is violated, when any Outrage is offer'd to those Drums and Trumpeters, who having a Passport from the General of an Army, or Governor of a Place, go from one Camp or Garrison to another, provided they carry publickly the Tokens of their Function, viz. The *Trumpeter his Trumpet*, the *Drummer his Drum*, and the *Herald his Coat of Arms*. Mary Queen of England, in the Year 1555, sent Norris her Herald to declare War against Henry II King of France. Norris had enter'd the Kingdom without making himself known, and indeed he was not provided with a Passport from his Mistress, for which Reasons the Duke de Montmorancy told him he deserv'd to be hang'd. However the King gave him Audience, in the Presence of the Nuncio, and of the Embassadors of Portugal, Venice, and of Ferrara, and told him that he accepted the Queen's Defiance, and as he had done nothing that could oblige the English to break with him, he had reason to hope that the End of the War would be fatal to 'em. He moreover added, that as the Herald had spoke to him from a Woman, he did not answer him as he would have done, if he had brought him such a Message from a Man. He would not suffer the Herald to reply, and commanded him to depart the Kingdom immediately. The King's Prophecy was verify'd in the Loss the English sustain'd of the Town of
Calai,

Calice, and of the little Countrey they had left in *France* It was a comical sort of a Herald that *Lewis* XI sent to *Edward* IV King of *England* The Stay the *English* Army made in *France*, gave great Uneasiness to *Lewis*, who defiring to send it to the other side of the Sea, bethought himself to make a Herald's Coat of the Banner of a Trumpet, and having cloth'd therewith a Groom belonging to one of his Noblemen, he difpatch'd him to the *English* Camp, where this pretended Herald made the first Overtures of an Accommodation, obtain'd a Paffport for the Deputies that were to negotiate it, and carry'd back with him a true Herald, who came to fetch a Paffport for the *English* Deputies This Groom who had been taught in a moment the Bufinefs of a Herald, had without doubt fomething fpiritual and fingular in him, which the King had taken notice of before he gave him this Commiffion

All thofe who have had any Knowledge of the *Law of Nations*, have ever had a great Confideration for *Trumpeters* and *Drums*, becaufe they in fome meafure difcharge the Functions of the *Fecales* and *Caduceators* of the Ancients. The Emperor *Charles* V having fummon'd a Diet at *Spires* in the Year 1544, *Francis* I, King of *France*, fent a Trumpeter to it, who was to ask a Paffport for the Embaffadors he intended to fend thither The Emperor caus'd the Trumpeter to be feiz'd, and having taken his Letter from him, made him be very ftrictly guarded But after having detain'd him four Days, he order'd his Letters to be reftor'd to him, and caus'd him to be conducted to *Nancy* by the fame Soldiers who had had him in Cuftody The Emperor faid, that the Trumpeter deferv'd to be hang'd, becaufe the King of *France* being his Enemy, he was not oblig'd to fuffer his Meffenger in the Empire, where he alone could give Safety to the Trumpeter and that he would have given it without difficulty, if he had addrefs'd himfelf to him, but that it was failing in the Refpect that was due to him, to fend a Trumpeter to the Deputies of the Diet while he was there in Perfon He was willing however to teftifie that he refpected the *Law of Nations*, by making the Trumpeter enjoy that Safety, which he ought to find in the King's Paffport

The Duke of *Alva* being encamp'd with his Army near the *Menfe*, the Prince of *Orange*, who was encamp'd on the other fide of the River, fent a Trumpeter to him, but the Duke caus'd him to be hang'd He faid he was not oblig'd to protect a Trumpeter, who brought him a Meffage from the Chief of the Rebels He was in the wrong, for although the *Law of Nations* does not protect thofe that violate it, by taking Arms againft their Prince, yet there is a great deal of difference betwixt a Deputy that comes from the Rebels, and a Trumpeter that ferves in their Army For the Deputy that accepts of a Commiffion from the Rebels, makes himfelf thereby an Accomplice of their Rebellion, whereas the Trumpeter is oblig'd to obey the Orders that are given him on pain of Death The fame Duke of *Alva*, while he was at the Head of *Philip* II's Army, in order to conquer *Portugal*, caus'd the Governor of *Cafcais* to be hang'd, becaufe he had fir'd upon the Trumpeter that had founded the Parley for the Summons to furrender Prince *Maurice* of *Naffau*, Captain General of the United Provinces, having caus'd *Tjendick* to be invefted, at the beginning of this Century, the Garrifon fir'd upon the Trumpeter that founded the *Chamade* The Prince refented it fo far, that he would not fo much as hear of a Capitulation fo that to fatisfie him, he had an *Italian* Soldier deliver'd up to him, who having deferv'd Death for other Crimes, was alfo accufed of this unwarrantable Act The *Italian* clear'd himfelf, and the Prince fent him back, and let the Governor know, *that the Violence that had been done to the Law of Nations, could not be expiated by the Death of a fingle Perfon* We read in the Hiftory of *Italy*, that *Fabritio Maramaldo* kill'd *Ferrucio* (who was Commiffary of the Republick of *Florence*) with his own Hand, becaufe that during the Siege of *Volterre* he had caus'd the Drummer to be hang'd, whom *Fabritio* had fent into the Place There are feveral Examples of Generals of Armies, that have caus'd Reparation to be made for Injuries done to Trumpeters and Drummers The two Armies of *Charles* V, and of *Henry* II, being in the Year 1554, encamp'd on the Frontiers of *Picardy* and the Low Countreys, a *French* Trumpeter, who had been fent to the Emperor's Camp to demand a Prifoner, fel into the hands of fome *Germans*, who difmounted him and left him in his Shirt The King having complain'd thereof the Duke of *Savoy*, who commanded the Imperial Army, caus'd a ftrict Inquiry to be made after the Authors of this Excefs, gave the Trumpeter a good Horfe out of his own Stable, and a new Coat and had him conducted fafe to the *French* Camp The Reparation made by the Duke, is a Token of the Refpect he had for the *Law of Nations*, by giving fo particular a Protection to a Trumpeter, who, excepting fome fmall Wages and this Privilege, had not the leaft Advantage over the leaft Party-man Indeed there are none but Princes, and thofe that are about 'em, that make it their Study, and come to the Knowledge of it, not in the Schools or at the Bar, but in the Management of Affairs, which have no more analogy to thofe that amufe the Judges and the litigious Crew, than there is betwixt the Materials that employ the Labour of a Goldfmith, and thofe that ferve the common Cobler

Now as none but the Sovereign, or the Perfon that reprefents him, and is impower'd by him, has the Right of fending Embaffadors, fo is there none but the Captain General, or he that in his abfence commands a Body or a Garrifon, that can give Paffports, or caufe a Place to be fummon'd by a Drum or a Trumpeter At the Siege that the *Admirante of Arragon* made of *Rhinberg* in the Year 1598, *Alfonfo d'Avalos*, Camp mafter of a *Spanifh* Regiment, caus'd the Garrifon to be fummon'd to furrender the Place, but the Governor fent Orders to the Drummer to withdraw, and that if any other Drummer or Trumpeter dar'd to come again, by the Order of any Colonel or Camp-mafter, he would caufe him to be hang'd

I think this a proper place to fay a word in reference to the Deputies of an Affembly, that the Sovereign calls together to take their Advice, or elfe to let 'em know his Pleafure concerning

cerning the Affairs of his Estate It is very certain there is a great deal of difference between these Deputies and publick Ministers But yet as they are publick Persons who represent the whole Body of the State, they ought to enjoy an inviolable Safety, as well going and coming, as during the stay they make in the Place where the Assembly is held So that it is not lawful for the Sovereign, and much less for him that is not such, to offer violence to their Persons, nor to molest 'em by Prosecutions, either for Debts or common Trespasses This is what is observ'd at the *Diets* of *Germany*, at the *Cortes* of *Spain*, in the Parliament of *England*, and in all the Assemblies of States wherever they are conven'd There are two Reasons for this The one is, That the Estates making one half, or the Trunk of a Body, whereof the Prince makes the other part and the Head, he cannot do otherwise than we see in natural Bodies, the Head does with respect to the other Members, which are obedient to a reasonable and lawful Will The other Reason is, That there is no Countrey, where the Estates have not Privileges, which being instead of Contracts between the Prince and his Subjects, he cannot violate 'em, without destroying the Foundation of Civil Society Admitting that *Henry* III King of *France* had taken no Oath, nor given any particular Assurances to the Duke, and Cardinal de *Guise*, the single general Security, which was due to all the Deputies, of which the States of *Bloise* were compos'd, was sufficient to protect their Persons from the Violence that was practis'd towards 'em It is true that the Regal Dignity, nor even the King's Life, were not safe, and I will not deny, but that the Life of the one depended on the Death of the other The King had receiv'd so many outragious Injuries, that they could not be aton'd for but by the violent Death of so powerful and dangerous a Subject, but that is no Argument, that the Security of the Estates, which ought to have been inviolate in all respects, was not violated by the Murther of those two Lords, and the Imprisonment of some others These *Strokes of State*, however necessary they may be sometimes, are accompany'd with Irregularities, that are not reconcileable either with Honour or Conscience The King having resolv'd to take off the Duke, would have made use of *Grillon*, Camp-master of the Regiment of Guardes He was a gallant Man, but being incapable of doing a cowardly Act, he offer'd the King to challenge the Duke by the way of Duel, to fight him without any advantage, and he assur'd him that he would do it with so much success, that he should soon find himself freed from the Anxieties this ambitious and rebel Prince created him continually The King would not consent to it, and *Grillon* would not do a foul Action There is but one thing that can save the King's Honour, which is the certain Advice he receiv'd, that it was the Duke's Intention to dethrone the King in that very Assembly, so that there were no measures to be observ'd with a Subject, who had made himself so powerful, that there was no proceeding against him by the ordinary ways of Justice, and of whom he could not rid himself, but by an extraordinary Violence Things being thus, and the Duke of *Guise* failing first in his Duty to his Sovereign, the King was not oblig'd to stick at any thing to save his Life and his Dignity

CHAP. IV.

The Princes of Germany have a Right to send Embassadors to represent them.

THE great Disputes the *Barberins* and the Duke of *Parma* had towards the latter end of the Pontificate of *Urban* VIII concerning the Dutchy of *Castro*, making it to be fear'd, that the continuation of the War might draw the main Forces of the two Crowns into *Italy*, *France* labour'd with application to compose the Difference The Pope, who receiv'd these Offices with Indignation, complaining one day to *Hugh de Lionne*, (who then negotiated without a Character, but has since been Secretary of State) told him, that the Duke of *Parma*, who being his Vassal, ought to come in Person and make his Submission, did not seem to take any notice of that Duty, and that instead of sending him ten Embassadors one after another, supposing he would admit of 'em, was for negotiating with him through the Mediation of a little Secretary of a subaltern Minister *Lionne* made answer, *That those Vassals, who by virtue of their first Investiture, receiv'd their Fiefs with all the Rights of Sovereignty, owe nothing to the Lord after the* simple *Homage, and may negotiate with him by the means of Embassadors* and as for the Minister of whom the Pope made mention, he was the Duke's Secretary, who as well as other Sovereign Princes, might give him what Quality he pleas'd, not being oblig'd to comply in that respect, with the Opinion or Capriciousness of the Prince to whom he employ'd him This Reply, which is so conformable to the *Law of Nations*, and to common Usage, is so contrary to the refusal the *French* make to admit the Ministers of the Princes of *Germany* in the Quality of Embassadors, that I find my self oblig'd, before I leave this matter, (which is the Subject of the two preceding Chapters) to give one to the Discussion of the Question, that is at this time in agitation at *Nimmeguen*, and in most of the Courts of *Europe*, to wit, whether the Princes of *Germany* have the Right of Embassy

I here speak of those Princes of *Germany* who have a Right to sit in the Diets, and I also comprehend the Electors, as well because *France* does

does not admit or acknowledge their Embassadors but in Congresses, not allowing them in its Court the Honours that are due to the Character, as because even in Congresses and Assemblies the Ministers of *France* do none to all the Embassadors of the Electors without Distinction, but absolutely refuse 'em to those of the other Princes. We shall find a proper Place elsewhere to tell after what manner they use 'em; I shall therefore only take notice here, that the said Honours cannot be refus'd to the Ministers of Princes, without disowning their Sovereignty, which would be by so much the less justifyable, that even those, who would undertake it, are for having it to have been established by the Peace of *Munster*, as it were by a Pragmatick Sanction, and have treated with the Princes of *Germany* as with Sovereigns.

As the King of *France* who reigns at present, possesses in the highest Degree, all the eminent Qualities that go to the forming a perfect Monarch, it is not to be doubted but he is also very civil, and that he is ever ready to shew to those foreign Princes who have no Dependence on him all the Civilities the Consideration they have for him can deserve, which makes 'em look upon him as the first and greatest King in *Christendom*. He not only suffers the Duke of *Savoy*, the great Duke of *Tuscany*, and the Dukes of *Mantua*, *Parma*, and *Modena*, to send him their Embassadors, but he also allows the same Princes at their own homes to take the place of Honour of his Embassadors. So that there is reason to wonder that this great Prince, who is otherwise so just, will not suffer the Princes of *Germany*, as the Dukes of *Newburg*, *Brunswick* and *Lunenburg*, and others of the same Dignity, to have even the Power of nominating Embassadors, and that he takes from them an Advantage which he grants to the Dukes of *Parma* and *Modena*.

Before I enter further into this Matter, I must lay down this Position as a thing certain, that the King does not hinder the Princes of *Germany* from sending him their Embassadors, but that he will not shew them the same Civilities which he does to the Embassadors of the Princes of *Italy*. When the Elector of *Bavaria* sent Count *Groensfeldt* and *Curtz* into *France*, in the Year 1683, their Quality of Embassadors was not disputed, but they would have treated 'em as they do the Embassadors of the *Swiss Cantons*, that is to say, lodge 'em in the Quality, but use 'em in reality like Ministers of the second Order. In the Month of *March* 1653, S *Kroll*, Chancellor of *Baden*, was sent to *France* with the Character of Embassador, to conclude the Marriage of the Prince, Son to the Marquis of *Baden*, with the Daughter of Prince *Thomas* of *Carignan*. He did not cover himself when he spoke to the King, but notwithstanding, the King stood all the time of the Audience, and also uncover'd. The Chancellor of *France* (whom the Embassador would likewise see) understanding that he was not cover'd when he spoke to the King, said that since it was so, he would neither give him the Place of Honour, nor the arm'd Chair at his House. And indeed the Chancellor receiv'd him only in the Hall, where they both were standing and uncover'd. The Chancellor, who did not fail to shew Civility to those to whom it is due,

behav'd himself after this manner, because he knew he oblig'd the Embassador more in treating him thus, than if he had us'd him altogether like a Minister of the second Order. The Masters of the Ceremonies were of Opinion that the Chancellor could not receive him the second time, because the Cardinal himself gave it even to Residents. They spoke the Truth, yet at the same time their Reasons were defective. For what the Cardinal did in this respect was not a thing of Obligation, and therefore his Example could not bind the Chancellor.

It is not my Intention to draw a Parallel between the Princes of *Germany* and those of *Italy*, but I think I may say without offending the latter, that the Families of *Germany*, or at least some of *France*, were not so noble as known when the Houses of *Bavaria* and *Brunswick* furnish'd Germany with Emperors. Those who do the greatest Honour to the Duke of *Savoy*, make him descended from a younger Brother of those Princes, of whom the Dukes of *Brunswick* and *Lunenburg* are the true and undoubted Posterity, and who, under the great *Henries*, extended their Dominions as far as *Alsire*, from the *Baltick* Sea to the Gulf of *Venice*. So that it is reasonable to believe that it is not on the account of the Antiquity of their Families, that the Princes of *Italy* ought to be preferr'd to those of *Germany*.

I cannot believe neither, that it is to be maintain'd, that those are more Sovereign and more independent than these. For besides that Sovereignty admits of no Comparative notwithstanding all Princes are not alike absolute, the Duke of *Savoy*, who is the first Prince of *Italy*, values himself so much on the Vicarship of the Empire, that he procur'd a Confirmation of it by the third Article of the Capitulation of the Emperor now reigning, and glories in being of the Number of his Princes. In the Year 1514, *Charles* Duke of *Savoy* sent his Embassadors to the Diet at *Spire*, where he complain'd of the Invasion the *Turks* had made in his Countrey, at the Instigation of the *French*. They represented that Matter had not wherein to contribute to the *Turkish* War, neither was it ooh to defray the Expences of his Journey, to appear in Person at the Diet, and therefore pray'd the Estates to protect him as a Member of the Empire. The great Duke of *Tuscany*, who has had a Confirmation of his Title from the Emperor, gives place to the Duke of *Savoy*, and the Dukes of *Mantua* and *Modena* hold their Dutchies as Fiefs of the Empire, as the Duke of *Parma* holds his of the See of *Rome*, notwithstanding which, the Pope himself admits of his Embassadors, and receives 'em with the same Civilities he shews to other Sovereign Princes. In the Year 1669, the Duke of *Parma* sent the Count de *Sint Secunde* to *Rome*, to complement *Clement X* upon his Exaltation. He was attended by eighteen Prelates to his Audience, and had a Cortege of one hundred and fifty Coaches, and the Pope receiv'd him in the Presence of eight Cardinals, whom he had sent for to his Chamber for that purpose. The Princes of *Italy* have no Sovereignty, which those of *Germany* have not, as good a Title too, as is absolute a manner, and to the same Degree as they. I shall not here make useless Enumeration thereof, but it is sufficient to say, that without being Sovereign a Prince cannot declare War and make Peace, cast Cannon, fortify Places, lay up Magazines, make Levies of Soldiers, treat of Alliances, as well within as without the Empire, coin Money, grant Pardons and Oblivions, and in a word, do all that a Sovereign does. This is so evident, that even France agrees thereto, and has acknowledg'd it on several Occasions, so that it would be superfluous to dwell longer upon it. It cannot therefore be on this Foundation, that Treaties to admit their Embassadors.

I can say, is much of the Forces, and Extent of the Estates of the one and the other. For although it is Sovereignty and not Power, that regulates the Rank and the Rights of Princes, I dare affirm nevertheless, that even on this account the Princes of Italy have no Advantage beyond those of Germany. The Kings of France were the First of all Christendom, at that very time that the English were in Possession of a considerable part of the Kingdom, and when Bigurdy, Britain, Dauphiné and Provence had their particular Lords. It is true, the Princes of Germany live upon their Demesn's, and raise neither Taxes, nor Customs, nor any other extraordinary Imposts from their Subjects, unless it be with the Consent of the Estates of their Country; but then that is the King of Great Britain's Case as well as theirs, and if we will believe Philip de Comines, that of all others, who ground their Actions upon Reason and Justice, and have the Safety and Welfare of their People for Motives of their Conduct. That Tract of Country, that between the two Rivers, the Elve and the Weser, extends it self from Magdeburg almost to the very Ocean, may it not be compar'd with the largest Provinces of Italy, as well for the Number and Quality of the Towns, as for the Importance of its strong Places, even without the Counties de Hoe and Depthold on this side and beyond the Weser? I'll be bold to say, that the two largest Provinces of Italy without excepting even those belonging to the Pope and the Republick of Venice, will not make together what the Countries of Brunswick and Lunenburg was done in the Year 1645. The Imperial Army having pass'd that of Swede, this Country serv'd for a Place of retreat to the latter, whose Cavalry was almost entirely dismounted, furnish'd it with very good Quarters all the Winter, without incommoding the Husbandman, and when it march'd out, supply'd it with fifteen thousand Horses. I cannot speak of the Armies that have been rais'd there, and which have been subsisted in't during an almost thirty Years War, as well as of those particularly which Duke George the Father of the three Princes that are now living, has commanded, and shall only say, that not one of the Princes of Italy, who ne suffer'd to give the Quality of Embassador to their Ministers, is able to do any thing like it. The War of the Barberins, against whom the Republick of Venice, the great Duke of Tuscany, and the Dukes of Parma and Modena, had exerted all their Strength, is a sufficient Proof thereof. It makes me affirm, that it is not likewise on this account that the Prince of Italy ought to be more consider'd than those of Germany.

Those that have any knowledge of the Affairs of the World, will not likewise say, that the first have done more for the Interest and Glory of France than the last. The Duke of Saxe, did not declare for France, till Spain either would not, or could no longer protect him, and all that he has done for it, is that he left off coming it my harm, when the Power rather turn'd him than the Will. The Duke of Mantua, who was oblig'd to France for the Preservation of his whole Estate, left the Memory, as well as grateful Sentiment thereof, is soon is the Troubles of the Kingdom gave him an Opportunity to show himself ungrateful and treacherous. There is no body but who is sensible of the disobliging Behaviour of the same Duke of Parma, who had been so mightily honour'd at Paris, in preference to the incomparable Duke of Saxe Weimar, and the Duke of Modena had no sooner declar'd for France, then he forc'd it to content to his reconciling himself with Spain. It cannot be deny'd, that all the Engagements, and all the Friendships of the Italian Princes, have always been accompany'd with Jealousies and Distrusts of which France has never been able to cure 'em. On the contrary, the Princes of Germany have always seconded, with Firmness and Courage, the Interests and Intentions of France, whilst it with Constancy oppos'd (ever since the Reign of Francis I, till the Peace of Westphalia) a predominate Power, which was going to establish it self in Europe. The Duke of Lunenburg whom I just now mention'd, has alone done more for the Success of the Arms of the Allies in Germany, than France could have expected from all the Princes of Italy together. And admitting that History took no notice of a great Number of German Princes, who have been well affected and very faithful to France, I need only oppose to all Italy that incomparable Amelia of Hanau, Princess Regent of Hesse, and the Heroine of our Age, who has plainly shewn, that, even for perfonal Merit, the Princes of Italy have no Advantage over those of Germany France, that is a competent Judge in this Matter, and that does judge of it with Freedom and Justice, will not scruple to own, that in all Ages Germany produces very great Princes, and that in one single Century there have been more of 'em seen at the Heads of Armies, than all Italy has afforded since the decay of the Roman Empire. Certainly, if the right of nominating I mould fors were annext to the Wit, Conduct, Generosity, and to all the other Qualities that to an extraordinary Princes, I would be bold to say, it were due to the Princes of Germany, preferably to those of Italy.

I know very well, that as at present most of the Princes of Germany are engag'd in a Party quite opposite to France, they will find it a difficult matter to obtain a Novelty, and an Advantage, which by being neglected is become of the last Importance. But as the King is a Prince, that is extremely reasonable in all his Actions, I with the profoundest respect beg his leave to examine whether he be so in this.

The Ignorance of the History of the ancient Roman Laws, and of the true Constitution of the present Affairs of Europe, has fill'd the greatest part of the Books of modern Lawyers with so many Paradoxes, that there is hardly any

any difference between their common Opinions and popular Errors. It is particularly remarkable in those of *Germany*, where one Doctor has no sooner struck into a prejudicate Opinion than all the rest fall into it likewise, with the same Fury that caus'd the two thousand *Gadarean* Swine to cast themselves headlong into the Sea. One would take it to be a kind of Enchantment, which produces the same effect in them, that *Circe*'s Potion wrought in the Companions of *Ulysses*. They find in History, that the *Roman* People gave up all their Rights of Sovereignty to the Emperor *Augustus*, who by degrees usurp'd also those that the Senate had reserv'd it self, and they apply to the Emperors of the House of *Austria*, the Commentaries and Glosses they make upon the ancient Constitutions, endeavouring to form an Idea of a fourth Monarchy. It is certain that the modern Emperors share the Sovereignty of the Empire in general with the Estates that compose it, and that they have none at all left in those Provinces that have particular Princes. The Emperor's Counsellors are excusable, and even those of the aulick Council, when they entertain these Sentiments. But this Fault is no way pardonable in those, who being of a Prince's Council, and oblig'd to speak in the behalf of the Rights of his Sovereignty, dare to declare themselves in favour of Maxims directly opposite to the Truth, and so prejudicial to their Master. The Ambition of Princes that have any thoughts of an universal Monarchy, does not want being excited by such pernicious Counsels, which would have made the Imperial Dignity hereditary, and the Power of the Emperor absolute, if *Charles* V could have transmitted it to his Successors, the Kings of *Spain*, in the Person of his Son *Philip*. It is also probable enough, that without the victorious Arms of *Gustavus Adolphus*, we should have seen in effect, that whereof there remains only an imperfect Idea in the wounded Imagination of some Pedants, who pretend that a Sovereign and absolute Power is resident in the Person of the Emperor of *Germany*. The Capitulations which have been made with *Ferdinand* III and *Leopold*, as well as the Treaties of *Westphalia*, have secur'd to the Princes of *Germany* those Rights that put 'em upon the Level with other Sovereigns, and set 'em in a Rank wherein they are oblig'd to yield but only to Crown'd Heads.

Yet nevertheless it is only on the false Maxims of those Doctors, that *France* can ground its refusal to admit the Embassadors of the Princes of *Germany*. It is but since the *Bohemian* War that the Council has taken a due Cognizance of the Affairs of the Empire, and as it is but since the Ministry of Cardinal *Richlieu* that any regard has been had thereto, so they have been very much neglected since his decease, as well as the Inclinations of the Princes, who out of a regard to their own particular Interest could not consent to the prevailing Power of the House of *Austria*. I shall add, that *France* thinking she should with more ease compass the Design she had, not to moderate, but even to pull down the Power of *Spain*, by attacking it in the Dutchy of *Milan*, or in the Kingdom of *Naples*, she shew'd a greater Consideration for the Princes of *Italy*, who were able to contribute or consent thereto, than to those of *Germany*, whose Friendship was not so useful to it, or at least not so necessary. It is what was very much forwarded by the Counsels of those Ministers, who to consecrate their own private Opinions, have acted contrary to the true Maxims, and have despis'd old Friends to make new ones, who were more able to second the Intention of those that were for raising the Grandeur of the *French* Monarchy upon the Ruins of that of *Spain*.

It cannot be deny'd also, that the King's Haughtiness will not easily suffer the Style and Conduct to be chang'd, especially now that he has carry'd the Glory of his Crown beyond the Pretensions, and even the Hopes of his Predecessors. It may be said again, that it is not without some Ground, that he will have all the Princes, be they who they will pay Him the same Respect they shew the Emperor, and will not allow them to exact more from the one, than they know will be granted by the other. He sees that the Princes of *Germany*, in writing to the Emperor, pay him the same Submissions they us'd to do when he was Sovereign, and when the Imperial Dignity was hereditary in the Houses of *Saxony*, of *Franconia*, and *Swabia*, and even greater than those the *French* themselves pay to their King. Hereupon he does not think himself oblig'd to treat as *Sovereigns*, those Persons the Emperor treats as *Subjects*.

I say *Subjects*, and to shew that I do not speak improperly, I might instance in the Submissions some Protestant Princes, and among the rest, the Landgrave of *Hesse* and the Duke of *Wirtemberg* made to the Emperor *Charles* V after the Battel of *Roglits*, who prostrating themselves at his Feet, and begging his pardon, tell him, *that they are his most humble and most obedient Servants, Vassals and Subjects*. But I consider that the Emperor, on this Occasion, behav'd himself as a victorious Prince, who having his Sword in his Hand gave Laws to all *Germany*, where he pretended to Reign as Sovereign and absolute Prince thereof. It was also an act of Sovereignty, when in the Year 1549 he confin'd (it *Placentia*) the Deputies or Embassadors of those Princes who had protested against the Decree of the Diet at *Spires*, and indeed it was not without some violence to the Law of *Nations*, or at least without breach of the Capitulation. There have been also Acts of the same strain in the Reigns of *Ferdinand* II, and *Ferdinand* III. When the first Discourse arose of negotiating a Peace at *Cologn*, and while the Emperor's Ministers and those of *France* were settling the Preliminaries at *Hamburg*, the King asking for Passports for his Allies, nam'd the *Swede*, the United Provinces, and the Princes of *Germany*. The Emperor made answer, that as for the *Swedes*, he had consented to a particular Congress, which was to be held at *Lubeck*, and that they ought themselves to ask for Passports if they would have any, that being in a Neutrality with the United Provinces, their Deputies had no occasion for any, and as to the Ministers of the Protestant Princes of *Germany*, he would not so much as suffer it to be mention'd, *That the Subjects of the Empire ought to ask the Emperor's pardon*, and not talk of Negotiation, more especially since the Door of Reconci-

Reconciliation was open to them by the Treaty of *Prague*. This Declaration of the Emperor oblig'd the *French* to change their Batteries; they said, that it was not the King's Intention to bring the Protestant Princes People to the Assembly as publick Ministers, but as private Persons, who were to instruct the Plenipotentiaries of *France*, in their Master's Interests. The Republick of *Venice* (whose Mediation had been accepted, and was chiefly to employ it self in what related to the Protestant Princes) not being able to prevail with the King of *France* not to insist, that at least they should be allow'd to send to the Assembly Persons in a private Capacity to sollicit their Interests, made two Overtures for that purpose. The one, that the Emperor should cause Passports to be dispatch'd for the safety of those, who as private Persons should recommend the Interests of their Masters to the Plenipotentiaries of *France*, and that he should grant them the privilege of sending and receiving Couriers; the other was, that in case the Emperor made any difficulty to give such Passports, he would make a general Declaration for the safety of all those whom the Parties interested in this War should send to the Assembly, with the aforesaid privilege of sending and receiving Couriers. The Emperor made answer, that there was no difference between the Passports to be given to the Ministers of the Protestant Princes, *Subjects of the Empire*, where the Quality of Minister should be express'd, and those where it was not, and that it was sufficient that the Princes duly inform'd the Plenipotentiaries of *France*, before they came to the Place appointed, and before they enter'd upon Business.

The King of *Poland* seconded the Instances of the King of *France*, in favour of the Protestant Princes, but the Emperor was angry thereat, and ask'd the Minister of *Poland*, what would be said in *France*, if the King his Master should desire Passports for the Count de Soissons, or for the Duke d'Espernon? That if the Rebel-Princes of *Germany* demanded Securities, they might find 'em in the Peace of *Prague*, by virtue of which they might lay themselves at his Feet, and obtain by their Submissions, not only the Restitution of their Estates, but also the Emperor's Favour and their own Quiet. But, said he, they despise the ample safe Conduct that the Treaty of *Prague* provides for 'em, and would have one that should warrant their stay in a neutral Place, where they might make their Pretensions, and dispute with the Emperor as with their Companion, to the end that Rebel-Subjects drawing their most merciful Lord and their Sovereign before a foreign Tribunal, might be able to treat with him as with their Equal, instead of having recourse to his Goodness, by Supplications and Remonstrances.

But as this jarring put a stop to the Negotiation of the Preliminaries, or at least serv'd for a Pretext to delay the same, the Emperor thought it advisable at last on the 21st of *April* 1638, to make a Declaration, by which he authoriz'd the Plenipotentiaries, who were on his part at *Cologn*, to issue out Passports for those whom the Princes and States that were not yet reconcil'd to him, should think fit to send to the Assembly, *where they should be consider'd as Attendants of the Embassadors of* France.

Cardinal *de Richelieu*, who was not over-forward to dispatch these, requir'd Passports in particular for the Ministers of Duke *Bernard de Weimar*, and those of the Landgrave of *Hesse*, because they had shewn a particular Inclination to the Interest of *France*, tho' he at the same time protested, *That it was not the King's Intention those Princes should send their Plenipotentiaries to the Congress, and did not scruple to own they had no right to send any*. The Emperor's Declaration before mention'd had a Clause in it to this effect, that the Passports of his Plenipotentiaries should be valid, even to those that should be guilty of High Treason. Now as this Crime can be committed only with respect to a Sovereign, the Emperor suppos'd that he was Sovereign, and that the Princes of *Germany* were his Subjects. But the Emperor's declining Condition having shaken his Resolution, and *France* being willing to make use of its then Prosperity, the King requir'd other Passports for the Elector *Palatin*, for the Dutchess of *Savoy* as Guardian and Regent, for the Elector of *Triers*, and for the Duke of *Brunswick* and *Lunenburg*, who he said were not less considerable than the Duke of *Weimar*, and the Landgrave of *Hesse*, and the Emperor not being able to resist so many pressing Instances, granted at last all the Passports that were requir'd of him.

These rude and improper Expressions furnish *France* with a specious Pretext, to refuse to the Princes of *Germany* that Honour which they pretend to be their due, and it may be said, that if we add thereto the different Usage the Emperor deals to the Ministers of foreign Princes, and to those of the Princes of *Germany*, they must be own'd to be the true Cause thereof. But this is what the King ought not to mind, and perhaps he would not really mind it in another Juncture of Affairs. We must dive to the bottom and search the Truth, and lay aside all outward Appearances. *John Frederick*, Elector of *Saxony*, and the same Landgrave of *Hesse*, of whom we spoke heretofore, put out a Manifesto in the Year 1546, before the Battel of *Roglutz*, for the Justification of their Arms, wherein they take notice, that as Princes of the Empire, *they can make Leagues defensive, as well with the other Princes of* Germany, *as with Strangers, and that they have Power to reform the Profession of Religion in their own Countrey*. *France* is sensible, that the Emperor is the Head, tho' not the Sovereign of the Empire, where his Authority is much less absolute than that of the King's in *Poland*. And indeed the Plenipotentiaries of *France* being at *Munster* in the Year 1644, wrote on the 6th of *April*, a circular Letter to the Princes of *Germany*, and concluded it in these Terms, *In fine, your Highness may assure your self, as well as all the other Princes of* Germany, *that it is here, and no where else, that they ought to recover their antient Dignity, their Rights and their Liberty, and where they will enjoy that Prosperity which they ought to promise themselves, which they communicate their Advice with ours in the present Assembly of this Place*. The whole Letter is fill'd with nothing but Protestations from *France*, that it only took Arms to restore to the Empire, and its Princes, their ancient Liberty; so that upon this Foundation *France* cannot consider them as the Emperor's Subjects, and cannot

30   *The* EMBASSADOR *and his* FUNCTIONS

not refuse 'em the same Honours, of which she is so prodigal to the Princes of *Italy*, who are Vassals and Feudataries of the Empire, and who are not more Sovereign than those of *Germany* France it self cannot dispute this, after the Declaration of its Ministers on the following Occasion In the Month of *October* 1644, there happen'd a mighty Contest at *Munster* about the Powers, and at last it was agreed, that the Ministers of the Emperor and of the other Crown'd Heads should prepare an Instrument, which they should cause to be accepted and sign'd in their respective Courts The *French* having communicated theirs to the Emperor's Plenipotentiaries, were told by these, that it was not their Master's Intention to treat with all the Princes, and all the Towns, that were engag'd in Alliance with a King, who was his Imperial Majesty's Enemy, because that would be a lessening to his Dignity But the Ministers of *France* obstinately maintain'd, *that the Princes of* Germany *might make Alliances with Strangers, without the Emperor's Consent,* and that his Approbation was not necessary, to make that lawful and valid, which they had contracted with *France* And in the Month of *June* or *July* 1646, the Counts *de Trantmansdorf* and *d'Avaux*, Plenipotentiaries of the Emperor and *France*, discoursing about the Treaty of Guaranty for the Observation of the Peace, that was negotiating at *Munster*, the first said, that the States of the Empire could not enter into this Guaranty without the Emperor's Consent, no more than *France* would suffer the Estates of that Kingdom to be Guarantees for it But *d'Avaux* made answer, that there was a great deal of difference between the two Estates, *because the one consisted of Sovereigns, and the other of Subjects.*

It is true there are two things that derogate in some measure from the Sovereignty of the Princes of *Germany*, viz The Appeals from their Sentences to the Chamber of *Spires*, or to the *Aulick* Council, and the Subsidies they pay to the Emperor, to the Payment whereof they may be compell'd, after they have consented thereto But then as much may be said of the United Provinces There is no Body so ignorant, as not to know that they are all Sovereign and Independent one of the other, and nevertheless that of *Zeeland* has no Court of Judicature, where Appeals are determin'd in *dernier ressort*, but only in that which is establish'd at the *Hague*, which however is no Prejudice to the Sovereignty of this Province, as well because that this Submission is made by virtue of a Contract with *Holland*, as because this Court, as well as the Great Council, is compos'd of *Assessors* nominated by both Provinces So that the Princes of *Germany* are not less Sovereigns, because the Sentence of their Judges may be either amended or annul'd by the Chamber of *Spires*, or by the *Aulick* Council, since that is done by virtue of the Constitutions and Ordinances made in the Diets, with the Princes Consent, as also because the Princes nominate the Counsellors and Assessors, of which these Courts are compos'd As for the Subsidies, the same may be said which I just took notice of with respect to the judicial part, *viz* That the United Provinces are liable to Executions, and may be compell'd to the Payment of those Subsidies to which they have consented and that by virtue of the Union or Treaty, without the least Prejudice to their Sovereignty

However I shall by someth of still more to the purpose, and which requires more in a more particular manner In the Month of *April* 1646, it was debated in the Council at *Vienna*, whether a Peace should be endeavour'd with the Emperor, tho' it the same time it could not be effected with *Spain* Ferdinand *Duke of Bavaria*, after having hindred the Question proposed at first, as he was us'd to do, concluded in the affirmative, and the whole Council with one unanimous Consent, resolv'd, amongst other things, that it *Alsace* were left to the King, on the same Conditions that *Sweden* pretended to have *Pomerania*, it would be more advantageous than prejudice it to contribute to the Accession of the Empire, provided they give the King usage and deliberating Vote in the Diet, and that is Quota, for all that *France* should publish in the Empire, did not exceed that of one of the Electors From whence we must necessarily conclude, that *France* it self is of Opinion, that the Subsidies, which are not levy'd in *Germany* but with the Consent of the Princes, and by way of Agreement made between the Emperor and the States, do not prejudice the latter And indeed, *France* it self, by making Treaties with the Princes of *Germany*, does acknowledge them to be Sovereigns

If the Princes of *Germany* knew themselves, and had Resolution enough to exalt Justice to be done 'em, they would make themselves be consider'd, and would take possession of a Right, that is their due by the very same Reasons that give it to the Electors but it is without that I find my self oblig'd to say, that if there be something obliging in the King's Procedure, there is also something very irregular in that of the Princes They cannot complain, without being at the same time liable to be reproach'd, and that with the greatest Justice too, that they do not do all they can and ought to do to support their Right, by making it appear that they deserve to have Embassadors, and that they are able to protect their Ministers

But however, as the Weakness of some cannot be imputed as a Crime to 'em all, it must be hop'd, that there will again be Princes, who will oppose with Vigour those, who shall dispute the Rank and Honour that cannot be refus'd to their Dignity The Duke of *Bavaria* refus'd to give place to the Republick of *Venice* at the Council of *Trent*, notwithstanding she carries it upon the level with Crown'd-Heads And in the Year 1620, he refus'd to see the Embassadors whom *France* had sent into *Germany* The Embassador of the Arch-Duke *Albert*, would not suffer the Embassador of *Venice* to be preferr'd to him at *London*, at the Marriage of the Elector *Palatine* and the Duke of *Nusburg* told the Minister of the United Provinces, that in his own House he gave place to none but the *Spanish* Embassador He was in the right of it in my Opinion, because he both could and ought to lay Claim to the same Respect that the Dukes of *Bavaria* and *Tuscany*, and even those of *Mantua* and *Parma* challenging in their own Houses I am not intended that *Boschot, Albert's* Embassador, was formaking his Master be consider'd on the account

of

The EMBASSADOR and his FUNCTIONS. 31

of the Provinces of the Low Countreys, which he possess'd in Sovereignty, and because he pretended to the Prerogatives of the ancient Dukes of *Burgundy*. But as he had not succeeded to their Grandeur, so it must be confess'd, that his chiefest Quality was that of Arch-Duke of *Austria*, which made him the first Prince of *Germany* after the Electors.

I also think I may here affirm, that it is not the Right, but the Possession, that *France* disputes with the Princes of *Germany* and for as much as it is certain, that it is only since the Congress at *Munster*, that the Civilities and Ceremonies that are shewn to the Ministers of the Electors have been regulated, one cannot maintain that those of the Princes enjoy'd the Quality and the Honours they pretend to at present before that time. All that can be said to their Advantage is, that the Qualities and Ceremonies were not so very well regulated in *Germany* a hundred Years ago, nor even in the beginning of this Century, and that the Titles of *Legatus* and *Ablegatus* have been frequently confounded, and apply'd without distinction, sometimes to Embassadors, and sometimes to Ministers of the Second Order of which an infinite Number of Examples may be drawn from History and the Archives. So that the Princes of *Germany*, who had but little Commerce with the Court of *France*, and none at all with those of *Italy*, were contented to entitle their Ministers to the Protection of the *Law of Nations*, under what publick Quality soever. But for as much as the Condition of the Electors was not much better than theirs at that time, I do not see why that of the Princes should be worse in this. I remember to have read, in the Relation that has been printed of the Travels of *William* Duke of *Saxe Weimar*, the Eldest of eight Brothers, that he cover'd himself in the Audience he had of King *Lewis* XIII, and of the Queen Mother. Duke *Bernard*, who was the Youngest of the eight Brothers, and who, tho' he wanted the Estate, had yet the Spirit of a Prince, seeing that the King suffer'd the Duke of *Parma* to be cover'd, made no difficulty to cover himself too, at the first Audience that the King gave him. The Court, that did not dream he would have Assurance enough to do it, did not give him any hint of the Matter, for fear of suggesting to him a Thought, which perhaps he might not otherwise have, and so did not dare to article with him. However he surpris'd it, and reap'd thereby an Advantage, to which he had not the least Pretension, if it had not been granted to a Prince, to whom he thought he ow'd no Preference. It all the Princes of *Germany* would act with this Resolution, and if they were always assisted with vigorous Counsels, they would not for a considerable time past, have been refus'd those Honours which the Electors have obtain'd. But there are some who are persuaded, that Easiness and Complaisance are more necessary for the Princes, than Generosity and Firmness, and that a lowly Weakness shall be more for their purpose, than that Elevation and Nobility of Soul, without which they have nothing of the Prince, but the bare Name and their Birth. It is about thirty Years since, that a certain Prince (who might be the first in all *Germany* if he would, and one of the most considerable in all *Europe*) being in *France*, where he was as it were *incognito*, would nevertheless see the King, who gave him Audience, and receiv'd him with great Civility, remaining in a standing Posture and uncover'd all the while the Prince spoke. But instead of stopping there, and carrying that Satisfaction home with him, he must needs visit the Duke of *Orleans*, notwithstanding the Declaration he caus'd to be made to him, that he would not suffer him to be cover'd before him. There was nothing could oblige this Prince to pay this Civility to the Duke of *Orleans* (who had suffer'd the Duke of *Wemar*, and even a younger Son of the House of *Wirtemberg*, and the Duke *de la Trimouille* to be cover'd before him and who though he was the Son and Brother of a King, was still a Subject) to receive from him those Incivilities that the Emperor himself would not have offer'd him, and the King had forborn. He had notice of it, but he was willing to receive an Affront, as I believe also, that the Ministers of the other Princes voluntarily neglected the Advantages which they might have obtain'd at *Munster*, where *France* stood in no less need of them than of the Electors. If the Meannesses, and sordid Acts that are committed, could be as easily excus'd or repair'd as done, it might be said, that this young Prince, who at that time had only a Pension of twelve or fifteen thousand Crowns, believ'd he risqu'd nothing. But I cannot justifie the Behaviour of the Marquis of *Baden Dourlach*. This Prince, who was the Head of his Family, and who struck into the Interests of *France* against the Emperor, when he came to Court in the Year 1635, was conducted to Audience by a Marshal of *France*, and by one of the Introducters of Embassadors, but he did not so much as pretend to cover himself in speaking to the King. All that can be said to it is, that this particular Action of a Prince, who stood in need of the King's Protection, cannot be any Prejudice to those who know themselves better, and who would not do that Wrong to their illustrious Houses, whose Antiquity may at least equal that of the first in *Europe*. I dare farther say, that they would not have been refus'd when they enter'd into the Alliance of the *Rhine*, nor even immediately before the War, which amongst other Inconveniencies gave also birth to this Difficulty, instead of carrying it Sword in Hand, and putting themselves in a Condition to extort with some Violence, what can only be hop'd for from an Accommodation. Moreover it will be requisite that the Emperor do, as he formerly did, with respect to the Electors, and that he exact of the Princes but only what they pay to the King of *France*, and by his Example to other Kings, who shall do them the same Honour. That the Princes on their part, cause that Respect to be paid them in the Empire, which is their due; and that they have no longer that Complaisance for the Emperor that is so prejudicial to their Sovereignty. A Cardinal Landgrave may enter into the particular Service of the Emperor, but it cannot be deny'd, that the Elector of *Triers*, the Bishop of *Strasbourg*, and the Marquis of *Baden*, who as Princes of the Empire had Seats in the Diets, did themselves a great deal of Prejudice, in taking

king upon them in the Year 1570, to conduct the Queen of *France*, who was Daughter of the Emperor *Maximilian* II, and that the Bishop of *Osnaburg*, who as Prince might send his Ministers to the Assembly of *Munster*, did a great deal of Wrong to the whole Order, in appearing there as Plenipotentiary of the Electoral College.

The Letter that is publish'd under the Title of *The Disinterested*, although it be nothing less, would make us believe that the Electors are the chief Opposers herein. Before I make the Reflections it deserves, I shall take notice, that in a Remonstrance printed in the Year 1673, wherein are represented to the Estates of *Germany*, the Dangers with which the Empire is threaten'd, with the Remedies that might be made use of to prevent the same, The Author says, That one of the things that disconcerts most the Union of the Princes, is the Superiority some of 'em pretend to have over the others. That the Electors distinguishing themselves from the other Princes, caus'd their Ministers to be treated with the Quality of Excellency. That the Electors themselves, giving Audience to the Ministers of the Princes, would be cover'd, and would not suffer these to be so. That at the last Diet of *Ratisbon* the Elector of *Cologn* behav'd himself after this manner, but that few Ministers visited him, and that some of those who did, cover'd themselves as soon as they saw the Elector cover'd, which oblig'd him to act after another manner, and to remain uncover'd during the Audience. The Emperor himself complain'd in the same Diet, of the excessive Honours which had been shewn to the Ministers of the Electors at *Munster*: and at the same time that he suffer'd 'em to be treated as Embassadors at the Congress, he would not acknowledge them in that Quality at *Vienna*. In the Year 1646, the Elector of *Bavaria* sent thither the Count *de Terri*, to make the Complements of Condolence for the Death of the Empress. He had the Quality of Embassador, yet they made him no Entry. The Emperor did not send him his Coach, and there was but one Gentleman to conduct him to Audience, not in the usual Hall, but in his Chamber, where the Emperor being always uncover'd, affected this Circumstance to oblige the Embassador to remain in the same State. The Ministers of the Elector of *Saxony*, contenting themselves with their Quality of *Ablegats*, rejected the Title of Excellency, which those of the Princes refus'd to give to the Plenipotentiaries of the Electors, tho' at the same time, these offer'd to do the like by them.

Wherefore after the Electoral College had taken a Resolution, which forbid their Embassadors to give place to those of *Venice*, the Princes came to one also in theirs, by which they ordain'd, that their first Plenipotentiaries should not give place to the second Plenipotentiaries of the Electors, to shew, that all the Advantage these have over those, is what the first has over the second, the second over the third, &c. And indeed, if the College of Electors constitutes the first Order of the States of the Empire, the Princes make the second, not as the free Cities make the third, of which those who are not altogether Strangers to the Affairs of *Germany* cannot doubt, but as a Body as powerful, and compos'd of Princes as Sovereign as the first.

This is not the Place to speak of the Origin of the Electoral Dignity, and it is not necessary to shew, that it is not from their first Institution that they hold the Advantage they take over the other Princes, but then again they ought not to take it ill, that these are zealous for the Preservation of their Rights, and of the Prerogatives that are inseparable from their Dignity, in order to hand 'em down to their Posterity, as entire as they receiv'd 'em from their Ancestors. By virtue of this Resolution of the Princes, the Plenipotentiaries of *Saltzburg* and of *Hildesheim*, who were at *Munster*, refus'd to give place in the publick Ceremonies, to the second Plenipotentiaries of *Mayence*, *Triers* and *Cologn*, and rather chose to quit their pontifical Habits and leave the Church, than to suffer the least Advantage to be taken over them.

The Letter of *The Disinterested* says, That the Pretension of the Princes is injurious to the Electors, that it is at the Instigation of *France* that they pursue it, and that it is the King's Intention to set the Electors and Princes at variance with the Emperor, by casting on him the Fault, of the Refusal that is made to acknowledge their Ministers as Embassadors. I agree with this Author, that the Electors have very eminent Rights, and that they have great Advantages over the other Princes, which have been confirm'd to them by the Treaty of *Westphalia*. And in truth one cannot speak with too much Respect of their august College, but they do not pretend themselves to be more Sovereign in their Countreys, than the others are in their Territories, so that there is nothing to weaken the Pretensions of these, or hinder 'em from asserting those Honours, which are due to them in the Rank they hold immediately after the Electors.

I must own, I cannot well comprehend how it is at the Instigation of *France*, that the Princes form these Pretensions, since it is she that opposes them most. I am willing to believe, that M. *Gravel*, who has been at leisure to study the Affairs of *Germany*, and has apply'd himself thereto, has perhaps strengthen'd the Pretensions of the Princes, and has represented to them, that they may assert to themselves, all the Honours that are due to Sovereigns, as well as the Electors, who enjoy the same as Princes and Sovereigns, and not as Electors, but that is all.

I have so much Respect for them, that I would not here repeat what has been written and publish'd on this Occasion, upon solid Principles enough, and convincing Proofs, but there seems to be something so opposite in what the Letter says of the Intention of *France*, to what is perceivable in the Actions of her Ministers, that I have some difficulty to adjust it in my Mind. If she looks upon the Pretensions of the Princes to be well grounded, and if she backs them against those of the Electors, how is it possible for her to elude them? and how can she refuse the Princes an Honour, which she her self thinks their due? It is said to be with a design to set 'em at variance with the Emperor, because she has a mind that the Court at *Vienna* should serve her as an Example. The

King

The EMBASSADOR and his FUNCTIONS.

King has no need of me to justifie his Intentions, but I cannot forbear saying, that those Intentions are not very sincere, that give an evil Interpretation to those that will admit of a very favourable one, and that upon Reasons, if not altogether demonstrable, at least very probable. When the Ministers of the Electors began to speak of their Pretentions at *Munster*, *France*, that could not hope to gain its Ends without their Consent, offer'd to do them the same Honours which are done to the Embassadors of *Venice* and *Holland*, upon this express Condition, That therein the King should do no more nor no less than what the Emperor would do in their behalf. This was look'd upon to be very just at that time, but now that the King holds the same Language, and will have the Princes have the same Consideration for him which they have for the Emperor, to whom the King pretends to owe nothing, he does it to set the Princes at variance with the Empire.

To conclude this Chapter, I shall lay down as a certain Truth that the Princes of *Germany* are in Possession of the Right of sending publick Ministers to all the Courts of *Europe*, which they could not do, if they were not Sovereigns, and since with the Right they have also the Possession, they cannot be hinder'd from giving them what Character they please, and they who refuse 'em the Honours which are their due, do not only fail in point of Civility, but also in what is a just Debt to the *Law of Nations.*

This is without doubt what the King will reflect upon, if he pleases to be put in mind, *that the late King acknowledg'a the Embassador of Duke* Charles *of* Lorrain, who had the Honour to be cover'd when he spoke to the King, and above all, that he suffer'd the Commanders, *de Form geres* and *de Forbin*, his Subjects and Officers, Embassadors from the great Master of *Maltha*, to be cover'd in the Audiences he gave them. So that the Princes of *Germany*, who ought to be consider'd after a clear different manner than the great Master of *Malter*, have reason to be offended at the refusal that is made 'em, of a thing that is so lawfully their due.

Notwithstanding which, the other Princes

make so good a Use of the Example of *France*, that they refuse to those of *Germany* the Honours they do to the Embassador of *Venice*, and to Sovereigns who cannot come in Competition with them. Clement VIII caus'd a solemn Entry to be made for the great Master of *Maltha*, to whom he gave Audience, making him sit above the last Cardinal Deacon. But one of the first Princes of *Germany*, after the Electors, being at *Rome* in the Year 1665, Alexander VII said, *He would not suffer him either to sit, or be cover'd at the Audience.*

There remains only to add here a Word or two, with reference to the Duke of *Lorrain* in particular, because it was upon his account that the Quality of Embassador was refus'd to the Ministers of the Princes of *Germany*. That the Marquis *de Ville*, the late Duke of *Lorrain*'s Minister, had that Quality, and was cover'd in speaking to the King, is what cannot be deny'd. He might do it as well for the Reason alledg'd in the beginning of the present Chapter, as because his Sovereignty is much less to be contested than that of the Princes of *Italy*. Charles IX King of *France*, oblig'd himself after a manner extraordinary enough, before two Notaries of the *Chastelet* of *Paris*, to yield to the Duke of *Lorrain* all the Rights of Sovereignty that the Kings his Predecessors had had over the Dutchy of *Bar*, which King Henry III confirm'd immediately after his return from *Poland*, and caus'd it to be ratify'd in Parliament. It was long before that, that *Anthony* had obtain'd of King *Francis* I. the Rights of the *Regalia*, for himself and his Son, and by the Agreement made at *Nuremberg*, between the Emperor Charles V. and the Estates of the Empire on the one part, and *Anthony* Duke of *Lorrain* on the other, the said Dutchy was declar'd a free Principality, exempt from Homage to the Emperor, and from the Sovereignty of the Empire, except in certain Cases. Since which time the Dukes of *Lorrain* have been consider'd as Sovereigns. They have been acknowledg'd as such in the Treaties the Crowns have made between themselves, and, as such, they have made Treaties with Crowns. So that their Sovereignty being indisputable, the Right of sending Embassadors ought to be so likewise

CHAP. V.

Of the Ministers of the Second Order.

ALL that have written of the publick Right unanimously agree, That the Ministers of the second Order, being compris'd under the Denomination of *Legati*, enjoy without any Contradiction all the Advantages that the *Law of Nations* bestows upon them. And the Declaration of the States of *Holland* the 29th of *March* 1651, of which we shall speak hereafter, is so express in this Point, that even if one would doubt of it elsewhere, it would be impossible to do it in a Countrey where the Law speaks so clearly. It names *Embassadors, Residents, Agents*, and comprehends all those that

have the Quality of *publick Ministers* on the part of what King, Prince, or Republick soever they are employ'd, that is to say, *Internuncios, Envoys Extraordinary, Plenipotentiaries, Commissioners, Secretaries of Embassies, &c* thereby condemning the Sentiments of the Court of Justice of the same Province, which in a Controversy it had in the Year 1644 with *Spiring*, Resident of *Sweden*, maintain'd that the *Law of Nations* protected only Embassadors, and does not reach the Ministers of the second Order. The Consent of Nations is the ground of the Declaration of the States of *Holland*,

K and

34   *The* EMBASSADOR *and his* FUNCTIONS

and renders this Protection by so much the more necessary, as Princes would be more inconvenienc'd from the want of these Ministers, than from that of Embassadors. The Electors and Princes of *Germany*, who have not yet been able to get the Character of Representative acknowledg'd in their Ministers, can have no other. The King of *France* himself, who cannot oblige the Court at *Vienna*, to give his Embassador the Rank which he holds every where else, sends thither only a Minister of the second Order, as well as to several other Places, whither his Dignity will not suffer him to send a Person characteris'd, as for instance, to *Liege*, *Hamburgh*, and even to the Diets, where an Embassador in Ordinary from *France* would be subject to be sometimes made uneasy. Others make use of 'em, either out of good Husbandry, or because the Affairs they have to negotiate are not of sufficient Importance to employ an Embassador. It is out of this Consideration that the Republick of *Venice* has a Resident with the *Swiss Cantons*, and that the States of the United Provinces have Ministers of the same Quality in *Spain*, *Sweden*, *Denmark*, *Vienna*, *Brussels*, and other Places, as also in the Armies of their Allies. The Emperor has only a Secretary or an Agent at *Venice*. La *Tuillerie*, Embassador from *France*, going from the *Hague* after the Peace of *Munster*, *Brasset* was left there in the Quality of Resident, as he had left *Chanut* in the same Quality at *Stockholm*, and *Chanut* left *Pâques* there, who having for some time negotiated the Affairs of *France* as *Agent*, had at last the Quality of *Resident*.

Besides this, Princes frequently chuse to make use of this kind of Minister, rather than of the splendid Quality of the other, as being more proper to carry on an Intrigue with Safety, where the Secret is more necessary than Pomp. They negotiate also with less trouble and more Success, they can go and come without much to do. They have no need to be so choice in their Steps, the Irregularity whereof does no Injury to the Dignity of their Master, provided they are neither false nor ridiculous. Now the Embassador is oblig'd to measure 'em, to concert all his Actions, to act according to Forms, and to preserve the Reputation of his Prince as well as his Interests. He must therefore demand his Audiences as well of the Sovereign as of the Ministers, whereas the Resident takes 'em of these when he finds an Opportunity, and being less incommodious and less formal than the Embassador, he finds a more easy access, and his Business dispatch'd with much more Expedition. I'll give here some Instances of what I say. The Victory gain'd by the Arms of the Emperor *Charles* V, before *Pavia*, in the Year 1524, so alarm'd all *Italy*, that Pope *Clement* VII, thinking himself sure of the Republick of *Florence*, made a League defensive with that of *Venice* into which the Allies pretended to bring *France* and *England*, the one being oppress'd by the Emperor, and the other jealous of his Power. The Allies had but just concluded it, when they understood that King *Francis* I had made the Treaty of *Madrid* for the recovery of his Liberty.

They were much surpriz'd thereat, but being soon inform'd that the King was not at all satisfy'd with the Emperor, as well on account of the ill Treatment he had receiv'd during his detention, as because he could not digest the severe Conditions of the Treaty, they resolv'd to perfect their Design of bringing him in with them. The *Venetians* intended to send two of their principal Senators into *France*, who, under the colour of complementing the King on the score of his Misfortunes and recover'd Liberty, should negotiate Affairs of much greater Consequence, but then, considering that some time must be giv'n to the Embassadors to prepare their Equipage, and judging that a subaltern Minister would do his Work with much less no se, and more effectually, they sent thither *Andrew Rosse*, Secretary of the Council de *Pregadi*. The Pope following then Example, dispatch'd thither *Paul Vettori*, and these two Ministers of the second Order happily concluded the Treaty, to the Satisfaction of the Parties concern'd. The Republick employ'd *Gaspar Spinelli* in *England*, at the same time, and for the same purpose. He was Secretary to *Laurence Orio*, their Embassador, who was dead at *London* some time before.

In the Year 1537, the same Republick seeing that *Francis* I, being disgusted at the Alliance and Assistance of the Great *Turk*, which made him odious to *Christendome*, and which had produc'd nothing under *Barberossa*, began to think of Peace, sent into *France*, *Francis Justinian*, not in the Quality of Embassador, but as an Envoy. And *Lewis Badouere* went to *Madrid* with the same Quality, notwithstanding he was an Embassador in Ordinary there on the part of the said Republick. These two Ministers without Character, dispos'd the two Monarchs to send their Plenipotentiaries to *Narbonne*, where the King of *France*, who first sent thither the Cardinal of *Lorrain*, caus'd him to be joyn'd by the King of *Navarr* his Brother-in-law.

I willingly make use of the Examples of this powerful and wise Republick, because there is Safety in following her, for which reason I shall take one or two more out of the History of it time. In the Year 1538, she employ'd at *Constantinople Laurence Gritti*, the natural Son of *Anarew*, altho' at the same time there was a *Bailo* or *Agent* at the Port. His Business was to negotiate a general Truce between the Emperor of the *Turks* and the Allies, who were Pope *Paul* III, the Emperor *Charles* V, and the Republick of *Venice*, but all he could obtain was a Suspension of Arms for three Months. *Jacomo Ragazzoni*, whom the Senate sent to *Constantinople* during the *Cyprian* War, had no Quality at all. *Selim* II having resolv'd to conquer this Island, and being inform'd that the *Chiaoux Cubat*, whom he had sent to *Venice* to demand it, had brought back an absolute Refusal, with a fix'd Resolution of the Senate to oppose any Violence that should be offer'd, set a guard upon the Agent *Mark Anthony Barbaro*, and caus'd the Consuls at *Alexandria* and *Aleppo* to be confin'd, but these last were soon set at liberty. This War was carry'd on contrary to the Advice, and against the Inclination

---

* *Certain Chief Senators of great Authority in* Venice.

of

of the first Vifier *Mehemet*, and the Republick, on her part, did not find its Interest in the Continuation of a Quarrel, in which the Christian Princes, her Allies, contributed nothing towards the easing of her, so that it was no very difficult Task to dispose both the one and the other to a Peace. The *Turks* fearing left a powerful League should be form'd amongst the Christians, which should hinder them from making a thorough Conquest of the Kingdom, after that of *Nicosia*, caus'd the *Bailo* or Agent to be sounded, whether he had not Orders to propose an Accommodation. And the first Vifier, finding his Constancy, did not condemn making the first Overtures of one to him. He took for Pretext the Complaints of some particular Persons, who had been taken, and whose Goods had been seiz'd since the Rupture, and caus'd the *Bailo* or Agent to use his Endeavours with the Senate, that the said Goods might be restor'd and the Prisoners set at liberty, since the *Venetian* Merchants continu'd to carry on their Commerce without any lett or hindrance, throughout all the Countreys belonging to the Grand Seigneur. He gave him leave and at the same time exhorted him to write and send an Express about it, giving him to understand by *Ibrahim Bey*, first Interpreter of the *Divan*, that he should be glad if the Senate would dispatch some Person to the Port, who, in speaking about the Commerce, should make some Proposals of Peace. The Agent dispatch'd his Steward and one of his Interpreters, and the Senate had so much the less Difficulty to comply therewith, because the *Turks* made the first Advances in the Matter. *Jacomo Ragazzoni*, who, being a Merchant, had an Interest in the Commerce, and who moreover had all the Qualities necessary for the Negotiation of an Affair of this nature, was sent to *Constantinople*. The Council of Ten gave him, with his Commission, a private Instruction to the *Bailo* or Agent, not to be shy, or keep off, if the Proposals the *Turks* should make to him were honourable and any way consistent with the Dignity of the Republick, and gave the full Power to *Ragazzoni*, in case the *Turks* should make any Difficulty to treat with the *Bailo* or Agent, on the account of his Confinement. But the *Divan*, pretending to gain by the Treaty, what their Arms had not yet conquer'd in the Island, the *Bailo* or Agent, who could not content thereto without exceeding his Orders, broke off the Negotiation, and sent back *Ragazzoni* to *Venice*, leaving even the Treaty of Commerce unfinish'd. In fine, the Senate seeing the whole Island lost, follow'd the Advice of *France* (which counsell'd her to put an end to the War by some good Accommodation) and gave the *Bailo* to understand its Intention. The *Turks* were as well inclin'd thereto as the *Venetians*, and nevertheless when the *Bailo* spoke to them of it, they doubled the Severities of his Prison, they darken'd the Windows of his Chamber, increas'd his Guards, and depriv'd him of the small Communication he had till then. This was done as well to oblige him to discover his last Orders, as to hinder him from conferring with the the Bishop of *Acs*, who was then come to *Constantinople* from *Charles* IX King of *France*, and of whom the *Barbarians* had entertain'd some Jealousy. But the first Vifier being well assur'd that this Minister did not know the Senate's Intention, and being apprehensive left *France* should intermeddle in the matter, in order to make it self necessary, let him alone and continu'd and concluded the Negotiation with the *Bailo*, by the Mediation of *Ibrahim Bey*, and by a *Jewish Physician* nam'd *Solomon*, who made an end of it the 15th of *March* 1573.

Francis I. often made use of this kind of Ministers. He sent to *Constantinople Cæsar Cantelmo*, a *Neapolitan*, who was banish'd for having follow'd the *French* Interest. He there had Audience of *Soliman*, and negotiated with the *Divan*, not as an Embassador, but as a Gentleman of the King's Houshold, because at that time the Quality of Envoy Extraordinary was not yet known. *Mervuille*, of whom we shall speak in the Tenth Chapter, was employ'd by the same King to the Duke of *Milan*, and it may be said, that the most important Affairs have been transacted by those *Philip de Commines* calls Embassadors or secret Ministers. *Francisco Bernardo*, a *Venetian* Gentleman, who resided at *London* on account of his own private Affairs, pass'd the Seas several times under that Pretext, and yet that did not hinder him from negotiating in *France*, on the part of *Henry* VIII King of *England*. *Paul Parista* says, that it was *Bernardo* that contributed most to the Treaty, that was concluded between *Henry* II and *Edward* VI, in the Year 1547. It was not *Francis de Montmorancy* Lord of *Rochepot*, Governor of *Picardy*, *Gaspar de Coligni*, Collonel of a Regiment of *French* Foot, nor the other Deputies of *France*, who made the Treaty with the Earl of *Bedford*, *William Paget*, and *William Peters*, by which *Boulogne* was restor'd to the *French* in the Year 1550, but it was *Anthony Guidotti*, a Gentleman of *Florence*, who, while he carry'd on his own Business in the two Kingdoms, transacted another that was not known, and yet was of great Importance, since it was he that adjusted in *Paris* the greatest Difficulties on the part of the same *Edward* VI. It was likewise *Guy Cavalcanti*, who in the beginning of Queen *Elizabeth*'s Reign had the greatest share in the Treaty which was made between *France* and *England*, after the Treaty of *Chateau Cambresis*. The Marshal *Destrades* knows, that one of the greatest Difficulties that hinder'd the Conclusion of the Treaty, which the States of the United Provinces were negotiating in *France* in the Years 1661, and 1662, was remov'd by a private Person, who does not boast of it, though the State is at the same time oblig'd to him. *Hugh de Lionne*, Secretary to the Queen of *France*, was sent to *Madrid* in the Year 1656, and had there dispos'd Matters so well, that if *Don Lewis de Haro* would at that time have comply'd a little with respect to the Prince of *Condé*'s Interest, he had transacted before he went away what *Anthony Pimentel* finish'd since at *Paris*, where he concluded the Treaty which the King of *Spain* ratify'd before the two Ministers came upon the Frontiers, where it received its last Perfection. Some Years before it had been twice discours'd of, that Cardinal *Mazarin* and Count *de Pegnaranda* were to have an Interview. The Cardinal made the Overture

Overture the first time, but the Count not doubting but it was the Intention of this first Minister, who was the most dextrous Negotiator in his time, to draw from it some great Advantage for the King his Master, caus'd him to be founded by *Friquet*, who talking with the Cardinal, soon found out that their conferring would be to no purpose. On the other side, when the Count defir'd to meet the Cardinal, when the Troubles of the Kingdom were at their height, *Lionne*, who went to the Count at *Cambray*, discover'd in the very first Conference, that his Intentions were not better than the Cardinals had been, and that if *France* would have Peace, the must purchafe it at the Expence of fome part of her Conquefts. Thefe fubaltern Ministers prevented, by their Dexterity, the Scandal which the Cardinal and the Count would inevitably have incurr'd, if they had parted difpleas'd, and notoriously diffatisfy'd after a publick Conference.

Of thefe Ministers of the fecond Order, fome have a publick Quality, as that of *Envoy*, *Refident*, *Commiffioner*, &c. and the others have not, as thofe I lately mention'd; but however the *Law of Nations* protects them all alike. The Emperor *Charles* V, to excufe the violent Execution that had been done in the Perfon of *Merveille*, faid, that a Minister could not enjoy the Privilege of the Miniftry unless his Quality appear'd publickly. It is true, he that offends an Embaffador or Minister, whofe Character is not confpicuous, does not violate the *Law of Nations*, but it cannot be deny'd, that the Prince (who has acknowledg'd the Minister in that Quality, and has negotiated with him) violates the fame *Law of Nations*, if he ufes violence to him, or fuffers any to be done him. *Francis Sforza*, Duke of *Milan*, had allow'd of *Merveille*, and had negotiated with him as with the King of *France*'s Minister, for which Reafon he was oblig'd to fecure him that Safety, which his Letters of Credence entitl'd him to. *Lomne* and *Pimentel* had no Quality, but they had a formal Power. *Deftraaes* had only the Quality of a Military Officer in *Holland*, when he negotiated the moft important Affairs that the United Provinces had with *France*. But the *Law of Nations* protected both the one and the other.

We muft however make fome Diftinction between the *Minister* and the *Negotiator*, becaufe every *Negotiator* is not a *Minister*. The Duke of *Longueville* being Prifoner of War in *England*, and *Andrew Gritti* being the fame in *France*, negotiated there. But they were not Ministers, becaufe they only made Overtures for a Negotiation, and did not in effect negotiate. The fame ought to be faid of *Bernardo*, *Guidotti*, and fome others; and I don't know if the fame ought not to be faid of *John Francis Valerio*. This *Venetian* Gentleman, having made fome ftay in *France*, had got there fuch good Acquaintance, that the firft Lords of the Kingdom made no difficulty to communicate to him the moft important Affairs. He acquainted the Senate therewith from time to time, and depending on his own Knowlege of things, he did not fcruple to affure it, that the King would caufe the Intereft of the Republick to be follicited at *Conftantinople*, and that if *Cantelmo*'s Negotiation had not the Succefs that was expected, he would fend thither other Ministers. He exhorted the Senate to confide in the King's Word, and to be affur'd of the Inclination his Majefty exprefs'd for the Good of the Republick, to bring it off with Reputation. *Valerio* was a Subject of the Republick and was not employ'd from it. The Republick it that time had no Union with *France*, tho' it had with the Emperor. It is alfo well known, that there is no State in the World more jealous of its Interefts than that of *Venice*, notwithftanding which, it approv'd of *Valerio*'s holding a Correfpondence with the chief Lords of the Court of *France*, for the Service of his Country.

To enter into a Detail of thefe Ministers of the fecond Order, we muft begin with the *Refidents* Embaffadors in Ordinary were formerly call'd *Refidents*, to diftinguish them from the Extraordinaries and it is after this manner the Quality of Refident, which is found in the Title of the Negotiations of *Francis Walfingham*, who was Embaffador in Ordinary in *France*, muft be underftood. This Word has a particular Signification within about fourfcore Years, and denotes a Minister who has not properly the reprefenting Character in the firft Degree, but who notwithftanding his a Quality that makes him enjoy the Protection of the *Law of Nations*, and makes him be confider'd as a publick Minister on the Sovereign's Account that employs him. The Declaration of the States of *Holland*, of which we fhall often make mention in this Treatife, puts Refidents in the Number of publick Ministers, and there is not any Court where this Quality is known, that does not grant 'em all the Advantages the *Law of Nations* fecures to them Officers, or that does not pay them all the Civilities, that do not partake of the Ceremonies properly belonging to Embaffadors. Thefe are fcarcely poffefs'd of any Right that the *Refidents* do not enjoy in common with them, and particularly the moft eminent of all, which is that of exercifing in their own Houfe, a Religion prohibited by the Laws of the State where they refide. We fhall bring fome Examples hereof in Chapter XXXVII, wherefore I fhall fay no more here, but that even in thofe Places where the Inquifition has erected its Tribunal this Liberty is not refus'd them, neither are they depriv'd of the other Rights, the *Law of Nations* gives to the Quality of publick Minister and Reprefentative. I know very well that he is this, in a Degree much inferior to that of an Embaffador, but it is after the fame manner as mitred Abbots are neverthelefs Prelates, tho' conftituted in a Dignity much inferior to that of Bifhop, and at a far greater diftance from that of Archbifhops, Patriarchs and Cardinals.

The Quality of *Envoy Extraordinary* is ftill more modern than that of *Refident*. It had its Origin from this, That Princes fometimes fent to foreign Courts Gentlemen of their Houfhold, in Affairs, the Negotiation whereof was neither long nor knotty, nor of that Importance as to employ an Embaffador, fo that the *Envoy* is as it were a *Refident Extraordinary*. In reality it is nothing elfe, and the Princes, that firft employ'd 'em, can have had no other Intention, notwithftanding that within fome time,

The EMBASSADOR and his FUNCTIONS.

time, the Ministers who have had this Quality, have been for raising themselves to something more, and making themselves be consider'd as little Embassadors. Never any body aim'd at this in a more haughty manner, nor with such ill Success, as the Marquis *Justiniani*, the first Minister in Ordinary that I know of, who has had the Quality of Envoy Extraordinary at the Court of *France* since the Honours have been regulated. He had the Assurance to hope he should be suffer'd to be cover'd when he spoke to the King, and he was preparing to enter the *Louvre* in his Coach. The Guards at the Gate, who were inform'd of his Intention, presented the Points of their Halberts to the Coach-man, and stop'd and put back his Horses in the View of the Publick. He had also the Mortification to find himself oblig'd to give place to to the Resident of *Brandenburg*, or at least to absent from the publick Assemblies, where they might have come in competition. The Master of the Ceremonies and the Introductors of Embassadors, know no Quality between the first Representative and the Resident, conformably to the Intention of the most Christian King, who observing that these new Pretentions might produce others, declar'd about ten or twelve Years since, that he did not pretend his Envoy Extraordinary at the Court of *Vienna*, should be consider'd after any other manner than as Resident in Ordinary. And as he did not require any other Honours should be shewn him, then what are usually done to those of this Quality, so he was likewise resolv'd to treat them both alike. Formerly *France* did Honours to Envoys, and they had the King's and Queen's Coaches to conduct them to their Audience, but in the Year 1638, the King of *England* being inform'd that this Honour had been done to *S Ravy* and to *Jermin*, whom the Queen and himself had sent to *France* on occasion of the Dauphin's Birth, he complain'd thereof. He said that if the King of *France* did so, he should be likewise oblig'd to do the same to those Gentlemen should be sent him, but that it would be necessary first to agree upon the whole, and make a particular Regulation upon that account. Whereupon it was resolv'd in *France*, that for the future, to begin with the Year 1639, no Honours should be done to this kind of Ministers, and accordingly no so have been done since.

M *Trevor* was Envoy Extraordinary at the Court of *France* in the Year 1668, for the Affairs of the Low Countreys, *Conrad Van Bennynguen* was there at the same time, and on the same account, in the Quality of Embassador Extraordinary from *Holland*. There is no Competitorship between *England* and the United Provinces, but the Quality of Envoy gave place without any dispute, to the Character of Embassador, as it would also yield to that of Resident, if this was vested in the Person of a Minister from a crown'd Head, and that in the Minister of a Republick, or some other Prince *Camprigt*, the Emperor's Resident, took place, without opposition, in the Envoys of *Denmark*, *Sweden*, and of those of all the other Princes, who could not pretend to take this advantage of him, without making a new Ceremonial. There is no place where the matter of Ceremony is less regulated than at the *Hague*, because no body there makes it his Study, and it is for that Reason, that this sort of Ministers have there obtain'd Advantages which are not their due. *George Downing*, having procur'd the King's Confirmation in the Employ *Cromwel* had conferr'd upon him in *Holland*, requir'd to be receiv'd at his Coach Door, that is to say, that he should receive the same Honours, that are done to Embassadors in Ordinary when they receive Audience, and he was back'd in his Pretensions by those who sought a Pretext for a Rupture. Upon advice at *Stockholm* 11 the Year 1652, that *Anthony Pimentel* was arriv'd at the *Dales* on the part of the King of *Spain*, the Count *de la Garde*, who had Orders to take care of his Reception in the Queen's Absence, sent two Coaches with six Horses each to meet him, as also some Officers of the Houshold to defray his Charges, and bring him to the Queen Mother's Palace which was fitted up for him. The Queen, being return'd to *Stockholm*, understanding that *Pimentel* had only the Quality of Envoy, was not well pleas'd with the Honours which had been done him. She said, that since he had only the Character of the second Order, they ought not to have sent to meet him, nor defray his Expences however since the thing was begun it ought to be pursu'd, and he was treated to the third Day after his first Audience. The Queen's Intention was to defray him all the time he should stay in *Sweden*, if he had had the Character of Embassador. This *Spanish* Minister got so great an Ascendant over the Mind of this Princess, that he even blotted out the very Remembrance of the Friendship she had promis'd, and really ow'd to *France*. She lodg'd him in the Castle, under her own Appartment, and bestow'd whole Nights upon his Conversation. At the Entry of the *English* Embassador, his Coach immediately follow'd the Queens, and preceded that of the Senators and Officers of the Crown. When he took his Audience of Leave, he insisted upon having the Coaches of the Crown, tho' at the same time he had so little way to go, that the Heads of the Postilion's Horses reach'd as far as the great Staircase, before the Coach began to move. *Pimentel* was a Man of Merit, but here was a little Ostentation on this Occasion, and we must think he had a mind to shew, that if *France* made Conquests in *Flanders*, *Spain* also made considerable ones in *Sweden*. These excessive Honours are not due to Ministers of the second Order, and cannot be pleasing to their Masters, who ought to desire there should be something reserv'd to the representing Character. In the Year 1633, Cardinal *de Richelieu* sent a Person whose Name was *la Grange aux Ormes*, the Son of a Physitian at *Metz*, to some of the Princes of *Germany*. He was but a bare Carrier of Letters, wherein the King complemented 'em on the Death of the King of *Sweden*. He was treated according to this Quality almost every where, but the Elector of *Saxony* made him wash first, plac'd him at the upper end of the Table, and did him the same Honours he would have been able to have shewn him, if he had had the Quality of Embassador. The Court of *France* was very angry hereat, and the Cardinal reproach'd *la Grange* with his Pride and Imprudence, banish'd him

L

him from Court, and remov'd him from all Employment. Whatever exceeds the ordinary Civilities, does not regard the Princes who make use of Ministers of the second Order, so that these Civilities cannot be made Precedents of, because they are either done out of a particular Consideration to the Person of the Minister, or else by such as do not understand the Ceremonial.

Sabran, Resident from France at London, having Letters of Credence for the Parliament, met with a great many Difficulties on account of the Honours he pretended to have done him, when he receiv'd Audience. But they were at last regulated after this manner, that the Parliament should appoint Deputies who should enter into Conference with him, and should at home do him the Honours of the House. The Parliament nam'd for this purpose, six Lords and twelve Deputies of the House of Commons, who in those Conferences that were held at their Houses, gave him an arm'd Chair at the upper End of the Table, and always sent two Deputies to him at home to communicate to him the Resolutions the Parliament took upon their Deliberations and Reports. The Deputies of the States General have at the Hague, repair'd to the House of the Ministers of Lunenburg, in order to confer with em, and that more than once, a thing however of so much the greater Consequence, that it was an Act of possession to these and that afterwards the Envoys and Residents of crown'd Heads might lay Claim to the sure Advantage. Both the one and the other have neglected the Benefit they might have reap'd therefrom, and the Deputies of the States have maintain'd themselves in the possession of holding the Conferences in one of the Chambers of their Apartment. I cannot tell out of what Motive they have renounc'd that which they also had, of taking there the place of Honour of the Ministers of the second Order. They first yielded it to those of crown'd Heads, and since have granted the Civility entire to all the rest. I have my self been there at several Conferences. But I must own I was much surpris'd to see (in the beginning of the Year 1675, when the Treaty with the Bishop of Ossaburg was sign'd) three of that Princes Ministers take the place of Honour. The loss of this kind of Advantages not being recoverable, the Sovereign ought never to consent thereto, and they who represent him cannot do it without a Crime, especially when it may be look'd upon as a Token of Weakness rather than of Generosity. Civility ought not to oblige a Sovereign State to renounce its Right, and to yield up a Possession it enjoy'd peaceably, and with Justice. The Prince Palatine, Charles Gustavus, being arriv'd at Stockholm a few Days before Queen Christina's Abdication, to whom he was going to succeed, all the foreign Ministers paid him Civility. Piques, the French Resident, was conducted to Audience by the Introductor of Embassadors in one of the Queen's Coaches, attended by several of the Prince's Footmen. The Marshal of the said Prince's Court receiv'd him at the top of the Staircase, and the Prince himself, passing through the Antichamber, receiv'd him in the middle of the Hall, and led him into the Chamber. The Audience being over, he reconducted the Resident to the same place where he had receiv'd him, and the Marshal and the Introductor accompany'd him likewise, the first to the top of the Staircase, and the other to his Lodgings. But here it may be said, that the Prince not being as yet Sovereign, he was not ty'd up to any Rules or Measures in the Dispensation of his Civilities. The same Piques, while he was only Agent in the Year 1651, went to visit the same Prince Palatin, who receiv'd him at the Entrance of the Hall, and conducted him into his Closet, where he offer'd him a Chair, but Piques excus'd himself, and refus'd to sit. He desir'd the Prince to take his Conveniency, while he read to him a Relation, that the Court of France had sent him, of the Retreat of the Prince of Conde, but he Prince kept standing and uncover'd. He had been declar'd presumptive Heir to the Crown, and as such he did not owe all these Civilities to the Agent, who on his side had not much, in desiring the Prince to sit, while he oblig'd him (by a rude Refusal of the Seat that was offer'd him) to be standing and uncover'd.

There are Envoys, and even Residents, who making no distinction between the representing Character, and the Quality of a subaltern Minister, affect being on the level with Persons of the first Quality, and are very forward to take all the Advantages imaginable over Earls and other Lords of very noble Birth. When M. de la Tuillerie, Embassador from France, made his Entry at the Hague, in November 1640, there was a great struggle for the Rank of their Coaches, between the Coachmen of M. de Brederode, Camp Marshal of the United Provinces, and of M. Spiring, Resident of Sweden. Brederode's Coachman having let the Embassador's Coach go by, advanc'd with a design to prevent Spiring's Coachman, and the better to affect it, the Postillion alighted and cut Spiring's Harness. This Minister seeing his Horses come back in this Condition, commanded other Harness to be put on, and sent his Coachman back with positive Orders to take advantage of the other, at any rate, but he did not succeed in it. Spiring complain'd to the Prince of Orange about it, who not being willing to meddle in the Matter, because M. de Brederode was his Brother-in-Law, sent him to the States-General, who regulated it after such a manner that the Resident was not very well satisfy'd with. When P. mentel's Coach follow'd the Queen's immediately, as I said before, the Senators protested, that they suffer'd it only out of obedience to the Queen's absolute Will, so that Spiring was in the wrong to dispute a Rank with a Lord, who besides his Place of Marshal de Camp, which gave him the Title of Excellency, was the first Gentleman in Holland, where he was as much consider'd as a Senator is in Sweden. We shall instance elsewhere in a more powerful Example on the like Occasion. The Minister of the second Order ought not to enter into Contests, the end whereof is not advantageous to his Master, but may very well do him harm. It is what he ought to avoid, and decline all Encounters that may embroil him.

An Agent is not, properly speaking, a publick Minister, and yet it is an hundred and fifty Years

Years since no other Minister was known, after an Embassador, than the Agent *Henry Stephanus* says, *There is also another Word come from Italy, relating to him, to whom only one half of the Honour due to an Embassador is shewn, for he is called Agent, and especially if he be sent to a Prince who is less than a King* At this time the Quality of *Resident* is much above that, because he has also the *representing Character*, tho' not in the first Degree The Signification of the word *Agent* declares, that he is only one that does Business M *Piques*, who is now a Counsellor in the Court of Aids in *Paris*, being Agent in *Sweden*, after *Chanut* was gone from thence, begg'd of the *Queen* that she would give him leave to entertain a Priest, that he might have Mass said in his House, by reason that since there was no Embassador from *France* nor *Portugal*, at *Stockholm*, neither his Domesticks, nor the *French* and *Italians* that were in the Queen's Service, had that Consolation The Queen said, *That Piques had no Qualification that gave him that Authority* But if the King his Master would write a Line to her, she assur'd him even then, that she would consent to it The Baron *de Rorté* and *Chanut*, being but *Residents* in *Sweden*, had caus'd Mass to be said there, even without the Queen's Permission, and that so publickly, that when she caus'd 'em to be spoke to about it, they did not scruple to make answer, *That their House being the King's House, they could protect the Exercise of their Religion* This *Agent* was not establish'd by any *Letter of Credence*, but only by *Chanut*, who in taking his Audience of Leave, told the Queen, *That he left* Piques, *who should manage Affairs till such time as the King should send a Minister* Some time after, *Piques* having deliver'd the Letters, by which the King gave him the Quality of *Resident*, the Queen told him, *She was glad to find that the King thought fit to entertain a Minister near her*, because it was a token of his Affection, and of his Inclination to hold a good Correspondence between the two Crowns It is not to say at the same time, that those Princes, to whom *Agents* are employ'd ought not to have some Consideration for them, as the Declaration of the States of *Holland* Ranks 'em amongst those who ought to enjoy the Protection of the *Law of Nations* But it is necessary also, that they who employ 'em should not make choice of People, who by their sordid and abject way of living bring Shame and Discredit on their Masters There have been *Agents* at *Paris* and the *Hague*, who kept publick Houses and that lodg'd in Chambers ready furnish'd Those Princes that suffer these meannesses, can have no reason to complain, if no Consideration be had for their *Agents*, and if they are not distinguish'd from others of the same Profession

The Quality of *Plenipotentiary* does not give a new Character to a Minister, it only denotes the extent of his Power and Authority If he has no other Character, he can be consider'd but as the Bearer of an Ample Procuration The Ministers who negotiated the Treaty of *Querusque* on the part of the Emperor, and that of the Preliminaries of *Westphalia*, had the Quality of *Commissioners*, and had a Full Power *Saavedra* and *le Brun* had only that of *Plenipotentiaries*, when they arriv'd at *Munster* D'avaux, who had treated with the Emperor's Plenipotentiary at *Hamburgh*, and who had done him the same Honours he had receiv'd, maintain'd that *Saavedra* and *le Brun* ought to be treated and consider'd as Embassadors, notwithstanding this Qualification was not taken notice of in their Powers *Servien*, who had brought the Court of *France* into his Sentiments, said on the contrary, that the Emperor and the King of *Spain*, by not giving the Quality of *Embassador* to their Ministers, might draw great Advantages therefrom, because they might be prodigal of their Civilities to the Embassadors from *France*, thereby to receive Honours to which they had no Claim, and by that means put the Ministers of the second Order, that is to say *Residents* and *Agents*, to whom Full Power may be given without the *character-z ng Quality*, in possession of Rights that belong only to *Representatives* That the Emperor often gave the Quality of *Plenipotentiary* to Ministers who assist the Embassadors, and who are like Counsellors to them whom for a l that he will not have consider'd as his Embassadors, because they are not of a Quality eminent enough to represent his Person That the Full Power had regard only to the Authority to treat, that it had nothing in common with the representing Quality, and that the Prince might make use of what Person he thought fit to treat but that every Body was not proper for the Character That *Spain* had reserv'd to it self the Power of giving the Character of Embassador to Don *Francisco de Melo*, or to the Marquess *de Castelrodrigo*, or else to the Duke of *Medina de las Torres*, leaving the Quality of Plenipotentiary to *Saavedra* and *le Brun*, who far from pretending to the Honours of the *Character*, did not dare to give one another the Stile of Excellency among themselves And as the Ministers of *France* made no difficulty to give place to those of the Emperor, who were vested with the same Quality, *so he of the Ministers of* France, *who together with the Quality of Plenipotentiary, should have also that of Embassador Extraordinary*, pretended a precedency to a *Commissioner*, Plenipotentiary *of the same Emperor*, who had it not This was one of the strongest Reasons for the altering of the Powers, to add to them the Quality of *Embassador Extraordinary* Those Princes who did not give the Quality of *Embassador* to their Ministers on the score of the Difficulties I made mention of in the preceding Chapter, gave them that of Plenipotentiary *Cinquenburg* and *Carissius* to whom the King of *Denmark* did not think fit to give the representing Character, had the Quality of Plenipotentiaries at the Assembly at *Breda*, in the Year 1667; they had that of *Envoys Extraordinary* at the *Hague*, and it was that which made 'em be consider'd by the Embassadors of Crown'd Heads, who treated them as Ministers of the second Order Cardinal *Mazarin* and *Don Lewis de Haro*, had only the Quality of Plenipotentiaries at the *Pyrenæan* Congress, but then they had another, which being much more eminent than that of Embassador, they could not acquire a new Lustre by the *Character* Even in the Year 1639, while the Preliminaries were a treating, the United Provinces met with some Difficulties relating to the Passports the *Spaniards* were to give them, and the States agreeing

ing with the Cardinal Infant, they were very much offended at the word *Deputy-Plenipotentiaries*, which was inferted inftead of that of *Embaffadors* But the *Spanifh* Minifters faid, That the States Pretenfions were by fo much the more ftrange, as this Quality was not to be found in the Paffports which the Emperor and the King of *Spain* had order'd for their own Minifters And that the Quality of Embaffador prefuppos'd a Sovereignty, which as yet was not allow'd them, and which could be regulated only at *Munfter*, as it has been already faid in the firft Chapter of this Book The Commiffioners, whom I lately mention'd, and who were at *Querafque* and *Hamburgh*, on the part of the Emperor, were publick Minifters beyond all difpute, and would have been fo even without their Quality of Plenipotentiaries *Servien* and *D'avaux*, who had treated with them, had confider'd them as fuch, and had paid 'em the fame Honours they would have done to the *reprefenting Character*, upon which however I muft obferve a very confiderable thing In this Affembly at *Querafque*, *Math as Baron de Galas* had the Quality of *Commiffioner* and *Plenipotentiary* from the Emperor *Ferdinand* And the Count *de la Roque*, who had the Character of Embaffador from *Spain*, pretended in this Quality to have the precedency of the Emperor's Minifter And in effect in the vifit they made to M *Servien*, the Count took the Hand of the Baron, and for this reafon the Marfhal *de Torras* and *Servien* pretended alfo to precede *Galas*, who had yielded to the Count *de la Roque*, who ought to yield to them This Pretenfion of the *French* Embaffadors oblig'd the Emperor's Minifters, and thofe of *Spain*, to come to this Agreement among themfelves, That for this once the Embaffador from *Spain* fhould give the Hand to the Emperor's Commiffioner, to the End that the *French* Embaffador's might do fo too, which was done In their Conferences they were feated in this Order The Nuncio *Pancirole* was feated at the upper end of the Table, having next to him on his left *Galas*, and after him on the fide of the Table *Servien* The *Marfhal* was on the Right, and had next to him the Prefident *de Rauts*, and the Secretary *Guichardi* was at the lower end of the Table The *French* Embaffadors made here a grofs Overfight, even according to *Servien*'s own Maxim, who on another Occafion maintain'd that the Quality of Plenipotentiary did not give the reprefenting Character, which however carry'd it, as I juft now faid

The two Northern Kings give alfo this Quality to the Minifters they fend upon the Frontiers, for the Affairs of the two Kingdoms And the Republick of *Venice* employs likewife *Commiffioners* in the Controverfies it fometimes has with the Houfe of *Auftria*, about their common Frontiers on the fide of *Frioul* and *Dalmatia* And there is no doubt to be made but thefe *Commiffioners* are publick Minifters

The Emperor frequently appoints *Commiffioners* for the Affairs which relate to the Empire, as has been feen in thofe of *Juliers*, *Mantua* and others In the Year 1574, the Emperor *Maximilian* fent two Councillors to *Genoa*, upon the Occafion of the Mifunderftandings that divided the ancient and new Nobility, and gave them the Quality of Commiffioners The Senate reprefented to him, that they could not acknowledge them in this Quality, Becaufe, faid they, *it is given to thofe whom Sovereigns employ to their Subjects* It is true this is fometimes done, but the Emperor confider'd this Republick as being dependant on the Empire, and as an *Arriere Fief* of the Dutchy of *Milan* The Eftates of the United Provinces give fometimes the Quality of *Commiffioners* to thofe they employ in foreign Courts, but then to judge whether they are publick Minifters we muft confider the nature of the Affairs they have to manage The Sieur *Heufft*, who refided thirty Years in this Quality at *Paris*, and there receiv'd the Subfidies, in order to remit the fame, was a good Banker and Partifan, who far from being confider'd as a publick Minifter, could not hinder his Succeffion from being tax'd as well as that of all the Financiers or Receivers, who had made their advantage of the diforder of the Times, and of the diffipation of the King's Money He was properly fpeaking, a Factor and Commiffioner, and the fame Name may be given to thofe Merchants, who at *Amfterdam* and *Hamburg* make intereft for this Quality with the Crowns of *Sweden* and *Denmark*, that thereby they may carry on their little Commerce with more eafe They have no Affairs of State to manage, neither do they refide near the Sovereign, who is he that can make 'em enjoy the Protection of the Law of Nations It feems alfo as if they laid no claim to it, any further than to be exempted from the extraordinary Subfidies which are raifed upon the other Subjects

This is what ought to be underftood alfo with relation to *Confuls*, and that for the fame reafon The Princes who employ them protect them, as Perfons concern'd in their Service, and as every good Mafter protects his Servants and Domefticks, but not as publick Minifters The Governor of *Cadiz*, having within feven or eight Months affronted and confin'd the *Dutch* Conful, the Eftates of the United Provinces complain'd thereof to the Court of *Madrid*, as of a Violence done to the *Law of Nations*, inftead of complaining of the Non-Execution of thofe Treaties, wherein they ought to find Safety and Security for their pretended Minifter, and not elfewhere Some Years fince they were for making the Conful (who refided on their part at *Genoa*) pafs for a publick Minifter, but the Senate wrote them word, that they did not acknowledge him for a publick Minifter, and that all that could be expected from them, was the peaceable fruition of thofe Rights and Privileges which Cuftom has beftow'd on this kind of Employment Confuls are only Merchants, who not withftanding their Office of *Judge in the Controverfies* that may arife among thofe of their own Nation, carry on at the fame time their own Traffick, and are liable to the Juftice of the Place where they refide, as well in civil as criminal Matters, which is altogether inconfiftent with the Quality of publick Minifter In the Year 1634, the Republick of *Venice* had like to have come to a Rupture with Pope *Urban* VIII, on account of the Violence the Governor of *Ancona* had offer'd to the Conful, who refided there on the part of the Senate

The

The EMBASSADOR and his FUNCTIONS.

The Consul's name was *Michael Oberti*, and he was a Native of *Bergamo*, his Family had discharg'd that Office for many years. The Governor, who suspected him to have given some Advices, upon which the Gallies of the Republick had taken some small vessels belonging to *Ragusa*, for having smugl'd the Duties that are paid in the Gulf, persecuted the Consul after such a manner, that he was forc'd to go to *Venice*, to acquaint the Senate therewith. He was no sooner gone, than the Governour put a Garrison into his House, and carry'd off his Furniture and Papers, even those which related to the Functions of his Employment. The Senate complain'd hereof, and demanded reparation with so much heat, that the *French* Embassador apprehending left they should proceed to an open Rupture with the Pope, endeavour'd to adjust the Difference, so as the Republick should be satisfy'd therewith. But before the Accommodation could be perfected, the Governor caus'd the Consul to be summon'd, and for Contumacy condemn'd him to Banishment, under the Pretext, that during the Contagion he had unladen Goods contrary to the Prohibition. There was more of Passion than Justice in this Sentence, since *Oberti* could prove, that he had done nothing without the Approbation of the Magistrate. So that the Senate was more offended at this last piece of Injustice, than at the first, and the *French* Embassador was forc'd to repeat his good Offices, to dispose the Minds of the Parties to an Accommodation. However he accomplish'd it at last, upon Condition, *that the Governor should repeal the Outlawry, and should suffer Oberti to be re-establish'd, and that the Senate, who should recall Oberti, should substitute in his Place whomsoever it plea'd*. Michael dying before all this could be executed, the Senate put his Brother in his room, but this last was no sooner arr'v'd at *Ancona*, than the Governor caus'd him to be put in Prison, and would not release him till he had given Security for his leaving the Town, and that he should not return. The *French* Ministers who had labour'd in the Reconciliation, and had engag'd their Words for the Execution of the Conditions, which allow'd the *Venetians* to nominate any other they should think fit, for Consul, were very much scandaliz'd at this Proceeding, and the Senate, to shew its Indignation, refus'd Audience to the Nuncio, and forbad its Embassador to take it of the Pope, till such time as they had receiv'd Satisfaction, which the Governor was forc'd to give. The Judges, Consuls of the Merchants at *Paris*, at *Lions*, and elsewhere, are quite a different thing.

As the Commissioner is a *Deputy*, employ'd by the Prince to his Subjects, so the *Deputy* may be said to be a Commissioner whom the Subjects employ to their Prince, and in this Signification he is no publick Minister, nor within the Protection of the *Law of Nations*, which has no room where the Civil Laws have a free Liberty to act. The same Word has a Signification more extensive, and denotes a Minister who has no other particular Quality, and then he may be a publick Minister, whether he be sent to a Congress, or to some Prince or Republick.

The President *Jeannin*, who does not trifle with Words, but goes directly to the solid part, gives this Quality to all the Ministers who were at the *Hague*, on the Negotiation of the Truce, tho' at the same time he confounds it with that of Embassador, in the Person of those who really had the representing Character. The Arch-Duke's Ministers, namely, the Marquis *Spinola*, President *Richardot*, Secretary *Mancidor*, Auditor *Verreyken*, and the Commissary General of the *Corashers*, had no Quality Care was taken not to give 'em that of Embassador, because the Arch-Duke consider'd the Estates of the United Provinces as Subjects and Rebels, and these Lords were not mean enough to pass for Ministers of the second Order. Yet it cannot be deny'd but they were publick Ministers, and that as such they had a Title to the Protection of the *Law of Nations*.

Prince *Maurice* of *Nassau*, accompany'd by Count *Henry* his Brother, Count *William* of *Nassau* Governor of *Frise*, and two other Lords of the same House, and follow'd by a great train of Officers *French* and *English*, went out to receive them at half a League's distance from the *Hague*, and they receiv'd the same Honours that would have been paid to the Character.

It is but within these few Years that mention has been made of *Deputies Extraordinary*, as of a new Species of Ministers, but then it is known only in *Holland*. And as they have met with a thousand Rubs, with reference to the Civilities they pretended to insist upon in foreign Courts, which do not easily strike into Novelties, there is no likelihood these Ministers should succeed under this new Quality. It will never be acknowledg'd in those Courts where the Ceremonies are regulated, and there is no Embassador who knows what is his due, that will make the least Difference between the *Deputy Extraordinary* and another *Envoy* or *Resident*. *Shering Rosenhan*, who had been a Minister at the Congress of *Westphalia* and *Lubeck*, (where the Quality of the Representatives had been nicely examin'd) and Embassador in *France*, and who was, in the Year 1654, Embassador Plenipotentiary from *Sweden* to *Germany*, made *Conrad Van Benningen*, & *Epo Bootma*, Deputies Extraordinary from the United Provinces, sensible he had learn'd enough, to know, that there was no publick Quality betwixt the Embassador and the Ministers of the second Order. To speak the truth, it was what they were not ignorant of themselves, since being arriv'd at *Stade*, instead of expecting the first Visit, they sent their *Letters of Credence* to *Rosenhan*, and paid him the Civility he ow'd them, if they had been any thing more than Ministers of the second Order. He sent 'em back the *Letter of Credence*, and caus'd 'em to be told, That he could not accept it, That the States, when they wrote to the Crown of *Sweden*, were accustom'd to make use of the *Latin* Tongue, and not of the *Flemish*, That it was moreover full of Cancellings, and unworthy to be presented to a person of Quality, and That he did not know the meaning of these two Characters V L in a Letter, where the Title of Excellency could not be refus'd to the Embassador of a crown'd Head. The Deputies extraordinary had no great Task to remove these Difficulties, but then they met with many others of greater Consequence, as well with reference to their Negotiation, as to the manner of their Reception.

Rosenhan receiv'd them in the middle of the Lobby, which serv'd him also for an Antechamber, took both the Hand and the Step of 'em, and being come into his Chamber, *he plac'd himself in the most honourable part thereof, next to an arm'd Chair, desiring the Deputies to sit down on Chairs with Backs, which were opposite to him, and in reconducting them back, he left them at the Door,* before they were got into their Coach. They were so much offended at this Procedure, that after they had din'd they sent him word by their Secretary, That, to prevent any Prejudice happening to the Dignity and Grandeur of their Principals, they were oblig'd to let him understand, That they could not be satisfy'd with the Reception they had had in the Morning. That they were Deputies at the Assembly of the States General, and that the Members of that Body, when they are deputed, although it be but verbally, to confer with Embassadors from crown'd Heads, are receiv'd at their alighting from their Coach, and reconducted back again to the Coach Door, and that this was the Practice even at the *Hague*. That upon much stronger Reasons was this Honour due to those, whom the States employ'd out of their Countrey in the Quality of *Deputies Extraordinary*, and provided with *Letters of Credence*. That for this Reason they hop'd his Excellency would make no Difficulty to consider them in that Quality, unless his Intention was to break off the Negotiation. *Rosenhan* made answer, That it was not his Intention to do any Prejudice to them, nor to their Principals. That he knew very well what he ow'd to the States Embassadors, but that *he did not understand what the Quality of Deputy Extraordinary meant. That he thought he ought to distinguish between the Character of Embassador and the Quality of Deputy*, and that if the Deputies requir'd to be us'd otherwise by him, they should have had the Quality of Embassadors in their Credentials. He sent 'em the same Message by his Secretary, when he desir'd to know what Hour they would be at leisure to receive the Visit he design'd to return 'em. The Deputies reply'd, that the Word *Deputy Extraordinary* was not new, and that the States of the United Provinces had employ'd that kind of Minister to the Northern Crowns, to the Elector of *Brandenburg*, to the Duke of *Neuburg*, and elsewhere, and that he, *Van Beuningen*, being in the same Quality in *Sweden*, the Embassadors had made no Difficulty to receive him at, and reconduct him to, the Coach. *Rosenhan* took no notice to them of it in his Visit, but only told them, they would do well to procure themselves the Quality of *Legati*. The Deputies made answer, That it did not depend on them, but on their Masters, to give them what Quality they thought convenient. They were in the right, and so was *Rosenhan* too, to maintain the Advantage his Character gave him over Ministers of the second Order. There is no Prince nor State that can, without the Consent of the other Potentates, introduce or set up a Quality (relating to mutual Correspondence) which is not known any where else; nor that can prescribe to the Embassadors of crown'd Heads, after what manner they ought to treat those Ministers, who have not the same Quality they themselves have. If in *Sweden* they did any thing beyond what they ought to *Van Beuningen*, they did it through Ignorance, or else out of some personal Consideration, which cannot oblige Embassadors to follow their Example. It is necessary also to observe, with reference to what these Gentlemen say concerning the Deputies whom the Estates send to those Embassadors that are at the *Hague*, that they are of the Body of the Assembly, and represent it when they go on these Commissions, whereas the *Deputies Extraordinary* who are sent out of the Countrey, are no longer of it after they have taken the Oath upon their Employ, and they become Ministers, who no longer make a part of the State, nor have any Seat in the Assembly, till after they have made a Report of their Employ. To which we must add, that this Quality of Deputy to the Assembly of the States General, is by so much the less considerable, that it is found in the Commission and Credentials of all the Embassadors, tho' there are some that do not appear there, but when they receive their Commission, and are sworn before their departure, and make a Report thereof at their return. This Quality is giv'n 'em, as the Republick of *Venice* gives to its Embassadors the Quality of *Grand Sage*, or *Sage of Terra firma*.

The Ceremonial was never very well settl'd in *Poland*, and yet they knew how to distinguish between the Embassador, and Minister of the second Order, by giving it to be understood, that nothing was due to the Quality of *Deputy Extraordinary*. John van den Honart, Magistrate of *Dort*, being vested therewith in the Year 1659, and being arriv'd near *Warsaw*, sent Advice toereof to the Chancellor. The Messenger was led to a sorry little House, which was design'd for his Lodgings, and answer was made him, that he might come when he pleas'd, for they did not intend to do him any Civilities. Accordingly he made his Entry without Ceremony, and after the Compliment, which the Chancellor sent to make him the next Day, he visited the Chancellor. He discours'd with him on the Subject of his Commission, desired him to procure him an Audience, and parted from him well enough satisfy'd, because the Chancellor had receiv'd him at, and reconducted him to, his Coach. The 2d of *July* the Chancellor signify'd to him by one of his Clerks, that the Day following the King and Queen would give him Audience about three of the Clock in the Afternoon, to which the *Deputy Extraordinary* made answer, that he would take care to be ready to be conducted to it after the usual Manner. The Clerk reporting these last Words, was sent back again, to learn of his Domesticks after what manner he pretended to be conducted, the Quality that his Letters gave him not being known in that Court. The *Deputy* sent him word, that the Character of *Deputy Extraordinary* was not a new thing, that his Masters the States had made use of them, for many Years past, to the *Northern Kings*, who treated 'em much after the rate of *Embassadors*.

The next day following, the same Clerk came and told him, that the Chancellor sent him thither, by the King's Order, to accompany him to his Audience, and he accordingly did accompany him to the Ante-chamber, which was full of all forts of People, not one of whom paid him the least Civility, except the first Comer. After he had waited there some time, one of the Grooms of the Bed-Chamber usher'd him into the place of Audience. Every body was put out, to give him the greater liberty to make his Compliment. After which the King told him, he was much oblig'd to his Masters the States, as well on the account of the Embassy M. Tibrants had discharg'd there for some time, as for this present Deputation. The King stood all the while, and uncover'd. The Queen did not shew him more Honour, to whom he was introduc'd by the same Clerk, and at his going out, the second Secretary accompany'd him to the middle of he Chamber. The Chancellor, who visited him the next Day, told him, that they could not give him any other Reception, because that Quality of Deputy Extraordinary was altogether unknown at that Court, where only one had been seen on the part of the King of Denmark, and to whom they had not done more Honour than they did to himself, altho' he had with that Quality, that of Plenipotentiary. Van den Honart could make no other answer, but that this Quality was not new in Holland. But then it did not belong to Holland, nor the States, to establish a new Character, and oblige the other Courts to acquiesce in a Novelty. They themselves make no Entries to Envoys Extraordinary, who are conducted to their first Audience only with two Coaches. However they order'd Van den Honart to have no more Conferences with the Ministers of Poland, unless they made Reparation for what was pass'd. It was repair'd in some measure within a few Days after his first Audience, before this Order came to his hands, and that by the Queen's Advice, who was oblig'd frequently to redress what was irregular in the King's Conduct. On the 27th of July, a Coach with two Gentlemen and four Footmen, was sent to conduct Van den Honart to Court and at his departure from thence to go to Dantzick, he was brought to Court again in a Coach with fix Horses, attended by two Gentlemen and four Footmen. When he came to the Castle, he was met by the Count de Donhof, one of the King's Chamberlains, and when he came into the Chamber, he found there two Arm'd Chairs of red Velvet, in the one of which the King seated himself, and invited the Deputy Extraordinary to sit down in the other, and to be cover'd. The Queen receiv'd him after the same manner. But then they went too far this second time, and not far enough the first. The King ought not to have made him be cover'd, and an Officer of the Court, who had understood his Business well, would not have advis'd the King to offer him an Arm'd Chair. On these Occasions recourse should be had, as I shall be often oblig'd to have, to what the Duke of Newburg us'd to say, that in those Courts that are remote from France and Italy, the Ceremonial is not so well regulated.

In the Year 1656, M. Van Ommeren, who was a Person of very great Merit and of an exemplary Probity, was sent to the Swiss Cantons in the same Quality, about the Affairs of the Valleys of Piedmont; but when he design'd to visit M. de la Barde, the French Embassador to those Parts, this last did not scruple to tell him, that he could not receive a Deputy Extraordinary with the same Honours he would shew to an Embassador. The French Embassador is expressly forbid to do it, and there is no doubt to be made, but the other Kings will follow his Example. The Embassador from Savoy, who was at that time employ'd to the Cantons, did not fail to do it. He gave Van Ommeren to understand, that he could not see him till he had seen the French Embassador, because he would inform himself of the manner of his Reception there. However they met in a third place, where the Deputy might give Precedency to the Embassador without scruple. Amongst all the Catholick Cantons, there was only that of Uri that caus'd Civilities to be done him, but the Protestants receiv'd him in a Body, at the Gate of the Town House; made him go first, and gave him the place of Honour and the Title of Excellency; that is to say, they did all they could have done to the representing Character. I can't believe there is in that Republick, any more than in Holland, an Academy, where Youth may apply themselves to the study of the Rules of Ceremonies, notwithstanding that the Hague is always adorn'd with a great Number of Ministers, and that there are several great Personages, who have discharg'd that Function in foreign Courts.

The Secretary of the Embassy has likewise a representing Quality. The Roman Ceremonial, which is the Rule of all Ceremonies, declares it positively, and moreover adds, that the Cardinals allow both Seat and Covering to those of the Embassies from crown'd Heads, and that of Venice, and do them the same Civilities they shew to the Residents of those Princes, to whom the Title of Most Serene is given. But if the Rule of Ceremonies did not explain it self so clearly, the Quality it self sufficiently intimates, that as the Secretary discharges part of the Embassador's Function, he is also a part of the Embassy; not as a Domestick Servant and Secretary to the Embassador, but as a Minister who depends on the Prince, and acts immediately by his Orders. It is true, he receives 'em sometimes from the Embassador, but then he does not receive them as from his Master, but as from a Minister of whom his Master makes use, as an Instrument, to let him know his Intention. And in reality there is a great deal of difference, between the Secretary of an Embassy, and that of an Embassador. The one is a domestick Officer, as I before took notice, whereas the other is a Minister of their common Prince, and his Representative in some measure. The Embassador chuses the one, and the Prince nominates the other. The one takes his Oath to, and receives his Wages from the Embassador, the other swears to the Prince, and has his Salary from him. The one writes only what

44   *The* EMBASSADOR *and his* FUNCTIONS.

what his Master dictates, while the other gives his Master Advice of whatever he thinks beneficial to his Service, and that even without the participation of the Embassador The one is the Embassador's menial Servant, whereas the other is in a manner his Controuler There is only the Republick of *Venice* that makes no distinction in the matter, and that because the Secretary of the Embassador is also Secretary of the Embassy, and is present at the Audiences, and at all the Embassador's publick Acts but then he stands behind his Chair In the Year 1641, there arriv'd at *London* two Embassadors from *Portugal*, who making their Visit to Prince *William* of *Orange*, who was there upon his Marriage, brought their Secretary with them, and made him sit down by them This was very incongruous in point of Civility, which does not allow the Servant to sit in the Presence of his Master The Prince indeed might have made him sit, if he had receiv'd any Message by him, on the part of his Masters. but in a Visit of Ceremony, where every Chair ought to be dispos'd in its proper place before the arrival of the Embassadors, the Number could neither be augmented, nor the Order chang'd, without confusion *France* has no Secretaries to the Embassy but only at *Rome* and *Constantinople* She had one at *Munster*, and in all Congresses where she employs more Embassadors than one, there is a Secretary that serves them all in general, besides him that each Embassador has in private The late M *Brasset*, after he had discharg'd the Office of Secretary to several Embassadors, had at last that of the Embassy, which serv'd him as a Recompence for his Merit, and he was made Resident in the beginning of the Assembly at *Munster* There was one along with M *de Thou*, while he was Embassador in *Holland*, but he did not discharge the Functions thereof He was a Priest, and Cardinal *Mazarine*, who esteem'd him for his Learning, procur'd this Employment for him, with a Pension of twelve hundred Livres, as being one of the greatest Mathematicians of those Times On the contrary M *Richara*, who at the *Hague* was Secretary of the Embassy from *Spain*, under Don *Esteran de Gamara*, was at the same time Secretary to the Embassador, and was within a little of discharging even the function of Embassador

The Secretary, who is left by Embassadors at any Court, upon their Departure from thence, or that stays there after the Death of an Embassador, cannot be consider'd as a publick Minister unless he has Letters of Credence which if he has, he then becomes *Agent* or Secretary of the Embassy, M *de Foix*, Embassador from *France*, being dead at *Rome*, M *de Villeroy* sent Orders to *Arnand Dossat*, who was Secretary to the Deceased, to be vigilant in the King's Interest, till such time as an other Embassador was sent It happen'd that none at all was sent, by reason of the Civil-Wars, the Decease of *Henry* III, and the little Consideration that *Rome* had at that time for *Henry* IV, it being before his Absolution yet for all that *Dossat* manag'd Affairs with admirable Success, but without any Quality He had none neither, even when he was joyn'd in the Commission which was given to *Du Perron*, to make the Submissions and receive the Penances Neither the one nor the other had any of the Qualities which have been spoken of in this Chapter which notwithstanding they were publick Ministers, and enjoy'd the Protection of the *Law of Nations* They were but *Procurators*, but being so to a very great King, and for a very extraordinary and solemn Action, and being themselves Prelates, they could not be consider'd as private Persons They had with their *Procuration*, Letters of Credence, which made them *publick Ministers*, tho' they had no Quality So that it is my Opinion, that this *Species* of *Procurators*, may be rank'd amongst the Ministers of the second Order

C H A P. VI.

To whom Embassadors are sent.

THE Right of *Embassy* being inseparable from *Sovereignty*, and this sort of *Correspondence* being held only among *Sovereigns*, we must from thence conclude, that the *Prince* or *State* that receives the *Embassador* ought to be *Sovereign*, as well as he that sends him When I made mention in the second Chapter of those Princes who have a Right to send Embassadors, I also took notice of those to whom they send 'em, so that it will be a difficult matter to say any thing new on that Subject in this I shall avoid also making Repetitions, and shall content my self with laying down as a simple Position, that Sovereigns neither send Embassadors to their own Subjects, nor to those of other Potentates, nor to the rebellious Subjects of a Prince whose Friendship they are chary of They send 'em to *Usurpers* when they have gain'd Possession, and to those Viceroys and Governors that have an absolute Authority Nay there are some Sovereigns, to whom they only send Ministers of the second Order *Charles Paschal*, who form'd his Embassador in the Mountains of the *Grisons*, upon the common Topick of *Legatus*, honours with that *Character* all Persons employ'd in any *Deputation* whatsoever But as we don't allow so great a Latitude either to the *Embassador*, nor even to the *modern publick Minister*, we shall not hinder him from diverting himself with his *Greek* and his *Latin*, while we shall (in treating of the Embassador and his Functions) deliver our selves in a Language that is commonly spoke at this time The King of *France* has his Embassadors in Ordinary at *Rome*, at *Venice* and at *Turin*, and upon certain Occasions he honours the Great Duke of *Tuscany* with *Embassies Extraordinary*, as also the Dukes of Mantua, Parma and Modena. The King of Spain on the contrary, employs none but Envoys or subaltern Ministers with the three last, who go to them with Letters from the Viceroy of Naples, or Governor of Milan. Neither France nor Spain have any Embassadors in Ordinary at Genoa, altho' the Embassadors of this Republick are receiv'd in France, and that, as well because it is but a very modern Sovereignty, as for this Reason, that she is not so absolute but France would dispute it with her, it she was in possession of the Dutchy of Milan, on which the City of Genoa formerly depended. The Consideration that they are oblig'd to have there for Spain, as well on account of the Interest of the most powerful of its Inhabitants, as by reason of its Vicinity to Milan and Final, is the Cause that France neglects her. I have elsewhere given the Reason why France has only a Minister of the second Order at Vienna, and it is only since the Peace at Munster, that she has there one in Ordinary, and another at the Diets of the Empire, on the score of the Interest Alsace, Lorrain and Brisac, make her have in the Affairs of Germany. While the War of the Empire lasted, she had continually a Minister with the General of the Swedish Army. And there is not any Court nor Assembly in all Germany, where she had not either her Ministers or Emissaries, ever since Cardinal Richelieu was at the head of Affairs.

Those Embassadors who are sent to Assemblies compos'd of several representing Ministers, are in reality sent to the Sovereigns those Ministers represent. Those who are sent to the Diets of Germany, are employ'd to the Emperor, and to the States of the Empire. The Diets of the Cantons, and the Assembly of the States-General, represent the Sovereignty of those two Republicks. When M. d'Avaux treated at Hamburgh with the Imperial Commissioner, he treated with the Emperor himself in a neutral Place. Hitherto crown'd Heads have not honour'd with their Embassies the Electors or particular Princes, but they have made no difficulty to send their Embassadors to the States of the Empire in general, and even to the Electoral College in a Body, as also to the Assemblies of some Princes united or joyn'd in Confederacy together, the Duke D'Engoulesme, the Count de Bethune, and M. de Chasteauneuf, to the Assembly at Ulm. Feuquieres, to that at Haslbron the Duke de Grammont, and Hugh de Lionne, to Francfort.

The same Reasons which hinder the King of France from receiving Embassadors from the Electors and Princes of Germany, hinder him also from sending any to them. So that as soon as that Difficulty is taken off on the one side, it will be likewise so on the other, and Embassadors will be seen in the Courts of the one as well as of the other, though at this time there be only Ministers of the second Order. The King of Great Britain, who has admitted at London the Embassadors of the Elector of Brandenburg, his not yet sent any that I know of to the Court at Berlin, and that, as I take it, for this Reason, that he will not make any step therein, which he does not see made by the Kings of France and Spain. If he has done otherwise, in acknowledging the Ministers of Brandenburg in this Quality, it is because he thought, he could not commit an Error by an excessive Civility, whereas by sending Embassadors, it would look like a sort of Submission.

The Northern Kings are not so shy but then again, they are not so exact and regular in the Point of Ceremonies, and they do not always distinguish, betwixt a Minister of the first, and one of the second Order that is to say, between the Legatus and the Ablegatus, or the Embassador and the Envoy. Those whom they make use of commonly in the Courts of the Princes of Germany are not Embassadors, whatever Qualities they give themselves, and whatever Honours are done them, they are but Envoys, who ought to be contented with the common Civilities. In the Year 1647, the Elector of Brandenburg sent Conrad de Burgstorf, his High Chamberlain and first Minister, to the Elector of Saxony, and the other Princes of the House of Brunswick and Lunenburg. He was a Gentleman, who with all his other Qualifications, had not one single one of those, that form a great Minister, and I dare be bold to say, that he did not know how to distinguish between the Embassador and the Envoy. He had with him the Retinue of a Prince, and he had the same Honours done him, as could have been shewn to the Elector himself. At his Arrival at Wolfembuttel he was saluted by the Cannons. The Duke gave him the Place of Honour at Table, in the Coach, and every where else, which sufficiently surpris'd me when I saw it, but I was still more surpris'd, when I understood that he had receiv'd the same Honours at Dresden. But as in those Courts the Rules of Ceremony are not well understood, they cannot be Precedents for what will be said in the sequel of this Work.

Sovereigns send their Embassadors only to Sovereigns, but as they are not link'd by Commerce nor Interest, to them all indifferently, so neither have they their Ministers, but with those with whom they have Affairs to negotiate. It is for this Reason, that no Prince whatever entertains a Minister with the great Master of Malta, neither do they send any Extraordinaries. As he is the Head of a religious Order, the Pope, who treats him in other things as he treats the Princes who have not the Title of Most Serene, sends only a Commissioner to Malta. On the other side, Sovereigns send Ministers sometimes to those Places where their Interest requires it, notwithstanding there is no Sovereign there for them to consider.

France has had a Resident at Hamburgh, not for any Affairs it had to adjust with the Magistrate, nor to facilitate the Correspondence it had with Sweden, but upon other particular Considerations. The Emperor has also a Resident there, who being employ'd to the Circle of the lower Saxony, has made choice of that City, as the most commodious Place, and not upon the score of the Affairs he has to negotiate, as with a Hanse Town, with which the Emperor has no Correspondence in this Quality.

Yet nevertheless these two Residents are publick Ministers, since they enjoy the Protection of the Law of Nations, and have the free

Exercise of their Religion in their own Houses, which they would not have, had they not *Letters of Credence* The Minister who is there from the States of the United Provinces, resides in that, as in a Town which almost alone supports the Remains of the Reputation of the *German* Free-Towns And if he resides there rather than at *Lubeck* or *Bremen*, it is on the account of the great Commerce those Provinces have with it, beyond what they have with the other Towns, and because it serves as a Line of Communication with the Kingdoms of *Denmark* and *Sweden* It is for this Reason also that they have a Commissioner at *Dantzick*, altho' this Town is not free, any more than that of *Hamburgh*, whatever Privileges it may have The Commissioner is a kind of Consul, who not having any *Letters of Credence* for the King, nor for the Senate of *Poland*, cannot be consider'd as a publick Minister The Resident that is employ'd by the said Estates at *Francfort* is the same, as is also the Resident the King of *France* entertains at *Strasburg* tho' it may be said, that this sort of Ministers are better supported by the Regard that is had for their Masters, than by any paid to their Character The King of *England* has a Minister at *Hamburgh*, to whom he gives the Quality of Resident, altho' he be in reality but a Commissioner or Consul, since he is establish'd there, only for the sake of the *English* Merchant Adventurers, who there carry on their Traffick under the Protection of the Court of *England* The Crown of *Sweden* had also one there till the last Rupture, who always enjoy'd the Benefit of the *Law of Nations*, and was consider'd and respected as a Minister, notwithstanding he was in his own Countrey, and was Brother to one of the Burgermasters of the same Town This is what I think my self oblig'd to take notice of, to the Confusion of our new and false Politicians, who have dar'd of their own private Authority, to abolish what has been introduced, and always inviolably observ'd, with the Consent of all the Nations of the Earth The Town of *Leige* is immediately subject to the Bishop, notwithstanding which, the King of *France* has frequently a Minister there, as he has at this present time

The Count *de Warfuse*, of the House of *Renesse*, when he caus'd the Burgermaster *Ruelle*, whom he had invited to Dinner to be murder'd, did not dare to violate the *Law of Nations*, tho' he had violated that of Hospitality which ought not to be less Sacred, notwithstanding it was no less his Interest to rid himself of the Abbot *de Monson* the French Minister, than of the other, who having been of the Feast ought to have tasted the Desert The Count did this black and perfidious Action to gratify the *Spaniards*, who being then at variance with *France* did not much regard its Minister but however, the Count respected his Character and siv'd him *Charles* IX, King of *France*, in the Year 1573 sent *Nicholas d'Angennes de Rambouillet* to the Senate of *Poland*, to thank it for the Choice it had made (on his Recommendation) of his Brother the Duke of *Anjou* But the Senate represents the Republick, that is to say, a Body, of which the King may be reckon'd the Head, tho' not the Sovereign.

The Embassador then being the Minister of one Sovereign to another Sovereign, and between two Princes or States that are really Sovereigns, or at least carry the Figure of being so, a Prince is not oblig'd to give the Protection of the *Law of Nations* to a Minister, that is sent by another Prince to his Subjects in Rebellion, to foment their Faction and Revolt Certainly there never was a more pernicious one, than that of the over-zealous *Catholicks*, or the League towards the end of the Reign of *Henry* III, King of *France* After his Decease, *Henry* IV was call'd to the Crown, by Laws which have beeen inviolably observ'd for many Ages *Philip* II, King of *Spain*, who could not be ignorant thereof, who had no business to meddle with other People's Affairs, and who meddled with 'em only to ruin his own in the Low Countreys, had notwithstanding his three *Embassadors* at *Paris* the Duke *de Feria*, Don *Diego d'Ibarra*, and *John Baptist Taxis* The Inhabitants of *Paris* had drove out *Henry* III, and did not acknowledge *Henry* IV, as those *Spanish* Ministers did not acknowledge him neither, even after his Absolution and Coronation On the contrary, they employ'd all their Money, Forces, or Artifice, *Spain* could furnish, to confirm the *French* in their Felony and Rebellion There is no doubt but the King might have treated them as declar'd Enemies, because these pretended Ministers, not having any *Letters of Credence* for himself, nor Orders to negotiate with his Council, he was not oblig'd to consider them as Embassadors I say the same of the *Legate*, and other Emissaries that the Pope had there at that time, and who did the King no better Service Yet nevertheless *Henry* suffer'd 'em to retire into Italy, or to *Brussels*, and after the reducing of *Paris* caus'd Civilities to be be shewn to the Legate But besides the excellent Nature of that good and great Prince, he had allow'd, that in the private Capitulation which was made with *M de Brissack*, some Articles should be inserted that gave 'em this Security, notwithstanding the Agreement was made without their Participation

During the last Commotions in *England*, most of the neighbouring Potentates had their Ministers there, but those that were there during the King's Life, had no other Object but the Reconciliation of the Subjects with their Sovereign and after his Decease, there appear'd but one Party which was powerful enough to oblige all the Neighbours to court its Friendship It is a thing most certain, that an Embassador ought to acknowledge no other Authority in the State where he negotiates, than that of the Sovereign, for whom he has *Letters of Credence*

La Ferté Imbault, who has been since known under the Quality of Marshal *Destampes*, being Embassador in *England* in the Year 1642, had been inform'd that *Roe*, who was at *Rat shon* on the part of the King of *England*, had there offer'd to make a League Offensive and Defensive with the House of *Austria*, if the Emperor would make Satisfaction to the King his Master with reference to the *Palatinate*, and the Electoral Dignity, *of which he complain'd to the Parliament* by means of the Earl of *Holland* The Parliament had never taken cogni

The EMBASSADOR and his FUNCTIONS. 47

cognizance of that kind of Affairs, and it was not to this Assembly that Embassadors were us'd to address themselves. The King therefore caus'd a Letter to be writ to *La Ferté* by one of his Secretaries of State, that the Embassador who had not been rightly inform'd of *Roe*'s Negotiation in *Germany*, had too easily believ'd and publish'd what he had heard. He likewise made him be ask'd, whether it was by the King his Master's Orders, that he had address'd himself to the Parliament, or *whether this Innovation was his own proper Act and Deed and also* whether he had oblig'd him thus to write his Sovereign. *La Ferté* made answer, that he had executed the Commands of the King his Master. It is very imprudent in this Minister to expose his Prince after this manner, and thereby render him the Object of the King of *Great Britain*'s Aversion, to whom a grosser Affront could not be offer'd. And accordingly he wrote into *France*, that if that Embassador was not immediately recall'd, he would take such measures as he should think proper for his Honour, and the Good of his Service. Hereupon he was recall'd, and after a manner that sufficiently declar'd he was look'd upon to be better qualify'd for War than Negotiations. In the Month of *May* 1665, the King of *France* caus'd the *Pope's Bull* to be register'd, by which he condemn'd what the *Jansenists* had written against his Infallibility. The *Nuncio* printed it of his own Authority, and therein took the Quality of *Nuncio* to the King and Kingdom of *France*, which was taken so ill, that the Parliament pass'd an Order against the Printer, and seiz'd all his Goods. The Parliament said, that if the *Nuncio* had been sent to the Kingdom, it would have been to exercise a *Jurisdiction*, whereas he had none; and that he was only sent to the King, that is to say, *to the Sovereign of the State*.

CHAP VII.

Of the Birth and Learning of an Embassador.

IN whatsoever Sense the Word Birth is taken, it is a great Ornament to the Embassador, if it be any thing considerable. If he derives it from an Illustrious House, or a noble Family, it gives a great Lustre to the Embassy, and if it be accompany'd by natural Parts that set it off, these render the Embassador so much the more proper for this eminent Employ. The one casts a bright Reflection on him, and the other is absolutely necessary, and gives him an Ability, without which it is impossible for him to succeed.

The Providence of God, which appears so manifestly in the whole Oeconomy of the Universe, is admirable in the Distribution of his Favours. The greatest part of those who possess Riches are not capable of acquiring any; and all that they can do by the means of their Wealth, is to raise themselves above the Condition of a Porter or Hackney-Coach-Man. There are but few Men that do Honour to the Dignity their Birth or Fortune has bestow'd upon them. Instead of making use of it to make themselves respected and lov'd, it only serves to make 'em despis'd and loath'd. If Virtue was Hereditary, there is no Employment but what would be preferably due to the Nobility. Would to God it was so, and that Gentlemen did not make their chiefest Virtue of that Bravery, which ever took delight in drowning in a Deluge of Blood, the Inhabitants of Towns and Provinces that have been destroy'd and laid waste by Fire, which has buried an infinite Number of Castles and Houses in their Ruins, which still reduces every Day so many Families, and so many Persons of all Ages and Sexes, to that Extremity of Miseries, that would strike the most barbarous Nations with Horror. *Valour* is the principal, or rather the only Virtue of those that are call'd Nobles, or Gentlemen, and who pretend to have mighty advantages over the Commonalty and that by the Conceit of an imaginary Quality, that one or other of their Predecessors has procur'd to all his Posterity, either by Favour or Merit. Their Inclination to War is neither acquir'd in the Academy nor in Hunting, but they there learn how it ought to be made, and by enuring themselves to Fatigues, that Exercise they go through in their Apprenticeship, becomes a Diversion to 'em when they know their Trade. There are but few of 'em who joyn Study thereto, and are happy enough to apply their Minds to that which can form 'em for the Management of Affairs, and is able to give 'em those Qualifications, without which it is impossible to be a Great Man. Those that do apply themselves thereto, or at their coming into the World bring along with them such natural Endowments, as can supply what they want in acquired Abilities, may succeed in either the one, or the other Profession. But then this is what seldom happens, and there are but few great Captains, that are at the same time able Ministers. The Count *de Dunois*, from whom the Dukes of *Longueville* are descended, whose Posterity fail'd but a few Years since, was without doubt one of the greatest Captains of his time, and he was also one of the most dextrous *Negotiators*. He was the natural Son of *Lewis* Duke of *Orleans*, who was Brother to *Charles* VI, King of *France*, but I do not believe I wrong his Memory, when I say, that he made himself greater than he was by his Birth, and that even without the Advantage of the latter, he would have been one of the greatest Men of his Age. The Mareshal *de Biron*, the Father, was as knowing as he was brave, and there is not any Countrey that has not produc'd this kind of Hero. Yet it is not the peculiar Lot of the Nobility. They are not all great Men. On the contrary, there are but few amongst
'em

'em that are so, or indeed would be so, or that would rather chuse to be virtuous and good Men, than bad Princes. I dare be bold to say, that there never was yet any King, that had such sublime and noble Sentiments, and that *Alfonsus* the *Magnanimous*, King of *Arragon* and *Naples*, was not really what he would fain have seem'd to be, when he said, that he found those Advantages in Learning, which Crowns could not bestow.

The Marshal *de Biron*, whom I just mention'd, express'd the Character of the Princes of the Blood in his time after such a manner, as plainly intimated, that if their Birth made them considerable, their Qualities made them contemptible. *Anthony* King of *Navarre*, was a very weak Prince, the Cardinals *de Borbon* and *de Vendosme*, were not very rational. The Princes of *Montpensier*, *de la Rochefoucaut*, and of *Conty*, and the Count *de Soissons* were Princes of the Blood, but then that was all could be said of 'em. There was only *Henry* King of *Navarre*, and *Lewis* Prince of *Condé*, that were really greater Men than they were Princes, and did full as much Honour to their Birth as they receiv'd from it.

This is not to say, that great Lords cannot be employ'd in Embassies, and to Advantage, but then it must be in those, where there is more of the Parade than of Negotiation. After the Death of *Henry* II, King of *France*, the Princes of *Condé*, and *de la Rochefoucaut*, were sent to the King of *Spain*, the one to be present at the Oath, for the Observation of the Treaty of *Chateau Cambresis*, and the other to carry the Order of St *Michael* Anthony, King of *Navarre*, and the Cardinal *de Bourbon*, conducted the Queen of *Spain* as far as the Frontiers. The Prince *Dauphin* was sent into *England*, to negotiate the Duke of *Alançon*'s Marriage. The Duke *de Mayenne* into *Spain*, for the double Marriage, and the Duke *de Cheverense* after that into *England* Princes, and those of the first Rank after them, give a great Lustre to Embassies of Ceremony, and are properer for them than more able Negotiators, because they represent the *Sovereign* after a more natural and lively manner, in an Embassy of Obedience, at a Marriage, a Christening, or at a Funeral, where there is something more splendid and less solid than in Negotiations. The Duke of *Longueville* was employ'd in that of *Munster*, not because he had more Capacity than *d'Avaux* and *Serwien*, but because it had been agreed with *Spain*, that an illustrious Personage should be at the Head of so illustrious an Embassy. He had good Seconds, which is the common Practice, when Princes are put at the Head of Negotiations. *Lewis* IX, when he sent Count *d'Eu*, one of the Princes of the Blood, to *Philip* Duke of *Burgundy*, joyn'd with him the Chancellor *Morvilliers*, and the Archbishop of *Narbonne* and to the Lord *de Cram*, who was a Man of the Sword, the Chancellor *Doriole*. *Philip* also on his side caus'd the Lord *de Crequi*, to be accompany'd by the Bishop of *Tournay*, and *Charles* sent him his Chancellor *Hugonet*, with the Lord of *Imbercourt*. *Henry* II, in the Negotiation of the Treaty that was concluded at *Vaucelles* in the Year 1556, made use of *Sebast an de l'Aubepine* with the Admiral *de Coligny*, as *Charles* V, and *Philip* his Son, sent along with *Charles* Count of *Lalain*, *Simon Renard*, *Charles Tisnaque*, *Philip de Bruxelles*, and *John Baptist Sciccus* a Lawyer. *Henry* III, when he sent, in the Year 1581, the Prince *Dauphin* Embassador to *England*, made him be accompany'd by several Persons of Quality, and among the rest, by *Pinart*, Secretary of State, and some other Gentlemen of the Gown, who were as his Council. They had in hand one of the nicest and most difficult Affairs, that can exercise the Mind and Industry of an Embassador, the Marriage of Queen *Elizabeth*.

It is not necessary to instance in Examples, after what has been seen at *Munster*, unless we will say, that he who is at present at *Nimeguen* at the head of the *French* Embassy, has all the Sufficiency of a Man of the Gown.

The Duke of *Longueville* had many good Qualifications. But they were more proper for the Title of Highness, than that of Excellency. In the Year 1647, *Serwien* being gone to the *Hague*, where he concluded I know not what Treaty of Guaranty, and *d'Avaux* being oblig'd to make some stay at *Osnaburg*, for the settling the Affair of *Pomerania* between the *Swedes* and the Elector of *Brandenburg*, the Duke, who was left alone at *Munster*, was for negotiating like a great Lord, and being no longer under the *Ferula* of his Pedagogues, proceeded after such a manner that Cardinal *Mazarine* began to apprehend the Consequences thereof. *Serwien*, who alone was acquainted with the first Minister's Intention, said, that the Duke was going to spoil all that *d'Avaux* trifled away his time at *Osnaburg*, while his Presence was altogether necessary at *Munster*, where there was occasion for a Man, who in discussing the Rights and Pretentions of the Crowns, was well acquainted with the Propriety and Force of Words, and could dexterously make use of those Subtleties of Grammar, which Princes and Noblemen are ignorant of, unless they learn 'em of their Secretaries. That it ought to be consider'd, that one single Person was not very proper for an Affair of that Nature, more especially if his high Birth exempted him in some measure, from that submissive and blind Obedience which Subalterns have for their Superiors. And in reality, when in the Year 1639, the Nuncio *Scotti* and *Argeio Cornaro*, Embassadors from *Venice*, press'd the King to nominate Plenipotentiaries for the Congress, which was to be held at *Cologn*, and was since transferr'd to *Munster*, the King told them, that *Charnace* and *Fuquieres*, who were design'd for this Employ, being dead, there were but few Noblemen in his Kingdom, who were quality'd for it. That the greatest part of those who wear the Sword, follow rather their own Whims, than the Orders which are given them, and that he was absolutely resolv'd to suffer it no longer, but to wash away the Faults of such Embassadors with their own Blood, so that some time was requisite to make Choice of such Persons, as had the necessary Qualities for so weighty a Concern.

If these Reasons hinder Kings and Sovereigns from entrusting their Affairs with Persons, who either want Ability, or have not Obedience enough to succeed in their Negotiation, there are others, which oblige 'em to employ them on certain Occasions, where they risque nothing, and where these Persons do more Honour to their Master, than can be done by those of a meaner Condition, and indeed where there is an indispensable Necessity for a great King to employ great Personages. The Kings of *France*, *Spain* and *Poland*, &c. when they cause their Obedience to be made to the Pope, give that Commission to Dukes, and Peers, to Grandees of *Spain*, and to Lords of the first Quality in their Kingdoms, but then to make it evident, that they are only sent to make a Figure, they have an *Orator* allow'd them, who makes the Speech for the Embassador, and pronounces it in his Presence.

Altho' great Personages are not altogether so fit for the important Affairs of Embassy, yet there is not less Inconvenience in employing People of mean Extraction, to represent a Sovereign in a foreign Court. As an ordinary Dawber cannot draw an excellent Picture, nor make a good Copy of an exquisite Original, so it is impossible for a Man of a vile Condition, duly to represent a great Prince, unless it be upon the Theatre, and to divert the People. It is what admits of no Contradiction nor Exception with respect to the Character, which ought not to be prostituted. Nay I could wish the same Consideration took place, in relation to Ministers of the second Order.

Lewis XI employ'd all sorts of People. But besides that Interest was the only Motive of all his Actions, it must not be believ'd, that *Olivier Daim*, his Barber, and Valet de Chambre, was an Embassador in the same Signification that is given at this time to the Character. In those Days, Honours were done at the Entries and Audience of Embassadors, yet none at all were done to *Olivier*. On the contrary, he arriv'd at *Ghent* without Ceremony, he staid there some time to carry on his Intrigues, and he did not speak to the Princes till he was oblig'd to make his Appearance and to speak *Lewis*'s Intention was to make use of him to stir up the Inhabitants of *Ghent* to Rebellion, in which he succeeded so ill, as well as in all the other Parts of his Embassy, that it was with great Difficulty he got safe out of the Hands of the Townsmen. When *Philip de Commes* gives the Quality of Embassador, to the Merchant whom *Galeas Sforza* Duke of *Milan* sent to *Lewis* XI, he talks in the Gibberish of those Times. This pretended Embassador being arriv'd without noise at *Lions*, where the Court then was, the King order'd him to repair to *Commes*, who understanding that the Merchant had Orders to make the Duke's Peace (who had quitted the King his Brother-in-law to enter into Alliance with the Duke of *Burgundy*) and that he had a hundred thousand Crowns of Gold to offer on that score, made his Report thereof, and procur'd Audience to the Embassador. The King would not receive his Money, was contented with the Satisfaction the Duke caus'd to be made to him, consented to the Reconciliation, and suffer'd it to be concluded, and publish'd the same Day. He told the Embassador, that he had three times the Revenues of the Duke, that he did not want his Money, and that if his Repentance was sincere, he was willing to be his Friend, as he had been before.

The same King, who employ'd all sorts of Persons indifferently, made it plain, that he knew how to distinguish those who were sent to himself, in the *Deputation*, which the States of the Low Countreys made to him after the Death of *Charles* the last Duke of *Burgundy*. The Inhabitants of *Ghent* had seiz'd the Princess *Mary*, his Daughter, and pretended to have the whole Direction of Affairs put into their Hands, in conjunction with the Estates of *Flanders*, and the neighbouring Provinces. The Deputies had procur'd themselves *Letters of Credence*, and believ'd they should be very acceptable to the King, when they propos'd this Princess in Marriage to the *Dauphin*. In presenting their Letters, they spoke very presumptuously of the Authority they had in the Countrey, of the Share they had in the Management of Affairs, and of the Deference the Princess had for the Advice of the States. The King, to make them sensible of their Folly, or rather to convince 'em that the Princess made a Jest of 'em, shew'd them a Letter, wherein *Mary* declar'd, she had entrusted *Margaret* her Mother-in-law, and Dowager of *Burgundy*, with the Direction of all her Affairs, with whom she had joyn'd *Adolphus* of *Cleves*, Lord of *Ravestein*, her near Relation, as also Chancellor *Hugonet* and the Lord *d'Imbercourt*, of whom the two last were with the King, having Letters of Creance with them from the Princess. *Commes* here adds, that *Lewis*'s Intention was to create a Misunderstanding between the *Flemings* and the *Burgundians*, that he might make his Advantage of their Divisions, and that as he look'd upon those that negotiated with him to differ little from Brutes, and to have no Correspondence but only with the Rabble and Scum of the People, he was resolv'd to put them out of Countenance, and out of possibility of making any Reply, for which Reason he shew'd them the Letter, which destroy'd at once all they had said of their Credit and Power.

Altho' it be not absolutely necessary, that the Embassador should be a Man of Birth, yet at the same time there must be nothing fordid nor mean in him, unless there be something that makes amends for that Imperfection, and supplies what commonly is wanting to the Education of those who have not that Advantage, so that the Prince may be able to give to Merit, what he would not bestow on Extraction. Cardinal *Dossat* was so meanly born that his Parents were never known, but then this Obscurity was illustrated by such excellent Qualities, that King *Henry* the Great, who had a perfect Knowledge of Men, after having employ'd him in his most important Affairs at *Rome* and elsewhere, procur'd him the Ecclesiastical Dignity after that of Pope. He had not exercis'd any Trade nor Profession that he could be upbraided with as scandalous, on the contrary, he had gone through his Studies, and quitted them only to apply himself to Business, in the House of *Paul de Foix*, Archbishop of *Thoulouse* and Embassador from *France* to *Rome*, and afterwards under the Cardinals *d'Este* and *Joyeuse*.

Peter Paul Reubens was no Shame to the King of *Spain*, neither by his Birth nor Profession. The one was neither vile nor abject; and the other serv'd only to represent on Canvase, much more naturally than on Paper, the Knowledge he had of polite Learning, and to express his rich Thought much more happily thereon, than he could have done it in a Book I am therefore far from putting him in the Number of those, whose Extraction ought to exclude 'em from this sort of Employment *Ragazzoni*, whom the Republick of *Venice* sent to *Constantinople*, was a Merchant but he was of the Body of those Citizens, out of which the Senate usually takes its Ministers, and of those whom it employs abroad in the Quality of Residents or Envoys, tho' commonly speaking, Merchants are not very proper for that purpose The *Florentines* apprehending lest the Interview Pope *Clement* VII, and the Emperor *Charles* V, were to have at *Boulogne* should terminate in the loss of their Liberty, because the Emperor had promis'd the Pope to lend him his Arms to reduce the Town, sent thither *Lewis Soderin*, *Andrew Nicholini* and *Robert Beazzy*, to whom the Republick gave the Quality of Embassadors The Pope receiv'd them very ill, and treated them with so much the more Contempt, because he said, *the Republick, instead of Senators, had sent him Merchants*, and not the most considerable amongst them These Embassadors plainly discover'd that they were really Merchants, for they had hid amongst their Baggage a great Quantity of Gold and Silver Thread, with a Design to smuggle the Customs thereof, that thereby they might be enabled to sell their Goods at so much the lower Price, but the Officers having detected the Fraud, the Pope and the Emperor were diverted therewith, who sent them back without any Answer We have seen in our Time, *Michael Particelli d'Emery*, from a Merchant at *Lions* become Embassador from *France* to the Duke of *Savoy*, and afterwards Superintendent of the Finances and one of the *Northern* Crowns has within these few Years had a Minister at the *Hague* who had been a Tapestry-maker however these two were successful, in a Profession so very different from their first Calling The History of *France* speaks much of one *James Cœur*, whom *Charles* VII, made his Cofferer. He was a Merchant, but after the same manner as the *Fuggers* were so at *Ausburg*, the *Wirtminsters* and *Vidmans* at *Venice*, and a great many of the best Families are so still at *Genoa* The King employ'd him in Embassies of great Importance, and amongst the rest in that to *Rome*, whither he went with *Tanneguy du Chastel*, and labour'd with success in suppressing the Schism between the Popes *Felix* and *Nicholas*, which very much incommoded the Church Neither *James Cœur* nor *d'Emery* were any longer Merchants when they commenced Embassadors, and I do not believe there can be one single Instance brought, where these two Qualifications have met at the same time, in the same Person The Duke of *Milan*'s was so, but in a strain'd Signification

The late King of *England* made one *Auger* his Resident in *France*; he was a *Frenchman* by Birth, and by Profession a Player on the Lute, that is to say, of a Calling that border'd upon the Comedian, as this Minister had no extraordinary Merit to recommend him, so was he the first that plainly made known, what ought to be expected from that sort of People, who have neither Honour to support, nor Estate to lose This Wretch forsook the King, and serv'd the Parliament against his Benefactor

I cannot tell whether the Men of Letters are fitter for Embassy than Tradesmen but I shall not scruple to say, that an *Embassadour* is not better form'd in the College than in the Shop It the one renders us Cowardly and Self-interested, the other makes us Clownish and Opiniated, and neither in the one nor in the other is learn'd what an Embassador ought to know. When I say Men of Letters, I would be understood to mean them, who have contracted too great a Familiarity with Books, who are too much wedded to the prejudicate Opinions of the Doctors, and have more Reading than good Sense in fine, to say all in one Word, who are either Pedants by Profession, or have pedantick Sentiments Before *Europe* beheld the Knowledge of the dead Languages revive, while Ignorance cover'd the face of the Earth for the most part, the Clergy or Men of the Gown were employ'd in Embassies or at least, there were very few, but had one or other of those they call'd Clerkes mix'd with them, and this because *Latin* was taught no where but in the Cloisters, and there were none but those who came out of them, that understood it H there we must refer the Custom, that still obtains at *Rome*, where the Embassadors of Obedience have their Orators at set Salaries, who make their *Latin* Speeches for them Some Embassadors carry them along with 'em, but there are also some Crowns, that allow for that purpose a certain Pension to some eminent Person, who makes it his Profession to declaime in the Consistory, and to make the Elogium of the Embassadors and Cardinals after their Decease *Marcus Antonius Muretus*, who spoke and wrote so elegantly in *Latin*, had hardly any other Subsistence than what *France* allow'd him on that Account An Embassador who should be as well skill'd in the *Latin* Tongue as *Muretus*, ought to conceal some part of that Perfection, for fear of falling into Pedantry, which is one of the most dangerous Rocks, against which his Reputation can split *Dossat* was Learned, and President *Jeannin* was a Man of Literature, and yet there is not one Word of *Latin* to be found in all their Dispatches, which are fill'd with nothing but important Advices, strong and judicious Reasonings, and with a series of Affairs, that shews they knew something beyond what they had learn'd at School *Walsingham* had study'd, as is plain to be seen by his Letters, tho' there is not any *Latin* mix'd with them, as there is in *Thomas Smith's*, who was employ'd with him at the Court of *France* *Charles Paschal*, who has form'd the Idea of an Embassador in his Book, did not represent him very well in his Embassy to the *Grisons* And even if *Philip Canaye*, Lord of *Fresne*, Embassador from *France* to *Venice*, did not speak of him as he does, yet his Embassador, and his Embassy, which he has made publick, ought to make one judge, that he knew a great deal of *Latin* and *Greek*, but was at the same time but a very Indifferent Minister Cardinal *Bessarion* was a very fit Man to fill a Professor's Chair, to teach the *Greek* Tongue, as in reality he was one of those, that reviv'd the primitive Knowledge of it In the most *Western* Parts

The EMBASSADOR and his FUNCTIONS. 51

Parts of *Europe*, in the fifteenth Century, but when he was put into another Profession, and was vested with the Quality of *Legate*, to negotiate with the first Princes of Christendom, he discover'd his Ignorance, and made it plain that he did not know the first Rudiments of it, by going to see the Duke of *Burgundy*, before he had visited the King of *France*.

Lewis XI, reproach'd him with it, in a very stinging Raillery, and refusing to negotiate with a Minister, that made no Distinction between the two Princes, he sent him back to the Pope, who found too late the Fault he had committed, in making choice of an impertinent and ridiculous Minister *John Lascaris*, whom *Lewis* XII sent Embassador to *Venice* in the Year 1503, was little better. He was descended from a Family that had given Great Princes to the Empire of *Constantinople*, and he was moreover very Learned, but then he had not the least Knowledge of the Affairs of the World. Besides which he made but a very indifferent Appearance; which together with his mean and sordid way of living was apt to make one believe, that instead of carrying it like an Embassador, and doing Honour to the King his Master, he affected to imitate the false Modesty of those, who abandon themselves entirely to contemplative Philosophy, and make profession of a study'd Poverty, partaking a little of the *Cynick*. His Commission was by so much the more difficult, that he had Orders to borrow Money, and to make an Alliance, at a time when the Inclinations of the Senate were not in the least dispos'd in favour of the *French*, because the King's Affairs in *Italy* were not in a very good State. *Laurence Suarez de Figneroa*, Embassador from *Ferdinand* the Catholick, and who did not fail to make his Advantage of the Republick's Dissatisfaction, which could not brook the King's sending a Pedant to them instead of an Embassador, said in the open Senate, That they might easily make a Judgment after what manner the King of *France* would treat them, if after the Conquest he pretended to make of *Naples*, he should set himself Master of his Affairs, and could tyrannize over *Italy* at his Pleasure, since in his ill Circumstances and Necessities, he shew'd such a Contempt for the Senate, *as to send them a* Greek *Philosopher newly come out of the College*.

I should not here make mention of the most learned and greatest Man of that Countrey, and of our Times, if I did not find my self oblig'd thereto by the Remarks that have been made at *Brussels*, upon what I have said relating to him in my Memoirs. I don't doubt but every body easily conceives, that it is *Hugh de Groot* I here speak of. I admire, with the rest of the World, the Wit, the Probity, and the Works of that great Personage: and moreover I have particular Reasons, that make me have a Veneration for his Memory, wherefore I was very cautious of saying any thing could in the least injure his high Reputation. So that the Remarker might very well have forbore reproaching me, with what I have written concerning his Application to Study. I know that such a Man as he could not take a more honourable, nor more solid Diversion, but I could have wish'd, with the rest of his Friends, that he had not made it his Business, especially in a Post that requir'd the whole Man. I am so far also from excluding all the Learned from this sort of Employment, that I could wish that all that enter upon it were learned, provided that with their Learning, they had also all the other necessary Qualifications. *William Buæus* knew as much *Greek* as Cardinal *Bessarion* and *Lascaris*, and indeed knew it better. He had even rummaged amongst the Dust of the College, but King *Francis* II took him out of it, made him one of his Council, and since sent him Embassador to Pope *Leo* X, who being the Person to whom *Europe* is partly oblig'd for the Restoration of polite Litterature, receiv'd him as a Man who was not so learned as he was able and experienc'd. *John Jovian Pontan* had a polite Learning, which did not savour of the *Pedant*, and he was skill'd in a a great many other things, besides those that are found in Books. He was Secretary of State, and Minister to *Ferdinand* of *Arragon*, natural Son and Successor of *Alphonsus* the Magnanimous, to the Kingdom of *Naples*, who knew how to Reign, altho' he made his Government detested and abominated by his Cruelties and tyrannical Acts. This Prince employ'd him to Pope *Alexander* VI, who was another Species of Monster, but who for all that had a Value for Men of Learning, when they were withall, Men of Parts, and who shew'd him much Esteem, not so much on the account of his Scholarship, as because he consider'd him as one of the most dextrous Negotiators of his time, which was a Qualification he had acquir'd at Court, and in the Management of Affairs, not in the College, nor among Books.

I am willing the Embassador should have had some Study, because it supplies sometimes what is wanting to natural Capacity, but then I would not have him give himself up to it as well because there is a Habit contracted in reading, which is directly opposite to the constant Activity of an Embassador, as because the School infects with a certain contradicting Humour, which is inconsistent with the Character of a well-bred Man. They who study only as much as is requisite to become such, and to make Learning subservient to their Profession, have thereby a great Advantage, tho' good Sense always relieves those who have not Study'd.

The Study of polite Literature ought to be a Foundation to all the Embassador's Knowledge: There true Morality is to be learn'd, not only in those Authors who make Profession of Philosophy, but also in those who teach it with more Efficacy than they do, who reduce it into Rules and Precepts. There is no Philosopher that teaches it more agreeably than *Horace*, nor that in a sporting manner declares it better,

Quid sit pulchrum, quid turpe, quid utile, quid non,
Plenius & melius Chrysippo & Crantor.

Provided we do not strike into Criticism nor Pedantry, we shall find there the Principles of Honesty, which ought to be the first Quality of the Embassador. The Knowledge of the Civil Law, if it be founded upon that of the History of the *Roman* Laws, is an admirable Ingredient for a Minister. But there are but few that apply

ply themselve to it, because to speak the Truth, the major Part of the Doctors that teach it, do not understand it, or if they do understand it, they will not give themselves the trouble to teach it their Scholars who on their part, are contented to imbibe a very light Tincture thereof, that they may not lose that time, they think better and more profitably employ'd on the Study of the wrangling part. There is nothing but the perfect Knowledge of the State of ancient *Rome*, and of the Occasions upon which the Laws were enacted, that can give a right Judgment of the Intention of the *Legiflators*, as well as of the Reasons, upon which so many great Men have grounded the Opinions, that compose the *Digefts* or *Pandects*, as the Decrees and Edicts of the Emperors make what is call'd the *Code*, and the *Authenticks*. I must add, that a Minifter employ'd in Ordinary at the Court of *Rome*, ought not to be ignorant of the *Canon Law*, since he has not always Affairs of State to negotiate, and almost all the rest relate only to the Difpatch of Benefices, and to the Differences one may have with the Expeditionaries, for the Rights of the Officers of that Court, which are all regulated by the Decrees, Decretals, and other particular Conftitutions, which are properly the Pope's Law.

But the chief Study of those that defign to be employ'd in Embaffies, ought to be that of *Hiftory*, I comprehend under that Name all that depends thereon, and is any way useful to it, as Memoirs, Inftructions and Negotiations, and particularly Treaties, which make one of the most effential and most confiderable Parts thereof. It may be faid of *Hiftory*, that there is none fo bad but fomething useful shall be found in it. But befides that Wrong that one does one's felf, as well as to the Publick, by wafting the time fo unprofitably, there is nothing fo irksom, as to be forc'd to turn over a large Volume, purpofely to meet with one fingle Paffage that fhall be rational. Wherefore one of the first Cares of him that propofes to form an Embassador, ought to be to point out to him the *Hiftorians* that are useful and even neceffary for him to read. He will without doubt have learn'd the Names of the Ancients in the College, and will have made use of some of them to form his Style. This is the ufe that is made of them in this Age, and to fill and clog the Memory of young People, while their Judgment is ripening, not only when they do not understand the *Greek* and *Latin*, but alfo when they are forward enough to penetrate into the Sentiments of Authors, and can reafon with them. All the ancient *Hiftorians* are known, and we may fay, that all those whofe Writings are still preferv'd, are good, altho' they are not all equally capable of contributing to the Perfection of an Embaffador. *Thucidides, Xenophon* and *Polybius* amongft the *Greeks, Titus Livius, Julius Cæfar, Salluftius, Velleius Paterculus* and *Tacitus* amongft the *Romans*, ought to be read and ftudy'd. Those that have writ since the Decay, or rather Ruin of the *Roman* Empire, cannot be put upon the level with the others, and scarce in many Ages, fince the Invafion of the *Goths, Vandals*, and other barbarous Nations, to the fifteenth or fixteenth Century, have there been one or two that can be rank'd amongst the tolerable ones. *Lipfius* recommends *Lambert a' Afchaffenburg*, and fpeaks advantageoufly of *Saxo Grammaticus* but all that can be faid of the laft is, that there is fome reafon to wonder, he has written in a Stile that partakes fo little of the Barbarian, in an Age where every body was fo. Since Men have begun to imitate the Politenefs and Elegancy of the Ancients, with more Succefs than their Sculpture, there is hardly any Countrey but what has afforded fome excellent Production on this matter. Let our Politicians give the first Place to *Tacitus* if they pleafe, for my own part I fhall be bold to fay, that upon an equitable and impartial Judgment, *Philip a Comines*, Lord of *Argenton*, is nothing inferior to him in any refpect whatever, being beyond Comparifon much more Faithful and more Judicious in what he writes of the Mafters he has ferv'd, as well as of the Tranfactions and Negotiations, where he has been concern'd, and of which he has been told to have a perfect Knowledge. There is not any Book fo useful to Princes and Minifters as the *Memoirs of Comines*. His Difinterestedness appears every where, he does Juftice to every Body, and there is not any remarkable Accident, of which he does not affign the firft Caufe to His Providence, who holds the Hearts of Kings in his Hand, that is to fay, the God of Battles, who alone difpofes of Crowns and Monarches.

Nicholas Matchiavel's Hiftory of *Florence* is a compleat Work, and almoft inimitable that of *Genoa* by *Hubert Foglietta*, *George Buchanan*'s Hiftory of *Scotland*, *Sleidan*'s State of Religion in *Germany*, *Fra Paolo*'s Hiftory of the Council of *Trent*, and those of the Low Countreys by *Hugh de Groot*, and *Everard de Reyd*, are admirable Peices in their kinds. *Don Carlos Coloma* has written with great Exactness and Judgment, what pafs'd in the faid Low Countreys from the Year 1588 to that of 1600. What *Pompeo Juftiniani* has written on that Subject is very good, altho' these two illuftrious Persons hardly take notice of any other Affairs than what relate to their own Calling. *Paul Faruta* and *Baptifta Nani*, both Procurators of St *Mark*, make it appear, that they were as capable of writing the Hiftory of their Country, as of serving it in the most important Junctures. They would doubtless stand in the firft Rank, were it not for the too frequent Speeches, (not one whereof being authentick, they cannot but have been made on purpofe to eftablish Pieces of falfe Eloquence, which ought not to be admitted in Hiftory) and the extreme Indulgence they shew for their Republick. *Hierome Conneftaggio* and *Peter John Capriata* are very good Hiftorians, and come very near the excellent manner of Writin', that recommends the two laft Tomes of *Hieronymo Zurita*, tho' they are not fo prolixe, nor fo fubject to Repetitions as this laft. The Prefident *de Thoa*'s Hiftory is very well writ, as well as that of *Francis Mezeray*, who would excell all the *French* Hiftorians, if he would but give us the Continuation of it, and beftow on the Memory of *Henry* IV, and *Lewis* XIII, the fame Pen he has fo happily employ'd for their Predeceffors. The Life of *Henry* IV, by the Bifhop *de Rhodez*, fince Archbifhop of *Paris*, is an extraordinary Work. That of *Henry* VII, King

The EMBASSADOR and his FUNCTIONS. 53

King of *England*, writ by *Bacon*, passes for a judicious Piece enough, and I might say the same of that of *Henry* VIII, if *Herbert* had not too much flatter'd the Memory of a Prince, who had very great Qualities, but a great many more bad ones than good. *Benjamin Priolo*, who has writ the History of the Minority of *Lewis* XIV, by copying *Tacitus* in many places, and imitating what is defective in him in others, has not acquir'd so great a Reputation as the Abbot *Vittorio Siri*, who under the Title of *Mercurius*, has oblig'd the Publick with several Volumes of the finest Memoirs that have yet appear'd. The History or *Narrative of the Affairs of State and War*, which has been writ in *Holland* in fourteen or fifteen Volumes, contains several Treaties, Resolutions, and other authentick Pieces, so that it may serve for an Inventory to those who have not access to the *Archives* of the State. But then what the Author adds of his own, is even inferior to a *Gazette*; which way soever it be taken. He has no Stile, his Language is barbarous, and the whole Composition is a mere *Chaos*. He has this in common with the greatest part of those of that Countrey, who presume to write Histories without Authority or Leave, and almost always without Judgment and Veracity.

As for Negotiations, they may be all read, but there are some that he ought always to keep in view, as well before as during the Embassy. Those of Cardinal *D'Ossat*, and of President *Jeannin*, are alone sufficient to instruct him, and make him an accomplish'd Minister. *Francis Wallingham* was such, and has left in his Dispatches, the Idea of an Embassador worthy of the Queen he serv'd, and of the first Minister under whom he acted. I dare be bold to say, that there is not a single Letter in the two first, where there is not something of which the most able Minister may make his Advantage. I wish I could say the same of the Negotiations of Cardinal *du Perron*, and that *D'Ossat* had not had so much Modesty, when he writ to *M. de Villeroy*, that he had learn'd a great deal of the other, not only in relation to Piety, but also to the Affairs of State. To speak the truth, he was but a mere *Braggadocio*, that mock'd God Almighty, and had no solid Knowledge of the Affairs of the World. To Negotiations I must subjoyn Treaties, which instruct wonderfully, because the Embassador learns by them, not only the true State of Affairs, but also the distinct Interests of Princes. And if he has ever so little Genius, he will likewise there discover that of the Parties, and form to himself thereby those Securities and Precautions that are necessary to be taken in Negotiations.

There are also Relations of the Condition and Circumstances of Courts where Embassadors have negotiated, of which we shall take more particular Notice in the sixteenth Chapter of the second Book, wherefore I shall say no more at present, but that they give a great Insight to those who know how to make a right use thereof.

I would here make mention of other Books very useful to an *Embassador*, but that I suppose him to have seen some of them, and as he has not leisure to apply himself with Assiduity to Reading, he ought to make choice of the most necessary. I shall mark him down but one more, which is the admirable Treatise of Count *Balthasar de Castillon*, because as the *Embassador* ought to be not only an able, but also a well-bred Man, or at least carry the Appearance of one, it is impossible for him to be so, or act the Part, unless he forms himself by the Rules of Civility and Good-breeding, which that gallant Man lays down in his Book. I say nothing of the Book of *Reflections and moral Maxims*, because one cannot speak of it, nor of its incomparable Author, without injuring the Merit of both the one and the other People will perhaps be scandaliz'd when I say, that all the Works of *Nicholas Machiavel* may be of mighty use to the *Embassador*. I do not pretend to apologize for that *Florentine Politician*, and I must own there are some Passages in him that are not very *Orthodox*, but then I shall not scruple to maintain, that there are some which are capable of a more favourable Explication, than what is commonly given them by *Pedants*. We must suppose him almost every where to say what Princes do, and not what they ought to do, and if he sometimes mingles Maxims that seem inconsistent with the Rules of the Christian Religion, it is to shew the Practice of *Usurpers* and *Tyrants*, and not how lawful Princes ought to behave themselves. I suppose the *Embassador* to have a Foundation of Honour, and that he is clear sighted enough to distinguish between Good and Evil, and that he has a sufficient Knowledge of both, to be able to embrace the first, and reject the latter.

CHAP. VIII.

What Age is proper for an Embassador.

THE Advantage of Birth, in the Signification I give it in the foregoing Chapter, is very different from that which Nature bestows on them that are not indebted to their Ancestors, and are really great Men, because they bring into the World with them the first Principles of Grandeur, which they are oblig'd to no body but themselves for. A noble Extraction is a singular Ornament to an Embassy. However, Strength of Genius, and an excellent Nature, are incomparably more necessary to the Embassador. But neither Birth, in what Sense soever it be taken, nor Study, can form an accomplish'd *Embassador* without Experience, which consummates what the others only began. So that as this Employ cannot be safely committed, but to those Persons whose Years have ripen'd their Understandings,

P

ings, I shall here say a word or two concerning the *Age requisite to an Embassador*.

The Republick of *Rome* had its particular Laws to regulate the Age of its Magistrates, and most Kingdoms to this Day have their own, with reference to those who are put into *Offices of Judicature*. At *Venice* none else are advanc'd to the most important Employments of the State, but *Senators* that have pass'd through the lesser, and have given Proof of their Zeal and Ability in a long Course of Years. So that notwithstanding there are no Rules in Politicks, nor Examples in History, on which one may ground a certain Maxim, in relation to the Age requisite to an *Embassador*, yet we may safely say, that it is in a mature Age only that a Man is qualified for *Embassy* as being a Function of great Difficulty, as well with respect to the Sovereign that is serv'd, as to the Court where the Negotiations are perform'd. Aged Shepherds are rarely mistaken in the Judgment they make in the Morning, of the Weather the rest of the Day will produce. It is true, that Prudence, which must serve the *Embassador* as the *Neecaie* to guide him in all his Actions, is not always limited to a certain Age. Judgment and common Sense which form it, often perform in a young Man of five and twenty or thirty Years of Age, what sometimes the Experience of a long Life cannot effect in a thick Beard of threescore Years Growth. There are certain Climates, where the Mind ripens and attains sooner to Perfection than in others. may there are some Constitutions of Body, where the Humours are so exactly mixt, that they form an admirable Temper, the Effects whereof are discoverable in the first *Juvenile* Years, and leave very fine Remains, even in a decrepit Age. It is commonly said, that the *Florentines* are cunninger and have more Wit than the *Venetians*, but that these have sounder and more solid Judgments than the *Florentines*, the Cause whereof is sought in the Subtilty and Grossness of the Air of the two Countreys. It is certain that at *Venice* the Judgment is sooner form'd than elsewhere, and that generally speaking, they are wiser there at Thirty, than in other Places at Fifty. since it is needless to seek the Cause thereof in physical Reasonings, since there is so evident a one to be found in the moral. There is no Countrey where so many Persons have a Share in the Affairs of the Publick as at *Venice*. Every where else they are communicated but to very few Deputies or Ministers, and there is no Countrey whatever, where they apply themselves thereto so young. The Conversation of a great Number of thorough-pac'd *Sages*, forms 'em early, and the Fathers, who know but one Trade, not being able to instruct their Children in any other, it is not to be wonder'd it, if they are found capable of Business, almost as soon as they begin to know themselves. The Republick has its particular Interests, which have nothing in common with those of the other Princes of Christendom. If we except the *Port*, where she has Affairs of great moment to negotiate, and where she, for the most part, employs only such Ministers, who have pass'd through all the other Embassys, her Embassadors have hardly any other Function in the Courts where they reside, (when she is not at War, and that *Italy* is not in danger of any) than to observe the Intrigues, and the common Course of general Affairs. She makes it also her care, to place young Gentlemen with her *Embassador*, who being of equal Quality with them, and aspiring in due time to the same Employment, make it their Endeavour to be capable thereof, by forming themselves early for Business.

The *Greeks* gave the Name of πρεσβυς, from whence that of *Presbyter* comes, which signifies Elder, to their Embassadors, to shew that these Employs ought not to be given to young Men. *Philip de Commes*, whose Authority I willingly borrow, is for having Princes make use on such Occasions, of Persons neither too old nor too young, and that for this Reason that if these are subject to lash out, and be hurry'd away with Passion, those have their Weaknesses that are much more dangerous. He says, that old Men are always timorous, that they are easily alarm'd, and that they often make Reports, that are capable of disconcerting all the Measures of a Council. But then this must be understood of those Elders, in whom Age has so far extinguish'd natural Heat, that they are no longer qualify'd for Negotiations, in which a moderate Warmth is no less necessary than the Coolness of Phlegm. However, as this Deficiency discovers it self immediately, the Prince is not able to be impos'd upon thereby, unless he be so voluntarily. He both may, and ought to know those he places in so eminent and important a Post. President *Jeannin* was upwards of sixty Years of Age, when he transacted that weighty and thorny Negotiation concerning the Truce of the Low Countreys, which was one of the most considerable and most knotty we any where read of, notwithstanding which, never any Minister shew'd greater Vigour, nor more Prudence in the Management thereof, in so much, that King *Henry* IV, who was Council, which was compos'd of the ablest Men of those Times, left the whole matter to his Conduct. Provided the Blood be not altogether frozen in the Veins, we may with Safety pursue the Maxim that says, *that cool Blood is the fittest for Counsel and the warm for Execution*. The Senate of *Venice*, which is equally prudent and happy in the Choice of its Ministers, had in the Year 1539 appointed Peter Zenon Embassador to *Constantinople*, who dying by the way, *Thomas Contarini*, *who was a Nobleman of somescore and some Years of Age*, was substituted in his Place. This ancient Gentleman perform'd the Journey, and had a very favourable Audience of the Great Turk. But the Divan having inform'd him, that the Republick should not have a Peace, if she did not yield up *Malvasia* and *Napoli de Romania* to the *Turks*, and adding thereto, that he would do well to go back to *Venice*, and acquaint the Senate with the Emperor's Intention, that he might there receive the Orders, which he said he had not, for the Concession of those two Towns. He immediately left *Constantinople*, and return'd no more. The said Senate, designing to compliment *Sultan Solyman*, at his return from the *Persian* Expedition in the Year 1550, chang'd *Catherino Zeno* with that Commission, who was fourscore and four Years of Age, as well as *Contarini*, and

The EMBASSADOR and his FUNCTIONS. 55

and altho' he had several weighty Matters to negotiate, after the Compliment perform'd, yet he did not refuse that laborious and tedious Journey, and succeeded in it to admiration. *Souman*, who was a mighty generous Prince, receiv'd him very well, did him several Favours, and consented on his account, that there should be no farther mention made of the Death of *Sabba Rays*, which the *Turks* were very eager to revenge.

We have a Relation, tho' imperfect, of the Embassy that *Garcia de Silva Figueroa* perform'd in *Persia* about sixty Years since. He was not so old as *Zenon* nor *Contarini*, but he had their Eye-sores and Imperfections, to wit, Gray-Hairs, no Teeth, and was subject to Transports, that shew'd the greatest Weakness imaginable, notwithstanding which, *Philip* III's Council engag'd the good Man in that tedious Voyage, wherein he was oblig'd to double the *Cape of Good Hope*, to pass and make some stay at *Ormus*, in the worst Climate of all *Asia*, to penetrate into the remotest Provinces of *Persia*, and to negotiate with *Sbah Abas*, the cunningest and most dexterous Prince of his time. Accordingly he perform'd nothing, except it was to condemn, by the issue of his Negotiation, the Choice the first Minister of *Spain* had made of the *Negotiator*. There are Laws, that not only exempt those of that Age from that sort of Employ, but also forbid 'em meddling with publick Affairs. At the same time, it Age has its Infirmities that render it incapable, it must be own'd, that Youth has its Failings, that are inconsistent with those Qualities which the Embassador ought of necessity to have. I dare venture to say, that it is the peculiar Happiness of *Venice*, to afford Subjects who may safely be entrusted with an Embassy in their green Years, and in the Extremity of old Age. The Noblemen there are both born and die Politicians, tho' at the same time this is not so universally true, but that there are Examples which make it plain, that it is much safer to employ the one than the other. In the Year 1605, a *Venetian* Embassador of the House of *Soranzo*, in his Return from *Madrid*, quarrell'd at *Barcelona* with a Tradesman or Leather Guilder, who wounded him very dangerously. *De Fresne Canaye* says, that the Gentlemen of that Family have the Character of being haughty, and tree of their Blows; and this being young, it is reasonable to think, that he must have been very outragious with the Tradesman, to bring upon himself, by a Transport of Youth, a Disgrace which he carry'd the Marks of as long as he liv'd. We do not say but other Climates may also produce Men, who by applying themselves to Politicks in their Youth, may succeed therein; may there is not any Country, that does not afford early Wits, that ripen even in the Spring of their Age, but then these are not very common. For the most part they have in their Studies more than one Object in view, or if they have but one, it is too vast and too extensive. One would think however, that it might be laid down as a general Maxim, that a vigorous old Age ought to be preferr'd to too green a Youth, and that the most proper Age for Embassy, is from forty to threescore. We must moreover add, that some Distinction may be made in the Affairs which the Embassador

has to negotiate, some whereof may be manag'd by an indifferent Capacity, whereas others shall require the consummate Experience of a perfect Politician. The Prince has no reason to be over scrupulous in the Choice of an Embassador, who has only a Compliment to make, who barely assists at Ceremony or that has Orders to negotiate an Affair, which he will not fail of concluding, if he keeps but within the Bounds of his Instructions. On the Occasions all Ages are proper, and I should even be desirous to have young Men employ'd therein, that they might, as in an Apprenticeship, qualify themselves for better things, so far am I from excluding them. There is not any Place where a young Minister can be better employ'd than at *Venice* because there is no Court where the Conduct of an Embassador is to be followed, and where he can better learn how to act with the utmost Circumspection. The ablest Minister in the World might make in Earnestly thither his *Masterpiece*, if he had Affairs of Importance to negotiate, as she is a proper School for a Novice, that he is afraid to form himself for the Management of Matters of greater moment. Every where else the Embassador visits the Ministers of State, and is visited by them, his Secretaries and Gentlemen have Opportunities of seeing the Clerks of the Secretaries of State, and he himself may contract Acquaintance that may give him a great Insight into things, if he have but Skill enough to behave himself as he ought, and to make his Advantage of the indifferent Answers and Replys, of the Mien, and even of Silence it self, which oftentimes is very declaratory in familiar Conversations. There are some Courts where an *Embassador* is oblig'd to visit the Ladies, who very often have a great Share in Intrigues. But the Secrets of the Republick of *Venice* are almost impenetrable. Publick Ministers have no manner of Commerce there, with those that have the direction of Affairs, and are privy to the Secrets of State. They never make mention of 'em, but in the *Senate*, or in the Assemblies that represent it, so that it is impossible to learn its Intention, but when it explains it self in its Resolutions. All the *Embassador* can do, is to judge by outward Appearances, and to get acquainted with the Clergy, or others, who not being themselves in great Offices, have either Friends or Relations that are, of whom they may perhaps learn something. And even this it self is so hard a matter to compass, that it is an extraordinary Happiness to be successful in it. *Francis of Carmagnole*, the *Venetian* General, being suspected to hold Intelligence with the *Turks*, the Senate resolv'd to put him to Death. Above a hundred and fifty Persons, and amongst the rest some of *Carmagnole*'s Relations and Friends, were privy to the Deliberations and Resolutions taken thereupon and yet for all that *Carmagnole* got no Knowledge of the matter during the eight Months he delay'd going to *Venice*. We may infer from the Treasons of the *Cavazzas* and *Abondio*, (the Particulars whereof shall be related in the 28th Chapter) that there are venal Souls at *Venice* as well as elsewhere. And that altho' it be no easie Task to penetrate there into the Secrets of the State, yet nevertheless it is not a thing absolutely impossible.

The

The Crown of *Sweden* employ'd in *France*, and in some other Courts, the Counts *Tott*, *Oxenstiern*, *Spar*, *Koningsmark*, and *Magnus de la Garde*, who were all very young. But, besides that the last was assisted by the S*eur Strasburg*, Son-in-law to *Camerarius*, who help'd him with his Counsel, It may be said with reference to him and all the rest, that in *Sweden* Employments are given to young Noblemen, because those that are in Years, and have a fix'd Settlement will not quit their Post, nor load themselves with an Expence that would sit heavy upon them. The Count de la Garde had no other Commission, but that of a Compliment on the Peace the *French* had effected between the two *Northern* Crowns by the Mediation of *la Tuillerie*, while the Gross of Affairs were discuss'd between the Ministers of the Allies at *Munster* and *Osnabrug*

The Conduct of the young Cardinal *Hypolito de Medicis*, of whom I shall say something in the 10th Chapter, was so rash and inconsiderate, that notwithstanding he was *Clement* VII's Legate, the Emperor *Charles* V, confin'd him That of *Charles Caraffa*, Nephew and Legate of *Paul* IV, was not much more prudent, neither in *France* nor *Spain* It is three and fifty Years since Cardinal *Francis Barbarin*, who is at present Dean of the College, was Legate in those two Kingdoms, and notwithstanding he was directed by the Counsel of *Pamphilio*, Auditor of the Legation, and who has since been Pope under the Name of *Innocent* X, yet he was guilty of some youthful Slips The Courts of *Vienna* and *Madrid* have within so ne Years seen a Minister, who had no more Hair upon his Face than in the Palm of his Hand and the *Hague* has had the Diversion of an Embassador, who being but a School-boy disguis'd, let every body perceive what he was in reality, by striking into those Vanities that turn'd his Brain, and degenerated into Extravagancies that have caus'd him to be shut up in a Madhouse

Whatever the Advantages of Birth may be, and what other natural Qualities soever come along with us into the World, it is Man must supply and rectify what is still wanting and imperfect and indeed You thought not to be employ'd but with the greatest Circumspection imaginable Its Slips and Inadvertencies are inseparable from it, till Experience has render'd it capable of the Management of Affairs It is for this Reason that the Republick of *Venice*, which for the most part has no great Interest to manage in the Courts of *France* and *Spain*, is not afraid of employing young Gentlemen there, that they may learn, and become capable of negotiating at *Rome*, and principally at *Constantinople*, where they employ only such Ministers as have given Proofs of their Ability in several other Embassies, whereof we have Examples in the Histories of *Venice*, which are full of them *France*, *England*, and almost all the other Potentates of Christendom, except the Emperor, who as King of *Hungary*, is a Neighbour, and reconcil'd Enemy of the *Turk*, have hardly any thing else to negotiate at the *Port*, excepting a bare Interest of Commerce for which Reason they sometimes there make use of Persons, whom they could not employ in other Courts, without prostituting their Interest, who notwithstanding make a good Figure in that There are Princes that are very reserv'd in this Point, and who fill that Post with such Subjects only, as can do them Honour, but it is not in those Countreys, where sometimes Favour, often Chance, and always Interest, but never the Choice and Judgment of the Master, disposes of the Embassies *France* has not always been happy herein, altho' she has had great Men there, who would have done her Honour in a Christian Court, as well as in the *Turkish* The Marquis de *Gnast*, Governor of *Milan*, who could discern Merit perfectly well, said of *Anthony Paulin*, Baron de la Garde, who in *Francis* I's time, was often employ'd to *Constantinople*, and was there related by *M de Langes*, Governor of *Piedmont*, that he was the wisest *French* Gentleman he had ever seen

M de Cesis was so great a Minister, that at ter two and twenty Years Embassy at *Constantinople*, where he had made himself admir'd, he was entrusted with the Education of the Duke of *Orleans*, Brother to *Lewis* XII The Character of *Achilles de Harley*, Baron de Sancy Successor and Kinsman of *M de Cesis*, is mention'd in the Relations of *Pietro della Valle*, who speaks of him these Terms " He was " a Nobleman of about thirty Years of Age, that " is to say, very young, and who at that Age " had gone through his Courses of Philoso- " phy, Divinity, and Law, as being destin'd " for the Gown but as he took to the Sword, " he apply'd himself to the Mathematicks, " wherein he made that Proficiency which got " him a very great Reputation, as he really " was one of the greatest Men of this Profes- " sion He had moreover a perfect Know- " leage of Simples, and had penetrated into " the most private Recesses of Chymistry As " for Languages, besides the *French* which was " natural to him, he knew the *Italian*, *Spanish* " and *German*, both the ancient and modern " *Greek* as well as the *Latin*, and in a little " time, with small Labour, he learn'd the *H - " brew* so well in *Constantinople*, that he un " derstood the *Rabbies*, and spoke it tolerably " All this in conjunction with what he knew " of the History of all Ages, and of all Nati- " ons, as well as of the separate Interests of " Princes, form'd a compleat Minister, at an " Age when others only begin to enter into " the Knowledge of Affairs I'll joyn to this *Embassador* him that his lately left *Venice*, where he has been for the space of some Years on the part of *France* He is mighty young, yet at the same time he is prudent in the highest Degree, and of a Capacity hardly to be attain'd to It is so indifferent Perfection that it will procure the Approbation of *Lewis* XIV And it is most certain, that ordinary Qualities would never have acquir'd him the Esteem of the wisest Senate in the World, to that degree as he possess'd it His Memoirs and Discourses express so great a Justness, he gives so admirable a Turn to his Thoughts, and he serves the King his Master with so punctual an Exactness, that the Success is much beyond what could be expected from a Minister of sixty Years of Age This will be less wonder'd at, when it is known, that he is the Son of a perfect Minister, and

all

all these fine Qualities are hereditary to him This is what cannot be said of *Julius Mazarine* He had learn'd nothing of his Father, and yet at twenty Years of Age he commenc'd Minister, and at seven and twenty he was able to give Instructions in Matter of Negotiations, so that it would be a difficult Point to fix the proper Age for an *Embassador*, which ought not so much to be regarded as his Merit Certainly if the Court may be look'd upon as a rough tempestuous Sea, full of Rocks and Shelves, and cover'd with Pirates and Rovers, it must be own'd to be requisite, that the Minister who engages himself in the one, and the Pilot who imbarks on the other, ought both to have, not only an undaunted Courage, but a consummate Experience, which is to be acquired only by Age

CHAP. IX

Whether Clergymen are proper for Embassies.

THE Author of the *Idea of the perfect Embassador*, declares for the Affirmative, and backs his Opinion with several Examples taken out of the Bible, and from History, which he would be glad to include entirely in his Book I shall not enquire into the Justness of the Examples, but I think I may say, he alledges very few that square with his Intention The Priests that slew the Victims and Sacrifices, and march'd at the head of the Armies of the People of *Israel*, were not Embassadors, neither did they do the Functions thereof Those religious Men whom Popes formerly sent to the Emperors were not so neither, because they were only Subjects who begg'd to have their Election confirm'd or implor'd the Protection and Justice of their Sovereign I also very much question what the same Author says, that there is no Law, either Human or Divine, that forbids the Clergy being employ'd in Embassies It is true, that since the spiritual Power has been confounded with the temporal Jurisdiction in the Person of the Pope since Cardinals are put upon the level with Kings, and Bishops are at the same time both Princes and Prelates, all the Clergy follow their Example, and imitate the Liberty they take, to meddle with all sorts of Affairs without distinction, but there are some among them who look upon it to be against God's Commands, and contrary to the Precepts of Christianity God would not allow the *Levites* to have any Share with the other Tribes, that their Affiduity and constant Attendance on the Service of the Altar, might not be interrupted by the Care they would be oblig'd to take to till their Lands, and preserve their Estates It is for this Reason he also says, he will be their Portion and their Inheritance Our Lord *Jesus Christ* says, his Kingdom is not of this World, that those who will follow him, must renounce all things, and cast off all Solicitude for temporal Goods, that they may with less Incumbrance travel on in the Path they are to follow during the whole Course of their Lives That he who has once set his Hand to the Plough must not look back, and that he who has once dedicated himself to the spiritual Ministry, is no more to intermeddle with the Affairs of the World There is no serving of two Masters, nor dividing the Heart, which has been once given and entirely devoted to God

At *Venice* the Clergy have no share in the Management of State Affairs, and it is to be admir'd that Princes should still employ *Prelates* to the Court of *Rome*, as well because they cannot prosecute a *Bishop*, who is sworn to, and depends on the Jurisdiction of the See of *Rome*, as because Prelates have more to hope for from the *Pope*, than from their *Master* A noble *Venetian*, whose Brother, Uncle or Nephew is a Cardinal, is excluded from all Deliberations relating to Ecclesiastical Affairs The Cardinals *d'Amboise* and *du Prat*, who were very disinterested *Prelates*, had a very great Hand in the Government, the one under *Lewis* XII, and the other under *Francis* I, but they would never be present at the Debates in Council on the Affairs relating to the *Pope* The Cardinal *de Lorain*'s Insolence was too excessive, to permit him to use the same Modesty, under *Francis* II, and *Charles* IX And the Cardinals *de la Rochefoucault*, *Richelieu*, and *Mazarine*, who were prime Ministers under *Lewis* XIII, and at the beginning of the present King's Reign, and had the absolute Disposal of Affairs, would also order such as related to the Pope, according as they were well or ill affected towards him Cardinal *Mazarine* was perfectly the Aversion of *Innocent* X, and *Alexander* VII, so that he could not be suspected to have too much Friendship or Complaisance for 'em and yet he was extraordinary careful to keep in with the Court of *Rome* *Richelieu* had a great Regard for *Urban* VIII, because he was no less affected to the Court of *France*

The Republick of *Venice*, which is admirable in all its Conduct, and in all its Maxims, is particularly so, *in not suffering Ecclesiasticks to enter the Senate* It considers that they who live in the State of Celibacy, not being sensible of that Tenderness marry'd Men have for their Children and Families, cannot have that natural Affection for a Countrey, which they cannot be succeeded in by their Posterity, as having none, and that those who take to the *Church*, become as it were Strangers, and Subjects to a foreign Power It is on this account that the *Venetians* will not allow their Gentry to accept of Benefices from the Pope, or to receive any Dignity from him, without the Consent or Recommendation of the *Senate* When *Mark Anthony Amulio* was *Embassador* at *Rome* from the *Republick*, Pope *Pius* IV, gave him a Bishoprick in the State of *Venice* The Senate was so offended at it, that Orders were immediately dispatch'd to the *Embassador*, to take his leave of the Court of *Rome*, and come away to give an account of his Actions. The Pope, who lov'd *Amulio*, perceiving he was become the Cause, tho' innocently, of his Friend's Disgrace, writ to the Senate, that *Amulio* was so far from asking the Bishoprick he had given him, that he did not so much as know his Intention therein, when he bestow'd it on him. To this he joyn'd such vehement and lively Protestations, that the Senate, to oblige the Pope, sent fresh Orders to *Amulio* to continue at *Rome*. He had already left that City upon his first Orders, but the Express meeting him on the way, oblig'd him to return thither again. Afterwards the *Senate* particularly charg'd him, to sollicit with the utmost Zeal and Diligence, the obtaining of a Cardinal's Cap for *John Grimani*, Patriarch of *Aquileia*, to which *Amulio* apply'd himself with all the Warmth and Affection imaginable, and the rather, because he hop'd by that Service to blot out the Memory of the Displeasure the Senate had express'd at the Pope's Proceeding. But some few Days before the great Promotion, which was made in *February* 1561, *Pius* acquainted him with the Reluctancy the *Inquisition* shew'd to the Promotion of *Grimani*, on account of his Sentiments touching Predestination, which were reported not to be very conformable to those of the Church of *Rome*. Whilst the Consistory, wherein the Promotion was to be made, was held, the Pope, who had sent for *Amulio*, caus'd him to be shut up in one of the Chambers of Cardinal *Boromeus*'s Apartment, till he had declar'd him Cardinal with the rest. *Amulio* would have excus'd himself, and alledg'd, that besides that Dignities being far above his Merit, he could not accept of it without leave from the Republick. But the Pope having commanded him to accept it, under pain of Disobedience, he thought himself no longer oblig'd to resist the gentle Compulsion, and answer'd, that being the Subject of a Republick, which professes the most profound Obedience to the Holy See, he thought it his Duty no longer to defer obeying the Pope. The *Senate*, which had been refus'd *Grimani*, and which had shew'd it self so highly displeas'd at the first Promotion of *Amulio*, had the less Reason to be satisfy'd with this, as being persuaded, that the Discontent express'd for the one, had drawn upon them the other. For this Reason, when the Senate sent one of its Secretaries to *Rome*, to thank the Pope for the Promotion of *Navager*, who had been honour'd with the Purple in the same Consistory, not one Word was said of *Amulio*, and his Relations were forbid making any Bonfires, or other publick Rejoycings, which are customary on the like Occasions.

There is still another powerful Reason, which ought to hinder Princes from employing Prelates or Clergymen of any Rank whatsoever on their Embassies. It may be said, that whatever Faults an Embassador commits, are in a manner criminous, and that they are not in reality always free from Guilt, and yet, the Prince who has no Jurisdiction over Ecclesiasticks, can neither punish nor chastise them, except only by Seizure of their temporal Estate. At the same time that *Henry* III, King of *France*, caus'd the Duke of *Guise* to be kill'd during the meeting of the States at *Blois*, and afterwards the Cardinal, Brother to the Duke, he also confin'd *Peter d'Espinac* Archbishop of *Lyons*, who was one of the Heads of the League. Some of the Duke's Domesticks had been also seiz'd at the same time, and upon their Depositions, the Archbishop was to have been examin'd by two Members of the Great Council, but he refus'd to answer. The King sent Cardinal *Gondy* Archbishop of *Paris* to him to oblige him to answer, but he said he would answer before the Pope, or such Commissioners as the Pope should appoint. However, if Cardinal *Morosin*, who was then Legate in *France*, and he the Cardinal *Gondy* were of Opinion, that he ought to answer before the Commissioners of the Great Council. He would do it, but that then they would be the Persons that infring'd the *Rights of the Church*, and that must be accountable for it to the Pope, and not he. The King's Council asserted, that in Cases of Treason, and especially those of the highest Nature, a Bishop was oblig'd to answer before the King's Judges and several Precedents is well Domestick as Foreign, were brought to warrant the same, which had been taken out of the Archives and Records of Parliament. Upon this Foundation *Nicholas Fumée*, Bishop of *Beauvais*, and *Beaulieu Ruse*, Secretary of State were sent to dispose him to submit to be examin'd. But the Archbishop told *Fumée*, that if he pretended to examine, as being himself a Prelate, he ought to consider, that as a Bishop he had no Superiority over him, who was an Archbishop, and his Primate, and that if it pretended to do it as a Peer of *France*, he could not be ignorant, that the *Jurisdiction* of the *Peers* did not extend to his *Person*. This was all the King could get from him, so that he was oblig'd to let him alone.

In like manner, when the same King sent the Bishop of *Mans* to *Rome*, to justify his Proceedings with respect to the Death of the Cardinal *de Guise*, the Pope told him, that he had nothing to say to him on account of the Duke's Death, who being the King's Subject, he had a Right, as his Sovereign, to execute Justice upon him, provided it were done in due form, but that he expected Satisfaction should be made him for the Death of the Cardinal, who was his Subject, and not the King's, *because all Cardinals are exempted from the Jurisdiction of Secular Princes, and become the Pope's Subjects, as well as Archbishops and Bishops, who take a particular Oath to that purpose*. That the King ought to have put the Cardinal into the Legate's Hands, who would have sent him to *Rome*, where he should have been try'd upon the Informations the King should have sent thither. Pope *Urban* VIII, said, that the Bishop of *Lamego* was his Subject, and having proceeded against him as such, caus'd him to be condemn'd.

The Cardinal *de Balue* had been convicted of having conspir'd with the Duke of *Guyenne*, Brother to *Lewis* XI, and with the Dukes of *Britany* and *Burgundy*, against the publick Tranquillity, and against the King's Person. He confess'd his Crime, and was sent to the *Bastille*, where he remain'd eleven Years, during which time, the Pope was continually making pressing Instances to have him put into his Hands, *because he was not under the King's Jurisdiction*. The King himself did not pretend to have a *Jurisdiction*

The EMBASSADOR and his Functions. 59

diction over the Person of the Cardinal, but he was for having the Pope to appoint Judges to try him within the Kingdom, and refus'd to send him to *Rome*. This Dispute was the cause of the Cardinal's long Detention, and yet the King never durst deliver him up to the secular Justice, nor indeed to the ordinary Judges of the Church. The Cardinal was born the King's Subject, besides which he was bound to him by a particular Oath, on account of the Temporalities of his Bishoprick, but only the Pope can appoint Judges to try a Bishop, and none but himself can preside at the Tryal of a Cardinal. The Cardinal *de Retz* was taken into Custody at the *Louvre*, and sent Prisoner to the Castle at *Vincennes* about the end of the Year 1652. But Cardinal *Mazarine* who was afraid of his Genius, and who had caus'd him to be apprehended out of a Jealousy of State, because he look'd upon him as the only Man in the whole Kingdom, who was most likely to dispossess him of the Post of first Minister, durst not nevertheless advise the King to appoint Judges to try him, tho' Pretexts are never wanting to those who are in Power. The Emperor *Ferdinand* I, caus'd *George Martinuzzi*, Cardinal of *Hungary*, to be put to Death. And in the Year 1618, *Ferdinand*, King or Bohemia and afterwards Emperor, concerted with *Maximilian*, Arch-Duke of *Austria*, the seizing of Cardinal *Clesel*, and caus'd him to be convey'd into *Tirol*; but Justice had no Share in those two Acts of Violence, no more than in the Imprisonment of Cardinal *de Retz*; and the Pope, justifying *Clesel*, adjudg'd the Authors of that Injustice that had been done him, to restore to him all that had been taken from him, under Pain of Excommunication, tho' it was six Months after the Fact, and upon a hearing of the Cause. Cardinal *Dossat*, who was a good Frenchman, faithful, and very zealous for the Service of the King, his Prince and Master, in his Letter to King *Henry* IV, of the 10th of February 1601, on the Subject of his Promotion, for which he was oblig'd to his Majesty, said, he could never have believ'd, that he would have procur'd him that Honour, since being thereby become the *Pope's Subject*, his Majesty might have reason to question his serving him for the future with the same Fidelity as he had done till then. A Consideration that worthy Man, and wise Politician, offer'd to the King, his Sovereign and Benefactor, to make him sensible, that the Oath the Cardinals take to the Pope, withdraws them from the Subjection they owe to their natural Princes on account of their Birth.

About the beginning of the Year 1645, Cardinal *de Valençay*, who had obtain'd the Purple without the King's Permission, nay even against his Intention, having left *Rome* without the Pope's Consent, in order to return to *France*, to use his Endeavours to make the Peace of the *Barberini*, who at that time were much out of favour at Court, the Queen Regent, who had been acquainted with his Journey by Cardinal *Bichi*, sent a Gentleman to meet, and tell him he must turn back, without coming any farther, and that if he had any private Business in *France*, he might give the Charge thereof to some of his Relations. The Cardinal, who suspected some such Orders might be sent him, declin'd meeting the Gentleman, embark'd on the River *Loire* at *Roane*, and came into *Paris* about Midnight. As soon as the Queen knew it she commanded him to leave the Town the same Day, and to depart the Kingdom in three Weeks. But the Person who carry'd the Order, not finding him very well dispos'd to obey the same, she resolv'd to confine him. However, before it went so far she sent for *M Bagny*, the Pope's Nuncio to whom she said, *she was sorry to find her self reduc'd to a Necessity of proceeding with rigor against Cardinal* Valençay, *to support the King's Authority, but that before she came to that Extremity, she was willing to give the Nuncio a Proof of the Respect the King had for the See of* Rome, *by communicating her Resolution to the Pope's Minister which she conceiv'd she had sufficiently comply'd with, since after having communicated her Design to the Nuncio, nothing could hinder the King from causing himself to be obey'd in his own Dominions* Bagny confess'd, that the Cardinal had justly drawn upon himself the King's Indignation by his Obstinacy, but he desir'd the *Queen* to suspend the Execution till he had spoken with *Valençay* Accordingly he spoke to him, and having dispos'd him to obey, obtain'd some few Days delay for his Return. He would not have been so positively press'd to depart *Paris*, had he shewn a little more Complaisance. He went to *Villeroy*, whither *Lionne*, and afterwards Cardinal *Mazarin* himself went to visit him, and concerted with him a Project of Reconciliation for the *Barberini*. He was a Frenchman, *born the King's Subject, and came to confer about a Matter, which at first was not very agreeable*, by reason of the Behaviour of the two Brothers, *Francis* and *Anthony*, and yet the Queen durst not proceed with rigor against him, without acquainting the Pope, tho' she knew *that his Negotiation could not be acceptable to his Holiness*. It is true the same Regard was afterwards had for the Cardinal *de Retz*, but besides that at that time, the Pope himself was not much regarded there, it concern'd the Peace of the first Minister, on whose Welfare, both the King and Kingdom then seem'd to depend.

Some Years since Cardinal *Imperiale*, being oblig'd to leave *Rome*, to make some Satisfaction to the King of *France*, who thought him an Accomplice in the Insolence of the *Corsican* Guards, and in the Neglect of Pope *Alexander* VII, and of the *Chigis* who had not punish'd the same, retir'd to *Genoa*, his native Country. The Senate apprehending lest his Residence there should create them some Troubles with *France*, endeavour'd to dispose him to a voluntary Retreat, and made use of the Mediation of his Brother *Carlo Imperiale* to that purpose. But the latter, who was himself a Senator, instead of going about it, told the Person who brought him the Message from the Republick, that it was not in the Power of the Senate, to oblige a Citizen of that Quality, who had committed no Crime, either against the State, or *against the Pope, his Sovereign*, to depart the City. That it was with his Holiness's Consent, and even by his Orders, that the Cardinal his Brother was come to *Genoa*, and that he could not retire elsewhere, without another express Order to that Effect. That besides, he

was

was a Clergyman, and as such, no way subject to the Orders of the Republick, which could not lay any Commands upon him. That his Brother would not withdraw, and that if he were necessitated to yield to violence, the Senate would be one day accountable for it. The Senate of Genoa by expelling the Cardinal, offended the Pope, but by suffering him to stay in their Town, they offended France, whose nearness and power they dreaded, and they knew that France would not fail to comprehend them in the accommodation that should be made with the Court of Rome. They were not oblig'd to suffer a Subject in their Town, who was so no longer, and who being become such to a foreign Prince, and yet no publick Minister, could no longer hope to be protected there, so that there was nothing to induce them to disoblige the King, who had it but too much in his power to resent the Retreat they should give to a Cardinal, whom he had compell'd to leave Rome, which render'd their apprehension much more lawful, than that of some Princes, who being afraid of their own Shadow, dare not give their own Minister that Protection, which they owe him by all the Laws of Honour and Justice. Whereupon there is one necessary Remark to be made against the position of those, who out of their Ignorance, judge, that nothing can free a Subject from the Jurisdiction of the Sovereign of the Country where he was born.

This exemption and independence of the Cardinals, together with the Rank they pretend to, and which they take above the first Princes after crown'd Heads, are the Cause why some Countries do not willingly suffer them. The King of Poland generally gives his nomination to Strangers, and the Republick of Venice think it enough barely to recommend those Subjects it would have vested with that Dignity. Neither does it take much pains to gain the friendship of the Cardinals, or to make Partisans in their College, which might make it regarded in the Elect on of Popes, tho' it is not less its Interest than that of the other Potentates of Italy, to keep a good understanding with the Court of Rome. It has a thousand ways to compass the same, but the Senate is of opinion that there are already but too many factions among the Cardinals, and being apprehensive lest those it should foment at Rome, might communicate their Contagion to Venice, and so infect the Republick, it has not thought fit to be concern'd therein, thus one of its first and gravest Senators delivers himself on that Head. I or the same Reason, Ferdinand King of Arragon, would not suffer Pope Alexander the Sixth to make a promotion of several Cardinals, who were most of 'em the King's Subjects, born in Catalonia, in Arragon, or in Valencia, and would not consent to it, till the Pope had promis'd him a Cap for the Bishop of Albi, who had contributed most towards disposing Charles VIII to restore Roussillon. Nay, even those Kings who affect and think it behoves them to have many Partisans in the College, are not for having it fill'd with their own Subjects, without their participation. Henry IV took it very ill, that Clement VIII had given a Cap to the Bishop of Lisieux, afterwards call'd the Cardinal de Givry, who was not in his favour. And the Court was not at all pleas'd with the promotion of the Cardinals de Marquemont, and Valença, under Urban VIII, tho' at last it consented to that of the first of them.

What I said above concerning the Archbishop of Lions, plainly shews, that the Cardinals are not the only Persons who enjoy this Exemption, but that it also extends to other Prelates, and particularly to Bishops. In the Year 1607, the Cantons of Uri and Lucern, sent to represent to Charles Paschal, the French Embassador, that it was a surprising thing to see the Bishop of Coire, who could acknowledge no other Judge than the Pope, subject to the Jurisdiction of a Tribunal the Grisons had erected extraordinary. The Judges of that Tribunal, to whom they had given the name of Straigerigt, according to the custom of all Incompetent Judges, did not scruple to proceed farther, and condemn'd the Bishop to pay the summ of twelve hundred Crowns, as well for Damages, as Fines and Charges. They made void and annull'd whatever he had done at Milan, except only what related to the Rights of his Bishoprick, and ordain'd, that his Person and temporal Estate should be subject to the three Leagues, with a prohibition to him not to meddle with the affairs of the State. On which Conditions, they promis'd to forget what was pass'd, and on the contrary, threatned to dispossess and to appoint him a Successor, if he did not abide by the Sentence. But all Men may plainly see, that this whole proceeding was violent, and unjust, as an usual consequence of those disorders, which are but too frequent in a State, where a predominant Faction oppresses the other, especially when Religion is concern'd, as it then happen'd amongst the Grisons, where that Stratgerigt, and whatever it had ordain'd, was soon abolish'd. A Roman Catholick King, let him be ever so absolute and despotick, can never cause a Bishop to be try'd by Regal Judges, that is to say, by the common Justice, but must desire the Pope to appoint Judges to try him.

When the Queen Mother Mary de Medicis, withdrew from Compiegne, to go into the Low Countries, she made use of a Coach, which one of the Noblemen of her Attendance had borrow'd of the Bishop of Leon in Britany. Cardinal Richelieu, who did not love that Prelate, and who was very revengeful, in the year 1632, obtain'd a Brief, by which the Pope appointed four Bishops, to Try all those Ecclesiasticks, of what Quality soever they might be, who should be found to have done any thing against the King's Person, or disturb'd the quiet of the Kingdom. Those four Bishops dispossess'd the Bishop of Leon, and sequester'd his Bishoprick. But after the Cardinal's death, the Bishop having made his Complaint to the General Assembly of the Clergy, where he represented the Irregularity of the four Bishop's proceedings, the King's Council thought fit that he should appeal to the Court of Rome, because the Assembly was of opinion, that the Sentence was not Canonical. The Bishop did so, and had the Sentence revers'd, the King and his Judges had no hand in it, on the contrary, his Majesty recommended his Subject's Case to a foreign Judge. Sebastian de Matos, Archbishop of Bra-

ga, was chief of the Conspirators, who had undertaken to kill *John* IV King of *Portugal*, at the beginning of his Reign. He was taken into Custody, *never was any Treason of the first Class better prov'd*. His Accomplices the Marquis *de Villareal*, the Duke *de Caminha*, the Count *d'Armamar*, and some others were executed, but the Archbishop, the Inquisitor General, and some other Clergy-men of a lesser Rank remain'd Prisoners, because there was no competent Judge to try them, without a particular Commission from the Pope for that purpose. This was afterwards one of the Causes, or Pretexts Pope *Urban* VIII made use of, not to admit the Bishop of *Lamego* Minister from *Portugal*, because the King detain'd in his Prisons several Prelates and Clergymen, whom he ought to put into the Pope's hands.

Never any Subject ow'd greater obligations to his Sovereign, than *Thomas Becket* did to *Henry* III King of *England*, the King had rais'd him from nothing, to the highest Dignities in his Kingdom, making him Chancellor, and afterwards Archbishop of *Canterbury*, and Primate of all *England*. Yet it may be said, that never was any Subject more obstinately rebellious, nor Prelate more insupportably proud. He delighted in opposing the foreign and unjust power of the Pope, to the lawful and sovereign Authority of his King, so that his Insolence being become very troublesom, the King prosecuted him with so much warmth, that he compell'd him to pass the Sea to seek his protection, whose unlawful Authority he had so often asserted against the King his lawful Sovereign *Henry*, who instead of putting his Subject into the hands of Justice, endeavour'd to bring him to his Duty by fair means, follow'd him into *France* (where the Archbishop had confer'd with the Pope) and allow'd the King of *France* to mediate an Accommodation so far, as that to overcome the obstinacy of that Man, he consented that the Clergy of *France* should take cognizance of the difference, and adjust it. But the Archbishop, who would admit of no other Judge nor Arbitrator than the Pope, whose Interest was the ground of the quarrel, refus'd to submit to it, and gave the King so much trouble, that he was oblig'd to let him return to his Diocese. This Clergyman was no sooner arriv'd in *England*, than he excommunicated the Archbishop of *York*, and refus'd to reconcile the other Prelates, who had sided with the King. So that *Henry* being out of patience, and not able to put him into the hands of Justice, grew at last so melancholy, that he could not forbear signifying in his familiar Conversations, that it would be a thing very acceptable to him, if any body would rid him of so vexatious and insufferable a Man. Whereupon some Gentlemen kill'd the Archbishop in his Church. But the Pope proceeded against them with so much Rigour, that the King for fear of being accounted an Accomplice, or Author of the Murther, disown'd it, and clear'd himself by Oath.

But to the end it may not be imagin'd, that none but Cardinals and Prelates enjoy the privilege of this Exemption, I lay it down as a Position, that they hold it in common with all other Clergymen, so that herein I comprise not only *the Commanders and Knights of the Order of St John of Jerusalem, or of Malta*, but also all Priests and Religious Persons, of what Quality or Order soever they are. There needs no other proof for what I have here said, than the Contest the Republick of *Venice* had with Pope *Paul* V in the first years of his Pontificate, and of that *Century*. The *Venetians* had no very good understanding with the See of *Rome*, by reason that what was transacting at *Venice* for the better preserving the Temporal Jurisdiction, was altogether ungrateful to the Pope. The Council of Ten, which judges sovereignly there of Criminal Matters, had caus'd a Canon, whose Name was *Vincent Scipio Sarasin*, to be taken into Custody, as also Count *Brandolin Valdemarino*, Abbot of *Nerveze*, whom they were preparing to try for enormous and heinous Crimes. The Prisoners desir'd to be refer'd to the Ecclesiastical Judge, and the Nuncio interposing, the Pope declar'd, he would not suffer the Council of Ten to take cognizance of the Crimes of the Clergy. And forasmuch as they continu'd at *Venice* to proceed on the Tryal of the Prisoners, the Pope had recourse to *Censures*, and afterwards to Excommunication, and to an Interdict. The difference was warmly debated on each side, and with so much obstinacy, that had it not been for the good offices *Henry* IV caus'd to be done by the Cardinals *Joyeuse* and *Perron*, and by *Bethune* and *du Fresne*, his Embassadors in ordinary at *Rome* and at *Venice*, it would have been a hard matter to have extinguish'd the fire the War was about to kindle in *Italy*. It was indeed prevented, but the Senate of *Venice* was oblig'd to deliver up to the Pope the two Prisoners, who were for that purpose brought to the Doge's Palace, and there put into the hands of a Doctor, and one of the Pope's Commissioners, before witnesses, of which a verbal Process was made, before the Censures were taken off. It cannot be deny'd, but that by such a solemn Act, after a Contest maintain'd with obstinacy for some years, the Republick renounc'd any Jurisdiction it could pretend to have over the Clergy.

Now to the end it may not be said that it was on account of the Dignity of the Abbot, and of the Canon, that the Pope would take cognizance of their Case, I shall here add that of a plain Monk. About the latter end of the year 1647, there was an Almanack sold about *Turin*, which, among other things, contain'd several dismal Predictions for the ensuing year, wherein the Prince's own Person was not spar'd. The Almanack was the product of a Monk of the Order of St *Bernard*, whose Name was *Don John Gandolfo*, and who had formerly been of the Order of the Reform'd *Augustin*'s. That crafty Monk, who knew more than the making of Almanacks, finding his Conscience trouble him, made his escape, but was seiz'd at *Ceva*, where he had hid himself in a Monastery, waiting for an opportunity to retire to *Savona*, which is in the Territory of *Genoa*. As soon as he was in Custody, he writ to the Dutchess of *Savoy*, that he had things of very great moment to discover to her, wherein her own Life, and that of the Duke her Son were concern'd. The Monk being carry'd to *Turin*, preparations were making

king for his Tryal, *in the presence of a Delegate from the Nuncio* He Impeach'd two of his Accomplices, one whereof dy'd in Prison, and the other was executed But the Nuncio not being willing that the Secular Judge should draw up his Indictment, had revok'd the power of his Commissioner, and the Pope making a difficulty to appoint another, *all proceedings against the Prisoner were superseded*, till the Nuncio had desir'd the Bishop of *Maurienne* to examine him, the Pope having consented thereto The Monk confess'd the Crime, and yet the Court of *Turin* thought fit to send the same Bishop to *Rome*, *to desire the Pope to appoint another Commissioner to assist at the Tryal of the Criminal* But the Pope would not consent, unless on such Conditions as the Council of *Turin* could not accept of However the Secular Judge proceeded to condemn the Criminal, as well on account of the nature of the Crime, which was of the utmost Consequence, as of the eminent Persons the Criminal would bring into it It was necessary to put to death the Author of so dangerous a Conspiracy, but is that could not be done according to the usual forms, by reason of the Incompetency of the Judge, he was executed in the Prison An infinite number of Instances of this sort might be produc'd

In *France* they have not the same regard for plain Priests and Religious Men in Cases of high Treason I take notice in another place, of Friar *Hilary*, a Capucin, who having left the Convent, in order to become a Secular Priest, conspir'd against the Life of the Queen-Mother, and was broken on the Wheel at *Paris* The Bishop of *Mans*, and the Marquis *de Pisani*, talking to Pope *Sixtus* V concerning the death of the Cardinal *de Guise*, gave him to understand, that in *France* the King can cause even Prelates to be try'd in Cases of high Treason, but the Pope did not agree to it, tho' the Ministers of *France* meant the Crime of high Treason in the first degree

These Examples do not properly belong to my Subject, and I have already said much, but I think I could not say too much, to support a Truth which I shall establish in Chap XI concerning the Exemption of publick Ministers Let us now see whether the *Clergy*, who ought not to suffer themselves to be employ'd on Embassies, are proper for them It must be own'd, there are some Prelates who have very worthily discharg'd that Office, and are very capable of it But these being two different Professions, and this Employment not being natural to Ecclesiasticks, it is but by meer chance that any of them make able Ministers Formerly almost all Embassies were bestow'd on Men of the Gown, or at least there were scarce any without a Prelate as chief, or some Monk as an associate It was generally thought that all Learning and Wisdom was either confin'd within the Cloisters, or else in the possession of the Clergy, and even at this time most Princes make no difficulty to employ them in their Embassies and Intrigues, but not without distinction All the Pope's Ministers are Prelates, most of the *Legates* are Cardinals, and the *Nuncios* and *Internuncio's* are Archbishops, Bishops, Abbots, or Officers of the Court, or of the Pope's Houshold Princes themselves sometimes employ Cardinals in their Embassies It is not very long since the Cardinal Landgrave of *Hesse*, was Embassador from the Emperor at *Rome* The Cardinal *de Joyeuse*, was so on the part of *Henry* IV, at *Rome* and *Venice*, upon the difference that was between Pope *Paul* V and the Republick, in the Years 1606, and 1607 Cardinal *Bichi* in the Year 1643, had the same Function in *Italy*, on account of the War the said Republick and some Princes of *Italy* made upon the *Barberins* The Cardinal of *Lyons* had been nominated for the Assembly that was to be held at *Cologn*, and Cardinal *Mazarin* had been also nominated for that at *Munster* Cardinal *d'Estrée*, who is a very worthy and illustrious Prelate, still negotiates for the King in *Italy* and *Germany* Since they may be Vice-Roys and Governors of Provinces, as they have been in several kingdoms of *Spain*, at *Naples*, in *Sicily*, at *Milan*, and in *Flanders* Since they have presided at the Diets in *Germany*, and at Councils in *Spain*, and that they are admitted to be prime Ministers, of which we have such great and successful Instances in *France*, it is reasonable to believe they have also the necessary qualifications for Embassies If they have been unfortunate in those eminent Posts in *Spain*, *Germany*, *England*, *Hungary*, *Transilvania*, and other Parts, where the Cardinals *d'Espinosa*, *Clesel*, *Wolsey*, *Martinuzzi*, *Bathory*, &c have either perish'd or been disgrac'd, it has happen'd rather thro' their Princes faults, than thro' their own

I cannot make mention of Archbishops and Bishops, without refreshing my memory with *M de Marquemont*, Archbishop of *Lyons*, Embassador from *France* at *Rome*, and since Cardinal The chief Minister judg'd the King was well serv'd, because this Prelate was very well with the Pope, and was for having him continu'd on at *Rome* But *Marquemont* writ him word, *That it was not the Business of an Archbishop of Lyons to spend his whole Life in a Court*, *and that what press'd him most to entreat his being recall'd*, *was the reproach his Conscience daily made him*, *and the grief he had to see himself depriv'd of the Consolations he should receive from a due discharge of his Archiepiscopal Functions* *Dossat* was no sooner consecrated Bishop of *Rennes*, than he writ to *Villeroy*, that the Duty of his *new Character would oblige him to Residence*, and that at *Rome* an Edict was every Year publish'd, by which the Bishops, and others, who have the Cure of Souls, were order'd to go and reside at their respective Churches Notwithstanding which, most Princes have formerly employ'd both the one and the other in their most momentous Negotiations, and there are some, that still do it at this time Here we may observe, that formerly when all Embassies were Extraordinary, a Prelate might absent himself from his Cure, during the little time that he employ'd in the Service of his King and Countrey, and might do the same without fundal But I cannot conceive how they, and all the rest, who have a charge of Souls, and who are oblig'd to Residence by the Divine Laws, can be allow'd any Dispensation to quit their Flocks, and be employ'd in Embassies *in Ordinary*, which take in several Years one after the other There have been some of them, who have no sooner perform'd perform'd one *Embaffie in Ordinary*, than they have enter'd upon another, and after that have been employ'd in a third. If they will live by the Altar, they ought to ferve it, and if they do not feed the Flock that has been committed to their Conduct, they thereby become *Apoftates*, and are oblig'd to account for it to the Almighty, unlefs they are employ'd for the fervice of the Church in general, or that of their own in particular, or are deputed to a Council, a Synod, or an Affembly of the Clergy. They cannot anfwer the abandoning their Flocks, to beftow themfelves on a Court, and to fhare in the Vices that reign there, and are infeparable therefrom. It may happen, that fome occafions may offer, wherein the good of the State (if not an abfolute neceffity) may require the fervice of a Prelate, either on account of his extraordinary Ability, or elfe by reafon of the Acquaintance and Intereft he has in the Court of the Prince to whom he may be fent, and then it is not unwarrantable to make ufe of their fervice in an *Embaffie Extraordinary*. But it feems as if that in *Ordinary* were inconfiftent with their Dignity, and with their *Ecclefiaftical Functions*. It cannot be deny'd but that they who act otherwife, have more *Ambition* than *Piety*, and that it is altogether impoffible, or at leaft very difficult, to be at the fame time an able and dextrous Minifter, and a good and pious Bifhop. I do not here fpeak of thofe, who inftead of being Minifters of Peace, become the Inftruments and Heralds of War. As that *Caraffa*, whofe Legation was fo pernicious to *France* under *Henry* II, who, at the requeft of that Prelate broke the Truce, which he had juft concluded at *Vancelles*; but of thofe, who intermeddle with Intrigues, that would be innocent, if they were but in the hands of skilful Perfons. One may fay of the Bifhop of *Bezers*, at prefent Cardinal *de Bonzy*, that were it not for his quality of Prelate, and his Epifcopal Dignity, the Character of *Embaffador* could not be given to a more worthy Minifter.

But after all, I cannot conceive how a Bifhop, who is able to make himfelf refpected at the Court of a Chriftian Potentate, can fubmit to be employ'd in that of *Conftantinople*, and that to an Infidel, who ought to be his abomination. *Francis* of *Noailles*, Bifhop of *Acs*, who was *Embaffador* on the part of *Charles* IX to *Selim* II, and *John* of *Monluc*, who was Protonotary when he was fent thither, and was fince promoted to the Archbifhoprick of *Vienne* in *Dauphine*, have not been the only Ecclefiafticks employ'd as *Embaffadors* at the Port, fince the Kings of *Hungary* have frequently fent fuch thither, and that *Ferdinand* of *Auftria* difpatch'd thither the Bifhop of *Agria*, in the Year 1556. It may be objected perchance, that a Prelate may, without fcruple, negotiate with a Prince, whofe friendfhip the Pope himfelf Courts. But then I cannot tell whether that Reafon will be fatisfactory to thofe, who do not approve of the correfpondence of the Pope, and who find fomething fo deteftable in it, that it cannot be juftify'd by the diftinction that is made between the Temporal Prince, and the Head of the Church. The Great Turk himfelf has fometimes employ'd Bifhops in his Embaffies. In the Year 1565, *Soliman* fent the Bifhop of *Harmftadt* into *Tranfilvania*, to the Emperor *Maximilian* II, to exhort him not to make War againft *John*, who being the Son of *John Zapoli*, took upon him the quality of King of *Hungary*, and Prince of *Tranfilvania*. There are feveral Examples of this kind in Hiftory, and particularly in the *Byzantine*. But then thefe Bifhops, who are in effect Slaves, and who are under a neceffity of obeying the Commands that are laid upon them, how tyrannical foever they may be, are by fo much the more excufable, as they are perfuaded that in thofe Employments they labour for the good of Chriftendom. However it muft be own'd that the Pope does not perform a very Religious Act, in entertaining a Correfpondence with the Great Turk, to oblige him to make War againft the Chriftians; unlefs there be the utmoft neceffity to countenance fuch procedure. Hiftory blufhes, when fhe makes mention of the Embaffie *Alexander* VI fent to *Conftantinople*, to impetrate Succour againft *Charles* VIII, King of *France*. He gave this Commiffion to *George Bouchard* of *Genoa*. *Bajazeth* fent back with him the *Chiaoux Daut*, who had the charge of a good fum of Money with him, and Orders to promife the augmentation of it to that off two hundred thoufand Crowns, if the Pope caus'd *Gemez* to be poifon'd, who was Brother to *Bajazeth*, and was guarded at *Rome*, from the time that *Lewis* XI King of *France* had fent him to *Alexander*. Thefe two Minifters of the Pope and the Turk, as they pafs'd from *Greece* into *Italy*, were taken at Sea by *John de la Ronere*, Brother to Cardinal of *St. Peter*, a declar'd Enemy of the Pope, and being plunder'd, were fet on fhore. The *Chiaoux* who had loft his Money, and had not wherewith to defray his Charges home, nor for his prefent fubfiftence, bethought himfelf of feeking relief from the Marquis of *Mantua*, who liv'd in a good underftanding with *Bajazeth*. The Marquis receiv'd him courteoufly, treated him handfomly, and fent him back to his Mafter, who in his turn, made the Marquis fenfible, that a well-plac'd Friendfhip can never be fufficiently requited nor valu'd. For he being fallen into the hands of the *Venetians*, who hated him mortally, he had never got out of them if it not been for the powerful interceffion of the Great *Turk*.

The other *Prelates*, and *Clergymen*, *who have not the Cure of Souls*, and who by confequence are not oblig'd to Refidence, nor by their vow to a reclufe Life, are at liberty to enter upon all kinds of Employments. For altho' there be not any Order, that by its firft Inftitution, does not oblige its Abbot to apply himfelt to any thing, rather than to the bufinefs of Negotiations, yet neverthelefs, as thefe Primitive Rules have not been obferv'd, and that moft Courts are fo pefter'd with this fort of Prelates, that they are no longer diftinguifh'd from other Courtiers, I do not fee why they may not be employ'd in Embaffies. For fince they are judg'd capable of all other Civil Offices and Functions, in the Council and every where elfe, they cannot be excluded thofe more eminent Employments, if they have the neceffary Qualifications to fucceed in them.

As for the *Religious*, we muft examine, firft, Whether their Profeffion ought not to exclude 'em from the Management of all publick Affairs. Secondly, Whether they are fit for them. And in the third place, Whether they ought to be consider'd as publick Ministers, and enjoy the Protection of the the *Law of Nations*. I might here make a Distinction betwixt those Monks who live upon the Funds and Revenues of their Convents, and the Mendicants, who ought not to have any other Income than that of their Wallet, did not their primitive Institution exclude both the one and the other from Embassies and Negotiations. All the Religious, when they enter the Convent, bid adieu to the World, and make a Vow to renounce whatever can give them any attach to it, in like manner as the primitive Monks did, who in order to avoid the Cruelty of Persecutions, or for some other Reason, retir'd into Deserts, that they might shun all Commerce with Men. They cannot be employ'd in Embassies, but they must shake off the Obedience they owe to their Superiors, dispense with their Vow of Poverty, and expose to the most violent Temptations, that Chastity, which makes 'em look upon Mariage it self as a State of Impurity and Pollution. I don't think I need here repeat what the Abbot of *Ursperg* says of the Mendicant Monks, nor what *M. Camus*, Bishop of *Bellay* (whose Zeal and Candor came near the Piety of the Bishops of the primitive Church) has writ and publish'd in several Volumes on that Subject, but I content my self to lay down this Position, that Monks do not only sin against the Rules of their Order, when they meddle with worldly Affairs, which renders them incapable of the Character, but also that they are not at all fit for Negotiation. When I say of Negotiation, I use the Word in its natural Signification, for the Management of publick Affairs, founded on a perfect Knowledge thereof, and on a Prudence altogether remote from those Artifices that degenerate often into a crafty Deceit and Treachery of which there are but too many Examples.

The Catholick Kings *Ferdinand* and *Isabella*, employ'd Religious almost in all their Affairs. Their Devotion was very interested, and favour'd strongly of Bigottry. The better to set off their false Piety, they had none but Monks for their Attendants, and employ'd no other in the Intrigues they had in all the Courts of the neighbouring Princes. Frier *John de Mauleon* negotiated constantly with *Charles* VIII, and obtain'd of him at last the Restitution of the County of *Roussillon*. Some *Religious of Montferrat* were employ'd there after the Revolution of the Affairs of *Naples*, and it was *John of Enguera*, a Monk of the Order of St *Bernard*, and Inquisitor of *Catalonia*, who made the first Proposals of the Marriage of *Germain de Foix*, Niece of *Lewis* XII, with *Ferdinand*, and he did not leave the Court of *France*, till he had concluded the Marriage of that Princess, and a League with the King. Prelates were the Ornament of all his Embassies, and the Religious were that of all his Negotiations, and particularly when he had a mind to trick and deceive, which was no very extraordinary thing with him. I should say no more, had not a certain Remarker of *Brussels*, Author of *The curious Treatise, concerning the carrying off Prince G. of* Furstemberg, (being very much scandaliz'd at what I have said elsewhere of the Infidelity of *Ferdinand* the Catholick) undertaken to vindicate his Memory, so that I cannot avoid adding here, that there is not any History of that Time, that does not speak of him, as of the most perfidious of all Princes. That of *Spain*, instead of justifying him, excuses him, on the Necessity he found himself reduc'd to, (by the Infidelity of those with whom he had to do) of preventing by his Treacheries, those that were intended to himself. *Hier Zurita*, who seems to have compos'd his History, that is to say the two last Tomes of his Works, to no other end but to make it serve for a Panegyrick to *Ferdinand*, cannot forbear speaking in these Terms. *Not only foreigners but those of the Countrey, have blam'd him very much for not keeping his Word nor Promises, and for always preferring the Consideration of his own particular Interest, to what was just and honest, since the true Foundation of Justice consists in the Constancy and Firmness of Works, and principally in that of Deeds. He that violates the good Faith, destroys all the universal Good of Men.* Zurita, to excuse him, does not deny it to be true, but says, that it is not just to charge a single Prince with a Fault, which all the Princes were guilty of. It is not my Intention to justify the other Princes. There is nothing that obliges me to it but it is a matter to be wonder'd at that the Histories of those Times, do not speak of these as they do of him, nor brand 'em with the same Infamy. *Ferdinand* could not brooke the Treachery of *Henry* VIII, king of *England*, his Son-in-law, yet nevertheless he deceiv'd him twice very villanously. But that I may not ingage my self in too long a Digression, I'll here draw his Picture with one Stroke of the Pensil, by relating the Story a *Spanish* Author tells of him, who has commented on the Memoirs of *Philip de Commines*. He says, that *Ferdinand* had sent his Secretary *Peter Quintana* to *Lewis* XII, King of *France*, to make some Overtures to him of an Alliance, but *Lewis* told him, that *Ferdinand*, who had deceiv'd him twice, should not deceive him the third time, and so sent him home. *Quintana*, when he gave an account of the ill Success of his Negotiation, had some difficulty to tell the true Cause of *Lewis*'s Refusal, and to take notice of the Reproach which had been made him of *Ferdinand*'s Infidelity. But finding himself press'd thereto by the King, he said at last, that *Lewis* had declar'd to him, that *Ferdinand* having deceiv'd him twice, he was far from any Inclination to treat with him again, lest he should furnish him with an Opportunity of doing it a third time. *Ferdinand* having paus'd a while on *Quintana*'s Report, ask'd him how many times does *Lewis* say I have deceiv'd him? twice? *by God the Drunkard lies, for I have deceiv'd him above ten times*. The Author, who speaks of it as of a pretty Repartee, adds, *by my Faith I believe* Ferdinand *spoke the truth*. I cannot tell whether after this I can be liable to stand a Tryal, for having maintain'd that true Piety and Sincerity were not the greatest Virtues of the Catholick King.

Besides that Monks are no longer look'd upon to make a part of the Civil Society, and that

The EMBASSADOR and his FUNCTIONS. 65

that they are in a Republick, but only what the Wasps are in a Bee-hive, *Ignavum pecus* Those mean Souls, who can stoop so low as to shut themselves up in a Convent, and wallow in Idleness, and in the Ordure and Filth of a *voluntary Mendicity*, cannot have that Elevation of Soul, that makes one of the most necessary and even constituent Parts of an Embassador Their Prudence is made up only of Artifices and little Wiles, that do not find Admittance in the Dealings of honest People Instead of that *noble Assurance* which so well becomes a publick Minister, they have a *Cynical Impudence*, which is proper in the utmost Degree to those of their Profession They are most commonly vain, indiscreet, imprudent and temerarious, and as such, more capable of marring Affairs than concluding them I am willing to believe that the *Capucins*, who are the most mortify'd of all the Religious, would not be guilty of a cheating Trick, nor of an Infidelity and I am as willing to enhance all that is said of the Ability of those, who have been seen to run up and down *Italy*, *France* and *Germany* during the Wars which had their beginning in *Bohemia* and *Mantua* But how is it possible not to have a very bad Opinion of a *Capucin*, who leaves his Convent to put himself at the Head of an Army of Rebels, as did Father *Ange de Joyeuse*? or to take upon himself all kinds of Affairs, politick and military, as did Father *Joseph*? or else to make such Overtures, as a Minister and a Man of Honour would not nor could not do? as did that *Capucin* who went to the Prince of *Orange* at the Siege of *Hulst*, of which I shall speak by and by or else again, to carry on other more dangerous Intrigues, as they did, who by their bloody Counsels have kindled and fomented a War in several Parts of *Europe* It is not necessary to name 'em, for fear of scandalizing an Order that does not approve of the Irregularities of some particular Persons, who like *Apostates*, would not submit to its Discipline

The *Capucin* whom I lately mention'd, was of one of the best Houses in the Low Countries, and having formerly been a Trooper, he thought he might be able to do the King of *Spain* Service in his own Profession Having therefore disguis'd himself, and receiv'd *Letters of Credence*, he went towards the end of the Year 1645 to the Prince of *Orange*'s Camp, who had besieg'd *Hulst* He told him, he had Orders to offer to the United Provinces, either a Peace or a Truce, at the Choice of the Prince, and on such Condition as the States themselves should think fit to express in Writing The Prince made answer, that the Matter being of the last Importance, he must take some time to think thereof, after which he would send him his answer As soon as the Monk was gone out, the Prince communicated his Negotiation to *Destrades*, who was in the King of *France*'s Interest, and the next Day he caus'd him to be shut up in a Closet, from whence he might hear the whole Conversation the Prince should have with the Monk He was made to repeat all he had said the Day before, concerning the Restitution of the Lands that belong to the House of *Orange* in the *Franche County*, which the King of *Spain* was

to let the Prince enjoy in full Sovereignty, and to augment the Revenues thereof to the Value of two hundred thousand Livres, to reimburse him what he had not enjoy'd therefrom during the War He likewise offer'd an absolute Sovereignty to the United Provinces, with the Arbitration of the Differences between the two Crowns, and concluded his Discourse, by representing the great Reason there was to apprehend the too near Neighbourhood of *France* After the *Capucin* had finish'd his Speech, the Prince told him, *he was very much scandaliz'd to see in that Apparel, a Man who had renounc'd the World, and who having oblig'd himself by Vow to the Service of God, ought not to meddle with th Affairs of that nature* That he had nothing more to say to him, but that it would not become himself to hearken to Proposals of Peace, while he was wholly taken up with the Siege of one of the strongest Places in *Flanders* This being done, the Prince caus'd *Destrades* to come in, to whom he gave a Copy of the Letters the Monk had brought him, and when he deliver'd to the Monk the Originals, he commanded him to depart from the Camp in six Hours time, and never return more This Commission was very suitable to a Monk, who might be disown'd, and with impunity charg'd with the Infamy and ill Success of the Negotiation There is an admirable Portraiture of a *Monk-Negotiator* in the Letter Cardinal *Dossat* writes to *Villeroy* on the 22d of *February* 1601, on the account of Frier *Hilary* of *Grenoble*, a *Capucin* The Monk had found out means to procure himself *Letters of Credence* from King *Henry* IV, to the Pope: But nothing was wanting on his part, to create to the King such Affairs as were capable of casting the Kingdom afresh into those Disorders and Troubles, which had requir'd so much pains to settle and compose them All that can be said of the Vanity, Temerity, Imprudence, of the Pride, Transports, and Impudence of the Monks, are found together in this *Capucin* in so high a Degree, that it might be sufficient alone to verify what I have said of all the other Monks This I am now speaking of, whose Name was *Travail*, some time after threw aside the Frock to become a secular Priest, and offer'd to *M de Luines* to contrive the Death of Marshal *d'Ancre* He insinuated himself so far in this Intrigue, that it was found necessary to communicate to him the Design that was taken, to get rid of the said Marshal but the Execution thereof having been perform'd without his having any Hand therein, and he being afraid, or at least willing to have it believ'd, that the Queen Mother would revenge on him the Death of the Marshal, he undertook to compass the Queen's Death, either by Stabbing or Poyson of which Crime being convicted, he was broken on the Wheel alive at *Paris* the 10th of *May* 1616 At the Place of Execution, he said, he would willingly have sacrific'd the Life of his Father or Mother to the Good of the State

This is what both they and the other Clergymen (I except the Prelates) are very subject to In the Year 1639, during the Contests between the *Hollanders* and the *Spaniards*, on account of Passports for the Ministers, who were to be employ'd in the Negotiations for a Peace,

S the

the Court of *Bruſſels*, ſent the Model of a Paſſport to the *Hague*, by the Rector of a Village, *within the Juriſdiction of the Mayor of* Boiſleduc Order requir'd it ſhould have been ſent to the *Venetian Embaſſador*, whoſe Mediation had been agreed on, that he might convey it to the States But for as much as the *Spaniards* would then have been oblig'd to warrant their Writing, after they had put it into the Hands of a publick Miniſter, and that they, on the contrary, had a mind to reſerve to themſelves the Liberty of diſowning it, if not intirely to diſown it, (it then Occaſions ſo requir'd) they charg'd a Prieſt therewith

Philip II, King of *Spain*, having form'd a Deſign to joyn the Crown of *Portugal* to the Monarchy of *Caſtile*, after the Deceaſe of King *Sebaſtian*, had ſent *Christopher ae Mora*, his Embaſſador Extraordinary to *Henry*, Succeſſor and Unkle to *Sebaſtian* But that he might make himſelf certainly ſure of the Succeſſion, it behov'd him to hinder *Henry*, who was already old, and a Prieſt, from marrying and not daring to open the Matter to him by a Perſon of Quality, he ſent a *Jacobin* Monk on the Errand, whoſe Name was *Ferdinand Caſtille* This Frock'd Negotiator repreſented to *Henry*, that he would give a great Advantage to Hereticks, and a great Scandal to all good Catholicks if he reſolv'd to marry *Henry* was devout even to Superſtition, for which Reaſon *Philip* thought he might ſafely employ a Religious to hold a Diſcourſe with him, which a Cavalier and a Man of Worth, would not ſo much as have ſpoken to him about, but *Henry*, who gave him a very bad Reception, ſpoke to him but once, and ſent him back without an Anſwer

They are Impudent beyond Imagination *Harold* having uſurp'd the Crown of *England* after the Death of *Edward*, the laſt King of the *Saxon* Line, *William* Duke of *Normandy* who pretended to it, in the Year 1066, paſs'd over the Sea with a powerful Army, and being encamp'd near *Haſtings*, within a little of *Harold*'s Camp, he ſent him word by a Monk, to reſign the Kingdom to him, according to his Oath to him to that purpoſe, ſome Years before, or at leaſt that he would do him Homage for the Kingdom, which he offer'd to let him have on that Condition but if he refuſ'd to comply with either of theſe Propoſals, their Difference might be decided by a ſingle Combate in the ſight of both Armies *Harold* made anſwer, that God alone could determine the Matter But the Monk reply'd audaciously, that if *Harold* pretended to conteſt *William*'s Right, he ought to have Recourſe to the Pope's Deciſion, *or elſe to the Chance of Arms* It is true, the Hiſtory of thoſe Times blames *Harold*, for not treating *William*'s Embaſſadors as their Character requir'd, but that does not juſtify the Monk, who ought not to have charg'd himſelf with any ſuch Commiſſion, nor to have carry'd a Meſſage of Defiance and Combate

In the Year 1292, after that *Peter*, King of *Arragon*, to whom the Hiſtories of the Countrey give the Surname of *Great*, had conquer'd the Kingdom of *Sicily*, *Charles*, Duke of *Anjou*, who had the Reputation of being the moſt valiant Prince in his time, ſent him word by a *Jacobin* M nk, of the Order of St *Dominick*, whoſe Name was *Simon de Lentin*, that *Peter* had not enter'd *Sicily* at the Door, but like a Thief, had obtain'd it by ill Means, ſince he, *Charles*, being neither his nor his Kingdom's Enemy, he had made War againſt him, without any previous Declaration thereof, or any open Denunce That he was therefore ready to maintain by ſingle Combate of Body to Body, that he detain'd his Kingdom unjuſtly, and that he had a ſurp'd and raiſh'd s like a Highwayman putting himſelf at the Head of a Rout of Rebels and Traytors *Peter* conſidering that *this Diſcourſe, which was made to him, with the Inciv lit, and Impudence of a Monk, was not a Meſſage to be carry'd by a Man of that Character, and not think worth, of any Anſwer, and ſo diſmiſs'd him*

In the Year 1309, *James* II, King of *Arragon*, ſent to Pope *Clement* V, *Peter de Marſile* a Monk of the ſame Order of St *Dominick*, and *Fortugno Mortinez*, to deſire Succour from him againſt the *Moors* The Monk deliver'd him ſelf with ſo little Reſpect, that the Pope put him into the Hands of the General of his Order, to have him puniſh'd

I do not ſay out Princes may employ them ſometime with Advantage, but then it is rather to diſpoſe the Parties to a Negotiation, than to negotiate. *Francis de Quignones*, General of *Cordeliers*, and ſince Cardinal de *St Croix*, went to and fro, between Pope *Clement* VII, and the Emperor *Charles* V, to diſpoſe them to the Accommodation that was agreed upon afterwards *Gabriel ae Guſman*, *Cordelier*, and Confeſſor to *Eleonora* of *Auſtria*, Queen of *France*, made the firſt Overtures of the Peace that was concluded in the Year 1544, between the ſame Emperor, and *Francis* I, King of *France* Theſe Princes were both weary of the War, and yet neither the one nor the other of them, could obtain of himſelf to make the firſt Overtures for a Peace, ſo that the Queen cauſ'd 'em to be made by this Monk After he had taken ſome few Journeys from the *French* Camp to that of the Emperor, where he ſettled the Preliminaries, that is to ſay, the Time and Place of the Congreſs *The High Admiral of France*, with *Bayard*, Secretary of State, on the one ſide, and *Don Ferdinand de Gonzague*, with *Granvell* on the other, met at *Cambray*, where they ſoon agreed on the Conditions of the Treaty, the Concluſion whereof was ſome what haſten'd, to deprive the Pope's Legates, who were on their way, of the Glory of it *Bonaventure Calatagironne*, General of the *Cordeliers*, was very buſy in the Negotiation of the Peace of *Vervins*, and *John Neyen* Commiſſary, General of the ſaid Order, in that of the Truce of the Low Countries but then they acted rather like Brokers than Merchants

When they intermeddle with Commerce it ſelf, they very rarely ſucceed *Don Garcia de Silva Figueroa*, (Embaſſador from *Philip* III, King of *Spain*, to the Court of *Perſia*) who was a very devout Nobleman, ſpeaking of the Employment that *Schach Abas* had given to a Religious, nam'd, *Brother Redempto de la Croix*, by making him be compriſ'd in the Commiſſion of *Robert Shirley*, whom he was ſending as Embaſſador to the King of *Spain*, ſays, that this Monk was a very good Man, and of an inno-

innocent Life enough, but yet it might be said, that by his meddling with Affairs, which had no relation with those of his Profession, he was the only Cause, of the deplorable Loss of *Ormus*, and that by his *Imprudence*, rather than by any *Malice*. Some time before the last Commotions in *Naples*, the Marquis of *Achaia* and of *Mont*, *Neapolitan* Noblemen, (having confederated with several other Persons of Quality, to cast off the Yoke of the *Spanish* Government) made use of a *Theatin Monk* nam'd *Andrew Paulucci*, whom they sent several times to Prince *Thomas* of *Savoy*, and to Cardinal *Mazarine*, but he prov'd so indiscreet in the carrying on his Intrigues, that upon the Discovery thereof, the Superior of his Order caus'd him to be seiz'd, and shut up in a Convent at *Ravenna*. Some of the Conspirators however found means to get him out, but distrusting his Conduct, they order'd him never to return to the Kingdom any more, but to give an account of his Negotiations, in pursuance of the Orders they should send him, by the way of Letter. Cardinal *Mazarine* caus'd him to be advis'd to take care of himself, and to be more reserv'd in his Discourse concerning his Negotiation, and to decline those Places where the *Spaniards* might take him by the Collar. But he neglected all this Counsel, and had the Temerity to go to *Naples*, during the few Days Quiet the Town enjoy'd after the Death of *Mas Aniello*. Here he was found disguis'd in a Soldier's Habit, seiz'd, guarded to the Castle, put upon the Rack, and executed. The Marquis of *Monts* suffer'd likewise, but the Marquis of *Achaia* found the Means to save himself in the Island of *Corfou*, and from thence retir'd to *Venice*. The discontented *Neapolitans* carry'd on their Intrigues with the Ministers who resided on the part of *France* at *Rome*, by the means of a *Jacobin* Monk, whose Name was Father *Capeci*, who was not more valuable than *Paulucci*, because he betray'd the King, his Sovereign Prince, as well as the other. In the Year 1548 the Pope having recall'd from the Emperor's Court, Cardinal *Sfondrati*, who had been Legate there, sent thither in the Quality of Nuncio, the Bishop of *Fano*, who was of the Order of St *Dominick*. The *French* Embassador, who pretended that the Pope ought to break off all Correspondence with *Charles* V, complain'd thereof, but the Pope caus'd him to be told, that in sending a Monk to the Emperor, he had done according to the Custom, in reference to those that are in their last Agony, to whom a Religious is sent to prepare them for Death; signifying thereby, that he sent this Minister to the Emperor for no other purpose, but to let him understand, that their Friendship, which was in a languishing State, would soon expire.

Formerly, while Superstition and Ignorance reign'd, the Religious were respected, but the Habit, and demure Mien, have long since lost their Influence, and the World will be no longer deceiv'd thereby; on the contrary, it is not without scruple, they are at present treated with, and there is a continual Distrust of their equivocal Meanings, as well as of the Intention of those Princes that employ them. They have not the Quality of Embassadors, because the Representation would participate of the Ridicule. But whether they have Letters of Credence, or that they are credited on their bare Word, if they are negotiated with, tho' they have not the Character of publick Ministers, they nevertheless enjoy the Protection of the Law of Nations, as on the other side, they cannot be too severely punish'd if they abuse their Habit and Profession, to contrive Treasons and Assassinations, with which one might fill up several Volumes. Father *Joseph*, who assisted *Leon Brulard* to conclude the Treaty of *Ratisbon*, had no Character.

CHAP. X.

Of Legates.

THere would be wanting something very Essential to this Treatise, if in speaking of *Embassadors* I did not bestow a Chapter also on *Legates*. There are two sorts of 'em. The one sort are Governors of Provinces or Towns, as of *Avignon*, *Ferrara*, *Urbine*, *Bologna*, &c. and may be created by the Pope's Brief, as well as in the Consistory. But the others are *Embassadors Extraordinary*, and *Plenipotentiaries*, and are always nominated by the Pope in the Consistory, that is to say, in the Assembly of Cardinals, that compose the Council of the Monarch, and the Senate of the Hierarchy. It is of these last I shall now speak. I cannot but put 'em in the Rank of *publick Ministers*, because the Pope sends his *Legates* on the same Accounts, for which temporal Princes send to one another their *Embassadors Extraordinary*. The Pope does not send any to Ladies. *Mary*, Sister to *Philip* II, and Widow of the Emperor *Maximilian* II, as she pass'd through *Italy* on her Journey to *Spain*, sent an *Embassador* to the Pope to kiss his Feet. *Frederick Madrucci*, Embassador from *Rodolfus*, and the Abbot of *Borsengues*, Agent for *Spain*, urg'd very much, that the Pope would send a *Legate* to the Empress. But they were answer'd, *that the Pope never sends any Legates to the Ladies*, unless they are Travelling through the Ecclesiastical Territories; and accordingly *Gregory* XIII, did no more than send her some Beads, and some *Agnus Dei's* by Father *Tolete* a Jesuit, whom she had sent for. It is true the Pope order'd Cardinal *Riario*, who was returning from his Legation in *Spain*, to present them to the Empress, but as this Prelate was already got too far from the Road she took, the Lord *Taverna*, who was going to *Spain* in the Quality of Nuncio, was charg'd with the Complement.

After the *Legate* is declar'd in the Consistory, the whole College accompanies him in Ceremony

remony out of the Gates of the Town, with their Families, Silver Maces and Cloak-bags, in the same manner as the Cavalcade is perform'd for a Cardinal who is going to receive the Hat from the Pope's hands. This done, the *Legate* may return to Town *Incognito*, but then he must neither appear any more in publick, nor receive any publick Visits. When he leaves the Town in good earnest, he cannot cause the Cross to be carry'd before him, 'till he is got forty Miles distant from the Town of *Rome*, because he does not till then shew the marks of his *Legation*, nor begin to execute the Functions thereof. At his Return they make him an Entry. The *Cardinals* send to meet him, and pay him their Visit in Ceremony. These *Legates* make Apostolical Protonotaries, Knights, and Doctors in all Faculties. They also legitimate Bastards, and have several other Powers, which not being very consistent with the Liberties of the *Gallican* Church, *Legates* are not receiv'd in *France*, 'till their *Bulls* have been examin'd and register'd in the Parliament of *Paris*, by virtue of a Letter that the King joyns to them, to order it to confirm and retine the Bulls, which is not done but with the following Modifications, which plainly shew the Power *Legates* have in other Kingdoms.

" That the *Legate* cannot, by virtue of his
" *Bulls*, exercise any Jurisdiction within
" the Kingdom, not even with the consent of
" the Parties, nor over those, who as being
" immediately Subjects of the See of *Rome*,
" are exempt from the ordinary Justice. But
" he shall be oblig'd to give them Judges on
" the place, who shall take cognizance of the
" matter, and regulate it. That the *Letters*
" *of Legitimation*, which he shall grant to Ba-
" stards, shall no farther be valid to them than
" to make 'em capable of being admitted into
" Orders, and that without prejudice to those
" Chapters and Colleges that do not receive
" Bastards, and these *Legitimates* shall have no
" part in Successions, nor be admitted into
" Civil Offices. That the *Legate* shall not
" Incorporate Benefices, but only nominate
" Judges according to the decrees of the Coun-
" cil of *Constance*. That he shall not dispense
" with the Years that are to be employ'd in
" Study by those, who by reason of their Qua-
" lity may be nominated to Benefices. That
" he shall not clog Benefices nor Prebends
" with Pensions, not even with the consent of
" those that possess them, unless it be for the
" profit of him that resigns 'em, or else to
" prevent Law Suits, and that he shall not
" suffer those that resign 'em, to reserve to
" themselves the whole Revenue, under the
" pretext of a Pension. That he shall not suf-
" fer those that possess Benefices, to alienate
" the Lands or Rents thereof, under any Ti-
" tle or any pretext whatsoever, even tho'
" such Benefices should not be depending on
" any Jurisdiction of the Kingdom, and should
" be immediately subject to the Pope, in
" which Case he shall be oblig'd to nominate
" Judges within the Kingdom, who shall pro-
" vide therein according to reason. That he
" shall not give Abbies either of Men or Women
" in *Commendam*, without the King's nomi-
" nation, who has a right thereto, by virtue
" of the Concordance or Agreement made with

" Pope *Leo* X. and that he shall not dispose
" of vacant Benefices, to the prejudice of the
" *Indulto* granted by the King to the Counsel-
" lors of Parliament. That he shall not ex-
" ercise any Jurisdiction between the King's
" Subjects, in the cases of Infidelity, Usury,
" or Divorce, concerning the restitution or
" the Portion, or for Goods unjustly acquir'd
" by unlawful Contracts. That he shall not
" take cognizance of the Crime of *Heresy*,
" when the publick Tranquillity shall be con-
" cern'd therein, and that the matter of Fact
" only is the thing in question, because the
" same belongs only to the King's Judges, and
" that in such case, he shall not presume to
" absolve the King's Subjects, except it be with
" reference to their Conscience, and the Ca-
" nonical Penance. That he shall not grant
" dispensations to those that have Benefices
" or are Religious, to make Wills to the pre-
" judice of the ordinary Customs of the King-
" dom, of the King's Edicts, and of the *Arrests*
" of Parliament. That he shall not be able to
" give dispensations to the prejudice of the lau-
" dable Customs and Privileges of Cathedral and
" Collegiate Churches, nor contrary to the
" Privileges granted to the Kings by Popes.
" That he shall not grant to the same Person
" a plurality of Benefices in the same Church,
" nor give to Executors of Testaments a long-
" er time than what is regulated by the Laws.
" That he shall not convert Pious Legacies to
" other uses, contrary to the Testator's Inten-
" tion, unless where the Will of the deceased
" cannot be fulfill'd, and provided that the
" same be employ'd to uses conformable to
" his mind. That he shall act nothing against
" the Rule *De Verisimili notitia, & publicandis*
" *resignationibus*. That he shall not compound
" for any profits receiv'd by those who have
" got possession of Benefices without a
" just Title, nor shall acquit them of 'em,
" because they ought to be restor'd to the
" Churches to whom of right they belong.
" That he shall not issue out any Ordinances,
" that in the collation of Benefices, regard
" shall only be had to his Letters, without
" producing the Procurations, by virtue of
" which the Benefices shall have been resign'd.
" That in his Letters he shall not make use of
" the *Clause anteferri*, nor of any the like
" Clauses, to the prejudice of the Right which
" is due to another. That he shall not order
" Ecclesiastical Causes to be brought before
" himself, nor take cognizance thereof, to
" the prejudice of the *Cap. de Causis*, nor
" shall use Sequestration. (*This Chapter de*
" *Causis, in the Agreements, says, that the Pope*
" *shall not commit the Causes of France, that*
" *are reserv'd to him, in partibus, that is to say*
" *to French Prelates*.) That he shall not take
" cognizance of those Crimes that are not
" purely Ecclesiastical, tho' they should be
" mix'd, if committed against the Laity, but
" only of such as are committed against the
" Clergy, and even in Crimes merely Eccle-
" siastical. He shall not condemn the Laity
" to pecuniary amercements, but the Eccle-
" siasticks only, and this pursuant to the Ca-
" nons, and provided, that it be without pre-
" judice to the Decrees of Councils inserted
" in the Canon Law. That he shall not issue
" out

"out Letters of Restitution or Rescission of
"Contracts That he shall not take cogni-
"zance of Actions real, whole Contracts shall
"have been pass'd between Lay Persons, or
"else between Ecclesiasticks, before Notary's
"Royal That he shall not rehabilitate Lay-
"Persons branded with Infamy, but only Ec-
"clesiasticks, with respect to their Function
"and Orders That he shall not suffer those
"who have resign'd their Benefices, to yield
"up to others the Pensions they had reserv'd
"to themselves That the disposition of those
"Benefices, of which the Legate has the col-
"lation, shall cease as soon as he shall be gone
"out of the Kingdom, and that before he
"shall depart from thence, he shall there leave
"the Act of his Legation In fine, he shall do
"nothing that can prejudice the holy Canons,
"the Agreements made between the Kings
"and Popes, the Oecumenical Councils, the
"Rights and Privileges of the Gallican Church,
"the Universities, and other publick Schools,
"of which he shall give an Assurance under
"his Hand This is what the Cardinals d'Amboise, Gouffier, du Prat, Farnese, Sadolet, Caraffa, of Ferrara, of St George, Verallo, and
and others have been oblig'd to promise.

Cardinal *Barberin*, when he came in the Quality of *Legate* into *France*, in the Year 1625, had sent his Bulls to the Nuncio *Spada*, to have the King's Letters annex'd to 'em, and to procure their being Register'd The Parliament ordain'd, that they should be Register'd with the Modifications, which should be express'd in an Act it would cause to be prepar'd for that purpose. But upon the *Nuncio*'s complaining thereof, the King order'd the Parliament to Register the Bulls in the same manner that those of Cardinal *de Medicis* had been in the Reign of *Henry* IV The Parliament obey'd, out for as much as the Pope's Officers had forgotten to insert the Title of King of *Navarr*, the Parliament rais'd fresh difficulties, and refus'd to Register the Bulls, unless the *Nuncio* procur'd others, or at least a Brief, that should rectify the omission, and that both he and the *Legate*, oblig'd themselves in Writing to comply herewith in a certain time The *Nuncio* would do nothing in it, and by his Importunities, he obtain'd other *coercive Letters*, that oblig'd the Parliament to proceed in their enregistring But it was ordain'd at the same time, that there should be writ upon the told thereof, *Read, Publish'd and Register'd, on the Conditions express'd in the Register*, and that at the Audience, where the Powers were to be publish'd, it should be declar'd *Vivâ Voce*, that it was without the approbation of the Council of *Trent*, and that the Bulls should not be restor'd to the *Legate*, 'till he brought a Brief that should supply this omission of the Kingdom of *Navarre* But the Pope chose rather to send other Bulls

The same Cardinal *Barberin* leaving the Court somewhat suddenly, and not without some incivility, took along with him the Register and Seal of his Legation, which he was oblig'd to leave with the Parliament The Attorney General being inform'd thereof, the Court order'd the King's Attorney of the Presidial Jurisdiction of *Lyons* to get both the one and the other from the *Datary*, and this Sub-

altern Officer taking along with him the Lieutenant General of the same Presidial, and being attended with about forty Pursevants, went to the Lodgings of the *under Datary*, who would fain have excus'd himself on account of the absence of his Master, but he was however oblig'd to promise in writing, that he would restore both the one and the other the next day following The Datary *Panfilio*, who has been since Pope under the Name of *Innocent* X told *M de Chremont*, who by the King's Order had attended the *Legate* to serve him, ever since he enter'd *France*, that the violence that had been offer'd to the *Legate* was insupportable, since at *Rome* no Officer dares approach the Palace of the French Embassador The thing was excus'd to the *Legate*, and the Lieutenant General with the King's Attorney had orders to come to Court, and there give an account of their Action, which was in reality a little irregular This was all that was done to satisfie the *Legate*, who sent the Seal and the Register of his *Legation*, by an express to the *Nuncio*, and He restor'd them to the Parliament

Whatever Regard Princes have for the See of *Rome*, and whatever benefit they need in the Pope's friendship, they will not suffer it to prejudice the rights of their Sovereignty, nor the interest of their Crown As soon as Pope *Paul* III was inform'd of the death of *Edward* VI King of *England*, he nominated Cardinal *Pool* to the *Legation* of that Kingdom However, not thinking it proper to expose the Authority of the See of *Rome*, till affairs were a little settled, He follow'd the advice of Queen *Mary*, who counsel'd him not to be too hasty, because the business of Religion could not be regulated but by the Parliament, which should be call'd together after her Coronation Wherefore the Pope giving another pretext to the *Legation*, sent the Cardinal forward, with orders to labour a Peace between the Emperor *Charles* V and *Henry* II King of *France*, till he had a convenient passage The Pope acquainted the two Princes therewith, and his intention was approv'd of in *France*, but the Bishop of *Arras* told the Abbot (whom the Cardinal had sent to *Bruxelles*, to give the Emperor advice of his Journey) that he was surpriz'd at the Pope's proceeding, who ought to have inform'd the Emperor thereof, before the *Legate* set out: That he did not see what could be hop'd for from the offices of one single Minister, since the two *Legates* the Pope had just recall'd, had not been able to effect any thing That this was but a Cloak to cover the *Legation* of *England* with, of which the Queen had so much the more reason to complain, as this Commission was of the last prejudice to her State and Interest That he knew she had not kept it hid from the *Legate* himself Which was a truth, but that did not hinder the Cardinal from continuing his Journey as far as the Countrey of *Wirtemberg*, after he had receiv'd the Duke's Passport, for which he waited some time at *Dillinguen* The Emperor being acquainted herewith, sent the *Legate* word by *Don John de Mendoza*, that for very important and weighty Reasons which he had communicated to the Pope, he could not suffer him to continue his

T Journey

remony out of the Gates of the Town, with their Families, Silver Maces and Cloak-bags, in the same manner as the Cavalcade is perform'd for a Cardinal who is going to receive the Hat from the Pope's hands. This done, the *Legate* may return to Town *Incognito*, but then he must neither appear any more in publick, nor receive any publick Visits. When he leaves the Town in good earnest, he cannot cause the Cross to be carry'd before him, 'till he is got forty Miles distant from the Town of *Rome*, because he does not till then shew the marks of his *Legation*, nor begin to execute the Functions thereof. At his Return they make him an Entry. The *Cardinals* send to meet him, and pay him their Visit in Ceremony. These *Legates* make Apostolical Protonotaries, Knights, and Doctors in all Faculties. They also legitimate Bastards, and have several other Powers, which not being very consistent with the Liberties of the *Gallican* Church, *Legates* are not receiv'd in *France*, 'till their *Bulls* have been examin'd and register'd in the Parliament of *Paris*, by virtue of a Letter that the King joyns to them, to order it to confirm and ratifie the Bulls, which is not done but with the following Modifications, which plainly shew the Power *Legates* have in other Kingdoms.

" That the *Legate* cannot, by virtue of his
" *Bulls*, exercise any Jurisdiction within
" the Kingdom, not even with the consent of
" the Parties, nor over those, who as being
" immediately Subjects of the See of *Rome*,
" are exempt from the ordinary Justice. But
" he shall be oblig'd to give them Judges on
" the place, who shall take cognizance of the
" matter, and regulate it. That the *Letters*
" *of Legitimation*, which he shall grant to Ba-
" stards, shall no farther be valid to them than
" to make 'em capable of being admitted into
" Orders, and that without prejudice to those
" Chapters and Colleges that do not receive
" Bastards, and these *Legitimates* shall have no
" part in Successions, nor be admitted into
" Civil Offices. That the *Legate* shall not
" Incorporate Benefices, but only nominate
" Judges according to the decrees of the Coun-
" cil of *Constance*. That he shall not dispense
" with the Years that are to be employ'd in
" Study by those, who by reason of their Qua-
" lity may be nominated to Benefices. That
" he shall not clog Benefices nor Prebends
" with Pensions, not even with the consent of
" those that possess them, unless it be for the
" profit of him that resigns 'em, or else to
" prevent Law Suits, and that he shall not
" suffer those that resign 'em, to reserve to
" themselves the whole Revenue, under the
" pretext of a Pension. That he shall not suf-
" fer those that possess Benefices, to alienate
" the Lands or Rents thereof, under any Ti-
" tle or any pretext whatsoever, even tho'
" such Benefices should not be depending on
" any Jurisdiction of the Kingdom, and should
" be immediately subject to the Pope, in
" which Case he shall be oblig'd to nominate
" Judges within the Kingdom, who shall pro-
" vide therein according to reason. That he
" shall not give Abbies either of Men or Women
" in *Commendam*, without the King's nomi-
" nation, who has a right thereto, by virtue
" of the Concordance or Agreement made with

" Pope *Leo* X. and that he shall not dispose
" of vacant Benefices, to the prejudice of the
" *Indulto* granted by the King to the Counsel-
" lors of Parliament. That he shall not ex-
" ercise any Jurisdiction between the King's
" Subjects, in the cases of Infidelity, Usury,
" or Divorce, concerning the restitution of
" the Portion, or for Goods unjustly acquir'd
" by unlawful Contracts. That he shall not
" take cognizance of the Crime of *Heresy*,
" when the publick Tranquillity shall be con-
" cern'd therein, and that the matter of Fact
" only is the thing in question, because the
" same belongs only to the King's Judges, and
" that in such case, he shall not presume to
" absolve the King's Subjects, except it be with
" reference to their Conscience, and the Ca-
" nonical Penance. That he shall not grant
" dispensations to those that have Benefices,
" or are Religious, to make Wills to the pre-
" judice of the ordinary Customs of the King-
" dom, of the King's Edicts, and of the *Arrests*
" of Parliament. That he shall not be able to
" give dispensations to the prejudice of the lau-
" dable Customs and Privileges of Cathedral and
" Collegiate Churches, nor contrary to the
" Privileges granted to the Kings by Popes.
" That he shall not grant to the same Person
" a plurality of Benefices in the same Church,
" nor give to Executors of Testaments a long-
" er time than what is regulated by the Laws.
" That he shall not convert Pious Legacies to
" other uses, contrary to the Testator's Inten-
" tion, unless where the Will of the deceased
" cannot be fulfill'd, and provided that the
" same be employ'd to uses conformable to
" his mind. That he shall act nothing against
" the Rule *De Verisimili notitia, & publicandis*
" *resignationibus*. That he shall not compound
" for any profits receiv'd by those who have
" got possession of Benefices without a
" just Title, nor shall acquit them of 'em,
" because they ought to be restor'd to the
" Churches to whom of right they belong.
" That he shall not issue out any Ordinances,
" that in the collation of Benefices, regard
" shall only be had to his Letters, without
" producing the Procurations, by virtue of
" which the Benefices shall have been resign'd.
" That in his Letters he shall not make use of
" the Clause *anteferri*, nor of any the like
" Clauses, to the prejudice of the Right which
" is due to another. That he shall not order
" Ecclesiastical Causes to be brought before
" himself, nor take cognizance thereof, to
" the prejudice of the *Cap. de Causis*, nor
" shall use Sequestration. (*This Chapter de*
" *Causis, in the Agreements*, says, *that the Pope*
" *shall not commit the Causes of* France, *that*
" *are reserv'd to him, in partibus, that is to say*
" *to French Prelates*.) That he shall not take
" cognizance of those Crimes that are not
" purely Ecclesiastical, tho' they should be
" mix'd, if committed against the Laity, but
" only of such as are committed against the
" Clergy, and even in Crimes merely Eccle-
" siastical. He shall not condemn the Laity
" to pecuniary amercements, but the Eccle-
" siasticks only, and this pursuant to the Ca-
" nons, and provided, that it be without pre-
" judice to the Decrees of Councils inserted
" in the Canon Law. That he shall not issue

" out

The EMBASSADOR and his FUNCTIONS

'out Letters of Restitution, or Rescission of
"Contracts: That he shall not take cogni-
"zance of Actions real, whole Contracts shall
"have been pass'd between Lay Persons, or
"else between Ecclesiasticks, before Notary's
"Royal: That he shall not rehabilitate Lay-
"Persons branded with Infamy, but only Ec-
"clesiasticks, with respect to their Function
"and Orders: That he shall not suffer those
'who have resign'd their Benefices, to yield
'up to others the Pensions they had reserv'd
"to hemselves: That the disposition of those
"Benefices, of which the *Legate* has the col-
"lation, shall cease as soon as he shall be gone
"out of the Kingdom, and that before he
"shall depart from thence, he shall there leave
"the *Acts* of his *Legation*. In fine, he shall do
"nothing that can prejudice the holy *Canons*,
"the Agreements made between the Kings
"and Popes, the Œcumenical Councils, the
"Rights and Privileges of the *Gallican* Church,
"the Universities, and other publick Schools,
"of which he shall give an Assurance under
"his Hand: This is what the Cardinals *d'Am-*
"*boise, Gouffier, du Prat, Faruese, Sadolet, Ca-*
"*raffa, of Ferrara, of St. George, Verallo,* and
and others have been oblig'd to promise.

Cardinal *Barberin,* when he came in the Quality of *Legate* into *France,* in the Year 1625, had sent his Bulls to the Nuncio *Spada,* to have the King's Letters annex'd to 'em, and to procure their being Register'd: The Parliament ordain'd, that they should be Register'd with the Modifications, which should be express'd in an Act it would cause to be prepar'd for that purpose. But upon the *Nuncio's* complaining thereof, the King order'd the Parliament to Register the Bulls in the same manner that those of Cardinal *de Medicis* had been in the Reign of *Henry IV.* The Parliament obey'd, but for as much as the Pope's Officers had forgotten to insert the Title of King of *Navarr,* the Parliament rais'd fresh difficulties, and refus'd to Register the Bulls, unless the *Nuncio* procur'd others, or at least a Brief, that should rectify the omission, and that both he and the *Legate,* oblig'd themselves in Writing to comply herewith in a certain time. The *Nuncio* would do nothing in it, and by his Importunities, he obtain'd other *coercive Letters,* that oblig'd the Parliament to proceed in their enregistring. But it was ordain'd at the same time, that there should be writ upon the fold thereof, *Read, Publish'd and Register'd, on the Conditions express'd in the Register,* and that at the Audience, where the Powers were to be publish'd, it should be declar'd *Vivâ Voce,* that it was without the approbation of the Council of *Trent,* and that the Bulls should not be restor'd to the *Legate,* 'till he brought a Brief that should supply this omission of the Kingdom of *Navarre.* But the Pope chose rather to send other Bulls.

The same Cardinal *Barberin* leaving the Court somewhat suddenly, and not without some incivility, took along with him the Register and Seal of his Legation, which he was oblig'd to leave with the Parliament. The Attorney General being inform'd thereof, the Court order'd the King's Attorney of the Presidial Jurisdiction of *Lyons* to get both the one and the other from the *Datary,* and this Sub-

altern Officer taking along with him the Lieutenant General of the same Presidial, and being attended with about forty Pursuivants, went to the Lodgings of the *under Datary,* who would fain have excus'd himself on account of the absence of his Master, but he was however oblig'd to promise in writing, that he would restore both the one and the other the next day following. The Datary *Panfilio,* who has been since Pope, under the Name of *Innocent X,* told *M. de Chaumont,* who by the King's Order had attended the *Legate* to serve him, ever since he enter'd *France,* that the violence that had been offer'd to the *Legate* was insupportable, since at *Rome no Officer dares approach the Palace of the French Embassador.* The thing was excus'd to the *Legate,* and the Lieutenant General with the King's Attorney had orders to come to Court, and there give an account of their Action, which was in reality a little irregular. This was all that was done to satisfie the *Legate,* who sent the Seal and the Register of his *Legation,* by an express to the *Nuncio,* and He restor'd them to the Parliament.

Whatever Regard Princes have for the See of *Rome,* and whatever benefit they find in the Pope's friendship, they will not suffer it to prejudice the rights of their Sovereignty, nor the interest of their Crown. As soon as Pope *Paul III.* was inform'd of the death of *Edward VI.* King of *England,* he nominated Cardinal *Pool* to the *Legation* of that Kingdom. However, not thinking it proper to expose the Authority of the See of *Rome,* till affairs were a little settled, He follow'd the advice of Queen *Mary,* who counsel'd him not to be too hasty, because the business of Religion could not be regulated but by the Parliament, which should be call'd together after her Coronation. Wherefore the Pope giving mother pretext to the *Legation,* sent the Cardinal forward, with orders to labour a Peace between the Emperor *Charles V.* and *Henry II.* King of *France,* till he had a convenient passage. The Pope acquainted the two Princes therewith, and his intention was approv'd of in *France,* but the Bishop of *Arras* told the Abbot (whom the Cardinal had sent to *Bruxelles,* to give the Emperor advice of his Journey) that he was surpriz'd at the Pope's proceeding, who ought to have inform'd the Emperor thereof, before the *Legate* set out: That he did not see what could be hop'd for from the offices of one single Minister, since the two *Legates* the Pope had just recall'd, had not been able to effect any thing. That this was but a Cloak to cover the *Legation* of *England* with, of which the Queen had so much the more reason to complain, as this Commission was of the last prejudice to her State and Interest. That he knew she had not kept it hid from the *Legate* himself. Which was a truth; but that did not hinder the Cardinal from continuing his Journey as far as the Countrey of *Wirtemberg,* after he had receiv'd the Duke's Passport, for which he waited some time at *Dillinguen.* The Emperor being acquainted herewith, sent the *Legate* word by *Don John de Mendoza,* that for very important and weighty Reasons which he had communicated to the Pope, he could not suffer him to continue his Journey

Journey to *Brussels*, so that he would do well to stay in the place where he actually was, or else in some other Town that lay in his way. He also added to what the Bishop of *Arras* had said to his Abbot, that since the Pope sent but one *Legate*, the Emperor could not approve of the Negotiations beginning where he was, because if it had not the Success the Pope promis'd himself from it, the Emperor might be thought to be the obstacle that hinder'd it. He also spoke to him concerning the Marriage, as of an Affair that was to be concluded previously to all others, and that with a stranger, in order to avoid the emulation of the English Noblemen. The *Legate* did not discover his sentiments on that subject, but he could not forbear making it known, that the opposition which was made to his Journey, affected him very sensibly. He said the Emperor thereby affronted the Holy See. That having orders to pursue his Journey, he did not see how any other Prince could oppose his so doing. That the Emperor would do well to speak plainly, and say it was not the *Legation*, but the Person of the *Legate* he did not like. *Menaoza* endeavour'd to cure him of this opinion, and to perswade him to pursue his Journey as far as *Liege*, where he might reside 'till he receiv'd the Pope's farther orders. The *Legate* thinking it more reputable for him to remain in *Germany*, than to reside in a Town so near the Court, where they would not receive him, And taking into consideration, that at *Liege* he should no longer have it in his power to make choice of his way to pass to *England*, chose rather to go back to *Dillinguen*, where he receiv'd orders from the Pope, not to stir from thence 'till the Emperor let him know what he intended to do. The *Legate* had sent another Abbot into *France*, where he found very favourable dispositions. But the same Abbot in making a report of his Journey, told the *Legate*, that as he came back through *Brussels*, he had very well understood that the Emperor would not be well pleas'd if the *Legate* should go first to *France* before he had seen him, because it was apprehended he would from thence pass into *England*. The Letters the *Legate* wrote to the Pope, to the Emperor, and even to Queen *Mary*, had no effect, till *Peter Soto*, who had been *Confessor* to *Charles*, took a turn to *Brussels*, and obtain'd leave for the *Legate* to continue his Journey, but this was not till after a certainty of the conclusion of *Philip*'s Marriage, the Emperor's Son, with the Queen of *England*. The Emperor sent the Duke of *Savoy* a good way into *Germany* to meet him, and conduct him to *Brussels*, where great honours were done him. However the dissatisfaction this Marriage occasion'd to a great many in *England*, had caus'd some Provinces to rise, and the *Legate*, who could not get thither, went to *France*, tho' with so little success, that at his return the Emperor did not scruple to say, *That he might very well have spar'd himself the pains of returning*. The *Legate* was so offended at these words, that he sent a Courrier on purpose to *Rome*, to desire the Pope to discharge him of the *Legation*, and dismiss him, but this was deny'd him. The Emperor was jealous of the Cardinal's Voyage to *England*, and indeed it was not without cause. He was perswaded that the *Legate* would enter into the sentiments of almost all the *English*, who had generally an aversion to the Marriage, because they look'd upon it as the beginning of a foreign Domination. The Queen her self had ask'd *Commendon*, when she saw him, soon after the death of *Edward* whether the Pope would make any difficulty to grant the Cardinal a dispensation that he might Marry. He had amongst his Attendance some Religious, who, being *English*, spoke freely of this Alliance, and it was observ'd that he himself did not explain himself very clear, when he was talk'd to about it. And even after the conclusion and consummation of the Marriage, he was not suffer'd to pass into *England*, till he had satisfy'd *Philip* concerning some difficulties he caus'd to be propos'd to him. He first made him be ask'd whether he was willing to come into the Kingdom without the marks of his *Legation*, Whether he pretended to make use of the power of his *Legation* as he thought fit himself, or else in concert with *Philip* and the Queen, and he signify'd to him, that it was necessary he should obtain a more simple power than what he had. That it was not sufficient to reconcile the inform, and to dispense with the marry'd Priests, upon condition they serv'd no longer at the Altar, and did not enjoy their Benefices, as also with the abstinence from certain Meats on prohibited days, and other things of the like nature. That the power the *Legate* had to transact and determine concerning the Ecclesiastical Revenues was useless, because that made People believe he design'd to erect a Tribunal, and to proceed against the Usurpers in a judicial manner, whereas it was necessary he should also have the power to yield 'em up, and leave them to those who possess'd 'em. That in case the *Legate* had any hopes of obtaining this Power from the Pope, he might come forthwith, but if he was doubtful in the matter, he would do well to stay at *Brussels* 'till he had procur'd it. The *Legate* made answer, that he could not have thought so many difficulties would have been rais'd concerning the Ceremonies of his Reception, after having made him wait so long. *That he sustain'd three Characters, that of his own Person, that of Embassador from the Pope, and that of Legate from the Apostolick See*. And notwithstanding he might justly pretend to the honours which are due to the last, yet he was willing to be contented with those which could not be refus'd to the second, since the Pope had order'd him to pass over all those Considerations, and to have nothing else in view, but the Salvation of those People. That his intention had always been to do nothing without their Majesty's participation. And as for the third point, that he had a particular Bull, by which the Pope permitted him to do whatever he should judge necessary for the Salvation of so many straying Souls, and that he did not doubt but the Pope would ratifie whatever he did, and even grant him a larger power, if he ask'd it of him. The Deputy whom *Philip* sent, having signify'd to the *Legate* that he was satisfy'd with that Answer, told him he had orders from the King and Queen to offer him the
Archbishop

Archbishoprick of *Canterbury*, with the Primacy of *England*. But the Cardinal reply'd, That being the Pope's Minister, he could accept of nothing without Orders from his Holiness. Besides, that it was far from his thoughts to talk of his own particular Interest, till that of the publick was regulated. After this Conference, he resolv'd to pass into *England* under the Conduct of my Lord *Hastings*, Master of the Horse, and of *William Paget*, whom the Queen had sent to meet him as far as *Brussels*. The Bishop of *Ely* and Viscount *Mountague* receiv'd him at his Landing at *Dover*, the Bishop of *Durham* and the Earl of *Shropshire* complemented him at *Gravesend*, and brought him to *London*. He did not till he came to *Gravesend* set up the Cross in the forepart of his Barge as a token of his Legation. The King who was at dinner when he was inform'd of the *Legate*'s being arriv'd, got up from the Table, and went to receive him at the *Tower-Key*, and the Queen receiv'd him at the top of the Stair-case. He went first to pay his respects to the King, who receiv'd him without his Chamber door, and the next day the King visited him.

In the Year 1537 the same Cardinal *Pool* had been sent by the Pope into *France*, to labour a Peace between the Emperor and the King. He was very honourably receiv'd in all the Towns through which he pass'd. But when he came to *Paris*, a Messenger came and told him from the King, who was then at *Hesdin*, That his Majesty was so far from suffering the Legate to come to Court, that he did not intend he should make any stay within the Kingdom. This was done out of complaisance to *Henry* VIII King of *England*, who was at great variance with the Pope, and was perswaded that he made use of the Cardinal to stir up his Subjects to an Insurrection. Wherefore he made pressing Instances to *Francis* the first, that he would send him to him a Prisoner, but finding that Prince was not capable of doing an action so base, and against the Law of Nations, he set a price upon the Cardinal's Head, and promis'd fifty thousand Crowns to the Person who should bring it him. Which oblig'd the Pope to call him back to *Rome*, and to give him Guards.

When the Cardinal of *Ferrara*, *Hippolytus d'Este* arriv'd in *France*, in the Reign of *Charles* IX the Chancellor of the Hospital refus'd to Seal his *Letters D'attache*, which the King usually annexes to the Pope's Bulls, to recommend the Registring of them in Parliament, and did not Seal 'em but with this addition, *That he did it by the King's express Commands, and against his own Opinion*. And this it self was not done till the Cardinal had made great submissions, and had promis'd *that he would not make use of his faculties to the prejudice of the Request the States of the Kingdom had made at Orleans, that it might be no longer allow'd the Pope to dispose of Benefices, nor to grant Dispensations against the Canons*, which the Parliament took care to Register.

About three hundred Years before, *viz* in the Year 1239 *Otto* Cardinal of *St Nicholas in Carcere Tulliano*, after he had made some stay in *England*, propos'd to pass into *Scotland*, there to reap his Harvest, as he had just done in *England*. But *Alexander* King of *Scotland* having advice thereof, went and met him on the frontiers, and told him, That if then, no Legate had ever been seen in his Kingdom, and that it could make a shift without 'em for the time to come, because all the Churches were in a very good Condition. Yet nevertheless, after great contestations, the King suffer'd him to enter *Scotland*, on condition *That it should be no prejudice to his Crown, and that it should not serve for a precedent, which he should promise in writing before he left the same*. The Cardinal perceiving he should not find his reckoning there, did not penetrate far into it, made no long stay there, nor did he see the King any more, who did not matter him.

When Cardinal *Caraffa* Nephew and *Legate* of Pope *Paul* IV arriv'd at *Brussels* the 13th of *December* 1558 *Philip* King of *Spain* receiv'd him at the City Gate, and plac'd him on his right hand. Some time after, the King having invited him to assist at the Ceremonies of the Festival of the Kings, went in Person to his Lodgings, conducted him to Mass, and afterwards made him Dine with him, which is a thing the Kings of *Spain* never do. He also order'd Turnaments and other diversions at *Brussels* out of respect to him, but he gave him so little satisfaction in reference to the affairs he had to negotiate, that the *Legate* to shew his discontent, retir'd into a Convent at a good distance from the Court, with an intention to return to *Rome*. *Philip* fearing lest this troublesome and violent Spirit should create him new broils, sent for him back, making him hope he would give the Pope better satisfaction by the Ministers he had at *Naples*, and other places in *Italy*, who were better acquainted with the affairs of those parts, than those he had with him at *Brussels*. Having given him this consolation, he sent him back to the Pope, who was not well pleas'd with his Nephew, no more than with *Philip*. *Philip* and *Charles* his Father had inherited that from *Ferdinand the Catholick*, who was the Prince of the World that knew best how to make Religion subservient to his Interest. In the preceding Chapter I said a word or two concerning the *Infidelity* of *Ferdinand*, in this I shall do the same, with reference to his *Hypocrisie*. The Remarker of *Brussels* can't endure the Memoirs should say he had more Devotion than Conscience, and endeavours to justifie him by the Testimony of *Father le Moine*, that is to say, *of the Author of the Treatise of easie Devotion*. This Father, to flatter bigotry, establishes in that Book a sort of Piety more conformable to the Rules of the *Alcoran*, than to the Doctrine of the Gospel, which, if you believe him, is not inconsistent with *Hypocrisie*, and that one may be a very good Christian, tho' swallow'd up in an abyss of Vices. Here is a proof of *Ferdinand*'s Devotion. Pope *Julius* II Sovereign Lord of the *Kingdom of Naples*, had caus'd an Officer of Justice to execute some Warrant relating to the exercise of a Jurisdiction which the Pope pretended to be his Right. *Ferdinand* having had advice thereof, order'd *Don John* of *Arragon*, *Count of Ribagorça* and *Vice-Roy of Naples*, his Nephew, *to seize that Officer of the Pope's, and to hang him up presently*, not as the Pope's Minister,

Minister, said he, but as the Officer of the immediate Lord of the Fief, and adding these express words, *Ellos al Papa, y vos a la Capa i e Others to the Pope, and you to the Cloak*. Is it not a very fine distinction, full of Devotion, and altogether Catholick? *Ferdinand* valu'd himself for his Infidelities, which the Author, whom I before mention'd, sometimes calls subtilties, and sometimes *Zorrerias*, which in good English signifies malice in grain, Treasons, and actions unworthy of a Prince, and a Man of honour.

I shall not say any thing of the usage *Clement* VII, and *Paul* IV receiv'd from *Charles* V and from *Philip* his Son, for fear of deviating too much from the matter I am upon, but I think I ought not to omit observing how *Charles* behav'd himself towards Cardinal *de Medicis*, Nephew of the said Pope *Clement*. *Soliman* Emperor of the Turks, had invaded *Germany*, and seeing there was no likelihood of making great Conquests, soon retir'd *Charles* on his side, having in his thoughts to take a Journey into *Spain*, and being willing to leave some *Italian* Regiments with *Ferdinand* his Brother, that he might make use of them in *Hungary*, gave them a foreign Leader, who was so ungrateful to them, that they tore their Colours to pieces, and disbanded themselves absolutely. It was *Peter Mary Rossi* an *Italian*, and Camp-Master, that had contribute most to the disorder. But Cardinal *de Medicis* who was with the Emperor in the quality of Legate, protected *Rossi*, and drew upon himself by that means a very foul disgrace. The *Emperor* had himself regulated his Stages, and the order of the march, according to which he was to set out first with the Van-Guard, and the *Legate* was to follow him two days after for the greater conveniency of Lodgings. This resolution had been taken at a Council of War, and was communicated to the *Legate*, who being egg'd on by youthful levity, did not stick to set out first, and go before, taking *Rossi* along with him, and so furnish'd the Emperor with an opportunity of shewing him his resentment. *They were both arrested*, and notwithstanding the *Legate* was set at liberty at the end of five days, and that *Charles* excus'd the proceeding at *Rome*, the Pope was so sensibly touch'd therewith, that he could not forbear shewing it by his tears.

All the other Princes have very little consideration for *Legates*, when they are not well pleas'd with those that send 'em. Pope *Julius* III having made a great many Cardinals at the nomination of *Charles* V, and having moreover spoke in the Consistory with little respect of *Henry* II King of *France*, this last oblig'd Cardinal *Verallo*, the *Pope's Legate*, to depart the Kingdom, and recall'd *M. de Termes* who was his Minister at *Rome*. *Lewis* XI us'd Cardinal *Bessarion* very ill, and the Emperor did not do over-well by Cardinal *de Visco*. Queen *Mary* of *England* would not admit *Petey* her *Confessor* to accept the Bulls of his *Legation*. She caus'd the Person to be arrested at *Calais*, and suffer'd his Boxes to be open'd, and Papers to be seiz'd, who was bringing *Petey* his Bulls, by virtue of which he was to succeed Cardinal *Pool* in his Legation.

Charles Pasibal says in his Treatise of the Embassador, that except the King of *France*, all the other Kings go out to meet the *Legate* at his Entry. It is true there are several Examples thereof in the Histories of *England* and *Spain*. In the Year 1237, *Henry* III King of *England*, went to meet the Cardinal *d' St Nicholas* (whom I above mention'd, as it is the place where he Landed, and made great submission to him, but then it was against the Opinion of the major part of the Noblemen of his Kingdom. In the Year 1473 *Rodrigues Borgia*, Cardinal of *Valencia*, and since Pope, under the Name of *Alexander* VI being *Legate* from *Sixtus* IV and making his publick Entry at *Madrid*, had not only *the Canopy given him, but the King in Person went out to meet him, and completed the Honour, by placing him on his right hand*. *Philip* II went to meet the Cardinals *Pool* and *Caraffa*, but it was not without some opposition on the part of the *English*, who judg'd he did too much. *Philip* IV went out to meet Cardinal *Barberin* in the Year 1626, tho' it the same time he us'd him after so disobliging a manner, that the Court of *Rome* has no reason to be proud of it. This King coming up to the *Legate* laid by the Gate through which he was to make his Entry, gave him a slender Salutation with his Hat, and speaking to him in the second Person, which is never done in *Spain*, but to Persons to whom no Honour is shewn at all, he as'd him *in what Condition he had left his Unkle, and how the Legate had his Health*, and having told him he was welcome, he plac'd him on his left hand, and conducted him to St Mary's Church Door, where he left him. The Commander *de Rula* had receiv'd the *Legate* at *Barcelona*, where he landed. The Count *d'Ognate* went to meet him as far as the Frontiers of *Castile*. The Cardinal *Infanta* sent a Gentleman of his Chamber to visit him at *Barajas*, and as soon as he arriv'd at St *Hierom's* of the Escurial, the King made him be Complemented by the Dukes of *Sessa* and of *Albuquerque*, and by the Marquis *de Liche*. But when the Honours were to be regulated, which he desir'd should be done him, they were absolutely refus'd. He pretended to have the Canopy at his Entry, and that the Princes of *Spain* should pay him the first Visit, but he obtain'd neither the one nor the other, because the Princes would have *the place of Honour in his own House*, and that he should treat them with the Title of *Highness*, while they only bestow'd on him that of *most Illustrious Lordship*. He maintain'd that they could not refuse him the Canopy, by reason they had given it to the *Prince of Wales* when he made his Entry at *Madrid*. To which answer was made, That it appear'd by the *Archives*, that heretofore the same Honour had been done to a Prince of *Castile* at *London*. That the Example of the *Prince of Wales* could not serve for his purpose, because that by the same Reason he might pretend to all the other Honours that were done to the Prince by a formal Resolution of Council, which ordain'd amongst other things, that he should take the upper hand of the King in all their Meetings. That he should make his Entry in the same manner, and with the same Ceremonies that are paid the King on the day of his Coronation. That he should have one of the best Apartments in the Palace. That a hundred Yeomen

Yeomen of the Guard should constantly attend his Person. That the Council should obey his Orders as they did the King's. That the Prisoners should be set at Liberty, and that the Declaration which had been publish'd against the excesses in Apparel should be revok'd. The Honours that are done to Sovereigns, and to presumptive Heirs of Crowns, ought not to be used as Precedents, nor communicated to Representatives, what Quality or Character soever they may have. I shall give here one more Example. The 25th of *November*, 1624, the *Arch-Duke Charles* arriv'd at *Madrid*, the *Admirante of Castile* went to meet him two days Journey off with a very fine *Cortege* of Noblemen, the two Princes, the King's Brothers, *Don Carlos* and the *Cardinal* went into the fields to meet him, and the King himself went out of Town, to receive him at two hundred paces distance from the Gate. He alighted, embrac'd the *Arch-Duke*, and plac'd him in the Coach next himself forward, while the two Princes sate backward next the Horses. The Duke of *Neubourg*, and the Earl Duke sate in one of the Boots, and the Admirante with the Emperor's Embassador in the other, the former taking the place of Honour of the latter, which is worth observation.

The *Spaniards* do not give the Canopy to *Legates* Francis Cardinal of *Diatrigstein*, nominated *Legate*, to go and Complement on the part of *Clement* VIII, the Arch-Duke *Albert*, and the *Infanta* his Wife, who were passing through *Italy*, in order to go to the Low-Countries, made pressing Instances to have the Canopy when he should make his Entry at *Milan*. But the *Constable of Castile*, Governor of the Dutchy, signify'd to him, that since the King had forbid him to give it to the *Arch-Dukes*, who were so dear and so nearly related to him, he could not grant to the *Legate* what the King refus'd to his Sister. The Cardinal stifly insisted upon it a long time, and yielded at last but to the firmness and resolution of the *Constable*, who oblig'd him to be contented with the Honour that the Arch-Duke and the Governor did him, to go and meet him, and take him between them to conduct him to the Church.

In *France* the usage is quite different, the King does not go to meet the *Legate*, and indeed does not always visit him. On the contrary, King *Henry* IV notify'd to Pope *Clement* VIII on account of the *Legation* of the Cardinal of *Florence*, that he would send the Prince of *Condé* to receive him at his Entry, it not being lawful for him to do him that Office in Person, and that notwithstanding it was the practice of the Kings his Predecessors to expect the *Legates* in the *Louvre*, yet he would visit the Cardinal before he enter'd into *Paris*. It is also but only since that King's Reign, that they are receiv'd and accompany'd by a Prince of the Blood at their Entry. *George* Cardinal *d'Amboise*, *Legate* from the Pope, and first Minister to *Lewis* XII. made his Entry into *Paris* the 16th of *February*, 1501. The Streets were hung with Tapestry; the Canopy was carried at first by the Sheriffs, and afterwards by some of the Companies of Merchants and Traders successively. The Parliament was there *by Deputies in black Gowns*,

and the Town-house and *Chastelet* in Bodies, and in their Habits of Ceremony. No mention is made there of the Duke of *Engoulesme*, who was then the only Prince of the Blood, of the branch of *Valois*, no more than at the Entry of Cardinal *Salviati*, which was perform'd on the 31st of *October* 1526. Cardinal *du Prat*, Archbishop of *Sens*, and Chancellor of *France*, made his the 27th of *December* 1530. He was accompany'd by the Cardinals *de Tournon* and *de Grammont*, and by some other Prelates. The Entry of Cardinal *Farnese* was on the 29th of *December*, 1539, that of Cardinal *Verallo* on the 13th of *December*, 1551, and that of Cardinal *Caraffa* on the 22d of *June*, 1556, all three without Princes of the Blood. I do not think neither that *Lewis* XI sent to meet Cardinal *Bessarion*, whom we before spoke of. *Henry* IV who was willing to oblige Pope *Clement* VII, and who was very well satisfy'd with the *Legate Alexander de Medicis*, made him a familiar Visit before he got to *Paris*, and would have the Prince of *Condé*, who was very young, and had but lately chang'd his Religion, go and meet him as far as St *James*'s Gate. Cardinal *Aldobrandin* Nephew and *Legate* of the same Pope, did not go so far as *Paris*, because the King was then at War with the Duke of *Savoy*; but when he arriv'd at *Chambery*, where there was a *French* Garrison at that time, he was receiv'd at the Gate of the Town by the Count *de Soissons*, and by the Duke of *Montpensier*, who was *a Prince of the Blood*. *La Busse* Governor of the Place, did him the Honour to go and take his Orders from him, altho' that belong'd to the Princes of the Blood. The King approv'd of what *La Busse* had done, notwithstanding the *Legate's* negotiation was not very acceptable to him. He did not visit him, on the contrary, he stay'd for him at the Capucin's Convent, where he gave him his first Audience, as well for the Reason I just mention'd, as because the Court of *Rome* might have claim'd a Title upon the possession. When Cardinal *Barberin* came into *France*, on the part of *Urban* VIII. in the Year 1625, Cardinal *Richelieu* was for having the King Visit the *Legate*, and in all likelihood he had prevail'd with him, if at that time he had had the Credit he has had since. The King excus'd himself on his Indisposition, and did him the civility of a Letter, reserving his Visit till he came to Court, which accordingly he perform'd while the *Legate* was at *Fountainbleau*. The Duke of *Orleans* the King's only Brother, receiv'd him at St. *James*'s Gate through which all *Legates* make their Entry; but it was with a great deal of reluctancy, finding it against the grain to do that Honour to a Representative. The Duke of *Orleans* only Brother to *Lewis* XIV, would not accompany Cardinal *Chigy* Legate from *Alexander* VII and upon his refusal, this Commission was given to the Prince of *Condé*, and to the Duke of *Enguien* his Son, Princes of the Blood. So that for the time to come, *Legates* must regulate their Pretensions on the Examples of *Henry* IV, and of *Lewis* XIV. The *Legate Barberin* yielded the place of Honour at his own House, to the Cardinals *Richelieu* and *la Valette*, as to his Seniors, and for the same Reason he yielded it also since to the Cardinal *Infant*

Infants in *Spain*, receiving him at the bottom of the Stayrs, and re-conducting him to his Coach.

At the Entry that was made to Cardinal *Aldobrandin* at *Chambery*, there happen'd a passage which, I think it necessary to take notice of. The Bishops of *Evreux* and of *Bayonne* had resolv'd to go and meet the *Legate* in their Pontifical Habits, but he gave 'em to understand, that in the Quality and Power he then was, he could not allow those Prelates to appear before him with the tokens of Jurisdiction and Episcopal Authority. The Bishop's made answer, that perhaps it might be the practice of *Legates* on the other side of the Mountains, but as they were in *France* (since *Chambery* was the *King's* Conquest) they pretended to make use of their Right, and of the Authority they held from God, that they might do nothing which the other Bishops their Brethren might lay to their Charge. The King who would not offend the *Legate*, as well because he was oblig'd to the Pope for his reconciliation to the See of *Rome*, and for the dissolution of his Marriage, as by reason he had still occasion for him in the Affair of *Savoy*, would not suffer the Bishops to go to meet the *Legate*; so that they were contented with paying him private Visits, in their usual Habits.

There happen'd something like this in the Legation of Cardinal *Barberin*, the *Legate* being arriv'd at *Orleans*, the Archbishop of *Tours*, and the Bishops of *Auxerre*, of *Nismes*, of *Malesais*, and of *Clermont* came thither with a design to Complement him, but the *Legate* would not suffer them to appear before him with their *Rochet* and * *Camail* open and uncover'd, because that according to the Ceremonial of *Rome*, Bishops ought not to appear before the *Legate* with any marks of Jurisdiction. The Bishops on their side maintain'd, that the Liberties of the *Gallican* Church allow'd them that Privilege, and finding they were not admitted, they went back without seeing him. Before he made his Entry into *Paris*, the Prelates who were there met, to a great number, offer'd to make him a Visit in their usual Habits, the Cassock and Cloak, and to accompany him at his Entry with their *Rochets*, and *Camails* open, which the *Legate* not approving of, it was agreed, that at this Ceremony the *Rochet* and *Camail* should be cover'd with the *Manteline* or *short Cloke*, which they should take off when they came to the Church of *Nôtre Dame*, after the same manner as the Bishops are us'd to do in the presence of the King. After this accommodation of the matter, the four Archbishops, and the thirty two Bishops who were in *Paris*, went to complement the *Legate*, and accompany'd him in this condition at his Entry. Yet nevertheless some time after, when the *Legate* would say Mass in *his Pontificalibus*, on our Lady's day in *August*, in the great Chappel at *Fontainbleau*, not one of the Prelates would assist at the Ceremony, because since his Entry he had scrupled to admit some Bishops, who would have visited him with their *Rochets* and *Camails* uncover'd; and because he said they ought not to have taken off their little Cloak in the Church, tho'

at the same time he had agreed thereto It was for this Reason also that they did not see him any more but in their ordinary Habits However he in the main receiv'd great Civilities Before he made his Entry into *Paris*, he was Lodg'd at *Chantelou*, whither the King wrote to him, that his indisposition hinder'd him from visiting him, as he otherwise would have done. The King had no such intention, and the *Legate* could not doubt but it was a meer excuse, but yet it was for all that very obliging. While he was at *Fontainbleau*, the King made him a visit in his Apartment. The *Legate* went to meet his Majesty as far as he could, and the Conversation lasted about half an hour. At his first publick Audience he caus'd the Cross to be born before him as far as the Antichamber, *and the King and he sate in equal Chairs*. Cardinal *de Richelieu*, M *de Schomberg* and *d'Harbant* Secretary of State, who were the King's Commissioners, negotiated with him at *Fontainbleau* in his Apartment, and in *Paris* at the *Hotel de Cligny*, where he was lodg'd. His Expences were defray'd during the whole time he stay'd in *France*, and the King's Officers treated him after the rate of two thousand five hundred livres *per day* for his Table. The King made him dine with himself, and the two Queens give him each of them a very magnificent Collation. After he had taken his audience of leave as *Legate*, he took another, as the Pope' Nephew.

No *Legate* is sent to *France*, but the Pope first gives advice to the King thereof, and has the Person design'd for the Legation first approv'd of by himself. This is also what is observ'd with reference to *Nuncio's*, of which we have an Example in the Bishop of *Mantua*, whom *Clement* VII had much ado to get accepted. He was suspected to be a *Spaniard* in inclination, and he was at last accepted, only because that of all the Competitors, he was the Man they had the least reason to complain of. In the course of his negotiation he gave none at all, so that it was without any uneasiness that he afterwards assisted with the *Legates* at the Assembly of *Verovns*. These *Nuncio's* are to the Pope, what *Embassadors* are to Secular Princes, there being of them both Ordinary, and Extraordinary *Anton Mary Gratiani*, who wrote the Life of Cardinal *Commendon*, when he speaks of the first Employment this Prelate had as *Nuncio*, expresses himself after a manner, that makes one infer, that in those times the word *Nuncio* was not so well known, or at least not so common as it has been since, especially in *Italy*. He says that in the Year 1555, *Commendon* was sent by the Pope to the Emperor in the Quality of Embassador, or to make use of the new Term, which is already much in use at *Rome*, says he, *he went as Nuncio from his Holiness*. Those that have but a slender knowledge of the Affairs of *France*, cannot be ignorant that *Nuncio's* had been there a long time talk'd of. The word is somewhat more Latin than that of Embassador, but it signifies the same thing, with this difference, that it denominates the Pope's Representing Minister particularly, as the *Internuncio* is his Envoy Extraordinary

* *A Camail is a purple Garment worn by a Bishop above his Rochet*

CHAP.

CHAP. XI.

The Prince may employ Strangers in his Embassies; even in their own Countrey.

I Shall not nave so hard a Task to make out this Position, as it is difficult to add any thing to what has been said already on that Subject, in the Memoirs. Nevertheless, seeing there are some Minds that are not yet fully convinc'd of this Truth, and that I find my self particularly oblig'd to establish it so firmly, that it may not be hereafter contested, I shall bestow this whole Chapter upon it, and treat distinctly of the two Parts of which the Thesis is compos'd. As for the first part, since the Sovereign may take his Ministers any where, even in the Cloisters, which are not of his Jurisdiction, he may also seek 'em among Strangers, and make choice there of Persons, upon whom he may exercise his ordinary Justice. Kings have in all Ages taken this Liberty, and have employ'd Strangers with success in their most important Negotiations. The King of *Persia* has employ'd in his Embassies, *Anthony* and *Robert Shirley*, and several Monks, *Castilians* and *Portuguese*. I shall hereafter have occasion to speak of *Ibrahim Strutzen*, and of *Bartholomew Cour*, who have been sent by the Great *Turk* to Christian Princes. *Lewis* XI, employ'd with Utility and Advantage *Philip de Commines*, at *Venice* and at *Florence*. *Lewis* XII, sent *Albert Pio*, Lord of *Carpi*, Embassador to *Rome*. *Cæsar Cantelmo*, a *Neapolitan*, negotiated for *Francis* I, at *Constantinople*, and *Francisco Bernardo*, a *Venetian* Gentleman, for *Henry* VIII, King of *England*, in *France*. *Stephen Battory*, King of *Poland*, sent in the Year 1582 *Dominick Alamanni*, a *Florentine*, to *John*, King of *Sweden*. Queen *Elizabeth* employ'd *Guy Cavalcanti*. *Philip* II, King of *Spain*, sent *Robert Kelley*, an *Englishman*, in Quality of Embassador to the Emperor *Maximilian* II. *Spain* does not want able Ministers, and one may say, that there are but too many in *France*; and nevertheless, Strangers have ever been made use of there, as well as in all the other Courts of Christendom. *Schomberg*, a *German*, and *Bassompierre*, a *Lorrainer*, have been employ'd in several Embassies. *Anthony Rincon* was a *Spaniard*; *Cæsar Fregose* was a *Genoese*; as was also *Claudio Marini*. *Mervelle* was a *Milanese*, Cardinal *Bichi* was a *Sienese*, *Mazarine* was a *Sicilian*, and the two last were the Pope's Subjects, by reason of their Dignity, but neither that nor their Birth, hinder'd them from serving foreign Princes. The King and Crown of *Sweden* have employ'd Strangers almost every where, even at the Assembly of *Westphalia*, and that of *Lubeck*, where *Salvius* had the chief Trust, to the exclusion of his Colleagues. The Popes have acted after the same manner; and there is not any Prince but does the same when occasion requires it. So that the general Consent of all Nations agreeing herein, it would be useless to dilate upon a Matter that is not contested.

The other part of the *Thesis* ought not to be so neither, after the many Examples that have been instanc'd in to confirm it, because that in reference to the *Law of Nations*, it is sufficient to know what is every where practis'd, without there being any Necessity to sift scrupulously into the Reason thereof. However, as there are People that are never satisfy'd, and that are so in love with their own prejudicate Opinions, that it is almost impossible to wean them from 'em, I shall endeavour at least to discover their Malady, and to hinder, by destroying their Principles, its communicating it self to those who are not prejudic'd with their false Notions. No body has hitherto doubted, that the Subject might discharge the Function of Embassador, to the Sovereign of the Place of his Birth. I know very well that *Bodin* maintains, *That the Subject who puts himself into the Service of a foreign Prince, against the Prohibition, or without the Permission of his Sovereign, may be claim'd by his Prince, and retain'd as a fugitive Servant, even tho' he should come to him in the Quality of Embassador.* But then I also know, that it is the private Opinion of *Bodin*, that is to say, of an Officer of Justice, who understood the Civil Law better than the *Law of Nations*: and who (since he does not confirm his Opinion, neither by Reasons nor Examples) cannot oblige me to have any Deference to it, to the Prejudice of the Reasons and Examples which I have to the contrary.

The Difficulty will be easily clear'd, after we have decided this Question, viz. Whether a Subject can, without a Crime, withdraw himself from the Subjection and Obedience, which he owes to the Sovereign of the Place of his Birth? It is certain he may free himself from the Jurisdiction of the Justice of his Sovereign, and I have heretofore demonstrated the same, by the Exemption of the Clergy. I shall only add thereto, that whereas Bishops and other Ecclesiasticks, who take an Oath to their Sovereign, on account of their temporal Estate, and enjoy his Protection, are also oblig'd to him in particular Duties. *The Knights of the Order of* Malta, become so much the Subjects of the Great Master, that they are oblig'd to obey him blindly, and to prefer the Service of the Order to that of their Countrey. Nevertheless there is no need of the Permission nor Acquiescence of the first Sovereign, either to enter into the said Order, or to go out of his said Sovereign's Subjection, tho' by making a Vow to the Order, a Man delivers himself up to a foreign Sovereign. This is what *Bodin* could not be ignorant of, nor also of what every body knows, *That the Air of* France *is so noble, that it gives Liberty to those who have it not; and suffers none to be Slaves, tho' they should enter the Kingdom in the Train of an Embassador.* He ought also to know by Experience, that the King never opposes the Will of those of his Sub-

Subjects, that leave *France* to go and settle themselves under another Sovereign. There are in a manner whole Colonies of 'em in *Holland*, and even *Spain* would be more unfrequented than it is, without the *French* Families that People some of its best Towns. In *Spain* it self there is a very ancient Custom, that permits the Subjects to renounce the Subjection which they owe to their Sovereign, and the Protection they hope for from him. Which being conformable to the *Law of Nature*, and the *Law of Nations*, it must be own'd, that this Liberty is common to all Men, unless it be in those Places where it has been alter'd by the Laws and Custom of the Countrey. Those of *Rome* cut it off in some measure, since they did not allow of Transmigrations, but upon condition to contribute to the municipal Charges of the Place from whence they departed. The *Czar of Muscovy* does not suffer his Subjects to go out of his Countrey without his leave, nay he does not allow them to change the Place of their Habitation. They are his Slaves, and cannot dispose of their Persons. At *Hamburgh* a Burgher cannot go and settle elsewhere, without leaving the tenth part of what he is worth to the Magistrate, and there are some Provinces in *Germany*, and in the *North*, where the Peasants, belonging in property to the Lord of the Mannor, cannot change their Place of Habitation, because they cannot change their Master nor Condition. But these are *Relicts of Pagan Servitude*. Every where else People enjoy the Liberty of Transmigration, according to the Opinion of *Groenwegen*, in his Treatise of the *abrogated Laws*; and of *Hugh de Groot* in his admirable Book, *De Jure Belli & pacis*. where he alledges the Saying of *Cicero*, in the Oration he made for *Balbus*, where he says, that it is the very Foundation of Liberty, *and that every one has a Right to dispose of his Person, without any Obligation or Constraint to be the Burgher of any Town any longer than he has a mind to it*. De Groot here adds, that this Liberty being in common, cannot prejudice the Sovereign, because if he loses one Subject, he may get ten for him from other Places. He only makes here two Exceptions *viz* That what is permitted to some particular Persons, is not permitted to a whole Community, as it is allowable to take Water out of a Brook or River, but it is not lawful to turn it another way, and also, that the Citizen of a Town which is incumber'd with Debts, and has been oblig'd to be at great Expences, cannot go and settle himself elsewhere, without paying his part of the Debt.

This is without doubt what the States of *Holland*, had a regard to, when they ordain'd, that those Inhabitants of the Province, that should go and settle in another during the War, should continue to contribute to the Charges as long as it lasted, because it is reasonable that they, who have enjoy'd the Benefit of the Protection of a Sovereign during the Peace, should likewise share in the Inconveniencies during the War. But they never forbad Transmigrations absolutely, nor hinder'd the Inhabitants of their Province to transplant themselves into another, which cannot be done without change of Sovereign, as well in the extent of those of the Union, as in going quite out of the Countrey. On the contrary, in obliging those that go and settle elsewhere, to continue to contribute to the Charges and Necessities of the State, they permit Transmigrations. So that it was what might have very well been let alone, the seeking to discover in a formal Resolution of the States of the Province, and of the Generality it self, a Paradox quite destitute of all appearance of Reason. Then it follows from hence, by an infallible Consequence, that he who can transplant himself and Family out of the Countrey, may, with much more reason, put himself in the Service of, or bind himself by Oath to, a foreign Prince, because he that can do a greater thing, can also do the less that is imply'd therein. If he does it with the Consent or Permission, express or tacit, of the Sovereign of the Place of his Birth, this looses, with the Jurisdiction, all the other Rights which he had over the Person of his Subject. The Reason thereof is very evident, because he that takes an Oath to a foreign Prince, is liable to his Jurisdiction, and is oblig'd to give him an account of his Actions.

This is an Obligation beyond Comparison much stronger than that of Birth, since the Subject can go out of a Countrey, and withdraw himself from the Subjection of his Sovereign, and as the *Spaniards* say, *desnaturarse*, without his Permission, but he that is sworn to a Prince cannot get off of it till he has procur'd his Discharge as the Soldier cannot leave the Standard, nor the Officer quit the Service, without a Licence, but he must at the same time become a Deserter, a Transfuge, and a Traitor. Now there is no being subject to two Sovereigns, nor accountable for our Actions to two different Princes, but by taking an Oath to the one, we get out of the Obligation we had to the other, for there is no serving two Masters, whose Interests may be quite different and contrary.

For this Reason I dare not maintain, that the Resolution the States General have taken within some Years, relating to those *Hollanders* that shall become Ministers to a foreign Prince, was concerted with their usual Prudence. Let them consider if they please, whether by ordaining, that their Subject, who in the Quality of a publick Minister, shall put himself in the Service of a foreign Prince, shall nevertheless remain subject to the Justice of the Province, they do not give an indirect Blow to the *Law of Nations*, which exempts him from it. To permit a Subject to pass into the Service of a foreign Prince, and at the same time to preserve a Jurisdiction over his Person, is rendering him useless to the Prince, and even depriving the said Prince of the Right of disposing of the Person of his Minister, and punishing him if he deserves it. On the other side, it is moreover destroying the Character of the Minister, by robbing him of the brightest of all his Privileges, *viz.* that of being exempt from the Jurisdiction of the Place where he resides, as we shall take notice hereafter. There is no Minister that knows himself, can be such a Coward, as to do so much Wrong to his Character: and there is not any Prince, that has a Dram of Honour, that will suffer any Justice besides his own to lay hands upon his Minister,

Minister, under any Pretext whatsoever Neither do I believe, that hitherto there has been one single Minister, that has acquiesc'd in a Resolution so prejudicial to his Dignity, and the Reputation of his Prince, or that would have accepted of so illustrious an Employment, on so abject and servile a Condition.

The States of *Holland* will, I hope, give me leave to say, that it does not belong to them to frustrate a publick Minister of the Advantages his Character bestows upon him, with the general Consent of all the Nations of the Earth. If they will have their Subject acknowledge their Jurisdiction, let them not admit him as a publick Minister: but when they have once admitted and acknowledg'd him in this Quality, let them not hinder him from enjoying all the Advantages that are inseparable from a Minister, of which the Exemption from the Justice of the Place, is the first and the most important. But of this we shall speak more fully in the 27¹ Chapter. So that I shall only add here to what I have already said, that I cannot tell whether the States of *Holland* have acted up to their Intention, when they pass'd a Resolution that hinders foreign Princes from employing a *Hollander* as a Minister, since by this means they oppose the good Disposition of any Prince, who by employing one of the Subjects of this Province to the States General, thinks to oblige them and give them particular Marks of his Friendship, by sending a Person that ought to be by so much the more acceptable to them, as it is impossible to wean our selves of the natural Love we have for our Countrey. If the Person of the Subject be not acceptable, as they make a part of the States General, and the most principal part too, they may oppose his being admitted, and if he becomes disagreeable during the time of his Negotiation, it is the business of the States General, to do what *Decorum* can warrant, to get rid of a troublesome and impertinent Minister.

In *England* the Subjects have a stronger and more particular Obligation to their Sovereign than elsewhere, by virtue of the *Right* which they call *Allegiance*. But that does not hinder the *English* from retiring out of the Kingdom, without the King's Permission: and when they have settled themselves elsewhere, neither the King's Authority, nor the Laws of the Kingdom, have any farther Power over them. In the Year 1644, *John Webster*, an *English* Merchant, living at *Amsterdam*, and some other Merchants of the same Nation, who assisted the King with their Money, were declar'd Enemies of the State, by the Parliament at *London*. Upon a Complaint made thereof by the States of Holland, in the Assembly of the States General, these order'd their Embassadors to inform themselves what Laws and Customs the Parliament pretended to make use of, to maintain, that an Englishman, residing out of the Kingdom, who has fix'd his Habitation in their Countrey, and is become a Burgess there, is still Subject to the Jurisdiction, and to the Laws of that Kingdom. We must therefore necessarily conclude, that even the States of *Holland* are of Opinion, that there are no Laws, either in *England* or elsewhere, that can hinder a Subject from transplanting his Habitation into another Countrey, and from giving himself another Sovereign, than what he had by reason of his Birth. This is confirm'd by the Answer the States of the United Provinces made at the beginning of this War, to the Manifesto the King of *Great Britain* publish'd to justifie his Arms, and particularly to that Article, where his Majesty promises all Safety and good Usage to the Inhabitants of those Provinces, that would come and settle themselves in *England*. The States might have said, according to the Opinion of some modern Politicians and Lawyers, that there were particular Laws that forbid the Inhabitants to transplant themselves elsewhere, without leave from their Sovereign, but instead of advancing so extravagant a Maxim, they only say, that their Countrey is not yet perceiv'd to grow thin of Inhabitants, by the frequent Transmigrations of the People, preferring the Gentleness of the *English* Government, to that of the United Provinces. From whence we ought certainly to judge, that the States are of Opinion, that those who believe they shall find more Gentleness and Conveniency in *England* than in their Countrey, may go and live there, without the leave of the Sovereign. We may likewise from thence conclude, that altho' *Bodin*'s Opinion could subsist in *France*, that is to say, in a Despotick Monarchy, yet it could not obtain in reference to *Holland*.

The Reasons I have just laid down sufficiently prove the impertinence of it, but that I may wholly destroy it, and make it appear to be false, even with respect to *France*, where he wrote, I shall here alledge, as in its proper place, the Example of *Claudius Marini*, and the Declaration King *Lewis* XIII made on his account, upon the Subject I treat of in this Chapter. This Gentleman being oblig'd to retire from *Genoa*, which was his native Countrey, was receiv'd in *France*, and employ'd by the King in the Quality of Embassador to the Court of *Turin*, at the time that the Duke of *Savoy* and the Constable *de Lesdiguieres* made War against that Republick. The Senate, which knew that *Marini* (who was not very well satisfy'd with those who had the chief Direction and Management of Affairs at *Genoa*) did it several Disservices, caus'd him to be indicted, condemn'd him for contumacy as a Rebel, raz'd his House, and set a Price upon his Head, promising eighteen thousand Crowns to him that should bring it to *Genoa*. The King, seeing his Minister treated after this manner, resented it, as all Princes ought to resent the Wrongs and Injuries that are done to those they honour with their Character. He order'd du *Fargis*, the *French* Embassador at *Madrid*, to procure to the Article of the Treaty of *Moncon*, which mention'd the recalling and re-establishing the Exiles, a particular Explication in favour of Marini. He requir'd, that therein it should be expressly said, that his Minister should be restored to his Honour, his Estate and Privileges, and that fifty thousand Livres should be paid him for Damages. The Count Duke d'*Olivares* not being able to engage for this particular Promise, without the consent of the *Genoese* Embassador, who had no Power at all on that Head, the King caus'd fifty Bales of Silk, that belong'd to *Genoese* Merchants, to be sold for the Benefit of *Marini*, and made him enjoy the Rents other *Genoese* had out of the

the Town-House of *Paris* Some time after, the King sent the Marquis *de Rambouillet* about the Regulation of some Points relating to the Execution of the same Treaty of *Monçon* And amongst other Articles of his Instructions, *the King recommended to him, after a very particular manner, the saving of* Marini *harmless* But as the Marquis could not obtain any thing with relation to the main Affair, and that he had no great Satisfaction at *Madrid*, he did not mention this particular Interest The King would even have *Marini* to be one of the *Arbitrators* of the Difference the Republick of *Genoa* had with the Duke of *Savoy*, on account of the Marquisate of *Zuccarello* And notwithstanding the Senate refus'd that, it was however oblig'd to annul his Outlawry, and to restore *Marini* to the Possession of his Estate and Honour The King's Declaration explains so well the *Law of Nations*, and the Question in hand, that I cannot forbear inserting it here at length It speaks in these Terms

"His Majesty being duly inform'd, that they, "who at present govern the Republick of *Ge-* "*noa, had by an unparallell'd Audaciousness, and* "*extraordinary Temerity, violated the Law of* "*Nations in the Person of the Sieur* Marini, *his* "*Majesty's Embassador in* Piedmont, by causing "a Sentence to be publish'd, by which they "declar'd him a Rebel in the highest Degree, "and as such condemn'd him to die, confisca- "ting all his Goods, Moveables and Immovea- "bles, within their Jurisdiction, and also de- "molishing his Houses, having moreover set "a Price upon his Head, *viz* eighteen thou- "sand Crowns His Majesty therefore taking "into Consideration, *how much his Dignity was* "*thereby offended, and the publick Laws violated,* "and resolving to have such Reparation made "as is suitable to such an Enterprize, his Ma- "jesty has taken, and put into his Protection "and Safeguard, the Person and Goods of the "said Sieur *Marini* his Embassador, in Conse- "quence whereof he has ordain'd, and does "ordain, That the *Effects, Merchandize and* "*Goods*, as well Moveables as Immoveables, "of all the *Genoese* within the Realm, *shall be* "*from the time present seiz'd*, in what Place "soever they may be, and a good and faithful "Inventory made by his Officers of the whole "*That the Persons of the said* Genoese *shall be* "*likewise arrested*, and put into the Royal Pri- "sons of the Places where they shall be taken, "to serve as Pledges for the Person and Goods "of the said Sieur *Marini*, and there to remain "till such time as it shall be otherwise ordain'd "by his Majesty, excepting however, in re- "ference to the Imprisonment of the Persons, "those of the *Genoese* who shall be found to "have Letters of Naturalization from his "Majesty, duly verify'd He moreover "wills, and intends, that for the better Exe- "cution of what is above mention'd, the "Books of Commerce of the said *Genoese* "be likewise seiz'd, the better to discover "all their Effects, and to prevent and hinder "their being conceal'd under the Names "of other Merchants Strictly charging and "commanding all his Subjects, of what Con- "dition or Quality soever, who shall have in "their Hands any Goods or Effects, or the "Persons of the said *Genoese*, or shall know "in what Place they are, to make known and "discover the same within eight Days from "the Day of the Publication of this present "Ordinance, on the Penalty to the *Contrave-* "*ners*, of the Confiscation of all their Goods, "one third whereof shall be apply'd to the Ho- "spitals of the Poor, another to his Majesty, "and the third to the Discoverer, declaring "that they who shall be any way aiding and "assisting to the Concealment of the said "Goods, Effects and Persons, shall thereby in- "cur the same Penalties And forasmuch as "his Majesty will, *upon so extraordinary and ir-* "*regular a Procedure of the Republick, by which* "*the publick Faith was violated*, make use of "extraordinary means, and such as are not "commonly practis'd in this Kingdom, for the "Reparation thereof His Majesty ordains "and promises a Reward of threescore thou "sand Livres to his Subjects, or other Per- "sons, of whatever Condition they may be, "who shall duly verify and make out their ha- "ving chastiz'd, and punish'd with Death, any "one of those who shall have assisted and been "present at the Judgement, and *temerarious* "*Sentence* given against the said Sieur *Marini* "his Embassador, and set a Price upon his "Head, which Sum his Majesty will cause to "be duly and punctually paid 'em out of his "Treasury His Majesty also ordains, that "this present Ordinance shall be publish'd "through all the parts of his Dominions, "where it shall be requisite, as also without the "same, charging and strictly commanding all "his Justices, Officers and Subjects, to be aid "ing and assisting in the Execution hereof "Given at *Fountainbleau* the fourth Day of "*October*, 1625." Sign'd *Lewis*, and under- neath *Lomenie*

In Pursuance of this Ordinance all the *Genoese* were put into Prison, in *Provence*, at *Lyons*, and at *Paris* But according to *Bodin's* Opinion, the Republick of *Genoa* was in the right, and could proceed against a Gentleman that was her Subject, and had put himself in the Service of a foreign Prince He had put himself there against the Will of his Sovereign He stirr'd up the Arms of *France* and *Savoy* against his Countrey, and notwithstanding that, the King says, That his Dignity is injur'd in the Person of his Embassador That the Sentence of the Senate was temerarious That the *Law of Nations* was violated thereby, and that the publick Laws were offended therein So that it is to be believ'd that the King, who judges that a Sovereign has not a Right to lay Claim to a Subject, that serves in the Quality of publick Minister to a foreign Prince in another Court, would never injure in his own, a *Frenchman*, that should be there employ'd by another Sovereign As in effect, it is judg'd in that Kingdom that the Character carries it, against Birth, and that neither the Civil Laws, nor Local Customs, any more than the particular Ordinances of Princes, can destroy a Right establish'd by the general Consent of all People

King *Francis* I employ'd *Anthony Rincon*, and *Cæsar Fregosa*, who were both Strangers The first was a *Spaniard*, that is to say, a Subject of the Emperor *Charles* V, who, according to *Bodin's* Maxim, might have laid Claim to him any ny where, and have treated him as a fugitive Servant, yet *Charles* was so far from making use of that pretended Right, that he did not dare to own the murdering of him, tho' it had been executed either by his express Order, or with his Approbation In the Year 1541, these two Ministers (the one of which was going to *Constantinople*, where he had already negotiated some Matters against the Emperors Service) believing they might with Safety pass through *Piedmont*, by reason of the Truce that had been agreed upon at *Nice*, embark'd themselves on the *Po*, in order to go by *Ferrara* to *Venice* The Marquis *du Guast*, Governor of *Milan*, being advis'd of their Passage, caus'd them to be murder'd by Soldiers he had laid in Ambuscade for that purpose, on the Bank of the River Some of their Retinue got away, and the rest were brought into the Castle of *Cremona*, so that there was not any room to doubt but the Fact was authoriz'd by the Governor of *Milan* King *Francis* I complain'd hereof to all the Courts of *Europe*, and requir'd Satisfaction of the Emperor, who instead of owning the Execution as an Act of Justice exercis'd upon his Subject, disown'd the same, and only said that *Rincon* and *Fregosa* not having made themselves known as publick Ministers, the *Law of Nations* had not been violated in Persons that had not made known their Character The Marquis *du Guast* defended himself by a *Manifesto* in print, and offer'd to fight any Person that should charge him with an Action, wherein he said he was not at all concern'd I must needs have been a black one, since the Emperor and the Marquis did not dare to own it, as without doubt they would have done, if *Charles* had believ'd he could have dispos'd of a Subject that had pass'd into the Service of, and taken an Oath to, a foreign Prince The Policy of the Authors of this Maxim is more modern, and was not yet known by those who believ'd they understood the *Law of Nations* in those times, and who in reality understood it perfectly well

After what I have said of the Liberty that almost all Christians enjoy, excepting the *Muscovite*, only, and some other Slaves, of transferring their Habitation out of the Place of their birth, there is no room to doubt but a Man may discharge the Function of Embassador in his own Countrey I or since there is no being the Subject of two Princes, as I before observ'd, and that he that goes out of the Place of his birth, goes at the same time out of the Subjection of his Sovereign, it follows, that he enters into that of a new Sovereign, whose Subject being become, he is oblig'd to obey him, and to serve him even against the Person of him who was his Sovereign, but being so no longer cannot desire of him any Duties to the Prejudice of the last, and consequently, he cannot hinder him from discharging the Functions of Embassador, nor from enjoying all the Advantages and Prerogatives that are dependent thereon.

Hereupon I shall take notice by the way, that a Subject of the States of *Holland*, who in the Quality of publick Minister passes into the Service of a foreign Prince, whether it be done with their Consent or not, transfers his Dwelling out of the Province, and is no longer their Subject For altho' he resides at the *Hague*, yet he is not there as in a Town of *Holland*, but he is there to attend the Court, as in a Place which the States of *Holland* have yielded up to the States General, to the end the Deputies they shall send thither may be there, as in a neutral Place, as they have formerly been at *Utrecht*, at *Bergen-op-zoom* and elsewhere, and that it may give to the Ministers of foreign Princes that Safety and Protection which is their due, by virtue of the *Law of Nations*, and *of the publick Faith* As on the other side, a *Hollander* who has put himself in the Service of a foreign Prince, in the Quality of a publick Minister, to be employ'd to the States General, is not an Embassador or Resident in his native Countrey, but he is such to a State or Power, of which *Holland* is but a part So that as the States of that Province cannot singly cause a Minister to be recall'd who is not acceptable to them, nor send him out of the Countrey, since that cannot be done but by the means of the States General, so likewise it does not belong to them, and still less to their Court of Justice, to proceed against a publick Minister, who as he owes them nothing, ought not to give an account of his Actions but to the Prince he serves, and to whom he has taken an Oath of Fidelity

There is no Prince that refuses to acknowledge his Subject in the Quality of Embassador, if he comes on the part of a Sovereign whom he has no reason to distrust, unless, for particular Reasons, the Person of the Embassador is not grateful to him. In the Year 1514, Pope *Leo* X sent to *Venice* Peter *Bembo*, a *Venetian* Gentleman, who there made a bold Speech enough, conformable to his Instructions, and the Pope's Intention The Sages of the College made their Report thereof to the Senate, who did not approve of the Nuncio's Harangue, but that did not hinder the *Doge* from telling him, that the Embassy the Pope had sent them was acceptable, *as well on the score of the Person of the Embassador, whose Merit was well known to the Senate, and the Affection he had for his native Countrey, as for the Love they had for the Prince that employ'd him* Paul IV sent at the same time Cardinal *Caraffa* his Nephew into *France*, and *Scipio Rebiba* to the Emperor, to whom he wrote, that he hop'd *that Legate would be by so much the more acceptable to him, as he was born his Subject* The Popes who gave the Quality of *Legate* to Cardinal *Wolsey* and Cardinal *Pool*, and afterwards to *Pesey*, the Queen's Confessor, did it because they thought those Ministers would be acceptable to the Court of *England*. *William* Archbishop of *Rheims* was not only a *Frenchman*, and Unkle by the Mother's side to King *Philip Augustus*, but he was also Regent in *France*, and withal Legate *Otto de Chasteauroux* was Legate in *France* under *Lewis* XI, and accompany'd him in his Expedition to the Holy Land Peter of *Luxemburg*, Bishop of *Mans* and of *Therouenne*, was Legate in *France* under *Philip de Valois* George *d'Amboise* was Archbishop of *Roane*, and first Minister of *Lewis* XII, and Legate: as Cardinal *du Prat* was Archbishop of *Sens*, Chancellor of *France*, and Legate, in the Reign of *Francis* I Pope *Clement* VI sent to Peter IV King of *Arragon* the Cardinal *de Rhodez*, of the

Title

Title of St *Cyriaque aux Thermes*, who was *Pagan*, and chief of the Embassie, with Frier *Bernard Oliver*, a Religious of the Order of St *Augustin*, and Bishop of *Huesca*, the one whereof was the Son of a *Catalan*, and the other was of *Valencia*, and *Peter's* Subject.

Julius III sent Cardinal *Mignelli* to *Sienna*, which was the place of his Birth, as judging him a very fit Person to regulate affairs there, by reason of the Credit his Birth gave him with that Republick. After the same manner *P—s V*, sending in the Year 1570, *Lewis de Torres Nuntio* into *Spain*, wrote to the King, that He, as being one of his Subjects, that he might repose the greater confidence in him. And accordingly, *Philip* took so much pleasure in the Conduct of this Prelate, that he gave him the Archbishoprick of *Montreal* in *Sicily*. Some Years since, the Cardinal Duke of *Mercoeur* was Legate in *France* at the Christening of the *Dauphine*, that is to say, to assist thereat, in the quality of Godfather on the part of the Pope.

In the Year 1294, Pope *Celestin* V sent *Raymond* Bishop of *Valence*, and *Boniface* of *Calamanzana*, Master of the Order of St *John* of *Jerusalem*, to *James* I. King of *Arragon*, tho' they were both of them the King's Subjects. In the Year 1423, *Alfonso* V. King of *Arragon* sent into *Castille* Don *Juan* of *Valeire* Bishop of *Lerida*, and *Gorsale Munroz*, in the Quality of Embassadors, altho' the Nobleman was a *Castilian*, born at *Salamanca*, but he had been Educated in *Arragon*, before *Alfonso* succeeded to the Crown. This Embassie was sent to the Queen of *Arragon*, who was at *Medina del Campo*, and not to the King of *Castile*, to whom it was not acceptable, notwithstanding which, the King suffer'd his Subject to enter the Kingdom in the quality of Embassador, and to be there in safety.

In the Year 1486, *Bernardin* of *Carvajal* was sent by Pope *Innocent* VIII. to *Ferdinand* and the *Catholicks*, a tho' he was that King's Subject. *Ladron de Guevara* a Gentleman of *Arragon*, was in the Year 1492, sent by *Philip* Arch-Duke of *Austria*, to *Ferdinand* and *Isabella* the Catholick Kings, notwithstanding he was their Subject. He there made the first overtures of the Marriage which has since been executed with *Jean* their Daughter. And some time after, *Maximilian* King of the Romans, and Father of *Philip*, sent thither *Caspar de Lantzau* his High-Steward, who was descended from one of the chief Houses of *Roussillon*, and as such, *Ladron*'s Subject, tho' he had from his youth attended upon *Maximilian*.

The Kings of *Sweden*, Predecessors of *Gustavus Adolphus*, had very little Correspondence with the rest of Europe. Their Subjects whose knowledge hardly went further than the Courts of the Baltick-Sea, knew nothing but the affairs of their own Countrey, and the interests of their King, which were not of any great extent. Wherefore King *Gustavus*, who after his glorious Performances in the Wars of *Muscovy*, *Denmark*, and *Poland*, made himself be consider'd as the only Hero capable of restoring the affairs of *Germany*, seeing that the Noblemen of his Countrey were better qualified to execute his Orders in the Army, than to bring about his Intentions in foreign Courts by negotiations and intrigues, took his Ministers indifferently where-ever he found any fit for his purpose. *Charles* his Father had already employ'd *Van Dyck*, and he continu'd to make use of him himself, and to employ differently *Hollanders* and *Germans* in *Holland*, *Germany*, *France*, and other places. Under Queen *Christina*, and under the Government of *Charles Gustavus* as also during the minority of the present King, the Crown of *Sweden* has employ'd *Hugh de Groot*, *Camerarius*, *Salvius*, *Salvburgius*, *Salvius*, and particularly *Spring*, *Christopher Delphque* Earl of *Dona* and *Vanoni*, *Non*, Hollanders, in *Holland* it self.

Cardinal *Alexander Bichi*, was by birth a Subject of the Great Duke of *Tuscany*, and was become the Pope's by his promotion, but neither his Birth nor his Dignity hinder'd the King of *France* from employing him both to the one and to the other, as he made use of *Feonnetto Justiniani*, a *Genoese*, in the Quality of publick Minister to the Republick of *Genoa*.

The Popes, who know how to procure to themselves whatever they believe to be their right, and even beyond it, suffer Princes to employ in the same Quality, not only Cardinals, but also *Romans*, who are born Subjects to the See of *Rome*. The Duke *Frederick Seelli*, a Roman Baron was Embassador to the Pope on the part of the Emperor *Ferdinand* III during the War with the *Barberins*, and he dar'd to speak to *Urban* in such bold Terms, that the Cardinal *Patron* complain'd thereof to Cardinal *Savelli* the Embassador's Brother. He told him that a Subject endu'd with the Character of Embassador, ought nevertheless to have a respect for his Sovereign. The Duke agreed thereto, but then he added, that this obligation was common to him, with all other publick Ministers, who ought to respect those Princes with whom they negotiate, but at the same time they are indispensibly oblig'd to execute punctually and with vigour the orders of the Master they serve, without any regard to the Prince with whom they negotiate, who is also oblig'd to respect *one* that speaks to him by his Embassador, notwithstanding the pretended obligation of Birth. And indeed *Cardinal Bichi*, whom I before mention'd, being come to *Rome* in the Quality of Embassador from *France*, went immediately to the Cardinal's *Barberini*, and declar'd to 'em that he would not leave them, 'till they had given him an answer in writing to all the Articles he had propos'd to them. He moreover added, he was inform'd that they despis'd to take Money out of the Treasury of the Castle of St *Angelo*, but he was willing to let them know, that if they did so, every body would have reason to believe that they did it with an intention to continue the War. *Bichi* was the Pope's Subject, he was moreover his Creature, and the *Barberins* were so powerful, or to speak the truth, so insolent at that time, that not one of the Cardinals would have dar'd to have spoke to 'em in such a strain, and *Bichi* himself would have been far from doing it without his Quality of Embassador, which put him out of the reach of their Insults. The same Duke *Savelli* having a great dispute with the Prince *Prefect* about Precedency, Pope *Innocent* X signify'd to him he should be glad if he did not come to the Chapel. But he made answer

That

The EMBASSADOR and his FUNCTIONS. 81

That should his Holiness command him not to come to the Throne, he would not scruple to come thither. By which it appears, that as Embassador he was more oblig'd to obey the Emperor, than as a Roman Baron to obey the Pope.

There cannot be any thing more bold, than the Example of *Abraham Strotzen*, who his Pride't figure at the Court of *Constantinople*, under the name of *Ibrahim Bey* as first Interpreter of *Solyman* and *Selim* II Emperors of the Turks. He was a *Polander*, and a Renegade, and nevertheless *Selim* sent him in the Year 1560, to *Sigismund* the August, King of *Poland*, concerning a passage for his Army which he was going to march against the *Muscovite*. He had a publick Audience, and afterwards several private Conferences with the King, who did not treat him as his Subject, but as the Minister of a Soveraign Prince, whose Character he respected.

In *France*, where sometimes the King employs Subjects to their Soveraigns, French men are also admitted in the Quality of Embassadors, *Bartholomaeus de Cocur* was a Physician, and a Provencial, but the great Turk sent him nevertheless with a Present to King *Henry* IV who did not treat him as a Subject, or a Renegade, notwithstanding the Laws of *France* are very severe against that kind of Criminal, but as a publick Minister. Perhaps it may be objected, that the King was oblig'd to on c a regard to the Power of the Prince that sent him, but that reason cannot be admitted with reference to a King, who did not act upon any such Principle, and who only had the *Law of Nations* for the guide of his behaviour in this case, which was always his and his Successor's practice towards their Subjects, when they have presented themselves to be cloath'd with the Character of Embassador not only from Crown'd Heads, but also from those Princes to whom the Quality of most Serenissmo is not given.

Shall bring for Example hereof, the Embassadors of *Malta*. The Great Master of the Order of St *Joan of Jerusalem* is a Sovereign Prince, and acknowledg'd as such by all the other Princes of Christendom. Notwithstanding which, neither himself nor his Embassadors are treated at *Rome*, as the *Duke of Savoy*, and the *Great Duke of Tuscany*, or their Ministers are; yet nevertheless the king of *France* makes 'em be cover'd at their Audience, even when they are his own Subjects, and notwithstanding the particular Oath they take to him as his Officers in his Wars. The Commander *de Hautjenill* Embassador from *Malta*, was a *Parisian*, and withal was a Lieutenant General in his Majesty's Army, actually serving when the King's there in Person; and nevertheless the King considers him as an Embassador, as he had consider'd in the same quality the Commander *de Souvré*, who preceded *Hautjenill*. But to the end it may be known how France behaves it self therein, I shall here give an Extract of some Memoirs that *M de Berlife* one of the Introductors of Embassadors has made of the function of his Office for the space of ten Years. He delivers himself thus " The " 30th of *January*, 1639, the Marescal de St " Luc, and the Sieur de Berlife went with the " King's and Queens Coaches as far as *Picquet*, " to meet the Bailiff de *Lombru*, Great

' Cross and Embassador Extraordinary from
" *Malta*, and conducted him to the *Hotel de
" Sillery*, where he was to Lodge, with a Cortege of sixty Coaches with six Horses. All
" the Princes, the Embassadors of the Romish
" Religion, and a great many other Noblemen
" having sent to meet him, having neither been
" lodg'd nor defray'd. The next day the Sieur
" *de Liancourt* first Gentleman of the Bed-
" Chamber went to visit him from the King.
" The 13th of *February* the Marescal de *St
" Luc*, and the Count *de Brulon* receiv'd him
" at his Lodgings, with the King's and Queen's
" Coaches, in order to conduct him to St
" *Germains* to receive Audience of their Majesties, before which the King gave him a
' Dinner. It was deliberated on, whether he
" should be Cover'd; which is worth remarking. In fine, the Count de *Brulon* spoke to
" the King about it, *and his Majesty remembring that the Commander de* Formigere, *Embassador Extraordinary from* Malta, *being likewise a French Man, and a Captain in the Regiment of Guard, had been Cover'a, resolv'd
" that he should also be cover'd, but that he
" should behave himself therein with modesty and
" respect*, which accordingly he did. For having
" made a short Speech to the King with his
" Hat on, he utterwards spoke again for some
' time to him uncover'd, as he did to the
" Queen. He also saw the *Dauphin*, it being the principal occasion of his coming, to
" congratulate the King on his Birth. He afterwards visited the Princes of the Blood,
" whom he Saluted, *Monseigneur tou Prince,
" who gave him toe hand, and the Title of Excellency*, and the Card inal *Richelieu*. The 10th
" of *April* he took his leave of their Majesty's,
" being conducted by the same Persons, and
" in the same manner to St *Germains*. The
" Count de *Brulon* brought him a Picture Box
" worth four thousand Livres, after which he
" set out, not to return to *Malta*, but to go
" *and Command the King's Galleys*, in the
' quality of Lieutenant General. Those Princes who know what respect is due to the *Law of Nations*, will always behave themselves after this manner, because they are sensible also that the service and publick acknowledgment of a foreign Prince frees the Minister not only from the duties of his Birth, but also from the obligation even of an Oath, which is much more binding than the other. This is what cannot be deny'd, for it an Oath of Fidelity did not add a fresh and even stronger obligation to that which is already due to the Sovereign on account of Birth, it would only be tender'd to foreign Officers and Soldiers, and not to those of the Country, and it would be needless to exact it from Officers of Justice, and those that are intrusted with the administration of publick affairs, did nor an Oath oblige 'em to a particular Duty. It is plain nevertheless that the dignity of *Embassador* is not inconsistent with the Commission of an Officer, and that out of the Functions that are purely Military, this latter always gives place to the former. What I have here said of the Commanders *Formigere*, *Souvré* and *Hautjenill* sufficiently confirms this Truth, tho' there were not a great many more Examples that might serve to that purpose. M *d'Aongun* was Colonel

Y m

in the *Swedish* Army in *Germany*, where he was a publick Minister; and Count *Konigsmarc* was a *Mareschal de Camp* in the *French* Army, and was at the same time Embassador from *Sweden* to the King. The *Baron de Charnacè* was Colonel of Foot, Captain of a Troop of light Horse, and Embassador from *France* in *Holland*. Every body that knew him, must needs be sensible of his ability; and he gave proof of his Courage, when he dy'd in the Trenches at the Siege of *Breda*.

The *Count Destrades*, who is at present a Mareschal of *France*, made all the Campaigns in *Holland* as a Military Officer till the Siege of *Hulst* inclusively, which did not hinder him from negotiating, and really being a Minister at the same time. And no body has hitherto dar'd to maintain that a Council of War could have proceeded against him, notwithstanding his quality of Minister. On the contrary, I am not afraid to say that a Council of War could not have proceeded against him, even in the case of Crimes purely Military, tho' at the same time he gave his consent that it should, because as he was the Depositary of the King's secret Intentions and Orders who was his Master, he could not submit himself to the jurisdiction of a Council of War, nor to any other, without doing injury to his dignity and service. I am not here speaking of the time when he was Embassador Extraordinary in *Holland*, because that altho' he had then also a Regiment, and had taken an Oath to the States, his Character put him undeniably above all the jurisdictions of the Countrey, even of that where he negotiated without any Quality, and where his Quality of Officer in the War serv'd as a Cloak to that of Minister, while he negotiated without seeming to do so, and was a Minister without being acknowledg'd as such by any but those with whom he negotiated; that is to say, by the Prince of *Orange*, and those of the *States* to whom he communicated his negotiation, and who were those that could secure him the protection of the *Law of Nations*. He actually enjoy'd it, since it was out of that consideration only that he came off so well in the difference he had with the Prince of *Orange* in the Year 1646 *Destrades* had orders to entrust the Prince with the Proposal which had been made for a Marriage betwixt the King and the *Infanta* of *Spain*, to whom the King her Father gave for Dowry, together with the Province of *Flanders*, the pretensions he had to the United Provinces. He desir'd the Prince to be very cautious how he communicated so important a Secret. But the Prince being of opinion he could not conceal it without wounding the fidelity he ow'd to the States, imparted it to his Masters. The States were for diving farther into the matter, but *Destrades* pretended to be ignorant, and said he knew nothing of it. The Prince of *Orange* was his Captain General, and he was in too high a consideration in the Countrey, to have the truth of what he said be doubted of; yet nevertheless he was forc'd to suffer the Lye in a manner to be given him by an Officer that was oblig'd to obey his Orders. It is reasonable to think the Prince would not have put up the affront, if he could have any way have shewn his resentment without losing the respect he ow'd to *Destrades*, as being the Minister of a great and powerful Monarch, who was the spring of all he acted on this occasion. This is what could not be unknown, since *Destrades* who was very reserv'd in all his actions, would have been far from advancing a proposition of that nature, without an express order for his so doing, and it is most certain he had one. The Prince of *Orange* on his side was very wise, and judg'd it was much better to dissemble the indirect proceedings of the *French* Ministers, who were the directors of *Destrades*'s actions, than to shew his own discontent, which wou'd only serve to increase his mortification. Cardinal *Mazarin* was for rendring the *Spaniards* intentions suspected to the States, who began already to listen to a particular Treaty, but it had a contrary effect in augmenting the jealousie that was already entertain'd of that neighbouring Power.

The regard Princes have to the Quality of *publick Ministers* is so great, that they even respect it in their own Subjects, and that sometimes when they are not oblig'd thereto. I do not say it is a lawful Cause for which a Prince can refuse to admit a Minister, on the contrary, I am of opinion that he cannot make use of that pretext, because a Subject by putting himself in the Service of a foreign Prince, passes out of the obedience and subjection of his natural Prince, but then there may be other circumstances that may occasion a Subject's being rejected, altho' he be vested with a publick Character. In the Year 1614 *Ferdinand* Duke of *Mantua*, sent *Scipio Pasquale* in the Quality of Embassador Extraordinary to the Court of *Madrid*. This Prelate was a Native of *Cosenza* in the Kingdom of *Naples*, and of course a Subject of the King of *Spain*, who might have said that the Duke fail'd in the respect he ow'd him, by sending a *Neapolitan* to him, and that for an affair wherein the Duke of *Savoy* the King's Brother-in-Law had so great an Interest, that he had sent the Prince his eldest Son into *Spain* to oppose *Pasquale's* Negotiation. But notwithstanding all this, the latter made himself be consider'd as an Embassador, and not as a Subject, and acquitted himself so well of his Function, that the success of his Negotiation was soon rewarded with the Bishoprick of *Casal*.

Had not the King of *France* sufficient reason to be offended, to see *Anger* a player on the Lute sent to him in the Quality of a publick Minister, as if *France* had been ransack'd on purpose to find out this mean wretch, and of a vile profession, to place him in so Illustrious an Employment in the Court of the first King in all Christendom? This would have been no far fetch'd, but a lawful Cause not to admit him, especially when he came into *France* on the part of the Parliament. However that did not hinder the King from receiving him, and considering him, not as a Subject, but as a publick Minister.

I shall lay hold on this occasion to rectifie what the Memoirs say of *Bernardo Bandini*, one of the Assassins of *Julian de Medicis* I have done it on the Testimony of an *Italian* Author, at a time when I had hardly any Books by me. I have not many at present, but however I have enough to inform me that

Bajazeth

Bajazeth was so far from sending *Baudini* to *Laurence de Medicis* as an *Embassador*, that he put him into his Hands as the Murderer of his Brother, and as a Token of the Esteem he had for *Laurence*, who was one of the illustrious Personages of his time. *Paul Jozius* says, that *Baudini* was hang'd. It is an Error, and I am sensible it is not the only one I have committed; but I do not for that deserve, that the Remarker of *Brussels* should accuse me of being guilty of Falshood, when I said that the Count *de Fuensaldagne*, was employ'd by the King of *Spain* in *Flanders*, under *D. John* of *Austria*. I own my Error, and my Infirmities; but as I am altogether incapable of committing a Falsification, so I am not afraid of saying, that the Remarks which have been publish'd at *Brussels* swarm therewith. I offer to prove what I say, whenever I shall be summon'd to do it, and to make it appear that the Author (if he has the Courage to own his Name) is an infamous Calumniator, a Sycophant that has no Honour, and strives to prepossess the World with an Infinity of Imposture against an innocent Man, and his Unworthiness is the greater, because he thought I was not in a Condition to defend my self. If he thinks I do him any Wrong, he may have recourse to Justice, in a Place, where hitherto there has been none for my Innocency. I say the same of him, who having disfigur'd, in his impertinent Histories, the illustrious Lives of the great *Gustavus Adolphus*, and of Cardinal *Mazarine*, has augmented the Number of his foolish Books with *Italian* Dialogues, which would have made fit Covers for the Almanacks of the Years 1674 and 1675.

Schach Abas, King of *Persia*, was one of the greatest Princes that has reign'd for many Ages. He had two powerful Neighbours, the Emperor of the *Turks*, and the Great Mogul, Emperor of *Indostban*, and he was in perpetual uneasiness on account of the first. To free himself thereof, and to give some Diversion to the *Turks*, he had several Negotiations in most of the Christian Princes Courts. He employ'd there particularly two Brothers, *Anthony* and *Robert Shirley*, who being of a Family considerable enough in *England*, and having provided a sufficient Fund to defray the Expence of their Voyage, settled themselves in the Court of *Ispahan*. I shall say nothing of the Eldest, who quitting at *Venice* his Quality of Embassador receiv'd there several Disgraces, but *Robert*, after having been employ'd to the Emperor, and at the Court of several other Princes of *Europe*, pass'd with the Quality of Embassador from *Schach*. King *James* made him be cover'd, and respected in his Subject the Character of Embassador. *Shirley* return'd thither in the Year 1613, with the same Qualification, and was again treated after the same manner. He was cloath'd after the *Persian* manner, and being conducted to Audience by the Earl of *Anglesey*, and by the Master of the Ceremonies, and having paid his Respects after the *Turkish* manner, he took off his *Turbant* and laid it at the King's Feet, but the King caus'd him to take it up *and be cover'd*. Some Days after he had Audience of the Prince of *Wales*, but he did not there so much as offer to touch his Turbant, notwithstanding the Prince put off his Hat as soon as he saw him enter the Room, and make his first Bow. He was there actually when King *James* dy'd. While he he staid at *London* there happen'd a very extraordinary thing, that might have oblig'd the King to exert his Justice towards his Subject, who did not sufficiently verify his Quality of Minister. There came into *England* a *Persian*, whose Name was *Magdibeg*, who likewise took upon him the Quality of Embassador, and who when he presented his *Letters of Credence*, maintain'd that those of *Robert Shirley* were false and supposititious. *Shirley* being desirous to clear this matter, and make out his Quality, went to the *Persian*, having with him some of his Relations, who were to be Witnesses of their Interview, but the *Persian*, instead of returning *Shirley*'s Civility, took his Letters, flung them on the Ground, and gave him a box on the Ear, and put him thereby so much out of Countenance and beyond Reply, that the *English* took occasion from thence, to make a very bad Judgment of the Sincerity of their Kinsman. *Magdibeg* wrote to the King of *Great-Britain*, that having the Honour to be the Embassador of a Monarch in friendship with his Majesty, he took the liberty to desire from him that Justice, which he would not refuse to the least of his Subjects. That being arriv'd in this Kingdom, he had been inform'd that a certain Person, who took upon himself the Quality of Embassador from the *Schach* his Master, had the Vanity to say, he had marry'd a Relation of his Highness. That he was so incens'd at the Insolence of this Discourse, that he could not forbear shewing his Resentment. But for as much as it behov'd him to justify his Proceeding to the Court of *Ispahan*, and that in order thereto, it was necessary he should have authentick Proofs of the Rumors *Shirley* had spread, he desir'd his Majesty would be pleas'd to order him an authentick Copy thereof. The King, whom it concern'd to know the truth of the Matter, might have caus'd a very exact Inquiry to be made of the same, if not by his ordinary Justice, at least by his Council, if he had believ'd his Jurisdiction could have reach'd his Subject, notwithstanding his Quality of Minister. But he would not meddle in it, and was contented to send the one and the other home in two different Ships, that the King of *Persia* might himself be judge of the Difference, and regulate the same between two Persons, each of whom took upon him the Quality of his Minister. He sent a Person of Quality along with them in another Ship, to bring him an account after what manner the Difference should be decided at the Court of *Ispahan*, but they all three dy'd in the Voyage.

I am of Opinion the Parliament of *Grenoble* would not have violated the *Law of Nations*, in punishing the Murder (in the Person of a pretended Minister) of which I shall make mention in the following Example. Colonel *Alard* of *Provence*, while he was in the Duke of *Savoy*'s Service, was, in the Year 1614, sent to Marshal *de Lesdiguieres*, Governor of *Dauphiné*, to ask Succour from him against the *Spaniards*, in the beginning of the *Mantuan* War. During the Stay he made at *Grenoble*, expecting the Orders the Court was to send the

Marſhal, ſome of his Attendants kill'd (by his Command) a Tradeſman of the Town, as he was returning from a Farm he had in the Countrey. This Murder being committed on the Highway, by People known to belong to the *Colonel*, oblig'd the Parliament to ſecure the Perſon of the Maſter. But the Marſhal, who was at one of his Countrey Seats near *Lyons*, being adviſ'd of what had paſs'd, came thither with all Diligence, and ſent to the Priſon to demand the Priſoner, *as being a publick Miniſter, whom the Duke of* Savoy *employ'd to him*. The Major of the Garriſon, who went to the Priſon, not being able to prevail with the Warden thereof to deliver him, *M de Leſdiguieres* went thither himſelf, and cauſ'd him to be ſet at Liberty. The Parliament being offended at ſo violent an Action, deputed the firſt Preſident, with ſome Counſellors and the Attorney General, to complain of *M de Leſdiguieres*, to *Leſdiguieres* himſelf and to repreſent the Conſequence of ſuch Proceedings, and deſire Reparation might be made for the ſame. They pray'd him to give the Judicature at leaſt this Satisfaction, to ſuffer the Colonel to be ſent back to Priſon, upon the Aſſurance they gave him, that he ſhould immediately be formally diſcharg'd, which would be for the Parliament's Reputation. But *Leſdiguieres* would not conſent thereto. He ſaid, that his Action juſtify'd it ſelf. That he had reaſon to complain of the Parliament, who being ſenſible he was actually within the Province, had nevertheleſs made a *Decree* without his Participation againſt a *publick Perſon*. That he could not avoid making uſe of extraordinary Means, becauſe he had a mind to oblige 'em to repair the Fault they had committed through their Precipitation, againſt the *Law of Nations*, in the Perſon of the *Colonel*, whom they knew to be the Duke of *Savoy*'s Agent, to whom *this Reſpect ought to be paid, not to touch his Miniſter without giving him Advice thereof*. The King approv'd of what Marſhal *de Leſdiguieres* had done, by a particular Declaration, which was ratify'd in the Parliament of *Grenoble*, in the Year 1615. Colonel *Alard* was a Frenchman, but for as much as he had no *Letters of Credence*, but to *Leſdiguieres*, he could not be conſider'd as a publick Miniſter, nor enjoy the Protection of the *Law of Nations*. For altho' I have ſaid above, that Princes ſometimes ſend to Viceroys and Governors, Perſons that are acknowledg'd to be publick Miniſters, that ought to be underſtood of thoſe Governors, who have an abſolute Power, and that govern without any other Dependence, but on the Sovereign only whom they repreſent. Which cannot be apply'd to the Governors of the Provinces of *France*, who ſhare their Power, not only with the Parliaments, but alſo with the King's Lieutenants, whoſe Function is independent on that of the Governor. So that one may ſay, that *Alard* was not a publick Miniſter, and even if he had been ſuch, the Governor of the Province, by compelling the Warden of the Priſon to ſurrender the Priſoner, committed an Act of Violence upon Juſtice, and ſtood in need of the King's Declaration, which ſhrowded him from the Reſentment the Parliament might otherwiſe have ſhewn. But *Leſdiguieres* was in the right to ſay, *That Juſtice it ſelf, owes that Reſpect to foreign Sovereigns, as not to meddle with their Miniſter, without giving them Advice thereof*. This is what ſhall be more fully diſcours'd of in the 27ᵗʰ Chapter.

Before I put an end to this, it will be neceſſary to make ſome Reflections on two or three Examples, whereby it will appear, that Miniſters have not always been very well treated in their native Countrey. In the Year 1644, the Parliament at *London* had publiſh'd an Order for all Roman Catholick to depart the City, and gave *Bruerton* leave to ſeize their Goods and apply the ſame to the Subſiſtence of the Army. *Anthony Forteſcue* perceiving how how roughly the Roman Catholicks were handled, and being one himſelf, endeavour'd to avoid the ill Treatment that was dealt to others, by declaring himſelf a *publick Miniſter and Reſident from the Duke of* Lorrain. The Parliament maintain'd, that as this Gentleman was an *Engliſhman* and by Birth a Subject of the State, he could not put himſelf in the Service of a foreign Prince, nor lay any Claim to the Protection of the *Law of Nations*. They moreover ſaid, that he had begg'd that Quality, while Affairs were in another State than they were then in. All he was worth was ſeiz'd, and a *French Prieſt* was taken up that had ſhelter'd himſelf in his Houſe, into which they put a Garriſon. But as to this Example, it may be ſaid, that the Authority the Parliament aſſum'd was illegal, ſince the King who is the Head thereof, and had call'd an other at *Oxford*, diſown'd it. It cannot be alſo deny'd, that it was compoſ'd of People wholly ignorant of the *Law of Nations*. That the Violence which was offer'd to *Forteſcue*, was but a part of thoſe that were done by it to all thoſe who did not approve of the brutiſh and blind Zeal of Rebellion, and preſerv'd ſtill ſome Reſpect for the Royal Dignity, and ſome Affection for the Perſon of the King. *Forteſcue* had been acknowledg'd as a publick Miniſter by his Sovereign and the Examples of *Wolſes*, *Pool*, *Shirley* and ſome others make it plain, that the Right of Allegiance, which is particular to *England*, does not hinder the *Engliſh* from putting themſelves into the Service of a foreign Prince, nor even to transfer their Dwelling out of the Kingdom. The Parliament pretended not to violate the *Law of Nations*, becauſe they did not acknowledge *Forteſcue* to be a publick Miniſter.

Francis Sforza, the laſt Duke of *Milan*, made uſe of the ſame Pretext to juſtify the Execution of *Merveille* or *Maraviglia*, a Gentleman of *Milan*, who reſided with him on the part of *Francis* I, King of *France*. *Sforza*, who had been reinſtated in the Dutchy by the Emperor *Charles* V, and knew very well he could not maintain himſelf in it without his Protection, did not dare to ſuffer a *French* Miniſter to appear publickly at his Court. However, as he was in a perpetual Diſtruſt of the Ambition and Power of *Charles*, who had a great fancy for the Dutchy, he was unwilling to neglect the King's Friendſhip, and permitted *Merveille* to ſpeak to him now and then about his Maſter's Affairs: and the Duke himſelf in writing to the King, referr'd himſelf to the Diſcourſe he had with that conceal'd Miniſter, till beginning to ſuſpect, that the Emperor had been inform'd of that private Correſpondence, he had

had a mind to clear himself, and deserve *Charles's* Favour by a little Stroke of State. A certain Person, whose Name was *Castillon*, had spoken of *Merveille* in abusive Terms enough, who by way of Revenge caus'd him to be kill'd by his Domesticks. The Duke took this occasion to rid himself of this Minister, and to oblige the Emperor to give him his Niece, who was Daughter to *Christierne* King of *Denmark*, and had been promis'd him, he caus'd him to be try'd, and had him executed in Prison. The King was so mightily offended hereat, that he complain'd of it to all the Princes in Christendom, and amongst the rest to the Emperor himself, whose Vassal the Duke was, and demanded Justice thereupon. The Emperor made answer, *that* Merveille *was not a Minister,* so that the Duke of *Milan* might cause him to be prosecuted as his Subject. Hereupon Letters were shewn him, wherein the Duke acknowledg'd the Deceas'd to be employ'd by the King, but the Emperor reply'd, *that a Minister could not insist upon his Quality, if he did not make it appear publickly.* The Emperor to be sure would not deliver himself in other Terms. He was glad he had broke off the Correspondence between the King and the Duke, who on account of this Execution were become irreconcileable. The Duke excus'd himself to the King, and signify'd to him, that he had never consider'd *Merveille* as a publick Minister, but as a private Person only who had no Character, nor any other Qualification than that of his Subject. Moreover that *Merveille* was of so disagreeable a Temper, that he had often notify'd to him to be gone. The King was not satisy'd with these Excuses; on the contrary he protested, that whenever he had an Opportunity, he would resent the Indignity had been done him in the Person of his Minister.

The Emperor and Duke both say, that *Merveille* had no Character, and that he could not be consider'd but as a private Person and a Subject. The King makes it appear, that the Duke had acknowledg'd him as a Minister, and that he had negotiated with him in that Quality, so that the Emperor being convinc'd thereof, has recourse to a very bad Reason, and asserts, that he was not a Minister, because he had not appear'd publickly as such. But this is what is of very little Importance for the establishing the Truth I lay down, that a publick Minister ought to enjoy the Privileges of the Ministry, even in his own Countrey, since the Emperor and the Duke not agreeing to the matter of Fact, that is to say, to the Quality of *Merveille*, do not dispute the Right, and tacitely confess, that if he had been a Minister the Duke could not have caus'd him to be executed, without violating the *Law of Nations.* The Duke's Excuses were impertinent. It was easy to convince him by his own Letters, that he had negotiated with *Merveille*. By causing him to be executed in the Night in Prison, he gave it to be understood, that he had been the Author of an Execution, that no body would have dar'd to have perform'd in the face of the Sun; and when he says, he had several times notify'd to him his Desire that he would withdraw, he confesses he consider'd him in another Capacity than that of a simple Subject,

since without his Quality of *Minister,* and the Consideration he had for the King his Master, he would easily have made him retire, without any Formality of Notice. However, the King, by maintaining that the *Law of Nations* had been violated in the Person of *Merveille* his *Minister,* lays down as a certain Truth that cannot be contested with him, *that his Quality of Minister exempted him from the Jurisdiction of the Sovereign of the Place of his Birth.* This is what neither the Emperor nor the Duke deny, but they are contented to say, that he was not a *Minister.*

The present Emperor and his Council justify, after the same manner, the carrying off of Prince *William* of *Furstemberg*, asserting that he had no Character. They said, he had neither Powers nor *Letters of Credence* that gave it him, or if he had any, he had not communicated them, so that it was what People might be ignorant of. They protest that they really are altogether ignorant of his having been Embassador, or publick Minister, and believe that he could not be such, since the Elector of *Cologn,* his Master, was himself upon the Place. The *French* Ministers said on the contrary, that the Prince had *Credentials,* that he had communicated the same, and that th it was sufficient, to put him in possession of all the Advantages and Prerogatives which the *Law of Nations* bestows on the Character. This is a Dispute that has divided all the Princes of Christendom, and surpasses my Knowledge and as they do not agree as to the Matter of Fact, it is impossible to regulate it by dint of Reason; besides which, I cannot undertake to speak to it here, since it does not belong to the Subject of this Chapter. The Prince of *Furstemberg*, if he was an Embassador, was not so in his native Countrey, nor to his Sovereign, but at *Cologn,* as in a neutral Place, and in an Assembly, of which the Emperor's Ministers made a part; so that he was not treated as an Embassador from a foreign Power, but was carry'd off as a rebellious Subject, in order to be put into the Hands of Justice. As therefore this Example is accompany'd with particular Circumstances, that are not found in those of *Fortescue* and *Merveille,* I shall defer dwelling on it any longer, till I can do it more to the purpose on another occasion. Only I cannot forbear saying here, that I could wish the Remarker of *Brussels*, who is so knowing in History, and polite, would satisfy the Curiosity of some Persons (who are not so knowing in the Affairs of *Germany* as he is) in a Scruple they have, with respect to the Emperor's Power. They are of Opinion that his Power does not extend so far, as to justify him in the carrying off, out of a Neutral Place, a Prince that is neither outlaw'd nor condemned, and who in his Quality of Prince is a Subject of the Empire, if I may be allow'd to speak so, and not of the Emperor. They also doubt, whether the Emperor could, as Arch-Duke, exercise so forcible an Authority, and which the *French* call violent, upon a Subject or Vassal, who is otherwise a Prince of the Empire. These are small Difficulties that the Remarker would do well to remove, that *France* might thereby be made sensible of

Z its

its Error, which as yet it is not. Thus we see, that of all the Examples hitherto alledg'd, there is not one that favours *Bodin*'s Opinion, and the bare *Opinionatrveness* of an Author, who is none of the most regular, is not sufficient to make me alter my Sentiment.

CHAP. XII.

Of the Fidelity of the Embassador

BY assigning to an Embassador a *mature* and *advanc'd Age*, I have also allotted him *Experience*, which is a necessary Consequence thereof. Wherefore it would be wide of my purpose to speak of this, as it would be likewise superfluous to make a particular Chapter of the Fidelity that ought to be united with Experience, in the Commissions of all Ministers, did not the *Remarker of Brussels* oblige me to make here a kind of Digression.

I own, I do not treat over-well in my Memoirs *Don Ferdinand Teiles de Faro*, Embassador from *Portugal* to the States of the United Provinces, because it went against me to justify a Minister, who not contented to abandon the Affairs that had been committed to him, betrays the several Interests, becomes a Deserter and a Transfuge, and goes over to the Party of his Master's Enemies. This Embassador, who arriv'd at the *Hague* in the Month of *July* 1658, made great use of the Mediation of the Ministers of *France* and *England* in the whole Course of his Negotiation, and this rather to penetrate into their Sentiments, than to discover his own to them. He entertain'd at the same time a strict Correspondence (but very privately) with *Don Estevan de Gamarra*, the *Spanish* Embassador, to reconcile him to the Court at *Madrid*, and to concert with him how to make his Retreat. Insomuch that he left the *Hague* in the Month of *April* 1659. He had not been above three Months in *Holland*, when he began to betray his Prince, and to be as a Spy upon the *French* Embassador, and the Resident of *England*. To justify his infamous Behaviour he publish'd a *Manifesto*, where he set forth how he had, ever since the Revolution of the Affairs of *Portugal*, preserv'd an inviolable Fidelity to his Catholick Majesty, as to him he look'd upon to be his Sovereign Prince. That he had been oblig'd to accept the Embassy of *Holland*, because as he had already excus'd himself from several Employments, he could not refuse this without rendering himself suspected. That the Power which had been vested in him at *Lisbon*, was so limited, that it was altogether impossible for him to succeed in his Negotiation on the Conditions contain'd therein. That *France* thwarted it, and that *M. de Thou* was the Person who oppos'd it most. And after all, that he did not believe any body would censure his Retreat, since what he did was only out of a Motive of Duty to his lawful Prince. The major part of his Servants retir'd to the *Spanish* Embassador's, who charg'd himself with the Payment of the Debts of the Fugitive. Some Days after, his Secretary presented a Memorial, wherein he spoke of this Action as of an abominable Treason, and represented that it stuck at *Don Ferdinand* only, that the Treaty was not concluded. The *Remarker of Brussels* makes his Apology, and says, That all the Crime of this *Embassador* was, that he did not approve of the Revolt of *Portugal*, nor of the Proceedings of him that was the Author thereof, and that he did no more than fling himself into the Arms of his natural and lawful King.

No body had compell'd *Ferdinand Teiles de Faro* to take an Oath of Fidelity to the Duke of *Braganza* at his Accession to the Crown. When he saw a Prince proclaim'd King whom he look'd upon to be an Usurper, he might have retir'd into *Castile* after the Example of several other *Portuguese* Noblemen. No body had forc'd him to charge himself with the Employment of Embassador, for the discharge whereof he had taken a particular Oath, and no body hinder'd him from taking the Road of *Germany*, and from thence passing into *Spain*, before he begun his Negotiation, as he did after he had engag'd himself therein. There is no *Spaniard*, that has ever so little Honour, who would be guilty of doing what this Embassador did for several Months, to wit, to sit the *French* and *English* Ministers, to no other End, but to have wherewith to entertain the *Spanish* Embassador. When it is said that an Embassador is an honourable Spy, it is to be understood of him that serves his Master, and not of him that betrays him. Out of this honourable Function, the Profession of a Spy is infamous, and he that meddles with it deserves to be hang'd. That of Advocate of Perfidiousness and Treason is no less detestable, and the *Panegyrist* of such foul Actions would, without doubt, be ready to act himself what he so much praises in another. He adds, That it was Necessity, and *France*, that oblig'd *Spain* to declare *Portugal* a free Crown, and that it was only the Effect of one of the hard Laws, to which Consent is given but with Reluctancy. This honest Man is very obliging to the *Portuguese*, in foretelling them what they are to expect from *Spain*, as soon as the Necessity which forc'd it to submit to such rigid Laws shall cease, and that *France* shall no longer intermeddle with their Interests. It may be said also, that this Warning may not be altogether unprofitable to the United Provinces, who have forc'd *Spain* by the like Necessity to undergo the Severity of those Laws which made 'em be acknowledg'd as a State so entirely independent, that they have not left the King the least token of the Sovereignty he had there formerly.

But

But if we will believe this great Politician, their Sovereignty will last no longer than *Spain* shall be engag'd in a War that hinders it from knowing it self. That Kingdom produces a great number of generous Men, that would be sorry these unworthy thoughts should be common to all the Nation, and that would not imitate the infidelity of that Traitor, nor the prevarication of him that justifies him. When he says the King of *Spain* was *Don Ferdinand*'s Master, either he knows not what he says, or if he has reflected on it, he advances a thing that is notoriously false. He might believe that the King of *Spain* was his Sovereign Prince, but he could not say he was his Master. The King of *Portugal*, to whom he had taken an Oath of Fidelity, of whom he held his Commission, and who gave him wherewithal to subsist, was his true Master. It was he had given him his *Letters of Credence*; t was for him he negotiated, and it was under his authority that he enjoy'd the protection of the *Law of Nations*. There is not any Treason so black, as not to be justifiable on the Principles of this gallant Man. The *Cordeliers of Metz*, who under the pretext of their General Assembly, had brought in Soldiers and Arms, and the *Religious of Maestricht*, who were for putting the Town into the hands of the *Spaniards*, did not only deserve his Praises, but also to be Canoniz'd.

Codignac the *French* Embassador at *Constantinople*, had made himself so intimate with the Ministers of the Port, that he gave a jealousie to *Henry* II his Master. The umbrage that was taken of his fidelity, was increas'd by the engagement he had in the Year 1556, with a *Greek* Gentlewoman who own'd two small Islands that were worth about two thousand Crowns per Ann. In the Year 1558, Orders were sent him to return to Court to give an account of his actions. But it was then he took off the Mask, and instead of passing into *France*, he declar'd himself for the King of *Spain*, and enter'd into his Service. The *Spaniards* had promis'd him the Embassie of *Constantinople*, where he had his Intrigues, and where he had for some time carried on his Negotiations under hand for his new Master. In the Year 1559, he procur'd Passports for the Minister whom the King of *Spain* should send thither as King of *Naples*. He had likewise a particular Correspondence with one of the Sons of the *Grand Seignior*, and it was prov'd that he carried on an Intelligence in *Montderis* and *Antibes*, to have them surrender'd to the *Spaniards*.

King *Henry* IV writing to M. de Maisse-Hurault his Embassador at *Venice*, on the 14th of March, 1590 complains very much of the Infidelity of the *Sieur de Lencome* his Embassador at *Constantinople*, and says he has several Proofs thereof, which he had receiv'd from the *Bassa*'s themselves. M. de Breves who succeeded him, caus'd him to be seiz'd and put into the Black Tower by the King's Orders. The Example of *Jerome Lipomano* is by so much the more memorable, as I reasons art no less rare among the Noble *Venetians*, than Monsters are elsewhere. He was *Baylo* at *Constantinople*, and being become suspected, *Laurence Bernardi* was substituted in his Place, in the Year 1591. As soon as *Lipomano* was embark'd on board the Galleys of the Republick, he had Guards set over him, and as soon as he came within sight of *Venice*, he cast himself into the Sea, or was thrown into it by the Order of those who would otherwise have shar'd in the infamy of his punishment.

No excuse can be made for the infidelity of a publick Minister. There is no difference between an Embassador that quits the Service of his Prince without his leave, to put himself into that of another Master, and between the Governor of a Town, who abandoning his Master's Service, sells the Place to the Enemy. Some Years ago the Minister who was on the part of the Elector of *Brandenburg* at *London*, quitted his Post to go and serve the Crown of *Sweden*. The Elector caus'd him to be declar'd infamous, and fix'd his name to the Gallows, notwithstanding this Minister excus'd himself on the extreme necessity he was reduc'd to. He had already been a Prisoner for Debt, and fearing to be so again, by reason they did not pay him his Salary, he had been forc'd to accept of the first offer that would afford him Bread. The misery of these Wretches seems to be consummate, for they are not only the aversion or the side they leave, but also the scorn and contempt of those they go to. So that the r Infamy may be said to be a sufficient punishment. And yet this sort of Traitors is not so dangerous as those Ministers who remaining in their Master's Service, ruine his affairs, by covering their evil intentions with the cloke of a false fidelity. Upon advice at *Florence* of the Negotiations *Lewis Sforza*, Sirnam'd *the Moor* (who had usurp'd the Dutchy of *Milan*) was carrying on with *Charles* VIII, and of the preparations that were making in *France* for the *Ital an* Expedition, *Peter de Medicis* chief of the Republick, prevail'd with it to send the Bishop of *Arezzo*, with *Peter Soderini* and *Peter Caponi* into *France*, to try to divert the storm with which *Italy* was threaten'd. *Peter de Medicis* had drawn up their Instructions conformably to his intentions. But *Soderini* and *Caponi* who were *Republicans* and Enemies to the power of the *Medicis*, instead of executing their Orders to obtain of *Charles* that the Republick might not be oblig'd to declare against the King of *Naples*, did *Peter* a great many ill offices. The *Florentines* had made a League with the Kings of *Naples*, even with the consent of *Lewis* XI, *Charles*'s Father, and pretended they could remain Neuters. But upon their being press'd to declare themselves, *Caponi* who was an inveterate Enemy of *Peter de Medicis*, whose Conduct was not altogether so regular as that of *Laurence* and *Cosmus* his Predecessors, told the *French* Ministers that the Intention of their Principals was very good, but that *Peter* hinder'd them from acting according to their inclination, and that to render him odious to the People, it would be requisite to banish all the *Florentine* Merchants and Bankers out of *France*, and give them to understand that they ow'd their disgrace to nothing but the evil disposition *Peter de Medicis* had for *France*. *Caponi*'s Infidelity succeeded, the *Florentines* had Orders to leave the Kingdom, and *Peter* was driven from *Florence*, but *Caponi* soon discover'd that he had quite another

ther defign than that of overthrowing the Authority of the *Medicis*, to introduce that of *France* He was for preferving the Liberty of his Countrey entire, as he did by an action altogether *Heroick*, of which we fhall have an opportunity to fpeak hereafter

Count *Albertin Bofchetto*, who was Steward of the Duke of *Mantua*'s Houfhold, and Commanded the Army of the Confederates in *Italy* againft *Charles* VIII, having met *Ph lip de Comines* at *Cafal*, made the firft Overtures to him of a Treaty, which was concluded fome time after To the end he might continue the Negotiation, he was fent to the King to defire the Paffports that were requifite for the Deputies who were to be of the Conference In the publick Audience he had, he fpoke of nothing but the fubject of his Commiffion, but having after that obtain'd a private Audience, *he advis'd the King not to grant the Paffports to the Confederates*, becaufe their Army was in fo bad a condition, and the Heads of it fo divided among themfelves, that it could not but be difpers'd in a few days What he faid was truth, and it was impoffible this fhould be a myftery to the *French* Generals, But the King would not follow the Councfl of a Traitor, who fome years after was executed for another Treafon, of which he had the management under *Ferdinand d'Efte*, and *Julius* his natural Brother, who confpir'd in the Year 1505, againft the Life of *Alfonfo* Duke of *Ferrara*

Ferdinand the Catholick, who oftner deceiv'd others, than he was deceiv'd himfelf, was neverthelefs very fcurvily dealt with by one *Lucena*, whom he fent Embaffador into *England* in the Year 1475 *Lewis* XI who never fail'd to make his advantage of opportunities when they prefented themfelves, caus'd him to be brought before him, and having found out the vanity and avaricious temper of the Man, he made fo very much of him, gave him fo many Prefents, and loaded him with fo many Promifes, even to the affuring him of a Cardinal's Hat, that he not only worm'd out the fecrets of his Inftructions, but alfo the whole fuccefs of his Negotiation, as he repafs'd thro' *France*, on his return home

Andrew Giezi, inftead of foliciting for Succour at the Court of *Conftantinople*, without which *Gabriel Battory* could not propofe to maintain himfelf in his Principality of *Tranfilvania*, againft the Arms of the Houfe of *Auftria*, was fo bafe as to betray him, and to make a Treaty with *Mahomet Belzergi* to drive out his Prince He promis'd to *Mahomet* that he would joyn the Troops he commanded for *Battory*, to the Turkifh Army, in order to make 'em Mafters of the whole Countrey, which he pretended to be afterwards invefted with by the *Great Turk* The *Baffa of Buda* prevented the execution thereof, and having reprefented to the *Divan* the confequences of the Rupture that would infallibly follow with the Emperor, he brought it to a Refolution, that Affairs fhould be left in the fame ftate they were then in, and that the fame Treaties fhould be confirm'd with *Matthias* (who was juft chofen in the room of *Rodolfus*) which had been concluded with his Predeceffor

There are fome Infidelities that are not altogether of fo deep a dye, nor fo capable of producing fuch ill effects, which neverthelefs are very dangerous, and even abominable in the perfon of a *Minifter*

They who have wrote the Intrigues of that Conclave wherein *Innocent* X was chofen, relate feveral particulars of the Infidelity of Cardinal *Anthony Barberin* He was Cardinal Protector of the Kingdom of *France*, in this Quality he had the fecret of the Conclave He had alfo exprefs Orders to caufe Cardinal *Pamfilio* to be put by, and he had feveral times promis'd both by word of mouth and writing, that he would never confent to his Exaltation, yet for all this, he confented thereto But what is moft to be wonder'd at in the fame Hiftory, is, that it does not diffemole, that the Marquis *de St Chaumont* who was Embaffador from *France*, and knew very well that *Pamfilio* was the verfion of the firft Minifter, and who had a point command to oppofe his Election, confented thereto for a fum of Money Cardinal *Mazarin* contented himfelf with calling him home, and caufing him to be confined to his Houfe, which was too great an Indulgence for fo black a Crime

The *French*, and thofe who upon their Memoirs have wrote what pafs'd at the *Congrefs of Weftphalia*, do not fcruple to fay pofitively that *Pau* and *Knuyt*, two of the Plenipotentiaries of the United Provinces were corrupted by *Spanifh* Money to prevail with their Mafters to make a feparate Treaty with *Spain*, exclufive of *France* One may believe it to be a Calumny, not only becaufe *Pau* has been juftify'd by a formal Declaration of the States of *Holland*, his Sovereigns, but alfo becaufe he could not act otherwife, without oppofing the intention of the fame States who were his Mafters Thefe accufations of declar'd Enemies, as the Minifters of *France* were to thefe two, are always to be fufpected, tho' they fhould be really true

In the beginning of this Century, the *Grifons* made a Treaty with the Count *de Fuentes* Governor of *Milan*, which could not fubfift with that they had made fome Years before with the Republick of *Venice*, and which was altogether inconfiftent with the ancient Alliance they had with *France* They did not confider the Confequences thereof, till they were fo far engag'd with the *Count*, that they could not fall off without breaking with *Spain* So that in order to qualifie the matter as well as they could, they were of Opinion to try to infert a Claufe in the Treaty of *Milan*, that it fhould not be any prejudice to the Treaties the *Leagues* had actually with *France*, and with the Republick of *Venice* They who had negotiated the Treaty of *Milan*, made ufe of this Artifice to get it approv'd of in *France*, and to have it Ratified with that referve In order hereunto, they entreated the *Canton of Zurich*, by an Embaffie on purpofe, to joyn with that of *Bern*, and to ufe their endeavours with the King of *France*, to the end that the Treaty of *Milan* fubfifting by his confent, the *Grifons* might get out of the *premunire* they had incurr'd The Embaffador of they *Grey Leagues*, inftead of keeping within the bounds of his Commiffion, did the contrary, and pray'd the two Cantons to employ their good Offices with the King, that he would oblige the *Grifons* to Ratifie the

Treaty

Treaty of *Milan* purely and simply, without Condition or Reserve, which he did, at the Instance of some Deputies, who, upon the breaking up of their *Pittag* or *Diet*, had remain'd at *Coire*, for the figning and difpatching the Refolutions that had been taken therein The two Cantons prefs'd by this Man's importunate urgency, wrote to the King, contrary to their own proper Sentiments, and against their Intereft The fame Embaffador being return'd to *Coire*, and giving an account of his Commiffion, had the impudence to fay that the Senate of *Zurich*, having feen the Refolution of the Communities of the *Grifons*, was at firft feiz'd with fome wonder thereat, but after it had been inform'd of the Reafons that had oblig'd 'em thereto, it acquiefced therein, and had refolv'd to write to the King, according to the defire and intention of the faid Communities He moreover added, that in a few days all the Cantons would have a general meeting at *Baden* about this Affair

Charles Pafchal, who fpeaks of this matter in his Embaffie, fays he will not fet down the Name of the Embaffador, for fear of branding his Pofterity with perpetual Infamy which perhaps might be the firft in abominating fo detestable an Infidelity There was no punifhing of it, without bringing the Countrey into the laft diforder and confufion, fo that it was thought more advifeable to diffemble the thing, than to detect a Crime which could not remain unpunifh'd, u made publick, and yet could not be punifh'd without troubling the tranquility of the State, which was to be preferv'd at all adventures

The difference that was like to kindle a War between *France* and *Spain*, for the Affair of the *Grifons*, almoft at the fame time as the Troubles of *Bohemia* gave a beginning to that of *Germany*, was in fome meafure accommodated by depofiting the *Valteline* into the hands of the Pope But for as much as it was not quite regulated and made an end of by that expedient, and that the two Kings could not be fatisfy'd therewith, any more than the *Grifons*, who were for having foreigners banifh'd out of a Countrey that belong'd to their Sovereignty, feveral overtures of agreement were made, as well at *Paris*, as at *Madrid*, and at *Rome* The Commander de *Sillery* Embaffador from *France* to the Pope, agreed to thofe which the *Spaniards* caus'd to be made by his Holinefs, and fign'd a Treaty that was in all appearance very advantagious to the Roman Catholick Religion, but in fact very prejudicial to the Reputation and Intereft of the King his Mafter The Council of *France* was fo incens'd thereat, that being of opinion that the Embaffador and the Chancellor his Brother, acted in concert with the Court of *Spain*, the one was recall'd, and the other was turn'd out, with his Son, who was Secretary of State It was at the fame time but a fufpicion which they would not fearch into, nor clear, by reafon of the Quality of the Perfons concern'd, who had been in *Henry* IV his time employ'd in the moft important Affairs of the Kingdom

The bare fufpicion of Infidelity is fufficient to remove a Minifter from all forts of Employments of this nature, becaufe that where there is a diftruft, the one can never give fatisfaction, nor the other be ever fatisfy'd *Albert Pio*, Lord of *Carpy*, Embaffador from *Lewis* XII. to Pope *Julius* II was fufpected not to Negotiate over fincerely between thofe two Princes, with reference to the difference they had on account of the protection that *Lewis* had promis'd to *Alfonfo* Duke of *Ferrara Albert* had no great kindnefs for the Duke, becaufe *Hercules*, *Alfonfo*'s Brother, having oblig'd *Gilbert Pio* to fell him one half of the County of *Carpy*, and to accept of other Lands in lieu thereof, he was afraid left he fhould be compell'd to fell alfo the other half For this Reafon he oppos'd whatever could farther contribute to the aggrandizing the Duke of *Ferrara* Yet neverthelefs, as the King was a Prince that did not love to change his Minifters, he continu'd him in his Poft, and was contented to have him ftrictly obferv'd

There is a kind of Infidelity that does not come up to Treafon, and yet produces the fame effect That *Minifter*, who does not know how to Husband his Mafter's Secrets, either through vanity or weaknefs, is not properly a Traitor, but for all that, he is guilty of Infidelity He is not fo Criminal, yet he is not lefs Dangerous than he that fells him, or expofes him through malice In the Year 1646, there was at *Stockholm* a *Refident from Portugal*, who by trufting the fecret of his Negotiation with *Chanut* the *French* Minifter, entirely ruin'd his own Bufinefs He told him that the Council of *Sweden* relifh'd very well the Propofal he had made to it, of fettling a Commerce between the two Nations, fo that the Merchandize and Goods that the two Kingdoms produce fhould pafs through the hands of the *Hollanders*, but the Veffels and Shipping fhould fail directly from *Stockholm*, to *Setubal* and *Lisbon* *Chanut*, who confider'd that by thefe means *Sweden* would contrive to have a great quantity of *French* Salt, which fold to a great Profit in that Kingdom, did not fail to make his advantage of this Information, and knew fo well how to thwart the Negotiation of the *Portuguefe*, that no mention was made thereof afterwards

That Embaffador that quits the Service of his Prince, during the time he is employ'd by him, although he does not betray his Mafter's Interefts, and does not fide with his Enemy, is notwithftanding unfaithful *Don John Emanuel* a *Spanifh* Nobleman, and of the Royal Houfe of *Caftile*, was Embaffador from *Ferdinand the Catholick*, to *Philip* Arch-Duke of *Auftria*, at the time that Queen *Ifabella* dy'd *Jean* the Wife of *Philip* was Heir to *Ifabella*, but that did not hinder *Ferdinand* from keeping Poffeffion of the Government of the Kingdom The *Caftilian Noblemen* did not like him very well, and *Don John Emanuel* was perpetually exhorting *Philip* to go and take poffeffion of a Crown which belong'd to him in right of his Wife Hereupon *Ferdinand*, who had advice of the ill offices his Embaffador did him, fent him Orders to go on his part to the Emperor *Maximilian*. *Don John* obey'd, but *Philip* who could not be without his Counfel, caus'd him to return, kept him with him, and made him one of his moft trufty Counfellors He excus'd himfelf for this difobedience, and wrote to to *Ferdinand*, that he might be affur'd, that the Stay he should make with *Philip* should do no Damage to his Affairs and that his Majesty could not doubt thereof, after so many Proofs he had given him of his Fidelity, tho' he had not been of the Number of those who had been best rewarded for the same. Whatever Name or Colour may be given to the Procedure of *Don John Emanuel*, it must be own'd that he was not very honest, and that it he cannot be accus'd of Treason, he cannot clear himself of a kind of Desertion which was somewhat criminal. The *Arch-Duke* was become his Sovereign, but however *Ferdinand* was for all that his Master, till such time as he had obtain'd, or at least ask'd his Discharge according to form. He did very ill Offices to his first Master, who sent the Bishop of *Palenzia* on purpose to the *Arch-Duke*, to demand his Minister. But this last refus'd to surrender him, and *Don John*, who had no great mind to return to *Ferdinand*, excus'd himself by Letter. The Character of *the Fidelity of a publick Minister*, is very well express'd in a Letter President *Jeannin* wrote to the Duke of *Sully*, on the 21st of *October* 1608, where he speaks of himself in these Terms " I have ever desir'd that the " King had a true Information of the State of " the Affairs of this Countrey And I have " all along for the time past given it faithfully, and without disguising any thing, " but it has not perhaps relish'd with those, " who being of an Opinion contrary to the " pursuit of what I was doing in his Majesty's " Name, requir'd of me a Dissimulation, and " an appearance of Duty, *instead of the true Effects of an honest Man, who is not satisfy'd with himself, if he does not seriously, and to the best of his Knowledge, execute what is commanded him*. All the Letters the King and *Villeroy* wrote to him, are so many *Encomiums* of his *Fidelity*, as well as of his Prudence.

Having spoken of the *Fidelity* the Minister owes to his Prince, it is likewise necessary to say a Word or two concerning that, which the Prince owes to his Minister. This Duty is reciprocal between 'em. Wherefore it behoves the Embassador, before he undertakes a Function which is the most difficult of all Functions, to be sure of the Intention, Countenance and Protection of the Prince he is going to serve, that he may not engage himself with a faint-hearted Prince, or that is unfaithful, and capable of betraying his Minister, and of destroying his Work. Pope *Clement* VII, endeavouring to persuade *Henry* IV, to make Peace with the King of *Spain*, notwithstanding the Alliance he had made with Queen *Elizabeth*, and the States of the United Provinces, quoted a Maxim of *Frances Mary* Duke of *Urbin*. That Prince was wont to say, that a Gentleman could not be worse than his Word, without making an irreparable Breach in his Honour, and without losing his Reputation, but that a Sovereign Prince ought to accommodate it to his Interest and that he might, without injuring himself, break his Word, lye, betray, and do any thing whatever he judg'd necessary for the Prosperity of his Affairs.

It is true, most Princes act after this manner, and what *Machiavel* says on this Subject is full as bold, but then he requires, that a Prince, how bad or false soever he may be, should always borrow the Mask of Piety and I mean, and that he carry at least a fair Appearance. his Reason is, that besides there being but few People, that are willing to be thought to be as bad as they really are, those that cover themselves with the Cloke of Virtue, may be so for a longer time, and with more safety. *Don Gonsales of Cordova* being Viceroy of *Naples*, after he had given a Passport in good form to *Cæsar Borgia*, Duke of *Valentinois*, caus'd him to be taken Prisoner but at the same time he sent to the Duke's House, and got away his Passport, lest so evident a Proof of his Perfidiousness should be produc'd against him. All those who have the least Modesty still left, will always endeavour to avoid the Reproaches that may be made to 'em of their Treachery, if they are gone too far in their Iniquity, to make themselves any. The Viceroy said he was oblig'd to obey the King his Master's Orders, whose Interest and Intention could receive no Prejudice from the Passport, and yet he suppress'd it, because he was sensible, that it might be a Reproach to him, that he could not be ignorant of the Intention of the *Catholick* King, and that he ought to have alledg'd the same, before he granted the Passport, which could not be violated, without violating at the same time the publick Faith and Safety.

Ferdinand the *Catholick* however own'd and approv'd this Infidelity, as well as the horrible Treachery that the same great Captain had dealt some Years before to *Ferdinand* Duke of *Calabria*, the Son of *Frederick* King of *Naples*. This young Prince finding himself besieg'd in *Tarento*, without any hopes of Succour, made a formal Treaty with *Gonsales* with reference to the Place, stipulating, amongst other things, expresly, that if the King his Father did not consent to all the Conditions of the Treaty, the Prince notwithstanding should have the Liberty to go whither he pleas'd, even into *France* if his Father desir'd it. He comply'd with all his Promises. But *Gonsales*, instead of executing the Treaty on his part, set a Guard upon the young Prince, would not suffer him to go off, and sent him at last into *Spain*. After all this the Remarker of *Brussels* cannot bear it should be said of *Ferdinand*, that with all his *Catholicism* he was a *Traytor* and an *Infidel*, tho' *Zurita* says, that in that, *Ansé, & verdad poria ser Notada y Amanzillada*.

Philip de Commines, who in the Person of *Lewis* XI, gives the Character of Infidelity, says, that the King being gone into *Guyenne*, upon Advice of the extreme Illness of the Duke his Brother, with a Design to make himself Master of the Province, and knowing that *Charles* Duke of *Burgundy* was with a powerful Army on the Frontiers of *Picardy*, with a Design to make a Diversion on that side in favour of the Dukes of *Guyenne* and *Brittany*, he sent to him the Lord *de Cran* and Chancellor *Doriole*, to amuse him with a Treaty which he would neither conclude nor execute. *Charles* had a longing desire to be repossess'd of the Towns on the River *Somme*, which had been engag'd to his Father *Philip the Good* by the Treaty of *Arras*, and had been redeem'd by *Lewis*, who flatter'd him with hopes of having them restor'd, tho' his Intention was only to

gain

gain a little time in expectation of his Brother's Death, which not being natural, the King could not be mistaken therein. The Duke receiv'd with Joy the Proposals of the Embassador's from *France*, and promis'd, that in case those Towns were restor'd to him, he would not only renounce the Alliance of the Dukes of *Guyenne* and *Britany*, but would moreover abandon them entirely, and leave them to the King's Disposal. The Treaty was concluded and sign'd, but the *French* Embassadors, who knew their Master, and did not believe it was really his Design to restore those Towns to *Charles*, told him, he would do well not to remove his Army far from the Frontiers, till the King had ratify'd the Treaty, and had sworn to the Observation thereof. The Duke follow'd their Counsel, and sent his Embassador to the King, to desire him to ratify the Treaty not the King who never wanted bad Pretexts, delay'd the Ratification, till such time as the Duke being dead, and all the Measures of the Duke of *Burgundy* being broken thereby, he plainly said, *he would do nothing in it*, *and that his Embassadors had exceeded their Power*. The Duke of *Burgundy* was no better than the King of *France* and notwithstanding he had not so much Wit, yet he was full as bad. He had sent *Simon de Quinsay* his Embassador to the Duke of *Britany*, to notify to him, that by virtue of the Treaty he had concluded with the King of *France*, he was oblig'd to renounce the Friendship and Alliance of the two Dukes. But amongst *Quinsay*'s Retinue, there was a certain Gentleman who had a *Letter of Credence*, which order'd him to assure the same Duke, that as soon as he should receive Advice of the Restitution of the Towns on the *Somme*, that far from abandoning him, he would assist him and the Duke of *Guyenne*, with his whole Power. *Lewis* thought to deceive his Embassadors, and the Duke was for deceiving the King, and his own Embassador, but found himself however the first deceiv'd by the Death of the Duke of *Guyenne*, which oblig'd him to alter all his Measures.

In the Year 1572, King *Charles* IX, who was not less Perfidious, but yet more cruel than *Lewis* XI, desired *Francis de la Noüe*, who was one of the wisest, honestest, and bravest Gentlemen of the Kingdom, to go to *Rochelle*, and endeavour to perswade the Inhabitants to comply with the King's Will. *La Noüe* excus'd himself at first, as being an Employment, that neither suited with his Humour, nor agreed with his Profession, but considering at last, that he had to do with a Prince that would not be contradicted, he said he would obey, but conjur'd his Majesty to believe, that it was impossible for him to second the Intention of those, who were for surprising, or betraying the *Rochellers* through his Means. The Horror of the Massacre of St *Bartholomew* was still present before the Eyes of the Religionaries, which created him some Difficulty to get Admittance into the Town, but as soon as he was got in, he had the Command of the Troops conferr'd upon him, of which the Garrison was compos'd. He did all he could to blot out of the Minds of the People, the just Distrust they had of the King, till at last perceiving his Person might become suspected, and his longer Stay unprofitable to the King, he withdrew. He could not answer for the Intention of a Prince, who had made himself execrable by the most inhuman Action, which was ever heard of: yet nevertheless his Conduct was so wise and so full of Honour, that both the Court and the Inhabitants of *Rochelle* remain'd equally satisfied of his Probity, and of the Sincerity of his Procedure.

Some without doubt will think I speak of this young Monarch in Terms a little too bold but I desire them to suspend their Judgment, till I have taken notice of a Passage in one of Cardinal *Dossat*'s Letters of the 22d of *December* 1599. He writes thus to M *de Villeroy*. " You will be pleas'd to know, that one
" Day the Pope told me, that when the Match
" was making betwixt *Henry* King of *Na-*
" *varre*, and *Margaret* of *Valois*, Cardinal *A-*
" *lexandrin*, who was Legate from Pope *Pi-*
" *us* V his Unkle, being in *France*, did all
" that he could to hinder it and after he had
" spoken several times to King *Charles* about it,
" his Majesty took him one Day by the Hand,
" and said to him, All that you say, Cardinal,
" is very good and I thank the Pope and you
" for it and *if I had any other Means to re-*
" *venge my self of my Enemies, I would not*
" *make this Match, but I have no other way but*
" *this* His Holiness added, that when the
" News of St *Bartholomew*'s Day came to
" *Rome*, the said Cardinal *Alexandrin* said ,
" Prais'd be God, the King of *France* has kept
" his Promise to me His Holiness said, He
" knew all this, because he was at that time
" Auditor to the said Cardinal, and was with
" him throughout the Journey he took into *Spain*
" first, and afterwards into *France* and that
" he himself had put all this down in Writing
" from that very time, and it might still be
" found among the Papers of the said Cardinal
" *Alexandrin*

Clement VIII, was a good Man enough But a good Christian would have been cautious of recommending so strongly the Maxim of the Duke of *Urbin*, and would not have utter'd himself in these Terms, on so horrible an Effusion of innocent Blood, and on so detestable a Perfidiousness, which have render'd the Reign and Memory of *Charles* IX, abominable

Henry III, Brother and Successor to *Charles* IX thinking it behov'd him to marry at his Return from *Poland*, sent *Claude Pinart*, one of the four Secretaries of State to *Stockholm*, to solicit a Match between him and the Princess *Elizabeth*, Sister of *John* King of *Sweden* His Negotiation was already in good Forwardness, and the Marriage was near being concluded, when the King calling to mind a Beauty he had seen at *Nancy*, as he was going to *Poland*, engag'd himself to her and wrote to *Pinart*, to return home, and leave the Negotiation in the State it was then in This was a gross Affront offer'd by this unconstant Prince, not only to the King, and to the Princess of *Sweden*, but even to his own Embassador, who was hard put to it, to get well off of so intricate an Affair, and to obtain leave to be gone

The worst of Infidelities would be the Refusal that a Prince (who being satisfy'd with the Services of his Minister) should make, to protect

protect him against an open Violence and a manifest Injustice. But this is what I shall not speak to, because I do not find any Instances thereof. On the contrary, *History* takes notice in many Places of the Firmness of Princes, who have not only oppos'd the Outrages done to their Ministers, but also the Wrongs and Injuries they were threatned with. The Marshal *d'Estree* had a furious Contention with the Court of *Rome* in the Year 1641. I shall relate the Particulars thereof in Chapter XXVIII, and shall here only say a word or two with relation to the pressing Instances the *Barberins* made at Court, to have a Man recall'd, who not only made his Character be respected, but also caus'd a dread of his Person and haughty Temper. The Nuncio *Scotti*, who had Orders to sollicit his Revocation, met at first with great Opposition, Cardinal *Richelieu* declaring to him, *That the King's Dignity was deeply concern'd therein, and that without doing him a signal Prejudice, no Consent could be given to the recalling an Embassador at the Pleasure of another Court where he was not acceptable, merely because he had with too much Firmness stuck to the Interest of the King his Master*, and because he had been outragiously dealt with Marshal *d'Estrée* had retir'd to *Caprarola*, which depends on the Duke of *Parma*, from whence he continu'd giving the *Barberins* so much Trouble and Uneasyness, that these repeating their Instances with more warmth than ever, the Cardinal at last resolv'd to recall this Minister, as well because he could no longer serve the King at *Rome*, as because he himself was not able to make so fierce and rough a Spirit act up to his Intentions. Notwithstanding which, he did it but on this Condition, that the Pope should likewise recall his *Nuncio*, that thereby the Court of *Rome* might have no Advantage over that of *France*.

The 17th of *August* 1657, the United Provinces resolv'd, at the Instance of those of *Holland*, who for that purpose came in a Body to the Assembly of the States General, that the King of *Sweden* should be requir'd to call home *Harald Appelboom*, his Resident, who had made use of some free and bold Expressions, in some Letters that had been intercepted in *Denmark*. The States, in writing to the King, did not only speak of *Appelboom*, as of an unprofitable Minister, and incapable of entertaining a good Correspondence between the Crown of *Sweden* and their State, but they also desir'd his Majesty to punish him, for having written things that were Reflections on the Government, and some of those of whom it was compos'd. They moreover added, that after a Month, to be counted from the Date of their Resolution, they would neither receive nor read his Memorials, and that no Answer should be made thereto, unless the Interest of the Crown of *Sweden*, and of the Estates of the Provinces, should require the same to be taken into Consideration. The King, who knew those Letters had been intercepted, wrote to his Resident, some time before the Resolution had been taken. That he did not doubt but they would make a noise, *but however he would not have him be uneasy on that account That he was well satisfy'd with his Service, and that he would stand by him*. And accordingly, the King was so far from recalling his Minister, that he requir'd Reparation to be made him, as well because they had declar'd him unprofitable and incapable, as because they had printed the intercepted Letters. He even protested, *that he would not grant any farther Audiences to the three Embassadors that resided with him on the part of the States, till his Resident was restor'd to the Function of his Employment, and Satisfaction had been made him*. The States were hereupon forc'd to bear with him, and to consider him as before. So that they might very well have forborn making this Step, to make a Retreat that was not very honourable. These Resolutions are often taken upon the Overtures, or on the Advice of Ministers, who with all their Ability have not a pertinent Knowledge of the *Law of Nations*, nor Experience enough, not to commit sometimes Irregularities in Affairs of this nature. Those who know what it is to offer to oblige a Prince, that has Courage and Honour, to so nice an Action, will never undertake it till they have well taken their Measures, and are well assur'd that the Prince, with whom they have to do, is willing to bear being ill us'd in the Person of his Minister.

There was in this Affair another Particular, of which I shall take notice, tho' it does not relate to the Subject, which I handle in this Chapter. The King of *Sweden* maintain'd, conformably to the Laws and Civil Right, that it was not his Minister had offended the Government, but that they should be taken to task who had publish'd and caus'd the intercepted Letters to be printed, because it is not they that write Pasquinades or Libels, but they that disperse them, that sin against the Laws, and are the true Criminals, which is very worthy of Observation, because some Ministers, although they were great Lawyers, and at one will believe them, great Politicians too, have committed very gross Faults on this Subject

I shall joyn to the Example of *Appelboom*, that of *Francis* Baron of *Lisola* Embassador on the part of the Emperor at *Warsaw* That Minister, who who had Wit, had made himself very acceptable to the King and Queen of *Poland*, who receiv'd from him considerable Services, till perceiving in the Year 1661 that the Queen undertook to cause a Successor to be chosen during the King's Life time, and that she endeavour'd to make the Election succeed in favour of a *French* Prince. He oppos'd openly enough the Intrigues that were forming for that purpose amongst the Senators. The Queen, who could not be ignorant of it, and who was at least as capable of governing as the King, caus'd it to be resolv'd, That the Bishop of *Warmia* and the Palatin of *Pomerania* should go to *Lisola*, and tell him, *That the Cabals he created in the Kingdom, hinder'd their Majesties from admitting him any more to Audience* Lisola to assure himself of their Intention, to find out whether there was any thing beyond the personal dislike, and whether these Prohibitions extended to the Negotiation he had to carry on, in the behalf of the Emperor his Master, ask'd to see the King, who sent him word, That if he had any thing to propose, he might do it in Writing Lisola refus'd to do it, and gave the Court at *Vienna* advice thereof, from whence he receiv'd in Answer, That the Emperor

peror was by so much the more surpriz'd at the Procedure of the King of *Poland*, that before he had recourse to Measures so opposite to that good Understanding that ought to be between neighbouring Princes, and such near Relations, and even to the Law of Nations, he ought to have made his Complaint The King of *Poland* wrote afterwards to the Emperor on that Subject, and his Resident, *Vespasian Landscoronsky*, seconded with his good Offices, the King his Master's Reasons But the Emperor, whose Interest it was to prevent the Election of a *French* Prince, approv'd of the Conduct of his Embassador However, as he could no longer do him any Service, in a Court where he had made himself disagreeable, he call'd him back at his own Request, and under another Colour *Lisola* went away without taking leave of either the King or the Queen, and the Emperor has ever since employ'd him in Negotiations of the utmost Importance, to which he apply'd himself with a great deal of Sufficiency, although frequently with small Success

These Examples would be sufficient, if it might not be said, with some Appearance of Truth, that the Consideration the Pope had for the King of *France*, the States of the United Provinces for the King of *Sweden*, and the King of *Poland* for the Emperor, hinder'd him the Ministers from being dismiss'd or sent home, but it is what cannot be said of the following Example, where a Republick has maintain'd its Minister, contrary to the Intention of the most powerful Monarch of *Christendom*, and against the Instances of Cardinal *Mazarin*, absolute Director and Manager of the Affairs of *France* It is not long since the States of the United Provinces had an Embassador there, who neither wanted Wit nor Knowledge, but he had not that Politeness which is necessary in all Courts, and without which it is impossible to succeed, in that particularly His Language was coarse, and his Expressions were so rude that his best Thoughts were disfigur'd thereby His too frequent *Sarcasms* had render'd him so odious, that the first Minister, who had been the principal Object thereof, resolv'd to make his utmost Efforts, to have him recall'd immediately after the Conclusion of the *Pyrenean* Treaty The Embassador had had a very hot Debate with Cardinal *Mazarin*, on account of the Depredations the *French* Privateers made in the *Mediterranean*, where they very much incommoded, or rather ruined the *Hollanders* Trade The Complaints the States had from time to time made thereof, had had no Effect, because that some of those who had the greatest Share in the Management of the Affairs of the Kingdom, had likewise the greatest in the Booty So that perceiving there was no other Remedy, they commanded their Admiral to oppose those Violences, and to seize those that did 'em, or had been guilty of 'em *De Ruiter*, their Vice-Admiral, took two of them on the Coast of *Italy*, and forasmuch as they were the King's Ships, though they had been arm'd and fitted out at the Expence of private Persons, the Court of *France*, judging that the Dignity of the Crown was concern'd therein, caus'd all the *Hollanders* Ships that were in the Ports of *France* to be seiz'd This extraordinary Procedure oblig'd the Embassador to demand a publick Audience, wherein he inveigh'd very much against this Violence, and justify'd, in some measure, what *de Ruiter* had done The King listen'd to him with a great deal of Patience, but when he began to speak of the Depredations, which were committed with the Approbation of the Court, and perhaps with the private Orders of the Ministry, the Cardinal interrupted him in the King's Presence, and us'd him with little Respect The Embassador made no other Reply, but that he had the Honour to speak to the King, and having made a low Bow to his Majesty, he pursu'd his Discourse with the same Vigour The Cardinal, who knew very well that what the Embassador said of the Piracies was but too true, and who could not brook the tacit Reproaches which were made him, as if he had a share therein, fell into a Passion, interrupted him twice more, and endeavour'd, tho' ineffectually, to hinder him from making an end But at the breaking up of the Audience he was so transported with Anger, that he gave him ill Language, to the great Scandal of those that consider'd what was due to the Character He went a great deal farther, for going down the back-stairs to the Queen's Apartment, he dispos'd her to signify to the Embassador, who was likewise going to receive Audience from her, that the Embassador having without doubt nothing to entertain her with, but what he had just told the King, it was not necessary for him to see her this time This Embassador was not at that time much in the favour with the States of *Holland*, who had nominated him to that Embassy That he might therefore restore himself to their former Esteem, he was willing to do something remarkable, for which he found a very favourable Opportunity For the Duke of *Orleans*, who had been confined to the Territories appropriated to the Support of his Dignity, having obtain'd leave to return to Court, was arriv'd there the same Day, and was come to pay his Duty to the King, at the Hour appointed for the Audience So that all the Princes and Noblemen that were then at *Paris* repair'd to the *Louvre*, to render the first Interview between the King and his Uncle so much the more solemn, and the Embassador could not have wish'd for a more splendid Juncture to display his Eloquence in The Affair made a great Noise *M de Thou* was sent into *Holland*, and during his stay there, he had Orders to labour to have the Embassador recall'd He communicated it to a Person he confided in, who having his own particular Views, gave him a very partial Advice, which, at the same time, the most dextrous Minister in the World would not have mistrusted This Confident, who was a Friend to him that was in *France*, counsell'd *M de Thou* to write to Cardinal *Mazarin*, That it being a matter of very great Importance, as well in it self, as by reason of the Uncertainty of the Issue thereof, he found himself oblig'd to represent to him, that the Embassador being in great Consideration with his Masters, it would be a difficult Point to dispossess him of his Employment, and that even if he succeeded therein, his being recall'd would be prejudicial to the Service and Interest of his Majesty, that the Intention of those that perhaps would consent thereto,

B b and

and give a helping hand to the bringing it to pass, was to have him succeeded by a Minister that depended entirely on the will of the predominant Faction, which was in possession of the administration of Affairs since the *Prince of Orange*'s death, so that the King would not find the Change to answer his purpose. The Cardinal who did not require Reasons, but a blind Obedience, and who at that very time design'd to have a strict union with those that should be judg'd most powerful in the State, according to the general Maxim and the true interest of Princes, could not acquiesce in *M. de Thou*'s Remostrance, and sent him fresh Orders to solicit the Revocation of the *Dutch* Embassador. *M. de Thou*, instead of executing these new Orders, had recourse again to the Advice of his Friend, who not being much concern'd what effects this disobedience might produce, Counsel'd him to continue his Remonstrances, and to oppose the same Advices to the same Orders. *De Thou* believ'd him, and the Cardinal being disgusted at this invincible obstinacy, call'd him Home. The safest way is not to declare ones self on these occasions, 'till the Prince has been sounded, whose Embassador is intended to be recall'd, because oftentimes Princes put on the Cloke of I know not what false Virtue, and stand obstinately by their Ministers, lest their Complaisance should pass for Weakness, and their Prudence for Timidity, as it frequently is in effect.

Thus the States-General, who had had a proof of the Fidelity of their Embassador in the execution of their Orders, were willing to give a Token of their own, by maintaining him in his Post, notwithstanding the instances of the King, and of an absolute Minister, who was very sensibly affected with what related to his own particular.

CHAP. XIII.

The Embassador ought to be Agreeable.

THE King of *France* sending the *Sieur Lamer* to *Lisbon* in the Year 1646, said in the first Article of his Instructions, that he honours him with that Employment, as well for other Considerations, as because he is sensible that being known to the King of *Portugal*, his *Person would be, for that reason, more acceptable to him*. On the contrary, *Sherwig Rosenham* had been Embassador from *Sweden*, in *France*, during the Commotions in *Paris*, and this Court was so little satisfy'd with his Conduct, that Queen *Christina* had been oblig'd to recall him. In the Year 1652, it was deliberated again in Council to send him back to *France* in the same Quality, and the Queen her self was for it. But it was represented to her, that there was no likelihood than a Minister, whose Person had not been very well approv'd of heretofore, should be afterwards acceptable, so that she delay'd giving him this Employment, 'till she was inform'd how he would be receiv'd in *France*. She was given to understand that he would not be very agreeable, for which Reason she thought no more of it.

Whatever Qualifications, whatever Perfections an Embassador may have, the success of his Negotiation will always be doubtful, if he be not agreeable to the Court where he is to Negotiate. That Prince that makes choice of a Minister whom he knows to be disagreeable, shews how is willing to offend the Prince to whom he sends him, or else he must be devoid of common sense, if he thinks to perswade him of the sincerity of his Intentions. On the other side, those of the Prince, who for particular Reasons receives a Minister whom he cannot relish, ought to be by so much the more suspected as dangerous, because he buries his just resentment in a deep dissimulation.

M. de Villeroy, who was a very dextrous and very able Minister said, that he that was on the King's part at *Rome*, ought to endeavour to hinder either a *Venetian* or *Florentine* from being employ'd in the Nuntiature of *France*, because it had trouble enough with the Embassadors of the Republick and of the great Duke, without having the Court perplex'd with *Nuncio*'s that had a dependence on either the one or the other. But it would be a difficult enterprize to undertake to exclude all the Subjects of two Potentates of *Italy*, for being incommodious to *France*, who yet are not its Enemies.

I shall set down what may displease in the Embassador, and in the Embassie, from whence it will be easie to judge what will render either the one or the other agreeable. The Embassador may be disagreeable on account of the Prince that employs him, or by reason of the business he has to Negotiate, or else because there is something that displeases in his Person. There are likewise Ministers, who being agreeable at first, become disagreeable and troublesome in the course of the Negotiation. I shall here speak of the one, and of the other, as well as of the manner how Princes are us'd to deal with those that are actually so, and with those that become so afterwards. As for the first, a Prince cannot admit of a Minister that is not agreeable to him, because the same *Law of Nations*, that does not permit any violence or injurious usage to be dealt to a Minister that had been admitted and acknowledg'd, allows Princes not to admit of a Minister from whom they may receive any displeasure.

I'll instance in some Examples. Pope *Clement* VIII had a kindness for the *Duke de Nevers*, and an esteem for the *Marquis of Pisani*, yet he notify'd to the one, that he would not acknow-

The EMBASSADOR and his FUNCTIONS.

acknowledge him in the quality of Embassador, and he forbid the other coming to Rome. King *Henry* IV, considering that he hazarded his Crown by delaying to change his Religion, turn'd Roman Catholick, and caus'd himself to be absolv'd from his pretended Heresy and Relapse by some Prelates of his own Kingdom. At which the Pope was so offended, that he call'd the action of the Bishops of *France*, an attempt upon the Pontifical Authority. Wherefore not being able, according to the maxims of the Court of *Rome*, to approve of what had been done at *St. Denis*, nor to acknowledge the King in that Quality, he neither would nor could admit his Embassador. But however, that he might not offend the King by too publick and scandalous a Refusal, he caus'd the Duke to be inform'd of his Intention, and that he did not consider him as an Embassador from the King of *France*. Father *Possevin* a Jesuite, whom the Pope employ'd on this occasion, having met *the Duke of Nevers* at *Poschiano*, which belongs to the *Grisons*, told him, by virtue of his *Letters of Credence*, that the Pope would not receive him, nor admit him as an Embassador, but only as *Duke of Nevers*, and *Prince of the House of Gonzaga*, to which he added, that his Holiness was very glad of the King's Conversion, and pray'd to God it might be sincere. The Duke, tho' very much surpriz'd at the Discourse, nevertheless pursu'd his Journey as far as *Mantua*, where the same Jesuite met him, and made the same declaration to him from the Pope, notwithstanding which, he in pursuance of his Orders, went directly to *Rome*. Before he reach'd that place, he was met again by Father *Possevin* at *Camoucha*, where he shew'd him a Letter, by which *Cardinal St. George*, one of the Pope's Nephews order'd him to declare to the Duke, *that the Pope expected he should come into Rome without any Train, and without any mark that could cause it to be thought he was a publick Minister, or hop'd to receive the least favour from his Holiness*, and moreover, that he should not stay there above ten days. The Duke at the same time was advis'd by his Friends, that the Pope had forbid the Cardinals to visit him, or to receive his visits. This rude and even insupportable usage to a Prince who was Embassador from the first King of Christendom, was very astonishing to him, but yet it did not hinder him from going to *Rome*. He arriv'd there upon Sunday the 21st of *November*, without any other Retinue than what he had brought along with him from *France*, which consisted in fifty Gentlemen, and three Prelates, whom the Clergy of *France* had joyn'd to the Embassie, to justifie what had pass'd in reference to the King's Absolution. He was admitted the same night to pay his respects to the Pope, and he entreated him not to limit the time of his stay at *Rome*, and not to be against his visiting the Cardinals, because he was oblig'd to deliver the King's Letters to them, and to acquaint them with the affairs he had to negotiate. He desir'd him moreover, to grant him audience in a full Consistory, in the presence of the Embassadors of *Spain*, and of the Deputies of the League, to the end he might justifie the proceedings of the King his Master. But the Pope was far from yielding to; and as for the other two Points, he said he would advise about 'em. On Tuesday the 23d of *November*, he had his first audience, and although it was not publick, yet he went to it attended by a Cortege of threescore and ten Gentlemen. He spoke in it very advantageously of the state of the King's affairs, and complain'd extremely of the impertinent and seditious procedure of the League. He was urgent with the Pope to give the King his Blessing, as a thing that could not be refus'd him after his Conversion, and pray'd him, with reference to his own Person, not to limit to so few days the time he had to stay at *Rome*. The Pope, who at that time was very much sway'd by the *Spaniards*, and who gave too much credit to the passionate advices the Cardinal of *Placentia* his Legate wrote him from *France*, would not explain himself neither to the one nor the other point. So that the Duke perceiving that it would be to no purpose to desire audience in the Consistory, deliver'd to the Pope the Letter the King had written to him, and accompany'd it with strong protestations of the Zeal his Majesty had for the Catholick Religion, and of the affection he had for the Person of the Pope, and for the House of the *Aldobrands*. He added that the King had sent along with him three Prelates, who having been present at his abjuration, were capable of giving his Holiness an account thereof, if he was willing he should introduce them to him. The Pope made no other answer to all this, but that he would consider of it. Saturday the 27th, the *Spanish* Embassador having obtain'd an Audience, went to it attended by Seventy Coaches, to equal the number of Persons the Duke brought with him to his. That audience of the *Spanish* Minister produc'd this effect, that the very Monday following the Pope signify'd to the Duke, that if he would see him once more, he would grant him a favourable Audience, but that he must be quick therein, because the stay he should continue to make at *Rome*, might give a jealousie to those he was oblig'd to have quite another consideration for, than what he could have for him. That being come to *Rome* but in a private Capacity, he had no occasion to visit the Cardinals. And as for the three *French* Prelates, that he could not admit 'em at his feet 'till they had seen the Cardinal of *St. Severine*, who was chief of the Inquisition, and Grand Penitentiary. The Duke observing all these Irregularities, that the Pope would not suffer him to see the Cardinals, and that the design was to embroil the three Prelates with the Inquisition, which is an endless work, desir'd the Pope's Chamberlain, who brought him this Message, to give him in writing what he had told him by word of mouth; and upon the other's telling him he had no Orders for that, he pray'd him to go and receive it from the Pope; to the end he might have leisure to consider what answer he should make. The Pope instead of sending the Chamberlain, sent Cardinal *Toledo* to him, who used the same Discourse, and carry'd back the same Answer, after very warm contests, which had no other effect, than that the Cardinal put an end to the Conversation, and said he would make

make a Report thereof to the Pope. On the 21st of *December*, the Chamberlain came and acquainted the Duke, that the Pope had not alter'd his Resolution, neither with respect to his visiting the Cardinals, nor concerning the three Prelates. And that he might have no room to doubt thereof, the Inquisition prosecuted them so earnestly, that all they could do was to save themselves in the Duke's Chamber, notwithstanding they had *Letters of Credence*, and *particular Instructions*, which might have made 'em be consider'd as *publick Ministers*. On the 6th of *December* the Duke had another Audience, and as he imagin'd it would be his last, he was willing also to make his utmost efforts on the Pope's Mind. He flung himself on his knees at the Pope's feet, and conjur'd him with the last submissions, accompany'd with tears, not to refuse his Blessing to the King, who presented himself before him as a penitent Sinner, whom the Church was not accustom'd to send away without Consolation. But finding the Pope inflexible, he got up, and changing his Note, he spoke to him with so moving an air, that the Pope was touch'd therewith, yet not so far as to grant the least hopes to the Duke, only he gave him leave to stay in *Rome* till the beginning of the Year following, 1594. The Duke at his departure from Audience, left a Memorial with the Pope, and towards the *Christmass-Holidays* he sent him another, making pressing Instances from time to time, to have an answer in Writing. He urg'd the the same thing again, in the Audience he had on the 2d of *January*, but he could obtain nothing, the Pope remaining inexorable, notwithstanding the lively Remonstrances the Duke made him, concerning the disorders the See of *Rome* had reason to apprehend from to cruel a denial, and the dissatisfaction the Pope would himself one day receive therefrom. The 6th of *January Cardinal Toleto* came and told the Duke, that the Pope did not think himself oblig'd to answer him in Writing, since he had given him nothing on the part of the King of *Navarr*, and that his Holiness had acquainted him, before he came to *Rome*, that he could consider him but as a private Person. The Duke grew angry hereat, and afterwards fell into a Conversation, wherein nothing was concluded. So that imagining his longer stay at *Rome* would be to no purpose, he took his Audience of Leave on the the 9th of *February*, and set out the 14th, having receiv'd the visits of the two Cardinals the Pope's Nephews. He made great complaints of the rigor of this procedure, and of the ill offices the Ministers that were on the part of his Holiness in *France*, did to the King, and to the Holy See it self, but I cannot tell whether it was with any great Justice.

The Pope had hinder'd the *Marquis of Pisani* from coming to *Rome*, and would not allow the *Duke of Nevers* to come thither in the Quality of Embassador. As a Sovereign Prince he could do both the one and the other, and as Pope he could do no otherwise. The King himself, who saw the Civilities the Pope shew'd his Enemies, and the assistance he gave them, could not be offended thereat, because that according to the Maxims of *Rome*, approv'd of and allow'd by those of the Religion his Majesty had just made profession of, he could not hope to be acknowledg'd for what he was in effect, 'till the Pope had himself absolv'd him from his pretended Heresie. As for the Duke, he could blame no body but himself for the ill success of his Negotiation, after the three successive notices which the Pope had given him, that he could not consider him but as Duke of *Nevers*, that is to say as a private Nobleman. He could not find fault with the Inquisition neither, because it might extend its Jurisdiction to Ecclesiasticks, who were found in the Company of a Nobleman that had no Character to protect 'em. Their *Credentials* and their *Instructions* were of no service to them, because the Pope did not acknowledge the Sovereignty of a Prince that had not as yet been receiv'd into the Roman Church, since he was not yet reconcil'd to him that could open him the door thereof, besides which, they came on the behalf of Prelates, who had encroach'd on the Pope's Jurisdiction, in a reserv'd Case. In this Example the *Duke of Nevers* was not disagreeable to *Clement*, but the Prince that employ'd him was, as well as the Subject of his Embassie. The following Example bears a great proportion to what I have now said.

After the Emperor *Charles* V. had resign'd the Imperial Dignity into the hands of the Electors, *Ferdinand* his Brother, who succeeded him in the Empire, thought himself oblig'd to notifie his Election to Pope *Paul* IV. who being in possession of the See of *Rome*, and pretending that the resignation of the Imperial Crown ought to have been made into his hands, and not into those of the Electors, refus'd to admit *Ferdinand's Embassador*. He maintain'd, that it was only in the case of Death that the Electors could proceed to a new Election, and that without that, the Election was faulty, because that amongst the Electors there were three Hereticks. He sent a Messenger to meet *Martin Gusman* (whom *Ferdinand* employ'd in that Embassie) to tell him he would do well *not to come to Rome*, 'till such time as the matter was adjusted by the seven Cardinals he had appointed to examine it, and who being all of 'em well affected to the House of *Austria*, would without doubt give satisfaction to *Ferdinand Gusman*, out of deference to the Pope's Orders, retir'd to *Tivoli*, from whence he gave the Emperor an account of what had happen'd to him; whereupon he receiv'd Orders to return home, if the Pope did not do him justice in few days. *Martin Gusman* instead of obeying, did notwithstanding go to *Rome*, not in the Quality of Embassador, as he said, but in a private Capacity, under a pretext of visiting the Holy Places and Churches. He even saw the Pope, who gave him Audience *in the presence of some of the Cardinals*. He therein represented the just ground the Emperor had to be angry, and to resent such unworthy usage. He told him *Ferdinand* had been chosen King of the *Romans*, not only with the participation of *Clement* VII. but even at his Suit. That afterwards he succeed in the Empire, it was not necessary to proceed to a new Election, because the King of the *Romans* succeeded in his

his own Right, as foon as ever there was an *Interregnum*, either by death, or otherwife That the Enemies of the Roman Catholick Religion would rejoyce at the mifunderftanding they fhould obferve between the Pope and the Emperor, who was the only caufe of the Devotion fome of the Princes of *Germany* ftill preferv'd for the See of *Rome*, and for the Catholick Church That *Ferdinand* could not without grief and indignation fuffer his Imperial Dignity to be difputed, which his Brother and himfelt had with fo much difficulty maintain'd againft fo great a number of Princes, and fo many People that had oppos'd the fame The Pope told him that the Affair being of the laft importance, he had laid it before an Affembly of Cardinals to examine into it, who would not fail to difcharge their Confcience *Martin Gufman* was hereupon forc'd to retire, and *Ferdinand* could get no other fatisfaction during the Life of *Paul* But immediately upon his deceafe, *Francis de la Tour* who had fucceeded in the room of *Gufman*, was acknowledg'd as the Emperor's Embaffador by the College of Cardinals, and by Pope *Pius IV* prefently after his exaltation The refufal *Paul IV* made to admit the Embaffador, was by fo much the more offenfive, as the Emperor and all the Empire were concern'd therein But however he did not thereby violate the *Law of Nations*, tho' it is true he ufurp'd and arrogated to himfelf a Temporal Authority that did not belong to him, whereas *Clement* made ufe of the Spiritual or Ecclefiaftical Power which the Canons and Poffeffion give the Pope This difference oblig'd *Philip II* King of *Spain*, who had a concern for the intereft of the Emperor his Unkle, to order *John of Figueroa* Governor of *Milan* to go to *Rome*, and to back *Martin Gufman*'s Endeavours *Figueroa* had fome time before caus'd a fmall Officer of the Jurifdiction of the Archbifhop of *Milan* to be Cudgel'd, whereupon he had incurr'd the Ecclefiaftical Cenfures, of which he had not been abfolv'd according to the formalities in that cafe This occafion'd the Pope to forbid his coming to *Rome*, which gave *Figueroa* fo fenfible a difpleafure, that retiring to *Gaeta*, he fell Sick, and dy'd a few days after Here it was the Perfon of the Embaffador that was not acceptable, and in whom there was fuch an impediment, which according to the Maxims of the Court of *Rome* was a lawful one, fo that not only the *Law of Nations* was not thereby offended, but the King likewife had no reafon to complain

In the Year 1600, the *Arch-Duke Albert* fent *Charles Count of Egmont*, and the *Prefident of the Council of Luxemburg*, to feveral Princes of *Germany*, to acquaint them with his acceffion to the States of *Flanders* and of *Burgundy*, to exhort them to live in a good underftanding with him, to caft on the United Provinces the Inconveniencies that were occafion'd by the vicinity of the War, and to excufe thofe they receiv'd from the Arms of *Spain* The *Elector Palatine* and the *Landgrave of Heffe* refus'd to hear them, and fent them back at the end of two days, notifying to them by their Counfellors, that if the *Arch-Duke* would have them think he had no hand in the diforders, of which the Empire had fo much reafon to complain, he ought to put an end to them, and punifh the Authors thereof Here it was not the Embaffadors that were diflik'd, but the Parties were not fatisfy'd with their Prince

Guftavus Adolphus King of *Sweden*, in order to juftifie his invading *Germany*, about fifty years ago, fays in his *Manifefto* among other things, that contrary to the *Law of Nations*, his Embaffadors had receiv'd the affront of being fent back, and that they had been refus'd admittance in *the Affembly at Lubeck*, without giving them leave to reprefent the Grievances they had orders from him to complain of That upon the firft advices of their arrival, it had not been thought enough to forbid 'em approaching the place where it was held, but that matters were carry'd to that pitch of infolence and bravado, *as to furb d' em entring into Germany, at the peril of their Lives* He fet forth that there was not any People fo barbarous as not to confefs that this it felf was a fufficient reafon to juftifie his refentment, whereupon one of the greateft Men of thofe times expreffes himfelf in thefe terms *A Prince muft be altogether infenfible not to refent fo grofs an affront, that violates the Law of Nations, and touches Sovereigns in the moft fenfible part* The Emperor could not hinder a foreign King from fending his Minifters to an Affembly of the Empire By making *Prohibitions on pain of Death* to the Embaffadors of a Prince who was not a declar'd Enemy of the Empire, he violated the *Law of Nations*, and even if he had not violated them, he fo grofly offended the Prince concern'd, that his Arms were fufficiently juftify'd thereby It is with reafon faid, that the outrage that is done to a publick Minifter, touches the Honour of the Mafter in the moft fenfible part If a Prince may be injur'd in his Picture, he with much more reafon may be fo in his Minifter, who reprefents him after a much more noble and lively manner I here give the fentiment of no lefs a Man than *Cardinal de Richelieu*

In the Year 1648 foon after the Conclufion of the Peace of *Munfter*, the *Commander de Souvré*, who was *Embaffador from the Order of St John of Jerufalem*, to *France*, went to *Holland* in the fame Capacity, to lay claim to the *Commanderies* that Order pretends to have a right to within the extent of the United Provinces The States liv'd in perfect Amity with the *Great Mafter*, who during the War, had given a fafe retreat in the Port of *Malta* to the *Dutch* Ships, and had handfomly treated thofe who Commanded them, fo that the States being fatisfied therewith, his Embaffador ought not to have been difagreeable to them, yet neverthelefs they could not have treated him in a more difobliging manner than they did The Embaffador being arriv'd at *Roterdam*, gave notice thereof to the States, and defir'd at the fame time, that they would give the neceffary Orders for his Reception The States firft fignify'd to him, that 'till then there had not been feen any Embaffador from the great Mafter in thofe Countries, fo that they could not refolve upon any thing relating to the Ceremonies of his Reception, without the advice of the States of the Provinces, their Principals However, they had no fooner made this Anfwer, swer, than they reflected, that it was deficient as to the Respect which is due to the *Law of Nations* and that, in sending back after this manner the Minister of a Prince that was acknowledg'd for Sovereign by all the World, who had oblig'd the State a thousand ways, and who reclaim'd his own after the usual Method in such Cases, they offended all the other Princes of Christendom, who interested themselves in the Welfare of the Order They, out of this Consideration, sent him word a few Days after, that they were ready to receive him with all the Honours due to his Character, but that they found themselves oblig'd to let him know, that they could not acknowledge the Great Master with reference to the Commanderies that are situate in those Provinces *Monsieur de Souvre*, exasperated at this Answer, which he said was unjust, and which at least was not very Civil, re-took the Road to *France*, after he had sent the States a formal Protestation against their Proceedings The States sent it him back again, and intreated him, at the same time, to come to the *Hague* and receive the Honours which were preparing for his Reception, but he that was to deliver this Message, did not find him at *Delft*, from whence he was gone in order to return to *France* The Complement was to be made without reserve but the States General however register'd the Reserve in the Archives of their secret Resolutions This Precaution was needless, since it could not give a Right to the Provinces, who were in Possession of several Commanderies without any Title, and, as it was said, without any Colour of Justice In this case it was nothing else, but the Subject-matter of the Embassy, that render'd the Embassador disagreeable, and that made him be sent back after so rude a manner, as would not have pass'd unresented, had it not been for the Civil Wars of *France*, which hinder'd it that time those Fleets to be fitted out, that have since done so much Mischief in the *Mediterranean*

When the Business an Embassador has to negotiate is odious, his Person cannot be acceptable Pope *Boniface* VIII intending in the Year 1296, to bring the *Sicilians* under the Obedience of *Charles* of *Anjou*, sent into the Island the Bishop of *Urgel*, and *Boniface* of *Calamendrana*, Master of the Order of St *John of Jerusalem*, accompany'd by the Archdeacon of the Church of *Urgel*, and by *John Perez de Navalis*, Embassadors from *James* II, King of *Arragon*, who were to exhort 'em to reconcile themselves with *Charles* But the Embassadors of the holy Father being enter'd into the Port of *Messina*, were not suffer'd to land, nor to enter the Town, to receive the Audience they had demanded The *Sicilian* Lords signify'd to them by a Gentleman, whose Name was *Peter d'Anse*, that the States of the Kingdom had resolv'd to acknowledge no other for their King than Prince *Don Frederick*, Brother to the King of *Arragon* This Gentleman, laying his Hand to his Sword, added to his Discourse, that that should give them Peace and that they would not be oblig'd to Parchment and Wax for it, which was what the Embassadors brought them That they should forthwith depart the Island, or prepare themselves to die immediately They were forc'd to be gone, for fear of trusting their Persons in a Place where the *Laws of Nations* would not have been much respected no great Consideration being had thereto, amidst the Disorders of Civil Wars The *Sicilians* violated it, not in refusing to admit the Embassadors, but in threatening their Lives

The Elector of *Brandenburgh*, who did not without Reluctancy enter into the Interest of the deceased King of *Sweden*, *Charles Gustavus*, quitted it, as soon as *Poland* (having recover'd it self from its first Surprize) found the means to make him change his Party, by promising him the Sovereignty of the Ducal *Prussia* He presently comply'd, but before he declar'd himself, the King and the Senate of *Poland* thought fit, that he should make an Overture of Agreement to the King of *Sweden*, in order to dispose him to a Peace He sent him for this end in the Year 1658, *Otto* Baron of *Swerin*, his first Minister, and *Daniel Weiman*, Chancellor of *Cleves* who being arriv'd at *Kiel* the 13th of May, were there visited by the Prince Palatine of *Sultsbach*, and by Count *Slippenbach*, who were come thither on purpose, the first from *Gottorp*, and the other from *Wismar* and within a few Days the King sent to desire them to come to him at *Flensburg* They arriv'd there on the 19th, and after they had communicated their *Letters of Credence*, the King sent one of the Gentlemen of his Houshold to complement them, but he still delay'd giving them Audience It was rumor'd, tho' falsly, that the Baron of *Swerin*, discoursing with the Prince of *Sultsbach*, had discover'd, that they had Orders to urge the King to restore the Royal *Prussia* to the Crown of *Poland* to take a Sum of Money in lieu thereof, and to fix the same as also to demand the Reimbursement of what Expences the Elector had been at in assisting him and that for the Discharge thereof he would yield up the Town and Bayliwick of *Stetin* It was moreover said, that the Embassadors were to declare to the King, that the Elector was so far engag'd with *Poland*, that he was oblig'd to risque his all with it *Swerin* had said nothing of all this, but the King of *Sweden*, who was but too well assur'd of the Engagement the Elector had enter'd into with *Poland*, imagining that the Intention of the Embassadors from *Brandenburg* was to declare War against him, if he did not grant all their Demands and fearing least in the Audience, Disputes might arise, that would only serve to provoke the already exasperated Minds, he was desirous to sound them a little, before he gave them Audience. To this purpose he employ'd three of his Ministers, and gave 'em to understand that he desir'd, that those of *Lunenburg* and *Hesse* should be present at the Audience they demanded *Swerin*, who was a Man of great Ability, said, it was not customary to enter upon Negotiation before Audience granted that they had Orders to ask it, and that they could not conceive, what could be the Design of having any other foreign Ministers by, who had no Qualification to be so, either as Witnesses or Parties The Ministers of *Sweden* said, that the King their Master, being persuaded the Elector had treated with the *Poles*, he could not give Audience to his Ministers without a previous Information Upon this Declaration the two Embassadors from the Elector resolv'd to retire But before they set out, they wrote to Count *Slippenbach*

penbach That the King of *Sweden* having invited them to come to him at *Flensburg*, they could not doubt of *their Persons being agreeable to him* that it was a thing without Precedent, to require they should declare their Commission to any other than his Majesty himself, that having no Orders to do so, they were on the point of returning, to give his Electoral Highness an account of what had pass'd and entreated the King to honour them with his Commands The Count made answer, that the King would not admit 'em to Audience, till they had a Full-power to restore a good Understanding between the Elector and him, because without that, he could consider the Embassadors but as his Enemies, or as Associates with them and that he would not suffer them to make mention of a Peace with *Poland* The Messenger that carry'd this Answer, did not come time enough to find the Embassadors, who had already left the Place, whereupon it was sent after them by a Trumpeter The Baron of *Suerin* and *Wetman* complain'd of this Procedure in a Writing, which was publish'd on the 14th of *August*, wherein they say, That in the manner they were treated, the *Law of Nations* had been violated The *Swedes* answer'd it about two Months after, in a kind of Manifesto, where they set forth That it was true, the King their Master had desir'd the Elector would send his Embassadors to his Majesty, to see if thereby he could cure himself of the Distrust he had of his Electoral Highness's Conduct that they had been receiv'd with Civility that his Ministers could not deny, that the Alliance had been violated on the part of the Elector, and that there had been already so many Overt-Hostilities on that side, that the King could not act otherwise than he did That he was sensible the Elector's Intention was very different from what his Ministers would have made it be believ'd this was the Reason he would not give them Audience, till he had div'd into the Secret of the Matter That the Embassadors finding themselves in an ill Case, had rather stolen away than retir'd That in delaying to give Audience to Embassadors that were Friends, *and in refusing it absolutely to Enemies, the Law of Nations was not violated* and that the Advices he receiv'd on all hands, oblig'd him to use a great deal of Circumspection The King of *Sweden* knew the Elector had treated with his Enemies, and that he was going to declare himself openly, because his Majesty would not grant him Conditions, which he look'd upon to be neither just nor honourable The King was too brave to comply with his Enemies Desires against his Inclination and indeed he did not yield to 'em, till he had lost his best Troops in the Island of *Funen*, which Misfortune affected him so sensibly, that it would not suffer him to survive the Disgrace It was not here the Embassadors that were disagreeable to him, but the Embassy it self did not please him

The King of *Sweden* did nothing that was offensive to the *Law of Nations* A Sovereign, who is absolute in his Dominions, cannot be compell'd to receive Ministers if they are not agreeable to him *Charles*, the last Duke of *Burgundy*, had sent into *Spain* the Protonotary *Artus de Bourbon*, and *Peter de Mirasmont*, who not being able to get Admittance into *Barcelona*, sent a Messenger to the States of *Catalonia*, to tell 'em, that they were oblig'd to give 'em Audience, as well out of respect to the Prince, who sent 'em to them particularly, as out of the Consideration they ought to have, and which the *Turks* themselves had, for the Ministers of Christian Princes But I can't tell whether it can be concluded from hence, that a Prince, who refuses to admit a Minister that is not agreeable to him, violates the *Law of Nations* He that is injurious to a publick Minister, is injurious also to the *Law of Nations*, but he that does not admit him, fails only in the Friendship and Civility which he owes to the Prince that sends him *Alphonso* V, King of *Arragon* and of the two *Sicilies*, surnam'd the *Magnanimous*, sent in the Year 1425 to the King of *Castile*, *Peter de Peralta*, Steward of his Houshold, *Francis Sarçuela*, *John Olzina* his Secretary, and *John Martinez de Burgos*, to be Witnesses to the signing of the Arbitration the two Kings had agreed upon, in the Person of *John*, King of *Navarre*, Brother to *Alphonso* The Intelligence these Embassadors had at the Court of *Castile*, giving the King strong Suspicions, *he would not permit them to enter into* Valladolid, where the Court then was, and he sent them word to go to *Medina del Campo*, and to stay there till further Orders *Alphonso* was offended hereat, and when he publish'd on the 4th of *June* in the same Year, a *Manifesto* for the Justification of his Arms, he takes notice of this Refusal, as of one of the Causes of the Rupture, but he does not say, that the King of *Castile* had violated the *Law of Nations* The same *Alphonso*, and *John* his Brother, being ready in the Year 1429, to enter *Castile* with an Army, gave the King an account why he did so, by *Don John de Luna*, Lord of *Illueca*, *Peter of Peralta*, *Francis* of *Sarçuela*, and *Garzia Aznar d'Anon* As soon as the Embassadors were arriv'd at Court, the King of *Castile* order'd them to go to a Village call'd *Atllon*, in which Place he would let them know his Intention and upon Advice some time after, that the King of *Arragon* had enter'd *Castile* with an Army, he sent them word, that they had nothing to do but to return home, and that he would not see them

It is sometimes matter of Prudence in a Prince not to admit him whom he shall be oblig'd to send back, and to prevent thereby a Scandal, for which it would be difficult to make Reparation. *George Villers*, Marquis and Duke of *Buckingham*, having procur'd to himself the Quality of Embassador Extraordinary, immediately after the Marriage of the Queen of *England*, notwithstanding there were already two Embassadors in *France* on the part of the King of *Great-Britain*, behav'd himself so little to the Satisfaction of the Court, that when he had a mind to return thither in the Year following, 1626, Cardinal *Richelieu* notify'd to him, not to give himself that trouble, because his Person would not be acceptable the Reasons why, were communicated to the Earl of *Holland*, who had remain'd in *Paris* ever since the Queen's Departure. The Earl represented to the Queen Mother, that to reject after that manner, a Minister that was all-powerful in his Court, would at once break off all good Correspondence betwixt the two Crowns: And that

that the little Complaisance that had been shewn to him in *France*, was the Cause of the *French* being so little consider'd in *England* But the Queen gave him no Satisfaction to his Complaint, and did not scruple to tell him, That the Court of *France* would sooner resolve upon a War than endure an Embassador, who, for very weighty Reasons, *could not be agreeable to the King* The Earl gave the Duke an Account thereof, and counsell'd him not to think of a Journey, from whence he could hope for nothing but Mortification If one has but ever so little Knowledge of the History of those Times, it is impossible to be ignorant of the Cause of the Rupture that follow'd soon after, or of the rash and impertinent Love the Duke was conceited with in his first Voyage His Design was to appear with so much Splendor and Magnificence in the second, that he might thereby make an Impression on some Persons of the first Rank and Quality of the Kingdom The Disappointment fill'd him with Spite and Malice, and he was so enrag'd to find his Thoughts discover'd, that he resolv'd upon a War which cost him his Life, and ruin'd the Party of the Religionaries in *France*

Some time after, the King of *Great Britain* having dismiss'd the *French* Domesticks belonging to the Queen, sent *Montague* to the King of *France*, to acquaint him with the Reason thereof, but he could not get Admittance In the Year 1627, after the Descent the *English* had made in the Island of *Ré*, the Duke of *Buckingham* imagining the Court of *France* would be glad to receive some Overture of an Accommodation, sent thither a Relation of his, nam'd *Ashburnham*, to make it This Gentleman had no *Letter of Credence* but from the Duke, who being at that time but only General of the *English* Army, his Minister was consider'd and treated but as a Drummer or Trumpeter would have been considered and treated The King would not see him, and it was resolv'd, he should not be spoke to from him On the contrary, he was strictly observ'd, and was sent away after such a manner, as gave sufficient Testimony how much his Master was hated and despised

It would be very difficult, or rather altogether impossible, to instance in all the Considerations that may render the Embassador or Embassy disagreeable, wherefore I shall content my self to stop at the Examples, and to make some Remarks thereupon, when they shall be necessary In the Year 1494, Pope *Alexander* VI sent *Francis Piccolomini*, Archbishop and Cardinal of *Siena*, in the Quality of Legate, to *Charles* VIII, to do him Honour at his Entrance into the Ecclesiastical State, but the King gave him to understand, that he would not suffer him to come to Court, and oblig'd him to return home This Cardinal, who has since been Pope under the Name of *Pius* III, being a Friend to the King of *Naples*, could not be so to *Charles*, nor, on that account, be acceptable to him In the Year 1480, the Pope gave the Quality of *Legate* to *Alfonso de Carillo*, Cardinal and Archbishop of *Toledo*, but *Ferdinand the Catholick* was so sensibly offended at the Procedure of the Pope, who had nominated him to the *Legation* without first acquainting him therewith, that he gave Orders to *Gonçale de Betete*, his Embassador at the Court of *Rome*, to take his leave of the Pope and come away, and to bring along with him all the *Spanish* Prelates The same *Ferdinand* would not admit the Bishop of *Arezzo*, Nuncio from *Julius* II, because he was a *Florentine*

The Pope has that Consideration for the Crowns of *France* and *Spain*, that, most commonly, he makes known to their Ministers the Qualities of the Nuncios he designs to employ in these two Courts *Alexander* VI, known by the Name of *Rodrigue Borgia* before his Exaltation, while he was Legate to *Sixtus* IV, had a mind to get into *Barcelona*, to try to dispose the Inhabitants to an Obedience *John* II, King of *Arragon*, who besieg'd the Town, gave his Consent thereto, but the Inhabitants would not admit him, but oppos'd him, and could not be prevail'd upon to let him enter the Place *Clement* VIII desiring, after the Absolution of King *Henry* IV, to settle a Minister near him, and having made choice of the Bishop of *Mantua* for that purpose, he made mention of him to *Dossat*, as of a Subject very capable of maintaining a good Correspondence between the Court of *France* and the See of *Rome* He did the same with reference to the Bishops of *Modena*, and of *Camerin*, who succeeded the Bishop of *Mantua* And when a Legate was to be sent into *France*, on occasion of the War in *Savoy*, Cardinal *Aldobrandin*, the Pope's first Minister, got a List of all the Cardinals, and examin'd, with Cardinal *Dossat*, the Qualities of those who were fit for it It is true he did not do this when he sent thither Cardinal *de Medicis*, because he knew that that Cardinal, who had openly enough distinguish'd his Zeal for the King's Interest, could not be disagreeable to him Cardinal *Dossat* says, on this Occasion, in the Letter he wrote to *M de Villeroy* on the 17th of *January* 1599, That there was a Discourse as if a Nuncio would be sent into *France*, and that he believ'd the Pope would talk with him about it before he nominated him *As he is wont to do with the King's Ministers on the like Occasions* When he does otherwise, it is reasonable to think that there is not a very good Understanding between the *Vatican* and the *Louvre* As for Example When in the beginning of the Pontificate of *Paul* V, the Lord *Ubaldini*, who was afterwards made a Cardinal, was sent Nuncio into *France*, altho' the King oppos'd his coming, because he knew him to be a Pensioner and Partisan of *Spain*, and since that, the Archbishoprick of *Urbin* has been refus'd him, notwithstanding both the King and Queen earnestly ask'd it for him Immediately after the Promotion of Cardinal *Ludovisio*, who took the Name of *Gregory* XV, the *French* Embassador made pressing Instances to the *Cardinal Nephew* to have either *Bagny*, *Luceliay*, or *Frangipani* nominated to the Nunciature of *France*, but as soon as ever he spoke to him about it, the *Cardinal Nephew* told him he had already giv'n his Word to *Corsini*, Clark of the Chamber, and pray'd him to get him accepted at Court The Embassador accordingly wrote about it, and represented, that it would be a difficult matter to oppose with Success the Intention of the *Cardinal Nephew*, and that it would not look very well to disoblige the *Cardinal Protector*, at the

the very beginning of his Uncle's Pontificate, since moreover that Prelate had *Qualifications that would render him agreeable*.

The Emperor refus'd to grant a Passport for the Cardinal of Lyons, who was to go on the part of *France* to the Congress at *Cologn*. There was no other Objection to his Person but his eminent Quality, which would have oblig'd the other Plenipotentiaries to have had too great a Deference to him. This Refusal was disobliging, and yet it never came into the Thoughts of *France* to say, that the Emperor had violated the *Law of Nations*.

The *Spaniards* being inform'd, after the Death of *Lewis* XIII, that that Court had some Thoughts of sending Cardinal *Mazarin* to the Assembly of *Westphalia*, oppos'd it, because it was he, as they said, who had manag'd the Intrigues that the Prince of *Sans* had carry'd on, to cause an Insurrection in the Kingdom of *Naples*. The *French* on their side shew'd a distrust of Cardinal *Rositti*, who was to perform the Function of Mediator between the two Crowns, and oblig'd the Pope to recall him from *Cologn*, on account of the Interest they said he had made in *England* with the *Queen Mother* of *France*, which had caus'd Cardinal *Richelieu* to suspect him. *Michael Ghislery*, while he was only a Dominican Frier, was sent to *Bergamo* in the Quality of Inquisitor, and executed his Function with so much Rigor and Severity, that he was not contented to examine into the Actions and Sentiments of his Predecessor, but was also for extending his Jurisdiction over *Vittorio Soranzo*, the Bishop of the said Town. It is well known that the Inquisition has not an absolute Ecclesiastical Power in the State of *Venice*, wherefore *Nicholas de Ponte*, who had the Office of *Podesta* there, not being able to bear the Insolence of the Frier, expell'd him out of his Government. Some Years after this, *Michael* being chosen Pope, under the Name of *Pius* V, the Republick, when it nominated the four Senators to go and make their Submission to him, put *Nicholas de Ponte* at the Head of this solemn Embassy. The Senate knew nothing of what had happen'd at *Bergamo*, neither did *Nicholas* remember any thing of it, or believ'd at least that the Pope had forgot it. But he remember'd it but too well. He would not see him, and oblig'd the other Embassadors to receive Audience without him. In the Year 1541, Pope *Paul* III sent *Michael de Silva*, Cardinal *de Visco*, in the Quality of Legate, to the Emperor *Charles* V, to endeavour to dispose him to make a Peace with *Francis* I. The Cardinal was very much out of the King of *Portugal*'s Favour, and the Emperor, who liv'd in the most intimate Confidence with that King, apprehending lest the Court of *Lisbon* should take Umbrage at this Legation, was very uneasy at it, and complain'd thereof, as if the Pope had a Design to set him at Variance with the King of *Portugal*. This oblig'd the Pope to recall not only the Legate, but also the Bishop of *Bergamo*, who had accompany'd him, and who, as being his Friend, was to have remain'd Nuncio at *Lisbon*. That Minister that is not agreeable to the Court where he negotiates, cannot be serviceable to him that employs him.

Zachary Delfinі, Nuncio to the Court of *Vienna*, and *John Francis Commendon*, Nuncio Extraordinary in *Germany*, were sent by Pope *Pius* IV to the Provinces in those Parts, to invite 'em to meet at the Council of *Trent*, either personally, or by their Deputies. The Princes and other Protestant States were assembled at *Naumburg* in *Misnia*, whither the two Nuncios resolv'd to go to them. I cannot tell whether they acquainted the Princes with their Intention, but this is certain, that no body went out to meet them, neither did they receive any Civilities at all at their Arrival. So that these Prelates, finding that in two Days time no body took notice of them, resolv'd between themselves, that the one should go to the Elector *Palatine*, and the other to the Elector of *Saxony*, and accordingly they desir'd Audience of these two Princes, who signify'd to them, that as they were but a part of the Body that was met about the publick Business, they could not grant 'em a particular Audience without first communicating it to the other Princes and Deputies. The Assembly hereupon resolv'd to give them a publick Audience, and that no particular Conferences should be had with them, because they were to be consider'd as Embassadors from the Enemy of their Party. Upon this Resolution they were sent for in a Coach, accompany'd by some Gentlemen, and several Guards, who march'd at the Head of the Horses. No body met 'em at their Arrival, they found no body in the Antichamber, and all the Honour that was done to 'em, was, that the whole Assembly rose as soon as the Nuncios enter'd, and no body offer'd to sit down till the Nuncios had taken their Places. They both spoke, one after another, but they receiv'd no other Answer than that they would take their Proposals into Consideration. They were carry'd back in the same Coach, and with the same Cortege, which had attended them to their Audience; and about an Hour after, some Counsellors, from so many Princes, brought back to the Nuncios the Pope's *Letters of Credence*, and told them, that the Assembly at their first receiving them, did not observe, that the Bishop of *Rome* styles the Princes their Masters, his Sons. That they did not acknowledge him for their Father, neither would they pass for his Sons, nor receive his Letters. Three Days after, the Assembly declar'd to them, by ten Deputies, that they had no other Answer to make them, but that the Princes their Masters would have no Communication with the Bishop of *Rome*. The two Nuncios, at their Departure from *Naumburg*, separated *Commendon*, whose Division comprehended *Saxony* and the Northern Kingdoms, went to *Brussels*, and from thence to *Lubeck*, under the Conduct of a Gentleman whose Name was *Gaspar de Schoneich*, whom the Emperor had given him, that he might travel with the greater Safety. Being come to *Lubeck*, and not being willing to run any risque after what had happen'd at *Naumburg*, they sent to desire *Frederick* II, King of *Denmark*, to send them a Passport. The King made no Answer to *Commendon*, but he wrote to *Schoneich*, that if he would come alone to *Copenhagnen*, he should be welcome, and that he should receive Honours on his account that

D d sent

sent him. As for the *Nuncio*, he found that in the time of the deceased King, no Correspondence had been held with the Court of *Rome*, so that not being able to enter on any Negotiation with the Pope's Nuncio, 'till he had deliberated with the States of his Kingdom, he could not at present admit him to Court, nor give him Audience He desir'd *Schoneich* to impart this to *Commendon*, and render it acceptable to him. *Eric* the Son of *Gustavus*, who Reign'd at that time in *Sweden*, had some thoughts of making his Addresses to *Elizabeth* Queen of *England*, and was just upon the point of setting out to explain himself to her in Person This oblig'd him to write to *Commendon*, that being ready to put to Sea, as soon as the wind would permit him, he was willing to give him notice thereof, to the end that if he thought it proper, he might come to him in *England*, where he might communicate to him the subject of his Commission He moreover added, that to facilitate his passage, he sent him a Passport, tho' he believ'd, that *Commendon*, being a *Publick Minister*, had no occasion for it Upon the receipt of this Letter, the Nuncio set out again for *Brussels*, with a design to take Shipping in *Flanders*, as soon as he should be inform'd of the passage of the King of *Sweden* He was in hopes the *Queen* would permit him to go to *London*, for the sake of so illustrious a Guest However, considering afterwards that the Queen might be against it, and that he ought to risque nothing, he alter'd his Mind, and went back to *Italy* The King of *Sweden* did not secure the Nuncio by writing to him that as *a publick Minister* he had no occasion for a Passport, for he thereby deceiv'd the *Nuncio*, and was deceiv'd himself

Commendon flatter'd himself with vain hopes, since the same Pope *Pius* IV designing to send the *Abbot Martinengue* into *England*, to exhort *Queen Elizabeth* to send her Deputies to *Trent*, order'd him to wait in *Flanders* for a Passport, which the *Spanish* Embassador was to procure him at *London* The *Queen* refus'd to send him one, and told the Embassador that three Reasons chiefly hinder'd her from admitting the *Pope's Nuncio* The first whereof was, that the Convocation and opening of the *Council* had not been notify'd to her, as it had been to other Princes The second, that the said Council was neither free nor Christian, and the third, that the *Nuncio* under the pretext of coming to desire her to send her Deputies to it, came in reality to animate her Subjects to a Revolt She added, that it was not without Example, that in preceding Reigns the Pope's Ministers had been refus'd admittance into *England*, since *Queen Mary*, tho' a Catholick, would not suffer him that was bringing the *Cardinals Hat to Pettey* to enter the Kingdom Which is worthy observation, because the *King of Sweden* says in his Letter to *Commendon*, that his *Character* would serve him for a Passport. However I shall not enlarge upon this now, by reason I shall speak more amply to it in Chapter 17 I shall only add here, that if these Ministers of the Pope were not acceptable to the respective Princes they were sent to, it was not on account of any defect in their own Persons, but because they would hold no correspondence with their Master, and that their Commission was not approv'd of

Delfini and *Commendon* had before them the Example of *Peter Paul Verger*, who being *Nuncio* in *Germany* some years before, obtain'd indeed a Passport, which permitted him to render himself at the *Assembly of Smalcald* But when he sent to demand Audience of the Elector of *Saxony*, this last signify'd to him, that whereas the Affair, about which he would confer with him, concern'd the general Interest of all the *Princes of the Union*, the particular Audience he might give him, would be of no manner of use So that the *Nuncio* might address himself to the *Assembly*, where the *Elector* would not fail to promote, to the utmost of his interest, whatever he should think would conduce to the glory of God, and the Establishment of the truth of the Gospel The *Nuncio* being come to *Smalcald*, obtain'd for all this a particular Audience of the Elector, to whom he deliver'd the two Briefs the Pope had written to him, the one as to an Elector, and the other, as to one of the Directors of the Circle of the upper *Saxony*, inviting him both in the one and in the other, to be present at the Council The *Elector* receiv'd the two Briefs, and having laid them upon a little Table, without opening them, He withdrew with some of his Counsellors into a Closet, from whence he sent word to the *Nuncio*, by the aforesaid Counsellors, that the Princes pressing him to come to the *Assembly*, upon Affairs of very great importance, the *Nuncio* ought to excuse the fault he committed against the Rules of Civility, but that he would soon let him know his intention concerning the two Briefs The same *Nuncio* could never obtain Audience of *Philip Landgrave of Hesse*, notwithstanding he ask'd it with Zeal and Earnestness

The States of the United Provinces have often refus'd, as well before as since the *Union of Utrecht*, to admit the Emperor's Embassadors, and those of several Princes of *Germany*, because they expected from 'em no other Proposals but such as were prejudicial to their Liberty and Interest In the Year 1579, *Charles Nutzel*, Lord of *Sunderpfull*, Counsellor to the Emperor in the Council of *Hungary*, being advanc'd as far as *Cologn*, with a design to pass into *Holland*, there to make some overtures of accommodation with the King of *Spain*, desir'd a Passport of the States They gave him to understand that they knew the subject of his Journey, that his Labour would be lost, and therefore he would do well not to give himself the trouble

This did not hinder him from going to the *Hague*, and presenting to the Assembly of the States General Letters from the Emperor and the Princes of the Empire, who were met at *Ratisbone*, but he was sent away with the same Answer that had formerly been given those who had made the like proposals In the Year 1599, *Salentin*, *who had been an Elector and Arch-Bishop of Cologn*, *Herman Count of Manderscheit*, and the said *Charles Nutzel*, solicited the States for a Passport, which they thought necessary to them for their better security in their Journey The States notified to them, that they knew the Contents of their Commiſſion, and that it was needleſs for them to come, becauſe they would receive no other Anſwer, than what had been already given to thoſe who had made the ſame propoſal. No Paſſport was ſent them, and they would not hazard themſelves without one. Nevertheleſs in the Year 1600, the States ſent a Paſſport to *Count de Manderſcheit*, and to *Charles Nutzel*, becauſe they did not come to make Propoſals of Peace, but only to treat about the Intereſts of the Princes and States of the *Lower Saxony*, who were very much incommoded by the Neighbourhood of the Arms of the United Provinces, as well as by thoſe of the Arch-Duke.

John II. King of *Arragon* in his own Right, and King of *Navarre* in Right of his Wife, did not ove *Charles* Prince of *Viana* his Son, to whom the Kingdom of *Navar* belong'd ſince the death of his Mother; and the Prince being continually Caballing againſt his Father, there was conſtantly one Negotiation or another between them. The *Catalonians* lov'd the Prince, and the King, to try to bring them over to his Intereſt, ſent to them in the Year 1641, the Protonotary *Anthony de Nogueras*, with Orders likewiſe to ſalute the Prince, after he had ſeen the Eſtates of the Province. But the States refus'd to hear him, till he had paid his Reſpects to the Prince, who, without giving *Nogueras* time to make his Complement, ſaid to him " I am ſurpriz'd at two things, *Nogueras*, the firſt is, that the King my Father " ſhould ſend you hither, *ſince the Perſons* " *ſent ſhould always be agreeable to thoſe to* " *whom they are ſent*; and the other, that you " ſhould be ſo audacious as to preſent your " ſelf before me, ſince when I was a Priſoner " in *Saragoſa*, you had the boldneſs to come " with Pen Ink and Paper to interrogate me, " urging me very much concerning the great " Crimes, and the pretended Treaſons of which " I was accus'd. I am willing you ſhould " underſtand, that it never comes into my " mind, but I am to mov'd thereat, that I am " no longer my ſelf. I am willing alſo to let " you know, that were it not for the reſpect " I have for my Father, and for ſome other " Conſiderations, you ſhould not go away " from hence with that Tongue that dar'd to " interrogate me, nor the Hand that wrote me " the Depoſitions. And that you may no " longer irritate my patience, I deſire and " command you to retire from before my " Eyes, becauſe they cannot bear the ſight of a " Man that would have laid ſo many Crimes " to my Charge. *Nogueras* would have reply'd, but the Prince ſilenc'd him, and made him retire, telling him that his Reply would only ſerve to provoke him the more, and therefore he would have him be gone. He had leave the next day however to come to the Aſſembly of the Eſtates, but the Prince would not admit him any more to his preſence. I am ſenſible that *Nogueras*, whom the King ſent to the States of *Catalonia* his Subjects, and to the Prince his Son, had not the Character of Embaſſador, properly ſpeaking, tho' at that time the *Catalonians* gave that Quality to their Miniſters, as well as to thoſe that were ſent to them. But that does not hinder this Example from being a very powerful confirmation of the poſition I laid down, that the Embaſſador ought to be agreeable.

I don't think there is any room to doubt of it, yet nevertheleſs I ſhall here ſet down what *Jerome Zurita* ſays of *Gutierre de Fuenſalida*. This Nobleman being in the Year 1505, Embaſſador from *Ferdinand* the *Catholick*, to the Arch-Duke *Philip*, and the *Princeſs Jean* his Wife, Son in-Law and Daughter to *Ferdinand*, took Audience one day of that Prince in the preſence of *Maximilian*, *Philip*'s Father, to whom, amongſt other things, he ſaid, that he had deſir'd the King his Maſter more than once to permit him to repair to him, *becauſe perceiving very well that his Perſon was not agreeable to his Highneſs, it was impoſſible for him to ſerve him in that Poſt*. That the King did did not make him any anſwer to that Article, till he wrote to him, that if his Majeſty did not grant him the liberty he begg'd, he would take it of himſelf, becauſe he was reſolv'd not to ſtay in a Court where they look'd over their ſhoulders at him. That hereupon the King had wrote to him, That he was far from commanding him to do a thing that was capable of receiving an evil interpretation, and that might make it be believ'd there was no great Love betwixt him and his Children, ſince he recall'd his Embaſſador. That therefore he would not do it, unleſs the *Arch-Duke* himſelf gave him to underſtand that he would no longer endure him, and that he ſtrictly forbid him going away without the expreſs leave of his Highneſs, who might order the matter as he thought fit, *ſince it could not be pleaſing to him to reſide in a Court where he imagin'd he was not acceptable*. The *Arch-Duke* made anſwer hereto That it depended on the King his Maſter to recall him, or let him remain, according as he ſhould think it proper. That if he had a mind his Embaſſador ſhould retire, he might go, and if he commanded him to ſtay, he might remain, and be aſſur'd he ſhould be well receiv'd, and well us'd. The *Arch-Duke* was not uneaſie to have this Miniſter recall'd, tho' he was diſagreeable to him, becauſe he was ſenſible he ſhould get nothing by the Change; and that *Ferdinand* would entertain near him an Embaſſador that ſhould obſerve the Counſels and Carriage of *Don John Manuel*, of whom we ſpoke in the preceeding Chapter, and that ſhould ſerve him as a Comptroller, a Cenſor, and a Pedagogue with thoſe Princes.

The Arch-Duke might eaſily have learn'd of the King his Father-in-Law, how to have rid himſelf of a vexatious Miniſter, and ſhut out an Embaſſador that is diſagreeable. *Ferdinand* had diſmiſs'd the ſame Year, tho' after a very obliging manner at leaſt in appearance, *Andrew del Burgo*, a *Cremoneſe*, who had negotiated with him on the part of *Maximilian the Emperor*, but he ſignified at the ſame time to the Emperor, that he deſir'd him (it for the future he thought fit to ſend any body to him) to make choice of a Miniſter whoſe intentions were good and ſincere, and that would not carry on Intrigues in his Court, to the prejudice of the quiet of his Kingdom. Some time after *Maximilian*, without reflecting on what *Ferdinand* had ſignify'd to him, ſent Orders to Andrew

Andrew del Burgo, who negotiated his affairs in *England*, to go from thence into *Spain*, to reside on his part in that Court: *Ferdinand* having Advice thereof, difpatch'd Orders to the Governors of all his Maritime Towns, that in what place foever *Andrew* should arrive, not to suffer him to come to Court, becaufe he would not admit him, nor fuffer him to refide in *Spain*. *Andrew* Landed at *Laredo*, where he was no fooner got on fhoar than the Governor feiz'd him, and having fet him and his Retinue on board another Veffel, he fent him back to *England*, notwithftanding the prefling inftances he made to let him be fent to Court, where he promis'd to give the King all the fatisfaction he could poffibly defire from *Maximilian*. But the Governor, who had his Orders what to do, executed them punctually. The Emperor was very much offended thereat, and *Don John Manuel* (who continu'd to do *Ferdinand* the fame ill Offices with him, which he had done him before with *Philip* who was dead) faid the Emperor ought to fend into *Spain* an Embaffador that fhould have fifty thoufand *Germans* at his heels, and then he would not be deny'd *what was not refus'd to the Turks or the Moors*, but might then Command as abfolutely there, as he did in *Germany Maximilian*, who was accuftom'd to make a great deal of noife, was contented to ufe fome menaces, and caus'd Propofals to be made in *England* for a League againft *Ferdinand*, but they vanifh'd into air. *Andrew del Burgo*, who was not agreeable at that time, was fince, after *Maximilian* and *Ferdinand* had come to an agreement concerning the Government of *Caftile*.

What *Don John Manuel* faid, that the *Turks* and *Moors* Embaffadors are not refus'd Admittance, is true, and he might have added, that thofe of declar'd Enemies are receiv'd, provided there be nothing in their Perfons, nor in their Commiffions, that can difpleafe or offend. The Inquifition that employs Fire and Sword againft pretended Hereticks, fuffers the very *Jews*, becaufe it fears the one more than the other. *Maximilian* fent back into *Spain* a Minifter, whom he knew, or ought to have known, was not agreeable there, for which Reafon he could blame no body but himfelf, for the Affront *Ferdinand* gave him, in fending back his Embaffador, becaufe he had been one of the principal Inftruments of the Divifions that oblig'd *Ferdinand* to go out of *Caftile*. There is no Prince but would have done the fame, and if *Ferdinand* could have juftify'd all his other Actions as well as this, he would have efcap'd many a fevere Line that blacken very much his Reputation, and have left Pofterity a very foul Portraiture of him. The *Law of Nations*, in protecting Minifters againft Violence, does not for that pretend to do any to Princes, nor does not pretend to take from them the Liberty of acting conformably to their Intereft, and of preferving the Quiet of their State, which might poffibly be difturb'd by an impertinent and vexatious Minifter. Neither does it hinder them from refenting the Wrong another Prince has done them, nor from fending away the Minifter of a Prince, that has not fhewn a due Refpect to theirs. *Philip* II. refus'd to give Audience to *William Wade* the Englifh Embaffador, becaufe Queen *Elizabeth* had difmifs'd *Don Bernardin de Mendofa*, Embaffador from *Spain*, for having carry'd on Intrigues againft the Tranquillity of the State, and prejudicial to the Safety of her Royal Perfon. The fame Queen would not fee *Alexander Humes*, Embaffador from *Scotland*, becaufe *Robert Bowes*, the *Englifh* Embaffador, had not been well treated in *Scotland*. In thefe Cafes the Embaffadors would be acceptable, if the Embaffy it felf was fo. In the Year 1672, at the beginning of the War, and in the height of the Diforders of the United Provinces, the States fent to the King of *France*, Mrs *de Ghent*, *de Groot*, and two others, of whom the one remain'd fick, or counterfeited being fo, and the other was difown'd by the States of his Province. Their Errand was to defire the King to give Peace to their State, but he would not fee them, but referr'd them to thofe of his Minifters, that had follow'd him. The two Perfons I juft nam'd, were very agreeable, and the Propofals they were to make, ought to have been fo likewife, but then their Principals were not fo.

That Prince that will not admit a Minifter becaufe he is not agreeable, ought to be more referv'd to the Embaffador, who being lik'd at his firft coming, becomes difagreeable in the Courfe of his Negotiation. The Refufal that is made to receive an Embaffador, may vex the Prince who fends him, but a Minifter that has been admitted cannot be difmifs'd without Scandal and the leaft Violence that is offer'd him, injures at the fame time the *Law of Nations*. The moft ufual, and moft natural way, as well as the moft warrantable, for Princes to get rid of Minifters that are difagreeable to them, is to complain of their Conduct to their refpective Mafters and if it be thought proper to proceed to fomething that fhews a greater Refentment, to refufe them Audience, till fuch time as their Mafters either re-call or juftify them. This has been the Practice of thofe Princes, that have diftinguifhed themfelves by their Equity and Moderation, even in Cafes, where the *Law of Nations*, allow'd them to do a great deal more. It was never the Intention of the Court of *Spain* to marry the *Infanta* to the Prince of *Wales*, and yet it could not endure, that the Court of *England* fhould fhew a Refentment, on the juft Occafion that of *Madrid* had given it. The Difficulty rais'd there concerning the Reftoration of the Elector *Palatine*, and the indirect Procedure of the firft Minifter, had oblig'd the King of *Great-Britain* to accommodate himfelf to the good Difpofition of his Parliament, fo that *Don John de Mendofa*, Marquis of *Inoyofa*, and *Don Carlos Coloma*, Embaffadors from *Spain*, knowing that the Duke of *Buckingham* had moft contributed thereto, refolv'd to ufe their utmoft Efforts to put him out of the King's Favour, for which purpofe they accus'd him of an abominable Treafon. They fpread a Rumor, and even carry'd it to the King's Ear, *That the Duke of Buckingham, with the Confent of the Prince of Wales, labour'd with the Parliament, to break off the Negotiation, which was carry'd on in Spain for the Marriage, and for the Reftitution of the Palatinate. That the Intention of the Prince and Duke, was to force the King to confent to a Rupture, and for default of Compliance therewith, to relegate*

gate him to one of his Countrey Houses, and to transfer the Royal Power into the Hands of the Prince, who was to be effectually put into Possession of the Regal Dignity. This Calumny, was not only capable of setting the King against the Prince his Son, and to change the whole face of Affairs, by removing him, who had the whole Management thereof, but also to cast the Kingdom into the utmost Confusion. The King slighted this Information of the Ministers of *Spain*, and the Duke dissembled their Treason, because he could not propose to punish it. However, on account of the Murmurs of the People, the Affair was laid before the Council, and from thence before the Parliament where some of the Members were of Opinion, that these Persons ought to be proceeded against, and that they ought no longer to enjoy the Benefit of their Character, which they had divested themselves of, by becoming Informers of a Crime, wherein the Publick had an Interest to know the Truth. In this kind of Assemblies, there are at any time but very few Members that have any Knowledge of the *Law of Nations* yet there were some who represented, *That they could not examine judicially, Persons that might shelter themselves under their Character of publick Ministers, and whom the King of* Spain *would not fail to own*. But that the Hainousness of their Crime ought to be represented to them, by the Speakers of both Houses that they should be urg'd to detect the Authors of this Calumny and given to understand, that for default thereof, they should be proceeded against as Impostors, and that they ought to be taken into Custody, till such time as their Master was made acquainted with the matter. Others were of Opinion that Satisfaction should be requir'd of the King of *Spain*, and in case of Refusal, War declar'd against him. But the King, who had no mind to embroil himself, was contented to make Complaints of it to the King of *Spain* and suffer'd the Embassadors to take their Audience of Leave with the usual Ceremonies. They desir'd another, wherein they pretended to justify themselves but one of the Secretaries of State was sent to 'em, to require they would explain themselves. They would not do it, and they were suffer'd to go away without receiving the King's Present, and without having the Coaches and Barges which generally conduct Embassadors, when the Court is satisfy'd with 'em. What they had done was approv'd of in *Spain*, where their Service was rewarded, instead of giving Satisfaction to the King of *England*.

The Marquis of *Mirabel*, Embassador from *Spain*, had been very busy in those Intrigues Cardinal *Richelieu* broke the neck of, on the Day call'd there-from, the Day of the *Dupes* or *Bubbles*, by removing the Queen Mother, and by the Disgrace of several Noblemen, some whereof were taken into Custody, and others quite discarded and banish'd, nay there were some that lost their Lives on the account. The Cardinal having no other way to shew his Resentment to the Embassador, sent him word by *M de Guron*, one of the Introductors, that the King not being satisfy'd with his Behaviour, expected he should make no Delay to return to *Spain*. and that if he had any particular Business, that requir'd he should make any longer stay in *France*, he might retire to *Orleans*. The King notify'd to him at the same time, that what he did in this matter, reserr'd only to the Person of the Marquis de Mirabel, and that in Consideration of his Master, with whom he would continue to keep a good Correspondence, he would give Orders that he should receive all the good Usage that was due to his Character. And accordingly, when two of his Sons, going from *Bourg la Reine* (where the Marquis was lodg'd) to see the House of *Berny*, had an unlucky Encounter with the Servant of a *French* Gentleman, in which the Embassador himself was hurt, care was taken to send him an *Exempt*, and two of the Life-Guards, to conduct him him safe to the Frontiers. Cardinal *de Richelieu* mingled in this Action a little particular Resentment, and would not have the patience, to wait for Satisfaction from the King of *Spain*.

What I just mention'd happen'd in the Year 1632. Two Years after, *Don Christoval de Benavides* and *Benavente*, who succeeded the Marquis *de Mirabel*, speaking one Day to *M Seguier*, Keeper of the Seals of *France*, concerning the Rupture that was likely to ensue between the two Crowns, and the Succour the King gave the *Hollanders*, express'd himself with heat against Cardinal *de Richelieu*, as against the only Cause, as he said, of this Misunderstanding and did not scruple to add, *that he was a Man that had neither Honour, Faith, nor Religion*. The *Keeper of the Seals*, who could not bear the first Minister should be us'd after this scurvy manner, as being not only his intimate Friend, but also his Benefactor, got up, and oblig'd the Embassador to withdraw *Don Christoval* being come to himself, and reflecting that his Passion might be of ill Consequence to him, was for justifying himself through the Mediation of the Emperor's Minister, but his Excuses were not allow'd of, and the Queen signify'd to him, that she would not see him, if he did not make the Cardinal Satisfaction. The Embassador would fain have had it believ'd, that *M Seguier* had not very well understood the *Spanish* Tongue, and deny'd what he said. But this was not sufficient, and upon Complaints the Cardinal made thereof, the King caus'd him to be reprimanded by *Bouthiller*, Secretary of State.

M de Blainville, who was first Gentleman of the Bed Chamber to *Lewis* XIII, and his Embassador to *Charles* I, King of *Great-Britain*, in the Year 1626, was of a very difficult and uneven Temper, and had every Day one Squabble or other at Court. But that which put him quite out of favour with the King, was his hindering the Queen from being present at the King's Coronation, on account of some Ceremonies, that the *Roman* Church does not approve of. It was also known, that it was he had persuaded the Queen not to be satisfy'd with the Place which was prepar'd for her to see the Cavalcade, when the King went to the Parliament at the first Meeting thereof: and that he fomented the Seeds of Divisions which some of the *French*, and especially the Clergymen, cast into the Mind of this Princess. For which Reasons the King of *England* signify'd to him, by my Lord *Conway*, one of the Secretaries of State, not to present himself any

more

more before him, and that he should likewise refrain visiting the Queen. Blainville made answer, that he did not receive his Orders from the King of England, that he was there to execute those of the King his Master, and that no body should hinder him from discharging his Function; he at last grew so angry, that he sent two or three times upon the heels one of the other, to demand Audience. The Refusal he receiv'd made him perfectly mad, so that the King, out of regard to the King of France, rather than to satisfie the Embassador, sent him word that he would make no difficulty to grant him Audience on any affairs relating to the King his Master, but if he offer'd to speak of any thing else, he would leave him, and not lend him an Ear. Blainville reply'd, that he was not in England for his own particular Affairs, but for those of the King his Master; and that the Refusal to give him Audience, did not refer to his own Person, but to the Prince that employ'd him. Till that Day he had been lodg'd and defray'd at the King of England's Expence; but after this Misunderstanding, he would neither be lodg'd nor treated, and so retir'd to Greenwich. He from thence dispatch'd a Courier to France, to acquaint the Court with what had happen'd to him; but he was prevented, and all the foreign Letters were stopp'd, till it was known what Effect those the King had sent thither had produc'd, which was this, that Blainville receiv'd Orders from his Master to have more Complaisance for the King of England, to accommodate himself to his Will, to get handsomly out of the present Misunderstanding, and then to take leave of the Court and return home. Blainville was forc'd to obey, and after he had seen the King twice privately, he took his Audience of Leave publickly. He was passionate in all his Conduct, and discover'd but little Reason in his Answer to the King, who had a Right to forbid him seeing the Queen, and refuse him Audience, till he had signify'd to the Court of France the just ground he had to complain of him. Nay he might have oblig'd him to leave the Kingdom where he was Sovereign; and if in so doing the King transgress'd either the Rules of Civility, or offended the Law of Nations, it was the King of France's business to resent it, and not the Embassadors to contend with a powerful Monarch. Princes are oblig'd to stand by their Ministers. Those that have Honour never fail to do it, and those that know themselves, know likewise how far they ought to carry their Resentment. The King of England did not offend the King of France. On the contrary, he made use of the Means all Princes ought to use, to get rid of a Minister that is disagreeable to them, by making him be recall'd by the Prince that employ'd him. The Constable of Montmorency, who was first Minister of France under Francis I, being sensible that the Nuncio sent his Court Advices, which were very prejudicial to the King's Service; and moreover did very ill Offices to the Constable in particular, complain'd thereof to the Pope, who recall'd this disagreeable Minister. The Minister of the United Provinces, of whom I spoke heretofore, was the Aversion of Cardinal Mazarin, who at that time had no reason to love his Masters, nor to cultivate their Friendship, and yet instead of causing him to retire, he made interest at the Hague to have him recall'd. It was by the same Means that he freed himself of Rosenhan, Embassador from Sweden, and that the Estates of the United Provinces would have rid themselves of Appleboom, and it ought to be the same way, that Princes should always free themselves, not only of disagreeable Ministers, but also of those that shall make themselves odious by Treasons, and by Crimes, which the Law of Nations does not protect. But for as much as I shall treat more amply on this Subject in Chapter XXIX, I shall end this with an Example, the Circumstances whereof are particular enough.

Philip de Commines takes notice, that some time after the Decease of Charles, the last Duke of Burgundy, the Emperor Frederick III, sent a solemn Embassy to the Low Countries, to conclude the Marriage between the Hereditary Princess of those rich Provinces, and his Son Maximilian, to whom she had been promis'd some Years before. The People of Ghent kept her in their own Town, where she was strictly observ'd, and withal, she was in a manner besieg'd with a Council, which was by so much the more troublesome, as the major part of those that compos'd it, oppos'd her Marriage. The Duke of Cleves, her near Relation, who design'd her for his Son, being inform'd that the Embassadors of Frederick, the Chief of whom were Lewis Duke of Bavaria and the Bishop of Metz, of the House of Baden, were arriv'd at Brussells, caus'd the Council to write to 'em, to remain there till further Orders, imagining that these Gentlemen being offended at the Affront, or disgusted at the Put-offs, with which they were to be amus'd, would return back to Vienna. But the Embassadors, who had a secret Intelligence in the Cabinet, and particularly with the Dutchess Dowager of Burgundy, Mother-in-law to the Princess, whose Intention they knew, pursu'd their Journey, arriv'd at Ghent, and demanded Audience, in which they secur'd themselves of the Success of their Negotiation. The Council would have oblig'd the Princess to remit the Embassadors to them, that they might there be inform'd of its Resolution and Will; but she was resolv'd to marry, and by that means get out of the Subjection of her Tutors, wherefore she acknowledg'd immediately the Letter she had written by her Father's Orders, to the Arch-Duke Maximilian, as also the Ring she had sent him and gave very well to be understood, that she would not go from the Promise she had formerly made. The Councils Refusal to admit the Embassadors, not being conformable to the Intention of the Sovereign, who was at Age to dispose of her Person and Inclinations, was impertinent; and the Authority it assum'd, to encroach upon the Rights of their Princess, was criminal. The Embassadors, the Embassy, and the Prince that sent them, were agreeable to the Princess, and they ought to have been so likewise to her Council, who had a greater Regard to their Interest than to their Duty

CHAP

CHAP. XIV.

Of Instructions.

IT is commonly said, that it is sufficient *to send an able Man, and let him act as he shall think fit* However, I don't believe that they who speak thus pretend by it that an *Embassador* ought to go upon his Commission, without *Instructions* It is requisite, and even necessary, he should know his Master's Intention, and be inform'd of his Will, in reference to the Affairs he is to negotiate, and all that ought to be expected from him, is, that the Prince should rely on the Ability of the Embassador for the Management and Execution thereof This, I must confess, is, what it is not necessary to say any thing to him of But altho' it be suppos'd that the Minister, whom the Prince pitches upon for an Employment of this Nature, possesses all the Qualifications requisite to form an accomplish'd Subject, and that he even has a perfect Knowledge of the Court where he is going to reside or negotiate, and that it be not doubted, but his Sufficiency may supply what may be wanting to his *Instructions*, which can never give him all the Light necessary for his Conduct, yet there are nevertheless several Particularities, of which he must of necessity be duly inform'd M de *Villeroy*, writing on the 30th of *May*, 1607, to President *Jeannin*, Embassador at that time from *France* to *Holland*, says, That in his Letter of the 14th he had given him an *Instruction*, but for all that, it was the King's Intention, and his, that he should make use of that, and all the others he should for the future send him, as he himself should think fit *Because being upon the Place*, says he, *you are better able to judge what is most expedient for the King's Service His Majesty has a full Confidence in you, and in those Gentlemen who assist you Wherefore he expects that you shall cut out, and pair off at your Discretion* Notwithstanding this, *Jeannin* and his Collegues had their *Instructions*, and from time to time receiv'd Orders, which made a part thereof, and were to regulate their Actions, to which they might give what Form and Turn they should think most proper, to accomplish the Intention of their Master The King himself makes use of much stronger Expressions in the Letter he writes to him, of the 17th of *April* 1608, where he says, *I put so much Confidence in you, and in the Care you have for the good of my Service, that you will make a better Choice of what shall be conducive to the Promotion of my Service, than I am able to prescribe, or command it you from hence.* The Terms of their first *Instruction*, which bears date on the 22d of *April* 1607, cannot be more formal, nor more expressive than they are. *His Majesty orders the present Memoir to be drawn up and deliver'd to them, to serve them as a Testimony of his Intentions and Commands, and not to prescribe to them any set Rule in what they are to execute* To which *Villeroy* adds, in the first Letter he writes to the President, *The King expects you should consult your self, for the principal Instructi-*

ons, *concerning what you shall have to do in this Journey* But all Princes are not so magnanimous, nor so knowing, as *Henry* IV was, neither are all Embassadors so wise and experienc'd as President *Jeannin* Notwithstanding which, he had two very good *Instructions* about him when he came to the *Hague* All Business is not of the same Nature, nor all Courts are not of the same Constitution I say, that the Orders the Prince gives, or sends from time to time to his Minister, make a part of his *Instructions* *Dossat* says, in one of his Letters to *Villeroy*, "The other Points of your " Letter which I do not particularize, are for " all that in as great, if not greater, Esteem " and Recommendation with me, each accor- " ding to its Importance But it is sufficient " I tell you in general, that I have taken good " notice of them for my *Instruction*, and that " I shall execute what they contain, as Occa- " sion shall require

The Marquis *de Fontenay-Mareüil* had been three Years Embassador in Ordinary at *Rome*, but when the King of *France* sent him thither, in the Year 1647, Cardinal *Mazarin* himself gave him the Memoirs of his *Instructions*, wherein he makes him sensible, that the State of Affairs was so alter'd, under the Pontificate of *Innocent* X, that having no manner of Resemblance with that wherein the Marquis left them under *Urban* VIII, he could not act any longer upon the same Principles. He was to negotiate there very intricate Matters, and very disagreeable to the Pope and his Ministers, the Reconciliation of the *Barberins*, the confignng *Beaupuy* into the King's Hands, and the Promotion of Cardinal *Mazarin*'s Brother The Pope mortally hated the Cardinal, and his Inclinations being altogether *Spanish*, it was necessary to let the Embassador know the State of the Court of *Rome*, and the Pope's Humor, by giving him notice, that he would succeed much better if he rather compell'd that timorous Mind than endeavour'd to persuade It, and that if he made a right use of the Discontent of the other Princes of *Italy*, who were not satisfy'd with *Innocent*, he would bring him to Reason The Cardinal, who knew the Affairs of those Parts, even better than he did those of *France*, and apply'd himself as much to them, fill'd his *Instructions* therewith, and without the Knowledge thereof it had been impossible for the Embassador to have serv'd the King, according to the Intention of the first Minister The same Genius may be observ'd in the *Instructions* he caus'd to be given to President *Gremonville*, to the Abbot of St *Nicholas*, to *Plessis Besançon*, to the Abbot *Bentevoglio*, &c for *Rome*, *Venice*, *Florence*, *Modena*, and *Parma* To say all in one Word The *Instructions* serve to inform the Embassador of the Will of the Prince, and of several things which he cannot learn elsewhere.

I am

I am willing to believe, that excepting the essential Particulars, which make the Subject of the Embassy, the most general *Instructions* are the best, to an able Minister. He knows that his Employment ought to have, for Object, the Preservation of Friendship between the two Princes. That it is he that presents the Letters, his Prince writes to him with whom he resides. That he is oblig'd to execute the Orders which are sent him. To take Care not to do any thing against his Master's Interest. That he must send continual and sincere Advices, and protect the Subjects of his Prince. These are things that it would be needless to recommend to an Embassador, tho' he knew his Business very indifferently. And on the other side, it is impossible to take notice in his *Instructions*, of all the Accidents that may happen, or of all the Precautions he should take, but then, this is what is supply'd by fresh Orders, which are sent him from time to time, as well in reference to the Advices he himself gives, as to those Occurrences that change the State of Affairs.

The Embassador indeed ought to desire his *Instructions* may be very particular, especially when he is charg'd with any intricate Negotiations. He ought to examine very scrupulously every Point thereof, to get explain'd to him what may be obscure and ambiguous; to procure the Alteration of what he judges may obstruct or hinder the Success of his Negotiation, to cause that to be put out which may render his Conduct suspected or odious, or his Person ridiculous, and get that inserted which may recommend either the one or the other, and procure a greater Satisfaction to his Master. He ought also to consider, that the more general his *Instructions* are, the more he has to answer for in reference to the Event of the Affairs he has to negotiate, because he is in a manner *Guarantee* for those, the Success whereof is expected from his Ability and Prudence.

In the Year 1570, Queen *Elizabeth* sent *Walsingham* (one of the compleatest Wits *England* has afforded) to *Charles* LX King of *France*, and she chiefly recommended to him the Interest of those of the reform'd Religion. It was a Matter of the greatest Nicety, and he had to do with a King and a Queen, who were the most distrustful and the most unfaithful of all Princes. The King of *Navarre*, the Prince of *Condé*, the Admiral *de Chastillon*, were their Aversion, and yet it was chiefly in their Favour that *Walsingham* was to act particularly. The *Instructions* the Queen gave him, at his entring upon his Employment, is a Piece so well turn'd that nothing can be seen stronger, nor more judiciously adapted to so difficult a Subject. Nothing came from the Queen but what was so, nor from the Minister in whom she confided, but as they contain'd a mixture of an Intrigue, which the King of *France* might consider as a *Domestick Affair*, in which she had no Concern, it was necessary to furnish the Embassador with a Mean that might make his Negotiation be born with, since it was not in it self agreeable. In this View she order'd him, in his *Instructions*, to make a Protestation at the very first, that it was not the Queen's Intention to protect another's Subjects, nor to speak in their Behalf to the Prejudice of their Sovereign's Interest, that what she did was out of an extraordinary Affection to the King's Person, and to the Tranquillity of his Kingdom, that she thought herself oblig'd to put him in mind how pernicious their Counsels were, who would willingly hinder him from granting Liberty of Conscience to an infinite Number of Persons, of all Qualities and Ages, to whom it had been already promis'd by formal Edicts, and who afterwards would not refuse to pay a blind Obedience to the Commands and Will of the King, that she was so fully perswaded that the Spirit of Rebellion had no Concern with the Actions of those People, that if she did at any time perceive but the least Appearance thereof, she would be the first herself, not only to condemn them, but also to unite her Arms to the King's, to help to punish and exterminate them. *Walsingham* having learn'd the Queen's Pleasure in his *Instructions*, desir'd to be inform'd of her Intention, in reference to some Particulars which were not taken notice of in them. He desir'd to know, whether, in case the King (who was infirm, and bestow'd a great deal of time on his Diversions) should remit him to the Queen his Mother, or to *Monsieur*, he should treat with them. That since the King had not Patience to be entertain'd long with serious Affairs, whether he might not negotiate in Writing, and by Memorials, those that were of Importance, and requir'd some length of Time and Application. And whether in that Case the Queen would not think it more proper for him to make use of the *Italian* or *Latin* Tongues, in order thereby to avoid evil Interpretations, that might be given to ill-turn'd *French* Phrases. After what manner he should govern himself towards the *English* Rebels which had retir'd into *France*. And what Rank he should take when he appear'd in publick Assemblies with the *Spanish* and *Portugal* Embassadors. This *Instruction* had no room, because the King of *France* gave his Subjects, who made Profession of the Protestant Religion, a Peace which was more fatal to them, than all the past Wars had been bloody, but that does not hinder the Discovery of many Tokens of the Queen's Address, and of *Walsingham*'s prudent Conduct. The second *Instruction* that was given to President *Jeannin* on the 6th of *August* 1608, is, in effect, nothing else than an *Illustration* of the Articles which he himself had propos'd to the King's Council, that he might thereby be the better inform'd of his Majesty's Intentions.

On the contrary, there is something very inconsiderate in the Procedure of the *Scotch Bishop*, who having receiv'd the impertinent *Instructions* of Queen *Mary* of *Scotland*, undertook to justify in *France* the Marriage she had contracted with the Earl of *Bothwel*, and was for making an Apology for both the one and the other, in an Audience the King gave him in the Presence of all the Court. The Ministers, who were on the part of *France* in *Scotland*, had inform'd the Queen Mother of the State of Affairs in that Kingdom. So that it was known there, that the carrying off the Queen, which she said was done by Violence, had nevertheless been concerted with herself, and that *Bothwel*, whom she had just marry'd, was

was one of the Assassins of her first Husband So that the Bishop made himself ridiculous, and only prostituted his own Reputation as well as the Queen's *Paul Dzialinski*, who got so little Credit by his Embassies to *Holland* and *England*, would not have been expos'd to the Affronts he there receiv'd, if he had well examin'd his *Instructions* before he charg'd himself therewith

After all, the *Instructions* are a secret Instrument which the Embassador is not oblig'd to communicate to the Court where he negotiates Nay, I dare affirm that he ought not to produce it, without a Necessity, and an express Order In the Year 1560, Queen *Elizabeth* sent into *Scotland Robert Bowes*, with Orders to make pressing Instances to have the Duke of *Lenox* remov'd from the King's Person, who was at that time very young Those of the Council of *Scotland* said, that it was so severe and unjust a thing, that not being able to believe the Queen had given him any such Orders, they desir'd to see them Bowes said, he would not shew them, and that all he could do, was to let the King and two or three of his Confidents see them The *Scotch* were not satisfy'd therewith But the Queen was so displeas'd at their Procedure, that she recall'd her Embassador, and refus'd to give Audience to him they sent to justify their Action

In the Year 1643, *Walter Strickland*, Minister from the Parliament of *London*, presented a Memorial to the States General wherein he spoke of the Prince of *Orange* with little Respect He was urg'd to shew his Orders, but it was a kind of Violence which could not well be justify'd They that did it, either did not reflect on what they did, or else they were very willing to offend his Masters We have seen within some Years a Minister, who having been sent by a powerful State to one of the first Princes of *Germany*, began his Negotiation by laying his *Instructions* on the Table But all that can be said of it is, that it was the Action of a Fool, in the utmost Extent of the Signification of that Epithet It is an unheard of thing, that a Minister has been compell'd to shew his Orders, and they who force him to do it offer Violence to the *Law of Nations*

The Publick would be very much oblig'd to him that would give it a Collection of *Instructions*, at least of the most important ones, of which Extracts may be found in History, and there are some curious Persons that have collected a great many For altho' they do not discov er to us the true Causes of the Motions, yet they contribute very much to the forming of the Judgment, and give us fine Precepts for politick Prudence The two *Instructions* Queen *Elizabeth* gave to *Francis Walsingham*, those the Duke of *Nevers* carry'd to *Rome* on the part of *Henry* IV, the two others the same King gave to president *Jeanning*, for the Negotiation of the Peace of the United Provinces, are very excellent Pieces Nothing can be added to the Instructions Pope *Urban* VIII gave to Cardinal *Ginetti* for the Assembly of *Cologn*, nor to those that were given in *France* to Mrs *d'Avaux* and *Servien* for the Congress of *Westphalia* I just now mention'd those Cardinal *Mazarin* gave the Marquis *de Fontenay Marueil*, which is a Product worthy of that Minister's Wit, whose Letters to the Embassadors, who were on the part of *France* at *Munster*, are so many curious *Instructions*

What I just now said concerning the Treatment *Walter Strickland* receiv ed at the *Hague*, is founded on the *Law of Nations*, because the Embassador (after he has presented his *Letters of Credence*, and had them approv'd) ought to enjoy the Effect thereof purely and simply, and has no farther Occasion to fortify or authorize his Negotiation, by producing other Instruments, unless he be invited, or that he himself desires to make a particular Treaty, for which he must necessarily have a *special Power* It is what I shall speak of, when I have said a Word or two concerning *Letters of Credence* in the following Chapter

CHAP. XV.

Of *Letters of Credence*.

THE Bulls the Popes give to their Legates serve them instead of *Letters of Credence*, and of *General Powers* They express their Character, and make known their Authority and Faculties, for which Reason I said, that *Legates* are as *Plenipotentiaries*, their Power being, by so much the greater, that thereby the Pope extends his own, even to the Prejudice of Sovereigns, upon whom he has already usurp'd but too much. *Credentials* are necessary to the Embassador, as well because they express his Character, and make him known to the Prince to whom he is sent, as because without them he is not able to negotiate. It is true, they are not so absolutely necessary, but that sometimes a Man may be a Publick Minister without them However this is what happens very rarely And then, to make good the Deficiency thereof, he must be provided with some other Instrument, Powers, Procuration, Passport, or what they call in *Holland Actus ad omnes Populos*, to make his Quality known and respected. *Albert*, Arch-Duke of *Austria*, and Sovereign, Prince of *Flanders*, gave to King *Henry* the Great the Quality of *My Lord*, and the Title of *Majesty*, but after the King's Death he chang'd his Stile, and refus'd the same Titles to his Successor; and upon this Difficulty the Court of *France* refus'd to admit his Embassador Nevertheless, as amongst the other Infirmities of the Government, which were remarkable during the Minority of *Lewis* XIII, there was also that of having too much Confidence in the Court of

Spain,

Spain, the Affair was put into negotiation, and it was resolv'd that Audience should be granted to the Arch-Duke's Embassador But that instead of presenting his *Letters of Credence to the King, he should communicate them to the Secretary of State*, to the end his Quality might not be unknown Likewise on the difficulty the Emperor made to give the Title of Majesty to the King of *France*, during the Negotiation at *Munster*, It was propos'd, amongst other Expedients, that in order to keep up to those Civilities Princes owe to one another, and which the Queen was oblig'd to observe on occasion of the death of the Empress, the Emperor should not write, but should notifie his affliction by a Gentleman sent for that purpose, who should have no Letters, but only a Passport containing the subject of his Journey

This is what depends on the Prince who receives the Minister, if he be perswaded of the intention of the Prince that sends him, it is sufficient He may acknowledge him as such, and even treat him as an Embassador, if he pleases, tho' the usual method is to give *Letters of Credence*, in which the Quality of the Minister is express'd In the Year 1643, *William Boreel*, and *John de Reede de Renswonde* being arriv'd at *London* in the beginning of *January*, went from thence to *Oxford*, they return'd to *London* in the Month of *March*, and notwithstanding they had no *Letters of Credence* from the Estates to the Parliament, yet they presented a Memorial to each of the two Houses This Memorial was not in due form, and yet the Parliament was so desirous to be acknowledg'd by a powerful Republick its Neighbour, that it gave the Embassadors of the States to understand, that if they had any thing to propose to the Lords and Commons in Parliament assembled, they would make them an answer The Embassadors did not explain themselves then, but being return'd from their second Journey to *Oxford*, from whence they came in the Month of *June*, they signify'd to both Houses that they had something to propose to them They were answer'd, that if they demanded Audience, they might present a Memorial, and it should be given them They desir'd it on the fifth of *July*, and had it on the eighteenth, and it was not till then they presented their *Letters of Credence* It was not much to the satisfaction either of the one or of the other But I observe in this Example, that the Parliament which had not treated the Embassadors very well, because they were suspected by it to be partial, being willing to justifie its proceedings, declar'd they would have negotiated with them, *even tho' they had had no Credentials for the Parliament*, because the Parliament being sensible they had the Character of Embassadors, could not doubt of their having orders to speak, nor of their being own'd

I have said, that the *Letter of Credence* makes known the Quality of the Minister, and particularly that of Embassador, which ought to be very expresly taken notice of in it. In the Year 1600, M. *d'Alincourt* was sent to *Rome*, to Compliment Pope *Clement* VIII He was a Knight of the Order, and Governor of *Lyons*, but what rais'd all his other qualities, was that of M. *de Villeroy* his Father, who was Secretary of State, and one of the chief Ministers to *Henry* IV His *Letter of Credence did not give him the Character of Embassador*, and yet the Pope not giving himself the leisure to read it, *made him sit down*, and treated him as an Embassador

The Pope having made this step, and perceiving afterwards that his *Credentials* did not give him that Character, spoke to Cardinal *Doffat* about it, who having foreseen what would happen, had entertain'd *M de Sillery* Embassador Extraordinary from *France* therewith, and it was agreed between 'em, that *M d'Alincourt* should pass for an Embassador They therefore told the Pope that it was no very extraordinary thing with *France* to omit expressing the Character in its *Letters of Credence*, more especially when the Birth or Dignity of the Minister did not admit of any Quality inferior to that of Embassador They satisfy'd the Pope so well hereof, that he acquiesced to it, and said he would then continue to treat him as he had begun He could not now be off of it, and the Cardinals were oblig'd to follow his Example All the Foreign Ministers made him the first Visit, and did him all the other usual Civilities, which they could not help doing, after what the Pope and the Cardinals had done before The King approv'd of the dexterity of his Ministers, and gave his consent that *d'Alincourt* should be consider'd as an Embassador But *Cardinal Doffat* will give me leave to doubt of what he says, that it is no very extraordinary thing in *France* to omit the Quality of the Minister in their *Credentials* On the contrary, it is what the Court of *France* is very exact and very punctual in, and I don't believe that *M de Villeroy* had omitted any thing through neglect in those of his Son The King was far from disallowing what *Cardinal Doffat* had done, because he had obtain'd an Honour for his Minister, which he did not pretend to

In the Year 1648 the *Elector of Brandenburg* sent to the *Hague*, *Philip Horn*, *Otto de Snerin*, *Wirich de Bernjau*, and *John Portman* They arriv'd there, without giving advice of their coming, they had no Entry made them, but they were Conducted to Audience with a greater Cortege than the States are accustom'd to give to any Ministers of the second Order They pretended to be treated as Embassadors, and were for having the Conferences held at their Houses, as is generally practis'd with those belonging to Crown'd Heads They were given to understand that there would be no difficulty in gratifying them, *but that the Character was not express'd in their Letters*, for which deficiency, they could not grant them all the Honours they desir'd They caus'd their *Letters of Credence* to be alter'd, and after that, the Conferences were held at their Houses

The Example of *De la Barde* may serve also to this purpose He had his *Letters of Credence*, which made him be consider'd at the Congress of *Westphalia*, as a Minister of the second Order The Court of *France* had nominated him to the Embassie of *Switzerland*, and the Embassadors Plenipotentiaries of that Crown, urg'd the *Nuncio* to give him the Style of Excellency

cellency, and to pay him the first Visit. But the *Nuncio* said, He could by no means comply with their Request, because he would not set an Example that no body else would follow. That *M. de la Barde* did very good Services to the Assembly, but should he grant what they desir'd, he would become altogether useless to it, since the other Ministers would never give him the Title of Excellency, and that he himself, after he had obtain'd it of the *Nuncio*, would be for obliging them to it. The *Venetian* Embassador refus'd it likewise for the same Reasons, so that *de la Barde* was forc'd to be contented with the Honours they were willing to do him. He made suit to the Ministers that were on the part of the Emperor at *Osnabourg*, to distinguish him from the other Ministers of the second Order. That since they could not treat him as Embassador, they at least would avoid treating him as a Resident, and that provided he was but treated in the third Person, after the *Italian* manner, he would not pretend to the place of Honour, either at Visits or Conferences. He had *Letter of Credence* to the *Swiss-Cantons*, which could not make him be consider'd at *Munster*, nor at *Osnabourg*.

In the Year 1613, the Republick of *Venice* sent *Gregory Barvarigo* Embassador to the *King of Great Britain*, and gave him *Letters of Credence* for him. The intention of the Republick, as well as its interest was to continue the Treaty it had concluded some Years before with the *Grey Leagues*, and therefore it had order'd *Barbarigo* to make some stay at *Coire*, and to try to renew the Negotiation as he pass'd by. During the stay *Barbarigo* made there it came to be known that he carry'd on Intrigues, which gave such a jealousie of him, that the People began to murmur thereat, and to threaten to offer violence to him. To prevent the same, he was for hiring the House of one of the Burger-Masters, who told him, that if he had orders to Negotiate with the *Grey Leagues*, and to reside in the Town, he ought to make it known, that the *Triumvirs* might be made acquainted therewith, who would give him Audience. *Barbarigo* answer'd, that he had nothing to negotiate with the *Leagues*, but had business to treat of with the *French* Embassador, and for that Reason he was oblig'd to make some stay at *Coire*.

He was born with for the sake of the *French* Embassador, and yet he gave no notice to the *Triumvirs*. He did no Civilities to the Magistracy, and information was given that he held Cabals very prejudicial to the quiet of the Countrey. He continu'd to live after this manner, till perceiving that the *Pittag* or General Assembly was going to order him to withdraw, because he was troublesome to 'em, and fearing lest he should be affronted, by reason that for want of Character he was not there in safety, and that he could not without hazarding his Person continue his Cabals, he bethought himself to demand Audience. He therein told 'em, that the Senate of *Venice*, who sent him into *England*, had thought fit to Command him by a new Order, to stop in some Town in his passage, and there wait for the Articles it had thought necessary to add to his Instructions. That he had for that purpose made choice of the Town of *Coire*, and that he laid hold of the opportunity of the present Assembly, to assure it of the affection the Republick had for the *State of the Leagues*. He that discharg'd the office of Interpreter to *Barbarigo*, added, that the Embassador desir'd the Assembly to grant him safety for his Person, and to take him into their protection, because the Senate would be apt to resent any violence offer'd to its Minister, against those of the *Grisons*, who either resided or pass'd through the State of *Venice*. The Assembly was surpriz'd at this discourse, and sent him word by the *Triumvirs*, accompany'd by a Deputy from each *League*, that the *Leagues* would always return the friendship the Republick express'd for it, but that the Embassadors actions and his words did not agree. That he give Treats, and had Conventicles, wherein such things were talk'd of, that might trouble the tranquillity of the State. That they would always discharge all the good offices could be expected or desired from their good Neighbourhood, provided the Republick did the like on its part, and that Affairs were left in the same state they were then in. After they had signify'd this Resolution to *Barbarigo*, it was left with him in Writing, and he retir'd into *Switzerland*. I was willing to set down all the particulars of this small History, because on this occasion the question was started, whether the *Law of Nations* would have been violated in his Person, in case he had not been treated with all the respect that is due to publick Ministers; and it was agreed, *That a Man is no publick Minister, if he has not Letters of Credence for the Sovereign of the place where he pretends to reside for some time, and by which he requires to be consider'd in that Quality*. *Barbarigo* at his going from *Coire*, had left his House Furnish'd, for which reason the *Triumvirs* who believ'd he would return, and desiring to be inform'd by the *Communities* how they should behave themselves if he did come back. They wrote them word, that if he should return, they should give him to understand, *That he was not to be born with any longer in that Countrey, after the Intrigues he had practis'd there against the publick quiet*. *Charles Paschal*, who was at that time Embassador from *France*, to the *Grisons*, and who has written a *Treatise of the Embassador*, highly approves of the Communities procedure.

The *Republick of Venice* had the same Notion, when she would not let the *Credentials* be deliver'd to *Andrew Gritti*, till he was ready to take upon him the Quality of publick Minister. *Andrew* had been made Prisoner of War at *Brescia*, and having been brought into *France*, his Wit and Conduct acquir'd him the esteem of the King, and the love of all the Nobility, insomuch that he was allow'd to come to Court, and appear there, not as a Prisoner, but almost like an Embassador. He receiv'd now and then Propositions there, which he communicated to the Senate, who not being satisfied with its Allies, hearken'd to them. He even laid the Scheme of an Alliance with *Ferrier*, whom *John James Trivulce* had sent to *Venice* with the King's participation. After the Project was concerted and approv'd of by both

both Parties, the Senate sent it into *France* by the Secretary of the Council of *Ten*, and at the same time gave him *Letters of Credence* for *Gritti*, who *notwithstanding was not to make use of them, unless he enjoy'd a perfect Liberty*. The King being inform'd of the Intention of the Senate, gave *Gritti* his Liberty, as soon as the Secretary arriv'd. It was then he took the Quality of Embassador, *by virtue of his Letters of Credence*; and that he concluded and sign'd the Treaty he had negotiated while he was Prisoner of War, and not as a Minister. To speak more exactly, we should say, that he had not negotiated; but that hearing the Propositions which were made him, and sending them in writing to the Senate, he had given an Opportunity for the Negotiation which was carry'd on at *Venice*, and was since finish'd in *France*.

The same ought to be said of all other Negotiations, which are perform'd without *Letters of Credence*, and without the express Orders of the Prince that is concern'd. *Enguelbert* Count of *Nassau*, who was in the Service of the Arch-Duke *Maximilian*, whose Subject he was, being made Prisoner of War in an Action near *Bethune*, was constantly telling the *French*, that if he was set at liberty, he would so well represent to *Maximilian*, how wrongfully he made War against the King, that he would dispose him to give his Majesty Satisfaction and he made so many Overtures to this purpose, that at last he had leave to pay his Ransom, and was dismiss'd. He had penetrated into the true Intentions of the Court of *France* so that at his Return into *Flanders*, he wrote to *Maximilian*, who was then at *Francfort*, and obtain'd leave of him to go back to *France* and conclude the Bargain. He came thither in the Company of the Lord *Desordes*, Marshal of *France*, and negotiated some time with the Duke and Dutchess of *Bourbon*, who had there the chief Direction of Affairs. He could not then conclude any thing, but upon the Assurance he gave, that he would dispose *Maximilian* to do whatever should be reasonable, they sent along with him the Bishop of *Lombez*, who was also Abbot of St *Denis*, the Lord *de la Roch-Choüart*, and *Peter de Sacierges*, Master of the Requests, who concluded the Treaty of *Francfort* the 20th of *July* 1489. The Count of *Nassau* was not a Minister while he was a Prisoner of War, and was so only after he return'd with *Letters of Credence*.

The Duke of *Longville* having been taken Prisoner at the Battel of *Guihegaste*, and carry'd into *England*, he there made the first Overtures of the Marriage between *Lewis* XII, and *Mary*, Sister to *Henry* VIII, but without *Credentials*. So that to that time he could be look'd upon but as a Prisoner of War, who having the Liberty to go and come upon his Parole, and leave to be every Day at Court, labour'd to reconcile the two Kings, out of a Motive of particular Affection. But after he had made it known in *France*, that the Discourse he had had in *England* relating to the Marriage, had not been disagreeable, and that *Letters of Credence* were sent him, with Power to conclude the same; he ought of necessity to be esteem'd a *Minister*, because it was only in this Quality, that he sign'd and concluded the Treaty. Thus the *Sieur de Bertonville*, being made a Prisoner, when the Emperor *Charles* V enter'd *Champain* with an Army, was set at liberty by *James de Medicis* and *Francis de Somali*, Counsellors to *Charles*, who told him at his Departure, that if in *France* there was any Dispositions to a Peace, there was a great deal on their side, by reason the Emperor was weary of the War. *Bertonville* acquainted *Annebault* therewith, and this last having made a Report thereof to the King, this Overture was relish'd, and *Bertonville* was sent back to *Flanders* with the Bailiff of *Dyon*, who brought it to be resolv'd, That *Annebault* and *Nucilly* on the one part, and *Gonzagues*, with *Granville* on the other, should have a Meeting, as accordingly they had, and concluded the Treaty. It is true, that *Gabriel de Guzman*, Confessor to Queen *Eleonora*, had gone some Journeys to and fro, and had prepar'd the Minds of the Parties.

If more modern Examples are requisite, the Marshal *de Grammont* having been taken Prisoner at the Battel of *Norlinguen*, on the 3d of *August* 1645, was conducted to *Ingolstad*, where his Exchange was regulated for the Count de *Glehen*, whom the *French* had taken in the same Action. But before the Prisoners were effectually exchang'd, and while the Marshal was still at *Ingolstad*, the Elector of *Bavaria* sent his Coach for him, and had him brought to *Munick*. The Prince of *Conde*, who did not know the Elector's Intention, sent him word by a Trumpeter, that if he did not send back the Marshal to *Ingolstad*, he would send the Count de *Glehen* to the *Bois de Vincennes*. But he was soon made easie. The Elector's Design was to entertain the Marshal with his true Interest, and to assure him how well he was affected to the King's, by that Mean laying the Foundation of that good Understanding, which some Years after restor'd Peace to *Germany* and acquir'd vast Advantages to *France*, which are to this Day very vexatious to the House of *Austria*. It cannot be said that the Marshal was a Minister, nor even that he negotiated, *because he had no Letters of Credence*. He did no more than hearken to the Overtures the Elector of *Bavaria* made him, in order to make a Report thereof at his Return into *France*.

The Count *de Liche* was a Prisoner of War at *Lisbon*, at the time Prince *Don Pedro* confin'd his Brother *Alphonso*, in order to take from him his Wife, Crown and Liberty. *Don Pedro* judg'd at first that Peace was absolutely necessary for his better Establishment, and the *Portuguese* desir'd it so ardently, that to obtain it, they had offer'd great Advantages to *Castile*, even to the leaving it some Marks of Sovereignty. But the Negotiation on that account not succeeding, *Don Pedro* renew'd it with the Count *de Liche*, who having begun the Treaty without *Credentials*, procur'd a Full-power from *Madrid* to labour it in Conjunction with the Earl of *Sandwich*, the *English* Embassador, who came to *Lisbon* for that purpose. The *French* Embassador would have oppos'd it, but that did not hinder the Treaty from being sign'd on the 31st of *January* 1668. Before the Count *de Liche* had receiv'd his *Letters of Credence* and *his Powers*, he was neither Embassador nor publick Minister, and after he had re-
cciv'd

The EMBASSADOR *and his* FUNCTIONS.   113

ceiv'd them, he was no longer a Prisoner of War, no more than *Andrew Gritti*, and the Duke of *Longueville* All that these Gentlemen did, *before they had their Letters of Credence*, could not be properly call'd Negotiation, but barely a Preparative to the true Negotiation, of which the publick Minister alone is capable

Not only a Prisoner cannot set up to be a Minister, be his Quality what it will, but also an Embassador (tho' he does not lose his Character, when he is made a Prisoner, to the Prejudice of the *Law of Nations*) cannot discharge his Functions of publick Minister, because he is depriv'd of the Liberty to execute his Master's Intentions   In the Year 1474, *John* II, King of *Arragon*, and *Ferdinand* and *Isabella*, Princes of *Castile*, sent to *Lewis* XI, King of *France*, *John Raimond Folch*, Count of *Cardona* and of *Prades*, *Bernard Hugh de Rocaberti*, Castellan of *Amposta*, and the Constable *Peter Peralta*, to try to terminate the Dispute *John* and *Lewis* had concerning the County of *Roussillon Lewis*, who was not at *Paris*, would not suffer the Embassadors to come to him, but oblig'd 'em to treat with his Council, but not being able to conclude any thing, they made their Protestation in their Master's Name, and went away   When they came to *Pont S Esprit*, they were forc'd to go back to *Lyons*, where a Guard was set over them, notwithstanding the Passport they had of the King Some Days after, they were told they might be gone, if they would revoke the Protestation they had made at *Paris*   They did revoke it, after they had protested afresh against the Violence that was offer'd them Hereupon they were suffer'd to depart, but they were stopp'd again at *Narbonne*, and during their Stay there, the King invited them several times to come to him where he was, giving them some hopes he would make Satisfaction to the King of *Arragon* but they return'd for answer, *That they had now no Power to negotiate, nor to hear any Overture of a Treaty: That the King their Master being inform'd of the Violence which had been offer'd them, and that they were not treated as Embassadors, had revok'd his Powers, and was resolv'd to reject whatever Propositions should be made, so long as they were Prisoners*

Private Persons may make and receive Overtures and Proposals of Accommodation, tho' they have neither *Letters of Credence* nor Commission, provided their Intention be good, and that their Design be to direct all they do to the Service of the Publick, and to the Advantage of the Sovereign   Every good Citizen, and every Man of Probity, is oblig'd to serve his Countrey with the Talent God has given him and provided he do not assume to himself a Power which he has not, not does not involve the publick Authority, he may enter upon Conferences, that have no other view than the Welfare of the State and of the Prince, and that cannot prejudice either the one or the other   In the Year 1612, the *Trivultes*, having a mind to alienate some Rights or Territories, which they had in the Countrey of the *Grisons*, the *Leagues* sent the Judge of one of their Communities to *Milan*, to treat with them about it The Partisans of *Spain* gave immediately Advice thereof to *Alphonso Cassati*, Embassador from the *Catholick* King to the Cantons, and to the *Leaguer*, who being then at *Milan*, caus'd the Judge to be so narrowly observ'd, that at his alighting from his Horse in the Inn, he was presently accosted by a Priest of his Acquaintance, who after the first Civilities, offer'd his Service to him, and would needs accompany him every where, to shew him the finest Palaces of the Town   The Priest having walk'd his Man up and down some time, contriv'd to bring him to the Palace of *Don John de Velasque*, Constable of *Castile* and Governor of *Milan*, just as he was coming from Mass, accompany'd by *Alphonso Cassati*   They stopp'd at our Stranger, and the Governor ask'd him, why the *Leagues* had refus'd a Passage to the *German* Troops which he had sent home   He added, that he desir'd to live in a friendly Correspondence with them, and after that he left him in the Hands of *Cassati*, who made an end of Catechising him   He told him, that the *Grisons* ought to make their Profit of the good Disposition the Governor had express'd to him That his Countrey might draw very great Advantages from so good a beginning, because if he was willing to burthen himself with the Intention and Orders of the Governor, the *Grisons* might make a beneficial Treaty with him, and obtain by it the Demolition of the Fort of *Fuentes* and that nothing but *France*, and the Protestant Ministers could hinder it   The Judge answer'd, *that he had not the Quality of a publick Person*, and that he came to *Milan* only upon some particular Affairs *Cassati* reply'd, that he was sensible of it, but however it need not hinder him from communicating to some of his Countreymen what he had entrusted him with   That he would thereby do a great piece of Service to his Countrey, and that he might acquaint him with the Sentiments of his Superiors at his Return to *Milan*, whither he knew he was to make a second Journey in some time   As soon as the Judge return'd to *Coire*, he did not fail to make a Report to the *French* Embassador, and to some of the Chief of the *Grisons* of the same Party, of the Conversation he had had with *Cassati*   The Embassador was very glad to see the *Spaniards* had met with a Man of that Integrity, and was for having *the Judge continue his private Negotiation when he came to* Milan, upon this Foundation however, that he should take away from *Cassati*, all hopes of ruining or altering the Alliance the *Grisons* had with the King his Master   The Judge was no sooner arriv'd at *Milan* the second time, than he saw *Cassati* in the Inn, but it was only to make him a small Compliment, deferring to the Day following to entertain him about Business, as he accordingly did, rendering himself at the Inn at the Hour he had appointed him   He at first shew'd him a Writing, containing the Conditions, upon which the Governor promis'd to demolish the Fort of *Fuentes*   The Judge seeing that one of the first was, that the *Grison*'s Passes should be open to the *Spaniards*, and shut up to all others, gave back the Writing to *Cassati*, and told him, he would by no means charge himself with Propositions which had been so often rejected by his Superiors   *Cassati*, instead of being disheartned, reply'd immediately, that some other Means must then be thought of, and that

G g   an an Agreement might be made, if it could but be known, what it was the Leagues defir'd of the Governor. The Judge made anfwer, That he could not tell, *That he was not a Minifter*, but however he believ'd he might with Safety fay, They requir'd nothing but the Execution of the Treaty made in the Year 1531. This Anfwer broke off the Negotiation. Charles *Pafchal*, who relates all thefe Particulars in his Embaffador, adds, That the Judge faid fo much at his Return home, that he, and the two Gentlemen to whom he communicated all that had pafs'd at *Milan*, were fenfible that it was only an Artifice in *Caffati*, who was endeavouring to get the Treaty, the *Grifons* had made with *France*, alter'd. And indeed the Orders he was to procure from *Spain*, for the Demolition of Fort *Fuentes*, did not come. So that Affairs remain'd in this State till in the Year 1627 the *Grifons* drove out the *French*, and flung themfelves into the Arms of the *Spaniards*. The Judge could, as a private Perfon, hear the Propofitions which were made to him for the Benefit of his Countrey, and might, without a Crime, fpeak his own Sentiments, fo long as he did not engage the State, and particularly in a Republick, where every Inhabitant has a greater fhare in Affairs than in a Monarchy.

Even Kings themfelves do not find fault with their Subjects and Officers for receiving innocent Propofitions, which do them no Prejudice, and which on the contrary may bring their Defigns to pafs. The Preliminaries of the Treaty, which was concluded on the 9th of *October* 1495, between King *Charles* VII on the one part, and the confederated Princes of *Italy* on the other, were regulated by People, who had neither *Letters of Credence*, nor *Powers*. *Charles* ftopp'd in *Piedmont* after the Battel of *Fornova*, and feeing there was no likelyhood of relieving the Duke of *Orleance*, who was befieg'd in *Novara*, let it be known that he had no Reluctancy to treat with the Confederates, who on their fide long'd to fee *Italy* freed from the *French*, but no body would make the firft Overture. It happen'd that *Charles* having fent *Philip de Commines* to *Cafal*, on occafion of the Death of the Marchionefs of *Montferrat*, at the fame time that Count *Albertin Bofchetto* came thither on the part of the Marquis of *Gonzagnes*, who commanded the Confederate Army, thefe two Deputies fell into a Difcourfe on the Subject of a Peace, and of the Benefit which would accrue to all *Chriftendom* therefrom. They carry'd it fo far, that the Count perceiving the *French* were well enough difpos'd, wrote to the Proveditors of the *Venetian* Troops about it, who lent an Ear thereto; and having communicated the Affair to the Duke of *Milan*'s General, they agreed at laft that the King fhould be defir'd to fend his Deputies to a Place between *Bolgari* and *Camariano*, which had been pitch'd upon as the moft commodious to both Parties. This was executed the Day following. *Gonzagues* and the Proveditor *Contarini* were fent on the part of the Republick, the Duke of *Milan* fent *Bernardin Vifconti*, and the King of *France* deputed thither the Cardinal St *Malo*, the Prince of *Orange*, the Marfhal *de Giez*, *Piennes* and *Commines*. This laft became a Minifter in this Commiffion, but he had no *Letters of Credence* when he regulated the Preliminaries with *Bofchetto*, who had none neither.

Suppofing then, that the *Credentials* confer the Character to the Minifter, and that they make him known to the Prince, to whom they are directed, that he may fecure him his own Protection, and that of the *Law of Nations*, it follows from thence, that thofe Princes, who have no Knowledge of the Character, are not oblig'd to refpect the Minifter. Neither do they violate the *Law of Nations*, if they treat him upon the level with other private Perfons. In the Year 1572, Queen *Elizabeth*, who was very jealous of all the Negotiations which were carry'd on in *Scotland*, had made an Agreement with the King of *France*, that the one fhould not negotiate there without the other, but Matters fhould be left in the State they were then in. However, is fhe had reafon to diftruft the Sincerity of Queen *Catherine* of *Medicis*, fhe caus'd all Paffengers to be fo ftrictly obferv'd, that, excepting Merchants, known to be fuch, and thofe who had Paffports, all that took that Road were ftopp'd. *Du Croc, who was going to* Scotland *in the Quality of Embaffador from* France, *had the fame Fortune, was taken into Cuftody, and brought up to* London. It made a great Noife in *France*, where it was talk'd of as of a Breach of the *Law of Nations*. But *Walfingham* told the Queen Mother that *Du Croc* having been taken into Cuftody but by virtue of a general Order, and of the Prohibition the Queen had made, that no body fhould go thither without a Paffport, he ought to blame himfelf for the Difgrace which had happen'd to him, becaufe he might have prevented it by taking a Paffport, and that the *Law of Nations* had not been violated at all in reference to him. Queen *Catherine*, who knew fhe had not obferv'd the Agreement, and that Queen *Elizabeth* had grounds to be jealous of *Du Croc*'s Negotion, found herfelf oblig'd to hearken to Reafon. An Embaffador, that does not make himfelf known in the Countrey through which he paffes, ought not to complain of the Occurrences that oppofe his Paffage. It is in this Cafe that what the Emperor *Charles* V faid in reference to *Merveille*, is acceptable, *viz* That there is no Obligation to refpect a Minifter if he does not make himfelf known publickly.

Henry II, King of *France*, fent the Order of St *Michael* to *Edward* VI King of *England*, by the Marfhal *de St André*. *Mary*, Queen Dowager of *Hungary*, Governefs of the Low Countries, endeavour'd to feize the Marfhal at his Return, as he pafs'd from *Dover* to *Calais*. *Henry*, coming to a Rupture fome time after with the King of *Spain*, takes notice in his *Manifefto*, that *Mary* had done an Action againft the Peace, but he does not however reproach her with having violated the *Law of Nations*, in offering to feize his Embaffador, becaufe the Marfhal was not fuch, in reference to *Mary*, nor to the King of *Spain*. *Selim* II, Emperor of the *Turks*, being on the point of breaking with the Republick of *Venice*, and having requir'd of it the Ifland of *Cyprus*, fent into *France* a *Chiaoux* nam'd *Mamut Bey*, to fee how his Enterprize was relifh'd there. He addrefs'd himfelf to *Ferrier*, Embaffador from *France* at *Venice*, who being unwilling to let

The EMBASSADOR *and his* FUNCTIONS 115

let him proceed in his Journey till he had himself been made acquainted with the Intention of his Court, dispatch'd an Express thither, but before the Courier came back, the Senate put the Chiaoux into Custody, and sent him a Prisoner to the Castle of *Verona*, where he remain'd till the Peace. The Embassador return'd him, and the King made pressing Instances for his Liberty, till being inform'd that the *Turk* had no other Commission but barely to try to penetrate into the Sentiments of the *French*, in reference to the *Cyprian* War, he acquiesc'd in the Reasons of the Republick, which represented to him, *that a Sovereign Power acknowledges no publick Minister who has not Letters of Credence to it.*

St *Amant*, who has made himself known by his Poems, being willing to make himself known also by his Negotiations, accepted in the Year 1650 of a Commission, which might give him Admittance to Queen *Christina* of *Sweden*. The Queen of *Poland* was brought to bed of a Princess, and he offer'd to carry the News thereof to *Stockholm*, but *he forgot to take Creaentials with him.* Whereupon *Chanut*, to whom he address'd himself, told him, he could not assume the Quality of Minister, and that his own Word was not sufficient to make him be treated as an Envoy. St *Amant*, by undertaking that Journey without *Letters of Credence*, acted more like a Poet than a publick Minister, and made it appear that there is a great deal of Difference between the Profession of the one and the Function of the other. These Examples make it plain, that the Embassador that negotiated for the Court of *Sweden*, in that of *Poland*, speaks very improperly, when he says, That the Elector of *Brandenburg*, who had threaten'd to have him cudgell'd, had thereby violated the *Law of Nations.* The Embassador cannot make himself be respected, but by the Prince, for whom he has *Letters of Credence*, the other Princes can only consider and treat him as a private Person. If they do any thing beyond that, it is only out of an Excess of Civility, which is not of Obligation.

Letters of Credence are, for the most part, dispatch'd out of the *Chance y*, that is to say, they are seal'd with the small Seal or Signet, and countersign'd by a Secretary of State, or by some other Minister who discharges that Function. However, that is not absolutely necessary, as well because in *Germany* and other Places, where the Princes sign the Dispatches themselves, they very rarely let them be countersign'd, as because it depends on the Prince to whom the Minister is sent, to content it self with the Form that is given them, and he may have the same Consideration for a Letter of the Cabinet as for a *Chancery* Dispatch.

When Princes employ a Confident in an Embassy, they sometimes add to the *Letter of Credence* a particular Letter of Recommendation, as a Token of their Confidence. Queens, tho' they are neither Regents nor *Tutrices*, charge sometimes the Embassador with their particular Letters, either to testify the Esteem they have for his Person, or the Friendship they have for the Prince to whom he is sent, but these cannot be properly call'd *Letters of Credence.* Those that Princes and Sovereign States write to Queens, or to Ministers of the Court where the Embassador goes to negotiate, are not so neither, they are only mere Letters of Civility, which often might be very well spar'd. The Court of *Spain* is very jealous of 'em, and will have that Honour reserv'd to the King alone, as being due to none but the Sovereign, exclusively of all others, which is very true. They have not been always so nice. *Vincent Trou* and *William Lippomano*, who went in the Year 1581 to compliment *Philip* II on his Succession, or on the Conquest of *Portugal*, carry'd Letters of Credence for the Cardinals of *Austria*, of *Toledo*, and of *Granvell*, for the Duke of *Alva*, &c.

The Embassadors whom Princes send to the *Switzers* have a Letter of Credence for all the *Cantons* in general, one for the Catholick *Cantons*, one for the Protestant *Cantons*, and one for each particular *Canton.* The Minister communicates his *Letters of Credence* by means of the Master of the Ceremonies, or of the Introductor of the Embassadors, to the Secretary of State, or to that Officer of the Prince's Houshold, who is to give Order for the Reception, which is what cannot be done till his Quality be known. In the Year 1638, the Sieur *Forbus* being arriv'd in *France*, on the part of the King of *Poland*, and insisting on being treated as an Embassador, the Count *de Brulon*, one of the Introductors, went to him, and desir'd to see his *Letters*, or *Passport.* It appear'd that in his *Letters* he had the Quality of *Nuncius.* He alledg'd that in his Countrey no Distinction was made between the Quality of *Nuncius* and that of *Legatus*, but the King of *France* understood it otherwise, and the Court treated him as an Envoy, as well in his Audiences, as in the present, which was only a Gold Chain worth about four or five hundred Crowns. In the same Year another *Polish* Gentleman, nam'd *Dembisky*, taking the Quality of Envoy Extraordinary, in order to forward his Business, which was to negotiate the Liberty of Prince *Casimir*, who was then a Prisoner at *Salon* in *Provence*, desir'd to see the King without Ceremony, and when he was for taking his Audience of leave, he pretended to be treated as an Envoy, but as his *Letters* did not give him any Quality, he receiv'd no Civility at all; nay, he was sent back without a present. It might be ask'd, whether the Pope ought not to have treated *d'Alincourt* after the same manner, being his *Letters of Credence* gave him no Character, any more than *Dossat*'s did to him, when in the Year 1598 he went on the King's part to *Venice*, and to *Florence*.

CHAP

CHAP. XVI.

Of the Embassador's Powers.

THE *Powers*, with respect to an Embassador, are nothing else, than what a Letter of Attorney is in reference to a private Person. The word is new in that acceptation, as well as that of *Plenipotentiary*, and it is not above eighty Years since Ministers did not disdain the Quality of *Procurators*, even in the Treaties they made on the part of Crown'd Heads. *Doffat* was a Bishop, and did the business of *France* at *Rome*, when in the Year 1598, he made a Treaty with the Great Duke of *Tuscany*, for the Restitution of the Islands of *If*, and of *Pomegus*, and yet he therein takes no other Quality than that of *Procurator*. The *Powers* are an essential Instrument of the Embassie, when a Treaty is either to be made or concluded, or a particular affair of Importance negotiated, in which case it behoves each Party to be sure of the other, as to the execution thereof. After the conclusion and execution of the Peace of *Munster* and *Ofnaburg*, *France* had often made an Overture to the Queen and Ministers of *Sweden*, for a new Alliance. *Chanut* never mention'd it at *Stockholm*, but he found there a strong inclination for it, and carry'd back formal assurances thereof. But as the Civil Wars in *France* (the success and consequences of which were apprehended in *Sweden*) chill'd very much the first heat for it, and *Chanut* receiv'd Orders to repair to the Assembly at *Lubeck*; he prevail'd with the Queen that the Alliance should be negotiated in that Place, and regulated betwixt him and *Salvius*. *Chanut* had indeed Orders to Treat, but he had not *Powers in a due form*. Wherefore at their beginning to talk of Affairs, *Salvius* desir'd to see his *Powers*. *Chanut* told him he had express Orders Sign'd by the Count *de Brienne*, Secretary of State, and shew'd 'em to him. *Salvius* reply'd, that those Orders were very good, but that they could be of no use but to the Bearer, and that it was necessary he should have formal *Powers*, without the Communication whereof he could not enter with him on a Negotiation for a Treaty of Alliance. The Queen of *Sweden* told the *French* Agent the same thing; and that on those occasions, it was requisite to be in possession of, and to communicate, *Powers* drawn up in good form. That there was a great deal of difference between a Minister who had no *Powers* at all, and he that has 'em, tho' they be imperfect; because that upon the ground of the one, the Negotiation may still be continued, and without the other, there was no making so much as a beginning.

What I have here said, has room also in reference to the *Legate*, because that although his Bulls and his Faculties give him a great Power, yet they are in reality no more than *Letters of Credence*, which give no Power to the Legate, except the Function of his Legation. Cardinal *Barberin* was Treated with, so long as he spoke only of a suspension of Arms, and of the Reparation the Pope demanded for the affront which had been offer'd him, in seizing some places which had been put into his hand by way of *Depositum*, in the *Valtelin*. But the minute he began to talke of the Securities that might be taken for the Roman Catholick Religion, which was to be preserv'd in the same Countrey, that is to say, of an essential Point, and which made one of the chief Articles of the Treaty of *Madrid*, which the Pope pretended to have alter'd. He was ask'd *whether he had a formal Power* for that Affair. He made answer that he had not, but he would engage that what he did should be approv'd of. The Pope said as much to the *French* Embassador, and on this assurance there was so much the less difficulty made to enter into Conference with him on that Subject, because the *French* Ministers did not intend to come to a Conclusion. The King by causing the *Legate* to be ask'd whether he had a formal Power for the Affair he negotiated, confirm'd what has been universally receiv'd. That a *General Power*, of what extent soever, and whatever Clauses may be added thereto, is not sufficient for a particular Treaty. *Jeannin* and *Russ* had very ample Power to Negotiate at the *Hague*, but when an Alliance between *France* and the United Provinces began to be talk'd of, the King sent them a special Power for that purpose on the 24th of *November*, 1607, tho' but six weeks before he had sent them the *Powers* of which I shall speak hereafter.

In ordinary Affairs the Embassador has no need of a *special Power*. The *Portugal* Embassador disputing the Rank with that of *Hungary* at the *Council of Trent*, said this latter had no *Authentick Powers*, but the Fathers of the Council declar'd, that the *Letters of Credence* were sufficient. And indeed there are a thousand occasions, and a thousand affairs, where in Powers are not only unnecessary, but also where they would be altogether of no use, and there are very few Embassies where it is requisite to employ Plenipotentiaries. For the most part, Embassies are only marks of an outward Friendship which Princes shew one to another, or else are only effects of their Civility, Curiosity, or Jealousie. Some are merely to observe the Prince to whom they are sent, or else to remove the Minister himself to a greater distance. The Employment that is given out of a Court to a Minister who has been its Confident, is an infallible sign of his disgrace, and the Embassie that is so given him, is no better than an honourable Banishment. The digression I shall make in alledging some Examples, shall not be very long. The Count *de Lude* being jealous of the Credit *Philip de Commines* had with *Lewis* XI procur'd him a Commission, which kept him

him some time employ'd on the Frontiers of *Poictou* and *Britany*, and his Embassie to *Venice* and *Florence* was only a consequence of the ill offices the Lord of *Chaumont* did him to the King, for having spoken in favour of the Inhabitants of *Dijon*. In the beginning of the Reign of *Francis* II the *Duke*, and Cardinal *de Guise* having a mind to remove the Princes of the Blood from Court, procur'd the Princes of *Condé*, and of *La Roche* upon *Yon*, to be sent to the King of *Spain*, and gave to the King of *Navarre*, and to the Cardinal of *Bourbon* the Conducting of the Queen, Wife to *Philip* II. *Roger de Saulary*, Lord of *Bellegarde*, and Mareschal of *France*, had been much in the favour of *Henry* III while he was Duke of *Anjou*, and King of *Poland*, but as the last Favourites had no great difficulty to remove the first, with this weak and unconstant Prince, the King to get rid of *Bellegarde*, nominated him to the Embassie of *Poland* giving him for Collegue *Guy du Faur de Pibrac*, with Orders to excuse his shameful retreat, and to endeavour to preserve a Crown to him, which he had despis'd and abandon'd. *Pibrac* went thither, but *Bellegarde* under a pretext to take a turn at Home, to settle his Domestick Affairs, retir'd to *Emanuel Philibert* Duke of *Savoy*, and laugh'd at the King. The Republick of *Venice* being persuaded that the Emperor *Charles* V would be able to bestow the Dutchy of *Milan* on some private Nobleman, after the death of *Francis Sforza*, resolv'd to make an Alliance with him, and to renounce that with *Francis* I which had been honourable and useful to it. *France* had its Partisans in the Senate, who had strongly oppos'd this Resolution, insomuch that the Senators who had been the cause of its being taken, and had procur'd themselves to be nominated, to go and acquaint *Charles* therewith, under the pretext of complimenting him on the Victory he had gain'd over the *Turks* at *Tunis*, being apprehensive that during their absence some alterations might be made in Affairs, procur'd the Embassie to *Rome* to be given to those of the greatest Credit and Interest amongst the opposite Party.

I don't think that this sort of Embassadors have any need of *Powers*. I moreover say that *Powers* are not so necessary to the Ministers who are the bearers thereof, as to the Commissioners or Embassadors that treat with them, and whom it behoves to be well assur'd that what they shall negotiate and treat of with the Plenipotentiaries, shall be approv'd of and ratify'd, although the *Powers* how ample and absolute soever they may be, have always some relation to the secret Orders the Ministers receive, which may be chang'd and alter'd, and often are, according to the Conjunctures and Revolutions of Affairs. The Embassador's Plenipotentiaries who were on the part of *France* at *Munster*, did not scruple to say upon all occurrences, that they had writ, or would write to the Court, and that they would wait for its fresh Orders. And notwithstanding those of *Sweden* boasted they had an absolute power to make Peace, on such Conditions as they themselves should think reasonable, yet it is certain that there did not a Mail arrive, but brought them fresh Orders; and that in affairs which were any whit of moment, they came to no Resolutions, till they had consulted the Queens pleasure, and the Opinion of the Senate at *Stockholm Chanut*, the *French* Embassador there, sometimes work'd a change in their Sentiments; and *Oxenstiern* did not make any step but under the conduct of the Chancellor his Father.

However, the *Powers* ought not to be limited at all, nor refer to the Instructions, because being Conditional, they would no longer be a *full* Power. The Cardinal *Spada* had Orders from Pope *Urban* VIII to treat with *Lionne* for the accommodating the difference the *Barberins* had with the Duke of *Parma*, concerning the Dutchy of *Castro*. They had let slip into the *Powers* of the Cardinal this Clause, *Servata Instructionis formâ*, but *Lionne* caus'd it to be taken out, because it destroy'd or impair'd the *Powers*. It is true at the same time, that the Prince may reserve to himself in the *Powers* the faculty of Ratifying. But even in that Case, the *Power* is not full, unless the Ratification be made mention of, as of a thing of course, which gives the last form to the Treaty. In Simple *Powers* generally this Clause is inserted, *That upon the advice the Embassador shall give of the State of the Negotiation or Treaty, the Prince shall deliberate on the directions he shall give him for the Conclusion thereof*, and then the Embassador's Power is limited, so that he cannot sign the Treaty, without receiving a more express Order than what his first *Powers* contain'd. On the first of *May*, 1572, Queen *Elizabeth* gave a Power to *Francis Walsingham* to enter upon a Negotiation with the Ministers of *France*, for a Treaty of Commerce, but she reserv'd to her self the faculty of signifying to him her last Intention, after the Negotiation should be in a greater forwardness.

It is most certain, that the *Powers* are at least as necessary to him that treats with the Minister, as to the Minister himself, as it will appear by the following Example. The Invasion with which *Philip* the Bold, King of *France*, threaten'd the Kingdom of *Arragon*, in the Year 1285, oblig'd the King, *Peter* the Great, to send to *Sancho* the Brave, King of *Castile*, a Gentleman whose Name was *Peter de Bolea*, to endeavour to bring him into his Interest. This Gentleman, who for all *Powers* had only a simple *Letter of Credence*, was at a great loss, finding the King of *Castile* very little dispos'd to act for the interest of the King of *Arragon*, insomuch that being apprehensive left he should declare in favour of *France*, he told him, that if he would but promise to remain neuter, the King of *Arragon* would give him the Town of *Calataynd*, after the War was at an end. *Sancho* remain'd neuter, and perceiving that *Peter* had made an advantageous Peace enough with *France*, he demanded of him the Town *Bolea* had promis'd him. The King of *Arragon* said, that the Gentleman he had sent him, had neither Order nor Power to promise any thing. But that he might not be wanting in any thing he ow'd to a King whose Friendship was dear to him, he sent him back the Gentleman, to be dispos'd of by him, as he pleas'd. *Bolea* acknowledg'd to the King of *Castile*, that he

H h   had

had no Orders to offer him any thing, but that it was the great Affection he had for the King his Master, which had oblig'd him to make those Offers, thereby to put him out of those Dangers, the Junction of the Arms of *France* with those of *Castile* made altogether inevitable. The King of *Castile* commended his Zeal, and what he had done, treated him, and sent him back to his Master. He could blame no body but himself, for having too lightly given Credit to the Saying of a Minister, who, according to the Rules of his Profession, did not scruple mingling a little Artifice with his Probity. Provided Embassadors do but gain their Point, they do not make much Scruple about the Means. The King of *Castile* ought to have had this Promise in Writing, and before he accepted of it, have had an authentick Copy of the *Power* by virtue of which it was made. And the King of *Arragon* on his side, who would have the King of *Castile* give Credit to what that Gentleman should say to him on his part, was not oblig'd to own all that his Envoy had done without Orders, and he did more than he was oblig'd to do, in putting into the Hands of the King of *Castile*, the Person of whom he might complain for having cheated him, but who, however, had done a very signal Service to his Master.

What was taken notice of in the beginning of this *Chapter*, in relation to Cardinal *Barbarin*, shews that sometimes a Minister may be treated with, although he have no *Powers*, provided he be of Quality sufficient to make what he does be approv'd, and that he have Authority enough for that purpose. After the Death of *Henry* III, King of *France*, the King of *Navarre*'s Right of Succession to the Crown could not be contested, because, as the Custom of *Paris* says, *the Dead gives Seisin to the Living*, and by that Mean all *Frenchmen* were become his Subjects. Yet nevertheless, as there was a Faction form'd in the State, and the King was willing to allow of Conferences with the Deputies of the Duke *du Maine* and of the *League*, there was a Necessity to consider them as publick Ministers, and to make them enjoy the Protection of the *Law of Nations*. In the Year 1593, the Ministers of both sides met in the Village of *Surene*, and before they enter'd upon Business, a Communication of *Powers* was requir'd. The King's Deputies produc'd a very ample one, but the Commission of the *Leaguers*, gave them no other *Powers*, but to *hear the Propositions, and to report the same*. So that some Difficulty was made to enter into Conference with them. But the Archbishop of *Bourges*, who was Chief of the King's Deputation, told his Collegues, that those of the *League* were Persons of that eminent Quality, and had so much Credit with the Party, that as it could not be doubted, but they would prevail with their Principals to approve of what they should agree to in the Conferences, he was of Opinion they might be safely treated with, and upon this Consideration the Conferences were continu'd. Among the Deputies whom the States of the United Provinces sent into *England* in the Year 1585, *Jacob de Grise*, Bailiff of *Escoutette of Bridges*, and *Noël Caron*, Burgermaster of the same Town, had no *Powers*, yet that did not hinder the Queen from admitting them with the rest, because she knew they would be own'd, and that their Principals would ratify what should be concluded with them.

For although there be no Safety at all to conclude with a Minister who has no *Powers*; and that there be none, even to enter into a Negotiation with him, whose *Powers* have not their due Form, yet it is sufficient however, that he who, notwithstanding that, is willing to negotiate with a Minister who has no *Powers*, or whose *Powers* are imperfect, is contented therewith. In the Year 1645, the Viscount *de Bregy*, Envoy from *France*, having regulated betwixt the King of *Poland* and himself, the Conditions of the Marriage with the Princess of *Mantua*, took Audience in the Senate, where the Contract was to be approv'd of, but he could not satisfy all the Senators, who said, that all the Princesses Estate was litigious, and that the King was not a Tie therein. *Bregy* reply'd, that being acknowledg'd in that Court for a publick Minister, he was ready to give all the Security that could be desir'd from a Man of his Character. He was answer'd, that they did not dispute his Quality, but that it was requisite to see, *whether he had a sufficient Power*, to give Security in so important an Affair. *Bregy* said, his *Power* was compris'd in his Instructions, which he drew out of his Pocket. His Instructions were very authentick, countersign'd by a Secretary of State, and the Senators would have been satisfy'd therewith, if he had shewn them the Article that mention'd the Queens Portion.

Bregy said, it was sufficient the King had seen it, and was satisfy'd therewith. Hereupon the Senators got up, in order to go and acquaint the King with what had pass'd in the Conference. But the King told them that there was some Incivility, in the Instance the Senators had made concerning the *Powers* that it was a Matter that related to himself, that he had seen them, was satisfy'd therewith, and safe therein. The Senators had reason to ask to see the *Powers*, because it belong'd to them to regulate the Queen's Dowry and they ought not to be contented with the Instructions, nor the Extract that *Bregy* might have given them thereof.

The *Spanish* Plenipotentiaries, who were at *Munster* in the Year 1644, instead of communicating *Powers* that were in common to 'em all, had each of them their respective *Powers*, which gave them a Faculty to negotiate and to conclude, *in conjunction with their Collegues*, whose Number or Names were not express'd therein. So that to retard or perplex the Negotiation, they needed but to excuse themselves on their *Powers*, which hinder'd them from acting without the other Plenipotentiaries their *Collegues*. The *Mediators* made the same Reflection, and oblig'd the *Spaniards* to get their *Powers* amended. But that they might not be oblig'd to enter into fresh Disputes on the account of Form, the Model of an Instrument was agreed upon, which the Emperor's Plenipotentiaries and those of *France* sign'd, and put into the Hands of the *Mediators*. It was also agreed amongst them, that upon a Declaration, which was made on all hands, that the *Powers* should be drawn up after that manner, the

the Negotiation should in the mean time be continu'd These *Powers* may serve for a Precedent to all those that may be given to Embassadors for the time to come They may be found amongst the Acts of the Negotiation of *Munster*, under the Date of the 20th of *September* 1643, which is that of the first *Powers*, which were not reform'd till the Year 1615

Those Princes that have a mind to get out of Perplexities, do not discontinue a Negotiation, tho' there be some Deficiency in the *Powers* The Embassadors, that were on the part of the Arch-Duke at *Vervins*, had *Powers*, wherein the *Spaniards* took notice that King *Henry* IV besought them for Peace The Ministers of *France* complain'd thereof but as that great Soul was above those little Artifices, he order'd his Embassadors to continue the Treaty, and that the *Powers* should be exchang'd and communicated, but just when the Treaty was ready to be sign'd

However, the surest and safest way is not to enter upon Business till the *Powers* are communicated *Francis* I, King of *France*, would not suffer his Mother, the Queen *Regent*, to go to *Cambray*, till he had sent to *Brussels* to know, whether *Margaret* of *Austria*, with whom she was to treat, had a sufficient *Power* for the purpose In the Year 1640, the Cardinal Infant, signify'd by Writing to the Nuncio *Scotti*, and to *Angel Cornaro*, Embassador from *Venice* to the Court of *France*, that if the King would send some Person to *Peronne* with due *Power*, he would likewise send his Plenipotentiary to *Cambray*, that they might together agree upon a Place where a Truce might be negotiated and concluded The King made answer, that he would not refuse deputing some body, but he would first send to *Brussels*, to be inform'd *whether the Cardinal Infant had Power* from the Emperor and the King of *Spain*, to treat of a Truce for ten or twelve Years In the Year 1642, the King of *Great-Britain* and the Elector *Palatin*, sent their Ministers to *Ratisbonne*, because mention was there to be made of an Accommodation for the Elector The Embassadors requir'd the Restitution of the upper and lower *Palatinate*, together with the Electoral Dignity, tho' at the same time there was no likelyhood at all of obtaining it, as well by reason of the Elector of *Bavaria*'s Opposition, as because it was against the Emperor's particular Interest, who had sufficiently explain'd himself on that Head Yet nevertheless the Emperor, to make it be believ'd he had a mind to gratifie the King of *England*, caus'd the Embassador to be ask'd, what the King his Master would do for the Empire, if the Elector was restor'd The Embassador made answer, that in such case, the King of *Great-Britain* would make an offensive and defensive Alliance with the Emperor and the Empire He was then ask'd, *whether he had Power for that*, and he was urg'd to shew them, but he said, he would not communicate them, till he was assur'd of the Restitution of both the *Palatinates*, with the Electoral Dignity The Emperor, apprehending lest the Embassador should be provided with a sufficient *Power*, and being surpris'd at so high a Demand, signify'd to him, that in the State the Affairs of *England* then were, the Power of the King alone would not be a sufficient Security, and that the Parliament must joyn therein The King of *Denmark*, and the Electors of *Saxony* and *Brandenburg*, who had manag'd this Affair as *Mediators*, offer'd to be *Guarantees for the Power*, but the Emperor, who had no reason to fear any thing from *England*, and who would not hear speak of Restitution, broke off the Negotiation, tho' it did not appear that the *Powers* were defective It was only a very bad Pretext The Emperor could not, without offending the King, require a *Power* from the Parliament When a Prince has a mind to do a thing he does not refuse entering upon Business, tho' it should happen that the *Powers* have not their due Form, as I said before, more especially when he has no room to doubt, that what the Minister does will be approv'd of

Ferdinand de Velasco, Constable of *Castile*, going at the beginning of this Century, to compliment King *James* on his Accession to the Crown of *England*, had also Orders to make an Alliance with him Instead of passing the Sea in Person, he sent to *London* President *Richardot*, the Count *de Taxis*, and two other Ministers, that they might get the Treaty in a Readiness to be sign'd at his Arrival The Council of *London*, examining into the *Powers* of these Embassadors, found that they were but *Subalterns* and *Subdelegates* and that they had no other *Power* than what the Constable had given them The *English* Commissioners made a Difficulty to enter into Conference with them, but the King would have the Negotiation carry'd on with these Ministers, and said, that they should not boggle at the Words, *to cause to be treated*, which were inserted in the Constable's *Powers* That it was the Business of Advocates to wrangle about Words, and that Princes ought to act after a more noble manner King *James* was for treating with *Spain* at any rate, for which reason he suffer'd himself to be easily perswaded, that the Constable's *Powers* had been drawn by those *Philip* II. had given for the Treaty of *Vervins* The *Spaniards* at first urg'd to have a League offensive, which they afterwards reduc'd to a defensive one, and at last were contented with a simple Treaty of Friendship and Commerce History takes notice, that in the Conferences the King's Commissioners yielded them the Place of Honour It was their Due, not only because they were Strangers, and that the Conferences were held in the Council Chamber, but also because they were consider'd as Embassadors from the King of *Spain*, and in the same Quality they had had at *Vervins*

John Zapoli, King of *Hungary*, being driven out of his Dominions by the Arms of *Ferdinand of Austria*, he retir'd into *Poland*, to *Jerome Laski* whose Birth, Merit and Estate, put him amongst the first Noblemen of the Kingdom *Sigismund* King of *Poland*, had had for his first Wife *John*'s Sister and on that account, as also because he had some Jealousy of the neighbouring Power of the House of *Austria*, he did not take ill the good Usage that unhappy Prince receiv'd without his Participation. *Laski*, who alone was at all the Expence, judging that none but *Soliman*, the Emperor of the *Turks*, could restore *John* to his Throne, or had Generosity enough to undertake it, resolv'd folv'd to go himself to *Conftantinople*, as Embaffador from the King of *Hungary* He had no other *Credentials*, nor other *Powers*, than fome Letters of Recommendation from *Sigifmund* to two or three *Baffha's* of the *Divan* *Ferdinand* fent thither *John Oberdanski*, a *Hungarian* Gentleman, that he might thwart *Lasky's* Negotiation, but he was not able to hinder him from obtaining the Inveftiture of *Hungary* for his Friend, *John* being to pay Homage for the fame to *Soliman* The *Turkifh* Army enter'd into *Hungary*, whither *John* went to the Grand Seignior, who promis'd to reftore to him all the Conquefts he fhould gain upon *Ferdinand* This was the Effect of the Interceffion and Negotiation of *Lasky*, who having made himfelf known at the Port, had no great Difficulty to acquire the Efteem of the *Turkifh* Emperor, who for certain was a very great Prince, and who was willing to give to the Merit of this Gentleman, the fame *Credence* he could have given to the *Letters*, or *Powers* of the King of *Poland*

Here it might be ask'd, Whether *the Faculty* the two Kings of *France* and *England*, *Francis* I and *Henry* VIII, gave to the Cardinal of *York*, to make a Treaty between thofe two Princes, on fuch Conditions as he himfelf fhould judge reafonable, was a *full Power*, fince he was rather their Arbitrator than their Plenipotentiary, and that it was rather a Submiffion which the two Kings made to him, than any *Power* that they gave him

Thus, when *Leo* X offer'd his Mediation for a Peace between *Maximilian* the Emperor and the Republick of *Venice*, he did not require a *Power* to negotiate, but that thofe two Potentates fhould abfolutely acquiefce in his Will The Pope having reprefented to both Parties the Intereft they had to put an end to fo long and vexatious a War, which ruined themfelves, and was the Deftruction of *Italy*, gave them to underftand, that if they approv'd of it he would take upon him the whole Management of the Negotiation, and that he would fo regulate their Interefts that they fhould be both fatisfy'd therewith The Senate confented to it at laft, tho' not without great Reluctancy The greateft Difficulty, which had till then hinder'd it from coming to an Agreement with the Emperor, was concerning the City of *Verona*, which the Emperor pretended to belong to the Empire, and relating to the Sum of Money the Republick was to pay, as well for the Charges of the War, as for the Places and Rights *Maximilian* was to yield up to it, either as Emperor or as Arch-Duke The Senate therefore caus'd a Compromife to be made, wherein mention was made of the Terms in which the faid Sum fhould be paid, and fent it to the Pope with the ufual Submiffion *Leo* was not contented herewith, but requir'd an *Abfolute Power*, without Condition or Reftriction, and fo well fatisfy'd the Republick, that he would have the fame Confideration for its Interefts, as if they were his own, that he would determine nothing without the Embaffador's Participation, that it fent him a very *full Power to make Peace on fuch Conditions as he fhould think juft and reafonable* The Embaffador, when he deliver'd thefe *Powers* into the Pope's Hands, told him, That the Senate knew there would be found fome Difficulties in the Affair, by fo much the greater, as their Enemies being fenfible of the Pope's ample Power, would perhaps be for preffing his Holinefs to grant them fuch Conditions, as it felf fhould judge to be neither juft nor reafonable And in effect the Pope met with fuch great Obftacles, that the Bifhop of *Gurc*, who came to *Rome* at the time the Pretenfions of the Parties were under Examination, judging that the Bufinefs was to be drawn out in length, the *Spaniards* had leifure to break off the Truce, which oblig'd the Republick to have Recourfe again to their Arms, and no farther mention was made of the *Power* the Pope had procur'd himfelf There is no colour to fay, that the Pope was a Plenipotentiary, becaufe it is well known that a Plenipotentiary is in effect but a Mandatary or Procurator, and the *Full Power* is nothing elfe but a Procuration *cum Libera* Nor can it be doubted, that the Plenipotentiary is oblig'd to give an Account of his Negotiation to the Prince who gave him the Power, by the fame Reafon which obliges a Procurator to give an account of his Adminiftration to his Mafter This is what could not be faid of the Pope, who would not have fubmitted to it, nor have had that Deference to the Republick He would not act as an Arbitrator neither So that it may be faid that he was a Mediator in effect, but fuch a Mediator as could oblige the Parties to receive the Law from him, and fuch as he pleas'd to give them It is well known, that Sovereigns have a great many ways to get out of thefe kind of Engagements, when they become prejudicial to their Interefts, but that does not hinder it from being very dangerous, to give too large a Power to a potent Mediator, and that, in Affairs where the Damage cannot be repair'd, neither by difowning, nor by the Death of the Plenipotentiary

Francis I being unwilling to let the Emperor *Charles* V annex the Dutchy of *Milan* to the Crown of *Spain* and yet loath to refolve upon a Rupture with him, difcharg'd his Refentment on *Charles* Duke of *Savoy*, and fent an Army into his Countrey under the Command of Admiral *Chabot*, who in a little time took all the beft Places the Duke had either on this fide or beyond the Mountains The Progrefs of his Arms was ftopp'd by the Cardinal of *Loraun*, whom the King had fent into *Italy* with a *very ample Power to make a Peace* The Emperor was there then, and the Cardinal was no fooner arriv'd, than he oblig'd *Chabot* to confent to a Sufpenfion of Arms, againft the Opinion of all the General Officers of the Army, and to the irreparable Damage of the King's Affairs The Cardinal went beyond his Power, and the Admiral did not know his, when he receiv'd Orders of this Nature from him, who had no Right to lay Commands on a General, who receives them only from his Sovereign immediately Indeed it prov'd of very ill Confequence to him The Fault he committed coft him his Eftate and his Reputation, and would have coft his Life, without the powerful Interceffion of his Relations and Friends, who obtain'd his Pardon The Cardinal's Crime remain'd unpunifh'd, on account of his Dignity, and alfo becaufe that even in thofe Days the Houfe of *Guife* was fo
powerful,

powerful, that King *Francis* made a very bad, but too true a Prognostick for the Kings his Successors

The *Powers* that are in common to several Plenipotentiaries ought of necessity to contain this Clause, *That in case of the Death or Absence of one or two of them, the other, or the rest of them may carry on the Negotiation*, because that for want thereof, the Death, or the Absence of one of them, makes all the *Power* useless When the Queen Regent of *France*, and *Margaret* of *Austria*, met at *Cambray*, the Republick of *Venice* deputed thither two Embassadors, *Justiniani* and *Navager*, but the last being dead, the Council of *France* did not think fit to let the other go to *Cambray*, but made him stay at *St Quintin* President *Jeannin*, *Buzanval* and *Russi* were compriz'd in the same *Powers*, with this Clause, *That all of them together, or two of them in the Absence of the third, might act, negotiate, &c* But forasmuch as the *Powers* took no notice of the Death of the third, *Jeannin* wrote to M de *Villeroy* immediately after the Death of *Buzanvel*, *That they were without Powers and without Commission*, and that of necessity they must either have fresh ones, or at least a Declaration by which the King should notify his Pleasure, that he and *Russi* should continue to negotiate according to his Intention, notwithstanding the Death of *Buzanval* This was judg'd so necessary, that new *Powers* were sent them on the 7th of *October* 1607, and this does not admit of any Dispute

At Congresses, where there are many Plenipotentiaries of several Parties, whose Interests are either opposite or different, the *Powers* are communicated by the Hands of the Mediators, as may be observ'd in many Places of this Treatise The Count of *Aversburg*, who was on the part of the Emperor at *Osnaburg*, refus'd to communicate his *Powers* to the Embassadors of *Sweden*, because the Mediators were at *Munster* The King of *Denmark* had been Mediator there for some time, but after the *Swedes* had invaded *Holstein*, and some other Provinces of *Denmark*, his Ministers had left the Congress The Imperialists, to excuse the Difficulty they made to communicate their *Powers* to the *Swedes* at *Osnaburg*, which was founded on the Absence of the *Danish* Ministers, said that this Communication was not necessary, because the *Powers* were drawn according to the Model agreed upon at *Hamburg* But the *French* Ministers reply'd, That admitting they were so, the Imperialists could not avoid communicating them, if it were but to compare them with the Model, and to see whether they were conformable thereto

The *Powers* are a particular Instrument which makes a part of the Treaty, after this has been ratify'd according to the Terms agreed upon So that although no Clauses ought to be suffer'd to slip in, that may be prejudicial to the Rights and Pretentions of any of the Parties concern'd, yet if it should happen that there did, they can have no Consequence, if there is not time to have them amended, because it is the Treaty it self that regulates those of the one and the other, and that alters or ratifies the Contents of the *Powers* The Embassadors from *Poland* and *Sweden* being met at *Lubeck*, in the Year 1652, to endeavour to prolong the Truce between the two Crowns, or to convert it into a perpetual Peace, put their *Powers* into the Hands of *Chanut* the *French* Embassador, who there discharg'd the Office of Mediator After they had been communicated on both sides, the *Swedes* found fault with the *Powers* of the *Poles*, because the King of *Poland* took therein the Quality of hereditary King of *Sweden*, and yet they were contented with the Promise the Embassadors of *Poland* made, that they would get them alter'd This Difficulty being taken away *Chanut*, believing there was now none left, was for entring upon Business, and putting the Matter in Agitation, but when he spoke to the *Swedes* about it, *Rosenhan* declar'd, *That they had express Orders not to begin to negotiate till the Powers were effectually exchang'd* On the other side, the *Poles* protested that they wou'd not part with their *Powers* till the Treaty was concluded *Chanut* would have had both Parties to have lodg'd them in his Hands till the Conclusion of the Treaty, but the *Swedes* Instructions and Orders were so precise in this Point, that they did not dare to admit the least Relaxation or Temperament thereupon, but constantly maintain'd that the *Powers* ought to be exchang'd before they enter'd upon Business This was mere *Chican*, because the *Powers* being lodg'd in the Hands of the Mediators, the *Swedes* would have been sure of being late They could not doubt, but the Defects observ'd in the *Polish Powers* would be rectify'd, because the Republick of *Poland* not being willing to engage it self in a fresh War for the King's separate Interest, and much less for an imaginary Title, there was nothing could hinder it from reforming the *Powers*

CHAP. XVII.
Of Passports and Safe-Conducts.

Notwithstanding the King of *Denmark*, writing to *Schoneich*, who had Orders from the Emperor to conduct *Commendon*, the Pope's Nuncio, through *Germany*, and from thence as far as the two *Northern* Kingdoms, takes notice in his Letter that *Schoneich*, as a publick Minister, had no Occasion for a Passport or Safe-Conduct, yet I think I may say with Authority, that there are infinite Encounters, where the Embassador would hazard his Person and his Master's Dignity, if he did not put himself under the Protection of the publick Faith by the mean of a *Passport* Those Princes only, to whom Embassadors and publick Ministers

sters are sent, are oblig'd to secure to them the protection of the *Law of Nations*.

The Republick of *Poland* designing to send Embassadors into *France*, to carry thither the decree of Election in favour of *Henry* Duke of *Anjou*, Brother to *Charles* IX, desired a *Passport* for them from the Emperor, and some of the Princes of *Germany*. However, taking into Consideration that the Emperor who had made Interest to procure that Crown for the Arch-Duke *Ernest* his Son, might refuse to grant one, and that the other Princes had without doubt respect enough for him, to make some difficulties in the matter, she let them set out. These Embassadors being arriv'd at *Leipsick*, wrote to *Augustus* Elector of *Saxony*, and excus'd themselves *for having enter'd his Countrey without giving him a previous notice thereof*. The Elector made answer to them, that he was much surpriz'd to understand they were advanc'd so far before they knew his Intention in reference to their passage. That he commanded his Officers to treat them with Civility, *but not to suffer them to depart from thence*. *Monluc* Bishop of *Valencia*, who had been Embassador from *France* to *Poland*, and who was the Person that had most contributed to the Election of *Henry*, was as a Conductor to the *Polish* Embassadors, and represented to them, that the respect the Elector had for the Emperor, would oblige him to make some wry faces, but that it was not his intention to stop them, and so well persuaded them thereof, that they pursu'd their Journey. Before they set out, they sent a Gentleman to the Elector, (who at a good distance from thence was taking the diversion of Hunting,) to desire a Passport from him, of which they did not design to make use, since, before the return of their Courrier, they had got through *Thuringia*, into the Countrey of *Hesse*, and *Monluc*, tho' he had the Quality of Embassador going to *Poland*, reflecting that neither his Character nor the *Law of Nations* could secure him from the violence he had reason to be apprehensive of in *Germany*, where he was liable to be stop'd, or otherwise outrageously dealt with for want of *Passports*, disguiz'd himself, and pass'd into *Poland incognito*, and with a small Retinue.

During the first Wars of the Low Countries, *Key* or *Carus Rantzou*, whom the King of *Denmark* had sent into *Spain*, taking with him a Convoy of *Spanish* Horse, was met between *Namur* and *Brussels* by a Party from *Berguesopzoom*, who having beaten their Enemies, carried *Rantzou* into their Garrison, without his making himself known to any but the Governor of the Place. There was found about him a Letter that the King of *Spain* wrote to the Duke of *Parma*, he was taken in an Enemy's Countrey, and without any *Passport* from the State to protect him from such sort of disgrace. Nevertheless the Governor of *Bergues* no sooner was inform'd of his Quality, than he set him at Liberty, that he might go to the *Hague*, where he made great complaints of the ill Treatment he had receiv'd. They endeavour'd to excuse what had happen'd, his Goods were restor'd to him, he receiv'd several other Civilities, and had since a Gold Chain sent him. All this did not hinder the King of *Denmark* from picking a Quarrel with the States. He said they had violated the *Law of Nations* in the Person of his Minister. He Arrested a Fleet of *Dutch* Merchant-Men in the *Sound*, and would not suffer it to pass, till the Proprietors had paid the Sum of thirty thousand Crowns for reparation of the Injury he said had been done to him. The King was very much a *Spaniard* at that time, and let slip no opportunity of affronting the States whenever he could. But they who made him believe that the *Law of Nations* had been violated on this occasion, were mistaken themselves, or else had a mind to impose upon him. The States could not divine the Quality of a Gentleman who had been found in an Enemy's Countrey, under the Convoy of Enemies, and who had no *Letters* for the State, where he pretended to be consider'd as a Publick Minister. The King of *Denmark* violated the publick Faith, by seizing the Ships of private Men, against whom he had issu'd out no *Letters of Reprizal*. The Count de *Harcourt* Embassador from *France* in *England*, being oblig'd to go to the King at *Oxford*, did not rely so much on his Character, but that he took a *Passport* from the Parliament of *London*. In Civil Wars no great consideration is had to the *Law of Nations*, and one cannot be too well provided against the Insolence of those who acknowledge neither Master nor Discipline.

But without that, a Prince is not oblig'd to admit the Embassador of his Enemy, nor to respect him in a place where his Arms may act according to the Laws of War, without violating the *Law of Nations*. There were not so many Years employ'd in Regulating the differences *France* and *Sweden* had with the Emperor, and to redress the Grievances of all the Princes of the Empire, as were consum'd in making the Treaty of the Preliminaries, of which the *Passports* of the Deputies were the most momentous part. I took notice in the fourth Chapter of this Book, that the Emperor made some difficulty to grant *Passports* to the Protestant Princes of *Germany*, notwithstanding the King of *France*, who desir'd 'em for them, as for his Allies, consented at first, that their Ministers should assist there but as private Persons. The *Nuncio's George Bolognetti*, and *Rannuces Scotti*, with *Aloysio Contarini* the *Venetian* Embassador, made pressing Instances to prevail with the King to desist from his demands in favour of the Protestant Princes. But perceiving that Cardinal *Richlieu* was obstinate in the matter, they made two Propositions that they believ'd ought to be acceptable to all Parties concern'd. The one was, that the Emperor should cause *Passports* to be dispatch'd for some particular Persons that should be nominated to the Assembly, who might there remain in safety with the *French* Plenipotentiaries, but should not appear as Publick Ministers, yet nevertheless should have the Liberty to send and receive Courriers. The other Proposition was, that the Emperor should cause a general *Passport* to be drawn, for all those who should have any Business at *Cologne*, where the Congress was to be held, with the same privilege of dispatching and receiving Expresses. But these two Overtures were

were not approv'd of at *Vienna*, and the third was also rejected, by which the Protestant Princes were permitted to acquaint the *French* Ministers with their Interests, by which means it would not be necessary they should themselves send Ministers to the Assembly *France* demanded *Passports* chiefly for the *Swedes* and for the *Hollanders* The Emperor said that the first were to meet at *Lubeck*, according to the first Proposal, and that if they had any need of *Passports* for that, they might demand them, and for the others, that they had no occasion for them, by reason of their Neutrality However the Emperor suffer'd himself to be overcome, granted the *Passports* that were ask'd him for the ones and the others, and declar'd that he would authorize the Plenipotentiaries, who were on his part at *Cologne*, to issue out *Passports* or *Safe-Conducts* for the Princes, who not being yet reconcil'd to him, would send their Ministers to *Cologne*, there to remain in the Retinue of the French Embassadors The Emperor rather chose to have those Princes depend altogether on *France*, and give themselves up to it, than to suffer they should treat immediately with him, and without the intervention of a Sovereign and equal Power This Declaration was made in the Month of *August*, 1638 but before these *Passports* were got ready, Cardinal *Richelieu* told *Angel Cornaro*, who had succeeded *Contarin* in the Embassy of *Venice*, that the King requir'd particular *Passports* for the Landgrave of *Hesse*, and for Duke *Bernard* of *Saxe-Weimar*, as being Princes whom *France* distinguish'd on account of their affection to the Good Cause, and the Services they did to his Crown, pretending however that they should not send their Ministers to *Cologne* France made two Objections to this Declaration The one was, that the Emperor issu'd out his *Passports* by his Plenipotentiaries, instead of having them dispatch'd in his Chancery, and Signing them himself, and the other, that no mention was made therein of the safety of the Expresses, which nevertheless was one of the beneficial parts of the *Passports* It moreover took notice, that the Declaration run, that the Ministers of the Protestant Princes should be in the Retinue of the French Plenipotentiaries, from whence they inferr'd, that out of that they would not be in safety As also that it spoke of the Crime of high Treason, and so treated the King's Allies as Subjects, and Rebels And in fine, that only those Princes of the Empire were admitted to the Congress, who were not as yet reconcil'd to the Emperor, and that thereby several of those who were most concern'd to be there, were excluded

The *Swedes* went a great deal farther, they demanded *Passports* for the Elector *Palatin*, for the Duke of *Wirtemberg*, and insisted on having all the Titles and all the Qualities of those Princes inserted in them But this heat abated, and they conform'd to the Sentiments of *France* The States of the United Provinces refus'd the Passport the King of *Spain* had dispatch'd for their Ministers, and *France* it self did not like it, on account of the words Licence, and Permission, which the *Spaniards* had slip'd into it, and which imply'd a Superiority that the States and their Allies could not admit All these Models of *Passports* except those of the *Swedes* and the *Hollanders*, express'd that they should enure to the Ministers of those Princes who should Negotiate their Interest by the Mediation of the *French* Plenipotentiaries The Emperor excluded in the General *Passport* the Elector *Palatin*, because he had been excluded at the Treaty of *Prague*, and he had caus'd two *Passports* to be prepar'd, which were particularly for the Landgrave of *Hesse*, and the Duke of *Weimar* But he would not allow the general *Passport* to be put into the hands of the Ministers of *France*, till the King deliver'd at the same time the *Passports* for the Emperor and his Allies, and namely for the Duke of *Lorrain* After this, *France* demanded *Passports* for the Elector of *Triers*, whom the Emperor still detain'd a Prisoner, and for the Dutchess of *Savoy*, to whom the Court of *Vienna* made difficulty to give the Quality of Regent and of Tutrix, because the Emperor had declar'd the Cardinal of *Savoy*, and Prince *Thomas* Regents The King requir'd also a Passport for the Dukes of *Brunswick* and *Lunenburg*, who he said were his new Allies, but being inform'd that these Princes had sent their Deputies to *Ratisbon*, in order to reconcile themselves with the Emperor, he superseded that Request for some time, till he knew that that Negotiation was broke off The Emperor at last resolv'd to issue out the General *Passport*, and to leave out the Clause of *Nondum Reconciliati*, which *France* insisted so much the more upon, because she conceiv'd it would suit better with her Intentions, to have all the Estates of the Empire meet at the Assembly, whose Number and Authority would weaken that of the Emperor's Ministers But the King not being contented with the General *Passport*, continu'd to press the dispatch of the *particular Passports* First, for the Dutchess Regent of *Savoy*, a second for the Landgrave of *Hesse*, a third for the Dukes of *Brunswick* and *Lunenburg*, a fourth for the Elector *Palatin*, and for the Princes his Brothers, a fifth for the Elector of *Triers*, and a sixth for the Resident who should be at *Munster* on the part of the Crown of *Sweden* He desir'd also that *Spain* should dispatch three, one for the *Plenipotentiaries*, who should go on his part to *Munster*, another for the Resident whom he should send to *Osnaburg*, and a third for the *Plenipotentiaries* of the United Provinces The Court of *Vienna* agreed at last thereto, and thereupon the Preliminary Treaty was concluded at *Hamburg*, the 24th of *December*, 1641 The Ministers of *France* signify'd their desire to have the *Passports* written upon Parchment, and they insisted on having the King of *Spain* himself sign those he should issue out, and that therein he should not make use of the Ministry of *Don Francisco de Melos*, who had been vested with Authority for that purpose, since the death of the *Cardinal Infant* But this was a very needless Scruple, because Parchment does not render those kinds of Instruments more Authentick than Paper, neither is it requisite that the King should sign them himself It is enough that a Secretary of State signs and countersigns them, and since the Prince can give his Minister the Power to make a Treaty, for certain he can also impower him to issue out *Passports*, as in effect

3   all

all the *Plenipotentiaries* that were at *Munster*, hourly gave them out, by virtue of a particular Power they had for that Purpose. The *Passports* that were dispatch'd for *Bellievre* and *Sillery*, Plenipotentiaries from *France*, at the Treaty of *Verovins*, were only sign'd by the Arch-Duke *Albert*, who had been authoriz'd for that purpose by the King of *Spain*. The Draught of the Emperor's *Passports*, which was approv'd of in *France*, was compris'd in the following Terms.

Ferdinandus Tertius, divinâ favente Clementia, Electus Romanorum Imperator, semper Augustus, ac Germaniæ, Hungariæ, Bohemiæ, Dalmatiæ, Croatiæ, Slavoniæ, Rex, Archidux Austriæ, Dux Burgundiæ, Stiriæ, Carinthia, Carniolæ & Wirtembergæ Comes Tirolis, &c. Universis & singulis, & sancti Romani Imperii Principibus, tam Ecclesiasticis quam secularibus Electoribus, Archiepiscopis, Episcopis, Ducibus, Marchionibus, Comitibus, Baronibus, Castellanis, Capitaneis, Militibus, Nobilibus, Clientibus, Gubernatoribus, Locumtenentibus, Ductoribus, Magistratibus, Exercituum Ductoribus Supremis, tam Equestrium, quam Pedestrium Copiarum, Legatis, Tribunis, aliisque Capitaneis, Vexilliferis, Centurionibus, atque aliis quibuscunque, militaria munera ac Officia gerentibus Burgi-magistris, Consulibus, Passuumque, Pontium ac Portuum quorumvis Custodibus, ac Classium & quarumcunque Præfectis Urbium, item Locorum, Terrarum & Communitatum Officialibus, ac quibuscumque nostris, ac sacri Romani Imperii, Regnorumque & Dominiorum Nostrorum Hæreditariorum subditis, ac fidelibus dilectis, gratiam nostram Cæsaream & omne bonum. Devotionibus & dilectionibus vestris ac vobis, clementer mandamus ac præcipimus, ut Deputatos a serenissimo Franciæ Rege Christianissimo, Affine ac Fratre nostro carissimo Plenipotentiarios Monasterium ad Tractatum Pacis ibidem instituendum, proficiscentes, videlicet N N N per Territoria ac Loca Potestati ac Jurisdictioni suæ & vestræ subjecta, una cum Comitibus, Familiaribus, Famulis, Equis, Curribus, Navibus, Rebus, sarcinis ac scripturis, quos secum habituri sunt, liberè, tuto, securè atque expeditè ire, transire, ac ibi commorari, & postmodum etiam a dicta Civitate Monasteriensi recedere & redire sinant & sinatis, neque permittant aut permittatis, ne tam in itu quam in reditu, quicquam Molestiæ aut Impedimenti afferatur. Quin potius quibuscumque rebus poterunt aut poteritis, si necessitas, aut ipsi ita postulaverint, juvent & juvetis. Mandamus quoque ut Cursores, qui vel Monasterium ad dictos Plenipotentiarios mittentur, vel inde ab ipsis expedientur, durantibus his Tractatibus, liberè, tuto, securè ac expeditè ire, transire sinant vel sinatis Spondente Fide,& Verbo Nostro Cæsareo, nullo Nos modo commissuros, ut per Nos dictorum Deputatorum securitas libertasque ullatenus turbetur, interpelleturve quin potius jam nunc serio ac strictè Mandamus omnibus & singulis Jurisdictionis nostræ Subjectis, ne cuiquam ex supradictis ullâ viâ ansint contravenire. Hæc est seria, expressa & omnimoda nostra voluntas. Harum vigore Litterarum Manu Nostra subscriptarum, & Sigilli Nostri Cæsarei appensione munitarum. Datæ in Civitate Nostra Vienna die 28 January, 1642.

The business of the *Passports* being regulated after this manner, the *Spaniards* would have the *French* Plenipotentiaries give them a Memorial, containing the Names and Qualities of all those they pretended to have compris'd therein. They were afraid in *Spain*, lest the *Portuguese* and the *Catalans* should send their Deputies in the Retinue of the Ministers of *France*, which gave them great Uneasiness. The *Spaniards* urg'd, that the *French* had us'd this Rigour in reference to the Retinue of the deceased Cardinal Infant, and that of *Don Diego Saavedra*, who had been oblig'd to give in a Catalogue of all the Persons they pretended to have compris'd in the *Passports*. But the *French* made answer, that far from begging *Passports*, as a thing merely depending on their Will, they requir'd 'em as an Effect, and a natural Consequence of the preliminary Treaty, which the *Spaniards* could not deny them. That as their Intention was not to make an Abuse thereof, and much less to render them useless to themselves, they expected they should be drawn with all the necessary Securities, for themselves and their Domesticks. That the *Passport* that had been demanded of the King their Master for the Retinue of the Cardinal Infant, and for *Don Diego de Saavedra*, was of another Nature. That it might be limited, and even quite refus'd. But for the *Passports* that were requir'd for the Congress, the *Spaniards* could do neither the one nor the other. That they would give in the Number of their Domesticks, and their Qualities and Functions in gross, but that they would not name them. They gave them the Satisfaction they demanded, and they passed in all Safety.

The Ministers of *France* spoke thus, because the *Spaniards* had said, that in *France* they had limited the *Passport*, that had there been granted for the Retinue of the Cardinal Infant, and for the Passage of *Saavedra*; and they had reason to say, that they should render the *Passport* useless to them, if they communicated that Benefit to Ministers, who were not their Domesticks, and who could not be compris'd therein. *Pignerana* would never suffer mention to be made to him of *Passports* for the Ministers of *Portugal* and *Catalonia*. The *Catalonians* did not demand any, because as they had deliver'd themselves up to the *French*, it belong'd to these to speak for their Interests. *Portugal* on the contrary had revolted, without the least participation of *France*. And indeed the reap'd no other Advantage from it, than that she found in the weakening of the *Spanish* Power. The King of *Portugal* neglected profiting of the Diversion the Arms of *France* give in *Catalonia*, in *Italy*, and in the Low Countries; for which Reason the King would not enter into an Alliance with him, that should lay an Obligation of having him compris'd in the Peace, or else to continue the War for his sake. Yet nevertheless *Servien* carry'd along with him one of the *Portuguese* Deputies, and one of the *Catalonians* to *Munster*, tho' with a great deal of Reluctancy, and merely out of Complaisance to Cardinal *Mazarine*, because he was sensible he run a great Risque, that he violated the publick Faith, and that he hazarded the Dignity of the King, his Master, in exposing himself to a very gross Affront, by so rash an Action.

Francisco d'Andrada Leitas, Embassador from *Por-*

Portugal at the *Hague*, receiv'd in the Year 1644 Orders from the King his Master, to go in the same Quality to *Munster* but fearing lest the *Spaniards* should insult him on his Journey, he defir'd the States to permit him to travel in the Company, and as it were in the Retinue, of their Plenipotentiaries They represented, of their Plenipotentiaries They represented to him, that it was what they could not do, *becaufe he being an Embaffador himfelf, he could not receive any Benefit from the Paffport of their Minifters* That he had nothing to fear on the Road, because they would give him so good a Convoy, that he might travel with the greatest Safety but that he would be oblig'd to seek it elsewhere than in their Guarantie, after his Arrival at *Munster*, where they could not protect him, nor make his Quarrel their own This did not hinder the King of *Portugal* from having his Ministers at *Munster* and at *Ofnaburg* and although the Mediators, and the Friends of the House of *Auftria*, did not consider them in this Quality, yet they enjoy'd a perfect Security under the Protection of the Plenipotentiaries of *France*, who gave them the Title of *Excellency* The *Portugefe* however, instead of being satisfy'd therewith, were obstinate in their Demands of *Paffports*, and Safe-conducts, and incessantly importun'd *Servien* and *d'Avaux* thereupon even when it was thought, that the Treaties were just upon Signing, between the Emp re and *France* They either did not, or would not consider, that *Spain* could not issue out *Paffports for them*, without acknowledging them for Ministers of a Sovereign Prince, and the Duke of *Braganza* to be lawful King of *Portugal*

France, for its part, would never grant a Passport for the Duke of *Lorrain's* Minister, because that Prince, in making the *Paris* Treaty in the Year 1641, had renounc'd the Alliance of the House of *Auftria*, so that the Emperor could no longer speak in his Behalf, as for an Ally And in reality, the Emperor's Minister, in settling the Preliminaries at *Hamburg*, had consented that no mention should be made of him, because his Affair had nothing in common with those of the Empire and *Spain* had no other Interest in him, than what she might have for a Prince who lent her his Troops, in consideration of the Subsidies she paid him for the same, and of the Quarters where he subsisted her Army

The Difficulty *France* has since made, to issue out Passports for the Ministers the present Duke of *Lorrain* had a mind to send to *Nimeguen*, does not appear so reasonable And indeed she soon yielded to Reason, the King having consider'd, that the Treaties, and the Dispositions of the deceased Duke *Charles*, could not prejudice this who by virtue of the Laws of the Country, has a Title to the Rights of a first Possessor by his Birth, and has re-united them in his Person, whether we suppose *Lorraine* to be subject to the *Salick* Law, or that the Succession thereto be laid open to Women It were to be wish'd, that the Council of *France* had been a little more steady on this Subject and that it had not undertaken to overthrow what had been establish'd in the last Reign, to introduce new Maxims, as the Productions of a Minister, who had full as much Wit as Judgement and Conscience.

The Pains that were taken and the Years that were employ'd to settle the *Paffports* for the Plenipotentiaries of *Munster*, sufficiently make out that they are sometimes necessary to the Embassador, and that his Character does not always make his whole Safety Cardinal *Pool* would not pass through the Countrey of *Wirtemberg*, without the Duke's *Safe-conduct* *Du Croc*, Embassador from *France* to *Scotland*, was stopp'd in *England* because he had none and Cardinal *Scipio Rebiba*, Legate from *Julius* III, would have been so in *Flanders*, if the Pope had not given him Advice of the Rupture he was going to have with the Emperor and if upon this Advice he had not quitted the Marks of his *Legation*, in order to save himself in the Countrey of *Liege* In the beginning of the Civil Wars in *France*, in the Year 1563, the Prince of *Conde* and the other Heads of the Religionaries, had put *Havre de Grace* into the Hands of the Queen of *England*, as a Pledge for the Money she had lent them But King *Charles* IX, having granted a sham Peace to those of the reform'd Religion, the same Prince of *Conde*, to give a Proof of his Zeal for the King's Service, join'd his Troops to those of the Constable *Monmorancy*, and help'd to besiege the *Havre*. The Queen sent into *France Nicholas Throgmorton*, who had been Embassador there, and offer'd to restore the *Havre*, provided she were put in possession of *Calais*, according to the Treaty she had made with *Charles* There was no War between the two Crowns, but that did not hinder the Artillery from making it self heard before the *Havre*, and great Preparations were making in *England* to succour it so that Throgmorton apprehending he should not be safe without a Passport, took one from the French Embassador at *London* notwithstanding which the French secur'd him, and did not set him at liberty till after the Reduction of the Place Throgmorton was the Man of all *England* most capable of carrying on an Intrigue, and in the Apprehension that was had of his Ability, they who had arrested him believ'd they did not violate the *Law of Nations*, because, as he had no *Credentials*, or had not yet deliver'd them, his Quality was not known It seems to be what he was afraid of himself, since he was willing to take a Passport Tho' being so able a Man as he was, he ought to have known, that a *Paffport* from the Embassador could not protect him, because as the Embassador's Power does not extend so far, unless he have a special Authority for that Purpose, his *Paffport* can only serve as a simple Letter of Recommendation In the Year 1601 Cardinal *Doffat*, who negotiated the Affairs of *France* at *Rome*, while there was no Embassador there, was desir'd by the Pope to to give a *Paffport* to an Embassador from *Perfia*, who had a mind to take *France* in his way to *Spain* The Cardinal, writing to King *Henry* IV about it, speaks of it as of a thing indifferent, which he was unwilling to refuse the Pope and says he had promis'd him such a *Paffport as he could give* that is to say, which should be no further respected, than should be thought convenient for the King's Service It belongs only to Sovereigns to give *Paffports*, because they only can secure the Effect of them, to those to whom they are granted. They

They that represent them as Viceroys, and Governors of Provinces, cannot insure their Validity any farther than the Extent of their Government. The Viceroy of *Naples*'s *Passports* are respected at *Milan*, and those of the Governor of *Milan* are respected at *Naples*, as also those of the *Spanish* Embassador at *Venice* serve throughout all *Italy*, because these three Ministers have the Direction of the Affairs of those parts.

On the other side, he that will enjoy the Benefit of a *Passport*, must keep within the Bounds therein prescrib'd him. The Couriers who were dispatch'd, or receiv'd by the Plenipotentiaries at *Munster*, had their Rout prescrib'd them, out of which their *Passports* were of no use to them. In the Year 1588, Queen *Elizabeth*, being willing to hearken to some Overtures of Accommodation, with which she was amus'd while in *Spain* the most powerful Fleet was fitting out that had been heard speak of, sent into *Flanders* the Earl of *Derby*, the Lord *Cobham* and *James Crofts*, with *Dale* and *Rogers*, Counsellors, to treat with Count *d'Aremberg*, *Champagny*, *Maas* and *Garbier*, whom the Duke of *Parma* had nominated on his part. The *Passport* that had been granted to the *English* was limited, insomuch that they were not allow'd to enter the Places where the Queen and the States had their Garrisons, nay, he would not give them *Passports* to warrant their entring into the Towns that were under the King of *Spain*'s Obedience, so that they were forc'd to encamp under Tents between *Ostend* and *Oudenlourg*. There was at first some Dispute about Precedency, which oblig'd the Earl of *Derby* to go to the Duke or *Parma* at *Brussels*. He was still there when that formidable naval Power appear'd in the Channel, but when he was for going away he was stopp'd. He made a very great Oversight in not making himself secure, and the Queen was not at all satisfy'd therewith.

The Archbishop of *Mechlin*, the Duke of *Areschot*, and some other Deputies of the Provinces of *Flanders*, having in the Year 1633 made some Overture of a Peace or Truce at the *Hague*, and their Proposition having been sent to the particular Estates of the United Provinces, they thought they might go and divert themselves in the other Towns of *Holland*, while they waited for their Resolution. But the States General being advis'd thereof, sent them Word by their Register, That in very few Days they should know the Intention of the Provinces, in the mean time, they desir'd the Deputies to seek their Diversion at the *Hague*. The Duke reply'd, That since it was but a thing desir'd, it lay in their Breast to acquiesce to it or not. But the Register made answer, That the Estates Desire, who represent the Sovereign, was equal to a Command. He moreover added, *That it did not belong to the Deputies to enlarge the Bounds of their Passport*, which only mention'd their Journey from *Brussels* to the *Hague*, and did not permit them to ramble elsewhere. And in fact, one of their Collegues having left the *Hague*, under the Pretext of going to buy Horses in *North-Holland*, an Express was sent after him to warn him to come back, and to set out at sight of the Letter, because it would be a difficult matter to secure him the Benefit of his Passport, and that he would expose himself to the Inconveniencies, which are unavoidable to those that have none.

A Prince is not oblig'd to grant Passports to the Ministers of another Prince with whom he is at War, or whose Intentions he has a Jealousy of, since sometimes they are refus'd even to Friends and indifferent Persons. King *Francis* I had no reason to be satisfy'd with the Emperor *Charles* V, who had not us'd him very well since the Battel of *Pavia*, so that he had no great Inclination to be civil to him. After that *Lewis* King of *Hungary* was kill'd by the *Turks*, at the Battel of *Mohats*, the Estates of the Empire, who were apprehensive of an Invasion from the Infidels, and who were of Opinion the Emperor's Presence might be necessary in *Germany*, desir'd a Passport of the King of *France*, for the Deputies they intended to send to him. The King who could not in point of Justice, nor without Incivility, refuse such a thing to Princes with whom he had no Quarrel, and who at the same time was willing to perplex the Emperor, granted them a *Passport*, but at the same time he made it useless to them, by limiting it to four Months, both for the Journey and Return. It would take the Deputies some time to prepare their Equipage, and they could not proceed therein as if they were riding post, so that they resolv'd to have no Obligation to the King, and contented themselves with representing to *Charles* the Necessity of his Presence, by Letters.

Pope *Pius* IV, when he invited all the Christian Princes to send their Deputies to the Council of *Trent*, was willing to do the same Honour to the Czar, or Great Duke of *Moscovy*. He had a mind to send thither *John Canobio* in the Quality of Nuncio, but *Sigismund Augustus*, King of *Poland*, notwithstanding he was a very Catholick Prince, would not allow of it. He told *Canobio*, that having laid the Matter before the Council of *Lithuania*, he had found it unanimously against it. That some of the Members thereof had offer'd one Reason, and others, another, but that they were all agreed that it was contrary to the Practice of all Antiquity, *to suffer the Embassadors of foreign Princes, even those of the Emperor, to pass through Lithuania to Moscovy during a War*. He also wrote about it to the Pope, and moreover told him, That even without that Difficulty, there was no likelihood that the Nuncio's Journey would be any way successful with such seditious People, who were Enemies to the *Latin* Church, and that the Countrey, which was either Desert, or peopled with *Barbarians*, would have expos'd the Person of the Nuncio to very great Inconveniencies and inevitable Dangers, which made him hope, that the Pope would not take ill *the Refusal he had made*, *to grant a Passport to Canobio*.

John Zapoli, King of *Hungary*, not being able to come to an Agreement with *Ferdinand* of *Austria*, who had marry'd the Sister of *Lewis*, *John*'s Predecessor, and who, on that account, pretended a Right of Succession to the Crown, had a mind to send *Jerome Lasky* to the Princes of *Germany* to desire Succour from them, but *Ferdinand* would not grant him a Passport, so that *Lasky* not thinking it proper to hazard his Person, altho' well character'd, remain'd in *Hungary*.

After

After the seventy Articles were sign'd, on the 8th of *January* 1647, between the Plenipotentiaries of *Spain* and those of the United Provinces, *Anthony le Brun*, one of the *Spanish* Plenipotentiaries, set out from *Munster* the very next Day, to carry the News thereof to *Brussels*. While he was there, he sent to the States to desire a *Passport* to go to the *Hague*. His Design was to observe, and to thwart *Servien*'s Negotiations, who was there contriving a Treaty of Guarantie, but *Servien* oppos'd the Dispatch of the *Passport*, and so order'd Matters that the States, after they had adv's'd with the Prince of *Orange*, refus'd to grant him one. This *Spanish* Minister, seeing he was deny'd, said, *That the Passport he had as Plenipotentiary from* Spain, *impower'd him also to go into* Holland, and indeed he went thither w thout Molestation. But the Estates being inform'd thereof, took it very ill, and oblig d him to return back. The *Passport* he had as Plenipotentiary could be of no use to him but only on his Journey, and at the Place of the Congress, and did not warrant his Proceeding into the Heart of the Country, there to carry on Intrigues and Cabals, contrary to the Intention of the States. This is what they made the Duke *d'Arescot* sensible of, and the other Deputies whom I above mention'd.

During the Negotiations of *Munster*, Count *Borgia*, Governor of the City of *Antwerp*, arrested there a Gentleman, who was the Minister of a Prince of *Germany*, who having taken at *Paris* a *Passport* for *Munster*, thought he was sufficiently authoriz'd thereby to pass into *Holland*. He us'd him civilly, and suffer'd him to see his Friends in the City, but he oblig'd him to procure another *Passport* from the Arch-Duke *France* having offer'd, and got approv'd, its Mediation for the Peace between the two Northern Crowns, and the two Kings having agreed to the Choice she had made of *M de la Tuillerie*, this last beginning to work on the Settlement of the Preliminaries, met at first with a very great Difficulty concerning the *Passports*. The Ministers of *Denmark* said, that their Commissioners would not be safe with the simple *Passports* of the *Swedes*, because there was no relying on their Word, their Signing, nor their Seal, unless the French Embassador would be Guarantie for the same, in the Name of the King his Master. *La Tuillerie* said, He would not by any means engage the Name and Authority of his King, without Orders, and withal, that he could not make this Proposition to the *Swedes*, without offending them irreconcileably, and without breaking off the Negotiation before it was begun. It was believing them to be capable of violating the *Law of Nations* and the publick Faith. Besides, *Sweden*, by putting her *Passports* into the Hands of the Mediator, in Order to their Transmission to *Denmark*, made the King of *France* Guarantie for the Safety the *Danes* were to find. I should be apt to say, that none but the Minister of King *Ferdinand the Catholick* was capable of offering so outragious a Violence to the *Law of Nations* as the great Captain offer'd to *Cæsar Borgia*, whom he caus'd to be arrested, notwithstanding the *Safe-Conduct* he had given him, if he had not had before him the Example of *Charles* the last Duke of *Burgundy*. This Prince had, with *Lewis* XI King of *France*, concerted the Death of the Constable *St Pol*, and these two Princes had mutually promis'd each the other, by a formal Treaty, that whichsoever of them should cause him to be seiz'd, should put him to Death, or else should deliver him up to the other, to be dispos'd of as he should think fit. After this Treaty the Duke sent him a *Safe-Conduct*, under the Security of which the Constable went to him in the *Low Countries*, but he caus'd him to be taken into Custody before he arriv'd at Court, and put him into the Hands of *Lewis*, who he knew would have no Compassion of this poor Wretch. The World is not less malicious at this present time, than it was in those Days, but however there are very few now that would be so, after that impudent manner. It is temerarious, and even a kind of Sacrilege, to carry our profane Thoughts into the Sanctuary of God's Secrets. And yet I think I may say, without sinning against the Laws of Christianity, and of Charity, that the continual Disgraces, which never forsook the Duke of *Burgundy* since that time, till he perish'd by the Perfidy of Count *Campobasso*, were a just Retribution for his own. It is overthrowing the very Principles of Honesty and of Civil Society, to fail in what has been solemnly promis'd in Writing, and to the publick Faith that is concern'd therein.

The Expedition of *Passports* not belonging to the Embassador, it would be useless to make here a Digression, to describe the Form they ought to have, and to represent with what Accuracy and Exactness the Titles and Qualities of those for whom the *Passports* are design'd, should be express'd. It is sufficient to have here inserted a Model, which may serve the Chancerres for a Precedent on all Occasions, *mutatis mutandis*.

CHAP. XVIII.

Of the Reception and Entry of the Embassador.

THE Civilities and Ceremonies that are done to Embassadors, making one of the most essential parts of the Embassy, I shall bestow upon them the three or four following Chapters, wherein I shall endeavour to lay down all that can be desir'd from him, who being depriv'd of the necessary assistance of Books, and the benefit of Conversation, can produce nothing but what must be very imperfect in all its parts.

" *Philip de Commines* says, that although
" Embassadors come from Princes that are
" either

" either secret or declar'd Enemies, or that
" are suspected Friends, one may have a dis-
" trust of them, but that must not hinder
" the Prince they are sent to, from receiving
" and treating them well, from sending to
" meet them, and lodging them, indeed he
" may place near them Men of noted wisdom
" to observe them In the Year 1627, the
States of the United Provinces sent into *Poland* Roch *Vanden Honart*, Counsellor in the
Great Council of *Holland* and *Zeeland*, *Andreas Bicker*, Burgermaster of the City of *Amsterdam*, and *Simon de Beaumont*, Penfionary of
the City of *Middleburg*, as Mediators between
the two Kings of *Poland* and *Sweden* King
Gustavus Adolphus shew'd them all the Civilities they could defire, but in *Poland* they receiv'd none at all When they came to *Warsaw*, no body went out to meet them, and
after they were set down at the House they
had hir'd, they were Complimented but only
in the Mareschal of the Kingdom's name, who,
as they were told, would acquaint them with
the hour defign'd for their Audience Three
days after, some refreshments of Meat, Poul-
try, Wine and Beer were sent them by the
King, who did not otherwise do them the least
Civility The Gentleman who came to them
from the Mareschal, told them amongst other
things, that in *Poland* they were not accustom'd
to make Entries to Embassadors He did not
say right, since there are several Examples of
very solemn and magnificent Entries which have
been made there, not only to the Count *de
Scafgots*, Embassador from the Emperor, and
to *Nassokin*, Embassador from the *Czar* of *Moscovy*, but also to the Ministers of *Brandenburg*
and of *Courland*, even when the Elector and
the Duke were Vassals of the Crown of *Poland* On the 10th of *October*, 1670, Mr *John
de Witt*, Embassador from the said United Provinces, made his Entry at *Warsaw*, and had
Civility shewn him The *Referendary* of the
Kingdom went to meet him in one of the
King's Coaches, follow'd by several other
Coches The Ministers of *Brandenburg* were
received by one of the General Officers, and
by the *Referendary* of *Lithuania*, who went to
meet them with a numerous Cortege They
infisted upon having *Palatins*, or at least *Ca-
stellans* come to meet them, but that was not
agreed to The Envoys of *Courland* were receiv'd by *Prasmonsky*, Secretary of the Crown,
in the King's Coach

The Civilities that are done to Embassadors
at their Reception, and at their Entry, are Regulated now almost in all Courts, but it is not
long since they were so Neither is it long
since proper Officers have been appointed to
Regulate the same, or to see the Regulations
Princes have made therein, executed The
Court of *Rome*, which is made up of Ceremonies, has had a Master of the Ceremonies for
several Ages It is but since the Year 1585
that there is a great Master of the Ceremonies
in *France*, and even he does not meddle with
what relates to Embassadors, no more than
the Master of the Ceremonies, unless it be in
the absence of the Introductors, or in some
very solemn and extraordinary Ceremony,
where he acts in concert with them The Introductors of Embassadors and foreign Princes, as by Title of Office, are still more modern At the Entry of Queen *Elizabeth* of
Austria, Wife to *Charles* IX into *Paris*, after
her Coronation on the 29th of *March*, 1571,
(where it is observ'd that the Nuncio and the
Embassadors of *Spain*, *Scotland*, and of *Venice*
were present) *the Sieur Jerome Gondy, who was
appointed to receive them*, went immediately before them, and they were Conducted, viz
the Nuncio, by the Abbot of *Vendofme*, the
Spanish Embassador by *M d'Espina*, the Embassador from *Scotland* by the Count *de Chaun*,
and the *Venetian* by *M de Meillant*, Knight of
the King's Order At the Entry of the same
Queen into *Masieres*, on the 26th of *November*,
1570, the same Embassadors were Conducted
and accompany'd by four of the eldest Counsellors of State, viz by *Messieurs de Mortil-
lers, de Travanes, de Lansac*, and *de Limoges*,
without any mention made of an Introductor
In the whole course of *Walsingham*'s Embassy,
no mention is made of an Introductor When
He, and *Norris* his Predecessor went to Audience on the 15th of *January*, 1571 no body
Conducted them At their arrival at the Castle of *Madrid*, they found there *M de Lansac*,
who entertain'd them, and kept them Company at their Dinner After that was over, another Nobleman came and entertain'd them,
and after that *Jero Gondy* came and acquainted them that the King was ready to give
them Audience, and had them into a Room,
where the King appear'd soon after *Lansac*
conducted them to them to the Audience of
the Queen Mother

At this day there are in *France* two Introductors, who serve half Yearly, and have for
Coadjutor or Lieutenant, an Officer that is
perpetual, and who executes his Function in
all the Civilities that are done to Embassadors,
on any occasion whatever There is likewise
an Introductor in *Spain*, but in most of the
other Courts there is none, and this Office is
confounded with that of Master of the Ceremonies As for Example, in those of *Stockholm, Copenhagen, Turin*, &c It is the *Chiaoux
Bachi*, or the Captain of the *Chiaoux* who discharges this Office at *Constantinople*, and *Moscovy* has her *Pristaves*, as *Persia* has her *Mihe-
manders*, who notwithstanding are only Commiffion'd for that single Action to which the
Sovereign appoints them

There is neither Master of the Ceremonies,
nor Introductor at *Vienna*, in *Poland*, in *Portugal*, nor even at *Venice*, yet nevertheless
there is no State where the Ceremonial is better regulated than in that Republick In the
United Provinces there is none neither, tho'
the Ceremonies are not by a great deal so well
regulated there, as at *Venice*, or in the other
Courts of *Europe*

I say that it is but of late that these Civilities are regulated, and it is for this Reason that
no notice is taken thereof in the History of
France It is but since the Reign of the deceafed King, that the Embassadors that arrive in
England, are no longer receiv'd nor defray'd
at their landing They are not now very nice
in the matter In *Spain*, tho' formerly no People exceeded them therein In the Month of
May, 1424, *Alfonso* the Magnanimous King of
Arragon, sent to *John* King of *Castile*, the Archbishop

The EMBASSADOR and his FUNCTIONS 129

bishop of *Tarragona*, and *Berenger Biraaxi*, Justice of *Arragon* These Embassadors being arriv'd at *St Clements*, a days Journey from *Villareal*, where the Court was, gave notice thereof to the King by their Gentlemen of the Horse *Don Alvaro de Luna*, who at that time govern'd the King of *Castile*, sent them word that they might remain where they were, till such time as they were inform'd where the King, who was going to leave *Villareal*, could give them Audience They stay'd there about a fortnight, and from thence went to the King, who was at *Ocagna* They were receiv'd without the Town by the *Constable*, by the *Admiral*, by the *Adelantado* of *Castile*, and by *Garci Alvarez*, Lord of *Oropeza* who were accompanied by several other *Noblemen* In the Year 1453, the same King of *Arragon* sent to the King of *Castile*, *Ferrier de la Nuça* Justice of *Arragon*, who being come within half a League of *Tordesillas*, where the Court was, was there receiv'd by Don *Diego Hurtade* de Mendoça, *Prior of St John's*, by the *Adelantado Parafan de Ribera*, by the *Son of the Master of the Order of* Alcantara, and by all the other Lords who had repair'd to Court on account of this Ceremony, except *Ruy Dias* the King's high Steward, who remain'd near his Person Henry King of *Castile*, sent in the Year 1456, *Lewis Gonçales* of *Asienca*, Dean of *Corduba*, and *Henry de Figueredo*, his Embassadors Extraordinary to the same *Alfonso*, King of *Arragon* and *Naples* These Gentlemen being come to *Aversa*, *Alfonso* sent out to meet them Marinus of *Marsan*, *Prince of* Rosano, *and Duke of* Sesa, *Felix Ursino Prince of Salerno*, Don *Inniguo de Guavarra*, Great *Seneschal*, Don *Diego Davalos* High *Chamberlain*, and several other Chief Noblemen of the Court, together with his Kings at Arms in their Ceremonial Apparel He receiv'd them in the new Castle of *Naples*, being accompany'd by the Duke of *Calabria*, his natural Son, who succeeded him since in the Kingdom of *Naples*, by Don *Arnaldus Rogerius de Pallas*, Patriarch of *Alexandria*, and by all the Embassadors of foreign Princes The Emperor *Maximilian* I went himself a League out of the Town of *Brugas*, to meet the Cardinal of *York*, Embassado from *Henry VIII* King of *England*

France it self has not always been so reserv'd as she is at present King *Henry II* being inform'd that the Duke of *Alva* (who came as Proxy from *Philip II* to Marry Madam *Elizabeth* his Daughter) drew near *Paris*, sent to meet him, *by the Prince of* Condé, *the Cardinals of* Loriain *and* Guise, *the Duke of* Lorrain, *the Duke* de Nemours, *Messieurs* de Guise *and* d'Aumale, *the Duke of* Bouillon, *Monsieur* de Nevers, *the Prince of* Ferrara, *and several other Noblemen, who had a Train of one hundred and fifty Pages, besides their other Domesticks* This Entry was made in the Month of *June*, 1559, no mention is made therein of Introductors, no more than at the Reception that was giv en in the Year 1564, to the Lord *Hudson*, Embassador Extraordinary from *England*, to meet whom, the King sent *the Duke* de Neveis, M de Bossy *Master of the Horse, the Count* de *Charny, and several other Lords and Gentlemen* At the Entry of Queen *Elizabeth* of *Austria*, whom I lately mention'd, she was accompany'd by the Elector of *Triers*, *the Bishop of* Strasburg, *the Marquis of* Baden, *and the Count* de Zolern Embassadors from the Emperor *Maximilian* II the Queen's Father No body was sent to meet them, because all the Princes went to meet the Queen, but as they march'd towards the Town, the Dukes of *Anjou*, and of *Alançon* the King's Brothers, took the Elector between them, the Bishop went between the Dukes of *Lorrain* and *Montpensier*, the Marquis between the Prince *Daufin* and *Monsieur d'Aumale*, and the Count between the Duke of *Guise*, and the Mareschal *de Montmorancy* In the Year 1598, not only several Princes and Noblemen, but also the Officers of the Town-House of *Paris*, went out to meet the Embassadors from *Spain*, who came to see the Treaty of *Vervins* sworn to They receiv'd Civilities, and were defray'd as soon as they enter'd the Kingdom, to the very day that *Henry* sworc to the execution of the Treaty After that, the Treating part ceas'd in reference to the Duke *d'Areschot*, the Admirant of *Arragon*, the Count *d'Aremberg*, and Don *Lewis de Velasco*, because as they remain'd as Hostages till the Restitution of the Places in *Picardy* and *Britan*, which were mention'd in the Treaty, was perform'd, their Quality of Embassador ceas'd The King sent them back on their Parole Chancelor *de Chiverny* says in his *Memoirs*, that the King acted thus by the Counsel of M *de Villeroy*, who had a mind thereby to acknowledge the Obligations he had to the King of *Spain*, and that ever since it has been brought into a Custom to treat Embassadors, which has been a heavy burthen on the Finances This is not very favourable to *Villeroy*, and I cannot tell whether on this occasion, we ought not to question *Chiverny*'s sincerity, since the Ceremonial of *France* says positively, that these Embassadors were not defray'd till the day of their arrival at *Paris* In the Year 1612 the Duke *de Mayenne* was sent into *Spain*, and the Duke of *Pastrana* came to *France* on account of the double Marriage which was solemnniz'd some Years after The Duke of *Pastrana* was not only receiv'd with great Civilities at his approach to *Paris*, but extraordinary Honours were done him as soon as he enter'd the Kingdom He came to *Bayonne* on the 16th of *July*, so late, that he was oblig'd to make his Entry by the light of Torches Four of the Chief Inhabitants of the Town went to meet him, as far as *St John de Luz* He was receiv'd with Ceremony, and entertain'd with all his Retinue, which consisted of above three hundred Persons, besides a great throng of Horses, Mules and Baggage All the Towns of *Guyenne* and *Poitou* follow'd this Example, 'till he came to *Orleans*, where the Mareschal *de la Chastre* Governor of the Town went out to meet him, with a Troop of two hundred Gentlemen The Marquis *de Ca nvres*, Governor of the Isle of *France*, had Orders to go and receive him at *Estampes*, but the Embassador made such long Stages, that he met him at *Linars*, from whence he conducted him to *Bourg la Reine*, and there left him to go and give the King an account thereof The next day the Marquis *d'Ancre*, the Queen's Chief Minister, went to Compliment him from the King The Dukes of *Nevers* and *de Piney*,

L l   attended

attended by four or five hundred Lords and Gentlemen, met him without the Suburbs of St *James*, on Post Horses. The Embassador and the two Dukes being met, alighted at the same time, and after their mutual Complements, the Embassador made use of the Horse the King had sent him. *Bonoeil* Introducter of the Embassadors having caus'd the *Spanish* and *French* Noblemen to mingle in their march, put himself immediately before the Embassador in ordinary of *Spain*, who had on his left the Duke *de Piney*, and was follow'd by the Duke *de Pastrana*, who was conducted by the Duke *de Nevers*. He was Lodg'd at the *Hotel de St. Paul*, where *M. de Bellegarde*, Master of the Horse came to him from the King, to give him to understand how acceptable his arrival was.

On the other side, the Duke of *Mayenne* had no sooner pass'd the River of *Bidassoa*, than he found the *Alcade* of the Town of St *Sevestian* (which is about three Leagues off of it) accompany'd by the King's Procurator, who brought him the Inquisition's Passport for himself, and his Retinue. The Officers of the Garrison and the Magistrate receiv'd him about a quarter of a League from the Town, where they made him an Entry, he had moreover the diversion of the Bull-fight, and Bonfires were made in all the Towns through which he pass'd. He found at *V. loria* some of the Officers of the King's Houshold, which were sent to meet him to prepare things for his more easy travelling, and more convenient supply of Provisions. At *Lerma* he was magnificently entertain'd by the Duke of that place. *M. de Vancelas*, the *French* Embassador in ordinary came to meet him as far as *Aranda del Duero*, and a Feaver having oblig'd the Duke to remain some days at *Torres de Laguna*, the King sent thither to him his Physicians and Apothecaries. While he was at the Castle of *Almeda*, where he made some stay, as well to recover his health, as to make preparation for his Entry, Two of Count *de Monsoreau*'s Footmen being got into a Plough'd field, the *Spaniard* to whom it belong'd, struck one of them with his stick, by whom he was kill'd upon the place. This Murther had like to have caus'd all the neighbouring Villages to rise, till in *Alcade* of *Madrid* (who gave an account thereof,) found that the *Spaniard* had been kill'd by two *French* Footmen. The Duke *de Mayenne* was for having them pursu'd, but the *Alcade* told him, the King had expresly forbid any prosecution to be made against the *French*. During the stay he made at *Almeda*, the King sent the Marquiss *d'Este* to him, to keep him Company, and attend him till the day of his Entry. It was made on the 17th of *July*, and he was met near *Madrid* by the Duke of *Alva*, whom the King had sent for that purpose, with the major part of the *Grandees* of the Court, and a great number of the other Nobility. These two Dukes at their meeting saluted one another, and the Duke of *Alva* made his Complement without dismounting. After which, having plac'd himself on the Embassador's left hand, he caus'd all the Noblemen of both Nations to march before them, and conducted him to the Palace of *Spinola*, which had been fitted up for him. Of all the *Spanish* Lords, none

but the Duke of *Alva* alighted off his Horse in the Court, and accompany'd the Embassador to his Apartment. This being done, he mounted his Horse again, and dismiss'd the Cavalcade. *The King forbid all his Justices to enter into the Houses where the French were lodg'd, for any Crime whatsoever*. The two days following were employ'd in receiving the Visits of the Nuncio, and other Foreign Ministers, is also those of the Nobility of the Court, and amongst the rest, that of the Archbishop Cardinal of *Toledo*, who does this Honour to none but the King.

These Extraordinary Occasions do not make a Rule, particularly in *Spain*, where they are not very apt to change the old Customs which have been establish'd since the Reign of *Charles V*. The Marquis *de Rambouillet* being nominated to the Embassy Extraordinary of *Spain*, towards the end of the Year 1626, there happen'd a considerable difficulty about his Reception. The Count *de Gondemar*, at his return from his Embassy in *England*, pass'd through *France*, and having *Letters of Credence* for the King, he was consider'd as in Embassador Extraordinary), and was receiv'd by a Mareschal of *France*. For which Reason it was pretended that the Marquiss *de Rambouillet* ought also to be receiv'd by a *Grandee* of *Spain*, or at least by some Nobleman of a Quality approaching to that. *Du Fargis*, who was Embassador in Ordinary at *Madrid*, urg'd it very much, but the Council oppos'd this pretension, and would not suffer the ancient usage to be chang'd or alter'd. It is said, that *it was the Custom to have the Nuncio and the Embassadors of the Emperor and of the King of France receiv'd by one of the Stewards of the King's Houshold* and that they would keep up to that practice. And accordingly, the Marquiss *de Formisan*, one of the Stewards of the King of *Spain*'s Houshold receiv'd the Embassador at his Entry, and conducted him to his Audience. The Civility that was shewn to Count *Gondemar* in *France*, might indeed invite but it could not oblige the *Spaniards* to follow that Example.

Now as a Court does not willingly change its Practice, so an Embassador ought not to suffer any Prejudice to be done to his Prince, and to the Ministers that may succeed him in his Employ, by any Alteration whatever, in the Honours that have been done to his Predecessors. *D'Argenson*, Master of the Requests, and Embassador of *France*, at his Arrival at *Venice* had an Occurrence, where his Address sav'd him from the Snare that had been laid for him in the beginning of his Embassy. The *Venetians* hoping to take advantage of him, and after his Example, of all the other *French* Embassadors, made him a Proposition which was altogether *Venetian*. The Rain, Hail, and whatever could render the Weather extremely bad, annoy'd the Preparations that had been made for his Entry, whereupon the *Senate* signify'd to him, that if he approv'd of it, they would not give him the trouble of going to the Convent of the Holy Ghost, which is three Miles from the City of *Venice*, and that he should be receiv'd in the Abby of St *George*. But *d'Argenson* made answer, that it should never be reproach'd to him, that he had impair'd the Rights and Honours of the Embassy. That since his

Predecessors had always been met at the Abby of the Holy Ghost, he was ready to go as far as *Chiozza*, if the Senate was willing to receive him there, without regarding either the Rain or Hail. It is true, his Fault would not have been a Precedent for his Successors, and *d'Argenson* might have recorded, that that Change should not prejudice the Rights of the King and his Ministers, but the surest way is, not to suffer any Innovation. I shall relate by and by how the Republick of *Venice* causes Embassadors to be receiv'd.

In *France* an Embassador at his Arrival gives notice thereof to him of the Secretaries that has the Province of foreign Affairs, and who having acquainted the King therewith receives his Orders, to deliver them to the Introductor, who is a Half-yearly Officer and this concerts with the Embassador the Day and Ceremonies of his Reception. Most commonly it is perform'd at St *Denis*, at *Piquepuce*, at *Ruth*, at the *Red-House*, or in some other Place near *Paris*, or the Palace where the King then resides. There is to be seen between the Castle of *Vincennes* and St *Anthony's-Gate*, which is the finest Avenue belonging to the Town, the Model of a Triumphal Arch, which is to serve for this Ceremony, and which will discover to Strangers, that what the present King undertakes and executes, is beyond Comp'rison greater than any thing that is perceivable of ancient *Rome* in its Ruins, or is read of the Actions of its Heroes in her History. Sometimes the Princes, sometimes Dukes and Peers, and sometimes Mareschals of *France*, are employ'd to go and receive Embassadors, but with this Distinction, that the Princes never discharge this Function but to Nuncio's, or the Embassadors of crown'd Heads, and that but seldom neither. In the Year 1634, the Count *d'Alais*, who was a Prince, and the Count *de Brulon*, one of the Introductors, went to receive M. *Bolognetti* Bishop of *Ascoli*, the Pope's Nuncio, at the Village of *Vannes*, and conducted him to his Lodgings. The next Day the King sent M *de Soevre*, first Gentleman of his Bed-chamber, to visit him, and the Queen sent the first Steward of her Houshold.

In the Month of *November* of the same Year, the aforesaid Count *d'Alais*, and *Bautru* Introductor, went to meet *Julius Mazarine*, Nuncio Extraordinary from the Pope, at *Picquepuce*. The Nuncio in Ordinary, the Count *d'Alais*, the Introductor, the Archbishops of *Tours* and of *Arles*, and the Bishop of *Bologne*, went into the King's Coach with him. The next Day M *de Liancourt*, one of the first Gentlemen of the Bed-chamber, complemented him from the King, and the Count *d'Urval* in the Queen's Name. He was not lodg'd in the Month of *April* 1635, the same Counts *d'Alais* and *de Brulon*, went to meet Chancellor *Oxenstiern*, Legate Plenipotentiary from *Sweden* in *Germany*, at two Leagues Distance from *Compiegne*, where the Court then was and conducted him to a House fitted up with the finest Furniture the King had, where he was treated all the time he stay'd there. About a Month before that, *Monsieur Grotius*, Embassador in Ordinary from *Sweden*, being arriv'd, the Marshal *d'Estrée* and the Count *de Brulon*, went in the King's and Queen's Coaches to receive him at St *Denis*, and conducted him to his Lodgings. It was much about the same time that the Viscount *Scudamore*, Embassador in Ordinary from *England*, arriv'd in *France* and by reason the King was to go a Progress, in which the Embassadors were not to follow him, he took his Audience of the King before he made his Entry. The King was at *Monceaux*, and the Embassador being at *Meaux*, the Duke *de Chevreuse*, and *Berlise* Introductor, went to receive him, and conducted him to Audience. After this he would still make his Entry, wherefore the Mareschal *du St Luc* and *Berlise*, went and receiv'd him at St *Denis*, and conducted him to his Lodging. No other Honour was done the Year following to the Earl of *Leicester*, Embassador Extraordinary from *England*, whom the Mareschal *de Chastillon* and the Count *de Brulon* went to receive at St *Dennis*, and conducted to the House appointed for Embassadors Extraordinary, where he receiv'd the usual Presents, and was visited by M *de Souvré* from the King. The same Year the Mareschal *de Chastillon* and *Berlise*, went to St *Denis* to meet *Zavaski*, Embassador Extraordinary from *Poland*, and conducted him to the House of St *Chaumont*, which was fitted up with the King's Furniture, where he was treated by the Officers of the Court till his first Audience. This is what is usually practic'd in reference to Embassadors only those of crown'd Heads are conducted to Audience by a Prince. In the Month of *October* 1634, the Mareschal *de Chastillon* and *Berlise*, went with the King's and Queen's Coaches to St *Denis*, to meet *Aloysio Contarini*, who succeeded *Soranzo* in the *Venetian* Embassy, and conducted him to his Lodgings behind the *Minims*. In *January* 1638, the same Mareschal and Count *de Brulon*, went with the King and Queen's Coach, to receive *Angel Cornaro*, Embassador from *Venice*, at the Chapel. The same Honours are done to the Embassadors of the United Provinces, as well Ordinary as Extraordinary, with this Difference however, that these, that is to say, the Extraordinaries, are treated till the Day of their Audience, and the others not. In the Month of *June* 1634, the Mareschal *de Chastillon* and the Count *de Brulon* went with the King and Queen's Coaches to St *Denis*, to meet the *Sieurs Pau* and *Knuit*, Embassadors Extraordinary from the States, and conducted them to the House appointed for the Extraordinaries, where they receiv'd the usual Presents. Some Years after, *viz.* in the Year 1637, *William de Lire* of *Osterwic*, Embassador in Ordinary from the same States, was receiv'd by the Mareschal *de la Force* at St *Denis* and the same Method has been observ'd, not only in reference to crown'd Heads, and those two powerful Republicks, but also in reference to the Embassadors of the Princes of *Italy*, *Savoy*, *Florence* and *Mantua*. In the Year 1638, in the Month of *February*, the Mareschal *de la Force* and the Count *de Brulon*, went to meet the *Sieur Agnelli*, Bishop of *Casal*, Embassador Extraordinary from *Mantua*, at *Piquepuce*, and conducted him to his Lodgings but he was neither lodg'd nor treated at the King's Charge. The Duke of *Savoy* pretends to something more than the other Princes of *Italy*, since he has taken the Quality of King of *Cyprus*, I speak of him elsewhere,

where, and as for the Great Duke of *Tuscany*, he has so well establish'd himself since the two Marriages of *Henry* II, and *Henry* IV, into that House, and its other great Alliances elsewhere, that he has much to do to yield to *Savoy* and his Embassadors are receiv'd by Mareschals of *France*, as those of the first Powers of *Europe*. In the Year 1643, M *Coisi* being come to the Court of *France*, to Complement it on the Death of King *Lewis* XIII, the Mareschal *de Bassompierre* went to receive him at *Piquepuce*, and the Mareschal *de Grammont* conducted him to Audience.

The same Honours are done to those of the Great Master of *Malta*, of which we have an Example in the *Bailly de Fourbin*, Great Cross, whom the Mareschal *de St Luc*, and the *Sieur de Berlise*, went to receive on the 30th of *January* 1639, at *Piquepuce*, with the King's and Queen's Coaches, and with a Cortege of above threescore other Coaches with six Horses, tho' he was at the same time the King's Subject and Officer, *viz.* Lieutenant General of his Galleys. There is some distinction shewn in reference to the Ministers of the Republick of *Genoa*. In the Month of *November*, 1637, the *Sieur Sauli*, then Embassador Extraordinary was receiv'd at *P quepuce*, not by a Mareschal of *France*, or any other Officer of the Crown, but by M *de Noailles*, who in his return from his Embassy at *Rome*, had receiv'd great Civilities at *Genoa*. The King also sent to visit him the next day, not by one of the first Gentlemen of his Bed-Chamber, but by the Marquiss *de Fourilles*, Great Harbinger, he was neither lodg'd nor defray'd. The Embassadors, whom all the *Cantons* send into *France* on the occasion of renewing their Alliance, are receiv'd at their entrance into the Kingdom, Honours and Civilities are done them in all the Towns through which they pass, and at their arrival in *Paris*, they receive more than are shewn to the Embassadors of crown'd Heads. But when any of the particular *Cantons* send thither, no more Honour is done them, than what is done to the Ministers of the *Second Order*. No Reception at all is made them, and they are accompany'd to their Audience only by the Introductor and M *de Villegeners*. In the Month of *March* 1634, *Reding* and *Znrloben*, Embassadors from the *Catholick Swiss Cantons*, arriv'd in *France*, but no other Honours were done them, except that of sending the King's Coaches for them, to conduct them to their Audience. In the Month of *December* of the same Year, the Embassadors of the three *Protestant Cantons*, *Zurich*, *Bern* and *Schafhouse*, were treated after the same manner I take notice elsewhere, that in those Times the same Honours were done to Envoys

Notwithstanding the Honours that are done to the Embassadors of the *Cantons*, yet there is a Distinction made between them, and those of crown'd Heads, and other Sovereigns. They are receiv'd neither by an Introductor, nor by a Prince, nor a Mareschal of *France*. The Mareschal *d'Aumont* goes to meet them, not as an Officer of the Crown, but as Governor of the City of *Paris* and the Lord Mayor and the Sheriffs receive them at fifty Paces from the Gate, to give them to understand that it is the Town, and not the King, that does them this Civility. *Henry* III, who took great delight in Ceremonies, was the first who on the 23th of *November* 1582, sent the Lord Mayor and the Sheriffs to meet the Deputies of the *Cantons*, and who caus'd them to be conducted directly to the Town-House, where they receiv'd every Day Presents of Pyes, Hipocras and of Torches. In those Days they had no other Quality given them than that of Deputies and to speak the truth, they are treated at this time as such. To make this out, I shall here give an Extract of what pass'd in the Embassy they sent into *France* in the Year 1663. On the 2d and 3d of *November* they arriv'd at *Charenton*, where Lodgings were prepar'd for them. On the 4th the Mareschal *d'Aumont* and *Berlise*, Introductor of the Embassadors, visited them from the King. On the 5th the Chancellor sent to Complement them, and the Judge or the Houshold went and settled the Rates of Provisions, because the Inhabitants over-sold them. The 7th the Embassadors signify'd, that they expected to cover themselves before the King, to be treated with the Title of Excellency, and that the Place of Honour should be yielded to them in the Visits they should make to the Princes and Ministers, but nothing of all this was granted them. On the 9th the King gave them a Dinner at *Vincennes*, where *de Barde*, who had made the Treaty, and *Sirex*, Counsellor of State, kept them Company, mounted near Horses with them after Dinner, and conducted them as far as the Entrance into the Suburbs of St *Anthony*, where they met the Mareschal *d'Aumont* an M *Josin* the Lord Mayor, who took the first Embassador between them as *Sil d'lia mie is* and the first Sheriff took the Second, and so on, a Nobleman and an Officer of the Town-House took the others They were conducted in this manner to St *Martin's-Street*, where Lodgings were provided for them. On the 10th the Lord Mayor and the Sheriffs sent to Complement them, and made them the Present of Wine, Hipocras, Pyes and Hams. On the same Day the Chancellor sent to invite them to Dinner for the next Day and notwithstanding the Embassadors had not as yet seen the King, it did not hinder them from sending four Deputies of their Body, to Complement the Chancellor, but as he happen'd to be ill of an *Erysipelas* in his Leg, they did not see him. On the 11th the Chancellor sent *Girauls*, with thirty Coaches, to bring them to his House, where Mrs *de Coaslin* and *de Rouisfort* receiv'd them at the top of the Steps, within the House, shook them all by the Hand, and took them into a Room till Dinner was serv'd up. At the upper End of the Table was an arm'd Chair for the Chancellor. The first Embassador plac'd himself on the Right hand, and the others in their Ranks below him, the Chancellor's Covert was taken away, and the Marquisses *de Coaslin* and *ae Rochefort* took his Place. Those of the Embassador's Retinue were dispos'd of in two other large Rooms, at two Tables with fifty Coverts each, which were serv'd at the same time. Each Embassador had behind him a Servant of the Town-House to attend him. The Marquis *de Coaslin* began all the Healths, *viz.* the *King's, the Queen Mother's, the Queen's, the Dauphin's, Monsieur's, that of M le Prince, and M le Duke, de*

Pr nce

The EMBASSADOR and his FUNCTIONS. 133

Prince of *Conty's*, the Cantons, the *Chancellor's*, the *Embassadors*, *Madam* de *Longueville's*, and the *Count* de *Soisson's* All these Healths were drank standing and bare Headed, the Trumpets sounding, and the Kettledrums and Drums beating Dinner being over, the Embassadors were led again into the Room where they had rested themselves at their Arrival, here it was that the Count *de Harcourt* came to them and conducted them to the King's Audience He saluted them all after the manner of their Countrey, but in going out, he took the Hand of them The Embassadors were all uncover'd while they spoke to the King, who himself was cover'd They were afterwards conducted to the *two Queens*, and to *Monsieur*, who was likewise cover'd, tho' the Embassadors remain'd bare headed *M le Prince*, and the Duke of *Enguien* were uncover'd, and conducted them to their Chamber door, both taking the Hand of them On the 12th, the Count *de Soissons* sent five and twenty Coaches to them, and gave them a Dinner, as being Colonel General of the *Suisse*, taking the Hand of them, as did also *M de Tourenne*, who likewise gave them a Dinner on the 13th The 14th they came about nine of the clock in the Morning, in hir'd Coaches, to the Chancellor's House, to enter into Conference with the King's Commissioners In the Gallery there was a large Table, at the upper end whereof, was a Chair for the King on the right hand were Chairs for the Commissioners, and on the left were nine and thirty for the Embassadors About half an hour after nine, *Mr de Villeroy* having taken the first Place in the Chancellor's absence, *Mrs de Brienne*, *le Tellier*, *L onne*, *Colbert*, and *la Barde* seated themselves after him They got up, and uncover'd themselves, without stirring out of their places, when they saw the Embassadors enter, who plac'd themselves on the other side of the Table But because they that were at the lower end, could not well hear what was said in the Conference, they remov'd their Chairs within a narrower Circle, so that that of the last Embassador touch'd almost that of *M de la Barde* This Conference, which was not long, being ended, the Embassadors withdrew in the same manner as they had enter'd, the Commissioners standing up as before, and uncover'd That day the *Mareschal de Grammont* gave them a Dinner, and the day following they had another Conference at the Chancellor's The 17th they held the last, where every thing was regulated and sign'd On the 18th the Treaty was sworn to, the 19th the King sent a Chain, and a Gold Medal to each Embassador, and twelve hundred Livres to defray their Journey The same day the Lord Mayor gave them a Dinner in the Town House, and on the 20th they Din'd once more at the King's expence at *Vincennes* The following Days they were entertain'd again On the 24th they made a Visit to the Chancellor, who receiv'd them in his Chamber, they spoke to him uncover'd, he being so likewise At their going away, he accompany'd them no farther than to the inside of the door of his Anti-chamber, always taking the Hand of them They employ'd some few days more in visiting the King's Commissioners, who all took the place of Honour in their own Houses of the Embassadors, after which, they set out one after the other They were not visited by any one of the Ministers

It is much after the manner I have above related, that these Civilities have been regulated in *France*, where formerly they were as excessive as any where else History observes, that in the Year 1457, *Ladislas* King of *Poland*, *Hungary* and *Bohemia*, sent into *France* a solemn Embassy, compos'd of several Noblemen of his three kingdoms, to desire *Magdalen* the Daughter of *Charles* VII in Marriage The Court being then at *Tours*, the King sent to meet the Embassadors at a Leagues distance from the Town, by the Duke of *Orleans*, Messieurs *d'Angoulesme*, *du Maine*, *de Foix*, *de Vendosme*, *de la March*, the Chancellor of France, and several other Noblemen The Marriage came to nothing, because on the same day that the Contract was to be sign'd, news was brought of the Death of *Ladislas* This oblig'd the Embassadors to depart from Court, and take the Road to *Germany*, yet nevertheless Entries were made them in all the Towns they pass'd through, and particularly at *Paris* They were receiv'd without the Town by the Count d'Eu, *Prince of the Blood*, by the *Arch-Bishop of Narbonne*, by the *Bishops of* Langres, Paris, Noyon, Rhodes, Meaux, Belier, *and of* St Brieu, *by the Count* d'Armagnac, *the Lord Mayor of Paris*, *the first President of the Parliament*, *attended by several Counsellors and other Officers*, *by the Chamber of Accounts*, *by the Superviors of the Monnoye*, *by the Electors or Assessors*, *and by the Sheriffs of the City* The Rector and the whole University in a Body went to meet them as far as the Convent of the Dominicans, near St *James's* Gate

These troublesome Entries are no longer in use, and if in that which was made for the Embassadors of *Poland*, in the Year 1645, there was any thing extraordinary, it was more owing to the Honour they did themselves, than to the Court, which did them no other, besides that of sending the Duke *d'Elbeuf*, a Prince of the House of *Lorrain* to receive them I am so much indebted to the memory of the late Queen of *Poland*, *Mary Louisa de Gonzague*, and the particularities of this Entry are so fine, and so odd, that it is absolutely necessary to say a word or two of the Honour this Princess receiv'd on this occasion

Sunday 29th of *October* being fix'd for this Ceremony, *Berlise*, one of the Introductors, went by eleven of the Clock in the Morning with the King's and Queen's Coaches to the *Hôtel d'Elbeuf*, because that Duke, and the Prince of *Harcourt* his Son, had Orders to go and receive the *Polish* Embassadors who had din'd at *Rully*, a House belonging to the *Sieur de Rambouillet*, about Cannon shot from St *Anthony's* Gate There arose some dispute between the Duke *d'Elbeuf* and the Embassadors, because the Duke pretended to meet them on the Road, whereas the Embassadors would not set out, nor get on Horseback, till the Duke had saluted them at *Rully* The Duke's pretension was altogether new, but it was necessary to regulate it, and before that could be done, the Day was almost spent, so that it began to be duskish when the Embassadors en-

M m ter'd

ter'd the Town at St *Anthony*'s Gate *Girault*, Affiftant to the Introducters, having drawn up the whole Troop that was on Horfeback, put himfelf at the head thereof, and made them march in this Order. The Captain of the *Heydukes*, or Guards of the *Palatin* of *Pofnania*, one of the Embaffadors, prefented himfelf firft. He was on Horfeback, drefs'd in a *Doloman* or clofe body'd Coat of yellow Satin, and over that he had a long Cloak lin'd with Sables, a Cap upon his Head of Cloth of Gold, with a Silver Ground, furr'd after the fame manner, and adorn'd with white Crane Feathers, which were faften'd to the Cap with a Buckle fet with precious Stones, holding in his Hand a *Bufdigan*, or *Pofican*, which is a Mace or Club made of *Indian* Wood, the end whereof had fix Angles, and was garnifh'd with Silver gilt, he had by his Side a Scimitar, the Scabbard whereof was of Silver, fet off with Turkifh Stones, his Saddle and Houfing was finely embroider'd with Gold and Silver Flowers, the Stirrops were of Siver, and very large, after the Polifh manner, the Bridle, Poitral and Crupper were made of Silver Links, very curioufly wrought, and at the Horfes Saddle, hung a long Sword in a Silver Scabbard, cover'd with Turkifh Stones. His Company, which confifted of thirty Men, were on foot. They were drefs'd in Caffocks of red Cloth, with flafh'd Sleeves, and over that, they had Cloaks of the fame Colour, and the fame Cloth tuck'd up over the fhoulder, and faften'd with eight Silver Buckles on each fide, their Caps were of the fame Cloth, furr'd, adorn'd with a Silver Plate inftead of Feathers, they carry'd a Carbine on their right Shoulders, and Battle-Axes on their left, their Heads were fhav'd all over, with the referve of a little Tuft on the top, and two large Whiskers, before them march'd four Men cloath'd in the fame Livery, carrying each a Colour, half red and half yellow, and they were follow'd by fix Fifers in the fame Livery. Afterwards march'd the Captain of the *Heydukes* of the Bifhop of *Warmia*, the other Embaffador, drefs'd in a Caffock of Crimfon Sattin, and a Velvet Cloak of the fame Colour, lin'd with Sables. His Cap, his Horfe, and the reft of his Equipage was like that of the other Captain. The *Heydukes* of his Company were cloath'd and arm'd as the others, with this exception, that their Cloaths were green, and inftead of eight Silver Buckles, they had fixteen on each fide. They were in all but five and twenty, and they had only five Fifers in the fame Livery. *Del Campo* follow'd him with the Gentlemen of his Band, and after them the Gentlemen of the Horfe, and Captain of the *Palatin* Embaffadors Carbineers in a Veft of Carnation Sattin, and a Cloak of green Velvet, his Cap was of the fame, garnifh'd with white Heron tops, and interfpers'd with precious Stones. He was mounted on a Horfe, whofe furniture was very magnificent, and had a rich Scimitar by his Side, and another hanging at his Saddle. His Troop confifted of fix and twenty Men, cloath'd in Red, their Saddles and Houfings were of Red Cloth, having with their Carbines both a Sword and a Scimitar. Then follow'd *de Vaux* Gentleman of the Horfe, with the Gentlemen of his Band, whofe Horfes were finely fet off with Knots of Ribbon. *Trezesky*, firft Gentleman of the Bed-Chamber to the faid Embaffador, follow'd him, having a Veft of Violet colour'd Sattin, and over that a Cloak without a Cape, of Tabby of the fame colour, lin'd with Sables. He held in his Hand a Steel Hammer, the handle whereof was Silver guilt, his Sword and Scimitar were bedeck'd with Turkifh Stones, the Saddle and Houfing were embroider'd with Silver, and the Bridle, Poitral and Crupper were compos'd of Silver Chains. He was follow'd by four and twenty Gentlemen of the Embaffador's Bedchamber, who had all of them a *Doloman* of yellow Sattin, and a Cloak of red Velvet lin'd with a yellow Sattin trimm'd with Buttons of Gold Wire, they were all very well mounted, and arm'd, and their Horfes Furniture was very rich. They had each of them a long Bow, and a Quiver finely adorn'd, and full of Arrows. *Arnolphs* and his Band who follow'd them, preceded the firft Gentleman of the Bifhop of *Warmia*'s Chamber, cloath'd in a Veft of white Sattin, and a Cloak of red Velvet, lin'd with Cloth of Silver, holding in his hand a Gold Mace, he was perfectly well mounted. He was follow'd by fixteen Gentlemen cloath'd with Vefts of a greyifh Sattin, and Cloaks and Caps of green Velvet, with white Crane Feathers, their Arms, ducking, and mounture were like the others. After thefe came *Memon* with his Band, and after them fix Trumpeters, three of the *Palatin*'s having Vefts of a yellow Sattin, and Cloaks and Caps of red Cloth, and the other three had Vefts of white Sattin, and Cloaks and Caps of a green Cloth, the Banners of the Trumpets were charg'd with the Arms of their Mafters, in Gold and Silver embroidery. *Biliaski* the *Palatin*'s Gentleman of the Horfe, had a white Turkifh Horfe led before him, he was cloath'd with a Veft of crimfon Sattin, and a Cloak of an iron grey Velvet, lin'd with Sables, he was mounted and equip'd like the others. The Saddle of the Turkifh Horfe was cover'd all over with Plates of Gold, thick fet with Rubies, Turkifh Stones, and Diamonds, his Houfing was embroider'd with Gold, his Bridle, Poitral and Crupper were made of Gold Chains cover'd with Plates of the fame Metal, fo curioufly wrought, that they were as pliable and flexible as if they had been made of Leather. His Shoes were of Silver, and on his Head he had a great Tuft of Heron Feathers, and on the Forehead a Star of Rubies and other precious Stones, and from his Saddle there hung a Sword, whofe Scabbard was of Silver gilt, fo thick fet with Turkifh Stones and Rubies, that the vacant part did not equal that which was fill'd up, as was alfo the guard. After this came three Muficians on Horfeback, cloath'd in Sattin, who were follow'd by feveral *Polifh* Gentlemen, that were at *Paris* as Travellers, and were drefs'd after the *French* Mode. The Count *de Noailles*, whom the Princefs *Louifa Mary* had fent to meet the Embaffadors, march'd at the Head of half *M de Poux*'s Academy, which was led by the Baron *de Biron*, in the abfence of the Gentleman of the Horfe, and the other half by the Count *de Barrault*, who was there likewife on the

The EMBASSADOR and his FUNCTIONS. 135

the part of the said Princess Then came *Szodrousky*, a *Polish* Colonel, and Captain of the *Palatin*'s Gentlemen of Honour, mounted on a white Turk, painted after the Turkish manner, his Saddle and Housing being of Gold and Silver Embroidery, cover'd with small Crescents of Silver gilt He was cloath'd with Cloth of Silver, and had upon his back a white Wing, so large, that it reach'd above his head, on which he wore a Cap of cloth of Silver, lin'd with Sable, adorn'd with a very fine plume of Crane Feathers, set off with several precious Stones, he had on each side of him a Foot-man cloath'd after the Turkish manner, with Gold Cassocks, and carrying long Axes in their hands Next appear'd some Noblemen, whom the King, the Queen, the Duke of *Orleans*, the Prince of *Conde*, and the Duke of *Enguien* had sent to meet the Embassadors, the rest placing themselves near the most remarkable among the Embassador's Retinue, viz. the Count *Opalinsky*, the *Palatin*'s Kinsman, *Alexander Sielsky*, the Bishop's Steward, and *Stanislas Kostka*, Count of *Steinberg*, dres'd in close body'd Coats, and Vests of Gold Brocade flower'd, with Buttons enrich'd with precious Stones, their Caps were adorn'd with Feathers, they were mounted on Turkish Horses, whose furniture was set off with plates of Gold bedeck'd with Diamonds, having about their necks three rounds of Gold Chain *Adrian Slupcki*, the Bishop's Nephew, *Enarist Belzeki*, *Francis Cifchinke*, *Stanislas Watta*, Chamberlain to the *Palatin* of *Posnania*, and Mareschal of the Embassy, mounted and cloath'd as those last mention'd *John Tragusky* habited in a Vest of of Gold Brocade lin'd with Sable, the Cap of the same, with a great Tuft of Heron Feathers, and a Sword hanging (like the rest) at the side of the Saddle, adorn'd with Gold and precious Stones This Horse did not cause so much admiration by his rich furniture, as by his docility, he that was upon him, making him fall down upon his knees, and bend his head to the very ground, as he pass'd by the Royal Palace, where the King and Queen were to see the Cavalcade Afterwards follow'd several other great Noblemen, amongst whom *Tzemberg*, the Count *de Morstein*, *Orzechucky*, the Bishop's Nephew, made as good an appearance as the others, having their Cassocks of Sattin, Velvet, and Brocade, and their Vests of the same, lin'd with Sables, Lynxes and other precious Furrs The Secretary of the Embassy very richly clad, and finely mounted, follow'd *Roncalgy*, Resident of *Poland*, his Horse's furniture was of black Velvet, and he was conducted by the Marquis *de Miossens* Lieutenant of the King's *Gens d'Arms*, then came *Cicklinsky*, Senator of *Poland*, clad in Cloth of Gold, lin'd with Lynxes Furrs, his Cap of the same, mounted on a Turkish Horse magnificently equipp'd After him follow'd two *Polish* Princes, *Radziwil*, and *Zamosky*, the last of whom, was Son to the deceas'd great Chancellor of *Poland*, very richly clad, after the *French* manner It was after these that the two Embassadors appear'd, having before them the *Sieur de Berlise*, and on their sides the Duke *d'Elbeuf*, and the Prince *de Harcourt* The Bishop, who had the Hand of his Colleague, was

dress'd in a violet Tabby, with a Hat, the band whereof was of Gold Wire, beset with Diamonds The *Palatin* had a close body'd Coat, and a Cassock of Gold Brocade, set off with a great many precious Stones, as well as his Scimitar, his Sword was cover'd all over with Turkish Stones, as were likewise his Stirrops, his Saddle and Housing were of Cloth or Gold, and his Horses shoes were of Gold, the one whereof was contriv'd to come off in the Street They had moreover several Coaches, two of which were very fine They were all fill'd with. Persons belonging to the Embassador's Retinue, viz their Confessors, their Physicians, some Jesuites, and other Ecclesiasticks, as well *Germans* as *Poles* Amongst the Horses there were forty Turks, three and twenty whereof were shod with Silver, besides that of the Embassador It was after this manner that they pass'd through the greatest part of *Paris* from *St Anthony*'s Gate, to the new Street of *St Honnoré*, where they were Lodg'd at *Vendosme* House As soon as they came thither, the king sent to complement 'em, by *Liancourt*, first Gentleman of his Bed-chamber, and the Queen, by the Count *d'Orval*, her first Gentleman of the House Two days after they had their first Audience, of which I shall perhaps have occasion to speak in the following Chapter I shall only add here, that a great deal more Honour was done in *France* to the Embassadors whom the Republick of *Poland* sent thither in the Year 1573, after the Election of *Henry* Duke of *Anjou* The Prince *Daufin*, Prince of the Blood, the Dukes of *Guise*, *Mayenne*, *d'Aumale*, with the Marquiss *d'Elbeuf*, all Princes of the House of *Lorrain*, receiv'd them without *St Martin*'s Gate, where *Paul de Foix* complemented them in these Princes Names The Embassy that *Sigismund* Father of *Uladislas* sent in the Year 1605, to the Emperor *Rodolfus* II and to *Charles* Arch-Duke of *Gratz*, for his second Marriage, had something in it that was more magnificent than this

The greatest Embassy, and for which *England* made the greatest Ceremonies, is that which *Henry* III King of *France* sent thither in the Year 1581 It had for Head the Prince *Daufin*, Son to the Duke *de Montpensier* Prince of the Blood, and was compos'd of the Duke *de Bovillon*, of Mareschal *de Cossé*, of *Mrs*, *de Lansac*, *de Carouge*, *de la Motte-fenelon*, and of *Pinart*, Secretary of State The Lord *Cobham* receiv'd them on the Queen's part, at their landing at *Dover*, having waited for them there eight days, with several Gentlemen appointed to serve them, and to defray them At their arrival at *Gravesend*, they found the Earls of *Northumberland*, *Bedford*, *Warwick*, and of *Arundel*, who conducted them in the Queen's Barges to *London*. When they drew near the Town, they were saluted by a hundred pieces of Cannon, which did not cease firing till they had pass'd the Bridge They landed at *Somerset-House*, all the Bells of the Town ringing for Joy, where Bonfires were made by the Queen's express Orders, who was willing to pay these outward Civilities to so many Persons of Quality, in an Affair wherein she was not very much dispos'd to give them any great satisfaction The House was very richly

richly furnish'd, she sent to them all the Lords that were then at *London*, and they were magnificently treated at Supper by the Queen's Officers, assisted by the Yeomen of the Guards in their usual Liveries, while the Musick diverted them, and the Artillery continu'd roaring from the *Tower*, and several other Places of the Town. The Queen having caus'd them to be treated three Days after this splendid manner, she notify'd to the Embassadors that she would give them Audience after she had din'd. They were conducted to it by the same Lords, who had receiv'd them at *Gravesend*. The Queen expected them in a large Timber-Hall which she had built on purpose for this Ceremony, and was hung with very rich Tapestries embroider'd with Gold and Silk, and rais'd with Brocade of Gold and Silver. The Roof of this Building was supported with several Pillars, painted and embellish'd with so many Devices and Emblems, that nothing could be prettier or more sublime. The Queen herself was magnificently dress'd, and gloriously set out with Jewels and precious Stones, amongst which there was in her Coiffure a Ruby, and an Emerald as large as the Palm of one's Hand. At the other end of the Hall, opposite to the Door, there was a kind of Theatre where the Queen was seated under a Canopy embroider'd with large Pearls. The Prince being come within ten or twelve Paces of her Majesty, she got up, and advancing as far as the first Step of the Theatre, she caus'd him to salute her, the other Noblemen kiss'd her Hand. After which, the first Complements were soon converted into Conversation, which ended with the Day-light. The same Lords who had conducted them to Audience reconducted them to their Lodgings. The next Day the Queen gave a Dinner to the Embassadors in the same Hall, and would have oblig'd the Prince *Daufin* to sit under the Canopy with her, but he excus'd himself, and sat at some Distance from her, having near him the Mareschal *de Cossé* and *M de Lansac*, the Duke of *Bouillon, la Motte-fenelon*, and *Pinart* were on the other side, and *Carongei* with *Mauvissiere*, Embassador in Ordinary from *France*, were at the end of the Table. There were besides, other Tables for the Lords and the Ladies of both Nations. Dinner being over there was a Ball, wherein the Queen danc'd with the Prince. After this Diversion, which lasted about two Hours, the Queen had the Embassadors into her Chamber, and from thence into a Gallery, where she had caus'd to be display'd whatever she had that was rich, exquisite and precious, and near these Rarities there was a large Table serv'd with a very sumptuous Collation. At Night they were again treated in their own Lodgings at the Queen's Expences. The Day following she invited them to take the Air upon the River, where she took the Prince with *Mrs de Bouillon* and *Marchimont* into her own Barge. The next Day the Earl of *Leicester* treated the Embassadors after the *English* manner, that is to say, very splendidly, there being so great a Profusion of all sorts of Viands and Sweetmeats, that all the *French* Noblemen were amaz'd thereat, and confess'd they had never seen so much at any one single Entertainment.

It is the Lord High Chamberlain that gives in *England* the necessary Orders for Entries, and for the Audiences of Embassadors, nominating to the Master of the Ceremonies (who in that Kingdom discharges the Function of Introductor of the Embassadors) the Lords who are to accompany them, either at the one or the other, and regulating the Number of Barges design'd to transport them from *Gravesend* or *Greenwich*, and that of the Coaches that are to bring them from the *Tower* to their Lodgings. This Office is generally perform'd by Earls, in reference to the Embassadors of crown'd Heads and Republicks, and by Barons in reference to those of other Princes. It was therefore taken notice of as a Fault committed by the great Chamberlain, when he caus'd the Abbot *Della Scaglia* (who was Embassador from *Savoy*) to be accompany'd by the Earl of *Carlisle*, as some time before he had caus'd the Marquiss *Pompeo Strozzi*, Embassador from the Duke of *Mantua*, to be conducted to Audience by the Earl of *Cleveland*. The Duke of *Savoy* being Brother-in-law to the King of *England*, there was room to do something more than ordinary for his Embassador, but there was nothing could oblige the great Chamberlain to do any thing extraordinary to the Embassador of *Mantua*, notwithstanding that in *France* he is also receiv'd by an Officer of the Crown.

In the Year 1660, the Estates of the United Provinces sent into *England Lewis* of *Nassau* Lord of *Beverweert*, *Simon Van Hoorn*, *Michael Van Gogh*, and *M de Ripperda de Farmsum*, to complement the King upon his Restoration, as also to conclude a stricter Union between the Crown and the Republick, according to the Hopes the King had giv'n the Estates before his Imbarkation in *Holland*. They arriv'd in *England* in the beginning of *November*, and after they had been some Days at *London incognito* they went to *Greenwich*, where the Lord *Richard* (whose eldest Brother was Son-in-law to the Sr *de Beverweert*) accompany'd by five or six Gentlemen of the King's Bed-Chamber, came on the part of his Majesty to do them Civilities, and brought Barges along with them to conduct them to *London*. They found at the *Tower* the Lord *Craven*, having with him about twenty Coaches with six Horses to each, who conducted them to the Sieur *Abraham Williams*, Master of the Ceremonies, where they were defrayed, and in all respects treated, as well at their Audience as on other Occasions, with the same Honours that are done to the Embassadors of crown'd Heads. The King had yet fresh in his Memory the Affection which had been shewn him in *Holland*, when he pass'd through it in order to his Imbarkation near the *Hague*, where the States of *Holland* had been at the Expence of two hundred and fifty thousand Crowns. The *Dutch* Author, who has written the History of his Time in a Jargon rather than in an intelligible Language, says, That this was the first time that the States Embassadors had been complemented by a Lord before their Arrival at *London*. So that it might be look'd upon to be from that time that they have been treated upon the level with those of crown'd Heads. However he ought to have remember'd what he had himself said, That in the Year 1644, *Boreel* and *Renswonde*, Embassadors

The EMBASSADOR and his FUNCTIONS. 137

sadors from the said Estates, were complemented at *Greenwich* by a Lord, and by two Deputies of the Lower House He ought then to have added, that That was the first time the Court did them this Honour, which indeed is true Queen *Elizabeth* contented her self with succouring them powerfully, and King *James*, who did not love them, affronted their Ministers on all Occasions instead of doing them Honour

In those times the Embassadors of crown'd Heads were receiv'd at their landing, were defray'd on their Journey, and supply'd with all necessary Carriages for themselves, for their Retinue, and for their Baggage, till they came to *London* The King sometimes would make them eat at his own Table, and in Assemblies, and other Diversions of the Court, he would have them under the same Canopy with himself But King *Charles* I finding his Embassadors did not receive the same Civilities in other Courts, and particularly that *France* was very reserv'd therein, lopt off all these superfluous Civilities, and made an Order, That for the future Embassadors should be receiv'd only at *Gravesend*, and conducted from thence in the King's Barges to the *Tower*, where the Coaches belonging to the Court should take them, to conduct them to their own Houses, or to the Lodgings provided for Extraordinary Embassadors This is now the Behaviour of almost all the other Courts, tho' sometimes there, as well as in that of *London* it self, these Regulations are dispens'd with When in the Year 1665 the Duke *de Verneuil* and M *Courtin* were sent into *England*, there to labour in Conjunction with the Count *de Courages*, Embassador in Ordinary from *France*, for an Accommodation with the United Provinces, they were not received at *Gravesend* according to the Regulation, but *Cotterel*, Master of the Ceremonies, went and receiv'd them at *Dover* It is very probable that the King had a mind to do Honour to the Duke, who was a legitimated natural Brother of the Queen of *England*, or else that he thought it proper to shew some particular Respect to *France*, whose Friendship was at that time necessary to him

It was at least as necessary to the Emperor *Ferdinand* II, at the beginning of the *Bohemian* War The Constable *de Luines*, who at that time govern'd the King and Kingdom of *France*, and who did not truly know the real Interest thereof, caus'd the Duke *d'Engouléme*, the Count *de Bethune*, and M *de Chasteauneuf*, who was call'd the Abbot *de Preaux* to be sent into *Germany*, to try if it were possible to dispose them to a Peace These Gentlemen being arriv'd in *Austria*, at the Distance of a Day's Journey from *Vienna*, met the Captain of the Emperor's Guards accompany'd by one of the first Noblemen of the Countrey, and by a great Number of Officers, to make 'em the first Complements At their getting out of the Barge, about half a League from the Town, they were receiv'd by the Marshal of the Emperor's Court, attended by three hundred Gentlemen, and by above fourscore Coaches with six Horses, who conducted them to the Lodgings that had been fitted up for them As soon as they alighted out of the Coach the Count *de Meggau*, great Chamberlain, came and paid them Civilities from his Imperial Majesty The Nuncio, and the Embassadors of *Spain* and *Venice*, complemented them without the Town, and those of *Florence*, *Modena* and *Malta*, visited them as soon as they came thither It is the Great Chamberlain, to this Day, who gives Orders in that Court for the Reception of Embassadors

The Court of *Rome* is not very prodigal of its Honours and Civilities, of which the Master of the Ceremonies keeps a very exact Register No Entry is made but to Embassadors of Obedience, for which Reason M *de Foix* Archbishop of *Thoulouse*, and Embassador from *France* to *Rome*, writing to the King his Master, takes notice that the Count *d'Olivares*, Embassador in Ordinary from *Spain*, having made it his Request to *Gregory* XIII, That the Vineyard of *Julius* III might be fitted up, in order to his being lodg'd there, and receiv'd at his Publick Entry The Pope signify'd to him, That he had nothing to do but to go directly to his Lodgings Nevertheless, he caus'd some Civilities to be paid him, because *Spain* made it self to be very much consider'd in those Days The Popes have always had a Consideration for those Potentates that know themselves, and insist upon having what is their due

The Emperor *Maximilian* I, in these important Affairs, made use of the bold and undertaking Spirit of *Matthew Langven*, and particularly in those of *Italy*, whither he sent him in the Year 1511, in order to mediate some Accommodation between *Julius* II and *Lewis* XII King of *France* The Ministers of these Princes were to meet at *Mantua*, but *Julius*, instead of sending thither any on his part, oblig'd *Matthew Langven*, who was Bishop of *Gurc*, to come to *Rome* with *Don Pedro d'Urrea*, Embassador from *Ferdinand* King of *Arragon*, and to leave at *Parma Stephen Poncher* Bishop of *Paris*, who was there on the part of *Lewis* The Pope, to gain the good Will of *Matthew*, who govern'd the Emperor his Master, resolv'd to load him with Honours, by going himself to *Ravenna*, and from thence to *Bologna*, as being a proper Place to entertain him well *Matthew* had with the Quality of Embassador that of Lieutenant General to the Emperor, and, as such, he had an Equipage suitable to the Magnificence of the Entry the Pope made him The whole Court went to meet him, and accompany'd him to the Consistory, where the Pope, attended by all the Cardinals, waited for him, and it was not till after this Publick Audience that he saw the Pope in his Chamber When the same Bishop of *Gurc* went to *Rome*, in the Year 1512, the same Pope (whose insufferable Pride gave so much Uneasiness to the King of *France*) making an Effort with his own natural Disposition, caus'd an Entry to be made him through all the Ecclesiastical State, and that with such unusal Honours, as had never been done to the Emperors Ministers since *Charlemagne* and *Otto the Great* He sent nine Prelates to meet him, with Orders to cause him to be supply'd with all things necessary Nay, *he would have oblig'd all the Cardinals to go and meet him in a Body, as far as the Gate of the City*, but they refus'd to do it, as being a thing without Precedent,

N n

cellent, and that would injure their Dignity. The two Cardinals of *Agen* and of *Strigonium* were forc'd to go and receive him at half a League's Distance from the City, where placing him between them, as being Lieutenant General to the Emperor, they conducted him to the Church of St *Mary del Populo*, that he might from thence repair with his Retinue to the Consistory.

I spoke in the thirteenth Chapter of the Journey the Duke *de Nevers* took to *Rome*, before the Absolution of *Henry* IV., and of the manner how he was receiv'd by Pope *Clement* VIII. In the Year 1608 the same King sent him again to *Rome*, to yield Obedience to *Paul* V. *Clement*'s Successor *Leo* XI. having liv'd very few Days after his Exaltation. The Duke being arriv'd at *Civita Vecchia* was saluted *on board the Galley by two Prelates in the Pope's Name*. The next Day *M. de Breves*, Embassador in Ordinary from *France*, met him at *Bracciano*, with a splendid Company of the Nobility of both Nations. Six Miles from *Rome* he met the Dukes of *Sforza*, *Conti*, *Sto Gemini*, the Prince *Peretti*, and even the Lord *Victor* the Pope's Nephew, who had six Coaches with six Horses each. The Cardinals *Gallo*, *Bevilacqua*, *Delfin* and *Serafin* went to meet him as far as *Pontemole*, and brought him along with them to *Rome*, where he arriv'd *incognito*. That Night he kiss'd the Pope's Feet. The Day following he visited the four Cardinals who had been to meet him, and employ'd the rest of the *Day in receiving the Visits of the other Cardinals, and even those of the Pope's Brothers*. On the 25th of *March* he made his Publick Entry. *John Baptista Borghese*, the Pope's Brother, went and receiv'd him at the Vineyard of *Leo Sforza*, and *in the Cavalcade he march'd immediately before the Embassador*. The two Patriarchs of *Jerusalem*, and of *Alexandria*, took him between them, and two Archbishops did the same Honour to the Embassador in Ordinary. His Retinue consisted of an hundred and twenty Gentlemen, besides others, and was one of the most magnificent that had been seen at *Rome*. He was lodg'd at the *Hostel de Russelay*, where he gave a Supper to all the Noblemen who honour'd his Entry with their Presence. On the 27th the Pope's Brother went and receiv'd him, in order to accompany him in the Cavalcade to his Audience; to which he went almost in the same Order that had been observ'd at his Entry, except that instead of Mules, and of the Family of the Cardinals, there were only Coaches. After he had rested himself a little in a Chamber very richly furnish'd, the two Patriarchs conducted him to the Royal Hall, where he found the Pope in the Consistory. After the Embassador had kiss'd his Feet, and that the Orator had made his Harangue, and had been answer'd, the Embassador kiss'd the Pope's Feet again, who then retir'd into his Chamber, the Embassador following him, and carrying the Train of his Cope. The Duke and the Embassador in Ordinary din'd with the Pope, with whom they had a pretty long Conversation before he dismiss'd them.

After this Precedent, there is no Embassador of Obedience (if he be a Prince, and comes on the part of a crown'd Head) but may pretend to the same Honours, or to whom they can be refus'd. Two Prelates go on the part of the Pope, and salute the Embassador in his Galley. The Pope's Nephew goes and meets him at six Miles distance from the Town. The Cardinals and the Pope's Nephews make him the first Visit. The Pope's Brother goes before him in his two Cavalcades, and it is likewise he that goes and receives him, to conduct him to his Audience. However, at this time, there is nothing like it practis'd. On the contrary the Pope's Relations pretend, That the Embassador owes them the first Visit, and those that are Cardinals will really have it.

It will not be altogether from the purpose, if I here relate the Particulars of an Entry, which tho' it were not made to an Embassador, has nevertheless some Analogy with what I just now mention'd. In the Year 1598, the Arch-Duchess, who was betroth'd to the Prince of *Spain*, being arriv'd at *Ferrara* whither the Pope was come to take possession of that Duchy, all the Court, and even all the Cardinals in a Body, went to meet her, and accompany'd her to the great Church, and from thence to the Palace where the Pope receiv'd her in full Consistory, without stirring from his Seat, or saying one Word. After she had kiss'd his Feet and Hand, she was plac'd on the Pope's left Hand within two Paces of him, after which the Arch-Duchess's Mother had the same Honour, and was plac'd near her Daughter, both of 'em standing. This done, the Arch-Duke *Albert* was also admitted to the same Ceremony. The Pope embrac'd him, and saluted him on each Cheek, after which he was plac'd on the other side, opposite to the Arch-Duchess. Presently after the Pope got up, gave them his Blessing, and retir'd leaving the Arch-Duke and the Arch-Duchesses where they had been plac'd, and there they convers'd for some time with the Cardinals, till they were conducted to the Appartments which had been prepar'd for them. The next Day the two Arch-Duchesses and the Arch Duke heard the Pope's Mass, and din'd with him after Dinner they receiv'd the Visits of the Ministers. This was on *Saturday* the 14th of *November*, and on *Sunday* the 15th, the Pope having celebrated Mass in his *Pontificalibus*, bless'd the Marriage of the Arch-Duchess with the King of *Spain*, who had made the Arch-Duke his Proxy on that occasion. This being done, the Pope marry'd the Arch-Duke with the Infanta, of whom the Duke *de Sessa*, Embassador from *Spain*, had care. The Pope gave the Sacrament to all the four with his own Hands; and Mass being over, he presented the Queen with the Rose, which the Popes, according to custom, send to great Princesses when they marry. Not one of them was admitted into the Choir during the Mass, but were plac'd at six or seaven Paces without the Choir, where two Pews or Tabernacles were prepar'd, one for the two Princesses, and the other for the Arch-Duke. The *Spanish* Embassador, nor the Constable of *Castille*, Governor of *Milan*, had no Rank assign'd them, but they stood by the Arch-Duke, as the Ladies did by the Princesses. The Embassadors of the Emperor and of *Venice*, were standing next to the Pope's Chair. There was then no Embassador

The EMBASSADOR and his FUNCTIONS. 139

fador from *France* for although *Doffat* discharg'd the Functions thereof, yet he had not the Character, so that he was present at the Ceremony but only as an Assistant These Princes were well enough lik'd, because they were contented with the Honours which were done them, and did not refuse the Cardinals those that were desir'd of them There was none but the Constable of *Castile*, who not being allow'd a Rank above the Cardinals at the Entry, left the Princes there, and did not accompany them

Philip de Commines says, that it is in *Italy* and at *Venice* chiefly, that the greatest Civilities are shewn to Embassadors And indeed it is not to be wonder'd at, because there are a great many Persons in that Senate, who have seen in that Quality most of the Courts of *Europe* When an Embassador from a crown'd Head is to be receiv'd, a *Knight of the Star* is nominated for that purpose, and most commonly, one that has been employ'd at that Court, which sends the Embassador that is to be receiv'd The Knight, accompany'd by threescore Senators in scarlet Robes, goes to the Embassador, who is at the Abby of the Holy Ghost, which is three Miles from the City, as I said before, where having complemented him on the part of the Republick, he conducts him to his Palace, in a *Gondola* richly furnish'd the Senators, his Companions, mixing themselves with those of the Embassador's Retinue, and giving them the Place of Honour, even to the very Pages The Knight Conductor, for there is no particular Officer for that at *Venice*, as he goes into the Embassador's Palace, gives him both the Hand and the Door, but at his coming away, he takes both the one and the other of him And after his Example, all the other Senators take them also of those of the Embassador's Retinue Notwithstanding which, the Lord *d'Argenson* complains, that he was not so well receiv'd in his second Embassy to *Venice*, as he had been in the first and altho' he does not give particular Instances, yet it is no hard matter to judge, that something was wanting at his Reception, the Circumstances whereof this wise Politician was not willing to make publick, for fear of injuring his own Reputation, and the Dignity of the King his Master The Senate is very exact in its Ceremonies, but for all that it sometimes does not strictly keep up to this Punctuality, but is more than ordinarily remiss therein, according to the Quality of the Persons that compose the Embassy

In the Year 1643, Cardinal *Bichi*, Embassador Extraordinary from *France*, having notify'd at *Venice*, that he had Orders from the King to go thither, to endeavour to accommodate the Difference that the Republick had with Pope *Urban* VIII, on account of the Duke of *Parma*'s Interest, the Senate commanded the *Podesta* of *Chiozza*, to go and meet him as far as the *Polisselle*, and to cause him to be magnificently treated every where He din'd at *Chiozza*, where he found several Boats laden with all forts of Refreshments and among the rest a gilt Boat, that was to bring him to the Convent of the Holy Ghost While he was there, the Chevalier *Landy*, accompany'd by *M des Hameaux*, Embassador in Ordinary from *France*, by a great many other Senators, and by all the Domesticks of Cardinal *Cornaro*, came and receiv'd him, and conducted him to that Cardinal's Palace, which had been prepar'd for him, and where the Senate had caus'd the Arms of *France* to be set over the Gate The Day following the same Chevalier *Landy*, attended by fourscore Senators, went and receiv'd him, in order to conduct him to Audience The Cardinal, who was cloath'd in Purple, on account of the Mourning for the Death of King *Lewis* XIII, waited for him *in the middle of the Hall*, having on his *Rochet* and *Camail* and after some Complements, they all descended, and went into the Boats the Senate had sent him there were three cover'd with Crimson Damask, in which the Cardinal, the Embassador in Ordinary, the Chevalier *Landy*, and some of the chief Senators took their Places, while the others, and the rest of his Retinue, got into the *Gondolas* which follow'd them At their landing at St *Mark*'s Place the Chevalier took the left Hand of the Cardinal, another Senator, that of the Embassador in Ordinary, and after their Example, the Senators of the Cortege did the same Honour to those of the Retinue of the two Embassadors *The Doge, accompany'd by all the Nobility, came and met him at the top of the Stair-case* and having saluted him, *by putting off his Ducal Cap*, he plac'd himself on the Cardinal's left Hand, and thus they went together to the College Hall, both uncover'd They ascended both at the same time, yet io neverthelefs, that the Cardinal was rather foremost He also took the first Place in the Doge's Seat, which had been made wider on purpose, that there might be room for both the one and the other After they were seated, the Cardinal presented his *Credentials* to the Doge, who caus'd them to be read by a Secretary, and after that the Cardinal made his Compliment, which was no sooner ended than they got up, and *the Doge, attended as before conducted him to the Stair-Case*, which is call'd the Gyant's Stair-Case and the Chevalier *Landy* accompany'd him even to his Chamber in the Palace Some Days after the *Doge and the Seigneurie return'd the Cardinal's Visit*, who receiv'd them in the Porch, *gave the Place of Honour to the Doge* and in re-conducting him, he accompany'd him to his Boat, refusing to withdraw till he had seen him go off This was an Excess of Civility, which did no prejudice however to the Dignity of the King of *France*, because he did not receive this Visit as Embassador, but as Cardinal and even is Embassador he ow'd this Honour to the Doge, after that he had receiv'd The Purple it self could not excuse him from it In the other particular Audiences, he was conducted by a great Sage, and by a Sage of *Terra firma*, but the most of the Conferences were held at his own Palace

The Senate had done as much to the Cardinal *de Joyeuse*, when in the Year 1607 he came to *Venice*, on account of the Difference the Republick had with Pope *Paul* V It was in the same Year, that *Charles Emmanuel*, Duke of *Savoy*, procur'd himself to be nominated by the Emperor to the Embassy of *Venice* of which I took notice in the first Chapter of this Book As soon as the Senate had Advice of the Duke's Design, they fell into a Debate, after what

man-

The EMBASSADOR and his FUNCTIONS.

manner they should receive that Prince, who is without doubt, the first of all *Italy*, and it was resolv'd, that the Doge, accompany'd by threescore Senators, should go and receive him with the *Bucentaure*, in St *Clement*'s Island, and should conduct him to his Palace But that the *Doge* should not go out of the *Bucentaure*, to shew thereby, that that Vessel was rather on the Doge's account than the Dukes That threescore Senators should conduct him to Audience, but that the Doge should place him on his left Hand, and should only give him the *Title of Excellency* This Embassy came to nothing but had the Duke seriously design'd to have perform'd it, the Resolution of the Senate, would have been sufficient to have made him change his, because the Senate had done as much for others, who in his Opinion were not so good as himself In the Year 1515, *Messieurs de Vendome* and *de Guise*, the Bishop of *Lavaure*, and some other Lords of the first Rank in the Court of *France*, laying hold on the Opportunity of the Journey King *Francis* I, took at that time to *Bologna*, to confer with Pope *Leo* X, had the Curiosity to go and see Town of *Venice* Upon Advice the Senate had thereof, *the Doge went in Person with the Bucentaure* to meet them, notwithstanding that in those Days this Vessel could not be row'd with Oars, as it is at present, but they were forc'd to tow it They were lodg'd in the finest Palaces of the Town Continual Feasts were made for them, and they receiv'd so much Honour and Civility otherwise, that they went away well satisfied It is probable the Doge would not have gone in Person, had it not been for the Duke of *Vendosme*, to whom he was willing to shew this Honour, as being a Prince of the Blood of *France* which is a Quality so much respected at *Venice*, that they are treated upon the Level with Sovereign Princes, the Infants of *Spain*, and the Cardinals, to whom the Doge does the Honour to take off his *Ducal Cap*, when they have Audience either in the Senate, or in the College I shall not here relate the Particulars of the Reception the Republick gave to King *Henry* III, when he pass'd through *Venice* in his Return from *Poland*, in the Year 1574 I shall only say, that this Prince, who was extremely affected with all sorts of Pleasures, never mention'd the Stay he made there, without distinguishing it by the particular Denomination of a continual Enchantment In the Year 1529, the Emperor *Charles* V, and King *Francis* I, intending to make it be believ'd, that they were going to have one common Interest, and joyn their Arms to make War against the *Turk*, sent together to *Venice*, the one *Don Alphonso d'Avalos*, Marquiss *du Guast*, Governor of *Milan*, and the other Admiral *Annebault*, Governor of *Piedmont*, who both arriv'd there on the 10th of *December* of the same Year The Senate sent to meet them, *an extraordinary Number of Senators, the Bucentaure*, seven Gallies, and an infinite Number of *Gondolas* They were lodg'd in a Palace splendidly furnish'd, and defray'd at the Expence of the Republick They had their first Audience in the Great Hall, in full Senate, where they made but one Complement In the private Audience they had afterwards in the College, the two Embassadors spoke one after the other but the Answer they receiv'd was so general, that these two Noblemen, finding they had to do with Persons, who were not to be impos'd upon by outward Appearances, took their Leaves at the same Audience, and went away

Count *de Vaudemont*, second Son to the Duke of *Lorrain*, having engag'd himself in the Service of the Republick, went to *Venice* in the Year 1603 He receiv'd great Civilities in all the Towns throughout that State But the *Podestras* took every where the Place of Honour of him, because they have the Representing Character Forty Senators, cloath'd in their Scarlet Robes, went to receive him at the *Saffousines* The same Number of Senators conducted him to his Audience, wherein the *Doge advanc'd five or six Paces to meet him, and took off his Ducal Cap* when he saluted him He was no Sovereign Prince, nor even the e'dest Son of a Sovereign, yet nevertheless the Duke did him an Honour, which he does not do to Embassadors, that are receiv'd and accompany'd to their Audience by threescore Senators

The Republick had, in the aforesaid Year 1603 made a very advantageous Treaty with the three *Grey Leagues*, who sent seven Embassadors to *Venice*, to see the Observation thereof sworn too They had a Retinue of a hundred and fifty Persons, and such great Honours were done them, that excepting those that were done to King *Henry* III, whom I lately mention'd, it may be said, that never any Ministers had been receiv'd with that Magnificence All the Towns sent out Horse and Foot to meet them, and they were every where defray'd even at *Venice*, where their Expences amounted to four hundred Crowns a Day But notwithstanding all this, they were receiv'd but by forty Gentlemen, where is Embassadors are receiv'd by threescore and these Gentlemen were not taken out of the *Pregad*, (which is compos'd of those Senators, who have gone through the principal Offices) according to the usual Custom, but out of the meanest Magistrates At *Venice* they are very cautious of Innovations, however there happen every Day Occurrences, where it is impossible to keep within the Bounds of a general Regulation

This Republick makes no Reception to Ministers of the second Order, and it is what is practic'd every where else, so that this Honour being due but only to the Character of an Embassador, it is impossible not to be surpris'd at that, which was done to Cardinal *Dossat* in the Year 1598 He was then but Bishop of *Bayeux*, and did the Business of *France* at *Rome*, without Quality, as I observ'd before in this very Chapter King *Henry* IV, commanded him to go to *Venice*, and to acquaint the Senate with the Peace he had just concluded with the King of *Spain*, and with the Duke of *Savoy* at *Vervins* He came to *Venice* as a Minister of the second Order But as soon as he had notify'd that he was come there by the King's Command, and that he had *Letters* for the Senate, two *Sages* were sent to him, *the one of Terra Firma, and the other of the Orders*, who told him, the Senate was very sorry, it was not advis'd of his coming, because it had not been able to give the necessary Orders for his *Reception,*

The EMBASSADOR and his FUNCTIONS. 141

Reception, which, had they had notice in time, should have been perform'd with the Honours that were due to the Minister of a King, for whom it had a very particular Veneration They added, That the Senate had commanded them to conduct him to a Lodging that had been fitted up and prepar'd for him; and accordingly they conducted him thither, notwithstanding the Opposition he made, and he was there treated at the Expence of the Republick

Philip de Commines says, That the first time King *Charles* VIII sent him to *Venice* the Republick made him an Entry, and caus'd him to be defray'd in all the Towns belonging to that State Five and twenty Gentlemen went to meet him as far as *Terra firma*, and conducted him to St *Andrew*'s Church, where five and twenty other Gentlemen, or Senators, joyn'd the first, so that the whole Company consisted of fifty Gentlemen They conducted him to St *George*'s Convent, where he was lodg'd and defray'd, the Republick being at the Expence, not only during the eight Days that *Commines* stay'd at *Venice*, but also as long as he remain'd within their State, and till he arriv'd at *Ferrara*

On the 7th of *July* 1670, the Lord *Falconbridge*, whom the King of *Great Britain* sent to some Princes and Potentates of *Italy*, made his Entry into *Venice* Sixty Senators cloath'd in their Scarlet Robes, with as many *Gondolas*, follow'd by above five hundred others, went and receiv'd him at the Convent of the Holy Ghost, and conducted him in *Morosini*'s *Gondola*, which was at the Head of the whole Parade, to the Lodgings he had hir'd and furnish'd *Morosini* having complemented him in the Name of the Senate, he and the Senators that accompany'd him took the Hand of the Embassador, who being at home was oblig'd to do them the Honours of his House The Embassador reconducted them to their *Gondola*'s, where he saw them all seated before he retir'd In the Evening the Senate sent him all sorts of Refreshments

Commines, to prove what he had said, that the Princes of *Italy* are honourable, and that they make Profession to know very well what Honours ought to be paid to Embassadors, takes notice, That he went in the Year 1495 to *Vigevano*, to *Lewis Sforza* Duke of *Milan*, by the King his Master's Order, and that this Prince went out of Town under the Pretext of going a hunting, but in reality to go and meet the King of *France*'s Minister.

The Great Duke of *Tuscany* has in that, as well as in many other things, a great advantage over most of the other Princes of *Italy*, and does honour to the Nation, by shewing excessive Civilities to the Ministers of foreign Princes *Paul de Foix* (who is often mention'd, and who cannot be too often spoke of in this Treatise,) being sent by King *Charles* IX, to the Princes of *Italy*, who had complemented him on the Election of his Brother to the Crown of *Poland*, and among the rest, to *Francis* Duke of *Florence*: This last went in Person to meet him with several Coaches It is true, that *Cosmus*, Father to *Francis*, was still living, but his Infirmities and Distempers having render'd him incapable of governing his Estates, he had resign'd them to his Son, and had only reserv'd to himself the Title thereof The same *M do Foix* was, in the Year 1547, sent again to *Florence* by King *Henry* III, and then the same Duke *Francis*, whose Father had been dead some Months, made him *the same Reception*

M *Dossat*, at his leaving *Venice*, had Orders to go to *Florence*, for the Negotiation of an Affair, of which mention is made elsewhere, being arriv'd at *Fiorenzole*, which is the first Town in *Toscany* on that side, he found there Count *Albert Castello*, whom the great Duke had sent thither to receive him The Count conducted him to the *Podesta*, where the great Mareschal of the Great Duke's Houshold waited for him, with a Great many of his Highness's Officers and Pages, in Order to treat him at Dinner, from thence he was conducted to the Palace the Great Duke has at the *Escarperie*, where he lay, and the next Day he went and din'd at the *Pratolin*, where *he was receiv'd by the Prince of* Toscany, *the Great Duke's eldest Son* As he drew near *Florence* in the Evening, he found, *at a good Distance from the Gate*, *the Lord* John de Medicis, with two Coaches, and a great many Gentlemen on Horseback, who conducted him into one of the finest Apartments of the Palace of *Piti*, where the Great Duke himself paid him a Visit immediately on his Arrival

My Lord *Falconbridge* did not receive greater, when he came to *Florence* from the King of *England* in the Year 1670 At his Arrival at *Leghorn* he found there two Coaches, and some of the Great Duke's Officers, who there waited for his Coming, and who every Day caus'd new Refreshments to be brought from Court: Four Miles off of *Florence* the Marquiss *Salviati* (who had been Embassador in *England*) waited for him with the Great Duke's Coaches The Great Duke's Brother complemented him at the City-Gate, made him go first into the Coach, seated him on his right Hand, and conducted him to his Apartment in the Palace Nothing more was done to *Falconbridge* than had been done to *Dossat*, notwithstanding this latter had not the Character the other had In the Year 1643, *Bertuccio Valieri*, Senator of *Venice*, was deputed by the Republick to the Army which the Confederates had rais'd for the Interest of the Duke of *Parma* And forasmuch as he was thereby become a Representant, as they say in *Italy*, the Great Duke did him the same Honours that would have been done to the Embassador of a crown'd Head *Valieri* found the Marquiss *de Jougny*, with the Officers of the Houshold, at the Boundaries of the Countrey ready to treat him Prince *Leopold de Medicis* went and receiv'd him without the Gate, and conducted him to his Apartment in the Palace At his Departure from *Florence*, the same Officers accompany'd him, and treated him as far as *Cortona*, where the Great Duke then was That Prince was then sick, so that he receiv'd him in his Bed, having before sent the Marquiss *do Conzague* to receive him without the Gates When, in the Year 1581, the Count *d'Olivares* went to *Rome* in the Quality of Embassador in Ordinary, the Great Duke went to meet him as far as *Leghorn*, but it is

O o very

very probable that the Great Duke did it because he is a Vassal to the King of Spain, on the account of *Siena*.

The Reception the Duke of *Savoy* gave my Lord *Falconbridge* is odd enough The Duke being inform'd that the Embassador drew near his State, sent Count *Miratore*, Master of the Ceremonies, to meet him, who having put three thousand Men under Arms, made him an Entry at *Veillane* by the Light of Torches At the Distance of three or four Miles from *Turin* he was complemented by the Gentlemen of the foreign Ministers, and of the Nobility of the Court, who sent their Coaches to meet him Some Paces without the Town the Marquiss *de St Germain*, Master of the Horse to the Duke of *Savoy*, Governor of *Turin*, and Knight of the Order of the *Annunciade*, waited for him with his Highness's Coach, which my Lord got into, and proceeded towards the Town, attended by two hundred and fourscore Guards on Horseback As soon as he alighted at the Palace which had been prepar'd for him, he was complemented from the Duke, and most of the Nobility visited him The next Day he receiv'd the Visits of the *French* and *Venetian* Embassadors, and the same Day he had Audience, to which he was conducted by the Marquiss *de St Germain*, and by the Master of the Ceremonies, who had brought him four Coaches belonging to the Court. The Duke receiv'd him at his Chamber-Door, and they remain'd both standing and uncover'd. That Prince who does not cover himself, does not treat the Minister like an Embassador, because he will not suffer the Minister to be cover'd It may be said, that the Duke of *Savoy* did him too much Honour at his Entry, to do him so little at his Audience.

Falconbridge, who went from *Turin* to *Genoa*, met near *Savona* the Master of the Ceremonies, and the Captain of the Galley which the Republick sent him to bring him to *Genoa* He was carry'd in a Chair, which he got out of as soon as he perceiv'd the Master of the Ceremonies draw near, but he soon got into it again, and pass'd through the Town after that manner to repair to the Galley, where the Governor of *Savona* went to salute him, and the Embassador did not go out of his Chamber to receive him, Being arriv'd within four Miles of *Genoa*, he was inform'd, by an Express, that four Senators were coming to salute him on the part of the Republick, as indeed they arriv'd almost at the same instant. The Embassador came out of the Poop to receive them, made them go in first, and gave them the Place of Honour. The Canon from the Town, and that of the Ships and Galleys that were in the Port, saluted him as he enter'd it, and at his landing he was presented with a Litter, which brought him to the Palace the Senate had caus'd to be fitted up for him, The next Day two Senators, cloath'd in damask Robes, and accompany'd by above two hundred Gentlemen, complemented him on the part of the Republick. He receiv'd them at the bottom of the Stair-Case, gave them the Hand, and the Stile of Excellency, and at their going away he accompany'd them to the Street Door Some may think it strange, that the Senators should take the Precedency in a Galley that belong'd to the Republick, but in so doing they did the Embassador the greater Honour, because they consider'd him as the Master of the Galley

Those Sovereigns that go themselves to meet Embassadors, as did the Emperor *Maximilian I* in reference to *Woolsey*, do too much, because there are not any that pretend to have this Honour done to their Ministers The Example of *Lewis Sforza* can be no Precedent, no more than that of the Duke of *Lorrain*, who went to meet the Duke *d'Engouleme*, the Count *de Bethune* and *M de Preaux*, Embassadors from *Lewis* XIII, who had also Credentials for him He receiv'd them without the Town of *Nancy*, and when they went away, he conducted them to the Place where he had receiv'd them; it is not on the Examples of these Princes that Civilities are regulated

In *Holland*, where the other Civilities are not very regular, those relating to the Entries of Embassadors are so in some measure The Embassadors that come from the Emperor, *France*, *Spain*, and from *England*, at their Arrival in the Countrey, may pass by *Rotteraam* and they that come from the *Northern* Kings, may without incommoding themselves, go to *Delf*. being these, they acquaint the States therewith, by the means of the weekly President, and there consent the Day of their Entry and Reception. The States have an Officer, to whom they give the Quality of Steward of the Houshold, who has no other Function, but to go to *Rotterdam*, or to *Delfs*, it the Embassador be there, to pay the Expence of his last Repast, and to conduct him with Boats, to within half a League of the *Hague*, where he causes the Embassador to arrive, at the same time that the Deputies of the States come there with a Cortege of thirty Coaches, with six, four, and two Horses The Embassador and the two Deputies, after the first Complements, go into the State's Coach, the Horses whereof notwithstanding, belong to private Persons, and are borrow'd, and conduct him to a House, which is hir'd of a private Person, to lodge Embassadors till their first Audience Formerly the Princes of *Orange* went themselves to meet Embassadors Did not the President *Jeannin* say in a Letter, that he writes to the King on the 29th of May 1607, that Prince *Maurice* went to meet him half a League from the *Hague* ? Yet there are so many Examples thereof, that it would be superfluous to alledge any here. Prince *Frederick Henry*, towards his latter end, excus'd himself therefrom, on the Infirmities of his Age, and the Gout, with which he was afflicted and the Prince, his Son, who had discharg'd this Function during his Father's Life, would do it no more after his Decease. After the King had given the Title of Highness to the Prince of *Orange*, this last might very well excuse himself from executing an Employment, that was so much beneath his Quality, Two Deputies of the States General, of two different Provinces, discharge this Office and as soon as the Embassador alights at his Lodgings, he is there complemented by eight Deputies, because that in all Deputations and Commissions the Province of *Holland* has always two. At every Repast, he takes at the Expence of the State,

two

two Deputies of the Assembly of States, or of the Council of State keep him Company. But for as much as those great and long Repasts are very often attended with some Excess, the Embassadors have found the means to be treated by Present, not as it is understood in *France*, when the King sends them raw Meats, to be dress'd by their own Domesticks, but by making them really a Present, of the Value of the Sum the Expence would amount to if the State bore it. So that this Office of Steward of the Houshold, which was not very necessary, is become altogether useless, but it is not the only one that is so.

They would make no Difficulty at the *Hague* to receive the Embassadors of the Electors with the same Civilities, which are there paid to those of crown'd Heads: but hitherto there has been none. Those that came thither in the Year 1648, from the Elector of *Brandenburg*, had not the Character at their Arrival; and when it was given them, they were no longer in a State to make their Entry, because their Negotiation being far advanc'd, without any great Prospect of Success, they would not make a great Appearance to do nothing. On the other side, as crown'd Heads do not send Embassadors to the Electors, it is hard to determin, whether these last would shew them greater Civilities, than to those of the United Provinces. In the Year 1658, the *Sieur Tibrants*, going in this Quality to *Berlin*, gave Advice thereof to the Baron *de Suerin*, the Elector of *Brandenburg*'s first Minister. Two Counsellors, and several Gentlemen, brought him five Coaches with six Horses each, within half a League of the Town, and conducted him to the Lodgings that had been fitted up for him, where he was every Day treated by the Elector's Officers. In the beginning of the Year 1633, the States sent *Gaspar de Vosbergue*, their Embassador to the Elector of *Cologn*, to the Duke of *Newburg*, and to the Bishop of *Osnaburg*. *Vosbergue* being come within a quarter of a League of the City of *Cologn*, where the Elector then was, met there two Counsellors, accompany'd by some Gentlemen, who had brought him two Coaches. He was conducted to the House of one of the Canons, which the Elector had caus'd to be fitted up with very fine Hangings, and a great Quantity of Plate. He had also sent thither a good Provision of Victuals and Refreshments, under the Dispensation of a Steward of the Houshold, who was assisted by several Gentlemen, some *Swissers* of his Guards, and Pages to serve him: so that there wanted nothing but the Canopy, which the Elector had formerly given him also at *Bonne*. The Electors have not always kept up to any one certain Method; and it is but within very few Years, that they have begun to regulate the Civilities and Ceremonies. In the Month of *October* 1627, *Van den Honart*, *Broker* and *Beaumont*, Embassadors from the United Provinces, went to see the Elector of *Brandenburg* at *Conningsberg*. They had no Entry made them, but as soon as they came to the Inn, the Elector sent them a Coach, which brought them to the Castle where they were lodg'd and defray'd.

The Dukes of *Bavaria* and *Newburg* have been more exact than the other Princes of *Germany*, because they live and are treated after their *Italian* manner. *Vosbergue*, whom I lately mention'd, at his Arrival in the Year 1633 at *Dusseldorp*, found at the Gate the Count *de Grevener*, the Prince of *Newburg*'s Governor, who waited for him with two Coaches, and several Gentlemen on Horseback, and conducted him to the Castle, the Duke's Guards lining the Streets through which he pass'd. When he alighted out of the Coach he was receiv'd and complemented by the Baron of *Wonsberm*, the Duke's Lieutenant General in the Government of all his Provinces. The Duke himself, and the Prince, came and met him in the Antichamber, where the Prince stay'd and the Duke led the Embassador through several Appartments, into a Chamber where he gave him Audience, taking every where the Hand and Precedency of him. There were several other Particularities, of which we shall make mention elsewhere, and which have been in part the Cause, that the States have been more reserv'd since that time, in giving the Character to the Ministers they send to those Princes, that entertain only Ministers of the second Order with them. *Mrs John*, Baron of *Ghent*, *James de Wassenaer d'Opdam*, *Anthony Parmentier de Heesswyeq*, and *Vander Beecke*, whom the Estates employ'd in the Year 1651, to the Elector of *Brandenburg*, and to the Duke of *Newburg*, had only the Quality of Deputies. No Reception was made them at *Cleves*, but as soon as they arriv'd, Count *Maurice de Nassau*, Governor of that Province for the Elector, paid them a Visit; and the Day following the Baron *de Suerin* did the same. They went from thence to *Dusseldorp*, where the Duke caus'd them to be receiv'd at the Gate by the Captain of his Guards, who brought them two Coaches, and conducted them to the Inn, because having refus'd to lodge in the Castle at *Cleves*, they would not receive that Honour at *Dusseldorp*.

The other Princes of *Germany* have regulated these Civilities, according to the Interest they had with the United Provinces. In the Year 1657, they sent to the Bishop of *Munster* three Deputies out of the Assembly of the States General, and one out of the Council of State. At their Arrival near the little Town of *Ahus*, where the Bishop then was, they were complemented by the *Drossart* of *Rhenen*, who alighting, made Excuses to them, that the Inconveniency of the Place hinder'd the Bishop from lodging them in the Castle, as he would gladly have done. They were no sooner set down at the Inn, than the Bishop sent three times to them to desire them to sup with him: and that he might oblige them thereto, he had forbid both the Town and the Inn to supply them with any Provisions. Notwithstanding which, they would not be prevail'd upon; nay they obstinately refus'd to receive a few Dishes, which he had caus'd his Cook to prepare for them, their Scruple going so far, as to make them resolve to fast, rather than break the Oath they had made, not to receive any Presents of any kind whatever. The next Day the Bishop sent the same *Drossart* to them, who conducted them to the Castle in a Coach with six Horses. *The Bishop himself receiv'd them at the bottom of the Stair-Case, gave them the Place of Honour, and led them into a Hall, where they all sate*

down

very probable that the Great Duke did it because he is a Vassal to the King of *Spain*, on the account of *Siena.*

The Reception the Duke of *Savoy* gave my Lord *Falconbridge* is odd enough. The Duke being inform'd that the Embassador drew near his State, sent Count *Miratore*, Master of the Ceremonies, to meet him, who having put three thousand Men under Arms, made him an Entry at *Veillane* by the Light of Torches. At the Distance of three or four Miles from *Turin* he was complemented by the Gentlemen of the foreign Ministers, and of the Nobility of the Court, who sent their Coaches to meet him. Some Paces without the Town the Marquifs *de St. Germain*, Master of the Horse to the Duke of *Savoy*, Governor of *Turin*, and Knight of the Order of the *Annonciade*, waited for him with his Highness's Coach, which my Lord got into, and proceeded towards the Town, attended by two hundred and fourscore Guards on Horseback. As foon as he alighted at the Palace which had been prepar'd for him, he was complemented from the Duke, and most of the Nobility visited him. The next Day he receiv'd the Visits of the *French* and *Venetian* Embassadors, and the same Day he had Audience, to which he was conducted by the Marquis *de St. Germain*, and by the Master of the Ceremonies, who had brought him four Coaches belonging to the Court. The Duke receiv'd him at his Chamber-Door, and they remain'd both standing and uncover'd. That Prince who does not cover himself, does not treat the Minister like an Embassador, because he will not suffer the Minister to be cover'd. It may be said, that the Duke of *Savoy* did him too much Honour at his Entry, to do him so little at his Audience.

Falconbridge, who went from *Turin* to *Genoa*, met near *Savona* the Master of the Ceremonies, and the Captain of the Galley which the Republick sent him to bring him to *Genoa*. He was carry'd in a Chair, which he got out of as foon as he perceiv'd the Master of the Ceremonies draw near, but he foon got into it again, and pass'd through the Town after that manner, to repair to the Galley, where the Governor of *Savona* went to salute him, and the Embassador did not go out of his Chamber to receive him. Being arriv'd within four Miles of *Genoa*, he was inform'd, by an Express, that four Senators were coming to salute him on the part of the Republick, as indeed they arriv'd almost at the same instant. The Embassador came out of the Poop to receive them, made them go in first, and gave them the Place of Honour. The Canon from the Town, and that of the Ships and Galleys that were in the Port, saluted him as he enter'd it, and at his landing he was presented with a Litter, which brought him to the Palace the Senate had caus'd to be fitted up for him. The next Day two Senators, cloath'd in damask Robes, and accompany'd by above two hundred Gentlemen, complemented him on the part of the Republick. He receiv'd them at the bottom of the Stair-Case, gave them the Hand, and the Stile of Excellency, and at their going away he accompany'd them to the Street-Door. Some may think it strange, that the Senators should take

the Precedency in a Galley that belong'd to the Republick, but in so doing they did the Embassador the greater Honour, because they consider'd him as the Master of the Galley.

Those Sovereigns that go themselves to meet Embassadors, as did the Emperor *Maximilian* I in reference to *Woolsey*, do too much, because there are not any that pretend to have this Honour done to their Ministers. The Example of *Lewis Sforza* can be no Precedent, no more than that of the Duke of *Lorrain*, who went to meet the Duke *d'Engoulême*, the Count *de Bethune* and *M. de Preaux*, Embassadors from *Lewis* XIII, who had also Credentials for him. He receiv'd them without the Town of *Nancy*, and when they went away, he conducted them to the Place where he had receiv'd them; it is not on the Examples of these Princes that Civilities are regulated.

In *Holland*, where the other Civilities are not very regular, those relating to the Entries of Embassadors are so in some measure. The Embassadors that come from the Emperor, *France*, *Spain* and from *England*, at their Arrival in the Countrey, may pass by *Rotterdam*; and they that come from the *Northern* Kings, may without incommoding themselves, go to *Delft*; being there, they acquaint the States therewith, by the means of the weekly President, and there concert the Day of their Entry and Reception. The States have an Officer, to whom they give the Quality of Steward of the Houshold, who has no other Function, but to go to *Rotterdam*, or to *Delft*, if the Embassador be there, to pay the Expence of his last Repast, and to conduct him with Boats, to within half a League of the *Hague*, where he causes the Embassador to arrive, at the same time that the Deputies of the States come there with a Cortege of thirty Coaches, with six, four, and two Horses. The Embassador and the two Deputies, after the first Complements, go into the State's Coach, the Horses whereof notwithstanding, belong to private Persons, and are borrow'd, and conduct him to a House, which is hir'd of a private Person, to lodge Embassadors till their first Audience. Formerly the Princes of *Orange* went themselves to meet Embassadors. Did not the President *Jeannin* say in a Letter, that he writes to the King on the 29th of *May* 1607, that Prince *Maurice* went to meet him half a League from the *Hague*? Yet there are so many Examples thereof, that it would be superfluous to alledge any here. Prince *Frederick Henry*, towards his latter end, excus'd himself therefrom, on the Infirmities of his Age, and the Gout, with which he was afflicted; and the Prince, his Son, who had discharg'd this Function during his Father's Life, would do it no more after his Decease. After the King had given the Title of Highness to the Prince of *Orange*, this last might very well excuse himself from executing an Employment, that was so much beneath his Quality. Two Deputies of the States General, of two different Provinces, discharge this Office; and as foon as the Embassador alights at his Lodgings, he is there complemented by eight Deputies, because that in all Deputations and Commissions the Province of *Holland* has always two. At every Repast he takes at the Expence of the State,

two

The EMBASSADOR *and his* FUNCTIONS.   143

two Deputies of the Assembly of States, or of the Council of State keep him Company. But for as much as those great and long Repasts are very often attended with some Excess, the Embassadors have found the means to be treated by Present not as it is understood in *France*, when the King sends them raw Meats, to be dress'd by their own Domesticks but by making them really a Present, of the Value of the Sum the Expence would amount to if the State bore it So that this Office of Steward of the Houshold, which was not very necessary, is become altogether useless, but it is not the only one that is so

They would make no Difficulty at the *Hague* to receive the Embassadors of the Electors with the same Civilities, which are there paid to those of crown'd Heads but hitherto there has been none Those that came thither in the Year 1648, from the Elector of *Brandenburg*, had not the Character at their Arrival and when it was given them, they were no longer in a State to make their Entry, because their Negotiation being far advanc'd, without any great Prospect of Success, they would not make a great Appearance to do nothing On the other side, as crown'd Heads do not send Embassadors to the Electors, it is hard to determin, whether these last would shew them greater Civilities, than to those of the United Provinces. In the Year 1658, the *Sieur Ybrants*, going in this Quality to *Berlin*, gave Advice thereof to the Baron *de Suerin*, the Elector of *Brandenburg*'s first Minister Two Counsellors, and several Gentlemen, brought him five Coaches with six Horses each, within half a League of the Town, and conducted him to the Lodgings that had been fitted up for him, where he was every Day treated by the Elector's Officers In the beginning of the Year 1633, the States sent *Gaspar de Vosbergue*, their Embassador to the Elector of *Cologn*, to the Duke of *Newburg*, and to the Bishop of *Ofnabrug* *Vosbergue* being come within a quarter of a League of the City of *Cologn*, where the Elector then was, met there two Counsellors, accompany'd by some Gentlemen, who had brought him two Coaches He was conducted to the House of one of the Canons, which the Elector had caus'd to be fitted up with very fine Hangings, and a great Quantity of Plate He had also sent thither a good Provision of Victuals and Refreshments, under the Dispensation of a Steward of the Houshold, who was assisted by several Gentlemen, some *Swissers* of his Guards, and Pages to serve him so that there wanted nothing but the Canopy, which the Elector had formerly given him also at *Bonne* The Electors have not always kept up to any one certain Method and it is but within very few Years, that they have begun to regulate the Civilities and Ceremonies In the Month of *October* 1627, *Van den Honart, Becker* and *Beaumont*, Embassadors from the United Provinces, went to see the Elector of *Brandenburg* at *Coningsberg* They had no Entry made them, but as soon as they came to the Inn, the Elector sent them a Coach, which brought them to the Castle where they were lodg'd and defray'd

The Dukes of *Bavaria* and *Newburg* have been more exact than the other Princes of *Germany*, because they live and are treated after then *Italian* manner. *Vosbergue*, whom I lately mention'd, at his Arrival in the Year 1633 at *Dusseldorp*, found at the Gate the Count *de Guevener*, the Prince of *Newburg*'s Governor, who waited for him with two Coaches, and several Gentlemen on Horseback, and conducted him to the Castle, the Duke's Guards lining the Streets through which he pass'd When he alighted out of the Coach he was receiv'd and complemented by the Baron of *Wonsheim*, the Duke's Lieutenant General in the Government of all his Provinces The Duke himself, and the Prince, came and met him in the Antichamber, where the Prince stay'd and the Duke led the Embassador through several Appartments, into a Chamber where he gave him Audience, taking every where the Hand and Precedency of him. There were several other Particularities, of which we shall make mention elsewhere, and which have been in part the Cause, that the States have been more reserv'd since that time, in giving the Character to the Ministers they send to those Princes, that entertain only Ministers of the second Order with them *Mrs John*, Baron of *Ghent*, *James de Wassenaer d'Opdam*, *Anthony Parmentier de Heeswyck*, and *Vander Beecke*, whom the Estates employ'd in the Year 1651, to the Elector of *Brandenburg*, and to the Duke of *Newbourg*, had only the Quality of Deputies No Reception was made them at *Cleves*, but as soon as they arriv'd, Count *Maurice de Nassau*, Governor of that Province for the Elector, paid them a Visit and the Day following the Baron *de Suerin* did the same. They went from thence to *Dusseldorp*, where the Duke caus'd them to be receiv'd at the Gate by the Captain of his Guards, who brought them two Coaches, and conducted them to the Inn because having refus'd to lodge in the Castle at *Cleves*, they would not receive that Honour at *Dusseldorp*

The other Princes of *Germany* have regulated these Civilities, according to the Interest they had with the United Provinces In the Year 1657, they sent to the Bishop of *Munster* three Deputies out of the Assembly of the States General, and one out of the Council of State At their Arrival near the little Town of *Abus*, where the Bishop then was, they were complemented by the *Drossart* of *Rhenen*, who a lighting, made Excuses to them, that the Inconveniency of the Place hinder'd the Bishop from lodging them in the Castle, as he would gladly have done They were no sooner set down at the Inn, than the Bishop sent three times to them to desire them to sup with him, and that he might oblige them thereto, he had forbid both the Town and the Inn to supply them with any Provisions Notwithstanding which, they would not be prevail'd upon, nay they obstinately refus'd to receive a few Dishes, which he had caus'd his Cook to prepare for them, their Scruple going so far, as to make them resolve to fast, rather than break the Oath they had made, not to receive any Presents of any kind whatever The next Day the Bishop sent the same *Drossart* to them, who conducted them to the Castle in a Coach with six Horses The Bishop himself receiv'd them at the bottom of the Stair-Case, gave them the Place of Honour, and led them into a Hall, where they all sate

down

down. In the Month of *April* 1668, *Godard de Reed d'Amerongue*, Deputy from the Province of *Utrecht* to the Assembly of the States General, was sent to the Bishop of *Munster*, to persuade him to grant a Passage for the Troops, which the Dukes of *Lunenburg* sent to the Assistance of the United Provinces. The Bishop, who was at *Lutguersbourg*, desir'd the Deputy to come thither, and sent to meet him, above a League off, by two Colonels, having with them six Coaches with six Horses each, twenty Heidukes, with some of the Yeomen of his Guard, and several Pages and Footmen. Within half a League of the Castle he was met by the Bishop's Coach, and a hundred and fifty Horse for his Convoy. Being arriv'd at *Lutguersbourg*, he was receiv'd at the Coach Door by four *Drossarts*, and at the bottom of the Stairs by the Bishop himself. At their going into the Hall they found two Chairs of red Velvet, in which they sate down, and after a quarter of an Hours Discourse, the Bishop had him conducted to the Appartment which he had caus'd to be prepar'd for him. He treated *M d'Amerongue* as his Relation, and was willing to have some Regard to his Birth, tho' he had very often shewn so little to his Principals, that their Ministers had but too much Reason to complain thereof. The same Deputies who had receiv'd such great Civilities from him at *Ahus*, being sent to him after the Reduction of the City of *Munster*, were not so very well treated by him; for in re-conducting them, he descended first, and took the Hand of them. However he made amends for this Fault the next Day, when they took their Audience of Leave, by receiving them as he had done the first time, and yielding them the Place of Honour every where. On other Occasions he has treated the Ministers of the States with so much Indignity, that without the Insensibility of a Stoick, it could not be dissembled. Hereupon a Question may be put, Whether the Bishop of *Munster*, who is a Prince of the Empire, and who, being a Clergyman, has the Precedency over almost all the secular Princes, is oblig'd to do to the Deputies of the United Provinces, that is to say, to Ministers of the second Order, any Honours that an Embassador would not shew them. *La Barde* and *Rosenhan*, Embassadors from *France* and *Sweden*, refus'd to give the Place of Honour to the Deputies Extraordinary of the United Provinces; and if regard be had to the present Regulations, with reference to Ministers of the second Order, they were in the right. I am therefore apt to doubt, whether that could be reasonably exacted of a Prince of the Empire, which would not be obtain'd of an Embassador, who was skill'd in his Profession. I do not in this derogate from the Dignity of the States, since they have it in their Power to make their Ministers be respected, provided they give them a Character that all Princes are oblig'd to consider.

It was at the Assembly of *Westphalia*, that the Rules of Civility were observ'd with the utmost Punctuality, particularly at the Entries. *Monsieur d'Avaux*, Embassador Plenipotentiary from *France*, arriv'd there on the 17th of *March* 1644. Colonel *Remond* Governor of the City, went to meet him in the Countrey, and paid him Civilities from the Magistrate. When he came near the City, two Gentlemen complemented him on the part of Count *Nassaw*, the Emperor's Plenipotentiary. After that two Gentlemen saluted him from *Saavedra* and *Zapata*, Plenipotentiaries from *Spain*; after which the Secretary of *Anthony le Brun*, third Plenipotentiary from *Spain*, and the Secretary of the *Venetian* Embassador, made him their Complements. They were all in Coaches, attended by a great number of their Masters Domesticks, who were distinguishable by their respective Liveries. The Embassador who made his Entry, alighted out of his Coach to receive the Complement.

On the 9th of *August*, 1657, the Mareschal *de Grammont* and *Lionne*, Embassadors from *France*, and the King's Plenipotentiaries throughout the whole extent of the Empire, and to the Kings of the North, made their Entry into *Francfort*. The Mareschal's Coach went first, and was follow'd by that of *Lionne*, after which came that of *Berenclau*, Embassador from *Sweden*, and then that of *Spoilsky*, Envoy from the same Crown. These were follow'd by three other Coaches belonging to the Mareschal and as many of *Lionne's*. This must be taken notice of, in opposition to the pretentions of *M de Thou*, concerning which we shall speak in the following Chapter.

In the Year 1645, *France* began to urge the States to send their Ministers to *Munster*, yet at the same time it rais'd a thousand difficulties relating to the Honours that should be done them in the view of this Illustrious Assembly, at last the matter was agreed in the following manner. At their arrival on the 11th of *January*, 1646, within half a League of *Munster*, they were met by the *French* Embassador's Coaches, and those of the Ministers of *Portugal*, accompany'd by some Gentlemen to complement them. The two Coaches belonging to the *Dutch* Embassadors, put themselves at the head of the rest. Three Companies of Foot were under their Arms near the Gate of the City, and hard by them some Companies of the Militia. The Embassadors of *Venice*, *Brunswick* and *Hesse* sent to complement them immediately on their arrival, and the *Venetian* particularly excus'd himself for not having sent his Coach to meet them, alledging the Resolution the Mediators had taken not to pay that Ceremony to the other Embassadors that should come thither.

At the Entry the Count *de Witgnestein* Plenipotentiary from *Brandenburg*, made at *Osnaburg* in the Year 1641, a great dispute arose between the Ministers of *Sweden*, and those of the Elector of *Mayence*, the consequence of which was to be dreaded. At the same time that the Horses were putting to, in order to go and meet the Count, advice was sent to the Plenipotentiaries of *Mayence*, that the *Swedes* pretended to send both their Coaches, and that both should take place of that of the Elector of *Mayence*. Count *Cratz*, first Plenipotentiary of that Elector, who had a mind to be Personally there, imagin'd he might prevent the intended affront, by desiring the Count *de Witgnestein* to go in his Coach, which by that means would go before those belonging to the *Swedes*, but he found an obstacle thereto. The Count *de Witgnestein* said, he was
oblig'd

oblig'd to make use of his own Coach, because the Elector had it made on purpose for the service of his first Embassador in this Ceremony. Hereupon Cratz bethought himself of another Expedient, and having put himself in Count Weigneftein's Coach, he sent his own back to Town, with so much haste, that that of Salvius could not get there before it. The Swedes had a mind to perp'ex the Matter, and complain'd also that Count Cratz did not get out of his Coach to receive the compliments of the Gentlemen they had sent to meet him, when he made his Entry.

The Plenipotentiaries of Bavaria stav'd above a Month in a Castle near Munster, waiting till the Ceremonies of their Entry were concerted, and the other Civilities they had a mind should be paid them. The Nuncio said he would send his Coach to meet them, and that he would not refuse the Title of Excellency to their first Plenipotentiary. The Spaniards were at first very peevish, they said they had comply'd with their Duty to the Electoral College, by sending to meet the Bishop of Osnaburg. They added, that perhaps they might be prevail'd upon to do something more in favour of Bavaria, in order thereby to increase the mortification of the Protestant Electors, but as soon as the Plenipotentiaries of France receiv'd Instructions to treat the Ministers of the Electors after the same manner that the Emperor's Plenipotentiaries should treat them, all these difficulties ceas'd, and the Ceremonies of their Entry were soon regulated. The Bishop of Osnaburg went in Person to meet them, got into the Coach belonging to the first, and plac'd him on his right hand. The Governor of the Town went likewise a good way farther into the Countrey than he had been for the Venetian Embassador, after the Coach belonging to the Plenipotentiaries of Bavaria follow'd six others with six Horses each, viz. that of the Nuncio, the two belonging to the Emperor's Plenipotentiaries, two of the French Embassadors, and that of the Embassador from Venice. The Gentlemen who accompany'd the Cortege, getting out of their Coaches, made their complements to the Plenipotentiaries who were making their Entry, and who had also alighted ought of theirs. The same Ceremonies were practis'd at the Entry of the Ministers of all the other Electors, and the Artillery saluted them as they enter'd into the Town. There were none but the Ministers of Saxony, who not valuing all that noise, arriv'd at Munster without Ceremonies.

Very few Princes at present will suffer the Ministers that reside near them, to intermeddle in the Civilities they do to Embassadors at their Entry, by reason of the contests and quarrels that happen'd about Precedency. The dispute that arose at London between the Count d'Estrades, and the Baron de Vatteville, Embassador from Spain, in the Year 1661, at the Entry of an Embassador from Sweden, oblig'd the King of Great Britain to exclude foreign Ministers from those Ceremonies. So many others arise also in other places, that the rest of the Princes thought it expedient to follow this Example, which they have done with good success, and great reason, since it belongs to them to do Honours in their own Dominions, and that Strangers have no business to have any concern therein. The Venetian Embassador, who was at London in the Year 1641, signify'd to those that were there on the part of the United Provinces, that he pretended to have his Coach go before theirs in the Cavalcade to their Audience. They made answer, that on all other occasions they would not dispute Precedency with the Embassador from Venice, but in this, which was a Solemnity that particularly related to themselves, they would make their Coach go immediately after the King's. It is not only amongst Embassadors that these quarrels happen, but also among the Ministers. M. de Thurenne's Coach took the rank of the Spanish Embassador's, and when the Count de Schafgots Embassador from the Emperor, had his Audience in the Senate of Poland on the 7th of June, 1669, the General and the Mareschal of the Crown would not suffer the Coaches of the Nuncio and the French Embassador's, to go before theirs, and oblig'd them to retire, which is worthy observation, because it is what would not be done elsewhere.

I should never have done, were I to fill up this Chapter with all that can be said on this Subject, but I suppose the Reader will not be displeas'd to see here the practice of those Courts, who notwithstanding they are not so civiliz'd as those I have already mention'd, yet are not wanting in the Honours that are due to Embassadors, and thereby sufficiently testifie, that in the height of their brutality, they have still more respect for the Law of Nations, than is shewn in some other parts of Europe. If the Turks are cruel, insolent and proud, the Muscovites are rude, barbarous and brutish. For although Birth makes some distinction among the last, yet they are all Slaves to the Czar, and in this servile and mean Education there is nothing to be seen but what is abject, gross and rustical. The Czar or Great Duke, causes all Embassadors to be receiv'd at the entrance into his Dominions, and defrays them as long as they stay there, but then this treatment, and the Honour that is done them, is accompanied with an arrogancy that is almost beastly. Whereas in the other Courts, the Masters of the Ceremonies, and the Introductors of Embassadors, do all the Civilities imaginable to Embassadors, and do the Honours of the House in the name of their Prince, the Muscovite Pristave does all he can to take the place of Honour, makes difficulty to alight from his Horse till the Embassador has quitted his; he with eagerness thrusts himself first into a Sled or Coach, to take possession of the most honourable place, and treats him with haughtiness on all occasions. There are several relations from those parts, and among the rest a very pertinent one of the Embassy the Duke of Holstein Gottorp sent thither, as also in Persia, in the Year 1633, and in the subsequent Years. But it is not any where that their impertinence is more lively represented, than in what we have of the Journey the Earl of Carlisle took thither in the Year 1663, being sent by the King of Great Britain. The Pristave, who receiv'd him at Archangel, took the hand of the Embassador, and would not yield it to him, till the

P p

the Governor of the Town commanded him to conform to the Earl's will, who was determin'd to maintain the Dignity of the King his Master. The day was appointed him for his Entry into *Moscow* He was on Horseback, and had travel'd about half a League, when they oblig'd him to delay it to the next day, and to go and lodge in the mean time at a forry Village near the City. The Embassador gave to understand that he was very much offended thereat, and complain'd thereof to the *Czar* in a Letter, in the strongest and most expressive terms, but instead of receiving any satisfaction, he had the mortification to have none, neither on this occasion, nor in reference to the subject of his Embassy; and moreover where he had reason to expect the greatest Honour, he on the contrary, receiv'd the grossest Affront. The *Czar* made him dine with him, but at a separate Table, and more remote from his own, than that which was provided for some *Boyares*, that is to say, for some of the *Czar's* Slaves, who were plac'd on the right, while the Embassador was plac'd on the left. This usage made him leave the Court very ill satisfy'd, insomuch that he refus'd the *Czar's* present, and having express'd his resentment with a great deal of warmth, the *Czar* thought fit to complain thereof to the King of Great Britain, by a particular Embassy for that purpose.

The *Turks* know very well what is due to Embassadors, and are not backward in doing them the Honours their Character challenges, when they are not incompatible with their interest, and in that sense there are also a great many *Turks* in *Christendom*. They who believe that the Port makes no distinction between Embassadors, and Ministers of the second Order, because they comprise both the one and the other under the general quality of *Elchi*, are mistaken. They distinguish very well between the Characters, as well as between the Merit of the Ministers, and between the Quality of the Princes that employ them. Those Ministers who reside there only on the account of Commerce, are very little consider'd, unless it be for the sake of their own personal Merit, of which the *Turks* judge equitably enough. To shew therefore that they make a difference between an Embassador, and a Minister of the second Order, I shall here set down the particulars of the Entry *Armory* or *Almeric Nam* Embassador and *Bailo* of *Venice* made at *Constantinople*, in the Year 1617. Being come within sight of the City, on the 11th of *February*, he saluted the *Seraglio* with all the Artillery belonging to the English Ship which had transported him from the Isle of *Chio* As soon as he was Landed, and before he came to his Lodgings, notwithstanding it began to be night, the *French* Embassador and the Ministers of the other Christian Princes sent their Secretaries to complement him, and the day following they went themselves with the usual Ceremonies, the *Internuncio* only excepted, who did not think himself oblig'd to pay this Civility, because he had already taken his Audience of Leave even of the *Bailo*, whom *Nam* came to succeed. He made his Entry on the 25th of the same Month, in the following manner

The two Embassadors, *Nam* and his Collegue or Predecessor, repair'd towards the Port on the side of *Galata*, and about two Miles from the City, which was the place of Rendezvous to all those that were to accompany him in this Cavalcade, the two Embassadors got on Horseback, and mov'd towards the Town, the Embassador's four *Janisaries* went first, not on Horseback, but on Foot, having over their Cassocks, which they call a *Doleman*, a Vest of Red Cloth, forty other *Janisaries* with their usual Habits and Arms, follow'd on Foot, commanded by their Captain, who follow'd them on Horseback, and preceded as many *Spahi's* or Troopers, who had no other Arms than Bows and Arrows, forty *Chiaorix* follow'd these, and after them the *Bailo's* Domesticks, that is to say, forty Courriers, or Letter-Carriers, who are all Subjects of the Republick, and serve to go and come from *Venice* to *Constantinople* They make these Journeys on foot, but yet they perform them with expedition enough They were all clad after the *Greek* manner, and in the Embassador's Livery, with a Vest and plaited Cap, after them march'd the Serjeants, and other Livery-Men, follow'd by the *Drogomans*, or the Republick's Interpreters, who were accompany'd by the *Drogomans* of all the other Christian Ministers, all on Horseback, and in the same Ranks which their Masters are us'd to keep among themselves. After them came the *Chiaoux Bachi*, that is to say, the Chief of the *Chiaoux*, who is like the Master of the Ceremonies, having on his right hand (which is the less honourable in *Turks*) a Captain of *Spahi's* These two Officers march'd immediately before the two Embassadors, the former of which had the place of Honour, because the other had not as yet enter'd on the exercise of his Employment, and they had a great number of Men in Livery near them The two Embassadors were follow'd by the Secretaries of the Embassadors of *France*, *Holland*, and *Venice*, this last doing Honour on this occasion to the other two. With the Secretaries march'd the two Sons, whom the new *Bailo* had brought along with him from *Venice*, and the *Roman* Gentleman, to whom we are oblig'd for this relation These last, that is to say, the three Secretaries, and the three Gentlemen march'd in two ranks three a breast, the *French* Secretary between the Embassador's two Sons, and the *Dutch* Secretary between the *Venetian* Secretary, and the *Roman* Gentleman, but when they came into narrow Streets, where it was necessary to file off, they march'd in two Columns, the three Secretaries keeping the right, and the three Gentlemen the left A great number of Gentlemen, the Domesticks of the other Embassadors, and of the Merchants of *Pera*, brought up the rear of the Procession, which was compos'd of two hundred and fifty Horse, besides those that were on Foot It was in this Order that the Embassadors took the way to *Galata*, and after having march'd partly round the same, they enter'd at one of the Gates, and went out at another, to go to the *Bailo's* Palace, which was without the Walls, where all the other Christian Ministers were Lodg'd. When they came to the Palace, the *Turks* who found their Dinner ready for them, instead of eating, shar'd the Victuals amongst themselves, and wen went away. The new *Bailo* made an Entertainment on this occasion, but of all the Foreign Ministers, only the Baron *de Sancy-Harlay*, Embassador from *France*, partook of the Dinner, and there happen'd nothing remarkable thereat.

If the Resident, who is on the part of the United Provinces at *Constantinople*, had sent the States a pertinent relation of the particulars of his Luxury, a Judgment might be form'd of the distinction that is made between the Ministers of the first and second Order, but as he did not do himself much Honour at his arrival at the Port, nor indeed to his Masters, he was cautious of mentioning in his Dispatches, an action that did not brighten his Reputation.

The same *Roman* Gentleman who has given the publick a relation of the Entry of the *Bailo Nani*, was also a witness to that, that shall conclude this Chapter, which I here set down, because there is something in it so very great, that nothing I have hitherto said, comes up to it.

In the Month of *April*, 1619, there arriv'd in *Persia* two *Muscovite* Embassadors, *Knez Juan Lostinski*, and *Juan Jnanowitz Schach Abas* was taken up with an Expedition he design'd against the *Turks*, so that not being able to give a Reception to the Embassadors at *Ardebil*, where they were in a constant alarm, their Entry was put off till the King should return to *Ispahan*. It was therefore perform'd on the 19th of *June*, in the same Year, and at the same time the *Indian* Embassador of the *Mogul*, and a *Turkish Chiaux* made theirs. The King desir'd *Don Garcia de Silva Figueroa*, Embassador from *Spain*, and the *English* Resident, to honour the Ceremony with their presence, and notify'd to them, that they might assist there in his Company, because he intended to go in Person to meet the Embassadors *Schach Abas*, to do them the greater Honour, or to make the greater ostentation of his Grandeur, had made a *Roll of threescore thousand effective Men*, whose Names he had a List of, and he had caus'd Arms to be distributed amongst them, notwithstanding most of them were only Artificers, Inhabitants of *Ispahan*, and the adjacent Villages. All this multitude was come early in the Morning to the *Maidan*, which is their Market, very well cloath'd, and dispos'd into several Companies and Battalions, under their Colours, commanded by their Captains, and other Officers, who had their Drums, Kettle Drums, Flutes, and other Instruments of Musick. The King caus'd these threescore thousand Men to be drawn up in two Files or equal Lines, which reach'd from the Palace Gate to the place where the Embassadors had Lodg'd the Night before, which was about twelve Miles from *Ispahan*, leaving between the Hayes a space sufficient to admit of the Embassador's Cavalcade. All the Instruments of Musick, which were in great number, resounded with such a noise, as would have drown'd that of the Thunder, and at every twenty paces distance, there were Men that left their Ranks to Dance, and make a kind of Ball, with which they diverted themselves, at least, as much as the Spectators. Besides this, there were in several places along the *Maidan*, and in the Streets, several young Men, very handsom, and neatly dress'd, who with Flagons and Cups of Gold, fill'd out Wine and Water refresh'd with Ice, to those that would drink. The King sent to the very Village where the Embassadors were Lodg'd, all the Nobility of his Court. They were all perfectly well mounted, and magnificently clad, so that there was nothing to be seen but Rich Stuffs, Saddles and Bits of massie Gold and Silver beset with precious Stones, as were also their Caps and Feathers which were very sumptuous. And notwithstanding, this had not the effect these Richesses were capable of producing, because these Noblemen only walk'd up and down the Town to shew themselves, yet there might be perceiv'd a very agreeable oddness even in this confusion. The *Schach* commanded also the *Jews* and the *Gavres*, who still make profession of the Religion of the ancient *Persian*, to go in Procession separately from the rest, but as for the Christians of the Suburbs of *Zulfa*, who had furnish'd seven hundred Men, they mingled with the other *Persians*. In fine, the King to do the Embassadors the greater Honour, caus'd twenty or five and twenty of the most beautiful *Courtesans* to appear there on Horseback, very richly dress'd, and bare-fac'd, which is the mark that distinguishes them from virtuous Women. The *Muscovian* Embassador who was the first, and who believ'd that the *Schach* would come and receive him in Person at his Quarters, waited a long time for him in the Village, dispatching Couriers from time to time, to be inform'd of his motion, but finding there was no likelihood of his coming, he mounted on Horseback, and the other Embassadors following his example, they put themselves in order, and mov'd towards the Town, each Embassador at the head of his Troop. Of all the other Foreign Ministers who had been invited to this Ceremony, only the *English* Resident went through to their Quarters, and that more out of Curiosity, than to do them Honour. The *Spanish* Embassador, who had set out finding the *Schach* did not come according to the assignation he had given him, return'd home very much incens'd that he had been oblig'd to go and meet the *Indian* Embassador, whom he call'd a Merchant, notwithstanding he was a near Relation of the *Mogul*, and that he had above fifteen hundred Persons in his Retinue. The other Embassadors, viz the *Mirjorite* (who was now single, his Collegue being deceas'd) and the *Turk*, were already arriv'd at the Palace, when *the King, who at last went to meet the Indian as far as the Gate of the City*, appear'd with him at the *Maidan*. As soon as he was got into the Palace (where *Figueroa* who had alter'd his mind, was likewise come) all the three Ministers presented to him Letters from their Masters. The whole Audience was employ'd therein, and in taking off some Cups of *Schiras* Wine, while the Conversation ran upon indifferent things, and was irregular enough. After two or three hours Entertainment, they all withdrew, without taking leave of the King, and without doing any Civility to one another. I have omitted taking notice, that when the Embassadors began to leave the Village, the sixty thousand Men, who as I said before, made a Lane from the Palace, to their Quarters, put themselves also in motion, falling in Routs,

Routs, and without Order, behind the Embaſſador's Retinue, and enter'd the Town in this confus'd manner, and ſo generally poſſeſs'd themſelves of all the Avenues that the *Indian* Embaſſador, who had a great Train of Baggage, could not get it into the Town that Day. The ſame Embaſſador, being inform'd that thoſe ſixty thouſand Men were moſt of them Tradeſmen, and had loſt their Day's Work for his ſake, order'd his Steward to give to each of them ten Sequins, which would have amounted to twelve hundred thouſand Crowns. But *Schach Abas*, who was none of the moſt liberal, and who was unwilling the *Indian* Embaſſador ſhould reproach his avaricious Temper, was angry thereat, and would not ſuffer it to be executed. As ſoon as the *Turkiſh* Embaſſador enter'd into *Perſia*, the *Schach* forbid on pain of Death to have any Communication with him, even under the Pretext of ſelling him Proviſions, but then he took Care to have him abundantly ſupply'd from his own Kitchin.

Theſe Entries and Receptions being made only to Embaſſadors, to the Excluſion of Miniſters of the ſecond Order, we muſt believe that *James Loffler* and *Philip Streif*, who arriv'd in *Paris* on the 16th of *October* 1634, were Embaſſadors. It was their own Faults that they were not receiv'd with Ceremony, and loaģ'd by the King's Appointment. They were treated with Preſents during the whole time of their ſtay at *Paris*. The Marquis *de Mortemar*, one of the firſt Gentlemen of the Bed-Chamber, viſited them from his Majeſty, and the Count *de Harcourt* with *M Barutri* conducted them to their Audience. It is true that the Count *de Bruloa* ſays in his Memoirs, That one of them was Embaſſador Extraordinary from *Sweden*, and the other from the four Circles of *Germany*. But beſides that *Loffler* had no Commiſſion from the Crown of *Sweden*, as I ſhall make it appear by and by, they were both treated alike on all Occaſions, as well in the Preſent as otherwiſe. To ſhew that they were both Embaſſadors from the four Circles of the Upper *Germany*, and that they had neither Powers nor Credentials from the Crown of *Sweden*, I need only produce their Declaration, wherein they ſay, *We* James Loffler, &c *and* Philip Streif, &c *by virtue of the Power given us by our Lords, the Princes and States of the four Circles of the Upper* Germany, *do ratify the aboveſaid Treaty*. Now theſe four Circles being compos'd only of Eccleſiaſtical and Secular Princes of *Germany*, of Prelates, of Counts, and of Cities, one would think it cou'd not be deny'd but on this Occaſion *France* acknowledg'd the Embaſſadors of the Princes in *Germany*.

CHAP. XIX.

Of Audiences

AUdiences are either publick and ſolemn, or private and for Buſineſs. Theſe making a part of the Embaſſadors Negotiation, ſhall alſo make a part of the ſecond Book of this Treatiſe, and the others ſhall be the Subject of this Chapter, by reaſon of the Ceremonies with which they are accompany'd. The *publick Audience* uſhers the Embaſſador into his Employment, and eſtabliſhes him in the Function of his Commiſſion, tho' it be not ſo abſolutely requiſite but he may negotiate without it. Thoſe Embaſſadors that are ſent to Congreſſes cannot take *Audience*, and only communicate their *Letters of Credence* to the Mediators, or Miniſters with whom they are to negotiate. It is true indeed that the Miniſter, to whom the Prince denies *Audience*, is incapable of negotiating, becauſe he is thereby given to underſtand that he will have no Commerce with him, as when the States of the United Provinces refus'd it to the *Portugal* Embaſſador, and the King of *Sweden* would not admit of thoſe of *Brandenburg*, but when any other Obſtacle or lawful Impediment hinders it, and that inſtead of refuſing it the *Audience* is only put off to another time, this Delay cannot hinder the Embaſſador from diſcharging all the Functions of his Office. Monſieur *de Baſſompierre*, being come to *Madrid* in the Year 1621, could not obtain *Audience* becauſe the King was ſick, but the ſame King notify'd to him, that if he would ſend him his *Credentials* he would nominate Commiſſioners who ſhould enter into Conference with him. Baſſompierre ſent him his *Letters* and the King accordingly appointed Commiſſioners, who ſo diligently apply'd themſelves during the King's Sickneſs, that the Treaty of *Madrid*, for the Affairs of the *Valteline*, was quickly concluded after his deceaſe. Baſſompierre took *Audience* of his Succeſſor with the uſual Ceremonies.

Theſe are almoſt every where regulated, as well as thoſe of the Entry, and they are all particular at *Rome*, where none but the Embaſſador of Obedience has *Audience* in the Conſiſtory, in a ſtanding Poſture and uncover'd, while an Orator, hir'd for that purpoſe, pronounces the Harangue in the Preſence of the Pope, and of the College of Cardinals. The Embaſſadors of the Emperor, of crown'd Heads, and of *Venice*, have theſe *Audiences* in the Royal Hall, but the Embaſſadors of other Princes have them in the Ducal Hall, and there are ſome to whom the Pope gives *Audience* only in his Chamber, where ſome Cardinals are preſent, but not enough to form a Conſiſtory. The Duke of *Savoy* pretends to the Royal Hall, ſince he has taken the Title of King of *Cyprus*, and becauſe he has not hitherto been able to obtain it, he forbears ſending any Embaſſadors of Obedience to *Rome*. The Republick of *Genoa* has offer'd ſome Millions to be admitted into the Royal Hall, but the Pope would not conſent

consent thereto, by reason of the Opposition the Senate of *Venice* made, which will not suffer this Equality. The Obedience being over, the Embassador follows the Pope, carries the Train of his Cope, and dines with him, as I observ'd before in the preceding Chapter, speaking of the *French* Embassador.

On the 13th of *September* 1582. arriv'd at *Rome* a *Moscovite* Embassador, for whom an Entry was made. He receiv'd his *Audience* in a spacious Hall, where the Pope was accompany'd by fifteen Cardinals, and not in the usual Hall for *Audiences*. The Embassador made the same Ceremonies that other Embassadors usually make, bowing three times, and kissing his Feet. He spoke in his own Tongue because he knew no other. The Pope presented him with three Vests of thin Brocade, a Chain of Gold, and gave some Chains likewise to those of his Retinue.

When the Pope gives *private Audiences* to the Embassadors of crown'd Heads, and those of *Venice*, he is seated in a Crimson Velvet Chair, with Gold and Silver Fringes, having under his Feet a scarlet Carpet. The Embassador is seated over against the Pope, on a Stool, and does not cover himself during the *Audience*. The Embassadors of other Princes are in a standing Posture, and most commonly the Pope walks up and down whilst they speak to him, or else he stands, leaning his Hand upon the Table, but at the beginning of the *Audience* he is seated in his Chair. The Prince that walks, while he gives *Audience* to a Minister, does him a little more Honour than if he slept, or spoke to him as he pass'd by him. When the Cardinals receive *Audience* from the Pope, they have a Chair with a Back to it. The *Venetian* Embassador always carries with him his Secretary, who stands behind his Master's Chair, which is likewise observ'd when he takes *Audience* of the Cardinals. These *Audiences* of the Cardinals are, properly speaking, but meer Visits, for which reason they might be more properly spoke to elsewhere. But as there are but two Words to be said on this Subject, I shall here add, That when the Secretary of a *Venetian* Embassador is to treat with a Cardinal, in the Absence of his Master, he is seated, as well as the Secretaries of the Embassadors of the Emperor, the Kings of *France* and *Spain*, and the same Honours are done him which are done to the Residents and Agents of Princes, to whom the Title of Most Serene is given. This is chiefly done to the Secretaries of the Embassy, because that these are also Ministers Representants. The Cardinals sent also the Secretaries of the Embassadors of *Savoy*, and of *Tuscany*. It must therefore be imagin'd that, in those parts, those important Employments are not given to Clarks or Copists, but to Ministers, that are as it were in their Apprenticeship; and who, having given Proof of their Merit, may aspire to the first Places in the State. The same Prelates, that is to say, the two Patriarchs that have receiv'd the Embassador at his Entry, conduct him also to his *Audience*.

It is only the first *Audience* that the Pope gives in full Consistory, and it is very rarely that Embassadors have there a second, even for extraordinary and very important Affairs. M. de *Termes*, Embassador from *France*, having obtain'd it in the Month of *May* 1551, takes particular notice in his Harangue, That he was sensible it was contrary to Custom, but that it was the King his Master's express Orders. He could not address himself to Pope *Julius* III because he was commanded to complain of him. He accompany'd his Discourse with a formal Protestation, after which he was to depart, and take along with him the Cardinals of *Ferrara* and of *Tournon*, who negotiated the King's Affairs at *Rome*. Some Years before, that is to say, in the Month of *December* 1547 *Don Diego Hurtado de Mendosse*, Embassador from the Emperor *Charles* V, took his *Audience* in the Consistory, on account of the Translation of the Council of *Trent*, and he was also call'd thither to hear the Answer the Pope was to make to his Proposition. He was there again on the 16th of *January* 1548, and made the same Protestation, that *Francis de Vargas* and *Martin de Velasque* made the same Day at *Bologna*, against the Translation of the Council. *Don Diego* express'd himself in Terms so strong, that the Pope, not daring to shew his Resentment, was for making it be believ'd that *M. ndosse*, in making this Protestation in the Consistory, had exceeded his Orders; since the Emperor had commanded him to complain of the Authors of the Translation, and not of the Pope, who had no Concern therein, as he said, the whole Affair relating only to the Legates and Prelates of the Council, who had judg'd the Translation necessary. We must also take notice, by the by, that the Pope gives no *Audience* in the Holy Week.

Some Distinction is made in *France*. But before I speak thereto, I must inform my Reader, that at *Vienna* the Officers of the Emperor's Houshold are employ'd in these Functions. There is neither Master of the Ceremonies nor Introductor of the Embassadors in that Court. It is the High Chamberlain that there regulates the Civilities, and that gives Orders for the Reception of publick Ministers. When the Duke *del Sesto*, Embassador from *Spain*, arriv'd at *Vienna* in the Month of *October* 1670, the Count *de Slabata* went and receiv'd him at his own House, in the Emperor's Coaches, when he came to the Palace he was receiv'd at the Entrance thereof by the Mareschal of the Court; the great Master receiv'd him the Knight's Hall; and at the going into the Antichamber he was receiv'd by the Count *de Lamberg*, Great Chamberlain.

In *France* the Nuntio's, and the Embassadors of crown'd Heads, are conducted to their *Audience* by Princes, and it is in that only, that the Embassadors of *Venice* are not treated as those of crown'd Heads. The last Day of *August* 1635, the Lord Viscount *Scudmore*, Embassador from *England*, being come to *Miaux*, in order to take his first *Audience* of the King, who was then at *Monceaux*, told *Berlise*, that he would not go to it if he was not conducted thereto by a Prince. There was none then at Court, so that *Girant* was sent Post to *Paris*, from whence he brought the next Day the Duke *de Chevreuse*, who discharg'd that Office. The Lord *Fielding*, Embassador Extraordinary from *England*, in the Year 1634, was conducted to *Audience* by the Count *d'Alais*, a Prince of the

House of *Valois* The Earl of *Leicester*, in the same Quality in the Year 1636, by the aforesaid Duke *de Chevreuse* Loffler and *Streyf*, Embassadors from the four Circles in the Year 1634, by the Count *de Harcourt*, Prince of the House of *Lorrain* Grotius, Embassador in Ordinary from *Sweden*, by the Duke *de Merseur*, Son to the Duke of *Vendosme* Savadsky, Embassador Extraordinary from *Poland* in the Year 1636, by the Duke *de Chevreuse* The Duke *de Joyeuse*, conducted to *Audience* the Bishop of *Warmia*, and the Palatine of *Posnania*, Embassadors Extraordinary from *Poland* in the Year 1645 It was accompany'd with the same Ceremonies which had been perform'd at their Entry, except that the two Embassadors, with the chief Noblemen of their Retinue, went in the King's and Queen's Coaches All the Princes and Nobility had receiv'd notice to render themselves at the Royal Palace, where their Majesties then were, and *de Rhodes*, great Master of the Ceremonies, was commanded to give the necessary Orders for this extraordinary *Audience* The Coaches having taken a Round in the second Court, they stopp'd before the Chamber of Descent, into which the Embassadors enter'd, and after they had retired themselves a little, and that all the *Poles* were arriv'd, they pass'd along the Court through a Lane made by the Grand Prevost's Guards under their Arms The *Great Master of the Ceremonies* receiv'd them at the foot of the Stair-Case, which was lin'd on both sides by the hundred *Switzers*, who made a Lane, the Drum beating, and *Ste Marte*, their Lieutenant, being at the Head of them At the Entrance into the Guard Room they were met by the Marquiss *de Chandenier*, Captain of the *Scotch* Guards who having caus'd part of the *Polish* Nobility to pass along, put himself before the Great-Master of the Ceremonies, and the Introductor, and after them follow'd the two Embassadors, conducted by the Duke *de Joyeuse*, they were follow'd by another Body of *Poles* The Body Guards made a Lane, the Antichamber was full of Nobility, and the Chamber was crowded with Lords, and Officers of the Houshold As fast as the *Polish* Lords enter'd the Gallery where the King and Queen were, the Great-Master rang'd them on both sides, to make a Passage for the Embassadors The Captain of the Guards, the Great-Master of the Ceremonies, and the Introductor having made their Bows, they open'd to give way to the Embassadors, who having likewise perform'd theirs, made their Complement in *Latin* the Bishop speaking first, and after him the *Palatine* This being done, they presented their *Credentials* to their Majesties, who gave them to the Count *de Brienne*, Secretary of State The rest of the *Audience* pass'd in indifferent Discourses, in which the Embassadors spoke *French* and after that, the *Polish* Lords made their Reverences to the King and Queen, and retir'd

From thence they went to the House of *Nevers*, to take their *Audience* of the Princess of *Mantua*, who receiv'd them at the Entrance of the Hall They spoke to her also in *Latin*, and made her a Present of a Cross of Diamonds worth a hundred thousand Crowns. The Bishop of *Orange* answer'd the Embassador's Harangue, and the Princess, their future Queen, conducted them to the middle of the Hall

After what I have said in the foregoing Chapter, of the Reception that was made in the Year 1611, to the Duke of *Mayenne* in *Spain*, and to the Duke of *Pastrana* in *France*, we must here add the Particulars of their *Audiences* The first had his on the 23d of *July*, and was conducted to it by the Duke *d'Usseda*, Son to the Duke of *Lerma*, who was accompany'd by the Dukes of *Alva* and of *Albuquerque*, and by several other Lords, who went and receiv'd him with a very numerous Cortege, at the Palace where he was lodg'd Having pass'd through several Galleries, where the *Spanish* Guards, the *Switzers* and *Burgundians* were drawn up in two Lanes, he was met at the Door of the *Audience-Hall*, by the Earls of *Casteh avio* and *Sidasan*, the King's High-Stewards, who conducted him pretty near the Throne where the King sate under a Canopy, having on his left Hand the Prince his Son, on his right the Duke of *Lerma* standing, and behind his Chair the Marquiss de la *Velade*, bare headed The *Embassador having made his first Bow, the King got up, at the second he took off his Hat, and at the third he embrac'd the Embassador, and made him be cover'd* After the Embassador had finish'd his Complement, he went and saluted the Prince, who embrac'd him But this was done but as it were by accident, because he was oblig'd to pay that Devoir to the *Infanta* first In the mean time the Prince of *Tingri*, the Embassador's Son, went and paid his Respects to the King, who made him be cover'd, and the other *French* Noblemen kiss'd his Hand From this *Audience* he went to that of the *Infanta*, to whom he made a Reverence, as to the Queen, because she had desir'd it, after which he saluted the Ladies The next Day he visited the Ministers, and Lords who had visited him and three Days after he went and deliver'd to the *Infanta* the Letter the King had written to her On the 22d of *August* he had another solemn *Audience*, at which the Contract of Marriage was read The Duke of *Lerma*, accompany'd by all the Grandees of the Court, went and receiv'd him at his Palace, and in conducting him, he caus'd all the Company to be so dispos'd, that all the *French* Nobility march'd first, two and two, and after them the Prince of *Tingri* alone After him came *M de Pusieux*, who had brought the Contract of Marriage, with *M de Vaucelas*, the Embassador in Ordinary, who went immediately before the Duke of *Mayenne* and of *Lerma* They found in the great Room the Nuncio *Cajetan*, who on this Occasion was to discharge the Function of Legate The Duke of *Mayenne* plac'd himself on the Nuncio's right Hand, the Duke of *Lerma* on his left, and by him sate the Count *Orsodelli*, Embassador from *Tuscany* Mrs *de Pusieux* and *de Vaucelas* fill'd the Bench of the other side There was another Bench for the Lords of the Council of State; and on that side the Duke of *Lerma* was of, there was a Forme for the Grandees of *Spain*, where sate the Duke *d'Usseda*, the Prince of *Tingri*, the Admirant of *Castile*, the Duke of *Maqueda*, the Count of *Peguera-da*, the Dukes of *Alva*, of *Sesse*, of *Feria*, of *Montalto*, of *Villahermosa* and of *Veragas* Before the Nuncio there was a Table cover'd with a Carpet of Crimson Velvet, by which on the was a Stool, on which sate *Don Antonio a' S rofequi*, Secretary of State, who read the Contract in the *Spanish* Tongue. The Duke of *Mayenne*, and *Mrs de Puisieux* and *du Vancelas*, as Procurators for the King and Queen Mother, sign'd the Contract first, which was couch'd in the *French* Language, and utter them the Duke of *Lerma*, as Procurator for the King and the *Infanta*, sign'd it, with *Arofequ*. The Duke of *Lerma* sign'd first the *Spanish* Contract, and the *French* Ministers sign'd it after him. At their going out of this Room, they enter'd into another, where they found the King seated betwixt the *Infanta* and the Prince. The Embassador complemented him on the Marriage, as also the *Infanta* and the Prince. This being done, a Lady was assign'd him for his Entertainment, and all the *French* Lords had each of them his. Some Days after, the King invited the Embassador to ride out with him, and then he let it liberty to the *French*, to be were in the Pleins, or on board the *Spanish* Gallies.

The Duke of *Pastrana*'s Audience, was not inferior to this in Solemnity. He receiv'd it on the 16th of *August* to conduct him to it, he had thirty Horses sent him out of the King's Stable, two Coaches with six Horses each, and is many with four, and two. The Duke of *Guise*, accompany'd by the Prince of *Joinville*, and the Chevalier *de Guise* his Brothers, by the Duke *d'Elbœuf*, by the Marquis *de Nermoustier*, *Le Nesle*, *de la Valette*, *d'Crequi*, *de St Luc*, a *Bassompierre*, *de Termes*, and by other Lords, went and receiv'd him at the Hotel of St *Paul*, and having caus'd three hundred *French* Gentlemen on Horseback to lead the Van, after them follow'd thirty *Spanish* Lords, each betwixt two *French* ones, in this Condition he conducted him to the *Louvre*. The Guards were rang'd on both sides of the way from the little *Bourbon*. The great Provost receiv'd him at the Gate, and the Captain of the hundred *Switzers* in the Court of the *Louvre*. The Captain of the King's Guards receiv'd him at the Entrance into the Guard-Room, and the Count *de Soissons*, Prince of the Blood, as he went out of that Room. The Passages were very light, because all the Pages of the little and great Stables, having each two Flambeaux of white Wax, convey'd him through the King's Chamber into the Gallery, where his Majesty expected him. The rais'd Floor where the King sate, was cover'd with a Velvet Carpet of a Violet Colour, interspers'd with *Flower-de-Luces* of Gold, under a Canopy, and in a Chair of the same, having on his left Hand the Queen Mother, seated in a Chair of black Velvet. The Embassador being come near, and having made three low Bows, presented to the King one of the *Letters* which he held betwixt his Fingers, and made a short Complement at the same time. After which the King arose, answer'd the Complement, and then embrac'd the Embassador, who after that went and spoke to the Queen, to whom he presented the other *Letter*, after which they enter'd into Conversation, the *Embassador being cover'd*. This being over the King return'd into his Chamber, whither the Embassador having follow'd him, he was conducted by the Duke of *Guise* to the Chamber of *Madam M le Premier*, and four Stewards of the Houshold receiv'd him in the Antichamber. As soon as he saw *Madam*, he made a profound Reverence, as he came under the Canopy he made a second, at which *Madam* got up, and at the third *he put one Knee upon the Ground*, and kiss'd her Hand in that Posture, she not offering to make him rise, till the Embassador in Ordinary put her in mind thereof, and pray'd her *to cause him to be cover'd*. At his Departure from hence, he went and saluted *Monsieur*, and the two other Princesses. From the 17th to the 21st, he receiv'd the Visits of the Princes and Lords of the Court, of the Cardinals *de Sourdis* and *du Perron*, and of the Chancellor and he imploy'd the following Days in returning the Visits, and assisting at the Entertainments which were made him by several of the Nobility. The Marriage Contract was read on the 25th, and it was the Prince of *Conti*, who went to fetch him in the King's Coach, follow'd by five and twenty others. The Embassador (who had in his Retinue forty Pages clad in Cloth of Silver) being enter'd into the Chamber, M *de Villeroy*, Secretary of State, read the Contract, which the King, the Queen and the Embassador sign'd and after that *M de Beaux*, another Secretary of State, had counter-sign'd it, it was put again into the Hands of *M de Villeroy*, in order to have the Seal fix'd to it.

I spoke a word or two above, concerning the Audience that Queen *Elizabeth* gave in the Year 1581, to the *French* Embassadors, as also concerning that the Duke of *Nevers* had at *Rome* in the Year 1608, and that of Cardinal *Bichi* at *Venice* in the Year 1643, &c. But as these extraordinary Occurrences can neither establish a Rule nor a Precedent, I shall refer 'em to the end of this Chapter, and acquaint my Reader here, that it is the Business of the Mareschals of *France*, and not of the Princes, to conduct the Embassadors of Republicks to their *Audience*. *Soranzo* and *Contarini*, were conducted to it in the Year 1634, by the Mareschal *de Chastillon*, who likewise in the Year 1638, conducted *Angel Cornaro*, Embassador from the same Republick, as also *Pau* and *Knuit*, Embassadors Extraordinary from the United Provinces. The Mareschal *de la Force* in the Year 1637. perform'd the same Office to the Sieur *d'Ostermo*, then Embassador in Ordinary, and in the same Year, the Mareschal *de St Luc* conducted the Lord *Sauli*, Embassador Extraordinary from *Genoa*, tho' at his Entry he had been only receiv'd by a Chevalier of the Order. None but the Embassadors from the *Swiss Cantons* are treated with some Inequality. Excessive Honours are done them when they come to confirm the Treaties of Alliance, as I have already taken notice in the foregoing Chapter, but at other times they receive but very moderate ones. No Reception at all was made to the Embassadors, whom the Catholick Cantons sent into *France* in the Month of *March* 1634, nor to those who came from the Protestant Cantons in the Month of *December* of the same Year and they were conducted to *Audience* but only by Knights of the Order, the first by *M de Villequiers*, Captain of the King's Guards, and the others by the Marquis *de Nesle*, Governor of *la Fere*.

The Republick of *Genoa* has not yet so well establish'd it self, but that her Ministers are distinguish'd from those of other Sovereigns, not only in *France*, but also in other Places. In the

the Year 1649, the Emperor's Sister passing through *Milan*, as she was going to be marry'd to the King of *Spain*, all the Potentates of *Italy* sent Embassadors to her. The Republick of *Genoa* sent also hers, whom the Queen caus'd to be conducted to *Audience* by *Don Rodrigno de Tappia*, one of her Gentlemen of the Horse, who also discharg'd the Funct on of Master of the Ceremonies. He brought them one of the Queen's Coaches with six Horses, into which the Embassadors got, and caus'd their own (which had also six Horses) to follow it. The Marquiss *de Caracena*, who was at the Window, seeing this last Coach enter into the Court, sent word to the Embassadors, that they should not be suffer'd to come up, nor to see the Queen, because they had been wanting in the Respect they ow'd her, by coming to the Place where she was, with a Coach and six Horses, contrary to the Custom of *Spain*. It was first insisted upon, that they should send back their Coach, but the Matter being discuss'd, and throughly examin'd, it was at last regulated in the following manner, viz. That in the light of all there present, two Horses should be taken off from their Coach, and sent home. They conform'd thereto, and afterwards were permitted to ascend, and make their Complement to the Queen.

The Embassador of *Savoy* has form'd great Pretensions, and particularly since the Duke has taken the Quality of King of *Cyprus*, and that he assumes the Title of Royal Highness, but hitherto he has not been able to obtain the least Advantage over the Embassador of the United Provinces. On the contrary, the King caus'd this to be visited by *M. de Liancourt*, first Gentleman of his Bed-Chamber, while he sent to the other the Count *de Nancy*, Master of the Wardrobe. It is also a Mareschal of *France*, that conducts the Embassadors of the the Great-Duke of *Tuscany* and of *Mantua* to Audience, as well as at their Entries.

The Count *de Druñent*, Embassador from *Savoy*, taking his *Audience* of Leave, receiv'd an extraordinary Honour, the Guards being under their Arms. The Count *de St Maurice*, who succeeded him in the Year 1633, insisted upon having the same Honour done him, but the Difficulties he met therein were so great, that he remain'd at *Paris* eight Months *Incognito*, before he appear'd as Embassador, and was at last forc'd to yield, and be contented with the usual Honours. He was conducted to *Audience*, on the 22d of *September* 1654, by the Mareschal *de Chastillon*, but the Guards were not under their Arms. They always take to 'em, for the *Nuncioes*, for the *Embassadors* of crown'd Heads, and for the *Venetian*. In the Year 1634, they were not under them for the Embassadors Extraordinary of the United Provinces and in 1637, only the hundred *Swifs*, and the Body Guards, took to them, for the Embassador in Ordinary. *William Boreel* came to *France* with the same Quality in the Year 1650, in the height of the Commotions of the Kingdom. The Court was then in *Guyenne*, occupy'd in the Reduction of the City of *Bourdeaux*, so that the Embassador being come to *Blaye*, *Saintot*, Master of the Ceremonies went thither from the King and Queen, to make him the first Complements, and the next day he brought thither the King and Queen's Coaches, and with them

the Duke *D'Amville* to Conduct him to *Bourg*, at his first *Audience*. He found there the *Guards under their Arms*, the hundred *Switzers*, and the Body Guards drawn up in two Lines, and he was receiv'd by the Captain of the Body Guards, and by the other Officers of the Houshold, at the entrance into the Hall, and of the Chamber. As soon as he had made his first bow, the King and the Queen rose up, the King and *Monsieur* uncover'd themselves, and stood all the time of the *Audience*, as did also the Queen. The Embassador put on his Hat at the King's second Request. As soon as he had finish'd his Complement, he presented his *Credentials*, and then made his Proposition. He had the same day *Audience* of Cardinal *Mazarin*, who receiv'd him with the same Civilities he was us'd to shew to the Embassadors of Crown'd Heads. The Officers and Domesticks of his Eminence receiv'd him at the Coach door, and Conducted him to the top of the Stair-case, where the Cardinal receiv'd him, and led him into his Chamber, taking as Cardinal, the place of Honour of him every where, the *Audience* being over, he conducted him to the place where he had receiv'd him. The Duke *d'Amville* treated him in the King's Name, but this is what is usually done, when the King is at any of his Countrey Houses, where the Embassador is not Lodg'd.

In *France* Civilities are done to Embassadors that only pass through the Kingdom, whether they have Letters for the King, as the Count *de Schaunbourg* had, who was going on the part of the Emperor, Embassador in ordinary to *Spain*, or have none, as *Falconiers*, who was going in the Quality of Nuncio to the Low-Countries, but with some difference. The first was consider'd as Embassador Extraordinary, was conducted to *Audience* by the Count *d'Alais*, treated at Dinner by the King's Officers, and presented with a pictur'd Box worth three thousand Crowns. The other was conducted to *Audience* by the Count *de Harcourt*, and treated at Dinner, but he had no Present.

The Embassadors of *Venice* take their first *Audience*, when their Predecessor takes his *Audience* of leave at the Court where he has resided. And after this Example, *Francis Walsingham*, Embassador from *England* to the Court of *France*, was presented in his first *Audience* to King *Charles* IX by *Henry Norris*, his Predecessor. As soon as *Norris* had given an account of *Walsingham*'s Quality, and the reason why he brought him thither, he caus'd him to draw near. And *Walsingham* having first perform'd the usual Ceremonies, and his Complement, deliver'd his *Letters of Credence*, which were read by the Secretary of State. He then said nothing else, but that he had Orders from the Queen his Mistress, to employ his best endeavours to strengthen the friendship of the two Crowns, and a good Correspondence between the Subjects. That he would apply himself thereto with heartiness and zeal, as well to discharge his duty, as because he was sensible it was the mutual interest of both Princes. The King having enquir'd of *Walsingham* after the Queen of *England*'s health, told him, he was very glad of the Choice her Majesty had made of so able a Minister, that

The EMBASSADOR *and his* FUNCTIONS. 153

he was welcome, and that he would give him *Audience,* whenever he fhould ask it, for the affairs of the Queen his Miftrefs After that, *Walfingham* defir'd to fee the Queen, who was Sick, and afterwards he faw the Queen Mother, and the Dukes of *Anjou* and *d'Alençon* tho' before that time, the Princes were us'd to be by the King, when Embaffadors receiv'd their firft *Audience*.

Notwithftanding there is fomething more refpectful in the Salutations and Reverences of the Oriental People, than there is in the taking off the Hat, or Cap, as is practis'd among the Chriftians of our *Europe*, yet it muft be confefs'd, that one of the greateft fubmiffions a Minifter can make to a Prince, is, not to be Cover'd when he fpeaks to him So that whatever Civility the Prince does to the Embaffador, yet if he does not caufe him to be Cover'd at his *Audience*, it cannot be faid that he treats him as an Embaffador All the Honours he is capable of doing him fignifie nothing, if he refufes him this, even tho' he were to be uncover'd himfelf There is none but the Pope, to whom the greateft Potentates of *Chriftendom* fhew this Refpect, not as to a Sovereign Prince, but as to the vifible Head of the Church All the other Princes ought to do Honour to Embaffadors, and allow them to be Cover'd In the Year 1627, *Roch Van den Honart*, Counfellor in the great Council of *Holland*, *Andrew Bicker* Bourgermafter of *Amfterdam*, and *Simon de Beaumont*, Counfellor Penfionary of *Zeland*, were fent into *Pruffia*, to endeavour an accommodation between the two Kings of *Poland*, and of *Sweden*

I fpake in the foregoing Chapter of the Reception that was made them at their Entry On the 6th of *July* the Carver of *Lithuania*, and the Staroft, or Caftellan, of *Warfaw*, came and receiv'd the Embaffadors, in order to conduct them to their *Audience*, having with them three of the King's Coaches The Marefchal of the Court came and took them at the Coach door, and having led them through the Guards, who made a double *Haye*, he brought them into the King's Apartment They found him in a great Room, leaning on his hand upon a Table And all the Civility he did them, was that after their third bow, he touch'd his Hat lightly, and put it on again immediately, *fuffering the Embaffadors to fpeake to him bare-headed, without giving them the leaft fign to be cover'd* The Queen did not receive them any better, contenting her felf with rifing a moment from her Seat, and then prefently fitting down again The Embaffadors gave to underftand, that they were very much fcandaliz'd at this procedure, but they were told, that that was all the civility the King could fhew them, becaufe that notwithftanding the Kings of *France* and *England* permitted the Embaffadors of the United Provinces to be cover'd when they fpake to them, it was only on account of the Alliance the States had with thofe Crowns, but that could not be a precedent for the King of *Poland*, who not having any with them, could not be oblig'd to have the fame confideration neither for their State, nor for their Embaffadors. This was a very bad excufe, becaufe the Kings of *France* and of *England* do not do this Honour to the Alliance they have with the United Provinces, but to the Sovereignty of their State, and it was the Sovereignty that had fent the Embaffy. It was thought the King was willing to do them this Incivility, by reafon of the ftrict Union he had with the Houfe of *Auftria* It was alfo difcours'd at Court, that it was not fatisfy'd with the Embaffadors having been firft to fee the King of *Sweden*, before they came to *Warfaw* The three days following they were entertain'd, the firft, by the Marefchal, the fecond, by the Vice-Chancellor, and the third, by *Gafpar de Donhof* the King's Chamberlain On the 9th of *July* they had Audience of Prince *Uladiflas*, who fent them three Coaches, and two of his Gentlemen caus'd them to be receiv'd at their alighting out of the Coach, and *made them be cover'd* On the 12th they had a Conference at the Vice-Chancellor's Houfe, who came and receiv'd them himfelf at the Coach door After the Conference was ended, the Embaffadors complain'd of *the Incivility the King and Queen had fhewn them at their Audience* They were told they fhould have fatisfaction made them, but that it could not be done juft then, becaufe they would not have it be believ'd that it was the King that made the reparation, having a mind to caft the blame on the Marefchal, who, as they faid, ought to have inform'd the King what he was to do That for this time they might depart with the Anfwer the King's Commiffaries fhould give them, and at their return, they fhould receive a greater fatisfaction with refpect to the Ceremonies On the 16th, the two Vice-Chancellors of *Poland*, and of *Lithuania*, the Marefchal and the Treafurer brought the Anfwer to the Embaffadors, and when they fet out, two Gentlemen brought them three Coaches which conducted them to the River, where they embark'd Their Negotiation being very knotty, and finding great difficulties and obftacles on both fides, the Embaffadors having Negotiated to no purpofe with the King of *Sweden*, refolv'd at laft to go away, and to take their Audience of Leave of the King of *Poland*, upon the affurance they had receiv'd, that they fhould be better treated than at their firft And indeed, the Great Marefchal of *Lithuania* having introduc'd them at their Return, the King receiv'd them very well, *making them be cover'd as foon as he had put on his Hat* However it was not a *publick Audience*, becaufe there were only prefent the Marefchal, who had accompany'd them, the King's firft Secretary, and the Embaffador's Gentlemen, who made their bows to his Majefty Thefe Gentlemen having been fo unworthily treated at their Entry, (for in *Poland* Entries are made to Embaffadors as well as elfewhere) ought to have concerted the Ceremonies of their *Audience*, or elfe have cover'd themfelves, without being bid Thofe Embaffadors that make thefe fubmiffions to Princes, proftitute the Dignity of their Mafter, and in fome meafure renounce his Sovereignty *Robert Shirley*, by putting his Turban at the King of *England's* feet, committed a Crime that could not be expiated but by Death, and the King in making him take it up, convinc'd the World that he knew better than this Embaffador, that the

R r Law

Laws of Nations makes it self be respected even by those, to whom otherwise too much respect cannot be paid.

I say that in *Poland* they know how to pay Civilities to Embassadors, as well as elsewhere *Commendon* was only Bishop and Nuncio in *Poland*, when King *Sigismund Augustus* sent a very great Cortege of Coaches to meet him three Leagues off of *Warsaw* And when the same *Commendon* being Cardinal, return'd thither as Legate, after the death of *Sigismund*, three Bishops, and as many Senators went and receiv'd him at his Lodgings, and when he alighted out of the Coach, at the opening of the Tent where the Senate was assembled, the two Mareschals of *Poland* and *Lithuania* receiv'd him; and having their Commanding staffs in their hands, made way for him, which is an Honour that is done only to the King's Person After he had saluted the Assembly, he took the first place between the Archbishop of *Gnesna*, and the Bishop of *Cracow* On this occasion they did an Honour to the Legate, which they would not have done to another Embassador. But if we consider that which the same Senate did in the Year 1670, to the Earl of *Schafgots* the Emperor's Embassador, we shall be oblig'd to own, that the *Poles* know very well what they owe to the Character, and that it is not through ignorance that they fail therein I took notice hereof in the foregoing Chapter

William Boreel, *Arbert Sonk*, and *Epo d'Ailua* Embassadors from the United Provinces to *Sweden*, in the Year 1640, were very well receiv'd there They were Lodg'd in a House very magnificently Furnish'd, each Embassador having a Canopy in his Chamber, besides that that was over their Table, where they eat in common, and were defray'd during the whole time of their stay at *Stockholm* On the 3ᵈ of *August* they had their first *Audience*

The Queen, who was seated in a kind of Throne, stood up at the Embassador's first bow, at the second she made a Courtesy, and at the third, *she descended to the first step of her Throne* They made their Harangue in the *Flemish* Language, and because the Queen did not after the first Complements, *make them be cover'd, they made no difficulty to put on their Hats*, taking them off at certain periods where the discourse was to be accompanied with some terms of respect The Senators yielded them the Hand, the Door, and the Chair in all their Conferences, but at first they made some difficulty to give the Title of Excellency to the Embassadors, *and were of Opinion that these last ought not to be covered at the Audience* However, all that was regulated to the satisfaction of the Embassadors The Queen was very young at this time, but the Senators, and particularly the Chancellor, ought to to have inform'd her of what she ought to do, and ought not to have been ignorant of the manner how the late King had treated the Embassadors of the United Provinces

La Tuillerie, Embassador from *France* to *Sweden*, was throughly skill'd in the management of what related to the dignity of the King his Master, and yet he never put on his Hat in the *Audiences* he had of Queen *Christina* When he left *Stockholm*, he left there *Chanut*, his Relation, who for some Years Negotiated the Affairs of *France* there, in the Quality of Resident, but with so much Capacity and Address, that he soon had the Character of Embassador given him In the first *Audience* that he had of the Queen in this Capacity, she would have o-blig'd him to be Cover'd, and urg'd him thereto He made answer, that he should not make any great difficulty to be Cover'd, were it but to shew that the King of *France* was willing to entertain a Minister of the first Rank near her Majesty, but that the King his Master was a Prince so Civil and well-bred, that without doubt he would not be cover'd himself, if he had the Honour to speak to the Queen, that is to say, to the Princess of the whole World, who most deserv'd to be serv'd and reverenc'd, so that he hop'd she would give him leave to persist in that respectful posture The Repartee was Spiritual, and Gallant We cannot pay too great submission to the Ladies, so that tho' all Embassadors were to imitate this action of *Chanut*, they would not be for so doing, either less worthy Persons, or less able Ministers I shall here add, that neither he, nor *la Tuillerie*, run the same risque that *Boreel* and his Collegues did, as well because the Senators of *Sweden* would never have thought of disputing the privilege of being Cover'd, with the *French* Embassadors, as because the Queen her self entreated them to be Cover'd, which she had not done in reference to the others May it not be said also, that *Boreel* had a great deal of Wit and Ability, but that Gallantry was neither his Virtue nor Vice?

In the Year 1626, *Bethlem Gabor*, Prince of *Transilvania*, sent into *England* a *German* Gentleman, nam'd *M Quaadt*, on account of the Wars, wherein the Elector *Palatin*, the King of *England*'s Son-in-Law, was very much concern'd This Minister's Retinue was but indifferent, for an Embassador that would consult his Master's Honour And on the other side, the Prince himself was not well enough known, nor sufficiently establish'd, to be able to pass for a Sovereign The King therefore, who shew'd him the usual Civilities, by making him be Conducted *to Audience by the Master of the Ceremonies, did not put on his Hat, thereby to oblige him to remain uncover'd* The Minister afterwards saw the Queen, who press'd him two or three times to be Cover'd, and indeed forc'd him to be so Hereupon the *English* blam'd him, and were of opinion he had committed a fault He had in reality committed one, but the *English* were guilty of the first, and the greatest, because they ought to have acquainted the Queen, that the King had not made him be Cover'd When the Master of the Ceremonies conducted this Gentleman to his *Audience* of leave, he ask'd him whether he intended to be Cover'd again when he spake to the Queen, but he made answer, that he would not put on his Hat, whatever instance the Queen might use to have him do it That he had put it on in his first *Audience*, at the Queen's repeated Instances, but because he then spake to her in his Master's Name, who had commanded him to see the Queen, where as when he took his leave of her, he executed a private duty.

The King look'd upon the Repartee to be Spiritual, but the Courtiers did not make the same Judgment of it. The Prince of *Transilvania*, by commanding his Minister to acquit himself in that Court of the usual Civilities, comprehended therein all the *Audiences*, the last as well as the first, so that it was in his Master's Name that he paid his Respects to the Queen, in the one, as well as in the other. The Duke of *Savoy*, by not Covering himself in the *Audience* he gave to my Lord *Falconbridge*, thereby to hinder him from being Cover'd, did not treat him like an Embassador.

The Marquiss *Pompey Strozzi*, Embassador from the Duke of *Mantua*, arriv'd at *London* in the Year 1627, at a time when there was no remembrance of there ever having been seen at that Court an Embassador from that Prince. The King would not at first consent to his being Cover'd, because he knew the Embassador of *Mantua* does not cover himself, when he speaks to the King of *Spain*. The Marquiss alledg'd, that his Master's Embassadors cover'd themselves in speaking to the Pope, to the Emperor, and to the King of *France*, and that he himself going to see the King of *France*, who was Sick in Bed, his Majesty had made him Sit, and be Cover'd. He did not mention the King of *Spain*, and he might have spar'd himself the trouble of naming the Pope, because that even the Embassador of *France* is not Cover'd when he speaks to the Pope. Neither does the Emperor allow the Embassador of *Mantua* to be Cover'd. But what he afterwards said of *France*, and that the Duke his Master does not visit the Embassadors of the first Kings of *Christendom*, nor give them the place of Honour at home, is true, and he has this in common with the Duke of *Savoy*, and the Great Duke, and within some Years with the Dukes of *Parma*, and *Modena*.

In the Year 1639, the *Bailo de Fourbin*, Great Cross, Embassador extraordinary from *Malta*, being arriv'd in *France*, Complemented the King upon the birth of the *Dauphine*, and having been receiv'd in the manner I related in the foregoing Chapter, the Mareschal *de St Luc* had Orders to Conduct him to Audience. The Court was at *St Germain*, and the Embassador being come thither, he was entertain'd at Dinner, during which time, *it was debated whether he should be Cover'd*. The King was spoke to about it, who remember'd that he had before suffer'd the Commander *de Formigere*, who was also Embassador from *Malta*, *to be Cover'd at his Audience, altho' he was a Captain in the Regiment of Guards*.

It was likewise represented to the King, that his Majesty had done the same Honour to the Marquiss *de Ville*, Embassador from Duke *Charles* of *Lorrain*, so that it was resolv'd that the *Bailo should be Cover'd*, but that he should make a modest and respectful use of that Liberty, which accordingly he did. After he had pronounc'd a short Harangue with his Hat on, he continu'd his discourse to the King for some time uncover'd, and he did not put on his Hat at all in speaking to the Queen. He visited the Princesses of the Blood, whom he Saluted. The Prince of *Condé*, and Cardinal *de Richelieu* gave him the Title of Excellency,

and the first gave him also the place of Honour. On the tenth of *April* he took his *Audience* of Leave with the same Ceremonies, and the King presented him with a Pictur'd Box worth four thousand Livres. When he set out from *Paris*, he did not go to *Malta*, to make a Report of his Embassy to the Great Master, but he went and Commanded the *French* Gallies, of which he was Lieutenant General.

Axel Baron d'*Oxenstiern*, Chancellor of *Sweden*, and Legate Plenipotentiary of the same Crown in *Germany*, not being able to reach the *Baltick*, to pass into *Sweden*, and finding himself oblig'd to take his way through *France*, arriv'd at *Compregne* on the 26th of *April*, 1635. The Count *d'Alass* and the Count *de Brulon* went to meet him with the King's and Queen's Coaches, and conducted him to one of the best Houses in the Town, which the King had caus'd to be fitted up for him. The same day he was visited by *M de la Meisterave*, Knight of the Order, and the next day the same Counts conducted him to his *Audience* of the King, *who made him be Cover'd*. The Regiments of Guards, the Grand Prevost's Men, the hundred *Swiss*, and the Body-Guards stood to their Arms. The Cardinal *de Richelieu* receiv'd him at the end of his Guard-Room, and reconducted him to the bottom of the Stairs. The Cardinal going two days after to see the Chancellor, this last receiv'd him as he alighted out of the Coach, and when he re-conducted him back, he did not retire till the Coach mov'd off. On the 30th of the same Month, he had his *Audience* of leave with the same Ceremonies. The King made him a Present of a Diamond worth twelve thousand Crowns, and sent him besides by the Introductor, a Box with his Picture of the value of six thousand Crowns. This Gentleman, who was one of the first Officers of the Crown of *Sweden*, had indeed the general and absolute direction of of the affairs of *Germany*, but he had no *Character* that could oblige the King to make him be Cover'd, since some Years after he would not allow that Privilege to a Prince, who was equal to the first in *Europe*, as well for Birth, as for Merit.

I speak of Duke *Bernard* of *Saxe Weimar*, and of the Journey he took to *Paris* in the Year 1636. The Duke of *Parma* was come thither some days before, and as he had receiv'd extraordinary Honours, the other believ'd he ought not to expect less, yet there was a great distinction made in the Reception of the one and of the other. The Duke of *Parma* was receiv'd at *Orleans*, whither were sent one of the Introductors, a Steward of the Houshold, a Comptroller, and two Gentlemen Waiters to treat him. The Mayor and the Sheriffs Harangu'd him, the Soldiers and Burgesses were under Arms, and the Magistrate made him the Present of Wine, and Sweetmeats. The Chapter and the University made him their Complements. The Duke *de la Valette* went with one of the Queen's Coaches, and thirty others went to meet him as far as *Chilly*. The Dukes of *Mercœur* and of *Beaufort* went with a great number of Lords and Gentlemen to receive him at *Bourg la Reine*, and conducted him to the *Louvre*, where the Regiments of Guards were under their Arms, and

...nd the *Switzers* and the Life-Guards were rang'd along the Stairs, and in the great Room He went directly to the King, who was in his Chamber, who advanc'd five or six steps towards him, and embrac'd him several times Monsieur, who was there, saluted him likewise, and then they all three put on their Hats.

The Duke of *Weimar* saw no body from the King till he came to *Lagny*, where the Count *de Guiche* went to see him with three or four of his Friends, one Steward, and one Comptroller, with some Officers of the King's Houshold, treated him at Dinner in the Camp, three or four Leagues from *Paris*, where the Duke *de la Trimouille* came to him with several Coaches, and brought him to the *Arsenal*, which had been fitted up with the King's Furniture He rested himself the Day following, and the next Day the Duke *de la Trimouille* conducted him to *Audience*, the King being then at St *Germains* The Duke of *Orleans*, who was present when *la Trimouille* acquainted the King that the Duke of *Weimar* was come, ask'd whether he was to be cover'd when he spoke to the King *La Trimouille* made answer that he could not tell, and that he had spoke to to Cardinal *de Richelieu* about it, who had told him he ought not to be cover'd Chavigny, who was there present, was urg'd to tell his Opinion He said that he ought not, and that if the King approv'd thereof, he would speak to the Duke of *Weimar* about it, but that he would not do it without an express Command, because that might make him have a Thought which perhaps he might not otherwise have That he was of the House of *Saxony* That he was sensible the Bishop of *Wirtsberg* was cover'd at *Metz*, and that he would, without doubt, think they could not refuse him what had been granted to the Duke of *Parma*

In fine, it was resolv'd at last, that he should not be spoke to The Duke of *Weimar* waited in the mean time in the Apartment of the Superintendent of the Finances, where word was brought him that he might see the King The Guards were not under their Arms when he arriv'd, but as he ascended into the King's Apartment, the *Switzers* and the Life-Guards made a Lane for him After he had made his Bows and his Complement, seeing the King put on his Hat, he put on his at the same time, which oblig'd the King to take his off, so that they talk'd for some time uncover'd, after which the King order'd the Duke to be conducted to Dinner As he went from *Audience*, Chavigny ask'd the Duke's Minister how his Master intended to behave himself before the Queen, and whether he pretended to be cover'd He was answer'd, that the Duke thought himself oblig'd to do what he did, after the Usage the Duke of *Parma* had had, but that he did not design to be cover'd in the Queen's Presence He was conducted to her, and afterwards to Monsieur, who made him be cover'd, but then he did the same Honour to the Duke *de la Trimouille*, and to the Prince of *Wirtenberg*, who accompany'd the Duke of *Weimar* Cardinal *de Richelieu* receiv'd him at the top of the Stair-Case, and offer'd him the Place of Honour, but took it after some Civilities At his going away, the Cardinal conducted him back to his Coach, into which the Duke would not enter till the Cardinal was withdrawn Before the Duke's Arrival at *Paris* it had been agreed with his Minister, that he should be cover'd when he spoke to the King, or else that he should be seated on a Stool before the Queen, so that when he desir'd to see the King after his *first Audience*, it was requisite to agree upon fresh Terms, and after several goings and comings it was at last determin'd that he should be contented with the Stool The Duke said, that for his part he was satisfy'd in having asserted what was due to his Birth, that those of his House might have nothing to reproach him And therefore for the future he was willing to conform to the King's Will and Pleasure After this Declaration the King gave him a noble Entertainment, remain'd uncover'd for half a quarter of an Hour, and then put on his Hat, but this was in his Closet, in the Presence of very few Confidents After Dinner he went to see the Queen, who order'd him the Stool, but he did not sit thereon above half a quarter of an Hour before he got up, and the Queen rose at the same time, they remain'd both standing till he retir'd, after the Conversation of half an Hour When he set out from *Paris*, he desir'd that one of the King's Coaches might carry him to *Chalon*, but Difficulties were objected on account of the Consequence, so that Cardinal *de Richelieu* gave him one of his The King's Officers treated him again at *Chalon* We shall have a farther Occasion hereafter to say something more, with reference to the Duke of *Parma*

Altho' what is done out of *Europe* does not always serve for a Precedent, yet it affords either matter of Instruction or Diversion - I shall therefore give here the History of an *Audience*, if not solemn, at least very extraordinary, which an Embassador had in one of the Quarters of the World, the most remote from our Climate In the Year 1623, that is to say, much about the time that *Garcia-de Figueroa* was Embassador in *Persia*, *Francisco de Gama*, Count *de Vidiguieira*, Viceroy of the Oriental *Indies*, sent Don *John Fernandis-Leitão* in the Quality of Embassador to *Venctapa Nasseka*, King of part of that Country, which the *Portuguese* call *Bisnaga* He had no Civilities at all done him at his Arrival at *Jekeri*, which is the Capital of this pretended Kingdom, neither did he receive the least Complement, only the next Day some Refreshments of small Value were sent him, as Sugar-Canes, Fruit, Sugar, and other Trifles, and withal he was told that the Day following he should be conducted to *Audience* The *Indians* came before the Hour appointed, so that the Embassador had not made an end of his Dinner, when a Messenger acquainted him that some *Indian* Lords waited for him in the Street, to conduct him to *Audience* He sent to desire them not to be *over-civil*, but to give him leave to make an end of his Dinner, and to dress himself, because in those hot Countries People consult their Ease during the excessive Heat of the Day The *Indians* having waited some time at the Door, went into the House, and there stay'd in the Entry, till the Embassador and his People were in a Condition to receive them. One of these *Indian* Lords had been Embassador to the Viceroy of *Goa*, from *Venctapa*, and was return'd with the *Portuguese*

tuguese Embassador, and the other had been General of his Army This laft, who had brought his Son along with him, made a Prefent to the *Portuguese* of a piece of fine painted Cloth, which is very common in those Parts, and the Embassador return'd his Present, by another of some Yards of Cloth While this little Commerce was going on, a publick Woman gave them the Diversion of a Dance The Company being got on Horseback, they proceeded in this Order First went two Men, having each of them a led Horse, one of which belong'd to the Embassador, and the other was a Present that the Viceroy sent to *Venctapa*, and after these follow'd some *Indians*, some of which were arm'd with Muskets, and the others with half Pikes, some were on Horseback and others on Foot, accompany'd with their usual Musick, compos'd of Drums and Flutes Then follow'd some Musqueteers, all cloth'd after the same manner, representing the Embassador's Guard A certain *Portuguese* nam'd *Hidalgo*, who on this Occasion did the Office of Captain of the Guards, march'd in their Rear on Horse-back, and well enough clad Immediately after him came the Embassador, accompany'd by the two *Ind an* Lords and four or five *Europeans*, mix'd with as many *Indians* (who were the Embassador's Gentlemen, and those of the Conductors) clos'd the Cavalcade Those of the Embassador's Retinue, who as I said, were in Number four or five, were on Horse-back, except one, who not finding any Horse to hire, was gone before, and waited for the others at the Palace-Gate, in order to get in with the rest The Palace was in a great Inclosure, hem'd in with several Walls and Ditches, so that there were several Bridges and Gates to pass over and through, before one came to the Body of the Place The Horsemen that compos'd the Cavalcade, having pass'd through the two first Gates, alighted, and as they went through the fourth Gate, they perceiv'd the King, who was seated in a little Court opposite to the Gate He was upon a rais'd Floor, under a Canopy mados'd like a Field bed, and supported by four Pillars of Wood gilt He had under him a sorry Carpet and a little Quilt, and was leaning against one of the Pillars, having at his Back two Cushions of Cotten Cloth, very fine and white His Sword, the Hilt whereof was Silver, lay by him upon another little Quilt, and on the other side of him, was a little Table of an Octogone Figure The lower Floor from the Canopy to the Gate was of Wood, having in the middle an Opening about the Wideness of the Mouth of a Well and they said, that underneath the Cover there was a Reservatory, that supply'd Water to a Fountain that was plac'd thereon during the violent Heats of Summer, which were not at the time we are speaking of very troublesome, for which Reason this Opening was so stopp'd, that it was a difficult matter to perceive there was one The King had by him, on his right Hand, several Noblemen, and among the rest, one that was cover'd with a very fine Cotton Cloth, and kept playing with a Fan to drive away the Flies All that were about the King were standing, except one single Person, who was said to be his Favourite, who was under the same Canopy against the Wall The Embassador, as soon as he set foot within the Court, made a Bow after the manner of the *Portuguese*, holding his Hat in his Hand, and he was feared it at an equal Distance from the King and the Favourite, the King remaining all the time as immoveable as a Statue One of the Lords Introductors, who was to serve as Interpreter, plac'd himself by one of the Pillars, which was opposite to that the King lean'd against The King having enquir'd after the Healths of the King of *Spain*, and of the Viceroy, and the Embassador having answer'd thereto, this last added that the Subject Matter of his Embasly was only a Visit of Civility, to entertain a good Understanding and Friendship with his Highness, and that the Viceroy as a Token thereof had sent him a Horse, which he desir'd he would accept of, till the Presents the King of *Spain* intended him should arrive, which were to be sent by the Opportunity of the first Ships, as would appear by the Viceroy's Letters I shall here observe by the by, that the *Portuguese* give the Title of *Highness* to all the Kings in those Parts, because that before the Union of the Crown of *Portugal* to that of *Castile* they gave no other to their own King, neither did the *Spaniards* themselves give the Title of Majesty to the King of *Castile*, before the Reign of *Charles V*

The Embassador having finish'd his Complement, he arose from his Place, put one Knee on the Ground, and presented his *Credentials* to the King, who without the least Inclination of his Body took them, and gave them to the Nobleman who serv'd as Interpreter, by whom they were delivered to the Secretary of State The Embassador had Letters also from the King of *Spain*, but he kept them for another *Audience* In the mean time the Viceroy's Present was brought, which consisted in some Fragments of Cloth of several Colours, and were put into a Bason of Wood gilt, which is a common Utensil among the *Ind ans*, and a Lance after the manner of the *Moors*, with a sharp Spike like that of a Pike, and a very pretty Target The Horse was likewise brought, cover'd with a Silk Housing After the King had view'd him, and handled the Lance a little, which the Embassador said was of the Fashion of *Portugal*, the Gentlemen of his Retinue were seated It is observ'd that the Embassador *did not cover himself during the Audience* And he that gives us this Relation, farther adds, *That this was a Precedent of so much the worse Consequence, as it was the first Embasly the* Portuguese *had sent to* Venctapa, *and so would serve as an Example to his Successors* That these Examples being capable of doing the greatest Prejudice, the *Minister* ought to be very cautious in what he does on these Occasions But that the Portuguese that are in the Indies *are very ignorant, and know nothing of what belongs to the Court, how knowing soever they may be, or think themselves to be, as this Embassador, for instance, who had a very great Opinion of his own Merit* It must be acknowledg'd that the *Portuguese* did too much, and that the Meannesses to which he stoop'd were criminal, even tho' he had had to do not with a *Venctapa*, but with a King of *Pegu*, or of *Siam*, the *Mogul*, or even the Emperor of *China*. He might also have forborn telling that little King,

King, that formerly he had been at that Court in a private Capacity, and that he had offer'd to fell him some Horses. The *Audience* being turn'd into Conversation, and it last into Feasting, the *Portuguese* Embassador ran every now and then into insupportable Extravagancies, even to the asking *Venezapa* to give him Letters of Recommendation to the King of *Spain*. The Conversation having lasted a considerable Time, the King caus'd a piece of Cloth of Gold to be brought him, of the largeness of a Toilet, and put it upon the Embassador's Shoulders, who retir'd with that Present.

I believe I may say, that it is perhaps the only Embassador who did not cover himself at an *Audience*, where he ought and might have done it. The Embassadors of the *Swiss Cantons*, who at their Entry had receiv'd Honours which are not done to those of the greatest Monarchs, could never obtain that which is not refus'd to the meanest Princes of *Italy*. After they had made their Entry into *Paris*, in the manner we have related in the foregoing Chapter, the Count *de Harcourt*, a Prince of the House of *Lorrain*, and the two Introductors, went and receiv'd them with the King's Coaches, at the Chancellor's, where they had din'd, in order to conduct them to *Audience*. The two Regiments of Guards were under their Arms. The Duke *d'Enguien*, Prince of the Blood, accompany'd by several Dukes and Peers, and by some Mareschals of *France*, receiv'd them at the bottom of the Stairs. The Marquiss *de Vardes*, Captain of the hundred *Switzers*, was at the Head of his Company, and the Marquiss *de Villequiers*, Captain of the Life-Guards, was at the Entrance into the King's Chamber. The King had by him the Duke of *Orleans*, the Prince of *Condé*, and the Officers of his Houshold. At their going from this *Audience*, they were conducted to the Queen's, and from thence went and paid their Respects to the *Dauphin*. *They had made pressing Instances, that they might be cover'd when they spoke to the King*, but it was refus'd them, and the King was resolv'd to keep Possession of the Advantage the Kings his Predecessors had acquir'd and left him, and the *Switzers*, who prefer Money to Honour, were willing to neglect the one to preserve the other. And indeed the King makes a great Difference betwixt the *Swiss* and his other Allies. He sometimes gives Subsidies to these, but he gives Pensions to those, the one's are his Friends, the other's are his Pensioners, he hires and buys Soldiers of the one's, and the others assist him by virtue of their Alliance.

There is a verbal Process, or an Act of the Oath that was taken at *Turin* in the beginning of the Year 1652, for the Execution of the Treaty of Alliance which was just renew'd between the Duke of *Savoy* and the nine Catholick Cantons, wherein it is expresly observ'd, that when the Duke went from under his Canopy, to go to the Table at which the Oath was to be taken, the Embassadors from the Cantons advance'd towards the other side, uncover'd, all the rest of the Assembly being in the same State, except the Duke, who was cover'd. Every body remain'd uncover'd, while *Hartman*, Secretary to the Cantons, made an Harangue, and while the Duke's Chancellor made an Answer in his Royal Highness's Name. They were cover'd while the Count *Nomis*, the Duke's Interpreter, explain'd the one and the other. But after the Duke and the Embassadors had taken the Oath, the Duke plac'd himself again under the Canopy, and put on his Hat, *the Embassadors and Lords of the Court remaining uncover'd*.

It is also observ'd in *France*, that when an Embassador enters into the Chamber, or Closet, where the King gives him *Audience*, the Door-keeper *opens both the Folds of the Door*, but if it be a Minister of the second Order, he then opens but one. As soon as the Embassador has put on his Hat, *all the Princes that are present at the Audience put on theirs likewise*. And it is not only the Princes of the Blood, nor those, who altho' descended from a sovereign House, have settl'd themselves in *France*, as those of *Savoy* and of *Lorrain*, that enjoy this Privilege, but also all those whom the King has declar'd to be Princes, as those of the House of *la Tour*, on the Score of the Territory of *Sedan*, which they have been in Possession of for some Years. The last Duke *d'Espernon*, whose Father was the first Lord of the Family, procur'd it, tho' he had no Principality, and that the Father, who thought he ow'd the King nothing, had never carry'd his Thoughts so high. When the Duke of *Parma* arriv'd at *Paris*, he cover'd himself before the King, and, to do him the greater Honour, the King forbad the Princes to be cover'd, and they accordingly obey'd. But then the Princes of the Blood would not be present. In *France* there is no particular Place appropriated to *Audiences*, the King most commonly gives them in his Chamber, by his Bed side, in his Closet, or in a Gallery, as Occasion happens. In *England* the King gives them to the Embassadors of crown'd Heads, and sometimes to the others, in the Presence-Chamber, and to Ministers of the second Order in some other Place, where he may happen to be. No Civilities are done them, except that formerly they were accompany'd by some Gentlemen of the Bed Chamber, but that is no longer practis'd.

The Respect that is due to Sovereigns, requires, that the Embassador at his *Audiences* speak with an intelligible Voice, but low. It is true this cannot be well perform'd in Republicks, where the *Audiences* are giv'n in Assemblies compos'd of many Persons, yet nevertheless, even on those Occasions, Discretion must be us'd, and he ought to direct his Discourse to the Doge, or to the President of the Assemblies, rather than to the whole Company. Neither ought his Speeches to be long, tedious, and wide from the purpose. It is a piece of Incivility to abuse the Patience of a private Person, and a Friend, but it is an unpardonable Imprudence to irritate that of a Prince. Nothing can be imagin'd more impertinent, than the Doctor, who being order'd to back the Negotiation the Duke of *Mecklenburg*'s younger Son was to carry on in *Sweden*, made an Harangue in *Latin* to Queen *Christina*, that lasted two Hours, extending himself on common Places, and every now and then touching on the *Italian* Politicks, which are opposite to the Rules of Christianity, in as much as they prefer *Utility* to *Honesty*. It was a great Tryal of the Discretion of a Princess, who could not endure either Pedants or Pedantry, since she was sensible of their Foible. They that know her, are convinc'd she is not a Wit can take delight in Common-places. It is said, that *Alphonso the Magnanimous*, King of *Arragon* and of *Naples*, took so much Pleasure in hearing *Jonas Manetti*, Embassador from *Florence*, that in his Attention he did not feel a Fly that settled on his Nose, at the beginning of his Harangue, and remain'd there till it was ended. It might be said, that perhaps it was not very long, but then it may be said again, that all Kings are not *Alphonsoes*, nor all the Embassadors *Manetties*.

I took notice in the Xth Chapter, that in the first *Audience Lewis* XIII. gave to Cardinal *Barberin* Legate from *Urban* VIII, he order'd him an Arm'd-Chair and I have elsewhere spoke of some King's of *Castile* and *Poland*, who have caus'd Embassadors to sit. But it is a long time that this has been left off in *Spain*, and the other Courts, where the Ceremonies are regulated. The Pope still causes the Embassadors of crown'd Heads to be seated, but every where else the Prince that gives Audience is standing, as well as the Embassador that receives it.

These Civilities therefore being almost equal amongst all the Princes, we must see a little what is practis'd in the two Republicks, where Princes have their Embassadors. At *Venice* they take their Audiences in the College, and they are conducted thither by the same Senators who have done them Honour at their Entry. The College is compos'd of the *Segniorie*, that is to say, of the Doge and his six Counsellors, of three Deputies of the *Quaranty* Criminal, of six Grand Sages, of five Sages of *Terra Firma*, and of five Sages of the *Orders*, making in all six and twenty Persons. As soon as the Embassador sets his Foot in the Hall, the whole Assembly rises, and all are uncover'd except the Doge, who takes off his Cap only to Sovereign Princes, to the *Infanta*'s of *Spain*, to the Princes of the Blood of *France*, and to Cardinals. The Embassador makes his three Bows, and three at each time, the first to the Doge, and the six Counsellors who are opposite to the Door, and the other two, to the Senators who are on each side, the Grand Sages with the Deputies of the Quaranty, being on the Right, and the Sages of *Terra Firma*, and of the *Orders*, on the left. The Embassador having taken his Place on the right Hand of the Doge, he presents his *Credentials*, which are read by a Secretary the Lecture being over, the Door is set open that any body may enter. The Embassador speaks to the Republick, and begins his Discourse with *Most Serene Duke, Most Excellent Lords* and this tho' the Doge be not present. This being done he retires, and the Chevalier that conducted him to *Audience*, re-conducts him back to his Palace, where he complements him afresh, and the Embassador sees him back to his Gondola, giving him the Place of Honour. The Embassadors of those Princes who have only the Quality of Duke are also seated on the right Hand of the Doge, but the College does not rise till they have made their second Bow, in the middle of the Hall. *Residents* are not suffer'd to sit not even the Emperor's, who for that Reason, has most commonly, only an Agent at *Venice* The Resident of *Tuscany* has his first *Audience* openly, which is an Advantage that he has over the other *Subaltern Ministers*, to whom *publick Audience* is not given

At the *Hague*, an Embassador is conducted to his first *Audience*, with the same Civilities which he has receiv'd at his Entry, that is to say, by two Deputies of the States-General, who go and receive him at his House, with a Cortege of thirty or forty Coaches, which follow a very large and fine Coach enough, belonging to the State, but the Horses that draw it belong to private Persons, and conduct him to the foot of the Stair-Case of the Great Hall of the Palace. There they alight, and go through the Hall, to the Appartment where the States meet. They all rise as soon as the Embassador enters, and remain standing and uncover'd till the Embassador sits down and is cover'd. He has an Arm'd-Chair of green Velvet, and a Cushion of the same, which are set directly over against that of the President, and the two Deputies that conducted him, place themselves on each side of him. The Embassadors address themselves to the Assembly, and most of 'em treat it, with *High and mighty Lords*. The Ministers of the Emperor, and of the King of *Spain*, who were not willing to do more than the Embassador of *France*, begin their Harangue by *Messieurs*, and treat the Estates with *Seigneuries* or *Lordships*. The King of *France*, even when he writes to them, gives them no other Quality than that of *Dear and Good Friends, Allies and Confederates*. He gives no other, either to the Republick of *Venice*, nor to the *Swiss Cantons* yet nevertheless, when his Embassadors speak to the College, they give the Doge the Stile of *Most Serene*, and the rest of the Senators that of *Most Excellent Lords*, and to the *Swiss Cantons* that of *Most Magnificent Lords*. The King of *Great-Britain*, and after his Example the *Northern* Kings, and all the other Princes and Sovereigns, give them the Stile of *High and Mighty Lords*. M d'*Estrades*, now Mareschal of *France*, at his first *Audience* in the Year 1662, began his Discourse by *Illustrious Lords*, but they were not pleas'd therewith. This Title, it is true, expresses something more than that of *Messieurs*, of which the King makes use when he speaks to the States of his Kingdom, and even to his Parliaments, that are his Subjects nay I am willing to think it rather more honourable than that of *High and Mighty* but they were of Opinion, that it was not necessary to change the Stile, to abridge them of any thing they could pretend to and at Court they were not satisfy'd with him neither, because he had done the States an Honour which his Predecessors were not us'd to give them. It appears in the Negotiation of President *Jeannin*, that the Arch-Duke was unwilling to suffer the States to take the Titles of *High and Mighty*, and that he gave them at the Treaty, that of *Illustrious*. However it must be acknowledg'd, that in the simple Title of *Messieurs*, there is something greater, than in all the Epithets that can be added to it. *Sire* in *France*, and *Sennor* in *Spain*, expresses better the Grandeur of those two *Monarchs*, than all the Titles of *Most Serene, Most Excellent*, &c. which other Princes assume, are able to do. The States of *Holland* take upon them

them the Titles of *Noble, Great, and Puiſſant Lords*, and thoſe of the other Provinces, the Quality ot *Noble and Puiſſant Lords* There is ground to wonder, that the Eſtates of thoſe Sovereign Provinces ſhould be contented with thoſe Titles which they have in common, not only with the Deputies of the States General, with thoſe of the Council of State, and even with their own Deputies, but alſo with the Court of Juſtice of *Holland*, whoſe Judges aſſume likewiſe the Title of *Noble and Puiſſant Lords*, tho' it be properly but a *Preſidial*, whoſe Sentences are ſubject to Caſſation and Reformation

After the Embaſſador has finiſh'd his Compliment, and that his *Letters of Credence* are read, the Preſident, who takes Advice of three or four Deputies, who ſit next him, makes an Anſwer and then the Embaſſador retires, and is conducted back to his Lodgings by the ſame Deputies who had brought him thither Envoys are alſo conducted to *Audience* by two Deputes But all their *Cortege* conſiſts in one Coach with four Horſes, and another with two, and the Arm'd-Chair he ſits in, is only of Cloth The Reſidents and Agents of Princes, who are not of the firſt Rank, have ſomething leſs and the Agents, as alſo the Deputies of the *Hanſeatick* Towns, are only conducted by one of the Regiſter's Clerks in a Coach with two Horſes

At the *Hague* they alſo make a Difference between the Embaſſadors *Extraordinary*, and thoſe in *Ordinary* Thoſe never receive *Audience*, but they are conducted to it with the ſame Ceremonies which were paid them at their firſt, but this Honour is done to thoſe in Ordinary, but only at their firſt and laſt at their other *Audiences*, they come in their Coach to the bottom of the Stairs, that lead to the Appartment of the States, who ſend two of their Deputies to receive them there as they cauſe the Miniſters of the ſecond Order to be receiv'd after the ſame manner, at the top of the Stairs

The Parliament at *London* had a mind to erect alſo a ſort of Republick, during the laſt Commotions in *England* The *Sieur de Sabran*, who reſided there on the part of *France*, endeavour'd to contract a Familiarity with ſome of the Deputies of the Parliament, in order to wipe away the Impreſſion, the *Spaniſh* Miniſter's Diſcourſes made there, to the Prejudice of the King his Maſter He had no *Credentials*, for which reaſon not one of the Members would admit him He procur'd *Letters of Credence*, and then he demanded *Audience* The Parliament granted it to him, but inſtead of giving it him in the uſual manner, and much after that the *Dutch* Embaſſador had been receiv'd he was told, that he ſhould have a Chair, in which he might ſit at his firſt coming but that the Parliament expected, *he ſhould make his Speech ſtanding and uncover'd* He refuſ'd *Audience* on theſe Terms, and had ſome Conferences thereupon None but Kings are allow'd to treat Miniſters of the ſecond Order after this haughty manner I or altho' theſe cannot pretend to the ſame Honours, that are paid to thoſe that are call'd *Characteriz'd*, ſince not only Sovereigns, but alſo Embaſſadors diſtinguiſh them, yet there is an Obligation, to conſider the Princes they repreſent, and no, to proſtitute their Grandeur or Dignity by Submiſſions, that are only due to crown'd Heads At *Venice* Reſidents are cover'd at the *Hague* they are not only cover'd, but ſit They have neither Entries nor Reception, but ſome Civilities are done them at their *Audiences* It is not long ſince they receiv'd conſiderable ones, not only at the *Northern* Courts, but alſo in that of *France* However ſince they have been aboliſh'd in this, they have not been continu'd in the others At *Copenhaguen* it was uſual to receive the Envoys of Electors in a Coach with ſix Horſes, till the preſent King alter'd this Cuſtom, as well in reference to the Envoys of the Electors, as to thoſe of crown'd Heads as he notify'd it to the Miniſter of *Brandenburg*, in the Month of *September* 1671 I have ſpoken more amply hereof in Chapter V

After the Marriage of the Prince of Conti, Cardinal *Mazarine*, Unkle to *Mademoiſelle Martinozzi*, whom the Prince had marry'd, ſignify'd to the foreign Miniſters, that he ſhould take it as a Favour if they paid ſome Civilities to the new-marry'd Couple To this the Reſident of *Brandenburg* made anſwer, that he ſhould be always ready to expreſs his Complaiſance to his Eminency, provided the uſual Method were obſerv'd, and that the Introductor of Embaſſadors, or his Aſſiſtant, notify'd the Marriage to him, and that the Civilities of the *Audience* were regulated He was given to underſtand, that it was hop'd he would not make any great Difficulty to remain uncover'd, while he ſpoke to a Prince of the Blood The Reſident reply'd, that the Cardinal himſelf did not exact this Submiſſion from him that his Eminency knew very well, how the Reſidents of Princes, that have the Title of *Moſt Serene*, are treated at *Rome* that he hop'd he ſhould not be oblig'd thereto in a *publick Audience*, and that it ſhould never be reproach'd him, that he had been guilty of ſo great a Meanneſs, while he was in the Service of a Prince, to whom the Prince of *Conti* would be oblig'd to give place every where The Cardinal was ſatisfy'd therewith, and ſaid, that in reality the Prince of *Conti* could not pretend to it with Juſtice

I have ſpoken in the foregoing *Chapter* of the Entry *Emery Nani*, Embaſſador from *Venice*, made at *Conſtantinople* in the Year 1615 I hope it will not be tedious to my Reader, to ſee in this, the Particulars of his firſt *Audience*, becauſe they have no manner of relation with thoſe Ceremonies, that are done in the other Courts of *Europe* The 27th of *May* being fix'd for that purpoſe, and thoſe that were to perform the *Cortege* being come before the Embaſſador's Palace, the two Bailos came out, and went on foot as far as the Arſenai, where they enter'd into a cover'd Barge, in which they paſs'd the Gulph that divides *Pera* from *Conſtantinople* They had on very rich Veſts of Gold Brocade, and all their Retinue were very fine At their landing near the *Jewry* Gate, they ſaw the *Grand Seignior*'s Horſes, and the *Chiaoux* who were to conduct them, accompany'd by a great many *Turks*, who do not fail to be preſent on theſe Occaſions, in expectation of getting a few *Aſpers* of the Embaſſadors It rain'd, wherefore the Embaſſadors, and thoſe

those of their Retinue having put on *Balandrans*, or Clokes for Rain, took the direct way to the *Seraglio* Having pass'd through the first Court, which is very large, and wherein was a great Number of *Spahees* o Horse-back, which were drawn up on both sides, They alighted at the Gate of the second Court, which no body enters on Horse-back, but only the *Grand Seignior* Here the Embassadors quitted their Clokes, as did also their Retinue, that they might shew their Vests, and their Peoples fine Clothes In this second Court there are two Allies of *Cypress* Trees, the one whereof leads from the Gate of the second Court, to the Gate, through which one enters in o what truly composes the *Seraglio*, or the *Sultan*'s Palace, and the other guides to the Gate of the *Divan*, that is to say, to the Place where the *Bachas Vizirs* meet about the Affairs of the State The Word *Divan* signifies the Council it self, as well as the Place where it assembles I our thousand *Janizaries* drawn up in order of Batte', were posted under a Gallery on the right side of the Gate of the *Divan*, and observ'd so profound a Silence, that a Mouse might have been heard to run along, and they remain'd as immoveable is so many Statues On the other side were to be seen several *Chaoux*, in the same Respect, and in the same Silence, the rest of the Court was so vacant that not one single Person was to be seen therein The two Embassadors, and their Retinue, pass'd through the middle of these *Chaoux*, and of these *Janizar s* and were receiv'd by the *Chiaoux-Bachi* at the Gate of the *Divan*, where the Vizirs were assembled The *Chiaoux-Bachi* was accompany'd by some other Officers, who had all of them a Silver Staff in their Hands, and he conducted the Embassadors into a Gallery, which serves as an Entry to the *Divan* The *Divan* it self is but an indifferent Building, having neither Hangings nor other Furniture The *Bacha*, or *Pacha*, (for so they call the Grand or First Vizir, by the way of Excellency) was sitting on a Bench opposite to the Door, under a little Grate, through which the Sultan can see and hear all that passes in the *Divan* On the same Bench, and on the right Hand of the First Vizir sate the other *Bachas* and on his left, but at some distance, the two *Cadileskers*, or Judges of *Romelia* and *Natolia*, that is to say, of *Europe* and *Asia* At the end of the Table which was before them, sate the two *Tefterdas*, or Super intendents of the Finances and behind them on a separate Bench, several Clarkes or Secretaries, who had all of them a Pen in their Hand, ready to write whatever should be commanded them And on the right side, opposite to the *Tefterdas*, sate the *Nascangi*, or Chancellor, who signs the Ordinances of the *Divan*, and the Will and Pleasure of the *Sultan* Not one of the Bashaws rose up when the Embassadors enter'd and they, on their part, did not so much as touch their Caps, nor those of their Retinue their Hats They were seated on two Stools right against the First Vizir and those of their Retinue, which the littleness of the Place did admit of, stood behind them After some Complements had pass'd on both sides, the First Vizir commanded the steward to cause Dinner to be serv'd up In the mean time the Vests were brought, which the Embassadors present the Bashaws with, but these gave it very well to be understood, that they receiv'd 'em as a Tribute, having the Impudence to make them be measur'd in the Presence of the *Bailos*, and reproaching them, that some of them were shorter than the others

Dinner being ready, a certain Officer came and cast here and there some Towels, like those they use in Convents instead or Napkins, but on this Occasion, they serv'd to wipe the Hands of the Company after they had wash'd over these Towels the same Officer put others of a streak'd Cloth, which serv'd instead of Napkins This being done, they plac'd before the First Vizir, on a low Stool, a Silver Ring, of the size of the bottom of a Hogshead, the Rim whereof had several pieces of Bread upon it, the Midale be ng void for a Dish, for there was but one serv'd up at a time At this first Table were two of the Bashaws with the First Vizir, and the two Embassadors Another Table like the first, was put before the other Bashaws a third before the *Cadileskers* one before the *Tefterdas*, and a fifth before the *Nascang* Each Table had thirty four Dishes serv'd upon it, most of them fill'd with Rice, and three or four Fowls roasted or boyl'd, with Sauces after their manner The last Services consisted of Pasties but they had neither Soop nor Intermesses, nor Fruit, nor Sweetmeats, because the *Turks* do not eat any either at Dinner or Supper, but only between Meals They don't drink till they have done eating so that the Sherbet was not brought till the latter end of the Repast There was of all sorts, and very excellent, which was serv'd in large silver Cups, because after the first had drunk, it pass'd from Hand to Hand till it was empty'd It was serv'd on a Plate, or tin Salver, and the Meats in Dishes of the same Metal Dinner being over, all was taken away except the Towels, which were left, till they had wash'd again, and dry'd their Hands The Embassadors having taken their leave of the *Divan*, went and sate down in the Court, near the Gate, through which one enters into the *Grand Seignior*'s Appartment, till such time as they should be introduc'd And it was here, that they put on the Vests the *Sultan* had presented them with The Ground of them was Red and Violet, interspers'd with Flowers of Gold, but the Workmanship was so mean, that the Embassadors usually bestow them on their *Valets de Chambre*, as they go from their Audience There were four and twenty on this Occasion, without reckoning the three the First Vizir had presented the two *Bailos* with, and the *Chiaoux* who had conducted the new one from *Venice*, and these were put over the others the Embassadors had already on While the two Embassadors were thus sitting in the Court, all the Officers of the *Divan* went to the *Audience* of the *Sultan*, the least Considerable taking it first, contrary to the Custom of *Europe*, where the best quality'd go first to Audience The *Aga* of the *Janizaries*, who went to it first, and who late just by the Door, instead of going directly in, took the Compass of the whole Court, passing by all the *Janizaries*, who saluted him with a very low Bow, remaining afterwards with their Arms across, and their Eyes downwards,

wards, till he was gone in Then the two *Cadileskers* went in together, he of *Romelia* taking the Place of Honour, both the one and the other carrying in their Looks the Tokens of Respect and Fear, that the approaching the *Grand Seignior* imprints in his Slaves After them all the *Vizirs* went together in a File, the first being Speaker for them all Their *Audience* was very short, and as soon as it was over, the two Embassadors were fetch'd, and some of their Retinue, in the following manner The old *Bailo* enter'd first, and after him the new one, then the Secretary of the old one, and the Secretary of the new one, the two Sons of this last, and after them some Gentlemen, who with the *Drogomans* made up seven and twenty in Number Going through the third Door, which is over against the second, and has a Gallery on both sides, there are seen in a little Passage between two Doors (which are every where double) some white Eunuchs, and some other Officers, who are the Keepers thereof, and who convey'd the Embassadors into a great Court, where nothing else was to be seen, except the Structure that makes the Hall, where the *Sultan* gives *Audience* It is an Appartment distinct from the Body of the Palace, the Entrance into it, is a kind of Gallery pav'd with black Marble The Door of this Building is so strait, that two Men have enough to do to go through it a Breast, and it has on each side a little Fountain, whose Water comes out of the Wall, which is all fac'd with black Marble, having here and there some *Turkish* and *Arabick* Characters Ye go up two Steps to the Door, which is so contriv'd, that to view it on the outside, one would think that it were in the middle of the Structure, and yet being got into it, it is found to be in one of the Corners of the Hall, having a Wall on the right adjoyning to the Door On the other side of the Hall, at that end which is most remote from the Door, there was a Glacis, or Slope cover'd with a *Persian* Carpet, the Ground whereof was Gold, and all the rest of the Floor was cover'd with a very fine *Turkish* Tapestry There was no other Ornament on the Walls, but little square Tyles painted and gilt, with *Flurons* after the *Arabian* manner The *Sultan* was sitting on the Glacis or rais'd Floor, with his Face turn'd towards the Vizirs, who were standing in order over against him, with a Meen and Countenance of Slaves so that the Embassadors and those of their Retinue, could have no sight of the *Grand Seignior* but in *profile* The Embassadors stopp'd at the Entrance, till those that were to follow them had join'd them, and that two *Capigibachis*, or Master-Porters, in order to lead them to the *Glacis*; had took them by the Hand, but as gently as the Physician does the Patient when he feels his Pulse The two Embassadors being brought after this manner pretty near the *Sultan*, but yet at some distance, made their Reverence to him, putting one Knee on the Ground, and advancing their Heads a little to kiss the Hem of his Vest, which one of the *Capigibachis* presented to their Mouths After they, and their Secretaries, and their Gentlemen had made their Reverence to the *Grand Seignior*, these last were led back, and made to go retrograde to the Door, and put into the

Court, while the Embassadors pronounc'd their Complement, which was very short The *Glacis*, on which the *Great Turk* sate, was not so high as our ordinary Benches, and notwithstanding the *Sultan* had a Stool with a Cushion under his Feet, yet he did not seem to be very much at his Ease, because the *Turks* may be said to squat rather than sit There stood by him, on a Stool, a very fine Standish, cover'd with Diamonds, his Waistcoat was of Cloth of Silver, and his Vest was a white Satin, lin'd with Sables He said not a Word to the two *Bailos*, but the First Vizir answer'd their Complement, telling the former, that the *Grand Seignior* wish'd him a good Voyage, and the new one, that he was welcome Being come out of the Hall they took off the Vests the *Grand Seignior* had given them, mounted their Horses, and return'd home in the same manner that they came

In the Year 1601, in the Reign of *Henry* IV, two *Turkish* Ministers came into *France*, *Barthelemy de Coeur*, a Provençal Renegade, and Physician of the *Grand Seignior*, who was follow'd by a *Chiaoux* in the Year 1607 But there was nothing extraordinary in their Audiences, as there was in that of *Soliman Mustafa Feraga*, which was very singular He arriv'd in *Provence* in the Year 1669, and having perform'd his Quarantine, by reason of the Plague which rag'd then at *Constantinople*, he was brought to *Paris*, where he was lodg'd at the House of the Extraordinaries *Lionne* visited him, and told him, that his *Letters* giving him no other Quality than that of *Eleki*, which is common to the Ministers of the first and second Order it created some Difficulty to consider him as Embassador *Mustafa Feraga* reply'd, that he had others, but that he was order'd on pain of Death, to deliver them to no other than the Emperor of the *French* in Person It was resolv'd he should be treated after the *Turkish* manner, and while things were preparing for that purpose, he was sent to lodge in one of those Houses of Pleasure, of which there are so many in the Village of *Issy*, two Leagues off of *Paris* On the 12th of *November* three Coaches with six Horses each were sent him which brought him to *Paris* to the Lodgings of *Lionne* At his getting out of the Coach he found no body in the Court to receive him but being ascended into an upper Hall, he there found *Lionne*'s first Clark, who advanc'd three or four Steps to meet him, seated him on a Stool, and plac'd himself by him, and order'd something to drink In the mean time *Mustafa Feraga*'s Interpreter, went to know of *Lionne*, when his Master might see him, and brought Word back, that that Minister had an Affair to dispatch, and as soon as ever it was done, he would let the *Turk* know it and accordingly he did, in a very little time after He was led through a little Gallery, which was full of Persons of Quality, and from thence into a small Room, where *Lionne*, who was entertaining himself with some of the Company, did no more than salute the *Turk* very slightly with his Hat, and having finish'd his Discourse, he went and plac'd himself on a Bed of Repose of Gold Brocade, which stood upon a *Persian* Carpet of Silk, the Ground whereof was Gold and Silver, leaning his Back against

against two Cushions of Gold Brocade, and caus'd *Muftafa Feraga* to be seated on a folding Stool of crimson Damask, with a Gold and Silver Fringe, which was plac'd before the Foot-Carpet *Lionne* told him, That he knew he had been made to believe that he, *Lionne*, was in *France*, what they call in *Turky Vizir-azem*, or First Vizir, but that he ought to be undeceiv'd, because the Emperor of *France* did not communicate his Authority to any body And as for himself, he was only one of the four little Secretaries, who serv'd to see the Commands of the Sovereign executed That after all, he did not know whether the King would give him *Audience* or not, by reason he brought him no Presents, which the Emperor his Master caus'd to be given him as a Tribute However he had *Audience*, and he was conducted to it by the Introductor, and by one of the Esquires of the great Stables The Guards, both Foot and Horse, were under their Arms, not to do him Honour, since he was not accompany'd by a Prince, nor a Mareschal of *France*, but to shew him the Grandeur of *France* The King was seated in a Throne at the end of the great Gallery of the new Castle of St *Germains*, and had on a Suit of Cloaths cover'd with precious Stones, worth above five Millions *Muftafa* began to make his Bows at the very beginning of the Gallery, and did not leave off till he had presented his *Credentials*, the King not so much as offering to touch his Hat all the time The King, who knows very well how to appear what he really is, did it perfectly well on this Occasion But *Lionne*, who was but one of the four little Secretaries, as he said, ought not to have play'd the *Vizir-azem* The first Minister of the Port, who has an Authority beyond Comparison, more absolute than that of the Minister of *France*, has some reason to treat the Embassadors of foreign Princes with Haughtiness, since even the Cardinals do not scruple to do it But *Lionne*, who was neither Cardinal nor first Minister, play'd but an indifferent part in this Comedy In all likelihood he was the Author of it, it is plain it savour'd of the *Turk*

There is something more extraordinary in the following Example, and indeed the one was only an Imitation, whereas the other was truly *Turkish* It is certain that the *Turks* treat Publick Ministers after so offensive a manner, that it is speaking improperly to say they do Civility to Embassadors In the Month of *May* 1677, the *French* Embassador being come to the First Vizir's, according to the Assignation which had been made him, they brought him into the Secretary's Chamber, where he waited three Hours before he was introduc'd into the Hall, where he was to have *Audience*, where he was amus'd again another good Hour There was plac'd upon an Alcove, rais'd about a Foot and half, a Velvet Chair embroider'd with Gold and Silver, for the First Vizir, and *at the Foot of the Alcove a Velvet Stool for the Embassador* The Embassador was so vex'd to see himself treated after this haughty and unequal manner, that he commanded his Interpreter to put the Stool upon the Alcove by the Vizir's Chair Hereupon one of the *Chiaoux* told him, that that was none of his Place, and that the Alcove was reserv'd for the Vizir, which put the Embassador into such a Passion, that he took himself the Stool, placed it on the Alcove, and seated himself thereon The First Vizir, being inform'd thereof, sent him word that his Pretensions were ill-grounded, and that Embassadors never had the Privilege of being on the Alcove; but the Embassador appearing obstinate in the matter, he gave his Commands to remove him from thence either by fair or foul means The *Chiaoux Bachi* being return'd into the Hall with this Order, told the Embassador, with a fierce and disdainful Air, to withdraw from thence, and because the Embassador was not over-hasty in retiring, he commanded some of his People to draw the Stool from under him, which was executed so suddenly, that all the Embassador could do, was to get up before they flung him down He thereupon retir'd, saying, that since he was so uncivilly us'd he had no Occasion for an *Audience* of the Vizir, who was so little concern'd thereat, that he signify'd to the Embassador, That since he would not receive his *Audience*, he might go and take that of the Devil

As those People are Slaves, and capable of the meanest Submissions, they think that all the rest of the World are so likewise, and that they may treat them with the same Superiority In the Year 1646, the Embassador of the *Cham* of *Tartary*, taking *Audience* of the King of *Poland*, appear'd there with his Vest of Taffata, which he wore over his Cassock of Sheep-Skins, the Wool whereof was outward The King was sitting under a Canopy, in a Chair that represented a kind of Throne, all of Gold Brocade The Embassador entring into the Hall, kneel'd *down on the Threshold of the Door, as did all those of his Retinue*, he did the same when he came *to the King's Feet, bowing his Head down to the very Floor before he kiss'd the Hem of the Royal Cloke* Because none but Christians are suffer'd to kiss his Hand After the Embassador had presented his *Credentials*, both he and his People retir'd on their Knees, as far as one of the Corners of the Room, where he made his Harangue These voluntary Meannesses, which are done by the Consent of the Prince who sends the Embassador, are pardonable in a People that make at best but a third Species between Men and Brutes

Too great Civilities degenerate into Submissions that are unworthy of a Publick Minister, and of the Prince who employs him The *Portugal* Embassador of the Viceroy of *Goa*, whom we before mention'd, who in presenting his *Letters of Credence* to a little *Indian* King, put one Knee on the Ground, and did not cover himself during the *Audience*, committed an inexcusable Incongruity *Don Garcia de Silva Figueroa*, Embassador from the King of *Spain*, in *Persia*, understood it much better On the Day he made his Entry at *Ispahan*, the two Governors of the Town, who accompany'd him in this Ceremony, led him through the *Maidan*, and would have oblig'd him to alight off his Horse to kiss the Step of the *Schach*'s Palace They said that it was a Custom, from the Observation of which, no body could be exempted, and that even the King's Sons were forc'd to pay that respect to the Palace of their Father But *Figueroa* made Answer, That he would not hinder them from acquitting themselves of their Ceremonies, but as for his own part he should be be very cautious of paying an Honour to the *Schach* which he would not pay to his own Master. So that altho' the two Governors and their Followers alighted from their Horses, the Embassador commanded his People not to quit theirs, and being come near the Palace, he contented himself with turning his Horse's Head towards the Gate, and to salute it with his Hat. The Honours the Embassadors pay to the *Grand Seignior*, and the profound Inclination of Body are forc'd from them, and have their Origin from the Adoration the Oriental Kings exact from those that approach them, of which we have an Instance in the History of the Wise Men, who came to pay their Adoration to our Saviour some time after his Birth. Their Adoration had not for Object the Divinity of *Jesus Christ*, but a humane Majesty, tho' very extraordinary. These Wise Men were not so much illuminated than St *John*, who was not so but from the Voice from Heaven, which declar'd, *This is my well-beloved Son, in whom I am well-pleased*. The *Chicane*, with which both the Church and the Inns of Court are infected, would be apt to make here a Distinction betwixt the Adoration of *Latria* and *Doulia*.

Africa has produc'd another kind of Monster. In the Year 1670, there arriv'd at *Paris* an Embassador from the King of the *Ardeans* in *Guinea*. His Name was *Matthias Lopez*, and was about seventy two Years of Age, however he had with him three Wives, of whom he had as many Sons, and he was besides well enough attended. When he made his Entry into *Paris*, he was in a Coach with six Horses, his Wives were in another, and these Coaches were follow'd by the King's, the Queen's, and those of the Princes. Twelve Negroes went before his Coach, the Captain whereof blow'd a Horn, instead of sounding a Trumpet. His Wives and Sons were cloath'd after the *French* Fashion, and they eat in publick. He was lodg'd in the House of *Luines*, and treated at the King's Expences. The Company of the *West Indies*, who promis'd themselves no small Advantages from this Embassy, provided them with Vests of Gold Brocade for their *Audience*. The Embassador, when he approach'd the King, saluted him after the manner of his Countrey, *by prostrating himself on the Ground*. He offer'd the King the Access and Entry into all the Ports and Harbours belonging to the Kingdom of *Ardea*, so that the *French* flatter'd themselves very much with the Hopes of a rich Commerce with that Coast, and believ'd they were already in Possession of all the Gold and Ivory of that Countrey, but not a Syllable has been heard of it since. The Monkeys of those Parts surpass in Malice and Infidelity those of the *Indies*, and all the rest of the World besides.

I could swell this Chapter with many more Examples, and even with the Particulars of the *Audiences* which the Kings of *England*, and of *Bohemia*, and some other Princes had a mind to take, at the *Hague* and elsewhere. But besides that Embassadors could not reduce 'em into Precedents, I think I am not here oblig'd to speak of things which do not properly belong to my Subject.

CHAP. XX.

Of the Honours and Civilities that Embassadors are oblig'd to pay, and of those that are done to Embassadors.

MEssieurs *d'Arpaionx*, and *de Bregy*, Embassadors of *France*, being in *Poland* during the *Interregnum*, after the Death of King *Uladislas*, gave the Title of Majesty to Prince *Casimir*, even before his Election. Queen *Christina*, who consider'd that this Title could not be given him, but by reason of his Pretension to the Crown of *Sweden*, was very angry thereat, and made great Expostulations thereupon to *Chanut*, the French Embassador at *Stockholm*. This Minister, who was much in her Favour, seeing his bad Excuses only serv'd to exasperate her, said at last that the Court of *France* had disown'd them. This satisfy'd the Queen in some Measure, but that she might be perfectly cur'd of her Inquietudes, she ask'd *Chanut* whether the King and the Queen Mother, when they wrote to Prince *Casimir*, gave him the Title of Majesty? And as *Chanut* said, at all Adventures, no, tho' he knew nothing of the matter, she reply'd, That then she had no reason to complain, *because the Civilities of Embassadors are not to be minded, being of no Consequence*. In the Treaty of the Truce that Monsieur *d'Avaux* had brought to a Conclusion between *Poland* and *Sweden*, the King of *Poland* had not taken the Quality of Hereditary King of *Sweden*, and had given that of Queen of *Sweden* to *Christina*, yet nevertheless, when the Ministers of the two Crowns met at *Lubeck*, in the Year 1551, the Embassadors of *Poland* were for giving the Quality of King Hereditary of *Sweden* to *Casimir*, and refus'd that of Queen of *Sweden* to *Christina*. Which was the most apparent Cause of the breaking up of the Assembly, tho' otherwise there was in either of the Parties but very little Disposition to an Accommodation. The Queen was in the right to say, *that the Civilities of Embassadors are of no Consequence*, when they are only mere Complements. But it must be own'd that they are of Consequence, when they are study'd and affected. As it is certain on the other side, that the Refusal an Embassador makes, to pay Civilities to those to whom he owes them, may have very vexatious Consequences. Now he owes them to the Prince to whom he is sent, to his Estate, and to his Ministers, and he cannot be wanting therein, without failing in his Duty. At his Arrival on the Frontiers he he ought to make himself known to the Governors, and pay, to the Places and Arms of the Sovereign, that Respect which cannot be refus'd him without offending him

The Count d'Averspergbeing, in the Year 1640, arriv'd at the *Hague*, on the part of the Emperor, instead of communicating his *Credentials* to the President of the Assembly of the States General, he caus'd them to be given to a Door-Keeper, who carry'd them into the Assembly The Inscription of them was fraught with magnificent Titles, *viz Illustribus, Generosis, Nobil bus & Honorabilibus nostris, & S Romani Imperii fidel bus Dilectis, N N Uramibus Un* 'arum Provinciarum Yet nevertheless nothing could be more offensive, than to use the Terms of Trusty and Well-beloved to a Sovereign and Independent State The States instead of opening the Letter sent it back to the Count, and signify'd to him by three Deputies, That they had ever been dispos'd to live in a good Intelligence with the Empire and the Emperor, and that they would always receive the Embassadors of his Imperial Majesty with Respect, but on the other side, they were oblig'd to maintain with Jealousy and Zeal the Rights of their Sovereignty That the Inscription of the Letter giving them a Suspicion, that the State was not better treated in the Text thereof, the Count would do well (in their Opinion) to go to himself to the Emperor, to inform his Council how they ought to be writ to, and to get his Letters reform'd Or else that he might retire into the Electorate of *Cologn*, or to some other neighbouring Place, till he had receiv'd others The Count of *Vienna* sent him others, but they again found something to cavil at in them, so that the Count, who all this while was at the *Hague*, perceiving they had a mind to be vexatious, and that he had no Hopes of succeeding in his Negotiation, retir'd, after he had stay'd there seven or eight Months to no purpose M *Frisuact*, who came and resided at the *Hague* on the part of the Emperor, in the Year 1658, brought Letters with the Inscription of *Chari Sui Amici* But besides that they did not carry the Air of Superiority, which is found in the Terms of *Nostris & S R Imperii Fidelibus Dilectis*, the Emperor did as the King of *France* does The Ignorance of those that have the Direction of the Chanceries, is the Cause of the Faults Princes commit on these Occasions As the Ignorance of the Publick Right makes others fall into Faults so gross and criminal, as to violate the Publick Safety in the Person of a Publick Minister

In the Year 1639, the *Palatin of Smolensko*, passing through the *Hague* in his way to *France*, whither he was going to sollicit the Liberty of Prince *Casimir*, desir'd Audience of the Estates, but as they knew his *Credentials* did not give them the Title of *Celsi & Præpotentes*, they would not admit him to Audience They remember'd how Prince *Janus Radzivil* had treated them in the Year 1633 This Prince study'd at *Leiden*, (where the Publick Right is not taught) when King *Uladislas* gave him the Quality of Embassador, to acquaint the States of the United Provinces with his Election The Inscription of his *Letters of Credence* was swell'd with the Titles of *Illustrissimis, Illustribus, Magnificis, Generosis, Nobilibus*, &c of which they are very prodigal in *Poland*, but then there was not any single one that express'd the Sovereignty of the State The Embassador, in making his Harangue, began with *Illustres, Magnifici*, speaking to the Prince of *Orange*, and the States, as if he had been talking to the Magistracy of some Town treating even the Prince of *Orange* less honourably than he would have done a *Palatin* of Poland By endeavouring to play the Embassador too much he made it plain that he knew nothing of the matter, being so rude as to leave in the Entry the Deputies the Estates had sent him, instead of accompanying them to the Coach He was oblig'd to make Reparation, and to acknowledge his Error

I neither will, nor am able to enter into a Discussion of the Rights of the King of *Great Britain*, who causes his Flag to be respected in the *Britannick* Seas, as far as the Coasts of *France* neither shall I dispute whether *Mansel*, V ce-Admiral of *England*, could under the Vice-Admiral of *France*, to no ft the Flag of the King his Master in the fight of *Calais* He did it by the Order of M *de Sully*, who was going to *England* in the Quality of Embassador, but *Mansel* made him take it down, and acknowledge the Sovereignty of the Sea to the *English* Flag It is well known what is due to the Ship of an Admiral, or to any that has the Tokens thereof, but in *France* they are of Opinion, that the King's Admiral may carry the Marks of the Sovereignty of his Master every where and that as at this time that the King's Maritime Forces are not inconsiderable, the *French* Admiral would make no difficulty to salute the Flag of the King of *Great-Britain* on the Coasts of *England* so would he expect the same Usage on the Coast of *France*, and an Equality of Honour in the open Sea, especially if their Strength was equal The *Swedish* Embassador, who refus'd to salute the *English* Flag on the River *Thames*, was in the wrong, since he thereby acquir'd no Right nor Advantage to the King his Master, and he inform'd the *English*, that when they came into the Roads and Harbours of *Sweden* they were not oblig'd to salute the King's Flag, even in his own Kingdom The Earl of *Essex*, Embassador Extraordinary from *England*, coming in a Man of War into the Sound, in the Month of *May* 1670, either neglected or disdain'd saluting the Castle of *Cronenbourg* Major General *Holke*, who commanded there, in order to remind the *English* of their Duty, fir'd three Guns at 'em with Balls The Embassador was scandaliz'd hereat, but *Holk* signify'd to him, That he was oblig'd to preserve the Rights of Sovereignty of the King his Master, who expected to have the same Respect paid him on his own Coasts, that the King of *England* exacted on those of his Kingdom The Earl obtain'd no other Satisfaction, no more than the Duke of *Sully* did, when he complain'd at *London* of *Mansel* Princes never disavow these Actions, especially when they have no reason to fear the Consequences thereof

Now if the Embassador, who refuses to acknowledge the Sovereign to whom he is sent, and to salute him at his Arrival on his Coasts, is wanting in Respect, what must be

U u said

said of a Minister that shall contest with the Sovereign, his Qualities and Titles, and who does his Endeavour to deprive him of them? It cannot be deny'd, that it is an Outrage of that Nature, that may oblige the Prince to pass over all the Considerations that ought otherwise to be had for a Publick Minister. The Republick of *Venice* was extremely offended that the Duke of *Savoy* had taken the Title of King of *Cyprus*. She had complain'd every where thereof, yet for all that the Count *de Bigliore*, the said Duke's Embassador, dar'd to set over the Gate of his Palace the Arms of his Master, *quarter'd with those of* Cyprus. Hereupon the Senate sent the Embassador Word, that if he did not cause those Arms to be taken down, he should have the Mortification to see them taken away, and broken to pieces before his Face. So that the Embassador chose rather to take them down, than to expose himself, and the Prince his Master, to an unavoidable Affront, which was at the same time irreparable.

There is also a Respect due to the Ministers, and to those that are most considerable in the State where the Embassador is employ'd. The Embassadors of *England* did not see Cardinal *Richelieu*, because he did not give them the Hand, and also because they had not for him the Consideration they ought to have. In the Month of *August* 1635, the Lord *Scudamore* Embassador from *England*, being ready to make his Entry into *Paris*, the Introductor ask'd the Cardinal whether he would send his Coach to meet him, the Cardinal made answer, That if the Embassador would see him he would send his Coach, but not otherwise. The Agent of *England* was consulted thereupon, who being urg'd thereto, said that *Scudamore* would do as his Predecessors had done, that is to say, that he would not see his Eminency. So that the Cardinal's Coach was not there. I may say for certain, that the Contempt the *English* had for that Minister, was one of the chief Causes of the King's Misfortune, and of the Disorders of the Kingdom.

Cardinal *d'Este*, Protector of *France*, who had obtain'd the Hat at the Emperor's Nomination, had quitted the Party of the House of *Austria* to side with that of *France*. The Admirant of *Castile*, Embassador of Obedience on the part of the King of *Spain*, in the Year 1646, when he sent to desire the Cardinals to do him Honour at his Entry, omitted asking Cardinal *d'Este*, and even declar'd that he would not visit him, nor cause his Coach to stop when he met him in the City. This Incivility was the Cause that not only the Cardinals *Grimaldi*, *de Valencay*, and *Theodoli*, Partisans of *France*, did not send their Families to meet him, but also of a very troublesome Dispute, in which the Admirant came very ill off. Cardinal *d'Este* said, he would find the means to procure himself the Respect that was due to him, and that he would take Care that the Admirant's Coach should be stop'd wheresoever he met it, and that he might not fail therein, he sent for Soldiers from *Modena* and other Places. The Admirant, on his side, sent for a thousand Men from *Naples*, and did not scruple to say, that he would take the Cardinal away by force out of his own Palace. This Animosity oblig'd the Pope to order Troops to repair to *Rome*, and all the other Cardinals resenting the Affront that was done to Cardinal *d'Este*, signify'd to the Admirant that *they would not admit of his Visit*, so that the Embassador finding the whole College declar'd against him, was forc'd to an Accommodation, and to pay Civility, and even make a kind of Reparation to the Cardinal *d'Este*. Those Embassadors, who create themselves Affairs of this Nature, ought to concert well their Measures, because the Interest and Dignity of the Prince suffers on these Occasions, and they besides make themselves odious in the Court where they reside.

The Emperor *Ferdinand* I, sending his Embassadors to *Trent* in the Year 1562, *forbid them to give the Hand to any Person whatever, except to the Legates only*. These Embassadors being one Day come to the Lodgings of the Senior Legate, with a Design to accompany him to the Church, gave to understand, that they would not give place to Cardinal *Madrucci* because he had not the Quality of Legate, conformably to the Orders particularly express'd in their Instructions. It was represented to them, that their Instructions being copy'd from those the Emperor *Charles* V had formerly given his Embassadors, when all the Cardinals that were at *Trent* were Legates, they ought to draw no Consequence therefrom to the Prejudice of Cardinal *Madrucci*. That they could not but know, *that all Cardinals take place of Embassadors every where*. And that hereunto might be added, that the same Embassadors of *Charles* V had yielded the Precedency in the same Place to the Cardinals of *Trent* and of *Jaen*, who were not Legates. The Embassadors of *Ferdinand* reply'd, That it was not their Business to explain the Emperor's Intention, contrary to the formal Words of their Instruction. So that the Cardinals *Hosius* and *Simonetta*, who expected the Embassadors in another Room, were forc'd to go to them, and remain Guarantees of the Approbation they assur'd the Emperor should give, to the Honour they should do to Cardinal *Madrucci*. The Emperor allow'd of what they did. However this Procedure ought not to serve for an Example, because nothing can warrant the Minister that acts contrary to his Instructions, if he be not otherwise assur'd of his Master's Intention.

These Occurrences are by so much the more inconvenient, that they at first imprint a very bad Opinion of the Conduct of the Embassador on the one side, as on the other side the Incivility that is done him ought to make him doubt of the Intention of the Prince, and of the Success of his Embassy.

The Admiral *de Chastillon* had nothing to negotiate at *Brussels*, when he was sent thither in the Year 1555, to see the Observation of the Truce, that had been concluded at *Vancelles*, sworn to. By the manner he was receiv'd, it was easy to judge that the Treaty had superseded the Animosities of the Princes, but had not quite extinguish'd them. The Admiral, who was Governor of *Picardy*, and Nephew to the Constable, was for appearing with a fine Retinue, but the Count *de Bossu*, whom the Emperor *Charles* V sent to meet him, rather to observe him than to do him Honour, told him at first, That the Town of *Brussels* was

was so throng'd, by reason of the Assembly of the States of all the Provinces of the *Low Countries*, whom the Emperor had there conven'd, that the Embassador's numerous Train, would not be able to find Lodgings there, so that he would do well to send back part of of it, as indeed he was oblig'd to do. When he was conducted to *Audience* he was led thro' the great Hall of the Palace, which was hung with Tapestry, wherein was represented, with the Battel of *Pavia*, one of the greatest Disgraces which ever happen'd to *France*. The Aamiral was very much offended thereat, and the Noblemen of his Retinue could not forbear shewing their Resentment. It must be own'd that after *Philip* King of *Spain*, who had also sign'd the Treaty, few Princes would be capable of receiving the Embassador of a great Monarch in so disobliging a manner.

After the Conclusion of the Treaty of *Vervins*, the Cardinal of *Florence*, (who had assisted there in the Quality of Legate) as he was returning from the Frontiers of *Picardy* in order to go back to *Rome*, express'd a Desire to see St *Germains*. The King having a mind to regale him, because he was a Prelate very well affected to *France*, gave his Orders, that the finest Furniture belonging to the Crown should be carry'd thither. The Queen of the Furniture accordingly did not fail to send thither a Bed and Hangings that Queen *Jean* ot *Navarre*, Mother of King *Henry* IV, *had embroider'd with her own Hands*, as being the richest Furniture he had in his keeping, and had caus'd the Room where the Legate was to lie, to be hung therewith. Good Fortune so order'd it, that the Marquis *de Rosni*, who had Orders to take care of his Treatment, having a mind to see whether the King's Intention had been fulfill'd, presently espy'd this Piece of Furniture, which he knew was fill'd with an Infinity of Devices against the Pope, and against the Clergy. He therefore had it taken away immediately, and so prevented a very strange Scandal. Some Years ago, one of the greatest and most powerful Cities of *Europe*, intending to give a splendid Entertainment to a certain Princess, caus'd to be represented at her Entry, all the Particulars of a horrible Tragedy, wherein the Father of this illustrious Lady, had acted the chief Part. The Mind must be strangely turn'd, to be able to think, that Objects so odious and frightful, can any way be grateful to a Person whom we design to divert and shew Respect to. These Incongruities are inconsistent with common Sense but yet they very frequently happen to those, that have more Lecture than Study, and who have travell'd, like *Jonas*, in the Body of a Beast. History observes as a very great Incivility what happen'd to the King of *Poland*, *Henry* of *Valois*, at *Heidelberg*. The Elector, who was otherwise a very civil Prince, and who could not be ignorant that the King was coming to see him, not only did not send any body to meet him, but did not so much as leave one single Person at home to compliment him at his coming to the Castle. In the Night he had a very warm Alarm, under the Pretext that one of the Apartments was on fire, and the Elector himself, as he conducted him through the Galleries and Chambers, shew'd him, and made him take notice of the Pictures of several Noblemen, who had been massacre'd on St *Bartholomew*'s Day, and among the rest, that of Admiral *Chastillon* Henry had been one of the chief Authors of the Muider, for which Reason the Elector express'd himself to him in such Terms, as serv'd for a cruel Reproach to those who had contributed to the Death of a Man, who was one of the worthiest Subjects the King of *France* had. But the Elector might have forborn treating after this manner a Prince, to whom he ought in his own Palace, to have shewn the Respect that was due to him, or else he should not have receiv'd him.

Commines has reason to say, that there is no City where more Civility is done to Embassadors, than at *Venice*, because there is not any, where they are more magnificently receiv'd. To which I must add, that there is not any State, where publick Ministers enjoy a greater Safety. When *Selim* II, Emperor of the *Turks*, sent *Crbat Chiaoux* to the Republick of *Venice*, to demand the Island of *Cyprus*, that is to say, to declare War against it, the Senate nevertheless paid him Civilities, he was conducted to Audience by Senators, and he had the most honourable Place given him, as the other Ministers of the *Port* always had. A Prince cannot shew too much Civility to a foreign Minister, but he may err in not doing enough. It is no less his business to make him be consider'd within his Dominions, than it is to see that his own Embassador be respected in the Court of another Prince. There is not any thing, that Princes who understand themselves are more sensible of, than of the Treatment that is dealt to those who represent them. It is what Princes ought not to be ignorant of, or if they are, they ought to have Officers that are knowing therein, for fear of being necessitated to make shameful Reparations, or not very honourable Excuses. As that King of *Poland*, who to excuse the Rusticity with which he had receiv'd the Embassadors of the United Provinces, had recourse to his Chamberlain, who as he said, ought to have inform'd him of what he had to do.

I have before observ'd in Chapter XVIII, that there is no *Master of the Ceremonies* at *Venice*, nor in Holland but he is for all that a very necessary Officer, and of great Importance, when he is an able Man. For as he is oblig'd to see the Embassadors often, as well on account of the Audiences, and publick Assemblies, as out of Civility, he may and ought to visit them from time to time, and in conversing with them, he cannot but receive some light, which tho' uncertain sometimes, yet does not fail to guide him to true ones.

As for the matter of Civility, even the *Turks*, when they have had either great Princes, or able Ministers, have paid it to Embassadors and have own'd that it was what could not be avoided, without destroying that Commerce, which is not less necessary to Sovereigns than to private Persons. After that *Roequnendoff*, who commanded the Arms of *Ferdinand* of *Austria*, had besieg'd *Buda* without Success, and that *Solıman* had made himself Master of that Town, which is the Capital of *Hungary*, *Ferdinand* sent to him *Nicholas de Salms* and *Sigismund de Ligtenstein*. There was an open

War between the two Princes, but that did not hinder *Soliman* from receiving the Embassadors perfectly well Soliman *caus'd them to be handsomely treated by the Bashaws, and those of their Retinue by Sangiacs, and after Dinner he had them conducted all over the Camp, that they might see it, and admire the Order, Discipline, Neatness and Silence thereof* And as for the Negotiation it self, he signify'd to them by *Rustan* his First Vizir, that he was ready to make Peace, if *Ferdinand* would restore all the Places that *Lewis* King of *Hungary*, Brother-in-law to *Ferdinand*, had been possess'd of If he withdrew all his Troops, and reimburs'd the Charges he had been at in the War, by paying for his Hereditary Lands of *Austria*, such a yearly Tribute as they should agree upon adding, that if these Conditions were not agreeable to *Ferdinand*, he had nothing to do but to resolve upon continuing on the War

But before we enter on a Detail of these Civilities we must lay down this Position, that those which are done to an Embassador, out of publick and solemn Actions, cannot be made use of as Precedents, neither by his Successors, nor other Ministers of the same Character Provided the Embassador has those Civilities paid him which are his due, he ought not to find fault with those that are done to another, out of particular and personal Considerations Queen *Elizabeth* was willing to honour the Mareschal *de Biron* so far, as to play on the Spinet before him, to dance to divert him, altho' she was not young, and to visit him at his own House, causing her Litter to stop before the Palace where he was lodg'd *Lewis Sforza*, Duke of *Milan*, being inform'd that *Lewis*, Duke of *Orleans*, had surpris'd *Navarra*, while *Charles* VIII, was in the Kingdom of *Naples*, went to see Jerome Leonne, the Venetian *Embassador, at his own House*, to pray him to represent to the Senate the Danger he was in, and to hasten the Succours he demanded King *James* I of *England*, was so familiar with Count *Gondemar*, the *Spanish* Embassador, that the Officers the most necessary about his Person, did not approach him with more liberty, than did that Embassador The late King of *Sweden, Charles Gustavus*, suffer'd the *French* Embassador to play the Companion with him, but then he took pleasure in him, as in a Person more capable to divert him, than to negotiate The present King of *Great-Britain* does not disdain going to the Entertainments Embassadors make him, and the *Northern* Kings sometimes do that Honour, not only to Embassadors, but also to Ministers of the second Order, the other Embassadors (with whom he does not live so familiarly) not being able to take offence thereat This is not practis'd in *Spain*, where no body eats at the King's Table and I don't think, that the present King of *France* has ever done it A Sovereign Prince, who neither gives the Hand, the Step, nor the Chair to Embassadors, is cautious of making them Visits at their own Houses. Henry IV, and *Lewis* XIII, Kings of *France*, and *Philip* II, King of *Spain*, have indeed visited the Legates, but then it was out of particular Considerations, and that has not been sufficient to make an Example *Lewis* XIV, and *Philip* IV, have not done it I often mention the Illustrious Embassy, that *France* sent into *Germany* in the Year 1620 Several Princes visited the Embassadors, and some of them, even prevented them in the first Visit The Embassadors understanding that the Duke of *Bavaria* did not intend to visit them, desir'd to know of the King their Master how they should govern themselves in reference to him They receiv'd for answer, that they might sound the Duke underhand, and that if they did not find him dispos'd to return their Visit, they should not go, but only send to him, to make their Excuse

Formerly when all Embassies were Extraordinary, Embassadors were defray'd *Philip de Commines* says, that the Republick of *Venice* knew what she was to give every Year to the Embassador of *Milan*, and the Duke of *Milan* knew what he was to furnish to the Embassador of *Venice*, and that he himself was defray'd for above a Year that he resided there This was practis'd every where and in some Places the Extraordinaries were still defray'd at the beginning of this Age The Senate of *Venice* allow'd *Don Francisco de Castro*, Embassador Extraordinary from *Spain*, two hundred Crowns a Day for his Table it offer'd the same to Cardinal *de Joyeuse*, who was there at the same time on the part of *France*, but he refus'd it I have said above, that in the Year 1640, the Embassadors Extraordinary of the United Provinces were defray'd in *Sweden*. But since most Embasses are become in Ordinary, and that even the Extraordinaries are often for several Years, Princes have thought fit to ease themselves of that Expence, and to change it into a Treat, which makes part of the Civilities they go to Embassadors It does not last for the most part above three or four Days, that is to say, the Day of their first Audience, or that ensuing it None but *Embassadors are treated in* France, *and not all of them neither* Those of the Princes of *Italy* are not, no more than those of the Republick of *Genoa Belisi*, one of the Introductors of Embassadors in *France*, to'd *Sauli*, Embassador from that Republick, that the King treated only the Embassadors of crown'd Heads but he did not explain himself well He ought to have added, that the King did that Honour also to the Republicks of *Venice*, and of the United Provinces, since he did it even before the Civilities were regulated in reference to these, as I have observ'd elsewhere, speaking of the Reception that was made to *Pau* and *Knut* in the Year 1634 The Embassadors are treated, either by a Comptroller, and by the other Officers of the King's Houshold, or else by Presents, that is to say, by sending them home such a Quantity of Meat and Fowls, that they may have them dress'd by their own Domesticks In this no Distinction is made between the Embassadors of crown'd Heads, and others because the Usage is sometimes one way, and sometimes another

The Duke of *Pastrana*, who came into *France* in the Year 1612, on the score of the double Marriage, *was treated by Presents*, during the Stay he made at *Paris*, and was treated by the King's Officers only at *Fontainbleau*, after he had took his Leave of the Court, which remain'd at *Paris* Several Entertainments were made for the Ministers of the Cantons, when they

The EMBASSADOR and his FUNCTIONS. 169

they came to *Paris* about the Renovation of the Alliance in 1602, and in 1663, but the King did not cause them to be treated during the time that preceded their Audience and not one of the Civilities was done them that are usually paid to Embassadors, except that the Guards were under their Arms, because it was thought proper to shew those Soldiers, to the Ministers of a Countrey that supplies *France* with so many. The Czar of *Moscovy* defrays all Embassadors, from the Day they enter into his Dominions, till they leave the same. The *Grand Seignior* and the Emperor defray also mutually the Embassadors they send each other, and treat them either by Presents, or else they give them Money.

He that was sent by *Sultan Ibrahim* to *Vienna* in the Year 1665, requir'd such a prodigious Quantity of Provisions for himself and those of his Retinue, that there was enough to furnish a whole Town. This will easily be believ'd, when it is known, that barely to make his Sauces, he requir'd to be furnish'd every Day with four Pounds of Pepper, four Pounds of Cloves, two Pounds of Saffron, sixty Pounds of Sugar, eighty Pounds of Honey, a hundred Pounds of Butter, and eighty Pounds of Almonds, &c.

It is only on extraordinary Occasions now, that Princes give Repasts to Embassadors after their first Audience, and that they make them dine with themselves, as I shall make it appear, after I have had a Word or two, concerning a Custom, which has been abolish'd in *France* but within some Years. It is not long since the Lord Mayor, and the Sheriffs of the City of *Paris*, were us'd to make a Present of Flambeaux of white Wax, of Sweet-meats, and of Wine to those Embassadors, who came thither about extraordinary and important Affairs. They paid this Civility to the Lord *Hayes*, who came to renew the Alliance in the Year 1616 and to the three Embassadors who were then on occasion of the Marriage of the late King and Queen of *England*. I do not find that those Civilities have been done to any other Embassadors since that time and is even that is were attended with some Circumstances particular enough, I shall here take notice of some of them.

It was in the Year 1625, that the Marriage was solemniz'd at *Paris* and the Queen of *England* being ready to set out, the King commanded the Lord Mayor and the Sheriffs to go and pay their Respects to her, and to carry her, is also to the Earl of *Carlisle*, and to the Lord *Rich*, since Earl of *Holland*, Embassadors Extraordinary from *England*, the usual Present of the City. These Officers of the Town, after they had saluted the Queen, went to see the Embassadors at their House, *and were receiv'd by 'em in the middle of the Stairs.* The Earl of *Carlisle*, who was the first, offer'd the Hand to the Lord Mayor and not being able to prevail with him to go first, they went into the Room together, the Lord *Rich* following them. At their going away, the Embassadors *conducted them to their very Coach,* and did not retire till the Lord Mayor and the Sheriffs were got in. Some Days after they made the same Present to the Duke of *Buckingham*, who was come thither after the Marriage. He receiv'd them in the middle of the Hall, where they made their Speech to him, and presented the Flambeaux, the Wine, and the Sweetmeats. He would have conducted them back to their Coach, but meeting the Duke *de Nemours* upon the Stairs, the Lord Mayor desir'd him to leave them to entertain the Duke, which accordingly he did, after several obliging Expressions, and having desir'd the Lords of *Carlisle* and *Rich* to conduct the Gentlemen of the City to their Coach.

It is thought somewhat strange, that the King of *Spain*, who did such great Honours to the Prince of *Wales* when he went to *Madrid*, did not once make him dine at his own Table. It is an Honour that the King or *Spain* does to no body. The other Kings who were us'd to do it to Embassadors, have left it off by degrees. In *France* and in *England* it is not done but at the Solemnities of a Marriage, or of an Oath for the Observation of Treaties and as those Oaths are out of date, by reason of the Ratification supplies the use thereof, these Entertainments are no longer practis'd neither. It is needless to repeat here what I as been said on that Head in the Memoirs, since even in the *North* they imitate in this and in several other things, what is practis'd in other Kingdoms. I have hitherto observ'd but the single Example of Cardinal *Caraffa*, Nephew to *Paul* IV, whom *Philip* II caus'd to dine with him at *Brussels*.

Embassadors Extraordinary are also lodg'd till the Day of their *Audience*, and in most Parts of the Kingdom there are Houses appointed for that purpose. Formerly the States of the United Provinces lodg'd even the Embassadors and Residents in Ordinary of crown'd Heads and the *French* Embassadors had their particular *Hostel* at the *Hague*, till the Year 1648. At that time *la Tuillerie* being Embassador in *Holland*, left it somewhat abruptly, that the separate Peace which had been concluded at *Munster* might not be publish'd in his Presence. Before he set out, he sent back the Keys of his House, which his Predecessors were us'd to leave in the Custody of the King's Agent, during the time there was no Embassador, and he gave the States to understand, that for the future the Commerce between the King and them would not be so great, but that it might be carry'd on by a Minister of the second Order. Whereupon the States resolv'd in the Month of *January* 1649, that for the time to come the Embassadors and Residents of crown'd Heads, should be no longer lodg'd at the Charge of the State.

I just now said, that the Extraordinaries are lodg'd till the Day of their *Audience*, and that is observ'd almost every where, but yet not so very regularly, but that sometimes Embassadors are suffer'd to continue there, more especially if they are not oblig'd to make room for a later Comer. And even on these Occasions, they cannot be dislodg'd handsomely, tho' at the same time it is a Piece of Incivility to stay there beyond the usual Term. The Earl of *Leicester*, Embassador from *England*, was lodg'd at *Paris* in the House of the Extraordinaries, when *Zavadsky*, Chamberlain and Embassador from *Poland*, arriv'd there in the Year 1636. Some were for dislodging the Earl, and Cardinal

X x

dinal *de Richelieu* insisted upon it so much the more, because the *English* Embassador did not visit him. But *Berlize* represented to the Cardinal the Consequence of affronting the Earl by dislodging him by force, and added, that infallibly the same Usage would be dealt to *M. de Seynezerre*, Embassador of France in *England*, who was there lodg'd at the King's Expence. The Cardinal acquiesc'd therefore, and *Zavadsky* was lodg'd at the *Hostel de St Chaumont. M Servien*, at his Arrival at the *Hague* in the Year 1647, found the House of the Extraordinaries occupy'd by the *Muscovite* Embassadors. The utmost Endeavours were us'd to dislodge them, but they could not be wrought upon to comply, so that the States were oblig'd to lodge *Servien* elsewhere. It would have been an Act of Injustice to dislodge the *Muscovites*, because the Czar lodges and defrays all Emoassadors.

It is again a necessary Civility that the Prince causes to be done to the Embassador, by having him visited on the same Day he arrives, or else the Day following. In which I said, there is also a Distinction made between the Embassadors of crown'd Heads, where I comprise also those of *Venice* and of *Holland*, and between those of the other Princes and Potentates of *Europe*. It is not done to those of the Cantons, and since they are not allow'd to be cover'd, that they have not the Title of Excellency, and that the Princes and Ministers do not yield them the Hand, it must be believ'd, that they are not treated as Embassadors. These two Civilities of the Title and the Hand, shall take up the greatest part of this Chapter, because all the others are granted without Difficulty to those that have the Quality of Embassador.

It is only since the latter end of the foregoing Century, that Embassadors have assum'd the Title of Excellency. *Lewis de Gonzagu*, Duke of *Nevers*, being sent to *Rome* by King *Henry* IV, in the Year 1593, the Pope would not own him as an Embassador, but the Ministers of the other Princes, who were well affected towards *France*, visited him notwithstanding, and as he was a Prince of the House of *Mantua*, they made no difficulty to give him the Title of Excellency.

The Partisans of *Spain*, who would not have the Embassador of that Crown to be inferior to the other, in any respect whatever, gave him the same Title *Foscarini*, who was at that time Embassador in *France* from the Republick of *Venice*, which is in Possession of a Right to be upon the Par with crown'd Heads, and to follow them immediately, bethought himself of being treated with the Title of Excellency by the *Sieur di Jacob*, Embassador from *Savoy*, and made no scruple to give him the same Quality. The Marquiss of St *Maurice*, who succeeded *Jacob*, follow'd the Example of his Predecessor, and these two Embassadors continu'd to treat one the other with this Equality, till *Contarini*, who succeeded *Foscarini*, refus'd to do this Honour to the Abbot of *Mante*, St *Maurice*'s Successor. The Pretext of his Refusal was, that he could not give the Title of *Excellency* to a Prelate of the second Order, while only that of *Most Reverend, and Most Illustrious Lordship* was given to Cardinals. However as it really was but a Pretext, the same *Contarini* refus'd it also to the Count *de Verrue*, Successor to the Abbot. He said he should be very cautious how he gave the Count a Quality, which he had refus'd to his Predecessor, by this means making his Game both of the one and the other, notwithstanding the Pope's Nuncioes, *Spada, Bichi* and *Ceva*, had given it him without any Difficulty. The Duke complain'd thereof, as well as of the Wrong he said the Doge did him, in refusing to insert in the Inscription of his Letters, the Title of Highness, which he gave him in the Text thereof.

There has always been a Jealousie between this Republick and the Dukes of *Savoy*, since near these two hundred Years. She formerly gave place to the Dukes, till *Emanuel Philibert*, seeing the Emperor *Charles* V, did not protect him powerfully enough against *Francis* I, reclaim'd the Protection of the Senate of *Venice*, and procur'd himself the Quality of Son of St *Mark*. Now as the Son could not with a good Grace take place of the Father, he yielded the Precedency to the Republick, on condition that at Visits and other Ceremonies, they should treat one another with Equality as to Titles. This is what was observ'd on both sides till the time above mention'd. The Duke Cardinal *Lmannel*, was so extremely offended at the Refusal of *Contarini*, that he would not see him, when he pass'd through *Savoy*, in his Return from his Embassy in *France*, and forbid doing him those Civilities, which were usually paid to the *Venetian* Embassadors when they pass'd through his Territories. The Animosities even went so far, that in the Year 1631 he expell'd the *Venetian* Embassador from his Court, under pretext, that he there carry'd on Intrigues against his Service. but this Hatred is become in a manner irreconcileable, since the Duke has taken the Quality or king of *Cyprus*, and has disputed it with the Republick, that possess'd that Kingdom when *Selim* II conquer'd it about a hundred Years ago. It would require too great and too tedious a Digression, to speak of the Rights and Pretentions of the Republick, and of the Duke of *Savoy*, for which Reason I shall not meddle therewith.

The Marquiss *de St Maurice*, Embassador Plenipotentiary of the same Duke of *Savoy*, at the Congress of *Westphalia*, would not make his Entry at *Munster*, till he knew first after what manner he should be treated. Before he left *Turin*, France had assur'd that Court, that he should not be distinguish'd from the Ministers of the United Provinces. The Nuncio signify'd to him, that he was ready to give him the Title of *Excellency*, provided he obtain'd it also from the Embassadors of the Emperor and of the crown'd Heads. At his Entry there were only the Nuncio, the Embassadors of *France*, the Bishop of *Osnaburg*, Plenipotentiary of the Electoral College, the Plenipotentiaries of *Bavaria*, and the Resident of *Sweden*, sent their Coaches to meet him. The Nuncio, and the same Ministers I just mention'd, paid him the first Visit. but *the said Nuncio, the Embassadors of the Emperor, and of* Spain, *refus'd to give him the Title of Excellency* for which he express'd so much the greater Resentment against those of *Spain*, because sometime after

after they were so prodigal thereof, to those to whom the Embassador of *Savoy* wou'd fain have given the Quality of Rebels, while they treated so unworthily a Prince that was near related to their Master. The Nuncio, who had made so many Steps, might very well have made one more, since *Pope Innocent* X. *ordain'd some time after, that the Embassadors of Savoy and of* Tuscany, *should have the Style of Excellency.*

It is not very long, since great Difficulties arose on this Subject. In the Year 1603, *Francisco de Castro*, Embassador Extraordinary from *Spain* to *Venice*, gave to understand that he would not give the Style of *Excellency* to the Embassadors in Ordinary that resided there, not even to him of *Spain*, but those from *France* and *England* signify'd to him, that if he refus'd to give them the Title which was due to their Character, they would not see him. That all the other Ministers, and even the Cardinals, making no Difficulty to give it them, they did not know under what Pretext the Embassador of *Spain* could refuse it them. Don *Francisco* was for backing his Design by the Example of the Constable of *Castile*, who going some time late to *England*, had not given it to the Ordinaries, however, Don *Francisco* was at last forc'd to yield, and do as the rest did.

The Emperor, tho' he order'd his Plenipotentiaries to pay to those of the Electors the same Honours they paid to the Embassador of *Venice* as well with Reference to the first Visit, as to the reconducting part, *would not at first allow them the Title of Excellency, because* it is not given to the Representants, which are on their part at the Diets, yet at last he alter'd his mind on this Article, and ca's'd it to be given them. *D'Avaux* and *la Tuillerie*, Embassadors from *France* to *Venice*, did not refuse to give the upper Hand in their own Houses, to the Embassadors of the United Provinces, neither did they make any Difficulty to reconduct them, *but yet they would not give them the Title of Excellency.* In which it must be confess'd, that there is something so very odd, that it is hard to comprehend the meaning of it. While Matters were settling with the States, in Reference to the Civilities that were to be done to their Embassadors at *Munster*, Cardinal *Mazarin*, who was willing to gratify them a little, *was of Opinion that the Style of Excellency might be given to their Embassadors, though at the same time they were deny'd the Hand.* He said that at *Rome* the Cardinals, and even the Cardinal Nephews, give *the Title of Excellency, to all Embassadors, and yet do not yield the Place of Honour to any one of them.*

In the Year 1644, *Borcel* and *Renswonde*, Embassadors from the United Provinces, in *England*, had a Dispute on this Subject with the Count *de Harcourt*, Embassador from *France*. They say, in the Report they make of their Embassy, that the Count had refus'd them *the Place of Honour, and the Title of Excellency*. The Count, on the contrary, said that he had refus'd them neither the one nor the other, and that he had made no other Answer to those who had spoke to him about it, than this, That he would give to Civility all that could be reasonably desir'd of him, and even more, but that he did not pretend to oblige himself thereto by a formal Contract or Stipulation, and that he had not explain'd himself more particularly thereon. The *Dutch* Embassadors were prudent enough not to contend any farther with the Count *de Harcourt*, who was more accustom'd to let the Prince and the Captain than the Embassador.

In the Year 1641, the States of the United Provinces sent to *London* that solemn Embassy of which we make mention elsewhere. The *Venetian* Embassador paid the usual Civilities to the Embassadors of the States, as soon as they arriv'd at *London*, but it is observ'd, that his Secretary never made use of the Word *Excellency*. He follow'd therein the Example of those of *France*, and particularly that of *d'Avaux* and of *la Tuillerie*, who being Embassadors at *Venice*, did not give the Title of *Excellency* to those of *Holland*, as I just now took notice.

However, we are sensible of the Contests the Emperor's Ministers and those of the King of *Spain* have had on this account, even with the Embassadors of *Venice*. In the Year 162 *Girolamo Landy*, Embassador from *Venice* at *London*, being inform'd that the Count *de Swartzemburg*, Embassador Extraordinary from the Emperor, was arriv'd there, sent his Secretary to complement him, and gave him to understand that he would soon acquit himself of his Devoirs to him in Person. But the Secretary observ'd that the Count, when he made mention of the *Venetian* Embassador, only gave him the Style of *Most Illustrious Lordship*, after the Example of Count *Gondemar* and of the Marquiss of *Inovosa*, *Embassadors from Spain*, who had behav'd themselves after the same manner. *Landy* being very much offended at the Procedure of the Count *de Swartzemburg*, who had sent no body to visit him, got the Master of the Ceremonies to speak to him about it, as well as concerning the Style of *Most Illustrious Lordship*. The Count made answer, That he could not treat other with a State that was so much below the Dignity of the Emperor his Master. *That he could not give him the Title of Excellency*, which he knew the *Spanish* Embassador did not give him. That what the other Embassadors had done equally to no Precedent to him, and if the Embassador of *Venice* pretended to make use of the Style of *Most Illustrious Lordship* to him, he would then give him but the bare Title of *Lordship*, and that he would always make some Distinction. That *Lanay* had no Reason neither, to complain of his not having return'd his Complement, because the Secretary had told him that his Master would immediately come and see him, and that he had expected him accordingly. These two Embassadors did not see one another, nor indeed could they, after what had happen'd. The Count *de Swartzemburg* did not understand Civility very well, or else he would not understand it.

At the same time that the Count treated *Girolamo Landy* after so offensive a manner at *London*, the Count *d'Ognate*, Embassador from *Spain*, did not use *Peter Gritti* better at *Vienna*, refusing to give him the Title of *Excellency*. The *Spaniards* were every powerful at that Court, and had the chief Direction of Affairs there, wherefore the Emperor not daring to oppose the

the Pride of the Count *d'Ognate*, could not hinder likewise *Gritti* from complaining to the Senate, who thereupon order'd him to retire, and leave a Secretary in that Post. These are often the Effects of the Capriciousness of the Minister, more than of the Will and Orders of the Master. In the Year 1624 the Count *de Kevenhuller*, the Emperor's Embassador at *Madrid*, refus'd to give the Title of *Excellency* to the Embassador of *Venice*. His Predecessor had given it, and the Count's Refusal had like to have been the Cause of a great Scandal, because the two Embassadors happening to meet one Day in the King's Antichamber, where none but the Embassadors of crown'd Heads have Admittance, they came at last to such high Words that they were just going to draw. They were however pacify'd, and prevail'd upon to salute one another with their Hats when they should chance to meet, but should not speak. The whole Matter was regulated in the Year 1636, when *France* and *Spain* having desir'd the Republick to endeavour an Accommodation between them, and she having nominated *John Pesaro* for that Purpose, the Ministers of the Emperor and of the King of *Spain* promis'd they would, for the future, treat the Embassadors of *Venice* as they did those of crown'd Heads.

The Count *Francis Nerli*, Plenipotentiary of the Duke of *Mantua* at *Munster*, pretended to have the Style of *Excellency*, and obtain'd it of the Embassadors of *France*, and of those of the Electors, which is worthy Observation. But the Nuncio, and the Emperor's Embassadors, absolutely refus'd to give him that Title. The *French* therefore declar'd to him, that if he did not likewise obtain it of the Emperor's Ministers, they would not continue to give it him neither. The Count, to maintain himself in his new Acquisition, pretended not to see the Emperor's Plenipotentiaries any more, but yet he under-hand entertain'd a Correspondence with them. His Wife dy'd, and he betook himself to the Church. So that not being able to lay any farther Claim to the Title of *Excellency* from the Nuncio, he was contented with that of *Most Illustrious Lordship*, with which even the Nuncio himself was forc'd to be satisfy'd.

In the Year 1639 the *Bailio de Forbin*, Great-Cross, came to *France* in the Quality of Embassador Extraordinary from *Malta*. He was a *French* Man, Lieutenant-General of the Galleys of *France*, and yet the King permitted him to be cover'd, the Prince of *Conde* and Cardinal *de Richelieu* gave him the Title of *Excellency*, and the Prince yielded to him the Place of Honour. There is no doubt but the Great Master of *Malta* is a Sovereign, but it is no Injustice to him to say that he is, properly speaking, but the General of a Religious Order. That his Sovereignty is confin'd within the Circumference of a Rock, and that his whole Strength consists in six or seven Galleys, which, instead of making War against the *Turks*, for the most part only infest private Persons by their Depredations, of which the Republick of *Venice*, and with her all *Christendom*, have had a sad Experience. I cannot forbear saying here, That it is surprizing enough to see the Embassadors of *France* give the Title of *Excellency* to a Minister, to whom those of the Emperor refuse it, and the King, who grants to his Officers and Subjects those Honours which he refuses to powerful Princes, whose Alliance he has not disdain'd. It is what is hard to comprehend. The Count Duke *d'Olivares*, first Minister of *Spain*, assum'd the Title of *Excellency*, as well on account of the Post he was in, as by reason of his Quality of *Grandee*, and nevertheless he had accustom'd the Embassadors to be contented with his giving them no other Title than that of *Lordship*. But fearing lest the Marquiss *de Rambouillet* (who was sent into *Spain* with the Quality of Embassador Extraordinary towards the end of the Year 1626) should not consent to this Inequality, he got *du Fargis*, Embassador in Ordinary from *France*, to speak to him about it. He assur'd the Marquiss, that it he granted him this Advantage, he would do him more Civility than he could otherwise pretend to, or hope for. The Marquiss did not explain himself any farther, but contented himself with answering in general Terms, That he would return the Civilities that should be done him, after that manner the Count Duke could desire he should. This general Answer, which signify'd nothing, giving reason to judge, that the Marquiss would not part with his Right. The Count Duke signify'd to him, that notwithstanding all the Grandees of *Spain* made Difficulty to be upon the Level with Embassadors in reference to Titles, That he was one of the Grandees, and that he had positive Orders to give no other Title to the Embassadors of crown'd Heads than that of *Lordship*, so that it was not in his Power to make any Alteration therein, yet he was willing nevertheless to establish that Equality betwixt the Marquiss and him, *that they should mutually treat one another with no other Style than that of* Signiorie *or* Lordship. The Marquiss acquiesced thereto, and it was very punctually observ'd. The Count Duke, hoping that an Excess of Civility might procure him an Advantage, which he could not promise himself of Right, went to see the Marquiss as soon as he understood he was arriv'd at *Madrid*, doing thereby an Honour to the Embassador of *France* that he had refus'd to the Legate. But he got nothing by it.

It is what will afford a great many Reflections. *The Princes of the Blood, in* France, *make no Difficulty to give the Style of* Excellency *to Embassadors, notwithstanding they have within some time refus'd to yield the Place of Honour to them*. The Cardinals make none neither, nor also the Sovereign *Princes of* Italy, tho' in their own Courts they take the Hand of 'em, for which Reason I cannot tell whether the Grandees of *Spain* have any Right to dispute with them the Title of *Excellency*. Moreover, I know very well that Kings do not give the Style of *Excellency* to Embassadors, but I cannot tell whether they can forbid their Ministers giving them that Title, and I do not make any Distinction here between the first and the others, for tho' the Confidence repos'd in Him gives him a greater Power, yet it does not give him a Quality that requires him a new Title. The Cardinal *Patrone* has all the Authority, but he has not for that a superior Quality, neither does he pretend to any other Title than that which is given to the other Cardinals. On the other side the Embassador ought not to suffer the Title of *Excellency* to be deny'd him, because it is given him as to the Representative of a Sovereign Prince. The Marquiss *de Rambouillet* might in some measure be satisfy'd, because the first Minister, who was a Duke and Grandee of *Spain*, pretended nothing from him, that he did not likewise grant him on his part, but *du Fargis* could not consent thereto, without injuring the Grandeur of the King his Master.

Philip IV, King of *Spain*, made difficulty to give the Title of *Sennor* to M *de Bassompierre*, Embassador Extraordinary from *France* at *Madrid* in the Year 1621. He said, he was only a Gentleman, who had not the Quality of Marquiss, nor of Count. But admitting *Bassompierre* had not been of a Birth Illustrious enough, and although even in the Court of *France* he had not been in the Rank of the first Lords of the Kingdom, after the Dukes and Peers and the Officers of the Crown, the King of *Spain* could not refuse the Title of Lord to his Character of Embassador Extraordinary. It is true the King of *Spain* has not that Civility for the Noblemen of his Court, which the King of *France* has for those of his. But it was necessary to have distinguish'd betwixt a Subject and a Stranger, betwixt a private Person and a publick Minister. *Philip* recover'd himself from his first Sentiment, and receiv'd *Bassompierre* so well, that the Day he made his Entry at *Madrid*, all the Prisons were open'd, not only to the Domesticks of the Embassadors in Ordinary of *France* and of *Venice*, who had committed any Outrages, but also to all other *Frenchmen*.

That Embassador who does not give to others the Title that is their due, has no reason to complain, if that of *Excellency* be not given him. In the Year 1603, the Duke of *Mantua* being come to *Venice*, the *Spanish* Embassador visited him, but instead of giving him the Title of *Highness*, he gave him that of *Serenity*, as being less esteem'd in *Spain*, where that of *Highness* was given only to the King, before *Charles* V's Reign, and even for some time afterwards. However, as that Title has given place to that of *Majesty* for a considerable time, and that even the King's natural Sons are allow'd the Title of *Highness*, the Duke perceiving that it was not the Embassador's Intention to do him Honour, he only gave him likewise the Title of *Signiory* or *Lordship*. The Doge of *Venice* thinks himself honour'd by the Title of *Serenity*, and the Elector of *Brandenburg*, has made pressing Instances to the Most Christian King, to give it him.

The Baron *de Haslang*, first Plenipotentiary to the Elector of *Bavaria*, not being able to obtain the Title of *Excellency* from the Embassadors of *France*, and yet being oblig'd to negotiate with them, he did not give them the Title, but only spoke to them in the third Person, after the manner of *Germany* and *Italy*, and they on their side did the like, as for example, M *d'Avaux* has said, M *le Baron* has said, *&c* This Matter has since been regulated in reference to the first Plenipotentiaries of the Electors, but the Embassadors of crown'd Heads, never gave the Title of *Excellency* to

the second, nor to their other Embassadors, and the Ministers of the Princes of *Germany* gave it neither to the one nor the other, that is to say, neither to the first nor second Electoral Embassadors.

This Title is become so common since the Assembly at *Munster*, that it can no longer be refus'd to those, whom the Sovereign has cloth'd with the Character of Embassador, tho' the Ministers of *France* pretend to adhere to the Regulation establish'd at *Munster*, and to give it only to the first. It is what I shall speak to hereafter in Chapter XXV. There is however an Exception to be made for those, who by reason of their Birth or Dignity, have a Quality above that which the Character gives them. Cardinal *Alexander Bichi* was Embassador Plenipotentiary from *France* in *Italy*, but that did not hinder him from having the Stile of *Eminency*, and those Honours were done to the Cardinal, which would not have been done to the Embassador. No body refus'd the Title of *Highness* to the Cardinal Lantgrave of *Hesse*, Embassador from the Emperor at *Rome*. The Ministers of *France* made no Difficulty to give the Title of *Highness* to the Bishop of *Osnabrug*, Plenipotentiary of the Electoral College, before they had Orders to give that of *Excellency* to the Plenipotentiaries of the Electors, and the Duke of *Nevers* himself had that Quality given him, as being a *Prince of the House of* Mantua, and not as Embassador of *France*. The Most Christian King, before he sent the Duke of *Longueville* to the Assembly of *Munster*, would have the Title of *Highness* given him, as well because he was in some manner of the Royal Blood, being descended from the Count of *Dunois*, natural Son of *Lewis* Duke of *Orleans*, who was Brother to *Charles* VI, as because he possess'd in Sovereignty the Territory of *Neufchastel* in *Switzerland*, but for all that the Duke met with very great Difficulties to have it given him at the Place of the Congress. The Plenipotentiaries of the Electors made none at all, because *France* had granted them the Title of *Excellency*, which was a great Novelty in the Empire. The Mediators, and the Emperor's Embassadors, refus'd to give it him even those of *Sweden*, judging that the Dignity of their Crown was concern'd therein, would do nothing but what they saw the rest do. On the same Day that the Duke arriv'd at *Munster*, the Nuncio, and the *Venetian* Embassador sent to complement him by two Gentlemen of their Retinue, but because they desir'd to speak with *M le Duke*, without mentioning the word *Highness*, he would not admit them, excusing himself on the *lassitude* he felt after the Fatigues of his Journey. So that the Mediators themselves did not see him, till after it was agreed, that it should not be esteem'd a formal Visit, nor of Ceremony, but should pass for a Conference of Business, where no Titles should be given on either side, and where they should talk to one another in the third Person, after the manner of *Italy*. The Count *de Pegnarande* being arriv'd at *Munster* some Days after, M *de Longueville*, who had as yet admitted no publick Visits, and who apprehended lest the Mediators should visit the Count first, signify'd to them, that notwithstanding he was not in a Condition to receive Visits, yet that should not hinder him from seeing those who would give themselves the trouble to come to him. The Mediators made answer, that they and the Emperor's Embassadors had already sent to desire Audience of *Pegnarande*, who had fix'd them an Hour the Day following after Dinner, and that otherwise they would not have fail'd to make him the first Visit, *as to him that came first*. The *French* Embassadors took it ill, however it had no farther Consequence. Eight Days after, the Mediators sent word to the Duke of *Longueville*, that the Count had communicated his Powers to them, and that they should be very glad to exchange them. He that brought the Message made no mention of *Highness*, for which Reason the Duke would not see him, but sent him an Answer by one of his Domesticks. The Secretary of the Embassy of *France*, going afterwards to see the Nuncio, to carry him the Duke of *Longueville*'s Powers, and having enter'd on the Discourse of Titles, the Nuncio told him, that when hereafter he should send any of his Gentlemen to the Duke, he would order him to give him the Title of *Highness*, provided that no Consequences were drawn therefrom, to the Prejudice of the Mediators themselves, as would be practis'd in *Italy*, where he that causes a Title to be given by his Domesticks, is deem'd to express his Intention to do the like himself. Accordingly, the Gentleman who carry'd to the Duke of *Longueville* the Powers of *Pegnarande*, on the part of the Nuncio, gave him the Title of *Highness Servien*, who carry'd back the same Powers to the Mediators, took an occasion to tell the Nuncio, that he could not comprehend, why any Person should make difficulty to do himself, what he caus'd to be done by one of his Gentlemen. That the Mediators had always said, they would follow therein 'the Example of the Emperor's Plenipotentiaries, and that *these had given the Title of Highness to the Duke of* Loguevelle. The Nuncio reply'd, that that was a thing not to be mention'd any farther, since when he offer'd the Secretary of the Embassy of *France*, to cause the Title of *Highness* to be given the Duke by his Gentleman, he had expressly added, that it should be on condition, that after that, nothing more should be requir'd of him, which he could not justify by the Example of the Count of *Nassaw Servien* said, that the Duke had heard nothing of any Condition, so that it was found necessary to come to a clearing of the Point with the Secretary of the Embassy. The Secretary therefore going to the Nuncio, put him in mind that he had said nothing else to him, than that what his Gentleman should do, should not be prejudicial to his own Person, but that no mention had been made of Conditions, nor of the Count of *Nassaw Servien* pretended, that since the Mediators had imitated the Plenipotentiaries of the Emperor, by giving the *Title of Highness to the Duke of* Longueville by a Gentleman, they might very well make one Step more, since he, of the Emperor's Plenipotentiaries, who was spokesman for them both, gave him the same Quality, but for all this the Mediators remain'd obstinate. *Servien* did not say all. It was not true, that the second Plenipotentiary of the Emperor had given the *Title of Highness to the Duke of* Longueville, when he had also spoken for the Count of *Nassaw*, and he had been disavow'd at *Vienna*, in the Advances he had made in his own particular. The Name of the Secretary of the Embassy of *France* was *Boulanger*, and he had an admirable Genius for that Function, accompany'd with a Probity, that had procur'd him the Esteem of all Men of Honour and Honesty. He was of all the *French*, the Person for whom the Nuncio had some Affection, and he continu'd to give him some Tokens thereof after his Promotion. Insomuch that *Boulanger*, promising himself a great Advantage from the Exaltation of *Fabio*, resolv'd to go and visit him at *Rome*. But Pope *Alexander* VII, soon gave him to understand, that in his new Dignity, he was not a better *Frenchman*, than he had been during his Nunciature, and that the Aversion the Pope had for all the Nation, extended as far as his own Person, which was the occasion of his remaining in *France*.

It might be here ask'd, whether the Most Christian King, who has a greater Power in his own Kingdom, than the Emperor has in the Empire, has not the same Faculty as he has, to create Princes? But that is not the thing in question. It was not the King's Intention to make the Duke of *Longueville* a Prince, when he gave him the Title of *Highness*, but only to declare, that since the Duke was Sovereign of *Neufchastel*, he could not be deny'd the Title of *Highness*. In the same manner, the King by ordering his Embassador to give the same Title to the Prince of Orange, did not declare him a Prince, nor did not erect *Orange* into a Principality or a Sovereignty, but he judg'd, that the Prince being a Sovereign, he ought to have the Title of *Highness*. It is true at the same time, that this Declaration cannot lay any Necessity on other Sovereigns to follow his Example, but then it cannot also be deny'd, that after the first King of Christendom, had shewn a Willingness to do this Honour to a Prince, the other Kings ought not to have refus'd it, and the Prince that receives it, ought not to suffer it to be taken from him.

I said before, that the Plenipotentiaries of *France* offer'd to give the Stile of *Highness* to the Bishop of *Osnaburg*, before they had receiv'd Orders to give that of *Excellency* to the Plenipotentiaries of the Electors, and they actually gave him the Title of *Grace*, or Dignity of Prince, to express what is call'd in the *German* Language *Jurstlizche Genade*, or *Burde*, and after the Duke of *Longueville* was arriv'd at *Munster*, they gave the Bishop the Title of *Highness*. I think my self oblig'd to say here, that as in *Italy* it is not given to all Princes without distinction, since the Republick of *Venice* gives only *that of Excellency to the Duke of* Parma, and that there are some Houses, where it is not given to the younger Children, so in *Germany* the Title of *Durchleuchtegheid*, which answers that of *Highness*, is not given to Bishops nor Prelates, nor even to those Electors, who are only Princes by reason of their Ecclesiastical Dignity, and are not so by Birth. Neither is it given to all Princes indifferently, but yet there are some, who notwithstanding they are not of the first Rank, have the Stile of *Jurstliche Gnade*. The word *Gnade* properly signi-

signifies Grace, Pardon, or Clemency But as the Word *Grace* signifies also Bounty, Favour, or good Disposition, it is also made use of in those Countries where the *French* Expression is adapted to the *German* Thought, to do Honour to those Princes who do not pretend to the Title of *Highness* The Queen *Margaret* of *Valois* says, in her Memoirs, That in passing through the Countrey of *Liege*, to go to the *Spaw* Waters, that Quality was given to the Bishop thereof, who is a Prince of the Empire This Quality of *Gnade* is so common in the *Upper Germany*, and particularly in *Austria*, and the neighbouring Provinces, that there is not a Baron that does not assume it as a Title inferior to that of *Excellency*. The *English* make use of it likewise, and give it to their Archbishops, and to Persons of the first Quality, after that of Princes, whereas the *Spaniards* give the Style of *Merced*, which has the same Signification, to Merchants, Artificers, and the most vile and abject Persons among the Commonalty Nevertheless in *Holland*, where the Word *Gnade* is understood only in its first Signification, they are so jealous of their Liberty (of which they have form'd such a strange Idea) that they cannot endure it, and in this Aversion the States themselves chuse rather to give the Title of *Highness* than that of *Grace*, to those who would be very well contented with the one, and have no Pretention to the other But this is not the only Irregularity that is there committed, in Reference to Honours and Civilities They think there, they do Honour to him to whom they give the Title of *Heres*, which in effect signifies no more than *Sr*, or *Lord* And they think they do still a greater Honour to those to whom they give the Quality of *Monsieur*, which certainly expresses something more than *Sieur* or *Lord*, which is the Title of Merchants in *Brabant* There are some young Women in *Germany*, and after their Example in *Holland*, who would think themselves affronted if they were stil'd *Damoiselles*, and if they were call'd *Fraulein*, which is a *German* Word, that has the same Signification and the same Etymology I or as in *France* the Word *Damoiselle* has been form'd of *Dame*, so in *Germany* the Word *Fraulein* is deriv'd from *Frau* In *France*, the King's Brother gives no other Style to his eldest Brother and Sovereign, than that of *Monsieur* And the first Princess of *France*, after the King's Daughters, and the richest in all *Europe*, glories in being also the first *Demoiselle* thereof

A great many things might be said on this Subject, but this is sufficient for a Digression I shall only add, that altho' the Difference of *Gnade* and of *Durchleuchtigheid* is observ'd also among the Electors, as I above took notice, yet at the Assembly of *Munster*, the Emperor thought fit that the Plenipotentiaries of the one's and the other's should have the same Style as those of *Venice* The Nuncio could never be brought to give the Title of *Highness* to the Bishop of *Osnaburg*, but he always gave him the Style of *Most Illustrious Lordship*, because the Bishop was not a Prince by Birth, and the Nuncio, who gave the Title of *Highness* only to those who were born Princes, and to those Cardinal's who were likewise Princes, was very cautious of giving it to the Bishop, who was not so

As when the Pope gave the Title of *Eminency* to Cardinals, he neither could, nor pretended to oblige crown'd Heads thereto, (amongst whom the Republick of *Venice* has been compris'd by a particular Declaration,) so Embassadors by procuring that of Excellency from their Equals or Inferiors, could not thereby oblige Sovereigns to treat them after the same manner Neither is there any King (at least among those who are knowing in the Matter of Civilities) that gives the Style of *Excellency* to Embassadors The Senate of *Venice* gives them only that of *Seigneurie* or *Lordship*, and the States General of the United Provinces are the only, to the best of my Knowledge, that give Embassadors the Stile of *Excellency* on all Occasions, by word of Mouth and in Writing The Arch-Duke *Leopold*, writing on the 24th of *May* 1620, to the Duke of *Engoulesme*, to the Count of *Bethune*, and to *Chasteauneuf*, Embassadors Extraordinary from *France* in *Germany*, gives to the Duke, who was a Prince, the Title of *Excellency*, and to the two others that of *Most Illustrious Lordship* After his Example the Duke of *Bavaria* deceas'd, writing to them on the 16 h and 20th of *June*, in the same Year, gives the Title of *Excellentissimus* to the Duke, and to the two others that of *Illustres* Thus the Duke of *Bavaria*, being Elector, and writing to the Embassadors Plenipotentiaries, who were on the part of *France* at *Munster*, on the 26th of *October* 1644, gives them only the Title of *M-ssieurs*, and of *Vous*, or *You*, the first Line without Civility, and in the Subscription, *Your Most Affectionate* It is true, the Duke of *Longueville* was not then come, however it looks as if there was a little Incivility in this manner of writing to Ministers Reprefentants, who had a full Power from the most powerful King in *Christendom*, who were not his Subjects, and whose Friendship was so necessary to him for the securing his most important Interests Sovereigns do not share their Dignity but with their Equals But I dare be bold to say, that there is nothing gives it a greater Lustre than the Civilities they bestow on those Persons, who owe them nothing but the Hat, and there is no Liberality that costs less It is true that the Duke, and the two other Plenipotentiaries on their side, us'd the Duke of *Bavaria* very Cavalierly in the Inscription of their Letters, directing them to *Monsieur, Monsieur the Duke of Bavaria*, and in the Subscription, which was no other than barely *Your very humble Servants* D'*Avaux* and *Servien* writing a Circular Letter to the Princes of *Germany*, on the 20th of *January*, 1645, give them the Title of *Most Serene*, and that of *Highness*, but in the Subscription, *Ready to serve your Highness* The Duke of *Angoulesme*, on the contrary, although a Prince by Birth, writing, with his Collegues, to the Count of *Hanau*, signs, *Your most affectionate Servant*

In the Year 1641, the King of *Spain* offer'd the Post of General of the Sea to Prince *Charles* of *Medicis*, Brother to the Great Duke of *Tuscany*, which was vacant by the Death of *Don Carlos* the King's Brother But the Great Duke would not suffer him to accept it, unless it was given him with all the Advantages that had been granted to Prince *Philibert* of *Savoy*:
He

He stipulated, amongst other things, that the Prince should not be oblig'd to yield the Hand, at home, to the Grandees of *Spain*, even tho' they had the Quality of Viceroy, or of Embassador. And all this was promis'd him. The Great Duke, at the same time, forgot to stipulate that the King should oblige the Grandees of *Spain* to go and visit the Prince, because without that it was very probable they would not do it, since they refus'd to give the Title of *Highness* to the younger Princes of the House of *Savoy*, who take place of those of *Tuscany*, and that they gave it to *Don John of Austria*, but on Condition that he should give them the Title of *Excellency*.

It is only within some Years, that the Ministers of the Court of *France*, and even the Secretaries of State, assume to themselves the Title of *Excellency*. It is from the Example of several other Courts of *Europe*, amongst whom that of *Sweden* pretends that it cannot be refus'd to the Senators, because they are not so much Members of the King's Council, as of the Senate of the Kingdom. The *Italians*, the *Spaniards*, and the *Germans*, speak almost always in the third Person, but the *French* find it hard to habituate themselves thereto, for which Reason those Titles are not very common there. The Prince of *Condé* cannot endure to have the Stile of *Highness*, since that Title, which belongs only to Sovereigns, has been prostituted to Persons who could hardly make out their Nobility. So that it was going to be almost as common as that of *Sir* is at *Lions*. *Royal Highness* is only spoke of since the first Journey the late Duke of *Orleans* took to *Brussels* in the Year 1631. It is only given to the Offspring of Kings, and the Duke of *Savoy* takes it but on account of his Pretensions to the Kingdom of *Cyprus*, tho' improperly enough. If that Kingdom be his, he is a King, and if it does not belong to him, he ought not to have the Title of *Royal Highness* neither.

When I spoke above, in the XVIIIth Chapter, of the Reception that was made to the *Swiss* Embassadors at *Paris*, I took notice that *Lionne*, Secretary of State, took at Home the Place of Honour, the Hand, the Door, and the Chair of them, which the Ministers do not do to the Embassador of the meanest Prince in *Italy*. The Embassadors, on their side, ought to do Honour to the Ministers, and to all the Persons of Quality that visit them on the part of the Prince. In the Year 1620, the Mareschal *de Cadenet*, who has since been known under the Quality of Duke and Mareschal *de Chaunes*, was sent into *England* on the Occasion of a Journey the late King, *Lewis* XIII, took to *Calais*, from whence he thought himself oblig'd to send to visit the King of *Great Britain*. The Mareschal being arriv'd at *Dover*, the Master of the Ceremonies brought him twenty Coaches and three hundred Horses. The Lord *Hunsdon* went to meet him as far as *Canterbury*, and the Earl of *Arundel* complemented him at *Gravesend* from the King. The Mareschal receiv'd him only at the top of the Stairs, and in reconducting him, he accompany'd him no farther than the Place where he had receiv'd him. The Earl was so scandaliz'd thereat, that when they were to set out the next Day, he would not see the Mareschal at his Lodgings, but sent him word that the Embassador's Retinue so fill'd the House where he was lodg'd, that his Person being thereby inaccessible, he would stay for him in the Street, in order to conduct him to the Barge. He accordingly waited for him, and being come to *Denmark*-House, where the Embassador was lodg'd, he took his leave of him at the Foot of the Stairs, leaving him in the Hands of some Gentlemen who accompany'd him into his Chamber. This was not all the Resentment the Earl shew'd. He complain'd thereof to the King, who caus'd it to be remonstrated to the Mareschal by the Comptroller of his Houshold, and oblig'd him to make Reparation. The Mareschal said that his Indisposition had hinder'd him from going to meet the Earl at *Gravesend*, and from reconducting him. But it was but a very bad Excuse, which would have been somewhat less deficient had he made it to the Earl himself. This Embassador was Brother to the Favourite, and it was in that Consideration that extraordinary Honours were done him. The Marquiss of *Buckingham*, and the Earls of *Dorset* and *Warwick*, conducted him to Audience, and some Days after the King made him dine with him.

La Villauxcleres de Lomenie, who has since been known under the Quality of Count of *Brienne*, went in the Year 1624 into *England*, as Embassador Extraordinary, for the Ratification of the Contract of Marriage between the Prince of *Wales* and *Henrietta* Daughter of *France*. Being arriv'd at *Gravesend* with the Marquiss *Deffiat*, who went as far as *Dover* to meet him, altho' he had the same Quality of Embassador Extraordinary, he was there complemented in the King's Name by the Earl of *Dorset*, who came thither with a Retinue of five and twenty Gentlemen, and with a Cortege of two and twenty Barges. The Earl being arriv'd at *Gravesend*, went directly to the Inn where the Embassadors were lodg'd, and was receiv'd at the bottom of the Stairs in the Entry, by the Marquiss de Rotelin, and by Monsieur de Massy, Brothers-in-law to La Villauxcleres, and by the two Embassadors at the top of the same Stairs. They paid one another great Civilities at the Chamber-Door, but at last the Earl was oblig'd to enter first. *La Villauxcleres* follow'd him. After him enter'd *Edward Herbert*, who had been Embassador in *France*, and the Marquiss *Deffiat* would do the Honours of the House. At his going away, the Earl refus'd a great while to take the Place of Honour, and did not take it but after great Contestations. The two Embassadors reconducted him to the House-Door. *La Villauxcleres* thought himself the Man of all *France*, who understood best the Business of Ceremonies. And it must be own'd, that after the inestimable Cabinet of the Count *de Bethune*, there was to be found with him a Collection of the finest Memoirs in the World. But one would think that on this Occasion neither he, nor all the others, knew very well what they did. The Earl of *Dorset* was deputed by the King of *England*, the Place of Honour was his due in the Embassador's Lodgings. He might indeed make some Refusals of it, out of Civility, but he could not suffer it to be taken from him. *La Villauxcleres* ought to send his Family to meet the Earl at the Street-Door, and ought to descend

The EMBASSADOR and his FUNCTIONS.

scend some Steps, to receive him on the Stairs. It was none of *Defhat*'s Business to do the Honours of the House. On the contrary, notwithstanding that *la Villauxcleres* had the Step and Hand of him, as being the last Comer, That could not take place at *la Villauxcleres*'s Lodgings, who was oblig'd at home to do Honour to his Collegue, who had the same Character he had himself. *Herbert* alone did well in receiving the Civility that was offer'd him. The *English*, going from thence, put it into deliberation, whether they should not signifie to the *French* Embassadors, that it was expected they should the next Day make a Visit to the Earl, and that if they fail'd therein, they on their part would not go to receive them, in order to conduct them to the River. This was certainly a very impertinent Proposition, and as such it was let drop.

Berlise, one of the Introductors of Embassadors in *France*, relates in his Memoirs, that going one Day from the King, to see the Viscount *Scudamore*, Embassador from *England*, and being about twenty Paces from the Inn, where the Viscount was lodg'd, he ask'd the *Sieur Girant*, whether the Embassador would not do by him as the other Embassadors had done by the other Conductors of Embassadors. That *Girant* indeed told him, there was no need to doubt it, and nevertheless he was willing to be inform'd therein by *M de Vic*, the *English* Agent, before he went in, and that *de Vic* told him, that *Wake*, *Scudamore*'s Predecessor, had been blam'd in *England* for having yielded the Place of Honour to the Introductor. That thereupon he had told *Girant*, that he who had been a long time in the Office, ought not to expose him that represented the King's Person. That that was the first time he had been surpris'd, and that it should be the last. It was therefore resolv'd immediately, that *Berlise* should see the Embassador in his Hall, without sitting down. That from that time he would not go to the Embassadors any more, and that Cardinal *de Richelieu* had told him, he did well to preserve the Dignity of his Office. *Berlise* adds, that he went to the Embassador from the King, and that on that account he ought to be consider'd and honour'd. If we take the pains to reason on what these Memoirs say, we shall be oblig'd to judge, that in this Example the Customs of *France* and *England* differ. Since this last takes it ill that *Wake* should yield at home the Place of Honour to the Conductor of Embassadors, it is reasonable to think, that Embassadors do not yield it to the Master of the Ceremonies at *London*. And that is most certain, as it is also certain, that the Introductors are in possession of a Right to insist upon having it in *France*. I have seen it more than once, and that the Embassadors conducted the Introductor to his Coach. However it looks as if there were some Deficiency in the Reasoning of *M de Berlise*, and there are so many other things to be observ'd on this Subject, that some would be apt to question the Right of the Conductors, and whether *England* has not more Reason of its side than *France*. *Berlise*, in saying that he went to see the Embassador from the King, says indeed the truth, but then he gives it a Turn which is not natural. He went as the King's Officer, and according to the Duty of his Office, so that he could not be consider'd as a First Gentleman of the Bed-Chamber, a Master of the Wardrobe, or some other Officer of the Houshold, whom the King employs to complement the Embassador. This Officer or Lord, who is a Representative, being a kind of Embassador, ought to be consider'd as the King's Deputy, but I do not think the same can be said of the Introductor, who only does what the Function of his Office obliges him to.

I am well assur'd that it will be a hard matter to reconcile the Pretentions of *M de Berlise*, with those of the President *de Bellievre*, who being Embassador from *France* in *Holland*, did a great deal more than the Viscount *Scudamore* did. He had been Embassador at *Venice* and in *England*. He was Grand Son to two Chancellors of *France*, he was a President *au Mortier*, and he had besides all this, a Merit that brighten'd very much what there was of Illustrious in his Office and Birth. His Predecessors had taken in their own Houses, the Hand and the Door of the Deputies of the States that went to see them. But the Rank and Titles had been regulated in the Assembly of *Munster*, and the State of the United Provinces had been acknowledg'd to be in such manner Sovereign, that the King of *Spain* had not only renounc'd his Right, but also his Titles, for which Reason the States, not being able to brook any longer their being us'd like the *Swifs Cantons*, represented to *M de Bellievre* the Reasons they had to insist upon having that Honour paid them in his own House, which was their Due, by his doing Civility to their Deputies, when they came to see him on their part. They took thereupon several very strong Resolutions, but the Embassador continu'd nevertheless to refuse them the Place of Honour in his House. He said he could not do it without Orders, and the Court not being in a Condition to think of those kinds of Affairs, he went from the *Hague*, where he did not leave any great Satisfaction of his Person. I should conceive that the Embassador of *England* might very well do in reference to an Introductor, (who is not one of the first Officers of the King's Houshold) what the Embassador of *France* did to the Deputies, who went to see him from the States, and who were of the Body of their Assembly *Chanut*, *de Thou*, *Destrades*, and *Pompone*, have done it without Contestation.

Moreover it looks like a Piece of Injustice to exact that Complaisance from foreign Embassadors, when the King won't suffer his to have it even for Princes. I do not here speak of those imaginary Princes, as, that of *Tarentum*, who refus'd to make the first Visit to *M Destrades*, Embassador from the King of *France*, whose Subject the Prince of *Tarentum* was, and who pretended to have the Hand, the Door and the Chair at the Embassador's House, but of those truly Princes, who have been oblig'd to yield to Embassadors all the Advantages imaginable, where-ever they chanc'd to meet, even in the Embassador's own Palace. The Duke of *Guise*, a Prince of the House of *Lorraine*, and Chief of that Branch that had taken Root in *France*, being at *Rome*, to try to annul the Marriage he had contracted with the Countess of *Bossu* at *Brussels*, and who had caus'd

the

the Family to lose above a hundred thousand Crowns in Benefices, made difficulty to go and visit the Marquis de Fontenay Mariel, Embassador from France, because this last refus'd to give him the Hand in his own House. Upon the Complaints the Embassador made thereof, the King wrote to the Duke of Guise on the 27th of *June*, 1644, "That the Refusal the " Duke made, to give Place to the Embassa- " dor, regarded his Royal Person, and gave " Strangers a very bad Opinion of the Respect " the Duke had for his Sovereign, and for the " Dignity of his Crown. That he therefore " commanded him, not to delay any longer paying " to his Embassador an Honour, that was so just- " ly his due. That the Prince of *Joinville*, eldest " Brother to the Duke, had acquitted himself " thereof without Reluctancy, to the *French* " Embassador in *Piedmont*. That all the World " was sufficiently satisfy'd, there could be no " Competition betwixt the Duke, and the Mar- " quis de *Fontenay*, as a private Person, but " at the same time he could not without Scan- " dal, continue his Contest with a Minister, " who represented his Person. So that he " hop'd, the Duke would without delay dis- " charge that Duty, and without any other " Concern, than what he might have for not " doing it sooner." Cardinal *Mazarine* added also a Letter which was at least as forcible, so that the Duke was oblig'd to obey. The Prince of *Tarentum* had this Example before his Eyes, yet nevertheless he continu'd obstinate not to see M *Destrades*, till he was necessitated to do by Force, what he might have done with a good Grace. Wherefore I shall say on this Occasion, that since Embassadors treat Princes after this Manner, the Ministers of the second Order have no great Reason to complain, when they receive either the same Honours, or Civilities that come near to those they pay to Princes. A great many more things might be said on this Subject, but what is for our present Purpose is, that it seems one might doubt, whether the Embassador, who does not in his own House yield the Place of Honour to a Prince, be oblig'd to give it to the Introductor of Embassadors.

The Lord Hollis, *Embassador from England, and the Embassador of* Venice, *would not in a third Place, yield Precedency to the Prince of* Conde. I won't say they were in the right. On the contrary, I am of Opinion that in *France*, something is due to the Princes of the Blood. I say something, but not all that the King has granted them within this little while. And I believe that the Embassador of *Venice* was by so much the more in the wrong, as he could not be ignorant of the Consideration which is had for the Princes of the Blood, even in his own Country, but I say it only on this account, that I think there is a great deal more reason to refuse the Place of Honour to a Conductor, than to dispute it with a Prince of the Blood, in a third Place. The Duke of *Savoy* would not permit *Prinly*, Embassador from *Venice*, to take the Precedency of Prince *Thomas* at the Procession of *Corpus Christi*, tho' at the same time he allow'd the Embassador of *Spain* to take this Advantage of him. The Republick resented it, and without doubt would not have suffer'd the same Prince to have taken the Place of Honour of the Embassador, in his own House.

The Pope's Nephews are not Princes of the Blood, because an Elective Sovereignty is not commun cable to Relations, for which Reason the Cardinals refus'd to give the Title of *Highness* to Prince *Casimir*, Cardinal of *Poland*. The Nephews, who are Cardinals, are consider'd on account of their Dignity, and *Thadeus Barberin* enter'd into Competition with the Embassadors, but only by reason of his Quality of Prefect of *Rome*. M *d'Urfé*, Embassador of *France*, writing to *Henry* II, on the 5th of *November* 1549, says, that on occasion of the Anniversary, he had been invited to the Entertainment the Pope gave to the Cardinals and Embassadors. That before they sate down to Table, the Steward and the Bishop of *Imola*, came and ask'd him from the Pope, and in his Presence, *if he pretended in this Ceremony to take Place of Duke* Horatio, *his Holiness's Nephew?* And that he made answer, Yes. That he expected that *Horatio*, as Duke of *Castro*, should sit below him. However he was willing to give him the Precedency, *not on account of his Quality of Duke, but because he was going to be Son in-law to the King his Master*: and to shew that it was merely on this score he yielded it to *Horatio*, he declar'd he would neither give the Hand, nor any other Advantage to *Octavio* his Brother. That he had desir'd the Master of the Ceremonies to register it accordingly, and at the same time he took *Horatio* by the Hand, and seated him above him. He moreover adds, *that this Procedure was look'd upon to be very gallant, because that, far from doing any Prejudice to his Character, he had made it known publickly, that had it not been for the Honour of the King's Alliance, to which* Horatio *pretended, he would not have given Place to the Quality of Duke*. That the Pope himself (not withstanding he was not over-pleas'd to see the Embassador's Pretensions, who took the Rank of his Nephews) had some Satisfaction in the Hopes that were given him of the Marriage.

As Civilities are not a Branch of the *Law of Nations*, they ought to be regulated by Custom, or according as the Occasion requires, but Embassadors will always do wisely to be free, or reserv'd therein, as shall be requisite to answer the Intention, and promote the Interest of their Masters. *Chanut*, Embassador from *France* in *Sweden*, had Orders to accommodate himself to the Will of Queen *Christina*, in reference to the Civilities he might pretend to; from the Prince *Palatine*, who was intended to succeed to the Crown, as well as in reference to those the Prince should desire from him when he was ask'd, whether he would give the Place of Honour to the Prince, and whether he would give him the Title of *Royal Highness*, *Chanut* made answer, that he would do whatever should be requir'd of him, but that he also expected to receive the same Honours, that the Princes of the Blood of *France* do to Embassadors. The Master of the Ceremonies reply'd, that as the Prince *Palatin* was the presumptive Successor to the Crown, the Embassador could pretend to no other Honours from him, than those the Duke of *Orleans* would do to a Minister of his Character. He added, that the Prince being nominated Successor, and having been declar'd such by an Act of the Estates, he was something

The EMBASSADOR and his FUNCTIONS. 179

thing more than the Duke of *Orleans* *Chanut* then told him, that *Monsieur* was the Son and Brother of a King, and that in that Quality he had an Advantage which the Prince *Palatine* had not. This Difficulty was the Cause that *Chanut* resolv'd not to visit the Prince. But at the very first Overture *Chanut* caus'd to be made to the Prince himself, he found him dispos'd to give him the Hand, the Door, and the Chair. He was therefore conducted to him by the Master of the Ceremonies. The Prince receiv'd him at the Coach Door, and re-conducted him to the same Place. Here he did too much. At the Entry that was made for Queen *Christina*, when she came to *Upsal*, the City where she was to be crown'd, the *French* Embassador's Coach gave place to the Prince *Palatin*'s: and at the Feast that follow'd after the Ceremony, the Embassador was seated immediately after the Prince, and the Embassadors of *Portugal* and of *Brandenburg* were likewise plac'd before the other Princes. *Chanut* pretended to no other Honour than that the Princes of the Blood pay to Embassadors. It is true, that at that time the Princes of the Blood yielded both the Hand and the Step to Embassadors, and not only to those of crown'd Heads, but also to those of the Republicks. The Count *de Brulon*, observes in his Memoirs, that in the Year 1639, the late Prince of *Condé* did this Honour to the *Baillo de Fouerbin*, Embassador of *Malta* and *Lionne* says in a Letter, that was intercepted about ten Years ago, that the Embassadors of *England* and *Venice*, refus'd to grant Precedency in a third Place, to the present Prince, as we have before observ'd. So that *Chanut* might pretend the same Advantage over the *Palatine*, who one may say was Prince of the Blood but by Adoption. In the Year 1667, *George d'Aubusson de la Feuillade*, Archbishop of *Embrun*, being Embassador at *Madrid*, went and paid a Visit to *Don John of Austria*, the King's natural Brother, before he had concerted the Civilities he might expect from him. *Don John* did him none, but in his own House took the Place of Honour of the Embassador with which the *French* Court was so disatisfy'd, that the Embassador was forbid continuing his Visits, unless the other gave him the Hand at home: and indeed they would not allow the Embassador to yield Precedency to *Don John* in a third Place. Natural Sons are much esteem'd in *Spain*, but for all that they cannot hold the same Rank there, that the Princes of the Blood hold in *France*, and nevertheless the Embassadors of *England* and of *Venice* refus'd them the Place of Honour and the Marquiss *de Fuentes*, Embassador of *Spain*, did not give it to the Duke of *Vendosme*. The Fault *M d'Embrun* committed was so much the greater, because he did more than the Emperor's Embassador had done, who would not visit *Don John* at his own House, by reason of his Pretensions. Within some Years the King has desir'd the Princes to behave themselves otherwise, and that at home they would take all Advantages of Embassadors. But as the Princes do not meddle in the Affairs of the State, I do not think that those Embassadors who have made difficulty to yield Precedency to them in a third Place, as *Lionne* remarks, will be over eager to visit *M le Prince* at home, there to be affronted. It is a refin'd Policy in those, who having a mind to remove the Princes of the Blood from all kinds of Affairs, deprive them also of the Communication they might have with foreign Ministers.

The Dukes of *Bavaria*, of *Neuburg*, of *Lorrain*, and all the Princes of *Italy*, to the Duke of *Parma* inclusively, take at home the Hand of the Embassadors of *France*, tho' there are some amongst them that give it to the Embassadors of the *Emperor*, and of *Spain*. I say a great deal more, That the younger Princes of the House of *Savoy* pretend to have it at home, and they have made it be given them in a third Place, as we shall observe elsewhere. I have heretofore spoken of the Reception the late Duke of *Nenburg* made in the Year 1633 to *Gaspar de Vosbergue*, Embassador from the United Provinces. That his Civility to him might be complete, he would have the Major of the Garrison go and receive his Orders from the Embassador. The Hour of Supper being come, the Duke went himself to his Appartment to fetch him, and conducted him to the Hall where Supper was serv'd, and caus'd him to wash at the same time with him, but the Duke took the first Place at Table. *Vosbergue* having express'd some Dissatisfaction thereat, the Duke signify'd to him, that he never had given the first Place to the Ministers of the United Provinces. That he had treated after the same manner the Count *de Grimbergue*, whom the *Infanta* had sent to him, and that at home he gave the Hand neither to the Embassadors of the House of *Austria*, nor even to the Nuncio, and that there was none but the Embassador of *Spain* to whom he granted that Advantage. That there was not one single Instance, that any of the Electors on the *Rhine* had done it, because being nearer to *France* and *Italy*, they were much more punctual in the matter of Ceremonies, than the Electors of *Saxony* and of *Brandenburg*. The Duke of *Neuburg* was in the right, to insist on having the same Respect paid him at home, that the Dukes of *Mantua* and of *Parma* assert to themselves in their own Palaces; but I know not how to reconcile what he says of the Nuncio, and of the Embassador of *Spain*, nor how he could refuse to the first, what he granted to the second. There is no likelihood, that there will be of a long time, any Embassadors from *France* seen at *Dusseldorp* or at *Nenbourg*: but if in the Revolution of Affairs, the King should think fit to send a Minister thither, he must at least be treated equally with him of *Spain* and other Kings have reason to expect the same Usage. He might very well say also, that in the Courts that are remote from those of *France* and *Italy*, they are not so scrupulous, tho' in that of *Berlin*, several things have been much better regulated, since the Baron of *Silerin* has there had the chief Direction of Affairs; but the Elector of *Saxony* will alter nothing in the ancient Customs.

He that gave to the Publick an Extract of the Negotiation the late *M Chanut* transacted in *Sweden*, and at *Lubeck*, says, It is observ'd in *Denmark*, that the King gives the Hand to the Embassadors of crown'd Heads, who have been particularly invited to the Ceremony. That that was the reason why, at *Copenhaguen*, *d'Avaux* and

and *la Tuillerie* had met with that Usage, and why the same had been done to *Benk* or *Benedict Schnt*, Embassador from the Queen of *Sweden*, who had been sent thither to present one of the Princesses to Baptism, that he never does this Honour to Embassadors in Ordinary He alledges for that, the Particulars of the Ceremonies that were perform'd at the Marriage of King *Frederick* II, in the Year 1575, and he observes that, at the Feast, the King sat at the upper end of the Table, having on his right Hand *Dauffay*, Embassador in Ordinary from *France*, and on his left *Augustus* Elector of *Saxony*. But one would hardly think this Example could be of any Use to the Intention of the Abbreviator, since the King being the Person that was marry'd, the first Place was his due even on that account. *James*, King of *England*, would not be present at the Marriage Feast of the Princess his Daughter, because he would have all the Honour of the Day paid to the Person marry'd, *viz.* the Elector *Palatin*. As for the Rank that is given in *Denmark* to the Embassador of *France*, above the Elector of *Saxony*, who ought not himself to give place to the Embassador at home, I must own I have not study'd the Ceremonial enough, to comprehend that Irregularity, and I am oblig'd to have recourse to the Duke of *Neubourg's* Principle, who says, that in the *Northern* Courts the Ceremonies are not so well regulated, as in those that are Neighbours of *France* and *Italy*. At the Feast that was made in the Year 1634, at *Copenhaguen*, on account of the Marriage of the Prince with the Princess of *Saxony*, the Honour was done to the new marry'd Couple. The King was not there, and the Embassadors were placed after Them, above all the Princes and Princesses. At the Supper of the third Day, the *Embassadors had the first Place, before the newly marry'd*, and at the Ball that ensu'd, *the King took the fourth Rank, after the three Embassadors*. Three Days after, was solemniz'd the Marriage of Count *Peus* with one of the King's natural Daughters, where *the Embassadors of the Emperor, and of France, conducted the Bridegroom, and the Embassador of Poland, with the King, the Bride*. At the *Carousel*, which was perform'd on the *Sunday* following, the *King took place again after the Embassadors*. They represented their Masters who had been expresly invited to the Prince's Wedding, but they had not been invited to the Marriage of the natural Daughter. So that the Reason, or rather the Distinction, which has been remark'd here above, cannot take place there, and much less in what I am going to say of *la Tuillerie*. This Minister, after having in the Year 1645 mediated a Conclusion of the Treaty of *Bromsebro*, between the two Crowns of the *North*, took his way through *Denmark*, to return to *Holland*. The King of *Denmark*, who had not gain'd his Ends in the Treaty, did him, for all that, all the Honours imaginable. The Artillery saluted him, and the Burghers were under their Arms in all the Towns through which he pass'd. The General of the Cavalry went to meet him with a thousand Horse, at some Leagues distance from *Copenhagnen*, and the Admiral of the Kingdom receiv'd him without the Town, with a great Cortege of Coaches.

The King himself did him a thousand Civilities, even to that Degree, that having made a great Feast on his account, *he plac'd him at the upper end of the Table*. The most Christian King had not been expresly invited to it, nor his Embassador, yet nevertheless he had an Honour done him which did not belong to him. I speak in another Place of *la Grange aux Ormes*, whom Cardinal *Richelieu* got banish'd from Court, because he had suffer'd the Elector of *Saxony* to set him above himself at Table. It is impossible in reading this, not to be seiz'd with Indignation at the Insolence of these Ministers, as well as at the Weakness of the Sovereigns, who knowing what they are, do not exact what is their due. It is the Business of the Gods to revenge the Injuries that are done to Gods. All Sovereigns have an Interest therein, and have an Interest to punish their Subjects, of what Quality or Character soever, if they fail in the Respect they owe to those in whom they see the Image and Character of the Grandeur and Dignity of their Prince.

I have seen in the Court of a Prince, who is the Head of one of the first and most powerful Houses of *Germany*, the Minister of an Elector, take the first Place every where, at Table, in Coach, at the Castle, and in the Town, as if he could pretend to it by an indisputable Right. Those who agree that the Princes of *Germany* have the Right of Embassy, in reference to foreign Princes, maintain that they have not the same Right in the Empire, because they are there as at home. But tho' an Elector should give the Character of Embassador to his Minister, how shall this dare to take the Place of Honour of a Prince in his own Palace, who would not give it to the Embassador of a crown'd Head, or at least ought not to give it?

In the Year 1530, Queen *Eleonora*, second Wife of *Francis* I, made her Entry into *Paris* after her Coronation, and at Night there was a Feast in the Palace, according to the Custom of those times, where the Queen, who sate at the middle of the Table, had on her right Hand the Cardinal of *Sens*, the Pope's Legate, and the Cardinals of *Grammont* and of *Trivulce*, *the Embassadors of the Pope, of the Emperor, of England, and of Venice, and on her left Hand were Princesses, and other Ladies*.

In the Order that was observ'd at the Feast of the Espousals of *Philip* II and *Elizabeth* of *France* in the Year 1559, the King and Queen sate at the middle of the Table, the betroth'd Lady on the King's right Hand, next to her the Duke of *Alva*, *Philip's* Embassador, then Madam, the King's Sister, and the Duke of *Lorrain*, and after them several other Princes, Princesses, and Cardinals, the Embassadors of the Pope, of *Portugal*, of *Venice*, of *Ferrara*, and of *Mantua*.

At the Feast that was made at *Maysiers*, in the Year 1570, on the Day of the Marriage of King *Charles* IX, and *Elizabeth* of *Austria*, the King sat at the middle of a great Table, having on his right Hand the Queen his Wife, and the Dukes of *Anjou* and of *Alençon*, his Brothers. On his left Hand were *the Queen his Mother, the Elector of Triers, who was one of the Emperor's Embassadors, the Dutchess of Lorrain, Madame the King's Sister, and the Duke*

The EMBASSADOR and his FUNCTIONS

Duke of Lorrain On the other side of the Table, over against the Elector, were seated *the Nuncio*, and *the Embassador of* Spain, *of* Scotland, *and of* Venice There were besides this two other Tables, at one of which were *the Cardinals of* Bourbon, *of* Lorrain, *and of* Guise, *the Bishop of* Strasbourg, *the Marquiss of* Baden, *and the Count of* Zolern, *Embassadors from the Emperor, the Dutchess of* Monpensier, *the Princess Dauph*n, *and Madam de* Nevers Where we must observe, that of the four Embassadors of the Emperor, only the first had a Place at the King's Table, with the Embassadors of the Pope, of *Spain*, of *Scotland*, and of *Venice* So that a great Distinction was made betwixt the first and the three others, tho' among these were two Princes of the Empire

When *Henry* IV was crown'd at *Chartres*, in the Year 1594, the Embassadors of *England*, and of *Venice*, who had been present at the Coronation, were also treated at the Feast The king's Table was plac'd upon an Alcove On the Right there was a Table for the Peers who were Ecclesiasticks, and on the Left one for the Secular Peers, and a little lower, one for the Embassadors, for the Chancellor, and for the other Officers of the Crown I cannot tell in what Order they sate, but we must believe they held the same, as to Rank, that was observ'd at the Coronation of *Lewis* XIII The Tables were dispos'd after the same manner, and the Embassadors were so seated, that the Nuncio, the Embassador of *Savoy*, and *Boneuil*, Introductor of the Embassadors, were on the Wall side, and the Embassador of *Venice*, with the Chancellor, on the other, all the Embassadors were, by this means, above the Chancellor *Boneuil* had a Place there on account of his Function, and not for the Dignity of his Office Where we must observe that the Peers, as well Ecclesiasticks as Secular, were there in their respective Functions, and made part of the Ceremony So that no body could be plac'd betwixt the King and them

Whether Embassadors are oblig'd to be present at all kinds of Ceremonies, is what we shall speak to in the following Chapter I shall only say in this, that when they are, they ought not to carry their Pretensions too high The Embassador of *France*, who was at *London* in the Year 1612, was invited to the Feast that was made there for the Marriage of the Princess of *England* and the Elector Palatin The King would not be there, because he would have the newly marry'd have all the Honour, for which Reason also they had arm'd Chairs, while the Prince of *Wales* had only a simple Chair, tho' he represented the nearest Relation of the Bride Nevertheless the *French* Embassador took a Fancy, as did also, by his Example, the *Venetian*, to insist upon having arm'd Chairs, and that the Carver, who was to serve the newly marry'd, should be below them But their Pretensions were judg'd to be so impertinent, that they were given to understand that their Absence would be dispens'd with, rather than gratify them therein The same Embassador of *Venice* was, the Year following, at the Marriage of a Lady of the Court, where he had an arm'd Chair, because the Prince of *Wales*, who was there too, had one The Count *de Bregy*, Son to *M de Flessilles*, President *in the Chamber of Accounts at* Paris, had made two Journies to *Uladislas* King of *Poland*, to whom he had made the first Overtures of a more strict Alliance with *France* It was confirm'd by the Marriage which the King contracted some time after with the Princess of *Mantua* And forasmuch as *Bregy* had been very instrumental thereto, the King of *France* order'd him to assist at the Ceremonies, as his Embassador *Uladislas* sent to meet the Queen, by Prince *Charles* his Brother, who receiv'd her on the King's part, in the *Cassube*, on this side *Dantzig*, and at the same time *Bregy*, who was there as Embassador, pretended to have the Rank of him It was a Pretension extravagant enough For admitting that *Charles* had not been born Prince of *Sweden*, as he was, (since *Casimir* renounc'd his Right but by the Treaty of *Oliva*, in the Year 1660) he was also Embassador on this Occasion, and was allotted a Function, in which no body could precede him, let his Quality be what it would The Mareschalless *de Guebriant*, Embassadrix in the conducting of the Queen of *Poland*, whom I just mention'd, form'd a Pretension wh ch was not less ridiculous She was for having *the same Rank, and the same Honours that had been done to the Arch-Dutchess, when she brought the Queen her Daughter into* Poland

The Cardinals are in Possession of a Right to take at home the Place of Honour of Embassadors It is what the Queen of *Sweden* was not so well inform'd of, as she is at present, when sending in the Year 1646, the Count *de la Garde*, Embassador Extraordinary, into *France*, she flatter'd her self with the Hopes that Cardinal *Mazarin* would yield to him this Advantage But as soon as she spoke thereof to *Chanut*, he told her that his Master had so particular a Consideration for her, that she might assure her self that whatever she could lawfully desire, would be granted to her Person, and to the Dignity of the Crown of *Sweden* But he let her know at the same time, that no Consideration could oblige the Cardinal to injure his Purple, for which he would be responsible to the whole College The Queen reply'd, That Chancellor *Oxenstiern* had no Character in reference to *France*, when he pass'd through it to return to *Sweden*, and that nevertheless, Cardinal *Richelieu* contriv'd so well the sharing of the Honours in the Visits they made each to the other, that it was hard to determin which of the two had the Advantage *Chanut* maintain'd that it had been entirely on the Cardinal's side, and he said right

The Count *de Tremes-posier*, and the Marquiss *Deffiat*, Embassadors Extraordinary from *France* at *London*, made Difficulty to assist at the Funeral of King *James*, because they were not allow'd to march in the same Rank with the King It was represented to him, that that was not practis'd neither in *France* nor *England*, nor elsewhere And at last they were prevail'd upon to let their Pretensions drop They march'd immediately after the Archbishop of *Canterbury* The Vanity of these Pretensions sufficiently declares that of the Embassador, who does not less prejudice his Master, in pretending to Honours that are not his due, than he would do in neglecting those which could not be refus'd him with Justice

A a a The

The Embassadors that are on the part of *France* and *Spain*, at *Rome*, do not at home yield the Place of Honour, but to the Embassadors of crown'd Heads, and to that of *Venice*, and to none else, not even to the Embassador of *Savoy* *D'Avaux*, who knew very well the Practice of *Rome*, in receiving at *Munster* the Visit of *Aloysio Contarini*, who was one of the Mediators, *descended but five Steps to meet him, and when he reconducted him, he accompany'd him but to the bottom of the Stairs* Contarini said that *d'Avaux* did not do him the Honour which was his due That he had receiv'd the Embassadors of the Emperor, and of the King of *Spain*, at the bottom of the Staircase That he had accompany'd them to their Coach, and that he ought to have done the same Civilities to him D'*Avaux* signify'd to him, That as *Contarini* had been Embassador at *Rome*, he might be suppos'd to know how the Matter of Civilities was regulated between the Embassadors of *France* and *Venice* in that Court, that the *Venetian* was only receiv'd at, and reconducted to, the top of the Staircase This was truth, as it is also true that the Embassador of *Venice* does not there shew greater Civilities to the Embassador of *France* However, as this Distinction of Treatments was very remarkable in the first Court of *Europe*, the Ministers of the Republick had endeavour'd to abolish that Custom, which was practis'd only at *Rome*, the Honours that were done every where else, to the Embassadors of crown'd Heads, and those of *Venice*, being equal, for which Reason *Contarini* rejoyn'd to *d'Avaux*, that the Embassadors of the Republick were in Possession of an absolute Equality with those of *France*, since the one's did not make a single Step more than the other's That it ought to be consider'd, that there was the same Equality between two Embassadors, who conducted each the other but to the top of the Stairs, as was between those who accompany'd one the other to the Coach That Messieurs *de Chasteauneuf* and *de Bassompierre*, Embassadors Extraordinary from *France* in *England*, had both accompany'd him to the Coach That it was none of M *d'Avaux*'s Business to make a Distinction between him and the Embassadors of the Emperor, and of *Spain*, and that what was particularly practis'd at *Rome*, could be no Precedent for *Munster* D'*Avaux* made Answer, That he could make no Alteration without express Orders from Court, and that it did not depend on him, but that he wonder'd *Contarini* should pretend to reap an Advantage from what had pass'd at *London*, rather than stick to what was practis'd at *Rome*, and much more that he should desire to alter a thing, wherein the Embassador of *France* had not the least Advantage over him of *Venice* *Contarini* not being satisfy'd with these Reasons, *d'Avaux* was oblig'd to write to Court, where he represented on one side the ill Effects that might attend the Displeasure of a Mediator, and on the other the Consequences that might be drawn therefrom for the Pretensions of the United Provinces, of the Electors, and several other Princes, to whom the same Honours could not be refus'd Before the Resolution of the Court arriv'd, *Contarini* receiv'd *d'Avaux* after the same manner that he receiv'd the other Embassadors of crown'd Heads, and accompany'd him to the Coach The Orders of the Court of *France* were conformable to the Desire and Intention of *Contarini*, who was more satisfy'd therewith than if he had made a great Conquest for the Republick

D'*Avaux* and *Servien*, going to the Assembly of *Munster*, had Orders to pass by the *Hague*, and there to adjust several things that the Council of *France* judg'd necessary to make the Treaty succeed to the common Advantage of the Allies, or at least according to the Intention of Cardinal *Mazarin* Among other Debates they had with the Deputies of the States, there were very warm ones concerning the Treatment should be dealt to the Ministers of the United Provinces when they should come to *Munster* They pretended to be treated like those of *Venice*, and did not dissemble that in case they had not the same Honours done them they would not go to the Congress, but would procure to themselves another Town, where they might appear in such manner as not to prejudice the Grandeur of their State, and hinted that they would agree with the *Spaniards* on a particular Assembly, which might be held at *Boisleauke* They said that King *Henry* IV had ordain'd, that the Embassadors of the United Provinces should immediately follow those of *Venice*, and that the same Honours should be done them That it was what had been practis'd till then, and that the present Design was to dispossess them of an Advantage which they had enjoy'd without Contestation, and particularly in *France* D'*Avaux* and *la Tuillerie*, the last of whom was Embassador in Ordinary at the *Hague*, said it was a new Pretension That while they themselves were Embassadors at *Venice*, they had made a Distinction between the Embassadors of crown'd Heads and those of the United Provinces, *to whom they had never given the Title of* Excellency, tho' they had never refus'd them the Place of Honour at the Visits they receiv'd from them That the States, who were oblig'd to *France* for the Civilities which were done every where to their Embassadors, ought not to make an Abuse thereof to the Prejudice of *France* it self, by extorting Advantages from it, which it could not grant without injuring it self That the Electors who dispute the Precedency with the States, and who exact it in the Empire, (whose Ministers notwithstanding are not cover'd when they speak to the King) would be for having them have the Title of *Excellency*, and would oblige *France* thereto, unless she would render her self incapable of negotiating with them That the Diversity of the Places where Assemblies are held, causes also some, in the Treatment of Ministers, and in the Ceremonies That at *Rome* the Embassadors of crown'd Heads do not yield the Hand at home to him of *Savoy*, and that even the Cardinals Nephews made some Distinction between the Embassadors that are at *Rome* and those that reside or negotiate in other Courts That the States had formerly ask'd *France* to give them place before the Arch-Duke, and before the Duke of *Savoy*, but that King *Henry* IV would not meddle therein, and had contented himself with treating them upon the Level with those Princes They concluded that the Queen could make no no Innovations during the King's Minority, to whom she was oblig'd to resign all his Rights, as intire and unimpair'd, as she had receiv'd them at the beginning of her Regency. D'Avaux and Servien left the Affair in this State, when they set out from the *Hague*, and it remain'd in the same till the beginning of the Year 1645. Then d'*Estrades*, who did the Business of *France* in *Holland* without Character, declar'd to the States, that the Queen Regent granted them what they had desir'd in reference to the Rank and Titles. I lately mention'd the Dispute d'*Avaux* had at *Munster* with *Contarini*, Embassador of *Venice*, wherein he did not remember what he here says, that the Diversity of Places, where the Ceremonies are perform'd, causes likewise a Difference in the Treatment of Embassadors.

I shall finish this Chapter with a word or two concerning the Honours that are done to Embassadrixes, in Consideration of the Embassadors, their Husbands Embassies being formerly all Extraordinary, and ending with the Business the Embassadors had to negotiate, they did not take their Wives with them, for which Reason no mention was made of Embassadrixes. Neither is it very long that they receive those Civilities, which rank them with those Ladies, who immediately follow Princesses. At least it is what is practis'd in *France*, where they are more consider'd than elsewhere. However it is but a little more than fifty Years, that the Queen allows them the Stool. The Marchioness of *Mirabel*, whose Husband was Embassador from *Spain*, was the first to whom the Queen, who was a *Spaniard*, granted this Honour in the Year 1621. The King consented thereto, provided the same Honour was done to the Embassadrix of *France* at *Madrid*, where they are very reserv'd in reference to those Kinds of Civilities, but especially if a Novelty is to be introduc'd. *Bassompierre*, who was at that time Embassador Extraordinary in *Spain*, ofter'd to *du Fargis* to speak to the Court about it, and to obtain it for the Embassadrix, his Wife. But *du Fargis* thank'd him, and told him he should find an Opportunity, and the Means to procure himself that Satisfaction, as accordingly he did some time after.

In the Year 1634, the Count *de Schauembourg*, who went in the Month of *August*, 1643, on the part of the Emperor, Embassador to *Spain*, as he pass'd through *France*, desir'd that his Lady might pay her Respects to the Queen. He had Letters for the King, who consider'd him as an Embassador Extraordinary. The Queen sent her Coach to the Embassadrix, who when she came to *Chantilly* was receiv'd at the bottom of the Stair-case by the Marchioness of *Senecy*, Lady of Honour to the Queen, who usher'd her into a Chamber, where they din'd together, after which she conducted her to the Queen, who order'd her the Stool. The King came thither, and saluted her, having first caus'd her to be consulted, whether she approv'd of it, because it was not the Custom of *Germany*. In the Month of *October*, 1635, the Queen receiv'd with the same Civilities the Viscountess *Scudamore*, and did her the same Honours; and on the 29th of *April*, 1647, the Wife of *Corfits Ulefelt*, Embassador Extraordinary from *Denmark*, receiv'd the same Civilities, and saw the Queen several times. Nay she was present at a Ball, where she had a Rank amongst the Dutchesses.

Madam *de Ghent*, who had accompany'd her Husband, who was Chief of that solemn Embassy which the States of the United Provinces sent into *France* in the Year 1660, having signify'd the Passion she had to pay her Respects to the Queen, one of the Introductors of Embassadors, accompany'd by *Girant*, Assistant or Lieutenant of the Introductors, (whom I have represented to be the Man in the World, that best understood the Point of Civilities) went to receive her at the House of the Embassadors, with the Queen's Coaches, and conducted her into the Antichamber, where she was receiv'd by the Lady of Honour, by the Attiring Lady, and the Maids of Honour. She had the Stool given her, but the Queen did not salute her, because it is an Honour that is reserv'd to the Princesses of the Blood. Her Husband and her self were two very handsome Personages, and as they were both come of a lustrious Families, their Carriage, that had something distinguishing in it, made them much consider'd at Court; and Madam *de Ghent* went away much esteem'd by both Queens. It was a long time since an Embassadrix from *Holland* had been seen at Court. Since the Death of Madam *de Languerac*, they had appear'd there but only at *Shrovetide*, and then they help'd to divert the Company, as much as the Players. Madam *de Groot*, whose Husband was Embassador in Ordinary from the United Provinces, was receiv'd there with the same Civilities Madam *de Ghent* had been, except that as the Court was at St *Germain*, she was conducted thither in the Queen's Coaches, was regal'd with a magnificent Dinner, and serv'd by the Queen's Officers.

Embassadrixes do not receive the same Civilities in *England*. The *French* think they do themselves Honour in shewing Civility to others, and particularly to Strangers. But this is what very few Nations imitate them in. While the Mareschal *de Cadenet* or *de Chaunes* was in *England*, on the part of Lewis XIII, he, and the Count *de Tillieres*, were invited to a Ball, and a great Feast, to which the Countess of *Buckingham*, Mother of the Favorite, had invited all the Beauties of the Court. She gave the first Place to the Marchioness of *Buckingham*, her Daughter in-law, the second to the Countess of *Tillieres*, and she took the third her self, to the great Scandal of the other *English* Countesses, who would have taken Place of the *French* Embassadrix. Some Days after the Lord Viscount *Doncaster* gave a Ball, and made an Entertainment also for the Embassadors. The King, who would be present thereat, had his particular Table, where sate the Prince of *Wales* on the King's right Hand, the Embassador Extraordinary on his left, and the Embassador in Ordinary at the end of the Table. There was another for the Lords and Ladies, at which the Marchioness of *Buckingham* had the first Place on the right side, a *French* Nobleman had the second, and the Countess of *Tillieres* the third. The Countess of *Warwick* had the first Place on the left side, a *French* Nobleman the second, and the Lady *Doncaster* the third, &c. The Countess of *Dorset* plac'd plac'd her self at the lower End of the Table, below several Ladies, who would have made no Difficulty to have yielded the upper Hand to her whether she did it out of Gallantry, or because she would not immediately follow the *French* Embassadrix, is uncertain. At the Feast, which was made in the Year 1612, for the Marriage of the Elector *Palatine* and the Princess of *England*, the High Chamberlain gave Orders, that the *French* Embassadrix should be plac'd after the last Countess, and before the first Baronness, but the Viscountess of *Effingham* would not give place to the Embassadrix, and chose rather to withdraw. The Honours that are done to Strangers are no Precedent, nor can have no Consequence, especially when they are rather done to the Quality, than the Person. In the Year 1614. the Wife of *M de Marais*, Embassador from *France*, having desir'd to pay her Respects to the Queen, one of the Substitutes of the Master of the Ceremonies, who also discharges the Function of Introductor, receiv'd her at the Gate of *Denmark* House, where the Embassadrix alighted out of her Coach, and he led her into a Chamber up one pair of Stairs, where she rested herself a little. As soon as the Queen was inform'd thereof, she sent thither the Countess of *Arundel*, and the Ladies *Sidney* and *Southwell*, Ladies of the Bed-Chamber, with one of the Maids of Honour to entertain the Embassadrix, and to conduct her to Audience. One of the Gentlemen in waiting, coming to give notice, that her Majesty was in the Presence Chamber, and there expected the Embassadrix, the Ladies conducted her thither the High-Chamberlain receiv'd her at the Chamber Door, and the Queen shew'd her great Civilities, but she did not make her sit down. At her going away the High-Chamberlain accompany'd her as far as the Guard Room, the Ladies conducted her to the Gallery of the first Court, and the Introductor led her to her Coach. In Civilities, it is, as in a great many other things, where if one has not all, one has nothing; tho' to speak the truth, they are but mere Civilities.

Embassadrixes have no share in the Character, and nothing is their due, but what cannot be refus'd to their Sex. It is true, the King of *France* requires a particular Respect to be paid to the Wives of his Embassadors, and that they be consider'd as Embassadrixes, that is to say, that extraordinary Honours be done them. But as they are not regulated, I shall delay speaking to them, till there is a new Ceremonial made for that purpose. In the mean time I shall take notice, that at *Munster*, and at *Osnaburg*, the Wives of the Embassadors, and of the Ministers of the second Order, observ'd in their Visits, the same Rank, and the same Rules, that the Husbands took and observ'd among themselves. For which Reason, when the Countess of *Saunazzare*, (whose Husband had succeeded to Count *Nerli*, in the Quality of Plenipotentiary of *Mantua*) would have visited Madam *Servien*, after having visited Madam *le Brun*, she was not admitted

---

CHAP. XXI.

Of the First Visit.

Monsieur *de Foix*, Archbishop of *Thoulouse*, Embassador from *France* at *Rome*, writing to King *Henry* III, his Master, on the 15th of *May*, 1581, says, that as soon as he was inform'd that Count *d'Olivares*, Embassador from *Spain*, was arriv'd, he had done him *Civility by a Secretary*, and had signify'd to him, that he would wait on him himself, as soon as the Count had receiv'd his first Audience of the Pope, *as Custom requires*, says he, *betwixt Embassadors of crown'd Heads*, to wit, *that the last Comer is visited by the first*. It is a general Rule that admits of no Exception, but only at *Rome*, where the Embassadors of the Emperor, of *France*, and of *Spain*, pay this Devoir but only to those of crown'd Heads, which is the Reason why *M de Foix* says, that it is *the Custom among the Embassadors of crown'd Heads*. He says, he had sent to complement the *Spanish* Embassador by a Secretary. This is a Civility that ought to be previous to that of the Visit, because it is as Essential. It serves to answer the Complement which the last Comer has made, to thank the Embassadors, who have sent their Coaches to meet him, or else to acquaint them with his Arrival. The new Comer returns it the very next Day, in the same Manner, and in the same Order he had receiv'd it. Count *d'Avaux* being arriv'd at *Munster*, sent the very next Day to complement the Count of *Nassau*, *Saavedra*, and *Zapata*, Plenipotentiaries of the Emperor and the King of *Spain*, by Gentlemen, and *le Brun*, and the Embassador of *Venice*, by one of his Secretaries. He thought he ought to make this Distinction, as well because *le Brun* was only the third Plenipotentiary, as because he was not of the Quality of the two others; and as for the *Venetian*, he was willing to do something less for the Republick than for crown'd Heads.

De Fresne Canaye, Embassador from *France* at *Venice*, had been employ'd in Embassies to *Germany* and *England*, where he ought to have learn'd the Ceremonial, and yet he was for taking advantage of the Custom of *Rome*, and refusing the first Visit to the Abbot of *Provane*, Embassador from *Savoy*. He wrote to *M de Villeroy* on the 12th of *July*, 1605, *that the Abbot, instead of being before-hand in the Point of Visits, as his Predecessor had done, expected the first, and insisted on having the Custom comply'd with. That the Spanish Embassador had done it, but that he, de Fresne, would not follow that Example, till he had receiv'd Orders so to do; because he knew what was practis'd at* Rome. *If it were left*

left to him, he would make the first Visit without any great Train, or much Noise That he should be glad to be instructed, because he knew th' *Duke of Savoy* was particularly inform'd of all that was done in these kind of Ceremonies The same *de Fresne*, who made the Difficulty with the Embassador of the Duke of *Savoy*, had been but too easy in the Dispute he had on the like Occasion with the Nuncio

Anthony Mary Grattian, Bishop of *Amelia*, who has written the Life of Cardinal *Commendon*, being Nuncio at *Venice* in the Pontificate of *Clement* VIII, *de Maisse Ihrault*, who had been there Embassador from *France*, took a Journey to Court, and return'd to *Venice* after the Absolution of *Henry* IV, and, as the last Comer, he pretended that the Nuncio should make him the first Visit The Nuncio said to it it was the same Person, and the same Embassy At that time the Nuncio, who had been in several Embassies, in the Retinue of *Commendon*, and who knew the Practice of all the other Courts, did not dispute the Right But he did not agree about the Matter of 1ist, and said that *de Maisse* was not the last Comer And indeed, by *Doyat*'s Letter of the last of *February*, 1596, we must believe that the Court was of that Opinion, and that *de Maisse* had Orders to pay the first Visit to the Bishop of *Amelia*, is to the last Comer, tho' they would have persuaded the Pope that it had been done out of Complaisance But the Bishop of *Malfetta* Nuncio at *Venice*, refus'd in the Year 1601 to make the first Visit to the *Spanish* Embassador, who on his side would not see the Nuncio Upon the Complaints the *Spaniards* made thereof at *Rome*, Cardinal *Aldobrandin*, the Pope's Nephew, was for being inform'd of the Matter by the Nuncio, who wrote him Word, That it was true, that formerly the Nuncio's did like the other Embassadors, and made the first Visit to the last Comer, but that within some time *they were in Possession at* Venice *of a Right to receive the first Visit by the last Comer* That Don *Diego de Mendossa*, who was arriv'd there since the Bishop of *Amelia*, had done it, the Duke of *Sesse*, who was Embassador from *Spain* at *Rome*, having written to him, That he ought to make no Difficulty to pay that Honour to the Nuncio, because there was no Danger of doing too much, to him who represented the common Father of all Roman Catholicks The Cardinal *Aldobrandin*, to justify the Nuncio's Proceeding, said he had, upon a diligent Examination, found that the Nuncio at *Madrid* behav'd himself after the same manner That he did not know what the Practice was elsewhere, and that he was willing to think, that even those of *Vienna* and *Paris* follow'd the Example of other Embassadors, but since he of *Venice* was in Possession, he was of Opinion he should maintain it In *France* they were of a different Sentiment When the President *de Villiers*, who succeeded *M de Maisse*, came to *Venice*, there was no Nuncio there, so that the President made no Difficulty to visit first him that was arriv'd after him *De Fresne Comaye* succeeded *Villiers*, and King *Henry* IV, foreseeing that his Embassador might have a Dispute with the Nuncio, gave him positive Commands not to visit the Nuncio, whom he should find at *Venice*, till he had receiv'd

the first Visit from him The Orders the Nuncio had were not less precise, and the two Ministers had a mind to see one another Whereupon several Propositions were made for that Purpose, and at last *de Fresne* agreed to that the Nuncio made, to visit the Embassadrix *De Fresne* said that his Appartment was so near his Wife's, that he could not visit her without visiting him also This was executed in the following manner The Nuncio went to see the Embassadrix, and the Embassador, who was at home, did the Honours of the House, in receiving and conducting the Nuncio, giving out, in the mean time, that the Nuncio had made him the first Visit The Nuncio said, on the contrary, that he had visited the Embassadrix, and for proof thereof, alledg'd that he went thither in his usual Habit, whereas if he had made a first Visit to the Embassador, he would have gone in the Habit suitable to his Quality, with the *Rocket* and *Camail* This did not hinder the Embassador from going to see the Nuncio He says, he went in his Cloke, and with a small Retinue, but as for the Nuncio's, he could not pretend to visit any body but the Nuncio, the Nuncio took it for a formal Visit, as in reality it was, and afterwards return'd a Visit to the Embassador with the usual Formalities, having on his *Rochet* and *Camail* They who printed *M de Fresne*'s Letters, have not left us the Idea of a great Genius And most certainly on this Occasion he committed an unpardonable Fault He ought not to have seen the Nuncio till this had made him a publick and solemn Visit, that all *Venice* might have beheld the Honour he did to the Embassador of the King of *France*, even tho' the Nuncio had not spread the Rumour that he had only visited the Embassadrix, and that if his Intention had been to visit the Embassador, he would have done it with the usual Formalities The Nuncio made the same Proposition to the *Spanish* Embassador, but this signify'd to him, that it was absolutely necessary to pass through his Appartment, to go to that of his Ladies I cannot tell on what account the Nuncio's can pretend to the first Visit from the last Comers, since they are in effect but Embassadors of the first Prince of *Christendom*, who in reference to Temporals has no Advantage over other Sovereigns, and if the Ministers of these yield the first Place to the Nuncio, it is because the Pope is their ghostly Father, but they do not pretend to grant him any Prerogative that carries a Mark of the least Superiority, or that can in the least prejudice their Sovereignty Formerly the Nuncio's were call'd Embassadors It is but a little above a hundred Years that the Term of *Nuncio* is in use, if we will believe *Henry Stephen*, *M de Branthome*, and the aforesaid Bishop of *Amelia*, tho' I remember to have found the same Quality in some of the Letters the Constable of *Montmorancy* wrote, in the Reign of *Francis* I, in the Year 1538 or 1539

Disirades arriv'd at the *Hague* towards the end of the Year 1662, with the Quality of Embassador Extraordinary, having but a little before discharg'd the same Function in *England* Don *Estevan de Gamarra*, Embassador of *Spain*, was gone at that time to *Brussels*, and being return'd at the end of two or three Months, he pretended that *Deftrades* ought to make him the firft Vifit, as to the laft Comer. A common Friend to both, at *Deftrades*'s Requeft, reprefented to *Don Eftevan*, That he ought to confider that he had refided at the *Hague* for feveral Years That he went every Year to *Bruffels*, either on account of his Affairs, or for his Diverfion. That it could not properly be faid he had been abfent, fince part of his Family remain'd at the *Hague*, and that his Houfe had been kept open, and was refpected as if he had been prefent. That at his going away he had not taken his *Audience of Leave*, and that at his Return he had not brought with him frefh *Credentials*. *Don Eftevan*, who was a very good Man indeed, and that was all, very capable of making good Chear to his Friends, but being otherwife but a middling kind of Minifter, remain'd obftinate for all this, and faid that if *Deftrades* expected the firft Vifit, he fhould not have it till the Day of Judgment. *Deftrades* gave an account thereof to the King his Mafter, who forthwith order'd his Embaffador at *Madrid* to declare to that Court, that if *Don Eftevan* did not do thofe things which had been regulated and agreed upon, his Majefty fhould be oblig'd to refent it. Hereupon the King of *Spain* commanded his Embaffador not to be refractary, in the Performance of a Ceremony which had been fettled between Embaffadors. So that *Don Eftevan* feeing it was impoffible for him to make any further Refufal, (yet diffembling his having receiv'd any Orders to follow the Cuftom) had a mind to make a piece of Gallantry of it, and fo fent to *Deftrades*, that, if he approv'd of it, he would come and dine with him. *Deftrades*, who knew his Bufinefs as well as any Man in the World, made anfwer, That he was of Opinion there would appear fomething very irregular, if after fo great a Coolnefs (which *Don Eftevan* had thought fit to make publick) they fhould jump on the fudden into fo great a Familiarity. That *Don Eftevan* might do as he thought fit, after he had paid him the firft Vifit with the ufual Formalities. *Don Eftevan*, who had feem'd to be fo fierce, as even to offend thofe who had countell'd him to make this Step with a good Grace, was neceffitated to do it *per* Force, and give *Deftrades* a much greater Advantage than that *Vateville* pretended to have over him at *London*. *Don Eftevan* thought to improve the Fault *Deftrades*'s Predeceffor had committed, who had paid him the firft Vifit after the *Pyrenean* Peace, though *Don Eftevan* had been there above two Years before him. He had alfo then been at *Bruffels*, and at his Return he had extorted this Civility from the *French* Embaffador. *Deftrades* underftood it otherwife, and had Reafon of his fide. When the Embaffy is compofed of a Plurality of Embaffadors, they muft be all vifited without Interruption, as fhall be faid hereafter in the XXVIth Chapter.

This Rule admitting no Exception from Embaffador to Embaffador, except at *Rome*, as I juft took notice, we muft believe, either that it was not very well eftablifh'd fix or feven fcore Years ago, or that the Lord *de Grignan*, Embaffador from *France* at *Rome*, under the Reign of *Francis* I, did not underftand his Bufinefs. He came into that Employment only through the Intereft of Cardinal *de Tournon*, whofe Niece he had marry'd, and the few Letters we have of his, fufficiently make known, that Negotiation was not his Excellency. In writing to the Conftable *Montmorancy*, firft Minifter of *France*, on the 9th of *November*, 1538, he fays, *That his Intention was to have made the firft Vifit to the Emperor's Embaffador, as foon as he had had his firft Audience of the Pope, but that he had been prevented*. That this Embaffudor had fent to know his Hour for the Vifit, the very next Day after his firft Audience. That he, *Grignan*, had declin'd it, and in order to hinder the Emperor's Minifter from being before-hand with him, he had fignify'd to him, that Affairs of Importance obliging him to go out immediately, he defir'd he would pardon him if he could not wait his coming. That he, at the fame time, order'd his Coach to be got ready, but before he could get out of the Court, he faw that of the Emperor's Embaffador enter. He adds, *that all* Rome *was aftonifh'd at this Civility, and fpoke of it, as of a thing that had never been done before*. For my part, I cannot but admire M *de Grignan*, who, being Embaffador at *Rome*, could believe that the Minifter of *Charles* V would pay to that of *Francis* I a Civility of this Nature, if he had not been oblig'd thereto by an indifpenfible Law. I dare not fay with *de Frefne Canaye*, that it makes a part of the *Law of Nations*, but I believe that this Cuftom is fo ancient, that *Grignan* ought not to have been ignorant of it, no more than of the Advantage he acquir'd to the King his Mafter, if the Emperor's Embaffador paid him a Civility which was not his due.

I juft now faid, that the Rule concerning the laft Comer is always to be minded by Embaffadors, and amongft them I comprife alfo the Nuncio's, who ought to obferve it as well as the reft. The Duke of *Crequy*, I ither to him who had the great Difpute with the *Ghyfi*, being gone to *Venice* in the Year 1633, after he had difcharg'd his Embaffy at *Rome*, the Nuncio vifited him firft, on the fame Day he had had his Audience in the Senate. The Nuncio at *Madrid* did the fame to the Duke of *Mayenne*, in the Year 1612, and it is certain that at *Paris*, and elfewhere, the Nuncio's follow the Example of other Embaffadors. But the Rule has its Exceptions in reference to fome other Perfons. The Cardinals ftand upon having the *firft Vifit*, and fome of the Pope's Nephews, who have pretended to this Honour, have obtain'd it, although they were not Cardinals. The Duke of *Crequy*, Embaffador Extraordinary from *France* at *Rome*, would not comply herein, and that Refufal was one of the Caufes (and perhaps the moft powerful) of the Difference he had with the *Ghyfi*. The Embaffadors of Obedience carry it very high, and *M de Crequy*, who was one of the haughtieft Lords of the Kingdom, judg'd that there ought to be a Diftinction made of thofe whom the Purple diftinguifh'd. That Embaffador of *France*, who when he gave the Hand to one of the Nephews of Pope *Paul* III, in Confideration of the Marriage he was in hopes of contracting with one of the King's natural Daughters, made it very plain, that it was for that only Reafon, he did not take the fame Advantage over the one,

which

which he actually took of the other Nevertheless *M. de Foix*, Embassador from *France* at *Rome*, says in one of his Letters, that immediately after his first Audience, he went to see Cardinal *Guastavillain*, and the Lord *Giacomo Boncompagno*, natural Son of *Gregory* XIII, tho' this last was no Clergyman One would think it might be said, that an Embassador does not owe the first Visit to him, to whom he is not oblig'd to yield Precedency in a third Place, as the Duke of *Crequy* did not owe it to *Don Sigismond Chisi*, no more than to the other Relations of *Alexander* VIII The Reason is still stronger why they should not owe it to those, of whom they take both the Hand and Step, wheresoever they meet them It was for this that *Fontenay Marnes* did not pay the first Visit to the Duke of *Guise* at *Rome*, nor *Destrades* to the Prince of *Tarento* at the *Hague* The King, writing in the Month of *August*, 1662, to Queen *Christina*, on account of the Action of the *Corsicans*, says, that the Duke of *Crequy* had delay'd for some time visiting the secular Relations of the Pope, because they who had preceded him, had behav'd themselves differently, but at last, he had paid them the first Visit, in pursuance of the Order he had sent him.

Destrades made difficulty to give the first Visit to the Lords of the House of *Naflaw*, who within some time had been declar'd Princes by the Emperor, and he did not do it till he had express Orders for that purpose. Formerly no great Difficulty was made on this account President *Jeannin* Embassador Extraordinary from *France* in *Holland*, writing to the King on the 19th of *June*, 1607, says, that *Count William of Naflaw, Governor of Frise, being arriv'd at the Hague, came to see him, before he could have leisure to prevent him* This shews the Intention *Jeannin* and his Collegues had, to pay the first Visit to the Count Those who could believe that *Jeannin* in that offended against the Rules, might be said not to have a due Knowledge of that Minister, and might undeceive themselves by the following Example He writes in one of his Letters, that there was advice, that the Arch-Duke was going to send to the *Hague* the great Auditor *Verreiken*, who was one of the chief Ministers at his Court, and had already been Embassador at *Vervins* and in *England*, but that the King's Embassadors would not see him, if he did not pay them the first Visit That they were sensible *they ow'd it him, as being the last Comer*, and the Embassador of a Prince in amity with their Master but that he came from a Prince, who was an Enemy to the State where they negotiated That they were of Opinion, they ought not to give any Umbrage to the States and withal, that there was *such a Disproportion betwixt the Dignity of the King, and that of the Arch-Duke*, that they thought they might wave that Civility They did not see *Verreiken*, but it was only because he had not the Character of Embassador The other Reasons might excuse in some measure, but they could not justifie the Incivility to the Embassadors of *France* And indeed they since alter'd their Minds, and *Ruffy-la place*, Embassador in Ordinary, went to see *Verreiken*, as soon as this last had taken his Audience The two Extraordinaries did not see him, because they apprehended lest he should not return their Civility, after he had given out that he would not visit any body *Verreiken* however gave *Ruffy* to understand, that he had also expected to be visited by the President

The Embassadors of crown'd Heads never have any Contest on this Subject, with the Princes of *Orange*, and have not made any Difficulty to make them the first Visit President *Jeannin* says, in his Letter of the 29th of *May* of the same Year, 1607, that *Prince Maurice came and met them at the Distance of half a League from the Hague* But no Consequence can be drawn therefrom, as well because that at that time Prince *Maurice*, being only the younger Brother of Prince *Philip*, who was Sovereign of the Principality of *Orange*, he could not come in competition with the Embassadors of *France*, since he even went to meet him on the part of the States, as because that within some Years, and chiefly since the King's Pleasure has been, that his Embassadors should give the Title of *Highness* to the Prince, they can no longer refuse him that Honour I do not speak of the Princes of the Blood, who insist upon having the first Visit paid them, out of the Chancellor of *France*, and of the Archbishop of *Toledo* in *Spain*, who receive the same Honours altho they are not more considerable at home, than the Prince of *Orange* is in the United Provinces, where he is the first, and most authoriz'd Person of the State Nay there are some Courts, where there are first Ministers, to whom the Embassador is oblig'd to pay the first Visit, and who, notwithstanding, never see the Embassador at his own House, unless they have some particular Considerat on for his Person, or are invited thither on some extraordinary Occasion The Archbishop of *Toledo*, and the Chancellor of *France*, who do not visit Embassadors, went however to see those, who in the Year 1612, were sent on account of the double Marriage into *France* and *Spain* For these fifty Years and more, that there has been no Constable in *France*, the Chancellor is there the first Officer of the Crown, as well as in *England*

De Fresne Canaye made a Scruple in reference to the Embassador of *Savoy*, but only because he did not look upon him to be well affected to *France* and he explain'd himself sufficiently, when he made no *Difficulty in the Year 1606, to do that Honour to the Marquess* Guicchardini, *Embassador of the Great Duke of* Tuscany The Court was not pleas'd with it, by reason he had refus'd it to that of *Savoy* and all he could alledge to excuse himself was, that he did it on account of the Great Duke's being the Queen's Unkle, as if Kings and Queens had any Relations The Embassador of *Spain*, who was then at *Venice*, said hereupon to *Fresne*, that he was ready to make the first Visit to the Embassador of *Tuscany*, if *Fresne* would promise to do the same Honour to the first Embassador that should come from the Duke of *Savoy* The French Embassador made answer, that he should be very sorry that he, the *Spanish* Embassador, should use violence to his Inclination, to do Honour to the Embassador of the Duke of *Tuscany*; and as for himself, that he would honour him of *Savoy*, according as he should know him to be well or ill affected to *France*

When

When *Alexander*, Abbot *della Scalgia*, Embassador Extraordinary from *Savoy*, arriv'd at *London*, in the Year 1627, of all the Embassadors, there was none but that of the United Provinces, would make him the first Visit The two Embassadors of *Denmark*, *Brake* and *Thomasson*, who were there at that time, excus'd themselves at first they said, the Indisposition of the one, hinder'd the other from acquitting himself of that Civility and afterwards they said, that having taken their Audience of Leave, they could not engage themselves in the Ceremony of Visits, which would be attended with other Inconveniencies that would be troublesome to them Which was a very lawful Excuse, because that after the Audience of Leave, the Embassador ought not to appear, but only to make his last Visits, and not to begin new ones

The Duke of *Savoy* was Father to the Brother-in-law of the King of *England*, and the Abbot went thither to carry on Negotiations against *France*, for which Reason the Court would have been glad to have had him receive Honours there, and caus'd the Embassadors of *Denmark* to be spoke to with some Warmth about it, but at last they flatly said, they would not comply therein, because it was a thing without Precedent, that the Embassador of a King, should pay the first Visit to that of a Duke I am apt to believe indeed, that in those Days there had been no Examples of any such Proceeding at *Copenhaguen*, but for all that, there had been Instances thereof in other Places, as may be seen in this Chapter The Earl of *Carlisle* said on this Occasion, that when he was Embassador at *Paris*, in the Year 1624, he had there paid the first Visit to the Embassador of *Savoy*, and that by the Example of the Nuncio, and the other Embassadors

It was represented to the Embassadors of *Denmark*, that in the beginning of this Century, there had been an Assembly of several Princes at *Dusseldorp*, for the Affairs of the Succession of *Juliers*, where the Embassador of *France* being arriv'd first, refus'd to make the first Visit to the Deputies of the States of the United Provinces, who were come there after him till perceiving that these obstinately absented from the Assembly, where nothing could be done without them, he at last did them the Honour of a Visit

But it was impossible to prevail with the *Danish* Embassadors, who did very well in their Refusal, but the Reason they alledg'd was worth nothing The Embassador of *Venice* did the like, by the Example of *M de Blamville*, who had behav'd himself after the same manner, to the Embassadors of *Savoy* and *Mantua*, who came to *London* while he was Embassador there. At this Day, that great Difficulties arise concerning many other things, none at all are made in reference to the Princes of *Italy*, whose Embassadors are visited the first, in all the Courts where they arrive last, except in that of *Rome* and of *Vienna*

I except also from the general Rule the Ministers of the Cantons They have none that have the Character, in the Courts of other Princes, and when they send thither Extraordinaries, they are not treated as Embassadors, with reference to this Civility, no more than in reference to the others Embassadors are very cautious not to pay the first Visit to these pretended Embassadors, whom all Ministers treat as their Inferiors, and who in reality are not Embassadors, since they have not the Privilege of being cover'd They perceive it very well themselves, and do not aspire to Honours they are not acquainted with The Embassadors whom the *Grisons* sent to *Venice* in the Year 1603, were treated throughout the State, but on the same Day they had their first Audience, they went and paid their Devoirs to the Embassador of *France* and that no Doubt might be made thereof, they went thither with the Tabour and Pipe The Plenipotentiaries of the Elector of *Saxony* have voluntarily excepted themselves from the general Rule instead of expecting the Visit of all the other Ministers at their Arrival at *Osnabourg*, they *prevented the Count of* Trautmansdorf, *the Emperor's first Plenipotentiary*, to whom they paid the first Visit, from whence those of *Sweden* took occasion to insist upon having the same Honours done them The same Ministers of *Saxony* being arriv'd since at *Munster*, were for changing their Conduct, and for having the first Visit from the Embassadors of crown'd Heads. *Pegnaranda* comply'd, but the Ministers of *France* did not see them, and pretended that they had at least a Right to the same Usage that had been dealt to the Plenipotentiaries of *Sweden*

The Embassador who pretends to this Honour, ought to give notice to the Ministers who owe it him, that he is arriv'd, or is near arriving, that they may send a Gentleman to complement him The Embassador that sends to pay Civility to the last Comer, before he has receiv'd any on his part, errs against Form and Method In the Year 1653, there was a second Assembly at *Lubeck*, concerning the Interests of *Poland* and *Sweden* As soon as *Chanut*, who was to discharge the Office of Mediator on the part of *France*, was arriv'd, *Shering Rosenhan*, first Plenipotentiary of *Sweden*, sent to know when he would be at leisure to receive the Visit he design'd to make him, his Intention being to prevent the *Polus Chanut*, who penetrated into his Meaning, signify'd to him that he receiv'd his Complement as a particular Civility, but that neither he, nor his House, were yet in a Condition to receive Visits of Ceremony as also, *that he d l not expect any from him, till he had notify'd his Arrival to him, because that was a Devoir which ought to be discharg'd first* This was what was very well known to the Embassadors of the United Provinces, who were to be concern'd in the same Negotiation, as Mediators with *Chanut*, but that did not hinder them from committing two very gross Faults The first was, that they gave notice of their Arrival to none but the Embassadors of *France*, and to the Chief of the Embassies of *Poland* and of *Sweden*, and the other was, that they accompany'd their ill digested Civility with a very ill favour'd Complement They repair'd the first, after *Chanut* had taken the liberty to remonstrate to 'em, that they ought also to have given notice to the other Embassadors, but they did not rectifie the other When they gave notice to the Embassadors of their Arrival,

Arrival, they added thereto, that they should not be in a Condition to receive Visits of three or four Days. It look'd as if they had a mind to refresh the Memory of those Gentlemen with their Duty, or to teach them their Business, by letting them know what they ought to do. Supposing they spoke to Persons who knew their Business, they ought to have signifi'd to them, that as soon as they were a little compos'd, and had recover'd themselves from the Fatigues of their Journey they would not fail to visit them. Their Complement had a smack of the Territory. We ought never to do Civilities by halves, nor corrupt it with Rusticities and Grossnesses, unworthy a Man who knows the World. The last Comer, in the notice he gives to the other Embassadors, ought to observe the Order in which he expects to be visited; for which Reason he ought to be nicely punctual, because as he is oblig'd to return the Visits in the same Order he has receiv'd them, he may in that, favour the ones more than the others.

The Bishop of Gure, first Plenipotentiary of the Emperor at the Congress of Nimineguen, having remain'd there some time incognito, began to appear in the beginning of the Month of September, 1677, and notify'd his Arrival to the other Ministers. The Spanish Embassadors were the first, but at the same time he put into the Hands of the Nuncio a Writing, wherein he signify'd, that he consider'd them on this Occasion as Ministers of the same House with the Emperor his Master, and that it should be of no Consequence in reference to the others. Those of Spain visited him the first Day. The next Day he gave Advice thereof *to the Nuncio, to the Mediators, to the Embassadors of the crown'd Heads, of the United Provinces, and of the Elector of* Brandenbourg, who all visited him the same Day, and the Day following he began to return the Visits.

The Plenipotentiaries of the Elector of Triers being arriv'd near Munster, those of France sent to desire them not to receive the Visit of the Embassadors of Spain, before theirs. Those of Triers made answer, that they could not send away any body, for which reason d'Avaux and Serwien visited them, as soon as they knew the Nuncio, and the Emperor's Embassadors had been there. The same Plenipotentiaries of Triers, in receiving the Nuncio's Visit ask'd him how they ought to govern themselves in this kind of Ceremony. The Nuncio told them, *that when they made the first Visit, they were oblig'd to have regard to the Rank of those they visited, but in returning the Visit to those who had made it to them, they ought to observe the same Order, in which they had receiv'd them.* Which is so true, that that is the chief Cause there is such a Strife, who shall make the first Visit to the last Comer. The Embassadors of Bavaria, after having receiv'd the Visit of all the other Ministers, visited the Nuncio, after him the Count of Nassau, and then the Plenipotentiaris of France first, both together at M d'Avaux's House, and then M Serwien at his own House separately, at which the Spaniards were very much mortify'd. I should think, that after what has been here said, it is easie to comprehend, that the Rule of the last Comer, ought not to be apply'd to the last arriv'd of two or three Embassadors, that come almost at the same time, so that the last of these two or three ought to be visited before those who came a Day or two before him have been visited. On the contrary, when the Mediators made the first Visit to *Pegneranda*, who was arriv'd some time after the Duke of *Longueville*, they sent word to the Duke, that they could no longer delay visiting the Count, altho' they were *sensible they ow'd him the first Visit, as being come first*, and that it had not stuck at them, but that the Duke would not admit the Person they sent, because they did not give him the Title of *Highness*.

At the Entry of the Count de Witgnestein, Plenipotentiary of Brandenburg, there happen'd a small Difference between the Ministers of Sweden, and those of the Elector of Mayence, which was the Cause that those of Sweden visited the Count before they went to see the other Count Cratz, Plenipotentiary of Mayence, made great Complaints thereof, as if the Count, in receiving the Swedes Visit, had done the utmost Prejudice to the Elector of Mayence, who he said was Dean of a College, where the Elector of Brandenburg had but the seventh Place. The Count said, that he would have wav'd it, but had been at last oblig'd to receive the Visit, because the Swedes, after having sent to him three times, had declar'd, that if he did not receive their Visit, they would not admit of his Cratz; however made a vexatious Affair of it to the Count of Witgnestein, which the Ministers of the other Electors had much ado to regulate. Cratz ought to have complain'd of the Swedes, who were they that disturb'd the Order of the Visits, and should not have quarrell'd with the Count of Witgnestein, who could not send away those who desir'd to see him, and who was not oblig'd to enquire, whether the Plenipotentiaries of Sweden had seen that of Mayence or not. As soon as d'Avaux was in a Condition to receive Visits at Munster, the Count of Nassaw Hademar came to him, and after him the three Plenipotentiaries of Spain made their Visit together, and receiv'd it in the same manner, meeting altogether at Saavedra's Lodgings for that purpose.

This Distinction is not always observ'd between the two last Comers; on the contrary, an Embassador of France, who should arrive at a Court two or three Days after an Embassador of Spain, would for all that pretend to the first Visit, by the same Reason, as at Rome he stands upon having the first Visit from a new Cardinal, even tho' this had receiv'd the first Visit from the Embassador of Spain. The Rule takes place only between the Minister who is already at a Court, and him who comes afterwards. It is customary for the Cardinals, and the Embassadors of crown'd Heads to visit the new Cardinals immediately after their Promotion. The new Cardinals do not return the Visits in the same Order they have receiv'd them, but after they have visited the Dean of the College, they see the other Cardinals without Order, and according as their Palaces lie in their way. As for the Embassadors, the Cardinals owe the first Visit to the Emperor's, and the second to that of France, even tho' the Embassador of Spain had prevented both the one and the other. Cardinal Savells,

C c c

velli, Archbishop of *Salerno*, had receiv'd the Hat in the same Promotion with the Archbishop of *Aix*; Brother to Cardinal *Mazarine*, on the 7th of *October*, 1647. The Count *d'Ognate* Embassador from *Spain*, endeavouring to win him over to the Interests of the House of *Austria*, to which that of *Savelli* was very much inclin'd, did not fail to be one of the first to visit him; and the Cardinal return'd his Visit, as soon as he had visited the Cardinals *Fontenay Marsell*, Embassador of *France*, being inform'd thereof, resented it after a manner that may be call'd cruel. As soon as he saw the Cardinal's Coaches stop in his Court, to set their Master down, he sent him word by the Groom of his Chamber, that the Embassador would not see him. The Cardinal, extremely surpriz'd at so strange an Occurrence, desir'd to know for what reason so gross an Affront was offer'd him. The Groom of the Chamber told him, that it was because, contrary to Custom, and against the Dignity of the Crown of *France*, he had made the first Visit to the Embassador of *Spain*. The Cardinal reply'd, that he ought to have been advis'd hereof, and not suffer'd to advance so far, to become the laughing Stock of the People; but he was answer'd, that he could blame no body but himself, because being a *Roman*, he ought to know the Custom of *Rome*, and what is due to the Embassador of *France*. The Embassador spoke to the Pope about it at his next Audience, who told him, that being inform'd of the Difference the Embassador had with Cardinal *Savelli*, he had had a mind to have the Opinion of six of the ancientest Cardinals thereupon, and that they had all with one Voice declar'd, that the new Cardinals observ'd no Order in their Visits, except in reference to the Dean *M de Fontenay* rejoyn'd, that he was sensible it was so, with respect to the Cardinals, but as for the Embassadors it was otherwise, the *French* Embassador being in possession of a Right to be preferr'd to the Embassador of *Spain* That in the Year 1641, a Cardinal *Montalto* had visited him, before he saw the Embassador of the Catholick King, and that otherwise he would not have admitted him That what had been always practis'd at *Rome*, ought not to be either chang'd or alter'd, at least that he would not suffer it to be done in his time That he himself, endeavouring to prevail with Cardinal *Bichi*, (who had obtain'd the Hat at the Nomination of the King his Master, and who was as Protector of *France*,) not to consider the Ministers of *Ferdinand* III, as Ministers of the Emperor, but only as Ministers of the King of *Hungary*, because he was acknowledg'd in *France* but only in this last Quality the Cardinal had told him, that he was at *Rome*, and that since the Pope acknowledg'd *Ferdinand* for Emperor, he, as Cardinal, could not avoid acknowledging his Ministers

Cardinal *Savelli* employ'd those that were Friends to both, to let *M de Fontenay* understand, that he was extremely concern'd at their Misintelligence, and protested it was not his Intention to offend *France*, nor the Embassador, but that he had follow'd the Advice of some Prelates, who had told him he ought to return the Visits in the same Order he had receiv'd them. That the Groom of the Chamber to *M de Fontenay*, might very well have done, as he that belong'd to Mareschal *d'Estrée* had formerly done, who had signify'd to the Duke of *Savelli*, his Father, Embassador from the Emperor, that if he saw the Duke of *Alanquerqu*, Embassador from *Spain*, before he paid him that Civility, he could not admit him That he had a great Esteem for the Person of *M de Fontenay*, and had a Veneration for his Character, and that on all accounts he covered to have a good Understanding with him The Cardinals, who think they may one Day stand fair for the Popedom, do not care to be at variance with those crown'd Heads, who may be Instrumental to their being excluded Cardinal *Savelli*, who knew how the Mareschal *d'Estrée* had us'd the Duke his Father ought not to have been ignorant of the Conduct he ought to have held with *M de Fontenay*

The Count *de Guldenleen*, who was Embassador Extraordinary from *Denmark* at *London*, in the Year 1669, being inform'd that *Jacob Boreel* was arriv'd thereon the part of the States of the United Provinces, as Embassador in Ordinary, sent his Secretary to complement him, and at the same time to know, when his Conveniency would permit him to receive his Visit, and *Boreel* appointed him the Hour of Three in the Afternoon the Day following On the same Day *M Colbert*, Embassador from *France*, did the same Civility to *Boreel*, who sent him word, that he could only appoint him the Hour of Four, having prefix'd that of Three to the Embassador of *Denmark* Colbert resolving to take his Advantage of this Answer in order to have the first Visit from *Boreel*, if he prevented the Embassador of *Denmark*, took his Measures so well, that he had ended his Visit, before this last had begun his But *de Guldenleen* being inform'd that *Colbert* had been there before him, and there being no room to doubt, that it was on purpose to exact the first Visit, by way of preference, he gave *Boreel* to understand, That as he had been the first to do him Civility, and had been punctual as to the Hour he had set him, he accordingly expected the Preference, and hop'd he would do him Justice, and pay him the first Visit, to the Exclusion of all others That he knew Boreel was so prudent, as not to pretend to regulate the Rank between crown'd Heads, but in case he should fail to observe the Order, he would not on his part fail to shew his Resentment, not only as an Embassador, but also as a Cavalier Boreel made answer, That it was not his Fault That he had appointed *M Colbert*'s Visit, after the Hour he had prefix'd to *Guldenleen*, and the other having anticipated the Hour, he could not send him away without seeing him However he found himself so perplex'd herein, that not knowing what Resolution to take, he did not dare to visit either the one or the other, till the King taking into Consideration, that this small Difference might be vexatious to all the three Embassadors, bethought himself of a Means to accommodate it, in such manner, that it might have no ill Consequence He therefore sent to desire the *Danish* Embassador to take some Days Diversion with him at *Windsor*, of which *Boreel* had notice, who contriv'd to be at *Guldenleen*'s Gate, at the very Hour he was just ready to get on Horseback,

Horſeback, in order to go to the King The Embaſſador of *Denmark*, ſurpriz'd at this Occurrence, or being willing to ſeem ſo, excus'd himſelf on the Neceſſity he was under to go and attend the King, who expected him. and ſignify'd to *Boreel*, that he was ſatisfy'd as to the Viſit, as if he had effectually receiv'd it, and that at his Return he would not fail to thank him for it. I cannot tell whether *Jeannin* and *Doſſat* would have acted like *Colbert* and *Guldenleew*. Thoſe prudent Men would have been fearful in engaging their Maſter in vexatious Affairs for Trifles, and would have rather choſe to decline the Diſpute, than to get out of it ſo cavalierly as theſe did *Boreel*, in returning the Viſits in the Order he had receiv'd them, would not have injur'd the Embaſſador nor the King of *France*, and *Colbert* gain'd no Advantage in dealing that foul Play to the Embaſſador of *Denmark*. The Plenipotentiaries of *France* did indeed ſignify to thoſe of the Emperor, that if they viſited the Count *de Pegneranda* before they diſcharg'd that Devoir to the Duke of *Longueville*, there ſhould be no more any Intercourſe of Viſits between them But this did not hinder the others from following the Example of the Mediators, and to viſit the Count. They ſent the Miniſters of *France* word, that they could not fall off, after they had deſir'd Audience, and that it ſhould be without prejudice to the Embaſſadors of *France*.

The Count of *Suartzenbourg*, the Emperor's Embaſſador in *England*, being arriv'd at *London* in the Year 1622, the Embaſſador of *France* paid him the uſual Civilities, and three Days after he viſited him, not doubting but the Count would return him the firſt Viſit, in Preference to the other Embaſſadors. But the Count did that Honour to the Embaſſador of *Spain*, as well becauſe this had been before-hand with the Embaſſador of *France*, as becauſe, according to the Order that is obſerv'd at *Vienna*, the Embaſſador of *Spain* is preferr'd to all the other Embaſſadors. Nevertheleſs the French Embaſſador was ſo offended thereat, that when the Count ſent to know whether he might ſee him after Dinner, he return'd for Anſwer, That the Weather having been very bad for ſome Days, and being now fair, he would take the Benefit of the fine Day, and go and take the Air in the Country. He was in the wrong, becauſe the Viſits are to be return'd in the Order they are receiv'd, and the Embaſſador of *Spain* had viſited the Count before the Embaſſador of *France*. It is a Civility that is due, and the Dignity of the Maſter is not concern'd therein.

The Embaſſador is oblig'd to conform to the Rules that have been agreed on for that purpoſe, and cannot fail therein without diſconcerting that Harmony, without which there can be no Converſation between publick Miniſters. But inaſmuch as the Dignity of the Maſter is not always concern'd in theſe Civilities, more eſpecially when there is no Competition, the Embaſſador may ſometimes diſpenſe himſelf from theſe Punctualities, and he ought to do ſo, if they are too incommodious, or if by the Diſpenſation he can acquire any Advantage to his Prince. The Count *de Lamberg*, Plenipotentiary of the Emperor, being arriv'd at *Munſter*, *Oxenſtiern* offer'd to make him the firſt Viſit, as to the laſt Comer, but before he actually made it, *Salvius* arriv'd alſo at *Munſter*; and, as the laſt Comer, he pretended to the firſt Viſit from the Count. This not knowing how to clear himſelf of this Intricacy, that he might offend neither the one nor the other, prevented them and went to ſee them all before *Oxenſtiern* had viſited him. The Count *de Lamberg* did herein the part of a gallant Man, but he was for finding Difficulty where there was none at all. He had nothing to do but to expect *Oxenſtiern*, and to return his Viſit, without any Conſideration for *Salvius*, who had no reaſon to complain of the Preference that was given to his Collegue, becauſe it was an Obligation wherein the Count was engag'd by receiving *Oxenſtiern*'s Viſit, and he ſatisfy'd *Salvius*, in viſiting him before he receiv'd his Viſit The Rule of the laſt Comer does not fix the time in which the Viſit is to be made, and only has room betwixt two Embaſſadors, the one of whom is upon the Place before the other arrives.

Chanut was very punctual, and the Miniſters of *Sweden* have ever been very difficult, and very ſenſible in the Matter of Civilities, nevertheleſs they had an Occurrence which was nice enough, at the Aſſembly that was held at *Lubeck* in the Year 1651. *Chanut* found there four Embaſſadors from *Poland*, and *Salvius* was there alone for the Crown of *Sweden*. The firſt having a mind to make their Viſit with great Ceremonies, were ſo long in their Preparations, that *Salvius* got the ſtart of them, *and paid his Viſit to* Chanut *before the others were ready*. He pretended, after that, that *Chanut* ought to return him the firſt Viſit by way of Preference, but the other would not conſent thereto, becauſe the *Poles* had ſent to him the firſt.

Embaſſadors owe alſo the firſt Viſit to thoſe Princes who come after them, provided the Princes are not Subjects of the Embaſſadors Maſter. I have touch'd upon this Matter above, and ſhall only add, that the three Embaſſadors of *France*, the Duke of *Engouleſme*, the Count of *Bethune*, and the Abbot *Preaux*, of whom the firſt was a Prince, and the two others had been employ'd in ſeveral Embaſſies, ſo that they might be ſuppos'd to know the Ceremonial; Theſe three Embaſſadors, I ſay, being at *Ulm*, and being inform'd that the Marquiſs of *Anſpach* and the Duke of *Wirtemberg* were come thither, ſent immediately to complement them, and to know the Hour of their Conveniency, *to make them a Viſit as to the laſt Comers* The Princes declin'd it, and prevented 'em, by viſiting them. Here they did themſelves great Wrong, and to all the other Princes of *Germany*, who at preſent do Penance for the Sins of their Anceſtors. The Refuſal they meet with, to be conſider'd as the Princes would deſire, is not very juſt, but it would ſtill be leſs ſo, if there were not amongſt them ſome, to whom too great Indignities cannot be offer'd, becauſe they cannot be guilty of more ſcandalous Meanneſſes.

All the Embaſſadors, who were at *Venice*, went to ſee the Duke of *Mantua*, when he arriv'd there in the Year 1602. *De Freſne* ſays, *That the Duke ſent'd him to be receiv'd at his landing*

landing from his Gondola, by Alexander Prince of Miranda, and by other Domesticks and that he receiv'd him himself at the top of the Staircase. That he yielded him the Hand. That he led him into his Closet, made him sit down, and reconducted him to the Place where he had receiv'd him. That when the Duke came to see him, he receiv'd him in the Entry, at some Paces from the Stairs, altho' his Predecessors had only receiv'd him at the bottom of the Stairs. I question what he says of the Hand, but not what he adds, that the Duke was not very well satisfy'd with the Reception the Embassador made him.

The English Embassador, that was at Paris in the Year 1640, did not refuse to make the first Visit to the Duke of Lorrain, but he requir'd that the Duke should, in reconducting him, accompany him to his Coach, because he had done that Honour to the Nuncio. The Ministers of Protestant Princes, who consider the Pope but as a temporal Prince only, will not pay any Deference to the Nuncio. And altho' the Embassadors of the Catholick Crowns give place to him, as to their First, they pretend nevertheless that the same Honour is due to them, wherefore those who were at Paris would not see the Duke of Lorrain for the same Reason.

The Visits, of which I have now spoken, are of Necessity, and make a part of the Ceremonies, which are inseparable from the Employment of Embassador. Those that are of mere Civility have their particular Rules, which are learn'd amongst the Great Ones, and not in Negotiations. The Embassador that takes a Journey, out of the Place of his Residence, for his own private Affairs, or for those of his Master, ought not to be consider'd at his Return as the last Comer, and the first Visit is not due to him but out of a mere Civility, as is also practis'd among private Persons on the like Occasions. If the Embassador receives new Credentials, by Reason of some Change in the State, by the Death of the Prince, or otherwise. On these Occasions Civilities are done him, not on account of his new Credentials, but of the Cause for which they were sent him.

The Visits that are made to Embassadors, who only pass by a Court, are of the same nature. The other Embassadors visit them most commonly, but it is without any Obligation.

Salagnac going Embassador to Constantinople on the part of France, pass'd through Venice, where all the other Embassadors visited him. There was none but the Nuncio that did not visit him, neither did he visit the Nuncio. De Fresne, Embassador of France, told him that what the other Embassadors had done, had been out of Civility, and not out of Devoir. So that as he could exact nothing from the Nuncio, he could neither prejudice himself nor the King, in doing him that Civility. There are some who would not have been of M. de Fresne's Sentiment. It was none of Salagnac's Business to make a Distinction, by doing an Honour to the Nuncio, that he did not do to the other Embassadors. And de Fresne was in the wrong to counsel Salagnac to do what he would not have dar'd to do himself, after the King's express Orders not to make the first Visit to the Nuncio.

This Civility of the first Visit, which is paid to the last Comer, is only practis'd between Embassador and Embassador, and does not regard the Minister of the second Order. However, it is certain that Dossat (who was only Bishop of Evreux, when he was at Venice, to communicate to the Senate the Conclusion of the Peace of Vervins) had not the representing Character, since his Letters of Credence did not mention it, but that did not hinder the Embassadors of Spain and of Savoy from making him the first Visit, as being the last Comer. This was not according to the Order, and at this time an Embassador would be cautious how he did it. All that can be said on this Head is, that Dossat was not a Minister of the second Order. His Quality of Bishop would not allow it, and it is reasonable to think, that the Republick consider'd him quite otherwise, since it caus'd him to be conducted to Audience by thirty Senators, and that its Intention was to give him both Reception and Entry. He was lodg'd and defray'd, and had those Honours done him, which are never done to Ministers of the second Order. One may here add, that in those times France was not over-punctual in expressing in the Credentials the Quality of the Embassador, of which we have so particular an Example in those of Alincourt, who was consider'd as an Embassador by the Pope, notwithstanding his Letters did not give him that Character.

CHAP. XXII.

Of some other Civilities which are done to Embassadors, or that Embassadors use towards one another.

Having spoken in some of the foregoing Chapters, of the Civilities that are of Obligation, and that are in some measure regulated, at least as much as things of this nature are capable of being so, I shall in this speak of some that are so but in part, or not at all. The Embassador, whose Prince has been solemnly invited to the Ceremony of a Christening, of a Marriage, or of a Funeral, ought to keep his Rank there, but if the Embassador that is upon the Place is only invited out of Civility, or if he assists there but only as the Minister of a Prince, or State, in Amity with that where he resides, or as a Spectator, there is no Obligation to give him the Rank, and it is sufficient to place him honourably and commo-

The EMBASSADOR and his FUNCTIONS.   193

commodiously Moreover, even when the Princes have been expresly invited, their Ministers cannot pretend the Rank before the Officers, whose Functions are necessary at the same Ceremony, when I have taken notice of to have been observ'd at the Coronation of Henry IV, and of Lewis XIII, where the Peers were plac'd before the Embassadors Formerly they were more expensive at Christenings and at Marriages than they are at this Time, unless it be in Germany and in the North, where still they invite a great many Strangers to these kinds of Ceremonies, with so profuse a Charge, that there is no Prince who can, without Inconveniencing himself, solemnize a Christening, a Marriage, and a Funeral, in the same Year It is also in those Parts that the Custom obtains of having several Godfathers assist at a Christening, and of inviting to it a great Number of Persons, without Distinction of Religion at what, however, the Roman Catholicks are more reserv'd than most of the Protestants, who ought to be more difficult in this Point than the others James, King of England, would not have caus'd one of his Children to be presented to Baptism by a Roman Catholick Prince, since he would not accept of the Civility King Henry IV did him, in desiring him to send some Person on his Part, to the Christening he made in the Year 1606, of the Dauphin, and some of the Princesses his Children De Fresne Canaye says, That th. King of England's Refusal contrary to what those of the reform'd Religion have always practis'd, and that it denotes a great Aversion for the Pope This Minister had formerly turn'd to the reform'd Religion, and had made Profession thereof thirty Years, but he did not for all that know very well the Dislipline of their Churches, as on the other side, Cardinal Dossat did not at all approve of the Resolution Henry IV wou'd have taken some Years before, to invite Queen Elizabeth to be Godmother to the Princess, the eldest Daughter of France, whom he would have had Christen'd with the Dauphin The Discipline of the Reform'd Churches of France obliges the Godfathers and Godmothers to breed up the Children they present to Baptism in the same Religion, for which Reason it does not admit of Heterodoxes

The Custom of making great Assemblies at Marriages, and to invite thither a great Number of Strangers, is abolish'd in most Courts a great while ago, and since they have left off making great Feasts on those Occasions, the Embassadors, whose Masters have no Interest in the Marriage, have not neither any Part at the least At that of the late King and Queen of England there were present with the Duke of Chevreuse, who represented the Bridegroom, only the Earls of Carlisle and Holland, who had negotiated the Affair, and sign'd the Contract They were present at the Celebration of the Marriage, but both they and the Duke retir'd during the Mass, because the King their Master was of a different Religion They were likewise invited to the Feast, and seated at the King's Table At the Marriage of Charles IX, and of Elizabeth of Austria, there was only the Elector of Triers had a Place at the King's Table, the three other Embassadors, the Bishop of Strasbourg, the Marquiss of Baden, and the Count of Zolern were seated at another Table I his had not been always the Practice, for which Reason it might be doubted, whether the four Embassadors of the United Provinces, who, in the Year 1641, had negotiated the Marriage of Prince William of Orange, were in the right to refuse dining at Court, because they knew they should not sit at the King's Table At the Marriage of the Elector Palatin and the Princess of England the Embassadors of France and Venice were invited to the Feast, and they had the Honour to eat at the Table of the newly marry'd, but the King was not there, altho' it was at a time that he us'd frequently to invite Embassadors to dine with him

I even now said, that there were only the Embassadors of England who were present at the Celebration of the Marriage I know very well that the Nuncio, and the Embassadors of Spain, of Venice, and of Savoy, were also there, but then they had no Rank There was none but the Baron of Languerac Embassador of the United Provinces, who, having a mind to make a Figure, desir'd he might march immediately after the Embassador of Venice, conformably to the Intention and Regulation of the late King But forasmuch as it was fear'd that the Embassador of Savoy would oppose it, and because the Embassador of Holland could not be present at Mass, it was thought proper that he should go along with the Duke de Chevreuse, and the two Embassadors of England. So that we went with them in the King's Coach, and march'd with them immediately before his Majesty

As for Funerals, it is only in those Places where they are accompany'd with great Feasts, that foreign Princes are invited, who otherwise would receive but a doleful and indifferent Diversion When the Embassadors upon the Place are invited to Ceremonies, they are for the most part plac'd after the Cardinals, and immediately after the Officers, who by their Functions are oblig'd to assist thereat This is observ'd at the Coronation of Kings and Queens, at the Oath that is taken for the Observation of a Treaty, or for the Renovation of an Alliance, at a Te Deum or Thanksgiving, at the Creation of Knights, at the opening of an Assembly of the States, and at all other Ceremonies of this Nature, as at the opening of the Parliament of England, &c The Ministers of Protestant Princes are hardly ever invited, because for the most part they are perform'd in those Places where they do not like to be, by reason of some Devotions which they do not approve of The Catholicks are not so scrupulous Trémes and Desshat, Embassadors of France, after they had accompany'd the Corpse into the Church of Westminster, at the Funeral of King James, would not assist at the Sermon, or Funeral Oration D'Avaux, who was a devout Catholick, conducted the Bride at the Marriage of the Prince of Denmark, and was present at the Ceremony Blainville said, He was willing to give his Conscience a scratch, to be present at the Coronation of the King of England The Queen of Sweden, when she sent to desire Chanut, Embassador of France, to assist at her Coronation, signify'd to him that there would be a Sermon, but that, that would not oblige him to any Religious Worship Chanut

D d d made

made answer, that he confider'd that Action but as a meer politick Ceremony, and that he should make no Difficulty to be prefent thereat, as he accordingly was, with the Embaffadors of *Portugal* and *Brandenbourg.*

The Oath that Princes take for the Execution and Obfervation of Treaties, is fo politick, that it is not neceffary it fhould be taken in a Church, notwithftanding Superftition fuggefts, that God (to whom the Oath is properly made) is there in a more particular manner than elfewhere. That which the *Grifons* took at *Venice* in the Year 1604, for the Execution of the Alliance they had made with the Republick, was executed in the Senate Hall, and the Pope approv'd of it. So likewife, when the King of *Spain* took the Oath for the Obfervation of the Treaty, the Conftable of *Caftile* had concluded in the Year 1604, at *London,* the Ceremonies thereof were perform'd at *Valladolid* in a Hall, between the Hands of the Archbifhop of *Toledo,* in the Prefence of *Charles Howard,* Earl of *Nottingham,* Admiral of *England.* Some of the Deputies of the *Grifons* were Proteftants, for which Reafon this Confideration was had for them at *Venice* and on the fame Account the fame Regard was had to the Admiral of *England* in *Spain.*

In the Year 1610, the Oath for the Confirmation of the Alliance between *France* and *Languana,* was taken in the Church of the *Feuillants* at *Paris,* and that for the Execution of the Peace in the Year 1629, in the Church of the Borough of St *Germans.* This Ceremony was formerly perform'd with great Solemnity, and extraordinary Honours were done to the Embaffadors who were fent on purpofe to affift thereat. When *Edmond,* Embaffador from *England,* enter'd into the Church of the Borough, the Guards were rang'd on both Sides of the Way, their Drums beating and Colours difplay'd, which he was given to underftand was in Honour, that is done only to Sovereigns. At prefent this is out of Date. Since Princes obferve their Word as religioufly as their Oaths, their Ratification is thought fufficient and it be ftill practis'd fometimes, it is only with the *Switzers,* who are ftill of Opinion, that there is more Security in an Oath, than in Parchment and Wax.

Thofe Princes that are truly Friends, or that maintain fome Appearance of Friendfhip among themfelves, make ufe of the Intermediation of their Embaffadors, to do one another Civilities on the good or evil Accidents that befall them, as thofe of the Birth, Marriage, or Death of a Prince, &c. And on thefe Occafions what I have faid before concerning the firft Vifit, ought to be obferv'd, to wit, that they who expect to have Civilities done them, muft be before-hand with thofe from whom they expect them, and notifie to them their good or bad Fortune. It is not to fay but there are Occafions, where they ought to get the Start of Advice, and where even the Embaffador ought to difcharge that Civility, without waiting for his Mafter's Orders, but he muft be fure always to take care, that the Dignity of his Prince be not prejudic'd thereby. After the I reafon of the Marechal *de Biron* was difcover'd, prov'd, and punifh'd in *France,* all the Minifters of the foreign Princes flock'd to the *Louvre,* to felicitate King *Henry* IV thereupon, becaufe they knew, that thofe who were true Friends would really rejoyce at it, and that the clandeftine Enemies who had been concern'd therein, lay under the greater Obligation to exprefs their Gladnefs, thereby to conceal their fruftrated evil Intentions. In fo extraordinary an Occurrence, of which the King would not give Advice to thofe Princes who were his Friends, for fear of fpeaking of thofe who had a Hand in fo flagitious a Defign, their Embaffadors ought not to wait for the Orders of their Principals. But in common Occurrences Cuftom muft be follow'd. The Queen of *Sweden* took it very ill, that *Uladiflas,* King of *Poland,* had not notify'd to her the Death of the Prince, of which the Queen his Confort had been deliver'd fome Days before, and took this Silence as a certain Mark of the Averfion the King had for her. On the other fide, the fame Queen thank'd the King of *Denmark,* who had given her Advice of his Affliction, after the Death of the Prince his eldeft Son and fhe went into Mourning for him, tho' fhe did not love the King of *Denmark* better than him of *Poland.*

In the Year 1672, the States General gave to the Prince of *Orange* the Poft of Captain General, that is to fay, the Command in Chief of the Armies of the Union, when they were out of the Territories of the United Provinces. The States of *Holland* conferr'd upon him at the fame time, the important Offices of Governor, Lieutenant, and Captain General of their Province, and of its Forces both by Sea and Land. The States General communicated their Refolution to the Minifters of the foreign Princes, but the States of *Holland,* and the Prince himfelf did not acquaint them with it. There were fome Minifters who went and complemented his Highnefs thereupon, but there were fome again, who did not think themfelves oblig'd to be over hafty, upon the bare Complement they had receiv'd by a Clark of the Notary of the States General. They therefore fent Advice thereof to their Mafters, and receiv'd Orders to expect the firft Civility from the Prince. Thofe Minifters who know their Bufinefs, do nothing that can prejudice the Dignity of their Mafter, as they would do, if they mingl'd in an Antichamber with a Crowd of Officers, and other People of lefs Confideration, and if they are not affur'd of the Civilities that are to be done to their Mafter, in their Perfon.

There is a great Deal to be obferv'd even with refpect to private Vifits. I fpeak elfewhere of the Conteft *Contarini* had with d'*Avaux* at *Munfter,* concerning the Civilities of a private Vifit; and it is what the Minifters of *Venice* are very punctual, or rather fuperftitious in. In the Month of *October,* 1668, the Embaffador of *Spain* going to fee that of *Venice* at *London,* being alighted out of his Coach, he went into a Hall, in expectation of the others coming to receive him, but the *Venetian* Embaffador fent him word, that he waited for him above. Hereupon the *Spaniard* afk'd if he was fick, and being told he was not, he fignify'd to him that he expected him below. The *Venetian* did not go down, and the other got into his Coach and went away home. Some Days after

after the Embaſſador of *Venice*, going to viſit the Embaſſador of *Spain*, this laſt ſent him word, that he could not admit him without the King his Maſter's Order, to whom he had ſent Advice of what had paſs'd between them The Embaſſadors of *France* and the United Provinces were forc'd to reconcile them The *Venetian* Embaſſador did this Incivility to that of *Spain*, becauſe this had treated him after the ſame manner, and as the Miniſters of *France* and *Venice* do the ſame Honours to one another, the Embaſſador of the Republick pretended the ſame from him of *Spain* and with Juſtice.

As for the Civilities Miniſters owe one to another at publick Ceremonies, they cannot be too difficult therein Formerly there was great talk of the Encounter the Marquiſs *de Trenel* had at *Rome* with the Embaſſador of *Spain*, in the Year 1625 The Marquiſs having made an Agreement to go and divert himſelf in the Countrey with ſome *French* Gentlemen, bethought himſelf before he took Coach, that it was a Holiday, and ask'd the Company whether it would not be proper to hear Maſs It was the Feaſt of St *James*, and the Church of the *Spaniards*, where it was chiefly obſerv'd, being in the Neighbourhood, they reſolv'd to go there, and even to take advantage of the Embaſſador of *Spain*, who was to do the Honours there The Embaſſador of *France* having got together what *French*men he could, went firſt to St *James*'s Church, having ſent his Cuſhion earlier by his eldeſt Footman The *Spaniſh* Embaſſador ſeeing the Footman enter, ask'd him, whether the *French* Embaſſador intended to honour the Feaſt of the Patron of their Nation with his Preſence and went to meet the Marquiſs *de Trenel*, and did him the Honours, as being the Maſter of the Place and of the Feaſt He would have got Reputation by it, if ſome Days after he had not gone himſelf to the Feaſt of the *French* at the Church of St *Lewis* If we will believe *M de Foix*, who underſtood wonderfully well the Matter of Ceremonies and Civilities, they both committed the Fault of a Novice He writes in one of his Letters to King *Henry* III, that Madrucci, *the Emperor's Embaſſador, had yielded the Place of Honour to the Embaſſador of* France, *in a publick Ceremony, and that he ſaid it was a Civility, which he thought himſelf oblig'd to do in a Church where he did the Honours, as he would have been oblig'd to do them in his own Houſe, if the Embaſſador of* France *had come to viſit him* But for as much as it was a publick Ceremony, ſays *M de Foix*, and a ſolemn Feaſt, where Madrucci *was at the Head of all the Nation, in the Preſence of ſeveral Cardinals, and of a great Number of other Perſons of Quality, he ought to have maintain'd his Rank, and every body judg'd that his Proceeding herein was irregular* For my part I have good Opinion enough of the Embaſſador of *Spain*, and of all the Nation, to believe that he would not have had ſo much Complaiſance for the Marquiſs *de Trenel*, if he had thought he could have avoided it, and declin'd the Scandal We may judge of it by the following Example

At the Canonization, which was perform'd at *Rome* in the Year 1588, *Don Diego d'Alcala*, the *Spaniſh* Embaſſador pretended to have the Precedency of the *French* Embaſſador, as in an Action which was done in Honour, and at the Expence or ſhould be the *Spaniſh* Nation But the Marquiſs *de Piſani*, Embaſſador from *France*, ſent him word, that he would not ſuffer him to remain in the Chapel after he had diſcharg'd his Function, if he did not come and place himſelf by him and below him The *Spaniſh* Embaſſador ſent to deſire him to permit him to take the firſt Place only for that one time, and that it ſhould be no Precedent The Marquiſs made anſwer, that he was willing to grant ſie him, but it ſhould be upon Condition, that the *Spaniſh* Embaſſador ſhould declare, that it ſhould be without Prejudice to the Right of the Embaſſador of *France*, and that he ſhould promiſe, that the next time the Pope ſhould come to Chapel, he ſhould come and place himſelf below him This was what the *Spaniſh* Embaſſador was far from doing, ſo that he choſe rather to go out of the Chapel, after he had diſcharg'd his Function

It will not be from the purpoſe, may be, to add here to what I have ſaid, what the ſame *M de Foix* obſerves in another Letter, That the Embaſſadors who are of the Church, have their Place in the Pope's Chapel near his Holineſs, before the Patriarchs, immediately after the Governor of *Rome* That formerly the ſecular Embaſſadors had their Place there alſo, but that they were ſtanding and uncover'd That Pope *Pius* IV, reſolving to keep theſe laſt Places for thoſe Princes, to whom the Title of *Moſt Serene* is not given, and who are not of Quality enough to be admitted amongſt the Cardinals, had in the Year 1575, order'd by a new Regulation, that the Lay Embaſſadors ſhould be ſeated and cover'd, in a Place more remote but that not one Embaſſador would conſent to it, and that from that time not one Embaſſador would do Honour to the Pope in the Chapel That this new Regulation gave a very great Advantage to the Embaſſador of *Spain* in this, that the ſame Pope, maintaining the *French* Embaſſador in poſſeſſion of the Precedency, that of *Spain* was no longer ſingular, ſo that his Abſence could be no longer taken notice of as an Advantage which he yielded to *France* *M de Grignan*, who relates to extraordinary a thing on account of the firſt Viſit, tells one no leſs ſurpriſing, in reference to the Pope's Chapel

The Letter he writes to the Conſtable *de Montmorancy* of the 22d of *April*, 1639, imports, *That the Embaſſy of Rome was much more proper for a Biſhop, than for a Man of his Profeſſion, That Prelates have where-with-all to ſupport the Expence of the Embaſſy, and that they do not grudge it, as well becauſe they have it out of Lands, of which they they have only the mean Profits, as becauſe it is a Mean to get other Benefices, and indeed to attain to the Cardinalſhip* He moreover adds, *That if the King thinks fit to employ there a Man of the Sword rather than a Prelate, that it ought to be a dignify'd Perſon, and that he have at leaſt the Quality of Marquiſs or of Count* For I aſſure you, my Lord, ſays he, *that it is grating to me, (conſidering the Grandeur of our Maſter) to ſee the Emperor's Embaſſador near the Pope, while I am at the bottom of the Chapel, with the Embaſſadors of* Venice *and of* Florence, *a thing I had great Debates about at firſt, but I found that the ſaid Embaſſador was*
then

there as Marquiss, and not as Embassador. The Count de Cifuentes had also obtain'd that Rank, as Count. When you shall send a Bishop thither, he will be in the Rank of Bishops, and so will not appear in the Rank of other Embassadors. There can be nothing said more directly opposite to what is practis'd at this Day, and even to Reason it self. According to the Principles of the Lord de Grignan, Embassadors do not take the Rank of the Masters they represent, but that which their own proper Quality gives them. This is an unheard-of thing, unknown even to those Ages that preceded that of M. de Grignan.

In the time of the same Pope Pius, the Embassador of Spain, had a Contest with the Senator of Rome, about the Precedency. This Senator is an Officer of Justice, who has under him Civil Judges, which are call'd Collaterals, and a Judge in Criminal Cases, who take the first Cognizance of all the Civil and Criminal Causes of the Inhabitants of Rome and an Appeal lies from their Sentences to the Captain of Appeals, who sits in the Capitol, as does also the Senator, with his Collaterals. The Senator ought to be a Stranger, and not a Roman: and on Days of Ceremony he appears in publick with a Vest of Gold Brocade, which almost trails on the Ground, is lin'd with a Crimson Silk, and his Ducal Sleeves, wearing about his Neck a Gold Chain after the manner of the Ancients. This Senator, who is only a subaltern Judge, as I have before taken notice, did not care to enter into Competition with the Embassador of Spain, but for all that he got the better of him, the Pope determining, by the Advice of the Master of the Ceremonies, that none but the Emperor's Embassador, could take place of the Senator in the Chapel.

I have spoken elsewhere of the Civilities the Cardinals do to Embassadors, and I touch'd a little on the Difference the Embassadors had with the Duke of Lorrain, concerning those they expected from him. It is what the ones and the others are very difficult in.

The Duke of Parma being in the Year 1641, gone to take a Turn in his Dutchy of Castro, he was told from the Pope, that his Holiness would take it well if he would make him a Visit at Rome, while he was in the Neighbourhood, and that it would, on the contrary, be taken ill, if he return'd into Lombardy without paying him that Devoir. The Duke consented to it, upon Condition that Thadeus Barberin, Prefect of Rome, should not be in the Town, during the Stay the Duke should make there, that so they might avoid the Competition they might otherwise have for the Rank. It was promis'd him, and notwithstanding he receiv'd Advice upon the Road, that the Pope did not keep his Word with him, and that the Prefect did not stir from Rome, yet he pursu'd his Journey. Don Thadeus did indeed offer to pay to the Duke all the Civilities he could expect from him, but then he requir'd that the Duke should return them, which the Duke would not do, nay he refus'd even to visit the Prefect's Lady, unless her Husband came and receiv'd him in his Coach, and did him all the other Honours of his House, since he was at home. This Contestation was succeeded by another much more violent, between the Duke, and the two Cardinals Barberins, concerning the same Civilities. The Cardinal Anthony, in reconducting the Duke, retir'd before this last was got into his Coach. The Duke return'd it, but after a much more offensive manner, for after the Cardinal had ended his Visit, and was got into his Coach, he still kept his Hat in his Hand, and intreated the Duke to retire, and not to incommode himself, altho' the Duke had been gone a good while, and had left him in the Entry. It was but a small beginning, but it was however the true Cause of the War between the Barberins and the Confederates, which in another Conjuncture would have drawn the Arms of the greatest Potentates of Europe into Italy.

The Embassadors, that reside in the same Court, on the part of two Princes at Enmity, do not visit one another, while there is open War, and even avoid the Occasions that might make them meet in a third Place. However, when it happens that they do meet by accident, they ought to be civil one to the other, because that as the greatest Acts of Generosity are done during the greatest Fervour of the War, so the Embassador ought always to follow the Intention and Inclination of Princes, whose Animosities are never brutish. He ought to distinguish betwixt the Persons and the Interests, and keep up to the Dignity of his Employment, after he has acquitted himself of what he owes to that of his Master. In the Year 1647, a Jacobin Monk, who concealed his true Name under that of Francis Taquet, had Orders to disburse to the Sum of Five hundred thousand Crowns, if he found the Means to set at liberty Don Duarte, Brother to the King of Portugal, but seeing that the Senate was not very well dispos'd to listen to the Propositions which he made on that score, he settl'd a Correspondence in the Cittadel of Milan, (where Don Duarte was kept Prisoner) tho' without Success, because the Marquiss de Fuentes, Embassador of Spain, observ'd the Actions of the Monk so narrowly, that he no sooner began an Intrigue, but it was immediately discover'd. This made the Monk resolve to rid him himself of the Embassador, by the Means of some Braves which he had at his Command. He communicated his Design to the President de Gremonville, Embassador from France, believing he might do it with Safety, by Reason of the good Wishes the Most Christian King had for the Interest of Portugal. But the President, who was a Man of too much Honour, to have any Concern in so mean and foul an Action, gave Advice thereof to the Marquiss de Fuentes, and thereby did him the same good Office, that he could have done him, if their Masters had been ever so good Friends. The Quality of Embassador is not inconsistent with that of a Man of Honour on the contrary, it seems to be inseparable from it.

Cardinal d'Este, Son of Renée of France, who was Daughter to Lewis XII, was Protector of France, and Christopher, Cardinal Madrucci, was so for Spain, so that they were Pensioners, declar'd Partisans, and Ministers of Princes who had quite different and opposite Interests, yet nevertheless they lov'd one another so well, that their Friendship may be com-

compar'd with that of those Personages, of whom so many Historians and Poets have fill'd their Books, there pass'd no Day that they had not three Hours Conversation together and even when at a Distance, they express'd so strong a Passion each for the other, that Cardinal *d'Este* being fallen sick at *Paris*, Madrucci, who was at *Rome*, dispatch'd every Day six Courriers to him, within three Hours one of another, that he might as often receive an Account of his Friend's Health Cardinal *d'Este* being return'd to *Rome*, had the Satisfaction to see this perfect Friend expire in his Arms I may be said that these two Prelates were Ministers, and they were without doubt confided in by the Kings their Masters, who were well assur'd of their Affection and Fidelity but except in the Secret of the Conclave, and of the ordinary Affairs of the Consistory, the Protector is no Embassador, nor representing Minister, neither is he responsible for the Success of the Negotiation, so that he cannot prejudice the Intention of the Prince, unless it be in contributing to the Election of a Pope, who was not acceptable to his Master, as did Cardinal *Anthony Barberin*, in consenting to the Exaltation of *Innocent* X, contrary to the Orders he had receiv'd from Court, and contrary to his Word and Promise And indeed he lost the Protection of *France* on that Account

The Embassador cannot go so far The Visits he should pay to the Embassador of a Prince at Enmity with his Master, would not be innocent and if they were not altogether criminal, they would always be extremely suspected, but when he accidentally meets him in a third Place, he ought not to refuse him the Civilities that are done to indifferent Persons The Officers and Soldiers of contrary Parties lay aside their Hostilities in a neutral Place, wherefore one would think, that an Embassacor, who certainly has something more noble in him, and that raises him above the Soldier, ought not to behave himself less civilly

In the Year 1615, the Count *de Gondemar*, Embassador from *Spain* at *London*, being invited to a Ball that was to be at Court, was very much surpriz'd, when he was told that Noel *Caron*, Embassador of the United Provinces, had been also invited to it, that he was just a coming, and that he was to sup with the King He told the Master of the Ceremonies, *That if he met M Caron in a particular Place, he would pay him Civility, but he could not suffer that the Minister of the King his Master's Subjects, who had revolted from him, should be treated on the Level with him, in a publick Assembly, in the Presence of the King and Queen, where every Body would be Witness of the Equality of Honours, that were done to the one and to the other That if he were not actually upon the Place, he should not have come, but since he was there, and that his Displeasure might disturb the Feast, he was willing to retire, provided Caron were oblig'd to do the same* It was represented to him, *That it would look ill in the King, to send away a publick Minister, whom he had solemnly invited*. That Don Alfonso de Velasco, the *Count's Predecessor*, had *suffer'd the Embassador of the States to eat with him at the King's Table, being satisfy'd with having the first Place on the right Hand, while the other had the second on the left* But it was impossible to overcome the Obstinacy of Count *Gondemar*, who retir'd with his Secretary, and one Footman, suffering his other Domesticks to remain at the Feast He was in the wrong to say that the States of the United Provinces were the Subjects of the King his Master, because the Catholick King had resign'd them, with those of *Flanders*, to the Arch Dukes, and these had treated with them, as well in their own Name, as by Virtue of the Power they had from the King of *Spain*, as with States and free People, over whom they had no Pretensions Perhaps in another Court than in that of King *James*, these two Embassadors would not have been invited to the same Feast The Count said, he would do Civility to *Caron*, if he met him in a third Place One Day *M Piques*, Resident of *France* in *Sweden*, going to see Mr *Whitlock*, Embassador of *England*, D *Anthony Pimentel*, Minister of *Spain*, came to visit the same Embassador, without giving him Notice thereof *Piques* kept his Place, and *Pimentel*, who knew the World very well, made him so obliging a Complement, that the Minister of *France*, who would not be indebted to the *Spanish* Civility, could not forbear returning it

The Ministers of Princes at Enmity, and of contrary Parties, see one another without Scruple, at Assemblies where Peace is negotiating One of the first things that *Contarini* did, after he came to *Munster*, was to dispose the Plenipotentiaries of the Emperor and of *Spain*, who came thither first, to visit the Embassadors of *France* as soon as they should arrive, and to receive the Visits of these, in the same Manner as the Ministers of the two Crowns were us'd to before the Rupture He represented to them, that they who met on so good an Account, ought to entertain among themselves at least some Resemblance of a Peace Those who have written pertinent Memoirs, of what pass'd in the Negotiation of *Munster*, take Notice, that on those Occasions, where the Civilities were not of mere Obligation, and where the Ministers, of what Party soever they were, visited one another, upon any good or bad Occurrence, they strove to be before-hand each with the other The Mediators, and the Plenipotentiaries of crown'd Heads, as well as those of the Electors, went to see the Count of *Nassau* upon the Death of the Empress, and the same Count, and the Plenipotentiaries of the Emperor and of *Spain*, visited the Duke of *Longueville*, upon the Death of the Prince of Conde, his Father-in-law *D'Avaux* and *Saavedra*, saw one another as Friends, in a third Place, without having any Dispute for the Rank, and without Ceremonies

The one did not pass by the others Door, but he sent to inquire after the Health of the Master of the House, but *d'Avaux* and *le Brun* could never agree, neither of the Place nor of the Civilities for an Interview in a third Place, because *d'Avaux* pretended to have an Advantage over the other They do not act otherwise at *Nimmeguen*

The Ministers of Protestant Princes do not see those of the Pope, because on the one Side they consider him but as a secular Prince, and on the other, the Pope will have no Communication with those he calls Hereticks The Embassadors Plenipotentiaries of the United

E e e Pro-

Provinces, at their Arrival at *Munster*, sent a Gentleman to the Nuncio, *Fabio Ghigy*, to let him know that they were come. The Gentleman was told that the Nuncio was not at Home, and when they sent him again, the Nuncio sent him Word, that being undress'd, he was not in a Condition to speak to him. The Nuncio had before declar'd, that he would have no Communication with Hereticks, and that he pretended to be Mediator only for the Roman Catholick Princes; so that the Embassador of a State, that has no Commerce at all with the Court of *Rome*, might very well have avoided doing him this Civility. Some Persons had endeavour'd to dispose him to do some to the Ministers of Protestant Princes, and to that purpose had alledg'd the Examples of the Cardinals *de la Valette*, *de Richelieu* and *Mazarin*, of *Ditrigstein*, and of some others. But he said, that the Post he was in oblig'd him to do as he did, and that if he had been sent to a Diet of the Empire, or to the Court of *Vienna*, or of *Paris*, where the meeting of Protestants is not to be avoided, perhaps he should not be so scrupulous as he was at *Munster*. The Nuncio who resides at the Court of *France*, has no Communication with the Ministers of Protestant Princes, but that does not hinder him from paying them Civilities when he accidentally meets them at the Louvre, or elsewhere. The Nuncio *Bagny* took occasion from hence to tell the Minister of one of the first Princes of *Germany*, that he grudg'd very much the Time that the Ministers, who for particular Reasons do not visit one another, spent at *Mademoiselle de Senneterre*'s two or three times a Week, where they entertain'd each the other, with great Freedom, on the Affairs of the World. That the Difference in point of Religion, ought not to hinder that Commerce, since the Catholicks and Protestants being both Christians, and hoping to be sav'd but *by the Death and Passion of Jesus Christ*, they ought not to shun one another like Turks and Pagans, and thereby destroy the main Principle of Christianity, which is Charity. It must be look'd upon as a strange Whim in *Fabio Ghigy*, and those that employ'd him, or else we must inquire into the Cause of what we see to Day, in the Pleasure Nature takes, to make her self admir'd, in her frequent and almost continual Oddnesses. *Bevilacqua*, who is Nuncio at the Congress of *Nimmeguen*, not only does not abhor the Conversation of the Ministers of Protestant Princes and States, but has offer'd to be before-hand with them in the Point of Civilities, if they would but promise to return them.

The Embassadors of *Denmark* and *Brandenburg*, made no Difficulty to do it; but they would have those of the United Provinces, who had granted a Passport to the Nuncio, shew them the Example. These have not been willing to do it hitherto, not out of Scruple of Conscience, but because they were apprehensive, lest the Allies should insensibly engage them, to admit of the Mediation of the Pope, and the Offices of his Nuncio, which would render that of the *English* less Considerable, and might offend them. So far is it from sticking at the Nuncio, that this strong Aversion should be laid aside, which is so uncharitable, so inhuman, and so contrary to civil Society. One would think that in *Holland*, where there is at least as many Bigots and Atheists, as good Christians, it ought not to be oppos'd out of Policy, since it is not done out of Conscience. Religion and Faction are synonymous, since the Priests are become Temporal Lords, and that the preaching Ministers are Flatterers and Mutineers.

Princes still keep up the Civility of inviting Embassadors, as also the Ministers of the second Order, to take part of the extraordinary Diversions of the Court. I lately mention'd the Ball, where King *James* invited the Embassadors of *Spain*, and of the United Provinces. In the Year 1635, King *Lewis* XIII. having prepar'd a very Magnificent one against *Easter*, the Embassadors desir'd to see it, and the King having order'd a List to be given him of all the Ministers that were at *Paris*, said they should all be there, and be invited to it as from himself. It was represented to him that some Disorder might arise therefrom, because there would not fail to be Disputes between some of them for the Rank, so that the King said none of them should be invited, but gave Orders to signify to them, that if they would be present there as private Persons, and not as Embassadors, they should be admitted without Ceremony. The Queen of *Sweden* did the same at a Ball where she danc'd, and told *Chanut* Embassador of *France*, that he might come there if he pleas'd, that he should have a commodious Place, but that it was not her Intention to settle the Rank between the Ministers, who should have none at this Assembly, of which she made only a Diversion and not a Ceremony. When Embassadors are invited, it must be done in such manner, that the Diversion be not interrupted by their Contestations and also that in obliging the ones, the others be not offended.

King *James*, who had a great Opinion of Count *de Gundemar*, and who had created himself an Affair with him, as I before took notice, made an ample Reparation to the *Spaniards*, in the Year 1620. *D'Aarstens*, *Bas*, and *Stavenisse*, Embassadors Extraordinary from the States, with *Caron* their Embassador in Ordinary, were invited from the King, to assist at the Feast of St *George*, to see the Ceremonies of the Order of the Garter; and they were told, they should be plac'd in a Pew on the Queen's side, as Don *Carlos Coloma*, Embassador of *Spain*, should be on the King's. The Master of the Ceremonies had no sooner made a Report of the Message, than the High-Chamberlain said, that the *Dutch* Embassadors could not be plac'd so near that of *Spain*, that there was but only the Partition of a thin Board between, with a Window which open'd on both sides, and that that might afford Matter of Scandal. Hereupon the Master of the Ceremonies went and told the Embassadors, that there was a Misunderstanding in the first Message they had receiv'd, because it was thought that neither the Embassador of *Spain*, nor even themselves, would like to be so near the one to the other; that they were therefore desir'd to approve of being present in the Morning at the Procession, in the usual Place, and at Night at the Evening Prayers, at which there would be be the same Ceremonies as at the Morning Service M *d'Aarsbens*, who was the chief of the Embassy, answer'd in the Name of all, That as they should take it as an Honour, and receive it as a Favour, whenever the King should be pleas'd to invite them to any Diversion or Ceremony, so they should submit without any Uneasiness to his Majesty's Will, whenever he should give them to understand that their Presence was not acceptable to him, as he now signify'd it to them by the Master of the Ceremonies, after having invited them solemnly That since the King judg'd his Favours would be better bestow'd elsewhere, and that he did not approve of their assisting at the Service of the Morning, they would absent themselves likewise from the Procession of the Evening, from which they desir'd to be excus'd

At *Shrovetide*, in the Year following, the same Embassadors receiv'd another Affront, and in a manner at the least as gross, and is shocking There was to be a Masquerade at Court, and it was not greatly desir'd that the *Dutch* Embassadors should partake of the Diversion, but as there was a sort of Obligation to invite them, they were indeed desir'd to be there, but, at the same time, so many Difficulties were rais'd, that they chose rather not to be there, than to be depriv'd of any Honour that was due to their State They were told at first that they should have a Box where they should be alone, but they said, that having till then had the Honour to be near the King's Person, with the Embassador of *France*, and the other Embassadors of crown'd Heads, even him of *Spain*, they could not accept of what was offer'd them The *English* reply'd, That the *Dutch* having lately sent Succours to the *Rochellers*, the Embassador of *France* would not be well pleas'd to see their Ministers so near him To this they made answer, That that Embassador had made a Declaration of the contrary, and that he had no Orders to decline meeting the Embassadors of the United Provinces Upon this the *English* bethought themselves of another Defeasance, and said there was a Necessity to give them a Box for themselves, because, as they were four, there would not be room for them all in the King's The Embassadors reply'd, That that Difficulty should be easily remov'd, because, if the King thought fit to invite them, only one should go for them all, that they might not incommode his Majesty The *English* having no more bad Reasons to offer after this, shew'd very plainly that they were not much concern'd to give Satisfaction to the Embassadors, since they were not invited at all The King, who had since his Accession to the Crown of *England*, made it sufficiently known that he did not love the State of the United Provinces, was not afraid of doing a thousand Indignities to its Ministers, more especially since the Match with *Spain* had ingross'd all his Thoughts

I do not think my self oblig'd to speak here of the extraordinary Civilities, which not being due cannot make a Rule, nor serve my Intention I have taken notice of some of them already, and I shall here add the Honour that *Don Lewis de Haro* did to *Hugues de Lionne*, who went to complement him from Cardinal *Mazarin* at St *Sebastian* He had no Quality, nor *Letters of Credence*, so that he could be consider'd but as one belonging to the Plenipotentiary of *France*, altho' he was also Minister of State *Don Lewis* sent to meet him at two Leagues Distance from the Town and lodg'd him in a House he had fitted up for that Purpose, he gave him the Title of *Excellency*, and caus'd it to be given him by all the Grandees, who do not willingly give it to Embassadors *Don Lewis* himself receiv'd him in the middle of his Guards Room, and gave him the first Place at his Table He did these Civilities to a Minister, who not only behav'd himself after the most submissive manner in the Cardinal's Presence, but who also under the Title of *Secretary of State*, discharg'd likewise the Function of Secretary to his Eminency

After that *M d'Avaux* had made his Entry at *Munster*, he sent two Gentlemen to the Count of *Nassau Hademar*, the Emperor's Embassador, to thank him for the Honour he had done him, in sending his Coach to meet him, and causing him to be complemented by two Gentlemen The Count in reconducting Mr *d'Avaux*'s Gentlemen, accompany'd them as far as the Street-Door The excessive Civilities which an Embassador does on these Occasions, where he is oblig'd to act the Embassador, are not very regular, and discover plainly that he does not very well know what he is, nor what he does

There was no Competition between Cardinal *Bichi* and the Commissioners who were at *Orange* on the part of the Elector of *Brandenbourg* Guardian to the Prince, in the Year 1652 The Cardinal, who was not very well with the Pope, had retir'd to his Bishoprick of *Carpentras*, where his eminent Qualities gave him as much Lustre as he receiv'd from the Purple, and where he was full as much respected as he would have been at *Rome* The Count *de Dona*, who had acquir'd the Friendship and Esteem of this Prelate, whose Counsels were a great Assistance to him, was for having the Commissioners of *Brandenburg* go and visit him in his Bishoprick The Cardinal receiv'd them with the same Civilities they could have hop'd for from one of his domestick Prelates He plac'd them at the upper end of the *Ruelle* of his Bed, gave them arm'd Chairs, and sate himself at the Entrance thereof on a Stool At Dinner they had arm'd Chairs, and in reconducting them he accompany'd them to their Coach, where he caus'd them to be serv'd with Wine at the Coach Door

Some time after, one of the Commissioners being return'd into *Holland*, the Cardinal went to see the other at the Castle of *Orange* He din'd there, but he would not sit down till arm'd Chairs were brought for the Governor and the Commissioner, who had order'd folding Stools for themselves Being inform'd that this Commissioner was gone to *Avignon*, incognito, to see the Ceremonies of a Procession of Penitents, he paid him the first Visit, being attended by above fourscore Gentlemen, and when he receiv'd it he order'd him an arm'd Chair, causing the Archbishop of *Avignon*, who came thither during the Visit, to sit upon a Form against the Wall Cardinal *Bichi*, in treating after this manner Persons who were infinitely inferior to him, and who had no publick

lick Quality in reference to him, and out of the Principality of *Orange*, did himself no Prejudice, because every body knew that he did them an Honour and a Favour which could not be made use of as a Precedent.

Those Princes who have gain'd the Knowledge of Men, know how to distinguish between the Merit of those Ministers who negotiate with them, by the Confidence they have in the one, and the Indifferency they have for the others. *Schach Abas*, King of *Persia*, was one of the ablest Princes of his time, and he was willing also to be thought a gallant Man. He did not design to gratify *Garcia de Silva Figueroa*, who was with him on the Part of the King of *Spain* in the Year 1619, for which Reason he did him a thousand Civilities and Courtesies, al'tho' the Conduct of that Minister was not very judicious, nor his Conversation very agreeable. One Day the *Scach*, having with him only two or three Persons, went to see the Embassador at his Lodgings, and to give him to understand that he intended to be very familiar with him, he saluted him after the *French* way, taking off his Turban. When he spoke to him he call'd him Father, or Grandfather, and *Figueroa* taking one Day the Liberty to tell him, That in their Conversation he receiv'd those Terms of Respect as an Honour the *Scach* thought fit to do his Master, hereupon *Scach Avas* signify'd to him, not by his Interpreter, but by a religious Man who was a *Spaniard*, and there present, that it was not the Consideration he had for the King of *Spain* that made him pay him these Civilities, but that he did them to him as to his Guest, and as to a Person whose Merit he esteem'd. In our *Europe* Kings do not make use of those Terms to express the Consideration they have for publick Ministers, and there is great likelihood that they would not be very well receiv'd neither.

Ferdinand de Velasque, Constable of *Castile*, whom *Philip* III sent in the beginning of this Century to King *James*, to complement him on his Accession to the Crown of *England*, had Wit, but he had not less Vanity, for which Reason the *English* perceiving that great Appearances pleas'd him, gave him thereof beyond Imagination, and what he could pretend to. The King being inform'd that the Constable kept his Bed, on Account of some slight Hurt he had got in his Foot, went himself to visit him, which put him into such an Extasie of Joy, that seeing the King come into his Room, he cry'd out, *Lord, I am not worthy thou should'st enter under my Roof.* As he went by *Paris*, at his Return from his Embassy in *England*, King *Henry* IV commanded *Zebastion Zamet* to give a Supper to the Constable, and as they were going to sit down, the King came in unexpectedly, and would make one amongst them. The Constable kneel'd down to present the Napkin to the King, but the King would not suffer it, and told him that he was brought to *Zamet*'s to receive Honours, and not to do them. The Constable was so tickled with these obliging Words, that he protested that all the Honours that had been done him in *England*, and all the rich Presents he had there receiv'd, were nothing to him, in Comparison of the Bounty with which he was treated by the greatest King of *Christendom*.

The Civilities that are done to Embassadors extend themselves sometimes to the Dead. *Don Francisco de Vera*, Embassador from *Spain* at *Venice*, dying there in the Year 1603, the Senate made him a Funeral, with the same Ceremonies that are usually done to the Doge, expending therein three thousand Crowns. In the Year 1607, *M de Buzanval*, one of the three Embassadors of *France*, dying at the *Hague*, the States were at the Expence of his Funeral. That Ceremony being over, a great Dinner was prepar'd at the Palace of the Princess of *Orange*, where the Deceas'd had lodg'd. Since President *Jeannin* thinks fit to give the King an Account of the Order that was observ'd there, I think my self oblig'd to say here a Word or two about it, because what he says of it deserves a little Reflection, that what has been practis'd since may be compar'd therewith. He says in his Letter of the 24th of September, That the Embassadors of *France* had the *first* and *most honourable Place*. In the second were the Deputies (they were Embassadors) of England, who did not express the least Thought of disputing the Precedency, tho' the Deputies of the States, who were sent to England, had told us at their Return from thence, that some of the King of England's Council had assur'd them they would Prince Maurice and Count William were next to them, and then Count Henry and Monsieur de Chatillon, and two other Lords of the same House of Nassaw. After these were the States in a Body, the Council of State, and then the other Corporations, one after the other, all two and two, and every one in deep Mourning. The same Order was observ'd at their Return, and at their sitting down to Dinner. There is no Prince that follows the Example of these two Republicks. I know very well that, within some Years, the Queen Regent of *Spain* was at the Expence of the Funeral of an Embassador that dy'd at *Madrid*, but then it was for particular Reasons, which will find a Place in the History of those Times, but must not make Part of this Work. I shall only make one Remark on what President *Jeannin* says in his Letter, *Concerning the Precedency the English Ministers pretended to*, That they had no Thoughts of entring into any Contestation on that Point, at this Time, where the Embassadors of *France* represented the nearest Relations of the Deceas'd, and where the States intended an Honour to the most Christian King.

Before I put an end to this Chapter, I must add a Line or two concerning what I said, That the Difference in Religion is an Obstacle sometimes to the Communication between Embassadors, but it is only between the least capable. *Pietro della Valla* says, in his Relations, *That a Resident of England being in the Year 1618 arriv'd at* Ispahan, (*which is the chief City of* Persia) *the European Catholicks, who are pretty numerous there, put it into debate how they should carry themselves towards him. The Religious of* Portugal, *who knew that the English came thither to incommode the Commerce of those of their Nation, were of Opinion that no Conversation at all should be had with the Resident. But the others again reply'd, That if the Portuguese had Reasons that hinder'd them from seeing him, they had none. That they ought not to give so much Scandal to a King that was an Infidel*, as to shew so bad an Understanding, so inconsistent with Christian Charity, in a Court where they were likely to see one another every Day. That all the Christians liv'd in so perfect an Union at Constantinople, that the English and Dutch (who were otherwise the most inveterated Enemies of of the Jesuits) had stickled to serve them who more fervour than the most zealous Catholicks That the Religious, whom the Pope sends into the remotest Parts of Asia, ought to have for Object the Conversion, not only of the Infidels, but also of the Heterodoxes, and that it was not the means to convert them, to decline their Company. Whereupon it was resolv'd, That they should visit the Resident of England with the same Indifferency with which they saw the other Christians.

Sovereigns have sometimes particular Reasons that oblige them to order their Ministers not to visit those of another Prince, and then it s something personal. In the Year 1620 the King of France forbid his three Embassadors, the Duke d'Engoulesme, the Count of Bethune, and the Abbot Des Preaux, to receive the Visit of M. d'Aarsens, who went on the Part of the States of the United Provinces to negotiate with some of the Princes of Germany and Italy, concerning the same Affairs of Bohemia, which were the Subject of the Embassy of France. The Order that was sent them expres'd that it was not on the States Account, with whom the King would continue to keep a good Understanding, but on M. d'Aarsens', account in particular, for having behav'd himself ill, in Reference to the Service and Dignity of his Majesty. They that have any Knowledge of the Affairs of those Times, cannot be ignorant that it was because that d'Aarsens had put himself at the Head of those who oppos'd, in the Year 1619, the Affair the King was negotiating with great Earnestness at the Hague, by Boissise and du Maurier, his Embassadors.

On the 29th of March, 1647, Adrian Pav, Sr. de Heemstede, one of the Plenipotentiaries of the United Provinces at Munster, having sent the Secretary of the Embassy to the Duke of Longueville, to know the Hour of his Conveniency to receive the Visit he intended to make him. The Duke told the Secretary, That the King his Master had forbid him having any Commerce with the Sieur de Heemstede, because it was he that had oblig'd the other Plenipotentiaries, his Colleagues, to sign the seventy Articles which had been concerted with the Ministers of Spain. That he every where gave Proofs of his ill Will to France, and particularly in a Writing he had sent to the States General, where he had endeavour'd to misrepresent, by his Lies, the Justice of the Complaints of the Ministers of France, and to put a bad Construction on their Intentions. That it was he also that had sent to the Hague a Writing of the Spaniards, which was a kind of Manifesto against France. And that all his Letters were fill'd with Gall against the Government, and against the Nation. The French publish'd at that time very bitter things against the Sr. de Heemsted, and their Books speak of him after such a manner, that they might injure his Memory if they did not mingle therein so much Passion.

One of the things that most hinders Embassadors from paying one another Civilities, is the Contest they have concerning the Honours and the Rank, not only on Account of the Competition of their Masters, but sometimes also by Reason of some Pretensions they have amongst themselves. The Embassadors of the United Provinces, and of Savoy, would make no Difficulty to pay one another the same Civilities, but they do not visit, because they could not see one another in a third Place, without disputing the Rank, concerning which their Masters are not agreed among themselves. The Embassador of Savoy and M. Van Omeren saw one another in a third Place in Switzerland, because this last not having the representing Character, he ow'd the Place of Honour to the other. It is very likely he would not have seen him at all, if he had not been oblig'd thereto on the Score of the Interest of the Inhabitants of the Valleys of Piedmont. The Elector of Bavaria's Plenipotentiary offer'd to make a Visit to the Plenipotentiaries of Sweden at Osnaburg, but Oxenstiern would not admit him, nor acknowledge his Master for Elector. It was not till three Years after that he receiv'd the Visit of the Minister of Bavaria, and that, at the Instance of the French Plenipotentiaries, who were Protectors of the Interests of Bavaria, as the Elector was the Solicitor of those of France.

This is not to say, but there are some Measures to be observ'd in the Countries they do to one another, or to the Ministers of the Place where they reside. Sir William Temple coming to the Hague in the Year 1668, in the Quality of Embassador Extraordinary, had Orders from the King of England to give the Hand to the Prince of Orange every where, even at his Highness's House, and at his Table. Which was by so much the more reasonable, that as the Prince was the King's Nephew, the Embassador ought to respect him as a Prince of the Blood of England, and as such could not do him too much Honour. In the Year 1674 he had procur'd another Order, which was not so reasonable, nor so easy to be executed. He was commanded to yield at Home the Place of Honour to the Counsellor Pensionary of Holland. Sir William Temple had already at that time publish'd his Remarks on the State of the United Provinces. So that it is to be wonder'd at, that he would suffer his Instructions to be clogg'd with an Article which might have been the Cause of infinite Disorders.

The Embassadors of crown'd Heads do not at Home give Place to the Ministers of the second Order, nor to the Deputies of the States General, nor to the States of Holland, unless they are particularly deputed from their respective Bodies. The Counsellor Pensionary has two Qualities, the one of Minister of the States of Holland, and the other of Deputy of the same Province to the States General. In the first he is the last of all the Assembly, and in the other he takes Place but after all the Deputies of Guelders and of Holland, and he his only the Step before all the Deputies of the five other Provinces. So that the Embassador cannot do him any Honour that the Deputies of Gelderland and Holland may not claim by the Way of Preference, and those of the other Provinces by Equality.

The Counsellor Pensionary of Zeeland, and all the Ministers, who under other Qualities
I i i   discharge

difcharge the fame Functions in the other Provinces, have the fame Pretenfions and the fame Rights so that the Embaffador not being able to refufe to the one, what he grants to the other, he ought to be very cautious in Reference to thefe Civilities more efpecially fince the Minifter of the fecond Order, who does not give place to the Counfellor Penfionary, may require them with more Juftice than he

CHAP. XXIII.

Of the Apparel and Expences of the Embaffador.

IF the Apparel and Expence of the Embaffador do not make a Part, they are at leaft a Confequence of the Civilities, which have been fpoken to in the foregoing Chapters, nay there are fome that would be defective, if the Apparel were wanting We have feen in one of the firft Courts of *Europe*, an Embaffador, who coming from his Kitchin Fire, was not afham'd to fhew himfelf without a Band, and in his Slippers, to Officers who came to him from the King No body can deny, but it was a very great Incivility Thefe Men difgrace their Character as well as their Sovereign, who ought never to give thefe eminent Employments to ill-bred Perfons, who do not fo much is know the very Rules of true Civility The Embaffador ought not to appear, nor fhew himfelf to thofe who have any thing to negotiate with him, till he is in a fuitable Condition, and drefs'd The late *M d'Avaux*, who knew fo well how to act the Embaffador, was fo punctual in this, that except thofe that ferv'd him in his Chamber, not one of his Domefticks faw him, till he was in the Condition, in which he receiv'd his moft folemn Vifits He never went out of his Chamber till he had his Cloke on, and he did not quit it till he return'd thither to go to Bed

As I am of Opinion that it is not neceffary the Embaffador fhould make himfelf known by his Clothes, becaufe his Character diftinguifhes him fufficiently, and that if he has a Mind to make an Appearance he may do it in his Retinue, and in the Expence of his Table, fo neither would I altogether condemn the Sentiment of thofe, who are for having all Perfons of Quality to make known the Difference thereof by the Diverfity of their Clothes It is what is almoft every where feen, there being no Countrey hardly, where the Habit does not diftinguifh the Officers of Juftice and Polity For although in *France* the Gown of Serge, and the fquare Cap, does not diftinguifh the Prefident from the Ufher, yet they notify that they are both Officers of Juftice It muft be acknowledg'd, that a grave Habit becomes a Magiftrate who is to regulate our Manners, and as it is his Bufinefs to prevent and fupprefs Luxury, with which the State might be infected, fo ought he to be an Example of Modefty to others, and not make himfelf ridiculous by light Perrukes, by Points of *Venice*, or of *Spain*, nor adorn himfelf with Robes of a ftrip'd, figur'd Work, and fo gay as not to be tolerable in Women, unlefs they are Young, or Coquets It is ftill more unfeemly to fee, in an Affembly met together on Important Affairs of State, fome Deputies, who inftead of appearing in a grave Habit, go thither without a Cloke, their Hats cock'd, with a Cane or Wand in their Hand, and in fuch a Condition as would be fhameful to the Clerks of a fubaltern Court

As for Embaffadors, I fhall firft of ferve that for the moft part they drefs themfelves after the Manner of the Countrey where they are employ'd, which muft be underftood particularly of Embaffadors Refidents, or in Ordinary There are only thofe of *Spain*, who efteeming their Fafhion to be better than all others, have fome Difficulty to accuftom themfelves to that of other Nations and it is not thought ftrange at *Rome*, *Venice*, *Turin*, nor at *Vienna* The *Mufcovites*, the *Poles*, and the other People who drefs after the *Afiatick* Manner, have no Minifters in Ordinary at the Court of the other Princes of Chriftendom

All the others drefs after the *French* Manner, or in a Mode that comes very near it *Julius Mazarin*, while he was ftill but a Negotiator, had Clothes of all Fafhions and as he fuited himfelf with an admirable Dexterity to the Humour of all forts of Perfons, he was alfo for fhewing himfelf Complaifant to all the Courts where he was employ'd, by imitating them in their Drefs, that he might appear a *Frenchman* with the *French*, a *Spaniard* with the *Spaniards*, &c Philip de Commines fays, that *Galeas de St Severin*, whom *Lewis Sforza* fent to *Charles* VIII, King of *France*, at his Arrival at Court, drefs'd himfelf after the *French* Manner, and ftruck into all the Gallantries of the Times The Embaffador who fhould appear at the Court of *France* in a ftrange Habit, would be fure to be gaz'd at by the *French*, and efpecially by the Ladies, but he would not thereby procure to himfelf the Efteem of neither the one, nor the other He that is willing to pafs for a Stranger in the Countrey where he negotiates, is willing alfo to be thought to have fomething fingular in his Mind, is well as in his Clothes Philip II, King of *Spain*, was not of a very complaifant Humour, and he had never been feen to drefs after the *Portuguefe* Fafhion, notwithftanding his Mother was, yet neverthelefs when he went to Lifbon, after the Conqueft of the Kingdom of *Portugal*, he would not appear there like the King of *Caftile*, but that he might render himfelf lefs difagreeable to the *Portuguefe*, he drefs'd himfelf after the Manner of the Countrey

As for the Colour and Trimming of their Clothes, Embaffadors act therein according to their Inclination, obferving always that Decency

cency that suits their Age, their Profession, and their Character, and dressing agreeably to the Occasions they are to be present at. There are Embassadors, that make one part of the Embassy to consist in a foolish Ostentation of the Grandeur of their Master, which they pretend to represent in their Apparel and Retinue, either to flatter the Humour of the Prince, or to gratify their own Vanity. It is not thereby that the Strength of a State is known, nor the true Magnificence of a Monarch. It is well known that they are all equally Sovereigns, but it is as well known that they are not all equally Powerful. We have seen them that were least so, affect the greatest Expences, even in those Courts, where it was well known, that the Minister did it, out of the Subsidies his Prince receiv'd from them. *Spain* is very Powerful, but it cannot be deny'd, that the Humour of the Nation is for making it appear still more Powerful than it really is. Its Embassies are Magnificent, and if I may be allow'd to say so, rather *really Sumptuous*. They that have been for imitating them, have not come near them. *Rome* has seen an Embassador of *Spain*, who, to accompany the Pope, (who was going to divert himself in the Countrey) had in his Equipage six Litters, as many Coaches with six Horses, two hundred Footmen, and threescore Waggons of Baggage. It was the Opinion of *France*, that the Plempotentiaries of *Sweden* would not come to *Munster*, lest the Splendor of the *French* Embassy, should outshine all the Expence *Sweden* could propose to be at: but the *French* were undeceiv'd, when at their Arrival at *Osnabrug*, they saw the *Sweaes* appear with so much Pomp and Magnificence, that nothing was to be seen like it at *Munster*. The Embassadors of *Sweden* made no Visit of Ceremony, but in the Queen's Coach, twelve Guards clad in Liveries, and arm'd with Halbards, went on both sides of the Coach, and before it march'd several Gentlemen, with a great Number of Pages and Footmen, having with them four Trumpetters and a Kettle-drum, which made themselves be heard, both going and coming.

The Duke of *Chevreuse*, who after the Marriage of the Queen of *England*, had Orders to conduct her, provided himself with the most glorious Equipage that had been ever seen in *France*. All the Men in Livery were clad in Crimson Velvet, with Sattin Waistcoats, except the Pages, whose Wastcoats were of Gold Brocade, as well as the Lining of their Clokes, which were cover'd with several Rowes of Gold and Silver Embroidery, so rich, and so clogg'd with these two Metals, that they were not able to serve, but only at a Ceremony of two or three Hours. The Footmen's Great Coats, and the Clokes of the Coachmen and Postillions were not less rich, and the Mules hardly wanted any other Burthen, so heavy was the Embroidery of their Capparisons. His Buffet of Vermillion gilt and carv'd, was compos'd of Basons, Barrels, Fountains, small Vats, and other Vessels of an extraordinary Weight; so that as they could not be of use even to a Sovereign, but on Occasions that very rarely or never happen, Cardinal *Mazarin* prevail'd with the King to buy what was left of it, for a Present, with some other fine Furniture, to the deceased King of *Sweden*. The *Chevalier de Terlon*, one of the Gentlemen of the Cardinal's Retinue, was the Person that was sent with it, and it was in this Employment, that he made himself so well known to that King, that he procur'd him the Quality of Embassador. The Cardinal never spoke of the Violence that had been done him, in obliging him to give the Representing Character to *Terlon*, but with the utmost Indignation. The Count *de la Garde*, the present Chancellor of *Sweden*, was in the Year 1646, sent into *France*, to thank the King and the Queen Regent for their Mediation, which had procur'd a Peace between the two Northern Crowns. The Subject of his Embassy was only a Compliment, and yet never any Embassador of *Sweden* appear'd with so magnificent a Retinue, nor ever made so fine an Expence.

Prelates, and Men of the Gown, when employ'd in Embassies, ought to be cloth'd in such manner, that their Profession may be known by their Garb. So likewise a Prince, a Grandee, or any other Person that wears the Sword, will always do himself Honour, by joyning to the Marks of his Embassy, those of his Profession. It is when they ought not to fail in, in Ceremonies and solemn Visits. When the Nuncio makes his first Visit to a Prince, or an Embassador, he ought to do it with his Rochet and Camail. Wherefore the Nuncio at *Venice*, who had been at M. *de Freyni*'s in his ordinary Dress, was in the right to say, that he had visited the Embassadrix, and not the Embassador. *Julius Mazarin*, being Nuncio Extraordinary in *France*, in the Year 1634, had a Dispute with the Prince of *Conae*, who being arriv'd at *Paris* after *Mazarin*, made some Difficulty to visit him first. They at last agreed, that this should go and see the Princess, and accordingly he did, but in his usual Habit. The Prince was there, and afterwards visited the Nuncio, who then return'd his Visit in his Rochet and Camail. He wore them also when he visited *Mademoiselle*: but in visiting the other Princesses, he had only his Cloke and Cassock. Cardinal *Richelieu* being inform'd that Cardinal *Bichi*, who was coming to take his Leave of him, and to present to him the Nuncio *Bolognetti*, his Successor, was in his Ceremonial Dress, he also put on his Pontifical Habit, and it was in this Garb that he receiv'd, and visited the Elector *Palatin* in the Year 1640. *Fabio Chigy*, who was Nuncio at *Munster*, receiv'd the Visits of the Embassadors of crown'd Heads, and of the first Plenipotentiaries of the Electors, in his Rochet and *Camail*, with his square Cap. In his other Visits he wore only the Camail, reserving the Rochet for Ecclesiastical Functions. When he made a Visit to the Chief of Embassies, he put on the Camail, the short Cloke, and Hat. He did not visit the other Plenipotentiaries till he had receiv'd theirs, and he receiv'd them but in his ordinary Habit, with his Night-Gown and square Cap. It is what the Clergy ought to be very exact in, as Cardinal *Dossat* observes very particularly, in the Visits he receiv'd and return'd at *Venice*, when he was sent thither in the Year 1598, being yet but a Prelate. He says, that being at *Venice*, when he receiv'd the Nuncio, and the

the Embaſſador of *Spain*, he receiv'd them with the Rochet and the little Cloke. And that Cardinal *Prioly*, Patriarch of *Venice*, making a Visit to *Doſſat*, had the same Habit that the Cardinals are us'd to wear when they go to the Pope. Here I shall take notice, that in *France* the Bishops do not use the *Mantelet* or little Cloke, as they do in *Italy*, but only the *Camail*. It is what all other Embaſſadors ought also to observe in all solemn Visits, as well active as paſſive, those of the Gown not to be without their Caſſocks, and long Cloke, or at least to be in a neat and decent Habit, and the military Men to have their Swords by their Side. The Duke of *Longueville*, intending to make the first Visit to the Emperor's Embaſſadors, pretended to take his Guards with him, but the Count de *Naſſau*, who had none, signify'd to him by the Mediators, That if the Duke brought his Guards with him, he should not be admitted. The having Guards is the Mark of a Superiority, which Embaſſadors do not acknowledge amongst themselves. Cardinal de *Richelieu* had his Guards, but when the King went to see him, the Captain of the King's Guards diſarm'd those of the Cardinal, and lock'd up their Arms, and did not restore the key thereof till the King was gone.

There are some Occasions where it is neceſſary that the Embaſſador should make an extraordinary Appearance in his Garb, as well as in his Retinue. In Embaſſies of Obedience, and in all others where the Embaſſador is oblig'd to aſſiſt at Aſſemblies, and solemn Ceremonies, he is also oblig'd to do Honour there, as well to the Prince he serves as to him to whom he is sent. The Embaſſador of *Venice*, of whom we have spoken elsewhere, being sensible that he should be invited to the Wedding of the Elector *Palatin*, and of the Princess of *England*, put his Servants into very fine new Liveries, to do Honour to his Republick as well as to the new marry'd Couple. The Earl of *Carliſle* and the Lord *Kensington*, who had negotiated the Marriage of the late King and Queen of *England*, appear'd there in Suits of Cloth of beaten Silver, their Hats and Clokes being adorn'd with precious Stones. The Baron de *Languerac*, Embaſſador of the United Provinces in *France*, was invited to aſſiſt at this Ceremony, but he was given to understand that he must lay aside his Mourning, and appear in such Clothes as would do Honour to the marry'd Couple.

Thus, on the Occaſion of a Mourning, the Embaſſador cannot avoid conforming, whether the Court where he resides gives it him, or that his Master is at the Expence thereof. But this is what requires a great deal of Caution. For besides the Diſtinction that ought to be made between the Persons for whom the Mourning is put on, the Embaſſador ought not to give it to those of his Domeſticks that wear Liveries, except it be for the Death of the Prince that employs him. On other Occaſions it ought not to go beyond his Person, and those of his Retinue that are allow'd to accompany him into the Antechamber. The greatest Mournings of a Court are not of long Duration, and as Princes conſole themselves easily, the Embaſſador ought not to affect to seem more afflicted than those of the Countrey.

King *Henry* IV, when he sent the Marquiſs de *Rosny* to *London*, to complement King *James* on his Acceſſion to the Crown of *England*, order'd him to appear in Mourning at his first Audience, becauſe he was alſo to make a Complement of Condolence on the Death of Queen *Elizabeth*. In pursuance of this Order, all the Lords and Gentlemen of the Embaſſador's House had put on Mourning the Day he was to receive Audience. But foraſmuch, as since the King's Arrival in *England*, not one *English* Man had appear'd before him in Mourning, the *English* Nobility (who were apprehensive that the Marquiſs, by appearing in that Condition, would in some meaſure reproach the Ingratitude to the Memory of the Queen, who was the greatest and best Princeſs that had ever wore a Crown) were ſo uneaſy'd thereat. They therefore signify'd to the Embaſſador, that the King, to whom the ſame Reproach might be made, as well as to all the Court, would take it very ill. So that the Embaſſador chang'd his Cloaths, and after his Example the Lords and Gentlemen of his Retinue chang'd theirs likewise.

The Dutcheſs of *Bar*, Sister to King *Henry* IV, being dead, all the Embaſſadors went into Mourning, and appear'd in that Condition before the King, to complement him on his Affliction. This Princeſs had made Profeſſion of the Proteſtant Religion ever since she was born, and would never apoſtatize notwithstanding all the Pope's Endeavours to that Purpoſe. This was the Reaſon why the Nuncio would not go into Mourning. The King let him word, that he might do as he pleaſ'd, but then he deſir'd he would forbear ſeeing him till the Mourning was over.

The Embaſſadors of *Venice* do not go into Mourning for the Death of their Doge, becauſe he is not the Sovereign, but only the first of their Republick. For which Reaſon the Senate aſſiſts at his Funeral Service in their Scarlet Gowns, and a Succeſſor is choſen in so few Days, that there is not Leiſure to make a Reflection on the Loſs the Republick has thereby sustain'd. The Chancellor of *France* never goes into Mourning, becauſe the King does not die in *France*, where *Death gives Seſſion to the Living*. So that there is no Interval between the Deceaſe of the one, and the Succeſſion of the other.

The ſaid Embaſſadors of *Venice* are commonly cloath'd in black, and they are always ſo when they receive Audience. And that they may appear with the greater Gravity, and like Senators, they quit the Cloke to take the Veſt, which is a ſort of Gown something like thoſe of the Councillors of State in *France*, which thoſe of the Court of Judicature in *Holland* imitate in ſome manner, except that theſe are ſomewhat ſhorter, and within ſome Years of Tabby, which is a Wear too airy and grave for the Councillors of the Preſidial. The Embaſſadors of crown'd Heads may wear a Sword at Audiences. And this is what has been done by thoſe who are not of the Profeſſion.

As the Religious that is diſguis'd loſes the Privilege and Exemption from secular Juriſdiction, ſo the Embaſſador diſguis'd derogates from his Character, and cannot enjoy the Protection of the *Law of Nations*. I do not here

here speak of the Embaſſador, who was found in his Court ready arm'd, becauſe the Officers of Juſtice could not be ignorant of his Quality but of the Embaſſador, that is found out of the Place of his Function and Reſidence, in a Dreſs very unſuitable to his Employment *M de Lanſac de St Gelais*, who had been Embaſſador at *Trent*, and who was ſo at *Rome* on the Part of *France*, receiv'd the King's Orders to go to *Siena* and to take upon him the Direction of Affairs, in the Abſence of *Strozzi* and *Maninc*, of whom the one was wounded, and the other was ſick. *Coſmus*, Duke of *Florence*, had ſo well poſſeſs'd himſelf of all the Avenues of the Town, that *Lanſac*, who was at *Mont-Alcino*, ſeeing there was no likelihood of getting in, diſguis'd himſelf like a Soldier, and ſet forwards with Guides, who deliv'r'd him into the Hands of the Enemy. *Don Franciſco* of *Toledo*, and *Don John Manriques*, who commanded the *Spaniſh* Troops, ſent him to *St Miniato*, and were for interrogating him formally upon the Intelligence the Prince of *Salerna* held in the Kingdom of *Naples*. In oppoſition to this, he did not alledge his Quality of Embaſſador, but inſiſted on his being a Priſoner of War. The King his Maſter reclaim'd him, and pretended to have him conſider'd, as if he ſtill manag'd the Affairs of *France* at *Rome*, becauſe he had not been recall'd, nor had not taken his Audience of Leave of the Pope. But for all this, he was not treated as an Embaſſador, and was ſet at Liberty, not by Virtue of the *Law of Nations* but by the Way of Exchange for *Aſcagne de la Corgne*. The *Spaniards*, to excuſe the Violence they offer'd, after the Battel of *Pavia*, to *Alexander* the Pope's Nuncio, alledg'd, that he was not in a becoming Habit, and that they did not know him. They did not ſpeak truth but however *Lanſac* could by no Means reclaim the Protection of the *Law of Nations* which the Pope could not ſecure to a diſguis'd Miniſter, who had been made a Priſoner out of the Eccleſiaſtical State and he could not hope for it from the King, while he was in the Hands of his Enemies, who might treat him as a Priſoner of War, even tho' he had not been diſguis'd. The Example of *Philip* of *Drenx*, Biſhop of *Beauvais*, ſufficiently ſhews, that there is no Right nor Privilege, that protects or favours diſguis'd Perſons.

After the Deceaſe of *Philip* of *Auſtria*, King of *Caſtile*, the Grandees of that Kingdom made a thouſand Cabals and Intrigues againſt *Ferdinand the Catholick*, who pretended to, and obtain'd at laſt the Government of that Kingdom, during the Indiſpoſition of the Queen his Daughter, and the Minority of *Charles* his Grandſon. Several of thoſe Grandees held Intelligence with the Emperor *Maximilian* I, who as Father to *Philip*, and Grandfather to *Charles*, pretended to the Guardianſhip of his Perſon, and to the Adminiſtration of his Kingdom, during his Minority. He kept for that Purpoſe a Correſpondence in *Caſtile*, whither he ſent in the Year 1508, *Don Pedro de Guevarra*, who having diſguis'd himſelf like a Footman, and put himſelf in the Retinue of another Nobleman, was diſcover'd, and taken at the Entrance into the Kingdom, by the Guards of the Frontiers. *Ferdinand* having cauſ'd him to be brought to the Caſtle of *Simancas*, had him put upon the Rack, and thereby extorted from him the Secret of all the Emperor's Intelligence with the Grandees of *Caſtile*, and eſpecially with the Great Captain, *Don Gonſales Ferdinandes* of *Cordoba*. *Maximilian* was ſo incens'd at the ill Treatment of his Miniſter, that he was for taking up all the *Spaniards* that were in *Antwerp*, and the other Towns of *Flanders*, and was near coming to a Rupture. But *Ferdinand* ſaid, that he could not be found fault with, for having proceeded in that Manner againſt a Man, who had been taken in a Habit, that gave reaſon to ſuſpect, he came rather to diſturb the Peace of the Kingdom, than to labour a good Correſpondence between the two Kings. Beſides, that he had no *Credentials*, nor any other Mark of a publick Miniſter.

In the ſecond Chapter Notice is taken of that Embaſſador who play'd ſo extravagant a Part in the Commotions of the City of *Naples*. They are one of the moſt remarkable Parts of the Hiſtory of thoſe Times, which particularly obſerves, that the Marquiſs de *Fonteney*, Embaſſador from *France* at *Rome*, gave the ſame Quality to *Lewis del Ferro*, impowering him to diſcharge the Function thereof with the pretended Republick of *Naples*, and gave him the Title of Excellency. This ſham Miniſter being inform'd that the Duke of *Guiſe* (who was arriv'd at *Naples*) was in Conference with *Gennaro Annuſe*, cauſ'd the Chamber Door to be open'd to him, as to the Embaſſador of *France*. He had no Hat, but two Pair of Beads about his Neck, one whereof he ſaid was to pray for the King of *France*, and the other for the People of *Naples*, and held his naked Sword in his Hand, and look'd more like one broke out of a Mad-Houſe, than a Miniſter. As ſoon as he perceiv'd the Duke, he flung his Sword away, and proſtrating himſelf on the Ground, he went and kiſs'd his Feet, and ſo eagerly embrac'd his Knees, that the Duke had ſome Difficulty to get rid of him. The Duke had Letters from *M de Fontenay* for this Embaſſador, but ſeeing a Man who had neither the Apparel, nor the Looks of one, he was dubious whether he ſhould deliver them to him or not. However, taking into Conſideration, that it was this Mad-man who had ſet all the People of *Naples* a madding, and had oblig'd them to have recourſe to the Protection of *France*, and the Aſſiſtance of the Duke himſelf, he reſolv'd to preſent them to him, and to do him Civility. The next Day he accompany'd the Duke to Maſs, carrying his Sword drawn before him, and bare Headed, having on a Perruke of Horſe-Hair, like thoſe the Furies wear in a Comedy. This chimerical Embaſſador, who was employ'd to a revolted Populace, by Virtue of a ridiculous Commiſſion, was in an Equipage ſutable to his Quality, and in a decent Habit.

It is Judgment that muſt regulate the Habit, the Livery, and the Expence of the Embaſſador. Such extraordinary Occaſions as thoſe I above mention'd, may and ought to excite him to do ſomething extraordinary eſpecially when Princes are employ'd, or Perſons of an eminent Quality, tho' they themſelves are liable to ſtrike into Exceſſes, as well as others. The Duke

Duke of *Paſtrana*, who came into *France* in the Year 1612, on Account of the double Marriage, had forty Pages cloth'd in Gold Brocade. The King himſelf had not ſo many, nor ſo richly clad, on the Day of his Marriage; neither is there any Monarch that will be at ſuch an Expence, unleſs it be for a Carouſel, or ſome other Diverſion of that Nature. The Duke of *Clevrenſe* was ſo inconvenienc'd by the Expence he was at in his Journey to *England*, that he felt it as long as he liv'd. It was neceſſary that his Table ſhould anſwer the Magnificence of the Clothes and Liveries; and it is what all Embaſſadors ought to take care of, who ſhould conſider, that the Honour of the Prince is in a manner proſtituted by ſo injudicious an Expence, and ſo heedleſs a Profuſion, even tho' it coſts his Maſter nothing. The publick Miniſter who obſerves others, is watch'd himſelf in his Turn, and cannot procure an Approbation of the Choice the Prince has made of him, but by a regular and ſteady Conduct. There have been Embaſſadors, who after a child iſh Diſſipation of their Subſtance, have been reduc'd to pawn their Plate, and even the Preſent that has been made them, which caus'd the Emouſſador to look little, and did no great Honour to his Maſter.

The Embaſſador that is irregular and extravagant in his Expences, tho' he bears the Charge himſelf, does ſometimes for ill that, prejudice the Service of his Prince. Amongſt the other Advantages the *Turks* obtain'd over the *Poles* by the Peace of *Chocem* in the Year 1623, the King of *Poland* oblig'd himſelf to ſend an Embaſſador Extraordinary, and to entertain one in Ordinary at *Conſtantinople* Chriſtopher *Zvarauſky*, who was nominated to the Embaſſy Extraordinary, appear'd there with a Retinue of Four hundred Perſons and was at ſo prodigious an Expence, that when *Sigiſmund* ſent thither in the Year 1630, *Alexander Piaſeczinſky*, the *Turks* would not at firſt acknowledge him for an Embaſſador, but conſider'd him only as a Letter-bearer, or at moſt but as a Miniſter of the ſecond Order, becauſe he had not wherewith to be at the ſame Expence. *Zbarauſky* had been at

The Trouble this gave to *Piaſeczianſky* at the beginning of his Negotiation, ſufficiently diſcover'd the Prejudice the exorbitant Expences of the other had done to his Maſter's Affairs. For which Reaſon Princes ſhould do well to reflect thereon, and regulate both the Equipage, and Expences of their Embaſſadors, which in effect add nothing to the true Grandeur of the Maſter.

Thoſe Princes who ſuffer Miniſters of the ſecond Order to be more Expenſive, than a well regulated Court would allow an Embaſſador to be, are not well adviſ'd. It is ſufficient that they who are not *Repreſentants* in the laſt Degree, have wherewith to ſubſiſt honourably, ſo as to do their Prince Credit, regulate their Equipage and Houſe in ſuch a Manner, as may diſtinguiſh them from private Perſons, and be an Inducement to the Prince, to advance them to other Employments, and recompence their Services. It is one of the Things Princes ought to be moſt careful of, ſince if they do not allow them honourable Salaries, and do not take particular Care to have them punctually paid, they cannot do themſelves Honour by them, nor receive thoſe Services from them, which they might otherwiſe reaſonably expect. The Miniſter who is ſtraiten'd in his Allowance, and is thereby oblig'd to employ all his Thoughts on the Means how to ſubſiſt, cannot labour with Application in the Affairs of his Maſter, who neglects him, as *Walſingham* very well repreſents in the Letter he writes to *Cecil*, on the 14th of *March*, 1571. Moreover the Miniſter ſo neglected is ſometimes reduc'd to Deſpair, an Inſtance whereof we have in that Reſident of *Brandenburg*, who having once been made a Priſoner for Debt, was forc'd to deſert, and eſpouſe the Intereſt of his Maſter's Foemies, that he might not incur the ſame Fate another time or at leaſt he is expos'd to Temptations capable of corrupting his Fidelity.

The Embaſſador ought to be well aſſur'd of the punctual Payment of his Salary before he takes the Employment upon him. But I muſt confeſs, that that was abſolutely impoſſible under the Miniſtry of Cardinal *Mazarin*. Amongſt the Funds that are ſettl'd in *France* at the beginning of the Year, that for the Embaſſadors is one of the Firſt, after the Expence of the King's Houſhold notwithſtanding which few Embaſſadors were paid, and not one punctually.

After the two Plenipotentiaries of the Crowns had ſign'd the *Pirenean* Treaty, the Mareſchal *de Grammont* was ſent to *Madrid*, to demand the *Infanta*, whoſe Marriage was the chief Article of the Treaty. He went Poſt thither, but altho' he rode the Journey like a Courier, that did not hinder him from being it a vaſt Expence at *Madrid*, and having a very magnificent Equipage. Herein he follow'd his own Humour, but that he might do ſomething the more, the Cardinal bid him ſpare nothing, and that he ſhould have wherewithal. That Miniſter was very prodigal of thoſe ſort of Promiſes, when he could find People that would believe him. This puts me in Mind of a Paſſage that happen'd in the Year 1652, betwixt him, and a Gentleman whoſe Name was *Gentillot*, and was well enough known in *Holland*, where he was Lieutenant Colonel of a Regiment of Foot. He was a very good Officer, and a Man of Honour, but I have not been ſufficiently acquainted with him, to be able to ſay whether he was alſo an able Negotiator. However Cardinal *Mazarin* thought fit to employ him in this Quality to *Cromwell*. During his Reſidence at *London*, he wrote to the Cardinal, that ſome Merchants had offer'd him to get Succours and Ammunition into *Dunkirk*, which was beſieg'd by the *Spaniards*; and that they requir'd for that Purpoſe but only the Sum of twenty thouſand Crowns. The Cardinal thank'd *Gentillot* very civilly for the important Service, and added, that he muſt not ſtick there, but that he ought to endeavour to raiſe that Sum, and ranſack his Pockets, or thoſe of his Friends, and that he would take care he ſhould be reimburs'd very ſpeedily. *Gentillot*, who was of *Guyenne*, and had finiſh'd his Accompliſhments in *Holland*, reply'd, That of Neceſſity his Eminency muſt not have known him very well, when he ſent him into *England*. That he was no Merchant, to be able to furniſh

nish twenty thousand Crowns out of his own Pocket, or by his Credit But even if he had both the one and the other, he must be thought a very great Fool, if he was suppos'd to be capable of advancing a Penny on his Eminency's Word

The Salaries the Republick of *Venice* allows its Embassadors, are very moderate, but they are settl'd, so that they know what they have to trust to, and what they can afford to spend They have what is necessary, and supply the superfluous Part out of their own, in hopes thereby to advance themselves to greater Dignities at home, and to more important Employments abroad The United Provinces allow Eighteen thousand Livres to the Embassadors in Ordinary, which they are paid very punctually The Extraordinaries know what they can expend a Day, and their Retinue is regulated according to a formal Resolution of the States for that purpose However, it is not so strictly observ'd, but that sometimes it is alter'd for particular Considerations France allows Six thousand Crowns to the Embassadors in Ordinary, and Twelve thousand to the Extraordinaries When Sir *William Temple* went to the *Hague* in the Year 1674, he had a hundred Pounds Sterling *per* Week, besides a very rich Buffet of Plate with the King of *Great Brittain*'s Arms upon it So that there was not any other Embassador's Table where so much was to be seen, nor that was cover'd with such large Dishes, and such fine Contrivances for Fruit and for Sweet meats When Cardinal *Aldobrandin* went Legate into *France*, in the Year 1600, he had a thousand Crowns *per Diem* to spend, besides the Revenue of his Benefices The King of *Spain* also allows his Embassadors and Ministers very well, though they are not always very punctually paid The Viceroy of *Naples* is oblig'd to pay those of *Rome*, *Venice*, and *Turin*

The Duke and the Cardinal *de Guise*, having a mind to remove the Princes of the Blood from Court, after the Death of *Henry* II, procur'd the Prince of *Condè* a Commission to go to *Spain*, in the quality of Embassadol Extraordinary, to be present at the Oath King *Philip* was to take for the Observation of the Peace The Cardinal who had the Direction of the Finances, order'd him a thousand Crowns to defray his Journey The Prince was very much shorten'd in his Affairs, and the same Sum would have been given to a Courrier, that had been sent so long a Journey, so that the Prince could not provide himself with an Equipage suitable to his Quality and Employment, without ruining himself, and without one, he must appear contemptible at the Court of *Spain* The Cardinal, who was not afraid of procuring an Affront to a Prince of the Blood, and who so little valu'd the Honour of an Embassador of *France*, prostituted that of the King and Crown

A Man of Parts, who with his Capacity has also a little Courage and Birth, will not willingly take upon him an Embassy, nor will not serve at his own Expences, unless the evil State of his Master's Affairs, and his own Zeal, oblige him to serve without any Regard to his own Interest for the present, in expectation of an infallible Reward hereafter Otherwise a Prince who has not wherewith to subsist his Minister, will be necessitated to employ the first that shall offer himself, and such Persons as are willing to purchase a false Honour at the Expence of the true Reputation of their Master A strange Havock was made of the Revenues of the Crown during the whole Reign of *Henry* III King of *France* All the Money he extorted from his Subjects, by an infinite number of Edicts, went into the Purse of his Favourites, as into an Abyss So that there never were any Funds for the necessary Expences, and particularly for those of Embassadors, which was the Cause, that for want of Persons of Merit and Quality, those Employments were given to such as had neither the one nor the other Of this Number was *Germigny de Germoles*, to whom the King gave the Embassy of *Constantinople*, as a Post which no Body but himself would accept of, without a Salary And truly he acquited himself very ill thereof, and particularly in an Occasion where he ought necessarily to have appear'd to preserve the King's Rank In the Year 1582, *Selim* II Emperor of the *Turks*, intending to circumcise his Son *Mahomet*, who was sixteen Years of Age, invited all the Embassadors who were at *Constantinople*, to be Spectators of the publick Ceremonies, which were to be previous to those of the Circumcision which was perform'd in the Sultan's Chamber, by the Bashaw *Mahomet*, who had formerly been *Selim*'s Barber All the Embassadors were present at the publick Ceremonies, except him of *France* The Author that has publish'd a Relation of those Ceremonies, is mistaken when he says, that the *French* Embassador would not be present thereat, because he would not give place to the Emperor *Rodulphus*'s Minister, which is not true, for the Embassador of *France* is the first of all Embassadors at *Constantinople*, the Emperor's being there consider'd but as the Embassador of the King of *Hungary* Germigny ought to have appear'd notwithstanding the Presence of the Embassador of *Poland*, because his Absence did not hinder this from being there, and he thereby gave the first Place to *Rodolphus*'s Embassador *Henry* III always took the Quality of King of *Poland*, as well as that of King of *France*, for which Reason *Germigny* would not be present at a publick Assembly with another Embassador of *Poland*

The Embassador Extraordinary cannot well avoid keeping an open Table, if he will do Honour to his Master At *Venice* a Senator is not suffer'd to have Communication with an Embassador, and in the Courts of *Rome*, *France* and *Spain*, the Ministers never make themselves so familiar with Embassadors, as to go and dine with them, unless they are invited on some extraordinary Occasion I speak of those Ministers that are of the Council, and who are concern'd in the Management of Affairs, and not of the Subalterns, as the Masters of the Ceremonies, and the Introducters of Embassadors, because these are oblig'd to visit the Embassadors sometimes, and to bear them Company at Dinner, as well out of Civility, and to do them Honour, as to try to benefit by their Conversation, from whence they may always gather something In the Courts of the North, where great Entertainments make part of the Negotiation,

tiation, this Expence is very necessary, as well as in *Holland*, where they take great Delight in Reasoning between two Trestles. The Fenns of the Country produce a multitude of Frogs. The major Part of Embassadors do not succeed therein, as well because every Body is not fit for it, as because it is contrary to the Dignity of the Character.

There are also but very few Embassadors that acquit themselves worthily of what they owe their Prince in this respect. There is none but *M. D'Estrades*, who, during the six Years of his Embassy Extraordinary in *Holland*, kept a splendid Table, magnificently and equally well serv'd, without suffering the Pretext of his Dispatches to hinder him from entertaining every Day at it, all the Persons of Quality who were willing to take part of his Good-cheer. There are some who affect a false Frugality, and others endeavour to lay up out of the Emoluments of the Embassy, but most of 'em ful therein, because the Officers they bring along with them know nothing of the matter. The Embassador's House is that of his Sovereign, and the Minister's Table ought to represent the Grandeur of his Master, by making known the honourable Salary he allows him. I have seen the Embassador Extraordinary of the most powerful Republick of *Europe*, who having been several times treated was resolv'd to give an Entertainment in his Turn. Amongst other Persons of great Quality, the Marefchals *de Chastillon* and of *la Meilleraye*, assisted thereat, but the Treat was so wretchedly fordid and pitiful, that there is not any Burgher in St *Denis*'s Street, but what treats his Neighbour or particular Friend better. And there is not any Country Wedding where they are not better serv'd. The Guests all star'd one at another, and going from this great Feast, the two Marefchals ask each the other, where they should go and dine. The same Embassador defir'd to have the King's Present in Bills of Exchange.

In the Year 1651, the Queen of *Sweden* nominated four Embassadors for the Assembly at *Lubeck*. The Count *de la Garde*, *Wachtmeister* Master of the Horse, *Salvius*, and *Rosenhan*, the two last of whom had been employ'd at the Congress of *Westphalia*. And forasmuch as the Treasury was almost exhausted, and that the Expence would have been prodigious, if they had all kept open Table, the Queen order'd, that there should be but one for the four Embassadors, and that they should be serv'd by the Officers of her Houshould, which were sent accordingly. But the Voyage and Employment of Count *de la Garde* having had no Consequence, *Salvius* would not confine himself to live in common, and so sent back the Queen's Officers.

There is another Expence which is very necessary, and which in Embassador cannot avoid. He is oblig'd to make Presents to the Officers who have serv'd and treated him in the Name of the Prince to whom he is employ'd. To the Drummers and Trumpeters, to the Coachmen and Footmen, not only on the Days of his Entry and of his Audience, but also on New-Year's Day and at solemn Feasts.

Philip de Comines says, that the Presents he had made to the Officers of the Republick of *Venice*, in his Passage through *Brescia*, *Verona*, *Vincenza*, and *Padua*, had cost him as much as if he had liv'd at his own Expences. But on these Occasions the Honour that is done to the Embassador must be consider'd, who on his part ought also to be honourable, and even magnificently so. However, Excess is here to be avoided as in all other Cases. Amongst the other Profusions, a certain Embassador was guilty of in *France*, it was observ'd that he order'd five hundred Pistoles to be given to the King's Trumpeters, who would have been very well contented with five. He deserv'd to have his ill-concerted Liberality trumpeted all over the Court, and throughout all *Europe*.

CHAP. XXIV.

Of the Competition between France *and* Spain

I Took Notice in Chapter XXII, that one of the Obstacles that hinder Embassadors from visiting one another, is the Contest they have about the Rank. They who cannot fee one another without Competition in a third Place, do not take any Pleasure neither in making one another familiar Visits.

If there had not been a War for these two last Ages, almost without Interruption, between *France* and *Spain*, which has in a manner caus'd a natural Aversion between the two Nations, and admitting that so many important and opposite Interests did not render these two Crowns almost irreconcileable, yet the Embassadors of the two Kings would never intervisit, unless they were oblig'd thereto by indispensable Devoirs. The King of *Spain* has indeed publickly declar'd by the Count *de Fuentes*, that his Embassador shall never be present in those Places where the Rank might be disputed between the two Ministers, but he has not for that oblig'd himself to yield it, nor to order his Embassador to assist at those Ceremonies where he would be oblig'd to give Place to him of *France*. On the contrary, he preserves it to himself still at *Vienna*, and his Embassador is very cautious of going to those Assemblies where that of *France* might put himself into an indisputable Possession, founded on a voluntary Cession. This is not to say that *France* is not so already, but that does not hinder the King of *Spain* from pretending that it has been unjustly adjudg'd to *France*, and he is inclin'd enough to contest it with her, if he were but able to do it

This

This Matter has been so often debated, that nothing can be added to what so many Doctors have written in the behalf of each of the Crowns. Neither is it my Intention to enter into the Discussion of their Pretensions, but only to give an historical and disinterested Narrative of what has pass'd on this Subject at *Venice*, at *Trent*, and at *Rome*. It is but since the Union of the Crowns of *Castile* and *Arragon*, and of the States and Kingdoms that depend thereon, with those of *Austria* and *Burgundy*, that the King of *Spain* thinks his Power ought to put him above the Level of all the other Princes of Christendom. And it is certain, that it was only in the Quality of Emperor, that *Charles* V had the Precedency of *Francis* I and *Henry* II Kings of *France*. At the Council of Constance, there was no Contest at all about Precedency between the Embassadors of *France* and those of the other Crowns. And on the 6*th* of *September* 1434, it was ordain'd at the Council of *Basil*, *That the Embassadors of Castile should immediately follow those of the most serene King of* France. Doctor *Medina*, and the Protonotary *Bernardin of Canasal*, being in the Year 1486 Embassadors at *Rome* from the Catholick Kings, had a warm Dispute in the Pope's Chapel, with the Embassador of *Maximilian* King of the *Romans*, about the Precedency. They had Orders (which must be well observ'd) not to pursue their Pretensions, if *Maximilian*'s Embassador took Place of him of *France*. But in case he did not precede him, not to suffer the Embassador of the King of the *Romans* to take Place of them next to the Embassador of *France*, because no Body could come between the Embassadors of *France* and *Castile*.

After the Emperor *Charles* V had abdicated, the Ministers of *France* immediately oppos'd the Pretensions of *Philip* his Son, and the first Dispute they had, was on the following Occasion *Francis ac Vargas*, who had been Embassador at *Venice* on the Part of *Charles*, had been recall'd by *Philip* as soon as *Charles* had resign'd the Imperial Dignity into the Hands of the Electors *Philip* in recalling *Vargas*, wrote to the Senate, that his Intention was to send him back in a little time, and yet he substituted *Dom N Layala* in his room. This new Comer was for maintaining himself in the Possession of what his Predecessor had enjoy'd as Embassador from the Emperor, but the Bishop of *Lodéne*, Embassador from *France*, oppos'd him so powerfully, that the other never dar'd to appear in any publick Action. When *Vargas* return'd to *Venice* in the Year 1557, he would not suffer the Senate to make him an Entry, in order to have it believ'd, that it was only a Continuation of his first Embassy, whereby he hop'd to maintain the same Rank he held while he was Embassador from the Emperor. He had taken a formal Leave of the Senate, and had receiv'd the usual Present at his Departure But admitting he had not taken his Leave, nor receiv'd the Present, and which is more, that he had not gone from *Venice*, he could not represent an Emperor that was no longer so, and who by his Abdication had annull'd the Power and Commission of his Embassador, so that *Vargas*, who could no longer act for *Charles*, could now be consider'd but as *Philip*'s Minister The Republick not being willing to offend *Spain*, endeavour'd to ease it self of the Decision of this Difference on the Pope, and in the mean time ordain'd, that the Embassadors should not appear at the publick Ceremonies, till the Difference was determin'd at *Rome* The Bishop of *Aes*, of the House of *Noailles*, who had succeeded the Bishop of *Lodéne*, made in the Month of *April*, 1558, fresh Instances to the Senate not to hinder him for the future, from assisting at the Ceremonies, and taking there the Place which was due to the Dignity of the King his Master, since *Vargas* could now no longer take the Quality of Embassador from the Emperor, since *Ferdinand* had succeeded to the Empire As soon as the two Embassadors began to contend on this Subject, the Senate order'd *Jacomo Soranzo*, its Embassador in *France*, to represent there the State of the Affair, and to endeavour to get that Court to approve of their having desir'd the *French* Embassador to refrain assisting at the Ceremonies, till such time as the Difference was regulated, but the Court would not at all acquiesce thereto Whereupon the Senate signify'd to the Bishop of *Acs*, That it was very very sorry to see the two Embassadors in this Contest, as well because their publick Acts were not honour'd by the Presence of the Ministers of two such great Monarchs, is because the Dispute was reviv'd in their State, and that it look'd as if the Decision thereof was requir'd of the Senate. That it hop'd the Difference would be made up elsewhere, and that in the mean time, the King would suffer Things to remain as they were, at least till the Ceremonial of *Rome* could be consulted about it, and the Senate be inform'd of the Practice of that Court The *French* Embassador made Answer, That he did not matter very much what the Ceremonial of *Rome* could say on that Head That his Intention was to maintain himself in the Possession of what the King his Master had enjoy'd for several Ages, yet nevertheless, he was willing not to trouble their publick Ceremonies, till those of the Ascension, at which he pretended to be present But being inform'd the next Day, that the Embassador of *Spain* had declar'd in a private Audience, which he had had that Day, *that he pretended to the Precedency, not as Embassador from the Emperor, but as Embassador from the King of* Spain He also desir'd Audience, and after that a Second, wherein he said, *That the Difference had chang'd its Nature, and that what* Vargas *had declar'd at his last Audience, being a new Pretension, of which no Mention had been made before, there was no longer Room for an Accommodation*, *but he was willing to let them know, that it was the Business of the Republick to maintain him in the Prerogative which the King his Master had been in Possession of Time immemorial, and confirm'd the Promise he had made, not to be present at publick Ceremonies till the Ascension* Some Days before this Festival, the Senate sent to desire him again to forbear this one Time, assisting at the Ceremonies, and not to force the Senate to decide a Difference which it ought not to take Cognizance of The Bishop had had Advice, that the Republick's Embassador at *Rome* had no Orders to consult the Ceremonial, but only to take notice of the Proceedings there concerning the Rank, in reference

rence to the French Embaſſador who was already there, and that of *Spain* who was ſhortly expected. He therefore proteſted he would make uſe of his Prerogative, and that he could no longer have any Deference to the Senates Deſire, to the Prejudice of the King his Maſter's poſitive Commands. The Deputies of the Senate reply'd, That it was not a Requeſt, but an Order of the Senate, which did not deſire the Embaſſador ſhould diſturb the Ceremony by his Preſence. The Embaſſador call'd together all the Domeſticks of Cardinal *Tournon*, who lodg'd with him, to be Witneſſes of the Meſſage the Senate ſent him, and gave an Account thereof to the King by his Letter of the 20th of *May*. Whereupon the King wrote to the Senate on the 11th of *June*, and gave Orders at the ſame Time to the Biſhop of *Acs* to declare to the Republick, that if ſhe continu'd any longer to make Difficulty to give him the Rank, which was his due, he would take his Audience of Leave, and retire. The Senate had already been inform'd thereof by its Embaſſador, to whom the King had explain'd himſelf, ſo that to prevent the Biſhop, in what he might ſay on that Head, it reſolv'd to ſend and deſire him to aſſiſt at the Ceremony, and at the ſolemn Proceſſion, which was to be perform'd on the Day of the Viſitation of the Virgin, where the Doge was to be accompany'd by thoſe Embaſſadors the Senate had invited. The *Spaniſh* Embaſſador was not deſir'd to be there, ſo that the Senate, by only inviting the French Embaſſador, *gave ſufficiently to be underſtood that the Precedency was adjudg'd to him*.

Lewis de Lanſac de St Gelais, of whom mention has been made in the foregoing Chapter, arriv'd at *Trent* on the 18th of *May*, 1562, in the Quality of Embaſſador from *France*. His Inſtructions, amongſt other things, contain'd alſo this, *That ſince the Spaniſh Embaſſador had diſputed with that of* France *the Rank which the King had always had, immediately after the Emperor, he was commanded not to ſuffer any other Place to be given to him or his Colleagues, either at the Council or elſewhere, or any the leaſt Alteration to be made therein, or that the Affair ſhould be ſo much as brought into Diſpute*. It was alſo enjoyn'd him, as alſo to the other Embaſſadors of *France*, *That in caſe ſo juſt a thing was refus'd them, to proteſt the Nullity of the Council, whoſe Decrees* France *would not receive in any manner whatever, to come away forthwith, and bring along with him all the* French *Prelates*. Thus it was that *Lanſac* began his Negotiation, and to give Uneaſineſs to the Legates.

The Marquiſs of *Peſcaire*, who had been at *Trent* as Embaſſador from *Philip*, but had not remain'd there long, had not only declar'd to the Legates that he would not be contented with the Place immediately after the French Embaſſadors, but he had likewiſe given them to underſtand that he would not obſtinately inſiſt on having the Precedency, but conſent to have ſome Expedient found out to modify the Matter. The Legates fearing leſt this Conteſt ſhould prove the Cauſe of great Diſorders, were for having the Pope make a Decree, That the Embaſſadors ſhould not aſſiſt at the Congregations, nor at the Seſſions, unleſs they were expreſly invited thither by one of the Meſſengers or Door-keepers of the Council, and that

the Embaſſador who ſhould appear there, with out being firſt invited thither, ſhould be oblig'd to give place to thoſe who ſhould have been invited. And foraſmuch as it concerned the Reputation of the Council, as well as that of the Embaſſadors, to have them all nam'd in the Acts, as well the Abſent as the Preſent, it was thought adviſeable to name them in the ſame Order that they arriv'd at *Trent*. But the French rejected theſe Overtures, as well as all the others that might render their Right problematical, or could ſo much as give the leaſt Ground to a Diſpute. Cardinal *Borromeus*, firſt Miniſter to *Pius* IV, made ſome other Propoſitions, but the Embaſſadors of *France* were unalterable in their Reſolution. And on the other Side, the King of *Spain* would not ſuffer the Count *de Lune*, his Embaſſador, to go to *Trent* till his Rank was regulated, as well in the Congregations as at the Seſſions. The Pope propos'd, as an Expedient to prevent all the Diſputes which were foreſeen to be unavoidable, that the ſame Method which was obſerv'd at *Rome* ſhould be follow'd, where the Embaſſador of *Spain* does not appear at the Ceremonies, when the *French* Embaſſador has a mind to be preſent, or elſe that the ſame Embaſſador ſhould tranſact the Affairs of the Emperor, and of the King of *Spain*. But this Overture not being approv'd by the *Spaniards*, and the Emperor not judging it proper to give a Commiſſion to the Count *de Lune*, becauſe *Germany* and *Spain* had different Intereſts to manage at *Trent*, it was found neceſſary to think of other Means, ſince *Philip* refus'd to ſend hither a Prelate who might have taken place amongſt the other Eccleſiaſtical Embaſſadors. The Pope continually exhorted the Legates to employ themſelves ſeduouſly in this Affair, but forbad them to mention it to *Lanſac* before the approaching Seſſion, for fear it ſhould be diſturb'd thereby, or retarded. For notwithſtanding it was his Intention to do nothing without the Participation of the Miniſters of *France*, or that could do the King their Maſter a Prejudice, either in the petitory or poſſeſſory Reſpect, yet he knew them to be ſo ſenſible in this Part, that they could not ſuffer the leaſt Propoſition of an Accommodation. This is what the Pope wrote to the Legates in general, but in a particular Diſpatch he ſent to the Cardinal of *Mantua*, he took notice, That *Franciſco de Vargas*, Embaſſador from Spain, had intimated to him, *as a great Secret, that the King his Maſter wrote him word, that rather than to diſturb or break off this holy Aſſembly, he would command his Embaſſador to give place to the laſt of all the Council*, proteſting however, at the ſame time, *that his Intention was, that this pure Complaiſance ſhould not prejudice his Rights nor Pretenſions*. *Vargas* had deſir'd the Pope alſo to make a Secret of it to the Legates, that they might not thereby be render'd more remiſs in their Endeavours for an Accommodation which they hop'd to bring the *French* to comply with. But *Pius* had not Diſcretion enough, to make a Secret of what he thought might very much facilitate the Progreſs of the Council, which might be otherwiſe very much retarded by Conteſts of this Nature.

Upon the Receipt of theſe Letters the Legates ſent for the *French* Embaſſadors, and re
preſented

presented to them how much it concern'd all *Christendom*, that the Council should be continu'd and brought to a Conclusion That the Offices of the Ministers of the two Crowns were necessary for that Purpose to effect which it was also requisite, that those of *France* should do for the King of *Spain* (who was their King's Brother-in-law) all that lay in their Power, provided they did not thereby prejudice the Dignity of the King their Master They propos'd to them at the same time two Means, both which preserv'd them their Rank immediately after the Emperor's Embassador The one was, *That the Embassador of Spain should have a Seat in the middle of the Hall, right against the Legates, in the same Place where that of Portugal had been seated in the Time of* Julius III, *on Account of the Contest he had with to it Embassador of the Emperor* Ferdinand, *who represented him as King of* Hungary The other was, *That the Count de* Lune *should have a Place on the Bench of the Ecclesiasticks after that Embassador of the Emperor, who was an Archbishop* The French Embassadors made Answer, *That they had no Propositions to make or receive That the Disorder proceeded only from those who were for introducing Novelties, and that the first way to prevent them was to leave Matters in the same State they had been in for many Ages That this was the King their Master's Order who commanded them to leave the Place, and to take along with them all the* French *Prelate, if the least Innovation was made That the Blame of all these Alterations was not to be laid on King* Philip, *but on certain ambitious Minds, who were restless, and Enemies to Quiet That they were so well satisfy'd of the good Intention of the King of* Spain, *that they knew that Prince was so far from designing any Prejudice to the King his Brother-in-law, during his Minority, that he would be always ready to assist him with all his Strength against the Rebels That* France *could not be satisfy'd with it self, if it did not answer that Friendship, but that the Laws of Gratitude did not oblige the King to impair his own Dignity*

The Cardinal of *Mantua* remonstrated to them, *That since they enjoy'd their Rank, they ought not to oppose the Satisfaction of others, at least if their Intentions were good, in Reference to the Council* The Embassadors reply'd, *That they should be very glad to contribute to the Satisfaction of others, provided it did no Injury to the Honour of their Prince That all these Propositions came from the* Spaniards, *who had no other Intention than to render doubtful and problematical, what it concern'd the Dignity of the Crown of* France *to lay down as a thing certain*, viz. *That the first Place, after the Emperor's, was due to the King That they could not be accus'd, nor even suspected, of any ill Will towards the Council, because they were for maintaining an ancient Possession, and would not consent to a Novelty* Then the Cardinal of *Mantua*, who knew the Secret, and would fain have concluded something more advantageous for the King of *Spain* than that of obliging his Embassador to take Place after that of *France*, ask'd the Embassadors of *France* what they would say, if the *Spanish* Embassador should go and seat himself below all the other Embassadors? and whether, in that Case, they would pretend to compell him to take a more honourable Place than that he chose himself? The Embassadors of *France*, surpriz'd at so extrordinary a Question, said they would consider of it The Legates desir'd them to think seriously thereof, and in the mean time, they endeavour'd to prevail with the Cardinal of *Lorrain*, to dispose the Embassadors to be more easy

The Cardinal said at first, *That the Embassadors ought to know what Orders they had That they were oblig'd to obey them, to keep to the ancient Usage, and that it was to the Court Recourse should be had, to try to find out some Modification.* Lansac, writing on this Subject to the *French* Embassador who was at *Rome*, did not scruple to say that nothing else should satisfy And as at that Time there was a Rumour, that *Lewis d'Avila*, the *Spanish* Embassador, had Orders to press the Pope to give the King his Master the Title of *Emperor of the Indies*, Lansac added in his Letter, *That the* Spaniards *must not imagine that that new Title would acquire a new Right to King* Philip, *who would not thereby oblige the Emperor of the* Gauls *to give Place to him*

The Pope being inform'd of what had pass'd in the first Conference, wrote to the Legates, *That he was not surpriz'd at the Answer of the* French, *and that he was pretty well satisfy'd that the Means he had propos'd would not succeed, but however, he had thought himself oblig'd to do all that depended on him That he had nothing more to say, than that in Case the* Spaniards *had a mind to protest, the Legates should receive their Protestation* This happen'd about the end of the Year 1562, and it was almost at the same Time that *Philip* wrote to the Pope, That, *in the present Conjuncture, he would not have too great a Regard to Precedency, because in the Post God had establish'd him, those vain Thoughts did not disquiet him, he being wholly intent on the Good of the Service of God, and of the Church* An Extract of this Letter having been communicated to the Legates, they immediately dispatch'd *Lancelot*, Advocate of the Council, to the Count de *Lune*, who was with the Emperor at the Diet of *Augsburg*, to invite him to come to *Trent* The Count said that he could not set out, till he was assur'd the Rank he was to have would be suitable to his Honour, without which Security he would not set forward, unless the King his Master sent him more express Orders for that Purpose than those he had already Lancelot then ask'd him what he meant by the Rank suitable to his Honour? The Count made Answer, That he thereby meant the first Place after the Emperor's Embassador, or else that immediately after the first Ecclesiastical Embassador, because the second represented *Ferdinand* as King of *Hungary* The Legates, who knew very well the *French* would reject entirely the first Proposition, were for obliging the Cardinal of *Lorrain* to prevail with them to condescend to the second But the Cardinal rejected that also, and told them that the Place of the Ecclesiasticks being more honourable than that of the Laity, it would only to serve to enhanse the Honours which were intended to the *Spaniards* There was still another Difficulty in the Matter, which was that *John de Morvilliers*, Bishop of *Orleans*, who in the Absence of *Lansac* discharg'd the Function of first Embassador, being a Clergyman

man, the Ministers of *France* had the upper Hand on both Benches, so that he of *Spain*, could not be seated without yielding the Precedency to the others. The Legates therefore resum'd their first Proposition, *viz.* to give to the *Spaniards* the Place, which had formerly been given to the *Portuguese*, right against the Legates, and the Cardinal *de Lorrain* was of Opinion, through a criminous Prevarication, that the *French* Embassadors, to whom was preserv'd the Place they had always had, immediately after the Emperor's Embassador, ought not to oppose the same. But the Embassadors were of a quite different Sentiment. They said, *That their Intention, as well as their Duty, was to preserve to the King their Master, the first Dignity after that of the Emperor, in such manner as it might be conspicuous to all the World and that no body might dispute it with them, as it might happen, if any other Place was allotted to the* Spanish *Embassador, than what was usual, which was that immediately next to the Embassador of* France *That they had no Orders to accept of any other Medium, and if they had not satisfaction on that Subject, they would be gone, and order all the* French *Prelates to retire, on pain of Disobedience, and Seizure of their Temporal Estates.* The Legates imagining that a vigorous Opposition would at last get the better of the Resolution of the *French*, told them, *That their inflexible Hardness and Obstinacy not being reasonable, they would have no Regard thereto, and would give to the Embassador of* Spain *the Place they had allotted him.* The *French* Embassadors were so much the more concern'd hereat, because they were apprehensive the Intention of the Legates was, to give that of *Spain* an extraordinary Place, not only in the Sessions, but also in the Congregations, where the Seats were to be dispos'd in such manner, that the Embassador of *Spain* would have the most honourable Place. They concluded that the Legates acted thus out of a Design to offend *France* so grievously, that she would be oblig'd to recall her Embassadors and Prelates, and thereby be the Cause of the Dissipation of the Council. Wherefore that the Dissolution of the Council might not draw after it a Rupture between the two Crowns, at a time when *France* did not care to provoke *Spain*, the Embassadors were for reducing the Legates to a Necessity of breaking with them first and resolv'd to send an Express to Court. As soon as the Legates were acquainted therewith by the Cardinal of *Lorrain*, they undeceiv'd the Embassadors, and signify'd to them, that their Thoughts went no farther than the Sessions and as to the Congregations, they would endeavour to dispose the Count *de Luna* to absent himself, as he might very well do, without prejudicing the Honour of the King his Master, since they were not publick Actions. This was the Colour that was given to the Acquiescence of the *French* Embassadors. But the truth is, that the Cardinal of *Lorrain*, in betraying the Honour and Interest of the King his Master, *compell'd them to consent to the Embassador of* Spain's *having an extraordinary Place.*

This being therefore in some Measure regulated, there remain'd still one Difficulty concerning the Rank he should have at the Processions, and at the Church Ceremonies, that is to say, in reference to the *Pax*, and the *Incense* at solemn Masses. The Cardinal of *Lorrain* said, he could find no other Accommodation in that Respect, but for the *Spanish* Embassador either to give place, or to absent with Protestation. He moreover added, that in his Opinion he might also have a Seat even at the Congregations, right against the Legates, but out of the Rank of the Embassadors, near the Secretary of the Council, to the end it might not be thought, that this Place had been given him by the Assembly, or by Order of the Presidents, upon which he might have form'd new Pretensions. But this was only the Cardinal's Sentiment, on which the Embassadors had not explain'd themselves. After he had conferr'd with them, in the beginning of the Month of *February*, 1563, he told the Legates, that the Embassadors were of Opinion, that during the King's Minority, the Ministers could not consent to the least Alteration, which might prejudice the Possession *France* was in, of preceding all the other Kings of *Christendom*, very where. That what would be done at *Trent*, would be of so much the greater Consequence, because the Eyes of the whole World would be intent on what should be regulated by the general Council. That the Services the Kings of *France* had done to the See of *Rome*, would not permit them to receive less Honour in this, than had been done them in former Councils. That whatever Place the *Spanish* Embassador might take, other than the usual one, immediately after that of *France*, even though he should take the last of all, might give Occasion to have the Right or the King their Master call'd in Question, and so would be a *Spolium*, which would oblige them to be gone. That the War the King sustain'd against the *Huguenots*, for the Churches and Religions sake, ought to prevail with the Fathers to imitate the Example of the Senate of *Venice*, which had maintain'd the King in the Possession of his Right. The Legates were the more surpris'd at this Discourse, by reason the King of *Spain* had given the Pope Hopes, that the good Offices he would do to the Court of *France*, would work upon it to send quite different Orders to its Embassadors.

Claudius de Quignones, Count *de Luna*, being arriv'd at *Trent* on the 11th of *April*, 1563, there arose a Contest about the Competition. He said, that if he could not obtain the Precedency over the Embassador of *France*, he would be contented if he were plac'd right against him, or on any other side, at the Choice of the *French* Embassador himself. He also declar'd, he would make no Difficulty to accept such other Place, as the Legates should assign him, provided it did not appear, that he yielded the Precedency to the *French* Embassador. But in case such a one was not given him, as he could accept of honourably, he would then pursue the Orders he had to withdraw. He really had such Orders. For notwithstanding *Philip* had written to the Pope, as we have before observ'd, that he would not amuse himself with these Vanities, nor carry on his Pretensions, these Sentiments were not over sincere, or else they must have alter'd very much since. In the mean time the Legates, considering that the Presence of the *Spanish* Embassador would add no small Lustre to the Council, and that it was even more necessary to it, than that of the Embassadors of *France*, by reason of the great Number of Prelates, Subjects, Creatures or Dependents of the King of *Spain*, resolv'd to execute what had been propos'd concerning the Place, and wrote about it to the Pope The Cardinal of *Lorrain* on his part wrote also to the Queen Mother, *Catherine de Medicis*, to know her Intention in this Matter She made answer, That she tenderly lov'd her Son the King of Spain, (it was so she call'd h m, tho' he was but her *Son-in-Law*) and that she would not only preserve his Honour to him, but also augment it it it lay in her Power That if he were in Possession of the Precedency, she would not so much as think of contesting it with him But that it was certain, the *French* Embassadors had always had, in all the Councils a Seat immediately after that of the Emperor, and particularly before that of Spain That in the Council of Constance, the famous John Gerson, Embassador of France, had had the first Place, and after him Raimond Folch, Count of Cardona, Embassador of Alphonso, King of Castile, and that at the Council of Lateran under Leo X, altho' Ferdinand possess'd in Spain the same Kingdoms that Philip is now possess'd of, William de Vic, his Embassador, had on all Occasions given place to John de Solurs, Embassador from Lewis XII, and especially in the 8th, 9th, and 10th Sessions That the King being very young, the Queen could not do any thing to the Prejudice of the King her Son, and against the Honour of the Nation Upon this Answer the Cardinal went to the Emperor at *Infpruck*, to desire him to prevail with the Count *de Lune* to come to an Accommodation, assuring him that afterwards the *French* Embassadors would do him all the Honours he could desire from them The Emperor told him, he would not meddle with those Pretensions, nor constitute himself Judge of the Rights of the two Kings, but that the Cardinal ought to remember what he himself had formerly said, That the *French* Embassadors did not divest themselves of their Possession, by suffering an extraordinary Place to be given to those of *Spain*, as long as they preserv'd their own That the wish'd the Embassadors would agree the Matter amicably among themselves, without engaging the Kings their Masters therein, to the Compassing of which he desir'd the Cardinal to employ his best Endeavours

The Pope, to whom the Legates had wrote about it, as I just now said, had the same Consideration for *Spain* that they had and judging that the offending of *Philip* would do the utmost Prejudice to the Affairs of the Council, resolv'd to procure him some Satisfaction And to the end the Legates might have the greater Authority and Courage to execute his Orders, he wrote to them, That the King of Spain urg'd him very much, and thought it strange, such Delays were made to assign a Place to his Embassador, as well at the Sessions, as in the Congregations That to him it seem'd reasonable and just, some Consideration should be had for so great a Monarch, and that some Expedient should be found to satisfy him, without prejudicing the Interest of the Parties That the Place he mark'd out to them in the Draught he sent them, appear'd to him honourable and to the purpose, and that he did not perceive what the French could therein complain of That that was what he intended, and that it was their Business to execute it with their wonted Dexterity, and that in case they met with any Opposition in their Endeavours, they should let them protest who had a mind to it, provided his Orders were executed, and that they did not fail therein. Cardinal *Boromeus* added hereunto a Letter in Cipher, wherein he told them, *That it was the Pope's Intention the Affair should remain a Secret till the time of its Execution*, that the French might be surpris'd That perhaps these might not be satisfy'd, but that they should let them protest, and even depart if they pleas'a But the Legates were commanded to execute the Order in all Respects Besides this general Letter, *Boromeus* wrote a private one to Cardinal *Moron* which imported as a great Secret, that *d'Avila* and *Vargas*, Embassadors from *Spain*, had put into the Hands of the Pope a Writing sign'd by them two, and seal'd with their Seal, by which they promis'd him in the King their Master's Name, that he would employ al his Forces, his Estates, and even his own Person, for the Defence, and for the Augmentation of the Authority of the Pope, of the Holy See, and of the Catholick Faith That it was the Pope's Pleasure that *Moron* should know this Particular, that he might judge thereby, that it was not without Reason he endeavour'd to procure Satisfaction to *Philip* The Legates, before they proceeded so far, were for making another Effort on the Minds of the *French* Embassadors, to dispose them to acquiesce to what was desir'd They succeeded indeed, but it was with a great deal of Difficulty, and through the Infidelity of the Cardinal of *Lorrain*, as we before observ'd When the Legates spoke thereof to the Count *de Lune*, this Minister (whether out of a Design to give the *French* to understand, that he was not oblig'd to them for it as a Favour, or that he would have it believ'd, that it the King his Master and himself acquiesce'd therein, it was out of a certain Deference the King was willing to have to the King of *France*, his Brother-in-Law) publish'd himself what the Pope had wrote on this Subject, without scrupling to alter a little of the Truth, and the Circumstances He moreover added, *That what the Pope did herein*, *was of his own mere Motion* The French were perfectly enrag'd hereat, and throughly perswaded, that the Intention of the Court of *Rome*, was to drive the Ministers and Prelates of *France* from *Trent*, in order to disperse the Council

The Count *de Lune*, not contented with the Place which was given him out of the Rank, in the Sessions as well as in the Congregations, was also for knowing whereabouts he should sit in the Church, from whence arose a greater Difficulty than the first, so that the Legates, notwithstanding the great Pains they took, could not bring the Embassadors of the two Crowns to an Agreement That of *Spain* refus'd to consent to whatever could give the least Idea of an Inequality, and those of *France* could not bear the very mentioning of an Equality This new Contest oblig'd the Legates to desire the Pope again, to order them what they should do and in case he thought fit also on this Occasion to favour *Spain*, that he would be pleas'd to lay his Commands upon them by a Letter on purpose, compris'd in such Terms, as might serve them for a Justification *Avila* and *Vargas* made pressing Instances also to him at *Rome*, so that the Pope seeing his first Orders had been so happily executed, as to be follow'd by no Disturbance nor Clamour, and hoping the second might be attended with the same Success, wrote to them, *That the Spanish Embassadors press'd him very much to settle the Rank, the Count de Lune was to have at solemn Masses which he could not decline, because as he had assign'd him his Place, it was requisite he should also do the like, in reference to the Pax and the Incense, unless he would suffer the Count to retire That in Consideration the King of Spain was the chief Support of the Catholick Religion, he desir'd the Legates would take care, that at the same time the Pax and Incense should be presented to the French Embassador, another Priest, or Ecclesiastical Minister, should do the same to that of Spain, and that they would proceed herein with so much Address, that the same might not be perceiv'd, till the very Moment of its Execution* He also told them his Intention was, that this Order should be executed, whatever the Consequence thereof might be, without Prejudice however to the Right of the Parties concern'd

The Cardinal *Boromeus* sent at the same time two Letters to them, the one whereof very much recommended the Secrecy of the Matter, (which was to be communicated by the Legates to none but the Count) the Address with which the Order was to be executed, and the Choice of the Ministers who were to be employ'd therein It also mark'd the Day for the Execution thereof, which was to be on the Eve or Feast of St *Peter* The other imported, that the Pope would not be pleas'd, if the Legates should in this, do as they had done in the Execution of the first Order, where they had publish'd, that it was his Holiness, who of his own Motion had directed them to act as they did, but he on the contrary expected that at the very time of Execution they should notify, that the Pope had order'd it at the Instance of the King of *Spain*, thereby to prevent the Count *de Lune* from going away and that that was the Reason why the Pope, who perceiv'd how things went in *France*, was unwilling to lose or risque *Spain* with her The Legates communicated their Order to the Count on the 22d of *June*, as he was just getting on Horseback, to go to the Emperor at *Inspruck* The Count told them he was satisfy'd, and that he believ'd there would be no great Reluctancy on the *French* side however that the Legates might, without disclosing the Secret, cause *the Expedient of the two Paxes and the two Censers*, to be propos'd by *Drascouitz*, one of the Emperor's Embassadors, as if it were a Thought of his Masters, in hopes to have it approv'd of *Drascouits* spoke to the Cardinal of *Lorrain* about it, and finding it was not at all lik'd, he propos'd another Modification, to wit, that on St *Peter*'s Day, neither the Pax nor the Incense should be given to either the one or the other, as had been practis'd in the Competition between the Embassadors of *Portugal* and of *Hungary*, under *Julius* III

But this Medium was also rejected by the Cardinal. Whereupon *Drascouitz* intreated him to speak to him freely, not as a Minister of *France*, but as a Cardinal, and a Person zealous for the Publick Good, and to tell him what he thought might and ought to be done Hereupon the Cardinal made him two Propositions The first was, *That the Embassador of Spain should not come to Church till towards the latter end of Mass, after the Ceremonies of the Pax and Incense were over* The other was, *That the Pax should not be presented to the Count, till it had been presented to all the Embassadors* He thereunto subjoyn'd, *That the last could no wise prejudice the Spanish Embassador, because being seated out of Rank, it was not requisite to observe any for him, which Omission would not injure him, since the Embassadors of the Emperor and of France, made no Difficulty to receive the Pax and Incense after the Embassadors of Poland and Savoy, who had their Place on the Bench of the Ecclesiasticks* But *Drascouitz* was not more satisfy'd with these Overtures, than the Cardinal was with those which had been made to him He therefore, when he made a Report to the Legates of his Negotiation, spoke of it as of a desperate Affair The Count *de Lune* return'd from *Inspruck* on the 27h, but so late, that not being able to speak with the Legates that Night, he went to see them the next Day, and learn'd from them what had pass'd between *Drascouitz* and the Cardinal of *Lorrain* They told him they were ready to execute the Pope's Orders He accepted their Offer, and moreover said, that he did not believe the *French* would make any Noise about it, provided they were surpris'd and that they would make still less, after the thing was done, because they would not be willing the World should believe, the *Spaniards* had got any Advantage over them, or that they had been Negligent in opposing the same but on the contrary, would be glad to have it thought, that nothing pass'd there to their Prejudice However at his rising from Dinner he would see the Legates again, and would talk to them more amply on the Matter He did not do it notwithstanding and in the mean time, in this Uncertainty of the Count's Intentions, they flatter'd themselves still with the Hopes, that at the Eve of the Execution of so important an Affair, he might perhaps reflect on the precise Orders he had, to avoid carefully all Causes and Occasions of a Rupture It was in this Uncertainty that the Feast of St *Peter* surpris'd them The Embassadors and a great Number of Prelates were come to the Legates, to accompany them to Church, but before they set forwards they were whisper'd in the Ear, that the *Spanish* Embassador intended to be there, and to bring thither some Prelates of his Nation Upon this Advice the Legates gave private Orders to the Master of the Ceremonies, to cause a Chair to be brought into the Vestry, and to have two strange Priests ready, to present at the same time the Pax to the two Embassadors

Those of *France* did not perceive it, but they had hardly taken their Place in the Church, when they saw the *Spanish* Embassador come in, before Mass was begun and at the same time a Seat was brought and plac'd out of Rank

Rank. The Place that was given him was not the same he had had in the Congregations, because the different Situation of the Theatre would not allow it, but the Chair was put in the Place which the Pope had mark'd out in his Letter, before a Pillar, above the Patriarchs, pretty near the Legates Chairs, and almost right against the Bench of the secular Embassadors. The *French* Embassadors were very much surpriz'd thereat, and the Cardinal of *Lorrain* complain'd of it to the Legates, and particularly that the Pope's Order had been kept a Secret from him, which made a Noise that spread it self throughout the whole Assembly. The said Embassadors having conferr'd among themselves, sent for the Master of the Ceremonies, and ask'd him how he pretended to act in reference to the *Pax* and the *Incense*. He told them his Orders, and thereupon they made very sharp Complaints to the Legates, and threaten'd to protest. The Cardinal of *Lorrain* who sate near the Legates, in seconding the Complaints of the Embassadors, said, That they were commanded to appeal to the Council, and to protest against Pope *Pius*, who the *French* said was not lawfully chosen, because he had been elected thro' *Simony*, and that the Queen had Letters under the Pope's Hand, which p ov d it plainly. After this first Transport, which made no Impression, the *French* said, that amputing the Pope were duly and canonically elected, they would appeal from him, as from a tyrannical Pope who deserv'd to be depos'd for the notorious Injustice he did in dispossessing a minor King of a Right which he had enjoy'd for many Ages, without Contestation, and that too without so much as giving him a Hearing. That *France* would separate from the See of *Rome*, till a juster Pope was plac'd therein, who should re-instate the King in the Possession of what he was so unjustly depriv'd. The Cardinal added, that all the *French* Prelates should depart, and that such Measures should be taken within the Kingdom, in reference to the Affairs of Religion, as should be thought proper by a National Synod, or otherwise. *Muglitz* and *Drascoutiz*, who as first Ecclesiastical Embassadors, were nearest the Legates, went to and from the Parties, and endeavour'd to calm their Minds, in which they labour'd during the Time the Lecture of the Gospel was finishing. But when the Preacher was beginning his Sermon, the Noise was so great, that the Legates to avoid a greater Scandal, retir'd into the Vestry, whither the Embassadors of the Emperor and of *Poland* follow'd them. The Cardinal of *Lorrain* went thither likewise, and took along with him *Regnant Ferrier* one of the *French* Embassadors, as also the Archbishop of *Sens*, and pray'd the Archbishop of *Granada* to be there present. This last inform'd him, that the Count *de Lune* desir'd nothing else, but to have the Orders of *Rome* executed, to which he referr'd himself. However the Legates, who knew that the King of *Spain* had charg'd the Count not to proceed to a Rupture, which the Archbishop of *Granada* had also assur'd them of, said that Precipitation ought to be avoided in an Affair of that Importance, and that they were oblig'd to skreen the Pope from the Reproach of being the Cause of the Dissipation of the Council,

which was to be apprehended from this Decision. Thus they talk'd to the *Spaniards*, while they answer'd the Threats of the *French*, and endeavour'd to allay their Fury, by representing to them, that what was done, was without Prejudice to their Rights and Pretensions. That Matters had been thus resolv'd upon from the very first Overture of the Council, and that the Pope express'd himself in those Terms in his Letters, which they offer'd to produce. They moreover urg'd, that there was no forcing the *Spanish* Embassador to give place to another, unless he were willing, and that since the *French* had consented to his being plac'd out of Rank, they might also very well suffer the *Pax* and *Incense* to be presented to him in an extraordinary manner. The *French* reply'd, that they could not take Words for Payment, that they were only Wind. Whereas in Actions there was Reality, and that as soon as any one is put in Possession, in what manner soever it be, he acquires a Title. The Legates to get out of this Perplexity, desir'd the Archbishop of *Granada* to know of the Count *de Luna*, if he were willing for t is one time, that the Ceremonies of the *Pax* and *Incense* should be omitted, letting him know at the same time, that they were ready to execute the Pope's Orders, if he absolutely requir'd it. The Count consented to their not being perform'd this time reserving to himself the Power of causing those Orders to be executed at the first Opportunity, which was to offer it self in three or four Days. But the Legates were in hopes they should find in the mean time some Expedient to settle the Difference, or at least, that the *Spanish* and *Italian* Prelates would have Leisure to prepare themselves to maintain the Pope's Act, which they had not been able to do, because it had not been communicated to them. But as the Pope's Orders were very positive, and that the Legates, who were oblig'd to have a particular Consideration for the King of *Spain*, were unwilling to have any thing reproach'd them, they desir'd Cardinal *Madrucci* to deliver the same Message to the Count *de Luna*, which the Archbishop of *Granada* had carry'd. The Cardinal did so in the Presence of *Drascoutiz* and of the Embassador of *Poland*, and brought the same Answer from him.

As for the *French*, it is true they had rejected the Proposition had been made them, concerning the Omission of the Ceremonies. But taking into Consideration, that by being obstinate, they would reduce the Legates to the Necessity of executing the Orders they had receiv'd, and lose at least in fact, a Thing of which they were for preserving the Right in all respects whatever, and that they broke with the Pope, which perhaps might not be for the Interest of the King their Master, they at last consented to the Modification. They consented that that Day, the Ceremonies should not be perform'd, not only to the Embassadors, but also to the Legates themselves. To which these last acquiesc'd the more readily, as not being willing to be the Cause, or Occasion of the Scandal that might arise therefrom. After that, the Embassador of *Spain* got up as soon as ever the Mass was ended, whereas before he was us'd to remain the last, and he went out even

even before the Legates Cross-bearer began to move

The same Day all the Embassadors repair'd to the Legates, some as being interested, and others as Mediators. The Legates told both the ones and the others, that being press'd thereto by the *Spanish* Embassador, they could no longer delay executing the Pope's Orders. And in effect, Cardinal *Simonetta* having sent for *Gabriel Palotta*, Auditor of the *Rota*, he bid him prepare the rough Draught of an Answer to the Protestation the Embassadors of *France* might make. *Palotta* made Answer, that he look'd upon it to be neither for the Service of God, nor that of the Pope, to kindle a Fire which perhaps might be hard to put out. That all the Prelates were extremely alarm'd with the Apprehension they had of the Schism of *France*, and that the Embassador of *Poland* had declar'd, that this Kingdom would infallibly follow the Example of that. The Cardinal reply'd, that the Orders from *Rome* were so precise and so absolute, that they did not leave to the Legates the Liberty to deliberate thereon. *Palotta* ingenuously reply'd, That he was resolv'd not to contribute to what might possibly prove the Ruine of the Church. That he had no Regard to the Pope's Command in this respect, but to God's, which expressly forbids giving Occasion to an apparent Schism in the Church. That all the Lawyers unanimously declar'd, that a Command is of no Force, when in the Execution thereof, there happen Changes which the Superior could not foresee. *Buencompagne* whom *Simonetta* sent for after *Palotta* was gone, was of the same Opinion, as well as *Navager* one of the Legates. So that all the Legates judg'd it proper to dispatch an Express to the Pope, to represent to him their Difficulties. Accordingly they did so, on the 1st of *July*, but to the end they might in the mean time bring the Minds of the Parties to some Moderation in the Matter, they made the utmost Secret of this Dispatch. They wrote to the Pope, that the Affair had been very ill receiv'd, not only by those who were interested therein, but also by the *Portuguese*, and even by some *Spaniards* who said it was not just to deprive a minor King of his ancient Possession, without hearing him. That *Ferdinand*, *Philip*'s Uncle, would not do it in his Court, nor even the Pope in his, where he might have done it with more Liberty than at the Council. That they were inform'd that the very next Day, the Embassadors of *France* design'd to come to them and declare, That the Liberty and Safety, which the Pope had so often promis'd them, was not to be found at the Council, since without the Advice of the Fathers, and without founding their Opinions, he acted so imperiously, and of his own Head and sole Authority made an Innovation so prejudicial to the King, the eldest Son of the Church, and acknowledg'd as such for many Ages, to whom so cruel an Outrage was offer'd in the Sight of the whole Council, to which he had sent his Embassadors and his Prelates. The Legates spoke of it as of an Action which was not only unjust, but also very pernicious. That the *French* had a Protestation ready for the next Sunday, on which they expected the Effect of the Menaces of the Legates. That they would there

speak with very little Respect of the Pope and the Pontificate, while at the same time they treated the King of *Spain* and his Embassador with great Civility, with a Design to lay all the Blame on *Pius*, and that this being done, they would immediately leave the Place. That they threaten'd to proceed against him as a *Simoniack* and a *Schismatick*, and that they would cause him to be depos'd, in which they were sensible all the North would back *France*. That among the Prelates who were at *Trent*, there were some malicious enough to believe, that the Pope made use of this Fetch to disperse the Council, that he might not be oblig'd to set a Hand to the Reformation.

It therefore belong'd to his Holiness to consider, whether it might not be proper to suspend the Execution of an Order from whence so great a Scandal might arise, and which they had not foreseen themselves when they had desir'd him to signifie his Pleasure to them, at a time when they did not believe the Execution would be accompany'd with so many Difficulties. The Cardinal of *Lorrain* dispatch'd also an Express, and wrote to the Pope in very strong Terms even to the telling him, that had it not been for the Piety and Prudence of the Count *de Lune*, and the Moderation of the *French* Ministers, the Legates had like to have made St *Peter*'s Festival the most unfortunate Day Christendom had ever seen. That the Rank he held in the Church, and the Zeal he had for the publick Good, oblig'd him to acquaint the Pope, that if his Order was executed, the *French* Embassadors would declare, that since he had laid aside the Office of Father, to take upon him the Quality of a Partizan, by giving Sentence without hearing him who was most interested, they would not abide by it, but would order their Affairs, by having Recourse to the Council, or otherwise as they should think convenient. That the Pope could not be ignorant, that the Resentment of great Princes, who know they are injur'd, makes them lose all manner of Consideration and Respect, and so he intreated him to reflect seriously thereon.

After the Legates had seal'd their Letters, they added one to the Cardinal *Boromeus* to whom they wrote, that they had just receiv'd Advice, that the Count *de Lune* was resolv'd to cause the Pope's Orders to be executed on the Sunday following, and that the Emperor's Ministers (who condemn'd the Obstinacy with which the Embassadors of *France* rejected the Modification) were come over to him. That the said Count finding his Endeavours with the Cardinal of *Lorrain* were fruitless, intended to signifie to him on the same Day by three Bishops, That he had resolv'd to cause the Orders of *Rome* to be executed. That he had Reason to complain of the Lukewarmness of the Legates, to the End this Complaint might serve them for a Justification as well as to the Pope, who, as the Count said, did not therein follow his own Motion, but acted at the Instance of the King of *Spain* his Master, tho' the *French* were for having the contrary believ'd. That the same Bishops were to add, that the Count had been inform'd, it was the Intention of the *French* to protest, but he could not believe it, nor that the Cardinal would suffer it, even to

the

the Embaſſadors were ſo diſpos'd. However if that ſhould happen, he would alſo proteſt on his Side, and would anſwer the diſreſpectful Terms they might uſe againſt the Pope, after ſuch a manner, as would ſufficiently convince the World that the King his Maſter will not ſuffer the reſpect to be loſt which is due to the common Father. That the King of *France* would ſome Day give Marks of his Reſentment and Indignation againſt thoſe, who ſhould have been the Cauſe of his Separation from the Church, and that if the *French* ſhould depart from *Trent*, that ſhould not hinder the Council from ſubſiſting and continuing. The Concluſion of the Letter was, That all this Procedure did not diminiſh the Perplexity they were in, and that they pray'd God to aſſiſt them with his Grace, whilſt they would do their utmoſt to diſpoſe the Parties to an Accommodation.

The Count had in Effect diſcours'd ſeveral Prelates well-affected to *Spain*, who had offer'd him all that lay in their Power, to maintain the King's Honour and the Pope's Authority. But he had alſo met with ſome *Spaniards*, who being wiſer and more reſolute than the reſt, had remonſtrated to him, That he ought to make a ſeriousReflection on theOrders the King had given him, not to come to a Rupture, and had even declar'd to him, that ſome Day they would reproach him with the Violation thereof in the Preſence of his Majeſty. The common Opinion was, That as in all the Aſſemblies which are compos'd of Men of the Gown, there is always a greater Inclination to Peace than to War, the Council would have been for waiting for freſh Orders from the Pope. His firſt Commands indeed contain'd, That the Legates ought not to heed the Menaces of the *French*, even tho' they ſhould retire from *Trent* But they made no mention of the Caſe where there might be likelihood of a Schiſm. The Pope therefore wrote to them, that if there was any Appearance of a Schiſm, it muſt be carefully avoided in all Reſpects, and laying aſide all Punctilio's, they ſhould remain within the Bounds preſcrib'd by the Laws and the Canons, and adhere to the Sentiments of the Holy Doctors. That it was his Opinion there was no Innovation in the Orders he had ſent to the Legates, and that it was not his Intention there ſhould be any for the future, but he would have them gain Time, and endeavour to bring the Matter to a Modification. And whatever happen'd, to offer to make the Council Judge of the Difference. That if the *French* had accepted the Condition, and the Count rejected it, he would be the Author of his own Wrong, and the Pope thereby diſcharg'd of his Obligation. That from the very beginning of his Pontificate the *Spaniards* had never ceas'd perſecuting him, and threatening him, that their King would recall his Embaſſador from *Rome*, and even from *Trent*, if the Pope did not do whatever they deſir'd him. That ſeeing ſo ſmall a Matter made him riſque the Friendſhip of ſo powerful and good a King, while the *French* were wanting in what they ow'd to God, by the Peace they had lately concluded with the Hereticks, and by their Edicts, which tolerated the Meetings in ſpite of the Catholicks, as alſo by the Alienation of the Revenues of the Church; without its Conſent and againſt its Will, he had been oblig'd to ſend them his firſt Orders, to the end he might not find himſelf abandon'd, without Friends and Support. That he had flatter'd himſelf the Execution thereof would have been perform'd without Noiſe or Clamour, as indeed the Count *de Luna* had made him believe, but ſeeing there was Danger of Schiſm therefrom, tho' he was perſuaded the *French* were otherwiſe inclin'd enough thereto, yet it was not proper to furniſh them with an Occaſion, or a Pretext for the ſame. So that they might delay the Execution of his Orders, taking Care at the ſame Time, not to diſcloſe the Secret of this, by which he ſuperſeded the former, till a Mean might be found out to reconcile the Parties, however, he refer'd himſelf to the Diſcretion of the Legates, to make it publick when they ſhould judge it convenient.

The general Diſpoſition of the Council was favourable to the *French*, inſomuch that the Emperor's Embaſſadors ſeeing they were blam'd on Account of their being too partial, excus'd themſelves thereupon to the Legates, by proteſting that they intermeddl'd therein, not as being any way concern'd, but only as Mediators. Nay, there were ſome Lawyers of the Legates Council, who maintain'd, *That as this Matter was entirely ſecular the Pope could not decide it without a Hearing, and even that, after a voluntary Submiſſion of the Parties.* Nevertheleſs, the Legates had made a formal Promiſe to the Count, to go through with it if he deſir'd it, and they could not juſtify themſelves to the King of *Spain*, if they fell off from their Word. So that they labour'd ſedulouſly, and with the utmoſt Application to accommodate the Affair, which was at laſt compaſs'd in the following manner. *That in the Seſſions the ſame Order ſhould be obſerv'd which had been kept on St Peter's Day. That on other ſolemn Days the Embaſſadors ſhould agree among themſelves, which of the two ſhould be preſent at the Ceremonies; whereby Things were thought to be ſo well adjuſted, that no Diſorder could ariſe therefrom, and that in the mean Time the two Kings ſhould be written to, to ſee if ſome Expedient might not be found to ſettle a fix'd Regulation therein.* The Cardinal of *Lorrain* diſpos'd, or rather compell'd the *French* Embaſſadors to a Compliance; and the Archbiſhop of *Grenada* made that of *Spain* acquieſce alſo, both of them aſſuring the Embaſſadors of the Approbation of the King their Maſter. It muſt be own'd that the Count *de Luna* obtain'd thereby all he could pretend to. Firſt, he did not give Place to the *French* Embaſſador; ſecondly, he had an honourable Place alloted him in all the Aſſemblies, which denoted a Competition between the two Crowns, and in the third Place his Conteſtations did not cauſe the Council to be diſpers'd, nor a Rupture with *France*, which is oblig'd to the Houſe of *Lorrain* for the Diſgrace.

In the mean Time the Difference about Precedency remain'd undecided at *Rome*. The *Spaniſh* Embaſſador made preſſing Inſtances there, that it might be determin'd by a definitive Sentence, and deſir'd to have the firſt Place on the Pope's Left Hand, leaving that on the Right to the Emperor's Embaſſador. He did not ſcruple to ſay, that if he were refus'd a Thing, which he ſaid was very juſt, the King his

his Master would not only recall his Embassador, but also command all his Subjects to leave the Ecclesiastical State. On the contrary, the *French* Embassador protested, That if he were molested in the quiet Possession he had been in for many Ages, to take Place immediately after the Emperor's Embassador, the King his Master would recall his Minister, and would, with all his Kingdom, shake off Obedience to the See of *Rome*. And in effect, the King had order'd his Embassador, that in Case the least thing were undertaken against his Right, to declare this Separation to the Pope, and to leave the City. The Pope being afraid, left *France* (where the Protestant Religion had already made a great Progress) should follow the Example of *England*, was in great Pain what to do. He had been sick, and under that Pretext he deferr'd going to Chapel, and when on *Holy Thursday* he gave his Blessing to the People from the Box in the Vatican, *he had so regulated the Rank, in Reference to the Embassadors of the two Crowns, that it could not be said which of them had the first*, excusing himself for so doing, that on those Days of Devotion none was given to any Body.

Loisel, Embassador from *France* at that Court, was so scandaliz'd hereat, that he took from thence an Occasion to ask his Audience of Leave, however his Departure was prevented, by giving him Hopes, that at the Chapel of *Whitsunday* he should receive Satisfaction. The Pope flatter'd himself that he might do it even with *Philip*'s Consent, who had wrote to him, as I before took Notice, that he would not amuse himself with those Vanities, and notwithstanding he had alter'd his Mind since, the Pope fed himself with the Hopes of bringing him back to his first Sentiment, by representing to him, that the greater and the more violent the Evils of *France* were, the greater Compassion *Philip* ought to have for it, and not stick at a little Smoke and Vain-Glory. But *Philip* made Answer to the two Nuncio's, who spoke to him about it, That too great a Progress had been made therein to let it drop, and that he referr'd the Matter to his Embassador, who had his Orders. *Ruy Gomez de Silva* rejected also the two Propositions which the same Nuncio's made to him, of having the *Spanish* Embassador absent himself from the publick Ceremonies, and said, that after what had happen'd at *Trent* the King would not stop here, but proceed farther. The Pope, that he might affront no Body, had in the mean time forbidden all the Embassadors to assist at the publick Ceremonies without his Order, and the better to oblige *France* to have a Deference thereto, he had desir'd the Emperor to command his Embassador to acquiesce to it. The Emperor did so, and his Embassador express'd a Readiness to absent from them, dissembling the Order he had receiv'd from Court, as being willing to have it believ'd, that what he did was only out of Deference to the Pope's Desire, thereby to oblige the *French* Embassador to follow his Example, but all this signify'd nothing. Upon the Advice they had in *France*, of what had pass'd at *Rome* on *Maunday Thursday*, the Queen-Mother told the *Nuncio*, That the King, young as he was, had nevertheless declar'd in full Council, that he would not suffer any Body to wrong him. That the Embassador had done very well in taking his Audience of Leave, but very ill in not coming away immediately. However, since the Affair was in that Condition, he might now continue there till *Whitsunday*. But that express Orders were sent him to come away, in Case Satisfaction were not given him at that Time, and to bring the Cardinal *de Bourdaisere* along with him. She moreover told him, she was willing to speak to him not as the King's Mother, and Regent, but as a Daughter of the Catholick Church, and let him know that, if the Pope fail'd herein, she foresaw a Fire kindling, of which the Enemies of the Church would make use, to irritate the more the King's Indignation, to the great Prejudice of Religion. The Cardinal of *Lorrain* spoke to him in the same Terms and thereupon the Nuncio wrote to *Rome*, That he was certain the good King *Philip* would not for so vain and frivolous a Pretension, be the Cause of the Loss of so many Souls, and of the Conflagration of a Kingdom in the Neighbourhood of his Estates of *Spain* and *Flanders*. That the King would think it an Honour to him to give here Marks of his own Prudence, and of that of his Council. After all, hath the Pope would only do therein what he was for doing formerly, and what the Republick of *Venice* did already, so that her Example might serve for a Justification to his Holiness.

The Pope had offer'd to leave the Decision of the Difference to the Council, or else to the *Rota*, but neither *France* nor *Spain* would submit thereto. The one because she would not have her Right call'd in Question, and the other because she distrusted hers. For which Reason he at last ordain'd, That without Prejudice to the Right each of the Parties might really have, the Embassador of *France* should be maintain'd in the Possession, and that he should have the Place which his Predecessors had always occupy'd, before *Charles* V Father to *Philip* had been elected Emperor, and which they had effectually enjoy'd, as well in the Chapel as at *Trent*. He offer'd at the same Time to refer the Cognizance of the Affair to the Council, or to the *Rota*, and in the mean Time to give a Place to the Embassador of *Spain*, separate from the other Embassadors, amongst the Cardinals, after the last Cardinal Priest. *Lewis de Cuniga*, and *de Requesens*, Great Commander of the Order of St *James* in *Castille*, since Governor of *Milan*, and afterwards of the Low Countries, where he dy'd, was so transported at this Declaration that the Pope told him in Anger, That it was a Civility, what he had offer'd him, to put him out of the Rank of the other Embassadors, but since he was not satisfy'd therewith, he might go even where he pleas'd, and that he would not revoke his Ordinance. He wrote also on this Subject to the Queen *Catherine de Medicis*, That what he had done had been out of a Motive of Justice, which had oblig'd him to regulate the Difference as he did. The *Spaniards* made a great Noise hereat, and gave out that *Philip* would employ his Arms to revenge himself. But all the Revenge he took was to recall his Embassador, and the Pope was willing to have it thought, that therein was more of Complaisance than of Resentment. Some Time before *Requesens* had, of his own Authority, caus'd a certain Licentiate to be carry'd off, and clap'd into Prison, which had so incens'd the Pope, that he had refus'd to give him Audience, and had desir'd *Philip*, by Cardinal *Pacheco*, to recall him, as being an unfit Minister to entertain a right Understanding between them. But herein he did not so much flatter himself, as he impos'd upon others.

The *Spaniards*, who were oblig'd to respect the Pope's Regulation at *Rome*, did not for that renounce their Pretensions on the contrary, they have ever since sought all Occasions, that might favour them, or could furnish them with some Title or Pretext. Don *Pedro Faxardo* being sent, some few Years after this Declaration of the Pope, to the Diet which had been call'd in *Poland*, for the Election of a new King upon the Death of *Sigismund Augustus*, and intending to go to the *Audience* the Senate gave to the Embassadors of all the Pretenders to the Crown, to recommend the Interest of their respective Masters, he joyn'd himself to the *Emperor's Embassador, and endeavour'd to enter with him into the Tent where the Senate was assembled*. He said, That the King of *Spain*, his Master, had no other Interest than that of the Emperor, and as he had no other Intention, than to recommend the Person of the Arch-Duke *Ernest*, *Maximilian*'s Son, he thought he might do it in the same Audience with the Emperor's Embassador: but *the Embassadors of* France *oppos'd it, and by causing him to withdraw, preserv'd to themselves the Rank which was due to the King their Master*.

There was another Dispute about Precedency, at the Assembly of *Vervins* in the Year 1598, between *Messieurs de Bellievre* and *de Sillery*, Embassadors of *France* on the one side, and *Messieurs Richardot*, *Taxis* and *Verreyken*, Embassadors from *Spain* on the other. The Cardinal of *Florence*, who was Legate there from *Clement* VIII, as Mediator, and who found himself very much perplex'd therein, propos'd several Expedients, which were all rejected by the *French*, as well as the Offer made by the *Spaniards*, to yield in the Quality of Embassadors from the Cardinal Arch-Duke, Governor of the Low Countries. *Bellievre* said, that he could not consider them but as Embassadors from the King of *Spain*, with whom the King his Master pretended to treat, and not with the Arch-Duke, nor with his Ministers, and insisted on their yielding to him in that Quality. To put an End to this Controversy, it was thought advisable so to order the Seats, that the Legate should be at the upper End of the Table. That the Bishop of *Mantua*, the Pope's Nuncio, should place himself on the Legates Right-Hand, and after that, the *French* should have the Choice of the Places, either the first on the Legate's Left-Hand, or the second on his Right, after the Nuncio. They took the first Place next the Legate, tho' it seems as if therein there were something that did not agree with the Maxim, *Of the last Place in the first Rank, being more honourable than the first in the second*. But besides that the having the Choice gave all the Advantage to the *French*, there were not two different Ranks on this Occasion, and the Places nearest to the first were the most honourable, since the two Places of the Embassadors of *France*, were reckon'd but for one, no more than the three of the Embassadors of *Spain*. Neither is there any Doubt to be made, but the *Spaniards* would have made the same Choice, if it had been left to them in which consisted almost all the Advantage.

The Count *de Tilliers*, Embassador in Ordinary from *France*, and the Count *de Gondemar*, Embassador Extraordinary from *Spain* in *England*, being invited to the Diversion of a Riding at the Ring, the Court desiring to please both Parties, had caus'd two Boxes to be built, which were plac'd in such manner, that it could not be said, that one of the Embassadors was more favour'd than the other. He of *France* said, *That it was not sufficient to place them both in an equal Degree of Honour, but that it was necessary every Body should be sensible, that* France *had the Precedency of* Spain: and that at least he ought to have the Choice of the Boxes. He could not obtain it, so that he would not be present at the Diversion, nor suffer his Lady to be there neither. The *Spanish* Embassador took Advantage hereof, as if he had got the better of the *French*. It cannot be deny'd, but then it is impossible for an Embassador to parry such Strokes, when the Prince with whom he resides, declares in favour of his Competitor. King *James* in his Inclinations was more a *Spaniard* than a *Frenchman*, if we will believe the History of those Times, and he diverted himself with the Count *de Gondemar*, who on his Part fed him with Hopes of the Marriage with the *Infanta*. There is a Difference between these Assemblies and solemn Ceremonies. The Embassador may absent himself from the ones, but he cannot avoid taking the Rank due to the King his Master at the others.

The Duke of *Longueville*, and the Count *de Pegneranda*, who were Chiefs of the Embassies of *France* and *Spain* at *Munster*, did not visit one another, not so much by Reason of the Count's Refusal to give the Title of Highness to the Duke, since this last declar'd, he did not pretend to it from the Count, and was willing their Conferences should run in the third Person without Title, but because it was very difficult for them to see one another, especially in a third Place, but the one would take Advantage of the other. The Count knew the *French* had boasted, that they would cause it to be given them, cost what it would, if an Occasion offer'd it self, for which Reason he was very cautious of exposing himself. *Diego de Saavedra*, and *Anthony le Brun*, often saw *d'Avaux* and *Servien* in the Conferences, sometimes at one of their Houses, and sometimes at the others, where they mutually gave the Style of Excellency each to the other, but they carefully avoided meeting in a third Place. M *d'Avaux*, who was one of the *French* Plenipotentiaries, happening to be alone at *Munster*, endeavour'd to dispose M *le Brun* to agree to an Assignation in the Capucin's Garden, but whatever Overtures were made, and Expedients propos'd to concert this Interview so that the Dignity of the two Crowns might not suffer thereby, it could never be brought to pass. *D'Avaux* had it represented to *le Brun*, that as he was the second in the Commission of the *French* Embassy, and the other the third in that of *Spain*, this would not injure himself very

very much if he granted him some small Advantage, but all was to no purpose This Jealousy even went so far, that the Assembly had like to have broke up, on the Difficulty which was started, *which of the two Kings should be first nam'd in the publick Acts* It was propos'd that neither the one nor the other should be nam'd, and that it should be simply said, *The two Crowns D'Avaux* relish'd this Overture well enough but *Servien*, who condemn'd whatever the other approv'd, rejected it, tho' he might have remember'd, if he had pleas'd, that it was what had been done at the Treaty of *Querasque*, which he had himself negotiated and sign'd, with the Mareschal *de Toiras*, in the Year 1631

The Encounter the Count *Destrades* and the Baron *de Vatteville*, Embassadors of *France* and *Spain*, had at *London*, in the Year 1661, made it very plain, that the *Spaniards* had not renounc'd their Pretensions, notwithstanding the Regulations of Pope *Pius* They were both to send their Coaches to meet Count *Brahe*, Embassador from *Sweden*, on the Day of his Entry And for as much as they made no doubt, but there would be a Contest about the Rank, they each of them took those Measures they judg'd necessary to procure the Advantage to his own side *Vatteville* sent for some Soldiers from *Ostend*, made sure of several *English*, and instead of Traces, had caus'd Chains of a moderate Thickness to be cover'd with Leather, that they might not be liable to be cut *Destrades* had indeed reinforc'd his Equipage a little, but not expecting things would come to such Extremities, he had not taken all the Precautions, which might have protected him from the Violence of others

The Duke of *York*, who fear'd and foresaw the Disorder, had caus'd a Troop of Horse, and three Companies of his Regiment of Foot to be drawn out but as the Officers had no Orders to meddle with the Quarrel of the Embassadors, all they could do, was to be Spectators of the Fight and Confusion Some of the *French* Embassador's Coach Horses were kill'd, as well as two or three of his People There were also some *Spaniards* who lost their Lives, but yet they carry'd the Day, because *Destrades* Coach could not move without Horses It was in Consequence of this Disorder, and of the Complaints *Destrades* made thereof, that the King of *England* ordain'd, that the foreign Ministers Coaches should not for the future attend at this kind of Ceremonies Upon the first Advice hereof in *France*, the King sent word to the Count *de Fuensaldagne*, Embassador of *Spain*, who had already begun to take his Leave, to be gone from Court in four and twenty Hours, and not to make any Stay in any of the Towns he should pass through, till he was got out of the Kingdom He moreover order'd the Archbishop of *Embrun*, his Embassador at *Madrid*, to require Satisfaction and Reparation, and unless he obtain'd both the one and the other, to retire The King of *Spain*, who was aged and sickly, promis'd he would comply with his Son-in-Law's Desire That he would recall Vatteville *from his Embassy in* England That he would give Orders to all his Embassadors, *not to be present at the Ceremonies, at which those of* France *should assist* That the Marquess of Fuentes, *who was nominated to the Embassy of* France, *should make a formal Declaration thereof to the King* He did so on the 24th of *March*, 1662, in the great Closet at the Louvre, whither the King had caus'd all the Embassadors and foreign Ministers then in *Paris* to come, in the Presence of the Duke of *Orleans*, the Prince of *Condé*, the Chancellor, and of several other Dukes and Peers, and of the four Secretaries of State, who registr'd the same It is in this State that the Affair is at present and one may say, That without a great Revolution, there is little likelyhood, that the Embassadors of *Spain* will be present at those Ceremonies, where they shall be oblig'd either to contest, or give up the Rank to those of *France*

Vatteville thought, without doubt, that he did a signal Service to the King of *Spain*, and instead thereof he created him a very pernicious Quarrel, from whence neither he nor his Master could draw any manner of Advantage Whatever Success he had in his Enterprise, he thereby acquired no Title to his King, nor Credit to himself

In the Month of *September*, 1667, the Duke *de Chaunes*, Embassador Extraordinary from *France* at *Rome*, had sent his Coach to meet the Embassador of *Malta*, to do him Honour at his Entry, but the Cavalcade being oblig'd to pass before the Palace of the *Spanish* Embassador, this last sent out all his Servants, and having caus'd the Horses of the *French* Embassador to be stop'd, made his own Coach take the Precedency The Duke complain'd thereof to the Pope, who spoke to the Embassador about it but this told him, That he had no Measures to observe with the Duke *de Chaunes*, since the King his Master had in two Respects as good as broke with the King of *Spain*, in succouring the *Portuguese*, and in carrying his Arms into *Flanders* That nothing could hinder him from revenging it on all Occasions This was a sorry Revenge, and a poor Comfort after the Loss of so many fine Towns in *Flanders*

CHAP. XXV.

Of several other Competitions.

THERE is not any thing the Embassador ought to be more jealous of, than of the Rights and Dignity of his Prince, and particularly of the Rank he holds amongst the other Princes, to the End he may preserve it to him in the Ceremonies and publick Assemblies It is what he cannot be negligent in on any Account or Consideration whatever,

and

and he cannot fail therein, but at the Expence of his Honour, and his Like Pope *Urban* VIII who had a great Indulgence for his Relations, would have all the Embassadors of crown'd Heads give place in the Chapels, and other publick Ceremonies, to *Thadeus Barberin*, Prefect of *Rome* They had this Complaisance for the Pope during his Pontificate or at least they avoided the Occasions where they must have enter'd into a Contest with his Nephew. But immediately after the Exaltation of *Innocent* X, the Duke *Savelli*, the Emperor's Embassador, although a Subject of the Pope, and the Count *de Sivella*, Embassador of *Spain*, caus'd it to be mention'd to the Marquiss *de St Chaumont*, Embassador from *France*, and they resolv'd together, to reassume the Rank over the Prefect The two first did not visit the third, because their Masters were at War, but they soon enter'd into the same Sentiments for the common Interest of their Honour *St Chaumont* kept his Bed, being sick of the Gout, but the two others took Possession of their ancient Right on the very Day of the Pope's Election, who not having yet forgot the Obligation he had to the deceased, and to the *Barberins*, who had been instrumental to the making him Pope, had some Difficulty to declare himself in Favour of the Embassadors He desir'd them by Cardinal *Capont*, not to assist at the Chapel that Day, signifying to them at the same time, that he would cause the Prefect to absent likewise So that nothing should pass to the Prejudice of their Rights, which should be preserv'd entire to them The Embassadors express'd a great deal of Surprize at this Proposition, which put them upon the Level with a private Man The *French* Embassador declar'd formally, *That nothing should hinder him from being there, tho' he were sure to lose his Life, because he had his Master's positive Orders for so doing* The Emperor's and the *Spanish* Embassadors made an Answer less vigorous, but after they had discuss'd the Matter with the Cardinals of the Party, it was resolv'd that *Savelli* should write a Billet to Cardinal *Caponi*, in which he should tell him positively, *That if the Pope himself should expressly forbid him to come to the Throne*, (the *Italians* call it *Solio*) *he would notwithstanding go and take his Place, whatever Opposition might be made him* St *Chaumont* added, that if he met the Prefect any where in the Town, he would oblige him to stop his Coach, and give him the way The Pope at last declar'd in Favour of the Embassadors, and gave the Prefect Leave to protest The Pope, when he sent to invite the Embassadors to assist at the Chapel, signify'd to them, that the Prefect would not be there, because he was gone out of Town about some Affairs. The Embassadors made Answer, That they would go and take their Places at the Throne, and did not trouble themselves whether the Prefect was at *Rome* or in the Countrey

It must be judg'd by *Savelli*'s Billet, that he would have had his Place at the Chapel, even tho' the Pope, instead of the Request he made him as to the Emperor's Embassador, had commanded him as his Subject, to refrain coming, that he would have preferr'd his Master's Service to the Orders of his Sovereign, how absolute soever they might have been Wherein we must observe, what is spoken of elsewhere concerning the Respect Sovereigns ought to have for the Character in any Person whatsoever It is true, a Sovereign Prince may make himself be obey'd, even by an Embassador, provided he does not violate the Law of Nations. But then as the Embassador on his side, acknowledges no other Orders than those of his Master, the Prince must see how he can justify himself to the Prince of the Embassador, if this last is not allow'd all the Liberty that is due to his Character In the Year 1558, the Senate of *Venice* signify'd to the Bishop of *Acs*, Embassador from *France*, that it was expected he would not be present at a Procession, where they would have been oblig'd to have invited also the Embassador of *Spain* The Bishop was so surpriz'd at this Message, that he would needs have all his own Domesticks, and those of Cardinal *de Tournon* (who was lodg'd with him) to be Witnesses thereof However this did not hinder him from having a Deference to the Request of the Senate, because the Sovereign may and ought to prevent by all possible means, whatever can disturb or ruffle the Tranquillity of the State The Kings of *France* and of *Great-Britain* have thought it adviseable, not to admit for the future, the Embassadors Coaches at the Entries of those who arrive, because as the Kings and Sovereigns do on these Occasions all the Honours, they are in the right not to approve of Strangers medling therein At *Rome* there is a particular Reason that obliges Embassadors to appear at the publick Ceremonies, because in their Absence others might be apt to take Possession of some Functions which are peculiar to them, as the carrying the Train of the Pope's Cope, or the Pall, or the marching in their Rank at solemn Processions It may be said on occasion of this Competition of the Embassadors, and the Prefect, that the Embassador who does not at home yeild the Place of Honour to a Prince of the House of *Lorrain*, will be far from doing it in a third Place to an imaginary Prince, though it may be also said, that Pope *Pius* adjudg'd the Precedency to the Senator of *Rome*, against the *Spanish* Embassador Those who have any Knowledge of History, know what the Authority of a Senator of *Rome* was for some Centuries after the tenth Pope Clement IV, to do Honour to *Charles* Duke of *Anjou*, Brother to *Lewis* IX, King of *France*, made him Senator of *Rome* Nicholas III ordain'd, That for the future, the Quality of Senator should not be given to any Prince of the Royal Blood So that at this time there remains only the Name of it

I have spoken at large in the foregoing Chapter, of the Difference the Embassadors of *France* and *Spain* had about the Rank, and after what manner it was regulated, as well at *Trent* as at *Rome* In the Year 1542, was reviv'd that the King of *France* had on the same Subject with the King of the *Romans*, and this on occasion of the Contest, the *Germans* and the *French* had concerning which of the two Kings should be nam'd first in the Decrees of the Council of *Trent* The *French* said, their King was Sovereign and Absolute, and was in Possession of following the Emperor immediately, and preceding all the other Kings in Christendom

Lll That

That the King of the *Romans* was only a Titular King, and Emperor in Expectancy, as Coadjutor of the Imperial Dignity. The *Germans* on the other side, maintain'd, that the King of the *Romans* had the same Authority which the Laws give the Emperor. That he dispos'd of the Fiefs, that it was from him Princes took their Investiture, and receiv'd the *Regalia*, and that in the Emperor's Absence, he sate in the Imperial Throne. That he conven'd the Diets, that he issu'd out Edicts, and in general did all that the Emperor could do. They added, that in the Emperor *Frederick* III's Time, the Embassadors of *Maximilian* King of the *Romans*, had preceded those of *Lewis* XII, King of *France*, in the Pope's Chapel. *D'Urfé*, *Ligneres*, and *Danais*, Embassadors from *France*, being arriv'd at *Trent*, some Time after were for knowing what Place they should have, as well at the Sessions as in the Congregations. Cardinal *Pacheco* told them, That in his Opinion, they made this Question very much out of Season, since he judg'd that the Embassadors of *France* would not enter into Competition with those of the Empire, and there were no others at *Trent*, and so there was no Body with whom they could have any Contestation about the Rank. Perhaps the Thing had ended here, had not the Archbishop of *Madera* thought fit to mention the King of the *Romans*, saying, That at the Council of *Lateran*, his Embassador had preceded that of *France*. The Archbishop of *Armac* made Answer, That at that Time *Maximilian* was not King of the *Romans*, but Emperor, and that he did not take the Quality thereof, because he was not yet crown'd by the Pope; whereas *Ferdinand* had only the bare Title. The Bishop of *Feltro* said, That the Examples of ancient History shew'd, that the Empire might at the same time have two Emperors of equal Power and Authority. But the Bishop of *Bitonto* took him up, and said, he had never heard say, nor read, that *Charles* and *Ferdinand* were both Emperors. The other Prelates would also speak their Sentiments, and the Contest had gone very far, had it not been for the Bishop of *Lucera*, who said, That it was not a Matter belonging to the Council, and that the Fathers ought not to take Cognizance thereof, but that it ought to be regulated by the Legates. All the Assembly acquiesc'd therein, tho' in such a manner as made it sufficiently known that the Council was favourably dispos'd to *France*. The Legates took here an Occasion to speak of a Decree which had been made soon after the Overture of the Council, whereby due Provision was made, that whatever should be done in reference to the Ceremonies, should do no Prejudice to the Parties, nor be any Precedent.

The Embassadors of *France* being inform'd of what had pass'd in that Conference, declar'd to the Legates, that if they did not assign them a certain and honourable Place among the Embassadors of the other Kings, they would be gone. The Legates made Answer, That they ought to have more Regard to the general Disposition of the Council, which was favourable to them, than to the Transports of two or three hair-brain'd Persons who abus'd the Liberty they had to speak, which the Place gave them.

That since the Embassadors of the Emperor were arriv'd at *Trent*, those of the King of the *Romans* had not appear'd, because the last Comers could act for both the one and the other. So that it was not necessary to begin a Process before the Possession was contested with them. The *French* Embassadors were not satisfy'd with this Answer, and the Legates appear'd to be so much the more perplex'd, because there was no likelihood of prevailing with either of the Parties to yield. They consider'd also, that the Council could not give Judgment in a thing, concerning which there was neither Law nor Custom, nor was not of its Jurisdiction. From whence it was reasonable to think, that even tho' the Fathers should determine the Matter upon good Principles, and an indisputable Right, they would not be able to put their Sentence in Execution nor to procure Obedience thereto. It seem'd as if the only Mean to remove these Difficulties, was to prevail with the Embassadors of *Ferdinand* not to be present at the publick Actions, because not having been there while the Emperor had no Embassadors at *Trent*, they might very well forbear it still, without any Suspicion of their doing so on the *French* Embassador's Account. The Legates apprehended besides, that the Embassadors of the Emperor, who is more especial Protector of the Council, pretended to some Pre-eminency there, would make Difficulty to suffer the *French* Embassadors to take Place immediately after them, but they made none, and those of *France* contenting themselves to keep the Rank which belong'd to them, immediately after the Emperor's Embassadors, acquiesc'd likewise. It is evident, that the Embassadors of *France* came off here with Advantage. For if the Pretensions of the King of the *Romans* were just and well founded, his Ministers did him an irreparable Prejudice, by not appearing at the publick Assemblies. They renounc'd their Master's Right, in suffering the *French* Embassadors to take Place next to those of the Emperor, never to relinquish the same after having gain'd Possession. And in effect, since the Embassadors of *Ferdinand* superseded the Execution of the Functions of their Employment, on the Appearance of the Emperor's Ministers, they sufficiently made known, that their Prince being only a Lieutenant, Vicar, or Coadjutor of his Brother, the Emperor's Presence eclips'd his Dignity, which in Reality had no Lustre but in the Absence of the Planet which gave it him.

It cannot be deny'd but the Ministers of the King of the *Romans* distrusted their Master's Right, since they had some Difficulty to maintain it in a Competition, which they had since with a much weaker Adversary. In the Year 1552, there arriv'd at *Trent* three Embassadors from *Portugal*, *James de Selva*, *James de Goves*, and *John Paez*, who immediately had a Difference about Precedency with the Embassadors of the King of the *Romans*. In Order to regulate the Contest, so as to preserve the Right of both Parties, it was order'd, That for the first Time the Speaker of the *Portugueze* should be seated on the Bench of the Ecclesiasticks, over against the Presidents or Legates. That in that Place he should declare his Obedience and

and in the mean time the Embassadors of *Ferdinand* should remain in a Room hard by But as this Provision did not decide the Difference, the Parties agreed among themselves to refer the Matter to the Pope, who took Cognizance thereof as Judge, and not as Arbitrator The Interessed, to render him favourable to them, try'd to make Friends at *Rome*, and had Recourse to the Intercession of those who had most Interest there The Ministers of *Ferdinand* writing on this Subject to some of the Pope's Officers, in recommending to them the Interest of their Master, desir'd they would furnish them with some Example that might oblige the Pope to pronounce in Favour of the King of the *Romans*, whether he consider'd *Ferdinand* in this Quality, or would give him the Advantage on Account of his Kingdom of *Hungary*, which was not a bare empty Title, but an effectual Possession Answer was made them, That after a due Enquiry it appear'd, *that the Difference had never been regulated in Reference to the Chapel* So that his Holiness could not determine the Difference, without hearing the Reasons of the Parties That his Advice was, that those Embassadors of *Ferdinand*, who were Bishops, should take their Places among the Ecclesiasticks, and put themselves at the Head of all the Prelates, while those of *Portugal* should be rank'd amongst the Seculars, and that if this Proposition did not please them they might accommodate the Matter with the Fathers of the Council, as they should think it proper On the 24th Day of *April* the Parties agreed among themselves, that in the general Assembly of that Day, where all the Embassadors were to be present, as also in those of the next Day, and of the 27th and 28th of the same Month, the Embassadors of *Portugal* should be seated opposite to those of the Emperor, that is to say, on the right Side, before the Legates, where those Electors who were Ecclesiasticks, and were gone, had been seated, and that those of *Ferdinand* should be plac'd by the Emperor's Embassadors on the left Hand The whole, for these Days only And to the End nothing might pass to the Prejudice of either Party, neither the Pax nor the Incense was presented to any of the Embassadors, of which those of *Portugal* caus'd an authentick Act to be given them Since that Time there has been no more Contests with the Embassadors of the King of the *Romans*, because *Ferdinand* having succeeded to the Empire, by the Resignation of *Charles*, he sent his Embassadors to *Trent* as Emperor He was also King of *Hungary*, and in that Quality he had also his Embassador

But before we speak of the Dispute this last had with the Embassador of the King of *Portugal*, I think my self oblig'd to say a Word or two concerning the Difference which happen'd at *Munster*, about the Quality of Majesty between the Emperor and the King of *France* In the Year 1646, the Queen Regent had sent to *Munster* the *Sieur de Mondevergues*, in Order to have him sent from thence, by the Plenipotentiaries to *Vienna*, to complement that Court on the Death of the Empress But forasmuch as in the Reign of *Lewis* XIII, the Emperor had been written to on such an Occasion, and had not answer'd the Letter, the Queen would not have this Gentleman set out, till it was certain that the Emperor would return the Civility which was intended him In the Conferences which the Plenipotentiaries of *France* had with those of the Emperor hereupon, the Count *de Trautmansdorf* told them no Answer had been made, because in those Letters the King gave no other Title to the Emperor than that of *Serenity* He was answer'd, That the King in that had follow'd the Emperor's Example, who had given the same Title to the King, in his So that the Council having deliberated thereupon, had resolv'd not to suffer the least Inequality betwixt the Emperor and the King That the King of *France* was Emperor within his own Dominions, even according to the Sentiments of the *German* Lawyers That they could make it appear, that this Equality had always been obferv'd amongst them, and that the Queen wou'd not suffer it to be alter'd in the least The Count reply'd, that, on the contrary they could prove, That King *Henry* IV, and the late King, had always given the Emperor the Style of *Majesty*, while this return'd them only that of *Serenity* They did not agree upon the Matter of Fact, wherefore several Means of Accommodation were propos'd The Mediators intermeddl'd, and it was thought the Parties might be satisfy'd if they gave one another the Style of *Majesty* or *Dilection*, or else that of *Imperial Majesty* and *Royal Majesty*, when the Emperor and the King wrote each to the other with their own Hand, or in the Style of the *Chancery* Letters were dispatch'd to *Vienna* and *Paris* about it, but as at that Time the two Courts had not much Complaisance one for the other, it was impossible to adjust the Difference The Emperor's *Chancery* was obstinate, and would not change its Style, and the Ministers of *France* could not suffer the King should be written to in a Style which was common to several Princes of *Germany*, and with the Doge of *Venice* They said that formerly none but the Kings of *France* were expressly nam'd in the Pope's Bulls, with the Emperors as their Equals, while they spoke of all the other Kings but in general, and without naming them, and that this Practice had been alter'd but since the Council of *Trent* That if it was necessary to trace Things up to their first Origin, it would be found, that the King of *France* was not oblig'd to take Place after the Emperor, but only after his Coronation by the Pope, because without this Ceremony he was properly but King of the *Romans* However, *it was at last agreed between* Trautmansdorf *and the Plenipotentiaries of* France, *by the Help of the Mediators, that when the Emperor and the King of* France *should write each to the other with their own Hands, they should give one to the other the Title of* Imperial Majesty *and* Royal Majesty

The Embassador I lately spoke of, who represented *Ferdinand* at *Trent* as King of *Hungary*, was nam'd *George Drascovitz*, and was Bishop of *Cinqeghses* He came thither incognito, but when *Anthony Mughtz*, Archbishop of *Prague*, one of the Emperor's Embassadors, made his Entry some Days after, *Drascovitz* went also out of Town, and an Entry was made to both of them; they being accompany'd by five Bishops who were sent to meet them.

them *Martin de Mafcaregnas*, Embaſſador from *Sebaſtian* King of *Portugal*, being arriv'd almoſt at the ſame Time within three Leagues of *Trent*, ſent Word to the Legates, That he would not allow the Embaſſador of the King of *Hungary* to have Audience before him, as well becauſe he had only ſimple *Letters of Credence* without any other Power, as becauſe he repreſented *Ferdinand* but only as King of *Hungary*, and that in that Quality he ought to give Place to the King of *Portugal*. From this Pretenſion of the *Portugueze* ſprung three Difficulties. The firſt, whether *Draſcoütz* ought to be receiv'd by Virtue of his Credentials, altho' he had no Powers. The other Difficulty was, whether his Audience ought to be put off till *Maſcaregnas* had taken his. And the third was how the Rank ſhould be regulated between them. The Fathers of the Council declar'd concerning the two firſt Points, That the Credentials were ſufficient to give the Character to *Draſcoütz*, and that as he was arriv'd before the Embaſſador of *Portugal*, he might alſo be firſt admitted to Audience. But the third Point, as the moſt difficult, was put into the Hands of ſome Prelates to examine. The Legates wrote about it to the Pope, and pray'd him, in the ſame Letter, not to refer the Cognizance thereof, either to them or the Council, no more than of that which was depending between the Embaſſadors of *France* and *Spain* on the ſame Subject, becauſe, as the *Spaniards* were there in great Number, there was no Room to doubt but they would determine it in Favour of their King. In the mean Time, the ſaid Legates conſidering that the Competition was not a Thing they could regulate of their own Authority, and as Judges, endeavour'd to diſpoſe the Parties to an Accommodation. They made an Order, by which they ordain'd, That thoſe Embaſſadors who were Prelates, or of the Church, ſhould be ſeated on a Bench on the Right Hand, at the Head of all the other Prelates, but in giving their Opinions upon the Matters propos'd, they ſhould declare their Sentiments according to their Seniority, in reference to their Promotion, becauſe then they diſcharg'd the Function of Biſhop, and not that of Embaſſador. As for the Lay-Embaſſadors, they ſhould have theirs on the Left Hand, and ſhould precede all the Prelates who were not Embaſſadors, except when they were clad in their Pontifical Habits, to execute ſome eccleſiaſtical Function, in which the Biſhops and miter'd Abbots ſhould go to the Altar before the Lay Embaſſadors, and that at ſolemn Proceſſions, theſe laſt ſhould march immediately before the Legates, which is the Rank they hold at *Rome* in the Proceſſions where the Pope aſſiſts in Perſon. What I have now related, was done in the Beginning of 1562. On the 26th of *February*, of the ſame Year, the Credentials of the Emperor's Embaſſador were read in the Aſſembly, and after that, thoſe of *Draſcoütz*, Embaſſador of *Ferdinand* King of *Hungary*. Then they ask'd *Maſcaregnas* for his, but he would not deliver them, pretending that the Council, by cauſing thoſe of the Embaſſador of *Hungary* to be read firſt, had prejudic'd the Rights of the King of *Portugal* his Maſter. The Secretary of the Council ſtept down from his Desk, to repreſent to *Maſcaregnas* that the Council had, in that, follow'd the Cuſtom of *Rome*, and of all the other Courts of *Europe*, where the firſt Comers are firſt heard. It was ſomewhat difficult to make him comprehend, and to perſuade him, that it was not the Intention of the Council to do any Prejudice to the King of *Portugal*, nor to his Embaſſador, becauſe there was no ſpeaking to him but by an Interpreter, but at laſt he agreed, and there was no Diſpute about the Rank. The one being of the Church, and the other a Lay-Perſon.

I ſhall here continue the Thread of my Diſcourſe (and perhaps not deviate from my Purpoſe) to ſome other Competitions, which frequently interrupted the ordinary Occupations of the Council. *John Strozzi*, Embaſſador from *Coſmus* Duke of *Florence*, who had not as yet the Quality of Great Duke of *Tuſcany*, arriv'd at *Trent* the 15th of *March*, 1562, and the next Day arriv'd *Melchior Lrſſy*, Embaſſador from the five little *Swiſs Cantons*. This laſt had expreſs Orders from his Superiors to take the next Rank immediately after the Embaſſador of *Venice*, and to precede all thoſe who ſhould give Place to the Republick. *Strozzi* oppos'd it, and the *Swiſs* Embaſſador proteſted, That if that Satisfaction were not giv'n him he would be gone. The Legates were ſo much the more perplex'd herein, becauſe there was no Accommodation to be hop'd for, and in breaking with either the one or the other the Council would be greatly prejudic'd thereby, and the Breach in Religion almoſt irreparable. They could not alſo be Judges in an Affair of this Nature, and ſuppoſing they were, they could not decide it without offending the Parties irreconcileably. To free themſelves from this Inquietude, they pray'd the Pope to take ſuch Meaſures that *Coſmus* might not enter into a Conteſt on that Head, but give up his Intereſt to the Good and Repoſe of *Chriſtendom*. *Coſmus* did ſo, by giving Orders to his Embaſſador to pretend ſome Occaſion to go into the Countrey, when he ſhould be inform'd that the *Swiſs* Embaſſador would be at the Aſſembly. If the *Cantons* at this Day enter'd into a Diſpute about the Rank with the Great Duke, they would not meet with the ſame Condeſcenſion. But this Competition can have no Room but at a Council, becauſe the *Swiſs* have no Embaſſadors in Ordinary in the Courts of Princes, and the Extraordinaries make ſo ſhort a Stay there, that they can have no great Communication with the other Embaſſadors, who have no Occaſion to meet with them in a third Place, neither do they ſeek it.

This Difference gave Birth to another, between the ſame *Swiſs* Embaſſador and *Auguſtin Baumgartner*, whom *Albert*, Duke of *Bavaria*, had ſent to *Trent* with the Quality of Embaſſador, with the Jeſuit *Cavillon*. They made no publick Entry, but when they ſaw the Legates, they told them, *That the Embaſſadors had Orders to give Place to none but to thoſe of crown'd Heads, and of the Electors*. The Legates made Anſwer, *That the Republick of* Venice *poſſeſs'd two Kingdoms*. The Miniſters of *Bavaria* reply'd, *That it was poſſible the Duke their Maſter, in mentioning the crown'd Heads, might alſo compriſe the Republick, but that it was not their Buſineſs to explain the Intention of their Maſter, ſince* he had not done it himself That they would write to him about it, and in the mean time, they defir'd the Legates to call together an Affembly, at which the Venetian Embaffadors might not affift, to the end they might therein shew their Credentials The Legates said, They could not do it, and defir'd the Bavarian Embaffadors to dispatch an Express to their Prince, that he might send them his last Orders They receiv'd them quickly, but in very positive Terms The Duke commanding Baumgartner to come away immediately from Trent, if he had not a Rank given him before the Embaffador of Venice There was no regulating this Competition to the Content of both Parties, and there was no disobliging either the one or the other, without hazarding Religion very much, the Duke being full as Considerable in Germany, as the Republick was so in Italy The Legates therefore pray'd the Pope to employ the Authority of Ferdinand, with the Duke of Bavaria his Son-in-Law, and to represent to him, that the Republick was a King in effect, and was in Possession of an indisputable Right to follow the crown'd Heads immediately But the Emperor, who would not meddle in a Negotiation of that Delicacy, kept within general Terms, and contented himself to send the Propositions of the Pope and the Legates, to the Duke his Son-in-Law Nevertheless the Bavarian Embaffador receiv'd a second Order to yield Precedency to the Embaffador of Venice protesting however at the same time, that it was for the sake of Peace, and without Prejudice to his Rights Baumgartner being afterwards admitted into the Congregation, there protested that the Precedency was due to the Prince his Master, because the Electoral Dignity was actually in his House, and the Imperial had been formerly Nicholas de Ponte, Embaffador of Venice, protested on the contrary, That it was neither through Courtefy nor Favour that he took the first Place, but of Right and Justice, not provisionally, but for ever They both requir'd to have their Protestations register'd, and the Animosity went so far, that the Embaffador of Bavaria refus'd to give a Copy of his Harangue, because he was inform'd the Venetian had not given any

Baumgartner could not form this Difficulty, without making himself a Controverfy with the Embaffadors of the Cantons and of Florence so that the Legates, to regulate in some Measure the Difference, prevail'd with the first of these two, to absent from the Congregations, till he had receiv'd fresh Orders on this Subject and Cosimus suffer'd himself to be perfuaded, to command his Embaffador not to be present thereat, even tho' the Embaffador of the Cantons should not be there But the Duke of Bavaria took it so hainously, that the Minister of the Cantons should presume to contest with his Embaffador, and that the Council should suffer it, that he commanded his Embaffador to leave Trent, and he accordingly went away The Legates gave him Affurance, that his Rank should be duly preferv'd to him in the Congregations, and that the Embaffador of the Cantons should never be invited thither, but he would not be satisfy'd therewith, without they made a formal Decree, which the Council did not think fit to do, for fear of offending the Swifs in too great a Manner

The Legates proceeded with so much the more Circumspection, because they had receiv'd Orders from Rome, to declare to the Embaffadors, that till the Answers were return'd from Bavaria and the Cantons, no Embaffador should affift at the Congregations, unless he were expressly invited, and that those who notwithstanding this should go, should give Place to those who were invited, and that they who should not be satisfy'd with this Regulation, might do as they thought fit The Swifs order'd their Embaffador to be contented with the Alternative, if he of Bavaria would consent thereto, but Baumgartner was set out when this Order came

The Bavarian Embaffador said right, that the Electoral Dignity was in his Master's House, but even if the Duke had been Elector himself, the Embaffador of Venice would notwithstanding that have disputed the Precedency with him The Contest which the Bishop of Osnaburg, Embaffador from the Electoral College, had at Munster with Aloysio Contarini, sufficiently shews, that the Republick is resolv'd to maintain it self in the Poffeffion she is in, in all the Courts, to follow the crown'd Heads immediately The Bishop alledg'd there amongst other Reasons, that at the Marriage of the Emperor Matthias, and of Anne of Bavaria, which was solemniz'd at Gratz in the Year 1600, the Embaffador of the Elector had preceded that of Venice Contarini, who did not allow it, said, That even if that were true, the Electors could not draw any Advantage therefrom, because the Palatine might have been there considerd, as a Relation of the Bride These particular Examples, where Princes regulate the Ceremonies as they please, are no Precedents When in the Year 1605, Sigifmond, King of Poland, solemniz'd the Marriage of Demetrius, the pretended Czar of Moscovy, with the Daughter of the Palatin of Sendomir, he seated at his own Table only the new marry'd Couple, the Queen, the Bride's Sifter, Wife to Sigifmond Battory, Prince of Transilvania, and the Embaffador of Muscovy There was another Table for the other Embaffadors, where that of the Elector of Brandenburg having been plac'd above the Embaffador of the Great Duke of Tuscany, this last was grievously vex'd thereat, but with so much the less Reason, as the Great Duke, who every where gives Place to the Duke of Savoy, makes no Difficulty to yield Precedency to the Electors, with whom the Duke of Savoy has no Competition, unless this last has new Pretensions, since he has given himself the Title of Royal Highness The Embaffador of Brandenburg had not more Reason to dispute the Rank with the Nuncio For altho' the Elector does not acknowledge the Pope in his Spiritual Capacity, and that he has no Commerce with him in reference to the Temporal, yet his Embaffador ought not to have been ignorant of the Rank the Nuncio holds in all the Catholick Courts

At this Day there is a Competition between all the Kings, because being all Sovereigns, they judge that their Rank ought not to be regulated by their Power, which is much greater, and more absolute in some than in others, but by their Sovereignty only, which admits of no Comparison. As soon as they began to settle the Preliminaries for the Congress of *Westphalia*, the *Swedes* declar'd, they would not yield to the Ministers of *France* in any thing, because the Crown of *Sweden*, altho' less Powerful than that of *France*, yet *possesses the same Dignity, in the same Degree, and so might justly pretend the same Rank.* And *France* on its part, not thinking it advisable to disoblige on this Account, a Crown whose Friendship was necessary to it, and not being able at the same Time, to renounce a Preheminency which she had enjoy'd for many Ages, another Expedient was thought of, and to avoid these Contestations, it was resolv'd that the Assembly should be held at two different Places, *viz.* at *Munster* and at *Osnaburg*. But from this Accommodation, sprung another Difficulty concerning the first Visit. It was absolutely necessary the Ministers should see one another often, because they could not separate their Interests, without ruining them. They therefore agreed at last, after many long and vexatious Debates, that the Conferences should be held at a third Place, in the Mid-way between *Munster* and *Osnaburg*, in two neighbouring Houses, *of which the French should have their Choice*. That the *Swedes* should come thither first, that they might make the first Visit to the *French*, as to the last Comers. But before all this could be executed, *Salvius*, one of the Plenipotentiaries of *Sweden*, having been oblig'd to make a Journey to *Munster*, the *French* paid him the first Visit, as to the last Comer. *Servien* went some Days after to *Osnaburg*, where he receiv'd also the first Visit. I shall speak in the second Part of this Work, of the Contest which arose between the two Crowns, concerning the Rank they should hold in signing the Treaty, which they were to negotiate with the Emperor, and the States of the Empire, as well as of the Difference *France* has had on the same Account with *England*.

In the Year 1607, *France* had three Embassadors at the *Hague*, and forasmuch as two were expected also from *England*, and that the first apprehended a Contest might arise among the Ministers, about the Rank, President *Jeannin* was for knowing from *M. de Villeroy*, how they were to govern themselves in reference to those of *England*, when they should be oblig'd to enter into Conference with them, either at the Lodgings of the *French* Embassadors, or in a third Place, at Prince *Maurice*'s, or elsewhere. Whereupon *M. de Villeroy* wrote on the 29th of *August* in these Terms. *We cannot believe that they* (the Embassadors of *England*) *will be so presumptuous as to dispute the Precedency with you, if they do it, it must be to thwart and perplex Matters. This Question was never contested between them and us, as it justly has by them with the Spaniards. For the English have formerly taken Place of the Castillians. When they come to your Houses, you ought to do them Honour, and give them the first Place by Courtesy. But when they shall come there, to treat in the Presence of the Deputies of the States, or others, you are not to give Place, either to them or any others, on any account whatever. This Contention would of it self be so prejudicial to the Dignity of the King our Master, that you ought to avoid engaging therein, or even to mention it, if it be possible. When you meet them at Prince Maurice's, or elsewhere, you are to take the most honourable Place. This is what the King has commanded me to write to you.* It is true when the Conferences were held at the *French* Embassadors, their Lodgings were to be consider'd as a neutral Place, but those of *England*, that they might not be reduc'd to the Necessity of yielding to the *French*, in the House of the *French* Embassadors, ought not to have suffer'd the Conferences to be held any where but in a third Place. The *English* said indeed, that they had Orders not to enter into a Contest with the *French* concerning the Rank, but that they thought also, that when they shew'd this Respect to the *French*, these ought on their part, to do them the Civility of giving them the first Place in their own Houses, when they should happen to be there with the Deputies of the States, and pay them the same Civilities which were shewn them at their private Visits. The Embassadors of *France* made answer, *That that would prejudice the Dignity of the King their Master, and would be contrary to the Protestation the English made, of being willing to yield, because that on those Occasions, their House would be a publick Place, destin'd to a solemn Assembly, for which Reason they would take the most honourable Place, as accordingly they did.* This would not be practis'd at this Day, since the Embassadors of *France*, yield in their own Houses the Place of Honour, even to the Deputies of the States, and with much more Reason would they do it to the Embassadors of *England*, who even without that, would be no longer so easy.

What *Villeroy* says, that *England* has formerly had the Precedency of *Castile*, is not without Foundation. King *Henry IV* having in the Year 1600, dispos'd *Spain* and *England* to to send their Ministers to *Bologne*, there to negotiate a Peace, it was consider'd in *England*, that the first Difficulty that would offer it self, would be concerning the Precedency. Queen *Elizabeth* having therefore caus'd an exact Search to be made of the Practice of Times past, it was found in the Ceremonial of *Rome*, that among the Kings, the first Place was due to the King of *France*, the second to the King of *England*, and the third to the King of *Castile*. That the *English* had peaceably enjoy'd this Advantage, at the Councils of *Constance*, of *Basil*, &c. Besides which, the Kingdom of *Castile*, which constitutes the first Title of the King of *Spain*, is altogether new in reference to *England* since before the Year 1017, it had no Kings, but only Counts and Pope *Julius* II had pronounc'd in favour of Henry VII, against Ferdinand *the Catholick*. In Conformity here unto, the Queen expresly commanded *Henry de Neufville*, her Embassador in Ordinary in *France*, *John Herbert*, *Robert Beale* and *Thomas Edmonds*, her Extraordinary Embassadors, not to yield Precedency to the Ministers of *Spain*. However, rather than to suffer the Negotiation to break off, to have recourse to *Lot*. After the Powers were communicated on both sides, the *English* pretended to the Precedency. The Ministers of *Spain* said, They were surpriz'd to see the *English*, who could not hope for an Equality with the Catholick King, pretend to the Precedency. The *English* reply'd, That their Right was notoriously plain; and that on all

The EMBASSADOR and his FUNCTIONS. 227

all Occasions their Embassadors ought to precede the Ministers of *Spain*, and of the Arch-Duke, who had only the Quality of Deputies but the *Spaniards* would not so much as hear this, and said, That the King of *Spain* would neither consent to the Precedency, nor even to an Equality They had no great mind to treat, and took this Pretext to break off the Negotiation, tho' the *English* offer'd to enter upon Business, without prejudicing this Pretension, and to negotiate by Writing

I had began to say, that there happen'd a great Contest concerning the Rank, between the Embassador of *Venice*, and that of the Electors I shall make make an end of it, when I have spoke a Word or two about that the Electors had with the Duke of *Burgundy* at the Council of *Basil* The Embassadors of *Philip the Good* said, That their Master was a Prince of the Blood, and the first Lay Peer of *France* That he was in Possession of *Burgundy*, which had formerly been a Kingdom, and with it, of six Dukedoms, fifteen Counties, and several other Sovereign Lordships, which gave him Rank immediately after the crown'd Heads *Philip* was in effect one of the most powerful Princes of Christendom and what he possess'd in *Burgundy* and in *Flanders*, were well worth the Kingdom of *France*, before *Charles* VII had reunited *Normandy* and *Guyenne* to it, and that *Lewis* XI, had joyn'd thereto *Burgundy* and *Province*, and *Charles* VIII, *Brittany* But all these Estates together could not give him a Dignity, that no one of his Provinces had in particular The Qualities of Prince of the Blood, and of first Peer, could not make him be consider'd any where but in *France*, and they were not what qualify'd him to send Embassadors to the Council The Dutchy of *Burgundy* being at this Day but a very small Part of what formerly made a large Kingdom enough, under that Name it could give him no other Rank than that of Duke It cannot be deny'd but the Electors and Princes of the Empire, ought to be at least as Considerable in the Empire, as the Cardinals are at *Rome*, because they are Sovereigns, and make a Part of the Empire, whereas the Cardinals are the Pope's Subjects, and only constitute his Council So that in this Quality, the Electors ought to precede all those who are not Sovereigns *Chopin* and *Chassagne*, *French* Lawyers, say, That the Fathers of the Council adjudg'd the Precedency to the Embassadors of the Duke of *Burgundy*, but the Truth of the Matter is, that after a Dispute of several Hours, these had a Place assign'd them right against that of the Emperor, on the Bench appointed for the Embassadors of crown'd Heads, and that the Electors kept theirs by the Emperor, as Members inseparable from their Head Neither was it the Council that regulated the Difference and the Rank among the Embassaors, but it was only done by way of Accommodation and Provision, as the Emperor *Sigismund* says very expressly, in a Letter which he writes on this Subject to the Fathers of the Council. So that one may say, That the Embassadors of the Duke of *Burgundy* reap'd no other Advantage thereby, than what was granted to the *Spanish* Embassador at *Trent*, where he had a Place given him out of Rank, while those of *France*

preserv'd the Place they had always had immediately after the Emperor It is true, that this Advantage was so much the greater to the *Spaniards*, and to the Duke of *Burgundy*, as in the Case of Precedency, *it is not sufficient to preserve ones own Rank, but it is also requisite, to oblige them who are to follow, to keep theirs likewise*

The Contest the Bishop of *Osnaburg* and the Embassador of *Venice* had at *Munster*, was considerable enough The Plenipotentiaries of *France* declar'd at first, That as the Bishop was a Prince of the Empire, they would make no Difficulty to pay him the first Visit, and to give him the Title of Highness and those of the Emperor struck into the same Sentiments But the Embassador of *Venice* fearing lest it might be a Precedent of ill Consequence to him, went and told the Ministers of *France*, That he very well perceiv'd the Intention of the Electoral College, was to dispossess the Republick of the Rank she had held for many Ages, immediately after the Crowns, from whence her Dignity and Reputation would receive a Prejudice, which he was oblig'd to oppose That the Precedency was due to the Republick, on the Account of its Antiquity, and of the Power and Extent of its Estates, having greater Revenues than all the Electors together as also on the Account of its Liberty, it acknowledging no other Superior but God alone, whereas the Electors take an Oath to the Emperor, and hold of him protesting that he should be oblig'd to withdraw, if Satisfaction was not given him The Bishop alledg'd for himself the Resolution the Electoral College had taken thereupon, and the Possession the Electors are in, of preceding all other Princes and States, except crown'd Heads He said, That if the Electors gave Place to *Venice*, the United Provinces would also pretend to the Precedency, and after that they should have the same Contestation with the *Swiss Cantons*, and with the Republick of *Genoa* That if *Contarini* would retire, it would not be the Elector's Fault, but the Injustice of his Pretentions that would be the Cause thereof The Bishop very much press'd the Plenipotentiaries of *France* to declare themselves for the Rights of the Electors, but they represented, that it was a Novelty, that it requir'd Deliberation, and that they ought not to proceed in it with Precipitancy, tho' he assur'd them, that the Count of *Nassau*, and *Volmar*, had Orders from the Emperor, to do the same Honours to the Embassadors of the Electors, as they did to those of *Venice Don Diego Saavedra*, who was then first Plenipotentiary of *Spain*, said at first, That what the Bishop demanded was neither Just nor Reasonable but as the Friendship of the Electors was more necessary to the King his Master, than that of the Republick, he soon resolv'd to do the same Honours to the Bishop, leaving the Difference of the Rank undecided The Ministers of *France* consented also thereto, upon Condition that those of the Electors should not do more Honour to the Emperor's Plenipotentiaries, than to those of the King signifying on another Occasion, that what was done at *Munster*, should be of no Consequence out of that Place. It is not long, since at *Vienna* more Honour was done to the Embassadors of *Venice* and of *Florence*, than

than to those of the Electors, and when Complaint was made thereof, the Count *de Trautmansdorf* said, *That in the Emperor's House the Electors were consider'd as an essential Part of it, and the Princes of* Italy *as Strangers, to whom more Civility was to be shewn than to Domesticks* To me the Comparison seems very familiar, and that *Trautmandorf* spoke like an Officer of the Emperor's Houshould But he did not thereby do much Honour to the Electors The Bull of *Charles* IV says, *That they are the Pillars, the Buttresses, the Luminaries of the Empire, of which they are an essential Part, and not of the Emperor's Houshold, where their Ministers ought to be preferr'd to those of all other Princes and States, except crown'd Heads, provided they have the same Character* I doubt whether those the Electors send to *Vienna* have that of Embassador, because there is no likelihood that their Embassadors would speak to the Emperor uncover'd, since they may avoid that Mortification, by giving to their Ministers the Quality of *Abgesanter*, instead of that of *Gesanter*, and if I am not mistaken, it is that which they most commonly give to them, tho' these two Words are often confounded in the Chanceries, as well as in Books The Resolution of the Electors, of which the Bishop of *Osnaburg* spoke, is conformable to the fourth Article of the Capitulation of the Emperor *Ferdinand* III, and to the Fifth of that of the present Emperor They both speak almost in the same Terms But as the Electors there renounce their own Interest, and have Regard only to the Empire, they cannot be strain'd beyond that to the Prejudice of other Sovereigns, who acknowledge neither the Laws nor the Decrees of the Princes of *Germany*

It will not be from the Purpose to observe here, what the Chancellor *de Chiverny* says of a Difficulty which happen'd at the Entry, which Queen *Elizabeth*, Daughter of the Emperor *Maximilian* II, (who came to be marry'd to King *Charles* IX) made at *Mezieres*, in the Year 1570 The King sent to meet her by the Duke of *Anjou* his Brother, and the Emperor had given the chief Charge of conducting his Daughter the Elector of *Triers* And forasmuch as there arose some Difficulty concerning the Rank these two Princes were to take, an Express was sent to Court to know the King's Intention, who said, that the Duke ought to yield to the Elector as to a Sovereign Prince, who was the Emperor's Embassador Chiverny says, that he who was then the Duke's Chancellor, knew so well how to represent to the Council the Wrong that was done to the first Prince of the Blood of *France*, and to the presumptive Heir of the Crown, who ought to give Place to crown'd Heads only, even out of the Kingdom, that Leave was given him to put the Affair in Negotiation, and to endeavour to bring the Elector to consent thereto, without being offended. That hereupon he, *Chiverny*, who had gain'd some Credit with the Elector, manag'd him so nicely, that he prevail'd with him to acquiesce; but that however, the Duke did him Civility, and offer'd him the Place of Honour, which the Elector refus'd This Passage is by so much the more remarkable, as the King himself judg'd that the Duke his Brother ought to yeild to the Elector, and that the Duke did not scruple to offer him the Place of Honour That the Ceremony was perform'd within the Kingdom, where Monsieur is without doubt, the second Person when there is no *Dauphin*, and that the Elector, who was not well vers'd in the Ceremonial, suffer'd himself to be hurry'd away with the Wheedles of *Chiverny*, who all along spoke for his Master's Interest After all, I cannot tell how he could maintain what he adds, that the first Prince of the Blood of *France* ought to precede all other Princes, except crown'd Heads, even out of the Kingdom Since soveriegn Princes, and particularly the Electors do not agree therein When in the Year 1640, the Elector *Palatine* came to *Paris*, the Duke of *Orleans* made Difficulty to give him the Place of Honour at his own House, for which Reason these two Princes did not visit The Duke of *Orleans* did not always reflect that he was a Subject, but Cardinal *de Richlieu* had an Opportunity more than once to make him know it

In the Year 1641, the States of the United Provinces sent into *England* an Embassy compos'd of the Lords of *Brederode, D'Aarsens*, and *de Hiemvliet*, about the Marriage of Prince *William* Son to the Prince of *Orange* One of the first Visits they made, was to the Elector *Palatine*, who was then at *London* The Elector who had carry'd it upon the Level with the Prince of *Orange*, the Son, took at his own House the upper Hand of the Embassadors, without boggling They thereupon signify'd to him, that they expected to be us'd after the same manner as he carry'd it to the Prince of *Orange* But he made Answer, that he was in Possession of the Precedency, and that he could not innovate, without knowing the King's Intention, but he did not visit the Embassadors There is room to wonder that *Aarsens*, who had been so long Embassador in *France*, who had been employ'd in so many Embassies in *Germany* and *Italy*, should not know that the Dukes of *Savoy, Florence*, and of *Mantua*, do not give at their own Palaces the Place of Honour to the Embassadors of crown'd Heads And yet these Princes have no Competition with the Electors However by the Elector *Palatine*'s Answer, it appears, *That he was willing to know the King's Intention*, that he pretended to this Prerogative as being a Prince of the Blood of *England*, rather than as Elector, tho' I can hardly believe that that was his Electoral Highness's Thought, because at that time, even the Princes of the Blood of *France*, made no Difficulty to give the Hand and Step to Embassadors, though at the same time they were very cautious of yeilding elsewhere the Advantage they enjoy'd in the first Court of *Europe*

It cannot be deny'd but the Electors have obtain'd a great Advantage, by obliging the King of *France*, to give them the Style of Brothers, because that in treating them thus upon the Level with the Dukes of *Savoy* and of *Lorrain*, one would think that his Majesty should not after that, make any Distinction neither, between the Ministers of the one and of the other I shall give no Occasion to be thought vain, when I say, that the Negotiation which was had on that Account, was my own Work,

Work, and that the Elector of *Brandenburg* is oblig'd for it to my Zeal, and to the Acquaintance I had at the Court of *France* *Fabian*, Count *de Donn*, who, with the eminent Qualities which are hereditary to his House, had a singular Merit, which brighten'd very much the Lustre of his Birth, being in the Year 1646 come into *France* on the Part of the Elector of *Brandenburg*, represented that that Prince, who possesses so many large Provinces that his Dominions extend from the Frontiers of *Gaul* to those of *Muscovy*, could not bear being treated on the Level, not only with the Dukes, Peers, and Officers of the Crown of *France*, but also with several little Counts of *Germany*, while the King at the same Time gave the Quality of *Brother* to the Dukes of *Savoy* and of *Lorrain*, who give Place to the Electors on all Occasions. He was told that it was the ancient Style of the *Chancery*, and that there was no altering of it during the King's Minority. That the Consequence thereof would be too great. That after that, the Elector would also pretend *to cause his Embassador to be cover'd*, and that his Example would give Birth to several other Pretensions, which a Regent would be cautious of meddling with. That the Duke of *Savoy* and of *Lorrain* gave the Title of Majesty to the King, which the Elector did not, notwithstanding some of his Predecessors had done it. However, it was added, that what could be done should be examin'd into, provided, the Elector would dispose the whole Electoral College to give the King the Title of *Majesty*, in which he would meet with so much the less Difficulty, because the three Ecclesiastical Electors, and the Elector of *Bavaria* did it already. The Count *de Doza* reply'd, That he had no Orders to engage the Elector in such a Negotiation. That he spoke only in Reference to his Master's Interest, and that what he ask'd was very just, but he could obtain nothing. And at his going away, he left me at that Court as Minister of the Elector, who sent me some Time after the necessary Letters and Commissions. The Year following, 1647, a Design was propos'd in the Electors Council to form a third Party in the Empire, with the Elector of *Saxony*, and the Princes of the House of *Brunswick* and *Lunenburg*. The Execution of this Project would have destroy'd the whole Work Cardinal *Mazarin* had been labouring at for so many Years at *Munster*, he therefore being very much alarm'd thereat, desir'd the Elector to approve of the King's making use of my Service, to offer him some Propositions, which he judg'd would indubitably be very advantageous to his Interests. I prepar'd to undertake the Journey, provided Letters were given me with the Quality of Brother. The Count *de Brienne*, whom I frequently saw, and familiarly enough, did not dissemble with me, that if the Matter was mention'd in Council he would oppose it with all his Power, and told me he would not sign the Letter, even tho' the Queen should lay her absolute Commands upon him to do it, and in effect he hinder'd the Council from coming to any Resolution in Favour of the Elector. But the Cardinal, who was liberal of any thing that did not cost Money, and who was willing to oblige the Elector, prevail'd with the Queen to write him a Letter with her own Hand, as did also the King, in both which they gave the Elector the Style of Brother. Immediately after the King had attain'd to the Years of Majority, the Cardinal seeing almost all the Kingdom rise against his Authority, and being desirous to make himself some Friends abroad, had no Difficulty to yield to the Instances I made, to have Letters dispatch'd out of the *Chancery* in the same Form. And the Count *de Brienne* was then oblig'd to execute the Orders the King gave him for that Purpose, after his Majority, as accordingly he did without Reluctancy.

The States of the United Provinces have Contests about the Rank not only with the Electors, but also with some other Princes of *Germany*. In the Year 1671, there was an Assembly of several Deputies of the Princes of the Circles of *Westphalia*, and of the *Lower Saxony* at *Bilefeld*, where the Chancellor of the Duke of *Newburg* having spread a Rumour, that he would not give Place to the Deputies of the United Provinces, these took the Alarm, and gave Advice thereof to their Principals. This caus'd great Uneasiness at the *Hague*, from whence a sharp Letter was written to the Duke on that Subject. The Duke did not answer it, but, some Time after, a Writing was publish'd, wherein the Pretensions of the States were examin'd and debated on the Duke's Part with great Animosity and Bitterness. Those Princes who constitute Branches, and as such have a Vote, and Seat in the Diets, are not oblig'd to give Place within the Empire to foreign Powers, except to crown'd Heads, and I dare be bold to say they ought to do it to none whatever, unless the Ministers have the Representing Character. Civilities may be done to the other, but they cannot pretend to the Precedency. The Electoral College, the Deputies whereof were assembl'd at *Ratisbone*, took in Occasion from this Dispute, in the Month of *August*, 1671, to make a Regulation in the following Terms, *That according to the ancient Custom, the Embassadors, the Envoys, and the Residents of the Electors, should precede as well at the Emperor's Court as in the other Courts, the Ministers of all Princes and Republicks, except those of crown'd Heads, and those of their Widows, and of their Children destin'd to the Succession when they shall come to Age.* What is said therein of the other Courts, is to be understood of the other Princes of *Germany*. For among the Princes of *Italy*, the Republick of *Venice* and the United Provinces are otherwise consider'd than the Electors.

It is true the Regulation says, That what obliges the Electoral College to make it, is, that it often happens that at the Emperor's Court, *and in those of other Kings*, and elsewhere, the Electors, their Embassadors, Deputies and Ministers, meet with the Embassadors, Deputies, and Residents of other Princes, and that it behoves them to maintain themselves in the Possession of the Precedency, which they have enjoy'd for many Ages. And that therefore they charge and command their Ministers, who shall be employ'd as well within the Empire as elsewhere, not to give Place to those of other Princes, except to those of crown'd Heads, &c. But this is what it is impos-

impossible to cause to be observ'd, even at the Court of *Vienna*, where the *Venetian* Embassador takes Place of the Ministers of all the Electors, altho' the Capitulation obliges the Emperor to secure to the Electors this Prerogative

At the Congress of *Westphalia* there happen'd a Dispute concerning the Rank, *between the United Provinces and the Duke of* Savoy, in what Order they should be nam'd in the Treaty The Estates were for being consider'd on Account of their Power, which is without doubt the greatest of all *Europe*, after that of the three first Crowns, and by Reason of the Extent of their Dominions, very much respected by several powerful Kings in the other Parts of the World The Duke alledg'd the Antiquity of his Principality, altho' the Dignity of most of the Provinces of the Low Countries is, beyond Comparison, more ancient than that of *Savoy*, the Advantage of his Birth, and the illustrious Alliances which he and some of his Predecessors have contracted in the first Houses of *Christendom*

This Dispute ceas'd, because the Duke caus'd himself to be put in the Number of the Princes of *Italy* The Great Duke of *Tuscany*, who thought the Duke of *Savoy* would rather have chosen to be plac'd amongst the Princes of *Germany*, pretended to be next in Rank to the Republick of *Venice* But the Duke, who knew that amongst the *Germans* he should be oblig'd to give Place to the Electors, and to the Arch-Dukes, and that the United Provinces, and some other Princes, would dispute the Rank with him, chose the other Party, and caus'd himself to be plac'd among the Princes of *Italy*, where his Rank was settl'd

It is somewhat strange, the Inequality of Treatments which was dealt at *Trent* to the Duke of *Bavaria*, and to the Ecclesiastical Princes, who, as it is well known, take Place of the Seculars *Martin de Roxas de Portalarabio*, Commander of *Malta*, and Embassador from the Great Master, arriv'd at *Trent* in the Month of *March*, 1563, and demanded a Place on the Bench of the Lay-Embassadors The Procurators of the Archbishop of *Saltzbourg*, of the Bishop of *Aichstat*, and of some other Prelates, *who had not been allow'd, no more than the Ecclesiastical Electors, to send Embassadors to the Council*, altho' with the Quality of Prelate, they have also that of Prince, oppos'd the Pretension of the Embassador of *Malta*, and said, That since they, whose Masters were Princes, had their Places among the Ecclesiasticks, the Embassador of an Order that is merely Ecclesiastical, as is that of St *John of Jerusalem*, ought to be seated there likewise The Embassador urg'd, That the Exercise of temporal War was inseparable from their Order, which had its Armies, coin'd Money, and did all that a Sovereign Prince can do, and which, for that Reason, had not its Procurators at the Council, as had the Archbishop of *Saltzbourg*, but its Embassador, and that by the Pope's express Orders, who had commanded it by his Brief, to send an Embassador, and not Procurators *That ever since the Pontificate of* Leo X, *the Embassadors of the Order had had a Place in the Pope's Chapel with the other Embassadors*. That the Ceremonial so order'd it, and that the Practice was not other in the Courts of the two first Kings of *Christendom* That the Bishops came to Council, to have their Vote there, and their Seat, and if together with their Bishoprick, they had also the Quality of Prince, or else were in actual Possession of some Principality, it was still but an Appendix, the Condition whereof could not be better then that of the Principal That for Proof thereof it was sufficient to alledge one Reason, to wit, That if the Archbishop of *Saltzbourg* had come to the Council in Person, he would have had Place only among the Ecclesiasticks, and in the Rank of his Promotion The Cognizance of the Contest was referr'd to the Pope, because the Debate was between Ecclesiasticks, and it was ordain'd that he should be seated among the Seculars, which was signify'd to the Archbishop of *Saltzbourg*

After this an Opposition was made by the Patriarchs, who wou'd not give Place to the Embassador of a Religious Order, notwithstanding the Legates had declar'd, that it should be without Prejudice to their Rights To remove all these Difficulties, the Legates wrote to the Pope, that the Embassador of *Malta* hiding himself very much perplex'd with all these Disputes, and his Person being of no great Assistance to the Council, his Holiness would do well to give him Orders to be gone The Pope did so, but before this Order arriv'd at *Trent*, the Legates chang'd their Minds, and did not think it proper to execute their Design, because they adjusted the Difference in such Manner, that the Embassador contented himself with the Place that was assigned him on the Bench of the Prelates, after the last Ecclesiastical Embassador of the Lay-Princes, of which he took Possession the 7th of *September* No Body disputes the Quality of Sovereign Prince with the Great Master of *Malta*

The Pope himself considers him as such, and was willing to testify the same in the Year 1581, when *John Bishop of la Cassiere*, who was Great Master of the Order, went to *Rome*, to justify himself of the Crimes of which he was accus'd by some of the Knights who had revolted against him. At his Arrival at *Rome*, the Families of the Pope and the Cardinals went to meet him, the Artillery of the Castle of St *Angelo* saluted him as he pass'd by, and all the Honours were done him that are usually done to Sovereigns The Cardinal *d'Este*, Protector of *France*, with whom he lodg'd, because the Great Master was a *French* Man, receiv'd him at the top of the Staircase, accompany'd by *M de Foix* the *French* Embassador, and four other Cardinals, either *French* Men by Birth or Inclination, waited for him in the Apartment which had been prepar'd for him The Pope did not receive him in the Consistory, but in his Chamber, whither he had caus'd twelve Cardinals to come to do him Honour, and he made him sit after the last Cardinal The Pope in giving him Audience in his Chamber, did him the same Honour which he does to the Embassadors of the Duke of *Mantua*, and of the other Princes of *Italy*, and that he would do to the Princes themselves, if they came thither in Person, except the Duke of *Savoy*, and the Great Duke of *Tuscany*, who have Audience in the Ducal Chamber The President

President *de Thou*, who is otherwise very exact and very faithful, says in his History, that the Pope *seated the Great Master after the fourth Caramal, before the eight others* But it seems to me, that there is more Verisimilitude to believe in this M. *de Foix*, who was at that Time Embassador at *Rome*, and who having a very particular Care of the Affairs of the Great Master, wrote to King *Henry* III, in the Terms I just mention'd And what makes me believe that *M de Thou*, or he that printed his Works after his Decease, forgot himself in this Point, is, that when *Cosmus*, Duke of *Florence*, arriv'd at *Rome* the 5th of *February*, 1560, he receiv'd a great many more Honours, than were done since to the Great-Master of *Malta* The Cardinals of St *Flora*, and of *Ferrara*, went as far as the City Gate to meet him at his Departure from Audience, which he had in the Ducal Chamber, the Pope gave him a Dinner, and to all the Cardinals but he was seated immediately before the last Cardinal Deacon He march'd also in the same Rank in the Procession, which was perform'd at *Rome* the 24th of the same Month Upon which I shall make this small Remark *en passant*, that when the Pope goes in Procession, the Embassadors carry the Pall to a certain Place, where they are reliev'd by the Barons

It will not be from the Purpose, to mention here the Competition some of the Princes of *Italy* have among themselves, and the Debates their Ministers have had on that Account The Duke of *Ferra*, Governor of *Milan*, did not do the same Civilities to the Ministers of the Duke of *Mantua*, which he did to those of *Savoy* whereupon these two Princes enter'd into great Contestations, not about Precedence, but about the Titles and Equality The Ministers of *Mantua* said, That the Governor was in the Wrong, because that at *Madrid*, and even at *Milan*, the Ministers of the two Princes had always been treated equally That the King of *Spain* would never give a Place in the Chapel to the Embassador of *Savoy*, notwithstanding the Duke's pressing Instances on that Account and that he would not suffer, that in reference to the Number of Horses to his Coach, and the other Honours, he should be distinguish'd from the Embassador of *Mantua* from that of *Genoa*, and of the other Princes of *Italy* That the Governors of *Milan*, Predecessors of the Duke of *Feria*, had not behav'd themselves otherwise, as well in respect to the Titles, as to the Chapel, and other publick Ceremonies, to which the Ministers of *Savoy* and of *Mantua* had always been invited by Turns That the *Savoyards* observ'd very well, that *Philip* II, King of *Spain*, had given their Duke the Title of *Highness*, when he went to *Madrid* on Account of his Marriage, but that they did not take Notice, that the Grandees of *Spain* had refus'd him that Title That it was true, that when the Duke went to *Madrid*, *the King went to meet him, and gave him the Honour of the Hand*, but that the very next Day after his Marriage, he treated him after the same Manner he had us'd to do before mention was made of that Alliance That it was only at the King's pressing Instances, that the Constable of *Castile*, and the other Grandees of *Spain* gave him the Title of *Highness* That in the Letters *Philip* II, and *Philip* III, had wrote to him, they had always styl'd him *Vos*, and at the beginning of the Letter *Sennor Hio, Sennor Hermano*, in the same Line, and without Civility That a Regulation had been made there since, by which it was ordain'd, that *the Prince, the Infantas, and their Brothers-in-Law, should have the Style of Highness*, but that the Duke could not draw any Advantage there-from, because that was done only, that more Honour might not be done to the Wife than to the Husband, whereas the Emperor himself had publickly given the Title of *Highness* to the Dutchess of *Mantua*, when she was at *Vienna*. But that the Ministers ought not to claim any thing from the Honours that are done to their Prince That since the Catholick King had been pleas'd to make no Distinction between the Dukes of *Savoy* and of *Mantua*, the Governor of *Milan* might have very well forborn making any there, where his King himself makes none

The Council of *Savoy* made Answer to this Writing by another, wherein they set forth, That there was no Comparison between the Dukes of *Savoy* and of *Mantua*, neither for Antiquity of Houses, nor for the Advantage of Alliances, of which a long Enumeration is there produc'd That the Governors of *Milan* had always given the Title of *Highness* to the Duke of *Savoy*, and that of *Excellency* to the Duke of *Mantua* That the Republick of *Venice* did the same That even the Duke *Emanuel Philibert* gave only the Style of *Excellency* to the Duke of *Mantua*, while this gave him that of *Highness* That *Saaforum* writes, That in his Time, of all the Princes of *Italy*, there was none but the Duke of *Savoy* to whom it was given That when the Duke *Charles Emanuel* went into *Spain* on the Score of his Marriage, the King *went to meet him, and gave him the Hand*, and that since the King himself gave him the Title of *Highness*, the Grandees of *Spain* could not refuse it him neither That notwithstanding the next Day after his Marriage, and since, he has been always treated with the Style of *Vos*, and of *Hio*, it was only to do him so much the more Honour, because therein he treated him upon the Level with the *Infantas*, and with the other Princes of his House That it is reasonable to believe that the King did not do it with any other Intention, since the Duke of *Savoy* being become his Son, it is probable he was willing to do him more Honour than before That it was true, that before mention was made of the Marriage, the King of *Spain* had only given him the Title of *Most Illustrious*, but that it was also true, that at that Time he gave only that of *Very Illustrious* to the Duke of *Mantua* That the Title of *Most Illustrious* had never been given to the Duke of *Mantua* before *Ferdinand*, who making his Advantage of the bad Understanding which was between *Spain* and *Savoy*, had begg'd it at *Madrid* That notwithstanding the said *Philip* did not think fit to give a Place in the Chapel to the Embassador of *Savoy*, altho' this might pretend to it with Justice, since he had it in those of *France*, of *Vienna*, and even of *Rome*, which is the first Court of *Christendom*, the Duke of *Mantua* could draw no Advantage from thence for himself, since it was not to take away the Difference

ference which is between these two Princes, the Duke of *Mantua* having no Place in the Chapel of the other Courts; and so, on that Account there was no Competition between them. That the King had signify'd to him, he should be glad not to be further importun'd about it, because what he did was to do him so much the more Honour, in treating him upon the Level with the other Princes of his House, and even with the Arch-Dukes. That before the Dukes of *Savoy* left off paying Obedience to the Pope, by reason of the well-grounded Pretension they have to perform it in the Royal Hall, they did it in the Ducal Chamber whereas even at this Day, the Dukes of *Mantua*, or their Ministers, do not perform it in the Consistory, but in the Pope's Chamber. That as for the Title of *Highness*, which the Emperor had given to the Dutchess of *Mantua* when he marry'd, at least if it was true, that he did really give it her, that possibly he might have Regard to the House, from whence the Dutchess was extracted, or to the Alliance she had with the Arch-Dutchess, Sister to the Emperor, whose Sister-in-Law she was, tho' it may be said, that it was a Civility which the Emperor was willing to do to a Lady, to whom the greatest Princes would think it a Glory to do Honour.

That it was certain, that if the Duke of Mantua had accompany'd his Sister into Germany, the Emperor would not have given him the Title of Highness, because he could not have done it, but to the Prejudice of those, who could pretend to it with more Justice than the Duke. But that it was a Piece of Prudence in him not to go thither, for fear he should there meet the Count d'Ognate, the Spanish Embassador, who pretended to take Place of the Duke, and that they should reciprocally give one the other the same Titles. That several Letters and Acts were to be found in the Archives of Savoy, wherein the Emperor gives the Title of Highness to the Dukes thereof. That it was impertinent to say, that the Honours which were done to Princes, draw no Consequences for the Ministers, since these regulate themselves by the Grandeur and Qualities of their Masters. And as for the Alternative, which was said to have been practis'd at Milan between the Ministers of the two Princes, that it imply'd a very gross Ignorance, or great Malice, in those who advanc'd Things which had so little Truth in them. That the Contrary was so notorious, that the Duke of Feria could not have done otherwise than he did, without introducing a Novelty which was both Offensive and Scandalous. It being certain that the Embassador of Mantua, had never appear'd there at the publick Assemblies, unless he of Savoy was either absent or sick. At this Day there is no Competition between the two Princes. The Duke of *Mantua* gives Place to that of *Savoy*, and they give one another reciprocally the Title of *Highness*.

There is no Competition neither between the Great Duke of *Tuscany* and the Duke of *Parma*, and nevertheless Prince *Francis*, the Son of *Cosmus*, being at *Madrid* in the Year 1562, had there a Contest with *Alexander Farnese*, Son of the Duke of *Parma*, and of *Margaret* of *Austria*, natural Sister to *Philip* II, King of *Spain*; *Cosmus*, who at that Time was negotiating a Match for his Son with one of the Emperor's Daughters, and who for that Purpose stood in need of the Favour of *Philip*, was willing his Son should yield him the Precedency, and should even dissemble his Displeasure.

It was almost at the same Time, there was a Contest at the Court of *France* for the Rank, between the Ministers of *Florence* and of *Ferrara*, and that those of *Florence* had the Advantage through the Favour of the Queen Mother, *Katherine de Medicis*. The Count *Ferdinand Scotti*, Plenipotentiary of *Edward* Duke of *Parma*, being in the Year 1643, at *Venice*, where he negotiated a League against the *Barberins*, said, he could not assist at the Conferences, because he had Orders not to give Place to the Minister of the Great Duke. He grounded on the Example of *Madrid* which I lately mention'd, as on a Title that justify'd his being in Possession. *Gussoni* and *Nani*, Deputies of the Senate, said, *That on these Occasions, there was an Obligation to follow what was practis'd in all the other Courts*, where the Ministers of the Great Duke have the Precedency of those of *Parma*, without Contestation, and that even at *Venice* these two Princes were treated with a great deal of Difference, since the Senate gave the Title of *Highness* to the one, and that of *Excellency* to the other. That a great many Things might be said, in reference to what had pass'd at *Madrid*, since it was only at the Instigation of some Enemies of the House of *Toledo*, which was straitly ally'd to that of the Great Duke, that this Quarrel had been created him.

At this Day there is no Duke of *Ferrara*, never since that Dukedom has been annex'd to the Pope's Mitre, as a Fee of the See of *Rome*, in the Time of *Clement* VIII, towards the End of the foregoing Century. However, to shew that there is nothing fix'd in most part of the Ranks of Princes, I shall here add a Word or two concerning the *Difference*, the *Minister of the Duke had with that of* Florence. *Cosmus* said, That the Republick of *Florence* had always preceded the Dutchy of *Ferrara*, and that she could not lose the Rank she had always held, under the Pretext, that she was now govern'd by a Sovereign Prince. The Duke of *Ferrara* maintain'd, That *Florence* having lost its first Dignity of ancient Republick, to become a new Principality, the Antiquity of the two Dutchies was no longer the Question. Pope *Pius* V, offer'd to regulate the Difference, but the Duke of *Ferrara* maintain'd, that it belong'd to the Emperor to decide it. The Duke of *Florence* acquiesc'd, and prevail'd with the Pope to consent thereto, but upon Condition that the Emperor should only do the Office of Arbitrator, and not that of Judge. *Maximilian* II was incens'd thereat and as both the Princes were nearly ally'd to him, he had no great Mind to speak his Opinion, and spun the Affair out in Length. The Duke of *Ferrara* in the mean Time procur'd the Difference to be regulated to his own Advantage at the Court of *France*, under *Francis* II, while the Duke of *Guise*, his Brother-in-Law, was there All-powerful. But his Pretentions being brought again upon the Stage, under *Charles* IX, on occasion of the Service, which was perform'd at *Paris* in the Year 1568, for the

the Prince of *Spain*, the Embassador of *Florence*, supported by the Credit of Queen *Catherine de Medicis*, demanded the next immediate Rank after that of *Venice*, and the Embassador of *Ferrara* oppos'd the same with so much Warmth, that the Dukes of *Anjou* and of *Alençon*, with the Cardinal of *Bourbon*, had much a-do to keep them from coming to an Engagement about it, and oblig'd them both to withdraw, leaving them the Liberty of protesting. *Cosmus* being made Great Duke of *Tuscany* some Time after, the Queen-Mother caus'd it be determin'd in his Favour.

It is necessary to add a Word more about what was lately hinted at concerning the Count *d'Ognate* Embassador of *Spain*, who pretended to have Precedency of the Duke of *Mantua*, and to treat him on the Level in reference to the Titles. He consider'd him as a Vassal of the Emperor, or of the Empire, and he knew that at the Court of *Madrid*, his *Minister is treated with some Difference from others*. But nowever, he holds the Rank of a sovereign Prince. He takes at home the Place of Honour of the Embassador of *France*, and his Embassador is cover'd when he speaks to the Kings of *France* and of *England*. If the Marquiss *de Fontenay* takes in his own House the Hand, the Door, and the Chair of the Duke of *Guise*, it is because he treats him as a Subject of the Prince he represents, but whatever Character a Minister may have, he cannot dispense himself from the Respect which is due to sovereign Princes, and he ought to make so much the less Difficulty here, because he makes none in reference to the Cardinals. It is true that Cardinals have the Precedency of Princes, but it is only at *Rome*, and in some other Courts where they are willing to suffer it. But they do not take Place of the Princes of the Blood of *France*, nor of the Princes or Infants of *Spain*. An ecclesiastical Elector wou'd not suffer a Cardinal to take the Upper-hand of him. A protestant Elector would suffer it still less. And I do not think that the Elector of *Bavaria* would permit it. Some Princes of *Italy* allow it, and perhaps those of *Germany* might do it, but both the one and the other are in the wrong.

In the Year 1642, some Electoral Ministers taking Audience of the Emperor, seem'd to be very much scandaliz'd that the Duke of *Neubourg* who was there present, was cover'd while they spoke to the Emperor uncover'd. I cannot tell whether they were in the right or not. The Princes of *Germany* ought to have at least the same Advantage with the Emperor, that the Grandees of *Spain* have with their King, that is to say, the Right of being cover'd in the Presence of the Emperor.

The Duke of *Neubourg* had it in effect, since the Emperor suffer'd it, and it did not belong to the Ministers of the Electors to put him in Mind of his Duty, if he fail'd therein. If they were really Embassadors, they ought to be cover'd, and if they were but Ministers of the second Order, why should they desire the Duke of *Neubourg* should have that Respect for them? I find my self oblig'd to repeat here what I said before, that the Electors and Princes of *Germany* do not give the true Character to the Ministers they employ to the Emperor. But if they do give it them, and withal suffer their Ministers not to be cover'd in speaking to the Emperor, they are in the wrong to complain of the Distinction which is made in *France* betwixt their Ministers and those of the Princes of *Italy*.

I must say still further, that the Duke of *Savoy* sends no more to pay Obedience to the Pope, and the Emperor has also left it off. When the Emperor still receiv'd the Imperial Crown at the Pope's Hands, they took an Oath to him, which was a kind of Liege-Homage, of which see a particular Example in *Lutharius II*

Rex venit ante fores, Jurans prius urbis honores
Mox homo fit Papæ, jemitque hoc aante Coronam.

But they have since been convinc'd, that they could not without injuring the Imperial Dignity, take an Oath to the Bishop of *Rome*, who according to the Order of Things, ought to make suit to them for a Confirmation of his Election, and take an Oath of Fidelity. Pope *Pius IV* said, That the Election of *Maximilian II*, was faulty, because that of all the Electors who were present thereat, there were but two that were lawful, since of the five others, three were Hereticks, he of *Cologn* was sick, and *Maximilian* himself was King of *Bohemia*. The Pope pretended moreover, that the Electors could not without his Consent, nominate a Successor to the Empire while the Emperor was still alive, but only during the Inter-regnum, and after his Decease. That they might indeed appoint a Coadjutor while the Emperor was still living, but that it did not depend on this Coadjutor, nor on the Electors, to change the Quality of King of the *Romans*, which the Election gave him, into that of Emperor, without the Pope, who ought to confirm the Election. He signify'd however, that he wou'd pass over all these Considerations, if *Maximilian* would take an Oath to him, and would send to *Rome* an Embassy of Obedience, as all other Christian Princes do, and as the Emperor *Ferdinand* his Father had done. The Pope even sent him the Form of an Oath, which he said had been copied from that of his Predecessors. *Maximilian* said, that he would not desire a Confirmation of his Election, unless it were made appear to him, that the other Emperors had done so before him. That the Oath which was exacted from him, was an Innovation, and that that which *Charles V* had taken, was applicable only to those Emperors who receive the Crown at the Pope's Hands. He moreover added, that it would not be found that *Charles* or *Ferdinand* had sent Embassadors of Obedience to *Rome*. That it was true indeed, that the Embassador of the Emperor his Father had done it, but then he had done it without Orders, and had suffer'd himself to be persuaded thereto by the Cardinals *Moron* and *Madrucci*, who had promis'd him to furnish him with Examples thereof, and that the Emperor had been so incens'd thereat, that if he had not more consider'd the Intention than the Action of his Embassador, he would have punish'd him severely for it. *Maximilian* indeed offer'd to pay Obedience for his Kingdoms of *Hungary* and *Bohemia*, and for his other hereditary Countries, as the Emperor *Maximilian han* I, his Great Grandfather had done, for the Provinces depending on the Succession of *Burgundy*, in the Name of his Son *Philip*, and that that was all *Julius* II had pretended from him, and it was also what *Pius* IV was forc'd to be contented with

The Cardinals have Competition with all Princes They pretend to be upon the Level with Kings, and to take Place of all other Princes, even those of the Blood of *France* In the Assembly which King *Henry* III had conven'd at St *Germains* in the Year 1583, there happen'd a Contest about the Rank, between *Charles* Cardinal of *Guise*, and *Charles* of *Bourbon*, Prince of the Blood, who had no other Quality than that The Cardinal *de Bourbon*, Archbishop of *Roan*, who had more of the Sentiments of a Priest, than of the Heart of a Prince, declar'd against *Charles* of *Bourbon*, his Nephew, and reproach'd him with Audaciousness, to dare to think of taking Place of a Cardinal, who was advanc'd in Years, and a Priest But however, the King gave it in favour of the Prince of the Blood, and adjudg'd him the Precedency, conformably to the Laws of the Kingdom The Cardinal *de Guise* would not therefore be present at the Assembly

Some Time after, the same *Charles* of *Bourbon*, having been made Cardinal, *Francis ae Joyeuse*, Archbishop of *Narbonne*, who was made Cardinal at the same Promotion, was for having the Precedency of *Charles*, who was call'd the Cardinal of *Vendosme*, because at *Rome*, the Cardinals who are Priests, take Place of the Deacons, and he would have carried it, through the Credit of the Duke of *Joyeuse* his Brother, if *John Lewis de Nogaret*, Duke *d'Epernon*, who shar'd the King's Favour with *Joyeuse*, had not represented the Consequence thereof to his Majesty, and had not reminded him of the Passage with the Cardinal *de Guise* After the Coronation of *Lewis* XIII, the King was for making a Promotion of the Knights of the Order There happen'd some Contest for the Rank among the Candidates, but particularly between the Prince of *Condé* and the Cardinal *de Joyeuse*, whom I just mention'd The Prince carried it, and the Cardinal chose rather to forego the Order than to yeild It must be own'd that a Clergyman is a haughty Animal, of what Religion soever he be Their Pride has succeeded that of the ancient Philosophers, whose Maxims they copy in all their Actions The Cardinals of *Retz* and of *la Rochefoucault*, Chiefs of the Council of *France*, had not Leisure to know themselves in that Post, but Cardinal *de Richlieu*, who was the fiercest of all the Ministers who had ever possess'd it, caus'd the same Submissions to be paid him in *France* that the Cardinals exact at *Rome* The Prince of *Condé*, who was wise, and who desir'd nothing but to compass his Ends, shew'd the utmost Complaisance to the Cardinal, but the Count *de Soisons*, who had not the same Prudence, said, that the Prince's Example did him no Prejudice, and by opposing the Regal Power and Authority which were lodg'd in the Cardinal's Hands, he was obliged to leave the Kingdom, and lost with his Life, the Fortune of his Friends in the Contestation The Embassadors of *England* would not negotiate with Cardinal *de Richlieu*, that they might not be oblig'd to give Place to him in his own House, but they did not advance their Masters Business thereby, and their Successors have known how to benefit by the ill Effects of these difficult and perplexing Scruples Cardinal *Mazarine* who enter'd into the Ministry during the King's Minority, could not do very well without the Friendship and Credit of the Prince of *Condé*, being himself a Foreigner, without Birth, and without any other Support than that of the Queen-Mother He was far from disputing the Rank with the Princes of the Blood, yet for all that he made himself be respected, and resented the Slights that were shewn him, by forcing the one to fling himself into the Arms of the *Spaniards*, and the other to submit so intirely to his Will, as even to marry one of his Nieces When the Duke of *Savoy*, the Father of him that now reigns, came to *Lions* in the Year 1659, he would not yield Precedency in a third Place to Cardinal *Mazarin* Those Princes who dare not at *Rome* raise any Difficulty with the Cardinals, who can do them neither Good nor Harm, ought to be much more cautious how they do it with a Cardinal, who is absolute Minister of a very powerful Kingdom Prince *Thomas*, Uncle to the Duke of *Savoy*, being inform'd that Cardinal *Zapata* had yielded the Hand and the Step to *Emanuel Philibert*, third Son of Duke *Charles*. *Emanuel*, whose fifth Son *Thomas* was, endeavour'd to take the same Advantage over Cardinal *Mazarin* But this prevented it so well, that he had no Reason to apprehend the Reproaches which the Court of *Rome* made to *Zapata* Don *John* of *Austria*, natural Son to *Charles* V, being come to *Rome* to receive the Pope's Benediction for the Expedition in which he was to command the naval Forces against the *Turks*, would not 1 ft. on single Cardinal, that he might not be oblig'd to pay them Honours which he did not think their due While he was at *Naples*, Cardinal *de Granvelle* gave him the Place of Honour every where, except at the single Ceremony which was perform'd in the Church of St *Claire*, where the Cardinal bless'd the Royal Standard On the contrary, Cardinal *Albert* of *Austria*, being at *Ferrara*, whither the Pope *Clement* VIII went after the Death of the last Duke, visited all the Cardinals, and did them all the Honours they could desire of him Don *John* of *Austria*, he who is at present the King of *Spain's* first Minister, being at *Naples* after the Reduction of that Town, would never grant Precedency to Cardinal *Filomarin*, Archbishop of the Place, except only in his Church

Cardinal *de Bourbon*, whom I lately mention'd, being in the Company of *Anthony* King of *Navarre*, his Brother, who was conducting *Isabella* of *France*, Queen of *Spain*, to the Frontiers of that Kingdom, had Orders to do Civilities to the *Spanish* Lords who came to receive her They were the Duke *de l'Infantade*, and the Cardinal *de Burgos*, his Brother, who were follow'd by a great Number of Persons of Quality, and among the rest, eleven titl'd Noblemen of the House of *Mendosse* The Cardinal receiv'd them at the Entrance into his Lodgings, and having conducted them through a large Ground-Room which was hung with Mourning, on account of the Death of *Henry* II,

und

The EMBASSADOR and his Functions. 235

and being feated in a Chair under a Canopy, between the Duke and the Cardinal, he caus'd a Lecture to be made of the Powers the Duke and Cardinal had to receive their Queen *After the reading of the Powers*, the Cardinal *de Bourbon* yielded the Place of Honour to the Cardinal *de Burgos*, as to his Senior. As they went up to the Apartment, where the Queen and the King of *Navarre* expected them, the Duke went first, and the Cardinal *de Burgo's* took the Hand of the Cardinal *de Bourbon*.

Philip Prince, and since King of *Spain*, thinking he could prevail with *Ferdinand* his Uncle to yield up to him his Quality of King of the *Romans*, went into *Germany* in the Year 1551, but his Journey proving fruitless, and having a Mind in his Return to pafs through *Italy*, he took *Trent* in his way, while the Council was there affembled. The Legate having Advice thereof, went with Cardinal *Madrucci* to meet him at the Diftance of three hundred Paces without the Town. *Philip* and the Legate embrac'd one another on Horfe-back, but the other Prelates alighted off their Horfes and kifs'd the Prince's Hand. The two Cardinals plac'd him between them, and conducted him to the Bifhop's Palace, where he was to lodge, and where the Legate took his Leave of him without alighting from his Horfe. The next Day *Philip* made the firft Vifit to the Legate, who came without the Gate of his Palace to receive him. His Vifit was very fhort. And going from thence he took the Legate along with him into an Ifland, which the *Adice* forms near the Town, where Cardinal *Madrucci* had caus'd a Timber Houfe to be built, which was very finely furnifh'd, and in which a moft magnificent Entertainment was prepar'd for him. *Philip*, the two Cardinals, and the Prince of *Savoy*, who accompany'd *Philip*, were all four at the upper end of the Table, and the other Prelates were on each Side. The next Day the Legate return'd *Philip's* Vifit, and the Day following, which was the 9th of *June*, the Prince left *Trent*. All the Prelates, except the Cardinals, conducted him without the Gate. Some Days after, *Maximilian*, King of *Bohemia*, who went to fetch his Wife from *Spain*, pafs'd alfo through *Trent*, but forafmuch as he had no Retinue, and that he pafs'd as it were *incognito*, no Entry was made him, nor any other Civility, except that *the Legate made him the firft Vifit*, and the next Day he return'd the fame. When *Albert*, and the Arch-Dutchefs who was going to be marry'd to the King of *Spain*, *Philip* III, arriv'd at *Ferrara*, all the College of Cardinals went in a Body to meet them.

There is no lawful Judge for the Competitions between Sovereigns, neither is it a Matter that belongs to a Council. And indeed there is no Prince that will undertake, or ever did undertake, to regulate the Rank between Minifters. The King of *England*, when he marry'd the Princefs his Daughter in the Year 1612, invited the Embaffadors of *France* and of *Venice* to the Feaft of the firft Day, and *Boifchot*, Embaffador of the Arch-Dukes *Albert* and *Ifabella*, to that of the Day following. *Boifchot* was much offended thereat, and faid, he could not fuffer that a Republick, which poffefs'd in a manner but a Foot of Land, in Comparifon of the Arch-Duke's great and vaft Provinces, fhould be preferr'd to them, fince fhe had never made Difficulty to yield to their Predeceffors, when they were yet but Dukes of *Burgundy*. The King fent him Word, *That it was not his Intention to erect himfelf as Judge of the Competition of Princes, nor to do any Prejudice to their Rights and Pretenfions, by regulating the Rank between their Minifters.* That he had invited the *Venetian* Embaffador firft, becaufe he had as good as invited himfelf above a Fortnight before; and that the Republick having been pleas'd to do fomething extraordinary, by ordering her Embaffador to make a magnificent Equipage, to do Honour to the new marry'd Couple, he had thought himfelf likewife oblig'd to do this Civility to her Embaffador. That all the Days fhould be equal, as well in the Entertainments as the Diverfions. And that he was even of Opinion that that of *Shrove-Tuefday*, to which *Boifchot* had been invited, would be the greateft of all, as being the Day of the greateft Rejoicing, protefting again, *That he did not undertake to fettle the Rank between the Minifters*, which he caus'd to be given him in Writing.

Queen *Chriftina* of *Sweden*, having defir'd the Elector of *Brandenburg* to fend his Minifters to *Lubeck*, to difcharge there the Office of Mediators between *Poland* and *Sweden*, together with *France*, *Venice*, and the United Provinces, *Ewald Cleyft*, the Elector's Embaffador, told the Queen, That he hop'd that the Parties who invited the Prince his Mafter to this Mediation, would alfo take Care to preferve him the Rank which was his Due. The Queen made Anfwer, *That it did not belong to her to regulate the Precedency among the Minifters*. And that the Elector, by making this Propofition, fubverted the Order of Things, by defiring the Parties interefted fhould become Mediators. *Cleyft* was a Minifter worthy of that Court, as it was then conftituted. Some time before he had told *Chanut*, the *French* Embaffador, that the Marquifs *Sigifmond*, the Elector's Embaffador, would have given a Box on the Ear to a Burghermafter of *Amfterdam*, who difputed the Precedency with him. There was a little Ignorance, and a great deal of Malice in this Tale. It was not a Burghermafter of *Amfterdam*, but a Counfellor of the Court of Juftice of *Frife*, that had the Difpute about the Rank with the Marquifs *Sigifmond*. And they did not proceed fo far as Menaces, nor nothing near it.

In the Year 1653, Queen *Chriftina* having invited all the foreign Minifters to a Ball, where fhe intended to dance, fhe told them, *Gentlemen, you fhall place your felves where you pleafe, for it is none of my Bufinefs to regulate your Ranks*. They all mingl'd with the Senators without Order. There was none but *Pimentel*, Minifter of *Spain*, who plac'd himfelf feparately from the reft, with *Radziensky* and *Blofeld*, who were Refugees from *Poland* and *Denmark*.

The King of *England* did not indeed regulate the Rank, but yet he diftinguifh'd between the Minifters, and that is done every where, tho' there is fomething very delicate in this Diftinction.

CHAP

CHAP. XXVI.

Of Embaſſies compos'd of ſeveral Embaſſadors.

Philip de Commines ſays, *That it is much better to ſend two or three Embaſſadors than one*; becauſe, what the one cannot find out the other does. He wrote in a Time when Embaſſies in Ordinary were not yet ſpoken of, which are never compos'd of a Plurality of Embaſſadors, and the Extraordinaries are not always neither. I do not here ſpeak of thoſe Extraordinary Embaſſadors, who have only the Name and Salary thereof, and who in effect diſcharge the Functions of Ordinaries, but of thoſe who are only employ'd to perform ſome Civility, to aſſiſt at a Ceremony, or to negotiate ſome particular Affair, the Concluſion whereof puts an end alſo to the Embaſſy. In an Obedience. To ſign a Contract of Marriage, the Articles whereof have been concerted, to preſent the Child of a Sovereign at Baptiſm, to make a Complement either on the Marriage or Death of a Prince, on his Acceſſion to the Crown, to ſee the Execution and Obſervation of a Treaty of Peace, or of an Alliance ſworn to, and for many other Affairs of this Nature, Princes frequently employ but a ſingle Perſon, whereas Republicks, on theſe Occaſions, almoſt always ſend a Plurality of Embaſſadors, tho' there is no certain Rule in this Caſe. After the Peace of Vervins, Henry IV ſent to Bruſſels the Mareſchal de Biron, who on this Occaſion was made Duke and Peer of France, to the end he might appear there with the greater Luſtre, and made him be accompany'd by Pompone de Bellievre and by Nicholas Brulart, who had negotiated the Treaty. The Arch-Duke ſent to Paris the Duke of Arſchot, the Count of Aremberg, the Admirant of Arragon, Don Lewis de Velaſque, Richardot, &c. which was a very extraordinary thing, and perhaps would not have been done if the Arch-Duke had not been oblig'd to ſend the Duke, the Count, the Admirant, and Don Lewis into France, there to remain as Hoſtages, till the Reſtitution of the Places which the Spaniards were to evacuate by Virtue of the Treaty, and Henry IV, who was the beſt and the civileſt Prince that ever was, was willing to return the Honour in Appearance which the Arch-Duke did him on the part of the King of Spain. The Republick of Venice commonly employs four Senators in Embaſſies of Obedience, and ſometimes ſhe increaſes, nay even doubles that Number. The States of the United Provinces make almoſt all their Extraordinary Embaſſies conſiſt of a Plurality of Perſons, becauſe their State being compos'd of ſeveral Sovereign Provinces, they will all have a Share in the Honours, as well as in the Affairs. Some Years ago the Swiſs Cantons ſent nine and thirty Embaſſadors or Deputies into France, to ſee the Confirmation of the Alliance ſworn to; and, in the Year 1602, they ſent about as many to King Henry IV.

The Republick of Venice, to do Honour to the Emperor Charles V, who came into Italy in the Year 1530, to confer with Pope Clement VII at Boulogne, ſent him ſix of its chiefeſt Senators, Mark Dandalo, Lewis Gradenigo, Lewis Mocenigo, Laurence Bragadin, Antony Suriano, and Nicholas Tiepolo, who having made their Complement, aſſiſted at the Ceremonies of his Coronation. Some Years before, in the firſt Journey Francis I took into Italy, ſhe ſent to the King George Cornaro, Andrew Gritti, Anthony Grimani, and Dominick Trevuſan, all four Procurators of St Mark, which is the firſt Dignity after that of the Doge, and ſhe commanded them to remain with the King as long as he ſhould ſtay in Italy. When Henry III, King of France, at his Return from Poland, enter'd into that part of Frioul which belongs to the Venetians, he was met there by Andrew Badouere, John Miqueli, John Soranzo, and James Foſcarini, who conducted him to Muran, where the Doge himſelf receiv'd him with Boats and Gondola's, and accompany'd him to the Palace of Foſcarini, which had been fitted up for him. Theſe four Senators did not leave him during the Stay he made in that Town, and conducted him throughout the whole State of the Republick, defraying him to the very Frontiers of the Dutchy of Ferrara. After the Death of Julius II, the Republick appointed ten Senators, of the graveſt and firſt Authority, to go and make their Obedience to Leo X, which ſhe ſignify'd to him by Foſcarini, her Embaſſador in Ordinary. The Intention of the Republick was, by doing this exceſſive Honour to the Pope, to prevail with him to enter into the Treaty which ſhe had juſt concluded with France. But finding Leo's Thoughts were otherwiſe diſpos'd, ſhe alſo laid aſide that of being at ſo extraordinary an Expence.

This great Number of Embaſſadors, which indeed ſerves for an Ornament to the Embaſſy, when it is intended to do Honour to a Prince, becomes neceſſary when they are employ'd in Negotiations that are knotty, intricate, and of Importance, more eſpecially, if ſeveral different Intereſts are mix'd therein; one ſingle Miniſter cannot always anſwer the Sufficiency of many, nor unravel alone all the Difficulties that attend it, nor charge himſelf with the Succeſs of an Infinity of Intrigues, which are but too common in ſuch Caſes. The Preſident Jeannin, ſpeaking of M. de Ruſſi his Collegue, ſays, That he is a very able Miniſter, and capable of ſupporting alone the Function and Dignity of an Embaſſy, but that the Affair they had to negotiate was ſo odd and intricate, that it would find full Employment for two Embaſſadors. That they had each of them their particular Acquaintance. And that notwithſtanding the King had given the Preſident Leave to take a Turn to Court, yet he was afraid of failing in the Service he ow'd his Majeſty, if he abſented while the Miniſters of the Arch-Duke continu'd their Conferences. In the Year 1647, d'Avaux going to Oſnaburg, to negotiate with the the Ministers of *Sweden*, and the States of the Empire, while *Servien* was at the *Hague*, the Duke of *Longueville*, who was left alone at *Munster*, proceeded after such a Manner as surpriz'd the whole Court, and oblig'd *Servien* to complain of the Leave which was granted to *d'Avaux*, to be so long away from a Place, where it was impossible for *a single Minister to acquit himself of the King's Service as he ought.* He said, that *M de Longueville* had like to have marr'd the Affairs. His Meaning was, that he had like to have made a Peace contrary to the Intention of the first Minister.

However, setting aside this Necessity, one would think that it were better to employ but one single Embassador. For if in the Plurality they are all equally Able, Contestation is inevitable. If among them there happens to be a strong and imperious Genius, he will be for regulating the Affairs after his own Whim, for transacting them alone, and for reaping singly all the Glory. The Embassy which *Henry IV* sent into *Holland* in the Year 1607, was compos'd of President *Jeannin, Buzanval* and *Russi*, who entertain'd a perfect Harmony among themselves, not so much by reason of the Superiority the President (who was one of the trustiest Ministers the King had) had over the two others, as chiefly because with his extraordinary Penetration, he had also a Modesty, and Sweetness of Temper not to be express'd. This Example is very rare, neither can it be deny'd, that after the Death of *Buzanval*, there was some small Misunderstanding between the other two. It cannot be deny'd neither, that the President was entrusted with all the Secret and all the Confidence, after what *Villeroy* writes to him of the 23d of *April*, 1607 *Buzanval* and *Russi* were both of the reform'd Religion, and so could not be confided in by *Villeroy*. Those Ministers who have the same Character, who see one another every Day, and who have frequent Consultations together, are not always in the same Sentiments, nor in a Humour to enter into those of their Collegues. Every one delights in maintaining his own Opinion. it is done sometimes with Warmth, and even with Obstinacy. from thence ensue Quarrels, and declar'd Enmities. It is impossible also but in the Number, one of them shall always have the Confidence of the Master, and shall thereby excite the Envy and Jealousy of his Companions.

Of the three Embassadors who were on the part of *France* at *Munster*, none but *Servien* was let into the Secret, because the two others were not capable of seconding the Artifices of him, who had the Direction of this Negotiation, as well as of all the Affairs of the Kingdom *D'Avaux*, who thought he ought to have this Advantage over his Collegue, was seiz'd with Jealousy thereat, which turn'd to a kind of Rage, since both Parties did not scruple to make their Animosities publick by printed Letters. This gave so great a Scandal to the whole Assembly, that the Duke of *Longueville* having in vain endeavour'd to reconcile them, the Nuncio and the *Venetian* Embassador signify'd to them, that the Pope and the Republick would be oblig'd to desire the King to send to *Munster* such Ministers, as were more capable of contributing to the Peace than they were. The King having dissembled the Scandal for some Time, recall'd *D'Avaux*, and left *Servien* alone at *Munster*. He concluded alone the Treaty of the Empire, is some Years before *d'Avaux* had meant'd alone the Truce between *Poland* and *Sweden*, and sett'd the Preliminaries for the Congress at *Munster*. *La Tuillerie* had alone concluded a Peace between the two Crowns of the *North*. Chanot was sent alone to *Lubeck*, to mediate a Peace between *Poland* and *Sweden*, and Queen *Christina*, who was a Queen indeed, explain'd her self very well at that Time, saying, That, in that kind of Negotiations, the great Number of Embassadors was troublesome.

The States of the United Provinces had Eight at *Munster*, but I cannot tell whether they were the better serv'd for it. There were two of them, who having been employ'd in several Negotiations, were for governing the rest, and making themselves necessary. The *French* said publickly, That the *Spanish* Gold and Silver had corrupted those two, and they don't scruple to say in their History, that some of them communicated the most private and most important Secrets of their Negotiation, to the Plenipotentiaries of *France*. They might very well have forborn prostituting thus in their Books, the Names and Memory of Persons of Quality, from whom they ought to have drawn such noble Services. But it is the Humour of the Nation, which finds more Satisfaction in publishing the Kindness that is done it, than in receiving it.

Oxenstiern and *Salvius*, who were on the Part of *Sweden* at *Osnaburg*, were not declar'd Enemies, as were *d'Avaux* and *Servien*, but they were almost always of contrary Sentiments. The first follow'd those of the Chancellor his Father, and the other depended entirely on the Queen, who confided in him. This appears on several Occasions, but particularly in a Conjuncture, wherein the Queen was pleas'd to shew the Esteem she had for the one, and how much she despis'd the other. The Elector of *Bavaria*, having in the Year 1647, almost as soon broke as concluded the Treaty of *Ulm*, which *France* had procur'd him, notwithstanding the Opposition of *Sweden*, *Oxenstiern* fell into such a Passion about it, that he was ready to conclude the Treaty with the Emperor, to the Exclusion of *France*, if *Salvius* would have sign'd it with him. *Oxenstiern* complain'd to the Queen of *Salvius*'s Refusal, and told her, that this last had been the only Hindrance, of his concluding a very advantageous Treaty with the Emperor. The Queen made a Jest of it, and sent *Oxenstiern*'s Letter to *Salvius*, who shew'd it to *Servien*, to destroy thereby, the Opinion the *French* might have of the Disposition of the Court of *Stockholm*, as if it were capable of treating without its Allies. Princes do not always meet with Ministers that merit their Confidence, as *Servien* and *Salvius* did, who had no other View than their own Interest, which they found in the Satisfaction of those who employ'd them.

Charnacé and *St Stephen*, being at the Court of *Bavaria* on the Part of *France*, in the Year 1632, proceeded to such Extremes, that they were for fighting a Duel, insomuch that their Divi-

Division render'd them useless with the Elector. In *England* there were three Embassadors from the United Provinces, who being lodg'd in the same House, had each of them their Kitchin and particular Table, and liv'd so ill together, that they were call'd, *the Disunited Embassadors as the United Provinces*, making themselves by that Means the Laughing-stocks and Contempt of those People, whom the Crime of Rebellion had so perfectly united against their Sovereign.

When in the Year 1570, the Pope, the King of *Spain*, and the Republick of *Venice* negotiated at *Rome* a League against *Selym* II, Emperor of the *Turks*, the Senate, which had for some Time employ'd therein *Suriano*, its Embassador in Ordinary, judg'd it adviseable to joyn *John Soranzo* with him, as Extraordinary. *Suriano* had had Occasion for all his Address, to overcome the Obstacles the Ministers of *Spain* were continually making; and as he had a great deal of Wit, they were easily persuaded at *Venice*, that he had too much Compliance for the others, and that he consented with too much Facility to those Things, which he ought to have debated with Vigour, and which the Senate had already rejected. He justify'd himself, and gave so good an Account of his Conduct, that *Soranzo*, who did not make any greater Progress therein than he, was soon recall'd.

It may fall out that a Prince, who has no great Confidence in the Capacity, or in the Fidelity of his Minister, may give him a Colleague, who may serve as a Comptroller and Supervisor, to observe his Actions. But then this so seldom happens, that it is hard to find one single Example thereof in History. Credit may be given to all that that of those Times says, of the dangerous Intrigues of *Henry de la Tour*, Duke of *Bouillon*. And yet I think my self oblig'd to acquaint the Reader, that it is after the Duke of *Sully*, who was not his Friend, that I say, That King *Henry* IV, finding himself very much press'd by the Duke of *Bouillon*, who was desirous to be sent into *England*, that he might there learn the true Sentiments Queen *Elizabeth* had in reference to *France*. And the King not being willing to refuse him, tho' he was in a continual Distrust of his Wit and his Intentions, spoke thereof to the Duke of *Sully*, and endeavour'd to dispose him to go into *England* with the other, that he might inspect his Actions; but the Duke de *Sully* excus'd himself.

In the Year 1623, there were at the same Time three Embassadors from *Spain* at *London*, two Extraordinaries, viz. the Marquis d'*Inojosa* and *Don Diego Hurtado de Mendossa*, and one in Ordinary, *Don Carlos Coloma*, besides *Don Diego Mexia*, who was there on the Part of the *Infanta*. The Marquiss, and *Don Diego de Mendosse*, differ'd about the Rank, and notwithstanding *Don Carlos* had a great deal of Deference to the Marquiss, yet their Humours were so opposite, that the Qualities of Oyl and Vinegar are not more contrary. The following Years 1624 and 1625, there were seven or eight Embassadors from *France* at *London*, the Duke de *Chevreuse*, Messieurs de la *Villeauxclercs*, de *Tremes*, *Deffiat*, de *Tilberos*, de *Chasteauneuf*, de *Blainville*, &c. *Augustin Gustiniani*,

Bishop of *Nebio*, says in his Annals, That in the Year 1494, the Republick of *Genoa* sent sixteen Embassadors to *Lewis le More*, Duke of *Milan*, and that in the Year 1499, she sent four and twenty to *Lewis* XII, King of *France*, *Alphonsus* the *Magnanimous*, King of *Arragon* and *Sicily*, being inform'd that *Alphonso Borgia* was elected Pope under the Name of *Calixtus* III, had so much Joy thereat, that he sent to pay him Obedience, by fifteen or sixteen, as well Prelates as Noblemen, of the best Quality in his Kingdoms, amongst whom were one Patriarch, three Archbishops, one Bishop, the Lord Chief Justice of *Sicily*, the Master of the Order of *Montesa*, and several other Persons of Note.

It is usual to send a Plurality of Embassadors to Congresses, which are appointed to negotiate a Peace between several Parties interested, of which we have many Instances, as well in ancient as in modern History. The Wars which have harras'd, and almost ruin'd a good part of *Christendom*, have afforded several. So that they who cannot remember what was done in *Westphalia*, cannot be ignorant of what pass'd at *Cologne*, and what is actually doing at *Nimeguen*. But I don't think mention was ever made of a more illustrious Assembly, than that which was conven'd at *Arras* in the Year 1435. The War which the *English* had carry'd on in *France* for several Years, had reduc'd the Kingdom to a very deplorable State, more especially after *Philip* Duke of *Burgundy*, (who was resolv'd to revenge his Father's Death, and did indeed revenge it in a very cruel Manner) had declar'd himself against the King. The Pope who saw *France* was perishing, thought himself oblig'd to exert his utmost Efforts, to try to bring the Minds of the contending Parties to reasonable Terms. The *English* had not well husbanded the Friendship of the Duke of *Burgundy*, since the Death of their King *Henry* V, so that the Duke (who had several Reasons to be dissatisfy'd) had no Difficulty to consent to the Place and Time which were appointed for the Congress. The Pope sent thither the Cardinals de *St Croix*, and of *Cyprus*, the Archbishop of *Auch*, the Bishops of *Acs*, of *Usez*, of *Auxerre*, of *Albania*, with some other Bishops and Prelates. On the Part of *Charles* VII, King of *France*, there were the Duke of *Bourbon*, Prince of the Blood, the Count de *Richemont*, Constable of *France*, *Christopher de Harcourt*, the Mareschal de la *Fayette*, *Adam de Cambray*, first President of the Parliament of *Paris*, and thirty other Lords and Persons of Distinction which History names. *Henry* VI, King of *England*, sent thither the Cardinal of *Winchester*, the Archbishop of *York*, the Bishops of *Lisieux*, of *Norwich* and of *St Davids*, the Earl of *Huntingdon*, with above fifty other Lords, Prelates, and Officers of the King's Houshold. The Embassadors of the Duke of *Burgundy*, were the Bishops of *Liege*, of *Cambray* and of *Arras*, *Nicholas Rollin*, his Chancellor, the Duke of *Gueldre*; the Counts d'*Estampes*, de *St Pol*, de *Ligny*, de *Nassau*, de *Vaudemont*, de *Nevers*, de *Montfort*, de *Valquenbourg*, de *Meguu*, the Prince of *Orange*'s Son, and several other Lords and Persons of Quality, the Dukes of *Brittany*, of *Alançon*, and of *Bar*. And the Provinces of *Brabant* and of *Holland*, had also their Deputies there. The Duke

The EMBASSADOR and his FUNCTIONS 239

Duke of *Burgundy*'s Harbinger, who kept a List of the Assembly, reported to his Master, that there were in the Town Five hundred Knights, and in all about *Nine or ten thousand Strangers*, comprehending therein above fifty Heralds, Pursuivants and Kings at Arms

Cardinal *Pool* having prevail'd with *Mary* Queen of *England* to offer her Mediation to reconcile the Differences that continu'd the War between the Emperor *Charles* V, her Father-in-law, and *Henry* II King of *France*, she brought them to consent to an Assembly of Embassadors, and to a Suspension of Arms She had caus'd a Timber-House to be built at *Marck*, two or three Leagues off of *Calice*, in which were three distinct Appartments for the Embassadors of the Emperor, for those of *France*, and the third for the Cardinal This Structure had its Conveniences for the Day, but at Night all the Embassadors retir'd to their own Homes, those of the Emperor to *Gravelins*, the *French* to *Ardres*, and the *English* to *Calice* In the middle of this Timber-House was a large Tent, to which the Embassadors might repair from their respective Appartments, through a long cover'd Gallery *John de la Cerda*, Duke of *Medina Celi*, *Charles* Count of *Salin*, *Anthony Pervot de Granvello*, Bishop of *Arras*, and keeper of the Seals to *Charles*, with *Viglius de Zuichem*, President of the Privy Council, and *Bravonus* President of the Parliament of *Mecklin*, assisted there on the Part of the Emperor The King of *France* sent thither *Charles* Cardinal of *Lorrain*, the Constable of *Montmorancy*, *Charles* of *Marillac*, Bishop of *Valence*, *John de Morvillers* Bishop of *Orleans*, and *Claudius de l'Aubepine*, Secretary of State Cardinal *Pool*, *Stephen Gardiner* Bishop of *Winchester*, and Chancellor of *England*, *William Arondel*, and *William Pages*, were on the Part of Queen *Mary* for the Mediation The Embassadors of the Emperor and of *France*, saw one another but once by the way of Civility, and the whole Negotiation was transacted through the Intermediation of the *English* They concluded nothing at this time But in the Month of *October*, 1558, there was another Assembly on the Part of *Henry*, and of *Philip* King of *Spain*, in the Abbey of *Cercamp*, whither came on the Part of *France*, the Cardinal of *Lorrain*, the Constable of *Montmorancy*, the Mareschal de *St André*, the Bishop of *Orleans*, and *Laubepine* And for *Spain*, *Ferdinand de Toledo*, Duke of *Alva*, *William Nassau*, Prince of *Orange*, *Ruy Gomez DeSilva* the Bishop of *Arras*, and *Ulrich Viglius de Zuichem*, who there laid the Scheme of the Treaty that was concluded the Year following at *Chasteau Cambresis* The Queen of *England* sent thither the Bishop of *Ely*, and *Thomas Howard* of *Effingham*, her Great Chamberlain When *Charles* of *Austria* su'd for the Imperial Crown, he employ'd in the Quality of Embassadors, the Archbishop of *Saltzbourg*, the Bishops of *Liege* and of *Trent*, *Frederick*, Count Palatin of the *Rhine*, *Casimir*, Marquiss of *Brandenbourg*, and *Henry*, Count of *Nassau*, accompany'd and assisted by some Counsellors

In the Embassies which are compos'd of several Ministers, all the Embassadors, in what Number soever they be, are inseparable, and make together but one Body, where the representing Character is like the Soul in the human Body, *entire in the Whole*, and *entire in each Part* It was after this Manner that the three Embassadors of *France* (who were sent into *Germany* in the Year 1620, on occasion of the Troubles of *Bohemia*) understood it And it was thus also that they who were on the Part of the same Crown at *Munster*, understood it, when they insisted on having the Visits paid to them all without Interruption, and that the same Honours should be done to each of them without Distinction In the Year 1645, at the beginning of the Negotiation of *Munster*, the Deputies of the Hanse Towns having sent to demand Audience of the Embassadors of *France*, at the *Hotel* of Monsieur *d'Avaux*, who was then the first, it was assign'd them on Sunday the 29th of *January*, *and it was signify'd to them at the same Time*, *that at their Departure from that Visit, or else the next Day after, they might also see* M *Servien*, who had a separate Lodging They were receiv'd in the Entry by M *d'Avaux*'s Domesticks, who fill'd the same, as well as the Stairs, up which they were conducted to the Chamber, where they also found M *Servien*, who did them the same Civility that M *d'Avaux* did, in taking them by the Hand, after the Custom of the Countrey They were seated on Chairs with Backs, and when they had finish'd their Complement, which they address'd to both of them, *d'Avaux* was for yeilding the Honour of the Answer to M *Servien*, who would not accept of the Civility, but oblig'd *d'Avaux* to make it, this last also conducted them alone to the bottom of the Staircase The Deputies thinking they had acquitted themselves of their Devoir to the Embassadors, were no sooner return'd home, than they sent to desire Audience of those of *Spain*, who gave it them on the Day following, in the same Manner as they had had it of the others On the last Day of *January* they sent to demand Audience of M *Servien* in particular, who appointed them the Hour of I we in the Afternoon The Domesticks receiv'd them in the Entry, and conducted them into a Chamber, where they remain'd some time alone Afterwards a Gentleman came and told them, That M *Servien*, it was true, had fix'd them an Hour, but at present he was taken up with other Affairs That he had also been inform'd, that the Day before they had paid their Visit to the Embassadors of *Spain* That that destroy'd the uncontested Right of the King of *France*, and that of M *Servien* in particular, who was Embassador in the same Degree, and in the same Dignity with M *d'Avaux* That he had Reason to be offended thereat, and could not acquit them without the King his Master's express Orders That they had sinn'd against their Principals, as well as against his Most Christian Majesty, and that they would find some Difficulty to clear themselves The Deputies, surpris'd at this Harangue, were for justifying their Proceeding, but their Excuse was not allow'd of So that finding there was no likelihood of speaking to *Servien*, they retir'd, the same Domesticks conducting them to their Coach The Deputies said for their Justification, That they had but one *Letter of Credence*, which address'd to both the Embassadors That the two Embassadors of *France* compos'd but one and the same Embassy, which was indivisible fible That they had fpoke both to the one and the other of them, before they vifited the Embaffadors of *Spain* That *M d'Avaux* had anfwer'd for them both, and that they thought they had difcharg'd their Duty in preferring *France* to *Spain*. They were fo fcandaliz'd at *Servien*'s Procedure, that they were for refenting it by a publick Writing, but they were hindred from doing it by the Minifters of *Heffe*, who adjufted the Difference to the Satisfaction of *Servien*, who going fome time after to *Ofnabourg*, fent word immediatly to the Deputies of the Hanfe Towns of his Arrival They vifited him, and he return'd their Vifit There was fome Appearance of Truth in what the Deputies faid, but it cannot be deny'd alfo, that they committed a great Fault If they believ'd they had had Audience of *M Servien* at *M d'Avaux's*, it was not neceffary to ask a Second, and if they did not think fo, they ought not to have interrupted their Vifits, to fee the Embaffadors of *Spain*, but they had to do with a Man, who did not diftinguifh between the Fault and the Crime In the beginning of the Affembly of *Munfter*, the Deputies of the Electors, of the Princes, and of the States of the Empire, were accuftom'd to vifit the two Embaffadors of *France* feparately, each at his own Lodgings But fome time after the Court ordain'd, That the two Embaffadors fhould repair to the Houfe of the Firft with their Retinue, to receive the firft Vifit, that in that Manner they might receive it with the greater Splendor, for the Dignity of the Embaffy, yet nevertheless that the Vifit fhould be continu'd to the Second without Interruption The Cardinal *Mazarin* was for imitating in that the Cuftom of *Rome*, where, when there are two Embaffadors from the fame Prince, they receive the firft Vifit at the Houfe of the Firft, where they both meet for that Purpofe It was no fmall Mortification for *Servien* who was the haughtieft of Mortals

The three Embaffadors of *France* whom I lately mention'd, met with the fame Difficulty, becaufe fome of the Princes of *Germany*, who were unwilling to offend *Spain*, were for obliging them to be contented with the alternative The Princes were willing to begin with *France* But they judg'd the *French* ought not to difapprove, that after they had firft vifited the Duke *d'Engoulefme*, they fhould vifit the *Spanifh* Embaffador, before they faw the Count *de Bethune*, and the fecond Embaffador of *Spain*, before they vifited *M Chafteauneuf*, but the *French* would never admit of this Separation, and refolv'd rather to receive the Vifits altogether in the fame Place, which was beyond Difpute the fafeft and moft reafonable Choice

The Lord *Wotton*, who was at that Time Embaffador, from *England* at *Vienna*, made the fame Difficulty He vifited the Duke *d'Engoulefme* the firft, and after that was for vifiting the *Spanifh* Embaffador, defigning when he had done fo to finifh his Vifits to *Mrs de Bethune* and *de Chafteauneuf* But they fignify'd to him, That if he faw the *Spanifh* Embaffador, before he made an End of his three Vifits, they would not fee him nor negotiate with him, and that none but *M d'Engoulefme* fhould treat with him Hereupon *Wotton* offer'd to vifit *M de Bethune* before *Chafteauneuf*, but they rejected again that Propofition, infomuch that he was oblig'd to vifit them all three before he went to fee the others

Cafpar of Geneva, Marquifs *de Lullins*, whom the Duke of *Savoy* had fent to the Affembly at *Vervins* in the Year 1598, was for taking Place after the two firft Embaffadors of *Spain*, and before the third He fuppos'd the two to be really the Embaffadors of *Spain*, and that the third was the Minifter of the Arch-Duke, Governor of the Low Countries The Truth is, They were all three Embaffadors from the King of *Spain*, who was the Party with whom *Henry* IV treated, and not with the Arch-Duke The Embaffadors of *Spain* oppos'd him herein and oblig'd that of *Savoy* to fit at the lower End of the Table, with the General of the *Cordeliers*, right againft the Legate

The fame Embaffadors of *France*, who were fo fenfible in this Point, and the fame *M Servien*, who treated fo outrageoufly the Deputies of the Hanfe Towns, did not fcruple to propofe to the States of the United Provinces, That at the Vifits their Plenipotentiaries fhould pay to thofe of *France* at *Munfter*, there fhould yield their Hand to the firft, or elfe to the two firft, and fhould take it of the others, which was look'd upon to be by fo much the more impertinent, as by that Mean not only the Union was injur'd, but a Diftinction was alfo made between the Provinces, which are all equally fovereign Neither would they hearken to this Overture And the *French* were oblig'd to do in Reference to the Embaffadors of the United Provinces, what they caus'd others to do to themfelves

Some People wonder that the Embaffadors Plenipotentiaries of *France*, who are now at *Nimeguen*, and who would not be willing a Diftinction fhould be made between the Mareschal *Deftrades* and *Mrs d'Avaux* and *Colbert*, notwithftanding the firft is an Officer of the Crown, fhould themfelves make a Diftinction between the firft Embaffador of the Electors and the fecond, by paying to the firft the Honours which they will not do to the others I am fenfible it is what was practis'd at the Congrefs of *Weftphalia*, but would one not think alfo, that fince *France* defir'd then, That what was there done in Reference to the Ceremonies fhould be no Precedent out of that Place, That no Precedent ought to be made neither, of what the Electors judge to have been done there, to the Prejudice of their lawful Pretenfions? So that one might fay, That all that has happen'd on that Subject can make neither Rule nor Example One may moreover add, That in thofe Times the Electors, and even the Emperor himfelf, fet at the Head of their Embaffies thofe Perfons, which they were willing fhould be confider'd after another Manner than their Colleagues The Emperor made fome Diftinction between the Count *de Naffan* and the Doctors *Crane* and *Volmar* The Elector of *Brandenburg* did himfelf diftinguifh between the Count *de Wuqueftein*, and the Doctors *Wefenbeeq* and *Frombold*, fo that they could not be offended at the Diftinction the *French*, and, after their Examples, the Mediators, made between the ones and the others But I cannot tell whether a Prince can give himfelf himself the Power of making a Distinction between the Ministers of another, which the Master himself does not make, more especially if these Ministers are of the same Quality, or at least pretty near it. However the Embassadors Plenipotentiaries of *France*, and after them, those of *Sweden* (who make no Difficulty to give the Title of Excellency, to yield the Hand, and to do to *M Sommtz* all the other Honours which they do to the Embassadors of the United Provinces) refuse the same to the *Sr Blaspel* his Collegue. The Embassadors of *England* at first did so too, but upon Reflection afterwards of what had pass'd at home, in the Embassy of Prince *Maurice* of *Nassaw*, and of *Daniel Weiman*, who, notwithstanding they were of very different Qualities, were nevertheless us'd alike at *London*, they chang'd their Conduct, and acquiesc'd to the Elector's Desires. Perhaps it may be said, That as the King of *Great Britain* may have had a particular Consideration for his Electoral Highness, for whom he has an Esteem, whom he has admitted into his Order, and with whom he has been willing to joyn in the Care of the Interests of the House of *Orange*, during the Minority of the Prince, so it is reasonable to believe, that a little Animosity has intermix'd with the Orders the Most Christian King gave to his Ministers on that Subject. There will be no great Difficulty to believe this, or at least to suspect, that no great Complaisance is to be hop'd for on that Side, if Reflection be but made on the Differences *France* has had with the Elector, since the Advantages the King has granted to the Elector, by the Treaty of *Vossen* in 1673, and on what the Ministers of the one have published against the Reputation of the other. There are also very opposite Interests between the King and the Elector, as well on the Account of *Pomerania*, as for other Reasons. So that no Wonder ought to be made at the little Disposition the two Kings have to be complaisant to his Electoral Highness.

But let us see whether he that has undertaken to unravel the Question has succeeded so well, as to leave the Assembly of *Nimeguen* well perswaded and convinc'd of the Strength of his Reasons, and whether this Cause, which ought to be debated with powerful Arguments, has not met (if not a Prevaricator) at least a very indifferent Advocate, and a very sorry Sophister.

In the first Place, what he collects from the History of the Mercury of the Abbot *Siri* is not much for his Advantage, neither does it serve his Intention. It was not very necessary to establish the Credit of that Author by the Quality of Counsellor of State, which he gives himself. There are above ten thousand Counsellors of State in *France*, besides those who are so in effect, and besides those who have the Quality thereof by Reason of their Offices, as have all the Presidents, all the Solicitors and Advocates General, the Masters of the Requests, &c. but who notwithstanding have no more Share in the Affairs, nor in the Honours that accompany them, than they who are actually in the *Indies*. I do not hereby pretend to weaken the Authority of the Abbot *Siri*, on the contrary, I am sensible that the late *Lionne* has communicated excellent Memoirs to him,

and that there is no Historian that speaks of the Affairs of *Munster* with greater Knowledge and Judgment than he. But what the Author of the *Unravelling* draws from thence, concerning the Title of Excellency, which was given at that Time to the Embassadors of the Electors, and the Orders those of *France* had to treat them upon the Level with the Embassadors of *Venice*, and of the United Provinces, is wide enough from the Purpose, because that relates only to the Treatment the *French* Embassadors had Orders to give to the first of the Electoral Embassadors, exclusively of the others. Reference is had to *Vittorio Siri*, whose Authority is so great with the *Unraveller*, that he is willing to be determin'd by his Arbitration, to whom the Plenipotentiaries of *France* will make no Difficulty neither to submit in this Respect.

I cannot tell neither, whether he is very reasonable himself, when he says, That it is not reasonable that the foreign Potentates, to whom the Electors send their Ministers, should make a Distinction which their Masters themselves do not make. That is not here the Question. The Electors do not send their Embassadors to the King of *France*, because he will not suffer them to be cover'd, but if he thought it proper to admit them, and to treat them as he does those of *Venice*, he could not be hinder'd from doing it. but upon Condition that they should send him but one Embassador a Time, or if several were sent, that he would do that Honour but to the first. If the *Unraveller* will say that that is unjust, we must enter into a Circle which has no End. At the same Time *France* has for Proof the Example of *Munster*, where the Emperor himself put it in Practice, and where all the Electors acquiesc'd thereto. There is again the late Example of *Hamburgh*, where the first Deputy of *Lunenburg* pretended to have the Precedency of the second of the Elector of *Brandenburg*. I at the same Time agree with him, that a Prince may give to his Minister what Quality he pleases, as *Lionne* told Pope *Urban* VIII. But for all that, the Prince to whom the Minister is sent, is not thereby oblig'd to treat him otherwise than he was us'd to do. The Emperor could not hinder the Commander *de Gremonville* from taking the Quality of Embassador, but he reserv'd to himself the Liberty of preserving the Rank to that of *Spain*. The King of *France* does not hinder the Ministers of the Cantons from taking the Quality of Embassador, but he hinders them from being cover'd at their Audience. He will not suffer his Secretaries of State to give them the Title of Excellency, nor to yield them the Hand and the Step. The Quality of Embassador was not disputed with the Count *de Gronsfelt* and *M Curtz*, but they were given to understand, that notwithstanding their Character, they must remain within the Bounds of Respect.

It is true, that in the Assemblies that are held out of the Empire, the Princes are not oblig'd to keep scrupulously up to the Order that is observ'd in the Diets, because the Electors are there at Home, but then may it not also be said, that Kings are not oblig'd to ratify all the Novelties the Electors have a Mind to introduce? And that it does not belong to the Electors, to prescribe to crown'd Heads, after what

Manner they will be treated? They follow in that the Style receiv'd in their Court, which they do not alter at the Pleasure of other People.

I shall say nothing of the Examples, that the Author of the *Unravelling* calls to his Assistance, except that that of the Assembly of *Lubeck*, where *Chanut* would follow the Order which had been observ'd at *Munster*, is against him. It is proper to know in what Terms *Lignage* speaks of it. He says, That in the Year 1653, there was an Assembly at *Lubeck*, for the reconciling the Differences, which according to all Appearances, could not be regulated but by Arms, if the Truce between the two Crowns of *Poland* and *Sweden* was not prolong'd, or else converted into a perpetual Peace. *France*, *Venice*, the United Provinces and *Brandenburg*, were to be concern'd therein as Mediators, and they accordingly sent their Embassadors thither. There were Three on the Part of the Elector, who being arriv'd at the Place of the Congress, met at first with a very great Obstacle, because *Chanut*, Embassador from *France*, would at home give the Place of Honour but only to the first Embassador, and refus'd to give the Title of Excellency to the two others. They complain'd very much thereof, but *Chanut* maintain'd his Procedure, by the Example of *Munster* and *Osnabourg*, which, as he said, ought to serve for a Rule on these Occasions. He moreover added, That he had the express Order of the King his Master, to act in this Manner. The Embassadors of *Poland* did the same Civilities to all the three Embassadors of *Brandenburg*, and treated them equally. Those of *Brandenburg* were for taking Advantage thereof, but *Chanut* told them, That the *Poles* could not give him the Law, and that *France* was not oblig'd to follow the Example of *Poland*. That the *North* not being well regulated in its Ceremonies, could not establish new ones without the Consent of other Sovereigns. The Ministers of *Sweden* follow'd *Chanut*'s Example, and those of *Venice*, and of the United Provinces, with whom the Embassadors of *Brandenburg* would come in Competition, said, They would not visit them, and that in their own Houses they would not give them the Hand. I cannot tell whether the Haughtiness of these last could be well justify'd, especially since the Ministers of *Brandenburg* had the Character of Embassadors; but I dare at the same Time say, That the *Unraveller* does not strengthen his Argument by this Example.

He does not act very sincerely neither, when he says, That the four Ministers, who in the Year 1648, were at the *Hague* on the Part of the Elector of *Brandenburg*, had not the Quality of Embassador at their first Journey. It is most certain on the contrary, that upon the Difficulty which was rais'd them about their Character, they caus'd their Credentials to be reform'd, without stirring from the *Hague*, and that of Embassador was given them before they left it. As for *M. de Lumbres*, he was President of the Magazine of Salt at *Monstruel* upon Sea, that is to say in a Place, and in a Function, where he had never heard speak of this sort of Affairs, when he was taken from his Post, at the Recommendation of the Duke of *Longueville*, to be employ'd to the Elector of *Brandenburg*. He was a mere Novice, who knew not what he did, who was disavow'd, and who, if he had not been so, could not prejudice the Rights nor Pretensions of the King his Master.

Whatever may be said, it is certain that the Honours, which are done to the Ministers of the Electors, were regulated only at the Congress of *Munster*. Before that Time the Quality of Embassador was given them but in a very general Signification. They did not cover themselves before crown'd Heads, neither did they so much as pretend to the Title of Excellency. The *Unraveller* ought to be more sincere, and acknowledge with the Author whom he quotes so often, that *France* expressly stipulated, that the new Honours which were done to the Electoral Ministers, should be reserv'd to the first, to the Exclusion of all others. He ought also to answer what the Abbreviator of the Negotiation of *Sweden* says, concerning what pass'd in the Assembly of *Lubeck* in the Year 1653, viz. That it was there observ'd, that when the Elector of *Brandenburg* caus'd the last Investiture to be taken for the Dutchy of *Prussia* in *Poland*, of the Elector's three Embassadors, none but the first had a Place given him on the side of the *King's Chair*, and that the two others were plac'd at some Distance, in another Line. He farther says, That at the Diet which was conven'd at *Ratisbon*, after the Peace of *Westphalia*, the Emperor complain'd very much of the excessive Honours which had been done to the Ministers of the Electors. To which I shall add, That the *Unraveller* does not reflect on what he says, when he speaks of the Embassadors of the Cantons. What Distinction could be made amongst them, when *Lionne* receiv'd them all at the top of the Staircase, and pretended to take the Hand and Step of the first, as well as of the others? They all spoke to the King, not as Embassadors, but as Deputies, uncover'd. He is not very well acquainted with *la Tuilleries* since he says, That that Embassador had at home yielded the Place of Honour to the Ministers of *Brandenburg*, who he says, were only Deputies. That Minister knew his Business too well, to commit a Fault of this Nature. It is wide from the Purpose also, that he speaks of the Honour which *Mrs. Colbert, Milet, St Geran, Furstemberg, Vauguyon, Verjus,* &c did to the Ministers of the Elector of *Brandenburg*, since neither the ones nor the others had the Character of Embassador, no more than *Downing, Vant* and *Loccard*, but if all these Ministers had been cloath'd with the Character, those of the Elector, to whom the Style of Excellency was given, by reason of the Rank they held in the Council, could be no Precedent for the Embassadors. I make no doubt of the *Unraveller's* being a very able Man, but I believe also, that he would have sooner found in his House wherewith to cut the Knot of the Question, than under his Perruke wherewith to unty it.

There are Persons of some Ability, who judge that those Ministers who stickle with so much Obstinacy for an Advantage of so little Importance, have therein more Regard to their own particular Glory (altho' imaginary) than to the true Interest of their Master. The Electors have therein no other, than to cause their Representatives to be acknowledg'd for Embassadors,

bassadors, and to procure them the same Civilities which are done to the Embassadors of *Venice* and of the United Provinces, and thereby to put themselves in possession of a Right which they neither had, nor did not pretend to fifty Years ago, and which was now become in common to them, with the first Potentates of Christendom. It is what *France* and *Sweden* offer to do, and they esteem that his Electoral Highness ought to be contented therewith, because that all he can pretend to beyond that, does not acquire more Honour to himself, but a great deal more Vanity to some one of his Ministers, who has such mighty Obligations to Fortune, that she might with more Reason complain of the Ingratitude of her Creature, if after the Example of other Wolves, she were not accustom'd to prostitute her self to the most unworthy. I may perhaps be mistaken, but I am perswaded that there is no Elector, that would not freely renounce the Advantage he pretends to for his second Embassador, if the King of *France* would at his Court, do to the first the same Civilities which he does to the Embassadors of the Princes of *Italy*.

When a Prince employs in the same Court two Embassadors, of whom the one is in Ordinary, and the other Extraordinary. This always has the Precedency of that, and if they are both Extraordinaries, the last Comer takes Place of the first. *Destiat* was Embassador Extraordinary at *London*, but *la Villeauxcleres*, who came thither after him, took the Precedency of him every where. In the Year 1623, *Don Carlos Coloma*, Governor of the City of *Cambray*, was Embassador in Ordinary from *Spain*, in *England*. *Don John de Mendosse* Marquiss *d'Inoyosa*, came thither some time after, in the Quality of Extraordinary, and at the same time that the Prince of *Wales* return'd from *Spain*, *Don Diego Hurtado de Mendosse* came thither in the same Quality. The Marquiss fearing lest *Don Diego*, as the last Comer, should pretend to the Precedency, and being sensible that he could not refuse it him with Justice, lodg'd him with himself, as being his Relation, and did him the Honours of the House. But *Don Diego* perceiving at last the Artifice, did not scruple to give the Marquiss to understand, that if there should at any Time happen any Occasion to appear in Publick together, *he should be the Man that would insist upon having the Rank which he judg'd was his due*. The Marquiss said indeed, that *Don Diego* could not take the first, because he was only sent to the Prince of *Wales*, and he had no other Business, than barely to carry back to the King his Master, the happy News of the Prince's safe Arrival. But for all that, he declin'd the Necessity of appearing with him at Court. He also said, that the King of *Spain* had regulated the Rank between them and to his Advantage; but yet he did not dare to accompany him to Audience, for fear of being oblig'd to give Place to him, and he let *Don Carlos Coloma* do this Office. *Don Diego* made no long Stay in *England*, and he was hardly set out from thence, when Letters arriv'd from the King of *Spain*, which reprimanded him severely for daring to dispute the Precedency with the Marquiss *d'Inoyosa*, and did not only revoke the Commission *Don Diego* had to see the Archduke and the King, as he pass'd through the Low-Countries and thro' *France*, but likewise commanded him to repair to his own House, and there to remain till farther Orders. The Court of *Madrid* was for having him respect the Quality of the Marquiss, who was of the Council of State, who had been Governor of *Milan*, and was actually Vice-Roy of *Navarre*, but this was what the Council should have expressly commanded him, because in Course *Don Diego* ought to take Place. In these Contestations the Concern was merely personal, the Dignity of the Prince having no Share therein.

Don Diego de Saavedra, Plenipotentiary of *Spain* at *Munster*, being inform'd that the Bishop of *Boisleduc* was nominated to negotiate there with him, was mightily concern'd thereat, *and did all that he could, to preserve to himself the first Place*, but in vain. The Bishop being arriv'd at *Munster*, sent to *Saavedra* the Seal and Cypher of the Embassy, in pursuance of an Order he had for that Purpose from the Marquiss *de Castelrodrigo*, which he communicated to him. But *Saavedra* signify'd to him, that in an Affair of that Importance, he receiv'd his Orders from none but the King immediately, and so would not comply. Their Quarrel lasted till *Pegneranda* being arrived at *Munster*, *Saavedra* put the Seal and Cypher into his Hands. It is reasonable to think, that formerly there was no Rule for that, since *Don Gutierre Gomez de Fuensolida*, being in the Year 1505, Embassador from *Ferdinand* the Catholick to *Ph lip* of *Austria*, his Son-in-Law, *Ferdinand* sent thither also another Embassador, nam'd *Don Pedro d'Ayalla*, notwithstanding which, *Don Gutiere* kept the Precedency, and was always the Speaker. History says expresly, that *Don Pedro* yeilded him this Honour, as to his Senior, and it is probable it makes this Remark, because at this Day, the quite contrary is practis'd.

In the Year 1607, King *Henry* IV sent President *Jeannin* to mediate there a Peace with *Spain*, at which he was to labour in Conjunction with the Sr *de Buzanval*, who was there Embassador in Ordinary. The King afterwards thought fit to substitute the Sr *de Russy* in the Office of Ordinary, and to comprehend him in the Commission with the two others. He arriv'd in *Holland* after them, but yet he had not the Precedency, as well because it was not the King's Intention, as because the two others were Extraordinaries, to whom the Ordinary is oblig'd to give Place. In these Cases Regard must be had to the Master's Intention. In the Year 1573, *Charles* IX, King of *France*, sent into *Poland John de Monluc*, Bishop of *Valencia*, to recommend there the Election of the Duke of *Anjou*. The Journey was dangerous, and it was apprehended that the Emperor, who solicited that Crown for his Son, would cause *Monluc* to be either kill'd, or taken up in *Germany*: For which Reason the Court sent after him, *Giles de Noailles* (he who succeeded since to the Bishop of *Acs*, his Brother, in the Embassy of *Constantinople*) to discharge the Function of Embassador to the Senate of *Poland*, in the Absence of *Monluc*, in case any Misfortune should happen to him, or otherwise conjointly with him. *Monluc*, who was not for having a Companion, and who consider'd that

the

the last Comer would pretend to have the Precedency, was at first mortify'd thereat But the other shew'd so much Deference to his Advice, in yielding to him every where, that *Monluc* seeing himself rather respected as a Master, than consider'd as a Colleague, suffer'd him without Reluctancy

Formerly there was not so much to do in the Matter *Philip de Commines* says, that *Ferdinand* the Catholick, finding himself in Possession of the *Rouffillon*, and having a Mind to make it be believ'd that his Intention was to make Reparation for his horrible Infidelity to *Charles* VIII, in arming all *Italy* against him, with a Design to oppose his Passage, at his Return from the Kingdom of *Naples*, had the Impudence to send him his usual Negotiator, Brother *John de Mauleon*, with some other religious of the Convent of *Montferrat* The Catholick Kings who had caus'd *Charles* to be driven out of *Italy*, and who had made him lose all the Kingdom of *Naples*, except *Gayette*, caus'd a Truce to be propos'd to him which might secure that important Place to him, which was the strongest of all *Charles* who was desirous to dive into the Intention of these Princes who had lately so villainously deceiv'd him, sent into *Spain*, *William* of *Poictiers*, Lord of *Clarieux*, but *Gayette* being taken before this Embassador could get to *Ferdinand*, so that the Affair was no longer in the same State Other Overtures were made to *Charles* about the Division of the Kingdom of *Naples*, and of all *Italy* Upon this Proposition *Charles* sent *Clarieux* back again with another Gentleman, nam'd *Michael de Clermont* Clarieux at his Return from the second Journey, reported, that *Ferdinand* and *Isabella* had declar'd to him, that their last Intention was to content themselves with that Part of the Kingdom of *Naples* which is nearest *Sicily*, that is to say, with *Calabria*, and that they would leave the rest to *Charles* *France* was very much surpriz'd at these liberal Offers from Princes whom it had so much Reason to distrust *Charles* therefore sent back the same Embassadors for the third time, and join'd with them *Imbert de Bertenay*, Lord *du Boccage*, who for having been approv'd of by *Lewis* XI, was the fitter to negotiate with *Ferdinand* and *Isabella*; who were the most subtile, and the most perfidious Princes of their Time But as soon as these three Embassadors were arriv'd, they were narrowly watch'd and observ'd, that they might have no Communication with any Body whatever, and they were soon sent back

In those Times there was no Notion of Embassadors in Ordinary, but forasmuch as *Clarieux* and *Clermont* had been employ'd at the Court of *Spain*, and about the same Affair, for which *du Boccage* was sent thither, they were compris'd in the same Commission This is what is almost always done So that when a Prince sends an Embassador Extraordinary to a Court where he has already one in Ordinary, he cannot exclude this from the Negotiation, without doing him wrong, and injuring himself In taking his Confidence from the Ordinary, he also lessens his Credit, without which it is impossible for him to succeed in the Affairs he has to negotiate The Republick of *Venice* when she sent in the Year 1581, *Vincent Tron* and *Hieronie Lippomano*, her Embassadors Extraordinary into *Spain*, to complement *Philip* II on his Succession to the Kingdom of *Portugal*, would have *Francis Morosini*, their Embassador in Ordinary, and *Matthew Zane*, who was to succeed him in the Embassy, to assist at all the Functions of the Extraordinary's I just now said, that *Buzanval* was Embassador in Ordinary in *Holland*, when *Jeannin* arriv'd there But he was compris'd in the same Commission, and he became Extraordinary as soon as *Ruffy* came to the *Hague*, and this labour'd there in Conjunction with the other two, although he was but in Ordinary *Dufargis* being Embassador in Ordinary from *France* at *Madrid*, was compris'd in the Commission of *Bassompierre*, and afterwards in that of the Marquiss of *Rambouillet* *William Borrel*, Embassador in Ordinary from the United Provinces at *Paris*, was in the Year 1660, compris'd in the Commission of *Mrs de Gnent*, *Van Beunningen* and *de Hubert*

Whereupon I shall make two or three more necessary Remarks First, That in the Commissions of an Embassy Extraordinary, where the Ordinary is compris'd with the Extraordinaries, they are distinguish'd in such Manner that the Prince makes known, that the Ordinary does not change his Quality, by saying in his *Credential Letter*, N N N *my Embassadors Extraordinary, with* N *my Embassador in Ordinary*, &c Secondly, It is requisite that the Ordinary (to be compris'd in the same Commission) have the same Character with the Extraordinary, because without that, he cannot pretend to it, neither can the Extraordinary suffer a Minister of the second Order to be associated with him M *de Baugy*, who has been known in the Quality of Embassador from *France* in *Holland*, being Resident at *Vienna* at the Beginning of the *Bohemian* War, made great Interest to be compris'd in the Commission of *Mrs d'Engoulesme*, *de Bethune*, and *de Chasteauneuf*, Embassadors Extraordinary with the Emperor, and he would not have been unserviceable to them, by Reason of the Knowledge he had of the Affairs of *Germany*, but the Court would never content thereto In the Year 1653, the King of *Denmark* sent an Embassador Extraordinary to *Stockholm*, to try to persuade the Queen of *Sweden* to succour the United Provinces against the *English*, or at least to get Assurance that she would not disturb the Kingdom of *Denmark*, while the King should employ his Forces in Favour of the *Hollanders* He had already a Minister of the second Order at that Court, whom he compris'd in the Commission of the Extraordinary Embassy, but he gave him the Character of Embassador, and order'd him to remain there in that Quality, after the Extraordinary was return'd home However, *Harald Appelboom*, Minister of the second Order from *Sweden*, sign'd with Count *de Dona*, Embassador Extraordinary from the same Crown, the Treaty which was concluded at the *Hague* the 23d of *Jannary* 1668, to serve as a Preliminary to the triple Alliance, but it was irregular, and the Count *de Dona* ought not to have suffer'd it

I shall further add to what I have already said, that *Paul Paruta*, in speaking of the four Procurators of St *Mark*, whom the Republick of *Venice* sent to King *Francis* I, says, That *Trevisan* was Spokesman, as being the youngest of 'em all. From whence we may infer, that it is the Custom at *Venice*, in Embassies compos'd of a Plurality of Embassadors, to have the youngest make the Harangues.

I might here also take Notice, That *the Embassador who has Collegues cannot negotiate alone, nor have particular Conferences without them* But as this properly belongs to the Function of the Embassador, we shall speak more pertinently thereto in the III^d Chapter of the Second Book of this Treatise. Before I finish this, I shall observe, that as on the one side a Prince may employ several Embassadors in the same Court, so on the other, one and the same Minister may serve several Princes. But this is what admits of a great many Exceptions and Distinctions. For two Princes never having all their Interests so in Common (what Alliance or Union soever may be between them) but their Friendship will be subject to Alterations and even to Rupture, it is impossible for one Minister to serve them both equally well, more especially if their Interests change their Nature. It is then the Evangelical Saying is verify'd, *That no Body can serve two Masters*. And this is the most natural Explication of the Passage. Several Allies may make Use of the same Minister, as to the Fact and the Interest of the Alliance, as the United Provinces make Use altogether of one and the same Minister, in all their Embassies in Ordinary, and in the major Part of their Commissions, but it is only for the common Interests of the whole Union. Without that, we must keep to the Saying of Holy Writ. *Nicholas de Bie*, Resident of *Poland* at the *Hague*, took upon him also the Management of the Affairs of the Duke of *Holstein Gottorp*, while this had none; neither with *Poland* nor the United Provinces. So that there was nothing incompatible in those two Employments. Some Time after, the King of *Sweden*, *Charles Gustavus*, having broke with the King of *Poland*, the Kings had both an Interest to preserve the Friendship of the United Provinces. *De Bie* was oblig'd to speak, not only for the King of *Poland*, but also for the Duke of *Holstein*, who being Father-in-Law to the King of *Sweden*, and having opposite Interests to those of the King of *Poland*, oblig'd his Minister to present Memorials, not very conformable to the Service of the King his Master, wherein he frequently contradicted himself, which did him an Injury, and promoted the Service neither of the one nor the other.

After the Decease of the Cardinal of *Mantua*, one of the Legates of the Council of *Trent*, where he died in the beginning of the Month of *March*, 1563, the Ministers and Prelates of *France*, and even those of the Emperor *Ferdinand*, cast their Eyes on *Charles* Cardinal of *Lorrain*, to procure him the Quality of Legate. But the Pope, who would have none that did not depend entirely on him, that he might thereby remain absolute Master of the Council, and whom it concern'd, that those who presided there should have no Dependence on any Body else, prevented the Intercession he knew the Emperor and the Prelates of the Council intended to make on that Subject, and nominated immediately the Cardinals *Moron* and *Navager*, Legates, to preside at the Council. The Cardinal of *Lorrain* was at *Trent* on the Part of *France*, and he was continually making Speeches for the Preservation of the Liberties of the *Gallican* Church, for the Superiority of the Council over the Pope, for the Communion in both Kinds, for the Liturgy in the vulgar Tongue, and for several other Things which were the Aversion of the Court of *Rome*, and very little conformable to the Sentiments of those who stickled for the Pope's Authority, as being paid for so doing. The Pope consider'd that it was impossible that the Cardinal of *Lorrain*, being in that Post, should not fail either in his Duty to *France*, or to the See of *Rome*, and particularly to his Holiness's self, who, in making him Legate, made him Depositary of his Secrets and Interests. The Cardinal *de Bourdaisiere*, who had penetrated into the Pope's Intention, made very pressing Instances in Favour of the Cardinal *de Lorrain*, before the Declaration was made in the Consistory. But the Pope told him plainly, That the Cardinal of *Lorrain* being the Head of a Party at *Trent*, could not officiate in the Post of Legate, which was proper only for a neutral and disinterested Minister, and *that there was no serving two Masters*. The Cardinal of *Lorrain* complain'd thereof, but with very little Justice.

Charles VIII. and *Ferdinand the Catholick*, both employ'd Brother *John de Mauleon*. *Ferdinand*, because he would deceive *Charles*, and *Charles*, because he was willing to be deceiv'd by *Ferdinand*. The one mightily coveted to be restor'd to the Possession of the *Roussillon* which his Father had mortgag'd to *France*, and the other, who had at least as much Passion for the Expedition to *Italy*, and for the Conquest of *Naples*, was impatient to discharge himself of that precious Pledge. He kept it a Mystery to his most faithful Servants, and perform'd the Negotiation by this Monk, who in serving two Masters, did the Business of the one, and ruin'd the Affairs of the other. *Don Diego Sarmiento d'Acugna*, Count *de Goudemar*, being Embassador of *Spain* in *England*, had made himself so agreeable to King *James*, that he not only liv'd with him in a Domestick Familiarity, but had also his Confidence in Affairs of the greatest Importance, and, among the rest, for the Conduct of the Negotiation of the Marriage of the Prince of *Wales*. It had been talk'd of several Years, and the King did not want Friends, and faithful Servants, who had told him from Time to Time, that the Court of *Madrid* thought of nothing less than of this Alliance, no more than of the Restitution of the *Palatinate*, which was to be one of the first Conditions thereof. But Count *de Goudemai* had so prepossess'd his Mind with these false Hopes, that he believ'd no other Oracle than what came out of the Mouth of that common Minister. The Count spoke of this Marriage as of a thing so certain, that the King made no Difficulty to send the Prince, his only Son, into *Spain*, and to entrust him with those who might have made away with him, if they had had such an Intention, as well as they had that to deceive him. The Count *de Goudemar*, who could not be ignorant that the Inquisition, and politick Interest, suggested invincible Obstacles against this Alliance, did nevertheless amuse the King therewith, and all the *English* Court, where he held a fort of Commerce, and finger'd before-hand Money for the Offices of the future Queen's Houshold And the King of *Spain* rewarded the Impostor with a Place in the Council of State

The Cardinals of *Richelieu* and *Mazarin* have frequently made a beneficial Use of the Service of the Ministers of the Princes of *Germany*, who resided at the Court of *France*, to their own Masters, and *Priandy*, Resident of *Mantua*, was the only Person that went to and fro for several Years about the Affairs of *Mantua*, notwithstanding he was the Duke's Minister But, on these Occasions, the Minister will do very well not to quit his Post without the express Leave of his Master, or being well assur'd that his Negotiation will be agreeable to the Prince he serves, or that he can answer for the Success thereof   *Roncaglio* negotiated the Affairs of the King of *Poland*, *Uladislas* IV, at the Court of *France*, at the Time that *Casimir*, Brother to *Uladislas*, resign'd the Cardinal's Hat with the same Levity with which he had accepted it, and with which he had some Time before taken and laid down the Habit of Jesuit Cardinal *Mazarin*, who had a Mind to cloath his Brother with the Purple, dispos'd *Roncaglio* to go to *Rome* to solicit the same, neither the one nor the other communicating it to the King of *Poland*, who being that *Roncaglio* manag'd his Affairs at *Paris*, came to be inform'd that he was negotiating there of Cardinal *Mazarin* at *Rome*.   This was an Irregularity that had no Example, but deserv'd very well to be made one

CHAP. XXVII.

Embassadors are inviolable in their Persons

THE Necessity of Embassies makes the Security of Embassadors, by the universal Consent of all the Nations of the Earth, and it is this general Consent that constitutes what is call'd the *Law of Nations*   It holds a *Medium* between the *Law of Nature* and the *Civil Law*, and is by so much the more considerable than the last, that it can neither be chang'd nor alter'd, but by the same unanimous Approbation of all People   There is no Sovereign that can assume the Authority to explain the Laws which compose this Right   Neither is there any Judge that can extend his Jurisdiction over those Persons whom this Law protects, because he would thereby disturb a Commerce, the Freedom whereof is founded on indispensable Necessity, and he would deprive Mankind of the Means of maintaining Society, which could not subsist without this Principle, which is more than Mathematical

I shall make this Chapter serve in some Measure as a Comment to the Law, *Si quis*, ff of *Legation*   It is not without Reluctancy that I mingle a little *Latin* in a Discourse, and in a Work, where I even affect to keep at a Distance from any thing that favours of ancient *Rome*, but having to do with People who are great Cavillers, and very bad Lawyers, I find my self oblig'd to shew the Publick, that those Judges who confine a publick Minister without a previous Information, and condemn him contrary to Form, do not less offend the Civil Law, of which they make Profession, than the *Law of Nations*, which they are ignorant of

Pomponius the Civilian says, in the Law I just quoted, That *he that outrages or beats the Embassador of an Enemy, violates the Law of Nations, because the Person of an Embassador is sacred   Wherefore those who are with us, and we declare War to the People who sent them, are nevertheless free. Insomuch that he who injures an Embassador, ought to be put into the Hands of him who sent him*   To this we may add what the *Jurisconsult*, *Ulpian*, says in the Law, *Lege Julia ff ad Leg 'ful de vi publica*, of those who beat or injure Embassadors, Orators, or those of their Retinue, and what the illustrious *Hugh de Groot* says on that Head, in his excellent Treatise *De Jure Belli & Pacis, lib 2 cap* 18 at the beginning   But there is no Explanation more natural and clear than that which the Illustrious, Great, and Puissant Estates of *Holland* and *Westfrise* give to these two Laws, in their Declaration of the 29ᵈ of *March*, 1651   They expect it shall serve for a Regulation and perpetual Edict, for which Reason they recommend the Observation and Execution thereof to the Court of Judicature of their Province, in the following Terms

" The Knights, Nobles, and the Cities of
" *Holland* and *Westfrise*, representing the E-
" states of the same Province, To all those
" who shall see or read these Presents, Greet-
" ing   Whereas according to the *Law of Na-*
" *tions*, and even that of *the Barbarians, the*
" *Persons of Embassadors, Residents, Agents,* and
" *of other the like publick Ministers of Kings,*
" *Princes and Republicks*, are every where held
" in such high Esteem, that no Person whate-
" ver dare offend, injure, or damnify them
" But on the contrary, they are in Possession
" of being respected, highly consider'd and ho-
" nour'd by every Body, nevertheless, foras-
" much as we are inform'd, that some *insolent,*
" *outragious, and dissolute Persons*, have dar'd to
" undertake and act the contrary to what is a-
" bove recited, in Reference to some publick
" Ministers who have been sent to this Estate,
" and who reside in our Province   We being
" willing to provide against the like Abuses
" for the future, have thought fit to ordain ve-
" ry expressly by this our Declaration, and to
" prohibit and forbid very seriously, as we do
" ordain, prohibit, and forbid very seriously
" by these Presents, *That no Person, of what*
" *Nation,*

"Nation, State, Quality or Condition foever, pre-
"fume to offend, endamage, injure by Word,
"Deed, or Look, the Embaffadors, Refidents, A-
"gents, or other Minifters of Kings, Princes, Re-
"publicks, &c. Others, having the Quality of pub-
"lick Minifters, or to offer them any Injury or
"Infult, directly or indirectly, in any manner or
"kind whatsoever, in their Perfons, Gentlemen
"of their Retinue, Servants, Houfes, Coaches,
"and other Things that may belong to them, or
"depend on them, under the Penalty of incur-
"ring our utmoft Indignation, and of being
"bodily punifh'd, as Violators of the Law of
"Nations, and Difturbers of the publick Quiet.
"The whole, according to the Nature and
"Exigency of the Cafe. Commanding all the
"Inhabitants of this Province, and all thofe
"who fhall there be prefent, that on the con-
"trary they fhew all manner of Honour, and
"pay all Refpect to this fort of Minifters,
"and even to give them, as alfo to their Do-
"mefticks, and to thofe of their Retinue, all
"Aid and Affiftance, and to contribute what-
"ever may be ferviceable to their Honour,
"and be aiding to their Service and Conveni-
"ency. Ordaining and commanding the firft,
"and the other Counfellors of the Court of this
"Province, as alfo all Officers, Juftices and
"Magiftrates, and all thofe to whom it fhall
"belong, to proceed againft the Tranfgreffors
"by the Execution of the Penalties above-
"mention'd, without any manner of Conni-
"vence or Diffimulation whatever. Done at
"the Hague, under our Great Seal, the 29 h or
March, 1651.

It is impoffible to make a more illuftrious Comment, and at the fame Time a more authentick and more authoritative Glofs upon the Law fi quis, than that the States of Holland give it by their Declaration, wherefore I fhall make fome Reflections both on the one and the other, which will ferve very much to clear the Matter, as well as what I have to fay on this Subject in the Sequel of this Chapter. And firft, one may conclude from the Law it felf, that thofe who offend and outrage a publick Minifter, do not only violate the Law of Nations, but that they alfo commit a capital Crime againft the Civil Laws. And that this Crime is Capital in the moft proper Signification, that is to fay, is punifhable with Death, appears evidently in this, that the Declaration of the States of Holland fays expreffly, That they ought to be punifh'd as Violators of the Law of Nations, and Difturbers of the publick Quiet. The Jurifconfult fays, they ought to be put into the Hands of him whofe Embaffador has been in-jur'd.

Secondly we muft know, That notwithftanding the Opinion of Pomponius is at this Day equivalent to a Law, yet he only expounds the Law of Nations. He does not tell what ought to be done, nor does not command and ordain, as the Declaration of the States of Holland does, but he only tells what is done, and what is practis'd, conformably to the Law of Nations. He moreover adds, That that part of the Law of Nations which protects Embaffadors, is fuperior to the other, which renders Prifoners of War Slaves, fince notwithftanding the Declaration of War, the Embaffadors of Enemies retain ftill their Liberty and Freedom;

from whence we muft neceffarily conclude, that it is alfo fuperior to all the Civil Law.

It may very well be allow'd me to quote an Example from the Roman Hiftory, to illuftrate a Roman Law. The Confuls who went with an Army into Africk in the third Punick War, had Orders from the Senate to demolifh the City of Carthage. As foon as the Army was landed, the Inhabitants of the City fent Embaffadors to the Confuls, who told them the Orders they had receiv'd from the Senate. Hereupon the Embaffadors gave Way to all that Grief and Indignation could dictate to defperate People. The Confuls let them make an end, and then Cenforinus, one of the Confuls told them, Withdraw, for you are ftill Legati, that is to fay Embaffadors, becaufe their City was not yet deftroy'd. The Conful gave thereby to underftand, That notwithftand they were Enemies, and that their Tranfport deferv'd fome Refentment, yet for all that, they were in Safety in the Roman Camp, by virtue of their Character, which protected them from all kinds of Infults. Teaching us by this Example, that fince the Law of Nations requires fuch Confiderat on fhould be had for the Embaffador of an Enemy, it is reafonable to believe, that he who lofes the Refpect which is due to the Embaffador of a Prince a Friend, does fomething worfe than violate the Law of Nations.

As for the Declaration of the States of Holland, there is hardly a Period in it, upon which fome Reflection may not be made. It fays at firft, That the Perfons of Embaffadors are privileg'd, even according to the Sentiment of the Barbarians, fo that they who violate them are worfe than Barbarians. 2. It extends the Protection of the Law of Nations to Minifters of the fecond Order, and even to Agents, who are not characteriz'd Minifters. This is what ought to be taken notice of, againft the Court of Juftice of Holland, which acting contrary to the Maxims eftablifh'd by the univerfal Confent of all People, was for maintaining in the Year 1644, That the Rule which fays, no Compulfion can be us'd to a publick Minifter, ought to be only apply'd to thofe who have the Character of Embaffador, and not to Minifters of the fecond Order. At leaft if it was ftill in that Error at that Time, it ought to be undeceiv'd fince the Year 1651, and it ought not to have in the Year 1675, proceeded againft the Refident of a Sovereign Prince, an Ally to that Eftate, and confin'd him a Prifoner without a previous Information, and without the other Formalities which are neceffary, even to the imprifoning a private Perfon. 3. The States ftyle Infolent, Outrageous, and Diffolute, thofe who dare offend or injure publick Minifters, directly or indirectly: from whence may be inferr'd, what ought to be faid of thofe, who offend and abufe directly and indirectly, the publick Minifter of a Prince who is a Friend and Ally of the State, after an unheard of Manner, and that has no Example in Hiftory. 4 The States of Holland ordain expreffly, that publick Minifters be refpected, not only in their Perfons, but alfo in their Houfe, in their Servants, and in their Coaches. 5 All thofe who thus act directly contrary to the Declaration of the States of Holland, fhew plainly that they have the utmoft Contempt for the higheft Indigna-

tion, with which they threaten the Transgressors of their Ordinance. 6 Ought not those to be put into the Number *of the Violators of the Law of Nations*, and of the Disturbers of the publick Quiet, who under any Pretext whatever, insult and injure a publick Minister, to the Prejudice of their express and rigorous Prohibitions? I shall not here observe, that the Declaration does not distinguish between the Minister who is born in the Countrey, and a Stranger, altho' the States of *Holland* cannot be ignorant of the Difference *Spring* had on that Account with the Court of Justice. I have treated this Matter so amply in Chapter II, that nothing can be added thereto.

The *Turks* say, Two Reasons oblige them to suffer the *Christian* Princes to have their Ministers at the Port. The first, That the *Grand Seignior* may have to whom to complain, and whom to come upon for the Infraction of Treaties. And the other, That they may have Hostages for the Execution of Treaties. It may be said they act like *Turks*, and in the Aversion their savage Natures have for *Christians*, they don't scruple to offend the Ministers of Sovereigns who reside with them; but then we ought to consider that it is contrary to their Law, the *Alcoran expressly forbidding to offend the Elchi*, that is to say the publick Minister, and that those among the *Turks*, that do not abandon themselves altogether to their Brutality, acknowledge that publick Ministers ought to be in Safety, even in the height of the War, and that they do not injure the Minister, till they have laid aside all Fear and Respect for the Master. They have given sufficient Testimony that they are not insensible in that Part, where the Prince that will not prostitute his Reputation, ought to be extremely sensible, and that they have known how to resent the Outrage that has been done to their Embassadors. *Selim* II, having open'd himself a Way to the Conquest of *Egypt*, by that of the Island of *Cyprus*, found in it at first considerable Obstacles enough, because the continual Encounters had so thinn'd his Troops, that he was not in a Condition to make any great Progress, for which Reason he would have been willing to have persuaded *Tomumbey, Soldan* or *Sultan* of *Egypt*, to get rid of the War by a good Accommodation. He therefore sent Embassadors to him, but the *Arabs* who serv'd in the Army of *Tomumbey*, believing they ought to be no longer afraid of *Selim*, murder'd them and *Tomumbey*, who could not punish People, who did not so much as know what Discipline was, was forc'd to dissemble this horrible Violence. But *Selim* being reinforc'd by a new Supply of other *Arabs*, gave Battel to *Tomumbey*, defeated him, and having taken him Prisoner after the Fight, he reproach'd him with the Murder of his Embassadors, and having caus'd him to be strangled by two Executioners, he order'd the Body to be hang'd up at the Gallows. *Tomumbey* did not approve of the Murder of the Embassadors, but by not punishing it, he became an Accomplice therein, and justify'd *Selim's* Resentment, since according to the Saying of Prince *Maurice* of *Nassau*, They who violate the *Law of Nations* cannot be too severely punish'd. He spoke it only on the Account of a Drummer or Trumpeter, who had been shot

at. What would he not have said of those, who losing all the Respect which is due to a Sovereign Prince, and to his Alliance, do to his Minister a more cruel Outrage than if they put him to Death?

All Sovereigns understand it thus, and have severely punish'd the Outrages their Subjects have offer'd to publick Ministers. In the Year 1601, *Soranzo*, who was returning from his Embassy in *Spain*, as he pass'd through *Barcelona*, where he was to Embark, had a great Dispute with a Leather Gilder, who had not serv'd him to his Mind. The *Spanish* Tradesman wounded the *Venetian* Embassador very dangerously in the Head, and in the Arm, and being afraid of Justice, he flung himself into a Church, which is in *Spain* the usual Retreat of Murderers. He pretended to enjoy the Protection of his Sanctuary, and the *Catalans* spoke warmly for the Privileges of the Place, and of the City of *Barcelona*. But the King made them pass over all those Considerations, and caus'd them to drag the Tradesman out of the Church, and punish him as a Violater of the *Law of Nations*, who ought not to find Impunity in the Privileges of a Church. Those Princes who lose the Respect which they owe to the *Law of Nations*, destroy the very Principles of Civil Society, and ought no more to be suffer'd there, than Wolves in a Sheepfold. *Ferdinand* of *Arragon*, King of *Naples*, was the worst Prince that had been for many Ages. The History of his Reign is fill'd with infinite Inhumanities, and speaks of him as of the most avaritious, most cruel, and most violent Man of his Time, and *Philip de Commines*, who makes his *Elogium*, says, He was a Glutton, unfaithful and profane, having neither Religion, Conscience nor Honour. It ought not therefore to be wonder'd at, that he should stain his Hands with the Blood of *James Trevulce*, Embassador from *Milan*, and convince the World that there was no Wickedness too black for him to perpetrate. He was the Son, but Bastard, of *Alphonso* V, King of *Arragon*, surnam'd the *Magnanimous*, who was without doubt one of the greatest and best Princes of the Age he liv'd in. The last *Greek* Emperors were either Fools or Wicked, and sometimes both, so that as other Histories are read for the sake of virtuous Examples, we need only read that of *Constantinople*, to see Vice represented on its Throne. The Christians of the other Parts of *Europe* had no greater Enemies than the *Greek* Emperors. Amongst other Horrors, with which History renders their Lives and Reigns abominable, we find that *Henry Dandolo*, a *Venetian* Gentleman, being sent to *Constantinople* by *Vital Micheli*, Doge of *Venice*, to make an end of the Treaty of Peace, which was begun to be negotiated, *Emanuel*, the *Greek* Emperor, led him into a Closet, where he compell'd him to look fixedly into a brass Bason made red-hot, till thereby he had lost his Sight. This is what History relates, tho' it does not agree with what it afterwards says, That *Dandolo* was made Doge of *Venice* in the Year 1194, after the Death of *Orio Malpiero*, and that he was so still, when he dy'd at *Constantinople* in the Year 1207. So that there is no great likelihood, that he had quite lost his Sight when he was there Embassador.

Here

Here one is apt to inquire, whether an Embassador is subject to the Jurisdiction of the Place of his Residence? and forasmuch as some maintain the Affirmative, I shall here set down some of their Reasons. The Court of *Spain* being at *Valladolid* in the Month of *July* 1601, the Servants of the Count *de Rochepot*, Embassador of *France*, quarrell'd with some *Spaniards*, of whom two were kill'd. Hereupon the Officers of Justice enter'd by force into the Embassador's Lodgings, where the Sergeants, and the People who enter'd with them, committed several Insolences, stole the Furniture and Plate, and carry'd off to Prison some of the Domesticks, among whom were the Embassador's Nephew, with a Design to have them try'd. Upon the Complaints the Count made at his Court, Orders were sent him to depart from that of *Madrid* and the King had not stop'd there, if the Pope had not oblig'd the King of *Spain* to send the Prisoners to *Rome*, to be there put into the Hands of his Holiness, and by him into those of the *French* Embassador. The Embassadors who were at that Time on the Part of *France* and *Spain* at *Venice*, falling into Discourse upon this Subject, he of *Spain* being willing to justify what the King his Master had done, said to that of *France*, That notwithstanding he did not make Profession of Letters, yet he thought he might alledge the Law, which lays down, that altho' an Embassador may desire to be remitted to his natural Judge for the Actions he might be liable to before his Embassy, yet he is oblig'd to answer before the Judge Resident upon the Place, for what shall befall him after his Embassy. But *de Fresne Canaye* answer'd him thus, That those Laws spoke only of such Embassadors as the Municipal Towns which were subject to the *Roman* Empire sent to *Rome*, who were Embassadors but in a very extensive Signification, which cannot be apply'd to the modern Character. Which is very true, and the *Spanish* Embassador was so well convinc'd thereof, that he could urge nothing else to justify what past at *Valladolid*, but that the King was forc'd to wink at the Magisterial Procedure, to prevent thereby a greater Disorder, and to give some Satisfaction to the People, who were ready to rise against the Regal Authority.

The Question was more formally debated at *London* in the Year 1571. The Council in the Trial of the Duke of *Norfolk*, found several very dangerous Intrigues which *John Lesley*, Bishop of *Rosse*, was machinating against the Queen's Person and the Tranquillity of the Kingdom. He had the Character of Embassador from Queen *Mary* of *Scotland*, who was at that Time a Prisoner in *England* and thinking he was allow'd to do every thing for the Good of the Queen his Mistress, by Reason *that his sacred and inviolable Character protected him from all Prosecutions which the Judicature might intend against him*, there was no Conspiracy of which he was not the Head, or one of the chief Accomplices. He had had private Conferences with the Earl of *Southampton*, and he kept a Correspondence with the Rebels, who were fled into *Flanders*, with the Duke of *Alva*, with the King of *Spain*, and with the Pope, to facilitate their invading *England*. Upon the Proofs had hereof, even by the Bishop's own Confession, the Council consulted the Opinion of *David Lewis*, *Valentine Dale*, *William Drury*, *William Aubry*, and of *Henry Jones*, who were five of the learnedest Civilians of the Kingdom, to whom it propos'd the four following Questions.

1. Whether the Embassador who stirs up a Rebellion against the Prince with whom he resides, ought to enjoy the Privileges of his Character, and whether he ought not to be punished and treated as an Enemy?

2. Whether the Minister or Sollicitor of a Prince, who has been depos'd by publick Authority, and in the Place of whom another has been crown'd, can enjoy the Privileges and Rights of Embassadors?

3. Whether a Prince who comes into the Kingdom of another Prince, and is there detained a Prisoner, can have a Minister there, and whether this shall be consider'd as an Embassador? And,

4. Whether if the Prince signifies to the Minister of his Master, who is detain'd a Prisoner, that for the future such Minister shall be no longer consider'd as Embassador, whether such Minister can pretend in Justice, to enjoy the Privileges of the Character?

These Civilians made Answer to the first Point That the Law of Nations as well as the Civil Law of the *Romans*, declare, that such a Minister has forfeited the Privileges of his Character, and that he is subject to the Penalties of the Laws.

2. That if that Prince be lawfully depos'd, the Minister can no longer enjoy the Privileges of the Character, since none but Sovereign Princes, and who have the Right of Majesty, can send Embassadors.

3. To the third That if such Prince has not lost his Sovereignty, he may have a Minister. But whether that Minister ought to be consider'd as an Embassador or not, depends on the Authority his Commission gives him. And,

4. That a Prince may hinder an Embassador from entering into his Kingdom, and may also oblige him to depart therefrom, if the Embassador does not remain within the Bounds of his Duty. But yet during the Time he is suffer'd to be there, he shall enjoy the Privileges of the Character.

Upon this Answer the Council sent for the Bishop, made him a severe Reprimand, and told him, that he should no longer be consider'd as Embassador, but should be punish'd as his Crimes deserv'd. The Bishop made Answer, *That he was the Embassador of a Sovereign Queen, who had been unjustly depos'd That according to his Duty, he had apply'd all his Endeavours to set his Princess at Liberty, and to procure the Good of both Kingdoms That he was come into England with a good Passport which he had produc'd, and with the Character and Authority of Embassador, whose sacred Right neither ought nor can in any manner be violated.* The Lord *Burleigh* reply'd, that there was no Law of Nations, nor any Passport or Letters of Safety, that can secure it to Embassadors who offend against the Majesty of the Prince, but that they are subject to the Penalties of the Law, since otherwise a wicked Embassador might with Impunity attempt upon the Life of the Prince. The Bishop maintain'd, that he had not violated the Law of Nations, and gave them to understand, that he hop'd they would not use him worse than *Throgmorton*, *Randolf*, and *Tamworth* had been

been us'd in *France* and in *Scotland*, where they had ftirr'd up and fomented Rebellions And yet all that had been done to them, was, that they were commanded to depart the Kingdom within a certain Time He was fent Prifoner to the *Tower*, where he was again interrogated, but they did not dare to try him He was fet at Liberty after a Detention of two Years, and he was oblig'd to depart the Kingdom

Since at the Expiration of fome Years, the Queen of *Scots* her felf was brought to her Trial, and that the Bifhop was not, by Reafon of his Character, it is reafonable to believe, that what the Lord *Burleigh* faid to him, was only by the way of Threat, and that the Council was not of the Opinion of the Civilians And indeed, there is Reafon to doubt whether they were not miftaken in their Anfwer to the firft Article, and whether the *Roman* Laws on which they ground, ought not to be apply'd to thofe Embaffadors whom the municipal Towns, or the *Roman* Colonies fent to the Senate, or to the Emperor As for the Law of Nations, of which they fpeak, it feems as if it were directly oppofite to what *Titus Livius* fays of the Embaffadors of *Tarquin*, who had contriv'd a Treafon in the City Thefe Embaffadors came from a King who had been driven out and depos'd It is probable they were *Romans*, and they had carry'd on Intrigues and Cabals, in order to change the Government, and to introduce Tyranny It was put in Debate, whether they fhould be proceeded againft as Traitors and Difturbers of the publick Quiet, *ana it was judg'd, that the Law of Nations protected them from all the Violence which could be offer'd them, under any Pretext whatever* The great *Hugo Grotius*, who ought not to be fpoke of without Veneration, in examining the Paffage where *Salluftius* fays, that *Bomilcar* was brought to Trial, who was of the Retinue of *Jugurtha*'s Embaffador, explains the Words *æquum & bonum* (to which greater Regard was had at *Rome* than to the Law of Nations) to be the Law of Nature in its propereft Signification So that *Salluftius* means thereby, that the Senate follow'd in that the Law of Nature, which permits the Punifhment of the Crime, where-ever the Criminal is to be found, rather than the Law of Nations, which excepts therefrom Embaffadors and fuch like Perfons, who ought to find their Safety in the publick Faith He farther adds, that it is to be thought that the Law of Nations gives to Embaffadors fomething more than what the Common Law gives to private Perfons, who would have the fame Advantage with publick Minifters, if the Character of thefe fecur'd them only againft Injuftice That altho' the Quality of Embaffador ought not to ferve for a Cover nor Impunity to his Crimes, yet the common Magiftrate ought not to take Cognizance thereof He is to be fent back to his Prince, who ought to punifh him, unlefs the Magiftrate will pafs for an Accomplice in the Outrage that is done him He at laft concludes with thefe noble Words *Quare omnino ita cenfeo placuiffe Gentibus, ut Communis mos, qui quemvis in alieno Territorio exiftentem ejus loci Territorio fubjicit, exceptionem pateretur in Legatis, ut qui ficut fictione quadam, habentur pro perfonis mittentium (Senatus faciem fecum attulerat, faciem Reipublicæ, ait de Legato quodam M Tullius) ita etiam fictione fimili conftituerentur quafi extra Territorium unde & Civilis Jure populi, apud quem vivunt, non tenentur* I infert thefe few *Latin* Words contrary to my Humour and Cuftom, to inftruct thofe who know as much bad *Latin* as good *French*, that they may thereby learn, *that the Embaffador or publick Minifter, who folicits the Affairs of a foreign Prince, and who is a-knowledg'd for fuch, is exempt from the Jurifdiction of the Place of his Refidence, becaufe his Actions ought to be confider'd as if the Prince himfelf had done them, till fuch time as he difavows them*

Indeed, the Reafon why the Law of Nations exempts the Publick Minifter from the Jurifdiction of the Place of his Refidence, is becaufe he reprefents a Sovereign, over whom another Sovereign has no Superiority nor Jurifdiction, for which Reafon he cannot extend it to his Embaffador neither Befides, that by this Means the Minifter would be fubject to two different Jurifdictions at the fame Time, and fo would become of no ufe to his Mafter, if any other could make him give an Account of his Actions *John de Vivonne*, Marquifs de *Piſans*, Embaffador from *France* at *Rome*, was without doubt, one of the greateft Men *France* has ever had for this fort of Employment He was Embaffador in Ordinary to *Sixtus V* when King *Henry III* fent to the Pope, *Claudius d'Angennes* Bifhop of *Mans*, to juftify his murdering the Cardinal *de Guife*, who had been kill'd at the Affembly of the States at *Blois* The Pope refus'd to abfolve the King, unlefs he afk'd him Abfolution by Writing, and in Form, and unlefs the Cardinal *de Bourbon* and the Archbifhop of *Lyons*, who were Prifoners, were put into his Hands The Bifhop and the Marquifs had feveral Audiences, and amongft the reft one, at which the Pope threaten'd the Bifhop to fend him to Prifon, becaufe he had fpoke with great Liberty for the Rights of the *Gallican* Church But the Marquifs interrupted the Pope, and told him in the Prefence of Cardinal *de Joyeufe*, that they were ready to pay him all the Refpect and all the Submiffions which were due to his Dignity, but that they were oblig'd to tell him, *That the Embaffadors of Sovereigns have ever been in Poffeffion of a Right to execute their Princes Orders in all Liberty and Safety, without any Fear of Prifon, or other Outrage* That they would make no Difficulty of kiffing the Ground on which the Pope trod, but at the fame time, he ought to be perfuaded, that neither the Dread of a Prifon, nor of Death it felf, fhould hinder them from fpeaking to him conformably to their Orders and Inftructions This generous Anfwer filenc'd the Pope, and ought to ferve for a Leffon to thofe Minifters, who through a falfe Prudence, and by a cowardly and criminous Complaifance, betray the Honour and Intereft of their Mafters

Certainly if the Canon Law exempts the Clergyman from the Jurifdiction of ordinary Juftice, as I have made it appear elfewhere If a Soldier when he enters into Service, fubjects himfelf to a foreign Juftice, even in his native Countrey, and if a Student of *Salamanca* who fhall commit a Murder, or any other Crime at *Madrid*, or elfewhere, may require to be fent before the Judge of the Univerfity The *Law* of *Nations*, which may be call'd the Privilege of Privileges, ought to exempt the publick Minister from the Jurisdiction of the Place of his Residence All Sovereigns have understood it so, and all Princes, who have had the Reputation of being wife and prudent, have confirm'd this Truth by their Example

We have a just instance'd in one, in the Person of the Bishop of *Roffe* He had been convinc'd, as well by unexceptionable Proofs, as by his own Confession, that he had carry'd on Intrigues which might have disturb'd the Tranquillity of the Kingdom, and the Success whereof might have cost the Queen of *England* her Life, and yet she was contented with sending him to *France*, where he continu'd to labour to procure the Liberty of the Queen of *Scotts* The same Queen *Elizabeth* being inform'd that *Don Bernardin de Mendossi*, Embassador of *Spain*, had been concern'd in all the Cabals that *Francis Throgmorton* and other Traytors had contriv'd against her Person and her State, made him be sharply reprimanded therefore by the Council, who commanded him in the Queen's Name to depart the Kingdom He did not make too much haste, for which Reason they set him on Board Captain *Hawkins*'s Vessel, who landed him at *Calais* It cannot be deny'd but the Embassadors, who become Authors or Accomplices of Treasons which threaten the Life of the Prince with whom they reside, or the State, with an inevitable or an apparent Revolution, go beyond the Sphere of their Function, and that not being neither secret Enemies, nor honourable Spies, but Traitors from whom there is no Fence, they violate the *Law of Nations*, and ought no longer to enjoy the Privilege of their Character Which is as indubitable as it is uncertain, not how the offended Prince may, but how he ought, to behave himself, *viz* Whether he ought to punish the Traitor himself, or whether he ought still to consider, in his Person, that of the Prince who employs him Those Princes, who have a Grain of Honour left, do not suffer any Outrage to be done to their Minister, on any Account, or under any Pretext whatever, because they look upon it to be a Respect due to them, to leave to themselves the Cognusance and the Punishment of the Crimes of their Minister, and that Complaint ought to be made to them, to the End that by doing Justice upon their Minister, they may give Satisfaction to the Prince who may demand it of them In which there is by so much the greater Appearance of Reason, that if Princes had the Liberty of Proceeding against the Embassador who negotiates with them on any Account, or under any Colour whatsoever, the Person of the Embassador would never be in Safety, because those who should have a Mind to make away with him would never want a Pretext And by that Mean the Prince, not being able to protect his Minister against all manner of Insults, would never be well serv'd

Philip II was so offended at the Violence, which he said had been done to his Embassador, that he would not see *William Waad*, whom Queen *Elizabeth* had sent to him to complain of *Mendosse*, and to verify the Necessity which had oblig'd her to send him out of *England Waad* left *Spain* also, because the King had remitted him to the Council He said his Orders were to address himself to the King, and since he would not admit him, he had nothing more to do in *Spain*

I cannot tell whether all History can furnish us with one single Prince who had so many eminent Qualities as King *Henry* IV had, and to whom Posterity has given and preserv'd the Sirname of *Great*, with more Justice It may be said that the Conquest of *France* was not his greatest Glory, but that the ten or twelve Years Peace, (which restor'd to *France* the Lustre it had lost since the Treaty of *Chasteau in Cambresis*, and since the Death of *Henry* II, which follow'd pretty near) gave sufficient Testimony, that the Virtues which preserve, are equivalent to those which perform the Conquests He had full as much Clemency, Magnanimity and Prudence, as Courage, and it is what I shall give two or three Examples of, suitable to the Subject of this Chapter

After the Death of the Dutchess of *Beaufort*, the King fell in Love with *Mademoiselle d'Entragues*, who was one of the most beautiful as well as of the most subtle Maidens of her Time. She affected to be very precise and finding her self much press'd by the King, she told him, She did not dare to grant him any thing, unless he promis'd her Marriage That it was not her Intention to make use of it, but that it was necessary to her to satisfy her Father and Relations The King comply'd with her, but this did not hinder him from getting divorc'd from Queen *Margaret*, by the Intervention and Authority of the Pope, and from marrying again, without *d'Entragues*'s making any Opposition And there was no Discourse of the Promise till after the Birth of the *Dauphin* I shall not relate all the Particulars of this Intrigue, but only that the Count *de Taxis*, and after him *Don Balthasar de Zuniga*, Embassadors from *Spain*, got in with the Father of the young Lady, and plotted with him and the Count *d'Auvergne*, or Duke *d'Engoulesme*, to make them pass with his Children into *Spain* The Ministers of *Spain* could have no other Intention than to have it believ'd, that the Marriage which the King had contracted with *Mary de Medicis*, contrary to the Promise he had made to *d'Entragues*, was not lawful And so that the Dauphin, and the other Princes which might be born of her, could not succeed to the Crown It was casting *France* into the utmost Confusion, to dispute the Birth of the presumptive Heir of the Kingdom It was impossible to devise a more dangerous Treason The Duke *d'Engoulesme* was try'd for it, and so was the Father and the Daughter, and there were convincing Proofs of the Treachery of the *Spanish* Embassadors Yet for all that, the King would not so much as suffer their Master to be mention'd

The same *Don Balthasar de Zuniga*, Embassador from *Spain*, tamper'd in the Height of Peace, with *John d'Alagon de Merargues*, to surrender the Town of *Marseilles* to the Catholick King This Gentleman was originally of the Kingdom of *Arragon*, but his Predecessors had establish'd themselves in *Provence*, where he had two Gallies always ready, and he was Procurator *Syndic* of the Province A Galley-

Galley-Slave, to whom he had disclos'd his Design, reveal'd it to the Duke of *Grusa*, who gave Advice thereof to the Court He was so narrowly watch'd, that he was surpris'd with *Bruneau*, Secretary to *Don Balthasar*, and they were both taken Prisoners There were found under *Bruneau*'s Garters a Discourse which contain'd the Particulars of the Execution of the Enterprize So that seeing himself convicted, and taken in the Fact, he made no Difficulty to confess all the Circumstances of the Treason. The Parliament brought *Merargues* to his Tryal, who had his Head cut off at the *Gréve*, and *Bruneau* was sent to the King, who deliver'd him up to the *Spanish* Embassador; causing him to be told at the same Time to send him out of the Kingdom The Embassador had made a great Noise, as soon as he knew that his Secretary was a Prisoner, and gave himself a great deal of Liberty when he spoke to the King on that Subject, even to the reproaching him that he violated the Peace, in assisting the *Hollanders* with Men and Money, and attempting to corrupt the Fidelity of some Ministers at *Brussels* The King, who could have reproach'd him with more Justice, answer'd him resolutely, and told him, That the Law of Nations did not oppose the confining a Minister, to prevent his doing Mischief Almost at the same Time was discover'd the Enterprize which was in Agitation against the City of *Metz*. The Authors thereof were punish'd And forasmuch as among the Accomplices there were two of the Arch-Duke's Subjects, the King would not suffer Justice to be done upon them, but sent them to him with the Tryal, no way doubting but he would cause them to be punish'd, if it were but to clear himself of the Suspicion he would otherwise be lyable to History observes, that King *Henry* IV had the Advice of the most learned and able Civilians in *Paris*, on the Affair of *Bruneau*, and that thereupon he restor'd him to his Master

Alfonso de la Cueva, Marquiss of *Bedmar*, form'd with *Peter Giron*, Duke of *Ossuna*, Viceroy of *Naples*, and *Peter de Toledo*, Marquiss of *Villefranche*, Governor of *Milan*, a *Triumvirate* for the Direction of the Affairs of *Italy*, under King *Philip* III, and under the Duke of *Lerma*, his first Minister The Marquiss *de Bedmar* was Embassador of *Spain* at *Venice*, and there was not any Hostility which he did not publickly exercise, nor Artifice that he did not underhand employ against the Service of the Republick The Procurator *Nani*, who speaks of it in those Terms, tells the Particulars of a Treason which the Marquiss had been the Contriver of, and which was in it self so detestable, that it render'd him unworthy of all the Considerations which ought to be had for a publick Minister A *French* Man, by Birth a *Norman*, and a Pirate by Profession, whose Name was *James la Pierre*, pretending to be dissatisfy'd with the Duke of *Ossuna*, retir'd to *Venice*, where he offer'd his Service to the Senate, with another *French* Man nam'd *Langlade*, who understood the making of Fire-Works These Men, who immediately found Employment, were introduc'd into the Arsenal, notwithstanding which they continu'd a Correspondence with the Embassador of *Spain*, to whom they had promis'd to set Fire to the Ammunition, and to some of the best Houses in the City In the mean Time the Duke of *Ossuna* had contracted with an *English* Man, nam'd *Halbot*, who had caus'd the Canals of *Venice* to be founded, into which he was to bring several Barks and Brigantins, which the Viceroy was to send into the Gulph, while the main Fleet should make towards the Coasts of *Istria*, in Order to augment the Confusion During which, Fire was to be set to the Mint, and some of the chief Noblemen of the Senate were to be kill'd This Design had been executed if *la Pierre* and *Langlade* had not been oblig'd to embark, to serve on Board the Fleet of the Republick, which was the Cause twas delay'd, and so sav'd the State For the Secret being in the mean Time communicated to several others, two *French* Gentlemen, the one whereof was of *Normandy*, and the other of *Dauphiné*, who had been made privy to the Treason, were struck with so much Horror thereat, that they reveal'd it to the Council of Ten Some of the Conspirators were taken and executed, and the Senate sent Orders to the Admiral, to put to Death *la Pierre* and *Langlade* La *Cueva*, who had had the whole Direction of the Intrigue, fearing to be insulted by the People, retir'd to *Milan*, after the Senate had already written to the King of *Spain*, to desire him to recall his Embassador Nothing more horrible nor more detestable could enter into the Thoughts of Man, because the Republick was utterly and inevitably ruin'd thereby And yet she shew'd no other Resentment than to complain thereof to the King, instead of abandoning the Embassador to the Peoples Fury, which would without doubt have reveng'd it in a cruel Manner *Capriata* makes great Excuses for the Embassador, and would have it believ'd that he had no Hand in the Treason, but I cannot believe that the Procurator *Nani*, who was a Man of Honour, and very will, would have offended the Memory of a Nobleman, who dy'd cloath'd with the Purple, and would have taken Pleasure to blacken, as one may say, a whole Nation by so heinous an Accusation, if he had not had good Proofs thereof, and unless he had thought himself oblig'd to insert those Circumstances as a Debt he ow'd to the Truth of his History.

The Marquiss *d'Inoyosa* and Dom *Carlos Coloma*, being Embassadors at *London*, undertook to ruin the Duke of *Buckingham* in the Mind of King *James*, and to sow the Seeds of so strong a Jealousy of the Intentions of the Prince of *Wales* his Son, that if they had succeeded, the Royal Family would have been so divided, that the Kingdom would have broke out into irreconcileable Factions The Parliament considr'd the ill Consequences thereof, and was for having the Heinousness of their Crime represented to them That they should be oblig'd to detect the Author of the Calumny, and that they should be given to understand, that, unless they did so, they should be taken to Task themselves, and esteemed as Impostors But the King and the Council, who did not follow the Motions of a passionate Assembly, were of Opinion that Complaint ought to be made to the King of *Spain*, and Satisfaction requir'd from him However, they were contented to let

let them be gone, and to signify to them, That their Conduct had not been grateful, by not making the usual Present to them, which is never omitted to Embassadors who have given no Distaste Nevertheless these Disgraces are often held as very meritorious, by the Masters of the Parties so disgrac'd

If an Embassador cannot be try'd for a Crime of State, much less can he be so for a common Offence, or the Fault of another, or be arrested for a civil Debt It is about thirty Years, since a *Spanish* Governor of a Province which borders on that of *Peru*, sent one of his Officers to *Constantinople*, to endeavour to procure to himself the Protection of the *Grand Seignior*, in the Design he had to erect his Government into a Sovereignty, paying such a yearly Tribute to the Port But the Divan abhorr'd the Governor's Perfidy, and caus'd his Messenger to be fasten'd to the Galley Chain, and did not take him from thence, till the *Spaniard* had renounc'd his Faith, and had promis'd to be Circumcis'd This was done in the Month of *September* 1646, and about a Month after the Renegade disappear'd, so that it was believ'd he was return'd to his own Countrey, or else was retir'd into some other Part of *Christendom* But the First Vizir being inform'd that he had been seen to go into the House of *Alexander Gr fenbec*, the Emperor's Resident, and that no Body had seen him come out, he sent on the last Day of *October* some Chiaoux, who in visiting all the Lodgings, discover'd the Place where the *Spaniard* had been interr'd Hereupon the Resident was seiz'd and brought before the Grand Vizir, to whom he confess'd the Murder, but he said he had been provok'd thereto by the Insolence of the Deceas'd, who had spoke disrespectfully of the Emperor his Master Yet it was found to be a premeditated Assassination, and that the Resident to compass his Ends the more privately, had sent all his Domesticks out of the way, excepting him who cut the Renegade's Throat The Resident was sent a Prisoner, not to the publick Prison, *as is practis'd elsewhere*, but to the House of one of the Chiaoux, with his Dragoman, and five or six of his Domesticks The *Turks* judg'd that the Emperor's Minister would not have dar'd to have undertaken so bold an Action, as that of assassinating in cool Blood, a *Mussulman* and a new Proselyte, without the express Orders of his Master, who without doubt had concerted the Matter with the King of *Spain*, they therefore proceeded very leisurely in his Affair, and gave him Time to employ his Friends to get out The French Embassador undertook the Solicitation thereof and notwithstanding the King his Master, and the Emperor were at War, he nevertheless spoke to the First Vizir about it, and represented to him, " That the Divan could not
" decline giving Advice to the Emperor of what
" had happen'd, before it came to any Resolution
" against a privileg'd Person, who could acknow-
" ledge no other Jurisdiction than that of the Em-
" peror his Master, and who indeed could neither
" be interrogated nor judg'd but by him. That
" the *Law of Nations* requir'd, that in those Ca-
" ses, where the publick Minister of a Prince
" who was a Friend or an Ally, commits a Fault
" or fails in his Duty, Advice should be given

" thereof to his Prince, to whom it belongs to
" punish him, and that the Emperor would
" without doubt do it, if recourse were had
" to him." The *Turks* took his Counsel in part, and dispatch'd an Express to *Vienna* But fearing that at the Return of the Courier they should be oblig'd to set the Resident at Liberty, if the Emperor approv'd of what his Minister had done, as he would without doubt, since it was by his Orders that the *Spaniard* had been kill'd, they chose rather to compound the Matter with him, and draw from him a Sum of Money His Irons were taken off at the Instance of the *French* Embassador, and of the Internuncio of *Poland*, and four Days after a *Jew* was sent to him, to let him know that he should be set at Liberty, if he would promise to pay within three Days, such a Sum as should be agreed on with him, and that the French Embassador would remain Security for the same The Resident made it his Request to the Embassador that he would, but he signify'd to him, that in his Post he could enter into no Obligation without the King his Master's Permission, more especially to People who have no Regard to the Character, nor to the *Laws of Nations* Upon the Embassador's Refusal, the *Jew* told him, that if the Resident would get out of his Troubles, he must oblige himself formally to procure the Payment of two hundred thousand Crowns, which were requir'd of the Emperor for the Renovation of the Peace, and withall, pay down presently thirty thousand Crowns The Resident represented, That not only he could not oblige the Emperor his Master, without becoming a Criminal, but besides that it would be to no purpose, because his Master would disown him, and not pay a Penny thereof, and that it was also impossible for him to raise the Sum of thirty thousand Crowns That all he could propose to raise, within a little Time, would amount at most but to ten thousand Crowns, with which the *Turks* were contented The *Jews* answer'd for it, and the Resident was set at Liberty I might add to this Example that of Colonel *Alard*, who having been sent by the Duke of *Savoy* to the Mareschal *Lesdiguieres*, caus'd a Burgess of *Grenoble* to be murder'd as he return'd from his Farm But as I have enlarg'd very much upon it in my Memoirs, and that after that, I might perhaps alledge several others, I don't think I ought to tire my Reader with a Multiplicity, after what I have remark'd on the Subject of this Example in Chapter II

After that in the Year 1644, the Gallies of *Malta* had taken the Galleon, wherein was found a Sultaness and her Son, the Divan caus'd the Embassadors of *France*, of *England* and of *Venice*, and the Resident of the United Provinces, to be summon'd before the two *Cadilessers* of *Romelia* and of *Natolia*, to be interrogated concerning this Depredation The French Embassador complain'd to the First Vizir, *Mehemet Bacha*, of so extraordinary a Procedure, and the Vizir own'd to him that it was certain, *That the Law of Nations was violated thereby*; *and that according to Order and Method, the Embassadors could not be summon'd before the Judges*; but he added at the same Time, That it was the Grand Seignior's Will, and that in the

whole

whole *Seraglio*, there was no body that dar'd to contradict it. The two Embassadors of *France* and of *Venice* appear'd, and said in their Deposition, That the Galleon having been taken in Seas very remote from *Constantinople*, they knew no other Particulars of it, than what they had learn'd from common Report. The *English* Embassador said, That the *English* made Profession of a Belief and Religion very contrary to that of the Knights of *Malta*, and that none of them were seen to wear the Cross, and that they had no Communication with them, nor any Concern with their Depredations. The Resident of *Holland* made answer, That the Island of *Malta* belong'd to the King of *Spain*, against whom the Estates his Masters had made War for these fourscore Years past, so that they could not be Responsible for the Actions of the Knights of that Order, nor oblig'd to make Reparation for a Violence in which they had no Hand, and of which they had not so much as heard any thing. The *Turks* who had escap'd out of the Hands of the *Maltese*, had reported, that most of the Knights concern'd in this Exploit were *French*, so that when the *French* Embassador was for justifying his Nation by a long Memorial, the *Cadilesker* told his *Dragoman*, that what the Embassador said signify'd no more than a Song. That he was willing to speak to him freely after his usual way, and declare, that the Emperor had resolv'd to go in Person to the Siege of *Malta*, and that if he discover'd that any Prince was so audacious, as to succour the Island either with Men, Provisions, Ammunition or Money, *he would lay hold of his Embassador, and would not be contented to put him to Death, but would make him expire in the cruellest and most exquisite Torments*. The Embassador gave an Account to his Court of the Procedure of the *Turk*. But the King, who was at War with the Emperor and King of *Spain*, sent him Orders to mingle so much Prudence with his Courage and Firmness, that no worse Disorder might ensue, since no Remedy could be apply'd thereto in the present State of Affairs and gave him to understand, that as he could not come to a Rupture with the Port, he, the Embassador, would do well to dissemble what was past, and not to shew any Resentment, as if he had been offended in his Character. He was oblig'd to drink this Cup, but this Patience, instead of moderating the Fury of the *Turks*, made them quite insolent, insomuch that they afterwards treated the Embassador himself after a strange Manner. M *de la Haye Vantelay*, Embassador of *France*, had resided five and twenty Years at *Constantinople*, and had done very good Offices to the Bailo of *Venice* since the Opening of the *Candian* War, tho' they had not always been very well acknowledg'd *Soranzo*, (which was the Bailo's Name) thinking he did a very important Service to the Republick, by obliging *France* to break with the Port, endeavour'd to render all the Actions of the Embassador suspected to the Ministers of that Court. This made *France* easily believe that it was by the Address of the Bailo, that a Letter in Cypher fell into the Hands of the *Turks*, whereby were discover'd several Intrigues which were carrying on against the Service of the *Grand Seignior*. The Letter being carry'd to *Adrianople*, where the Court was, Orders were dispatch'd immediately to *la Haye* to repair thither in all Diligence, but his Age, the Gout, and his other Indispositions, hindering him from being able to perform the Journey, he sent thither his Son, assisted by the Secretary of the *French* Merchants. As soon as they were arriv'd, the First Vizir sent for them to come to him, and spoke to 'em about the Letter in such haughty and offensive Terms, that the young *la Haye*, losing both Patience and Respect, told him he did not fear his Menaces. That he had a Master, who if he could not prevent the Effects thereof, would not fail to take ample Revenge for them. This so incens'd the First Vizier, who was very brutish, and an Enemy to the *French*, that he commanded one of the Chiaoux to strike him on the Face, and this Command was so well executed, that *la Haye* had two of his Teeth broke, and afterwards was dragg'd with the Secretary into a Dungeon. The Vizir's Cruelty not being satisfy'd herewith, would needs have the Embassador make the Journey in Person, and flung him also into Prison. He and his Son were set at Liberty at the End of two Months, by the Help of Money and Submissions, but it was only to receive other ill Treatments, which oblig'd him at last to quit that Post, and to repair to *France* with the King his Master's Leave.

The Emperor's Resident had committed a Murder on the Person of a Proselyte, which is one of the greatest Crimes that can be committed against the Alcoran. The Loss of the Galleon, the Outrage done to the Sultaness, and the carrying off her Son, disturb'd the Reason of the *Grand Seignior*. And it was not altogether without Cause, that the Vizir was so transported against *la Haye*, because it was very certain, that he held an Intelligence with some *Greek* Bishops, to stir up an Insurrection in the *Morea*, and yet it must be own'd, that the Vizir's Behaviour was *Turkish*. We shall see how they behave themselves elsewhere, when I shall have shewn, that the *English* would not violate the *Law of Nations* in this Respect, even at a Time when no other Laws were acknowleg'd, than those that might be serviceable to the Establishment of Usurpation and Tyranny. In the Year 1654, M *de Bas*, Envoy from *France* to *England*, was accus'd to have been concern'd in a Conspiracy, which had been contriv'd against the Person of *Cromwell*. One *Naudin*, a Physician of *Paris*, had put him in the Number of the Accomplices, and there were otherwise such strong Proofs against *de Bas*, that the Council having sent for him, to hear what he had to say, read to him the Depositions of the Witnesses. But when the Counsellors were for interrogating him, in order to know the Truth from his own Mouth, he told them, That he could safely answer them, and declare he had no knowledge of the Affair, in which he had no Hand. That he would make no Difficulty neither to inform *Cromwell* privately, by the way of giving him an Insight, as far as he knew, but *that he was not oblig'd to undergo an Interrogatory before a Judge, nor to answer in a Course of Justice, because being a publick Minister, he should thereby Sin against the Dignity of the King his Master*,

Master, to whom alone he was oblig'd to give an Account of his Actions. Whereupon *Cromwell*, and five of the seven Counsellors which compos'd the Council, withdrawing into another Chamber, and returning some time after, they ask'd *de Bas* if he persisted in his Resolution not to answer, and because he said *he would not answer*, he was order'd to depart the Kingdom in twice four and twenty Hours. He was sufficiently convicted to have conspir'd against *Cromwell*, yet for all that, this Usurper, who had plainly shewn on other Occasions, that he did not much regard Embassadors, and who at that time had not more need of *France* than *France* had of him, judg'd that all that could be done to *de Bas*, without violating the *Law of Nations*, was to make him depart the Island.

In the Year 1618, one *la Chesnaye*, who had been Domestick to *M. des Maretz*, the *French* Embassador, and who was so then to *M. le Clerc*, who had remain'd at *London* in the Quality of Agent for that Crown, had confess'd that there was a Design to send Sir *Walter Raleigh* into *France*, and that the Design had been communicated to the Agent. The Service of the King of *England* was concern'd therein, for which Reason *le Clerc* was sent for, to hear what he had to say. *Le Clerc* said, he would not speak unless he was seated and cover'd, because *la Berchere* was treated so, who did the Business of *England* in *France*. The Counsellors made answer, That each Countrey had its Customs, and that in *England* they were not oblig'd to follow those of *France*. Nevertheless *le Clerc* remain'd so obstinate, that it was resolv'd they should all go into another Room, which not being appropriated to the Council, they should be standing, and that it should not pass for a judicial Action, but that the Affair of *Raleigh* should be talk'd of by the way of Discourse and Conversation. *Le Clerc* at first swore bitterly that he knew nothing of the Matter till being convicted by the Confession and Confronting of *la Chesnaye*, he likewise confess'd it with the utmost Confusion. Hereupon the Council told him, that the King would not permit him to meddle any more with the Management of Affairs, nor to present himself before him, till it should be known, at the Return of the Courrier who had been sent into *France*, whether the King his Master would own him or not. The Court of *France* would have been willing to maintain its Minister, and to that end, sent him a Packet, with Orders *to deliver it into the Hands of the King of England*, to see if it was possible to regain him Access to the Court: but the King would not admit him, so that he was forc'd to retire into *France*, where he was not much consider'd since.

Now if an Embassador cannot be brought to Tryal for a Crime, and particularly for a common Offence, much less can he be subject to the Justice of the Place of his Residence in a Civil Action, or arrested for Debt. Some Years ago the Court of Justice in *Holland* caus'd the Resident of *Portugal* to be arrested for Debt, because they had been contracted during his Ministry. It grounded on those Laws, which as I said before, can be only apply'd to that kind of Embassadors, which at present are call'd Deputies, which the Towns subject to the Empire sent to *Rome*, and not at all to those who have the true Character, or the Quality of a publick Minister, who represents the Person of a Sovereign Prince. For if the Deputies of a Town in *Holland* cannot be arrested for Debt, while they are Members of the Assembly, with much more Reason ought that Respect to be had to the Representative of a foreign Sovereign Prince, who ought to be inviolable, because he cannot be hinder'd from acting, but his Master's Service must suffer thereby. *Don Francisco de Melos*, Embassador from *Portugal*, did not do any great Offices for the Liberty of the Resident, because in the Procedure of this, there was something so very infamous, that they were cautious of making a Noise about the Matter, for fear the Minister's Roguery should injure the Dignity of the Prince that employ'd him.

I am not afraid of saying after *M. de Groot*, that since the Judicature cannot seize the Furniture of a publick Minister for Debt, much less can it imprison his Person, because he ought to be free from all Constraint, as well in reference to his Person, as to his Goods, for without that he cannot maintain the Dignity of his Character. Those who give him Credit, ought to take their Security before they do it, and blame themselves if they do not do so. Tradesmen trust every Day, and hazard their Goods, in hope of gaining thereby. They know that it is not without the Risque of Bankrupcy, which they have as much Reason to fear in an Embassador, as in a private Person. Sovereigns every Day ruin those who give them Credit, and the Minister is not better than his Master.

In the Year 1646, the Divan sent a Summons by a Chiaoux to the *English* Embassador, at the Request of some *English* Merchants of *Constantinople*, to see himself condemn'd to the Restitution of some Money, which they said had been unjustly exacted from them. The Embassador to gain a little Time pretended to be sick, and in the mean while desir'd that of *France*, to represent to the First Vizir the Incongruity of the Divan's Procedure, and the Impertinency of the *English* Merchants, in causing an Embassador to be cited before a *Turkish* Judge, where the *French*, who have there peculiar Judges, are not oblig'd to appear. The Vizir agreed herein, and said, *That he knew it was an unheard of Thing to summon an Embassador before the Divan; and that not only the Privileges of Embassadors were thereby destroy'd, but also the Law of Nations*. That the *English* Merchants had gain'd the two Cadileskers. That the Embassador's irregular Procedure deserv'd very well some Correction, and that he would do wisely to make up the Matter with the Parties, and to get clear of the Affair without Noise. That he had a Consideration for the Intercession of the *French* Embassador, who might take it upon himself, and be *Arbitrator* in the Case if he pleas'd, and the Parties concern'd were willing, because the *Turkish* Judges never refer any Causes that are brought before them. The Embassador reply'd, That if the Vizir thought fit to use his Authority with the *English* Merchants, there would be no Difficulty in adjusting the rest, since it was in Effect but a Sequel of their Disobedience. The Vizir went
about

about it, and succeeded, by reconciling the Embassador with the Merchants, but this Peace lasted no longer than till the Arrival of the first News from London. The *English* at *Constantinople*, being animated by the same Spirit of Rebellion which had set all *England* almost in an Uproar, gave themselves no Rest till they had driven away the Embassador, after such a Manner that sufficiently demonstrates, there are some Christians capable of exceeding the Uncircumcis'd in Brutality, who would not have been so inhuman without the Instigation of the *English*. The Parliament sent another Embassador to *Constantinople*, and the First Vizir, by taking Cognizance of the Difference that was between the two *English* Embassadors, erected himself as a competent Judge, and by causing the one to be taken away, he violated the publick Faith, his Word, which he had given to the *French* Embassador, and whatever there is most Sacred in the Commerce of Men: He even lost the Respect which he ow'd to the Sea, by compelling the Embassadrix to embark in a sorry little Vessel, and he order'd the Embassador to be put on board an *English* Ship at *Smyrna*, that he might be deliver'd into the Hands of the Parliament.

The Declaration of the States of *Holland* says, That they who offend Embassadors or publick Ministers, by Look or by Word, *violate also the Law of Nations*. In the Year 1472, the Constable *de St Pol* went to *Roye*, from King *Lewis* XI, to confer there with the Chancellor of *Burgundy*, and with the Lord *d'Imbercourt*, Embassadors from the Duke of *Burgundy*, with whom *Lewis* had constantly some Difference. The Constable, who was a haughty Man, being transported in the Heat of the Contest, gave the Lye to *Imbercourt*. *Philip de Commines*, in speaking of this Nobleman, says, that he was the discreetest Gentleman he ever knew and most certainly he gave good Proof thereof on this Occasion, for he made no other Answer to the Constable, than *that he did not take the Lye from him as Constable, but as from the proper Person of the King of France, whom the Constable represented, and who had promis'd him Security in all Respects, as he on his side, did not look upon this Affront as given to Imbercourt, but as done to the Duke of Burgundy himself, whom he represented, and to whom he would report the same*. This Spurt of a Gendarm, unworthy of a Minister, had a very ill Effect, and was the chief Cause of the Loss of the Constable, who being some time after deliver'd into the Hands of *d'Imbercourt*, and by him into those of the King of *France*, had his Head cut off. This Gentleman in his wise and prudent Answer, gives a necessary Lesson to *Princes, who ought to learn thereby, that no Outrage can be done to the Minister, but is done at the same time to the Master himself, whose Person he represents. That it belongs to the Prince to resent it, if he has any Honour, and that he ought not to be either easie or insensible on these Occasions, if he has any Regard to his Reputation in the World*. A private Countrey Gentleman protects his Domestick, and does not suffer even his Dog to be injur'd.

In the Year 1627, *Paul Rosencrants*, Embassador from *Denmark* at *London*, being oblig'd to take a Journey to the Court of *France* about the Affairs of the King his Master, and to make some Stay there, made an Agreement with a *German* who liv'd at *London*, and who made it his Business to conduct Persons of Quality from *London* to *Paris*, and from *Paris* to *London*. He agreed to give him a hundred and fifty Crowns *per* Month, as also for the Conveyance and Food for himself and his People, after the Rate of five and twenty Crowns *per* Head, which he accordingly paid him at his Return to *London*. Two Days after, the *German* seeming not to be satisfy'd, form'd new Pretentions, which were impertinent enough, and addressing himself to the Embassador in Person, said several very offensive things, and had even the Impudence to leave them with him in Writing. The Embassador hereupon complain'd to the High Chamberlain, and the King being inform'd thereof, order'd the Lord President of the Council, the High Chamberlain, and the Vice Chamberlain, to hear the Person who brought the Complaint from the Embassador, as well as the *German*, and to take Cognizance of the Affair. They did so, *and condemn'd* Philip Weisman (that was the *German*'s Name) *to be in prison'd till he had given Satisfaction and made Reparation, unless the Embassador had rather conveigh him to the King his Master, that he might punish him*. *Philip* remain'd five or six Days confin'd in the House of a Sergeant but for asmuch as he was obstinate in the Point of not giving Satisfaction, an Instrument was deliver'd to the Embassador, by which *Leave was given him to transfer his Man into a publick Prison, and to cause him to be kept there, till he had a Conveniency to Ship him off for Hamburg, and from thence to Denmark*. The *German* seeing the Embassador intended he should make the Voyage, and that he might possibly be ill us'd, resolv'd to make Reparation, both by Word of Mouth and in Writing.

General *Spar*, and *Giles de Haze*, whom the last Wars in *Germany* have made sufficiently known, hated one the other mortally, so that as soon as the last put himself in the Service of the Republick of *Venice*, the other went and serv'd the Pope and the *Barberins* during the War of *Castro*, towards the End of the Year 1643. *Spar* seeing his Enemy in the Protection of the Republick, wrote a very impertinent Letter to the Embassador of *Venice* at *Vienna*. Upon the Complaint this Minister made there of to the Emperor, *Spar was taken up, and guarded by fifteen Musqueteers at his own Expence, and the Doctor who had advis'd him to write the Letter was put in Irons*. Moreover, the Emperor order'd him to send two Persons of Quality to the Embassador, to ask him Pardon, and to offer him the Satisfaction which was due to him. He signify'd to the Embassador at the same time, that if he was not satisfy'd with the Reparation which *Spar* should make him, he would oblige him to make such a one as should serve for a convincing Proof of the Esteem he had for the Republick, and for the Person of the Embassador. *Spar* sent to ask him Pardon by the Counts *Magnis* and *Montecuculi*, accompany'd by the Baron *de Roqueendolf*: but forasmuch as the Embassador seem'd not to be satisfy'd with this forc'd Reparation, the Emperor put it into Deliberation, what was fitting to be done more to satisfy him. The Council declar'd,

The EMBASSADOR and his FUNCTIONS. 257

declar'd, *That the Reparation* Spar *had made being very great, by Reason of his Quality, of his Merit, and of the great Employments he had had, the Embassador might be contented therewith, and that the Emperor could not well enjoyn a greater Penalty, after he had been seven Weeks confin'd, if his Majesty intended there should be any Proportion betwixt the Punishment and the Offence, and that the same might be said in Reference to the Doctor* But the Emperor going in Person to the Council, and having caus'd the Affair to be put in Deliberation in his Presence, *condemn'd* Spar *to be conducted to* Neustadt, *and there to be confin'd with two Servants, till such Time as the Embassador was satisfy'd, and the Doctor to be banish'd from Court and all the hereditary Provinces* Spain was enrag'd that he was going to be shut up in a Place that he said was a Prison only for Traytors, and the whole Court indeed was mov'd with Indignation thereat It tomuch that the Embassador, fearing lest his too great Rigour should render him odious to the Nation, came one Day to the Emperor's Miss, and going from thence he thank'd his Imperial Majesty for the Consideration he had been pleas'd to have, as well for the Dignity of his Character, as for the Reputation of the Republick He farther added, That he might venture to assure his Majesty, that the Senate would not esteem her self less oblig'd to him for his gracious Pardon to General *Spar*, than for the Mortification he had given him, intreating him to accept of his Intercession The Emperor having answer'd the Embassador's Compliment, told him, *He was very glad he was satisfy'd That as he was willing to punish* Spar *in Consideration of him, so likewise was he ready to pardon him for his Sake That* Spar *had committed a great Fault, and that he was willing he should serve for an Example to those who should be wanting in the Respect that is due to publick Ministers* When the Embassador went from Audience, every Body caress'd him, and express'd Civility to him, the Court never tiring in the Praise of his Generosity In the Evening the Count de Ketzenbuller, one of the Council of State, and first Steward of the Empress *Mary*, came with a great Cortege of *Traineaux*, or Sleds, fill'd with Ladies, to renew the Complements of the whole Court to the Embassador, and two Days after, *Spar, accompany'd by the Count de* Wolkestein *Master of the Horse to the Emperor, came to pay him his Devoirs* The Doctor was no so soon set at Liberty, because being inform'd that the Council of State had not approv'd the Emperor's great Severity, he had presented a Petition to the *Aulick* Council, which had been taken ill

There is to be observ'd in these two last Examples, That it is not the ordinary Justice that takes Cognizance of the Injury which has been done to an Embassador, but in *England* the King refers the Cognizance thereof to his Privy Council, and at *Vienna*, the Emperor not being satisfy'd with the Sentiments of his Council of State, sits as Judge himself, and pronounces the Sentence From whence we may conclude, That it is great Temerity and Presumption in a subaltern or presidial Court, to undertake to try the publick and character'iz'd Minister of a Sovereign Prince, and an Ally to the State where he resides We must moreover observe, and particularly in the Example of *Rosencrantz*, that the Council of *England* ordain'd, That the *German*, who had offended him, should be put into the Hands of the King of *Denmark*, conformably to the Law of which I spoke in the beginning of this Chapter

Imbercourt tells the Constable *de St Pol*, That it belongs to the King of *France* to make him enjoy the Safety which is due to his Character, and gives thereby to understand, that it is the Prince's Duty with whom the publick Minister resides, or with whom he negotiates, to protect him against all Injuries, Insults, and Violences, as in Effect the King of *England* and the Emperor highly protected the Embassadors of *Denmark* and of *Venice* This is what the States of *Holland* are very sensible of, when they take the Embassadors and publick Ministers into their particular Protection, by their illustrious Declaration in the Year 1651 M *Hugues de Groot* says, on this Subject, *That as soon as the Prince admits and a knowledges a publick Minister, he obliges himself to protect him, and to secure him the Enjoyment of the Benefit of the Law of Nations, by a kind of Agreement or tacit Contract* So that one cannot make any very favourable Judgment of those Princes, who, instead of protecting the Embassadors and Ministers who reside with them, persecute and injure them Pope *Julius* II caus'd the Embassador of *Charles* III, Duke of *Savoy*, *to be put in Prison, and made him be tortur'd, because he had told him, That the Duke his Master would be willing to use his Endeavours to reconcile him and the King of* France The Pope treated him like a Spy and a Traytor But *Julius* was the proudest and most insolent Man in the World, and when the Fumes of the Wine had disturb'd his Brain, which happen'd pretty often, he did not know what he did His violent and outrageous Behaviour oblig'd *Lewis* XII to convene a Council against him at *Pisa*, and to coin those *Escus d'Ors*, which we still see with this Inscription, *Nomen Babylonis perdam* The Marquiss de *Pisani*, Embassador from *France* at *Rome*, said of Pope *Sixtus* V, That he was the worst Monk he had ever seen He would not have said so if he had known *Sixtus* IV, who was a Monk also, and a much worse Man than *Sixtus* V If in his whole Life he had done no other ill Action than to conspire against the Life of *Laurence*, and of *Julian de Medicis*, and to consent that they should be kill'd in the Church, and that the Elevation of the Host should serve for a Signal to the Conspirators, it must be own'd, that he was not only a very bad Monk, but also a most detestable Pope The Count *Jerome de Riario* his Nephew, or his Son, who seconded these Violences, had the Insolence to tell some Embassadors, That the Pope would cause them to be flung into the *Tiber* A Catholick Author says of *Julius* II, That he was born for the Ruin of the Church And the judicious Author of the History of *Florence*, in giving the Character of *Sixtus* IV, has left a strange Idea of him to Posterity

The unhappy and tragical End of the *Caraffa*'s is a manifest Proof of their disorderly Government The *Spaniards*, who could not be ignorant of the Negotiations Pope *Paul* IV carry'd carry'd on in *France*, were for preventing the Effect thereof by the Means of the Duke of *Alva*, Viceroy of *Naples* The Duke, who knew that the *Caraffa*'s had an Eye upon the Kingdom, had Couriers constantly on the Road, and held a very close Correspondence with the Ministers of *Spain* who were at *Rome* It happen'd one Day, that the Courier whom the Count *de Taxis*, the Emperor's Post-Master, had sent to *Naples*, was discover'd at *Terracina*, and was the more narrowly observ'd, because having quitted the Marks of his Function, his Journey became very much suspected by the Governor, who took him up and sent him to *Rome* A great many Letters were found about him, which being almost all written in Cypher, increas'd the Suspicion that was already conceiv'd of him The Pope having a Mind to dive into the Mystery, caus'd *the Count de Taxis to be taken up* As soon as the Marquiss *de Sarria*, the Emperor's Embassador, was inform'd thereof, he demanded Audience, with a Design to complain of the Violence that was done to one of the Emperor's Officers The Marquiss had brought along with him *Garci lasso de la Vega, who did the Affairs of Philip, King of Naples, with the Pope, and was he that had made the Dispatches which were found upon the Courier, for which Reason the Cardinal* Carassa *had him taken out of the Pope's Antichamber, and sent him Prisoner to the Castle of St Angelo* The Embassador understanding, at his coming from Audience, that a second Affront had been offer'd him, desir'd to go in again, and to speak to the Pope But he was deny'd Admittance The Letters being decypher'd, it appear'd that the Duke of *Alva* was invited to come and invade the State of the Church, while the Pope was without an Army, and the Towns were without Defence The Pope being willing to justify his Procedure, held a Consistory on the 27th of *July*, 1555, in which he summon'd the Advocate and Attorney Generals, who said in the Presence of several Officers of Justice, That the Ministers of the Emperor, and of King *Philip*, and particularly the Viceroy of *Naples*, were forming very dangerous Designs against the State of the Church, and desir'd that some Cardinals might be appointed to examine into the same, and that afterwards the Princes and their Ministers might be excommunicated That the Fiefs they held of the Church might be declar'd Escheats, and themselves depriv'd of their Estates, Honours, and Dignities, which was resolv'd upon in the Consistory The Duke of *Alva*, fearing lest the Pope, whose excessive Transports drew near to Fury and Rage, should should put *Garcilasso* to Death, *since he had order'd him to be try'd*, sent the Count de la Tolfe, to complain of *the Violence that was offer'd to publick Ministers* The Marquiss *de Sarria*, on the other side, having demanded his Audience of Leave, in Pursuance of the Order he had receiv'd to retire, the Pope, who consider'd that it would be no easy Matter to renew the Negotiation when the Embassador was gone, delay'd giving it him, and at last bethought himself to make a Feast, to which he invited twelve Cardinals of those he most confided in, the Duke *de Palliano* his Nephew, and the Emperor's Embassador. Dinner being over, the Pope told him,

That understanding he had a Mind to be gone, and that it was in Order thereunto he had desir'd Audience, he pray'd him to tell before the Company what he had to propose to him The Marquiss did so And after he had complain'd in very strong Terms, of the Violences that were offer'd to his Princes and their Ministers, he added that he had positive Orders to take his Leave and depart The Cardinals represented to the Marquiss, That altho' he could not be hinder'd from going away, without Violation of the *Law of Nations*, yet they conceiv'd he would do well to delay his Journey to some Days, if he could do it without Prejudice to the Obedience he ow'd to the Orders of the Emperor his Master The Embassador reply'd, They were too express for that, and that he was oblig'd to obey Hereupon he was sent into another Room, with the Duke de *Palliano*, to the end the Pope and the Cardinals might concert among themselves with the greater Freedom the Answer they were to make him The Opinion of the Cardinals was, That according to the *Law of Nations* he could not be hinder'd from going away, however such Instances ought to be made to him to prolong his Stay After the Embassador was call'd in, the Pope told him the Sentiments of the Company, with so much Civility, that the Embassador tnought himself oblig'd to answer, That upon his Return to his Lodgings he would examine his Orders again, and see what he could possibly do, without offending the Emperor his Master But he set out the next Day, and went to *Naples*, that he might not seem to consent, in some Measure, to the Proceeding of the Pope's Officers, and of the Attorney General The King of *Spain* resented the Outrage which had been done to his Ministers, and caus'd Reparation to be made him

That Justice which extends its Jurisdiction over the sacred Person of a publick Minister, and that Violence which is destitute of all Formality are equally criminous, and destructive of the *Law of Nations*, as well the one as the other The Court of Justice, that threatens to torture the publick Minister of a Prince, who is an Ally, to compel him (not to name the Accomplices of a Conspiracy which had been contriv'd against the Repose of the State, or to discover the Secret of a criminous Correspondence,) but to force him to declare the Intelligence he might hold in the State it self, to procure that Insight which was necessary to him for the Service of the Prince his Master, commits an abominable Crime, which cannot be expiated but by the severest Punishment of those incompetent and unjust Judges

None but a *Ferdinand of Arragon*, a *Cæsar Borgia*, a *Jerome of Riario*, and such like other Monsters, are capable of offering Violence to publick Ministers, but neither they, nor the *Turks* themselves, do not exercise their Brutishness, but on the Embassadors of their Enemies Whereas a few Judges of a Presidial (yet I must except those who would have no Hand in the Injustice and irregular Proceedings of the rest) were so audacious, as to treat with the utmost Ignominy the Minister of the most faithful, and most disinterested Ally the State had The whole History thereof shall be given in a particular Treatise

Ir

In the Year 1672, after the Bishop of *Munster* had rais'd the Siege of *Groninguen*, the Magistrate of the Town took up a Gentleman of the Countrey, brought him to his Tryal, and condemn'd him to perpetual Imprisonment. The States of the Province of *Groninguen* are compos'd of the Magistrate of the Town on the one part, and of the Gentry and Proprietors of the circumjacent Countrey on the other, which make the two Branches thereof. This Province is as Sovereign, as are all the Rest that compose the Union, but then the Assembly of the States General is Judge of the Differences which may arise between the Members of the said Province.

For which Reason those of the circumjacent Countrey, after they had given another Turn to the Affair, by the Means of their Syndic, brought the Matter in the Year 1677, before the Assembly of the States General, where they maintain'd, that the Town could not alone try a Gentleman but that the Deputies of the other Branch ought to have been present, without whom the Judges of the Town were neither Competent nor Lawful. The States General in the Year 1678 annull'd the Sentence of the Town, and set the Gentleman at Liberty, and restor'd him to his Estate, Honours, and Dignities. But this was not done till the Affair had been discuss'd with great Warmth, particularly in the Assembly of the States of *Holland*, where after a sharp Contestation, it was judg'd, that they ought to espouse the Interest of the circumjacent Countrey, against the Sentiments of the Town, and that it might bear its own Blame, it was declar'd that the *Law of Nations* had been violated in the Person of the Gentleman, Prisoner. It was no small Surprise to the Rest, the Thought of those, who back'd their Opinion with the *Law of Nations*, to which on other Occasions so little Regard has been shewn.

The speaking in the Behalf of the *Sieur Renguers*, was no great Justification of the Procedure of a subaltern Court of Judicature, against a publick Minister, who had the representing Character from a sovereign Prince, who was an Ally of the State. One would think also, that the *Law of Nations* was not very properly apply'd to an Affair purely Domestick, wherein the other United Provinces had no other Concern, than what they thought they ought to have for the Quiet of their Neighbours and Allies, out of a Reason of State, and not out of Regard to the common Interest of all People. To speak the Truth, they forgot themselves, in not distinguishing between the *publick Faith*, and the *Law of Nations*. The one gives Safety to the Deputy, and the other to the Minister. A Passport or Safeconduct may, and indeed ought to entitle one to the publick Safety, as ought also a Contract, an Alliance, and an Union, but a publick Minister enjoys it, on Account of his Character, by virtue of the *Law of Nations*. The Deputies whom the United Provinces send to the Assembly of the States, ought there to enjoy the publick Safety, not by virtue of the *Law of Nations*, which has no room but among Strangers, but by virtue of their Union, because they altogether make but one Body of a State. The Reason is still stronger why the Deputies of the same Province, whether it have two or more Members, cannot pretend to enjoy the publick Safety by virtue of the *Law of Nations*; but only by virtue of the Treaties which the Members have made among themselves, and of the Union they have together. In the same Manner the Sovereign who convenes the States of his Kingdom or Province, is oblig'd to secure Safety to the Deputies, and yet I don't think it can be said, that the Deputies have a Right to it by virtue of the *Law of Nations*. King *Henry* III, in causing the Duke and Cardinal *de Guise* to be kill'd at the States of *Blois*, violated the publick Faith but he could not be said to violate the *Law of Nations* by putting his Subjects to Death, as I said in Chapter III.

The Deputies whom the Princes and States of the Empire send to the Diets, or to the Emperor's Court, are of another sort. The Emperor, as Emperor, is not Sovereign, and yet there is not a Prince of the Empire but is so, provided he be in Possession of a Principality that gives him a Vote and Seat in the Diets and nevertheless there are fundamental Laws of the Empire, which make these Princes be consider'd as Members of the same Body in the Empire it self. For which Reason their Ministers are only consider'd as Deputies, and not as Embassadors at the Diets, where they enjoy an entire Safety, by virtue of the *publick Faith*, and not by virtue of the *Law of Nations*. In the Year 1529, the Elector of *Saxony*, *George* Marquiss of *Brandenburg*, *Ernest* and *Francis* Dukes of *Lunenburg*, the Lantgrave of *Hesse*, the Prince of *Anhalt*, and some other Princes and Towns having protested against the Decree of the Assembly at *Spire*, sent three Deputies to the Emperor *Charles* V, to represent the Grievances which oblig'd them to oppose the Execution of the Decree, and to appeal. The Deputies found the Emperor at *Placentia* in *Lombardie*, where they presented the Protestation and Appeal of the Princes, and spoke to him with so much Firmness and Liberty, as well by Word of Mouth as in Writing, that the Emperor being offended thereat, caus'd them to be taken up at their Inn, and forbid them on pain of Death, to write to the Princes, or to notify to them by any indirect way, that they were under Confinement. In the Relation these Ministers give of what pass'd on this Occasion, they say, That the Emperor, who had sworn at his Coronation that he would preserve the Rights and Liberties of the Princes of the Empire, was oblig'd to hearken to their Remonstrances, and to admit their Ministers, whom he could not put under Arrest, without infringing his Oath, and violating the *Law of Nations*. They also protested formally against it, before one of their Colleagues, who was a Notary, and they made a solemn Appeal. The Emperor himself considering, that this Violence would be ill taken in the Empire, caus'd them to be set at Liberty at the End of a Fortnight, and sent them back into *Germany*. He had violated his Oath, and the publick Faith, but he did not violate the *Law of Nations*, to which these Deputies give too great an Extent.

It is not to say but that *Law of Nations* may be sometimes violated in the Person of those who have not the Character, but then they must be Foreigners and notwithstanding they have

have not a publick Character, they must have some particular Quality, that intitles them to the Protection of the *Law of Nations* *Calatagironne*, who was concern'd in the Treaty of *Vervins*, and who had before made several Journeys to and fro, had not the Quality of Embassador, nor was not compris'd in the Pope's Commission Father *John Neyen*, who had so great a Share in the Negotiation of the Truce of the Low Countries, and Father *Joseph* who help'd to make the Treaty of *Ratisbone*, had no Quality, yet that did not hinder them from enjoying all the Protection of the *Law of Nations* At the Assembly of *Crespy* in *Valois*, there was a *Jacobin* Fryar, who negotiated there by the Consent of *Charles*, and of *Francis* I *Stephen de Nueilly*, Master of the Requests, entering into Dispute with the Fryar, gave him a Box on the Ear *Nueilly* violated thereby the *Law of Nations*, and did himself so much harm by this Action, that when some time after there was a Discourse of making him Chancellor of *France*, the Cardinal of *Tournon* oppos'd it, and said, That so violent a Spirit was not fit for the first Dignity of the Gown, nor to be a Minister, who (as he was at the Head of Affairs) ought to serve for an Example of Moderation to the Rest The Maxim of Cardinal *de Tournon* is not well founded every where There are some Ministers who recommend themselves no other way than by their Violence, who being rebuk'd by the Affairs of which they are not capable, domineer over every Body, and cause that to be done by Force, which they cannot attempt by Reason But as they are not Embassadors, we shall not speak of them in this Treatise

At the beginning of the Negotiation of *Munster*, the Plenipotentiaries of *France*, in examining the Powers of the Emperor's Plenipotentiaries, observ'd amongst other Defects therein, that these had not caus'd the Quality of Embassador to be given them, and press'd them very much to get it added to that of Plenipotentiary The Counts of *Nassaw* and *Volmar*, said, That that did not depend on them, and that the *French* might if they pleas'd, get the Quality of Embassador taken away *D'Avaux* and *Servien* judg'd on the contrary, That they ought not to get it remov'd, as well because they were not oblig'd to have any Complaisance for those who had none for them, as because it was the ordinary Style of *France* They further said, That being in an Enemy's Country, where they might receive Orders to treat of Alliances with some of the Princes of *Germany*, and to carry on Negotiations that would have nothing in common with those of *Munster*, and which perhaps would not be very conformable to the Emperor's Intention, the Character of Embassador was very necessary to them, as well to give the greater Authority to what they should treat about, *as for the greater Security of their Persons*, *if they were discover'd to carry on Negotiations which had no Relation with those of the Assembly*, *because the Character of Embassador being venerable amongst all Nations*, *it was respected*, &c Upon which it might be said, That supposing the Character of Embassador gives an entire Security to him that is cloth'd therewith, it seems as if the *French* Ministers would make it be believ'd, that that of Plenipotentiary does not, and that the Ministers of the second Order, ought not to enjoy the Protection of the *Law of Nations*, which nevertheless is contrary to the Intention, and Consent of all People The Declaration of the States of *Holland* is express thereupon and I make the Observation the more willingly, because it is reasonable to think they were surpriz'd by some strange Artifice, to make them consent to the scandalous Outrage, their Court of Judicature did to a publick Minister in their very Sight So that to give a true Explication to this Passage, we must necessarily say, that the Embassadors of *France* had therein a Regard, not to those Princes nor Ministers who know what the *Law of Nations* is, and what is due to all those that represent a Sovereign Prince, whatever their Character or Quality may be, but that they had then in their Thoughts, those People, who know no other Representative than the Embassador, it being very certain, that where the Quality of Plenipotentiary would not secure them from Violence and Insults, the Character of Embassador would not protect them neither I have spoken in the first Chapter of this Book, of the Instance the United Provinces made, that the *French* Ministers would raise the Quality of Embassador out of their Powers They would not do it, but they don't alledge the Reason that is mention'd here

It was much about the time that the States of *Holland* publish'd their Declaration, that they made it plain, they knew how to practise themselves what they ordain'd to others, and cause their Intention to be executed by the Court of Justice *Don Antonio de Sousa*, *de Macedo*, Embassador from *John* King of *Portugal*, making some Propositions which the State did not think very reasonable, they gave him to understand, that they would have no more Conferences with him, and that for the future, *they would not consider him as an Embassador*, *but as a private Person* *Don Antonio* made answer, *That it depended on the State*, *to continue the Conferences*, *or to break 'em off*, *but as for the Quality of Embassador*, *that he did not hold it of them*, *and so they could not deprive him of it neither* *That Facility being reserv'd to the King his Master*, *exclusively of all other Sovereigns*, *that the Law of Nations oblig'd the States to acknowledge him for such*, *notwithstanding he was not acceptable to them* That he own'd, that the same *Law of Nations* permitted them to compel him to leave the Country, if they had a mind to come to a Rupture with the King his Master, but that he hop'd for quite the contrary from their Prudence That even in such case, *They ought to give him leisure to depart*, *and acknowledge him for Embassador*, *till he was arriv'd at* Lisbon And indeed, when his Creditors and those of his Predecessor, for whom he stood engag'd, presented a Petition to put him under Arrest as a private Person, the Court of Justice, which at that time was fill'd with People of Worth, and grave Persons, refus'd to do it till it knew first the Sentiments of the States of *Holland* in so important an Affair They declar'd, that the Judicature ought not to regard the Resolution of the States General, because that had only in view the Negotiation of the Embassador of *Portugal*, *and could not hinder the* Law of Nations *from being*

being consider'd and preserv'd in his Person, nor his Character from being respected.

Mrs Slingelant, de Masdam, de Hubert and Tibrants, Embassadors from the United Provinces, being in the Month of April, 1656, arriv'd at Loüenburg, a Town belonging either to Cassubia or Pomerania, the Governor of the Place, who was a Swede, hindering them from pursuing their Journey, they protested *That the Law of Nations was violated in their Persons* The Governor said, He did not put them under Arrest, but that he could not suffer them to pass, because of the general Prohibition he had not to let any Body pass They sent to make their Complaints to the Chancellor of *Sweden*, who signify'd to them, That it was not the Intention of the King his Master to arrest them, but he only desir'd the Embassadors would let him see them, before they went to *Dantzig*, yet nevertheless he left them the Liberty of taking what Road they pleas'd They took that of *Dantzig*, according to their Orders, and arriv'd there the 24th of the same Month The Dutch Embassadors said, That by hindring them from passing, the *Law of Nations was violated, Quia omnis Coactio debet abesse a Legato*, and the Court of Justice in Holland shall not be said to violate the said *Law of Nations* in putting a publick Minister in Prison A publick Minister who had been admitted by the States General, by the Consent of the States of all the United Provinces, and by Consequence there was a formal Obligation to protect him Whereas the Dutch Embassadors, whom I just mention'd, had not as yet presented their *Letters of Credence*, and had not been yet admitted by the King of *Sweden*, who, if he respected their Character, it was because he would not break with the States, and not out of Deference to the *Law of Nations*, which was not violated by what he did, but in a very extensive and improper Signification

The same King of *Sweden* might rather be said to violate the *Law of Nations*, in an Encounter he had with the same Dutch Embassadors in the following Month of *May* *Sidney*, *Honywood*, and *Bond*, Embassadors from *England*, who were to labour in Conjunction with them, at a Peace in the *North*, had demanded Audience for them all And after *Sidney*, who was Spokesman, had finish'd his Discourse, and deliver'd to the King the Project on which *France*, *England*, and the States pretended to conclude the Accommodation, the King said, I know very well what this Paper contains, but I wonder that you *English*, who are my Friends, should think it fitting to give me the Law I accept of you, not as Arbitrators but as Mediators, provided you do not do any thing that is against the Rules of Friendship Then turning himself towards the *Hollanders*, he told them, And for your Parts, *I refuse you for Mediators, because you are my Enemies* *I might have us'd you as the King of* Denmark *us'd my Embassador, the Baron* Bielke. This Baron had been detain'd a Prisoner at *Copenhaguen*, so that the King of *Sweden*, by threatening to imprison Embassadors, to whom he could not refuse the publick Safety, lost the Respect he ow'd to the *Law of Nations*, and violated it in Effect. The Pope *Sixtus* V told the *Spanish* Embassador, who desir'd him to accommodate the King his Master with part of his Treasures, to make War against the Hereticks of *France*, That if he spoke to him any more on that Matter, he would cause his Head to be cut off. He knew not how to jest, and as he mortally hated the *Spaniards*, the *Spanish* Embassador ought not to have jested with him But it must be own'd, that (if it is allowable to speak so of a Pope) he was guilty of a Brutality which would not have remain'd unpunish'd, if his Passion had proceeded to the Effect of his Menaces As for the King of *Sweden*, who was not in a Condition to offend the United Provinces, by arresting their Embassadors, he might very well have spar'd threatening them When Princes, who are Conquerors, are merely Soldiers, they are very subject to these Transports

Sixtus IV, not being able to brook the Liberty with which the Bishop of *Osma*, Embassador from *Ferdinand the Catholick* spoke to him, sent him to Prison But *Ferdinand* signify'd to the Pope by *Diego de Vadillo*, one of the Gentlemen of his Houshold, That if he did not set his Embassador at Liberty, he would come himself and release him This was speaking and acting like a Prince, who was sensible how much it concern'd his Reputation to protect his Minister

I should think it were giving too great an Extent to the *Law of Nations*, to maintain that it was violated by a lowring Look at an Embassador Yet one may be wanting in the Respect that is due to his Character, without injuring his Person The Mareschal *d'Estrée*, Embassador from *France* at *Rome*, had seiz'd upon the Inheritance of a Judge, who being a French Man, was dead without leaving any Issue, and the Count *de Chasteauvillain*, who had retir'd to *Rome* under the Pontificate of *Urban* VIII, to whom he was related, protected a Man, who said he was one of the Deceased's Creditors The Mareschal took it ill, insomuch that they came to such Words as the Embassador thought himself oblig'd to resent It happen'd on the 25th of *March*, 1641, that the Count going to see the Count *de Fiesque*, this last told him, that he expected the *French* Embassador, who had sent him Notice of his coming, this oblig'd the Count *de Chasteauvillain* to take his Leave, and to order his Coachman to go directly Home, but he could not avoid meeting the Embassador's Coach And notwithstanding, according to the Custom of *Rome*, he stopp'd, and even stood up, with his Hat in his Hand, to salute the Embassador, this last pass'd on, and even threaten'd him The Count was so enrag'd thereat, that being come Home, altho' he was of the Church, he put it into Deliberation whether he should not send a Challenge to the Mareschal, or whether his Son should not challenge the other's. However taking into Consideration what he ow'd to the Character, he resolv'd to wait for another Opportunity, and in the mean Time, he never went about the Town without a good Number of arm'd Men, always avoiding nevertheless passing before the Embassador's Palace. The Embassador complain'd to the Pope, who, to give him some Satisfaction, sent the Count a Prisoner to the Castle of St *Angelo*, but he was soon taken from thence, and sent to *Viterbo*, rather to protect him from the Violence of that Minister, than by the way of Punishment.

Steno Bielke, of whom the King of *Sweden* made mention, was sent by him to *Copenhagen*, with *Peter Julius Coyet*, to look after the Interest of the Duke of *Holstein Gottorp*, the King's Father-in-Law, conformably to the 21st Article of the Treaty of *Roschild*. They were still there, when the said King resolv'd to complete the Conquest of the Kingdom of *Denmark*. *Coyet*, who knew his Person would not be safe after this second Rupture, went away, under the Pretext to go and facilitate the Execution of the Treaty with the King his Master, promising to return in a Fortnight. In the mean Time the *Swedish* Army being enter'd again into the Isle of *Zeeland*, and *Bielke* fearing lest the People of *Copenhaguen* should insult him, bought up Arms, and augmented the Number of his Domesticks, with a Design to oppose any Violence that might be offer'd him. However, seeing that this weak Resistance would only hasten his Ruin, he had Recourse to the King's Protection against the Fury of the People, and was glad to find his Safety in one of the Apartments of the Royal Garden, where he had Guards appointed him, and where he remain'd a Prisoner till the Month of *August*, 1659. It is a great Question, whether the King of *Denmark*, in confining *Steno Bielke*, violated the *Law of Nations* or not, and whether he was oblig'd to secure him the publick Safety, as well during the Time of his Residence, as in his going and coming, since he had admitted him, or whether he could use him as an Enemy, since the King his Master broke the Treaty which he had just concluded, and invaded the Kingdom, without any previous Declaration. But it may be said, that the King of *Sweden* alledg'd *Steno Bielke* improperly, because if the King of *Denmark* was in the right to confine him, the King of *Sweden* was in the wrong to complain thereof. And if the King of *Denmark*, in so doing, offended the *Law of Nations*, the King of *Sweden* injur'd himself in discovering that he was capable of making an Arrest, which he look'd upon himself to be unjust and violent. He could not arrest the *Dutch* Embassadors without violating the *Law of Nations*, because he had admitted them, and acknowledg'd them, as the Embassadors of a State in Friendship with him. Their Masters had done no Act of Hostility against him, and if any thing had otherwise happen'd, with which he had Reason to be dissatisfy'd, he might oblige them to retire.

The ill Usage that is offer'd to an Embassador in a popular Commotion, it is true, violates the *Law of Nations*, but as in those Cases the Protection of the Prince is useless to him, this ought not to fail to revenge him, if it be in his Power, or at least he ought to shew, that it does not stick at him that it is not repair'd. When *Francis Sforza*, General of the Army of the City of *Milan*, made himself Prince of the whole Dutchy, by the Favour of the People, *Leonard Veneto*, Embassador of *Venice*, was kill'd with some other Persons of Quality who oppos'd the Peoples Fury. After the Sticklers for Liberty were taken off, the Sovereignty was offer'd to *Sforza*, who was far from punishing the Authors of the Murder of the Embassador, since the same Rascals were the Authors of his Fortune, which his accurs'd Posterity did not enjoy long.

In Republicks, where the Magistrate makes a part of the People, both the one and the other are answerable for the Violence which is done to the publick Minister. The *Switzers*, who invaded *France* in the Year 1513, at the same time that the Emperor *Maximilian* and *Henry* VIII King of *England* were upon the Frontiers with powerful Armies, had besieg'd *Dijon*, and in taking that Town there was nothing could hinder them from penetrating into the Heart of the Kingdom. The Lord *de la Trimouille* sav'd himself, in all likelihood, by the Treaty he made with them, promising them six hundred thousand Ducats. That the King should no longer protect the Council he had conven'd at *Pisa*, and should renounce his Pretensions to the Dutchy of *Milan*. *Lewis* XII was not at all satisfy'd with this Treaty, and particularly with the last Article, so that he refus'd to ratify it. The *Switzers* enrag'd at this Refusal, and to see themselves frustrated of so considerable a Sum, because the Hostages, which had been given as Pledges for the Execution of the Treaty, had made their Escape, rejected with Disdain all the Proposals the King made them. Tho' excepting the Renunciation of his Right to the Duchy of *Milan*, he offer'd them incomparably greater Advantages than those they had stipulated by the Treaty. In their Fury they compell'd those of *Geneva* to deliver into their Hands the President of *Grenoble*, whom the King sent to treat with them, and having caus'd him to be brought to them, they put him on the Rack, to extort from his own Mouth who they were the King his Master gave Pensions to, or had any secret Correspondence with him. All the *Switzers* were guilty of the Outrage that was done to a publick Minister. All the *Grisons*, as well the Magistrates as the People, were answerable for the Disorders which happen'd in the Year 1617, to *John Baptista Padavin*, Secretary to the Republick of *Venice* in the *Agnedine*. The People rising against him, employ'd the Arms of the Publick to compel him to save himself at *Morbegno*, and from thence in the State of *Venice*.

Even in the Year 1513, the same Senate had sent to the Cantons *Peter Stella*, Secretary of the Council of the *Pregadi*, to endeavour to bring them into the League the Republick had made with *France* against the Emperor *Maximilian*, and against the other Princes, who had a Design upon the Liberty of *Italy*. But as soon as *Stella* began to mention at *Zurich* the renewing Friendship with *France*, the People enter'd into a perfect Fury, and losing the Respect that reasonable Persons have for the *Law of Nations*, it fell upon this publick Minister, who had much ado to save himself from the Hand of these Furies, by the Means of some of the Magistrates, who order'd him a Guard. The Council was summon'd at the same time, wherein it was resolv'd to make War with *France*, which was done with so much Precipitation, that the raising of the Troops, their confus'd March, the Defeat of the *French* who were beaten at *Novarra*, and the Re-establishment of *Francis Sforza*, had hardly any Interval. The Resolutions that are taken in this sort of Assem-

The EMBASSADOR and his FUNCTIONS. 263

Assemblies, resemble the Disorders and Irregularities, which are caus'd by popular Insurrections, where the *Law of Nations* is not more consider'd than the Common Law. An Embassador is not secur'd by his Character against the Insolence of a People in Rebellion, and a publick Minister has in vain Recourse to the Protection of the Magistracy which has lost its Authority.

It is an Offence against the Civil Laws, and is a Crime to intercept the Letters of a private Person, because the publick Safety is disturb'd thereby, but there is no intercepting those of an Embassador without violating the *Law of Nations* The President *Richardot* going from the *Hague*, where he had negotiated as a publick Minister on the part of the Arch-Duke *Albert*, left in the Drawer of his Table the original Instruction which his Master had given him The Landlord of the House having found it, gave it to the Count *John de Nassaw* and this having caus'd it to fall into the Hands of Prince *Maurice*, who communicated it to the States, it was immediately sent to the Provinces, and made publick. *Richardot* being advis'd thereof, wrote to President *Jeannin* on the 7th of *October*, 1608, in these Terms *It is violating both the* Jus Hospitii, *and the religious Respect which is due to Embassadors, whose Persons and Goods ought to be in an entire Safety, and Reason would have requir'd, they should have sent 'em to me, instead of making a Trophy of them* No Body ever doubted, that the Security which is due to publick Persons, extends it self also to their Letters The President *Jeannin*, Embassador from *France* in *Holland*, had intrusted his Dispatches to a Man of his Acquaintance, to carry them to the Posthouse This Man had the Confidence to open the Letter, and to make an Extract of it, the Copy of which being communicated to several Persons, fell at last into the Hands of the Embassador He complain'd thereof to the States, who offer'd to punish exemplarily the Infidelity of a Man, *who had violated the* Law of Nations, *by unsealing the Letters of a publick Minister*, but M *Jeannin* would not name him, for fear of exposing him to the Scandal of a Scaffold.

Aloisio Contarini, being Embassador from *Venice* in *England* in the Year 1625, sent a Packet of Letters to *Dover*, to the two Embassadors of *Denmark*, who were going into *France*, and who had promis'd to deliver it to the Embassador, who was on the Part of the Republick at *Paris* The Lieutenant of *Dover* Castle being inform'd thereof, sent to the Embassadors to desire they would transmit the Packet to him, that he might only see it, because, as he said, it was a Deference that was due to his Office, but as soon as their Secretary had deliver'd it to him, he told him he would himself take care it should come to hand, and instead of sending it into *France*, he sent it back to *London* After the Packet had been open'd at Court, and those Letters had been taken out which it had a mind to see, it was restor'd to the Embassador of *Venice* He complain'd thereof to the King, and told him, He would absent from the Court, till he should receive the Directions of the Senate on so extraordinary an Occasion However he remain'd there, the King having given him some Satisfaction, and caus'd his Letters to be restor'd to him but for all that, he acquainted the Senate therewith, which some time after sent him Orders *to forbear taking Audience of the King or the Council, till he should effectually have receiv'd a publick Reparation*

In the Year 1646, in the Height of the Commotions of *England*, some Letters (which an extraordinary Courrier was carrying to *Sabran*, Resident from *France* at *London*) were intercepted at *Rochester* This Minister having Advice thereof sent to demand his Letters, and made pressing Instances to have Reparation made for the Insult, which had been offer'd to a publick Minister, by intercepting his Letters Upon the Information the *French* had, that the Courrier had been carry'd to the Earl of *Northumberland*'s House, as were also the Letters, *Monstrueil* (who did there the Affairs of *France*, but chiefly with the King and the *Scots*) immediately went thither and going up into a Room above Stairs, he found upon the Table, amongst a great many other Packets, that, in which the Courier said, the Letters which were taken from him had been inclos'd *Monstrueil* took it up, and having open'd the Packet, put the Letters into his Pocket, with some others which were address'd to *Sabran* and himself. The Earl's Domesticks being surpris'd at so bold an Action, said nothing, but the Earl himself coming into the Room soon after, *Monstrevil* in his Transport of Passion made him bitter Reproaches, for *having, contrary to the* Law of Nations, *stop'd his Courrier, and taking from him the Letters which the King his Master had sent him, for which Action he demanded Reparation* The Earl made answer, That it was not his Fault, and that the Letters had been brought to his House, in order to be convey'd to the Deputies of the two Nations, to whom he was oblig'd to be answerable for the same That he would communicate his Complaints to them, but that he would not conceal from him, that he thought it very strange, that in his own House, he, *Monstrevl*, had taken and open'd a Packet that was not directed to him *Monstrevil* reply'd, That he thought it much stranger, that the *English* should detain a whole Day, the Letters of the King of *France*, and that his Minister should not have the Liberty to open a Paper in which they were wrapp'd up, to retake them The Earl desir'd him to restore them to him But *Monstrevil* told him, *That the Affront the Earl offer'd him, in thinking him capable of so infamous an Action; and in believing him to have so mean a Soul, as to betray the Secrets and Interests of the King his Master, as he should do if he gave to any other, the Letters which were directed to himself, was still more offensive than that he had offer'd him; in arresting his Courier, and intercepting his Letters That he was so far from any such Thought, that there was no Peril to which he would not expose himself, to hinder them from being taken from him, or to go and take them out of the Hands of him, that should offer to detain them.* Sabran, on his part, being inform'd of what was doing at *Northumberland* House, presently ran thither, and there told the Earl, That if his Letters were in the Hands of a Sovereign, he would not scruple to wrest them from him The Earl was against *Monstrevil*'s taking the Courier along him, unless

Sabran

Sebray remain'd a Pledge for his forth coming, whenever it should be requir'd. But the two French Ministers, far from giving him this Satisfaction, said, They expected Reparation, and that they would cause it to be made them. During the Dispute, which was pretty warm, the Earl's Domesticks, had taken care to shut the Street-Door, so that when the French were for going out they found themselves stop'd, but the Earl caus'd it to be open'd to them. On the same Day he sent to the Deputies of the two Nations, an Account of the Contest and as in the Confusion and Change of Government, great Violences are Things of Course, there were some of the Deputies, who were for having Monstreuil brought before a Council of War, in order to be try'd. Others were for having an Enquiry made into the Cause of his Stay at London, and that no doubt there would be found sufficient Matter to make him a Criminal. But the Earl of Lauderdale, who was there alone on the Part of the Scots, said, He could not consent to the being wanting in Respect to the Minister of so great a King as was that of France. He represented alone the whole Nation, as I just now said, so that his single Opinion making a Division, the Deputies could come to no Resolution, but remitted the Affair to the Parliament, who was glad not to meddle therewith, and judg'd it proper not to make any farther Mention thereof. He that collected the Particulars I have here set down, out of the very Dispatches of those Ministers, farther adds, *That perhaps it might not be thought to be to the Purpose, to swell a regular History with all these minute Particulars; but that he gives this Detail with a Design, that this Action may serve for an Example and Rule to Ministers, who may thereby learn, with what Courage and Intrepidity they ought to act, to maintain the Dignity of their Employment, by conserving the Honour, the Grandeur and the Reputation of their Master as Princes may therein learn, to what the Law of Nations obliges them, in reference to the Ministers of foreign Princes.*

The Minister who will preserve himself inviolate, ought to make known his Character, as I shall take notice in Chapter XXIX. To conclude this, which is already too long, I shall add, That all sorts of ill Treatment to a publick Minister, do not violate the Law of Nations. The Deputies whom the Cantons of Zurich and Glaris sent to the Grisons at the beginning of this Century, were very ill receiv'd. No Civility at all was done them, nay it was forbid to have any manner of Communication with them, and when they were sent away, no other Answer was made them, except that nothing of what they desir'd should be comply'd with. Hereupon the Switzers said, That the Grisons violated the Law of Nations by this Manner of Procedure. They were mistaken. It was indeed a Rusticity, and an odd Behaviour enough, towards the Deputies of a State, which forms almost one Republick with them. But the Matter of Civilities is not a part of the Law of Nations.

I here comprise under the Name of publick Minister, not only those who have a publick Quality, as Embassadors, Envoys, Residents, &c. but also those who negotiate without a Character, provided the Prince admits them, and negotiates with them. *Merveille* ought to have enjoy'd the Protection of the Law of Nations, which extends it self to the Monks, as I said before. In the Year 1579, *Simier* was employ'd in England, to prosecute on the Part of the Duke of Alençon his Marriage with Queen Elizabeth. He was at London, not in the Behalf of a Sovereign, but of the Brother of a Sovereign and yet as soon as the Queen was inform'd that some of the Nobility had a Design upon his Life, she gave them to understand, that her Intention was, *That besides the particular Protection which she gave him, he should also enjoy that of the Law of Nations*, and thus it is that all Princes ought to act.

It is not necessary to add here, that Princes have always been extremely sensible of the Injuries done to their Ministers, because they know they are done to their Persons but I cannot forbear saying, That those who have no Sense thereof do not deserve the Name of Prince. All who have written concerning the publick Right, agree, that a Sovereign cannot have a more lawful Cause to make War so that there is Reason to wonder at the Ignorance and Stupidity of a Minister, whose History I think my self oblig'd to give. He was a pretended Excellency, but it did not go beyond his own Domesticks, because he was not acknowledg'd in the Quality of Embassador. It was represented to him, the Injury the Prince his Master did himself, in suffering a thousand Indignities to be done him, in the Person of his Minister, and in shewing so much Indifferency in an Affair, where his Reputation was so much concern'd. He reply'd, That it must not be imagin'd, that his Prince would put on his Armour, or make War for the Quarrel of his Minister. It is certain, this impertinent and ignorant Embassador, did not do his Master any great Honour, nor himself. He ought to have stifl'd in his abject and mean Soul, so vile a Thought, and pity'd those Ministers, who are unhappy enough to serve such Princes as abandon them, and make it publickly known, that they have neither the Heart, nor the Power, nor perhaps the Will, to protect them against Violations, which have no Example in History.

See what *Cicero* says of the War the Romans made with *Mithridates* but particularly the Reparation, which the most Christian King caus'd to be made him in the Year 1663, by Pope *Alexander* VII, for the Insolence the *Corsican* Guards had been guilty of the Year before, to the Duke *de Crequey*, Embassador of France. That Minister was Haughty, and the Pope's Ministers were Insolent, insomuch that with these Dispositions, they soon pass'd, from Coolness and Indifferency for each other, to great Enmity, of which the *Ghigy*, Relations of the Pope, gave a Proof on the 20th of *August*, 1662. The Embassadors Domesticks had had a Difference with the Corsican Guards, who fir'd several Shot into the Coach of the Embassadrix, kill'd one of her Pages, and pursu'd her with their Arms to her very Palace, where she had much adoe to save her self, in great Disorder and Precipitation. The Duke being angry to see himself so unworthily treated by these People, laid the Blame on the Pope's Relations, and after he had conferr'd with the *French* Cardinals,

nals, he left *Rome*, and retir'd into the Territories of the Great Duke of *Tuscany* Notwithstanding the Offices the Pope caus'd to be done to him and to his Lady, to hinder him from going The Pope himself wrote to the King about it, and offer'd to punish severely the Authors of the Disorder But the Satisfaction the Pope offer'd, bearing no Proportion with that the King requir'd, the Nuncio felt the first Effects of the King's Resentment He was order'd to go to *Meaux*, and there to wait the King's Pleasure, who being inform'd that the Nuncio, instead of taking the Road to *Meaux*, was gone to St *Denis*, sent thither forty Musqueteers of his Guards on Horseback, who possess'd themselves of all the Avenues of the Convent, to which the Nuncio was retir'd, they accompany'd him every where, and watch'd him so narrowly, that excepting his Domesticks no body could speak to him This was the first Treatment he had, upon Advice of what had happen'd on the 20th of *August* But as soon as it was known in *France*, that the Duke was gone out of the Ecclesiastical Territories, ten more Musqueteers were added to the first, who made the Nuncio set forward, and in their March took his Coach in the middle of them, so that one half of them were before the Horses, and the other half behind the Coach, they conducted him in this manner to the Entrance into *Savoy* The Nuncio arriv'd at *Rome*, almost at the same time that the Duke of *Crequy* return'd to *France* Some Overtures of an Accommodation were made indeed, but the King taking the usual Slowness of the Court of *Rome*, as a Mark of the evil Disposition of the Pope's Relations, caus'd some Troops to file off towards *Italy*, seiz'd upon *Avignon* and its Dependencies, and gave out that he was going to pass the *Alpes* in Person *Alexander* VII, who had done Honour to his Post while he was Nuncio at *Munster*, and who had acquir'd Reputation being Cardinal, had lost it all since he was Pope, insomuch that finding no Friends to stand by him against *France*, he was forc'd to an Accommodation The first thing the King stipulated, was, that the Treaty should not be at *Rome* But *Pisa* was pitch'd upon, whither the Pope sent *Cæsar Rasponi*, Referendary of both the one and the other Signatures And the King employ'd there the Abbot *de Bourlemont*, Auditor of the *Rota*, who concluded the Treaty on the 22d of *February*, 1664 It was indeed a Treaty, but upon very unequal Terms The Pope thereby oblig'd himself to a Reparation, which might be call'd *amende honorable*, since he promises to send the Cardinal his Nephew in the Quality of Legate, who should protest that it was not his Intention to offend the King, nor his Embassador That neither himself, nor any of his Family, had any Concern in the Outrage, and that for the future they would give the King Proofs of their Zeal, of their Obedience, and of their Fidelity That *Don Mario Ghigy* should make the same Protestation, and should depart from *Rome*, till the Legate had given the King this Satisfaction, and that the whole Nation of *Corsica* should be declar'd incapable of serving for the time to come, not only at *Rome*, but also throughout the whole Ecclesiastical State And *that a Pyramid should be erected right against their ancient Guard-Room, with an Inscription which should contain this Declaration* Since the King pass'd over all the Consideration, which all the Catholick Potentates us'd to have for the Pope, and that he reveng'd so severely the Outrage which had been done to his Embassador, we must believe that Princes (who ought to consider their Ministers as their own Image) ought to employ all the Courage and Strength they have to revenge the Injury which is done them in the Person of their Minister

Give me leave to make here one single Reflection upon the carrying off of Prince *William* of *Furstemberg*, and to observe that among those who undertake to justify that Action, there are two sorts of Advocates The ones defend the Emperor's Right, and maintain that he could with Justice cause his Subject and Vassal to be seiz'd and carry'd off, even in a Place where he was employ'd with the Character of a publick Minister by a foreign Sovereign The others will not enter into an Examination of this Question, but keep within the Bounds of the Fact, and suppose as a thing certain that he had no Character, or at least that he did not make it known, so that the Emperor was not oblig'd to respect him It is most certain that the Prince, to enjoy the Protection of the *Law of Nations*, ought to have produc'd his Credentials, or else to have communicated his Powers to the whole Assembly, and it is also as certain that he did not do it So that it ought to be acknowledg'd, that even with this Advantage it was not necessary to render problematical an uncontested Maxim, which declares that there is no violating the Person of an Embassador, or publick Minister, who is acknowledg'd for such, (wherever he may be) without Violation of the *Law of Nations*.

CHAP. XXVIII.

The House and Domesticks of an Embassador are inviolable.

WIlliam *Pelissier*, Bishop of *Montpellier*, Embassador at *Venice*, in the Reign of King *Francis* I, making use of the Mediation of *Cæsar Fregose*, (he that was kill'd some time after with *Anthony Rincon*) had won over to his Interest *Constantin* and *Nicholas Gavazza*, of whom the one was Secretary of the Council of Ten, and the other of the Council of the *Pregadi*, *Maffeo Leone*, Sage of *Terra firma*; *Augustin Abondio*, and *John Francis Valerio*, who discover'd to him all they could learn of the Secrets of the Republick *Girolamo Martelosso*, *telojjo*, a *Venetian* Gentleman, who kept Company with the Wife of *Abondio*, having one Day found in the Closet of this last some Letters from *Nicholas Cavazza*, which run upon Affairs of the State, communicated them to the Council of Ten, where the Hand of *Cavazza* being known, they had no great Difficulty to trace the Treason up to its Source *Maffée Leone* and *Constantin Cavazza* had time enough to make their Escape, and the three others took Sanctuary in the House of the *French* Embassador. The Senate sent thither *Bernard Georgio*, one of the Avogadors of the Commons, (which is a very considerable Magistrate at *Venice*) to desire the Embassador to deliver up the Traitors into the Hands of Justice. But the Domesticks hinder'd him from speaking to him, and even offer'd some Violence to those the Council of Ten had sent along with the Avogador to aid and assist him. This Resistance oblig'd him to go out of the House, but Guards were immediately posted at all the Avenues thereof, and two little Pieces of Canon were brought thither in a Boat, in Order to batter and beat down the Gate. The Embassador seeing these Preparations, and fearing lest this Violence should be follow'd by a greater, yielded, and surrender'd the Criminals. The King said, They had violated the *Law of Nations*, in forcing the House of his Minister. And express'd his Resentment therefore, by refusing for some Months to admit to his Presence *Anthony Venier*, Embassador from the Republick. But some time after, the King having besieg'd *Perpignan*, whither *Venier* had follow'd him, he sent for him, and said nothing that was harsh to him, but only ask'd him, What he would say if he was treated after the same manner his Embassador had been treated at *Venice*? *Venier* made answer, That if the Traytors and Rebels to his Majesty took Shelter in his House, he would take them himself by the Arm to deliver them into the Hands of Justice, because if he did not do it the Senate would not fail to punish him severely. The Answer was worthy of an Embassador and a Senator of *Venice*, and could not be more discreet, because they referr'd to the Words, and not to the Intention of the King. Since it is reasonable to think, that the Senate would not punish its Embassador for having harbour'd, or even favour'd the Escape of Traitors who had serv'd it.

It may be said, upon this Example, that according to the *Law of Nations* the House of an Embassador can afford Safety to none but himself and his Domesticks, and cannot serve as an *Asylum* to Strangers, but with the Consent of the Sovereign of the Place, who may extend or restrain that Privilege as he pleases, because it does not make part of the *Law of Nations*. The Auditor of the Legate *Barberin* said indeed to the King's Attorney at *Lions*, (who ask'd him for the Seal and the Register of his Legation a little uncivilly) That at *Rome* an Officer of Justice dares not so much as approach the Palace of the *French* Embassador. Which is true. And it is well known, that in *Spain* the Houses of publick Ministers did enjoy very considerable Liberties and Immunities. But forasmuch as they abus'd what they possess'd without a Title, and by the Indulgence of the Kings only, it was reasonable to deprive them thereof, and to make them be contented with some other Advantages, more proportionate to those they enjoy in other Courts. The present Pope is in the right also to try to take away that enormous Licence which the Embassadors of crown'd Heads give themselves, to extend their Protection to whole Quarters, to make them serve for a Retreat, to all kinds of profligate Wretches, from Justice. There are some, however, who think that the Embassadors on their part have Reason to maintain themselves in the Possession of a Right which they have enjoy'd a long Time, especially under a Prince who has no other Title to his Sovereignty than a bare Possession.

To speak in general. The House of the Embassador ought not to protect those Persons, who by their Crimes disturb and overthrow Civil Society, which the Publick Right endeavours to protect and preserve, since even according to the Law of *Moses*, the most sacred Places ought to be Sanctuaries and Asylums to none but the Unfortunate. It is Superstition that has open'd them to all sorts of Criminals without Distinction, who are there protected by an incompetent and unlawful Power. So that I think I may say, that if the *French* Embassador could not handsomely abandon those Persons he had corrupted, neither could he protect, against the Justice of the Place, the Subjects of the Republick, amongst whom there were some who ow'd a more particular Fidelity to the State by Reason of their Offices. As a Sovereign cannot substract the Embassador from the Justice of his own Prince, so neither can the Embassadors substract the Subjects from the Justice of their Sovereign, nor hinder him from executing his Justice upon them, without doing him Wrong, and infringing the Rights of his Crown. On other Occasions, the House of the Embassador ought to be respected, as if it were the Palace of the Prince himself. For it is so in Effect, or at least it is in his particular Protection, as well as his Person. It is on this Account, that in several Courts of *Europe* the Embassadors set up the Arms of their Master over the Gate of their Palace. And almost every where they have a Chair of State, which denotes the Presence of the Master of the House. At the Congress of *Westphalia*, the Houses of the Embassadors and Plenipotentiaries were known by the Arms of the Sovereigns whom they represented, not only those of crown'd Heads, of Republicks, and of the Electors, but also those of the Princes of *Germany* and *Italy*. The Embassadors of the United Provinces, writing to the States General, do not fail to date their Letters, *From the House of their High Mightinesses*, not so much because they defray the Expences of the Embassy, and pay the Rent of the House, as chiefly because it is their Representative that lodges there.

In fine, the Embassador ought to enjoy in his House so great a Liberty, that no body can there controul his Actions, nor even hinder him from exercising the Religion of his Prince, notwithstanding it be prohibited by the Laws of the Countrey where he is employ'd. In the Year 1644, the Parliament of *London* sent some Deputies to the *Spanish* Embassador, with Orders to search his House for two *Irish* Friars or Priests, to whom it was said the Embassador gave Shelter. The Embassador told 'em, He would not suffer his House to be search'd, and that he had rather lose his Life in opposing the same, than to have his Head cut off in *Spain*, for not knowing how to support the Dignity of his Character, nor the Honour of *the King, to whom the House belong'd, and not to him*. As for the Priests he entertain'd for his Service, that he would give an Account of them to the Parliament. It was believ'd he had been assisting to the Evasion of two *Irish* Lords, who had made their Escape out of the *Tower* of *London*, or at least that the *Irish* Priests, to whom the Embassador gave a Retreat, were aiding thereto which was the Cause that the People threaten'd to plunder the House. It would have been almost impossible to save it, had not the *Irish* Noblemen chanc'd to be retaken at the same time.

It was in the same Year, that the Parliament having taken up the Landlady of *Sabran* Resident of *France*, and committed her to Prison, sent a Garrison into her House. *Sabran* complain'd thereof, but the Parliament said, That the Gentlewoman was *English* that the House did not belong to the Resident, but to her, and that her Crime was prov'd so that the Resident, who had only some Chambers there, could not hinder the Law from proceeding against her. Nevertheless as it made a Noise, and that the other publick Ministers concern'd themselves in the Affair, the Parliament thought fit to justify it self to *France*, and it was on this Account chiefly, that it sent thither that Player on the Lute, whom we have mention'd elsewhere.

The States of *Sweden* being assembl'd at *Stockholm* in the Year 1648, the Bishops and Ministers, who are there to a great Number, and have Credit with the People, as they have every where else, made great Complaints against the Foreigners, who were every Day seen to go to Mass at *M Channt*'s House, who then was only Resident of *France*. The Queen, who was oblig'd to have some Complaisance for those People, signify'd to *Channt*, *That she would not take from him the Exercise of his Religion in his House, but she desir'd him not to admit there so many Strangers, because the People were scandaliz'd thereat.* The Secretary *Guldenclau*, who had deliver'd the Message, having spoke in somewhat a lofty Tone, *Channt* made answer, *That he was not oblig'd to the Queen for the Liberty he had to exercise his Religion in his own House, and for his Family, but that he held it from the King that employ'd him, and from the Law of Nations, and therefore he would not shut the Door upon those Catholicks, who should repair thither.* That the Law of *Sweden* could not abolish the Law of Nations, (which must be well observ'd, against the new Politicians) nor the Privileges it gives to the House and Person of the Embassador, or publick Minister, and that it could not extend so far as to Strangers, who were come into the Kingdom on the publick Faith. That he saw no Swedes in his Chapel, whereas in Paris all sorts of People repair'd to the Lutheran Minister, who was tolerated there for the Queen's sake. That the Baron de Rorté, his Predecessor, had given the same Answer to those who had held him the same Discourse on the Part of the Directors

of the Kingdom. That the House was the King's and not his. And that he would not hinder the Foreigners, and particularly the French from coming there. The Secretary reply'd, That if the Resident did not take some Course therein, there was Reason to apprehend that the People, who were scandaliz'd at it, would proceed to some Violence. *Channt* rejoyn'd, That the Queen was so well obey'd in her Kingdom, and the King his Master so much consider'd there, that he could not apprehend any Disorder therefrom. He complain'd to the Queen, who told him, That the Secretary had exceeded his Orders, and had done more than he had been commanded. That she was oblig'd to have some Complaisance for the States of the Kingdom, and that she desir'd him to have a little for her, while they were assembled, and that after they broke up, he might do as he was us'd to do, and with the same Liberty as before.

In the Year 1603, the Nuncio who was at *Venice*, complain'd of the Liberty the *English* Embassador took, to have publick Preaching in his House. The Nuncio said, That the Sermons were in *English*, but it might one Day happen, that they might be preach'd in *Italian*, and that all sorts of Persons might repair to them. That the Embassador ought to be oblig'd to go and reside at *Muran*, or in some other By-place, to avoid the Scandal. These Complaints being carry'd to the Senate, it was there said, *That the King of England was so great a Prince, that the Republick not being able to be without his Friendship, it could not hinder his Minister from exercising at home the Religion of his Master*, but that he should be desir'd not to admit Foreigners there. It is certain that amongst the other Rights which the publick Minister ought to enjoy, is compris'd that of exercising in his own House the Religion which he professes, or rather that of the Prince that employs him. As therein the Sovereign is consider'd whom the Minister represents, so likewise is it to his Religion, that this Respect is shewn. So that there is room to doubt, whether the Embassador, who should profess a Religion that should have no Analogy to that of his Master, nor to the prevailing Religion of the Country where he resides, could exercise it publickly in his own House. But one would think it might be here said, That if the Prince (who would not have his Minister an Atheist, and who would rather he should be of any Religion, than of none at all) permits him to exercise it in his House, the Sovereign with whom he resides ought not to oppose him in it. Princes seldom employ Ministers that make Profession of a Religion different from their own; but when they do, they commonly make Choice of such as profess the Religion of the Prince to whom they send them. *Mirembeau*, whom *Henry* III, King of *France*, employ'd to the Protestant Princes of *Germany*, was of their Religion. *Segur*, *Calignon*, le Duke de *Bouillon*, le Marquis de *Rosny*, *Buzenval*, *la Place*, *du Maurier*, whom *Henry* IV, and *Lewis* XIII, have employ'd in *Germany*, *England* and *Holland* as also the Counts de *Zinkendorf* and de *Windischgratz*, whom the Emperor employ'd for some Years, were Protestants, so that it was not necessary they should have Preaching in in their own Houses, yet nevertheless, if the Princes who employ'd them and who were Catholicks, had desir'd they should cause Mass to be said at their own Homes, it would not have been oppos'd

The Ministers of the second Order enjoy this Right, as well as many others, equally with Embassadors The Residents of the King of *Great Britain*, have enjoy'd it every where without Contradiction and the Residents of the United Provinces, have the free Liberty of having Preachings in their own Houses, not only at the Courts of *Lutheran* Princes, where the Exercise of that Religion that is call'd the Reform'd, is not less severely prohibited, than that of the *Roman* Catholicks, but also at *Constantinople*, at *Brussels*, and even at *Lisbon* and at *Madrid*, in the very face of the Inquisition

But this is a Privilege which in reality ought not to extend it self beyond the Person of the Embassador and his Domesticks For notwithstanding he cannot be hinder'd from admitting all the Foreigners that shall present themselves at his Gate, yet the Sovereign may forbid his Subjects, and even all those Foreigners who are oblig'd to respect the Laws of his State, to repair to the Embassadors, or to have any Communication with them, as well in the Matter of Religion as otherwise Those Princes therefore who are not willing the Laws of their Countrey should be alter'd, do not suffer their Subjects to frequent those Assemblies, nor the Embassadors to have the Service perform'd in any other Tongue, than in that of their Master The Inquisition has made Provision in this Case, in *France* and *Spain*, as well as in the United Provinces and notwithstanding the reform'd Religion is establish'd by Edict in the one, and that in the others there is a great Indulgence shewn to those of the *Roman* Profession, yet the Subjects are severely forbidden to frequent such unlawful Assemblies Philip II, of *Spain*, would not permit the Embassador of Queen *Elizabeth* to serve God after his own Way in his own House, and compell'd his Domesticks to go to Mass, but his Successors have made it sufficiently known, that the Devotion of Princes, how Religious soever they may be, is never so sincere, as not to have a Mixture of State Interest in it, and that this very often prevails over the other

Supposing then that the House of the Embassador be also in the Protection of the *Law of Nations*, it ought to be inviolable so that it cannot be subject to be search'd, unless he makes it serve for a Sanctuary to profligate wicked People, for the *Law of Nations* does not protect it so far as that Upon this Foundation *M de Bye*, Resident of *Poland*, ought not to have suffer'd the States of the United Provinces, or those of *Holland*, to cause his House to be search'd for a Gentleman, Subject to the King of *Poland*, his Master neither is it probable he would have suffer'd it, if they had not come in arm'd, and us'd Violence This *Polish* Gentleman having been oblig'd to go out of his Countrey, on the Account of a Disgrace which had there happen'd to him, had retir'd into *Moscovy*, and had put himself in the Retinue of two Embassadors whom the Czar sent into *Holland* but his Design was, not to return into a Countrey where all are Slaves He therefore stole away from the Embassadors, and retir'd to the Resident's of *Poland*, who apprehending what afterwards follow'd, conveigh'd him away The *Muscovites* made so much Noise about it, that the States of *Holland*, having set a Guard at all the Avenues of his House, sent some Officers and Soldiers in to the same to search for the Fugitive They found no such Person there, and yet they offer'd this Affront to the publick Minister of the King of *Poland* The *Pole* was not born a Slave to the Czar, and if he was become such, by going to reside in *Muscovy*, he recover'd his natural Liberty the Moment he set Foot in a Countrey which does not nourish any Slaves, and where it ought not to be so much as known, what Servitude and Slavery is The *French* Lawyers say, *That the Air of* France *is so good and so benign, that as soon as a Slave enters into the Kingdom, tho' it be in the Retinue of an Embassador, he breaths nothing but Liberty, and recovers it immediately* There is still a stronger Reason why the State of the United Provinces (which ought to subsist but by Liberty and Justice, and which ought to protect those whom Tyranny would persecute and oppress) cannot excuse it self for this Treatment to the House of the Resident of *Poland*

In the Year 1642, *Francisco Andrada Leitao*, Embassador from *Portugal* at the *Hague*, having been cheated by a Horse Courser, detain'd him a Prisoner in his House The Horse Courser's Wife hereupon made a great Clamour, at which the Rabble getting together, at first broke the Windows with Stones, then broke open the Door next the Street, afterwards forc'd all the other Doors, and riff'd all the Boxes and Trunks, taking away all the Plate and pretious Furniture, with so much Disorder and Confusion, that all that the Embassador and his Domesticks could do, was to save themselves through the Garden to the neighbouring Houses The Burghers took to their Arms, and the Court of Justice, with the Magistracy of the *Hague*, repair'd to the Place, to stop the Progress of the Tumult The Embassador having complain'd of this Outrage to the States General, some of the Deputies were of Opinion, that they ought to indemnify and save him harmless, that thereby the State might be discharg'd of the otherwise just Reproach which might be made it, for having suffer'd the *Law of Nations* to be violated in his Person, and in his House But the *Law of Nations* was again neglected in this Point, and the Embassador was forc'd to be contented with the bad Excuse, the States made him by three of its Deputies The Embassador who had publickly taught the Law, ought to have known, that he was not allow'd to make a Prison of his House and it was a great Piece of Imprudence in him, to expose himself to a Rabble, that knows no Medium between the most dissolute Licence, and the most ignominious Servitude But for all that, the State was oblig'd of Right to make Reparation for a Violence which it could not punish, and to indemnify him, for what he had lost in that popular Insurrection

There happen'd something like this in the Year 1601, to *Anthony de Silly*, Count de *Rochepot*, Embassador of *France* in *Spain* The Court was at *Valladolid*, where the Inhabitants not being

The EMBASSADOR and his FUNCTIONS

being much accustom'd to the Sight of French Men, committed several Insolencies to those of the Embassador's Retinue, even to that Degree as to oblige the Embassador to get out of his Coach, and draw his Sword against those who abus'd his People, and who had kill'd one of his Footmen behind his Coach, without his being able to get Satisfaction therefore. After this some of his Gentlemen going one Night to take the Air, the People began to call them Names, and among the rest, *Veliacos Borachos*, and *Lutheranos*, so that the French drawing their Swords, kill'd two of them upon the Spot. But they were no sooner got home, than they found themselves invested by the People, assisted by a good Number of Officers of Justice, who under the Pretext of preventing a greater Disorder, forc'd the House in several Places, broke open the Chamber Doors, plunder'd and carry'd off the Plate and other Furniture, beat and abus'd the Domesticks, and took away the Gentlemen Prisoners, and with them the Embassador's Nephew. Some Days after they restor'd to him what could be recover'd of what had been taken from him, but the Gentlemen were detain'd Prisoners. Upon the Advice the Embassador gave the King his Master thereof, he was order'd to retire from the Court of *Spain*. The King forbad all Commerce with that Kingdom, and the two Crowns in all likelihood were upon the Point of coming to a Rupture, had not the Pope interceded, and caus'd the Prisoners to be brought and deliver'd up to him, who put them into the Hands of the *French* Embassador, who was then at *Rome Du Fargis*, while he was Embassador from *France* at the Court of *Madrid*, had almost the like Encounter in the Year 1621, and it would have produc'd the like Effect, if the Mareschal *de Bassompierre*, who arriv'd there at that Juncture of Time, in the Quality of Extraordinary, had not accommodated the Difference.

The Judicature of *Valladolid* violated the *Law of Nations* two Ways, by forcing the House of the Embassador, and by carrying off his Domesticks, and the King of *Spain* in consenting to the one and to the other, was not altogether Innocent. His Ministers flung the Fault upon the People, which being got together in a tumultuary Manner, there was a Necessity to give them some Satisfaction, and this would have been somewhat plausible, if the Gentlemen had not remain'd Prisoners, and in Irons, till they were taken off at *Rome*. The King's Business was to have demanded of the Embassador, those who had kill'd the *Spaniards*, or else to have urg'd him to have done Justice upon them himself, and for Default of both these, to have requir'd Satisfaction of the King of *France*. Some time after, and even before the Prisoners were deliver'd into the Hands of the Pope, which was not done till ten Months were expir'd, the Servants of the *Venetian* Embassador kill'd two *Spaniards* at *Madrid* but the King of *Spain* forbad taking them either in the House, or while they attended the Embassador in any Place whatsoever, either in the Town or Countrey. These Prohibitions were agreeable to the *Law of Nations*, and it was thus that they acted in *Holland*, while they had any Respect there for the said *Law*. On the

same Day that *M. de Thou*, Embassador from *France*, arriv'd at the *Hague* towards the latter End of *April*, 1657, one of his Domesticks was for offering Violence to a Woman that he met in the Street. The Patrole prevented him, and carry'd him away to the Guard House, with a Design, in the Morning, to put him into the Hands of Justice. The Embassador being inform'd thereof, reclaim'd his Domestick and the Counsellors Deputies of *Holland*, who represent the Sovereign of the Province in the Absence of the States, caus'd him to be surrender'd to him, that he might punish him himself. *De Thou* was in the Right to speak in the Behalf of his Domestick, and to shew at his Entrance upon his Employment, that he was not unworthy of the Character with which the King, had honour'd him, since he knew how to support the Dignity thereof. And the States of *Holland* on their Part, made it plain that they had a Respect for the *Law of Nations*.

Wherefore no Precedent ought to be made of *Oliver Cromwell*'s Action, who in the Year 1654, took up *Pantaleon de Sa & Menses*, out of the House of the Count *de Penagion*, Embassador of *Portugal*, his Brother, and made him be publickly executed at *London*. It is true that *Pantaleon* had committed a great Crime, in killing wrongfully an *Englishman* who was walking with his future Bride, in a Place they call the *New Exchange*. It is also true, that the *English* were extremely irritated at this Action, which was capable of raising the whole Town, and that it was necessary to give them some Satisfaction. But then it is also true, that *Cromwell* might have satisfy'd them with Appearances, and that he ought to have done any thing rather than violate the *Law of Nations*. However he was willing to sacrifice it with this Gentleman to his Ambition and after he had committed a Parricide, he did not scruple the committing a Sacriledge.

The Offer *M. de Thou* made to punish his Domestick, and the Acquiescence of the States of *Holland* therein, confirm what is said of the Right an Embassador has to do Justice in his own House, upon those who depend on him. In the Year 1602, *Henry* IV sent the Marquiss *de Rosny* to King *James*, to Complement him on his Accession to the Crown of *England* The same Day that the Embassador arriv'd at *London*, some of his Gentlemen went to a dissolute House, where they quarrell'd with some *English*, and kill'd one of them. The People clamour'd thereat, and threaten'd the *French* to come and attack them at home, so that they all made their Escape to the Embassador's Palace, who was lodg'd at *Arundel* House. These Commotions could not be made with so little Disorder, but the Embassador must be sensible of them, and at the same time be inform'd of the Cause thereof. He therefore immediately secur'd the Author of the Murder, and retiring into a Room with some *French* Noblemen, who had accompany'd him in his Embassy, he condemn'd the Party to suffer Death, on the Confession he drew from his own Mouth. The Criminal was the Son of one of the great Auditors of the Chancery, and of one of the best Families of *Paris* yet nevertheless the Embassador, who was otherwise of a severe Temper enough, being willing to oblige the People of *London*, sent word to the Mayor that he had try'd the Murderer, and had condemn'd him to suffer Death, and that the Officers might come and take him away, in order to see the Sentence executed.

The Mayor accordingly sent for him, and had him away. But the Count *de Beaumont-Harlay*, Embassador in Ordinary from *France*, who had strongly oppos'd the Resolution *M. de Rosny* had taken, to deliver this young Gentleman up to the *English*, went in the mean time to the King of *England*, obtain'd the Criminal's Pardon, and caus'd him to be set at Liberty. *Henry* IV, who approv'd of all the Marquifs *de Rhosny*'s Actions, commended this also, tho' contrary to the Sentiment of the Council, and of all *France*, which maintain'd that none but the natural Sovereign of the Criminal could give him a Pardon, and that the King of *England*, who had no Jurisdiction over the Domestick of the Embassador, could much less dispose of the Life of the said Domestick. All that the King of *Great Britain* could do, was to supersede the Execution, and to give Advice to the King of *France*, of the State of the Affair, and to leave to him the Disposal of his Subject, who was come into *England* with his Embassador, or else to send him back to the Embassador, that he might himself cause his Sentence to be executed, for which the King of *England* was not oblig'd to lend his Officers, who ought to serve no other Judges than those to whom they had sworn.

The Embassador is by so much the more particularly oblig'd to protect his Domesticks, because they cannot be injur'd, but his own Person must be injur'd at the same time. One of the Pages of *Francis Miquels*, Embassador from *Venice* at *Turin*, having drawn his Sword in the Duke's Antichamber, against *Don Antonio* of *Savoy*, the Duke was for having the Embassador put the Page into his Hands, that he might cause him to be punish'd, but *Miqueli* refus'd to do it, notwithstanding the Displeasure the Duke shew'd thereat. The Senate of *Venice*, which fear'd left the Duke should proceed to some violent Resentment, there not being a perfect good Understanding at that time between the Republick and the Court of *Savoy*, recall'd its Embassador, and by that means the Correspondence between the Republick and the Duke was quite at an end. The Count *de Bigliore*, who was on the part of the Duke of *Savoy* at *Venice*, took also his Audience of Leave at the College, and set out the next Day, that he might not be oblig'd to take the usual Present which is made to Embassadors. The Count was not otherwise very well satisfy'd with the *Venetians*, who had forc'd him to take down from over his Gate the Arms of the Prince his Master, because he had quarter'd them with those of *Cyprus*.

In the Year 1626, the Coachman of *M. d'Espasses*, Embassador from *France* at the *Hague*, having affronted a *French* Captain, this last obtain'd no other Reparation, upon the Complaints he made to the Embassador, but this impertinent Answer, That the Coachman of an Embassador of *France* was as good as the Captain of a *French* Company in *Holland*. The other Captains, who were most of 'em Persons of Birth, resented it by caning the Coachman before the Embassador's Face, who, as he was making a Visit, had the Mortification to see through the Window the Affront that was offer'd to himself in the Person of his Domestick. He complain'd thereof to the King his Master, who wrote to the States, and gave them to understand by an Express, that he would have those Officers sent Prisoners to him, who had committed this Outrage to his Embassador, and that the Refusal the States should make to comply with him herein, would hinder him from sending them any Embassadors for the future, and even from continuing the Subsidies. The *Captains were the King's Subjects*, and had Pensions from him, yet all the Satisfaction he receiv'd was, that they suspended them for some time. The Embassador was not contented therewith, but shew'd his Resentment now and then, and did not even spare the State in an offensive and scandalous Memorial, which the States sent to the Extraordinary Embassadors who were on their Part in *France*, and desir'd the King to order his Embassador to treat with more Civility, a State which his Majesty honour'd with his Alliance, and to keep within the Bounds of the Respect which Allies usually pay one to another, instead of importuning them with his Memorials fill'd with Injuries and Reproaches. They likewise signify'd their Resentment to the Embassador himself, who, being recover'd from his first Transport, was for excusing himself, but he had been too violent, and he had made himself so many Enemies, that it prov'd no hard Matter to have him recall'd.

Spiring, Resident of *Sweden* at the *Hague*, that is to say, in his native Countrey, maintain'd that the Court of Justice had no Jurisdiction over his Person, and that it ought to leave to himself, that over his Domesticks. It would not explain it self then in Reference to the Question which was propos'd, viz. Whether a publick Minister could be oblig'd to answer for any Crime before the Judge of the Place of his Residence. However, it has since explain'd it self in the Case of the Resident of *Lunenburg*, contrary to the unanimous Opinion of all those who have written concerning the publick Right. But it seems as if it had Reason to make Difficulty concerning the Right the Resident arrogated to himself, to exercise a Jurisdiction over his Domesticks. The Sovereign himself is but a private Person, and has no Jurisdiction in the Territories of another, so that one would think his Representative cannot pretend to it neither. There seems also to be a great Incongruity, to allow an Embassador, or a Minister of the second Order, to exercise a Jurisdiction over his Domesticks, because not being accompany'd with a sufficient Number of Judges, he cannot proceed against them in Form, and after he shall have condemn'd them he has no Ministers of Justice to execute his Sentence. But forasmuch as the Embassador's House is the House of the Prince whom he represents, there is no doubt but he has a Jurisdiction within his own Walls, and may dispose of his Domesticks, within the Extent of the Authority his Master has given him for that Purpose. The Formalities of Justice are not of the *Law of Nature*, which the Embassador may follow, and he is not oblig'd to conform to the Civil Law. Or if he have any Scruple in the Matter, he may send the Criminal into his Countrey, and there have him judg'd by the Judicature of his Prince

It might again be doubted, whether the Embassador can extend his Jurisdiction on over those of his Domesticks, who are Subjects of the Sovereign with whom he resides But it seems it ought to be determin'd in the Affirmative For if the Sovereign permits his Subject to put himself in the Service of a Prince, or other Person, who has Power of Jurisdiction over all those that are in his Service, he abandons them also to that foreign Jurisdiction Spring uses the Court of Justice of *Holland* very ill in his Protestations, tho' he is in the wrong in the main, because the Court of Justice might and ought to take into its Protection and special Safeguard the Inhabitants of the *Hague*, to screen 'em from the Insolences with which the Domesticks of the Resident threaten'd them

From whence I shall take Occasion to say That as the Embassador ought to protect his Domesticks, so is he oblig'd in some measure to answer for their Actions I or which reason he ought to be very difficult in his Choice of them, not only on account of the Disorders which dissolute and irregular Persons are lyable to cause, but also because that under the Name of Domesticks, Spies may creep in, and even disguis'd Enemies, who may thwart his Negotiations under-hand, and betray his own Interests, as well as those of his Master In the Year 1567, the Emperor *Maximilian* II sent into *England* the Count de *Stolberg*, to propose a Match betwixt the Arch-Duke *Charles*, his Son, and Queen *Elizabeth* The Queen being willing to return the Civility, (altho' her Intentions were very contrary to the Marriage) sent the Earl of *Sussex* to carry the Garter to the Emperor, and to acquaint him with the many Difficulties which occur'd in this Proposal The Earl, who had an Inclination for this Match, would fain have put it in Negotiation, and have brought it to a Conclusion But the Earl of *Leicester*, who had himself some Hopes of marrying the Queen, and was for breaking off the Negotiation with *Vienna*, introduc'd the Baron *North* (who was an ingenious Man, and a great Confident of the Earl of *Leicester*'s) into the Embassador's Family The Baron's Birth easily procur'd him the Familiarity of the Earl of *Sussex*, which afforded him the Means to penetrate into all the Intrigues, and all the Secrets of the Negotiation, which he did not fail to communicate to his Friend in *England*

The Domesticks of Embassadors do but too often make their just Liberty degenerate into Licentiousness, the Consequences whereof may be very dangerous In the beginning of the Year 1563, there happen'd a very great Disorder at *Trent*, on account of a Quarrel between the Domesticks of two Bishops (the one of which was a *French* Man, and the other a *Spaniard*) in which the *French* Bishop's Domestick receiv'd his Death's Wound Some *Italians*, who were present at the Encounter, judging there had been some foul Play, because several *Spaniards* had drawn their Swords against one single *French* Man, espous'd the Matter, by which Means the Quarrel became national, betwixt the *French* and *Italians* on one Side, and the *Spaniards* on the other

It went so far, that they never met, but those, who thought they had an Advantage over the others, attack'd the weakest, it not being in the Power of the Legates, notwithstanding their utmost Care, to hinder the Massacre So that on the 12th of *March* there was an Engagement, in which several were kill'd and wounded on both Sides The Governor and Garrison of the Town had much ado to part them, and the Legates were so alarm'd thereat that they did not dare to stir out of their Houses They were for having the Cardinal of *Lorrain* (who had the greatest Authority among the *French* Ministers) to disarm his Domesticks, but he told them, That as his Person was not in Safety, it was requisite his Servants should be arm'd And *Lansac*, one of the *French* Embassadors, maintain'd, That his Quality allow'd him to be accompany'd by what Number of Domesticks he thought fit The *Spaniards*, who were proud and haughty, would not disarm neither, so that for six Days together there was no Assembly, the Prelates not daring to appear in the Streets for fear of being ill us'd The Legates, seeing here was no other Remedy, sent for the Embassadors, and represented to 'em, *That it was impossible to continue the Council, unless Peace could be maintain'd within the Town, and that that was not to be hop'd for, in such great Animosities, unless they all disarm d That in another Conjuncture the Embassadors might enjoy their Privileges, which were intended rather to give a Lustre to their Character, than to shed Blood* The Embassadors had a Deference to this Remonstrance, and agreed, *That none but themselves, and a certain Number of their Retinue (a List of whose Names should be given to the Magistrate of the Town) should go arm'd That the Number should not be reduc'd to so few Persons, in Reference to the Cardinal of Lorrain, but that however it should be regulated, and that he should be also oblig'd to give in their Names to the Magistrate, with a Prohibition to all the others, to go arm'd* The Legates, to shew Example to the rest, disarm'd first

The Legates were in the right to give the Term of Privilege to the Permission the Domesticks of Embassadors have to go arm'd, because they have it not by virtue of the *Law of Nations* Since it protects them, as well as their Masters, against all Insults and Violences, it ought to disarm them instead of giving them Arms, which can only serve to offend others, and not to defend those who are in the Protection of the publick Faith In *France* the Footmen have been frequently forbid wearing of Swords, and yet we have seen heretofore, that Embassadors caus'd theirs to be distinguish'd from the rest Because these Ordinances were slighted, and almost as soon abolish'd as publish'd. But since *Lewis* XIV has found the Means to be obey'd, and to disarm this Rabble, Embassadors no longer pretend to a Privilege for their Footmen. If all the rest were allow'd to wear Swords, the Domesticks of Embassadors ought to seek their Security in nothing but the Dignity and Character of their Master

All the Ministers agreed at *Munster*, that the Cognizance of the Crimes of their Domesticks, should belong to the Jurisdiction of the Magistrate

strate of the Town, which being done by a voluntary Submission, could not prejudice their Character, nor the Dignity of their Masters, and at the same time it serv'd for a Curb to the Insolence of their Domesticks. The Count of *Nassau*, Chief of the Emperor's Embassy, and *Contarins*, who was one of the Mediators, put some of their People into the Hands of the Magistrate, having first taken away their Liveries, to shew that they no longer belong'd to them. The same Method is observ'd at *Nimeguen*. At *Breda*, where the Garrison might be apt to have Quarrels with the Domesticks, all the Embassadors made a Regulation with the Governor, and ordain'd that the Livery Men should carry no short Arms that might be hid, and that it should not be lawful for them to oppose the Patrole. That this, when it found in the Night any of the Domesticks or an Embassador, making a Noise or Disturbance, should conduct them mildly to their respective Homes, and in Case of Resistance, should carry them to the main Guard, where they should be kept till the next Day, to be deliver'd up to their Masters, to the End he might punish them himself. There was not here the same Reason to apprehend Inconveniencies as in other Places, as well because the Assembly was not so numerous, as because it did not last so long as those of *Munster* and *Nimeguen*.

The Dragomans or Interpreters whom the Embassadors of Christian Princes make use of at *Constantinople*, enjoy also the Privileges of their other Domesticks, so that if the *Turks* do not always respect 'em as they ought, it is an Effect of their Brutality, which has no great Consideration for the Embassadors themselves. The First Vizir commonly employs a Chiaoux, when he sends any Message to an Embassador. But in the Year 1647, *Saits Bacha* took a fancy to send a Janizary to that of *France*, to desire of him certain Machines of Glass, with which the Candles were cover'd to prevent the Agitation of the Wind. But because the Embassador's Interpreter did not come soon enough to receive his Message, and also because he had not what he came for, he committed several Insolences there, and at his going from thence, he went and complain'd first, as if he had been very ill us'd. The Dragoman going afterwards to the Vizir from the Embassador to complain of the Janizary's Insolence, was very ill receiv'd and put in Prison. The Embassador was no sooner acquainted therewith, than he sent his Secretary to him, but he had not time allow'd him to justify the Dragoman. They put him away, and threaten'd to Cudgel him, and send him to the Gallies, which is the usual Complement of these Gentlemen. The Embassador complain'd thereof to the Aga Ali, who promis'd him his Domestick should be surrender'd to him, and told him, he would even do it in spight of the Vizir, if he were not afraid this last would on other Occasions revenge himself upon the *French*. Some Days after the Dragoman sent Word to the Embassador, that the Chiaoux Bassi being come to see him, had told him, that the Vizir, who was recover'd from his first Precipitation, would consent to his having his Liberty, if a Memorial were presented to him to that Effect. The Embassador, who did not think it adviseable to break with the First Minister, took that Method, and obtain'd the Liberty of his Interpreter, but the Vizir forbad this last ever setting Foot into the Divan for the future. *This is a Copy drawn from the Original of the* Turk's *Humour,* (says the Author of this History) *and the Character of a barbarous Nation, which transported by the first Motions of its Passion, tho' it sometimes repents it, yet will never consess it, and instead of making Reparation, seeks always but Pretexts to Cloak it with, and endeavours to justify it by fresh Injustices.* These Outrages were formerly peculiar to the *Turks*, but within some time they have so infected Christendom, that the Circumstan'd might come thither, to learn something more than what they know.

The Declaration of the States of *Holland*, mentions moreover the Coach of the Embassador and publick Minister, as it that were also in the Protection of the *Law of Nations*, with the other Dependencies of the Embassy. It ought to be inviolable in Effect, whether it be empty, or that the Embassador has a Mind to secure thereby some Person who is under his Protection. The Marquiss *de Fontenay Mareuil* Embassador from *France* at *Rome*, gave a Retreat to the Exiles and Rebels of *Naples*, during the last Commotions in that Kingdom. But forasmuch as he found it hard to be reimburs'd the Expences he was at on that Account, he was willing to get rid of them, by sending them back to *Naples*, where they would be more Serviceable than at *Rome*, and for that Purpose he made use of some Ships and Gallies that had brought Prince *Thomas* of *Savoy* to the Coast of *Tuscany*. The Embassador's Coaches, and those of Cardinal *Barberin*, guided by some of the Embassadors Domesticks, under the Conduct of the Chief Gentleman of his Chamber, were to carry them to the Place of their Imbarcation. But as they were going out of the Town, they found themselves attack'd by a great Number of the Corsi, belonging to the Pope's Guard, who had hid themselves in some of the neighbouring Houses, so with all the Resistance they could make, they could not hinder *Hippolytus Pastena*, one of the Chief Rebels of *Naples*, and sixteen others, from being hurry'd away to Prison. The Embassador was grievously offended at the Insult had been offer'd to his Coach, and having deliberated with the Cardinals *Barberin* and *Ursin*, gave out, that he was going to imbark on Prince *Thomas*'s Ships, and order'd his Daughter to prepare her self for the Voyage, and sent to desire Audience of the Pope, that he might acquaint him with the Subject of his Discontent, and Retreat. Being admitted to Audience, he declaim'd warmly against the Violence which had been offer'd to his People and Coach. He told the Pope that it was an unheard of thing, which offended not only the Dignity of the King his Master, but also the *Law of Nations*, and was capable of extinguishing all Commerce between Princes, and that he could not think it could be done by Order from his Holiness, but at the Instigation of some of his Ministers over-devoted to the *Spanish* Party. He therefore demanded of him, the *Liberty of the Prisoners, and Reparation for the Affront*. The Pope own'd, that it was by his Order that this Execu-

Execution had been made; and that he meant thereby to seize those Persons, whom the Embassador had help'd to escape out of Prison That since the Embassador gave himself the Liberty to protect Profligates, and whatever was Criminal within the Ecclesiastical State, it ought at least to be allow'd him, as Sovereign thereof, to cause them to be retaken where-ever they could be found, *it not being reasonable the Rights and Privileges of Embassadors should extend so far*, more especially since he had warn'd him thereof The Embassador reply'd, That it would not appear he had harbour'd any of the Pope's Subjects, but only some *Neapolitans*, whom he might lawfully protect against the Persecution of the *Spaniards* After some Dispute upon the Matter, the Pope consented that those whom the Embassador should name, should be set at Liberty But *M de Fontenay* was not satisfy'd therewith, but still insisted, That exemplary Punishment should be made on those *who had done that Outrage to the King, to violate the Coach of his Embassador* The Pope maintain'd, That it was the Embassador himself, that had furnish'd the Occasion *of losing the Respect which was due to his Coach*, by making it instrumental to the Evasion of Prisoners After great Contestations, which proceeded even to Threats on both sides, *M de Fontenay* (whose Interest it was to send back the *Neapolitans*, and who was afraid lest Pope *Innocent*, who was extremely obstinate, and more a *Spaniard* than a *Frenchman*, should become resolute at last,) accepted the Terms that all the Prisoners should be set at Liberty, and that the Nuncio who was at *Paris*, should regulate with the King the Reparation the Embassador demanded *on account of the Violence that had been done to his Coach* Here all the Advantage was on the Embassador's side, since the Pope, by surrendring the Prisoners, tacitely own'd he had done better not to have arrested them, and that he had made a Noise for nothing

In *Holland* the Embassadors enjoy an Exemption from all Duties, that are rais'd on all Commodities that are consum'd, but they are oblig'd to pay those of Entry, and Exportation, from which none are exempt In *France*, where the King himself is oblig'd to discount with the Farmer of the Customs, those Duties that are payable for all those Things which he Imports for his own Use, the Embassador can pretend to no more, than that the King will do him the Favour to satisfy the Farmer for him, but then he is oblig'd to declare what he Imports, or what he Exports on his own Account In the Year 1561, Queen *Elizabeth* sent *Thomas Chaloner* her Embassador into *Spain*, who not being able to brook the Affront the Commissioners of the Customs had put upon him, in opening his Chests and Boxes to search them, complain'd thereof to the Queen his Mistress, and desir'd to be recall'd from a Place where Embassadors were treated with so much Incivility But the Queen wrote to him, *That an Embassador was oblig'd to wink at whatever did not directly offend the Dignity of his Sovereign* The *Law of Nations* was not violated thereby,

for which Reason he could not complain, but only of an Incivility, which the Queen could resent if she thought it proper

The Embassador that obliges himself in a Contract before a Publick Notary in the Place where he resides, obliges himself likewise to the Execution of the Contract, because he subjects himself also to the Jurisdiction of the Sovereign of the Place But as he cannot do it without the Consent of the Prince his Master, whose Dignity is concern'd, at least for what regards his Person, one might here make a *Quere*, whether in some particular Cases his Goods and Furniture are not liable to an Execution as for Instance, for the Rent of his House, or otherwise The Embassador that has hir'd a House, is oblig'd to leave it when his Lease is out, if he will not renew it, and if he refuses to do it, he is compellable thereto by the Justice of the Place, because the Proprietor who has let his House to another, or has a mind to come and live in it himself, being oblig'd to fulfil what he has promis'd to another, or not being able to lie in the Streets himself, the Embassador ought to comply with the Contract, and may even be forc'd to it But notwithstanding in the foregoing Case no Violence is done to the *Law of Nations*, yet as these Executions are never serv'd without offending the Master of the Embassador, the surest way is not to contract with the Embassador, without the Security of some Citizen, on whom an Execution may be serv'd without offending the *Law of Nations* directly or indirectly

The Pope was in the Right to say, That the Privilege of Embassadors does not warrant their giving Protection to all sorts of People without Distinction Because *they do not hold it of the Law of Nations, but only of the Indulgence of Princes, who cannot be thought to have made them any Grant to the Prejudice of their Sovereignty* For which Reason the Embassador ought to be very Cautious therein, unless he will run the Risque of being affronted, and of causing his Master to be so too He ought to be as reserv'd in this Point as in that of Passports *Montaigne*, who was a trusty Minister of the late Queen of *England*, had cross'd the Sea with the Count *de Harcourt*, Embassador of *France* In landing at *Dover*, he had no Difficulty to mingle with the Count's Domesticks, but when he was setting out from thence, in order to go to *London*, and from thence to the King at *Oxford*, he was known, taken up, and sent to the *Tower* The Count *de Harcourt* reclaim'd him, and made pressing Instances to have him restor'd to him, but to no purpose He could not protect him who was not his Domestick, no more than a publick Minister can give Safety to another publick Minister, nor even to a Foreigner, who should pretend to enjoy the Benefit of his Passport, neither was he taken in the Embassador's Retinue, nor found to have any of his Dispatches about him but he had indeed some Letters that the Queen wrote to the King, with whom the Party that caus'd *Mountaigne* to be taken up, was at War.

Aaaa CHAP

CHAP XXIX.

Embassadors are not always inviolable.

THE Embassadors Plenipotentiaries of *France*, being arriv'd at *Munster* in the Month of *April*, 1644, wrote a Circular Letter to all the Princes of *Germany*, and another to the Deputies of the Assembly of *Franckfort*, to exhort the States of the Empire to send their Ministers to the Congress, in order to labour, as they said, in the Recovery of that Liberty, which the Emperor had wrested from them. The Court at *Vienna* was mightily offended at this Procedure, and said, That the French turn'd all Germany topsy-turvy, that their Ministers overthrew the very Principles of the Government establish'd in the Empire, and that they debauch'd the Subjects from the Obedience they ow'd their Sovereign. It maintain'd that the Law of Nations would not be violated, if having taken their Passports from them, they were punish'd according to the Rigour of the Laws. That the Passports had not been granted them, that they should make use thereof to the Prejudice of the Repose of the Empire, and to stir up a Rebellion, by causing an Insurrection of the Subjects against their Magistrate, but to the End they might labour at a General Peace. If this Resentment of the Court of *Vienna* was just, we must say, that the Person of the Embassador is not always inviolable. This is what is very certain, but it is not so easy a Matter to determine, to what Degree it is so, or to say in what Cases it is not nor also by whom, and after what manner the Embassador ought to be punish'd, when having violated the *Law of Nations*, he in vain reclaims its Protection.

He that has given the Publick a Treatise, under the Title of *The Idea of a perfect Embassador*, says, That the Embassador of one of the first Potentates of Italy, having at Madrid given Shelter to a Criminal, whom the Officers of Justice pursu'd, and having invited the Prevost or Sheriff to come into his Palace, caus'd him to be beaten and ill us'd by his Domesticks. That upon the Complaints of the Prevost, the President of Castile sent thither other Officers of Justice, who finding the Embassador in his Court, with his Sword in his Hand, and his Shield upon his Arm, they seiz'd him gently, and carry'd him into a neighbouring House, while they took up some of his Domesticks. That they were brought to a Tryal. That the Embassador's Gentleman who had broke the Prevost's Wand, was condemn'd to have his Hand cut off. That some of his Footmen were sentenc'd to be hang'd, and others to be sent to the Gallies. That the King of Spain having communicated this Process to the Master of the Embassador, would not suffer the Sentence to be executed, being contented to expel the Guilty out of the Kingdom; That he wrote afterwards to that Prince, and to all the other Potentates; That he expected, if any of his Embassadors committed Actions unworthy of their Quality and Employment, that they should not enjoy the Benefit of the Law of Nations, nor the Priviledges of their Character, but that they should be try'd, according to the Laws of the Countrey where they resided. I must own I know no more of this History, than what the Author relates of it. Indeed there is something like it, in the Violence which was done at *Valladolid* to the *French* Embassador in the Year 1601, and which we mention'd in the foregoing Chapter, tho' at the same Time the Issue was very different because the King of *Spain* made Reparation to the King of *France*, and was oblig'd to send the Prisoners to *Rome*, where the Pope put them into the Hands of the Count *de Bethune*. Publick Ministers ought to respect the Justice of the Place where they reside, but the Officers of Justice are also oblig'd to have a Veneration for the Character, and these last ought not always to follow their Zeal, which is not at all Times inseparable from Prudence and Moderation. On the contrary, these People are the more liable to be hurry'd away with Transport and Passion, because they look upon themselves to be above the Laws, and that no Body can judge them. Wherefore it cannot be deny'd, that if it be true the King of *Spain* explain'd himself after this manner, it was a very strange Expression. For if a Sovereign be suffer'd to proceed against the Minister whom another Sovereign sends to him, and that even in the Case of common Offences, not only the *Law of Nations* is thereby destroy'd, which exempts the publick Minister from the Jurisdiction of the ordinary Justice of the Place of his Residence, but he that permits it acts also against his own Dignity. If this Leave be given to Princes, not one Embassador nor publick Minister will be in Safety, and not one Sovereign will be able to protect his Minister, nor to assure himself of his Fidelity How is it possible for an Embassador to penetrate into the Secret of Affairs, which however is one of the principal Parts of his Function, if his Intrigues are made Crimes of State, and if the Judge of the Place be allow'd to take Cognizance thereof, and to proceed against him? We know there is no such thing as Friendship among Princes, and that the Appearances thereof being often more dangerous than declar'd Enmities, it would be impossible for the Embassador who stood in fear of the Inquiry of one of the Princes, to avoid the Reproaches of the other. What would have become of so many Embassadors, who have caus'd the Subjects to revolt against their Prince, who have furnish'd the Money and Arms with which they made War against their Sovereign, who have carry'd on Intrigues to surprise Places in a profound Peace, who have form'd and fomented Treasons, the bare Remembrance of which strikes one with Horror, and who have even attempted the Life of the Princes with whom they resided? Nevertheless after Queen *Elizabeth* had sent away *Bernardin de Mendosse*, Embassador from *Spain*, for having been concern'd in *Throgmorton*'s Conspiracy, *Philip* II took it so ill, that he would not see *William Waad*,

Waad, whom the Queen sent to him to justify her Procedure, and to make Complaints against *Mendoffe*. *Philip* was of Opinion, That the Queen was oblig'd to signify to him the Cause she had not to be satisfy'd with the Conduct of his Embassador, before she dismiss'd him. It is true, in an ordinary Affair she ought to have done so, and it is what Princes usually do, but then it must be consider'd, that there are Occurrences, where not only there is no Obligation to observe these Measures, but where also it would be very dangerous to take all these Precautions. *Francis Throgmorton* had conspir'd against the Queen's Person, whose Life was very precious, and of great Importance to the State. *Mendoffe* had had a Hand therein, and it was under his Name that the Treason had been form'd, and his Presence might have fomented the Conspiracy, and animated the Plotters. So that it cannot be deny'd but it had been the utmost Imprudence to suffer him in the Kingdom till she had written into *Spain*, and receiv'd *Philip*'s Answer. Besides, by making him retire he was skreen'd from the Violence of the People, of whom the Magistrate is not always the Master. It was the same *Bernardin de Mendoffe*, who treated with *Henry* IV, (while he was yet but King of *Navarr*) on the part of *Philip* II, who promis'd him four hundred thousand Crowns if he would take up Arms against *Henry* III, and who, after the Death of this, was one of the greatest Incendiaries of the War which the League continu'd to make with his Successor. The Republick of *Venice* did not send away *Alfonso de la Cueva* after the Treason which would have overturn'd its very Foundations. It was contented to desire the King of *Spain* to recall him, but it was when there was nothing more to fear. And this Moderation is peculiar to the wisest and gravest Senate in the World. *Don Alfonso* knew that the *Law of Nations* could not protect him, at least not against a People justly provok'd, for which Reason he retir'd to *Milan* without taking of Leave.

That Embassador, who violates first the *Law of Nations*, is in the wrong to desire its Protection. I do not willingly make use of Examples out of ancient History, but there is one in *Titus Livius*, that is so remarkable, that it may very well find a Place among the most eminent in modern History. The *Gauls* having penetrated as far as *Tuscany*, where they had besieg'd the Town of *Clusy*, the Senate of *Rome* sent *Fabius* thither, with two Colleagues of the same Family, to desire the *Gauls* to draw off their Army, and not to molest the Republick's Allies. The Embassadors, instead of acquitting themselves of the Office of Peace-Makers, sided with those of *Clusy*, and were present at several Engagements they had with the Besiegers. The *Gauls* sent to complain at *Rome* of the Violence their Embassadors had done to the *Law of Nations*, but the *Romans*, far from delivering them up to the *Gauls*, who requir'd them in order to punish them, confer'd upon them the Year following the first Dignities of the City, under the Name of Military Tribunes with the Consular Power, which so provok'd the *Gauls*, that they march'd directly to *Rome*, took the Town, and would have destroy'd it so entirely, that the Name of it would not have been known at this Day, had it not been for the Resistance they met with at the Capitol. All Embassadors, that take a Side, lose the Privilege of their Character, as well as the Ecclesiasticks that are taken in Arms. I have spoken elsewhere of the Bishop of *Beauvais*.

Francis, the last Duke of *Burgundy*, held an Intelligence with *Richard* III, King of *England*, so that there was a very intimate Correspondence between them. *Lewis* XI, who had good Information thereof, and who had found the Means to intercept several of his Letters, with *Richard*'s Answers, seeing that the Duke, and *Peter Landais*, a Minister he confided in, deceiv'd him, and carry'd on in *England* very dangerous Intrigues against him, he caus'd the Chancellor of *Britain*, and six other Counsellors whom the Duke sent to him, to be put *into so many separate Prisons, where he kept them twelve Days*. After that, he shew'd the original Letters to the Chancellor, and suffer'd him to take them away with him, that the Duke might see, the King was very well inform'd of his evil Intentions, and of the Artifices of his Minister, justifying thereby the Violence he had done to his Deputies, in treating them as Spies, and not as Embassadors. Yet as they were come under the publick Faith, they ought to have been consider'd and treated as Ministers. The King might have sent them back, or else not have suffer'd them to come into the Kingdom. But *Lewis* XI, who was not very regular in all his Actions, was not so neither in this, and was willing to affront the Ministers, because he did not fear the Resentment of the Prince their Master. *Selim* II sent in the Year 1570, to *Venice*, *Cubat Chiaoux*, to demand the Island of *Cyprus*, and in case of Refusal to declare War against the Republick. *Selim* had arrested the *Venetian* Embassador, *Mark Anthony Barbaro*, so that *Cubat* himself did not think he was safe in the Town, and apprehended some Violence from the People. But the Senate perceiving his Uneasiness, were so far from confining him, that they encourag'd him, and told him, *That the Republick had never suffer'd its Subjects to violate the Law of Nations, by injuring or offending an Embassador, so that he had nothing to fear on that part, and that he should be reconducted in all Safety the same way that he came*. It were to be wish'd that all Republicks would take Example from the just, prudent, and generous Procedure of the Senate, who would not do to the Minister of a *Turk* and an Enemy, what was done in *Holland* to the Minister of a Prince who was an Ally, and succour'd the States with his Arms.

The *Law of Nations* does not protect those Crimes which Nature abhors, because it is not its Intention to destroy it, nor to lend its Authority to Wretches who ought to have no Share in Civil Society. Nevertheless it seems as if Sovereigns ow'd that Respect one to the other, that not believing themselves capable of such Thoughts as are always disavow'd, more especially when they don't succeed, they may take Satisfaction of the Ministers, yet they do still better to complain to the Masters, to the end they may punish them, since they are oblig'd to answer for their Actions. But as these Complaints are not commonly made by Princes that have any great Kindness one for the other, and that those Princes who have opposite Interests are always Enemies disguis'd, and do not much perplex themselves whether they are satisfy'd one with the other or not, the Prince that is offended, not caring to make fruitless Complaints, and being willing at the same time to preserve some Respect for the *Law of Nations*, dismisses the Minister, without giving his Master time to recall him.

King *Henry* IV, in taking up *Bruneau*, Secretary to *Don Balthasar de Zuniga*, and putting him into the Hands of the Parliament, did not offend the *Law of Nations*. *Bruneau* was taken in the Fact, bargaining with one of the King's Subjects, in a profound Peace, for one of the most important Towns in the Kingdom. It behov'd the King to know the Truth of the Matter, and to convict *Merargues*, which could not be done but from the Mouth of *Bruneau*. And he comply'd with the *Law of Nations*, by hindering the Parliament from condemning him. He contented himself with proving the Crime, and discovering the Authors thereof.

It is observ'd, and more particularly in the History of *England*, because those Crimes have been more frequent, and less dissembl'd in that Kingdom than elsewhere, that it has been the Council of State for the most part, that has taken Cognizance of that kind of Affairs, and not the ordinary Justice. The Reason is, because publick Ministers neither can nor ought to acknowledge it. As also because these Differences, wherein the Sovereigns are directly concern'd, cannot be regulated but by themselves, or by their Privy Council. The Lawyers, of whom the Courts of Justice are generally compos'd, may probably know, what Penalties are appointed for Criminals of State, but yet I very much doubt whether they know how to distinguish betwixt a Criminal of State and a common Delinquent. The Court of *Holland* maintain'd that the *Sieur Sois*, heretofore Advocate for the *English* Nation at the *Hague*, had, by wounding a Man in the Streets, violated the *Law of Nations*. Nothing more impertinent could be said. It ought to have said, That he had violated the publick Safety. But in saying that he had violated the *Law of Nations*, it plainly shew'd, that it had not much study'd a Law, which does not make a part of its Profession. Those who rob upon the High Way, or that break open Houses in the Night, tho' they are not so dangerous as another sort of People that I know, *violate indeed the publick Safety*. But hitherto not one of those who have written of the publick Right, has rank'd these Crimes amongst those that are committed against the *Law of Nations*. As on the contrary there is not one, that does not place amongst the Violators of the *Law of Nations*, those who are guilty of what the States of *Holland* prohibit so rigorously in their Declaration.

The Marquiss of *Sarria*, Embassador from the Emperor *Charles* V, at *Rome*, had obtain'd of the Count *de Montorio*, Pope *Paul* IV's Nephew, the Permission to go out of the Town at what Hour of the Night he pleas'd. He frequently went a Hunting, and being come one Day to the Gate very early, the Captain of the Guard, who knew nothing of the Count's Order, would not open the Gate. So that the Embassador, who was well attended, caus'd the Soldiers to be driven away, and the Gate to be open'd *per Force*. It was a treasonable Crime, for which

Fraterno primum maduerunt sanguine Muri,

but it was not a Crime against the *Law of Nations*. The Pope and his Nephews made great Complaints thereof, and the Embassador, to justify himself, demanded Audience with great Earnestness. But Cardinal *Caraffa* signify'd to him, That he would do well not to be so urgent in the Matter, because it was the Pope's Intention to have him taken up, and perhaps to do something still worse to him. The Pope could not do it without violating the *Law of Nations*, which would not have been violated if the Embassador had been confin'd, or even kill'd in the Action, *while he was driving away the Guards, and forcing the Gates of the City*. According to the *Law of Nature*, *Violence may be oppos'd by Violence*, and it does not consider the Embassador that goes out of the Bounds of his Function to disturb the publick Quiet, but as a private Person in the Heat of Action, as I shall more particularly take notice by and by. *Diego de Mendosse* caus'd the *Barrizel*, or Prevost of *Rome*, to be beaten. The Mareschal *d'Estree* caus'd the Register of the Consistory to be cudgell'd in the middle of the Day, and his Gentleman of the Horse broke the Galley-Slaves Chain. And yet of all those that mention these Actions, there is not one that says the *Law of Nations* was violated there by, on the contrary the Register of *Como* was banish'd, because in the Sentence of *M. d'Estree's* Gentleman of the Horse, he had spoken of him as of a Domestick of the Embassador of *France*.

I say still more. That unless the Danger be apparent, or that the Prince, with whom the publick Minister resides, has a Design to break with the Master, Sovereigns owe one another this Respect, that he, who is not satisfy'd with the Conduct of a Minister, ought to complain to his Master before he dismisses the Minister, reserving to himself to shew his Resentment against him who refuses to do him Justice. In the Year 1563, Queen *Elizabeth* being inform'd that *Alvaro de Quadra*, Embassador from *Spain*, carry'd on very dangerous Cabals in her Kingdom, desir'd *Philip* II to recall him. *Philip* told the Queen's Embassador (who made pressing Instances to that Purpose) that he could not gratify her in that Point. That the Condition of Princes would be very unhappy, if they were oblig'd to recall their Minister, whenever his Conduct shall not square with the Humour or Interest of those with whom he negotiates. Hereupon the Queen, who had not otherwise any great Reason to be satisfy'd with the King of *Spain*, not relishing at all this Answer, set a Guard upon *Don Alvaro*, and caus'd him to be *interrogated by the Lords of the Council*. This Embassador had treated the Queen with little Respect, for which Reason she, on her part, had not much for his Character, but caus'd him to be us'd so roughly that he sicken'd upon it, and dy'd with Grief. He must of Necessity have offended her highly, since these Severities

verities were not natural to her, and that since that Time she would not violate the *Law of Nations*, in the Person of the Bishop of *Rosse*, who had done full as much Mischief, as the Queen of *Scots*, his Mistress *Philip* caus'd grievous Reproaches to be made to the Queen, on this Account, by *Diego Gusman de Silva*, who succeeded *Don Alvaro* in the Embassy This Action was one of the first Marks of the bad Understanding, which never ceas'd between these two Princes, as long as they liv'd *Philip* reveng'd himself by the Employment he gave to *Robert Shelley*, (who was the Queen's Aversion) sending him Embassador to *Vienna* to the Emperor *Maximilian* The Queen had done all she was oblig'd to do, in desiring *Philip* to recall his Embassador

In the Year 1626 there was a very dangerous Conspiracy in *France*, where the Intention of the Plotters was; not only to change the Ministry, but also to dethrone the King, and to set up the Duke of *Orleance* in his Place The Count *de Soissons* and the two Brothers of *Vendosme*, were concern'd therein but the Spring of all the Motion in this Machine was the Duke of *Savoy* He was not at all satisfy'd with the Treaty of *Monçon* And as his Mind fed on nothing but Intrigues, he was for revenging himself on the Court of *France*, in putting it into such Confusion, that he might make an Advantage of its Disorders The Abbot *Alexander Scaglia*, his Embassador, and one of his trustiest Ministers, seconded his Intentions to Admiration, and engag'd so many Persons of Quality in his Design, that without an Accident which discover'd the Secret of the Conspirators, the Project was infallible The first Minister was to be kill'd at *Fleury*, where he lodg'd The Count *de Chalais*, whom the others had employ'd, was executed The Abbot *Scaglia*, who knew very well that Cardinal *de Richelieu* would never pardon him, prevail'd with his Master to send him into *England*, where he perswaded the Duke of *Buckingham* to discard all the *French* from the Queen's Service, and was in part the Cause of the military Preparations that were since made there, for those of the Religion in *France*, whom the King of *Great Britain* took into his Protection The Embassador by meddling with so horrible a Conspiracy, exceeded the Bounds of his Function, and violated the *Law of Nations* Cardinal *de Richelieu*, who knew the Abbot had acted nothing, but by his Master's Orders, and that this was not dispos'd to give the King Satisfaction, who on his Part was not in a Condition to go to War with the Duke, would not have fail'd to have satisfy'd himself, and would not have so much consulted the *Law of Nations*, as his own Resentment

It seems as if one might say on this Subject, that there is no Case where the ordinary Justice can extend its Jurisdiction over the publick Ministers, and that with so much the more Assurance, that I find it to be the Sentiment of M *Hugh de Groot* It is what is indisputable in reference to common Offences And as for Crimes of State, where the Embassador violates the *Law of Nations*, and particularly if he attempts the Life of the Prince with whom he resides, the Sovereign alone, or the Council of State on his Part, can take Cognizance thereof, arrest the Traitor in his House, and send him afterwards, with the Informations, to the Prince his Master, that he may punish him We do not find that for above an Age past Princes have proceeded with so much Rigour, but they have been contented to send these dangerous Ministers out of their States It is after this Manner the Kings of *France*, of *England*, and the Republick of *Venice*, have dealt with those Embassadors, who have been convicted of Treasons so black, that the *Law of Nations* could not protect them The most benign Course, the most civil, and I dare say the most necessary, and almost the only one, is to desire the Prince to recall his Minister *Don Alphonso de la Cueva* was the greatest Enemy the Republick of *Venice* had It is to him she is oblig'd for the Scrutiny which calls her Liberty in question, and nothing can be imagin'd more horrible, than the Fire that would have consum'd the Town, the Blood that would have drown'd its Inhabitants, and the Confusion which would have subverted the State, if two *French* Gentlemen had not sav'd the Republick by discovering the Danger to the Senate and yet it chose rather to get him recall'd, than to send him away

The King of *Great Britain* is the First in his Kingdoms, by reason of his Dignity and his Birth, and he deserves likewise to be so, on account of his Goodness and Civility wherefore we must think it was not without Cause, that he sent an Order to *Don Bernardo de Salinas*, Minister of *Spain*, in *March*, 1677, to be gone from his Court in four and twenty Hours, and to depart the Kingdom in twenty Days He acquainted the King of *Spain*, and the Duke *de Vilhermosa*, Governor of the Low Countries, with the Reasons of his Procedure What I have been able to learn of it in the Place where I am, is that the King complains of the Cabals which *Don Bernardo* practis'd against the Repose of his Kingdom and assures him that without that Provocation he had not proceeded to such an Extremity The Duke of *Vilhermosa* made no other Answer to the *English* Resident, who spoke to him about it, Than that he knew not what to say to it, because he had had no Advice of it from *Don Bernardo de Salinas* but that he thought it was a very hasty way of Proceeding with the Minister of a Great Monarch *Don Bernardo* said, he would not go out of *England* without a positive Command to that Purpose from the King his Master, whose Orders he had executed according to his Intention The Divisions of the Court of *Madrid*, and the Disorders of the Low Countries hinder'd the King of *Spain* from shewing his Resentment

I said before, that it is the Sovereign with whom the Minister resides, who ought to secure him that Safety, which the *Law of Nations* and the publick Faith intitle him to, because that after he has admitted the Minister, he enters into a kind of *tacit* Contract, which indispensably obliges him thereto But the Prince who arrests an Embassador in his Dominions, who comes there, or passes through them, without his Leave, does not violate the *Law of Nations* *Anthony Rinçon* and *Cæsar Fregose*, of whom the one was going to *Constantinople*, and the other to *Venice*, on the Part of King *Francis* I, *ris* I, were kill'd upon the *Po*, on which they were embark'd for *Ferrara* The King said, That the Marquiss *du Guast*, Governor of *Milan*, had caus'd them to be taken upon the River That he had tortur'd them, and put them to Death, after he had extorted from them the Secret of their Negotiation He said, The Marquiss had violated the *Law of Nations*, and press'd the Emperor to do Justice for the Murder, unless he would have it believ'd, he intended to break the Truce The Pope, *Paul* III, fearing lest this Accident should break it in effect, or should serve at least for a Pretext to the Rupture, sent into *France William Dandin*, at that time his Secretary, and since a Cardinal, to make some Overtures of an Accommodation But the King still insisted upon having Satisfaction, for the Outrage he said had been done to him by the Death of his Ministers, and in order to have it effectually, he arrested at *Lions George* of *Austria*, Archbishop of *Valencia* in *Spain*, who was the Emperor's natural Unkle, and detain'd him a Prisoner till the Nuncio *Ardinghello*, whom the Pope sent on purpose into *France*, procur'd him his Liberty The Nuncio represented to the King, *That this Prelate (who as Archbishop was the Pope's Subject) had had no Hand in the Affair of* Rinçon*, and that it was not Just to make him suffer for an Evil which he had not committed* The Emperor writing since to the Pope on that Subject, says in his Letter, *That King Francis made use of the Pretext of the Death of* Rinçon *and I* regose, *to make War in Italy, and on the Frontiers of Spain and the Low Countries That they had been, kill'd in* Piedmont, *as they were passing, not with the Retinue of Embassadors, but as Spies That as they did not make themselves known, it was not a thing of Obligation to acknowledge them neither, nor to consider them as publick Ministers* Rinçon had already negotiated and concerted a Treaty at *Constantinople*, and at his Return by *Venice*, he had given an Account to the Senate of the Disposition in which he had found and left the Port, so that the Emperor could not be ignorant of it and *Rinçon* did not think himself so safe under his Quality of Embassador in a strange Countrey, but at his setting out from *Venice* he procur'd a Guard to convoy him to the Frontiers of the State, that he might pass securely into *France* *Paul Jove* said, *Francis* I was in the wrong to complain of the Death of *Rinçon*, as well because he was kill'd in an Enemy's Countrey, as because he had as a Deserter been condemn'd, and banish'd in *Spain* for Contumacy and that for that Reason, he ought not to have appear'd in the Emperor's Territories He moreover says, That *Camille*, *Fregose*'s Lieutenant, and the Watermen, who were to conduct these two Ministers to *Ferrara*, were carry'd to Prison to the Castle of *Cremona*, so that it could not be doubted, that the Governor of *Milan* was the Author of the Assassination This last justify'd himself in a printed Apology, offering to fight all those who should accuse him of so base an Action *Paul Jove* does not justify the Emperor at all *Piedmont* did not belong to him, nor was not an Enemy's Countrey, during the Truce On the other side, if *Rinçon* was a Traytor and Deserter, the Emperor might have as easily secur'd him, as he made him be kill'd, and might have brought him to his Tryal But then again, King *Francis* could not say, that the Emperor had violated the *Law of Nations*, because *Rinçon* and *Fregose* were not publick Ministers in reference to him, yet he violated the *Publick Faith*, by causing to be assassinated those Persons, who ought to have enjoy'd the Benefit of the Truce We must distinguish between the *Law of Nations* and the *Publick Faith*, because they are in effect two very different Things Mary Queen of *Scots*, being compell'd to abdicate, and finding her self still persecuted, made her Escape into *England*, where she remain'd a Prisoner *France*, which stickled very much for her, was also for having a Share in the Direction of the Affairs of *Scotland* and with that Design had concerted with the Ministers, who were on the Part of Queen *Elizabeth* at *Paris*, an Instruction on with which *du Croc* was intrusted, who was sent thither in the Quality of Embassador *Du Croc*, as he pass'd through *England*, making Instances to have Leave to see the Queen, who was a Prisoner It was in the Year 1572, at the Time that *Seton* a *Scotch* Lord, (whom a Storm had oblig'd to land at *Harwich*) having disguis'd himself, had pass'd through *England*, and had flung himself into the Castle of *Edinbourg*, which held out for the Queen of *Scots* This Occurrence, and the Earnestness with which *du Croc* desir'd to see her, made him suspected, so that Queen *Elizabeth* oppos'd this Visit, as well as his continuing his Journey He complain'd thereof as of a Violation of the Law of Nations and Queen *Catherine*, speaking on this Subject to the *English* Embassador, told him, *That it was an unheard of thing, that the Embassador of a Prince who was a Friend, should be arrested in a neutral Countrey* The Queen signify'd to her, That she had sent arrested *du Croc* That he was at Liberty to go and come, and even to return to *France*, but that she had oppos'd his Passage, because she could not consent to his going into *Scotland*, till she had an Answer to what she had caus'd to be represented to the Court of *France*, relating to this Journey That he had been arrested on the Frontiers, by Virtue of the General Orders the Officers of those Parts had, not to let any Body pass without a Passport That the Court of *France* had oblig'd it self to carry on no Negotiation in *Scotland*, without the Participation of *England* Queen *Catherine*, who was not willing to have it believ'd she had any Hand in the Intrigues which were on foot in Favour of the Queen of *Scotland*, for fear the *French Protestants* should find Protection in *England*, hearken'd to the Reason of Queen *Elizabeth*, and acquiesc'd thereto

Henry IV, while he was yet but King of *Navarre*, sent in the Year 1583, *James Segur de Pardaillan*, and *Geoffroy de Calignon*, into *England*, and from thence into *Denmark*, and to the Princes of *Germany*, to endeavour to dispose the Protestants to agree among themselves, on the Points that divided them in the Matter of Religion The Emperor, incens'd to see at the Courts of the Electors, and in the Empire, foreign Embassadors who did not address themselves to him, and who by uniting the Protestants among themselves, weaken'd the Catholick Party, order'd the Duke of *Bavaria*, and Count

Count *de Solms*, to arrest them if they could, as People who fomented Cabals against the publick Quiet *Segur* having Advice thereof, wrote to the Emperor, That being inform'd he was blam'd for entring into the Empire as a publick Minister, without making himself known to him, who was the Head of it, and that it was said he carry'd on Intrigues with some Princes to the Prejudice of the Repose of *Germany*, and against the Dignity of his Imperial Majesty, he thought himself oblig'd to tell him, That he had believ'd he might enter into *Germany* without a Passport, under the Benefit of the Peace the Empire had with *France* That it was by the express Order of the King of *Navarre* his Master, that he had begun his Negotiation with the Electors of *Saxony* and *Brandenburg*, that they might be Witnesses of the Sincerity of his Proceedings, and certify to the Emperor, that there was nothing therein could disturb the Tranquillity of the Empire For the Truth whereof he referr'd himself to those Princes whom he had seen as he pass'd But as *Segur* was somewhat visionary and fanciful, and that the Princes of *Germany* were not much inclin'd to second the Intentions of the King of *Navarre*, who notwithstanding his Zeal for Religion had a great many other Views, the Negotiation of these Embassadors had not the Success which he had promis'd himself, and as they were not safe in *Germany* they did not stay long there, but went home by different Ways The King of *Navarre*, as a King, had the Faculty of sending Embassadors, but yet he had none in any of the other Courts of *Europe*, and had it not been for the Sake of Religion, he had not hazarded these, because he was not consider'd nor treated as a Sovereign in that of *France* The Emperor was of Opinion, that all Embassadors ought to address themselves to him, and no where else, if they would enjoy the Benefit of the *Law of Nations*, and be inviolate People were not at that time sufficiently undeceiv'd of his pretended Sovereignty, and it was upon this Foundation that the Emperor *Charles* V arrested and sent back the Trumpeter *Francis* I had sent to the States of the Empire

It is moreover certain that the Embassador is not inviolable when he commits a Violence, because in that Case the *Law of Nature* is preferable to the *Law of Nations* I do' even then Care should be taken to keep within the Bounds of a lawful and necessary Defence, that is to say, rather to oppose such Violence than offer any One of the Domesticks of *Don Balthasar de la Cueva*, Embassador from *Spain* at *Vienna*, having spoken some insolent Words to the Count *de Kevenhuller*, chief Huntsman to the Emperor in the *Upper Austria*, had for his Reward a good caning The disguis'd *Spaniard* not being able to digest the Affront, made an Agreement with some of the other Domesticks of the Embassador, and attack'd the Count one Night in his Coach, with their Swords and Pistols, and that with so much Heat, that all the Coachman could do (who was himself dangerously wounded) was to drive the Coach across the Entrance of a narrow Street, so that the Count had an Opportunity to get out, and take Shelter in his Mother's House The Uproar brought together several Persons of Quality, who dispers'd the *Spaniards*, yet so, that nine of them got into the Town-House, and there barricaded themselves so strongly, that they could not be forc'd till two of them were disabled Upon the Advice the Embassador receiv'd, that his Men were attack'd in the Town-House, he ran thither in Person, and was preparing to assist them, but the main Guard, which was doubled, oblig'd him to retire The next Day he went in great Fury to the Emperor's Palace, where he made loud Complaints of the Violence which had been done to his Domesticks, and demanded Reparation The Emperor would not see him, so that the Embassador taking into Consideration that he had to do with a strong Party, and that his Procedure had been more violent than judicious, endeavour'd an Accommodation through the Means of the *Confessarius* of the Empress, and found it the more difficult to accomplish, because the Circumstances were not agreed to The Emperor and the Embassador dispatch'd Expresses, who were to carry the Justification and Complaint of the Parties to the Court of *Madrid*, but the Embassador's Courier was arrested at some Leagues Distance from *Vienna* Don *Balthasar* was in the mean time guarded in his House, the Avenues of which were poss'ss'd by forty Musqueteers Wherefore he desir'd the Nuncio to tell the Emperor, That since his Majesty had twice refus'd to give him Audience, he would not ask it of him any more, till he himself offer'd it, unless he presently set his Domesticks at Liberty, and caus'd the Musqueteers (who besieg'd his House) to be taken away They came at last to a Composition, and the Accommodation was concluded The Embassador made his Excuse to the Emperor, and the Count *de Kevenhuller* declar'd, upon his Faith and Conscience, in the Presence of the Embassador, and of some Deputies who were nominated for that Purpose, that he did not know that the Person he had can'd belong'd to the *Spanish* Embassador His Servants were set at Liberty, the Embassador appear'd at Court, and the Count having paid the first Visit to the Embassador, receiv'd also that of his Excellency The Embassador, in permitting his People to commit so great a Violence, did himself by so much the greater Wrong, as he had thereby no longer a Right to complain of that which had been done to one of his Domesticks And by going in Person to succour his Men, he justify'd all that happen'd to him afterwards, and all that the Emperor could do against a Minister, who prostituting his Character himself, ought to expect all the Oppositions that could be made to his Violences That Embassador, who is reduc'd to the Necessity of making Excuses, does no great Honour, neither to his Quality nor to his Master

I have spoken elsewhere of the Civility the *Muscovites* do to foreign Ministers, but when the *Poles* have an Advantage over them, they give themselves mighty Airs Some time after the Czar's Army was defeated before *Smolensko*, the King of *Poland* sent a solemn Embassy into *Muscovy* This *Polish* Embassador oblig'd the *Muscovite Priestaves* to yield him the Precedency every where, and in every Respect. He made his Proposition sitting, and when, at his naming the King his Master, with all his Titles, he perceiv'd the *Boyares* did not uncover themselves, he stopp'd, till the Czar commanded them to take off their Bonnets. The King of *Poland* sent no Present to the Czar, but the Embassador, in his own Particular, made him a Present of a very fine Coach. After he had taken his Audience of Leave, the Czar sent him a very rich Present of Martins, but he would not accept of it, for which Reason they also sent him back his Coach. And the Embassador, who flipp'd no Opportunity of shewing the Contempt he had for the Nation, took from thence an Occasion to fling the Priestave headlong down the Stairs. This was an Affront done to the Czar himself, who had great Reason to resent it against a Minister, who by so insufferable an Insolence render'd himself unworthy of the Protection of the *Law of Nations*. The Embassador had to do with a Nation that does not always respect the Character, but it had been so grievously mortify'd before *Smolensko*, that it was incapable of expressing any Resentment. However, the Czar signify'd to the Embassador, *That he did not know whether it was by his King's Orders he committed these Excesses, or whether it was of his own Motion that he gave himself these Airs. That if the King his Master had order'd him to deal after this outrageous manner with him, he must bear it patiently, till God enabled him to revenge it. That the Event of Battels was in his Hand, and that he might hope it would some Day be favourable to him. But if the Embassador had done it without Orders, he would complain to the King of* Poland, *and demand Justice to be done him*. Want of Power made this Prince act conformably to the *Law of Nations*, which he otherwise would not have done by Reason.

The Duke *Frederick* of *Holstein-Gottorp* had several great Designs, and amongst others, that of settling the Commerce of *Persian* Silks in *Germany*, by the way of *Tartary* and *Muscovy*. To compass his Intention, he sent somewhat above forty Years ago to *Moscow* and *Ispahan*, two Embassadors, the one of which was an Advocate and the other a Merchant, and as they were of different Professions, so likewise were they of quite contrary Humours. During the Stay they made at *Ispahan*, the Merchant-Embassador picking a frivolous Quarrel with one of the Gentlemen of their Retinue, caus'd him to be put in Irons. The Gentleman found the Means to make his Escape, and to fling himself into an Asylum, which the *Persians* call *Alla Capi*. The Embassadors made it their Request to have him surrender'd to them, and said that he had robb'd them. The Schach signify'd to them, *That if what the Embassadors said they had been robb'd of was found upon the Fugitive, it should be restor'd to them, but that it was not in his Power to take the Man out of the Freedom of the Place, not even if he had committed a Crime against his Royal Person*. Brugman (that was the Merchant-Embassador's Name) was so transported with Anger at this Answer, that he said he would have his Domestick, and that he would kill him even if he found him in the Arms of the Schach. He was not contented with giving this Loose to his Passion, but he suborn'd an *Armenian* to persuade the Gentleman to go out of the Asylum by Night, and seek his Safety with the Agent of *Holland*, and, in the mean time, he sent several of his Servants to the Gate of *Alla Capi*, in order to seize him or kill him at his going out. His Collegue did all he could to hinder this Violence, but his Opposition signify'd nothing. So that the Executioners of his Brutishness, finding that the Gentleman did not come out, were preparing to force the Asylum, and to charge the Soldiers who kept Guard there. They made so great a Noise, that the Schach, being waken'd therewith, commanded the Gate of *Alla Capi* to be shut, which was what had not been seen time immemorial. The King was so exasperated at what had happen'd, that as soon as he rose the next Day he told the Lords of his Council, That not being safe in his Palace by reason of the *Germans*, who disturb'd even his Rest, it was requisite that either he or they should leave the City. Brugman did also another thing, which was by so much the more dangerous, because he engag'd therein all the Christians, and had to do with a Prince, who having lost all the Sentiments of Nature to his own Blood, and nearest Relations, would have no great Consideration for the Embassadors of a Duke of *Holstein*. He took the ready way to have the Throats of the whole Embassy cut. And therein the Schach's Resentment would have been by so much the juster, that no Prince is oblig'd to suffer the publick Violence of an Embassador, but he may and ought to oppose the same with the Strength God and Nature has given him, thereby to maintain his Dignity, and protect his Subjects.

I say the same of private Persons, who, notwithstanding the Respect they owe to the Character, may defend themselves against the Embassador that injures them, and repell Violence by Violence. The *Law of Nations* protects a Minister against any Violence that may be offer'd him, but it does not for that authorise his Excesses and Insolences. That Embassador who compels a private Person to measure his Sword with him, makes himself a private Person, and can lay the Blame of the Disgraces that may befall him on these Occasions, on no body but himself, for having had Recourse to Violence for that Protection, which he ought to have found no where but in the *Law of Nations*. *Julius Mazarin*, whom Pope *Urban* VIII employ'd as a publick Minister for the Affairs of *Mantua*, had mediated a Suspension of Arms between the *French* and the *Spaniards*, and thinking himself oblig'd to see it punctually observ'd, he came to high Words with Don *Martin* of *Arragon*, a Camp-Marechal, and Lieutenant General of the Horse, who in Prejudice of the Truce caus'd the Intrenchment that cover'd his Quarter to be reinforc'd. Don *Martin*, who could not brook *Mazarin's* Reproaches, said several very offensive things to him, as well against the Pope as against his Minister, even so far as to tell him, That the Journeys and Negotiations of that Minister had done more Mischief to *Spain* than the Invasion of the *Moors*. *Mazarin* finding himself much injur'd by this Discourse, and remembring still that he had been a Captain under *Torquato Conti*, drew his Sword and attack'd Don *Martin*, who on his part repell'd the Assault with Vigour, insomuch that great Disorder would have ensu'd, had

had not the Duke of *Lerma* and *Piccolomini*, (who came timely in) parted them. They oblig'd *Don Martin* to make Reparation, *not for having drawn his Sword in his own Defence*, but for, what he had spoken offensively of the Pope and his Minister. By this Means *Mazarin* came off Cavalierly enough, but by drawing his Sword first, and forcing *Don Martin* to defend himself, he risqu'd his Character, and expos'd himself to the Hazard of an Affront, for which he could not have demanded Reparation. The *Spaniards* have Expressions which are peculiar to themselves. In that of *Don Martin* there was a great deal of the Hyperbole, but I think one may say at present with a greater Appearance of Truth, what he spoke in the Transport of his Anger. The Acquisition of *Pignerol*, which takes from the *Spaniards* the predominant Power in *Italy*, that of *Sedan*, the Conquest of several important Places in *Flanders*, and in fine, the *Pyrenean* Peace are the Work of *Mazarin*; and I am not afraid to say, that the Treaties of *Portugal* and of *Aix la Chapelle* are Consequences thereof, and that the great Designs which have been executed since, have been form'd upon his Plan. So that what was Hyperbole then, may very well be Truth at this time.

The Embassador ought never to fight in Duel, on any Account whatever. He is paid to serve his Master with his Wit and Tongue, and not with his Sword. Princes make use of their Ministers to argue for their Rights and Interests, but it is the Business of the Generals of their Armies to decide their Quarrels, and to revenge the Injuries which have been done them. The Memoirs relating to Embassadors and publick Ministers, make mention of a Challenge from the Count *de Soissons* to the Lord *Kensington*, since Earl of *Holland*, Embassador from *England* at *Paris*. The Author has therein rely'd on the Credit of the *French* History. But that Lord himself writing to the Duke of *Buckingham*, concerning this Occurrence, complains indeed of the Incivility of the Count *de Soissons*, in the Terms the *French* History takes notice of, but he does not say one single Word of the pretended Duel. On the contrary, he says, That he shew'd no other Resentment thereof, than that he caus'd the Marquiss *de la Valette* to reproach the Count *de Soissons* therewith, to whom the Count made the Answer that is found in the Memoirs. He adds, *That some Days after, the Count* de Lude *having signify'd to him, that he had something to say to him from a great Prince, and that he (not doubting but he brought him a Challenge from the Count* de Soissons*) having caus'd him to enter, the Count* de Lude*, after a very civil Complement, had said nothing else to him, but that the Count* de Soissons *had seen one of his English Horses, which he would be glad to buy if the Embassador would set a Price upon him. That he had made Answer, That if the Count* de Soissons *would do him the Honour to speak to him himself about it, he would willingly make him a Present of it, and without that the Horse should not go out of his Stable.* He moreover says, *That since then the Count* de Soissons *had saluted him very civilly on all Occasions*. I know very well that within some Years, a Minister of the second Order, thinking he had been affronted by an Embassador in one of the Nor-

thern Courts, was for resenting it, and gave the Embassador to understand that he pretended to satisfy himself like a Cavalier: and that the Embassador sent him Word, He should be always ready to give him Satisfaction in an honourable Way. But they must both excuse me, if I say, that it was imprudently enough done on either side. Those cholerick Motions and brisk Actions, partake a little of the Romance. The Embassador may, and indeed ought to be somewhat a Comedian, but he ought never to act the Part of a Stage-Captain.

Before I put an End to this Chapter, I shall touch upon what happen'd within this little while, betwixt a great Prince, and the Embassador of a crown'd Head, in reference to what I observ'd above, *that the Embassador is only inviolable in respect of the Prince with whom he resides*. M *Lelienhouc*, Embassador from the Crown of *Sweden* to the King of *Poland*, had, by Order of the King his Master, publish'd there several Things, which reflected very much on the Reputation of the Elector of *Brandenburg*. This Prince was so highly offended thereat, that he let slip this Expression, *That he would cause* Lelienhouc *to be cudgell'd.* This last complain'd thereof in Writing to the King of *Poland*, where he says, *He will cudgel the Elector*, who, as he asserts, has violated the *Law of Nations*, by threatening a *Characteriz'd Person*. I shall not examine whether there was any Excess in the Resentment of the one or the other, but let us see whether the Elector violated the *Law of Nations*, in threatening the Embassador that resided at the Court of a neutral Prince, and I am not afraid to say, That he did not violate it at all. The Embassador's Master being a declar'd Enemy of the Elector, the Embassador was so likewise, and this not having any Character in reference to the Elector, the Elector was not oblig'd to have any Consideration for him, but might treat him as an Enemy where-ever he met him, without violating the *Law of Nations*. Lelienhouc had a Right to claim the Protection of the King of *Poland*, against the Violence with which he was threaten'd, and it was the Duty of the said King of *Poland*, to secure him Safety at his Court, for which the Elector ought to have a Respect. The Elector in violating this Respect offended the King of *Poland*, and oblig'd him to undertake the Protection of the Embassador who resided with him, and so might have drawn the Arms of *Poland* upon him. But he did not violate the *Law of Nations*: nay he did not so much as violate the publick Safety, in causing Lelienhouc to be cudgell'd, except in reference to the King of *Poland*. So that I think I may conclude, that the Person of an Embassador is not always inviolable.

I have spoken elsewhere of those Embassadors who happen to be in a Countrey, without having Credentials for the Sovereign of the Place: I shall therefore only add here, That such an Embassador can be consider'd but only as a private Person by the said Sovereign. In the Year 1641, an Embassador whom the King of *Portugal* sent into *Holland*, as he pass'd through *England* desir'd to see the King, who made no Difficulty to give him Audience, but he signify'd to him, that he would give it him

C c c c but

but as to a private Person, and that he would not allow him to be cover'd. The Embassador would not accept of the Audience on these Conditions. The King of *Great Britain* was not oblig'd to treat him otherwise. He was ignorant of the Character of this Stranger, who had no Credential Letters for him, and therefore could not insist upon being consider'd as a publick Minister. Those Embassadors who are to pass through the Territories of another Sovereign, ought to be provided either with Credentials or a Passport that may make them known. In the Year 1634 the Count *de Schauenbourg*, who was going to reside in *Spain* on the part of the Emperor, took *France* in his Way, and having Credential Letters for the King, he procur'd himself Audience, and had a fine Present made him. Some Time after *Falconieri*, as he pass'd through *France* to go in the Quality of Nuncio to *Flanders*, ask'd to see the King, who gave him Audience, tho' he had no Letters for him, but it was through the Means of the Nuncio in Ordinary *Bolognetti* (who conducted him to the same) that he obtain'd it. He receiv'd no Present, because he had no Letters.

There is something still more singular in the following Example. *Ferdinand the Catholick* after the Death of his Wife pretended to have the same Share in the Administration of the Affairs of the Kingdom of *Castile*, that he had had during the Queen's Life. *Philip* of *Austria*, his Son-in-Law, oppos'd it, and was for being declar'd King of *Castile*, as being the Husband of the Queen his Wife, who was the undoubted Heir thereof. *Ferdinand* being inform'd that *Philip* was sending *Anthony d'Acugna* to *Rome*, to justify his Right, gave Orders to *Gonçales Hernandes* (who was call'd the Great Captain) to take up this Embassador, either upon the Road, or even at *Rome* it self. They miss'd him, notwithstanding the Lord *de Piombino* had giv'n Notice to *Don Gonçales*, That the Embassador having landed, in passing from *Savona* to *Portohercule*, it was an easie Matter to surprise him. *Don Gonçales* excus'd himself, and said it had been impossible for him to take him on the Road, because that *Prosper Colomne*, who had had those Orders before him, had giv'n Advice thereof to *d'Acugna*, by the Cardinal *Colomne*, who was his intimate Friend, and that the Embassador stood so well upon his Guard at *Rome*, that there was no taking him without an open Violence, and a publick Scandal, which he could not find in his Heart to be guilty of. And in effect the Great Captain by such Violence would have broke with the Pope, who was oblig'd to protect the Embassador, and would have giv'n an abominable Scandal to all those who have any Respect for the *Law of Nations*, which protected *d'Acugna* in the Place of his Residence, in Reference to the Pope

CHAP. XXX.
When the Embassador's Function ceases.

ALtho' I reserve the Function of the Embassador for the Subject of the next Book, yet I think my self oblig'd to inform my Reader at the End of this, how the Embassador ceases to be a Minister. It is certain that the same Causes that put an End to Power, in private Concerns, conclude the Commission of a publick Minister In publick Affairs. The Power of the Embassador ceases, when the Prince who employs him is no longer in a Condition to act, or that He to whom he is employ'd, is no longer in a Capacity to carry on Negotiations with him, that is to say, by the Death of either the one or the other. In the Year 1566 the Emperor *Maximilian* II. sent to *Constantinople*, in the Quality of Embassador, an *Hungarian* Lord, who hearing of the Death of *Soliman*, to whom he had been sent, did not proceed in his Journey, but return'd home. On his Way he met *Selim, Soliman's* second Son and his Successor He spoke to the First Vizir *Mehemet*, and desir'd to pay his Respects to the *Grand Seignior* But the First Vizir told him, That since the Emperor his Master had sent him to *Soliman*, who was no longer in Being, he could not negotiate with *Selim*, for whom he had no Letters That he would give him Leave to see the *Grand Seignior*, but he should not speak to him, and that if *Maximilian* had any thing to communicate to him, he might either send another Embassador, or else other Credentials to him to whom he spoke *John Mocenigo* was Embassador of *Venice* in *France*, at the Time that Henry III was kill'd, and notwithstanding, according to the Laws of the Kingdom, *France* is never without a King, because the dead one gives Seizin to the Living, as I have elsewhere observ'd, and that the next Prince of the Blood succeeds immediately, nevertheless the Embassador remain'd without Function and Character. On the other side, *de Maisse Hurault*, who was Embassador of *France* at *Venice*, was in the same Condition, till the Senate had provided in that Case. The said Senate unanimously resolv'd, that the King of *Navarre* should be acknowledg'd for King of *France*, and signify'd at the same Time to *M. de Maisse*, that he might continue to discharge his Office, and that he should be consider'd as he was in the deceased King's Time, till he could procure himself other Credentials. It may be said that the Republick made a *French* Embassador on this Occasion, which she would have been very cautious of doing at another Juncture. But it was sensible it would thereby oblige *Henry* IV by acknowledging him for King of *France* in the Person of his Minister, as she sent at the same Time Orders to *Mocenigo*, to continue to discharge his Function with *Henry* IV. This Action was of so great Importance, that the Pope us'd his utmost Efforts to hinder the Senate from taking this Resolution, and the King of *Spain*, who for the Space of eighteen Years had had no Embassador at *Venice*, sent one thither on the same Account. The Pope even made use of Threats, if the Republick acknowledg'd a King whom the Holy See had condemn'd and excommunicated as an Heretick. In the Year 1621 *Bassompierre* was sent to *Madrid* about the Affair of the *Valtelin*. He was hardly come thither but the King fell sick and dy'd. He had Letters of Credence for *Philip* III, but the Ministers of *Philip* IV did not scruple to have Conferences with him as well as with *du Farges* Embassador in Ordinary from *France*, tho' according to Rule fresh Credentials were necessary both to the one and the other under this Pretext, which was not only specious, but also lawful, the *Spaniards* might have spun Things out in Length, but they chose rather to make a Treaty which they had no mind to execute, than to stick out by refusing to negotiate with Ministers who had neither Letters nor Powers

The Power of the Embassador ceases also when he is recall'd, and when he has gone through the Time of his Service. That of Embassadors in Ordinary is almost every where regulated to three Years, yet for all that it is not lawful for an Embassador to depart from a Court where he resides without an express Order, or the Leave of his Prince. At *Venice* they are so punctual in this, that an Embassador is not allow'd to depart from the Court where he resides, till his Successor be arriv'd; which is another Proof of the consummate and imitable Prudence of this Republick, which by obliging the Embassador to instruct his Successor in the State of the Affairs of the Court where he is to negotiate, and to put into his Hands all the Memoirs of his Embassy, shews that in the Change of the Persons, there is no Change in the Procedure and Genius, no more than in the Maxims and Conduct of the Senate, or in the Form of their Government. An Embassador of *Venice*, who at the Expiration of the Years of his Service should quit his Post without expecting his Successor, would be consider'd and punish'd as a Deserter, as much as if he had abandon'd it in the middle of his Time All Republicks are not so nice as this is. In the Year 1647, the States of the United Provinces sent an Order to the Embassadors Plenipotentiaries who were on their Part at *Munster*, not to leave the Place, yet nevertheless three of them without any Regard thereto went away. They had Interest enough in their Provinces, to get their Disobedience approv'd by the States General, and to procure their being sent back to the Congress. They had before them the Example of another Embassador of the same Country, who being employ'd to the Northern Kings, and being tir'd with his Business, left it on the sudden, and went home. I believe that besides these Examples few others will be found. The Republick of *Venice* would punish with the last Severity so shameful a Desertion, and a Monarch would never pardon so horrible a Contempt. There are in *Holland* Persons very capable of Negotiation, but then they are not in any great Number, and as there is no Law that obliges those who have any Share in the Government of the State to take upon them

this sort of Employment, they accept of it for the most part but upon Condition to leave it when they please, and they remain in it, in effect, no longer than they find it for their Purpose

There are no such Stipulations made with Princes. Their Minister is oblig'd to remain in his Post till they send to relieve him, or give him Leave to quit it. *Mortfontaine Hotman*, Embassador from *France* to the Cantons, seeing in the Year 1598 that the King his Master was likely to lose those important and necessary Allies, unless they were speedily satisfy'd, resolv'd to go himself to Court, without waiting for the King's Permission. The Council look'd upon this as a very ill Action, and said, *That an Embassador that left his Employment but for a Moment, was not less criminal than a Centinel that abandon'd his Post*. The King said, on the contrary, *That Regard should be had to the Intention of the Embassador, and to the dangerous State the Alliance was in*. It was also consider'd that *Mortfontaine*'s Journey hinder'd the Cantons from sending their Embassadors to Court, which would have found it harder to content them, after they had been at the Expence of the Journey, than the Embassador did, who at his Return satisfy'd them with a very reasonable Sum

The Marquis *de Fontenay Mareuil* succeeding in the Embassy of *Rome* to the Mareschal d'*Estrée*, had Orders to negotiate chiefly the Reception of the *Portugal* Embassador, and the Accommodation of the Difference the Duke of *Parma* had with the *Barberins* concerning the Dutchy of *Castro*. He did not succeed either in the one or the other, and was vex'd at the Court of *Rome*, because the Pope had annull'd what the General Chapter of the *Jacobins* had done at *Genoa*, where Father *Mazarin*, the Cardinal's Brother, had been elected General of the Order. The Mortification he receiv'd therefrom made him *leave Rome and retire into the Countrey*. The Court of *France* was very angry thereat, it express'd indeed to the Nuncio its Concern at the Pope's Procedure, but that did not hinder it from having still more at the Embassador's, whom the King commanded to return to his Function at *Rome*. However, that this might be done with some Reputation to the Crown, and to the Embassador himself, it was agreed to accept the Offer *Justinian*, Embassador of *Venice*, made, of the Mediation of the Republick. It did employ its good Offices tho' with some Reluctancy, as well because it had only a Resident at *Rome*, where a Matter of this Importance could not be negotiated by a Minister of the second Order, as because it was not satisfy'd with the Offer, its Embassador had made without its Participation. At last however, she approv'd of the Office of *Justinian*, and her Mediation produc'd a very good Effect. At *Rome* they maintain'd that they were not oblig'd to give Satisfaction to *M de Fontenay*, because as he retur'd without Orders, and contrary to the King's Intention, his Majesty's Reputation was not concern'd therein Nevertheless, to give him some Satisfaction in Appearance, the Pope contented Father *Mazarin*, by making him Master of the sacred Palace. The Embassador who knew the Cardinal would not have it believ'd that he and his

his Brother had any Share in thefe Difcontents, thank'd Cardinal *Barbarin* for the new Dignity with which the Fryar had been honour'd, and fignify'd to him, that in a few Days he would return to *Rome*, to continue there the Functions of his Embaffy.

An Embaffador may go from his Poft when in his Perfon the Prince whom he reprefents is injur'd, fo that he is oblig'd to fhew his Refentment, and to demand Reparation. The Marefchal *d'Eftrée*, and the Duke of *Crequy* Embaffadors of *France* at *Rome*, both left that Court, but on very different Accounts, as well as with different Succefs. The Marefchal protected his Gentleman of the Horfe, who in breaking the Chain of the Galley Slaves, had violated the publick Juftice and Safety. They who were Depofitaries of the Sovereign Authority at *Rome*, caus'd the Gentleman of the Horfe to be kill'd, and fet his Head upon the Bridge of St *Angelo* among thofe of other Criminals and Banditti. A greater Affront could not be offer'd to the Embaffador, but forafmuch as he had drawn it upon himfelf, by protecting a Domeftick, whom he ought to have punifh'd or convey'd away, he receiv'd no manner of Satisfaction therefore. The King his Mafter did not refent it, and was fo far from approving what he had done, that the *Barberins* had the Satisfaction to fee him recall'd at their Suit. The Duke de *Crequy*, on the contrary, was highly protected, becaufe the Difference he had with the *Ghify* did not deferve that fo cruel an Outrage fhould be offer'd him, in the Perfon of the Embaffadrix his Lady. The King's Dignity was injur'd thereby, fo that he could not continue to execute the Functions of his Employment, without a Reparation proportionate to the Affront he had receiv'd, and unlefs the King his Mafter had Satisfaction made him, who was much more concern'd therein than himfelf. This was what he could not expect from the Pope's Relations, and as the King was to fend him his Orders thereupon, he immediately went out of the Ecclefiaftical State, and did not return to *Rome*, till after the Treaty of *Pifa* had regulated the publick Reparation the Pope was to make to the King, the Embaffador, and his Lady.

The Prince who has Reafon to be fatisfy'd with the Conduct of his Embaffador, fhews it by continuing his Employment to him after the Expiration of the ordinary Time. In *Holland*, where all the Subjects are not very fit for this fort of Employment, (I fpeak of thofe who have a Share in the Management of Affairs,) becaufe fome want Ability, and others have not that commendable Ambition, which almoft every where elfe caufes thefe glorious Pofts to be fought after, they are for the moft part continu'd to thofe that have them, and know how to find their own Intereft therein, by making fome Benefit thereof.

Thofe Princes who recal their Minifters before the Time of their Service is expir'd, either do it of their own mere Motion, becaufe they are not fatisfy'd with them, or elfe to advance them to other Employments, or at the Requeft of thofe Princes with whom they refide. M *Deftampes*, Brother to the Cardinal *de Valencay*, and to the Archbifhop of *Rheims*, and Embaffador from *France* in *Holland*, was recall'd abruptly enough, becaufe he had not negotiated according to the Intention of the firft Minifter. M *de Pompone* was remov'd from the Embaffy in *Holland*, to be employ'd in *Sweden*, where he was more neceffary, and he did not leave that Court, but to take Poffeffion of the Place of Secretary of State. M *Peter de Groot* was Embaffador from the United Provinces in *Sweden*, where his Service was fo ufeful, that by continuing him in his Employment, they might have affur'd themfelves of the Friendfhip of that Crown, and yet they recall'd him, to fend him into *France*, where he was altogether ufelefs, becaufe that Court had taken Meafures with the King of *England* to make War with the States. *Blainville* was recall'd for no other Reafon but becaufe he was not acceptable to the King of *England*, and his Humour was look'd upon to be fomewhat harfh and untractable, and not fit for Negotiation.

That Prince who obliges a Minifter to depart from his Court, do's indeed put an End to the Function of his Employment, but do's not thereby take away his Character. I hat Embaffador of *Portugal*, whom we have fpoken of elfewhere, to whom the States of the United Provinces notify'd, That they no longer acknowledg'd him for an Embaffador, and that they would have no more Conferences with him, made a very wife Anfwer in telling them, *That the one depended on the States, but that the other depended intirely on the King his Mafter only. That it was he who had giv'n him the Character, and that none but he could take it from him, and that it was into his Hands he would furrender it*.

Princes fometimes oblige Minifters to go part out of their States, and caufe them to be carry'd away by main Force. Queen *Elizabeth* caus'd *Don Bernardin de Mendoffe*, Embaffador from *Spain*, and the Bifhop of *Roffe*, Embaffador from the Queen of *Scots*, to be put on Shipboard, but then both of them had carry'd on Intrigues againft her Life, and againft the Tranquillity of her State. The Nuncio whom the prefent King of *France* caus'd to be guarded to the *Frontiers* of *Savoy*, felt the firft Effects of the King's juft Indignation at the violent Procedure of the Pope's Relations. The King of *Portugal* not being able to get his Minifters admitted at the Court of *Rome*, would no longer fuffer the Pope's Minifter in his Dominions, from whence the Holy See however drew its ufual Revenues. Having therefore fent for the Vicecollector towards the End of the Year 1646, he told him, That fince the Pope would not acknowledge him for what the whole Kingdom had made him, that is to fay, for King of *Portugal*, he was not oblig'd neither to fuffer a Minifter of *Rome* to refide at his Court. That he (the Vicecollector) was more capable than any other to inform his Holinefs of the true State of the Churches of *Portugal*, and of the Neceffity to provide them with Paftors. That whenever his Holinefs would admit his Minifters, he fhould be alfo ready to receive thofe of *Rome* with open Arms, and that it would be with Pleafure he fhould fee the Vicecollector return with the Quality of Nuncio. That he had giv'n the neceffary Orders for the Convenien cy of his Voyage, and that there was a Ship ready to tranfport him to *Italy* He was forc'd to go on Board the Night following, and be gone. It was six Years that his Ministers had been refus'd Admittance at *Rome*, for which Reason he was not oblig'd to respect those of the Pope. In the Year 1659, under the Ministry of Cardinal *Mazarin*, *the Resident of* Brandenburg *receiv'd a Message to depart the Kingdom with his Family*. Some Days after, he was permitted to continue there a Month longer, and to this Purpose a Passport was drawn in Form for him, sign'd *le Terrier*. But before the Term was expir'd he was sent to the *Bastile*, and, at the end of some Weeks, he was taken from thence to be conducted to *Calais*, and there shipp'd off. Princes do not treat Ministers after this manner, (unless they have been offended by their Masters) if they have any Consideration for the one and the other. The Cardinal was afterwards sorry he had treated with so much Rigour a Minister, of whom he had no Reason to complain, and he shew'd it by offering him very great Advantages, to invite him to return to *France*.

The Minister is not always oblig'd to retire when he is given to understand that his Person is not agreeable. The Prince that is for having him withdraw, ought to apply to the Master of the Embassador, and procure him to be recall'd, because the Minister cannot leave his Post, but by his Orders who plac'd him there. *Ferdinand the Catholick* having got the County of *Roussillon* out of the Hands of *Charles* VIII, was moreover for hindering him from going into *Italy*, to attempt the Conquest of the Kingdom of *Naples*. He sent to him for this Purpose *Don Alfonso de Silva* (Brother to the Count *de Cifuentes*) who made himself so disagreeable by his continual Remonstrances, that the King signify'd to him, That he might be gone as soon as he pleas'd. This was dismissing him in very intelligible Terms: But *Don Alphonso* reply'd, That he thought he was negotiating with a Prince, who was Brother and Ally to the King his Master, whose Affairs he sollicited, without which he would instantly depart. That if the King of *France* would notify his Intentions to the King his Master, either by his Means, or by an Express, he might do it, but as for himself he should stay till farther Orders. He stay'd in effect, and follow'd the King into *Italy*, till finding a thousand Indignities were put upon him, and apprehending still greater Insults, after he had been warn'd to depart the Court, he retir'd to *Genoa*, giving *Charles* to understand, before he set out, that *Ferdinand* could not avoid sending to the Pope the Assistance he desir'd. The Archbishop of *Embrun*, Embassador of *France* at *Madrid*, being in the Month of *October*, 1662, in the King of *Spain*'s Antichamber, enter'd into a Discourse with a *Spanish* Lord, who was very well at Court, concerning the Affairs of *Portugal*, and as *M. d'Embrun* had a great deal of Zeal and Warmth, he was not contented to say, That the King his Master would employ the whole Strength of his Kingdom to oppose the Conquest of *Portugal*, but he had also the Assurance to maintain it in the Presence of the King of *Spain*, insomuch that he was commanded to depart the Court. The Embassador reply'd, That he would retire when he should receive the King his Master's Orders for that Purpose, and not before. The King of *Spain* complain'd thereof, and desir'd the King his Son-in-law to recall his Embassador, because he had on another Occasion talk'd very high, for being refus'd the Surrender of a *French* Cordelier, who, as it was said, carry'd on Intrigues against the King's Service. But the Complaints of the Marquiss *de Fuentes* were eluded, and the King maintain'd his Minister. He said that the *Spaniards* had not well understood the Embassador's *French*, or that this last had not well express'd himself in *Spanish*. However after that, in the Year 1667, the same King had enter'd into the Low Countries, the Queen-Regent of *Spain* sent Orders to the said Archbishop to be gone, and would not suffer him to wait in *Madrid*, for the Letters the first Courier was to bring him. All he could obtain was leave to wait for them at *Alcala*. He receiv'd them there, with Orders from the King to leave the Court of *Spain*, as soon as he should have receiv'd the Passports that were necessary for his safe travelling.

Hostilities also determine Embassies. The *Law of Nations* is not violated in the Person of the Minister of a Prince, who breaks with him, with whom such Minister resides, because that after a Declaration, and an open War, the Minister of the Prince that is an Enemy becomes an Enemy likewise, and can no longer enjoy the publick Safety. But whether the Master of the Minister, or the Prince with whom the Minister resides, makes the Rupture or declares War, the Minister ought always to have leisure to retire. If it be the Embassador's Master that is going to declare the War, or break without a previous Declaration, he ought to give his Minister notice thereof, and recall him in time. As on the other side, if the Prince with whom he resides declares it, the Minister ought to enjoy the Protection of the *Law of Nations*, till he be got out of his Dominions. The Republick of *Venice*, the Great Duke of *Tuscany*, and the Duke of *Modena*, having in the Year 1643 made a League to procure the Restitution of the Dutchy of *Castro* to the Duke of *Parma*, the Senate order'd Secretary *Bon*, who did the Business of the Republick at *Rome*, to retire, and the Great Duke sent the like Order to *Nicolini*, his Embassador. The *Spanish* Cardinals, who would have been glad to have lent a Hand to an Accommodation, would have prevail'd with *Nicolini* to have staid, but he told them, *He had his Orders, and withall, that he would not expose himself to the Affronts he might be lyable to after the Rupture*. Princes sometimes however permit the Minister of an Enemy to remain with them, notwithstanding the Rupture, but that is for the most part done against Reason, and contrary to the Rules of Prudence. After the first Rupture with the *English*, in the Year 1665, the Embassador of the United Provinces remain'd still at *London*, and the Minister of the King of *England* continu'd at the *Hague*, but with very bad Success. The States had the Mortification to see the Embassador's Secretary taken up, and to find themselves in a manner necessitated to take up the Secretary of the *English* Minister. They both recall'd their respective Ministers, after they had both violated the *Law of Nations*. Upon the last Rupture

Rupture the States left again a Minister at *London*, and one at *Paris*, but with very little Advantage, and if at present they have still one at *Stockholm*, it is because the United Provinces treat the King of *Sweden* as an Enemy, but only on account that he is so to their Allies, and not properly theirs. I cannot comprehend why they left a Minister at *Paris*, in a Court that is so jealous of all Correspondences, that even in the Height of Peace, it causes all Letters to be open'd, that are, but the least suspected, and so that Minister who could not do the least Service, only augmented the Jealousy was conceiv'd at his Stay, because he could not give the least Advice, but he expos'd himself to an inevitable Affront.

To prevent all these Vexations, those Princes that are regular in their Conduct, recall their Embassador when they are upon the Point of a Rupture, or immediately after, as I just now said. After the Emperor, the King of *Spain*, the Republick of *Venice*, and the Duke of *Milan* had concluded their League against *Charles* VIII, the Senate told *Philip de Commines*, the French Embassador, That it had order'd *Dominick Trevisan*, and *Dominick Lorisdan*, Embassadors on the part of the Republick to *Charles* at *Naples*, to return Home, because it was going to break with the King. In the Year 1646, the King of *France* sent twelve Men of War, to the Assistance of the Republick, under the Conduct of the Commandor *de Nenschaise*. He was order'd to set up the Standard of St *Mark* as soon as he should reach the Isle of *Corfou*, lest appearing in the *Venetian* Fleet under the French Colours, the *Turks* should take there-from an Occasion of Rupture. Nevertheless as it was well known, that the *Venetians* themselves would be glad that the *Turks* should be inform'd of the French Succours, thereby to oblige 'em to shew some Resentment, which might engage the French also, the King sent Orders to his Embassador, *That if he thought those Barbarians would offer any Affront to him, or that he did not look upon himself to be in Safety at* Constantinople, *to steal away as well as he could, and try to make his Escape to* France. There are but few Examples, where Princes have been forc'd to send such Orders to their Ministers, and have done it, except in reference to the *Turks*. Some have retur'd without waiting for their Master's Orders, because their Uneasiness would not permit them to do it, as *Don Alphonso de la Cueva*, after the Treason at *Venice* was discover'd, in which he had had so great a Hand that he had Reason to dread the People's Resentment. It is very probable that for the Time to come, those Princes who shall send their Ministers to the *Hague*, will take the same Precautions for their Safety, as being necessary.

All that has been hitherto said ought chiefly to be apply'd, to Embassies in Ordinary, since the Extraordinaries end with the Negotiation of the Affair, that is the Subject of the Embassador's Employment. Examples hereof are to be found every where, and therein may be observ'd, that most of 'em have been of short Duration, nay there are some, the Affairs whereof have been regulated in less than four and twenty Hours. *Philip de Commines* relates, that *Lewis* XI, judging that he ought to make an Advantage of the War, *Charles* Duke of *Burgundy*, was engag'd in against the People of *Liege*, and that in the mean time he might safely attack the Duke of *Brittany*, who had been one of the chief Actors in the War for the publick Good, sent the Cardinal *de Balue* and the Constable St *Pol* to *Charles*. These Embassadors told the Duke of *Burgundy*, That the People of *Liege* being compris'd in the Treaty the King their Master had made with the Duke, he could not make War against them without violating the Peace, unless he also suffer'd the King to make War against the Duke of *Brittain*. That the King would abandon the People of *Liege*, if the Duke would abandon the *Britton Charles* made Answer, That the War he made with the *Liegese*, was Defensive in respect to him. That they had broke the Treaty, for the Observation of which they had given him three Hundred Hostages, and that he cou'd not suffer the King to make War with the Duke of *Brittain*, who was his Ally. *These Embassadors did their Business, and were dispatch'd in a very few Hours.* *Charles* told them when he dismiss'd them, that he was going to give Battel to the *Liegese*, that if he was defeated the King might do as he thought fit in reference to the Duke of *Brittain*, but if he return'd victorious, the King would do well to let the *Britton* alone. This was not the Maxim of *Schach Abas*, King of *Persia*, who said that in dispatching Embassadors with so much Precipitation, they were not treated like Ministers, but like Couriers. The Duke follow'd that of our Lord of *Argentos*, who is of Opinion, that the Embassadors either of declar'd or secret Enemies ought to be quickly dismiss'd.

When the late King of *England* sent the Order of the Garter to Prince *Henry* of *Nassau*, the Resident who was on his Part with the States of the United Provinces, had a Commission to assist at the Ceremony in the Quality of Embassador Extraordinary, as accordingly he did, but he laid down the Character the same Day. In the same manner the two Bishops, that assisted at the Marriage of *Uladislas* King of *Poland*, as Embassadors of the Dukes of *Neubourg* and of *Mantua*, had the Character but for that Day. After the Peace of *Verum*, the Arch-Duke sent to *Paris* the Duke *d'Arescbot*, the *Admirant of Arragon*, the President *Richardot*, the Count *d'Aremberg*, Don *Lewis de Velasco*, and the Auditor *Verreycken*, to see the Execution and Observation of the Treaty sworn to. Immediately after the Ceremonies *Richardot* and *Verreycken* return'd to *Brussels*, and the other four remain'd at *Paris*, but their Character of Embassador ceas'd, and they were no longer consider'd but as Hostages for the Restitution of those Places which the King of *Spain* held still in *France*.

A Prince may recall his Minister when he pleases, and the Prince with whom the Minister resides, may also make Instances to have him recall'd, when his Conduct is suspected by him or is not agreeable to him. But a Prince who is not the Master of the Minister, and who is nothing to negotiate with him, cannot oblige the Prince that employs him to recall him, without incroaching upon his Sovereignty, and without arrogating to himself in a foreign Court,

Court, an Authority that does not belong to him *John Francis Belletsa*, Senator of *Turin*, did the Business of the Duke of *Savoy* at *Munster*, in conjunction with the Marquiss of *St. Germain*, not as Embassador, but as a subaltern Minister. He was disagreeable at the Court of *France*, because they had Advice there, that he intended to bring the Affair of *Pignerol* upon the Stage for which Reason it press'd the Dutchess Regent of *Savoy* to recall him. She was very much offended thereat, as a thing that concern'd the Sovereignty of the Prince her Son, which she said was deposited with her during her Regency, and the Minority of the Prince. The Marquiss *de Pianezza*, Chief Minister of the Court of *Turin*, told the Marquiss *du Plessis Pralin*, who commanded the Arms of *France* in *Italy*, that the Dutchess would sooner see her self reduc'd to the last Extremity, than suffer this Impair to be made in the Sovereignty of the Prince her Son. The Queen Regent of *France*, and Cardinal *Mazarin*, pass'd over all these Considerations, and recall'd the *Sieur d'Asguebonne*, Embassador of *France* at *Turin*, and refus'd to give Audience to the Abbot *de Veruë*, Embassador from *Savoy*. The Dutchess had a *French* Army in the Heart of her Countrey, and the Cardinal to intimidate her still more, spread a Rumour that more Troops were marching thither. The Abbot gave Advice thereof by an Express, and so throughly alarm'd the Dutchess, that to avoid coming to a Rupture with *France*, she at last resolv'd to recall *Belletsa*. However, that this might be done with some Reputation to her self and him, she made use of the Pretext of the Embassy of *Poland*, whither she sent him to complement King *Uladislas* upon his Marriage with the Princess of *Mantua*. No Prince will ever attempt to imitate this Action, but he will be willing that the whole Universe should know, he has no great Consideration for him, whom he obliges to do an Action so unworthy of a Sovereign.

The Embassador surrenders his Character into the Hands of him who gave it him, at his Return from his Embassy. In the Year 1645, the States of the United Provinces gave *d'Avaux* and *Servien* to understand, that they were surpris'd, that in their Commission of Plenipotentiaries, the King should give them the Quality of Embassadors, to the Prejudice of what had been concerted with the *Spaniards*, that on all sides only that of Plenipotentiary should be made use of. The Ministers of *France* said, They were no less amaz'd at the Remark the States made thereon; and that they were ignorant of what the States had agreed upon with the *Spaniards*. That the same Quality of Embassador was in the Powers they had communicated at the *Hague*, where no Notice had been taken thereof. *That since they had that Quality when they were in Holland, they could not lay it down, till they surrender'd it into the Hands of the King, at their Return to France.* I have spoken elsewhere of *Don Antonio de Sousa de Macedo*, and of the Answer he made the same States. That is so great a Truth, that even if there had been an open War declar'd between the King of *Portugal* and the States, and that *Don Antonio* had been taken upon the Sea before he arriv'd at *Lisbon*, he could not have been declar'd a good Prize.

Ancient History makes mention of a *Roman*, who being arriv'd at *Rome*, at his Return from his Embassy, was kill'd before he had made his Report. The Murderer said, he had not violated the *Law of Nations* in killing a Man, who being return'd from his Embassy, could no longer be consider'd as an Embassador, and that as he was otherwise the Son of an Outlaw, he might be kill'd with Impunity. The Murderer was condemn'd as a Violator of the *Law of Nations*, because the Embassador ought to be in Safety, and in the Protection of the *Law of Nations*, till such Time as he has made his Report, and is discharg'd of the Embassy. However I am of Opinion they ought to have distinguish'd on this Occasion between the *Publick Safety* and the *Law of Nations*.

But as we shall speak more particularly of the Report, in the second Part of this Treatile, I shall only say here, That the Embassadors whom the United Provinces employ, take their Seat in the Assembly of the States General, that they may have the Quality of Deputy to the Assembly, which represents the whole Union and they are consider'd as such, till they have sworn to their Commission. After that they are no longer consider'd but as Ministers of the State, and they have no Seat in the Assembly. Even at their Return, when they make a Report of their Embassy, they are seated out of Rank, behind the other Deputies of which the Assembly is compos'd. It is true that when *M. de Groot*, who was Embassador in *France*, came to the *Hague* in the Year 1671, to inform the State of the Preparations which were making in *France*, and of the Designs that were forming there against the United Provinces, he was allow'd to take his usual Place in the Assembly of the States General, but it was by express Order of the States of *Holland*, his Sovereigns, who can depute thither whom they please extraordinarily, not only by virtue of Credential Letters, but also by the Mouth of the other Deputies of the same Province. But then he did not make a Report of his Embassy, but only gave there Information of some Particulars which it concern'd the State to know. Those of whom the Republick of *Venice* makes use in the like Employments, have the Quality of Sages but they have no Share in the Government, and even at their Return from their Embassy, they cannot be admitted therein till after a fresh Balloting.

Queen *Christina* of *Sweden* had acknowledg'd the King of *Portugal*, and had made an Allyance with him. She had acknowledg'd his Minister, and had done him Honour at the Ceremonies of her Coronation. Nevertheless some Days before her Abdication, she bethought her self of commanding the Master of the Ceremonies to go to *Anthony de Silva* and *Sousa*, Resident of *Portugal*, with a seal'd Letter, and Orders not to open it but in the Presence of the Resident to read it to him, and to bring back the Original to her, leaving him a Copy thereof if he desir'd one. This Letter contain'd, That as the Queen acknowledg'd no other King of *Portugal* than *Philip* IV. King of *Spain*, she signify'd to the Resident of the Duke of *Braganza*, pre-

pretended King of *Portugal*, that his Employment being of no Utility at that Court, he might retire as soon as he pleas'd, because for the future his Master should be consider'd there but as an Usurper However, that since the Resident was come into *Sweden* under the *Publick Faith, she would see that he enjoy'd the inviolable Protection of the Law of Nations* The Resident notwithstanding this remain'd at *Stockholm*, enjoy'd the aforesaid Protection effectually, and was restor'd to the Function of his Employment under the Reign of *Charles Gustavus* It did not belong to the Queen to take away his Quality, no more than it is in the Power of a Presidial Court to take away the Character which the Resident of the Duke of *Lunenburg* has from a foreign Sovereign Power, that continues it to him, and who alone can dispose of the Character of his Minister

The Embassador that goes from a Court where he leaves some Satisfaction of his Conduct, receives Marks thereof at his Departure, and after he has taken his Audience of Leave, he is presented according to the Esteem is had of his Merit, or the Consideration the Prince his Master is in, and sometimes also according to the Importance of the Affair that is the Subject of his Embassy There are some Courts where some Civility is done to the Embassador when he goes away, but it is now but rarely done At the *Hague* he is conducted to the same Place where he was receiv'd In *England* they have Barges order'd them, which carry them on Board the Ship appointed for their Transportation but in the Execution of all this there is little or no Ceremony us'd

It is a great Point that of the Presents, because the Republick of *Venice* takes it for a great Affront if her Embassador is not presented, and the United Provinces forbid their Embassadors taking any under the Penalty of Disgrace In the Year 1603 *Priuly*, Embassador from *Venice* at *Turin*, not being very well with the Duke of *Savoy*, on account of some Jealousy of Women, could not obtain his Audience of Leave, and was oblig'd to go away without a Present The Senate was so angry thereat, that when the Nuncio offer'd to intermeddle in the Accommodation of their Difference, the Republick insisted upon three Things That the Duke should send first an Embassador to *Venice*. That he should settle the Rank between the Princes his Children and the Embassadors of the Republick, and in the third Place, *That he should send to Priuly the Present that was due to him as Embassador of* Venice The same Senate judging that it was none of his Province to abolish a Custom which obtains in all the Courts of the World, and that its Embassadors ought not to refuse the Honour that other Princes do to those who represent the Republick, has esteem'd, on the other side, that the Present which is made them, as to its Ministers, ought not to be converted to their own private Advantage, and has ordain'd therefore, that the Present they shall receive shall be brought to the Senate; to be dispos'd of as it shall think fit. The Embassadors do so, and altho' generally speaking the Senate restores it to them, it does not always do it, but it always gives them to understand, that it is to their Sovereign they are oblig'd for it, more than to the foreign Potentate In the Year 1530 the Republick sent to Pope *Clement* VII, and to the Emperor *Charles* V six of its chiefest Senators, who assisted at the Coronation of *Charles*, after they had made their Complement on the Place, these two Princes had just concluded between themselves, which was properly the Subject of their Embassy At their Departure *the Emperor made them a Present of five hundred* Portugal *Doubles, of the Value of ten Crowns each but the Senate caus'd them to be put into the Treasury of St* Mark, *to be employ'd in the Service* of the Republick The Emperor return'd the Civility of this Embassy with another, compos'd of three of his Counsellors, who were very well receiv'd at *Venice, and presented each with a Gold Cup of the Value of a thousand Crowns*

In most of the Courts of *Europe* a particular Honour is done to the Embassadors of *Venice*. For if it be their first Embassy, they are ask'd, whether they will be made Knights In *France* this Order is call'd *l'Accollade*, and the King confers it on the Embassador in a private Audience, after he has taken his Leave publickly It is done without Ceremony, one of the first *Valets de Chamber* or of the Wardrobe lays a Cushion at the King's Feet, on which the Embassador kneels down The King draws his Sword, makes him a Knight, and gives him at the same time a Sword, and a Shoulder Belt The Pope do's it also sometimes and thereupon happen'd a remarkable Occurrence enough in the Year 1601 The Pope *Clement* VIII, having confer'd Knighthood on the Embassadors of *Venice*, the Ordinary and the Extraordinary, it appear'd the one of them *John Mocenigo* had already been Knighted by King *Henry* IV There were some who said, That it was a Thing without Precedent, and that perhaps the Pope had done it designedly, because he look'd upon what the King had done before his Absolution to be null But others said on the contrary, that when *Mocenigo* understood that the Pope intended to Knight him, he had said he was one already by the Hand of the King of *France* But the Affair being put under Examination, it was alledg'd that Pope *Sixtus* V had confer'd Knighthood on the four Embassadors of Obedience whom the Republick had sent to him, notwithstanding *Foscarini*, who was one of the Number, had already been Knighted at *Venice* by King *Henry* III who was lodg'd at his House, so that it was concluded that the Pope's Knighthood was not inconsistent with that of the other Christian Princes, because they have no Competition with his Holiness

In the Year 1646 *John Tiepolo* went on the part of the Republick into *Poland*, to endeavour to persuade the King to break with the *Turk*, in order to make a Diversion in Favour of the Isle of *Candia*. The King *Uladislas* had rais'd some foreign Troops, under Pretext of the necessary Defence of the Frontiers of his Kingdom, but with a Design to break with the *Turk*, and to engage *Poland* in an offensive War So that *Tiepolo* found there such favourable Dispositions, that he had Reason to hope for a happy Issue of his Negotiation, if they had not been alter'd by the Umbrage the *Poles* took at the King's Arming, because as he had done it without the Consent of the States of the Kingdom, they were apprehensive he did it with a Design
to

to change the Form of the Government. They complain'd thereof at the Diet, and oblig'd the King to disband all the foreign Troops, of whom he thought to compose a Body of five and twenty thousand Men, which with the Friends and Partizans he had in the Army of the Countrey, might have done an irreparable Damage to the Liberty of *Poland*. *Tiepolo* therefore finding it was impossible to persuade that Nation to a Rupture, took his Audience of Leave. At this Audience the King Knighted him, in the Presence of the Queen and the whole Court. He oblig'd the new Knight to charge the Arms of his Family with an Eagle and a Sheaf, which are the Arms of *Poland*, and of the Royal House of *Sweden*, from whence the King was descended. This is one of the principal Ornaments of the first Nobility of *Venice*, amongst whom these are distinguish'd, who appear in Publick with a Star, for which Reason they are call'd *The Knights of the Star*. In the Year 1603 the Grey Leagues sent seven Embassadors to *Venice* to see the Observation of the Alliance that had been concluded between these two Republicks sworn to. The Oath was taken in the Great Council Chamber, and when they took their Audience of Leave, the Doge made them all seven Knights, by striking them gently on the Shoulder and the Head, while their Gilt Spurs were putting on, and each of them was presented with a Gold Chain, and a Medal of the Value of five hundred Crowns

At *Venice* the Laws are very rigorous against those who receive Benefices, or take Pensions from a foreign Sovereign. But at the same Time the Republick is so far from being offended at the Presents that are made to her Embassadors, or from forbidding them to receive any at the Conclusion of their Embassy, that it takes it ill when they have none, and would be apt to call them to an Account for their Behaviour, which had render'd them unworthy of the Benevolence of the Prince they came from *Anthony Foscarini*, he that was since strangl'd in Prison for Crimes against the State, of which he was afterwards found to be innocent, had been six Years Embassador at *London* and being sensible that his Predecessors had receiv'd very fine Presents there, he expected one at least as valuable as that which had been made to the last Embassador, who had resided there but three Years, but he was mightily surpris'd to see them bring him one not worth above half as much. He complain'd of it, but he was told it was the King's Pleasure, who had reduc'd the Presents to half their former Value, and that was all his Remedy.

As the Prince who makes a Present to an Embassador at the End of his Employment, considers not only the Person of the Minister, but also that of the Sovereign he represents, so the Embassador in accepting the Present, ought to have as much Consideration for his Master's Interest, and for the Satisfaction he reaps from his Embassy, as for that he leaves of his Conduct at the Court where he was employ'd. It is on this Account that there are so many Examples of Embassadors, and even of the politest and best qualify'd, that have refus'd the Presents of those Princes, who did not answer what the Minister had reason to hope from his Negotiation. *Octavian Bon*, Embassador Extraordinary from *Venice* at *Madrid*, not having been able to procure Justice for some Depredations that the *Spaniards* had committed on the Subjects of the Republick, and being willing to express how little satisfy'd he went away, refus'd the Present that was brought him from the King.

After the League of *Cambray* had been concluded between Pope *Julius* II, the Emperor *Maximilian*, *Lewis* XII King of *France*, and *Ferdinand* the *Catholick*, *Lewis* signify'd to *Anthony Condolmer* Embassador from *Venice*, that he did not desire he should attend him in his Journey to *Italy*, but that he would have him go to *Lions*, where he would let him know what he had to do. The King sent him at the same time a very fine Present. But forasmuch as these Civilities are done to Embassadors only at their Departure, *Condolmer*, who concluded from thence that he was dismiss'd, would not accept it, and said, *That his Life was at Stake if he receiv'd the Present of a King who was going to make War with the Republick*. After the Lord *Hollis*, Embassador from *England* to *France*, had taken his Audience of Leave in the Year 1666, the King sent him a Diamond of the Value of five and twenty thousand Livres. The two Kings were upon the point of declaring War, on account of that the King of *England* actually made with the United Provinces, for which Reason *Hollis* refus'd the Present. He said he did not come into *France* to inrich himself, and that moreover he had not receiv'd Satisfaction for the Affront the Princess of *Carignan* had offer'd to his Wife. It was represented to him that it was a Token of the Esteem the King had for his Person, and that it was the Custom of *France*, where a Present from the King could not be refus'd without Incivility. It was none in the State the Affairs of the two Crowns were then in, where the Embassador might very well commit one, in reference to a Prince who was not a Friend to his Master.

In the Year 1595, *Clement* VIII sent *John Francis Aldobrandin*, his Nephew, into *Spain*, to try to persuade the King to send a powerful Succour against the *Turks* in *Hungary*. He made a very short Stay at *Madrid*, and at his going away, the King, the Prince, and the Infant, offer'd him very considerable Presents, but the Pope had forbidden him taking any. The Pope was not for having his Relations oblig'd to crown'd Heads. And as he does not himself make very magnificent Presents to Embassadors, his Incivility was of no great Consequence.

These Presents are also refus'd, when the Master of the Embassador is not satisfy'd with the Prince with whom the Embassador has negotiated, or when the Embassador will not be oblig'd to the Civility of a Prince, of whom he is not otherwise satisfy'd, as I just now said. In the Year 1483, *Ferdinand* and *Isabella* sent to *Charles* VIII *John de Ribera*, Lord of *Montemayor*, to demand the Restitution of the *Roussillon*. He did not succeed, for which Reason he refus'd to accept the Plate the King would have presented him with. The *French* said it was an Incivility, and that it was never known in *France* that any body refus'd the King's Present. *Ribera* only made this Answer,

4 E *That*

That it was never known in Spain, that an Embassador receiv'd the Present of a King, with whom the Prince the Embassador serv'd had no Reason to be satisfy'd. I should think one might here call to mind those *Roman* Embassadors, who refus'd the Presents *Ptolomy* King of *Egypt* would have made them, but however, at a Feast the King gave them, they suffer'd Gold Crowns to be put upon their Heads. Instead of rejecting with Rusticity the Honour the King did them, they receiv'd the Crowns, and the next Day they went and plac'd 'em on the Heads of the Statues of the Kings which were in *Jupiter's* Temple. *Charles Howard*, Earl of *Carlisle*, being sent Embassador Extraordinary from *England* to the Czar of *Muscovy*, in the Year 1664, was but indifferently us'd, so that not receiving any Satisfaction, neither in Reference to the Affair he had to negotiate, or to the Complaints he made of the Incivilities that had been offer'd him, he express'd his Uneasiness thereat on all Occasions, but chiefly some Days before he left that Court. The Czar had sent him a Present of Martins, of the Value of two thousand Crowns, another of fourteen hundred Crowns, for his Lady, and a third of a thousand Crowns, for his Son, besides the other Presents for his Domesticks. But he refus'd to accept them, and was coarse enough in his Behaviour to the Nobleman that accompany'd them. The Czar sent another Person of Quality to him, to be inform'd of the Cause from the Embassador, who told the *Muscovite*, *That he did not think he ought to carry away any Tokens of his Czarrish Majesty's Benevolence, while he gave so little Satisfaction to the King his Master.* The Czar was contented with this Answer, and being well enough pleas'd to keep his Skins, he sent back the Present the Embassador had made him from himself, which the Embassador also re-accepted.

When there is no lawful Ground, the Embassador cannot refuse without Rusticity, and without affronting the Prince, the Present he sends him. In the Year 1632, *Don Gonçales* of *Corduba*, Embassador Extraordinary from *Spain*, receiv'd great Civilities in *France*, where he made no long Stay. At his Departure the King presented him with a Sword, which with the Belt was esteem'd worth ten thousand Crowns. He would not accept it, and yet sent a Present to the Count *de Guron*, one of the Introductors of the Embassador, but the Count told the Secretary, who brought it him, That he would not receive any Present from a Minister of *Spain*, who had had the Incivility to refuse the Effects of the King's Liberality. M *Dossat* being still but a Bishop, had Orders to go to *Venice*, and to communicate to the Senate the Peace which had been lately concluded at *Vervins*. At his going away the Senate sent him a thousand Crowns, in four Baggs of red Cloth. He would have refus'd them, but it was represented to him, *That it would not only be an Incivility, but even an Affront, that would offend the Republick, and oblige it to forbid its Ministers ever receiving any thing from the King.* After the President *Jeannin* had almost finish'd the Negotiation for the twelve Years Truce, the Arch-Duke signify'd to him by Letter, that he intended to present him, and the other Embassadors who had labour'd with him, with a considerable Sum of Money, which he refus'd to accept, but he made no Difficulty to accept the two Suits of Hangings which the Arch-Duke sent him. Altho' he was a Minister whose Integrity was without Reproach or Suspicion, and that he had not negotiated with the Arch-Duke but with his Enemies.

Don Antonio Pimentel having concluded at *Paris* the Treaty, which since receiv'd its last Perfection at the *Pyrenean* Mountains, and having procur'd the Ratification of what he had negotiated, and brought together the first Ministers of the two Crowns on the Frontiers, Cardinal *Mazarin* sent him a Hatband of Diamonds, and Ear-pendents for his Lady. He refus'd the Present, and signify'd to the Cardinal, that since the Affair was not perfectly concluded, he intreated his Eminence to delay making him feel the Effects of the King's Liberality. That he was not rude enough to refuse them, when he should see what he had promis'd on the part of the King his Master, and his first Minister accomplish'd. I cannot forbear making here a Comparison of this Procedure, with that of a certain Minister, who having discharg'd at the *Hague* the Function of a Herald, rather than that of an Embassador, and having declar'd that his Character was extinct, even to the refusing the Memorial the States would have sent him, did notwithstanding all this take his Audience of Leave publickly, thereby to procure to himself the Present of six thousand Livres, which the States for some time have given to the Embassadors of crown'd Heads, tho' he could not be ignorant that his King was going to make War with them. He was the Aversion of the *Hollanders* when he came into the Countrey, and he was their Detestation when he left it, whereas *Pimentel* left in *France* the Reputation of a very honest, very gallant, and very able Man. It was the same Minister, who while he resided some Years before in *Sweden*, had so extinguish'd in the Queen's Mind all the Affection and Esteem she had for *France*, and left in the room thereof Inclinations so contrary, that that great Princess was no longer known but by the Lineaments of her Face, which was not the part that made her great.

All Princes are not equally liberal and magnificent on these Occasions. Some of 'em consider therein the Master of the Embassador, some again have a Regard to the personal Merit of the Embassador, and there are others also, that make Reflection on the Subject of the Embassy, and on the Importance of the Negotiation. It cannot be deny'd neither, that there are some Princes who make their Liberality subservient to their Ambition, or to some other By-Design, thereby to bring over to their Interests those, to whom the Presents are only as it were an Earnest of what they may hope for hereafter. The Mareschal *de Biron* went to *Brussels*, to see the Observation of the Peace of *Vervins* sworn to, and brought away Presents that engag'd him in very pernicious Affairs. In *France* the Present to the Nuncio most commonly consists in a Side-Board of Plate, of the Value of ten thousand Livres, and if he be made Cardinal during his Nunciature, it amounts to seven or eight thousand Crowns. The Presents to Embassadors in Ordinary are regulated to about two thousand Crowns, for

those

The EMBASSADOR and his FUNCTIONS. 291

those of crown'd Heads and of *Venice*, but sometimes they receive an additional Present extraordinary, and even their usual Present is augmented as the Occasions seem to require There is nothing fix'd in this Point, in Reference to the Extraordinaries, but Regard is therein had to the Prince that sends them, to the Person of the Embassador, and to the Affair he negotiates When *M de Bassompierre* went into *England*, in the Year 1626, he receiv'd a Present of the Value of seven thousand Pound Sterling, and the Mareschal *de Grammont*, who went in the Year 1659, to demand the Infant in Marriage, was presented with a Hatband of Diamonds worth thirty thousand Crowns

But a great deal of Roguery is committed on these Occasions, more especially when the Present is made in Jewels *John Zavadsky*, Embassador of *Poland*, after he had been at the *Hague*, *Brussels*, and at *London*, arriv'd at *Paris* in the Month of *March* 1636 The Affair he had to negotiate was of no great Importance And forasmuch as he was consider'd but as a circular Embassador, and that *M d'Avaux* who had been twice with the King of *Poland*, had been but indifferently presented, it was likewise resolv'd to make him but a slender Present However, after he had shewn that which the Cardinal Infant had made him, which was well worth twenty thousand Livres, it was resolv'd to bestow sixteen thousand Livres in that the King intended him *Berlize* carry'd him a Diamond, and a pictur'd Box which was told him to have cost fifteen thousand Livres *Zavadzky* fell sick, and being, after his Recovery, ready to set out, *Berlize* went to see him to pay him the last Complements, and to excuse, on the Absence of the Court, his not having been overwell receiv'd and treated during his Stay at *Paris*, but the Embassador taking him aside, told him, That he had been written to from Court, that the King had order'd him a Present of the Value of six thousand Crowns, and that that which he had receiv'd was not worth above two at most That if there had been but two or three thousand Livres Difference, he would have took no Notice of it, and that what he did say, was not by the way of Complaint, but to shew how Embassadors were us'd, and how the King was serv'd in *France*. That for certain it would be written into *Poland*, that he had receiv'd a Present worth six thousand Crowns, so that he should be liable to be suspected of Artifice, if he produc'd that which had been brought him, because it would never be believ'd that the King of *France* had made him so sorry a Present, after those he had receiv'd in *England* and at *Bruxelles* *Berlize* who was not capable of doing an ill Action, had no Difficulty to justifie himself But those Persons of Quality who had deliver'd the Jewels to him, did not get any great Reputation thereby After *Zavadzky* was gone, a Gold Chain was sent to him of the Value of a thousand Crowns The two *Dutch* Embassadors were much cunninger For they prefer'd good Bills of Exchange, in which they would not be impos'd upon, and where there was nothing to be lost by the Fashion, as there is in Jewels and Plate, of which they had their Choice The Protector *Cromwell* was for making a Present of a Service of Plate of the Value of twenty thousand Livres to *William Nieuport*, Embassador of the United Provinces at *London* The express Prohibition that is made to Embassadors in *Holland* to take any Presents, oblig'd *Nieuport* to refuse this, even after his Return home, and after he had made a Report of his Embassy He that had Orders to offer it him at the *Hague*, having a mind to make an Advantage of the other's Refusal and Probity, kept it, and *Cromwell* dying some Time after, he remain'd possess'd thereof, and would have been so still, if after the King's Restoration an ungrateful and treacherous Friend, had not discover'd it to a Person in Power, who oblig'd him to make Restitution of what he did not possess with a very good Title

To prevent these Frauds, Persons of Confidence are employ'd on such Occasions, viz either the Masters of the Ceremonies, or the Introductors of Embassadors, who receive the Present either from the King's own Hand, or else from that of one of the Officers of his Houshold, the Super-intendent of the Revenues, or the Secretary of State for foreign Affairs In the Year 1636 the Marquiss of *St Germain*, Envoy Extraordinary from *Savoy*, having taken his Audience of Leave, *M de Chavigny*, Secretary of State, sent him the King's Present by *la Barde*, his first Clerk *Berlize* looking upon that to be prejudicial to his Function, had a mind to complain thereof But not daring to offend a Secretary of State, who was in great Credit with Cardinal *Richelieu*, he thought it better to inform himself from *Chavigny* how it came to pass, and therefore ask'd him, if it was by the King's Order that he had employ'd therein a Person who did not belong to his Majesty, and done that Prejudice to his Office? *Chavigny* made Answer, That it should have no Consequence, and that if *Berlize* complain'd thereof, he would say, That the Introductor not coming himself to receive them at his Hands, he was not willing to intrust 'em with a Person whose Substance was not answerable for the Presents, which are sometimes of very great Value That he had done it only on this Account, and not at all to offend *Berlize*, or to *make any Innovation in his Office* This was a Reparation, but a very bad Excuse, because he to whom *Chavigny* had refus'd to deliver the Presents, was the King's Officer as his Father had been before him, had a great deal of Honour, and much more than they who had made their Profit of *Zavadzky*'s Present, whom *Chavigny* might very well know

I just mention'd the rich Present that was made to *M de Bassompierre*, when he was Embassador in *England* They have there an Officer of Importance, who has the keeping of all the Plate, and of all the King's Jewels that are not set. This Officer pretended that it belong'd to him to carry the Present to the Embassador, and had so strengthen'd his Party at Court, that the Duke of *Buckingham* had declar'd in his Favour. But the Master of the Ceremonies and his Assistant, being inform'd thereof, represented their Interest to the Earl of *Montgomery*, Great Chamberlain, and afterwards to the Earl of *Pembrook*, High Steward of the King's Houshold, and left them so well satisfy'd of their Right, that they likewise brought over the Duke of *Buckingham* to their Sentiment,

ment; so that it was resolv'd, that the Master of the Ceremonies should carry the Present, as accordingly he did. The King himself told the Master of the Ceremonies, (when this last came to acquaint him how the Embassador had receiv'd the Present, and thank'd his Majesty for the Favour he had done him in giving him this Commission) that it belong'd to the Master of the Ceremonies to carry the Presents of Jewels to Embassadors, to the Exclusion of all others.

This Custom of making a Present to an Embassador at his Departure from a Court, having succeeded to that of Defraying him, and being so well establish'd that it is of as great an Extent as the *Law of Nations* it self, there is Reason to be surpris'd at the Regulation that has been made on that Subject in *Holland*. The States of the United Provinces being assembled extraordinarily in the Year 1651, on the Occasion of the Death of the Prince of *Orange*, Father of him that governs now, came on the 10th of *August* to a Resolution, by which they forbad those Ministers who should be employ'd on their Part to foreign Potentates, to take any Presents directly or indirectly, in any manner or way whatever. These Prohibitions are so scrupulously observ'd, that there is no Minister that does not refuse the Civilities Princes offer him, even the very Refreshments they send him when he passes through their Countrey. I never could yet learn the true Cause that has oblig'd so wise and prudent a State, to make a Regulation that absolutely destroys the very Principles of a Civility that is receiv'd amongst all the Nations of the World. I before observ'd that the Republick of *Venice* would try an Embassador who should return home without a Present, whereas that of *Holland* would declare him infamous that should bring one, or barely receive a Plate of Fruit or other Refreshments. I cannot tell whether the Authors of this Regulation pretended to found a Republick of *Plato* in their Fens and Marshes, but it cannot be deny'd, that they thereby condemn the Sentiments of all the other Kings and Potentates of the Universe, who are of Opinion they ought to express to the Embassador the Consideration they have for his Prince, the Esteem they have of his own Person, and the Satisfaction they have from his Conduct and Behaviour. It must also be own'd, that they who could come to so singular a Resolution, could not but have a very bad Opinion of the Ministers they employ'd, since they look'd upon 'em to be so easily Corruptible, that a Dish of Meat or of Fruit, or a Bottle of Wine should be able to make them fail in their Fidelity to their Countrey. I am willing to believe that there are mean Souls, selfish and unfaithful enough, to suffer themselves to be corrupted, but I cannot see how an Embassador can be corrupted by the Present he receives, when he is no longer in a Condition to negotiate, nor to betray the Interest of his Prince, even if he were dispos'd to do it; and by a Present that cannot serve for a Reward, not only of a Disloyalty and Treason, but even of a small Service. I dare not at the same time say, that so powerful and glorious a State has done it out of a Principle of Thriftiness and good Husbandry, since it does not hinder it from making very considerable Presents to foreign Embassadors, and doing them that Honour, which it will not suffer its own Ministers to receive.

I could wish the History of the Times had not taken notice of the Difficulty the States of *Holland* made in the Year 1654, to consent to a Present of five hundred Crowns, which the States General were for making to the *Sieur Brasset*, Resident of *France*. He was an able and agreeable Minister, who having lost his Sight in the Service of his Master, was going to retire, and it was in debate to make him the usual Present. The Deputies of *Holland* were against it, not thinking it reasonable to make Presents to foreign Ministers, while those of that State were not allow'd to receive any in the other Courts. They were of the same Opinion, when it was propos'd to make the usual Present to the Heirs of *M. le Brun*, Embassador from *Spain*, who dy'd at the *Hague*, and to the *Sieur Stockar*, Envoy of the Protestant Cantons, but at last the other Provinces carry'd it, and caus'd the Presents to be made. A Prince or State may make what Regulations they please for their own Subjects, but it is not just to impose them on those of another Prince, and to pretend to regulate in reference to them, the Civilities that have been universally receiv'd. *Spinola*, Minister of *Genoa*, said, he would have his Present, and would be treated as *Jacomo Negrone*, his Predecessor, had been. The Prince that is not satisfy'd with the Conduct and Behaviour of a foreign Minister, is not oblig'd to give him Marks of his Benevolence, of which there are several Examples, and among the rest a very powerful one, in the Person of the Marquiss *d'Inoyosa* and of *Don Carlo Coloma*, Embassadors of *Spain* in *England*, who having grievously offended the the Prince of *Wales* and the Duke of *Buckingham*, had in deed their Audience of Leave, but went away without Presents. In the Year 1647, *Serviru* made a Treaty of Guaranty at the *Hague*, but his manner of Negotiating being insupportable, the States of *Holland* would not suffer the usual Present to be made him. He had had great Differences with the Minister, who was on the Part of this Province at *Munster*, for which Reason no Opportunity was slip'd to let him know that he was not belov'd, nor was held in any great Consideration.

I do not perceive that hitherto this Regulation has procur'd any great Advantages to the State, but on the contrary, that it has brought several Disgraces upon it. In the Year 1652, the Parliament made use of this Pretext, to forbid *St. John* and *Strickland* receiving the Presents the States had sent them, for having negotiated some time in *Holland*. Those Ministers did since very bad Offices to the United Provinces, and were in part the Cause of the War they soon after engag'd in with this new Republick. In the Year 1662, *Mrs. de Ghent*, *Van Buningen* and *de Hubert*, with the Embassador in Ordinary *Boreel*, concluded a Treaty at *Paris*, which in all likelihood would have renew'd Friendship between *France* and the United Provinces. The King sent very rich Presents to the four Embassadors, who refus'd them. The King took no notice thereof, but forbad the six or seven Commissioners, who had

The EMBASSADOR and his FUNCTIONS.

labour'd at the Treaty, to receive the Presents the States would have made them, by which Means the States made themselves so many Enemies in the King of *France*'s Council.

When the Embassador has receiv'd his Present, and has perform'd his last Visits, he is oblig'd to make a Present also to the Introductor, and he is guided therein by the Value of the Present he has receiv'd, or by the Trouble that he has had in conducting him to his Audiences. *M. de Bassompierre* made no long Stay at *London*, but yet he receiv'd so noble a Present, that he sent one of three hundred *Jacobuses* to the Master of the Ceremonies. There are some Nations, and even some Ministers, that are more sordid and niggardly than others, and there are some Embassadors, who having no Honour themselves, know not how to do any to their Masters. One can hardly forbear blushing, when one reads in the Memoirs of *England*, the printed Names of some Embassadors, who after having been fourteen Months at *London*, and having in that time had above sixty Audiences, were so narrow-Soul'd as to send the Master of the Ceremonies a Present of sixscore Ducats, notwithstanding he had carry'd them very rich Presents from the King.

Altho' it is not my Intention to speak here of the Presents Princes make to one another, no more than of those which Embassadors make at the Courts where they negotiate, I shall however take notice that they are so essential a Part of the Embassy in the Oriental Courts, that there are Princes who send Embassadors to one another, on no other Account but to accompany their Presents, of which they make a kind of Commerce. In the Year 1621, the *Indian* King of *Decan*, sent an Embassador to *Schach Abas*, King of *Persia*, only to present to him some Pieces of Cotton, which is manufactur'd in his Countrey, which were in some Measure to pay for the Horses, the *Schach* had sent him some time before. But what they miscall Present, is properly speaking a Traffick, because on both sides they are so exact in adjusting the Value, that there is no Advantage to him that makes, or to him that receives the Present, and they regulate it, as a thing wherein their Reputation is concern'd. A great deal might be said hereupon, but as t does not belong to my Subject, I shall finish here the first Part of this Treatise.

The End of the First BOOK.

Ffff   THE

THE EMBASSADOR AND HIS FUNCTIONS.

BOOK II.

CHAP. I.

Of the Function of the Embassador in general.

 Make use of this Word on purpose to distinguish between the Functions and the Actions of an Embassador, because the ones have a nearer Relation to the Character, and the others to the Person. The Embassador does not always negotiate, that is to say, he ought not always to act the Embassador every where, and on all Occasions I said elsewhere, that he ought to have a Tincture of the Comedian, and I must here add, That perhaps in the whole Commerce of the World, there is not a more comical Personage than the Embassador There is not a more illustrious Theatre than a Court, neither is there any Comedy, where the Actors seem less what they are in effect, than Embassadors do in their Negotiation, and there is none that represents more important Personages But as the best Actor is not always upon the Stage, but changes his manner of Behaviour after the Curtain is drawn, so the Embassador who has play'd his part well in the Functions of his Character, ought to act the Man of Honour and the Gentleman, when he ceases to act the Comedian.

At Assemblies of Ceremony he cannot quit his Rank without a Crime and even at his Table, where he gives a Scantling of the Grandeur and Magnificence of his Prince, he may represent him in some measure But as Kings them selves sometimes lay aside that burthensome and incommodious Gravity, and, like *Moses*, put sometimes a Vail over their Faces, to the end their Majesty may not dazle the Eyes of those that approach them, so the Embassador cannot without blotting out the Character of a Gentleman and well bred Person, continually keep on that of a publick Minister This Compound of Formalities, Decencies and Circumspections may indeed form a politick Pedant, but not a perfect Embassador, who ought to be a consummate gallant Man, that is to say, a Man fram'd to the Mode of the Court Nothing hinders an Embassador from seeing and entertaining the Ladies, but if on these Occasions, where even Kings themselves shew themselves communicative and familiar, he should affect to be grave, and keep up the Character of Embassador, I would not say that he would thereby render himself ridiculous, but he would not be far from it *Chanut* who seem'd to be born for this eminent Employment, would not put

on

on his Hat, when he receiv'd Audience of Queen *Christina* of *Sweden* He knew what was due to the Monarch he reprefented but he did more Honour to the King his Mafter, in telling the Queen the Reafon of his not being cover'd, than if he really had been fo. The Embaffador that pays Civilities to the Ladies, and to thofe who have no Competition with him, fhews that his Mafter is not deceiv'd in his Choice, and that his Minifter knows how to live, as well as how to negotiate It is impoffible but the Embaffador, who will always act the Embaffador, muft be very uneafy to himfelf, and his Dignity prove a Burthen to him, as thofe Clothes are which are only for folemn Occafions, and for a Ceremony of fhort Duration, which one neither would nor could put on every Day That Embaffador that will exert his Character in all his Actions, ought firft to renounce all the Devoirs of Civility, and not that, but alfo all the Laws of Friendfhip, and whatever there is moft agreeable and delightful in Life, *viz.* Society and Converfation, which may be faid to be one of the pleafanteft Parts, nay even the Soul of Life

This is what I thought my felf oblig'd to fay, before I enter'd upon the Functions of a Minifter, who cannot be ufeful to his Prince, nor even be confider'd at the Court where he refides, if he be not in that which employs him What Efteem can Strangers have of him, who is not efteem'd in his own Country? And what Credit can be given to the Offices and Words of the Embaffador, who is not confided in by his Mafter? The Plenipotentiaries who were at *Munfter* on the part of *France*, faid, There was no Appearance that the Houfe of *Auftria* defign'd to make a Peace, *fince of all the Minifters fhe had at the Congrefs, there was not one that had the Confidence of his Mafter, or that had the Qualities neceffary for a Negotiation of that Importance* That every body knew that the Count de *Naffaw* had only the Advantage of Birth to quality him for that Employment That he had been four or five Years at *Cologn*, for no other End but to make a Figure, while there was nothing to negotiate That *Savedra* had had fome Refidence, from whence he had been transferr'd all on the fudden, and as it were *per faltum*, to the firft Affembly of *Europe* That Count *Zapata* was confider'd on the account of his Learning, more than for his other Qualities, and that *le Brun*, who was only Attorney General in a provincial Court, being a Stranger, *could not know the true Intentions of the Court of* Madrid, *nor have its Confidence* That *France*, on the contrary, had fent thither the Duke of *Longueville*, who was the firft, and chiefeft Nobleman of the Kingdom after the Princes, with the Counts *d'Avaux* and *Servien* The firft of which, after his Embaffies at *Venice* and in *Denmark*, had, as Mediator, concluded the Truce between *Poland* and *Sweden*, and had afterwards negotiated and concluded the Preliminaries at *Hamburg* And the other, after having manag'd and negotiated very weighty and important Affairs in *Italy*, had had in *France* the Direction of the military Affairs, under Cardinal *de Richelieu*, in the Quality of Secretary of State, which is an Office of the laft Confidence So that if a Comparifon were made of the Qualities of all thefe Minifters on both fides, it might be eafy to judge which of the two Crowns had the greateft Inclination for a Peace The Embaffador who is affur'd of the Confidence of his Mafter, or at leaft of his Efteem, goes on with Firmnefs, acts with Vigour, and procures in his own Perfon a Confideration and Efteem for that of his Prince, in the whole Sequel of his Negotiation

Thofe Perfons of Quality whom Princes employ in their Embaffies, in order to remove 'em from Court, ought to be confider'd as honourable Exiles, and are not very capable of Serving, neither is it the Intention of the Prince they fhould do much, who in removing under any Colour whatever, a Perfon that is difagreeable to him, has only a mind to get rid of him, and therein imitates the Phyficians, who in purging the Body carry off the fuperfluous Humours as well as the dangerous There are fome Princes that make ufe of the honourable Pretext of Embaffy, to cover the ignominious Caufe of the Removal of the Embaffador, of which there are but too many Examples in Hiftory And then it is, that the wretched Minifter becomes the Object of the Contempt, or Compaffion of the Prince, to whom he is employ'd, unlefs this has Generofity enough to beftow his Efteem on the perfonal Merit of a Minifter, whom Violence, Injuftice, and even Brutality perfecutes In thefe Cafes the Perfon is more confider'd than the Character, which is not only ufelefs, but even a Burden to the difgrac'd and banifh'd Minifter So that I fhall not put him in the Number of thofe, whofe Function is to make the other Part of my Treatife

I exclude alfo from Embaffy all thofe pretended Embaffadors, who are only fit for the Stage, and are only produc'd like dumb Perfonages in a Comedy or a Farce The Jefuits, who delight very much in thefe Diverfions, and are themfelves great Comedians, even to that Degree as to convert into Pomp and Oftentation all the Divine Service, bethought themfelves, about a hundred Years ago, of procuring a folemn Embaffy of *Japannefes* to be fent to *Rome*, towards the latter end of the Pontificate of *Gregory* XIII Thofe Fathers had in effect made a great Number of Profelytes in *Japan*, at leaft if this Quality can be given to thofe, that are help'd out of Idolatry and Paganifm, to be plung'd into an Abyfs of Ignorance, and caft into a Gulph of Superftitions, which are little better than thofe of the Pagans, from whence they are borrow'd, to fhew in *Europe* what they were capable of doing in the remoteft Parts of *Afia* They oblig'd thefe miferable Wretches to depute fome amongft 'em, to acknowledge the Pope as vifible Head of the univerfal Church They were three Years on their Way They receiv'd extraordinary Honours every where, but particularly at *Rome*, from whence they carry'd nothing but the Pope's Bleffing, which was not follow'd by that of Heaven All the Perfecutions of the firft Ages of the Church, cannot be brought into a Parallel with the Cruelty and Horror of the Torments which thefe poor Ideots were made to fuffer, who were only Chriftians by name, and who had nothing more of the Religion of *Rome* it self, but an implicit Faith that is to say, a gross Ignorance of the first, and most necessary Articles of the true Faith. Under the Pontificate of *Clement* VII, there came to *Rome* a pretended Embassador from the King of the *Abyssins*, about the Union of the Schismatick Churches in those Parts with that of *Rome*, of which however nothing more has been heard of since. In the Beginning of the Year 1595, under *Clement* VIII, came to *Rome Abdel Missias* and *Joseph*, Monks of the Desert of St *Macarius* in *Egypt*, with *Barjus* the Archdeacon, who said they were sent by *Gabriel*, Patriarch of *Alexandria*, to make Abjuration between the Hands of the Pope, of the Error in which the Greek Church is, concerning the Procession of the Holy Ghost, as accordingly they did, casting themselves at the Feet of his Holiness. But this Embassy was in effect but a Comedy, because it was soon known, that *Gabriel* was not the Name of the Patriarch of *Alexandria*, nor of his Predecessor *Ambo Johannes*, but that the Patriarch's Name was *Meletius*, and his Sirname *Pegas*, he was a *Candiote*, whose Thoughts were very far from a Reconciliation with the Church of *Rome*.

Embassies Extraordinary have for Object, either the Negotiation of an Affair, or a Ceremony, where the Embassador only represents the Person of the Prince. In the Embassies of Obedience, the Embassador makes the same Figure that a mute Personage makes in a Comedy. His Orator speaks for him, and provided that the Embassador does but know when to make his Reverences and Bows, he is not too capable for this Function. In the other Ceremonies, of a Christening, a Marriage, a Funeral, the seeing the Observation of a Treaty of Peace sworn to, or of a Visit that Princes make one to another by their Embassadors (when they in Person approach their common Frontiers) they are always Persons of the first Quality that are employ'd, and it is very well done, but it would be still better, if on these Occasions the handsomest Personages were pitch'd upon, tho' they had but little Wit, because the one is necessary and the other is not. *Henry* IV had no occasion to send the Duke of *Biron* to *Bruxelles* after the Peace of *Vervins*. But that Prince was so generous, that he could not tell how to distrust those who were oblig'd to him for all their Fortune.

The Embassador in Ordinary has several various Objects, which cannot be plac'd under certain Titles. It may be said in general, *That his chief Function consists in his entertaining a good Correspondence between the two Princes in his delivering the Letters his Master writes to the Prince with whom he resides, in soliciting an Answer thereto in his observing all that passes at the Court where he negotiates in protecting the Subjects, and in preserving the Interest of his Master.* He serves as an Interpreter to the two Princes, and as a Broker in the Commerce that is between them. That of their Letters is entertain'd among Princes, but by the Means of their Ministers, who accompany them with a Discourse suitable to the Subject thereof, and conformable to the Orders that are sent them.

I have spoken in the fourteenth Chapter of the first Book, of the Instruction Queen *Eliza*beth gave in the Year 1570 to *Francis Walsingham*, who went on her Part in the Quality of Embassador into *France*. It contains almost all the general Duties of an Embassador in Ordinary, for which Reason I think I may here set down some Periods of that excellent Piece. *After you shall have deliver'd your Letters*, says she, *and that you shall have been presented by our Embassador, to whom you are to succeed, who will not fail to give you the necessary Advices, and to recommend your Person to the King, to the Queen Mother, and to all the others it shall be requisite, you shall speak to them in Terms that shall make them sensible, that you have express Orders to make your Ministry subservient to the entertaining the good Friendship that is between us and the King, and consequently, to entertain Union, and a reciprocal Commerce between the Subjects of the one and the other, conformably to the Treaties which have been made between us on that Subject. Wherefore being resolv'd to follow those Orders, as well by reason of the Duty of your Employment, as in Consideration of the Good the two Kingdoms ought to promise themselves therefrom, you shall require them, that in case any thing happens that may alter the good Opinion they ought to have of us, (which we assure our selves will not happen, and still less, that you should give them any Subject) they suspend the Judgment that might be made to our Prejudice, till they have inform'd themselves of the Truth, by the satisfactory Answer we shall give them.* She farther adds, *You shall observe all the Actions of the King, and the Queen Regent, as well private as publick, which might be prejudicial to us and to our State of which you shall give us Advice with all the Diligence and Secrecy necessary. And that you may succeed better in, you shall inform your self from our Embassador, your Predecessor, of the Means by which you may be able to learn those Things which it concerns us to know.*

In these few Lines you find the two first Functions of an Embassador, who is represented there as a *Messenger of Peace* on one side, and as an *honourable Spy* on the other. He ought to make it his chief Business to entertain a good Correspondence between the Prince that employs him, and him with whom he resides, which is chiefly done, when the Embassador explains the Intentions of his Master after a good manner, when he persuades the Prince with whom he negotiates, of the Sincerity of his own, when he removes the Umbrages that Prince might have, and prevents those he might take, or might be given him from other Hands. *Justin* speaking, in the second Book of his History, of the Embassadors that *Vexoris* King of *Egypt* sent to the *Scythians*, he calls them *Lenones*. The Commentator says expressly, *Leno, id est Mediator, qui apud Italos dicitur Ambasciator*.

One of the first Things that the Embassador ought to do, to succeed in the Profession of a Spy, is to study well the Humour and Genius of the Ministers that compose the Council of the Prince with whom he is to negotiate, because without that it is impossible for him to take sure Measures for his Negotiation. All Ministers are Men, and as such they have their *Foible*, that is to say their Passions and their Interests, which the Embassador ought to know if he will do himself Honour, and likewise to his

The EMBASSADOR and his FUNCTIONS. 297

his Master He may to this purpose contract an Acquaintance with those Embassadors who have resided there before him, and particularly with the Ministers of the second Order, who having a more easy Access, and less to be suspected than that of Embassadors, have also more Opportunities to penetrate into Affairs An Embassador ought to suppose that no Prince is willing his Minister should create him Troubles Those who have a mind to have any, never want the Means to procure them, whenever they please, and sometimes they have them from so many Quarters, that their Ministers may very well forbear creating them any new ones All Princes are not like *Lewis* XI or *Charles* Duke of *Burgundy*, the one of which could not live without Intrigues, and the other never put an End to one War, but in order to enter upon another And indeed it cannot be said, that it was their Ministers engag'd them in their Troubles, which were only the Effects of their perverse Inclinations, and restless Tempers The one was himself his whole Council, and the other was the Chief of his

On the contrary, there is hardly any Prince, who (excepting the Time of Rupture, and of War declar'd) would not wish to be well with his Neighbours And I dare say, that there are none, but would be willing to avoid all disgusting Appearances, even with his false Friends, and secret Enemies There may be a Friendship between the Kings of *France* and of *England*, as much as Kings and Princes are capable thereof, but there will never be any between the two Nations There was none at all between *Catherine* of *Medicis*, and Queen *Elizabeth*, neither could there be any between such opposite Humours and Inclinations The Negotiation that was on Foot at that Time for the Marriage of Queen *Elizabeth* with the Duke of *Anjou*, and for the Alliance that was concluded at *Blois*, only serv'd to decoy the *Huguenots* into the Snare they fell into on St *Bartholomew*'s Day in the Year 1572 That horrible Infidelity, and that bloody and execrable Execution, did not hinder the two Princes from having their Embassadors each at the other's Court, nor from preserving some Appearance of Friendship, and good Understanding between them The *Pyrenean* Peace, and the Marriage which was the Cause or a Consequence of the Treaty, did not re-establish between *France* and *Spain* that Friendship, to which the two Nations had been Strangers for almost two hundred Years And the King of *Spain* could not consider that of *France* but as a Son-in-Law, who having extorted his Daughter from him, and compell'd him to make a disadvantageous Peace, continu'd to succour his Enemies, and to arm his rebellious Subjects against him, which the *Spaniards* said was directly contrary to the Treaty Nevertheless there was an Embassador of *France* at *Madrid*, and one of *Spain* at *Paris*, and this Appearance of Friendship continu'd, till in the Year 1667 the *French* Army enter'd into *Flanders*, without any previous Declaration of War The King said he did not in reality make War, but only took Possession of what belong'd to the Queen his Wife, by virtue of the Right of Devolution That acknowledging no Judge before whom he could plead his Case, he made use of the Cannon, and would do himself Justice

Nay there are some Princes, who judging it beneficial to their Interest to have it believ'd they are very well, and even act in Concert with those who have Embassadors with them, affect to establish a sort of Confidence with the Ministers of the Sovereign, whose Friendship can give Reputation to their Affairs *Henry* II King of *France*, having resolv'd in the Year 1551 to put himself at the Head of a powerful Army, and to enter in Person into *Germany*, communicated his Design to *John Capello*, Embassador from *Venice*, and gave him to understand he should take it well if he would accompany him in this Expedition The King's Intention was to make the Emperor believe by this Appearance, that he was perfectly well with the Republick, and that she approv'd of what he did The Senate on its Part was glad also to give a little Jealousy to the Emperor, who gave a great deal to all *Italy* in the Affair of *Parma*, from whence the Republick might very well have taken a Ground or a Pretext to renew a strict Intelligence with *France* Capello obtain'd the Consent of the Senate, which was by so much the more necessary to him, as it seems, as if the Sovereign, that allows an Embassador to attend an Expedition, approves of, and justifies it in some measure The *Spaniards* pretended they did not know *Alexander*, the Pope's Nuncio, when they found him and us'd him very ill in the *French* Camp before *Pavia*, but it was a very bad Excuse They did what they did on purpose, because all that are found in an Enemy's Army, are Enemies by Contagion

Unless the Embassador has an express Order to attend this sort of Expeditions, he ought not to be very forward in doing it and the Princes themselves ought to be very reserv'd therein *Martin Justiniani*, Embassador of *Venice*, follow'd the Emperor *Charles* V in that of *Algiers*, where he dy'd of Sickness and Fatigue, tho' that was what he ought to have least apprehended He would have been much more unfortunate, had he fallen into the Hands of the *Africans*, who not having less Fierceness than those furious Animals the Climate produces in such great Numbers, would have took Pleasure to have exerted it with Advantage on this Occasion by reason of his Character In these Conjunctures, where there is no Room for Negotiation, and where all the Embassador can do is to give Advice to his Master of what passes, the Prince would do much better to employ a military Officer, who being capable of judging of martial Actions, can give a better Account of them than a Man of the Robe; it not being necessary for this to vest him with the Representing Character, which the Prince ought never to expose without Necessity *Sultan Mahomet* having rais'd a powerful Army towards the End of the last Century, with a Design to carry the War into *Hungary*, would have the Embassadors of *France* and *England* follow him in this Expedition They had not Time to acquaint their Masters therewith, nor to expect their Orders, and I cannot tell whether they would have been allow'd to deliberate on the Signification of the Will of the *Turkish* Emperor, who thinks he acts conformably to the *Law of Nations*, when he deals to Embassadors somewhat better Usage than he does to

G g g g his

his Slaves. The *Sultan*, to enable the Embassadors to subsist in their attending the Army, sent every Day to each of them five Sheep, twenty Pullets or Capons, two hundred Loaves of Bread, twelve Pounds of Sugar, and as much Honey and Butter, a Pound of Pepper, and as much Ginger and Cloves, twelve Pounds of Candles, and as many Wax Tapers, a Sack of Rice, two Horse-Loads of Wood, as much Hay, and a sufficient Quantity of Barley to keep their Horses, and twenty Camels to carry their Baggage. I do not here speak of the Hermaphrodite Embassadors, who are at the same time publick Ministers and War-Officers, because these two Professions being directly contrary one to the other, and their Functions incompatible, of Necessity the Function of the one supersedes that of the other. *Charnace*, *Destrades*, *d'Avogour*, *Konigsmark*, *Hautefeuille* were at the same time Embassadors and Officers of War, but they were not consider'd as Embassadors in the Army, nor as Officers of War at the Court where they negotiated. I have spoken of them elsewhere, for which Reason I shall continue to make out what I before advanc'd, That one of the chief Functions of the Embassador is *to act the Spy*.

Philip de Commines says a Distinction ought to be made, between the Embassadors that come from real Friends, and those that false Friends or covert Enemies send. The ones are contented to observe the Court where they reside, so that nothing may pass to the Prejudice of their Masters, and the others are errant Spies. Those serve their Master without offending the Prince with whom they reside, while these are not afraid of offending the Prince with whom they negotiate, provided they compass the Ends of him that employs them. This is what Queen *Elizabeth* expresses so well in *Walsingham*'s Instructions, that I may safely say upon that Foundation, That the Embassador ought to labour with Application to entertain a good Correspondence between the two Princes, and have no other View in observing the Actions of the Court where he resides, than to prevent the Prejudice they might do to the Affairs of his Master. But as Sincerity is not a Virtue that is much known at Court, and that there are but very few Princes that have a true Friendship one for the other, so neither are there many Ministers that confine themselves within these Bounds. For the most part they are wholly taken up in Intrigues, and they propose no other Interest in the Actions of the neighbouring Princes, but only to take Occasion therefrom to disturb their Quiet, and to kindle in their Countrey a Fire, at which their Master may warm himself. The Embassadors *France* sent into *England* under the Ministry of Cardinal *de Richelieu*, and the Agents it employ'd in *Scotland*, did not a little contribute to the Commotions of those two Kingdoms, where they did not only serve as Spies, but where they became also the first Springs of those Machines that made such strange Changes in the State. The imprudent and rash Procedure of the first Minister, the Queen's passionate and offensive Expressions, Cardinal *de Richelieu*'s Resentment, and the Ministers he caus'd to be sent thither, ruin'd the King, and had like to have abolish'd ev'n Royalty it self.

This Function of the Embassador, *to act the Spy*, is by so much the harder to execute, as it is not natural. As he is suspected, he ought also to suspect every Body, and ought not lightly to credit the Advices that are given him. A Man of Honour will not be apt to furnish a Stranger with Advices, to the Prejudice of his Countrey's Good, and a Traytor may be double. He may get his Treason rewarded by the Embassador, and may procure to himself another Reward for discovering it the first. The Needy and Interessed ought always to be suspected, and even those who are not, ought not to be admitted by the Embassador without Distinction. Princes have their Agents, who make it their Business to acquire the Confidence of the Embassador, by giving him some Advices, the Truth of which passes off a great deal of false News, which give him a prejudicate Opinion against the Truth. The Embassador, who was on the part of the United Provinces at *London*, in the Year 1671, that is to say, at the time the King of *Great Britain* made a Treaty with that of *France* to engage in a War against them, held a Correspondence with those People that were sent on purpose to him, to inspire him (under the Colour of the utmost Confidence) with such Sentiments as it was coveted he should have of the King's Intentions. He was a very new Minister, and otherwise of a Capacity below that of middling, so that upon the Report of these suborn'd Persons, he assur'd the States his Masters, that the King was very far from the thoughts of making War against them, and that he would without doubt declare for them, if they did but give him Satisfaction on some Points, which, as he said, were of no great Importance. Perhaps in all *England* this Embassador was the only Person that was ignorant of the War's being resolv'd upon, and yet all his Dispatches ridicul'd those who gave their Common Matters Information, that the two Kings had concerted to attack the United Provinces, tho' their Advice was accompany'd with Particulars which did not admit of the least doubt of the Truth thereof. As indeed it would not have been doubted of, had it not been for the brutish Passion of some, and the fatal Blindness of others, who represented the true Informations that were sent from *France*, as the Productions of those that made use thereof against the Preferment of the Prince of *Orange*.

In the beginning of the Year 1588, after the Condemnation, and before the Execution of the Queen of *Scotts*, *l'Aubepine Chasteauneuf*, Embassador in Ordinary from *France*, seeing the Offices he did to obtain the Queen's Liberty were of no Utility, was for making use of other Means to procure it, by talking of Queen *Elizabeth*. He communicated his Design first to one *Stafford*, whose Brother was Embassador from *England* in *France*. And because this refus'd to defile his Hands with the Blood of his Sovereign Queen, he, by the Mediation of his Secretary, treated with a profligate Wretch who was to be got out of Jayl, where he was detain'd for Crimes. *Stafford*, who had been a Witness to the Conference the Secretary and the Criminal had had, about the manner of taking the Queen off, reported all the Particulars

lars thereof to the Council Chasteauneuf's Secretary, who was going to France was stop'd in his way thither and thereupon the Embassador was sent for to Cecil's House, where he was told the Reason why his Secretary had been taken up, with all the Circumstances of the Conspiracy. The Lord Treasurer having finish'd his Discourse, was for having *Stafford*, the Secretary, and the Criminal, brought thither, that by their Depositions they might confirm what had been alledg'd; but the Embassador getting up in Anger, said, That he would not hearken to any Accusation whatever, to the Prejudice of his Character, and of the Dignity of the King his Master. Those of the Queen's Council, viz. the Treasurer, the Earl of *Leicester*, *Christopher Hatton* Vice-Chamberlain, and Secretary *Davison*, having represented to him, that it was not to produce Informers and Accusers, that these People were sent for, but only to make him sensible that it was no Forgery, or contriv'd thing, but a Truth, he acquiesc'd. As soon as the Embassador saw *Stafford* enter, he did not suffer him to speak; but reproach'd him with having been the first Proposer of this abominable Design, and that he, the Embassador, had threaten'd to send him manacl'd and fetter'd to the Queen, if he did not desist from his damnable Enterprise, and that if he did not give Information thereof, it was for the sake of his Mother and Brother. *Stafford* hearing this flung himself upon his Knees, and protested with the greatest Imprecations imaginable, that it was the Embassador who had made the first Overture of this detestable Undertaking. Whereupon the Embassador was so transported, that *Stafford* was taken away, and the others were not produc'd.

The Treasurer having from the Embassador's own Words gain'd this Truth, that he had a Knowledge of the Conspiracy, reproach'd him therewith. The Embassador reply'd, *That even if he had had a Knowledge of the Matter, he was not, as an Embassador, oblig'd to reveal it to any but the King his Master*. The Treasurer made answer, *That admitting the Embassador was not oblig'd (which however was not a thing agreed to) to discover to the Prince with whom he resided, the Conspiracies that were forming against his Person and Life, yet it was the Duty of a Christian to warn his Neighbour of the Evil with which he was threaten'd L'Aubepine reply'd, That the Dignity of his Function oblig'd him to another particular Behaviour. That an Embassador of France understanding that a Conspiracy was forming against the King of* Spain, *had not acquainted him therewith, but had given the King his Master Advice thereof, who had approv'd his Conduct*. The Treasurer then exhorted him to take care not to offend the Queen for the future, to remember what he ow'd to his Character, and the Queen's Clemency, who by letting wicked Embassadors go unpunish'd, did not intend to give a bad Example to the good, and told him he ought to consider, *That Impunity is not always a Proof of Innocency*.

L'Aubepine did not labour to entertain a good Understanding between the two Princes; he on the contrary destroy'd it, and instead of proceeding like a Spy, he acted the Part of a Traytor. And indeed, he could not be said to serve the King his Master according to his Intentions, and his Interest, but he executed the secret Orders of the Chiefs of the League, of whom King *Henry* III had already taken some Jealousies, which did not cease but with the Life of the ones and the others. The Embassador was Brother-in-Law to *M de Villeroy*, who was got so deep in the League, that he could not avoid the Suspicion of having had a Hand in the Death of the King his Benefactor. *L'Aubepine*'s Treasons were so far from relieving the Queen of *Scots*, that they hasten'd the Execution of her Sentence, and did not only render him suspected, but altogether incapable of negotiating with a Queen, whose Death he had contriv'd. These Intrigues are unworthy a Man of Honour, and inconsistent with the Prudence of a Minister who intends to serve his Master.

Those Violences of which we have spoken in Chapter XXIX of the first Book, are also incompatible with the Functions of an Embassador, who in violating the publick Safety, becomes unworthy the Protection of the Law of Nations. *Robert Bowes*, who was Embassador from Queen *Elizabeth*, to *James* King of the *Scots*, in the Year 1599, perceiv'd that one *Achfield* had very good Acquaintance at that Court, and fearing lest they should prove prejudicial to the Repose of the Queen his Mistress, he found the Means to make him drunk by his Domesticks, and to have him carry'd off to *Berwick*. The King, who was extremely offended at this Violence, set a Guard upon the Embassador, and was for obliging him to cause *Achfield* to be brought back. He sent to demand him of the Governor of *Berwick*, who said he could not surrender him without the Queen's Orders, and the Embassador discharg'd himself thereof on his Domesticks, who, as he said, had carry'd off *Achfield* without his Participation; but the King was not satisfy'd with this lame Excuse, and would not see *Bowes* any more, who was oblig'd to retire. King *James*, who was presumptive Heir of the Crown of *England*, the Succession whereof depended in part on the Declaration of Queen *Elizabeth*, had Considerations for her, which hinder'd him from shewing a greater Resentment, which might have gone so far as to detain the Embassador, and compel him to procure *Achfield* to be brought back, whom he had caus'd to be carry'd off, and this without violating the Law of Nations.

In the Year 1639, the Marquiss *de Castelrodrigue*, Embassador from *Spain* at *Rome*, laying hold on the Disorders of the midnight Mass, which is said in the Night before *Christmas-Day*, caus'd the Prince of *Sans* to be carry'd off, and had him conducted to *Naples*, where he was publickly beheaded. This Nobleman was of the House of *Doreficr*, and had negotiated with the Ministers of *France*, to the Prejudice of the King of *Spain's* Interest, not without the Pope's Participation. The two Courts of *Rome* and *Madrid* were not very well together at that Time, so that the Ministers had no great Regard one for the other; and the *Barberini*, as being the Weaker, did not dare to shew their Resentment, but by Affronts that were not so publick, tho' they were not less sensible than those they receiv'd. It is not long since the Minister of *Brandenburg* caus'd Colonel

nel *Kaleſtein* to be carry'd off from *Warſaw*, and had him conducted into *Pruſſia*, where he was try'd. The Miniſter got clear of it by diſowning the Violence, but then he had to do with an inſenſible King. A Prince that is neither weak in Power nor altogether ſtupid, ought to revenge this ſort of Affronts, as the Embaſſador on his ſide ought to take his Meaſures very well, not only in reference to the Prince who makes him commit the Violence, but alſo to him who cannot reſent it but in a publick Manner, for fear of being accus'd to have violated the *Law of Nations*, at leaſt by uſing ſuch Means as he may diſown, and which Princes never want. Cardinal *de Richelieu*, when he caus'd in the Year 1640, Count *Philip d'Aglié* to be carry'd off at *Turin*, did not employ the *French* Embaſſador, that he might not expoſe his Character, but he made uſe of the Governor of the Citadel, as being more capable of juſtifying an Action of that Nature.

Commines ſpeaks very ingenuouſly, as he commonly does, and with a great deal of Judgment, of the Embaſſadors who perform'd the Negotiations between King *Lewis* XI, and the Dukes of *Normandy* and *Brittany*. He ſays, *That Embaſſadors were continually going and coming, between the King and the Dukes, as alſo between the King and the Duke of* Burgundy. *Not in order to unite them, or to procure a good Underſtanding between them, but ſome to get Informations, others to give Advices, and ſome again, to gain, ſuborn and corrupt People, all making uſe of every kind of Artifice to trick and deceive, under the noble Pretext of ſincere Honeſty, and the honourable Title of Embaſſy.* Theſe ſame Artifices and Impoſtures make at this very Day the beſt part of Embaſſies. They do not deceive ſo groſly nor ſo impudently as they did then, but the Embaſſador's Artifices for being more ſubtle and of a finer Thread, are not for that leſs dangerous. *Lewis* XI, *Ferdinand the Catholick*, the Duke of *Burgundy*, and the major part of the Princes of thoſe Times, did not ſo much as know what Honeſty and Sincerity meant and as they were not very ſolicitous for their own Reputation, they made no Difficulty to proſtitute that of their Miniſters, who not finding any Credit in the Courts where they reſided, could not poſſibly bring to paſs their Maſter's Intentions. *Lewis* XI had carry'd on ſeveral Negotiations with the Emperor *Frederick* III, and had promis'd him very powerful Succours againſt the Duke of *Burgundy*, and yet had done nothing. At laſt he bethought himſelf of ſending *John Tiercelin*, Lord of *la Broſſe*, who promis'd the Emperor to divide the Duke's Dominions with him, if he would declare War againſt him. The Emperor made him no anſwer, but ſent him back with the Tale of the three Companions, who had run up a good Reckoning upon the Skin of the Bear, they had neither yet taken nor kill'd.

Commines ſays, there is not any Court but has Malecontents in it, and I think I may add, that there are none without Traytors, but as the Embaſſador muſt diſtruſt theſe, ſo he ought not indifferently and without Diſtinction to put his Confidence in thoſe. Some are diſſatisfy'd becauſe they are kept out of thoſe Employments they think they are intitl'd to by their Merit or their Services, and there are others that retire of their own accord from Buſineſs, becauſe they don't approve of the Conduct of the Miniſtry. There are often amongſt both theſe, Perſons of Quality, who are very well affected to the State, and who notwithſtanding their good Intentions, ſometimes diſcover their Diſcontent, and ſpeak with Freedom of the true State of Affairs, and of the *Foible* of the Government. It is from this ſort of People, that the Embaſſador may get great Lights, provided he do but know how to diſtinguiſh the true from the falſe. It requires a great Penetration to ſee to the Bottom of the Heart of Man, which is impenetrable to all other Underſtandings but the Divine. It is what no Rules nor Inſtructions can be given for, except in general, that the Embaſſador ought to form himſelf by his own Experience. He ought chiefly to apply himſelf to the Study of the Prince's Genius, and the Humour of the Miniſters with whom he is to negotiate. For as their Intentions are not to be div'd into, there is no judging thereof, any more than of their Actions, but by their Character. It is that which produces the ones, and makes the others known very naturally. There is hardly any Letter in the Negotiations of Cardinal *Doſſat*, that does not contain ſome Strokes of the Idea he gives of *Clement* VIII, and of Cardinal *Aldobrandin* his firſt Miniſter, and there is no Painter that can repreſent a Face ſo naturally, as Preſident *Jeannin* does the Character of Prince *Maurice* of *Naſſau*, and of the Sieur *Oldenbarnevelt*. On the contrary, *Francis Walſingham* was a very skilful and very able Miniſter, and yet *Charles* IX knew ſo well how to conceal his true Sentiments from him, and the utter Averſion he had for the Admiral *Chaſtillon*, that he deceiv'd this clearſighted Miniſter, who did not ſcruple to write to Queen *Elizabeth*, *That he was well aſſur'd, that amongſt all the King's Subjects there was none the King had ſo great an Opinion of as of the Admiral, and that there was Room to believe, his Majeſty would employ him in Affairs of the greateſt Confidence.* Never did Miniſter apply himſelf more to the Study of a Court, never was Miniſter more diſtruſtful, and never had Miniſter more Reaſon to diſtruſt, and yet never did Miniſter ſucceed ſo ill in the Buſineſs of a Spy, to a young King, who perfectly bubbl'd him, becauſe *Walſingham* who was a Man of Probity, as much as it is poſſible to be ſo, in the Profeſſion of Embaſſador and of Miniſter, could not believe that ſo young a King could be ſo abominably perfidious, as to cover under ſuch fine Words, and ſuch vehement Proteſtations, ſuch black and deteſtable Thoughts. *Charles* IX had been bred up under a Mother who had infected the Court and the whole Kingdom with the moſt dangerous Vices of her Countrey. The Count *Lewis* of *Naſſau* (Brother to *William* Prince of *Orange*) whom the King deceiv'd firſt, help'd very much to deceive *Walſingham*. What would have become of *France*, if this Prince, who at three and twenty Years of Age was a greater Diſſembler than *Tiberius*, and more cruel than *Herod*, had attain'd the Years of thoſe two Monſters of Inhumanity? Embaſſadors had on the contrary a great Advantage, to negotiate with King *Henry* IV and Queen *Elizabeth*. They found in the one a great Soul and an open Heart, and in the other an an equal and steady Conduct (*semper eadem*) a vigorous Prudence, without any Mixture of those Artifices and Wiles, which are the chief Excellencies of most Women. This made Pope *Sixtus* V say, That there was only those two Princes that were capable of reigning, and with whom he would unite in Interests, if they were not Hereticks.

What *Commines* says of the Artifices of the Embassadors of *Lewis* XI, and of those of the Dukes of *Normandy*, *Brittany* and *Burgundy*, shall be hereafter more amply explain'd in Chapter VI. To conclude this I shall only add, that altho' one of the principal Functions of an Embassador is to be continually upon the Watch, in what regards his Master's Interest, that he may be able to give him a faithful and exact Account thereof, yet he ought not to neglect informing himself sedulously of the Affairs which the other Princes are negotiating at the Court where he resides. For notwithstanding it seems as if his Prince was not concern'd therein, and that in reality he has none directly, yet they may indirectly have some Reflection upon him. Besides, the Curiosity of Princes is such, that they are for knowing even the most indifferent Things, of which they who are wise, and understand their Interest, can tell how to make their Advantage. *Lewis* IX, who first settl'd the Posts in *France*, was for knowing every thing. It is true it concern'd him to be punctually and quickly advis'd of the Success of the Duke of *Burgundy*'s Arms, whose Prosperity occasion'd all his Uneasiness, but he moreover had his Intrigues in all the other Courts, and was for being inform'd of what pass'd in all the rest of the World.

CHAP. II.

With whom the Embassador ought to negotiate.

I Said in the sixth Chapter of the first Book, that the Embassador can acknowledge but one Sovereign in the State where he resides, so that he can negotiate only with him. But forasmuch as he cannot always negotiate with the Prince immediately, it may be proper to speak here of those that treat with the Embassador, on the Part and under the Authority of the Prince.

Master *Oliver Daim*, *Lewis* XI's Barber and Valet de Chambre going in the Quality of Embassador to *Mary*, Heiress of *Burgundy* and of the Low Countries, had Orders to speak to her alone and in private. *Oliver* was a *Flemming*, born in a little Village near *Ghent* and because he had some Acquaintance in this great Town, he was to carry on Intrigues to make it rise against that Princess. This is what he busy'd himself with instead of demanding Audience, and acting the Embassador, so that his Stay there becoming suspected, the Council signify'd to him, That if he did not make his Character known, he should not be suffer'd any longer in the Town. Being therefore admitted to Audience, he found the Princess accompany'd by *Adolphus* Duke of *Cleves*, *Lewis* of *Bourbon*, Bishop of *Liege*, and the other Lords of her Council. After he had deliver'd his Credentials, and perform'd the first Civilities, they were for obliging him to make known his Commission, but he said, *His Orders were to acquaint none but the Princess therewith*. Hereupon it was represented to him, That it was neither the Custom, nor even decent, to suffer a Man to entertain in private a young Princess who was still to marry, and that if he did not tell what he came to negotiate, he should be made to speak. This resolute Declaration startl'd *Oliver*, who having nothing that was good to say, or to negotiate, still persisted *to speak with the Princess alone*, and that with so much Obstinacy, that it plainly appear'd he could not depart from the Audience without Confusion. He made but a short Stay in the Town after his Audience, because the People were for flinging him into the River. It was an odd way enough of negotiating, to pretend to make a Secret of his Negotiation to the Ministers of a Princess, who the King knew very well was not in a State to act of her own Head. Those Ministers who are to negotiate at a Court, where the Prince is as well the Soul as the Head of his Council, are very happy, because the Prince taking himself Cognizance of his Affairs, and making himself easy of Access, the Embassador has not so much Difficulty, and is at the same time sure that the Intentions, which do not pass through the Organs of others, can receive no Alteration. A grave Personage, who has deserv'd by his Services one of the highest Dignities of the first Republick of *Europe*, says, That *Lewis* XI King of *France*, instead of imitating other Princes, who for the most part love Ostentation and Pomp, despis'd outward Appearance, and only minded his Closet, and those Ministers that negotiated without Shew and Noise, to the end he might entertain them familiarly. They had no occasion to demand Audience. They needed only to give a Scratch at the King's Chamber Door, and they were admitted. *Henry* III was a Lover of Ceremonies and Formalities, but instead of doing his Business, and compassing his Ends, others did theirs at his Expence. *Henry* IV, on the contrary, was free, and no way ceremonious: He was for knowing all, and in transacting his Affairs himself, he was sure they were both done and according to his Mind. The Embassadors who negotiated in *France* at that Time, and the Ministers who were there employ'd, acted upon Principles that could not deceive them.

There are some Courts where the Affairs are transacted in the Prince's Cabinet, as in *France*, and others, where the Minister must address himself to the Council, as in *Spain*, and in the Courts

Courts of almost all the Princes of *Germany* in *England* Embassadors treat sometimes with the King immediately, and sometimes with the Council, as Occasion, and the Nature of Affairs require. I suppose there is no Embassador so much a Novice and a Stranger in his Business, as not to know before he arrives at a Court, with whom he is to negotiate when he comes there. He ought to know who it is that has the chief Direction and Management of Affairs, not only under the Prince, but also under the first Minister, if there be one, that he may know to whom he is to apply himself after his first Audience. The Embassador ought to contract an Acquaintance first with the Master of the Ceremonies, or with the Introductor of the Embassadors, in those Courts where these two Offices are distinct. It is from them that he may learn more particularly the Names and Qualities of the Ministers he ought to see, and it is they also that can mark out to him the foreign Ministers with whom he may have some Commerce either of Affairs or Civility. In *France*, and in *Spain*, these two Officers have their distinct Functions; but in *England* the same Officer discharges those of both. It is but within these few Years that these Officers are known in the Northern Kingdoms. The Electors have none, neither is there any either at *Venice* or at the *Hague*. There is indeed at *Venice* an Officer that is call'd The *Doge's Knight*, who has a Salary from the Republick, and has no other Function but to receive Embassadors at the Entrance of the Palace, and conduct them to the Doge's Apartment, when they are invited thither on the Account of some publick Assembly or Ceremony. The Civilities of Receptions and Audiences are well enough regulated in *Holland*, but for want of an Officer skill'd therein, they are sometimes alter'd to the great Prejudice of the Dignity of the State. Besides that on those Occasions where the States are oblig'd to make some extraordinary Complement, they make use of the Register's Clerk, whereas in these Conjunctures they ought to employ some Person that would do them Honour, as well as to the Princes to whom they would shew Civility in the Person of their Minister. I say the same of the Prince of *Orange*, who having made the Offices and Dignities of his Predecessors hereditary to his Family, the State ought to allow him an Officer, to whom foreign Ministers should apply themselves, to to know by his Means his Highness's Hour, who would thereby be less incommoded, and would give greater Satisfaction to those who are to negotiate with him.

There are some Courts which are almost never without a first Minister, and even those Princes who do not leave the whole Management of their Affairs to one single Minister, have nevertheless one whom they put a greater Confidence in, than in the others; and it is to these Persons that Embassadors ought to address themselves in the Intervals of their Audiences, with which Princes will not be importun'd every Day. The first Minister, who for the most part is, at least as hard of Access as the Prince himself, has his Subordinate Ministers, who are of more easy Access, and have more Leisure to digest the Affairs, before they are carry'd to the Patron. There is nothing that perplexes more an Embassador, than the Orders he receives not to negotiate with the first Minister. The Earl of *Leicester*, Embassador Extraordinary from *England*, and *M. de Groot*, the Father, Embassador from *Sweden*, did not see Cardinal *de Richelieu*, because they were of Opinion that he ought not to take any Advantage over them, on the Account of his Purple. This was only the Pretext thereof, and not the true Cause. *England* neglected very much the Friendship of *France* at that Time, and the Queen of *Great Britain*, instead of cultivating the Cardinal's, struck into the Interest and Passion of the Queen Mother, and did not scruple to offend the first Minister irreconcileably, by provoking him with outrageous Sayings, of which she had Leisure to repent. As for *Sweden*, the Chancellor *Oxenstiern*, who govern'd it during the Queen's Minority, was not satisfy'd with the Civilities the Cardinal had paid him, when he pass'd by the Court of *France*, in his Return to *Sweden*. He was also desirous to draw all the Negotiation to *Stockholm*, and to transact the most important of all with the Generals in *Germany*, so that *M. de Groot* had no great Matters to unravel with Cardinal *de Richelieu*. *Edward* Duke of *Parma* had all the *French* Inclinations, but he not tally hated Cardinal *Mazarin* and out of that Aversion he forbad the Minister that solicited his Affairs at *Paris*, seeing the first Minister on any Account whatever. He was a Prince of an odd Temper, who gave himself up to his capricious Humours, and who in breaking with the Cardinal, would without doubt have broken with the Court it self, could he have found his Account with the *Spaniards*. The Pope *Innocent* X. took Pleasure likewise to vent his ill Humours on Cardinal *Mazarin*. There was a domestick Enmity, besides a natural Antipathy, between him and the Pope, who did not otherwise much care for *France*, and was not afraid of being at Variance with her, provided she did but know it was only for her first Minister's sake. The Cardinal was ven'd hereat, but he gave also a thousand Mortifications and Uneasinesses to the Pope, and the most sensible ones he felt during the whole Course of his Pontificate. The two Cardinals, *de Richelieu* and *Mazarin* were absolute Masters of Affairs, so that it was impossible to dispatch any at Court without them, and much more to succeed in any without their Participation and Consent; and it was even Folly to undertake it. Princes themselves are apt to look upon the Contempt that is shewn their Minister, as a Condemnation of their Choice, and take it as an Injury done to their Person.

The Popes who most commonly attain to that Dignity, but in an advanc'd and almost decrepid Age, are desirous to enjoy it as long as they can, for which Reason they discharge themselves willingly of the Burthen of Affairs, and more especially of those that can alter their Health, or disturb their Repose, on some of their Relations, or some other *Cardinal in whom they confide*, to whom they give the Quality of *Cardinal Patron*, because he is the Comptroller of Affairs, of which he has the Direction and Supervisorship. Such were Cardinal *Borgias* under *Alexander* IV. *Farnese* under *Paul* III. *Caraffa* under *Paul* IV. *Boromeus* under

The EMBASSADOR *and his* FUNCTIONS. 303

der *Pius* IV *Aldobrandin* under *Clement* VIII *Borghese* under *Paul* V *Ghisi*, under *Alexander* VII *Rospigliosi* under *Clement* IX *Altieri* under *Cibo* under the present Pope, and several others, of whom the History of Nepotism makes a long Enumeration. It is from them that all the Legates, and all the Nuncios receive their Instructions, and to whom they give an Account of their Negotiations as it is also to them, that all the foreign Ministers address themselves for those Affairs they have to negotiate at the Court of *Rome*. There is also a Cardinal, who has the Quality of Secretary of State, and who has the dispatching of all Letters and Packets, but he is but a subaltern Minister, who receives his Orders from the *Cardinal Patron*, as from the first Minister.

At the Court of *Constantinople* the Embassadors don't at all negotiate with the Sultan. The Pride of the *Turks*, and the Custom of the *Asiatick* Princes, do not suffer him to be communicative, except it be to the Women, and to the Officers of the Seraglio. The Grand Seignior eases himself of the Direction and Chagrin of Affairs, upon the first Vizir, who is call'd by Excellency the *Pacha*. It is he that is the absolute Master of all the Affairs that are transacted throughout the whole *Turkish* Empire. For tho' his Authority be precarious, and that his Power, and even his Life depend on the Sultan's Wink, who makes no Distinction between his first Ministers, and the last of his Slaves, yet he has that absolute Command out of the Seraglio, that his Orders are not less respected, nor less punctually executed than those of the Sultan himself. It is with him that all the Embassadors negotiate, either personally or by their Interpreters. In the Absence of the first Vizir they treat with the Divan, and sometimes with the Kaimacan, the Bashaw of the Sea, or some other Officer of the Seraglio, whose Friendship and Confidence they may purchase. The two first Vizirs, Father and Son, the Predecessors of this that is now, maintain'd themselves in Credit till they dy'd, which is a Thing without Precedent in that Court.

Altho' there be no first Minister at *Vienna*, the Emperors have always had some Minister in whom they repos'd a greater Confidence than in the rest, to whom Embassadors apply'd themselves in reference to the Affairs they had to negotiate. *Maximilian* I had, amongst others, his *Mathew Languen*, who from Secretary became Bishop of *Gure*, Cardinal, and Lieutenant General to the Emperor in *Italy*. *Charles* V had his *Mercurin* of *Gattinara*, and the two *Granvelles*, Father and Son, and some other Ministers, to whom he intrusted the foreign Dispatches and Affairs. The Emperors his Successors have also had their chief Ministers *Rodolphus* and *Matthias* had Occasion for them. The two *Ferdinands* were not without theirs neither, and it were easy to name above twelve Noblemen who had the chief Management of Affairs under them, and under the present Emperor, without comprising amongst them the Prince of *Lobkowits*, the Remembrance of whom is still fresh. Embassadors carry it at *Vienna* after another manner than they do elsewhere, and a Distinction ought indeed to be made amongst them, by reason of the Advantage that of *Spain* has of making himself be consider'd there as a Domestick, and of procuring Audience from the Emperor, and from the Council whenever he presents himself before them. The other Embassadors have also a very great Facility to negotiate with the Emperor himself, as well because he is frequently at Council in Person, as because they may every Day repair to the Antichamber, and accompany him to his Devotions, and at his Return, they have almost always an Opportunity of speaking to him, either about indifferent Matters, or those they have in Charge to negotiate. Excepting these Occasions, as well the Embassadors as the Ministers of the second Order, negotiate with the Council, and particularly with the President thereof, who is for the most part one the chief Officers of the Emperor's Houshold. The Ministers whom the Grand Seignior sends, always negotiate with the President of the Council of War, because the Disorders that happen on the Frontiers of *Hungary* are their whole Business.

The Functions of Ministers being regulated in the Courts of *France* and *Spain*, as well as in almost all the others, the Embassador cannot be ignorant with whom he is to negotiate. There is no King nor Prince but would have it believ'd he understands his Affairs perfectly well, and is capable of transacting them himself. But it cannot be deny'd but some of them apply themselves more thereto than others. There has been no King of *France* since *Lewis* XI to *Henry* IV, but who has had his Minister, and suffer'd himself to be govern'd. *Briçonnet* and *de Vers* were the chief Ministers to *Charles* VIII. Cardinal *d'Amboise* govern'd all under *Lewis* XII. The Constable *de Montmorancy* had all the Power under *Francis* I and *Henry* II, under whom the *Guises* began to get into Authority. Under *Francis* II, *Charles* IX, and *Henry* III, all Embassadors negotiated with the Queen Mother *Catherine de Medicis*, who was Regent during the Minority, or rather absolute Mistress of the Wills of the Kings her Sons, who to speak the Truth were little better than the last Kings of the two first Lines. *Henry* IV was a King, and reign'd in effect. In his Time there was no such thing as a first Minister. His Council was compos'd of very able Men, but yet he was the ablest amongst his Council. He listen'd to their Advices, but after he had heard them, he follow'd the Light of his own Judgment. He delighted in the Conversation of the Embassadors and Ministers of those Princes and Republicks he lov'd, because they had lov'd him before he was in Circumstances to make himself consider'd. The Embassadors of Queen *Elizabeth*, of *Venice*, and of the United Provinces saw him familiarly, notwithstanding they, and the other Ministers negotiated commonly with *Villeroy*, who was he of the four Secretaries that had the Province of foreign Affairs. After the Death of *Henry*, the Queen Regent *Mary de Medicis* put the Management of Affairs into the Hands of the Marquiss *d'Ancre*, who had for Successor under *Lewis* XIII *M. de Luines*, who dy'd Constable of *France*. His Administration did not procure any great Reputation to the Affairs of that Crown, which retiev'd themselves but after the King had given the

Direction

Direction thereof to Cardinal *de Richelieu*, who made himself Comptroller thereof under the Quality of first Minister. They all pass'd through his Hands, so that of course the foreign Ministers must do so to. They negotiated also sometimes with Father *Joseph* a Capucin, but commonly with *Boutillier* and *Chavigny* his Son, who as Secretaries of State one after the other, had the Province of the foreign Affairs. The Count *de Brienne* succeeded to *M. de Chavigny* at the Beginning of the last Regency, and of Cardinal *Mazarin*'s Ministry, and it was to him the foreign Ministers address'd themselves concerning those Affairs that were to be brought before the Council, but as for those that were determin'd in the Cabinet, the Cardinal had reserv'd the Cognizance thereof to himself and as he was become inaccessible, recourse was had to him through the Intermediation of *Hugues de Lionne*, who by this Mean drew to himself all the foreign Ministers, and was in effect what the Count *de Brienne* was only in Appearance. The Count resign'd his Office to his Son, who was oblig'd to sell it to *Lionne*, and this left it by his Death to a Successor, who has discharg'd it with infinite Merit, and has beyond Comparison more Honour and Probity, than his Predecessor Mons *Colbert*, who was prefer'd to the King by the Hands of Cardinal *Mazarin*, who has an intire Confidence in him, is present at all the Deliberations for foreign Affairs, and yet he will by no means speak to an Embassador, as well because his other Occupations, which are but too great of themselves, hinder him from doing it, as because he will not incroach upon another's Province.

Philip II. King of *Spain* had his Ministers, but he had no first Minister. On the contrary, he was so apprehensive lest it should be thought he suffer'd himself to be govern'd, or that another had the Direction of Affairs, that he remov'd the Cardinal *d'Espinosa* from Court, because he took too much upon him in the Council. *Philip* III gave himself up intirely to *Don Francisco de Sandoval de Roxas* Duke of *Lerma*. After the Death of *Philip* III *Don Balthasar* of *Zuniga*, and *Don Gaspar de Guzman*, Count of *Olivares*, enjoy'd either the Favour or the Credit, which the *Spaniards* call *Privança*, but *Don Balthasar* dying soon after the King, the Count of *Olivares* remain'd alone all-powerful with *Philip* IV, and it was with him that Embassadors negotiated, as after his Disgrace, they did with *Don Lewis de Haro*. Before that Time, and since the tragical Death of *D Alvaro de Luna*, Constable of *Castile*, no mention had been made of a first Minister. *Ferdinand the Catholick* was himself his first Minister, and knew more than all his Council. *Philip* his Son-in-Law would have suffer'd himself to have been govern'd had he liv'd. *Charles*, Son to *Philip* I made use of the Cardinal *de Ximenez*, not as of a first Minister, but as of a Lieutenant General in his Absence. He and *Philip* II his Son, follow'd their own Judgments, and as they chose their Ministers, they knew also how to distinguish their Advice, and their Counsels, of which these two Kings were always the Masters. The President of the Privy Council, and that of *Castile*, are two Ministers of great Trust, and above the Secretaries of State there is one for the Dispatches, and it is to these three Ministers Embassadors resort, when there is no first Minister. *D John of Austria* is above what they call *Privança*, being the King's natural Brother, and having plac'd himself in the Post he is in, he would not suffer any Comparison to be made betwixt him and the Privado's of the two last Reigns but for all that, he discharges their Functions; so that it is impossible for Embassadors to succeed at the Court of *Madrid* without him.

On this Occasion I shall here relate what pass'd in the Reign of *Philip* III, betwixt the Duke of *Lerma*, his first Minister, and *Petr Gritti*, Embassador from *Venice*. The Republick found it self extremely perplex'd with the War she had with the House of *Austria*, on the account of the *Uscoques*, while she was besides engag'd in that the Duke of *Savoy* had with *Spain*, order'd *Gritti*, who was on her part at *Madrid*, to endeavour to dispose that Court to a Peace. He found the first Minister so well dispos'd, that the King of *Spain* interceded at *Vienna*, and dispos'd the Emperor also to it *Christopher de Kevenhuller*, Count *de Fauquenberg*, who arriv'd at *Madrid* with Powers from the Arch-Duke *Ferdinand*, (who had Affairs of greater Importance in *Germany*) soon agreed to a Peace which was honourable, and in every Respect advantageous to the Republick But as soon as the Treaty was communicated to *Gritti*, and that he saw the King of *Spain* took upon him to be *Arbitrator*, and did not speak like a Mediator, insomuch that it was rather a definitive Sentence than a Treaty, he said it was not in his Power to consent thereto That there had been no Submission on his part That he had desir'd the Duke of *Lerma* to employ the King's Authority to procure a Peace to *Italy*, and that all he could do was to send a Copy of the Treaty to *Venice*, that the Senate might examin it and ratify it if it thought fit The Duke of *Lerma*, seeing they were going to expose the Dignity of the King his Master, who had engag'd very far with the Emperor and the Arch-Duke, sent for *Gritti*, and desir'd all the Embassadors who were at *Madrid*, to be present when he spoke to the *Venetian* Embassador, that they might one Day be witness thereof He reproach'd *Gritti* with the Duplicity of his Procedure but *Gritti* remain'd firm, and maintain'd to the first Minister that there had been no Submission That none had been desir'd from him, and indeed that there could be none, because he had no Orders for that, so that he was far from consenting thereto I shall relate hereafter how this Difference was ended, and only here observe, that the King of *Spain* took the part of his first Minister, and was so offended at the Procedure of the *Venetian* Embassador, that he would not concern himself in the Affair

The King of *Great Britain* allows Embassadors to mingle with the Nobles of his Court, to be present, as private Persons, at the publick Assemblies and Diversions, and to seek Opportunities of speaking to him, and taking Audience without asking it, and without Ceremony But that does not hinder Embassadors from knowing, that there is a proper Organ, by which they ought to make their Master's Intentions known to the King, and that in form

The

The EMBASSADOR and his FUNCTIONS.

The two Secretaries serve for this purpose which are call'd principal Secretaries. They have their distinct Provinces, so that there is no Embassador, that does not know to which of the two he is to apply himself, for the Affairs of his Master. There is no first Minister in *England* since the Death of *George Villiars*, Duke of *Buckingham*, Father to him that is now living. The late King did indeed repose a peculiar Confidence in some Ministers, as in the Archbishop of *Canterbury* and the Earl of *Strafford*. And this has Chancellor *Hyde*, and at present the Lord *Latimer*, Great Treasurer, but one cannot say that they are first Ministers, nor that they have the whole Management of Affairs. The present King has no need of any, no more than that of *France*, whose Ability is but too great for his Neighbours, and too formidable for his Enemies.

During the Minority of Queen *Christina*, certain Senators of *Sweden* transacted, with the other Affairs of the State, those that regarded the Interests of the Crown had to settle with Foreigners, the chief Authority residing in the Chancellor *Oxenstiern*, as well on the Account of that he had had under the late King, whose whole Council he had been, as because at that Time he had more Knowledge of the foreign Affairs, than all the other Senators together. Besides that with the Office of Chancellor he also discharg'd that of Secretary of State. The Queen had no sooner attain'd the Age requisite by the Laws to act of her own Head, than she made it plain that she had also the necessary Capacity for it, and yet the Chancellor's Credit was so considerable even in the Queen's Majority, that *Chanut*, Minister of *France*, was cautious of shewing, that he would sooner follow the Queen's Sentiments than those of her first Minister. The Queen did not love *Oxenstiern* nor his Family, but as it is one of the most powerful, and best ally'd of the whole Kingdom, and that she could not be without his Advice, nor his Service, so neither could she hinder the foreign Ministers from negotiating with him, as with him that executed the Office of Secretary of State, as I just now said. The Queen's Successor, who had too much Wit, and too much Ambition for *Sweden*, was far from suffering himself to be govern'd: and during the Minority of the King his Son, the Senators, who had a Share in the Regency and Guardianship with the Queen, negotiated also with the foreign Ministers, to whom they appointed Commissioners to enter into Conferences with them, where the Chancellor bore always the greatest Sway. *Pimentel*, Minister of *Spain* in *Sweden*, was lodg'd in the Castle at *Stockholm*, and negotiated with the Queen immediately, and pass'd whole Nights in her Closet.

But this can be no Precedent, no more than the Liberty *Terlon*, the *French* Embassador, took with King *Charles Gustavus*, and in *Denmark* with the late King. In that Kingdom, as well as in *Sweden*, the King converses familiarly enough with the Ministers of those Princes and States: he has no Reason to distrust, especially when the Minister has a personal Merit, that intitles him to the King's Esteem, or else some Quality that diverts him. The King of *Denmark* most commonly gives the chief Management of his Affairs either to his Chancellor or to some other Nobleman, to whom he gives the Title of Vicar, or Lieutenant General, which is call'd in the *German* Language, *Stadsbalter*. There have been several under the late King, and even in this Prince's Reign, who notwithstanding they had not the Quality of first Minister, had nevertheless an Authority that came pretty near that which first Ministers assume to themselves in other Courts. In these two Kingdoms there is hardly any Affair negotiated which is not laid before and resolv'd in Council; altho' the present King of *Denmark* acts with a more absolute Authority than his Predecessors did.

The Republick of *Venice* negotiates with Embassadors in an Assembly which is call'd the *College*, which is compos'd of the Nobles, and the Deputies of some other Magistrates, and it is there that the Senate signifies its Intentions to 'em, after the manner I shall lay down in the following Chapter, having given an Account in the nineteenth of the first Book how they receive Audience. I shall therefore add nothing here, except that when an Embassador has any particular Affair that relates to his Person, his Domesticks or his Friends, he does not apply himself to the *College*, which represents the Sovereignty of the Republick, and which concerns it self only with the Affairs of the State, but to the great Sages by the Means of their Secretary, or by the Intercourse of the Consul of the Nation. There is no Senator at *Venice*, nor Minister, that is employ'd in the Service of the Republick, that dares to have the least Communication with an Embassador, or a foreign Prince, on Pain of Death. This Law reaches even the Doge. *Philip de Commines* says indeed, that when he was Embassador at *Venice* on the part of *Charles* VIII, he had a private Conference with the Doge, who had a mind to make use of him, to persuade his Master to leave the Kingdom of *Naples* to the *Arragonians*, in Consideration of an annual Acknowledgment: but we must believe that the Doge had an express Leave for so extraordinary an Action.

In those Republicks where Laws govern, or at least where they ought to govern, rather than the Magistrates, no other Power is acknowledg'd but the Sovereign. It cannot be communicated to any Person whatever, because this kind of States, not being subject to personal Infirmities, nor to Minorities, it is not necessary to support the sovereign Power by a borrow'd and subaltern Authority. The Ministers whom Republicks employ, ought to be Ministers in effect, and cannot extend their Authority beyond the Bounds of their Instructions. However, when they are allow'd to hear foreign Ministers, and to negotiate with them, the Embassador is oblig'd to conform thereto, and he would not do his Master any Service, if he address'd himself to any other Minister. Those Princes and States, that send their Embassadors or Ministers to the State of the United Provinces, give them Credentials for a College, (if I may be allow'd to use the Term) which is call'd *the Assembly of the States General*, because it is compos'd of the Deputies of the Seven Provinces that form the Union.

I should

I should make too great a Digreſſion if I undertook to treat here of the Form of Government of this State, wherefore I ſhall be contented to ſay, That the Number of its Deputies is not ſettl'd, becauſe each Province may ſend as many as it pleaſes, ſince they do not vote by Perſons, but by Provinces, and each Province preſides there a Week, taking it by Turns He that preſides there on the part of a Province, and is call'd the Preſident of the Week, is alſo he to whom the Embaſſador muſt apply himſelf for the Affairs he has to negotiate Theſe Deputies at the Beginning of the Year divide the Affairs amongſt themſelves, and are as it were perpetual Commiſſioners for that Year, of thoſe that are fall'n to their Share by Lot And as there are none of any Importance which the Aſſembly does not refer to them, to be examin'd and digeſted by them, the Embaſſador may inform himſelf of the Regiſter of the Names of thoſe who are concern'd in the Affairs of his Maſter And as the Province of Holland aſſumes to it ſelf a very great Direction in the Government of a State, of which ſhe makes ſo conſiderable a Part, and that her Miniſter, who is in effect but the Syndic of the States of this Province, is alſo on their Part perpetual Deputy to the Aſſembly of the States General, inſomuch that nothing is there reſolv'd but what he has propos'd or approv'd, on the Part of his Maſters, the foreign Miniſters are glad to be before-hand with him, and to prepare him, becauſe as his Approbation is capable of procuring them the Succeſs they deſire, ſo his Oppoſition is alſo capable of ruining and deſtroying their Intentions

Since the firſt beginning of this Republick the States General, and even thoſe of the particular Provinces, excepting thoſe of Friſe and Groninguen, have neither done, nor debated any thing of Importance, without the Advice of the Prince of Orange, their Captain General, and Governor of moſt of the ſaid Provinces, and it has ſucceeded well enough with them, particularly the Oracles of Prince Henry, the greateſt Captain, and the ableſt Politician of our Age So that there is no foreign Miniſter, but who having paid his Civilities to the States, pays alſo his Devoirs to the Prince, has Credential Letters for him, and communicates to him his Maſter's Concerns, as well to give him a Knowledge thereof, as thereby to procure his Favour The firſt Miniſter of the United Provinces is the Treaſurer General, who is the Orderer of the Finances under the Council of State the ſecond is the Regiſter of the States General, and the third the Secretary of the Council of State, who are all three Officers of Truſt, but none of 'em meddles with foreign Affairs, and the Embaſſador does not negotiate with them The States of Holland have their particular Miniſters, viz their Counſello. Penſionary, who is the firſt, and who on ſome Occaſions diſcharges the Office of Secretary of State, and a Secretary They have alſo a Keeper of the Seals, but he only fixes the Seal, and has no Share in the Affairs, nor in the Deliberations in this Quality

CHAP. III
How the Embaſſadors ought to negotiate.

THERE is no Rule to be given for the Manner of Negotiation, whether it ought to be executed by word of Mouth, or in Writing In this the Embaſſador muſt follow the Cuſtom of the Court where he is, and accommodate himſelf to what is there practis'd I am ſenſible it is not from Turkey nor Perſia that the Embaſſador muſt borrow Examples, eſpecially when he would form to himſelf Precepts of Civility or Juſtice but it cannot be deny'd, that it is not in the Power of an Embaſſador to change in a Court, the Manner of Negotiating which he finds eſtabliſh'd, and that he cannot condemn it without Injuſtice Vincenzio de Gli Aleſſandri, whom the Republick of Venice ſent into Perſia in the time of the Cyprian War, was oblig'd to negotiate with Sultan Caſdar Mirza, third Son, and firſt Miniſter to Schach Tamas The Venetian Miniſter had no great Difficulty to obtain Audience, and the Prince promiſ'd him to make a Report thereof to the King his Father Three Months elapſ'd after his Audience, before the Mirza ſignify'd to him, that the King had very well comprehended the Subject of his Commiſſion, but judg'd that in an Affair of that Importance, precipitation ought to be avoided, and that ſince the Alliance the Republick had a mind to make was to be perpetual, they ſhould be able to ſee in two or three Years time what Courſe Affairs would take, and thereupon form Reſolutions ſuitable to the common Intereſt of the Allies That other King of Perſia, Schach Abas ſaid, That to diſpatch publick Miniſters very ſoon, were to uſe them like Couriers, and not like Embaſſadors Each Court, and even each King has its particular Manner of acting, and it is thereby that the Embaſſador muſt govern himſelf The Author of the Treatiſe of The Idea of a perfect Embaſſador, alledges the Examples of the Embaſſadors in Homer and Virgil, to ſhew how the Embaſſador ought to negotiate He alſo borrows ſome from Arioſto and from Taſſo, but it is without doubt to form an Embaſſador altogether as Chimerical as are the Heroes of thoſe Poets

At Venice, where Embaſſadors have no Commerce at all with thoſe who are there concern'd in the Management of Affairs, and where there is no Miniſter whom they can entertain with their Maſter's Intereſts, they are oblig'd to explain themſelves in Writing to the College The Senate alſo anſwers the Memorial of Embaſſadors in Writing, and ſends for them to the College to hear the Anſwer read to them, or elſe it ſends it to them by a Secretary, who reads it to the Embassador, or dictates it to his Secretary, and carrys back the Original, it being forbidden him at the Peril of his Life, to leave it with the Embassador, which is without doubt the Effect of a very refin'd Policy, because Occurrences might happen, where the Senate might disavow what it had done, and maintain that the Copy which the Embassador produces had been alter'd by his Secretary, since that of the Republick does not sign it.

Publick Ministers negotiate also by Memorials in *Holland*, where within some Years they have made it an Obligation to do so, by a Resolution they were forc'd to come to, on the account of a certain foreign Minister, who made no Difficulty to unsay what he had signify'd by the President of the Week, or some other Deputy, or to give to his Discourses a Sense so contrary to his first Intentions, that there was no laying any Stress on what he said. The Register, or one of the Clarks of the Protonotary, whom they call Agent, placing himself behind the President's Chair, reads the Memorials the foreign Ministers present. They are generally put into the Hands of Commissioners, who examin them, and make a Report thereof to the Assembly of the States General, giving their Opinions at the same time, upon which the States form their Resolution. This Resolution being fix'd, register'd and sign'd by the President, and countersign'd by the Register, is put into the Hands of the Agent, who communicates it to the Embassador.

In other Courts where the Practice is different, the Embassador ought to be very cautious of committing his Thoughts to Paper. I said in Chapter XIV, of the first Book, that *Francis Walsingham*, desiring to be inform'd concerning some Points of the Instructions Queen *Elizabeth* gave him in the Year 1670, ask'd, amongst other things, *Whether he might not be permitted, in Affairs of Importance, to give his Reasons in Writing? And in case the Queen approv'd it, Whether he might not express himself in Latin or Italian, because he was better skill'd in them than in the* French, *as also because the* French *would by that Means have no Advantage over him?* The same Queen says in the Instruction she gives him on the 23d of *February*, 1571, That *Walsingham*, thinking he shall have some Difficulty to express himself in his Audiences to his Mind, may desire leave of the King to read his Thoughts, as he shall have put them in Writing, and translated them into *French*, since the *French* Embassador did the same to her. That the King ought to take it less ill in an *Englishman*, who does not make use of his Mother Tongue, because it is allow'd the other, who is a *Frenchman*. However, *that her Intention is not,* (in case it be granted him) *that he shall leave a Copy with the King, or suffer it to be copy'd, but that he should keep it, unless it were earnestly requir'd*.

Paul de Foix, Embassador of *France* at *Rome*, made great Complaints in the Year 1582, of *John Vitelli*, (natural Son to *Chiapin*, Marquifs of *Ceton*) who commanded the Pope's Forces at *Avignon*, and did not treat very well the King's Subjects in his Provinces of *Dauphiné* and *Province*. These Complaints were accompany'd with such pressing Instances from *Henry* III, for the Revocation of *Vitelli*, that the Pope finding himself necessitated to make some Reflection thereon, signify'd to the Embassador, that he should be glad to have down in Writing, what the Embassador had told him by word of Mouth, that he might take it into Consideration at his leisure, while he pass'd some Days in the Countrey. *M de Foix*, told the Pope's Secretary, who brought him the Message, *That he thought that Demand was altogether new, because it had been always the Custom to treat of Affairs by word of Mouth, however that he would think of it.* This Embassador writing on this Subject to the King his Master, says, *That he had been willing to gratify the Pope for that one time, and that he had sent him a Paper which was not sign'd, and did not bear his Name.* This is what he writes in his Dispatch of *April* 3, 1582. And in that of *June* 2, of the same Year, he says, *That he will wait for his Majesty's Orders, whether he ought to negotiate in Writing or not*.

Bernardin Bochetel, Bishop of *Rennes*, Embassador of *France* at *Vienna*, had Orders to negotiate a Match between King *Charles* IX, and *Elizabeth* of *Austria*, Daughter of the Emperor *Maximilian* II. He made the Demand in form, and the Emperor having taken the Advice of his Council, made him a very offensive Answer, because *Chantonnay Granvelle*, Embassador of *Philip* II, and some other Partizans of *Spain*, form'd a great many Objections against this Alliance. The Emperor after some Words of Civility, which serv'd for an Introduction to the Answer, very much extoll'd the Advantage that all *Christendom* would receive from this High Alliance, and said, he would consent to the Marriage on the following Conditions. *That the King should forthwith restore the Towns of* Metz, Toul *and* Verdun, *to the State they were in when* Henry II *took them. That he should renounce the Friendship of the* Turk, *and should make a League with the Emperor against the common Enemy. That in the present Conjuncture, the King should send a powerful Army to his Assistance, and that if it should happen hereafter, that any Difference should arise between the two Kings of* Spain *and of* France, *this last should allow the Emperor to declare for the other: upon all which he would expect his Master's Sentiments.* The Embassador made an Answer thereunto the very next Day, but by word of Mouth. *That it was three Years since he first mention'd this Marriage, and that he had hop'd, that since the Emperor had not the Disposal of his Children in Marriage, as he should think fit, with reference to the Honour and Advantage of his House, that he would at least have made use of a more honourable Expression and Excuse, with which the King his Master might have been satisfy'd. But instead of communicating to him the Articles of a Contract of Marriage, he prescrib'd such Conditions to him, and gave him such Laws, that a Conqueror would hardly impose on him he had subdu'd. That the King was not reduc'd to those Extremities the* Spaniards *imagin'd. That he was willing to succour* Christendom *against the common Enemy, but he did not pretend it should be more oblig'd to his Wife therefore than to himself,* &c. All the rest of the Embassador's Answer was of the same Force, and he concluded it by saying, *that no farther mention should be made of the Marriage.* And in fact he was forbidden prosecuting that Negotiation, which never-

nevertheless was concluded some Years after The Bishop was press'd to give his Answer in writing; but he refus'd to do it.

In the Year 1586, some of the Electors, Princes, and Towns of *Germany*, sent a very solemn Embassy to King *Henry* III, to entreat him to abate a little of the rigorous Persecution of those of the Reform'd Religion The Embassadors were somewhat too vehement in their Discourse for the Ears of a King, who was accustom'd to the grossest Flatteries, *and left it him in Writing* The next Day the King sent them an Answer by one of his Secretaries of State, who read it in the Presence of the Embassadors; but *he refus'd to leave them a Copy of it*, tho' they urg'd it very much In the Year 1589, the same King (who had rid himself at *Blois* of the Duke, and Cardinal *de Guise*) being touch'd a little with the Death of the Cardinal, sent to *Rome* the Bishop of *Mans*, who in Conjunction with the Cardinal *de Joyeuse*, and the Marquiss *de Pisani*, Embassador in Ordinary from *France*, was to justify that Action, and prevail with the Pope to approve of it: But *he expressly forbad him to offer any thing in Writing; to the End the Pope might not imagin, that the King would address himself to him by the way of Request, or that his Intention was to sue for an Absolution from the Censures, which he did not think he had incurr'd* Thus the Pope *Clement* VIII *would never give any thing in Writing to the Duke of* Nevers, whom King *Henry* IV had sent to *Rome*, to desire Absolution of the Pope, who had refus'd to receive the King's Letters, or to do any thing that could give ground to believe he acknowledg'd the King in that Quality.

At present the Negotiation by Memorial is become more in vogue than it was formerly, not only at the Court of *Madrid*, where it is now very usual, but also in that of *France* He of the Secretaries of State, who has there the Province of the foreign Affairs, had some Difficulty to accustom himself to it, and even at this Day, he does not carry the Memorials of Embassadors to the upper Council, unless he be oblig'd thereto for his Discharge, neither are they answer'd in Writing, unless the King gives his express Orders for that Purpose. This is what is also practis'd elsewhere; especially when the Writings may have farther Consequences We have spoken above of the Discontent *Boischot*, Embassador from the Arch-Duke *Albert* at *London*, had on the Account of the *Venetian* Embassador's being preferr'd to him, at the Feast that was made there, at the Marriage of the Princess with the Elector *Palatin*, to which the one had been invited the first Day, and the other on the second *Boischot* made great Complaints about it to the Master of the Ceremonies, and sent a Writing to the Lord Chamberlain, who is he that regulates the Civilities in *England*, in which he alledg'd several Reasons, why he should be preferr'd to the Embassador of *Venice* The Lord Chamberlain having read the Writing, restor'd it to *Boischot*'s Secretary, who carry'd it back. Some Days after the King caus'd an Answer to be made thereto, which was also put in Writing, wherein he justify'd his Procedure, and protested that it was not his Intention to regulate the Rank amongst the foreign Ministers. After the Master of the Ceremonies had caus'd the Writing to be read to the Embassador, he was for having it back, but *Boischot refus'd to return it, and said, that his Secretary had not brought back to him that which he had sent to the Lord Chamberlain* Which the Master of the Ceremonies having reported to the Lord Chamberlain, this last sent him back immediately, and signify'd to the Embassador, that he had return'd his Writing to his Secretary, and *that he likewise would have the King's from him* *Boischot* having inform'd himself of his Secretary, what was become of his Writing, and understanding he had brought it away, *sent back also the other* The King was in the right to withdraw a Writing, which discover'd that his Procedure had stood in need of a Justification

The Negotiations that are made in Assemblies in neutral Towns, or that are consider'd as such, and by the Ministers of several Princes who are at War, have their particular Forms, and the Practice and Manner of them is not always the same Sometimes the Embassadors, or Plenipotentiaries meet to negotiate, and treat in effect, and then the Negotiation s per form'd by the help of Mediators, at least for the most part, notwithstanding the Parties are agreed as to the most essential Points, as at *Munster*, at Cologne, at *Nimeguen*, and at the Congresses, which have been made within these many Years for Treaties of Peace between the *Northern* Crowns But when all things are agreed upon so that there is nothing in all likelihood that can break off the Negotiation, the Meeting is only to conclude, and finish the Treaty with more Solemnity *Lionne* had begun to treat at *Madrid*, and *Pimentel* had made an End at *Paris*, so that the two first Ministers being well assur'd that they should not separate till they had given the last Perfection to the Treaty, made no Difficulty to repair to the Frontiers of the two Kingdoms, to confer and to settle between themselves certain Points upon which they knew very well no Rupture would ensue The Mediators who were at *Vervins*, and at *Aix la Chappelle*, had adjusted the most difficult Articles, nay almost all, before the Ministers of the Princes concern'd came to the Place appointed for the Congress, and were there chiefly, but to the End that by signing the Treaty with the Embassadors of the Parties, they might reap the Honour that was due to their glorious Labour *Commines* in-larges pretty much on the Particulars of an Assembly and Negotiation, which happen'd on the part of *Charles* VIII, and the Confederate Princes of *Italy*, after the unfortunate Expedition of *Naples*: but as this Matter is different from that which is treated in this Chapter, I shall reserve it for another

I shall make hereafter some Reflections on the Negotiation at *Munster*, but I think my self oblig'd to say here, *That the first Propositions that* d'Avaux *and* Servien *made there, were communicated to the Mediators in Writing* But forasmuch as on both sides they began to be long-winded in their Discourses, and to make Answers and Replies, as in a juridical and formal Process; *the Court of* France *sent Orders to its Plenipotentiaries, to negotiate no more by Writing*, and barely to communicate the Demands and the Pretensions; reserving to themselves to

The EMBASSADOR and his FUNCTIONS.   309

to back their Reasons by Word of Mouth, when they spoke to the Mediators. Those of *Sweden* declar'd, on the contrary, that they could negotiate no other way than in Writing, as well because it was the Custom of *Sweden*, and of all the North, as because that at *Ofnabourg* there were no Mediators to whom they might give their Reasons by Word of Mouth, to have them reported to the Parties. The Embassadors of *France* reply'd, That their Orders did not permit them to negotiate in Writing. That the *Swedes* might indeed follow therein the Custom of their Countrey, but that they could not pretend to subject *France* thereto. So that on each side they should be allow'd to do what they thought fit in that respect. They represented to the Ministers of *Sweden*, that those Writings would take up a great deal of Time, and that that Method of Proceeding would partake more of the Chicane and Cavil than of Negotiation. The *Swedes* at last said, that it was not their Intention to spin out Affairs in Length, but that they were oblig'd to make the principal Propositions in Writing, as well to gratify the Allies, who made pressing Instances that it might be so, as because the Interest of both Crowns was concern'd therein.

In the Year 1646, the same Plenipotentiaries of *France*, perceiving that the Difference that was between the Ministers of *Sweden* and *Brandenburg* concerning *Pomerania*, was a powerful Obstacle to the Peace, resolv'd to write into *Sweden*, in order to prevail with the Queen to abate a little of that Rigour with which she treated the Elector. A Peace was desir'd in *France* with the greater Earnestness, because the Finances there were in a bad Condition, and that it had agreed with the Elector of *Bavaria* concerning the Satisfaction of that Crown. *D'Avaux*, who took Delight in Writing, and who express'd himself well in Latin, made afterwards the Draught of a long Letter, which the Plenipotentiaries were to write to the Queen of *Sweden*. But *Servien*, who found Fault with every thing that came from the Pen or Wit of his Collegue, said, *That the King had expressly forbidden them to negotiate in Writing*. That he had had but too much Complaisance, when he sign'd the circular Letters they had written immediately after the opening of the Assembly at *Munster*, which had had so ill an Effect. That indeed it had been resolv'd between them, that a Letter should be sent into *Sweden*, but that that might be done without writing to the Queen. That the King had his Embassadors at *Stockholm*, to whom a Letter might be written. That the Letter of which *d'Avaux* had made a Draught not being capable of being alter'd nor favourably interpreted, might pass there for an Invective, and be consider'd as a Justification of the Procedure of their common Enemies, to the Prejudice of their Allies. That the Embassador might tell by Word of Mouth the whole Contents of the Letter, and that with more Success, because he might do it either all at once, and at the same Time, or at his Conveniency, and according to the Impression he found his Discourse made upon the Queen's Mind. That he might rectify those Passages he should find too strong or too violent, whereas the Letter might produce a quite contrary Effect, even with those, who being convinc'd by the Strength of the Reasons and of the Truth, yet would not be able to approve of the Manner of acting of the *French* Plenipotentiaries.

La Tuillerie, the *French* Embassador, having prevail'd with the two Northern Kings to send their Commissioners with full Power to *Bremsebro*, on the Frontiers of both Kingdoms, in order to treat there of a Peace, brought them to agree mutually to three Things. The first, that at their first Interview they should take one another by the Hand, and should pay each to the other the Civilities that should be concerted between them. The second was, that their Powers should be exchang'd by the Hands of *la Tuillerie*, and the third, that they should approve of the Manner of negotiating, of which he should make use in this Assembly. He desir'd and obtain'd of the Parties, *that they should negotiate in Writing*, and that the Propositions should be lodg'd in his Hands, for fear lest in the Contestation they should be transported to Resentments more capable of breaking than concluding the Treaty.

We have spoken of the Instructions in the first Part of this Treatise, where we observ'd that it was a private Instrument, which the Embassador ought not to communicate. I here say the same of all the Orders that are sent him, because they make a part of his Instructions. This is what the Minister ought to observe in the whole Course of his Employment, and he ought even to avoid giving Copies of his Letters. *Dossat* having receiv'd a Letter, which he thought might please the Pope, resolv'd to read it to him. However, as he therein committed an Irregularity against his Function, he was desirous to justify himself to the King, to whom he wrote in the following Terms. *Altho' it be not a thing customary, nor that ought to be easily done, and which I should be less liable to do than any body else, yet for this Time, which shall be no Precedent, I thought I ought to do as I did, &c. to avoid having it said in* France, *that I had omitted remonstrating any thing they had a mind I should remonstrate, or being calumniated here, for having added any thing of my own.* Cardinal *Aldobrandin* ask'd him for a Copy of the Letter, and *Dossat* said, that he made no Difficulty to give it *for that once, which should be no Precedent in other Cases*. From whence one may conclude, that a publick Minister cannot be compell'd to shew his Orders, without doing Violence to the *Law of Nations*, and without injuring the Prince, whose *Credentials* he presented at the Entry of his Embassy.

The Embassador that negotiates by word of Mouth, does it either with the Prince himself in private Audiences, or with the first Minister, with the Secretary of State, or with some other Minister, or with the Council, or with Commissioners at Conferences. In Chapter VII of the first Part, I recommended to the Embassador, or to him that pretends to take this Employment upon him, the Reflexions, and moral Maxims of one of the first and most illustrious Personages of our Time. To shew how the Minister may benefit thereby, in reference to this Chapter, I shall here set down the 141 Maxim, where he says, "That there is scarce "any Body, but who thinks rather on what

K k k k "he

"he has to say, than of answering precisely to what is said to him, and that the most capable and most complaisant are contented to shew an attentive Mien, at the same Time that one may see in their Eyes, and in their Mind, an Inattention to what is said to them, and a kind of longing to return to what they have to say, instead of considering that it is but a bad Mean to get the Good-will of others, or to persuade them, to seek so eagerly to please ones self, and that to hearken well, and to answer well is one of the greatest Perfections of Conversation." The Moral here has only for Object, Conversation, and endeavours to form a well-bred Gentleman, but in my Opinion one may extend this Maxim even to Politicks, and say, that it is a necessary part in a publick Minister, who will never pass for a Man of Ability, nor reasonable, unless he has in Conferences and Audiences the same Command of himself that a well bred Gentleman ought to have in private Meetings The Precipitancy in answering, of which *M L D D L R* speaks in this Maxim, is not equally common to all Nations The *French* are a little more subject to it than the others, and yet we ought to admire the Attention of *Dossat*, not only in the Audiences he has of the Pope, and his Ministers, where he takes notice of all the Circumstances, and even the least Words but the same Attention is to be observ'd, and the same Patience, and the same Reservedness and Modesty in the Audiences he gives

The Embassador ought never to present himself to Audience till he has desir'd it, and he has had an Hour assign'd him for that purpose The Duke de *Monteleon*, Embassador of *Spain* in *France*, was so assiduous at the *Louvre*, that there did not pass a Day, that he did not see the Queen Mother, Mary de *Medicis* The Day that the Mareschal *d'Ancre* was kill'd he came into the *Louvre* on Foot, but *Vitri*, who observ'd that he took the Way to the Apartment of the Queen Mother, call'd to him and told him, it was not to that but to the King's he ought to repair, which he was oblig'd to do He was at the same Time given to understand by *Villeroy*, that it was not reasonable he should be seen so often at the *Louvre* That it was sufficient for him to come thither once a Week for ordinary Audiences, and when he had a mind to have extraordinary ones, he might make an extraordinary Demand for them. That the other Embassadors took theirs but once a Fortnight, and that the Court was dispos'd to have a particular Consideration for him The Duke made Answer, That it was not as Embassador, but as *Majordomo Major* to the Queen Regnant, that he came so often to the *Louvre* Hereupon he was told, That the Quality of *Majordomo* was not known in *France*, and that it did not belong to the King of *Spain* to assign Officers to the Queen of *France*, and that he would not be allow'd to take a greater Liberty than was given to the *French* Embassador at *Madrid* At present there is no set Day for Audiences, and Embassadors have none, unless they demand 'em The Minister of the second Order, who has not a Character that obliges him to concert with so much Exactness all his Steps, and all his Actions, ought not however to expose himself, but he may seek an Occasion to speak to the Prince, or his Minister, provided he do not occasion himself to be repuls'd, and that in his Person no Affront is offer'd through his Means to his Master This is what ought to be understood of a regular Court, where every Body knows what is due to foreign Ministers, because the most consummate Prudence cannot secure an Embassador, or other Minister, from the Insult of a violent Prince, or of an ignorant and passionate Minister, who instead of being scrupulous in declining all Occasions of Scandal, runs to meet them, and is not afraid of offending those sacred Persons

Charles Sforza, Prior of *Lombardy*, commanded three Galleys in the Service of *Henry* II King of *France*, and in the Design he had to retire to follow his Brother's Fortunes who were in the Emperor's Interest, he thought he should make himself more valuable to the Party, and to his new Friends, by being guilty of an ill Action, and carrying off the three Galleys, and presenting them to the Emperor *Sforza* despair'd of bringing into his Measures *Nicholas l'Alleman*, who commanded the Galleys under him, so that not daring to speak to him of it, he oblig'd him to conduct them to *Civita Vecchia* under Pretext to refit them there, before he brought them into *Provence* to be laid up While they were in the Port, *Charles*'s Brothers made themselves Masters of 'em, and were for sending them to *Naples*, to *Bernardin de Mendosse*, who commanded there in the Absence of the Duke of *Alva* But the commanding Officer would not suffer it without an express Order from the Count *de Montorio*, the Pope's Nephew, who was chief Governor of *Civita Vecchia* The Count gave his Leave for the carrying off the Galleys, but the *French* Ministers complain'd thereof so loudly that the Pope signify'd to the Cardinal *de St Flore*, Brother to *Charles*, that if the Galleys were not restor'd he would come upon him for them The Cardinal instead of obeying got together the Night following all his Friends, all the Imperial and *Spanish* Cardinals, the Marquiss of *Sarria*, the Emperor's Embassador, the Count *de Chincon*, Embassador of Obedience from *Philip*, and all the Partisans of the House of *Austria*. In this Assembly the Pope was spoke of with so much Passion and Insolence, that *Paul* IV was no sooner inform'd thereof the next Day, than he resolv'd to resent it In the mean time the Count *de Montorio* fearing the obstinate and irreconcileable Humour of his Unkle, found a Mean to withdraw the Order he had sent to the Governor of *Civita Vecchia* in reference to the three Galleys, and to put in the Room thereof one which charg'd *Losin* with this Seizure This *Lotin* was Secretary of the Cardinal *de St Flore*, (who as it was said had chang'd it against the Count's Intention) which oblig'd the Pope to send the Secretary to Prison The Emperor's Embassador, being advis'd thereof, Sent to desire An dience, and altho' it was refus'd him, yet he order'd his Coach to be got ready, and repair'd to the Antichamber to demand it himself, but it was refus'd him again, so that he was forc'd to retire Upon this Affront he sent an Express to the Emperor, who order'd him to leave *Rome*, a
wel

well on this Account, as for several other Affronts which were offer'd at that Time to those who had an Affection for Spain. The Cardinal de St Flore was one of those who felt the first Effects thereof Cardinal Caraffa under the Pretext of taking him, and carrying him to take the Air, got him out of his House, and conducted him to the Castle of St Angelo, where he left him, till he had oblig'd Mendoffe to send back the Galleys, which were restor'd to Nicholas l'Alleman

The Marquis of Sarria had no Reason to complain of the Refusal the Pope had made to give him Audience at the Moment he ask'd it, because that depends on the Prince, who consults his Conveniency on that Point. And it is the Practice of all Courts to do so, tho' there are some Occasions where Audience can neither be refus'd nor delay'd, unless a Rupture be design'd. And this was the Intention of Paul IV, who had already arrested the Abbots Berfegue and Nanni, the first of whom was Agent to the Duke of Alva, Viceroy of Naples, and Lieutenant General to the Emperor in Italy He had also arrested Garcilaffo de la Vega, who did the King of Spain's Business at Rome But the Pope said, that the two Abbots being Ecclesiasticks, he had a Jurisdiction over their Persons, and could cause them to be prosecuted in Form That the Abbot Berfegue did no longer act for the Duke, and that Garcilaffo had first violated the Law of Nations, which forbids publick Ministers undertaking any thing against the Quiet of the State where they reside, because as the Minister finds his Safety in the Protection of the Law of Nations, so ought the Prince to find his in the Conduct of the Minister

What I have here said of private Audiences, may be also apply'd to the publick, which may be deferr'd, and even refus'd without Violation of the Law of Nations, nay without so much as offending against Civility In the Year 1638, the Pope sent Nuncios into France and Spain, to exhort the two Kings to a Peace The Nuncio Scotti who was in France could not obtain Admittance, because it was known there, that the Nuncio who was to go to Spain was not yet set out from Rome and the King would not have the World think that he was less inclin'd to a Peace than the King of Spain, and so wanted more Exhortation thereto than the other It may be said that the Prince that does not admit the Minister of another Prince, or who after having admitted him delays or refuses to give him Audience, offends against Custom and against Civility, but I dare not warrant that these Refusals or Delays violate the Law of Nations, unless a very large Signification be given to the Words Violate and Violence, tho' it cannot be deny'd that he that despises the Minister, offends at the same Time the Master In the Year 1658, the Ministers of Brandenburg, who had been sent to the King of Sweden the Year before, not being able to obtain Audience, gave out, That the Law of Nations had been violated in their Persons, by the Refusal the King of Sweden made to hear them, after having admitted them. On the contrary, the Ministers of Sweden said, That it was not only lawful for the King their Master to act as he had done, but also that it would have been a great Imprudence to have heard them That he had been inform'd, that the Elector had treated with the King of Poland, and being thereto become his Enemy, nothing could oblige him to do Civilities to the Ministers of a Prince with whom he was going to break, and with whom he had no longer any Measures to observe That the King their Master had not refus'd the Audience to the Elector's Ministers, but had a mind to be satisfy'd, before he granted it, how he ought to treat them, whether as Friends or as Enemies, and that the Embassadors, for fear of being oblig'd to explain themselves, had rather stoll'n away than return'd That the Law of Nations had not been violated, because all Princes take their own Conveniency for Audiences That the King might delay for some Days that of the Ministers of a Prince, who had treated with their common Enemy, who had committed Hostilities against him That it is true, the Embassador of an Enemy may be admitted, but there is no Obligation to do it, and that Audience might be refus'd him without Violation of the Law of Nations, whose Protection extends no farther than to the Safety of the Embassador's Person, and of his Retinue, since he may be even forc'd to depart out of the Countrey, as has been said in Chapter XXX of the first Book

The Prince who has a mind to live in a good Understanding with another Prince, shall receive his Minister very well, shall hear him favourably, and do him Civility but on the contrary he that does not fear offending the other, shall shew no Consideration for his Minister, without violating for that the Law of Nations. In the Year 1586, Fredrick Duke of Wirtemberg, the Count de Montbeliard, Wolfgang Count d'Jembourg, and some other Noblemen of the first Quality, were sent into France on the part of several Princes and States of the Empire King Henry III, having Advice that these Embassadors came to speak to him, concerning the Interest of his Protestant Subjects, remov'd from Paris under the Pretext of going to drink the Waters of Bourbon, and sent the Queen to Chemonceaux The Embassadors being arriv'd at Paris, were told they must have a little Patience, till the King return'd, who would be back in three Months The Duke and the Count seeing they were treated so unworthily, wrote to the King, that their domestick Affairs not permitting them to make so long a Stay in France, they were oblig'd to ask Leave to be gone, and set out forthwith Their Collegues who waited for the King's Return, were very ill us'd, but neither the ones nor the others complain'd that the Law of Nations had been violated in reference to them

The Emperor Charles V had sent to Trent Nicholas Perenot de Granvelle, one of his trustiest Ministers, and Anthony de Granvelle, Bishop of Arras, the Son of Nicholas These Embassadors demanded Audience as soon as they arriv'd, but the Legates who judg'd that this publick Action would be an Opening of the Council, which they had a mind to delay for some time, made some Difficulty to grant it them, and told them the Reason why. representing to them, that there were as yet so few Prelates at Trent, that they could not make the Appearance nunce of an Oecumenical Council Granvelle, furpriz'd and incens'd at the Refusal, told the Legates, *That they could not oppose their having Audience, unless they had a mind to affront the Emperor and his Embassadors*, who represented the first Monarch of *Christendom*, and a King who was Lord of a great Part of the World, since *they could not refuse it to the Minister of any Prince whatsoever* That if they continu'd to refuse it to them, they would fasten a Writing on the great Gate of the Cathedral Church, wherein they would protest the Nullity of the Council The Legates finding themselves urg'd in this manner, gave them Audience the very next Day, but it was in a great Room at Cardinal *Parisious*, who was the antientest Legate, and not in the Place where the Prelates were to assemble for the Council The Threats of their Protestation were founded on the Emperor's being Protector of the Council, and that he, and *Philip* his Son, had been nominally invited to send their Embassadors thither They did not say, that by such Refusal the *Law of Nations* was violated, but *that their Masters were affronted thereby*

These Refusals happen every Day, and one might compile a Volume of Examples of them In the Year 1614, the Queen Regent of *France* sent the Marquis *de Coeuvres*, known since under the Quality of Mareschal *d'Estree*, to the Princes of *Italy*, on the Occasion of the War of *Montserrat* The Duke of *Savoy*, *Charles Emmanuel*, who knew that this Embassador had nothing that was very agreeable to say to him, went to *Nice* to avoid seeing him, and by that means did not give him Audience, till after the Difference he had with the Duke of *Mantua* had been in some Measure adjusted, and when the Marquis, having seen the other Princes of *Italy*, was returning back to the Court of *France* In the Year 1641, the Emperor being at the Diet at *Ratisbonne*, refus'd to give Audience to the Embassador of *Denmark*, because the King did not in his Credentials give him the Title of Majesty, but only that of *Imperial Dignity* The King of *Denmark*, gives to all the other Kings the Title of *Royal Dignity*, at least it was his Practice some Years agoe, and even the Princes of the Empire made use of this Style, but they have since chang'd it, because they think there is full as much Civility as Deference, in the Honours they pay to crown'd Heads The Kings of *Denmark* have not always been so difficult Letters may be produc'd, where they give the Title of Majesty to the King of *France*, for above sixscore Years past The Manner of Speaking and Writing, in reference to Titles, change so often, that the most knowing Princes have hardly ever subjected themselves thereto, but have been very prodigal of Civilities when they have been of any Utility to them There is no kind of Liberality that incommodes less, and acquires more Friends

The subaltern Representants, or those of the second Order, do not so often see the Sovereigns as Embassadors do, but they are nevertheless sometimes admitted to Audiences, and invited to solemn Assemblies There is only the Pope that thinks it beneath him to treat with this sort of Minister At the beginning of the War of *Castro*, the Republick of *Venice* had no Embassador at *Rome*, by reason of the Difference the last Embassador had had with the Prince Prefect, so that she caus'd her Affairs to be done by a Secretary, to whom she had given the Quality of *Resident* This Secretary obtain'd Audience of the Pope, upon the Orders the Senate sent him to represent to his Holiness the dismal Consequences of the War But Cardinal *Barberin*, writing on this Subject to the Nuncio, order'd him to signify to the Senate, that it was a Favour the Pope had done him, *since it was not the Custom to give Audience to Residents*, nor to negotiate with Ministers of that Quality Notwithstanding which the Pope gave him several Audiences since The Master of the Chamber refus'd to demand Audience of the Pope for the Secretary Monguidi, whom the Duke of *Parma* had left at *Rome*, to solicite his Affairs there, and the Pope complain'd since to *Lionne*, of the Duke's making use of a Secretary to negotiate with him But *Lionne* made answer, That it was at the Liberty of Princes to make Choice of their Ministers, and to give 'em what Quality or Character they pleas'd The Abbot of St *Nicolas* was no Embassador, and yet for all that he negotiated with the Pope

After all, it is not in publick Audiences that the main part of a Negotiation is perform'd They for the most part consist only in Ceremonies, and only serve to make a Complement, or at most to make some Declaration to the Prince, or to get one from him That which the Embassador of the United Provinces had in the Year 1657, on the Account of the Depredations the *French* made in the Mediterranean, and that which the Marquis *de Fuentes*, Embassador of *Spain*, had in the Year 1662, concerning the Satisfaction the Catholic King gave to the King of *France*, about the Precedency, are very remarkable, but yet not so much as the Circumstances of an Audience, which *Henry* III, King of *England* gave to the Pope's Nuncio The Ministers who were on the part of the See of *Rome* in *England*, were so insolent, that their Tyranny was one of the principal Causes of the continual Insurrections that disturb'd the Tranquillity of his Reign, so that for fear of being dethron'd by his Subjects, he was sometimes necessitated to deliver up the Nuncio's to them, who liv'd there as in a conquer'd Countrey The Pope had sent thither one Master *Martin*, whom the *English* nick-nam'd Master *Mastin*, (which in *English* signifys a Mastiff-Dog) because he was continually gaping after Benefices and Prebends This Man had render'd himself so odious by his Pillagings and Rapines, that some Noblemen sent him word by a Gentleman, that if he did not leave the Kingdom in three Days, he should be cut in Pieces with all his People Hereupon he demanded Audience, to get from the King a Declaration, whether it was by his Order that Message had been brought him The King told him he knew nothing of it, but that the Actions of the Pope's Ministers had so incens'd his People, and especially the Nobility, that being ready to take up Arms against him, he was of Opinion that the Nuncio's Life was not in Safety Hereupon the Nuncio intreated the King to give him some Person of Quality to conduct him safe as far as *Dover*, but the King told

told him, That he gave him the Devil, who should conduct him to Hell However he gave him a Gentleman, who conducted him to the Place of his Imbarcation

The Embassador, whether he negotiates by Memorial, or treats by word of Mouth, ought not to play the Orator, nor affect to be Eloquent, his Discourse and his Reasoning ought to be nervous and succinct He that takes Delight in being heard, or in hearing himself, or that makes Harangues, or is too verbose, often contradicts himself, or makes Overtures which cannot be agreeable to his Prince The Word *Dicerie*, which the *Italians* give to this kind of Discourse, expresses wonderfully well the Vanity thereof He must have a great deal, who can imagin, that he has alone Wit enough to bring into his Sentiments, not a Crowd of People, which is easily won by the Ear, but five or six Ministers, whom a wise Prince has chosen out of his Council, to preserve and secure his Interest and Reputation against the Pretensions of Foreigners The Strength of Reason is lost in the Multiplicity of Words, and in Confusion and besides that this Flux of the Mouth is ungrateful, it is putting the Mind upon the Rack, to undertake to drag it along *per force*, instead of bringing it over by a gentle and insinuating Violence I took notice in Chapter VII of the first part of this Treatise, that the Negotiations of Cardinal *Dossat*, and of President *Jeannin*, are almost alone capable of forming a perfect Embassador and I have given Proof thereof when Occasion has offer'd, and as she offers her self very favourably here, I shall observe another Place which affords him two important Lessons *Dossat* was yet but Minister of *France*, when Pope *Clement* VIII spoke to him of the Peace which *Henry* IV was about making with the King of *Spain*, and of the Conquest of *England* which *Philip* II was to undertake And upon *Dossat*'s representing to him, that the King could not break the Alliance he had lately made with the Queen of *England*, the Pope let slip from him several pernicious Maxims, which were unworthy of any honest Man Whereupon *Dossat*, writing to *Villeroy* on the 1st of *February*, 1597, says, He had but too much to reply to all that, but that he thought he ought not to stop in so slippery a Place thereby instructing all Ministers, and teaching them, not to take notice to the Prince who speaks to them, that they have observ'd either the Weakness of his Reasoning, or his dangerous Maxims, far from dwelling on them as it were to reproach him therewith The other Lesson which he gives to new Embassadors is, That they let the Prince have the last Saying, that they may not pass for obstinate and uncivil After the he has related in the same Letter all the Pope's Discourse, and what Answer he had made, he adds, *I could have reply'd to all that, as to many other things, but I would not have the last Word, as well to observe that Civility and Reverence which became me, more especially at a time where nothing was to be decided, as also to preserve in him that Facility of Communicating himself, and making known his Intentions* Where we must take notice of what *Dossat* says by the by, *That they were deciding nothing*, giving thereby to understand, that in the Case of Decision it is allowable to reply strenuously, provided the Embassador keeps within the Bounds of Respect and Civility, and takes care to avoid Cavils and obstinate Contestations, which are of no Utility, but unworthy an honest and well-bred Gentleman He therefore says in another Place, That when he treats or negotiates, *he grants at the very first what he finds to be reasonable and just*, but besides that, nothing can be obtain'd from him if he treats for another

There are a great many things to be said concerning the Language which Embassadors and publick Ministers make use of in their Negotiation There is hardly any Court where there is not a different Practice, as well in publick Audiences, as in Memorials and private Negotiations At the Court of *Constantinople* all the Ministers have their Dragomans The *Turks* know no other Tongue than their own, neither do they admit any other The Harangue which the Embassador of Obedience makes in the Consistory, or that he causes to be made there, is in *Latin* but all the Negotiations that are carry'd on, as well with the Pope as with the Cardinal Nephews, are express'd in *Italian* In *France* all the Ministers negotiate in *French*, and speak all *French* in their Audiences, and in their Memorials The Count *de la Garde*, Embassador of *Sweden*, spoke in the *Swedish* Language in the first Harangue he made to the King and to the Queen Regent, in which he did something for the Dignity of the Crown of *Sweden* in appearance, but it was found fault with, that he should make use of a Language which not one of the King's Subjects could understand nor interpret He afterwards made a long Discourse to the Duke of *Orleans*, the King's Lieutenant General throughout his whole Kingdom, and he spoke nothing but *French* in all the Sequel of his Negotiation In *England* almost all the Ministers negotiate in *French*, which is allow'd there, as well because it was formerly the Language of the Countrey, as because the *French* Tongue has in some manner succeeded to the *Latin*, and is become common At *Madrid* they negotiate in *Spanish*, tho' the *French* Embassador makes use of the Language of his own Countrey, and the Minister of the United Provinces, who have no Commerce with the King of *Spain*, but as he is Duke of *Burgundy*, presents his Memorials either in *Flemish* or in *French*, with a *Spanish* Translation In this the Minister must follow the Custom of the Court where he resides, and accommodate himself to the Practice thereof *M de la Court*, who had also the Quality of Embassador of *France* at *Munster*, but not that of Plenipotentiary, having one Day presented to the Deputies of the States of the Empire a Memorial in *French*, they were very much scandaliz'd thereat, and made a great Murmuring against the Deputies of the Elector of *Mayence*, who having the Direction of the Chancery, had receiv'd and carry'd it to the Assembly They resolv'd it should be signify'd to the *French* Ministers, *That it was an ancient and inviolable Custom of the Diets of the Empire, not to hear any Proposition made either by word of Mouth or in Writing, unless it were express'd in the Language of the Countrey, or else in Latin*, because if they should admit of the *French* Tongue likewise, the *Spaniards*, the *Italians*, and afterwards the *Hungarians* and the *Swedes*, would also pretend to utter themselves in their own Language. At *Vienna* the *German* and the *Latin* Tongue is us'd, and sometimes the *Italian*, which is there familiar enough. At the Northern Courts the foreign Ministers never make use of the Language of the Country, but of their own, the *German* or the *Latin*. The *Latin* Tongue is familiarly spoken in *Poland*, and Embassadors make use of no other, and sometimes of the *Italian*, but rarely, except it be in Conversation. At the *Hague*, where there are Ministers almost from all the Parts of *Europe*, the *French* Tongue is most made use of than any other. Those Ministers who are skill'd in it use no other. *Le Brun*, Embassador of *Spain*, *Friquet* and *Lisola*, the Emperor's Ministers, were all three *Burgundians*, so that the *French* Tongue being natural to them, they us'd no other in all their Negotiations. Those of *Spain* express themselves in their own Language, in their Memorials, but then they accompany them with a *French* Copy. The *English* Ministers speak also *English* and *French*, wherefore the States, in communicating their Resolutions to the Emperor's Ministers, and those of those three Crowns, cause them also to be translated into *French*. The Envoys and Residents of *Sweden* and of *Denmark*, have sometimes spoken *French*, sometimes *Latin*, and sometimes also *Flemish*, or *German* with a *Flemish* Translation.

Princes very much affect to speak in their own Tongue in Treaties, or at least to make use of a Language that is commonly spoken. In the Year 1647, when they began at *Munster* to set down some Articles in Writing relating to the Peace which was to be made between the two Crowns, the Count de *Pegneranda* urg'd very much that they might also be put into *Spanish*. The Duke of *Longueville* said, That therein, nor in such like Matters, *France* did not pretend any Advantage over *Spain*, but also that he would not suffer a Novelty to be introduc'd, nor that any thing should be done contrary to what had been practis'd in all former Treaties, which had been all express'd in the *French* Tongue, as would appear, recourse being had to the Collection thereof, which was printed at *Antwerp*. The *Spaniards* reply'd, That of all the Treaties that had been concluded between *France* and *Spain*, only that of *Vervins* had been compris'd in *French*, and that too, because it was not the King who had treated therein directly, but the Arch-Duke with the King's *Procuration*. This was a very weak Reason. That King who gives a Power to treat, altho' he gives it to a Prince, or to an Embassador directly and immediately, does nevertheless treat in Person. *Philip* II treated at *Vervins* as well as at *Chateau* in *Cambresis*, and they were his Embassadors, and not those of the Arch-Duke, that contested the Precedency with the Embassadors of *France*. The Duke of *Longueville* had Reason to alledge the *Antwerp* Collection, because therein are to be found several Treaties which were concluded between the Emperor *Charles* V and King *Francis* I, who follow'd therein the Example of the Kings of *France*, and of the Dukes of *Burgundy* their Predecessors. The *Pyrenean* Treaty was put into both Languages, and it is certain it is what has been observ'd on many other Occasions; as well in reference to *France*, as to several other Kings and States, and it is what cannot be refus'd when the Parties are of equal Dignity.

The Embassador, whose Collegues are compris'd in the same Commission with him, cannot negotiate without their Participation, nor even receive Overtures but in their Presence, without committing a Crime. The Duke of *Holstein-Gottorp* caus'd *Otto Brugman* to be try'd, and to have his Head cut off at his Return from his Embassy at *Persia*, and one of his greatest Crimes was to have negotiated without his Collegue, as well at *Ispahan* as in *Moscow*. In the Year 1646, the Count de *Pegneranda* signify'd to the Duke of *Longueville*, that if he would receive, under the Promise of Secrecy, the Proposition he would make him, he would tell him in Confidence upon what Foot a Peace might be made between the two Crowns. The Duke made Answer, *That he could not receive it without communicating it to his Collegues*, and that he would be also Security for their Secrecy. But this was what the Count would not be contented with, so that it came to nothing. In President *Jeannin*'s Negotiations the Minister is frequently seen in Conferences, and in private Visits with Prince *Maurice* and with Count *William* of *Nassau*, with the first Minister of *Holland*, even with *Richardot* and with others. But besides that he was one of the trusted Ministers *Henry* IV had, he had also the Secret of the Embassy, and express Orders for those private Negotiations. In the same manner President *Richardot*, in whom the Arch-Duke put his chief Confidence (notwithstanding the Marquis *Spinola* was the Head of the Deputation, and that *Mancidor* acted for the King of *Spain*) paid every Day private Visits to President *Jeannin*, and had secret Meetings with him. But then the Arch Duke approv'd thereof and would not have his Collegues privy to these Conversations, wherein those two able Ministers made the greatest Progress in Affairs. It is also customary for all the Embassadors to sign, not only the Treaties they conclude, but also the Memorials they present, and the Letters they dispatch in common. However it is what is not so absolutely necessary, in reference to Memorials, but that they may do otherwise if they think fit. While the Marriage of Prince *William* of *Orange* was negotiating in *England*, in the Year 1641, none but *Aarssens* alone sign'd the Memorials, because, as *Brederode* and *Heemvliet* were no great Clerks, they rely'd upon their Collegue, who drawing them up alone, sign'd them also alone.

Here would be a proper Place to speak of the Advantage Princes have to negotiate their most important Affairs, by Ministers of the second Order, if I had not spoken thereof in Chapter V of the first Book. There I have told the Reasons why, and alledg'd Examples thereof. So that I shall add nothing to what I have there said, but that whoever has the least Knowledge of what passes in the World, will find that the greatest part of the most important Affairs have been transacted or prepar'd by unknown Persons, or subaltern Ministers. *Lewis* XI and *Charles* Count of *Chatolois* not being able to adjust the Differences between them, employ'd therein two Gentlemen, Subjects to the Duke

Duke of *Burgundy*. They had been in *Charles's* Service, who had been oblig'd to difmifs them to gratify his Father, and *Lewis* had receiv'd them and entertain'd them very well So that being agreeable both to the King and to the Count, they made up the Differences between those two Princes The Emperor *Maximilian*, and *Ferdinand the Catholick* had fubmitted to *Lewis XII*, and the Cardinal of *Rouen*, the Difference that was between them for the Regency of *Caftile*, during the Minority of the Arch-Duke *Charles* their Grandfon, after the Death of *Philip*, who was Son to the one, and Son-in-Law to the other But the Princefs *Margaret*, *Philip's* Sifter, caus'd this Affair to be negotiated under-hand by 1 Gentleman whofe Name was *Claudius de Chilly* This Minifter without Quality going to *Ferdinand*, adjufted the Difference fo well, that the King of *France* and the Cardinal had no Concern therein, nor any thing left to do, but to pronounce on what *Ferdinand* had already agreed to It is not to the Plenipotentiaries of the Emperor, and thofe of the Crowns of *France* and *Sweden*, that *Germany* was oblig'd for the Peace that was concluded at *Munfter* about thirty Years ago It was to the fecret Negotiations which the Elector of *Bavaria* carry'd on at *Paris* by his Confeffarius, by the Nuncios, and by other clandefline Minifters, that this great Work was owing, becaufe without them the Emperor would never have confented to the Conditions, which were the Caufe of the Peace between the Parties The Affembly at *Nimeguen* is compos'd of as great Perfonages as have been feen in any other, but I don't believe that they pretend to regulate the Differences between the Princes at Variance They may perhaps fign the Peace, but they fhall not be the Authors of it They are terrible Minifters that are concern'd therein

On thefe Occafions Princes ought not to employ all Perfons indifferently, but they ought to make Choice of able Men, efpecially when they are to fpeak, or give any Advice by Word of Mouth The Duke of *Brittany* made ufe of a Footman to acquaint the Duke of *Burgundy* with the Intelligence, he faid *Lewis XI* had in the Towns of *Bruges*, *Antwerp* and *Bruffells* This Footman, who had no Credentials, meeting the Duke of *Burgundy* in the Fields, deliver'd this important Meffage *Charles* was extremely angry hereat, and faid nothing elfe to the Meffenger but that he fhould tell his Mafter, that he was not well inform'd of his Intentions, nor of the State and Condition of his Towns *Philip de Commines* takes notice of it as of a grofs Overfight, and a very imprudent Neglect in the Duke of *Brittany*, and fays elfewhere, that the fame Duke of *Burgundy*, while he was ftill but Count of *Charolois*, caus'd his Interefts to be negotiated with *Lewis* by two Perfons of very mean Condition, during the War for the publick Good, and that the Princes his Allies were fo fcandaliz'd thereat, that they met two or three Times without the Count, and would have abandon'd him if he had not chang'd his Conduct The Gentlemen here meant were thofe I juft fpoke of

What we have hitherto faid is concerning the Form of Negotiation, but as for the Effence thereof, there is neither Precept nor Example to be given, becaufe it changes with the Affairs the Embaffador has to negotiate, which are innumerable, and almoft all of a different Nature However, as the Embaffador ought not only to fecure the Interefts of his Mafter, but alfo do his beft for that of his Subjects, I am of Opinion that the Embaffador may make fome Diftinction therein, and that he ought to follow the Counfel the Cardinal of *Florence* gave to *Doffat* in the Year 1599 *Henry* IV made continual Inftances to have the Archbifhop of *Bourges* transfer'd to the Archbifhoprick of *Sens* This Prelate had given Abfolution to the King at St *Denys*, and was thereby become the Pope's Averfion, who look'd upon him to have incroach'd upon his Authority, fo that he could hardly bear the very mentioning of it to him The Cardinal who knew that the Pope would never Confent to this Tranflation, unlefs he were forc'd thereto, faid to *Doffat*, who folicited for it, *That all Affairs ought not to be treated after the fame manner That thofe of private Perfons ought to be treated as private, and thofe of the King and Kingdom as regal and publick* Becaufe it often happen'd, that by obtaining a Favour for private Perfons an Obligation was incurr'd, which ought to have been referv'd for Occafions of Importance This Remonftrance made fo ftrong an Impreffion on the King's Mind, that he defifted from the Profecution he had begun in Favour of the Archbifhop The Embaffador may make his Advantage hereof if he thinks it proper

---

CHAP. IV.

The Embaffador ought not to meddle with the Domeftick Affairs of the State where he negotiates.

Queen *Elizabeth*, from whom the wifeft Princes may borrow Examples of Prudence and Circumfpection, intending in the Year 1570, to fend *Francis Walfingham* to the Court of *France*, recommended to him particularly the Intereft of thofe of the Reform'd Religion This was a domeftick Matter, and a very nice one, fo that notwithftanding fhe put it into the Hands of a very able Minifter, yet fhe thought fit to give him an Inftruction, which carry'd the Face as if it were out of an Excefs of Affection which the Queen had for the King in particular, and the Good of his Kingdom, that fhe fpoke in the Behalf of the King

King of *Navarre*, the Prince of *Condé*, and the other Lords, who made Profeſſion of the Proteſtant Religion King *Charles* IX, with whom *Walſingham* was to negotiate, was ſo ſenſible in this part, that when the Embaſſadors or Deputies of the Princes of *Germany* repreſented to him the Intereſt he had to preſerve and ſpare his Proteſtant Subjects, he told them, That being the moſt Chriſtian King, and born a Catholick, he was oblig'd to ſecure the Religion in which he had been educated That he could not be hinder'd from employing the ordinary Method of Juſtice againſt Hereticks, who under the Colour of Religion were contriving a Rebellion in his Kingdom, and *that he did not want Tutors to teach him how he ought to govern at home* Some Princes of *Germany* were for doing the ſame Offices with King *Henry* III, in the Year 1586, but they were not better receiv'd than the others The German Miniſters having obtain'd Audience at St *Germain in Laye*, told the King, That Liberty of Conſcience was taken away from thoſe of the Religion in *France* to gratify the Pope's Ambition, and that of ſome other Lords of the Kingdom, in Prejudice of the Promiſe which had been made them, and of the Edicts which had been granted them, and intreated his Majeſty to give them Peace, and to lay thereby the Foundations of that everlaſting Friendſhip which the Princes intereſted in the Cauſe of Religion pretended to entertain with *France* The King, who was very much offended at this Diſcourſe, and at the Reproach of being worſe than his Word, anſwer'd them in a haughty manner, *That he was reſponſible for his Actions to none but God That he could give Laws to his Subjects and aboliſh them, as he ſhould think fit That till then he had reign'd with Sovereignty, and without Dependence, and that he pretended to do ſo ſtill, and that thoſe who ſaid he had been worſe than his Word, ly'd* That that was all the Anſwer he had to make them, and that they ſhould forthwith depart out of his Dominions

There is no Prince to whom this ſort of Offices are not ungrateful, and who can patiently ſuffer foreign Princes to interceed for his Subjects The Cardinal *de Richelieu* being inform'd that the Count *de Soiſſons* had deſir'd the Nuncio *Scotti* to uſe his Intereſt with the Pope, that he would intercede with the King for him, told the Nuncio, That the King would not take it well that his Holineſs ſhould concern himſelf in this Affair, *which being merely domeſtick, his Majeſty would never ſuffer any Perſon whatever to interpoſe between him and his Subjects* The Nuncio, before he wrote to the Pope, *was willing to know the Cardinal's Intention*, who made him the foregoing Anſwer All Miniſters ought to follow the Example of this Nuncio, and if they are prevented by their Maſter's Orders, they ought to ſtudy well the Humour of the Prince to whom they are to ſpeak, and make Choice of Terms altogether inoffenſive It is not very eaſy to determine, whether there were more of the Crime or of Imprudence in the Conduct of the Duke of *Bouillon* after the Death of the Marſhal *de Biron*, or whether the Duke had more Reaſon to diſtruſt the Intentions of King *Henry* IV, or his own Conſcience. While he voluntarily condemn'd himſelf to be baniſh'd for ſeveral Years, the Queen of *England*, and the major part of the Proteſtant Princes of *Germany* interceded for him with the King, who receiv'd the Miniſters of the ones with ſome Concern, and thoſe of the others with Indifferency, but he gave a very favourable Anſwer to the Deputies of the Reform'd Cantons, who join'd their good Offices to thoſe of the other Potentates The Intentions of thoſe good Companions could give him no Suſpicion, and their Requeſt was compris'd in ſuch ſubmiſſive Terms, that the King thought fit to anſwer them in Writing, That their Interceſſion was acceptable to him, becauſe he was not only ſenſible they were perſuaded of the Duke's Innocency, but alſo that it was their Affection to the Welfare of his State that made them ſpeak That therefore he took it kindly of them, and thank'd them That they ought to know that the Duke of *Bouillon* was not ſo innocent as they believ'd him, and that he was very ſorry he could not do for their Sakes, what he would otherwiſe do of his own Inclination but that they might be aſſur'd, that the Duke might in all Safety have Recourſe either to his Juſtice or to his Clemency, and that he would find his Eaſe and Satisfaction in the one or in the other

Sovereigns have always an Averſion for Offices of this Nature, becauſe it is a kind of Protection that Foreigners give to Subjects, and that it ſeems as if they would have a Share in the Government of the State where they thus employ their Miniſters The Marquis *de Fontenay Maruëil*, being Embaſſador of *France* at *Rome* in the Year 1641, had to negotiate, amongſt other Affairs, an Accommodation of the Difference the Pope had with the Duke of *Parma*, concerning the Dutchy of *Caſtro* But when the Embaſſador began to mention it, the Pope told him, that he expected the Duke ſhould humble himſelf in Perſon That it would be of pernicious Conſequence to ſuffer a Subject to treat with his Sovereign upon the Level, and to pretend to have him ſpoken to of Compoſition and Agreement, by the Mediation of a third Perſon That he deſir'd the Duke himſelf ſhould pay him that Obedience and Submiſſion which was his Due *That he was very much ſurpriz'd to ſee that the King of* France *ſhould pretend that the Subjects of another Sovereign ſhould behave themſelves after ſuch a manner, which he would not approve of when he was ſpoke to in the Behalf of the Dukes of* Guiſe, Montmorancy, *of* Lorrain *and others That the King had forgot the Anſwer he had given his Nuncio, when he offer'd to ſpeak in the Affair of the Count de* Soiſſons *Innocent* X ſpoke in a more lofty Tone when *France* gave its Protection to the *Barberins*, and that the King interceded for their Re eſtabliſhment The Pope ſaid, *That it was a domeſtick Affair which had been put into the Hands of the ordinary Juſtice, and that he hop'd the King would not meddle therewith, as he on his part would not intermeddle in the Affairs of his Kingdom* He yielded at laſt to the repeated Efforts of the *French* Miniſters, (which were powerfully ſeconded by the continual Inſtances of the Republick of *Venice* and of the Great Duke of *Tuſcany*) rather than to Reaſon and Juſtice, which were on the Pope's Side. The *Barberins* were his Subjects, who could not without a Crime have Recourſe to a foreign

reign Power, of whom they had no Dependence, nor reclaim its Protection. The Pope shew'd sufficiently that he yielded only to the Importunities of the *French* Ministers, when he told those of *Venice*, and of the Great Duke of *Tuscany*, That he would never admit of their Mediation nor Offices, *and that it was as much as he could do to suffer the Intercession of* France, *for whose Sake he was willing to pardon the Barberins, but not to enter into a Capitulation with them.* So that seeing after their Return the *French* Embassador did not leave off speaking in their Behalf, he told *M. de Gremonville*, That *it did not belong to Foreigners to meddle with his domestick Affairs,* and spoke to him in such strong Terms, *that the Embassador was so getting up, and going away, very little satisfy'd with the Pope.*

Queen *Christina* of *Sweden*, who could distinguish extraordinary Subjects, who admir'd them, and who had a very particular Esteem for the Prince of *Conde*, and for his Virtues and heroick Actions, being inform'd that during the Troubles of *Paris* he had been confin'd to the Castle of *Vincennes*, with the Prince of *Conti* and the Duke of *Longueville*, she was touch'd with Compassion for him, and signify'd that she should be glad to intercede for his Liberty, and use her good Offices to reconcile him with the first Minister, if the Queen Regent approv'd of it. But *Chanut*, the *French* Embassador, who had a great deal of Power over the Queen's Mind, made her lay aside that Thought, and the frequent Revolutions that happen'd in *France* took away the Opportunity of executing it. But at last the Prince being set at Liberty, retir'd to his House at St. *Maur*, and from thence out of the Kingdom, and then she desir'd the Sieur *Piques*, Resident of *France*, to try to know whether the Queen Regent would like that she should use her Endeavours to adjust the Differences that divided *France*, and gave such great Advantages to her Enemies. *Piques* wrote about it, and receiv'd Orders to thank Queen *Christina* for her good Will, and to tell her that the Affairs of the Kingdom being on the Point of an Accommodation, it was not necessary that her Majesty should give her self any Trouble therein. She was sensibly touch'd hereat, and said, That since the most Christian King did not approve of her meddling therewith, she would say no more of it. Some time after, the *French* Resident discoursing on this Subject with *Salvius*, one of the Senators of *Sweden*, and one of the Ministers the Queen repos'd the greatest Confidence in, this last told him frankly, That it had not been by his Advice that the Queen had offer'd to do this Office, and that it was not his Opinion the King ought to accept it, *because a Prince ought never to suffer a foreign Prince to intermeddle in his domestick Affairs.*

M. *Chanut*, Embassador in *Sweden*, who was a very able Minister, and a zealous Catholick on the Principles of *Descartes*, knew how to excuse himself from the Offices some People would have put him upon, for the Advancement of the *Roman* Religion, which they were for introducing into that Kingdom, *because it was a domestick Affair*. Those of the Congregation, which is call'd *de propaganda fide*, having resolv'd at *Rome* to send into that Kingdom three Jacobins disguis'd, as Missionaries, got *Gueffier*, Resident of *France* at *Rome*, to desire *Chanut* to second their good Intentions. *Chanut* made answer, That he could not give a Retreat to these Religious without the express Orders of the King his Master, who without doubt would not send him any, in the State Affairs were then in. That he look'd upon it to be a domestick Affair, and that it was dangerous to hazard, *under the Name and Authority of the King, a Mission which would be of no Utility.* That the Chancellor Oxenstiern, who had always endeavour'd to stifle the ill will he had for *France*, would not fail to shew it on this Occasion, to render the very Name of a *French* Man odious there, and to recommend his Person and Zeal to the Clergy of the Country. That the same Reason that had oblig'd the *Swedes* to abolish the ancient Religion would oblige them to maintain the new one, which was so well establish'd in the Kingdom, that it seem'd as if there had never been any other there: That not one of the native Inhabitants was suffer'd to make Profession of the *Roman Catholick* Religion, insomuch that, among so many Millions of Souls, he knew but one that had the Sentiments thereof. That the Ignorance of the Language of the Country was absolutely against the Design which was form'd at *Rome*. That the Court of *Stockholm* not being accustom'd to the Sight of a great Confluence of Strangers, those Religious would no sooner appear than their new and unknown Face, would excite the Curiosity of those, who would be for knowing their Profession, as well as the Subject of their Voyage thither, and if at any time they should enter upon Controversy, which is very severely forbidden by the Laws of the Kingdom, they would expose their Persons to manifest Dangers, and the King's Authority to an inevitable Affront. That all the Favour that could then be obtain'd for them, would be to have them expell'd the Country with Shame and Scandal. That withall, the Crown of *Sweden* would have Reason to complain of the King for suffering his Embassador to intrude himself into the domestick Affairs of the Kingdom, and instead of labouring to preserve a good Understanding among the Allies, to give Sanctuary and Shelter to Persons who were capable of troubling the Quiet of the State, even against the Interest of *France* it self. Of all the Affairs that can employ an Embassador, those that regard Religion and the Religious are the nicest. The *Latin* Patriarch of *Constantinople*, intending to send some Jesuites to *Pera*, pray'd *Dossat* to recommend them to *de Breves*, the *French* Embassador, that they might find a Protection in his Character. *Dossat* made answer, That he did not dare to write on that Subject without the King's Orders, and that if he did write, *Breves* would have no Regard to his Letters, nor ought not to have any, till he had inform'd himself of the King's Pleasure. That the Jesuites had the Character of being Partisans of *Spain*, and that the *Turk* being at War with the House of *Austria*, it was probable their Religious would be no very agreeable Sight at *Constantinople*.

Before I leave *Sweden*, I shall take notice of an Affair in which it bore a good part. The beginning of the Troubles of *France* were by so much the more dangerous, that the King having left *Paris* on the Eve of the *Epiphany*, laid Siege to that Town, the Capital of the Kingdom. *Shering Rosenhan*, Embassador of *Sweden*,

Sweden, apprehending lest these Disorders should hinder the Exchange of the Ratifications, and the Execution of the Treaty of *Munster*, while *France* was still at War with *Spain*, and that *Sweden* should remain alone expos'd to the Emperor's Resentment, spoke thereof with so much Warmth to Cardinal *Mazarin*, that this told him, he question'd very much whether the Queen of *Sweden* would stand by him in all he advanc'd. *Rosenhan* was for obliging the Queen Regent to come to an Accommodation with the Parliament, and with those who had declar'd against the Court, and that upon Conditions which incroach'd upon the Royal Authority. The Cardinal hereupon wrote to *Chanut*, who spoke of it to Queen *Christina*, but in such general Terms, that the Queen not being able to comprehend by his Discourse what had happen'd between the two Ministers, only made this Answer, That she hop'd *Rosenhan* had neither said nor advis'd the Queen Regent to any thing that could make it be thought he had a greater Consideration for the Subjects Interest than for the King's Dignity, and that if he had, *or offer'd to meddle with what did not belong to his Ministry, she disavow'd him*. She also offer'd her Mediation to reconcile the Difference between the Court and the Parliament of *Paris*. But *Chanut* did not declare himself upon those Offers, as well because he had no Orders to that Purpose, as because he judg'd *that those foreign Mediations were disagreeable in domestick Affairs*.

They are so in effect. Nay, it is very dangerous to admit a foreign Minister to the important Deliberations of a State, whatever may be the Link of Friendship or Interest with its Master. The Counts of *Gayazze* and of *Beljoyeuse*, Embassadors from *Lewis Sforza*, Regent of the Dutchy of *Milan*, were present at all the Councils *Charles* VIII held about the Affairs of *Italy*. The two Ministers which then govern'd the King, viz *Stephen Devers* and *Briçonnet*, did not only suffer them to be there, but even summon'd them thereto, till they perceiv'd that *Lewis* (who had brought the Arms of *France* into *Italy* but only for his own particular Interest) betray'd the King, and cross'd the Designs which had been founded on his own Advices and Counsels, by the Means of those treacherous Counsellors who had been corrupted by *Lewis*'s Money. *Commines* says, That these two Counts were not suspected till *Lewis* withdrew from Court, to go and take Possession of the Dutchy of *Milan*, and that it was then it was resolv'd to exclude them from the Council, after they had done all the Mischief they could. The Council of State, which makes so considerable a part of the United Provinces, was not less incommoded by the Presence of the *English* Embassador, during the time he was allow'd to sit there, than a natural Body may be suppos'd to be, when a foreign and unnatural Body crowds in, or is bred there.

At the beginning of the last Commotions in *England*, the Pope sent *John Baptista Rainuccini*, Archbishop of *Fermo*, into *Ireland*, who in a little time acquir'd so much Credit amongst the Clergy of that Countrey, (which is the most ignorant and the most superstitious of all *Europe*) that he prevail'd with their Assembly to protest against the Peace which some Catholicks there had agreed to, with those of the King of *Great Britain*'s Party, and even went so far as to excommunicate those who had consented thereto. This was not all, but he afterwards remov'd with the whole Assembly to *Kilkenny*, and there summon'd the Generals of the Army, and having with them compos'd a Council for the Direction of Affairs, as well Civil as Military, *he made himself the Head thereof*, contrary to the Pope's express Orders, who had forbidden him exceeding the Bounds of his Profession. He had procur'd to himself the Disposal of all the Revenues, of all the Places and Employments, and he acted with so much Empire, that of his own Authority he committed to Prison the Baron of *Monjquerry*, Brother-in-Law to the Marquiss of *Ormond*, with eight other Catholick Lords who had consented to the Peace, and it was only by a kind of Miracle that the Viceroy (making his Escape) depriv'd him of the Means or bestowing *Ireland* on whom he pleas'd. But the ill Success of the Siege of *Dublin*, which he had advis'd, his unequal and irregular Conduct, the Aversion the People had to the Government of a Priest, and chiefly the Liberty and Justification of the Noblemen he had caus'd to be took up, made him lose his Authority, and ruin'd his Credit with the Parliament, as well as the Hopes that were entertain'd at *Rome* of the Re-union of that Kingdom. So that the Nuncio being become the Aversion and Contempt of the People, a thousand Insults and Affronts were offer'd him, to that Degree, as even to break his Windows. *This Minister did not only go beyond the Sphere of his Orders, but also of the Functions of his Embassy, which did not allow him to make himself the Head of a Party, and to constitute himself President of the Council of State, in a Countrey where he was a Stranger, and where his Master had no Command*.

This is what an Embassador ought to avoid, as the most dangerous Rock in the whole Course of his Negotiation. He is not allow'd to concern himself in the Parties that are form'd in a Court, nor to enter into the Factions that divide a State where he negotiates. He ought to have no Communication with the Party that declares against the Sovereign or against his first Minister. In the Year 1584, Pope *Sixtus* V having recall'd *James Ragazzoni* Bishop of *Bergamo*, his Nuncio in *France*, sent in his room *Fabio Muorto de Frangipani*, Archbishop of *Nazareth*, who had been Nuncio there before King *Henry* III, who was not pleas'd with the Nomination of this Prelate, as well because he was a *Neapolitan*, and a Subject of the King of *Spain*, as because in his first Nunciature he had not carry'd himself satisfactorily, sent Orders to the Cardinal *d'Este*, and to the Marquiss of *Pisani*, his Embassadors, to desire the Pope to send him a Minister whom he had not so much Reason to suspect, he not being able to bear with this, on the account of his violent Temper. The Pope told them, That he could not be hinder'd from employing what Minister he thought fit, and so notwithstanding the King's Request let him set out, protesting at the same time, that if the King did not admit him, he would not give any farther Audience to his Embassador. *Henry* believ'd that the Nuncio was very much inclin'd to the Party of the League

League, wherefore upon the Advice he had that he had set out from *Rome*, he sent an Express to meet him, to desire him to stop at the Place where the Courier should find him, and not to leave it till farther Orders. The Nuncio, who was come to *Lyons*, was surpris'd thereat, but taking into Consideration, that on the one side he had to do with a Master that would be obey'd, and on the other with a Prince who was as easy as he was unconstant, he gave Advice to the Pope of what had happen'd, and wrote to the King, that he knew his Orders, and that nevertheless he would pursue his Journey, as accordingly he did. As soon as the Pope understood the Encounter his Nuncio had met with, he sent word to the Marquis *de Pisani*, to depart from his Dominions in three Days. The Marquis made answer, to the Person who brought him the Message, That the Pope's Territories were not so large, but he could get out of them in four and twenty Hours, and went away in effect. The Pope having recover'd himself from his Transport, employ'd *Horace Rucellay* to negotiate the Marquis's Return. In *France* also the Nuncio's Business was made up, and he carry'd himself so fairly, and with that Moderation, that the King had Reason to be satisfy'd therewith. After the Death of *Henry* III the same Pope sent Cardinal *Cajetan* into *France* in the Quality of Legate. But this Minister of the pretended common Father, instead of visiting the Cardinals *de Vendome* and *de Lenoncourt*, (who notwithstanding they had declar'd themselves for *Henry* IV, their lawful Sovereign, did nevertheless apply themselves to the Preservation of the *Roman Catholick* Religion) wou'd have no Conference nor Communication with any, but the Prelates a d Lords who belong'd to the League, and consulted none but the *Spanish* Ministers, who fomented the Rebellion of the *Parisians*, and of most of the other Towns of the Kingdom. The King meeting one Day in the Fields, as it were by accident, with *Mark Anthony Mocenigo*, Bishop of *Ceneda*, complain'd to him very much of the Partiality of the Legate, with whom the Bishop was come into *France*, and told him, That tho' the Legate had no Credentials for him, it was not probable that the Pope should have order'd him to act as he did. That it could never be the Pope's Intention, that his Minister, coming into the Kingdom, should declare himself the King's Enemy, and join with a Crowd of seditious People, in order to foment a Rebellion, instead of suppressing it. So that far from doing the Office of Mediator, and extinguishing the Fire of Civil War, he pour'd Oyl therein. This Minister did not only exceed the Bounds of his Employment and Function, but as he had no Credentials to the King, so neither had he any Character that could make him be consider'd as a publick Minister. And even it he had had one, yet by his declaring himself openly against the Sovereign, he had no Right to the Protection of the Law of Nations, from a Prince whom he himself did not acknowledge. The Queens *Catherine* and *Mary de Medicis*, were both weak enough to believe, that the Counsels and Power of the Court of *Madrid* were necessary to them, to maintain their own particular Authority against the Princes of the Blood, who had reason to pretend to the Regency in a Kingdom where the *Salick Law* is as it were the Foundation of all the rest. However it may be said with Truth, that the *Civil Wars*, with which *France* has been harrass'd since the Death of *Henry* II till the Peace of *Vervins*, or within a little thereof, were the Effects of the Counsels Catherine took from the Ministers of Spain. One Day this Princess discoursing with *Thomas de Perenot de Chantonne*, Embassador from *Philip* II, she ask'd his Advice, in reference to the Troubles that disturb'd the Kingdom under *Francis* II. That Minister told her, he thought there was but one way to put an End to them, which was to remove the Duke and Cardinal *de Guise* from the Management of the publick Affairs, and to restore the Constable *de Montmorancy*, to the Authority he had had under the late King. This Advice was very faithful in all Appearance, but was in effect very dangerous. The *Spanish* Embassador hated the Constable mortally, and he gave the Queen this Counsel to no other End, than to bring *France* into the utmost Confusion. She did not believe him, because she did not love the Constable, and did not yet fear the *Guises*. But she since gave but too much Credit to the Counsels Cardinal *de Granvelle* and the Duke of *Alva* gave her, when he confer'd with her at *Bayonne*. *Philip*, who despis'd this Woman and her Government, had the Assurance to signify to her, that he could not approve of what had pass'd at the Conference at *Poissy*, at which she had caus'd some Protestant Doctors to assist, and that it belong'd to him to hinder (during the King's Minority) any thing from being done to the Prejudice of his Brother-in-Law. The Queen was weak, and imprudent enough to send into *Spain James de Momborron*, Lord of *Aufance*, to give an Account to *Philip* of what had pass'd at *Poissy*. *Philip* arrogated to himself the Guardianship of *Charles* IX, altho' all the Laws, as well general as particular, were against his having an Administration, which could not fall into worse nor more dangerous Hands.

I said above, that the Prince who forbids his Embassador having any Commerce with the first Minister of the Court where he is to negotiate, prejudices his Affairs, but that Embassador who offends the first Minister ruins them, and renders himself incapable of negotiating. The Marquis *d'Inojosa* and Don *Carlos Coloma*, Embassadors of *Spain* at *London*, undertook to ruin the Duke of *Buckingham*, King *James's* first Minister and Favourite, in the Mind of his Master, and this by an Accusation, destitute not only of all the necessary Proofs, but also of all the Appearances They presented to the King, and communicated to several Lords of the Council, a Memorial, where they set forth, "That the King did not "enjoy a greater Liberty than did *John* King "of *France*, when he was a Prisoner in *England*, or than *Francis* I did at *Madrid*, because he was believ'd and surrounded by the "Servants and Creatures of the Duke of *Buckingham*. That the Embassadors had been in-"form'd, and knew very well, that four "Months were elaps'd since the King was to "have been confin'd to one of his Countrey "Houses, to divert himself, while the Govern-
"ment

" ment was put into other Hands, and that
" the Duke of *Buckingham's* Friends made no
" longer a Secret of it That the said Duke
" secur'd himself of all those he knew to be
" Enemies to the present Government That
" he took them out of Prison, or got them re-
" call'd from their Exile, in order to strengthen
" his Party in the Parliament, as for Instance,
" the Lords of *Oxford*, of *Southampton* and
" *Say* That the Duke, to make himself be
" consider'd, and to lessen the King, had often
" boasted in Parliament, That he had made
" the King do this or that That the three
" Kingdoms were not govern'd by one single
" Monarch, but by a Triumvirate, of which
" the Duke was the first and the chief, the
" Prince of *Wales* the second, and the King
" the last, and that every Bodies Eyes were
" turn'd towards the rising Sun That the
" King, who was the eldest and wisest Prince
" in *Europe*, ought to be so in Effect, and free
" himself from his Captivity, and deliver him-
" self from the Danger with which he was
" threaten'd That he had no other way to do
" this, but by ridding himself of him whose
" Grandeur ought to be no less suspected than
" his Affectation to make himself popular was
" dangerous That they should be glad if his
" Majesty would be chary of the Secret of this
" Advice, which could not take Vent, but it
" must expose them to inevitable Dangers
" That nevertheless, if he thought it proper
" for the Good of his Service to communi-
" cate it, they willingly consented thereto, be-
" cause they were ready to sacrifice their Lives
" for him " There was nothing that one might
not expect from the Marquiss's irregular and
passionate Temper, but I cannot imagin how
he prevail'd with *Coloma* to consent thereto,
who was a wise and sober Man, and an Enemy to Irregularity and Violence There is no
Likelihood that the Court of *Madrid* should
give them Orders to injure the Duke so cruelly, who was all-powerful with the King, and
to bring the Prince himself into so horrible an
Accusation, which was capable of setting the
Father against the Son, and casting the whole
Kingdom into the utmost Confusion They
would not have done it with Impunity if they
had address'd themselves to Cardinal *de Richelieu*, who in an Accusation or Calumny of this
Nature would not have much consider'd their
Character, nor the Order of the King their
Master, even if they had had an express one

I have elsewhere spoken of the Count *de Benavente*, Embassador from *Spain*, who discoursing with the Chancellor of *France*, had
let some Words slip, with which Cardinal *de
Richelieu*, first Minister of that Court, had Reason to be offended, altho' he had said nothing
that could render his Fidelity suspected Nevertheless the Cardinal caus'd Reparation to be
done him, and oblig'd the Embassador to retire
sooner than he would otherwise have done
Walter Strickland the Parliament of *England*'s
Minister at the *Hague*, having presented a Memorial to the States, wherein he offended
the Prince of *Orange*, they sent for him into
one of the Anti Rooms, where they ask'd him,
Whether it was of his own mere Motion, or
by express Orders, that he had presented that
Memorial, which spoke in such offensive Terms

of the Prince At first he told them he was
not oblig'd to make any such Declaration, and
that if in his Memorial there was any Thing
that did not please, they might complain thereof to his Principals, to whom he was oblig'd
to give an Account of his Actions, and not to
the States However, finding himself press'd
by the Deputies, he drew a Paper out of his
Pocket, which as he said contain'd the Parliaments Order The States not being satisfy'd
with this, declar'd by their Resolution of
May 7, 1643, *That what the Memorial contain'd
relating to the Prince of* Orange *was false, forg'd,
and contrary to the Truth That a Letter should
be written to the Parliament to demand Reparation, and that in the mean Time they would receive no more Memorials from* Strickland The
King of *Poland* signify'd to the Baron *de Lisola*
the Emperor's Embassador, *That he would admit him no more to Audience, on the Account of
the Cabals he fomented in his Kingdom* When
Robert Bowes, Embassador from *England*, made
Instance in *Scotland* to have the Duke of *Lenox*
remov'd from the King, the Council of *Scotland* said, *It was an unheard of thing that a Prince
should take upon him to regulate the Council in the
Kingdom of another Sovereign* That they could
not believe the Queen had given any such Orders to her Embassador, and desir'd to see it
Bowes, who would not do that Wrong to the
Queen's Dignity, as to produce her Instructions, chose rather to retire without taking
Leave of the King

Blainville, the *French* Embassador, very much
forgot himself, when he flatter'd the Queen of
England's little Displeasures, and fomented the
domestick Divisions, which were the Cause at
last of removing all the *French* from the Queen's
Retinue, and were one of the first Causes of
the War that ensu'd between the two Crowns
The Court of *France* disavow'd the Conduct of
this Minister, and recall'd him, because that
contrary to the Duty of his Office, *he had intermeddled with the domestick Affairs of the King
of* England It is what a prudent Minister will
carefully avoid, and will ever delight in imitating that wise Embassador of *Spain* who being employ'd in one of the first Courts of *Europe*, refus'd to gratify the Queen, who was for
having him speak to the King *concerning a domestick Affair*, which was very nice He told
her he had no Orders for that purpose, but e-
ven if he had a very precise one, he should
make a Difficulty to execute it, and would re
present to the King his Master, that he might
possibly receive an Answer which might shut
his Mouth, and cause his Majesty to repent
the having given him Orders so contrary to his
Interests

In the Year 1571, the Duke of *Norfolk*, who
had carry'd on Intrigues for the Liberty of the
Queen of *Scots*, whom he pretended to marry,
and who had caus'd some Noblemen in the
Northern Provinces of *England* to take up
Arms, was himself taken up and executed At
his Tryal it was prov'd, that *la Motte Fenelon*,
the *French* Embassador, had sent Money to the
Duke's Party, and that there was a very strict
Intelligence between them Queen *Elizabeth*,
instead of expressing any Resentment, was contented to complain thereof, as well as of the
Zeal with which the Embassador prosecuted
the

The EMBASSADOR and his FUNCTIONS. 321

the Queen of *Scots* Liberty *Walsingham*, who had Orders to make these Complaints, having spoke thereof to Queen *Catherine*, added, That he could not forbear telling her Majesty, that it was certain that *la Motte* had had Intrigues with the Duke of *Norfolk*, who was a very dangerous Subject, and that he spoke so warmly for the Liberty of the Queen of *Scots*, who was a sworn Enemy to the Queen his Mistress, that it was reasonable to think he did not act without the express Orders of the Court, in an Affair of that Importance from whence it might be inferr'd, *That France was for intermedaling in the domestick Affairs of* England. The Queen excus'd the Intentions and Procedure of *la Motte*, and said, That if he had done any thing which could displease Queen *Elizabeth*, it was contrary to the King his Master's Orders, and that the Good-will he might have in his own particular for the Queen of *Scots*, should not be prejudicial to the Service of the Queen of *England*.

Here may be added to what I have already said, *the Example of* Alfonso *King of* Castile, *and of* Peter IV *King of* Arragon, of whom mention is made in the Memoirs. *Peter* had resolv'd to punish severely the Rebellion of the Inhabitants of *Valencia*, but *Alfonso* caus'd him to be desir'd, by *Gomez Fernandez de Sorta*, to defer the Execution of his Resolution, till he had sent him the *Infant Don Ferdinand*, and the Count *Lurique*, his Sons, who were to intercede for the Rebels. *Peter* made Answer to *Gomez Fernandez*, That he was very much surpriz'd the King of *Castile* should send him an Embassy on this Account, since as well he as all the other Princes of the World, ought to commend the Resolution he had taken to punish his rebellious Subjects, instead of hindering him from doing it. *That they were his Subjects, and that the Disposal of them ought to be left to himself*.

In the Year 1650, there arose some Difference between the Prince of *Orange* and the States of *Holland*. Some of their Deputies were sent Prisoners to the Castle of *Loevestein*, and the Prince carry'd the Arms of the State before the City of *Amsterdam*. Anthony *le Brua*, Embassador from *Spain*, who was otherwise an able and wise Minister, thinking he did a very grateful Thing to the Prince, went and offer'd him the Arms of the King his Master, for the more speedy Reduction of the Place, but the Prince answer'd him, *That the King of* Spain *had nothing to do to medale with the domestick Affairs of the Countrey, and that neither he nor the States had any Occasion for his Arms. That if the King should cause his Troops to advance, their little Misunderstandings would soon cease, and all the Forces of the State will be seen to unite to oppose the Foreigners*. They soon ceas'd in Effect, and the same Embassador, endeavouring to repair his first Fault, made a second, by demanding Audience of the States, to complement them on the Reconciliation. It was granted him, but as soon as they were inform'd of the Subject of it, they sent him Word (tho' he was already at the Bottom of the Stairs, where their Deputies were to receive him) That they were oblig'd to desire him to approve of their remitting him to another Time, so that he went away with a kind of Affront, for having had a mind to concern himself in a domestick Affair, of which he ought not to have taken any Cognizance.

It was for the same Reason that the Dukes of *Brunswick* and *Lunenburg* refus'd, in the Year 1670, to admit of the Mediation of the States of the United Provinces, for the Accommodation of the Differences they had with the Capital City of their Countrey. It cannot be deny'd that it is subject immediately to the Princes of this House, but as she had obtain'd great Privileges from their Predecessors, (and being one of the most considerable of the *Teutonick Hanse*) she had by little and little withdrawn her self from the Obedience which she ow'd them, and had had the Assurance to oppose their Entrance. All the Princes of that House were in Arms on the Occasion of a Difference they had with the Bishop of *Munster*, for the Protection of the Town of *Hoxer*, and being sensible that the Town of *Brunswick* was not in a Condition to make any great Resistance, they laid Siege to it. The States of the United Provinces, who have I know not what Treaties with the Hanseatick Towns, from which notwithstanding they have never yet receiv'd the least Advantage, had formerly caus'd the Siege of the said Town to be rais'd, and imagining they should succeed again, they sent thither for all Succour, a solemn Deputation, and offer'd their Mediation for the agreeing the Differences. The Princes signify'd to the Deputies, *That as the r High Mightinesses would not be glad that they should take Cognizance of the Differences they might have with their Subjects, so they hop'd likewise they would not intermeddle in the Disputes they had with theirs, nor concern themselves with their domestick Affairs*. They would not so much as suffer the Deputies to send their Letters by a Trumpeter into the Town, and this with so much the greater Justice, because the States had done the same on so many Occasions, that the Deputies (who could not be ignorant of it) might very well have forborn desiring any such Thing.

In the Month of *March* 1644, Messieurs d'*Avaux* and *Servien*, Embassadors Extraordinary from *France*, taking their Audience of Leave in the Assembly of the States General, to go to *Munster*, intreated them to have a little Compassion and Moderation for those Inhabitants of the United Provinces, who made Profession of the Roman Catholick Religion. They had hinted some Days before that they would speak to that effect, and they had been desir'd not to do it, and to consider that their Intercession would do at least as much Harm as good to the Roman Catholicks. So that the States seeing the Embassadors had nevertheless follow'd their own Sentiments, rather than the Counsel which had been given them, express'd their Displeasure at it, and declar'd, by a formal Resolution, that this Proposition was contrary to the fundamental Laws of the State and its Repose. That they were surpriz'd thereat, and to prevent the Disorders and Mischiefs that might ensue, they would make such rigorous Regulations, and such severe Ordinances, that the Insolence of the Roman Catholicks, who had begg'd this foreign Intercession, should have Cause to repent it. *It was a domestick Matter*, which being of the last Importance,

oblig'd

oblig'd the States to send this their Resolution to the Embassadors by eight Deputies, who added thereto by Word of Mouth, what the Resolution did not express in Terms strong enough. D'*Avaux* had a little too much Devotion for a Man of his Profession, and *Servien*, who adapted his to the Nature of Affairs, had been for following the Advice of those who were the most moderate among the States, who had counsell'd them to risque nothing in an Adventure, where there was nothing to be hop'd for. He had represented to d'*Avaux*, that what they should do, would prove but a vain Ostentation, of no Utility to the Catholicks, and which might produce a very ill Effect, and that it were better to be moderate in the Execution of the Orders the King had given them, by converting their publick Recommendations into private Offices, for the Relief of the Catholicks. These two Embassadors, and those who had given them these Orders, ought to have reflected on the Answer, *Charles* IX, and *Henry* III, had given to the Protestant Princes of *Germany*, who had been for doing the like Offices for those of the Religion in *France*.

The Embassador who has acquir'd the Confidence of the Court where he resides, either by his own Merit, or by the Consideration of the common Interest of the two Princes, may intrude himself into the Affairs of the Countrey where he resides, if it be desir'd of him. *Angelo Cornaro*, Embassador from *Venice* at *Paris*, had made himself so acceptable to that Court, that Cardinal *de Richelieu* finding his Counsels were very useful to him, made them even necessary, and desir'd the Republick to continue him in the Embassy, when the Term of Years for his Service should be expir'd: but on these Occasions the Minister, instead of discharging the Function of an Embassador, does that of a Counsellor, and of a particular Friend. The King of *Portugal*, who dy'd last, had accepted the Crown, but only because he suppos'd it would cost him nothing to maintain himself in that Dignity, as long as *France* and *Spain* should be at War, and that whenever *France* should make a Peace, it would comprise him therein. He was undeceiv'd, as well by the Opposition the *Spaniards* made against it at *Munster*, as by the Difficulty Cardinal *Mazarin* express'd, to engage the King his Master in an Alliance that could oblige him thereto. He therefore bethought himself of resigning the Crown, for the Benefit of the Duke of *Orleans*, or of some other Prince that *France* should nominate, and of retiring himself to the *Terceres*. He caus'd one of his Secretaries of State *to communicate this Thought to* Lanier, who resided on the Part of *France* at *Lisbon*. The Embassador considering that it was not a random Thought that had accidentally come into the King's Head, but a fix'd Resolution, which had been communicated to the Queen, and to some of the Lords of the Council, told the Secretary his Sentiments thereof, and added, that he would speak to the King about it. He did so, and represented to him, as well as to the Queen, That the King his Master would be much surpriz'd to understand, that his Majesty had been capable of taking a Resolution so unsuitable to his Honour and Interest, and that without doubt by the Advice of Persons very indifferently affected to the Good of his Service, and to see him entertain Thoughts so prejudicial to the Interest of both Crowns. That he would be far from imparting any thing thereof to his Court, but since the King had been pleas'd to intrust him with it, he would take the Liberty to tell him. That the Design his Majesty had to desire Mademoiselle, or else the Duke of *Longueville*'s Daughter, for the Prince his Son, would not succeed, and that he must not so much as think of giving the Command of his Army to some Prince or Lord of *France*, as well as the Direction of the Affairs of his Kingdom, but that he must commit both the one and the other to the Prince his Son, when he came to Age. That the King of *France*'s Interest could not suffer the Crown of *Portugal* to be re-united to that of *Castile*, and that he would without all doubt make a last Effort to hinder it, but that it was also necessary the King of *Portugal* should help himself, and not forsake his Interest. That he had no other way to secure himself than by acting on his Part with Vigour, while *France* assisted him with Men and Money, and made a powerful Diversion, as well in *Catalonia* as in *Italy* and *Flanders*. The Revolt of the City of *Palermo*, and the Insurrection of *Naples* were what confirm'd the King of *Portugal* and not Lanier's Reasons, who on this Occasion did not make any Offer to intermeddle with the domestick Affairs of the King of *Portugal*, but only told his own private Sentiments on the Proposition the King had made him.

CHAP. V.

The Embassador ought to execute his Orders, and how.

THE Embassador is indispensably oblig'd to execute punctually the Orders of his Prince, when they are express and reiterated, unless he be well assur'd he shall commit a greater Evil, and shall render himself more criminal in executing them, than by delaying to obey them. The *Roman*, who seeing the Ladders rear'd, and the Enemies in a Condition to surprize the Town, had no Regard to the Law that forbad him at the Peril of his Life to approach the Rampart, but ran to the Danger, repuls'd the Enemies, and flung down their Ladders. And the Magistrate, instead of punishing him according to the Rigour of the Laws, commended his Zeal, approv'd his Action, and rewarded the Service this good Citizen

tizen had done his Countrey *Walsingham* writing on the 2d of *April*, 1571, to the Lord *Burleigh*, makes use of this Example, and says, That considering he could not execute the Queen's Orders, without failing in the Zeal and Fidelity he ow'd her, he had chosen rather to decline it, *and thereby expose himself to the Hazard of being reproach'd thereupon.* Cardinal *Dossat*, speaking of the Orders *Henry* IV sent him, does not scruple to say more than once, That they are Orders which he cannot execute, till his Majesty has explain'd himself more expressly on the Remonstrances he shall make, or has made to his Majesty. And on the other side, he did not fear hazarding something beyond his Orders whenever he thought he cou'd exceed them, without prejudicing the King's Interest. The Negotiation he had Orders to carry on with the Great Duke of *Tuscany*, for the Restitution of the Islands of *Pomeques* and of *If*, was by so much the more difficult, as they could not be got out of the Hands of the Great Duke, without reimbursing him a good Sum of Money. The King who had no Money, had no Credit neither with the Great Duke, so that *Dossat*, that these Places might not be left in strange Hands, oblig'd himself to procure twelve Sureties, or Pledges for the Reimbursement of that Sum. He had no Orders for that, and he says, he confesses it was a bold Stroke, what he had done, but he adds, That he had learn'd, that in grand Affairs, to decline a great Evil, and obtain a great Good, one must dare to do something, and take a good Resolution to get out of a bad Case, as well, and as soon as one can. He justifies himself afterwards, and says he did it to set the King's Mind at Ease, and to secure the Coasts of *Provence*, which would be expos'd to the Discretion of Foreigners, if the King did not repossess himself of those Islands.

Not only the Embassador is not oblig'd, but he even ought not to execute all the Orders that are sent him, if he judges that he should become more criminal by obeying, than by representing to his Prince the Reasons which hinder him from obeying. King *Henry* IV's would have transferr'd the Archbishop of *Bourges* to the Archbishoprick of *Sens*, and caus'd pressing Instances be made for that Purpose. Pope *Clement* VIII, who did not love that Prelate, because it was he had given Absolution to the King at St *Denis*, would not consent thereto. The King, on his side, growing weary of the Pope's continu'd Refusals, wrote with his own Hand to *Dossat*, That he would not ask any more Favours of the Pope till he had obtain'd this, commanding him to read the Letter to his Holiness. *Dossat* was preparing to do it, but the Pope not having the Patience to hear it, commanded him to tell him the Contents thereof. *Dossat* did so, but he did not say one Word to the Pope of the Declaration the King made therein, that he would ask no more Favours. Writing to *Villeroy*, he says, He omitted it on Purpose, as well because this Declaration might be made at any time, as because that when such Expressions are slipt from a great Prince, they must either be maintain'd and kept up to, to the Detriment of several private Persons as well as of the publick, or else act contrary to them with little Reputation.

In such Cases the Embassador must consult his Prudence, and the Nature of the Affair he has to manage. The Ministers who dispatch the Prince's Orders, sometimes mingle their Passion or Interest therewith, nay the Prince himself does not always follow Reason, and his true Interest so close, but that he sometimes loses the Sight of them. His Intentions, how good and just soever they may be, may be alter'd by prejudicate Opinions, or by evil Counsels. This is the Reason why the King of *France*, who is the most absolute of all the Monarchs of *Christendom*, will have his Edicts verify'd, and register'd in Parliament, and that his Orders pass through the Hands of the Governors of Provinces, who before they join their Letters thereto, which authorize the Execution thereof within their Governments, observe whether the King's Orders have their due Forms, and whether they do not contain any thing contrary to his Interests, to Justice, and to the Laws of the Kingdom. The King suffers also his Parliament to make Remonstrances to him, and the Governors to represent either the Injustice that resides in the Orders, or the Difficulty that will be found in the Execution of them. In the same manner a Prince, that sends his Orders to his Embassador, is willing he should examine them, and judge whether they can be executed without prejudicing his Affairs, that he may not ruin them by an imprudent Zeal, or by a giddy and blind Obedience. King *Henry* IV knew full as much as the ablest of his Ministers, and *Villeroy*, who had the principal Direction of the foreign Affairs under him, was a consummate Minister, and nevertheless when they send Orders to President *Jeannin*, they almost always tell him, That such is their Opinion, and that it is his Business to judge whether they are consistent with the State of the Affair he has to negotiate. Provided the Embassador does not exceed the Bounds of his Power, and that he does not act contrary to the Intentions, and against the Dignity of his Prince, he ought to shew himself easy, and avoid Cavilling and Contestation. The Affair of *Henry* IV's Absolution was very nice, because the Interest and Reputation of the Crown of *France* was to be taken Care of, and it was necessary at the same time to give to the See of *Rome* what was its due. Wherefore the King's Sollicitors (without exceeding their Power, and securing the Dignity of the King, and of the Crown of *France*,) say, They had refus'd nothing of what belong'd to the Dignity of the Holy See, and of the Pope, as far as their Power could extend. As in effect an Embassador who has Merit, and understands his Business well, will pass over a great many small Matters, which would stop and puzzle an ignorant Head, or a slender Ability.

Pope *Pius* V, who could not wean himself of the ill Habits he had contracted in his Convent, being inform'd that some Regulations were to be made in Reference to Religion, at the Diet which had been summon'd at *Ausburg*, in the Year 1566, wrote to Cardinal *Commendon*, who was with the Emperor, to protest against whatever should be done there, and to declare to the Ecclesiastical Princes, That he would make use of the Spiritual Sword against them, and against the Emperor first of all.

That

That he would deprive him of the Imperial Dignity, dispossess him of his Kingdoms and hereditary Countreys, and would declare him incapable of succeeding to the Crown of *Spain*, when the Succession should happen *Commendon*, who was a *Venetian*, that is to say, neither giddy-brain'd, nor a Bigot, judging that the Execution of the Pope's Orders would only serve to exasperate the Minds still more, communicated them to the Emperor, and it was agreed between them that he should write to the Pope, *That he was of Opinion, That after the Assurance the Emperor had given him, that no mention should be made of Religion in the Diet, it was not proper to make a Protestation, which would be of no Utility* The Pope, who could not endure a Contradiction, repeated his Orders to him, and added thereto, That if the Emperor suffer'd Religion to be so much as spoke of in the Diet, altho' they came to no Resolution therein, he should excommunicate the Emperor immediately; with all the other Catholick Princes *Commendon however did nothing of all this*, but behav'd himself with the same Prudence, of which we see so many Instances in all his Negotiations, where may be discover'd throughout the whole, the Air and Genius of his Countrey It is true that, before the Arrival of the last Orders, it had been resolv'd, That the Affair of Religion shou'd be referr'd to another Diet, but it did not stick at the Pope, that the Cardinal, by executing his precipitate Orders, had caus'd all the Catholick Princes of *Germany* to revolt against the See of *Rome*

In fact, the Embassador may do as much Harm to his Master's Affairs, by executing his Orders with too much Precipitation and Exactness, as in eluding them by an affected Disobedience The Count *de Trautmansdorf*, the Emperor's chief Embassador at the Congress of *Westphalia*, labour'd with a continual Application, and with success enough at the Peace of the Empire There was no Advantage which he did not offer to the *Swedish* Ministers, out of a Design, and in hopes of separating that Crown from the Interest of its Allies, to the end there might be no Obligation given to *France* the Satisfaction the Elector of *Bavaria* made it hope for He met therein almost insuperable Obstacles But in the Year 1647 he lighted on so favourable a Conjuncture that he might in a manner have been sure of the Success of his Negotiation *France* had very particular, and very strict Engagements with the Court of *Munich*, of which the *Swedes* were so jealous, that *Oxenstiern* did not scruple to say, That *Sweden* would rather chuse to have the Imperial Dignity perpetuated in the House of *Austria*, than to see it pass into that of *Bavaria*, while this had so close an Union with *France* Moreover the *Swedish* Army was so embarass'd in *Bohemia*, that it was doubted whether it could well disengage it self, and Cardinal *Mazarin*, who was ever a good Husband, and sparing out of Season, had signify'd to the Court of *Sweden*, That *France* was not in a Condition to continue to it the Payment of the Subsidies This Declaration, which incommoded and provok'd the *Swedes*, was contrary to the Treaties, whereby *France* oblig'd it self to pay them till the Peace was concluded

So that *Trautmansdorf* might have made an Advantage of this Discontent, and have been in Hopes of bringing the *Swedes* to consent to a separate Treaty, had it not been for the Order the Emperor sent him by an Express, to delay the Conclusion thereof, because he had already corrupted *John de Weert*, and he believ'd he should be able to bring over to his Service all the Troops of the Elector of *Bavaria*, the absolute Disposal of whom, promis'd him infallible Progresses in the Empire, and incomparable Advantages over his Enemies The Count obey'd punctually his Master's Orders, whose Affairs receiv'd irreparable Prejudice by this Punctuality, because he thereby lost the Opportunity he had of gaining the *Swedes*, and of fortifying the bad Understanding, which was then considerable between the Ministers of the two Crowns *Trautmansdorf* was so much in the Favour of the Emperor his Master, that notwithstanding his Remoteness, the *Spaniards* who did not love him, could not ruin his Credit at the Court of *Vienna*, but yet he did not dare to run the risque of delaying the Execution of his Orders, altho' by making a separate Treaty with *Sweden*, he would have acqui'rd to himself a glorious and everlasting Reputation, and to his Master an Advantage, that could neither be sufficiently rewarded nor acknowledg'd

The Embassador who has a perfect Knowledge of the Interest and Humour of his Prince, of that of his first Minister, and of the Constitution of his Council, may take his Measures, and judge to what Degree he ought to defer to the Orders of the one or the other The Duke of *Alva*, Viceroy of *Naples*, and Lieutenant General to *Philip* II in *Italy*, had resolv'd to break with the *Caraffas*, who had done a thousand Indignities to the Emperor's Ministers and those of the King of *Spain*, and having a mind that every body should believe he was forc'd thereto by Pope *Paul* IV, he sent to *Rome* P rro *Loffredi*, Marquis of *Trevico*, to make some Overtures of an Accommodation to the Pope and to the Cardinals *The Duke gave him express Orders to remain at Rome but four Days, whether he had an Answer or not* But the Pope (who expected every Day an Account of the Success of the Negotiation he was practising in *France*, not daring neither to break nor conclude with the Marquiss) represented to him, that it was impossible to give him an Answer in four Days to the Propositions he had made him, because being oblig'd to communicate them to all the Cardinals, it would require some time to confute the Sentiments of those who were not well intention'd This Minister, who did not know the Viceroy's Design, and who vainly flatter'd himself with the Hopes of reconciling the jarring Minds, suffer'd himself to be persuaded to remain some Days longer at *Rome*, beyond the Term his Master had allotted him The Duke who had not the least Thought of coming to an Agreement with the Pope, seeing his Man did not come back at the End of four Days, invaded the Ecclesiastical State Hereupon the Pope arrested the Marquiss, as the Minister of him who made War with him without any previous Declaration, and at the same time that he amus'd him with a Negotiation. The Minister who did not execute

ecute his Orders, by remaining at *Rome* beyond the Term which had been prescrib'd him, and who might thereby have disconcerted all his Master's Designs, was become a Criminal, and justify'd also the Pope's Procedure, who was not oblig'd to consider him as a publick Minister, after the Hostilities his Master committed, and after the Declaration he had himself made, that his Commission was but for four Days.

King *Henry* IV had reduc'd the Duke of *Savoy* to such great Extremities, that without the Pope's Consideration, he had forc'd him, not only to treat with him, but to receive what Law the Victor pleas'd. In this Condition the Duke sent to the King *Francis* d'*Arconnas*, Count de *Tousaine*, and *René de Lucinge*, Lord des *Alymes* his first Steward, with Power to make an Exchange for the Marquisate of *Saluzzo*, and he even sent them Orders to sign the Project which had been drawn up for that Purpose, *but three Days after he alter'd his Mind and recall'd it.* Cardinal *Aldobrandin*, who was there as Mediator on the part of the Pope, considering that the Duke's Procedure might be capable of rekindling the War between the two Crowns, was so disharten'd thereat, that he declar'd to the Embassadors of *Savoy*, that he would meddle no more in the Affair, till they had promis'd him in Writing to sign whatever he should settle with the King's Commissioners. The Embassadors had no sooner made this Promise, than they receiv'd *fresh Prohibitions not to sign any thing*, and accordingly, after the Legate had concluded the Treaty, they refus'd to sign it. The Legate was extremely dissatisfy'd, and us'd all sorts of Promises, Threats and Commands, to oblige them to sign, but all to no Purpose, but at last he bethought himself to promise them in Writing, that he would prevail with the Duke to approve of, and ratify whatever they should sign. That he would secure to them their Offices and Dignities. That he would protect them from any Persecutions they might apprehend, and to declare that what they had done had been *per force*, and in pursuance of the Order they had receiv'd, to submit to the Cardinal's Authority.

The Embassadors sign'd at last the Treaty, but they soon repented it, because the Duke disavow'd them, and was so incens'd at the Disobedience of his Ministers, that *Arconnas* had much ado to resolve to present himself before him, and des *Alymes*, who was become the Subject of the King of *France*, on account of the Lands he held in *Bugey*, would return no more to *Savoy*.

The Treaty which had been made at *Vienna* in the Year 1602, concerning the Affair of the *Uscoques*, and that which was concluded some Years after at *Ast* about the *Monferrat*, not having been executed, *France* fearing lest she should be oblig'd to carry her Arms into *Italy*, to oppose the predominant Power of *Spain*, made the Court of *Madrid* consent to a Treaty, which was finish'd at *Paris* in the Year 1617. The Republick of *Venice* was very much interested therein, and she found her Ends in the Treaty, but *Ottavio Bon* and *Vincent Gussoni*, her Embassadors, had Orders to sign nothing, without an effectual Restitution of what Depredations had been made upon their Subjects in the Gulf. The King of *France* promis'd them to use such pressing Instances with the King of *Spain*, his Father-in-Law, that they need not doubt of the Restitution, but this Assurance was not able to make them go beyond their Orders. However the same Embassadors considering since, that if the Duke of *Savoy*, who found his Account in the Treaty, should accept it, the Republick would remain alone expos'd to the Resentment of the Arch-Duke, and of the King of *Spain*, resolv'd to sign it. They were very glad of it at *Venice*; because she got out of Trouble with all imaginable Advantages, and yet for all that, the Senate deliberating on the Circumstances of the Negotiation, and judging that the Marks of Obedience were wanting which Embassadors owe to the Republick, sent them Orders to surrender themselves Prisoners to answer for their Disobedience. It also sent the Chevalier *Simon Contarini*, as Embassador Extraordinary to the King, to acquaint him with the Reason that oblig'd it to proceed in this Manner against *Bon* and *Gussoni*, but the King order'd *Contarini* to remain at *Lions*, till the Senate had given up her Resentment to the Intercession his Majesty made for the Embassadors, whose Intentions had not only been innocent, but also beneficial. The Senate was contented to recall the Embassadors, and to ratify the Treaty in the Manner we shall relate hereafter. The Embassador can find his Safety only in the punctual Execution of his Orders. There is no Warranty that can skreen him from the just Indignation of the Prince, which he shall draw upon himself by his Disobedience.

As on the one side the Embassador who has express and precise Orders, ought to execute them punctually, if he is very well persuaded of the Intention and constant Will of his Master, so ought he on the other, to act with great Circumspection, and with great Reservedness, *in those Affairs concerning which he has no Orders at all*. In the beginning of the *Candian* War, *la Haye Vantelay*, Embassador of *France*, had gain'd a *Turkish Dragoman*, who govern'd the First Vizir, and had dispos'd him to hearken to some Propositions on the part of the Republick, so far that the First Vizir ask'd the Interpreter, what the Senate of *Venice* would give in Lands and Money for a Peace. The *French* Embassador, who manag'd this Intrigue, thinking he had procur'd a mighty Advantage to the Republick by the Vizir's Declaration, communicated it to the Baylo, and this answer'd haughtily enough, That it belong'd to the Grand Seignior, who had begun the War, to say what he pretended to have. *La Haye* look'd upon this to be reasonable, and that it was what was practis'd every where else, but he thought likewise that the Affair would be far advanc'd in the Seraglio, if the Embassador gave him the Power to ask for Peace in the Name of the Republick, to the End he might carry the Project thereof to the first Minister. The Baylo reply'd that that was impossible, *That he had no Orders to demand a Peace*, and so he should be far from making any such Advance. Hereupon the *French* Embassador declar'd, That neither he nor the Interpreter who had acted the Mediator, could meddle no farther in this Affair, because there was no likelihood that the *Turkish* Emperor would consent to a Peace,

O o o o if

if he was not befought thereto with the Refpect he thought was due to his Grandeur The Baylo Soranço allow'd it to be true, but he faid, *He had no Orders*, and that the Affair muft remain as it was till he had given Advice thereof to the Senate There are no Minifters more fcrupulous on this Subject than thofe of *Venice*, becaufe the Republick exacts from them an Obedience by fo much the more punctual, that the leaft Indulgence fhe fhould have for thofe who are all equal by Birth, would difconcert the Harmony by which fhe fubfifts I have fpoken elfewhere, and fhall fpeak again hereafter of *Octavian Bon* and of *Vincent Guffoni*, whofe Hiftory is very fingular in all its Circumftances

In the Year 1558, the States of *Scotland* fent into *France* the Archbifhop of *Glafcow*, the Bifhop of *Orkney*, and the Earls of *Rothefay* and of *Caffelles*, with feveral other Noblemen, to be prefent at the Marriage of their Queen, who was to efpoufe the *Dauphin*, eldeft Son to *Henry* II After the Confummation of the Marriage, the Embaffadors were fent for to the Council, where they were told, That the King defir'd they would caufe the Crown and other Ornaments to be brought to *France*, becaufe he had a mind to have his Son crown'd King of *Scotland* The Embaffadors having made Anfwer, *That they had no Orders concerning that Affair*, thofe of the Council reply'd, That what the King defir'd now of them, was that they would give their Word, that when the Matter fhould be debated in the Council or in the Parliament of *Scotland*, they would back the King's Intention with their Votes, and that they would fign a Writing that fhould be offer'd them to this Purpofe The Embaffadors faid, *They had their Orders, and that they could not exceed them* That they would willingly do what the *French*, their ancient and faithful Friends and Allies, fhould defire of them, but that they hop'd alfo, That nothing would be requir'd of them that could prejudice their Honour or Confcience

The Minifter who undertakes an Affair for which he has no Orders, is refponfible for the Succefs thereof, whereas he who only executes the Orders that are given him, how unjuft or unreafonable foever they may be, charges his Mafter therewith I cannot tell how *Gabriel d'Aramont* could juftify himfelf to King *Henry* II, in reference to the Commiffion he took in the Year 1551, of the Great Mafter of *Malta*. *Gabriel* was returning to *Conftantinople*, where he had already been in the Quality of Embaffador, and having in his Voyage put into the Harbour of *Malta*, the Great Mafter pray'd him to go to *Sinan Bacha* and *Dragut*, who befieg'd the Town of *Tripoli*, and to prevail with them to raife the Siege There was an Alliance between *Henry* and *Soliman* but I muft own I cannot comprehend, how *d'Aramont* could imagin, that at his Inftance thofe two Generals fhould raife the Siege of an important Place, without neceffity, and without their Prince's Orders, upon the bare Requeft of an Embaffador, who had no Powers in that Refpect from the King his Mafter, nor any Credentials for them And indeed he receiv'd an Affront for his Pains, and brought one upon the King, becaufe *Sinan* continu'd the Siege, and oblig'd

d'Aramont to remain as a Prifoner in the Camp, till after the Reduction of the Place

There are however fome Occafions where the Embaffador ought to rifque fomething, becaufe it is impoffible for the Prince to forefee all Accidents, and all Occurrences, fo as to be able to inftruct his Embaffador concerning all that may happen And fometimes he has not leifure allow'd him to wait for his Prince's Orders, but is oblig'd to make a Choice, and it is on thefe Occafions that the Minifter fhews what he is good for, and what he can do In the Year 1645, the States of the United Provinces put it in debate, Whether they fhould not Intereft themfelves in the *Norbern* War, and whether they fhould not change their Mediation into a Rupture *D'Eftrades*, who at that time difcharg'd the Function of Embaffador, tho' he had not the Character, reprefented to the States, That the Treaties they were ingag'd in with *France*, oblig'd them to employ all their Forces againft the *Spaniards*, and that they would very much weaken thofe they had in *Flanders*, if they fent any of them into Par's fo remote from the Frontiers of *France*, and made them comprehend fo well the Prejudice they would thereby do to the Common Caufe, that he made them lay afide the Thoughts they had to declare themfelves The Court of *France* drew a very great Advantage therefrom, and yet it feem'd not to be much fatisfy'd with fome Expreffions which he had been forc'd to make ufe of, and which were not very obliging to a Crown ally'd to *France* But befides that *d'Eftrades* had acted therein in concert with the Prince of *Orange*, the Council of *France* it felf confefs'd, that he had not only done a fignal Service to the King, but alfo that it was impoffible to have proceeded with more Addrefs and Prudence He had no Orders, but if he had not fpoke the States had declar'd themfelves and *Sweden* would have been oblig'd to have drawn its Forces out of *Germany*, where they would no longer have been able to fecond the Arms and Intentions of *France*

The Embaffador ought chiefly to take care not to engage himfelf, without exprefs Orders, in Negotiations, the Confequences whereof may be of great Importance, and the Succefs uncertain, and to confider that the Effects of a falfe Zeal and of Imprudence, are often as dangerous as thofe of Infidelity The Emperor *Ferdinand* II told *Don Balthafar de Zuniga*, Embaffador of *Spain*, and fignify'd the fame to the King of *Spain* himfelf by Father *Hyacinte*, that the Elector *Palatin* could not be reftor'd, but the *Roman* Religion muft fuffer extremely by it, and to confider that the Houfe of *Auftria* receive the utmoft Prejudice thereby It is what the Earl of *Briftol*, Embaffador of *England* at *Madrid*, could not be ignorant of He knew alfo that *Ferdinand* had effectually difpos'd of the Upper *Palatinate*, and of the Electoral Dignity it felf: That he could not difpoffefs the Elector of *Bavaria* thereof, without reimburfing him feveral Millions of Crowns, which he had lent him fince the Troubles of *Bohemia*, and that the *Spaniards* themfelves had no great mind to quit the lower *Palatinate* which they were in poffeffion of He knew likewife that the Marriage of the Prince of *Wales* with the *Infanta* of *Spain* would come to nothing without this Reftitution,

The EMBASSADOR and his FUNCTIONS. 327

tion, and unless on the other side the *Roman Catholicks* of *England* were allow'd the Exercise of their Religion. These Difficulties were invincible, but yet they did not hinder the Earl from putting the Affair of the Marriage in Negotiation, and from hearkening to the Propositions the Duke of *Lerma* made him on that Subject, as a thing which he thought he could bring about, and of which he created himself a Difference with the Count *d'Olivarés* under *Philip* IV. The Passion the Earl of *Bristol* had to oblige the *English* of his Religion, and to render his Person necessary, was so great, that he engag'd the Prince, presumptive Heir of the Crown of *Great-Britain*, to travel into *Spain*, and to put himself into the Hands of People who hated his Religion, and could not love his Person. He had never got from 'em, if his Destiny had not reserv'd him for a more unhappy End, and if the Court of *Madrid* had not made it known on this Occasion, (from whence she might have drawn incomparable Advantages) that she preferr'd this Appearance of Honour to all other Considerations. I would not say the Earl of *Bristol's* Intention was bad, but it cannot be deny'd, that his Procedure was very imprudent, and that the Negotiation he continu'd to carry on after the Prince was gone from *Spain* was criminous. He was well enough acquainted with the Court of *Madrid*, to have no room to doubt, that the Difficulty the Court of *Rome* made concerning the Dispensation, was only an Artifice of the *Spaniards*, it being certain that there was no other, than what the *Spanish* Inquisition and the Count *Duk* caus'd to be started. The Marriage of *Margaret* of *Valois* with *Henry* King of *Navarre*, that of *Catherine*, Sister to the said *Henry*, with the Prince of *Lorrain*, of *Henrietta* of *France* with the aforesaid Prince of *Wales*, and of the Princess of *Portugal* with the King of *England*, make it plain enough that the Difference of Religions does not hinder the Court of *Rome* from giving its Dispensations, when they are demanded regularly and in form.

If the Embassador ought not to act without Orders, and if he cannot, without necessity, avoid executing those that are given him, he cannot, without a Crime and without Treason, act directly contrary to his Master's Orders. The Count *Albertin de Bossehetto*, whom the Confederate Princes of *Italy* sent to the Camp of *Charles* VIII, under the Pretext of going to see his Son, who serv'd in the *French* Army under *John James Trivulce*, he might desire a Passport for the Deputies who were to assist at the Congress, after he had shewn his Commission to the King, demanded a private Audience, wherein he inform'd him of the bad State of the Confederates Army, and of the Divisions of the Generals, and exhorted him to grant them nothing, because their Troops would disperse themselves in a few Days, and they would be oblig'd to raise the Siege of *Novarra*. This Minister, whose business it was to promote a Peace, endeavour'd to break off the Treaty before it was begun.

There is nothing risqu'd in following the Example of M *Chanut*, because he was a wise and skilful Minister, I shall therefore set down what was his Practice, in Reference to the Orders which were sent him. He was yet but Resident in *Sweden*, when he was commanded to feel the Pulse of that Court, and endeavour to find out whether it would approve of *France's* making a Treaty of Friendship with the King of *Poland*, and allowing him Subsidies to carry on a War against the *Tartars*. The Queen of *Sweden* liv'd in a perpetual Distrust of *Poland*, and had even desir'd *Chanut* not to speak of an Accommodation, because she would have none with the King, till a Peace had regulated the Affairs of *Germany*. *Chanut*, on his part, was every Day telling the Queen of the Difficulties *France* had to find Money, because she was continually talking to him of the Subsidies, which she pretended to have augmented, and made pressing Instances at that Court for that Purpose. So that *Chanut*, judging that he should expose himself if he said that *France* would assist the King of *Poland* with Money, at the same time that he was every Day protesting that it had none to pay the *Swedish* Subsidies, had a great Mind to say nothing of it to the Queen, but taking it afterwards into Consideration, *that the Orders he had receiv'd were very express*, he resolv'd to speak to her about it, and succeeded therein better than he expected. The Queen, who knew Cardinal *Mazarin's* Humour, and who was sensible he was not a Man that would give Money to the King of *Poland* to do nothing, while *France* had so much Difficulty to pay what it ow'd to *Sweden*, whose Friendship was so necessary to it, made Answer, That she was glad that *France* made it self Friends, and that she should not at all be jealous of a Treaty, which would have a greater Appearance than Effect. *Chanut* knew that the Cardinal would have the Orders he gave in the King's Name executed, for which Reason he also maintain'd himself better than that other Minister, who neglected executing the reiterated Orders which where sent him, to use his Endeavours to procure the Revocation of an Embassador, who was not agreeable at the Court. Almost at the same time that *Chanut* spoke to the Queen about the Alliance of *Poland*, he receiv'd also Orders to urge, that the two thousand *German* Horse of Mareschal *de Turenne's* Army, (who having mutiny'd, had joyn'd that of *Sweden*) might return to the King's Service. He spoke accordingly to the Prince *Palatin* about it, who was going into *Germany* in the Quality of Generalissimo of the Armies of that Crown, and he found him inclin'd enough to gratify *France* therein, in pursuance of a Command the Queen had given him to that Effect. But upon the Prince's adding, That the readiest Means to bring those Mutineers to their Duty, would be to assure them that they should never be call'd to an Account for this Mutiny and Desertion, any way whatever, and that he, *Chanut*, should remain as a Pledge for the Execution of what Promises the King should make them; Here *Chanut* would promise nothing, but said, *He had no Orders for that*. He did not doubt of the King's granting them an Amnesty, and he consider'd also that it would be a Mean to gain the Affection of the *German* Troops, who after the Empire was in Peace, might go into the King of *Spain's* Service, but then he also reflected, that the King's Word did not want a Security, and that he could make no Promises

mises without express Orders La Haye Vantelay, Embassador of France at Constantinople, signify'd to the Emperor's Resident, that he could not remain Security for a private Debt without the King his Master's Orders

The same Chanut had been nominated in the Year 1651 to the Embassy of Lubeck, to do there the Office of Mediator on the Part of France between Poland and Sweden, but forasmuch as it was not believ'd at Paris that the Embassadors of the Parties concern'd would be very punctual in their coming to the Place of the Congress, they had neglected in France sending him the necessary Orders for his setting out In the mean Time Advice came to Stockholm, that the Ministers of Poland were set out from Dantzick, so that the Queen fearing left they should be out of Patience (if at their Arrival at Lubeck they found neither Swedish Embassador nor Mediator,) and so return home again, desir'd and press'd Chanut to set out She represented to him, That having been nominated to this Embassy, and knowing it was the Intention of the King his Master, that he should go thither, he ought to make no Difficulty to set out, nor delay his Voyage, under Pretext that he had not yet receiv'd his Orders for that Purpose, since without all doubt he would find them either at Lubeck or at Hamburgh But he told the Queen, That as he was far from going about an Action of this Importance without express Orders, and without Instructions, all that he could do was to hold himself ready, and to set forwards as soon as he should have receiv'd them, and that in the mean Time he would send a Secretary to Lubeck, to assure the Polish Ministers that he was ready to follow And in Fact he did not set out till he had receiv'd his Orders

Cardinal Mazarin's Orders were sometimes admirable, but very perplexing This Minister being willing to make an Advantage of the last Commotions in Naples, and at the same Time unwilling the World should believe his Intention was to make use of this Occasion, to retard the Conclusion of the Peace that was negotiating at Munster, wrote to the Marquis de Fontenay Marsueil, That if he thought he could do the King any Service by going in Person to Naples, without hazarding at the same Time the Dignity of his Character, he might transport himself thither in a Man of War which he would give Orders to be ready for him, and that those who manag'd the King's Affairs in Italy, and commanded there his Armies, as Cardinal Grimaldi, the Duke of Modena, Destrades, &c should be order'd to give him all the Assistance he should require of Men, Provisions and Ammunition The Cardinal, after he had tack'd to this odd Order an Instruction relating to the Manner in which he was to speak of the Affair of Naples to the Pope, and how he was to deal with the Great Duke of Tuscany, the Dukes of Parma and Modena, and the Republick of Venice, says, He must not be overhasty in concluding a Treaty with the People of Naples, till Affairs were better settl'd than they then were. However, as he referr'd to him the Matter of the Voyage, so likewise did he that of hastening or retarding the Treaty as well because being almost upon the Place he was a better Judge therein than they could be at Paris, as because the King would nevertheless do for the Neapolitans, without Agreement, all that could be stipulated with his Majesty by a formal Treaty But he must above all things take care, that the Negotiation of Munster was not thereby disturb'd or delay'd The Cardinal recommended the same thing to him in a Letter he wrote to him with his own Hand, Representing to him however, that such an Opportunity ought not to be let slip, from whence France might draw so many great Advantages He moreover own'd, that there was some Contradiction in his Orders, but he hop'd the Embassador's Prudence would distinguish it and take it right It was not the Consideration of the Treaty of Munster which hinder'd the Cardinal from engaging in the Affair of Naples, but it was because he did not see to the Bottom of all those Commotions Some Measures had been taken with some Neapolitan Noblemen, but they were broke by the Insurrection of the People, who were more furiously transported against the Nobility than against the Spaniards But what most displeas'd the first Minister was the Duke of Guise's going thither, which made it apprehended in France lest he should either mart the Affairs, or make himself Master of the Kingdom Those Orders wherein there is a Contradiction, Obscurity or Ambiguity, perplex an Embassador, if he has not Leisure granted him to be better inform'd but when the Execution of such Orders depends on the Embassador, and that it is left to his own Choice to take the surest side, it is no very hard Matter for him to elude the Intention of those who would be for charging him with the Event of a bad Business One of the Orders, the Execution whereof is very difficult, is that which is given to an Embassador to dispose of a certain Sum of Money, which is put into his Hands to be employ'd as he shall think fit, without any particular Directions, because there is no Oeconomy so nice, as to be able to satisfy the Mind of a Prince ever so little saving and distrustful Cardinal Mazarin, who dispos'd of so many Millions by his Testament, and who had given such vast Fortunes to his Nieces, said, He could not find in his Heart to lay out one hundred Crowns of the King's Money, unless he knew that they were well employ'd He had order'd three thousand Pistoles to be given to the Abbot Bentivoglio, which were to be laid out in buying up Horses for the Recruits of the Army in Italy, and were also to serve to gain some Ministers of the Princes in those Parts The Abbot was likewise to take the Expences of his Journey out of this Sum, and nevertheless the Cardinal recommended to him not to be at any unuseful Expence King Lewis XI, was extremely mistrustful and saving, but then he was prodigal, and entrusted his Money with any body when he had a Mind to gain any foreign Minister

CHAP. VI.

Of Prudence and Cunning.

IN the foregoing Chapter I have said that the Embassador in receiving his Prince's Orders, ought to consult his Prudence before he executes them. I shall add in this, that it ought to serve him for a North Pole in the whole Course of his Negotiation. It is she alone can make it successful, and it is she alone is capable of forming a perfect Embassador. She holds the first Rank among political Virtues, and can alone supply all that is wanting in the Embassador, so that one may very well say with the Poet, *Nullum numen abest si sit Prudentia*. But as it is sometimes difficult to distinguish true Virtue from Appearance, so it is easy to be mistaken in this, by taking Cunning for Prudence. The one is a great Virtue, and the other is a Vice, which partakes very much of Cowardise. Cunning is in effect but a bastard Prudence, a false Niceness, and the Product of a lowly and abject Mind, incapable of great Things. *Bonjamin Gianfighazzi*, Embassador of the Duke of *Florence* at *Rome*, was a very prudent and very skilful Minister, and made the first Breach in the Fortune of the *Caraffa*'s. *Cosmus* his Master, who was not less dextrous than himself, and who had a mind to join the Town of *Siena* to what he already possess'd in *Tuscany*, happily made Use of the Prudence of this Minister, to compass his Intention. *Cosmus* had contributed very much to the driving the *French* Garrison out of that Town, by the Means of his Troops, his Provisions, and Ammunition, and by advancing considerable Sums of Money, which he had lent to the Emperor *Charles* V, and *Philip* his Son, from whom he now and then demanded the Repayment thereof. These two Princes grew weary of the Expence they were oblig'd to be at for the Subsistence of the Garrison of *Siena*, they therefore willingly hearken'd to the Propositions of those who counsell'd them to sell the Town to the *Caraffa*'s, and thereby gain the Friendship of *Paul* IV. *Cosmus* being inform'd thereof by the Duke of *Alva*, who was his Wife's Relation, represented to *Philip* by *Alfonso Tornabon*, who resided with him in *England*, the Wrong that was done him by such Advice, and the Prejudice he did to his Affairs, in preferring to his sincere Friends and Servants insolent and haughty People, who would requite him with Ingratitude. It was no hard Matter for him to break off this Bargain, because at that Time the *Caraffa*'s were ingag'd in the *French* Interest, but all the Difficulty was to prevail with *Philip* to give *Siena* to *Cosmus*, who to remove it made use of the dextrous Prudence of *Gianfighazzi*. This Minister, to make *Philip* believe that *Cosmus* intended to enter into the King of *France*'s Interest, made there some Overtures of an Accommodation, and desir'd the Pope to be Mediator therein, recommending to him particularly to get it speedily concluded, and above all Things to keep the Secret, that the *Spaniards* (whose Neighbourhood was troublesome to him, by reason of the Places they held on the Coast of *Tuscany*) might not take Umbrage thereat, nor be inform'd thereof till after the Affair was concluded. The Pope, who did not distrust *Cosmus*, communicated the whole Negotiation to the *French* Ministers, who did not fail to dispatch an Express to the King about it, and press him to send some Person speedily, who might have Power to grant the Duke whatever he desir'd. *Charles de Marillac*, Archbishop of *Vienne*, whom the King caus'd to set out immediately, was no sooner come to *Rome*, than the *French*, who imagin'd that *Cosmus* could not fall off when the Negotiation should be made publick, spoke of it as of a Thing agreed upon. This answer'd the Intention of the Duke of *Florence*, and made his Minister's Game, because *they desir'd the King of Spain might hear of it, and be alarm'd thereat*, that thereby they might gain their Ends, and the Advantage they immediately reap'd from it. For *Philip* being inform'd of the Rumour of this Negotiation, and fearing lest *Cosmus* should conclude his Treaty with *France*, resolv'd to put him in Possession of *Siena*, and to this effect gave Orders to Cardinal *de Burgos* (who commanded there) to march out the *Spanish* Garrison. The Cardinal obey'd, but not without Regret.

These Dexterities, far from being criminal, are very commendable, and these Artifices, provided they are not accompany'd with Roguery and Knavery, acquire a great Reputation to the Embassador. Cardinal *Alexander Bichi* had a particular Genius for Negotiation, and a Prudence that made him be admit'd. Pope *Urban* VIII. did not dare to admit the Bishop of *Lamego*, Embassador from the new King of *Portugal*, nor would not suffer him to enter *Rome*, for fear of offending *Spain*. *France* was for having him admitted, and employ'd for that purpose the Marquiss de *Fontenay Mareuil* to the Pope, but he that procur'd him Leave to come to *Rome* was Cardinal *Bichi*. He was Com-protector of *France*, and being sensible that the Pope was very uneasy since the Bishop's Arrival at *Civita Vecchia*, he went to the Pope and told him, *That being inform'd that the Bishop intended to come to Rome, and that the Pope had resolv'd not to admit him, he was willing to acquaint his Holiness, That if he caus'd the Bishop to be lodg'd in the Countrey, he would be oblig'd to allow him Guards, to protect him against the Insults the Spaniards might offer him, unless he would suffer his Dignity to be violated in the Person of this Prelate. That it must be own'd the King of Portugal did not know very well yet how to act the King, since he employ'd in this Embassy the Money which he might have laid out to greater Advantage, in buying of Arms, and fortifying his Frontiers. That there was also some Imprudence in his sending this Embassy, before he had taken Care to know whether it would be agree-*

able or not. But that at the same Time it must be acknowledg'd that this Simplicity was a Token of an extraordinary Devotion, from whence the Holy See rece v'd the Satisfaction to behold this Prince pass over all those important Considerations of State, to give an illustrious Proof of the Respect and Veneration he had for the See of Rome, out of a Design to make it known to the World, that he would begin his Reign by so conspicuous an Action of Piety, That in order to secure the Bishop from the Violence of the Spaniards, and to quiet his Holiness's Mind, there was no better way than to permit the Bishop to come to Rome, and that thereby his Holiness would ease himself of a great Expence, which he would be oblig'd to be at, in allowing the Bishop a Guard in the Countrey. There can be nothing more prudent nor more ingenious. All the Cardinal's Reasoning was grounded on this Principle, That the Bishop of *Lamego* would not be in Safety out of the City of *Rome*. It seems as if this Principle was not very true, because the *Spaniards* had no other Interest than to hinder the Bishop from coming to *Rome*, and appearing there in the Quality of a publick Minister, because by that Mean the Pope declar'd himself against the Usurpation. The more he blames the Precipitation and Imprudence of the King of *Portugal*, the more he heightens his Zeal and Piety, and obliges the Pope to make a serious Reflection thereon. The Bishop came to *Rome* in effect, but he would have been safer in the Countrey.

The Treaty of *Vervins*, wherein *Charles Emanuel* Duke of *Savoy* had caus'd himself to be compris'd, made the Pope Arbitrator of the Difference the Duke had with the King about the Marquisate of *Saluzzo*, and the King caus'd his Interests to be solicited at *Rome* by the Marquiss of *Sillery Brulart*. The two Princes concern'd were in equal Apprehension lest the Pope should desire to have the Marquisate put into his Hands by way of Sequestration. and *Sillery* dreading every Thing from the Duke's Wit and Artifices, prevented him in this manner. *He gave out that the King's Intention was to invest one of the Pope's Nephews with the Marquisate, as soon as he should have gotten Possession thereof.* This so alarm'd the Duke of *Savoy*, that he order'd his Embassador to tell the Pope, That he was in hopes his Holiness would have made no Difficulty to pronounce on the Possession, and to maintain him in it. The Pope made Answer, He would do what Justice requir'd, and upon that Foundation he would endeavour to preserve Union between the Christian Princes. The Embassador of *Savoy* not being satisfy'd with this general Answer, reply'd, That if his Holiness adjudg'd the Marquisate to the Duke, he might dispose of it in favour of one of his Nephews, or of some of his other Relations. This so offended the Pope, who thereby judg'd that the Duke of *Savoy* thought him capable of being corrupted, that he declar'd, That from that very Moment he was no longer Arbitrator, nor would be any farther concern'd in the Matter, since he was thought partial and interested. *Sillery's* Address had a good Effect, and occasion'd the Duke to commit a Fault gross enough, for a Prince who had a great deal of Wit, and who was willing to know that he had it.

Cosmus and his Minister made use of very lawful Means to oblige the King of *Spain* to withdraw his Garrison from *Siena*. *Philip* could not pretend to keep that Town, as well because it was of no Utility to him, as because he could not enlarge his Dominions that way without giving a Jealousy to all the rest of *Italy*. *Cosmus* had contributed very much to the Reduction of the Town, and had lent considerable Sums of Money to *Philip*, as I said before. It was not Cardinal *Bichi*'s Intention to deceive the Pope, when he advis'd him to let the Bishop of *Lamego* come to *Rome*, and *Sillery* only prevented the Duke of *Savoy*'s Artifices. These are Strokes of Dexterity that are allow'd, and even necessary to the Embassador.

The two following Examples are taken from the Negotiation of a Minister, whose Probity and Ability were without Reproach. His publick Employment under *Henry* IV. began from an Order that was given him to penetrate into the Pope's Sentiments, as well in reference to the Absolution which the King had resolv'd to sue for, as concerning the Conditions under which he might have the same. The Letters which were written to him on this Subject, pass'd through the Hands of the Great Duke of *Tuscany*, who recommended to him the Secret thereof, as of a Thing on which depended the whole Success of the Affair. The Pope and Cardinal *Aldobrandin* told him as much, so that he spoke to no Body of the Dispatches he had receiv'd. But Cardinal *de Gondy* having written to two Persons of Quality, and very well affected to *France*, that such Orders had been sent to *Dossat*, and even that the Letters made mention of the Conditions of the Absolution, of all which he had taken no notice neither to the Pope, nor to the *Cardinal Patron*, because he had receiv'd no Orders for that purpose, *Dossat* found himself in so much the greater Perplexities, because these two Gentlemen were for speaking both to the one and the other of it. A Minister less prudent and less able had not known what to do. He had kept the Secret very religiously, even to the using Violence to his own Judgment, in persisting to deny that he had receiv'd the Letters, of which Cardinal *de Gondy* made mention in his. But what gave him the greatest Uneasiness was, the Fear he had that the Pope and his Minister should take a Handle from thence to doubt of his Sincerity, because when they learnt from other Hands those Things which he had not imparted to them, they might either think him double, by reason of his disguising the King's real Sentiments to them, or else Coward enough not to dare to execute the Orders he had receiv'd. To shew that he was neither the one nor the other, and that together with his Sincerity and Courage, he had Dexterity and Prudence enough to get out of so intricate an Affair, he went to Cardinal *Aldobrandin*, and told him, That being oblig'd to keep the Secret, to the King his Master, to the Pope and to himself, who was first Minister to his Holiness, to whom he had promis'd it, he found himself reduc'd to the Necessity of going beyond the King's Commands, and to communicate to him some Particulars of his Dispatches to clear himself of the Suspicion which

which might be otherwife had of his Sincerity That were it not for this he would not take the Liberty to fpeak without Orders, of thofe Things which he had been written to about, but only to know his own particular Sentiments, and of which he could not have difcours'd with his Holinefs, without being wanting in fome meafure to the Refpect that he ow'd him After that he enlarg'd very much on the Doubts the Court of France had, that the Court of Rome intended to tack to the Affair of the Abfolution certain Conditions, which neither the King nor the Kingdom could accept of Doffat's Difcourfe was very well receiv'd, he div'd into the Pope's Intentions, and carry'd off from his Conference the Satisfaction he had reafon to promife himfelf from his Prudence

It was moreover apprehended in France, and not without Caufe, that the Pope, when he gave his Abfolution, would annull that which the Prelates of France had given the King at St Denis Doffat fear'd it likewife, and very much diftrufted the Intentions of the Court of Rome in that refpect He therefore gives the King feveral Precautions which might be taken againft the Artifices of thofe People I fhall here fet down only two of them, which denote a refin'd Prudence The one relates to the Terms of the Act of Abfolution, and the other to the Procuration the King's Minifters were to bring to Rome As to the firft, he fays, That the King's Sollicitors, after having debated all the Words of the Abfolution, might carry it away, fuch as it was given them, and that after fome Time the Attorney General might provide in Parliament againft the prejudicial Claufes the Court of Rome fhould have flipt into the Bull, or elfe make the States of the Kingdom interpofe to have them taken out Doffat adds, that this Expedient is not according to his Humour, but that in Affairs of this Nature there is fometimes a Neceffity to make ufe of worfe Means than this He likewife fays, in reference to the Procuration, That the King may caufe the Abfolution to be ask'd for, pure and fimple, fo that no Prejudice could be drawn from thence againft the firft Abfolution and to the End the Court of Rome might take no Advantage of thofe general Terms, the King might explain his Intention by a fecret Act, which he fhould pafs before his Embaffadors fet out But forafmuch as this manner of acting is not very natural to Doffat, he fays, That it is not without fome Confufion that he mentions this Act, becaufe he knows that the King's Magnanimity and Generofity will not without Difficulty confent thereto but when one has to do with People who deal in nothing but Artifices, there is a Neceffity to make ufe of other Artifices to deftroy theirs, as one may make ufe of offenfive Arms, and even kill with Impunity, while one remains within the Bounds of a lawful and neceffary Defence, fo in cafe of Neceffity one may employ Means which would not be allowable nor lawful without that

It is a Stroke of the moft refin'd Prudence, to make it be believ'd that one neglects thofe Things which one moft defires, that one looks upon them with Indifferency, and that even one has fome Averfion for them If I might be allow'd to make ufe of the familiar Comparifon of the Rowers, who turn their Backs to the Place they defign to land at, I think it may be very well apply'd here Cardinal Mazarin help'd himfelf wonderfully by this Artifice, and he gave an excellent Proof thereof, at the Congrefs of the Pyrenees In the Treaty Pimentel had adjufted at Paris with Lionne, the Interefts of the Prince of Condé had alfo been regulated, and it was agreed to that he fhould return to France, and fhould be repoffefs'd of his Eftate, but not of his Employments and Governments Don Lewis de Haro had given his Word to the Prince, that he would procure him both the ones and the others, and the Negotiation Lionne had carry'd on fome Years before at Madrid was broke off, but on account of this Difficulty When the two Minifters met upon the Frontiers, to put the laft Hand to the Treaty, and to concert the Execution of what had been refolv'd on at Paris, Don Lewis made again frefh Inftances for the entire Reftoration of the Prince The Cardinal exprefs'd fuch a Reluctancy to that, that D Lewis told him, in the Heat of the Debate, that the King his Mafter would ratify without any Difficulty what Pimentel had agreed to, but at the fame Time his Majefty could not be hinder'd from rewarding the Prince, by giving him fome Places in Sovereignty on the Frontiers of the Kingdom and of the Low Countries This Reply amaz'd and perplex'd the Cardinal He confider'd that the Prince who was to return to France by virtue of the Treaty, could not live there in a private Capacity That the Government of Burgundy, which he had before that of Guyenne was given him, was no great matter That his Place of Great-Mafter did not make him more confiderable than his Quality of firft Prince of the Blood That by reftoring him to his Places and Dignities he was more ftrongly link'd to the King's Service, and that if he refum'd them by his Mediation, he, the Prince, would be oblig'd to him, and become his Friend, for which Reafons *he paffionately defir'd to do him this good Office* But that he might draw from thence fome Advantage to the King, *He protefted he would never confent thereto, and exprefs'd an utter Averfion to all the Overtures fhould be made him on that Subject* This manner of acting was fo natural to Cardinal Mazarin, that he had no Difficulty to perfuade the firft Minifter of Spain, that to difingage his Word which he had given the Prince of Condé, it fhould coft the King his Mafter fomething, as in effect it did, for to obtain a Reftoration, which no way incommoded France, and which the Cardinal defir'd at leaft as much as Don Lewis, this laft yielded up fome other Places, which cover'd the new Conquefts I cannot tell whether one might not fay that it coft the King of France at leaft as much, who had declar'd, He had rather be without the Peace and Marriage, than fuffer the Spaniards to have the Advantage of reftoring the Prince of Condé yet neverthelefs they had it, and thereby were too many for the Cardinal's refin'd Policy. If this Minifter had negotiated the private Intereft of the Prince with the Prince himfelf, he had thereby gain'd the Friendfhip of fo great a Subject, and had procur'd the King an Advantage incomparably greater than that which he receiv'd from the Acqui-

Acquisition of two or three sorry Places, which his Arms would have reduc'd in the Year 1667, without the least Resistance.

Prudence has that in common with all other Virtues, that there is no separating from it ever so little, without striking into Vice, and making it dwindle into Timidity, or degenerate into *Cunning*, and even into *Roguery*. In the beginning of the Year 1573, King *Charles* IX. sent into *England Albert de Gondy*, Count *de Retz*. He was an ingenious *Florentine*, who, under the Pretext of getting the Treaty confirm'd, which had been concluded at *Blois* the Year before, had Orders to justify what had pass'd at the Massacre of St *Bartlemy*. He found Queen *Elizabeth* at *Canterbury*, where the Birth-Day of that Princess was to be celebrated by the Archbishop of the Place, who gave her a magnificent Entertainment. The *French* Embassador, who was invited to it, found an Opportunity to put the Queen upon the Discourse of that horrible Day, and had the Art to give so admirable a Turn to that inhuman Action (the Cause whereof he cast upon those of the Religion) that the Queen remain'd in a manner convinc'd of what he said, or at least she was willing to make it be believ'd she was, that she might thereby have a Pretext not to succour the *French* Protestants, of whom she was not very well satisfy'd. This Action of *Charles* IX. could not be justify'd, and a Man of Honour would not have undertook to do it. What the Pope *Clement* VIII says thereof to Cardinal *Dossat*, makes it appear to be the basest Treason that ever was heard of.

In the Year 1583, the Duke *de Joyeuse*, one of *Henry* III's Favourites, having a Design to procure to himself a Settlement suitable to his Fortune, cast his Eye upon the Government of *Languedoc*, and not being able to prevail with the Duke *de Montmorancy* to part with it, he try'd to dispossess him of it by indirect Means, by making the Pope believe that that Nobleman was a Friend and Partizan of the King of *Navarre*, and of the Prince of *Condé*, who were Enemies to the Roman Catholick Religion. The King, and Queen-Mother, who did not love the House of *Montmorancy*, and who had a Mind the Duke *de Joyeuse* should appear in *Italy* with distinguishing Marks of Favour, seconded his Designs, and gave him Letters of Recommendation to the Pope, and to all the other Potentates in those Parts. The Duke speaking to the Pope, told him, That the King his Master's Thoughts were wholly intent upon the Preservation of the Catholick Religion, and the Authority of the Holy See, but *that his good Intentions were always cross'd or eluded, and that chiefly by the Duke of* Montmorancy, *who suffer'd the Hugonot Religion to settle it self in his Government, with more Liberty than at* Geneva. That the King had for a long time been thinking how he ought to express his Resentment, but would not come to any Resolution without the Pope's Participation, and without taking his Advice, in Reference to the Conduct he ought to observe therein. The Pope, who had had Advice of the Subject of the Embassy, and of the Intention of the Embassador, told him, after some Words of Civility, That he believ'd the King had not been rightly inform'd about the Duke of *Montmorancy*. That he was not to be impos'd upon, who had a perfect Knowledge of the Duke's Piety, and Proofs of his Zeal. Insomuch that he would joyn his Prayers to those of all Persons of Worth, that the King, by continuing to honour the Duke with the Affection his Services and those of his Predecessors deserv'd, might not reduce him to the Necessity of casting himself into the Arms of the Enemies of Religion, and there to seek his Safety. The Pope said so much to *Joyeuse*, that that young Nobleman, seeing the Court of *Rome* had not the same Consideration for him, nor the same Sentiments as that of *France* had, remain'd without Reply, and retir'd with Confusion. He had the Quality of Embassador, but the Subject of his Embassy was not very honourable, nor his manner of acting very prudent.

D'Avaux and *Servien* were, without doubt, very great Ministers, who, in the whole Course of the Negotiation of *Munster*, gave every Day fresh Proofs of their Sufficiency, but they one Day bethought themselves of an Artifice, wherein there was at least as much Cunning and Subtilty as Prudence. They had written Circular Letters to all the Princes, and all the States of *Germany*, to desire them to send their Deputies to the Assembly, that they might there deliberate with them on the Means that might restore them to their ancient Dignity and Liberty. After some of the Deputies were arriv'd at *Munster*, an odd Thought enough came into the Heads of the *French* Plenipotentiaries, who imagin'd they should shew a fine Stroke of State Policy, if they declar'd that the King their Master, to give the Princes of *Germany* an illustrious Mark of his Disinterestedness, and of his Royal Benevolence, offer'd to withdraw all the Troops he had in the Empire, if the Emperor on his Side would grant a general Amnesty, and consent that Affairs should be put in the same State they were in, in the Year 1618, and that Means should be agreed upon for the Security of the Execution, and Duration of the Peace. They suppos'd they hazarded nothing, because they were well assur'd that the Emperor and Duke of *Bavaria* would never consent thereto, that nevertheless, by these specious Offers they should procure to the King their Master the Affection of the Princes of *Germany*, and by making him Guarantee for the Execution of the Treaty, make him Arbitrator of the Affairs of the Empire. However as the *Swedes* were very much concern'd therein, since this Proposition sent them back to the other side of the *Baltick*, the *French* Ministers judg'd, that they ought not to proceed without the Participation of their Allies, nor indeed without the Advice of their Court. But the Cardinal, who had his particular Views, and was at least as refin'd as themselves, represented to them, That these Offers could not be made without offending the Duke of *Bavaria*, and without unlinking him quite from the King's Interest, because they depriv'd him of the Electoral Dignity, of the *Upper Palatinate*, and of all the Advantages he had acquir'd during the War. That the said Offers would be suspected, and appear ridiculous, even to those who would hardly believe that *France* would be so complaisant as to restore *Brisac*, and all the other Places of *Germany*, and who knew that

that *Pomerania* was offer'd to the *Swede*, with with some Maritim Towns, besides a good Sum of Money. That he was indeed of Opinion the Emperor would not approve of it, but however he believ'd that the Council of *Vienna* would be artificial enough to give out that he accepted the Condition, on purpose to put the *French* upon a Necessity of contradicting themselves, or else to make some foul Step, which would blacken their Intentions, and fully their whole Conduct. He thereunto added many other Reasons, which plainly discover'd the Vanity of this Artifice, which would be so far from perswading the World of any Inclination *France* said she had for a Peace, that it would convince 'em of quite the contrary. *Dossat*, at his first Entrance on the Negotiation of the Affairs of *France*, not being able to demand Audience of the Pope without giving some Umbrage to the *Spaniards*, desir'd it as if he had Occasion to speak to the Pope on the Part of the Queen *Dowager* of *France*, who had given him in Charge the Solicitation of the Honours she had a Mind to pay to the Memory of the deceas'd King. When he was at the Pope's Feet, he told him, He had made use of this Pretext, that under the Colour thereof he might have Access to his Holiness, without any wise alarming the *Spaniards*, but that he had Orders from the King to speak to him about his Concerns. However, that he might not pass for an Impostor in the Pope's Thoughts, and even in the King's, he told him, That he had really receiv'd, within four Days, the Queen's Commands to make fresh Instances, so that what he had caus'd to be said to his Holiness was true, as it would be also, when he should say at his going from his Audience, That he had spoke to him of the Queen's Business. There are but few Ministers, at this Day, that would make that Scruple.

There is a Species of Address, that is rather Roguery than either Cunning or Artifice. In the Year 1662, the Count *d'Ognate*, Embassador of *Spain* at *Rome*, when he did Homage for the Kingdom of *Naples* on St. *Peter*'s Eve, presented indeed the *Spanish Gennet*, but the seven thousand Crowns, which ought to have accompany'd it, were not ready. The Treasurer of the Apostolick Chamber acquainted the Pope therewith, and moreover said, That the Embassador had assur'd him that nothing was wanting to the Bill of Exchange but the signing, but that he would sign it, and the Money should be forthwith paid, in the mean time he humbly intreated the Pope to accept of the *Spanish Gonnet*, without Prejudice to his Rights. The Embassador's Intention was to gain thereby a Title, which should free the Kingdom of *Naples* from that annual Tribute. But the Pope made Answer, That he would not do that Wrong to the Apostolical Chamber, and that the Embassador should pay the seven thousand Crowns immediately, or else he might take away the *Spanish Gennet*, and that he would not receive the Homage without the Money. That the Banker *Sacchets*, who was there present, should take upon him to pay the Money, not in Consideration of the Pope, but should take the Embassador's Security, without which, he would do nothing in it. The Embassador, who thought to bubble the Pope, procur'd to himself a great Affront, being forc'd to make use of the Credit of a Banker to get out of an unlucky Business, wherein a Minister, more prudent and less cunning, would have been far from engaging himself.

From these little Tricks and Knaveries, which one endeavours to palm upon the World for Gallantries, one easily passes to grosser Impostures, which are unworthy of a Minister who has ever so little Honour and Reputation to husband. For if the Embassador is unhappy enough to lose that, and to pass once for an Impostor or a Lyar, he can no longer either negotiate or appear, because he has thereby lost all Confidence and Credit, which is the Foundation of all the Commerce that passes among Men, of what Nature soever it may be. Where there are perpetual Distrusts, there is a Design to deceive, or an Apprehension of being deceiv'd, so that it is impossible to be successful in a Negotiation where they have any Share. I or whether the Embassador follows therein his Prince's Orders, or acts in Conformity to his own Humour and Genius, it is impossible but he must be suspected and thereby become incapable of negotiating. The Embassador is not oblig'd to discover all his Thoughts, and he is allow'd, or rather under a Necessity, to disguise them sometimes, but I don't know whether he be allow'd, on any Occasion whatever, to act contrary to the Principles of Honour, that is to say, whether he can destroy the Truth by a Lye. *Philip de Commines* being Embassador from *France* at *Venice*, and observing Couriers continually going and coming, had no great Difficulty to guess that there were Intrigues on Foot against King *Charles* VIII, his Master. For his better Information he endeavour'd to make some Discovery by the Means of the Embassadors of the Duke of *Milan*, who was *Charles*'s Ally. These Gentlemen were not contented to counterfeit the Ignorants, and to signify to *Commines*, That they were not less surpriz'd than he was, at the Goings and Comings of so many Embassadors, but they even ask'd him, What the *Spanish* Embassador had to do at *Venice*, tho' they knew he had pass'd through *Milan*, and that he had there conferr'd with the Duke. At last, finding themselves press'd to tell what they knew of the Negotiation which was carry'd on at *Venice*, because *Commines* declar'd to them, That he would acquaint the King his Master with what pass'd there, *They protested, with a great many Oaths, that there was nothing negotiating against the King's Interest*. *Commines* says *they ly'd*, that is to say, that they were guilty of an infamous Action, unworthy of a Minister or an honest Man.

Cardinal *d'Amboise* coming to the Emperor *Maximilian* I at *Trent*, in the Year 1509, it was put into Debate what should be done with the Republick of *Venice*. The Cardinal was for having it destroy'd utterly. It was not the Opinion of *Ferdinand the Catholick*, who had given Orders to *Jomes de Conchillos*, Bishop of *Catania*, his Embassador, to propose to the Emperor an Accommodation with the Pope, and with the Republick, in Order to stop the Progress of *Lewis* XII's Arms, who had already made great Conquests in *Italy*, before the other Allies had put themselves in a Condition to execute the Treaty of *Cambray*,

Cambray, excepting the Pope, who had taken some Places in *Romania*. This Embassador who had his Orders, who knew the Intentions of the King his Master, and who was very resolv'd to follow them, was nevertheless of the Cardinal's Opinion, with a Design to deceive him, and to keep from him the true Sentiments of the Catholick King, who betray'd the King of *France*. He knew he could do no Prejudice to his Master, because he was assur'd that the Pope would never consent to the Ruin of the Republick; but that did not hinder there being in his Procedure an Insincerity unworthy of an honest Man.

The same *Commines*, speaking of himself, says, That while he was yet in the Service of the Duke of *Burgundy*, he was sent to *Calais*, where he found that *Vauclerc* Governor of the Place, and all the *English* Officers had taken the Earl of *Warwick*'s Device, which was a black Staff. That they made this open Declaration, because they had been assur'd that King *Edward* IV had been kill'd in the Battel he had given the Earl. *Commines* adds, *That he told them this News was true, altho' he knew the contrary, and that he was sure Edward was in Holland*. He had no Difficulty to cause what he said to be believ'd, because every Body knew that the first News the Duke of *Burgundy* had receiv'd of the Defeat of *Edward*, had been accompany'd with that of his Death. But I cannot tell whether his Procedure can be justify'd. The Embassador may and ought to dissemble and instead of being oblig'd to tell all, his Silence makes a part of his Fidelity. He may conceal a Truth that would be prejudicial to his Master's Service, but I should think a Lye can never be justify'd.

In the Year 1646, the Embassador of *Spain*, who was at *Venice* at that time, having procur'd Audience in the College, on the Account of the Descent the *French* had made on the Coast of *Tuscany*, and of the Passage the Republick of *Genoa* gave to their Troops, says, That now was come to pass what he had foretold long before, concerning the Intention of the *French*: That they had no other, than to weaken the Forces of the Princes of *Italy*, thereby to put them out of a Condition to oppose those of the *Grand Seignior, with whom they had resolv'd upon the War of* Candia. So gross and imprudent a Falsity strips the Embassador at once of all his Credit, and all his Reputation. *Dossat*, who utters nothing but Oracles for those who have the Management of Affairs, or pretend to be concern'd therein, says, in the Letter he writes to the King on the 23d of *December* 1594, That after the Promise he had made to the Pope and to Cardinal *Aldobrandin*, to speak to no body of the Dispatch he had receiv'd from the King, he had thought himself oblig'd to be as good as his Word, thereby to give them Reason to believe he would never deceive them. That he was secret and true. That for the time to come they might speak to him with the same Confidence and Assurance they had done. And in fact, it is impossible that the Embassador should acquire the least Credit or Belief in the Court where he negotiates, if he wants either of these two Qualities. I know very well *that all Men are Lyars*; and that *Dossat*, who with the Qualities of an able Minister, had also that of a Man of Honour, says in his Letter of the 4th of *January* 1595, that he had firmly deny'd to *Lomelin* and to *Dalbene* to have receiv'd the Dispatch, the Contents whereof he had communicated to the Pope: which seems not to be very suitable to the prudent Man, of which he made Profession, and of which he gives so many Tokens in the whole Course of his Negotiation. But I am not afraid to say, That in that he did not injure his Reputation. And I dare add, without acting the Casuist, That we must distinguish first between the Habit and the Action. Secondly, It is one thing to deny a Truth, and another to tell a Lye. In the third Place we must consider, That *Dossat* in disguising the Truth offended no body. And finally, That he must either have been unfaithful to the King his Master, and not have kept his Word, or must not have told the Truth which is not lying, except it be in a Signification improper enough.

There are Embassadors who think themselves very prudent, and that they do an important Service to their Prince in spreading false Rumours, imagining thereby to get a great Advantage over their Enemies. *D. Bernardin de Mendosse*, Embassador of *Spain*, came to the very *Louvre* to assure the King, that that formidable Fleet of the Year 1588, had made a Descent in *England*, that the whole Kingdom was up in Arms against Queen *Elizabeth*, and that the Conquest of the whole Island was certain. A *Spanish* Religious, preaching at *Milan* in the Presence of the Governor and the Magistracy, told it as Gospel, and yet every body knew the contrary. There are others who do not scruple to give out Letters, which they pretend to have been intercepted, to lessen the Circumstances, and disparage the Conduct of those whose Prosperity is troublesome to them. During the *Barberin*'s War, the *Spanish* Embassador dispers'd a Letter in *Venice*, wherein Cardinal *Mazarin* exhorted Cardinal *Bichi* to act with Address in his Negotiation, and to precipitate nothing, to the End, that the Princes of *Italy* consuming and devouring one another, *France* might gain its Point. These Letters were sent to all the Courts of *Europe*, but the Roguery was soon discover'd, because it was not the Interest of *France* to protract the War in *Italy*, where she would have been oblig'd to have taken a Side, and to have employ'd some part of her Troops. *Le Brun*, Embassador of *Spain* at *Munster*, proceeded there with greater Dexterity, but with as little Success. He knew the *French* Plenipotentiaries were not satisfy'd with those of *Sweden*, and that they would not fail to express it in their first Dispatches to Court, wherefore he found the Means to get one of them, which spake in very high Terms of the Humour and Procedure of *Oxenstiern*, and of the Chancellor his Father. *Le Brun* thought he ought to aggravate what the Letter said, for which Reason he alter'd some Passages thereof so that it was not only capable of offending extremely those two Ministers, but also of setting the two Crowns in Alliance, at variance. He did too much, and gave by that Means a great Advantage to the *French*, who being easily able to discover what was false therein, had no Difficulty to render all the rest suspected,

suspected, and to make it be believ'd it was all imposture.

At the beginning of the War with which *Christendom* is still afflicted, a Minister of the Court of *Vienna* contriv'd a very scandalous Writing, under the Title of a Discourse, which the Commander *de Gremonville*, the *French* Minister, had made to the Emperor's Council against the State of the United Provinces. But it was soon found to be nothing but a very gross Piece of Roguery, and that it was the Work of a Man, all whose Products shew'd a great deal of Wit, and Knowledge enough, but very little Judgement and Conduct. The Embassador ought to seek his Master's Glory and Advantage on all Occasions. He may magnify the Success of his Arms, conceal and dissemble his Losses and Disgraces, but he cannot forge nor contrive false Pieces, without dishonouring his Character. A publick Minister ought to detest such Impostures, and criminal Artifices, and he ought to be above those little Cunnings and Duplicities, which are only the Products of a weak and ill turn'd Mind.

Towards the End of the last Century *Sigismund Battory*, not being able to maintain himself in the Principality of *Transilvania*, resign'd it to Cardinal *Andrew Battory* his Relation. The Emperor *Rodolphus*, who had a Mind to annex this Province to his Kingdom of *Hungary*, made use of *Michael*, Lord of *Walachia*, to hinder him from taking possession thereof. The Cardinal on his side employ'd the Pope's Nuncio, to endeavour to persuade *Michael* not to intermeddle in this War. The Nuncio to succeed therein, *told* Michael *that he had an Order from the Emperor, wherein he desir'd the Cardinal might not be disturb'd in his Possession*. *Michael* having desir'd to see the Order, the Nuncio told him, he had left it in the Cardinal's Hands, that he would go and fetch it in a few Days, and that at the same time he would dispose the Cardinal to come to an Accommodation with the Emperor. The Nuncio's ill Luck would have it, that *Michael* receiv'd an Order by which the Emperor commanded him to drive out the Cardinal, so that he was preparing to give him Battel. The Nuncio oppos'd him again, and going into all the Quarters of the Army, and representing to the Officers the Horror of the Effusion of so much Christian Blood, endeavour'd to hinder them from consenting to a Battel. But *Michael*, to remove from before his Eyes an Object that hinder'd him from executing the Emperor's Orders, gently seiz'd the Person of the Nuncio, had him led to his Quarters, and commanded his Son to guard him during the Fight, which was fatal to the Cardinal. The Nuncio ly'd against his Honour and withall took a Side contrary to his Instructions. He was disavow'd for his Pains, and relegated to his Bishoprick.

The Prudence of an Embassador consists chiefly in knowing how to elude the cunning Strokes of others, and to avoid the Snares that are prepar'd for him. That is to say, to hinder his being deceiv'd and impos'd upon. He is not always deceiv'd, tho' he be deceiv'd in effect. He is not deceiv'd, when discovering the Artifice of the Impostor, he gives him to understand, that Violence may be offer'd to him, but that his Ability is not to be surpris'd. *Corvitz Ulefeld*, Great-Master of *Denmark*, being oblig'd to make his Escape, found his Safety at *Stockholm*, in the powerful Protection of Queen *Christina* of *Sweden*, who receiv'd and caress'd all Strangers, and was very liable to bestow her Esteem on the last Comer. She did not make a Mystery of it to the *Danish* Embassador, who was extremely scandaliz'd thereat; but one Day she bethought her self of sending the Master of the Ceremonies to the said Embassador, and to signify to him, That she had effectually found out, that *Ulefeld* was an ill Man and a Rascal, unworthy of her Protection. That she was resolv'd to withdraw it, and to declare it to him herself in the Embassador's Presence, if he would come to Court the next Day. *The Embassador seem'd to be very much surpriz'd at a Discourse so different from that the Queen had held to him some Days before, and did not dissemble to the Master of the Ceremonies, the Distrust he had of the Queen's Intention*, however he told him, That he would not fail to be at the Castle, because he assur'd himself that the Queen's Intentions were sincere, and that she would not suffer *Ulefeld* to justify himself, nor to say any thing against the Honour and Reputation of the King his Master. On the same Day he receiv'd Advice that the Queen had been at *Ulefeld*'s Lodgings, had taken him in her Coach, and carry'd him to take the Air; he therefore sent for the Master of the Ceremonies, and made the same Protestations to him which he had already made, that he would not suffer *Ulefeld* to do any thing to the Prejudice of the King his Master. He told him likewise the Grounds he had to distrust the Queen's Intention. Nevertheless upon the fresh Assurances the Master of the Ceremonies gave him, he went the next Day to the Castle, but he was hardly got into the Queen's Chamber, when she sent for *Ulefeld*, to whom she gave leave to justify himself, to the great Astonishment of the Embassador, who not being able to get out of the Room, because he was hinder'd by some Noblemen who guarded the Door, he went to a Window, and there fell a raving till *Ulefeld* had made an end of reading a Paper. Afterwards he went out and retir'd to his Lodgings, without saying one word of the Cause of the Assembly, but he complain'd loudly to some of the Senators of the Queen's Procedure. She did not deceive him; because he distrusted her One is deceiv'd and cheated, but when one believes one is not Prudence, how consummate soever it may be, cannot warrant us from Treachery, but he that publish'd this History did not very much oblige this great Princess. There is no Occasion for a great deal of Wit and Refinedness for so gross an Artifice.

What the Dispatches of the *French* Plenipotentiaries say, of the shameful Artifices with which the Ministers of the United Provinces cover'd the Intrigues they carry'd on with those of *Spain* at *Munster*, is so scandalous, that I wonder that hitherto no body has undertook to justify their Procedure, to vindicate the Honour of the State. A modern Author speaks of 'em in these Terms. *Whatever Warmth might be remark'd in the Conduct of the* French *Plenipotentiaries, might be excus'd, if after all* the Lenitives they had employ'd strong Medicines, with People who were resolv'd to conclude at any rate, and who, not remembring the Obligations they had to France, nor the Treaties which ought to have hinder'd them from thinking of a separate Treaty, carry'd themselves so disobligingly to her. If on the contrary, they might by more safe and honourable Means obtain with the general Applause of the whole World, all their Pretensions, they ought not, by indirect and uncertain Ways, draw upon themselves the Aversion and Detestation of all honest People, by leaving to th jo ill a Grace a Friendship and Alliance, which was so much for their Purpose, and even necessary to them. If while they thirsted after Repose, they jung'd that the first Minister of France oppos'd it, and if they believ'd in fine, that the prodigious Greatness of that Crown was a Misfortune to them, they might have found their Account after a more honourable Way, without having Recourse to a kind of Felony and Perjury, and without giving to the Universe so ill an Opinion of their Duplicity. With what Horror will Posterity read in History, the Infamy with which these People, their Ministers, their Deputies and the Chief of their State, ly'd and took false Oaths every Moment, and committed Treacheries every time the French Ministers claim'd the Execution of the Treaties they had made with the King? It is true that the Plenipotentiaries who were on the part of the United Provinces at Munster, did themselves a great deal of Wrong on many Occasions, where they made very solemn Protestations of the Sincerity of their Intention, tho' their Actions gave them openly the Lye. Whatever Treaties the States might have with France, they were not oblig'd to make them Instruments of the Ruin of their Republick, but they might have got off of their Engagement, by following the Example of Henry IV, who having a Mind to treat with Spain, signify'd to the Queen of England, and the United Provinces, his Allies, that the State of his Affairs did not permit him to continue the War. That Prince who would have his Ally ruin himself for his sake, would be unjust, and he that should ruin his Subjects for the sake of his Allies, would not be less so.

One of the things the Embassador ought to be most cautious of in his Negotiation, is not to be mistaken. I mean, that he must not suffer himself to be amus'd in the Conferences he has with the Ministers, or at the Audiences the Prince gives him; All the Civilities, all the Caresses, all the Digressions that baffle and elude his Instances, all the sharp Puts-off, all the Protestations, and with much more Reason, all the ambiguous Answers, ought to be suspected by him. Nay he ought to look upon all Entertainments and Diversions, as so many Obstacles that are oppos'd to the Execution of his Orders. Whitlock, who was Embassador from England in Sweden in the Year 1683, complain'd to every body, that in his Audiences the Queen spoke to him of nothing but Philosophy, and entertain'd him with nothing but her Balls and her Diversions, and that she never said to him neither Yes nor No; The Duke of Guise says in his Memoirs, That Tears cost Pope Innocent X. nothing, and speaks of him as of a Man that acted very well all kinds of Personages. Cardinal Mazarin, who knew him perfectly well, recommended constantly to the Abbot de St Nicolas, afterwards Bishop of Angers, who solicited the King's Affairs at Rome, Not to suffer himself to be deceiv'd to put up his Transports, and to applaud the Discourses, the Flatteries and Protestations of the Pope but to take in payment nothing but Effects, to pursue his Point, and not to leave him till he had explain'd himself, and had got a categorical Answer from him. If it was ever necessary for an Embassador to take these Measures, it was with the said Cardinal Mazarin. He did not give Audience to foreign Ministers till they had ask'd it several times, and till he saw, as one may say, the Doors of his Appartment force'd. And when he admitted them, instead of giving them Audience he began to speak first, and did not leave off entertaining them with indifferent things, to gain time, and to deprive the Minister of the Leisure and Means to do their Master's Business. He would take a Turn round Europe, and relate all sorts of News, shewing a great deal of Countrey to those who would follow him. So that for the most part the Embassadors and Ministers, had much ado to find a Moment to acquaint him with a very small Part of their Affairs. He was besides, the closest Man in the World; His Thoughts and his Intentions were impenetrable to his greatest Confidents; neither was there any Certainty in his Word, nor in his Oaths how great soever they might be. This is what Vittorio Siri says of him, and I know part of it to be true by Experience.

In the Year 1646, the Abbot Bentivoglio, one of Cardinal Mazarin's greatest Confidents, after Zongo Ondedei, was sent to some Princes in Italy, to prevail with them to enter into the King's Interests, while the Arms of France should act upon the Coast of Tuscany. He had Orders to do the same Offices with the Great Duke, who was the most wary and most reserv'd Prince in the World, who told him, That he requir'd some time to deliberate concerning the Propositions the Abbot had made him, and to reflect on the Advantages, he had told him the Princes of Italy would find in the Neighbourhood of the Arms of France. That if they were imploy'd in the Kingdom of Naples or in Sicily, perhaps he might not meddle, but if they attack'd any Place on the Coast of Tuscany, the Treaties he had with Spain, and the Obligation he had on the Account of the Town of Siena, would hinder him from explaining himself so soon concerning the Neutrality France solicited him for. That he had Lands in the Kingdom of Naples, and that the King of Spain ow'd him five Millions of Gold, which perplex'd him, and oblig'd him to think of him. The Abbot answer'd him, That he desir'd his Resolution, and not Words. That he did not know what the Naval Forces were to undertake. But he was willing to let him know, That in what Place soever it landed, they would treat as Enemies all those who should have directly or indirectly succour'd the King's Enemies.

I'll give an Instance of what I just said concerning Entertainments and Diversions. After the Death of Henry King of Portugal, the Pope Gregory XIII. sent into Spain Cardinal Riario, in the Quality of Legate. The Count de Sastago, Viceroy of Arragon, treated him so magnificently as soon as ever he enter'd into his Government, that the Cardinal intrusted him

him with the Secret of his Legation The Pope's Intention was to make himself Judge, and to pronounce definitively concerning the Right of the Princes who pretended to the Crown of *Portugal* The Count gave the King Advice thereof, who on his part gave Orders to make him a solemn Entry in all the Towns through which he pass'd, where they made such vast Preparations, so many Entertainments, so many Bull Fights, and gave so many other Diversions, that the King had the Leisure to enter into *Portugal*, and to push his Conquests before the Cardinal could come up with him

In the Beginning of the Year 1660, two Embassadors of one of the Northern Crowns, being in *Holland*, to endeavour to prevail with the United Provinces to declare themselves in Favour of the King their Master, went to *Amsterdam*, in order to dispose the Magistrates of that Town to forward their Pretensions in the Assembly of the States of the Province They were very well receiv'd, they were feasted, defray'd, carry'd to the Play-house, and entertain'd with several other Diversions, and as for the matter of their Negotiation, they were sent back with very general Assurances of the good Intention of the Magistrates but they were but indifferently satisfy'd with the Treaty which was concluded afterwards, at the Instance of the Crowns of *France* and *England*, and with the Consent of the States The Entertainments and Diversions were all the Embassadors got for the Fatigue of their Journey, and the King for the Honour he had done the Town to write to it.

There is another Vice very contrary to Prudence, and which nevertheless masks it self with it sometimes, *viz* Timidity, when the Embassador has not the Assurance to execute the Orders he receives, and to deliver them with all the Vigour he owes to his Employment This is properly speaking an infamous Cowardice, and unworthy of the Character *I would not*, says *Dossat*, *have the Pope believe me Coward enough not to dare to carry him the King's Commands in the same Terms I receiv'd them* And in Fact, the Minister who has so mean a Soul as not to follow the Orders which are given him, is so far from passing for prudent, that he does not deserve the Post with which he is honour'd He says in another Place, I am preparing my self to execute the Commands your Majesty sends me by *M du Perron*, in order to serve your Majesty under him with all the Powers of my Soul In which Service, Fidelity, Integrity and Zeal shall never be wanting in me, nor (whatever Difficulty I may apprehend therein) Boldness neither On the contrary, one cannot enough esteem the Generosity of those who speak with Freedom and Courage for the Interest and Dignity of their Master of which we shall have occasion to speak in the following Chapter

The Embassador mistakes, and may be said to run Riot, not only when he suffers himself to be amus'd, but also when he is disheartn'd and tires Cardinal *Barberin* own'd, That it was one of the Secrets of his Ministry, as well as of the Government of the Pope his Uncle, to know how to free themselves from the Importunity of publick Ministers, by tiring them out with Refusals which were not very reasonable, or else by Procrastinations and affected Delays For which Reason Cardinal *Mazarin*, who was the ablest Negotiator in the World, recommended very much to the Abbot of St *Nicolas*, whom I lately mention'd, not to seem to be uneasy at the Pope's tiresome way of Proceeding, or to shew that it was capable of discouraging him so far as to lay aside going to Audience, because he could not please the Pope better

It is also a great piece of Prudence to know how to palliate or hide an Evil which one cannot remedy The Embassador who is among Barbarians who have no Respect for the *Law of Nations*, cannot always avoid those Injuries and Outrages, which he would have no Reason to fear in a civiliz'd Nation, but he must be cautious of demanding Reparation, unless he be sure of obtaining it In dissembling the Matter, he suffers, but in demanding Reparation he engages the Name and Dignity of his Master and if he obtains nothing, he makes him receive an Affront, which obliges the Prince to shew a Resentment, and the Minister to retire The Turks had compell'd the Embassadors of France, of England, and of Venice to appear before the Judges in Ordinary A greater Affront could not be offer'd neither to the Sovereigns nor to the Ministers, but the Court of *France* wrote to the Embassador, to dissemble the Matter, because the King's Affairs would not permit him to resent it The Earl of *Carlisle*, Embassador from *England* in *Moscovy*, being already on Horseback, and having advanc'd some part of the Way towards making his Publick Entry, was interrupted, and oblig'd to go and lodge in a sorry Village near the Town. He complain'd thereof in Writing, and demanded Reparation and by requiring Reason from those who had none, and by procuring a Denial, he made a real Affront of that which was before but a piece of Clownishness and Rusticity, which a prudent Dissimulation would have pass'd off for an Oversight or a Blunder We shall have an Occasion hereafter in Chapter X, to speak of the false Prudence of an Embassador, who for want of making a Report of what the Emperor had said to him, made his Master receive a very gross Affront. But then true Prudence does not permit an Embassador to write to his Prince all that passes *M. de Foix* says, it is sufficient to acquaint one of the Ministers, in whom the Prince has the greatest Confidence therewith, till his Address supplies him with a Remedy On *June* 2, 1616, King *Lewis* XIII, sent for the Duke *de Monteleon*, the *Spanish* Embassador, and told him, That as he was Guarantee for the Execution of the Treaty of *Ast*, he could not suffer the Catholick King to disturb the Duke of *Savoy*, and that he was resolv'd to succour him, since his good Offices for the Continuation of the Repose of *Italy* had been ineffectual The Embassador made Answer, That he would always contribute as much as lay in his Power to Peace; but as for the Declaration his Majesty had made to him, that he would send Succours to the Duke of *Savoy*, he intreated him to impart It to his Master by some other Hand, because he could not change his Quality of Embassador into that of a Herald, especially to

Rrrr the

the Prince he ſerv'd The King reply'd, That he had told him his Intention, and he might acquaint the King of *Spain* therewith if he thought fit The Embaſſador's Anſwer was very prudent, becauſe the King of *France* ought to have given that Commiſſion to the Miniſter who was on his part at *Madrid*, but however the Embaſſador could not avoid giving Advice thereof to the Duke of *Lerma*

Prudence has ſo vaſt an Object, that one may ſay it is almoſt infinite The Embaſſador ought not only to conſider that the Principles of Reaſoning in Policy are as uncertain, as thoſe of the Mathematicks are infallible, but he ought to know alſo, that the ſtrongeſt Reaſons, and which are in a manner demonſtrative, are not always concluding It is a fundamental Maxim in the Government of the United Provinces, that thoſe Reſolutions that are taken with the Conſent and expreſs Order of all the Provinces, cannot be alter'd nor annull'd but with their unanimous Conſent, and expreſs Order The Inſtructions their Plenipotentiaries carry'd to *Munſter*, had been examin'd by all the Provinces, regulated and fix'd by their Order and unanimous Conſent It is certain that theſe Inſtructions order'd the Plenipotentiaries to obſerve punctually the Treaty of the Year 1644, and to conclude nothing without *France* Upon theſe Principles la *Tuillerie*, Embaſſador of *France*, maintain'd, That the States Plenipotentiaries did not dare, nor could not make a particular Treaty with *Spain* He ſaid that the whole State was not corrupted That there were in it ſome Perſons of ſound Judgment, and of Quality, who would not allow of ſo villainous a Failure to *France*, to the Friendſhip the State ow'd it, and to the Promiſe had been made to it, eſpecially ſince the States had not Guarantee for all that *Spain* promis'd them by the Treaty, and that the Plenipotentiaries would not expoſe themſelves to Diſgrace, nor to the Enquiry might be made therein His reaſoning was good, and becoming a Man of Underſtanding, but for all that he was miſtaken, becauſe they did conclude excluſively of *France*

There are numberleſs Advices to be given to an Embaſſador on the account of Prudence, but I dare be bold to ſay, that there is no need to give any to a Miniſter to whom this Virtue is natural, or acquir'd by a long Habit He forms his Conduct on his own Maxims, and behaves himſelf as Occaſions ſeem to require He will not fail to take down in Writing whatever his Prince orders or recommends to him by word of Mouth, as well to eaſe his Memory, as for the Juſtification of his Procedure He will be very cautious of ſpeaking too freely in a ſuſpicious Place, and will always believe that the very Walls have Ears, but he will particulary take into Conſideration what the illuſtrious Author of the excellent moral Reflections ſays, *viz That the moſt conſummate Prudence cannot aſſure us of the leaſt Effect imaginable, becauſe, working upon a Matter ſo changeable and inconſtant, and ſo unknown as Man is, it cannot execute with any Security any of its Projects* To this I muſt add, That there is not any that can divine, nor prevent the Artifices malicious Minds ſhall make uſe of to ſurpriſe it. I own that *Creville*, who was Gentleman,

and *Richer*, who was Secretary to the Conſtable *de St Pol*, were not great Miniſters, but it muſt alſo be allow'd, that there was no Prudence, how refin'd ſoever it might be, that could avoid the Snares *Lewis* XI had laid for them Their Deſign was to ruin the Duke of *Burgundy* in the Opinion of *Lewis*, and even render him ridiculous if they could The King who hated them both alike, and had a mind to undo them, endeavour'd to render them irreconcileable, by diſcovering to the one the Duplicities and Perfidies of the other The Sieur *de Contay* was with him on the part of the Duke, and to convince him of the Conſtable's evil Intentions, he hid this Gentleman behind a Skreen in the Chamber where he was to give Audience to theſe Miniſters They had already told a hundred Stories of the Duke of *Burgundy*, and to the end his Miniſter might make a faithful Report thereof, the King put them upon the ſame Diſcourſe, and made them repeat the Railleries the Duke made of the King of *England*, and how much he reſented the Peace *Edward* had concluded with the King They ſaid ſo much that there was no need of any more to perſuade *Contay* of the Conſtable's Duplicity, and to give the Duke a Diſtruſt of that Nobleman of which he could never after be cur'd

Stephen Taverna was a very able Miniſter, but yet with all his Prudence he could not elude the Artifices of *Peter de Medicis* This laſt was in the firſt Authority at *Florence*, and that of the Republick was very conſiderable in a Conjuncture where *Charles* VIII was going to enter into *Italy* in order to conquer *Naples Lewis le More*, who brought thither the Arms of *France*, did it only that he might not remain expos'd to the Diſcretion of *Alfonſo*, eldeſt Son to *Ferdinand* King of *Naples*, who could not ſuffer that *Lewis* ſhould uſurp the Ducheſs of *Milan* from *John Galeas* his Son-in-Law, and Nephew to *Lewis* IV Conſidering therefore that the Victories of the *French* might be his Ruin, he endeavour'd to prevail with *Peter de Medicis* to diſpoſe *Alfonſo* not to meddle with the Affairs of his Son-in-Law And it was to this purpoſe that he ſent *Stephen Taverna* to him *Peter*, who diſtruſted *Lewis*'s Intentions, who was in effect one of the moſt dangerous Men of his Time, gave Advice thereof to *Alfonſo*, and agreed with him to make known *Lewis*'s Perfidy and Treachery to *John Mattaron* the *French* Embaſſador, in order to let him ſee upon what Grounds his Maſter form'd his Reſolution to paſs into *Italy* and to the End the Embaſſador might not doubt of the true Intentions of *Lewis*, *Peter* put him into a Cloſet which was next to the Ruel of his Bed, where he kept, under the Pretext of ſome Indiſpoſition The Embaſſador of *Milan* being come, *Peter de Medicis* told him, that he could not diſſemble to him, that he had great Reaſon to diſtruſt *Lewis*'s Intention, becauſe he was aſſur'd that he continu'd his Negotiations at the Court of *France*, and preſs'd *Charles* to invade *Italy* That this oblig'd him to be diffident of him, and to take ſuch Meaſures as might ſhelter him from the Storm which was going to fall upon his Head *Taverna* made Anſwer, That there was no Room to doubt of the Sincerity of what he ſaid on the part of

his

his Master, since it could not be doubted that he had as much Reason to apprehend the Success of the Arms of *France*, and no less Interest to oppose them, than the other Princes of *Italy*, and urg'd *Peter* very much to entertain a good Disposition for their common Country, which otherwise would inevitably fall under a foreign Bondage. The *French* Embassador did not fail to give Advice hereof immediately to the King his Master, but the Advice wrought a quite contrary Effect to what it would have done in a more reasonable Mind, and less prejudic'd than that of *Charles* was *Lewis* seeing his Treachery was discover'd, justify'd himself by renewing his Instances for the Invasion, as well as his Offers to assist him with Men and Money. The *French* Council was unhappy enough to neglect this important Advice, and to enter into the Sentiments of a Traytor, who was the first to declare himself against the King, and to take up Arms to hinder him from getting out of *Italy*.

Jerome Moron, Chancellor to *Francis Sforza* the last Duke of *Milan*, had the Reputation of being one of the ablest Ministers of State of his Time. The Duke his Master was in a continual Uneasiness and Distrust of the Emperor *Charles* V, who had a great longing to make himself Master of the Dutchy, as the most commodious Post for the Communication, and even for the Junction of his States of *Italy*, and *Spain* to those of *Germany*. In order therefore to employ him elsewhere, the Pope, the Republick of *Venice*, and he, treated with *Don Alfonso Davalos*, Marquiss of *Pescarre*, to prevail with him to make himself Master of the Kingdom of *Naples*. This Nobleman was confided in by the Emperor. The Army respected him, and he had full as much Ambition as Courage and Conduct, so that it was thought that the Offer which was made him of a Crown would not be disagreeable to him. It is very probable that it was not at first, since he went a great way in the Negotiation, but whether he found some Impossibility in the Execution, or that he look'd upon the Action it self not to be honourable, he resolv'd to discover the whole Intrigue to the Emperor, in such a manner that he should not be able to doubt of it. He therefore hid *Anthony de Leiva* in a Place, where without being seen, he might learn all the Particulars from the Mouth of *Moron*, who was the Person that manag'd all this Affair. It cost *Moron* his Life, and *Francis Sforza* the Dutchy.

We have a more modern Example in the Duke of *Ossuna*, Viceroy of *Naples*. This Nobleman, who had a great deal of Wit, and still more Ambition, endeavour'd to make himself King of *Naples*, and to this effect he held a Correspondence with the Crown of *France*, by means of the Mareschal *de Lesdiguieres*, and with the Duke of *Savoy De Veyne*, a Gentleman of *Dauphine*, who was the Broker in this Commerce, had Orders to apply himself concerning this Affair to *Deagent*, who had a great Interest at Court at that Time, but the Duke *de Luines*, who under the Name of Favourite discharg'd the Functions of first Minister, being become jealous of *Deagent*, caus'd him to be remov'd, and by that Mean ruin'd this great Design, which was just ready to be put in Execution. The Duke of *Ossuna* not being now able to execute it on his side, and having a Mind to justify himself to the *Spanish* Ministers, who were but too well convinc'd of his Intention, had hid two *Spaniards* behind the Hangings of the Room where *de Veyne* was to speak to him. But this Gentleman, being at his Arrival at *Naples* inform'd that he would not find there the Dispositions he had left, said nothing that could make it be believ'd the Court of *France* had any Hand in this Intrigue.

CHAP. VII.
Of the Liberty of Speaking.

THE Liberty of Speaking is one of the first Parts, and one of the principal Rights of an Embassador, but then it is also that in which he had most need of his Prudence. There is nothing that recommends him so much, and is so necessary to him as this Assurance, by which he dares to speak up for the Interest of the Prince his Master, and execute his Orders, how high soever they may run: but there is a great deal of Difference between the Liberty of Speaking and Petulancy, between a free and witty Repartee and an offensive Sarcasm, between lawful and respectful Complaints and gross Reproaches, which partake of Rusticity and Impudence. The Embassador is indispensably oblig'd to execute his Master's Orders, but he may do it in such a manner as may soften the Harshness of his Action, and justify his Conduct, altho' his Master's Intention be not approv'd of. He ought to keep within the Bounds of Respect, notwithstanding his Prince commands him to express himself in Words which cannot be agreeable. The Embassador that loses the Respect which is due to Sovereigns, does not only expose himself to the Affronts he ought to expect from a Prince who is not over-patient, but he also runs the Risque of being disavow'd. The Action of *Anthony Fonseca*, Embassador from *Ferdinand the Catholick*, who tore the Treaty in the Presence of *Charles* VIII, was insolent, and deserv'd to be requited with some mortifying Affront. *Lewis* XI sent the Count *d'Eu* and Chancellor *Morvilliers* to *Philip* Duke of *Burgundy*, but with a Design to have some offensive Expressions deliver'd to the Count *de Charolois*. The Chancellor did it, but the Count told him, or the Archbishop of *Narbonne*, who was the third Embassador, that the King should repent it, and indeed he made

made him repent it so heartily, that he was forc'd to disavow, and put away the Chancellor his Embassador.

The least that can happen to him is to extort some vexatious Answer, which does the Master as much Damage as the Minister. Henry VIII, King of England, was a Prince that was irregular enough, and thought he ought to be the Umpire of the Affairs of Europe. He was angry at the Refusal the Emperor *Charles* V. made to deliver up to him an *English* Nobleman, who had taken Refuge in the Low Countries, and, in his Anger, he sent Orders to his Embassador to reproach the Emperor therewith. The Embassador being either too punctual in executing his Orders, or else carrying his Master's Resentment a little too far, let slip the Word *Ingratitude*. Hereupon *Charles*, who had till then given him a very favourable Audience, took up the Word *Ingratitude*, and ask'd him who it was that he pretended to accuse thereof? And the *Englishman* making Answer, That it was of himself and of the King of *France* he spoke, the Emperor reply'd, That he did not doubt but the King of *France* would justify himself very well. That as for himself, he was willing the Embassador should know that it did not belong to him, nor even to his Master, to tax him with *Ingratitude*. That the King of *England* had never done any thing, nor indeed could not do any thing, for him, that could render him an *Ingrate*, and that if he had done any small Matter for him, he had return'd it double to him. After all, *That the Word* Ingratitude, *which the Embassador made use of, might indeed pass between Persons of equal Quality or Dignity, or from a Superior to an Inferior, but could not be allow'd of in him the Embassador, who was neither the one nor the other, and that he did not believe his Master would stand by him in it*.

Paul *Dzialinski*, Embassador from *Sigismund* III, King of *Poland*, was sent to the States of the United Provinces, and afterwards to the Queen of *England*. This Embassador, who came from a King, who had caus'd himself to be driven out of *Sweden*, and who was not very much consider'd in *Poland* itself, had no great Success in *Holland*. And going from thence to *England*, he told the Queen, That the *English* did not only disturb the Commerce of the Merchants of *Poland* and *Prussia*, but also, that contrary to the *Law of Nations*, they hinder'd them from trafficking in *Spain*. That the King his Master, who was so strictly ally'd to the House of *Austria* and the King of *Spain*, could not suffer his Subjects to be treated after that manner, and that unless the Queen caus'd their Shipping and Goods to be restor'd to them, and permitted them to traffick freely with *Spain*, he would do himself Justice, so that the Authors of these Disorders should have Reason to repent it. The Queen answer'd him immediately, *How much am I mistaken! I expected an Embassador, and he proves a Herald. Since the Hour I was born, I never heard so insolent and inconsiderate a Discourse.* "If you have this "Commission from your King, of which however I very much doubt, he must have but "very little Knowledge of what has pass'd be- "tween the Kings his Predecessors and us. As "for your own Part, you seem to have read

"more Books than you have learn'd Politicks. "For since you speak so much of the *Law of* "*Nations*, you must know, that when there is "a War between two Princes, the *Law of* "*Nations*, as well as the *Law of Nature*, al- "lows the hindering of any Succour to be gi- "ven to the Enemy. And as for the Alliance "you boast your King has with the House of "*Austria*, you may call to Mind that some of "that House were for depriving him of the "Crown. As for the rest, I shall signify my "Pleasure to you by my Council." This said, she retir'd into her Closet, and left the Embassador. In the Conferences he had with the Council he excus'd himself, and said, That the Harangue had been given him in Writing. He did not see the Queen any more, and he was dismiss'd with an Answer which he had no great Reason to be satisfy'd with.

There have been Princes who have caus'd very offensive things to be said to the Popes. *Calixtus* III was born the Subject of *Alonso*, the *Magnanimous*, and ow'd all his Fortune to that Prince, and yet he made Difficulty to invest him with the Kingdom of *Naples*. *Ximenes Perez Corolla*, Count of *Contentayna*, Embassador from *Alfonsus*, seeing the Pope persisted in refusing the Investiture, told him, *That he ought to remember his mean Extraction, and the Place from whence he came*, and added so many other Reproaches, that the Pope, who could not resent it otherwise, gave him his Curse.

Nothing can be haughtier than what *Charles* VIII, King of *France*, caus'd to be said to *Alexander* VI, from whom he also ask'd the Investiture of the Kingdom of *Naples*. His Embassador told him, *That the Pope ought to consider, that the King having contracted an Alliance with the King of the* Romans, *it would always be in his Power to dispossess him of the Papal Dignity, not only by his Arms, but also by the Force of Reason and Justice, by calling a General Council. That it might be prov'd by good Evidence, that he had been elected through* Simony. *That he was prophane in his Life and Manners. That it was rumour'd he was guilty of several Murders, and that it could be made out he was an Heretick.* The Pope, who very well deserv'd this Reproach, and something more, did not resent it against the Embassador, because the King was coming with a powerful Army into *Italy*, but he soon found an Opportunity to revenge himself on the King, by making him lose the Kingdom of *Naples*.

Ferdinand the Catholick, as devout as he was, did not use the same Pope any better, because not being able to hinder him from consenting to *Lewis* XII being divorc'd from *Jean* of *France*, his first Wife, to marry *Anne* of *Britain*, he signify'd to him by *Garcilasso de la Vega*, his Embassador, that he ought to think of a Reformation of the Scandals the Court of *Rome* gave every Day. And that the Pope might know that he spoke to him in these Terms, by his Master's express Commands, he read to him the Order he had receiv'd in Writing. The Pope thereupon flew into such a Passion that he snatch'd the Paper out of the Embassador's Hands, and threaten'd him, as if he had exceeded his Orders. *Garcilasso* hereupon told the Pope, That he neither said not did

did any thing but what an Embassador, and an honest Man, was oblig'd to say and to do, for the Service of his Prince. That he was willing the Pope should know, that, as long as he should remain at his Court, he would tell him with great Freedom whatever he should be commanded to tell him, and what he should think conducive to the Good of Christendom. That if the Pope was disturb'd thereat, he might cause him to be recall'd, and that he should be glad of it, because he was very sensible that his Stay there was to no Purpose.

It was in the same Year, 1497, and in the Year 1498, that the same King *Ferdinand*, and *Emanuel* King of *Portugal*, reiterated their Instances for a Reformation, by *Don Inigo de Cordoba, Philip Ponce, Don Rodrigue da Castro,* and *Don Henry Coutinho,* their Embassadors. The Pope, instead of hearkening to their Remonstrances, *gave them injurious Language,* and did not even spare their Masters. They had a second Audience towards the end of *December*, and perceiv'd very well, as they went in, that the Guards were reinforc'd, but that did not hinder them from telling the Pope, *That every body was sensible of the unlawful Means he had us'd to make himself be chosen, and that his Election was scandalous and vicious.* The Pope interrupting their Discourse, made Answer, That the King and Queen of *Spain* did not hold their Kingdoms by so just a Title as he did the See of *Rome.* That they had usurp'd 'em, whereas he had been canonically chosen. Afterwards addressing himself particularly to *Philip Ponce,* he told him, That he would chastise him as a Madman, for having dar'd to speak reflectingly of his Election. *Inigo* thereupon spoke, and told the Pope, That Embassadors were not to be us'd after that manner, and especially those who represented such powerful Princes. The Pope then told him, he would excommunicate *Ferdinand* in *Cœna Domini.* The Embassadors had Orders to make, in a full Consistory, the same Declaration they had made to the Pope, to whom they gave a formal Summons the 23d of *January,* 1499, in the Presence of the Cardinals *de St Croix* and *Sforza*, which put him into so violent a Passion, that he said, *That if the Duke of Valentinois was there, they would not dare to hold him that Language. That in the time of Pope Sixtus, the Count Jerome de Rinnio had not scrupled to tell the Embassadors of Spain, That he would cause them to be flung into the Tiber. That they had told him several times the same things, and that he would hear no more of that sort. That they should take great Care not to mention any such thing in the Consistory, because they would obtain nothing there, and would come off but ill.* These Embassadors had their express Orders, which they were oblig'd to follow, notwithstanding they knew they had to do with a Man, who, after he had violated the *Laws of Nature* in all its Parts, would have no great Consideration for the *Law of Nations.* That there was not more Security at *Rome* for Embassadors, than there was amongst the *Tartars* of *Daguestan*, and that the Duke of *Valentinois* was full as dangerous at least as Count *Jerome of Riario.*

The Embassador, who receives such Orders, ought to know whether the Prince who gives him them has the Heart and the Power to maintain and protect him, because he cannot be ignorant, that a Prince who knows his Power is not offended with Impunity, if he be ever so little sensible to Reproaches, especially if they are made in publick, and with some Appearance of Truth. The Princes of *Germany* must needs have had a very bad Opinion of King *Henry* III, since they caus'd so offensive a Discourse to be made to him towards the end of the Year 1586. They had put it in Writing, that the Embassadors might read it at their Audience. As accordingly they did. They said in it, That the Princes their Masters were very much surpriz'd at the Temerity of some particular Persons, who of their own private Authority had had the Assurance to disturb the Peace the King had granted to those of the Reform'd Religion in his Kingdom, altho' he had confirm'd it with a solemn Oath. That what increas'd their Displeasure was to find the King changed. That his Majesty, after having written to the Governors of the Provinces, That his Intention was to cause the Peace to be observ'd and executed, had struck into quite the contrary Sentiments, by forbidding the Exercise of the same Religion. That the King cast the Cause of the new War upon the Religionaries, altho' he heretofore had declar'd the contrary, and had promis'd upon his Word they should enjoy the Benefit of his Edicts. That they did not see what Advantage the King could reap from a Change that disturb'd the Repose of his Kingdom, and sully'd his Majesty's Reputation, to whom nothing ought to be so valuable as his Promise and his Word. That God never suffer'd the Violation thereof to go unpunish'd, and that he who persecutes and oppresses those he knows to be innocent, cannot be innocent himself. That the Princes their Masters intreated the King to consider, That the end of an unjust War could not be happy, and that he would do well to give Peace to his Subjects who had a Veneration for his Person, and readily obey'd his Commands. That he ought to stop his Ears to the Counsels of the Court of *Rome*, and of its Emissaries, who had no other Intention but to weaken the King's Authority and Strength, in Order to disturb the legitimate Order of the Succession, to make way for a strange one. *Henry* III hated his Protestant Subjects, and fear'd the Leaguers; but he most hated those, and fear'd these most; finding therefore an Opportunity to give a Mark of his Hatred and Resentment to the first, he made to the Embassadors the Answer which I have observ'd in Chapter IV. Those Princes might very well have forborn expressing themselves to the King in those Terms, because they were not in a Condition to support their Embassadors, nor to resent the Affront which might be offer'd them, and which was offer'd them in Effect. It must be own'd that there was in their Discourse a Grossness which border'd upon Impudence, and deserv'd very well that the King should have caus'd them to be put out of his Presence, besides, it did not belong to the Princes of *Germany* to meddle with the Affairs of the Religionaries of *France*, since they would not have suffer'd the King to intercede for their Roman Catholick Subjects.

If the Embassador ought to be reserv'd on these Occasions, with all Princes, he ought with more Reason to be so with those whose Pride cannot suffer Reproaches nor Remonstrances *Jerome Laski*, who was without doubt one of the most illustrious Personages of the last Age, had giv'n a Retreat to *John Zapoli*, King of *Hungary*, who had been oblig'd to yield to the Arms of *Ferdinand* of *Austria* Laski had at his own Expences discharg'd the Function of Embassador at *Constantinople*, and had there obtain'd the Restoration of *John* under the Protection of Sultan *Soliman* Some time after he fell out with *John*, and quitted his Party to side with *Ferdinand*, who employ'd him in his turn to negotiate his Interest at the Port, tho' he had not the same Success *Soliman*, who was really a very great Prince, and who was for having it believ'd that Justice and Generosity were the Motives of all his Actions, signify'd to *Ferdinand*'s Embassadors, That the Protection he had promis'd to *John Zapoli*, who was dead, oblig'd him to continue it to his Widow and Son, who was his Vassal and Tributary That his Intention was, that the Son should reign after his Father, and that he had sufficiently explain'd himself in the Letters of Investiture And in Effect *Soliman*, to shew that he confirm'd to the Son the Protection he had given the Father, had sent him a Vest of Brocade, a Mace, and some other Presents which the *Turks* are us'd to make on the like Occasions *Laski*, finding the Affair in this State at his coming to *Constantinople*, said, with a *Polish* Liberty, *That the Emperor and* Ferdinand *his Brother would resent the Wrong that was done them* He said too much in a Court, where no Distinction is made between Violence and Justice, and where the Ministers cannot endure to be reproach'd The first Vizir said, *Laski* deserv'd Death, and sent him to Prison, but *Soliman*, who lov'd great Men, soon set him at Liberty

Pope *Sixtus* V, whom Fortune had rais'd from the lowest Meanness to the highest Dignity of *Christendom*, was not so much oblig'd to Fortune for it as to his Merit, it being certain that for some Ages the See of *Rome* had not been fill'd with so great a Personage He had a Value for those Persons in whom he discover'd any thing extraordinary, and notwithstanding he had no great Reason to love them, yet he granted them his Esteem He had always some Difference with the Marquiss of *Pisani*, and he banish'd him out of the Ecclesiastical State but he soon recall'd him, because he admir'd in him that Greatness of Soul, which ranks him amongst the greatest Ministers that have ever been He had a high Dispute with *Pius* V, concerning the Count *de Gayazze*, whom the Pope had put into the Inquisition King *Charles* IX, who lov'd that Gentlemen, sent Orders to *Pisani* to reclaim him as his Subject and Officer, and to procure him his Liberty The Marquiss having spoke several times to the Pope about it to no Purpose, told him at last, *That he gave him eight Days longer, and if he did not in that Time set the Count at Liberty, he should be oblig'd to do what would not be pleasing to the Pope Pisani*, not finding himself gain any Ground at the end of the eight Days, told the Pope, *That if in four and twenty Hours he did not set the Count at Liberty he would leave Rome, and would take along with him the Embassador in Ordinary*, which would interrupt the Commerce the Court of *Rome* had with that of *France*, for the Dispatch of the Benefices The Pope, who was interessed, follow'd the Counsel of those Cardinals; who advis'd him to deliver up the Prisoner

When the Glory and Interest of a Prince is concern'd, and the Embassador has Orders to speak with Freedom, he ought to execute them without Scruple, because then there is not either to deliberate upon, nor to hesitate at *Jam* Amiot, Abbot of *Bellosane*, and since Bishop of *Auxerre*, and Great Almoner of *France*, was sent to the Council of *Trent* in the Year 1551 His Letters were not address'd to the Council, but to the Assembly (*Conventus*) of *Trent*, at which the Fathers were so scandaliz'd, that they put it to Debate whether they should receive the Letters, and whether they should give Audience to the Embassador Amiot having at last obtain'd the one and the other, said at his Audience, "That it was a strange thing to see " the Pope, who gave himself the Title or " Common Father, turn Partizan That the " King his Master had hoped, that after the " Death of *Paul* III, *Julius* his Successor would " have labour'd at the Preservation of the Liberty of *Italy*, by protecting the House of " *Farnese*, and maintaining it in *Parma*, but " that the Pope had join'd his Counsels and " his Arms to those who were Enemies of " both, and not contented therewith had " caus'd *Mirandola* to be attack'd by *John Baptista del Monte*, who had there committed " Cruelties unheard of, even amongst *Barbarians*. That instead of making use of the " Sword of the Word of God, at a time when " the Common Enemy threaten'd *Christendom*, " whose Tranquillity was otherwise disturb'd " by very dangerous Divisions, he attack'd " with real Arms the Vassals of the Church, " and even the most Christian King himself " That this Procedure was unworthy of him " who honour'd himself with the Quality of " Servant of the Servants of God, and of Vicar on Earth of Jesus Christ, that pacifick " Lamb That the King was very much surpriz'd to see the Pope call a Council, at a " Time where he united his Arms with those " of the Emperor, to fight him, and that, to " the End the Prelates of *France*, who could " not come thither by reason of the War, might " not inform against the Head, as well as " against the Members, and might not help " to reform the Corruptions thereof, as well " in Morals as in Doctrine That he had no " Orders to complain of the War that was " made against the King, as well because this " was not the Place where that Matter was to " be treated, as because his Majesty had wherewith to do himself Justice, and even strike " Terror into those who threaten'd him But " that his Majesty could not suffer Ambition " to cover it self with the Veil of Piety, and " Religion to be made subservient to the Avidity with which the Goods of others were " ravenously made a Prey of, nor tamely behold the horrible Confusion of all things sacred and prophane That the King, as eldest " Son of the Church, declar'd for that Reason, " That he could not suffer the Bishops of his

"Kingdom to go to the Council of *Trent*, while an unjust War was carry'd on against him, nor hold that Assembly for an OEcumenical Council, and lawfully conven'd, but as a private Assembly, to whose Decrees, neither he nor his Kingdom would have any Deference He desir'd the Fathers to excuse the Freedom of his Discourse, and to cause his Protestation to be register'd, of which he left them a Copy

Some Years after, *viz* in the Year 1563, *Arnaud de Ferrier* Embassador from *France* to *Trent*, made there, about the Month of *September*, a Discourse as high at least as that of *Amiot* It was on the Subject of the Rank that was given to the *Spanish* Embassador He says, "That *Pius* IV, like an unnatural Father, had "dispossess'd the most Christian King, his "eldest Son, against all Form, of the Advan- "tage he always had, of preceding all the o- "ther Kings of *Christendom* That the same "*Pius*, erecting himself as Judge in his own "Cause, had rais'd his particular Authority a- "bove that of the Council That under the "Pretext of uniting the Church and the Chri- "stian Princes, he disturb'd the Peace, and set "the two Brothers-in-Law at variance, by "changing by force, and a notorious Wick- "edness, the Ordinance of the Councils of "*Constance*, of *Basil*, and of *Lateran*. That 'this Procedure oblig'd the Embassadors of "*France* to remove from a Place, where *Pius* "depriv'd the Laws of their Force, the Ca- "nons of their Authority, and the Council of "its Liberty That the Fathers neither re- "solv'd upon, nor publish'd any thing, that "had not before been resolv'd upon at *Rome*, "and after they had receiv'd the Pope's Or- "ders That all the Delays, and all the Pro- "crastinations were caus'd by that *Pius*, who "knew that the Abuses of the Church could "not be corrected, unless they were reform'd "in its Head, as well as in its Members" He added hereunto "It is against this *Pius* that "we particularly protest We have spilt our "Blood for the Church and for the Popes, "and we have a Veneration for them, but "we neither acknowledge *Pius* nor his Au- "thority, and we reject all his Decrees and "all his Ordinances He is neither Vicar of "Jesus Christ, nor Successor of St *Peter* "And forasmuch as the Decrees are form'd "at *Rome*, and are not made at *Trent*, we have "reason to look upon them as the Declarati- "ons of *Pius*, rather than as the Canons of an "OEcumenical Council And we protest and "declare, that what is there resolv'd, or shall "hereafter be resolv'd in this Assembly, shall "not be approv'd of by the King, nor consi- "der'd by the *Gallican* Church, as the Decrees "of a Council lawfully conven'd In the "mean time, I exhort you the Archbishops, "Bishops and Prelates of *France*, and I com- "mand you in the King's Name to leave this "Place, and not to return to it, till the Out- "rage that has been done to his Majesty has "been repair'd" These two Harangues were very high it is certain, but it cannot be deny'd, but there was something of a higher Strain in the Embassador's Discourses, who spoke to the Pope himself, and to such Popes as had Courage enough to resent it. nay I dare not say for certain, that *Ferrier*'s Harangue was actually pronounc'd Don *Pedro* of *Arragon*, Embassador of *Spain* at *Rome* in the Year 1665, having let slip some Words of Resentment a- gainst the Court, which favour'd the Affairs of the King of *Portugal*, in what related to the Churches of that Kingdom, Pope *Alexander* VII, who had been inform'd thereof, told him, That he was an ill Man, and a Minister incapable of serving the King his Master The Embassador made answer, That the Pope had reason to accuse him of Negligence and Incapacity, since he had been willing to omit executing the King's Order, when a Treaty was carrying on to his Prejudice with the Minister of *Portugal* That the Pope, in making him that Reproach, upbraided him with his good Nature, but that he was in the wrong to say, he was an ill Man and that he could with more Justice say, that *Fabio Chisy* was an ill Man, since he forc'd him to execute the King his Master's Order's, and to desire the College of Cardinals to consider, Whether the See of *Rome* was more concern'd to do something for four Bishopricks in *Portugal*, than to hazard a hundred and thirty Bishopricks and sixty Abbies in *Spain* The Pope told him also, That the Assemblies he held at home were very dangerous, and might furnish an Occasion of pillaging the Town The Embassador reply'd, That if that were his Intention, he needed only to retire with all the Subjects of the King his Master, because those who would then remain not being able to subsist, would commit that Disorder which could not be apprehended from him

What I have said of the Embassador who has express Orders is plain I must add, That he may also speak with Freedom without Orders, when he judges it necessary for the Honour and Service of his Master, and that he is sure he shall not be disavow'd The Count *de Bethune*, being on the part of *France* at *Rome*, about the Affair of the *Valteline*, Cardinal *Magalotti* came and told him, That the Pope had resolv'd to send *Torquato Conti* into the *Valteline* with Troops, in order to make himself Master of the Forts which had been given in *depositum* to his Predecessor The Count answer'd him, That he could hardly believe what the Cardinal told him concerning the Pope's Resolution That the imaginary Reputation, on which the Cardinal said the Pope grounded his Resolution, was a Consideration for a temporal Prince, and not for the Head of the Church, who would always glory more in suffering and enduring, than in shewing Resentment for a thing, wherein he had not been offended and that even if he had, the Example of his primitive Predecessors ought to invite him to forget Injuries That his Holiness exceeded the Bounds of Neutrality, and renounc'd the Quality of common Father, in employing his Forces against the King's, who would without doubt be displeas'd, that the Pope should take so strange a Resolution That it was not the way to maintain a good Correspondence with his Majesty to threaten him That he would then be oblig'd to hearken to the Propositions the Hereticks made him, to make a strict Alliance with them, the Effects whereof would be a just Reproach to the Pope and instead of making Peace, would finish the Work of kindling the Fire of War throughout *Christendom*, to the Prejudice of the Catholick Religion. The Embassador said indeed, that he had no Orders to speak this, and that it was his Zeal for the Service of the King his Master, and the Affection he had for the Pope, that made him express himself in this manner, from whence the Pope took a Pretext to say, That it was not the King's Intention nor Sentiment. But the Count knew what he did, and got himself avow'd.

However he did very well to tell the Cardinal, that he did not speak by his Master's Orders, but that it was his own private Sentiment. In the Years 1572, and 1573, there was a great Discourse of the Marriage of Queen *Elizabeth* and the Duke of *Alançon*. The Queen order'd *Walsingham* to give 'em to understand in *France* that she could not think of marrying a Prince she had never seen, nor also suffer him to have any Exercise of a Religion which she judg'd to be contrary to the Word of God, as it was to the Laws of the Kingdom. The Queen Mother made answer, That there was no likelihood that the Duke her Son would go over to *England*, unless he were certain of succeeding in his Courtship, and ask'd *Walsingham* what the Queen of *England* meant, that the Duke should not have the Exercise of his Religion? *Walsingham* said, It was not for him to interpret the Queen's Intention, *but in his own private Capacity, he thought the Queen would not suffer the Exercise of a Religion prohibited by the Laws of the Kingdom*. The Queen Mother reply'd, That she desir'd nothing else, than that Queen *Elizabeth* would assure her, by a Word under her Hand, of the Success of the Marriage, before she engag'd her Son to pass the Sea; and as for the Matter of Religion, That her Son desir'd only the Exercise of it for himself and some of his Domesticks, to the Exclusion of all the *English*. *Walsingham* said, He would acquaint the Queen his Mistress herewith, but *that he did not believe she would grant either the one or the other*.

To take from the Embassador the Liberty of Speaking, is to deprive him of one of the principal Functions of his Employment, and on the other side, the Prince cannot enough esteem a Minister, who has the noble Assurance of daring to execute his Orders with vigour. *Michael John Gralla*, High-Steward to *Ferdinand the Catholick*, and his Embassador to *Lewis* XII, with *Diego Perez*, taking one Day Audience of the King and his Council, there arose a warm Dispute on the Execution or Inexecution of the Treaties that were between the two Kings. *Gralla* said, That the King his Master had executed them punctually on his part. The King answer'd, That he had done the like on his part, and would continue to do it for the time to come; upon which he was ready to fight the King of *Spain*, and the King of the *Romans*. *Gralla* reply'd, *That his King was as just a Prince, and as accomplish'd as any the World afforded, and that for the Defence of his Person and his Honour, he would fight his Majesty, and as many Princes as should present themselves, and should be of equal Dignity with him*. *Lewis* then said, He believ'd the King of *Spain* did not pretend to be better than he. Nor *you* don't pretend to better than the King *my Master*, answer'd *Gralla*. An Embassador's Repartee could not go further, without losing the Respect he ow'd the King.

Princes should not expose themselves to their sharp Returns, nor oblige the Embassador to lose that Respect that is due to the Sovereign, because he owes none to him, who loses it to the Master that employs him. *Ulefeld*, Great-Master of *Denmark*, retiring to *Sweden*, was there powerfully protected by the Queen. The Embassador of *Denmark*, to shew that this Gentleman was unworthy this Protection, told the Queen one Day, That the Great-Master had converted to his own particular Profit a Sum of five and twenty thousand Crowns, which the King had remitted to him, to assist the King of *England* in his Necessity. The Queen said, That if the Great-Master assur'd her he had caus'd that Sum to be paid to the King of *England*, she would believe him, and that if this should deny it, she would say he ly'd, and that if twelve more such Kings should say the same, she would affirm that all the twelve ly'd. That since the King of *Denmark* would not restore the Great-Master to the Possession of his Estate, she would give him so good a one, that he should have no Occasion to grieve at what he lost in *Denmark*. The Embassador boldly reply'd, That her Majesty might give him half her Kingdom, if she pleas'd, without his Master's finding fault therewith, but *that would not hinder him from thinking* Ulefeld *the basest and most perfidious of all Mankind*. This happen'd in the Year 1654, a little before the Queen's Abdication, and when it was no longer in her Power to dispose of any thing, so that she might very well have forborn drawing this Repartee upon her self.

Anthony Donati, Embassador of *Venice* at *Rome*, discoursing one Day familiarly with *Paul* V, the Pope having a mind to rally the Republick, ask'd him where she kept the Charters and Titles, that justify'd the Possession of so many Towns she had in *Lombardy*, and elsewhere on *Terra firma*? *Donati* was not at all surpriz'd, but answer'd, *That they would be found on the back of the Donation of* Constantine *the Great*. The Repartee silenc'd the Pope, by reproaching the See of *Rome* with an Usurpation, of which the Pope would have accus'd the Republick. They had nothing to reproach themselves with, either the one or the other. The Republick possesses *Brescia* and *Bergamo*, but by virtue of a Treaty made with *Francis Sforza*, Usurper of the Dutchy of *Milan*, and it was only the barbarous Cruelties and Perfidies of the Duke of *Valentinois*, that gave to the See of *Rome*, after the Death of *Alexander* VI, and under *Julius* II, all that the Pope possesses in *Romania*. These sharp and witty Repartees give a great Reputation to a Minister. But as they are the Effects of a Presence and Vivacity of Mind, which does not fall to every bodies Share, every Embassador is not capable of them. The Repartee of *Peter Danais*, Embassador of *France* at the Council of *Trent*, was admirable. He had made a Speech concerning a Reformation, which not being very agreeable to the Pope, an *Italian* Prelate said, by way of Contempt, *Gallus cantat*, A Cock crows: but he presently reply'd, *Utinam*

Utinam ad istum Galli cantum Petrus resipisceret! Would to God *Peter* would repent at the crowing of this Cock! There is nothing in the Apophthegms of the Ancients that comes near it.

Catarin Belegne, Embassador on the part of the Republick of *Venice* at *Turin*, being one Day in a Conversation where the Count *Philip a'Aglié*, the most authoriz'd Minister of that Court, spoke very advantageously of the Right the Duke of *Savoy* has to the Kingdom of *Cyprus*, he answer'd him and said, That the Senate would give a great deal that that Island was in the Hands of the Duke of *Savoy*, because it would not continue so two Months. He said true, because all the Naval Forces the Duke could oppose to those of *Venice* consists only in two Galleys, which he entertains at *Nice*, and which for the most part are not mann'd.

The Embassador does not go beyond the Bounds of Prudence, in justifying his Actions, and speaking for his Honour in strong Terms and with Warmth. The President *Jeannin* being inform'd that *Lambert*, at that Time a Captain in *Holland*, and since very much consider'd in *France*, had reported to the Court, that the President was not belov'd at the *Hague*, because he labour'd with too much Zeal for the Truce, says, in the Letter he writes to *M. de Villeroy* on *November* 22, 1608, that it is an impudent Lye, and that he is more honour'd and respected in *Holland* than ever any Body was in that Employment. He repeats the same Words in another Period of the same Letter, which he continues, and concludes it with the same Strength.

Anthony Donati, of whom I just spoke, being Embassador of *Venice* at *Turin* at the Beginning of the War in *Piedmont*, had the Management of the Subsidies the Republick allow'd to *Charles Emanuel* Duke of *Savoy*. The Duke complain'd of the Embassador, as if he made an Advantage of the Money which pass'd through his Hands; and he even demanded some Arrears after *Donati* had gone through the Term of his Service. The Senate, who had seen the Accounts of its Embassador, and had pass'd them, made Answer to the Duke, That it appear'd there was nothing due to him, and to prove it, sent him a Letter which *Donati* had written to *Venice* during his Embassy, in which he gave the Duke of *Savoy* three Times the Lye. The *Venetians* were not at all satisfy'd with the Duke's Conduct, for which reason they were not afraid of offending him. *Donati* sent the Republick's Answer to the Duke by an Express, and offer'd him to come in Person to *Turin*, in order to make an end of settling his Accounts, but the Duke would not see his Man.

Cardinal *Mazarin* could not consent to a Peace, unless it united the Provinces of *Flanders* to the Crown of *France*. To succeed therein, there was no kind of Artifice which he did not make use of to prevail with the United Provinces to continue the War with *Spain*. But not being able to hinder them from making a separate Peace, because they apprehended becoming Frontiers to *France*, he turn'd his Thoughts towards *Germany*, and us'd his utmost Efforts to make a Treaty which should hinder the Emperor from assisting *Spain* against *France*. The Cardinal and his Confidents did in the mean time all they could to persuade the World of the Sincerity of his Intentions, and of the Inclination he had to make a Peace with *Spain*. But *Servien* complaining one Day to the Mediators of the fresh Difficulties the Ministers of the House of *Austria* were continually starting, *Contarini*, Embassador of *Venice*, and one of the Mediators, could not forbear saying, That it was not the Ministers of the House of *Austria*, but those of *France* that created these Difficulties and to speak the Truth, That it was he, *Servien*, who alone gave Birth to all the Obstacle. That it was he who for three Years past had form'd all the Impediments that obstructed the Peace, and that by the secret Orders of some Persons who did not desire it, of which he would say more if it were necessary *Servien* reply'd, That *Contarini*'s Procedure was strange, and unworthy of a Mediator, who ought to carry himself with Moderation, and not fly into Passions against the Parties. That he, *Servien*, spoke on the part of a great King, as his Minister and Plenipotentiary, and that it did not belong to a Mediator to use him after that manner. That it was a long time that he, *Contarini*, made use of this Artifice, and every where spoke of those secret Orders, with a Design to sow Division among the *French* Ministers. That the Council's Intentions were upright and sincere, and that Peace was passionately desir'd by it. The Nuncio and *d'Avaux*, who were present at this Conversation, said nothing either the one or the other, as well because they were persuaded of the Justice of *Contarini*'s Reproaches, as because the last only expressed the Nuncio's Thoughts, who had explain'd himself on several Occasions. It is not probable that it was out of any Affection *Contarini* had for *Spain*, that he spoke after this manner. It cannot be said neither that this Minister, who had acquir'd so great a Reputation in the Embassies he had gone through in most Courts of *Europe*, should err through Imprudence. The Zeal he had for the Preservation of his Countrey, which was engag'd in the vexatious and troublesome *Candian* War, forc'd these Expressions from him, and oblig'd him to disburthen his Heart against those who by delaying to make Peace, hinder'd the other Christian Princes from assisting the Republick against the Infidels. *Servien* was in the right to say that *France* passionately desir'd Peace, and might say the same of the Cardinal, but that was not the Difference he had with *Contarini* France was for having Peace after its own way, but she did not agree with *Spain*, nor even with the Mediators, as to the Justice and Equity of the Conditions.

The Freedom of Speaking extends it self also to the Complaints of Embassadors, and to their Solicitations, which ought neither to be unjust nor importunate, but always lawful and necessary. *Anthony Paulin* Baron *de la Garde* had been bred up under *M. de Langeay*, Governor of *Piedmont*, one of the greatest Men of his Age, and *Paulin* had made so great a Proficiency in this School, that the Marquiss *de Gnast*, who did not judge of him like a Novice, but was arriv'd to a great Knowledge in Men, said of him, that he was the ablest *French-man*

man he had ever convers'd with King Francis I employ'd him to Soliman Emperor of the Turks, and he had already negotiated at Constantinople, when he was sent again to second the Instances of the Bishop of *Acs*, who was there Embassador in Ordinary, for which reason he ought to know the Air of that Court, and the Humour of the Ministers At his Arrival at *Constantinople* he found, that not only they were not arming by Sea, but that there was no Preparation to divert the Emperor *Charles V*'s Forces, while the King should attack him in *Spain* and in *Flanders*, so that these two Ministers, the one of whom was to carry the Resolution of the Divan into *France*, shew'd their Dissatisfaction so publickly, that the first Vizir, thinking himself oblig'd to justify his Prince's Procedure, sent for 'em to the Council, and spoke to them in these Terms "We " meet every Day in this Place, appointed by " the Grand Seignior for the Deliberation of " his most Important Affairs, and we, his " Slaves, do not bring hither our Passions, that " we may speak with so much the greater Liberty, but I would not have this Liberty, " the faithful Companion of Truth, offend " you, or incommode you For ever since " the King your Master has made an Alliance " with the *Ottoman* House, we have not fail'd " to do him all the good Offices which he " could desire from us, because the Grand " Seignior loves you, and would willingly " contribute all that depends on his Power to " establish yours, at the Expence of your Enemies But there is so little Reason and E" quity in your Demands, that we may say they " are neither just nor honest, and they who " do not love you so well as we do, might " say, *That they are impertinent, and even im*" *pudent, since you violate your selves with so* " *much Insolence the Laws of Friendship* Allies make Alliances subsist in sharing the Danger and Expence among them, but they are " soon destroy'd if there be a Neglect in maintaining them by mutual Offices It is you, " Gentlemen *Frenchmen*, who being always " negligent and drowsy in our Dangers, and " ever urgent and awake in your own, have " never strengthen'd our Friendship with effectual Succours, but only with Words and " useless Embassies Tell us, pray now, what " Proof have you given us of your Friendship that could make the least Diversion to " our common Enemies, while *Charles* had " drawn all the Forces of the West into *Austria* and *Hungary*, during the Siege of *Cortona* and of *Pairas*, the Attack and Reduction of *Tunis*? We are willing to pardon " you this Fault, but we cannot bear that " you should not compassionate our Afflictions, " and instead of resenting the Outrages that " were done us, you should be so complaisant " as to complement the Author of 'em Our " General was advanc'd as far as *Aulona*, with a " Design to pass into *Italy* for your Service, " but we did not find in the *Pastille* the Friends " and Intelligence you so much boasted of, " and you even lay still in the mean Time in " the other Parts of *Italy*, where you ought to " have made so powerful a Diversion So " that while you were no way serviceable to " us, and altogether of no Utility to your

" selves, you always lost the Opportunities of " doing well, tho' at that Time we neither " wanted your Advice nor Assistance, nor have " not since stood in need of them The Republick of *Venice* has felt the Effects of our " Power, and has had Proofs of our Fidelity, " and our Arms have done us Justice, while " you were making of Truces with our common Enemy, and imprudently seconding the " Designs they were forming against us It is " without your Assistance that we repuls'd the " Efforts of our Enemies, that *Barberossa* dispers'd the rival Forces, that he destroy'd " the *Spanish* Pirates, and that he made new " Conquests after the Reduction of our Towns " We are therefore willing you should know " that we have no Obligation to you, but we " chuse rather not to remember all this, than " to fail in the point of Friendship We will " readily give you Marks of our Affection, " but we must also consider the Season, the " Dangers and Conjunctures, that we may not " abandon our selves too much to Fortune " You are come so late, that it wou'd be temerity in us to expose a Fleet to the Seas " The Summer is too far spent, and Autumn " is so near at hand, that it is impossible for " us to furnish our Galleys with their Crew, " and our Ships with their necessary Complements Those who are not accustom'd to " long Voyages are subject to inevitable Maladies The Wrack *Barberossa* sustain'd in " the Mouth of *August*, sufficiently shews " how treacherous the Sea is in this Season " The Winter ought to be employ'd in arming, " the Spring is the Time to put to Sea, and " an Army is to be made use of in Summer, " in order to retire at the Beginning of Autumn I hope you have not taken ill that I " have spoken to you with as much Freedom " as Affection, referring my self for the rest " to what the Grand Seignior shall think fit " to resolve upon in reference to your Demands "

There is nothing barbarous in this reasoning, and if there be some vigorous Expressions in it, it must be acknowledg'd that the *French* deserv'd them very well

This Freedom of Speech may extend it self likewise to those who have not the Character of Embassador or of publick Minister, as to the Deputies Towns and Communities send to their Sovereigns However as these cannot enjoy the Protection of the *Law of Nations*, but only the Security of the publick Faith, which is not of so great an Extent, their Liberty ought not to be so neither The Embassador may sometimes go beyond that great Respect which is due to all Princes, but the Deputy ought always to keep within the Bounds of the Submission he owes his Sovereign, and if the Zeal he has for his Countrey obliges him to speak with some Warmth, it ought to be so respectful, that the Prince may not be offended thereby The *Spanish* Troops which were quarter'd in the *Milaneze* had mutiny'd for want of their Pay, and committed insufferable Insolencies there The Magistrate of *Milan* sent Deputies to the Emperor *Charles V* to complain thereof Baptista *Archinto*, Chief of the Deputation, after he had represented the People's Misery, and spoke of the Proofs all the Inhabitants

bitants gave continually of their Affection for the House of *Austria*, said in the Conclusion of his Speech, *That it was an easy matter to put an End to these Disorders, but that there were but two Ways to do it The one was to pay forthwith the Musters that were due to the Soldiers, and the other, in case there was none due, to permit the Milanese to revenge the Outrages they had receiv'd from them, and to employ their Arms against Thieves, who shew'd neither Obedience to their General, nor Respect to the Emperor himself* Charles, who was not in a Condition to do the one, nor disposed to suffer the other, and who was very much offended at the *Freedom of the Speech*, referr'd him to Granvelle, to whom he sent Orders at the same Time to give him a severe Reprimand Granvelle, who was a Master at that, did not fail to do it, but *Archinto* told him that the Emperor ought not to be offended at the Freedom of the Speech which a feeling Sense of the Evil had forc'd from him, and that he was oblig'd to add, *That if the Grievance were not redress'd, the Actions of the Milanese would be much more forcible than this Words had been And how can you suffer*, says he to *Granvelle*, *you, who have the chief Management of the Emperor's Affairs, that the Excesses and Abuses of a Rout of Thieves and mutinous Soldiers should ruin a Town that enriches you, and has supply'd the Emperor's House and Kitchin with all Necessaries for so many Years?* *Archinto* was not the worse us'd for this Freedom, nor the State of *Milan* any whit the better for it, but there was no hindering these poor Wretches from bemoaning their hard Fate and Complaining

One cannot say too much in Commendation of *Nicolas Machiavel's* History of *Florence* and yet I am of Opinion that the same Judgment ought to be made of his Harangues, which curious Writers make of those with which some of the best Historians disfigure their excellent Works This is not however any Obstacle to our believing that the Deputies (whom the City of *Milan* sent to Count *Francis Sforza*, after the Peace he had concluded with the *Venetians*) had Orders to make very sharp Reproaches to him He was General of the Army of *Milan* against the Republick of *Venice*, and he of his own Head made a Treaty with her, at the Expence of the Liberty of the State of *Milan*, of which he made himself Sovereign Prince The *Milanese*, who could no longer doubt of his Intention after so visible an Effect, sent Deputies to him, who said all that a just Resentment, Rage and Despair could dictate to People who found themselves betray'd by him who was oblig'd to defend them, and oppress'd by him that should have protected them They reproach'd him with his Avarice, his Ambition, his Pride, his Cruelty, his Ingratitude, his Infidelity, his Deceits, his Treachery, and in fine all that could be said of the wickedest of Men Indeed too much could not be said of him, any more than of *Galeas*, and of *Lewis the Moor* his Sons, the one of whom was kill'd in St *Stephen's* Church at *Milan*, and the other dy'd a Prisoner in the Castle of *Loches* in *Touraine*

The Embassador ought not to mingle Insolence with this Liberty, as I have already said, for fear of bringing on himself those Disgraces, of which we have given some Examples

In the Year 1469, *Stephen*, Prince or Waivode of *Walachia*, having defeated the *Tartars* in Battel, and the Cham's Son being taken Prisoner, the Father sent to demand him, by an Embassy compos'd of a hundred Persons These Barbarians, instead of demanding their Prince in civil Terms, threaten'd *Stephen* to ravage and lay Waste his Country if he did not restore their Prince, but the Waivode, far from being surpris'd at their Threats, commanded the Prisoner to be brought before him, and having caus'd him to be cut into four Quarters in their Presence, order'd all the Embassadors to be empaled except one, whose Nose and Ears he made to be cut off, and sent him back in that Condition to the Cham, to give him an Account of the Issue of the Embassy I would not have this brutish Action serve for an Example, but yet it may be of Use to shew, that there is no Security for the Embassador who lashes out into Transports of Passion, altogether inconsistent with his Function If he does not always meet with such excessive Disgraces, he draws upon himself Repartees which put him in Disorder The Clergy, and especially the Monks and Fryars, are very subject thereto In Chapter IX of the first Book mention is made of two Jacobin Fryars, *Simon Lentin* and *Peter de Marsilio*, the one of which made a very insolent Discourse to *Peter the Great*, King of *Arragon*, and the other to Pope *Clement* V *Peter* us'd his disdainfully, and then dismiss'd him, but *Clement* put his into the Hands of his Superior, in order to be punish'd Princes will not suffer the Clergy to insult them *Philip Augustus*, King of *France*, and *Richard* Earl of *Poictou*, made War with *Henry* II, King of *England* The Pope, *Clement*, who was for obliging them all to carry their Arms against the Infidels in the Holy Land (which was for some Ages the Madness both of Princes and People) sent Cardinal *d'Agname* to them to reconcile them The Legate finding that his Authority and Menaces made no Impression on the Mind of *Philip*, told him at last he would excommunicate him and put his Kingdom under an Interdiction, unless he made a Peace with the King of *England* *Philip* made Answer to him, *That he did not fear his Fulminations, as well because they were unjust, as because it was not the Business of the Church of Rome to proceed by Censures against a King of France, who had taken Arms but only against his disobedient and rebellious Subjects*

Towards the latter end of the Life of *Clement* VIII, the Republick of *Venice* began to have several Disputes with the See of *Rome*, and the Pope, who was not for giving himself any Uneasiness, appointed Cardinal *Borghese* to treat about them, with *Leonard Donati*, the *Venetian* Embassador The Cardinal, who was a great Canonist, and spoke mightily for the Rights of the Church, perceiving that *Donati* defended with great Firmness those of the Republick, told him one Day, That if he was Pope, he would not trifle away so much time in talking, but *he would excommunicate the Doge*

Doge and the Senate. And for my part, answer'd *Donati*, if I was Doge, I would not heed your Excommunications. The Cardinal was chosen Pope, and *Donati* Doge, and they both prov'd as good as their Words. *Paul* V excommunicated the Doge and the Senate, and the Doge and the Senate laugh'd at the Excommunication, and came off with Glory.

These sensible and resolute Answers, and the courageous Actions of the Embassador, proceeding from the same Principle, I think my self oblig'd to say a Word or two concerning them in this Chapter. Both the ones and the others ought to be equally esteem'd, provided the Words be free from Petulancy, and the Actions from Insolence. That of *Anthony de Fonseca*, who tore the Treaty in the Presence of *Charles* VIII, and several of the Nobility, was altogether impudent. He was for doing something remarkable, but he very well deserv'd to be grosly affronted for it, since the *Law of Nations* protected him from Violence. On the contrary, what *Peter Caponi* did, might have been the Occasion of some Violence being offer'd to him, but did not deserve an Affront, because it was generous and honourable. *Charles* VIII, King of *France*, did not use the *Florentins* very well, after they had receiv'd him into their Town, but requir'd things of 'em very prejudicial to their Liberty. *Peter Caponi*, who was one of the four Deputies who were to treat with the *French* Commissioners, being one Day in Conference with them in the King's Presence, and seeing the *French* insisted on Conditions which were very hard and unjust, snatch'd the Paper which contain'd them out of the Hands of the Counsellor who had propos'd them, and tearing them before the King, said, *Since you persist in demanding such unreasonable things, you may even sound your Trumpets, and we'll ring our Bells, and then see who will remain Master*. His Person might have been violated, without prejudicing the *Law of Nations*, because he was not a publick Minister; but by reason his Action was glorious, and done for the Preservation of the Liberty of his Country, he did not deserve to be affronted. It succeeded to his Wish, for the *French*, surpriz'd at so brave a Resolution, moderated their Demands, and agreed with the *Florentins*.

Sultan *Ibrahim* was so incens'd at the Loss of the Galeon, which was taken by the Gallies of *Malta*, that he swore he would put to Death all the Christians that could be found within his Dominions, and that he would not so much as spare the sacred Persons of the Embassadors. The Grand Seigneur's Visits are fatal to those who receive them. *Ibrahim* had said, He would go and visit his good Friends, the Embassadors of *France* and of *Venice*, and this Resolution was so well taken, that the last had Advice thereof by a Bostangi. The *Hogia*, that is to say, the Doctor, or Preceptor to *Ibrahim*, who had a Friendship for the *French* Embassador, gave him an Account of it, and signify'd to him, that he would do well to be gone, till the Storm were blown threaten'd all the Christians was over. *La Hay Vantelay*, who had that Post at this time, return'd the Hogia Thanks for his good Will, and farther said, *That he should be far from making use of his Counsel. That the Duty of his Employment, and his own Honour, would not suffer him to retire in the present Juncture of Affairs, without the Consent and Order of the King his Master. That he was so far from thinking of making his Escape, that he should on the contrary think himself injur'd if his Majesty should simply his Place by any other, and intreat him to delay the Execution of such Design to another time, and not to envy him the Glory of sacrificing his Life for the Service of his Prince. Besides, that he could not imagine that the Embassador of the King of France, who was a Friend and Ally of the Ottoman House, ought to be in any Apprehension of being insulted or outrag'd, under the Reign of so just an Emperor as* Ibrahim *was, and who was serv'd by so prudent and wise a Council, compos'd of so many sage Ministers who would not fail to represent to him of what Importance the Friendship of the King of* France *was to him*. The Hogia prais'd his Resolution, and said he wish'd all the *Turks* were like him, but not all the Christians.

There happen'd something like this, much about the same time, to *Soranzo*, Embassador or Bailo of *Venice* at *Constantinople*. The same *French* Embassador, who had answer'd the *Turkish* Doctor with so much Bravery, gave information to *Soranzo*, That it had been resolv'd in the Seraglio to shut him up in the Seven Towers, or in some other dismal Prison, or else to put him to Death, and exhorted him to prevent the Danger, he could declare no other way than by retiring, and he offer'd him at the same time his Assistance for his getting safe out of *Constantinople*. *Soranzo* sent him his Thanks, and gave him to understand, That he did not doubt but he ran a great risque in continuing at *Constantinople*, and yet he would not retire without the Republick's express Order. When there is a Greatness of Soul to answer these Expressions which may be call'd sublime, the Embassador who possesses it, is an inestimable Treasure to the Prince that employs him. There is less Honour got by lending a forlorn Hope in an Attack, or in taking a View of a Breach, in the Breach it self, than there is in so honourable and dangerous a Post. There are thousands of Soldiers capable of the one, but there are no Generals, and but very few Ministers, capable of the other.

Lewis the *Moor*, Usurper of the Dutchy of *Milan*, was too wicked to be very able. He was known, and so distrusted. After *Charles* VIII had conquer'd the Kingdom of *Naples*, the Princes and Potentates of *Italy*, who had engag'd in an Alliance against him, were for bringing into the same the Republick of *Florence*, and the better to prevail with it, they fed it with the Hopes of being put in Possession of the Town of *Pisa*. The *Florent* knew that the *Venetians*, and the Duke of *Milan*, pretended each to have it for themselves, and that they sollicited the Declaration of *Florence* but only to deceive her. They therefore sent Embassadors to the Emperor *Maximilian*, to try to obtain his Consent. The Emperor referr'd them to the Pope's Legate, and this last told them, It was from *Lewis* that they must learn the Sentiments of the Allies. They went to *Milan*, and had demanded Audience, when the Republick sent them Orders to ask nothing of the Duke of *Milan*. The Duke intended to make

make a Jest of the Embassadors, and having to that Purpose sent for several Persons of Quality to be present thereat, he was much surpriz'd at the Complement the Embassadors made him. They said nothing else to him, but that as they were passing through his State to return home, they had thought themselves oblig'd to pay their Devoirs to him. The Duke ask'd them what Answer the Emperor had given them. To which they answer'd, That the Laws of their State did not allow them to reveal the Secrets of their Embassy. This Answer having put the Duke to a *Nonplus*, he ask'd them, Whether they would give him the hearing, if he told them the Emperor's Answer. They reply'd, That they were not forbid hearing what should be told them, and that they could not hinder him from speaking. The Duke then said, He wou'd tell them the Emperor's Answer, but that they must first tell him what they had propos'd to him. To this they reply'd, That he must excuse them, for the Reason before alledg'd, as also because it was of no Utility, since it was improbable that the Emperor, who had signify'd to him the Answer he had made them, should not also have inform'd him of their Proposition. The Duke having no more to say, remain'd confounded, said several injurious things to the Embassadors, and so dismiss'd them.

I make mention in the second Chapter of the first Book, of the Speech *Gutierre Gomez de Fuensalida*, Embassador from *Ferdinand the Catholick* made to the Arch-Duke *Philip*, when he thought his Person was not agreeable to that Prince. *Don Pedro d'Ayala* succeeded *Gutierre*. But he was not acceptable to *Philip* neither, who had a general Aversion for all his Father-in-Law's Ministers. *Ayala*, after he had been employ'd to the King of *England*, went into *Spain* with *Philip*, who told him one Day, That till then he had declin'd taking Notice to him of what he had negotiated in *England* and in *Flanders*, to his Prejudice, but now that he was in *Spain*, he ought to consider that he was his Wife's Subject, and his, and that he ought to take his Measures accordingly. *Don Pedro* made Answer, *That wherever he had been, he had always acquitted himself of his Duty like a good* Castilian. *That he would continue to act after the same manner, and that he believ'd no worse would come of it, than what had hitherto happen'd. That if his Highness thought that the Stay he should make at his Court would be prejudicial, either to his Person, or Kingdoms, he would acquaint the King his Master therewith, and be gone.* The Arch-Duke, who took upon him the Quality of King of *Castile*, and who was so in Effect, in the Behalf of his Wife, being pleas'd with this Freedom, reply'd, That he had rather he should stay there than any Body else, but as he was his Subject, he ought to be cautious of doing any thing against his Interest. I have spoken of the Obligation which a Minister, who is employ'd by a foreign Prince, is under to his natural Prince, in the same second Chapter of the first Book.

A Minister of *Venice* shall conclude this Chapter. *Morosini* being Embassador on the part of the Republick at *Constantinople*, had some Difficulty to justify the Disorder which had happen'd in the Year 1569, in the Island of *Corfu*, where several *Turks* had been kill'd, unwarrantably enough. The Grand Seigneur resented it so highly that he swore, that not only the Republick, but all *Christendom*, should have Cause to repent it. *Morosini*, who knew that the Action was inexcusable, endeavour'd to elude the Effect of the *Turks* Threats, but finding they were resolv'd to have Satisfaction, he told them, That they could pretend to no other than to have the *Podesta* of *Corfu* put into their Hands, and promis'd it should be done. He wrote at the same time to the Senate, to make away with the Podesta, that the *Turks* might not have such an Advantage. The Senate hereupon caus'd the Podesta to be put on Board a Ship, in Order to come and give an Account of his Behaviour, but in the Voyage he was flung into the Sea. And it was given out that he had leap'd into it himself, to avoid the Punishment the *Turks* would have inflicted upon him. The Port was contented therewith, and by this Mean the Republick avoided a notorious publick Reparation. *Morosini* gain'd thereby so great a Reputation, and the Senate was so well pleas'd, that upon his declaring at his Return Home that he would never marry, the Bishoprick of *Verona* was conferr'd upon him, and *Sixtus* V, who was skill'd in, and esteem'd extraordinary Men, made him a Cardinal.

CHAP. VIII.
Of Moderation.

I Do not here mean that *Moderation*, of which the illustrious Author of the Reflections, Sentences, and moral Maxims, gives so excellent a Character, and of which the Wisest have but an Appearance, but of that Phlegm and Coolness, either study'd or natural, which is so necessary to those who enter upon the Management of publick Affairs. I do not pretend to act the Philosopher, and shall content my self with saying, That Moderation, whether it be an Effect or a part of Prudence, is a Quality by so much the more requisite to the Embassador, as he that does not possess himself, gives a mighty Advantage to him with whom he negotiates. *Julius Mazarin* being but twenty Years of Age, had the Address to put the Duke of *Feria*, Governor of *Milan*, into a Passion, and to discover by that Mean his true Sentiments. Those Minds that are compos'd of Salt-peter and Sulphur, which the least Spark sets on fire, are very liable to mar Affairs by their Transports, because it is an eafy Master to excite their Anger, and put them in a Rage, during which they know not what they do. I have obferv'd in the foregoing Chapter, that *Contarini* having reproach'd *Servien*; that it was he particularly who form'd all the Obstacles that retarded the Peace *Servien* told him, That it was not the Bufinefs of a Mediator to fpeak with Paffion, but he ought to have Moderation What he fays of the Mediator ought to be apply'd to all Embaffadors without Diftinction *Servien* was a Man of no mean Talent There was not any Affair but what he was capable of managing, neither was there any Poft that he could not worthily fill but then he was fo ftormy in his Humour, that there was no Negotiation that did not rifque being embroil'd and fpoil'd in his Hands by his paffionate Tranfports In the Year 1647, Cardinal *Mazarin* fent him Orders to go to the *Hague*, to treat about a Guaranty with the States of the United Provinces, for the Execution of the Peace which was negotiating at *Munfter* but he behav'd himfelf after fo imperious and haughty a manner, that inftead of endeavouring to gain thofe Republicans, accuftom'd to be treated gently, it feem'd as if he would play the Dictator, and extort from them, by mere Force and Authority, what was purely voluntary, and what he could not hope for, but by making them comprehend the Reafon thereof, and their own proper Intereft He fpoke to the Deputies of the States, not as to the King his Mafter's Allies, but as to his Subjects His Collegues could not approve of his Procedure, and efpecially *la Tuillerie* (who feconded his Negotiation in *Holland*, and who was not himfelf either cold or ftupid, but a refolute and vigorous Minifter) reprefented to him the Prejudice he did to the King's Affairs, by irritating a People, whofe Alliance had not always been unferviceable to *France*

They who have written the Hiftory of thofe Times in *France* it felf, do not fcruple to own, that the two Plenipotentiaries, who at their Arrival at the *Hague* in the Year 1644, had marr'd all by their Pride and imperious Behaviour, made an End to extirpate, by the furious Tranfports with which their Letters were fill'd, the little Remains of Affection thofe People ftill had for *France* That Prudence indeed requir'd they fhould apply fome Remedies to prevent the Evil they had reafon to apprehend, and to cure that which already appear'd, but then they fhould have made ufe of Lenitives and fuch Medicines as would affwage and mitigate the Diftemper, and not of thofe that vifibly inflam'd it, or render'd it altogether incurable, by making the Impoftume break too foon, and out of feafon It was reprefented, that if the Levity of thefe People wanted to be kept under, they might have made ufe of a Cavefon, and that too fevere in Correction would produce the fame Effect, which too ftrong Medicins have in a Cacochymical Body that abounds with ill Humours. *La Tuillory* (who as I juft faid blam'd fince *Servien*'s Conduct, and who was at leaft as hot as he) had contributed very much to the Exafperation of the People's Minds before *Servien* came to the *Hague* in the Year 1647. He perceiv'd it, and chang'd his Behaviour, when he found *Servien* was for outdoing him.

On the contrary, never was there feen any thing fo mild and fo engaging, as Prefident *Jeannin*'s Humour I fhould be in the wrong to fay, he had Moderation, he was Moderation it felf It was very difficult to withftand the Force of his Reafoning, but it was altogether impoffible not to yield to the infinuating Manner that accompany'd it He committed a fort of gentle and agreeable Rape upon the Mind, which one neither could, nor was willing to refift In all his Memorials, and in all his Conferences, we find a Minifter without Paffion, and without Intereft, who referr'd all things to the Advantage of the State where he negotiated, infomuch that he caus'd thofe Propofitions to be relifh'd, and even embrac'd, which had been rejected fince the Beginning of the Troubles King *Henry* IV was extremely incens'd at the firft Sufpenfion of Arms the States had agreed to with the *Spaniards* in the Years 1607, without his Participation, and order'd *Jeannin* to fignify to them his Refentment, which was great and juft In his firft Audience *Jeannin* reprefented the Reafon the King had to be angry, that he was fo neglected by the States, after the Proofs they had receiv'd of his Affection, and while he actually affifted them with fuch confiderable Sums. He farther faid, That it was not fo much the Refolution they had taken, to fufpend the Hoftilities, that offended the King, (fince they look'd upon it to be neceffary for the Good of their State) as the Manner thereof and Form, which were indeed outrageous, becaufe they ought not to have made a Secret of it to him, who of all Princes was moft concern'd either in their good or ill Fortune

Thofe Minifters who are oblig'd to their Temper and Conftitution for this Moderation are happy, but they who acquire it but with great Difficulty, and by ufing Violence to themfelves, while they endeavour to conquer their Paffion, and keep down the turbulent Vapours of a Choler adult, or parch'd Blood, deferve a great deal more Glory There is hardly any body but has heard of Marefchal *d'Eftrée*'s Hastinefs, and who does not know a Minifter of the fame Quality, who has negotiated above thefe forty Years, and is ftill at this Day at the Head of one of the firft Embaffies of *Europe* It cannot be faid that his Brain is troubl'd with Indifpofitions of this Nature but yet his Mind is lively, and he is fubject to fuch Emotions of Choler, that his Domefticks have fometimes much adoe to avoid the Effects thereof, yet neverthelefs in Conferences and Negotiations he is never puzzl'd nor diforder'd He is then fo Cool, has fuch an Evennefs of Temper, and fo much Moderation, that he never lafhes out, let the Conteft he is engag'd in be ever fo great and he is fo much Mafter of himfelf, that there is not any Object, that can put him out of the Way he has propos'd to himfelf to obtain his Ends

I am not afraid of giving the fame Extent to Moderation which I have heretofore given to Prudence, nay I dare affert, That it is the fame Virtue under another Name. They have both the fame Ends and the fame Objects. When I fay the Embaffador ought to be moderate in his Difcourfe; That he ought not to fally, nor offend any body That he ought to be be moderate in his Expences, and not render himself ridiculous by his Profusions, or by the Vanity and Extravagancy of his Apparel, or by the excessive Number of his Domesticks, do I not say at the same time, that he must be wise and prudent? When I say that violent Transports (which are so opposite to Moderation) are the Rocks that endanger Negotiation, and sink Reputation, do I not say, That Prudence ought to be his Guide throughout his whole Conduct? It is about thirty Years since an Embassador, who had little else to support his Expences but the Money he got in the Place where he was employ'd, made such prodigious ones, that after he had squander'd away, in less than six Weeks or two Months, above two hundred and fifty thousand Crowns, was oblig'd to pawn his Plate, and even the Present he had receiv'd after his Audience of Leave It was well known that the Prince he serv'd was not in a Condition to make him make a Figure, and it was commonly said, That a little Moderation would have done more Honour to the Master and the Minister, who would not then have been necessitated to borrow Money every where to carry himself home

The Embassador from the United Provinces, had Orders to signify to the Court of France, That they could no longer bear the Depredations its Privateers committed in the Mediterranean, and forasmuch as they were persuaded that some of the Ministers were concern'd therein, he was commanded to speak to the King himself To speak the Truth, the Depredations were insufferable And as the Embassador had no great Kindness for Cardinal Mazarin, (who had as little for him) he sought or rather met with an Opportunity to do him a very bad Turn, in an Audience where the whole Court was present I cannot tell whether it was his Master's Intention that he should affront the first Minister, and offend him irreconcileably, who at that time reign'd more absolutely than the King himself However the Embassador was happy enough to be avow'd, and the States came to very high Resolutions on that Subject, but nevertheless it seems as if it was neither their Interest nor their Intention to execute them The Arms of France were victorious every where, and made a great Progress in Flanders The Protector seconded them The States were mightily perplex'd with the Northern War They might very well have reflected, that if the Depredations disturb'd the Commerce, a War destroy'd it, and that they could not break with France without hazarding their All One would think a private Audience, or a vigorous Memorial, strong in Reasons, would not have made so much Noise, and yet would have been full as effectual The moderate Embassador would have took that Method, and would not have brought upon himself the Affront the Cardinal gave this at his Departure from Audience

The Marquiss du Fargis, Embassador of France in Spain, was far from having that Moderation which makes one of the chief Qualifications of an accomplish'd Minister. His Haughtiness was ill supported, and had more in it of Pride than of that Greatness of Soul which is express'd by the Word Haughtiness, when we

make it a good Quality He was in continual Transports, and there was not the least Moderation in his Speeches Having in the Year 1623, follow'd the Court of Spain to Barcelona, where the King had call'd together the States of Catalonia, who were not very much inclin'd to grant the Subsidies which were demanded of them He said the King his Master would be always ready to come and assist the King of Spain his Brother-in-Law with an Army of twenty thousand Men, to punish his rebellious Subjects This Speech so incens'd the Catalans, that they were upon the Point of taking Arms, with a Design to kill du Fargis The King, who was inform'd of the Danger du Fargis was in, desir'd the Emperor's Embassador not to leave him, but to take along with him some of the King's Guards, and see him safe home but du Fargis, instead of moderating his Heat, and not exposing himself as he had done two Years before, gave a greater Loose to his Passion, and vented several other more extravagant Rodomontades, which were as displeasing to the Court of France, as they were to the States of Catalonia

A moderate Minister would have done quite otherwise, than did Don Balthasar de la Cueva, Embassador of Spain at Vienna, in the Year 1666 Some of his Domesticks had committed a great Outrage to one of the chief Officers of the Emperor's Court They had been driven, and forc'd to save themselves in the Town House, where they continu'd to resist the Guard The Embassador, instead of blaming the Insolence of his People, and endeavouring to get them off, thought fit to authorize their Violence by his Presence, and made the Court ring with his unjust Complaints The Emperor was so scandaliz'd thereat, that he set a Guard upon the Embassador, refus'd to give him Audience, and oblig'd him to excuse himself The Minister that is reduc'd to this, does no great Honour, neither to his Character nor Master

The Embassador ought to shew his Moderation in all his Conduct, and every Day, when he can find an Opportunity, of which we have an illustrious Example in Cardinal Dossat, and in the Difference he had with Brother Hilary of Grenoble a Capucin, and one of the most impertinent Friars the Cloisters ever afforded. The Cardinal relates the Particulars thereof in the Letter he wrote to M de Villeroy, on the 22d of February, 1601. This Friar, who was Vanity it self, having entertain'd the Cardinal with several things that were false, desir'd him to procure him Audience from the Pope Dossat promis'd to do it, and accordingly spoke himself about it to the Master of the Chamber, whereas had it been for himself, he would have sent one of his Attendants to demand it, or else one of his Gentlemen · But the Pope's Indisposition having hinder'd him from giving it for some time to the Cardinals and Embassadors, there was no likelihood he would prefer a Capucin to them So that Dossat signify'd to the Friar, That he must have a little Patience The Friar was offended at it, fell into a Passion, and told several Persons of Quality, That he would obtain Audience without the Cardinal's Meditation, and upon the handsome Message the Cardinal sent him on the same Subject, he made this Answer, That he should quickly

quickly return to *France* and the King would then send him back with other Letters, but they should not be for the Cardinal, who was remiss in his Majesty's Affairs, and was not capable of discharging them, no more than *M. de Sillery.* All the Resentment *M. Dossat* shew'd, was to speak of it with Contempt, as coming from a mere Friar, and to say, he was not afraid that the Judgment the King would form of his Zeal and Actions would depend on the Report of that insignificant Capucin, nor of that of all the Capucins and Friars in the World. I should never have done, if I was to bring Proofs from his other Letters, as well as from those of President *Jeannin*, because there is hardly one but what will furnish an Example. However I think my self oblig'd to add here two other Proofs of the Moderation of *M. Dossat.* He was a Domestick to the Cardinal *de Joyeuse*, and had, under him, solicited the Affairs of *France*, with so much Judgment and Success, that King *Henry* III had a mind to have him near his Person, and to give him the Place of Secretary of State. He refus'd it, tho' he had not any Employment nor Benefice to subsist by. The other Proof is, That the Cardinal *d'Este*, who had receiv'd great Services from *Dossat*, and knew his Probity, being on his Death-bed, left him four thousand Crowns: but fearing left *Dossat* should find some Difficulty to get that Sum from the Duke of *Modena*, he was for giving him a Jewel worth twenty thousand Crowns, that it might serve for a Pledge, till he was paid the four thousand; but his Moderation would not suffer him to take Security for a Gift that was altogether gratuitous and voluntary, tho' he was needy enough at that time, as well as all the rest of his Life. This Necessity it self is another Mark of his Moderation.

This Virtue is more familiar to Ministers of the Robe, than to those of the Sword, because these do not always distinguish between the Embassador and the Captain. In the Year 1651, during the Commotions of *Paris*, the Mareschal *de Thurenne*, who had declar'd for the Princes, endeavour'd to bring to their Assistance the Troops he commanded in *Germany*. The Baron *d'Avaugour*, Minister of *France* in the *Swedish* Army, had obtain'd of the Prince *Palatin*, who commanded it as Generalissimo, two thousand Horse, who were to joyn Colonel *Erloch* and oppose *M. de Thurenne*'s Passage. The Mareschal *Wrangel* had given Orders to the Officer who was to command those two thousand Horse, not to go out of *Germany*, and not to fight neither the *Germans* or the *Lorrainers D'Avaugour*, who look'd upon this Restriction to be prejudicial to his Master's Service, came to high Words with *Wrangel* about it, who being Mareschal de Camp, the other as Colonel ow'd him Respect and Obedience, and yet they were both going to draw in the Generalissimo's Antichamber, who coming out of his Closet at the Noise, commanded *Wrangel* to withdraw: but he told d'*Avaugour*, That he exceeded the Bounds of his Ministry and of Moderation, *which ought to be inseparable from his Character, and that it did not belong to him to fly into Passions, and to have recourse to Arms to support his Master's Interest.* This did not hinder the Prince (when the Baron was retir'd) from comending the Zeal this Minister shew'd for the Service of his King.

The King of *France* had granted his Protection to the *Barberins* against the Persecutions of Pope *Innocent*, and had procur'd a Peace between them, and the Princes and States of *Italy*, who had taken Arms for the Recovery of the Dutchy of *Castro*. The Republick of *Venice*, who was for the League, had caus'd all the Revenues the *Barberins* had in the State of *Venice* to be seiz'd and altho' after the Peace the Senate ought to have put them in possession of their Estates again, yet it did not do it, and receiv'd but coldly, and with Indifferency enough, the Offices the King caus'd to be done for their Reestablishment. The President *ac Gremonville*, who was Embassador there, having receiv'd Orders to procure a positive Answer on that Head, instead of the indefinite and uncertain ones which were made to his Instances, press'd the Senate so much thereupon, that it at last consented to their Restoration. It was oblig'd thereto by virtue of the Treaty, and yet it did it so late, and with so ill a Grace, that some were for persuading the Embassador, that if he did not resent the Senate's ill Treatment, he ought at least to forbear complementing it. He made Answer, That it was the King his Master's Business to signify to the *Venetian* Embassador, that the Senate might have behav'd it self otherwise than it had done, but as for his part, he would not fail in what he ow'd to Moderation and Civility and resolv'd to complement the Senate.

I say moreover, that since Moderation ought to accompany all the Embassador's Actions and every part thereof, it may be allow'd the same Extent, which I have before assign'd to Prudence, and one may say that it is a Retinue which ought inseparably to attend his whole Conduct. He ought to be very jealous and, extremely scrupulous in reference to the Honours which cannot be refus'd him, as the Representative of a Sovereign Prince, but he ought not to give way to Extravagancy, nor pretend to Honours which are neither due to his Person nor Character. He may take Place of a Prince, who notwithstanding he be born of a Sovereign House, is become the Subject of another Sovereign Prince, but he ought not to dispute it with a Sovereign. The Princes of the Houses of *Savoy* and *Lorrain*, who have settl'd in *France*, who have, as one may say, taken rooting there, and who are really Subjects, cannot enter into Competition with the Embassadors of Crown'd Heads. I say the same of the Princes of *Italy*, who are younger Sons, (altho' those of *Savoy*, and within some Time those of *Tuscany* dispute it with them) and of those of *Germany*, who having only a simple Appennage or Maintenance, have no Seat in the Diets of the Empire, and so have no Share in the Sovereignty. But the Embassador who would pretend to take Precedency of a Sovereign, or of his presumptive Heir, or else to be upon the Level with the Sons or Brothers of Crown'd Heads, offends against Moderation. Those Embassadors who were for having arm'd Chairs at an Entertainment where the Prince of *Wales* had none; he that made Difficulty to give Place to the hereditary Prince of of *Sweden*, Brother to the King of *Poland*, and the Mareschaless of *Guebriant*, who pretended to be paid the same Honours which had formerly been done to the Arch-Dutchess of *Tirol*, were guilty of an unpardonable Impertinency, and brought an Affront upon their Masters. The Embassador represents the Sovereign, but he is not the Sovereign, for which reason he ought to give Place to those who have that Prerogative, wherever he meets them. It is the only Reason why the King of *France* is willing to suffer the Princes of *Italy*, who are acknowledg'd for Sovereigns, to take the Place of Honour at Home of his Embassadors. Nay a Sovereign ought not to desire excessive Honours should be done to his Embassador, because they oblige him to do the same, and these Civilities are dear to them who do not owe them, and are not paid without Reluctancy.

CHAP. IX.

It is lawful for an Embassador to corrupt the Ministers of the Court where he resides.

I Have spoken in the last Chapter of the first Book, of the Presents the Prince makes to Embassadors when they go out of their Employment, as well to shew the Esteem he has for their Persons, and that he is satisfy'd with their Conduct, as to manifest the Consideration he has for their Master. I shall here speak of those Presents which the Embassadors themselves make, and of the other Means they make use of to bring over to their Prince's Interest the Ministers of the Court where they negotiate. This is one of those Functions of the Embassador that he never acquits himself of without express Orders, or unless he be very sure he shall be avow'd, since there is no Embassador who without that would be at the Expence thereof, or run the Risque of creating himself Troubles with the Sovereign of the Place where he resides. When King *Henry* IV caus'd Secretary *Bruneau* to be taken up, for having been discover'd to treat with *Merargues* about the surprising of *Marseilles*, the *Spanish* Embassador reclaim'd the Secretary as his Domestick, and reproach'd the King amongst other things that his Ministers had endeavour'd to corrupt those of the Court at *Brussels*. The King told him, *That that was what an Embassador might lawfully do, in order to discover thereby the Intrigues which were carry'd on against his Master's Service, and that the Business of Marseilles, Metz, and other Places, made it plain that he had reason to endeavour to penetrate into the Designs which were forming at Brussels against the Repose of his Kingdom.* Philip de Commines is never tir'd of speaking of the Address with which *Lewis* XI, and his Ministers, gain'd those of other Princes. He was not dishearten'd at the first Refusal, he renew'd his Instances, and never left off promising Money, Revenues, Offices and Benefices, till he had gain'd his Point. *Commines* might speak hereof by Experience, because he had suffer'd himself to be debauch'd from the Service of the Duke of *Burgundy* to enter into the King's, who was not deceiv'd in the Choice of that Minister. The King by these Means made himself a great many Friends, and got out of many a troublesome Affair, by his Liberalities, rather than his Address, notwithstanding he had a great deal. As soon as he observ'd either Parts or Merit in a Man, he never rested till he had gain'd him. A Gentleman of *Gascony*, who was in the King of *England*'s Service, being one Day discoursing with *Commines*, told him, that King *Edward* IV had been present in seven Battels, where he had fought on I oot, and come off victorious from them all, but that he had lost one, which had sully'd the Lustre of the Glory he had acquir'd in all the former, and that was the Peace he had lately concluded with the King of *France*. The King was no sooner inform'd of the Particulars of this Conversation, than he commanded *Commines* to bring the *Gascon* Gentleman to him, whom he caus'd to dine with him, and there said so many Things to him that he brought him over to his Service.

During the Congress of *Westphalia* the Duke of *Longueville* offer'd a considerable Present to the Sieur *de Reede de Nederhorst*, one of the Deputies of the United Provinces on the Part of the States of *Utrecht*, and he offer'd one likewise to the Secretary of the Embassy, because they were well affected to *France*. They both refus'd to accept it, and said, That after the Conclusion of the Peace they would not refuse the Tokens of the King's Liberality if his Majesty judg'd they had deserv'd them; but that they ought to be excus'd from doing it during the Negotiation. The United Provinces made a particular Treaty, and the *French* who did not conclude theirs of above eleven Years after, thought no more of the good Offices they had receiv'd from those Ministers. On the contrary, they have suffer'd one of them to be dishonour'd after his Death by one of their best Historians, who does not scruple to say, that he reveal'd to the *French* Plenipotentiaries the most secret Sentiments of his Collegues. It is what they might very well have forborn, as *Servien* on his part has acquir'd no great Reputation of Prudence in accusing *Pau de Heemstede* and *Kunst*, two of the Plenipotentiaries of the United Provinces, to have been corrupted by *Spanish* Money. They were two Ministers who were in effect what they call *at Florence Misero*, but as there is nothing so easy as to justify ones self of a Crime that has no Witnesses, they clear'd themselves by their Oath, and reap'd Honour

nour from the Accusation of their greatest Enemy.

In the height of the Negotiation of *Munster*, *Nourmont*, Agent of the *Spanish* Ministers, and Broker in the private Commerce they had with those of the United Provinces, told *Knuit*, who manag'd the Prince of *Orange*'s Interest, that the King of *Spain* intended to make a Present to the Prince of the Towns of *Venlo* and *Ruremonde*, and that if his Highness desir'd it, the Town of *Guelder* should also be added, and that the Ratification thereof should be sent from *Spain* as soon as the Prince should have explain'd himself. *Servien* fearing lest these Offers should make an Impression in the Mind of the Prince, whose Judgment was extremely weaken'd by Age and continual Indispositions, dispatch'd his Nephew to Court in all Haste, to procure Orders to be sent him, to offer the Prince the Town of *Bruges* (if he took it during that Campaign) in full Sovereignty with some other neighbouring Villages, on Condition he took the Investiture from the King, and left the Catholick Religion in the State it was then in; but above all things, on Condition that the States should not separate from the *French* Interest. *D'Estrades* had formerly offer'd the Prince the Exchange of the Town of *Antwerp* for the Principality of *Orange*, and to yield him some other Rights and imaginary Pretensions, but the Prince, instead of accepting these Offers, had rejected them, and they produc'd a very ill effect. *Servien* moreover said, That it was necessary to gain the Princess of *Orange*, and at the same time he and his Collegues try'd to gain some of the Plenipotentiaries who were at *Munster*, but all this came to nothing. The Ministers of the two Crowns acted therein conformably to their Master's Interest, and made use of such Means to gain their Ends, as were very lawful in reference to them. *D'Estrades* was sworn to, and in the Service of the States, and yet that did not hinder him from making (as a publick Minister) such Offers as were capable of corrupting the first Person in the State, if he had met with a corruptible Subject. The Deputies whom the Arch-Dukes sent to the *Hague* in the Year 1607, to make Proposals of a Peace, which was since converted into a Truce of twelve Years, employ'd a *Cordelier*, whom they had with them, to corrupt the Fidelity of the Register of the States General, who was a Minister of great Authority at that Time, and made him an Offer of very considerable Presents. He acquainted Prince *Maurice* therewith, and the Sieur *d'Oldenbarnevelt* first Minister of the Province of *Holland*, who advis'd him to take the Present, and to put it into a third Hand. They gave him a very fine Diamond of the Value of six thousand Crowns, a Bill of Exchange of fifteen thousand, and a Promise of thirty five thousand more, which he was to receive after the Conclusion of the Peace. The Estates were very much scandaliz'd at this Procedure, and the Archduke disavow'd it. *M. de Villeroy* says, in one of his Dispatches, That the *Cordelier*'s Action was disavow'd, because he had behav'd himself therein like a Fryar, that is to say, after too gross a manner. There were but too many Persons of Quality and Authority in *Holland*, who did not approve of the Negotiation of Brother *John Neyen*, who not having any Character of a publick Minister, could not pretend to take upon him to corrupt one of the chief Ministers of the State, without acting contrary to the Tenor of his Passport, which was all the Security he had, and yet instead of affronting him, they were contented to give some Confusion to the other Deputies, and to the *Cordelier* as much Shame as Friars and Monks are capable of. Some time after the *Cordelier* took a Journey into *Spain*, and at his Return he sent to the States to desire a Passport for himself, and the Auditor *Verreiken*, who was to bring to the *Hague* the King of *Spain*'s Ratification, in the Form the States had desir'd it. It was put into Debate, whether they ought not to refuse a Passport to him who would have corrupted the Register, but at last it was resolv'd it should be sent him. He return'd to the *Hague*, and continu'd to act the Negotiator, notwithstanding his former Intrigue.

Edward IV, whom I lately mention'd, was sensible that the chief Lords of his Court had Pensions from *Lewis* XI. *Commines* names a good many of them, and relates how *Howard*, Great Chamberlain of *England*, did not refuse the Pension of *France*, that he put the fine Pieces stampt with the Sun into his Sleeve, but that he would not give any Acquittance for the same, that his Name might not be seen in the Registers of the Chamber of Accounts at *Paris*. It is not there indeed, but it is very plainly to be seen in the Memoirs of *Philip de Commines*, which are much more publick, and deserve full as much Credit as the Registers of the Chamber of Accounts. It is said, that one Day an *English* Gentleman signify'd to King *James* that he had a Matter of very great Importance to impart to him, but that his Majesty must assure him of his Protection in a particular manner, because without that his Life would be in great Danger. After he had taken his necessary Precautions he told him, That several Noblemen of his Court and Council receiv'd Pensions from *Spain*, and that he could make it out. The King answer'd him, That he knew it very well, and made a Jest of it. He moreover said, he wish'd the King of *Spain* would give them ten times as much, because this unprofitable Expence would render him less able to make War against him. The *French* who take Pleasure in publishing the Good they do, as well as the Favours they receive, have endeavour'd to make it be believ'd, that the Ministers of the Court of *England* were not very difficult on that Subject, not long since Queen *Elizabeth* would not have suffer'd it. *Henry* IV. had given the Order of St *Michael* to *Nicolas Clifford*, and to *Anthony Sherley*, on the Account of the Services they had done him in the War. These two Gentlemen being return'd into *England*, the Queen sent them to Prison, and commanded them to send back the Order, and to cause their Names to be rau'd out of the Registers. She said, *That as a virtuous Woman ought to look on none but her Husband, so a Subject ought not to cast his Eyes on any other Sovereign than him God had set over him. I will not*, said she, *have my Sheep mark'd with a strange Brand, nor suffer them to follow the Pipe of a strange Shepherd.* Queen *Christina* would

would not permit the Prince *Palatin* to receive the Order of the Garter, nor the Count *de la Garde* to be made a Prince of the Empire These two Queens were in the right to hinder their Subjects from entering into Engagements with foreign Princes They cannot share out their Affection, nor their Zeal without robbing their Sovereign of all that Portion they so bestow, who ought to be as jealous thereof, as a Husband is of his Wife's Honour It was a kind of Corruption, the Office which *la Tuilerie* the *French* Embassador did to the Princess of *Orange*, in the Year 1646 He told her, that after the Death of the Prince her Husband, who in all likelihood would not live long, the King would not fail to protect and support her That if before the Conclusion of the Peace any thing could be done for the Interest of her House, his Majesty would not only employ his good Offices therein, but also his Arms, to obtain for it all possible Advantages He gave her to understand, That the King would not suffer *Holland* to disturb her, for having oppos'd a Peace, which would separate the United Provinces from the Interest of *France* Nay, *La Tuilerie* had Orders to confirm to her the Offer had been made to the Prince, to leave him *Antwerp*, and to assure her, the King would joyn his Arms to those of the State for the reducing of that Place The Prince had positively declar'd, That he would not hearken to any Treaty for his own particular Interests, but the Princess taking advantage of the Infirmities of her Husband, dispos'd him to whatever she pleas'd, and made him consent to a Treaty, by which the King of *Spain* gave to the Princess the Territories of *Turnhout* and of *Sevenbergue* She expected nothing like that, from *France*, and she chose rather to suit her self to the Sentiments of *Holland* Besides which, there were Domestick Considerations which made her take that side

Philip de Commines says, That it is a mighty Advantage to an Embassador, to be able to dive into the Affairs of a Prince by the Means of his Minister And indeed, it may be said to be one of the most important Services an Embassador can do his Master, That of acquiring him one of the Ministers of the Court where he negotiates For as he is an honourable Spy, it is not only a sure way to penetrate into the Secret, but also to give Affairs that Turn which his Master desires, and which conduces most to his Interest Now that an Embassador, who gains or corrupts a Minister, does not violate the *Law of Nations*, and keeps within the Bounds of his Function, is what all the World is agreed in But then this Liberty, which is allow'd the Embassador, is not of infinite Extent The same *Henry* IV, who told *Don Balthasar de Zuniga*, That an Embassador may gain or corrupt a Minister, in order to discover the Secrets of the Court where he resides, caus'd *Bruneau* to be taken up, who was debauching *Merargues* The *Spaniards* had corrupted one of M *de Villeroy*'s Clerks, and learn'd from him the most momentous Secrets of the State The King did not come upon the Ministers of *Spain* for it, because that Commerce is allow'd of, tho' sometimes under the Colour of this Permission, they pass off Contraband Goods True Friends seldom make use of it, and never abuse it *William Polissier*, Bishop of *Montpellier*, Embassador of *France* at *Venice*, had corrupted *Maffée Leone*, the two Brothers *Canaffes*, and some others, either Ministers or Subjects of the Republick of *Venice*, who communicated to him Secrets, which he imparted to the Court of *Constantinople* The Senate punish'd the Traytors severely, but it did not complain of the Embassador And if some time after it sollicited the King to recall this Minister, it was only because he did them many ill Offices, and gave out false Reports, capable of altering the good Correspondence the Republick was willing to hold with the King

Yet I can hardly believe that the *Law of Nations*, which ought to serve only to the Preservation of Civil Society, would protect those who destroy the very Principles thereof, by forming Treasons, and contriving Plots against the Person of the Prince with whom they reside, by fomenting a Rebellion, by disturbing the Repose of the State, or by favouring Hostilities in the height of Peace The Bishop of *Rosse*, *Don Bernardin de Mendossi*, the Abbot *Scaglia*, and some other Embassadors whom I have mentioned elsewhere, carry'd on a Commerce which the *Law of Nations* does not allow of They did not corrupt the Ministers to learn their Secret, but they caball'd and contriv'd Treasons against the Prince and the State *Philip de Commines* is of Opinion, That a wise Prince ought to rid himself of this sort of wicked and vexatious Ministers

Ministers are corrupted, not only by Presents, but also by several other Means The Vanity of the ones is attack'd by Flattery, and the Ambition of others is excited by Praises and extraordinary Encomiums To some a great Fortune is promis'd, and the Dissatisfaction of others is fomented by entring into their Interest, against the Prince, by whom they think they are either neglected or despised The Ministers of *Spain* and of *Savoy* employ'd all these Means to debauch and ruin the Duke of *Biron* King *Henry* IV sent him to *Brussels*, to see the Peace of *Vervins* sworn to The Arch-Duke made Presents to him, not as to an Embassador, or an Officer of the Crown, whom the King mightily consider'd, but as to a Man he had a Mind to gain, and who could not be purchas'd at too dear a Rate The *Spaniards* poison'd his Mind with extravagant Praises, and with the Hopes of an imaginary Sovereignty The Duke of *Savoy* made an end to win him by the Promises of a high Alliance, but chiefly by malicious Reports of the little Esteem the King had for his Person He thought the King could not sufficiently acknowledge his Services, but by dividing his Kingdom with him So that finding himself plac'd in the Rank with other Subjects, tho' the most illustrious ones, he forgot himself so far, that he undertook to conspire against the Life of his Sovereign, who was the best Prince that had been for many Ages The Count *de Fresque*, Embassador of *Savoy*, in the Complement he made to the King on the Discovery of *Biron*'s Conspiracy, was for justifying his Master, but his Justification was not well receiv'd The King, far from complaining of those Ministers who had been concern'd therein, would not so much as suffer

fer either them or their Princes to be accus'd. Those who have ever so little Generosity, do not defile themselves with this sort of Treasons, and they who have the least Grain of Prudence, ought not to make it known that they are capable of them.

Mention is made elsewhere of an Embassador, who far from gaining any Minister of the Court of *France*, in Order to learn the Secrets thereof, reveal'd those of *Ferdinand the Catholick* to *Lewis* XI. These Infidelities do not belong to the Subject of this Chapter. I shall only say that those Princes, who have not the Means to make these Acquisitions, lose a great Advantage, and a fine Opportunity of compassing their End. The States of the United Provinces do not afford their Ministers these Means, they have no Funds for that Purpose. So that not being able to be at the Expence of these Intrigues, without the Participation of a great Number of Persons, who are not all capable of Secrecy, they would not be likely to succeed in it very well, tho' they should undertake it, unless they left the whole Management thereof to the Prince of *Orange*, as they have intrusted him with that of their most important Affairs. I could instance in Conjunctures, where the Expence of fifty thousand Crowns would have sav'd them Millions. It cannot be deny'd but it is one of the greatest Infirmities of their Government, that Persons of all Ranks and Conditions are concern'd therein. But this belongs to History, and has nothing in common with the Matter I treat of.

To make out what is contain'd in this Chapter, it will not be amiss to see the Instruction President *Jeannin* gives to *M. de Preaux*, on the 2d of *April*, 1609, which is very particular on this Subject, with the Instruction the Sieur de *Preaux* brought back from Court. In the first he speaks in these Terms.

" For the particular Service of his Majesty,
" it is requisite to know his Intention. It is
" well known, in the first Place, that it is to
" strengthen as much as may be the Authority
" of Prince *Maurice*, and of those private Per-
" sons which are known to be most against
" the *Spanish* Power, and to acquire there,
" and entertain Servants, who shall take Care,
" and be oblig'd to remind the Estates, of his
" Majesty's Kindness to them, and Deserts from
" them. Which cannot be done but by employing
" every Year some Money to engage them, and
" gain their Affection. For when only the Bo-
" dy of a Republick in general is oblig'd, it
" often quits the Obligation of its Debts by In-
" gratitude, but the particular Persons who
" are engag'd, being Men of Credit and Ca-
" pacity, are of great Utility and Service, and
" in this State it is esteem'd necessary, foras-
" much as it is well known, that they are
" ready to receive the Conveniency and Ad-
" vantages one is willing to offer them. And
" what ought the rather to invite his Majesty
" to think hereof, is, that it is probable that
" the King of *Spain* (who has made a Treaty
" which many look upon to be shameful to
" him) had no other Inducement thereto be-
" sides Necessity, (which is put for a chief
" Cause) but the Hopes he had, or rather the
" Assurance, that he might settle some Corre-
" spondence amongst them, by *scattering* there

" every Year some considerable Sum, in order to
" change them, and make them return from
" whence they went. Now there is no better
" Mean, besides the good and wise Con-
" duct of the State in general, but for his Ma-
" jesty to oblige some Servants to oppose such Pra-
" ctices and Corruption, in which one Crown
" from him will do more to secure them, and ren-
" der them well affected to his Crown, than a
" hundred from the King of *Spain* will do, to
" bring them over to him. His Majesty ha-
" ving acquir'd some Servants, and settled
" a Correspondence for some time, may, if
" he should desire any thing farther, explain
" himself.

The King, in Answer to this Article of *Jeannin*'s Instruction, says, *It is his Majesty's Intention, and shall be his Care, to preserve and increase for the future, at much as he shall be able, the Credit and Authority, the Assistance he has given to the said Estates, and his Benevolence, have acquir'd him heretofore amongst 'em, as well tha, h may have the Means to continue to do them Good, and render his Counsels more acceptable to them, as for the Benefit and Advantage his Kingdom may also receive therefrom, and for the other good Reasons, Hopes, and Considerations, which the said Sieur Jeannin had represented to him by the said Sieur de Preaux. To effect this, his Majesty has thought fit to employ on that side the Sum of one hundred thousand Livers in Pensions and Benefits, to be dispens'd by the said Sieur* Jeannin, *whether by the way of annual Pensions, or gratuitous Gifts, to those he shall judge deserving of such Gratification, and to have a Power to serve his Majesty. Wherefore the said Sieur* Jeannin *may, by virtue of the present Memorial, which is sign'd by his Hand, and countersign'd by his Oracle, promise and grant from this present, and before he leaves the Countrey, the said Pensions and Benefits, as far as the said Sum shall go, in that Form he shall think the best, his Majesty referring himself herein entirely to his Prudence and Loyalty. Only he must know, that his Majesty has prais'd and approv'd the Project the said Sieur* de Preaux *brought him, and which he has already made in regard to the Quality and Conditions of the Persons, on whom he has cast his Eyes for this Purpose, whom he shall agree to treat and favour according to their Merit and Power, amongst which his Majesty thinks, that he ought not to omit making an Offer to Prince* Maurice *by way of Pension, or other Gift, worthy him, even tho' it were known he would not accept the same, if it were but to testify to him more and more the Esteem his Majesty has for him. It is thought it cannot be less than thirty thousand Livers. However, his Majesty refers it to the Judgment of the Sieur* Jeannin, *as likewise does all that concerns the intire Distribution of the said Sum, in which the said Sieur* de Barnevelt *ought to have a Share worthy his Merit, as the said Sieur* de Preaux *is charg'd to acquaint the said Sieur* Jeannin *more particularly. The said Sum of a hundred thousand Livers shall be sent thither at two Terms, with the other Monies his Majesty designs to expend in the Payment of the aforesaid Men at Arms, to be put into the Hands of him, the said Sieur* Jeannin *shall judge proper to make a Distribution thereof, according to what he shall have fix'd and determin'd, to the End all things may be manag'd secretly and faithfully, as it is requisite in such Cases.*

CHAP

CHAP. X.

Of Letters and Dispatches.

I Shall not here trouble my felf to fay, that the Embaffador ought to be very careful in keeping the Minutes of his Letters, and to lay them up according to the Order of their Date, that he may be able to find them readily whenever he fhall have Occafion which is what he alfo ought to obferve in reference to the Difpatches he receives, becaufe it is the proper Function of the Secretary, who ought to title both the ones and the others, and put them in order, before either he or his Mafter locks them up This is what Cardinal *Mazarin* was fo exact in, that his Domefticks could not fail of cafting their Eye, and laying their Hand immediately on the Paper he ask'd them for The Punctuality of the late *M de Witt*, firft Minifter of *Holland*, came very near this, and he was therein perfectly well feconded by the Clark of *Holland*, who ferv'd under him But I fhould think one might fay, That the Embaffador who is exact and punctual, does not fail to fet down at the Head of his Difpatches, the Dates of thofe he had fent before, to which he has receiv'd no Anfwer As alfo thofe of the Letters he has receiv'd fince his laft When he writes about Affairs of Importance, and the Ways are not very fafe, it is proper to fend Duplicates He ought alfo to write on all Occafions, as well Ordinary as Extraordinary, wherefoever he happens to be, both to fatisfy his Prince's Curiofity, and to give Proofs of his Diligence

As for the Difpatches themfelves, there are many Rules to be given, and many Obfervations to be made, but the moft univerfal Rule is, That the Embaffador therein muft accommodate himfelf to the Humour and Will of his Mafter There is no Prince that underftands his Affairs, but will require his Embaffador fhould write to himfelf immediately If he has a firft Minifter, the Embaffador cannot avoid writing to him alfo, upon all Occafions that fhall offer, as well as to the Secretary who is intrufted with that kind of Affairs, and fends him Anfwers to his Difpatches, on the part of the Prince In the Reign of *Henry* IV the Embaffadors wrote only to the King himfelf, and to him of the Secretaries of State, who had the Province of foreign Affairs All Cardinal *Doffat*'s Letters, and thofe of Cardinal *du Perron*, of Prefident *Jeannin*, and of *de Fresne Canay*, are addrefs'd to the King himfelf or to *M de Villeroy* at leaft thofe that make a Part of the Courfe of their Negotiation, becaufe the King, who was the Head and Mafter of his Council, would have all Affairs pafs through his Hands and Mind While the Duke *de Luines* was in favour, all the Embaffadors wrote to him, but not conftantly, as they have fince done under the Miniftry of the Cardinals *de Richelieu* and *Mazarin*, to whom a more exact Account was given of the Negotiations, than even to the King himfelf, and the Secretary of State, who at that time was in effect but a fubaltern Minifter under the firft In *Spain*, *England*, and all the other Courts of *Europe*, the Practice s the fame The *Turks*, who have no Minifters in Ordinary in foreign Courts, have no great Commerce of Letters Their Chiaoux, who very often can neither read nor write, are only Meffengers, who having deliver'd their Meffage, return home, and make their Report to the Vizir by word of Mouth All the Negotiations and all the Treaties the Grand Seignior caufes to be made, are made at *Conftantinople* with the Divan, or elfe in the Countrey with the Firft Vizir, or with fome Bacha, and always in their own Tongue The Embaffadors of *Venice* addrefs their Letters to the Doge, tho' properly fpeaking they write to the Republick it felf, for which Reafon the Seigneury reads them, or elfe they are read at the College, which communicates them to the Council of *Pregadi*, or elfe to the Senate it felf, if the Matter requires it The Embaffadors and Minifters, which the United Provinces employ abroad, write to the States General, but very often their Letters are not worth the Paper they blot and blur, and much lefs the Poftage If they have any important Affair to communicate, they addrefs their Letters to the Regifter of the States, who reads it in the Affembly, or elfe to thofe amongft 'em who are appointed for fecret Affairs Of thefe Difpatches fome are communicated by Copies which are fent to the Provinces, and the others are put under Lock and Key, with other fecret Inftruments, of which it is forbid to give any Copy There are fome Embaffadors who write alfo to the Prince of *Orange*, and to the States of the Province which nominated them to the Embaffy This Refpect is due to the Prince of *Orange*, becaufe, as the moft important Refolutions are form'd on his Judgment and Opinion, it is neceffary he fhould be punctually inform'd of the Particulars of all the Negotiations which are carrying on in foreign Courts The Embaffador who is employ'd at the Nomination of the States of *Holland*, writes to the firft Minifter of that Province, which as it has always fome Perfon belonging to it, in all the Embaffies that are compos'd of a Plurality of Embaffadors, the States of this Province are more particularly inform'd than the others, of what is negotiating abroad

It often happens that the Prince who has no firft Minifter has nevertheless put a particular Confidence in one or other of his Council, and then the Embaffador to fecure the Friendfhip of this Confident, ought to write often to him, that he may be protected by him in his Abfence, and that he may alfo be more particularly inform'd of the Prince's Intentions In *Henry* IV's Reign there was no Embaffador that did not hold fome Correfpondence with the Duke of *Sully*, as well becaufe he had a greater Share of the Confidence of that Prince than any other Minifter, as becaufe it was by

Y y y y   his

his Orders only that their Salaries were paid them. There was only Cardinal *Doſſat* (who either on the account of his Religion, or becauſe he held no Correſpondence but only with *M. de Villeroy*) did not write to him at all. *Walſingham* wrote to the Earl of *Leiceſter*, the Miniſter Queen *Elizabeth* confided in, almoſt as often as to the Queen her ſelf, or elſe to the Secretary of State, and he did not omit writing to the Lord *Burleigh*, after this was promoted to the Office of High Treaſurer of the Kingdom, altho' he had not the Quality of firſt Miniſter, nor was not ſo in effect, under a Queen that govern'd, and did not ſuffer her ſelf to be governed. The Miniſters of the Court of *Rome* write to the Pope, but they never fail to write alſo to the Cardinal *Patron*.

As to the Quality of Diſpatches, the Embaſſador muſt know the Humour of the Prince, and that of the firſt Miniſter who has the Direction of his Affairs. *Doſſat*, who knew that King *Henry* IV. took himſelf Cognizance of his Affairs, and that he would be very particularly inform'd thereof, writing to him on *December* 22, 1594, which is the firſt Letter that is found among the Diſpatches he ſent the King, expreſſes himſelf in theſe Terms. *Foraſmuch as it concerns your Majeſty's Satisfaction to be inform'd particularly how every thing paſs'd at my Audience, and indeed that by ſeveral Particulars you may the more eaſily judge of the Pope's Diſpoſition, it is alſo my Duty to ſhew very minutely, how I behav'd my ſelf, what I ſaid, and what was anſwer'd me.* The Diſpatch which follows deſerves to be read and ſtudy'd, becauſe it may ſerve for a Model, even to a very able Miniſter. What may be ſaid of Diſpatches in general is, That there is no Prince but loves they ſhould be ſtrong rather than prolix, and indeed moſt Miniſters require Things, and not unprofitable Words. King *Henry* IV. took ſo much Pleaſure in reading the well-reaſon'd Letters of Preſident *Jeannin*, that he made *Villeroy* write to him on *October* 8, 1607, *That his Letters could not be too long. That there was not any thing unprofitable or ſuperfluous to be found in them, ſo that he ſhould continue to extend them, and to particularize as he had begun. That the King deſir'd it, and had commanded him to ſignify the ſame to him, and that his Letters were moſt certainly very agreeable to his Majeſty.* It may be ſaid with Truth of Preſident *Jeannin*'s Letters, what is ſaid of the Epiſtles of an ancient Author, That the longeſt are the fineſt. King *Henry* IV. was very knowing himſelf, but it is certain that never any Prince had ſuch able Miniſters, nor any Miniſters ſo great a Maſter, nor ſo equitable a Valuer of their Merit. *Jeannin* could not pretend to a more glorious Reward for his Services, than ſo authentick an Approbation of ſo good and ſo powerful a Monarch. Cardinal *Mazarin*, who took Delight in letting his Mind take a long Range, and who never tir'd with reaſoning, requir'd alſo that the Embaſſadors ſhould enlarge upon their Subjects. He often made uſe of *Silhon*'s Pen for his Diſpatches, eſpecially for the Affairs of *Germany* and *Sweden*, and *Silhon*, who pretended to Politicks and Eloquence, ſeconded very well the Intentions of his Eminence *D'Avaux* and *Servien* anſwer'd them perfectly, and might be ſaid to write Volumes rather than Letters. It cannot be deny'd but there is Matter in them, and almoſt all of them are fill'd with ſolid Reaſons, which Study and Application ſupply'd the one with, and Nature the other, but it muſt alſo be acknowledg'd, that the moſt prolix Diſcourſes are not the ſtrongeſt, and that it is impoſſible but in a great Number of Reaſons there muſt be ſome weak ones, which inſtead of convincing the Mind, perplex it.

The Nuncio and *Venetian* Embaſſador reproach'd one Day *d'Avaux* and *Servien* the *French* Plenipotentiaries, That they ſent every Week large Diſpatches to their Court. That it was impoſſible but in ſuch Prolixity there muſt be often things of greater Appearance than Truth, and that they would do better to be more conciſe and more reſerv'd. *Longueville* and *d'Avaux* made no Anſwer to theſe Reproaches, but *Servien*, who was never without a Reply, told them, That the youngeſt of them three was above fifty Years old, and that they ought not to be taught at that Age how to make their Diſpatches. That their Intention was to ſatisfy the Queen and the firſt Miniſter, that they had ſucceeded therein hitherto, and hop'd they ſhould do it likewiſe for the time to come, without ſtanding in need of any body's Advice for that purpoſe. They could not make their Diſpatches leſs, becauſe as they were to give an Account of whatever paſs'd in the Negotiations, which were of a vaſt Extent, and to anſwer all the Articles and all the Reaſons of the Cardinal's Letters, which were very long, and often accompany'd with large Memorials, they were oblig'd to make Reflections on the ones and the others. And indeed the Embaſſador's Letters cannot be too prolix, when the State of the Affairs he has to negotiate obliges him thereto. The *French* Plenipotentiaries had to negotiate with the Emperor's Miniſters, with thoſe of *Spain*, of *Sweden*, of *Bavaria*, and with thoſe of almoſt all the Princes of *Germany* and *Italy*, beſides thoſe of the United Provinces. They had the Intereſts of *Portugal* and *Catalonia* to ſupport, where they met with inſuperable Difficulties and Obſtacles, ſo that they could not poſſibly make little Diſpatches. Whatever may be ſaid, their longeſt Letters are not tedious, and are much more agreeable than thoſe of ſome others, who notwithſtanding paſs for great Men, tho' at the ſame time their Letters are only fill'd with Trifles and Fooleries, fitter to take up ſome Pages in a Dictionary, than the Mind of a reaſonable Perſon. There is nothing ſo tireſome as the Length of the ones, nor nothing ſo troubleſome as the falſe Eloquence of the others. *Baſſompierre* being Embaſſador Extraordinary in *Spain* in the Year 1621, ſays in the Letter he writes to *M. de Puiſieux* on *April* 27, that he will keep within the Rules all Embaſſadors ought to obſerve, *To make a very ſuccinct Diſpatch to the Miniſter, where they make a long one to their Maſter.* But this is no general Rule, for they muſt therein accommodate themſelves to the Humour of the Prince, and to the Authority of the Miniſter. The King whom *Baſſompierre* ſerv'd did not love to read long Letters, and notwithſtanding he was jealous of an Authority he was not acquainted with, as the Duke of *Rohan* ſays,

says, yet he lik'd better to have the Contents of Letters reported to him, than to be oblig'd to read them himself.

It is not necessary that the Style of the Embassador should be very polite. It is sufficient it is clear and intelligible, so that it be not disfigur'd with Solecisms and Barbarisms. Nay I should rather be for his not having the utmost Clearness, than to see him forc'd and affected. The Negligence of a Cavalier becomes an Embassador much better than the Affectation of a Pedant or an Advocate. Provided he have ever so little Capacity and Use of Writing, he will have no Difficulty to express his Sentiments after he has conceiv'd 'em well, and digested them in his Mind, so that if he understands himself well, he will make himself easily understood to others. That he may do it in an orderly manner, he may disburthen his Memory on a Table Book or in short Memorandums, from whence he may take, and place in its due Order on Paper what he has to write, as well concerning general Affairs, as those of his Commission, especially when at his going from an Audience or a Conference, he has his Memory still fill'd with what was either said or done. President *Jeannin* says in one of his Letters, that he wrote down every Day what pass'd, and caus'd it to be put into Cypher, to send it at that instant if an Opportunity offer'd. That by this Mean his Letter was swell'd, not being able to omit any thing that merited to be inserted in it. He ought to know whom he may intrust the Secret with, and judge whether he ought to write it all with his own Hand, or whether he may transmit it by that of his Secretary. This, as I said before, is one of the most important Parts of an Embassador. He must also know what he ought to write to the Prince himself, and what ought to be reserv'd for the Secretary of State, or such other Minister to whom he has Orders to address his Dispatches. It is his Business again to judge what he ought to write in Cypher, and when the Importance of an Affair is such as to deserve an Express. There is no Rule to be given on all these Heads, because the Embassador must therein consult himself, who alone can judge of the Importance of the Affair, and of the Curiosity or Interest of his Prince. *Lewis* XI, who first establish'd the Posts in *France*, was for knowing all, and being the first inform'd. There are Occurrences where he ought not to grudge the Expence of an extraordinary Courier, because sometimes the Moments of a first Advice cannot be too dearly paid for, since in a surprising Accident they may afford very great Advantages, or irreparable Damages. In what, the Embassador ought not to distinguish between good and bad News, on the contrary he ought to be so much the readier to write the bad, when his Master is concern'd therein, because an Advice sent in time is of the last Importance, by reason of the Consequences bad Successes may have. It is not necessary, in my Opinion, to add here, that in such cases the Embassador ought to have the Prudence to pass his Letters through the Hands of a Minister, who being in Credit with the Prince, can prepare his Mind to receive a vexatious Account, and represent to him the Service his Embassador does him in giving it him; because he gives him the Means and the Leisure to repair what is pass'd, and to prevent what otherwise would have been inevitable.

This is not the Place to treat of Cyphers, because it would lead us into too great a Digression to speak of so ample a Matter. However I'll say a Word or two about it. Entire Treatises have been written on that Subject, and a Sovereign Prince, to shew that his large Library had not been unuseful to him, has written a great Volume thereon. But he has done what is usual enough to those who write such sort of Books, where, instead of exhausting the Matter, they pass very lightly over what is most essential in the Subject they pretend to treat of, and while they say nothing but what is most common therein, they only repeat and copy what others have written, and what almost all the World knows. One may say that Cypher (it is so they call the secret way of Writing, by reason for the most part those Characters of modern Arithmetick which have been brought from the *Indies* are made use of) is a kind of Magick. *Trithemius* Abbot of *Spanheim* has reduc'd it into a sort of *Cabala*, and yet there is nothing more easy than to unravel this Appearance of Charm by the Help of the Key. Nay there are some People who decypher without Difficulty all sorts of Characters, how hard, obscure and odd soever they may be, and find out the Key thereof with so much Ease, that one would think they had it about them. *Rossignol*, who serv'd Cardinal *Richelieu* in this Function, and made his Fortune thereby, was so dextrous and successful in it, that he decypher'd without much Pains all the Letters that were brought him, not only those which were written in a Language he understood, but also those that were written in a Tongue to which he was an utter Stranger, and whereof he had not the least Knowledge. It is no hard matter to invent a Million of new Cyphers, but it is almost impossible to find out any that cannot be unravel'd by those who have a little Genius that way, and a great deal of Use. During the Wars and Disorders of the League, the *Spaniards* made use of a Cypher which was compos'd of above five hundred Characters, so that there was no body could decypher their Letters. At last, those that were intercepted were sent to *Francis Vietta*, a famous Mathematician of those Times. He had never apply'd himself to that kind of Study, and had never so much as heard of those Cyphers which are made use of in Letters, and yet after he had consider'd a little thereon, he found out the Key of them, and decypher'd them easily. The *Spaniards* did not know till two Years after, that their Secret was discover'd, and when they perceiv'd it by intercepted Letters, they were so amaz'd thereat, that they said, King *Henry* IV, had made use of Magick to find out the Key of their Cypher. They who are skill'd therein, know in what the Secret consists. The Jargon that was formerly much more us'd than it is at present, was in my Opinion of little Utility, whether it was intermix'd with a Cypher or not. As soon as the Tenour of an Affair is known, and the Court where it is negotiated, there is no Difficulty to find out the Persons whom Dispatches speak of.

When

When Embassies are compos'd of many Embassadors, they for the most part make a Dispatch in common, besides which they also send each a Letter in particular, but this is not always practis'd. There is not one single particular Dispatch to be seen in the Embassy the Duke d'*Engoulesme*, the Count *de Bethune* and the Abbot *d'Espreanx* perform'd in *Germany* in the Year 1621. *Du Perron* and *Dossat* were only Solicitors, when they negotiated the Absolution of *Henry* IV, with *Clement* VIII, but yet that did not hinder them from being publick Ministers, and notwithstanding they had an Affair to manage in common, yet they both made particular Dispatches. *Oxenstiern* and *Salvius*, Plenipotentiaries of *Sweden* at *Osnaburg*, wrote each of them to the Queen and to the Senate, besides their Letter in common. The Ministers who were on the part of *France* at *Munster* made one common Dispatch by the Secretary of the Embassy for the Queen Regent and for the Secretary of State, besides which they wrote in private to Cardinal *Mazarin* *Norris* and *Walsingham*, *Smith* and *Walsingham*, and the said *Walsingham* with *Cobham* and *Sommers*, wrote in Conjunction to the Queen and to the Ministers of *England*. If a Prince sends an Embassador Extraordinary to a Court where there is already one in Ordinary, altho' this be compris'd in the same Commission, yet the Extraordinary makes particular Dispatches for those Affairs which he is particularly charg'd with. This is to be seen in President *Jeannin*'s Negotiation, who gives himself a particular and exact Account of all Circumstances, altho' the King had other Ministers besides him at the *Hague*, who solicited the same Affair with the President *Bassompierre*, Embassador Extraordinary from *France*, and *du Fargis*, Embassador in Ordinary at *Madrid*, negotiated in Conjunction the Affair of the *Valteline*. They sometimes made a Dispatch in common, but for the most part they each of them made a particular one.

There are some Embassadors who make two sorts of Dispatches, the one for the Affairs they have to negotiate, and where the Prince their Master is interested, and the other for general News, which they are oblig'd to inform themselves of, that they may acquaint their Master therewith. Some act one way and some another, for my part I should think a Distinction might be made, and that the Embassador might swell his Dispatches with some important Affairs, notwithstanding they have nothing in common with his Negotiation, but for common News, I should rather be for his putting them in a Sheet by themselves, and sending them rather to the Minister than to the Prince. *M de Foix*, *Dossat*, *Walsingham*, and several others, mingle general Affairs with the particular, and I do not find that the Princes to whom they wrote found fault therewith. The skilful Embassador will not content himself to transmit in Writing the Grand Affairs, but he will penetrate into the Reasons and Motives thereof. For some Ages there had not happen'd a more important Affair to the See of *Rome* than that of *Ferrara*, after the Decease of the last Duke *Alfonso d'Este* had taken Possession thereof, and had caus'd the Inhabitants to swear Allegiance to him, besides which, most of the Potentates of *Italy* favour'd his Pretensions; insomuch that it was fear'd the Pope would find a strong Opposition, and yet he met with none at all But that they might not be surpris'd hereat in *France*, *Dossat* sets down the Reasons thereof, which are very strong and convincing. Those Ministers who shall have the same Penetration, will do themselves Honour in imitating his Example.

The Embassador cannot be well inform'd of general Affairs if he does not hold a Correspondence, not only with the other Ministers the Prince their Master employs in other Courts (which is expressly injoyn'd him by his Instructions) but also with all sorts of Persons without Distinctions, provided he does not offend against his Prince's Interest. For if he be allow'd to corrupt the Ministers of the Court where he resides, as I observ'd in the foregoing Chapter, with much greater Reason shall he be allow'd to debauch those of the Court of an Enemy, provided he can procure thereby any Advantage to his Master's Service, which very well deserves a particular Remark and Reflexion. The Resident who was on the part of the Elector of *Brandenburgh* at *Stockholm* in the Year 1653, wrote duly as well to the Minister his Master entertain'd at *Vienna*, as to other Friends he had at that Court. Queen *Christina*, who had still her first Sentiments for *France*, and was not well satisfy'd with the Emperor, signify'd to the Resident that he could not suffer that Correspondence, and that he should desist from continuing it. The Resident made Answer, That no Body could hinder him from holding it. *That he enjoy'd this Liberty by virtue of the Law of Nations*, and that it behov'd him to inform himself of what pass'd elsewhere, that he might be the better able to serve the Elector his Master, who had commanded him to write to his other Ministers what pass'd at the Court of *Sweden*, and to receive from them the Informations they were capable of giving him. That he did not believe that *Sweden* would pretend to regulate his Correspondence, and hinder him from holding it with whom he thought fit. The other publick Ministers approv'd of the Resident's Repartee, and their Approbation shut the Mouth of his Controulers. And indeed since the Subject of an Ally may lawfully traffick with the Subject of another Ally, provided he do not furnish him with Arms and other contraband Goods, I do not see how the publick Minister of a Prince an Ally can be hinder'd from entertaining a Correspondence with the Enemy of the Prince with whom he resides, especially if he does not supply him with contraband Goods, that is to say, if he does not send him any Advice that can prejudice the Affairs of the last. But if that happens, the same must be done that is practis'd in reference to those who carry on a Commerce of contraband Merchandize it must be confiscated, but the Confiscation does not reach the Ships, nor even the other Merchandize that is found on Board the same Ship, and much less the Master or Proprietors thereof. The Prince who intercepts Letters that are prejudicial to his Service, cannot come upon the Minister who has written them, but he ought to complain to the Prince who employs such Minister, and he must procure

cure himself Justice by those Means Sovereigns are us'd to take on the like Occasions. Queen *Christina* her self had experienc'd in another occasion, that a publick Minister may hold a Correspondence in a Court which is not very well affected to that where he resides. In the Year 1651, she resolv'd to send *Berenclau* to *Vienna*, to excuse the Delay of the Embassy which was to receive the Investiture of the new Conquests the Crown of *Sweden* had made in *Germany*. Berenclau taking Notice of his Employment to *Chanut*, desir'd him to make a Complement for him to *Servien*, and to tell him, that if he could serve him where he was going, he would do it with Affection, on account of the particular Esteem he had for his Person. *Chanut*, thinking that these Offers of Civility might reach to the carrying on a Correspondence with *Servien*, was for confirming him in his good Sentiments, but *Berenclau* undeceiv'd him, and told him, he ought not to give so great an Extent to his Intention, and he did not indeed engage in this Correspondence till the Queen had, at *Chanut's* Suit, oblig'd him thereto. As the Embassador's chief Application ought to be to entertain Friendship and a good Understanding between the two Princes, he ought not always to criminalize, or render the Intentions, or even the Words of the Prince with whom he negotiates suspected. I have elsewhere given the Reason thereof, where I say that there is no Prince that likes his Minister should create him Troubles. Besides, there is Imprudence and even Malice to give a bad Sense to Expressions, which are much more natural when a favourable one is given them. Cardinal *Dossat* had receiv'd an Audience, in which the Pope had expres's'd a great Resentment at the Registring and Publication of the Edict of *Nants*. His Fidelity oblig'd him to make an exact Report of all that had pass'd there, but before he begins to recite the Particulars, he tells King *Henry* IV, that he hopes his Majesty will excuse the Pope, because his Intentions are not bad, and that it is his Zeal for the Catholick Religion, as well as what he owes to his own Reputation, that make him speak. The Pope had been violent enough, and yet *Dossat*, by praying the King to excuse him, excuses him first himself.

The Embassador cannot be too reserv'd in writing of News either general or particular. He ought to be very punctual in sending that which comes to his Knowledge, but he ought to distinguish well between the doubtful and the certain, lest mingling the false with the true, the Falshess of the one should destroy the Credit that is due to the other. He ought to be still more reserv'd in telling his Sentiment in reference to the State of Affairs, and particularly concerning the Success of his Negotiation, whatever Assurance he may have given him of it. If Men are not Deceivers, they may be deceived themselves, and there may every Moment Accidents happen, that may ruin the finest Appearances: sometimes there is no believing even what one sees. *Vidit, aut vidisse putat*. The *Sieur de Ste Aldegonde*, who did the Business of the States of the Low Countries at the Court of *London* in the Year 1581, being come one Night into the Queen's Chamber, saw her conversing with the Duke of Alençon. The Lords and Ladies were so far off that they could not partake therein, but all that were there, were Witnesses of an Action, from which great Consequences might be drawn. The Queen taking a Ring off her Finger put it upon the Duke's, who soon after retir'd with a Joy that shew'd his Satisfaction, as if he carry'd with him the Earnest and Assurance of his Marriage. *Ste Aldegonde*, who look'd upon this Action to be of the last Importance for his Masters, gave them Advice thereof by an Express which he sent away that very Night. The Noise of the Bells, and the Cannons, and the Fires which were made in all the Towns throughout the Low Countries, discover'd sufficiently the Joy they had there on the Account of an Advice that prov'd to be false. The Queen reproach'd *Ste Aldegonde* with having been too precipitate in giving an Advice, concerning which he might have been better inform'd, and undeceiv'd in a few Hours. In *June* 1646, the Secretary of the Embassy that was on the part of *Sweden* at *Osnaburg*, wrote to the Prince *Palatin*, *Charles Gustavus*, that a Truce was sign'd between the *Spaniards* and the *Hollanders*, and that it had been publish'd at *Amsterdam*. This Advice, which was given by a publick Minister, who ought to be well inform'd in an Affair of that Nature, was capable of alarming very much the Court of *Sweden*, and would have alarm'd it in effect, if *Chanut* had not produc'd Letters from the *Hague* of a fresher Date by four Days than those of *Osnaburg*, which made known the Vanity of the Secretary's Advices.

I should freely follow the Sentiment of those, who would have the Embassador make a naked and simple Narrative of what passes in his Negotiation, without any Mixture of his own Opinions or Counsels without forgetting however any thing that can strengthen the Particulars of his Relations. Cardinal *Dossat* is very exact in remarking those of all the Audiences, where he had Affairs of Importance to negotiate, even to the observing the Smiles, the Meen and the Gestures of Pope *Clement* VIII, that the King might be the better able to judge of the Thoughts and Intentions of his Holiness, the Tone of his Voice, the Warmth or Indifferency of his Discourse, and all the Circumstances that could contribute to the forming a Judgment, whether the Words were study'd or natural, which shews the Sincerity, or discovers the Artifice, and makes one distinguish Complements from sincere Expressions. I say I would not have the Embassador crowd in his own Sentiments, unless his Master requires them, for then he ought to tell him his Opinion frankly, and like a Man of Honour, without Interest or Passion. *I should be too ignorant and simple*, says *Dossat* to King *Henry* IV, *if I thought otherwise and too disloyal, and unworthy the Office with which you are pleas'd to honour me, if I wrote to you otherwise than what I think*. If he says any thing of his own Motion, he may excuse himself upon his Zeal, which makes him speak, or else he may make his own particular Opinion pass for the general Sentiment, and he may add, That being upon the Place, he thinks he may with some probability spend his Judgment on those things which are under his Sight. My Author, whom I would give for a Pattern to all Ministers, often expresses his own Sentiments by other Mouths. In the Letter he wrote to *M. de Villeroy*, on the 15th of *July*, 1602, concerning the Duke of *Biron*, he says, He can tell him nothing of his own, but he will represent to him what he has heard others say. At the same time they are only the same Sentiments, with which he fills the Letter he writes to the King on the same Subject. This is his Practice in many other Places. It is certain, that unless the Prince employs mere Blockheads, of the grossest Stupidity, as it sometimes happens, he is oblig'd often to follow the Hints his Embassador gives him, who may be clearer sighted than they who have not the Opportunity of seeing Affairs in their proper Light. *M. de Villeroy* was one of the most dextrous and ablest Ministers *France* ever had, and yet he often asks Cardinal *Dossat*'s Advice, and he, as well as *Henry* IV, often resign'd Affairs to the Conduct and Judgment of President *Jeannin*, who had sometimes executed Orders before he had receiv'd them. Cardinal *Mazarin*, who was willing to be thought to have Wit, and indeed who had to spare, often ask'd the Advice of the *French* Embassadors who were at *Munster*, and left to them the Disposal of the King's Affairs and Interests. But then he did thus but after he had told them his own Sentiments, and to make them responsible for the Success.

It is not enough that the Advices the Embassador gives be true, but he must likewise have a great Regard to the Prince and Ministers of the Court where he negotiates, and take Care of saying any thing in his Letters that can offend them; unless his Master's Service be concern'd, in which Case he ought to pass over all other Considerations, and respect no body. But without this Necessity he cannot shew too much Modesty. For notwithstanding he is accountable for his Actions to none but the Prince that employs him, yet he with whom he negotiates may complain of him, and demand Reparation. And as most Princes are at this Day dispos'd, they had rather expose, if not abandon a Minister, than create themselves any Trouble. *Channt* had said in one of his Letters to the *French* Plenipotentiaries at *Munster*, that Chancellor *Oxenstiern* did not second very well the Inclination the Queen of *Sweden* had for the Peace of *Germany*, and the Ministers, writing to Court on that Subject, enlarg'd very much thereon, and inveigh'd against the Chancellor. The *Spaniards* had corrupted one of the Clerks of the Secretaryship of the *French* Embassadors, who, in communicating to them Copies of all the Letters the Embassadors had receiv'd from their Court, or that they had sent thither within the Space of seven Months, gave them also one of this. They did not fail to shew it to the Embassadors of *Sweden* who were at *Osnaburg*, and particularly to *Oxenstiern*, whose Indignation thereat was so much the greater, because he thereby discover'd the Intrigues which were carry'd on between the two Courts of *France* and *Sweden*, to procure the Disgrace and Removal of the Chancellor his Father. This piece of Roguery did not produce the Effect the *Spaniards* had promis'd themselves from it, because the Chancellor judging that he could not resent it, without incurring the Queen's Displeasure, and without embroiling *Sweden* with *France*, was willing to sacrifice his Resentment to the publick Interest, and so spoke of it as of a fictitious Instrument. The Queen took no other Notice thereof than this, that supposing *Channt* had done the Chancellor Wrong, by giving an ill Turn to his Sentiments, yet it did not belong to her to reproach him with it. That he had a Master, to whom alone he was oblig'd to give an Account of his Actions, and to no body else.

Nevertheless the same Queen did not scruple to make a very bitter Reproach to the Minister of the United Provinces, who had given an extravagant Information enough to his Masters. He had written to them that there was a Negotiation on foot at *Stockholm* for a strict Alliance between *France* and *Sweden*; That the Design was to maintain a certain Number of Men of War in the Ports of *Dunkirk* and *Gottenbourg*, but that *France* had made Answer, That there was no likelihood of making a new Treaty, till the Kingdom was restor'd to Quiet, and as for the Ships, there was no Conveniency at all at *Dunkirk*. The Queen having seen a Copy of these Letters, sent him word to forbear for the future giving way to such idle Notions. This Minister was very subject thereto, and another, who had had more Wisdom, would not have written them, as on the other side, one more resolute would not have remain'd without Reply. But he was such a sorry Tool of a Man, that there was not ever so insignificant a Clerk, but was more capable than he, of discharging the Function of a publick Minister.

At the beginning of the last Troubles in *France*, from which there was Reason to apprehend as dreadful Consequences as had been seen in those of *England*, *Shering Rosenhan*, Embassador of *Sweden*, considering that a Civil War in that Kingdom might very well hinder the Execution of the Peace of *Germany*, and incommode *Sweden*, was not contented to press Cardinal *Mazarin* continually to come to an Accommodation with the Parliament. But as he was persuaded that the King, nor his Dignity, was not what was aim'd at, and that the Difference was properly only between the Cardinal and the Princes who actuated the Parliament, he fill'd all his Letters with Reasons that justify'd these, and condemn'd all the Actions of the other. He also sent along with his Dispatches all the Libels that were printed, and dispers'd up and down at that time, against the Queen Regent, against the Cardinal, and indirectly against even the Regal Authority. Complaint was made thereof, not to *Rosenhan*, but the Queen of *Sweden*, who was oblig'd to recall her Minister, notwithstanding she was very well satisfy'd with his Services. I said a little before, that Queen *Elizabeth* made a sharp Reprimand to *Sir Aldegonde*, on the account of the precipitate Advice he had sent the States, and the Prince of *Orange*, about her Marriage with the Duke of *Alençon*. But then this Advice concern'd her, and was of great Importance to her in particular, and moreover the Queen's Authority was so great with the States, that she might very well speak a Word of Resentment to their Minister.

This Precaution is so much the more necessary to the Embassador, not only because there are a thousand Accidents which may make his Letters miscarry, or cause them to be intercepted, and that the Infidelity of a Domestick may communicate them, but also because there are some Places where there is an Obligation to make Copies of them, and where it is almost impossible to secure the greatest Secrets. There is no Minister who negotiates a Fortnight at the *Hague*, that does not know how they govern there. In *Sweden* the Letters are read in the Senate, which is compos'd of a great number of Officers of the Crown, and other Ministers. Even in those Courts where the Council is reduc'd to a very few Persons, there is no hindering the greatest part of the Dispatches from passing through the Hands of the Clerks, whose Fidelity is not always proof. The most important of all are decypher'd by Persons, who may be mercenary or interessed. After the Example of *l'Hoste*, Godson and Clerk to *Villeroy*, who sold his Master's Secrets to the *Spaniards*, there is no need to seek for others. It is not long since one of *Lionne*'s Clerks was hang'd at *Paris*, for carrying on the same Commerce, but all are not hang'd that are guilty thereof. The Embassador ought not to be less reserv'd in giving his Advice to his Master, and telling him his Sentiments when he does not require them, than he ought to acquit himself with Fidelity therein, when his Prince asks him his Opinion. Cardinal *Dossat* had not the Quality of Embassador, and yet he discharg'd the Functions of one. One may see in all his Dispatches, with what Firmness he gives his Advice when it is ask'd him. King *Henry* IV, and *Villeroy* his trusty Minister, observing the indirect Procedure of the Duke of *Savoy*, in reference to the Marquisate of *Saluzzo*, were for knowing the Cardinal's Judgment, in reference to the Conduct he thought the King of *Spain* would hold in that Conjuncture, and concerning what the King ought to do in case *Spain* should declare it self. There is nothing can be stronger, nor more judicious, than the Advice *Dossat* gives on this Affair in his Letter of the 23d of *September*, 1600. The King and *Villeroy*, who were the first Personages in *Europe* for Politicks, condescended to take the Advice of a Priest, in a Conjuncture of that Niceness and Difficulty, where the King had already enter'd *Savoy* with an Army. On the contrary, the same Minister's Modesty is admirable, when he gives his Opinion of his own Accord. The Duke of *Mercœur* did not desist from carrying on his Rebellion in *Britany*, even after the King was reconcil'd to the See of *Rome*. *Dossat* was for having the King carry his Arms on that side, leaving the Frontiers of *Picardy* well guarded. And this Advice was so conformable to the King's Reason and Intentions, that it was follow'd. However *Dossat*, speaking to that Affair in his Letter of the 12th of *February*, 1597, says, That most People judge, that is what ought to be done. And that if he meddles with what does not belong to his Profession, it is out of an Excess of Zeal for the King's Service. And again, after he has spoken very pertinently of the Affair with the Duke of *Savoy*, in the same Letter, he adds, *But I forget my self*, says he, *yet I shall not be sorry the King sees that my Impertinence, which proceeds only from the Zeal I have for his Service and the Safety and Repose of my Countrey*;

I ought to have begun this Chapter with what I shall conclude it, viz. That the Embassador is oblig'd to give an Account, in his first Dispatches, of the Reception was given him at his Arrival at the Court where he is to negotiate, especially if he has had any extraordinary Honours done him. President *Jeannin* says, in the Letter he wrote to the King on the 22d of *May*, 1607, That the Governor and Magistrate of *Flushing* had receiv'd him in the Port. That he was saluted with twenty Pieces of Cannon, and that he found the Garrison under Arms, and drawn up in two Lines, from the Gate to his Lodgings. And in that of the 29th of the same Month, he writes, That in all the Towns through which he had pass'd, the Magistrate had visited him, and that Prince *Maurice*, with seven Deputies of the States, came to receive him at a Village half a League distant from the *Hague*. King *Henry* IV, in his Answer to some other Letters, tells him, It was a great Satisfaction to him to learn, from his Dispatches, the Civilities the Magistrates of the Towns in *Holland*, which he had seen, had done him, as well as the Acknowledgment they express'd for the Favours they had receiv'd from *France*. *Dossat* does not omit any one particular of the Reception he had, when he went to *Venice* and *Florence* on the part of the same King, and does not fail to mention the Presents the Republick and the Great Duke made him. Which is by so much the more necessary, as these Honours are only done to the Minister, to shew the Consideration is had for the Master, but what he writes, on the Subject of what has been said in this Chapter, in his Letter of the 16th of *January*, 1597, deserves a very particular Reflection. *Villeroy* had written to him, That the Court was inform'd that the Cardinals *Sforza* and *Aquaviva* were going to pass into the Interest of *Spain*. To which he makes Answer in these Terms, *Those who gave you Advice that the first had sided with Spain, and that the other would do the same, signify'd it to my self at the same time, and I hear others say as much. But in things that are not urgent, and where there is no Danger to stay a little, to be better inform'd, I am not usually in hast to write to you about them, and especially if the Matter in Hand be to give you an ill Impression of Persons of Honour, and to see you in an Alarm.* After he has justify'd the Intentions of those two Cardinals, he adds, *I should have thought I had done some Disservice to his Majesty, if without good Grounds I should have suggested an ill Thought to him, and given him any handle to distrust either the One or the other. Nay, I even was afraid, lest you should hearken to any thing that might reach their Ears, there being nothing that could provoke them more, who have generous and noble Souls, than to see themselves misbeliev'd and misconstru'd by you and me, to be something else than what they really are. Should I write to you those things which are whisper'd about, which I don't believe, or know to be false, and send you the Refutations of them, I should never have done, there does not pass a Day that my Ears are not stunn'd therewith.* If all the Dispatches of this great Man were not fill'd with Marks of an extraordinary Prudence, I would

would fay that this Paſſage is admirable, but forafmuch as his whole Negotiation is ſo, it is fufficient to apply it to the prefent Chapter, and make it ſerve for a Leſſon to the Embaſſador, who will never be liable to ramble nor go out of his Way, if he does but follow the Steps of this able Politician

CHAP. XI.
Of Mediation, and of Embaſſadors Mediators.

THE Quality of Mediator is one of the moſt difficult the Embaſſador has to ſuſtain, and Mediation is one of his moſt perplexing Employments The Prince whom he repreſents ought to be without Intereſt, and his Miniſter without Paſſion, which is not very eaſy nor very uſual, ſince we are ſeldom without, even in reference to thoſe Things and Perſons which are moſt indifferent to us Wherefore the one ought to be very circumſpect in offering his Mediation, and the Conduct of the other ſo regular, that he may not be ſuſpected of Partiality in any reſpect whatever In the Year 1645, *France* offer'd its Mediation to the two *Northern* Crowns, who were at variance She was ſo ſtrictly ally'd to *Sweden*, that their Intereſts were almoſt inſeparable, and particularly in *Germany* and this Conſideration was the Cauſe, that the King of *Denmark* receiv'd thoſe Offers with ſuch Uneaſineſs, that he would have rejected them, had it not been for the ill State of his Affairs, and the Reflection he made that the Advantages the *Swedes* had over him, would make them be apt to abandon their Conqueſts in *Germany*, to purſue and ſecure thoſe they made with ſo much Succeſs on the Frontiers of their Kingdom He conſider'd likewiſe, that the *French* could have no other Intention than that of making a Peace, becauſe this new War gave a powerful Diverſion to the Arms they employ'd in the Empire, and deſtroy'd in the Graſs, the Harveſt they hop'd to reap, after ſo many Victories they had there obtain'd The King of *Denmark* conſented at laſt, becauſe he could not otherwiſe get out of a War, the Beginnings whereof had been very unſucceſsful to him, and the End of which might be very fatal In the Year 1651, there was a Diſcourſe of having an Aſſembly of the Plenipotentiaries of *Poland* and of *Sweden*, in one of the Towns of *Germany*, in the Neighbourhood of the two Kingdoms, and at laſt *Lubeck* was pitch'd upon *France*, the Republick of *Venice*, the States of the United Provinces, the Elector of *Brandenburg*, and the Duke of *Courlande*, were to be Mediators The *Poles* would not ſuffer *France* to employ the Viſcount *de Bregy*, its Embaſſador in *Poland*, becauſe he was ſuſpected by them, and *Chanut* had ſome Difficulty to take this Mediation upon him, becauſe he judg'd he ought not to be leſs ſuſpected by *Poland* than the other, by reaſon of the long Stay he had made at the Court of *Sweden*, where he had not only acquir'd the Eſteem, but alſo the Confidence of the Queen. However the Reputation of his Probity was ſo well eſtabliſh'd, that the *Poles* approv'd of him without Difficulty, even when after the ineffectual Concluſion of the firſt Aſſembly, a ſecond was conven'd in the Year 1652 In the Year 1655, during the Rupture between the Crowns of *Polana* and *Sweden*, the Emperor ſent to offer his Mediation to the laſt, by the Count *de Pottinguen*, Vice-Chancellor of *Bohemia* They had begun to treat without a Mediator The *Swedes* were perſuaded that the Emperor's Intention was rather to exaſperate Matters than to accommodate them They were ſenſible that if the Negotiation was to be perform'd by Mediators, they could not avoid making uſe of thoſe who had been concern'd at *Lubeck* That the Emperor had endeavour'd to prevail with the *Muſcovite* to declare War with *Sweden*, and even that *Leſſinsky* whom the King of *Poland* had ſent to *Vienna*, had brought from thence ſome Aſſurance of Succour The Count arriv'd at *Thorn* in the Month of *December*, but by reaſon the King was continually in Motion, he could not ſpeak to him till the 5th of *April* of the following Year, and he did not ſee him any more after that time and repairing with *Liſola* to the *Poliſh* Army, he of his own accord renounc'd the Quality of Mediator

Some Years after, viz in the Year 1672, the two Kings of *France* and *England* having declar'd War againſt the United Provinces, *Sweden*, inſtead of aſſiſting theſe, as they were oblig'd by virtue of the Treaties which were between them and particularly by that of the triple Alliance, was contented to offer its Mediation The King of *Great Britain* accepted it immediately, and with a good Grace, at the ſame time that he rejected with Haughtineſs that of the Elector of *Brandenburg* This Prince, who had offer'd his Mediation to the King of *France* before the Rupture, bethought himſelf of offering it to that of *England*, after he had concluded his Treaty with the United Provinces, and when he was actually in the Field with a powerful Army to ſuccour them The King of *England* therefore receiv'd with Indignation the Memorial which the Miniſter of *Brandenburg* preſented him on that account, and cauſ'd an Anſwer to be made him in writing, in bad *French* enough, but in very intelligible Terms, where he ſaid, " That the Miniſter of *Brandenburg* ought not to be ſurpriſ'd, to find his Majeſty ſo ſenſibly touch'd, " when he ſaw his Electoral Highneſs, his " ancient Ally, become the chief Support of " his Enemies, and that he could not but look " upon it to be a very bad Effect of an Alliance ſo long cheriſh'd, to find his Electoral " Highneſs joyn with his Majeſty in time of " Peace, and complain of the States General, " and

The EMBASSADOR and his FUNCTIONS.

" and in time of War always unite his Arms
" with those of the said States against h s Ma-
" jesty As for what is offer'd at the End of
" the Memorial, to wit, his Electoral High-
" ness s Mediation, that his Majesty could no
" way condescend to it For altho' the En-
" voy Extraordinary makes use of the soft
" Term of Mediation, yet all those who are
" impartial, who shall consider it as accompa-
" ny'd with such a Treaty, will judge it to be
" no other than an Arbitration, and it would
" not be otherwise interpreted in his Majesty,
" should he accept of such Offer, and admit
" of such a Treaty as he desires, than as a Sub-
" mission to whatever his Electoral Highness
" should determine For which Reasons *his*
" *Majesty accepts the Mediation of the King of*
" *Sweden, as being unarm'd and disinterested,*
" *and cannot admit of that of his Electoral High-*
" *ness, whom he looks upon to be arm'd, and en-*
" *gag'd with his Enemies*" I wis willing to set
down here the proper Words of the King of
England, and leave it to the Reader's Judgment, whether it was not out of season, that
the Elector offer'd his Mediation to the King,
who had just broke with the United Provinces after such a Manner, as sufficiently made
known, that it was not any Consideration for
his Electoral Highness, that could reconcile
him with them

In the Beginning of the Month of *November*, 1674, the Emperor's Commissioners being
in Conference with the Minister of *Sweden*,
on the Subject of the same Mediation, told him
by word of Mouth and in Writing, " That
" his Imperial Majesty accepted the Mediation
" of the Crown of *Sweden*, provided it de-
" clar'd, that during the present War it would
" not assist either Party and promis'd not to
" lay down the Office of Mediation till the
" War was at an End, far from committing
" any Act of Hostility against the Emperor, a-
" gainst his Allies, or against the Empire" In
Consideration whereof, the Emperor offer'd,
as well for himself, as in the Name of his Allies, the reciprocal Sureties for the Guaranty
of the Treaty of *Westphalia*, in reference to
Sweden

I said before, that the Minister Mediator
ought to be disinterested as well as the Prince
who employs him Pope *Urban* VIII had nominated the Cardinal *Rossetti*, to discharge the
Function of Mediator at the Congress of *Cologne*, which was afterwards transferr'd to
Munster, but forasmuch as *France* was not at
all satisfy'd with his Conduct, on the Account
of the Correspondence he had had at *Brussels*
and in *England*, with the Queen Mother, *Mary de Medicis*, his Mediation was rejected, and
the Pope was oblig'd to recall him Cardinal
Alexander Bichi, was an *Italian*, a Creature of
the *Barberins*, and a Cardinal, that is to say
oblig'd, as well by Oath, as by particular Duty, to prefer the Interest and Advantage of the
See of *Rome*, to all the Considerations he could
have for his Countrey, for his Friends and Relations, and for whatever could be dear to him
in the World, so that it seem'd, as if the Republick of *Venice* ought to make Difficulty to
admit of his Mediation, in a Difference she
actually had with the Pope concerning the
Temporal, of which she is extremely jealous

Nevertheless she accepted it, as well for the
Knowledge she had of his Merit, as because
he acted by the Order, and according to the
Intention of *France*, which could not be suspected by her

The Count *Servien*, speaking of the Mediators who kill'd themselves at *Munster* with doing nothing, said, " He could not comprehend
" why *France* should make Difficulty to nego-
" tiate immediately with the Ministers of the
" Emperor and of the King of *Spain*, since he
" had always found a greater Light, and met
" with more Facility in Affairs in treating di-
" rectly with them, than when they pass'd
" through the Hands of Mediators That the
" Ministers of *France* had never made the least
" Concession on any Point, but the Mediators
" run immediately to the others, to communi-
" cate it to them, without improving it, or
" drawing the least Advantage therefrom for
" *France* That it was observ'd, that the Se-
" crets which had been intrusted to the Medi-
" ators, had been publish'd by them in remote
" Places, to the Prejudice of the Interest of
" the Crown That whenever the Parties
" charg'd the Mediators with any Saying,
" these only made use thereof to do the *French*
" a Mischief That there was Artifice in all
" their Procedure, in this, that they never dis-
" cover'd but a Part of what they were im-
" power'd to offer *France*, and even before
" they made any Offers, they would stipulate
" something or other, and that they never
" ceas'd speaking of the Complaisance of the
" *Austrians*, so far as to say it was necessary
" to hold them in, that they might not preci-
" pitously grant whatever the *French* demand-
" ed, &c That the Nuncio, one of the Me-
" diators, being a Creature of Pope *Urban*, and
" having a mind to ingratiate himself with the
" Court of *Rome*, cross'd the Intentions of
" *France*, the Prosperity of which giving a
" Jealousy to the Republick of *Venice*, there
" was no room to hope for any great Matters
" from the good Offices of its Minister, who
" was the other Mediator" *Servien* could not
say in plainer Terms, that the two Princes
Mediators were interessed, and that their Ministers were so likewise

Cardinal *Mazarine* himself, writing on the
same Subject to the *French* Plenipotentiaries in
the Year 1646, speaks of the Mediators in
these Terms, " The Ministers of *Spain* them-
" selves, says he, are not so animated against
" *France* as the Mediators They are jealous
" of the Affection the Elector of *Bavaria* has
" for the Crown, as well as of the Prosperity
" of his Arms They press the Count *de Peg-
" neranda* to conclude a particular Treaty with
" the United Provinces If the Nuncio ap-
" ply'd himself with Zeal to reconcile the
" two Crowns, that they might unite their
" Arms against the Infidels and Hereticks, he
" would do the Office of a true Mediator, and
" of a Minister of the Apostolick See, which
" ought to have no other View than the Ad-
" vantage and Augmentation of the Catholick
" Religion But that in labouring to procure
" all Advantages to the Hereticks, to invite
" them to a particular Peace, and in obtain-
" ing for the Elector *Palatin*, those they are
" for taking from the Elector of *Bavaria*, he

5 A " *neither*

"neither difcharg'd the Duty of a good Mediator, "nor of a Nuncio of the Holy See. That he "gave out, that the Nuncio at *Paris* had written "him Word, that the Queen's Intentions were "very good, but that they were poyſon'd by "the pernicious Counſels of the firſt Mini- "ſter, who juggling with *Servien*, oppos'd her "Majeſty's good Deſires. That the *Venetian* "Embaſſador could have no other Motive, "than the Thought with which the Repub- "lick was ſtrongly poſſeſs'd, of reducing the "Power of the two Crowns to an Equality, "capable of enſuring the Repoſe of *Chriſten- "dom*. So that it the main Points were but "ſufficiently agreed on with the Emperor and "the King of *Spain*, that it might not be thought "the Manner of proceeding was chang'd, in "order to retard the Concluſion of the Trea- "ty, he ſhould be *for laying aſide the Mediators "quite*, thereby to revenge the Wrong their "Procedure did to *France*.

To ſpeak the Truth, the Mediators had a great deal of Trouble at *Munſter*, but little Succeſs, and ſtill leſs Honour. Their Intentions were good, but they met every where with ſuch inflexible Obdurateneſs, that the ſtrongeſt Reaſons in the World were not able to ſoften. Being therefore oblig'd to ſpeak ſometimes in a lofty Tone, and particularly to the *French* Plenipotentiaries, who were for enjoying the Benefit of the Proſperity of their Maſter's Arms, they made themſelves ſuſpected by the ones, and diſagreeable to the others. In the Affairs of the Empire it ſelf, where Peace was at laſt concluded, the Satisfaction of the Crowns in Alliance (which was the moſt eſſential Article) was adjuſted without them, by the Offices and Inſtances of the Duke of *Bavaria*. The Intention of the *French* was to exclude the Mediators intirely, and they would have excluded them in effect, had it not been for the Apprehenſion they were in, that ſuch Procedure would confirm the Opinion People had already, of the ſmall Inclination they had for a Peace.

It may be ſaid with truth. That it is not the Mediators who make Treaties, and that it is the good Diſpoſition of the Parties which brings them to a Concluſion. The Peace which was made at *Munſter* between *Spain* and the United Provinces in the Year 1648, was not the Work of the Nuncio, nor of the *Venetian* Embaſſador, no more than that which was made ſome Months after, between the Empire and the two Crowns of *France* and *Sweden*. The Mediators did not ſucceed in that of *Spain*, tho' they had ſpent many Years to no purpoſe therein, ſo that the two Kings were forc'd to agree between themſelves, by the Mediation of two ſubaltern Miniſters, without the Intervention of the Pope, and of the Republick, and even without the Mediation of the Electors, who had offer'd it. *France* would have employ'd its Mediation at *Conſtantinople*, in order to reconcile the Republick of *Venice* and the Port, in hopes of ſaving *Candia*, in the whole or in part, but ſhe made her Peace with the Grand Seignior, when no body intermeddled therein. They were ſtrange Mediators, who in the Year 1660, concluded a Peace between *Charles Guſtavus*, and *Frederick* III, Kings of *Sweden* and *Denmark*. and the ſame may be ſaid of thoſe who were inſtrumental to the Treaty of *Aix la Chapelle* in the Year 1668, tho' all the Mediators did not fare equally well thereby.

Pope *Innocent* X. ſeeing one Day from his Window two Boys fight at boxing, would not ſuffer them to be parted. He ſaid they would leave off of themſelves when they were tir'd with fighting, and that the ſame thing would happen to the two Kings of *France* and *Spain*, who would put an end to the War when both ſides ſhould be weary thereof, without the Neceſſity of my body's being concern'd. The Plenipotentiaries of the United Provinces, who had a greater Deſire than thoſe of *France* to forward and conclude their Negotiation would not paſs through the Hands of the Mediators, but on May 5, 1646 agreed with the Miniſters of *Spain* to act without them, that they ſhou'd treat immediately between themſelves, and that the Conferences ſhould be held alternately, one Day at the Houſe of the Plenipotentiaries of *Spain*, and the next at that of thoſe of *Holland*, and that they at whoſe Houſe the Conferences ſhould be held, ſhould do the Honours of the Houſe to the others, &c. The United Provinces perceiving that the Mediators made no Progreſs between *France* and *Spain*, look'd upon them to be of no Utility to them. But when once a Mediation has been admitted, it can be no longer rejected, without a Deſign to offend the Mediator. Cardinal *Mazarin*, who, as I ſaid before, did not find his Ends with the Nuncio and the *Venetian* Embaſſador, wrote to the *French* Plenipotentiaries to negotiate without them, but *d'Avaux* ſaid, *That there was no excluding from the Mediation (without Scandal) Miniſters who had labour'd for three Years paſt there in*, becauſe it would make the World talk, and give it Reaſon to believe, that *France* intended to break off the Negotiation, at a time when it was thought that Peace was juſt upon a Concluſion. And indeed the Plenipotentiaries wrote to the Cardinal, *That there was no offering that Affront to the Mediators*, who not withſtanding their diſobliging Procedure, had done ſeveral good Offices to *France*, and that they would continue to make uſe of them as Perſons neceſſary, altho' they ſuſpected them. This had not always been *Servien*'s Opinion, but his Collegues were more moderate.

The Plenipotentiaries who were on the part of the United Provinces at *Munſter*, after they had adjuſted the greateſt Difficulties of their Treaty with the *Spaniſh* Miniſters, expreſs'd ſo great a Paſſion for an Accommodation of the Differences, which till then had not been able to be regulated between the two Crowns, that the *French* Miniſters gave them Leave at laſt, tho' with great Reluctancy, to employ their Offices, to try to bring them nearer to an Agreement. They made ſeveral Goings and Comings, but beſides that there was no Diſpoſition on either ſide, theſe pretended Mediators did not go about it as they ought. The Nuncio, who was vex'd that the *French* and *Spaniards* neglected him, to make uſe of Miniſters who had no Concern in the Mediation, complain'd thereof to thoſe of *France*. The Duke of *Longueville* told him, That they would receive indifferently from every body thoſe Offices that could any way contribute to the adjuſting of their

their Differences, but when they should come to join Issue, they would make use of the ordinary way, and would receive the Conclusion from no other Hands than the Mediators which makes it plain that the *Dutch* Ministers were not Mediators, altho' they did the Functions thereof, and that even with more Success than the Nuncio and *Venetian* Embassador had done, insomuch that there was a Likelihood that in a very few Days they would have made a great Progress therein, if *Pegneranda*, who was sure of the separate Treaty, had not had so great an Aversion for that with *France* His Obstinacy and Price cost the King of *Spain* the best part of the *Low Countries*.

I made mention in the Beginning of this Chapter of the Mediation *France* offer'd to the two Northern Crowns in the Year 1645 *Gaspar Coquet de la Tuillerie*, who was to labour therein, met with a very great Difficulty at his entring upon the Mediation, to wit, in the Jealousy might be taken from his first Visit in *Sweden*, as well as in *Denmark* He was Embassador in *Holland*, and could not go to *Sweden* but through the Kingdom of *Denmark*, unless he went by Sea, which was what he could not think of, and even if he did, he should be oblig'd to pass along the Coast of *Jutland*, and perhaps through the Sound The Queen of *Sweden* however insisted on the Embassador Mediator's paying her the first Visit He found the Means to get out of this Perplexity, by seeking the Friendship of General *Tortenson*, Plenipotentiary of *Sweden*, and Commander of the Forces of that Crown in *Germany*, He made him a Visit as he pass'd by his Quarters, and told him, That his Master's Intention was to use his Endeavours to put an End to the War between the two Kings of *Sweden* and of *Denmark*, thereby the better to enable the first of those Crowns to succour its Friends in *Germany*, desiring him to second, with his good Offices, the Letter which he sent by a Gentleman to the Queen, to beg of her not to take it ill that he went to *Copenhagen* before he came to *Stockholm* The Prince *Rodrigue* of *Wirtemberg* was gone thither some time before on the part of the Queen Regent of *France*, in order to do the same Office, but his Person not being very agreeable there, la *Tuillerie* was forc'd to have recourse to his Address *Lewis* XI affronted Cardinal *Bessarion*, because intending to do the Office of Mediator between him and the Duke of *Burgundy*, he had paid the first Visit to the Duke

The Abbot *de Branthome* of the House of *Bourdeilles*, makes mention thereof in his Memoirs, in the Life of *Charles* VIII, in these Terms Pope *Eugenius* having sent to King *Lewis* XI a great, learned and able Person of the Countrey of *Greece*, and Archbishop of *Nice*, whose Name was *Bessarion*, in the Quality of Legate, to mediate a Peace between him and *Charles* Duke of *Burgundy* This good Man, not being so much a Courtier as a Philosopher, and not distinguishing between the Grandeur of the one and the other, and between the Lord and the Vassal, went first to the Duke, from whom having receiv'd his Dispatch, he very innocently went to the King, who look'd upon the Procedure of this poor Philosopher to be very odd and strange, in visiting the Vassal before the Lord, and imagin'd he did it out of Contempt Nevertheless he lent a tolerable Attention to his philosophical Harangue, after which with a Countenance half angry, but accompany'd with a disdainful Smile, he laid his Hand gently on his reverential Beard, and said to him, Reverend Sir, *Barbara Græct, genus ret nem, quod habere solebant* and without any farther Answer left him there quite astonish'd, and by and by sent him word by some other Person, That he might retire, for he should have no other Answer nor Dispatch *Branthome* hereupon makes Reflections worthy of himself, and put afterwards the Question, Whether the Embassadors ought to go first to the greatest or the least of the two Princes with whom he is to negotiate, and handles it very problematically, after his usual manner I do not pretend to decide it, nor to give Rules for this sort of Visits Paul III sent *Alexander Farnese* his Nephew first to King *Francis* I, and afterwards to the Emperor *Charles* V Pius V, on the contrary, sent Cardinal *Alexandrin* his Nephew first to *Philip* II, King of *Spain*, and afterwards to *Charles* IX, King of *France*, without this last's taking it ill There is more Difficulty therein at present It is certain the Embassador ought to distinguish between the Princes, when their Dignity distinguishes them, and when there is a Competition between them, he must carry it so to the one, that the other may not be offended thereat, and that the Honour he does to the one, may not give the other any Jealousy Some Rules may be form'd from the Examples alledg'd in this Chapter

It is certain the Embassador, or Minister Mediator, ought necessarily to distinguish between the Princes he is to reconcile, especially if their Dignity distinguishes them Cardinal *Pool* not being able to obtain Leave of the Emperor *Charles* V, to pursue his Journey to *England*, would fain have gone into *France*, in order to sound there his Intentions concerning his Mediation, but *Charles* would not consent to it During the War about *Castro*, Hugh de *Lionne* had Orders to use his Endeavours to adjust the Differences between the *Barberins* and the Princes of *Italy* *Lionne* before he went to *Rome* to confer with the Pope, whose Arms, as well temporal as spiritual, might be said to have taken the Field, went to the Duke of *Parma*, as well because he was the most concern'd, as because he was in his way To excuse himself herein, he said he discharg'd the Office of Intercessor, rather than that of Mediator, so that it was necessary for him to know the Intentions and Dispositions of the Duke, who was Vassal of the See of *Rome*, before he could assure the Pope of the Submissions he was to expect from him Nevertheless, when after the Peace, which was concluded in the Year 1644, *Venice* had some Thoughts of sending an Embassador Extraordinary into *France*, to thank the King for his Mediation, *Gussoni*, one of the Deputies of the Senate, who was against this Expence, said, That the two Mediators, Cardinal *Bichi* and *Lionne* had been both at *Rome* before they came to *Venice*, whither one of them at least ought to have come before he went to *Rome*, whereas, on the contrary, the Republick had not seen them till they had concerted with the *Barberins* whatever they

they had a mind to. The Senate was not very well satisfy'd with this Peace, tho', as it had not acted with that Vigour which was expected from the Reputation of its Arms, and those of the Allies having been employ'd but with much Disorder and Confusion, the Republick could not hope for any great Advantages therefrom. She pretended to the Honour of the first Visit, because she maintain'd that she had no Difference to unravel with the Holy See, or with the Pope, but only with the *Barberins*.

I believe I may say on this occasion that in the Year 1625, Pope *Urban* finding himself perplex'd with the Affair of the *Valtelline*, sent the Cardinal *Francis Barberin* one of his Nephews into *France*, to endeavour to regulate the Difference between the two Crowns. The Cardinal did not meet there with any great Satisfaction, for which reason the Pope was for having him go to *Spain*, to see whether he should not there find a greater Disposition to an Accommodation, but the *Spaniards* protested they would not receive this Legation, because they look'd upon it as the Sequel of that of *France*, and this Opposition oblig'd the Pope to recall the Cardinal back to *Rome*, in order to send him from thence to *Spain*. And forasmuch as the *Spaniards* were not satisfy'd therewith, *because the Legate had been in* France *before he came to* Spain, it was necessary to find some other Pretext for his Journey, and give it out, That the Cardinal went thither only to stand for the Pope at the Christening of the Princess the Queen of *Spain* was lately deliver'd of. The *Spaniards* are not the only People who are vain enough to suffer themselves to be deceiv'd, and to deceive themselves by outward Appearances, which they and every body else knows to be false and ridiculous. When in the Year 1651, *Chanut* was at *Lubeck*, as Mediator on the part of *France*, he was ask'd whether he had his Powers. He answer'd, that he had, and that he was ready to communicate them, but that he would not give a Copy thereof to the Parties. I cannot tell whether the Powers are of absolute Necessity in this Case, because the Prince who employs the Mediator not being oblig'd to ratify any thing, it seems as if it were sufficient that the Minister verifies his Quality by any publick Act whatever, and that the Powers are only made use of because this Verification cannot well be perform'd by Credential Letters, which the Prince Mediator cannot address to Deputies, of whom the Assembly is compos'd. And that they were not formal Powers, appears by the Speech *Chanut* made at that time, wherein he maintain'd, That it was not necessary that they should be dispatch'd under the Great Seal, and that those Princes to whom the Mediation of *France* might be useful or convenient, ought not to be accustom'd thereto.

It must be observ'd that *Aloysio Contarini*, being Mediator on the part of the Republick of *Venice* at *Munster*, did not pretend to any Advantage, Prerogative or Precedency, on the account of his Quality of Mediator, over the Embassadors of Crown'd Heads, so that when he happen'd to be in a third Place, with the Nuncio and other Embassadors, the Nuncio took indeed the first Place, but *Contarini* took his only after these, and not immediately after the Nuncio. And on any Occasions, where the Princes and States of the Empire sent a Deputation to the Mediators, in the Presence of the Embassadors of the Emperor and of the King of *France*, the Deputies first saluted the Nuncio, and after him the Emperor's Embassadors and those of *France*, and the *Venetian* last. The Embassadors of Crown'd Heads do Honour to the Mediator, if his Master is of the same Dignity with theirs. At the Congress of *Breda* they all yielded the Precedency to the *Swedish* Embassadors. But as the Christian Kings consider the Emperor but as the first amongst them, the Embassadors who are on the part of the King of *Great Britain* at *Nimeguen*, *pretend that the Bishop of* Gure *and his Colleagues, Embassadors from the Emperor, should have the same Deference for them.* They say they have their Master's express Orders for the same, and their Difference will be by so much the harder to adjust, as there is no Medium to take, and they cannot therein submit to the Arbitration of a third Person, because not one King will refer himself to the Pope, and all the other Princes are interested. What seems most grievous herein is, left the King of *Great Britain* carrying it so high, should pretend to treat the Princes of *Germany* as the Emperor does.

Altho' the *Venetian* Embassador was consider'd and honour'd at *Munster* as a Mediator, yet nevertheless the Nuncio pretended that this Quality was only due to him, because the Catholicks had desir'd no other Mediation than the Pope's. He said his Briefs made no mention of any other Mediator, and that even *Contarini*'s Credentials express'd nothing more than that he should be aiding and assisting to the Nuncio in this Negotiation, and that upon the first Overture that *France* had made to admit the *Venetians*, these had employ'd their Friends at *Vienna*, at *Paris*, and at *Madrid*, to get themselves accepted. And in Fact all the Writings, Propositions, Answers and Replies were address'd only to the Nuncio, and he kept them at Home, it was he that communicated them to the Parties, and that alone sign'd the Answers. He never went to see the *Venetian* Embassador for Affairs of this nature, but sent for him to come to him. Neither did he suffer the other to sign any thing with him, and if he communicated any Instrument to him, it was only a Copy, which the Signature of his Auditor or Secretary, or else the Seal of the Nunciature render'd authentick, insomuch that he almost pass'd for the only Mediator with the Catholicks. The Plenipotentiaries of the Catholick Princes held their Conferences in the Nuncio's House, having first obtain'd from him the Hour of their Audience or Visit, at which the *Venetian* Embassador was present also; this last came likewise to the Nuncio's, when they were to visit together the Plenipotentiaries of the Crown'd Heads. It was observ'd that the Embassador of *Venice* had been above eight hundred times at the Nuncio's House, who said, that he acted thus by way of Precaution, to the end, that in Affairs of that Importance he might have an unexceptionable Witness of his Actions, as well as of his Words, against the Equivocations of the Parties, and against

The EMBASSADOR and his FUNCTIONS. 369

against the Doubts that might be had of his Sincerity. What I have now said *of the Nuncio's Brief, and of the Venetian Embassador's Credentials*, confirms what I had observ'd before, that the Powers are not absolutely necessary to a Mediator, since these two Ministers had none.

The Word Mediator sufficiently expresses his Function, which consists properly in putting himself in the middle, to bring the Parties at Variance nearer together; whereof I shall here give a very singular Instance. I have already spoken several times of the Mediation *France* offer'd to the two Northern Crowns in the Year 1644. La *Tuillerie* having oblig'd the two Kings, in the beginning of the following Year, to send their Commissioners to *Bremsebro*, on the Frontiers of the two Kingdoms, made both sides consent to the lodging their Powers in his Hands, to be communicated by him to the Parties: That in case the Powers were found good and sufficient, the Deputies of *Sweden* and of *Denmark* should meet in the middle of the Bridge which makes the Frontier of the two Kingdoms, and should take one another by the Hand. After the Powers were approv'd and exchang'd, the Embassador Mediator made them agree on the Terms they should make use of in their Complement at their first Interview. This being done, the *Swedish* Deputies came within half a League of *Bremsebro*, and the *Danes* to *Christianople*, and forasmuch as these (who according to Custom ought, as the first Comers, to have acquainted the others therewith) fail'd therein, the *Sweder* supply'd it, by notifying to the *Danes*, that they should be at *Bremsebro* at half an Hour after one of the Clock in the Afternoon. The Tents of the ones and of the others were pitch'd at both Ends of the Bridge, and *la Tuillerie* having plac'd himself in the middle of the Bridge, by a Stone which denotes the Frontiers of the two Kingdoms, put himself in the middle of the four Embassadors of the United Provinces, who were there also as Mediators, and as the Gout hinder'd him from going himself to fetch the Deputies, to bring them to this Stone, and also because he did not know which of the two he should fetch first, he caus'd a Trumpet to be founded, and at this Signal all the Deputies came out of their Tents at the same time, and march'd to the middle of the Bridge, counting their Steps, &c. After this first Interview the Mediators went backwards and forwards between the Parties, receiv'd and communicated the Propositions and Answers, and at last brought the Treaty to a Conclusion.

The Emperor's Ministers, and those of the two Kings of *France* and *Spain*, having agreed at *Munster* of the manner of treating, they, on *December* 4, 1644, put their first Demand into the Hands of the Mediators, to whom those of *Spain* signify'd on the same Day, that if the Proposition of the *French* was not conformable to theirs, and that they had no other Intention than to talk of certain Preliminaries, there was no occasion to do any more than to send them back those they had given in, without communicating them to the *French* Plenipotentiaries. Whereupon the Mediators went to the *Spanish* Plenipotentiaries, where those

from the Emperor happen'd to be also, and told them, "That it did not belong to them to
"judge of the Propositions: That the Office of
" Mediation permitted them only to make a
" faithful Report of what was told them, with-
" out adding any thing of their own, except
" Exhortations to do what is just and reasona-
" ble. But as for the making a Judgment of
" the Equity and Justice of the Propositions,
" or to say which Propositions would be pro-
" perest to forward the Treaty, that that ex-
" ceeded the Power of their Employment.
" That it was absolutely necessary their Pro-
" positions should be communicated to the
" *French*, or else that they should all be restor'd
" on both sides.

If the Mediators are requir'd by one of the Parties to make a Proposition to the other, they ought to make no Difficulty therein, how grievous soever it might be. In the Beginning of the Year 1646, the Plenipotentiaries of *France* urg'd the Mediators to demand a Passport of the *Spanish* Ministers for the Embassadors of *Portugal*, and the Liberty of *Don Duarte* of *Braganca*. The Mediators knew that this Proposition would be ill receiv'd, but that did not hinder them from making it to the Count *de Pegneranda*, and whereas this gave a loose to his Passion as soon as the Nuncio began to mention *Portugal*, *Contarini*, who on his part easily took Fire, told him, "That it was not
" the way to negotiate to give way to such
" Transports: That the Office of Mediator
" oblig'd them to report punctually the Propo-
" sition the other had charg'd them with, and
" as they should make no Scruple to demand
" the City of *Paris* of the *French*, it the *Spaniards*
" desir'd it, so neither would they make any
" Difficulty to ask *Madrid* of the *Spaniards*, if
" the *French* requir'd them so to do.

The Instructions the Court of *Rome* gave to Cardinal *Ginetti*, when it sent him in the Quality of Legate Mediator to the Congress at *Cologne*, are very considerable. For besides that they inform him particularly of all the Affairs which were there to be discuss'd, where almost all *Europe* was concern'd, they instruct him perfectly in all he was to do in that Quality. They recommend to him first, and above all things, Indifferency, without which all his Offices would be useless, in which the Legate ought to be so exact that not only no Partiality should be discover'd in his Conduct, but also that none should be observable either in the Actions or Words of his Domesticks. 2. That he should not make any Proposition, because he might make such as might not be agreeable to one of the Parties, and by that Mean would become suspected and of no Utility, and that he should content himself with making a faithful Report of what should be told him. 3. That in the Contest between two equal Powers, where neither is willing to make the first Proposition, because that shews some Weakness or Deference, the Mediator ought to oblige them both to deliver their Propositions to him at the same time. 4. That he must endeavour to acquire the Confidence of the Parties, that they may discover to him their true Sentiments. 5. That he be secret, and communicate to either Party but what the other would have him. 6. That he do not take upon him any Arbitration, nor

5 B   suffer

suffer any to be put upon the Pope, because then instead of Mediator he would become Judge 7 That he do not dispatch any Courier to either of the Princes interested because if that Prince cannot consent to what is desir'd of him, he will be angry that an Express was sent him, but let him cause the Ministers themselves to send him, and that he write by the same Hand to the Nuncio who resides with the Prince, that he may discharge that Office 8 That he decline as much as may be any Jealousy or Umbrage he might give by sending in Express to the Pope 9 They recommend to him Moderation and Patience

Princes do not always accept the Mediation is offer'd them Of which I have before given an Example, where the King of *England* refus'd that of the Elector of *Brandenburg*, because this was interested The Emperor's Plenipotentiaries, and the Ministers of *Denmark*, considering that the King of *Denmark* could no longer do the Office of Mediator, after the Rupture between the two *Northern* Crowns, *Contarini* represented to the Ministers of *France*, that it was necessary to substitute another Mediator in his Place, because the *Swedes* not having any at *Osnaburg*, they could not carry on their Negotiation, which also put a Stop to that which was to be at *Munster*, since according to the preliminary Treaty, *France* and *Sweden* were to go the same Pace Upon this Difficulty it was propos'd to perform the Mediation of *Osnaburg* by the Republick of *Venice* but the Emperor would not consent thereto, and excluded *Contarini* The Pretext was, that he would not disoblige the King of *Denmark*, who might reassume the Mediation, after the Peace should be concluded in the *North*, but the true reason was, that the Emperor would not have any Mediator between him and the Protestant Princes, because he pretended to treat them as his Subjects

The States of the United Provinces, when they sent their Plenipotentiaries to *Munster* commanded them to avoid the Occasions which might oblige them to negotiate by the means of the Mediators, and that if any Difference chanc'd to arise, which they could not regulate with the *Spaniards* immediately, they might apply themselves to the *French* Embassadors, or else to that of *Venice*, and discourse with them about it by the way of Conversation, That like Mediators they might propose some Means of Accommodation But for the rest, that they should always meet together with the *Spanish* Ministers directly, at the Town house, or in some other publick Place, without Mediators and there take one side of the Table, leaving the *Spaniards* the Choice of the other I take notice elsewhere that they met alternately at their own Houses

Cardinal *Francis Barberin* was sent into *France* in the Year 1625, to endeavour to accommodate the Difference that was between the two Crowns about the *Valteline* He did nothing in it because the King insisted, that according to the Treaty of *Madrid*, the *Valteline* should be restor'd to the *Grisons*, with all the Rights of Superiority which they had there, before the Insurrection of those of the Valley In the Year 1626, the same Cardinal went into *Spain*, with a Design to bring there to a good Issue the Mediation, which had not succeeded in *France*, but the *Spaniards* despis'd or neglected him so much, that they concluded the Treaty of *Monçon*, after the Legate was already arriv'd in *Spain*, but to the end he might not think they had any Intention to affront him they antedated the Treaty wherein he had no Concern

A Peace being concluded between *France* and *England* in the Year 1629, the Instruments thereof on both sides were put into the Hands of some Embassadors, who had been concern'd there in his Peace makers, and not as Mediators, to keep them by way of Deposition, till the Ratifications should be exchang'd It cannot be said neither, that the Archbishop of *Pisa* Embassador from the Great Duke of *Tuscany* at *Madrid*, was a Mediator, notwithstanding *Bassompierre* and *du Fargis*, Embassadors from *France*, suffer'd him to assist at the Conferences, in order to discharge the Office of Pacifier of the Differences the *French* Embassadors might have with the *Spanish* Commissioners The Great Duke had not offer'd his Mediation, neither had it been accepted of in *France*, and to speak the Truth it was not very necessary, considering the Disposition the *Spaniards* were in to satisfy the *French*, by granting them a Treaty they had no mind to execute He Embassadors made a bold Step in admitting the Embassador of *Tuscany* to the Conferences without an express Order from their Court altho' they were persuaded of the Intention of a Minister, whose Master had an Interest not to have the Repose of *Italy*, disturb'd on the account of the *Valteline*

The King of *Sweden*, *Charles Gustavus*, could not or that the States of the United Provinces should intervene as Mediators, in the Treaty they were for having him make with the King of *Denmark*, not after his own Way, but conformably to the Intention of *France*, *England*, and the said United Provinces, who had all erected themselves as Mediators, That a Treaty might be made which should hinder the King of *Sweden* from ruining his Grandeur on the Ruins of the King of *Denmark* He told the Embassadors of the States, that he rejected their Mediation, that he look'd upon them as his Enemies, and that he might perhaps treat them as such *France* and *England* had indeed an Interest to oppose the vast Designs of the King of *Sweden*, but yet they meddl'd but faintly, and would rather have declar'd for him than for the King of *Denmark* so that we must believe that had it not been for the Loss of the Battel of *Funen*, which very much mortify'd the King of *Sweden*, if it was not the real Cause of his Death, their Mediation would not have produc'd the Effect it did utter his Death It was not without Reluctancy and Regret that the King of *France* admitted of the Mediation of *England*, *Sweden* and of the United Provinces in the Year 1668 And it is very probable he would not have admitted thereof if he had not been assur'd that he should be allow'd by the Treaty to keep all the Conquests he had made, and had a mind to make When he enter'd the Low Countries in the Year 1667, he had protested that he had no other Intention than to pursue the Rights of the Queen
his

his Wife, and to put himself in Possession of what accru'd to him by the Devolution, or of an Equivalent And this is what he obtain'd by the Treaty of *Aix la Chapelle* As for the Choice he left to the *Spaniards*, these got no Advantage at all thereby, because in yielding to *France* the Places she desir'd, they enlarg'd and cover'd the Frontiers of that Kingdom, and by leaving him the Towns he had conquer'd, they impair'd their own Frontiers, and gave the *French* Entrance into their Countrey, even to the Heart of *Brabant*, and to the very Gates of *Brussels* It is true, that in all this, as well as in the tripple Alliance, and in the defensive Alliance, which was since concluded between *England* and the United Provinces, there is something so odd, and so mysterious, that it is very hard to unravel

CHAP. XII.

Of Treaties.

IT is none of the Embassador's Business to inform himself, whether the Prince, who commands him to make a Treaty, can oblige his Successor to the Execution thereof He has nothing to do but to pursue his Orders, and to keep within the Bounds of his Instructions and Powers I shall not therefore enter into the Examination of this Question, but shall only say, That, according to the Opinion of *Bodin*, the King of *France* cannot in any manner oblige his Successor to the Execution of the Treaties he shall make during his Reign He grounds his Position on this Principle, That the King, altho' he be the most absolute of all the Monarchs in *Christendom*, is only a Tenant or Usufructuary of his Kingdom, and so his Power ends with his Life That his Successor not being call'd to the Crown by the Will, nor by the Disposal of his Predecessor, but succeeding thereto in his own Right, by virtue of the fundamental Law of the Kingdom, he is not oblig'd to follow his Sentiments, to the Prejudice of that Liberty which his Predecessor cannot take from him Upon this Maxim two Conclusions may be form'd, and in my Opinion very pertinent ones The first is, That whatever Treaties Princes make, they subsist no longer, (even amongst the most Religious, and most Jealous of their Word) than during their Life The other Conclusion is, That if the Kings, who are Usufructuaries, cannot oblige their Successors and Heirs, those who have the Management of Affairs in an Aristocratical or Democratical State, not for Life, nor as Usufructuaries, but only for a certain time, and as Administrators by Election, can much less oblige their Posterity, that is to say, those who succeed them in their Functions, either during their Life, or after their Decease, but they are oblig'd to leave Affairs in the State, where they found them, and to their Successors the intire Liberty of Deliberations, as they receiv'd it from their Ancestors However, it is daily seen that Princes and Republicks oblige themselves every Day in Treaties, as well for themselves as for their Heirs and Successors The Renovations of Alliance, which were made with the *Swiss Cantons* in the Reign of *Henry* IV, and within some Years with the present King, extend themselves to the Decease of their Successor, and even beyond it, and those Treaties, which one may say are to subsist but three Days, speak of a Friendship and Confederacy, which is to be perpetual between the Kings and their Children, born and to be born, their Successors and Heirs, Kingdoms and States, &c The *Pyrenean* Treaty may serve for an Example thereof But this is what the Embassador ought not to be uneasy at The Execution of the Treaty is none of his Business, the Conclusion only is what he can answer for, by taking Care therein of his Master's Interest

But I think my self oblig'd to say, That as the Contracts that pass between private Persons are founded on the Civil Laws, so the Treaties which are made between Sovereigns are founded on the *Law of Nations* So that it would be ridiculous to desire the Rescision thereof, for the same Causes, for which the Civil Law restores the private Person, who is injur'd, to the State he was in before the Contract I shall add farther, That Princes make no Treaties but with this tacit Condition, That they will observe them no longer than they can do it without prejudicing their Interest Their Intention is to extract all the Profit thereof, and to leave all the Inconveniencies, and all the Danger, to their Companion if they can It was not long that King *Henry* IV had made a very strong Alliance with the Queen of *England*, and the States of the United Provinces, when he lent an Ear to the Overtures the Pope caus'd to be made to him for a Peace, which was afterwards concluded at *Vervins* Clement VIII, talking one Day of this Affair to *Dossat*, about the beginning of the Year 1597, that is to say, a very few Months after the Alliance was concluded with the Queen of *England*, he told him, That the King, who had made an Oath to an Heretick, had another Oath to God, and to him the Pope He added thereto, that *Francis Mary*, Duke of *Urbin*, was us'd to say, That a simple Gentleman, or a Nobleman who was no Sovereign, could not break his Word without sullying his Honour and Reputation, but that Sovereign Princes could, for Reasons of State, make Treaties and break them, make Alliances and leave them, lye, betray, and do all the like things, without prejudicing their Honour I know not whether the Pope had much, in alledging this fine Maxim of the Duke of *Urbin* It was not *Henry* IV's Principle, but he represented to the Queen, by *Hurault de Maisse*, his Embassador, that the State of his Kingdom not permitting

permitting him to continue a War which would be ruinous to his Subjects, he was of Opinion that it no less concern'd his Allies than himself, that he should take Care of his Preservation, to the End, that after he had settled his own Affairs, he might be able to give his Friends that Assistance which they ought to promise themselves from his good Will, and assur'd her that the Peace he was going to make would be as beneficial and useful to his Allies, as it was necessary to his Kingdom. The French Embassador added hereto what I just observ'd of the tacit Condition, which is inseparable from all the Treaties and Alliances of Princes. The Reason hereof is, That Princes have an Obligation to their Subjects, which is beyond Comparison much stronger, than that they enter into by any Alliance, How strict soever it may be. It may again be said, That it is much better to put an end to the Alliance by a separate Treaty, provided Baseness and Perfidy do not mingle therein, than to suffer an Ally to be destroy'd by a powerful Enemy. But to renounce a formal Treaty without Necessity, and to declare loudly that one will not execute it, is to offend the publick Faith, and to subvert the Foundations of all the Commerce Princes are oblig'd to entertain among themselves.

Count *Eric Oxenstiern*, who afterwards succeeded his Father in the Office of Chancellor of *Sweden*, discoursing one Day with the Resident of *Denmark*, on the Subject of the War the United Provinces had with the *English*, told him, That indeed there were I readies which seem'd to oblige the Crown of *Sweden* to assist the *Hollanders* against the Parliamentarians of *England*. That when they were made, the times requir'd it, but that Affairs were very much alter'd since. The Chancellor said the same to the *French* Resident, who was for recommending to him the Interest of the United Provinces. The late King of *Sweden* did not fear saying, That he did not know what kind of Animal a Treaty was. And to speak the truth, considering how the Parties have behav'd themselves since the triple Alliance, which was concluded in the Year 1668, between *England*, *Sweden*, and the United Provinces, it must be confess'd that Princes observe Treaties but as far as they please, and that it is Interest or Whim, and not Honesty of Principle, that guides their Actions. The Wax and Parchment do not bind faster than a Chain of Straw, and they seem to glory in out-doing the *Florentin* Politician, in all he says, concerning the most pernicious Maxims of the worst of Men. It is not my Design to speak here of the Intentions and Sentiments of Princes, but only of the manner how they cause Treaties to be made by their Embassadors.

When I speak of Treaties, I comprehend therein the preliminary ones, which often give more trouble, and take up more time, than is employ'd in adjusting the Differences themselves. The Town of *Hamburg* saw, for seven Years together, Ministers who had nothing else to do but to regulate the Time and Place of the Congress, and the Passports of the Ministers, of which the Assembly was to be compos'd. I have spoken in the XXVIIth Chapter of the first Book, of the Difficulties that occurr'd concerning the Passports, there was not any about the Time, but they were whole Years a settling the Place of the Congress. The Pope *Urban* VIII desir'd that the Peace might be negotiated at *Rome*. The Council of *France*, on the contrary, was not for having this Negotiation transacted under the Pope's Eyes, and to avoid it, they said, it was impossible, because they were going to labour at a Peace, which could not be general, unless the Interests of several Protestant Princes were thereby regular d, who would not, nor could not send their Ministers to *Rome*. The Emperor, who was desirous to negotiate in a Place whither the Protestant Princes, and even several who were Catholicks, would not send, because he should by that Mean, become Master of their Interests, consented that the Treaty should be made at *Rome*, and promis'd to prevail with Spain to agree thereto. *France* having refus'd this Overture, the Emperor propos'd *Spires*, *Augsburg*, *Constance*, and *Trent*. But this Proposition was likewise rejected by the King of *France*, as well because those Towns depended on the Emperor, as because he judg'd it was against his Dignity, to suffer himself to be carry'd any way by other Peoples Sentiments, and especially those of the Emperor, who might have drawn Advantages therefrom, which *France* could not allow him. At last it was agreed, that the Catholicks should meet at *Cologn*, and the Protestants at *Hamburg* or at *Lubeck*. But forasmuch as the *Swedes* judg'd that *Cologn* and *Hamburg* were too far distant one from the other, and that the frequent and almost continual Communication of the Allies would thereby be much incommoded, by Reason of the Distance of the Places from the *Rhine* to the *Baltick Sea* side, they desir'd *M d'Avaux* to propose *Munster* and *Osnaburg*, as Towns equally commodious to all the Parties concern'd. The States of the Empire, who were at that time assembled at *Ratisbone*, approv'd the Choice, and the Emperor consented likewise thereto, tho' he would have been better pleas'd they had pitch'd upon *Spire* and *Worms*.

Some Princes have been very difficult on this Point, whereas others have not been so in the least. In the Year 1559, the Kings of *France* and *Spain* sent their Ministers first to *Lisle*, but the Constable *Montmorancy* refus'd to conclude the Treaty in a Town in Subjection to the King of *Spain*, because he would not have the World believe that the King of *France* had sollicited the King of *Spain*, even as far as his own House for a Peace. For which Reason the Embassadors of the two Kings met afterwards in the Abbey of *Cereamp*, and sign'd the Treaty at *Chasteau* in *Cambresis*, as in a neutral Place. During the War about *Castro*, the Cardinals *Donghi* and *Bichi* (of whom the one was the Pope's Plenipotentiary, and the other was Embassador Extraordinary, and Mediator on the part of *France*) discoursing about the Place, where the Ministers of the Parties concern'd might meet, to treat of Peace, *Bichi* said It would be proper to leave the Choice thereof to the Princes in Alliance, thereby to express some Confidence in them. But *Donghi* answer'd, *That the Negotiation ought to be perform'd in some Town belonging to the Ecclesiastical State, that the Reputation of the Holy See was concern'd*
there

therein, and that the *Princes* ow'd that *Respect to the Pope* The first thing the most Christian King propos'd, when mention was first made of accommodating the Difference he had with *Alexander* VII, on the Account of the *Corsican* Guards, was, *That the Treaty should not be negotiated at* Rome, *but in a neutral Place* And in fact the Treaty was fin (sh'd and sign'd at *Pisa* In the Year 1598, the two Kings agreed upon the little Town of *Vervins*, as a Place situated at almost an equal Distance from *Paris* and *Brussels*, and equally commodious to *Henry* IV, and to the Arch-Duke *Albert*, who had a Procuration from the King of *Spain* The Truce between the same Arch-Duke and the United Provinces, was at first negotiated at the *Hague*, but when it was to be concluded, the Deputies on both sides met at *Antwerp* *Bentivoglio* says, That the *Spaniards* insisted on the Treaties being sign'd in that Town, on the Account of its Reputation in the World *France* has made no Difficulty to negotiate, and to make Treaties for the Affairs of *Germany*, in *Germany* it self, at *Brwalde*, at *Ratisbone*, at *Hailorom*, at *Ulm*, at *Munster*, &c as for those of *Italy*, in *Italy*, at *Querasque*, at *Turin*, and elsewhere Nay she has condescended even to treat in *Spain*, at *Madrid*, at *Monçon*, &c

The Negotiation for the Peace, which was concluded between the two Crowns in the Year 1659, was begun in the Year 1656, by *Lionne* at *Madrid*, continu'd and finish'd by *Pimentel* at *Paris*, and in fine sign'd at the *Pyrenees*, that is to say, on the Frontiers of the two Kingdoms, and that, for the Dignity of the two Crowns, in a Place almost equally distant from *Paris* and *Madrid* To this purpose such exact Measures were taken, in an Island that parts the two Kingdoms, that each of the two first Ministers might say, That he treated in the King his Master's Territories, and did not yield the least Advantage to his Companion After the Invasion the *French* Arms made in the Low Countries in the Year 1667, and after the Alliances *England*, *Sweden* and the United Provinces made, to stop the Progress thereof, *Spain*, which did not despair of prevailing with the Allies to break with *France*, and had besides some Difficulty to consent to a Peace, to which it was in a Manner forc'd by the Arms of the Allies, stickl'd very much to have it negotiated at *Rome*, in the Presence, and by the Mediation of the Pope, or that the two Kings should send their Ministers to the *Pyrenees*, since the Matter in hand was the Execution of the Treaty which had been made there in the Year 1659 But *France* said, That it was an Affair which related to the Provinces of *Flanders* immediately, and so that the Treaty could not be made but on the Frontiers on that side, more especially since *England*, *Sweden* and the United Provinces concern'd themselves therein I shall here observe by the by, that in the *Pheasant* Island, in the Place where the two first Ministers met, there was a Table for each, the one of which was on the Territory of *France*, and the other on that of *Spain*, and each of them sign'd upon his own, but the Contract of Marriage was sign'd upon the Table of Don *Lewis de Haro*, because that Honour was due to the *Infanta*, whom the King of *France* courted

There is never any Difference on this Subject between the two *Northern* Kings, because most commonly the Deputies or Commissioners meet on the Frontiers of the two Kingdoms, or else in some Place which is at an equal Distance from both *Bremsebro*, where the Treaty between *Sweden* and *Denmark* was concluded in the Year 1645, is between *Colmar* and *Christianople* And if since that time Treaties have been made at *Roschild* and at *Tosturp*, and since that at *Copenhaguen*, it was because the two Kings were upon the Place In the Year 1651, the Ministers of *Poland*, who were to assemble in order to procure a Prolongation of their Truce, or else to convert it into a perpetual Peace, had great Debates concerning the Place of the Congress The *Poles* were for meeting at *Francfort* on the *Oder*, or at *Landsberg*, and the *Swedes* propos'd *Lubeck* or *Hamburg*, and they at last agreed to meet at *Lubeck* but nothing was done there, and the Treaty was not concluded till several Years after, at the Convent of *Oliva* near *Danzick*, as being a Place convenient to both

Those Princes between whom there is a Competition, make sometimes a Point of Honour of it but they who are above the Competition do not stop at these small Difficulties The King of *Great Britain*, whom the States of the United Provinces had courted even in *Whitehall*, to conclude there the Treaty of the Year 1662, offer'd in the Year 1667, to send his Embassadors to the very *Hague*, there to negotiate a Peace, and sent them in effect to *Breda*, where it was concluded, altho' the Town belongs to the Sovereignty of the States As soon as mention was made of renewing the Negotiation, which the carrying off of Prince *William* of *Furstemberg* had broke off at *Cologn*, the King of *France* offer'd to send his Plenipotentiaries to such Town as should be nam'd, out of *Germany*, because he judg'd by what had happen'd at *Cologn*, that there was no Safety for them in the Empire And in reality as soon as *Nimeguen* was nominated, he acquiesc'd thereto, notwithstanding it be the first Town of *Gueldre*, within the State of the United Provinces The Towns where these Kinds of Assemblies are held, ought to enjoy a perfect Neutrality, in reference to all Parties concern'd, that their Ministers may there enjoy the same Liberty and Safety, they would have at home After it was resolv'd that the Assembly should be transferr'd from *Cologn* to *Munster*, *John Crane*, Counsellor in the *Aulick* Council to the Emperor, went thither, and return'd to the Magistrate the Oath of Fidelity it had made to the Empire, (for the Time the Assembly should last) to the End the Ministers of the Princes concern'd might repair thither, go and stay without scruple, as in a neutral Place Which was done solemnly at the Town House, and an Act was taken thereof before a Notary

After the Princes have agreed on the Place of the Assembly, and that their Ministers are come thither, these sometimes start Difficulties concerning the Form and Manner of the Negotiation Whether it shall be perform'd by word of Mouth, or in Writing? If there be a Mediator, which shall first deliver their Propositions into his Hands? Whether the Embassadors fadors shall visit one the other? How, and where they shall meet, when they shall begin their Conferences? And how all things shall be accommodated, so that there be an exact Equality between those who have the same Character, and between whom there is a Competition? There was not formerly so much scruple on these Accounts, as there is at present Charles VIII having almost at the same time conquer'd and lost the Kingdom of *Naples*, and seeing all the Potentates of *Italy* confederated and arm'd against him, judg'd there was no better way to disengage the Duke of *Orleance*, who was reduc'd to the last Extremities in *Novarra*, than to make a Peace with the Confederates. The Preliminaries having been regulated with little Trouble, the Deputies on all sides repair'd to *Vercelli*, and met every Day in the House where the Duke of *Milan* was lodg'd. When the *French* Deputies came there, the Duke himself receiv'd them at the Gate of his House. The Dutchess came to meet them at the Entrance of a large Gallery, and then the *French* Noblemen, to do her Honour, march'd before her, and conducted her to her Husband's Appartment, where the Conferences were held. In the Room there were two Rows of Chairs, one for the Deputies of the Confederates, and the other for those of *France*. The first had at their Head one of the Emperor's Counsellors, who was follow'd by the *Spanish* Embassador, next to whom sat the Marquiss of *Gouzague*, General of the *Venetian* Army, follow'd by the Proveditors and Embassador of *Venice*. The Duke and Dutchess of *Milan* were seated after them, before the Embassador of *Ferrara*, who was last of all. There was none but the Duke of *Milan* who spoke for all the Confederates, and who caus'd Silence, when the *French*, according to their Custom, were for speaking two or three at a time. After Affairs had been discuss'd, and digested for some Days, and that they were in such a Condition that the Articles could be put down in Writing, the Deputies sent for two Secretaries, one of each Party, who wrote down what had been agreed to, each in his own Tongue, and after these had made an end of writing one Article, they read it aloud. In the next Session the same Secretaries read over again what had been fix'd in the preceding, that it might appear whether any thing had been chang'd or alter'd. This was the Practice till the Conclusion of the Treaty, and by this Means all the Differences were regulated in a very few Days. Before they began the Conferences, the Deputies of the Confederates oblig'd those of *France* to swear, they would treat *bona fide*, and with Sincerity, and to protest that their Intention was to make a Peace, and not to be double in their Procedure, in order to get the Duke of *Orleance* out of *Novarra*, and then to unsay what they had before agreed to. It was necessary here that the Confederates should believe the *French* to be honester People than themselves, since they referr'd themselves to their Oath, of which the *Italians* would not have made any great Scruple.

I was willing to remark these Particulars after *Philip de Commines*, to shew that we are not so easy in our present Time. The least Difficulties often become invincible Obstacles. In the Year 1651, there was at *Lubeck* an Assembly of Ministers from *Polana* and from *Sweden*, of which I spoke before *Chanut*, who was Mediator there on the part of *France*, met at first with so great Obstacles, that it was resolv'd, *the Plenipotentiaries of the two Crowns should not see one another, till after Affairs were regulated*. That they should all pass through the Hands of the Mediators, and that in the mean time the *Poles* and the *Swedes* should reciprocally pay each other a Visit of Civility. However this was not done, because the *Poles* refus'd to give the Quality of Queen of *Sweden* to Queen *Christina*, altho' she was in fact. In the Treaty of *Stumpsdorf*, where the Truce was concluded, for the Prolongation of which the Assembly of *Lubeck* was held, the King of *Poland* gave it her, and nevertheless the Ministers of the same Crown refus'd to give it her, in speaking of her. The *Poles* finding that the *Swedish* Plenipotentiaries would not admit their Visit without it, signify'd to *Chanut* that they would pass over that Consideration, and in speaking of the Queen they would expresly call her Queen of *Sweden*. Their Intention was to do nothing therein, and to deceive *Chanut* as well as the *Swedish* Ministers, but as they had to do with a skilful Negotiator, who div'd into their Meaning, he represented to them, that this base Piece of Cunning would occasion their receiving a gross Affront, for if they fail'd in what they had promis'd, the *Swedes* would not return the Honour the *Poles* had done them, in visiting them. The *Swedes* on their side would not suffer the Ministers of *Poland* to give their King the Quality of King of *Sweden*, and refus'd to admit of any Modification therein. It was therefore at last agreed on, that there should be no Visit made on either side, and they approv'd of *Chanut*'s Proposal, to see one the other at an Entertainment. But hereupon fresh Difficulties arose, because the *Poles* would regale the *Swedes* first, and these, who judg'd that the first Visit was due to them, as to the last Comers, pretended to have the Preference, as in effect they had by *Chanut*'s Advice. *Salvius*, who was the Chief of the *Swedish* Embassy, treated first all the other Ministers, who saw one another afterwards at several other Entertainments, where things pass'd well enough, but however they did not enter upon Negotiation in this Assembly, no more than in that which was held at the same Place in the Year 1653, where great Difficulties happen'd concerning the Powers, of which we have spoken in Chapter XVI of the first Book.

At the Congress of *Bremsebro*, the Ministers of *Sweden* and of *Denmark*, at their meeting in the Middle of the Bridge, which serves as a common Frontier to the two Kingdoms, saluted indeed the Mediators, but they did not pay any Civility each to the other, but were contented to take one the other by the Hand, as it had been before agreed upon, and after that both sides withdrew. This first Interview having pass'd in this manner, they deliver'd their Propositions into the Hands of *la Tuillerie*, and this was the Beginning of the Negotiation which produc'd at last a Peace.

At the Congress of *Breda* the Embassadors of all the Parties concern'd visited one another first of all with great Civility, in the Order they had come thither and after the Powers were communicated by the Hands of the Mediator, the opening of the Assembly and of the Negotiation was begun in the Castle on the 4th of *June*, 1667 The Ministers of *Denmark*, who had indeed the Quality of Plenipotentiaries, but had not the Character of Embassador, repair'd thither the first Those of the United Provinces follow'd them pretty near The Embassadors of *France*, who were lodg'd hard by the Castle, went after them, and a foot The Embassadors of *Sweden*, who were the Mediators, went thither in their Coaches, as did likewise those of *England*, who were the last At their Arrival at the Castle Gate they found the Governor, who after some Words of Civility, conducted them to the Appartments which had been prepar'd for them There was a particular Room for each Embassy, and one for the Deputies of the States General, but these assembl'd after that, as did also the Ministers of *Denmark*, in the *French* Embassador's Appartment as Allies, while the *English* were in their own All the Chambers answer'd to a great Room wherein were the Mediators, who went to the ones and to the others The first Conference lasted from Nine a Clock in the Morning till One in the Afternoon They observ'd no Order in going out, except that the last come went out first After this the Mediators reduc'd the Propositions of the Parties to certain Articles, of which the Treaty was compos'd, which was concluded on the last of *July*

All the Conditions of the Treaty, which was made between the two Crowns in the Year 1659, had been adjusted, and even sign'd at *Paris*, out to reduce them into the Form of a Treaty, and to concert the Execution thereof the two first Ministers repair'd to the Frontiers, where all Formalities were observ'd with that Equality which I observ'd before Cardinal *Mazarin* had with him *Hugh de Lionne*, Minister and Secretary of State and *Don Lewis de Haro* made use of *Coloma*, Secretary of State for *Spain*, who both enter'd into the Room where the Conferences were held, after the two Ministers had agreed to any Article that was to be put into Writing The next Day after, these two subaltern Ministers met at *Fontarabia*, or at *Andaya*, alternately, where they collated what had been agreed to in the last Conference, and then it was made a formal Article of the Treaty This was the Manner of Proceeding till it was concluded

The Treaties which are made between Princes who are not at variance are not liable to all these Difficulties The Places for the Assembly are indifferent to them, and there is no Competition on that Account The *French* have made Treaties in *England*, and the *English* have done the same in *France* The pretended triple Alliance, and afterwards the defensive Alliance between *England* and the United Provinces, were made at the *Hague*, some time after the Treaty of *Breda* *France* has also made Treaties there, as well before the twelve Years Truce, as since The Alliances the States of the United Provinces have made with other Potentates, have been negotiated, sometimes at the *Hague*, and sometimes where those Kings

resided whose Friendship and Protection they courted When these Negotiations are perform'd at the Hague, the States nominate eight Deputies of their Assembly, viz two of the Province of *Holland*, and one of each of the other Provinces, for whom a Commission is dispatch'd, or else a Power under the Great Seal After which they begin the Conferences with the foreign Ministers If the Minister is provided with the Character of first Representant, the Conferences are held at his Lodgings, but the Ministers of the second Order are oblig'd to repair to one of the great Rooms, or Antichambers of the States General, where they enter into Conference with them They are receiv'd by two Deputies at the top of the Stair-case, and after the Conference is over they are re-conducted back to the same Place This Civility is paid them at all the Conferences, and at all their Audiences, except the first and the last, for which they are fetch'd from home in a Coach with four Horses, follow'd by another with two, to which the foreign Minister may joyn as many more as he pleases at his own Expences I cannot find in History the Reason why the Conferences for the Negotiation of the Truce for twelve Years, were held in one of the Antichambers of the States General, which is still to this Day call'd by the Name of the Chamber of the Truce It is true several of them were held at President *Jeannin's*, who was Chief of the *French* Embassy, whither came the Ministers of *England*, of *Denmark*, and of some Princes of *Germany*, but there was not so much as one single one held at the *Spanish* Ministers It may be said they had not the Character of Embassador, because the King of *Spain* and the Arch-Duke were far from giving that Quality to the Ministers they sent to the States, whom they did not acknowledge to be Sovereigns but then it seems also, that after the Honours which were paid them at their Entry, they might very well have done them this also

At *Venice* the Conferences are held at the Palace, in one of the Senate's Rooms, which do not belong to the Doge's Appartment The Princes of *Italy*, who were interessed in the the War about *Castro*, having sent their Ministers to *Venice*, to agree upon a Confederacy to oppose the *Barberins*, the Senate deputed *Baptista Nani*, and *Vincent Gussoni*, to enter into Negotiation with them, and all the Conferences were held at the Palace After the Arrival of Cardinal *Bichi*, they were sometimes held at his House, but most commonly at the Palace

In *France* Embassadors and publick Ministers repair to the Chancellor's, who is the first Commissioner in all Affairs of this Nature, and who by reason of the Dignity of his Office never repairs any where else, except it be to the King's Palace Neither does he visit any Body, unless it be *Monsieur* the King's Brother, and the Princes of the Blood, and these but very rarely His House is consider'd as the King's, because the Seal is kept there One of the hundred *Swiss* Guards his Gate, and two of the Grand Prevost's Guards always attend his Person The late Mr *Seguier*, who seem'd to be born for this eminent Dignity, and who enjoy'd it above thirty Years, held at his own House, under the Reign of the late King, and under

under Cardinal *de Richelieu*'s Ministry, the Council relating to the Finances, or the King's Revenues, at which the Prince of *Conde*, first Prince of the Blood, did not think much to be present

In *England* the Conferences are held in one of the Council Chambers at *Whitehall*, or in some other of the King's Palaces When the Marquiss *de Rosny* went thither in the Quality of Embassador Extraordinary on the part of *Henry* IV, he had several Conferences at his own House with the King's Commissioners, who were willing to do him that Honour, on account of the Confidence with which the King his Master honour'd him

M de Bassompierre being come in the Year 1621 to *Madrid*, at the time that *Philip* III fell sick, could not receive his publick Audience, yet that did not hinder him from treating, by virtue of his Credentials which he had sent to the King Wherefore the Commissioners, who for that reason could not send for him to the Palace, went nevertheless to his own House, and there treated But the Count *de Benevente*, who was one of the Commissioners, refus'd to be there, and insisted on having the Conferences held at the Palace After the Death of the King, *Bassompierre* took his publick Audience, notwithstanding he had not fresh Credentials, but from that time all the Conferences were held at St *Jerome*'s Convent, or else at the Palace

In the beginning of the Year 1646, the *French* Plenipotentiaries, having a mind to negotiate with the States of the Empire immediately, without the Intervention of the Emperor's Ministers, signify'd to those of the Electors, Princes and Towns, that if they would send their Deputies to the Duke of *Longueville*'s Palace, they should have communicated to them the Reply the *French* would make to the Emperor's Answer The Imperial Ministers perceiving what was doing, represented the Consequences thereof to the Electors Plenipotentiaries, who did not require much Pains to be persuaded, that the Honour of the Empire was concern'd in that of their Masters Insomuch that they signify'd to the *French* Plenipotentiaries, that when the Emperor himself had any thing to propose to the States of the Empire in the Diets, he did not send for them to come to his Palace, but had them spoken to in the usual Place of their Assembly by his Commissioners or Representants That they were ready to be complaisant to the *French* Plenipotentiaries, but they were of Opinion, that they could not without wronging themselves, resort to the Duke of *Longueville*'s Palace at their simple Request That they did not doubt but the Embassador of *Venice* would make the same Difficulty they did, so that *if the Plenipotentiaries of* France *had any thing to communicate to them, they might repair to the Place, and at the Hour, the States of the Empire are accustom'd to assemble* That in the Year 1630, *M de Leon Brulard* had observ'd this Method in the Diet at *Ratisbon*, and that the Embassadors of *Poland* in the Year 1636, and those of *England* had follow'd the same Custom in the same Place in the Year 1641 Whereupon it was resolv'd that the Replies should be put into the Hands of the Mediators, to be communicated there according to the usual Method Here the Business was with the States of the Empire in a Body, that is to say, with the Deputies of the three Orders, of the Electors, the Princes, and free Towns but when the Plenipotentiaries of an Elector, or of a Prince, or the Deputies of a Town, had any thing to negotiate with the Embassadors of *France*, they made no Difficulty to repair to their Houses On the contrary, *d'Avaux* being come to *Osnaburg*, in order to confer with the Ministers of *Sweden*, and with the Deputies of the Protestant Princes, those of *Magdeburg*, of *Sax Weimar*, of *Saxe Lawemberg*, of *Baden-Dorlach*, and of some Towns, went to his o n House to talk to him, but all separat. y I think it may not be from the purpose to mention here a Passage remarkable enough When *George Frederick* Count of *Waldeck* went into the Service of the United Provinces in the Year 1672, as *Mareschal de Camp*, he had no manner of Knowledge of the Constitution of that State, where he pretended to be able to restore his Affairs by a Policy peculiar to himself He made no Distinction between the States General and the particular States of the Provinces, and not knowing what was the Power of the Council of State, nor what Authority the Magistrates have in the Towns, he had form'd to himself an odd Idea thereof In these Thoughts he undertook to regulate every thing, and to command, not according to Method and Custom, but as a Chief in War with the Staff, and imperiously Being one Day come to *Amsterdam*, where he had occasion to ask for something requisite for the Execution of a Design in the Neighbourhood, he sent to the Burgher Masters to come to him to the Inn where he was quarter'd, but he receiv'd for Answer, That the Burgher-Masters were us'd to assemble at the Town-house, and that if the Count had any thing to propose, he might repair thither, and they would give him Audience

By a particular Act, which was sign'd on May 5, 1646, the Plenipotentiaries of *Spain* and of the United Provinces agreed, that the Conferences should be held alternately at each of their Houses, and that they at whose House the Conferences were held, should do the Honours of the House

As for the Form of Negotiation it is very various, and it is commonly agreed upon in the first Conferences In the beginning of the Treaty at *Munster* and at *Osnaburg*, the Plenipotentiaries of *France* and of *Sweden* agreed, that each Party should pursue that Method it lik'd best These were for making their Propositions in Writing, and giving in the Reasons with which they back'd them The *French*, on the contrary, were for having only the naked Propositions put in Writing The *Swedes* desir'd also that the first Proposition the Allies should make, to enter upon Business, might be general, that is to say, that it might comprehend all the Articles of the Treaty The *French* oppos'd it, as a thing contrary to the Custom of *France*, where all the Articles are examin'd one after another, and all are agreed to before they are reduc'd into the Form of a Treaty Wherefore they agreed at last, that the Propositions should be made in the most general

general Terms could be thought of, because they could afterwards infert whatever Particulars they had a mind to

M de Baffompierre being Embaffador Extraordinary at Madrid in the Year 1621, wrote to the King his Mafter on *March* 18, that being ready to enter into Conference with the King of *Spain*'s Commiffioners, the Embaffador in Ordinary and himfelf had been of Opinion, *That they ought to except againft the Count de Benevente*, becaufe being Unkle to the Duke of *Ferra*'s Wife, who was himfelf Governor of *Milan*, and made the Affair of the *Valteline* his own, he would not in all Likelihood be very favourable to them in the Conferences, but however they judg'd at laft that it was better to bear with him than to offend by fuch Exception a great Nobleman, who was very powerful at Court It was very great Prudence in thefe Minifters not to irritate a Perfon of that Quality, but I cannot tell whether there was not full as much in not undertaking an Affair, in which perhaps they would not have fucceeded The Laws indeed allow Parties to except againft a Judge for certain lawful Caufes, but to pretend to regulate the Will of a Prince, concerning the Nomination of his Commiffioners whom he choofes amongft the ableft and faithfulleft of his Council, is what I can find no Example of and I am of Opinion that they who would undertake any fuch thing with Princes who know themfelves, would not be very well receiv'd

The Earl of *Carlifle*, Embaffador from the King of Great Britain to the Czar of *Mufcovy* in the Year 1663, not receiving any great Satisfaction in that Court, laid the Blame thereof particularly on a *Mufcovite* Nobleman, call'd *Pronchiffoff*, who was one of the Czar's Commiffioners, and difcharg'd with the Embaffador the Office of *Priftave*, that is to fay, of Introductor The Earl did not fcruple to accufe this *Mufcovite* Lord, in a publick Audience, of feveral Impoftures and Falfhoods, and endeavour'd to have him put out of the Commiffion, as a fufpected Perfon, and an Enemy to the Embaffador and his Negotiation But this did not hinder him from being maintain'd in his Functions, as well becaufe the Czar believ'd his Dignity was concern'd therein, as becaufe he was not at all fatisfy'd with the Earl's Conduct, who after that had the Mortification to fee every Day near his Perfon a Minifter whom he would have remov'd, but who notwithftanding was kept in againft his Will The *Spanifh* Embaffador made preffing Inftance at *Paris*, that he might be attended at his Audience of Leave by another Introductor than he who was in Waiting, becaufe, as he faid, he had been affronted by him but it was judg'd that they ought not to have fo much Complaifance for a foreign Minifter, as for his fake to difpoffefs the King's Officer of the Function of his Employment

During the Affembly at *Munfter* there were mighty Difputes about the Rank and Titles fhould be given to the Emperor, and to the two Kings of *France* and of *Spain*, in the Treaty, and in the Writings and Projects which their Minifters fhould communicate each to the others by the Hands of the Mediators The Emperor's Plenipotentiaries apprehended left thofe of *France* fhould renew their former Pretenfions, and that the King of *France* would precede the Emperor, becaufe the *French* had formerly maintain'd, that the Election gave him no other Quality than that of King of the *Romans*, and that the Imperial Dignity depended on the Crown, which the Elect was to receive from the Hands of the Pope, and that fince *Charles* V, who was crown'd at *Bologne*, not one of his Succeffors had endeavour'd to receive this Honour at *Rome* The *Spanifh* Minifters fear'd on their fide, left thofe of *France* fhould infift on having the Name of their King plac'd in fuch manner, that there could no longer be any Doubt concerning the Precedency The *Imperialifts* therefore confented, that there fhould never be in the fame Inftrument thefe Words, *The Emperor and the Crown*, as alfo, that after the Emperor fhould be nam'd therein, the Quality of Majefty which fhould follow, fhould be common to the Emperor and the King, who fhould be there mention'd with him, *and that in the Projects which the Plenipotentiaries of France fhould caufe to be communicated to thofe of the Emperor, they fhould fign in the moft honourable Place*

On this Occafion I fhall fpeak of the Signature of Treaties, where the Embaffador ought to be very fcrupulous in preferving the Rank that belongs to the Prince his Mafter At the Contract of Marriage which was to be between Queen *Elizabeth* of *England* with the Duke of *Anjou*, whereof a Draught was made in the Year 1581, the *French* and *Englifh* Minifters had fome Difficulty to agree upon the Rank they fhould obferve at the figning The *Englifh* Commiffioners, who had drawn up the Articles, had put their Names before thofe of the *French* Embaffadors, and thefe maintain'd, *That the Precedency was due to them*, as well in thofe Deeds they fhould carry away with them, as in thofe that fhould remain in *England* They faid it was what was due to the Dignity of the King of *France*, and that it was what had been obferv'd without Contradiction at the Treaty which had been concluded at *Blois* in the Year 1572 The *Englifh* faid, on the contrary, that in all the Writings they had prepar'd or exchang'd, even with the Emperor's Minifters, the *Englifh* Commiffioners had fign'd before the others, and that their Names preceded every where, throughout the Text as well as in the Signature That this was what had been obferv'd alfo with the *French*, and offer'd for this purpofe to produce the Original Deeds of the Treaties made between *Edward* VI and *Francis* I in the Year 1546, between the fame *Edward* and *Henry* II in the Year 1551, and that of *Chafteau* in *Cambrefis* in the Year 1559 "They " at laft agreed that the Names, Signatures and " Seals of the *French* Embaffadors fhould pre" cede thofe of the *Englifh* Commiffioners, as " well in the Marriage Contract as in the o" ther Deeds the faid Embaffadors fhould de" liver to the Englifh Commiffioners, and " that reciprocally the Names, Signatures and " Seals of the *Englifh* Commiffioners fhould " be firft in the Duplicates thefe fhould give " to the *French* Embaffadors And this with" out Prejudice to thefe, and on Condition " the *Englifh* fhould make out that fuch had " been the Practice in times paft in all the

5 D "Treaties,

"Treaties, except that of *Blois*, where the *English* acknowledg'd they had committed an Oversight, notwithstanding it was *Walsingham* who had negotiated and concluded it, who was not very much accustom'd to make any." In the Year 1596, the Duke of *Bouillon la Tour* concluded an Alliance in the Name of King *Henry* IV, with the same Queen, and with the States of the United Provinces, but when these Instruments were to be communicated and exchang'd, the Duke refus'd to receive that of the *English* Commissioners, because they had sign'd in the most honourable Place He said, that the King his Master was in Possession of the first Place, which had never been disputed him in all the Treaties which had been made between the two Crowns, and alledg'd amongst others that of *Blois*, which I before mention'd It is certain it had been the Practice, while the Kings of *England* were Vassals to the Crown of *France*, on the account of the Dutchies of *Normandy* and of *Guyenne*, and that they had never disputed the Rank with the King of *France* at the Councils or elsewhere So that there is no reason to wonder that *Walsingham* and his Collegues suffer'd themselves to be carry'd away by what was customary after so many Examples, of which we find a Collection printed by the Care of *John du Tillet*, chief Register in the Parliament of *Paris* But as in the Year 1581, the *English* Commissioners carry'd it against the *French* Embassadors, so likewise did they carry it this time against the Duke *of Bouillon*, who had Orders to yield, because the Queen's Friendship was necessary to the King his Master

This Difficulty was reviv'd in the Year 1624, on account of the Marriage of the Prince of *Wales* with the Daughter of *France*, and it was regulated after the same manner as above, after the *English* Embassadors had given a Writing under their Hands, which deserves to be inserted here in its proper Terms "We the underwritten Embassadors Extraordinary, Procurators and Deputies of the most serene King of Great Britain, &c to treat about the Marriage of the Prince of *Wales* his Son with *Henrietta Maria*, Sister to the most Christian King, do acknowledge and own, that in passing the Articles of the said Contract of Marriage, the Commissioners and Deputies of the most Christian King made Difficulty, and refus'd to sign two Copies of the said Articles, by reason we pretended in one thereof to put our Names first, maintaining that their Names ought to be prepos'd to ours, as well in the Instrument which was to be deliver'd by us to them, to remain in *France*, as in the other Instrument sign'd by them, and deliver'd to us, to be carry'd into *England* grounding herein on the Dignity, Prerogative and Preheminency of the said most Christian King whom they represent Alledging also that in the Treaty made in the Year 1572, at *Blois* on the *Loire*, it was so done and observ'd between the Deputies of their most Christian and most Serene Majesties To which we the above mention'd Embassadors of *Great Britain* answer'd and maintain'd on the contrary That as for any Writings which have been deliver'd by the Embassadors or Deputies of our said Kings or Queens, to the Commissioners of any Prince whatever, even of the Emperors themselves, the Embassadors or Deputies of our said Kings or Queens, have always us'd to prepose their own Names or Signatures, in the Writings by them given or their Parts to the Commissioners of other Princes, and that it so appears by the original Deeds of the Treaties, by them sign'd and deliver'd to the said Commissioners and Deputies of foreign Princes, even by those which were made in the Year 1546, between King *Edward* VI, King of *England*, and *Francis* I, the most Christian King, in the Year 1551, between the said King *Edward* and King *Henry* II, and in the Year 1559, at the Treaty of *Chasteau in Cambresis* in all which in their signing and sealing, the Commissioners of *England* have been prepos'd to those of *France*, in those which were by the said Commissioners of *England* given and deliver'd To which we refer our selves intirely for our Direction on this Occasion, and do agree to hold our Right by the same Whereupon it has been thought advisable that pursuant to the said Form, and ancient Usage by us alledg'd, the Names, Signings, and Seals of the said Commissioners of the said most Christian King shall precede ours in the said Articles, and other Deeds that depend thereon, which shall be given and deliver'd to us by them, as also that our Names shall precede theirs in the Deeds which we shall deliver to them, as we say it has been customary heretofore in the like Cases, without Prejudice to the Pretensions of the said Lords Commissioners of the said most Christian King And moreover on Condition, that where, by the said Treaties and Contracts heretofore pass'd between the Deputies of our said Kings and Queens, with those of the said most Christian Kings (excepting nevertheless the Treaty made at *Blois* in the Year 1572, which we say, if so it be, to have been pass'd through Error and Inadvertency) it will not be found nor appear, that the Names and Signings of the Deputies of our Kings and Queens shall have been put or plac'd after those of the Deputies of the said most Christian Kings In this Case, as well from this present as then, we consent and agree that the said Articles by us sign'd and deliver'd to the said Commissioners of *France*, shall be reform'd in that respect, and our Names and Signs postpon'd to those of the said Commissioners Under which Conditions, Charges and Reformations the said Articles have been respectively sign'd in the Form as above In Witness whereof we have sign'd these Presents the twentieth Day of *November* one thousand six hundred and twenty four Sign'd *Carlisle, Holland*

When they began to put down in Writing the Project of a Treaty the Crowns of *France* and of *Sweden* were to make with the Emperor and with the Empire, the *Swedes* did not fail to give themselves therein the most honourable Place Since the Reign of *Gustavus Adolphus*, *Sweden* had always acted in such manner with *France*, that there was not the least Inequality between the two Crowns in all the Treaties,

Treaties, and the Ministers of *France* had suffer'd those of *Sweden* to sign the first in all the Treaties they provided. But they judg'd also, that this ought not to have Place in a Treaty which they should make with a third Party, and which would be seen by all the World. Nevertheless as they would not offend *Sweden*, they consented that the two Crowns should do as they should think fit for the Preservation of their respective Dignity, in the Instruments they should give to the Emperor's Ministers, to the end there might be an exact Equality observ'd between them. But when after the Peace of *Westphalia* it was propos'd to renew the Alliance between the two Crowns, *Chanut* was order'd to secure punctually to *France* the Advantages which were due to it, and to yield nothing to the *Swedes*, who were very difficult on this Subject. It is true that all Kings are equal as to Dignity, but then they are not so in the point of Power, and there is nothing that can hinder one to be first in Rank, even among those who are otherwise equal.

There is hardly at present any Dispute about the Signature. In the Year 1642, two *Muscovite* Embassadors, who were at *Copenhagen*, press'd very much the King of *Denmark* to finish the Treaty, which had been talk'd of eleven Years before, concerning the Renovation of the Alliances between the two Crowns. But after all the Articles of the Treaty had been regulated, the *Muscovites* were obstinate as to the nominating the Czar first in both Instruments. They founded their Pretension on Example, and said, That it was what had been done in the time of King *Frederick*, Father of the King Regnant. The *Danish* Commissioners answer'd, *That it was a general Custom for every Sovereign Prince to name himself first in the Instrument he gives to the other*, and that if this had not been observ'd in the late King's Time, the fault must be laid on the Ignorance of the Secretary, who had made the Draught of the Treaty, from whence no Consequence could be drawn. And in reality it is what is observ'd at this Day between Sovereigns who are of equal Dignity; so that it admits of no Exception in reference to Crown'd Heads, who always observe this Equality amongst themselves, but not in reference to Republicks, whom Kings consider as their Inferiors, whatever Honours they may otherwise do them. The United Provinces have gain'd this Equality with the Northern Crowns, and they have likewise agreed it with the Electors.

There was some Contest about the Signature of the Treaty, which *d'Avaux*, *Servien* and *la Tuillerie* made at the *Hague* in the Year 1644. The Deputies of the States did not dispute the Rank with the *French* Ministers, but they were for having them all three sign in one and the same Column, and not in the same Line. They alledg'd, that at the Treaty of *Compeigne* in the Year 1624, the Mareschal *de Lesdigueres*, and the Marquiss *de la Vieuville* had indeed sign'd in the first Line, but that *Bulion*, who was the third Commissioner, had sign'd in the second. and that in the same manner *Charnace* had sign'd in the second Line, after the other Commissioners in the Year 1635, and that the Ministers of the United Provinces had sign'd in the first. But *d'Avaux*, *Servien* and *la Tuillerie* would not so much as hear it mention'd, and they all sign'd in the same Line, but in so small a Character, that the first Deputy had still Room enough left to sign. The Pretention of these was not well grounded, and the others Difficulty was of no Utility, because the Treaty being made from Sovereign to Sovereign, and all the Embassadors representing together but one single Prince or State, whether they all sign in the same Line, or in a Column, those in the first Rank were all in a more honourable Place than those of the second, by this Rule, that the last of the first Order precedes the first of the second. Neither do I believe that the Ministers of the United Provinces, who had sign'd the Treaties of the Year 1624, and that of 1635, imagin'd they had any Advantage over *Bulion* and *Charnace*. In the Year 1662, there were so many Commissioners on the part of the King of *France*, that they could not all sign in the same Line, but they sign'd on both sides in Columns, however I don't think that *M. de Ghent*, who was the first in the second Column, conceiv'd himself to be in a more honourable Place than the Duke and Mareschal *de Villeroy*, who was the second in the first.

What I have here observ'd will be easily illustrated by the following Example. At the Treaty which was concluded at *Breda July* 31, 1667, between *France* and *England* separately, the Mediators, *George Fleming* and *Christopher Delfiane de Dona*, Embassadors of *Sweden*, sign'd in the most honourable Place, and in a Column *D'Estrades* and *Courtin*, Embassadors of *France*, sign'd utter them in the same manner, and *Hollis* and *Coventry* the *English* Embassadors, sign'd in the Place that remain'd vacant, as the others had done. By this mean *Fleming*, *d'Estrades* and *Hollis* were upon the same Line, but neither *d'Estrades* nor *Hollis* pretended to have sign'd in a more honourable Place than Count *de Dona*, to whom they yielded Precedency as to one of the Mediators, and *Hollis* did not pretend to precede there *Courtin*. *The last Place of the first Rank is more honourable than the first of the second, and the last of the second is more honourable than the first of the third*. It seems therefore that the Dispute the *French* Embassadors had at the *Hague* with the Commissioners of the States was very needless. *Charnace*, in signing in the second Line, at the Treaty of 1635, sign'd nevertheless in a more honourable Place than that which was left to the first of the *Dutch* Embassadors in the first. There was something of Humour in it on both sides, and it seems as if the *French* Embassadors made a Point of Honour of it, only because the Commissioners of the States had a mind to make a matter of it.

The Great Duke of *Tuscany*, who had no mind to enter upon a Negotiation with *Dossat*, Bishop of *Rennes*, finding himself at last so much press'd thereto by him, that he could no longer put him off, fix'd certain Articles, which were agreed to on both Sides. But after they were reduc'd into the Form of a Treaty, the Great Duke refus'd to sign it, and said, That since the Bishop had only a Procuration from the King, he would likewise give one to *Vinta*, Secretary of State of *Florence*, who should sign for

for the Great Duke. *Dossat* would not acquiesce hereto, nor even accept the Offer which was made him, to have the Treaty sign'd by the Great Dutchess, and both Sides remain'd so obstinate, that the Great Duke comply'd at last, but on *Dossat*'s declaring to him, that the Moment his Highness should tell him positively he would not sign, he would mount his Horse and be gone. *Dossat* was in the right, because, as the Great Duke was there present, his refusing to sign gave a Suspicion of his Intentions.

There are a World of Remarks to be made on the Terms which are commonly made use of in Treaties, but as that would also prove an infinite and unprofitable Labour, I shall here content my self to make some, which, in my Opinion, deserve very well to be reflected on by the Embassador. First then, he ought not to suffer those Words of Form (which it concerns the Prince his Master to have express'd) to be compris'd or stifled under general Terms, because this Negligence affords Princes, who adhere rather to the Gloss than to the Text, the Advantage of making thereof an Explanation more conformable to their Interest, than to the Intention of the Embassador's Master. He ought not neither to suffer an essential Clause, or important Condition, to be made a separate or secret Article, unless it be there expressly said, That such Article shall have the same Force, as if it had been inserted Word for Word in the Treaty. While Queen *Elizabeth* was negotiating in the Year 1572, the Defensive Alliance which I before mention'd, she was for having it positively said therein, That the King of *France* should give her such Assistance as should be agreed upon, *even if she were attack'd for the Cause, or under the Pretext of Religion*. The Ministers of *France* said, That the General Terms of succouring the Queen, for any Cause, or under any Pretext whatever she should be attack'd, were sufficient, and comprehended also that which the Queen was for having expressly inserted. They moreover said, That if the Queen was not satisfy'd therewith, the King would give her a particular Assurance thereof, by a Letter under the Privy Signet, by a Brief, or else by a separate Article. But the *English* affirm'd, That neither the Letter, nor the Brief, nor the separate Article, did secure them, unless this Article were sign'd by the King, and dispatch'd under the Great Seal, as well as the Treaty it self. After very great Debates hereupon, the Queen order'd her Embassadors to have a little more Complaisance for the King, and to be contented with a particular Declaration. She did it on the Assurance her Ministers gave her of that Prince's Sincerity, who was the greatest Dissembler, and the most perfidious of all the Kings *France* ever had. The only Difficulty which so long delay'd the Conclusion of the Treaty, between the King of *France* and the United Provinces, in the Year 1662, arose from the *Dutch* Embassadors insisting on *the King's being Guarantee expressly for the Fishery*. The Council of *France*, who was unwilling to offend the King of *Great Britain*, maintain'd that the General Guaranty which was mention'd in the Treaty comprehended also this, and that it was not necessary for a superfluous Expression, which was of no Utility, to create a Quarrel with a powerful King, who was a Friend and near Relation of that of *France*, and it stopp'd here with so much Firmness, that there was nothing but the single Consideration of the Union the said Provinces might enter into with the House of *Austria*, that oblig'd the *French* Commissioners to give way, in a Point which they thought to be very nice and full of Difficulty. The three Embassadors, who were concern'd in this Negotiation, are still living, as well as the Mareschal *d'Estrades*, and they cannot be ignorant, that it was much forwarded by a private Person, who had no Concern in the Matter, and who nevertheless was very serviceable therein, tho' he was not very well rewarded for his Pains.

One of the Points which prov'd the hardest to adjust, at the Treaty of the Truce of the Year 1609, was the Continuation *of the Navigation, and of the Commerce with the Indies*, for which the Estates requir'd an express Article in the Treaty. The *Spanish* Ministers, and those of the Arch Duke, would not consent thereto, and asserted that the States ought to be contented with the general Expression, which allow'd the Commerce every where. But while both sides were so obstinate on this Article, that they were on the Point of breaking off, the Mediators, that is to say, the Embassadors of *France* and *England*, bethought themselves of proposing an Expedient, and to declare by a particular Deed sign'd by themselves, That notwithstanding the Commerce of the *Indies* was not namely express'd in the Treaty, yet nevertheless the *Spanish* Ministers had declar'd, That it was the Intention of the King their Master, to comprise it in the General Expression, but that the Regard to the said King's Reputation had not permitted it to be more particularly explain'd in Writing. So that the Embassadors Mediators remain'd Depositaries of the Words of those Deputies, and formally prom's'd, That the Kings their Masters should warrant the Execution of this Article, as well as of all the others. Those who have the least Knowledge of the Affairs of those Times, cannot be ignorant how much Pains were taken, to give a good Turn to the Words Liberty and Sovereignty, which nevertheless were the Grounds of the whole Treaty.

Likewise it is not sufficient that in a Treaty, one of the Princes concern'd makes a general Cession of all the Conquests the other shall have gain'd over him, but *it is necessary to express the particular Names of all the Towns and Places so yielded, with their Appurtenances and Dependencies*, which it would do well to specify also, if it was possible, and that in such Terms, as may leave no Scruple or Doubt in the Mind, to the end it may be known precisely what is pretended to be compris'd under the Word Dependencies, and in what they consist. It is what the *French* Plenipotentiaries particularly insisted upon, when, in the Year 1647, there was some Talk of signing some Articles which were to make part of the Treaty, which was hop'd might be concluded between the two Crowns. They said that the King their Master pretended that *Spain*, in yielding to *France* a Town which was the chief of a Castellany, or of a Bayliwick, yielded to it also all that depended penned on the same Castellany or Bayliwick, excepting those Places which were fortify'd, and wherein there was a Garrison. There can be nothing seen more exact on this Head, than the Contents of the 35th, 36th, and 37th Articles, and those that follow, to the 49th inclusively, of the *Pyrenean* Treaty. It was the Work of Cardinal *Mazarin*, who understood the Chicane of Negotiation better than any Man in the World. Yet nevertheless every body knows, that, after the Treaty of *Aix la Chapelle*, the *French* rais'd fresh Difficulties about the Dependencies of the Places which *Spain* yielded to them by the same Treaty, and that they were the Seeds of a new War, which was only delay'd because *France* had a mind to declare it against the United Provinces. *The Saluting of the Flag*, of which mention is made in several Treaties, between *England* and the said Provinces, was never so well explain'd in any, but it has been divers Times the Cause, or Pretext of the bad Understanding between the two Nations, till at last the Matter was so well regulated by the Treaty of the Month of *February*, in the Year 1675, that there is no Room left to cavil on that Subject.

The Embassador ought not to be less exact in causing to be set down precisely, and specifying the Succour, to which the Allies mutually oblige themselves. There are every where Examples hereof. In the Treaties made between *Francis* I, and *Henry* VIII, in the Year 1532, between the Emperor *Charles* V, and the same *Henry*, in the Year 1543, and 1548, and in many others, but particularly, and more lately, in those the States of the United Provinces have made with *France*, since the Year 1624 to the Year 1662. In this last the King promises to assist the States with twelve thousand Men at his own Expences, and the States, on their Side, oblige themselves to assist the King with six thousand Foot also, at their Expences, leaving to the Choice of the Party attack'd, to receive the said Succour in Men, Money, or in Ammunition, in the whole or in part. Likewise in the Year 1668, the same States made a Defensive Alliance with the King of *Great Britain*, where the Allies reciprocally oblige themselves to assist one the other with forty Men of War, whose Rate, Mounture, and Equipage, are there specify'd, and besides that, with six thousand Foot and four hundred Horse. The whole, at the Expences of the Party attack'd, who notwithstanding should not be oblig'd to refund the Charges, and reimburse his Ally, till three Years after the War should be ended. It must be own'd these two Treaties were very punctually executed between *France* and *England*, in the Year 1672. In the Alliance which was concluded at *Brunswick*, on the 22d of *September* of the same Year, between the Emperor, the King of *Denmark*, the Elector of *Brandenburg*, the Dukes of *Brunswick* and *Lunenburg*, *Zell* and *Wolfembuttel*, and the *Landgrave* of *Hesse Castle*, the Succour was regulated at three thousand Horse and six thousand Foot for each of the three first, at twelve hundred Foot and six hundred Horse for *Zell*, at a thousand Foot and four hundred Horse for *Wolfenbuttel*, and at four hundred Horse and eight hundred Foot for the *Landgrave*. Which I set down on purpose, that the Reader may observe the Proportion the Princes themselves settled amongst them.

The General Terms, which are commonly made use of to confirm foregoing Treaties, are not Precautions sufficient against the Artifices of those who are for eluding the Effects thereof, unless it be expresly said That they should be executed according their Form and Tenor, as if they had been inserted Word for Word in the present Treaty. And if in the preceding Treaties there be a particular Clause, or any essential Article, which ought to be inserted in the following Treaty, or that ought to be executed at its making, it cannot be neglected, without running the risque of losing the Effect of the first. On the 15th of *March*, 1638, a Treaty of Guaranty was sign'd at *Hamburg*, between *d'Avaux* and *Salvius*, Plenipotentiaries of *France* and *Sweden*, the 15th Article whereof bore, *That the same Article should be inserted Word for Word in the Treaty of Peace, which was going to be negotiated in* Germany, *and that such Treaty of Peace should be sign'd respectively by the Plenipotentiaries of both Crowns*. Which was however so far neglected in the Year 1648, that the *French* did not sign the Treaty of *Sweden*, nor the *Swedes* that of *France*. And this 15th Article not being inserted, neither in the one nor in the other, the Obligation into which the two Crowns were enter'd for the Guaranty was extinct. So that it was judg'd that, in the Necessity which oblig'd them to a reciprocal Guaranty of the Conquests they had made in *Germany*, it was requisite to make a new Treaty of Guaranty, which notwithstanding was not done till some Years after.

If it be intended that the Alliance should extend beyond the Life of the Princes who treat, it is absolutely necessary that the Words, Heirs and Successors, should be express'd in the Treaty, and it is not enough to say that it shall be perpetual. This is what *Chanut* maintain'd, when, in the Year 1651, he was concern'd with *Salvius* in the Renovation of the Alliance between the two Crowns of *France* and *Sweden*. On the other side, *Chanut* would not suffer the Words, *the King and Kingdom of* France, to be inserted. He urg'd that this manner of speaking would make it be believ'd, That the Kingdom could have or represent a Body separate from its Head, or that it could have some Distinct Right or Action. He farther said, That perhaps this had not been so scrupulously observ'd heretofore, but that he was oblig'd to be careful therein, and to hinder its being put at the Head of a solemn Treaty, and that too, at a Time when there were but too many who encroach'd upon the Regal Authority. *Salvius*, on the contrary, would have the Words, *the Kingdom of* Sweden, particularly express'd, as making a separate Body, and, notwithstanding he was a *German*, he could not bear that in the Treaty, the *Swedes* should be consider'd as Subjects; in so great a Submission as the *French Chanut's* Scruple partook a little of Superstition, and has not been approv'd, at least his Example has not been follow'd in the *Pyrenean* Treaty, which says, That there shall be a Peace between *the two Kings, their Kingdoms, States, Countries and Subjects*, &c. That is to say, That the Kingdoms, States, Countries and Subjects, shall enjoy the Peace

5 E the

the two Kings were making. Which is in my Opinion, the most natural Explication that can be given to this sort of Expression.

In like Manner, in the making a Treaty of Friendship or Alliance, it is usual to insert this Clause, *That this Treaty shall not derogate from preceding Treaties, which the Allies may have made before between them, or with others.* Queen *Elizabeth* says, in one of her Instructions to her Embassadors, who negotiated an Alliance in *France*, That it is an ancient Custom to comprise therein the Friends in common to both Parties, or the particular Friends of each Ally. But then it is necessary, that the Parties should explain themselves before the signing of the Treaty, because it may happen, that the one may be for excluding him, whom the other would have compris'd. Queen *Elizabeth* would not suffer the Pope and the See of *Rome* to be nam'd in the Treaty she concluded at *Blois* in the Year 1572. The 122d Article of the *Pyrenean* Treaty carrys, that besides the Princes and Potentates which are therein nam'd, all those shall be compris'd, who *by the Consent of both Kings*, shall have a mind to be comprehended within a Year after the Publication of the Peace. Where may be remark'd by the by, That the King of *Spain* caus'd to be comprehended on his part, the States of the United Provinces, but *France*, who remember'd, and will perhaps for a long time remember the separate Treaty of *Munster*, said nothing at all of it.

It is not very necessary, in my Opinion, to add to what I have here said, that if equivocal Terms and Ambiguities are troublesome in Conversation, they ought with much more Reason be banish'd from Treaties, where it is impossible to speak too clearly, and where such Words should be made use of, as do not leave the least Scruple or Doubt in the Mind, nor the least room for an Explication contrary to the Intention of those who treat. For as Distrust is the Mother of Safety, it is but too lawful, in the very bad, and nevertheless very true Opinion, which ought to be had of the major part of those, with whom Princes intrust the Management of their Affairs. It is what the Embassador ought to be by so much the more exact and nice in, as by giving a little Turn to a Period, and by putting a Word in a certain Place, it is possible to give it quite another Sense, and directly contrary to the Intention and Interest of the Prince who employs him.

In the Year 1607, the Arch-Duke had agreed with the States of the United Provinces for a Suspension of Arms, with a Design to treat of a Peace, which should secure Liberty and Sovereignty to the Provinces, as well on his part, as in the Name of the King of *Spain*. The King indeed acquiesc'd to the Suspension of Arms, but he would not consent to the Liberty nor Sovereignty, unless the States granted to the *Roman Catholicks* the free Exercise of their Religion, and renounc'd the Commerce to the *Indies.* These Conditions were impossible, so that the Negotiation which was on foot for a Peace, but at first with very little appearance of Success, because the Provinces insisted on their Liberty and Sovereignty, of which they had had formal Assurances. The Arch-Duke's Ministers said, That their Master could not renounce the Sovereignty, because the End of the Truce put Affairs again in the same State they were in before. The *French* Embassadors were for having these Words put into the Treaty, *The Arch-Dukes declare, as well in their own Name, as in the Name of the King of Spain, That they hold and acknowledg the United Provinces for free States and Countries over whom they pretend nothing, and in this Quality treat with them.* But the Deputies of *Flanders* chang'd the Period after the following Manner, *The Arch-Dukes declare, that they are willing to treat with the United Provinces, as holding and acknowledging them for free Estates and Countries over whom they pretend nothing, and in this Quality they offer to make a Truce with them.*

There are often very great Contests concerning the Titles. The Arch-Duke's Deputies would never permit, that in the Treaty of the Truce the Titles of *High and Mighty* should be given to the States of the United Provinces, and oblig'd them to be contented with that of *Illustrious.* The Embassadors who made the Treaty of the Year 1635, suffer'd to be put therein simply, *The States General of the United Provinces* whereas the Treaties of the Year 1608, and 1624, say, *Messieurs the States General,* and that of the Year 1610, *High and Mighty.* Those who have made Treaties since the Year 1635, have therein made use of the same Terms, till in the Year 1644, *d'Avaux, Servien* and *la Tuillerie,* being for using the same Style, the Deputies of the States oppos'd it, and obtain'd the Title of Lords to be let slip in. The States General, to whom most of the Christian Kings gave the Quality of *High and Mighty Lords*, do not assume it themselves, but they call themselves *Hoog Mogende,* that is to say, *Highly Powerful,* tho' they have explain'd themselves otherwise in the Titles they require foreign Princes should give them. The Quality of *High and Puissant* is so common in *France* that the Dukes, Peers, and Mareschals of *France* disdain it; and there is not any pretended Marquiss, who does not assume it in the Acts he passes before a Notary. The Ministers of *France* are very difficult therein, and sometimes too scrupulous. The same Embassadors of *France*, whom I lately mention'd, seeing that one of the Deputies of the States took the Quality of Counsellor to his Highness Monsieur the Prince of *Orange*, would not suffer the Quality of *Highness* to appear in an Act where the King spoke so that it was taken away, leaving simply *Monsieur the Prince* of Orange. In which these Embassadors had by so much the more Reason, as the King does not treat otherwise the Dukes of *Savoy* and of *Lorrain* and in speaking of the Dutchess of *Savoy,* his Sister, he only says, *Madam the Dutchess of Savoy*. But it is to be wonder'd at, that the same Embassadors should make Difficulty to give the Quality of *Messieurs* to the States General, while they gave that of *Monsieur* to the Prince of *Orange*, and that of *Messieurs* to the younger Sons of the House of *Savoy.* There is no Reason to be found for it but in the Irregularity, which is remarkable in all Acts of this Nature. The Marquiss *de St Chaumont*, Embassador of *France,* making a Treaty with *William*, Lantgrave of *Hesse*, on the 21st of *October*, 1630, takes the Qualities of *Most Illustrious, and Most*

Ex-

Excellent, and gives only that of *Very Illustrious*, and *Puissant* to the *Lantgrave*, that is to say, to a Prince who treated as Sovereign to Sovereign, with the King, who for Antiquity, might go upon the Level with the first Princes of the Empire, and who had had some in his House, before the Marquiss had had Gentlemen in his Family.

It is not the Business of a Novice, that of negotiating a Treaty of Alliance on the part of a Prince, who is already in Rupture, to engage therein another Prince, whose chief Interest consists in enjoying Quiet, and the Benefit of a Neutrality. I have said, that in the War about *Castro*, the *Barberins* employ'd both the Temporal and Spiritual Arms of the Pope, with which the Duke of *Parma* could not pretend to cope. The Great Duke of *Tuscany*, and the Duke of *Modena*, were his Brothers-in-Law, and the Republick of *Venice* beheld but with regret, the Motions that bid fair to disturb all *Italy*. *France* favour'd the Duke under hand, and *Spain* had an Interest to prevent a War, which was kindling in the Neighbourhood of the Kingdom of *Naples*, and which would not fail to communicate its ill Effects to *Lombardy* and the Dutchy of *Milan*. But the two Crowns, who were employing all their Forces in *Germany*, in *Flanders*, and on the Frontiers of *Spain*, could not succour the Duke but with their Wishes and good Offices, while the Princes of *Italy* were neither in the Humour nor Condition to declare themselves, for fear of drawing into their Countrey those Arms, which did not as yet threaten their Frontiers. It concern'd both the ones and the others to smother the Fire in its Ashes, before it set all *Italy* in a Flame, yet not one of them would declare. The Duke of *Parma* sent to *Venice* the Count *Ferdinand Scotti*, who was a very able Negotiator, who represented to the Senate, not only the Glory the Republick might thereby acquire, but also the Interest it had to oppose the powerful Arming of the *Barberins*, in the face of the whole World, to disperse the Troops which were gathering on the Frontiers, and to hinder the Fortifications of several Posts of the *Ferrarese*, almost under the Canon of the Places belonging to the Republick. It was neither the Interest nor Inclination of the Republick to break with the Pope, and thereby give Birth to a War, whose Consequences would be very dismal, as well as of long Duration. The Senate distrusted also the fiery Spirit, and the irregular Procedure of the Duke of *Parma*, as well as the Thoughts he might have, to bring foreign Troops to his Assistance, which was of all things what *Venice* apprehended most. Insomuch that the Senate before it engag'd it self, was for being sure of the Intentions of the Great Duke, and of the Duke of *Modena*, who had full as much Concern therein as the Republick. For which Reason Count *Scotti*, at his Arrival at *Venice*, found the Senate so little dispos'd to comply with the Duke, that far from obtaining an open Declaration, it did not give him the least Hopes of any Succour, either in Men or Money. All he could get from it was, that the Senate promis'd him to do him powerful and efficacious Offices with the Pope, but there were by so much the less Hopes of any good Effect, as the Pope, who was of an obstinate Temper enough, was become insolent, haughty and inflexible, after the Reduction of *Castro*. Nevertheless it was this rigorous Disposition and the little Consideration they had at *Rome* for the Intercession of this powerful Republick, which contributed most to the Success of *Scotti*'s Negotiation. In order to make it successful, and to engage the Republick, at least indirectly, he desir'd the Senate to send Orders to its Resident at *Rome*, to employ his Offices, that the Embassador the Duke his Master had a mind to send thither might be admitted. From whence the Duke drew this Advantage, that if his Minister was admitted the *Barberins* open'd an Ear to an Accommodation, and if the Pope refus'd to admit him, he thereby offended in the highest Degree, and irritated the Republick, which had Power from the Duke, to offer to his Holiness all the Submissions could reasonably be requir'd from him. The Nuncio *Vitelli*, who often took Audience at the College, endeavour'd to justify the Pope's Intention, and the Actions of his Nephews, and did not fail to exaggerate the Duke of *Parma*'s Obstinacy, who as the Nuncio said, did not shew any Disposition to humble himself, nor to give his Holiness Satisfaction. The Senate was very much offended at the Procedure of the *Barberins*, and at the Contempt they express'd for all the Intercessions and Instances it was continually making for the Duke of *Parma*, but it was also of Opinion that the Dutchy of *Castro* was not of so great Importance, that it should, for its sake break with the Pope, and trouble the Repose of *Italy*. It also made Reflection on the Indifferency of the Princes, who besides the general Interest, had also that of their own Houses, and who nevertheless did not declare themselves, so that it persisted with greater Firmness than ever, to refuse any Succour to the Duke, and to engage with him, expressing an Aversion to an open Declaration. The fear the *Venetians* had, lest Stubbornness or Despair should make the Duke fling himself into the Arms of some foreign Power, shook indeed, but did not overcome their Resolution; and it is very certain that Count *Scotti*, as able a Man as he was, would have effected nothing at *Venice*, if the *Barberins* had not spoil'd all at *Rome*, and if they had been wise enough to husband the Friendship of the Republick, and not to give it any Jealousy, as they did by advancing their Arms towards *Lombardy*. This Temerity extorted from the Senate the Declaration, which neither *Scotti*'s Ability, nor the Strength of the other Ministers Reasons could not have wrested from it.

I might here add something concerning the Treaties of Guaranty, but forasmuch as the Embassador negotiates them in the same manner as he does all other Treaties, I shall only say, that there is no Guaranty nor Precaution that can procure Security in a Treaty, unless the Guarantee and Guaranted have the same Interest. It was not without the utmost Reluctancy that *Charles Emanuel* Duke of *Savoy* consented to the Treaty which was made at *Ast* in the Year 1615, and he refus'd to ratify it, unless *France*, *England*, and the Republick of *Venice* would be Guarantees for the Execution of it, as they were, and that after a very extraordinary

dinary manner For the King of *Spain* suffer'd to have it express'd in one of the Articles, that in Cafe of Infraction the Marefchal *de Lefdiguerres* Governor of *Dauphine*, should have Power to fuccour the Duke with the Troops of his Government, and thofe of the neighbouring Provinces, without ftanding in need for that purpofe, of any frefh Orders from Court The fixteenth Article of the Treaty of *Ratisbone* fays, that for the better Security of the Execution of the Treaty, Hoftages fhould be given on both fides That of *Querafque* fays the fame, but as the Pope refus'd to charge himfelf with the Guard of the Hoftages, it was neceffary to have recourfe to other Means Above two Years were fpent at *Nuremberg* in regulating the Execution of the Treaties of *Weftphalia* During the Negotiation which was carry'd on in the beginning of this Century with the United Provinces, about a Peace which was afterwards turn'd into a Truce of twelve Years, the Eftates requir'd that they who were under the Obedience of the King of *Spain*, fhould remain Guarantees for the Obfervation and Execution of the Treaty Prefident *Jeannin* remonftrated to them, that not only this Demand was unjuft, but alfo that this Precaution was altogether of no Utility, becaufe Subjects act only according to their Princes Pleafure, and thofe cannot oblige thefe to act contrary to their Intereft and Intention The Emperor's Minifters made the like Propofition to thofe of *France*, during the Negotiation of *Munfter*, but *d'Avaux* and *Servien* faid that there was no Nobleman in *France* that was able to interpofe in the Treaty as Guarantee or Security, and that the Verification of Treaties which is done in Parliament, is only a bare Regiftring and a kind of Publication, to the end they may be executed with the greater Facility within the Diftrict of its Jurifdiction In like manner the Treaties that relate to Commerce, are regifter'd in the Parliaments of *Rouen*, *Bourdeaux*, *Rennes*, and *Aix* in *Provence*, as well as in that of *Paris*, on account of the Traffick which is carry'd on on the *Seine*, the *Garone*, the *Loire*, and in the *Mediterranean* Sea In the particular Treaty which was made at *Munfter* for the Intereft of the Houfe of *Orange*, feveral Prelates of *Brabant* were concern'd by the way of Sureties, but was it the better executed for that?

For which reafon the Minifter ought to be very cautious of obliging his Mafter to give any other Sureties than thofe of his Word, his Signature and Seal *Doffat* having receiv'd the King's Commands to treat with the Great Duke of *Tufcany* about the Reftitution of the Iflands of *If*, *Rateneau* and *Pomegues*, on the Coafts of *Provence*, met therein with fo many Difficulties, that not to leave his Negotiation imperfect, and thofe Iflands in foreign Hands, he prevail'd with the King to give Security for the Sums of Money which were to be repaid to the Great Duke, and that fuch twelve Perfons as the Duke fhould name fhould be engag'd for the fame *Doffat* writing on this Subject to the King on *May* 5, 1598, confeffes that it was a bold Stroke in him to pafs the Article of Sureties, but that without it he could have done nothing That he had learnt that in Affairs of Importance, to avoid a great Evil and to obtain a great Good, fomething muft be rifqu'd, in order to get out of the Perplexity the beft way one can He juftifies his Procedure by feveral other Reafons, but he fufficiently makes known, that the Minifter ought not inconfiderately to involve his Prince in fuch Engagements, and that it is a very nice matter to venture to engage him without exprefs Orders

What *Philip de Commines* fays of a Treaty which was made in the Year 1472, at *Bovines* near *Namur*, between *Lewis* XI, King of *France*, and *Charles* Duke of *Burgundy*, is without Example The Embaffadors of thefe two Princes had agreed between themfelves that the Conftable *de St Pol* fhould be publickly declar'd an Enemy to the King and the Duke, and that he of the two Princes that could firft caufe him to be taken, fhould be oblig'd to put him to Death in eight Days, or to deliver him into the Hands of the other, that he might do what he would with him The Conftable who could not doubt but this Affembly was held on his account, as well becaufe he knew the Intention of the Princes, as becaufe the Embaffadors were his declar'd Enemies, knew fo well how to wheedle with the King, and to perfuade him that the Duke intended to deceive him, that *Lewis* fent Orders to his Embaffadors to ftop, and leave the Affair in the State it was in, without concluding it But when the Courier arriv'd at *Bovines* the Bufinefs was done, the Treaty was fign'd, and according to the Cuftom of thofe Times, the Embaffadors had exchang'd the Inftruments in Form, and had taken the Oath for the Execution thereof However they were fo good Friends, that the King's Embaffadors prevail'd with thofe of the Duke to confent, that they fhould be reftor'd on both fides, and that they fhould feparate without doing any thing The *French* executed the Orders and Intention of the King their Mafter, but the *Burgundians* plaid a bold Stroke

CHAP

CHAP. XIII.

Of the Treaties of Munster and Osnaburg.

FOR many Ages past there has not been any Negotiation where so many Monarchs, Potentates and Princes were concern'd, where so many Difficulties were to be overcome, where so many different and opposite Interests met, and where so many able Ministers were employ'd, as at the Congress of *Westphalia*. I therefore thought I should do a thing neither disagreeable nor unprofitable to those who design themselves for publick Employs, if I related the most essential Particulars in a separate Chapter from that which shall speak of the principal Treaties which have been made within these fourscore Years. The Emperor, to whom were join'd, with the Elector of *Bavaria*, the Princes and Catholick States of *Germany*, the King of *France*, the King of *Spain*, the Crown of *Sweden*, who spoke for the Protestants of *Germany*, and the States of the United Provinces, were the Heads of the Parties. The King of *Denmark* had offer'd his Mediation to the Emperor and to the Crown of *Sweden*, and it had been agreed to. But that King having made himself suspected by the secret Intelligence he entertain'd at the Court of *Vienna*, and by the Negotiations he carry'd on in *Muscovy*, where he had but too much discover'd the Jealousy he had of the Prosperity and Grandeur of the neighbouring Crown, the *Swedes* were for disingaging themselves from this Mediation, and did disingage themselves after a terrible manner, by an open Rupture in the Year 1644. By this means the whole Mediation remain'd in the Pope, and in some measure in the Republick of *Venice*, who made use of the Talents of *Fabio Ghisy* and of *Aloisio Contarini*, to bring to Perfection so glorious a Work. The first had amongst many other great Qualities that of knowing perfectly well how to cover his bad ones, and that with so admirable an Artifice, that the whole College of Cardinals did not perceive them till after he was chosen Pope. The other was a Man of Honour, and he had come off with Reputation in so many Embassies, that he had acquir'd that of being one of the ablest Negotiators of his Time. It was the Interest of both of them to bring the Negotiation to a good Issue, as well for their own Honour, as because *Ghisy* thereby open'd himself a Way to greater Dignities, and that *Contarini*, by procuring a Peace, gave to the major part of the Christian Princes the Means to succour the Republick against the *Turks*, who had made a Descent in *Candia*. But it was all an Opera.

The Kings of *France* and *Sweden* were declar'd Enemies to the Emperor, and in open Rupture with him. The Lantgrave of *Hesse Cassel*, who had treated with *France*, even in the Year 1630, had also an Army in the Field against the Emperor. All the Protestant Princes, except the Elector of *Saxony*, and the Lantgrave of *Hesse Darmstadt* his Son-in-Law, were not satisfy'd with the Court of *Vienna*, and even the Elector of *Bavaria*, Brother-in-Law to the Emperor, being jealous of the Grandeur of the House of *Austria*, which was rais'd to a formidable Power, after the Conquest of the Dutchies of *Mecklenburg* and of *Pomeran'a*, not only did not pursue his Interest, but even pretended to regulate them. *France* demanded for Satisfaction, and to indemnify it, the Town of *Brisac* with the *Brisgau*, *Alsace*, *Philipsburg*, and the Bishopricks of *Metz*, *Toul* and *Verdun*, that is to say, all that its Arms had seiz'd or conquer'd from the Empire during almost a hundred Years. So that it dismember'd a very considerable Province from it, and it took from the House of *Austria* one of its best and most important Places, with a good part of its Territory. *Sweden* pretended to both *Pomerania*'s, to the Town of *Wismar* in the Dutchy of *Mecklenburg*, to the Archbishoprick of *Breme*, and Bishoprick of *Verden*, besides several Millions of Crowns for the defraying the Expences of its Army. The Elector of *Brandenburgh*, who had very lawful Pretensions to *Pomerania*, oppos'd that of the *Swedes*, who moreover demanded the Bishoprick of *Paderborn* for the Lantgrave of *Hesse*, with some other Advantages. The Ministers of *Sweden* were rather for giving him this Recompence at the Expence of the Clergy, than consenting to his taking it from the Lantgrave of *Darmstadt*, because this last being a Lutheran, they were for favouring a Prince who made Profession of the same Religion with them. They also insisted on the Restoration of the Elector *Palatin* to the Electoral Dignity, as well as to both the *Palatinates*, and on the free and publick Exercise of the Protestant Religion, as well in the Emperor's Hereditary Provinces, as throughout the whole Empire, where it had been suffer'd in the Year 1618. The Duke of *Mecklenburg* could by no means consent that the Town of *Wismar* should be lopp'd off from his Demesne, and the King of *Denmark* pretended that they could not refuse to his Son the Restitution of the Archbishoprick of *Breme*. There were long and very vexatious Contestations about *Pomerania*, between *Sweden* and the Elector of *Brandenburgh*, at first for the whole Province, and afterwards for the Partition, and finally for the Recompence should be given to the Elector. The *Swedes* were for having him recompenc'd in Bishopricks, to which should be added the Dutchies of *Jaguersdorf*, of *Segan* and of *Glogau* in *Silesia*. The Ministers of *Spain* exhorted the Elector to stand firm, and not to yield up *Pomerania*. They gave him Hopes of Succours from the Kings of *Poland* and *Denmark*, and they promis'd him the whole Strength of their Master, when at the same time he was not able to hinder the *French* from making a very great Progress in the *Low Countries*, the Preservation whereof was of greater Importance to the King of *Spain*, than that of *Pomerania* was to the Elector

5 F

The

The Intention of *Spain* was to oblige the Elector to declare for the House of *Austria*, but such was the Constitution of his Council at that time, that he could do no Good to his Friends, nor any Harm to his Enemies, but indeed a great deal to himself, by giving to *Sweden* a plausible Pretext to deprive him of all *Pomerania*, and obliging it to frustrate him of all the Recompence it was for procuring him elsewhere. *France* acquir'd an incomparable Advantage by the Cession of *Alsace*, and of two important Places on the *Rhine*, because she thereby secur'd *Lorrain*, *Brisac* serv'd it for a Line of Communication with the Elector of *Bavaria*, and *Philipsburg* was a Curb to the four Electors on the *Rhine*.

The Emperor considering that these Satisfactions dismember'd the Empire, even to the disfiguring it, and that the perfect Union between the Crowns of *France* and *Sweden*, took from him all Hopes of getting clear of the War with Advantage, endeavour'd to separate their Interests, and particularly to gain *Sweden*. He therefore gave it Hopes of a greater Satisfaction than it could lawfully pretend to, if it would join with those who should oppose the Demands of *France*, which the Emperor's Ministers said were so exorbitant, that they ought to be suspected even by the *Swedes* themselves. The Count *de Trautmansdorf*, who manag'd this Intrigue particularly, would have succeeded therein, if he had known how to make his Advantage of the Conjunctures which were very favourable to him. *Oxenstiern*, one of the *Swedish* Plenipotentiaries, had no great Affection for *France*, no more than the Chancellor his Father, and he was offer'd such advantageous Conditions, that he believes he could not refuse them without prejudicing the Crown of *Sweden*. But the Count *de Trautmansdorf* lost the Opportunity very unseasonably, and render'd (by his imprudent Obedience which was precipitate, and truly blind) the Interests and Councils of the two Crowns inseparable. However all the Firmness of the Plenipotentiaries of the Allies, would not have been able to have extorted from the Emperor the extravagant Satisfactions they demanded, if the Duke of *Bavaria* had not thwarted his Designs. During the *Bohemian* War, he had lent the Emperor the Sum of Nine millions of Crowns, and had the *Upper Austria* engag'd for the same, so that the Emperor, to reimburse him at the Expence of others, and to clear at the same time so important a Province, gave him the *Upper Palatinate*, together with the Electoral Dignity, which he had confiscated from *Frederick* King of *Bohemia*. The Elector of *Bavaria* was so advanc'd in Years, and his Son so young, that he could not hope to continue the Electoral Dignity in his House, unless he settl'd it during his Life. The Emperor was become a very bad Guarantee to him, since the Progress the Arms of the *French* and *Swedes* had made in *Germany*, as well because the Court of *Vienna* was not in a Condition to protect him against the Arms of the Allies, while they should continue to act in Conjunction, as because he was in continual Fears, lest the Emperor should make an Accommodation with the Crowns to his Exclusion. *Sweden* at first made mighty Instances for the Restoration of the Elector *Palatin*, in which it was seconded by the Duke of *Newburgh*, presumptive Heir to the Electoral Dignity, for want of Issue Male in the Branch of *Heidelberg*. Wherefore the Elector of *Bavaria*, having recourse to Religion, which is a mighty Help to those who have Address enough to make a good Use of it, sent his *Confessarius* to the Court of *France*, where he represented how much it concern'd the Roman Catholick Religion, that the Electoral Dignity should not be conferr'd on a Prince who was an Heretick, and that the same Religion which had been introduc'd into the *Upper Palatinate* might be preserv'd there. There is no Court where Religion finds fewer Bubbles than in that of *France*, but the Queen Mother was so devout, that it was but making Religion the Pretext, to any Impression one would give her; and Cardinal *Mazarin*, altho' he was neither superstitious, nor excessively devout, had no great Difficulty to enter into the same Sentiments; as well because it was requisite to grant something to the Religion of the Prince, and to the Queen's Devotion, as chiefly because the Declaration of the *Bavarian* was an inestimable Advantage to *France*. This *Confessarius* assur'd the first Minister, that the Elector his Master would oblige the Emperor to give Peace to the Empire, and Satisfaction to the two Crowns. The Elector of *Bavaria* was the *Swedes* Aversion, who not only consider'd him as the Head of the Catholick Party in *Germany*, but also as him whose Friendship would render theirs despicable; or at least that *France* being secure of the Elector's Intention, who was the most powerful and the wisest of all the Princes of the Empire, would for the time to come oppose their Wills with more Firmness, when the *French* Ministers said were always very absolute, and sometimes not very reasonable. The *French* on their side could not consent to the Ruin of that Prince, because it drew along with it that of all the Catholicks, and in all Appearance that of the Religion it self throughout *Germany*, and that it would put *Sweden* in a Condition to have no need of the *French* Troops nor Subsidies. Insomuch that it was no small Task that *d'Avaux* and *Servien* undertook to get this new Union approv'd of at *Osnaburg*; but after they had obtain'd the first Acquiescence, by the Assurance they gave the *Swedish* Ministers, that their Queen would find her Account in it, and that *France* would accept of no Satisfaction till *Sweden* had hers, they no longer thought of that Zeal for Religion, which had made them speak in the Behalf of the Elector *Palatin*. His Interest was forsaken, and the House of *Bavaria* was declar'd for. It was agreed that the *Upper Palatinate* should remain to the Duke, as a Province which he could better preserve than the *Upper Austria*, which the Emperor might at any time withdraw, either by reimbursing the Elector, or by indemnifying him otherwise. Before that this Prince had made sure of *France*, and by its Means of *Sweden*, it was propos'd to transfer the Electoral Dignity of *Bohemia* to the House of *Bavaria*, or else to make that of the *Palatin* alternative to the two Branches of *Heidelberg* and *Munich*, or else to leave it to the Duke during his Life, and to revert after his Death to the Princes *Palatins*, but after this Reconciliation it was resolv'd to gratify him with it and all his Posterity, and to create an eighth Electorate for the *Palatin*.

I just took notice of the strongest Motives *France* had to declare for the Elector of *Bavaria*, but she nevertheless gave out that there were a great many others which oblig'd her not to concern her self for the *Palatin* House, which she said was but indifferently affected towards that Crown. They were quite of a different Opinion in King *Henry* IV's Time, and it was well known, that had it not been for the Duke of *Bavaria*, the House of *Austria* would have been reduc'd to the last Extremities in *Germany*, for which Reason *France* would not have it thought that she oppos'd his Satisfaction, but, on the contrary, that it was to her that the *Palatin* should be oblig'd for the Advantages which his other Friends should obtain for him, or that Fortune should fling in his Way. She protested however, and said she was resolv'd, that in Case *Sweden* and the other Protestant Princes obstinately persisted to demand the Restoration of the Elector *Palatin*, so as make it unavoidable, she would join with them, and would second them with Zeal, giving the *Swedish* Ministers to understand nevertheless, that the more they demanded for the Elector *Palatin*, the less would they obtain for themselves. Which *Servien*'s Address knew so well how to represent to them, that in *Sweden* all the Resolutions were chang'd which had been taken there on this Subject, and she took the part of her greatest Enemy.

There were moreover other Jealousies between the two confederated Crowns. The Landgrave of *Hesse*, who had a particular Treaty with *France*, and who receiv'd Subsidies from it, was the only one of all the Protestant Princes, who having taken that side openly, depended more on her than of *Sweden*. The Elector of *Triers*, and some Bishops of *Franconia*, whom the Emperor could not defend against the Arms of *Sweden*, reclaim'd the Protection of *France*. The Elector of *Brandenburgh*, who had nothing to hope for from *Sweden*, and nothing to fear from the Emperor, courted also the Friendship of that powerful Crown. All these Jealousies serv'd only to augment that which was already conceiv'd in *Sweden*, of the Intrigues which were on Foot between the Courts of *Paris* and of *Munich*. There were more than one Minister in the Senate of *Stockholm*, who were persuaded that the Alliance of *France* was not very necessary, nor even very advantageous to that Crown, and that after the Peace in *Germany* it would not be any way beneficial to it, in what however they were very much deceiv'd. They were of Opinion that the *French* Plenipotentiaries ought to moderate their Demands a little, and contenting themselves with the three Bishopricks, the *Lower Alsace*, *Brisac* and *Philipsburg*, not form any higher Pretensions. They said, that *France* was unjust, in desiring to tye up the Emperor from succouring the King of *Spain*, while at the same time she reserv'd to her self the Liberty of assisting the King of *Portugal*, altho' she was not oblig'd thereto by any Consideration either of Parentage or Alliance. That it ought not to hinder the Emperor from interceding for the Duke of *Lorrain*, nor from comprising the Circle of *Burgundy* in the Empire. This was the Reason why *France* strengthen'd it self with the Duke of *Bavaria* against *Sweden*, which on its side fortify'd it self with the Protestant Princes. So that it would have been no very hard matter for it to have acquir'd a great Advantage in the Empire over the *French*, more especially if in the Continuation of the Prosperity of its Arms, she had gain'd some signal Victory over the other Party, because then she would have stood in no need of *France*. The *Swedes* also were not a little vex'd, as well as reasonably, at the Violence *France* offer'd them, in obliging them to consent to a Truce, which the Elector of *Bavaria* broke immediately after he had concluded it. But notwithstanding all these Jealousies, Distrusts and Dissatisfactions, the two Crowns so well consider'd, that their Divisions ruin'd the Interest of both the one and the other, that they resolv'd to seek and to find their mutual Good in an indissoluble Union. The Emperor's Ministers endeavour'd to gain the Princes of *Germany*, and especially the Protestants, and particularly the Princess Regent of *Hesse*, who was the Honour of her Sex, and the Heroine of her Age; but they met with an invincible Resistance which forc'd them to yield to the Necessity the Emperor found himself reduc'd to by the Elector of *Bavaria*'s Menaces. He was for leaving to his Son, together with Quiet, an indisputable Possession of all his Acquisitions and Conquests, of which the Electoral Dignity made a part, under the Protection of *France*, accompany'd with the Guaranty of the whole Empire, which were Advantages he could not hope for either from a Continuation of the War, or from the Friendship of the Emperor his Brother-in-Law.

The Duke *Charles* of *Lorrain* was a great Obstacle to the Peace, at least they who were not for having it on the Conditions the confederated Crowns demanded it, made use of his Pretensions to keep it off. The Duke had been dispossess'd of his Estates, or to speak properly, of those of his Wife, for having taken the Emperor's part against the late King of *Sweden*, contrary to the Intentions and Interest of *France*. His Troops acted still in Conjunction with those of *Spain*, and one part of *Lorrain* was held of the Empire, so that it seem'd that his Friends had reason to urge that his Interests might be consider'd at *Munster*. The Ministers of *France* asserted, on the contrary, that they had nothing in common with the Affairs of *Germany*. That the Duke had made several Treaties with the King, without the Consent, and even without the Participation of the Emperor and the States of the Empire. That the King intended to execute them on his part, and to cause them to be executed by the Duke; and that for that reason he had never suffer'd in the Preliminary Treaties Passports to be granted to the Dukes Ministers, because he was not to be concern'd in what was to be negotiated at the Congress. The King had an Interest to secure *Lorrain*, which serv'd him as a Line of Communication with *Alsace*, and with the other Conquests of *Germany*, which it was a hard matter to preserve without that, as it was almost impossible for the Duke of *Lorrain* to preserve his former Inclinations for the House of *Austria*, while the King should remain Master of *Brisac*. I have seen the Original of a Letter the Duke of *Lorrain* wrote a few Days after the Duke of *Weimar* had made himself Master of that Place, where he said, That it was high time to lay by the Profession of Arms, and put on a religious Habit, since they had not been able to succour the most important Place the House of *Austria* had, in all its hereditary Countries. After the Treaty he had made on *March* 29, 1641, and that he had caus'd the King solemnly to swear to the Observation of between the Hands of the Bishop of *Meaux*, and which the Duke had violated three Days after he had sign'd it, there was no Likelihood that the King would suffer such a Prince as the Duke of *Lorrain* to make a Jest of him. And in effect the *French* Plenipotentiaries had Resolution enough to get granted to them what they demanded, and to cause the Duke to be excluded the Negotiation and Treaty of *Munster*. This is not the Place to relate how he was us'd in that of the *Pyrenees*, where he was not more consider'd by his pretended Friends, than by his real Enemies.

France was willing to conclude with the Emperor, because there had appear'd some Beginnings of Troubles at *Paris*, the Consequences whereof might be very dangerous in the Continuation of the War with *Germany*. She consum'd a vast Fund in Subsidies, which were given to *Sweden*, to the Lantgrave, and elsewhere. Her Armies might be more usefully employ'd in the Low Countries, and she was in a continual Uneasiness, lest some Whim or Dissatisfaction should oblige the *Swedes* to make a Party with the Protestants of *Germany*, which might establish them so powerfully in the Empire, that the *French* Interest should be no longer consider'd, and that of the Catholicks be quite ruin'd. Wherefore that this might not be too much weaken'd in the Person of the Elector of *Bavaria*, who was the Head thereof, as I even now said, *France* made the *Swedes* consent to a Suspension of Arms, by representing to the Ministers of *Sweden*, That the King not being able to supply any longer the excessive Charges of the War, nor even of the Subsidies, it was time to make a Peace, since thereby the two Crowns would get all the Advantages they could promise themselves, from all the Hostilities which a Continuation of the War might extort from the Emperor. *France* look'd upon it as her Right to cause this Suspension of Arms, since the *Swedes* had not scrupled to make one with the Elector of *Saxony*, without the Participation of their Allies. The Elector of *Bavaria* was in great Perplexities. He had constantly sided with the Emperor, who was his nearest Relation, and his Brother in-Law, and he was oblig'd to the House of *Austria* for the Electoral Dignity, and, as one may say, for all his Fortune. There was also some likelihood that it was from her he was to hope for the Preservation thereof, instead of expecting it from a strange Crown, from whence he could receive but very uncertain Sureties. He was sensible that the Emperor could not be lost, nor the Empire dissipated, but he must be involv'd in the same Fate with them. His Intention was to make himself equally considerable at *Vienna* and at *Paris*, and to put himself in such a Condition as to be able to turn the Scale on which side soever he should declare. He therefore, when he concluded a Suspension of Arms with *France*, was for reserving to himself the Liberty of assisting the Emperor against *Sweden*. And forasmuch as *France* neither could, nor would consent thereto, he immediately broke the Truce, and did not renew the Negotiation with *France*, till this had assur'd him that the *Swedes* should joyn with her, to procure him all the Advantages he could hope for for his House, and that they would endeavour to procure Satisfaction to the Elector *Palatin* some other way.

France had a great Advantage in the Congress, because she was equally consider'd and respected there by the Protestants, and by the Catholicks. These had been always zealous Partizans to the House of *Austria*, and Enemies to the *French*, who had been the Cause of *Sweden*'s arming against the Empire, and were the true Occasion of the Misfortunes with which *Germany* had been afflicted for so many Years. Nevertheless, such was their Aversion to the Protestants, who had a Design against their Religion and their Benefices, that they desir'd Satisfaction might be given to *France*, because they hop'd to be protected by it. On the other side, the Protestants expected no Good from the Union *France* was going to make with the Catholicks, contrary to the ancient Maxims of that Crown, and could willingly have wish'd that all the Satisfaction might be given to *Sweden*, but they were afraid of making it known, because they had been so ill us'd by the House of *Austria*, that they stood in need of a powerful Protection against it. The *Spaniards* press'd the Emperor's Ministers to grant to the Protestants whatever they should demand, and if *Trautmansdorf* had had the Power, or Resolution enough to have done it, he had greatly perplex'd Cardinal *Mazarin*'s Policy, and that of the Ministers who acted by his Orders.

The Differences between the two Crowns of *France* and *Spain* were not so easy to be adjusted. *Portugal*, *Catalonia*, *Lorrain* and *Casal* were powerful Obstacles, but the greatest of all was Cardinal *Mazarin*'s little or no Inclination thereto, who could not consent to a Peace, if there by he did not unite the Provinces of *Flanders* to the Crown of *France*. He had imagin'd that *Spain*, to recover *Catalonia*, and to procure *Portugal*'s being forsaken, would make no Difficulty to give up the Low Countries. But this was what there was so much the less likelihood of, that the *French* judg'd themselves it would be impossible for them to keep *Catalonia*, where they were not better belov'd than the *Spaniards*, and there was nothing oblig'd them to protect the *Portuguese* but the Design the Cardinal had and continu'd to have after the *Pyrenean* Peace, to stir up there a new War against *Spain*. Moreover the Measures the Count *de Pegneranda* took with the *Dutch*, to make 'em consent to a separate Peace, broke those of the Cardinal. The Count, who was a Minister without Experience, and without Genius, had imagin'd that *Spain*, having made a Peace with the United Provinces, would be able to oppose equal Forces to *France*, when those of the Low Countries

Countries should no longer be diverted by the *Hollanders*, and he still flatter'd himself with the Hopes of a great Revolution, with which he thought *France* infallibly threaten'd There was no Diligence omitted by the Ministers of the two Crowns, nor any Artifices which they did not employ, either to preserve or acquire the Friendship of this Republick But the *Hollanders*, who could not bear the imperious Deportment of the *French* Ministers, and who dreading the Neighbourhood of a powerful Monarch, and of a warlike and restless Nation, were not less sensibly touch'd with the Progress the Arms of *France* continu'd to make in *Flanders* than the *Spaniards* themselves, willingly lent an Ear to a separate Agreement They conceiv'd that *France* having declar'd a War with *Spain*, but for their Sakes, would rather chuse to make a Peace than to continue to carry on a War alone, in a Countrey where each single Place would take them up at least a Campaign, and that by that mean there would be always a strong Barrier between the Frontiers of *France* and the United Provinces But they, as well as the *Spaniards*, have had the Leisure to undeceive themselves, and to know, that the Strength of the Kingdom of *France* is able to oppose that of all the rest of *Europe*, under so great a Monarch as he who now reigns there, The Cardinal, who was unwilling to bring upon himself the Hatred of all *Christendom*, which thirsted after Peace, was for having it believ'd he passionately desir'd it

The Plenipotentiaries of *France* judg'd that the King their Master ought to be contented, if he was allow'd to keep the County of *Roussillon*, with the Town of *Roses*, all *Artois*, comprehending therein *Aire* and *St Omer*, *Gravelines*, *Buxbourg*, *Thionville*, *Cambray* and the *Cambresis*, and that in Consideration thereof he might abandon *Catalonia*, as being a Province very hard to keep, and even restore *Damvilliers*, *Landrecy*, and some other Places in *Flanders*, and in the County of *Burgundy* The Reason was, That *France*, by the Acquisition of those Places on the side of *Picardy* and the *Boulognese*, of the three Bishopricks on the side of *Champagne*, of the best part of *Lorrain*, with *Brisac* and *Philipsburg*, enlarg'd very much the Frontiers of the Kingdom, and gave the City of *Paris* a noble outside But the *Spaniards*, who were assur'd of the Intention of the *Dutch*, had no mind to treat with *France*, and much less to yield to it *Cambray*, *Aire*, and *St Omer*, which do not only cover the Low Countries, but also give an Entrance into *France* The Cardinal, on his part, was for profiting of the Prosperity of the King's Arms, and reducing *Spain* to such a Condition as should hinder it from breaking the Treaty whenever it should think fit, and he did not scruple to say, That that was the only Guaranty for the Execution of the Peace *France* did not dare to propose the Exchange of *Catalonia* for some other Province, lest the *Catalans*, who were not very well satisfy'd with the *French* Government, should prevent it, and reconcile themselves to their natural King For which Reason they were made to believe, That the King offer'd to restore six of the best Towns in the Low Countries, in Exchange for those the *Spaniards* possess'd in *Catalonia*, thereby to unite the whole Province to the Crown of *France* But this is what had not been mention'd, because it was too well known in *France*, that *Spain* would be far from yielding up one of the best peopled Provinces of the Kingdom, and which is so necessary to it for a Communication with *Italy* *France* was for keeping all her Conquests, unless *Spain* would restore to her those she had made in former Wars, and amongst the rest the Kingdom of *Navarr* Her Ministers gave out, that she would besides pretend to the Dutchy of *Milan*, and perhaps also to the Kingdom of *Naples* *Piombino* and *Portolongone* were also amongst the greatest Difficulties The *Spaniards* would by no means suffer the *French* to have strong Places on the Coast of *Tuscany*, from whence they might extremely incommode the Kingdom of *Naples*, and demanded in Explication of the Treaties of *Monçon* and *Querasque*, They insisted on a Regulation concerning *Caffal* That Satisfaction should be given to the Duke of *Lorrain*, and that the *French* should leave off assisting *Portugal* The *French* said it was not their Intention to keep *Caffal*, but they would however have good Security, that at no Time, and in no Case, this Place should be liable to fall into the Hands of the *Spaniards* And this Security was a very Chimerical Thing, concerning which it was impossible to agree There was nothing could oblige the *French* to speak in the Behalf of the King of *Portugal*, as I said before There was no Alliance between the two Kings, and that of *Portugal*, not only had not done any thing for *France* since his Accession to the Crown, but had not so much as known how to make an Advantage of the powerful Diversions *France* had made to the Arms of *Spain*, even into *Spain* it self The *Dutch*, who had no Reason to be satisfy'd with the *Portugueze*, on the Account of what had pass'd in *Brasil*, joyn'd with the *Spaniards* against them Insomuch that the *French* Plenipotentiaries had not only the invincible Resistance of those who were their Enemies to deal with, but also the Dissatisfaction of those who were their Friends, and who could not suffer they should speak in the Favour of the *Portugueze*, because the *Spaniards* gave them Hopes that, by means of the separate Treaty which was negotiating with them, they should easily re-enter into the Possession of *Brasil*

The Cardinal, who contriv'd all these Perplexities, who delighted therein, and gain'd his Point thereby, was for clearing himself however, and, to make it be believ'd that it was both his Intention and Interest to make a Peace, consented that for some Time the Plenipotentiaries of the United Provinces should do the Office of Mediators between *France* and *Spain*, but as he had quite another View, so many fresh Difficulties were started every Day, that the *Hollanders*, seeing they were made a Jest of, laid down their pretended Mediation as a thing ridiculous, and of no manner of Utility The Cardinal was at the same time for having every Body believe that Peace was not only his Inclination, but also his Interest And he spoke so often of it, and in such strong Terms, that he was almost himself persuaded that he desir'd a thing which was his Aversion, and which he could not covet for many Considerations, which

5 G   they

they cannot be ignorant of; who have a particular Knowledge of the Affairs of those Times. They who believ'd that *Servien* knew his real Intentions were deceiv'd. He knew indeed more thereof than his Collegues, but he could not boast of having the Confidence of the Cardinal, who intrusted no body therewith, hardly himself especially in those things he coveted should be kept a Secret, or wherein it concern'd him to disguise the Truth, so consummate a Dissembler he was, or to express it better in *Italian*, *Cupo*, with his most confident Friends. He was sensible he could not keep himself altogether impenetrable to the piercing Sight of *Servien*. M' *Colbert* serv'd him in his most important Concerns. *Ondedei* had some Interest with him, and the Cardinal could not intirely conceal himself to *Lionne*, and the Abbot *Bentivoglio*, who had a great Share in the Affairs of *Italy*, to which he apply'd himself more, than to those of *France*. But amongst all these, there was not one for whom he had not some Reserve, so that what has been known of his Intentions, has been only by Conjectures, which do not always fail those who have some Capacity. One Day discoursing a considerable time with the Minister of one of the first Princes of *Germany*, who had receiv'd Orders to repair to his Master, he told him, That he knew very well that there was a Talk there of forming a third Party between the Electors of *Saxony* and *Brandenburg*, and the House of *Brunswick* and *Lunenburg*, which would oblige the Emperor and the Crowns to make a Peace in the Empire, but he did not doubt, but all those Princes were perswaded that *France* desir'd it and as for himself in particular, that it was his Passion. That Foreigners might indeed believe he was wicked, but he hop'd they had not a bad Opinion enough of him, to believe he was either a Fool or a Mad-man. That it was requisite he should be something more than all that, if he prefer'd the Vexations and Uneasiness the ill State of the King's Revenues gave him, while the War exhausted them all, to the Repose and Satisfaction he should find in the Plenty Peace would bring to the Kingdom. This is what he would have all the foreign Ministers believe, yet nevertheless it is certain, that it was only with the utmost Unwillingness, that he consented to the Peace which was concluded since at the *Pyrenees*, eleven Years after the Congress of *Westphalia*, at a Time when the intire Conquest of the Low Countries was much more probable, than during the Negotiation of *Munster*. The Kingdom enjoy'd a perfect Tranquility within, and abroad a Prosperity which made its Power to be both respected and fear'd. But the Queen was for preserving to the King her Brother what he had still left him of the Provinces of *Flanders*, she was for having the Satisfaction of procuring Peace to *France*, and her strongest Passion was to see the King her Son, marry'd to the *Infanta* of *Spain* her Niece. The Cardinal oppos'd it at first with Warmth, and represented the incomparable Advantages *France* might infallibly promise it self from a Continuation of the War, and he yielded at last but to the pressing and repeated Instances of the Queen, but with so much Concern, that he did not scruple to tell her, That by entring into her Majesty's Sentiments on a Point of this Importance, at a Time when there was no Doubt to be made of a complete Conquest of all the Provinces of *Flanders*, he quitted all the Obligations he had to her, which were neither small, nor few in Number. This Reluctancy, which he shew'd in the Course of so many Years, and the strict Union he made with the Usurper of the *English* Crown, made an End to undeceive those the Cardinal might have impos'd upon concerning the Sincerity of his Intention in reference to Peace. The Duke of *Longueville* saw into it, wherefore perceiving that *Servien* was the King's chief Instrument, or rather the Cardinals, and that the *Dutch* had concluded their Treaty with *Spain*, he desir'd to be recall'd, and return'd to *France*. D'*Avaux* was recall'd because he was not agreeable nor complaisant enough to justify the whole Procedure, and all the Intentions of the first Minister and after these two Plenipotentiaries were withdrawn, *Servien* remain'd sole Master of the Negotiation and he made an end of it so far as it related to the Affairs of *Germany*, conformably to the Cardinal's Project.

The United Provinces had a mind to treat with *Spain*, but every body was not perswaded they could do it, without violating the Treaties they had with *France*. They did not agree about the Explication of the foregoing Treaties, which were many, but that which regulated Affairs most, was the Treaty *Charnacé* had made at the *Hague* the 16th of *April*, 1634. The King therein oblig'd himself to assist the States with a Million and three hundred thousand Livers every Year, besides the Million he gave them by the Treaty of the Year 1630. He also promis'd to break with the King of *Spain*, if he violated the Peace or the Truce, which the States might make with him, and the States oblig'd themselves on their side, not to treat with the King of *Spain*, without the Intervention of the King of *France*, and to break with the first, it he attack'd *France*, in the States, Towns or Places, she possess'd at the time of the Treaty. From whence the Ministers of *France* concluded, as well as from the Memorial *Charnacé* had given in at that time, that the *Hollanders* were oblig'd to break with the King of *Spain*, in case the King of *France* was attack'd in the Countrey of the *Grisons*, in the *Valteline*, on the Account of the Affair of *Mantua*, *Casal*, *Pignerol*, and of *Lorrain*, and generally in all his other States They said, that the King's Thoughts could not then be confin'd to the Low Countries, where there was as yet no War, and where he possess'd nothing. That since in that case the United Provinces were to break with the King of *Spain*, even altho' they should have made a Peace with him, with much more Reason were they oblig'd not to treat with him, without the Consent of *France*. That the Term of seven Years, which the Treaties of the Years 1630, and 1634, spoke of, had been extended by that of the Year 1635, till the Conclusion of a Peace, or till the *Spaniards* were utterly expell'd the Low Countries. That the King, who had the Choice either of continuing the Subsidies, or of breaking with *Spain*, had chosen the last. That the *Dutch* themselves had insisted on the King's breaking with that Crown, and

and that the Treaty of 1635, does not only regulate the Actions of the Armies, and the Partition of the Conquests, but that it also provides, that the States shall not treat with Spain but in Conjunction with France, and that they shall be oblig'd to come to a Rupture with the Spaniards, if they attack the King That this Rupture being general, altho' the greatest Effort was made in the Low Countries, the mutual Guaranty ought to be so too, in reference to all the Conquests, on which side soever they were made In Holland they asserted, That the the seven Years, of which mention is made in the Treaty of the Year 1634, being expir'd, and that of the Year 1635, not taking any notice of the Interest France had in the Affairs of the Grisons, of Mantua, &c the United Provinces could not be oblig'd but to the Guaranty of the Conquests, which should be made in the Low Countries But the French Ministers reply'd, That the last Treaty was so far from destroying the former, that it confirm'd it, and gave it a greater Extent in reference to Time Some thought they could silence the French by saying, that the secret Article, which serves as an Explanation to the 9th Article of the Treaty of the Year 1635, oblig'd the Allies to make War only in the Low Countries But therein was a little Sophistry, because that that Article, in speaking of the principal Employments of the Armies of the Allies, did not excuse France from the general Rupture, and could not hinder the King of Spain from attacking her every where, nor the United Provinces from succouring her, if she was attack'd elsewhere The French Ministers urg'd, That the Diversions the Arms of France would make in Italy and in Spain, would have the same Effect, and afford the same Advantages to the Hollanders, as if she caus'd them to act in Flanders That the secret Article did not provide against making War in any other Parts of Europe, but only took notice, that it might be more usefully made in the Low Countries than in Italy or in Spain The United Provinces believ'd they had a Right to hinder France from concluding separately with the Emperor without their Consent But forasmuch as they had refus'd to break with him, when in the Year 1636, he sent an Army into Burgundy under Galas, and after that another into Piccardy under Piccolomini, they did not dare to oppose it, for fear of drawing on themselves a Reproach, which would have been but too just Of all the Provinces, that of Holland was most tir'd with the War They were all jealous of the continual Victories of the French, and dreaded more their Neighbourhood, than the remote Power of Spain, so that they resolv'd at last to make a separate Treaty with this, since France could not consent to a general Peace, wherein she did not find all the Advantages she could promise herself from the Prosperity of her Arms D'Avaux and Servien had made a Treaty at the Hague on the 1st of March, 1644, by which the Estates had enter'd into a new Obligation not to treat, but in Conjunction with France, so that it seem'd as if by making a separate Treaty, they fail'd in all that they ow'd to France, and in what they ow'd themselves, unless they were (for the Preservation of their Republick) necessitated to get rid of a War, that exhausted them, and entirely ruin'd them France on its part resolv'd to continue it even after the Hollanders should have concluded their Treaty, and she has made it plain, that for that purpose, she had no need either of the Assistance or of the Diversion of the Arms of the United Provinces who were sensible but too late, that neither they nor their Allies were able to hinder the most Christian King from making Conquests, which would in the End unite the Provinces of Flanders to his Crown, unless he were prevented by a good Peace, as he indeed was

CHAP. XIV.

The most considerable Treaties relating to the Affairs of this Age.

I Have said in the VIth Chapter of the first Part of this Book, that the Study of the modern Treaties ought to make the strongest Application of the Embassador A Collection of the Treaties which have been made since the beginning of this Century, would be an excellent and very useful Work, and would serve for a general Instruction to a publick Minister, because he would there find a Plan of those Affairs, which he ought not to be ignorant of, if he will succeed in his Employment I do not scruple to say, That the Publick would have no small Obligation to him who should present it with such a Work especially if he put at the Head of the Treaties, those Occurrences which were the Occasion of their being made, with the most remarkable Particulars of the Negotiations which were carry'd on for that Purpose John du Tillet, chief Register to the Parliament of Paris, and Keeper of the Charters of France, has printed a Continuation of the ancient Treaties, which have been made between the Kings of France and England My Intention was to follow his Example, and to communicate to the Publick all the Treaties which have been made in our Time, and have the greatest Analogy with the present Affairs, wherein those, who should one Day apply themselves to the writing a History, might have discover'd great Lights to guide them in the Course they were to hold therein But the Court of Justice of Holland having seiz'd all my Papers and Memorials without distinction, without causing the least Inventory to be made thereof, (which ought to be observ'd) and having since dissipated and dispers'd them, without the Participation of those who have most Interest therein, I have

I have lost, together with the Work of several Years Labour, both the Mind and the Means of continuing it. Insomuch that all I can do in the Condition I am in, is to lay down in this Chapter the Project of a Work which perhaps might not have been unserviceable nor disagreeable to those who delight in this kind of Study, which is one of the most necessary a publick Minister can apply himself to.

The Treaty of *Vervins* made the Beginning of the Work, as it was the Beginning of the Repose. Christendom was going to enjoy towards the End of the last Century, if it had not been disturb'd by other Accidents, which happen'd some Years after a Peace was made between *France* and *Spain*. *Charles Emanuel* Duke of *Savoy* had desir'd to be compris'd therein, but he was against its regulating the Difference he had with the King about the Marquisate of *Saluzzo*. Both sides referr'd themselves to the Pope, who as Arbitrator was to decide it in a Year. The Duke who had usurp'd the Marquisate during the Disorders of the League, and who could not hope for a favourable Determination, contriv'd so well to disgust the Pope, that he would no longer meddle in the Affair. The Duke, who did not want Wit, and who knew that King *Henry* IV, had a great deal of Generosity, went to see him at *Fontainbleau*, and made him several Propositions, which would not have been rejected by a King less clear sighted than this, and less devoted to an Interest which in this Conjuncture was inseparable from true Glory. He declar'd to the Duke, that all the Overtures that could be made him, before the Restitution of the Marquisate, would be to no purpose: and this Firmness oblig'd the Duke to make the Treaty of *Paris* on *February* 27, 1600, by which he promis'd to restore the Marquisate, or else to give the King the *Bressan*, with some other Territories in the Neighbourhood of *Burgundy*. The Duke being return'd back to *Savoy*, repented himself of the Treaty, and refus'd to execute it. So that the King to compel him thereto made use of his Arms, and having conquer'd in a few Days all that the Duke possess'd on this side the *Alps*, he obtain'd at last the *Bressan*, with the Bayliwick of *Gez*, *Veromay*, &c. by the Treaty which was made at *Lions*, *January* 17, 1601.

After this there was no other War talk'd of but that of the *Low Countries*. King *Henry* IV, who was willing to have it believ'd that all his Thoughts were bent on Peace, and who grew weary of assisting the United Provinces with the considerable Subsidies he supply'd 'em with towards the Support of the Charge of the *Spanish* War, while all his Thoughts were intent on accumulating Treasures for some secret Design, made pressing Instances to the States to hearken to the Overtures of Peace which the Arch-Duke *Albert* made them. But forasmuch as the *Spaniards* were for inserting therein Conditions which were hard enough, as the Exercise of the Roman Catholick Religion, and a Prohibition of Commerce with the *Indies*, no farther mention was made of a Peace: but the Parties were brought to consent to a Truce of twelve Years, which was concluded at *Antwerp* on *April* 9, 1609.

Before this Negotiation was finish'd, the King of *France* was willing to make a Treaty of Alliance defensive, with the said Provinces on *January* 23, 1608, and by his Example *James* King of *Great Britain* concluded one with them on *June* 26, in the same Year 1608. After the Arch-Duke had treated with these Provinces, as with a free State, over which neither the King of *Spain* nor he pretended any thing, *France* and *England* made another more particular Treaty with them at the *Hague*, *July* 17, 1609.

King *Henry* IV being kill'd in the Month of *May* 1610, all his great Designs vanish'd, and *France* thought on nothing else but of being well with *Spain*, and keeping so. So that from the Year 1598, there was no Treaty made between those two Crowns till the Peace of *Munster*, of which we shall speak hereafter. Only on *November* 13 of the said Year 1610, there was concluded at *Paris* a Treaty of Neutrality, between the *Franche Compte* on the one side, and the Viscounty of *Auxonne*, with the Countrey of *Bassigny* on the other. And on *September* 27 1614, a Treaty was concluded at *Madrid*, about a Difference between the two Crowns concerning the Frontiers of the *Upper* and *Lower Navarre*, wherein the *Spaniards* had all the Advantage, and made their Benefit of the Weakness of the *French* Government under Queen *Mary* of *Medicis*, and afterwards under the Ministry of the Duke *de Lu nes*.

While the Truce was negotiating in *Holland*, and before it was concluded, there appear'd the Grounds of a new War in *Germany*, where the Duke of *Cleves* dying without Issue, left a very rich Inheritance, but it was disputed by so great a number of Heirs and Pretenders, that there was no room to doubt that the Sword must decide the Right of the ones, and regulate the Pretensions of the others. The Elector of *Brandenburgh* and the Duke of *Newburgh* were the next Heirs. The Elector of *Saxony*, the Marquis *de Burgon*, of the House of *Austria*, pretended also thereto, and the Emperor was for disposing of it as of a Fief which escheated to the Empire for want of Heirs Male. He accordingly sent thither the Arch-Duke *Leopold* to take Possession thereof, as Imperial Commissioner. *France* could not suffer that the House of *Austria* should unite to its Power Provinces which might serve for a Line of Communication between the Low Countries and *Germany*, for which reason *Henry* IV thought himself oblig'd to oppose this Establishment: and it was partly the Cause or the Pretext of the Preparations he made for some Years before his Death. He had openly enough declar'd for the two Princes of *Brandenburgh* and of *Newburgh*, who were both Protestants, and who on *May* 31, 1609, had concluded the Treaty of *Dartmont*, and on *July* 14 of the same Year that of *Dourbourg* for their common Interest, and again a third at *Hall* in *Swabia* on *January* 27, 1619. *France* which found it self concern'd therein, as I just said, *England*, and the United Provinces, who fear'd lest Interest might alter the Friendship of those Princes, made them conclude the Treaty of *Santen* on *November* 12, 1614. But this Treaty was not executed, notwithstanding the Offices of the two Crowns and of the States. On the contrary, those two Princes having

since

since enter'd into different and opposite Interests, and having even declar'd War, it was found difficult enough to supersede now and then their Hostilities by provisional Treaties the most remarkable whereof are the three Treaties which were concluded at *Driffeldorp* on *May* 11, 1624, on *March* 9, 1629, and on *April* 8, 1647, for the Partition of the Inheritance, till their Difference could be regulated On *October* 11, 1651, there was another made at *Effen*, where was concluded on *September* 9, 1666, a Treaty, which converted all the provisional Treaties into an effective Partition, with a Design to settle an indissoluble Friendship between these two Princes At least if it can be believ'd of two Relations, who pretending each to the whole Inheritance, were oblig'd to be contented with half thereof On *February* 15, 1645, the States of *Juliers* and of *Cleves*, &c made a Treaty between them at *Cologn*

The Alliance the Duke of *Newburgh* took to in the House of *Bavaria*, of which he was a Branch, making it believ'd that he would seek for Support in the Catholick Party, as he had embrac'd its Religion, the Elector sought with so much the more Earnestness the Friendship of the Protestant Princes, and amongst the rest that of the United Provinces, with whom he had made a Treaty *April* 25, in the Year 1605 On *December* 23, 1618, there was again a Treaty made at the *Hague* for the Succession of *Juliers*, between the States General and some Protestant Princes, who were assembl'd at *Hailborn* After the Duke of *Newburgh* had declar'd openly, the Elector did the same on his side, strengthening himself by means of the Treaties he made with the States, as in the Year 1616, for the Loan of a hundred thousand Crowns, which were advanc'd under the Name of one *Hoefyfer* After that was made the Treaty of the *Hague* of *October* 23, 1624 That of *July* 31, 1629, for the Repayment of the Sum of a hundred thousand Crowns, with the Interest, and the Interest of the Interest Another on *April* 2, 1632, and another on *September* 4, 1636, for the same Debt On *July* 27, 1655, was concluded at the *Hague* a Treaty of Alliance, and since another in the Month of *December* 1665 The Treaty of *Cleves* was made *February* 16, 1666, with the separate Article for the Toll of *Guennep*, and a particular Treaty for a stricter Alliance On *January* 6, 1667, there was another made at the *Hague*, on account of the War with which *France* threaten'd the *Low Countries* On *May* 6, 1672, while the *French* Armies were already marching to attack the United Provinces, they made a Treaty of Alliance at *Berlin*, for the raising and subsisting an Army of twenty thousand Men, with which the Elector was to assist the States, who had two powerful Enemies upon them, to wit, the Kings of *France* and of *England*

The Princes of *Germany*, the Roman Catholicks on one side, and Protestants on the other, liv'd in continual and incurable Distrusts Even before the Peace of *Vervins* there was a Schism in the Chapter of *Strasburg*, where some had chosen *Charles* Cardinal of *Lorrain*, and the others *John George* Marquiss of *Brandenburg*, who took to Arms about it, till a provisional Treaty was made on that account at *Hague-nau*, *November* 22, 1604, and since confirm'd by a Treaty at the same Place, *February* 22, 1620 The Protestants had for a long time complain'd of the Judgments and Decrees the Chamber of *Spires* and the Aulick Council gave, out of Hatred to the Religion, concerning the Church Lands, which the Catholicks usurp'd contrary to the Treaty of *Paffaw*, but chiefly about the Proscription of the Town of *Donawert*, which the Duke of *Bavaria* executed rather with Cruelty than Rigour They had often complain'd thereof but to no purpose, so that fearing lest the House of *Austria* and the Catholick Party should benefit themselves by the Succession of *Juliers* and above all, taking Umbrage at the part *Spain* assum'd in the Management of the Affairs of the Empire, as it had already but too much Authority in the Council of *Vienna*, they met at *Hall* in *Swabia*, where they made on *January* 17, 1610 that Union, which made it self so much talk'd of at the Beginning of the first Wars of *Germany*, and of the Commotions of *Bohemia* It was follow'd by a Treaty which the same Princes made at the same Place with the United Provinces on the eleventh of *February* of the same Year, which was confirm'd by the King of *France* at *Paris* the 23d ensuing, by that of *Hailbron* of *September* 20, by another which some Electors made with the United Provinces, *December* 23 of the same Year, and afterwards by another Treaty which was made at the *Hague*, *May* 16, 1613

The Catholick Princes oppos'd this Union by the League they made at *Mulhausen* the

One may say that it was what sav'd the Emperor, and preserv'd the Imperial Dignity of the House of *Austria* From the Year 1606, *Spain* had made a private Treaty with the Arch-Dukes *Matthias*, *Maximilian*, and *Ferdinand*, by which they had agreed, that they should endeavour to raise to the Empire him amongst them, which was the oldest Prince of that House to which the King of *Spain* consented, on Condition, That for Default of Heirs Male, he should succeed to the Kingdoms of *Hungary* and *Bohemia* This Treaty was afterwards renew'd and enlarg'd at *Prague*, *June* 6, 1617, where *Ferdinand* consented, that for Default of Male Issue, *Spain* should succeed to all the Hereditary Countries, and by this mean they render'd their Interest one and the same

The Arch-Duke *Ferdinand* had for his Appennage, together with *Stiria*, *Carinthia*, *Carniola* and the *Frioul*, at least that part of this Province which belongs to the House of *Austria*, on which account he had an unlucky Difference enough with the Republick of *Venice* He protected the *Uscoques*, who not only committed several Depredations in the Gulph, but also very much annoy'd the *Turks*, who resented it to the *Venetians*, who were Guarantees for the Safety of the *Adriatick* Sea. The Emperor accommodated the Difference by a Treaty which was concluded at *Vienna* in the Year 1612 But *Ferdinand* neglecting to execute it, both sides took to Arms, and the War which at first was confin'd to *Frioul* and *Dalmatia*, communicated it self to the rest of *Italy*, on the Score of the Difference the Duke of *Savoy* had with that of *Mantua*

5 H   The

The Duke of *Savoy* had Pretensions to the *Montferrat*, and in marrying his Daughter to *Francis*, Duke of *Mantua*, he allow'd that no mention should be made thereof. But *Francis* dying in the Year 1612, and leaving but one only Daughter very young, and the Cardinal of *Mantua* having succeeded to the Dutchy, the Duke of *Savoy* reviv'd his old Pretensions. He sent for his Daughter, the Widow of the deceased, and requir'd that the young Princess, his Grand-Daughter (whom he consider'd as Heiress of the *Montferrat*) should be put into his Hands. The Duke of *Mantua* oppos'd it, and declar'd himself Guardian to his Niece, who was but three Years old. He refus'd her even to *Don John de Mendose*, Marquiss of *Inoyosa*, Governor of *Milan*, who demanded her of him in the Name of the King of *Spain*. The Duke of *Savoy* enter'd the *Montferrat* with an Army in the Month of *April* 1613, and thereby equally offended the King of *Spain*, who pretended to be, if not Judge, at least Arbitrator of the Differences of all the Princes of *Italy*, and the Queen Regent of *France*, who was for protecting the Duke of *Mantua* her Nephew. The Treaties which had been made at *Chasteau* in *Cambresis* in the Year 1559, and at *Vervins* in the Year 1598, contain'd expressly, that neither of the two Kings should attack the Estates of the Duke of *Mantua*, nor suffer the Duke of *Savoy* to prosecute his Pretensions against the *Montferrat*. So that the Governor of *Milan*, apprehending lest the *French* should make use of this occasion to send Troops into *Italy*, oblig'd the Duke of *Savoy* to acquiesce to the King of *Spain*'s Desires. But forasmuch as the Treaty which was sign'd for that purpose at ―― had been made without the Participation of the Duke of *Mantua*, and that the *Spaniards* had tack'd Conditions thereto, which both his Honour and Interest hinder'd him from fulfilling, there ensu'd a second Rupture, which lasted till the Treaty of *Ast*, which was concluded *June* 1615.

Some Months after, the Republick of *Venice* came to a Rupture with the Arch-Duke *Ferdinand* on the Account of the *Uscoques*, as I before observ'd. To give a Diversion to the Forces of *Ferdinand*, whom *Spain* was going to succour, she resolv'd to furnish Employment to the Governour of *Milan*, who was he that could incommode her most. To this Effect she treated with the Duke of *Savoy*, who complain'd of the Inexecution of the Treaty of *Ast*, of which he accus'd the *Spaniards*, so that finding himself assur'd of very considerable Subsidies from the *Venetians*, he refus'd to hearken to the Propositions of Accommodation which the Pope and *France* made to him. The Council of *Paris* had no great Mind to engage the King in the *Italian* War, neither was the Chief Minister of the Court of *Madrid* inclin'd thereto, and the Arms of *Spain* not making any great Progress in *Piedmont*, no more than those of the *Venetians* in the *Friouli*, the Parties easily consented to a Negotiation, which produc'd the Treaty of *Madrid* in the Year 1617. But forasmuch as the King of *Spain* spoke there like a Master and an Arbitrator, the Embassador of *Venice* would not accept of him, and the Pope refusing to meddle therein on the Conditions which the Duke of *Savoy* annex'd to his Submission, the Affair was at last carry'd to *Paris*, where the Treaty was concluded *September* 6, 1617, as shall be related in the following Chapter. The Court of *Madrid* confirm'd it towards the End of the same Month and in the Month of *October* in the same Year a Treaty was made between the Duke of *Savoy* and the Governor of *Milan* at *Pavia*, for the Execution of the Treaty of *Paris*. The Duke of *Savoy* was no sooner got clear of this War, than he engag'd in new Intrigues with those who labour'd to stir up *Bohemia* to an Insurrection, as well as the other Hereditary Provinces of *Ferdinand*. The Republick of *Venice* had the same Interest and the same Intention, and it was in this View that she made an Alliance with the United Provinces, by the Treaty which was concluded at the *Hague*, *December* 31, 1619, and confirm'd by another which was made at the same Place, *April* 18, 1620.

Before I speak of the Commotions of *Bohemia*, which were the Cause of a very fatal War, that produc'd a great many Treaties, it is necessary to speak of those of the *Grisons*, which some People look upon to have been the Source of those Disorders which have harrass'd *Europe* for above these threescore Years. The Disputes the Duke of *Savoy* had with the Republick of *Genoa*, about the Marquisate of *Zuccarello*, and the Duke of *Modena* with the Republick of *Lucca*, about the *Garfagnana*, do not deserve to be dwelt upon, because those trifling Wars which were made on those Accounts, began and ended almost at the same time. King *Henry* IV, when he renew'd in the Year 1602, the Alliance with the *Swiss Cantons*, and the *Grey Leagues*, had reserv'd to himself a Passage through the *Valteline* for himself and his Friends. The *Valteline* is a Valley which reaches from the Lake *Como*, and the Dutchy of *Milan*, of which it was formerly a part, as far as *Tirol*. So that that Passage which is of two and twenty Leagues extent, is very commodious for a Communication of the States the House of *Austria* possesses in *Germany*, with those which the King of *Spain* holds in *Italy*. The *Valtelines* are Subjects to the *Grey Leagues*, but the Duke of *Feria*, Governor of *Milan*, under the Pretext of maintaining the Roman Catholick Religion in the *Valteline*, and of protecting the Inhabitants against the *Grisons* their Sovereigns, seiz'd the whole Valley, and even compell'd the *Leagues* to conclude the Treaty of *Coire* with him on *March* 19, 1617, and after that another on *October* 15, 1619, which were both very prejudicial to *France*. King *Lewis* XIII finding himself dispossess'd of an Advantage which the King his Father had acquir'd and left him, and considering withal that this Usurpation made an end to establish the predominate Power of the *Spaniards* in *Italy*, complain'd thereof to the Pope, and sent *M. de Bassompierre* into *Spain*, with Orders to procure a Redress of the Encroachment. *Bassompierre* arriv'd at *Madrid* a few Days before *Philip* III dy'd, but yet that did not hinder him from entring upon, and continuing his Negotiation, and notwithstanding he had no Power to make a Treaty, yet he concluded that of *Madrid*, *April* 25, 1621. That Treaty regulated in some measure the Affair of the *Valteline*, it secur'd there the Roman Catholick

The EMBASSADOR and his FUNCTIONS. 395

Catholick Religion, and the Sovereignty to the *Grisons* But the *Spaniards*, who had shewn themselves very easy to conclude the Treaty, rais'd a thousand Difficulties about the Execution of it The Duke of *Feria*, instead of following the Orders which were sent him from *Madrid*, sent for the Deputies of the *Grisons* to *Milan*, and oblig'd them in the Month of *January*, 1622, to make a Treaty, by which they renounc'd the Sovereignty of the *Valteline* And in *September* of the same Year, the Arch-Duke caus'd them to sign another Treaty at *Lindau*, by which the *Grisons* yielded up to him the League of the Ten Jurisdictions, with the Seigneury of *Mayenfelt*

On *May* 3, 1622, there was indeed another Treaty concluded at *Madrid*, but he that had made it without Order was disavow'd in *France*, because thereby the Passage of the *Valteline* was granted to all the Catholick Princes and States without Distinction The Refusal the *Spaniards* made, to execute the first Treaty of *Madrid*, oblig'd the King to make, in the Year 1623, a Treaty with the Republick of *Venice* and the Duke of *Savoy* It was equally fear'd at *Rome* and at *Madrid*, that, in this Disposition of Humours, the two Crowns would come to a Rupture, wherefore the *Spaniards* employ'd the Pope, who, in the Year 1624, engag'd the Commander de *Sillery*, Embassador of *France* at *Rome*, in a Project of a Treaty which was disavow'd in *France*, because the Embassador did therein an irreparable Prejudice to the Sovereignty of the *Grisons*, and that he had neither Order nor Power to treat, so that to give a publick Testimony how little it was satisfy'd with his Conduct, he was recall'd It was on the same Account that *Urban* VIII sent Cardinal *Barberin* into *France*, where he effected nothing Cardinal *de Richelieu*, who at that time had been made first Minister, was of Opinion that the King's Honour was not less engag'd therein than the Interest of the Leagues, and was very angry with *du Fargis*, Embassador of *France* in *Spain*, who from a familiar Conversation, which he had with the Count Duke *d'Olivares*, had enter'd into a formal Negotiation However, as the Party of the Religionaries was still very considerable in the Kingdom, it was not thought adviseable to break with *Spain*, nor to disavow the Treaty, but Orders were sent to *du Fargis* to get some of its Articles reform'd, of which, after several Debates, a formal Treaty was made, which was sign'd at *Monçon*, March 5, 1626, at least it was dated from that Day That Cardinal *Barberin*, who arriv'd in *Spain*, when it was just upon the Point of being concluded, might have no Hand therein This Treaty was made without the Participation of the Prince of *Savoy*, who was in *France* at that time, neither was any mention made of it to the *Venetian* Embassador, so that the Republick and the Duke were very much offended thereat The King endeavour'd to justify his Procedure by Embassadors Extraordinary, whom he sent to *Venice* and *Turin*. But forasmuch as the *Grisons* themselves rejected the Treaty, which had been made without them, because they were not therein treated very much like Sovereigns; and that it was not otherwise very punctually executed by either of the Parties, the King of *France*, while he was at the Siege of *Rochell*, in the Year 1629, made a Declaration, which was to serve as an Explanation to several Articles of the Treaty of *Monçon* The *Imperialists* said, That it did not belong to *France* to explain alone a Treaty which had been made for the Common Interest, and carry'd their Arms, which they held ready in *Germany* for that Purpose, into the *Valteline*, of which they made themselves Masters Hereupon it was found necessary to enter upon fresh Negotiations, which the Elector of *Bavaria* brought to Perfection at *Ratisbone*, where was concluded *October* 13, 1630, a Treaty between the Emperor *Ferdinand* II and *Lewis* XIII, it contain'd, That the *Grisons* and the *Valtelines* should be restor'd to their former State But this Treaty not being executed in Reference to the 12th and 13th Articles, which speak of the *Valteline*, two Treaties were made at *Querasque* in *Piedmont*, *April* 6 and *June* 19, 1631, which provided for the Execution of that of *Ratisbone*, as well concerning the Affairs of *Mantua*, as those of the *Valteline*, from whence the Emperor withdrew his Arms, because he had Occasion for them against the King of *Sweden*

The Course of the War in *Bohemia* had brought them into *Germany*, where they who had the chief Management of the Affairs of *France* were for being concern'd, but upon Principles very different from those on which King *Henry* IV had grounded his Maxims They dispatch'd a solemn Embassy, compos'd of the Duke of *Engoulesme*, of the Count *de Bethune*, and of *M de Chasteauneuf*, who, instead of entering into the Interests of the ancient Friends of *France*, concluded the Treaty of *Ulm*, *July* 13, 1620 This Treaty contain'd, That no Elector, or Prince of either Party; that is to say, of the Union and of the League, should attack directly or indirectly any Electorate, Principality, Province or Town, under any Pretext whatever The Ministers of *France* imagin'd they had play'd a fine Stroke of State, and nevertheless thereby they gave the Duke of *Bavaria* the Means to joyn his Troops to those of the Emperor in *Bohemia*, and to procure him, together with the Victory of *Prague*, all the other Advantages which the Arms of *Ferdinand* acquir'd since in *Germany* The first which he reap'd, from the Success of this Battel, was the Reduction of *Hungary*, where *Gabor Bethlehem* had caus'd himself to be proclaim'd King *Bethlehem* had made an Alliance with *Frederick* King of *Bohemia*, by a Treaty which had been concluded at Presburg in the Year 1620 But after the Loss of this Battel, and after the precipitate Retreat of the King of *Bohemia*, he lent an Ear to the Proposals for an Accommodation, which the Court of *Vienna* made to him, and he demanded Passports for the Deputies he was to send to the Conferences, where the *French* Embassadors assisted as Mediators This was not the Emperor's Intention, who having overcome his Difficulties, and having no longer any Consideration for *France*, continu'd the Negotiation with *Bethlehem*, and at last concluded the Treaty with him at Vienna, May 5, 1624

While the Emperor, and the Duke of *Bavaria*, made an end to reduce *Bohemia*, and the Provinces that depend thereon, the *Spaniards* enter'd into the *Palatinate*, of which they made them-

themselves Masters in a very little time, and so terrify'd the United Princes, who were not in a Condition to oppose them, that to prevent being driven out of their Countries, they were forc'd to make an Agreement with the Marquiss *Spinola*, who there commanded the Arms of *Spain*. The Lantgrave of *Hesse* was the first that made his Treaty at *Bingue*, *April* 5, 1621, and the other Princes of the Union concluded their Treaties with the said Marquiss, at *Mayence*, the twelfth of the same Month.

James, King of *Great Britain*, had not approv'd of the Resolution of his Son-in-Law, and was of Opinion that that which *Bohemia* had taken, to call him to the Crown, was a declar'd Revolt, but yet he could not bear that the Emperor should deprive the *Palatine* of the Electoral Dignity, nor that the *Spaniards* and the Duke of *Bavaria* should dispossess him of his hereditary Estates. However, as War was neither the King's Talent nor Inclination, he made use of no other Means than that of Negotiation, and endeavour'd to procure his Reestablishment by the way of Embassies, which he sometimes sent to the Emperor, sometimes to the Diets, and sometimes to *Madrid* and *Brussels*. The Infant sent him also her Ministers, accompany'd by those of the King of *Spain*, who made two Treaties at *London*, on *March* 29 and *April* 14, 1623, the one for the Restitution of the *Palatinate*, and the other for the Sequestration of the Town of *Frankendal*. The *Spaniards*, who knew King *James*, and did not fear him, neglected him, and *France*, and the United Provinces, whom it behov'd to oppose all the Prosperities and prodigious Grandeur to which the House of *Austria* was arriv'd, expected nothing vigorous from him. But as they were extremely jealous of the said Grandeur, and that a great many other Potentates besides, took Umbrage thereat, *France* and the United Provinces enter'd into a stricter Union, (of which we shall speak hereafter,) and on *August* 8, 1624, a Treaty was concluded at *Paris* for the Recovery of the *Palatinate* and the *Valteline*, between *France*, *England*, *Sweden*, *Denmark*, *Venice*, the United Provinces, and the Duke of *Savoy*.

In the Year 1621, the Ministers of *England*, *Denmark*, *Sweden*, of the United Provinces, of the Elector of *Brandenburgh*, of the Dukes of *Brunswick*, *Lunenburg*, *Holstein*, *Pomerania*, and of the States of the Circle of the Lower *Saxony*, had concluded the Treaty of *Segneberg*, in the Countrey of *Holstein*; after another Treaty which the States of the United Provinces had caus'd to be made at *London*, on *June* 15, 1624, in Favour of the Elector Palatin. The particular Treaty which was concluded at the *Hague*, on *August* 1 of the following Year 1625, with King *Charles*, had no other Object, no more than that which was made at *Titchfield* on the twenty fifth of the same Month. On *December* 9, of the same Year, another Treaty was again made at the *Hague*, on the same Account, and the King of *Denmark* was brought into the same. It was after this Treaty that this last declar'd War against the Emperor, but his good Intentions were so ill pursu'd, and his Arms were attended with so little Fortune, that to get clear of all these Disgraces he made an Accommodation with *Ferdinand* II, by the Treaty which was concluded at *Lubeck*, on *May* 22, 1629. He had from *March* 25, 1625, concluded the Treaty of *Lawemburg* with the Archbishops of *Magdeburg* and of *Bremen*, with the Duke of *Brunswick Wolfembuttel*, with *Adolphus Frederick* and *John Albert* Dukes of *Mecklenburg*, and with *Frederick* Duke of *Holstein*, for the Preservation of the Lower *Saxony*. But it was this Treaty that drew thither *Tilly*'s Army, and was the Cause of the Proscription of the Dukes of *Mecklenburg*, whose Dutchy was given to the Duke of *Fridland*.

The bad Success of the King of *Denmark*'s Enterprize making *France* apprehend lest her ancient Allies in the Empire should be opprest'd by the Power of the House of *Austria*, she labour'd at an Accommodation between the Kings of *Poland* and *Sweden*, which was effected at *Warsaw*, *October* 8, 1622, in Order to afford the Great *Gustavus Adolphus* the Means, and Leisure to apply himself to the Affairs of *Germany*. The Emperor had carry'd his Conquests as far as the *Baltick* Sea. He had taken all the *Mecklenburg* from its Princes, and in all *Pomerania* there was only the Town of *Stralsund* that refus'd to receive an Imperial Garrison. This Town had put it self under the Protection of the King of *Sweden*, by a Treaty made from *January* 23, 1628. So that when General *Arnhem* being'd it, it made so vigorous a Defence, that she gave the King time to disengage himself from the War with *Poland*, and to pass into *Germany*. It was by the Treaty that was concluded at *Tiegenhof*, *February* 28, 1630, and in the same Year he began to treat with *France*, who employ'd therein *Hercules* Baron of *Charnacé*, with whom he concluded, on *January* 23 of the following Year, the Treaty of *Berwald* for five Years. On *August* 12, of the same Year, 1631, the same King made a Treaty of Alliance with *William* Lantgrave of *Hesse*, and afterwards with the Elector of *Saxony*, and some other Protestant Princes, to whom the Emperor oppos'd an Alliance, which he had contracted with some Catholick Princes at *Vienna*, on *February* 14, 1632. *Gustavus Adolphus* being kill'd at the Battel of *Lutzen*, *November* 16 of the same Year, the Alliance between *France* and *Sweden* was renew'd with Queen *Christina*, by the Treaty which was concluded at *Hailbron*, *April* 13, 1633, and this Alliance was to last till there was a Peace. On *September* 17, 1634, there was another Treaty made at *Franckfort* with Chancellor *Oxenstiern*, Director General of the Affairs, and of the Arms of *Sweden* in *Germany*, and with the other Confederates, whose Deputies were assembled in that Place. This Treaty was since confirm'd and enlarg'd by another Treaty, which was concluded at *Paris* on *November* 1 of the same Year. The Chancellor going afterwards through *France*, made again another Treaty at *Compiegne*, *April* 28, 1635. The Plenipotentiaries of the two Crowns made on *March* 20, 1636, another Treaty at *Wismar*, but this Treaty not being ratify'd in *Sweden*, and the Emperor *Ferdinand* II, against whom the Allies had taken Arms, being dead, it was judg'd necessary to renew the Alliances by a Treaty, which *d'Avaux* and *Salvius*, Embassadors of *France* and *Sweden*, made at *Hamburgh*, *March* 6, 1638. This Treaty, which was only made for

three

three Years, was to expire *March* 15, 1641 On *January* 30, of the same Year 1641, another Treaty was concluded by the same Ministers at the same Place, which was to last till there was a Peace

The Preliminary Treaty for a General Peace was at last concluded at *Hamburgh, December* 25 of the same Year 1641 The Emperor on the one Part, and *France* with her Allies on the other, came there to an Agreement concerning the Time and Place for the Assembly, as also about the Passports for their Ministers Since that Time to the Conclusion of the Peace of *Westphalia*, there was not any Treaty between the two Crowns of *France* and *Sweden March* 14, there was indeed a Treaty made at *Ulm* with the Elector of *Bavaria*, who had also Power from the Elector of *Cologn*, wherein was also compris'd the Lantgrave of *Hesse*, but it was as soon broke as concluded, and had like to have created a very bad Understanding between the two Crowns Since the Peace of *Germany*, *France* has made several Treaties with *Sweden*, and particularly since the Abdication of Queen *Christina*, and the Death of *Charles Gustavus*, and among the rest that of *Fontainbleau*, of *September* 22, 1661, that of *Stockholm*, of *December* 30, 1662, concerning the Commerce, and particularly that which *M de Pomponne* made at *Stockholm*, on *April* 14, 1672

The Congress of *Westphalia* produc'd the Treaty which was concluded at *Munster, January* 30, 1648, between *Spain* and the United Provinces, that which was sign'd at the same Place on *October* 28, of the same Year, between the Emperor and the King of *France*, another between the Emperor and *Sweden*, at *Osnaburg*, *October* 28, 1648, and at last that of *Neuremberg*, of *July* 2, 1650, for the Execution of the Treaties of *Westphalia*

Before *France* declar'd it self against the House of *Austria*, Cardinal *de Richelieu*, who was for stirring up Enemies to *Spain* on all sides, undertook to give it a powerful Diversion by Means of the *Hollanders*, who were again engag'd in a War with the *Spaniards*, since the Expiration of the Truce of twelve Years To this Effect a Treaty was concluded at *Compiegne*, *April* 1, 1624, with a separate Article *June* 18, of the same Year On *April* 12, of the following Year, a particular Treaty was made concerning some Ships which were to be employ'd under Vice-Admiral *Hautain* at the Siege of *Rochelle*, on *August* 28, 1617, a Treaty was indeed concluded at *Paris* for nine Years, but it was not ratify'd, and on *June* 17, 1634, a more particular Treaty was made at the *Hague*, for the Subsidies, and for a stricter Alliance, which was confirm'd and enlarg'd by another Treaty concluded by the Baron *de Charnaed* at the *Hague*, *April* 15, 1634, and was to last seven Years The States General, who then thought they should reap greater Advantages from a Continuation of the War, if *France* was engag'd therein with them, oblig'd the King to declare against *Spain*, after the Treaty that was concluded at *Paris*, *February* 8, 1635, for a perpetual Alliance Since that time, there has hardly pass'd a Year, till the Peace of *Munster*, in which there was not some Treaty made between *France* and the United Provinces As that of *March* 16, of the same Year, concerning the Word and the Order which should be given in the Army, that of the *Hague*, on *September* 6, 1636, for the Supply of fifteen hundred thousand Livres, that of the same Place, on *December* 17, 1637, for a Subsidy of twelve hundred thousand Livres, and of *April* 26, 1639, at St *Germains*, for Subsidies, that of *Paris*, on *February* 14, 1641, for Subsidies, that of the *Hague*, on *March* 8, 1642, for thirty Companies of Foot, that of *Paris*, on *March* 30, 1633, which was renew'd *May* 16, following, that of the *Hague*, of *February* 29, 1644, for Subsidies, that for a Guaranty, on *March* 1, of the same Year, that of the *Hague*, on *April* 20, 1645, for the Campaign, those of *Paris*, on *April* 6, 1646, for Subsidies; that concerning the *Marine*, concluded at *Paris*, *April* 18, 1646, which serv'd for a Model for all the Treaties of that Nature, which have been made since that time, and, in fine, that for a Guaranty, on *July* 29, 1647

The United Provinces having, at the beginning of the following Year, made a separate Treaty with *Spain* at *Munster*, on *January* 30, 1648, have had no great Commerce of Affairs with *France* since then, but on the contrary, a very great Difference, on the Account of the continual Depredations which the *French* Privateers committed in the *Mediterranean*, which gave Occasion to Reprisals, and afterwards to a kind of Treaty, which was made at the *Hague* with *M de Thou*, in the Year 1657 On *May* 20, 1659, another Treaty was concluded at the *Hague*, between the Ministers of *France*, *England*, and the Deputies of the States, for the Affairs of the *North*, which was not executed at all on the part of *France*, and but very faintly on that of *England*, as well for other Considerations, as by Reason of the Change which happen'd in the Government after the Death of *Oliver Cromwell* On *April* 27, 1662, another Alliance was concluded at *Paris*, between *France* and the United Provinces, by virtue of which the King assisted them against *England*, and against the Bishop of *Munster* During this War with *England*, another Treaty was concluded on *May* 5, 1667, which was particularly for the Junction of the Fleets, which however was not done, because the *French* employ'd theirs on the Coast of *Portugal*

In the heighth of the War in *Germany*, and almost at the same time that *France* had treated with the King of *Sweden*, it labour'd to unlink the Elector of *Bavaria* from the Interest of the House of *Austria*, and to this Effect the Treaty of *Munich* was concluded with him, on *May* 8, 1631 The King promis'd the *Bavarian* by this Treaty, to secure the Electoral Dignity to his Person and House, and neither to assist with his Arms nor Money, those who should make War against him There was in this Treaty something very opposite to that which *France* had lately concluded with the King of *Sweden*, who considering the Duke of *Bavaria* as the Head of the *Catholick* League, and as him who had alone retriev'd the Emperor's Affairs, by the powerful Succours he had from time to time sent him, was not at all satisfy'd therewith, no more than with that which *la Saludie* concluded at *Ehrenbretstein*, with *Philip*, Archbishop and Elector of *Triers*, on *April* 9, 1632, because this Treaty con-

tain'd

tain'd amongst other things, That the King of *France* should employ his Forces, to drive out the *Swedes* that should be found within the Archbishoprick *France* made another particular Alliance with him at *Fontainbleau*, on *October* 12, 1661.

France, to strengthen its Party in the Empire after the Death of King *Gustavus Adolphus*, made on *April* 13, 1633, a Treaty at *Halbron*, with the Princes and States of the four Circles of the Upper and Lower *Rhine*, of *Francomia* and *Suabia*. On *September* 17, 1634, was concluded another, which we have before made mention of, as well as of that which was transacted at *Paris* on *November* 1 following, for the Continuation of the War with the Empire. The Emperor on his Part concluded on *May* 30, 1635, the Treaty of *Prague* with the Elector of *Saxony*, who therein stipulated certain Conditions for himself, and for the other *Protestant* Princes who would come into the same. On *October* 21, 1636, a Treaty was concluded at *Wefel*, between the Marquess of St *Chaumont*, Embassador of *France*, and *William*, Landgrave of *Hesse*, after another Treaty which had been made at *Minden*, *June* 12. preceeding; but had not its Perfection for want of being ratify'd, as also by reason of some Conditions which had been agreed to at the *Hague*, *September* 13, of the same Year, for raising the Siege of *Ehrenbreistein* or *Hermestein*. The Lantgrave promises therein to raise the Siege of that Fortress, and to maintain seven thousand Foot and three thousand Horse, for the Service of the common Cause, and the King promises to remit to him every Year a Subsidy of two hundred thousand Crowns. This Treaty was to last till there was a Peace. It was renew'd after the Death of this Prince, with *Amelia* of *Hannu*, his Widow, Regent of *Hesse*, by a Treaty concluded at *Dorsten*, *October* 22, 1639, on the same Conditions with the preceeding Treaty. On the 30th of the same Month the same Princess made a Treaty at *Minden* upon the *Werre*, with the Princes of *Brunswick* and *Lunenbourg*. Even from *October* 26, 1635, a Treaty had been concluded at St *Germain en Laye*, between *Ponica*, Minister of *Bernard*, Duke of *Saxe Weimar*, and the King's Commissaries, for the raising and subsisting of twelve thousand Foot, and five thousand Horse, in Consideration of four millions of Livres per Ann. On *October* 17, 1637, the Duke made another Treaty at *Paris*; but it was only to settle the Arrears that were due to him. This Prince dying in the Year 1639, *France* made a Treaty at *Brisac* with the Directors of the Army of the Deceas'd, in the Month of *October*.

Next to the Duke of *Bavaria*, there was no Prince that shew'd more Zeal or those Affection for the Interest of the House of *Austria*, than *Charles* Duke of *Lorrain*. For which Reason the Emperor made pressing Instances, while the Preliminaries were negotiating at *Hambourg*, that Passports might be granted to the Deputies the Duke pretended to send to the Assembly, which was to meet about a general Peace; but *France* would never consent thereto, by reason of the particular Treaties he had concluded with the King, without the Intervention of the Emperor, and of the King of *Spain*. And in fact, on *January* 6, 1632, the Duke of *Lorrain* had made the Treaty of *Vic*, by which he renounc'd all the Alliances, and all the Treaties, which he had made contrary to the Intentions and Interest of the King. But forasmuch as the Duke did not make good the same, but oblig'd the King to carry his Arms into *Lorrain*, the King would not restore the Places which had been conquer'd from him, till he put into his Hands the Towns of *Stenay*, *Jametz* and *Clermont*, which were to remain so for the Space of four Years, and serve as a Pledge for the Promise he made, never to depart from the Interest of his Majesty. This Treaty was made at *Liverdun*, *June* 26, 1632. This same Treaty not being able to hinder the Duke from continuing his Correspondence with the House of *Austria*, as well in *Spain* as in *Germany*, the King, to prevent the *Swedes*, (who threaten'd *Lorrain*) was forc'd to enter it again with a powerful Army in the Year 1633, and besieg'd *Nancy*, compelling the Duke to receive a *French* Garrison, by a Treaty which was concluded in the Camp before *Nancy*, *September* 6, of the same Year. Some private Articles were added thereto, which were agreed upon at *Charmes* the 20th of the same Month. The Duke of *Lorrain*, instead of executing these Treaties bona fide, flung himself openly into the Party of the House of *Austria*, and declar'd against *France*. He remain'd so till in the Year 1641, he came into *France*, whether because he was really disheartn'd by the continual Improsperity of the Emperor's Arms, and those of the King of *Spain*, or that his Intention was to make better Terms for himself with them, and he there concluded the Treaty of *Paris*, on *March* 29, of the same Year 1641. By this Treaty he yielded up the Towns of *Stenay*, *Jametz*, *Clermont* and *Dun*, to be annex'd to the Crown of *France* for ever, together with their Appurtenances and Dependencies, and consented that the King should put a *French* Garrison into *Nancy* till a Peace should be concluded. But this Treaty was almost as soon violated as made, and the Duke return'd immediately to his first Maxims and true Inclinations. Even from *January* 19, 1634, he had yielded up the Dutchy of *Lorrain* to the Cardinal his Brother, but with the Design to reserve still the Sovereignty and Revenue thereof to himself. As in effect, treating with *France* in the Year 1641, he speaks in the Quality of Duke and of Sovereign. Some Years after he was for renewing with her, and passing with his Troops into the King's Service, but the *Spaniards* prevented him, stopp'd him at *Brussels*, and sent him a Prisoner to the Cittadel of *Antwerp*, from whence they convey'd him into *Spain*. He remain'd a Prisoner there till the Peace of the *Pyrenees*, in which he was compris'd; but in such a Manner as oblig'd him to make a particular Treaty with *France*, which was concluded at *Paris* the last Day of *February*, 1661. And after that another, of *February* 6, 1662, by which he yields up *Lorrain* to *France*, on Condition that the Princes of his House, should be acknowledg'd for Princes of the Blood of *France*, after those of the House of *Bourbon*. This was the Work of *M de Lionne*, but it was not what made him deserve the Encomium *M D, S E,* gives him, as to the most accomplish'd Politician of our Age. He

He did not know him fo well as others have done fince the Year 1636 By the Treaty of *Metz*, which was concluded on the laſt of *Auguſt*, 1643, the King reinſtates the Duke in the Poſſeſſion of *Lorrain*, in the Condition it was reſtor'd him by the Treaty of 1661, with an Exception of the Town of *Marſal*, for which there was a particular Covenant in this Treaty The *French* accus'd the Duke of *Lorrain* of Duplicity, even after theſe two laſt Treaties, for which reaſon the King was for ſeizing him But as he liv'd in a continual Diſtruſt, he took the Alarm from the firſt Advice he receiv'd of the Motion of the Troops of *France*, and made his Eſcape to die in Exile, much regretted by his Subjects, tho' his reſtleſs Humour and Imprudence had reduc'd them to the utmoſt Miſery

Charles Emanuel, Duke of *Savoy*, not having receiv'd from the King of *Spain*, neither the Aſſiſtance nor the Protection he had promis'd himſelf from him, in the Difference he had with *Henry* IV about the Marquiſate of *Saluzzo*, joyn'd in Intereſt with *France*, but the Death of *Henry*, and of the Duke of *Mantua*, oblig'd him to take other Meaſures *France* aſſiſted him againſt the Republick of *Genoa*, as we ſaid before and on *December* 14, 1616, ſhe mediated an Accommodation between the Duke, and the Duke of *Nemours*, who being of the ſame Houſe, had rais'd Troops in order to procure to himſelf a larger Appennage The Duke of *Savoy* was not ſatisfy'd with the Treaty of *Moncon*, for which reaſon he created a thouſand Troubles to Cardinal *de Richelieu*, and croſs'd all the Deſigns of *France* on the ſide of *Italy* The Treaty of *Suſa* was indeed concluded with him on *March* 11, 1629, and afterwards that of *Mireſleur*, on *October* 19, 1631, but they did not alter the Duke's Inclination, who hated the Cardinal full as much as he was hated by him, and oppos'd all his Intentions Inſomuch that he ſuffer'd the Miniſters of *Spain* to accommodate the Difference of *Zuccarello* by the Treaty of *Madrid*, of *November* 27, without the Participation of *France* On the other ſide *Spain* had no Share in the Treaty, which the Mareſchal *de Torras* and *Servien* (who had negotiated that of *Queraſque*) concluded at *Turin* on *October* 19, 1631, for the *depoſitum* of *Pignerol* during ſix Months and on *July* 5, 1632, with *Victor Amadeus* Duke of *Savoy*, for the Town and Cittadel of *Pignerol* On *July* 11, 1635, a Treaty was made at *Rivolles*, for a League offenſive and defenſive, between *Lewis* XIII, and the ſame Duke, who dying ſometime after, this Alliance was renew'd with the Dutcheſs his Widow at *Turin*, *June* 13, 1638 She was Mother and Guardian to the young Duke, but the Guardianſhip and the Regency were diſputed with her, by the Cardinal of *Savoy* and the Prince of *Carignan*, Brothers to the late Duke, who took to Arms, and made War againſt her, till ſuch time as the Difference was adjuſted by the Mediation of *France*, which procur'd the Treaty of *Turin* on *June* 14, 1642. There had been a Treaty concluded there with Prince *Thomas* of *Carignan*, on *December* 8, 1640. But he went from it, and did not execute it

The States of the United Provinces, before they intermeddl'd in the War of *Germany* with the King of *Sweden*, had made a Treaty with him at the *Hague*, on *April* 5, and *December* 11, 1614, which was follow'd by another Treaty of *December* 11, 1616, by which the King oblig'd himſelf to furniſh a certain Quantity of Copper, and this again was follow'd by a third Treaty on *November* 26, 1618, for the Loan of the Sum of ſeven hundred fifty ſix thouſand, five hundred and four Livres, thirteen Sols After the King of *Denmark* had loſt the Battel of *Lutern*, and had concluded the Treaty of *Lubeck*, of which we have before made mention, ſeveral Princes and States treated with *Guſtavus* King of *Sweden* The States of the United Provinces were among the firſt, and concluded the Treaty of   Some Years after the Death of the King, they renew'd this Treaty with Queen *Chriſtina*, Daughter of the late King, and with thoſe who had the Management of the Affairs of the Kingdom, on *September* 1, 1640, at *Stockholm* This Treaty was follow'd by a Treaty of Guaranty, which was concluded at *Suderocra*, *Auguſt* 15, 1645 On *September* 11, 1656, was concluded with *Charles Guſtavus*, Succeſſor to *Chriſtina*, the Treaty of *Elbing*, which the States of the United Provinces refus'd to ratify, unleſs ſome Articles were explain'd, which was adjuſted at *Elſenore*, *December* 29, 1659 The King of *Sweden* conform'd thereto, becauſe as he had procur'd himſelf but too many Enemies, he was oblig'd to yield to Neceſſity Some Years after his Demiſe, to wit, in the Year 1665, a Treaty was made at the *Hague*, which regulated the Differences which the *Weſt-India* Company of *Holland* had with the *African* Company of *Sweden*, and the Commerce of the *Guinea* Coaſt On *July* 16, 1667, a preliminary Treaty was concluded, and the 18th of the ſame Month a Treaty for the Renovation of Friendſhip Towards the End of the ſame Year, Count *Chriſtopher de Dona*, who had been concern'd as Mediator in the Peace of *Breda*, caus'd alſo the Treaty of *Elbing* to be redreſs'd, ſome Articles whereof had been alter'd, contrary to the Intention of the King of *Sweden* On *January* 23, 1668, was concluded with the ſame Count, the Treaty for a Peace between the two Crowns of *France* and *Spain* On *April* 25, 1668, was concluded at *London* the Treaty for a triple Alliance, of which the King of *England* had caus'd a Propoſition to be made at the *Hague* towards the End of the foregoing Year, but it had no effect On the contrary, *England* attack'd the United Provinces directly, and *Sweden* endeavour'd to divert their Forces, by attacking their Allies On *November* 16, 1675, a Treaty of Commerce was concluded at Stockholm with the aforeſaid Provinces

It was during the War in *Germany*, that the Rupture happen'd between *France* and *England* The Marriage of the King of *Great Britain*, inſtead of promoting a good Underſtanding between the two Crowns, caus'd ſuch an Alteration in their Friendſhip, that the two Kings came to a Rupture upon it Their Confidence had not been very great, each in the other, ſince the Death of Queen *Elizabeth*, and the Treaties which had been made between them did not reach farther than Decency, as the Treaty which was made with King *James* in the Year 1603, ſoon after his Acceſſion to the

Crown

Crown of *England* That which was made at *Fontainbleau* on *April* 14, 1623, was only a simple Treaty of Commerce, and the Treaty of *Paris* of *November* 20, confirm'd by King *Charles*, *May* 21, 1625, referr'd only to his Marriage Their good Understanding was soon at an End, by the Descent the *English* made in the Island of *Ré*, and by the Protection they promis'd since to the *Rochellers*, by the Treaty of *January* 28, 1628 But their Arms having been unfortunate, and the Duke of *Buckingham*, who was in part the Cause of the bad Understanding between the two Kings, being kill'd, it was no very hard Matter to cement their Friendship, and dispose them to a Peace the Treaty whereof was concluded at *Sufa* on *April* 24, 1629 On *March* 29, 1632, a Treaty of Commerce was made at St *Germain* between *France* and *England* Since that time this Kingdom was so harrass'd by Civil Wars, that the King had hardly any farther Commerce with foreign Powers After his Death, a kind of Republick or rather Anarchy was form'd, of which *Oliver Cromwell* was the Head, under the Quality of Protector

It was with him that the United Provinces engag'd in a War in the Year 1652, and afterwards made a Peace at *London*, *April* 5, 1654 On *April* 11, of the same Year, a Treaty was concluded at *Upsale*, between *Christina* of *Sweden* and the same Protector, who suffer'd a Treaty to be made between him and the King of *Portugal* on *July* 10 of the same Year The King of *Denmark* treated with him at *Westminster*, *September* 15 of the same Year 1654 *France* came in but late, and concluded its Treaty at *London* but on *November* 3, 1655, and she found her Account therein. It being certain that it is to this Treaty chiefly, that she is oblig'd for the Conquests she has since made in *Flanders* On *February* 6, 1659, another Treaty was made at the *Hague*, for adjusting the Differences between the *East-India* Companies of both Nations, and on the 27th the Sum was fix'd which the *Hollanders* should give to the *English*, after a Treaty which had been made the 3d of the same Month for the Affairs of the *North*

Immediately after the Restoration of the present King, all the Princes of *Christendom* courted his Friendship, and almost all of them treated with him There had been no Interruption of Friendship between the Kings of *France* and *England*, for which Reason they were contented to make a simple Treaty of Commerce, which was concluded at *Fontainbleau*, *October* 15, 1661 The King of *Great Britain*, at his embarking in *Holland* in order to go to *England*, made such mighty Protestations of an everlasting Acknowledgment for the Affection the States express'd to him in his Passage through their Country, that they thought themselves oblig'd to send a solemn Embassy after him, which was however above two Years a negotiating a Treaty of simple Friendship or to speak more properly, of mere Indifferency, which was not sign'd at *London* till *September* 14, 1662 As it is easy to pass from Coolness and Indifferency to an overt Enmity, the two Nations engag'd in a very cruel War the End whereof not proving so successful as the Beginning seem'd to promise, the King of *England* consented at last, that a Peace should be concluded at *Breda*, *July* 31, 1667, as well with the United Provinces, as with the Kings of *France* and of *Denmark*, their Allies, who made there particular Treaties of the same Date

Before we speak of the Invasion the Arms of *France* made the same Year into *Flanders*, which will lead us to the Peace which was lately concluded at *Nimeguen*, and which shall also put an end to this Chapter, we must say a word or two concerning the War of *Castro*, which arm'd a good part of the Potentates of *Italy* against the *Barberins*, towards the end of the Pontificate of *Urban* VIII The Republick of *Venice* enter'd into it with Reluctancy, and the same may be said of the Great Duke of *Tuscany*, and of the Duke of *Modena*, who got out of the same with Joy, by the Treaty which was made at *Ferrara*, *March* 31, 1644. The Invasion *Charles Gustavus* King of *Sweden* made into *Poland* in the Year 1655, was the Cause of a great Revolution in the Affairs of the World Before that time in *May* 1652, a Treaty had been made at *Stettin* for the Partition of *Pomerania*, between the King of *Sweden* and the Elector of *Brandenburg*, and after this Rupture the King had oblig'd the Elector to come into his Interests, first by the Treaty which these two Princes made at *Coningsberg* on *January* 17, 1556, which was follow'd by another Treaty, concluded at *Marienburg* *June* 15, 1656, with separate Articles of the same Month *November* 20 and 23 following the King and the Elector made another Treaty at *Liban* in *Prussia* But the *Swedish* Conquests becoming inconvenient to the Elector, this last reconcil'd himself with *Poland* by the Treaty which was concluded at *Welau*, *September* 19, 1657, and since again by another made at *Brisgotz* on *November* 6, 1659, where the Elector stipulated pretty considerable Advantages The King of *Denmark* having broke with that of *Sweden*, while the Arms of the last were employ'd elsewhere, he made an Alliance with *Poland*, by a Treaty which was concluded at *Copenhagen*, *July* 28, 1657, and after that another at *Cologn* on the *Spree*, *January* 17, 1658, between the same King of *Denmark* and the Elector, by virtue whereof the Arms of *Brandenburg* being advanc'd into *Holstein*, a Treaty of Neutrality was concluded on *November* 25, 1658 at *Flensburg*, between the Elector and the Duke of *Holstein Gottorp* Some Time before, the King of *Poland* had made a Treaty at *Vienna* with the King of *Hungary* on *May* 27, 1657, for the Assistance this last should furnish against *Sweden*, and on *February* 14 of the following Year, the Elector of *Brandenburg* made a Treaty with the same King of *Hungary* to the same effect Nevertheless the victorious Arms of the King of *Sweden* oblig'd the King of *Denmark* to conclude two Treaties with him, one at *Tostrup* on the 18th, and the other at *Roschild*, *February* 26, 1658 But these two Treaties being violated almost as soon as they were made, Hostilities began afresh on both sides, and ended but with the Life of the King of *Sweden* For it was not till after his Death that the Treaty of *Olivia* was concluded, *May* 3, 1660, which gave Peace to *Poland* as the Treaty of *Copenhagen*, which was concluded *June* 6, of the same Year, procur'd it to *Denmark*

France

The EMBASSADOR and his FUNCTIONS. 401

France, *England* and the United Provinces concern'd themselves very much in all those Treaties. The first, seeing the *Muscovite* attack'd the King of *Sweden* in *Livonia*, and that the two Kings of *Hungary* and of *Poland*, with the Elector of *Brandenburg*, diverted his Arms in *Pomerania*, while he had occasion for them in *Denmark*, fear'd left he should be ftrip'd of his Conquests in *Germany*. The *English* were for having it believ'd, that the Interest of the Proteftant Religion oblig'd them to labour at the Reconciliation of the two Northern Kings, tho' it was not out of that Motive that they made a Treaty with *France* in relation to those Affairs at *Westminster*, *February* 3, 1659. The United Provinces, which had therein a truer and more fenfible Intereft, viz. that of their Commerce, and of juft Apprehenfion of feeing the two Powers of thofe Parts reunited in the Perfon of a fingle Prince, concluded on *May* 21, of the fame Year 1659, a Treaty at the *Hague* with the Minifters of *France* and *England*, and afterwards thofe of *Auguft* 4, and of *September* 12 following, in order to put an end to that War. Hiftory will give an account how thofe Treaties were executed, as well as that which was made at *London*, *July* 29, of the fame Year.

The United Provinces were not only extremely incommoded in their Commerce, but they were alfo oblig'd to oppofe the prevailing Power of *Sweden*, as well out of Intereft, as on the account of feveral Treaties which they had with the Crown of *Denmark*. Amongft the moft remarkable which have been made fince the Beginning of this Century are, the Treaty which was made at the *Hague* on *May* 14, 1621. That of *October* 6, 1625, for a Supply of three thoufand Men. That of *May* 13, 1645, for the Duties that are paid in the *Sound*. That of *Chriftianople* of *Auguft* 13, of the fame Year 1645, for the Duties that are rais'd in *Norway*, at the *Hague* of *February* 12, 1646. That of the *Hague* of *February* 12, 1647, concerning the Duties which are paid in *Norway*. The Treaty of Alliance made at the *Hague*, *October* 9, of the fame Year 1647, and another of the fame Date for the Redemption or Forfeiture of the Toll Duties in the *Sound*. That of *Copenhagen* of *February* 18, 1649, and another of *September* 26, of the fame Year, made at the *Hague* for the Suppreffion of the Treaty of *October* 9, 1649, with a Treaty for a defenfive Alliance of the fame Date, concerning the Forfeiture of the Duty in the *Sound*. Another of *February* 8, for an Alliance, and of *September* 27, 1653, for the fame Toll. Another concluded at *Copenhagen*, *Auguft* 16, 1656, againft *Sweden*, with its Enlargement, of *July* 17, 1657. Another relating to the Gaging of Ships, of *April* 15, 1658. The Alliance made at the *Hague* between the King of *Denmark* and the United Provinces, on *February* 11, 1666, with the feparate Articles, relating to the *Weft India* Company, and the Affiftance of eight Men of War. Another Treaty concerning the Duties which are rais'd on Timber in *Norway*. A Treaty of Guaranty between *France*, *Denmark*, and the United Provinces. On *October* 25, 1666, the Quadruple Alliance was concluded at the *Hague* between the King of *Denmark*, the United Provinces, the Elector of *Brandenburg*, and the Dukes of *Brunfwick* and *Lunenburg*, *Zell* and *Ofnaburg*. And finally, on *July* 10, 1674, the Treaty for fuccouring the United Provinces was concluded at *Copenhagen*.

The two Crowns of *Sweden* and *Denmark* have been almoft in continual Wars, which have furnifh'd occafion for feveral Treaties, of which fome have been taken notice of before. There was one made in the Year 1613. The *Swedes* fearing left King *Chriftian* IV. fhould declare againft them, or fhould form a third Party in the Year 1644, when the War in *Germany* was at its height, were for preventing him, and compell'd him to accept the hard Conditions they impos'd upon him, by the Treaty which was concluded at Bremfebro, *Auguft* 13, 1645. This Treaty was follow'd by another, which was made at *Copenhagen*, *November* 5, of the fame Year, with *M. de la Tuillerie*, Embaffador of *France*. On *March* 19, 1641, the fame King made a Treaty of Commerce with *Spain*. The Difference the King of *Denmark* has with the City of *Hamburgh*, which he pretends is a Dependance of the Dutchy of *Holftein*, has alfo caus'd fome Treaties, whereof that which he made at *Seernburg*, *July* 18, 1621, is the moft confiderable, after that he had made with the *Hanfeatick* Towns at *Odenzee*, in the Year 1616. Both the one and the other are founded on the Treaty which was concluded at *Copenhagen* with the *Vandalick* Towns, on the Eve of St *Bartholomew*, 1441, and on that which was made at *Odenzee*, *July* 20, 1560. The Treaty which the Archbifhop of *Breme*, Son to *Chriftian* IV, made at *Stade* on *October* 1639, is of the fame Nature. In the Year 1660, immediately after the Reftoration of the prefent King, a Treaty was made between the Kings of *England* and *Denmark*, and another at Breda, *July* 31, 1667. Befides the Treaties which the Affairs of *Germany* caus'd *Sweden* to make with *France* and the United Provinces, and whereof we have before made mention, fhe concluded a Treaty with *England* in *Cromwell*'s time. And fince, between the two prefent Kings, firft at *London*, on *October* 23, 1661, and another at the fame Place on *April* 11, 1644, and afterwards a third on *February* 16, 1666, and in fine that of the triple Alliance, of which we have fpoken elfewhere. One between *Sweden* and *Poland* for a Truce of fix Years in the Month of *June* 1629, which being expir'd in the Year 1635, another Treaty was made for a Truce of many Years, which was concluded at *Stumpfdorf* on *September* 12, 1635, and was to laft till *July* 11, 1661. It was not yet expir'd when in the Year 1656, *Charles Guftavus* enter'd into *Poland*, as has been faid, which gave occafion to the Treaty of *Oliva*. On *February* 18, 1630, a Treaty was concluded at *Dirfhau* between *Sweden* and the Town of *Dantzick*. And forafmuch as by the Peace of *Weftphalia* the Principality of *Breme* remain'd to the *Swedes*, who thereupon form'd Pretenfions over the Capital thereof, this, relying on its Privileges, oppos'd the *Swedifh* Arms; fo that at laft both Parties came to a Treaty, which was concluded at *Habenhanfen* on *November* 28, 1654. But frefh Differences arifing between the Crown of *Sweden* and the fame Town, it was neceffary to proceed to another Treaty, which was finifh'd at *Stade*, *November*

5 K ber

ber 25, 1666 On *July* 6, of the same Year a Treaty had been made at *Hall*, between *Sweden* and the Princes of the House of *Saxony*.

The United Provinces have made a great many Treaties with their Neighbours, especially since the King of *Spain* has renounc'd his pretended Sovereignty over them, by the Treaty which was concluded at *Munster*, *January* 30, 1648 They had long before, to wit, on *June* 26, 1608, made a Treaty of Alliance with *England*, and on *September* 17, of the same Year, for the Sum which Queen *Elizabeth* had lent them On *May* 21, 1616, the Treaty of *Greenwich* for the Restitution of *Flushing*, &c and those of *London*, of *June* 5, 1624, and of the *Hague*, of *August* 5, 1625 Since the Peace of *Munster* the King of *Spain* himself has treated with them as with Sovereigns as in the *Treaty of Commerce, and Matters relating to the Sea*, which was made at the *Hague*, *December* 17, 1650 The Treaty for the *Provisional Partition of the Countries on the other side the* Meuse, on *March* 27, 1658, and *concerning the Estate of the* Carthusians *of August* 28, of the same Year On *December* 26, 1661, was at last concluded *the Partition of the Countries beyond the* Meuse, and on *September* 20, 1664, the Treaty was made which settl'd the Limits of the County of *Flanders* On *April* 29, 1665, a Treaty was made for the Suppression of the Bipartite Court of Justice, whose Judges were half Roman Catholicks, and half Protestants On *April* 9, 1668, that for the Loan of two Millions, but it was neither ratify'd nor executed On *August* 30, 1673, was concluded at the *Hague* a Treaty of Alliance against *France* for five and twenty Years, and on *October* 16, 1675, one was made with *Spain*, and the Bishop of *Munster*. The Irruption the *French* made into *Flanders* in the Year 1667, and the War they made in the Year 1672, against the United Provinces, occasion'd these three last Treaties, as well as several others, which we have taken notice of above The Treaties which were made with the Admirant of *Arragon* in the Year 1603, and with *Spinola* at *Calmthout* on *October* 18, 1622, relate only to the Quarters of the Prisoners of War

Since the Peace of *Vervins* there had been no Treaty between *France* and *Spain*, for the Interest of the two Crowns directly, till on *November* 7, 1659, was concluded that of the *Pyrenees* in the Island of *Pheasants*, and the Treaty which was agreed to by the Ministers of *England* and *Holland* at *St Germain en Laye* on *April* 25, 1668, and afterwards sign'd and concluded at *Aix la Chapelle* on *May* 2, of the same Year. This last Treaty subsisted only till the Year 1673, and the Rupture lasted till the Peace, which was concluded at *Nimeguen*, *September* 17, 1678. I have above made mention of a little Treaty which was concluded at *Madrid* in the Year 1614, and of some other Treaties which related to the Affairs of *Mantua* and of the *Valteline*.

There were great Discontents between the two Crowns, even before they broke out in the Year 1635. They have not fail'd of improving the Occasions whereby other of them could create Troubles to the other The Duke of *Rohan* caus'd a Treaty to be made with the Court of *Madrid*, *May* 3, 1629. The Marquiss d'*Aytone*, who commanded the Arms of the King of *Spain* in the *Low Countries*, made a Treaty with the Duke of *Orleans* on *May* 12, 1632 On *March* 13, 1642, *Fontrailles* negotiated a Treaty at *Madrid* for the same Duke of *Orleans*, and the Count de *Soissons*, and in the Beginning of the Year 1643, another for the Duke of *Orleans*, the Duke of *Bouillon*, *Cinq Mars*, &c France return'd the Kindness when it had an Opportunity, as for Instance, When she took the *Catalans* into her Protection, by the Treaty which was made at *Paris*, *September* 18, 1641 It is true that at that time she was at War with *Spain*, and that she was going to enter into the same when she concluded the Treaty of *Lisbon* on *March* 31, 1667, for an Alliance with the King of *Portugal* That Treaty, and the Invasion the Arms of *France* made in *Flanders* in the Year 1667, were the Cause of that which was concluded at *Madrid* on *January* 5, of the following Year 1668, between *Spain* and *Portugal*

The said Rupture between *France* and *Spain* gave occasion to the triple Alliance, which was concluded at the *Hague*, *January* 23, 1668, between *England*, *Sweden*, and the United Provinces On the same Day, and at the same Place, was made a *Treaty of Defensive Alliance* between *England* and the United Provinces, to which was join'd a *Treaty of Commerce and Marine*, *February* 17 It seem'd as if the Treaty of *Breda*, and these fine and great Alliances, which were concluded but on the Overtures the *English* made thereof, were only intended to render the United Provinces irreconcileable with *France*, since even in the Year 1671, or at the beginning of the Year 1672, the King of *England* made a League with it for the Conquest of those Provinces, against whom he made War, without any previous Declaration However perceiving soon that his Subjects grew weary of a War that incommoded their Commerce, while *France* alone gain'd by his Conquests, he at last yielded to the Sentiments of the Parliament, and suffer'd the King of *Spain* to mediate a Treaty, which was concluded at *London*, *February* 19, 1674

Among the Princes of *Germany* there was only the Elector of *Cologn* and the Bishop of *Munster* that sided with *France* The first had a Difference with the States about the Town of *Rhineberg*, but what animated him most against them, were the interested Counsels of the two Bishops of *Strasburg* and *Metz* of the House of *Furstemberg* But as soon as the Emperor had concluded his Treaty with the States at *Cologn*, on *April* 22, 1674, for the Junction of their Arms against *France*, the Elector concluded also his Treaty with them, on *May* 11, in the same Year 1674

The Bishop of *Munster* had soon after his Election a Difference with the capital City of his Diocese, wherein the States General engag'd themselves so far in behalf of the City, that the Bishop never forgave them He reduc'd the City in some measure after a Treaty which was concluded at *Schonvelt* on *February* 25, 1655, and made himself quite Master thereof by the Treaty which was made at *Geysteyn*, *October* 24, 1657 The same States interested themselves also for the Prince of *Ostfrise* against the said Bishop, who had proceeded to an Execution against the same Prince for a Sum of Money which he ow'd to the Prince of *Ligtenstein* This Difference was accommodated, but notwithstanding the Accommodation, he engag'd in a League with the King of *England*, to cause a Diversion to the *Hollanders* The Alliance these made with the Dukes of *Lunenburg*, and afterwards with the Elector of *Brandenburg*, oblig'd him to make the Treaty which was concluded at *Cleves*, April 18, 1666, into which the Dukes of *Lunenburg*, *Zell* and of *Osnaburg* enter'd These Princes had from *September* 9, 1665, made a Treaty at the *Hague*, with the United Provinces, by which they promis'd to raise and subsist four thousand Horse, and eight thousand Foot They en er'd afterwards into the quadruple Alliance, which was concluded at the *Hague*, *October* 25, 1666, and on *March* 16, 1668, they again made a particular Treaty with the United Provinces On *August* 22, 1667, was concluded a Treaty of Alliance at *Brunswick*, between the Electors of *Cologn* and *Brandenburg*, the Bishop of *Osnaburg*, the Dukes of *Brunswick* and *Lunenburg*, *Zell* and *Wolfenbuttel*, and the Lantgrave of *Hesse Cassel* After the Rupture in the Year 1672, several Treaties were made, whereof the first was concluded at *Berlin* on *May* 6, with the Elector of *Brandenburg*, for the raising and subsisting of twelve thousand Foot and eight thousand Horse On *September* 22, of the same Year 1672, a Treaty of Alliance defensive was concluded at *Brunswick*, between the Emperor, the King of *Denmark*, the Elector of *Brandenburg*, the Dukes of *Brunswick* and *Lunenburg*, and the Lantgrave of *Hesse Cassel*, after a Treaty which had been made at the same Place, *August* 22, 1667, between the Princes and States of the Circle of *Lower Saxony* But these two Treaties were, if not destroy'd, at least very much invalidated, by that which the Elector made with *France* at the Camp at *Vosten* on *April* 23, 1673 On *August* 30, of the same Year a Treaty was made at the *Hague*, between the King of *Spain* and the United Provinces as also a third between those three Allies and the Duke of *Lorrain* The Elector engag'd himself again since with the States, in a Treaty which was concluded at *Berlin*, on *July* 1, 1674 The Elector of *Cologn* reconcil'd himself with the Emperor, and with the States of the United Provinces by the Treaty of *Cologn* of *May* 11, 1674 The Bishop of *Munster* had also made his Accommodation, and the Dukes of *Brunswick* and *Lunenburg*, *Zell* and *Wolfenbuttel* had likewise treated with them. On *March* 9, 1675, was concluded at *Munich* a Treaty of Alliance for three Years, between the Crown of *Sweden* and the Elector of *Bavaria*, and on *September* 18 of the same Year, a Treaty of Neutrality was concluded between the King of *Denmark*, the Elector of *Brandenburg*, and the Bishop of *Munster*, they engaging for the Emperor, with *John Frederick* Duke of *Brunswick* and *Lunenburg*

What chiefly caus'd the Elector of *Brandenburg* to make a fresh Engagement with the States of the United Provinces, was the Treaty which had been made at *London* the 29th of *February* preceding, 1675, between the two *East India* Companies of *England* and *Holland*. The Elector had contracted a particular Intimacy with the King of *England*, during the Stay this last made in *Germany* and *Flanders*, under the Tyranny of *Cromwell* So that after the King's Restoration, a Treaty of Alliance was concluded between them at *London*, *July* 20, 1661 It was by the Mediation of his Ministers, that in the said City of *London* a Treaty was concluded on *May* 17 preceding, in the Name of the Princess Dowager of *Orange*, for the Guardianship of the Prince her Grandson

Altho' the Prince of *Orange* be not of the Number of those Sovereigns that at this time contend in War nevertheless the Merit of some of his Predecessors, and the Post this holds in most of the United Provinces, obliges me touch upon some Treaties which have been made for his particular Interest as for Instance, that which was concluded at *Ruel* with Cardinal *de Richelieu*, *November* 24, 1639 *January* 8, 1647, a Treaty was made at *Munster* between the Plenipotentiaries of *Spain* and those of the Prince of *Orange*, which was confirm'd after the Death of Prince *Frederick Henry*, *December* 17, of the same Year but it was new model'd by the Treaty which was concluded at the *Hague* on *October* 12, 1651, with the Guardians of the young Prince On *February* 15, 1659, a Treaty was made at *Coesfelt*, between the Bishop of *Munster* and the Guardians of the Prince for the Estate of *Bevergarden*

We may reckon amongst these particular Treaties, that which was made on *December* 4, 1616, between the Dukes of *Savoy* and *Nemours*. This last pretended to a larger Portion, and had made some Levies with *Spanish* Money, but *France* interceded, and reconcil'd these two Princes It was in the same Year that the Count *de Bueil*, a Nobleman of *Savoy*, put himself under the Protection of the Crown of *France* But this was not properly a Treaty, no more than the Agreement which the said Count made since with the Governor of *Milan*, to put himself into the Protection of the King of *Spain* On *July* 8, 1641, a Treaty was made at *Perone*, for *Monaco* On *August* 31, 1643, a Treaty of Alliance was made at *Venice* between the Republick, the Great Duke of *Tuscany*, and the Duke of *Modena*, against the *Barberins* Their Difference was made up by the Treaty, which was sign'd as I said above, at *Ferrara*, on *March* 31, 1644, by the Cardinals *Dongbi* and *Bichy*, Plenipotentiaries from the Pope and the King of *France*, and by the Allies at *Venice* the same Day The Treaty of defensive Alliance, which was made at *Cologn* on *December* 25, 1651, between some Princes of *Germany*, is of the same Nature, as also that which the Estates of *Cleves* made among themselves at *Mehr*, *July* 24, 1646 Here we may add the Treaties which were made between the two *East-India* Companies of *England* and *Holland* at *London*, *June* 2, and *July* 17, 1619, as also that of the *Hague* of *February* 6, 1659, together with that which was made with the Deputies of *St Malo* at the *Hague*, *October* 20, 1629 The Treaty made at *Avignon*, *March* 20, 1660, with the Count *de Dona*, for the Principality of *Orange* That which the two Provinces of *Holland* and *Zeland* concluded at the *Hague* on *September* 21, 1661, for their Court of Juſtice, and the Office of Captain General On *July* 21. 1668, another Treaty was made at the *Hague*, between the Deputies of *South-Holland* and thoſe of *North-Holland*, for their Quota towards the Contributions of the Province, which could not be regulated ſince the Union. The United Provinces made alſo a particular Treaty with the Elector of *Cologn* at the *Hague*, on *February* 14, 1667, and another of *December* 22, of the ſame Year, for the Town of *Rhyneberg*. I muſt hereunto add, the Treaty which the States of *Pruſſia* made with the Elector of *Brandenburg* at *Martenbourg*, on *November* 12, 1651, and that which was made at *Paris*, *December* 16, 1660, between the King of *France* and the Arch-Duke of *Inſpruck*, for *Alſace*, which properly ſpeaking, only facilitated the Execution of one of the Articles of the Treaty of *Weſtphalia*. The Treaty of *Piſa*, which was concluded *February* 12, 1664, between the Pope and the King of *France*, is ſingular and very conſiderable in all its Points, but it may be ſaid, to be an Inſtrument out of the way, becauſe it has nothing common with the general Affairs, no more than the Treaty which was made at *Tillemont* between *Maximilian Henry*, Elector and Archbiſhop of *Cologne*, and the Arch-Duke *Leopold William*, Governor of the *Low Countries*, for the Quarters of the Duke of *Lorrain*'s Troops, which was concluded on *March* 17, 1654. And in *December* the ſame Year one was made at *Cologn* on the ſame account, between the Electors and the Princes of the *Rhine*.

The United Provinces were the firſt that acknowledg'd the Duke of *Braganza* after his Acceſſion to the Crown of *Portugal*, and concluded with him on *June* 13, 1641, the Treaty of the *Hague*, as well for the Good of both States, as for that of the *Eaſt India* Company. This Treaty, as well as all the others, which the States have made with the King of *Portugal*, were concluded at the *Hague*, as was alſo that of *March* 27, 1645, for Fort *Galle* in the Iſland of *Ceylon*; and the Treaty of Peace which was concluded on *Auguſt* 16, 1661.

The ſaid United Provinces were concern'd as Guarantees in the Treaties and Agreements which have been made from time to time between the Counts and Princes of *Oſtfriſe* on the one part, and the States of the ſame Province on the other. There are ſo many of them, that whole Volumes might be made thereof, and the Information I might give of them, or the Enumeration I might make of the ſame, would be uſeful only to thoſe who are employ'd in thoſe Affairs, and delight in Conteſts and Cavils. It is ſufficient to obſerve in general, that the Treaty of *January* 2, 1624, made Count *Mansfelt*'s Army leave thoſe Quarters. And foraſmuch as ſome Years after, the Lantgrave of *Heſſe* had quarter'd his there, it was requiſite to treat again with him, as had been done at *Leeroort*, *September* 23, 1637.

The Treaties which the States have made with the Hanſe Towns in general, or with ſome of them in particular, have procur'd no Advantage at all to the United Provinces. In the Month of *May*, 1613, they made one at the *Hague* with the Town of *Lubeck*. In *December*, 1615, they made one with the Hanſe Towns, likewiſe at the *Hague*. On *Auguſt* 4, 1645, they made one with the Towns of *Breme* and *Hamburgh*, and on *November* 14, 1641, one with the Towns of *Lubeck*, *Breme* and *Hamburgh*, both at the *Hague*. On *July* 10, 1656, a Treaty was made at the *Hague* with the Town of *Dantzick*, occaſion'd by the War the King of *Sweden* was making in *Poland*. To which I ſhall add, that the ſame Hanſe Towns, that is to ſay, *Lubeck*, *Breme* and *Hamburgh* obtain'd on *May* 10, 1655, the Confirmation of their Privileges, from the moſt Chriſtian King, for thirteen Years, to which they give the Name of Treaty. It was founded on a Privilege King *Lewis* XI had granted them at *Amboiſe* in the Month of *September*, 1483, and confirm'd by King *Henry* IV at *Fontainbleau*, *December* 2, 1604. Theſe three I owns had made a particular Alliance on *November* 24, 1614. One might compoſe a Volume of the Treaties which the *Swiſs Cantons* have made, either among themſelves or with their Neighbours, and particularly with *France* and *Spain*. With this laſt for the Defence of the Dutchy of *Milan*, as alſo with the Houſe of *Auſtria* for the Foreſt Towns, with the *Griſons*, &c. which have very little or no relation to general Affairs, if we except thoſe which have been made for the *Valteline*, which we have touch'd upon above.

Many Princes and Chriſtian States have made Treaties, as well with the Port as with the Pirates of *Africa*. On *July* 17, 1662, the King of *England* cauſ'd a Treaty to be made with the *Algerines*. On *October* 5 following, another with thoſe of *Tunis*, and finally a third on the 18th of the ſame Month, and one with thoſe of *Tripoli*. On *April* 2, 1666, a Treaty was made at *Tangier* with *Cid Hamet Haaer Gailant*. On *December* 24, 1610, a Treaty was made at the *Hague* with the King of *Morocco*. In the beginning of *June* 1612, a Treaty was concluded at *Conſtantinople* with the Grand Seignior. In the Month of *May* 1617, and in *June* 1629, the States treated with thoſe of *Algiers*, as alſo on *January* 30, 1626. On *February* 7, 1631, a Treaty was made at the *Hague* with the King of *Perſia*. On *February* 9, 1651, a Treaty was made in the Ship *Leewarden*, with the Town of *Sally*, in the Road of the ſaid Town, and another Treaty at the *Hague*, *March* 25, 1657, with the Deputies of *Sally*, and an Explanation of the ſame Treaty on *October* 22, 1659. On *March* 26, 1662, one was made with thoſe of *Algiers*, and *November* 2, of the ſame Year, another with thoſe of *Tunis*. In the Year 1674, the *Algerines* made an Overture for a new Treaty with the United Provinces, but after great Negotiations they could come to no Concluſion, but concerning the Redemption of Slaves of which a Treaty was made in the Year 1677, and ratify'd by the States *September* 25, of the ſame Year.

The moſt conſiderable Treaties *Poland* has made in our Time with the *Turks*, are, firſt that which *Staniſlaus Zolskiensky* made in the Year 1617, with *Skinder Bacha* near the Town of *Buſſa*. He had neither Orders nor Power to treat with the *Turks*, and much leſs to yield to them ſo conſiderable a Province as is that of *Moldavia*, which cover'd *Poland* againſt the Incurſions of the *Tartars*. The other Treaty is that which was made *October* 9, 1621, near *Chocim*, and is beyond Compariſon more honourable

nourable than the first, but the *Turks* nevertheless preserv'd therein the Advantages which the other Treaty had procur'd them On *October* 18, 1672, was made in the open Field the last Treaty between the Grand Seigneur and the King of *Poland*
In the Year 1640 was concluded a Treaty between *France* and *Poland*, but it speaks only of the Liberty of Prince *Casimir*, Brother to the King of *Poland*, and on *July* 13, 1656, a Treaty was made at the *Hague*, between the King of *Poland* and the United Provinces, but it had no Consequence

CHAP. XV.
Of Ratifications.

PResident *Jeannin*, Embassador Extraordinary from *France* in *Holland*, for the Negotiation of the Truce of twelve Years, writing to *M de Villeroy*, on *September* 6, 1608, says something very remarkable on the Subject of Ratifications He there takes notice, that he had represented to President *Richardot*, Embassador from the Arch-Dukes, That his Master having a good and sufficient Procuration from the King of *Spain*, had no need of fresh Powers, to grant to the States of the United Provinces the Declaration they demanded concerning the Liberty of their Republick That although there might possibly be something contrary thereto in his Instructions, it was very likely, that if the Arch-Dukes could resolve to take that Counsel, the King of *Spain* would rather chuse to wink at it, and even to ratify the same, than to consent expresly thereto before the thing was done *That admitting the States should have only this Treaty, without the King of* Spain's *Ratification in Form, yet this last would nevertheless be formally oblig'd in reference to them, because a Procuration is a sufficient Obligation* Whereas at the time of the Suspension of Arms the Arch-Dukes had none, yet having promis'd to get it ratify'd, they were oblig'd to deliver the Ratification in good Form

I willingly quote this Passage, to shew that the Ratification is not an essential part of a Treaty, which is by so much the more evident, not only because a Treaty is a common and publick Instrument, and the Ratification a private and particular one, but also because a Treaty would be good, and subsist without the Ratification, if it were certain that the Treaty, and he that has made it, would not be disavow'd The Treaty of *Vervins* was concluded and sign'd *May* 2, 1598, the Peace was publish'd at *Paris*, *June* 12, and the Oath for the Observation and Execution of the Treaty, which supply'd the Place of a Ratification, was not perform'd till the 21st of the same Month The present King, writing to the States of the United Provinces, on *June* 30, 1678, says, That Custom would require that things should remain in the same State they were then in, till a Peace was thoroughly confirm'd by the exchange of the Ratifications, and by the Publication of the Treaties, but that nevertheless, at the Desire of the States, he is willing to supersede the Hostilities in the Low Countries The King says, *That Custom would require*, but in causing the Hostilities to cease, he shews, that it is not absolutely necessary It is true, one might maintain by the same Reason, That the signing of the Treaty was not necessary, since the Treaty was not yet sign'd, but the King supposes it was, since the Estates had assur'd him it should be so by the latter end of *June*, of which the 30th was the last Day So that in all likelihood, the Orders he gave for a Cessation of Hostilities, could not be brought to the Generals till after the signing The Treaty which was sign'd at *Paris*, *April* 27, 1662, was not ratify'd by the King till *March* 20, of the following Year

After that, in the Year 1598, *Dossat* had treated with the Great Duke about the Restitution of the Islands of *If* and *Porregues*, and that the Treaty was ratify'd in *France*, the Great Duke told him, That if he would take along with him, or send back to the King the Letters of Ratification, he would be contented with his Majesty's bare Word He signify'd the same to him by the Chevalier *Vinta*, his Secretary, but *Dossat* nevertheless put the Ratification into his Hands Neither did I make use of this Example, but only to shew that the Great Duke did not doubt the Execution of the Treaty, even without the Ratification

The Treaty which was made at *Nimeguen*, between *France* and *Spain*, on *September* 17, 1678, contains, That after the Ratifications shall have been deliver'd, the most Christian King shall swear to the Observation of the Treaty on the Cross and the Gospel In my Opinion, this is a needless Precaution, since the Prince who shall have engag'd his Faith in the Signature, and his Honour in the Ratification, if he violates either the one or the other, will make no Scruple to wound his Conscience, which was not less concern'd (in those that have any) in their Word Here I must add, that the Ratification would not be at all necessary, if the Treaty was made and sign'd by the Princes themselves, or if there was a Certainty, that the Instructions Princes give to their Ministers were conformable to the Powers these communicate to those who treat with them

In the Year 1449, the Count *de Dunois*, Courtroy Admiral of *France*, the Lord of *Retz*, and *Bertram de Beauvau*, Lord of *Precigny*, made a Treaty with the Duke of *Britany*, on the Part of *Charles* VII, King of *France* As soon as the Treaty was concluded, *the Duke vaut'd his Letters Patents to be prepar'd, which he sign'd with his own Hand, and made them be sign'd and seal'd by the Barons of his Countrey* Besides this,

5 L the

the said Duke, and the Barons and Noblemen of *Britany*, promis'd to do and fulfill religiously and punctually the Contents of the Letters Patents, and never to act any thing contrary to their Tenor; of which they gave their Faith and Word solemnly, by touching the French Embassadors in the Hand, according to the Custom of those Times. This was not a Ratification, but a kind of Guaranty, because the Ratification being nothing else but the Approbation of the Action of another, it was not necessary that the Barons should ratify what they had done and sign'd themselves. In like manner, when the Lord *de Cran*, and the Chancellor *Doriole*, made that fine Treaty with *Charles* Duke of *Burgundy*, which we have spoke of elsewhere, the Duke gave his Letters Patents, and the Embassadors of *France* promis'd, that the King their Master should swear to the Observation thereof.

However, notwithstanding that the Ratification is no essential part of a Treaty, nor even of the Function of the Embassador, yet it seems to be become a necessary Appendix to the one and the other, since it is by it that a Treaty receives its last Perfection, and that without it there is no Security that it shall be executed. This is one of the Reasons why the Publication of Treaties is not perform'd, till after the Ratifications have been exchang'd, tho' it is what is not always nicely observ'd, for the Reason I have just now alleg'd, That the Ratification is not of the Essence of a Treaty, nor does not make a part thereof. As soon as in the Year 1571, the League was concluded against the *Turk*, betwen the Pope, *Spain*, and the Republick of *Venice*, Pope *Pius* V immediately swore to the Execution of the same. Cardinal *Pacheco* did the like for the King of *Spain*, and the Embassador of *Venice* having also sworn to it, after their Example, the Treaty was publish'd the next Day. The League was concluded at *Rome*, on *May* 20, the Embassadors did not sign it, nor fix their Seals thereto, till after they had sworn to the Observation thereof, and it was not publish'd at *Venice* till *July* 2, that is to say, six Weeks after it had been publish'd at *Rome*, and before it had been ratify'd in *Spain*. The Embassadors who have negotiated and concluded a Treaty, are oblig'd in Honour to get it ratify'd, because that Prince that refuses to ratify a Treaty, disavows his Minister, or tacitly accuses him of having exceeded his Powers.

John de Monluc, Bishop of *Valence*, and Embassador of King *Charles* IX in *Poland*, that he might succeed in the Election of the Duke of *Anjou*, which he had begun to negotiate, promis'd amongst other things, That for the sake of the *Polish* Lords, (who made Profession of the Protestant Religion, and who were pretty numerous at that time) great Advantages should be granted to those of the Religion in *France*. The Embassadors of *Poland*, who carry'd the Decree of Election into *France*, amongst whom were some very zealous Protestants, insisted with Warmth on the Execution of that Point. The King's Council told them, That *Monluc* had had no Orders to promise any thing in Favour of those of the Religion, and *Monluc* confess'd that neither his Powers, nor his Instructions, made any mention thereof. But he said, That he had receiv'd a general Order to procure the Election at any rate, and that seeing it was impossible to answer the King's Intentions therein, unless the Protestant *Polish* Nobility were assur'd that neither the King nor the Duke of *Anjou* had had any part in the Massacre of St *Bartholomew*, he had not scrupled to say, That the King was so far from consenting to this Action, that he would cause the Authors thereof to be punish'd, and would give very good Treatment to those of the Religion in his Kingdom. But that it was a thing in which *Poland* had no Interest, so that the King was not oblig'd to ratify what his Embassadors had promis'd without Orders.

This Expression of the Bishop of *Valence* is a little too general, and if he takes the Word, Order, for that of Instruction, it is absolutely false. For if the Embassador does not exceed the Bounds of his Powers, altho' he does not keep within those of his Instructions, the Prince is oblig'd to approve of him, and to ratify what has been negotiated in his Name, and by virtue of his Powers. The Reason is because the Minister to whom the Powers are communicated, and to whom an authentick Copy thereof is given, supposing that the Embassador with whom he treats is fully inform'd of the Intention of his Master, and that he acts conformably to the one and the other, makes no Scruple to enter into a Negotiation, and to conclude with him, who is the Bearer of a full Power, and who ought to know what Latitude his Instructions allow him. But he that treats with a Minister, who has no Power at all, ought to expect a Disapprobation, and has no Reason to complain if the Master refuses to ratify what his Embassador has done without Orders, and without Power. The *Spaniards* would not execute the Treaty which M. *du Bassompierre* had made at *Madrid*, in the Year 1621. And *France*, on its part, not approving the Articles which had been concerted with the Commander *Sillery* at *Rome*, concerning the *Valteline*, the Count Duke *d'Olivares*, fearing lest *France* should do it self Justice by the way of Arms, engag'd *du Fargis*, Embassador of *France* at *Madrid*, in a Negotiation, which at last produc'd the Treaty which was sign'd at *Monçon*, in the Year 1626. Upon the Advice that *du Fargis* gave to this Court, of the Overtures that had been made to him, and of the Advantages he hop'd to obtain thereby for the King, if Orders were sent him, or only a bare Permission to enter into a Negotiation, he receiv'd for Answer, That he might answer with Civility to fine Words that were given him at *Madrid*, and even signify that the King was not against the Accommodation, if honourable Conditions were propos'd for the same, and a full Security He was given to understand in what these honourable Conditions, and this Security consisted, to wit, in preserving to the *Grisons* the Sovereignty of the *Valtuline*, and the Passage for those Troops the King should at any time send into *Italy*, conformably to the Treaty of *Madrid*. And forasmuch as the *French* were in continual Distrusts of the Intention of the *Spaniards*, *du Fargis* had Orders sent him, by another express Dispatch, to be very reserv'd therein, and not to engage till he was well assur'd to come off with Advantage. Whereunto

unto was added an express Prohibition to make any Answers, from which the *Spaniards* might draw any Advantage. Nevertheless on *January* 1, 1626, he sign'd the Project of a Treaty with the Count Duke, and had the Assurance to send it to Court; but his Procedure was so ill receiv'd there, that in its first Resentment, it was propos'd to recall immediately an Embassador, that had been so audacious as to make a Treaty without Orders and without Powers. Nay some of the Council were even for having him brought to his Tryal. However, as the Affairs of that Kingdom were not yet very well prepar'd for a Rupture, it was resolv'd that the Fault should be wink'd at, and *that instead of ratifying* what *du Fargis* had done, another Project should be sent him, by which he should cause the first to be reform'd. He did it with some Advantage to the Interest of the King his Master, but yet not altogether conformable to the Intention of the first Minister, insomuch that a third Project was sent him, *to which was annex'd the King's Ratification*, to make the Exchange thereof, if he could get it approv'd at *Madrid*, where it was agreed to, as we have said elsewhere.

I have related in Chapter VIII of this Book, how the Republick of *Venice* got out of the Difference she had with the House of *Austria*, on the Account of the Depredations of the *Uscoques*, and of the Engagement she was enter'd into with the Duke of *Savoy* against *Spain*. The Treaty which was made at *Madrid* in the Year 1617 would have brought it off gloriously, if the Duke of *Lerma*, first Minister of *Spain*, had not made the King his Master speak therein more like an Arbitrator than a Mediator. The *Venetian* Embassador protested that he had made no Submission, and that he had been very cautious of making any, because he had no Power for that Purpose. This Difference was debated between the Duke and the Embassador with so much Warmth, that the Duke would needs have all the Embassadors that were then at *Madrid* witnesses thereof, and the King was so very angry thereat, that he would not meddle any more in the Matter, but remitted it to the Pope. The Duke of *Savoy* being inform'd thereof by the Abbot *Scaglia*, who did his Affairs at *Rome*, commanded him to assure the Pope, that he approv'd of and ratify'd all that had been done at *Madrid* by *Peter Grotti*, who had been impower'd by him, provided the Execution of the Treaty of *Ast* was likewise secur'd, and that the Republick found its Safety therein. These Conditions giving the Pope to understand that the Duke would satisfy nothing in effect, and that he did not allow him the same Liberty which the King of *Spain* gave him, refus'd to take Cognizance of the Affair. The Senate of *Venice*, which beheld a foreign naval Army in the Gulf, and the Preparations the Duke of *Ossuna* continu'd to make at *Naples*, agreed to and approv'd the Treaty of *Madrid*, protesting at the same time, that it receiv'd it as from the Mediation, and not from the Arbitration of the King of *Spain*. It also dispatch'd an Express, with Power to *Octavio Bon*, and to *Vincent Gussoni*, who were on its part at the Court of *France*, to conclude the same Articles with the Ministers of the King, giving them Power to substitute *Peter Grotti*,

that he might give the last Perfection thereto in *Spain*. I shall not enlarge on the Reasons that oblig'd the Republick to act after this Manner, but shall only say, That the Court of *France* was so pleas'd to be consider'd in *Italy* as Arbitrator of so important a Difference, that it adjusted all the Difficulties of the Treaty with the Embassadors of *Venice*, and regulated all things with them without the Participation of the Embassadors of *Spain* and *Savoy*, notwithstanding the Duke, to hinder the Governor of *Milan* from carrying his Arms into the State of *Venice*, had not scrupl'd to draw them into his own Countrey. The Republick found therein its Advantage, and was glad to extricate it self after this Manner; but considering that the Indifferency she express'd for the Duke's Interest, sully'd the Reputation she had in the World, and apprehending lest she should one Day be made to repent the Contempt she had shewn for the good Disposition of the King of *Spain*, she made as if she disapprov'd what had been done at *Paris*, and *refus'd to ratify it*. She took for Pretext, that the Treaty did not make mention of certain *Mahones* which had been taken by the Ships of the Viceroy of *Naples*, tho' the King had formally promis'd, he would prevail with the Court of *Madrid* to restore them, as also that the Embassador of *Spain* had no Powers concerning the Restitution. This was the Pretext the Senate made use of *to refuse to ratify*. It disavow'd the Embassadors, who had so happily extricated the Republick out of so troublesome an Affair, and sent them Orders to come and render themselves Prisoners, to answer for what they had done. *Simon Contarini* was sent to *France* at the same time, to acquaint the King with the Reasons which oblig'd the Republick to proceed with so much Rigour against the two Embassadors, who, as she said, could not justify their Conduct. In the mean time it was given out at *Venice*, *That the Senate would not ratify what had been done at* Paris. But the King laugh'd at these slight Wiles, and commanded *Contarini* not to stir from *Lions* till the Republick had ratify'd the Treaty which the two Embassadors had sign'd, and till she had approv'd their Conduct. *Baptist Nani*, Procurator of St *Mark*, who has wrote the History of his Countrey, is very tender of the Senate's Reputation on this Occasion, and relates but very few of the Particulars; for which Reason I was willing to dwell a little longer thereupon.

The Prince that will have nothing to reproach to himself, cannot refuse to ratify the Treaty which his Plenipotentiary has made and sign'd, unless he disavows him openly, and punishes him for having exceeded his Power. He owes that Satisfaction, and something more, to the Prince whom his Minister has impos'd upon, and he owes it even to his own Honour, which does not allow him to go from his Word, which he has given him in his full Powers. Most commonly those Terms are inserted therein, *We promise on the Faith and Word of a King, or Prince, and under the Obligation and Pledge of all our Estates, present and to come, to hold for good, firm and stable, and to fulfil whatever shall have been so stipulated, granted and agreed by our Plenipotentiaries, and to cause our Letters of Ratification*

tification to be dispatch'd within the time they shall have oblig'd themselves to procure them

I just now said, That the bare disowning a Minister who has exceeded his Power, is no satisfaction to the Prince who has treated *bona fide* with the Plenipotentiary. As the Civil Laws oblige a private Person to ratify what his Mandatary has done by virtue of his Procuration, so the *Law of Nations* obliges the Prince to ratify what his Minister has done by virtue of his Powers, especially if the Powers are full and absolute, without any Clause or Condition, to limit or restrain the same. For which reason I cannot tell whether one can well justify the Refusal, the States of the United Provinces made in the Year 1659, to ratify the Treaty, which their Embassadors Plenipotentiaries had made with the King of *Sweden* at *Elbing*. It is certain that the Ministers had their Powers in good Form, and that they had not exceeded them, since they had not made one single Step therein, nor fix'd any one Article, without the Participation and Consent of their Principals. It is also certain that the Deputies of the States, who examin'd the Treaty, found it conformable to the Orders and Instructions of the Embassadors. The States themselves had communicated it to the Ministers of their Allies, to the King of *Denmark* and to the Protector of *England*, insomuch that it was not doubted but it would be ratify'd by the unanimous Consent of all the Provinces.

Nevertheless the States of *Holland* were willing to give a Proof of their Ability, if what is said be true. *That ablest Men affect to decline exerting the cunning Part for a long time, in order to make use of it on some great Occasion, and for some mighty Interest.* They did not only refuse to ratify the Treaty of *Elbing*, as being inconsistent with their Interest, but they likewise brought over the Deputies of the other Provinces to their Sentiments, and made it be resolv'd, that before they ratify'd the Treaty, they should demand of the *Swedes* an Explanation of some Points, which were thought to be of the utmost Importance to the Commerce. The King of *Sweden* offer'd them this Satisfaction, provided they assur'd him, that that being done they would ratify the Treaty, but this was what they refus'd to be plain in, so that it sufficiently appear'd, that it was not their Intention to ratify it, notwithstanding the States of *Zeeland* and *Frise*, which had had their Embassadors upon the Place, were for having it ratify'd purely and simply. Some time after a kind of Treaty was made, to which the Title of *Elucidation* was given, a Term altogether as new, as the Manner of acting was strange, in a Countrey which had always affected to appear religious in executing what it had promis'd. It was but a Piece of Cunning in effect, and a Subtilty, which are but false Virtues, and the utter Aversion of honest and able Men. The States were oblig'd to acknowledge the same, and to renounce the Advantages which the *Elucidation* gave them, when in the Year 1667, and 1668, they were willing to purchase the Friendship of *Sweden*, to bring it into the triple Alliance.

Cardinal *Mazarin*, who was no Slave to his Word, and who was willing it should be known that he was not, had regulated, or caus'd to be regulated at *Paris* with *Don Antonio Pimentel*, all the Articles of which the Treaty of the *Pyrenees* was since compos'd. He had not ingag'd in this Negotiation, till *Don Antonio* had shew'd him Powers in good form, as some Years before, the King of *France* had sign'd such another Instrument for *Lionne* in the Presence of the Person the King of *Spain* confided in. But being sensible that what *Lionne* had done at *Madrid*, had been broken off, but on account of the Difficulty which was found therein concerning the Interest of the Prince of *Condé*, and fearing lest *Don Lewis de Haro* (who was extremely jealous of his Word) would fulfil that which he had given to the Prince, and disavow *Pimentel*, as the Cardinal would have made no scruple to prostitute a subaltern Minister, and even an Embassador for so important a Concern, he set out from *Paris* full of Fears, determin'd not to repair to the Frontiers, nor even to go beyond *Poictiers*, unless he receiv'd the Ratification of what had been agreed on at *Paris*, which was longer a coming, than the Term *Pimentel* had taken to procure the same. It was brought to him before he reach'd *Amboise*, and thereupon he continu'd his Journey to the Place appointed for the Conference, where the first Minister of *Spain* render'd himself at the same time, and avow'd all that *Pimentel* had concluded at *Paris*. And notwithstanding some Alterations were made therein, in reference to the Interest of the Prince of *Condé*, yet it was only with the Cardinal's Consent, who had full as much Address as *Don Lewis*, and full as much Power in his Court, but *Don Lewis*, in making the Cardinal consent to the Restoration of the Prince, and in executing his Word punctually, shew'd that he did not want Wit, and that he had Probity enough to cause to be ratify'd *bona fide*, what had been agreed to, on the Powers of *Pimentel*.

At the beginning of the Year 1646, some *Neapolitan* Noblemen sent the Abbot *Laudati* to *Rome*, and signify'd to the Marquifs *de Fontenay Maruesl*, Embassador of *France*, that they would have no foreign King, but if *France* would be contented to see the Crown of *Naples* wrested from the Head of the King of *Spain*, to transfer it into one of the chief Families of that Kingdom, they would endeavour to bring it about, and she should have the Diversion thereof. The Embassador receiv'd and approv'd the Abbot's Proposition, but he told him, it would be requisite that some of those Noblemen should put themselves at the Head of the People, which was already up in several Provinces of the Kingdom, in order to dispose it to receive the King the Nobility should give it. The *Neapolitan* Lords made answer, That the Embassador was in the right, but that it was also just, that he should promise them in his Master's Name, by a Writing under his Hand, that if they had the ill Fortune to miscarry in their Enterprise, and that their good Intentions should not produce the Effect they had reason to hope for, they should be indemnify'd and sav'd harmless, and have as much Revenues bestow'd on them in *France*, as they should lose in *Naples*, either in Lands or Benefices. The Embassador made no Difficulty

at

at all to do it, and gave them all Obligations, to some of ten, to others of twelve or fifteen thousand Crowns in Revenue. The Embassador, who had no Order nor Power to oblige the King, gave them in effect but only blank Papers. He neither oblig'd the King thereby nor himself, because he had caus'd the Obligations to be drawn in the King's Name, who had given him no Orders for that purpose, and he promis'd nothing in his own particular. The *Neapolitan* Lords could not complain thereof neither, because they knew, or ought to have known, that the Embassador had no Procuration, that he would be disavow'd, and that *his Master would not ratify* what had been done without his Order.

In the Year 1644, *Leonard Torstenson*, Legate Plenipotentiary of the Crown of *Sweden*, and General of the Armies she had in *Germany*, made with *Ragotski*, Prince of *Transilvania*, a Treaty, which was by so much the more odd, not to say extravagant, because he had neither Order nor Powers from the King of *France*, who did not so much as know what was negotiating with *Ragotski*. He oblig'd him to the Payment of some Subsidies, and to several other things to which the King neither would nor could consent. So that *there was no likelihood that the King would ratify a Treaty*, in which he had had no part, and which had been made contrary to his Intention. And indeed the King, instead of ratifying it, caus'd another Treaty to be made with *Ragotski* by *Croissy*, who promis'd him a Subsidy of a hundred thousand Crowns, payable at *Constantinople*. Whereupon happen'd two things which were extraordinary enough. The one, That the Queen of *Sweden*, *instead of ratifying in Form the Treaty* which her Minister had made, was contented to write a Letter to *Ragotski*, wherein she assur'd him, that *Torstenson* should not fail to execute what he had promis'd him. *Torstenson* accordingly did it effectually, even beyond the Queen's Intentions. For notwithstanding he was inform'd that *Ragotski* treated with the Emperor, and that the Treaty was near a Conclusion, yet that did not hinder him from causing the Subsidies to be paid, tho' he run the Risque of being disavow'd. The other is, That *Croissy* on his part perceiving the double Procedure of this Prince, stop'd at *Dantzick* the Bills of Exchange which he was to send to *Constantinople* on *Ragotski's* Account. *Torstenson* said, That for a little Money they ought not to lose the Opportunity of preserving a good Friend, who seeing himself compell'd by the Necessity of his Affairs, acted contrary to his Inclination, and that he would not fail to fulfil his Promise to him. This History puts me in mind of another, of which I shall say a word or two, without making any great Digression. St *Aulnais*, Governor of *Laucatte*, sharing the Disgrace of the Mareschal *de Torras* his Unkle, was so forsaken by the Cardinal *de Richelieu*, that it seem'd as if he intended to let him perish in his Post, or at least to cause him to receive an Affront. This reduc'd him to such great Extremities, that he treated with the Court of *Madrid*, and promis'd to surrender *Laucatte* to the *Spaniards*, if the King his Master did not send him by a certain Day, wherewith to pay his Garrison. He at the same time sent Advice thereof to the Cardinal, who remitted Money to him at the Day prefix'd, and continu'd him in the Place which he would before have dispossess'd him of. The same Day on which St *Aulnais* receiv'd the Money of *France*, or the next, a *Spanish* Commissary arriv'd at *Laucatte* with the Sum which he had demanded of the Court of *Madrid*. St *Aulnais* told him, that he was no longer in a Condition to receive it, because the King his Master had sent him wherewith to pay his Garrison. The *Spanish* Commissary reply'd, That it was not the Custom of the King of *Spain* to return into his Coffers the Money which he had once taken out of them. That the Sum which he had destin'd to St *Aulnais* should remain with him, and that he would not carry it back. I know not how St *Aulnais* behav'd himself then, but this I know, that continuing to render himself suspected to the Court of *France*, she also continu'd to persecute him, so that being tir'd at last therewith, he accepted the advantageous Conditions the *Spaniards* offer'd him, and retir'd into *Spain*, where he dy'd, after he had done very great Services against his Countrey.

It is but after all Authors, without excepting even the *Spaniards* themselves, that I speak of the Infidelity of *Ferdinand the Catholick*. He deceiv'd all the Princes who treated with him, but in the following Example we shall see whether he had more Consideration for his Son-in-Law than for the others. *Zurita* says, That he drove out *Frederick* King of *Naples* after an abominable manner, and that he did not shew more Honesty in the Partition he made of the same Kingdom with *Lewis* XII, King of *France*. *Philip* of *Austria* his Son-in-Law, considering that a Rupture between those two Kings would communicate its Evils to his Provinces in *Flanders*, endeavour'd to prevent it. He procur'd a very ample Power, for the Accommodation he pretended to effect between the two Crowns. *Ferdinand* sent along with him two Embassadors, who were to assist him with their Counsel, and have the greatest Share in the Negotiation, where the Arch-Duke could conclude nothing without them. It was by their Advice that the Treaty was made, and that the Parties agreed, that the Provinces of the Kingdom of *Naples*, which were the occasion of the Difference, should be put into the Hands of the Arch-Duke, and that all the Kingdom should be given to *Charles*, Duke of *Luxemburg*, his Son, who should espouse the Daughter of *Lewis*. This Treaty was sent into *Italy*, with Orders to the Generals of both Armies to cause a Cessation of all Hostilities. The Duke *de Nemours*, who commanded that of *France*, obey'd the same, but *Gonçale Fernandez*, who was call'd the Great Captain, having a mind to improve the Advantages he had over the *French*, answer'd, That he would receive no Orders unless they came from *Spain*, and that till such time as he should receive them, he would continue to pursue the War. And indeed he carry'd it on so well, that he made himself Master of the whole Kingdom, while *Lewis*, expecting the Effect of the Treaty he had just concluded with the Arch-Duke, neglected to succour it. The Arch-Duke, who was not less incens'd at the Refusal of the Great Captain, than *Lewis* was at the Artifices

fices and Infidelities of the Catholick King, protested he would have no Hand therein, and offer'd to remain at the Court of France, till what he had negotiated should be ratify'd and executed. He made continual Instances for that purpose to Ferdinand, but all to no purpose, because that King, who through the Disguise of his Devotion had no other Religion than his Interest, made use sometimes of one, sometimes of another Pretext, to delay dispatching the Ratification, till seeing himself sure of the Conquest of the whole Kingdom of Naples, he resolved not to keep his said Treaty, also to his Son-in-Law. He made, during that Philip had excused himself, That it was indeed true, that to do him the greatest Honour he had given him ample Powers, but that he was limited by his Instructions, which he was order'd to follow. Philip maintain'd, on the contrary, That his Instructions were at least as ample as his Powers. That before he set out from the Court of Spain, the King and Queen had positively declar'd, that their Intention was that it cause should be made by his Mediation, and that they had both made Oath on the holy Gospel, and on the Cross to observe religiously and execute punctually all that should be there negotiated and concluded. That although he might have made use of his Power in its full Latitude, yet he had not done it, but had neither granted nor resolv'd any thing without the Advice of the two Embassadors. Lewis was very well satisfy'd with the Procedure of Philip, who is a good Flemming, and a downright honest Man. But Ferdinand having sent two other Embassadors to him to execute what was pass'd, and make an Overture of some other Accommodation, he gave them a publick Audience, wherein he told them in the Presence of the whole Court, That he would not hearken to any Proposition, till Ferdinand had ratify'd and executed the Treaty of Blois, and that for and that he had made Amends for what was past. That it not only appear'd strange to him, but also a thing abominable and detestable, that two Princes, who had just procur'd to themselves the Name of Catholicks, should have so little regard to their Faith, their Honour, their Oath and Religion, also that they had sworn little Consideration for that Son-in-Law who was one of the great, powerful and to Princes of Europe, then Son and presumptive Heir. And after this he order'd the Embassadors to depart the Court the same Day.

There is no occasion to wonder if the Apology which a certain Observator of Brussels makes in the behalf of this Catholick King, since he does not scruple to make that of the Duke of Alva, and that of the Portugal Embassador, who was infamous enough to betray the Interest of the King his Master, and to enter publickly into the Party of his Enemy, becoming at the same time Deserter and Traytor. If this had been Ferdinand's first Perfidy, it might have been, if not justify'd, it least excus'd, by the Example of other Princes, amongst whom one may say, that there is not so much as one whole Honour and Conscience as Proof against a Crown.

I have said in Chapter XII of this Book, that Sovereign Magistrates, That a King or a Prince

is not oblig'd to execute the Treaty his Predecessor has made, if he finds therein any thing contrary to his Interest. And indeed 'tis usual to have all Treaties renew'd or confirm'd by the Successor, notwithstanding he was oblig'd thereto by his Predecessor. Upon this Foundation it may be said, that there is a great deal more reason why a Successor shall not be oblig'd to finish a Treaty, which his Predecessor had left imperfect, for want of the Ratification. Anthony Isealan Adamar Paulin, Baron de la Garde, having been sent by King Henry II to Constantinople, was afterwards sent into England, where he made a Treaty with Henry VIII. This King being dead, and France desiring soon after before the Treaty was ratify'd the Guardians of Edward VI, who had succeeded Henry, and had sent John Bi and his Embassador into France, to congratulate him upon his Accession to the Crown, caused him in just in case to be made for the Ratification of the Treaty which had been made between the Kings their Fathers. But Ibars made Answer, That he would not ratify it, as well because it contain'd several unjust things, as because he was not oblig'd to do what the King his Father had refus'd or delay'd to do.

I shall not here repeat what I said before of the Obligation the Prince enters into by his full Powers he gives his Minister. Indeed it is not properly the Business of an Embassador, who has finish'd his Negotiation, in concluding and signing the Treaty. Neither is it necessary that the Embassador should remain at the Place of the Congress till the Ratification is made. The Exchange, which is to be made there of, is not of Obligation to be made there. On the contrary it is often made elsewhere by subaltern Ministers, or by the Mediators if they think fit to give themselves the Trouble to write for it. After that the Truillenr had made the Treaty between the two Northern Crowns at Bromsebro, in the Year 1645, the Ratification at the one and of the other was sent to the Hands of Philibert Hennequin Resident from the at Copenhagen, who made the Exchange of it in a Village on the Frontiers of the two Kingdoms, whether the Deputies on both sides repair'd, and gave their Receipt for the same. When there are to Mediators the Ratification is deliver'd to the Embassador in Ordinary or else to some other Minister, who sends it to the Prince his Master. The Treaty which was made at Blois in the Year 1572 between Charles IX, King of France, and Queen Elizabeth of England, contain'd, that it should be ratify'd on both sides within four Months, and that the Queen's Ratification should be put into the Hands of the Embassador in Ordinary of France, who should be particularly author'd for that purpose. For which reason he order'd Walsingham to inform himself precisely of the Court of France, in what time it desir'd the Exchange should be made.

When a Treaty is made between Princes and Potentates between whom there is no Competition, as when Crown'd Heads ratify Treaty to be made with other Princes or with Republicks, sometimes that Respect is shewn to the first, that the Ratification is communicated to them before the Exchange thereof is made. Cardinal D'Ossat, Plenipotentiary

The EMBASSADOR *and his* FUNCTIONS 411

tentiary of *Urban* VIII, at the Treaty which was made between the Princes of *Italy* and the *Barberins* at the End of the War of *Castro*, writing to Cardinal *Bichi*, Plenipotentiary of *France*, speaks to him in these Terms *Tho' Duty and Custom obliges Princes to give in their Ratifications first, that the Pope, who ought to be the last in presenting it, may be able to make the necessary Reflection thereon, he knows nevertheless that without the Consideration of* Castro, *Bichi would not fail to me all suitable Precautions that they are as full as may be, and that they may be conformable to that of the Pope.* The Republick found Fault with this, because it contain'd a Clause, that oblig'd the Successors also to the Execution of the Treaty, and said, That her State being perpetual, no mention ought to be made of Successors in the Ratification. The *Barberins* answer'd, That this was a mere Cavil, and not a Difficulty, because the same Clause appear'd in the Treaty which had been made at *Bologne* in the Year 1630. That the Doge, who is nam'd therein, being mortal, they might and ought to mention also the Successors, since it was an usual Clause even of the Republick, which says in its Acts, *Nos, cum nostro Senatu, pro nobis, nostrisque Successoribus*, *Dominusque nostri*, or else, *Præsentibus Successoribus, & Republica Juste*. But there was found therein a greater Difficulty on the part of all the Allies, who would not suffer that the Ratification should make the World believe that they were the Authors of the War, and desir'd a Peace occasion'd both the one and the other was false. They said, that the *Barberins* had begun the War, not only by the Invasion of the Duchy of *Castro*, but also by the Preparations they had made to carry their Arms into *Lombardy*. That it was requisite the Pope should cause that Clause to be left out of his Ratification or else suffer the Republick and the other Allies to slip into those same Clauses which would not please him. And indeed the Senate caus'd a Ratification to be drawn, which made the *Barberins* the Cause of the War, which had oblig'd the Princes to enter into a League, and to oppose the Violence of the Court of *Rome*. This Resolution so alarm'd Cardinal *Bichi*, who discharg'd the Office of Mediator that he declin'd to the Great Duke and to the Duke of *Modena*, That this Ratification would never be approv'd of at *Rome*, and desir'd them to prevail with the Senate to alter those Terms. He had a Conference with the Deputies of the Republick on the same Account, but all he could obtain from them was, *That the Pope should any pinch not simply*, by leaving out those Words which could not be agreed to, or if it needs must make mention of the War, only their Words should be inserted, *That to set an End to the present War the Parties had agreed to the Treaty,* &c. which he ratify'd And this was what the Pope was contented with. In effect the shortest Ratifications, and the most general are the best, provided they are drawn up in Form. It is sufficient that they shew and approve of what is contain'd in the Treaty, and that in express and efficacious Terms.

I say in good Form because it is necessary that the Ratification should be despatch'd under the Great Seal, and in the same manner as the Treaty it self. The States of the United Provinces, before the, enter'd into a formal Negotiation with the Ministers of the Arch-Duke *Albert*, in the Year 1607, contented to a Suspension of Arms, which the King of *Spain* was to approve of and ratify, as well as the Point that related to the Liberty and Sovereignty of their State. The Council of *Spain*, tho' it passionately desir'd a Peace, or at least a Cessation of Arms in the *Low Countries*, where all its Revenues were finking as in an Abyss, had some Difficulty to ratify what the Arch-Duke had promis'd and granted to obtain the Suspension of Arms, but not being willing to go from the Prince's Word, and the Monarchy of *Spain* not being in a Condition to continue a War which was burthensome to it, the King of *Spain* caus'd at last an Act of Ratification to be dispatch'd. The Auditor *Verreycas* brought it to the *Hague*, where it was found to defective that they had much to do to suffer him to remain there a few Days, during which he promis'd to get it mended. The States found Fault that the Ratification was only wrote on Paper, and that it was sign'd *Yo el Rey*; whereas it ought to have been on Parchment, and sign'd with the King's Name, who acts thus with all Foreigners, who are independent of him. They were also of Opinion, that it was not less defective in Substance than in Form. Provided the Ratification be express'd in Terms that are simple and general, and that the whole Treaty be inserted therein, one cannot be deceiv'd in it.

It was a kind of Treaty, the Absolution of *Henry* IV, which *du Perron* and *Dusse* had negotiated at *Rome*, and it was necessary that the King should ratify what they had done there. The Court of *Rome*, who is not contented to make Kings lay themselves at the Pope's Feet, but will have him also trample on their Belief, insisted, That in the Letters Patents of Ratification the whole Act of Absolution should be inserted, to the end the King might have the Mortification to make in express Acknowledgment thereof. But *Dossat* wrote, That the King had nothing else to do but to take into his Hand the Letters Patents of Ratification and to tell the Legate, *That he has ratify'd and approv'd, and does ratify and approve all that his been done at* Rome, *by his Procurators*, in reference to his Absolution, and that he has caus'd his Letters of Ratification to be dispatch'd *in forma probante* and authentical, which he continu'd and deliver'd to him, desiring him to send them to our holy Father the Pope. He adds thereto, *That it is the strictest and most ample Form, and as is different*.

The Treaty of *Breda* having been sign'd on the last of *July* 1667, between the Kings of *France* and of *Denmark*, and the Estates of the United Provinces on the one part, and the King of *Great Britain* on the other, all the Embassadors, except those of the Country, who took their turn home, remain'd at the Place, expecting the Ratifications from their Masters. That of *England* being arriv'd *August* 12, the 24th was pitch'd upon to make the Exchange thereof, which was done in the following manner. The Horse and Foot of the Garrison being drawn up in Order of Battle before the Castle the two Embassadors of *France* repair'd thither about eleven of the Clock in the Forenoon, and went into the Room, where during the Negotiation they were us'd to rest themselves, before they enter'd into Conference. The Plenipotentiaries of the United Provinces follow'd them soon after, and went into the Room which was appropriated to them, as did also those of *Denmark*, and afterwards the Embassadors of *Sweden*, who were Mediators, each into their respective Apartment. The *English* Embassadors came the last. As soon as these were come, the Mediators went into the Conference Chamber, where the Ministers of the three Allies being also come, these put the *Treaties with the Ratifications* into the Hands of the Mediators, who went afterwards with the Ministers of *France*, *Denmark* and the United Provinces, into the Room of the Embassadors of *France*, from whence those of *Sweden* went out immediately to go into that of the Embassadors of *England*, who deliver'd to them the *Treaties with the Ratification* of the King of *Great Britain*. After that their Secretary had collated them, and that the Embassadors of *England* had sign'd and seal'd them, the Mediators carry'd them to the Ministers of the three Allies, who read them, and collated them again. This being done, these repair'd to the Conference Chamber, whither the Mediators also conducted the Embassadors of *England*, who were receiv'd with great Civilities by the others, and after some Complements they separated. The Publication of the Peace was perform'd the same Day at *Breda*, as in a Town whose Neutrality had been expressly stipulated for the whole Negotiation, and for all its Consequences, and this by virtue of a Power which the Embassadors of all the Parties concern'd had for that effect. Those of *England* and of the United Provinces caus'd it to be done with Solemnity at the Sound of the Trumpet, but those of *France* and of *Denmark* were contented to do it by Placaerts, which they caus'd to be posted on the Gates of their Houses. There was no delaying the Publication, because there were remote Places, where Hostilities were not to cease but in a certain time after the Publication.

The Treaty of *Osnaburg* being just on the point of Signing, *Servien* had agreed with the Plenipotentiaries of *Sweden*, that these should take care to have the Ratification sent them before-hand, that the Exchange thereof might be made immediately after the Signing, because the Ministers of *France*, who were for getting clear of the War in *Germany*, in order to prosecute it with so much the greater Vigor against *Spain*, were in continual Distrusts of the Intentions of the Court of *Stockholm*, as well as of those of the Court of *Vienna*. They gave Orders to *Chanut* to speak about it, but the Chancellor *Oxenstiern* told him, that the Queen and the Senate judg'd it would be a thing of no Utility to send into *Sweden* a Treaty which the Ministers of the Princes concern'd therein had not yet sign'd, *and that it was mere Madness to believe that the Queen would give her Ratification upon the bare Copy of an Act, which had not as yet receiv'd its Forms*. That her Majesty was too prudent of her self, and assisted with a Council too well experienc'd in Affairs to act after that manner. That there was no Haste. That there would be time enough to observe Order. That this Peace could not be executed in a Fortnight's Time, &c. The States of the Empire made instance, about that time, that *Sweden* should disband her Forces immediately after the signing of the Treaty, but the *Swedes* said, *That the Treaty was not perfect till after the Ratification*. When in the Year 1647, *Servien* made a Treaty of Guaranty at the *Hague*, amongst other Difficulties, this was propos'd, to wit, Whether after the signing of the Treaty, which was negotiating at *Munster*, there should be a Cessation of Hostilities or not? The States said, *That the bare signing a d not supersede Hostilities*, but that after the Signature, it might be debated whether it were proper to make them cease, before the Ratification and Publication were executed.

This is not to say but sometimes Treaties do subsist, notwithstanding they are not ratify'd, because, as I said before, the Ratification is not an essential part thereof. The Truce which was concluded in the Year 1609, between *Spain* and the Arch-Dukes on the one part, and the United Provinces on the other, was never ratify'd according to Form. And it was not much heeded, because the States had good Guarantees. It was three Years before the Court of *Madrid* ratify'd the Treaty of *Vervins*, but King *Henry* IV. did not trouble himself much thereat, because that did not hinder the Arch Duke from executing it, nor from drawing the *Spanish* Garrisons out of those Places which were to be restor'd, and were so in effect by virtue of the Treaty. The Death of *Philip* II was in part the Cause of this Delay, his Successor, who was young, thinking he ought to shew that he did not approve what his Father had done towards his latter Days, was very shy and nice in the matter.

It is true that the Prince who refuses to ratify, hinders the Execution of the Treaty, of which I have just given some Examples. In the Year 1624, the Commander *Sillery*, Embassador of *France* at *Rome*, having approv'd of some Articles which the Pope had caus'd to be put in Writing concerning the Affair of the *Valteline*, with the Consent of the Duke of *Pastrana*, Embassador of *Spain*, he sent them by an Express to Court, to have them ratify'd. The Courier, at his Arrival at *Paris*, found that the Chancellor, and Monsieur *de Puisieux*, the Secretary of State, Brother and Nephew of the Commander, were disgrac'd, and that the Court was not at all dispos'd to ratify the Articles which had been concerted at *Rome*. The Nuncios *Corsini* and *Spada* were told, *That the King disavow'd the Commander, and would not ratify what his Embassador had done without Orders and without Powers*. To which was added, That there was nothing as yet sign'd, so that the Affair was still entire, and withal, that the Embassador had approv'd the Articles, but since he had been inform'd of the Disgrace and Banishment of his Brother. Orders were also sent to Cardinal *la Valette*, and to the Archbishop of *Lions*, who were at *Rome*, to speak to the Pope about it in the same Terms, and to make pressing Instances for the Execution of the Treaty that *Bassompierre* had made at *Madrid* in the Year 1621, where we must however

however observe, that it was not properly a Ratification, which the Commander *de Sillery* demanded, but only an Approbation of what he had done, since there was no Treaty, and that till such Time as something was sign'd, there could be no Talk of a Ratification. The Pope, and the Duke of *Pastrana*, who had treated with a Minister who had no Power, had no Reason to complain of the Refusal of *France*.

The Procedure of Cardinal *de Richelieu* was not so sincere, in reference to the Treaty of *Ratisbonne*. This first Minister apprehending lest the Intrigues of the Cabinet should ruine him, since the Queen-Mother, who had declared her self, had made a powerful Party against him, while the Affairs of *Germany* and *Italy* engross'd his Thoughts, and afforded a great Advantage to his Enemies, gave a private Order to *Charles de Loon Brulard*, and to Father *Joseph* a Capucin, who knew the last Intentions of the first Minister, to conclude the Treaty of *Ratisbonne* at any rate. They concluded it in Effect, but the Cardinal no sooner perceiv'd himself Master of Affairs within the Kingdom, than he disavow'd what had been done in *Germany*. The King refus'd to ratify it, and said, That his Ministers had exceeded their Power. That they had blended the Affairs of the Empire, and of *Lorrain*, with those of *Italy*. That the Republick of *Venice* was compris'd therein, but in weak and ambiguous Terms, and, in fine, That the Interest of the *Grisons* was not thereby secur'd. But it seems as if these Reproaches might be made to the Ministers the King had employ'd, and not to the Emperor, who had treated *bona fide* with them, in Consideration of their full Power, which they had communicated to him. For which Reason he ought not to suffer thereby, and the Malice, or Imprudence of others, could not be imputed to him.

Before I finish this Chapter, I shall here relate an Example, which I look upon to be singular in its kind. The Abbot *Bentivoglio*, who was the Confident of Cardinal *Mazarin*, having, in the Year 1646, concluded a Treaty of Neutrality with the Great Duke of *Tuscany*, the Great Duke requir'd, That Prince *Thomas* of *Savoy*, who commanded the Arms of *France* in *Italy*, should ratify it. That Prince ratify'd it in Effect, by an Act of *May* 20, of the same Year, and the King approv'd of it after that. This was a thing altogether extraordinary. For since it was necessary that the King should ratify the Negotiation and the Treaty of his Minister, who was wary enough not to sign any thing contrary to his Orders, the Ratification of Prince *Thomas* was of no Utility, and could not secure the Great Duke.

What Cardinal *Dossat* says, concerning the Ratification of the Absolution of King *Henry* IV, in the Letter he wrote to *M de Villeroy*, on *September* 18, 1596, which is all on that Subject, deserves very well to be seen and consider'd by those, who may perhaps think that I do not say enough about it in the present Chapter. To which may be joyn'd a remarkable Passage enough of his Letter of *August* 4, 1598, where he speaks of the Offer that *Ferdinand*, Great Duke of *Tuscany*, made to surrender the Ratification, which the same King *Henry* IV had made of the Treaty, which had been transacted for the Restitution of the Castle and Isle of *If*, and of the Forts and Island of *Pomegues*, by the Mediation of the Sieur *Dossat*, Bishop of *Rennes*, on *May* 1, of the same Year 1598.

CHAP. XVI.

Of the Report the Embassador makes of his Negotiation.

There is a great deal of Difference between the Report which the Embassador makes of his Negotiation and Embassy, and the Relation he gives of the Constitution of the State, and of the Court where he has negotiated. All Embassadors make a Report, but there are so few that make a pertinent Relation of the State wherein they have resided, that it seems to be particular to those of *Venice*, who have made very fine ones, especially of the Court of *Rome*, and of some other Courts of *Italy*.

Philip de Commines says, "That the Prince " ought not to suffer his Embassador to make " his Report in publick, but ought to cause it " to be made to himself alone, or in the Pre- " sence of very few Persons, for fear that the " ill News, which they may bring, should in- " timidate the Council, or teerify the People. He farther says, " That the Prince ought to " acquaint his Minister with what he is wil- " ling should be made publick thereof, and " what he is to answer to those, who may dif- " course him about the Success of his Nego- " tiation." *Commines* wrote in a time when all Embassies were Extraordinary, and when, for the most part, one single Affair made the Subject of the Embassy. The Journies, and Residence of Embassadors, were most commonly very short. So that at their Return they did not fatigue the Prince much in giving him an Account of the Affair, of which they had had the Management and Conduct. But this Precaution is not very necessary at this Day, because there is no Sovereign but will have his Embassador make a Report of his Negotiation to himself only, notwithstanding all his Dispatches have been communicated to him, and that he cannot be ignorant of what pass'd therein. So that altho' it rarely happens that he learns from the Mouth of his Embassador, any thing else but what he has seen in his Letters, yet nevertheless he requires that Respect to be paid him, *ut rursu ipsi reddatur*. Besides, it is just and necessary that the Minister should resign his Character into the Hands of the Sovereign from whom he receiv'd it.

In those Kingdoms and States where the Sovereign shares in some Measure the Management and Disposition of Affairs, either with the first Minister, or with his Council, or else with the Senate, the Embassador makes also his Report to those who have a part in the first Authority. Republicks have their Councils, or their Assemblies, where the Embassadors make their Report. At *Venice* they generally make it to the College, or to the Council of *Pregadi*, and sometimes, if the Affair be of Importance, to the Council of Ten. In *Holland* the Embassador makes a general and succinct Report in the Assembly of the States General, where, if he has any thing particular to say, the Secret whereof ought to be prudently manag'd, he has Commissioners appointed him. And as the Embassadors are only taken out of the Body of the States General, the Embassador makes sometimes his Report in the Province which deputed him to the General Assembly. When the Embassador makes his Report, he is still a Minister, and as such he does not sit down with the other Deputies at the Council-Board, but he has a Seat given him at some Distance from the Table, behind the Deputies, who are seated right against the President, but as soon as he has finish'd his Report, and that he has been thank'd, he resumes his Place among the other Deputies of his Province. At *Venice* the Embassadors make an Extract of all that has pass'd during their Embassy, and add thereto an exact Relation of the Constitution of the State where they have been employ'd. But in *Holland* the Embassadors make a kind of verbal Process, where they say nothing but what they have said in their Dispatches, which are found there inserted Word for Word, and by this means nothing is to be met with but what was known before, and what would be found with the same Facility in the Letters themselves, if they were bound up in a Volume. However, the Embassadors cause themselves to be paid for the Pains they take to compose these verbal Processes, and get them copy'd, which frequently enough take up not Quires only, but whole Reams of Paper, which only serve to fill the Archives with monstrous and useless Registers.

There is no hindering the best intention'd Embassadors from discovering, in their Report, their own Sentiments, while they make others speak, nor from justifying and rectifying whatever pass'd in the Embassy. That is to say, there is an Obligation to suffer them to make a Report after their own way. But there are very few Examples of Embassadors that have made a false Report, and directly contrary to the Success of their Negotiation. Nevertheless there is one, which, being singular enough, deserves I should say a Word or two of it. The *Florentines*, hoping they should preserve their Republick, and their Liberty, sent in the Year 1530, four Embassadors to the Emperor *Charles* V. who was then come to *Genoa*. These Embassadors having ask'd Pardon for the Fault they had committed, in declaring for *France*, and recommended to the Emperor the Preservation of their Liberty, obtain'd no other Answer from him, than, That they should be pardon'd what was pass'd, provided they gave Satisfaction to the Pope, and restor'd the House of *Medicis* to the State they were in before the last Insurrection of the People. The four Persons of whom this Embassy was compos'd, considering that the Emperor's Answer would not be very agreeable to the People, had no great Mind to go back to *Florence* to make their Report. *Matthew Strozzi*, who was the first, instead of returning thither went to *Venice*; *Thomas Soderini*, pretending to be sick, stay'd at one of his Countrey Houses, and *Nicholas Capponi* dy'd in the Commission, so that there was none but *Raphael Jerome*, who went alone to give an Account of their common Negotiation. Being come to *Florence*, he did not give himself the Leisure to change his Clothes, but suffer'd himself to be conducted streight to the Town-House, where he told the People who had follow'd him from the Gate of the City, That Affairs were not in so bad a Condition as was thought. That the Emperor had brought but a small Army with him. That the Invasion with which the *Turk* threaten'd *Hungary*, and the evil Disposition of Minds in *Germany*, would oblige him to succour *Ferdinand* his Brother, and would hinder him from undertaking any thing against the Republick of *Florence*, except it were with a very indifferent Army, and no way proportionable to so great an Enterprize. So that the Republick might resolve upon a War, and be assur'd to come off with Advantage. This false Report made the *Florentines* resolve upon a War, and cast them into those Misfortunes which ended but with their Liberty, which they lost however but to enjoy a more happy State, under a lawful Sovereignty. I have spoken in the XIIth Chapter of the First Book, of an Embassador of the *Grisons*, and of the Report he made at his Return from the Canton of *Zurich* What he related was as false, as all that he had done by virtue of his Commission was unfaithful.

On the contrary, a faithful, judicious, and disinterested Report, denotes a Probity and Greatness of Soul, which very much recommends the Embassador. The Lord *Montgomery* was a mortal Enemy to *Matthew Stuart*, Earl of *Lenox*, whom King *Francis* I. had sent into *Scotland*, in Order to promote the Divisions with which the Kingdom was harrass'd by troublesome Factions, which were forming there, under the Queen and the Cardinal of St *Andrew*, on the one side, and *James Hamilton* on the other. The Earl of *Lenox* was not very acceptable to the Queen, for which reason she did him very ill Offices at the Court of *France*, and the King being prejudic'd by her Advice, was incens'd against the Earl, caus'd *d'Aubigny* his Brother to be put into the Bastile, and made use of *Montgomery*, as being the Earl's declar'd Enemy, to inform against him in *Scotland*. *Montgomery* went thither, but having learn'd that this *Scotch* Nobleman was a Criminal, only because the Queen had a Mind to rid her self of him, he made very sharp Reproaches to the Cardinal of St *Andrew* about it, and being return'd to *France*, he there made so favourable a Report of the Earl of *Lenox*, that the King being entirely satisfy'd therewith, caus'd *d'Aubigny* to be set at Liberty.

Altho' the *Venetian* Embassadors make, at the end of their Embassy, a Relation of the Genius,

Genius, the Inclinations, the Virtues and the Vices of Princes, as also of the Humour and Interests of the Ministers of the Court, as well as of the Disposition of the People of the Place where they have negotiated, I esteem nevertheless, that that ought to make a part of their Employment, rather than of their Report. It seems to be the Minister's Business to inform himself of all those things, in the Course of his Negotiation, and that he is oblig'd to communicate the same to his Master, because they may give a great Insight, and may serve to regulate the Measures the Prince is to take. During the Time that *Chanut* negotiated at *Stockholm*, for the Court of *France*, the Queen order'd him to send her the Picture of Queen *Christina* of *Sweden*. He mention'd it to this, who was very well pleas'd thereat, and set one about it, but before it was finish'd, *Chanut* drew her Portraiture, or Character, in a Letter, wherein he so well represented what was agreeable in her Face, and what was great and charming in the Mind of that Princess, that the skilful Pencil of *Bourdon*, did not so well satisfy the Curiosity of the Court of *France*, and of the Queen Regent, as did the admirable Pen of that able Minister. There has appear'd within some Years in *Holland* a Relation of the Resident, whom the United Provinces entertain at *Constantinople*. This Minister, who knew nothing but a little of the cavilling Part of the Law, coming into this new Employment, bethought himself of making the Plan of a Court, where he was but newly arriv'd, and sent to the States his Masters so impertinent and gross a Relation thereof, and even so injurious and offensive, that I am amaz'd they should suffer it to be printed, since the Work might be capable of drawing the Indignation of the Grand Seigneur, not only on the Head of the Minister, but likewise on the whole Nation.

The Embassador, in making his Report, ought to be so faithful and punctual, as not to omit any thing that it behoves his Master to know, nor conceal, nor disguise any thing, of all that has been told him. King *Francis* I, being return'd into *France*, after having been a Prisoner in *Spain*, sent Word to the Emperor *Charles* V, by the President of *Bourdeaux*, That several Reasons hinder'd him from executing some Articles of the Treaty of *Madrid*. The Emperor told the President, that the King his Master did not act *bona fide*, and that he did not proceed like a Man of Honour, which he was ready to maintain to him after what manner he pleas'd. The President, in making his Report, did not say one Word of all this Discourse, notwithstanding it was the real Answer of the Emperor. Insomuch that when *Francis* I, and *Henry* VIII, sent sometime after to bid Defiance to *Charles*, this told the Herald, That, without doubt, the King his Master had not been inform'd of the Answer he had made to the President of *Bourdeaux*. That he had told him, That he desir'd the King to remember the last Discourse he had held to him at their parting, *viz*. That if the King fall'd in the Promise he had made him, he, the Emperor, would maintain to him, That he did not act like a Man of Honour, and that he had acquitted himself of his Word better than the King. This Answer, which the Emperor made to the Herald, in the Presence a great many Persons of Quality, was shameful to the King, who had avoided it, if the President had made him a faithful Report of his Embassy.

Embassadors do not always stay till the Expiration of their Embassies to make their Report. There are sometimes extraordinary Occasions, where it concerns them to inform their Masters by Word of Mouth, in a more particular manner than they can do it by their Dispatches. It is impossible to find any more ample, and more judicious, than those which President *Jeannin* wrote, while he negotiated in *Holland* King *Henry* IV, and *M de Villeroy*, are never tir'd with speaking of them with Satisfaction, and with all the Encomiums they justly deserve, yet nevertheless, the said King, judging that that Minister from whom he had learn'd so many fine things wou'd still tell him something more, would needs have him come to him, and press'd him thereto now and then with so much Earnestness, that he did not scruple to say, That he expected him with Impatience. The President went at last, and, upon his Report were form'd the last Instructions, which he carry'd away from Court.

M de Puisieux, Secretary of State for foreign Affairs, writing to *M de Bassompierre*, Embassador Extraordinary in *Spain*, in the Year 1621, told him, That the King would take his Measures, on the Report he shall make of his Negotiation. Which makes it plain that the Report is sometimes by so much the more necessary, as let the Dispatches be ever so ample, the Embassador is able to tell his Master or his Council more at one Audience, concerning the true Constitution of Affairs, than he can write in a hundred Letters. During the Negotiation for a Peace, at *Munster*, the Plenipotentiaries of the United Provinces took several Journies to the *Hague*, as did those of *Spain* now and then to *Brussels*. In the Year 1646, in the Height of the Negotiation, which was carry'd on between the Ministers of *Spain* and the United Provinces, the Court of *France* was so very uneasy thereat, that the better to inform it self of the Intention of the States, she order'd *la Tuillerie* to come and satisfy it by Word of Mouth. This Minister being on the Point of setting out, presented a Memorial on *August* 7, wherein he set forth, That being oblig'd, at his Arrival at Court, to make a Report of the State, in which he had left the Affairs of those Provinces, it concern'd him to know what Answer he might make to the King and the Queen Regent, when they should ask him (as to be sure they would not fail to do) what were the true Intentions of the States after the Rumours that were spread, of the Accommodation they were making with the *Spaniards*, contrary to the Faith of the Treaties they had concluded with *France*. They made him an Answer, which was more satisfactory in Appearance than it was in Effect, and *la Tuillerie* (who knew his Business better than any Man living) made as if he acquiesc'd thereto, and was very well satisfy'd, since he could assure the King of the Sincerity of the Intentions of the States, tho' he was so little persuaded thereof, that his Journey serv'd chiefly to make an end to undeceive the Court of *France* of the good Opinion it might still entertain of them

In the Year 1671, *Peter de Groot*, Embassador of the United Provinces in *France*, had in a very little time got such good Intelligence in that Court, that he was very punctually inform'd of the Resolutions which were taken there, against the State of his Masters. He acquainted them from time to time therewith, but not daring, nor being able to write all, and perceiving however, that his Letters did not make the Impression they ought, he desir'd leave to take a Turn into *Holland*, that he might there make a pertinent Report of the true State of Affairs, and of the Intentions of *France*. It was granted him, and I know that he made a Report, which might have secur'd the United Provinces from the Insults, which were offer'd them the Year following, in the very Heart of their State, if the Divisions on the Account of the Prince of *Orange*'s Employment, and the prejudicate Opinions of some, who could not perswade themselves that *England* was capable of breaking with those Provinces, had not corrupted the Effect of that Minister's good and salutary Informations. But on these Occasions the Embassador neither ought nor can abandon his Post without Orders, or at least without the leave of his Master.

The Relation *Lazarus Mocenigo* has made of the Court of the Duke of *Urbin*, and that which *Jerome Lippomano* has made of the Court of the Duke of *Savoy*, are very fine and very particular, as well as that which the Chevalier *Cornaro* has given of the Court of *Rome*, such as it was in the time of *Alexander* VII. It were to be wish'd that all Embassadors would follow the Example of those of *Venice*, because it would be one of the best Services they could do to their Successors, as well as to their Princes. The Remarks which Sir *William Temple* has made of the State of the United Provinces, will be inimitable when he shall have put the last Hand to them, of which they have by so much the more need, as during the time of his Employment since at the *Hague*, he has without doubt learnt things, of which he could not have a perfect Knowledge when he publish'd his Book.

CHAP. XVII.

Of some illustrious Embassadors of our Time.

MY Intention was to look back as far as into the last Century, and to pay to some of the great Men of that Time, the Honour that is due to their Memory. But considering that History does them Justice, and finding my self destitute of what would be most necessary to me, for the Execution of so vast a Design, my Books and Memoirs having been scatter'd and dissipated, I have confin'd my self to the Embassadors of our Time, who have distinguish'd themselves by their Negotiations, and who certainly deserve that Posterity should have for them, the Veneration that ought to be inseparable from those Actions, which the Sword and the Gown render equally illustrious. There would be no less Pleasure to speak of *Philip de Commines*, of *Lansac de St Gelais*, of the Marquiss of *Pisani*, of *Paul de Foix*, Archbishop of *Thoulouse*, of *Laurence Suarez de Figueroa*, of *Garcilasso de la Vega* his Brother, of *Francis Walsingham*, and of several other Personages who have negotiated heretofore with Success in the first Courts of *Europe*, than there would be to remark those Passages of their Life, that have acquir'd them the Reputation they have left behind them. I shall perhaps find an Opportunity to give elsewhere some Incense to their *Manes*, and in the mean time I shall say something of some of those who have distinguish'd themselves, or do first render themselves conspicuous in the most important Negotiations of our Age. Now as there is nothing so difficult as to regulate the Rank amongst Embassadors, I shall therein observe no other Order, than that which has been given to the Alphabet.

Abel Servien, Embassador Plenipotentiary of *France* at *Munster*, with the Duke of *Longueville*, and *Claudius de Mesmes*, Count *d'Avaux*, was a very great Minister, and one of the ablest of the Profession. But to give a just Character of him, and at the same time that of M. *d'Avaux* his Collegue, I shall make use of the Parallel that *Victorio Siri* makes of those two Personages, that therein may be seen the Portraicture and Qualities of both the one and the other. He says, That *d'Avaux* had as much Merit as any other Minister of the Kingdom, and that in his continual Employments, he had acquir'd an Experience, and a Prudence which render'd him capable of the Management of the most important Affairs. That he had given Proofs thereof, while he was Embassador at *Venice*, where he concluded an Alliance for the Interests of the Duke of *Mantua*, in the Truce he caus'd to be concluded between *Poland* and *Sweden*, and in the long and tedious Negotiation of the Preliminary Treaty, which he caus'd to be concluded at *Hamburg*, but particularly in the Sequel of the Negotiation of *Munster*, of which that which he perform'd at the *Hague* in the Year 1644, made a part. Insomuch that he was thought to be a March for all manner of Affairs, how difficult and tedious soever they might be. But that he was heavy and rude, rather than brisk and polite, tho' he repair'd that Defect by an indefatigable Application, employing sometimes whole Weeks in revising and giving the finishing Strokes to his Works, altho' they sometimes consisted but of a few Lines. That he had a very good Opinion of himself, and that he could not suffer any body to be put in Comparison, or on the Level with him. That *Servien* on the contrary, had the Reputation of being one of the ablest Men of the Kingdom. That he had dif discharg'd the Office of Secretary of State, under the difficult Ministry of Cardinal *de Richelieu*, with a very great Sufficiency, as well as that of Embassador Extraordinary at the Treaties of *Querasque*, which he had brought to a Conclusion with admirable Address. That his Mind was lively, present, and all Fire, proper for the Humour and Genius of the Nation. That that was the Cause that made him have some Uneasiness to give place to *d'Avaux*, who was his Senior in the Employment, and also more considerable on the account of his Relations, who possess'd the first Offices of the Gown. So that it might be said of them, what was formerly said of *Cæsar* and *Pompey*, That it the one could not endure an Equal, the other would not acknowledge a Superior. The one had too ardent a Zeal for the *Roman Catholick* Religion, and the other was too distrustful, hasty, and violent: but they were both haughty and proud to excess. Those who may think I don't give a natural Air enough to their Portraictures, need only to read the Letters they have written to each other, and which they did not scruple to publish, notwithstanding they don't do themselves any great Honour therein, nor to the King their Master. It must be own'd, that if there was any thing troublesome in *d'Avaux*, there was something insupportable in *Servien*. This last had not the Probity nor the Disinterestedness of the other, and if *Servien* has left a Great Reputation behind him, *d'Avaux* has left a much Better. The Count *d'Avaux* his Nephew, will add a new Lustre to the Memory of him I just spoke of, and will augment the Number of the Great-Men the House of the *Mesmes* has produc'd. He must have a very extraordinary Merit, to be employ'd at the Congress of *Nimeguen*, where the Interests of almost all the Sovereigns of *Christendom* were discuss'd and regulated, and to have been able to oblige the King his Master, to put him into an Employment at least as difficult as the other, in honouring him with the Embassy Extraordinary of *Holland*. This is not an illustrious Theatre enough for his eminent Qualities, but as in the important Employments, in which the King his Master has made use of him, he has given Proofs of a great Capacity, so does he give Tokens of his Address in this, which is not indeed so glorious as the former were, but at least as considerable for its Consequences.

I have spoken in Chapter VIII of the first Book, of *Achilles de Harlay*, Baron *de Sancy*, Embassador of *France* at *Constantinople*, and as he there faithfully copy'd the Portraicture that *Pier della Valle* draws of him in his Letters, I shall say no more of him here, but that he ought necessarily to be put in the Number of the most illustrious Embassadors, since he had all the Qualities requisite for that Purpose. I say as much of *M. de Harlay*, Count *de Cely*, Predecessor to *Achilles*, who during the two and twenty Years of his Embassy, made his Conduct be so admir'd, that having gain'd the Esteem of the Divan, and the Friendship of most of the Vizirs and Bashaws, there was not any Affair, tho' ever so difficult, but he brought it to a good Issue through his Prudence, as well for the Service of the King his Master, as for the Satisfaction of most of the other Christian Princes, whose Subjects that had any Business at the Port, found a powerful Protector in the Person of this Minister. They who know the Particulars of his Procedure agree, that upon his Manner of acting and negotiating the Idea of a perfect Embassador might be better form'd, than it is found in the Books of those who have made a great Collection of common Places, to represent quite another thing than what they promise.

Adrian Paau, *Sieur de Heemstede*, &c. has had several Employments, as well in *Holland* his native Countrey, as elsewhere in very considerable Embassies. The Town of *Amsterdam*, where his Father was a Burgomaster, made him its Pensionary, and in this Quality he accompany'd the Deputies of the said Town to the Assemblies of the States of *Holland*. He has discharg'd several Embassies in *France*, *England*, and elsewhere, where he has discover'd through a Grossness and Sordidness, which were peculiar to him, and which were accompany'd with other Qualities little becoming an Embassador, that with those Imperfections a Man may sometimes have a great Sense and a solid Judgment. One may say, that the Treaty that caus'd a Rupture between the two Crowns of *France* and *Spain* in the Year 1635, was chiefly his Work, but it was in the Negotiation of *Munster* that his Talent shew'd it self most. It cannot be deny'd but it was he particularly, who following the Orders of the States of his Province, concluded there the separate Peace with *Spain*, carrying himself therein with so much Firmness, mix'd with a little Artifice, that the Ministers of *France*, who had no great reason to love him, and who did not esteem him to be a very good Man, could not forbear speaking of his Capacity. The King at that time forbad his Plenipotentiaries having any Conversation with him. It was after the Conclusion of the Peace of *Munster*, and after the Death of the late King of *Great Britain*, that he was employ'd to the Parliament of *London*, and that he was made for the second time first Minister of the States of *Holland*, under the Quality of Counsellor Pensionary. He had quitted this Office, to enter into the Chamber of Accounts for the Demesne of the same Province, but as after the Death of *Jacob Catz*, who in his Employment of Pensionary had been very soft and negligent, she had occasion for a stronger Head, and a more understanding Man, she oblig'd *Paau* to put himself again at the Head of Affairs. He dy'd in that Office in the beginning of the Year 1653, and was by so much the less regretted as he made room for a Successor, whose extraordinary Merit has eclips'd all the Glory and Reputation his Predecessors had acquir'd in that Post.

Alexander Cardinal *Bichi* seem'd to be born for Negotiation, so that if together with his Ability, he had been a little more knavish than he was, he might perhaps have had with Cardinal *Richelieu*, the Post which *Julius Mazarin* had since. While he was Nuncio in *France*, his Conduct was so much approv'd, that it was not less at the King's Instance, than by the Inclination of the Pope who was his Relation, that he found himself honour'd with the Purple towards the End of his Nunciature. The King consider'd him as a Prelate very well affected to him, and the *Barberins* look'd upon him, as on one that would some Day be capable of doing very signal Services to their House, and to the See of *Rome*. *France* made use of his Advice and Counsels in several weighty Affairs, but particularly in the Accommodation of the Difference the *Barberins* had with the Duke of *Parma*, and on his Account with the Republick of *Venice*, and some other Princes of *Italy*. He was oblig'd to the *Barberins*, as I just said, but having in this Conjuncture accepted the Embassy Extraordinary of *France*, he labour'd to bring about the King's Intention, without any Regard to what he ow'd to the Pope and the *Barberins*. He was grave without Affectation, prudent without Cunning, diligent without Hurry, and a Friend without Interest. The civilest and the best of Men. During his Residence at his Bishoprick of *Carpentras*, under the Pontificate of *Innocent* X, he so vigorously protected the Count *de Dona*, Governor of *Orange*, and after so engaging a Manner, that I find my self oblig'd to say, (as having been an ocular Witness thereof) That it is to his good Offices, and to his Authority, that the Principality is indebted, for the Repose it has enjoy'd during the Minority of the Prince, and the Heat of the Contention between the two Princesses.

Alexander Abbot of *Scaglia*, Brother to the Count of *Caluse*, Minister of *Charles Emanuel* Duke of *Savoy*, had not the Qualities of Cardinal *Buchi*, but the common Proverb of *Like Master, like Man*, may be very well apply'd to him. The Duke, who was the most ambitious and the most restless of all Princes, had made him his Confident, and employ'd him in his nicest Negotiations. He solicited the Affairs of *Savoy* with Pope *Paul* V, in the Quality of Embassador, when *Philip* III, King of *Spain*, sent to the Court of *Rome* to take Cognizance of the Difference the *Venetians* and the Duke of *Savoy* had with the House of *Austria* and he had the Address to start so many Difficulties, that the Pope would not meddle therein in doing whereof he executed the Orders and Intention of his Master. In the Year 1626, he was Embassador in *France*, where he had a great Hand in the Intrigues, which caus'd the Count *de Chalais* to be executed at *Nants*, and threaten'd the King and Kingdom with a horrible Revolution, if the Prudence and good Fortune of Cardinal *de Richelieu* had not prevented the same. The Abbot not being able after that, to remain in a Court where he would have ruin'd the first Minister, went into *Holland*, and from thence into *England*, with a Design to stir up new Enemies to *France*, and create fresh Troubles to the Cardinal, by endeavouring to procure Succours to be sent to the *Rochellers*, and to the other Religionaries of the Kingdom. After that, the Duke of *Savoy* sent him to *Madrid*, where he did very ill Offices to the Marquiss of *Spinola*, who did not act in the Affair of *Mantua* according to the Humour of that Prince. The Abbot had Wit, but he was a mere Perturbator as well as his Master, and fitter to create Troubles, than to unravel and put an End to them. So that tho' he cannot be rank'd amongst the wisest Embassadors, he ought however to have a Place amongst the most Ingenious.

Alphonsa de la Cueva, Marquiss of *Bedmar*, Embassador of *Spain* at *Venice*, was no ordinary Man, but he was the greatest, and the most dangerous Enemy the Republick had. Those that make him the Author of the Book call'd, *The Scrutiny*, or, *The Examination of the Liberty of Venice*, bring but a weak Proof enough thereof, tho' there appears in it a very great Knowledge, and still a greater Animosity against the State. But I cannot tell how *Capriata* can justify him in that execrable Treason, which had destroy'd the Town and the Republick, if two *French* Gentlemen had not discover'd the Particulars thereof to the Senate. It is certain, that after what the Procurator *Nani* has publish'd on that Matter, from what he found in the Archives of the Republick, there there is no longer any room to doubt that *Don Alphonso* was the principal Contriver of the same. So that one may say, That as able a Man as he was, he was no great Embassador, since by so foul an Act on he render'd himself unworthy of the Protection of the *Law of Nations*, and expos'd himself to the Mercy or a People justly incens'd, by so abominable an Attempt. The King of *Spain*, who recall'd him at the Request of the Senate, nevertheless acknowledg'd his Merit, and the Service he would have done him in that Conjuncture, first by sending him Embassador into *Flanders* to the Arch-Dukes, and afterwards by procuring him a Cardinal's Hat, and the Superintendency of the Affairs of the Low Countries under the *Infanta*.

Aloysio, or *Lewis Contarini*, was so form'd for Negotiation, that his whole Life was almost but one continual Embassy. In the Year 1627, he was sent Embassador on the part of the Republick to *London*, where he labour'd successfully enough, at the Reconciliation of the Differences, which had caus'd *France* to come to a Rupture with *England*. In the Year 1629, he was Embassador in Ordinary at *Paris*, and in 1632, at *Rome*. In the Year 1638, he was Bailo, or Embassador at *Constantinople*. At that time the *Venetians* attack'd and destroy'd in the Harbour of *Valone* several Gallies, which the Pyrates of *Algiers* had brought thither. These Pyrates made great Complaints thereof at the Port, and the *Turks* would without doubt have resented it, if the *Grand Seignior*, *Amurath* IV, had not been engag'd in the *Persian* War. In his Absence however the Caimacan put the Bailo under Arrest, and confin'd him in a little sorry House in *Galata*. He also put a Garrison into the Palace of the Embassador, but he suffer'd him to receive the Visits of his Friends. The Matter was made up the Year following, and he was sent back to his Palace. In the Year 1643, he was nominated to the Embassy of *Munster*, to discharge there the Office of Mediator on the part of the Republick, in Conjunction with the Pope's Nuncio. He was very sedulous therein, and it must be own'd that he acquitted himself worthily of his Employment, notwithstanding he did not satisfy the Ministers of *France*, it being certain that during that Congress, he assisted at about eight hundred Conferences, which were all of no Utility in reference to the two Crowns of *France* and *Spain*. and altho' he contributed very much to the Peace of *Germany*, yet it was not

not thought fit to mention him in the Treaty, no more than the Nuncio, becaufe the Pope not being able to confent to the Advantages which were thereby granted to the Proteſtants, would not fuffer his Nuncio to be nam'd therein.

Angel Contarini poſſeſs'd all the neceſſary Qualities for an Embaſſador, altho' the Republick of *Venice* employ'd him rather in Embaſſies of Solemnity, than in great Negotiations. He was firſt ſent into *England* with *Anthony Cornaro*, to complement King *Charles* I on his Acceſſion to the Throne. In the Year 1629, he was ſent to Pope *Urban* VIII, who had a particular Eſteem for him, and in the Year 1637, he went Embaſſador Extraordinary to the Emperor *Ferdinand* III. The Behaviour of his Succeſſor in the Year 1643, towards General *Spar*, who had offended him, ſhews that he was a true Embaſſador, and knew very well what belong'd to the Dignity of his Character.

Angel Cornaro, Embaſſador on the part of the Republick at *Paris*, was ſo able a Subject, that Cardinal *de Richelieu*, who was the greateſt Miniſter *France* has had ſince the Foundation of that Monarchy, conſulted him, and made uſe of his Advice in the moſt perplexing Conjunctures. He even ſuffer'd this foreign Miniſter to intercede for the Reconciliation of the Count *de Soiſſons*, and of the Duke of *Guiſe*, (which was a very nice Affair) for whom the Pope was not allow'd to make Interceſſion, and he certainly had effected an Accommodation for the laſt, but for the violent Tranſports of that Prince, which were the Cauſe of his Ruine, and had like to have been that of his whole Houſe. *Cornaro* had render'd himſelf ſo agreeable, and even neceſſary to this firſt Miniſter, that the time of his Embaſſy, which is regulated at *Venice*, being expir'd, the King wrote with his own Hand to the Senate, to deſire it to excuſe the Embaſſador from the Rigour of the Laws of the State, and to continue him in his Employment for ſome Years longer, to which the Senate acquieſced. He muſt have been endow'd with very extraordinary Qualities, to be able in that Poſt to acquire not only the Eſteem, but alſo the Confidence of a Miniſter (who was not prodigal of either) even to communicate to him the moſt ſecret Affairs, and to employ him in foreign Courts for the King's Service.

Anthony le Brun, Solicitor General to the Parliament of *Dol*, was the laſt, but the ableſt of the Plenipotentiaries the King of *Spain* had at *Munſter*. He had more Knowledge of the Affairs of the Low Countries than any of his Collegues as his Humour was alſo more complaiſant, and his Converſation more agreeable, he was likewiſe fitter for Negotiation. So that one may ſay, that it was chiefly to him that the King of *Spain* was oblig'd for the Peace the *Dutch* made there exclusively of *France*. This Service was acknowledg'd by his being ſent Embaſſador to the States of the United Provinces, and afterwards by a conſiderable Office in the Exchequer at *Bruſſells*. He expreſs'd himſelf well either by word of Mouth or in Writing. And as he was born in the County of *Burgundy*, that is to ſay, in the Low Countries themſelves, he had no Difficulty to accommodate himſelf to the Humour of the People, which had ſome Reſemblance with his Genius and his manner of Living. The Inhabitants of all the Low Countries are tractable enough, provided they are govern'd with a gentle Rein and conformable to Reaſon, then they follow without Reſiſtance thoſe that lead them, but they oppoſe thoſe who are for dragging them along by Force. He was belov'd at the *Hague*, and would have been a uſeful Servant to the King his Maſter, if his Employment had not ended with his Life, when he began to be well known, and his Merit to be eſteem'd.

I have nothing to ſay of *Arnauld Doſſat* Cardinal, becauſe one cannot ſpeak of him without doing him Wrong, ſince *Anthony Muretus*, the moſt eloquent Man of his Time, ſtops ſhort when he would make his Encomium in his Funeral Oration. I ſhall only ſay of him, that never did any Miniſter exert in his Employment ſo much Affection, ſo much Zeal, ſo much Application, nor ſo much Fidelity for the Service of the King his Maſter, as did that Prelate. As for his Ability, we may judge of it by what we have of his Negotiations. For which is well as for many other Treatiſes, the Publick is oblig'd to the late Meſſieurs *au Puy*, the Honour and Ornament of our Age. We have Proofs of his Ability in the Negotiation he concluded with the Great Duke of *Tuſcany*, for the Reſtitution of the Iſle of *If*. In that he perform'd with *Clement* VIII, for the Reconciliation of King *Henry* IV to the Church of *Rome*. For the Declaration of the Nullity of the Marriage of the ſame King, which had laſted almoſt thirty Years with Queen *Margaret* of *Valois*. For the Diſpenſation of the Marriage of *Catherine de Bourbon*, Siſter to *Henry* IV, with the Duke *de Bar*, and for ſeveral other Affairs of very great Importance, and very intricate. His Diſpatches are not leſs neceſſary to an Embaſſador that pretends to ſucceed in his Employment, than the Bible and a Courſe of the Law are to Divines and Civilians, who will ſucceed in their Profeſſion.

All I can ſay of M S *Arnauld*, Lord of *Pompone*, is that the King his Maſter would not of his own Motion have advanc'd him to one of the firſt and moſt conſiderable Places in the Kingdom, by making him Secretary of State for Foreign Affairs, if this Miniſter had not made known his extraordinary Capacity in the Embaſſies wherein he was employ'd for ſeveral Years. He had been Embaſſador in *Sweden* and in *Holland*, and had been ſent for the ſecond time into *Sweden*, when the moſt Chriſtian King call'd him home, to come and diſcharge an Office which cannot be poſſeſs'd without enjoying alſo the Confidence of the Maſter. Which this great Monarch, who knows ſo well how to chuſe his Miniſters, would never have done, if he had not been very well ſatisfy'd with the Conduct of this, and if he had not judg'd that *M. Arnauld* underſtood ſo well Affairs of this Nature, that he might ſafely entruſt him with the Direction of thoſe which make the principal Occupation of the Council above. In his firſt Embaſſy to *Sweden* he had only ordinary Affairs to negotiate. He made ſo ſhort a Stay in *Holland*, that it was impoſſible for him to re-unite thoſe Minds which

which the triple Alliance had render'd irreconcileable, but his last Embassy in *Sweden* secur'd that Crown to *France*, whom it concern'd so much that the *Swedes* should not espouse the Interest of the United Provinces, that without that Assurance the King would have been unwilling to resolve upon the War that begun in the Year 1671. *M. Arnauld* is of a Family which has produc'd a great many illustrious Personages in all Professions; and as for his own particular, it must be acknowledg'd that he has, together with that Merit which is as it were hereditary to him, a rich Stock of Probity, on which those who negotiate with him may safely rely. I wish I cou'd say as much of his Predecessor.

All that can be said to the Advantage of all the Embassadors in general, may be apply'd to *M. de Barillon* alone. I don't speak of his Virtue, nor of his Honesty, which are familiar and hereditary to him, but I cannot forbear saying, that to represent an Idea of a truly Man of Worth, and of a great Embassador, it would be sufficient to draw the Portraicture and Character of this great Minister. His Name is illustrious, but his personal Merit has procur'd him a particular Veneration, and the Esteem of the greatest King in Christendom. He serv'd with Reputation and Success at the Congress of *Cologn*, after which his Majesty employ'd him in *England*, in a very difficult Conjuncture of Affairs. He succeeded after the manner the King his Master desir'd and there is no doubt but he will reap therefrom, that Glory and Honour which is due to his incomparable Ability.

The Character of *Baptista Nani*, Procurator of St *Mark*, is to be found in the History of his Countrey, and of the Affairs that happen'd in his Time in *Italy*. He has written it with so much Skill and Judgment, that if he had given no other Proof of his Sufficiency, he will always pass for a very great Man, with those who have any Taste. But he has besides acquir'd so high a Reputation in all his Embassies, and particularly in that of *France*, that it would be a piece of Injustice to him, not to place him amongst the greatest Embassadors, and amongst the ablest Ministers, since it is impossible but he must know perfectly well the Affairs he has so judiciously written. The late Emperor, who had been a Witness of his Negotiations at *Vienna*, held him in great Esteem and the Republick her self has thought fit to express to what Degree she valu'd him, in honouring his Merit with the first Dignity after the Ducal.

The Count *de Bethune* was full as illustrious by his fine Qualities as by his Family, which is without doubt one of the first and most ancient of the Low Countries. The Duke of *Sully*, his Brother, who was one of those Ministers in whom King *Henry* IV. put the greatest Confidence, brought him into Business; but at his first Entrance therein, he made it plain that he was very capable thereof. He did Honour to the King his Master, in his Embassy at *Rome*, where he acquitted himself so well of what was expected from him, that he was hardly ever without Employment from that Time. The Duke his Brother was out of all, when after the Death of *Henry* the Count was sent to *Milan* and *Turin*, to labour at an Accommodation of the Differences the Duke of *Savoy* and the Governor of *Milan* had about the *Montferrat*. In the Year 1620, he was sent with the Duke *d'Engoulesme* and the *S Depreaux* into *Germany*, on the account of the Commotions in *Bohemia*. He was the Soul, as one may say, of that Embassy, and he would have done great Services to *France*, if the Duke *de Luines*, who had the entire Management of Affairs, had let them rowl on the ancient Maxims of that Crown. He had not so good an Appearance, but he had full as much Wit and Capacity as the Duke his Brother, and he may be rank'd amongst the greatest Men and the ablest Negotiators of his Time. The Count his Son had as much Merit as any Lord of the Kingdom, but he had too much Honour to stoop to a Dependence on the Ministers, who were not for having Friends, or Servants, but Slaves. He never had any Employment, tho' he was very capable thereof.

Cardinal *de Bonzy* left off being in Embassador, at an Age when others begin to take that Employment upon them, and shew'd that he was capable of that eminent Employment before he enter'd upon it. *Venice*, which is commonly the School of new Embassadors, serv'd him as a Theatre, where he display'd his incomparable Qualities. The Court of *Madrid*, which is very shy of shewing its Esteem for Foreigners, could not refuse it him, and has admir'd his Eloquence, his Judgment, his Wit and his Conduct: but all these great Qualities shew'd themselves with much more Lustre in his Embassy to *Poland*, where he had insurmountable Difficulties to struggle with and overcome. Never did any Minister negotiate with more Facility, or greater Success, and never did Embassador leave his Master more satisfy'd with his Conduct and manner of Acting, but then he serv'd a Prince, who is not only knowing in Men, but likewise knows perfectly well how to recompence their Services, and who could not give a more illustrious Mark thereof, than in obtaining for him the Purple, which gives him a Place immediately after the Princes of the Blood, before all the other Princes and Lords of the Kingdom, and which for the future will acquire him in the Council, in the Consistory, and in the Conclave, as much Reputation as he has gain'd and left in foreign Courts.

Chasteauneuf d'Aubespine was the Son of a Master, but he made his Apprenticeship under one of the greatest Men that ever was employ'd in Affairs of State. He was yet but Abbot *de Preaux*, when *M de Villeroy*, his Unkle, put him with President *Jeannin*, who was going to negotiate a Peace, and conclude a Truce in *Holland*. He there serv'd as a subaltern Minister, and succeeded well enough in the Journeys the President made him take now and then, as well to the Arch-Duke *Albert* as to the King. In the Year 1620, he was sent into *Germany* with the Duke *d'Engoulesme* and the Count *de Bethune*, for the Accommodation of the Affairs of *Bohemia* and the *Palatinate*, but was too limited in his Orders to be able to succeed in a Negotiation, the Importance whereof was not at that Time sufficiently weigh'd by the first Minister. In the Year 1626, he he was fent to *Venice*, to juftify the King's Intention, and to get the Reafons relifh'd which had oblig'd *France* to approve of the Treaty of *Monçon* The Republick receiv'd the bad Excufes of a thing it could not remedy, but the *Swifs Cantons*, to whom he went afterwards on the fame Account, were not at all fatisfy'd with what had been done in reference to the *Valtelline* In the Year 1629, he was Embaffador Extraordinary in *England*, to fee the Peace fworn to After that the Cardinal procur'd him the Seals, but he foon took them from him, and fent him Prifoner to the Caftle of *Engoulifme*, as a Man of an infufferable Sp rit, and unfaithful to his Benefactor They were reftor'd to him during the laft Com notions of *Paris* but his Humour not being agreeable to the Court, and ftill lefs to Cardinal *Mazarin*, againft whom he was continually caballing, he was relegated to tne *Red-houfe*, where he dy'd fome Years after He was a great Minifter, who became his Poft very well, and a very able Negotiator, but then he was fo haughty and proud, that in all his Actions he behav'd himfelf like a great V zir, rather than like the Minifter of the Court of *France*, which is the moft polite and the civileft of all *Europe*

Chriftopher de Baffompierre, Marefchal of *France*, has left us, with the Memoirs of his Life, Relations of the Embaffies he has perform'd in *Spain*, in *England*, and to the *Swifs Cantons* for which reafon I might forbear faying any thing of h m, and content my felf with adding his Name to thofe Embaffadors, of whom I have undertaken to give fome Account in this Chapter But as I had the Opportunity of contracting a particular Acquaintance with him, fo far as to obtain the Communication of his Memoirs, which have been publifh'd but fince his Deceafe, I think my felf oblig'd to give a fhort Account of what I have perceiv'd extraordinary in this Nobleman What has been printed of his Works, fufficiently fhews that Negotiation was not his Talent He had indeed other Qualities which render'd him highly confiderable It was impoffible to fee a finer Man than *M de Baffompierre*, nor that had a greater Prefence of Mind, or was more agreeable He was withal fplendid in his Expence, and rather magnificent than liberal The moft civil and the moft generous Man in the World So that with thefe Qualities, and the Intereft he had in the Houfe of *Guife*, it was not very difficult for him to get to be confider'd at Court, under the Regency of *Mary of Medicis* Cardinal de *Richelieu* lov'd him, but coming to know that he was one of the Cabal of Noblemen who confpir'd at *Lions*, (where the King lay fick to Extremity) againft his Fortune and Life, he caus'd him to be put into the *Baftille*, where he remain'd till after the Death of that Minifter He was reftor'd to his Poft of Colonel General of the *Swifs*, but he did not enjoy it long, for one Morning he was found dead in his Bed

Chriftopher Kevenhuller, Count of *Frankenberg*, Embaffador of the Emperor *Matthias*, and of the Arch-Duke *Ferdinand* at *Madrid*, was a very worthy Minifter At the fame time that *Ferdinand* was call'd to the Crown of *Bohemia*, *Kevenhuller* happily adjufted the Difference the Republick of *Venice* had with the Houfe of *Auftria* concerning the *Ufcoques*. That Treaty did not take Place, as I have obferv'd elfewhere, and particularly in Chapter XV of this Book, till it was finifh'd at *Paris*, and the King of *France* had oblig'd the *Venetians* to ratify it. *Kevenhuller* has written his Negotiations, and has publifh'd one part of 'em in the *German* Tongue, but the other has been fuppref's'd of Thofe that have feen what is publick are of Opinion, that he was one of the ableft Negotiators the Court of *Vienna* has afforded and employ'd, and that nothing can be added to the Delicacy which appears in all his Procedure They fpeak ftill of him there with Refpect, and his Memory and Works are in very great Efteem

M Colbert is very much indebted to his eldeft Brother, who introduc'd him into Affairs, and into the great World, but he is ftill more indebted to his own Virtue and Merit, fince he has maintain'd himfelf there, and ftill continues to do fo by his Services, and by his own Sufficiency The feveral Negotiations he has heretofore perform'd in *Germany*, particularly at *Cleves* and at *Aix la Chapelle*, as a Minifter of the fecond Order, have procur'd him fome Reputation, and ufher'd him into Embaffies In that to *England* he out-did himfelf, and was the Admiration of that Court, which has not much for Foreigners They who know what has been negotiated between the two Courts fince the triple Alliance, and particularly fince the Rupture in the Year 1672, and the Treaty of *London* in 1674, cannot be ignorant that he has had Affairs of the laft Importance to negotiate He behav'd himfelf fo well therein, that the King his Mafter judg'd he could not make a better Choice than of this Minifter, to labour in Conjunction with the Marefchal *d'Eftrades* and Count *d'Avaux* at the general Peace And it is probable he will not leave *Nimeguen*, till he has help'd to give the laft Perfection to a Work which is to give Repofe to *Chriftendom*

If I ought not to fpeak without Scruple of thofe Embaffadors who are ftill living, and in Employment, I ought to have a great deal when I write the Elogium of *Conrad van Beuninguen*, Burgo-Mafter of the City of *Amfterdam*, as well becaufe I am not altogether difinterefted, as becaufe amongft all the Embaffadors, of whom I here make a fmall Catalogue, there is hardly any one that has been fo often, and fo continually employ'd in foreign Negotiations The Courts of *Copenhagen* and of *Stockholm* have feen him, during the ruinous War the United Provinces had with *Oliver Cromwell* till the Year 1654 It was he chiefly, who with *M Trevor*, Minifter of *England*, fettled in the Year 1668, at *St Germain en Laye*, the Articles on which the Treaty of *Aix la Chapelle* was afterwards concluded In the Year 1654, he had been fent to *Breme*, to adjuft the Difference which that Town had with the Crown of *Sweden* He has fince negotiated with the Count *do Monterey* at *Bruffells*, and he has been for fome Years in *England* He has a great Vivacity of Mind, an inimitable Facility of expreffing himfelf, and an inexhauftible Fund of Reafons, with which his Difcourfes are conftantly fill'd He has a great deal of Study, and a great Inclination to Philofophy, sophy, as well in his Sentiments as in his Morals. From whence I infer, That he may be rank'd, not only in the Number of the Illustrious Embassadors, but also amongst the Learned Men of our Time.

I should not satisfy the Publick, nor my self, if I did not bestow a few Lines on *M. Honnoré Courtin*, and if I did not say a Word or two of the great and considerable Employments which the King his Master has intrusted him with. I shall say nothing of those he has had at home, where he made his Apprenticeship in those Employments, which are given to them who are destin'd to the first Places of the Gown, viz. In the Parliament, and in the Council, as that of Master of the Requests, and in the Provinces, as those of Intendant of Justice, and of the Revenues. *M. Courtin* had pass'd through them all, when after the Conclusion of the Peace of the *Pyrenees*, he was deputed to regulate the Limits of the new Conquests on the side of the Low Countries. In the Year 1665, he was sent with the Duke *de Vernueil* into *England*, to try to prevail with the King to put an end to the Hostilities with which the *English* disturb'd the Repose of the United Provinces. In the Year 1667, he was sent with *M. d'Estrades* to the Congress of *Breda*, as Embassador Extraordinary and Plenipotentiary, after having been employ'd in *Germany* for the Accommodation of the Difference the Elector *Palatin* had with the Electors of *Mayence*, of *Triers*, and of *Cologn*, &c. and concerning the Right of *Wildfang*. In the Year 1673, he was sent with the same Quality to *Cologne*, with the Duke *de Chaulne* and *M. de Barillon*, and this Assembly being dissipated, on the Account of the carrying off of Prince *William* of *Furstemberg*, the King his Master employ'd him in the Embassy Extraordinary to *England*. His Wit and Conduct appear'd in this Embassy, as well as in all those that preceded it, with so much Lustre, that it cannot be deny'd but he was one of the able Embassadors of our Time, and that his Services cannot be sufficiently acknowledg'd, unless he be rewarded with one of the most considerable Posts in the Court, the Council, or the Parliament.

The House of *d'Estrée*, which is one of the most Illustrious Ones of *France*, has produc'd a great many Hero's, of whom *M. le Cardinal de Laon* is without doubt one of the first. The Mareschal *d'Estrée*, his Father, had very great Qualities, which made him be consider'd by Cardinal *Richelieu*, as a Nobleman very capable of serving the King, not only at the Head of his Armies, but also in the knottyest Affairs, and most intricate Negotiations. Out of this Consideration he caus'd him to be sent Embassador to *Rome*, and to the *Swiss Cantons*. Those who knew him, and who know with what Air he acted in all his Employments, agree that he was much fitter for the Field than the Closet. He had Courage, and was the Man in the World the most capable of doing a brave Action; but when he had to do with skilful Heads, he did not dispute the Ground with the same Advantage, as where he was to act with Vigour and Courage. He was born a Captain, and in that Humour he was for commanding, and could not bear in Conferences where he was to negotiate with his Equals or with his Superiors, that they should not treat him with that Respect he requir'd should be shewn him every where. The Cardinal did not perceive it till it was too late, after the Mareschal had embroil'd himself with the Pope's Nephews, without Hopes of Reconciliation. They caus'd the Head of the Gentleman of the Horse to the Embassador of *France*, to be put amongst those of several others of the Banditti, and Rogues, so that there was but too much handle to quarrel with the Court of *Rome*. After several violent Transports he refus'd to go, and give an Account of his Actions at Court. Those Noblemen who are of this Temper, and who undertake to protect their Domesticks, let their Crimes be ever so outrageous, are not at all fit for the Ministry, because an Embassador ought always to avoid the Occasions that create Troubles to his Master. It is not necessary to alledge any other Examples, after those which are to be found in this Treatise. The Cardinal, his Son, would not behave himself after this manner. He is a great Man, a wise Prelate, and a very able Minister and Negotiator.

They who have written an Account of all that pass'd in the Difference, that arm'd the Republick of *Venice*, and some other Potentates of *Italy*, against the *Barberins*, about forty Years ago, cannot sufficiently admire the Ingenuity and Prudence of Count *Ferdinand Scotti*, who negotiated the Interest of the Duke of *Parma* with the Senate. I don't find that he has meddl'd with any other publick Affairs, but it must be acknowledg'd that he did in this (which was very intricate, and wherein he had to struggle with the natural, and almost invincible Obstinacy of a Republick, which would not so much as suffer a Rupture with the Pope to be mention'd to it) beyond whatever could be expected from the most consummate Prudence of the most skilful Minister. Those that will take the Pains to read with Application all that pass'd in this Negotiation, and particularly at *Venice*, will agree, that I do not sufficiently praise a Man who succeeded so well, in a Profession he had never before been concern'd in. This is however what is not very extraordinary in *Italy*.

The Marquiss *de Fontenay Maruezl* had so well satisfy'd the King, and the first Minister, in his first Embassy at *Rome*, that Cardinal *Mazarin*, who made his Advantage of the Affairs the King caus'd to be negotiated with the Pope, during the last Commotions of the Kingdom of *Naples*, employ'd him again in this Conjuncture, as being a Minister very capable of governing the Mind of Pope *Innocent* X. The Marquiss apply'd himself therein with Zeal and Affection, but there was a domestick and irreconcileable Hatred between the Pope and the Cardinal. Besides which, *Innocent* was very strongly inclin'd to the *Spaniards*. So that the Duke of *Guise*, whose Conduct was irregular enough, crossing his Undertaking, it was impossible for *M. de Fontenay* to do any thing to the Advantage of *France*. The Embassador had Orders to oppose the Duke's Designs, which were not approv'd of at Court, and this was what he had no Difficulty to succeed in, because it was impossible for the Duke, who had neither Troops, Money, nor Ammunition, to
drive

drive the *Spaniards* out of *Naples*, while the People perfecuted with Fury the Nobility and Barons, who were they that could contribute moſt thereto. M *de Fontenay*, who was a very able Miniſter, did not however ſatisfy Cardinal *Mazarin* in this laſt Embaſſy, notwithſtanding it was the Pope's Inflexibility which fruſtrated the Embaſſador's Induſtry and Application. Nevertheleſs, tho' he did not loſe in this Employment the Reputation which he firſt had procur'd him, and which he had acquir'd in *England* where he had alſo been Embaſſador. Yet he loſt the Fruits of his Labour, and with them the Friendſhip of the firſt Miniſter, who did not employ him any more after that Time.

Francois d'Aerſens, Lord of *Someldick*, of *Spyck*, &c. was one of the greateſt Miniſters the United Provinces have had for Negotiation. His Father, who was alſo a Man of great Parts, was in a Poſt where it was an eaſy matter for him to procure his Son Employment. *John d'Oldenbarnvelt*, of whom I ſhall ſpeak by and by, who had then the chief Management of the Affairs of *Holland*, and of all the United Provinces, got him to be ſent into *France*, in the Quality of Agent. It was there that he learnt to negotiate with thoſe Great Maſters, *Henry* IV, *Villeroy*, *Roſny*, *Sillery*, *Jeannin*, &c. and he ſucceeded ſo well therein as to have his Conduct approv'd by them. He had afterwards the Character of Embaſſador, and was the firſt that was conſider'd in that Quality at that Court, and in whoſe Time King *Henry* IV declar'd, That the Embaſſador of the United Provinces ſhould take Place immediately after that of *Venice*. He was afterwards employ'd to that Republick, and to ſeveral Princes of *Germany* and *Italy*, on the Account of the Commotions of *Bohemia*. He has moreover been ſeveral Times Embaſſador Extraordinary in *France* and in *England*, of which he has made a very exact and judicious Collection. I have ſeen them, and have obſerv'd therein, that all the Inſtructions the State gave him, and all the Credentials he carry'd with him in his laſt Embaſſies, are all of his own Faſhion. So that we muſt believe that he was the Perſon, of all the Countrey, who knew beſt, not only how to negotiate, but alſo how to inſtruct an Embaſſador in what he had to negotiate. And indeed he has done Honour to the State in all his Embaſſies, as well as to the Character with which his Sovereigns have inveſted him, tho' neither he nor his Poſterity have any Reaſon to repine at the the Time he employ'd in the Service of his Countrey.

I know not whether the Count *de Fuenſaldagne* has ſerv'd in any other Embaſſies than in that of *France*, but from the manner he behav'd himſelf in this, we muſt believe that one Embaſſy is ſufficient to procure a high Reputation to an Embaſſador. He had given Proofs of his Ability, while he had the chief Management of the Affairs of the Low Countries under the Arch-Duke *Leopold*, and afterwards in the Government of *Milan*. As he knew the ill State of thoſe Provinces, he was the firſt that undeceiv'd *Don Lewis de Haro*, in the vain Hopes the Council of *Spain* had conceiv'd, of being able to ſave them from the Arms of *France*, and it was he that adviſ'd him to make a Peace at any Rate. It was with this Intention that he began, while he was ſtill at *Bruſſels*, to entertain a Correſpondence with Cardinal *Mazarin*, and that he oppos'd all the Prince of *Condé*'s Contrivances to exaſperate *France* ſtill more. Being Governor of *Milan*, he continu'd this Correſpondence. So that as he was the Perſon who had procur'd the firſt Diſpoſition to a Peace, he was look'd upon, after that was concluded at the *Pyrenees*, to be the moſt proper Perſon to preſerve the Fruit he had planted and cultivated, for which Reaſon he was ſent Embaſſador Extraordinary to *Paris*. He had ſo worthily diſcharg'd the great Employments he had been entruſted with, that he had no Difficulty to ſucceed in this, wherein his Conduct was ſo wiſe and even, that he was ſoon as well belov'd at the Court of *France*, as he was eſteem'd in that of *Spain*. I cou'd inſtance in very conſiderable Particulars thereof, if I might be allow'd to make the leaſt Digreſſion, in a Chapter wherein I have ſpoken of ſo many great Perſonages. I have given an Account how he left the Court of *France*, and how being arriv'd in the Low Countries he dy'd in the firſt Poſt there, and on the firſt Day of his Government.

I ſhall ſpeak of *Gaſpar de Bracamonte*, Count *de Pegneranda*, but only becauſe he was the Chief of that ſolemn Embaſſy when the King of *Spain* ſent to *Munſter*. He then juſt began to enter upon Buſineſs, and had not the neceſſary Experience to come off with Succeſs, in a Negotiation of that Importance. He had only ſeen the Court of *Spain*, ſo that not having had Lerſure to unlearn the ill Habits which are in a manner natural to thoſe who have never been out of their own Countrey, of what Nation ſoever they may be, he was proud and obſtinate, and ſo prepoſſeſs'd in Favour of his own Sentiments, that it was impoſſible to cure him thereof. He was perſuaded that the Emperor did not dare to treat without *Spain*: That *France* was threaten'd with an inevitable Revolution, and that having concluded a ſeparate Treaty with the United Provinces, there ought to be no Apprehenſion of the Arms of *France* making any farther Progreſs into *Flanders*. And upon theſe wild Notions, he rejected all the Propoſitions that could forward an Accommodation between the two Crowns. He did not acquire at *Munſter* the Reputation of an able Negotiator, becauſe being paſſionate and obſtinate, as I juſt now ſaid, he adviſ'd with no body, nor would hearken to no other Conditions than what were agreeable to the Conceptions he had of the imaginary Grandeur of the King his Maſter, who is oblig'd to him for all the Loſſes he has ſuſtain'd in the Low Countries ſince that Time, that is to ſay, ſince the Rupture of the Negotiation of *Munſter*. He has been ſince employ'd in the Council of *Spain*, where he acquitted himſelf worthily of his Poſt, and made it appear that he only wanted a little Experience, to make him capable of Affairs.

Gaſpar Coignet de la Thuillerie had both natural and acquir'd Parts, which made him be conſider'd as one of the ableſt Men of *France*. He had a Mien that ſet off his Character, and he was withal civil, inſinuating, reaſonable, moderate, good Company, ſtrong in his Arguments,

guments, eloquent beyond what is usual, firm, and solid Being Embassador at *Venice*, he there work'd happily at the Accommodation of the Differences the Republick had with the Pope, concerning their common Frontiers, on the side of the *Ferrarese*, towards the Mouth of the *Po* He was Embassador in *Holland* in the Year 1645, when the King his Master dispatch'd him to act the part of Mediator between the two *Northern* Powers He succeeded so well therein, that both sides remain'd very well satisfy'd with his good Offices The Queen of *Sweden* was so, because the Peace that was concluded at *Bremsebro*, gave the *Swedes* the Means to pursue their Designs in *Germany*, and to second there those of *France* And altho' the King of *Denmark* did not find his Account in it, he was however glad to be able to preserve a good part of his Dominions, when he ran the risque of losing them all He went afterwards to *Stockholm*, where he serv'd the King his Master perfectly well, as he also did at his Return to *Holland*. He remain'd there till the United Provinces having concluded a separate Treaty with *Spain*, and made a kind of Divorce with *France*, he retir'd in 1648, to *Paris*, where he was design'd for greater Employments, but for the Troubles of the Kingdom, during which he dy'd

I wish I had not so much reason to speak of *Godefroy* Count *d'Estrades*, Mareschal of *France*, and Knight of the King's Orders, &c I shall not here consider him as an Officer of the Crown, who rais'd himself to this Dignity by his own Merit and Services, without the least Favour, which seems inseparable from the Fortune of the Court The most Christian King, who is very just in all his Actions, did an extraordinary Piece of Justice, when he honour'd *M d'Estrades* with this eminent Dignity, in so advanc'd an Age, that he could no longer delay giving him so illustrious a Mark of his Esteem But this does not belong to my Subject I here speak of him as of an able Minister, and not as of the General of an Army He had no sooner taken upon him this Profession, than he was put upon Negotiation by the greatest Man that ever had the Management of the Affairs of a great State, and he answer'd so well what Cardinal *de Richelieu* had promis'd himself from his Ability, that it may be said, that from that time he shar'd with the Embassadors the Confidence of those Affairs, which have been negotiated in *Holland* by Cardinal *Mazarin*, and the Ministers who have succeeded him, could not do without this Negotiator of the Camp, in the most intricate Conjunctures It is impossible to imagin more perplexing ones, than those which constantly employ'd him, during the Negotiations of *Munster* and of *Osnaburg*, and especially in the Precipitation with which the *Hollanders* ran to a Peace, during the Sickness and Infirmities of the Prince of *Orange* The History of those Times relates the Particulars of the Intrigues of the whole Negotiation, and takes notice of the part *M d'Estrades* had therein, for which reason I shall say nothing of it, no more than of what pass'd, and was negotiated by his Means in *Italy*, while he there commanded the *French* Army But is it possible, without

Admiration, to refresh one's Memory with the Address he shew'd, in acquiring to *France* the Town of *Dunkirk*? Not that little sorry Place which was taken and retaken several times before the *Pyrenean* Peace, but that Place which *Cromwell* had caus'd to be fortify'd at a prodigious Expence, and which was to serve as a Door for the *English* to enter *France* at whenever they pleas'd I should never have done, if I enter'd upon a Detail of all that was transacted in *Holland*, during the six Years of his Embassy Extraordinary there It is sufficient to say, That his King was so well satisfy'd therewith, that he has not only acknowledg'd his Services on all Occasions, but also put him at the Head of that illustrious Embassy, which was to restore Peace to the United Provinces And as in that his Majesty consider'd *M d'Estrades*, as the most capable Person of his Kingdom to bring about his Intentions, for the Glory of his Reign, and for the Repose of *Christendom* so there is no room to doubt, but this Minister will crown so many fine Actions of his illustrious Life with the most glorious of all, by not leaving *Nimeguen*, till he has concluded a general Peace

The Marquiss of *Grana* and of *Final*, Father to him who during these last Wars, was one of those who acquir'd the greatest Reputation, either for Arms or Negotiation, did not make himself less consider'd in the Council of *Vienna*, than in the Armies where he had the chiefest Employments next to the first But in the Embassy he perform'd at *Madrid* in the Year 1641, which is (if I mistake not) the only one he ever was employ'd in, he play'd a Stroke of the ablest Man that ever undertook to negotiate *Philip* IV, King of *Spain*, had left the whole Conduct of his Affairs to the Count Duke *d'Olivares*, but whether his Capacity or his Genius was inferior to that of Cardinal *de Richelieu*, he succeeded in nothing on the contrary several Provinces revolted, and whole Kingdoms withdrew themselves from the Crown of *Castille* The *Low Countries* were on the Point of being lost, and the Evil communicating it self to *Germany*, the Marquiss of *Grana*, considering the common Interest of the House, undertook to represent to the King of *Spain* the deplorable State of his Affairs, and took for that purpose such Measures with the Queen, who understood things very well, that they remov'd the Count This was a bold and artful Stroke of a Minister, who was capable of a great deal more, and who thereby did a very signal Service to the Emperor, and to all the House of *Austria*

The Republick of *Venice* would alone furnish wherewithal to make a great Volume of illustrious Embassadors So that tho' I instance but in a few *Venetians*, it is not my Intention to wrong those that do not occur to my Memory, but I should injure those who make so considerable a part of modern History, if I did not insert them in this Catalogue Of this Number is *William Soranzo*, who in the Year 1612, concluded the Treaty of *Vienna*, concerning the Affair of the *Uscoques* In the Year 1618, he made another Treaty at *Rome* with Cardinal *Borgia*, about the Restitution of some Ships, which had been taken by
those

those belonging to the Duke of *Ussuna*, Viceroy of *Naples* In the Year 1621, he was sent Embassador Extraordinary to *Madrid*, to complement *Philip* IV on his Accession to the Crown In the Year 1623, he went in the same Quality to *Rome*, on the occasion of the Exaltation of *Urban* VIII In the Year 1629, he was sent Embassador Extraordinary into *France*, on the account of the War of *Savoy*, because the Duke oppos'd the Passage of the *French* Army In the Year 1630, Cardinal *de Richelieu* desir'd him to take a Journey to *Turin*, and afterwards to *Casal*, for the Regulation of the Garrison of that Place with the *Spaniards*, wherein he succeeded to the Satisfaction of both Crowns, and in the Year 1653, he was employ'd with *Nani* to settle the Limits between the State of the Church and the Republick

Hercules, Baron of *Charnace*, was also of the Choice of Cardinal *de Richelieu*, which of it self ought to give a very favourable Opinion of an Embassador But he I am speaking of did not stand in need of this Prepossession His Negotiations with *Gustavus Adolphus*, King of *Sweden*, which produc'd the Treaty of *Berwalde* on *January* 23, 1631, and which caus'd so great an effect in *Germany*, are very convincing Proofs thereof, if there were no other It was he that brought the Arms of *Sweden* into the Empire, and laid the first Foundations of that Alliance, which has been so useful and so glorious to the two Crowns, and is so still to that of *Sweden* He continu'd to negotiate with the same King, and with Chancellor *Oxenstiern*, till after the Battel of *Lutzen*, which made him retire into *France* He had also negotiated with the Elector of *Bavaria* at *Munich*, but with little Success, by reason of the ill Humour of *St Stephen*, a Relation of Father *Joseph*'s, who being jealous to see in that Court an abler Man than himself, thwarted all his Negotiations, to the great Prejudice of the Affairs of the King his Master It was *Charnace* who sign'd on the fifteenth Day of *April*, 1634, the Treaty of the *Hague*, after which it was judg'd proper to make that of the eighth of *January* of the following Year, where he was concern'd as one of the King's Commissioners By the Treaty of 1634, the King promis'd to raise and to entertain in the Service of the States a Regiment of Foot, and a Troop of Horse, the Command whereof was given to *Charnace*, who mingling the Profession of Colonel with the Function of Embassador, would needs be present at the last Siege of *Breda*, where he was kill'd in the Trenches

Jerome Beverning is without doubt one of the first Men of the United Provinces for Negotiation The Town of *Goude*, which does not want great Subjects, has more than once deputed him to the Assemblies of the States of the Province of *Holland*, and to the Colleges of the Generality And he has always perfectly well answer'd whatever could be expected from his Ability It was he who in the Year 1654, concluded with *Oliver Cromwell* the Treaty which gave Peace to the United Provinces, but which had like to have brought them into a Civil War, on the Score of the Prince of *Orange*'s Interest, which according to the Opinion of some, had not beeen sufficiently consider'd therein *Holland* in it's own particular was so well satisfy'd with the Service he had done it on this occasion, that it procur'd him the Office of Treasurer General, that is to say, of first Minister of the United Provinces There is not that Affair of ever so perplex'd an Intricacy, but he disintangles it, if he will apply himself If Proofs thereof are requisite, it is but looking into the Treaty he caus'd to be concluded at *Cleves* with the Bishop of *Munster* in the Year 1666, and he did not negotiate with less Success at *Madrid*, concerning the important Interest of the Provinces of *Flanders* If he did not succeed at *Cologn*, the Fault must be laid on the evil Disposition of the Parties, and on the bad Conjuncture of Affairs, rather than on his Manner of Acting, which was always uniform and equally vigorous On which account he was entrusted with the whole Negotiation that was carry'd on at *Nimeguen*, and he was the Person the States pitch'd upon to go and finish it with the most Christian King near *Ghent* He finds himself cloy'd with Employments, insomuch that whereas others seek them, he declines them; chusing rather to enjoy himself in a rural Solitude, than to cherish the Uneasiness that accompanies Business, and which often is not less vexatious to himself than to those who have to negotiate with him To give the Character of *Beverning* would require another guess Pen than mine, because if we examine well all the Parts thereof, it will appear, that setting aside some small Unevenness in his Humour, there is nothing therein but what is consummate

John Baron of *Ghent*, Lord of *Osterwede*, Deputy on the part of the Province of *Guelder* to the Assembly of the States General for these forty Years or upwards, was employ'd in the Year 1651, in the Accommodation of the Differences which had embroil'd the Elector of *Brandenburg* with the Duke of *Newburg* In the Year 1660, he was sent with *Conrade van Beuningnen*, of whom I have before made mention, and with *Justus de Hubert*, now Secretary to the States of *Zeland*, to go and complement the most Christian King on the Peace of the *Pyrenees*, and on his Marriage These Embassadors had Orders to renew the Alliance between that Crown and the United Provinces, which was very much alter'd since the Peace of *Munster* It was concluded but in the Year 1662, so that *M de Ghent* had Time enough to make make his Talent known He is a Gentleman very handsome in his Person, and who is a perfect Master of the *French* Tongue ' And as it belong'd to him, as chief of the Embassy, to make all the Harangues, and all the Complements, he acquitted himself so well thereof, that that Court, which is the most polite', but at the same Time the most difficult of all Courts, could never be weary of admiring the Politeness of this Foreigner In the Year 1672, he was deputed with some other Gentlemen of the Assembly of the States General, to see on what Conditions the King would grant a Peace to the United Provinces Of the four Ministers this Deputation was compos'd of, there was one that counter-

counterfeited being sick. Another was difavow'd by the States of his Province, so that being come back with the first Resolution, the Ministers of *France* had given them, he return'd thither no more. *M. de Groot*, who was concern'd on the part of the States of *Holland*, took indeed a second Journey to the *French* Army, but perceiving that it would be requisite to make a third, he excus'd himself. *M. de Ghent*, who in the mean Time remain'd at the Court of *France*, expecting the Return of his Collegues, was oblig'd to follow it to *Paris*. He was narrowly observ'd, but also very well treated in the Journey. And as soon as he was come to *Paris* he had Liberty to see and receive all sorts of Persons, and he there also receiv'd several Marks of the Esteem was had for his Person. The *Dauphin*, the Duke of *Orleans*, and all the Noblemen of the Court entertain'd him very kindly. Since his Return he has return'd his Post in the Assembly of the States General, and he is at present in such an Age, and has acquir'd so much Glory, that he ought not to have any farther Ambition for foreign Employments.

John Knuit, deputed on the part of the Province of *Zeland* to the Assembly of the States General, as representing the Prince of *Orange*, the first and only Nobleman of that Province, was employ'd in very important Negotiations, amongst the rest, in that which occasion'd the Rupture in the Year 1635, and in that which procur'd the separate Peace at *Munster* in the Year 1648. He and *Pau* were the chief Architects of both those Works. He had a daring and enterprizing Spirit, and was withal subtil and indefatigable. The Prince of *Orange*, *Frederick Henry*, employ'd him in very nice Conjunctures with Success, particularly in the Affair of the Principality of *Orange*, the Governor whereof had treated with a foreign Power. He disguis'd himself like a Merchant, let Soldiers into the Town, cut off the Governor's Retreat, who was gone out of the Castle, and attack'd him in a private House, whither he had retir'd: and by that means sav'd a State to a House, which without it would not produce any Princes. It was in Recompence of this Service, that the Prince gave him the chief Direction of the Affairs of *Zeland*, and put him in a Post, which procur'd him every Day new Commissions, either within the State or out of the Countrey, the greatest part whereof he discharg'd very happily. In the Year 1647, he made the Treaty for the Interest of the House of *Orange* with the Plenipotentiaries of *Spain*. As his Extraction was mean enough, he could not break himself of certain Habits, which are contracted in a bad Education. He had nothing in him that was Great, all was Cunning and Artifice, and he was so extremely sordid; and what the *Florentines* call *Misero*, that Rules might have been laid down for the most wretched Stinginess, from those of his Oeconomy.

The Life of *John Oldenbarnevelt* has been illustrious enough to deserve a pretty large Volume. I shall not examin his private Actions, neither shall I give my self the Trouble to justify his Memory, because I consider him here but as an Embassador, who, in that Quality, has done such great Services to his Countrey, that it might very well have forborn putting him to Death by the Hands of the Hangman, upon the Sentence of a great Number of incompetent and illegal Judges. In the Year 1585, while he was yet but Pensionary of the Town of *Roteradam*, he was sent with other Deputies into *England*, to offer to Queen *Elizabeth* the Sovereignty of the United Provinces, and he obtain'd of her a considerable Supply of Men and Money, on the Security of some Towns in *Holland* and *Zeland*, which were mortgag'd for the Time. In the Year 1597, he was sent with *Justin de Nassau* to King *Henry* IV, to endeavour to make him lay aside the Thoughts of treating with the King of *Spain*. But the Resolution was already taken, the King had given his Reasons for so doing to the Queen of *England*, and the Peace was effectually concluded the Year following at *Vervins*. In this Embassy the King thought fit to confer with this Minister privately, and to satisfy him of the Reasons which oblig'd him to put an End to a War that ruin'd his Kingdom, and he assur'd him of the Constancy of his Affection to the State of the United Provinces, of which he promis'd to give Marks by considerable Subsidies. *Justin de Nassau*, and the Sieur *Oldenbarnevelt*, at their Departure from the Court of *France*, pass'd into *England*, where they made a Report to the Queen of the Disposition in which they had left *Henry* IV, and they got from her a very favourable Declaration, notwithstanding the Lord *Burleigh*, who was an Enemy to War, approv'd the Resolution which had been taken in *France* to make a Peace with *Spain*. He had been made first Minister of *Holland*, under the Quality of Advocate of the Province, in the Year 1586, and in that same Quality he had the Secret of all the Embassies in which he was employ'd since that Time, as in that which the States General sent into *England* in the Year 1598, to regulate with the Queen the Sums to which the Money she had assisted them with amounted. This was the third Embassy he had perform'd to the Queen: and notwithstanding he had several Collegues, yet she desir'd to have a private Conference with *Oldenbarnevelt*. In the Year 1603, he was sent, with Prince *Frederick Henry* of *Nassau*, with the Lord *Brederode*, and with some other Persons of Quality, to complement King *James* on his Accession to the Crown of *Great Britain*. In this Embassy the Sieur *d'Oldenbarnevelt* had again a private Conference with the King, and therein he so well justify'd the Intention of his Masters, and the Reasons they had to continue the War with *Spain*, that the King remain'd satisfy'd therewith. He had acquir'd Credit enough in his Province to prevail with it to consent to the Truce of twelve Years, against the Opinion of Prince *Maurice* of *Nassau*, who from thence conceiv'd so great a Hatred for this Minister, that he did not rest, till he had procur'd his Death after the manner I before mention'd.

After the Parallel *Vitorio Siri* makes of Messieurs *d'Avaux* and *Servien*, I think I ought not to make any Difficulty to make one of two others, who liv'd at *Osnaburg* almost after the same manner as those I just spoke of, liv'd at *Munster*,

Munster, tho' with a great deal less Scandal, since they were very careful not to print their Quarrels. It is *John Oxenstiern* and *John Adoler Salvius*, Embassadors Plenipotentiaries of *Sweden* at the Congress of *Westphalia*, I mean to speak of. The first, whose Father was Chancellor, and great Director of the Affairs of that Kingdom, had, together with that great Name, the Advantage of an illustrious Birth, and that of the Advice and continual Counsels of a Father, who had not his Fellow for Negotiation, and who had a thorough Knowledge of the Affairs of *Germany*. The other was not so well born, but he was full as subtil and artificial as *Oxenstiern*, and as being the Queen's Creature, he had the Confidence of that Princess, who did not love the Chancellor, and who for his sake had a Prejudice to all his House. So that these two Ministers receiving sometimes different and even contrary Instructions, it must not be wonder'd at, if in the Course of the Negotiation they were so often seen in different and opposite Sentiments. The *Oxenstierns*, as well the Father as the Son, did not love *France* nor the *French*. The Queen, on the contrary, at that Time could not endure the other Nations. For which Reasons the Embassador *Oxenstiern* always press'd for an Accommodation with the Emperor, and that *Sweden* should seek its Satisfaction, even to the Prejudice of *France*. *Salvius*, who follow'd the Inclination and Orders of the Queen, would not consent to what would have prejudic'd a Crown so strictly ally'd, to which she was oblig'd for all the Advantages that *Sweden* possess'd in *Germany*. *Oxenstiern* was rough, and sometimes obstinate. *Salvius* was gentle and complaisant, but so timorous, that *Servien* said, it would not be so hard a Task for him to overcome the Obstinacy of the one, as to fix the Irresolution of the other. Moreover *Salvius* was very selfish, and not altogether incorruptible; whereof *Oxenstiern* could not be suspected, he being actually in Possession of a great deal of Wealth, and in Expectation of a great deal more, tho' *Salvius* on his part was not without, having rais'd himself to a very good Fortune for a Man of his Condition. The Queen continu'd her Favour to him after the Conclusion of the Peace of *Westphalia*. She employ'd him for the Execution of the Treaty, and since again at the Assembly of *Lubeck*. From whence being return'd, and just ready to take another Voyage, he dy'd at *Stockholm*. *Oxenstiern* had no other Employment, and to speak the Truth, the Queen was not at all satisfy'd with that he had had in *Germany*.

John Richardot, President of the Council of the Arch-Duke *Albert*, had the Confidence of his Prince, who made use of his Advice in all his Affairs, and employ'd his Person in those of the greatest Moment. He was Chief of the Embassy which the said Arch-Duke sent in the Name of the King of *Spain* to *Vervins*, where a Peace was concluded between the two Crowns in the Year 1598. Some Years after King *Philip* III sent the Constable of *Castile* into *England*, to complement King *James*, on his Accession to the Crown, and to make a Treaty of Alliance with him. The Constable, who was no extraordinary Negotiator, substituted *Richardot*, and some others of the Arch-Duke's Ministers whom he sent into *England*, where they prepar'd the whole Treaty, so that there wanted nothing but the signing when the Constable arriv'd at *London*, tho' it was but a simple Treaty of Friendship and Commerce. *Richardot* gave very great Proofs of his Ability, in the Negotiation which was perform'd at the *Hague* in the beginning of this Century, about the Truce for twelve Years. For altho' he was not the Chief of the Embassy, while the Marquiss *Spinola* was there, yet that did not hinder him from having the Confidence of the Arch-Duke, and knowing his true Design, having Leave from him to have private Conferences with President *Jeannin*. So that one may say, that the main part of the Negotiation, for what related to the Interest of the King of *Spain*, and of the Arch-Duke, was transacted by these two Ministers. He was a Man of Honour, and it sometimes there was a Mixture of Artifice in some of his Actions, it was not without doing Violence to his own Nature.

The whole Life of Cardinal *Joyeuse* carries with it so many Marks of an extraordinary Merit, that it cannot be deny'd but he was more oblig'd to himself than to his Brother's Favour, who procur'd him the Purple, at the Request of *Henry* III, during this King's Life, and particularly after the Death of the Duke and Cardinal *de Guise*, he was employ'd to the Pope, with the Bishop of *Mans* and the Marquiss of *Pisani*, to endeavour to procure an Absolution for the Violence which had been done to the Cardinal; but he had not the Quality of Publick Minister and Embassador, till he was employ'd as Mediator on the part of *Henry* IV, for the Accommodation of the Difference between Pope *Paul* V, and the Republick of *Venice*. Some of the Particulars of his Negotiation are to be seen in *M. de Fresne Canaye*'s Letters, which discover that he was a very skilful and able Embassador, especially in this, that he manag'd the matter so, that the *Spanish* Ministers had no Hand at all in the Treaty, and that he preserv'd the whole Glory thereof to *France*. The Republick was very well satisfy'd with his manner of acting, and express'd its Acknowledgment by the excessive Honours the Senate did him at his coming to *Venice*, to put the last Hand to his Work. On this occasion I shall say a word or two, *en passant*, concerning *do Fresne Canaye*. They who after his Death publish'd the Dispatches he had made during his Embassy at *Venice*, have not done any great Honour to his Memory. He must needs have been a Man of Merit, since King *Henry* IV had employ'd him in *Germany* and *England*, where he had negotiated before his Embassy to *Venice*; but as he came afterwards to a Place where there was nothing to negotiate, we ought not to wonder at the little matter that is found in his Letters. But as I just said, the Compiler might have spar'd himself the Trouble of giving them to the Publick, and of making three large Volumes of what might have been compris'd in ten or twelve Sheets.

Isaac Volmar, Baron of *Rieden*, one of the Embassadors Plenipotentiaries at the Congress of *Westphalia*, was one of the ablest Ministers of the Assembly. He understood perfectly well the Interest of the House of *Austria*, and knew how to manage it, so that it may be said, that he was one of those who did the greatest Service there

there, to that Party. Most of the Civilians of *Germany*, have their own particular Principles, which not being always very conformable to common Sense, form also of that Set of Men a sort of Politicians that are esteem'd no where, but in those Courts where no others are known, and where they teach the same Principles. *Volmar* had study'd after the manner of *Germany*, but he had un'earn'd the pedantick part, and the School Maxims betimes, at least as much as it is possible to be cured of a Gangrene, that penetrates to the very Bone, and even infects the Marrow. He was civil and moderate, and had form'd himself at the Court of *Vienna*, where are constantly seen a great Number of *Spanish* and *Italian* Noblemen and Ministers. He would certainly have done more useful Services to his Master the Emperor, and to his Countrey, than he did if he could have acted according to his own Genius, and have freed himself of the Dependence, the Emperor's Ministers have of those of *Spain*. He was since deputed on the part of the Emperor *Leopold*, to the Assembly of *Franckfort* in the Year 1657, and following, and at last to *Ratisbone*, where he dy'd on *October* 13, 1612, being 76 Years of Age.

Peter Chanut was a Relation of *M. de la Tuillerie*, (whom I have before spoken of) and train'd up by him. It was *la Tuillerie*, who carry'd him to *Sweden*, left him there, and procur'd him the Quality of publick Minister of the second Order. This it self would be sufficient to recommend any other Embassador than *Chanut*. But he was somewhat more oblig'd to himself, than to his Relation and Patron. He was one of the learnedst Men of his Time, and amongst the first Disciples of *Des Cartes*. He express'd himself perfectly well in most of those Languages that are most in use, as well the Living as the Dead. He had travell'd very much, and having improv'd himself thereby, he had acquir'd that Knowledge, which procur'd him at first, not only the Esteem, but also the Confidence of Queen *Christina* of *Sweden*. He had withal a great deal of Honour, and much Zeal for the *Roman Catholick* Religion, tho' not very conformable to the *Cartesian* Philosophy. All these Qualities, and amongst the rest, the Art he had to govern the Queen's Mind, procur'd him the Quality of Representative in the first Rank. He took no Vanity therefrom in his Person, nor in his Conduct. While he was still but Resident he had negotiated with the Ability of an Embassador, and when he was Embassador, he carry'd himself with the Modesty of a Resident; not but that on several Occasions (some whereof I have instanc'd in) he knew very well how to vindicate what was due to the Dignity of his Character. *Sweden* and the United Provinces are sensible of, and will for a long time remember the Merit of this great Personage. He assisted as Mediator on the part of *France*, at the two Assemblies of *Lubeck* in the Year 1651, and 1652, and one may say, That of all the Ministers of that Congress, none but *Chanut* made a Figure there, all the rest being like so many mute Personages on the Theatre. He may be said to have been an Embassador of the first Class, and that there are but very few that can take place of him. His Friends could have wish'd, that having discharg'd so many illustrious Employments, which he had had in *Sweden*, in *Germany*, and in *Holland*, he had not addicted himself to a Minister, who amongst his other insupportable Vanities, had a mind to have that of being follow'd, by a Minister who had a Place in the Council as well as himself. His Negotiations, maim'd and disfigur'd as they are, do however carry the Marks of what he was in effect, altho' he that has publish'd them in that lame Condition has done him irreparable Damage. They who thus assume the Authority of retrenching from the Works of such great Men, what they think ought not to be communicated, would do much better to give nothing to the Publick, than to print their imperfect Extracts, devoid of Judgment, and wherein neither the Air nor Genius of the Minister is to be discover'd.

Peter de Groot, Son to the great *Hugh*, was not so learned as his Father, but I think I may say, That he was every whit at least as able a Minister. After he had successfully serv'd the Elector *Palatin*, and some other Princes of *Germany* at the *Hague*, he devoted himself entirely to the Service of his Countrey. As Pensionary of the City of *Amsterdam* he had Admittance into the Assembly of the States of *Holland*, and after some Years, he was sent with the Quality of Embassador in Ordinary, to the Court of *Stockholm*, where the States were us'd to entertain only a Minister of the second Order, but it was thought necessary to do something extraordinary for so extraordinary a Personage. He was so happy in his Negotiation, that there was room to hope, that he would have render'd the Interest of the Crown of *Sweden*, inseparable from that of the United Provinces, if he had not been recall'd, in order to be sent to *France*. It was at a time when the King being very much incens'd at the triple Alliance, the States had caus'd to be made for the Defence of the Provinces of *Flanders*, which are under the Obedience of the King of *Spain*, had resolv'd to resent it, and to make War against the United Provinces. It may be said of *M. de Groot*, That never did so ill made a Body, lodge so beautiful and great a Soul. He had an admirable Presence of Mind, a charming Conversation, a clear and solid Judgment, Sentiments that were just and equitable, a great Knowledge of all sorts of Affairs, as well domestick as foreign and above all, what the *French* call the Art of pleasing. His Name was known at the Court of *France*, where he was immediately consider'd as the only Minister capable of reconciling the disagreeing Minds, if they had not been altogether irreconcileable. I have spoken elsewhere of the Civilities the King caus'd to be done him, to the very Day before the Declaration. After the Rupture in the Year 1672, he was sent to the King, with *M. de Ghent*, and some other Deputies, whom History will make known, to endeavour to bring Affairs to an Accommodation, but the Revolution which happen'd in the Countrey, broke off the Series of that Negotiation, and forc'd him to seek elsewhere an *Asylum* for his Innocence, which

was

was not safe at home. His Enemies and mine, did not cease persecuting him, even after that the Court of Justice of *Holland*, (which did not dare to commit two Violences, on the Heels one of the other) had justify'd him in form. I dare say no more of him, tho' there is no saying too much of a Man, who was above all Encomiums. I am writing this at the very time I am inform'd of his Decease. I cannot but pity *Holland* for having lost a Man, who would have help'd to repair the Breaches, which Disorders have caus'd in the State within some Years.

There are some Men that one can reap no Honour from, in speaking of them, because one can say nothing of them but what is infinitely below their Merit. Peter *Jeannin* is of the Number of these Great Men. He had been Counsellor to the Duke of *Mayenne*, while this was Head of the League, and he had justify'd the Procedure of his Master, at the Court of *Madrid*, at a Time when the Blame of all the Disgraces that happen'd to the Party were laid upon that Prince. After the Duke's Reconciliation, King *Henry* IV receiv'd him into his Service, and made him one of his trustiest Ministers. The King lov'd him, because he knew that it was by *Jeannin*'s Counsels chiefly, that the Designs of those, who were for calling in a Stranger to the Crown, were overthrown. The Encomium that is put at the Head of the Negotiation he had transacted in *Holland*, contains nothing comparable to what is to be found in the Negotiation it self, where it appears that King *Henry* IV and *M. de Villeroy*, what a King, and what a Minister take more Pleasure to follow his Counsels, than they have Difficulty to instruct him in their Intentions, and to regulate his Conduct. If President *Jeannin* had done nothing else in his whole Life, than to bring to a Conclusion the twelve Years Truce, notwithstanding the Difficulties and Oppositions he met with on all Sides, and to have founded that powerful State of the United Provinces, it cannot be deny'd but it was a kind of Miracle, and that he deserves to be put in the Rank of the greatest and most illustrious Embassadors that ever were. I could willingly make a Parallel between Cardinal *Dossat* and President *Jeannin*, but as I find in both of them Qualities equally great, a profound Learning, a Mind extremely inlighten'd, a clear and solid Judgment, a prudent and disinterested Zeal, an incomparable Fidelity, and an Address and Application not to be found any where else, I must own, that I could not say any thing of the one, which would not also in Justice be due to the other. The Force of their Reasoning, the Sweetness of their Humour, and of their Moderation, shew themselves with so much Lustre in all their Dispatches, that it seems as if, being employ'd under the same Monarch, they had also brought the same Talents to his Service, in Order to deserve from him the same Esteem, and the same Recompences, each in his Profession. Altho' *Henry* IV had not the Reputation to have bestow'd very great ones upon them.

The Father and Grandfather of *Pompone de Bellievre*, having been employ'd in several Embassies, it may be said of him that he was the Son of a Master. As he was the Grandson, by his Father and Mother, of two Chancellors of *France*, and the Son of a President *au Mortier*, the Gown did not afford a more illustrious Personage than himself. In the Year 1635, soon after the Rupture between the two Crowns, he was sent in the Quality of Embassador Extraordinary into *Italy*, to inform the Republick of *Venice*, and the other Potentates of those Parts, of the Justice of the King's Arms, and to try to prevail with some of them to engage in the Party. He was already President of the Parliament, when in the Year 1645 he was sent into *England* with the same Quality, on the Account of the Commotions of that Kingdom, but he found the Parties so exasperated, that there was no likelihood of reconciling them. In the Year 1651, after the Decease of the late Prince of *Orange* (the Father of him that now lives) he was sent into *Holland*, as well to complement the States on that Conjuncture, as to see what would be deliberated in the great Assembly which had been summon'd at the *Hague*, because most of the Provinces were without a Governor, and the State had no Captain General. He found there at the very first, and indeed started himself so many Difficulties, on the Score of the Ceremonies and Civilities, which the Deputies of the States insisted upon, since the Congress of *Westphalia*, that seeing withal, that the foreign Ministers would have no Share in the Deliberations of the Great Assembly, and that he had every Day bad Accidents to encounter with on the Score of the Ceremonial, he took his Leave, and return'd to *France*. Two or three Years after, he had the Place of first President of the Parliament of *Paris* given him, which is the first belonging to the Gown, after that of Chancellor. It has always been fill'd with great Men, but there had not yet been any in it, that had done it so much Honour as he did, nor that had discharg'd it with so much Gravity, and so much Sufficiency. He did not enjoy it long enough to exert his whole Talent, Death envying the Parliament a Head that was all its Glory, and that knew very well how to preserve its Dignity and Prerogatives.

The Queen of *Sweden* being sensible of the good Qualities of *Shering Rosenhan*, gave him at first a very honourable Employment, and of great Trust. She sent him to *Munster* with the Quality of Resident, to assist on the part of the Crown of *Sweden*, at the Conferences which the Plenipotentiaries of *France* were to have with the Emperor's Ministers, that is to say, to observe their Actions and Proceedings. Nay, he had himself there some Intrigues with the Ministers of *Spain*, which procur'd him Reproaches from *d'Avaux* and *Servien*, who were jealous thereof. They were not yet quite cur'd of their Jealousy, when being Embassador in *France*, during the last Commotions of *Paris*, he press'd Cardinal *Mazarin* to make an Accommodation with the Parliament, even tho' he somewhat impair'd the Royal Authority. The Cardinal, who knew that such Accommodation could not be made, but at the Expence of his Fortune, complain'd thereof in *Sweden*, and made him be recall'd. Queen *Christina* was willing to shew that Complaisance to the Queen Regent of *France*, but as she was sensible

sensible that *Rosenhan*'s Intentions were good, (for he was apprehensive lest the Disturbances in *France*, should hinder the Execution of the Peace of *Germany*, or should rekindle a new War) she did not condemn his Procedure, and having an Esteem for the Prince of *Condé*, she did not approve of the Cardinal's Since that Time she continu'd to employ *Rosenhan* at *Lubeck*, and elsewhere And after her Abdication, the King, her Successor, had an Esteem for the Merit of this Minister, and made use of him in the Affairs of *Breme*, and on other Occasions He was a very understanding Minister, had a great Fund of Study, and a great Knowledge of Affairs; and who, notwithstanding he was born in one of the coldest Climates of *Europe*, had nevertheless Qualities which are not very common, even in the hottest There was neither Affectation nor Artifice in his Actions, and yet there was something in them so subtil and refin'd, that it was a hard Matter to be sufficiently guarded against him He had besides, a natural Freedom which denoted a Greatness of Soul, worthy of a true Embassador

The Count *de Trautmansdorf* had the chief Confidence of his Master, when he procur'd himself to be sent Embassador to *Munster* He knew that there is nothing impairs Favour so easily as Absence, and he could not be ignorant that the *Spanish* Ministers would do him all the ill Offices imaginable, during his remote Employ, in Order to deprive him of the Credit he had at the Court of *Vienna*, yet nevertheless he voluntarily quitted that Post, to endeavour to procure a Peace to *Germany*. The Emperor had upon him the two Powers of *France* and *Sweden*, but he was not less incommoded by the Friendship of his nearest Relations and Allies, the King of *Spain* and the Elector of *Bavaria* *Trautmansdorf*, to free his Master of all these Inquietudes, resolv'd to disintangle his Sovereign's Interest from those of his Relations, and to make a Peace with one of the two Crowns He was open enough; but, with his Sincerity, he had also Ability and Address enough to manage the most important Affairs, and to guard himself against the Artifices of those Ministers he negotiated with He was of Opinion that the King of *Spain*'s Interest ought not to make a part of the Emperor's or Empires, and with this Notion he apply'd himself so heartily to this Negotiation, that it cannot be deny'd but *Germany* is oblig'd to him for the Peace which was concluded with the Crowns of *France* and *Sweden* in the Year 1648 And it is to him also that *France* is oblig'd, for the Advantages she gain'd by that Treaty, because he lost the Opportunity of concluding with *Sweden* without *France*, as I have said elsewhere

Sir *William Temple* was a Creature of the Lord *Arlington*'s who being Secretary of State, and entrusted with the Confidence of the King his Master, procur'd this Friend to be sent Resident to *Brussels* It was by this Employment that he enter'd into Affairs, of which he gained some Knowledge under the Protection of that great Statesman From *Brussels* he went into *Holland*, at a Time when the *French* having invaded the Low Countries, seem'd to render the Interest of *England* and the United Provinces inseparable When *M Temple* came to the *Hague* he found the first Minister dispos'd to hearken to all the Overtures that could contribute to put a stop to the Progress of the Arms of *France*, and to receive with Gladness the Propositions he there made for a new Alliance It was propos'd, negotiated, and concluded in four or five Days The Deputies of the Assembly of the States General, judging that in that Conjuncture, where the Matter in Hand was to gain the King of *England* to their Interest, they might very well pass over some Formalities, and act a little cavalierly *M Temple*, after that, labour'd at a Triple Alliance, into which *Sweden* was brought And after that again, at a particular defensive Alliance between the King his Master and those Provinces But all these Treaties were hardly concluded, when the King of *Great Britain* entering into fresh Engagements with that of *France*, this caus'd *Temple* to be recall'd, who from that Time remain'd without Employment, till a Peace being concluded between *England* and the United Provinces, in the Year 1674, the Lord *Arlington*, who continu'd to him his Protection, got him to be sent to the *Hague* as Embassador Extraordinary, and afterwards to *Nimeguen*, with the Quality of Embassador Plenipotentiary for a General Peace He was there about a Year, at the end of which he had either Orders or Leave to retire into *England*, where he is still at this Time The Remarks he has made on the States of the United Provinces, and some other Works which he has communicated only to his Friends, sufficiently discover that he is a Minister of very great Parts, and that he is capable of serving his Master in Employments of this Nature He publish'd his Remarks after his first Embassy, which makes it be believ'd that we shall see them augmented, and rectify'd in some Places, after the second

My Intention was to say something more, concerning him, and indeed to speak of several other Embassadors, as also of some Ministers of the Second Order, and particularly of all those that are at present at *Nimeguen*, amongst whom there are some very Illustrious Ones. But having already given but too much Extent to my Work, and my Mind not having the Liberty requisite to give it a greater Perfection, while my Body is confin'd in a very rigorous Prison, I am forc'd to put an End to it Perhaps somebody or other, that has a greater Capacity, and better Means than I have, may give another Turn to what I have begun, and make a complete Treatise of *The Embassador and his Functions*.

AN
Historical Discourse
OF THE
ELECTION
OF THE
EMPEROR,
And of the
Electors of the Empire.

TO

My Lord *SEGUIER*,

DUKE, and PEER, and CHANCELLOR

OF

FRANCE.

MY LORD,

HE Employment with which one of the first and greatest Princes of the Empire has thought fit to honour me, having induc'd me to get a particular Knowledge of the Affairs of *Germany*, I was composing a general History thereof, on the Memoirs, which I have with great Care collected, of the same; and I was finishing that Work, when the Curiosity of some Persons of Quality oblig'd me to discontinue it, and to make a Discourse concerning the Election of the Emperor, on occasion of the approaching Electoral Diet *France* had had so small a Share in those which have been been held within these hundred and twenty Years, that it had quite neglected the Study of a Matter, the Knowledge whereof seem'd to be of no Use, and which it had no Occasion to learn. But of late, the Revolutions with which *Germany* has been threaten'd, after an *Interregnum* which afforded the Interested time to carry on several Negotiations, stir'd up in the Curious, a Desire to inform themselves of the State of Affairs in those Parts, and of the Particulars of one of the most celebrated Actions that is perform'd in *Europe*. So that they who had prevail'd with me to undertake this Work, have also been able to persuade me, that I could give nothing so bad on this Occasion, but it would be lik'd, and receiv'd with Satisfaction by the Publick I am sensible, My Lord, that this Discourse does not deserve the Honour of Your Approbation, and that in presenting it to You, I expose it to the Cen-

sure

Epistle Dedicatory.

sure of so clear-sighted a Judgment, that You will discover all the Faults thereof at the first View. And in reality, there are but very few Things sufficiently finish'd, not to appear imperfect in some respect or other, to the consummate Knowledge of that great Genius, which King *Lewis* the Just, judg'd alone capable of supporting worthily the two eminent Qualities of Chief Justice, and of Minister of State. Neither had I, My Lord, taken the Liberty to offer You this small Treatise, amongst the excellent Works that Three of the ablest Men of our Age produce every Day under the Honour of Your Patronage, if You had not done me the Favour to give me to understand, that it would not be unacceptable to You, and that You would have for it the same Bounty, with which You have suffer'd me to approach You for so many Years. It is therefore, My Lord, that I am so far from believing I can improve this Conjuncture to the acquitting my self of the great Obligations I have to You, that I am forc'd to acknowledge I thereby contract new ones, by begging You will be pleas'd to honour it with the same Protection You have vouchsaf'd to bestow on its Author. It must be own'd, My Lord, that *France* beholds in all Your Conduct a perfect Idea of a great Magistrate, and that she is infinitely delighted in the Justice You so equally dispense to all sorts of Persons: But as to my own particular, I have felt such favourable Effects thereof, that I shall be for ever oblig'd to You for the Care You were pleas'd to take, to secure me my Right in an Affair of very great Importance. Your Lordship, out of Your excessive Goodness, would needs add thereto the Favour of putting me in the Number of those You receive into Your House, as into the Sanctuary of the Learned, and even of Learning it self, and to consider me rather as a Person that honours and admires You, than as a publick Person. I have not Vanity enough to persuade my self, that I possess any Quality that merits the Honour of Your Favour: But I ought to believe that if You have found in me any thing that could prevail with You to grant it me, it must without doubt be the Respect and Veneration, which I have in a greater Degree for Your self, than for Your Dignity. Insomuch, that I dare be bold to say, that it will be an Effect of Your Justice, as well as of Your Bounty, when You shall be entirely persuaded, that I am very truly,

My Lord,
Your very Humble, and
very Obedient Servant,

D. W. R. D. B.

TO THE
READER.

IT fares with Politicks as with Physick. Every body tampers therewith, and very few succeed therein. Both the one and the other have Bodies to preserve, and Maladies to cure. Both stand in need of Study and Experience, and both have Doctors, who teach and practise according to the Rules of Art. But then both have also their Quacks, who are for curing the Distemper before they know the Causes thereof, and the Constitution of the Body. Of this Number are those who have written concerning the approaching Diet, as well in Italy as in France and Germany, like Politicians rather than Historians, and who have rather endeavour'd to regulate the Choice the Princes Electors ought to make, than to treat of the Institution of the Electoral College, of the State it is at present in, of the Princes that compose the same, and of the essential Circumstances which the Law requires should be observ'd in the Election.

The Author of the present Discourse has acted quite otherwise. He has confin'd himself within the Bounds of the Truth of History, on which he grounds all his Arguments, without Passion, and without Interest. While he keeps within these Limits he will not be liable to say with one of those Authors, That the Eagle took its Flight even into the East, so long as the Monarchy of the Empire was moderated by the Electors. Since in the Time of Conrade III, of Frederick I, and Frederick II, who made War against the Infidels of the East, the Quality of Elector was not yet known. He will not give that of Collegue to the King of the Romans, who is chosen in the Emperor's Life-time, since the Capitulation expressly forbids him meddling with the Administration of the Affairs of the Empire, and that that Author says himself, That the Austrian Cæsars have only left an empty Name without Power to the King of the Romans. He will not put William of Nassaw in the Catalogue of the Emperors, and he will be asham'd to say that Ferdinand II, was Unkle to the Emperor Matthias, his Predecessor. He will be cautious of advancing that Hungary has been lopp'd off from the Empire. That William of Holland, Alfonsus of Castile, and Richard of Cornwal have shar'd the Empire amongst them. That the Pope bestows the Empire. That the Emperor owes Homage to the See of Rome. That formerly the Kings of the Romans were only created in case of the Emperor's Absence or Indisposition, and that they had an ordinary Power: That the Electors depriv'd the Houses of Saxony, of Franconia, and of Suabia, of the Imperial Dignity, thereby to stifle all the Pretensions of those Families to

The Preface.

an Hereditary Succession. That Austria *was usurp'd from* Ottocarius, *King of* Bohemia. *That* Wenceslas *was as soon dispossess'd as chosen, and that* Maximilian *I*, Rodolphus *II, and* Matthias *caus'd their Successors to be elected. He will avoid discovering such gross Ignorance, which is inexcusable in a Man who boasts to have compos'd a large Treatise on the most important Affairs of the Empire, and who might have said on that Subject an Infinity of other things of greater Moment and Truth towards the maintaining the good Cause. But he will take Care to support all that he shall say with publick Proofs, and those so strong and forcible, that he believes all those who are well vers'd in the Knowledge of the History and Affairs of* Germany, *will agree therein.*

At first he had only made some Memoirs on this Subject, which he communicated to three or four of his Friends, but they were without Form, and such as the Work of a few Days might be suppos'd to be. But having been since desir'd to publish them, he undertook to make a kind of Treatise thereof, and to observe some Method therein, at least as much as the Nature of the Matter would permit.

To speak orderly in the same, it was requisite to shew that the Empire has not always been Elective. That the Electoral College, which is compos'd of a certain Number of Princes, Ecclesiasticks and Seculars, was not instituted at the same Time that the Election began to take Place in Germany, *but that the first Elections were made by all the States of the Empire assembl'd in a Body, and that by little and little the Electors were reduc'd to the Number limited by the* Golden Bull. *That it was* Charles *IV. who fix'd the Number, and made a fundamental Law, of what was before but a Custom, who confirm'd the Rights of the Electors, and regulated the Ceremonies of the Election. It was necessary to speak of the Electors in general, and of the Family and Person of each Elector in Particular, to be able thereby to judge of their Interests, and of the Consideration will be had for them in the approaching Diet, before we speak of the Election; which is here consider'd, either in its Preliminaries, which are the essential Circumstances which precede it, or in it self; or else in its effect, which is the Creation of an Emperor.*

He chose not to make this Discourse so large as the Copiousness of the Matter would have allow'd him; because his Intention was to write only for the Interregnum, and to adapt it only to the Election. But this is not what has hinder'd the Author from giving that Turn and Perfection to his Style, which is what is most admir'd at this Day in any Book. For besides that it is very difficult to put the German *Instruments into good* French (*which however he was oblig'd to insert in this Treatise*) *as for instance the* Golden Bull *and the* Capitulation, &c. *he that writes this is a Foreigner who neither would nor could disguise himself, and who makes no Difficulty to own, that all he has been able to do was to make himself intelligible. However he thinks he may safely promise, that in a little time he will publish something more perfect, if he may have Leave to hope, that the Imperfections of his Expression may be made Amends for, by the Insight he gives into the Affairs he handles.*

OF THE ELECTION OF THE EMPEROR,

And of the

Electors of the Empire.

CHAP. I.

That the Empire was hereditary in Charlemagne's Time.

E might presuppose, as a thing very certain, that the Empire, whether it be taken for the Imperial Dignity, or for the Body of the Empire it self, that is to say, the States and Provinces of which the Empire is compos'd, was hereditary in the House of *Charlemagne.* But forasmuch as there are Persons of very eminent Learning, who do not scruple to call this Truth into doubt, we shall shew by the Authority of contemporary Historians, and by the Series of History, that a free Election was not absolutely establish'd in the Empire, till after the Death of the Emperor *Frederick* II. It is evident that recourse has been had to Election, when Heirs have fail'd in the Family of the Prince reigning, but an hereditary State, does not for that become elective. There is no Monarchy wherein the Royal Family has not fail'd, and where it may not fail again, but that Default of Princes in the Royal Family, has not render'd the State that was hereditary, elective, notwithstanding recourse has been there had to Election several times, as appears by the History of the first Monarchy of *Europe*, where the Crown has pass'd from the Family of the *Merovingians*, into that of the *Carlovingians*, and from this, to the Posterity of *Hugues Capet*, and yet it cannot be said for that to become elective. For as the Succession of

5 T seve-

several Princes of the same Family does not make a State hereditary, when they succeed by virtue of an Election, so several Elections do not render a State elective, provided a presumptive Heir can interrupt the Election by right of hereditary Succession.

Charlemagne possess'd France by the same Title as the Kings his Predecessors had possess'd it One part of Germany was annex'd thereto, and the other was conquer'd by him, as well as Lombardy, and the other Provinces of Italy. Now there needs but a slender Knowledge of History, to know that the State of France has ever been hereditary, even under the Kings of the first Race. Childeric dying in the Year 484, Clovis his Son, succeeded by virtue of hereditary Right * Clovis left his Sons Heirs to the Kingdom † Clotharius, the Son of Clovis, dying in the Year 565, left the Kingdom to his Sons, as Aimon says, and afterwards ‡ Now the Sons, Heirs to the Kingdom, were call'd, &c. And this Form of Succession continu'd, till there were no Princes left of the Posterity of Meroveus in France.

This is so great a Truth, that it cannot even be said, That Pepin, who procur'd himself to be substituted to Childeric, the last King of the first Race, was elected. He was already King in effect, and was absolute Master of the State, because he had succeeded in that Power to his Father and Grand-father, when he made use of the Authority of Pope Zachary to obtain a Title, for which it was not necessary to proceed to an Election. But as for Charlemagne and his Successors, it is certain that the Right of hereditary Succession was so well secur'd in them, as well in the Empire, as in the Kingdoms of France, Germany and Italy, that even Bastards have succeeded to their Fathers, and their nearest Relations. For notwithstanding the Consent of the States of the Empire was sometimes concern'd therein, as when in the Year 889, * the Emperor Arnulfus not having as yet any lawful Issue, oblig'd the Eastern Francs to take an Oath of Fidelity to Sneutibold and Ratold, his natural Sons, yet that has nothing in common with an Election which is nothing but the Choice, which the universal Consent, or that of the major Part of the Princes, makes of another Prince, who without that could not pretend to the Empire.

There is not any body so ignorant as not to know, that the Imperial Dignity has always pass'd from Father to Son, or to the nearest Relation, as long as it remain'd in the House of Charlemagne. Lewis the Debonnaire, who had succeeded in the Empire to his Father, left it to Lotharius his eldest Son, and this left it to his Son Lewis II, who had for Successor Charles the Bald his Unkle To Charles II, succeeded Charles III, call'd the Gross, his Nephew, who had for Successor Arnulphus, natural Son to his Brother Carloman, King of Bavaria, to whom succeeded Lewis III, his Son, who was the last Prince of the House of Charlemagne, of the German Branch.

But to make the Right of hereditary Succession to the Empire in this Family more evident, it must be known after what Manner those Princes succeeded one to the other. History says, that Charlemagne associated Lewis his Son to the Empire, and caus'd him to be crown'd in the Year 813, † with the Imperial Crown. The Ceremonies of his Coronation were very remarkable in this, that he would have every body to acknowledge, that he held the Empire of God only, and by right of hereditary Succession, and not by the Choice of the Princes, since their Dignities were not as yet hereditary at that time To this Purpose he caus'd the Imperial Crown to be set upon the Altar, and order'd Lewis to go and take it, and crown himself therewith Lewis the Debonnaire did the like by Lotharius his eldest Son causing him to be crown'd, and associating him to the Empire in the Year 81- † so that altho' Lotharius was in Italy when his Father dy'd, and that his two Brothers might have taken an Advantage from his Absence yet the Imperial Dignity was secur'd to him, because his Father had declar'd him Emperor, and had sent to him, as he lay dying, the Honours or Ornaments of the Empire, that is to say, the Scepter and Crown Charles the Bald having made himself Master of the Town of Metz, which is the Capital of Lorrain, after the Death of Lotharius his Nephew, * he took the Quality of Emperor and of August, as being King of two Kingdoms and after the Death of Lewis II, Brother to this Lotharius, he was effectually crown'd Emperor at Rome, † without any Election on the part of the Princes of Germany, any more than in the Succession of Charles the Gross, of Arnulphus, and of Lewis III, his Successors. So that it may be said, that the Empire was merely hereditary, as long there were Princes of the Posterity of Charlemagne in Germany. And it is what almost all Authors agree in. But the Succession being laid open by the Death of Lewis III, who dy'd without Issue, on January 21, 912, the States of Germany found themselves oblig'd to proceed to the Nomination of a Successor by the way of Election which being an undoubted Truth, there remains that we examin whether this Election render'd the Empire elective, which shall be the Subject of the following Chapter.

* Aimon Lib. 1 c 11 † Id. lib. 1 c ult ‡ Lib 1, c ult * Annal, Fuld † Annal Francos ‡ Ibid.
* In 169. ‡ In 877

CHAP.

CHAP. II.

When the Empire began to be Elective.

EVery body knows that the modern Empire is elective, and that the Emperors succeed thereto by virtue of the Election and Choice which the Princes Electors make of him they think capable thereof For altho' we see the Imperial Dignity continu'd in the House of *Austria* for above these two hundred Years, to wit, since *Albert* II to *Ferdinand* III, who was the tenth Emperor of this House without Interruption, yet these Princes dare not say they have any Pretenfions thereto, by virtue of hereditary Right On the contrary, the Emperor Elect, is oblig'd to protest solemnly immediately after he is chosen, that he has no Pretenfions at all thereto and to swear that he will never do any thing that may render the Empire hereditary to himself or his Family, but will take care that himself, and his Children, and Succeffors shall, according to the ancient Custom, the Constitution of the *Golden Bull*, and the Laws of the Empire *maintain the Princes Electors in their Right of Election*, and Vicarship during the *Interregnum*, freely consenting that whatever he or his Succeffors shall at any time do or undertake to the Prejudice of this Oath, shall be null and of no effect And it is for this reason that the Archbishop, who officiates at the Coronation, does not fail to say to the Emperor, when he puts the Crown upon his Head, *Hold and receive the Empire, not by hereditary Right, but by the Consent of the eight Electors*

But forasmuch as the Number of Electors was not regulated till several Centuries after the Election took place, it will not be improper to shew at what Time the Empire began to be elective, before we speak of the Creation of the Electors, and of the Institution of the Electoral College We shall here make use of the word Election in its proper and natural Signification, and according to the Definition we have given of it in the foregoing Chapter, and not for a simple Approbation and Consent, as *Gregory* of *Tours* and *Aymons* take it, when they speak of the Succeffion of the Kings of *France* of the first Race And it is so that we ought to understand what *Sigebert*, and the Abbot of *Urfperg* say, *That Pepin was elected after the manner of the* French, since it is certain that the *French* did not elect their Kings, but were contented to lift upon a Buckler, and carry about the Affembly, the Prince who succeeded to the Crown by virtue only of the fundamental Law of the Kingdom

To find therefore the beginning of this Election, it must of necessity be sought where hereditary Succeffion ended Some say, *that Charlemagne instituted the College of Electors, and so that the Election began by Lewis the Debonnair*, quoting even the Year of this pretended Institution, which they say was publish'd in the Year 769 But this Opinion is impertinent and ridiculous For besides that we have shewn, that *Lewis* succeeded by virtue of hereditary Right, it is certain that *Charlemagne* was not yet Emperor at that Time and there is not any Likelihood at all, that *Charles* would institute the Electoral Dignity, or change his Hereditary States into elective, to the Prejudice of those Children he might still have, and really had since to a good Number, so as not to be oblig'd to seek for a Succeffor out of his own House And we accordingly see hereditary Succeffion continu'd in his Family from Father to Son, and Relation to Relation, without any Interruption, as well in *Germany* as in *France*, till such time as his Posterity failing in one of the Branches, and degenerating so in the other, that the Princes thereof were no longer known, but by the Sirnames they contracted from their Weakness, it was found absolutely requisite to make them be succeeded by Strangers

To fix then the beginning of a free Election in the Empire, we must by the way of Preliminary prove two things The First, That the Posterity of *Charlemagne*, in the *German* Branch, fail'd in the Person of *Lewis* III And the other, That even after the Death of *Lewis* III, the Empire did not become so elective, but great regard was had to the Nomination of the deceas'd Emperor, and even to Confanguinity it self which was so very much consider'd in most of his Succeffors, that we made no Difficulty to say it the beginning of this Treatife, that the Empire did not become absolutely elective till after the Death of the Emperor *Frederick* II

Altho' it be indubitable that the Emperor *Lewis* III dy'd without Children, and left no Heirs, yet there are some who say, that *Arnulphus*, his Father, had two Sons, our *Lewis*, and *Conrade*, Father to *Conrade* who succeeded to the Empire in the Year 921, after the Death of *Lewis* his pretended Unkle Others give to *Lewis* two Daughters, and marry one of them to *Conrade*, and the other to *Henry* I, his Succeffor maintaining that both the one and the other came to the Empire in Consideration of this Alliance, and by virtue of hereditary Right But we shall endeavour to shew the Impossibility of this Relation, as of a thing that is directly contrary to the Order of Nature, without trifling away our Time to bring the Testimony of the contemporary Authors, who all say, that *Lewis* III died without Issue, and that the Posterity of *Charlemagne*, in the *German* Branch, fail'd in his Person And that the Reader's Mind may intirely acquiesce to the Demonstration we shall give thereof, at least as much as the Force of Arguments drawn from the Truth of History can afford, we shall employ, against the Opinion of those who are for making the Empire purely hereditary to

---

* Lindenbr in vita Car Magni Jordan & Spangenberg in Chronicis.

the Death of *Henry* II, (they ought to say *Henry* V, since *Conrade* II, *Henry* III, *Henry* IV, and *Henry* V, were of the *Saxon* House, as well as *Henry* II, as we shall see hereafter) but only such Reasons, the Solidity whereof we shall leave to the Judgment of those who shall take the Pains to examin them.

The History of those Times says expressly, that in the Year 889, the Emperor *Arnulphus* had not yet any lawful Issue, when he was for obliging the States of the Empire, assembl'd at *Forgheim*, to take the Oath of Allegiance to *Suendebold* and *Ratold*, who were his natural Sons. Those of *Bavaria* did it, but those of *Franconia* oppos'd it, and consented at last, but on Condition, that the Oath they should so take should not bind them, unless the Emperor dy'd without lawful Issue. From whence we must conclude, that at that time *Arnulphus* had none. And in Fact the *Annales Francorum*, publish'd by *Pithou*, and since by *Freherus*, and afterwards by *du Chesne*, under the Title of *The Annals of Fuld*, of *St Bertin*, and of *Metz*, say, that *Lewis* was not born till the Year 893, and that he was baptiz'd by *Hatton*, Archbishop of *Mayence*, who had succeeded to that Dignity but in the Year 891, that is to say, in the same Year that *Sunderold*, his Predecessor, was kill'd by the *Normans*. So that *Lewis* could at most be but seven Years old, when he succeeded his Father on *November* 29, 899, and nineteen when he dy'd, on *January* 21, 912. And this is what cannot be doubted of, without overthrowing all the Principles of History, which require that Credit should be given to what Authors write concerning the Affairs of their Times, and of which they may have been as it were ocular Witnesses, unless they relate things incredible in themselves, or that the Truth thereof be contested by others better inform'd than they. Now the Histories of the same Time, and of the first following Centuries, all say, that *Lewis* III was very young when he came to the Empire. Nay there are some who take notice of the Age of seven Years, and farther add, that by reason of his Infancy the Administration of Affairs was given to *Hatton*, Archbishop of *Mentz*, and to *Otho*, Duke of *Saxony*, there not being one single Author that says the contrary. His Epitaph expresses how old he was when he dy'd in the following Lines

Quatuor vix lustra videbam,
Injecit rapidas cum mihi Parca manus.

This being presuppos'd, we say that *Lewis* was the eldest Son of *Arnulphus*, since he succeeded his Father in the Empire, to the Prejudice of his pretended Brother, the Father of *Conrade* I, and that there is no Likelihood that a Child of seven Years of Age would have been suffer'd to succeed, while there was one who by reason of his more advanc'd Age was more capable of governing. Now if *Conrade*, the Father of *Conrade* I, was the younger Brother of *Lewis* III, it is certain, that when *Arnulphus* died he could not be above six Years old, and when his Son succeeded in the Empire to *Lewis* III, eighteen at most, an Age at which it was impossible for him to have had a Son capable of succeeding in the Empire. Moreover the History of those Times says in express Terms, That *Conrade* was chosen at the Refusal of *Otho*, Duke of *Saxony*, on the account of his Courage, and the Experience he had in War, in order to oppose the Incursions of the *Normans* and *Hungarians*, who had over-run all *Germany*, during the Reign of *Lewis* III, and that the Emperor *Conrade* I, was Son to *Conrade*, Duke of *Franconia*, who was kill'd *February* 25, 905, by *Albert* Count of *Bamberg*, who, if he had been the younger Brother of *Lewis*, could not at that time be above eleven Years old, nor be the Head of a Party, and still less have a Son able to govern the State seven Years after. We could confirm this Truth by several other Reasons, and a Multitude of Passages, did we not fear to swell our Discourse too much, which Consideration obliges us to pass to the Alliance which some will have between *Lewis*, *Conrade* I, and *Henry* the Fowler, when we shall have first repeated here, what we just now said, that *Lewis* III dy'd at nineteen Years of Age, at which it was impossible he should have any Daughter marry'd to *Conrade* his Successor, who therefore could not be his Son-in-Law.

The same Impossibility occurs in *Henry* I, he succeeded in the Empire to *Conrade* I, in the Year 919, that is to say, above seven Years after the Death of *Lewis* III, who at that Time could not be above six or seven and twenty Years of Age at most, and nevertheless he must then have been a Grandfather, since it is certain that *Henry* I, his pretended Son-in-Law, had actually Children when he succeeded to *Conrade* I. For it is certain that *Otho* his Son was marry'd in the Year 930, *or according to others in 932, in which he was of necessity fourteen Years old at least, and consequently that he could not be born since the Year 918, that is to say, since his Father's Accession to the Crown, and the rather because *William*, *Otho*'s natural Son, who was nominated to the Archbishoprick of *Mayence* in the Year 954, was born in 928, † at which Time *Otho* ought of necessity to be fourteen Years old, to be capable of getting Children, and to be born in the Year 914, in which *Lewis* III, his pretended Grandfather, could not be above one or two and twenty Years of Age at most. To which we may subjoin the Testimonies of all the Classicks, ‡ who all say, that *Henry the Fowler* marry'd for his first Wife, *Hateburge*, of whom was born *Tanquard*, and for second *Mahault*, the Daughter of *Thierry* Count of *Aldembourg*, of whom he had *Otho*, *Henry* Duke of *Bavaria*, *Brunon* Archbishop of *Cologn*, and the Daughters, whom we make known elsewhere.

There are others, who considering the Impossibility of this Alliance, and yet being willing to establish a Continuation of hereditary Succession of the House of *Charlemagne*, to that of *Saxony*, say, * That *Otho*, Duke of *Saxony*, Father of *Henry* I, marry'd *Luitgarde*, the Daughter of *Arnulphus*, and Sister to *Lewis* III,

---

* *The Continuer of Reginon and Luitpr lib 4 cap 5 Bishop of Mersbourg, and De Witikind of Corbie.*
‡ *Contin of Reginon*
‡ *Amongst others De Ditmar*
* *Aventin Annal Bojor lib 4*

Emperors To know whether this is possible, we must learn from History, that *Henry* I dy'd on *July* 2, 936, being sixty Years of Age, from whence it follows, that he must necessarily be born in the Year 876, since the Birth of *O S* in which *Arnulphus*, who dy'd on *November* 29, 899, in the fiftieth Year of his Age, could not be above seven and twenty Years old It is true, he might possibly be a Grandfather at that Age, provided he had marry'd his Daughter as soon as she was marriageable, and that he himself had also marry'd as soon as he was capable of getting Children But this is what we are not oblig'd to believe, unless forc'd thereto by the other Circumstances of History But they are so far from making mention thereof, that on the contrary there appears so great an Inequality of Age between *Lewis* and *Lutgarde*, his pretended Sister, that she might be rather taken for his Mother, it being certain that *Lutgarde* ought to be at least fifty Years old, when *Lewis* dy'd at the Age of twenty, considering the Age of *Henry* I, who at that Time was at least six and thirty Years old

But let us pre-suppose that this pretended Alliance be true, yet that will not hinder the hereditary Succession from having been interrupted in the Person of *Conrade* I, after whose Death it was requisite to proceed to an Election, not to have any Regard to *Everard* Duke of *Franconia*, his Brother, and therefore we say, that there would be no Alliance near enough between *Lewis*, *Conrade* and *Henry*, to found thereon Pretensions to the Imperial Crown by Right of Hereditary Succession, and that the Election began to take place in the Person of *Conrade* I

CHAP III.

Of what Nature was the first Election of the Emperors of Germany.

IT will not be very difficult to shew, that the Election of those Princes, who succeeded immediately to the Emperors of the House of *Charlemagne*, had nothing in common with that which is now in Use, neither is there indeed any Author hardly, except those we have hinted at above, but who refers the Institution of the Electors to the tenth Century but it is almost impossible to say of what Nature was the Election of *Conrade* I, after the Death of *Lewis* III The Authors of that Time say nothing at all of it There were none but the Clergy and Religious concern'd in writing the History, and those good Fathers, being more solicitous for the Interest of their Convent, than to fill their Books with Things that might have oblig'd Posterity, instead of making mention of what was most important, are contented to speak of the Fertility of the Seasons, and to write Fables and Legends rather than what properly belongs to History All that one can gather from them is, that after the Death of the Emperor, all the Princes of the Empire, as well Seculars as Ecclesiasticks, assisted at the Election of the Successor, which however had not so great an Influence, but there was still a great deal of Deference shewn to the Will of the deceased, and to the Nomination he had made This was the Cause that there still appear'd a kind of lawful hereditary Succession, at least a testamentary one, so that it may be doubted in some measure, whether the Succession depended more on the Election of the Princes, or on the last Will of the Predecessor We have not any Particulars at all of the Election of *Conrade* I They who speak the most pertinently of it say, that the Royal Line being extinct in the Person of *Lewis* III, Conrade, the Son of *Conrade* of *Franconia*, who was kill'd by *Albert* Count of *Bamberg*, succeeded to the Empire *Lustprand*, * an Author almost contemporary, says, he was chosen by the whole People, that is to say, by all the States of *Germany* at the same time one cannot determin whether it was on the mere Consideration of his Merits, or whether regard was had therein to the Recommendation of the deceas'd Emperor

The Election of *Henry* I is attended with more Particulars in History It says, That *Conrade*, being on his Death-bed, and considering that the Authority *Henry*, Duke of *Saxony*, had in the Empire, hinder'd him entirely from continuing the Imperial Dignity in his House, sent for *Eberhard*, his Brother, Duke of *Franconia* And having represented to him, in the Presence of several Princes and Noblemen, how hard it would be for him to establish himself in the Empire, he advis'd him to yield it to *Henry*, Duke of *Saxony*, to be before-hand with him in his Submissions, and to secure himself of his Favour, by carrying to him himself, the Honours or Imperial Ornaments Intreating at the same time the Princes and Noblemen there present to approve the Choice he had made, and to confer the Imperial Dignity on *Henry*, Duke of *Saxony*, as to him in whose Person were to be found all the Qualities necessary for so high an Administration *Conrade* dying after this Declaration, the Princes of *Franconia*, *Suabia*, *Saxony* and *Bavaria* elected *Henry*, and confirm'd by such their Choice, the Nomination the deceased had made of his Person

We learn from the Circumstances of this Election, first, That it was in effect only a Con-

* Lib 2 cap 7

firmation

firmation of the last Will of *Conrade* I, secondly, That at this Election were present the Dukes of *Suabia* and of *Franconia* Provinces which at present have no Princes that can assist at the Elections, since it is near four hundred Years since *Suabia* has had any particular Prince, and the House of *Austria*, who has that Title, is in Possession but of a small Portion thereof, as the Bishop of *Wurtzbourg* is only titular Prince of *Franconia* Thirdly, That no mention is made therein of the King of *Bohemia*, no more than of the Count *Palatine* of the *Rhine*, nor of the Marquis of *Brandenbourg*, who was not known at that Time And fourthly, That not only the Heads of Families were present at this Election, as is customary with the modern Electors, but all the Princes in general Which is evident, not only from the Testimony of *Wittikind* and *Luitprand*, who say so in express Terms, but also from the Circumstances of the History of that Time, by which we are inform'd that *Arnoul* Duke of *Bavaria* was in *Hungary*, that *Henry* was in *Saxony*, and that *Burghard*, Duke of *Suabia*, oppos'd his Election, and took Arms against him, while the other Princes authoriz'd him by their Presence From whence we must conclude, that there were other Princes of *Bavaria*, of *Saxony* and *Suabia*, who assisted at this Election, which was by that Means very different from that which has been introduc'd since

We see the same Manner of electing in *Otho* I, and in the two other *Otho*'s his Successors *Wittikind*, who was a Religious in the Convent of *Corbie* in *Saxony*, and who liv'd in their Time, and has dedicated his History to *Matilda*, or *Mahault*, Abbess of *Quedlinbourg*, Daughter of the Emperor *Otho* I, and of *Adelaide* of *Burgundy*, his second Wife, says * that the Emperor *Henry* I being sick, conven'd the People, *and appointed his Son King, and dying some Time after, all the People of* Franconia *and* Saxony *chose* Otho *his Son, whom the Father had nominated for his Successor* The Circumstances which the said *Wittikind* adds, are so remarkable, that they are worthy to be inserted here He says then, † "That after the Death of *Henry*, the Eastern *French* and the *Saxons* having " agreed that the Election should be made at " *Aix la Chapelle*, the Dukes and chief Noble-" men repair'd thither, and being with the o-" ther Princes, and the rest of the Nobility, " assembled in a Gallery, which joyns to the " great Church built by *Charlemagne*, they seat-" ed the young Prince on a Throne prepar'd " on purpose, chose him King, and took an " Oath of Fidelity to him, touching him in the " Hand, and promising him to assist him against " all his Enemies While the Princes and o-" ther Lords were employ'd in this Election, " the chief Prelate (that is to say, the Arch-" bishop of *Mentz*) cloath'd in his *Pontificali-" bus*, and attended by the Clergy, waited for " him in the Church, and seeing him come " out of the Gallery, went to meet him, took " him by the left Hand, carrying the Crosier

" in his right, and having conducted him to " the middle of the Body of the Church, stop'd " there, and turning to the People who had " flock'd thither, he said, *Behold, I here bring " you* Otho, *whom God has chosen, the late " King has nominated, and the Princes have " made King If this Election pleases you, de-" clare it, by lifting up your Hands*

And that it may not be thought that *Wittikind*, in speaking of the Princes, meant those who at present enjoy the Electoral Dignity, he names some of them, and makes them discharge their respective Offices, at the Feast that was made to *Otho*, after the Ceremonies of his Coronation He instances in *Giselbert* Duke of *Lorrain*, *Eberhard* Duke of *Franconia*, Brother to the Emperor *Conrade* I, *Herman* Duke of *Suabia*, and *Arnoul* Duke of *Bavaria*, and yet it is certain that the Emperor *Charles* IV, in regulating the Number of the Electors in the *Golden Bull*, does not so much as name one of these Princes, and consequently that this Election has nothing in common with that which is at present in Force And indeed our main Scope, in alledging this Passage, is only to shew that great Deference was had to the Nomination of the Predecessor, which restrain'd the Election of the Princes to the single Person of his Son

The Continuer of *Reg non* says, That the Emperor *Otho* I, designing to go into *Italy* in the Year 966, conven'd the States of the Empire at *Worms*, where his Son *Otho was chosen by the universal Consent of all the Princes, and of the whole People* He says he was chosen, but the Particulars of the History make it plain that this Election was only an Approbation of the Will of the Emperor, who had a mind to secure the Empire to his Son, in Order to avoid the Oppositions he had himself met with, at his Accession to the Crown This appears plainly by what *Wittikind* and *Ditmar* say, That *Otho* II was again elected after the Death of his Father, by all the People The Word *Collaudare*, which *Ditmar* makes use of, instead of that of *Eligere*, is a full Confirmation of what we just now said

Otho III was elected after the same manner during his Father's Life, who having summon'd the States of the Empire at *Verona*, in the Year 983, caus'd his Son to be chosen there, who then could not be above eleven Years old But that did not hinder the same *Otho* (being on his Death-Bed) from disposing, by his Will and Testament, of the Imperial Dignity in Favour of his Son, which is by so much the more remarkable, that such Disposal would have been ridiculous, had the Succession depended absolutely on the Election of the Princes and the People It is to this *Otho* that is ascrib'd the Institution of the Electoral College, such as it was before the Treaty of *Munster* had augmented the Number of the Electors But whether this Opinion is agreeable to the Truth of History, is what we shall see in the following Chapter

* *At the end of Book* 1 † *Lib* 2

CHAP. IV.

That the Electoral College was not instituted by the Emperor Otho III, *nor in his Time.*

WE have made it appear very plainly, that the Election began to take Place immediately after the Death of the Emperor *Lewis* III, who was the last Prince of the House of *Charlemagne* in *Germany*, but that it was very different from that which is in force at present, so that there remains still to know, When the Modern Election had its Beginning, when the College of Electors was instituted, when it was reduc'd to the Number of seven, and when the Electoral Dignity was appropriated to the Archiepiscopal Sees of *Mentz*, *Triers*, and *Cologne*, to the Kingdom of *Bohemia*, to the Palatinate of the *Rhine*, (to *Bavaria*,) to the Dutchy of *Saxony*, and Marquisate of *Brandenburg*, to the Exclusion of all the other Principalities of *Germany*.

The Cardinals *Bellarmin* and *Baronius* ascribe the Institution of the College of Electors to Pope *Gregory* V, and the major part of Authors, as well ancient as modern, *Italians* and *Germans*, say, That the Electors were instituted and reduc'd to the Number of seven in the said *Gregory*'s Time, and that of the Emperor *Otho* III, but they dispute amongst themselves, whether this Regulation was made by the Pope, or by the Emperor with the Pope's Authority.

It is the Opinion of all the Canonists, and even of some of the exactest Historians, as of the Centuriators, of *Sleidan*, and of the President *de Thou*. The Acts of the Church of *Aquileia* attribute this Institution to Pope *Silvester* II, *Theod*. of *Niem*, to *Conrade* II, and there are some who ascribe it to *Otho* IV, which is what *Goldast* would make us believe, when he relates the Fragment of the Constitution he made for that Purpose, in the Diet conven'd at *Franckfort* in the Year 1208.

It is not our Intention to reconcile these different Opinions, but only to shew, that the Institution of the Electoral College, to the Number seven, was not made till above two hundred Years after the Death of *Gregory* and *Otho*, and so that this Honour is not due to either the one or the other.

It cannot be deny'd, but the College of Electors is the most considerable, the most illustrious, and the most august Society, not only in *Germany*, but also of all *Europe*, as being compos'd of Prelates and Princes, who pretend to, and may, carry it on the Level with crown'd Heads. For which Reason there is Ground to wonder, that hitherto there does not appear any authentick Act of its Institution, and that since the Death of *Otho* III, to *Martinus Polonus*, who wrote above two hundred and fifty Years after, there is not any Author to be found that makes mention thereof, or that even knows the Quality of Elector. We might take some Advantage from this Silence, as being an invincible Proof against the pretended Institution of *Otho* III and *Gregory* V, and content our selves with the bare denying a thing, for which no warrantable Testimony can be produc'd, and that with so much the more Reason, as there is no History that speaks of the Electors before the Reign of *Frederick* I, or if it makes a particular Dignity thereof, before that of *Frederick* II his Grandson.

On the contrary, if we do but bring ever so little Attention to the Lecture of the History of those Times, we shall find, that of all the modern secular Electors, there was not any one known in the Time of *Otho* III, besides the Duke of *Saxony*. *Bohemia* was not yet erected into a Kingdom, and its Dukes were so little concern'd in the Affairs of the Empire, that *Dubravius* Bishop of *Olmuts*, who wrote the History thereof, and is of the Opinion of those who ascribe the Institution of the Electoral College to *Otho* III, seeing it was impossible to bring the King of *Bohemia* into the same, says that that Emperor made but six, and that it was *Rodolphus* I, who liv'd near three hundred Years after this pretended Institution, who augmented the Number thereof, by adding thereto the King of *Bohemia*, as well to do Honour to *Wenceslas* his Son-in-law, as to prevent the Disorders which are but too frequent, when the Votes may be equally divided. The Counts Palatin of the *Rhine* were not yet known, because the Palatinate made a part of *Franconia*, and the Marquiss of *Brandenburg* did not yet hold the Rank of Prince, but was only a simple Governor of a Frontier, which was still intirely Pagan, and depended wholly on the Duke of *Saxony*. These Reasons are, in my Apprehension, strong enough to confute the Opinion of those who ascribe the Institution of the Electoral College to *Otho* III, or to *Gregory* V.

But forasmuch as we cannot establish this Truth by more convincing Arguments, than those which the History of those Times affords, we shall examin the Elections of the following Emperors, who succeeded *Otho* III, that we may see whether there is any thing to be found therein, that comes near to what is practis'd at this Day. When we shall have first observ'd, that there is no likelihood at all that the Emperor *Otho* III, who was not above twenty five or twenty six Years old, when Pope *Gregory* V dy'd in the Year 998, should have been for making the Empire merely elective, at a Time when he might still have Children capable of succeeding, and when he had Relations near enough, not to be willing to frustrate them of what they might in some Measure hope to have by Right of hereditary Succession. For besides *Henry* of *Saxony*, Duke of *Bavaria*, who succeeded him in the Empire, there were the Sons of *Otho*, who was the Son of *Lutolfe*, Duke of *Suabia*, eldest Son to the Emperor *Otho* I, and of *Edgid* or *Judith* of *England*, his first Wife, and *Brunou*, Unkle to *Henry*,

444 *Of the* ELECTION *of the* EMPEROR, *and*

Henry, and younger Son of *Henry* I, Duke of *Saxony*, who was the second Son of the Emperor *Henry* I, and Brother of *Otho* I

And in fact, there is not any thing in the Election of *Henry* II, who succeeded immediately to *Otho* III, that refers to what is practis'd at this Day He was not chosen by a certain Number of Princes, which are call'd Electors on the contrary, they who are for maintaining his Election are oblig'd to allow, that he was elected by almost all the Princes of the Empire, who in effect did nothing more, than confirm his Pretensions against those of the other Princes of the same House He was the Son *Henry* the Mutineer, Duke of *Bavaria*, who was Grandson to *Henry* I, who was also Duke of *Bavaria*, and so Great-Grandson to the Emperor *Henry* I, as well as *Otho* III, his Predecessor But there were other Relations as near as he, to wit, *Henry*, Father of the Emperor *Conrade* II, and *Conrade* the Father of *Conrade*, Duke of *Franconia*, Brother to Pope *Gregory* V, and to *William* Bishop *Strasbourg*, who had not less Right thereto than himself, as being descended from the eldest Son of the Emperor *Otho* I, so that the Election that the Princes made of the Person of *Henry*, Duke of *Bavaria*, was not an Election, but rather a Regulation of the Pretensions of the Relations in the same Degree

Henry pretended that the Crown was due to him, as to the nearest Relation of the Deceas'd, because the Descendents of *Lutolfe*, the eldest Son of *Otho*, had been excluded by *Otho* II, his younger Brother, and it was in this Quality that he was consider'd, not by seven Electors, (altho' the pretended Institution of the Electoral College ought to have been then in its greatest Force) but by all the States of the Empire *Ditmar* Bishop of *Mersbourg*, who liv'd at that time, and dy'd in the Reign of *Henry* II, in the Year 1018, says, " *That* Henry, *Duke of* Ba-
" varia, *having caus'd the Imperial Ornaments to*
" *be given him immediately after the Death of*
" Otho III, *was for securing to himself the Suf-*
" *frage of* Sigfrid, *Archbishop of* Cologn, *who*
" *protested to him that he could promise him no-*
" *thing, but that he would follow the Sentiment*
" *of all the People, and that being inform'd that*
" *the Princes of* Saxony, *to wit* Giseler, *Arch-*
" *bishop of* Magdebourg, *with the other Bishops*
" *of the Countrey* Duke Bernard *of* Saxony, *the*
" *Marquisses* Lotharius, Eggard *and* Geron, *and*
" *the other Princes of* Germany, *were assembled*
" *at* Werle, *where were present also* Sophia *and*
" Adelheida, *Abbesses of* Gandersheim *and of*
" Quedlinbourg, *his Cousins, Daughters of the*
" *Emperor* Otho II, *and of* Theophania *of*
" Greece, *he sent to them a Gentleman, who*
" *having made known his Master's Intentions to*
" *these Princesses, negotiated so happily through*
" *their Means, and by the Promises he made to*
" *those who could be serviceable to him on this Oc-*
" *casion, that all the Assembly declar'd with one*
" *Voice, that* Henry *should reign by the Grace of*
" God, *and by hereditary Right*

Whatever there was in it, he drew great Advantages from his Birth, but even if he were not oblig'd for the Imperial Dignity, to the Rank he held in the Empire, and to the Honour he

had to be a near Relation to the Emperor *Otho*, and that he held it only from the mere Election of the Princes, it is certain that by those Princes cannot be understood the seven Electors, but all the Princes of the Empire, as well Ecclesiasticks as Seculars, since *Ditmar* names some of them, and says expressly, that *Omnes Regni Optimates*, all the Great Men of the Kingdom were present at his Election, and after him *Otho*, Bishop of *Frisingen*, says positively, † *That all the Lords of the Kingdom chose him* An Election, which in effect did no more than confirm the Right he had already thereto

Let us look into the Particulars of the Election of ‡ *Conrade* II, Successor to *Henry* The said Bishop of *Frisingen* * says, That he was chosen *by all the States of the Kingdom* who were for confirming by their Election, the Esteem *Henry* had express'd for his Person But we go a great deal farther, and say, That his Birth was not therein less consider'd than his Merit, and the Judgment of his Predecessor The Quality of Duke of *Franconia*, which the Histories give him, has given room to the common Error which has slip'd into the Minds of all those who have undertook to speak of the Affairs of *Germany*, *that after the Death of* Henry II, *the Imperial Dignity pass'd from the House of* Saxony *into that of* Franconia tho' it be very true, that *Conrade* II was of the same House of *Saxony*, descended in a direct and Male Line from the Emperors *Henry*, and *Otho* I We have very strong Conjectures for this in History, but the Testimony of *Wippo*, a contemporary Author, and Chaplain to the Emperor *Henry* III, Son and Successor of *Conrade* II, is unexceptionable, and a convincing Proof He says then, That *Conrade* Duke of *Franconia*, call'd the Eldest, and *Conrade* the Younger, his Competitor for the Empire, were Cousin Germans, Sons of two Brothers, the one of which was call'd *Hetzel* or *Henry*, and the other *Cuno* or *Conrade*, and that these two Brothers were Sons of *Otho*, Duke of *Franconia* (and of *Suabia*,) and Brothers to *Brunon*, who was Pope under the Name of *Gregory* V, and to *William* Bishop of *Strasbourg* Then it appears, that *Conrade* II was Great-Grandson to the Emperor *Otho* I, and so a Prince of the House of *Saxony* Now that it may not be thought that *Otho*, to whom *Wippo* gives the Quality of Duke of *Franconia*, is another than he who succeed to *Lutolfe*, his Father, in the Dutchy of *Suabia*, we must observe what the Bishop of *Mersbourg* says, to wit, That the Emperor *Otho* III, being come to *Rome*, made *Bruno* his Nephew, (he was the Son of his Cousin German) Son of Duke *Otho*, (of *Suabia*) Pope in the place of *John* who was dead

This being establish'd, we might maintain that *Conrade* II succeeded to the Empire by virtue of hereditary Right, and that the States of *Germany* met after the Death of *Henry* II, but only to regulate the Difference between the two Cousin Germans, who were Relations in the same Degree to the deceas'd Emperor But it is sufficient that we are able to to shew, that the Circumstances of his Election, destroy entirely the Opinion of those, who refer the Institution of the Electoral College to the

* Lib 5 p 52. † Lib 6 c 27 ‡ Conrade II * Ibid c 28

Time

of the ELECTORS of the EMPIRE.   445

Time of the Emperor *Otho* III The Abbot of *Urſperg*, makes preſent at the Election of *Conrade* II, *Eberhard* Biſhop of *Bamberg*, and makes him be ſo very much conſider'd in the Aſſembly, that it is to his Authority chiefly, and that of *Aribo* Archbiſhop of *Mentz*, that he aſcribes the Promotion of that Prince But let us ſee all the Particulars of it in *Wippo*, whom we juſt quoted, who has wrote his Life, and dedicated it to the Emperor *Henry* III, his Son He ſpeaks thus of it

" It is proper to name here ſome Princes,
" as well Eccleſiaſticks as Seculars, who liv'd
" then, *and by the Advice of whom* (the *Laſtern*)
" France *is accuſtom'd to chuſe its Kings* At
" that Time (*ſc* in the Year 1024) *Aribo* go-
" vern'd the Archbiſhoprick of *Mentz* *Pele-*
" *rin*, a Relation to *Aribo*, govern'd that of
" *Cologn*, and *Poppo*, Brother to Duke *Erneſt*,
" (*ſc* of *Suabia*) was Archbiſhop of *Triers*, ha-
" ving under his Guardianſhip his Nephew *Er-*
" *neſt*, his Brother's Son *Eberhara* was Biſhop
" of *Bamberg*, *Hetmo* of *Conſtance*, *Werner* of
" *Strasbourg*, *Mercelin* of *Wurtzbourg*, *Bruno*,
" Brother to the Emperor *Henry* II of *Augſ-*
" *bourg*, *Gunther*, Brother to the Counts *Eg-*
" *hard* and *Herman*, was Archbiſhop of *Saltz-*
" *bourg*, *Burghard* was Biſhop of *Ratisbon*, *Al-*
" *bert* of *Friſingen* *Many other Biſhops and Ab-*
" *bots were preſent with theſe at the Election* I
" decline making mention of the Prelates of
" *Saxony*, becauſe not having my Knowledge
" of their Merits, I would not here ſet down
" their Names without Encomiums, *tho' I am*
" *ſenſible they have a Right to aſſiſt at thoſe Aſ-*
" *ſemblies, to deliberate there, and cooperate with*
" *the others* I ſay nothing of the Prelates of
' Italy, who could not repair thither by reaſon
" of the Shortneſs of Time The Dukes who
" liv'd at that Time were, *Benno* Duke of *Sax-*
" *ony*, *Adelbert* of *Iſtria*, (it is *Carinthia*) *Hetz-*
" *lo* (*Henry*) of *Bavaria*, *Erneſt* of *Suevia*, *Fri-*
" *derick* of *Lorrain*, *Gothelo* of *Moſellane*, *Con-*
" *rade* of *Worms*, Duke of *Francoma*, *Ulric* of
" *Bohemia* Theſe Biſhops and Dukes whom
" we have juſt nam'd, endeavour'd to effect
" that the Republick might not remain long
' without a Head, &c Afterwards he goes
" on Between *Worms* and *Mentz*, there is a
" Place where all the Great Men, and as one
" may ſay, all the Forces, and all the Bowels
" of the Kingdom, aſſembl'd and encamp'd a-
" long the *Rhine* on the part of *Germany* came
" thither the *Saxons*, the *Slavonians*, the *Eaſtern*
" *Francs*, the *Norici*, (*Bavarians*) and the *Sua-*
" *bians* and on the ſide of the *Gaules*, the
" *French* who inhabit on the *Rhine*, the *Ripua-*
" *rii*, and the *Lorrainers* After that the Num-
" ber of thoſe *who could pretend to the Empire*
" (as the Princes of the Houſe of *Saxony*, de-
" ſcended in a Right and Male Line from *Bru-*
" *no*, younger Son of *Henry*, the firſt Duke of
" *Bavaria* of this Family, whoſe Poſterity did
" not fail, till it did ſo in *Henry the Groſs*, Son
" of *Otho*, Count of *Northeim*, who dy'd in
" the Year 1100,) was reduc'd to a few Per-
" ſons, and that again to Two, viz Two
" *Comrades*, Dukes of *Franconia*, Couſin Ger-
" mans The Eldeſt of the Two addreſſing
" himſelf to the other, repreſented to him the

" Advantages they might reap from the Eſteem
" the whole Aſſembly had for them, to the
" Excluſion of all others, and the Injury they
" would do themſelves, if they ruin'd this high
" Reputation by their irregular Ambition
" praying him to acquieſce to the Choice the
" Princes ſhould make of one of them, and
" having diſpos'd him to what he had deſir'd
" of him, they both reaſſum'd their Places
" Then the People having aſk'd the Archbiſhop
" of *Mentz*, (*whoſe Right it is to Vote firſt*)
" which of the two he made Choice of, he pre-
" ſently nam'd *Conrade* the Elder, and his Ad-
" vice was follow'd *by all the Archbiſhops, and*
" *by all the other Prelates* There was only
" the Archbiſhop of *Cologn*, and the Duke of
" *Lorrain*, who expreſs'd ſome Diſſatisfaction
" thereat, but they alſo came into the Senti-
" ment of the reſt

Such was the Election of *Conrade* II, and ſuch was the Cuſtom and the Manner of chuſing the Emperors, for above two hundred Years after the Death of *Conrade*, which is what Cardinal *Baronius* himſelf does not make any Difficulty to own † And yet nothing like this is to be ſeen in the modern Election The Relations and Friends make Intereſt, the People have a Share therein, and conſult the Suffrage of the Archbiſhop of *Mentz* The *Eaſtern Francs*, the *Suabians*, and *Lorrainers*, whom the *Golden Bull* does not acknowledge, make the beſt part of the Aſſembly, and at this Day the Dukes of *Suab a*, *Franconia* and *Lorrain*, have no Right to be preſent at the Elections Beſides the Archbiſhop of *Mentz*, *Cologn* and *Triers*, there are other Biſhops who give their Votes, and the Majority of Suffrages in this great Aſſembly gives the Empire

The ſame *Conrade* II had for Succeſſor in the Empire *Henry* III, his Son, ſo that the Imperial Dignity began again to be, as it were, hereditary in his Houſe Hiſtory ſays, That his Father cauſ'd him to be crown'd in the Year 1028, *with the Approbation of all the Princes, and of all the People* Words by ſo much the more remarkable, that the Word Approbation expreſſes a great deal leſs than that of Election or Confirmation, and that therein no mention is made of the ſeven Electors, *but of all the Princes, and of all the People* The Authors of the Time ſpeak almoſt in the ſame Terms, of the Election which *Henry* III, cauſ'd to be made ‡ of *Henry* IV, his Son, (who was not then above two Years old) by all the States of the Empire aſſembled at *Triers*

* In the Year 1077, a good Number of Princes, particularly of *Saxony* and *Suabia*, being aſſembled at *Forchaim* in *Franconia*, they proceeded to the Election of an Emperor againſt *Henry* IV, and choſe *Rodolfus* of *Rhinfeld*, Duke of *Suabia* It is true that this Election was made in a very tumultuary Manner, and contrary to the Forms but there is not one Author that ſays, That they who were preſent thereat, had not a Right to chooſe And yet they name *Bertold*, Duke of *Zeringen*, and the Biſhops of *Wurtzbourg* and of *Metz* But what was there moſt remarkable was, that the ſame Princes made a Decree, which imported, That the Imperial Dignity ſhould no

† Annal Tom 10. § 36 & ſeq   ‡ Henry IV   * Rodolphus of Rhinfeld

longer

longer descend to Children by hereditary Right, *as had been practis'd in Time past*, but that it should by a free Election, be conferr'd on the most Worthy. Insomuch, that if the People did not think the Emperor's Son had all the Qualities requisite, or that it had otherwise an Aversion to his Person, it should be at liberty to chuse whomsoever it should think fit. Nothing can be said more expressly against the pretended Institution of the Electoral College in the Time of *Otho* III, and to prove that the Empire was not so absolutely elective, but great Consideration was had to the Birth of the Elect.

Bertold, a Priest of the Diocese of *Constance*, who liv'd in the Time of the Emperor *Henry*, and who was himself employ'd by the Pope in the Difference he had with the Emperor, says, That after the Death of *Rodolphus* of *Rhinfeld*, the Princes of *Germany*, to wit, the *Archbishops, Bishops, Dukes, Marquisses* and *Counts*, being assembl'd, chose † *Herman* of *Luxembourg*. And we read in History, that at the Election of *Henry* V, Son and Successor of *Henry* IV, were present fifty two Princes, who proceeded to the Election, notwithstanding the Absence of the Duke of *Saxony*.

It was in the Person of *Henry* V, who dy'd at *Utrecht, May* 22, 1125, that the Male Line of the Princes of *Saxony*, descended from the Emperor *Henry* I, fail'd. So that the Royal Race being wholly extinct, it was necessary to look for a Successor in another Family, which not being to be done, but by the way of Election, we must see whether that of *Lotharius* II, Successor to *Henry* V, was perform'd by the seven Electors, so as to allow us to say, that the Electoral College was already instituted at that Time, and this is what we shall examine in the following Chapter.

CHAP. V.

Whether the Election of the Emperors, Successors to Henry V, *was perform'd by seven Electors, and whether the Electoral College was instituted under the Emperors of the House of* Suabia.

IT is certain that after the Death of *Henry* V, the Imperial Dignity pass'd into a strange Family, by the Election the Princes of *Germany* made of the Person of *Lotharius* II. He was the Son of *Gebhard*, Count of *Supplinbourg*, and had mary'd *Rixe*, Daughter to *Henry* of *Saxony*, sirnam'd the *Fat*, Count of *Northeim*, descended in a direct and Male Line from *Henry*, Duke of *Bavaria*, younger Son of the Emperor *Henry* I. So that it may be still said, That the Princes of the Empire in calling him to the Crown, had some Regard to the Alliance, by which he had been as it were grafted into the Family of the Emperors of the House of *Saxony*, however it must be own'd, that whereas in the foregoing Time great Consideration had been had to Birth, (the Princes making no Choice, but out of the Royal House) on this Occasion the Elect is almost entirely oblig'd for his Election, to the sole Will of the Electors. For which Reason * the Bishop of *Frisingen*, speaking of the Emperors of his *Time*, says in very express Terms, that the Imperial Dignity has this peculiar to it self, that it is not to be attain'd by Right of hereditary Succession, but by the sole Election of the Princes.

When we here mention the Election of the Princes, we thereby mean all the Princes of *Germany*. The Continuer of *Sigebert*, who liv'd at that Time, says, That at the Election of *Lotharius* II, were present a great Number of Princes, and that he was chosen, *by two Archbishops, two Bishops, and many other Prelates, and Lords of* Germany. Goldast, *in his first Tomo of the Imp Constitut p 259*, produces Convocatory Letters for the Election of an Emperor, after the Death of *Henry* V, sign'd by *Adelbert* Archbishop of *Mentz*, *Frederick* Archbishop of *Cologn*, by the Bishops of *Constance*, of *Worms* and *Spires*, by the Abbot of *Fuld*, by the Dukes of *Bavaria* and *Suabia*, by the Counts *Palatin* of the *Rhine*, and the Count of *Sultzbach*. They summon *Otho*, Bishop of *Bamberg*, to be present at *Mentz*, towards St *Bartholomew*'s Day, in order to proceed with them to the Election. *Albert Crantz*, a grave and exact Author, speaking of this same Election †, makes it appear by its Circumstances, that it was executed in a full Assembly of the States. That the *Eastern Francs* and the *Suabians*, who have no Elector at this Time, proceeded separately to the Election of *Conrade* of *Suabia*, Duke of *Franconia*, and were for having that of *Lotharius* declar'd faulty.

Otho, Bishop of *Frisingen*, says, That ‡ *Conrade* III, Successor to *Lotharius* II, was chosen by several Princes, and yet we are inform'd by the History of those Times, that *Henry* Duke of *Bavaria* and *Saxony*, Son-in-Law to the deceas'd Emperor, who made Interest to be Emperor himself, was not summon'd thereto, and that the See of *Mentz* was vacant. There was no King of *Bohemia* at that Time. *Conrade* was Duke of *Franconia* and Count *Palatine* of the *Rhine*, and the Marquisate of *Brandenburg* had not been yet separated from the Dutchy of *Saxony*. So that of all the modern Electors, there were only the Archbishops of *Cologn* and of *Triers* who were present at this Election

† *Herman of Luxembourg*   * *In his Chron* Ald, 152   † *Saxon*. lib 8 c. 1   ‡ *Conrade* III Election

of the ELECTORS of the EMPIRE. 447

Election ‡ That of *Frederick* I, Nephew and Successor to *Conrade* III, is more circumstantiated. The same Bishop of *Frisingen*, who was his near Relation, and who has written part of his Life, says, * That all the Princes of *Germany*, and even some Noblemen of *Italy* were present at his Election, in so great a Number, that it seem'd almost incredible that in so short a time so great a Multitude should be call'd together, since between the Death of *Conrade* III, who dy'd *February* 15, and the Election of *Frederick* I, which was perform'd on *March* 14, there was the Interval but of eighteen Days. The Poet *Gunther*, who liv'd at the same time, and has written the Life of that Prince, says, that all the Prelates and Princes of the Empire assisted at his Election, and speaks thereof almost in the same Terms that *Wippo* speaks of that of the Emperor *Conrade* II. The natural Simplicity of his Verses, which are not impertinent for the Time in which he wrote, deserves very well that those he has made on the Subject of our Discourse, should be inserted here † He says then,

" *Orbaque Regni*
" *Teutonici sedes Conradi morte vacabat*
" *Acturi Sacra de Successore Coronæ*
" *Conveniunt proceres, totius viscera Regni,*
" *Sede satis nota, rapido quæ proxima Mago*

§ §

" *Huc sacri celebresque Viri, quos laude serena*
' *Insula, vel Gladius mundo facit esse verendos,*
" *Ex omni Regione fluunt ad commoda Regni*
" *Publica, de summis agere ac disponere rebus*
" *Exacta ratione parant*
" *Sic postquam sedere Duces, dubioq, voluntant*
" *Pectora, cui tanti Regni tribuantur honores*
" *Saxones & quorum Ripuana nomine Tellus,*
" *Westphaliæque Urbes, & Norica Regna*
" *regentes,*
" *Allobrogumque Duces coeunt, Cymbrique*
" *feroces,*
" *Vindelici, Rhætique ruunt, quos Suevia*
" *nutrit,*
" *Quosque Carentinis collimant Austria Campis,*
" *Quas Lycus & tumidis Ister prælabitur oris*

§ §

" *Tandem quid peteret Regni fortuna, per*
" *unum*
" *Dignata est aperire virum, qui nomine clarus,*
" *Dux, Comes, aut Præsul,*
" *Sic ubi mellisflua, quisquis fuit illo disertus,*
" *Voce peroravit, concordi protinus omnes*
" *Assensere sono læto sermone cietur*
" *Dux puer in Regem*

The Particulars of this Election are by so much the more remarkable, that there is not so much as one that can give any Ground to think it was made by a regulated Number of seven Electors, or has any relation with what is practis'd at this Day. Those who would say that this Author writes like a Poet, and as such enriches the Subject he handles, ought to consider that he writes the History of the Emperor *Frederick* I, while he was still living, and with so much Exactness, that there is not one single Circumstance that partakes of the Fable. Which will be demonstratively evident, if it be compar'd with what we have before alledg'd from *Otho* Bishop of *Frisingen*, and with what is related in the Chronicle of *Ulric* and of *St Afre*, ‡ That *Frederick* I was elected by the common Vote and Consent of all the Princes. To which we think our selves oblig'd to add, That *Conrade* III, and *Frederick*.I, were very near Relations of the last Emperors of the House of *Saxony*, and that the first was very much consider'd on that account, after the Death of *Henry* V, his Unkle on the Mother's side, as being the Son of *Frederick* of *Staufen*, first Duke of *Suabia* of this Family, and of *Agnes* Daughter of the Emperor *Henry*.IV From the same Marriage of *Frederick* and *Agnes* was born *Frederick* Duke of *Suabia*, Father of the Emperor *Frederick* I, who by that Mean was great Grandson to the Emperor *Henry* IV. So that one may say, that in the Election of these two Princes their Birth was not less consider'd than their Merit. And in Fact we shall see, that the Empire was again become in some measure hereditary.

We have no Particulars of the Election of *Henry* VI, but *Otho* of *S Blasio*, who has continu'd the History of *Otho* of *Frisingen*, says, * That the Emperor *Frederick* I, when he allotted the Portions of his Children, appointed *Henry*, his eldest Son, King, as if the Royal Dignity had made a part of his future Inheritance. And in effect being on the point of setting out, in order to go to the Holy Land, and being willing to put his Sons in Possession of the Partition he had made amongst them many Years before, he gave † the *Regalia*, that is to say, the Regal Ornaments to *Henry*.

The same Emperor *Henry* VI, reflecting on the Inconveniences and Disorders that disturb'd the Repose of the Empire during the *Interregnum*, before the Suffrages of so great a Number of Princes could agree in the Choice of one single Person, ordain'd, that there should be no more Elections, but that the Succession should go by hereditary Right, so that the nearest Relation of the deceased should be Emperor. And to begin by his Son *Frederick*, he ordain'd that the Kingdoms of *Sicily*, *Calabria*, *Apulia*, and the Principality of *Capua*, which his Son possess'd as a particular Demesne in Right of his Mother, should be united to the Empire. He ordain'd also, that in Default of Males, Women should succeed, and this Ordinance was ratify'd, not only by the Court of *Rome*, but also by the fifty two Princes who are wont to chuse the Emperor. They are the very Words which the Author of the great *Belgick* Chronicle has taken from *Joannes Monachus*. ‡ And that the Reader may not be surpriz'd that this prodigious Number of Electors, we must see what *Conrade* of *Lichtenau*, Abbot of *Ursperg*, who liv'd under the Emperor *Frederick*, says of the Election of *Henry* V, to wit, * That at the Diet of *Mentz* were present fifty two Princes, who elected *Henry*, which is conformable to what all the others say, concerning

the

† Fredericus * Lib 2 cap 1 de gestis Frederici ‡ Inter Authores Hist Germ à Rubero editos,
pag 210 † In the Year 1152 * Chap. 21. ‡ Ibid. l 12 ‡ Pag 205
* In the Year 1106

the Nomination of *Frederick* II, to which befides the Authority of the Father, they bring the concurring Confent of all the Princes of *Germany*.

But that we may the better eftablifh this Truth, that under the ‡ Emperors of the Houfe of *Suabia*, the Election was quite different from what it is at prefent, we fhall reprefent the Particulars of the Schifm which had like to have ruin'd the Empire after the Death of *Henry* VI And to this effect we fhall relate here what two contemporary Authors fay thereof, *viz*. *Otho* of *S Blafio*, whom we before quoted, and *Godfrey*, a Monk of Saint *Pantaleon*'s at *Cologn*; The firft fpeaks thus * "The Eaftern " Princes, to wit, the Duke of *Bavaria*, and " *Bernard* of *Saxony*, with the other Lords, " and the Bifhops of *Magdeburg* and *Saltzburg*, " with the other Eafterlings, prefix'd a Day to " meet at *Arnsberg* in *Thuringia* Philip (Duke " of *Suabia*) being come thither, it was there " refolv'd, that he fhould be made Adminiftra- " tor of the Empire, till fuch time as *Frederick*, " his Nephew (Son to *Henry* VI) who had " been elected by the other Princes, fhould ar- " rive in *Germany* But the Archbifhops of *Co- " logn* and *Triers*, with fome Bifhops, and " *Henry* Count *Palatine* of the *Rhine*, with " many other Lords of thofe Parts, being " met together, annull'd this Election, and " fent for *Bertold*, Duke of *Zeringen*, with a " Defign to make him King. *Bertold* comply'd " with the Difpofition of the Princes, but he " foon chang'd his Mind, fo that the Princes " fent for *Otho*; the Son of *Henry*, heretofore " Duke of *Saxony* and *Bavaria*, and chofe him " by the Confent of fome Towns in thofe Parts " Thofe Princes who had not been prefent at " thefe Elections (they had therefore a Right " to affift thereat) engag'd fome on the one " fide, and fome on the other, to wit, *Leo- " pold* Duke of *Auftria*, the King of *Bohemia*, " the Landgrave of *Thuringia*, and *Bertold* of " *Zeringen*, with *Philip*; and the Duke of *Bra- " bant* and fome others with *Otho*

The Circumstances are more remarkable in *Godfrey*, † who fays, "The Archbifhops of " *Cologn* and of *Triers*, pretending to be in " Poffeffion of a Right to elect, being met at " *Andernach*, with *Bernard* Duke of *Saxony*, " and feveral other Bifhops, Counts and Lords, " they fix'd a Day to meet at *Cologn*, where " they fent for *Bertold* Duke of *Zeringen*, with " a Defign to make him King But the Eaftern " Marquiffes (of *Mifnia*) and *Bernard* Duke " of *Saxony*, the Archbifhop of *Magdeburg*, and " many other Princes of the *Upper Germany*, " inftead of repairing to *Cologn*, met at *Erfort* " Which the others being inform'd of, they " fent *Herman* Bifhop of *Munfter* to thofe Prin- " ces, to defire them not to proceed to an E- " lection in their Abfence, but to nominate a " place whither they might repair on both fides, " that they might there with the common Con- " fent of all proceed to the Election of a pro- " per Perfon But before they got to *Erfort*, " they were inform'd of the Election there of " *Philip* Duke of *Suabia*, Brother to the late " Emperor deceas'd, at which they were by " fo much the more offended, as it was with- " out Precedent or Example, that the Princes " of *Saxony* had made a King, and proceed " ing on their fide to an Election, they chofe " *Bertold* of *Zeringen*, and upon his Refufal, " *Otho*, Count of *Poictou*, Son to *Henry* Duke " of *Saxony* and of *Bavaria*

Both Parties intending to procure their Election to be confirm'd by the Pope *Innocent* III, wrote Letters to him, which are ftill to be found intire in the Canon Law and elfewhere, but they are fo far from fpeaking of feven Electors, that they fay in exprefs Terms, *We the Princes and Barons* of Germany, *as well Secu-* lar as Ecclefiaftical, have elected And in the Subfcription, I *Adolphus* Archbifhop of *Cologn* have elected and fign'd, I *Bernard* Bifhop of *Paderlorn* have elected and fign'd, and fo of the others, *viz* I *Thietmar* Bifhop of *Minden*, I *Hittikind* Abbot of *Corbie* on the *Wefer*, I *Gerard* Abbot of *Thuits*, I *Heribert* Abbot of *Verdon*, I *Henry* Duke of *Lorrain* and of *Brabant*, Marqu fs of the Holy Empire, have elected and fign'd, I *Henry* Count of *Cuyck* have elected and fign'd In thofe Letters which the Partifans of *Philip* fent to the Pope, are nam'd, the Archbifhops of *Magdeburg* and of *Befançon*, the Bifhops of *Ratisbonne*, of *Frifingen*, of *Augsburg*, of *Conftance*, of *Hildefheim* The Abbots of *Fuld*, of *Heftald* and of *Tergent* The King of *Bohemia*, the Duke of *Saxony*, the Duke of *Bavaria*, the Duke of *Auftria*, the Duke of *Moravia*, and the Marquifs of *Ravensberg*

This is of that Force, that Cardinal *Baronius*, who maintains that the Electoral Colledge was inftituted by *Otho* III, (but that his Ordinance was not executed,) is obl g'd to fay, ‡ that *Leo Oftienfis* is miftaken, when he would have it believ'd (in explaining the decretal *Venerabilem*) that in the Time of *Innocent* III, there were but feven Electors, it being certain, fays he, that it appears by thofe Letters, that at that Time all the Vaffals of the Empire, as well Ecclefiafticks, to wit, the Archbifhops, Bifhops and Abbots, as the Secular Princes, to wit, the Dukes, Marquiffes, Counts and Barons, were lawful Electors of the kings of the *Romans*, defign'd to be Emperors To which he adds, that this is fo true, that there is a very evident Proof of the fame in the Election of *Frederick* II

* The Emperor *Philip* being kill'd on *June* 2, 1208, *Otho* of *Saxony*, Count of *Poictou*, was again propos'd, whofe Election was perform'd with the Particulars obferv'd by *Arnoul*, Prefident of the Cathedral Church of *Hildefheim*, and fince Abbot of *Lubeck*, who has continu'd the Chronicles of the *Slavonians* by *Helmold* Prieft of *Buzou*, who liv'd at that Time They are alone capable of blotting out of the Mind of the Reader, whatever may ftill remain there in Favour of the Opinion of thofe who are for the Inftitution of the Electoral College to the Emperor *Otho* For which reafon we fhall with Pleafure infert 'em here word for word He expreffes himfelf in this manner concerning them † " *Otho* being willing to make ufe " of the Occafion of the Death of *Philip*, had " Thoughts of taking Arms againft h s Suc-

‡ *Philip and Otho* IV   * Cap 16   ‡ *Page* 261 *Tom* 1 *of Freherus*   † *Tom* 10 Ann 996 § 56
* *Otho* IV   ‖ *Lib* 7 c 15

of the ELECTORS *of the* EMPIRE.

" mus, when the Archbishop of *Magdeburg*
" and Duke *Bernard* of *Saxony* exhorted him
" not to employ Force, but rather to endea-
" vour to get together an Assemby of Princes,
" and to desire them to proceed to the Election
" of his Person He therefore summon'd the
" Princes to meet at *Halberstadt*, whither most
" of the Prelates and Princes of *Saxony* repair'd,
" as well as the Bishop of *Wurtzburg* These
" Pr nces elected with one unanimous Voice and
" with one common Consent, as if they had been
" inspir'd by God, *Otho* King of the *Romans*,
" always August, in the Name of the Father,
" of the Son, and of the Holy Ghost " The
Archbishop of *Magdeburg*, to whom it belong'd
to vote first, as it seem'd, began, and all the
others follow'd, as the Marquiss of *Misnia*,
the Lantgrave of *Thuringia*, and all the others
who had a Right to elect No mention is
made of the three Ecclesiastical Electors, no
more than of the King of *Bohemia*, and of the
Marquiss of *Brandenburg*, and the Archbishop
of *Magdeburg* and the Bishop of *Wurtzburg* are
said to be present, and two other Electors of
Saxony, viz the Lantgrave of *Thuringia* and
the Marquiss of *Misnia*

* *Frederick* II was nominated to the Empire
while he was still in the Cradle by the Emperor *Henry* IV his Father And we have seen

above, that in Consideration thereof the Princes were of Opinion, after the Death of *Henry*, that *Philip* ought to be contented with the
Administration or Regency during the Absence
of his Nephew, who by that means was acknowledg'd for Emperor, yet nevertheless
Otho IV being excommunicated by the Pope,
and the Princes of *Germany* being disgusted at
his Government, *Sigfrid* Archbishop of *Mentz*
was for having them proceed to a new Flection For this purpose he desir'd the King
of *Bohemia*, the Duke of *Bavaria*, the Duke of
Austria, the Lantgrave of *Thuringia*, and divers other Princes to repair to *Bamberg*, where he
caus'd to be chosen *Frederick* King of *Sicily* † He
summon'd to this Election the Duke of *Bavaria* (who had no Share there n before the last
Wars of *Germany*) the Duke of *Austria*, and
the Lantgrave of *Thuringia*, whom the *Golden
Bull* does not know , and neglects to call
thereto the Count *Palatin* of the *Rhine* (who
was Brother to *Otho*) and the Archbishops of
Cologn and of *Triers*, because they were in the
same Party, and nevertheless that does not
hinder them from proceeding to an Election

But this is dwelling too long on the Refu-
tation of an Ordinance which is not produc'd,
and which it is confess'd was never executed

CHAP. VI.

Whether the Electoral College was instituted to the Number of seven, before the Publication of the Golden Bull.

WE are of Opinion that those who shall have taken the Pains to examin what we have said in the two last foregoing Chapters, against the Sentiment of those who refer the Institution of the Electoral College to *Otho* III, will be oblig'd to acquiesce to the Truth we have there establish'd, by indubitable Proofs drawn from the Series of ‡ History Hitherto we have contended with obstinate and ignorant People, but now we have to do with Persons of a very great Reputation, and of a very profound Knowledge in History *Onuphrius Panvinius*, the Honour of the Order of St *Augustin*, having found that it is impossible to maintain the Opinion of those who ascribe the Institution of the Electoral College to *Gregory* V, and to *Otho* III, says, * That the Number of Electors was regulated as it was forty Years ago, in the thirteenth Century, from the Year 1250, to the Year 1280, that is to say, above two hundred and fifty Years after the Death of *O-
tho* III, and makes a last Effort to prove that the Honour of this Institution is due to Pope *Gregory* V But as his eminent Learning is accompany'd with a rare Sincerity, he acknowledges ingenuously that it is only a Conjecture, which he would not maintain against the Truth of History, in which he was not able to find in what Time, by whom, and in what Council or Diet the College of Electors was instituted to the Number of seven

Goldast gives us the Extract of an Ordinance publish'd at *Franckfort*, in the Year 1609, by the Emperor *Otho* IV, † in the Presence of *Hugo-
lin* Cardinal of *Ostia*, and of *Leo* Cardinal of *Sabin*, with the Consent of the fifty Princes who were present at his Election, importing that for the future the Empire should no longer be hereditary, but that the Emperor should be chosen by three Ecclesiastical Princes, to wit, by the Archbishops of *Mentz*, of *Triers*, and of *Cologn* , and by three secular Princes, to wit, the Count *Palatin* of the *Rhine*, the Duke of *Saxony*, and the Marquiss of *Brandenburg*, who, in case of an Equality of Votes, should call thereto the King of *Bohemia* *Trithemius*, Abbot of *Spanheim*, says, That at the Election of *William* of *Holland*, Successor of *Frederick* II, the seven Electors were present, and discharg'd the Functions of their respective Offices But as *Trithemius* is a very bad Warrant for what he says without Authority, we may say in Opposition to the Extract of this Ordinance or Constitution, which is no where produc'd, that it is only the Invention of his Brain who

† *Frederick* II ‡ Urspeig An 1210. ‡ Gewold in his Treatise De Septemviratu c 7.
* In his Treatise De Comitus c 9 † Seth Calvis Chronolog A 1209

utters

450 *Of the* ELECTION *of the* EMPEROR, *and*

utters it, and that there is no likelihood that an Emperor, who might have Children, would deprive them of the Hopes of succeeding him, and that fifty Princes, who had a Right to assist at the Elections, would dispossess themselves thereof, in Favour of a very small Number of them, to the Exclusion of the rest.

It is also certain, that in the subsequent Elections there is no Appearance of any Regulation. It is true, some Mention is begun to be made of Electors in the thirteenth Century, but that Quality was not as yet annex'd to the Principalities, and the Number was not yet fix'd. To represent this in a clear Light, we must put the Reader in Mind of what we said before, ‡ to wit, That the Duke of *Austria* was present at the second Election of the Emperor *Fredrick* II, which was perform'd in the Year 1210, and in the Quality of Elector. Now that no Doubt may be made hereof, it is requisite to know, that *Primislas* II, sirnam'd *Ottocarns*, King of *Bohemia*, having made himself Master of *Austria* (which he pretended belong'd to him in Right of his Wife, who was Daughter to *Leopold* VII, Duke of *Austria*, altho' he had poison'd her, and had no Children by her) maintain'd still, in the Time of the Emperor *Rodolphus* I, that is to say, above sixty Years after the Election of *Frederick* II, that he ought to have two Votes at the Election, one as King of *Bohemia*, and the other as Duke of *Austria*, and disputed it obstinately with *Henry* Duke of *Bavaria*, who maintain'd that the Electoral Dignity was annex'd to his Dutchy. It is true that the Emperor *Rodolphus* pronounc'd in favour of the Duke, by commanding the King of *Bohemia* to be contented with one Suffrage, but that does not hinder the Electoral Right from being still litigious at that Time. And the Emperor, in pronouncing in favour of *Bavaria*, confirms what we just now said, to wit, That the Number of Electors was not yet regulated, and that in allowing *Bavaria*, there must be at least eight, besides that the *Golden Bull* retrenches him absolutely.

* After the Death of *William*, the Princes of the Empire had several Assemblies about the Election, but not being able to agree, they at last fix'd a Day, and resolv'd to meet at *Franckfort* immediately after the *Epiphany*. The Archbishops of *Mentz* and of *Cologn*, *Lewis* Count Palatin of the *Rhine*, and his Brother *Henry* Duke of *Bavaria*, came thither and elected *Richard* Duke of *Cornwall*, Brother to *John* and *Henry* Kings of *England*. But the Archbishop of *Triers*, and some other Princes, not approving of this Election, met about the middle of *Lent*, and finding themselves authoriz'd by the Letters and Powers of the King of *Bohemia*, the Duke of *Saxony*, and of the Marquisses of *Brandenburg* and divers other Princes, they elected *Alphonsus* King of *Castile*. They are the very Words of *Henry Stero*, † a Monk of *Altaisch*, who liv'd in the Time of *Rodolphus* I, of *Adolphus* of *Nassau*, and of *Albert* I, Emperors, that is to say, much about the Time we are speaking of. Notwithstanding which, there does not appear any thing regulated concerning the Number of the Electors, since besides the Princes whom *Stero* does not name (tho' the Archbishop of *Triers* made use of their Powers) he names at least nine, to wit, the three Archbishops, two Princes of the House of *Bavaria* and *Saxony*, and at least two of the House of *Brandenburg*, since he speaks in the Plural Number.

‡ *Eberhard*, Archdeacon of *Ratisbone*, who liv'd at the same Time, and has written Annals of *Austria*, of *Suabia*, and of *Bavaria*, from the Year 1273, in which *Rodolphus* I was chosen, to that of 1305, * speaks almost in the same Terms, when he says, † That *Adolphus*, King of the *Romans*, being ready to enter with his Army into *France*, was hinder'd from doing so by the Archbishop of *Mentz*, by the King of *Bohemia*, by *Albert* Duke of *Saxon*, and by two Marquisses of *Brandenburg*, which is a sufficient Testimony, that, notwithstanding the Electoral Dignity began then to be secur'd to certain Families, the Number of Electors was not yet regulated.

We have very considerable Proofs hereof in what happen'd immediately before the Election of the Emperor *Charles* IV, Author of the *Golden Bull*. *Albert* of *Austria*, who succeeded to *Adolphus* of *Nassau*, being kill'd *May* 1, 1308, *Henry* ‡ of *Luxemburg* succeeded him. But forasmuch as History says nothing of the Particulars of his Election, we shall pass it by, and shall speak of that which was made by Schism, of *Lewis* Duke of *Bavaria*, and of *Frederick le Bel* Duke of *Austria*, Cousin Germans, and both Grandsons to the Emperor *Rodolphus* I. The Emperor *Henry* of *Luxemburg* being dead of Poison on *August* 24, 1313, there was an *Interregnum* of above a Year. At last two were chosen in the Year 1314, that is to say, above three hundred and twelve Years after the Death of *Otho* III. And nevertheless at these Elections were present at least nine Electors, viz. the three Ecclesiasticks, *Rodolphus* Count Palatin of the *Rhine*, and *Lewis* Duke of *Bavaria* his Brother, *John* of *Bohemia*, *Volmar* Marquiss of *Brandenburg*, *Rodolphus* the Son of *Albert* I Duke of *Saxony*, and *Erick* Son to *John* III Duke of the *Lower Saxony*.

But there is not any thing more convincing than what pass'd at the Election of * *Charles* IV, that is to say, immediately before the Publication of the *Golden Bull*. *Lewis* IV had preserv'd the Rights of the Empire with great Vigour against the Attempts of the Popes, who, on their part, had created him so many Enemies, that, in the Year 1346, some Princes proceeded to the Election of *Charles* of *Luxemburg*, Grandson to the Emperor *Henry* VII. But he could not so well establish himself, but, after the Death of *Lewis*, an Attempt was made to dispossess him of the Imperial Dignity. *Albert* of *Strasburg*, who liv'd at that Time, and who has written a Chronicle from the Reign of *Rodolphus* I to the Death of *Charles* IV, speaks thereof in such Terms, as will sufficiently make known, That the Number of Electors was not regulated

---

‡ In Chron preced.   * *Richard* of *Cornwall*, and *Alphonsus*   † In Chron An 1257   ‡ *Albert* I
* H. Canis has publish'd it, Tom 1 Antiq Lect   , In the Year 1259.   ‡ *Henry* VII   * *Charles* IV

of the ELECTORS of the EMPIRE. 451

regulated before the Publication of the *Golden Bull* He writes thus †
"After the Death of *Lewis* IV, *Henry* Archbishop of *Mentz*, *Lewis* Marquiss of *Brandenburg*, *Rupert* Count *Palatin* of the *Rhine*, as well for himself, as by virtue of the Power he had receiv'd from *Rodolphus*, and *Rupert* of *Bavaria*, his Cousins, and from *Eric* Duke of *Saxony*, who had likewise a Right to elect, because his Father was the eldest Son of *Rodolphus*, also Duke of *Saxony*, who had elected *Charles* IV, met in order to elect *Edward* King of *England*, who excusing himself on the Differences he had to decide with the King of *France*, they chose *Frederick* Marquiss of *Misnia*." And afterwards speaking of the Election of *Gunther* Count of *Suartzemburg*, he says, ‡ "That the Count consented to their Proceeding to the Election of his Person, provided that the Princes and Lords who were assembled at *Franckfort*, declar'd the Empire vacant, and that the major part of the Princes, who should be judg'd to have a Right to elect, should agree thereupon among themselves." So that four Princes, and a good Number of Lords being met, and having declar'd the Empire vacant, and that those four had a Right to elect, *Henry* of *Wirneburg* Archbishop of *Mentz*, *Lewis* Marquiss of *Brandenburg*, *Rodolphus* Duke of the *Rhine*, who was a Prisoner, and *Eric* Duke of *Saxony*, elected on the Day of the Purification *Gunther* Count of *Suartzemburg*." At the first Election was present *Rupert* Count *Palatin* of the *Rhine*, with Powers from *Rodolphus* and *Rupert* his Cousins At the second, *Rodolphus* elects, with the Consent of the two Ruperts Wherein we must observe, not only that two Princes of the same House, and of the same Branch, discharge the Functions of Elector, and assist at the Election in this Quality, but also that they have Power from the absent, who by that Means have a Share in the Electoral Dignity We even see two Electors in the House of *Saxony*, the one whereof chuses *Charles* IV, and the other *Edward* King of *England*, and *Gunther* Count of *Suartzemburg* From whence we must conclude that the Number of Electors was not yet regulated immediately before the Publication of the *Golden Bull*, and that this Regulation was very necessary to avoid Schisms, and to give Repose to the Empire of *Germany*

What we have now said is so notorious, that even those who refer the Institution of the College of Electors to the Emperor *Otho* III, and to Pope *Gregory* V, are forc'd to agree to a Truth which they are not able to contest We have seen above the Confession of Cardinal *Baronius* But, that no Advantage may be drawn therefrom, they say it is indeed true, that, before the Publication of the *Golden Bull*, all the Princes of the Empire were call'd to the Elections, but that they had no definitive Voice, and so only a Right of Presentation, or of Nomination, and not that of Election, which was reserv'd to the seven Electors, excluding all the other Princes of *Germany*, that is to say, That when all the Princes, as well Ecclesiasticks and Seculars, and even the Counts and Barons, were assembled, the seven Electors retir'd into a Chamber appointed for the Election, while the other Princes and Lords deliberated in another Apartment on the Nomination of one or more Persons, endow'd with all the Qualities necessary for this high Dignity, and that this Nomination being perform'd by a Plurality of Votes, the same was put into Writing, to be presented to the Electors, who afterwards examin'd among themselves, and in private, into the Merits of the Persons so nam'd, and elected him they thought the best qualify'd

They alledge for this a Passage out of *Roger* * *Hoveden*, which says, *That, after the Death of the Emperor, the Archbishops, Bishops, Abbots, Dukes, Counts, and other Lords, meet, and nominate twelve Persons, out of which Number they will have the Emperor chosen, and present them to the Archbishops of* Mentz *and of* Cologn, *to the Duke of* Saxony, *and the Count* Palatin, *so that he of the twelve so nominated, that is chosen by these four Princes, is Emperor* But who does not here see that *Hoveden* speaks like an *Englishman*, that is to say, like a Foreigner who has no Knowledge at all of the Affairs of *Germany*? He does not deserve we should reflect on what he says, because there is nothing like it in all the History of the Times, and we have instance'd in the contrary, when we spoke of the Election of the Emperor *Philip*, which was perform'd in the Time *Hoveden* speaks of We shall only take notice, that what he says signifies nothing to the Institution of the Electoral College by *Otho* III, or *Gregory* V, inasmuch as he reduces the Electors to four in Number, and excludes therefrom the Archbishop of *Triers*, the King of *Bohemia*, and the Marquiss of *Brandenburg*

We shall therefore oppose his Testimony with that of *Matthew Paris*, who liv'd almost at the same Time, and who being of the Council of *Richard* Duke of *Cornwall*, who was call'd to the Empire after the Death of *William* of *Holland*, might have an Insight into the Affairs of *Germany*, which the other had not Speaking of the Election of *Richard*, he says, † "The chief Lords, on whom depends the Election of the King of the *Romans*, the future Emperor, are the Archbishop of *Cologn*, the Archbishop of *Mentz*, the Archbishop of *Triers*, the King of *Bohemia*, the Count *Palatin* of the *Rhine*, the Duke of *Austria*, the Duke of *Poland*, the Marquiss of *Miche*, the Marquiss of *Brandenburg*, the Duke of *Saxony*, the Duke of *Brunswick*, the Duke of *Carinthia*, the Duke of *Melay*, the Duke of *Brabant*, who is also Duke of *Lovain*, the Lantgrave of *Thuringia*, and the Marquiss of *Misnia*" It is true, it may be said of him what we said above of *Roger Hoveden*, that is to say, That he does not treat of foreign Affairs with the same Exactness he brings to the History of *England*, but yet we may gather from him this certain Truth, That in his Time, that is to say, about fifty Years after that of *Hoveden*, there was no Talk of four Electors,

‡ An 1348 pag 145 Tom 2 of *Ursic* † An 1349 pag 150
* *Cap Defuncto itaq, Imper Annal narre post* 776 ‡ An 1257 *sub Henrico* III *Anglia Rege*

nor

nor of the Electoral College, in the State it is now in.

Simon Schardius, Counsellor to *Wolfgang-William*, Duke of *Newburg*, who has written a Treatise of the Electors, to which he has given the Title *De Septemviratu*, with a Design to shew that they were instituted in the Time of *Gregory* V, and of *Otho* III, says, That he has a Cannon, with which he can batter all the Arguments that can be objected to this pretended Institution, and alledges for this Purpose the Canon *Venerabilem extr de Electo & Electi potest* and particularly these Words of Pope *Innocent*, *Jus Principum nobis noluimus vendicare, verum illis Principibus, jus & potestatem Eligendi Regem in Imperatorem promovendum, recognoscimus, ad quos de Jure, & antiqua Consuetudine, noscimus pertinere*, that is to say, That so far are we from being inclin'd to usurp the Right of the Electors, that on the contrary we acknowledge that it belongs to those who actually possess it with a good Title, and from all Antiquity. But Cardinal *Baronius* answers for us in the Place we have before quoted, ‡ and says, That they who believe that the Pope here means the seven Electors, are mistaken, it being certain that in his Time all the Princes of *Germany* were Electors. And in Reality it is impossible to draw from those Words any Consequence for the *Septemviratu*, for, that it may not be thought the Pope speaks of seven Electors, we must see what the same Pope says elsewhere, to wit, That the Princes of *Germany*, who are not Electors, are the King of *Bohemia*, the Duke of *Lorrain*, the Duke of *Brunswick*, the Duke of *Suabia*, the Lantgrave of *Thuringia*, the Duke of *Limbourg*, the Duke of *Carinthia*, the Duke of *Saxony*, and the Duke of *Gueldres*. That the Secular Electoral Princes are the Duke of *Austria*, the Duke of *Bavaria*, the Duke of the *Saxons*, the Duke of *Brabant*, and of *Lovain*, and that the Prelates are the Archbishops of *Mentz*, of *Cologn*, and of *Saltzbourg*.

He says expressly, that the King of *Bohemia* and the Duke of *Saxony* are not Electors, and that the Archbishop of *Saltzbourg*, the Dukes *Austria*, of *Bavaria*, of *Suabia* and of *Brabant* are, there being no room to reproach him with Ignorance in the Affairs of *Germany*, for his excluding from the Election, the King of *Bohemia*, and the Duke of *Saxony*, so as to render his Testimony invalid. For besides that in his Time there were several Dukes of *Saxony*, some of whom began to be excluded from the Election, while the others maintain'd their Right, as appears by the same Passage, where he puts the Duke of the *Saxons* in the Number of the Electors, it may be said, that the Electoral Dignity was not as yet annex'd to the Kingdom of *Bohemia*, and that it was not so, till the Declaration the Emperor *Rodolphus* I made on that Account in favour of *Wenceslas*, his Son-in-law, as we shall make it appear elsewhere, when we shall speak of the King of *Bohemia* in particular. We indeed acknowledge that there is some Contradiction to be found between *Innocent* IV, and *Matthew Paris*, but it is sufficient for us to shew, that they agree in this, that they make the Number of Electors much greater than it is at present.

Cardinal *Bellarmin*, who has compos'd a Treatise, *De Translatione Imperii*, against *Flaccius Illyricus*, who had written one on the same Subject, considering that the Authority of *Martinus Polonus*, who is the first that has written of the Institution of the seven Electors, *Gregory* V, is not of Force enough to be oppos'd to that of Pope *Innocent* his Master. That the Book, *De Regimine Principum*, which is ascrib'd to *Thomas Aquinas*, is supposititious, and that the Testimonies of modern Authors cannot be compar'd with the Truth gather'd from the Particulars of History, he explains himself, and as if he had liv'd six hundred Years ago, pronounces confidently, and as if he had the Original of the pretended Ordinance of *Gregory* V by him, says, * That the Decree of *Gregory* contain'd four Points. First, That he made the Empire, which till then had been hereditary, elective. Secondly, That he took away the Right of Election from the People, who enjoy'd it before, in Concurrence with the Prelates and Princes. Thirdly, That he excluded from the Election the *Italians*, who had a Share therein before. And, Fourthly, That he reduc'd the Number of the Electors, which was before confus'd and uncertain, to that of Seven. To all which he adds, That this Ordinance of *Gregory* was very punctually executed, immediately after the Death of *Otho* III, in reference to the three first Points, but as to the Fourth, to wit, the Reduction of the Electors to the Number of Seven, it was not so, by reason of the Opposition made by the other Princes.

But this Shift destroys it self in this, That as to the first Point it makes the Empire hereditary to the Time of *Gregory*. And as to the Second and Third, the Cardinal confesses that before the Publication of this pretended Ordinance, the People, and even that of *Italy*, had a Share in the Election. Now if it was hereditary, how could the People elect? And if it was elective, how can the first Point subsist? Besides that the Third is directly contrary to the Truth of History, since we have made it appear above, that the *Italians* were present at several posterior Elections, and particularly at those of *Conrade* II, and of *Frideric* I. And as for the fourth Point, which *Bellarmin* confesses was not executed, we think that this ingenuous Confession makes altogether for the Opinion which we establish, since by owning that all the other Princes oppos'd the Reduction to the Number of Seven, and that in effect the Right of electing remain'd common to all, he ought to produce the Ordinance it self, or at least alledge some contemporary Author who makes mention of it. But forasmuch as we find a profound Silence therein for above two hundred Years after the Death of *Otho*, without any Author's speaking of the Electors, and still less of the Ordinance of *Gregory*, we think we may take Advantage therefrom, and absolutely deny that *Gregory* V, and *Otho* III, regulated the Number of the Electors, and may be bold to say, that it was not so, till the Time of the Emperor *Charles* IV

‡ *Chap.* V.   * Lib 3 cap 2

CHAP.

CHAP. VII.

The Golden Bull.

What we have said in the foregoing Chapters, only serves for a Preliminary to the Treatise of the Election, and of the Electors, which being grounded chiefly on the *Golden Bull*, we have thought it proper to insert it here at length, as being in a manner the sole Foundation of all we shall treat of hereafter

IN the Name of the holy and undivided Trinity Amen CHARLES, by the Grace of God, Emperor of the *Romans*, always August, and King of *Bohemia*, to all present and to come

That Kingdom that is divided in it self shall be desolate, for its Princes have made themselves Accomplices of Robbers And it is for that Reason that God has sent amongst them the Spirit of Stupefaction, that they may go groping their way when the Sun is in its Meridian, as if they walk'd in a profound Darkness, and he has taken from them their Lights, that they may become blind themselves, and Leaders of the Blind They who travel in Darkness stumble, and they who are blind in their Understanding sow Division and Enmity, the sole Springs of all other Wickedness Say, Prince, how would'st thou have reign'd in *Lucifer*, if thou hadst not call'd Dissension to thy Assistance? Say, *Satan*, how thou would'st have driven *Adam* from *Paradise*, if thou had'st not debauch'd him from the Obedience which he ow'd to his Creator Say, Anger, how could'st thou have ruin'd the *Roman* Empire, if Division had not arm'd *Pompey* against *Cæsar*, and if it had not fill'd the whole Empire with Civil Wars? Say, Luxury, how thou would'st have destroy'd the City of *Troy*, it Dissension had not ravish'd *Helen* from her Husband? And thou, Envy, how many times hast thou us'd thy utmost Efforts, to try to ruin this Empire, which God has founded on these three theological Virtues, Faith, Hope and Charity, as on a holy and undivided Trinity, by sowing, as the old Serpent did, the Venom of Dissension among the Electors? Among the Electors, I say, who are the Supporters and Buttresses of that Structure, the main Branches, and chief Members of the Empire, who like seven Flambeaus ought to give it Light and Splendor, by the Union of their Minds and Sentiments, and by a perfect good Understanding amongst themselves Wherefore finding our selves oblig'd to hinder these Disorders from happening for the future, as well on the Account of the Imperial Dignity with which we are invested, as of the Electoral which we enjoy as King of *Bohemia*, after having caus'd this Affair to be maturely deliberated in our Court or solemn Diet assembl'd at *Nurembourg*, where were present all the Electors, as well Ecclesiasticks as Seculars, and several other Princes, Counts, Barons, Lords, Gentlemen and Deputies of Free-Towns, by the Advice of whom, and by our full Power, and Imperial Authority, being seated in the Throne of the Empire, cloth'd with the Imperial Robes, and having the Imperial Crown on our Head, and holding the Ornaments in our Hands We have publish'd the present Edict, and have thought fit to prevent by the following Laws, those Disorders and Dissensions, which might for the future disturb the Tranquillity of the Empire Given in the Year of Grace, One Thousand Three Hundred Fifty Six Indict IX *January* 10 Of our Reign the Tenth, and of our Empire the First

CHAPTER I

Of the Safe-conduct of the Electors, and by whom they ought to be guarded

§ 1 WE therefore will and ordain, by this perpetual and irrevocable Edict, of our certain Knowledge, and full Imperial Power, that whenever there shall be Occasion for the Election of a King of the *Romans*, future Emperor, and that according to the ancient and laudable Custom, the Princes Electors shall set out, in order to repair to the Place of the Election, the Electors, through whose Countries the other Electors or their Deputies shall have Occasion to pass, being well and duly requir'd thereto, shall be oblig'd to conduct them safely through the Countries under their Jurisdiction and Obedience, or farther if it be necessary, and to give them a Safe-conduct without any Fraud, to the Place of the Election, as well going as coming, under the Penalty of being perjur'd, and of losing their Vote and Suffrage, and the Share they should have had in the Election, for that Time only, without any need of other Declaration than the present, against those who in this shall have shewn themselves negligent, or Rebels

§ 2 We also ordain, and give notice to all the other Princes who hold of the Empire, of what Quality or Condition they may be, as also to all Counts, Barons, Vassals and Subjects, as well Nobles as Plebeians, to the Inhabitants and Communities of Towns, Burroughs, and Places of the Empire, under the Penalties hereafter express'd, That they guard, and give Safe-conduct to the Electors, or to the Deputies they shall send to the Election, through their Countries and Territories, or farther if possible, without any Fraud And for default in doing this, the said Counts, Barons, Vassals, and noble Subjects, as Perjurers, shall be depriv'd not only of the Fiefs they hold of the Empire, but also of all their other Estates, of what Quality soever they may be And as for the Inhabitants and Communities of Towns, they shall not only forfeit all their Privileges, Liberties,

Immunities and Favours they hold of the Empire, but shall also be deem'd proscrib'd Perjurers, and put in the Ban of the Empire, as in such Case we from this present put them, as well as then permitting all our Subjects in general, and each of them in particular, to fall upon them, and to attack, offend and injure the Proscrib'd, without having need for this Effect to obtain any Permission from the Judicature, or that in such Case the Aggressor need to apprehend any Punishment on the part of the Empire, which is far from revenging those, who like Perjurers, Rebels, disobedient and perfidious Wretches, shall have been so audacious as to disturb the Repose of the State, and to offend the Dignity of the Empire.

§ 3. We ordain and give notice to all the Inhabitants and Communities of Towns, that they sell to the Electors, or to the Deputies they shall send to the Election, as well going as coming, at a reasonable Rate, those Provisions they shall have occasion for, as well for themselves as for those of their Retinue. And all this without Fraud, and under the same Penalties.

§ 4. If any Prince, Count, Baron, Vassal and Subject, Noble or Plebeian, Inhabitant or Community of a Town is temerarious enough to undertake or attempt any thing against the Electors or their Deputies, going or coming, to offend them in their Persons, or in their Retinue and Attendants, he shall be subject to the same Penalties.

§ 5. If it happens that an Elector has a Quarrel with some of his Collegues, their Difference shall not hinder them (upon being requir'd thereto) from giving him the necessary Safe-conduct, under the Penalty of losing their Votes in the Election for that time only, as we said before.

§ 6. In like Manner, if the other Princes, Counts, Barons, Officers and Vassals, Nobles or Plebeians, Inhabitants and Communities of Towns, have a Quarrel, or are at War amongst themselves, or with any one of the Electors, yet they shall not fail of giving the necessary Safe-conduct, if they will avoid the Penalties with which this present Edict threatens them.

§ 7. And to the End this our Will may be executed in every Point, we will and ordain, That the Princes, Counts, Barons, Gentlemen, Towns and Communities, give for this Effect, their Letters sign'd and seal'd in good Form, and that they oblige themselves by Oath not to contravene the same, in any Manner whatever, ordaining the same Penalties against those, who shall refuse to give their Letters in good Form.

§ 8. It it happens that an Elector, or other Prince, holding of the Empire, of what Quality or Condition soever he may be, Count, Baron, or their Heirs or Successors, holding Fiefs of the Empire, refuses to obey our Laws and Constitutions. If he be an Elector, the other Princes his Collegues shall expel him their College, and shall deprive him of his Vote, and Electoral Dignity, and of the Fiefs he holds of the Empire. And if it be any other Prince or Lord, not only he shall be refus'd the Investiture of his Fiefs, but he shall also be declar'd subject to the Penalties before-mention'd.

§ 9. Now notwithstanding our Will is to oblige to this Safe-conduct, indifferently, all Princes, Counts, Barons, Gentlemen, and Communities, yet we have thought fit to assign to each Elector particular Safe-conducts, Escorts, and Convoyes, according to the Places and Territories through which they are to pass, in the following manner.

§ 10. First, The King of *Bohemia*, Great Cup-bearer of the Empire, shall be conducted by the Archbishop of *Mentz*, and by the Bishops of *Bamberg* and of *Wurtzbourg*, by the Burgraves of *Nurembourg*, by the Counts of *Hohenlo*, of *Wertheim*, of *Bruneck* and of *Hanau*, and by the Towns of *Nuremberg*, of *Rotembourg* on the *Tauber*, and of *Winsheim*.

§ 11. The Archbishop of *Cologn*, Great Chancellor of the Empire in *Italy*, shall be conducted by the Archbishops of *Mayence* and of *Triers*, by the Count *Palatin*, by the Lantgrave of *Hesse*, by the Counts of *Catznetlebogen*, of *Nassau*, of *Dietz*, of *Isembourg*, of *Westerbourg*, of *Runkel*, of *Limbourg* and of *Falkenstein* and by the Towns of *Wetzlar*, *Gelnhausen* and *Fn. slar*.

§ 12. The Archbishop of *Triers*, Great Chancellor of the Empire amongst the *Gauls*, and in the Kingdom of *Arles*, shall be conducted by the Archbishop of *Mentz*, and by the Count *Palatin*, by the Counts of *Spanheim*, *Veldentz*, *Catznellebogen*, *Nassau*, *Dietz*, *Isembourg*, *Westerbourg*, *Runkel*, *Falkenstien*, *Eppenstein*, and by the Town of *Mentz*.

§ 13. The Count *Palatin* of the *Rhine*, High Steward of the Empire, shall be conducted by the Archbishop of *Mentz*.

§ 14. The Duke of *Saxony*, Great Mareschal of the Empire, shall be conducted by the King of *Bohemia*, by the Archbishops of *Mentz* and of *Magdebourg*, by the Bishops of *Bamberg* and of *Wurtzbourg*, by the Marquiss of *Misnia*, by the Lantgrave of *Hesse*, by the Abbots of *Fuld* and of *Hirtsfelt*, by the Burggraves of *Nuremberg*, by the Counts of *Hohenlo*, of *Wertheim*, of *Bruneck*, of *Hanau* and of *Falkenstein*, and by the Towns of *Erfort*, *Mulhausen*, *Nuremberg*, *Rotembourg* on the *Tauber*, and of *Wertheim*.

§ 15. All those we have now nam'd, shall all conduct together with the Elector of *Saxony*, the Marquiss of *Brandenbourg*, Great Chamberlain of the Empire.

§ 16. Our Will is, and we ordain very expressly, That whosoever of the Electors shall have a mind to make use of these Escorts and Safe-conducts, shall make it duly known to those from whom he would require them, and signify to them what Road he intends to take, to the End, that they who shall be nominated for such Convoy or Safe-conduct, may have due Time to prepare themselves for the same.

§ 17. However what we have now said of Safe-conducts ought to be so understood, that they whom we have mention'd, and all the others, shall not be oblig'd to give any Escort or Safe conduct, except on their own Territories, and within their own Countrey, and so far as they can do it conveniently, and no further, the whole without Fraud.

§ 18. It is also our Will, and we ordain, that the Archbishop of *Mentz* for the Time being, shall send Expresses to all the other Electors his

his Collegues, and shall invite 'em to assist at the Election by his Letters Patents, which shall express and name the Day on which the said Letters in all Likelihood may be deliver'd to them, to the end that in three Months, reckoning from the said Day, they may repair in Person, or else send their Deputies to *Francfort* on the *Main*, provided with a good Procuration sign'd with their Hand, and seal'd, in order to proceed to the Election of a King of the *Romans*, future Emperor. Now what these Letters ought to be, and in what Terms are to be conceiv'd the Procuration and Powers of the Embassadors, or Deputies the Electors shall think fit to send to the Election, is what shall be explain'd hereafter, when we shall speak of the Form we require should be observ'd therein.

§ 19 And the said Archbishop of *Mentz* shall be oblig'd to summon by his Letters Patents the other Electors his Collegues, within a Month after he shall be inform'd of the Death of the Emperor, which if he does not do, the other Electors may, and shall be oblig'd by virtue of the Oath they have taken to the Empire, to meet at *Francfort* within the first three Months following, in order to proceed there to the Election of a King of the *Romans*, future Emperor, as we have said above.

§ 20 And each Elector or his Embassador, shall not enter the Town of *Francfort* but with the Retinue of two hundred Horse only, amongst whom he may have fifty Men at Arms and no more.

§ 21 That Elector, who after having been duly summon'd and invited to the Election of a King of the *Romans*, future Emperor, shall refuse or neglect to come thither, or to send his Embassadors or Deputies, provided with a good Procuration sign'd and seal'd in good Form, or who being come to the Place, or having sent thither his Deputies, if he or they leave the Town before the Election is executed, he shall for that Time lose the Vote and Share he had there.

§ 22 We command the Magistrates and Inhabitants of the said Town of *Francfort*, and signify to them to take into their Protection all the said Electors, as well in general as every of them in particular, and the ones against the others, in case of any Difference or Quarel amongst them, and this towards and against all, as well their Persons as their Domesticks, compris'd in the Number of two hundred which we have assign'd them. And this by the Oath which we ordain them to take for this effect on the holy Gospels. And in case they fail therein, we declare them from this present Time, as well as then, Perjurers and Traitors, and as such to have forfeited all the Rights, Privileges and Immunities which they hold, or may hold of the Empire, proscribing them, and putting them in the Ban of the Empire and as such we expose them to the Discretion of the first Comer, to be with Impunity attack'd, injur'd and kill'd as Traitors, perfidious and unfaithful to the Empire, without the Aggressor's being liable to be punish'd or accountable to Justice for the same. Likewise the Inhabitants of the said Town of *Francfort* shall not suffer any Stranger, unless he be of the Retinue of the Electors to enter into the Town during the whole Time of the Election, of what Condition or Quality soever he may be. And if there is found any other Stranger in the Town, besides the Number of two hundred, of which the Retinue of the Electors ought to be compos'd, the said Inhabitants shall be oblig'd by virtue of the Oath they have taken to the Empire, and of that which we command them to take expressly for that, to make him depart thence immediately and without Delay.

CHAP II
Of the Election of the King of the Romans

§ 1 After that the Electors, or their Deputies, shall be come to *Francfort*, they shall not fail to repair the very next Day in the Morning to the Church of Saint *Bartholomew*, where they shall cause to be said in their Presence a Mass to invoke the Holy Ghost, to the end that the same Holy Ghost, illuminating their Minds, and strengthening them with his Grace, they may be able to make Choice of a good and just Prince, and worthy to be elected King of the *Romans*, future Emperor, for the Good of all *Christendom*. After that the Mass shall be ended, the the Electors, follow'd by their Attendants, but without Arms, shall march up to the Altar, on which Mass shall have been said, and there shall take the Oath on the Gospel of St *John*, *In principio erat Verbum*, which shall be laid before them, the Ecclesiasticks by putting their Hand on their Stomach, and the Seculars by actually touching the Gospel. The Archbishop of *Mentz* shall present to them the Form of the Oath, which he shall take with them, and they or their Deputies with him, much after this manner.

§ 2 "I Marquiss of *Brandenburg*, Great "Chamberlain of the Empire, Prince Ele- "ctor, do swear on the holy Gospels put "here effectually before me, by the Faith I "owe to God, and by the Oath I have ta- "ken to the holy Empire, that by the Help "of God, with all my Understanding, and "all the Force of my Judgment, I will chuse "for the temporal Head of *Christendom*, "that is to say, for King of the *Romans*, "future Emperor, him I shall judge in my "Conscience to be most worthy thereof, and "I promise oh the same Faith, that I will give "my Vote and Suffrage in the said Election, "without any Hope of Profit, Pension, Pro- "mise or particular Interest. So help me God, "and all his Saints.

§ 3 After the Electors, and the Embassadors of those absent, shall have taken the Oath in the Form above mention'd, they shall go no more out of the Town of *Francfort*, nor shall not separate till the Election be ended, and till they have chosen a temporal Head to the World, or to *Christendom*, to wit, a King of the *Romans*, future Emperor. And if they do not perform the same within a Month, to reckon from the Day they shall have taken the Oath, they shall have no other Food but Bread and Water. And we very expressly forbid

456   *Of the* ELECTION *of the* EMPEROR, *and*

bid them to go out of the said Town of *Francfort*, till they all, or the major part of them, shall have chosen a temporal Head to *Christendom*, that is to say, a King of the *Romans*, future Emperor

§ 4 The Election which shall have been made by the Consent of the major part of the Electors, and by a Plurality of Votes, shall be of the same Force as if it been made by all of them unanimously. Likewise if any one of the Electors, or his Embassadors or Deputies shall come to *Francfort* after the Election shall be begun, they shall be admitted, the Election remaining in the same State it shall be in at the Time of their Arrival

§ 5 And forasmuch as by an ancient and laudable Custom it has been so at all Times inviolably observ'd, it is also our Will, and we ordain by our full Power, that for the time to come, he who shall be so chosen King of the *Romans*, shall be oblig'd to confirm to the Electors, as to the chief Members of the Empire, all the Rights, Privileges, Liberties, Favours, Exemptions, Dignities and Advantages which they hold of the holy Empire, which they enjoy, and shall have enjoy'd till then, and this without any Delay or put off, immediately after his Election, and before he can be capable of meddling with the Administration of the Affairs of the Empire And this the elected King of the *Romans* shall be oblig'd to confirm to them by his Letters Patents, sign'd and seal'd in good Form, immediately after he shall be crown'd Emperor

§ 6 Which Confirmation shall be made by the Elect, to each of the Electors in particular, in the Quality of King of the *Romans*, and afterwards shall be by him renew'd in the Quality of Emperor, promising that he will give them no Trouble or Lett in the Functions of their Dignities, or in the Enjoyment of their Rights, Privileges and Preheminences, but on the contrary will generously maintain them therein

§ 7 Finally, we ordain, that in case three Electors present, or the Deputies or Embassadors of the absent, give their Vote and Suffrage to any one of their Collegues to elect him King of the *Romans*, the Vote of the fourth, if he be there in Person, or that of his Embassador in his Absence, shall have the same Force and Virtue as that of the others, shall augment the Number of the Chusers, and effect that Plurality which is necessary for the Election

---

CHAP III
Of the Place of the Archbishops of Triers, Cologn *and* Mayence.

IN *the Name of the holy and undivided Trinity Amen*

CHARLES, by the Grace of God, Emperor of the *Romans*, always August, and King of *Bohemia*, to all present and to come

§ 1 The Glory and Majesty of the Empire, the Honour of the Emperor, and the State it self subsists but by the Union and good Understanding between the venerable and illustrious Princes Electors, who like Buttresses support that sacred Structure by the ingenious Piety of their Prudence, by which they strengthen the Power of the Imperial Arm So that the closer the Knot of their mutual Friendship is knit, the firmer is the Peace of *Christendom*, and the more secure and unshakeable

§ 2 Therefore to remove and take away for ever all Subject of Quarrel and Jealousy which might arise amongst the venerable Archbishops of *Mentz*, of *Triers*, and of *Cologn*, on the Score of Precedency in the Royal and Imperial Courts, and to the end, living in a good Understanding among themselves, they may with one Heart labour to promote the Good of the State, and apply all their Thoughts to the Affairs of the Empire, for the Consolation of all *Christendom*, we have, by the Advice and Counsel of all the Electors, as well Ecclesiasticks as Seculars, ordain'd and determin'd, and do ordain and determine by this present Edict, which is to be perpetual and irrevocable, that the Reverend the Archbishops abovenam'd shall take their Places as follows, to wit, that of *Triers* over-against the Emperor, that of *Mayence* within his Diocese and Province, and even out of his Province, within the whole Extent of his Chancery, except within the Province of *Cologn* only, on the Right Hand of the Emperor, as in like manner the Archbishop of *Cologn* shall have it within his Province, and out of his Province all over *Italy* and amongst the *Gauls* and this in all publick Actions and Ceremonies, as Judgments, Conferences, Collations, and Investitures of Fiefs, Entertainments, Councils, and in all other Assemblies where they shall be present about the Affairs of the Empire And it is our Will that this Order of Place be observ'd amongst the said Archbishops of *Triers*, *Cologn*, and *Mayence*, and between their Successors perpetually, and it shall not be in the Power of any Person or Persons whatever to change or alter the same, for any Cause or Occasion whatsoever

---

CHAP IV
Of the Princes Electors in General

§ 1 WE ordain also that in all the Imperial Courts, or Assemblies, where the Emperor and the Princes shall be present in Person, as well in Council as at Table, the King of *Bohemia*, as a Prince crown'd and sacred, shall take Place immediately after the Archbishop, who, according to the Place where the Assembly shall be held, shall be seated on the Right Hand of the Emperor, by virtue of this present Ordinance And after him on the same side shall sit the Count *Palatin* of the *Rhine* On the Left Hand, and immediately after the Archbishop, who shall be on that side, the Duke of *Saxony* shall take Place, and after him the Marquiss of *Brandenburg*

§ 2 The

of the ELECTORS of the EMPIRE.

§ 2. The Archbishop of *Mentz* shall have Power and Right, as he has at all Times had it, to call together his Collegues whenever the Empire shall become vacant. In like manner none but the said Archbishop only shall have Power to put Things to the Vote, collect the Suffrages, and ask the Opinions in the following manner.

§ 3. First he shall ask the Opinion of the Archbishop of *Triers*, who shall have the first Vote, according to what has been it all Times practis'd in this respect. After that he shall ask that of the Archbishop of *Cologn*, whose Office it is to crown the King of the *Romans*. The King of *Bohemia* shall vote in the third Place, as being the first of the Secular Electors, on the account of his Regal Dignity. The Count Palatin of the *Rhine* shall have the fourth Vote. The fifth shall belong to the Duke of *Saxony*, and the sixth to the Marquis of *Brandenburg*. This being done, the other Princes Electors shall in their Turn ask the Archbishop of *Majence* his Vote and Suffrage.

§ 4. We also ordain that at the Ceremonies of the Imperial Court, the Marquis of *Brandenburg* shall give the Emperor, or the King of the *Romans*, Water to wash with. The King of *Bohemia* shall serve him when he would drink the first Time, it being left to his Choice to do the same with the Royal Crown on his Head or not, and the Duke of *Saxony* shall do his Office as he has been us'd to do.

CHAP V.

Of the Right of the Count Palatin of the Rhine, and of the Duke of Saxony.

§ 1. WHen the Empire shall happen to be vacant, the illustrious Count *Palatin*, High Steward of the holy Empire, shall be Vicar of the Empire in *Suabia*, in *Franconia*, and on the *Rhine*, on the account of his Principality, or by virtue of the Privilege particularly belonging to the *Palatinate*, with Power to administer Justice, to nominate to Benefices, to receive the Revenue of the Empire, to counterfeits, and to receive Fealty and Homage in the Name of the Emperor, except those Fiefs, the Investiture whereof is given with the Standard, which therefore we reserve to the Emperor only, or to the King of the *Romans* to whom also of Obligation shall be renew'd the Loyalty and Homage which shall have been made to the Vicar during the *Interregnum*. Forbidding nevertheless very expressly the said Count *Palatin*, to alienate or mortgage any thing belonging to the Empire, during the Time of his Vicarship.

§ 2. It is also our Will that the illustrious Duke of *Saxony*, Great Marshal, do enjoy the same Right of Vicarship in those Countries where the *Saxon* Law takes place, in the same manner, and on the same Conditions above mention'd.

§ 3. And altho' by a very ancient Custom the King of the *Romans* or the Emperor be oblig'd to be accountable to the Law, and to answer before the Count *Palatin* High Steward and Prince Elector of the holy Empire, yet the Count *Palatin* shall not exercise this Jurisdiction, unless it be in a Diet or Imperial Court where the Emperor or King of the *Romans* is personally present.

CHAP VI.

Of the Comparison of the Electors with the other Princes.

WE ordain that in all the Ceremonies and publick Assemblies of the Empire, the said Princes Electors, as well Ecclesiasticks as Seculars, shall be seated in the manner, and according to the Order above prescrib'd, and that no other Prince, of what Dignity, State, Condition or Quality soever he may be, shall pretend to any Precedency there. We ordain particularly in reference to the King of *Bohemia*, that he shall precede, without any Contestation, all the other Kings and Princes how powerful and considerable soever they may be, and whatever be the Cause that obliges them to be present at the Diets and publick and general Assemblies of the Empire.

CHAP VII.

Of the Succession of the Princes.

§ 1. AMidst the many Applications we bestow on the Affairs of the Empire, there is not any that affords us more Labour than that we employ Night and Day for the Preservation of Peace and a good Understanding between the Princes Electors, because we know that we cannot make use of their Prudence in the Administration of the Affairs of the Empire, if we do not remove from them all Subjects of Hatred and Rancour amongst themselves, which we propose to do by declaring and justifying the Rights of every one of them.

§ 2. Indeed it is manifest and notorious to all the World, and there is no body who does not know that the illustrious King of *Bohemia*, the Count Palatin of the *Rhine*, the Duke of *Saxony*, and the Marquiss of *Brandenburg* have a Right of Vote and Place at the Election of the King of the *Romans*, future Emperor, by virtue of their Reign, and of their Principalities, as well as the Ecclesiastical Electors their Collegues, with whom they are reputed, and are in effect true and lawful Princes Electors of the holy Empire. Now that for the time to come there may happen no Scandal or Division among the Children of the said Secular Princes Electors, and that the publick Welfare and Tranquillity may not be in Danger of being disturb'd or retarded, we have been willing to remove the Cause thereof by this perpetual and irrevocable Edict, and for this purpose we ordain that the said Secular Electors, or any one of them happening

6 A to

to dye, the Right, Vote and Power of Election shall belong, without any Difficulty or Contestation, to his eldest Son, who shall be lawfully born, and a Layman, and in Default of him to his next Brother, who shall be, as we said before, lawfully begotten, and a Layman And if it shall happen that the said eldest Son dyes without Issue lawfully begotten, the Right, Vote and Power of Election shall belong, by virtue of the present Edict to his Brother by the Father's Side in a direct and lawful Line And it is our Will that this Succession of the eldest Sons be inviolably observ'd for ever among the Heirs of the Electors, yet so nevertheless, that in case the said Prince Elector or his eldest Son happens to dye, leaving Children in the State of Minority, the eldest of the Brothers of such Elector, or of such eldest Son, shall be Guardian and Administrator of the young Elector, till he has attain'd the Age of eighteen Years complete, and then the Guardian or Administrator shall be oblig'd to surrender immediately and without delay, to his Pupil, the Right of Election, which he shall have enjoy'd till then

§ 3 And if it shall happen that any of the Principalities come to be vacant, to the Profit of the Empire, the Emperor, or the King of the *Romans*, may dispose thereof, as of a thing escheated to him, and to the holy Empire, without Prejudice however to the Rights, Priviledges, and Customs, which our Kingdom of *Bohemia* has obtain'd from the Emperors our Predecessors, by virtue of which, the Inhabitants of our said Kingdom may chuse to themselves a King when the Kingdom shall be vacant Neither do we pretend to prejudice those Rights, but, on the contrary, we understand and will, very expressly, that our said Kingdom be maintain'd therein, and that its Priviledges be preserv'd in every Point, according to their Form and Tenour

CHAP VIII

Of the Exemption of the King of Bohemia, and of the Inhabitants of the said Kingdom

AND forasmuch as by a Priviledge which the Emperors and Kings, our Predecessors, have granted to the Illustrious Kings of *Bohemia*, our Ancestors and Predecessors, to the Kingdom and Crown of *Bohemia*, as also it has been there practis'd in all Times, without this Custom being interrupted by any Action, or Custom to the contrary, that no Prince, Baron, Gentleman, Soldier, Vassal, Burgess, or other Inhabitant of that Kingdom, of what Condition or Quality soever he may be, can for any Cause, or under any Pretext whatever, be cited before any other Judge than before the King of *Bohemia*: We, being minded to renew the said Grant and Priviledge, do ordain, of our full Imperial Power, by this perpetual and irrevocable Constitution, that, if notwithstanding that Priviledge, any Prince, Baron, Nobleman, Vassal, Burgess or Peasant, is summon'd out of the Kingdom for any Cause whatever, civil or criminal, he shall not be deem'd lyable to such Jurisdiction, or to appear either in Person or by his Attorney And if it shall happen that the foreign Judge, not residing within the Kingdom, shall proceed in such Cause to a Sentence interlocutory or definitive, it is our Will, and we ordain by our full Imperial Power, that all Defaults and Orders, issu'd out by such Judges, as also the Sentences and Executions, shall be declar'd null, and that it shall not be allowable by virtue of those Sentences to execute or attempt any thing to the Prejudice of the present Priviledge We likewise very expressly forbid all Princes, Barons, Nobles, Vassals, Burgesses, Peasants, and all other Persons, of what Condition or Quality soever they may be, to appeal from the Decrees or Sentences, interlocutory or definitive, given by the king or his Judges, on Pain of Nullity, or Loss of their Cause

CHAP IX

Of Mines of Gold, Silver, and other Mettals

WE ordain also, and declare, by this perpetual and irrevocable Edict, by the same Imperial Power, and of our certain Knowledge, that our Successors Kings of *Bohemia*, and all the other Electors, as well Ecclesiasticks as Seculars, may possess all the Mines of Gold, Silver, Tinn, Copper, Brass, Lead, and of all other Mettals, as also all the Salt-Pits already discover'd, and that shall be hereafter discover'd, as well in our said Kingdom, and the Provinces thereunto annex'd, as in the Territories and Principalities of the other Princes Electors, without their being oblig'd to pay any Duties for the same, in any manner or way whatever They may also receive the Duties and Customs which are already establish'd, and harbour the Jews, as the Kings of *Bohemia*, our Ancestors and Predecessors, have formerly done, as also the other Electors have at all Times had a Right to do the same

CHAP X

Concerning the Coyn

WE also ordain that the King of *Bohemia*, who shall after us succeed to the Kingdom, shall be able to coyn Money of Gold and Silver, in such part of his Kingdom, and in such Places under his Obedience, as he shall think fit, and in such Manner and Form as has been at all Times observ'd in our said Kingdom, and this pursuant to the Right the Kings our Predecessors have at all Times enjoy'd

We also understand, and ordain by this present Imperial Constitution, and perpetual Bounty, that the Kings of *Bohemia* may purchase from other Princes and Lords, and even from all other Persons, Lands, Castles and Inheritances, of what Kind or Nature soever they may be, and even receive them by Gift and by Mortgage, on Condition however, that they shall

shall be oblig'd to leave them in the same Nature as they found them, the Fiefs, as Fiefs, and the Freeholds and alodial Lands, as such, &c. and to pay the ordinary Duties to the Empire. Which present Constitution we also extend to all the other Electors, as well Ecclesiasticks as Seculars, their lawful Successors and Heirs, the whole on the Terms and Conditions above-mention'd.

CHAP XI

Of the Exemption of the Princes Electors

§ 1. WE also ordain that the Counts, Barons, Gentlemen, Nobles, Vassals, Officers, Soldiers, Burgesses, and all other Persons, of what Condition or Quality soever they may be, Subjects of the Churches of Cologn, Mayence and Triers, shall not be forc'd out of the Jurisdiction of the said Churches at the Instance of any Plaintiff, nor oblig'd to appear, and be impleadable, before any other Judges than before the Ordinary Judges of the Archbishop of Mayence, of Triers, and of Cologn, as we find it has been at all Times observ'd. And if it shall happen, that notwithstanding this present Edict, any of the Subjects of the Churches of Mayence, of Triers, and of Cologn, be summon'd before any other Judge, for any Cause whatever, civil or criminal, the Person so summon'd shall not be oblig'd to appear. But we ordain, that whatever shall have been done against such Persons not appearing, by the Judges residing out of the District or Extent of the Jurisdiction of the said Churches, shall be null and of no Effect.

§ 2. To all which we add very expressly, That the Counts, Barons, Gentlemen, Noblemen, Vassals, Burgesses and Inhabitants, Subjects of the said Churches, of what Condition soever they may be, cannot appeal from the Sentences, definitive or interlocutory of the Officials, or of the secular Judges of the said Archbishops, and of the said Churches, unless it be in the Case of Denial of Justice, prohibiting and forbidding all other Judges to receive such Appeals, and to take Cognizance thereof, on Pain of Nullity. And in Case of Denial of Justice, we permit them to appeal, not indifferently to all other Judges in Ordinary, or Subdelegates, but immediately to the Imperial Court, and to the Judge who shall there preside, cassing and annulling whatever shall be done contrary to this present Constitution.

§ 3. The which we extend also by this Imperial Law, to the Illustrious Count Palatin Duke of Saxony, and Marquiss of Brandenburg, and to their lawful Successors and Heirs, in the Manner and Form above-mention'd.

CHAP XII

Of the Assembly of the Princes

§ 1. THE Cares which continually take up our Thoughts, for the Good of the State, have made our Imperial Highness consider that it is necessary the Princes Electors, who are the unshakeable Foundations, and the immoveable Bases of the Empire, being remote one from another, should meet oftner than they have us'd to do, to the End that having made a Report to the Assembly of the Faults and Disorders they shall have observ'd at home, and in their Neighbourhood, they may be able to apply a Remedy thereto by their common Advice, and by their prudent Counsels prescribe and ordain the necessary Reformation.

§ 2. We have therefore resolv'd, in the solemn Assembly of the Princes Electors, as well Ecclesiasticks as Seculars, and of many other Princes and Lords, and by their Advice we have thought fit to ordain, That for the Time to come the said Princes Electors shall meet personally once in the Year, in one of our Imperial Towns, within a Month after Easter. And to this Purpose we desire that the Assembly of this present Year may be made in our Imperial City of Metz, there to resolve in what Place it may conveniently be held the next Year. And this present Ordinance shall take Place no longer than it shall please us and them, we taking into our Protection and Safeguard the said Princes Electors, as well going and coming, as during the Stay they shall make at these Assemblies.

And forasmuch as the Dispatch of Affairs is most commonly retarded by the Feasts and Entertainments, which are made at the Assemblies of Princes, we ordain with their Consent, That, during the said Assemblies, there shall be no general Feast made, but yet there may be particular Ones, which do not prejudice the Dispatch of Affairs.

CHAP XIII

Of the Revocation of Privileges

WE likewise ordain by this Imperial Edict, perpetual and irrevocable, That all the Privileges, and all the Letters which we or the Emperors our Predecessors shall have granted de motu proprio, or otherwise, to all sorts of Persons, of what Condition or Quality soever they may be, even to Towns and Communities, for Rights, Customs, Favours, and Exemptions, and even those which we or the Emperors our Successors shall grant for the time to come, shall not prejudice or derogate in any manner whatever, from the Rights, Honours, and Dignities of the Lords Princes Electors, as well Ecclesiasticks as Seculars, altho' it should, by the said Privileges and Letters, be expressly said, That they could not be revok'd or made void, unless the said Letters be entirely inserted in the Revocation, and that it makes a particular mention thereof. Which said Privileges and Letters, inasmuch as they prejudice and derogate from the Liberties, Jurisdictions, Rights, Honours, and Dignities of the said Princes Electors, or of any of them, we now annull and revoke, of our certain Knowledge, and hold them as annull'd and revok'd by our full Imperial Power.

CHAP XIV.

Of those from whom Fiefs are taken away, as being unworthy thereof.

AND forasmuch as in many Places the Vassals and Feudataries make a verbal Resignation, out of Season, and maliciously, of the Fiefs they hold of their Lords, to the end they may be able to defy them, and that under the Pretext of a War, or declar'd Enmity, they may attack, invade, and take Possession of the said Fiefs and Lands, we declare by this perpetual and irrevocable Edict, That such Resignations and Renunciations shall be deem'd as not made, unless they shall have been made frankly and really. So that the Lords have been put into real and effectual Possession of the said Fiefs, with Protestation to leave it free to the said Lords, without troubling or molesting them in any manner or way whatever. We ordain at the same Time, That those who shall give any Disturbance to their Lords in the Possession of those Fiefs so resign'd, or not resign'd, shall be declar'd infamous, and put in the Ban of the Empire, without it being ever in their Power to re-enter under any Pretext whatever, and we declare, That the Investiture, which shall be given to the Prejudice of the present Constitution, shall be null. We ordain also that the same Penalties shall be executed against all those who shall dare to attempt any thing against their Lords, or shall do any thing maliciously to their Disservice, without any previous Defiance or Renunciation.

CHAP XV.

Of Conspiracies.

§ 1. WE also disapprove and condemn all Leagues and unlawful Conspiracies, and all private Assemblies, forbid by the Laws between Towns and Towns, and private Man and private Man, or between a Town and a private Person, under Pretext of Parentage, or of the Protection of Burgesses and Inhabitants, and under any other Colour that may be given to such Alliances and Confederacies, which we by these Presents declare to be null. As also all those which the private Inhabitants and Subjects of the Princes and Lords might make, with any other Prince, Town or Community, without the Consent of their Lords, and without excepting them in their Treaties. All which we ordain, in Execution of the Constitutions of the Emperors our Predecessors.

§ 2. We except nevertheless the Confederacies, Leagues and Alliances, which are known to be made by Princes and Towns for the Preservation of the publick Peace.

§ 3. We condemn all private Persons, who shall have dar'd to make Leagues and Confederacies against the express Tenor of this Law, in three and twenty Marks of Gold by the way of Fine, besides the Penalty above express'd, and the Note of Infamy, and each Town, besides the Loss of its Privileges, Rights and Liberties, in two hundred Marks of Gold, whereof one half shall be confiscated to our Profit, and the other half to the Profit of the Lord to whose Prejudice the Alliance or League shall have been made.

CHAP XVI.

Of the Pfalburgers.

§ 1. AND forasmuch as several Burghers, who are Subjects of Barons, having a Mind to shake off the Yoke of the ordinary Subjection, procure to themselves the Right of Burghers elsewhere, pretending to be protected by those who give them such Right, and enjoy the Liberties and Privileges of the Places where they procure the same, while they nevertheless remain and reside effectively in the Place of their first Abode, and under their ancient Lords, which Burghers are call'd in the German Tongue *Pfalburger*, and because it is not just that any should receive Benefit from their Malice, we having taking hereupon the Advice of all the Electors, as well Ecclesiasticks as Seculars, of our full Imperial Power and certain Knowledge have ordain'd, and do ordain by this perpetual and irrevocable Edict, That those Burghers and Inhabitants, who shall after this manner make a Jest of those under whom they remain, shall not in any way whatever enjoy the Rights, Privileges, and Liberties of the Towns where they shall so have acquir'd the Right of Burghers, unless they actually live there, and do all those things which the Inhabitants of those Places are oblig'd to do.

§ 2. And those who are already receiv'd, or shall be receiv'd hereafter, contrary to the Tenor of this Law, shall not in any manner whatever enjoy the Right of such Reception, nor the Privileges of those Places where they shall pretend to have been receiv'd. And this notwithstanding all Privileges, Letters, or Customs to the contrary hereof, which they may have already obtain'd, or might obtain hereafter. The which, by reason they are contrary to this Ordinance, we revoke by these Presents, and declare them to be void and of no Effect, except the Rights which the Lords, who shall have been so abandon'd, have over the Persons and Goods of their Subjects. And we forbid all other Lords, Towns and Communities, to receive the Subjects of another, and command them to send back those they shall have receiv'd amongst them, within a Month after the Signification of these Presents, under the Penalty of a hundred Marks of pure Gold, the one half whereof to be apply'd to our Treasury, and the other to the Lords of such as shall have been so receiv'd.

CHAP XVII.

Of Defiances.

WE declare that they who having Cause to bid Defiance to any one, or shall pretend
to

to have it, shall send to challenge or defy him, any where else than at the Place of his Abode, or at a Place where he does not commonly reside, cannot with Honour ravage his Lands, nor burn his Houses, or otherwise damnify his Estate And forasmuch as it is not reasonable any Advantage should be reap'd from Malice we ordain, by this perpetual and irrevocable Edict, that no Person whatever shall, under the Pretext of Defiance, lay waste, burn or outrage a Lord or any other Person with whom he has liv'd familiarly, or in a friendly and civil Manner, till three Days after the Defiance shall have been signify'd to the Person, or at the Place of Abode of him he shall have a mind to defy Whoever shall undertake to do otherwise shall be declar'd Infamous, and punish'd by the Law as a Traitor, in the same Manner as if he had been the Aggressor without any Defiance

We also forbid and condemn all forts of unjust Wars and Quarrels, as likewise all undue Burnings, Ravages, Violence and Impositions, as also the Exactions which have been usually practis'd, for Safe conducts, and Safeguards which are forc'd on my Person The Whole under the Penalties appointed by the Laws

CHAP XVIII
The Form of a Summons, or Letters of Intimation

Obis Illustri & Magnifico Principi, Domino Marchioni Brandeburgenii, Sacri Imperii Archicamerario, Coelectori & amico nostro charissimo, Electionem Romani Regis, quæ ex rationabilibus causis imminet facienda, præsentibus intimamus, vosque ex Officii nostri debito ad Electionem præfatam rite vocamus, quatenus a die tali, &c infra tres menses continuo computandos, per vos, seu Nuncios aut Procuratores vestros, unum vel plures sufficiens mandatum habentes, ea locum debitum, juxta formam sacrarum Legum super hoc editarum, venire curetis, deliberaturi, tractaturi, & concordaturi cum aliis Comprincipibus & Coelectoribus vestris, & nostris de Electione futuri Regis Romanorum, in Imperatorem postmodum, favente Deo, promovendi In eodem mansuri usque ad plenam Confirmationem Electionis hujusmodi & alias facturi & processuri, prout in sacris Legibus super hoc deliberate editis invenitur expressum alias non obstante vestra, seu vestrorum absentia, in præmissis una cum aliis Comprincipibus, & Coelectoribus vestris, prout Legum ipsarum sancivit Authoritas, finaliter procedimus

CHAP XIX
The Form of the Procuration

*NOS N Dei Gratia Comes Palatinus Rheni, Sacri Imperii Archidapifer, Princeps Elector Notum facimus tenore præsentium universis, quod cum Electio Romanorum Regis ex rationabilibus Causis immineat facienda nos ac Honore & Statu Sacri Imperii sollicitudine debita intmacre cupientes, ne tam gravioribus dispendiis periculose subjaceat, de fide & Circumspectionis Industria dilectorum nobis talis, &c fiducium nostrorum obtinentes utique præsumptionis indubiæ fiduciam singularem ipsos, & quemlibet eorum in solidum, ita quod non sit melior Conditio occupantis, sed quod per unum inceptum fuerit, per alium finiri valeat, & licet terminari, omni jure, modo & forma, quibus melius & efficacius possumus, seu valemus, nostros veros & legitimos Procuratores, & Nuncios speciales facimus, constituimus, & ordinamus, ad tractandum ubi bet una cum eis Comprincipibus & Coelectoribus nostris, tam Ecclesiasticis quam Secularibus, & cum ipsis concordabunt * & concludent de quacumque persona habili & Idonea in Regem Romanorum Eligenda, & ipsis tractatis super Electione tali persona habendis, pro nobis, loco & nomine nostris, intereffendum, tractandum & deliberandum, nec non vice & nomine nostris eardem personam nominandum, & in ipsam consentendum, ac etiam in Regem Romanorum Eligendum, ad Sacrum Imperium promovendum, ac in animam nstr. in præstandum quodcumque Juramentum acceptorium, devotum & Consuetum fuerit, circa præmissa & quodlibet præmissorum, alium vel alios Procuratores in solidum subs tuendum & revocandum, & omnia & singula faciendum qu a in præmissis & in ea pro in sa, etiam usque ad Consummationem Tractatuum, Nominationis, Deliberationis & Electionis hujusmodi de præsenti facienda necessaria aut utilia fuerint, seu et in quomodolibet opportuna, etiamsi præm ssa, vel eorum quodlibet, mandatum exigant speciale, etiamsi majora vel magis singularia fuerint supradictis, & quæ nosmetipsi facere possemus, si hujusmodi Tractatuum, Deliberationis, Nominationis, & Electionis futuræ Negotiis præsentes & personaliter adessemus Gratum & ratum habentes & habere volentes, & nos perpetuo habituros firmiter promittentes, quicquid per antedictos Procuratores seu Nuncios nostros, nec non Substitutos & Substituendos, ab ipsis seu ipsorum altero, in præmissis seu præmissorum quolibet, actum, gestum, seu factum fuerit, aut quomodolibet ordinatum*

CHAP XX
Of the Union between the Princes Electors, and of the Rights which particularly belong to them

FOR as much as it is well known that all the Principalities, by virtue of which the secular Princes Electors have a Right and Vote in the Election of the King of the Romans, future Emperor, are so annex'd and link'd to the Rights, Offices, Dignities and other Prerogatives, that they are inseparably united in themselves so that the Right and Vote, the Office and Dignity, can only belong to him who possesses effectually the said Principalities, with their Territories, Vassallages, Fiefs and Demesnes, We ordain by this Imperial Edict, perpetual and irrevocable, that for the future the said Principalities shall be so

* Here there is a Fault in the Original

united

united to the Electoral Dignity, that whoever shall be peaceable Possessor of one of the said Principalities, shall likewise be so of the Electoral Dignity, and shall be esteem'd by all, true and lawful Elector: and as such, shall of Obligation be invited to the Elections of the Kings of the *Romans*, and to all the Assemblies that shall be conven'd, for the Honour and Dignity of the Empire, and for the Good of the State, without possibility of separating the Electoral Dignity from the Principalities, at any Time, or on any Account whatever, and without Possibility of suing for, or recovering the one, without the other, either by Law or otherwise. We requiring, that all Hearing shall be deny'd to him, who shall sue for the one without the other. And if it shall happen, that by surprise or otherwise, a Hearing be given to those who shall sue for the one without the other, or even that an Order or Sentence has been given in that Respect, the whole shall be null, and of no effect.

CHAP XXI
Of the Order to be obſerv'd by the Archbiſhops in any Proceſſion

WE have said in the beginning of this present Constitution, that it was necessary to regulate the Order and Rank the Electors ought to keep, as well in Councils as at Processions, and even at Table in the Diets and other publick Assemblies, thereby to avoid the Inconveniences which might ensue therefrom. For which Reason we have resolv'd to assign to each of them, the Rank they shall hold at Processions and in their March, and we ordain by this perpetual Edict, That every time the Emperor, or the King of the *Romans*, shall think fit to go out in Publick, and in Ceremony, during the Diets and General Assemblies, and will have the Regalia or Ornaments carry'd before him, the Archbishop of *Triers* shall march first and alone, so that between him and the Emperor shall be none but the Princes who bear the Regalia. But if the Emperor does not cause them to be carry'd, then the said Archbishop shall march in the same Rank, but immediately before the Emperor, at whose sides the two other Archbishops shall march, each in the Place which has been above assign'd him according to the Province in which they shall happen to be.

CHAP XXII
Of the Order the Secular Princes ſhall obſerve who carry the Regalia

AND that we may settle the Rank the secular Princes Electors shall hold in marching with the Emperor in Publick and in Ceremony, We ordain, That when the Emperor, or the King of the *Romans*, shall be present at any Diet or General Assembly, where it shall be requisite for the Princes Electors to bear the Regalia or Imperial Ornaments before him, at his going in Publick, or at a Procession, the Elector of *Saxony*, who carrys the Imperial or Royal Sword, shall march immediately before the Emperor, between him and the Archbishop of *Triers*, and shall have on his Right-Hand the Count *Palatin* carrying the Ball, and on his Left the Marquiss of *Brandenburg* bearing the Scepter, going all three a breast. The King of *Bohemia* shall follow the Emperor immediately, no body to go between him and the Emperor.

CHAP XXIII
Of the Functions of the Archbiſhops in the Preſence of the Emperor

WHen Mass shall be to be said before the Emperor, or the King of the *Romans*, and that the Archbishops of *Mayence*, of *Triers*, and of *Cologn*, or two of them shall be present, in that Case shall be observ'd, at the Confession which is made at the beginning of Mass, at the kissing of the Gospel, and the Pax, and even when a Blessing is crav'd at Table, as also at the Graces which are said after Meals, the Order we have thought fit to establish therein by their Advice and Consent, to wit, That the First shall have that Honour the first Day, the Second the second Day, and the Third the third Day, establishing the Order of Primacy among the Archbishops, according to the Order and Time of their Consecration. And to the End they may prevent one the other in the Point of Honour and Civility, and that by their Example they may oblige the others to do the like among themselves, It is our Will, That he to whom it shall belong to officiate, shall do to his Collegues the Honour of an Offer of his Place, and that he do not officiate till the others shall have refus'd the same.

The following LAWS were publiſh'd by CHARLES IV, *Emperor Auguſt, King of* Bohemia, *in the Diet of* Metz, *on* Chriſtmas-Day, 1356, *aſſiſted by all the Princes Electors of the Holy Empire, and in the Preſence of the Reverend Father in God* T *Biſhop of* Alba, *Cardinal of the Holy See, and of* Charles *the eldeſt Son of* France, *Duke of* Normandy, *and Dolphin of the* Viennese

CHAP XXIV

§ 1 WE ordain, That he who shall have been so wicked as to attempt, or to promise to attempt, with Princes, Gentlemen, or private Persons, or even with Plebeians, against the Life of the Reverend and Illustrious Prin

Princes Electors of the Holy *Roman* Empire, as well Ecclesiasticks as Seculars, (who are as the Members of our Body) or of any of them, shall perish by the Sword as being guilty of High Treason, and that his Goods and Estate shall be confiscated, because on these Occasions the Laws punish with the same Severity, the Will, as the Crime it self And altho' it were just, that the Sons of such Person should dye the same Death, because the same Examples may be apprehended from them, yet nevertheless we by a particular Bounty give them their Lives, but it is our Will, that they be depriv'd of their maternal Inheritance and of all the Goods and Estates they might hope for from their other Relations and Friends, to the End that being always poor and necessitous, they may always have before their Eyes the Infamy of their Father, and being depriv'd of all sorts of Honours and Dignities, they may languish in a perpetual Want, so as to find the in Comfort in Death, and their Torment in Life

§ 2 It is also our Will, That they who shall dare to intercede for such kind of Persons, be branded with perpetual Infamy

§ 3 As for the Daughters of such Criminals, in what Number soever they may be, we ordain, That they shall have the *falcidian* Allowance out of their Mother's Estate, whether she have made a Will or not, to the End they may be contented with a bare Sustenance, and may not enjoy either the Advantage of the Inheritance, nor the Quality of Heiresses, because the Sentence ought to be by so much the more moderate in reference to them, as we are persuaded that the Infirmity and Weakness of their Sex, will hinder them from committing Crimes of this Nature

§ 4 We declare also, That the Emancipations such Persons shall have made of their Sons or their Daughters since the Publication of the present Law, shall be null and of no Effect

§ 5 In like Manner we declare null and of no Validity all Constitutions or Settlements of Portions, Donations, and all other Alienations which shall have been made by Fraud, and even of Right, from the Time they shall have begun to lay the first Project of these Conspirations

§ 6 We indeed allow the Wives of such Persons to withdraw their Portion, but if the Dowry their Husbands have made them, and whereof they have receiv'd the Revenue and Profits, is to return to their Sons, it is our Will that whatever is so to be restor'd to the Sons, be apply'd to our Treasury, and even that the Daughters have out of the same, only the falcidian Allowance

§ 7 What we have here said concerning these Criminals and their Sons, ought to be understood also of their Attendants, Accomplices and Ministers, as also of their Sons However if any one of the Accomplices, being touch'd with a Desire of true Glory, shall discover the Conspiracy in its beginning, he may assure himself of an honourable Reward from us But those who shall have had a Hand in these Conspiracies, and shall reveal them but very late, yet before they have been detected, may be assur'd of the Pardon of their Crime We also ordain, That even after the Death of the Criminal it shall be lawful to inquire into what has been acted against the Persons of the said Princes Electors, as well Seculars as Ecclesiasticks The Question may also be given in this Crime, to the Servants and Domesticks against their Masters

§ 8 We likewise ordain by this Imperial Edict, and it is our Will, That an Information be taken even after the Death of the Criminal, to the End that the Crime being prov'd, the Memory of the Deceas'd may be condemn'd, and his Goods confiscated For as soon as any Person resolves on a Wickedness of this Nature, he is guilty thereof in his Soul, and tormented in his Conscience Wherefore it is our Will, That as soon as any one shall be guilty of this Crime, he shall be no longer able to sell, alienate, nor give Liberty to his Slaves, neither shall it be lawful to pay him what is due to him

§ 9 We ordain, That for these Crimes the Question may be given to the Servants and Domesticks of the Criminals, and that they may be forc'd to depose against their Masters, because too great an Abhorrence and Detestation cannot be had, of the Attempts that are made against the Princes Electors, as well Ecclesiasticks as Seculars And if any one of these Criminals dyes while his Tryal is preparing it is our Will that the Estates which might come to him by Succession, be put into the Hands of the Law, till it be known to whom they ought to belong

CHAP XXV
Of the Preservation of the Principalities of the Electors entire

IF it be good that all the other Principalities be preserv'd entire, to the End Justice may thereby be corroborated, and that the good and lawful Subjects may enjoy a great Repose and a profound Peace, it is beyond Comparison still more just, that the great Principalities, Demesnes, Honours and Rights of the Princes Electors, should remain unimpair'd and entire For where the Danger is greatest, there the strongest Remedies must be apply'd, lest the Pillars being beat down, the whole Structure should fall to ruin

§ 1 It is therefore our Will, and we ordain by this perpetual Edict, That for the Time to come, the large and magnificent Principalities, to wit, the Kingdom of *Bohemia*, the County Palatin of the *Rhine*, the Dutchy of *Saxony*, and the Marquisate of *Brandenburg*, their Lands, Districts, Homages and Vassalages, with their Appurtenances and Dependences, shall not be liable to be shar'd, divided or dismember'd, in any way whatever, but that they remain perpetually whole, and be preserv'd entire

§ 2 It is our Will that the eldest Son shall succeed thereto, and that the whole Demesne, and the whole Right belong to him alone, unless he be a Fool, or have some such other notable Imperfection, that shall absolutely hinder him from governing In which Case we deprive him of the Inheritance, and call thereto the second Son, if there be any in the same Line, if
not,

not, the eldest of the Brothers or such other Relation on the Father's side who shall appear to be nearest in a direct and Male Line, who shall be oblig'd to give Proofs of his Bounty and Piety to his other Brothers and Sisters, by contributing to their Subsistence according as God shall inspire him, and to the Wealth he shall have, but we expressly forbid all Partition, Division or Dismembring of the Principalities of the Electors, and of their Appurtenances and Dependences in any manner whatever.

CHAP XXVI

Of the Imperial Court, and of the Meeting or Session

§ 1 ON the Day the Emperor, or the King of the *Romans*, shall think fit to hold a solemn Court the Princes Electors, as well Ecclesiasticks as Seculars, shall repair by one of the Clock or thereabout, to the Imperial or Royal Lodgings, where the Emperor or King of the Romans, being cloth'd in his Imperial Garments, shall mount on Horseback with all the Princes Electors, who shall accompany him to the Place prepar'd for the Session, in the Order and Manner we have above prescrib'd, in the Ordinance that regulates the Order of Processions.

§ 2 In this Procession the Arch-Councellor, in whose Chancery the Imperial Court shall be held, shall carry at the end of a Silver Rod, all the Imperial and Royal Seals

§ 3 But the Secular Princes shall carry the Scepter, the Ball, and the Sword in such manner as we have said elsewhere

§ 4 Some other Princes, the Nomination of whom shall depend on the Will of the Emperor, shall carry the Crown of *Aix-la-Chapelle*, and that of *Milan*, immediately before the Archbishop of *Triers*, who shall march in the Rank we have allotted him above However this Ceremony shall be only perform'd before the Emperor crown'd, and not before the King of the *Romans*

§ 5 The Empress, or Queen of the *Romans*, being cloth'd in her Royal Apparel and Ornaments, shall march immediately after the Emperor, or the King of the *Romans*, but at the distance of some Paces, and shall march so to the place of the Assembly, accompany'd by her Ladies and Maids of Honour

CHAP XXVII

Of the Functions of the Princes Electors in the solemn Courts of the Emperors, or of the Kings of the Romans

WE ordain, that in what Place soever the Emperor or the King of the *Romans* shall think fit to keep his solemn Courts, where the Princes Electors shall be oblig'd to do their Functions and discharge their Offices, the following Order shall be observ'd

§ 1 First the Emperor, or the King of the *Romans*, being seated in his Royal Chair, or Imperial Throne, the Duke of *Saxony* shall do his Office in the manner we shall hereafter express There shall be put before the Imperial or Royal Lodgings, a Heap of Oats which shall reach to the Belly or Saddle of the Horse, on which the Duke shall be mounted, and the Duke holding a Silver Staff in his Hand, and a Measure or Bushel of Silver of the Weight of twelve Marks, and being on Horseback, shall fill his Bushel with Oats, and shall give the same to the first Groom that shall be there easily, and having planted the Staff in the Heap of Oats, he shall withdraw, and leave the Oats to the Lord of *Pappenheim*, Vice-Marshal, and in his Absence to the Marshal of the Imperial Court, who shall permit the same to be pillag'd

§ 2 As soon as the Emperor, or King of the *Romans*, shall be seated at Table, the Ecclesiastical Princes Electors, that is to say, the Archbishops, standing up before the Table with the other Prelates, shall crave a Blessing on the same, according to the Order we have before prescrib'd The Blessing being crav'd, all the Archbishops, if they are present, or else one or two of them, shall take the Imperial or Royal Seals from the Hands of the Emperor's Chancellor And he in whose Arch Chancery the solemn Court is held, having at his Sides the other two Archbishops, who shall with him have their Hands on the Silver Staff, from which the Seals shall hang, shall advance, and making a low Bow, shall put the Seals on the Table before the Emperor, who shall restore them presently, and he, in whose Arch-Chancery the Ceremonies shall be perform'd, shall put the Great Seal about his Neck, and shall wear it in that manner all the time of Dinner, and after Dinner on Horseback from the Palace to his Lodgings Now the Staff of which we now speak ought to be of Silver, to the Weight of twelve Marks, and the three Archbishops shall cause it to be made at their Expence, each bearing a third part thereof The Staff and the Seals shall remain to the Chancellor of the Court, who shall dispose thereof as he pleases For as soon as one of the Archbishops to whom it shall belong to carry the Seals about his Neck from the Palace to his Lodgings, sha'l be come there, he shall send back the Seal and the Horse to the Chancellor of the Court, to whom Decency requires he should also give the Horse, that he may thereby give a Testimony of the Affection he has for him, and of the Value he has for his Person

§ 3 After that, the Marquiss of *Brandenburg*, being on Horseback, shall approach, and having in his Hand a Bason, and an Ewer of Silver of the Weight of twelve Marks, with Water and a fine Napkin, and lighting off his Horse, shall pour out Water for the Emperor, or the King of the *Romans*, to wash with

§ 4 The Count *Palatin* of the *Rhine* shall enter on Horseback, carrying four Dishes of Silver, with Meat in them, each Dish weighing three Marks, and lighting off his Horse, shall set the Dishes on the Table, before the Emperor, or the King of the *Romans*

§ 5 Then

§ 5 Then shall come the King of *Bohemia*, Great Cup-bearer, being also on Horseback, and holding in his Hand a Silver Cup or Goblet cover'd, weighing twelve Marks, and full of Wine and Water, and alighting from his Horse, shall present the same to the Emperor, or the King of the *Romans*, to drink

§ 6 We also ordain, that pursuant to what has been hitherto practis'd, the Lord of *Falquenstein*, Vice-Chamberlain, shall have the Horse, the Bason, and the Ewer of the Marquifs of *Brandenburg* The Lord of *Nortemberg*, Steward, the Horse and the Dishes of the Count *Palatin* of the *Rhine* The Deputy Cupbearer of *Limburg*, the Horse and Cup of the King of *Bohemia*, and the Vice-Marshal *Pappenheim* the Horse, the Staff, and Measure of the Duke of *Saxony* Provided still that these Officers are personally present at the Imperial or Royal Court, and there do the Functions of their Offices, but if they are all absent, or some of them, then the Officers in Ordinary of the Emperor, or of the King of the *Romans*, shall serve in their Absence each in his Office and as they discharge the Functions thereof, so they shall also enjoy the Emoluments

that there is no Memory to the contrary, that it has been at all Times happily obferv'd, that the Election of a King of the *Romans*, future Emperor, ought to be perform'd in the Town of *Francfort*, and the Coronation at *Aix-la-Chapelle*, and that the Emperor Elect ought to hold his first Court at *Nuremberg* It is our Will, for many Reasons, that the same be practis'd for the future, unless there happens some lawful Impediment

§ 6 When also any of the Electors, not being able to come in Person to these solemn Courts, shall send thither an Embaffador or Deputy, this Embaffador, of what Condition or Quality foever he may be, shall indeed be admitted to the Affemblies by virtue of his Powers, but he shall not fit at the Table which shall have been prepar'd for him that fent him

§ 7 In fine, all the Ceremonies of the Imperial or Royal Court being ended, all the Scaffolds and Structure of Wood, which shall have been made for the Meeting, and for the Tables of the Emperor, or of the King of the *Romans*, and of the Princes Electors aflembl'd for a solemn Court, or to give the Investiture of the Fiefs, shall belong to the Steward

CHAP XXVIII
Of the Imperial and Electoral Tables

§ 1 THE Imperial or Royal Table ought to be so dispos'd, that it may be six Foot higher than the other Tables of the Room, and on Days of solemn Courts, none shall sit there, except the Emperor, or the King of the *Romans*, alone

§ 2 But the Place or Table of the Emprefs, or Queen, shall be prepar'd on one side, and lower than that of the Emperor, or of the King of the *Romans*, by three Foot, and higher than that of the Electors by three Foot but the Tables and Places of the Princes Electors shall be all of the same height

§ 3 Tables shall be prepar'd for the seven Electors, Ecclesiasticks as well as Seculars, at the bottom of the Imperial Table, to wit, three on the right, and three others on the left, and the seventh right against the Emperor, or the King of the *Romans*, in the same Order we have laid down before in the Chapter of the Places and Order to be observ'd by the Princes Electors, so that no Person or any Condition or Quality whatever, shall place themselves in the intermediate Space, or at their Tables

§ 4 However the abovesaid Secular Princes Electors, or any of them, shall not fit down at Table, till all the other Electors their Collegues shall have discharg'd their Offices, but as soon as any one of them shall have perform'd his, he shall retire to his Table, and shall there remain standing till all the others have executed the Functions of their Offices, and then they shall all fit down at the same time, each at his Table

§ 5 And forasmuch as we find by very certain Relations, and by Traditions so ancient,

CHAP XXIX
Of the Rights of the Officers, when the Princes do Homage for their Fiefs to the Emperor, or to the King of the Romans

§ 1 WF ordain by this present Imperial Edict, that when the Princes Electors, as well Ecclesiasticks as Seculars, shall receive their Fiefs or *Regalia* from the Hands of the Emperor, or the King of the *Romans*, they shall not be oblig'd to pay or give any thing for the same For the Money which is given for Investitures being due to the Officers, and the Princes Electors being the first Officers of the Court, where they have their Substitutes establish'd and paid by the Emperors, it would be impertinent for the Substitutes to require Money or Prefents from their Superiors, unless the said Princes Electors will give them any thing of their own good Will, and by the way of Liberality

§ 2 But all the other Princes of the Empire, as well Ecclesiasticks as Seculars, in receiving their Fiefs, as we just now said, from the Emperor, or of the King of the *Romans*, shall give to the Officers of the Court, each sixty three Marks and one Quarter of Silver, unless they can prove their Exemption, and shew by Imperial or Royal Privileges, that they are dispens'd with from paying the said Sum, and all the other Fees which have been us'd to be paid at the receiving an Investiture And it shall be the Steward of the Houshold to the Emperor, or to the King of the *Romans*, who shall make a Partition of the said Sum of sixty three Marks, and one Quarter of Silver, in the following manner First having taken ten Marks for himself, he shall give as much to the Chancellor of the Emperor, or of the King of the

6 C *Romans*

Romans To the Secretaries, Notaries and Inditers he shall give three Marks, to the Sealer for the Wax a quarter of a Mark, the Chancellor or the Secretaries not being oblig'd to give for the same any more than a Certificate, and simple Letters of Investiture. In like manner the Steward shall give the said Sum of ten Marks to the Cup-bearer of *Limburg*, ten to the Steward of *Nortemberg*, ten to the Vice-Mareschal of *Pappenheim*, and ten to the Vice-Chamberlain of *Falquensteur* provided that they are personally present at these Investitures, and that they there'd scharge the Functions of their Offices, otherwise, and in their Absence, the Officers of the Court of the Emperor, or of the King of the *Romans*, who shall do the Office of the absent, and who shall have had the Trouble thereof, shall also receive the Profit and Emoluments thence accruing.

§ 3 But the Horse, or such other Beast, on which shall be mounted the Prince who does Homage to the Emperor, or to the King of the *Romans*, whatever it may be, shall belong to the Great Mareschal, that is to say, to the Duke of *Saxony*, if he be there present; if not, to the Lord of *Pappenheim* his Vice-Mareschal, and in his Absence to the Mareschal of the Emperor's Court.

CHAP XXX
Of the Instruction of the Princes Electors in Languages

§ 1 FOrasmuch as the Largeness of the *Roman* Empire is oblig'd to give Laws to, and command People of different Nations, varying in their Morals, manner of Living and Languages, it is just, and those endu'd with the most Wisdom think it so, that the Princes Electors, who are the Columns and Buttresses of the Empire, should be instructed in such manner as to speak several Languages, because as they are oblig'd to assist the Emperor in its most important Affairs, it is necessary they should understand Variety of Persons, and also that they should be able to make themselves understood by them.

§ 2 Wherefore we ordain, that the Sons, the Heirs and Successors of the illustrious Princes Electors, to wit, of the King of *Bohemia*, of the Count Palatin of the *Rhine*, of the Duke of *Saxony*, and of the Marquiss of *Branaenburg*, who in all Likelihood know the *German* Tongue, because they ought to have learn'd it from their Infancy, having attain'd the Age of seven Years, shall be instructed in the *Latin* Tongue, the *Italian*, and *Sclavonian* that by the Time they have attain'd that of fourteen they may be skill'd therein. Which is what we esteem not only to be useful, but also necessary, by reason the use of these Languages is very common in the Empire, for the Management of its most momentous Affairs.

§ 3 However we leave it to the Discretion of the Fathers to direct the Particulars of this Instruction, so that it shall depend on them to send their Sons or their Relations whom they shall think likely to succeed them in the Electorate, to such Places where they may learn those Languages with Ease, or to assign them such Preceptors and Companions, by whose Instructions and Conversation they may render themselves perfect therein.

CHAP. VIII.
Several Remarks on the Golden Bull.

* FOrmerly the Emperors caus'd their Edicts to be seal'd with a Golden Seal, which was call'd *Bulla*, or *Bull*, which is a barbarous Word in its Signification, rather than in its Etymology, but the Title of *Golden Bull* is by Excellency given to the Edict which the Emperor *Charles* IV, Duke of *Luxemburg* and King of *Bohemia*, made in the Year 1356, to regulate the Rights, Privileges, Prerogatives, and Preheminences of the Princes Electors, and that, by reason of the Advantage this Edict has over all the others, serving as a pragmatick Sanction, or rather as a fundamental Law to the Empire, a Basis to the Grandeur of the Electors, and a Lustre to the Electoral Dignity. The Original of this Edict, which is conceiv'd in *Latin*, written on Vellum, is kept in the Town-house of *Francfort* on the *Main*, bound up in red Parchment, being a *Quarto* of about an Inch thick. At the Back of the Book on which it is sow'd, there pass several Nooses or sliding Knots of black and yellow Silk, at the end of which hangs a Golden Seal of the Thickness and Largeness of a Silver Crown, which is said to be hollow, and fill'd with Wax. On the one side whereof is to be seen the Emperor seated in a Chair, in the manner of a Throne, holding in his Right Hand the Scepter, and in the Left a Golden Ball, with this Motto in the Circumference. *Carolus Quartus, Divina favente Clementia, Romanorum Imperator semper Augustus* and for want of Room, there is put in the Body of the Medal, near the King's Effigies, on the one side, *Bohemia*, and on the other, *Rex*. On the Reverse is a Castle with three Towers, or Belfreys, much like the Arms of the City of *Hamburgh*, which denotes a great Church, or a City, on the Gate are these Words, *Aurea Roma*; and in the Circumference,

Roma Caput mundi regit orbis frœna Rotundi,

without Subscription

---

*] *Remark, the* Golden Bull, *or Seal*

The Golden Seal is here a Mark of Sovereignty in the Person of the Emperor His Successors preserv'd to themselves this Right down to Frederick III, and to Maximilian I, as appears by the Constitutions of the Years 1495, and 1497, which are only seal'd with the Emperor's Seal But when the Sovereign Power began to be curb'd by Capitulations at the Election of the Emperor Charles V, this Custom was alter'd, as well as the Terms the Emperors were us'd to insert in their Edicts, *of our certain Knowledge, Authority and Imperial Power*, of which the Emperor Charles IV makes use in several Places of his *Golden Bull* Formerly the States of the Empire approv'd, and authoriz'd in some measure the Resolutions which were taken at the Diets, but then the Sole Will of the Emperor gave them the Force and Virtue of a thing determin'd *Res singulæ, ad effectum producte, glo iosi Principis anditui, in sacris ejus obtutibus exponebantur, & quicquid nata a Deo sapientia eligeret, omnes sequebantur*, says Hincmar Maximilian I, from the Year 1500, inserted in his Letters these Words *with the Consent of the Electors* But at this Day they go a great deal further There is now no Edict nor Constitution made but with the Consent of the States, and in the General Diets of the Empire, by way of Contract and reciprocal Obligation between the Emperor and the Empire, who not taking any Resolutions till they have been agreed upon on both sides, there is no longer any mention made of Imperial Power, but this Clause is inserted *We have agreed with the States, and the States with us, on what follows* So that when in the last Diet at Ratisbone, which broke up on May 19, 1654, the Emperor had slipt into the Resolution this Clause, *of our full Power and Imperial Authority*, there arose so great a Confusion thereupon, that the Emperor, to cover his Fault, was oblig'd to cast it on the Ignorance of the Clerk who had drawn up the Instrument

As for the Seal, it is not long since it was customary to seal the Resolutions which have the Force of a Law in the Empire, in such manner that the Emperor's Seal was at the Head of the silken Nooses, which afterwards made two Ends, of which that on the right had first of all the Seal of the Elector of Mentz, and in his Absence that of Mother Ecclesiastical Elector, who was there present After that the Seal of the first Ecclesiastical Prince, or that of his Deputy and afterwards that of the first Prelate, who was not a Prince On that on the left, was first the Seal of the first Secular Elector, or of his Deputy, after that, that of the first Prince, and afterwards that of a Count of the Empire This Honour being alternately shar'd between the Counts of Swabia and of Wetteravia After which the two Ends were join'd, to apply thereto the Seal of the Town where the Diet was held

But this Order was chang'd in the last Diet of Ratisbone, which we before mention'd, so that the Nooses or running Knots having pass'd through the Emperor's Seal, had six Seals on each end, to wit, on the right side, 1 That of Mayence, 2 That of the Elector of Bavaria, 3 That of the Archbishop of Saltzburg, 4 That of the Duke of Bavaria, 5 One for the Prelates who were not Princes, and, 6. The Seal of the City of Cologn On the left side were the Seals, 1 Of the Elector of Saxony, 2 Of the Elector of Brandenburg, 3 Of the Archbishop of Magdeburg, 4 Of the Count Palatin of Lauteren, 5 Of the Counts of Wetteravia, and, 6 The Seal of the Town of Ratisbone With this Difference nevertheless, that the Embassadors of the Electors of Bavaria, of Saxony, and of Brandenburg, and of the Archbishop of Saltzburg, put there the Seals of their Princes The Deputies of the Archbishop of Magdeburg, of the Palatin of Lauteren, put their own Seals, and the others were theie present To which we must farther add, that when the Emperors seal'd in Gold, the Kings of the Romans seal'd only in Wax

We must take notice that the * *Golden Bull* makes no mention of any other Edict, or of any other Law or Constitution that has regulated the Number and the Dignity of the Electors, but only of an ancient and laudable Custom, overthrowing by that means the Opinion of those who ascribe the Institution of the Electoral College to Gregory V, and to Otho III And indeed we have before made it appear, † that at the Time of the Election of Charles IV, Author of the *Golden Bull*, the Number of Electors was not yet regulated Wherefore we are not afraid to say, that there is great Likelihood the Electoral Dignity, or the Right of Electing, was by degrees usurp'd by the Archbishops of Mentz, of Triers, and of Cologn, by the King of Bohemia, by the Count Palatin of the Rhine, by the Duke of Saxony, and by the Marquiss of Brandenburg as well by the express Exclusion of the Duke of Austria, who was foreclos'd in the Time of the Emperor Rodolphus I, and by the Deprivation of several illustrious Families, whose Princes had a Right to assist at the Elections, as the Dukes of Suabia, of Franconia and Carinthia, as by the Reunion of several Principalities, which had all of them a Right to elect in the same Family As for Instance, Bavaria and the Palatinate, Misnia and Thuringia, Moravia and Silesia, which last made a part of Poland, with Bohemia, and by the Alienation of several Provinces which have been separated from the Interest and Obedience of the Empire, as all Italy, Poland, Lorrain, the Dutchies of Guelder, of Brabant, Luxemburg, and others and that so the modern Electors, who had made themselves extremely powerful and considerable, as well by reason of the Extent of their States, as by their Alliances, have by little and little arrogated to themselves the Right of Election to the Exclusion of all the other Princes of Germany, establishing themselves in this Dignity, and setting themselves up for Electors, by a Custom insensibly introduc'd, especially during the Schisms which began to ruin the Empire under and after the Reign of Frederick II, so that this Custom did not pass into a fundamental Law, till it did so by the Publication of the *Golden Bull*

We see therein, that ‡ the Number of Electors

---

* III *The Golden Bull is the first Constitution that mentions Electors*   ‡ Chap 6
† IV *The Number of the Electors*

ctors is regulated, and fix'd to that of seven, and the Electoral College remain'd in this State till these last Wars of *Germany* *Frederick* V, Elector *Palatin*, being put in the Ban of the Empire for having accepted of the Crown of *Bohemia*, the Emperor *Ferdinand* II. dispos'd in the Year 1623 of the Electoral Dignity, appropriated by the *Golden Bull* to the Counts *Palatins* of the *Rhine*, as being the eldest Branch of the House of *Bavaria*, in Favour of *Maximilian* Duke of *Bavaria* of the Branch of *Munichen*, but during the Negotiation of the Peace of *Germany*, the Crown of *Sweden* and the Protestant Princes made Instances that that Honour might be restor'd to the *Palatin* House, so that by the Treaty concluded at *Munster* and at *Osnaburg*, in the Month of *October*, 1648, an eighth Electorate was created for *Charles Lewis*, Count *Palatin* of the *Rhine*, and his Relations, and lawful Heirs in the Male Line. The Article says, *As for what relates to the* Palatin *House, the Emperor, and the Empire, for the publick Good and Tranquillity, consent, That by virtue of the present Agreement an eighth Electorate be establish'd, which shall be enjoy'd for the Time to come by the Lord* Charles Lewis, *Count* Palatin *of the* Rhine, *and his Heirs and Relations on the Father's Side, descending from the Branch of* Rodolphus, *according to the Order of succeeding, express'd in the* Golden Bull. From thence it follows, that, instead of seven Electors mention'd in the *Caroline* Constitution, there are at this Day eight, to wit, the Archbishops of *Mayence*, of *Triers*, and of *Cologn*, the King of *Bohemia*, the Duke of *Bavaria*, the Duke of *Saxony*, the Marquiss of *Brandenburg*, and the Count *Palatin* of the *Rhine*. We shall hereafter speak of each of them in particular.

* From what we have now said, one might conclude, that the Order establish'd by the *Golden Bull* may be chang'd, and so would not be a fundamental Law of the Empire. And this is indubitable, because we see that not only in many things the Regulation of the *Golden Bull* is not observ'd, but also that the same has been derogated from, by several Constitutions contrary thereunto, and that in what was most essential therein, as in the Number of the Electors, which had been fix'd to seven by the Emperor *Charles* IV, in order to avoid an Equality of Votes, and the Disorders that are as it were an inevitable Consequence thereof. However this Change does not hinder the *Golden Bull* from serving still as a fundamental Law to the State, but on the contrary, since this Change was not made but by the general Consent of all the States of the Empire, which might even change the whole Form of the Government, we must believe that the Regulation made by the *Golden Bull* cannot be chang'd, at least as to what is of the Essence of the Election, but by a Power, of which the States of the Empire are the only Depositaries, to the Exclusion even of the Electoral College, which cannot alone abolish what has been establish'd by all the States together.

It is also certain, that the Electors alone may alter the Regulations which relate to them in particular, and which were only made with their Consent, as the Emperor *Charles* IV expresses himself in the Text of the *Golden Bull*, when he treats of the Functions of the three Ecclesiastical Electors. So that if they think fit to change amongst themselves the Rank, they may do it, because they are alone concern'd therein, and that it is of no Importance at all to the Publick, that they march or sit after one manner sooner than another. Provided such Change or Alteration be made by the Consent of all of them, and without any Opposition, forasmuch as the Contradiction of any one of them would absolutely hinder the same. The Reason of what we have now said, is, That he that can do the greater can also do the lesser, so that if the Electors can of their Authority change the Place and Time of the Election, they may also alter the Rank among themselves. But with this Difference, that the one may be done by a Plurality of Votes, and to the other the Consent of all is absolutely necessary, by this Rule of the Civil Law, *That two cannot dispose of the Right of a third, and to his Prejudice, without his Consent.* Now it is not necessary to prove that the Electors may change the Place or Election, contrary to the express Direction of the Law, since there are so many Examples thereof, and as for the Time, we see, that even at this Day they do not proceed to the Election, altho' the Day of their Intimation be elaps'd above these four Months. Which nevertheless is so contrary to the *Golden Bull*, that if two or three, or at most four Electors, oppos'd this Delay, and met at *Franckfort* in order to proceed to an Election, they might do it without Possibility of declaring the same faulty, because the voluntary Absence of the Persons summon'd, can do no Prejudice to the Right of the present, as the Text expresses it in formal Terms, *Ch* 1 § 21. And it is for this Reason that such Delays are by so much the more dangerous, that they, who are the Cause thereof, would be answerable for the Schism, which might ensue therefrom in the Empire.

† Having then presuppos'd, as we now said, that what the *Golden Bull* contains concerning the Essence of the Election, cannot be alter'd but with the Consent of all the States of the Empire, there remains to examine, Whether contrary to the express Direction of the Law the Elector of *Mayence* can convene the Electors his Collegues, for the Election of a King of the *Romans* during the Emperor's Life. It is evident that all that the *Golden Bull* says of the Election, can have no Room, unless the Empire be vacant. The Passages are too express, and too formal on that Subject, in the first Chapter, *Concerning the Safe-conduct of the Electors*, § 19. *And the said Archbishop shall be oblig'd to summons the other Electors his Collegues within a Month after he shall be inform'd of the Death of the Emperor.* Chap IV *Concerning the Electors in general*, § 2. *Whenever the Empire shall become vacant*, the Archbishop of *Mayence* shall have Power and a Right to convene. And Chap V *Concerning the Right of the Count* Palatin, § 1. *When the holy Empire shall become vacant*, &c. It is in Effect the Intention of the Legislator, and the true Sense of the Law, in which nothing is to be found that can give a-

---

* V *Changes contrary to the* Golden Bull.   † VI *Whether there can be any Election when the Empire is not vacant.*

ny Suspicion of the contrary For so far are the Words, *Electionem, quæ ex rationabilibus Causis imminet facienda*, which are to be found in the Form of the Letters of Intimation, and that of the Procuration, from being able to suggest that the Election has room, even when the Empire is not vacant, that, on the contrary, they signify properly, *The Election to which it is necessary to proceed, for very weighty and important Causes*, that is to say, on the Account of the Death of the Emperor Which will plainly appear, if they are compar'd with the Passage we before alledg'd, and which says in formal Terms, That the Archbishop of *Mayence* shall have Power and Right to call together the Electors his Collegues, *when the Empire shall be vacant* From whence it necessarily follows, that when the Empire shall not be vacant, the Archbishop shall have no Right to convene

And that this Law has been always understood after this manner in the Empire, appears evidently by the Reasons the Princes alledg'd, to procure the Election of *Ferdinand* I to be declar'd vicious About the latter End of the Year 1530, *Albert* of *Brandenburg*, Archbishop and Elector of *Mayence*, summon'd the Electors, and invited them to repair by a certain Day to *Cologn*, in order to proceed to the Election of a King of the *Romans John*, Elector of *Saxony*, who was otherwise dissatisfy'd with the Emperor, would not come thither, but the other six Electors (*Ferdinand* himself being compris'd) did, notwithstanding his Absence, proceed, and elected on *January* 5, 1531, *Ferdinand*, Brother to the Emperor *Charles* V, King of the *Romans* The Elector of *Saxony*, and with him *Ernest* Duke of *Lunenburg*, *Philip* Landgrave of *Hesse*, *William* and *Lewis* Dukes of *Bavaria*, complain'd of that Procedure, maintaining, all, that this Election could not subsist, for the many Defects that occurr'd therein, but chiefly because the Archbishop of *Mentz*, in convening the Electors, had exceeded his Power, since the *Golden Bull* gives it him but only when the Empire is vacant And therefore when the Electors of *Mentz* and *Palatin* were for entring into a Negotiation with them, to oblige them to acknowledge *Ferdinand*, the Elector of *Saxony*, and the other Princes, gave them to understand, That they were ready to allow of what was pass'd, provided an Ordinance was made, that for the future, before any Procedure to the Election of a King of the *Romans*, during the Life of the Emperor, the Archbishop of *Mayence* should be oblig'd to call together the six Electors (because the King of *Bohemia* has no Share in the Affairs of the Empire out of the Election, nor even in the Deliberations which are had on the Necessity of an Election) and six secular Princes, in order to deliberate and consult with them, whether it be necessary to proceed to an Election during the Life of the Emperor, and that he should be even oblig'd to take their Consent in good Form, for the Convocation The Accommodation was not made, till the Treaty which was concluded at *Caden* in *Bohemia, June* 29, 1534, and one of its chief Articles contain'd in express Terms, * That the Elector of *Saxony* should acknowledge *Ferdinand* for King of the *Romans*, but that *Ferdinand* should be oblig'd, on his part, to procure that the Emperor, and the other Electors, should pass an Ordinance, That for the Time to come, whenever there should be Occasion to proceed to the Election of a King of the *Romans*, during the Life of the Emperor, the Electors should be oblig'd to meet, to deliberate on the Necessity of such Election

Moreover we maintain, That the Princes Electors, as Electors, cannot take a Resolution of that Importance, and which destroys one of the most momentous Parts of the fundamental Law of the Empire, but that it is the Electoral College that alone, as first Member of the Empire, can do it, because it can dispense in the Matter of Common Law, by a sovereign Power, with the tacit Consent of the two others, which have not oppos'd the Possession the Electoral College has by little and little acquir'd of the Sovereignty of the Empire, in part of its most important Functions, of which the Election of a King of the *Romans*, during the Life of the Emperor, is not the least And as it is impossible it should be perform'd, but the Emperor must have a greater Hand therein than the Electors, and his Authority deprive them, in some Measure, of the Liberty which ancient Custom and the *Golden Bull* gives them, the whole Empire has an Interest to hinder the Imperial Dignity from becoming hereditary, or that there should be several Heads of the Empire at the same Time

It is also plain, that they who have caus'd Coadjutors (as one may say) to be given them during their Life, have done it out of a Design to render the Empire hereditary in their Family It was so under *Charlemagne*, and the Emperors of his House, as we have said elsewhere So that they could cause Successors to be nominated during their Life, and those of the House of *Saxony* and *Suabia* were willing it should be known that they endeavour'd to establish a kind of hereditary Succession in their Families But there is Room to wonder, that the Emperor *Charles* IV should dare to desire the Electors to proceed to the Election of his Son, contrary to the express Declaration of the Law he had just publish'd The History of that Time says, That he alienated a part of the Demesne of the Empire, to corrupt those who without that would not have betray'd their Honour, nor cast their Eyes on a Prince who brought so many ill Qualities to the Government of the Empire, that the Electors were forc'd to do, out of the last Necessity, what they had before done by Corruption, that is to say, to proceed to the Election, and to substitute in his Place, not a King of the *Romans*, but an Emperor, during his Life In the other Elections of this Nature, so much Deference was had to the Will of the Emperors who had caus'd the same, that one may say, that not only the Directions of the *Golden Bull* were not consider'd therein, but also that even the Electors themselves did not enjoy all the Liberty, which they are entitled to by the fundamental Law of the Empire, and with-

---
* Sleidan l 9.

out which the whole Election is faulty

It is true that by the Articles 34, and 38, of the Capitulations of *Ferdinand* II, and III, the Emperor permits the Electors to proceed to the Election of a King of the *Romans*, during the Life of the Emperor, nay without his Consent, when they shall judge it necessary for the Good of the Affairs of the Empire but the Law * in that Case presupposes a manifest Necessity, notorious to all the Empire, and declar'd such by the Electors, before the Archbishop of *Mayence* can summon his Collegues
† In what we have now said, the Quality of King of the *Romans* has a Signification very different from that which the *Golden Bull* gives it and that the Difference thereof may appear, it is requisite to know, that that Quality was not so much as known in the House of *Charlemagne* There were indeed to be found therein Kings of *Italy*, of *Germany*, of *Bavaria*, of *Lorrain*, of *Arles*, &c but no King of the *Romans* This Quality was at that Time inseparable from that of Emperor, who was Sovereign Prince of the City of *Rome* It is also certain that the Emperors of the House of *Saxony*, down to *Henry* V, when they procur'd their Sons to be nominated to the Succession of the Empire, caus'd the Quality of King to be given them, but without the Denomination of any particular Province and they were only call'd Kings and not Kings of the *Romans*, or Kings of *Germany* It is since the Reign of *Friderit*, sirnam'd *Red-beard*, that Histories begin to speak of a King of the *Romans* but in the Signification in which that Quality is taken at this Day, that is to say, to denote thereby the presumptive Heir of the Empire whereas the *Golden Bull*, when it speaks of the King of the *Romans*, means the Prince who is chosen by the Consent of the Electors, after the Death of the Emperor, and to whom nothing is wanting but the Papal Coronation, to take the Quality of Emperor

Charles the *Bald* having usurp'd the Imperial Dignity after the Death of the Emperor *Lewis* II, his Nephew, and having oblig'd Pope *John* VIII to crown him, to the Prejudice of *Lewis* the *German*, his eldest Brother, was the first that began to reckon the Years of his Empire separately from those of his Reign, not so much to signify that he held the Imperial Dignity from the Pope, as because being King of *France* from the Year 840, he could not confound the Years of his Reign with those of the Empire, to which he had succeeded but since the Death of *Lewis* II, who did not dye of thirty five Years after that Time So that one might say, That this Distinction did not begin from the Day on which he was crown'd by the Pope, but from the Day he had taken possession of the Empire, which was vacant by the Death of his Nephew if one was not oblig'd to acknowledge, that the too scrupulous Devotion of some Emperors, and the Softness of others, has yielded to the Popes an Advantage which they had not, and whereof they have made so good a use, that they not only pretended to have the Imperial Dignity at their Disposal, but have also found the Means to share the Empire with them, and make themselves Masters of its Capital City

We shall see elsewhere whether it be the Pope or the Election that bestows the Empire and it is sufficient to acknowledge here, that most of the Emperors have had that Deference to the Popes, as to be contented with the Quality of King, till they were crown'd by the Pope, notwithstanding they were in full possession of the Sovereignty, and actually discharg'd all the Functions thereof, so that they wanted only the bare Name And it is in this Sense we must understand the *Golden Bull*, when it speaks of the King of the *Romans*, future Emperor that is to say, of the Sovereign Prince of the Empire, who only takes the Quality of King, but is in effect Emperor, and who will take the Quality thereof immediately after the Ceremonies of the Coronation by the Pope From whence we may conclude, That there can be no room absolutely for the Election of a King of the *Romans*, but when the Empire is vacant; because the same State cannot have two Sovereigns at the same Time But at this Day, the King of the *Romans* is nothing else, than the Prince who is nominated by the Electors during the Life of the Emperor, with Power to administer Affairs, in the Emperor's Absence, and in his Name and to succeed to the Empire immediately after the Death of the Emperor, without any need of a farther Election or Confirmation Whereof we have an Example in *Rodolphus* II, who having been elected King of the *Romans* during the Life of the Emperor *Maximilian* II, his Father, and being present at the Diet of *Ratisbone*, where the Emperor dy'd *October* 12, 1576, caus'd immediately the Inscription of his Lodgings to be alter'd, and instead of *Royal Majesty*, made be put, *for his Imperial Majesty* And it is by this Means that they endeavour to save their Honour, who make no Difficulty to elect a King of the *Romans* during the Life of the Emperor, when they say, That the Law speaks only of the Election of a King of the *Romans*, who is Emperor in effect but that the modern Elections are properly no more than Nominations of a Successor and so are not within the Bounds of the Law But this Shift does not destroy the Reason we have before alledg'd, drawn from the same *Golden Bull*, which by giving to the Archbishop of *Mayence* the Power to convene the Electors his Collegues, in order to an Election, declares expressly, That he cannot make use of the same, but when the Empire is vacant so that to have a Convocation of the Electors, for the Election of a King of the *Romans* during the Life of the Emperor, the Archbishop of *Mayence* is oblig'd to get himself authoriz'd by those who have Power to do it in default of the Law, that is to say, by the States of the Empire, or by the College of Electors, who represent them, when this Election gives only the Survivorship, and as one may say, the Coadjutorship And thus it is we must understand the 38th Article of the Capitulation of the Emperor who dy'd last, which says, That the Electors may meet for the Election of a King of the *Romans*, whenever they shall judge it

* Chap. I   † VII *The Quality of King of the* Romans

necessary

necessary for the Good of the Affairs of the Empire, even during the Life of the Emperor, with, or without his Consent. For to make a King of the *Romans* in the Sense of the *Golden Bull*, during the Life of the Emperor, is what is impossible, unless there has been a previous Proceeding for the Deposition of the Emperor reigning, as has been said before.

CHAP. IX.

Of the Electoral College, and of the Dignity and Power of the Princes Electors in general.

WE have said in the foregoing Chapter, that there is no room for an Election, properly speaking, but when the Empire is vacant: but before we speak of the Election it self, we shall treat of the Electoral College, and of the Princes Electors in general, as also of some Preliminaries which precede the Election, and make one of the principal Parts thereof.

We have shewn, that the College of Electors, and the Electoral Dignity, had their Beginning but about the Time that the Emperor *Charles* IV regulated their Number, and confirm'd their Rights, Privileges and Prerogatives, by his perpetual and irrevocable Edict, which is call'd the *Golden Bull*, which speaking of the Princes Electors, says, That they are *the Flambeaus that gave Light to the Empire, its Buttresses, Pillars and Bases, the most necessary Members of the Emperor, the Prop which by an ingenious Prudence supports the whole Fabrick, and the main Force of the Imperial Arm, that he may by their Counsel govern the perpetual Inconstancy of the Affairs of the World.* And the Emperor *Rodolphus* II, in his Decree of *July* 17, 1590, says, *That the Eminence of the Princes Electors is so inseparable from the Eminence of the Imperial Power, that the one cannot subsist without the other.* And indeed, whether we consider the Electoral College, as the first, and most powerful Member of the Empire, and the Electors, as the only hereditary Officers of the Empire, or look upon 'em as the Princes, who can bestow the Crown of *Germany* on whom they please, and can deprive the Emperor of his Dignity, if they judge it necessary for the Good of the Affairs of the Empire, we shall be oblig'd to acknowledge, that if in all *Europe* there be a Body that can be put in parallel with what there was most August in the ancient *Roman* Empire, it is without doubt the Electoral College, which is compos'd of so many Senators, Consuls, and Dictators, or rather of so many Sovereigns, as there are Princes Electors.

* It is certain that the first Institution of the Electoral College confin'd it to the Number Seven, but it would be folly to seek for the Reason of this Number, in the imaginary Efficacy, which is by a superstitious Observation bestow'd on the Septenary Number, since it is to be found only in the Inequality of Votes, which was esteem'd necessary to avoid those Divisions and Schisms, which were but too common in the Empire. *Simon Schardius* says, That the Author of the Institution of the Electoral College, was oblig'd to fix it to the Number Seven, rather than to that of Three or Five, as well because he could not refuse that Honour to the Three Archbishops, who were already Great Chancellors of the Empire, as thereby to give some Satisfaction to all the Orders of the ancient Electors, which were compos'd of Kings, Dukes, Marquisses and Counts. He presupposes that the Electoral College was instituted by the Emperor *Otho* III, and agrees that the Empire became elective but only after the Death of *Lewis* III. So that those pretended Electors of whom he speaks, can only be consider'd from the Year 912, to 1002, in which *Otho* III dy'd, and yet it will not be found that during that Time there were any Kings present at the Elections, not even the King of *Bohemia*, whose Regal Dignity is only known since the Year 1086. Moreover, the Dutchies and Counties were not as yet hereditary, and most of the Marquisates were only erected by *Henry* I. So that it cannot be said, That at his Election there were any Marquisses present, no more than at that of *Conrade* I his Predecessor. And we have shewn elsewhere, that the Succession of the Three *Othos* was rather hereditary than elective.

There are others who say, that *Otho* III made choice of those Prelates and Princes, to the end the Archbishop of *Mentz*, Great Chancellor of the Empire in *Germany*, might chuse for the *Germans*; the Archbishop of *Triers*, as Great Chancellor of the Empire amongst the *Gauls*, and in the Kingdom of *Arles* for *France*; the Archbishop of *Cologn*, as Great Chancellor of the Empire in *Italy*, for the *Italians*; the King of *Bohemia* for the *Slavonians*, and the Duke of *Saxony* for the *Saxons*. But this Reason is by so much the more impertinent, as by that means the Count *Palatin* of the *Rhine* and the Marquiss of *Brandenburg* would represent no body, besides that it is ridiculous to say, that the Archbishop of *Triers* speaks there in the Behalf of the *French*, since for these many Ages past *France* does not acknowledge the Empire, and does not intermeddle in its Affairs as being a part thereof, nay she would not allow at the last Treaty of *Munster*, that *Alsace*, which was given it to reimburse the Charges of the War, should continue in the Dependence of the Empire.

* *The Reason of the Septenary Number.*

We say then, that the Truth of the Matter is, that those Princes had no great Difficulty to exclude all the rest; as well for the Reasons heretofore alledg'd, * as because that the Archbishops of *Mentz*, of *Triers*, and of *Cologn*, being the most powerful Prelates of *Germany*, who had had a good Share in the former Elections, there was an Obligation to consider them, as well as the King of *Bohemia*, who was very potent, and without doubt the first Prince of *Germany*, not only on the account of his Regal Dignity, but also of the many Provinces he possess'd, a good part of which he had annex'd to his Crown. The Count Palatin of the *Rhine* was one of the first Princes of the Empire, not only by reason of his Estates, which were the finest and largest of all *Germany*, and because he had the Quality of the Emperor's Judge, but also as being the eldest of the House of *Bavaria*, as Grandson to the Emperor *Adolphus* of *Nassaw*, and as Unkle to the Emperor *Charles* IV, who had marry'd in the Year 1353, for his second Wife, *Agnes* of *Bavaria*, Daughter of *Rodolphus* III, Count Palatin of the *Rhine*. The Duke of *Saxony* possess'd the first Dutchy of the Empire, and had for Grandfather by the Mother's side the Emperor *Rodolphus* I. And the Marquisate of *Brandenburg* was in the Hands of the Princes of the House of *Bavaria*, Sons of the Emperor *Lewis* IV. So that we must not wonder if these Princes seiz'd the Honour and Authority of electing the Emperors to themselves, at a Time when the other Princes of the Empire were not in a Condition to dispute it with them.

Neither must we wonder that the Number of the Secular Electors is greater than that of the Ecclesiasticks. For since these last assist at the Elections but only in the Quality of Princes, it is very reasonable to allow some Advantage to those who are so in effect, and since the matter is to elect a Secular Prince, or, as the *Golden Bull* says, a Temporal Head to the Empire, it is just that the Seculars should have the best Share in the Election, even if there were not reason to fear, lest the Ecclesiasticks (who depend in some measure on a Foreign Power) should labour to establish the Pope's Authority, to the Prejudice of the Dignity of the Empire.

† As for the Dignity of the Electors, besides the Epithets the *Golden Bull* gives them, it must be own'd to be so great, that to make them Kings, they only want the Title and Regal Crown. The Law it self gives them, in some measure, the Majestick Dignity, when it says, that they who undertake any thing against the Person of an Elector, are guilty of High Treason, because their Dignity constitutes a part of the Imperial Dignity, and is inseparable from it, as we have said in the beginning of this Chapter.

‡ And it is for this reason that the Electors precede all the other Princes, of what Condition or Quality soever they may be. The *Golden Bull* says expresly, * *That in all the publick Ceremonies and Assemblies of the Empire, the Princes Electors, as well Ecclesiasticks as Seculars, shall hold their Place and Rank, and that no other Prince, of what Dignity, Estate, Condition, or Quality he may be, shall pretend to any Precedency.* And this Rule admits of no Exception in reference to the Diets and General Assemblies of the Empire, nor even with respect to the Electoral Assemblies, where the Electors represent the Sovereignty. This is so true, that altho' the same Text seems to make an Exception of Foreign Kings, when it says, *That particularly the King of* Bohemia *shall precede, without any Contestation, all other Kings, how powerful soever they may be*, yet nevertheless all the other Electors lay claim to the same Advantage, and enjoy it in effect: nay they do not suffer (even out of the Diets) any Foreigner to precede them in *Germany*. We shall say nothing of the manner how *Lewis* IV, Elector *Palatin*, receiv'd *Henry* Duke of *Anjou* in his Journey to *Poland*, altho' he was a King Elect, and Brother of the first King of *Christendom*. For he made it but too plain that he was at home, and one may say, that he us'd that great Prince with a little Incivility. But we have an illustrious Example in *Joachim* II, Elector of *Brandenburg*, who refus'd to yield Precedency to *Rodolphus* of *Austria*, notwithstanding he was Son to the Emperor then reigning, crown'd King of *Hungary*, and destin'd to the Empire, to which he attain'd some Years after.

It is true that the Fathers of the Council of *Basil* would needs take Cognizance of the Difference which happen'd there about Precedency between the Electors and the Bishop of *Chalon*, Embassador from *Philip the Good*, Duke of *Burgundy*, and that they were imprudent enough to pronounce in Favour of the Bishop, by the Decree they made on *May* 23, 1437. But this Sentence being given by incompetent Judges, had so little Force, that when the Embassadors of *Charles the Bold*, the Son of *Philip*, would have taken Advantage thereof, and pretended to the Precedency in the Diet of *Ratisbone* in the Year 1471, the Electors oppos'd it, and oblig'd the Embassadors to take their Seat out of the Rank, on a Bench design'd for Foreign Embassadors, right against the Emperor, while they themselves kept their Places, by the Emperor's side, and in the same Line. The Electors were in the right to act after this manner; because the Duke of *Burgundy*, notwithstanding he possess'd several Dutchies and Counties, and was a Prince of the Blood, and Dean of the Secular Peers of *France*, could not be consider'd but in two respects, to wit, either as a Foreign Prince, and in that Quality he could not pretend to Rank or Place before, nor amongst the Electors, or else, as Prince of the Empire, on the account of his Dutchies of *Brabant*, of *Limburg*, and of *Luxemburg*, and in this Quality he was oblig'd to give Place to the Electors. Besides, he could not dispute Precedency with them, because, as he possess'd no Territories in Sovereignty, he could not refuse the Hand to the Electors, † who are Sovereign Princes, as we shall see presently, altho' they do Homage, because in doing it to the Empire, they only do it to themselves. This was the reason why the Pope's Nuncio

---

* Chap. 1. Rem. 3.
" Chap. 6.
† *High Treason is committed against the Electors*
‡ *Holland and Zeland had been Members of the Empire*
‡ *The Precedency of the Electors*

and the Embassador of *England*, knowing very well that the Electors would not yield Precedency to them, would not be present at the first Coronation of the Emperor *Charles* V As in effect, they would have been so far from giving Place to the Nuncio, that *Adolphus* of *Schauemburg*, Elector of *Cologn*, absolutely refus'd to yield Precedency to Cardinal *Moron*, the Pope's Legate at the Diet of *Ratisbone* in the Year 1556 It is true that in the Council of *Trent* the Ecclesiastical Electors plac'd themselves after the Legates, but then we must consider, that it was an Assembly merely Ecclesiastical, and that the Electors, by being immediately after the Legates, had without doubt the most honourable Place after those who represented the Pope's Person, in the Quality he gives himself of Head of the Church, and before all the other Secular Princes

* We don't deny that every where else but in the Empire the Electors have a great deal of Deference for Crown'd Heads, and we believe that even in *Germany* it self they would make no Difficulty to pay some Respect to Kings, especially to him who is in Possession of preceding all the other Kings of *Christendom*, since the fourth Article of the Capitulation of the Emperor that dy'd last declares expressly, that the Embassadors of the Electors shall give Place to those of Crown'd Heads ev'n at the Court of the Emperor, but then we say also, that excepting Kings, there is no Prince but who is oblig'd to yield them the Precedency The Duke of *Savoy* is one of the first Princes of *Europe* · He takes the Quality of King of *Cyprus*, and his Embassadors are treated in *France* as those of Crown'd Heads yet nevertheless the Duke *Charles Emanuel* (the Prince in the World who knew best how to procure himself what he thought his Due) Grandson by the Mother's side to *Francis* I, King of *France*, Son-in-Law to *Philip* II, and Brother-in-Law to *Philip* III King of *Spain*, being one Day at Table with the late Cardinal *de la Vallette*, and the Duke of *Longueville*, and this last having ask'd him after what manner he carry'd it in reference to the Electors, he took off his Hat, and said, That he respected them as his Masters and Superiors, because being Vicar of the Empire, he was oblig'd to acknowledge them for such An Answer that ought to give Confusion to those who not being acknowledg'd for Princes, and not being so in effect, will however carry it on the Level with the Electors, and fail in the Respect they owe them

† We said before that the Princes the Electors are Sovereigns, and it is without doubt this Sovereignty which gives the greatest Lustre to the Electoral Dignity It is true this will appear a Paradox to those who believe that the Sovereignty of the Empire resides in the Person of the Emperor, as Head of the fourth universal Monarchy But besides that this Opinion is very ill establish'd, we shall content our selves with this previous Supposition, as being a certain Truth, that he that possesses all the Rights of Sovereignty is a Sovereign, and to shew that the Princes Electors possess them all In the *first* place they make Laws, Statutes and Constitutions They abolish the old ones, and establish new ones, without the Emperor's Leave, and with so absolute a Power, that the Chamber of *Spire* is oblig'd to have regard thereto in the Judgments it gives between their Subjects, even tho' these Laws and Constitutions should derogate from the Common Law *Secondly*, They exact an Oath of Fidelity from their Subjects, and by that means oblige them more strictly to themselves than to the Emperor, to whom the Electors are only oblig'd in a simple Acknowledgment of Vassallage, which they pay him as to the first Person of the Empire *Thirdly*, They create Officers for the Administration of Justice They make Regulations for the Civil Government, and have their Chancellors, their Parliaments, their Counsellors of State, their Treasurers, and all the other Officers of State, Jurisdiction, Polity, and Revenues, that Sovereign Princes are us'd to have But *Fourthly*, the most illustrious Mark of Sovereignty is the Power they have of making War, and to be able with Impunity to handle the Sword which God puts into the Hands of none but Sovereigns Private Persons in making War with one another, are liable to the Penalties which the Laws ordain against the Seditious, who disturb the Tranquility of the State, and violate the publick Peace And if they take Arms against their Prince, they are Rebels and Criminals of High Treason There is no Pretext that can justify the Arms which a Subject takes against his Prince, and it is not a War, but a Revolt, and an actual Rebellion, the Guilt whereof cannot be expiated but by Death, If sometimes the Title of Peace is given to the Treaties Sovereigns make with their Subjects, to oblige them to lay down their Arms, it is an Abuse Peace is only the Conclusion of a lawful War, declar'd by a Prince to a Prince, and by a Sovereign to a Sovereign whereas Rebellions can be quell'd by nothing but the Death of the Rebels, or by the Pardon which the Goodness of the Prince has granted them But the Electors apprehend nothing of all this They declare and make War whenever they please and to this purpose they make Levies of Soldiers, as well for their own Defence as for the Assistance of their Friends and Allies They appoint Places of Arms, and of Rendezvous They lay up Magazines of Provisions and Ammunition They cast Cannon, fortify their Towns, and build Forts on their Frontiers And that they may make themselves more powerful and more considerable, they make Leagues and Alliances amongst themselves, and with Strangers, and the Emperor cannot be offended thereat Whereof we have not only Examples in the Confederacy of *Smalkalden*, which the Elector of *Saxony* and some other Protestant Princes engag'd in about six score Years ago, and in the Union the said Protestants made some Years before these last Wars of *Germany*, but also the Laws and Constitutions of the Empire allow thereof, and are very express on this Subject, particularly those of the Years 1555, 1564, and 1570 And it is for this Reason that the Electors treat with the Emperor on

---

* *The Electors give Place to Crown'd Heads every where else but in Diets they have in common with other Princes*

† *The Rights of Sovereignty of the Electors, which they have in common with other Princes*

6 E the

474   *Of the* Election *of the* EMPEROR, *and*

the Level, and make no mention of Pardon or Abolition but of an Amnesty, or General Oblivion, or what has been done on both sides. We have an Example hereof in the Treaty which the late Duke of *Saxe* made with the Emperor *Ferdinand* II, in the Month of *May*, 1635, which is commonly call'd, *The Peace of Prague*, wherein the Elector speaks and treats like a Sovereign as well as the Emperor *Itself*. I. The Electors have high, middling, and low Jurisdictions, not only as the other Lords who have a supream Jurisdiction, but in a much more eminent Degree, since they judge *in dernier ressort*, especially in Criminal Causes where they proceed to an Execution notwithstanding an Appeal. We shall hereafter have occasion to enlarge on what relates to Civil Proceedings. *2dly*, They harbour and give Protection to the *Jews*, *3dly*, They grant Letters of Pardon of Grace or Remission, and of Abolition, of Revocation of the Ban, and of Restitution to Honours and Estates, and generally all others for the Dispatch whereof there is a Necessity to have recourse to the Sovereign Power. *4thly*, They grant the Rights and Privileges of Fairs and publick Markets. *Amb ... 5thly*, They raise Impotes and Taxes, as well personal as real, and establish Forces and Duties. *7thly*, They permit and forbid Hunting and Fishing in the Forests and Rivers within the Extent of their Power, and have for his purpose all the necessary Justice and Jurisdiction *in forreft*. They have the Rights of Waifs and Strays, of Shipwracks, and of Treasures for what ever Heirs deceas'd. They coin Money both of Gold and Silver with what Stamp and Title they please. They enjoy so in that hence worth and profit out that of their Neighbours Coining, carried within their Jurisdiction. *Thirdly*, They take the Tithes of Mines and Salt-pits, which private Persons discover in their Territories. They have a Share in the Treasures that are found, and pay no more of it than to the Emperor *Quanieme*. They find their Embassadors to Kings, Princes and foreign States. *Ifdtwo*. They contract Marriage as well within as without the Empire without asking Permission for the same. *Seventh*, They grant Dispensations for Marriages in the Degrees forbidden by the Canons. And *Iawfally*, They even change the State of Religion within their Countries. To say all in a word, They do every thing that a Sovereign can do and all that a King can do in his Dominions. We do not want Examples nor Authorities to confirm what we have here said, but for as much as no body can doubt hereof, and to impress it on the Princes of the Empire enjoy the Rights and Privileges of what is the Electors, we shall content our selves with remitting the Curiosity of the Reader to the whole Volume, which have been written on that Subject, by *Isannus* in his Treatise *De Regalibus Herr Aruiacus, & Jure Maieftatis, Math. Stephanus in Jurisdictione, Ursuinus in Re duking in Regiminis Scientia & Ecclesiastico, Arumaeus, Beforosus, Hermundus de Trenburg, Daniel Otto* &c. and shall speak now of those Rights and Privileges which are peculiar to the Princes Electors.

The Electoral College may be consider'd, either as the first Member of the States of the Empire, whereof the two others are the Princes and free Cities, or else as an Assembly compos'd of Princes, who do not have a right to elect an Emperor, and to call to the Empire him they judge most worthy thereof. As one of the Members of the Empire it was compos'd (before the Number was augmented by the Treaty of *Munster*,) but of six Princes, to wit of the Archbishops of *Mayence* of *Triers*, and of *Cologn*, of the Count Palatin of the *Rhine*, and since the Year 1623, of the Duke of *Bavaria*, who was put in his place of the Duke of *Saxony* and of the Marquis of *Brandenburg*. At this Day it is compos'd of seven Princes, because two Electorates have been made of *Bavaria* where before there was but one but the Electoral College is such, that is to say, compos'd of Princes which are consider'd in the Quality of Electors comprehensibly, together with those which are mention'd, the King of *Bohemia* who, notwithstanding he has no Share in the Affairs of the Empire, is nevertheless an Elector and has a Right to assist at the Election as to the without him the Electoral College, convoked for an Election, would not be complete, because if it were neglected, he might cause it to be declar'd void, as we shall say hereafter.

* Under eight Princes have alone the Right to make an Emperor and to call to the Empire, by the way of Election, a Prince who without that could not pretend thereto and is that is the first and chief Function of these Princes, they were called Electors because they have a Right to elect, to the exclusion of all the other Princes of *Germany*. When we say that the Electors alone have a Right to elect we do not only exclude therefrom all the other Princes, but even the Emperor, who cannot be present at the Election that is made of a King of the *Romans* during his Life, when the absolute Necessity of the Affairs of the Empire obliges the Elector to proceed thereto, but we also give to understand, that the Right of electing an Emperor is peculiar, and, as the Schools term it, proper to the Princes Electors. We shall speak more amply thereof elsewhere, when we shall treat of the Election itself.

‡ The Princes Electors are in Possession, for above these six score Years, not to make an end of the Election till they have limited the Power of the future Emperor, by Conditions put down in Writing and whereof a sort of Treaty is made which is call'd the *Capitulation*, by which the Emperor elect renounces to almost all the Rights of Sovereignty which the former Emperors enjoy'd. We also make up a whole Chapter thereof in the Sequel of this Treatise. Wherefore we shall proceed.

‖ The Right of electing belongs to the Electors by the Fundamental Law, and the States of the Empire have referr'd to them that of setting Bounds to the Sovereignty of the Emperor; and they do both the one and the other in the Name of the whole Empire, because they have succeeded in that to the Right which all the Princes, Prelates and Free Towns en-

juy'd

joy'd formerly, but the Question is to know Whether the said Princes Electors have also the Power to depose him they have chosen. This is what might be doubted. First, because it seems as if the Power of the Electors consisted only in the Election, which being performed, they have executed all the Power of their Office. Secondly, because the Law that gives them a Power to elect, does not give them that of deposing, since there should have been a particular Expression for that Purpose, because the Law cannot be strain'd to things that are odious. Thirdly, because that the Emperor is the Lord of the Universe, and, as such, above the Laws. That it belongs only to God to judge Sovereigns. That the Emperor becomes such, immediately after the Election, and so the Power of the Electors cannot reach his Person. Fourthly, because the same Law that obliges the Emperor to appear, and be accountable to the Laws, before the Count Palatin of the Rhine, ordains very expresly, That the Count Palatin shall not take Cognizance thereof, but in a Diet or General Assembly, and in Conjunction with all the States of the Empire in a Body, who alone can judge him, and therefore that the Princes Electors cannot assume a Right which the States of the Empire have reserv'd to themselves.

We willingly own that the Law, which gives to the Electors a Right to elect, does not give them the Power to depose, but it does not follow from thence that the Electors cannot depose. Rights are not always acquir'd by an express Law, for if that were the States themselves of the Empire could no depose the Emperor. And yet it is certain nevertheless that they can, and there are Examples thereof in Charles the Gross, and in Adolphus of Nassau because that Right is natural to them, and as such they have reign'd it by a tacit Content to the Electors, who have exerted it without any Opposition from the States. It is true also that a Subject cannot dethrone their Sovereign. But that in elective States, they, who have a Right to elect, have also the Power to depose, unless the Election is perform'd by the States assembled in a Body, but we are so far from supposing, that the Emperor is Emperor, is Sovereign, that on the contrary we have just before said, that there is not any Elector but who is Sovereign. Now it is impossible to establish a Plurality of Sovereignties in the same State, is to give several Suns to the World. And since the Emperor is oblig'd to acknowledge the Count Palatin for Judge, it is evident that he may be judg'd, and by Consequence that he may be also depos'd, for it would be to no Purpose to judge him, it the Judgment cannot be executed, and if he can be depos'd by the State, he may there will be so by the Electors, to whom the States have resign'd their Power. They are very much mistaken, who believe that the Electors have fulfill'd the whole Duty of their Office by the sole Act of Election, since the Golden Bull ordains very expresly, * That the Electors shall meet every Year, to make a Report to the Assembly of those Differences they have debated in their respective Provinces, and to remedy the same among themselves, and to reform what shall be found amiss, even in the Person of the Emperor. We have alledg'd the Examples of Charles the Gross, and of Adolphus of Nassau. The first was depos'd by the States, in a Body, because the Empire being still at that Time hereditary, it was of Necessity requisite that all the States should meet in a Body to proceed to an Action of that Importance. Adolphus of Nassau was depos'd by those who had then a Right to elect, whose Number (it being as yet regulated, it may be said, that those Princes and Prelates who were present, represented in some Measure the States of the Empire. But there is not any room left to doubt of the Right of the Electors after the Deposition of Wenceslas. He was Son to the Emperor Charles IV, and had been elected since the Publication of the Golden Bull so that the Order that was observ'd in his Deposition, is sufficient alone to resolve the Right which we attribute to the Electors, by reason of the Sanctity held therein. We have the several Procels thereof and the Judgment, amongst the Imperial Constitutions publish'd by Goldast, where John Archbishop of Mentz speaks of the same, in the VIIIth Article in these Terms, † Nos ergo Joannes Archiepiscopus, in nomine sacri Romani Dominion Sacri Romani Imperii Coadjutor, cum consensu, tractatu & consilio confratrum dignitatis & Electorum, non a nobis repraesentata, quae pragmatica, doaris in seriam procedimus Dominum Wenceslaum, ceu in tibram, negligentem, dissipatorem, a indignum Sacri Romani Imperii administratorem Romani Imperii, omni causa Gratia, Dignitate, a Dominio absoluto nudamus, privamus, & habitus causa &c. That the Archbishop had said before, That it was in Consequence of the Complaints, of the Princes, Prelates, and free Cities had made against the Conduct of Wenceslas, that the Electors had put this important Affair in Deliberation, but he does not say that the Princes, Prelates, and free Towns, had any Share therein. And when he pronounces the Sentence of Deposition, as it occurring y belonging to him to publish the Election, or the Quality of Dean of the Electoral College, he makes no mention at all of the States of the Empire, but only speaks in the Name of the Electors his Colleagues. However, since the said verbal Process divests the of the Complaints of the Princes, Towns, it would not be amiss to bring for this Presumption, That at the very Occasion of the Extremities, the Advice of some of the most considerable Princes of the Empire was taken after which the Electors met. In order to judge of the Necessity of the Deposition, that they might authorize the Archbishop of Mentz to send for out his Summons for the Convocation, which he has not otherwise the Power to do, but when the Empire is vacant, since the Emperor himself cannot cause it without the express Permission and Consent of the Electors, and that by the Example of what was practis'd at the Proceeding to the Deposition of the Emperor Henry IV. This Prince protested against the Proceedings of those who would effectually do Violence to him, and said, That he ought it least to be allow'd the Time to call together the Archbishops of *Mentz*, of *Triers*, and of *Breme*, the Bishops of *Frisingen*, of *Augsburg*, of *Coire*, and of *Basil*, the Duke *Magnus* and the Duke *Thierry*, the Duke of *Bohemia*, the Counts of *Flanders* and of *Burgundy*, and the others; that they might take Cognizance with them who were already assembled, of the Cause of the Deposition.

It might here be doubted, whether in the Case of Deposition, it would be necessary to summon thereto the King of *Bohemia*. We make no Difficulty to conclude in the negative; not so much because the King of *Bohemia* was not present at the Deposition of *Wenceslas*, for that could not be, *Wenceslas* being himself King of *Bohemia*, as because the King of *Bohemia* is an Elector for the Election only, and has nothing to do with the Deliberations which regard the Affairs of the Empire, which alone has an Interest, it should be well govern'd, and because the Electoral College is consider'd in this Action, as first Member of the States of the Empire, rather than as merely electoral.¹ It is also certain that the Right of electing is only a bare Honour, which the Emperor *Charles* IV had a Mind to annex to his Crown of *Bohemia*, and this Advantage cannot be strain'd to the Prejudice of the other Electors, whose Authority is by so much the greater, as the Number of the Electors is lesser.

‡ The XIIth Chapter of the *Golden Bull*, which we lately quoted, says, *That it is necessary the Princes Electors (who are the unshakeable Foundations, and the immoveable Bases of the Empire) being remote one from another, should meet oftner than they were us'd to do, to the end, that having made a Report to the Assembly of what is wanting, and of the Disorders they shall have observ'd at home, and in their Neighbourhood, they may be able to remedy the same by their common Advice, and ordain by the Prudence of their Counsels the necessary Reformation.* The Emperor adds, *That they shall meet once a Year in Person, and in one of the Imperial Towns.* The Necessity which the Law imposes on the Electors of meeting every Year, and in Person, was rather an Injunction, and a Service, than a Right or a Privilege. They could not dispense therewith, but with the Emperor's Permission, and the common Consent of all the Electors. But at this day there is nothing that obliges them, to meet, except the sole Necessity of the publick Affairs, which may move and invite them but cannot compel them. There is no Time now limited, nor Place fix'd for that Purpose, neither is there any thing that can absolutely oblige them to be personally present at these Assemblies. The Capitulation of the Emperor *Charles* V, confirm'd by the Capitulations of all the other following Emperors, says, *We also permit the six Princes Electors above-nam'd to meet, by virtue of the Golden Bull, as often as they shall have a Conveniency to do it, and shall judge it necessary for the Good of the Affairs of the Empire, that they may deliberate and consult, without our being able to hinder the same, or on that Account to conceive any Indignation against the said Electors in general, or against any one of them in particular.* This Capitulation, as also all the others, speaks but of six Electors, and by that means tacitly excludes the King of *Bohemia* from the Electoral Assemblies, for the Reasons we shall have Occasion to touch upon hereafter, when we shall speak of the King of *Bohemia* in particular.

These Assemblies are call'd *Collegiate Diets*, to distinguish them from those which are held only on the Score of the Election, and which are for that Reason call'd *Electoral Diets*. * *Goldaste* thinks that these Collegiate Diets have had their Beginning during the Interregnum, under *Alphonsus* of *Castile* and *Richard* of *Cornwall*, but the express Words of the Emperor *Charles* IV, when he says, That he ordains, that for the Time to come the Electors shall meet every Year, and that this Ordinance shall last as long as it shall please him and the Electors, sufficiently shew that they have no other Foundation than the *Golden Bull*. Since that Time, the six Electors have made several Treaties amongst themselves, for the Preservation of this Right, and particularly that which they made at *Worms* in the Year 1521, by which they ordain, That the Archbishop of *Mayence* shall have Power to convene the other Electors his Colleagues, by his Letters Patents, (which shall contain the Subject of the Convocation) only when the Remoteness of the Electors shall have hinder'd them from agreeing on the Affair that is propos'd, in which Case the Elector of *Mentz* shall assign them a Day, by which they shall repair to *Mayence*, *Franckfort*, *Gelnhausen*, or to *Fuld*. But at this Day the Practice is otherwise. The Convocation is not perform'd till the Electors have judg'd it necessary. There is no set Place for these Assemblies, and they are often made at the Instance of the Emperor, who sometimes is there present, either in his own Person, or else by his Commissioners. It is not that he has any Right to be there, but the Electors suffer it. As for the Affairs that are there treated off, they are without doubt the most important of the Empire, as appear'd by the Collegiate Diet, which was conven'd at *Ratisbone*, in the Year 1630, where the Electors oblig'd the Emperor *Ferdinand* II to dismiss the the Duke of *Wallestein*, to disband part of his Army, to supersede the Contributions, gave Audience to the Embassadors of *France* and *England*, who acted there contrary to the Emperor's Intentions, and forc'd him to consent to a Treaty that was very glorious to *France*, and very disadvantageous to the House of *Austria*, concerning the Succession to the Dutchy of *Mantua*.

† The Convocation of the States General of the Empire, or of the Imperial Diets, belongs only to the Sovereign, and forasmuch as the Emperor represents the Sovereign Magistrate in the Empire, it also belongs to him to convene the Diets. We say that the Emperor represents the Sovereign, but because he is not so in effect, since the Empire of *Germany* is not a Monarchical State, the Power of convening the States has been so limited in his

---

‡ IV *Of meeting about the Affairs of the Empire.*
† V *To give their Consent to the Convocation of the General Diets.*

* In Tractatu de Regno Bohem. Lib. 3 C. 6 n. 7

Person

of the ELECTORS of the EMPIRE

Perfon by all the Capitulations, that he cannot do it without the Confent of the Electors. The Capitulation of the Emperor *Ferdinand* III, fays very expreſly, *We will not undertake to ſummon a Diet, or General Aſſembly, till we have firſt ſent an expreſs Deputation, to deſire the Conſent and Agreement of the ſix Electors.* The Confent of the Electors muſt be expreſs, and to be ſuch, the Emperor muſt make known to the Electors the Exigency of Affairs that obliges him to call a Diet, requiring the Advice and Confent of each of them, even with reference to the Time and Place of the Aſſembly, which is ſo abſolutely neceſſary, that if the Emperor omits asking the Advice and Confent of any one of them, the whole Convocation will thereby be defective and null. The Electors ſend their Confent in the Form of *Letters Patents*, ſign'd under their Hand, and ſeal'd with the Great Seal. Where we muſt obſerve, That therein the Plurality of Votes is conſider'd as well as at the Elections, as well for the *negative* as the *affirmative*: ſo that the Oppoſition of two or of three would not hinder the Emperor from proceeding, but that of four would, becauſe it would divide the Suffrages, and hinder the Convocation.

* The Confent of the Princes Electors, is not only requiſite for the Convocation of the Diets, but alſo to all the other Acts by which the Emperor might arrogate to himſelf any Right of Sovereignty. The Right of making Treaties of Alliance, and of Leagues offenſive and defenſive, without doubt belongs to none but Sovereigns: but ſo far is the Emperor (as Emperor) from having that Power, that on the contrary, by the Capitulations which have been made with the laſt Emperors, it is very expreſly ſaid, that the Emperor ſhall make no League nor Alliance, as well in *Germany* with the Princes of the Empire, as elſewhere with foreign Princes and States, without the Confent of the ſix Electors: it not being ſufficient to obtain for that, the Confent or Declaration in Writing, of each Elector in particular, but the Emperor is oblig'd to make the Propoſal thereof in a Collegiate Diet, expreſly conceiv'd for that Purpoſe. And foraſmuch as it was otherwiſe acted, in the Negotiation of the Treaty of *Prague* in the Year 1635, it was declar'd by the Treaty it ſelf, and by the Capitulation made the Year following with *Ferdinand* III, that it ſhould not be a Precedent: but that the former Capitulations ſhould be inviolably obſerv'd for the future, without any Diſpenſation to the Emperor, except in the utmoſt Neceſſity, and for very weighty and preſſing Cauſes, in Confideration whereof, he may delay convening the Collegiate Diet, but he ſhall nevertheleſs ask the Confent of the Princes Electors in particular.

† The Electors, as Sovereign Princes, can raiſe Taxes, and lay Duties on their Subjects but they cannot lay, nor raiſe any Duties on Strangers who paſs through their Countrey, but with the Confent of all the other Electors aſſembled in a Collegiate Diet. The Reaſon is, becauſe their Sovereignty does not extend beyond the Places under their Obedience: and foraſmuch as the Electors and their Subjects enjoy a general Exemption, of all Duties of Entries, or carrying out, Tolls, &c. it was thought fit that the raiſing of thoſe Duties, and the ſetling the Impoſts, ſhould not be done but by the general Confent of 'em all, as the laſt Emperor promiſes in his Capitulation, Article 20, &c. That he will not ſuffer any Perſon, of what Condition or Quality ſoever he may be, to lay new Impoſts, or to inhance and continue thoſe already eſtabliſh'd, without the Confent of the ſix Electors, obtain'd in a Collegiate Diet, nor can the Emperor for that Effect, give Letters of Recommendation to the Electors.

‡ The Empire had formerly its Revenues, and the Emperor had his Demeſnes, the Revenues whereof were capable not only of ſupplying the ordinary Expences of his Court, but alſo of furniſhing the extraordinary Charges of the War. But for above theſe two hundred Years laſt paſt, the Emperors have liv'd only on the Revenues of their hereditary Countries, and made War but with the Contributions which they have rais'd on all the States of the Empire, purſuant to the Taxation or Aſſeſſment of the Regiſter. When the Emperors went to receive the Imperial Crown at *Rome*, all the Eſtates of the Empire were oblig'd to ſend along with him a certain Number of Men at Arms, to wit, twenty thouſand Foot and four thouſand Horſe: and in default of the Supply of Men, that Duty was converted into Money, at the Rate of four Florins, that is to ſay, of eight Livres of *French* Money for each Foot Soldier, and of twelve Florins, or of four and twenty Livres per Month for each Trooper. It is true that this Number was moderated in the Diet of *Worms*, in the Year 1557, to three thouſand ſix hundred and four Horſe, and to ſixteen thouſand four hundred forty nine Foot, whoſe Pay, at the Rate we before laid down, amounts to near two hundred and twenty thouſand Livres per Month, which being multiply'd (for they ſometimes grant a hundred, or ſixſcore thouſand) amounts to very conſiderable Sums. This Collection of Money is what we call Contributions, and in the *German* Phraſe, the *Journies to* Rome: and they are demanded by the way of Subſidy. The Electors in giving their Confent thereto, might authoriſe the raiſing thereof, but ſince the laſt Diet ſome Alterations have been made, and it has been thought reaſonable, that ſince all the States were charg'd therewith, all the States ſhould likewiſe conſent to the raiſing of the ſame.

* We have ſaid before in this Chapter, that the Electors have a Right to coin Money, and that they can even regulate the Standard thereof, but that the ſame is in common to 'em with all the other Princes and free States of the Empire. And therefore that is not the Right or Privilege which we pretend to ſpeak of here, but of that the Electors have to hinder the Emperor from giving the Privilege of coining Money, to thoſe who had it not before, without the Confent of the ſix Electors. We ſpeak of that Right of coining Money,

---

† VI To hinder the Emperor from making Alliances without their Confent.
‡ VIII To hinder the Emperor from making Gatherings, or raiſing Contributions.
| VII They give leave to raiſe Impoſts.
* IX To give their Confent for the Privilege of coining Money.

which

which the Emperor can grant with the Consent of the Princes Electors, and not of that of regulating the Standard thereof, which the Emperor, as Emperor, has not, nor cannot grant, because it is inseparably annex'd to the Sovereignty

† The Proscription, or banishing out of the Empire, which succeeded to the Interdiction of Fire and Water of the ancient *Romans*, is without doubt one of the most illustrious Marks of Sovereignty For which Reason it was not thought adviseable to leave it to the Discretion of the Emperor Formerly it was done only by the Estates assembled in a Body, as appears in the Proscriptions of the two *Henrys*, Father and Son, Dukes of *Saxony*, and of *Bavaria*, because the Proscription, which is call'd in *Germany* the Imperial Ban, being a Penalty that extends to the Children, so as to deprive 'em even of the Estates which they do not inherit from their Fathers, but to which they succeed by virtue of the first Investiture, and which cannot be alienated by Contract, it is just that this Alteration, which destroys in some Measure the Nature of the Fiefs, be done with the Approbation of all the States of the Empire, or with a right Information of the Cause by the Imperial Chamber, which represents them tho' it seems as if the Text of the *Golden Bull* (which speaks of the Misfortune of the Sons, who are depriv'd of their paternal Inheritance) ought not to be understood, but of the Confiscation which is made in the Case of High Treason, in the first Degree But it is not in the Proscriptions that are made according to the Forms and ordinary Procedures, that the Consent of the Electors is requir'd It is necessary, only when in notorious Cases the Criminal is proceeded against in an extraordinary Manner, whereof there are two very remarkable Instances The first in the Proscription of *John Frideric*, Elector of *Saxony*, by the Emperor *Charles* V And the other in that of the Elector *Palatin* who dy'd last, by the Emperor *Ferdinand* II This last gave Occasion to the Complaints which the Electors of *Saxony* and of *Brandenburg* made of the Precipitancy with which the same was done so that to prevent the like Disorders for the future, that Article was inserted in the Capitulation of *Ferdinand* III, which says, That the Emperor shall not be able to put any body into the Ban of the Empire, even in notorious Cases, without the Knowledge, Advice and Consent of the Princes Electors, provided those against whom such Proceeding is, be of the States immediately subject to the Empire it being certain that they who are not, may be proscrib'd by the Lords on whom they depend

‡ And forasmuch as the Procedures we have now spoken of, were sometimes executed by the Council which happens to be in Authority near the Person of the Emperor, which frequently encroach'd also on the Jurisdiction of the Chamber of *Spire*, it has been thought adviseable to stipulate by the Capitulation made with the late Emperor, That a Regulation should be made for the *Aulick Council* of the Empire, with the Consent of the six Electors, according to which the Emperor should be oblig'd to reform the same

* The Electors have also this Advantage over the other Princes of the Empire, that they pay nothing for the Investitures, which they are oblig'd to desire a Confirmation of at every Change, for which all the other Princes, as well Ecclesiasticks as Seculars, are oblig'd to pay sixty three Marks of Silver and a quarter, to the Officers of the Emperor's Court, and to the Vicars of the Electors, according to the Direction of the *Golden Bull* and the Prince who receives the Investiture, is to leave the Horse he was mounted on at that Time to the Great Mareschal of the Empire, or to his Deputy, and in their Absence to the Mareschal of the Emperor's Court

Charles IV, in regulating the Duties which the Princes of the Empire are to pay when they do Homage for their Fiefs, to sixty three Marks and a quarter of Silver, excepts therefrom the Electors, ¶ because that Sum being due to the Deputy Officers, or to the Officers of the Emperor's Court, and the Electors being hereditary Officers of the Empire, it would not be just that the Substitutes should exact Money or Presents from their Superiors But this is what we shall have Occasion to speak more amply of elsewhere, in Chap XI of this Discourse

All these Rights and Privileges are so annex'd to ‡ the Electoral Dignity, that they are inseparable therefrom, just as the Electoral Dignity is inseparable from the three Archbishopricks of *Mentz*, *Triers* and *Cologn*, and from the Principalities to which the *Golden Bull* appropriates the same So that he who is in a peaceable Possession of the Kingdom of *Bohemia*, of *Bavaria*, of the Dutchy of *Saxony*, of the Marquisate of *Brandenburg*, and of the County *Palatin* of the *Rhine*, is Elector, and ought to be summon'd to the Election, without possibility of separating the Electoral Dignity from the Principalities, at any Time, or for any Cause whatever, and without possibility of the one being su'd for, or recover'd without the other, in Law or otherwise, agreeably to the *Caroline* Constitution, which is express therein, in Chap 30

* Now that the Princes Electors might have wherewith to support this high Dignity, which gives them so much Advantage over the other Princes, the Emperor *Charles* IV thought fit that their Principalities should be indivisible, and forbad the Partition, or dismembring thereof in such plain Terms, that none but the Eldest alone can succeed thereto Formerly, and before the Number of Electors was regulated, the Practice was otherwise, because the Electoral Dignity being shareable among the Princes of the same House, it was necessary the Principality should be so too And in fact we see several Princes of the House of *Bavaria*, several Dukes of *Saxony*, and several Marquisses of *Brandenburg* at the Elections, at the same Time, and who in effect possess'd together with the Title, the Principalities and the Electoral Dignity it self

At this Day the *Golden Bull* is exactly observ'd in that Respect For notwithstanding

---

‡ X *No Proscription to be made without their Consent*
* XII *To receive the Investitures gratis* † *Chap* 30
* *The Principalities are indivisible*

‡ XI *To consent to the Ordinances of the Aulick Council*
¶ *The Electoral Dignity is appropriated to the Principalities*

there

there are above ten Branches in the *Palatin* Houſe, ſix or ſeven in that of *Saxony*, and three in that of *Brandenburg*, yet it will not appear that the Ducal *Saxony*, the *Palatinate* of the *Rhine*, or the Marquiſate of *Brandenburg*, to which the Electoral Dignity is appropriated, have been diſmember'd *Luſatia* was ſeparated from *Bohemia* by the Treaty of *Prague*, and that of *Munſter* gives the *Upper Palatinate* to the Elector of *Bavaria* But then *Luſatia* does not make a Part of the Kingdom of *Bohemia*, nor the *Upper Palatinate* a Part of the *Palatinate* of the *Rhine*, on the Account whereof the *Palatin* is an Elector of the Empire In like Manner the Elector of *Saxony* has given Portions to his Brothers in *Luſatia* and *Thuringia*, but then thoſe Provinces have nothing in common with the Dutchy of *Saxony*, to which the Electoral Dignity was annex'd before it enter'd into the Houſe of *Miſnia* The Marquiſſes of *Anſpach* and of *Culmbach*, are younger Brothers of the Houſe of *Brandenburg*, and have had their Portions in *Prutland* and *Franconia*, but they had none in the Marquiſate of *Brandenburg*, by virtue whereof the Prince who enjoys it at this Day is Elector We don't ſpeak here of the Right of Elderſhip, or Primogeniture, which ſeveral other Princes of *Germany* have eſtabliſh'd in their Families, by a Cuſtom inſenſibly introduc'd, or by particular and domeſtick Ordinances, and by teſtamentary Diſpoſitions, confirm'd by the Emperor, becauſe it does not belong to the Subject of our Diſcourſe, and therefore we ſhall content our ſelves with ſaying here by the by, that the Right of Elderſhip takes place in the Houſe of *Auſtria*, in that of *Bavaria*, in the Dutchy of *Wirtemberg*, in that of *Brunſwick* and of *Lunenburg*, where nevertheleſs there are three Branches, in the Houſe of *Heſſe*, where it has been eſtabliſh'd of late, in the two Branches of *Caſſel* and *Darmſtad*, and in that of *Guſtrau* and *Suerin* in the Dutchy of *Mecklemburg*

After what we have ſaid of the Grandeur, Dignity and Rights of the Princes Electors, we think we may add, That ſince theſe Princes enjoy, within the Extent of their States, all the Advantages the Emperors poſſeſs'd there, when they were ſtill Sovereign Lords of *Germany*, they have Reaſon to put at the Head of their Titles, *by the Grace of God*, which is an Honour reſerv'd to them only, who are acknowledg'd for Sovereigns, and who in effect hold only of God and their Sword And as the Author of a Book entitl'd, *An Enquiry into the Rights of the King, and of the Crown* of France, might very well have forborn ſaying, *That the Electors hold of the Sovereignty of our Crown, and own themſelves Vaſſals, and liege Men of the Kings of France*, wherefore the King was willing to do them the Juſtice to diſtinguiſh them, and conſider them in quite another Manner than he does almoſt all the other Princes of *Europe*, in order to oblige them to give him the Title of *Majeſty*, which the Princes Electors gave formerly to the Emperor only They gave to all foreign Kings the Style of *Royal Dignity*, and ſaid they were in poſſeſſion of ſo doing, by virtue of a very ancient Cuſtom * as they repreſent it in their Letters to the King of *Sweden*, of *Auguſt* 13, 1630, on the Complaints that Prince had made, in writing to the Electors, on *April* 25, in the ſame Year, that in giving him the Style of *Royal Dignity*, they had not given him the Title, which he held from God and his Anceſtors

During the Negotiation of the Peace at *Munſter* and *Oſnaburg*, the Plenipotentiaries of *France* had ſignify'd, that the King could no longer ſuffer that they ſhould refuſe him the Title which the greateſt Monarchs of the World made no Difficulty to give him, but if the Princes Electors would change their Style, his Majeſty would alſo change that which levell'd 'em with the Dukes, and Peers, and Mareſchals of *France*, and even with the Counts of *Germany* The Elector of *Bavaria*, who could not hope to maintain himſelf in the Electoral Dignity which was but juſt come into his Houſe, without the good Offices which he expected from *France*, had done it, and after his Example the Elector of *Cologn* his Brother The two other Eccleſiaſtical Electors, who are not born Princes, and who had given the Title of Highneſs to a General of an Army, might very well give that of Majeſty to the King, and the Prince *Palatin* was not acknowledg'd as an Elector So that in the whole Electoral College there remain'd only *Saxony* and *Brandenburg* who had not yet had that Deference to the King, The laſt made an Offer of it by a Perſon of Quality, whom he ſent on purpoſe to the Court at the beginning of the Year 1646, but foraſmuch as the Elector of *Saxony* continu'd to proteſt, that he would not change the Style, the Court ſignify'd alſo that the King would not do it neither, unleſs all the Electors did ſo, becauſe in writing to the Electoral College there would be an Obligation to Honour otherwiſe thoſe who gave the King the Style of Majeſty, than thoſe that ſhould not, which was what could not be done in the ſame Letter However when it was repreſented, that even tho' all the Electors ſhould comply with what the King deſir'd of them, it would not be juſt the ſame Honour ſhould be done to the Eccleſiaſtical Electors who are not Princes by Birth, as to thoſe that are, ſince the Emperor and the Electors themſelves us'd them differently, and accordingly the King would always make a Diſtinction, Reaſon began to be hearken'd to, and in the Year 1647, the Queen, who was then Regent, was pleas'd to write with her own Hand to the Elector of *Brandenburg*, and ſtyle him Brother The King follow'd this Example in the Year 1654, and the Year following the *Sieur de Lumbres*, being ſent from Court to his Electoral Highneſs, carry'd Letters with him, which were conceiv'd in the ſame Terms, and counter-ſign'd by a Secretary of State ſo that at preſent no Difficulty is made therein But notwithſtanding the Elector of *Brandenburg* gives the King the Style of *Majeſty*, yet he does not do the ſame to the other Kings of *Europe*, not even to the King of *Spain*, to whom he continues the Style of *Royal Dignity* Which is ſo true, that altho' as Duke of *Pruſſia*, he was a Vaſſal of the Crown of *Poland*, (before he had obtain'd the Sovereignty thereof by the Treaty he has lately concluded) he gave

* Lundorp. Act Pub Tom III Lib I Tract II, & 12

no other Style than that of *Royal Dignity*, to the King of *Poland*, when he was in *Germany* and styl'd him *Majesty*, only when he was in *Prussia*, where he consider'd him as his Sovereign

After this it cannot be doubted that the Princes Electors have a Right to send Embassadors, since the *Golden Bull* gives this Quality to the Ministers whom they employ out of the Empire, and that they ought to be treated in the Courts of foreign Kings like the Embassadors of Crown'd Heads Since those of *Savoy*, which cannot enter into Competition with the Electors, enjoy that Advantage in the Court of *France*, which serves for a Rule to all the other Courts of *Europe*, without its being in the Power of any other Prince whatever to refuse them this Honour Here we take the word Embassador in its proper and common Signification, and not improperly, as was done when it was suffer'd to be slipt into the Treaty that was made three Years ago by the Deputies of the City of *Hamburgh*, for the Freedom of Commerce, tho' with this Difference, that therein the Quality of *Embassadors deputed* is given them, that is to say, of simple Envoys of a Town, whose Freedom is still contested, as one of the principal and most understanding Ministers of the Court answer'd very pertinently, when he was ask'd Audience for these pretended Embassadors But this is what we shall have an Opportunity to make a particular Discourse about, in the General State of the Empire of *Germany*, which shall follow in a little Time, if this finds Approbation

CHAP X.

Of the Ecclesiastical Electors.

WE have said before that the Electoral Dignity of the Ecclesiasticks is not less appropriated to the three Archbishopricks, than that of the Seculars is to the four Principalities which the Emperor names in the *Golden Bull* So that he who says, the Archbishop of *Mentz*, of *Triers*, and of *Cologn*, denominates at the same time so many Princes Electors of the Holy Empire, however with this Difference, that whereas the Secular Electors succeed to the Electoral Dignity by hereditary Right, and by virtue of the Investiture of the first Acquirer, the Ecclesiasticks hold theirs but by the Choice which the Chapter makes of their Persons by the way of Election The Clergy and the People have ever had a Right to elect their Bishops in *Germany*, but the Chapters of the Cathedral Churches, have by little and little usurp'd the same, to the Exclusion not only of the Laity, but likewise of all the rest of the Clergy of the same Diocese, tho' without Prejudice to the Confirmation of the Emperor, of whom the Archbishop or Bishop elect was oblig'd to receive the Investiture by a Ring and a Wand, till Pope *Gregory* VII undertook to brand with Simony the Duty the new Bishops paid to their Sovereign. This was one of the chief Grounds of the Civil Wars in the Reign of the Emperor *Henry* IV, who saw his own Son in Arms against him, under a Pretext which the Malice of the Clergy, and the Superstition of those Times had render'd plausible However the same Son having attain'd to the Empire, and taking into Consideration that this Attempt robb'd him of one of the most valuable Jewels of his Crown, he oppos'd it with all the Vigour imaginable, till finding himself threaten'd with the same Disorders which had cost his Father both the Empire and his Life, he was forc'd to accommodate the Matter by the Treaty he made with the Pope *Calixtus* III, in the Year 1122, by which he renounc'd the Right of Investiture by the Ring and Wand, contenting himself with the Homage the Bishops were to do for their Temporals, and for the Fiefs which hold of the Empire But by the *Concordat* made between the Pope *Nicolas* V, and the Emperor *Frederick* III, in the Month of *April* 1447, the Pope does not only reserve to himself the Right of confirming the Election of the Prelates, but also the Power of judging of the Validity of the Election, of declaring it faulty, and to provide for the Churches, if it shall appear that the Election was not Canonical, or if the *Elect* shall fail to take out the Papal Confirmation within a Month and twenty Days, without which the Emperor cannot admit him to his Oath for the Temporal

This Election is perform'd by a Plurality of the Votes of the Chapter, and it is not enough that the *Elect* has more Suffrages in reference to those who may be set up by others, but the Plurality of Votes must be consider'd with respect to the whole Chapter As for instance, if of thirty Canons or Prebendaries, of which the Chapter is compos'd, eight chuse *Peter*, ten *Paul*, and twelve *James*, notwithstanding the Number of those who elect *James* is greater by half than that of those who nominate *Peter*, and greater also than that of those who elect *Paul*, yet *James* shall not be Archbishop, but *James* must have more Votes alone than the two others together, and the Suffrages of the major part of the Chapter, that is to say, that at least sixteen must concur to his Election to make it Canonical But when one part of the Chapter elects, and the other postulates, the Number of the Postulants must be at least twice as great as that of the Chusers, that is to say, there must be at least twenty Postulants against six Chusers, to make the Postulation succeed Now we call Postulation the Nomination of a Person who cannot be elected according to the Canons, either for some Defect in his Person, Age, Birth, or otherwise, or because he is already provided with a Bishoprick For inasmuch as the Canons forbid the nominating to a Bishoprick a Minor and a Bastard, and that it is not allow'd to possess two Bishopricks at the same time, and so the Election that should be made of a Person in whom these Defects should be found, would be vicious, the manner of Proceeding therein is by the way of Postulation, that is to say, that the Chapter prays him, who has the Right of confirming the Election, to approve the Nomination it has made of a Person whose Election would not otherwise be canonical, and in such case the Catholicks apply to the Pope, and the Protestants to the Emperor

But we here speak of the three Catholick Electors, who are all Catholicks, in reference to whom the Treaty of *Passau* made in the Year 1555, declares in express Terms, That so far are the Chapters of *Mayence*, of *Triers*, and *Cologn* from being able to make Choice of a Protestant, that on the contrary, if it shall happen that a Catholick Archbishop or Bishop of a Catholick Diocese changes his Religion, he is oblig'd also to change his Condition, and to leave the Archbishoprick to a Catholick Whereof we have Examples in *Herman* of *Weda*, and in *Gebhard* of *Thruchses*, Archbishops and Electors of *Cologn*, who were depos'd on the account of Religion

It is certain that we do not here consider the Ecclesiastical Electors as Archbishops, but as Princes of the Empire, and Electors, and in this Quality they are oblig'd to receive the Investiture from the Emperor So that it seems that one might say, properly speaking, that the Chapter only makes the Archbishop, and that it is the Emperor who makes the Elector from whence one might conclude, that the three Ecclesiastical Electors cannot be present at the Elections before the Investiture And indeed this Opinion is so well establish'd in the Schools, that the Doctors make it pass for common, tho' Reason, and even Experience, are manifestly against it For the *Thesis* that says, that the Election of the Chapter makes the Archbishop, and that the Investiture makes the Prince Elector, is false, and directly contrary to the Disposition of the *Golden Bull*, which says, That the Electoral Dignity of the Ecclesiasticks is annex'd to the Archbishopricks of *Mayence*, of *Triers*, and of *Cologn*, from whence it follows, that the *Elect* cannot be Elector, unless he be Archbishop, and that he cannot be Archbishop but he must be both Prince and Elector at the same Time, because they are inseparable Qualities in those three Ecclesiastical Electors, who assist at the Elections not only as Princes, but also as Prelates, to whom the Electoral Dignity is so appropriated, that it cannot be communicated to seculars, whose Number is regulated and fix'd, as well as that of the Ecclesiasticks

We know very well that it is the Consecration that properly makes the Bishop or the Archbishop, but this is what no regard is had to in *Germany*, where it is sufficient to have been elected by the Chapter, confirm'd by the Pope, invested of the Temporal by the Emperor, and to have the Administration of the Archbishoprick, to be Archbishop, and to be able to discharge the Functions thereof, altho' the Pope's Confirmation be not altogether so necessary, but that the *Elect* may without it discharge all the Electoral Functions, as we shall see in the Examples we shall produce anon, when we shall have prov'd that the *Elect* by the Chapter may assist at the Elections, even before he has receiv'd the Investiture from the Emperor, that is to say, before he has taken the Oath of Fidelity for his Temporals The Reason is, that the Election gives to the Elect, what the Entrance on an Inheritance gives the Heir, where the Dead gives Seisin to the Living, and where after the Death of a Secular Elector, his Son, his Brother, or other nearest Relation by the Father, succeeds by virtue of the Law, and by reason of the Investiture he has receiv'd in the Person of the first Acquirer So that the Successor being Elector, as soon as he takes Possession of the Principality, from which the Secular Electoral Dignity is inseparable, it follows necessarily that the Elect by the Chapter is Elector as soon as he is in Possession of the Archbishoprick, from which the Ecclesiastical Electoral Dignity is also inseparable Besides, since even according to the Canon Law, the Elect has the Administration of the Temporals, and the Enjoyment of the Fruits, by the sole Virtue of the Election, before the Pope's Confirmation, and even before the Investiture, he has also the Right of giving his Vote at the Elections, which is one of the principal Effects of the Administration, and one of the first Prerogatives and Preeminencies of the Archiepiscopal Dignity I or without that there would ensue such Inconveniencies as it would be impossible to remedy particularly if it happen'd that the Archbishop of *Mayence* should dye, after the Emperor's Decease, and before he had summon'd the Electors his Collegues to the future Election In which Case, if it was necessary that he who should be chosen during the *Interregnum*, should receive the Investiture before he could do any of the Electoral Functions, there could be no Election, since the Vicars cannot give the Investitures of this nature during the *Interregnum*, and so the Ordinance which the *Golden Bull* has made concerning the Election, could not be executed in any one single Point The Electors might indeed meet without the Convocation of the Archbishop of *Mayence*, but the same Archbishop could not be summon'd to the Election, which however he might cause to be declar'd vicious, for his being neglected and the whole Order of the Election would be overthrown, since there would be no body to tender the Oath to the other Electors, to take their Votes, and to pronounce the Decree of the Election, because the Law gives these Functions to the Archbishop of *Mentz*, to the Exclusion of the other two Ecclesiastical Electors, who are not authoriz'd by the Law for that purpose And it signifies nothing to say, that the Ecclesiastical Electors, in taking the Oath at the beginning of the Election, are oblig'd to keep to the Form which is prescrib'd them in the *Golden Bull*, and to swear *by the Oath they have taken to the Empire*, and that they take no Oath to the Emperor, but when they receive the Investiture of their Temporals, and therefore that they must have taken it, before they can be admitted to the Election. For besides that we can destroy the Force of such Reasoning, and shew that it makes entirely for us, because the secular Electors are oblig'd to take the same Oath,

6 G

in the same Terms, and yet notwithstanding that, it is certain they can assist at the Election before they have receiv'd the Investiture of their Fiefs, as we shall see in the following Chapter, we say that the Word Oath, in the *Golden Bull*, is taken in a very extensive Signification, for the Duty and Obligation which all the Subjects owe to the Empire, otherwise this Form of Speech, *I swear by the Oath*, would be altogether incongruous and impertinent

To which we must add, That if the Archbishops, who have been elected by the Chapter, can do the Functions of Prince before the Investiture, they may also do those of Prince Elector Now it is indubitable, that the Archbishops of *Mayence*, of *Triers*, and of *Cologn*, assist at the General Diets of the Empire, in the same Quality that gives them Admittance into the Collegiate Diets, and even to the Elections themselves They there hold the Rank of Princes Electors, and as such assist at the Deliberations which the Electors, as well Ecclesiasticks as Seculars, have amongst themselves It was in this Quality that *Daniel Brendel* of *Hamburgh*, who was elected Archbishop of *Mayence* on *April* 18, 1555, assisted the same Year at the Diet of *Augsburg*, and at all the Deliberations of the other Electors, before he had taken the Oath of Fidelity, and receiv'd the Investiture from the Emperor *Jacob d'Els* was elected Archbishop of *Triers* in the Month of *April*, 1567, and yet he was present the same Year at the Diet of *Ratisbone*, in the Quality of Elector, altho' he had not as yet obtain'd the Investiture from the Emperor But let us come to the Elections The Emperor *Ferdinand* I finding himself in Years, and being willing to secure the Imperial Dignity to his House, resolv'd to cause his Son *Maximilian* to be chosen King of the *Romans*, about the latter end of the Year 1562, in which *John Gebhard* of *Mantsfeld*, Archbishop and Elector of *Cologn*, dying on *November* 2, the Emperor sent Orders to the Chapter, to proceed to the Nomination of another Archbishop, to the end that might not retard the Election of his Son The Chapter did so, and elected *Frederick* Count of *Weda*, who assisted at the Election of *Maximilian* II, tho' he had neither the Pope's Confirmation, nor the Investiture from the Emperor The Emperor *Rodolphus* II dy'd *February* 10, 1612, and during the *Interregnum*, to wit, on the 17th of the same Month, dy'd also *Ernest* of *Bavaria*, Elector of *Cologn* *Ferdinand* his Nephew succeeded him on *March* 12, so that the Empire being vacant, he could not receive the Investiture Yet nevertheless he assisted at the Election of the Emperor *Matthias*, which was perform'd on *June* 13, of the same Year Moreover, the same *Ferdinand*, who enjoy'd together with the Archbishoprick of *Cologn*, the Bishopricks of *Liege*, *Munster*, *Hildesheim*, and *Paderborn*, till *September* 13, 1650, never so much as went about getting himself consecrated, and has made it plain by his Example, That to be Elector, the sole Possession of the Archbishoprick is sufficient, and that the Consecration, and the Investiture, are not at all necessary thereto

* The Emperor *Charles* IV, who during the whole Time of his Reign labour'd only to ruin the Empire, insomuch that *Maximilian* I, making Reflection on the Havock and Waste which was committed in his Time, even to the Ruin of some of the best Provinces, and of the principal Rights of the Empire, was us'd to say, That *Charles* had ruin'd it to enrich his Kingdom of *Bohemia*, and that the Empire of *Germany*, since its first Foundation, had not had a more dangerous Prince than he The same *Charles* (I say) who reduc'd the Empire into the State we see it in at this Day, had nevertheless the Vanity to surround the Emperor's Throne, with a Splendor which dazl'd the Eyes of those who can be amus'd with an Exterior, and took Delight in being attended by Princes, who not only on the Score of their Birth, but also in Consideration of the Electoral Dignity, shew something more august and great, than what is seen in all the other Courts of *Europe* And that nothing might be wanting to this apparent Grandeur of the Emperor, he was not contented to give him for Officers all the secular Electors, but he likewise gave him Great Chancellors, whose Functions he distributed through *Germany*, *Italy*, and the *Gauls*, as if he had still possess'd that vast Power which the Emperor *Charlemagne* had seen reunited in his own Person

It would be of no Utility to treat here of the Origin of the Word, after what has been said thereof by so many learned Men, and particularly by *Spelman* in his *Archæology*, and it is impossible to find out in History the Beginning of this Dignity of Arch-Chancellor, and at what Time it was appropriated to the Sees of *Mayence*, of *Triers*, and of *Cologn*, at least if we pretend to go beyond the Publication of the *Golden Bull*

It is certain that the Archbishops of *Mayence* have taken the Quality of *Apocrisiarius*, of *Capellanus*, of *Custos Palatii*, of *Archi-Capellanus*, of *Referendarius*, and of *Archi-Cancellarius*, long before the *Golden Bull* had regulated the Number, Dignity, and Functions of the Electors As for instance, *Robert* Archbishop of *Mayence*, under the Emperor *Otho* I, *Willigise* under *Otho* III, and under *Henry* II his Successor, *Aribon* under the same *Henry*, and *Conrade* II, *Bardo* under the same *Conrade*, and under *Henry* III, *Luitpold* and *Sigfrid* under *Henry* IV, *Aldebert* I under *Lotharius* II, and *Aldebert* II under *Conrade* III, and *Henry* under the same *Conrade* III, and under *Frederick* I, and we might instance in a great many others, if it were necessary to enlarge upon this Subject But we say, That it will not appear that the Archbishops of *Mayence* have taken the Quality of Great Chancellor of the Empire of *Germany*, exclusively of the other Parts of the Empire, or that their Functions were so annex'd to *Germany*, but that they also discharg'd their Office in *Italy* and elsewhere, when they were there in the Emperor's Retinue, nor that the Archbishops of *Triers* and of *Cologn* have taken the Quality of Great Chancellors of the *Gauls* and of *Italy*, except when they were personally present with the Emperor in *Burgundy*, or in *Italy* On the contrary, the Archbishops of *Mayence* have taken the Quality of Great Chan-

---

* The Offices of the Crown of the Empire, are so many Proofs of the Vanity of the Emperor *Charles* IV

cellor simply, without limiting the Office to the Affairs of *Germany*, sooner than to those of *Italy* And the Reason thereof is evident For the Empire being hereditary and monarchical under *Charlemagne*, and indeed, in some Measure, under the Emperors of the House of *Saxony*, and of *Suabia*, they were rather Chancellors of the Emperor than of the Empire Whereas at this Day they are Chancellors of the Empire, and would not like to be call'd Chancellors of the Emperor, and for Proof thereof, *Hildebert* and *Bruno* Archbishops of *Cologn* have taken that Quality under *Charlemagne*, and under *Otho* I, *Helisachar*, Abbot of *Jumieges*, under *Lewis the Debonnaire*, *Agilmar* Bishop of *Vienna*, and *Hilduin* Abbot of *St Denis*, under *Lotharius* I, *Luttard* Bishop of *Verceil*, under *Charles the Gross*, &c

It is true also, that under the Emperor *Frederick* I, who often pass'd the *Alpes*, on the Account of the Rebellion of the Towns in *Lombardy*, the Archbishop of *Cologn*, who was with him, discharg'd the Office of Chancellor, even with some particular Propriety to the Affairs of *Italy* But we dare not say that these Dignities were appropriated to the Archiepiscopal Sees of *Mayence* and of *Cologn*, and still less to that of *Triers*, since there is not to be found any one Act before the Publication of the *Golden Bull*, where the Archbishop of *Triers* has sign'd in the Quality of Great Chancellor, except the Inscription of the Letter which the Archbishops of *Mayence*, of *Triers*, and of *Cologn*, the Marquiss of *Brandenburg*, the Count *Palatin* of the *Rhine*, and the Duke of *Saxony*, wrote to Pope *Bennet* XII, in the Time of the Emperor *Lewis* IV, where *Baldwin* Archbishop of *Triers* takes the Quality of Chancellor of the *Gauls*, which is very much suspected. On the contrary, there are several where the Archbishops of *Vienna* have sign'd in the Quality of Arch-Chancellors of the Kingdom of *Burgundy* We shall hereafter speak of the Functions of the Office of Arch-Chancellor, when we shall treat of the Archbishop of *Mayence*, who is he that at this Day discharges alone the Office of Great Chancellor, since the Empire is confin'd within the Bounds of *Germany* We shall likewise have Occasion to speak of the Rank which the *Golden Bull* gives to the Ecclesiasticks, and of the Function they discharge at the Ceremonies, when we shall treat of the Election and Coronation of the Emperor

We have said heretofore, when we spoke of the Dignity and Rights of the Electors, that the King, in Consideration of the Advantages they have over all the other Princes of the Empire, was willing to distinguish them, and give them the Style of Brothers. The King has not yet done that Honour to the Elector of *Saxony*, for the Reasons we shall elsewhere relate, but he does not do it at all, neither is there any likelihood that he ever will do It, to the Electors of *Mayence* and of *Triers*, who are not Princes by Birth, because, for almost these hundred Years, these two Chapters do not admit of Princes, and by that Means lopp off from the Princes the Hope of attaining to a Dignity, which, next to the Emperor's, is the first in *Germany*, contenting themselves with calling thereto Gentlemen, who can account for four Descents This is the Reason why the Emperor, in writing to them, treats them with some sort of Superiority, by giving them the Quality of Nephew instead of that of Unkle, which he gives to the secular Electors, or to those among the Ecclesiasticks, who are Princes by Birth The same Difference is to be remark'd in the Letters which the secular Electors write to those of *Mayence*, and of *Triers* For whereas in writing to the secular Princes, or to the Ecclesiasticks when they are born Princes, they give them the Quality of *Most Serene*, and style them *Cousins* and *Brothers*, they give the others only that of *Most Reverend*, and the Style of *Most dear and good Friend* And so far are the Ecclesiastical Electors from being offended thereat, that they even suffer their Inferiors and Subjects to give them the Style of *Electoral Clemency* or *Grace*, † whereas the others do not allow any other Style to be given them than that of *Most Serene Highness* Where we must observe, that this Quality of *Grace* and of *Clemency* is given in *Germany* to every Count, and even to some Barons, especially when they are immediate Subjects of the Empire It is true that Pope *Urban* VIII, in ordaining, in the Year 1628, That the Cardinals should insist upon the Title of *Eminence*, would have it be in common to them with the Ecclesiastical Princes Electors, and with the Great Master of the Order of *Malta* But as at that Time the Cardinals of *Savoy* and of *Lorrain* continu'd to claim the Title of *Highness*, so the Ecclesiastical Electors, when they are Princes by Birth, do not suffer the Title of *Eminence* to be given them, but insist upon that of *Most Serene Highness* And the Protestant Electors, who have no great Deference to the Pope's Regulations, still give to the others the same Titles which were given them before the Bull of *Urban* VIII However this Custom of admitting in the Chapter, none but Gentlemen of four Descents, is not so ancient, but that, since the Institution of that Archbishoprick, Persons of very mean Condition have been rais'd thereto *Peter d'Aichspad* was Physician to *Henry* of *Luxemburg*, before he was Emperor, and was born at *Triers* of very poor Parents *Henry Gurtelknop* was the Son of a Baker of *Isne* in *Suabia*, and was taken out of the Convent of the *Cordeliers* to be made Bishop of *Basil*, from whence he was call'd to the Archbishoprick of *Mayence* And *Willigise*, Chancellor to the Emperors *Otho* III and *Henry* II, and Archbishop of *Mayence*, was the Son of a Cartwright in the Village of *Schoningen*, in the Countrey of *Brunswick* An Example which we instance in, on purpose to make known to Posterity the Modesty with which this Prelate liv'd, in so elevated a Fortune, wherein he made the Meanness of his Extraction to be constantly before his Eyes, by the Wheels he caus'd to be painted in the Windows, and in so many other Places, that they gave a Beginning to the Arms of the Archbishoprick of *Mayence*. Which shews that at that Time Merit was still rewarded, with what is now ap-

---

† *It is after this manner that Queen Margaret made use of the German Word* Gnade, *when she speaks in her Memoirs of the Bishop of* Liege

propriated

propriated to Birth tho' otherwife there is Reafon to wonder, that for fo many Ages there have hardly been feven or eight Princes, who have fought after this high Dignity

* The Archbifhop of *Mayence* is not only the firft of the Ecclefiaftical Electors, but he is as it were Dean of the whole Electoral College It is in this Quality, and as Great Chancellor of the Empire in *Germany*, that he takes place of all the other Electors his Colleagues, that he fummons them to the Electoral Diet, that he gives them the Oath, that he takes their Votes, and that he pronounces the Decree of the Election which Advantages have oblig'd *Sleidan* to call him the *perpetual Conful* of the Electors When we fay that he precedes all the other Electors his Colleagues, we do not pretend to fpeak of the Archbifhop of *Triers*, who almoft always has a Place out of Rank, nor of the Elector of *Cologn*, to whom the *Golden Bull* gives the Precedency within his Diocefe, and within the whole Extent of his *Archicancellarate*, in what neverthelefs cannot be comprehended, the Bifhopricks which the Archbifhop of *Cologn* poffeffes out of his Metropolitan

That of *Mayence* formerly made a part of the Archbifhoprick of *Triers*, from which the Pope *Zachary* feparated it, to erect it into a Metropolitan about the Year 748, in favour of *Bonface*, who is commonly call'd the Apoftle of *Germany*, or rather of *Frife* The Letters the Pope writes him on this Subject, give him but five *Suffragans*, to wit *Tongres*, or *Liege*, *Cologn*, *Worms*, *Spire* and *Utrecht* but it is certain that his Metropolitan extended its Jurifdiction over all the Churches of *Germany* on the other fide of the *Rhine*, where at that time there was no Bifhoprick, becaufe it was ftill in a manner all *Pagan* but the two following Centuries have fo peopl'd it with *Chriftians*, that *Charlemagne*, and the Emperors his Succeffors, were oblig'd to found feveral other Bifhopricks, which have for the moft part been fubjected to the Archbifhoprick of *Mayence* fo that he has at this Day for † Suffragans the Bifhops of *Wurtzburg*, of *Worms*, of *Spires*, of *Strasburg*, of *Augsburg*, of *Coire*, of *Aichftad*, of *Conftance*, of *Hildefheim*, of *Verden*, of *Paderborn*, and of *Halberftad*

‡ As for the Rights, Privileges and Preeminencies, that are peculiar to the Archbifhop of *Mayence*, we have already touch'd upon fome of them, and fhall fpeak more amply thereof when we treat of the Election of the Emperor, where we fhall fee, *Firft*, That it is he alone that has a Right to convene the Electors his Colleagues for the Election, and to appoint the Day for the opening of the Electoral Diet *Secondly*, He tenders the Oath to the other Electors *Thirdly*, He takes the Votes, and votes laft himfelf ! *Fourthly*, He pronounces the Decree of the Election *Fifthly*, It is his Right to crown the Emperor, when the Ceremonies are perform'd any where elfe than in the Metropolitan of the Archbifhop of *Cologn*, as it was judg'd in his Favour in the Year 1653, in the Coronation of the King of the *Romans* who dy'd laft *Sixthly*, As Great Chancellor of the Empire in *Germany*, he is Keeper of the Seals of the Empire, and Warden and Depofitary of all the Acts, Archives, Charters, and even of the Regifter or Matricular Book of the Empire It is in this Quality that he counterfigns all the Refolutions that are taken at the Diets, or General Affemblies, and all the Acts that are publifh'd in the Name of the Empire But forafmuch as he cannot be perfonally prefent at all that is done at the Emperor's Court, he allows the Emperor's Chancellor to fign the Acts in his Abfence, in the Quality of Vice Chancellor, and as Vicar to the Archbifhop of *Mayence*, between whofe Hands the faid Vice Chancellor is oblig'd to take the Oath of Fidelity which he owes to the Empire, and even to the Archbifhop, who in writing to him ftyles him *Trufty* *Seventhly*, It is to the Archbifhop of *Mayence* that the Embaffadors and Deputies, which the Electors, the Princes, and the other Eftates of the Empire, fend to the Diets and General Affemblies, are oblig'd to addrefs themfelves, and to communicate their Powers and Credentials, to have them regifter'd In like manner, when the fame Deputies have a mind to leave the Place of the Affembly before the States break up, they are oblig'd to afk his Leave It is alfo before him, and in the Chancery of *Mayence* that all Summonfes, Proteftations, and all the other important Acts of the Empire are executed *Eighthly*, It is of the Archbifhop of *Mayence*, that Revifals of the Caufes judg'd by the Chamber of *Spires* muft be demanded, unlefs they are demanded againft Judgments given by the Archbifhop of *Mayence* or that the faid Archbifhop himfelf demands them, or that he has otherwife an Intereft in the Affair in which Cafes Application is made to the Archbifhop of *Triers*, who caufes the Civil Requeft to be difpatch'd *Ninthly*, Formerly the Archbifhop of *Mayence* enjoy'd the Right which the *Golden Bull* gives to all the Electors, to judge and determin in *dernier Refort*, with a Prohibition to all their Subjects, of what Condition or Quality foever, to appeal from their Sentences, either definitive or interlocutory, except in the Cafe of denial of Juftice but he does not enjoy that Privilege now, no more than the three Electors his Neighbours and at this Day his Subjects appeal to the Chamber of *Spire*, if the principal Sum exceeds four hundred Florins, which make eight hundred Livres, *French* Money *Tenthly*, It is certain that formerly the Archbifhop of *Mayence* had the Right of crowning the King of *Bohemia* * *Trithemius* and *Brucfius* fay, That it was *Henry* of *Virtenburg*, who fucceeded in the Archbifhoprick of *Mayence* in the Year 1328, that fold that Right to the Church of *Prague* but *Albertus Argentinenfis*, fays, with a greater Appearance of Truth, That the Emperor *Charles* IV, when he erected the See of *Prague* into an Archbifhoprick, annex'd thereto the Right of crowning the King of *Bohemia*

† We muft here add, That the Cathedral Church of *Mayence* has forty two Canons, comprehending in that Number the Prevoft, the Dean, the Great Warden, the Scholaftick and the Chaunter, of whom Four and Twenty

compose what we call the Chapter, and have the Right of chusing an Archbishop, and of giving a Prince Elector to the Empire, to the Exclusion of the other Eighteen, who are admitted into the Chapter, by the Death or Resignation of one of the Capitularies, and that not according to the Order of their Reception, but by the Election of the Chapter

The Electoral and Archiepiscopal Dignity of *Mayence*, is at this Day possess'd by the Right Reverend *John Philip* of *Schonborn*, who having succeeded in the Bishoprick of *Wurtzburg* to *Francis* of *Hatsfeldt*, who dy'd *July* 30, 1647, was elected Archbishop of *Mayence*, on *November* 19, 1642, after the Death of *Anselm Casimir Wambolt* of *Umbstadt*, who had succeeded therein in the Year 1629 It might be said of this Prince, as well as of the two other Ecclesiasticks his Colleagues, what is said of most Prelates, to wit, That they are for enjoying their Benefices, and that they make no other use thereof, than for the Grandeur of their House But we know that we do not speak here ot an ordinary Man He is a Prince who might very well expect from the eminent Qualities he possesses, the Rank his Dignity gives him in the Electoral College He form'd himself on the great Examples of his Predecessors, and particularly on that of the Great *Albert* of *Brandenburg*, whose Memory is still in Veneration in *Germany*, for having preserv'd the Empire against the Disorders with which it was threatend during the *Interregnum* after the Death of the Emperor *Maximilian* I He is one of the wisest Princes of his Time, and loves his Countrey, wherefore we must believe that all his Counsels will tend to the Preservation of the Tranquillity of the Empire, and consequently to the Execution of the Treaty of *Munster*, tho' one may say, That at his Election, the Chapter did not less consider the good Disposition the King had for him, than the extraordinary Merit which entitl'd him to this high Dignity and therefore that he will acknowledge the Obligations he has to *France*, especially while she continues to cooperate to the strengthening of the Peace of *Germany*

‡ The Archbishop of *Triers* precedes the Archbishop of *Cologn*, on account of the Antiquity of his Church, which is said to have been founded a few Years after the Death of our Saviour, tho' *Sulpitius Severus* says, That it was very late before *Christianity* made any Progress on this side the *Alpes* · which hinders us from taking any notice of what has been written of its first Bishops But we say, That the City of *Triers*, which * *Ammian Marcellinus* calls the Habitation of Princes, and † *Solinus*, the largest of all the Cities on this side the *Alpes*, was very considerable in the third and fourth Century, its Diocese extending it self over all the first and second *Belgia*, and over all the first and second *Germany*, these two last Provinces having remain'd under the spiritual Jurisdiction of the Archbishop of *Triers*, till the Pope *Zachary* lopp'd from it in the eighth Century, the Cities of *Mayence*, *Cologn*, *Liege* and *Utrecht* in the second *Germany*, and those of *Strasburg*, *Worms* and *Spires* in the first, in favour of *Bonifacius*, and of the Archbishop of *Mayence* his Successors, as we said before, at this Day it has only ‡ three Suffragans, which are the Bishops of *Metz*, of *Toul* and of *Verdun*, all three Subjects to the King So that the first Church of all *Germany*, which is the Mother of all the rest, was sirnam'd the second *Rome*, and had procur'd to its Archbishop the Sirname of Heir to Saint *Peter*, sees it self at this Day, as it were barren and forsaken, and the least of all the Metropolitans of *Germany*

* The Archbishop of *Triers* does however possess, as to his own particular, several fine Rights and great Advantages, besides those which he has in common with the other Electors his Colleagues He is Great Chancellor of the Empire among the *Gauls*, and in the Kingdom of *Arles* but forasmuch as we have spoken of this Quality before, we shall not trifle away our our Time to examin, whether his Arch-Chancellorship extends it self over all the *Gauls*, or only over the Kingdom of *Arles*, which formerly comprehended *Provence*, *Dauphine*, *Savoy*, the County of *Burgundy* and the *Swisser*, and we shall content our selves to say, That the Archbishop of *Triers* has only the bare Name thereof, without any Functions, since his Office cannot be executed in a Countrey where the Empire of *Germany* is not at all acknowledg'd 2 What he enjoys effectually, is the Honour to vote first in the Elections, pursuant to the express Directions of the *Golden Bull*, which says, first he (to wit, the Archbishop of *Mayence*) shall ask the Opinion of the Archbishop of *Triers*, who shall vote first 3 It is he that takes the Vote of the Archbishop of *Mayence*, after all the others And, 4 that tenders him the Oath, which the Electors are oblig'd to take before the Election 5 He is seated out of Rank, and right against the Emperor, in all the Assemblies, as well Electoral as General, without any Distinction of Places, and without any Pretention of Claim to any other Seat, even in his own Metropolitan, or within the Extent of his Chancery, if it should happen that any Assemblies should be held there 6 He can of his own Authority proscribe, and put into the Ban of the Empire those he is excommunicated, and who do not reconcile themselves within a Year after the Excommunication has been publish'd · and this Proscription has the same Force as if it had been made by the Chamber of *Spires*, or by the States of the Empire 7 He can take into his own Hands, and reunite to the *Demesne* of his Church, all the Fiefs situated in his Diocese, and that hold of the Empire, for default of Homage within the Time limited by the Ordinances 8 All the Fiefs that hold of the See of *Triers* return to the same, by the same Means by which the Imperial I iefs return to the Empire, and particularly for want of Issue Male, unless the Heirs can produce Proofs of their Privilege 9 But the most illustrious of all the Advantages the Archbishop of *Triers* possesses, is that of the *Guard-Noble*, whereby he has the Wardship of all the Minors of his Metropolitan, which neither the other Electors, nor even the Emperor himself can pretend over their Subjects.

‡ *The Elector of Triers* * Lib 15 † Lib. 3 ‡ *His Suffragans* * *His Rights*

He that at this Day is in Possession of the Electoral and Archiepiscopal Dignity of *Triers* is call'd *Charles Gasper* of *Leyen*, who is a Gentleman of the Countrey, and was chosen after the Death of *Philip Christopher* of *Soteren*, who had succeeded in this Dignity to *Lotharius* of *Metternich*, who dy'd September 7, 1623.

The Elector of *Triers* has some Interest in *France*, as well because his three Suffragans, to wit, the Bishops of *Mets*, *Toul* and *Verdun* are Subjects to the King, as because he is a near Neighbour of it, and that being Chancellor of the Empire among the *Gauls*, he would be in great Consideration, and would have great Advantages over his Collegues, if the King should be call'd to the Empire. *Richard* of *Grieffenclau*, Archbishop of *Triers*, was very much consider'd during the *Interregnum* after the Death of *Maximilian* I. But he spoke against the Election of *Charles* V, and for that of *Francis* I, with so much Vigour, that his Passion weaken'd the Force of his Reasoning, and made him be suspected to have been corrupted by *French* Money. Yet nevertheless, if his Courage had been seconded by those who had engag'd their Words to King *Francis* I, *Franco* had without doubt had a good Share in that Election, at least it would have prevail'd so far as to have had *Charles* excluded, which was what the King endeavour'd, more than to procure the Election of his own Person. The Elector who dy'd last sacrific'd himself wholly to the Indignation of the House of *Austria*, for having sought the Protection of *France*, at a Time when that of the Emperor would not only have been of no Utility to him, but also very prejudicial. He was already dissatisfy'd, because in the Year 1625, the Emperor had espous'd the Interest of the Abbot of St *Maximin* against him, when *Gustavus Adolphus*, King of *Sweden*, enter'd into *Germany* in the Year 1630. The Elector seeing that that Prince had pass'd through *Germany* like Lightning, and had treated as declar'd Enemies those who did not declare themselves, was forc'd to take a Side. The Emperor was too remote, too weak, and too much involv'd, to be able to succour him against a powerful and victorious Enemy, who was near at hand, and the Elector not caring to declare for a Prince of a contrary Religion, cast himself into the Arms of the late King, and put himself under the Protection of *France*. This Prelate was very much consider'd, as well on the account of the Rank he held in the Electoral College and in the Empire, as of the Fortresses of *Hermstein* and of *Philipsburg*, which are Places of very great Importance on the *Rhine*. But the Chapter being compos'd mostly of Partisans of the House of *Austria*, hinder'd him from acting according to his good Intentions; which oblig'd the King to command the Count of *Suiza* and M. *d'Arpajou* to secure the City of *Triers*. The *Spaniards* dissembl'd this Affront till after the first Advantage which they obtain'd in the first Battel, of *Norlinguen*, they thought they might declare themselves, and seize the City of *Triers*, which the Count *d'Embden* surpriz'd March 26, 1635, and made the Elector Prisoner.

The Resentment *France* shew'd hereupon, in taking from thence occasion to declare War against the King of *Spain*, might prevail with his Successor to follow his Example, rather than the Necessity he is thought under, of taking a Side on the Score of *Philipsburgh*, or the Hopes it is said might be given him of the Restitution of that important Place, since it does not belong to him, but to the Demesne of the Bishoprick of *Spires*, which the last Elector possess'd, together with the Archbishoprick of *Triers*, but since his Death the Chapter of *Spires* has chosen *Lotharius Frederick* of *Metternich*, who enjoys at present the Propriety of the Place, and the Revenue of the Demesne of *Philipsburgh*, in execution of the Treaty of *Munster*, which Article however imports no more, than that the King shall not pretend to any thing else than to the Protection and Lodgment of his Garrison in the Castle of *Philipsburgh*, but that the Propriety of the Place, with all its Jurisdiction and Possession, together with all the Emoluments, Fruits, Acquisitions, &c. shall belong, and shall be preserv'd to the Chapter of *Spires*.

There is great Likelihood that he will act in Concert with the two other Ecclesiastical Electors in the next Election, or at least that he will not come to a Rupture with those two Princes, who are his Neighbours, and beyond Comparison more powerful than himself. He has a great deal of Deference to the Elector of *Mayence*, who is his Relation and he treats him with some kind of Respect, on the account of the high Reputation that Prelate has procur'd himself in the Empire. He has not less for that of *Cologn*, as well on the score of his Birth, as because he is Cousin German to the Elector of *Bavaria*, with whom he has a common Interest.

*The Archbishop of *Cologn* has his Place on the Emperor's left hand, and so he yields Precedency to that of *Mayence* every where but in his Metropolitan, and within the Extent of his Chancery. He gives place also in some respect to the Archbishop of *Triers*, who has his Seat out of Rank, as we said before. The Archiepiscopal See of *Cologn* depended formerly on the Archbishoprick of *Triers*, and afterwards on that of *Mayence* but the Christian Religion making great Progresses under *Pepin* and *Charlemagne*, it was requisite to found every Day new Bishopricks, and to augment the Number of the Metropolitans. The Archbishop of *Cologn* is without doubt the most ancient of all *Germany*, after those of *Triers* and *Mayence*, and his Church is so rich, especially since it has join'd to its Demesne the Dutchies of *Westphalia* and *Angaria*, which were confiscated from *Henry the Lyon* Duke of *Saxony* and of *Bavaria*, in the Time of the Emperor *Frederick* II, that its Prelates had no great Difficulty to preserve to it the Right of Election, and to make it be compris'd in the Number of the Electors, regulated by the *Golden Bull*. †This Church has this Peculiar to it self, that it admits into its Chapter Princes by Birth, and even eight Doctors in Divinity, and the Canon Law, with this Difference however, that the Chapter which has a Right to chuse the Arch-

---

* The Elector of Cologn   † The Chapter of Cologn is compos'd of 10 Canons

bishop

bishop, and is compos'd of five and twenty Canons, whom they call Capitularies, does not admit of any ignoble Persons, but these eight Graduates are Supernumeraries, and do not make a part of the Number of the other five and twenty Canons, out of which as of a Seminary, they take those that are to fill up the vacant Places of the Chapter. There are at this Day among the Canons, besides *Francis* of *Lorrain* Bishop of *Verdun*, who is Dean of the Chapter, two Princes of the House of *Austria*, two of *Florence*, one of the House of *Hesse*, one of that of *Baden*, one of that of *Bavaria*, two of the House of *Nassau*, and one Prince of *Arnberg*. But the Capitularies who would willingly follow the Example of those of *Mayence* and of *Triers*, or at least communicate this high Dignity to Counts, do not willingly fill the vacant Places with Persons of that Condition.

‡ The Suffragans of the Archbishop of *Cologn* are the Bishops of *Munster*, of *Liege*, of *Minden*, and of *Osnaburg*. The Bishop of *Utrecht* who was the fifth, was taken from it, and his See erected into an Archbishoprick in the Year 1559, at the Instance of *Philip* II, King of *Spain*. The Bishoprick of *Minden* was converted into a Temporal Principality by the Treaty of *Munster*, and makes part of the Equivalent which was given to the Elector of *Brandenburg*, in recompence for that part of *Pomerania* which was yielded to the Crown of *Sweden*. The same Treaty of *Munster*, by making the Bishoprick of *Osnaburg* alternative between a Catholick Prelate, and one of the Princes of the House of *Brunswick Lunenburg*, who are Protestants as well as most of the Inhabitants, withdraws it in some measure from the Metropolitan of *Cologn*, which therefore at this Day has only two Suffragans, to wit, *Liege* and *Munster*.

* 1 The Elector of *Cologn* is Arch-Chancellor of the Empire in *Italy*, but without any Function, as well as that of *Triers*. For altho' there are Principalities in *Italy* which still acknowledge the Empire, yet they are govern'd by Lords who have the Quality of Vicars perpetual, who within their own Jurisdiction do what the Emperor could do, or else the Dispatches are made at the Emperor's Court by the Vice-Chancellor, who does the Office of the Archbishop of *Mayence*, and it is for this reason that the Archives which concern *Italy* are also kept by the said Archbishop in his Chancery, with the other Deeds of the Empire of *Germany*. 2. He precedes the Archbishop of *Mayence* within the whole Extent of his Metropolitan, as also in *Italy* and among the *Gauls*; where he takes his Place on the Right Hand of the Emperor, leaving the Left to the Archbishop of *Mayence*, according to the Direction of the *Golden Bull*. Which 3 assigns him likewise the second Vote in the Electoral College, and requires he should vote immediately after the Archbishop of *Triers*. 4. The same *Golden Bull* says, Chap. 4 § 3. That the Archbishop of *Cologn* has the Office and Right to crown the King of the *Romans*. Where we must observe that it does not give him that Right, but only says that he has it. Tho' it is certain that formerly, and down to the Emperor *Henry* III, almost all the Emperors were crown'd by the Archbishops of *Mayence*. There is an illustrious Example thereof at the Coronation of *Otho* I, where the two Archbishops of *Triers* and of *Cologn* enter'd into a Contestation concerning this Right. The first pretended to it on the Score of the Antiquity of his Church, and the other, because the Ceremonies were perform'd in his Diocese: but they both yielded it to *Hildebert* Archbishop of *Mayence*, who discharg'd it at Function, notwithstanding it was in the Diocese of another. Most of the following Emperors have been crown'd at *Aix la Chapelle*, where the Archbishops of *Cologn* would not suffer their Jurisdiction to be encroach'd upon. So that we must not wonder that the *Golden Bull* speaks thereof as of a Right appropriated to the Archbishop of *Cologn*: but the Explanation that has been given to the Law, since the Coronation of the King of the *Romans* who dy'd last, makes it plain that it is his Right only when the Coronation is perform'd in his Diocese. The Coronations of *Matthias*, of *Ferdinand* II, and of *Ferdinand* III, were perform'd by the Archbishop of *Mayence*, without any Opposition on the part of the Archbishop of *Cologn*, but besides that the Cities of *Francfort* and of *Ratisbon*, were pitch'd upon for that purpose, which Cities do not belong to the Metropolitan of *Cologn*, the Archbishop was not *in Sacris*; and by Consequence was not in a Condition to give the Emperor that Unction which he had not himself. This was the main Reason the Elector of *Cologn* alledg'd, together with the Text of the *Golden Bull*, for the Justification of his Right, at the last Coronation, notwithstanding which the Emperor pronounc'd in Favour of the Elector of *Mentz*. We here make use of the word Unction, because we properly mean here the Anointing or Consecration, whereof the Coronation is only a part, and is perform'd by the three Archbishops Electors together, all three having their Hand on the Crown, when it is put on the Emperor's Head. 5. The Subjects of the Archbishop of *Cologn* cannot be summon'd in the first Instance before the Chamber of *Rotweil*, and they cannot appeal from his Sentences, unless the Sum in Dispute exceeds that of five hundred Florins, or of a thousand Livres *French* Money, in Principal. Nay the Appeals must be sued out within six Months after the Pronunciation of the Sentence, and the Appellant is oblig'd to give sufficient Security for what has been adjudg'd. 6. The Archbishop has the Power of judging Malefactors within the City of *Cologn*, which he executes by his Officers; tho' this City be free, and subject immediately to the Empire, and so independent of the Archbishop, that she suffers him to remain these but very few Days, and with a regulated Retinue.

Maximilian Henry, who at this Time possesses the Archbishoprick and the Electoral Dignity of *Cologn*, is the Son of *Albert* Duke of *Bavaria*, who is still living, and of *Mahault* of *Leuchtenberg*. *Ferdinand* of *Bavaria*, his Unkle and Predecessor, caus'd him to be chosen Coadjutor on *February* 16, 1642, and left

‡ *His Suffragans.* * *The Rights of the Elector of Cologn.*

him

him the See vacant by his Death in the Year 1650. He also succeeded to his Unkle in the Bishoprick of *Liege*, and in that of *Hildesheim*, and in the Prevostship of *Berchtesgaden* in *Bavaria*, by virtue whereof he is also a Prince of the Empire. But the Chapters of *Munster* and of *Paderborn* which the Unkle possess'd, together with the Bishopricks we have already nam'd, have given themselves Bishops out of their own Body. The first, *Christopher Bernard* of *Gaalen*, and the other, *Thierry Adolphus* of *Reck*, who are Gentlemen of the Countrey. This Prince was born *October* 8, 1621. So that at present he is but six and thirty Years of Age, however he is very sickly, and does not promise a long Life, tho' this infirm Habit of Body does not hinder him from having vast Thoughts, and from projecting Designs capable of changing intirely the present State of Affairs in *Germany*. He has always listen'd to the Propositions that have been made in against the Establishment of the Grandeur of the House of *Austria*, and there is no doubt out he will follow the Sentiment of those who are for removing the Imperial Dignity out of it, as well because he may hope to procure it to his own, as on the account of the Resentment he has for the Affront he thinks was offer'd him at the last Coronation. It is he in effect who will have it believ'd, that he declares the most openly against the Pretensions of the King of *Hungary*, and is most capable of bringing about the Negotiation that is in Hand in Favour of the Duke of *Bavaria*, at least if it be the Interest of the Empire to chuse an Emperor elsewhere, than amongst the Successors of those who have been in Possession thereof for above these two hundred Years.

CHAP. XI.

Of the Secular Princes Electors in general.

BEfore we speak of the new Succession and Investiture, by which the Secular Princes Electors acquire the Electoral Dignity, as the Ecclesiasticks do by their Election, we shall say by the way, that whereas at the Time of the Publication of the *Golden Bull*, there were but four Secular Electors, there are at this Day five. The States of the Empire being assembl'd at *Munster* in the Year 1648, having judg'd it proper for the publick Good and Tranquillity, to create an eighth Electorate, in Consideration of *Charles Lewis* Count *Palatin* of the *Rhine*, as we have said before * Of these five Princes two, to wit, those of *Bohemia* and *Bavaria* are Catholicks, the three others are Protestants, and of these three two, to wit, *Brandenburg* and the *Palatin* are of the Reform'd Religion, and the third, to wit, *Saxony*, is of the Confession of *Augsburg* or *Lutheran*.

They who have a particular Knowledge of the Affairs of *Germany*, are sensible, that the Proscription of the Elector *Palatin* who dy'd last, and the Change that ensu'd by the Translation of the Electoral Dignity to the Person of the Duke of *Bavaria*, is of the last Importance. For before that Time the Electoral College, for what regards the other Affairs of the Empire, which have nothing in common with those of the Election, was compos'd of six Electors, three whereof being Protestants, there could be no Apprehension of any thing being done to the Prejudice of the Liberty of the Princes of *Germany*, or of their Allies. Wherefore it was a great Surprize to see the great Embassy enter *Germany*, which was compos'd of the Duke of *Angoulesme*, the Count *de Bethune*, and of *M de Chasteauneuf*, to act directly against the Interest of *France*, and to labour at the Confirmation of a Greatness, which it will be very hard to lower at present.

To repair in some measure this Fault, Instance was made at *Munster*, that the Number of the Electors might be augmented with an eighth, in order to strengthen the Party of those who could not hate *France*, wherein they seem not to have succeeded ill, at least in reference to the future Election.

The Translation of the Electoral Dignity from one Family to another, which we have just instanc'd in, confirms what we have said at the beginning of this Chapter of the new Investiture. For altho' the *Golden Bull* seems not to speak thereof in express Terms, yet it is evident that an Electoral Family being so far extinct as not to have any Heir, and that the Principality being escheated to the Empire by right of Fief, the Emperor can, and ought to fill the vacant Place, by substituting therein another Prince by a new Investiture. In like manner it may happen, that for want of Heirs in an Electoral House, the Elector who sees himself without Heirs, resigns his States and his Dignity to the Empire, as also that having Heirs, he obliges them to consent to his Alienation thereof, for the Good of his Affairs, by the Agreement of the Emperor and of the other Electors, and to his selling them to a Prince of another Family. And in all these Cases there must be a new Investiture, as well as when by Proscription, or otherwise, the Principality with the Electoral Dignity is confiscated. To which we must add, the Necessity of a new Investiture, when by virtue of a Treaty of mutual Succession, the Principality to which the Electoral Dignity is annex'd, passes into another Family.

We do not find that since the Publication of the *Golden Bull* the Electoral Dignity has pass'd from one Family to another for want of Heirs. For altho' it is enter'd into the House of *Misnia*, and into that of the Burgraves of

* Ch 8 Rem 4

Nuremberg,

of the ELECTORS of the EMPIRE.

Nuremberg, or of *Zollern*, since that time, yet it cannot be said that there were no Princes left of the House of *Saxony*, when *Frederick* Marquiss of *Misnia* was invested therewith, since it is certain that those of *Anhalt* and of *Saxe Lauemburg* are of the same Family in which the Electoral Dignity was in the Time of the Emperor *Charles* IV, and of the Publication of the *Golden Bull* And notwithstanding the Emperor *Sigismund* had no Children when he treated about the Marquisate of *Brandenburg*, and the Electoral Dignity with *Frederick* Burgrave of *Nuremberg*, yet he might still hope for some So that it could not be acquir'd by any other Title than that of Resignation, tho' it may be said, in reference to the Dukes of *Saxony*, that the Collaterals were not compris'd in the Investiture of the Electoral Dignity, when it was given to Princes, who were in effect of the same House, but of another Branch which is what the Electors of *Saxony* of the House of *Misnia* did not fail to alledge, in the Difference they had on that Subject with the Dukes of *Saxe Lauemburg*, whereof we shall have occasion to speak in Chap VI We have an Example of a new Investiture by Confiscation in the same House of *Saxony*, and another in that of the *Palatin* But as we shall speak of them elsewhere, we shall enlarge no farther on that Subject, and shall pass on to the Treaties several Princes of *Germany* make among themselves for the mutual Succession of one Family to another

* The Emperors *Ferdinand* II and III promise in their Capitulations, that they will not for the future bestow on private Persons the Fiefs which shall become vacant to the Profit of the Empire, but that they will re-unite them to the Empire, to serve by the way of Demesne to the Emperor, and that they will not give the Hopes or Reversion thereof to any body so that the Emperor could not for the time to come confirm the Treaties which the Princes Electors or others might make for a mutual Succession, for want of Heirs Male in either of the Families, tho' he cannot hinder the Execution of that which subsists for these several Ages, between the Houses of *Saxony* and of *Hesse*, and was confirm'd by the Emperor *Charles* IV, and by the other Emperors his Successors, even by the Treaty of *Prague* in the Year 1635

The Foundations of the Treaty of mutual Succession between *Saxony* and *Hesse*, were laid in the Partition which *Henry the Illustrious*, Marquiss of *Misnia*, and *Henry* of *Brabant*, styl'd *the Infant*, made of the Inheritance of *Henry Raspe*, last Lantgrave of *Thuringia*, by which *Thuringia* being enter'd into the House of *Misnia*, and *Hesse* falling to *Henry the Infant*, these Princes made in the Year 1274 a Treaty, by which it was agreed, that for want of Heirs Male in either of the two Families, the other should succeed It is true that at that Time the Marquisses of *Misnia* were not Dukes of *Saxony* · That the Electoral Dignity was not appropriated to that Family, and that there is not any one Treaty that speaks of the Electorate, so that it might be doubted whether the Electoral *Saxony* and the Dignity be compris'd in the Treaty of mutual Succession, but forasmuch as there is nothing reserv'd in the Treaty, no more than in the Imperial Confirmation, which have been renew'd from time to time, and comprehend all the Estates, present and future, without any Exception, there is nothing that can hinder us from believing, that if the Princes happen'd to fail in the House of *Saxony*, those of *Hesse* would succeed in the Electoral Dignity, as well as in all the other Estates which the Duke of *Saxony* is at present in Possession of And that there may be no room to doubt of the Intention of the Princes, it is requisite to see the Treaty they made in the Year 1587, in which the Electoral Dignity was expressly compris'd but particularly, and in much stronger Terms in the Treaty of Alliance and mutual Succession, made at *Naumburg* in *Thuringia*, March 30, 1614, between *John George* and *John Sigismund*, Electors of *Saxony* and of *Brandenburg*, and *Maurice* Lantgrave of *Hesse*, with all the other Princes of those three Houses, which imports, That the Male Line happening to fail in the House of *Brandenburg*, the Princes of the two Houses of *Saxony* and of *Hesse* shall have equal Shares of all the Estates of the last Prince of *Brandenburg*, in such manner, that the Electoral Dignity shall be compris'd in that part which shall fall to *Hesse* but if it shall happen that the Male Line fails in the House of *Saxony*, the Elector and the Princes of *Brandenburg* shall have only one third part of all the Estates, and those of the House of *Hesse* shall have the other two thirds, together with the Electoral Dignity

This Alliance between these three Houses subsists still, tho' it is hard to say at what time precisely *Brandenburg* came into the same, since all the Treaties made between *Saxony* and *Brandenburg* before the Year 1614, make mention but of one hereditary Alliance between those two Families, and do not regulate the Succession Moreover the Dukes of *Saxony* made in the Year 1555, another Treaty of mutual Succession with the Counts of *Henneberg*, with the Consent of the Lantgraves of *Hesse* But forasmuch as there is no Proportion between this County and the Dutchy of *Saxony*, it was stipulated that the Princes happening to fail in the House of *Saxony*, the Counts of *Henneberg* should inherit only what the Dukes of *Saxony* possess'd in *Franconia*, and has been since given to *John Casimir*, Duke of *Saxony* at *Coburg*, and is at this Day possess'd by the Dukes of *Saxony* of the Branch of *Altemburg* This Treaty with the Counts of *Henneberg* which we have just mention'd, has had its effect in this, that *George Ernest*, Count and Prince of *Henneberg*, dying without Issue Male on *December* 22, 1583, and all the Male Line being extinct with his Person, the Dukes of *Saxony* have succeeded in the County which they still enjoy It is true that at this Day there are so many Princes in those three Houses, that there is not any likelihood of the Male Line failing of a long time So that the new Investiture, by which the Electoral Dignity is acquir'd for want of Heirs, being what happens very rare, we shall proceed farther tho' there is not

---

* *Treaty of mutual Succession*

any thing that one ought not to apprehend, after we have seen ten Princes of the House of *Pomerania* dye without Issue, notwithstanding they had all attain'd to Man's Estate. There are very few Princes of the House of *Bavaria*. The Elector has no Children, his Brother is not marry'd. And of the two Sons of Duke *Albert*, the one is Archbishop of *Cologn*, and a Priest, and the other is of the Church, and a Bishop. So that there is great likelihood that the new Investiture may, for want of Heirs, take Place in this House sooner than in any other. It the same Treaty, by which the eighth Electorate was created, had not provided in such Case, by ordaining that for want of Male Issue, in the House of *Bavaria*, the new Electoral Dignity shall remain extinct, and that of *Bavaria* be reunited to the *Palatin* Branch.

† The new Investiture, which is given after the Confiscation of the Electoral Dignity from a Prince proscrib'd, is not so extraordinary, altho' since the Publication of the *Golden Bull*, we have in all but two Examples thereof. I or *Rupert*, Count *Palatin* of the *Rhine*, who was put into the Ban of the Empire by the Emperor *Maximilian* I, was only the second Son of the Elector *Philip*, and *Lewis* V, his eldest Brother, and nevertheless succeed his Father in the Electoral Dignity. All that was irregular therein, was that after the Death of *Lewis* V, who dy'd without Issue, on *March* 15, 1544, *Frederick*, the third Son of *Philip*, and Brother to *Lewis*, succeeded in the Electoral Dignity, to the Prejudice of *Otho-Henry*, Son of the second Son of the said *Philip*, contrary to the express Direction of the *Golden Bull*, which calls to the Succession the second Brother of the deceas'd, and his Children *in infinitum*, before that the third can lay any Claim thereto. But this happen'd because that after the Proscription of *Rupert*, it was necessary his Son should be rehabilitated, which was done, but on Condition that he should not possess the Electoral Dignity till after the Death of his Uncle, who had marry'd the Emperor *Charles* V's Niece, and who had no Children.

The two Proscriptions that have given Occasion for new Investitures, are those of *John Frederick* Elector of *Saxony*, and of *Frederick* V Elector *Palatin*. The first was put in the Ban of the Empire, *July* 20, 1546, by the Emperor *Charles* V, but forasmuch as the Proscription was executed contrary to Form, by the sole Power of the Emperor, and without having heard the Elector, the Electoral Dignity was not dispos'd of till after that *John Frederick* being fall'n into the Hands of the Emperor, after the Loss of a Battel, and seeing himself in the Discretion of his Enemy, who had condemn'd him to dye, he was necessitated to redeem his Life by consenting to a Translation of the Electoral Dignity to *Maurice* Duke of *Saxony*, his Relation, who was invested therewith *February* 24, 1548.

The Proscription of the Elector *Palatin* was executed in our Time, and every body knows the Cause, Particulars, and Consequences thereof, but there is in it something remarkable. That whereas in the Translation of the Electoral Dignity from the Person of *John Frederick* to that of *Maurice*, it was left annex'd to the Principality, that is to say, to the Electoral *Saxony*, which was transferr'd also with the Dignity. In this last, on the contrary, the the Procedure was directly against the *Golden Bull*, which appropriates the Electoral Dignity to the *Palatinate*, which Dignity is at this Time annex'd to *Bavaria*, whereof we shall speak more amply elsewhere.

* *Sleidan* represents the Ceremonies of the new Investiture of *Maurice*, in so few Lines, that the Reader cannot be displeas'd to see them here, as a thing entirely depending on the Matter we treat of. He says, " That *February* 24, the Birth-Day of *Charles* V having " been fix'd for this Ceremony, the Emperor, " accompany'd by the Electors, repair'd about " three in the Afternoon to a large Timber " Building, which had been erected for that " Purpose in the middle of the Market-Place. " They all withdrew from it, to put on their " Garments of Ceremony in a House hard by, " from whence they presently return'd to take " their Seats, the Emperor in the Throne " which had been prepar'd for him, and the " Electors in their usual Places. *Maurice* was " in the mean time on Horseback, with a " good Number of Princes and Lords, in a " Street right against the aforesaid Building, " and having detach'd some Cavaliers, who rode " round the Theatre upon a Gallop, he caus'd " to advance *Henry* Duke of *Brunswick*, *Wolfgang* Count *Palatin* of the *Rhine*, Brother " to the Elector, and *Albert* Duke of *Bavaria*, " who being come up on the Gallop alighted " off their Horses, and, having made three low " Bows, cast themselves upon their Knees, and " pray'd the Emperor to vouchsafe to grant to " *Maurice* the Investiture of the Electoral Dignity, and of the Principalities which depend " thereon. The Emperor, after having taken " the Advice of the Electors, made Answer " by the Archbishop of *Mayence*, That he very " well remember'd the Promise he had made to " *Maurice*, and that he was ready to admit him to " Homage, and to give him the Investiture of " the Election, if he came in Person to ask it. " These three Princes having thank'd the Emperor, made their Report thereof to *Maurice*, " who thereupon immediately advanc'd with " the rest of his Retinue, having before him " twelve Trumpets two pair of Kettle-Drums, " and ten Standards, carry'd by as many Princes or Counts, and representing the Provinces of which he demanded the Investiture " He dismounted at the Foot of the Theatre, " and having ascended the same, with all the " Princes who were there present to do him " Honour, and having made three low Bows, " he cast himself upon his Knees before the " Emperor, having behind him likewise on " their Knees the three Princes, (who had demanded the Investiture for him, and *Hoyer* " Count of *Mansfild*, who ask'd it for *Augustus* Duke of *Saxony* his Brother) and there " demanded in Person what he had before made " suit for by others. The Emperor answer'd, " That in Consideration of the Services, which " he and his Brother had done to him and to the " holy Empire, it was requisite to invest him

---

† *Translation of the Electoral Dignity after Confiscation*   * *The Ceremonies of the new Investiture,* Lib. 20   " and

"and his Children, and for want of Male Issue, the Duke *Augustus*, and his, with the Electoral Dignity, and the Principalities confiscated from the Duke *John Frederick*, they all taking in him the Oath which the Electors and Princes owe to the Emperor and the Empire After which the Archbishop having laid the Book on the Emperor's Knees, read the Oath, which *Maurice* repeated Word for Word And after that, the Emperor, having taken the Sword from the Hands of the Count of *Pappenheim*, gave it to *Maurice*, and invested him by that Mean with the Electoral Dignity, and with the Office of Great Mareschal of the Empire The Investiture of the Principalities was perform'd by the Means of the Standards which the Emperor took from the Princes who carry'd them, to give them to *Maurice* one after the other, the Count of *Mansfield* putting his Hand to all of them, for Duke *Augustus* After that, *Maurice* took his Place among the Electors, and the Standards being flung amongst the People, the Emperor and the five Electors went and chang'd their Cloaths at the House where they had taken them But *Maurice* kept on his, and return'd back to his Lodgings with the same Noblemen who had accompany'd him at this Ceremony

The Ceremonies of the Investiture which was given to *Maximilian* Duke of *Bavaria*, of the *Palatin* Electoral Dignity, on *February* 25, 1623, are very different from these, and have this Particularity, that instead of the Standards which *Maurice* receiv'd from the Hand of *Charles* V, *Maximilian* only kiss'd the Pommel of the Sword the Emperor held in his Hand But forasmuch as the Electoral Dignity was only conferr'd on the Person of *Maximilian*, who had no Children, it was perform'd almost like a private Action in the Emperor's Antichamber

The Investiture which we have now spoken of is very different from that which the Secular Electors take at the ordinary Changes, and even from that which the Ecclesiasticks take after their Election, in this, that the new Investiture gives Possession of the Electorate, so that the Candidate or Nominee has no Electoral Function without it Whereas the Heirs of the Secular Electors finding themselves seiz'd of the Electoral Dignity, by the Death of the Predecessor, are truly Electors, and may assist at the Elections before the Investiture, as well as the Ecclesiasticks, immediately after they have been elected by the Chapter, as we have said before

*As for the Succession, which is the most usual Mean of acquiring the Electoral Dignity, the *Golden Bull* makes three Degrees thereof, the first, from the Father to the Son, the second, from Brother to Brother, and the third, for Default of the one and the other, to the next Relation by the Father's Side, descended from Male to Male from the first invested The Law §, in saying, That any one of the Secular Electors happening to die, the Right, Vote, and Power of Electing shall belong, without any Difficulty or Contradiction, to his eldest Son, lawfully born, and a Lay Man, and in Default of him, to his eldest Son, also lawfully born, and Lay, ‡ extends the Succession in a direct Line unlimitedly, and excludes therefrom all Collaterals, as long as there is any lawful Male left of the Branch of the eldest Son of the deceas'd Elector, to which the *Golden Bull* appropriates the Electoral Dignity, contrary to the ancient Custom, which made it common to several Princes of the same Family, altho' of different Branches, as we have made it appear, when we spoke * of the Election of *Charles* IV, at which were present three Princes of the *Palatin* House, and two of that of *Saxony*

The Question that is here made by most of the Civilians, to wit, whether the second Son, born of a Father who was already Elector, ought to be preferr'd to his eldest Brother, not born before the Father was Elector, is altogether frivolous For besides that it has been long since decided in favour of the eldest Son, by the *Golden Bull*, which makes no Distinction at all, one might ask by the same Reason, Whether a younger Son ought solely to inherit the Acquisitions his Father may have made since the Birth of the eldest Son, and before that of the second, which would be ridiculous There is besides this a particular Reason, and at the same time invincible, in favour of the eldest Sons of Electors, in what State soever they are born, because they do not succeed as Heirs to their Fathers, but by virtue of the Investiture which they receiv'd with the first Acquirer, which has given a Right to all his Posterity, according to the Order of their Birth, and even entitles to the Succession, and Electoral Dignity, the Nephews or † Grandsons of the Electors, altho' their Father never were in Possession thereof And it is impossible that this Order, establish'd by the Nature of the Fief, and by the Law it self, should be alter'd by any testamentary Disposition, or by any particular Statutes, which the Princes of *Germany* are accustom'd to make for the Preservation of their Houses

‡ It seems however, that this Order may be chang'd by the voluntary Resignation of the eldest Son, and that he may renounce a Right which is introduc'd in his Favour, after the Example of what has formerly been done in the House of *Brandenburg* *Frederick*, first Elector of *Brandenburg*, of the House of the *Burgraves* of *Nuremburg*, had two Sons *John* and *Frederick*, *John*, who was the eldest, was of a singular Temper, and not very fit for the Management of Affairs *Frederick*, on the contrary, was an active and vigorous Prince, who had from his first Youth acquir'd so high a Reputation, that at the Age of one and twenty Years he was made Protector of the Council of *Basil* The Father, who was for preserving in his Family that Dignity he had introduc'd therein, apprehending lest it should sink in the Hands of *John*, who employ'd himself continually in searching into Secrets, which procur'd him the Sirname of the *Chymist*, was very desirous to transfer it to the Person of *Frederick* He found no great Difficulty to prevail with his eldest Son to give his Consent thereto, and suffer his younger Brother to succeed in

* *The Succession of the Secular Electors* † Chap 7 § 2 ‡ *The direct Line,* * *Here above, Chap* 6
† *Nepotes,* ‡ *The eldest Son may renounce his Right*

the Electoral Dignity But this Example is of no force against the Order establish'd by the *Golden Bull* For *John*'s Renunciation was personal, and could not do any Prejudice to the Right of his Sons, of whom the Eldest would indubitably have been lawful Elector after the Death of the Father, notwithstanding his Renunciation, and notwithstanding the actual Possession of *Frederick*; but both the Brothers dy'd without any Male Issue so that there was no Dispute between their Heirs about the Succession in the Electoral Dignity To which we may add, That it appears by History, that when the Renunciation of *John* took effect, which was at the Death of the Father, he had no Son, and was not in a Condition to have any, since he marry'd his Daughter to *Christopher* of *Bavaria* King of *Denmark* the very next Year following, in which *Rodolphus* his Son, who liv'd but nine Months, dy'd So that the Example we have now alledg'd, being of no moment against the *General Rule*, no more than that of *Frederick* II, of which we have spoken in this same Chapter, and who was preferr'd in the *Palatin* Electoral Dignity to *Otho Henry* his Nephew, who was the Son of a proscrib'd Father, we say that it admits of no Exception That the Collaterals are never call'd to the Succession while there are any Heirs qualify'd to succeed in the direct Line That the Unkle cannot be preferr'd to the Nephew, under any Pretext, or for any Cause whatever, and that no regard is ever had therein to Age or to Proximity, but to the Order establish'd by the Law, and Nature it self For both the one and the other hinder the younger Brother from succeeding, unless there are no Descendents left of the Eldest, and call the Brother to the Succession, but only when there are no Sons left And thus it is that we must understand the *Golden Bull*, when it says, * *If it happens that the eldest Son dyes, without leaving any male Issue lawfully begotten, and Lay, the Right, Vote and Power of Election shall belong, by virtue of this present Edict, to his Brother, descended in a direct and lawful Line, by the Father's-side, and after him to his eldest Son, Lay and lawfully begotten* Where it formally excludes the Brother, as long as there are any Sons, that is to say Descendents, the Word *Son* being here taken in the full Extent of the Signification which the Civilians give it, and for want of Descendents it calls to the Succession the Brother and his Sons, *in infinitum*, and in the same Order which it had establish'd in the Branch of the eldest Son so that as long as there are Descendents in the Branch of the second, the third Brother, altho' a nearer Relation to the Eldest, than his Nephews or Great-Nephews born of the second Brother, cannot be call'd to the Succession

But forasmuch as the collateral Kindred do not succeed in the Electorate, but only by virtue of the Investiture of the first Elector, who has acquir'd that Right to all his Posterity, so that no body can take from him what the Law, the Quality of the Fief, and even Nature it self give him, it follows that the Brother of the first invested, whose Father was not Elector, cannot succeed in the Electoral Dignity, even tho' his Brother should dye without Children, unless he be compris'd in the first Investiture We have an Example thereof in what we have said above, concerning that of *Maurice* Elector of *Saxony*, who caus'd his Brother *Augustus* to be compris'd therein, whose Posterity is still at this Day in peaceable Possession of the Electoral Dignity of *Saxony*, by virtue of this first Investiture In like manner, in the Translation of the *Palatin* Electorate to the Person of *Maximilian*, Duke of *Bavaria*, the Investiture extends to *Albert* his Brother, and to his Descendents to perpetuity, who without that would have no part in the Electoral Dignity

Since then this first Investiture extends to all the Posterity of the first invested, it is evident that the Law calls to the Succession, not only the Sons and the Brothers, but also all the other Relations descended from him in the Male Line, how remote soever the Degree may be by which they are related to the deceased, having regard however to the Proximity of the Branches, and not to that of the Persons For Example, All the Marquisses of *Brandenburg* who live at this Day, are descended from *John George* Great-Great-Grandfather of the present Elector, who left amongst other Children, *Joachim Frederick*, who succeeded to the Father in the Electorate, *Christian* who had his *Appennage* at *Culmbach*, and *Joachim-Ernest*, who had his at *Anspach* *Joachim Frederick* left *John Sigismund* Elector, *John George*, who had his *Appennage* or Portion at *Jagerndorf*, but who left no Issue, and *Christian*, who was Administrator of *Magdeburg*, and is still living *John Sigismund* left only *George William*, Father of the present Elector Altho' this Prince be in the Flower of his Age, and enjoys a perfect Health, he thought fit nevertheless to have the Succession regulated some Years ago, before he had the Children God has since give him but the Right of the Administrator was never call'd in question, tho' he be only a Great Unkle and next to him (because he is in a decrepit Age, and has no Children) that of *Ermand Augustus* Marquiss of *Culmbach*, was secur'd, and in case of Death, to *Christian Ernest* his Son, notwithstanding this last be more remote by one Degree than *Albert*, the Son of *Joachim Ernest*, Marquiss of *Brandenburg* at *Anspach*, who acquiesc'd to this Sentiment, as to a thing that could not be disputed in *Germany* The Degrees of this Parentage will be better seen in the following Table

* Loco sub. cit

of the ELECTORS of the EMPIRE.

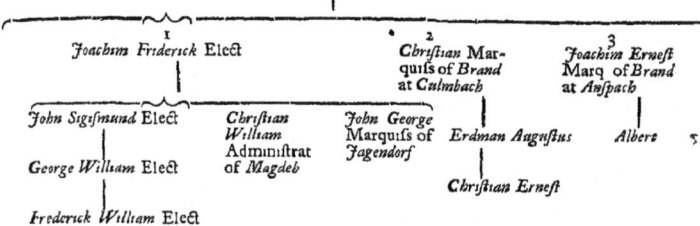

* The Emperor *Charles* IV, in regulating the Order of the Succession for the secular Electors, after the Manner we have said, comprehends nominally amongst them the King of *Bohemia* and nevertheless at the End of the same Chapter, it seems as if he would except him, when he says, That his Intention is to preserve to the Kingdom of *Bohemia* its *Privileges*, which permit the Inhabitants to elect a King, when the Kingdom is vacant. The Sense of the Law, in which the Emperor explains himself very clearly every where else, is by so much the more obscure in this Place, as there is a Contradiction therein, in what he says of the Right the Inhabitants of the Kingdom of *Bohemia* have to chuse themselves a King when the Throne is vacant, and the Order of Succession which he pretends to establish in the Royal Family of *Bohemia*. The greatest Difficulty resides in the Word *Vacant*, and to know when the Kingdom of *Bohemia* is so. In hereditary Kingdoms, where *the Dead gives Seizin to the Living*, the Kingdom is not vacant but only when Heirs fail in the Royal Family, but in elective Kingdoms, the Death of the King makes the *Interregnum* so that to know when the Kingdom of *Bohemia* is vacant, it is requisite first to know, whether it be hereditary or elective. There are some who say it is hereditary, and that the Emperor in saying that the Inhabitants have a Right to give themselves a King, means that the Kingdom is vacant for want of Heirs in the Royal Family, and that whereas in that Case the other Electorates escheat to the Empire, and the Emperor may dispose thereof, as of all the other Fiefs of the Empire, the Inhabitants of the Kingdom of *Bohemia* proceed to an Election, without deferring to the Will of the Emperor. But so far are they from resolving the Difficulty, that on the contrary they give birth to a much greater, in this, That supposing the Succession be hereditary in *Bohemia*, it must of necessity extend to Women, since they have often transferr'd the Crown to foreign Houses, even since the Publication of the *Golden Bull* Which is contrary to the Intention of the Legislator, who will appropriate the Succession of the Electoral Dignity to the Males, and to the Eldest thereof. To unravel therefore all these Difficulties, we must say, That the Kingdom of *Bohemia* has always been elective, as we shall see elsewhere in the irregular Successions of its Princes, and in the Sureties they have given to the Inhabitants for the Preservation of their Right of Election and that the Intention of *Charles* IV, being to make it hereditary in his Family, he would needs regulate the Succession thereof, and flatter nevertheless the *Bohemians*, in leaving them the Enjoyment of their Privileges concerning the Election, in appearance rather than in effect.

† The *Golden Bull* in calling to the Succession the Eldest, requires he should be *lawfully born*, and *Lay*, but what it adds in reference to the Age of the Elector does not relate to the Succession, but to the Function of the Electoral Dignity. It is certain that Bastards are excluded from the Succession, without its being in the Power of the Prince, to correct by his Letters Patents the Defects of Birth, in any Manner whatever. Priests are also incapable of succeeding in the Electoral Dignity, and even those Prelates who have only the minor Orders, because the Law will not have the Number of the Ecclesiastical Electors to increase to the Prejudice of the Seculars. But if the Prelate resigns his Benefices, and becomes secular by the Pope's Dispensation, it is certain he may succeed as being Lay. The Condition of *Protestant* Princes, who make no Vows, and who do not take Orders, has a great Advantage in this, over that of the *Roman Catholicks*, because there is nothing that can hinder them from possessing together with the Electoral Dignity, both Abbies and Bishopricks, since the Examples we have thereof in *Saxony* and *Brandenburg* testify that they nevertheless remain within the Limitations of the Law, are Lay, and have all the Qualities necessary to habilitate them to succeed. We then conclude, That as an Ecclesiastical Elector who changes his Religion, is oblig'd to quit his Archbishoprick together with the Electoral Dignity, so a *Catholick* Prelate that embraces the *Protestant* Religion, and so becomes Lay, is capable of succeeding in a Secular Electorate, if he has otherwise all the other Qualities necessary to enable him to succeed.

‡ As for the Age the Emperor requires in a secular Elector to be capable to elect, the Text says, *In case a Prince Elector, or his eldest Son*,

* *Whether the Order of hereditary Succession takes place in Bohemia?* † *The Qualities necessary to the Secular Electors* ‡ *His Age comes*

6 K

comes to dye, leaving Children that are Minors, the eldest of the Brothers of such Elector, or of such eldest Son, shall remain Guardian and Administrator to the young Elector, till he has attain'd the Age of eighteen Years complete, and then the Guardian or Administrator shall be oblig'd to surrender, immediately and without delay, to his Pupil, the Rights, Vote, and Power of the Election, with its Appurtenances and Dependencies, which he shall have enjoy'd till that Time. The Emperor does here two Things, first he regulates the Age of the Secular Elector; and in the second Place he assigns him a Guardian during his Minority. The Minority of the Elector is regulated to eighteen Years complete, and this is what the Text is so clear in, that hitherto there has not been known any Elector to have assisted at an Election before that Age, tho' there have been some who have govern'd their States before the Age of eighteen Years complete, but contrary to the Intention of the Law, which regulates the Time of Majority in very express Terms, and annexes the Electoral Dignity to the Estates and Principalities of the Secular Electors inseparably, for that the one cannot subsist without the other. The Examples that are alledg'd of Frederick IV, Elector Palatin, and of Joachim I, Elector of Brandenburg, have this Irregularity, that both the one and the other were without a Guardian before the Time ordain'd by the Golden Bull, but then they have this Particular also, That the first, who was born March 5, 1574, being very young when Lewis VI his Father dy'd, on October 12, 1583, remain'd under the Guardianship of John Casimir his Unkle, who dying also on January 16, 1592, it was not thought necessary to appoint another Guardian or Administrator, for the remaining six Weeks which were wanting to the Majority of Frederick. The Example of the Elector of Brandenburg is more remarkable. He was born February 21, 1484, and could not yet be sixteen Years old, when his Father dy'd in the Year 1499. The Law conferr'd the Administration of the Electorate, and of the Provinces that depend thereon, on Frederick Marquiss of Brandenburg at Anspach, his Unkle, who had Moderation enough to advise his Pupil to ask the Opinion of the other Electors concerning the Administration. The Elector of Mayence made answer, That the Article of the Golden Bull, which regulates the Majority of the Secular Electors to eighteen Years complete, related to the Election only, and to what depends thereon, but that he might govern his Estates, and take upon him the Administration of Affairs, without any Difficulty. One cannot very well say, whether this was the true Sentiment of the Archbishop of Mayence, or whether he had a mind to shew a Complaisance to the young Prince, but it is certain that the Law, which regulates the Succession of the Electors, and all that depends thereon, in very clear Terms, does not allow of that Exposition, and that without the Easiness which is found in the Mind of the Prince, whom the said Law call'd to the Administration, and who could renounce his Right, there would have been an Obligation to remain within the Terms express'd in the Golden Bull, and to leave the whole Conduct of Affairs to the Administrator

* It is so they call at this Day, the Guardian the Law gives to the Elector while a Minor. It says, that the eldest of the Brothers of the Elector, or of the eldest Son, who dyes leaving a minor Son, shall be Guardian to the young Elector, observing therein the same Order it observ'd before in regulating the Succession, and calling to the Guardianship the nearest Relation by the Father's side, and the most capable of succeeding, who is to continue Administrator, and as it were Regent of the Electorate, and of the Electoral Dignity, till the young Elector his Pupil shall attain to the Age of eighteen Years complete. The Administrator has a Right to do, during the Minority, all that an Elector at Age, and in possession of his Rights can do: not as Procurator or Manager for his Pupil, or as the Representative of the Person of the young Elector, but of his own Power, and by virtue of the fundamental Law of the Empire, which gives him all the Authority, and all the Rights the Electors themselves possess. It is in their Name that all Dispatches are made during the Minority of the young Elector. They, and not the Pupils, are invited to the Elections, and they appear there, and take their Rank, not in a common Habit, and after all the Electors present, as the Embassadors and Plenipotentiaries of the absent do, but in the Electoral Apparel, and in the same Place their Pupil would hold, if he were at Age. and thus, whereas other Guardianships are burthensome and incommodious, this is honourable, and by so much the more profitable, as the Administrator holds the Rank of Elector, and supports the Dignity thereof at the Expence of his Pupil: for which Reason the Law regulates the Majority at eighteen Years of Age, rather than to twenty, or five and twenty, that the Administrators may not have the Leisure so to habituate themselves to this Grandeur which they enjoy as one may say but by the way of Loan, and that they may not get such firm Footing there, by too long a Course of Years, as not to be liable to be dispossess'd.

When we say that the Administrator enjoys these Advantages by virtue of the Fundamental Law of the Empire, we suppose that there is no Testamentary Disposition that can change this Order, establish'd for the Guardianship as well as for the Succession. For altho' the same Frederick IV, Elector Palatin, whom we before spoke of, had ordain'd by his Testament, that Philip Lewis, Palatin of the Rhine at Newburg, notwithstanding he was his nearest Relation by the Father's Side, should be excluded the Administration of his Son, who at the Death of his Father was but fourteen Years old, and that in consequence thereof John II, Count Palatin of the Rhine at Deuxponts, who was a more remote Relation, and Nephew to Philip Lewis, was admitted, yet it cannot be inferr'd from thence, that the Direction of the Law takes Place only when there is no Testament: on the contrary, most of the other Electors, and the Emperor himself, declar'd that it was a manifest Contravention to the Golden Bull,

* The Guardian of the Elector in Minority

and

and that it was tolerated but only out of particular Confiderations, and without Prejudice to the Right the Relations of the Electors are int tl'd to by the Law

Now whereas the Adminiftrator has not only the Right to elect during the Minority of the young Elector, but alfo to the Adminiftration of all his Eftates and Principalities, fo is he oblig'd to furrender both the one and the others to his Pupil immediately after the eighteen Years complete And this is fo undoubted a Truth, that when *Richard*, Count *Palatin* of the *Rhine* at *Zimmeren* (who pretended to the Adminiftration of *Frederick* V, after the Death of *John Cafimir*) was for keeping the Government of the Countrey, till his pretended Pupil had attain'd the Age of five and twenty Years, explaining the Text of the *Golden Bull*, which fays, *That immediately after the Age of eighteen Years, the Adminiftrator fhall furrender to his Pupil the Rights of the Elect on, with what depends thereon*, of the fole Faculty of Electing, of the Office of the Vicufhip, and of what depends on this Function, he was efteem'd ridiculous, and was oblig'd to leave to the Elector, who had attain'd the Age limited by the Bull, the Government, and the Enjoyment of all his Eftates The Law which makes the Electoral Dignity, and the Principality to which it is annex'd, infeparable one from the other, is exprefs enough on that Subject But it might be doubted whether the Majority of an Elector would extend alfo to the other Provinces he poffeffes out of the Electorate fo that if together with the Electorate he poffeffes other Provinces which do not depend thereon, and where the Majority is regulated by the Common Law to five and twenty Years, he fhall be deem'd a Major at eighteen But we refolutely affirm, that an Elector that has attain'd the Age of eighteen Years complete, is a Major every where becaufe the Elector being capable of being prefent at the Collegiate Diets, in which the moft important Affairs of the Empire pafs through the Hands of feven Electors, he may alfo, and with more Reafon, affift at the Affemblies of the Princes, who only fecond the Cares of the Electors, and who meet in fo great a Number, that the Youth of one Prince cannot do much Damage to the Deliberations Befides which, it would be impertinent that an Elector who is at Age in reference to his Electorate, fhould be under Guardianfhip with refpect to his other Provinces And indeed, if we except the Example of *Richard*, whom we juft inftanc'd in, it will not appear that ever any Adminiftrator made any Difficulty to furrender to his Pupil all his Principalities, of what Nature foever they were, immediately after the eighteen Years complete The Elector of *Brandenburg* that is now living was but twenty Years old when his Father dy'd in the Year 1640 And fo it might be faid, that he was not yet at Age in reference to the Dutchy of *Pruffia*, and to the Eftates of the Succeffion of *Cleves* and *Julters* but that did not hinder him from taking upon him the free Adminiftration of the ones and the others, without ever its entring into any body's Thoughts to give him an Adminiftrator for thofe Provinces which do not depend on the Electoral Dignity

We have faid before in this Chapter, that the Emperor in regulating the Succeffion of the Secular Electors, protefts that his Intention is not to prejudice the Rights the Inhabitants of *Bohemia* have to chufe themfelves a King when the Kingdom is vacant From whence it neceffarily follows, That if there be an Exception for the Succeffion, in reference to the Kingdom of *Bohemia*, there is alfo one for the Guardianfhip, and that if the States of *Bohemia* have a Right to elect a King, they have alfo that of affigning a Tutor or Guardian to the King in his Minority And indeed, when in the Year 1519, after the Death of the Emperor *Maximilian* I, the Empire would proceed to an Election, it was not *Sigifmund* King of *Polana*, Unkle by the Father's fide to King *Lewis*, who was then but thirteen Years old, but the Eftates of the Kingdom that deputed to the Election In the Year 1619, at the Election of *Ferdinand* II, the fame States, writing to the Elector of *Mayence*, faid, That during the Minority of their King, the Benefit and Adminiftration of the Electoral Rights, do not belong to the neareft Relations, but to the Eftates and Grandees of the Kingdom It is true that *Ferdinand* made them this Anfwer, That the States of *Bohemia* were not call'd to the Election of *Charles* V, but the King himfelf was invited thereto, who fent thither the Baron of *Sternburg* and that it was he that was prefent at the Election, and not the Deputies of the States But this Anfwer fignifies nothing, becaufe according to the Prefcription of the Law it was requifite that the Adminiftrator of *Lewis* fhould affift at the Flection, and not the Embaffador of the King, who being then a Minor had no Right to depute, fince as he could not elect in Perfon before the Age of eighteen Years complete, fo neither could he before that Time elect by Proxy or Embaffador As this Day it is no longer liable to thefe Difputes For the Kingdom of *Bohemia* is acknowledg'd for hereditary fince the Peace of *Munfter*, and the King's neareft Relation by the Father's fide is Adminiftrator of the Electoral Dignity in *Bohemia* as well as in *Bavaria*, in *Saxony*, in *Brandenburg*, and in the *Palatinate*, as we fhall fee hereafter

* Now the Queftion is, whether the fame Elector can poffefs two Electorates to the Prejudice of the Difpofition of the Law, which fixes the Number of the Electors in fuch manner, that it feems as if it could not be diminifh'd, as it has not hitherto been augmented, but for very urgent and weighty Reafons, and by a general Refolution of all the States of the Empire We fay that the Law regulates the Number of the Suffrages or Votes, rather than that of the Electors, and that it is certain that as the fame Prince may poffefs feveral Principalities, he may alfo acquire feveral Electorates For it is evident that that might happen by the Extinction of all the Princes of the Houfes of *Saxony* or of *Brandenburg* In which cafe, fuppofing alfo that there were none left neither in the Houfe of *Heffe*, the Electoral Dignity would pafs into the furviving Family,

* One Elector may poffefs two Electorates

the chief of which would without doubt possess two Electorates, and would re-unite them in his Person And if the Arms of the last Elector *Palatin* had had the Success in *Bohemia* which might reasonably have been hop'd for, it is certain he had also had two Votes in the Electoral College.

* The same Reason that hinders the young Elector from doing the Electoral Functions before the Age of eighteen Years complete, removes from the Succession him who is not *Compos Mentis*, or that some other natural Defect renders incapable of acting For whereas the Law ordains Guardians to private Persons, when they are Fools or mad, the *Golden Bull* gives Successors to those Princes whom the Infirmity of Mind disables from performing those Functions that are inseparable from this high Dignity It expresses it self thus † *Nevertheless it is our Will, that the eldest Son succeed, and that all the Demesne and all the Right belong to him alone unless he be a Fool, or has some such other notable Defect, which absolutely disables him from governing In which case we deprive him of the Succession, to which we call the second Son if there be any, &c* The Law makes no mention of those who become Fools after the Succession So that as it does not say, that a Prince may be depos'd for Imbecillity of Mind, it seems as if in such case the Direction of the Common Law ought to be observ'd, and their Example follow'd, who during their Princes Folly or Disability have given the Administration of Affairs to their nearest Relations by the Father's side, in the same manner as the Law ordains concerning the Guardianship during their Minority

‡ Notwithstanding the Electors are true and lawful Princes Electors of the Holy Empire by virtue of their Principalities, * and that the Right, Vote, and Power of the Election belongs without any Difficulty or Contestation to the eldest Son, who shall be Lay and lawfully born , yet the Elector who finds himself seiz'd of the real Possession of the Electorate by the Death of his Predecessor, and who effectually enjoys all its Rights by virtue of the Investiture given to the first Acquirer, is nevertheless oblig'd to renew the Investiture, and to receive a Confirmation thereof within a Year and a Day after his Accession to his Estates, and to reiterate the Oath which he owes to the Empire at every Change that shall happen But forasmuch as it is, properly speaking, but a mere Ceremony, so it is only done for Forms sake For whereas in the new Investiture he that demands it is oblig'd to take it in Person, and get himself accompany'd by Peers of the Empire, as we have seen in that of *Maurice* Elector of *Saxony*, and in that of *Maximilian* Elector of *Bavaria*, who was accompany'd in the Year 1623 by the Archbishop of *Saltzburg*, and by Duke *Albert* of *Bavaria* his Brother, the Investiture which is given at the Change of the Emperors, or of the Electors, may be demanded by Proxy, and it is sufficient to have usual Witnesses to this Action, because it is of so little Importance, that it gives no new Quality to the Elector, who without it does nevertheless assist at the Elections, and do all the other Electoral Functions

† We shall speak of the Offices of the Secular Electors, and of their Functions, when we treat of each Elector in particular and we shall content our selves to say here, for what relates to them in general, That their Offices were for a long time ambulatory, and that they were appropriated to the Electors, but only when the Electoral Dignity was annex'd to the States and Principalities, from which it is now inseparable Which is what is very certain, if we look back to the Time of *Charlemagne*, and of the Emperors of his House, under whom the Dutchies and Counties were not as yet hereditary The Duke was not Governor of a Province, but as the Count was Governor of a single Town, and he held the Government only at the Will of the Emperor At the Coronation of the Emperor *Otho* I, which was perform'd at *Aix la Chapelle* in the Year 936, *Giselbert*, Duke of *Lorrain*, discharg'd the Office of Great Chamberlain, *Eberhard*, Duke of *Franconia*, that of High Steward, *Herman*, Duke of *Suabia* that of Great Cup-bearer, and *Arnauld* Duke of *Bavaria* that of Great Mareschal although *Sigefrid*, to whom *Wittikind* ‡ gives the Quality of *Optimus Saxonum*, that is to say, of the chief Nobleman of *Saxony*, is there personally present, and might have executed his Office, if at that Time it had been annex'd to his Family or Principality No mention is made there of the King of *Bohemia*, of the Count *Palatin* of the *Rhine*, nor of the Marquis of *Brandenburg* * *Mesico* and *Boleslas*, Dukes of *Bohemia*, were present at the Diet the Emperor *Otho* III had conven'd at *Quedlimburg* in the Year 985 But they did not discharge the Office of Cup-bearer, on the contrary, the Emperor caus'd it to be executed by *Hetzelon*, Count *Palatin*, while *Henry* I Duke of *Bavaria* discharg'd that of High Steward, *Conrade* Duke of *Franconia* that of Great Chamberlain, and *Bernard* Duke of *Saxony*, that of Master of the Horse, or Great Mareschal And indeed it will not appear that the Kings of *Bohemia* have executed the Office of Great Cup-bearer before the Coronation of the Emperor *William* of *Holland*, where *Wenceslas* King of *Bohemia* officiated in the Ceremonies thereof, as *Joannes à Beka* says, who was a contemporary Author, and after him *Trithemius*, and other more modern Authors The same may be said of the three other Secular Electors, and that it is only since the Publication of the *Golden Bull*, that they take the Quality of Officers of the Empire While the Electoral Dignity of *Saxony* remain'd in the House of *Anhalt*, its Princes were contented to take the Quality of Great Mareschal of the Empire and in the Bull publish'd by the Emperor *Rodolphus* I, in Favour of the King of *Bohemia* his Son-in-Law , *Rupert* Count *Palatin* of the *Rhine*, and *Rodolphus* the eldest Son of the Duke of *Saxony*, take the Quality of Lord High Steward, and of Great Mareschal of the Empire, and do not speak at all of that of Elector, which at that Time was consider'd as a Faculty, rather than as a particular Dignity *Albinus*, who has

---

* *A Fool cannot succeed in the Electorate*
† *Of the Offices of the Secular Electors*
‡ Chap XXV § 1
* Ditmar Hist Sax Lb 4
* Conр VII § 21
† Investiture
‡ Lib 2

written the Chronicles of *Misnia*, says, That *Albert* sirnam'd the *German Achilles*, who dy'd in the Year 1486, was the first Prince of the House of *Brandenburg*, that took the Quality of Elector in his Letters At this Day they all assume the Quality of their Offices, and add thereto that of *Prince Elector of the Holy Empire* but in the Subscriptions they only make use of their Christian Names, and of the Quality of Elector Within some Years the Office of hereditary Great Treasurer of the Empire has been created in Favour of the Elector *Palatin* of the *Rhine*

The Secular Electors, as hereditary Officers of the Empire, have their Vicars, whose Offices are also perpetual and hereditary, and who do the Functions thereof, in the Absence of the Electors But forasmuch as we here speak only of the Electors, and that this Chapter is already but too large, we shall reserve that for a particular Discourse hereafter But we shall here observe by the way the Error of those who believe and teach, that the Secular Electors hold of the Bishoprick of *Bamberg* on the account of their hereditary Offices The Truth being, that they are not only hereditary Officers of the Crown of the Empire, of which they hold by reason of their Offices, as well as on the score of their Principalities, and of the Electoral Dignity, but they are also hereditary Officers of the Bishoprick of *Bamberg*, where they have also perpetual Vicars, but very different from those they have in the Empire, as we shall shew in the following Chapter

* The *Golden Bull* establishes two different Orders for the Rank among the Secular Electors the one as to their Seat, and the other in Processions It regulates their Seat in Chapter IV, where it says, *That in all the Courts, or Imperial Assemblies, where the Emperor and the Princes are personally present, as well in the Council as at Table, the King of* Bohemia*, as being a Crown'd Head, and Sacred, shall take Place immediately after that Archbishop who, according to the Place of the Assembly, shall be on the Emperor's Right Hand, by virtue of the present Ordinance and after him on the same Side shall be seated the Count* Palatin *of the* Rhine *On the Left Hand, immediately after the Archbishop who shall be on that side, shall be seated the Duke of* Saxony*, and after him the Marquiss of* Brandenburg So that at the General Assemblies, where the Electors place themselves in the same Line with the Emperor, they form'd the following Figure

| Palatin | Bohemia | Mayence | The Emperor Triers | Cologn | Saxony | Brandenburg |

And in the particular Assemblies, and at solemn Feasts, this

	The Emperor	
Mayence		Cologn
	Triers	
Bohemia		Saxony
Palatin		Brandenburg

But the same *Golden Bull* requires, that at Processions, and in Marching, the Electors shall observe the Order which it prescribes in Chap XXII to wit, *That the Duke of* Saxony, *carrying the Imperial Sword, shall go immediately before the Emperor, having before him the Archbishop of* Triers On *his Right the Count* Palatin *of the* Rhine *carrying the Ball or Globe; and on his Left the Marquiss of* Brandenburg, *carrying the Scepter The King of* Bohemia *shall march immediately after the Emperor, which will represent the following Figure*

	Cologn	Brandenburg	
Bohemia	The Emperor	Saxony	Triers
	Mayence	Palatin	

But forasmuch as this Order cannot be observ'd at this Day, because by the Peace of *Munster* in eighth Elector has been created, to whom there was a Necessity to give a Place, the States of the Empire assembl'd at *Ratisbone* in the Year 1653, and 54, taking into Consideration that at the augmenting the Number of the Electors, Care had not been taken to regulate the Rank of the eighth For want whereof those Disorders might ensue, which the Emperor *Charles* IV intended to prevent by his Ordinance, they desir'd the Electoral College to make a Regulation for their Ranks and Seats, as well at the general Diets as at the particular Assemblies, where the Electors meet for the Affairs of the Empire, and for the Election of an Emperor, or of a King of the *Romans* We shall not deviate from our Subject, and shall only speak here of the Electoral Diets, where the Electors will have the following Order observ'd

† When the Princes Electors shall be assembl'd for the Election of an Emperor, or of a King of the *Romans*, they shall take their Seats in such manner, that *Mayence* shall have the first Place, *Triers* and *Cologn* the second and third alternately, *Bohemia* alternately after the Ecclesiasticks, *Bavaria* the fifth, *Saxony* the sixth, *Brandenburg* the seventh, and the *Palatin* the eighth, all in a Line Provided always, and be it to be understood, that this shall be observ'd when all the Electors shall be personally present at the Election, or when they

---

* *The Order of Precedency among the Secular Electors.*
† *The Order in which the Electors shall sit when all present*

shall all send thither their Deputies or Embassadors, and that so there be an Equality amongst all that are present. * For if it shall happen that some shall come in Person, and the others send their Deputies or Embassadors, it is certain that all the Electors present shall precede all the Embassadors of the absent

† Formerly the Electors, in accompanying the Emperor, or the King of the *Romans*, to the Church, or to other publick Assemblies after his Election, march'd in the Order prescrib'd by the *Golden Bull*; in the manner we have represented before, but there was a Necessity to change it intirely, on the account of the eighth Electorate and the Electors have agreed, that at this Day *Triers* shall nevertheless march first, and alone as before, but that after him shall march *Bavaria*, carrying the Globe, having on his Right *Brandenburg* with the Scepter, and on his Left the *Palatin*, carrying the Crown. After them shall come the Elector of *Saxony* alone, bearing the Sword immediately before the Emperor, who shall have by his Sides *Mayence* and *Cologn*, and after him the King of *Bohemia* in the following manner

	Cologn		Palatin	
The King of *Bohemia*	The Emperor	*Saxony*	*Bavaria*.	*Triers*
	Mayence		*Brandenburg*	

‡ But when there shall be only the Elector of *Saxony*, who carries the Sword before the Emperor, without the other Electors bearing the other Regalia or Ornaments of the Empire, there shall be some Alteration in their March, for the Elector of *Triers*, who before march'd at the Head of the Procession, shall take Place after the Electors of *Bavaria*, of *Brandenburg* and *Palatin*, who shall march first, and a breast, and after them *Triers* alone, before *Saxony*, who shall march in his Rank as well as the others, thus

	Cologn			Palatin
Bohemia	The Emperor	*Saxony*	*Triers*	*Bavaria*
	Mayence			*Brandenburg*

It is true that formerly the Elector of *Triers* march'd immediately before the Emperor, betwixt him and the three Secular Electors, when they did not carry the Regalia or Imperial Ornaments, nor the Elector of *Saxony* the Sword but forasmuch as the Number of the Electors has been augmented, and that it was difficult to make all the four Secular Electors march a breast, it was agreed that for the future they should march two and two, to wit, *Brandenburg* and *Palatin* first, after them *Bavaria* and *Saxony*, and then *Triers*, who is to march alone immediately before the Emperor The Archbishops of *Mayence* and of *Cologn* shall be in their Places on each side of his Imperial Majesty, and the King of *Bohemia* in his usual Rank after him, so that they will then form the following Figure

	Cologn		*Saxony*	*Palatin*
Bohemia	The Emperor	*Triers*		
	Mayence		*Bavaria*	*Brandenburg*

* However if it happens that all the Electors are not all personally present at the Elections, but that some of them are there by their Proxies or Embassadors, it is certain that then all the Electors who shall be present shall precede the Embassadors of the absent So that if the *Palatin*, who is the last of all, happens to be the only of the Seculars present at the Election, which is not very extraordinary, because the others are very remote, he shall without any Difficulty have the Precedency of all the Embassadors of the absent, and shall march immediately after the Ecclesiastical Electors, who are oblig'd to be there in Person, by reason of the Functions of their Offices, which are personal This must be understood of the Seats and the Rank the Electors hold, when they are not oblig'd to carry the Regalia or Imperial Ornaments. For when they carry them, the Embassadors of the absent do not take the Place of their Masters, since they rather represent the hereditary Officers of the Crown of the Empire on this occasion, than the Electors, but their Vicars, to whom the Law appropriates the Function of those Offices in the Absence of the Electors; and who march in the same Rank the Electors would hold, if they were there present We shall add here, that the

* *Rank of the Embassadors of absent Electors without the Regalia.* † *Order of Marching with the Regalia,* ‡ *Order of Marching*
  * *Rank of the Embassadors of the absent Electors*

Emperor

Emperor requires the Secular Electors should cause their Sons and presumptive Heirs to be instructed, when they are seven Years old, in foreign Languages, especially in the *Latin*, *Italian*, and *Sclavonian*, that they may thereby become so much the more capable of assisting the Emperor in the Government of the Empire. He names the *Latin*, as being the most universal, the *Sclavonian*, because that in *Bohemia*, and the Provinces which depend thereon, it is common and familiar, and the *Italian*, because several Princes of those Parts still acknowledge the Empire, tho' by the Word which the *German* Text of the *Golden Bull* makes use of, may also be understood the *French* Tongue; which was familiar, and, as it were, natural to the Emperor *Charles IV*.

CHAP. XII.

Of the Vicars of the Empire, and of the Vicars of the Electors.

THE preceding Chapter, in treating of the Secular Electors in General, not having permitted us to speak of the Vicarship of the Empire, during the *Interregnum*, because that Dignity is appropriated to the Count *Palatin* of the *Rhine*, and to the Duke of *Saxony*, to the Exclusion of the others, we find our selves oblig'd to bestow a particular Chapter thereon. At the beginning of which we shall say, That notwithstanding it seems as if the *Golden Bull*, when it says, That * *when the Empire shall become vacant*, *the Illustrious Count Palatin of the* Rhine, *Great Steward of the holy Empire, shall be Vicar of the Empire in* Suabia, *&c.* would infer, that the Vicarship of the Count *Palatin*, and of the Duke of *Saxony*, cannot take Place but only when the Empire is vacant, that is to say, after the Death of the Emperor, and during the *Interregnum*. Yet this must be understood to extend to the Absence the Emperor, † who not being in a Condition to administer Affairs, and to govern in his own Person, these two Electors have a Right to do their Office of Vicars, in the same manner as if the Empire was vacant. The Reason thereof is, because these two Vicars have not a delegated or transitory, but an ordinary and perpetual Power, which they hold of the Law directly, without any Dependence on the Will of the Emperor, who cannot put Vicars in their Room, at his going out of the Empire, unless it be with their Consent. To which refers the Constitution ‡ of the Emperor *Rupert* of *Bavaria*, who designing to pass into *Italy* in the Year 1401, left the Vicarship of the Empire to *Lewis*, Count *Palatin* of the *Rhine*, his Son, because, says he, he had a perfect Knowledge of his Fidelity and Conduct, but *Præcipuè advertentes, a Divis Romanis Imperatoribus & Regibus, Prædecessoribus nostris, hactenus fuisse observatum, ac etiam de Jure Comitatûs* Palatinatus Rheni *fuisse, & esse, quod cum Romanus Imperator, vel Rex, ultra Montes in* Italiam *ingressus fuerit, in ipsius absentia Vicariatum Imperii in* Germania, Gallia, *& Regno* Arelatensi, *ad Comitem* Palatinum Rheni *pertinuisse & pertinere, &c.* For altho' the same Emperor adds, That he makes this Nomination of his Son by the Advice of the States, and after having put the Affair in Deliberation with the Electors, Princes, and other Lords of the Empire, of his certain Knowledge and imperial Authority, which would not be necessary if the Right of the Vicarship belong'd to the *Palatin* and Palatinate by virtue of the Law, yet it may be said, that he was oblig'd to do so, not only because the Power which he gives him exceeds that which the *Golden Bull* gives to the Vicars, but also because he extends it to all *Germany*, even to those Provinces where the Duke of *Saxony* is indubitably entitled to it during the *Interregnum*.

It is a hard Matter to say precisely, when this Right began to be annex'd to the *Palatinate*, or whether it be a Consequence of the Jurisdiction the Count *Palatin* had formerly in the imperial Court, and which the *Golden Bull* says * belongs to him by a very ancient Custom, in reference to the Person of the Emperor himself. But they who have spoken thereof, with Advantage to the *Palatin*, agree that it cannot be fetch'd higher than from the *Interregnum* between the Death of *Rodolphus* I. and the Election of *Adolphus* of *Nassau*, tho' it be certain that from that Time, he has so well maintain'd himself in this Right, that when the Emperors have been for giving Vicars to the Empire, to administer the Affairs thereof in their Absence, they have been oblig'd to secure to the Elector *Palatin* the Preservation of his Right by their Letters Patents. The Emperor *Charles* V. intending to establish his Brother *Ferdinand* Vicar of the Empire, during his Absence, was oblig'd to assure the Count *Palatin*, that that Action should not prejudice him. The Constitutions of the Empire, of 1566, and of 69, under *Ferdinand* and *Maximilian* II, of 1575, 78, 85, and of 1594, under *Rodolphus* II, and of 1612, under *Matthias*, confirm this Right to the *Palatin*. And it is only within some Years, and since the Beginning of this Century, that it has begun to be asserted, That this Advantage, as well as the Palatine Electoral Dignity, is due to the Dutchy of *Bavaria*. But this Dispute never came out of the School, till after the Death of the late Emperor, the Elector of *Bavaria* pretended that this Right had been transfer'd to him, together with the Electoral Dignity, by the Treaty of *Munster*, when it said, † *That the Electoral Dignity*, *which the*

---

* Palatin and Saxony, *Vicars of the Empire.*   † *Vicars during the Emperor's Absence.*
‡ Goldast Constit. Imp. Tom 1. pag. 381.   * Chap v § 1.   * § And first.

Electors Palatin *have heretofore possess'd, together with all their Offices, Regalia, Precedencies, Arms and Rights, whatever they may be, depending on this Dignity, without excepting any, shall remain to the Lord* Maximilian, *Count* Palatin *of the* Rhine, *Duke of* Bavaria, *and to his Childrens* &c

The *Palatin*, on the contrary, maintain'd, That the Right of Vicarship was not annex'd to the Electoral Dignity, and so it could not pass along with it to another Family But that the Law and ancient Custom appropriated that Right to the *Palatinate*, and that he was Vicar of the Empire, not as Elector, but as Count Palatin of the *Rhine*, which Quality gave him also that of Judge of the Emperor It is true that the *Golden Bull* says very expressly, That the Count Palatin, *Great Steward of the Empire, is Vicar of the Empire, on the Account of his Principality, or by virtue of the Privilege particularly annex'd to the* Palatinate But the Elector of *Bavaria* answers, That the Emperor speaks in those Terms, because the Electoral Dignity was also annex'd to the *Palatinate*, from which Dignity the Right of Vicarship being inseparable, it ought to pass with it to his Person and Family And indeed, all the other Electors declar'd in favour of *Bavaria*, and the Chamber of *Spires* it self suffer'd *Bavaria* and *Saxony* to compose, with their joint Arms, the Seal which it makes use of during the *Interregnum*, and it makes use of their Names to authorize the Edicts it issues out at present

‡ The Extent of the Vicariate of the *Palatin* comprehends *Suabia, Franconia*, and the Course of the *Rhine*, that is to say, all *Germany*, from the Source of the *Rhine* and the *Danube* to the Low Countries, comprising therein all that still acknowledges the Empire in *Italy*, *Savoy*, and *Burgundy* And that of *Saxony* comprehends not only the Provinces where the *Saxon* Law takes Place, but also all the others that are situate within the Circles of the Upper and Lower *Saxony*, as the Dutchies of *Brunswick* and of *Lunenburg*, of *Pomerania, Mecklenburg*, and of *Breme*, which make use of the Common Law

* The Power of the Vicars is so great, that excepting the Investiture of the Principalities, they can do all that the Emperor could do in Person, with this Difference nevertheless, that what they have done stands in need of the Confirmation of the Emperor, who, at his Accession to the Crown, generally confirms all that the Vicars have done during the *Interregnum*, and that they who have done Homage to the Vicars, are oblig'd to renew the same to the Emperor's self, because it is a Duty that cannot be refus'd to the Person They exercise their Power separately, each in the Provinces which the Law assigns him, unless it be in the Chamber of *Spires*, the which administring Justice in the Name of all the Estates of the Empire, acknowledges both the Vicars, because by excluding the one, she would thereby acknowledge the other for sole Vicar of the whole Empire When we say that their Power has the same Extent as that of the Emperor himself, we conclude therefrom, That the perpetual Vicars, as the Dukes of *Savoy*, of *Mantua*, and others, who acknowledge the Authority of the Emperor, ought to acknowledge that of the Vicars during the *Interregnum*, which is what is indubitable

The chief Advantages of the Vicars are, 1 The Right of Regalia, or to nominate to Benefices, which the *Germans* call, *Jus primariarum precum*, which belongs to the Emperor, to the Exclusion of all the other Princes 2 To receive the Revenues of the Demesne of the Empire, and to dispose thereof for the Publick Good 3 To receive Fealty and Homage from the Vassals of the Empire, unless the Fiefs are of the Nature of those which we shall speak of by and by 4 To judge Causes in the first Instance, concerning which Recourse may be had to the *Aulick* Council, to the Exclusion of the Chamber of *Spires*, and generally all the other Advantages which the Emperor enjoys as Emperor

The two Cases reserv'd by the Law are, The Alienation of the Demesne of the Empire, and the Investiture which is given by the Standard and by the Sceptre As for the first, it is not in the Power of the Emperor himself, to alienate or mortgage the Demesne of the Empire without the express Consent of the Electors And as for the other, it is not just that they, who are Members depending on the Empire immediately, and who enjoy all the Rights of Regalia, as well as the Vicars, should do Submissions to any body else than the Emperor in Person, to whom they are reserv'd by the express Disposition of the Law

The Vicarship which begins presently after the Death, and with the Absence of the Emperor, ends at his Return, and by a new Election

† The Vicars of the Electors are hereditary Officers of the Empire, substituted to the Officers of the Crown of the Empire, to discharge their Offices in their Absence The King of *Bohemia*, the Duke of *Bavaria*, who has succeeded in the *Palatin* Electoral Dignity, the Duke of *Saxony* and the Marquiss of *Brandenburg*, have each of them theirs The King of *Bohemia*, as Great Cup-bearer of the Empire, has for Vicar the Baron of *Limburg*, and in the Office of Great Cup-bearer of the Bishoprick of *Bamberg*, the Lord of *Auffas* At the Time of the Publication of the *Golden Bull*, the Lord of *Norremberg* was Vicar to the Count Palatin of the *Rhine*, in the Office of Great Steward of the Empire, and in that of ‡ Great Steward of the Bishoprick of *Bamberg*, he has for Vicar the Lord *Truchses**, of *Pommerfelden* The Baron of *Selnick*, or of *Seldech*, did this Office at the Coronation of the Emperor *Maximilian* I, and at this Day it belongs to the Family of *Waltbourg*, which bears also the Name or Quality of *Truchses* The Count of *Pappenheim* is Vicar of the Duke of *Saxony*, as Great Mareschal of the Empire, who in his Office of Great Mareschal of the Bishoprick of *Bamberg*, has for Vicar the Lord of *Ebnen* The Marquiss of *Brandenburg*, as Great Chamberlain, has for Vicar in the Empire the Count of *Hohenzollern*, who succeeded in that Office

---

† *The Extent of the Vicariate*
‡ *Vicars of the Bishoprick of* Bamberg
* *The Power of the Vicars*
* *The Word signifies properly a Sewer, or the Office which is call'd in* Italy, Scalco
† *Vicars of the Electors*

to the Count of *Falquenstein*, and to the Baron of *Winsverg*, whose Families are extinct, and in the Bishoprick of *Bamberg*, the Lord of *Rottenban*. The Count *Palatin* of the *Rhine*, as Great Treasurer of the Emperor, has no Function nor Vicar in the Empire, no more than in the Bishoprick of *Bamberg*.

The Secular Electors are oblig'd to do Homage to the Bishop of *Bamberg*, for the hereditary Offices of his Church, but that it is performed by Proxy, and without Ceremonies. The Proxy only saying, that he presents himself there to demand the Investiture, and the Bishop making Answer, That he gives it according to the usual Custom. Their Vicars in the Bishoprick discharge their Offices at the Entries of the new Bishops, and do Homage for the same to the Electors. But the Vicars of the Electors of the Empire, hold also of the Empire, which has establish'd them in their Offices. So that if an Elector, when he sends an Embassador to the Diet, or to the Election, should give him in express Power to do the Functions of his Office, he would not be admitted, because the Vicars are the proper Officers in the Absence of the Electors. And thus it was judg'd in the Year 1486, at the Coronation of *Maximilian* I, where the Baron of *Winsberg* was maintain'd in the Exercise of his Office of Chamberlain, against the Pretensions of the Embassador of the Elector of *Brandenburg*. And for the Baron of *Limburg*, against the Embassadors of *Bohemia* at the Coronation of *Charles* V, at *Aix la Chapelle*. And even in Favour of the Count of *Pappenheim*, against the Pretensions of the Prince of *Anhalt*, who was present at *Cologn*, at the Coronation of the same Emperor *Charles*, in the Name, and as Embassador from the Elector of *Saxony*, Great Mareschal hereditary of the Empire. Examples, that were follow'd at the Coronations of *Maximilian* II, of *Rodolphus* II, of *Matthias*, of *Ferdinand* II, where there was not so much as one Secular Elector present, of *Ferdinand* III, where there was only the Duke of *Bavaria*, and of the King of the *Romans*, who dy'd last.

We must however observe, in these three last Coronations, that the Kings of *Bohemia* had not their Embassadors there, but were present, and were there chosen Emperors, so that there was an absolute Necessity their Offices should be discharg'd by the Vicars. And it is to what we may refer the Example of *Charles* IV, who being King of *Bohemia*, and not being able to execute the Office of Great Cup-bearer, because he was chosen Emperor, he caus'd it to be perform'd by *Valram* Duke of *Brabant* and of *Luxemburg*. But at this Day the Vicars are in Possession of discharging the Functions of the Offices in the Absence of the Electors.

‡ When the Electors are personally present at the Election, or Coronation of the Emperor, they execute their Offices themselves, in the manner we shall see hereafter, and then their Vicars have no Function at all; nay, they are not any way assisting to them in the Execution of their Offices, except that they wait for the Electors at the Gate of the Town-House of *Franckfort*, or of the Place where the Imperial Court is prepar'd, in order to help each their Elector to get on Horseback, and dismount and in Acknowledgment of this small Service, the Elector gives the Horse he rode upon, and the Place it was employ'd in the Exercise of his Office, to the Vicar that is substituted to him.

* There is only Count *Pappenheim*, Vicar to the Elector of *Saxony*, in his Office of Great Mareschal of the Empire, whose Function is of a greater Extent, for he performs his Office first at the Diets which are convened for the general Affairs of the Empire. Secondly, at the particular Assemblies the Electors have about the Election. Thirdly at the Coronations. Fourthly, at the Journeys the Emperors formerly took into *Italy*, in order to receive the Imperial Crown at *Rome*. And fifthly, in the Army where the Emperor commands in Person.

When these Occasions offer, the Elector of *Saxony* sends Word to the eldest of the Counts of *Pappenheim*, or else he writes to all the Counts of the same House in general, that is to say, to those who are concern'd in the Castle of *Pappenheim*, and have not had their Portion elsewhere, to take care that nothing may be wanting that depends on the Functions of his Office, which consist chiefly, first, in the Discharge of the Functions of Master of the Ceremonies, to introduce the Princes and other Estates of the Empire to the Emperor, and into the Room where the Assembly is held. Secondly, to cause a Throne to be prepar'd for the Emperor. As also, thirdly, to dispose the Seats and Benches for the Electors, Princes, and Deputies of the Free Towns. Fourthly, formerly, he regulated the Seats of the Princes, and took each Prince by the Arm to conduct him to his Place. But the Accident that happen'd at the Diet of *Augsburg*, under the Emperor *Frederick* III, where *Sigismund*, Count of *Pappenheim*, having preferr'd *Albert* Duke of *Saxony* to *George* of *Bavaria*, this last was so offended thereat, that he sent a Challenge to the Count thereupon. The Emperor prevented the Combat, but yet this Accident gave Occasion to change the ancient Custom, and it was ordain'd that the Emperor should, for the future, regulate the Order of the Session among the Princes. Fifthly, it is his Care to signify to the Princes, and Deputies of the Towns, the Hour fix'd for the Assembly. Sixthly, in the particular Assemblies which the Princes have at the Diets, he takes the Votes, and computes the Suffrages. Seventhly, at the time of the Election he disposes the Guards at the Gates of the Town, and at the Chamber where the Electors are assembled. And eighthly, he keeps the Key of the Door of the Place where the Electors are shut up during the Election.

The Count of *Pappenheim* is oblig'd to be personally present at all the Assemblies, where the Emperor or the Elector of *Saxony* are present, and in his Absence, the Mareschal of the Emperor's Court executes the Office, which is what he has in common with all the other Vi-

---

‡ *The Vicars, and not the Embassadors, do the Office of the Electors.*
* *The Office of the Count of* Pappenheim.
‡ *The Vicars have no Functions in the Presence of the Electors.*

ears of the Electors, to whom the Officers of the Court are substituted in their Absence, each in his respective Office.

The Count of *Pappenheim* has moreover this peculiar to him, that he can appoint a Lieutenant, which he can nominate of his own Authority, and send him to the Town where the Diet is convén'd, (when he can't go thither in Person) with *Credentials* from the Elector of *Saxony* to the Magistrate of the Place, to see into the Conveniency of Lodgings, and of the room where the Assembly is to be held, to inform himself of the Goodness of the Air, and whether the Town be not infected with any contagious Malady, or whether it be not incommoded with Soldiers, as also of the Price and Conveniency of Provisions, and if he finds any Difficulty, he gives Advice thereof to the Emperor and to the Duke of *Saxony*.

Formerly the Count of *Pappenheim* did not settle the Lodgings, without an Assistant appointed by the Magistracy of the Place of the Assembly; but by the Agreement made between the Count and the Imperial Towns, in the Diet assembl'd at *Augsburg* in the Year 1614, they yielded to him the marking of them, whose Authority therein is so absolute, that even the Embassadors of foreign Princes are not allow'd to cause Lodgings to be secur'd to them, nay even those Princes who have Houses in the Town where the Diet is held, cannot make use of them without the Count of *Pappenheim*'s Permission, tho' he cannot refuse to give them his Mark, if requir'd so to do. At present the Lodgings are prepar'd by Agreement between the Count and the Emperor's Harbingers, and those of the Electors and of the other Princes of the Empire.

The chief Function of the Count of *Pappenheim*, is to carry the Sword before the Emperor in the Absence of the Elector of *Saxony*, even to the Exclusion of his Embassadors, as we before observ'd, tho' they should have the Quality of Princes, which is not impossible, as we saw just now in the Person of the Prince of *Anhalt*, who assisted at the Coronation of the Emperor *Charles* V. And at the next Election, Prince *Maurice* of *Nassau* will be there, in the Quality of Embassador from the Elector of *Brandenburg*. However, if the Prince who is presumptive Heir of the Electoral Dignity represents the Person of his Father, the Count owes him that Deference, as to suffer him to do the Functions of his Office on two or three Occasions. It depend's on the Emperor to give Orders to have the Sword carry'd before him; then the Count ought to carry it naked, and himself uncover'd, having his right Hand on his Stomach, in such manner that the Point of the Sword may appear above his Shoulder. He ought not to suffer the Pope's Cross bearer, or that of a Cardinal Legate *a Latere* to march by his side, even tho' the Pope, or the Cardinal Legate should march on the Emperor's side, because he ought to have a free use of the Sword, unless the other Regalia or Imperial Ornaments are also born, as the Globe or Golden Ball, and the Scepter; for then he may and ought to suffer the Bearers to march a breast with him. In the Church, and in the other Places of Ceremony, he holds the Sword with both Hands on his Stomach. At the Elevation of the Sacrament he grounds the Point of his Sword, having his right Hand on the Pummel of the Guard, and holds his left Hand lifted towards Heaven, with his Face always towards the Emperor.

When the Elector of *Saxony* causes the Sword to be carry'd before him, this Honour is also due to the Count of *Pappenheim*, who carries it before the Elector every where else, but in *Saxony*, and those Provinces that are annex'd thereto, where the Mareschal of the Court performs his Functions. He that is the eldest of all the Counts of *Pappenheim*, provided he have a Share in the Castle, as we have already said, may either execute this Office in Person, or nominate any one of his Relations of the same House, on whom he has a mind to confer this Honour. When the Elector of *Saxony* discharges his Office in Person, the Count of *Pappenheim*, instead of bearing the Sword, marches at the Head of all the Procession, having by his side the Mareschal of the Emperor's Court, if he be there present; if he be not there, he marches alone, holding the commanding Staff in his Hand.

He has this in common with the other Vicars, that of the sixty three Marks and one Quarter, Silver, which the Princes and other Lords, as well Ecclesiasticks as Seculars, except the Electors, pay for the Investiture, ten belong to him; provided he executes in Person the Functions of his Office, because in his absence this Right belongs to the Mareschal of the Emperor's Court, as well as the Horse on which the Prince who receives the Investiture is mounted. However if the Elector of *Saxony* be there in Person the Horse belongs to him, to the Exclusion of the others.

CHAP. XIII.

Of the King of Bohemia, Prince Elector of the Holy Empire.

After having treated of the Electoral Dignity, of the Rights, Advantages, Prerogatives and Preemencies of the Electors; of the three Ecclesiastical Electors, and of the Secular Electors in general, the Order of our Discourse requires we should now speak of each Secular Elector in particular. We shall begin with the King of *Bohemia*, who is without doubt the first of the Secular Electors, on the Account of his Royal Dignity.

of the ELECTORS of the EMPIRE. 503

And that we may proceed therein with some Order, we shall say a word or two concerning the Kingdom it self, and its Princes

* There is not any Province in all *Germany*, whose Etymology is more indubitable than that of *Bohemia*. The Word *Bohemia* signifies the Habitation of the *Boy*, People amongst the *Gauls*, who having penetrated into *Germany* under the Conduct of *Sigovesus*, Nephew to *Ambigatus*, in the Time of *Tarquinius Priscus* King of *Rome*, about the Year 587, before the Birth of our Saviour, drove out the *Hermunduri* and the *Nemetes* from those Parts, and settled in that Place which the neighbouring People call'd *Bohemia*. *Marobduus* having made himself the Head of the *Marcomanni*, under the first Emperors, and having a Design to make himself King of those People of old *Suabia*, he cast his Eyes on *Bohemia*, which is a Province situate at the Extremity of *Germany*, and incompass'd with an impenetrable Forest, as on a Place where he should be shelter'd from the Persecution of the *Roman* Arms, and drove from thence the *Boy*, whom he oblig'd to retire to the Countrey, which is call'd still at this Day from their Name *Bavaria*. † The *Sclavy* succeeded the *Marcomanni*, but their Invasion, which happen'd about the Year 454, after the Birth of *Jesus Christ*, did not occasion the Name which the *Boy* had given that Province to be chang'd. Those *Barbarians* were come out of *Scythia*, or from those Places which are inhabitated at present by the *Muscovites* and the *Tartars* and having shar'd their Conquests amongst them, they cast the Foundations of the two new States, which at this Day are call'd *Poland* and *Bohemia*. The *Sclavonians*, who inhabit there still, call it indeed in their Language *Cheskazeme*, that is to say, Countrey of the *Chez*, or of the Posterity of *Checus*; but it is a Name unknown, and the *Sclavonians* themselves make use thereof but very rarely.

When we say that the *Sclavy* enter'd into *Germany* in the fifth Century, we follow the Opinion of *Cromer* and of *Neugebaur*, who say in their History of *Poland*, and with a great deal of Probability, that the *Sclavy*, who had quitted *Scythia* to enter into *Muscovy* a good while before, advanc'd into *Poland*, and afterwards into *Germany* and *Bohemia*, in the Time, and under the Favour of the March of *Attila*, King of the *Huns*, tho' a great many other grave Authors refer the Transmigration of the *Northern* People to the Time of the Emperor *Maurice*, who began his Reign in the Year 611, and *Calvisius* puts it in the Year 645. However it be, it is certain that the Inhabitants of *Bohemia* are *Sclavonians* originally, and not *Germans*. This is also one of the Reasons, on which is founded the Opinion of those, who maintain that *Bohemia* does not constitute a part of *Germany*. That this Kingdom is no Member of the Empire, and by Consequence that its King cannot be an Elector. It is the common Opinion of the Doctors on *C. Venerabilem extr de El post* supported by Cardinal *Bellarmin*, in his Treatise, *De Translatione Imperii*, where he says, that *Bohemia is not compris'd in any Circle, that its Inhabitants are Strangers, that they do not submit to the Resolutions of the General Diets, and that they do not contribute to the Charges of the Empire*: so that to secure to the King of *Bohemia* his Electoral Dignity, it is necessary first to shew that *Bohemia* makes a part of *Germany*, and that its Kings are Princes of the Empire.

‡ Every body knows that *Bohemia* is situate in the Heart of *Germany*, and is encompass'd by the Forest *Hercynia*, on all sides like a Wall, and which separates it towards the *East* from *Silesia* and *Moravia*, towards the *North* from *Misnia* and *Lusatia*, towards the *South* from *Austria* and the *Upper Palatinate*, and towards the *West* from *Franconia* and the *Voitland*, which are all Provinces of *Germany*. It is true its Inhabitants are *Sclavy*, and Foreigners originally, but that does not hinder *Bohemia* from making a Part of *Germany*, and of the Empire it self. The People of *Lombardy* were *Germans*, and have for many Ages had Kings of their Countrey, Laws, and a particular Government, notwithstanding which no body yet has question'd whether *Lombardy* makes a Part of *Italy*. In like manner the *Normans*, who are *Danes* and *Swedes* originally, settl'd in *France* several Ages after the *Sclavy* came into *Bohemia*. But *Normandy* is neverthelefs one of the most considerable Provinces of the Kingdom of *France*. The same *Sclavi* possess'd *Pomerania*, the Dutchy of *Mecklenburg*, and a good part of the Marches of *Brandenburg*; and it is certain that most of the Inhabitants of those Provinces are *Sclavy* originally, as well as those of *Bohemia*; but that yet does not hinder them from making a Part of *Germany*, and from depending on the Empire.

* It is indeed true, that *Bohemia* is not compris'd under any Circle, and that the Emperor *Maximilian* I, when he regulated the Circles to Six in Number, in the Diet conven'd at *Augsburg*, in the Year 1500, did not comprehend therein *Bohemia*, no more than at the Regulation he made at *Cologn* in the Year 1512, where he augmented the Number thereof to Ten. But it is true also, that the Emperor *Wenceslas*, in making the first Regulation for the Circles at *Merguetheim* in the Year 1387, made only Four, whereof *Bohemia*, with the Provinces which depend thereon, made the first; and that to be a Member of the Empire it is not necessary to be compris'd in any Circle, since it is certain that in the Time of the same Emperor *Maximilian*, the Great Master of the Order of *Prussia* was a Prince of the Empire, and yet he does not so much as mention *Prussia* at all in the Ordinances he made for the Circles.

But to speak pertinently thereof, we must presuppose, as a thing that cannot be contested, That the Princes and Kings of *Bohemia* acknowledg'd the Empire even in the Time of *Charlemagne*, that they did Homage to the Kings and Emperors of *Germany*, and that they have even had some Respect for *France*, before its Princes had attain'd to the Imperial Dignity. We shall bring some Instances thereof out of History, for the better understanding of what we shall say hereafter.

---

* *The Origin of the Name of the Empire.*   † *The Sclavonians possess Bohemia.*   ‡ *Bohemia makes a part of Germany.*   * *And*

We

We read there, that about the Year 600, *Childebert* and *Dagobert*, Kings of both the *Gallia*, that is to say, of the *Oriental* and *Occidental*, commanded the *Bavarians* to make War against the *Bohemians*, who had revolted. And *Cosmas* of *Prague* says, That *Pepin* King of *France*, and Father to *Charlemagne*, impos'd upon them a Tribute of six score Oxen, and of six hundred Marks of Silver. The Princes of *Bohemia* have ever acknowledg'd the Emperors of *Germany* as their Sovereign Lords. In the Person of *Charlemagne* in the Year 806, and in that of *Lewis* the *Debonnair* his Son in the Year 830. † They did Homage to *Lewis* the *German*, King of *Germany*, Son to *Lewis* the *Deboonair*, in 848, 849, 856, 857, 869, 871, and 874. To *Charles* the *Gross* in 880. To *Arnoul* or *Arnulfus*, who gave *Bohemia* to *Zuentibold* King of *Moravia*, in 890, 893, and 897, and to *Henry* I, in 920, 921, 922, 928, and in 930, The same Emperor *Henry* I, gave leave to *Wenceslas*, a *Bohemian* Lord, to take the Quality of Prince and Duke, and granted to his Subjects the same Rights, Privileges and Liberties, that the *Bavarians* and *Saxons* enjoy'd at that Time. St *Wenceslas*, and *Boleslas* his Brother, did Homage to the Emperor *Otho* I, and *Boleslas* and *Mesico* to *Otho* III. The Emperor *Henry* II, took *Bohemia* from *Boleslas* II, and invested therewith *Ulaaman*, Marquis of *Mizen*. *Uratislas*, and *Spitigeneus* his Son, did Homage to the Emperor *Henry* III. *Henry* IV gave the Quality of King to *Uratislas* in the Year 1086, and in 1099, he gave the Investiture thereof to *Borivoy*. In 1127, *Sobieslas* did Homage for *Bohemia* to *Lotharius* II, and being present in 1138, at the Diet of *Bamberg*, he intreated the Emperor *Conrade* III, to give the Investiture thereof to *Boleslar* his Nephew. The same *Boleslas* did Homage therefore in 1140, to *Conrade*, and in 1158, to *Frederick Barbarossa*, his Successor in the Empire, who took away the Crown of *Bohemia* from *Sobieslas*, and invested therewith *Freaerick*, who reign'd till the Year 1190. *Henry* Bishop of *Prague*, who was the Son of *Uladislas* I, being call'd to the Crown of *Bohemia* in 1192, was oblig'd to demand the Investiture thereof from *Henry* VI, and obtain'd it by the Means of a good Sum of Money. The Emperor *Philip* of *Suabia*, having put *Primislas Othocarus* King of *Bohemia* in the Ban of the Empire, took *Theobald* from School, and invested him with the Kingdom in the Year 1212. *Primislas Othocarus* II, did in the Year 1277, Homage to the Emperor *Rodulfu.* of *Habspurg* for the Kingdom of *Bohemia*, at the Head of the whole Army. *Henry* VII being at *Spires* in 1309, invested therewith *John* of *Luxemburg* his Son, and the same King *John* did Homage therefore to *Lewis* of *Bavaria*, who had succeeded his Father in the Empire. *George* of *Podiebrach*, and *Uladislas*, Sons to *Casimir* King of *Poland*, did Homage for the Kingdom of *Bohemia* to *Frederick* III. And *Ferdinand* and *Matthias* Kings of *Bohemia*, paid the same Devoirs to the Emperors *Charles* V, and *Rodolphus* II, their Brothers. Which we think sufficient to verify the Dependence *Bohemia* has of the Empire. We shall add thereto, That the Princes and Kings of *Bohemia* were oblig'd to accompany the Emperor with three hundred Lances or Spears, in the Journey he us'd to take formerly into *Italy*, in order to receive there the Imperial Crown at *Rome*. That they were proceeded against when they attempted to withdraw themselves from the Obedience of the Empire, and that they were oblig'd to be present at the Diets.

† It is as Prince of the Empire, that *Boleslas* was present in the Year 973, at the Diet which the Emperor *Otho* II had conven'd at *Quedlinburg*, and that he was put in the Ban of the Empire, for having refus'd to assist at the Diet, the same Emperor had call'd together at *Hamar* in the Year 975. This oblig'd him to be personally present at that of *Aysle* in *Thuringia* in 977. *Mesico* and *Boleslas* were present at the Diet of *Quedlinburg*, under the Emperor *Otho* III, in the Year 985. *Boleslas* III, appear'd in the Year 1003, at that which the Emperor *Henry* II had conven'd at *Merebu*. *Uheres* t that of *Ma*, &c in 1025, under *Conrade* II. The same *Uheres* having kill'd his Brother *J...* in the Year 1028, the Emperor *Conrade* summon'd him before him, and put him in the Ban of the Empire. Some Years after he pardon'd him, and oblig'd him to do him Homage. *Sbeislas* or *Bretislas* was put in the Ban of the Empire by *Henry* III, who caus'd him to be try'd with Circumstances which are very remarkable. Moreover *Preceslas* Duke of *Bohemia*, having made Incursions into *Poland*, from whence he had brought great Riches, the same Emperor *Henry* pretended, that he ought to dispose thereof as Sovereign Prince of *Bohemia* and upon *Preceslas* his Refusal to acknowledge the Empire on this Occasion, *Henry* declar'd War against him. The *Bohemians* seeing themselves threaten'd with this Storm, sent their Deputies to meet the Emperor, to whom they spoke in these Terms. *We have always liv'd*, said they, *and we shall live under the Empire of Charles, (the Great) and of his Successors. This People never rebell'd, but is ever has been, and as well for ever he, saith it to thee in all thy Wars, if thou wilt do us Justice*. *Henry* for all this advanc'd his Army, and as he was only for punishing the Stubbornness of *Preceslas*, he compell'd him to come and lay himself at his Feet, and to do him those Submissions which drew from him these Words, *What Triumph do you hope for from a War, which you make against a Countrey and a People that belong to you?* The same *Preceslas* was at the Diet of *Ratisbone* in the Year 1048, at that of *Goslar* in 1050, and at that of *Mayence* in 1051, which were all call'd by the same Emperor. There happen'd a thing very remarkable about the Year 1067, under *Henry* IV, *Wratislas* Duke of *Bohemia*, was for confirming (of his own Authority) the Election the Chapter of *Prague* had made of a Bishop nam'd *Lanco*, a Native of *Saxony*. But *Corat*, Son to *Ufebor*, one of the Palatins of *Bohemia*, not being able to bear the Wrong that was done to *Jaromir*, the Son of *Bretislas*, oppos'd it, and spoke in these Terms. *Let the Emperor live, as thanks be to God he does yet. But thou makest thy self Emperor, when by giving the Investiture by the Ring and the Wand, thou usurp'st the Right that be-*

---

† *The Kings of* Bohemia *do Homage to the Emperor.*   ‡ *They appear at the Diets of the Empire.*

longs

of the ELECTORS *of the* EMPIRE   505

longs to him And in effect the Emperor confirm'd the Election of *Jaromir*, and invested him with the Bishoprick *June* 28, 1068 The same Emperor gave the Title of King to *Uratiſlas*, as we said before And that it might appear that *Uratiſlas* held the Crown immediately of him, he would needs put it on his Head, and caus'd him to be anointed by *Engelbert*, Archbishop of *Triers* The same Emperor, writing to *Uratiſlas* after he was King, styles him Trusty and it was he that in the Year 1092, gave the Bishoprick of *Prague* to *Coſmas*, who has written the History of *Bohemia* In 1098, he commanded *Preceſlas* to repair to him at *Ratisbone*, where he gave him the Investiture by the Standard of the Crown of *Bohemia*, for *Borivoy* his Brother The same *Borivoy* having been driven out of the Countrey by *Suendebold*, complain'd thereof to *Henry* V, who sent for *Suendebold*, and put him under Confinement in the Year 1107 *Suendebold* dying the Year following, or according to others in 1109, the Emperor gave the *Bohemians* leave to chuse themselves another Prince They elected *Uladiſlas*, who had for Competitor *Borivoy* but the Emperor having sent for both of them, put *Borivoy* in Prison, and caus'd the Eyes of some of his Partisans to be put out The same *Uladiſlas* was at the Diet of *Bamberg* in the Year 1124 *Ulricus* at that of *Merſburg* in 1127, and at that of *Ratisbone* in 1130, under *Lotharius* II *Sobieſlas* was at that of *Magdeburg* in 1134, under the same *Lotharius*, and in 1138, at that of *Bamberg* under *Conrade* III *Uladiſlas* was present in 1156, at the Diet of *Ratisbone* under *Frederick* I and pronounc'd the Decree, by which the Marquisate of *Auſtria* was erected into a Dutchy In the Year 1157, he sent his Brother *Theobald* to the Diet of *Arbois* in the County of *Burgundy*, and was personally present at that of *Bamberg* and of *Wurtzburg* in the same Year, as also it that or *Ratisbone* in 1158, at that of *Augsburg* in 1159, at that of *Erfurt* in 1160, at that of *Lodi* in Lombardy in 1161, at that of *Bizançon* in 1162, and at that of *Bamberg* in 1169 *Frederick* I, Emperor, gave *Bohemia* to *Frederick*, to the Prejudice of *Sobieſlas*, who was his eldest Son The same *Frederick*, King of *Bohemia*, was present at the Diets of *Ratisbone* in 1179, and 1182, and at that of *Bamberg* in the same Year *Wenceſlas* being driven out by *Primiſlas*, the Son of *Uladiſlas* IV, after the Death of *Frederick*, and of *Conrade* his Successor, the Emperor *Henry* VI, summon'd him before him, as a *Perturbator* of the publick Tranquility, and an Infringer of the Peace of the Empire *Othocarius* was present at the Diet of *Mayence* in 1199, and at that of *Boppard* in the Year 1200, under the Emperor *Philip* of *Suabia* *Primiſlas Othocarius* assisted at that of *Mersburg* in 1203, and sent his Brother *Wenceſlas* to that of *Mayence* in 1209, under *Otho* IV In the same Year he was personally present at that of *Naumburg*, and in 1211, at that of *Baſil*, and in 1212, at that of *Baſil*, and in 1213, at that of *Egra*, under *Frederick* II *Wenceſlas* was present at that of *Egra* in 1217, at that of *Bamberg* in 1223, and in 1235 *Othocarius* II, was in 1247, at the Diet of *Aix la Chappelle*, in 1274, at that of *Nuremberg*, and in 1275, at that of *Wurtzburg*, under *Rodolphus* I *Wenceſlas* his Son, was at that of *Erfort* in 1280, and in 1294, at that of *Grubenheim*, under *Adolphus* of *Naſſaw*, and in 1299, at that of *Nuremberg*, under *Albert* I *John* of *Luxemburg* King of *Bohemia*, presided at the Diet of *Bamberg* in 1313, in the Name of *Henry* VII his Father, which is what he could not have done, if he had not been a Prince of the Empire He was personally present at that of *Egra* in 1318, at that of *Ratisbone* in 1324, and at that of *Francfort* in 1328, under *Lewis* IV

From whence we must conclude, that the Dukes and Kings of *Bohemia*, who have been present at so many General Assemblies, are Princes of the Empire, and that *Bohemia* is one of its principal Members as the Emperor *Rodolphus* II says in express Terms, in the Edict for the Peace of Religion in the Empire in the Year 1609 And indeed, to say Elector, is to say Prince, because it is so impossible to be the one without the other, that the *Germans* have no Word that simply signifies Elector, and that that of which all the Electors make use to express their Quality, is that of *Prince Elector of the Holy Empire*

* It is true, that for above these two hundred Years the Kings of *Bohemia* are not call'd to the General Diets, nor even to the Assemblies which the Electors have amongst themselves concerning the Affairs of the Empire, distinct from those that are for the Election of an Emperor, or of a King of the *Romans* but that does not hinder them from contributing to the Charges of the War against the *Turks*, and to the other Expences of the Empire For by the Resolution taken in the Year 1471, at *Ratisbone*, and concerning the War against the *Turks*, it was said in express Terms, that *Bohemia*, and the Provinces which are annex'd thereto, should be tax'd as all the other States of the Empire Which has been confirm'd by the Resolutions taken at the Diets of *Augsburg* in the Year 1500, under the Emperor *Maximilian* I, in 1522, at *Nuremberg*, in 1541, at *Ratisbone*, in 1542, at *Spires* and *Nuremberg*, and again at *Spires* in 1544, under the Emperor *Charles* V And if it does not appear that the Kings of *Bohemia* have since that Time been invited to the Diets, either general or particular, it is because the Qualities of Emperor and of King of *Bohemia* meeting in the same Person, they could not invite themselves besides which the Kingdom of *Bohemia*, and the Imperial Dignity, having been for a long Course of Years in the House of *Auſtria*, which is more concern'd in the Preservation of *Hungary*, where the *Turkish* Arms are most dreaded, of all the Provinces of *Germany*, it draws from *Bohemia* beyond comparison more Succour, than could be requir'd from it, by the Regulations made at the Diets Tho' it nevertheless makes use of all Opportunities, that can contribute to the exempting this Kingdom from being subject to the Empire

† It began to separate from it in the Time of the Council of *Conſtance*, and on the account of the execution of *John Hus*, and *Jerome* of *Prague* They were burnt contrary to the

---

* *Now they no longer are present there* † *Since when and for what they ſeparated from the Empire*

Pro-

Promife and Safe-conduct which had been given them and the *Bohemians*, who had for the moft part imbib'd the Doctrine of thefe two learned Men, purfu'd the Revenge of their Death with fo much Animofity, and fo much Succefs, that the Victories they gain'd over the Emperor *Sigifmund* and the other Princes who were for intermeddling in the Quarrel, put them in a Condition not only to require a Liberty of Confcience, but alfo to hope for that of their State The Diforders of thofe Civil Wars, and the Difference in Religion, had render'd the *Bohemians* fo odious to the *Germans*, who had already a great Averfion to them, that they were no longer fo'licitous of calling to the Diets thofe who had already feparated from the Communion of their Church, and who refus'd to obey the Laws of the Empire, and the Refolutions the *Germans* took in their General Affemblies

* But as for the Electoral Dignity, the Kings of *Bohemia* have at all Times been fo jealous thereof, that they have not been lefs careful of preferving the Right of the Election, than they had fhewn themfelves defirous to get into the Number of the Electors, as foon as it begin to be a particular Quality in the Empire We muft not wonder that Pope *Innocent* IV puts the King of *Bohemia* at the Head of thofe Princes who are not Electors, as we have feen elfewhere, † becaufe the Quality of Elector was not as yet annex'd to the Kingdom of *Bohemia*, no more than to the other Principalities to which it is at this Day appropriated And it is to that Time muft be referr'd what the Commentators *in c venerabilem extr de Elect & El pot* and the Mirrors of the Law of *Saxony* and of *Suabia* pofitively affirm, when they fay, that the King of *Bohemia* is Great Cupbearer of the Empire, but does not elect, becaufe he is not a *German* But the Moderns, is Cardinal *Bellarmin*, and even feveral German Doctors, who ftrike into the fame Error, or who affirm, that the King of *Bohemia* is not call'd to the Elections but when there is an equality of Votes, and when a Schifm is apprehended in the Empire, are inexcufable The Quality of Elector might have been difputed with the King of *Bohemia* before the Publication of the *Golden Bull*, becaufe it was not fo well fecur'd to him, but *Wenceflas* II found himfelf oblig'd to procure for that purpofe from the Emperor *Rodolphus* I his Father-in-Law, Letters which we fhall infert in this Chapter, and which would not have been neceffary, if his Right had been above Controverfy, and inconteftable, but at prefent it can no longer be call'd to queftion, fince *Charles* IV, who was Emperor and King of *Bohemia*, has render'd it infeparable from his Kingdom He fays, ‡ *That it is manifeft and notorious to all the World, and that there is no body who does not know, that the illuftrious King of* Bohemia *has a Right, Vote, and Seat at the Election of the King of the Romans, future Emperor, by virtue of his Reign, and that he is reputed, and is in effect true and lawful Prince Elector of the Empire* * *That he is the firft of the Secular Electors, by reafon of his Regal Dignity* † *That he fhall take place immediately after the Archbifhop, who, according to the place of the Affembly, fhall be on the Emperor's right Hand, and,* ‡ *That he fhall vote after the Archbifhop of* Cologn, *and before all the other Secular Electors* * Which is fo true, that even before the Publication of the *Golden Bull*, and when the Electoral Dignity was not yet fix'd to certain Principalities and Families, the Kings of *Bohemia* were prefent at feveral Elections whereof we have Examples in *Bolefas*, Duke of *Bohemia*, who affifted at the Election of the Emperor *Henry* II, *Ulric* at that of *Conrade* the *Salique*, *Sobeflas* at that of *Conrade* III, and *Udiflas* II at that of *Frederick* I *Primiflas Othocarius* is nam'd firft among the Secular Princes, who elected *Philip* of *Suabia* And *Frederick* II fays very expreffly, that the fame *Primiflas Othocarius* adher'd conftantly to the Election of his Perfon The fame *Primiflas* fent in the Year 1222, *Bretiflas*, Duke of *Skale*, his Relation, to the Diet of *Strafburg*, to affift at the Election of *Henry* of *Suabia*, the Son of *Frederick* II In the Year 1248, *Othocarius* II was prefent at the Election of *William* of *Holland* and in 1257, he gave his Suffrage to *Alfonfus* King of *Caftile*, againft *Richard* of *Cornwall* *Wenceflas* II refus'd the Imperial Crown which was offer'd to him, and tl would the Election of *Adolphus* or *Naffau* It is true that he was not there in Perfon, but it is certain that he was fo well acknowledg'd for Elector, that *Albert* Duke of *Saxony* order'd his Embaffadors to give his Voice to him that fhould be nominated by the King of *Bohemia*, who on his fide defir'd the Archbifhop of *Mayence* to reprefent his Perfon in this Action, purfuant to the Cuftom of the Times, when the abfent Princes intrufted fome of thofe who were prefent to act for them, and their Embaffadors had nothing to do but to juftify the Caufe of the Abfence of their Mifters The fame *Wenceflas* faid that *Albert* I was oblig'd to him for the Imperial Dignity and *John* of *Luxemburg* was prefent at the Election of *Lewis* of *Bavaria* and of *Charles* IV his Succeffor

There is no likelihood that after the Paffages of the *Golden Bull*, which we have quoted, and which are fo clear and fo exprefs on that Subject, and after fo many Examples, any body can ftill doubt of the Right of the King of *Bohemia* but that no Scruple at all may remain in the moft difficult Minds, we fhall here relate two Teftimonies, the Originals whereof are kept in the Archives of the Kingdom of *Bohemia*, and are of fo great Authority, that it may in fome meafure be preferr'd to that of the *Golden Bull* The firft is of the Emperor *Rodolphus* I, which we have tranflated Word for Word in thefe Terms " *Rodolphus*, by " the Grace of God, King of the *Romans*, to " all thofe to whom thefe Prefents fhall come, " Greeting Being willing to remove from " Pofterity ill Ground of Quarrel and Con- " teftation, in proving the Right of the Prin- " ces, we have caus'd a very exact and very " curious Search to be made of the Right which " our moft dear Son and Prince, the illuftrious " King of *Bohemia* and his Heirs, may have in

of the ELECTORS of the EMPIRE. 507

" the Empire, and in the Election of the King
" of the Romans, and we have found by the
" Deposition, and by the Testimony of all the
" Princes, Barons, Nobles, and Lords of the
" Empire, as also by that of divers other aged
" Persons, that the King of *Bohemia* ought to
" be, and is in effect, Cup-bearer of the Em-
" pire, and that the Rights of the Office of
" Cup-bearer belong to him and to his Heirs,
" by right of hereditary Succession. We have
" also sufficiently verify'd, that the King of
" *Bohemia* and his Heirs ought to have a Right
" and Vote in the Election of the King of the
" *Romans*, future Emperor, as well, and in the
" same Quality, as the other Electors. We
" therefore say, that the Rights of Great Cup-
" bearer, and of Elector, do not only belong
" to the King of *Bohemia* and to his Heirs, but
" but also that they did before belong to his
" Predecessors, Father, Grand-Father, Great-
" Grand-Father, and Great-Great-Grand Fa-
" ther. And therefore desiring to provide
" that the King of *Bohemia*, or his Heirs, may
" not be disturb'd therein for the future,
" we say, acknowledge and declare by these
" Presents, that the Rights and the Office of
" Great Cup-bearer belong to the King of *Bo-
" hemia* and to his Successors, to the exclu-
" sion of all others, as well as the Vote and
" Session in the Election of the King of the
" *Romans*, future Emperor. And to the end
" that Calumny, Malice and Imposture may
" find nothing to object for the future, we
" have of our full Power and Royal Authori-
" ty caus'd these Presents to be prepar'd, to
" which we have caus'd the Seal of our Arms
" to be affix'd. Given at *Erfort*, *September* 26,
" 1290, and of our Reign the 17th.

The other Testimony is of *Rupert* Count Palatin of the *Rhine*, and Prince Elector of the Holy Empire, in the Form of a Certificate, made at *Mezz* in the same Year that the *Golden Bull* was publish'd by the Emperor *Charles* IV in the following manner.

" Altho' there has never been any doubt of
" the Rights which the Illustrious King of *Bo-
" hemia*, our Coelector and Collegue, has in-
" herited from his Predecessors, Father, Grand-
" Father, Great-Grand-Father, and Great-
" Great-Grand-Father, and that he still pos-
" sesses it this present, as well of Right, as in
" effect as well as we, and the other Princes
" our Coelectors, the Power of raising the
" King of the *Romans* to the Imperial Digni-
" ty, and that this is more clear than the Sun,
" yet there have been Sons of Darkness, who
" taking Pleasure to go groping at Noon Day,
" dare declare War against Virtue, and by a
" diabolical Envy and Malice call Darkness
" Light, and Light Darkness. Wherefore oc-
" ing willing to take care that nothing like this
" may happen in reference to the most serene
" Prince the King of *Bohemia*, or to his Heirs
" and Successors Kings of *Bohemia* and that
" we may take from the wicked all handle of
" Slander, we say, and declare in Conscience,
" not lightly nor with Precipitation, but after
" a mature Deliberation, and after a very exact
" Search and Enquiry which we have made
" with the other Princes, our Coelectors and
" Collegues, that the most serene Princes
" Kings of *Bohemia*, and their Predecessors,
" have had from Time immemorial, and ought
" to have, a Right and Vote in the Election
' of the King of the *Romans* and of the Em-
" peror, as well as we, and the Princes our
" Coelectors, as well Seculars as Ecclesia-
" sticks. So that when the Election takes place,
' the most serene Prince the King of *Bohem a*
" ought to be solemnly invited to the Election,
" and there enjoy, as well in Person as by his
" Deputies or Embassadors, whom he shall
" send thereto, all the Rights that is to say,
" of Vote and Session, and of all the other
" Privileges, in the same manner as we, and
" and the other Princes our Coelectors and
" Collegues, have accustom'd to enjoy the
" same. We also verify that the most serene
' Prince the King of *Bohemia* is Great Cup-
" bearer of the Holy Roman Empire, and that
" he is not oblig'd to execute the Office of
" Great Cup-bearer under the Royal Crown
" in all the Ceremonies, even in the Presence
" of the Emperor, standing, sitting or march-
' ing, according to the laudable Custom of the
" most serene Princes the Lords Kings of *Bo-
" hemia* his Ancestors and Predecessors. In
" Testimony whereof we have caus'd these
" Presents to be dispatch'd under the Seal of
' our Arms. Given at *Metz* in the Year 1356,
' the *Sunday* before St *Lucy's* Day.

* The *Gold n Bull* in giving to the King of *Bohemia* his Rank amongst the Electors, and in ordaining that he shall vote immediately after the Archbishops of *Triers* and of *Cologn*, confounds the Error of those who write that the King of *Bohemia* has no Vote except in the Case of an Equality amongst the other Electors *Petrus de Andlo* Canon of *Colmar*, who has written a Treatise of the Roman Empire, of the Creation, Coronation, and Dignity of the Emperor, and has dedicated his Work to *Frederick* III, says, † *De Consuetudine tamen Rex Bohemiæ ad Electionem non vocatur, nisi cum vota aliorum sunt æqualia numero, & sic hodie practicatur* that is to say, Custom requires that the King of *Bohem a* should not be call'd to the Election, but when there is an equality of Votes among the others and this is what is practis'd at this Day. But there is reason to wonder that a Man who understood the publick Law of *Germany*, who chose it for the chief Object of his Meditations, and who alledges the Text of the *Golden Bull* in Favour of the King of *Bohemia*, should say that he is not invited to the Elections, but only when the Votes are equally divided amongst the other Electors. It is possible that by Neglect the King of *Bohemia* was not invited to the Elections of *Rupert* of *Bavaria*, of *Sigismund*, of *Albert* II, and of *Frederick* III, Successors of *Charles* IV, because there was no likelihood that *Wenceslas*, who had been depos'd, should be call'd to the Elections of *Rupert* and of *Sigismund*, whom he could not authorize by his Pretence but with the last Infamy. *Albert* II was himself King of *Bohemia*, and at the time of the Election of *Frederick* III, under whom *Petrus de Andlo* wrote, *Ladyslas* King of *Bohemia* was so young, that there was no thought

* *The King of Bohemia has the third Vote in the Lateral College*. † *Lib. Cap. 2* of inviting him. But it will not appear that the King of *Bohemia* was ever call'd after the Election was begun, or that the Equality of the other Electors Votes has oblig'd them to wait his coming. On the contrary, since the *Golden Bull* assigns him his Rank, and regulates the Order in which he is to vote, it is impossible he should depend on an equal Division. For *Triers* voting first, *Cologn* the second, and *Bohemia* the third, there must of necessity four vote after him, to wit, the three other Secular Electors, and *Mayence*, and at this Day five, by reason of the eighth Electorate, and so it is in his Power to nominate such Prince as he shall think fit, without expecting an equal Division, or the Sentiments of his Collegues.

‡ And indeed it is not the Equality of Votes, but the Law that calls the King of *Bohemia* to the Election. So that if the Archbishop of *Mayence* fails to invite him with the other Electors, the whole Election may be declar'd faulty. We have a very illustrious Example thereof in the Election of *Maximilian I. Frederick III*, his Father, liv'd at great variance with *Uladislas* King of *Bohemia*, and hated him to that degree, that he could not resolve to set him at the Election of his Son, to which he nevertheless proceeded, notwithstanding he had not caus'd him to be invited. But *Uladislas* was so very much offended thereat, that he was for having the Election declar'd vicious, and ready to take to Arms for the execution of the *Golden Bull*. An Accommodation was motion'd to him, with considerable Advantages enough, but he insisted upon being discharg'd from the Obligation the Kings of *Bohemia* are under to accompany the Emperor in his Journey to *Rome* with three hundred Lances; to which the other Electors not being willing to consent, a Medium was found at last to satisfy him, by promising him that for the future there should be no Election either of Emperor, or King of the *Romans*, without the King of *Bohemia*'s being invited to be present thereat in Person, or to send his Deputies or Embassadors to the same, in default whereof all the other Electors should be oblig'd to pay him five hundred Marks of Gold each. To which if we add the Particulars of all the Elections since *Maximilian* I, to the Emperor who dy'd last, it will appear that the King of the *Bohemia* has been invited thereto with the other Electors his Collegues, and that he had therein the Vote and Rank which the Law gives him. So that his Right cannot be call'd in question.

* After all, it is almost impossible to say at what Time the Electoral Dignity was annex'd to the Crown of *Bohemia*; and he that would undertake to enquire into it, would meet with as much Difficulty as we have seen Clearness in the Truth we have now establish'd. We have destroy'd elsewhere the Opinion of those who have been for making it believ'd that the King of *Bohemia*, and the other Electors his Collegues, were nominated by Pope *Gregory* V, and by the Emperor *Otho* III, and we have shewn, that he cannot have been added to the Electoral College by the Emperor *Henry* III. They who ascribe the Institution thereof to *Otho* IV, make the Electoral Dignity of the Kings of *Bohemia* begin from that Time. And *Dubravius* Bishop of *Olmutz* in *Moravia*, an exact Author, and very zealous for the Interest of his Princes, says, That the Kings of *Bohemia* hold the Electoral Dignity from the Emperor *Rodolphus* I, who secur'd it to the King of *Bohemia* in the Person of *Wenceslas* II, who had marry'd his Daughter, and in Consideration of this Alliance. There are others who maintain, that the Kings of *Bohemia* had no Share in the Election before the Publication of the *Golden Bull*: but this is what is directly contrary to the Truth of History, the Particulars whereof we have seen in this Chapter. The Letters Patents of the Emperor *Rodolphus*, and the Declaration of *Rupert* Count *Palatin*, say very expressly, that the Kings of *Bohemia* are Electors, and that even in the thirteenth Century they held the Faculty of electing from their Predecessors Great Grand Fathers and Great-Great-Grand-Fathers. And the *Golden Bull* it self founds the Right of the King of *Bohemia*, is well as that of the other Electors, on ancient Custom. And notwithstanding it seems as if what we now say were directly contrary to what we have establish'd elsewhere, to wit, That the Institution of the Electoral College is not so ancient as the Acts of *Rodolphus* and of *Rupert*, and even the *Golden Bull*, would make us believe; yet if we give our selves but the Trouble of comparing their Words, with the Circumstances of the History, it will be very easy to reconcile them. For it is certain that the Kings of *Bohemia* had a Right to elect, and did effectually elect several Emperors and Kings of the *Romans* even in the twelfth Century and before, yet not as Electors, because this Quality only began to be known, and was still new in the Time of the Emperor *Rodolphus* I, but is Princes of the Empire. From whence it follows, that the Intention of *Rodolphus* was to secure this new Quality to *Wenceslas* and his Kingdom, and not to confer on him the Right of Electing, which the Kings of *Bohemia*, as Princes of the Empire, possess'd already by virtue of their Quality of Prince. And it is thus we must understand the Words of the Emperor *Charles* IV, when he says, That the King of *Bohemia*, the Count *Palatin* of the *Rhine*, the Duke of *Saxony*, and the Marquiss of *Brandenburg* have always been in Possession of the Right of Election, because he will not speak of the Quality of Elector, which was not known before *Frederick* II, but of the Right they had as Princes of the Empire to be present at the Elections with the rest, that it might not be thought he would advance to this Dignity Princes who had no Share therein before, to the exclusion of many others who assisted thereat before the Publication of the *Golden Bull*. Wherefore we are not afraid to say of the Kings of *Bohemia*, what we have said of all the other Electors in general, to wit, That as Princes of the Empire they have always elected with the others, and that they have made themselves very considerable in *Germany*, as well on the account of their Quality of King, as by the great extent of their States, particularly during

---

‡ *He is invited to the Election with the other Electors.* * *When the Electoral Dignity was annex'd to the Crown of Bohemia.*
† *Chap. IV.*

the

of the ELECTORS of the EMPIRE.

the Schisms with which the Empire was afflicted after the Death of *Frederick* II. They were capable of taking a Rank among those to whom Custom, confirm'd by the *Golden Bull*, had by Degrees appropriated the Electoral Dignity to the Exclusion of the others

* The Emperor *Charles* IV. having appropriated the Electoral Dignity to the Princes he names in the *Golden Bull*, requires that the said Princes should have a more particular Care of the Affairs of the Empire than the rest, and that in order thereto, † *They meet once a Year in one of the Imperial Towns, within a Month after Easter, to the End that having there made a Report of what is wanting, and of the Disorders they shall have observ'd at home, and in their Neighbourhood they may remedy the same by their common Ad ice, and ordain by their Prudence and their Counsels the necessary Reformation* At this Day the Assemblies the Electors hold in particular for the Affairs of the Empire, are call'd *Collegiate Diets*, to distinguish them from the *Electoral*, where they only treat of the Election The Emperor *Charles* IV, as well as all the Electors, Ecclesiasticks and Seculars, assisted indifferently at both But at this Day, and for above these two hundred Years, the Kings of *Bohemia* are excluded the first Goldaste, who has written a large Volume of the Kingdom of *Bohemia*, says, That they are injur'd, and that such Procedure is contrary to the Disposition of the fundamental Law of the Empire, which calls thereto the Kings of *Bohemia*, as well as the other Electors, which is indubitable But it is also true that the same Law removes Strangers from the Knowledge of the Affairs of the Empire, and that the *Kings of Bohem a* having study'd to separate themselves from its Interest, they ought also to bear with their being removed from the Deliberations which are had concerning Affairs, in which they have no Concern They have endeavour'd to be admitted, and the Cardinal *Clesel*, whom the Arch-Duke *Matthias* had sent to the Electors assembled at *Nuremberg*, in the Year 1611, made pressing Instance to be receiv'd in the Electoral College, and to be admitted at the Deliberations, in the Name of his Master who was King of *Bohemia*, but he could obtain nothing, no more than *Matthias* himself, when he urg'd it to the Electors assembled at *Franckfort* in the Year 1612 They permitted him nevertheless at the last Session to take his Place in the College, which communicated to him the Resolutions which had been taken there, and allow'd him to give his Opinion thereupon but without any other Suffrage, or Vote decisive, or deliberative, wherewith he was forc'd to be contented *Ferdinand* II, Emperor and King of *Bohemia*, met with the same Difficulties at the College of Electors, assembl'd at *Franckfort* in the Year 1609, who would not admit him, altho' he was more interested than the others on the Account of the Disturbances in his Kingdom, for which this Assembly had been chiefly call'd, and at this Day the same Refusal is made to the Prince of *Lobkovitz*, whom the King of *Bohemia* had sent to *Franckfort*, because the Diet that has been call'd for the Election is not yet open, and that the King of *Bohemia* has no Share in the Deliberations which are had for the other Affairs of the Empire

‡ The King of *Bohemia* is Great Cup-bearer hereditary of the Empire, and his Function consists in presenting to the King of the *Romans*, or to the Emperor, a Silver Cup, weighing twelve Ounces, cover'd, and full of Wine and Water, the first time he asks to drink, * and he may do this *devoir* to the Emperor having his Regal Crown on his Head, or without it, the Law leaving it to his Choice to do therein as he himself shall think fit, † and not obliging him to this Function, but when the Emperor eats in publick, and in Ceremony, which at this Day is only practis'd immediately after the Coronation We have said in Chap XI, That the Offices of the Crown of the Empire were appropriated to the Princes who possess them at this Day, at the same time that the Electoral Dignity was annex'd to the Principalities And forasmuch as we have spoken of that of the King of *Bohemia* in particular, we shall only add, that, as Great Cup-bearer, he has for Arms Gules, a Lyon Argent, crown'd, arm'd and langued Or, the Tail forked, having on his Breast a Gold Cup

The Advantages the King of *Bohemia* has above the other Electors his Collegues, are,

1 That he has the Quality of King, that he is anointed and crown'd, and has the Style of Majesty, tho' the Electors give him only the Quality, or, as they term it, the predicate of the Royal Dignity *Bohemia* was formerly, in part, subject to the Kingdom of *Moravia*, and its Princes for a long time were contented with the Quality of Duke The Emperor *Otho* I offer'd that of King to *S Wenceslas*, but he refus'd it And it was *Henry* IV who gave it first to *Uratislas*, the Son of *Bretislas*, in the Diet conven'd at *Mayence*, in the Year 1086 His Successors despis'd it, till *Uladislas* II got a Confirmation thereof from the Emperor *Frederick* I, in the Diet of *Ratisbone*, An 1158 But it was *Primislas Othocarus* who annex'd the Royal Dignity to his Successors and Kingdom, under the Emperor *Philip* of *Suabia*, about the Year 1198 And it is from that time that they enjoy it, till now

2 It is on the Account of his Regal Dignity, that he takes Place immediately after the Archbishop, who is on the Emperor's Right

3 That he marches out of Rank, and alone, immediately after the Emperor The *Golden Bull* ordains it in very express Terms, ‡ and it is at this Day observ'd without any Difficulty, notwithstanding what the same *Golden Bull* says, Chap XXVI, That the Empress is to march immediately after the Emperor, from whence some have been for proving that there was a Contradiction in the Law But it is so only in the Imagination of some sickly Minds, who might resolve the Difficulty they form to themselves by the Law it self, which says that the Empress ought to follow the Emperor immediately, but at some Paces distance And it is in this distant Interval, that not only the King of *Bohemia* takes his Place, but where likewise are the domestick Officers of the Electors, who

---
* *The King of Bohemia is not call'd to the Collegiate Diets*   † Chap xii   ‡ *The particular Right of the King of* Bohemia
* *Golden Bull*, Chap XXVII § 1   † Chap iv § 4   ‡ Chap xii

cannot

cannot be far from their Masters, and even those of the Empress, whereof there are several that precede her

4. That he has the fourth Vote in the Election.

5 That he takes Place of all the other Kings and Princes of *Christendom*, not only in the Diets, where the other Electors have the same Advantage, but also every where else within the Empire

6 By the particular Privilege granted by the Emperor *Frederick* II to the King of *Bohemia*, he is not oblig'd to take the Investiture of his Kingdom, unless the Emperor advances as far as *Nuremberg* or *Bamberg*, or some other Town near his Frontiers The Letters of this Privilege are dated at *Basil*, in the Year 1212, and have been confirm'd by the Letters of the Emperor *Frederick* III, given at *Neustad* in *Austria*, *An* 1462

7 The Emperor is oblig'd to give to the King of *Bohemia*, when he comes to receive the Investiture, a Guard and Safe-conduct, as well going as coming

8 Whereas, at the Investiture of other Princes, the Standards and Banners that represent the Arms of the Provinces for which they do Homage, are torn to pieces, and flung to the People, those of the King of *Bohemia* are preserv'd, who has them born before him at the Return of his Cavalcade to the Emperor's Palace

9 Formerly, and before that *Bohemia* was hereditary in the House of *Austria*, the King and Elector of *Bohemia*, who had not attain'd the Age of eighteen Years complete, had no Administrator, as the other Princes, the secular Electors, have, during their Minority, but the States of the Kingdom had Care of the Education of the Prince, and took upon them the Administration of Affairs during his Minority

10 The Kingdom of *Bohemia* had also this Advantage, That whereas the Emperor dispos'd of the Fiefs escheated to the Empire for want of Heirs Male, by Confiscation, or otherwise, the Kingdom of *Bohemia* being vacant, it belong'd to the States to proceed to an Election, and to call to the Crown him they judg'd best qualify'd for the same

* On which Occasion we make no Difficulty to say, That whatever the Emperor *Charles* IV has ordain'd relating to the Succession of the secular Electors, even in reference to the King of *Bohemia*, this Kingdom was formerly elective And forasmuch as for the Decision of Questions about Fact, there can be nothing stronger than authentick Testimonies, we shall employ for the Support of the Truth of our Thesis, but only Examples which we have taken out of History, the Truth whereof was never contested by those who have establish'd an hereditary Succession in that Kingdom, by the sole Success of their Arms, confirm'd by the last Treaty of *Munster* But so far was the Kingdom from being hereditary, before it enter'd into the House of *Austria*, that, on the contrary, there never was seen in it a very regular Succession *Uratislas*, who dy'd in the Year 1093, left five Sons, notwithstanding which, the States proceeded to an Election, and call'd to the Succession *Conrade* Duke of *Moravia*, his Brother The same *Conrade* being dead a few Months after his Election, the States, without having any Regard to his Sons, elected *Bretislas*, the Son of *Uratislas Dubravius* says that *Ulric*, the Son of *Conrade*, made his Complaints thereof to the Emperor, and prevail'd with him to declare in his Favour, but that it was on Condition that the *Bohemians* should have the Liberty to chuse him they should judge most capable, and the best qualify'd for the Government In like manner when *Suendebold*, the Son of *Otho* Duke of *Olmutz*, usurp'd the Kingdom from *Borivoy* Brother to *Bretislas*, the Great Men of the Kingdom counsell'd him to have Recourse to the Emperor, and to remonstrate to him, that the Complaints *Borivoy* would have prevented him with, were very ill grounded, because the States of the Countrey, who have a Right to call to the Crown whom they please, had cast their Eyes on him, and had preferr'd him to *Borivoy* And indeed he procur'd himself to be maintain'd by the Emperor, in the Possession of the Kingdom, in which the Election had establish'd him *Uladislas*, the Brother of *Borivoy* and of *Bretsla*, was preferr'd by the same States of the Kingdom to *Otho*, Brother and presumptive Heir to *Snendebold*, who was only Cousin-German to *Uladislas* To this must be referr'd the Answer which the same *Uladislas* made to those, who demanded of him the Restitution of the Crown, on the Part of *Borivoy* his eldest Brother, who had been driven out by *Suendevola*, to wit, that it was not of him they ought to ask it, but of the States of the Kingdom, who alone had a Right to dispose thereof The same *Uladislas* left when he dy'd three Sons, and yet he had for Successor *Sobieslas*, his Brother At that Time *Otho*, Brother to *Suendevold*, had made himself Master of the Castle of *Vissegard*, and would not surrender it till he first knew the Declaration the States of the Kingdom had, by one common Consent, made in Favour of *Sobieslas*, who had also for Successor *Uladislas* II, his Nephew, notwithstanding he had left Children capable of the Government *Uladislas* II, being willing to resign the Kingdom to his Son *Frederick*, address'd himself for that Purpose to the Emperor *Frederick* I, to obtain his Leave for the same, but the Emperor signify'd to him, That he should either govern the Kingdom himself, or leave the free Election to the States And indeed the same *Uladislas*, who had both Sons and Brothers, had for Successor *Sobieslas*, his Cousin-German The Elections of *Henry* Bishop of *Prague*, during the Detention of his Brother *Wenceslas*, and that of *Uladislas*, Son to *Uladislas* II, admit of no Contradiction, no more than that of *Henry* Duke of *Carinthia*, after the Death of *Wenceslas* IV To which one might add several Letters Patents, by which the Kings of *Bohemia*, even the last of them, have secur'd the Right of Election to the States of the Kingdom, if it were not certain, that since the House of *Austria* is in Possession thereof, in a manner by Right of Conquest, it has chang'd its Condition, and is become merely hereditary

---

* *The Kingdom of Bohemia was formerly elective.*

of the ELECTORS of the EMPIRE.   511

‡ It is in this Quality it is at this Day possess'd, by *Leopold Ignatius* Arch-Duke of *Austria*, the eldest Son of the last Emperor, and of *Mary* of *Austria*, Daughter to *Philip* III, King of *Spain*, who is at present King and Elector of *Bohemia* But forasmuch as his is born but since *June* 8, 1640, and so has not attain'd eighteen Years complete, to which Age the *Golden Bull* regulates the Majority of the Princes Electors, it is certain that he cannot discharge the Functions thereof, if the Election be made before *June* 9, of the current Year, and that even the College cannot admit the Embassador he might send in his Name, because the Law calls to the Guardianship of the Elector in his minority, † and to the Functions of the Electorate, the nearest Relation by the Father's side, without its being in the Power of the Pupil to frustrate him, or to do any thing to his Prejudice His nearest Relation and Unkle on the Father's side, is *Leopold William* Arch-Duke of *Austria*, ‡ the only Brother of the late Emperor and it is he whom the Law would without doubt call to the Administration, if there did not meet in his Person a Difficulty that absolutely excludes him The *Golden Bull* gives the Guardianship of the minor Elector, and the Administration of the Electorate, to the nearest Relation of the deceas'd, provided he have all the Qualities requisite to succeed, if the deceas'd has left no Children, that is to say, provided he be lawfully born, eighteen Years old complete, and Lay The Arch-Duke has without doubt the two first Qualities, but then he has not the last, for he is Ecclesiastick, and possesses several Bishopricks, which hinder him from taking the Quality of Administrator of the Electorate, during the Minority of his Nephew He would augment the Number of the Ecclesiastical Electors, which the *Golden Bull* has limited to Three, and consequently would disturb the whole OEconomy of the Election, so that to supply his Place, there would be a Necessity to consider the Arch-Duke *Ferdinand Charles*, Arch-Duke of *Austria* at *Inspruck*, who is Coutin German to the deceased Emperor, unless the Election be put off till the Majority of the King of *Bohemia*, or that his Age be dispens'd with by the Electoral College, as it is the Representative of the Sovereignty of the Empire or else that the Friends of the House of *Austria*, esteeming themselves strong enough in the Diet to compass the Election of the King of *Bohemia* without the Assistance of his Suffrage, think fit to proceed therein without him, because his voluntary Absence cannot render the Election vicious

* What we have here said concerning the active Vote of the King of *Bohemia*, is indubitable, but let us see whether he can have the passive in the next Election That is to say, Whether altho' he cannot elect by reason of his Minority, he can nevertheless be elected, notwithstanding the Defect of his Age If all that the *Golden Bull* says of the Electors were to extend to the Emperors, and if all the Qualities it requires in the ones, were likewise necessary in the others, it is most certain that the King of *Bohemia* could not aspire to the Empire, till he were eighteen Years old complete, because there is not less Capacity requisite to reign than to elect But there is no necessary Consequence from the one to the other, and the Law not regulating the Age of the Emperor, no body whatever can assume the Authority to regulate it It speaks only of the Age of the Electors, and leaves to their Discretion, the Judgment of the Capacity of him they are to elect, according to the Condition the Affairs of the Empire are in, at the Time of the Election. And this has at all Times been the Practice of *Germany*, when it has been judg'd more adviseable to elect an Infant, than to leave the Empire without a Head, thereby to prevent the Ambition of those, who taking advantage of the *Interregnum*, might disturb and ruffle its Tranquillity and Repose, and attempt to encroach upon its Liberty There are Examples thereof in *Otho* II, and in *Otho* III, who was so young when he succeeded to his Father, that he was from thence sirnam'd the Infant *Henry* III was but twelve Years old when he was appointed Emperor *Henry* IV was but five, and was not as yet baptiz'd, when he was nominated Emperor *Henry* VI was very young, and *Frederick* II, his Son, was still in the Cradle when he was chosen *Henry* and *Conrade*, both Sons of *Frederick* II, were not thirteen Years of Age, when their Father caus'd them to be nominated Kings of the *Romans*, successively one after the other So that if there is no other Defect in the Person of the King of *Bohemia*, we must not think it can be sufficient to hinder his Election, since he is actually in an Age, at which the King who now reigns, had already exceeded five Years of majority

† And accordingly it is certain, that he is one of the Subjects that will be most consider'd at the next Election. There are very great ones, and a great many of them among the *Protestant* Princes of *Germany*, but among the *Roman Catholicks*, there is hardly two or three that could be pitch'd upon, because that altho' the others have all the necessary Qualities for the Administration of the Government, they have not wherewith to supply the Expences requisite to support the Imperial Dignity But as we acknowledge that the *Protestant* Princes are absolutely excluded by their Religion, since there is no likelihood that the five *Roman Catholick* Electors will chuse a Prince of a contrary Religion so we believe that the King of *Bohemia* will receive a great Advantage from his, not so much on the Account of the Profession he makes of the *Catholick*, as because most of the *Roman Catholicks* of *Germany* are prepossess'd of this Opinion, that the House of *Austria* is as it were the Asylum and Preservatrix thereof

He has again this Advantage, that his Friends and Partisans have found the Means to persuade the *Catholicks* of *Germany*, that the Imperial Dignity cannot be remov'd from the House of *Austria*, without ruining the Religion, by setting the *Catholicks* at variance among themselves, and without endangering the Repose of

---

‡ *The present King and Elector of* Bohemia   † *Is a Minor*   ‡ *Whether the Arch-Duke can be Administrator?*
* *The King of* Bohemia *being a minor may be elected*   † *Will be consider'd at the next Election.*

the Empire, becaufe the King of *Bohemia* having a powerful Army on foot, would be apt to refent the Neglect might be had of his Perfon.

Befides the Kingdom of *Hungary*, which ferves as a Bullwark to *Germany* againft the *Turk*, he poffeffes that of *Bohemia* with the Provinces, that depend thereon, as *Silefia* and *Moravia*, *Auftria*, *Stiria*, *Carinthia*, *Croatia*, *Carniola*, &c having for his Neighbours in the Empire the Electors of *Bavaria*, of *Saxony* and of *Brandenburg*, the Archbifhop of *Saltsburg*, and the Arch-Duke of *Tirol* and out of *Germany*, the Emperor of the *Turks*, the King of *Poland*, and the Republick of *Venice*. Hitherto he has liv'd in a perfect good Underftanding with the Llector of *Bavaria*, who is his Coufin German, and who without doubt will procure him the Empire, if he does not afpire thereto himfelf, becaufe he will not fuffer the Imperial Dignity to be remov'd from the Houfe of *Auftria*, to be introduc'd into another, with which he would not have that Union of Intereft and Parentage which he has with the firft. The Elector of *Saxony* has given his whole Affection to the King of *Bohemia*, as well on the Account of the Obligation his Houfe has to that of *Auftria*, as by reafon of the little Commerce he has with thofe, who meant thwart the Negotiation that is on foot for the Election of his Perfon. The Elector of *Brandenburg*, in treating with the King of *Sweden*, feem'd to have engag'd in a contrary Intereft to that of the Houfe of *Auftria*. But the Treaty he has lately concluded with the King of *Poland*, plainly difcovers that he paffionately defires a Peace, and affords ground to think, that he will follow the Sentiments of thofe who labour to reftore Tranquility to the Empire.

The King of *Bohemia* is very well with *Poland*, and the Republick has always had a great Refpect for the Houfe of *Auftria*. It is true that the *Turk* appears in Arms on the Frontiers of its Eftates, but it is not her he threatens and provided the King of *Bohemia* will abandon the common Interefts of *Chriftendom*, the other will not break with him.

It is alfo true, that as the great Eftates he poffeffes will afford him wherewith to fupport the Imperial Dignity, in cafe he fhould be call'd thereto, fo likewife it might be fear'd, left he fhould make ufe thereof, after the Example of fome of his Predeceffors, to oppreſs the Liberty of the Princes of *Germany*. And it may happen, that as the good Qualities of Body and Mind which meet in his Perfon will contribute very much to his Election, they may be alfo judg'd more proper to a Monarch, than to the Head of a Free-State, and that the fame Power of the Houfe of *Auftria*, that will make him be confider'd in the approaching Election, may alfo prove an Obftacle to him, on the Account of the Umbrage it gives to all thofe who have reafon to apprehend it. But it may be faid, that what would have ruin'd his Pretenfions at another Time, will forward his Election in the prefent Occafion. He has alone more Troops than all the other Princes together, but his Friends have had the Intereft and Addrefs to perfuade, that he cannot do a more important Service to the State, than to fubfift at his own Expence, and within his hereditary Countries, an Army able to oppofe the *Turk's* Paffage, and to preferve Peace in the Empire. That the Power of the Houfe of *Auftria*, which had formerly made it felf formidable to all *Europe*, is at prefent become a neceffary Remedy againft the Evils the Empire has reafon to be apprehenfive of from that of Foreigners, whofe Grandeur is much better eftablifh'd than that of *Spain* and whereas fo long a Series of Emperors, as the Houfe of *Auftria* has given to *Germany* within thefe two hundred Years, ought to terrifie, they have been able to perfuade, that the Merit of fo many Predeceffors has acquir'd Obligations on the Empire, which all Pofterity ought to acknowledge and fo, without the laft Ingratitude towards the Memory of fo many great Princes, an Emperor cannot be fought for out of the Houfe of *Auftria* in the *German* Branch, whereof the King of *Bohemia* is at this Day the Chief.

It is certain that fome of the Ecclefiaftical Electors have the fame Sentiments, and that *France* it felf will contribute its Wifhes for the Election of a Prince, who is the Queen's Nephew, Coufin German to the King, and much of the fame Age, and adorn'd with the fame fine Qualities that fhine fo brightly in his Majefty and which might promife to the one and the other, at another Time, and without fo ftrong a Competition, the Empire of the whole World.

* The Crown of *Bohemia* remain'd in the Pofterity of *Primiflas*, firft Duke of *Bohemia*, down to *Wenceflas* III, who being kill'd on *Auguft* 3, 1306, as he was going to take poffeffion of the Crown of *Poland*, the States of the Kingdom call'd thereto *Henry* Duke of *Carinthia*, who had marry'd *Anne* the eldeft Sifter of *Wenceflas* III. But the Emperor *Albert* I, who pretended a Right thereto, as well by virtue of the Treaty made between the Emperor *Rodolphus* I, and *Wenceflas* II King of *Bohemia*, by which it had been faid, That *Wenceflas*, or his Son, happening to dye without male Iffue, his Son *Roudolphus*, who had marry'd *Agnes*, the Sifter of *Wenceflas*, or his Heirs, fhould fucceed in *Bohemia*, to the Exclufion of all others that might pretend thereto, as becaufe he confider'd that Kingdom as a Fief efcheated to the Empire, for want of Males in the Royal Family, carry'd thither his Son *Rodolphus*, and the better to fecure him abfolutely of the Crown, he made him marry *Elizabeth* of *Poland*, *Wenceflas*'s Widdow. But *Rodolphus* did not reign there a Year, and dy'd *June* 28, 1308. After his Death *Henry* of *Carinthia* return'd to *Bohemia*, where he reign'd till fuch time as *Henry* of *Luxembourg*, having attain'd to the Empire, confifcated *Bohemia* from him for default of Homage, and receiving the Inveftiture from the Emperor He fubftituted in his room *John* of *Luxemburg* his Son, who marry'd *Elizabeth*, younger Sifter of *Wenceflas* III, and caus'd him to be crown'd on *Candlemas* Day, 1310. Queen *Elizabeth* dying *September* 28, 1339, he marry'd in *December* 1344, *Beatrix*, Daughter to *Lewis* I, Duke of *Bour-*

---

* *How* Bohemia *came in to the Houfe of* Auftria

bon,

bon, and of *Mary* of *Hainault* Towards the latter end of his Days he became blind but neither his Age nor Affliction hinder'd him from being present at the Battel which *Philip* of *Valois*, King of *France*, gave to *Edward* King of *England* near *Cressy* in *Picardy*, where he was kill'd *August* 26, 1346 He had by his first Wife,

Wenceslas, since call'd *Charles*, Emperor and King of *Bohemia*

Primislas, who was born *November* 22, 1318, and dy'd *April* 20, 1320

John Henry, Duke of *Moravia*

Bona, who was betroth'd to *Frederick the Severe*, Marquiss of *Misnia* but she marry'd *John* Duke of *Normandy*, who succeeded *Philip* his Father in the Kingdom of *France*

Margaret, the Wife of *Henry*, who was the Son of *Henry* Duke of *Bavaria*, and of *Elizabeth* of *Hungary*

Anne, a Twin with *Elizabeth*, marry'd *Otho the Beau*, Duke of *Austria*, Son to the Emperor *Albert* I

Elizabeth her Sister, dy'd young

By the second Wife he had,

Wenceslas, who had for his Share the Dutchy of *Luxemburg*, and succeeded since in *Brabant* He is said to have had another Son, nam'd *Nicholas*, who was made Patriarch of *Aquileia* in the Month of *October* 1350, and held that See seven Years and nine Months, but he that has made Remarks on the History of *Luxemburg* by *Vignier*, says, that he cannot learn whether *Nicholas* was by the first or second *Venter* and *Ferdinand Ughelli*, who has some Years since publish'd *Italia Sacra*, says, that he was a Bastard

Wenceslas, who at his Confirmation was nam'd *Charles* by *Charles the Bel* King of *France*, was the eldest Son of *John* of *Luxemburg* and of *Elizabeth* of *Bohemia*, and was born *May* 14, 1316 He was chosen Emperor during the Life of his Father, in opposition to *Lewis* of *Bavaria*, who dying in the Year 1387, he took Possession of the Imperial Dignity He marry'd for first Wife *Blanche*, the Daughter of *Charles* Count of *Valois*, and of *Mahaud de Chastillon*, by whom he had no Children, no more than by *Agnes* of *Bavaria*, the Daughter of *Rodolphus* II, Count Palatin of the *Rhine*, his second Wife He had for third Wife, *Anne* Daughter to *Henry* II, Duke of *Jaur*, who was Brother to *Boleslas* II, Duke of *Suevinis* and his fourth Wife was *Elizabeth* Daughter to *Rognslas* V, Duke of *Pomerania*, and of *Elizabeth* of *Poland* He dy'd *March* 27, 1378 The Particulars of his Reign make a part of the General History, for which reason we shall say nothing of them here, except that it is he that is the *Author of the Golden Bull*, and that he had by his third Wife,

Wenceslas, who succeeded his Father in the Kingdom of *Bohemia* and in the Empire He marry'd for first Wife *Jean* of *Bavaria*, Daughter of *Albert*, Count of *Hainault* and of *Holland* and for second, *Sophia*, the Daughter of *John* Duke of *Bavaria* at *Munich*, and of *Elizabeth* of *Gorlitz* but he had no Children by either, and dy'd of an Apoplexy *August* 10, 1419

Catherine, who marry'd *Rodolphus the Magnanimous*, Duke of *Austria*, eldest Son of the Emperor *Albert* II

He had by his fourth Wife,

Sigismund, who succeeded in *Bohemia* and in the Empire

John, Count of *Gorlitz*

Elizabeth, Wife to *Albert* III, Duke of *Austria*

Margaret, the Wife of *Lewis* King of *Hungary*

Elizabeth, Wife to *John Galeaz Visconti* Duke of *Milan* and of this Marriage was born *Valentine*, who was Wife to *Lewis*, Duke of *Orleans*, Grand-Father to *Lewis* XII, and Great-Grand-Father to *Francis* I, Kings of *France*

Margaret, the Wife of *John* II, Burgrave of *Nuremberg*

Anna, Wife to *Otho* of *Bavaria*, Marquiss of *Brandenburg*, Son to the Emperor *Lewis* IV

Helen, who was marry'd to *Richard* II, King of *England* *Polydore Virgil* says her Name was *Anne*, that she was Daughter to *Wenceslas*, and that the Marriage was solemniz'd in the Year 1387 but that cannot be, because *Wenceslas* was then but 26 Years old, and could not have a Daughter at Age to be marry'd

Agnes, who was betroth'd to *William the Ambitious*, Duke of *Austria* and *Carinthia*

Margaret, second Wife to *Amadeus le Vert*, Count of *Savoy*

Sigismund, Son to the Emperor *Charles* IV, and *Elizabeth* of *Pomerania*, his fourth Wife, succeeded his Brother *Wenceslas* in the Kingdom of *Bohemia* But the *Bohemian*, being incens'd at the Death of *John Hus* and *Jerome* of *Prague*, hinder'd him from taking peaceable Possession of the Kingdom He marry'd for first Wife *Mary* the Daughter of *Lewis* King of *Hungary*, and for second *Barbe*, Daughter to *Herman* Count of *Ciliey*, and dy'd *December* 9, 1437, leaving by his first Wife,

Elizabeth, who was marry'd in 1422 to *Albert*, the Son of *Albert* IV, Duke of *Austria*, and of *Jean* of *Bavaria*, who succeeded his Father-in-Law in the Kingdoms of *Bohemia* and *Hungary*, notwithstanding the Opposition of the *Taborites*, who had call'd to the Crown of *Bohemia Casimir* King of *Poland* He succeeded also to *Sigismund* in the Empire but he did not long enjoy all these Dignities, and dy'd *October* 28, 1439 He had by *Elizabeth* of *Luxemburg*,

Gregory, who dy'd *February* 16, 1435, being very young

Anna, the Wife of *William*, who was Son to *Frederick the Warrior*, first Elector of *Saxony*, of the House of *Misnia*

Elizabeth, marry'd to *Casimir* IV, King of *Poland*, and

Ladislas, whose Infancy fill'd *Bohemia* with Troubles and Disorders (which are inseparable from the Minority of Princes) till such time as the Administration of Affairs was given to *George de Podiebrach*, a Gentleman of the Countrey, who acquitted himself thereof with all the Fidelity he ow'd to his native Countrey *Ladislas* was crown'd at *Prague*, *October* 28, 1453, and was betroth'd to *Magdalen* Daughter to *Charles* VII, King of *France* but he dy'd before the Marriage was solemniz'd of a Sickness which lasted but 36 Hours

After the Death of *Ladislas*, the Emperor *Frederick* III was for disposing of *Bohemia* as of a Fief escheated to the Empire, because

6 P

Ladislas

Ladiſlas had neglected to do Homage for the ſame *William* Duke of *Saxony,* and *Caſimir* King of *Poland* pretended thereto in Right of their Wives, who were Siſters to the deceaſed *Sigiſmund* and *Albert,* Arch-Dukes of *Auſtria,* demanded it in Execution of the Treaty made between the Emperor *Rodolphus* I, and *Wenceſlas* II, King of *Bohemia,* which we ſpoke of before. and *Charles* VII, King of *France,* ſaid, that *Bohemia* belong'd to him by virtue of the Marriage Contract made between *Ladiſlas* and his Daughter *Magdalen.* But the States of the Kingdom maintain'd, that the Election ought to take place, and call'd to the Crown the ſame *George Podiebrach,* who had given ſo many Proofs of his Conduct during the Regency. He dy'd *March* 22, 1471, his Poſterity did not ſucceed in *Bohemia,* but it poſſeſs'd a long time the Dutchies of *Munſterberg* and of *Ols* in *Sileſia.*

The Emperor *Frederick* III, *Caſimir* King of *Poland,* and *Matthias* King of *Hungary* made Intereſt for the Crown of *Bohemia* after the Death of *George Podiebrach.* Some were for calling thereto *Albert* Duke of *Saxony,* Son-in-Law to *George.* But *Caſimir* carry'd it for his Son *Uladiſlas,* who was Grandſon to the Emperor *Albert* II and *Elizabeth* of *Luxemburg,* Daughter and Heireſs to the Emperor *Sigiſmund,* King of *Hungary* and *Bohemia. Uladiſlas* was but fifteen Years old when he was choſen King of *Bohemia, May.* 25, 1471. *Matthias* King of *Hungary* dying in the Year 1490,

Beatrix his Widow, imagining that if ſhe could obtain the Crown of *Hungary* for *Uladiſlas,* he would make no Difficulty to marry her, labour'd ſo ſucceſsfully therein, that ſhe procur'd him to be elected, but he marry'd *Anne,* the Daughter of *Gaſton* IV, Count *de Foix,* and of *Catherine* of *Candale,* and dy'd at *Buda* in *Hungary, March* 12, 1516, leaving

Lewis and *Anne*

Lewis, the Son of *Uladiſlas,* King of *Hungary* and *Bohemia,* and of *Anne de Foix,* was born *July* 1, 1506, and was crown'd at *Prague, March* 11, 1509, while his Father was ſtill living, to whom he ſucceeded in the Kingdom of *Hungary* and *Bohemia, An* 1516. He marry'd *Mary,* Daughter to *Philip* of *Auſtria* Duke of *Burgundy,* and of *Jean* of *Spain.* He was found ſtiff'd in a Moraſs, after the Battel he loſt againſt the *Turks* near *Mohatz, Auguſt* 29, 1526, and left no Children.

Anne, Siſter to *Lewis,* marry'd *Ferdinand* of *Auſtria,* Brother to the Emperor *Charles* V, who was crown'd King of *Bohemia* in the Year 1527, and ſo the Crown of *Bohemia* return'd again to the Houſe of *Auſtria,* where it ſtill remains at this Day. *Maximilian* II, Son to *Ferdinand* I, *Rodolphus* II, *Matthias, Ferdinand* II, *Ferdinand* III, and *Leopold Ignatius* having ſucceeded therein without Interruption, and even without Conteſtation, excepting that which was the occaſion of the laſt War in *Germany.*

CHAP. XIV.

Of the Duke of Bavaria Prince Elector of the Holy Empire.

THE Emperor *Maximilian* I was us'd to ſay, he had this Advantage over all the other Monarchs of *Europe,* That he reign'd over Kings. He, of whom we have juſt treated in the foregoing Chapter, has both the Character and Quality thereof, and thoſe we are going to ſpeak of at preſent, have the Rights and Power thereunto belonging. The firſt that preſents himſelf to us is the Duke of *Bavaria,* who has taken the Place of the Count *Palatin* of the *Rhine,* whom the *Golden Bull* cauſes to march immediately after the King of *Bohemia.* This Change, which is without doubt the moſt remarkable that has happen'd in the Empire ſince the Publication of the *Golden Bull,* by reaſon it unlinks the Electoral Dignity from the County *Palatin* of the *Rhine,* to which it was inſeparably annex'd, obliges us to aſcend to the firſt Cauſe of this Tranſlation of the Electorate from the *Palatin* Branch to that of *Bavaria,* of which we ſhall ſpeak in this Chapter.

The Treaty made at *Paſſaw* in the Year 1555, between the Emperor *Charles* V and *Ferdinand,* King of the *Romans* his Brother on the one part, and the Proteſtant Princes of *Germany,* on the other, permitted the Members immediately ſubject to the Empire, to eſtabliſh within their Juriſdiction, ſuch Practice of Religion

as they ſhould judge moſt conducive to the Repoſe of their Subjects. The Kingdom of *Bohemia,* and the Provinces thereon depending, as principal Members of the Empire, were for making their Advantage thereof, and ſettling ſome Regulations in Favour of thoſe who are call'd in thoſe Parts, *ſub utraque,* becauſe they receive the Communion under both Species. But the Council of *Vienna* oppos'd it, and ſaid, that *Bohemia* being a Province hereditary in the Houſe of *Auſtria,* the Emperor might eſtabliſh there the Catholick Religion, even by virtue of the Treaty of *Paſſaw,* provided he left the Proteſtants within the Limitations of the Treaties they had made with the Emperor *Sigiſmund,* and the Kings of *Bohemia* his Predeceſſors. However the Proteſtants being numerous enough to enable them to hope from their Strength, what was refuſ'd to their Intreaties, and *Rodolphus* II, who reign'd then, apprehending leſt they ſhould ſide with his Brother *Matthias,* who had taken Arms againſt him, he gave them Leave by his Letters Patents of *July* 9, 1609, to build Temples, Church-yards, Hoſpitals and Schools on their own Lands, and at their own Expences, in what Juriſdiction ſoever they were ſituated and that even without the Permiſſion of the Lord of the Fief, or of the Chief Juſticiary,

In all the rest of the Empire the Protestants complain'd of the ill Treatment they said was shewn them, and in order to procure to themselves Satisfaction, some of them enter'd into a strict Alliance, to which they gave the Name of *Union*, and to those Princes who engag'd therein, that of *Correspondents*. The first Foundations of this Alliance were laid in the Assembly of *Ahausen*, *May* 4, 1608. But it was not concluded till the Year 1609, at *Hall* in *Suabia*, where it chose for its Head the Elector *Palatin*. The Catholicks on their side oppos'd thereto another Alliance, which they made, as they said, for the Preservation of the Roman Catholick Religion, and gave it the Name of the *Catholick League*, and for Head, *Maximilian* Duke of *Bavaria*. But Affairs remain'd in this Condition on both sides, without proceeding to any greater Extremities, till the beginning of the *Bohemian* War in the Year 1618, under the Reign of *Matthias*. The Subject or Pretext of these Troubles was, that the Archbishop of *Prague* had caus'd a Temple to be demolish'd, which the Protestants had built in a place call'd *Clostergrab*, and had shut up another at *Brunau*. They complain'd thereof at *Vienna*, but they were answer'd, that nothing had been done against the Privileges of the Countrey, nor contrary to the Emperor's Edicts. Upon this Answer the States of the Kingdom were conven'd, whereof the Emperor being inform'd he forbad their Proceeding any farther. But the matter was resolv'd upon, and the Opening of the States being perform'd *May* 21 1618, two Days after, several Lords and Deputies of the Towns went to the Council, where they made their Remonstrances, and demanded Justice, but with somewhat less Respect than was becoming Suppliants. For seeing that the Lord of *Scabata*, President of the Council, the Sieur *Martinits*, and the Secretary of State did not receive their Petitions, with that favourable Disposition as they had promis'd themselves from the Equity of their Cause, they flung them out at the Windows from two Stories high. The States sent immediately Commissions for the raising of Men throughout the whole Kingdom, that they might thereby be in a Condition to maintain an Action of that Consequence. And in order to justify what they had done, they publish'd a *Manifesto*, in which they gave to understand that in the aforesaid Execution they had follow'd the good and laudable ancient Custom, which allows of such Procedure against Traitors of the Countrey, and Disturbers of the publick Quiet. The Emperor who was disarm'd, express'd at first no other Resentment thereof, except that he caus'd the *Manifesto* to be answer'd, tho' he was fully resolv'd to chastise this Rebellion, and to send a considerable Army into *Bohemia*, under the Conduct of the Count of *Bucquoy*, who had under him the Counts of *Dampierre*, of *Bougghem*, and of *Collalto*. The *Bohemians* gave the Command of their Army to *Ernest* of *Mansfeldt*, who was just come out of the Service of the Duke of *Savoy*, against the King *Spain*, and who brought them a good Number of Officers, that were broken since the Conclusion of a Peace between those two Princes in *Italy*. The Count de *Bucquoy* being enter'd into *Bohemia*, suffer'd his Soldiers to exercise such Cruelties and Insolencies, which not only made an end of exasperating the Minds, but even stirr'd up Pity in the neighbouring States. *Silesia* was the first that declar'd for the *Bohemians*, and the united Princes being assembl'd at *Rotemburg* on the *Tarver*, sent to intreat the Emperor to consider, that such was the Importance of this Affair, as not only to relate to *Bohemia*, but also to all the Protestants of *Germany*, and pray'd him to recal his Army, and remove by that means the Umbrage all *Germany* took at so violent a Procedure. The Affair was put into Negotiation, and the Archbishop of *Mayence*, the Electors *Palatin* and of *Saxony*, and the Duke of *Bavaria* were nominated to labour at an Accommodation, which was hinder'd by Delays, which are but too common in matters of this nature, but chiefly by the Death of the Emperor *Matthias*, who dy'd *March* 20, 1619.

The Aversion the *Bohemians* had conceiv'd against the Government of the last Emperors, did not end with the Life of *Matthias*, on the contrary, the Troubles which began during his Life, continu'd with much more Vehemence after his Death. For the States of the Kingdom being inform'd that *Ferdinand* of *Austria* had been invited to the Election as King of *Bohemia*, they wrote to the Archbishop of *Mayence*, and represented by their Deputies to the Electoral College, That *Ferdinand* not being in peaceable Possession of the Kingdom of *Bohemia*, he could not have any hand in the Election. But the Electors, without having any regard to these Remonstrances, admitted him nevertheless to all the Deliberations they held for the Election, nay they even chose him Emperor *August* 27, 1619, almost at the same time as the *Bohemians* invited the Elector *Palatin*, *Frederick* V, to wear their Crown. This last Election preceded that of *Ferdinand* by only one Day, and so alarm'd all *Germany*, that the very first Accounts were had thereof, serv'd as the first Sound of the Trumpet to those who were engag'd in one of the two Parties. The new King of *Bohemia*, knowing that the Partisans of the House of *Austria* would not fail to take to their Arms, for the Preservation of what it possess'd in the Empire, which depended intirely on the Issue of this War, arm'd powerfully, and endeavour'd to bring into the Quarrel as well the united Princes, of whom he was the Head, as all his Relations and Allies, who were of the most powerful of *Europe*. The Catholicks, who on their side consider'd, that if the Protestants acquir'd by this mean a fourth Vote in the Electoral College, they would not fail in time to place the Imperial Crown on the Head of a Prince of their Party, could not dissemble their Apprehension, and caus'd Levies to be made throughout the whole Extent of their Jurisdiction. But the Emperor, who had a mind to make a publick Matter of a particular Quarrel, altho' the Elector *Palatin* had taken Arms against *Ferdinand*, when he was still but Arch-Duke of *Austria* and King of *Bohemia*, and before he had attain'd to the Empire, styl'd him Rebel, and put him into the Ban of the Empire, as guilty of High Treason, without

without any Form of Process, contrary to the Laws of the State, and contrary to the Capitulation the Electors had made with him at his Accession to the Crown. The Execution of this Proscription was committed to *Maximilian* Duke of *Bavaria*, Head of the Catholick League, and to the Marquiss of *Spinola*, who commanded the *Spanish* Troops which the Arch-Duke *Albert* had sent to the Assistance of the Emperor. The Duke of *Bavaria* had supply'd *Ferdinand* with a good Sum of Money, which, together with the Interest thereof, amounted to several Millions of Gold, for the Repayment of which he had a Mortgage on the *Upper Austria*, besides the Emperor's Word, who had promis'd him at the beginning of the War to bestow on him the Spoils of the Elector *Palatin*. And in effect on *February* 25, 1623, he gave him the Investiture of the *Palatin* Electoral Dignity. But forasmuch as the Electors of *Saxony* and of *Brandenburg* found fault with this precipitate and irregular Procedure, as being directly contrary to the Disposition of the *Golden Bull*, which annexes the Electoral Dignity to the *Palatinate* inseparably, it was given out at first, that it was intended only to the Person of *Maximilian*, who being already advanc'd in Years, and having no Children, there was room to hope that no Wrong would be done to those of the *Palatin*, who having had no hand in the pretended Crime of their Father, could not have any neither in his Disgrace. *Maximilian* himself publish'd that he receiv'd this Dignity for his Person only, and gave Assurance thereof to the Emperor in Writing. But as soon as he saw the Affairs of *Germany* in such a State, that the Protestants could no longer make themselves fear'd, he declar'd himself, by making it known that the Electoral Dignity standing him in stead of a very considerable Reimbursement, he pretended to have purchas'd it for himself, and all his House. And that he might interest *France* in the Preservation of this fine Conquest, he engag'd in several Treaties with it, which tho' they produc'd no effect, but only that of Confusion and Trouble to those who were concern'd therein, yet they were in part the Cause, that by the Peace of *Munster* was confirm'd to him, and to all the Princes of his House, descended from *William* Duke of *Bavaria*, his Father, the Electoral Dignity, which was before possess'd by the Counts Palatins of the *Rhine*. The Article of the Treaty of *Munster* speaks thus, *And first, as for what relates to the House of* Bavaria, *the Electoral Dignity which the Electors* Palatins *have hitherto possess'd, with all its Rights, Regalia, Offices, Precedencies, Arms, &c whatever, belonging to that Dignity, without any manner of exception as also all the* Upper Palatinate, *and the Earldom of* Cham, *with all their Appurtenances and Dependences, Rights, and Regalia, shall remain for the time to come to the Lord* Maximilian, *Count Palatin of the* Rhine, *Duke of* Bavaria, *and to his Children, and to all the Line of* William, *so long as there shall be any Male Issue therein. In Consideration whereof the Lord Elector of* Bavaria *shall renounce intirely for himself, his Heirs and Successors, to the Debt of thirteen Millions, and to all the Pretensions he can have to the Upper* Austria, &c *And a little after, That if it shall happen that all the Branch of* William, *as to the Male, comes to fail, and be wholly extinct (the* Palatin *Branch still subsisting) not only the Upper* Palatinate, *but also the Electoral Dignity, which now belongs to the Duke of* Bavaria, *shall return to the* Palatins *who shall be then living. And in the mean time they shall enjoy, as well as the Dukes of* Bavaria, *the effect of the pretended Investiture.*

* Before the Treaty of *Munster* had thus regulated the Right of these two Princes, the Duke of *Bavaria*, considering that this Translation of the Electoral Dignity from one Branch to the other, was defective and faulty in all its Circumstances, and having Reason to fear lest one Day Posterity might declare it so, suffer'd some Civilians to undertake to persuade the World, That the Dukes of *Bavaria* were the Electors, and that the Electoral Dignity was annex'd to *Bavaria*, and not to the *Palatinate*. They who have written on this Subject, strengthen their Opinion with Reasons so plausible and specious, that it is difficult to discover the Weakness thereof, unless they are confronted with the Truth of History.

It is certain that not only the Dukes of *Bavaria* have assisted at several Elections before the Publication of the *Golden Bull*, but that they have also discharg'd the Office of Great Steward of the Empire, which is inseparable from the Electoral Dignity. And we even say with the Emperor *Rodolphus* I, that the Duke of *Bavaria* was an Elector on the account of his Dutchy. But we say also that the Election does not make the Elector, for if it did, the Administrators of the Electors during their Minority, who assist at the Elections by virtue of the fundamental Law, in their own Right, and not as Guardians of their Pupils, would be Electors, but that it is the real Possession of the Principality, to which the Electoral Dignity is annex'd, that gives this Quality, so that to prove, that the Duke of *Bavaria* was an Elector, it must be known whether the Dutchy was an Electorate since the Publication of the *Golden Bull*.

When the Emperor *Rodolphus* I says that the Duke of *Bavaria* was an Elector on the Score of his Dutchy, he speaks of a Time in which the Number of the Electors was not regulated, nor the Electoral Dignity annex'd to particular Principalities, is it was afterwards by the *Golden Bull*. Moreover to comprehend the Intention of *Rodolphus*, it is requisite to know that the Difference was between *Othocarus* King of *Bohemia* (who had usurp'd the Dutchy of *Austria*) and *Henry* Duke of *Bavaria* *Othocarus* pretended he had a Right to two Votes, the one on the Account of his Kingdom of *Bohemia*, and the other on the Score of *Austria*, but *Henry* maintain'd, that, as Duke of *Austria*, he had no Right to elect, and that it belong'd to himself on the Account of *Bavaria*, of which *Austria* was formerly but a part, and that if *Henry*, who succeeded his Brother *Leo-*

---

* *The Electoral Dignity was annex'd to the Palatinate by the Golden Bull, and not to Bavaria*

pold,

of the ELECTORS of the EMPIRE. 517

pold, in *Austria* and in *Bavaria*, was present at the Election of the Emperor *Frederick* I, it was in the Quality of Duke of *Bavaria*, rather than as Marquiss of *Austria*. It is true, that since *Austria* has been erected into a Dutchy by the said Emperor *Frederick* I, its Princes have assisted at the Elections of several Emperors, as at those of *Henry* VI, of *Philip* of *Suabia*, of *Otho* IV, of *Frederick* II, and of several others. But for all that, when the Number of the Electors (which was very confus'd and uncertain in the Time of *Frederick* I, and of the Emperors his Successors) was reduc'd to a smaller, and more regular, the Duke of *Bavaria* (who was one of the most powerful Princes of *Germany*) was preferr'd to that of *Austria*, who did not begin to be known under that Quality, but in the Time of the said Emperor. But this does not hinder the Counts *Palatins* of the *Rhine*, who were Vicars of the Empire during the *Interregnum*, sole Judges of the Emperor's Person, and consequently the first Princes of the Empire, from having had a Right to elect, as well as the Dukes of *Bavaria*.

Moreover, even if what these Doctors presuppose was true, to wit, That the Electoral College was instituted by the Emperor *Otho* III, and that from that Time the Electoral Dignity was annex'd to certain Principalities, the Counts *Palatins* would nevertheless be Electors. Because, as the eldest of the Family, they inherited those Provinces to which the Dignity was appropriated, and it was in this Quality that *Rodolphus*, Son to *Lewis the Severe*, Count *Palatin* of the *Rhine*, and Duke of *Bavaria*, succeeded in the *Palatinate*, and in the Electoral Dignity, leaving *Bavaria* to *Lewis* his younger Brother. The same *Lewis* having attain'd to the Empire, and having proscrib'd his Brother *Rodolphus* for having sided with *Frederick* Duke of *Austria* against him, did not dare to dispossess his Nephews of the Electoral Dignity, even after the Proscription, but all the Advantage he reap'd from the Disgrace of *Rodolphus*, and the Misfortunes of his Children, was, that by the Treaty which he made with them at *Pavia*, in the Year 1329, he oblig'd them to consent that the Electoral Dignity should be in common to both Branches, and that the Functions thereof should be executed by both alternately, with which the Emperor, who had the Power in his own Hands, and who had confiscated all his Brother's Estate, would not have been contented, if he had believ'd that the Electoral Dignity had been annex'd to *Bavaria*, and not to the *Palatinate*. But let us see what Right the Dukes of *Bavaria* can claim from this Transaction, and whether by virtue of this Consent they were call'd or invited to the Elections. There is no body so ignorant, as not to know that this sort of Contracts, made between the Guardian and the Pupil, or between a Man who is arm'd with Power, and him who has just Reason to fear, is of no Effect, especially when the Wrong is so outragious, that the Law does not refuse to restore the Party aggriev'd to the State he was in before the Contract, and consequently that such Transaction is null, admitting that it were not directly contrary to the fundamental Law of the Empire, as it really

s For whether the Institution of the Electoral College be ascrib'd to *Otho* III, in which Case the Parties could not derogate from the Law, or to *Charles* IV, and then it must be own'd that this Transaction was annull'd by a posterior Law, which annexes the Electoral Dignity, and the Office of Great Steward of the Empire, to the *Palatinat*, in such express Terms, and so often repeated, that it plainly appears that it excludes therefrom *Bavaria* and all its Princes. In Chap VII § 2 it says, *Certainly, it is manifest, and notorious to all the World, and there is not any body who does not know, that the Illustrious Count* Palatin *of the* Rhine *has a Right, Vote, and Seat at the Election of a King of the* Romans *future Emperor, by virtue of his Principality*. Chap I § 13 *The Count* Palatin *of the* Rhine, *Great Steward of the Empire, shall be conducted by the Archbishop* of Mayence, Chap IV § 1 *The King of* Bohemia *shall take place*, &c and after him, on the same side, *shall sit the Count* Palatin *of the* Rhine. And in the same Chap § 3 *In the fourth place shall vote the Count* Palatin *of the* Rhine. Chap V § 1 *When the Empire shall become vacant, the Illustrious Count* Palatin *of the* Rhine, *Great Steward of the holy Empire, shall be Vicar of the Empire in* Suabia, *in* Franconia, *and on the* Rhine, *on the Account of his Principality, or by virtue of the Privilege annex'd to the* Palatinate. Chap VI § 3 *By a very ancient Custom, the King of the* Romans, *or the Emperor, shall be impleadable, and oblig'd to answer before the Count* Palatin *of the* Rhine, *Great Steward, and Prince Elector of the holy Empire*. Chap II § 3 *Which Constitution we extend by this Imperial Law, to the Illustrious Count* Palatin *of the* Rhine, &c. And so afterwards, in Chap XXII, XXV, § 1 XXVII, § 4 and Chap XXX § 2 where it speaks always of the Count *Palatin* of the *Rhine*, and never of the Duke of *Bavaria*. There are Letters of the said Emperor *Charles* IV, dated before the Publication of the *Golden Bull*, *June* 1, 1354, at *Keysersberg*, in which he quotes some Letters of *John* King of *Bohemia*, his Father, dated at *Franckfort* the *Friday* before *Palm-Sunday*, *An* 1339, which say very expressly, That even at that Time *Rodolphus*, Count *Palatin* of the *Rhine*, was true and lawful Elector, and that he enjoy'd the Right of Electing, on the account of the *Palatinate*. The same Emperor, speaking of the Count *Palatin Rupert*, in his Letters given at *Nuremberg* in the same Year that the *Golden Bull* was publish'd, says, *Because he is in Possession of a Vote in the Election of the King of the* Romans, *as also in Possession of the* Palatin *Principality, and of the Office of Great Steward, of the Jurisdiction, Vassallages, Appurtenances and Dependencies, on which the Right and the Suffrage of the Electors is founded*. And afterwards, *We find that the Vote, the Right, and the Election are so founded on the* Palatinate, *and in the Office of Great Steward, that the one cannot subsist without the other*. In the same Year all the Electors issu'd out their Letters Patents, by which they secure and confirm the Electoral Dignity to one another, and, among the rest, *Lewis the Roman*, Marquiss and Elector of *Brandenburg*, notwithstanding he was of the House of *Bavaria*, and Son to the Emperor *Lewis* IV, does nevertheless acknowledge the Count *Palatin* for Elector, without making a-

6 Q ny

ny mention of the pretended Right of the Duke of *Bavaria* But there is nothing more express on this Subject, than what the Emperor *Sigismund* says, in his Letters Patents of the Year 1418, where he expresses himself thus, in § 2 *Sane cum alias per Literas omnium Principum Electorum, nominatim divæ Retordationis, serenissimi Princip s ac Domini, Domini Caroli IV Romanorum Imperatoris, & Bohemiæ Regis, genitoris nostri carissimi, velut Bohemiæ Regis, venerabilium Gerlaci Moguntini, per Alemaniam, Boemundi Trevirensis, per Galliam, ac Regnum Arelatense, Wilhelmi Coloniensis, per Italiam sacri Romani Imperii Archicancellariorum, Archiepiscoporum, Rudolphi Ducis Saxoniæ, sacri Romani Imperii Archimareschalli, & Ludovici, dicti Romer, quondam Imperatoris Ludovici filii, Marchionis Brandeburgensis sacri Romani Imperii Archicamerarii Ac etiam Principibus, Comitibus, Baronibus, Nobilibus, Proceribus, & multis aliis nostris & Sacri Imperii fidelibus, informationem certissimam, & Luce Testimonii clariora, nostra suscepit Imperialis Celsitudo, qualiter felicis memoriæ Rupertus præsenior, quondam Comes Palatinus Rheni, S R I Archidapifer, & Bavariæ Dux, Patruus illustris Ludovici, Comitis Palatini Rheni, S R I Archidapiferi, Principis Electoris, nec non Bavariæ Ducis, Avunculi nostri carissimi, & post prædictum Rupertum præseniorem, Rupertus senior, Avus jam dicti Avunculi nostri Ludovici, & post eundem Rupertum seniorem, Rupertus Pater jam dicti Avunculi nostri Ludovici, successive tanquam Archidapiferi ejusdem Imperii, & veri Principes Electores, ab omnibus aliis eorum Coelectoribus semper habiti & reputati fuerunt ac etiam voluntate, consensu & votis aliorum suorum Coelectorum Principum unanimiter accedentibus, claræ memoriæ serenissimos quondam Romanorum Reges prædecessores nostros, temporibus suis, & rationaliter, juxta Sacri Romani Imperii observantiam, in Romanorum Reges elegerunt, ad Imperatoriam Celsitudinem promovendos Ac subsequenter idem modernus Ludovicus, cum aliis Coelectoribus suis modernis, retroactis temporibus, nos in Romanorum Regem elegit, qui disponente eo, a quo bona cuncta procedunt Rege Regum, & Domino Dominorum, Coronam Imperialem suscepimus* " *Quodque prædicti Rupertus præsenior,*
" *Patruus, ac Rupertus, Pater dicti Ludovici,*
" *quondam Comites Palatini Rheni, diuturna*
" *temporum præscriptione inconcussæ habuerunt &*
" *possederunt, prout etiam ipse Ludovicus impræ-*
" *sentiarum, ad instar illorum, ex successione pa-*
" *terna & hereditaria, dignoscitur justo Titulo*
" *possidere jus, vocem, dignitatim, & potestatem*
" *Eligendi Romanorum Regem, in Imperatorem*
" *promovendum, quemadmodum in nostris Lite-*
" *ris declaratoriis, sub Regali Romanorum Ti-*
" *tulo desuper editis ac promulgatis plenius conti-*
" *netur Et quod longinquitate sæpe fit Tempo-*
" *ris, quod res Clara præsentibus, redditur per*
" *oblivionem obscura, &c*

If any one would maliciously shut his Eyes against the Clearness of this Truth, which is much brighter than that of the Sun at Noon-Day, we could render it palpable in the Succession of so great a Number of Electors, continu'd for above three hundred Years in the *Palatin* House, without its being interrupted by any Contest or Protestation on the part of the Dukes of *Bavaria*, excepting that which *William* Duke of *Bavaria* made, in the Year 1544 when he oppos'd the Investiture of *Frederick* II But the Emperor *Charles* V had no Regard thereto, but gave it notwithstanding *William* founded his Pretensions on this, That *Rupert*, the eldest Son of *Philip* Elector *Palatin*, had been put in the Ban of the Empire He had marry'd *Isabella*, the only Daughter of *George the Rich*, Duke of *Bavaria* at *Landshut*, and pretended that all the Inheritance of the Father-in-Law belong'd to him, as well by virtue of the Testament of the deceas'd, as by his Contract of Marriage But *Albert*, Duke of *Bavaria* at *Munichen*, who had marry'd the Sister of the Emperor *Maximilian* I, oppos'd it, and making use of the Advantage of this Alliance, he procur'd *Rupert* to be put in the Ban of the Empire This Disgrace serv'd for a Foundation to the Hopes which the Dukes of *Bavaria* began to have from that Time, that they might contrive to have the *Palatin* Electoral Dignity transferr'd to their Family, but they vanish'd immediately, by the Peace which *Lewis* and *Frederick*, Brothers to *Rupert*, made with the Emperor *William*, the Son of *Albert*, seeing his Hopes driven so far backward, had Recourse to Artifice, and under the Pretext of renewing a mutual Friendship between the two Branches, by means whereof the Princes of the *Palatin* Branch might retrieve their Affairs he engag'd the two Brothers to make a Treaty with him, into which this Article was slipp'd, That, by that Treaty, all the former Treaties made between the Princes of the two Branches, should remain confirm'd And it is upon this Article that he grounded his Pretensions, as if those two Princes had, by Words so general, particularly confirm'd the Treaty of *Pavia*, made between the Emperor *Lewis* IV and the Sons of the Elector *Palatin*, *Rodolphus* his Nephews, by which the Electoral Dignity had been render'd alternative to the two Branches, tho' he knew that it was not in their Power to make an Alteration of that Nature in the Electoral College, contrary to the express Direction of the fundamental Law of the Empire, which, by calling to the Succession of the Electoral Dignity, the eldest of Families to the Exclusion of the younger, annexes it to the Counts *Palatins*, who are the eldest of the House, and excluded therefrom the Dukes of *Bavaria*, who are a younger Branch

But forasmuch as the Plenipotentiaries of the Electors, and of the other Princes of *Germany* assembled at *Munster*, and representing the Sovereignty of the Empire, thought fit to change the Order establish'd by the *Golden Bull* And to convey the *Palatin* Electoral Dignity to the *Bavarian* Branch, we shall finish this Chapter with speaking of the Dutchy of *Bavaria*, and of its Princes, as being at this Day Electors of the holy Empire

* We have said, in the foregoing Chapter, that the *Boy*, a People of the *Gauls*, enter'd into *Germany* under the Conduct of *Sigovesus*, at the same Time that another part of the same People march'd into *Italy*, under *Bellovesus*, in the Reign of *Tarquinius Priscus*, King of the *Romans*, and that they there took Possession of that Countrey, which at present is call'd from

* *The Origin of the Word Bavaria.*

their

of the ELECTORS of the EMPIRE.

their Name, *Bohemia*, and remain'd there till the *Marcomans* forc'd them to seek another Habitation elsewhere, and to retire into that Part of the ancient *Noricum*, which is at present call'd *Bavaria* Ior as the neighbouring People had call'd the first *Boyenheim*, that is to say, Habitation of the *Boy*, so they nam'd the last *Boyenland*, that is to say, the Countrey or Land of *Boy*, and in process of Time, *Boyeren*, or *Bayeren*, which has been chang'd to *Bajoaria*, *Bavvaria*, and afterwards into *Bavaria* The Name of the Province has been known but since the latter end of the sixth Century, when *Garibald*, King of *Bavaria*, gave his Daughter *Theodelinda* in Marriage to *Antharis*, King of *Lombardy*, and that of *Bavaria* is hardly to be met with in History, before the Time of the Emperor *Frederick* II

* It has for its Neighbours on the *North* side, *Franconia* and the *Upper Palatinate*, towards the *East*, *Bohemia* and *Austria*, to the *Southward* the *Alps* of *Tirol*, and towards the *West*, *Suabia* The River *Leck*, which rises out of the same *Alps*, and after having wash'd the Walls of *Fuessen*, of *Schonga* and of *Augsburg*, discharges its Waters into the *Danube* near *Rain*, below *Donawert*, divides it into the Upper and Lower *Bavaria* The principal Towns of the Upper are *Munchen*, where for the most part its Princes reside, *Ingolstadt* a strong Town, and honour'd with an University which is famous enough, and *Frysingen*, an Episcopal City Those of the Lower are *Ratisbone*, an Imperial City, *Passaw*, a Bishop's See, *Lantshut* and *Straubingen*, and some others of less note, which make in all about five and thirty, besides fourscore and fourteen Burroughs enclos'd with Walls It makes alone one of the Circles of the Empire, and comprehends its Elector, the Archbishop of *Saltsburg*, the Bishops of *Ratisbone*, of *Frysingen* and of *Passaw* The Abbots of *Waltsassen*, of St *Emeran* at *Ratisbone*, and of *Keizersheim* The Abbesses of the Upper and Lower *Moustier* of *Ratisbone*, the Prevost of *Berchtolsgaden*, the Duke of *Bavaria*, the Counts Palatins of the *Rhine* at *Neuburg* and at *Sultsbach*, the Lantgrave of *Leuchtemberg*, the Prince d'*Eggenberg*, Duke of *Crumaut*, the Prince of *Lobkoitiz*, the Counts of *Ottemburg*, some Barons, immediate Subjects of the Empire, and the Town of *Ratisbone* *Andreas Ratisponensis* says, That *Bavaria* receiv'd the *Christian* Religion about the Year 182, after the Birth of *Jesus Christ* but it is certain that it was still *Pagan*, when *Childebert* King of *France*, drove the *Huns* and the *Sclavy* out of it, above four hundred Years after that Time † It had then its particular Kings, but *Childebert* reduc'd it into a Province, and made *Tassilon* Governor thereof, in the Quality of Duke After him govern'd *Tendo*, and after him *Theodebert*, *Theudo* II, and *Odilon* After him *Odilon* II, who marry'd *Suanahilde*, Daughter or Niece to *Charles Martel*, Mayor of the Palace in *France*, and who was driven out by *Pepin* and *Carloman*, the Sons of *Charles Martel* These Princes gave *Bavaria* to *Tassilon* II, who having revolted against *Charlemagne*, in favour of *Didier* King of the *Lombards*, his Father in-law, was depriv'd of his Estates, and shut up with his Son in the Convent of *Laurisheim* by which means *Bavaria* was again reunited to the Crown of *France*

It remain'd annex'd to it till it was again separated from it by the Partition which was made between the Sons of *Lewis* the *Debonnaire*, in the Year 843, by which it fell to *Lewis* sirnam'd the *German*, his second Son ‡ *Carloman*, the Son of *Lewis*, had it after the Death of his Father, and left it to *Arnoul* his natural Son, who having attain'd to the Empire, gave the Government of *Bavaria*, under the Title of a Dutchy, to *Leopold*, who was kill'd by the *Hungarians* in the Year 907 He left two Sons, *Arnoul*, call'd the *Bad*, and *Bertold* The first succeeded in the Dutchy of *Bavaria*, but he took up Arms against the Emperor *Conrade* I, who compell'd him to retire into *Hungary* After the Death of *Arnoul*, *Bertold* his Brother succeeded in *Bavaria*, and after him *Henry*, Brother to the Emperor *Otho* I, who had marry'd the Daughter of *Arnoul* * *Bavaria* continu'd in the *Saxon* House, till the Emperor *Henry*, Grandson to *Henry* I, gave it to *Henry* or *Hetzel*, Brother to the Emperess *Cunigonde*, who held the Dutchy till he dy'd The Emperor *Conrade* II, gave it to his Son *Henry*, who at his Accession to the Crown reunited it to the Empire, and gave it afterwards to *Conrade* his younger Son, who dying in the Year 1056, the Emperor *Henry* IV, gave it to *Agnes* his Mother, who govern'd the Dutchy in Person, till the Year 1061 Then she gave it to *Otho*, Count of *Northeim*, of the House of *Saxony*, as being descended in a direct and male Line from *Bruno*, the third Son of *Henry*, first Duke of *Bavaria*, of that Family This Prince having taken Arms against the Emperor with the other rebellious *Saxons*, *Henry* gave *Bavaria* to *Guelfe* IV, the Son of *Azzon*, Marquiss of *Este* *Guelfe* IV, had marry'd for first Wife *Ethelinda*, the Daughter of *Otho*, Count of *Northeim*, Duke of *Bavaria* but he divorc'd her out of Complaisance to the Emperor, and marry'd for second Wife *Judith*, Daughter to *Bandouin*, sirnam'd from *Lisle*, Count of *Flanaers*, which *Judith* was the Widow of *Toste*, or *Tostique*, Son to *Godwin*, Earl of *Northumberland*, and eldest Brother to *Harold*, King of *England*, and of this Marriage was born *Guelfe* V, and *Henry* the *Black*, Dukes of *Bavaria* This last marry'd *Wulfilda*, the Daughter of *Magnus* Duke of *Saxony*, and had by her amongst other Children, *Henry* the *Proud*, who succeeded in the Dutchy of *Bavaria*, and in part of *Saxony*, in Consideration of his Marriage with *Gertrude*, Daughter to the Emperor *Lotharius* II He oppos'd the Election of the Emperor *Conrade* III, after the Death of *Lotharius*, with so much Obstinacy, that he thereby lost his Estates, and even his Life *Conrade* gave *Bavaria* to *Leopold* Marquiss of *Austria*, his Brother by the Mother's side, and after his Death to *Henry* his Brother, who marry'd *Gertrude*, the Widow of *Henry* the *Proud* † But *Frederick* I, sirnam'd *Red-beard*, having attain'd to the Empire, accommodated the Difference between the two *Henry*s, so that *Bavaria* was

---

* *The Frontiers of Bavaria* † *Its Princes before Charlemagne* ‡ *Under the Successors of Charlemagne*
* *Under the Emperors of the Saxon House* † *The Emperor Frederick I lops off Austria from it*

restor'd

Of the ELECTION of the EMPEROR, and

restor'd to *Henry* the *Lyon*, the Son of *Henry* the *Proud*, except that part of the Dutchy, which is between the Rivers *In* and *Ens*, which was annex'd to *Austria*, which was likewise erected into a Dutchy and by that Means withdrawn from the Subjection and Jurisdiction of the Dukes of *Bavaria*

‡ *Henry* the *Lyon*, Duke of *Bavaria* and *Saxony*, marry'd for first Wife *Clementia*, the Daughter of *Conrade* Duke of *Zeringen*, whom he divorc'd under the Pretext of Parentage, and had by her only one Daughter nam'd *Clementia*, who was marry'd to *Frederick* of *Suabia*, Son to the Emperor *Conrade* III, and after his Death to *Canutus*, Son to *Volmar* I, King of *Denmark* He had for second Wife *Mahault* or *Mathilda*, Daughter to *Henry* II, King of *England*, of whom he had several Children, and among the rest *Otho* IV, Emperor, and *William*, from whom sprung the Dukes of *Brunswick* and of *Lunenburg*, who are now living *Henry*'s haughty Temper, and the Power he had in *Germany*, where his Estates extended from the *Baltick* as far as *Italy*, carry'd him beyond the Bounds of his Duty towards the Emperor, who caus'd him to be put in the Ban of the Empire, and confiscated all his Estates and among the rest *Bavar a*, which he gave in the Year 1080, to *Otho*, * Count *Palatin* of *Wittelspach*, Father to *Lewis* I, from whom sprung all the Counts *Palatins* and Dukes of *Bavaria*, whom we shall treat of at present

† Both the ones and the others descend from *Otho*, Count of *Schiren*, Son to *Brabon*, Count *d'Abensperg*, who liv'd about the Year 1048, and presented to the Emperor *Henry* III, two and thirty Sons at *Mans* Estate *Otho* III, Grandson to *Otho* I, Count of *Schiren*, built the Castle of *Wittelspach*, which began from that Time to change the Name of the Family, and left *Otho* IV, Father of *Otho* V, who introduc'd *Bavaria* into this House *Lewis* his Son left *Otho* VI, sirnam'd the *Illustrious*, who marry'd *Agnes*, Daughter to *Henry* of *Saxony*, who was Son to *Henry* the *Lyon* and by this Marriage he brought the *Palatinate* into the House of *Bavaria* He left two Sons, *Henry*, whose Posterity fail'd in the Person of *Otho*, Son to *Stephen*, who dy'd in the Year 1335, and *Lewis*, sirnam'd the *Severe*, for having too hastily executed his Wife for a false Suspicion of Adultery *Lewis* marry'd for third Wife *Mahault*, Daughter of the Emperor *Rodolphus* I, and had by her *Rodolphus*, common Father to all the Electors, and Princes *Palatins*, and *Lewis*, who was elected Emperor, *October* 18, 1314 The Emperor *Lewis* had by *Beatrix* of *Glogan* his first Wife, *Lewis*, Father to *Menard*, Count of *Tirol*, who dy'd without Children, and *Stephen* By *Marguerit*, Heiress of the Counties of *Hainault*, and of *Holland*, he had several Children and amongst others *Albert*, Father to *William*, who left only one Daughter nam'd *Jaquelme*, who yielded up her Estates of *Hainault*, and of *Holland*, to *Philip* the *Good*, Duke of *Burgundy*, and left no Posterity

Stephen, the second Son of the Emperor *Lewis* of *Bavaria*, and of *Beatrix* of *Glogan*, his first Wife, had by *Elizabeth*, Daughter to *Lewis* II, King of *Hungary* and *Naples*, *Stephen* I,

who left, by *Thadea Visconti*, *Isabella* Queen of *France*, Wife to *Charles* VI, and *Lewis*, Father to *Lewis* the *Hunch-back'd*, who dy'd without Children in the Year 1445 2 *Frederick*, and 3 *John*

2 *Frederick*, second Son to *Stephen*, and *Elizabeth* of *Hungary*, had by *Marguerit* of *Austria*, Daughter to *Albert* IV, *Henry*, who had for his Portion *Lantshut* and *Ingolstadt*, and was Father to *George* the *Rich*, who left only one Daughter nam'd *Elizabeth*, who was marry'd to *Rupert*, Count *Palatin* of the *Rhine*

3. *John*, the third Son of *Stephen* the eldest Brother, and of *Elizabeth* of *Hungary*, had for his Share *Munichen*, and dy'd *August* 8, 1397, leaving *Ernestus*, who had by *Elizabeth Visconti*, *Albert*, who had by *Ann* of *Brunswick*, *Albert* the *Wise* This last was born *December* 15, 1440, and marry'd in 1487, *Cunegunda* of *Austria*, Daughter of the Emperor *Frederick* III, and of *Leonora* of *Portugal* It was he that contested with *Rupert*, Count *Palatin* of the *Rhine*, the Inheritance of *George* the *Rich*, and finding himself supported by the Arms and Authority of the Emperor *Maximilian* I, his Brother-in-law, he had no great Difficulty to triumph over his Enemies, and to reunite all *Bavaria* in his Person, except what the *Palatins* of *Neuburg* possess on the *Danube* He dy'd *March* 18, 1508, leaving *Lewis*, who had no Issue, and *William* *William*, the Son of *Albert* the *Wise*, and of *Cunegunda* of *Austria*, made Instance after the Death of *Philip*, Elector *Palatin*, that the Electoral Dignity might be conferr'd on himself, by virtue of the Treaty of *Pavia*, made between the Emperor *Lewis* of *Bavaria*, and the Children of *Rodolphus*, Elector *Palatin*, but the Emperor *Charles* V, would not hearken thereto He also with the Elector of *Saxony* oppos'd the Election of *Ferdinand* I, and left, by *Mary Jacob*, the Daughter of *Philip*, Marquiss of *Baden*, *Albert*, who was born *February* 28, 1528, and marry'd on *July* 4, 1546, *Anne*, Daughter to the Emperor *Ferdinand* I, and of *Anne* of *Hungary*, and dy'd *October* 24, 1579, leaving besides *Charles*, *Frederick* and *Mary Maximiliana*, who dy'd young, *William Ferdinand*, who never marry'd, but left a natural Son nam'd *Francis William*, who is at this Day Bishop of *Osnaburg*, *Ernest* Archbishop and Elector of *Cologn*, Bishop of *Liege*, *Hildesheim* and *Frisingen*, who dy'd *February* 17, 1612, and *Mary*, the Wife of *Charles* of *Austria*, and consequently Grand mother to the Emperor who dy'd last, to *Philip* IV, King of *Spain*, and to the Queen, Mother of *Lewis* XIV

William, the eldest Son of *Albert*, and of *Anne* of *Austria*, was born *September* 29, 1548, and marry'd on *February* 22, 1565, *Renée*, the Daughter of *Francis* Duke of *Lorrain*, and of *Christian* of *Denmark* He resign'd the Government of the Dutchy to his Son *Maximilian*, and retir'd into the Charter-House at *Ratisbone*, where he dy'd *May* 23, 1626, being 78 Years of Age His Children are, *Chrystopher*, who dy'd young, *Maximilian Philip*, Cardinal and Bishop of *Ratisbone*, *Ferdinand*, who succeeded in the Year 1612, to *Ernest* his Unkle in the Archbishoprick of *Cologn*, and to the Bishop-

---

† *It is confiscated from Henry the Lyon.*   * *It enters into the House of Schiren*   † *The Queen of these Princes*

ricks

ricks of *Liege* and of *Hildesheim*, and dy'd September 13, 1650, having possess'd those Bishopricks, together with those of *Munster*, and of *Paderborn* thirty eight Years, without being a Priest *Charles*, who dy'd young *Albert*, of whom we shall speak by and by, and several Daughters among the rest, *Anne-Mary*, first Wife of the Emperor *Ferdinand* II, and Mother to *Ferdinand* III And *Magdalen* Wife to *Wolfgang William* of *Bavaria*, Count Palatin of the *Rhine* at *Newburg*

Maximilian, the eldest Son of *William* and of *René* of *Lorrain*, was born *April* 17, 1575, and marry'd in *February* 1595, for first Wife *Elizabeth*, the Daughter of *Charles* III, Duke of *Lorrain*, and of *Claud* of *France* who dying without Children in the Year 1634, he marry'd on *Feb* 15, 1635, *Anne-Mary* of *Austria*, Daughter to the Emperor *Ferdinand* II, and *Anne-Mary* of *Bavaria* his Sister It is he that procur'd the Electoral Dignity to be transferr'd from the Palat a Branch to that of *Bavaria* in the Year 1623 He dy'd *August* 27, 1651, and has left *Ferdinand-Mary-Francis-Ignatius-Wolfgang*, born *October* 21, 1636, who has succeeded his Father in the Dignity which he still enjoys at this Day, and marry'd on *January* 12, 1652, *Adelaide*, Daughter to *Victor Amadeus*, Duke of *Savoy*, and *Christina* of *France*, and *Philip-Max in Emanuel Hierosme*, born *September* 30, 1638

Albert, the second Son of *William*, and *René* of *Lorrain*, was born *April* 13, 1584, and marry'd on *February* 26, 1612, *Malaut*, Daughter to *George Lewis*, Landgrave of *Leuchtenberg*, and of *Mary-Salome* of *Baden*, by whom he had several Children, but those who are still living are *Maximilian Henry*, Archbishop and Elector of *Cologn*, of whom we have spoken elsewhere, and *Albert Sigismund*, who is Bishop of *Frisingen*, but he is not yet consecrated, and has some Thoughts of Matrimony, because the Elector of *Bavaria* has no Children, and so there is of the whole House only himself and the Elector left to keep up the *Wilhelmin* Line, to which the Electoral Dignity is annex'd

* As for the Rights, Privileges, Prerogatives, and Preeminences which the Duke of *Bavaria* enjoys as Elector, and which cannot be contested with him, since the Electoral Dignity of the Count Palatin of the *Rhine* has been transferr'd to him, They are, first, That he is the fifth in the Electoral College, and the second among the Seculars but in voting he is the fourth, and speaks his Opinion immediately after the King of *Bohemia*, after whom he also takes Place in publick Assemblies tho' in marching he sometimes goes between *Brandenburg* and the *Palatin*, and sometimes on the Right of the *Saxon*, as we have seen in Chap XI 2 At those Ceremonies where the Electors carry the Regalia or Ornaments of the Empire, the Elector of *Bavaria* carries the *Golden Ball*, which represents the World, and which he also bears in his Arms, which are quarterly, in the first and fourth, which are Sable a Lyon crown'd Or, langued and arm'd Gules, in the second and third Bendy Argent and Azure of one and twenty Pieces, and over the whole, Gules a Globe Or But of all the Dukes of *Bavaria*, none but he of the Family that is honour'd with the Electoral Dignity, bears over the whole the Golden Globe, as the Elector of *Bohemia* does the Cup, the Elector of *Saxony* the two handed Sword, the Elector of *Brandenburg* the Scepter, and the Elector Palatin the Crown *Frederick* II, Elector Palatin, was the first that bore it in his Arms, in the Time, and with the Permission of the Emperor *Charles* V 3 He is Great Steward hereditary of the Empire, and in this Quality he officiates at the Imperial Feasts after the Coronation The only Function of this Office is, that the Elector of *Bavaria* goes into the Emperor's Kitchen and there takes Meat in four Silver Dishes of the Weight of three Marks each, which he carries on Horseback to the Gate of the Imperial Palace, where he alights and going up to the Room prepar'd for the Feast, he sets them on the Table before the Emperor He is assisted in this Function by the Baron of *Walsbourg*, is Vicar in the Office of Great Steward, who lends him his Hand when he mounts on Horseback, and when he alights, and in Consideration of this Service, the Silver Dishes and the Horse on which the Elector rode belong to him He is also Great Steward of the Bishoprick of *Bamberg*, and on the account of this Office he holds in Fee the Castle of *Hohenstein*, and the Bailwicks of *Harspruck*, of *Velck* of *Aurlpach*, of *Pagents*, and of *Vellen* The Lord *Trevelfes* of *Pommersfelden* is his Vicar in the Bishoprick The Advantage the Elector of *Bavaria* has over the King of *Bohemia* (the Office of Great Steward being beyond Comparison more honourable than that of Great Cup-bearer) makes known that these Offices were not instituted, nor annex'd to the Principalities at the same time but that that of Great Steward was in the House of *Bavaria*, of which the *Palatins* are the eldest Branch, before the King of *Bohemia* was provided with that of Great Cup-bearer, because without doubt the most honourable Office would have been appropriated to the Regal Dignity 4 At the beginning of the present Interregnum, the Electors of *Bavaria* and *Palatin* had a Contest about the Quality of Vicar, which the *Golden Bull* seems to annex to the Palatinate inseparably, rather than to the Electoral Dignity, when it says, † " That when " the Empire shall become vacant, the illu- " strious Count *Palatin*, Great Steward of the " Holy Empire, shall be Vicar of the Empire " in *Suabia*, in *Franconia*, and on the *Rhine*, on " the account of his Principality, or by virtue of " the Privilege annex'd to the Palatinate But the Elector of *Bavaria* maintain'd, that the *Palatin* Electoral Dignity having pass'd into his House, with all its Appurtenances and Dependencies, the Quality and Functions of Vicar ought to be compris'd therein And thus the other Electors, and the Imperial Chamber of *Spires* have explain'd that Article of the Treaty of *Munster*, that speaks of this Translation

The *Golden Bull*, in saying ‡ That the King of the *Romans*, or the Emperor, is implendable, and oblig'd to answer before the Count *Palatin* by a very ancient Custom, shews that the Count *Palatin* was the Emperor's Judge, be-

* *The Rights of the Elector of Bavaria* † *Chap 5 § 1* ‡ *Chap 5 § 3*

6 R   fore

fore the Electoral Dignity was annex'd to the *Palatinate* And indeed, the Term of Count *Palatin* signifies nothing else but Judge of the Palace, of which the Emperor makes the principal part So that one may doubt, whether this Quality pass'd into the House of *Bavaria* with the Electoral Dignity, as one of its Dependencies, as well as the other particular Advantages which the Counts *Palatins* enjoy'd, and of which we shall speak in Chapter XVII For since the Electoral College has not as yet determin'd the matter, so neither shall we, but we shall content our selves with saying, that as they are not Rights inseparable from the Electoral Dignity, if nevertheless it be thought fit to gratify the Elector of *Bavaria* therewith, it might be so order'd that they might be in common to him and to the Elector *Palatin* but this last cannot be absolutely depriv'd thereof, without some sort of Injustice

* Let us now see how the Elector will be consider'd in the next Diet, and whether there be any Likelihood that the Negotiation which is on foot for the Election of his Person will succeed The Advantages he has are, 1 That of his Age, having pass'd the one and twentieth Year thereof, and not yet attain'd to that of two and twenty 2 The Qualities of Body and Mind, with which he is endow'd 3 His Birth, which is without doubt amongst the most Illustrious of all *Germany*, as coming from a House that has given a great many Electors to the Empire, and which gave it formerly for Head, the great *Lewis* of *Bavaria*, who preserv'd the Rights thereof against the Attempts of Foreigners, with a Vigour that has no Example in all History 4 His Estates and Wealth, which are capable of supporting the Imperial Dignity, as they have preserv'd it in the House of *Austria*, by the Loan which *Maximilian* made of so many Millions to the Emperor *Ferdinand* II 5 His Relations and Allies, being Chief of the House of *Bavaria*, Cousin German to the King of *Bohemia*, and to the Elector of *Cologn*, who shews a greater Inclination for him than for the House of *Austria*, a very near Relation of that of *Lorrain*, and Brother-in-law to the Duke of *Savoy* 6 His Religion, which has made the House of *Bavaria* be consider'd as the Head of the Catholick Party in *Germany*, if the House of *Austria* should fail 7 He will likewise have the Interest of *France*, and that of all its Friends in the Empire, who will without doubt make an utmost Effort to bring about his Election

As soon as the Design was form'd there of removing the Imperial Dignity out of the House of *Austria*, it presently cast its Eyes on *Bavaria*, as on the sole Support of the Roman Catholick Religion in those Parts and there is no body but knows, that at the same Time the King of *Sweden* was brought into *Germany*, the Elector of *Bavaria* was treated with, and had those Hopes given him then, which might now produce their Effects, if the Affairs of *Germany* were but duly dispos'd But all the Endeavours that have hitherto been us'd to win him, have had no Effect, and as yet it has been impossible to alienate the Elector of *Bavaria* from the Interest of the House of *Austria* Neither is there any Probability of succeeding therein at present, since there is not any of his attaining to the Empire At the Age he is now in, he might very well have Ambition enough to aspire to it, and it is likely enough that in the Electoral College there are Princes who wish it him, but they are neither powerful enough, nor enow in Number to be able to surmount all the Obstacles they might meet therein Most of the Electors believe, or would have it believ'd, that the Imperial Dignity cannot be remov'd from the House of *Austria*, without kindling the War afresh in *Germany* Some of them are entirely persuaded thereof, and those that are in the Interest of that House make use of the Pretext of the publick Good, and of the Affection they have for the Repose of the Empire, to cover that which they really have for the Party, so that both the ones and the others would be sure to oppose the Election of *Bavaria*, and proceed directly to that of the King of *Bohemia* They who declare for him, and who listen'd to the Propositions which were made in Favour of *Bavaria*, before the Queen of *Spain* was brought to bed of a Prince, are at present skreen'd from the just Reproach that might have been made them, had they call'd to the Imperial Crown a Prince who might in all Appearance join to it that of *Spain* and have no longer occasion to fear being accus'd of having betray'd the Liberty of their Country

The great Qualities of the Elector of *Bavaria* might be consider'd, at a time when they were not to be found in a more eminent Degree in the Person of his Competitor His House is Illustrious, but that of *Austria* is interior to it in nothing And if he reckons one or two Emperors among his Ancestors, the King of *Bohemia* can count twelve amongst his Predecessors His Riches, and the Extent of his Estates, cannot be compar'd with those of a Prince who possesses two Kingdoms, and several other very large and very considerable Provinces If the Relations of the one and the other are to be consider'd, we shall find that the King of *Bohemia* has for Cousin German, and for Unkle, the two first Kings of *Christendom*, and is ally'd to most of the Sovereigns of *Europe*

The Elector of *Bavaria* has without doubt a very great Advantage, to see three Princes of his House in the Electoral College, so that to bring about his Election, there would want but two more to be brought over as might be thought and we are willing to believe, that he may hope for the Suffrage of the Elector of *Cologn*, who is his Cousin German, tho' there is no very good Understanding between them But as for the Elector *Palatin*, who is of the same House, and the eldest Branch thereof, we must look back as far as the thirteenth Century to find out the beginning of the Relation Besides which there is an inveterate Aversion between the Princes of the two Branches, since the time that *Rodolphus* (the Stock from whence the Electors *Palatins* descend) elected Emperor of *Austria*, preferably to *Lewis* of *Bavaria* his Brother, who did not spare him in his turn, but drove him out of the Country, and com-

* Whoever he can aspire to the Empire

of the ELECTORS of the EMPIRE.

pell'd him to retire into *England*, where he dy'd in Exile. And this Hatred is become irreconcileable since the last Wars in *Germany*, by the Translation of the Electoral Dignity. Some are of Opinion that a Reconciliation might be wrought by restoring Affairs to the same State they were in before the Troubles of *Bohemia*. But besides that there is no likelihood that the Elector of *Bavaria* would purchase at too rate an imaginary Honour, and which would only pass through his House, it is not in his Power to dispose of the Electoral Dignity, nor of the *Upper Palatinate*, with their Appurtenances and Dependencies, without the Consent of all the Princes of *Bavaria* of the Posterity of *William*, which will be far from renouncing a Right that belongs to it as well as to the Elector, who is only the Depositary thereof. The same Religion from whence he might reap very great Advantages, will be what will do him the greatest Prejudice, because the Catholick Party having preserv'd it self during the last Wars in *Germany*, but by a good Understanding between the Princes who make Profession of that Religion, there is no room to doubt but it would be ruin'd entirely, if the same Princes should come to a Rupture amongst themselves, and the Roman Catholick Religion would find its Grave, where it thought to seek for an *Asylum*. It is true that the King has great and powerful Friends in *Germany*, and particularly among the Protestants. He may even have some in the Electoral College, who would side with his Interest there, but then it is to be presum'd that the King of *Bohemia*, who is a German Prince, whose Predecessors have had Leisure to establish themselves, and to acquire Friends in the Empire, will find there a greater Number, who will all oppose the Election of the Duke of *Bavaria*.

* But supposing the Elector of *Bavaria* to be able to aspire to the Imperial Dignity, let us see whether he ought to accept of it even tho' it were offer'd him. The *Italian* Letter which was sent hither from *Rome*, fill'd with bad Prognosticks for the future Election, says, That his Mother, and his first Minister, would hinder him from taking any strong Resolution on this Subject, because they are in the Interest of the House of *Austria*. But as we easily believe with the Author of this Letter, that the Relations and Ministers of the Elector of *Bavaria* would not advise him to charge himself with so burthensome a Dignity, so we cannot be persuaded that their Counsel is grounded on the Reason which he adds. The Electoress Dowager of *Bavaria* is of the House of *Austria*, and Sister of the late Emperor, it is true, but is she unnatural enough to prefer the Interest of her Nephew to that of her Son? Or is it a greater Advantage to her to have the Quality of Mother of a Prince Elector, than to be consider'd as the Emperor's Mother? The Queen Mother of King *Lewis* XIV is

of the same House, and Sister to the King of *Spain*, but that did not hinder her from sacrificing her Brother's Interest to the Glory of the King her Son, and to the Advantage of the Crown of *France*. It cannot be deny'd that Count *Curtz* has some Affection for the Court of *Vienna*, and we are willing to believe that his Counsels are not altogether disinterested, but we also say, that there is no Minister whose Imprudence and Meanness, or as the *Italians* say with more Emphasis, the *Dapoccagne* is great enough to make him neglect the Grandeur of his Prince, when he finds an Opportunity to establish it and raise his own Fortune under the Shade of his Master's. So that we must believe that Count *Curtz*, who is in the Dependence of a foreign and predominate Court, would endeavour to withdraw himself from it, and make himself the Arbitrator of Affairs, if he judg'd it to be for the Advantage of his Prince. But the Counsel which he gives him, as well as the Princess his Mother, to shut his Ears to the Propositions might be made him concerning the Exaltation of his Person, is founded, in their Opinion, upon Considerations very prudent, and of a refin'd Policy, which will not suffer the Elector of *Bavaria* to introduce into his House a Dignity which he cannot acquire but with a great deal of Difficulty, and which he could not support without an Expence that would ruin him even tho' he had no reason to apprehend the effect of the just Resentment of the King of *Bohemia*, who finding himself put back from a Dignity, which he looks upon to be due to the Merit of his Predecessors, and to which the State of Affairs seem'd to call him (were it not for the Intrigues that should be carry'd on in Favour of *Bavaria*) and being powerfully arm'd, might dispute with him the Possession of that Empire, which he esteem'd to be wrested from his House by unjust and illegal Means.

† We have now to see in the Close of this Chapter to whom the Elector of *Bavaria* will in all likelihood give his Vote, if he cannot hope to bring about his own Election, or does not think it proper to have it endeavour'd. It is certain that in the Electoral College there is only himself and the King of *Bohemia*, on whom it can cast its Eyes, because the six others are either Ecclesiasticks or Protestants. Out of the College, and in the Empire there are none but who are either Protestants, or out of a Condition to support the Imperial Dignity, and the Electors will never think of seeking an Emperor in *France* or in *Italy*, as long as they shall have in *Germany* Persons adorn'd with all the Qualities necessary to fill worthily the Throne of the Empire. So that there is no room to doubt that *Bavaria* will give his Vote to the King of *Bohemia*, who is his Neighbour, his nearest Relation, and the Head of a Family, that has introduc'd into his own all the Grandeur it is in Possession of

---

* *Whether he would aspire to it if he could?*   † *To whom he will give his Vote.*

CHAP.

CHAP. XV.

Of the Duke of Saxony Prince Elector of the Holy Empire.

* THE Origin of the Word *Saxony* is by so much the harder to find, as it cannot be said whether it be *German*, *Sclavonian*, or *Gothick*. *Wittikind*, Abbot of *Corbie* on the *Weser*, will have it that the *Saxons* descend from certain *Macedonians*, who having remain'd in *Asia* after the Death of *Alexander the Great*, embark'd with a Design to return home, but were by tempestuous Weather cast on the Coast of *Germany*, where they gave themselves the Name of *Saxons* from the Place of their Imbarkation; and by that means the Word would be *Asiatick*, or corrupted *Greek*. This is a ridiculous Notion, but it has for all that been so well receiv'd in the Cloisters, where they take Delight to canonize Tales of this nature, that there is hardly any Author who has written before the sixth Century, that does not begin the History of *Saxony* by this Fable, as they do that of *France* by the pretended Princes of *Troy*. Of the same kind is again the Invention of those who derive this Word from a certain Prince, whose Name was *Saxo*, who they say was the Son of *Nugnon*, and Brother to *Vandalus*. There are some who would have it believ'd that even in the eighth Century the Use of the *Latin* Tongue was well establish'd in the extreme Parts of *Germany* to the Northward, and that these People were call'd *Saxons* from the Word *Saxum*, by reason of their Invincible Temper, as if they would thereby intimate that these People were as hard and as untractable as a Rock. Others seek for the Etymology of the Word in a certain kind of Arms, which these People us'd, and alledge for that these Verses

Quippe brevis Glad us aprid illos Saxa vocatur
Unde sibi nomen Saxo traxisse putatur

And this Invention is so very agreeable to *Pontanus*, in his Treatise of the Origin of the *French*, that he does not scruple to say, † That the Swords that are in the Arms of *Saxony*, serve as an infallible Proof of the Truth of this Etymology. But it is but reasonable to forgive this great Man one Oversight, who very rarely makes any one who might without a Crime be ignorant that the Swords cross-wise in the Arms of *Saxony* are a Token of the Dignity of hereditary Great Marshal of the Empire, and that they particularly belong to the Arms of the Elector, who alone makes use of them, to the Exclusion of all the other Princes of the same House. It might be said with some greater Appearance of Reason, that whereas the ancient *Saxony* comprehended only the Lower *Saxony* and *Westphalia*, where the Pronunciation is not so strong as in *Thuringia* and *Misnia*, which at this time make the greatest part of the *Upper Saxony*, the true Name of these

People was formerly *Saffen*, and that they had given themselves this Name, because their Habitation was fix'd and determin'd, whereas the *Vandals*, *Sclavonians*, *Lombards*, and *Burgundians* chang'd theirs from time to time, after the Example of the Inhabitants of the most Northern Parts of *Asia*, from whence they came. But to speak ingenuously, it must be own'd that this People is so ancient, that there is not any Author that speaks of its Origin, and that it is impossible to give with any Truth the Etymology of its Name, tho' we will not condemn *Camden's* Opinion, who says, That the *Saxons* have their Name and Origin from the *Sace*, a People of *Asia* who leaving by little and little *Scythia* and *Sarmatia* in *Asia*, pass'd into *Europe* with the *Suevi*, *Massagetæ* and *Daci*, since it is observable that those People did for a long time preserve among themselves in *Europe*, the same Neighbourhood they had before in *Asia*. *Ptolomæus Alexandrinus*, who liv'd in the Time of the Emperor *Trajan*, is the first that speaks of them, but he does but barely name them.

Their first Habitation was in the *Peninsula*, which the Ancients call'd *Cimbrica Chersonesus*, where are *Jutland*, the Dutchies of *Slefwick* and of *Holstein*, *Suormaria* and the *Ditmark*, from whence they by degrees gain'd Ground upon the *Suevi* and the *French*, as the ones retir'd towards the *Upper German*, and the others pass'd the *Rhine*, to possess themselves of *Gaul*. They made themselves at first known by the Incursions and Pyracies they committed on the Coasts of the *Gauls*, which made them so considerable, that in the Year 428, in the time of the Emperor *Theodosius* the younger, the *Britons* call'd them to their Assistance against the *Picts*. † The *Saxons* assisted them so well, that they drove out both their Friends and their Enemies, and remain'd Masters of that part of the Island of *Britain*, which is still at this Day call'd *England*, on the account of the *English*, a *Saxon* People, who went thither under their Generals *Hengist* and *Horsa*, Brothers and Companions in their Fortune.

In the Year 451, the *Saxons* gave Proofs of their Valour, in the Battel in which *Attila* was defeated by *Ætius*. In 524 they assisted *Thierry* King of *Austrasia*, against *Ermenfroy* King of *Thuringia*, and in 630, *Bertold* their Prince was kill'd in the Battel the *French* gave them under the Conduct of *Dagobert* King of *Metz*. After this Loss they began to pay Tribute to *France*, but they were not entirely subdu'd but under * *Charlemagne*, who made an end of reducing them after a War of thirty three Years. † It is only from that time that we have any knowledge of the Inhabitants and of the Country of *Saxony* which had then for its Frontiers towards the East the *Elbe* and the *Sala*,

---
* *The Etymology of its Name* † *Lib. II. Chap. II* ‡ *The Saxons possess themselves of England*
* *Charlemagne subdues them* † *The Frontiers of ancient Saxony*

of the ELECTORS of the EMPIRE.

and for Neighbours on that fide the *Henedes* or *Vinides*, and the *Sorabs*, towards the *South*, the Mountains which feparate it from *Thuringia* and *Heſſe*, towards the *Weſt*, the *Rhine* from its Mouth to *Duis*, over againſt *Cologn*, and towards the *North*, the Ocean from the ſaid Mouth of the *Rhine* to the River *Eider*, in the Dutchy of *Holſtein*

‡ Its Inhabitants were divided into *Oſtphalians*, *Weſtphalians*, and *Angarians*. The *Oſtphalians* poſſeſs'd the Countrey, where are at preſent the Dutchies of *Brunſwick* and *Lunenburg*, between the *Elbe* and the *Weſer*, from the Sea to the Foreſt *Hercynia* The *Weſtphalians* and *Angarians* remain'd on this ſide the *Weſer*, the firſt, as being the moſt *Weſtern* of all the *Saxons*, towards the *Rhine*, where are the Dutchy of *Berg*, the County of *Merc*, the Imperial Town of *Dortmont*, part of the Dutchy of *Cleves*, the Counties of *Benthem* and of *Tecklenburg*, the Biſhoprick of *Munſter* and *Tranſiſulania*, and the others in the Place where are the Towns of *Wildeſhuſen*, *Minden*, and *Hervorden*, near which is the Town of *Engueren*, famous for the Tomb of *Wittikind the Great*, Prince of *Saxony*, and for having given a Name to this People, thoſe of *Lemgon*, *Oſnaburg*, and of *Soeſt*, the Counties of *Diepholt*, of *Waldec*, and of *Arnsberg*, and the Countrey of *Snrland*

The Modern *Saxony* is beyond Compariſon larger, and if we compriſe *Weſtphalia* therein, it makes without doubt above one third of *Germany*, ſince without this Province it forms two of the largeſt Circles of the Empire, which are thoſe of the *Upper* and *Lower Saxony* The Circle of the *Upper Saxony* comprehends the two Electorates of *Saxony* and *Brandenburg*, the Biſhopricks of *Meiſſen*, *Merſburg*, *Naubnrg*, *Brandenburg*, *Havelberg*, of *Lubus*, and of *Camin*, the Dutchy of *Pomerania*, the Abbeys of *Quedlinburg*, and of *Gerenrode*, whoſe Abbeſſes are Princeſſes of the Empire, the Marquiſate of *Miſnia*, and the Lantgraviate of *Thuringia*, the Principality of *Anhalt*, the Abbeys of *Walkenried* and *Salfeld*, the Counties of *Suartzenburg*, of *Mantsfelt*, of *Stolberg*, and of *Barby*, and ſeveral other Counties and Lordſhips which are falı'n to other Families In the Circle of the *Lower Saxony* are comprehended the King of *Denmark* as Duke of *Holſtein* and Lord of *Stormaria*, and of *Ditmark*, the other Dukes of *Holſtein*, the Archbiſhops of *Magdeburg* and of *Bremen*, the Biſhops of *Halberſtad*, *Hildeſheim*, *Lubeck*, *Suerin*, and *Ratzeburg*, the Dukes of *Brunſwick* and of *Lunenburg*, of *Mecklenburg* and *Saxe-Lauenburg*, and the Towns of *Lubeck*, *Mulhauſen*, *Goſlar* and *Northauſen*

We ſhall in this Chapter ſpeak only of the *Upper Saxony*, or rather of what the Elector of *Saxony* poſſeſſes there, and we ſhall reſerve, for the following Chapter, what relates to the Elector of *Brandenburg*, who has his Marquiſate in the ſame Circle

By the Frontiers we have juſt given to ancient *Saxony*, it appears that the *Upper* was not compris'd therein And indeed the Poſſeſſors of the Electoral *Saxony* did not make themſelves known under the Quality of Dukes of *Saxony*, but ſince the Princes of the Houſe of *Anhalt* have join'd thereto the *Lower Saxony*, after it had been confiſcated from *Henry the Lion* It is of that part chiefly that *Ludolphus* was Duke or Governor, who is ſaid to have been Nephew to *Wittikind the Great*, and who dy'd in the Year 869, leaving *Bruno* and *Tanquard*, who built the Town of *Brunſwick*, and *Otho* Father to *Henry*, who ſucceeded *An* 918 to *Conrade* I in the Empire, and dy'd *July* 2, 936 He left *Otho*, *Bruno*, who was Archbiſhop of *Cologn*, and Arch-Duke of *Lorrain*, and *Henry*, who had *Bavaria* for his Share, and left *Henry* and *Bruno* The firſt ſucceeded in *Bavaria*, and was Father of the Emperor *Henry* II, who dy'd without Iſſue, *July* 13, 1024 *Bruno* had his Portion in *Saxony*, and the Quality of Marquiſs *Bruno* II, his Son, was Father to *Ludolphus*, who left *Bruno* III, the Father of *Hetzel* or *Henry* Biſhop of *Hildeſheim*, *Herman*, Palatin of *Saxony*, who dy'd without Children, and *Otho*, who had his Portion on the River *Weſer*, and was Count of *Northeim* and of *Gottinguen* The Emperor *Henry* IV gave him, in the Year 1061, the Dutchy of *Bavaria*, but he loſt it, together with his Life, in the Battel he was engag'd in againſt the ſaid Emperor, *June* 9, 1075 Of the four Sons he left, there were only two that had Children But *Henry*, firnam'd the *Fat*, who was the eldeſt, had only Daughters, and *Egbert*, his younger Brother, one Son of the ſame Name, who dy'd without Iſſue in the Year 1090 *Gertrude*, the eldeſt Daughter of *Henry the Fat*, was marry'd to *Conrade*, Count Palatin of the *Rhine*, and the other, whoſe Name was *Rixa*, marry'd *Lotharius*, the Son of *Gebhard* Count of *Supplinburg*, who ſucceeded in the Year 1100, in that Part of the *Lower Saxony*, which the Poſterity of *Henry* Duke of *Bavaria*, Brother to the Emperor *Otho* I, had poſſeſs'd, to which he re-united ſince all the Inheritance of the Princes of the Houſe of *Billinguen*, in the manner we ſhall ſee hereafter

Otho ſucceeded to his Father in the Empire, and erected a new Dutchy of *Saxony*, in favour of *Herman* of *Billinguen*, Lord of *Stubikeſhorn*, to whom he gave that part of *Saxony* which had been conquer'd from the *Nortalbingnians*, and from the *Sclavi*, towards the Countrey of *Holſtein*, and where is at preſent that of the Dukes of *Saxe-Lanemburg* He was a Gentleman who had rais'd himſelf to this Dignity by his Merit, tho' it was at firſt only a Government, which the Emperor did not give him in Fief till the Year 966 We ſhall ſpeak of his Poſterity, when we ſhall have firſt acquainted the Reader, that *Otho* marry'd for firſt Wife *Judith*, or *Edgith*, Daughter to *Edward* I King of *England*, and for ſecond *Adelheida*, the Daughter to *Rodolphus* II. King of *Burgundy*, and Widow of *Lotharius* King of *Italy* He had by this ſecond Match *Otho* II, who ſucceeded him in the Empire, and who left when he dy'd, *December* 10, 985, *Otho* III, Emperor, and laſt Duke of *Saxony* of this Branch, who dy'd without Children, *January* 24, 1002 *Lutolphus*, the eldeſt Son of the Emperor *Otho* I, and of *Edgid* of *England*, dy'd before the Father, *September* 6, 957, leaving *Otho*, who was Duke of *Suabia* and *Franconia*, and Father to *Bruno*, who was Pope under the Name of *Gregory* V,

‡ *Its Iphobitants*

to

to *William* Bishop of *Strasburg*, and to *Henry* and *Conrade*, the first of which had a Son nam'd *Conrade*, who was chosen Emperor after the Death of *Henry* II, and his Posterity ended but in *Henry* V, who dy'd without Children, *May* 23, 1123 This we say with *Wippo*, a contemporary Author, and Chaplain to the Emperor *Conrade* II, in Opposition to the Opinion of those who make him come of the House of *Franconia*, and who, contrary to the Truth of History, speak of *Henry* II, as of the last Emperor of the House of *Saxony*

Herman of *Billinguen*, who gave beginning to another Family, as we said before, join'd to that part of *Saxony* which he possess'd with the Title of a Dutchy, the Countrey which is at present the Dutchy of *Lunenburg*, and several other Lands and Rights on this side the *Elbe*, and dy'd *April* 1, 973, leaving for Issue *Benno*, the Father of *Bernard*, who dy'd in the Year 1062, and left amongst others *Ortulphus* or *Otho*, Father to *Magnus*, who marry'd *Sophia*, Daughter to *Geise* King of *Hungary*, and had by her *Heilike*, who was was marry'd to *Otho* of *Ballenstad*, Count of *Anhalt*, and *Wulsild*, who marry'd *Henry* the *Black*, Duke of *Bavaria*

* *Magnus* dying in the Year 1106, without leaving any Male-Issue, the Emperor *Henry* V, who pretended that the Dutchy was escheated to the Empire, and who otherwise had no great Reason to be satisfy'd with the deceas'd, gave the Lower *Saxony* to *Lotharius* of *Supplinburg*, who was already in Possession of part thereof, as we said before † *Lotharius* was call'd to the Empire after the Death of *Henry* V, and gave *Gertrude*, his only Daughter, in Marriage, with *Saxony*, to *Henry the Proud*, Duke of *Bavaria*, who by that Means re-united these two great Estates in his Person, in which he maintain'd himself peaceably under the Protection of the Emperor his Father-in-Law But *Lotharius* dying, *December* 6, 1137, and *Henry* having pretended to the Empire, *Albert* the *Bear*, Prince of *Anhalt*, Son to *Otho* of *Ballenstad*, and so Grandson to *Magnus* the last Duke of *Saxony*, of the Male Posterity of *Herman* of *Billinguen*, as well as *Henry*, desir'd a Partition, and made so good an Use of the Jealousy the Emperor *Conrade* III had conceiv'd of his Competitor, that he found a mean to seize the Lower *Saxony* *Henry* retook it from him, but finding himself disgrac'd by the Emperor, driven out of *Bavaria*, and in Danger of losing *Saxony* again, he dy'd with Grief, *September* 19, 1139. The Emperor *Frederick* I, who succeeded *Conrade* III his Unkle, *March* 4, 1152, began his Reign with restoring Tranquillity to the Empire, by the Accommodation he made between *Henry the Lion*, Son to *Henry the Proud*, on the one part, and *Henry* of *Austria*, and *Albert the Bear* on the other. He caus'd *Bavaria* and *Saxony* to be restor'd to the first, having first lopp'd off *Austria* from the one, as we said in the foregoing Chapter, and from the other the Countrey of *Brandenburg*, which he erected into an hereditary Marquisate, in favour of *Albert the Bear* *Henry*, instead of acknowledging the Bounty the Emperor had

shewn him, abandon'd him at the Siege he had laid before *Alexandria*, in the Year 1175, and thereby oblig'd him to resent his Ingratitude, at the Instances of most of the Princes of *Germany*, who complain'd of his Violence, whereupon he was summon'd to appear, found guilty of Contumacy, and put in the Ban of the Empire, and had all his Estate confiscated All his Neighbours benefited by his Disgrace *Otho* of *Wittelspach* had *Bavaria*, ‡ and *Bernard* Prince of *Anhalt*, Son to *Albert the Bear*, had *Saxony*, to which he then join'd the Town of *Wittemberg*, with the Countrey which at this Day makes the Electorate of *Saxony* The Archbishop of *Cologn* annex'd to his Crosier what his Successors still possess in *Westphalia*, those of *Magdeburg*, and of *Bremen*, took what lay convenient for them in the Neighbourhood

Henry indeed made his Peace after some Years, by the Mediation of the King of *England* his Father-in-Law, but he obtain'd only the Restitution of that Countrey which is known at this Day under the Name of the Dutchies of *Brunswick* and *Lunenburg*, the Title of Duke of *Saxony* remaining to the Princes of the House of *Anhalt*, altho of all this rich Spoil there remain'd to them but a very small Portion of *Saxony* on the other side of the *Elbe*, which became the Share of a younger Brother of the same House *Bernard* was so, and had left, by the Partition which had been made of his Father's Inheritance, the Marquisate of *Brandenburg* to *Otho* his eldest Brother, of whom we shall have Occasion to speak in the following Chapter He had by *Judith*, the Daughter of *Canutus* Duke of *Sleswic*, who was the Son of *Canutus* IV King of *Denmark*, *Albert* and *Henry*, being Common Father to the Princes of *Anhalt*. *Albert*, the eldest Son of *Bernard*, marry'd *Helen*, Daughter to *Otho the Infant*, first Duke of *Brunswick*, and had by her *Albert* II, *John*, of whom are descended the Dukes of the Lower *Saxony*, who are generally known by the Title of *Saxe-Lauenburg*, *Rodolphus*, (who had amongst other Children *Albert*, Great Master of *Rhodes*) and *Frederick* Bishop of *Merseburg*

Albert II. had, by *Agnes* of *Habsburg*, Daughter to the Emperor *Rodolphus* I, *Rodolphus*, who had by *Judith*, Daughter to *Otho the Tall*, Marquis of *Brandenburg*, *Otho*, and by *Agnes* of *Rupin*, his third Wife, *Wenceslas* *Otho* left *Albert* the third, who was kill'd by a Stone from a Sling, at the Siege of the Castle of *Rieblinguen*, *June* 28, 1385, and left but one Daughter, nam'd *Helen*, who marry'd *Girard* Count of *Hoye*

Wenceslas had by *Cecilia* of *Carrara*, Daughter to *Francis* Prince of *Padua*, amongst others, *Wenceslas* Archbishop of *Magdeburg*, *Rodolphus* III, who saw all his Children die before him, of whom two, viz *Wenceslas* and *Sigismund*, were bury'd under the Ruins of a Tower in the Town of *Suentz*, *An* 1406, and *Albert* IV, who had none at all, and dy'd in the Year 1422.

The Succession being open by his Death, *Frederick*, Marquiss and Elector of *Brandenburg*, took Possession of the *Upper Saxony*, in

---

* *Saxony* enters into the House of *Supplinburg*
‡ *Saxony* enters into the House of *Anhalt*

† *It goes on of as to enter into that of the Guelfs*

the

the Name of the Emperor *Sigifmund*, to the Prejudice of the Right of *Eric* V, Duke of *Saxe-Lauenburg*, who being defcended in a direct Male-Line from *John*, the younger Son of *Albert* I, and Brother to *Albert* III, Dukes of *Saxony*, pretended that the Electoral Durchy of *Saxony* belong'd to him, as to the neareft Male Heir of the deceafed But the Emperor, taking into Confideration that the Countrey ftood in need of a powerful Prince, who could defend it againft the Incurfions of the *Bohemians*, who had taken Arms for Religion, and having withal a Mind to acknowledge the Servaces *Frederick the Warrior*, Marquifs of *Mifnia*, had done him againft thofe very Enemies, he gave him the Inveftiture of the Electoral *Saxony*, *January* 6, 1423 *Eric* oppos'd it, receiv'd the Inveftiture of the Office of hereditary Marefchal of the Bifhop of *Bamberg*, and went in Perfon to the Emperor who was then in *Hungary*, to try to obtain the Electoral Dignity and the Dutchy of *Saxony*, and to reprefent to him his Right, founded on the *Golden Bull*, and acknowledg'd by the Letters Patents, by which the Emperor had affur'd him of the Succeffion from the Year 1414 All the Comfort he receiv'd, was, that the Emperor told him, That he had believ'd he might difpofe of the Electorate of *Saxony*, as of a Fief efcheated to the Empire, but if he could be made fenfible that the Fief was not efcheatable, he would fecure him his Right, and would do him Juftice, when he fhould have made out his Pretenfions to the Electoral College, to whom he referr'd the Cognizance of the Matter In the mean time he confirm'd the Inveftiture he had given to *Frederick* of *Mifnia*, by other Letters dated on *St Peter*'s Day, 1425 The Electors heard the Reafons of the Parties, tho' they would not determin the Difference, but contented themfelves with remitting them to the Emperor This concluded the Affair, the Marquifs of *Mifnia* was in Poffeffion of the Electorate, and it was in a manner impoffible to difpoffefs him, for which Reafon *Sigifmund*, who found every Day new Pretexts to elude the Purfuit of *Eric*, referr'd him in the Year 1426 to the States of the Empire, who were to meet at *Nuremberg* But as the Emperor did not come thither in Perfon, and there were but two Electors prefent, the others would not meddle in the Matter, and gave *Eric* very well to underftand, that he had nothing to hope for He afterwards addrefs'd himfelf to the Pope, *Eugenius* IV, who gave him Letters to the Council of *Bafil*, to whom he referr'd the Cognizance of this Caufe But the Emperor was fo offended at the Proceedings of the one and the other, that he would no longer give the Title of Duke of *Saxony* to *Eric*, but ftyl'd him only Duke of *Lauenburg*, and wrote fo forcible a Letter to the Council which had given him the Quality of Elector, That the Fathers would no longer be concern'd in the thing which they referr'd to the Emperor, to be by him determin'd in fix Months *Eric* dy'd in that Time, without Children, and his Brother *Bernard*, feeing that all the Pains the deceafed had taken had been to no purpofe, acquiefc'd to what had been done, and was contented with the *Lower Saxony*. *John*, his Son, was for renewing the Profecutions under the Emperor *Frede-*

rick III, but he did not fucceed better than his Unkle, fo that the *Upper Saxony*, together with the Electoral Dignity, remain'd in the Houfe of *Mifnia*

There is room to wonder that the Emperor *Sigifmund* would transfer the Electoral Dignity from the Houfe of *Anhalt* to that of *Mifnia*, while there were ftill Heirs in the firft, contrary to the exprefs Difpofition of the *Golden Bull*, which calls to the Succeffion of the Principality, and of the Flectorate, the neareft Relation by the Father's fide, how remote foever he may be, and that by virtue of the Inveftiture given to the firft Acquirer, who receiv'd it in the Behalf of all his Pofterity *in infinitum* So that if the Emperor *Frederick* I, when he gave *Saxony* to *Bernard* Prince of *Anhalt*, did annex thereto the Electoral Dignity, it was not in the Power of *Sigifmund* to difpofe thereof; not only to the Prejudice of *Saxe-Lauenburg*, but alfo without wronging the Princes of *Anhalt*, fince they would all have been compris'd in the firft Inveftiture And both the ones and the others would have had great Reafon to complain of the Injuftice *Sigifmund* would have done them But we have prov'd elfewhere, that the Electoral Dignity was not appropriated to the Principalities to which it is at this Day annex'd, till a long Time after the Death of *Frederick* I And fo, as the Princes of *Anhalt*, and the Dukes of *Saxe-Lauenburg*, had already ftruck into Branches, and form'd particular Families, a great while before the Dignity was fix'd to *Saxony*, they could not complain of the Emperor's difpofing thereof, as of a Fief efcheated to the Empire, fince they were not compris'd in the firft Inveftiture

The Princes of the Houfe of *Mifnia* add, in their Behalf, another Reafon, and fay, that the Emperor *Sigifmund* did them Juftice, in reftoring *Saxony* to them, which belongs to them as Princes defcended in a direct Male Line from *Wittikind the Great*, Prince of *Saxony*, to wit, from *Wittikind* II, his younger Son, the Father of *Ditgrem*, and Grandfather of *Ditmar*, who left amongft other Sons *Thierry*, Count of *Mersburg*

Dedon, Son to *Thierry* I, dy'd in the Year 1009, and left *Thierry* II, who dy'd in the Year 1034, and left feveral Children, amongft whom was *Dedon* II, whofe Male Pofterity ended in his Sons, and *Timon*, the Father of *Conrade the Great*, Count of *Wittin* and of *Meriburg*, who dy'd *February* 5, 1156, leaving by *Lutgard* of *Suabia*, Sifter to the Emperor *Conrade* III, *Otho* and *Thierry* III. This laft had by two Wives five Sons, but their Pofterity did not reach beyond the third Generation *Otho* Count of *Wettin*, and Marquifs of *Mifnia*, was firnam'd the *Rich*, becaufe that in his Time the Silver Mines began to be difcover'd, of which we fhall fay fomething in the Clofe of this Chapter He dy'd *February* 18, 1189, leaving by *Avoye* of *Anhalt*, Daughter to *Albert the Bear*, Marquifs of *Brandenburg*, *Albert*, who dy'd without Iffue, *June* 24, 1195, and *Thierry* IV, Father to *Henry the Illuftrious*

Henry, the Son of *Thierry* IV, Marquifs of *Mifnia*, and of *Judith*, Daughter to *Herman*, Langgrave of *Thuringia*, being very young when his Father dy'd, *Lewis* VI, Lantgrave of *Thuringia*, took care to educate him in his Court

Lewis

Lewis dying in the Year 1227, his Son *Herman* succeeded him, but he dy'd soon after without Issue, and left *Thuringia* to his Unkle *Henry*, Brother to *Judith*, and so Unkle by the Mother's side to *Henry the Illustrious*. *Henry*, Landgrave of *Thuringia*, dying also without Children *February* 16, 1248, the Succession was contested by *Henry the Illustrious*, who was the Son of a Sister of the two Landgraves, *Lewis* and *Henry*, and Grandson to *Herman* I, on the one part, and by *Henry*, Duke of *Brabant*, the Son of *Sophia*, who was Daughter to *Lewis* II, of the other. *Sophia* carry'd her Son upon the Place, and made an Alliance with *Albert*, Duke of *Brunswick*, but she gain'd nothing by so doing; for the Success of their Arms not answering their Hopes, she made an Agreement with *Henry the Illustrious*, and left him *Thuringia*, which enter'd by that Means into the House of *Misnia* and the Countrey of *Hesse* remain'd to *Henry* of *Brabant*, on Condition that the Male Line failing in one of the two Families, the other should succeed and it is this Treaty that begins the Alliance of mutual Succession, which still subsists between the Houses of *Saxony* and of *Hesse*. *Henry*, Marquiss of *Misnia*, had by *Constance*, Daughter to *Leopold* VII, Duke of *Austria*, *Albert* and *Thierry* V, and dy'd *February* 25, 1288. *Thierry* V had a Son nam'd *Frederick*, who dy'd without Children in the Year 1291, and two Daughters, Nuns at *Weissenfels*.

Albert marry'd *Marguerit* of *Suabia*, Daughter to the Emperor *Frederick* II. But falling in love with a young Lady who was in his Wifes Retinue, he resolv'd to get rid of the one, in order to enjoy the other with the greater Freedom, and so often attempted on his Wifes Life, that she was forc'd to make her escape. She went out of the House on foot in the Night, on *June* 24, 1270, and retir'd to *Francfort*, where she dy'd *April* 18, the Year following. The bad Usage he shew'd his Wife, and his Severity to the Sons of this first Match, whom he was for disinheriting, gave him the sirname of *Unnatural*, and drew upon him the Arms of his Children, who drove him out of his Estates, and compell'd him to retire to *Erfort*, where he dy'd in the Year 1314.

Frederick, his eldest Son, only left Posterity. He was sirnam'd the *Bitten*, because his Mother being resolv'd to retire, and not being able to take her Children along with her, they being very young, bit him on the Cheek, thereby to leave him the last and perpetual Marks of her Tenderness, which her Tears and Kisses could not sufficiently express. He dy'd *April* 25, 1325, and left *Frederick*, sirnam'd the *Grave*, who marry'd *Mahault* of *Bavaria*, Daughter to the Emperor *Lewis* IV, and of *Beatrix* of *Poland*, and had by her *Frederick the Valiant*, *Balthasar*, who had for Portion *Thuringia*, and left a Son nam'd *Frederick*, who dy'd without Issue in the Year 1439, *Lewis*, Bishop of *Halberstad*, and Archbishop of *Mayence* and of *Magdeburg*, *William*, who had no Children, and *Sigismund*, Bishop of *Mersburg*.

Frederick the Valiant, marry'd in 1448, *Catherine*, Daughter to *Henry* XII, Count of *Henneberg*, who brought him in Marriage the Town of *Coburg* in *Franconia*, and had by her *Frederick*, sirnam'd the *Warrior*, who introduc'd the Electoral Dignity of *Saxony* into the House of *Misnia*. He dy'd *January* 5, 1428, and left, by *Catherine*, the Daughter of *Henry* Duke of *Brunswick* and *Lunenburg*, *Frederick* II, *William*, who left only two Daughters, and *Sigismund*, Bishop of *Wurtsburg*.

Frederick II, second Elector of *Saxony* of the House of *Misna*, call'd the *Peaceable*, marry'd *Marguerit* of *Austria*, Sister to the Emperor *Frederick* III, and dy'd *September* 7, 1464. He had amongst other Children two Sons, *Ernest* and *Albert*, whom we shall make known in their Posterity, which still subsists at this Day.

Ernest, the eldest Son of *Frederick* II, succeeded his Father in the Electorate, and had by *Elizabeth*, Daughter to *Albert* III, Duke of *Bavaria*, at *Munichen*, *Frederick* III, who succeeded in the Electoral Dignity, but he never marry'd, and dy'd *May* 5, 1525, *John Ernest*, Archbishop of *Magdeburg*, and Bishop of *Halberstad*, and *Albert*, Archbishop and Elector of *Mayence*.

John, Son to *Ernest*, succeeded *Frederick* III, his Brother, in the Electoral Dignity, and in the Year 1531, he oppos'd the Election of *Ferdinand* I. It was he that presented to the Emperor *Charles* V the Confession of Faith of the Protestants of *Germany*, which is commonly call'd the Confession of *Augsburg*, and that took *Luther* into his particular Protection. He dy'd *August* 16, 1532, leaving, by *Sophia*, the Daughter of *Magnus* III, Duke of *Mecklenburg*, his first Wife, *John Frederick*, and *John Ernest*, who had his Portion at *Coburg*, but he dy'd without Children.

John Frederick, the Son of *John*, was born at *Torgan June* 30, 1503, and succeeded to his Father in the Electorate of *Saxony*. In the Year 1527, he marry'd *Sybylla*, Daughter to *John* III, Duke of *Cleves*, and to *Mary*, Heiress of *Juliers*, and it was mention'd in the Contract of Marriage, that if the Male Line happen'd to fail in the House of *Cleves*, that of *Saxony* should succeed therein. It is on this, that the Dukes of *Saxony* found the Pretensions they have to the Inheritance of *Cleves* and *Juliers*, against the Elector of *Brandenburg*, and the *Palatin* of *Neuburg*. In the Year 1536, he made himself Head of the Confederacy of *Smalcalden*, in which were engag'd with him, *Philip*, *Ernest* and *Francis*, Dukes of *Brunswick* and *Lunenburg*, *Ulric*, Duke of *Wirtemberg*, *Philip*, Landgrave of *Hesse*, *Barmin* and *Philip*, Dukes of *Pomerania*, *Wolfgang*, *John*, *George* and *Joachim*, Princes of *Anhalt*, *Gebhard* and *Albert*, Counts of *Mansfelt*, and the Free-Cities and *Hanse*-Towns, *Strasburg*, *Augsburg*, *Constance*, *Ulm*, *Eslingen*, *Reutlinguen*, *Memmingen*, *Kempten*, *Lindau*, *Biberach*, *Isne*, *Magdeburg*, *Bremen*, *Brunswick*, *Goslar*, *Hannover*, *Gottingen*, *Eimbeck*, *Hamburgh*, *Lubeck* and *Minden*: but having taken Arms against the Emperor *Charles* V, he was defeated in the Battel which was fought near *Mulberg* on the *Elbe*, *April* 24, 1547, in which he remain'd Prisoner with the Emperor, who depriv'd him of the Electoral Dignity, and invested therewith *Maurice*, Duke of *Saxony*, his Relation. He dy'd *March* 3, 1554, leaving Issue, *John Frederick* I, *John Frederick* II, who never marry'd, and dy'd *October* 31, 1565, and *John William*.

of the ELECTORS of the EMPIRE.

John Frederick, the eldest Son of the Elector of the same Name, having given Retreat to *William* of *Grumbach* and his Accomplices, who had murder'd *Melchior Zobel*, Bishop of *Wurtzburg*, was put in the Ban of the Empire. *John William* his Brother, and *Augustus*, Elector of *Saxony*, executed the Sentence of Proscription, besieg'd him in *Gotha*, and compell'd him to surrender at Discretion, after four Months Siege. He was carry'd Prisoner to *Dresden*, and from thence to *Vienna* and *Presburg*, and at last to *Neustad*, where he dy'd *May* 9, 1595, after nineteen Years of Captivity. He left Issue, by *Elizabeth* of *Bavaria*, Daughter to *Frederick* III, Elector Palatin, *John Casimir*, who had his Portion at *Coburg*, and dy'd without Children *July* 16, 1633, and *John Ernest*, who had his at *Eisenach*, where he dy'd also without Issue, *October* 23, 1638. The Inheritance of these two Brothers was divided between the Dukes of *Altemburg* and *Weimar*, descended from *John William*, the younger Son of the Elector *John Frederick*, who dy'd *March* 12, 1573, leaving by *Susanna Dorothea* of *Bavaria*, Daughter to *Frederick* III, Elector *Palatin*, *Frederick William*, and *John*.

Frederick William, the eldest Son of *John William*, had his Portion at *Altemburg*. He marry'd on *May* 5, 1583, for first Wife *Sophia*, Daughter to *Christopher*, Duke of *Wirtemberg*, and *Anne Mary* of *Brandenburg*; but all the Issue he had by this Match being dead, except two Daughters, the one of which dy'd a Maid in the Year 1626, and the other who was Abbess of *Quedlinburg*, *February* 10, 1645, and the Mother dying on *July* 2, 1590, he marry'd *August* 29, 1595, for second Wife, *Anne Mary* of *Bavaria*, the Daughter of *Philip Lewis*, Count Palatin of the *Rhine* at *Neuburg*, and of *Anne* of *Cleves*, and dy'd *July* 7, 1602. The Children of this second Bed are, 1 *John Philip*, who was born *January* 25, 1597, and marry'd on *October* 24, 1618, to *Elizabeth*, the Daughter of *Henry Julius*, Duke of *Brunswick* and *Lunenburg*, and dy'd *April* 11, 1639, leaving *Elizabeth Sophia*, who was marry'd on *October* 24, 1636, to *Ernest*, Duke of *Saxe-Weimar*, at *Gotha*, 2 *Frederick*, who was born *February* 12, 1569, and was kill'd *October* 25, 1625, near *Hannover*, (by an Imperial Party) being in the Service of the King of *Denmark*, 3 *John William*, who was also in the Service of the King of *Denmark*, and dy'd without Issue on *December* 2, 1642, 4 *Frederick William* II, 5 *Anne Sophia*, marry'd to *Frederick*, Duke of *Munsterberg* in *Silesia*. And, 6 *Dorothy*, who was marry'd to *Albert*, Duke of *Saxony* at *Eisenach*.

Frederick William II, is the only one of all the Brothers that is alive at present. He was born *February* 22, 1603, above six Months after the Death of his Father, and marry'd on *September* 18, 1638, for first Wife, *Sophia Elizabeth* of *Brandenburg*, Daughter to *Christian William*, heretofore Administrator of *Magdeburg*, by whom he had no Children. His second Wife, who is still living, is *Magdalen Sibylla*, Daughter to *John George*, Elector of *Saxony*, and to *Magdalen Sibylla* of *Brandenburg*, and the Widow of *Christian*, Prince of *Denmark*, eldest Brother to the present King, by whom he has several Children.

John, the second Son of *John William*, was born *May* 22, 1570, and had for Portion the Town of *Weimar*. He marry'd on *January* 8, 1593, *Mary Dorothy*, the Daughter of *Joachim Ernest*, Prince of *Anhalt*, and of *Eleonora* of *Wirtemberg*, and dy'd *October* 31, 1605, leaving Issue, 1 *John Ernest*, who was born *February* 21, 1594, he did not marry, and dy'd *December* 4, 1626, in *Silesia*, where he commanded a Body of Men against the Emperor *Ferdinand* II, 2 *Frederick*, who was born *March* 1, 1596, and was kill'd *August* 19, 1622, in the Battel of *Fleury*, commanding a Regiment under Count *Mansfelt*, 3 *William*, 4 *Albert*, who was born *July* 27, 1599. He marry'd on *June* 24, 1633, *Dorothy*, Daughter to *Frederick William* Duke of *Saxony*, at *Altemburg*, but he had no Children by her, and dy'd *December* 20, 1644, 5 *John Frederick*, who was born *September* 19, 1600, and dy'd *October* 12, 1628. His Brothers had caus'd him to be shut up in a House at *Weimar*, which is still uninhibited, 6 *Ernest*, 7 *Frederick William*, who was born *February* 7, 1603, and dy'd *August* 16, 1619, And, 8 *Bernard*, who was born *August* 6, 1604, and dy'd *July* 8, 1639, at *Neuburg* on the *Rhine*. He was the greatest Prince that *Germany* has produc'd for many Ages, and would have rais'd the Glory of his House, had he liv'd but a few Years longer.

2 *William*, third Son to *John*, is living still at *Weimar*. He was born *April* 11, 1598, and marry'd on *May* 25, 1625, *Eleonora Dorothea*, the Daughter of *John George*, Duke of *Anhalt* at *Dessau*, and of *Dorothy* of *Mansfelt*, by whom he has several Children.

3 *Ernest*, his Brother, was born *December* 25, 1601. He has his Portion at *Gotha*, and marry'd on *October* 24, 1636, *Elizabeth Sophia*, the Daughter of *John Philip*, Duke of *Saxony* at *Altemburg*, and of *Elizabeth* of *Brunswick*, by whom he has five or six Sons, and three or four Daughters.

Let us now run back to *Albert*, the younger Son of *Frederick* II, Elector of *Saxony*, and of *Margueret* of *Austria*, and let us see how the Electoral Dignity pass'd to his Posterity, to the Prejudice of that of the Eldest. *Albert* was born *August* 1, 1443, and marry'd in the Year 1459, *Zedene*, the Daughter of *George* of *Podiebrach*, King of *Bohemia*. The Emperor *Maximilian* I, gave him, under the Title of Hereditary Governor, that part of *Frise*, which at this Day makes one of the United Provinces, between the Rivers *Isel* and *Ems*. He dy'd *September* 12, 1500, leaving Issue, *George*, who had no Children, *Frederick*, Master of the *Teutonic* Order in *Prussia*, and since Conjutor to the Archbishop of *Magdeburg*, and *Henry*.

Henry was born *March* 16, 1473, succeeded his Brother *George* in the Year 1539, and reform'd Religion in his Countrey. He dy'd *August* 18, 1541, leaving, by *Catherine*, the Daughter of *Magnus* III, Duke of *Mecklenburg*, and of *Sophia* of *Pomerania*, *Maurice* and *Augustus*.

Maurice, the eldest Son of *Henry*, was born *March* 21, 1521. He sided with the Emperor *Charles* V, against the Confederates of *Smalcalden*, and against the Interest of his Religion. He receiv'd for recompence, from him, the Electoral Dignity, which had been confiscated from

6 T   *John*

John Frederick, and he was invested therewith on *February* 24, 1548 In the Year 1550, he besieg'd the Town of *Magdeburg* in the Name of the Empire but he made an Agreement with it, after a Siege of fourteen Months, thereby to have it in his Power to make use of his Army for the Liberty of *Philip*, Lantgrave of *Hesse*, his Father-in-law He forc'd the Emperor to retire from *Inspruck* in disorder, and oblig'd him to grant to the Protestants the Advantages they obtain'd by the Treaty of *Passau*, which still holds the Rank of a perpetual Edict for the Affairs of Religion in the Empire On *July* 9, 1553, he gave Battel to *Albert*, Marquiss of *Brandenburg*, and gain'd over him a complete Victory but he therein receiv'd a Musket Shot, of which he dy'd three Days after, leaving only one Daughter nam'd *Anne*, who was second Wife to *William* of *Nassau*, and Mother to *Maurice*, Prince of *Orange*

Augustus was born *July* 31, 1526, and succeeded his Brother in the Electoral Dignity In the Year 1554, he came to an Agreement with the Sons of *John Frederick* Elector, in reference to the Differences he might have with them, concerning the Translation of the Electoral Dignity, and the Lands thereon depending He also renew'd with them conjoyntly, the Treaty of mutual Succession between the Houses of *Saxony* and *Hesse* In 1558, he confirm'd the Election of *Ferdinand* I, and was personally present at the Elections of *Maximilian* II, and of *Rodolphus* his Son In 1576, he yielded to *Joachim Frederick*, Administrator of *Magdeburg*, the Viscountship of the Town, and the Rights that depend thereon, referving only the Title to himself In his time dy'd also without Children *George Ernest*, Count of *Henneberg*, and so the Earldom came to the House of *Saxony*, by virtue of the Treaty of mutual Succession, of which we have spoken in Chap II *Augustus* dy'd *February* 11, 1586, leaving by *Anne*, the Daughter of *Christian* III, King of *Denmark*, and of *Dorothy* of *Saxe-Lauenburg*, *Christian* I

Christian, Elector of *Saxony*, was born *October* 29, 1560, and marry'd on *April* 21, 1582, *Sophia*, the Daughter of *John George*, Elector of *Brandenburg*, and of *Sabina* also of *Brandenburg* He dy'd *September* 25, 1591, and left *Christian* II, *John George*, and *Augustus* who dy'd without Issue on *January* 15, 1616

Christian II succeeded his Father in the Electorate, and marry'd *Avoye*, the Daughter of *Frederick* II, King of *Denmark* but he had no Children by her, and dy'd *July* 15, 1611.

John George, younger Son of *Christian* I, and of *Sophia* of *Brandenburg*, was born *March* 5, 1585, and succeeded his Brother in the Electoral Dignity On *September* 16, 1640, he marry'd for first Wife *Elizabeth Sibylla*, the Daughter of *Frederick*, Duke of *Wirtemberg*, who dying without Issue on *January* 20, 1606, he marry'd on *July* 17, 1607, for second Wife, *Magdalen Sibylla*, Daughter to *Albert Frederick*, Marquiss of *Brandenburg* and Duke of *Prussia*, and to *Mary Eleonor* of *Juliers*, and dy'd *October* 18, 1656 The Children that surviv'd him, and are still living, are,

1 *John George*, who was born *May* 13, 1613, and marry'd on *November* 13, 1638, *Magdalen Sibylla*, the Daughter of *Christian*, Marquiss of *Brandenburg* at *Anspach*, and of *Mary* of *Brandenburg*, by whom he has a Son nam'd *John George*, born *September* 20, 1647 It is this Prince who is at present Elector of *Saxony*,

2 *Augustus*, who was born *August* 13, 1614, and was made Administrator of *Magdeburg* by the Treaty of *Prague* in the Year 1634, but forasmuch as this Archbishoprick has been converted into a Dutchy by the Treaty of *Munster*, in favour of the Elector of *Brandenburg*, who is to succeed therein after the Death of *Augustus*, the Elector his Brother has been oblig'd to assign him a Portion elsewhere He has since the Year 1646, marry'd *Anne Mary*, the Daughter of *Albert Frederick*, Duke of *Meklenburg* at *Suerin*, and of *Anne Mary* of *Ostfrise*, by whom he has several Children amongst others *John Adolphus*, born *November* 2, 1648, *Augustus*, born *December* 3, 1650, and *Christian*, born *January* 25, 1652,

3 *Christian*, who was born *October* 27, 1616, and marry'd in *November* 1650, *Christina*, the Daughter of *Philip*, Duke of *Holstein* at *Glucsburg*, and of *Sophia Avoye* of *Saxe-Lauenburg*, by whom he has Children,

4 *Maurice*, who was born *March* 28, 1619, he had marry'd for first Wife *Sophia Avoye*, the Daughter of *Philip*, Duke of *Holstein* at *Glucsburg*, and of *Sophia Avoye* of *Saxe-Lauenburg*, who dy'd in the Year 1657 On *July* 13, 1656, he marry'd for second Wife *Dorothy Mary*, the Daughter of *William*, Duke of *Saxony* at *Weimar*,

5 *Sophia Eleonora*, who was born *November* 21, 1609, and was marry'd on *April* 1, 1627, to *George*, Lantgrave of *Hesse Darmstadt*,

6 *Mary Elizabeth*, who was born *November* 22, 1610, and was marry'd on *February* 21, 1630, to *Frederick*, Duke of *Holstein Gottorp*,

7 *Magdalen Sibylla*, who was born *December* 23, 1617, and was marry'd in 1634 to *Christian*, the eldest Son of *Christian* IV, King of *Denmark*, who dying *June* 4, 1647, she marry'd in 1652, for second Husband, *Frederick William* II, Duke of *Saxony* at *Altemburg*

The Elector has made a Partition with his Brothers, and has yielded to them part of *Lusatia*, and of what the Father possess'd in *Thuringia*, and in the County of *Henneberg*, together with the Bishopricks of *Naumburg* and of *Mersburg*, so that if they have all Children, as it is very likely they will, the Electoral Branch of *Saxony* will be subdivided into several other Branches, which will make it least seven with that of *Altemburg*, (where there is but one at present) and that of *Weimar*, in which there are two, the one at *Weimar*, and the other at *Gotha* These last, altho' descended from *John*, a younger Brother of *John William*, Grandfather to the Duke of *Altemburg*, have always murmur'd at the Translation of the Electoral Dignity, from the Person of *John Frederick*, to that of *Maurice* and this Branch has produc'd such great Princes, that the Electors have believ'd that they might one Day make good their Pretensions to the Electorate It might be said with Truth, that the strong Jealousy the late Elector had of the Conduct of the Protestant Army, which was given to Duke *Bernard* of *Weimar*, after the Death of the late King of *Sweden*, was one of the greatest Causes of his Change, and of the Treaty he made with the Emperor at *Prague*, *An* 1635

And

And in effect the Princes of the eldest Branch maintain, That the Translation of the Electoral Dignity, made by the Emperor Charles V, is faulty in all its Circumstances, and that if it ought to subsist, it can only be by virtue of the Treaty of Naumburg. For Maurice dying in the Year 1553, John Frederick, who had resum'd the Quality of Elector, considering that the Emperor Charles V, and Ferdinand his Brother (who seem'd inclin'd to favour this Enterprize, out of Hatred to Maurice, who had us'd them ill, and on the account of the Umbrage they took from the Alliance Augustus his Brother had lately contracted with the King of Denmark) countenanc'd his Interest but only with a Design to set the Princes of Saxony at Variance amongst themselves, and thereby to ruin the whole House, he came to an Agreement with Augustus by a Treaty which was made at Naumburg in the Month of February 1554. John Frederick and his three Sons, who were all at Age, renounc'd by that Treaty for themselves and for their Heirs to the Electoral Dignity, upon Condition that the Father should, during his own Life, take the Title of Elector born. And to recompence in some measure those Princes for the Loss they sustain'd, Augustus yielded to them some Towns and Territories, the Revenue whereof amounted to pretty near that of the Electoral Saxony. Ferdinand King of the Romans, Christian III, King of Denmark, Joachim Elector of Brandenburg, William Duke of Juliers, Philip Duke of Pomerania, Philip Lantgrave of Hesse, and the Deputies of the States of all the Towns of Saxony were present at this Transaction, and sign'd it. But if the Electoral Dignity is appropriated to the Heirs without Reserve, by virtue of the first Acquirer and by the Provision of the Prince who gave the first Investiture thereof, it is certain that this Transaction could not alienate a Right, which is acquir'd to all Posterity in infinitum.

After all, the Dukes of Altemburg have constantly adher'd to the Interest of the Electoral Court of Dresden, but those of Weimar have express'd a little more Vigour. Of the eight Brothers, four have dy'd with their Arms in their Hand against a House that has ruin'd theirs and of the four others, two were indispos'd in their Health, and of the two others who are still living, the eldest has for a long time commanded the Armies in the Quality of Lieutenant General under the King of Sweden, and the other who lives now at Gotha, commanded a Regiment of Horse in the same War, under Duke Bernard h s Brother

As for the Elector himself, it is certain that he will have no passive Vote in the future Election, because his Religion excludes him, tho' otherwise he possesses all the necessary Qualities for it. He has so openly declar'd for the House of Austria, that it cannot be doubted that he will give his Suffrage to the King of Bohemia, and that he will employ all his Ability of Wit, Credit and Friends for his Election.

The Electors of Saxony are for preserving themselves by the same Means which they made use of to establish themselves. They owe their Grandeur to the Emperor Charles V, and they maintain themselves by an inseparable Adhesion to the Interest of his House. The same Maurice, who transferr'd the Electoral Dignity to the younger Branch, took up Arms against his Benefactor, and strengthen'd himself by an Alliance with France against him, but as soon as he had secur'd his Interest, he effected his Reconciliation without Henry II, who seem'd to resent his Behaviour, and from that Time the Electors of Saxony have had so little Commerce with France, that hitherto they have not thought fit to give the King the Title of Majesty.

The Rights and Prerogatives which are peculiar to the Elector of Saxony, are 1. That he is hereditary Great Mareschal of the Empire They who have a moderate Knowledge of the German Tongue, know that the Word Mareschal is synonymous with that of Esquire, of Cavallerizze, and of Constable and it is probable that this Office was only created in Favour of him who had the Care of the Stable, when the Prince call'd the Constable to more important Employments, and to more elevated Functions. The Golden Bull regulates those of the Elector of Saxony to two Ceremonies, whereof the one is to carry the Sword before the Emperor when he goes in Procession the Day of his Coronation, or with all the Princes and States of the Empire, at the opening or concluding of a Diet, and the other is never done but at the Imperial Feast, which is also made on the score of the Coronation. And then the Elector of Saxony, after having accompany'd the Emperor to the Town House of Franckfort, or else to the House where the Feast is to be made, he remounts his Horse, and rides him into a Heap of Oats, in which the Horse being up to his Belly, the Elector fills a Silver Bushel therewith, into which he plants a Staff also of Silver, and which together with the Bushel ought to weigh twelve Marks, and so gives it to the first Groom of the Emperor's Stable, who is there present to take it from him.

However this Right of carrying the Sword before the Emperor, has not been always so appropriated to the Office of Great Mareschal of the Empire, but that it has been often disputed with the Elector of Saxony, as when the Emperor Charles IV, in judging the Difference which arose on that account between Wenceslas of Luxemburg, Duke of Brabant his Brother, and Rodolphus of Saxony in the Diet of Metz, An 1357, pronounc'd in Favour of Rodolphus, but with this Condition, that it should be but for that time only, and without any farther Consequence, because Wenceslas had not then done Homage for his Dutchy. And in effect at the Diet of Franckfort, where Wenceslas, Son to the same Emperor, was chosen King of the Romans in the Year 1377, the Emperor caus'd the Sword to be carry'd by his Son Sigismund, who was Marquiss of Brandenburg. But the Elector of Saxony, as Great Mareschal, has other Rights much more essential than those, as for instance, that of having the Command of those Forces that are in Garrison in the Place where the Diet is held, insomuch that the Emperor himself cannot regulate the Guard of the Town without him nay the Emperor Charles V having set a Guard at the Gates of the City of Augsburg, during the Diet

Diet that was held there in the Year 1530, *John* Elector of *Saxony* complain'd thereof, and oblig'd the Emperor to withdraw his Soldiers, and to assure the Elector, that for the future he would not do so any more, but would leave him the Disposition thereof, as being Great Mareschal hereditary of the Empire.

As such it is his Right to indicate the Assemblies which are held in the Diets, as well general as particular, nay even in the Electoral Diets, and in all others of what nature soever they may be, excepting the Collegial Diets, where it belongs to the Elector of *Mayence* to convene them. So that when the Electors, Princes, and Free Cities, or their Deputies who assist at the Diet, are oblig'd to hold Assemblies, each Member in particular, or all the States in a Body, it the Elector of *Saxony* be there present, the Archbishop of *Mayence* is oblig'd to give him Notice, either in Person, or by a Letter which he sends to his Chancery, that there is to be an Assembly; whereupon the Elector of *Saxony* dispatches his Order, by which he enjoins the Count of *Pappenheim* to notify to the other Electors, Princes and States of the Empire the Hour of the Assembly. But if the Elector of *Saxony* be not personally present at the Diet, the Archbishop of *Mentz* sends his Order to the Count of *Pappenheim*, and convenes the Assembly in his own Name. And this is observ'd even at those Diets that are summon'd for the Election, where the Elector of *Saxony* gives his Orders, to notify to the other Electors the Hour that is fix'd for the Deliberations. Pursuant to the Regulation that was made for this purpose at *Franckfort*, between *Daniel Brendel* Archbishop and Elector of *Mayence*, and *Augustus* Elector of *Saxony* in the Year 1562.

The Duke of *Saxony*, as hereditary Great Mareschal of the Empire, bears Coupé Argent and Sable, two Swords Gules Salter wise. The Arms of the Elector * of *Saxony* are quarterly of all the Provinces he possesses, and even of those to which he pretends a Right, as of the Dutchies of *Juliers*, *Cleves* and *Berg* but those which are commonly call'd the Arms of *Saxony*, which the Princes of the House of *Misnia* have borrow'd from those of *Anhalt* are,

† The *Golden Bull*, Chap 4 § 3 gives him the fifth Vote in the Electoral College, and ordains that he shall vote immediately after the Count *Palatin* of the *Rhine*, to whom the Duke of *Bavaria* has been substituted, and before the Marquiss of *Brandenburgh* For which reason he takes place between those two Electors, when all the Electors are assembl'd about the Election, and when they are all in a Line, pursuant to the last Regulation made at *Ratisbone*. In marching his Rank is immediately before the Emperor, when he carries the Imperial Sword, whether the other Electors bear the Ornaments or Regalia of the Empire or not: but when he does not carry the Sword, the Archbishop of *Triers* takes his Place, and he then has his on the left Hand of the Elector of *Bavaria*.

‡ The Elector of *Saxony* is Vicar of the Empire during the *Interregnum*, not only throughout all those Provinces where the *Saxon* Law prevails, but every where else out of the Extent of the Count *Palatin* of the *Rhine*'s Vicariate. We have spoken thereof in Chapter XII

The *Golden Bull*, Chapter II, gives to all the Electors two Privileges. The first is, that their Subjects cannot be forc'd out of their Jurisdiction, to answer the Law before any other Judges and the other, that the said Subjects cannot appeal from the Sentences given by the Electors, or by their Judges, but the Electors of *Saxony* and *Brandenburg* are the only that have taken Care to preserve, and have confirm'd to them from time to time these Privileges, which the others have lost through their own Neglect. As for the Elector of *Saxony*, the Emperor *Ferdinand* I declares by his Letters Patents, given at *Augsburg*, *May* 2, 1559, that all the Dukes of *Saxony* are Judges in *dernier Resort* of all their Subjects Causes, as well civil as criminal, by virtue of the long Possession they are in, not to defer to Appeals, but to proceed on to an Execution, notwithstanding any Opposition or Appeal whatsoever, forbidding the Judges of the Chamber to receive the Appeals, except in Cases where Justice is deny'd. Those Causes are likewise excepted, whose Cognizance belongs at first to the Imperial Chamber, as also those of the Inhabitants of the three Bishopricks of *Mersburg*, *Naumburg*, and of *Merssen* which it is true were incorporated to *Saxony*, but without Prejudice to the Rights of the Empire, of whom the Bishops of those three Dioceses held heretofore immediately

They who say, that the Elector of *Saxony* is Director of all the Ecclesiastical Affairs of the Protestants, and that the Elector *Palatin* has the Direction of their civil Affairs, are mistaken *John*, and *John-Frederick*, Electors of *Saxony*, took *Luther* into their Protection and the last of them presented the Confession of the Protestants to the Emperor *Charles* V, in the Diet of *Augsburg*, *An* 1530 It was also *Maurice* Elector of *Saxony*, who procur'd the Treaty of *Passaw* for the Liberty of Religion in the Empire, but then they did it out of a particular Zeal and so far are the Electors of *Saxony* from having any Title or particular Character for that, that on the contrary they have been known to act with the same Zeal, but somewhat less considerate, against those who, notwithstanding they have particular Sentiments, are nevertheless of the same Religion with them As in effect the Elector of *Saxony* has no Advantage over the other two Protestant Electors, and cannot meddle with the Direction of the Affairs of Religion, but in Conjunction with them, and particularly with the Consent of the Elector of *Brandenburg*, who has as much Interest therein as he, if not more, as we shall shew in the following Chapter

We promis'd at the beginning of this Chapter to say a word or two of the Silver Mines the Elector of *Saxony* has in his Countrey of *Misnia* He has several, but the richest, and which might formerly have vy'd with the Mines of *Potosi*, are those of *Sneberg* They were dis-

---
* *The Arms of the Elector of Saxony* † *His Rank* ‡ *He is Vicar of the Empire*

cover'd

cover'd in the Year 1471, and yielded so much Money at first, that the bare Tyth thereof was worth to the Duke of *Saxony* in thirty Years, that is to say, to the Year 1501, five hundred and ten Millions of Gold, and nine hundred thousand Crowns, and from the Year 1501, to that of 1537, three hundred and eighty Millions of Gold, and eight hundred thousand Crowns They have not yielded so much since that Time but yet they are not so exhausted but the Elector still draws a great deal from thence, tho' the War has in a manner ruin'd and destroy'd them

CHAP. XVI.

Of the Marquiss of Brandenburg, *Prince Elector of the Holy Empire.*

THE Province that is known at this Day under the Name of the *Marc-Brandenburg*, made formerly a part of the old *Suabia* Its People were forc'd to make room for their Neighbours, and to seek a Habitation elsewhere, in the Time of the Emperor *Augustus*, who permitted them to settle on the *Rhine*, and to take Possession of that part of *Rhætia*, and of the Countrey which is still call'd by their Name *Suabia* The *Sclavi*, and the *Henets* occupy'd in the beginning of the sixth Century that part of *Germany* that is between the *Danube* and the Source of the *Elbe*, and from thence along the *Elbe* to the Countrey of *Holstein* betwixt the same River and the *Baltick* Sea, comprising *Silesia*, *Bohemia*, part of the *Marc-Brandenburg*, *Pomerania*, and the Dutchy of *Mecklenburg*

The whole Province takes its Name from the capital City, but they who say that this City was built by *Brennus*, the Leader of those *Gauls* who took and sack'd *Rome*, about two hundred Years before the Birth of our Saviour, and that it was at first call'd *Brennebnrg*, look for its Origin among Fables, it being certain that this Name is of a much later Date, and that in the Year 928, the Inhabitants of the Countrey call'd it still by the *Sclavonian* Name *Schorlitz* It was in that Time that the Emperor *Henry* I fortify'd it against the *Sclavi*, the *Hennets*, and the *Obotritæ*, and establish'd therein a Marquiss or Governor of the Frontiers and it is since that Time that it has by little and little communicated its Name to the Conquests, according as the *Germans* made any over those *Barbarians*, which being beyond Comparison more considerable than those they gain'd over the *Hungarians* in *Austria*, the *Bohemians* in *Misnia*, and over the *Poles* in *Moravia*, we must not wonder that the Marquisate of *Brandenburg* is become the greatest and the first of the whole Empire

And indeed it may be said to be the largest Province of *Germany*, being at least seven Days Journey in length, and as many in breadth, and extending from *Poland* and *Silesia*, as far as the Dutchy of *Mecklenburg* about ten or twelve Leagues from *Hamburgh* The Provinces that border upon it are, the Dutchies of *Pomerania* and of *Mecklenburg* towards the North That of *Lunenburg* towards the North-East *Brunswick* towards the West The Dutchy of *Magdeburg* towards the South-West The Principality of *Anhalt* and of *Lusatia* towards the South *Silesia* towards the South-East *Poland* towards the East, and the *Pomerelle*, with the *Royal Prussia*, towards the North-East

It is divided into the Old, the Middle, and the New *Marc* The first extends it self from the Dutchy of *Lunenburg* to the River *Elbe*, the other from the *Elbe* to the River *Oder*, and the third from the *Oder* as far as *Poland* The Rivers that run across it are the *Elbe*, the *Oder*, the *Spree*, the *Havel*, and the *Wartha*, which are all navigable Its chief Towns are *Brandenburg*, an Episcopal City, *Berlin*, the usual Residence of the Elector, *Franckfort* on the *Oder*, an University, *Havelberg*, a Bishop's See, *Custrin*, an impregnable City and Fortress on the Confluence of the *Oder* and of the *Wartha*, *Spandau*, a very strong Place within two Leagues of *Berlin*, on the *Spree*, *Peitz*, a Fortress also on the same River on the side of *Lusatia*, *Libus*, an Episcopal City, *Sonneburg*, the Seat of the Provincial Master of the Order of St *John of Jerusalem*, &c

* The Emperor *Henry* I gave the Government of this Frontier, with the Title of Marquiss to *Sigfrid* Count of *Ringelheim*, Brother to the Empress, whom *Reusner* makes descend in a direct Male Line from *Wittikind the Great*, Prince of *Saxony* who dying in the Year 940, the Emperor *Otho* I gave the Marquisate to *Geron*, Count of *Altemburg* and *Mersburg*, who dy'd in the Year 965 After him succeeded in the Marquisate of *Brandenburg Bruno*, Count of *Wettin*, the Father of *Hugues*, who was made first hereditary Marquiss of *Brandenburg* by the Emperor *Otho* III. *Hugues* dy'd in the Year 1001, at *Pistoia* in *Italy*, being Governor of *Tuscany*, and left the Marquisate to *Thierry* his Nephew, who was driven out by the *Sclavi*, for having offended *Mistivoy*, Prince of *Mecklenburg*, and dy'd in Exile at *Magdeburg*

The Emperor *Conrade* II gave the Marquisate to *Udo* or *Otho*, the Son of *Sigfrid* II, Count of *Stade*, and Nephew to *Thierry*, who had for Successor in the Marquisate *Udo* II, his Son, and after him *Rodolphus* his younger Son This last left it to his Son *Udo* III, who having

* *Its first Princes*

taken

taken Arms with the other *Saxons* against *Henry* IV the Emperor, who was not in a Condition to punish him, gave Leave to the *Sclavy* to occupy all that Countrey, as far as the River *Havel*

The Emperor *Henry* V gave the Title of Marquiss of *Brandenburg* to *Otho the Rich*, Marquiss of *Soltuedel*, who had marry'd *Heslike*, the Daughter of *Magnus*, last Duke of *Saxony*, of the Posterity of *Herman* of *Bilingen* *But the Marquisate remain'd in the Hands of the *Barbarians* till the Reign of the Emperor *Frederick* I, who gave it to *Albert the Bear*, the Son of *Otho* of *Soltuedel*, and *Ball ngstadt* Count of *Anhalt* This Prince peopl'd the Countrey of *Brandenburg* with *Flemmings* and *Dutch*, and strengthen'd himself against the *Sclavis* by the Help of Colonies He marry'd for first Wife *Sophia* the Daughter of *Otho* Count of *Reinee*, and for second *Adelheide*, who was Daughter to *Conrade* the Great Marquiss of *Misnia*, but he had no Children by her, and dy'd November 18, 1169, leaving Issue by the first *Otho*; *Bernard*, who was made Duke of *Saxony*, *Sigfred* Bishop of *Brandenburg*, and Archbishop of *Breme*, *Henry* Prevost of the Church of *Magdeburg*, *Anselm* Bishop of *Havelberg*, &c

Otho his Son dy'd in the Year 1198, and left Issue *Albert* II, who dy'd in the Year 1221, and had by *Mahault* the Daughter of *Conrade* III, last Count of *Rochlitz*, and of *Mary* of *Poland*, *John* and *Otho* III, who both left Posterity, *Mahault* who was marry'd to *Otho the Infant*, first Duke of *Brunswick*, *Anne* who marry'd *Nicholas* III, Prince of *Mecklenburg*, and *Agnes* the Wife of *Eric* III, King of *Denmark* *Otho* III, call'd *the Pious*, younger Son to *Albert* II, had four Sons, who all liv'd to be Men, and marry'd but there was but one of them that left a Son call'd *Otho* IV, and sirnam'd *the Tall*, who had three Sons, two of which dy'd without Issue, and the third, nam'd *Herman*, left one Son, in whom the Posterity of *Otho* III fail'd

John the eldest Son of *Albert* II dy'd April 4, 1266, leaving 1 *John* II, who had three Sons, but they all dy'd without Issue, 2 *Otho*, who also dy'd without Issue, 3. *Conrade*, 4 *Eric* Archbishop of *Magdeburg*, and some Daughters *Conrade*, the younger Son of *John* I, left when he dy'd *An* 1304, *John* III, who had no Children, *Conrade* Master of the Teutonick Order, *Otho* a Knight Templar, *Volmar*, who left only two Daughters, who were marry'd into House of *Brunswick*, and *Henry*

Henry dy'd in the Year 1318, and left *Volmar* II, who marry'd *Anne* Daughter to the the Emperor *Albert* I, but he had no Issue by her, and dy'd in the Year 1323, and *John* IV, who possess'd the Marquisate of *Brandenburg* but fifteen Days after the Death of his Brother, and dy'd in the same Year 1323, without Issue

† The Posterity of *Otho* I, Marquiss of *Brandenburg* having fail'd in *John* IV, because *Bernard* the Brother of *Otho* had had his Portion in *Saxony*. So that the Dukes of *Saxe-Lauenburg*, and the Princes of *Anhalt*, who descend from him, could have no Pretensions on *Brandenburg*, because they were not compris'd in the Investiture of *Otho* And the Marquisate, being escheated to the Empire for want of Male Issue, the Emperor *Lewis* of *Bavaria* gave it to *Lewis* his eldest Son, who resign'd it in the Month of February 1352, to *Lewis the Roman* his Brother *Lewis the Roman* marry'd *Ingelberge*, the Daughter of *Albert* first Duke of *Mecklenburg*, and of *Eufemia* of *Sweden*, Widow to *John* IV, last Marquiss of *Brandenburg*, of the House of *Anhalt* but he had no Children by her, and dy'd in the Year 1356 *Otho* of *Bavaria* his Brother succeeded in the Marquisate, and marry'd for second Wife *Anne* of *Luxemburg*, the Daughter of the Emperor *Charles* IV, to whom he sold the Marquisate of *Brandenburg*, for two hundred thousand Ducats of *Hungary*. ‡ *Charles* gave it to his Son *Wenceslas*, and this gave it to *Sigismund* his Brother, who sold it to *Josse* of *Luxemburg*, Marquiss of *Moravia*, and *Josse* sold it to *William the Rich*, *Marquiss of *Misnia* But *Sigismund* having attain'd to the Empire, withdrew the Marquisate of *Brandenburg* from the Hands of *William*, and sold it to *Frederick* of *Hohenzollern* Burgrave of *Nuremberg*, who paid for the same Four hundred thousand Florins, or Eight hundred thousand Livres *French* Money which is certainly a very inconsiderable Sum, in comparison of those that private Persons at this Day lay out for the Purchase of a single Lordship, or of a House of Pleasure *Frederick* to make up the Sum of Four hundred thousand Florins, which was a very great one in an Age less corrupt than this in which we live, was forc'd to sell to the Town of *Nuremberg* his Rights of Viscount, excepting only the Title, and of two Forests which he possess'd in the Neighbourhood

He was a Prince of the Empire, Count Burgrave of *Nuremberg*, and was descended in a direct and Male Line from *Estol Frederick* Count of *Hohenzollern*, who had marry'd *Elizabeth* of *Habspurg*, Sister to the Emperor *Rodolphus* I, who made him Burgrave of *Nuremberg*, after the Family of the first Burgraves was extinct, by the Death of *Henry* last Count of *Vohbourg*, about the Year 1274 Of this Marriage were born *Frederick*, *Estol Frederick*, from whom descend the Counts and Princes of *Hohenzollern*, and *Frederick* II, Bishop of *Constance*

Frederick I had several Children, but none of them but *Frederick* II left Posterity He follow'd the Party of *Lewis* of *Bavaria*, against *Frederick* of *Austria*, whom he made a Prisoner with his own Hand in the Battel of *Muldorf* He marry'd *Margaret* the Daughter of *Ulric* Duke of *Carinthia* and Count of *Tirol*, and left *John*, *Bertold*, Commander of the Teutonick Order, and Chancellor to the Emperor *Lewis* IV, *Frederick*, who was nominated to the Bishoprick of *Ratisbone*, and *Albert*, who had no Issue *John*, the Son of *Frederick* II, bought the Town of *Culmbach*, and dy'd October 7, 1357, leaving by *Elizabeth* of *Henneberg* *Frederick* III, who marry'd for first Wife *Elizabeth*, the Daughter of *Frederick the Severe*,

---

* *The Marquisate enters into the House of* Anhalt † *The Marquisate enters into the House of* Bavaria
‡ *It enters into the House of* Luxemburg   * *It enters into the House of* Misnia

Marquiss

of the ELECTORS of the EMPIRE. 535

Marquifs of *Mifnia*, and of *Mahault* of *Bavaria*, and for fecond, *Ingelburg*, the only Daughter of *Lewis the Roman*, Duke of *Bavaria*, and Marquifs of *Brandenburg*. He had by this fecond Marriage only Daughters, but he had by the firft *John* II, who left by *Margaret* of *Luxemburg*, Daughter to the Emperor *Charles* IV, only *Elizabeth*, Wife to *Everard* IV, Count of *Wirtemberg*, *Frederick* IV, who fucceeded his Father, *Elizabeth*, who was marry'd to *Rupert* of *Bavaria*, Count Palatin of the *Rhine*, and Emperor, and *Beatrix*, the Wife of *Albert* III, Son to *Albert the Wife*, Duke of *Auftria*.

Frederick IV, the Son of *Frederick* III, and of *Elizabeth* of *Mifnia*, his firft Wife, acquir'd in the Year 1411, the Marquifate of *Brandenburg* from the Emperor *Sigifmund*, but it was only by the way of Mortgage. On *April* 30, 1415, he was declar'd Elector by the Confent of the whole Electoral College, but he did not take the Inveftiture thereof till *April* 10, 1417, at the Council of *Conftance*. The Emperor then made him pay a very confiderable Sum, and referv'd to himfelf and to his Brother the Privilege of vacating the Agreement, by reimburfing him, and the Condition that it fhould return for want of Male Iffue. He marry'd *Ifabella* the Daughter of *Frederick* Duke of *Bavaria* at *Landfhut*, and of *Magdalen Vifcontti*, and dy'd *September* 21, 1440, leaving four Sons and eight Daughters. *John*, his eldeft Son, renounc'd his Right of Primogeniture, and refign'd the Electoral Dignity, to which he was call'd by the *Golden Bull*, to *Frederick* his Brother. He had no Iffue Male, fo that the Renunciation being perfonal, and not extending to his Pofterity, there was no body could pretend in Intereft to oppofe it, and fo he confirm'd, by his Example, what we have faid elfewhere, to wit, That the eldeft Brother can renounce the Right which the Law gives him, provided it be without Prejudice to his Children, whom the fame Law entitles to the Succeffion of the Electoral Dignity, not as Heirs to the Father, but by virtue of the Inveftiture of the firft Acquirer.

Frederick, fecond Son to *Frederick* I, fucceeded his Father in the Electoral Dignity. He was but 21 Years old when he was made Protector of the Council of *Bafil*, and it was he that acquir'd to the Houfe of *Brandenburg* the Rights it has fince gain'd over the Dutchy of *Pomerania*. The Princes of *Pomerania*, as well thofe of the Branch of *Wolgaft*, as thofe of *Stettin*, began to acknowledge the Empire but in the Time of the Emperor *Frederick* I, who erected this Province into a Dutchy, in favour of *Boguflas* I, and *Cafimir* his Brother, who were Sons to *Wartiflas* I, who did him Homage therefore according in the ufual Manner and Form. But their Succeffors having neglected to pay thefe Devoirs to the Empire for a long Courfe of Years, *Lewis the Roman*, Marquifs of *Brandenburg*, Son to the Emperor *Lewis* of *Bavaria*, begg'd the Confifcation of the Dutchy of his Father. The Pretenfions which he founded on this Confifcation, pafs'd with the Marquifate of *Brandenburg* into the Houfe of *Luxemburg*, and afterwards into that of *Hohenzollern*. *Frederick* II was for purfuing them, on the Occafion of the Death of *Otho*, laft Duke of *Pomerania* at *Stettin*, of the Pofterity of *Otho* the younger Son of *Barnim* I, who dying without Iffue, in the Year 1464, *Frederick*, relying on the Tranfaction at *Franckfort* on the *Oder*, in the Year 1338, between *Lewis the Roman* and *Barnim* III Duke of *Pomerania*, obtain'd the Inveftiture thereof from the Emperor *Frederick* III. But when he was for taking Poffeffion thereof, *Eric* and *Wartiflas* X, Dukes of *Pomerania*, oppos'd the fame, and oblig'd him to come to an Accommodation, by which the Dukes of *Pomerania* allow'd him to take the Title and the Arms of *Pomerania*. It was alfo mention'd in the fame Treaty, That for want of Male Iffue in the Houfe of *Pomerania*, the Princes of *Brandenburg* fhould fucceed therein, and in effect he receiv'd the Inveftiture thereof, jointly with the Dukes of *Pomerania*, from the fame Emperor *Frederick*. Our Elector of the fame Name was betroth'd to *Avoye*, the Daughter of *Uladiflas* King of *Poland*, and was on this Confideration call'd to the Crown. But *Avoye* dying before the Marriage was confummated, he would not accept of it. He had by *Catherine*, the Daughter of *Frederick the Warrior*, Elector of *Saxony*, but two Sons, who dy'd young, and two Daughters.

The third Son of *Frederick*, firft Elector of *Brandenburg*, of the Houfe of *Hohenzollern*, was nam'd alfo *Frederick*, and left only two Daughters, but *Albert*, his fourth Son, left Pofterity. He was born *November* 24, 1414, and fucceeded his Brother in the Electoral Dignity. *Æneas Sylvius*, who was fince Pope under the Name of *Pius* II, calls him the *German Achilles* and the *Teutonick Ulyffes*, on the Account of his Courage, Prudence, and Eloquence. He made War againft the Dukes of *Pomerania*, and oblig'd them to do him Homage for the Town of *Stettin*, and it was he that commanded the Imperial Army againft *Charles the Bold*, Duke of *Burgundy*, who had befieg'd *Nuys*. After he had given great Proofs of his Conduct, on feveral Occafions, he was for giving one of his Moderation, by refigning the Government of his Eftates, and the Adminiftration of his Affairs, to his Son, tho' at the Age of fixty two Years, which he had feen when he made this Refignation, *June* 25, 1476, he had ftill Vigour enough left to govern in Perfon. He referv'd to himfelf the Electoral Dignity, which he was refolv'd to keep till his Death. And in effect being at *Franckfort*, at the Election of *Maximilian* I, he dy'd there *March* 11, 1486, at feventy two Years of Age. He marry'd for firft Wife *Margaret*, the Daughter of *James* Marquifs of *Baden*, and of *Margaret* of *Lorrain*, by whom he had *John*. And he had for fecond Wife *Anne*, the Daughter of *Frederick the Peaceable*, Elector of *Saxony*, and of *Margaret* of *Auftria*, by whom he had *Frederick*, who had his Portion in *Voitland*, and whofe Pofterity brought *Pruffia* into the Houfe of *Brandenburg*, as we fhall fee when we fhall have made an end to fpeak of the Electors.

John, the eldeft Son of *Albert*, and of *Margaret* of *Baden*, fucceeded his Father in the Electoral Dignity, and marry'd *Margaret* the Daughter of *William* (who was Son to *Frederick* I Elector of *Saxony*) and of *Anne* of *Auftria*, by whom he left, when he dy'd, in the Year

536   *Of the* ELECTION *of the* EMPEROR, *and*

Year 1499, 1 *Joachim*, who succeeded his Father, 2 *Albert*, who was born *June* 28, 1490 He was first a Canon of *Triers* and *Mayence* In the Year 1513, he was chosen Bishop of *Halberstad*, and Archbishop of *Magdeburg March* 9, 1514, he was chosen Archbishop and Elector of *Mayence*, and *August* 1, 1518, he was made Cardinal, by the Title of *S Chrysogone*, which he afterwards chang'd for that of *St Peter ad Vincula* Altho' he was but nine and twenty Years old at the Time of the Election of *Charles* V, yet nevertheless he had the greatest Hand therein, and brought the rest of the College into his Sentiments He dy'd during the Diet of *Ausgburg*, *September* 24, 1545 Of *John*'s two Daughters, the eldest, whose Name was *Anne*, marry'd in 1502, *Frederick*, Duke of *Holstein*, who was afterwards King of *Denmark*, and the other, whose Name was *Ursula*, was marry'd in 1506, to *Henry the Peaceable*, Duke of *Mecklenburg*

Joachim I, the eldest Son of *John*, was born *February* 21, 1484 So that as he could not be above sixteen Years old when his Father dy'd, the States of the Countrey were for offering the Administration of the Affairs of the Marquisate to *Frederick* Marquiss of *Anspach*, his Unkle, but he advis'd his Nephew to consult the Opinion of the other Electors Thereupon the Elector of *Mayence* sent him Word, that the Article of the *Golden Bull*, which gives the Guardianship of the Elector, during his Minority, to the nearest Relation by the Father's side, till he has attain'd eighteen Years complete, related to the Election only, and what depends thereon, but that his Age ought not to hinder him from taking upon him the Administration of the Affairs of his State He re-united to his Estates that part of the Marquisate which is between the *Oder* and *Poland*, and is call'd the *New Marc* Lewis of *Erlichausen*, Great Master of the *Teutonick* Order in *Prussia*, had formerly mortgag'd it to *Frederick* II Elector, but *Albert* of *Brandenburg*, great Master of the same Order, perfected the Alienation thereof in favour of *Joachim*, in the Year 1517, and yielded it up entirely, to be hereditary in the House of *Brandenburg* In the Year 1524, he join'd thereto the Earldom of *Rupin*, by Right of Fief, and for want of Issue Male It was he also who, by the Mediation of *Eric* Duke of *Brunswick*, and of *Albert* Duke of *Mecklenburg*, concluded the last Transaction with the Dukes of *Pomerania*, which contain'd, That for the future the Marquisses of *Brandenburg* should not hinder the Dukes of *Pomerania* from receiving the Investiture from the Emperor, but that the Dukes should also suffer the Marquisses of *Brandenburg* to be compris'd in the same Investitures, in order to succeed in *Pomerania* when the Male Line should happen to fail in that Family; and that to this Effect, the three Estates of this Province should be oblig'd to take the Oath of Fidelity to the Marquisses of *Brandenburg*, and to renew the same at every Change of Lords, that he might be intitl'd to the Succession upon Occasion He was present at the Election of the Emperor *Charles* V, but he had more Affection for King *Francis* I, with whom he held always a very good Correspondence, as well as with the Pope *Leo* X He marry'd, in the Month of *May*, 1502, *Elizabeth* the Daughter of *John* King of *Denmark*, and of *Christina* of *Saxony*, and dy'd *July* 11, 1535, leaving Issue, 1 *Joachim* II, who succeeded his Father, 2 *John*, who left by *Catherine* of *Brunswick* only two Daughters, 3 *Anne*, who was marry'd to *Albert* III Duke of *Mecklenourg*, 4 *Elizabeth*, the Wife of *Eric* Duke of *Brunswick*, and by a second Marriage of *Poppon* XVIII Count of *Henneberg*, 5 *Margaret*, marry'd to *George* Duke of *Pomerania*, and by a second Match to *John* Prince of *Anhalt*

Joachim II was born *January* 9, 1503 He reform'd Religion in the Marquisate, and receiv'd the Communion himself under both Kinds, *November* 1, 1539 He was appointed General of the Army which the Empire sent against the *Turks*, in the Year 1542, and he follow'd the Emperor *Charles* V's Party against the Confederates of *Smalcalden* But he underhand favour'd that of *Maurice* Elector of *Saxony*, against the same Emperor, on Account of the ill Treatment he dealt to *Philip* Landgrave of *Hesse*, contrary to the Promise he had sent him by our Elector After that, he renew'd in 1551, the hereditary Alliance with the Houses of *Saxony* and *Hesse* The Emperor *Ferdinand* I set him in Possession of the Dutchy of *Crossen* in *Silesia*, and his Brother-in-Law, *Sigismund Augustus* King of *Poland*, confirm'd to him that of the Dutchy of *Prussia* It was he that began the Fortifications of *Spandau*, but they were not finish'd but under *John George* his Son, by *Francis Giramella*, and the Count de *Linares* He also built the stately Palace, which is to be seen at this Day, cover'd with Brass, at *Berlin* He was present at the Confirmation of the Election of *Ferdinand* I, and elected, with his Collegues, *Maximilian* II his Son He dy'd *January* 2, 1571, of Poyson He had marry'd for first Wife *Magdalen*, the Daughter of *George the Rich*, Duke of *Saxony*, and of *Barbe* of *Poland*, and for second, *Avoye*, Daughter to *Sigismund* King of *Poland*, by *Barbe* of *Sepuse* He had by the first, amongst other Children, *John George*, and *Frederick* Archbishop of *Magdeburg*, and Bishop of *Halberstad*, who dy'd in the first Year of his Pontificate, and by the second, *Sigismund*, who succeeded his Brother in the Archbishoprick of *Magdeburg*

John George, the eldest Son of *Joachim* II, was born *September* 11, 1525, and succeeded to his Father in the Electoral Dignity, *An* 1571 The Memory of this Prince is still in Veneration in the Countrey, on account of the numerous and illustrious Posterity he left, as well in the Marquisate and Electorate of *Brandenburg*, as in *Franconia* and *Vortland*, where his Posterity reign still at this Day His first Wife was *Sophia*, Daughter to *Frederick* II, Duke of *Brig* and *Lignits*, and to *Sophia* of *Brandenburg*, by whom he had *Joachim Frederick*, who succeeded him in the Electoral Dignity He marry'd for second Wife *Sabina*, the Daughter of *George the Pious*, Marquiss of *Brandenburg* at *Auspach*, and of *Avoye*, of *Munsterberg*, by whom he had several Children, but they all dy'd young, excepting three Daughters, who were marry'd, to wit, *Ermuda* to *John Frederick*, Duke of *Pomerania* at *Stettin*, *Anne Mary* to *Barnim*, also Duke of *Pomerania* at *Stettin*, and *Sophia* to *Christian* I, Elector of *Saxony* He had by *Elizabeth*

of the ELECTORS of the EMPIRE. 537

Elizabeth, the Daughter of *Joachim Ernest*, Prince of *Anhalt*, and of *Elizabeth* of *Barby* his third Wife, *Christian*, who had his Portion at *Barerth* and *Culmbach*, *Joachim Ernest*, who had his at *Anspach*, and have both left Posterity, *Frederick*, *George Albert*, *Sigismund John*, and *John George*, who dy'd without Issue, *Magdalen*, Wife to *Lewis*, Lantgrave of *Hesse Darmstadt*, *Agnes*, marry'd to *Philip*, Duke of *Pomerania* at *Wolgast*, and by a second Match to *Francis Charles*, Duke of *Saxe-Lauenburg*, *Elizabeth Sophia*, who was marry'd to *Janus Radzivil*, Duke of *Breze*, &c and afterwards to *Julius Henry*, Duke of *Saxe-Lauenburg*, *Dorothea Sibylla*, marry'd to *John Christian*, Duke of *Lignits* *John George*, the Father of all these Children, dy'd *January* 8, 1598

Joachim Frederick, Elector of *Brandenburg*, Son to *John George*, by *Sophia* of *Lignits*, his first Wife, was born *January* 27, 1546 Whilst his Father was still living he was was nominated to the Bishopricks of *Havelberg* and of *Libus*, and succeeded his Unkle in the Archbishoprick of *Magdeburg* He succeeded in the Electoral Dignity in the Year 1598, and dy'd *July* 18, 1608 He had marry'd on *January* 8, 1570, *Catherin*, the Daughter of *John*, Marquiss of *Brandenburg*, his Great-Unkle by the Father's side, and of *Catherin* of *Brunswick*, who departing this World on *September* 30, 1602, he marry'd for second Wife *Eleonor*, the Daughter of *Albert Frederick* of *Brandenburg*, Duke of *Prussia*, and of *Mary Eleonor* of *Cleves* He had by his first Wife, 1 *John Sigismund*, Elector, 2 *John George*, who was born on *December* 16, 1577 On *May* 20, 1592, he was chosen Bishop of *Strasburg* by a Division, against *Leopold*, Arch-Duke of *Austria* On *July* 31, 1616, he was made Provincial Master of the Order of St *John* of *Jerusalem*, and had for Appennage or Portion the Dutchy of *Jagerndorf* in *Silesia* On *June* 14, 1610, he marry'd *Eve Christina*, the Daughter of *Frederick*, Duke of *Wirtemberg*, and of *Sibylla* of *Anhalt*, but he had no Children by her, and dy'd *March* 12, 1624 He was put in the Ban of the Empire, for having taken Arms against the Emperor in the beginning of the last Wars in *Germany*, for which Reason the Dutchy of *Jagersdorf* was confiscated from him but the Elector of *Brandenburg* demands it as an Appennage, that ought to be reunited to his Demesne, 3 *Augustus*, who dy'd at the Age of twenty one, 4 *Albert Frederick*, who dy'd at nineteen Years of Age, 5 *Joachim*, and, 6 *Ernest*, who were Twins, and dy'd both without Issue, the first at seventeen Years of Age, and the other at thirty, 7 *Christian William*, who was born *April* 28, 1587, he was nominated to the Archbishoprick of *Magdeburg*, *April* 26, 1598, and marry'd on *January* 1, 1615, *Dorothy*, the Daughter of *Henry Julius*, Duke of *Brunswick* and *Lunenburg*, and of *Elizabeth* of *Denmark*, by whom he had in the Year 1616, *Sophia Elizabeth*, who was marry'd to *Frederick William* II, Duke of *Saxony* at *Altemburg* This Prince fell into the Hands of the Imperialists at the taking of *Magdeburg*, on *May* 20, 1630, and was carry'd to *Vienna*, where he chang'd his Religion, and accepted the Office of Great-Huntsman to the Emperor He marry'd for second Wife, a Daughter of the Count *de Martinitz* in *Bohemia*, and is still living, 8 *Anne Catherin*, marry'd to *Christian* VI, King of *Denmark*, and Mother of the present King, and *Barba Sophia*, who was marry'd to *Frederick*, and was Mother to *Eberhard*, *Frederick* and *Ulrick*, Dukes of *Wirtemberg* *Joachim Frederick* had by a second Wife *Mary Eleonor*, who was marry'd in 1632, to *Philip Lewis* of *Bavaria*, Count *Palatin* of the *Rhine* at *Zimmeren*

John Sigismund, Elector of *Brandenburg*, was born *November* 8, 1572, and succeeded in the Year 1608, to his Father in the Electoral Dignity He marry'd on *October* 20, 1594, *Anne*, the Daughter of *Albert Frederick* of *Brandenburg*, Duke of *Prussia*, and of *Mary Eleonor* of *Cleves* The Mother of *Anne* was eldest Daughter to *William*, Duke of *Juliers*, *Cleves* and *Berg*, so that *John William*, his Brother, dying without Issue *March* 25 1609, *John Sigismund*, who had marry'd the eldest Daughter of *Anne*, was for taking possession of this large Inheritance in the Name of his Wife, but it it was contested with him by *Wolfgang William*, Count *Palatin* of the *Rhine* at *Neuburg*, who was Son to *Anne*, the second Daughter of *William*, Duke of *Cleves*, and pretended to be preferr'd to his Cousin, as being the nearest Male Heir of the last Duke of *Cleves* At present the Heirs of those two Princes have made a provisional Partition of all the Inheritance, by which the Elector of *Brandenburg* enjoys the Dutchy of *Cleves*, and the Counties of *Marc* and *Ravensberg*, and the Duke of *Neuburg*, the Dutchies of *Juliers* and *Berg*, and the Lordship of *Ravestein*, till such time as the Cause shall be judg'd between the Parties In 1610, *John Sigismund* sign'd the Union that several Protestant Princes had enter'd into in *Germany* In 1611, he did Homage to the King of *Poland* for the Dutchy of *Prussia*, and receiv'd the Investiture thereof for himself, and his Male Descendents, as also for his Brothers, and their Issue Male, which had been granted before but to *Albert* and his Brothers, and their Descendents in a direct Male Line In 1614, he made an End of reforming Religion, and made Profession of that which the reform'd Churches teach in *France*, the Low Countries, and in *Switzerland* The same Year he renew'd the Treaty of mutual Succession with the Princes of *Saxony* and *Hesse*. and in the Year 1618, he had a Fit of an Apoplexy, which turning to a Palsy, oblig'd him to yield up the Government of his Estates, and of the Electoral Dignity it self, to his Son He liv'd but a Month after this Resignation, and dy'd *December* 23, 1619 He had by his Wife, 1 *George William*, who succeeded his Father, 2 *Joachim Sigismund*, who dy'd at thirteen Years of Age, 3 *John Frederick*, and, 4 *Albert Christian*, who both dy'd young, 5 *Anne Sophia*, who was marry'd to *Frederick Ulrick*, Duke of *Brunswick* at *Wolfembuttel*, and is still living, but is retir'd to *Berlin* on the Account of her Indisposition, 6 *Mary Eleonor*, marry'd to *Gustavus Adolphus*, King of *Sweden*, and Mother to Queen *Christina*, 7 *Catherin*, the Wife of *Bethlehem Gabor*, Prince of *Transilvania*, and afterwards of *Francis Charles*, Duke of *Saxe-Lauenburg*, and, 8 *Agnes*, who dy'd young.

George William, Elector of *Brandenburg*, was born at *Berlin*, *November* 3, 1595, *John George* his Great Grandfather, being still alive He

6 X

succeeded in 1619, to his Father in the Electoral Dignity, and he possess'd fine Qualities enough to make him be consider'd in the Empire, if the War in *Germany* had not involv'd him in its Disorders and Misfortunes, by the ill Conduct of a first Minister, to whom he had entrusted the Management of the Affairs of his State, under his Authority He marry'd on *July* 14, 1616, *Elizabeth Charlot* of *Bavaria*, the Daughter of *Frederick* IV, Elector *Palatin*, and of *Louise Julian* of *Nassau Orange*, who is still living in the Dutchy of *Crossen* in *Silesia*, where she has her Dowry, and dy'd *December* 1, 1640, leaving *Frederick William*, *Louise Charlott*, who marry'd *James* Duke of *Curland*, and *Avoye Sophia*, who was Wife to *William* V, Lantgrave of *Hesse Cassel*.

Frederick William was born *February* 16, 1620, and succeeded his Father in the Electoral Dignity, *An* 1640 He marry'd *Louise* of *Nassau*, the Daughter of *Frederick Henry*, Prince of *Orange*, by whom he has *Charles Emile*, who was born *February* 16, 1655, and *Frederick*, who was born in *June* 1657 It is this Prince who is at this Day Elector of *Brandenburg*, and we shall speak of him, after we have made known the other Princes of the same House, amongst whom the first is *Christian*, ∗ Son to *John George*, Elector of *Brandenburg*, by *Elizabeth* of *Anhalt*, his third Wife. He had for Portion *Culmbach* and *Bareith*, and marry'd on *April* 29, 1604, *Mary*, the Daughter of *Albert Frederick* of *Brandenburg*, Duke of *Prussia*, and dy'd *May* 1655 Of this Marriage was born, amongst others, 1 *Erdman Augustus*, who came into the World *October* 29, 1615, and has marry'd *Sophia*, the Daughter of *Joachim Ernest*, Marquiss of *Brandenburg* at *Anspach*, and of *Sophia* of *Solms*, by whom he has Children, among the rest *Christian Ernest*, &c 2 *George Albert*, who was born *March* 10, 1619, and has marry'd *Mary Elizabeth*, Daughter to *Philip*, Duke of *Holstein* at *Glucsburg*, 3 *Anne Mary*, marry'd to *John Anthony* of *Cruman*, Prince of *Eggenberg*, and, 4 *Magdalen Sibylla*, marry'd to *John George*, present Elector of *Saxony*

† *Joachim Ernest*, Brother to *Christian*, and second Son to *John George*, Elector of *Brandenburg*, by *Elizabeth* of *Anhalt*, his third Wife, had for his Portion *Anspach* It was he that commanded the Army of the United Princes at the beginning of the last Wars in *Germany*, but with little Success, and still less Reputation He marry'd on *October* 14, 1613, *Sophia*, the Daughter of *John George*, Count of *Solms*, by whom he left when he dy'd in the Year 1625, *Albert* and *Sophia*, who was marry'd to *Erdman Augustus*, Marquiss of *Brandenburg* at *Culmbach*.

Albert was born *September* 28, 1629, and marry'd in 1642, for first Wife, *Henrietta Louise*, the Daughter of *Lewis Frederick*, Duke of *Wirtemberg* at *Montbeliard:* who dying in 1651, he marry'd for second Wife, *Sophia Marguerit*, the Daughter of *Joachim Ernest*, Count of *Ottingen* He has by his first Wife a Daughter, and by the second, a Son nam'd *John Frederick*, born in the Year 1655

‡ We have said before, that *Albert*, Elector of *Brandenburg* had by *Anne* of *Saxony*, his second Wife, a Son nam'd *Frederick*, who had his Portion in *Poland* It is true that his Posterity is intirely extinct, and his Branch is reunited to the main Stock in the Person of the present Elector but forasmuch is it is requisite to know how *Prussia* came in to the House of *Brandenburg*, we shall take notice that *Frederick* dy'd *May* 2, 1536, and had by *Sophia*, Daughter to *Casimir* III, King of *Poland*, by *Elizabeth* of *Austria*, 1 *Casimir*, the Father of *Albert*, who distinguish'd himself so much in the first Wars of the Protestants in *Germany*, and dy'd without Issue, *January* 8, 1557, 2 *George*, the Father of *George Frederick*, who dy'd *May* 6, 1603, without Issue, 3 *Albert*, Duke of *Prussia*, 4 *John*, who was Governor of *Valencia* for the Emperor *Charles* V, and marry'd *Germaine de Foix*, the Widow of *Ferdinand*, King of *Arragon*, and dy'd without Issue in the Year 1524, *Frederick*, who dy'd also without Issue in 1536, 6 *William*, Bishop of *Riga* in *Livonia*, 7 *Gumbert*, Chamberlain to Pope *Leo* X, 8 *Elizabeth*, who marry'd *Ernest*, Marquiss of *Baden Dourlach*, 9 *Marguerit*, third Wife to *Boguslas* X, Duke of *Pomerania*, 10 *Sophia*, marry'd to *Frederick* II, Duke of *Lignitz*, 11 *Anne*, who marry'd *Wenceslas* III, Duke of *Thesse*, &c

Albert, third Son to *Frederick*, by *Sophia* of *Poland*, was elected in the Year 1511, Great-Master of the Teutonick Order in *Prussia*, after the Death of *Frederick* of *Saxony* And in this Quality he made his Entry into *Koningsberg* on *November* 22 of the same Year, being then but one and twenty Years old The King and the Senate of *Poland* approv'd his Election, but on this Condition, That he should take an Oath of Fidelity to the Crown *Albert* excus'd himself on the Injunction he said the Pope and the Emperor had laid upon him to the contrary and that he might be in a Condition to oppose the *Poles*, he desir'd Succour from the Princes of the Empire, and borrow'd Money of his Friends, amongst others of *Gualtier* of *Plettenberg*, Provincial Master of the Teutonick Order in *Livonia*, who by the Means of a Sum of Money, had freed himself from the Subjection and Dependence, which the Master of *Livonia* paid before to the Great-Master of *Prussia* *Sigismund*, King of *Poland*, was at War then with the *Muscovites* and the *Tartars*; so that *Albert* remain'd undisturb'd for some Years But *Sigismund* at last declar'd War against him in the Year 1519 However the Year following the Parties agreed upon a Truce of four Years, during which time the Emperor *Charles* V, *Lewis* King of *Hungary*, the Cardinals of *Saltsburg*, and of *Strigonia*, *George* Duke of *Saxony*, and the Bishop of the five Churches in *Hungary*, should endeavour to reconcile them, or else should decide their Difference as Arbitrators But the Truce being expir'd, without the Arbitrators offering to determin the Matter, *Albert*, who judg'd very well, that he could not hope for Succour, while the Emperor was at open War with *France*, and the *Turks* had got possession of some part of *Hungary*, and that *Germany* it self was harrass'd by

---

∗ *Marquiss of Brandenburg at Culmbach, denburg Dukes of Prussia.*   † *Marquiss of Brandenburg at Anspach*   ‡ *The Marquisses of Brandenburg Dukes of Prussia.*

of the ELECTORS of the EMPIRE.

an almost general Insurrection, desir'd *George* Marquiss of *Brandenburgh* his Brother, and *Albert* Duke of *Lignits*, to endeavour to accommodate the Affair at the Court of *Poland*. They succeeded so well in their Negotiation, that *Albert* going himself to *Cracou*, concluded there his Treaty, by which it was agreed that the Eastern part of *Prussia* should remain to him, with all the Towns, Castles, Burroughs, Appurtenances and Dependencies, to hold the same by the Title of a Dutchy, by Fealty and Homage to the King and the Crown of *Poland*. In this Investiture were compris'd *Casimir*, *George* and *John*, Brothers to *Albert*, and their lawful Male Issue, on Condition it should return to the Crown for want of Males. I or which the States of the Province gave their Letters, which they call *Reversals*, in good Form. The said Treaty, which was sign'd *April* 8, 1525, contain'd moreover, that the Duke of *Prussia*, as first *Palatin* of *Poland*, should have the first Place in the Diets and Assemblies, except in those which are held for the Election of a King. In the Year 1526, he marry'd *Dorothy* the Daughter of *Frederick* I, King of *Denmark*, by *Anne of Brandenburg*, from whence *Gualtier* of *Cronenburg*, who had procur'd himself to be substituted in his Dignity of Great Master, took occasion to complain to the Emperor *Charles* V, who being at *Augsburg* in the Year 1530, repeal'd and annull'd all that *Albert* had done with the King of *Poland*, pretending that *Prussia* being a Member and Fief of the Empire, the King of *Poland* could not dispose thereof, and that the Great Master of the Teutonick Order, as a Prince of the Empire, could not withdraw himself from the Obedience which he owes him. The Chamber of *Spires* likewise took Cognizance of this Affair, and put *Albert* in the Ban of the Empire in the Year 1532. The King of *Poland* made pressing Instances to try to get the Proscription repeal'd, and sent, for that purpose, *Stanislaus Lasens* to the Diet conven'd at *Augsburg* in 1548, but he could obtain nothing. As on the other side the States of the Empire could not put their Decree in Execution. But the Marquisses of *Brandenburg* have since that time maintain'd themselves in the peaceable Possession of *Prussia*, under the Protection of the Crown of *Poland*. At this Day, and by the Treaty of the Elector of *Brandenburg* has made lately with the King and the Crown of *Poland*, he possesses this Province in full Sovereignty. *Albert* first Duke of *Prussia* marry'd for second Wife *Anne Mary*, the Daughter of *Eric* the elder Duke of *Brunswick*, and of *Elizabeth of Brandenburg*, and dy'd *March* 19, 1568. He had by his first Wife several Children, who all dy'd young except two Daughters, the one of which did not marry, and the other, nam'd *Anne Sophia*, was marry'd. *October* 24, 1555, to *John Albert* Duke of *Mecklenburg*. By his second Wife he had *Albert Frederick*, who succeeded in the Dutchy of *Prussia*, and marry'd on *October* 14, 1573, *Mary Eleonor*, the eldest Daughter of *William*, Duke of *Juliers*, of *Cleves* and of *Berg*, &c. and of *Mary of Austria*, by whom he had amongst others *Anne* his eldest Daughter, who marry'd in the Year 1594, *John*

Sigismund, Grandfather to the Elector of *Brandenburg* who is now living.

* By what we have here said it is easy to judge in what Consideration a Prince ought to be, who possesses so many Principalities, and such a vast extent of Provinces, that within a small matter he can traverse all *Germany* from West to East, without going out of his own Estates. But his Interest will be best known, and what will be his Sentiments in all Likelihood in the next Diet, by the account we shall give of his Neighbours, who are, on the side of the Dutchy of *Cleves*, and those Provinces that depend thereon, the States of the United Provinces, the King of *Spain* as Duke of *Brabant* and Lord of the upper part of *Guelders*, the Elector of *Cologn*, as Archbishop, as well as Bishop of *Liege*, the Duke of *Neuburg*, the Lantgrave of *Hesse*, the Bishops of *Munster* and *Ofnaburg*, and the Dukes of *Brunswick* and *Lunenburg*, who are also his Neighbours on the score of the Principalities of *Minden* and *Halberstad*. He has a common Interest with the States, and the King of *Spain* considers him as well on that account, as for the Influence he can give to the Affairs of *Germany*. He holds a very good Intelligence with the Lantgrave, who is his Brother-in-Law, and with all the other Princes, except the Duke of *Neuburg*, who disputes with him the Succession of *Juliers* and *Cleves*. In the Marc of *Brandenburg* he has for Neighbours the same Dukes of *Brunswick Lunenburg*, the Duke of *Brunswick* at *Wolfenbuttel*, the Princes of *Anhalt*, the Elector of *Saxony*, and his Brothers on the score of the Archbishoprick of *Magdeburg* and of *Lusatia*. The King of *Bohemia* on the account of *Silesia*, the King of *Poland*, the King of *Sweden*, as Duke of *Pomerania*, and the Duke of *Mecklenburg*. At present the Elector is very well with all these Princes, and one might say that he has no Enemies, secret or declar'd, did not the Treaty he has lately concluded with the King of *Poland* give some Umbrage to the *Swede*, who is also his Neighbour in *Prussia* on the side of *Livonia*, and even in the Royal *Prussia* it self, by the Places the King has taken within these two Years from *Poland*.

† They who believe that the Elector of *Brandenburg* can hardly forget the ill Treatment he receiv'd it *Munster*, when the best part of *Pomerania* was given to the Crown of *Sweden*, whereas this last might have taken ‡ its Satisfaction of those against whom it had taken Arms, the late King of *Sweden* having protested that he would never demand that Province, to the Prejudice of the Rights the House of *Brandenburg* might have thereto. They, I say, who make this Judgment of our Elector, do not know him. He gave up all his Resentments to the Repose of the Empire, and he is too generous to entertain a secret Hatred, since he is in a Condition to declare himself even with Advantage. But if he does not blindly follow all the Sentiments of the King of *Sweden*, especially those he may have concerning the next Election, we must believe that he suffers himself to be carry'd away by the Motions of Tenderness which he has for his Country, and Prudence inspires him, by representing

---

* *The neighbouring Princes of the Elector of Brandenburg.* † *His Sentiments for the ensuing Election.* ‡ *Satisfaction.*

ing to him all other Evils more tolerable than that of a Civil War.

The Elector of *Brandenburg* is the oldest Elector of the whole College, having succeeded his Father in the Electoral Dignity in the Year 1640, whereas all the others have attain'd thereto but several Years since. He cannot aspire to the Imperial Dignity by reason of his Religion, and even if he could, he has too much Judgment to desire it, at the Expence of his own Repose and of that of the Empire But as he is at present powerfully arm'd, and and finds himself strengthen'd by the Friendship of the most powerful Princes of those Parts, there is no doubt but his Suffrage will be mightily consider'd by those who shall labour with him in the Execution of the Treaties of *Munster* and *Osnaburg*, and in the Preservation of the Peace of the Empire

* As for the Electoral Dignity of *Brandenburg*, it is hard to say at what time precisely it was annex'd to the Marquisate For there is no Likelihood at all that the Marquisses assisted at the Elections, when the Marquisate of *Brandenburg* made still a part of the Dutchy of *Saxony*, and did not hold immediately of the Empire, and it is certain that when the Marquisate enter'd into the House of *Anhalt*, its Princes were present at the Elections, not as Marquisses of *Brandenburg*, but as having otherwise the Quality of Princes of the Empire It is also indubitable, that when afterwards the Marquisate became the Portion of an elder Brother, and that the Principality of *Anhalt* remain'd to the younger, the Marquisses continu'd to be Princes, notwithstanding they no longer possess'd their first Principality, and that as such they were Electors with the other Princes of the Empire But the Faculty of Electing was not as yet appropriated to certain Princes, to the Exclusion of the others, and that Right did yet bestow a Dignity annex'd to the Principality, from which it was so far from being inseparable, that even a few Years before the Publication of the *Golden Bull*, and in the same Century, *Lewis*, the eldest Son of the Emperor *Lewis* of *Bavaria*, in resigning the Marquisate of *Brandenburg* to *Lewis the Roman* his Brother, reserv'd to himself the Right of Electing, at a time when the Number of the Electors was not yet so well regulated as it was afterwards by the *Golden Bull*, which also annex'd the Electoral Dignity to the House, and to the Principality of *Brandenburg*

† To the Quality of Elector, and to the Marquisate of *Brandenburg*, is annex'd the Office of hereditary Great Chamberlain of the Holy Empire The *Annales Francorum* in the Year 782, call him *Cubicularius*, and in the Year 828, in speaking of *Bernard* Count of *Barcelona, Camerarius* Gregory *of Tours*, Lib 4 Cap 24 calls him *Præpositus Regalis Cameræ*, and he had the Administration of the Revenues and of the King's Demesne At present he has no Function, because the Empire has no Demesne that is not alienated, and the Emperor, as Emperor, has no Revenues of which he can give the Management to the Great Chamberlain

‡ In this Quality he carries the Scepter, when he marches in Procession before the Emperor, and he takes the Right Hand of the Elector Palatin He therefore charges his Arms therewith, which are quarterly of all the Provinces he possesses, and over which he pretends a Right, bearing over the whole Azure a Scepter Or It is not that the Electors of *Brandenburg* have always been in such Possession of this Right to bear the Scepter, but at the Coronation of the Emperor *Charles* IV, the Marquis of *Juliers* seiz'd it, but then the Marquis of *Brandenburg* snatch'd it from him, and thereby gave occasion to the Regulation by which the same Emperor ordain'd, that at the Coronation of the Emperor, the Marquis of *Brandenburg* should alone have a Right to carry the Scepter, but that at other Ceremonies, as of Investitures and other Solemnities, another Marquis might discharge this Function

In the same Quality he pours out Water to the Emperor or King of the *Romans* to wash with, at the Feast he gives to the Electors after his Coronation, in the manner prescrib'd by the *Golden Bull*, which says, Chap XXVII § 3 That after the Ecclesiastical Electors shall have bless'd the Imperial Table, the Marquis of *Brandenburg* shall draw near, and holding a Silver Bason and Ewer of the Weight of twelve Marks, and a fine Napkin, he shall pour out Water to the Emperor, or King of the *Romans*, to wash with The Bason and Ewer, as also the Horse which the Elector of *Brandenburg* rode upon, belong to the Count of *Hohenzollern*, his perpetual and hereditary Vicar in the Office of Great Chamberlain

The Elector of *Brandenburg* has the same Advantage which the Elector of *Saxony* enjoys, his Subjects not being allow'd to appeal from his Sentences, definitive or interlocutory as well by virtue of the ancient Custom, which was confirm'd by the *Golden Bull*, as by the special Privilege of the Emperor *Maximilian* II in the Year 1568

It is true that all the other Secular Electors have Prerogatives and Preeminencies which are peculiar to them, as for instance, the King of *Bohemia* has the Advantage to be a Crown'd Head The Duke of *Bavaria* and the Duke of *Saxony* are Vicars of the Empire during the *Interregnum*, and the Count Palatin is the Emperor's Judge But the Elector of *Brandenburg* has this Advantage over the King of *Bohemia*, that he has a Right to assist at the Collegiate Diets, and at all the other Assemblies, as well general as particular, and he is not afraid that the Princes of his House will dispute the Electoral Dignity with him, or that younger Branches should be preferr'd to him, as in the Houses of *Saxony* and *Bavaria*

---

* *When the Electoral Dignity was annex'd to the Marquisate.* ‡ *His Rank and his Arms.*

† *The Prerogatives of the Elector of Brandenburg*

CHAP

CHAP. XVII.

Of the Count Palatin of the Rhine, Prince Elector of the Holy Empire.

THE Elector *Palatin*, as being the eldest Branch of the House of *Bavaria*, ought to hold the Rank which the *Golden Bull* gives him immediately after the King of *Bohemia*, and it is on his account that we ought to speak of the Dukes and Dutchy of *Bavaria* but as we were oblig'd to follow the Sentiments of all the States of the Empire, who have thought fit, for the sake of the publick Tranquillity, to change that Order, and to transfer the Electoral Dignity from the eldest Branch to the younger, we have given the junior the Rank which he at present holds in the Electoral College And forasmuch as he is known under the Quality of Elector of *Bavaria*, notwithstanding he holds the Place, and does the Functions of the *Palatin*, we have spoken of the Electorate, and of the Princes of *Bavaria* above in Chapter XIV, and have reserv'd this for the Elector *Palatin*, who at this Day has his Rank after all the rest

* The Word *Palatin* is without doubt *Latin* originally, and it is certain that in the time of *Charlemagne*, and long after, the Count *Palatin*, or *Comes Palatii*, was the Judge of the Palace for ordinary Causes This is what we might confirm by several authentick Testimonies, if the whole Treatises which *Hubert Thomas Leodius*, *Pithon*, and *Marq Freherus* have written on this Subject, did not afford so many, that they may very well spare us this Trouble This Dignity which had at first its Functions but only in the Emperor's Palace, and where the Court was, became in time hereditary in certain Families as in one of the *Saxon* Branches, in that of *Wittelspach* in *Bavaria*, in that of *Tubingen* in *Suabia*, &c which had all their Counts *Palatins* And it continu'd therein till those being re-united to more considerable Principalities, this Title was lost every where elfe but in the *Palatinate* of the *Rhine*

The Province which is at this time call'd by that Name, and which extends on the Western side from the Dutchy of *Deuxponts* as far as *Franconia* and the Dutchy of *Wirtemberg* towards the East, and from the *Mein* towards the North, as far as *Alsace* on the South side, had no Advantage over the other *Palatinates* about five or six hundred Years ago, and it made part of *Franconia*, as *Wittelspach* of *Bavaria*, and *Tubingen* of *Suabia*, but it began to distinguish it self from the others, under the Emperor *Frederick* I, who gave the *Palatinate* of the *Rhine* to *Conrade* of *Suabia*, his Brother by the Father's side, who had marry'd *Elizabeth*, Daughter to *Herman*, the last Count *Palatin* of the *Rhine* By this Marriage he had *Clementia* his only Daughter, who was marry'd to *Henry* of *Saxony*, the Son of *Henry* the *Lion*, and Brother to the Emperor *Otho* IV, who by this means succeeded in the *Palatinate* but he left also but one only Daughter, who marry'd in the Year 1215, *Otho* the *Illustrious*, Son to *Lewis* Duke of *Bavaria* We have shewn elsewhere, that this *Otho* descends in a direct and Male Line from *Otho* Count of *Schiren*, and and that he left two Sons, to wit *Henry*, whose Posterity fail'd in *Otho*, who dy'd in the Year 1335, and *Lewis*, common Father to all the Dukes of *Bavaria*, and all the Counts *Palatins* of the *Rhine* who are now living

Lewis, the eldest Son of *Otho* the *Illustrious*, and of *Agnes* of *Saxony*, Heiress of the *Palatinate*, was born *April* 3, 1229, and had for Portion the *Palatinate* of the *Rhine*, and part of the *Upper Bavaria* He marry'd for first Wife *Mary*, the Daughter of *Henry* II, Duke of *Brabant*, and of *Mary* of *Suabia*, whom he caus'd to be beheaded on *January* 11, 1256, for Suspicion of Adultery, without so much as giving her a Hearing, and with so much Precipitation, that he caus'd a young Lady to be kill'd at the same time, who was a Confident of the Dutchess, made her Woman be flung Headlong from the top of a Tower, and the Traitor who brought him the false Report, to be knock'd on the Head This Execution gave him the Name of *Severe* But he was so sorry for it, that he made Reparation to the Brother of the Dutchess, and to justify her Memory, he built the Convent of *Furstenfeld*, where the following Verses are still to be seen at this Day

Conjugis innocuæ fusi monumenta cruoris,
Pro culpa pretium templa sacrata vides

He marry'd for second Wife *Anne* the Daughter of *Conrade* Duke of *Massovia*, by whom he had no Issue and for third *Mahault*, the Daughter of the Emperor *Rodolphus* I, and of *Anne* of *Hohenberg* His Reputation was so great in the Empire, that the Princes not being able to agree in the Choice of an Emperor during the Division between *Alfonsus* King of *Castile*, and *Richard* of *Cornwal*, they refer'd themselves to *Lewis* Duke of *Bavaria*, who nominated *Rodolphus* of *Habspurg*, whose Daughter he afterwards marry'd He dy'd *February* 2, 1295, leaving Issue *Rodolphus*, from whom sprung the Electors *Palatins*, *Lewis* Emperor and Duke of *Bavaria*, of whose Posterity we have spoken elsewhere, *Mahault*, marry'd to *Otho* the *Severe*, who was Son to *John* Duke of *Lunenburg*; *Anne*, third Wife to *Henry* the *Infant*, first Lantgrave of *Hesse*, and *Agnes*, who was marry'd to *Henry* Marquiss of *Landsberg*

---

* The Origin of the Palatinate

Rodolphus, the eldest Son of *Lewis the Severe*, and of *Mahault* of *Habspurg*, his third Wife, was born *October* 4, 1274, and had for his Portion the *Palatinate* of the *Rhine*, and part of the *Upper Bavaria*, which he shar'd with his Brother *Lewis*. But *Lewis*, who was but seven Years old when this Partition was made, oblig'd his Brother to enlarge his Portion, by a Treaty they made *An* 1313. However this Accommodation did not so well reconcile their Minds, but *Rodolphus* oppos'd the Election of his Brother, and openly declar'd in favour of *Frederick* of *Austria*, his Competitor. *Lewis*, on his part, resented these ill Offices, drove his Brother out of his Estates, and forc'd him to retire into *England*, where he dy'd in Exile, *April* 11, 1319. He had marry'd *Mahault*, the Daughter of the Emperor *Adolphus* of *Nassau*, and of *Imagine* of *Limburg*, by whom he had *Adolphus*, who left Posterity, *Radolphus* II, and *Rupert*, who had no Children, and *Mahault*, marry'd to *John* Count of *Spanheim*.

Adolphus, the eldest Son of *Rodolphus* I, and of *Mahault* of *Nassau*, was born *September* 27, 1300, and made, in the Year 1329, a Treaty with the Emperor his Unkle, who was then at *Pavia*, which contain'd, That the Electoral Dignity should for the future be alternative in the two Branches of the House of *Bavaria*, to begin by the Offspring of *Rodolphus*, as being the eldest Branch. But this is what the Emperor *Charles* IV had no Regard to, but ordain'd by the *Golden Bull* that it should be inseparable from the *Palatinate* of the *Rhine*. It was said in the same Treaty, That the Emperor should restore to his Nephews that part of *Bavaria* which at present is call'd the *Upper Palatinate*, which has ever since remain'd to the *Palatins*, till the last War in *Germany*. He had by *Irmengard* of *Ottinguen*, *Rupert*, who had by *Beatrix* the Daughter of *Frederick* III, King of *Sicily*, and of *Eleonor* of *Anjou*, *Rupert* II, who succeeded in the Electoral Dignity, and was elected Emperor after the Deposition of *Wenceslas*, *An* 1400. He dy'd *May* 18, 1410, leaving by his second Wife, who was *Elizabeth*, Daughter to *Frederick* III, Burgrave of *Nuremberg*, 1 *Lewis*, who left Issue, 2 *John*, who marry'd *Catherine* the Daughter of *Wartislas* VII, Duke of *Pomerania* at *Wolgast*, by whom he had, amongst others, *Christopher*, who was call'd to the Crown of *Sweden*, *An* 1439, and dy'd *January* 6, 1448, without Issue, as well as all his Brothers, 3 *Frederick*, who had no Children, 4 *Otho*, Father to *Rupert* Bishop of *Ratisbone*, to *Albert* Bishop of *Strasburg*, to two other Sons who had no Issue, and to four Daughters, 5 *Stephen*, whose Posterity is still living, 6 *Margaret*, marry'd to *Charles* II, Duke of *Lorrain*, 7 *Elizabeth*, who was marry'd to *Frederick*, the third Son of *Leopold the Good*, Arch-Duke of *Austria*, and 8 *Agnes*, who marry'd *Adolphus* first Duke of *Cleves*.

Lewis III, the eldest Son of the Emperor *Rupert*, succeeded his Father in the Electoral Dignity. He was Vicar in the Empire, during the Journey the Emperor his Father took to *Italy*, and the Council of *Constance* desir'd him to take Care of its Safety. He marry'd for first Wife *Blanche*, the Daughter of *Henry* Duke of *Lancaster*, and Earl of *Darby*, who usurp'd the Kingdom of *England* from *Richard* II, his Cousin-German, by whom he had *Rupert*, call'd the *English*, who dy'd without Issue in the Year 1426. He marry'd in 1418, for second Wife, *Mahault*, the Daughter of *Amadeus* of *Savoy*, Prince of *Achaia*, and of *Catherine* who was Daughter to *Amadeus* Count of *Geneva*, by *Mahault* of *Boulogne*, and dy'd *December* 30, 1436, leaving Issue, 1 *Lewis* IV, 2 *Frederick*, who was born *August* 1, 1425, and was firnam'd the *Victorious*, on account of the Battel he gain'd in the Year 1462, over *Ulric* Count of *Wirtemberg*, 3 *Charles*, Marquis of *Baden*, and *George*, Bishop of *Metz*, his Brother. After the Death of his eldest Brother he serv'd the Electoral Dignity, to the Prejudice of his Nephew, contrary to the Direction of the *Golden Bull*, and even against the Protestations of the Emperor *Frederick* III. But he agreed the Matter with his Nephew, and, the better to secure him the Succession, he adopted him, and marry'd a Gentlewoman nam'd *Clare* of *Tettinguen*, by whom he had two Sons, *Frederick*, who dy'd before the Father in the Year 1474, and *Lewis*, from whom are descended the Counts of *Leisenstein*, *Wertheim*, and *Rochfort*. *Trithemius* has compos'd a particular Treatise of the Life of this Prince, who dy'd *December* 12, 1476, 3 *Rupert*, who was chosen Archbishop of *Cologn* in the Year 1463, and was dispossess'd by *Herman* Lantgrave of *Hesse*, in the Year 1480, 4 *Mahault*, marry'd to *Lewis* Count of *Wirtemberg*, and in a second Match to *Albert* of *Austria*, Brother to the Emperor *Frederick* III.

Lewis IV, eldest Son to *Lewis* III, by *Mahault* of *Savoy*, marry'd *Emilia*, the Daughter of *Albert* Elector of *Brandenburg*, and of *Anne* of *Saxony*, and dy'd *August* 13, 1446, leaving his Wife with Child of a Son, who was nam'd *Philip*.

Philip, the posthumous Son of *Lewis* IV, Elector *Palatin*, and of *Emilia* of *Brandenburg*, marry'd, *March* 11, 1474, *Margaret*, Daughter to *Lewis the Rich*, Duke of *Bavaria*. He succeeded in the Electoral Dignity, and dy'd *March* 17, 1508. He had by that Marriage, 1 *Lewis* V, who was born *July* 2, 1478. He was present at the Election of the Emperor *Charles* V, and dy'd *March* 15, 1544, leaving no Issue by *Sibylla*, Daughter to *Albert* IV, Duke of *Bavaria*, 2 *Rupert*, who marry'd *Elizabeth*, the Daughter of *George the Rich*, Duke of *Bavaria*, and of *Avoye* of *Poland*. By the Contract of Marriage, it was agreed, That *Rupert*, and his Wife who was an only Daughter, should inherit all the Goods, moveable and immoveable, of *George*, who confirm'd the Contract by his Testament, of which he made *Lewis* XII, King of *France*, and *Uladyslas*, King of *Poland*, Executors, but *Albert* IV, Duke of *Bavaria* at *Munichen*, who had marry'd *Cunegunda*, the Daughter of the Emperor *Frederick* III, maintain'd that *Bavaria*, being a Masculin Fief, could not fall to the Distaff, and obtain'd the Investiture thereof from the Emperor *Maximilian* I, his Brother-in-Law, who considering nevertheless, that the Electors *Palatins* had been very much wrong'd by the Treaty which the Emperor *Lewis* IV had made with his Nephews, was for bringing the Parties to an Agreement, so that *Albert* was contented with one Third of the Inheritance of *George*, and left the

the two other Thirds to *Rupert* for his Life, after which, his Heirs should be oblig'd to restore another Third. But *Rupert* rejected these Conditions, and engag'd himself in a War, which made him be put in the Ban of the Empire, and he was unfortunate enough to fall into the Hands of the Emperor, who caus'd him to be poyson'd, with his Wife and Son. His second Son, nam'd *Otho Henry*, succeeded *Frederick* II, his Unkle, in the Electoral Dignity. The Emperor *Maximilian* I. restor'd him to that part of *Bavaria*, which the Duke of *Neuburg*, and the other Princes of the same Branch, possess at present. He had no Children, no more than *Philip* his Brother, who distinguish'd himself by his Courage and Conduct, of which he gave such signal Proofs, in defending the City of *Vienna*, which the Emperor *Soliman* had besieg'd in the Year 1529. He never marry'd, and dy'd *July* 4, 1541. 3 *Frederick* II, the third Son of *Philip*, was born *December* 9, 1482. At eighteen Years of Age he put himself in the Retinue of *Philip* of *Austria*, King of *Spain*, and, since that Time, did very great Services to the Emperors *Maximilian* I and *Charles* V, particularly by commanding the Army of the Empire, while *Philip* his Brother defended the City of *Vienna*. He was rewarded with the great Pretensions which *Dorothy*, Daughter to *Christian* II, King of *Denmark*, brought him in Marriage. He succeeded in the Electoral Dignity, to the Prejudice of the Children of *Rupert*, his eldest Brother, but he had no Issue, and dy'd *February* 26, 1556. 4 *Philip*, who was elected Bishop of *Frisinguen* in the Year 1496, and of *Naumburg* in 1517, and dy'd in the Year 1540, 5 *George*, who was Bishop of *Spires*, 6 *Henry*, who was chosen Bishop of *Worms*, *An* 1529, and the Year following he succeeded *Philip* of *Burgundy* in the Bishoprick of *Utrecht*, the Temporal and Sovereignty whereof he sold to the Emperor *Charles* V, *November* 15, 1527, 7 *John*, who was chosen Bishop of *Ratisbone* in the Year 1507, and dy'd in 1538, 8 *Wolfgang*, who never marry'd, and dy'd *April* 4, 1558.

So all the Posterity of *Lewis*, the eldest Son of the Emperor *Rupert*, failing with the Children of *Philip*, the *Palatinate* and the Electoral Dignity fell to the Descendents of *Stephen*, the last Son of the same Emperor, who had for Appennage the Town of *Zimmeren*, and marry'd *June* 16, 1410, *Anne*, the only Daughter and Heiress of *Frederick* Count of *Veldents*. He dy'd in the Year 1451, and left Issue, 1 *Frederick*, who left Posterity, 2 *Lewis* V, who form'd the Branch of *Deuxponts*, 3 *Rupert*, who was chosen Bishop of *Strasburg*, but was forc'd to yield to his Competitor, 4 *John*, Bishop of *Munster* and Archbishop of *Magdeburg*, 5 *Stephen*, Dean of the Cathedral Church of *Cologn*, 6 *John* II, Prebendary of *Strasburg*.

Frederick, the eldest Son of *Stephen*, was born in the Year 1417, and marry'd, in 1454, *Margaret d'Egmont*, Daughter to *Arnoul* Duke of *Geldre*, by *Catherine* of *Cleves*, and dy'd *November* 21, 1480, leaving Issue, 1 *John*, who had Offspring, 2 *Rupert*, Bishop of *Ratisbone*, 3 *Stephen*, Prevost of the Church of *Cologn*, 4 *William*, Prebendary of *Triers*, 5 *Frederick*, Prebendary of *Cologn*.

John, the Son of *Frederick*, marry'd *Jean*, the Daughter of *John* Count of *Nassau* at *Sarbrucken*, and dy'd 1509, leaving *John* II, who had Issue, and *Frederick*, who dy'd young.

John II was born *March* 20, 1492, and marry'd for first Wife *Beatrix*, the Daughter of *Christopher* Marquiss of *Baden*, and of *Ottilia* of *Catznelbogen*, who dying *May* 1, 1535, he marry'd for second Wife *Mary Jaqueline* Countess of *Ottinguen*, and dy'd *May* 18, 1557. He had, by his first Wife, 1 *Frederick* III, Elector, 2 *George*, who had no Issue, 3 *Richard*, who dy'd also without Children, 4 *William*, who dy'd young, and several Daughters, amongst the rest *Sabina*, marry'd to *Lamoral* Count of *Egmont*, who was executed at *Brussels*, *An* 1568, and *Magdalen*, who was marry'd to *Philip* Count of *Hanau*.

Frederick III, Son to *John* II, by *Beatrix* of *Baden*, was born *February* 14, 1515, and succeeded in the Electorate, *An* 1559, as being the nearest Relation, by the Father's side, of *Otho Henry*, and descended in a direct Male Line from *Stephen*, the youngest Son of the Emperor *Rupert*, and Brother to *Lewis* III, who was Great Grandfather to *Otho Henry*. In this Quality he assisted at the Election of the Emperor *Maximilian* II, in the Year 1562. He had marry'd, *June* 12, 1537, *Mary* Daughter of *Casimir* Marquiss of *Brandenburg*, and of *Susanna* of *Bavaria*, who dying *October* 31, 1567, he marry'd *April* 25, 1569, for second Wife, *Emilia*, Daughter to *Humbert* III, Count of *Muns* and *Nnenar*, who was the Widow of *Henry* Baron of *Brederode*, by whom he had no Issue. He dy'd *October* 26, 1576, and had by his first Wife, 1 *Albert*, who dy'd young, 2 *Lewis* VI, Elector, 3 *Herman Lewis*, who was drown'd near *Bourges*, *July* 1, 1556, being fifteen Years old, 4 *John Casimir*, who was born *March* 14, 1543, and was Administrator of the Electorate, during the Minority of *Frederick* IV. He led two Armies into *France*, to the Assistance of the King of *Navar* and of the Prince of *Conde*, in 1568 and 1575, and Queen *Elizabeth* of *England* honour'd him with the Order of the Garter. He dy'd *January* 15, 1592, leaving by *Elizabeth*, the Daughter of *Augustus*, Elector of *Saxony*, and of *Anne* of *Denmark*, only one Daughter, nam'd *Dorothy*, who was marry'd to *John George* Prince of *Anhalt* at *Dessau*, 5 *Christopher*, who was kill'd in the Battel of *Moock*, bearing Arms for the States of the Low Countries against the King of *Spain*, *April* 17, 1574, and left no Issue. *Frederick* III had three other Sons, who dy'd young, and his Daughters were marry'd, to wit, the first, nam'd *Elizabeth*, to *John Frederick* II, Duke of *Saxony*, *Susanna Dorothy* to *John William*, also Duke of *Saxony*, Brother to *John Frederick*, *Anne Elizabeth* marry'd *Philip* II, Lantgrave of *Hesse* at *Rhinfels*, and in a second Match *John Augustus* of *Bavaria*, Count *Palatin* of the *Rhine* at *Lutzelstein*, and *Cunegunda Jacoba* marry'd *John*, Count of *Nassau* at *Dillemburg*, Brother to *William* Prince of *Orange*.

Lewis IV, Elector Palatin, eldest Son to *Frederick* III, was born *July* 4, 1539, and marry'd in 1560, *Elizabeth*, the Daughter of *Philip* Lantgrave of *Hesse*, and of *Christina* of *Saxony*, who dying, *March* 11, 1582, he marry'd *July* 2, 1583, for second Wife, *Anne* Daughter to *Edward*

544   *Of the* ELECTION *of the* EMPEROR, *and*

zard II, Count of *Ooftfrife*, by *Catherine* of *Sweden*, but he dy'd *October* 12, of the same Year He had several Children by his first Wife, but they all dy'd young; except *Frederick* IV, who succeeded in the Electoral Dignity, and *Anne Mary*, marry'd to *Charles* Duke of *Summerland*, (who made himself King of *Sweden*) Father to *Guftavus Adolphus*

Frederick IV, Elector *Palatin*, Son to *Lewis* VI, was born *March* 5, 1574, and remain'd, during his Minority, under the Guardianship and Administration of *John Casimir*, his Unkle, till the Year 1592 On *June* 14, 1593, he marry'd *Louise Julian*, the Daughter of *William* of *Naffau* Prince of *Orange*, and of *Charlott* of *Montpenfier*, his third Wife, and dy'd *September* 18, 1610, leaving, 1 *Frederick* V, who succeeded in the Electorate, 2 *Philip Lewis*, who was born *November* 26, 1602, and marry'd, in 1632, *Mary Eleonor*, Daughter to *Joachim Frederick* Elector of *Brandenburg*, by *Eleonor* of *Pruffia*, by whom he left when he dy'd, in the Year 1654, *Lewis-Henry-Maurice-Francis*, Duke of *Zimmeren*, and two Daughters; 3 *Louise Julian*, marry'd to *John* II, Count *Palatin* of the *Rhine*, at *Deuxponts*, Administrator of the Electorate during the Minority of *Frederick* V, 4 *Catherine Sophia*, who is not marry'd, and is still living, 5 *Elizabeth Charlott*, who was born *November* 7, 1597, and marry'd *July* 16, 1616, *George William* Elector of *Brandenburg* She had also some other Children, who dy'd young

Frederick V, Elector *Palatin*, the Son of *Frederick* IV, and of *Louise Julian*, of *Naffau*, was born *August* 16, 1596 He was educated for some time at *Sedan*, under the Care of the Mareschal *de Bouillon*, who had marry'd his Aunt by the Mother's Side February 14, 1613, he marry'd *Elizabeth*, the Daughter of *James* King of *Great Britain*, by *Anne* of *Denmark* In the Year 1619, he was call'd to the Crown of *Bohemia*, but the Lofs of one single Battel took all from him, and oblig'd him to retire into *Holland* The just and victorious Arms of the late King of *Sweden* invited him to take a Journey into *Germany*, in the Year 1632, but the Lofs he sustain'd, in the Person of that Great Prince, afflicted him in so sensible a manner, that he dy'd thereof a Fortnight after He departed this Life at the Castle of *Mayence*, November 29, of the same Year He has left several Children, to wit, three Sons, and as many Daughters The Sons are, 1 *Charles Lewis*, Elector, 2 *Robert*, who was born *October* 17, 1619 This Prince had acquir'd great Reputation in Arms, and was in the Service of the King of *Hungary*, 3 *Edward*, who was born *October* 5, 1624, and marry'd *April* 24, 1645, *Anne* of *Gonzague*, the Daughter of *Charles* Duke of *Mantua*, and of *Catherine* of *Lorrain* The Daughters are, 1 *Elizabeth*, who was born *December* 26, 1618 This Princess never marry'd, and apply'd her self wholly to the Study of the *Belles Lettres*, 2 *Louise Hollandine*, who was born *April* 18, 1622 She withdrew from the Queen of *Bohemia*, her Mother, under the Pretext of Religion, no body knowing what is become of her, 3 *Henrietta*, who was born *July* 7, 1626 She has

liv'd w n tne Electrix Dowager of *Brandenburg*, her Aunt

Charles Lewis, the eldest Son of *Frederick* V, and of *Elizabeth* of *England*, was born *December* 22, 1617, and has marry'd since, in the Year 1650, *Charlotte*, the Daughter of *William* V, Lantgrave of *Heffe Caffel*, and of *Amelia* of *Hanau*, by whom he has Children, among the rest, *Charles*, born *March* 3, 1651, *Louise*, born *May*, 1652, &c It was in Consideration of him, that the Deputies of the States of the Empire, assembled at *Munster* and *Ofnaburg*, created an eighth Electorate, by the Treaty which was concluded *October* 24, 1648, and it is this Prince who is at this Day in Possession of the *Palatin* Electoral Dignity We shall speak of him hereafter, when we shall have made known the different Branches of this Family

* We have hitherto spoken of the Electoral, and of a Branch that came out of it, and which took its Rise in the Person of *Philip Lewis*, Brother to the late Elector, who has left but one Son, as we said before, who takes the Quality of Duke of *Simmeren* All the others came from *Lewis*, call'd the *Black*, the younger Son of *Stephen*, Son to the Emperor *Rupert*   *Lewis* had for his Share *Deuxponts*, and the County of *Veldentz*, and marry'd *Jean* of *Croy*, the Daughter of *Anthony* Count of *Porcean*, and of *Margaret* of *Lorrain*, by whom he had several Children, to wit, 1 *David*, who dy'd young, 2 *Gaspar*, who marry'd *Emilia*, the Daughter of *Albert* Elector of *Brandenburg*, and of *Anne* of *Saxony*, but he dismember'd himself, out of Rage to find himself impotent, for which Reason his Wife left him, and *Alexander*, his Brother, confin'd him as being mad, 3 *Alexander*, who left Issue, 4 *Albert*, Bishop of *Strasburg*, 5 *Philip*, Prebendary of *Strasburg*, 6 *John*, Canon of *Cologn*, 7 *Sampson*, who fell from a Tower, and dy'd on the Spot, and some Daughters

Alexander marry'd *Margaret*, the Daughter of *Craft* or *Crato* V, Count of *Hohenlo*, and of *Helen* of *Wirtemberg*, and dy'd *October* 31, 1514, leaving Issue, 1 *Lewis*, who had Offspring, 2 *George*, Prebendary of *Triers* and of *Cologn*, 3 *Rupert*, from whom descend the *Palatins* of *Lutzelftein*, or of *la petite Pierre*, of whom we shall speak hereafter, and some Daughters

Lewis, the Son of *Alexander*, was born in 1502, and marry'd, *October* 10, 1525, *Elizabeth*, Daughter to *William the Eldeft*, Lantgrave of *Heffe*, by *Anne* of *Brunfwick*, and dy'd *December* 3, 1532, leaving *Wolfgang*

Wolfgang, Son to *Lewis*, was born *September* 26, 1526 He succeeded, after the Death of *Otho Henry* Elector *Palatin*, by the Confent of the Princes of the Electoral Line, in that part of *Bavaria* which the Emperor *Maximilian* I had reftor'd to the Children of *Rupert*, who dy'd in Prifon, whereof the Town of *Neuburg* on the *Danube* is Capital He marry'd, *September* 6, 1544, *Anne*, the Daughter of *Philip* Lantgrave of *Heffe*, and of *Chriftina* of *Saxony*, and dy'd *June* 11, 1569, in his March to *France*, whither he was leading seven thousand

* The Palatins of Deuxponts

Foot,

of the ELECTORS *of the* EMPIRE.   545

Foot and five hundred Horse, to the Assistance of the Prince of *Condé*, and of the Admiral *de Coligny*, leaving Issue *Philip Lewis*, from whom are descended the Dukes of *Neuburg*, 2 *John*, Duke of *Bavaria* at *Deuxponts*; 3 *Otho Henry*, who left only one Daughter, nam'd *Dorothy*, marry'd to *George John* II, Count *Palatin* of *Lutzelstein*, 4 *Frederick*, who left no Issue, 5 *Charles*, who made a Branch, and his Posterity live still at *Birkenfeld* He had also several Daughters, but most of them dy'd young, and the others did not marry very considerably

Philip Lewis, the eldest Son of *Wolfgang*, Count *Palatin* of the *Rhine* at *Deuxponts*, and of *Anne* of *Hesse*, was born *October* 2, 1547, and had for Portion *Neuburg*, and some other Towns on the *Daunbe* He marry'd on *September* 27, 1574, *Anne*, the Daughter of *William*, Duke of *Juliers, Cleves* and *Berg*, &c and of *Mary* of *Austria*, and dy'd *August* 12, 1614 He had by his Wife, besides those Children that dy'd young, 1 *Wolfgang William*, 2 *Augustus*, who had his Portion at *Sultzbach*, 3 *John Frederick*, who had his at *Hippolstein*, 4 *Anne Mary*, marry'd to *Frederick William*, Duke of *Saxony*, at *Altemburg*

Wolfgang William, the eldest Son of *Philip Lewis*, and of *Anne* of *Juliers*, disputed this rich Inheritance with the Elector of *Brandenburg*, as being the Son of a younger Daughter, whereas the Elector had only the Right of a Daughter of the eldest Daughter He was born *October* 25, 1578, and marry'd on *November* 11, 1613, *Magdalen*, the Daughter of *William*, Duke of *Bavaria*, and of *Renée* of *Lorrain* who dying in the Year 1628, he marry'd for second Wife, on *November* 11, 1631, *Elizabeth Charlotte* of *Bavaria*, the Daughter of *John* II, Duke of *Deuxponts*, and on *May* 7, 1651, he marry'd for third Wife *Mary Frances*, the Daughter of *Francis Egon*, Count of *Furstemb* and dy'd *March* 20, 1653, leaving Issue only one Son

Philip William, the Son of *Wolfgang William*, and of *Magdalen* of *Bavaria*, was born *November* 14, 1615 He marry'd for first Wife *Catherin Constance*, the Daughter of *Sigismund*, King of *Poland*, and of *Constance* of *Austria*, who dying on *October* 9, 1651, without Children, he has since marry'd in the Year 1653, *Elizabeth Amelia*, the Daughter of *George*, Landgrave of *Hesse* at *Darmstad* They who had a Design to get the Imperial Dignity out of the House of *Austria*, consider'd this Prince, as him who might aspire to the Empire upon the Duke of *Bavaria*'s Refusal but the little likelihood there was of Success in this Negotiation, was the Cause it was not undertaken And indeed he would have been excluded by all the secular Electors, who would never have suffer'd a Prince to be call'd to that Dignity, who had not wherewith to support it.

Augustus, the second Son of *Philip Lewis*, Count *Palatin* of the *Rhine*, and Duke of *Bavaria* at *Neuburg*, was born *October* 2, 1582, and had his Portion at *Sultzbach*, and marry'd *July* 2, 1620, *Avoye*, the Daughter of *John Adolphus*, Duke of *Holstein Gottorp*, and of *Augusta* of *Denmark* He dy'd *August* 14, 1632 His Children are, 1 *Christian Augustus*, who was born *July* 16, 1622, and marry'd in 1653, *Amelia*, the Daughter of *John*, Count of *Nassau*, the Widow of *Wrangel*, a *Swedish* General, 2 *Philip*, who was born *January* 19, 1630, and two other Sons, who dy'd young, 3 *Emilia Sophia*, who was marry'd to *Joachim*, Count of *Ottingnen*, 4 *Augusta Sophia*, marry'd to *Wenceslas Poppel*, Prince of *Lobkowitz*.

John Frederick, the third Son of *Philip Lewis*, was born *August* 23, 1587, and had for Portion *Hippolstein* He marry'd *November* 7, 1624, *Sophia Agnes*, the Daughter of *Lewis*, Lantgrave of *Hesse Darmstad*, and of *Magdalen* of *Branaenburg*, by whom he had several Children, but they all dy'd young so that this Branch was extinct when he dy'd, which he did on *October* 9, 1644

John, second Son to *Wolfgang*, and younger Brother to *Philip Lewis*, Count *Palatin* of the *Rhine*, and Duke of *Bavaria* at *Neuburg*, was born *March* 18, 1550, and had for Portion *Deuxponts* He marry'd on *October* 4, 1579, *Magdalen*, the Daughter of *William*, Duke of *Juliers, Cleves*, and *Berg*, and of *Mary* of *Austria*, and dy'd *August* 12, 1604 The Children who liv'd are, 1 *John* II, who left Issue, 2 *Frederick Casimir*, who made a particular Branch of the *Palatins* of *Landsberg*, 3 *John Casimir*, whose Posterity is still living in *Sweden*, 4 *Mary Elizabeth*, who marry'd on *May* 18, 1601, *George Gustavus* of *Bavaria*, Count *Palatin* at *Lautrec*

John II, the Son of *John* I, was born *March* 26, 1584, and marry'd in the Year 1604, *Catherin*, the Daughter of *René* II, Duke of *Rohan*, and of *Catherin* of *Parthenay* and on *May* 4, 1612, he marry'd for second Wife *Louise Julian* of *Bavaria*, the Daughter of *Frederick* IV, Elector *Palatin*, and of *Louise Julian* of *Nassau*, and dy'd *July* 30, 1635 He had by his first Wife only *Magdalen Catherin*, who was marry'd to *Christian* of *Bavaria*, Count *Palatin* at *Birkenfelt* He had by the second, 1 *Frederick*; 2 *Catherin Charlotte*, who was marry'd to *Wolfgang William* of *Bavaria*, Count *Palatin* of the *Rhine* at *Neuburg*, 3 *Julian Magdalen*, who was marry'd in the Year 1645, to *Frederick Lewis* of *Bavaria*, Count *Palatin* of the *Rhine* at *Landsperg*, her Cousin, and several other Daughters

Frederick Casimir, the second Son of *John*, Count *Palatin* of the *Rhine* at *Deuxponts*, was born *June* 10, 1585, and had for Portion *Landsperg* He marry'd in the Year 1616, *Emilia* of *Nassau*, the Daughter of *William*, Prince of *Orange*; and dy'd *September* 20, 1645, leaving Issue *Frederick Lewis*

Frederick Lewis, the Son of *Frederick Casimir*, and of *Emilia* of *Nassau*, was born *October* 17, 1619, and marry'd on *November* 17, 1645, *Julian Magdalen* of *Bavaria*, Daughter to *John* II, Count *Palatin* of the *Rhine* at *Deuxponts*, by whom he has Children, amongst others *Lewis William*, born *February* 13, 1648 As Cousin German of the late Prince of *Orange*, he was for being concern'd in the Guardianship of his Posthumous Son; but it was given to the Mother and Grandmother, in Conjunction with the Elector of *Brandenburg*, Unkle of the Pupil by the Mother's side

John Casimir, the third Son of *John*, Duke of *Deuxponts*, was born *April* 12, 1589 And as he could not hope for any great Provision

6 Z

in *Germany*, he retir'd to *Sweden*, where he marry'd on *June* 11, 1615, *Catherin*, the Daughter of *Charles*, King of *Sweden*, and had by her, 1 *Charles Gustavus*, 2 *John Adolphus*, born in the Year 1629. He was Generalissimo to the King of *Sweden* his Brother, in *Prussia*, 3 *Christina Magdalen*, who was born *March* 17, 1616, and marry'd in the Year 1642, to *Frederick*, Marquiss of *Baden Dourlach*, 4 *Mary Euphrosyne*, who was born *February* 4, 1625, and marry'd in 1647, to the Count *Magnus Gabriel de la Garde*, 5 *Eleonor Catherin*, who was born *May* 27, 1626. She is at present the Relict of *Frederick*, Lantgrave of *Hesse*, who was kill'd in *Poland*.

Charles Gustavus of *Bavaria*, the Son of *John Casimir*, was born *November* 8, 1622. He has since *June* 16, 1654, succeeded to the Crown of *Sweden*, by the Resignation of Queen *Christina*, his Cousin German, and marry'd in the Year following *Avoye Eleonor*, the Daughter of *Frederick*, Duke of *Holstein Gottorp*, by *Mary Elizabeth* of *Saxony*, by whom he had one Son.

We have said before that *Charles*, the fifth Son of *Wolfgang*, Count Palatin of the *Rhine* at *Deuxponts*, and of *Anne* of *Hesse*, made also a particular Branch. He was born *December* 4, 1560, and had for his Portion *Birkenfeld*. He marry'd on *February* 25, 1586, *Dorothy*, the Daughter of *William the Young*, Duke of *Brunswick* and *Lunenburg*, and of *Dorothy* of *Denmark*, and dy'd on *December* 6, 1600, leaving Issue, 1 *George William*, 2 *Frederick*, who was born *October* 19, 1594, and dy'd in the Year 1626, without Issue, 3 *Christian*, 4 *Sophia*, who has marry'd *Craft*, Count of *Hohenlo*.

George William, the eldest Son of *Charles*, was born *August* 6, 1591, and marry'd on *December* 1, 1616, *Dorothy*, the Daughter of *Otho*, Count of *Solms* at *Sonneuald*. He has marry'd for second Wife *Julian*, Rhingrave of *Grumbach*, whom he has divorc'd; and for third, *Anne Elizabeth*, the Daughter of *Lewis Eberhard*, Count of *Ottingnen*. He had no Children but by his first Wife, to wit, *Charles Otho*, born *August* 26, 1625, and three Daughters, amongst the rest *Mary Magdalen*, who was marry'd to *Anthony Gunther*, Count of *Swartzenburg* at *Sunderhausel*.

Christian, the second Son of *Charles*, Count Palatin of the *Rhine* at *Birkenfeld*, was born *August* 24, 1598, and has his Residence at *Bischweiler*. He was General of the Horse under the late King of *Sweden*, and marry'd for first Wife *Magdalen Catharin*, Daughter to *John* of *Bavaria*, who dying in the Year 1648, he marry'd the Year following for second Wife, *Mary*, Countess of *Helfenstein*, the Relict of the Lantgrave of *Leuchtemberg*. He had by the first Match, 1 *Christian*, born *June* 22, 1637, 2 *John Charles*, born *October* 17, 1638, 3 *Dorothy Catharin*, who marry'd *John Lewis*, Count of *Nassau*, and two other Daughters.

Having shewn how the *Palatins* of *Newburg*, *Salzbach*, *Deuxponts*, *Landsberg*, *Sweden*, *Birkenfeld*, and of *Bischweiler*, descend from *Lewis*, eldest Son to *Alexander*, Count Palatin of the *Rhine* at *Deuxponts*, we must give an Account of the Posterity of *Rupert*, younger Son to the same *Alexander*, by *Margaret* of *Hohenlo*, who had for Portion *Lutzelstein* or *La Petite-pierre*. He marry'd *Ursula*, the Daughter of *John* VII Rhingrave, and of *Jean de Meurs*, and dy'd in the Year 1544, leaving *George John*, who left Issue, *Anne*, second Wife to *Charles* II, Marquiss of *Baden*, and *Ursula*, marry'd to *Wiric*, Count of *Falkenstein*.

George John, the Son of *Rupert*, was born *April* 11, 1543. He built the Town of *Lutzelstein*, which is commonly call'd in *France*, *La Petite-pierre*, in *English* the *Little Stone*. He marry'd *Anne Mary*, the Daughter of *Gustavus* King of *Sweden*, and of *Margaret*, who was Daughter to *Abraham* Lord of *Loholm*, and dy'd on *May* 16, 1592, leaving Issue, 1 *George Gustavus*, who has also left Issue, 2 *John Augustus*, who marry'd in the Year 1599, *Anne Elizabeth*, Daughter to *Frederick* III, Elector Palatin, by *Mary* of *Brandenburg*, Widow of *Philip*, Lantgrave of *Hesse* at *Rhinfels*, and dy'd *September* 18, 1611, without Issue, 3 *Lewis Philip*, who was kill'd by the Splinter of a Lance in a Turnament at *Heidelberg*, on *October* 14, 1601, 4 *George John*, who also left Issue, 5 *Ursula*, second Wife to *Lewis* Duke of *Wirtemberg*, 6 *Anne Margaret*, third Wife to *Richard* of *Bavaria*, Count Palatin of the *Rhine* at *Simmeren*.

George Gustavus, the eldest Son of *George John*, was born *February* 8, 1564, and marry'd in the Year 1586, for first Wife, *Elizabeth*, the Daughter of *Christopher* Duke of *Wirtemberg*, the Widow of *George Ernest*, Prince of *Henneberg*. On *May* 18, 1601, he marry'd for second Wife, *Elizabeth* of *Bavaria*, the Daughter of *John* I, Count Palatin of the *Rhine* at *Deuxponts*, and of *Magdalen* of *Juliers*, and dy'd in the Month of *July*, 1634. His Children are, 1 *John Frederick*, who was born *January* 12, 1604, and had betroth'd *Sophia Catherin*, Daughter to *Charles* Duke of *Munsterberg*, but he dy'd before the Marriage, serving under the late King of *Sweden* in the Year 1632, 2 *Charles Lewis*, who was born *February* 5, 1607, and was wounded on *July* 17, 1631, in a Battel near *Werben*, being also in the Service of the King of *Sweden*, whereof he dy'd a few Days after; 3 *Leopold Lewis*, who was born *February* 1, 1625, and marry'd on *July* 4, 1648, *Agatha Christina*, Daughter to *Philip Wolfgang*, Count of *Hanau*, and some Daughters, amongst others *Anne Magdalen*, who was marry'd to *Henry Wenceslas*, Duke of *Munsterberg*.

George John II, the younger Son of *George John* I, was born in the Year 1586, and marry'd in 1613, *Dorothy Susanna*, Daughter to *Otho Henry*, Count Palatin of the *Rhine* at *Sulesbach*, by whom he has Children.

These are all the Princes of the Posterity of *Rodolphus*, Count Palatin of the *Rhine*, and Duke of *Bavaria*, eldest Son to *Lewis the Severe*, who are compris'd in the General Investiture, and who may all hope for the Electoral Dignity, for default of Sons, or other nearer Relations, not by virtue of the Investiture given to the first Elector of this Branch because it is the Duke of *Bavaria* who is at present invested therewith, but in Execution of the Treaty of *Munster*; which contains, That *Charles Lewis*, and his Heirs and Relations by the Father's side, descended from *Rodolphus*, shall possess the eighth Electorate, which was then created, and shall enjoy the same according to the

of the ELECTORS of the EMPIRE.

the Order of the *Golden Bull*. And according to this Constitution the Princes *Palatins* are intitl'd to the Succession of the Electorate in the following Order, 1 The Sons of the present Elector, 2 His two Brothers succesively, and if they dye without Issue, 3 The Duke of *Simmeren*, Son to the Brother of *Frederick* V, Father to the Elector; 4 The Duke of *Neuburg*, as being the eldest of the Princes descended in a direct and Male Line from *Lewis the Black*, the younger Son of *Stephen*, and Brother to *Frederick*, from whom came the Electors, 5 The Count *Palatin* of *Sultzbach*, junior of the House of *Neuburg*, 6 The Duke of *Deuxponts*, as the eldest of the Princes descended from *John*, the second Son of *Wolfgang*, and younger Brother to *Philip Lewis*, Duke of *Neuburg*, 7 The Duke of *Lansperg*, as coming from *Frederick Casimir*, second Son of *John*, 8 The King of *Sweden*, as being the eldest of the Princes descended from *John Casimir*, third Son of the said *John* Duke of *Deuxponts*, 9 The *Palatin* of *Birkenfeld*, as coming from *Charles*, fifth Son of *Wolfgang*, and third Brother of *Philip Lewis*, Duke of *Neuburg*, 10 The *Palatin Christian* of *Bischweiler*, his Brother, 11 And in the last place the *Palatin* of *Lautrec*, and of *La Petite-pierre*, descended from *Rupert*, the younger Son of *Alexander*, and Brother to *Lewis*, the common Father of all the Dukes and *Palatins*, except those of the Electoral Branch.

All these Princes take in their Titles the Quality of Count *Palatin* of the *Rhine*, and of Duke of *Bavaria*, because being of the House of *Bavaria*, they all assume the Quality thereof, according to the Custom of *Germany*, where the eldest Brothers are not distinguish'd from the younger by their Qualities. It is not to say but *Deuxponts* and *Neuburg* are Dutchies, but, as the Lords of those Territories are Princes of the House of *Bavaria*, by that sort of Abbreviation is meant, that they are Dukes of the House of *Bavaria*, dwelling at *Neuburg* or at *Deuxponts*. In the same Manner as the Title of Dukes of *Altemburg*, of *Weimar* and of *Gotha*, and that of Marquiss of *Culmbach* and *Anspach*, is given to those Dukes of *Saxony*, who reside at *Altemburg*, *Weimar*, and at *Gotha*, and to those Marquisses of *Brandenburg* who reside at *Culmbach* and *Anspach*.

1 We must own that there seems to be some Inconsistency in the Partitions we have here spoken of, with what we have said elsewhere, That not only the Electoral Dignity cannot be separated from the Principality to which it is annex'd, but also that the Principality is it self indivisible. But this Contradiction is only in appearance; since in effect there is no Partition made of that part of the *Palatinate*, which the Elector *Palatin* possess'd at the Time of the Publication of the *Golden Bull*, or when the Electoral Dignity was annex'd to the *Palatinate*, but of those Counties and other Territories which have been acquir'd by the Electors, Successors to *Rodolphus*, as the Counties of *Spanheim* and of *Deuxponts*, under which almost all the others are compris'd, which were not united to the *Palatinate* but in the time of the Emperor *Rupert*, and of his Successors Counts

Palatins of the *Rhine*. And therefore the Princes who possess those Counties, wholly or in part, by the way of Partition or Lot, and not as a simple Appennage, have a Right to assist at the Diets, as Princes of the Empire; nay even with this Advantage, that altho' the ancient *Palatine* Electoral Dignity be gone out of their Branch, yet they nevertheless preserve the Rank they had formerly, and have Precedency of the younger Princes of the Electoral Houses of *Saxony* and of *Brandenburg*, for they take Place on the side of the Secular Princes, to wit, *Lautern*, who is Brother to the Elector, *Simmeren* and *Neuburg* immediately after *Bavaria*, and before *Bremi*, and *Deuxponts*, and *Veldens*, or *Birkenfeld*, after *Breme*, and before the Princes of *Saxony*. It was in the beginning of this last War in *Germany* that this fine Coat without Seam was torn, and that contrary to the Constitution of the *Golden Bull* this Principality was dismember'd, when the *Palatinate* on this side the *Rhine* was given to the King of *Spain*, the Bailywick of *Germersheim* to the Arch-Duke, the Bailywicks of *Urtiberg* and of *Umbstadt* to the Lantgrave of *Darmstadt*; and to the Bishops of *Worms* and *Spires*, and to the Great Master of the Teutonick Order, what they found lie conveniently for them. But the Peace of *Munster* has reunited again what the War had dissipated, and has bury'd in an eternal Oblivion, all that had been done against the Laws of the State, and to the Prejudice of the Liberty of the Empire.

* As for the Person of the Elector *Palatin*, he possesses without doubt very great Qualities both of Body and Mind, a perfect Knowledge of several Languages, and has such an Experience in Affairs, that is capable of forming a compleate Prince. He has for near Relations the Kings of *Great Britain* and of *Denmark*, the Elector of *Brandenburg* and the Prince of *Orange*. The Lantgrave of *Hesse Cassel* is his Brother-in-law, and he has liv'd long enough in *Holland* and in *England*, to have been able to make himself Friends there. The King of *Sweden* is a younger Branch of his House, as well as the Electors of *Bavaria* and *Cologn*, so that he might make himself be consider'd, if Affairs were otherwise dispos'd for that Purpose. But his Religion excludes him absolutely, and he is so ill with *Mayence* and *Bavaria*, and by consequence also with *Cologn*, that he cannot hope for their Suffrages, no more than for that of the King of *Bohemia*, even tho' his Religion should be no Obstacle, and tho' all the Friends of the House of *Austria* should not declare against him on such Occasion. The good Offices the King of *Bohemia* has done to the Elector of *Bavaria*, by securing to him the Vicarship, give room to believe, that the Elector *Palatin* might labour to remove the Imperial Dignity from the House of *Austria*, if he thought he could procure it to fall into the Hands of a Prince, whom he had less reason to hate than the Duke of *Bavaria*. But this is what there is no likelihood of, and so it would be hard to conjecture what will be the Success of the Negotiation, which the Elector *Palatin* carrys on out of the Empire, and which Party he will side with in the approaching Diet; except that

---

* *The Person of the Elector Palatin.*

one

one may say, that having the seventh Vote in the Electoral College, he will in all appearance be oblig'd to follow the Plurality unless he should have Interest enough to form a particular Opinion, and make it successful

* At the Treaty of *Munster*, which we before mention'd, it was thought sufficient to make some Satisfaction to the Prince *Palatin* of the *Rhine*, in restoring him to the *Lower Palatinate*, and in creating in his Favour an eighth Electorate But the States of the Empire assembl'd at *Ratisbone* in the Year 1653, and 54, taking into Consideration that there is no Elector, but who has also an Office inseparable from the Electoral Dignity, they instituted in Favour of the same Elector *Palatin* the Office of Great Treasurer hereditary, but without any Function, except that of carrying the Golden Crown at the Processions Formerly he took his Place, and voted immediately after the King of *Bohemia*, and before all the other Secular Electors, and in the Collegiate Diets he held the first Rank amongst them But the Elector of *Bavaria* has at present his Place, and enjoys all the other Advantages which formerly belong'd to the Elector *Palatin* as Elector, so that he is at this Day the last of all, and votes after all his Collegues, except the Archbishop of *Mayence*, who votes last

The Vicarship has been adjudg'd to the Elector of *Bavaria*, but there is room to doubt whether the Quality of Judge of the Emperor (which the Elector *Palatin* did not hold as Elector, but as Count *Palatin*, on account of the *Palatinate* of the *Rhine*) can be taken from the Elector *Palatin*. The *Golden Bull* says, Chap V § 3 That it is by a very ancient Custom that the Emperor, or the King of the *Romans*, is oblig'd to be accountable to the Law, and to answer it before the Count *Palatin* of the *Rhine* It is true that it adds thereto the Quality of Great Steward and of Prince Elector of the Holy Empire, so that it seems as if all those Qualities were inseparable But we have shewn before, and it is most certain, that the word *Count-Palatin* signifies Judge of the Palace, and that in that Quality he is also Judge of the Emperor, and not as Great Steward or Elector So that this Quality of Judge not depending on the Electoral Dignity, it cannot pass with it to the Branch of *Bavaria*, unless at the same time the Quality of Count *Palatin*, and the *Palatinate* it self, to which the Quality of Judge of the Emperor is annex'd, be taken from the Elector of *Heidelberg*

The Elector *Palatin* alone has the Privilege of retracting or re-purchasing the Demesne of the Empire which has been alienated, by reimbursing the Purchaser the just Sum he had paid for the same

The Count *Palatin* of the *Rhine*, that is to say, the Head of that Family, has also another Advantage, to wit, That of being born General of the Armies of the Empire And it is in this Quality that *Frederick* II commanded the Army of the Empire against the *Turks*, while his Brother *Philip* defended the Town of *Vienna* against *Soliman* their Emperor in the Year 1522 But they who say that it was on this Consideration, and because the Duke of *Bavaria* had succeeded in the *Palatin* Electoral Dignity, that he had the Command of the Army in the Year 1630, are mistaken, for it was done because the Elector *Palatin* was proscrib'd, and all the Princes of his House being concern'd in his Quarrel, except the Duke of *Nenburg*, there was a kind of Necessity to confer the Command thereof on him that was already Master of the Troops of the League, and who had giv'n to understand (by his obliging the Emperor to take it from the Duke of *Fridland*) that he was a Man that would take of his own Head, what could not be giv'n to another without his Consent

CHAP. XVIII

Of the Preliminaries of the Election, and of the Capitulation.

Hitherto we have spoken of the beginning of the Election, and of the Origin of the Electors, and we have shewn that the Election began to take place in *Conrade* I, immediately after the Death of *Lewis* III, last Emperor of the House of *Charlemagne* That at first all the Princes had a Right to assist at the Elections. That the Quality of Elector did not begin to be known but under the Emperor *Frederick* II That by degrees it became a particular Dignity. That the Electors seiz'd this Prerogative by a Custom insensibly introduc'd, and that their Number and their Privileges were not regulated by an express Law, but in the Time of the Emperor *Charles* IV, in the Year 1356. But altho' in speaking of the Emperors, we have in some measure touch'd upon the Election it self, yet to speak of it pertinently, it is requisite to represent it with all its Circumstances and that we may do this with some Order, we shall treat first of several essential Particulars which precede the Election, and are as it were the Preliminaries thereof This done, we shall speak of the Election it self, and afterwards of its effect, which is the Creation of an Emperor We shall finish our Discourse by the Coronation of the Emperor, which is so inseparable from the Election, that the Emperor *Charles* IV, who has employ'd several Chapters of the *Golden Bull* in the Regulation of this Ceremony, makes it an essential part thereof

We find our selves oblig'd to repeat here what we have said elsewhere, to wit, That to proceed to the Election of a King of the *Romans*, in the Signification which the *Golden Bull*

* *His Rights and Prerogatives*

of the ELECTORS of the EMPIRE.

gives to this Quality, it is absolutely requisite that the Empire be vacant. For in this Signification the Quality of King of the *Romans*, and that of Emperor being synonymous, because the Emperor not being any longer crown'd at *Rome*, he is only King of the *Romans* in the signification which the *Golden Bull* gives to this Quality, altho' he be Emperor in effect, and takes the Quality thereof, there is no creating of an Emperor, or giving a Head to the Empire, under any Name or Title whatever, unless the Empire be vacant by the Death, by the Deposition, or by the voluntary Abdication of the Predecessor. We have said also, that to proceed to the Election of a King of the *Romans* in the modern Signification, that is to say, to give a Coadjutor to the Emperor in being, the Archbishop of *Mayence* must be authoriz'd by the States of the Empire, or by the Electoral College which represents them, before he can convene the other Electors. But we here speak of the free Election of an Emperor, which ought to be done according to the Forms prescrib'd by the *Golden Bull*, which ordains *,

† That the Empire becoming vacant, the Archbishop of *Mayence* for the time being, as Great Chancellor of the Empire in *Germany*, shall send Expresses to all the other Electors his Collegues, and invite them to repair to the Election. It is certain that the Archbishop of *Mayence* has possess'd this Right long before the Publication of the *Golden Bull*, tho' it seems as if the Emperor gave it him by a new Constitution, when he says, *It is our Will*. Whereas in several other Places, where he ought not to speak with so much Assurance, he grounds on the ancient Custom. For *Otho* of *Frisingen*, ‡ speaking of the Election of *Lotharius* II, after the Death of *Henry* V, says, that *Adelbert* Archbishop of *Mayence* conven'd the Princes at *Mayence*, because according to the ancient Custom, that Prelate has a Right to call together the Princes when the Empire is become vacant. It is true that there is no mounting any higher, but we shall find this Privilege ill enough establish'd, for *Lambert* of *Aschaffenburg* *, speaking of the Election of *Rodolphus* of *Rhinfelden*, against *Henry* IV, says, that the Archbishop of *Mayence* conven'd the Princes, because he has the Right to chuse and consecrate the Emperor, on account of the Primacy of his See. So that if his Right of convening were grounded only on that he had to elect, the other Princes, who had a Right to elect as well as he, ought also to have that of convening for the Election. As in effect, notwithstanding *Adelbert* conven'd the Princes for the Election of *Lotharius* II, the circular Letters, related by *Goldast* †, shew that *Frederick* Archbishop of *Cologn*, the Bishops of *Constance*, *Worms*, and of *Spires*, the Abbot of *Fuld*, the Dukes of *Bavaria* and *Suabia*, and the Count *Palatin* of the *Rhine*, had also sign'd them as well as he. And it appears that formerly the Count *Palatin* of the *Rhine* sent his Circular Letters to the Princes as well as the Archbishop of *Mayence*. But at present, and since the Publication of the *Golden Bull*, this Right is appropriated to the Archbishop of *Mayence*, as to the Dean of the Electoral College, and Great Chancellor of the Empire in *Germany*, without there being any Instance that since that time any other Elector has intermeddl'd in that Function. Wherefore it would be to very little purpose to dispute here whether the Chapter has that Right when the See is vacant. It is appropriated to the Person of the Archbishop. There is no Law that gives this Power to the Canons, neither is there any Example that the Chapter ever made use of it.

The Archbishop of *Mayence* is oblig'd to summon to the Election all the other Electors, as well Ecclesiasticks as Seculars. This is what is so necessary, that even tho' all the Electors should be actually present at the Place of the Election about other Affairs, the Archbishop would be nevertheless oblig'd to summon them by his Letters. Whereof we have a very remarkable Instance in the Emperor *Frederick* III, who intending to procure his Son *Maximilian* to be elected in the Year 1486, conven'd the Electors, first at *Wurtzburg*, and after that at *Franckfort*, without intimating to them the Subject of their Meeting. But when he had finish'd the Negotiation he had on Foot for that purpose, and that the Electors had consented to the Election, the Archbishop of *Mayence* did nevertheless send his Circular Letters to the Electors, tho' they were there present. And it is so essential to the Election, that all the Electors be invited, that if the Archbishop of *Mayence* forgets or neglects any one of them, he that shall have been so neglected or forgotten, may cause the Election to be declar'd null and defective. It is not that such Election would be null in it self, so that an Elector who had been duly summon'd, and would not repair thither, or who being there, should have refus'd his Suffrage to the Person elected, could cause it to be declar'd null, under pretext that another had not been summon'd thereto: but none but the Party alone that has been neglected, can cause it to be declar'd faulty, as appears by the Resentment *Ladislas* King of *Bohemia* shew'd for the Contempt which had been had of his Person, at the Election of *Maximilian* I, when *Ferdinand* II caus'd the Electors to be call'd together about the Election of *Ferdinand* III, his Son. The Archbishop of *Triers* was a Prisoner, and unless it were in open Derision of him, he could not be summon'd to an Election, to which he had not the Liberty to repair, so that it was resolv'd to proceed therein without him. But this Contempt had like to have had a very pernicious effect, because the Enemies of the House of *Austria* took from thence an occasion to accuse his Election of Nullity, and *France* refus'd to give the Quality of Emperor to *Ferdinand* III, till the Preliminaries of the Treaty of *Munster* and *Osnaburg* had been concerted.

The Archbishop of *Mayence* sends his Letters by one of the Gentlemen of his Court, and causes him to be accompany'd by a Secretary or Notary, who takes an account of the Delivery of the same, and draws up a verbal Process of the Reddition of the Letters. He is

---

* *Chap 1 § 19* † *The Archbishop of Mayence convenes* ‡ *De Gest Frid 1, Lib 4 Cap 16*
* *In the Year 10, 3.* † *Constit Imper Tom. 1 pag 259*

not oblig'd to direct them to any other Place than that of the usual Residence of the Electors, to wit, Those for the Archbishop of *Triers* at the City of *Triers*, those for the Archbishop of *Cologn* at Bonne, those for the Duke of *Bavaria* at *Munich*, for the Duke of *Saxony* at *Dresden*, for the Marquifs of *Brandenburgh* at *Berlin*, and those for the Count *Palatin* at *Heidelberg*, unless he out of Civility causes them to be repair'd to wherever they happen to be.

The Convocation ought to be perform'd within a Month after the Archbishop of *Mayence* has had Advice of the Death of the Emperor, and the Archbishop ought to appoint the opening of the Electoral Diet within three Months, counting from the Day of the Delivery of the Letters, so that allowing about fifteen Days for the Gentleman's Journey who carries them, he fixes the Day of the opening to that Day three Months and a half after the Date of the Letters. For Example, the Emperor *Ferdinand* III dy'd *April* 2, 1657, the Archbishop of *Mayence* might have Advice of his Death the 12th, He sent his Circular Letters about the latter end of the same Month, and fix'd the Convocation at the end of *August*. This is what is so essential to the Election, that it is not in the Power of the Archbishop of *Mayence* to grant a longer Delay by his Circular Letters, but he can prorogue the time of opening the Diet, with the Consent of all the Electors, and not of his own Motion. The *Golden Bull* prescribes the Terms in which these Circular Letters ought to be conceiv'd, and sets down the Form thereof*, but this is what is no longer observ'd now. For we find amongst the Acts publish'd by *Lundorp*, those which the Archbishop of *Mayence* sent for the Election of the late Emperor, which are in the *German* Tongue, and have nothing in common, at least as to the Style and Form, with those that are to be seen in the *Golden Bull*.

† If the Archbishop of *Mayence* fails to convene the Electors within the Time prescrib'd by the Law, they may repair to the Place of Election *ex Officio* and of their own Motion, nay they are even oblig'd to be there, by the Oath they have taken to the Empire‡, because they do not hold their Right from the Archbishop of *Mayence*, but of the Law, and of the first Investiture, by virtue whereof they assist at the Election, even without being invited to it, and before they have receiv'd the Investiture from the Emperor, as we have said elsewhere *

† The Law requires that the Election be perform'd at *Franckfort*, but before the Publication of the *Golden Bull*, there was no particular Town fix'd for the Election on the contrary, when all the Princes had still a Share therein, they held an Assembly at *Rens*, where they resolv'd upon the Day and Place for the Election. And indeed, if we look over History, we shall not find therein three Emperors that have been elected at *Franckfort* before the Emperor *Frederick* II. *Conrade* I was chosen at *Forcheim*, *Henry* I at *Fritzlar*, *Otho* I at *Aix la Chapelle*, *Otho* II at *Worms*, *Otho* III at *Rome*, *Henry* II at *Mayence*, *Conrade* II in a Plain between *Worms* and *Mayence*, *Conrade* III at *Coblents*, *Frederick* I at *Franckfort*, *Henry* VI at *Bamberg*, and *Philip* at *Erfurt*. However, since the *Golden Bull* has appointed a certain Place for that purpose, it is not in the Power of the Archbishop of *Mayence* to make the Convocation elsewhere. Wherefore, when in the Year 1530, the Archbishop conven'd the Electors at *Cologn*, in order to proceed to the Election of *Ferdinand* I, the Elector of *Saxony* oppos'd it, and accus'd the Election of Nullity, for having been perform'd any where but at *Franckfort*, which is the Place appointed for that purpose by the Law, so that it cannot be alter'd but by the general Consent of all the Electors, who allow'd the Elections of *Rodolphus* II, and of *Ferdinand* III, to be perform'd at *Ratisbone*, and that of the late King of the *Romans* at *Augsburg*.

† The Electors either go thither in Person, or else send their Embassadors, with an ample and general Power, and not particular for any single Subject. And to the end no Mistake may be made in the Form, the *Golden Bull* sets it down, * such as it ought to be. and the Embassadors on their Arrival at the Place of Election, are oblig'd to communicate their Powers, and to cause them to be register'd in the Chancery at *Mayence*, which gives a Copy thereof to all the other Electors. Where we must observe, that if an Elector sends several Embassadors, there is only one of them that takes Place in the Electoral College, and assists at the Deliberations. Formerly the Emperor elect, or King of the *Romans*, paid Four thousand five hundred Marks of Silver to each of the Princes who had assisted at his Election. And then they who could not be there in Person gave Power to some other Prince to elect for them, giving them Security for that Sum, as may be seen by the Offer which *Albert* Duke of *Saxony* makes to *Wenceslas* King of *Bohemia*, to consent to the Election of the Person the King shall nominate, giving him the Hostages he requires for the Security of his Payment.

The same *Golden Bull*, intending to provide for the Safety of the Electors, as well going to the Election, as in their return home, is not contented to forbid under very express Penalties the giving them any Trouble or Hindrance. But it wills also and ordains, that the other Electors, Princes, Counts, Barons, Gentlemen, Free Towns, and Vassals of the Empire, being requir'd thereto, do conduct and guard them going and coming through all the Countries and Territories under their Jurisdiction and Obedience, after the manner express'd in the first Chapter, which hardly speaks of any thing else but of the Convoy and Safe-conduct of the Electors.

The Request must be made in Letters on purpose, which mark the Day and Place where the Requirer desires to be receiv'd by the Convoy, and the Number of Horses he has in his Retinue, and he that gives it, is oblig'd to give his Safe-conduct in Writing and in Form, con-

* Chap. XVIII   † In default of a Summons the Electors meet   ‡ Chap 1 § 29   * Chap X
† The Place of the Election   ‡ The Electors may send thither their Embassadors   * Chap XIX

of the ELECTORS of the EMPIRE.   551

taining Safety for the Person of the Elector and his Retinue, with Orders to the Bailiffs of his District, and to the Governors of the Places under his Obedience to provide for his Safety.

That Elector who after having been thus duly invited to the Election by the Letters of the Archbishop of *Mayence*, and who after having obtain'd the Safe-conducts and Convoys necessary for the Safety of his Journey, neglects to repair to the Place of Election, either in Person or by his Embassadors, or who leaves the Diet before the Election is over, loses his Right and Suffrage but for that Time only, because his Neglect is not a Crime, and cannot prejudice those who have a Right in the Election by virtue of the first Investiture. The Case of the Elector that arrives at *Franckfort* after the opening of the Diet is less grievous, but forasmuch as it is not reasonable that all the others should wait for him, he may finish with them the Election, which remains in the same State he found it in at his Arrival. Hereupon a Difficulty might be form'd, to wit, whether if of the eight Electors two should voluntarily absent, and of the six present four should chuse a capable Person, the Election would be lawful. There is room to doubt it, because for the due Performance of the Election, the Plurality of the Votes of the whole College is requisite. But notwithstanding that, we may say that the voluntary Absence of some of the Electors would not render the Election faulty, because the Obstinacy of the absent cannot deprive the present of their Right, nor prejudice the State, which would suffer by a long *Interregnum*.

The Constitution of the *Golden Bull* regulates the Retinue and Attendance of the Electors, in going to the Election, to two hundred Horse, comprehending therein fifty Men at Arms, which they are allow'd to have for the Guard of their Persons, and forbids very expressly the Magistrates of *Franckfort* to suffer them to enter the Town with a larger Retinue, thereby to prevent the Disorders which might otherwise hinder the Freedom of the Election, if the Electors were allow'd to be attended by what number of Forces they should think fit. And nevertheless this Regulation is no longer observ'd at all: on the contrary, there is not any Secular Elector who can reduce him' If to so small a number of Domesticks, and who does not bring along with him a Train of five or six hundred Horse to the Election.

The Electors, or their Embassadors, being arriv'd at *Franckfort*, oblige the Magistrates and the Inhabitants of the Town to take the Oath which the Law exacts from them under the Penalty of Proscription, and by which they promise to take into their Protection and Safeguard the Electors and their Retinue, and to put out and remove from the Town all Strangers, of what Quality or Condition soever they may be. In order thereto the Magistrate causes Proclamation to be made to that effect by beat of Drum through all the Streets of the Town, and at the same time to the Inhabitants to repair the next Day to the Place before the Town house, where they swear to the Electors

As for the removing of Strangers during the Election, it has been executed with more or less Rigour, according to the Disposition of Affairs, and the Humour of the Electors. In the time of the Election of the Emperor *Charles* V, the Embassadors of *France* and *Spain* remain'd in the Neighbourhood, and in that of the late Emperor *Ferdinand* II, his Father, who was still living, proceeded therein even to Threats with the Embassador of *Spain*, who refus'd to go out of the City of *Ratisbone*, and sent him word, That if he would not defer to the Constitution of the *Golden Bull*, by going voluntarily out of the Town, he should be oblig'd to make him do it by Force. But that depends in part on the extent the Electors give to the time of the Election. The *Golden Bull* requires * that the Electors open the Electoral Diet the very next Day after their Arrival, that for this effect they repair to St *Bartholomew*'s Church, that they begin the Election by the Mass of the Holy Ghost, and by the Oath, and that they make an end of it in a Month, † reckoning from the Day they are sworn. But at present the Practice is different. For the Electors take what Time they please for their Deliberations, as well on the Election it self, and on the Person they are to elect, as on the Capitulation and Conditions they intend to stipulate from him, whom they call to the Imperial Dignity which being concluded, and they agreed on all things, they set a Day for the Election, which they begin and end afterwards in one Morning as we shall see in the following Chapter. So that it is in the Power of the Electors to send the Strangers out of the City of *Franckfort* as soon as they begin to deliberate on the Affairs of the Election, or to suffer them to abide there till the very Day of the Election. It is probable they will make a Reflection on the Honour which the Kings of *France* and *Spain* do them, in deputing to them so illustrious an Embassy, of which the Marschal *de Grammont* and the Count *de Pegneranda* are the Chiefs, and that they will not suffer them to go out of the Town, but only for the very Day of the Election, if it were but out of Consideration that they cannot exclude the one without the other, nor shew Respect to one of the Crowns on this occasion, without doing as much to the other.

‡ The Capitulation, which we have before mention'd, is of the Essence of the Election, and of so much the more Importance, as it regulates the whole Reign of the future Emperor, and gives the Form to the Government in this, that it makes an end to destroy what still remain'd Monarchical in the Empire. It formerly made one of the principal Parts of the Election, before it was made a Preliminary, and before that was made a mere Ceremony, which at this Day is call'd Election. There is no body but who knows that the words, to Capitulate, and Parley, are synonymous, and signify to propose and debate certain Conditions, compris'd in several Articles or little Chapters, which must be agreed on before the Treaty can be perfected, for which they are propos'd. And so we say, that the Capitulation is nothing else than the Contents of certain Conditions which the Electors cause to be propos'd, and which

---

* Cap II § 1   † Ibid § 4   ‡ Tit. Cap. II § 1

he

he that aspires to the Imperial Dignity is oblig'd to accept of, before the Electors proceed to the Publication of the Election, and to confirm immediately after. The *German* Authors, when they will speak *Latin*, call it *Lex Regia*, but in a Signification very different from that which is given to the Law, by which the *Roman* People formerly yielded up all its Rights of Sovereignty to the Emperor; since this serves as a Curb to that great Power, and endeavours to reduce it within the Bounds of an Aristocratical Government, if we may be allow'd to speak thus, with one of the greatest Princes *Germany* has produc'd for many Ages.

They who refer the Origin thereof to the Emperor *Conrade* I, and say, that at the time of his Election Conditions were propos'd to him, under which he was oblig'd to accept the Empire, make themselves ridiculous. For the States of *Germany* were forc'd to chuse themselves a Prince, not because the Empire was elective, but because the Posterity of *Charlemagne*, which had fail'd in *Germany*, could not afford them one, but there is no likelihood he had any Conditions prescrib'd to him, since there was no ground to complain of the Government of the last Emperors. And indeed no Alteration appears in the Procedure of those who came after. They have all reign'd like Sovereigns, and have all govern'd with an absolute Power, but not despotical. The Truth is, there will no Capitulation be found, before the sixteenth Century, and it is certain that it was *Frederick* Duke of *Saxony*, who having refus'd the Empire himself, and given his Vote to *Charles* of *Austria*, said it was necessary to secure the Liberty of *Germany*, before his Election was publish'd, and skreen it from those Dangers which it seem'd to be lyable to, from the great Power of *Spain*, and the Obligation *Charles* was under to visit often his hereditary Kingdoms, by such Laws as should moderate the one, and remedy the others. That it was on this Proposition, that some Days were employ'd in drawing up certain Articles, which were sent to the Embassadors of *Charles*, and that the Name of *Capitulation* was given to these Articles. Since that Time there has been no Election, but there has been at the same Time a new Capitulation. But forasmuch as the last comprehends all the former, and that it is impossible to know the true State of the present Affairs of *Germany* without it, we shall here insert that which was made in the Year 1636, with the late Emperor, which is by so much the more remarkable, as it is much more ample than the others, and that it was made at a Time when the Emperor's too great Authority stood in need of being moderated by new Laws, and by a stronger Capitulation. The Tenor whereof is as follows.

We *Ferdinand* III, by the Grace of God, elected King of the *Romans*, always August, King of *Germany*, *Hungary*, *Bohemia*, and of *Dalmatia*, *Croatia*, and *Sclavonia*, Arch-Duke of *Austria*, Duke of *Burgundy*, Marquiss of *Moravia* and *Lusatia*, Duke of *Luxemburg*, *Silesia*, *Stiria*, *Carinthia*, *Crain*, and of *Wirtemberg*, Count of *Habspourg*, and of *Tirol*, &c. do acknowledge by these Letters Patents, and do make known to all Persons, That having been call'd and rais'd, within these few Days, to the Dignity and Name, and constituted in the Honour and Power of King of the *Romans*, by the Providence of God, and by the lawful Election of the most Reverend and most Illustrious *Anselm Casimir*, Archbishop of *Mayence*, *Ferdinand*, Archbishop of *Cologn*, *Maximilian*, Count *Palatin* of the *Rhine*, Duke of the *Upper* and *Lower Bavaria*, of *Frederick Metsch*, Lord of *Reichenbach* and of *Frise*, of *Adam* Count of *Suartzemburg*, Lord of the *Upper Landberg*, and of *Gimborn*, Master Provincial of the Order of St *John* in the *Marc-Brandenburg*, *Saxony*, *Pomerania*, and *Vandalia*, Embassadors Plenipotentiaries, in the Name and on the Part of *John George* Duke of *Saxony*, *Juliers*, *Cleves* and *Berg*, Burgrave of *Nuremberg*, and of *George William* Marquiss of *Brandenburg*, respectively Great Chancellors of the Empire, in *Germany* and in *Italy*, and Great Steward, Great Mareschal, and Great Chamberlain of the holy Empire, our dear Nephews, Unkles, and Princes Electors. With which Dignity we having thought fit to charge our selves, to the Praise and Glory of God, and for the universal Good of all *Christendom*, and particularly for that of the *German* Nation. We have agreed and granted, *by Form of Contract, and reciprocal Obligation*, of our good and free Will, with our said Nephews, Unkles, and Princes Electors. And we have consented, accepted and promis'd, the whole of our own Knowledge, and by virtue of these Presents, as follows.

1 First, That as Advocate of the Christian Church, we will take the said Church, the See of *Rome*, and the Person of the Pope, into our Protection, and will protect and defend them faithfully during the whole Time of our Reign. That we will establish Peace and Union in the Church, and that we will cause Justice to be administer'd in such manner, that it shall have its entire Freedom, to the End that all, as well Poor as Rich, may be indifferently protected by it, pursuant to the Ordinances, Liberties, and ancient Customs of the Empire. However, our two Unkles, the Electors of *Saxony* and of *Brandenburg*, have declar'd very expressly to us, That for what relates to this Article, as also to the eighteenth of this present Obligation, in what they contain in reference to the See of *Rome*, and to the Person of the Pope, that they do not consent thereto, neither do they pretend to oblige us in that Respect.

2 It is also our Will, and we promise to observe inviolably the *Golden Bull*, and whatever has been ordain'd, receiv'd, and resolv'd, concerning the publick Peace of the Empire, as well in what relates to Religion, as to what regards things temporal and prophane, nor only in the Diet of *Augsburg*, held in the Year 1555, but also by the Ordinances, Constitutions, and Resolutions of the other Diets, provided they contain nothing contrary to the Resolution of the Diet of *Augsburg*, and to all that shall appear to have been repeated, corrected, augmented and confirm'd, by the following Diets, to the Prejudice of which, we will molest no body, nor suffer any body to be molested. On the contrary, we shall take Care to confirm all the Resolutions, and, it need be, we will renew and amend them, by the Counsel and Advice of the Princes Electors and

and of the other Princes and States of the Empire, according as the State of Affairs shall require

3 We will maintain in all Respects, and by all Means, the *German* Nation, the holy *Roman* Empire, and the Princes Electors, as its chief Members, as also all the other Princes, Counts, Barons, and Estates, in their Pre-eminencies, Dignities, Rights and Customs, Goods, Honours and Power, each according to his Condition and Quality, and we will not suffer any Trouble or Lett to be offer'd them therein. It is also our Will, and we oblige our selves, to confirm to them without any Delay their Rights of *Regalia*, and of Superiority, their Liberties, Privileges, and Mortgages, is also all the Rights, Usages, and Customs which they have enjoy'd, and which they have, and do enjoy at this present. And as King of the *Romans*, we will maintain, defend and protect them therein, in reference to, and against all, without Prejudice to the Right of others

4 And forasmuch as, for some Time past, the Embassadors of foreign Princes have dar'd to pretend to a Precedency over the Embassadors of the Electors, at the Court and Chapels of the Emperor, and of the King of the *Romans*, we hereby declare that we will not suffer it for the Time to come, unless the Competition falls between the Embassadors of Electors and those of crown'd Heads, or of foreign Kings, their Widows, or their minor Children, being still Pupils, but such, that they may hope to succeed to the Crown as soon as they shall have attain'd to Majority, in which Case they shall have the Precedency of the Embassadors of the Electors

5 We also allow the six Electors to meet by virtue of the Power which the *Golden Bull* gives them, whenever they shall judge it necessary for the Good of the Affairs of the Empire, as also for their particular Necessities, and to deliberate on, and determine, what shall be requisite, without its being in our Power to offer to impede or obstruct them, or that we will on that Account conceive any Indignation, or Displeasure against them in general, or against any one of them in particular, but we promise that in that Respect, and in all other things, we will execute sincerely and *bona fide* whatever is contain'd in the *Golden Bull*, confirming for this Purpose, and approving on our Part, in all their Points and Articles, as much as is necessary, the Alliances and Leagues which have been made with the Consent and Approbation of the Emperors our Predecessors, between the Electors, and particularly between those of the Circle of the *Rhine*

6 We will oppose all sorts of Societies, Leagues and Confederacies, which the Subjects, as well Nobles as Commoners, shall endeavour to form against the Electors, Princes, and other Estates of the Empire. We will dissipate those which are already contriv'd, and will make use of the Counsel, and Forces of the Electors, Princes, and States of the Empire, for the preventing those which shall be attempted for the Time to come

7 We also declare, That in the Quality of King of the *Romans*, we cannot in our own Name, nor for the Affairs of the Empire, make any Treaty, League or Alliance, with Foreign Princes and States, nor in the Empire it self, till we have first conven'd the six Electors in a certain Place, and at a certain Day, and till we have obtain'd from them, or the major part of them, the necessary Consent and Permission for that Purpose. With this Proviso however, That we shall be oblig'd to ask such Permission in a Collegiate Diet, and not by particular Declarations, which the said Electors might give us, unless it should happen that the State of Affairs, and the publick Interest should not allow of such Delay. And we do not pretend that what pass'd in the Peace of *Prague*, can be drawn to any Consequence or Prejudice for the future, as has been sufficiently provided against by the said Treaty

8 We will take Care that all the Electors, Princes and Lords, as well Ecclesiasticks as Seculars, who sha'l be found to have been spoliated or dispossess'd by Violence, as well in their own Persons as in those of their Ancestors and Predecessors, of their Rights, Goods, Territories and Lordships, be restor'd by the ordinary Means of the Law, and will maintain them therein, defend and protect them in Justice, without any Delay or Procrastination

9 But above all things, we will not undertake to seize, sell, mortgage or engage, charge or alienate, in any manner or way whatever, the Estates belonging to the Empire, without the express Consent of all the Electors in general, and of each of them in particular. On the contrary, we will do all that we can, and will make use of all sorts of Means to re-unite to the Demesne of the Empire all the Provinces, Lands, Principalities and Lordships, which have been lopp'd from it by Confiscation or otherwise, and which are for the most part unjustly possess'd by Strangers. In which we will always make use of the Counsel, Advice, and Assistance of the Electors, Princes, and States of the Empire, and the rather because we are sensible, that several Demesnes and considerable Fiefs, as well in *Italy* as elsewhere, are in the Hands of Foreigners. For which Reason we shall cause a very exact Search and Enquiry to be made therein, (if that be not done during the Life of the present Emperor) and thereby endeavour to have a very particular Knowledge of those Alienations, whereof we shall cause a Report to be made to the Chancery of *Mayence* within a Year infallibly, reckoning from the Day of our Accession to the Crown. In which, as also in all that we have now said, we will make use of the Counsel and Assistance of the six Princes Electors, and of the other Princes and States of the Empire, to the end we may undertake nothing but what we and they shall judge together to be proper and advisable, just and useful. The whole, without Prejudice to the Privileges, Rights, and Liberties of others

10 And if it shall appear that we, and ours, are in Possession of Demesnes belonging to the Empire, which have not been given to us in Fief, or which we do not otherwise possess with a good Title, we promise, by the Duty we owe to the Empire, to restore them immediately, and without Delay, at the first Summons we shall receive on that Account, on the part of the Electors

11 We

11. We promise that during all the Time of our Reign we will live in Peace, and good Understanding with the Kings and Princes our Neighbours, and with all the other Christian Estates, and that we will not undertake to declare War, or send any Defiance, as well within as without the Empire, or to bring into it any Troops from abroad, without the Knowledge, Advice, and Consent of the States of the Empire, and at least without that of the six Electors. And if any of the Princes, or other States of the Empire, should introduce any, we will oblige 'em to disband them forthwith. However, if it should happen that the Empire be attack'd, or that a War be made against our Person on the Account of the Empire, it shall be allow'd us in such Case, to make use of the Assistance of all our Friends and Allies.

12. We promise likewise, and give our Faith and Word, that the Armies which are at present on foot, or may hereafter be rais'd for the Defence of the Empire, shall not go out of the same without the Knowledge and Consent of the Princes Electors, but that we will employ them for the Defence and Relief of the affected and oppress'd States. And if we make any Levies, or permit others to make any, for the Service of any foreign Princes, we will order it so, that the Princes Electors, and the other Princes and States of the Empire shall not be burthen'd with Quartering, or the Passage of Soldiers, or with Rendezvous, or Places of assembling, contrary to the Constitutions of the Empire, during their March, or the Time of their Abode or Sojournment, and that even those which are already in Germany be disbanded, as soon as God shall have given Peace to the Empire.

13. In like manner we will not charge the Princes Electors, nor the other Estates of the Empire, with the Convocations of Diets, Journeys, Contributions for the Expences of the Chancery, nor with other Impost or Collections, if necessity does not oblige us thereto, for very weighty Causes and important Affairs, even for which we shall not be able to convene Diets, nor demand Contributions, or establish Imposts, without the Knowledge and Permission of the six Electors. We promise particularly, That we will not convene any Diet out of the Bounds of Germany, and even that we will not resolve to call any within the Empire till we have first ask'd thereupon, (by a Deputation on purpose) and obtain'd the Consent and Approbation of the Princes Electors. Neither will we employ the Money that shall be rais'd by the Consent of the States, but to the Usage to which it shall be destin'd.

14. When the Necessity of the Affairs of the Empire shall oblige us to demand Contributions of the States of the Empire, we will do it by the ordinary Ways and Means, in the Diets, and in the Assemblies of the Circles, or if the State of Affairs cannot suffer any Delay, by the Advice and Consent of the six Electors. And forasmuch as during the present War, the fundamental Laws of the Empire, and the good ancient Customs have been many ways violated in the Execution and Payment of the Contributions, our Intention is that these Excesses shall no way prejudice the Constitutions of the Empire, and shall be no Precedents for the Time to come.

15. It shall not be in our Power to bestow the Imperial or Royal Offices, as well at Court as in the Empire, nor even those of the Army, or of the Council of War, but only to natural Germans, and to Persons of Condition and of Quality, as, to Princes, Counts, Barons and Gentlemen, illustrious by their Birth, and recommendable by their Merit, particularly as for the Employments of the Council of War, and in the War it self, shall be presented with foreign Subjects, such Germans as shall possess the same Qualities, and who are oblig'd by Oath, or any other Duty, to none but us and to the holy Empire. And we also promise that we will preserve the said Offices in their Honours, Dignities, Rights, Liberties, and Preeminencies, without taking any thing from them, and without making any Alteration therein, in any manner or way whatever.

16. We will make use of no other Language in our Letters and Acts, than of the German, or of the Latin, unless it be in those Places where these Languages are not us'd, and there we may make use of that which is in use.

17. We will not suffer the Electors, Princes, Counts, Barons, Gentlemen, or other Estates, and Subjects of the Empire, to be cited or summon'd out of Germany or elsewhere, before any but their ordinary Judges. But pursuant to the express Constitution of the Golden Bull, and the other Ordinances and Laws of the Empire, we will leave the first Cognizance to their natural Judges. And whereas the Princes Electors, as being the chief Members of the Empire, have particularly this Advantage over all the other Estates, not only by the Golden Bull, but also by sundry other Privileges, to be exempt from all foreign Jurisdiction, and namely from that of the Chamber of Rotweil, as well in their Persons as their Domesticks and Subjects. And notwithstanding that, they are nevertheless vex'd by the Procedures of this Chamber, we will take such Measures, that it shall cease and forbear them for the future. And it is our Will, That if the said Chamber continues to vex or molest them, the Princes Electors may not only hinder their Subjects from being impleadable there, but may also punish, according to the Exigency of the Cases, those, who contrary to the present Prohibitions shall dare to undertake to give them Citations thither.

18. And whereas the Court of Rome, by its Gifts without Form, Rescriptions of the Annates of Churches, Reservations and Dispentations, and by the great Number and Multiplication of Offices, and by sundry other different Means, overburdens the German Churches, and the Clergy, contrary to the Privileges by them obtain'd, to the Prejudice of the Rights of Patronage, and of the feudal Lords, and contrary to the Concordates and Treaties, made between the Church, the See, and the Pope of Rome, on the one part, and the Princes of Germany, on the other; and that in consequence thereof, several Societies, Fraternities, Contracts, and unlawful Acquisitions are made, it is our Will, and we are oblig'd to use such Means with our holy Father the Pope, and with

with the See of *Rome*, by the Council and Advice of the Electors, Princes and States of the Empire, that the same may be remedy'd for the future. And we will take care that the Concordates and Treaties made with the Princes, and their Privileges and Liberties be not violated, but that they be maintain'd and preserv'd in their full Force and Virtue. And we will labour to put an End to the Disorders and Abuses which have hitherto been committed therein, and will take due Care that nothing be done for the time to come, without the Counsel and Advice of the Princes Electors the whole pursuant to the Resolution taken at the Diet of *Augsburg*, in the Year 1530.

19. We will earnestly endeavour that the burdensom Societies, and Monopolies of Merchants, who have so much afflicted the whole Empire by their Usury, and by the extraordinary Dearth they have caus'd of all sorts of Commodities, be abolish'd. Wherein we will make use of the Counsel of the Electors and Princes.

20. And whereas all *Germany*, and the holy *Roman* Empire, is over-burthen'd with Imposts and Duties, which are levy'd as well by Water as by Land, We will not suffer any new one to be establish'd for the time to come, or that those which are already est blish'd be enhanc'd or continued nay as for what regards our Person, We promise, that we will not establish any new ones, neither will we continue or enhaunce those which are already establish'd, unless it be with the Knowledge, Advice and Consent of the six Electors, given in a Collegiate Diet so that we shall refer to the first Collegiate Diet, all such as shall desire our leave to set up new Imposts, or to enhance or continue the old ones, and shall exhort them in the mean time to leave Affairs in the State they shall be in. And whereas the Word Impost is not always made use of, because it is too odious, but that of the Duty of Discharge, or of Estapes and that under this Pretext the same or greater Sums are nevertheless exacted from Ships and Goods. It is our Will, that all the Duties that are rais'd after this Manner, under what Name, Colour or Pretext soever, without the express leave of the Electoral College, be abolish'd and suppress'd as Usurpations, and if any of the Electors are burthen'd therewith in their own particular, we permit him to abolish them, by such Means as he shall judge most expeditious for that Purpose.

21. In like Manner, it is our Will that the States (who have obtain'd of the Emperors our Predecessors, with the Consent of the Electors, the Permission to establish Imposts, or to enhanse and continue those which are already establish'd, with this Condition and Reservation, that the Princes Electors, their Subjects, Domesticks, and Factors, or other free Persons, even their Furniture and Baggage shall not be chargeable therewith, but as well themselves, as their Furniture and Goods, shall freely pass and repass through their Dutchies and Territories, without paying any Duties for the same) do give for this Effect in Writing the necessary Securities to the Electors; and that they who have not yet oblig'd themselves thereto, do do it immediately, and without delay, and that they lodge those Securities in the Hands of the Electors. Accordingly we shall not permit, that they, who shall hereafter obtain leave to set up, continue or enhanse the Imposts, shall take out their requisit Instruments from the Chancery, till they have before given the necessary Securities to the Electors.

22. And whereas it is known, that on the Occasion of the last Wars in the Low Countries, the whole Course of the *Rhine*, particularly towards the nether Part, has been so clogg'd with Imposts, that the Revenue of the Princes Electors on that side, and the Traffick of the Subjects and Factors, is thereby diminish'd and incommoded to that Degree, that the Commerce ceases, and is ruin'd entirely and that moreover, Ships of War and Frigates have been sent into that River, without the Consent of the Electors, and to the Prejudice of their Rights of Sovereignty, and that they visit the said Merchant Ships, and require insupportable Extortions, without its having been hitherto possible to make them withdraw, whatever Instances the Electors have made for that purpose, we will do whatever shall be in our Power, as well of our own Motion, as by the Counsel of the Princes Electors, to free the Empire thereof, and to procure the Abolition and Suppression of the Duties which are there exacted.

23. Moreover, we shall not give either Hopes, or any Letters of Recommendation to the Electors, to those who shall address to us, in order to obtain by our Intercession, the Establishment or Continuation of those Duties.

24. And if it shall happen that any Person, of what Rank or Quality soever he may be, undertakes of his own Motion, without our Permission, and without the Consent of the Electors, to establish new Imposts in his Countries, Principalities, Demesnes or Territories, we will hinder him therefrom by very express Prohibitions, and by all other due and reasonable Means, at the first Knowledge we shall have thereof, and as soon as we have Advice of the same. And we will not permit any Person whatever to attempt to set up by Violence, and of his own Motion, new Imposts or Duties, or to enhanse and usurp them, in any Manner whatever.

25. And if it should happen, that by the Establishment of these new Imposts, the Duties of the Princes Electors should be lessen'd, or entirely suppress'd, so that they should be oblig'd to have recourse to the Law on that account, either as Plaintiffs or Defendants, forasmuch as the Permission of laying new Imposts cannot be obtain'd but from the Emperor, or the King of the *Romans*, by and with the Consent of the six Electors of the holy Empire, and so the Judgment of the Suits which may arise therefrom, belongs only to us. It is our Will, that they be decided before us, without their being oblig'd to suffer our Imperial Chamber, or any other Court in ordinary, to take Cognizance thereof and hereof we shall not fail to advertise the Chamber.

26. And whereas the Exemptions, which have been given within some Time to divers Persons, of the Duties which are payable on the *Rhine* and on the *Danube*, lessen the Duties and

and Revenues of the Princes Electors, we shall endeavour to get them abolish'd, as being importable, neither will we suffer for the future, any Letters of Recommendation to be ask'd of us, by virtue of which they may be claim'd

27 If any Elector, Prince, or other Person of Condition, is molested or troubl'd in the Possession of his *Regalia*, Liberties, Privileges, Rights and Prerogatives, or if any body offers to deprive them thereof, or to lessen or abolish them, so that he be thereby oblig'd to have recourse on that account, to the ordinary Proceedings at Law with his Adversary, or be already engag'd therein, we will leave a free Course to Justice, without giving him any Let or Hinderance, directly or indirectly

28 We likewise promise, and give our Word, that we will leave to the Princes Electors, and to the other Estates of the Empire, the free and entire Disposition of the Fiefs, in what Place soever they are situate, which shall have been confiscated from their Subjects and Vassals, on the account of High Treason, or otherwise, in any Manner whatever, without applying them to the Imperial Treasury, and without obliging them to receive those Vassals, or any others that shall be presented to them We shall do the like in reference to free Tenures, which shall have been confiscated in the Manner we have now express'd, for Crimes of High Treason, or otherwise, which we will not take from the Electors, or other States of the Empire, who have a Right of Confiscation, by an ancient Custom, or otherwise but we will leave the entire Disposal thereof, and Confiscation, to the Lords of the Territory where they are situate

29 We will do no Violence to the Electors, Princes, Prelates, Counts, Barons, or other Estates of the Empire, neither will we suffer any to be done to them by others but if we, or any others, have Pretensions against them all in general, or against any one of them in particular, we will prosecute them by the ordinary way of Justice, in order to avoid that of Violence, and all Rebellion, Division and Disorder in the Empire We will not suffer neither, that they who offer to be accountable to Law, be attack'd, wrong'd, damnify'd, surpriz'd or burden'd, under any Colour or Pretext whatever, by Arms or Pillage, Defiance or War nor even by the Passage, or Quartering of Soldiers, without the utmost Necessity, and through the Ignorance of the Colonel of the Circle, and of his Assistants, and of the other States of the Empire

30 We will not suffer neither, for the future, any Person to be proceeded against by Proscription, of what Condition or Quality soever he may be, Elector, Prince or other, in any Manner, or for any Cause whatever, without his being heard, and without the Knowledge, Advice and Consent of the Princes Electors of the holy Empire But we will take care that the Procedure be by the ordinary Ways of Justice, pursuant to the Constitutions of the holy Empire, and conformably to the Order of the Procedures of the Chamber of *Spires*, reform'd in the Year 1555, and confirm'd by the Resolution of the same Year, without Prejudice however to the Defence allow'd to the Party offended, by the publick Peace unless the Act was publick and notorious, and that the Violater of the publick Tranquillity should continue obstinately in his Violence, in which Case, it would not be very necessary to proceed therein by the ordinary Means but we will nevertheless be oblig'd to call thereto those of the Princes Electors of the holy Empire, who shall not be interested in the Affair, and we will not procede on to a Proscription without their Participation

31 And whereas the *Roman* Empire is very much impair'd and decay'd, We promise that we will endeavour to reunite thereto the Contributions of the Cities, and the other Rights, which are at present engag'd to foreign Persons and we will cause a Memorial to be made, or a List of the Persons who are at present in Possession thereof, which we will send into the Chancery of the Archbishop of *Mayence* within six Months, if it sha'l appear that that has not been done before our Accession to the Crown and we will not suffer the Empire and the Publick to be frustrated thereof, contrary to all Reason and Justice, unless these Engagements or Alienations appear to have been made with the Consent of the six Electors

32 We will not give the Investiture or Reversion of those Fiefs which may become vacant, or escheate to us, and to the Empire, during the Time of our Reign, especially if they are of any Consideration, as Principalities, Counties, Baronies and Towns But we will re-unite them to the Body of the Empire, for the Maintenance and Support of the Imperial Dignity, in our own Person, and in that of our Successors, Emperors and Kings of the *Romans*, till it be entirely restor'd to its first Grandeur The whole without Prejudice to the Rights which we have in our hereditary Countries, and to those of others in all Respects

33 Above all, we will endeavour to preserve all the Fiefs belonging to the Empire, in whatever Place they are situate, as well in *Germany* as elsewhere and we will cause the Homages to be renew'd at every Change, so that if even after our Accession to the Crown, it should appear that we are in possession of any, it is our Intention to do Homage therefore, or if that cannot well be done, we will give such Sureties to the Princes Electors thereof, that the Empire shall have reason to be satisfy'd therewith

34 If it shall happen hereafter that any Principality, County, Barony, * *Emphyteose*, or other Lands which owe Duties and Services, Rents, or Contributions to the Empire, or which are otherwise subjected to it, fall into our Hands (after the Death of those who actually possess them) by Right of Succession or if we give 'em to others or if we possess them our selves, it is our Intention that it shall be on Condition, that they shall continue to pay to the Empire the same Duties, Services and Contributions, without any Regard to the pretended Exemptions, which might be alledg'd

---

* Lands let by a long Lease, as from ten to a hundred Years, in order to be improv'd.

35. We will also reunite, and apply to the Empire, whatever we shall recover or acquire by the Counsel, and with the Aid and Assistance of the Princes Electors. And altho' the Electors, Princes and States of the Empire be not oblig'd to succour us, in what we shall undertake without their Knowledge, and without their Consent, we will nevertheless reunite to the Empire what we shall have so acquir'd without their Assistance.

36. And whereas hitherto the Empire has been extremely incommoded by the Disorders which are committed in reference to the Coin, we will apply our utmost Care, that they may be remedy'd by the Counsel of the Electors, Princes and other Estates of the Empire. And that a good Order may be observ'd therein for the future, we will make use of the Means ordain'd by the Resolution of the Diet in the Year 1603, and of the other preceding Diets; and we will not fail to employ all the Means by which the like Disorders may be prevented for the time to come.

37. We will not give the Right of coyning Money to any Person whatever, without the express Consent of the six Electors. And if we find that they who enjoy this Right of Kingly Prerogative and Privilege at present, do abuse the same contrary to the Edicts publish'd on the Score of the Coyn, we shall not be contented barely to interdict them, by virtue of the Constitutions of the Empire, but also if it shall appear that they have obtain'd it without the Consent of the Electors, we will absolutely dispossess them thereof, and will not permit them to be restor'd thereto, without the Consent of the said Electors. We will particularly repeal and annul the Privileges, which shall have been granted to such States as are not subject immediately to the Empire, to whom we will not for the Time to come grant those Privileges or the like, without the Consent of the Electors, especially if they prejudice the Rights of the Electors.

38. But chiefly we shall have a great Care not to pretend that the Empire belongs to us by Right of hereditary Succession, neither will we do any thing that can make it be believ'd that we intend to hold it by that Title, and as hereditary, leave it to our Children, Heirs and Successors: but we promise, as well for us, as for our said Children, Heirs and Successors, that we will leave the Princes Electors, their Heirs and Successors, in what Degree soever they may be, in the possession of the Right of electing a King of the *Romans*, so that they may proceed to the Election of a King of the *Romans*, as often as they shall judge it necessary for the Good of the Empire, and for the Ease and Relief of the Emperor during his Life, with his Consent, and even without it, if having been requested thereto by the Electors, for urgent Causes, he refuses to give his Consent. We also promise, that we will maintain the Vicars in their Power, and in the Enjoyment of the Rights they possess, by virtue of the ancient Custom of the *Golden Bull*, of the Canon Law, and of the other Laws and Constitutions of the Empire, whenever the Necessity of Affairs shall require it, or Occasion shall offer it self for that Purpose: and we will not suffer them to be troubl'd or molested, nor their Vicarships, or the Rights that depend thereon, to be contested by any Person whatever, it being our Will that all that has been done against the Electors, and to their Prejudice, be declar'd null, and of no validity.

39. As King of the *Romans* we pretend to take the Royal Crown, and we promise, that we will use all possible Diligence, to endeavour to obtain also the Imperial. We will also reside (as long as the State of Affairs shall permit) and we will establish our Court in the Empire of the *German* Nation, for the Honour and Utility, and for the Relief of all its Members, Estates and Subjects. We will also invite the Princes Electors to our Coronation, and in all other things we will act in such Manner, that there shall be no reason to complain of us.

40. We will give no Letters, Rescriptions or Orders, neither will we suffer any to be issu'd out, to the Prejudice of the present Capitulation, of the *Golden Bull*, of the Constitutions of the Empire, or to the Prejudice of the publick Peace, establish'd as well for Religion, as for temporal Things, or against the Ordinance made for the Regulation of the Chamber of *Spires* in the Year 1555, or against the other Laws and Constitutions already made, or to be made hereafter, in any manner or way whatever. Nay we will not oblige the Princes to grant us any thing that is contrary to the *Golden Bull*, the Liberties of the Empire, and to the Laws, Constitutions and Treaties which we have now mention'd, directly or indirectly. And if it shall happen that we obtain any thing like it, we will not make use thereof in any manner whatever.

41. And if it should happen that any Person should have obtain'd Letters contrary to what we have here said, or to the foregoing Articles, it is our Will that they be ras'd, cancell'd and suppress'd, and as null and of no effect we declare them to be void even now, as well as then, and we promise, in case of need, to give for this effect all the necessary Declarations the whole without Fraud.

42. We promise that we will grant to the Electors, Princes, and other States of the Empire, and to their Embassadors and Deputies, the Audiences they shall ask of us, and that we will dispatch them speedily. And that we will not refuse them the Investitures of their Fiefs, nor the Letters necessary thereto, and that in Affairs of Importance, we will make use of the Advice and Counsel of the Princes Electors.

43. Particularly we promise to take care that the Privy Council of the Empire, establish'd in our Court, be compos'd of Princes, Counts, Barons, Gentlemen, and of other Persons of Quality which we will chuse, not only amongst our Vassals and Subjects, but also most of them among those who are born, and possess Estates in the other Provinces of the Empire of the *German* Nation, who have been train'd up in Business, and whose Reputation is so well establish'd, that every body may hope to receive good Justice from them.

44. We will also make a Regulation, and a particular Instruction for the Council of the Empire, establish'd in our Court, and will communicate it in the first Diet (if that be not done during the Life of the present Emperor)

to the Princes Electors, in order to have their Opinion thereupon. We will revise the same every Year, or at least every two Year, in the Presence of the Archbishop of *Mayence*, as Great Chancellor of the Empire in *Germany*. But above all things, we will put into Consideration the Remonstrance made by the Electors in the last Assembly of *Nuremberg*, concerning the Administration of Justice, to which we shall have regard. In like manner we promise that we will alter nothing of what shall have been resolv'd and determin'd in our said Council by peremptory Judgment, neither will we suffer any Person whatever to take Cognizance of the same, or hinder the Execution thereof.

45. We also promise, that we will execute, and cause to be executed, the Regulation which the Emperor or we may make, by the Advice of the Princes Electors, for the Council of the Empire establish'd in our Court, and against the Disorders and Abuses which have crept into the same, and we will not allow of any Contravention thereto in any manner whatever.

46. We shall also have very particular Care, and we will not suffer, that the Favours we shall dispense, as King of the *Romans*, and future Emperor, especially for the Titles of Duke, Count, and Baron, and even for Patents to ennoble, and those for *Palatinates*, or for Privileges and Exemptions, be dispatch'd any where else than in the Chanceries of the Empire, pursuant to the good ancient Custom, and will not cause the *Golden Bull* (which the Emperors regnant are accustom'd to make use of) to be put to any Letters, but such as shall have been dispatch'd in the Chancery of the Empire.

47. In like manner we will not give the Title of Duke and Count but to Persons of high Merit, who reside effectually in the Empire, and have wherewith to support the Dignity with which they desire to be invested.

48. And whereas we are oblig'd to have a particular Consideration for the Princes Electors of the Holy Empire, as our precious Members, and as the Buttresses of the Empire, we will take care that their Vicars and hereditary Officers, who shall be at Court, be also consider'd, and that they discharge their Offices, as well at the Elections, as at the Diets and other Assemblies, general or particular, where they can lay Claim to this Honour, and shall not permit the Officers of our Court to encroach upon their Functions. And if it shall happen that the Officers of our Court be oblig'd, for certain Reasons, to execute them, the Vicars and hereditary Officers of the Electors shall nevertheless enjoy the Fruits and Emoluments of their Offices, in the same manner as if they had done the Functions thereof.

49. We will not meddle with the Government of the Empire, nor with the Administration of Affairs, during the Life of the Emperor, but with his Permission, and when he shall call us thereto, neither will we encroach upon the Sovereignty and Imperial Dignity in any manner or way whatever.

50. And whereas for particular and very weighty Reasons, the Elector of *Triers* cannot assist at the present Election, neither in Person nor by his Embassadors, our Intention is, that his Absence shall not have any Consequence, nor do any Prejudice for the future, as in effect we do not thereby mean to violate the *Golden Bull*, nor the good ancient Custom.

51. And to the end those of our Council, as also those of the Council of the Empire, establish'd in our Court, may have a perfect Knowledge of the Contents of the present Capitulation, and that it may serve for a Rule to their Deliberations and Resolutions, we shall not content our selves with communicating it to them, but we will oblige them to promise expressly, by taking an Oath of Fidelity, that they will not counsel us, nor ever do any thing but what shall be conformable to this Capitulation.

All which things above mention'd in general, and each of them in particular, we the above-nam'd King of the *Romans* have granted and promis'd, upon our Honour, and upon our Faith and Royal Word, to the above-nam'd Princes and Electors, and do grant and promise them by virtue of these present Letters, and have promis'd by a solemn Oath to God, on the Holy Gospel, to observe and execute them firmly and inviolably, without contravening thereto our selves, or suffering any thing to be acted to the contrary, directly or indirectly, in any manner or way whatever.

In Testimony whereof we have caus'd six Letters to be dispatch'd of the same Tenor, and have caus'd them to be seal'd with our Arms. Given at our Imperial City of *Ratisbone*, *December* 24, in the Year of our Lord and Saviour Jesus Christ, 1636. Of our Reigns, of *Rome* the first, of *Hungary* the second, and of *Bohemia* the tenth. And was sign'd *Ferdinand*, and underneath *Ferdinand Curtz*, Baron of *Senftenau*.

The Capitulation serves as a fundamental Law to the Empire, as well as the *Golden Bull*, and indeed is in some manner of more Importance than the *Caroline Constitution*, because the Electors, who represent in this Action the States and Sovereignty of the Empire, may derogate therefrom by the *Capitulation*. So that it hardly contains any one Article, on which some Reflection may not be made. But this is what cannot be done without making a Treatise that should comprehend the State of all the Affairs of *Germany*. For which Reason we shall keep within the Bounds of our Discourse, which speaks only of the Electors, and of the Election. Only we will take notice, that the number of the Electors had not yet been augmented, at the time of the Capitulation of *Ferdinand* III, and the King of *Bohemia* having no Concern in the Affairs of the Empire out of the Election, it could speak but of six Electors, whereas at this Day, and since the Creation of an eighth Electorate, there is an Obligation to mention seven Electors. The Resolutions of the Diets, of which the Capitulation speaks, are the Ordinances, Decrees and Regulations which the States of the Empire make in their General Assemblies. They make use for that of a *German* Word *, which is synonymous with that of *Congé*, or *Leave*,

---

* *The* German *word is* Abscheid.

in whatever Sense it can be taken, and their Doctors express it, tho' very improperly, by the *Latin* word *recessus*, because these Resolutions conclude the States, and are not form'd but at their separating, and when they take Leave one of the other.

As for the Exception which the Protestant Electors make to the first Article, which speaks of the Pope, and of the See of *Rome*, it was in the Capitulation of *Maximilian* II, that they began to protest, That it was not their Intention to oblige the Emperor to protect the Pope, who having declar'd against them and their Doctrine, their Interest would not permit them to speak in the behalf of his, and that they could do nothing for the Pope but what would be contrary to the Advantages they had had so much Difficulty to obtain by the Treaty of *Passau*.

We shall moreover add, at the end of this Chapter, that the word *Palatinate*, whereof mention is made in Article 46 of the present Capitulation, has nothing in common with the *Palatinate* of the *Rhine*, but is only a Dignity with which the Emperor sometimes honours Men of Learning, who obtain the same through Favour, and oftner for Money than by Merit. These Persons are call'd *Counts Palatins*, and they can make Doctors, create Notaries, legitimate Bastards, &c. But as these Counts are not very much respected, their Productions are still less consider'd, which are all venal, as well as the Dignity it self.

C H A P. XIX.

Of the Election of the Emperor.

WE have said in the foregoing Chapter, that the Deliberations that are had concerning the Election, and which we have plac'd among the Preliminaries, made formerly one of its principal Parts, and indeed the *Golden Bull* requires †, that the Electors being come to *Franckfort*, do repair the very next Day to St *Bartholomew*'s Church, that they there begin the Deliberations about the Election, and that they put an End to it in a Month. But there is not any Legislator, whose Intention is not eluded presently after the Publication of the Law. The Electors, to exempt themselves from those Penalties which the Law imposes on them, if they do not finish the Election in a Month (reckoning from the Day they are sworn) have found a Means to make the Election last six Months, and longer if they think fit, without apprehending to incur thereby the Penalties ordain'd by the *Golden Bull*, and to be reduc'd to Bread and Water for all Nourishment. And for this purpose they have distinguish'd the Deliberations (which make the principal part of the Election, and which may retard the Conclusion thereof) from the Election it self. In that of *Charles* V, so great a Difference is to be seen between the Deliberations and the Election, notwithstanding the Electors had caus'd the Mass of the Holy Ghost to be said before they enter'd upon Business, that the Archbishop of *Mayence* himself, in opening the Diet, seeing that it might be reproach'd to him that he acted contrary to the Order establish'd by the *Golden Bull*, protests, *That they are not there assembled to speak their Opinions, or to give their Suffrages, but only to discourse together in an amicable manner concerning the future Election.* That is to say, that they were not there to elect, but to deliberate, as in effect the Archbishop of *Mayence*, who ought to give his Opinion last, spoke first, and concluded his Discourse by the Nomination of *Charles*. *Triers*, who ought to vote the first, spoke his Opinion the second, and *Sleidan* observes, that he took that Rank but on the account of the great Reputation he had in the Empire for his Prudence and the Duke of *Saxony*, who ought to have spoken the fifth, gave his Opinion before *Bohemia* and the *Palatin* (who ought to have preceded him,) because he was so very much consider'd in the College, that his Colleagues did not only yield up that Honour to him, but they call'd him to the Empire, and had preferr'd him to *Charles*, if he had had Ambition enough to accept the Dignity which was offer'd him. And indeed they did not give their Suffrages, but they only spoke their Opinions, and they did not elect, but they deliberated on the Election, which was perform'd some Days after, and according to the Forms prescrib'd by the *Golden Bull*, as *Goldast* represents it in his publick Acts, publish'd in the *German* Tongue *An* 1614 ‡. The Archbishop of *Triers* therein voted first, conformably to the *Golden Bull*, and gave his Suffrage to *Charles*: whereas in the Deliberation he was for excluding *Charles*, and was for having *Francis* I, King of *France* chosen. The other Electors voted in the Order regulated by the *Golden Bull*, and the Archbishop of *Mayence* last of all. The like has been practis'd in all the subsequent Elections, which are accompany'd with all the Circumstances of Forms, which the *Golden Bull* requires should be observ'd therein, but it is only by the way of Ceremony. But forasmuch as they are so absolutely necessary, that the Election would be vicious without them, we shall set down in this Chapter how the Emperors are chosen, according to the Regulation made by the *Golden Bull*.

These Ceremonies are only perform'd when the Election is resolv'd upon, so that when the Electors are agreed in reference to the Person they have a mind to call to the Imperial Crown, they fix a Day for the Election, or rather for the Publication they intend to make thereof. The Day being come, the Electors

† *Chap.* II § 1.   ‡ Part I Tit 16 pag. 41

repair

repair in the Morning to the Town-house, without Order, with their Retinue and usual Apparel Being all of them met together, they retire each into a separate Room, where they put on their Electoral Habits * to wit, the three Ecclesiasticks, Robes and Caps of Scarlet, lin'd with Ermin, and the Secular Electors, Robes and Caps of Crimson Velvet, lin'd with the same Furs Being come out of the Town-house they mount on Horseback, to repair to St *Bartholomew*'s Church the Place nominated in the Circular Letters, and destin'd to the Election

† The *Golden Bull* does not regulate the Order which the Electors are to observe in this Cavalcade, for which reason a great Variety is to be found therein, almost in all the Elections In that of *Maximilian* I, they observ'd the following Order The Count *Palatin* of the *Rhine* march'd first, having on his left *Maximilian*, who was only titular Arch-Duke of *Austria* After them march'd the Archbishop of *Triers* alone, and after him the Duke of *Saxony* also alone, carrying the Sword drawn before the Emperor, who had on his right Hand the Archbishop of *Mayence*, and on his left that of *Cologn* The King of *Bohemia* had not been invited thereto, and the Marquiss of *Brandenburg*, who was ill of the Gout, was carry'd to the Church in a Chair, and did not take any Rank with the rest In that of *Maximilian* II, An 1562, *Mayence* and *Triers* march'd first, after them *Cologn* and *Bohemia*, and after them the *Palatin*, *Saxony*, and *Brandenburg* abreast, the *Palatin* being in the middle, *Saxony* on the Right, and *Brandenburg* on the left The same Order was observ'd in the Cavalcade which was perform'd for the Election of *Matthias* in the Year 1612 The Archbishop of *Triers* did not assist at the Election of *Ferdinand* III, wherefore the Order was chang'd, so that the Archbishops of *Mayence* and *Cologn* march'd first, after them the King of *Bohemia* and the Duke of *Bavaria*, and then the Embassadors of *Saxony* and *Brandenburg* At this Day *Mayence* and *Triers* march first, after them *Cologn* and *Bohemia*, then *Bavaria* and *Saxony*, and finally *Brandenburg* and the *Palatin*

In this Cavalcade all the Electors have the hereditary Mareschals of their Archbishopricks or Principalities, or else of their Court, marching before them, and carrying the Sword Those of the Ecclesiasticks in Scabbards adorn'd with Silver Gilt and the Seculars in Scabbards of Crimson Velvet, set off with Silver The Embassadors of the absent Electors have nothing of all this They have only their usual Apparel, they have no Officers before them, and take their Rank only after all the Electors present, but the Administrators or Guardians of the Electors in their Minority, enjoy all the Honours and all the Preeminences which the Law gives to the Electors themselves and the Elector of *Saxony* has this in particular, that it is not the hereditary Mareschal of the Dutchy of *Saxony*, but the Count of *Pappenheim* that carries the Sword before him

‡ The Electors being arriv'd at the Church Door, and alighting from their Horses, enter the Church in Procession as far as the Choir, where they find their Chairs prepar'd and dispos'd according to the Rank they hold in the Electoral College, each having an Inscription in large Characters, expressing the Name of the Elector it is intended for At the Election of *Maximilian* I, the Emperor his Father, who was there present, took his Place before the Altar, having on his right Hand the Archbishop of *Mayence*, the Count *Palatin* of the *Rhine*, and *Maximilian* of *Austria* And on his left the Archbishop of *Cologn*, the Duke of *Saxony*, and the Marquiss of *Brandenburg* and *Triers* sate above the Electors, by the Wall towards the Altar In those of *Maximilian* II, of *Matthias*, and of the other following Emperors, *Mayence*, *Bohemia*, and the *Palatin* took the right side, and *Cologn*, *Saxony*, and *Brandenburg* the left But since the Creation of the eighth Electorate the Practice is otherwise, for *Mayence*, *Bohemia* and *Saxony* take the right, and *Cologn*, *Bavaria*, *Brandenburg*, and the *Palatin* the left, and *Triers* the middle As soon as the Electors have taken their Places, some Princes and Counts, and the Counsellors of the Electors are let in, and then the Count of *Pappenheim* shuts the Door and takes the keys, which being done, the Prelate who is to officiate begins the Hymn, *Veni Creator Spiritus*, during which, as also during the Mass, the Officers belonging to the Electors stand before them, holding the Sword rested on their Shoulder, tho' it is observable in the Election of *Maximilian* I, that the Officers retir'd, and laid the Swords on Velvet Cushions before the Electors The Musicians having ended the Hymn, Mass begins, during which the Protestant Electors withdraw, and do not return till it is over, and then the Hymn, *Veni Creator*, is repeated

After that all the Electors rise, and being come near the Altar (their Officers marching, and carrying the naked Sword before them) they turn towards the Princes who are in the Choir, and then the Archbishop of *Mayence* makes a Speech to this effect, That since they are come thither to chuse a temporal Head to *Christendom*, pursuant to the Direction of the *Golden Bull*, he is willing to believe, that the Electors his Colleagues will make no Difficulty to take the Oath, which the same *Golden Bull* ordains should be taken before they proceed to the Election After which he puts the Gospel into the Hands of the Archbishop of *Triers*, who dictates to him the Form of the Oath When the Archbishop of *Mayence* has taken it, all the other Electors do the same in his Hands, one after another The Seculars by putting their Hand on the Gospel, and the Ecclesiasticks laying it on their Stomach The Form of the Oath is taken from Chap II § 2 of the *Golden Bull*, and is compris'd in these Terms.

I——Prince Elector of the Holy Empire, swear on the Holy Gospel, put here really before me, by the Faith I owe to God and to the Holy Roman Empire, that by the Help of God, and the whole Strength of my Mind and Understanding, I will chuse for Temporal Head of Christendom, *that is to say, for King of the* Romans *future Emperor, him that I shall judge in my Conscience to be most capable thereof. promising on the same*

* *The Habits of the Electors*   † *The Cavalcade*   ‡ *Their Places in the Church*

Faith,

Faith, that I will give my Vote and Suffrage in the said Election, without any hope of Profit, Pension, Promise, Recompence, or other Acknowledgment of any nature whatever The Golden Bull adds thereto, *So help me God and his Holy Gospel* The Archbishop of *Mayence* causes in account hereof to be taken down in Writing by two Notaries, who are there present or by two of his Secretaries, authoriz'd for this effect, who take for Witness for the same, the Princes and Lords who were admitted into the Chancel

The Electors being sworn resume their Places, and the Hymn, *Veni Creator Spiritus*, is sung for the third time which being ended, the Electors retire into the Conclave or Place prepar'd for the Election At *Franckfort* there is a Place destin'd particularly to that purpose, which is a little vaulted Gallery, into which there is an Entry out of the Chancel it self Here it is that they observe very exactly the Order which the *Golden Bull* requires should be observ'd at the Election of a King of the *Romans*, without the least Variation, excepting the Rank and Place which was regulated in the last Diet of *Ratisbone*, after the manner we have before related in Chap II It was there ordain'd, that when the Electors shall be assembl'd for the Election of a King of the *Romans*, or of an Emperor, they shall take their Places in such manner, that *Mayence* shall have the first, *Triers* and *Cologn* the second and third alternately, *Bohemia* the fourth, *Bavaria* the fifth, *Saxony* the sixth, *Brandenburg* the seventh, and the *Palatin* the eighth, all in the same Line, provided they be all there present For when some of them are there personally present, and the others represented by their Embassadors, the Embassadors of the absent fall in the Rear, and place themselves after all the Electors present After the Electors have taken their Places the Count of *Pappenheim* shuts the Conclave, and puts the Keys in such a place where the Electors may be Masters of them

It is then they execute indispensably the Regulation of the *Golden Bull* in Chap IV § 2 which requires that the Archbishop of *Mayence* should collect the Votes, and ask the Suffrages, giving his own last of all Formerly he voted the first, of which we have an Infinity of Proofs in History, and amongst the rest the illustrious Testimony of the Emperor *Frederick* I, who says very expressly to the Legates of Pope *Adrian* IV, *We give the first Vote at the Election to the Archbishop of* Mayence and *Gunther Ligurinus* says,

———*Ad proceres Electio pertinet, in qua Præcipuam vocem præsul, de more vetusto, Moguntinus habet*———

But at this time the Regulation of the *Golden Bull* is observ'd in all its Circumstances and Ceremonies, for which reason the Archbishop of *Mayence* follows also very exactly the Order establish'd by the *Golden Bull* in asking the Suffrages, 1 of the Archbishop of *Triers*, 2 of the Archbishop of *Cologn*, 3 of the King of *Bohemia*, who votes in his Rank, and not in the Case of a Division only, 4 of the Duke of *Bavaria*, 5 of the Duke of *Saxony*, 6 of the Marquiss of *Brandenburg*, and 7 of the Count *Palatin* of the *Rhine* This done, the Elector of *Triers* takes the Vote of the Archbishop of *Mayenco*

We have said elsewhere, that the Plurality of Votes makes an Emperor, or a King of the *Romans*, and that an Election made by the Consent of the major part of the Electors, has the same Force as if it had been made by the unanimous Consent of all of them, pursuant to the Tenor of the *Golden Bull*, Chap II § and we have observ'd, that by the Plurality of Votes is understood, that of the whole College, so that to make an Emperor now that there are eight Electors, it is requisite that five Suffrages should concur to his Election And it is also true, that if the Person nominated to the Empire be likewise an Elector, he may assist himself with his own Suffrage, augment the Number of the Chusers, and make the requisite Plurality of Votes, by the Addition of his own so that if there are four Electors who nominate him, he may conclude and finish the Election by his own Suffrage, which will make the fifth, by which he shall be Emperor pursuant to the Tenor of the *Golden Bull* in the same Chapter, § 7 On this Occasion is alledg'd the Example of *Sigismund* of *Luxemburg*, King of *Hungary*, and Marquiss of *Brandenburg*, who was desir'd by the other Electors, at the time of the Election, after the Death of the Emperor *Rupert* of *Bavaria*, to nominate to the Empire him of the Princes whom he should in his Conscience judge to have all the Qualities necessary for that high Dignity He answer'd thereto, that the other Electors, in shewing that Deference to his Judgment in an Affair of that Importance, put him upon the necessity of declaring, that he had not a sufficient Knowledge of the particular Merits of the others, to charge his Conscience therewith, but that he knew himself so perfectly well, that he might safely say, they would not be mistaken in the Choice of himself, and so according to the Power that the Electors his Collegues had given him, he nominated himself to the Empire *Dubravius* Bishop of *Orinutz* speaks hereof as of a true History, but it is certain, that *Sigismund* assisted at the Election but by his Embassadors, and that he was in his Kingdom of *Hungary* when he was chosen Emperor Be it as it will, the Text is formal therein, and it is a thing which is not at all doubted of

And that nothing may be wanting to Shew and Ceremony, the Electors being thus shut up, send for their Chancellors and principal Counsellors, as if they had occasion for their Advice upon the Difficulties which occur in the Election, and then put them out to continue their Deliberations, but this is all Grimace, since they begin and finish in less than an Hour the Election of the first Person of *Christendom*

The Election being ended, the Electors cause their chief Ministers of State to re-enter, and the Chancellor of the Archbishop of *Mayence*, together with the Chancellor of another Secular Elector, having reckon'd up the Suffrages, set the same down in Writing, and draw up a verbal Process, which all the Electors sign, and cause to be seal'd with the Great Seal

7 D of

of their Arms This being done the Electors go out of the Conclave, and go streight to the high Altar, on which they seat the new Elect, and then the Archbishop of *Mayence* having recommended to him the Interest of the Empire, and caus'd him to sign the Conditions under which he has been rais'd to that Dignity, he obliges him to confirm to the Electors all the Rights, Privileges, Sovereignties, Prerogatives and Preeminencies which they enjoy, and after that he causes a Publication of the Election

This Confirmation of the Electors Rights is so necessary, that without it the new Elect cannot meddle with the Administration of the Affairs of the Empire, and he is oblig'd to give one to each Elector, in the Form of Letters Patents, sign'd and seal'd with the Great Seal This Confirmation was formerly executed near *Coblentz*, between *Rens* and *Capel*, at a Place that is still at this Day call'd *Konigstul*, that is to say, *Royal Seat* It was a Structure erected in an Orchard, under seven great Walnut Trees, where there were Seats of Free Stone for the Emperor and the seven Electors, built on Pillars join'd together by so many Arches But this Building is altogether ruin'd, and the Confirmation is at this Day perform'd at the Place of the Election

But we cannot better represent all the Particulars of this Ceremony, than in the Election of the late Emperor, which was perform'd at *Ratisbone*, in the following manner

On *December* 22, 1636, about seven a Clock in the Morning, the Embassadors of *Brandenburg*, then those of *Saxony*, after them the Archbishop of *Cologn*, after him the King of *Bohemia* and *Hungary*, and the Duke of *Bavaria*, and last of all the Archbishop of *Mayence*, came to the Town-House, and repair'd all to the ordinary Council Chamber, except the King of *Bohemia*, who went into a particular Room, where he put on his Electoral Garments The Electors of *Cologn* and *Bavaria* went also, and put on their Robes in a Chamber destin'd to that Use, and the Elector of *Mayence* put on his in the Antichamber Those of the Electors of *Mayence* and of *Cologn* were of Scarlet, and those of the King of *Bohemia* and of the Elector of *Bavaria* were of Crimson Velvet, lin'd with Ermins After they had put on their Robes, and the King of *Bohemia* having the Crown upon his Head, they return'd to the Council Chamber, but they made no longer stay there, than to march out together At the Gate of the Town-House they all mounted their Horses, in order to proceed to the Cathedral Church, as to the Place appointed for the Election by the Circular Letters *Mayence* and *Cologn* march'd at the Head, after them the King of *Bohemia* and the Duke of *Bavaria*, and the Embassadors of *Saxony* and *Brandenburg* came last, but in their ordinary Habits, neither had they any Officers before them, as the Electors, who had before them the hereditary Mareschals of their Electorates, or the Mareschals in Ordinary of their Courts, who were likewise on Horseback, and carry'd a Sword for the Ecclesiasticks, in a Scabbard of Silver gilt, and for the Seculars, in a Scabbard of Crimson Velvet

They dismounted at the Church Door, and march'd in the same Order into the Chancel, their Officers going before them, and carrying the Sword rested on their Right Shoulder The Chancel was all hung with Crimson Velvet, having on the Right Hand as you go in, and on the Left of the high Altar, against the Wall, three Chairs cover'd with the same, and as many on the other side, with an Inscription in very large Characters, for *Mayence*, *Cologn*, *Bohemia*, *Bavaria*, *Saxony* and *Brandenburg* The Electors of *Mayence*, of *Bohemia*, and of *Bavaria*, took their Seats on the left side of the Altar, and the Elector of *Cologn*, with the Embassadors of *Saxony* and of *Brandenburg*, plac'd themselves in the three other Chairs on the Right Side of the high Altar Right against it, in the middle of the Chancel, there was a seventh Chair empty for the Elector of *Triers*, who was absent The Officers were standing before each Elector, having the Sword rested on their Shoulders

As soon as the Electors had taken their Places, the Bishop of *Ratisbone*, a Prince of the Empire, who was already cloath'd in his Pontifical Habit, and who only waited for the Electors, advanc'd to the high Altar, being follow'd by *Hugues Eberhard Cratz* of *Scharfenstein*, Chantor of the Church of *Mayence*, Archdeacon of *Triers*, and Prevost of the Church of *Wormes*, and by *John Valentine de Gotz*, call'd *Sinsig*, Prevost of the Church of *Spire*, by *Sebastian Tengt*, Dean of *Ratisbone*, and by *Gaspar George* of *Heguenberg*, with their Chaplains as Assistants, to receive the Mitre and Crosier of the officiating Bishop, who began the Service by the *Antiphone*, *Veni Creator Spiritus*, and the Emperor's Musick finish'd it * While the Bishop sung the Verses and the Collects, the Electors, and the Embassador of *Brandenburg*, who was a Catholick, kneel'd down, but that of *Saxony* kept standing

After that, began the Mass of the Holy Ghost (pursuant to the Constitution of the *Golden Bull*) accompany'd with the Emperor's Musick The Sieur *de Gortz* sung the Gospel, and the Sieur *de Cratz* the Epistle After the Gospel, the two Assistants, follow'd by several Ecclesiasticks, and preceded by two of the Emperor's Pages, carrying Flambeaux of white Wax, having taken the Censer and the Gospel, came up to the Elector of *Mayence*, and, after three profound Reverences, gave him Incense as many times, and after him to the Elector of *Cologn*, to the King of *Bohemia*, to the Duke of *Bavaria*, and to the Embassador of *Brandenburg* one after the other, and presented to them the Gospel to kiss in the same Order After the Bishop who officiated had made an end of the *Introitus*, and said, *per omnia secula seculorum*, the Embassador of *Saxony* withdrew, and did not return till Mass was ended During the *Agnus Dei*, the Assistants carry'd a Silver Cross, or the *Pax*, to be kiss'd by the Electors and Embassador of *Brandenburg* After the Mass was ended, and that the Embassador of *Saxony* had resum'd his Place,

---

* It was the Count of Suartzemburg

of the ELECTORS of the EMPIRE.

the Bishop unvested himself before the Altar, put on a Cope, and kneeling down, began the Hymn, *Veni Creator Spiritus*, which was ended by the Musick.

This being done, the Bishop of *Ratisbone* withdrew with his Assistants, and the Electors, and the Embassadors of the Absent, observing the same Order with which they enter'd into the Church, approach'd the Altar, on which the Gospels lay open, and the Archbishop of *Mayence* addrefs'd himself to his Collegues, and told them, That since they had agreed to proceed that Day to the Election of a King of the *Romans*, and that pursuant to the Constitution of the *Golden Bull*, and to the laudable ancient Custom, it was necessary that the Mass of the Holy Ghost being ended, all the Electors should take the usual Oath. That he was thoroughly persuaded that the Electors his Collegues, and the Embassadors of the Absent would make no Difficulty to do it, and having put the Tenor of the Oath into the Hands of the Archbishop of *Cologn*, who read it over to him, he took the said Oath in the following manner

I, Anselm Casimir, *by the Grace of God, Archbishop of* Mayence, *Great Chancellor of the holy* Roman Empire, *in* Germany, *Prince Elector*, &c *do swear on the holy Gospels, here really put before me, by the Faith which I owe to God and to the holy* Roman Empire, *That with the help of God, and the whole Strength of my Mind and Understanding, I will chuse for the temporal Head of* Christendom, *that is to say, for King of the* Romans, *future Emperor, him I shall think in my Conscience to be the most capable thereof, promising, on the same Faith, that I will give my Vote and Suffrage in this Election, without any Hope of Profit, Pension, Promise, Recompence, or other Acknowledgment So help me God, and his holy Gospel.*

After him, all the Electors took the Oath in the Hands of the Archbishop of *Mayence*, who read to them the Text of the *Golden Bull*, changing only the Names and Qualities, and gave to each an authentick Copy thereof without any Alteration, except in the last Words, as we have said before. The Ecclesiastick Electors, in taking the Oath, laid their Right Hand upon their Breast, and the King of *Bohemia*, as also the Elector of *Bavaria*, and the Embassadors of *Saxony*, and *Brandenburg*, put two Fingers of their Right Hand on the Book

The Oath being taken, the Archbishop of *Mayence* order'd two of his Secretaries, who were requir'd thereto instead of Notaries, to draw up a verbal Process, and take an Act of the same, which they did in the usual Forms.

This being done, the Electors and Embassadors resum'd their Places, till the Hymn, *Veni Creator Spiritus*, with the Versicles and Collects belonging thereto, was sung again, which being ended, they went into one of the Chapels in the Chancel which was appointed for the Election, and which on that Account was hung with a very rich Tapestry, and adorn'd with a little Altar. They also took in along with them their Chancellors, and some of their Council, and the two Secretaries of the Archbishop of *Mayence*, to do the Functions of Notaries. The Count of *Pappenheim*, hereditary Mareschal of the Empire, who stood at the Door, immediately lock'd the Chancel and the Chapel, and hung the Keys of the Gates of the Town, which were all in a Leathern Bag, at one of the Cross-bars of the Chapel

After that the Electors had taken their Places in Chairs of red Velvet, which were plac'd on the Right Hand, at the Entrance into the Chapel, the Archbishop of *Mayence* ask'd the other Electors and Embassadors, If any of them knew any thing that could hinder them from proceeding to the Election, defiring them to declare themselves thereupon, and the Electors having all answer'd, That they knew of nothing that could hinder or retard the Election *Mayence* continu'd, and said, That the Electors might remember, that within some Days a certain Capitulation had been contriv'd, and several Articles put down in Writing, which the Electors and Embassadors had approv'd, but that the ancient Custom requir'd that this Capitulation should be read again in the Conclave, and that afterwards the Electors should promise one to another, touching each the other's Hand, to observe them firmly and inviolably, and that if it should happen that one of their College should be rais'd to the Dignity of King of the *Romans*, he should be oblig'd to take the Oath in the Form it was conceiv'd, and should swear to observe punctually the Capitulation, and all the Conditions which they had jointly agreed to As also, That the Election which should be made by the Plurality of Votes, should be of the same Force as if they had all consented thereto unanimously, and that the Elect should be proclaim'd King of the *Romans*, and held for such, in the same manner as if he had been elected with one general Voice, and therefore he hop'd they would make no Difficulty to promise it, and to give their Word for the same, which should be instead of a solemn Oath

The Ecclesiastical Electors, the King of *Bohemia*, the Duke of *Bavaria*, and the two Embassadors, said that they consented thereto, and that they promis'd it, and they touch'd each the other's Hand Whereof the Archbishop of *Mayence* requir'd the Notaries to draw up their verbal Process, and to make one or more formal Instruments of the same if it were necessary

The Notaries took to witness all that were there present, and made their verbal Process After which the Archbishop of *Mayence* caus'd all the Chancellors and Counsellors, who had serv'd as Witnesses, to withdraw, and order'd the Count *de Pappenheim* to shut the Chapel Door, who took the Keys thereof, and then the Electors proceeded to the Election, which lasted about three Quarters of an Hour The Election being ended, the Chancellors and Counsellors were call'd in again, and a solemn Deputation was made to the Emperor to give him Advice thereof The Elector of *Mayence* sent the Sieur *de Mitternich*, Prevost of his Cathedral Church, the Archbishop of *Cologn*, the Count *de Komgfeck*, the King of *Bohemia*, the Count *de Martinis*, his Vicechancellor, the Duke of *Bavaria*, the Count *Dornig*, the Embassador of *Saxony*, Doctor *Tuntzel*, and that of *Brandenburg*, the Sieur *de Knefebeck*, who pray'd his Imperial Majesty to take the Pains to go to the Conclave, to hear the Resolution which

which had been taken there concerning the Election. In the mean time the Elector of *Mayence,* as well for himself as in the Name of the Electors present, and of the Embassadors of the absent, represented to the Counsellors and Notaries, who had been recall'd into the Chapel, That the Electors had judg'd it necessary, in Consideration of the present State of Affairs, to give to the Empire, by a solemn Election, a Subject capable and qualify'd, and that having all of one Agreement, and by a common Consent acknowledg'd, That *Ferdinand* III, King of *Hungary* and *Bohemia,* possess'd all the Qualities requisite to a King of the *Romans,* who was one Day to succeed in the Empire to his Imperial Majesty, to whom God send a long and happy Life, they had elected, and did elect all, with one Voice, the said *Ferdinand* III. King of the *Romans.* But whereas his Royal Dignity made Difficulty to accept that Honour without the Consent of the Emperor his Father, it was proper to keep the Election secret till his Imperial Majesty's Pleasure should be known.

Whereupon the Archbishop of *Mayence,* having ask'd the other Electors, and the Embassadors, If that were not their Intention, Will and Sentiment, and they having answer'd, Yes He requir'd the Notaries, by virtue of the Power which the other Electors had given him, to draw up their verbal Process thereof, to make and deliver one or more Instruments in form, of the same, if Need required it, which the Notaries promis'd to do, and for this Effect they took the Counsellors there present as Witnesses.

The Deputies of the Electors return'd back within a little half Hour, and made their Report, That the Emperor would repair forthwith to the Church, as accordingly he did, and that with so much Diligence, that the Electors, who intended to have met him in the middle of the Body of the Church, found he had already enter'd the Chancel. They march'd in the same Order they had observ'd in coming into the Church, except that their Mareschals carry'd the Sword with the Point downwards. As soon as the Emperor perceiv'd them, he got out of the Chair in which he was carry'd, having before him *Wolfgang William* Count of *Pappenheim,* who discharg'd the Office of hereditary Mareschal, in the absence of the eldest of that House, who was indispos'd. The Electors having first complemented the Emperor, conducted him into a Chapel right against the Conclave, where the Imperial Garments lay ready, and the *Regalia* of the Empire, and then they retir'd into the Conclave. As soon as they knew that the Emperor was Robed, they went and receiv'd him in the Chapel, and conducted him into the Conclave, the Secular Electors marching first, and carrying the *Regalia,* and the Ecclesiasticks after. As soon as the Emperor had seated himself in a Chair, right against those of the Electors, and that the Chancellors and Counsellors were let in, the Archbishop of *Mayence* standing up, made his Report of the Election which had been made of the Person of *Ferdinand* III.

After the Archbishop had resum'd his Seat, the new King of the *Romans* went and seated himself in a Chair, which was plac'd on the Right of the Emperor's, in such manner nevertheless, that with Respect to the Altar, the Emperor still retain'd the first Place. Immediately after they went out of the Conclave, and the Emperor plac'd himself in a Chair under a Canopy, having before him an Oratory, where he kneel'd while Prayers were saying, during which Time he had caus'd his Crown to be taken off by the Count *Kiesel,* first Gentleman of his Bed-Chamber. He had by him the Count of *Wolfseck,* who held the Globe, the Prince of *Hohenzollern,* who held the Sceptre, and a young Count of *Pappenheim* who held the Sword, and on his Right Hand were five Heralds at Arms dress'd in their Jackets. The Electors and the Embassadors conducted the King of the *Romans* streight to the High Altar, and after the Embassador of *Brandenburg* had taken off his Crown, which the Baron of *Limburg* receiv'd on a Velvet Cushion, the Bishop of *Ratisbone,* who had said the Mass of the Holy Ghost, pronounc'd some Prayers, during which, the Emperor, the King of the *Romans,* the Electors, and the Embassador of *Brandenburg,* kneel'd down, but that of *Saxony* kept standing.

Prayers being over, the Embassador of *Brandenburg* put the Crown again on the Head of the King of the *Romans,* and all the Electors and Embassadors plac'd him upon the Altar, assisting themselves therein with two Steps cover'd with Velvet, which had been made on purpose for that Use, and *Te Deum* was sung to the Sound of the Trumpets and Kettle-Drums, and follow'd by the Discharge of all the Canon of the Town, and several Volleys from the Burghers, who were under Arms.

After this the King of the *Romans,* and the Electors and Embassadors retir'd from the Altar, and went up into a Gallery erected in the Body of the Church, adjoyning to the Door of the Chancel, and cover'd with a very rich Tapestry. First march'd the Heralds with their Maces and Jackets. After them came some Lords, Counts and Barons, and then the hereditary Mareschals of the Electors. After that follow'd the Duke of *Bavaria,* who carry'd the Globe, having on his Right the Embassador of *Saxony,* and on his Left that of *Brandenburg,* who carry'd the Scepter. Then came the young Count of *Pappenheim,* who bore the naked Sword before the Emperor, who was carry'd in a Chair, dress'd in his Imperial Garments, and having the Imperial Crown on his Head. The King of the *Romans* march'd last, having on his Right the Archbishop of *Mayence,* and on his Left the Archbishop of *Cologn.* In the Gallery were five Chairs of Crimson Velvet, two on the Right Hand, for the Electors of *Mayence* and of *Bavaria,* and three on the Left Hand, for the Elector of *Cologn,* and for the Embassadors of *Saxony* and *Brandenburg.* In the middle were on an Alcove, rais'd about two Foot, two Chairs cover'd with Cloth of Gold and Silver, the one for the Emperor, and the other, which was about a Foot and Half backwarder than the first, for the King of the *Romans.*

When they had taken their Places, the Archbishop of *Mayence* order'd *John Regnault,* Baron of *Metternich,* Provost of the Cathedral Church, to proclaim the Election to the People.

ple and at the same time the King of the Romans, the Electors and the Embassadors stood up, but the Emperor remain'd sitting, while the Baron of *Metternich* made the Proclamation according to the Tenor of what had been given him in writing, and was to this effect

The most Reverend, and most Serene, my most Gracious Lords, the Princes Electors of the Holy Empire, having judg'd it necessary, for very pressing and important Causes, to proceed to the Choice and Election of a King of the Romans, *their Graces and Electoral Highnesses, and the Embassadors of the absent, have, after a mature and serious Deliberation, to the Honour and Glory of Almighty God, and for the Benefit and Advantage of the Holy Empire, and of all Christendom, elected in the Name of God, and nominated by one common Agreement, and with one Voice, for King of the* Romans, *the most Serene and most Powerful Prince and Lord,* Ferdinand III, *King of* Hungary *and* Bohemia, *Arch-Duke of* Austria, *&c our most Gracious Lord, as being born Arch-Duke of* Austria, *and their Coelector, in the Quality of King of* Bohemia, *to be Emperor, as soon as the Empire shall become vacant, which may it please God to delay for many Years Which Election, so unanimously made, I publish and declare in the Name of the most Gracious Lords, the Princes Electors, and the Embassadors of the absents commanding every one to acknowledge for such the said Lord* Ferdinand III, *King of* Hungary *and* Bohemia, *&c and to pay him the Honour and Respect which is due to him*

After the Baron of *Metternich* had read the Proclamation, he cry'd first, *God save the King*, and made a Sign to the People to do the same so that in a moment, the whole Church rung with Acclamations of Joy, which were accompany'd with the Sound of Trumpets and Kettle-Drums These Ceremonies were ended but very late, and the Assembly did not separate till it was past two a Clock in the Afternoon

They went out of the Church in the following Order

The Magistrates of *Ratisbone* had caus'd a Wooden Bridge to be made, adorn'd with Ballusters, and cover'd with Cloth, from the Church to the Bishop's Palace The Domesticks of the Emperor, of the King of the *Romans*, of the Electors, and of the other Princes, with the Counts, Barons and Gentlemen, march'd first After them came the Trumpets and Kettle Drums, and then the five Heralds at Arms, all uncover'd The Elector of *Bavaria* march'd next, between the Embassadors of *Saxony* and *Brandenburg* Then follow'd the young Count of *Pappenheim* alone, carrying the Sword drawn before the Emperor, who was carry'd in a Chair by reason of his Indisposition Going out of the Church, four Senators of the City of *Ratisbone* receiv'd him under a Canopy of Yellow Taffaty, having in the Top thereof on the Inside, an Eagle embroider'd in Black Silk The King of the *Romans* was on his Left Hand, but a little backwarder, and had at his Sides the Electors of *Mayence* and of *Cologn*, who also let him go half a Pace before them Some Persons of great Quality, Prelates and others follow'd them, and the Yeomen of the Guard, and the Body Guards, clos'd the Procession

The Emperor was cloth'd in his Imperial Garments, and had the Imperial Crown on his Head The King of the *Romans* had also his, but he had not chang'd his Clothes, and had on the same Electoral Robe, which he had when he went into the Conclave The Embassadors had their ordinary Habits, and cover'd themselves at their going out of the Church, as well as the Electors, who caus'd the Sword to be carry'd before them, but in the Scabbard, and the Point downward The Emperor and the King of the *Romans* enter'd into their Appartment, where they thank'd and dismiss'd the Electors, who retir'd to their Lodgings

---

CHAP. XX.

Of the Effect of the Election.

WE have given to understand in the whole Sequel of this Discourse, that the Princes who are call'd Electors, have this Quality but only because they are in Possession of the Right of chusing a Head to the Empire and we have shewn, that the Plurality of Votes in the Electoral College makes an Emperor, so that it seems as if there was no room to doubt of the Effect of the Election. But they who shall consider that the same *Golden Bull*, which has serv'd for Foundation to this Treatise, never speaks of the Election of an Emperor, and gives no other Power to the Electors, than to make a King of the *Romans*, future Emperor that is to say, a Prince who is not to take the Quality of Emperor, till he has been crown'd by the Pope, will easily allow, that it is not without Reason that we make a particular Chapter of the Effect of the Election, to know whether the Elect ought to be contented with the Quality of King, or whether he can take that of Emperor immediately after his Election

There are two Opinions quite different on this Subject, the one maintains that the Pope is in possession of the Right, not only to give the Title of Emperor to the Elect, but also the Empire it self and that the Election receives its Force from the Confirmation of the Pope The other says on the contrary, that the bare Election makes the Emperor, and that it is not necessary the Pope's Authority should intervene directly or indirectly

There was formerly to be seen in a Picture in the Great-Hall of the *Lateran*, the Ceremonies of the Coronation of the Emperor *Lotharius* II, where the Pope *Innocent* II. had caus'd the Emperor to be represented at his Feet, to receive the Imperial Crown, and do him Homage for the Empire And that his Intention might not be doubted of, he had caus'd Verses to be added thereto, which said very expressly, that *Lotharius* became there the Pope's Man, that is to say, his Vassal

Rex venit ante fores, jurans prius urbis honores
Post homo fit Papæ, sumit quo dante Coronam

Pope *Adrian* IV, think ng he had some Reason to be dissatisfy'd with *Freder ck* I, was willing to lay hold of the Opportunity, and see whether that Emperor would suffer him to corroborate thereby, the Pretensions of his Predecessors He nad contriv'd (in reproaching him with his Ingratitude, and that he did not acknow'edge the Obligations he had to him) to slip into his Letters the Word *Beneficium*, with a Design to explain it to his Advantage, it it was over-look'd, and to make it believ'd that the Emperor own'd the Empire to be a I ief of the See of *Rome*, or to maintain his Pretensions, it the Emperor offer'd to dispute them with him And indeed, his Legates did not dissemble the Matter, and shew'd very well that the Word *Beneficium* signify'd I ief, when they said, *Of whom then does the Emperor hold the Empire, if he does not hold it of the Pope?* *John* XXII, and *Clement* V, explain themselves much better, when they say, *That the Kings of the Romans, who are chosen in Germany, are not look'd upon as Emperors, and that they cannot discharge the Functions thereof, till they have receiv'd the Power, together with the Crown, from the Hands of the Pope, to whom the Administration of the Affairs of the Empire belongs, during the Interregnum* That the Empire holds of the See of Rome That the Election of the Princes of Germany *has no other Force, than what it receives from the Authority and Confirmation of the Pope* That the Elect *cannot meddle with the Affairs of the Empire, but under the good liking of the Divinity* (numine) *of the Vicar and Lieutenant of God, and that the Empire becoming vacant, the Pope can dispose of it absolutely, as of a Fief of the See of Rome*

The Doctors who stand up for the Interest of that Court, ground the Power they assign the Popes, not so much on that of tying and untying which our Saviour gives to St *Peter*, and to the other Apostles, (because they are oblig'd to acknowledge that that Power is only Spiritual,) as on the Possession of the Right which they say the Popes have to transfer States and Empires They alledge for this Purpose the Examples of *Zachary*, and *Leo* III, and say, that the first transferr'd the Kingdom of *France* from the House of *Merovens* to that of *Pepin*, and that the other took away the *Roman* Empire from the *Greeks*, to bestow it on the Eastern and Western *French*, in the Person of *Charlemagne* That the major part of the Princes who have been call'd to the Empire, did not take the Quality of Emperor till they had receiv'd the Imperial Crown from the Hands of the Pope That they cannot after their Election assume any other Quality than that of King, and that they reckon'd the Years of their Empire, but from the Day of their Coronation at *Rome* That *Charlemagne* himself would not dispose of the Empire, without the Pope's Permission, since he thought fit to send his Will and Testament as far as *Rome*, to have it sign'd and confirm'd by him, who alone has a Right on Earth to dispose of the Empire That the Emperor *Albert* I, intreated the Pope *Boniface* VIII, to make the Empire hereditary in his House, which he would not have done, if he had not believ'd that the Pope had a Power to dispose of the same That *Emanuel Comnenus*, Emperor of *Constantinople*, offer'd a good Sum of Money to the Pope, and a very considerable Army against his Enemies, and to reunite the *Greek* Church to the *Latin*, it he would reunite the Empires of the East and West in his Person

But they who speak for the Emperor's Interest, answer to this, That the Examples of *Zachary* and of *Leo* III, are of no use to the Intention of those that alledge them That indeed it is true, that several Authors, * almost Contemporaries with them, say very expressly, That the Deposition of *Childerick*, and the Exaltation of *Pepin*, was the Work of the Pope, and that it was done by *Zachary's* Authority But then it must be consider'd that they are most of them Strangers, and as Ecclesiasticks, interessed in the Pope's Cause Besides which, they are often contented to copy one another Word for Word, and their Language is not so pure, to allow all their Expressions to be taken in their proper and natural Signification That this appears evidently by the Testimony of a great Number of other Historians, at least as knowing, and beyond comparison more exact than the first, who all say, That *Childerick* was shav'd, and that *Pepin* was plac'd up the Throne by the Election of the *French* Amongst the Authors they alledge for this, there are two that are irreproachable, to wit, *Ado* and *Sigebert* The first, who was Archbishop of *Vienna*, and liv'd under *Charles the Bald*, and under *Lewis* his Son, says, † That *Pepin* having sent Burghard, Bishop of *Wurtzburg* to *Rome*, to consult the Pope concerning the State of the Affairs of the Kingdom, *Zachary* made answer to him, That it was better to call to the Crown him that appear'd capable of reigning, whereupon *the* French *gave themselves a King, pursuant to the Pope's Advice, and that of the Embassadors* Sigebert, *a Monk in the Abbey of* Gemblours *in* Brabant, *who liv'd under the Emperor* Henry IV, says, ‡ That Prince *Pepin* was crown'd by *Boniface*, Archbishop of *Mayence* by Apostolick Authority, *and by the Choice of the* French And that no doubt may be made hereof, they say, That the most affectionate to the Interest of the Court of *Rome*, the Prelates, Religious, and the *Italians*, agree that the Pope interven'd in this Action, but only to favour the Change the *French* design'd to make, and did really make with the Consent of the States of the Kingdom *Flavius Blondus*, Secretary to Pope *Eugenius* IV, does not scruple to speak thus of it, * " I find in *Alcuin*, in *Paulus Diaconus*, " and in most of those who have written the " History of *France*, That the Lords and Peo-

---

* Blondel *names them all in his Treatise*, De Formula Regnante Christo Sect - § 16   † Ann 749   ‡ Ann 750
* Decad 1 lib. 10 p 148

" ple

"ple of the Kingdom, making a Comparison of the great Qualities of *Pepin*, with the Impertinencies of *Childerick*, sent to the Pope to ask him, Whether they were oblig'd to suffer the Idleness of the one, and frustrate the other of the Honour which was due to his Merit? And that after the Pope had answer'd, That it was proper to acknowledge for King, him, who was most capable of supporting the Regal Dignity, *The* French *declar'd* Pepin *King, and put* Childerick *into a Convent, by the Advice of all the People* Antoninus, Archbishop of *Florence*, says, † That *Pepin*, Mayor of the Palace, considering the Incapacity of his King, sent a solemn Embassy to Pope *Zachary*, and defir'd to know of him who best deserv'd to be King, He who had all the Qualities requisite thereto, and had the whole Administration of the Government, or he, who spending all his Time in Drunkenness and Sloth, had only the bare Name thereof." To which, it is said, the Pope made this Answer, That he who knew the Art of Reigning, ought to reign in effect, and that these Embassadors having made their Report in *France* of the Pope's Answer, *a General Assembly was held of the Princes and Prelates, who depos'd* Childerick, *and elected, with one common Consent*, Pepin, *whom they caus'd to reign over them* P *Maturus*, a Jesuite, who has made Annotations upon *Antoninus*, adds, That the Pope had no Share in the Change, except that he made Answer to the Embassador's Questions, in the common Sense, and that *the whole Affair was begun, and finish'd by the* French *themselves* Nauclerus ‡, and *Sabellicus* *, do not speak otherwise thereof But no body is more express on this Subject than *Michael Coccinius*, in his Treatise *De Translatione Imperij*, when he says, That *Childerick*, the last King of *France* of *Merovens*'s Posterity, was depos'd because he was incapable of reigning, and that *Pepin*, who was a Native of *Gallia Belgica*, was made King by the Pope Now it is reasonable to believe, says he, that this Deposition of *Childerick*, and the Exaltation of *Pepin* had their chief Force from the Consent and Authority of the *French* I or by what we read that it was the Pope who depos'd the one, and substituted the other, must be understood, that he consented to those who depos'd and substituted, and that he freed them from their Oath of Fidelity, conformably to the Explication which the Gloss gives *in q 6 c alius*, where it says, *Deposuit, hoc est, deponentibus Consensit*

They add to the Testimony of these Authors, the Particulars of the History of this Deposition, and say, That *Pepin* was substituted in the Place of *Childerick*, without the Intervention of the Pope's Authority, directly or indirectly, at least if the Word *Authority* be taken in its true Signification, for the Power of him who can command, and without which the *French* would not have dar'd, nor could not have proceeded to the Deposition of the King, and to the Election of another For all those who in speaking of this Action, have accompany'd it with some Circumstances, make it sufficiently known, that the *French* did not intreat the Pope's Permission, for an Action of this Importance but that it was *Pepin*, who had himself Occasion for it, to give a Colour to his Usurpation And all that he did was to send *Burghard*, Bishop of *Wurtzburg*, to Pope *Zachary*, to ask in general Terms, which of the two best deserv'd to be King, he who had only the bare Name thereof, and abus'd that Quality, to pass his Life in a continu'd Idleness, or else he, who under the Name of a private Person, possess'd Qualities which were truly Regal, and employ'd his whole Care, and all his Thoughts in the Conduct and Management of the Affairs of the Kingdom and that the Pope did no more than make a very general Answer, and such a one as might reasonably be expected from a Man of Sense

For which Reason *Claude de Seissel*, who was a great Statesman under *Lewis* XII, speaking of this Action, says, That *Pepin*, considering that this Question, and the Answer which common Sense would oblige the Pope to make, would be capable of raising in *Zachary*, hopes of several Advantages against the Kings of *Lombardy*, had Address enough to wrest by this mean, a tacit Consent from the Pope to authorize his Usurpation But if, says *Claude Fauchet* *, he had ask'd the Pope, whether it was lawful for *Pepin* to make use of the Weakness of his Prince, to take the Crown off of his King's Head to place it on his own? There is no likelihood that a good Pope, who had the least Tincture of divine and human Right, would have made an Answer in favour of *Pepin* From whence they conclude, That *Zachary* did not back *Pepin* with his Authority, but was contented to favour his Pretensions under-hand So that it cannot be said, it was the Pope who transferr'd the Regal Crown of *France* from one Family to the other, but that this Change is owing only to the universal Consent, and unanimous Agreement of the States of the Kingdom

They produce against the Example of *Leo* III, the same Testimonies which we have just alledg'd against that of *Zachary*, but it will be sufficient to say with them, that in what *Leo* did there was no Translation of the Empire, because the word *Transfer* signifies to take from one Place or Person, to carry to, or give to another, so that the thing transferr'd is no longer where it was, but is found to be where before it was not But *Leo* III took nothing from the *Greeks*, not even so much as the Title of Emperor, which remain'd to the Princes of *Constantinople*, till such time as the *Turks* made themselves Masters thereof, and he gave no Empire to *Charlemagne*, who gain'd nothing in the West by his Coronation but the bare Title This is what Cardinal *Bellarmin* restrains all the Power of the Pope to, at least in the Example of *Leo* III, when he says, That it is certain that *Charlemagne* was in Possession before his Coronation of all *France*, *Germany*, and *Italy*, either by Right of Succession, or by that of Conquest, and that the Pope gave him only the bare Title of Emperor. The others on the contrary say, that the Pope did not so much as give him the Title but that it was the Senate and People of *Rome* who would

† *Part Hist* 2 Tit 18 cap 1 § 2   ‡ *Gener* 26 Art 750.   * *Ænead* 8 lib 8   † *Antiq Gaul* libr 6 chap 1

needs

Of the ELECTION *of the* EMPEROR, *and*

needs honour with an extraordinary Quality their Sovereign, who possess'd too many Kingdoms to be contented with that of King and that the same Pope, who as being *Charlemagne*'s Subject, could not arrogate to himself the Authority of undertaking of his own Head an Affair of this nature, discharg'd no other Function at his Coronation than that which the Custom of *France* gives to the Archbishop of *Rheims*. They alledge for that, *Sigebert*, who says on this account, * " That the *Romans* being grown " weary of the Government of their Emperors " who resided at *Constantinople*, and laying hold " of the occasion they had from the Infolence of " a Woman, who had caus'd the Eyes of the " Emperor her Son to be put out, in order to " reign her self, saluted King *Charles* Emperor " with one common Consent, crown'd him by " the Hands of the Pope, and call'd him Empe- " ror and August." *Godefroy de Viterbe* †, explaining these words, *Crown'd by God*, which the *Roman* People mingl'd with their Acclamations at the Coronation of *Charlemagne*, says, That the Pope indeed crown'd *Charles*, but that it was God who anointed him, and that he was consecrated by a Hand which is only visible to the Heart, alledging for that the Passage of Holy Writ, where God says, That it is he has anointed *David* to make it appear that *Charlemagne* held the Imperial Dignity of none but God immediately. And it is for this purpose they relate what the learned *Onuphrius Panvinius* says, ‡ That *Charles* having been declar'd Emperor by the Senate and the *Roman* People, was anointed and crown'd by the Pope, with a Diadem or Crown of Gold, because he was the first Prelate of the World after the Example of the Emperors of the East, who caus'd themselves to be crown'd by the Patriarchs of *Constantinople*, who were the first Prelates of the whole *Greek* Empire.

They find that nothing is more easy than to answer the Objections the first make concerning *Charlemagne*, *Albert* I, and *Emanuel Comnenus*. For first, as to *Charlemagne*, they say, that he made his Testament in the Year 806, and that he does not therein so much as mention the Empire, nor his Son *Lewis*, and that in reality he could not then have any thought of him, since both *Charles* and *Pepin* his Elder Brothers were still living, and excluded *Lewis* from the Imperial Dignity. That *Charlemagne* did indeed send his Will to the Pope, and desir'd him to sign it: but that he likewise did the same Honour to all the Metropolitans, and to divers other Bishops of his Empire. And that he was so far from intending by this Civility to beg the Imperial Dignity for his Son, that on the contrary the circumstances of *Lewis*'s Coronation, whereof we have spoken heretofore, * make it very plain that he had a mind all the World should know, that he held the Empire of God immediately, and by Right of hereditary Succession.

As for *Albert* I, the Truth is, that this Emperor finding himself press'd by *Boniface* VIII, to declare War against *Philip le Bel* King of *France*, he gave him to understand, That he was ready to take Arms against *France*, but it was necessary to consider, that he might perish in the War, and so leave his Children to the Mercy of the Enemies of his House so that to give him both the Means and Courage to undertake it, it would be proper to confirm the Empire to his Son, and to make it hereditary to his Posterity. There would indeed be room to speak with Advantage in Favour of the Pope's Authority, in the Election of the Emperors, if *Boniface* had alter'd the elective State of the Empire, and made it hereditary, and if the Princes and States of *Germany* had approv'd the Change either by a publick Acknowledgment or a tacit Consent. But there is no possibility of grounding it on the bare Demand of a Prince, who had a mind to rid himself of the Pope's Importunity, and who laugh'd at the Gift he offer'd him of the Kingdom of *France*, if he would but conquer it. However *Boniface*, who did not scruple to maintain that all Crowns held of his Mitre, was not so imprudent notwithstanding as to undertake an Affair of that Importance, and the Refusal he made to *Albert*, is an infallible Proof of his Impotency, and of the Apprehension he had of offending the Princes of the Empire, who would have had Courage enough to have employ'd against him the same Means which *Philip* was oblig'd to make use of for the Preservation of the Rights of his Crown

That the Offers of *Emanuel Comnenus* were not founded on the Opinion he had of the Pope's Power, but on the Knowledge he had of the Weakness of the Minds of those Times, which were so devoted to the Pope's Will, that they made no Difference between the Decrees of the Court of *Rome*, and the Oracles of the Sanctuary. But notwithstanding all this, it will not appear that the Advantage he offer'd the Pope (which was the greatest the See of *Rome* can ever obtain, to wit, the Re-union of the Eastern and Western Churches) could prevail with the Pope to grant the *Greek* Emperor what he demanded

As to what the first say, that those Princes of *Germany* which have not been crown'd by the Popes, ought not to be plac'd in the Catalogue of the Emperors, the others answer, that they cannot deny but the following Emperors are commonly left out of the said Catalogue, to wit, *Lewis* III, *Conrade* I, *Henry* I, *Conrade* III, *Philip* of *Suabia*, *William* of *Holland*, *Alphonsus* of *Castile*, *Richard* of *Cornwal*, *Rodolphus* I, *Adolphus* of *Nassau*, *Albert* I, *Wenceslas*, *Rupert*, and *Albert* II But that it is by an Abuse and the mere Caprice of the *Italian* Writers, who insert in the place of *Lewis* III, and of some of his Successors, several Usurpers, who caus'd themselves to be crown'd at *Rome* in those Times, tho' they possess'd but a very small part or what formerly made the Empire of *Germany*. And to shew that they have Reason to speak thus, they say against the Objection which the first make here, concerning *Lewis le Begue* (who was crown'd Emperor, and was the third of the Name, and so *Lewis* of *Bavaria* would have been the fifth, if *Lewis* the Son of *Arnulphus* had been Emperor) that *Lewis le Begue* never took the Quality of Emperor, and that he was crown'd at *Troyes* by Pope *John* but only as King of *France*. So that

* Ann. 801   † Part 17   ‡ In his Treatise de Comitiis, cap 5   * Chap 1

if he be taken from the Number of the Emperors, which muſt of neceſſity be done, Lewis of Bavaria will not be the fourth, but the third of that Name, if Lewis the Son of Arnulphus was not Emperor. They moreover ſay, that even the Canons, in ſaying that Henry Duke of Bavaria, who ſucceeded to the Empire to Otho III, is the ſecond Emperor of that Name, ſufficiently declare that they believe Henry the Fowler was the firſt, and Emperor, and that if the Quality of Emperor be not given to Lewis III, Conrade I, and Henry the Fowler, it is not becauſe they were not crown'd at Rome, but becauſe they did not reign in Italy, where was the Seat of the Empire under Lotharius I, Lewis II, and Charles the Bald.

That it is true alſo, that the ſame Charles the Bald was he who began to diſtinguiſh between the Years of his Empire and thoſe of his Reign, but that he could not do otherwiſe, becauſe he was King of France long before he attain'd the Empire, and that it was not ſo much the Coronation that gave him the Quality of Emperor, as the Poſſeſſion of Italy, to which this Quality had been annex'd under Lewis II, his Predeceſſor, as we obſerv'd before. So that if he took the Title thereof but from the Day of his Coronation, it was becauſe he could not be certain whether Lewis the German his eldeſt Brother would get the ſtart of him, and make ſure of Italy, and the City of Rome before him. That thus Otho I did not aſſume the Quality of Emperor but from the Day he was crown'd at Rome, becauſe he judg'd that he took Poſſeſſion of Italy by this Ceremony. But that it cannot be ſaid that therefore the Pope gave him the Empire, or even the Title of Emperor, ſince Otho could not hold that Dignity or a Prelate, whom he treated as a Subject, and from whom he took the Pontificate ſome Days after. That the ſaid Poſſeſſion of Italy, and of the City of Rome, has obig'd moſt of Otho's Succeſſors to diſtinguiſh between the Years of their Reign and thoſe of their Empire, and yet that this Cuſtom has not been ſo univerſal, but that amongſt ſo many Emperors, there are ſeveral to be found who have taken the Quality of Emperor and of Auguſt preſently after their Election, and before their Coronation. For Frederick II was not crown'd by Hugolin Biſhop of Oſtia, and Legate from Honorius III, till November 22, 1220, and yet there are Letters of April 19 foregoing, by which he confirms to the Biſhop of Utrecht certain Rights and Privileges, which had been granted to him before by his Predeceſſors, wherein he aſſumes the Quality of Emperor of the Romans, and of Auguſt. William of Holland makes a Donation to John d'Avênes, dated June 9, 1252, and in the fourth Year of his Empire, where he makes uſe of the word Empire, tho' he was never crown'd by the Pope. Rodolphus I takes the Quality of Auguſt in the Act, by which he confirms to Reginald Earl of Gueldres the right of coining Money, from the Year 1282. Adolphus of Naſſau takes alſo the Quality of Auguſt in the Act, by which he confirms to the ſaid Reginald the leave to build the Town of Staveren in Friſe. Albert I takes the ſame Quality of Auguſt, in the Letters which confirm to Reginald of Gueldres the Inveſtiture Rodolphus I had given him of the Eaſtern Friſe, which is at preſent call'd the Weſtern, in reſpect to that which is ſituate beyond the River Ems. They are dated at Boppard, Apr. 24, 1299, and thoſe from Rodolphus are inſerted therein, dated July 29, 1290. Henry of Luxemburg was not crown'd at Rome till the Year 1212, yet neverthelesſs he aſſumes the Quality of Auguſt in 1210. Wenceſlas was not crown'd at all in Italy, and yet that does not hinder him from taking the Quality of Emperor of the Romans, always Auguſt, in his Letters of Inveſtiture of the Dutchy of Guelders for William of Juliers, dated October 18, 1383. And it is with the ſame Indifferency that ſeveral other Emperors reckon the Years of their Empire ſometimes from the Day of their Election, and ſometimes from that of their Coronation.

That all the Emperors who have reign'd ſince Charles V, have reckon'd the Years of their Empire from the Day of their Election, and have neglected receiving the Imperial Crown from the Hands of the Pope, becauſe they look'd upon this Action to be a mere Ceremony, which their Predeceſſors had made uſe of, only to give the greater Luſtre to the Imperial Dignity, or elſe thereby to take as it were a civil Poſſeſſion of Italy, over which they pretended by this mean to preſerve their Rights. And that it appears manifeſtly that it is but a Ceremony, not only in this, that divers Princes who did not pretend to the Empire, would needs be crown'd by the Pope, but alſo becauſe ſome Emperors have reiterated this Ceremony in their own Perſons, tho' the Quality of Emperor was not conteſted with them. There are Examples thereof in Pepin King of France, who cauſ'd himſelf to be crown'd with his Sons in the Year 753, by Pope Stephen II, tho' he had in the Year 750 been crown'd by Boniface Archbiſhop of Mayence. Charles and Carloman Sons to Pepin, were nevertheleſs crown'd at their Acceſſion to the Crown, tho' they had already been crown'd with their Father by Pope Stephen. Lewis le Begne cauſ'd himſelf to be crown'd by Pope John VII, and yet he did not take the Quality of Emperor for all that. Lewis the Debonnair, who had been crown'd during his Father's Life in the Year 812, was ſo again by Stephen IV, in the Year 816. Lewis II was crown'd by Sergius II, in the Year 864, and by Adrian II the fifth of June 871. Otho I by John XII in the Year 962, and by Leo VIII in 968. Henry V by Paſcal II, in the Year 1111, and by the Biſhop of Braccara, whom he had cauſ'd to be choſen in oppoſition to Gelaſius II in 1118. Otho IV by Guy de Poré, Legate from Pope Innocent III, in the Year 1203, and Innocent himſelf in the Year 1209. Charles IV by Peter Bermandy and Giles, Cardinals of Oſtia and of Sabine, Legates from Innocent VI, in 1355, and by Urban V, in the Year 1364. They oppoſe to the Advantage the firſt may gain from the Decrees of John XXII, and thoſe of Clement V, the expreſs Proteſtations of ſeveral Emperors, who poſitively ſay, That they hold their Dignity but of the Election only, which gives to the Elect all that Succeſſion gives to the Heir. Frederick I made Anſwer to the Legates of Pope Adrian, That the Crown of the Empire is free. That it holds of God immediately

mediately. That the Emperor holds his Dignity of the Election of the Princes of *Germany*, and that the Pope's Unction is but a mere Ceremony, as well as that of the Archbishop of Cologn. *Rodolphus* I. spoke to those who press'd him to go, and receive the Imperial Crown at *Rome*, in these Terms *Italy has consirm'd several Kings of Germany, I shall not go to Rome, I am King, I am Emperor, and promise my self to govern my Estates with as much Conduct, as if I had been crown'd at* Rome. And the Emperor *Maximilian*, who would never be crown'd by the Pope, tho' he took several Journies to *Italy*, did not scruple to tell the Legate, who was at the Diet of *Constance* in the Year 1507, *That it is but a mere Ceremony, and that it is of no Utility to receive the Imperial Crown from the Hands of the Pope, since all the Authority and Power of the Emperor depends absolutely of the Electors and States of the Empire*.

These are mostly the Reasons of both Parties, of which every one may judge. But it seems to many of the most learned in this matter, that those of the Emperors are strongest and best grounded in the Truth of History, since Pope *Innocent* in C. *Venerabilem de Electio & Elect. potestate*, makes no Difficulty to say *It is our Opinion however, that if the Emperor cannot receive the Crown at* Rome, *he nevertheless receives the Authority to administer the Affairs of the Empire from the Archbishop of* Cologn, *or even from the Power which the Election it self gives him, without the Coronation*.

And therefore we shall finish this Discourse with the formal Words of the Constitution of the Emperor *Lewis* IV, which declares, by the Advice and Consent of all the Princes and States of the Empire, That *he who is chosen by all the Princes unanimously, or by the Plurality of Votes, ought to be reputed and nam'd, and is in effect true and lawful King and Emperor of the* Romans. That all the Subjects ought to respect him in this Quality, and that immediately after his Election he can administer the Affairs of the Empire, without its being requisite that the Consent, Authority, Approbation, or Confirmation of the Pope, of the Apostolick See, or of any other foreign Power whatever, should intervene directly or indirectly.

FINIS.

INDEX.

A

	Page
Abas, King of *Persia*	55, 83, 147
Abbot *Bentivoglio*, Minister of *France* in *Italy*	107
Confident of Card *Mazarine*	390
Abbot *de Bersegne*	311
Abbot *Bourlemont*, Minister of *France* at the Treaty of *Pisa*	265
Abbot of *Brantholme*	368
Abbot *Martinengue*, Minister of the Pope	192
Abbot *Nanny*, Agent of *Spain*	311
Abbot *de St Nicholas*, Minister of *France* at *Rome*	312
Abbot *de Provane*, Embassador of *Savoy* at *Venice*	184
Abbot *Alexandre della Scaglia* 188 Embassador of *Savoy* in *France* 277 In *England*	136
Abbot *Sirs*	241
Abbot of *Vendome*	128
Abbot of *Verrue*, Embassador of *Savoy* in *France*	276
Abbot of *Ursperg*	64
Abgesanter is Deputy	228
Ablegatus and Deputy are Synonymous Terms	15, 32
Abraham Williams, Master of the Ceremonies in *England*	135
Absolution of *Henry* IV	331
Acceptable, an Embassador ought to be so	94
Achilles de Harlay de Sancy, Embassador of *France* at the Port	56, 417
Address of the *Swedish* Embassador unsuccessful	198
Admiral *Chabot*	117
Admiral *de Chastillon* See *Jaspar de Coligny*	
Admirant of *Arragon*, Embassador of *Spain* in *France*	129, 236
Admirant of *Castille*	166
Adolphus, Duke of *Cleves*	301
Adoration of the *Eastern* Kings	164
Adrian, Pau	417
Advices of Embassadors	362
Affairs Domestick	315
Aga of the *Janisaries*	161
Age of an Embassador	63, &c.
Agent, a Publick Minister	2, 33, 247
not properly a Representative Minister	38
Agent of the *Anseatick* Towns, how treated at the *Hague*	15
Agent of the States of *Holland*	307
Agent of *France*, refuses to answer in a Court of Justice	254
Alard, Coll and Agent of *Savoy*	19
Albert Pio Signeur de Carpy, Embassador of *France* at *Rome*	75, 89
Alberto Boschetto, a Traytor	88, 114
Alcala Diego canoniz d	195
Alcoran protects Publick Ministers	248
Aldobrandini, first Minister of Pope *Clement* VIII	100
Legate in *France*	74
The Expence of his Legation	207
Alexander, the Pope's Nuntio	205, 297
Alexander Bichi See Cardinal *Bichi*	
Alexander VI Pope, demands Succour of the *Turk*	65
Sends a Legate to *Charles* VIII	100
Alexander VII refuses to let a *German* Prince sit or cover in his Presence 32 Obliged to give Satisfaction to *Lewis* XIV 264 See	343

	Page
Alexander Farnese	231
Alexander Grisenber, Resident for the Emperor at the Port	253
Alexander Humes, the *Scots* Embassador in *England*	103
Alexander Piaseczinsky, Embassador of *Poland* at the Port	206
Alexandri de gli Vincent, Minister of *Venice* in *Persia*	306
Alincourt, Minister of *France* at *Rome*	110
Alla Capi, an *Asylum* at *Ispahan*	280
Allegiance	77
Allies may make use of the same Minister	244
Alliance between *France* and the United Provinces	371
Aloysio Contarini, Embassador of *Venice* in *England*	263
In *France*	123
Alphonso Borgia See Cardinal *Borgia*	
Alphonso Casati, Embassador in *Switzerland*	21, 114
Alphonso de la Cueva, Embassador of *Spain* at *Venice*	232, 277, 286
Alphonso, Duke of *Ferrara*	88
Alphonso de Cardenas, Embassador of *Spain* in *England*	17
Alphonso de Valasco, Embassador of *Spain* in *England*	197
Alphonso, Prince of *Naples*	338
Alphonso, King of *Castille*	321
Alphonso of *Este*	360
Alphonso the Magnanimous	340
Alphonso Tornabon, Minister of *France* in *England*	329
His Character	418
Alvaro de Luna, Constable of *Castille*, Favourite of the King of *Spain* 129 His Tragical End	304
Alvaro de Quadra, Embassador of *Spain* at *London*	276
Amboise See Cardinal d *Amboise*	
Amelia de Hanau, Princess Regent of *Hesse*	28
Andrew Badouere, Envoy from the Senate of *Venice* to *Henry* III	236
Andrew Bicker, Embassador from the United Provinces in *Poland* and *Sweden*, to the Elector of *Brandenburgh*	142
Andrew del Borgo, Embassador from the Emperor in *Spain*	103
Andrew Chitzi, an Embassador and Traytor	88
Andrew Gritti, a Prisoner of War negotiates	111
Andrew Mauriquez, Minister of the Governour of *Milan*	22
Andrew Nicolini, Embassador of *Florence* to the Pope and the Emperor	49
Andrew Paulucci, a Monk, negotiates	67
Andrew Roffe, Envoy from the Republick of *Venice* in *France*	34
Ange de Joyeuse, a Capuchin	65
Angelo Cornaro, Embassador of *Venice* in *France*	48, 119, 123, 131, 151, 322
His Character	419
Angelo Contarini, his Character	ibid
Anjou, Duke of	129, 233
Ann of *Bretagne*	49
Annebaut, Admiral of *France*	140
D'*Anse Peter*	58
Anthony d *Acugna*, Minister of the Archduke *Philip*	282

Anthony

INDEX.

Anthony Arosequi, Secretary of State in Spain 151
Anthony Donati, Embassador of Venice at Rome 54
Anthony Condolmer, Embassador of Venice in *France*, refuses the King's Present 289
Anthony de Fonseca, Embassador of *Spain* at *Venice* 18, 339, 348
Anthony Fortesch, Minister of the Duke of *Lorain* in *England* 84
Anthony Gurdotti, Minister without a Character 35
Anthony Maria Gratian, Bishop of *Amalia*, Nuncio at *Venice* 74, 185
Anthony de Noguerres, Minister of the King of *Arragon* 103
Anthony Parmentier de Heesfwicq, Deputy of the United Provinces to the Elector of *Brandenburgh* 143
Anthony, Paulin, Baron *de la Garde*, Embassador of *France* at the *Port* 56, 345, 410
Anthony Rincon, Embassador of *France* at the *Port*'s Kill'd 78, 278
Anthony, King of *Navarre*, Embassador 20
a weak Prince 48
Anthony Shirley, Embassador of *Persia* 75, 354
Anthony de Sylva and *Sousa*, Resident of *Portugal* in *Sueden* 28
Anthony de Sousa de Mazedo, Embassador of *Portugal* at the *Hague* ibid
Anthony Veniero, Embassador of *Venice* in *France* 266
Apology of *Ferdinand* the Catholick 410
Appellations 30
Applications principal of the Embassadors 300
Appointments of Embassadors 207
Those of *Venice* ibid
Archbishop of *Arimac* 222
Archbishop of *Auch*, sent by the Pope to the Congress at *Arras* 238
Archbishop of *Bourges* 118, 323
Archbishop of *Braga* made Prisoner 61
of *Canterbury* kill'd ibid
Archbishop of *Embrun*, Embassador of the Queen Regent of *France* in *Spain* 22
Archbishop of *Embrun*, *George Aubusson de la Feuillade*, Embassador of *France* in *Spain* 220, 285
Gives Precedence to Don *John* of *Austria* in a third Place,
Obliged to depart 285
Archbishop of *Fermo*, Nuncio in *Ireland* 318
Archbishop of *Glascow*, Embassador of *Scotland* in *France* 326
of *Granada* 215
of *Lion*, Prisoner, refuses to answer 58
Archbishop of *Madera* 222
Archbishop of *Mecklin*, *Joseph de Bergagne*, Plenipotentiary of *Spain* at *Munster* 224
Deputed to the *Hague* 285
Archbishop of *Narbonne* 133 Embassador from *Lewis* XI. to the Duke of *Burgundy* 16, 48, 339
Francis de Joyeuse See Cardinal *de Joyeuse*
Archbishop of *Nazareth*, Nuncio in *France* 319
of *Pisa*, Embassador from the Great Duke at *Madrid* 370
Archbishop of *Saltzburgh*, Embassador from the Emperor in *Spain* 239
Archbishop of *Sens* 215
Archbishop of *Tarragona*, Embassador of *Arragon* to the King of *Castille* 128
of *Toledo*, does not visit Embassadors 123
Alphonso de Corillo, Legate in *Spain* 100
of *Toulouse*, *Paul de Foix*, Embassador of *France* at *Rome* 137, 184
at *Florence* 141
Pays the first Visit to the Pope's natural Son 187
Harangues the *Polish* Embassadors 135

of *Tours*, waits on the Pope's Legate 74
of *Valentia*, *George of Austria*, Prisoner 278
of *Vienne* *Charles de Marillac*, Embassador of *France* at *Rome* 329
Archbishop of *York* 239
Archduke *Albert*, makes the first Overtures of Peace 6
Gives the *French* King the Titles of *Monseigneur* and *Majesty* 127
Sends Embassadors, though only a Governour 21
Gives Place to Cardinals 233
His Embassador refuses Precedence to the Embassador of *Venice* 6
Sovereign of the Low Countries 97
Archduke *Charles* 73, 270
Archduke *Philip* 103, 282
Argenson, Embassador of *France* at *Venice* 130
Arnaud de Ferrier, Embassador of *France* at *Trent* 51
Arnauld Simon de Pomponne, Embassador in *Holland* and *Sweaen* 277
Arnauld Roger de Palas, Patriarch of *Alexandria* 128
Arpajoux, Embassador of *France* in *Poland* 164
Arthur of *Bourbon*, Minister of the Duke of *Burgundy* 99
Article, separate of a Treaty 350
Artifice of the Queen of *Sueden* 43
Of the Plenipotentiaries of *France* 41
Arundel, Earl of, uncivil to the *French* Embassador 17
Meets the Embassador of *France* 135
Ashburnham, Minister of the Duke of *Buckingham* 100
Assembly of Nobles in *France* 11
Assembly at *Arras* 238
Avalos Diego 129
Avaugour, Minister of *France*, and Colonel in the Army of *Sueden* 81, 298, 352
Avaux, Embassador of *France*, and Plenipotentiary at *Munster* 30, 176, 189, 219
Embassador of *France* in *Denmark* 181, 194
at *Venice* 171
at the *Hague* 182
at *Osnaburg* 173
his Exactness in Dress 202
his Quarrel with *Servien* 239
concludes the Treaty between *Poland* and *Sweden* ibid
See Pages 295, 309, 321, 332, 338, 366, 379
Audiences 148 See 310
Audiences of the *Polish* Embassadors at *Paris* 134
of Cardinal *Bichi* at *Venice* 151
the College gives them at *Venice* 159
how the Pope gives them 148
his private Audiences ibid
Audiences of Cardinals ibid
Audience of the Duke of *Mayenne* in *Spain* 150
of the Duke of *Pastrana* in *France* ibid.
of the Embassadors of the *Cantons* 158
of the Embassador of the *Cham* of *Tartary* 163
how it is given in *Holland* 159
Embassadors ought to speak low at it 158
Audience publick refused to the Minister of the Parliament of *England* 7
the Pope gives it only in Consistory 84
Audience of the King's Brothers 153
Audiences of Embassadors extraordinary at the *Hague* 159
Auger, a Player on the Lute, Minister of *Charles* I of *England* in *France* 50
Augustin Baumgartner, Embassador of the Duke of *Bavaria* at *Trent* 224
Augustin Justiniani, Bishop of *Nebio*, his History of *Genoa* 238
Austria

INDEX.

Austria See Cardinal of
Axel Oxenstiern, Plenipotentiary of *Sweden* in
 Germany 23
   arrives in *Compeigne* 132
   the King makes him be cover'd 155

B

Bacha or Pacha 161
Bachas Visiers ibid
Bacon, wrote the History of *Henry* VII King of
 England 53
Badouere *Lewis*, Minister of *Venice* at *Madrid* 34
Bagni, Nuncio in *France* 56, 198
Bailly o. Forbin, Embassador of *Malta* 81, 132
   is cover'd speaking to the King 155
   has the Title of Excellency 172
   the Prince of *Conde* gives him the Hand 179
Ballue See Cardinal de Ballue
Balthasar de Castiglion, his Courtier 53
Balthasar de la Ceuva, Embassador of *Spain* at
 Vienna 179, 351
Balthasar de Zuniga, Minister of *Spain* 304
Balthasar de Zuniga, Embassador of *Spain* at *Venice* 326
Baly See Bajlo
Baptisms 193
Baptista Archinto, Deputy of *Milan* 346
Baptista Nani, Minister of *Venice* 375, 418
   his Character 356
Barberigo Gregory, Embassador of *Venice* in *England* 110
Barberini, not well with the Court of *France* 59
La Barde, Embassador of *France* to the Cantons
 43, 132
   at *Munster* without Letters of Credence 110
   Minister of State in *France* 133
   first Clerk to *Chavigni* 291
Barillon 356
Barons of *Catalonia* 14
Bartholomew de la Caur, Embassador from the
 Port in *France* 81, 162
Bas Dudenic, Embassador of the United Provinces
 in *England* 198
De Bas, Envoy of *France* in *England* 254
Bassompierre Francis, Embassador of *France* in
 Spain   48, 151, 173, 183, 244
   in *England* 122, 291, 293, 358, 360, 370,
    376, 377, 415
   his Character 421
Battel of *Guinegaste* 112
Battel of *Nerlinguen* ibid
Battel of *Mortheac* 103
Battory See Cardinal Battory
Bavaria, comes to an Accommodation with
 France 32
Baugy, Resident of *France* at *Venice*, and Embassador in *Holland* 244
Bautru, Introducer of Embassadors 131
Baylo, the Embassador of *Venice* at the Port so called 9, 326
Beale Robert, Embassador of *England* in *France* 226
Beaulieu Rufe, Secretary of State 58
Beaupuy 107
Bedford, Earl of 135
Bellegarde, Mareschal of *France* 117
   Master of the Horse in *France* 130
Bellievre, Embassador of *France* at *Verdun* 219
   at *Brussels* 236
Bellievre, Embassador of *France* in *Holland*, refuses the Place of Honour to the States Deputies 277
Bembo Peter, Embassador in his own Countrey 79
Benedict Sehut, Embassador of *Sweden* in *Denmark* 180
Berchere, Agent of *England* in *France* 255
Berenclau, Embassador of *Sweden* at *Frankfort* 144
   at *Vienna* 361
Berenger de Bardaxi, Judge of *Arragon*, Embassador in *Castille* 129
Bergeyck *John Baptist de Broucoven*, Minister of
 Spain at *Aix la Chapelle* 22
Berlise, Introducer of Embassadors in *France*, writes
 Memoirs 2, 131, 291
   claims Precedence of the *English* Embassador 177
Bernard Bandini, assassinates *Julio de Medicis* 82
Bernard Hugo de Rocaberti, Embassador of *Spain* in
 France 113
Bernard Giorgio, Avogador of the Commons at
 Venice 266
Bernard Oliver, a Monk, a Negotiator 80
Bernard de Salinas, Embassador of *Spain* in *England* 277
Bernard of Saxony See Duke Weimar
Bernardi Laurence, Embassador of *Venice* at the
 Port 87
   at *Vienna* 236
Bernardin de Carvajal, Minister of *Innocent* VIII 80
   Embassador of *Spain* at *Rome* 209
Bernardin de Mendoza, Embassador of *Spain* in
 England 104, 251
   driven out of the Kingdom ibid See 310,
    334, 355
Bernardin Visconti, Minister of *Milan* 114
Bertonville, Prisoner of War negotiates 112
Betruccio Valieri, Minister of *Venice* 142
Bessarion See Cardinal Bessarion
Bethlem Gabor, Prince of *Transylvania* 155
Beveue, Secretary to the *Swedish* Embassy 311
Bevilacqua See Cardinal Bevil
Bevilacqua, Nuncio at *Nimeguen* 198
De Bie Nicholas, Minister of *Holstein* 245
Birth of Embassadors 17
   of Cardinal *Dossat* 49
Biron, Duke Mareschal, Embassador of *France* in
 England, receives extraordinary Honours there 68
   Embassador at *Brussels* 236
Bishop of *Aes*, Embassador of *France* at the
 Port 35
   at *Venice* 211
   at *Arras*, on the Part of the Pope 238
   of *France*, at *Constantinople*, 63, 346
Bishop of *Agria*, Embassador at the Port 63
Bishop of *Arezzo*, Nuncio in *Spain*, not admitted 100
Bishop of *Arras*, Francis Peronet de Granvelle 69,
    239
   Embassador at *Trent* 311
Bishop of *Auxerre* 74, 238
Bishop of *Bayonne* 74
Bishop of *Beauvais* 59
 Philip de Dreux 105
Bishop of *Bellay* 64
Bishop of *Bergamo*, Nuncio in *France* 318
Bishop of *Bexieres Bonzy*, Embassador 63
Bishop of *Cambray* 238
Bishop of *Camerin*, Nuncio in *France* 100
Bishop of *Casal*, Embassador of *Mantua* in *France* 131
Bishop of *Catania*, Embassador of *Spain* to the
 Emperor 333
Bishop of *Ceneda* 319
Bishop of *Coimbra*, Embassador of the Regents of
 Portugal 22
Bishop of *Coire* 60
Bishop of *Durham* 71
Bishop of *Ely* 70
Bishop of *Evreux* 74
Bishop of *Fano*, Nuncio to the Emperor 66
Bishop of *Ferro* 222

7 G Bishop

INDEX.

Bishop of *Gurc*, Maximilian, first Minister in Italy
    120, 303
    Embassador from the Emperor at Nime-
loguen   189
Bishop of *Hermestadt*, Embassador from the Tur-
kish Emperor   63
Bishop of *Lamego*, Embassador of Portugal at
Rome   59
    the Pope afraid to admit him   329
Bishop of *Leon*   66
Bishop of *Liege*   301
Bishop of *Limoges*, Sebastian l'Aubepine, Embassa-
dor of France in Spain   20
Bishop of *Lisieux*   60
Bishop of *Lodeve*, Embassador of France at Ve-
nice   209
Bishop of *Lombes*, Embassador of France to Maxi-
milian   211
Bishop of *Lucena*   211
Bishop of *Malefais*   74
Bishop of *Malfette*, Nuncio at Venice   185
Bishop of *Mans*, Claude d'Angennes, Embassador
of France at Rome   59, 251, 308
Bishop of *Mantua*, Nuncio in France   74, 219
Bishop of *Metz*, Embassador from the Emperor   106
Bishop of *Modena*, Nuncio in France   100
Bishop of *Montpellier*, Embassador of France at
Venice   355
Bishop of *Munster*, how he receives the Deputies
of the United Provinces   143
Bishop of *Nismes*   74
Bishop of *Norwich*   238
Bishop of *Orange*   150
Bishop of *Orkney*   21
    Embassador of Scotland in France   326
Bishop of *Osma*, Embassador of Ferdinand the Ca-
tholick   261
Bishop of *Osnaburg*, Embassador of the Electoral
College   3, 109
Bishop of *Rennes*, Embassador to the Emperor   308
Bishop of *Rosse*, John Lesley, Embassador from the
Scots Queen   21
    corresponds with the English Rebels   149
    shipp'd off by Command of Queen Eliza-
beth 184   See 355
Bishop of *St David*   238
Bishop of *Strasbourg*, Embassador from the Em-
peror   129, 181
Bishop of *Tarascon*   79
Bishop of *Tournay*, Embassador from Philip Duke
of Burgundy to Lewis XI   16
Bishop of *Trent*   239
Bishop of *Urgel*, Minister of Innocent VIII   98
Bishop of *Uses*   238
Bishop of *Warmia*, Embassador of Poland in
France   150
Bishop of *Winchester*, Stephen Gardiner   239
Bishop of *Wirtzbourg*, covers himself   156
Bishops are the Pope's Subjects   19
Bishops *in partibus*   8
Bishops of France use the *Camail* instead of the
Little Cloak   204
Bishop John of la Cassiere, Great Master of Mal-
ta   130
Blainville, Embassador of France in England 163,
194, 320
Blum John   75, 78
Boyard of Muscovy   280
Boischot, the Archduke's Embassador in England
30, 236, 308
Boissise, Embassador of France in England   201
Boissy, Master of the Horse in France   249
De Boles, Peter John, Embassador in his own
Country   117
Bologna   See Cardinal of Bologna.
Bolognetti George, Nuncio in France   122, 131

Bon Octavio, Embassador of Venice at Madrid   29
Bonaventura Calatagironni, General of the Corde-
liers, a Negotiator   66, 259
Boncompagno, Auditor of the Rota   216
Bond, Embassador of England to the King of
Sweden   261
Bonjans Gianfigliazzi, Embassador of Florence at
Rome   329
Boniface VIII Pope   98
Boniface de Calamandrana, Minister of the Pope in
Arragon   80, 98
Bonzy, Embassador of Florence   50
Bonoeil de Thou, Introducer of Embassadors in
France   129
Boreel William, Embassador of the United Provinces
123, 151, 154, 171, 244
Borromee   See Cardinal Bor
Bostangi   348
Boswel, the King of England's Resident at the
Hague   7
Bothwel, Earl of   106
Boulanger, Secretary to the Embassy of France at
Munster   175
Bourbon   See Cardinal of Bourbon
Bourdaisiere   See Cardinal of Bourdaisiere
Bouthiller, Secretary of State in France   106
Bowes Robert, Embassador in Scotland from Eng-
land   109
Bracciano   See Duke of Bracciano
Brabo, Embassador of Denmark at London   187
Brand, Deputy of the Anseatick Towns in Eng-
land   15
Brasset, Resident of France at the Hague   34, 292
Bruvenus, President of Mechlin, Minister of
Charles V   239
Brederode, Embassador of the United Provinces in
England   228, 314
Bregy, Viscount de   117, 118
Bregy, Embassador of France in Poland   254
Breves, Embassador of France at Rome   138
Brian John, Embassador from Edward VI. in
France   410
Briconet, Minister and Confident of Charles VII
303
Bristol, Earl of   326
Brulard Nicholas, Secretary of State to Henry III   12
    See Sillery
Le Brun Anthony, Embassador at Munster and the
Hague   295, 314, 321, 334
    his Character   419
Bruneau, Secretary to the Embassador of Spain ar-
rested   252, 276, 353
Bude William, a learned and able Minister   51
Bucentaure   140
Buchanan George, writes the History of Scotland   52
Buckingham   See Duke of Buckingham
Bugwald Godscale, Embassador of Denmark at the
Hague   379
Bulson, Minister of France   ibid
Bulls of Legates should be register'd   68
Burgos   See Cardinal of
Burleigh, Minister and Confident of Queen Eliza-
beth   358
Buzanval, Embassador of France in Holland 120,
244
    his Death   200

C

Cadelasquior, or Cadilesker, Judge in Turky 162, 254
Candar Sultan Nizza, Prince of Persia   306
Caimacan   303
Calignon Godfry, Minister of the King of Navarre
167, 278
Calixtus III Pope   238, 340
Camerarius, Embassador of Sweden at the Hague
124
Canassos,

INDEX.

	Page
Canassos, Traytors	355
Cantons Swifs, have no Embassadors in ordinary	10
send thirty nine Embassadors to *France*	23
Protestant *Cantons*, give a Minister of the second Order the Title of Excellency	43
Capel Father, a Monk, a Negotiator	66
Capigi Bachi	175
Capitulations of *Ferdinand* III and the Emperor *Leopold*	28, 228
Caponi Nicholas, Embassador of *Florence*	414
Caponi See Cardinal *Caponi*	
Caponi Peter, Minister of *Florence*	151
his Boldness	348
Capriata Peter John, writes a History	53
Character protects Embassadors	105
surrender d into the Hands of Sovereigns at Return	267
Caraffas, the r Fortune	257
Cardinal, has the Hand and Precedency of an Embassador	171
Cardinal, gives Place of Honour to the Doge of *Venice* in his Palace	151
Cardinal *Patrone*, has no higher Dignity than another Cardinal	172
Cardinals are Subjects to the Pope	58
will have the first Visit	138, 186
wait on the Archdutchess in a Body	138
have not the Canopy in *France*	73
Cardinals have not the Canopy in *Spain*	ibid
Cardinals, Protectors	3
Cardinal of *Agen*	138
Albornos	19
Cardinal *Aldobrandin*, Legate in *France*	73
the Expences of his Legation	207
first Minister to *Clement* VIII	100, 185, 300, 309, 325, 330
Cardinal *Alexandrin*, Legate in *France*	90, 367
Cardinal of *Amboise, George*, first Minister and Legate in *France*	57, 73, 79, 315, 333
Cardinal of *Anagnia*	347
Cardinal of *Aquaviva*	363
Cardinal of *Austria*	116
Cardinal of *Ballue*, Minister to *Lewis* XI and the Duke of *Burgundy*	286
conspires against the King	12
Cardinal *Barberino, Francis*, Legate in *France*	56, 69, 73, 116
in *Spain*	73
first Minister of *Urban* VIII	12
does Honours to the Cardinals his Elders	9
See 312, 337, 368, 370	
Cardinal *Barberino, Anthony*, his Infidelity	88, 197
protects the Bishop of *Lamego*	19
quarrels with the Duke of *Parma*	208
Cardinal *Battori* disgrac'd	62, 340
Cardinal *Bessarion*	51, 73, 368
Cardinal *Bevilacqua*	138
Cardinal *Biobi, Alexander*, Embassador in *France*	3, 62, 75, 80, 170, 173
gives Advice of the Journey of the Cardinal *de Valencay*	59
Comprotector of *France*	190
retires to his Bishoprick	199, 200, 329, 365, 372, 411
his Character	417
Cardinal of *Bologna*	126
Cardinal of *Bonzy*	420
Cardinal of *Borghese*	346
Cardinal of *Borgia, Alphonso*, Pope *Calixtus* III	238
of *Borgia, Rodorigo*, Legate in *Spain*	100
Cardinal *Borromeus*, first Minister of *Pius* IV	214, 216
Cardinal *Bourbon*, Embassador	3, 48, 117, 233
his Presumption	234
Cardinal *Bourdaisiere*	218, 245
Cardinal of *Burgos*	234, 324

	Page
Cardinal *Cajetan*, Legate in *France*	349
Cardinal *Capont*	22
Cardinal *Caraffa, Charles*, Legate in *France* and *Brussels*	56, 69, 71, 311
dines with *Ph lip* II	169
Cardinal *Casimir* of *Poland*	187
Cardinal of *Ceva*	170
Cardinal *Clesel* arrested	58
Cardinal *Colonna*	282
Cardinal *Commendon*, Legate in *Poland*	157, 324
Cardinal *Cornaro*	139
Cardinal *Cyprus*, Legate at *Arras*	239
Cardinal of *Dandin*	278
Cardinal *Delsino Zachary*	138
Cardinal *Didrigstein*	73, 198
Cardinal *Denghi*	272, 411
Cardinal *d Ossat*	18, 125, 309, 310, 330, 348, 351, 358, 360, 380, 384, 405
his Character	419
Cardinal *d Espinosa*	51, 304
Cardinal *Este*, Protector of *France*	166, 197, 230, 351
Cardinal *d Estree*, Embassador	25, 422
Cardinal *Farnese*, Legate in *France*	69, 73, 149, 373
Cardinal of *Ferrara, Hippolyto d Este*, Legate in *France*	69, 249, 251
Cardinal *Filomarini*	234
Cardinal of *Florence*	315
Cardinal *Gallo*	138
Cardinal *Ghigi*, Legate in *France*	73
Cardinal *Ghinetti*, Legate at *Cologne*	109, 369
Cardinal *Gondi*	330
Cardinal *Gouffier*	169
Cardinal of *Grammont*	73, 181
Cardinal *Granville*	115, 310
Cardinal *Grimaldi*	328
Cardinal of *Guise*	234, 329
Cardinal *Gustavilain*	187
Cardinal of *Hesse, Frederick*, Embassador from the Emperor at *Rome*	3, 173
Cardinal of *Hungary, George Martinuzzi*	59, 62
Cardinal *Hosius*	166
Cardinal of *Jaen*	ibid
Cardinal *Imperials* obliged to go to *France*	59
Cardinal *Infanta*	72, 119
Cardinal of *Joyeuse*, sent to *Rome* by the League	7, 62, 140, 308, 351
Cardinal of *Lenoncourt*	319
Cardinal of *Lion*, nam d Embassador at *Munster*	62, 100
Cardinal of *Lorrain*	57, 120, 212, 214, 218, 245
Cardinal *Ludovisio*	100
Cardinal of *Madrucci*	166, 234
Cardinal of *Magalotti*	196, 203, 343
Cardinal of *Mantua*, Legate at *Ferrara*	211
Cardinal of *Marquemont*	62
Cardinal *Mazarin*	57, 75, 198
Plenipotentiary of *France* at the *Pyrenees*	30
gives Place to the Princes of the Blood	234, 246, 302, 318, 328, 331, 336, 337, 345, 351, 365, 389, 406
Cardinal of *Medicis, Alexander*, Legate in *France*	73, 167, 219
of *Medicis, Hippolyto*	56
Legate to *Charles* V	69, 71
Cardinal of *Mercoeur*, Legate in *France*	70
Cardinal *Mignelli*, Legate at *Sienna*	ibid
Cardinal *Monsalto*	196
Cardinal of *Moron*, Legate at *Trent*	214, 233
Cardinal *Morosini*	340
Cardinal *Navager*, Legate at *Trent*	216, 245
Cardinal *Otho*, of St *Nicholas in Carcere Tulliano*	71
Cardinal *Pacheco*	219, 222, 405
Cardinal *Pamphilio*	88
Cardinal *Parisio*	312
Cardinal *du Perrone*, his Negotiation	52, 151
Cardinal of *Piacentia*	95

Cardinal

INDEX.

Cardinal *Poole*, Legate in *England* 69, 71, 79, 125, 239, 367
  Legate in *France* 71
Cardinal *du Prat* 57, 73, 79
Cardinal *Prouli* 204
Cardinal *Rebiba*, Legate with the Emperor 79, 125
Cardinal of *Retz* 59, 234
Cardinal of *Rhodes* 79
Cardinal of *Riario* 67
  Legate in *Spain* 336
Cardinal of *Richelieu* 57, 60, 73, 105, 166, 198
Cardinal of *Roma* 18
Cardinal *Rossetti* 12, 100, 365
Cardinal *Sadolet* 69
Cardinal of St *Andrew* 414
Cardinal of St. *Crofs*, Legate at *Arras* 238, 341
Cardinal of St *Flore* 231, 310
Cardinal of St *Malo* 111
Cardinal of St *Severine*, Grand Penitentiary 95
Cardinal *Salviati*, Legate in *France* 73
Cardinal *Savelli* 190
Cardinal of *Savoy* 123
Cardinal of *Sens* 181
Cardinal of St *George*, Nephew of *Clement* VIII 69
Cardinal of *Serafin* 138
Cardinal *Sfondrati* 66
Cardinal *Sforza* 341
Cardinal of *Sienna*, *Francis de Picolomini*, Legate, not admitted 100
Cardinal *Simonetta*, Legate at *Trent* 167, 216
Cardinal of *Sourdis* 151
Cardinal of *Thadoli* 166
Cardinal of *Toledo* 115
Cardinal *Tolete* 95
Cardinal of *Tournon* 73, 148, 186, 259
Cardinal of *Trent* 166
Cardinal *Trevulci* 181
Cardinal of *Valancay* 159, 166, 284
Cardinal of *Valentia*, *Rodrigo Borgia* 72
Cardinal of *la Valette* 73, 198, 412
Cardinal of *Vendome* 48, 234, 319
Cardinal *Verallo*, Legate in *France* 69, 72, 74
Cardinal of *Visco*, *Michael de Silva* 72, 101
Cardinal *Ursin* 272
Cardinal of *Winchester* 177
Cardinal *Wolfey*, Legate in *England* 79
  Embassador in *France* 120
Cardinal *Ximenes* 304
Cardinal *Zapara* 234
Cardinals, Patrons 358
Carlos Coloma, writes a History 52
  Embassador of *Spain* in *England* 104, 198, 292, 319
Caron See *Noel Caron*
Carlifle, Earl of See among the Counts
Carongei, Embassador of *France* in *England* 135
Casimir, Prince of *Poland*, Prisoner 115
  King of *Poland* abdicates 20
Casimir, Marquis of *Brandenburg*, Embassador of *Charles* of *Austria* King of *Spain* 239
Cassels, Earl of, Embassador of *Scotland* in *France* 32
Catalans, pretend to send Embassadors 13
  their Ministers deny'd Passports 124
Catalonia necessary to *Spain* 389
Catholicks zealous 46
Cauza, *Constantine* and *Nicholas*, Traytors 55, 266
Cercle of *Burgundy* 387
Ceremonial at *Rome* 209
Ceremonies not regulated in all Courts 179
  those of Entries are regulated 142
  Great Master of 128
  receives Embassadors in *Poland* 150
Cesar Borgia arrested 127, 258
Cesar Cantelino, Minister at the Port 75

Cesar Fregosa, Embassador of *France* at the Port Kill'd 75, 85
Cesar Rasponi, Minister of Pope *Alexander* VII 265
Cesis de Harlay, Embassador of *France* at the Port 56
Chabot Philip, Admiral of *France* 120
Chaloner Thomas, Embassador of *England* in *Spain* 273
Cham of *Tartary*, sends Embassadors to *Poland* 163
Champigny 125
Chancellor of *France* does not visit Embassadors 187
  does not go into Mourning 204
  is First Commissioner 375
Chantonnay Granvelle, Embassador of *Spain* at *Vienna* 308
  in *France* 319
Coanut, Minister of *France* in *Sweden*, obliges the Prince Palatine to give him the Place or Honour 179
  Resident of *France* in *Sweden* 34, 151, 267
  does a gallant Action 152
  is very punctual 191
  Embassador at the Assembly at *Lubeck* 116, 121, 188, 305, 318, 364, 368, 428
Chappel, the Pope's 195
Charisius Peter, Plenipotentiary of *Denmark* at *Breda* 39
Charles of *Anjou*, Senator of *Rome* 221
Charles, Duke of *Burgundy* 297, 367, 384
Charles V Emperor 140, 173
  takes place of the *French* King only as Emperor 209, 303, 314, 414
Charles VI King of *France* 14
Charles VII King of *France* 49, 163, 238
Charles VIII King of *France* 88, 114, 244, 318, 338
Charles IX King of *France*, a cruel Prince 90, 303, 331, 340, 411
Charles I King of *England* 134
Charles of *Bourbon* 234
Charles, King of *Sweden* 89
Charles Gustavus, king of *Sweden* 305, 365, 369
Charles, Duke of *Sudermania*, usurps the Crown of *Sweden* 309
Charles Amanuel, Duke of *Savoy* 3, 231
Charles, Brother of the King of *Poland* 181
Charles III Duke of *Savoy* 120
  sends Deputies to the Diet of the Empire 16
Charles Gustavus, Prince of *Sweden*, does Honour to the Agent of *France* 61, 179
  King of *Sweden* 168
Charles of *Marillac*, Bishop of *Valence*, Minister of *France* 239
Charles of *Medicis*, will not give the Place of Honour in his own House to the Grandees of *Spain* 175
Charles Nutzel, the Emperor's Embassador at the *Hague* 102
Charles Paschal, Embassador of *France* to the *Grifons*, writes a Treatise concerning an Embassador 45, 113
  has more Learning than Ability 50
Charles, Regent of *France* 22
Charles Sforza 310
Charles Tisnaque, Embassador of *Charles* V in *France* 48
Charnace Hercules, Embassador and Colonel 50
  design'd for the Embassy of *Munster* 48
  Minister of *France* in *Bavaria* 238, 379, 424
Chasteauneuf l'Aubepine, Embassador of *France* in *Germany* 49, 137
  in *England* 182
Chavigny Bouthiller, Secretary of State 156, 291
La Chesnoy 255
  Chevalier

INDEX.

Chevalier de l Accolade 288
— de Cornaro, Embassador of Venice at Rome 416
— de Guise 151
— Ierlon, one of Cardinal Mazarine's Retinue 203
Chiaoux Barhi, Introducer of Embassadors in Turky 128, 146, 161, 163, 357
Chiaoux 146
Chiverny, Chancellor of France, writes Memoirs 129
— Chancellor to the Duke of Anjou 228
Christiern, King of Denmark, expell'd his Dominions 19
Christina, Queen of Sweden 163, 181
— affronts the Minister of Portugal 18
— her Merit 155
— cou'd not endure Pedants 158
— wou'd not regulate Rank among Ministers 198, 235
— abdicates 70
— See 305, 318, 355
Christopher Delhque Dona, Embassador of Sweden at the Hague 129
Christopher de Moura, Embassador of Castille in Portugal 8
Christopher Sbaransky, Embassador of Poland at the Port 206
Christoval de Benavides and Benevente, Embassador of Spain in France 105
Civilities of Embassadors not to be drawn into Consequence 164
Civilities done to Embassadors 127, & seq
— great at Venice 139
— none done in France to the Swiss Embassadors, except at their Entry 168
— are not due by the Law of Nations 179
— equal between the Embassadors of France and Venice 182
Civilities of Embassadors have been regulated but within these few Years 128, 144
— not regulated among the Electors 143
Civilities of little or no Obligation 192
Claude de l'Aubepine, Secretary of State in France 239
Claude de Chilly, a Minister without Character 315
Claude Martini, Embassador of France at Turin 78
Clement IV Pope 221
Clement V Pope 347
Clement VI Pope 79
Clement VII Pope, ill us'd by the Emperor 72, 97, 236
Clement VIII refuses to admit the Duke of Nevers 95, 100, 138 See 295, 300, 411
— would oblige Henry IV to break his Word with the Queen of England 90
— sends a Nuncio to France 100
Clarieux, Embassador of France in Spain 244
Le Clerc, Agent of France in England 236
Clemens Lewald, Minister of Brandenburgh 235
Clifford Nicholas 354
Clinguenbergh Paul, Minister of Denmark at Breda 39
Coach, Chanuts, gives place to the Prince of Sweden's 179
Coaches of Ministers do not now attend at the Entries of Embassadors 145
Coachman, the Embassador of France's, assaulted at the Hague 270
Coachman of the Mareschal de Turenne, cuts the Coach of the French Embassador 135
Cobham, Minister of England in the Low Countries 125
Coetivi, Admiral of France 117
Colbert John Baptist, Minister of France 133, 421

Colbert Charles, Embassador of France in England 190
Coligni Jasper de, Admiral de Chastillon 48, 166
College of Venice 159, 305
Comer first See Visit
Commanders of Malta 61
Commander de Formigeres, Embassador and Captain of the Guards 33, 81
Commander de Gremonville 334
Commander de Hautefeuille, Embassador and Lieutenant General 81
Commander de Neufochaise 287
Commander de Sillery, Embassador of France at Rome 89, 112
Commander de Souvre, Embassador of Malta in France 97
— in Holland ibid
Commendon John Francis, Minister of the Pope in England 70
— Nuncio in Germany 100
— Nuncio in Poland 154
Commentators of Cæsar 52
Commerce, none between the Nuncio and the Protestants 197, 214
Commines Philip de, Minister of Lewis XI 49
— writes Memoirs 52
— Embassador at Venice 139, 287
— Envoy at Casal 114
— disgrac'd 117, 300, 305, 333, &c
Commissary Geneneral of the Cordeliers 41, 259
Commissioners 33
— are Publick Ministers 40
— not always so 47
— Commissioners 41, 373
Competition between France and Spain 208
— between the King of France and the King of the Romans 222
— between Spain and England 216
— between the Embassadors of Portugal and the King of the Romans 224
— between the Embassadors of Hungary and Portugal ibid
— between the Electors and the Duke of Burgundy 227
— between Venice and Bavaria 225
— between the five Cantons and the Duke of Bavaria 224
— between the five Cantons and the Duke of Florence ibid
— between France and Sweden 226
— between Savoy and Mantua 231
— between Florence and Ferrara 232
— between the Embassador of Malta and the Minister of Saltzburgh 230
— between the Embassador of Malta and the Patriarchs ibid
— between the Nuncio and the Embassador of Brandenburg 226
— between Embassadors and the Prefect of Rome ibid
— between the Cardinals and Princes 234
— between the Embassador of Spain and the Duke of Mantua 235
Conclave may send Embassadors 22
Concordat between the Pope and the French King 68
Conestaggio Jerom, writes a History 52
Confederacy of Princes 357
Conference at the House of the Ministers of Lunenbourg 38
Conferences 221
Confessor of the Elector of Bavaria, a Negotiator 317
Congress of Munster 386

INDEX

	Page
of *Arras*	238
of *Nimeguen*	ibid
Congresses	308, 331, 369, 375
Conrade Van Beuningen, Embassador of the United Provinces in *France*	37, 244
Constable of St *Paul*, Embassador of *Lewis* XI to the Duke of *Burgundy*	286
arrested and executed	127, 157
wheedles *Lewis* XI	384
Constable of *Castille*	129
Governor of *Milan*	139
Constable of *Lunes*, first Minister of *France*	137
Constable of *Montmorancy*, first Minister of *France*	185
refuses to treat in a Town belonging to the King of *Spain*	372
Deputy-Extraordinary	41
his Character	421
Conrade de Burgstoff, Minister of *Brandenburg*	45
Consistory	148
Consuls of *Alexandria* and *Aleppo* arrested	34
Constance Embassador of *Venice*	318
Consul *Dutch*, arrested	40
Consul not a Minister	ibid
Contai, Minister of the Duke of *Burgundy*	338
Contarini, Proveditore of *Venice*	114
Mediator at *Munster*	345
his Character	418
Contarini Thomas, Embassador at 84 Years old	54
Contests for the Title of Excellency, between the States of the United Provinces, and the Embassador of *France*	182
between the Duke of *Lorrain*, and the Embassador of *England*	192
between the Embassador of *France* and *Venice*	ibid
between the Embassador of *Spain*, and the Senator of *Rome*	196
between the Duke of *Parma*, and the Senator of *Rome*	ibid
between the United Provinces and *Savoy*	201
between the Nuntio and the Prince of *Condé*, for the first Visit	204
between the Embassadors of *France* and *Spain*, at *Venice*	209
at *Trent*	211
between the Embassadors of *France* and *Spain*, at *Vervins*	219
between the Embassador of *Venice*, and the Bishop of *Osnaburg*	225
at *Munster*, about Powers	30
Conway, Earl of, Secretary of State in *England*	105
Cordeliers of *Metz*	87
Corfitz Ulfeld, Embassador of *Denmark* in *France*	183, 336
great Master of *Denmark*	335
Coronation, a politick Ceremony	195
Coronation of *Henry* IV and *Lewis* XIII	181
Correspondence of Embassadors	358
Corruptions	357
Corsi, Embassador from the Great Duke of *Tuscany*	132
Corsican, Guards at *Rome*, insult the *French* Embassador	264
Corsini, Clerk of the Chamber	100
Nuntio in *France*	113
Cosmo, Duke of *Florence*	141, 230
how he is receiv'd at *Rome*	231
an Enemy to the *French*	329
Cotterel, Sir *Charles*, Master of the Ceremonies in *England*	137
Council *Aulick*	28
Council of Ten, makes out the Processes of Ecclesiasticks	61

	Page
Council of State in *Holland*	318
Council of *Pregadi*	414
Council general, ought to take no Cognizance of the Rank of Princes	222
of *Constance*	67
of *Basil*	209
of *Lateran*	214
of *Trent*	69, 126, 210, 322, 234
transferred to *Bologna*	148
d *Aglie*	300, 344
Count *d Alais* goes to meet the Popes Nuntio	131
Count *Oxenstiern*	ibid
d *Aremberg*, the Duke of *Parmas* Deputy,	125
Embassador of *Spain* in *France*	129, 136
Aversperg, Embassador from the Emperor, at *Osnaburg*	120
at the Hague	165
obliged to depart	ibid
Count *Barlament*, Embassador of the Archduke *Albert*	21
Count *de Beaumont Harlay*, Embassador of *France* in *England*	269
de Beloyeuse, Minister of *Milan*	318
Count *de Benavente Benavides*	329, 377
de Bethune, Embassador of *France* in *England*	45, 138
at *Rome*	61, 343
His Character	421
Count *de Bigliore*, Embassador of *Savoy* at *Venice*	270
obliged to take down the Arms at his Door	166
Count *del Borgia*, Governor of the Citadel of *Antwerp*	127
Count *de Boschetto*	327
Bothwel, Earl of,	108
Count *de Brahe*, Embassador of *Sweden* at *London*	220
de Brienne Secretary of State	116, 133
Count *de Brulon* Introductor of Embassadors in *France*	115, 130
writes Memoirs	2
Count *de Gantecroix*, Embassador from the Emperor to the Republick of *Venice*	4
Carlisle, Earl of, Embassador from *England* in *France*	169, 188, 104
introduces the *Savoy* Embassador	136
Embassador in *Muscovy*	145, 290, See 377
Count *de Castelruvio* High Steward of the Houshold of the King of *Spain*	150
Count *de Cecis*	56, 105, 417
Count *de Charnry*	129
Count *de Charolois*	339
Count *de Chincon*, Embassador of *Spain* at *Rome*	310
Count *de Cifuentes*, Embassador of *Spain* at *Rome*	195
Cleveland, Earl of	136
Count *Cratz*, Plenipotentiary of *Mentz* at *Munster*	144
Count *de Dona*	129
Count *de Drouent*, Embassador of *Savoy* in *France*	151
Count *de Dunois*	48, 173, 405
Count *de Egmont*, Embassador from the Archduke in *Germany*	97
Count *de Eu*, Embassador from *Lewis* XI to the Duke of *Burgundy*	48, 339
Count *de Fiesque*	161
Embassador of *Savoy* in *France*	355
Count *de Fuensaldagne*, Embassador of *Spain* in *France*	220
again	423
Count *de Fuentes*, Governor of *Milan*	88
Count *de la Garde Magnus*, Embassador of *Sweden* in

INDEX.

	Page
in France	56
again	312
his Expence	204
design'd Embassador at *Lubeck*	209
Count de Gayazza, Minister of *Milan*	318
Count de Glehen	112
Count Gondomer, Diego Sarmiento de Acugna, Embassador of *Spain* in *England*	130
is agreeable to King *James* I	168
his Rencounter with the Embassador of the United Provinces	197
Civilities done him in *France*	168
obliges the *French* Embassador to give way to him	219
Count de Gribergue, Embassador from the *Infanta*, to the Duke of *Neubourg*	179
Count de Gronsfelt, Embassador of *Bavaria* in *France*	26
Count de Guldenlieu, Embassador of *Denmark* in *England*	190
Count de Harcourt, Henry, of *Lorrain*, Embassador of *France* in *England*, refuses to do Civilities to the Embassadors of the United Provinces	171
takes a Passport of the Parliament	122
conducts the *Swiss* to Audience	132
Count Isembourg, Embassador in *France*	311
Count de Kevenhuller, Embassador of the Emperor, in *Spain*	172
Kevenhuller, chief Huntsman to the Emperor in *Austria*	279
Count de Konigsmarc, Embassador of *Sweden*, and an Officer in *France*	82
Count de Lalain, Charles, Embassador from *Philip* of *Austria*, in *France*	48
Count de Lamberg, Great Chamberlain to the Emperor	149
Plenipotentiary at *Munster*	191
Count de Lanoy, Viceroy of *Naples*, sends an Envoy Embassador to *Rome*	21
Count de Legny	239
Count de Lude	117
Count de Lune, Claude de *Quignones*, Embassador of *Spain* at the Council of *Trent*	314
Count de Manderscheidt, Embassador of the Emperor at the Hague	102
Count de Meggau, Great Chamberlain to the Emperor	137
Count de Meguen	238
Count de Montecuculi	256
Count de Montfort	238
Count de Monterie	310
Count de Mura tore, Master of the Ceremonies in *Savoy*	242
Count de Nancey, Master of the Wardrobe	151
Count de Nassau Engelbert, Negotiator	112
Henry, Embassador of *Charles* of *Austria*, King of *Spain*	239
Maurice, Governor of *Cleves*	143
Embassador of *Brandenburg*, at *London*	241
Hadamar, Plenipotentiary of the Emperor at *Munster* 185, 199 again	295
Lewis	300
William, Governor of *Frizeland*	187
Count de Nerli Francis, Plenipotentiary of *Mantua*, at *Munster*	172
Count de Neyers	238
Count de Ognati, goes to meet the Legate	72
refuses the Title of Excellency to the *Venetian* Embassador	172
Embassador of *Spain*, at *Vienna*, will not give Place to the Duke of *Mantua*	213
Embassador of *Spain* at *Rome*	333
Count de Olivares, Embassador of *Spain*, at *Rome*	137, 327
his Policy	406

	Page
Count Duc d'Olivares, first Minister of *Spain*	172
Favourite to *Philip* IV	304
Count de Orsodelli, Embassador of *Tuscany*, in *Spain*	150
Count Oxenstiern	40
ibid	
Count de Pegnaranda Gaspar de Braramonte, Plenipotentiary of *Spain*, at *Munster*	22
a Subdelegate	
sees not the Duke of *Longueville*	273
would have the Treaty with *France* in the *Spanish* Tongue	314
Count de Raconitz, Philip of *Savoy*, General of an Army	23
Count de Retz, Embassador of *France*, in *England*	331
Count de Riba Gorca, John of *Arragon*	71
Count de Richmont	238
Count de la Roque, Embassador of *Spain*, at *Querasque*	40
Count de St Paul	238
Count de Salasar, High-Steward of the Houshold to the King of *Spain*	150
Count de Sannazare, Plenipotentiary of *Mantua*, at *Munster*	184
Count de Saspago, Viceroy of *Arragon*	336
Count de Schafgotz, Embassador from the Emperor, in *Poland*	145
Count de Schauembourg, Embassador from the Emperor, in *Spain*	152
Count Scotti Ferdinando, Minister of *Parma*	422
Count de Siruella, Embassador of *Spain*, at *Rome*	221
Count de Slabata	148
Count de Slippenbach, Minister of the King of *Sweden*	98
Count de Soissons, Prince of the Blood	48
goes to meet the Legate	73
receives the *Spanish* Embassador	151
his Quarrel with the *English* Embassador	281
Count de Soissons Savoy, Colonel General of the *Swiss*	167
Count Spar, Embassador of *Sweden*, in *France*	56
Count de Swartzenbourg, Embassador from the Emperor, at *London*, his Quarrel with the *Venetian* Embassador	172
and the *French* Embassador	190
Count Terri, Embassador of *Bavaria*, at *Venice*	32
Count de Tillieres, Embassador of *France*, in *England*	183, 220
Count de la Tolfe, Minister of the Duke of *Alba*, at *Rome*	258
Count de Tort, Embassador of *Sweden*, in *France*	56
Count de Tousaine, Embassador of *Savoy*, in *France*	325
Count Trautsmansdorf, first Plenipotentiary of the Emperor 30,	188
an Officer of his Houshold	218
in Favour with his Master	324
his Conduct	430
again	386
Count de Tremes Potur, Embassador of *France*, in *England*	181, 194
Count de Valquenbourgh	238
Count de Vaudemont	141, 238
Count de Verrue, Embassador of *Savoy*, in *France*	170
Count de Waldeck	376
Count de Witgnenstein, Embassador of *Brandenburg*, at *Osnaburgh*	189
Count de Zollern, Embassador from the Emperor, in *France*	129, 181
Couriers of Embassadors, and their Safety	123
Court of *England* protects *Hamburgh*	46
Court Provincial of *Holland*, does not understand publick Right	36, 247

INDEX.

its Counsellors Disturbers of the publick Peace 248
Court of *Rome* difpenfes Marriages with the Heterodox 327
La Court, Embaffador of France, at *Munfter* 313
Courtin, Embaffador of France in *England* 137
at Breda 379
Coyet Peter Julius, de, the Minifter of *Sweden* in Denmark 262
Crampright, Refident of the Emperor at the *Hague* 37
Cran, Embaffador from *Lewis* XI to the Duke of *Burgundy* 48 See 313
Crane, Embaffador from the Emperor, at *Munfter* 240
Craven, Lord 136
Crequi, Embaffador from the Duke of *Burgundy*, in France 16
Crequi, Marquis 150
Creville, the Conftable of St *Paul*'s Minifter 338
Du Croc, Embaffador of France, in Scotland 114, 125, 278
Crofts, James, Minifter of *England* in the Low-Countries 126
Cubat Chiaoux finds entire Security at *Venice* 34, 167
De Cuniga and Requefens Lewis, Embaffador of Spain, at *Rome* 219
Curtz, Embaffador of *Bavaria*, in France 26
Cyphers 377
Czar of *Mufcovy* fends no Embaffadors in Ordinary 11
defrays the Expence of all Embaffadors 145
is convened to the Council of *Trent* 126
See 379

D

Dame, Damoifelle form'd of it 175
Dunoits Peter, Embaffador of France, at *Trent* 222
a fine Repartee of his againft the Pope 344, 345
Dandin William, Secretary to Pope Paul III 278
Darmftadt Heffe, Landgrave of 97
Datary of a Legate, affronted 69
Dauffay, Embaffador of France in Denmark, takes place of the Elector of *Saxony* 180
Dauphine of France fends Embaffadors 11, 22
See 325, 326
Daut Chiaoux 63
Declaration of the States of Holland 246
Deffiat, Embaffador of France in *England* 194
Delphin Zachary, Nuncio in *Germany* 101
Dembifky, a pretended Minifter 115
Demetrius, a pretended Czar of *Mufcovy* 225
Denmark, King of, gives place to Embaffadors 180
is Mediator 121
Quarrels with the *Dutch* 122
See alfo 305, 364, 369
Dependencies 380
Depredations of the French 351
Deputies of the States of the Low-Countries 12, 49
treated as Publick Minifters 12
Deputies that compofe the Affembly of the States-General 17
Deputies of the Archduke, at the *Hague* 351
Deputies that are not Embaffadors 377
Deputies of the Princes of *Germany*, arrefted 28, 259
Deputies fent by the States to the Bifhop of *Munfter* 144
Deputies Extraordinary, 41 & feq
are allowed to be covered 43
Deputies of the *Anfeatick* Towns, 15, 239
Deputy, a Quality very general 41
Derby, Earl of, Minifter of *England*, in the Low-Countries 126
Defcordes, Marefchal of France 112

Deftrades, a Minifter without Quality 5, 35, 183, 186
Embaffador and Colonel 82, 185
Difference with the Spanifh Embaffador 145, 185
at a great Expence 208 See 328, 351, 380
Devotion falfe 71
Dexterity in Minifters, commendable 329
Difference between the Minifters of *Sweden* and *Metz* 189
between the Embaffador of France, and the Prince of *Orange* 82
between the Embaffadors of France and Spain 145
Difference between the Pope and the Republick of *Venice* 347
between France and Spain 388
for Rank 377, & feq.
for the Marquifate of *Saluces* 324, 333
Difficulty about the Quality of Embaffador in Powers 6
about Paffports 123, 124, 372
about the Entry of the Plenipotentiaries of *Bavaria* 145
Dignity Imperial 377
Dilection, a Title in *Germany* 223
Difobedience 282
Difpatches, or Letters 357 & feq
Difpute between Paul V and the Republick of *Venice* 3, 61
between Cardinal *de l'Efte*, and the Embaffador of Spain 166
between the Embaffadors of Spain and *Venice* 171
between *Urban* VIII and the Duke of Parma 139
Divan 161
their Refolution 346
Doctors German, have falfe Maxims 28
Doctor, impertinent 158
Doctor Medina, Embaffador of Spain, at *Rome* 200
Doge of *Venice* does Honour to a Cardinal Embaffador 140
muft have no Communication with an Embaffador 305
Dombes, a Sovereignty 11
Domefticks of an Embaffador are inviolable 266, 269
Embaffadors ought to be careful in the Choice of them 270
Dominick Alamanni, Embaffador of *Tranfylvania* 44
Dominick Loredan, Embaffador of *Venice*, to Charles VIII 286
Dominick Trevifan, Embaffador of *Venice* to Charles VIII 286
Doncafter, Vifcount of 183
Dorislaus Ifaac, Minifter of the Parliament of *England*, affaffinated 8
Doriole, Chancellor of France, Embaffador to the Duke of *Burgundy* 48, 90 See alfo 411
Dorfet, Earl of, complements the *French* Embaffador 176
Doffat Arnauld, Minifter without Quality 5
Secretary to the Embaffador of *France* 44
his obfcure Birth 49
learned 50
Bifhop of *Rennes* 78
Minifter at *Venice* 204
at *Florence* 141
See Cardinal *Doffat*
Downing Sir George, *Englifh* Envoy at the *Hague* 37
Dragomans 162
are Domefticks to Embaffadors 272
See again 313

Draught,

INDEX.

	Page
Dragut, a *Turkish* General	326
Drafcoutsz *George*, the Emperors Embassador at Trent	215
Drummers, under the Protection of the Law of Nations	24
Duarte Don, Brother to the King of *Portugal*	196
Duels, Ministers not to fight them	281
Dukes and Peers conduct Embassadors	131
Duke of *Alva*, Viceroy of *Naples*, sends an Embassador to *Rome*	21
orders the Governor of *Cafcais* to be taken	24
Minister at the Assembly at *Cercamp*	239
Embassador of *Spain*, in *France*	1–9
his ill Counsels	319
Duke of *Albuquerque*	72, 190
Duke of *Alençon* 129, 239, 263 See	362
Duke d'*Amville*	152
Duke d'*Anjou*	129
Duke of *Arschot*, Deputy at the *Hague*	126
Embassador of *Spain*, in *France*	129
Duke of *Bar*	239
Duke of *Bavaria* descends of Emperors	26
will not give place to *Venice*	30
Embassador from the Emperor	106
punctual in Civilities	143
Duke of *Biron*, Embassador of *France*, at *Brussels*	236
in *England*	108
Duke of *Bouillon la Marc*, meets the *Spanish* Embassador	129
Embassador in *England*	135
his ill Conduct	316
yields to the *English* Commissioners	378
Duke of *Bouillon*, *Henry de la Tour*, Embassador in *England*	238
declared Prince	11
Duke of *Bourbon*, Minister of *France*	112
His Wife's Power	ibid
Embassador at the Congress of *Arras*	238
Duke of *Bretagne* 238 See also	405
Duke of *Breze*	3
Duke of *Brunswick* descends of Emperors	26
France demands Passports for the Dukes of his Family	123
they refuse the Mediation of the States General	321
Duke of *Buckingham* 99, 100, 104	
first Minister in *England*	305
the *Spanish* Embassador contrives to ruin him	319
Duke of *Camina* executed	61
Duke de *Chaulnes*, Embassador of *France*, at *Rome*	220
Duke of *Cheureuse*, Embassador of *France*, in *England*	48
his Train and Livery	203
goes to meet the *English* Embassadors	131
Duke of *Cleves*	106
Duke of *Conti*	138
Duke of *Courland*	364
Duke of *Crequi*, Embassador of *France*, at *Rome*, refuses the first Visit to the Pope's Relations	187
his Rencounter with the *Ghisi*	264
Embassador to *Cromwell*	18
Duke d'*Elbeuf* goes to meet the Embassadors of *Poland*	133, 150
Duke d'*Engoulesme*	251
Embassador of *France*, in *Germany*	70, 137
Duke d'*Epernon*, *John Lewis de Nogaret*, covers himself as a Prince	158
in great Favour with *Henry* III	234
Duke of *Feria*, Embassador of *Spain*, in *France*	4
Governor of *Milan*	7, 231, 394
of *Ferrara*	233

	Page
Duke of *Grammont*, Embassador of *France*, in *Germany*	45
Duke of *Guise* goes to meet the Emperor's Embassadors 129 See also	319
Duke of *Guise* killed at *Blois*	58
Duke of *Guise* obliged to give place to the Embassador of *France*	179, 233
Duke of *Guyenne*	90
Duke of *Holstein Gottorp* 280 See also	314
Duke de l'*Infantada*, Embassador of *Spain*, in *France*	234
Duke de *Joyeuse*, Embassador at *Rome*, introduces the *Polish* Embassadors	133
his Treachery	332
Duke of *Lerma* 150, 281 See also 304, 327	
Duke of *Longueville*, Prisoner of War, negotiates	36, 113
Plenipotentiary at *Munster*	219, 295
his Visits	204
Duke of *Lorrain* goes to meet the Embassadors of *France*	142
sends Ministers to the Congress, though dispossessed of his Countrey	20
his Minister acknowledg'd as an Embassador	33
he is no Obstacle to the Peace	387
Duke de *Lunes*, Constable of *France*	127
See also	357
Duke of *Luxembourg*, no Embassador	7
Duke of *Mantua* sends Embassadors	10
his Contest with the Duke of *Savoy*	331
gives place to *Savoy*	ibid
is ungrateful to *France*	27
visits the *French* Embassador at *Venice*	191
Duke of *Mantua*, *Ferdinand*	82
Duke of *Maqueda*	150
Duke of *Mayenne*, Lieutenant of the League	118
Embassador of *France*, in *Spain* 48, 129, 150	
Duke of *Medina Celi*, *John de la Cerda*	239
Duke of *Medina de los Torres*, design'd Embassador at *Munster*	39
Duke of *Meklenburg*	385
Duke of *Mercœur*	363
Duke of *Milan*	375
Duke of *Modena* sends Embassadors comes to an Accommodation with the *Spaniards* 27 See also	10, 328
Duke of *Montalto*	150
Duke of *Mentelon*	310
Duke of *Montmorancy*, Constable of *France*	106
Duke of *Montpensier*	48
goes to meet the Legate	129
Duke of *Nemours* goes to meet the *Spanish* Embassador	ibid
commands the *French* Army	409
Duke of *Neuburg* hath place of Embassadors	179
Heir to the Elector *Palatin*	386
punctual in his Civilities	143
covers in the Emperor's Presence	233
Duke of *Nevers*, *Lewis de Gonzaga*, the first Embassador that had the Title of Excellency	170
the Pope refuses to admit it	138
goes to meet the *Spanish* Embassador	129
Duke of *Orleans* goes to meet the Legate	73
besieged in *Novarra*	175
Lieutenant-General of the Kingdom	23
Duke de *Ossuna*, *Peter Giron*, Viceroy of *Naples*	252
Duke of *Palliano*, Nephew of Pope *Paul* IV	258
Duke of *Parma* sends Embassadors	10
as Governor of the Low-Countries	21
how he is receiv'd in *France*	155
covers himself	158
his Difference with the *Barberini*	196
gives place to the Great Duke	231

The

INDEX.

The Republick of *Venice* gives him the Title of Excellency 231
   goes to *Rome* 196
Duke *Edward*, mortally hates Cardinal *Mazarin* 302, 368
Duke of *Paftrana*, Embaffador of *Spain* in France 129
   his Prefents 168
   the Civilities done him 129
   See alfo 413
Duke of *Piney* 129
Duke of *Santo Gemini* 138
Duke *Savelli*, *Frederick*, the Emperor's Embaffador at *Rome* 80, 190, 221
Duke of *Savoy*, where he has Embaffadors 10
   demands to be Embaffador 3
   caufes himfelf to be nam'd for the Embaffy of *Venice* 3, 149
   pretends to the Royal Hall 148
   takes the Quality of King of *Cyprus* 148, 170
   orders the *Venetian* Embaffador to leave his Court *ibid*
   wou'd diftinguifh himfelf 151
   will not give Cardinal *Mazarine* Precedency in a third Place 234
   avoids the *French* Embaffador 312, 330, 345, 383
Duke of *Seffa*, Embaffador of *Spain* at *Rome* 72, 129, 138, 150
Duke of *Sefto*, Embaffador of *Spain* at *Venice* 149
Duke of *Sully*, Embaffador of *France* in England 165
   refufes to go with the Duke of *Bouillon* 238
   Confident of *Henry IV* 357
Duke *de la Trimouille* 11
Duke of *Vendome* 140
Duke of *Veraguas* 150
Duke of *Verneuil*, Embaffador of *France* in England 137
Duke of *Villa Hermofa* 150, 277
Duke of *Uffeda* 150
Duke of *Urbin* 371
Duke of *Weimar* 123, 155
Duke of *Wirtemberg* 28, 191
Dupes, the Day of 105
Dutchefs of *Bar* 204
Dutchefs of *Beaufort* 251
Dutchefs of *Savoy*, Regent and Guardian 29
Dutchy of *Caftro* 196, 285
Dutchy of *Ferrara* 231

E

Ebrahim Bey, or *Abraham Strotzen*, firft Interpreter at the Port 35
   Embaffador in *Poland* 75, 81
Ebrahim, Sultan 169
Ecclefiafticks, exempt from Secular Jurifdiction 61
   their Pride 234, 235
Edmonds Thomas, Embaffador of *England* in France 194
Edward IV ufurps the Crown of *England* 17
   falfe News of his Death 334
   his Courtiers *French* Penfioners 354
Edward VI King of *England* 114
   his Treaty with *Francis I* 377
   not ratify'd 410
Ecclefiaftick Minifters 50
   whether proper 57
   not fuffer'd to enter the Senate of *Venice* *ib*
Elbing, Treaty of, refus'd to be ratify'd 408
Electors have Eminent Rights 32
   are the firft Order of the States of the Empire *ibid*
   fend no Embaffadors but to Congreffes 143, 178, & *feq*
   the *French* King ftyles them Brothers 228

their Plenipotentiaries treated alike at *Munfter* 175
Effingham Thomas Howard, Lord Chamberlain 239
   Lady, will not give place to the *French* Embaffadrefs 182
Elector of *Bavaria* writes to the Embaffadors of *France* at *Munfter* 175
   negotiates with the Marefchal *de Grammont* 112
   in the *French* Intereft 365
   to promote Popery 386
Elector of *Brandenburg* fends Plenipotentiaries to *Sueden* before a War 98
   offers to guaranty the King of *England*'s Powers 119
   claims the Title of Sereniry 120
   quits Parties 98
   fends Embaffadors to the *Hague* 110
   contefts with *Sueden* about *Pomerania* 385
   courts France 367
Elector of *Cologne* does not let Minifters cover in his Prefence 32
Elector of *Mentz*, Dean of the College 144
Elector *Palatine*, refufes to hear the Archduke's Embaffador 91
   excluded the General Paffport 123
   refufes to do Civilities to the Embaffadors of the United Provinces 194
   lofes his Dominions 385
Elector of *Saxony*, *Auguftus*, gives place to the *French* Embaffador 180
   will not give Audience to the Nuncio 102
   his Plenipotentiaries give the firft Vifit to the Emperor's 88
   his Minifters refufe the Title of Excellency 32
   and other Civilities 144
   John Frederick, his Manifefto againft *Char V* Emperor 30
Elector of *Saxony*, offers to guaranty the King of *England*'s Powers 119
   reconcil'd to the Emperor 385
   claims the Dutchy of *Cleves* 392
Elector of *Triers*, Embaffador from the Emperor 31, 129, 181 See alfo 387
Leonora of *Auftria*, Queen of France 5
Elchi, Name of Minifters in *Turky* 146
Elizabeth of *Auftria* 129
Elizabeth of France *ibid*
Elizabeth, Queen of *England*, employs a Stranger as an Embaffador 75
   fends *Walfingham* to France 108
   and *Throgmorton* 125
   receives a great Embaffy from *France* 135, 136
   honours the Marefchal *de Biron* 168
   her Proceedings againft the Bifhop of *Roffe*, the *Scots* Queen's Minifters 249
   orders the *Spanifh* Embaffador to depart 251
   ufes another *Spanifh* Embaffador roughly 276
   her Inclinations oppofite to thofe of *Katherine de Medicis* 297
   her Inftructions to *Walfingham* 298
   Walfingham's Letter to her from *France* 300
   her Zeal for the Proteftant Religion 315
   what fhe faid of marrying the Duke of *Alonçon* 344
   will not allow her Subjects to receive Honours from a Foreign Prince 354
   her Treaty with *Charles IX* 410
Elucidations 408
Emanuel, Emperor of *Conftantinople* 248
Emanuel, King of *Portugal* 211
Emanuel Philibert, Duke of *Savoy*, gives place to the Republick of *Venice* 170, 249, 173
Embaffador, the Etymology of the Word 2

INDEX.

	Page
is a publick Minister	ibid
of Obedience	4, 148
Embassador first distinguish'd	181
Embassador, a necessary Minister	1
in Ordinary, not appointed by the Law of Nations	6
Embassador Ordinary and Extraordinary	4
distinguish'd at the Hague	160
Extraordinary, has Precedence of the Ordinary	243
Embassador, is a Player	10
should have a noble Exterior and Appearance	4
this Quality given formerly to all publick Ministers	2
Embassadors that are Deputies of Towns, Ministers of the second Order	15
Embassadors treated by the King's Officers	168
their Presents	ibid
Embassadors Residents, Ministers of the second Order	15
Embassadors are Representatives	2
more Advantage to send than to receive them	11
are not cover'd at Audiences of the Pope	118
Embassador cannot make a Deputy	22
Embassador, without Character, and without Function	4
Embassador, Merchant	436
Imaginary	164
Circular	290
of a Day	286
a Traytor	88
Embassadors are inviolable in their Persons 246, &c.	
when they are not so	274
call'd to answer	253
oblig'd by a Contract before a Notary Publick	273
their Expences formerly born	168
their Lodging defray'd	170
Embassador of France took place of the Embassadors of other Kings at the Councils of Constance and Basil	209
Embassador of France had a Palace at the Hague 170	
takes the Hand of Princes at his own House	176
is affronted in Turky	183
Embassador is obliged to notify his Arrival	185
Embassador is exempted from the Jurisdiction of the Place of his Residence	249
may exercise the Religion of his Prince	266
whether he may do Justice on his Domesticks	269
Embassador of an Elector takes the Place of Honour of a Sovereign Prince	176
Embassador of England does not cover himself	142
does not fee the Cardinal de Richlieu	166
Embassador takes place of a Daughter of France	181
of a Chancellor of France	ibid
makes a Difficulty of giving it to Cardinals	166
Embassadors of France write to the Duke of Bavaria	176
Embassador of Spain obtains an extraordinary Place at the Council of Trent	211, 212
after the Cardinal Priest	219
Embassador of Sweden refuses to salute the English Flag	165
Embassador of the United Provinces offends Cardinal Mazarine	93, 94
Embassadors of the Cantons do not cover themselves	138
how they are treated	132
Embassadors of the United Provinces at Munster	137
go immediately after those of Venice	178

	Page
Embassadors, not all of them are treated in France	168
Embassadors of Princes who are Enemies do not visit	196
Embassadors of England refuse to treat with Cardinal Richlieu	233
Embassador of Malta	132
has a Place in the Chapel	169
does not cover speaking of the King of Spain	155
Embassador of Mantua has no Place in the Chapel	231
Embassador of Venice refuses the Title of Excellency to the Embassador of the United Provinces	169
will not treat with the Embassadors of Portugal	18
his unjust Pretension	148
will not give place to the Prince of Condé	178
Embassador of Muscovy in Persia	147
Embassador of Genoa	132
Embassador of Spain gives place to the Emperor's Commissioner	40
magnificent	203
Embassador of the Mogul	147, 148
Embassador of Turky interested	169
Embassadors of Catalonia, Syndics only	14
Embassador of Parma and his Audience	26, 27
Embassador of the King of Egypt	296
Embassador of Japan at Rome	295
Embassador Hermaphrodite	298
Embassador, not to act the Part of a Herald	337
Embassador of France too imperious	388, 389
Embassador is an Actor	295
ought to be a gallant Man	ibid
ought to be respected in his Master's Court	ibid
is the Messenger of Peace	296
an Honourable Spy	ibid
ought not to talk with too much Assurance of the Success of his Negotiation	361
ought not to refuse Commissioners	ibid
Embassadors of the Republick of Florence	414
Embassador of the United Provinces	351
address their Letters to the States General	357
Embassadors of Venice address their Letters to the Doge	358
Embassadors of England pass an Act touching Rank	377
Embassadors illustrious	416, &seq
Embassadresses	183
a new Quality	5
the Queen of France gives the Stool to the Spanish Embassadress	183
the Rank given them in England	184
Embassadresses at Munster treated like their Husbands	ibid
Embassies, and their Necessity	2
solemn	10
from Germany to France	308
of the Swiss Cantons	132
of the King of Hungary	134
of France in England	135
compos'd of several Persons	236
extraordinary	295
Chimerical	ibid
Eminency	175
Emperor, treats the Princes of Germany as Subjects	29, 30
as also the States of the United Provinces	165
where he has Ministers	8
Protector of General Councils	222
Emperor, offers his Mediation to Sweden, consents to treat at Rome	364, 372
Emperor, Turkish, sends no Embassadors in ordinary	10

INDEX.

	Page
Emperor's great Chamberlain, regulates the Ceremonies of Embassadors	150
Empire, was formerly Hereditary	20, 30
Enemies send Embassadors	18
England, King of, sends away the Domesticks of his Queen	99, 100
has not had an Embassador at the Hague till within these few Years	9, 10
has Embassadors at Paris	ibid
Vassal to the Crown of France for Normandy and Gayenne	16
admits the Embassadors of Brandenbourg	45
rejects their Masters Mediation	364
his Embassadors at Breda carry it high	368
England, has Embassadors every where	9
England, High Chamberlain of, regulates the Ceremonies of Embassadors	136
d Enguera John, a Monk and Negotiator	64
Enterview between the Pope and the French King	140
d Entragues, Damoiselle, her Intrigue	251
Entry of an Embassador	127, &c seq
of the King of Hungary's Embassadors	133
of the Embassadors of Poland	ibid
of an Indian Embassador	147
Entry remarkable	138
Entry of a Venetian Embassador	147
another of the same	136
Entry of Cardinal Bichi	ibid
Entry, none at Rome but to Embassadors of Obedience	137
Envoy Extraordinary	4, 33, 36
is a new Quality	36
nothing but a Resident Extraordinary	ibid
Civilities done him	159, 160
Envoy of Courland, receiv'd with Ceremonies in Poland	128
Epo Aaiza, Embassador of the United Provinces in Sweden	154
Epo Bootsman, Deputy Extraordinary	41
Eric, King of Sweden	120
Erlach, Colonel	352
Espesses, Embassador of France at the Hague	470
Essex, Earl of, Embassador from King Charles II to the King of Denmark, refuses to salute the Castle of Cronembourg	165
Estampes, Embassador of France at the Hague	284
Estree See Marechal d Estree	
Everard de Reyd, writes a History of the Low Countries	52
Eugenius Pope	367
Excellency a new Quality	170
the Embassador of Venice assumes it	ibid
given to the Duke of Mantua	231
the Republick of Venice give it to the Duke of Parma	ibid
Innocent X gives it to the Embassadors of Savoy and Tuscany	170, 171
The Emperor will not allow it to be given to the Electors Ministers	171, 172
The Embassadors of France refuse it to those of the United Provinces	171
The Nuncio refuses it to the Savoy Embassador	170
Expence of the Embassador	201
often prostitutes the Reputation of the Prince	206
Experience is the finishing Qualification of an Embassador	53, 56, 86

F

Fabian de Dohb, Minister of Brandenburg	229
Fabio Chisi, Nuncio at Munster	198
how he receives Embassadors See	343
his Qualifications	385

	Page
Fabritio Marenalfo, kills Fabritio Commissary of the Republick of Florence	24
Faction	7, 8
Faculties of Legate	116
Falconbridge, Lord Viscount, Cromwell's Embassador in France	17
from the King of England at Venice	141
at Florence	219
at Genoa	220
his Reception at Turin	ibid.
Falconieri, Nuncio at Brussels, his Audience of the French King, with Letters of Credence	282
ality of the Spanish Embassador at Venice	334
Du Fargis, Embassador of France in Spain	78, 108, 144
wants Moderation	351, 370
Farnese, a modern House	26
Feria, a false Prudence	337
Fectales	24
Felix de Ursins, Prince of Salernum	129
Ferdinand of Castille, a Monk a Negotiator	66
Ferdinand the Catholick, will not suffer his Subjects to be made Cardinals	60
Hypocrite	71
a great Cheat	64, 144
accents d himself	88
See 304, 315, 333	
his bold Message to the Pope	340
Ferdinand I Empero	96, 166
Ferdinand II Empero.	137
his Favourites	303
Ferdinand III Emperor	80
his Favourites	303
Ferdinand, King of Naples	338
Ferdinand, King of the Romans	342
Ferdinand Diaz of Toledo	187
Ferdinand, Duke of Calabria	90
Ferdinand Scotti, Plenipotentiary of Parma at Venice	232
Ferdinand de Sylva, Embassador of Portugal in Castille	22
Ferdinand Telles de Faro, Embassador of Portugal, a Deserter	86
Ferdinand de Velasco, Constable of Castille, Embassador of Spain in England	200
Ferdinand Gonzague, Minister of Charles V	66
Ferrier de la Nuca, Embassador of Arragon in Castille	129
Ferrier, Regnauld, Embassador of France at Venice	114
at Trent	14, 215
Ferro, del Levius a ridiculous Embassador	205
La Ferte, Imbault, Embassador of France in England	46
Fenquieres, Embassador of France in Germany	45
design'd for the Embassy of Munster	48
Fidelity	4, 86
its Character	89
Fielding, Lord, Embassador of England in France	149
Figuera, John de, Governour of Milan	97
Finet, John, Master of the Ceremonies in England, writes Memoirs	1
Flag of England to be respected	165
Flemming, George, Embassador of Sweden	154
Florence, gives Precedency to Parma	232
Florentines, are cunning	ibid
send Embassadors to the Pope	50
make an Alliance with the King of Naples	87
De Foix, Matthieu, Count	14
Fontenay Marueil, Embassador of France at Rome	19
obliges the Duke of Guise to give him Hand in his own House	178
his Instruction	107
affronts Cardinal Spivelli	190
leaves

INDEX

	Page		Page
leaves *Rome* without Orders	283	his first Audience	152
his Negotiations there	316	*Fran Fraulein*	175
the perplexing Orders he receiv'd from *Mazarine*	328, 422	Fraud	201
Forbus, Minister of *Poland* in *France*	116	*Frederick* II King of *Denmark*	180
Fort of *Fuentes*	113	*Frederick* III King of *Denmark*	366
Foscarini James, meets *Henry* III of *France*	236	*Frederick* III Emperor,	106, 222
Foscarini Anthony, Embassador of *Venice*, in *France*	170	deceived by *Lewis* XI	370
in *England*	288	*Frederick*, Count de *Dona*, Governor of *Orange*	199
Knighted by *Henry* III who lodg'd at his House	288	*Frederick*, Prince *Palatine*, Embassador of *Charles* King of *Spain*	239
strangled in Prison	289	*Frederick*, Duke of *Wirtemburg*, Embassador in *France*	311
France has Ministers every where	8	*Fresnoy Canaye*, *Philip de*, Embassador of *France*, at *Venice*	50
in the *Swedish* Army	45	in *Germany* and *England*	185
sends Embassadors to the Diets	ibid	commits a great Fault	ibid
has a Resident at *Hamburgh*	46	gives the first Visit to the Embassador of *Tuscany*	187
boasts of her Liberty	75	his Letters	357
mediates between the Northern Crowns	364	Friendship of *German* Princes, useless to *France*	28
sends Embassadors to *Munster*	385	Friendship of the Cardinals *d'Este*, and *de Medicis*	197
Francis I	84, 119, 120, 140, 236	Friendship between the Republicks of the United Provinces and *Venice*, broken	22
causes the Legate to depart the Kingdom	71		
makes himself Master of *Savoy*	110	*Friquet John*, Minister without Character	35, 100
refuses a Passport to the Princes of *Germany*	123	the Emperor's Minister at the *Hague*	ibid
employs Strangers	142, 377	uses the *French* Tongue	314
sends a Defiance to *Charles* V	415	*Fromhold*, Minister of *Brandenburg*, at *Osnaburg*	240
Francis II	319	Functions of an Embassador	295
Francis, the last Duke of *Bretagne*	275	different from his Actions	ibid
Francis of *Aarssens*, first Embassador of the United Provinces, in *France*	55	Functions of Embassadors in Ordinary	297
Embassador in *England*	198, 228	Funerals	194
the Court of *France* disgusted with him	201	**G**	
his Character	423	*Gabriel de Aramont*, Embassador of *France*, at the Port	316
Francis Andrada Lietao, Embassador of *Portugal*, at the *Hague*	124	*Gabriel de Guzman*, a Cordelier, a Negotiator	112
Francis Bernardo, Minister without Character	35	*Gabriel Galotta* Auditor of the Rota	216
Francis de Carmagnole	56	*Cajetan*, Nuncio in *Spain*	150
Francis de Castro, Embassador of *Spain*, at *Venice*	168, 171	*Galeas de St Severin*, Embassador of the Duke of *Milan*	202
Francis Duke of *Florence*	141	*Galeas Sforza*, Duke of *Milan*	49
Francis de Gama, Viceroy of the *Indies*	156	*Galas Matthias*, Commissioner for the Emperor, at *Querasque*	39
Francis Justiniani, Minister of *Venice*, in *France*	34	*Garbier*	125
Francis I Isola, Embassador from the Emperor, in *Poland*	79	*Garcia d'Aznar d'Anon*	99
Francis Maria, de la *Rovera*, Duke of *Urbin*	89	*Garcia d Alvarez*	119
Francisco de Melo, nam'd for the Embassie at *Munster*	38	*Garcia de Silva Figueroa*, Embassador of *Spain*, in *Persia*	54, 163
Francisco de Melo, Embassador of *Portugal*, at the *Hague*	255	*Garcilasso de la Vega*, Minister of *Spain*, at *Rome*	257
Francis Miqueli, Embassador of *Venice*, at *Turin*	269	arrested	310
Francis Morosini, Embassador of *Venice*, in *Spain*	244	*Gascon*, Gentleman	353
Francis de la Noue	90	*Gaspar de Bracamonte*. See Count de *Pegnaranda*	
Francis de Quignone, General of the Cordeliers, a Negotiator	66	*Gaspar de Coligni*, Colonel of the *French* Infantry	35
Francis Sarcuela, Minister of *Arragon*	99	*Gaspar de Donhof*, Chamberlain to the King of *Poland*	153
Francis Sforza, General of the Army of the *Milanese*	261	*Gaspar de Geneva*, Marquifs *de Iullins*, Embassador of *Savoy*, at *Vervins*	240
Duke of *Milan*	35, 84	*Gaspar de Lupian*, Minister of the Archduke *Philip*	80
betrays the *Milanese*	347	*Gaspar Spinelli*, Embassador of *Venice*, at *London*	34
Francis de Somale, Minister of *Charles* V	112	*Gaspar de Vospergue*, Embassador from the United Provinces, to the Elector of *Cologne*	143
Francis of *Toledo*	105	*Gaures*, *Persian* Peasants	147
Francis de la Tour, Embassador of the Emperor, at *Rome*	96	*Gemer*, Brothel to *Bajazet*	63
Francis Throgmorton, a Traytor	249, 251, 275	*Genaro Annese*, Chief of the *Neapolitan* Rebels	205
Francis de Vargas, Embassador of *Charles* V at *Venice*	209	Generals of Armies, employ'd as Ministers	23
at *Bologne*	149	*Genoa* sends Embassadors	10
Francis de Vera, Embassador of *Spain*, at *Venice*	200	to the Duke of *Milan*	238
Francis Vietto, Mathematician	69	her Ministers treated with some Difference	151
Francis Walsingham, learned	50	*Genoa* pretends to the Royal Hall	148
Embassador of *England*, in *France*	108	her Embassador affronted	151
his Instructions	107	sends sixteen Embassadors to the Duke of *Milan*	238

7 K twenty

INDEX

	Page		Page
twenty four to *Lewis* XII	235	*Groenhouse*, a Civilian	7
Gentillor, Minister of France, in *England*	207	*Gror neuen* City of, does not violate the Law of Nations in prosecuting the Sieur *Renguers*	21
Gentlemen	48, 160	*Groo*, Madam de, her Reception in France	183
George Duke of *Lunenburg*	27	*Grotius Hugo*, Embassador of *Sweden*, in *France*	23, 302
George Bouchard, the Pope's Minister at *Constantinople*	63	one of the greatest Men of the Age	51
George Fleming, Embassador of *Sweden*, at *Breda*	379	writes History,	52
Germigny de Germoles, Embassador of *France* at the Port	20	writes a Treatise of the Law of Nations	2,6
Ghent, John de, his Character	425	his admirable Writings	52, 76, 104
Madam *de*, her Reception in *France*	183	*Grotius Peter*, his Son	428
Ghigy, affront the French Embassador at *Rome*	264	his Character	*ibid*
Ghislery Michael, a Monk	100	Embassador of the United Provinces, in *France*	104, 287
Giles de Noailles, Minister of *France*, in *Poland*, and at *Constantinople*	343	Guaranty of the King of *England's* Powers	119
Girard, Bishop of *St Flour*, Embassador of *France*, in *Arragon*	14	Guaranty for the Fishery	380
Girault, Deputy-Introductor of Embassadors	134	Guards did not take to their Arms for the Embassadors of the United Provinces	151
Girolamo Landy, Embassador of *Venice*, in *England*	171	they do now	*ibid*
Girolamo Martloffo, a Noble *Venetian*	206	*Gueffer*, Resident of *France*, at *Rome*	318
Gnade, a German Title	175	*Guron* Introductor of Embassadors, refuses the *Spanish* Embassador's Present	290
Godard de Reed, d'Ameronge, Deputy of the United Provinces, to the Bishop of *Munster*	144	*Guffoni Vincent*, Minister of *Venice* 231 See 3,6	
Gogh Michael Van, Embassador of the United Provinces, in *England*	136	*Gustavus Adolphus*, King of *Sweden*	79, 97
Gondy Jerom, exercises the Office of Master of the Ceremonies	128	*Gutierre Gomes de Fuensalida*,	10,
Gonsalo de Betete, Embassador of *Ferdinand* the Catholick, at *Rome*	100	Embassador of *Spain* to the Archduke	3,9
Gonsalo d'Asienca Leuis, Embassador of *Castille*, in *Arragon*	129	*Guy Cavalcanti*, Minister without Character	35
Gonsalo Fernandez de Cordoua, Viceroy of *Naples*, his Perfidiousness	90, 262	*Guy de Fann, de Pibrac*, Embassador of *France*, in *Poland*	117
his Conquests	409	*Guy de Rochfort*, Chancellor of *France*, Embassador to the Archduke *Philip*	16
Gonsalo de Monroy, Minister of *Arragon*	79	*Guzman Martin de*, Embassador from the Emperor at *Rome*	97
Governours in Chief, send Embassadors	21		
Governour of *Milan*, sends and receives Embassadors	*ibid*	**H**	
Govia Juces, de, Embassador of *Portugal*, at *Trent*	222	Habit decent, for the first Visit	185
		Habits of an Embassador	201
		Haga Cornelis, Orator of the United Provinces, at the Port	10
Grace, a Title given in *England*	175	Hall Royal, and Hall Ducal	148
Gradinego Lewis, Embassador of *Venice*, to the Emperor	236	*Hamburgh* is not an Imperial Town	14, 165
Gralla Michael John	344	*Hamburgh* and *Lubeck* proposed for a Congress	372
Grammont Duke and Mareschal, arrives at *Frankfort*	45	*Hameaux des*, Embassador of *France*, at *Venice*	139
Grandees of *Spain*	173	Hans Towns are no State	15, 46
La Grange aux Ormes, a Physician's Son sent to *Germany* by Cardinal *Richlieu*	37	*Haro Lewis de*, first Minister and Plenipotentiary of *Spain*, at the *Pyrenees*	17, 199, 304
Honours done him by the Elector of *Saxony*	38	his Saying about the Prince of *Condé*	331, 375, 408
Granvelle Nicholas, Minister of the Emperor, at *Trent*	311	*Harold Appleboom*, Minister of *Sweden*, at the Hague	92
Gravelle, Minister of *France*, in *Germany*	32	*Harold*, King of *England*	66
Greatness of Soul, necessary to an Embassador	64	*Hartman*, Secretary of the Popish Cantons	158
Gregory XIII gives Audience to the Embassador of *Navarre*	20	*Hasland*, Plenipotentiary of *Bavaria*, at *Munster*	185
will not allow the *Spanish* Embassador a Publick Entry	137	*Hastings*, Great Chamberlain of *England*	123
receives Embassadors from *Japan*	295	*Hatton*, Vice-Chamberlain of *England*	299
his Legate imposed upon in *Spain*	336	*Hautefeuille*	298
Gremonville, President, Embassador of *France*, at *Venice*	352	*La Haye Vantelay*, Embassador of *France*, at the Port	395
his Moderation	*ibid*	endeavours to procure a Peace for the *Venetians*	325
Gremonvilles, Commander, Minister of *France*, at *Venice*	33	Hay Lord, Embassador of *England*, in *France*	169
Grignan, Embassador of *France*, at *Rome*	196	*Heemvliet*, Embassador of the United Provinces, in *England*	228
Grisons, the State of their Republick	7, 89	*Hennequin*, Resident of *France*, at *Copenhagen*	411
they send Embassadors	7, 204	*Henry* II, King of *England*, his Wars with the *French*	347
are a Soveraign State	10		
drive away the *French*	143	*Henry* III King of *England*, meets the Cardinal of *St Nicholas*	72
Gritti Laurence, Minister of *Venice*, at the Port	34	the Audience he gave the Pope's Nuncio	312
Gritti Peter, Embassador of *Venice*, at *Vienna*	171	*Henry* V King of *England*, in League with the Duke of *Burgundy*	238
in *Spain*	304, 407	*Henry* VIII King of *England*	170

INDEX.

in League with the Emperor *Maximilian*,
against *France* 262
would be Umpire of the Affairs of *Europe* 340
his Treaty with *Francis* I not ratify'd 410
challenges *Charles* V 414
Henry II King of *France*, sends the Order of St *Michael*, to *Edward* V King of *England* 114, 297
his Inconstancy 91, 132, 140, 236
a Lover of Ceremonies 301
how Embassadors negotiated under him 303, 311
Henry III finds out the ill Designs of the Leaguers 12
Henry IV his great Civility to the *Spanish* Embassador and the Pope's Legate, who did not own him to be King 46
gives great Priviledges to the Hans Towns 14
sends the Duke of *Nevers* to *Rome* 95
crowned at *Chartres* 181
his Goodness 135, 236
Henry IV his great Soul 300
not ceremonious 301
has no Minister 303
angry with the Pope 323
reduces the Duke of *Savoy* to a low Condition 325
gives the Order of St *Michael* to two *English* Gentlemen 354
his flying of Embassadors corrupting Ministers of State 355
his Embassadors wrote to himself only 357
the Pope obstinate against him 361
his Alliance with Queen *Elizabeth* 371
Henry, King of *Castile* 128, 129
Henry, King of *Portugal* 22, 66 See 336
Henry, Prince of *Orange* 306
Henry Cotinho, Embassador of *Portugal*, at *Rome* 341
Henry Dandalo 248
Henry de Figueredo, Embassador of *Castille*, in *Arragon* 129
Henry de Neufville, Embassador from Queen *Elizabeth*, in *France* 226
Henry de Marle, first President and Embassador 13
Henrietta of *France*, Queen of *England* 15, 327
Heralds enjoy the Protection of the Law of Nations 23, 24
Herald of *Jesus* XI ibid
Herald, a Groom made one 24
Herbaut, Secretary of State in *France* 74
Herbert John, Embassador of *England*, in *France* 226
Herbert Edward, Minister of *England*, in *France* 176
Herbert Lord, his History of *Henry* VIII 53
Highness, a higher Title than that of Eminency 173
given formerly to the Kings of *Spain* ibid
France gives it to the Prince of *Orange* 174
most Serene given to the Rebels at *Naples* 14
Royal 176
the Cardinals refuse to give the Title to the Cardinal of *Poland* 178
Highness, a Quality rejected in a Treaty 383
Hilary, Fryer of *Grenoble*, a Capuchine 65
his Difference with Cardinal *Dossat* 351
History of *Florence* 346
History of the *Roman* Law 51
History the principal Study of an Embassador 52
History of *Henry* IV ibid
History of *Aitzema* ibid
Histories to be read by Embassadors ibid
Hogia, Preceptor to the Grand Segnior 348
Holke obliges the *English* Embassador to salute *Cronenburg* 165
Hollander ceases to be a Subject of the States General, when Minister for a foreign Prince at the *Hague* 79
Hollis Lord, Embassador of *England*, in *France*, refuses the King's Present 289
refuses to give place to the Prince of *Conde* 178
Embassador of *England* at *Breda* 379
Honeywood, Embassador of *England*, to the King of *Sweden* 261
Honnore Courtin, his Character 422
Honours extraordinary are of no Consequence 168
done to a Minister of the second Order 149
more than are due, sometimes paid 199
Horace, a great Philosopher 51
Horatio Farnese, Duke of *Castro* 178
Horn Philip, Minister of *Brandenburg*, at the *Hague* 110
Hosle, Clerk to Monsieur *de Villeroy*, a Traytor 355, 363
Hostilities put an End to the Functions of an Embassador 285
House of an Embassador, inviolable 69, 266
is his Prince's 323
House of *Brunswick* 27
Houshold, Steward of, in *Spain* receives Embassadors 130
Howard, Great Chamberlain of *England*, a Pensioner of *France* 354
Hubert Jeste de, Embassador of the United Provinces, in *France*, 244
Hubert Foglietti writes his History of *Genoa* 52
Hubert Peter de, Embassador of the United Provinces, to the King of *Sweden* 260
Hudson, Embassador of *England*, in *France* 129
Hugh de Burgo, Deputy of the *Irish* Papists 8
Hugonet, Chancellor of *Burgundy*, Embassador to *Lewis* XI 48
Hurault de Maisse, Embassador of *France*, in *England* 371
Hyacinthe a Monk and Negotiator 326

I

Jacob Catz, Pensionary of *Holland* 417
Jacob, Embassador of *Savoy* 170
Jacob de Grise, Bailiff of *Bruges* 118
Jacob de Wassenar, Deputy of the United Provinces, to the Elector of *Brandenburg* 113
Jacomo Buoncampagno, natural Son of *Gregory* VIII 250
Jacomo Negrone, Minister of *Genoa*, at the *Hague* 292
Jacomo Soranzo, Embassador of *Venice*, in *France* 209
James, King of *England*, makes *Shirley* be covered 83
refuses to be Godfather to the Children of *France* 193
treats the Embassador of *Holland* ill 199
does not love the *Dutch* ibid
lives familiarly with the Embassador of *Spain* 168
inclines to the *Spaniards* 219
when, King of the *Scots*, will not see Queen *Elizabeth*'s Embassador 299 See 351
James II King of *Arragon*, his Embassador us'd ill by the Pope 66
JamesCœur, Minister of *Charles* VII a Merchant 50
Jane of *Castille*, Wife of the Archduke *Philip* 89
Jane of *France*, Wife of *Lewis* XII 340
Jane of *Navarre* 167
Janisaries 146
d'Ibarra Diego, Embassador of *Spain*, in *France* 46
Ibrahim See *Ebrahim*, enrag'd against the Christians 348
Idea of a perfect Embassador 306
Jealousie between the Republick of *Venice* and the Duke of *Savoy* 170

Jeannetin

INDEX

Jeannetin Justiniani, Minister of France at Genoa 60
Jeann'n See Peter Jeannin
Jeannin, Embassador of France at the Hague 300, 314, 415
Jermyn, Mr Embassador of England in France 37
Jewish Physician, a Negotiator 35
Imbercourt, Embassador of the Duke of Burgundy 48, 237
 Deputy to the Dutchess of Burgundy 49
Imbert de Bertenay, Sieur de Boccage, Embassador of France in Spain
Imprudence of the Embassador of France 47
 of the Resident of Portugal 102
Imprudence as dangerous as Infidelity 326
Impudence of a Turkish Minister 169
Impudence of Monks 66
Incivility of the Muscovites 145
 of the Spaniards 167
 of the Embassadors of Holland 188
 of the Embassado of Spain 195
 of a German Prince 167
 of the King of Poland 153
Infidelity 88, 89
Inigo de Cordona, Embassador of Spain at Rome 341
Innocent X Pope 79, 107, 197, 220
 took pleasure to mortify Cardinal Mazarin 302 See 336
Inquisitor General arrested 61
Inquisition of Rome 96
Instruction 106, & seq
 should be kept secret 309
 of Cardinal Gine ti 369
 of Walsingham 296, 297
Intercepter of Letters 263
Interest of the Muscovite 11
Interest, causes an Usurper to be acknowledg'd 18
Internuncio 2, 8, 74
Interregnum, none in Hereditary Kingdoms 22
Introductor of Embassadors, a new Office 128
 whether he may have the Place of Honour at an Embassadors 177
 none at Vienna 128, 149
 the Doge's Knight receives them at Venice 302

John I King of Arragon 14
John II King of Navarre 98
John, King of Sweden 75
John of Austria, Son of Charles V sends Embassadors 21
 does not give place to Cardinals 234
John of Austria, Son of Philip IV ibid
John Baptiste Borghese, Brother to Paul V 138
John Capello, Embassador of Venice in France 297
John Galeas, Duke of Milan 338
John Baptist Gattinara, Embassador of the Viceroy of Naples 21
John Baptiste Taxis, Minister of Spain in France 46
John Borcel, Embassador of the United Provinces in England 190
John Canobio, Nuncio 125
John de Chimmazzero, Embassador of Spain at Rome 17
John Francis Aldobrandin, Nephew of Clement VIII Minister in Spain 289
John Francis Valerio, Minister without Character 36
John Francis Valerio, a Traytor 266
John Frederick, Elector of Saxony 29
John Gondolfo, a Monk executed 61
John Gerson, Embassador of France at the Council of Constance 214
John Grimani, Patriarch of Aquileia 58
John de Ghent, Embassador of the United Provinces in France 104, 244
 Deputy to the Elector of Brandenburg 144
John Cnuit, Embassador of the United Provinces at Munster 88

in France 151
John Emanuel Don, Embassador of Ferdinand to Philip of Austria 89
Joinville, Prince of 150, 178
Joseph, Father, a Capuchin, and Minister of State 65
 was an Embassador at Ratisbonne 66, 259
 disavow'd by Cardinal Mazarin 413
Isabella, Queen of Castille 64
Italy Princes of, not to be preferr'd to those of Germany 27
 take the Hand of Embassadors at their own Houses 119
Juanouitz, John, Embassador of Muscovy in Persia 147
Julius II Pope 71, 226
 enlarges his Territories by Violence and Cruelty 344
Julius III Pope 72, 79 See 342
Julius Cæsar 52
Justiniani, Embassador of Venice in France 120, 283

K

Kaleste'n, Colonel 300
Katherine of Bourbon, Princess of Loraine 35
Katherine de Medicis, Queen of France 114, 214, 219, 232 319
Katherino Zeno, Embassador at the Age of 84 54
Katherino Belegno, Embassador of Venice at Turin 345
Keeper of the Seal in Holland 306
Kensington, Lord Rich, Embassador of England in France 99
 Earl of Holland ibid
Kevenhuller, Embassador of the Emperor in Spain 304
 his Character 421
Killegrew, Embassador of England at the Hague 9
King of France does not visit the Legate 168
Kings of England and France send to visit Embassadors the Day they arrive 170
Knight of the Doge 302
Knight of the Star 139
Knights of Malta, exempted from ordinary Jurisdiction 61
Knuit, Minister of the States General, falsely accus'd 353
Koningsmark, an Embassador and Officer of War 298
Krebs, Embassador of the Marquis of Baden in France 26

L

Ladislaus, King of Hungary 133
Ladron de Guevara, Minister of the Archduke Philip 80
Lambert d'Ascaffembourg 52
Lancelot, Advocate of the Council of Trent 211
Landais, Peter de, Minister of the Duke of Bretagne 275
Landgrave of Hesse submits to the Emperor claims the Bishoprick of Paderborn 385
Langey, Governour of Piedmont 56
Languerac, Embassador of the United Provinces in France 204
Lanier, Embassador of France in Portugal 93
 communicates his private Thoughts to that King 322
Languien, Minister of the Emperor in Italy 138
 See also 303
Lansac, Lewis de St Gelais 128
 Embassador of France in England 135
 at Rome 205
 at Trent 210
 taken in Disguise 205
 a great Minister 416

Lascaris,

INDEX.

Lascaris, John, Embassador of France at *Venice* 51
Laski, Jerom, Embassador from *Zapoli*, King of
   Hungary to the Princes of *Germany* 126
   to the *Grand Seignior* 20, 119
   changes Sides 342
Law, *Siquis ff de Legatis* 246
Law, *Lege Julia ad Leg Jul, de Vi publica* 346
Law Canon 51
Law of Nations protects Embassadors 1, 7
   extends to Ministers of the second Order 2, 33
   is ill apply'd 17
   does not protect Rebels 8
   is the Privilege of Privileges 250
Law of Nations, the Foundation of Treaties 371
Lawyers Civil, their Opinion about the Law of Nations 249, 250
Layala, Embassador of *Spain* at *Venice* 209
Lazari, a Rabble at *Naples* so call'd 14
League of *France* 118
League of *Cambray* 289
League *Grison* See *Grisons*,
Legatus 2
Leicester, Earl of, Minister of *England* 251
   Embassador of *England* in *France* 131
   Governour of the United Provinces 9
Leitao, John Fernandez de, a ridiculous Embassador 156
Lelienhove, Embassador of *Sweden* in *Poland* 281
Lencome, Embassador of *France* at the Port 87
Lenox, Earl of, *Matthew Stuart* 125
Lenox, Duke of 109
Leo Brulard, Embassador of *France* at *Ratisbon* 376
Leo X Pope 79, 118
Leo XI Pope 138
Leonardo Donati, Embassador of *Venice* at *Rome* 345
Leonardo Venieso, Embassador of *Venice* kill'd 262
Leone Jerom, Embassador of *Venice* at *Milan* 268
Lescun 20
Lesley John See Bishop of *Rosse*
Lessinsky, Embassador of *Poland* at *Vienna* 364
Letters of Embassadors inviolable 262
Letters Circular 30, 274
Letters Credential 109, 115
   for the *Cantons* ibid
Letters of Recommendation ibid
Letter, entituled the *Disinterested*, a Tract 32
Letters, Men of 50
Letters of *Dossat, Jeannin, &c* 357
Lewis XI will not admit the Embassadors of the Usurper *Richard* III 17
   makes use of all sorts of Persons 49
   rallies Cardinal *Bessarion* 51, 88
   is perfidious 90
   joins *Burgundy* and *Provence* to *France* 227
   See 297, 300
   will know every thing 301, 314, 339, 353, 384
Lewis XII of *France* 219, 222, 238, 257
Lewis XIV 163, 168
Lewis, King of *Hungary* 126
Lewis, Duke of *Orleans* 173
Lewis, Prince of *Conde* 48
Lewis Sforza, Duke of *Milan* 238
   goes to meet *Philip de Comines* 141
   visits the Embassador of *Venice* 142
   great with *Charles* VIII. of *France* 318
   See 338, 347
Liancourt, first Gentleman of the Chamber 192, 151
Liberty of Speech 339, &c seq
Liege, City, subject to its Bishop 46
Liguieres, Embassador of *France* at *Trent* 222
Lionne, Hugh de, Minister without Character 35
   Minister of *France* 133
   takes place of the *Swiss* Embassadors 176
   Embassador of *France* in *Germany* 45
   arrives at *Frankfort* 144

   gives Audience to *Mustapha Foraga* 163
   Minister of Cardinal *Mazarine* 199
   See 308, 368, 377, 389, 408
Lipomano William, Embassador of *Venice* in *Spain* 115
Lipomano Jerom, Embassador of *Venice* at the Port 87
   at *Turin* 416
Lipsius 52
Lisola 364
Livius Titus 52
Lobconits 303
Lockhart, Embassador for the Protector of *England* 17
   highly honour'd in *France* ibid
Loffler James, Embassador of the four Circles in *France* 148
Loffredi Peter, Embassador of the Viceroy of *Naples* 21
See *Pierro Loffredi*
Lopez Matthew, an *African* Embassador 164
Loisel, Embassador of *France* at *Rome* 218
Lords Great, not the properest for Embassies, and why 48, 49
Lorrame, a free Principality 33
   the Succession there 125
Lotharius II Emperor 233
Lucena, an Embassador and Traytor 88
Lumbres, Monsieur de, Embassador of *France* in the North 242
Lumes, Constable of 137
Luna, John de, Minister at *Arragon* 99
Lundsman, Deputy of the Hanse Towns in *London* 14
Lunenburg Brunswick, House of 27
Lussy Melchior, Embassador of the five little Cantons at *Trent* 225
Luxemburg, Peter de, Legate in *France* 79

M

Maes 125
Matchiavel Nicholas 52, 53
Madam, and *Mademoiselle* 175
Madrucci Frederick, Embassador of the Emperor at *Rome* 67
Magdalen of *France* 133
Magdebeg, Minister of *Persia* 83
Magnificence of an *Indian* Embassador 147, 148
   of the Plenipotentiaries of *Sweden* 203
Mahomet, Sultan 297
Majesty 223
Maisse Hurault, Embassador of *France* at *Venice* 185
Malta, Great Master of, a Soveraign 81, 230
   makes his Entry at *Rome* 33, 230
Mamus Bey 113
Manciender, Minister of *Spain* 41
   Embassador at the *Hague* 314
Manon James, Embassador of *Florence* 158
Mansel, Vice-Admiral of *England* 165
Marais de, Embassador of *France* in *England* 184
Marchioness of *Mirabel*, has the Honour of the Stool 383
Marchioness *de Senecy*, Lady of Honour to the Queen, Wife of *Lewis* XIII. 183
Mareschal *de Bassompierre* 132
   de *Bellegarde, Roger de Saint Iary* 117
   de *Chastillon* 131, 208
   de la *Chastre*, Governour of *Orleans* 194
   de *Chaune*, Embassador of *France* in *England* 186, &c seq
   de *Cosse*, Embassador of *France* in *England* 135
   d'*Estampes*, Embassador of *France* in *England* 46
   d'*Estrades*, his Character 424
   d'*Estree*, Embassador of *France* at *Rome* 92
   has

L

INDEX.

	Page
has a Quarrel there	261
goes to meet the Embaſſador of *Sweden*	131
his Character	422
de *Giez*	114
de *Grammont*	112
de les *Diguieres*	339, 352
de St *Andrew*	114
de St *Luc*	131
de la *Meilleraye*	208
de *Strozzi*	205
de *Toiras*	40
de *Turenne*	11
he takes Arms againſt the King	252
Mareſchalleſs de *Guebriant*, Embaſſatrix	5
claims Precedence of the Archdutcheſs	181
ſtands on her Privilege	353
Mareſchals of *France*, conduct Embaſſadors of Republicks	151
Margaret of *Auſtria*	120, 315
Margaret, Dutcheſs of *Alençon*	5
Margaret, Widow of *Maximilian* II	67
Margaret, Dowager of *Burgundy*	49
Margaret de Valois, Queen of *France*	251
Margaret de Valois, Queen of *Navarre*	327
Marriage double	150
of *Charles* IX and *Elizabeth* of *Auſtria*	181, 193
of *Philip* III and *Margaret* of *Auſtria*	5
of *Philip* II and *Mary* of *England*	70
of *Henry* IV and *Margaret* of *Valois*	91
of the Prince of *Conti*, and Mademoiſelle de *Martinozzi*	160
of the King of *England*, and *Henrietta* of *France*	176
of the Prince of *Wales*	88
Marriages	181
Marquis d'*Athaia*	66
d'*Ancre*	65, 129
d *Anſpach*	191
of *Baden*, Embaſſador from the Emperor *France*	31, 129, 181
ſends an Embaſſador to *France*	26
Marquis of *Baden Dourlach*, does not cover himſelf	31, 252
Marquis of *Bedmar* See *Alphonſo de la Cueva*	
Marquis of *Bergues Opzoom*	12
Marquis de *Bourgou*	392
of *Caracena*	151
of *Caſtel Rodrigo*	221
Embaſſador of *Spain* at *Rome*	299
Marquis de *Chandenier*, Captain of the *Scots* Guard de *Corps*	150
de *Cœuvres*, Governour of the Iſle of *Franc*	119
Embaſſador of *France* in *Italy*	31
Marquis d'*Effiat*, Embaſſador of *France* in *England*	177, 181
de *Formiſtan*, Steward of the Houſhold to the King of *Spain*	130
de *Fourilles*, Great Harbinger	132
Marquis de la *Fuentes*, Embaſſador of *Spain* in *France*	179
at *Venice*	197
his Audience about Precedency	312
Marquis du *Guaſt*, *Alphonſo de Gonzalos*	
d'*Avalos*, Governour of *Milan*	56
cauſes two Miniſters to be murder'd	79
Embaſſador at *Venice*	140
Marquis de *Gonzagua*, General of the Confederates	114
their Plenipotentiary	ibid.
	See alſo 375
Marquis de *Guicciardin*, Embaſſador of *Tuſcany*	187
de *Grana*	414
Marquis *Juſtiniani*, Envoy of *Genoa*	37
de *Litcho*	72
Priſoner and Negotiator	112

	Page
de *Lullins* See *Gaſpar de Geneva*	210
de *Mantua*, Priſoner	63
de *Mirabel*, Embaſſador of *Spain* in *France*	105
de *Monte*, executed at *Naples*	66
de *Mortemar*, firſt Gentleman of the Bedchamber	148
de *Neſle*, Governour of *le Fere*	150
de *Noirmonſtier*	ibid.
de *Peſcara*, Embaſſador of *Spain* at *Trent*	210
tempted to make himſelf Maſter of the Kingdom of *Naples*	339
de *Pianezza*	287
de *Piſani*	308
baniſh'd by the Pope	342, 416
du *Pleſſis Praſlin* See *Piſani*	287
de *Rambouillet*, *Nicholas d Angennes*, Embaſſador to the Senate of *Poland*	46
in *Spain*	78
treated on an Equality with the Count Duke	172
Marquis de *Roſny*, Embaſſador without Letters	2
Embaſſador in *England*	204, 269
honour d there	376
de *Rotelin*	176
de St *Chaumont*, Embaſſador of *France* at *Rome*	88, 220
in *Germany*	382
his Inſolence	383
de St *Germain*, Governour of *Turin*	140, 142
Plenipotentiary of *Savoy* at *Munſter*	287
Marquis de St *Maurice*, Embaſſador of *Savoy* in *France*	151, 170
at *Munſter*	170
Marquis de *Salviati*	141
de *Sarria*, Embaſſador from the Emperor at *Rome*	276
complains of the Pope without Cauſe	311
Marquis *Spinola*, a publick Miniſter	41
a meaner Man more truſted in a Negotiation	314
Marquis de *Trenel*, Embaſſador of *France* at *Rome*	195
de *Velada*	150
de *Vieuville*	379
de *Villareal*, executed	61
de *Villa Francha*, Peter of *Toledo*	252
de *Ville*, Embaſſador of the Duke of *Lorain* in *France*	33
honour d there	ibid.
de los *Velez*, Embaſſador of *Spain* at *Rome*	19
Marſilio, *Peter de*, a *Jacobin* Fryar and Negotiator	347
Martin, king of *Arragon*	14
Martin of *Arragon*	ibid
his Difference with the Pope's Nuncio	280
Mary, Queen of *England*	69, 239
Mary, Queen of *Scotland*	108, 278
Mary Louiſa, Queen of *Poland*	133
Mary de Medicis	319, 365
Mary Ghigy	264
Marin Juſtiniani, Embaſſador of *Venice* to the Emperor	297
Marin de Marſin, Prince of *Roſſano*	129
Maſcaregnas, *Martin de*, Embaſſador of *Portugal* at *Trent*	223
Maſdam Dorp, Embaſſador from the United Provinces to the King of *Sweden*	260
Maſter of the Chamber to the Pope	95
Maſter of Ceremonies at the Coun of *Trent*	128, 167
Maſter of the Ceremonies 301 See alſo	303
Mattarſon, *John*, Embaſſador of *France* at *Florence*	338
Matthias, Emperor	215
Mauleon, *John de*, a Monk and Negotiator	64, 145
du *Maurier*, Embaſſador of *France* at the *Hagua*	201
Mauriquez, *John*, General of the *Spaniſh* Army	205
	Maxims

INDEX.

	Page
Maxims Moral	53
Maximilian, King of the Romans	209, 222
meets the Cardinal of York	129, 142
Emperor	261, 315
Maximilian, King of Bohemia	234
Maximilian II Emperor	232
Mazarin, Julius, Cardinal, a young Negotiator	57, 349
Nuncio Extraordinary in France	131
has Clothes of all Fashions	202
employ'd by Pope Urban VIII.	280
Mediators, give the first Visit to the Count de Pegnaranda	174
refuse to admit the Minister of Portugal	18
communicate their Powers	120
See also 364, & seq
Mediators interested	365
Mediation of Brandenburg rejected	364
of Venice	370
of the United Provinces	321, 376
Mediation of England, Sweden, and the United Provinces	371
Medicis, Laurence de	82
Medicis, Peter de, Chief of the Republick of Florence 87	See also 338
Mahomet Basha, Prime Vizier	253, 282
Memoirs of Philip de Comines	52
Memoirs concerning Embassadors	1
Mendoza de Diego, Minister of Spain at Venice	186
Mendoza de Diego, Hurtado de	129
Embassador of Charles V at Rome	149
of Philip IV in England	238
Mendoza, John de, Marquis of Inoyosa, Embassador of Spain in England	104, 243, 252, 292
See 43 Governour of Milan	394
Merargues, John of Arragon, a Traytor	251
contrives to surprize Marseilles	353
Merced, a Title very common in Spain	175
Merveille, Minister of France at Milan	35
Mexia Diego, Embassador from the Infanta at London	238
Mezeray, Francis, writes the History of France 52
Mien, shocking	256
Minister, impertinent	109
Minister of Brandenburg, a Deserter	87
Ministers Publick, are inviolable	264
Ministers of the second Order	2, 33
are more convenient than Embassadors	33, 34
Ministers of the German Princes, consider'd as Attendants on the French Embassadors	29
Ministers of State, take on them the Title of Excellency	176
Minister of the Pope ill used	312
Minister of Brandenburg not admitted	311
Ministers of France, their Jealousie	180
Minister first	302
Ministry of Cardinal Richlieu, and Cardinal Mazarine	357
Miquely, John, sent to wait upon Henry IIII of France	236
Miramont, Peter de, Minister of the Duke of Burgundy	99
Mirembeau, Minister of Henry III in Germany	267
Misuro, Corruption in Ministers	353
Mocenigo, Embassador of Venice in France	286
at Rome	288
Mocenigo, Lazarus, Embassador of Venice at Urbin	416
Mocenigo, Lewis, Embassador of Venice to the Emperor	236
Moderation	349, & seq
Modification of the Faculties of a Legate	69
Le Moin, Father	71
Momberon James de, Minister of France in Spain	319
Monks, are passionate	346

	Page
Monks, do not make a Part of Civil Society	64
claim the Protection of the Law of Nations, if employ'd as Negotiators	66
Monk, Jacobin, a Negotiator	65
Monks, dangerous	196
ill used	259
Monluc, John de, Prothonotary Minister at the Port	62
disguises himself	122
Embassador of France in Poland	ibid
exceeds his Instructions	406
Monsieur the Dauphin, cover'd when he gave Audience to the Swiss	132
Monsieur, means more than Heer in Flemish, or Herr in German	175
Monstreul, Minister of France in England	263
Montagù, Minister of England in France	100
Montgomery, Minister of France in Scotland	125
Montigny, sent to Spain by the States of the Low Countries	12
Morfontaine Hofman, Embassador of France in Swisserland	283
Morosini, Embassador of Venice at Constantinople	319
Morvilliers, Chancellor of France, Embassador	48, 339
Morvilliers, John, Bishop of Orleans, Embassador of France at Trent	217
Minister	239
La Motte Fenelon, Embassador of France in England	135 See also 321
Mourning	204
Muglitz, Embassador of the Emperor at Trent 315, 223
Munster and Osnabrug, nam'd for the Congress	372
Muscovites, have Commerce with the English and Dutch	11
are Slaves	145
are uncivil and barbarous	ibid
Mustapha Feraga, Minister of the Port in France	162
See Solomon Mustaseraga
Muller, Dideric, Deputy of the Anseatik Towns in France	14

N

Nani, Baptist, Procurator of St Mark, writes a History	52, 251
Ministers of the Republick of Venice	232
Nani, Almory, Embassador of Venice at the Port, his Entry	146
his Audience	160
Nantua, Embassador of France at the Port	11
Naples, a Fief of the See of Rome, and Sovereignty	17
Naples, King of, sends Embassadors to Rome	ibid
Nasciangi, Chancellor of the Grand Seignior	160
Navarre, King of, sends Embassadors to Germany	178
de Nassau de Beverweart, Lewis, Embassador of the United Provinces in England	136
de Nassau, Maurice, Embassador of Brandenburg in London	241
Nassokin, Embassador of Muscovy in Poland	128
Navager, Embassador of Venice in France	120
Nederhost	353
Negotiation of Bavaria in France	97
Negotiation, Form of it	376
Negotiation of Munster	308
Negotiations of Dossat and Jeannin, sufficient to instruct a Minister 53 See also	313
Negotiations, when carry'd on at Constantinople, not for the Merchant's Interest	56
Negotiator, not always an Embassador	4, 35
Nephew of the Pope, gives Embassadors the Title of Excellency	175
is no Prince of the Blood	178
receives

INDEX

	Page
receives Embassadors	138
Neutrality of the United Provinces with the Empire	28
News, how to be written by an Embassador	360
Neyers, John, a Cordelier and Negotiator	259, 351, 354
Nicholas III Pope	221
Nicolini, Embassador of Tuscany at Rome	285
Nobility	47
Noel de Caron, first Embassador of the United Provinces in England	6
his meeting with the Spanish Embassador	197
Burgomaster of Bruges	118
Noirmont, Minister of Spain, in Holland	353
Norfolk, Duke of 349 See also	321
Norris, the English Herald in France, ill us'd	73
Norris Henry, Embassador of England, in France	152
Northumberland, Earl of	135, 263
Notifications ought to precede Complements	194
Nottingham, Earl of, Embassador of England, in Spain	194
Nuncius is deputed, or sent	115
Nuncii terrestres	123
Nuncio is an Embassador	2, 8
is a new Quality	74
has no Pretence to the first Visit	185
makes the first Visit	186
how he makes Visits	204
sent to the King, and not to the Kingdom of France	47
Nuncio the sole Mediator	366, 369

O

Oath for the Observation of Treaties	194
Obedience, Embassador of	6, 148
the Emperor sends none to the Pope	133
the Duke of Savoy sends none to him	ibid
d'Obersdansky, Embassador from Ferdinand, to the Pope	180
Oberti Michael, Consul of Venice, at Ancona	40
Octavio Fon, Embassador of Venice, in France 326,	377
Octavio Farnese	178
Odaux, Minister of the King of Navarre, in Spain	30
Officers of the Town-house of Paris, goe to meet the Spanish Embassadors	129
Old Man subject to Weaknesses	54
Oldenbarnevelt John	300, 351
Oliver Cromwell, great Honours paid him	17, 18
Oliver Daun	393
Barber and Embassador	49
d'Olzina John, Minister of Arragon	99
Ommeren, Deputy Extraordinary	43
Ondedei, Confident of the Cardinal Mazarin	100
Orange, Princes of, Maurice and Henry, will meet Embassadors	80
receive the first Visit of them	142
Orange Maurice, Prince of	300, 351
Orange, Prince of	302, 321
William, Minister of the Emperor	239
Orator	148
Order of the Garter	198
Orders, how an Embassador should execute them	312, &c. seq
Orders of the States of Catalonia	14
Orders of Princes, make part of their Instructions	106
Orio Laurence, Embassador of Venice, at London	34
Ormond, Duke of, Minister of England	17
d'Ostervick William de Lier, Embassador of the United Provinces, at Venice	10
in France	151
Otho de Chasteauroux, Legate in France	79
Otho Brugman	314

	Page
Otho de Swerin, Embassador of Brandenburg to the King of Sweden	98
first Minister	143
at the Hague	110
Oxenstiern John, Plenipotentiary, Embassador of Sweden, at Osnaburg	324
refuses the Visit of the Minister of Bavaria	201
his Difference with Salvius his Collegue	237
has no Love for the French	386
rough and obstinate	427
Oxenstiern Axel	305
rough and obstinate	427

P

Raau Adrien	417
Embassador of the United Provinces, in France	131
conducted by the Mareschal of France	151
his Aversion to France	261
Pacificators	370
Padavin, John Baptist, Secretary of Venice	261
Paer John de, Embassador of Portugal at Trent	222
Paget William, receives the Pope's Legate	71
Palatine of Posnania Embassador of Poland, in France	150
Pamphilio, Datary to the Legate	69
Pancirole, Nuncio at Querasque	40
Paolo Fra, writes the History of the Council of Trent	52
Parallel between d'Avaux and Servien	416
Parliament of England	7
how they treated the French Embassador	160
Particelli Michael, Embassador of France, at Turin	50
a Merchant	ibid.
Barosa Paul, his History	52
Passports, who may give them 24, 21, &c. seq.	
the Emperor refuses them to the German Princes	28
grants them	30
Projects of Passports	119
France refuses them to the Duke of Lorrain	129
cannot be extended	ibid
Passport of the Inquisition	130
Pastina Hippolyto, Chief of the Neapolitan Rebels	272
Paternulus Valms	52
Patriarchs claim Precedence of the Embassador of Malta	236
conduct Embassadors at Rome	138
Paul III Pope 69 See also	342
Paul IV Pope	71, 79
his Stubbornness	311
Paul V Pope	3, 138
Paulin Baron de la Gaude See Anthony Paulin	
Peace, the Interest of the Venetians	9
Peace separate, made by the Dutch	388
Pedantry	4, 9, 51
Pedro d'Ayala 243 See 349,	426
Pedro d'Arragon, Embassador of Spain, at Rome	343
Pedro Faxarda, Embassador of Spain, in Poland	319
Pedro de Guevara, arrested	204
Pedro de Marsilio, a Monk and Negotiator	66
Pedro, a Prince of Portugal	19
Pedro de Toledo, Governour of Milan	21
Pedro de Urrea, Embassador of Ferdinand, in Italy	138
Peinena de Castro Lewis, Embassador of Portugal, at Rome	28

Pelissier

INDEX.

	Page
Pelisier William, Bishop of *Montpellier*, Embassador of *France*, at *Venice*	266
Penshorn David, Deputy of the *Anseatick* Towns, in *France*	14
Pension paid by the King of *Spain* to the Cantons	10
Pension design'd for the Prince of *Orange*	356
Penitionary Counsellor of *Holland*, is the last of the Deputies 201 See	306
Peralta, Peter de, Minister of *Spain*	99
Peretti, Prince	213
Perez Diego, Embassador of *Spain*, in *France*	344
Perez de Navales John, Embassador of *Arragon*, in *Sicily*	29
Perfect Embassador	1
du Perron, Minister of *France*, at *Rome*	360
Persecutions of *Japan*	295
Peter le Grand, King of *Arragon*	66
uses two insolent Fryers roughly	347
Peter Jeannin, a learned able Man	50
aged	54
Embassador of *France* at the *Hague* 106, 185, 244, 262	
acts in an extraordinary Manner about the Visit	187
Peter, Prince of *Moldavia*	5
Petey, or *Peto* nam'd, Legate in *England*	79
Philibert, Prince of *Savoy*	1-6
Philip of *Austria*	304, 315
Philip II King of *Spain*	97
marries a Daughter of *France*	119
wants Complacency	203
Philip II and *Philip* III 231 See also	304
Philip III and IV Kings of *Spain* 173, 182 See also	327
Philip the Hardy, King of *France*	117
Philip Augustus, King of *France*	347
Philip, Prince of *Spain*	234
Philip of *Bruxels*, Embassador from the Emperor in *France*	48
Philip Chabot, Sieur de *Biron*, Embassador from the Regent of *France*, in *Spain*	22
Philip Duke of *Burgundy*, sends Embassadors	16
sends Embassadors to the Council of *Basil*	226
separates from the *English*	238
Pimentel Anthony, Minister without Character	35
sent from *Spain* to *Sueden*	37, 197
refuses the *French* king's Present	290 See 305, 308
his Treaty at *Paris* now d	408
Pinart Claude, Secretary of State in *France*	48, 135
Embassador in *England*	ibid
in *Sueden*	91
Piquet, Agent and Resident of *France*, in *Sweden*	34, 197
Pirro Loffreds, Marquis of *Treviso*, arrested by the Pope	324
Pisani John Vivonne, Embassador of *France*, at *Rome*	62
a great Minister	250
Pisaro John, Embassador of *Venice*, at *Vienna*	171
Pistag, the General Assembly of the *Grisons*	111
Pius IV Pope, invites the Czar of *Muscovy* to the Council of *Trent*	110
regulates the Seat of Embassadors	195
his Difference with *Maximilian* II	233
his Tyranny	343
Pius V	79, 324
his Dispute with the Marquis *Pisani*	342
Place the most honourable, given to the Ministers of *Lunenburgh*	38
which is the most honourable	219
Player of the Lute, a Minister	82
Plenipotentiary	2

	Page
is but a Mandatary	120
the first of the Princes of *Germany*, not to give place to the Second of the Electors	32
gives no new Character	39
Plenipotentiaries of *Spain*	118
Plenipotentiaries give Passports	123, 124
Plenipotentiaries *Dutch*, Mediators	389
Plenipotent aries that are not Embassadors	375
Plesis Besançon, Minister of *France*, in *Italy*	107
Podestates	4
Podestat of *Corfu* crown'd	349
Polybius	52
Pomponne du Bellievre	429
Pompeo Justiniani, writes the History of the Low-Countries	82
Pompeo Strozzi, Embassador of *Mantua*, in *England*	136, 155
Pomponne Simon Arnauld de	419
Ponce Philip, Embassador of *Spain*, at *Rome*	341
Pontan John Jovian, Minister of the King of *Naples*, at *Rome*	51
Ponte Nicholas da, Podestat of *Bergamo*, and Embassador of *Venice*, at *Rome*	101
at *Trent*	225
Pope, has his Ministers in all Catholick Courts	8
Pope, a Mediator	95
Pope's Brother receives an Embassador	9
Por., has no Ministers in Ordinary in foreign Courts	10
Portugal, Embassadors of, not acknowledged	18, 19
Portugal, king of, has his Ministers at *Munster*	125
assisted by *France*	322
Portman John, Minister of *Brandenburgh*, at the *Hague*	110
Possession makes Princes considered	18
Possevin Anthony, a Jesuit	95
forbids the *French* Embassador to come to *Rome*	ibid
Power for the Princes of *Germany*	30
Power limited	117
of the Ministers at *Munster*	118
are a part of the Treaty	121
communicated by Mediators	ibid
Power necessary to an Embassador	368
Prasmansky, Secretary of State in *Poland*	128
Prefect of *Rome*	196
Pregadi of *Venice*	140
Prelate, an Embassador	63, 64
Preliminaries	114, 372
Presents	292
Presents Embassadors should make	208
Embassador of *England* refuses the Czar's	145
Presents of Embassadors	353
President of the Week, in *Holland*	306
President of the Council, at *Vienna*	303
Pretensions of *France*	389
of the *Muscovite* Embassadors	379
Pretensions ridiculous, of an Embassador	181
Priandi Minister of *Mantua*, in *France*	245
Pride of Churchmen	234
Princes conduct Embassadors of crowned Heads, to Audience	151
Princes, Subjects	11
titulary	ibid 12
Princes covered at Audiences of Embassadors	158
Princes of *Germany* treated as Subjects	29
have Right to send Embassadors	25 & seq
Prince of *Conde*	106
gives the Hand to the Embassador of *Maltha* 179 See	331
Prince of *Conti*	151
Prince Dauphin	48, 132
Embassador in *France*	135

7 M   Princes

INDEX.

Princes younger, of *Savoy*, pretend to have Precedency of Embassadors 179
Prince *Palatine*, Generalissimo of *Sweden* 327
Prince of *Savoy* and *Lorrain*, Subjects, 352
Princes of *Italy*, younger Sons 352
Principles of Policy, uncertain 337, 338
Priolo Benjamin, writes a History 52
Prisoners of War, whether they may be Ministers 36
Pristaves, Introductor of Embassadors in *Muscovy* 128, 179
are uncivil 145 See also 377
Privanca Privados, in *Spain* 304
Priuli, Embassador of *Venice*, at *Turin* 178
the Republick will have the Duke of *Savoy* make him the usual Present 288
Private persons may make and receive Overtures of Accommodation 113
Proayre, Embassador of *Arragon* 14
Procurators of St *Mark* 236
Procurators, publick Ministers 44
Prodigality of a Minister 351
Protestant Princes courted by the *Spaniards* 388
Protestation of *France* against the Council of *Trent* 343
Proveditores of *Venice* 4
Provinces United, have their Ministers every where 10
are Sovereigns 17
their Embassadors offend against the Rules of Civility 190 See 337, 370
Provost of the Merchants of *Paris* 132
Prudence, an Embassadors chief Guide 54
of the Embassador of *Spain* 185
See 321, 329, & *seq*
Publication of Treaties 405
Publick Persons are not always publick Ministers 12, 13
Puisieux, Secretary of State in *France* 151, 358
in Disgrace 412

Q

Quality much consider'd by the King of *Spain* 172
Queen, Regent of *France* 114, 214, 319
Queen, Regent of *Spain* 200
Querasque Congress, Rank of the Ministers there 40
Quintana Peter de, Minister of *Ferdinand* the Catholick 64
Quinsay Simon de, Minister of the Duke of *Burgundy* 90

R

Rack, the President of *Grenoble*, Embassador of *France* put upon it 262
Radzwil Janus, Embassador of *Poland*, at the *Hague* 165
Rawleigh, Sir *Walter* 255
Randolph, Embassador of *England*, in *Scotland* 349
Rank of the Embassadors of the United Provinces, regulated 182, 183
of the Embassadors of *France* and *Spain*, at *Vervins* 219
Princes could not regulate it 198
adjudged in *France* 218 & *seq*
Rank in signing Treaties 377
Raphael Jerom, Embassador of *Florence* 414
Ratifications of Treaties 405 & *seq*
Ratifications of the Treaty of *Elbing* refus'd 408
Reasons why *France* was for Peace 98
Reception of Embassadors 62, 137
at *Venice* 138
at the *Hague* 142 See also 363
Rector of the University of *Paris*, goes to meet Embassadors 134
Redanto de la Croix, a Monk and Negociator 66
Reding, Embassador of the Catholick Cantons 132

Reduction of *Siena* 329
de *Reede* de *Renswoude John*, Embassador of the United Provinces, in *England* 110, 171
Regent of *France* 110, 120
Regents send Embassadors 22
Registring of Treaties 384
Register Clerk in *Holland*, what Office he exercises 302
his Diligence 357
Register of *Cano* banish'd by the Pope, an account of the *French* Embassador 276
Report false, of an Embassador 414, 415
Relations of Embassies 52
of the Travels of the Duke *de Saxe Weimar* 31
of *Muscovy*, by *Olearius* 145
of *Persia*, by *Figueroa* 55
of *Peter de la Valla* 56
of the Embassie of the Earl of *Carlisle* 145
Relations of an Embassador 413
of the Courts of *Savoy* and *Urbin* 416
of Sir *William Temple* *ibid*
Religion and Faction synonimous 198
Religious of *Montferrat*, Negociators 64
Religious are not proper for Embassies *ibid*
Religious in Disguise, lose their Privilege 205
Religious of *Maestricht* 87
Remark considerable touching the first Visit 191, 368
Remarker of *Brussels* 410
Remonstrance of the Princes of *Germany* 340
Renard Simon, Embassador of the Emperor in *France* 48
Rencounter of *Destrades* and *Vatteville*, at *London* 220
Renegado 253
Rene de Lucinge, Embassador of *Savoy* 325
Rengners, a Magistrate of *Groninguen*, his rash Proceeding 259
Repartee, a good one 344
Report of an Embassador 413 & *seq*
Representations 4
Representations impertinent 167
Republicks of *Genoa*, *Luca*, and *Ragusa* 10
Republick of *Venice* 305, 364
Residents 2, 33
France has one at *Vienna* 34
they are not admitted to sit at *Venice* 159
they sit before the Cardinals 148
cover themselves at *Venice*, and the *Hague* 178
Resident, a new Quality 36
the Signification of the Word *ibid*
is a publick Minister *ibid* 37
Residents at *Hamburgh* 45
Resident of *Brandenburgh* deserts 206
Resident of *Portugal* arrested 255
Riario Jerom de 341
Nephew of *Sextus* IV 257
Ribera John de, Embassador of *Spain*, in *France* 289
Richard III King of *England* 17
Rich Embassador of *England* See *Kensington*
Richardot, Embassador of *Spain*, at *Vervins*, and in *France* 22, 219
the Archduke's Minister 314
Right of Devolution 297
Right of Embassy, a Mark of Sovereignty 1
why it is 7
Right of Burghership may be renounc'd 76
Right of War and Peace *ibid*
Ripporda de *Tarmsum*, Embassador of the United Provinces, in *England* 136
Rech Sur'yon, Prince de la 48
Roch Van den Honart, Embassador of the United Provinces, in *Poland* and *Sweden* 128

Roche-

INDEX.

Rochepot, Francis de Montmorancy, Governour of Picardy 35
Rodolphus the Emperor 303
Rosencrans, Paul, Embassador of Denmark in England and France 256
Rothsay, Earl of, Embassador of Scotland in France 34
de la Rovere, John 62
Row, Embassador of England in Germany 46
de Royas de Portalarabia, Embassador of Maltha at Trent 230
Rubens, Sir Peter Paul the Painter, Minister for the King of Spain in England 49
his Merit 50
Russy, Embassador of France at the Hague 120, 187, 244
Rustan, Prime Vizier 168
Ruy Diaz 128
Ruy Gomez de Silva 239

S

Saavedra, Diego de, Plenipotentiary of Spain at Munster 22, 228, 282
h s Passport 22
his Difference with the Bishop of Boisleduc 143
Sabran, Minister of France in England 263
Sacrificers, not Embassadors among the Jews 57
Safe Conduct 121, & seq
Sadler, Minister of Sweden 80
St Aldegonde, Embassador of the United Provinces in England, writes false News 361
St Amant, Poet and Minister 113
St John, Embassador of England in Holland 287, 292
St Paul, Constable of 127, 157
St Ravy, Minister of France in England 57
St Stephen, Minister of France in Bavaria 238
Saintot, Master of the Ceremonies 151
Salius, Nicholas de, Minister of the Emperor at the Port 168
Salomon, a Jewish Physician 35
Sallust, the Historian 5
Salvius, Embassador of Sweden at Osnaburg 80
chief of the Swedish Ministers at Lubeck 134
Saluting the Flag settled between England and Holland 381
Sancho the Brave, King of Castille 117
Sancy, Achilles de Harlay, Embassador of France at the Port 56
Sandwich, Earl of 113
Sans, Prince of 101
carry'd off 299
Saobadsky, John, Embassador of Poland in France 170
Sarasin, Vincent Scipio, arrested 61
Sarmiento d Acugna Diego See Count de Gondemar
Sas, the English Advocate at the Hague 276
Satisfaction of France 385
of Sweden ibid
Sauly, Embassador of Genoa in France 132
Scipio Pasquale, Embassador of Mantua in Spain 82
Scotti Rainuccio, Nuncio in France 48, 92
Scudamore, Viscount of, Embassador of England in France 131
his Contest with Berlise 177
Sdialinski Paul, Embassador of Poland in Holland and England 109 See also 340
de Seaux, Secretary of State in France 151
Secretaries of State assume the Title of Excellency 176
Secretary of the Council of State in Holland 306
Secretary of Embassies and Embassadors 2, 43
Secretary of Embassadors sits at Cardinals 149
Secretary of the Viceroy of Naples complements the Pope 21

Secretary of the Portugal Embassador sits 43
Secretary of the Embassador of Venice ibid
Seguier, Peter, Keeper of the Great Seal in France 106
Chancellor 26
treats the Swiss Deputies 132 See 375
Segur, James de Segur de Pardaillan, Embassador from the King of Navarre 279
Selim, Emperor of the Turks 115
Selva, James de, Embassador of Portugal at Trent 222
Selva, John de, first President and Embassador 22
Senate of Poland sends Embassadors ibid,
Senate of Venice, gives the Rank to France 209, 210
Senator of Rome 196
Senators of Sweden, assume the Title of Excellency 176
Senecy, sent to Rome by the League 7
Senneterre, Embassador of France in England 170
Serbet 162
Signiory of Venice 159
their Secrecy 56
Serenissimo, a Title given the Doge of Venice 159
Sere uty 173
Servien, Embassador of France at Munster 176, 231
makes a Treaty of Guaranty at the Hague 48, 231, 292 See 321, 345, 365
Shering Rosenhan, Minister at the Congress of Westphalia 41
Embassador, Plenipotentiary in Germany ib.
is disagreeable to France 93
is recalled 106
nam d Embassador at Lubeck 208
is Embassador there 188
See also 318, 364
Shirley, Sir Robert, Embassador to his own Soveraign 148
Shrewsbury, Earl of 71 de le Shropshire
Sicily, King of, Prince of the Blood of France 11
Sidney, Algernoon, Embassador of England to the King of Sweden 261
Siege of Brunswick 321
Siege of Novara 327
Sigismund, King of Poland 17, 125
Sigismund, Augustus, King of Poland 116
uncivil to the Dutch Embassadors 128
Sigismund, Battori, Prince of Transylvania 125
See also 334
Sigismund, Marquis of Brandenburg, Embassador of the Elector 235
Sigismund III King of Poland 340
Sigismund de Ligthenstem, Minister of the Emperor to Soliman 168
Signing of Treaties 376
Silhon, Secretary to Cardinal Mazarin 358
Sillery, Nicholas Brulard, Embassador of France at Vervins 219
at Brussels 236
Simie, Minister of the Duke of Alenson 264
Simon, Van Beaumont, Embassador from the United Provinces to the King of Poland 128
to the Elector of Brandenburg 143
Simon Contarini, Embassador of Venice in France 325
Simon Van Horn, Embassador of the United Provinces in England 136
Simon de Lentin, a Monk and Negotiator 66
See also 346
Sinan Bassa 326
Sixtus IV an ill Pope 72, 257
arrests the Spanish Embassador 261
Sixtus V Pope 250, 257 See also 300, 319
Sleidan, John, writes a History 52
Slingelant, Godfrey, Embassador from the United Provinces in Sweden 261
Smith, Thomas, Embassador of England in France 50
Snoilsky

INDEX.

	Page		Page
Snoilsky, Minister of *Sweden* at *Frankfort*	144	his Character	416
Sóderin, Minister of *Florence*	49, 414	Subjects cannot send Embassadors	12
Soliman, Emperor of the Turks	54, 120	may exempt themselves from the Jurisdiction of their Sovereigns	60, 75
Soliman, *Mustafraga*	162	may change Countrey	76
Solio 221 a Throne	ibid	Succours, ought to be speci-y d in Treaties	381
Soler, John, Embassador of *France* at the Lateran Council	214	Sultan	303
Sonk, Albert, Embassador of the United Provinces in Sweden	154	Sultan *Soliman*	341
Soranzo, Embassador of *Venice* in *Spain*	248	Surety for a *Turkish* Minister at Venice	167
in France	151	for the Deputies of the States	25
at *Rome*	238	Suspicion	89
is Bailo at *Constantinople* 254. See also	348	*Sussex*, Earl of, Embassador of *England* to the Emperor	271
Soranzo, William	424	Sweden, offers her Mediation at *Vienna*	364
Sovereigns give Passports	125	Sweden, Kings of, have little Commerce with the rest of *Europe*	80
do not give Embassadors the Title of Excellency	175	King of, has Embassadors at *Munster*	385
Spies	86	*Sweden*, demands Passports	123
Sovereignty of the Princes of *Germany*	26	*Swedes*, allow no Catholicks	318
Spada, Nuncio in *France*	412	*Swifs*, put a *French* Minister to the Torture	262
Spahis	145		
Spain, where she has Embassadors	8	**T**	
Spain, King of, his Embassadors at *Rome*	9	Table of Embassador	207
Spaniards, make Profession of Sincerity	19	*Tacitus*	52
Spar, offends the *Venetian* Embassador	256	*Tamas Schahar*, King of *Persia*	306
Spinola. See Marquis *Spinola*		*Tamworth*, Embassador of *England* in *Scotland*	349
Spinola, Minister of *Genoa* in *Holland*	292	*Iannequi de Castel*, Embassador of *France* at *Rome*	257
Spiring, Peter, Resident of *Sweden* at the Hague	38	*Tarante*, Prince of	178
pretends to have Jurisdiction over his Domesticks	270	*Taxis*, Postmaster of *Rome*	257
Stafford, Earl of	7, 14	*Testarda*, Treasurer in *Turky*	162
Stadtholder	305	*Le Tellier*, Minister of State in *France*	133
States of the Empire are Sovereigns	30	*Terlon*, carries a Present to *Sweden*	204
States of *Arragon*	13, 14	Embassador of *France* there	305
States General, where they have Embassadors	10	*Temple*, Sir *William*, his Remarks on the United Provinces 416	See 43
have a Commissioner at *Dantzick*	46	his Allowance	207
refuse to admit the Emperor s Embassador	102	Embassador of *England* at the *Hague*	9
refuse the Passports of *Spain*	113	gives Place to the Prince of *Orange*	101
States General	305, 364	gives Place to the Pensionary	ibid
States of *Holland*, name an Embassador to *France*	10	See also	430
and extraordinary Embassadors	ibid	*Termes*, Embassador of *France* at *Rome*	72
their Resolution contrary to the Law of Nations	76	*Thadeo Barberino*, Prefect at *Rome*	178, 220
See also	357	Third Party in *Germany*	389
States of *Zealand* name an Embassador for *England*	10	*Thomas* of *Savoy*, Prince of *Carignan*	3
Stavenisse, Embassador of the United Provinces in *England*	198	*Thomasson*, Embassador of *Denmark* at *London*	191
Stella, Peter, Secretary of *Venice*	262	*de Thou, Christopher*, his History	5
Steno Bielke, Embassador of *Sweden* in *Denmark*	261	*Thou, James Augustus de*, Embassador of *France* at the *Hague*	269
Stephen Gamarra, Embassador of *Spain* at the Hague	86	*Throgmorton, Nicholas*, Embassador of *England* in *Scotland*	21
Stephen Despot of *Wallachia*	347	in France	125
Stephen Battory, Prince of *Transylvania*	75	*Thucydides*	52
Stephen of *Neuvilly*	259	*Tiepoli, John*, Minister of *Venice* in *Poland*	288
Stephen Poncher, Bishop of *Paris*, Embassador of *France* in *Italy*	138	*Tiercelin, John*, Embassador of *France* to the Emperor	300
Stephen, Prince of *Moldavia*	5	*du Tillet, John*	378
Stephen Tavara, Embassador of *Milan* at *Florence*	338	*Tingry*, Prince of	150
Stile of Embassador's Letters	358	Title of Serenity not known	173
Stoccar, Minister of the *Cantons* at the *Hague*	118	Title of High and Mighty	160
Strasueriths, Judges in *Swifferland*	60	Title, the Archduke gives the Embassadors of *France*	175
Strangers employ d in Embassies	75	*Titus Livius*	52, 250
Strasburg, one of the *Swedish* Embassy in *France*	56	*Tolet*, Jesuit	67
Streiff, Philip, Embassador of the four Circles	148	*Tomumbey*, Sultan of *Egypt*	248
Strickland, Walter, Minister of the Parliament of *England* at the *Hague*	8, 109, 292	hang'd	ibid
Strozzi, John, Embassador of *Florence* at *Trent*	214	*Torquato Conti*	281, 343
Strozzi, Matthew, Embassador of *Florence*	414	*Torres, de Lewis*, Nuncio in *Spain*	79
Study of an Embassador	47	*de la Tour d Auvergne*, Princes of that House	11, 158
of Treaties worthy the Application of an Embassador	391	Towns, *Anseatick*, send no Deputies	15
Suarez de Figueroa, Laurence, Embassador of *Spain* at *Venice*	51	their Commerce with *England*	ibid
		Train, Magnificent of a *Spanish* Embassador	223
		of a *Swedish*	ibid
		Transmigration, or changing Countrey	75
		Traytors	87, 251
			Treason

INDEX.

	Page		Page
Treason	275	of Munster	161, 397, 402
Treaty of Aix la Chapelle	19, 402	Treaty of Nancy	398, 303
of Amboise	403	of Nimeguen	400, 402
of Arras	90	Treaty of Odemzeo	401
of Asi	394	of Oliva	181, 400
of Avignon	403	of Osnaburg	396, 415
Treaty of Berlin	393, 394, 403	Treaty of Paris	392, 394, 396, 404
of Berwalde	396	of Pavia	394
of Bergue	395	of Peronne	403
of Bisigotz	400	of Pisa	264, 403
of Blois	377, 411	of Prague	29, 398
of Bologna	411	of Presburg	395
of Bovines	384	of Pyrenees	19, 398
of Breda	399, 402	Treaty of Querasque	220, 395
of Brisac	398	Treaty of Ratisbon	384
of Bromsebro	180, 373, 401	of Rivolles	399
of Brunswick	403	of Roschild	261
of Brussels	402	of Ruel	403
of Bussa	404	Treaty of St Germain	397, 398
Treaty of Calimthout	402	of Savoy and the Catholick Cantons	158
of Charmes	398	of Sansen	393
of Chasteau in Cambresis	19, 377, 394	of Schonolidt	402
of Chochim	206, 404	of Segueberg	396
of Christianople	401	of Staden	401
of Cleves	393, 403	of Sternberg	ibid.
of Coire	394	of Stetin	400
of Cologne	393, 402, 403	of Stockholm	399
of Cologne on the Spree	400	of Stumsdorf	401
of Compiegne	396, 397	of Suderocra	399
of Coningsberg	400	of Susa	398
of Copenhagen	401	Treaty of Tangier	404
of Coutsalt	403	of Tichfield	396
Treaty of Dirshau	401	of Tiquenhof	ibid
of Dorsten	398	of Tostrup	400
of Dortmont	392	of Tunis	404
of Dusseldorp	393	of Turin	399
Treaty of Ehrebresstein	397	Treaty of Vaucelles	45, 166
of Elbing	399	between Venice and the Grisons	140
of Elsenor	398	of Venice	403
of Essen	399	of Verouns	19, 314, 330, 391, 393, 400
Treaty of Ferrara	400	of Vic	398
of Flensbourg	401	of Vienna	393, 395, 396
of Fontambleau	397, 398, 404	of Ulm	238, 395, 396
of Frankfort	312	of Vossin	241
Treaty of Guaranty	48, 383, 397	of Vosten	403
of Greepwich	401	of Upsale	400
of Gueissen	402	Treaty of Warsaw	396
Treaty of Habenhausen	401	of Welean	400
of the Hague	144, 390, 391, 392, 393, 394, 396, 397, 399, 401, 403, 404	of Wesel	398
		of Westphalia	384
Treaty of Haguenau		of Westminster	400, 401
of Hailbron	396, 398	of Wismar	396
of Hall in Swabia	393	Treasurer General, first Minister of the United Provinces	306
of Hall in Saxony	401		
of Hamburgh	396, 397	Treaties, their Study necessary for Embassadors	52
Treaty of Labrau	401	Trevisan, Procurator of St Mark, Embassador of Venice to Francis I	345
of Lawemburg	396		
of Lindau	294	Trevor, Envoy of England in France	37
of Lion	392	Trimouille, Governour of Burgundy	261
of Liras	404	Triple Alliance	364, 402
of Lisbon	113, 402	Trithemius, Abbot of Spanheim	359
of Liverdun	398	Trivulco, James, Embassador of Milan, kill'd at Naples	248
of London	194, 400, 401, 403		
of Lubeck	399	Trivulco, John James, a Milanese, serves the French King	327
Treaty of Madrid	34, 399		
of Marine	397	Trivulse	113
of Marienburg	404	Trumpeters, protected by the Law of Nations	23
of Mehr	403	Trumpeter arrested	23, 24
of Mentz	396	hang'd	ibid
of Metz	399	Truce of twelve Years	380, 386
of Minden	398	La Tuillerie, Embassador of France at the Hague	169, 182
of Mirefleur	399		
of Mouton	394, 399	Mediator in the North	127
of Mulhausen	393	is not cover'd at Audience in Sweden	154
of Munden	398	Embassador of France at Venice	171
of Munich	397, 403	in Denmark 180 See also 309, 380, 415	

INDEX

	Page
Turk Grand, his Seraglio	161, 162
Turks, violent Proceedings with Ministers	337
distinguish between Ministers	146
call some Elchi, or Eltchi, and some Houlak, that is, Envoys	ibid
treat Embassadors ill	163
Tuscany, Great Duke of	132
he goes to receive Embassadors	141

V

	Page
Vadillo, Diego de, Minister of Spain at Rome	261
de la Valla, Peter,	56
what he says of an English Resident in Persia	200
of Achilles de Harlay	416
Valour	48
Valour of the Swifs	10
Valteline, rises	7
Vander Honart, John, Deputy Extraordinary in Poland	42
Vander Noot, Minister of Sweden in Holland	80
Vandyke, Jacob, Minister of Sweden	17
Vassal, sends no Embassador to his Lord	16
unless he holds his Fee in Sovereignty	17
Vatteville, Embassador of Spain at London	220
Vaucelas, Embassador of France in Spain	151
Vauclere, Lieutenant Governour of Calais	5
declares against Edward IV	334
Ubaldini, Nuncio in France	100
de Velasco, John, Governour of Milan	113
de Velasco, Lewis, Embassador of Spain in France	129, 136
de Velasco, Martin, Embassador from the Emperor at the Council of Bologna	149
Venctapa Najeka, an Indian King	156
Venice, where she has Embassadors	9
gives them the Title of Sage	ibid
formerly gave place to the Duke of Savoy	171
composes Embassies extraordinary of several Persons	236
excommunicated	61
Venetians, are wise betimes	54
Verger, Peter Paul, Nuncio in Germany	102
Verreyken, Embassador of Spain at Vervins	22, 219
Vettori, Paul, sent to the Pope	34
Vic, William de, Embassador of Castille at the Council of Lateran	213
Viglius de Zuichem, Minister of Charles V	239
Villaquier, Captain of the Gardes du Corps	151
Villiers, Embassador of France at Venice	185
Villeroy, Minister of France	351, 412
Vinta, Secretary of State at Florence	379
Visit first	184, 368
Visits	184
first due to the last Comer	132
paid according as they are received	188, 189
Cardinal visits the first	138
Visits of the Plenipotentiaries of France	189
of the Grison Embassadors	188
of the Duke of Milan to the Embassador of Venice	168
of the Embassador of Bavaria	189
of new Cardinals	190
first paid to Ministers of the second Order	187
all the Embassadors of the same Prince to be visited	186
first refus'd to the Minister of Savoy	187
paid him by the English Minister	188
refus'd to the Embassadors of Savoy and Mantua	187
not paid to the Swiss Cantons	188
due to Princes	191
Vizier Prime	161, 162, 336

	Page
what he said of Lanski, the Transylvanian Envoy	340
Volmar, Isaac, Plenipotentiary of the Emperor at Munster	240
Vorinsky, John, Embassador of Muscovy in Persia	147
Urban VIII Pope	16
d'Urfe, Embassador of France at Rome	178
at Trent	222

W

	Page
Wachtmeister, Embassador for Lubeck Congress	108
Wade, William, Embassador of England in Spain	251
Walachia, Michael, Despot of	334
Wales, Prince of	104
bubbled in Spain	326
Walsingham, Minister of England	142, 300, 307, 315, 322, 358
War of the Barberins, shews the Weakness of the Princes of Italy	27, 383
War of Castro	383, 411
War of the Uscoques	325
Warwick, Earl of	135
his Device	334
Webster, John, an Englishman, settled in Holland, supplies King Charles I with Money	77
Werman, Daniel, Embassador of Brandenburg to the King of Sweden	98
in England	248
Wesenbeck, Minister of Brandenburg at Osnaburg	240
Whitlock, Embassador of England in Sweden	197
William the Conquerour	66
William of Furstemberg, whether he was a Minister	85
seiz'd and carry'd off	265
William, Landgrave of Hesse	383
Wirtemberg, Prince of, covers before Monsieur in France	156
de Wit, John, Embassador from the United Provinces in Poland	128
first Minister of Holland	357
Wirquestein, Count, Minister at Osnaburg	240
Wootton, Sir Henry, Embassador of England at Venice	ibid
Wrangel, Mareschal	352

X

	Page
Xenophon	52
Ximen Perez Corella, Embassador of the King of Arragon and Naples	340
Ximenes, Cardinal	304

Y

	Page
York, Archbishop of, excommunicated	61
York, Duke of, his Care to prevent a Quarrel between the French and Spanish Embassadors	220
Youth, not proper for Embassies	54
Tsbrants, Embassador of the United Provinces to the Elector of Brandenburg	143
to the King of Sweden	261

Z

	Page
Zani, Matthew, Embassador of Venice in Spain	244
Zapara, Cardinal	234
Zapata, Plenipotentiary of Spain at Munster	185
is learned	295
Zapoli, John, King of Hungary	19
driven out of his Kingdom	119, 126
protected by the Turks	312
Zeno, Peter, Embassador of Venice at the Port	54
Zuniga, Balthasar, Embassador of Spain in France	252, 276
Zurita, Jerom, his History	52, 64
Zurlauben, Embassador of the Catholick Cantons	132

FINIS.

Lightning Source UK Ltd.
Milton Keynes UK
UKHW020430100123
415073UK00005B/465